P9-BJT-197

NOTABLE NAMES
in
AMERICAN HISTORY

A Tabulated Register

Third Edition
of
White's Conspectus of American Biography

James T. White & Company
1973

Library of Congress Cataloging in Publication Data
Main entry under title:

Notable names in American history.

1. United States – Biography I. White's conspectus of American biography.
E176.N89 1973 920'.073 73-6885
ISBN 0-88371-002-1

Printed in the United States of America

James T. White & Company
Clifton, New Jersey 07013

TABLE OF CONTENTS

I THE COLONIAL ERA 1
Signers of important documents, delegates to principal convocations, and governing officials

II THE UNITED STATES GOVERNMENT: EXECUTIVE BRANCH 11
Presidents and Vice Presidents of the United States of America, Presidential and Vice-Presidential candidates, and first ladies

III CABINETS 21
Presidential Cabinets and Cabinet members

IV THE UNITED STATES GOVERNMENT: LEGISLATIVE BRANCH 49
Members of the Senate and House of Representatives

V THE UNITED STATES GOVERNMENT: JUDICIAL BRANCH 267
Supreme Court and appellate court justices of the United States

VI STATES OF THE UNION 275
Governors, United States senators, and state chief justices

VII THE CONFEDERACY 389
Leaders of the Confederate States government and military forces

VIII THE MILITARY 397
Deputy secretaries of defense, secretaries of the services, and commanders of the armed forces

IX THE FOREIGN SERVICE 421
United States diplomatic representatives

X THE FEDERAL SERVICES 441
Chiefs of government bureaus and agencies

XI LOCAL GOVERNMENT 447
Mayors of noteworthy cities of the United States

XII HIGHER EDUCATION 463
Presidents of leading colleges and universities

XIII AMERICAN FOUNDATIONS 489
Presidents of leading non-profit organizations

XIV ART AND SCIENCE COLLECTIONS 495
Directors of museums and art galleries

XV RELIGION IN AMERICA 503
Leaders of principal church bodies and denominations

XVI COMMERCE AND INDUSTRY 541
Chief executives of leading companies

XVII ORGANIZED LABOR 555
Presidents of unions and guilds

XVIII NATIONAL ASSOCIATIONS 561
Presidents of academies, institutes, fraternal organizations, and other societies

XIX LAUREATES 581
Recipients of awards, prizes, and honors

INDEX 615

PREFACE

The editors who prepared the antecedents of this volume were motivated by the need for a source book in the form of a tabulated record that would provide simply and quickly answers to many basic questions in the fields of American biography and history. *The Conspectus of American Biography* (1906) and *White's Conspectus of American Biography* (1937), containing as they did many and variously arranged listings of the names of noteworthy men of achievement in the United States, each claimed an important place as a reference tool on shelves and desks in libraries throughout the country. Now, the demand for a new edition to include the names of the makers of recent American history is met by the publication of the present work.

The title *Notable Names in American History* has been chosen to reflect the fact that the current edition has been completely revised and brought up to date and that its scope has been greatly enhanced by the addition of new listings, the total now embracing virtually all fields of endeavor. In addition, several tabulations have been set forth in two different ways; Cabinet officers, for instance, are recorded in chronological order under the departments they head and in groups under each presidency. The Table of Contents indicates the rich storehouse of information contained herein, a broad panorama reaching from the list of signers of the Mayflower Compact to the most current data on contemporary noteworthy Americans.

Significantly, the present edition boasts the added feature of a complete Index of more than 50,000 separate entries. An awesome editorial task, the compilation of this Index was undertaken in the belief that it would constitute a vital contribution to the usefulness of the volume. *Notable Names* answers the question, "When was Charles Evans Hughes chief justice of the United States?" and also, through the Index, the query "What other positions did Charles Evans Hughes hold in his lifetime?" Thus, the volume has been made doubly helpful by providing two distinct approaches for locating the information contained in its pages.

The current volume is designed as a primary handbook for students, research workers, editors and writers, public officials, teachers, librarians, and others seeking data concerning this nation's prominent citizens, past and present.

The compilations that make up the body of this work have been drawn from original and authentic sources and their verification has involved consultation and extensive correspondence with officials of a multitude of public and private organizations; many federal, state, and municipal bureaus; and a wide range of American institutions. The publication, because of the painstaking care expended upon it, is uniquely comprehensive and bears the stamp of authority.

Like their predecessors at the start of the century, the present editors have prepared a volume they feel fills a vital reference need. The editors' labors will be amply rewarded if the researcher's query on where to locate names and dates in American history is answered simply: "Look in *Notable Names*"!

Notable Names in American History

I

THE COLONIAL ERA

Signers of important documents, delegates to principal convocations, and Colonial state officials from the year of the Mayflower Compact to 1789.

THE COLONIAL ERA

SIGNERS OF THE MAYFLOWER COMPACT

December 21, 1620

John Alden
Isaac Allerton
John Allerton
John Billington
William Bradford
William Brewster
Richard Britteridge
Peter Brown
John Carver
James Chilton
Richard Clarke
Francis Cooke
John Crackston
Edward Doty
Francis Eaton
Thomas English
Moses Fletcher
Edward Fuller
Samuel Fuller
Richard Gardiner
John Goodman
Stephen Hopkins
John Howland
Edward Lister
Edmund Margeson
Christopher Martin
William Mullins
Degory Priest
John Ridgedale
Thomas Rogers
George Soule
Myles Standish
Edward Tilley
John Tilley
Thomas Tinker
John Turner
Richard Warren
William White
Thomas Williams
Edward Winslow
Gilbert Winslow

DELEGATES TO THE FIRST COLONIAL CONGRESS

New York City, 1690

Etienne Delancey (N.Y.)
Nathan Gold (Conn.)
Jacob Leisler (N.Y.)
William Pitkin (Conn.)
Samuel Sewall (Mass.)
William Stoughton (Mass.)
John Wolley (Plymouth)

DELEGATES TO THE SECOND COLONIAL CONGRESS

Albany, N.Y., 1754

Theodore Atkinson (N.H.)
Abraham Barnes (Md.)
John Chambers (N.Y.)
John Chandler (Mass.)
James Delancey (N.Y.)
Benjamin Franklin (Pa.)
Stephen Hopkins (R.I.)
Martin Howard, Jr. (R.I.)
Sir William Johnson (N.Y.)
Joseph Murray (N.Y.)
Isaac Norris (Pa.)
Oliver Partridge (Mass.)
John Penn (Pa.)
Richard Peters (Pa.)
William Pitkin (Conn.)
Henry Sherburne, Jr. (N.H.)
William Smith (N.Y.)
Benjamin Tasker (Md.)
Meshech Weare (N.H.)
Samuel Welles (Mass.)
Richard Wibird (N.H.)
Elisha Williams (Conn.)
Roger Wolcott (Conn.)
John Worthington (Mass.)

DELEGATES TO THE STAMP ACT CONGRESS

New York City, 1765

William Bayard (N.Y.)
Joseph Borden (N.J.)
Metcalf Bowler (R.I.)
George Bryan (Pa.)
John Cruger (N.Y.)
John Dickinson (Pa.)
Eliphalet Dyer (Conn.)
Hendrick Fisher (N.J.)
Christopher Gadsden (S.C.)
William S. Johnson (Conn.)
Leonard Lispenard (N.Y.)
Philip Livingston (N.Y.)
Robert R. Livingston (N.Y.)
Thomas Lynch (S.C.)
Thomas McKean (Del.)
John Merton (Pa.)
William Murdock (Md.)
Robert Ogden (N.J.)
James Otis (Mass.)
Oliver Partridge (Mass.)
Thomas Ringgold (Md.)
Caesar Rodney (Del.)
David Rowland (Conn.)
Timothy Ruggles (Mass.)
John Rutledge (S.C.)
Edward Tilghman (Md.)
Henry Ward (R.I.)

SIGNERS OF THE DECLARATION OF INDEPENDENCE

July 4, 1776

CONNECTICUT

Samuel Huntington
Roger Sherman
William Williams
Oliver Wolcott

DELAWARE

Thomas McKean
George Read
Caesar Rodney

GEORGIA

Button Gwinnett
Lyman Hall
George Walton

MARYLAND

Charles Carroll
of Carrollton
Samuel Chase
William Paca
Thomas Stone

MASSACHUSETTS

John Adams
Samuel Adams
Elbridge Gerry
John Hancock
Robert Treat Paine

NEW HAMPSHIRE

Josiah Bartlett
Matthew Thornton
William Whipple

NEW JERSEY

Abraham Clark
John Hart
Francis Hopkinson
Richard Stockton
John Witherspoon

NEW YORK

William Floyd
Francis Lewis
Philip Livingston
Lewis Morris

NORTH CAROLINA

Joseph Hewes
William Hooper
John Penn

PENNSYLVANIA

George Clymer
Benjamin Franklin
Robert Morris
John Morton
George Ross
Benjamin Rush
James Smith
George Taylor
James Wilson

RHODE ISLAND

William Ellery
Stephen Hopkins

SOUTH CAROLINA

Thomas Heyward, Jr.
Thomas Lynch, Jr.
Arthur Middleton
Edward Rutledge

VIRGINIA

Carter Braxton
Benjamin Harrison
Thomas Jefferson
Francis Lightfoot Lee
Richard Henry Lee
Thomas Nelson, Jr.
George Wythe

MEMBERS OF THE COMMITTEE THAT PREPARED THE ARTICLES OF CONFEDERATION

1776

Samuel Adams (Mass.)
Josiah Bartlett (N.H.)
John Dickinson (Chairman; Pa.)
Button Gwinnett (Ga.)
Joseph Hewes (N.C.)
Stephen Hopkins (R.I.)
Francis Hopkinson (N.J.)
Robert R. Livingston (N.Y.)
Thomas McKean (Del.)
Thomas Nelson, Jr. (Va.)
Edward Rutledge (S.C.)
Roger Sherman (Conn.)
Thomas Stone (Md.)

SIGNERS OF THE ARTICLES OF CONFEDERATION

Adopted November 15, 1777

CONNECTICUT

Andrew Adams
Titus Hosmer
Samuel Huntington
Roger Sherman
Oliver Wolcott

DELAWARE

John Dickinson
Thomas McKean
Nicholas Van Dyke

GEORGIA

Edward Langworthy
Edward Telfair
George Walton

MARYLAND

Daniel Carroll
John Hanson

MASSACHUSETTS

Samuel Adams
Francis Dana
Elbridge Gerry
John Hancock
Samuel Holten
James Lovell

NEW HAMPSHIRE

Josiah Bartlett
John Wentworth

NEW JERSEY

Nathaniel Scudder
John Witherspoon

NEW YORK

James Duane
William Duer
Francis Lewis
Gouverneur Morris

NORTH CAROLINA

Cornelius Harnett
John Penn
John Williams

PENNSYLVANIA

William Clingan
Joseph Reed
Daniel Roberdeau
Jonathan Bayard Smith

RHODE ISLAND

John Collins
William Ellery
Henry Marchant

SOUTH CAROLINA

William Henry Drayton
Thomas Heyward, Jr.
Richard Hutson
Henry Laurens
John Mathews

VIRGINIA

John Banister
John Harvie
Francis Lightfoot Lee
Richard Henry Lee

DELEGATES TO THE CONSTITUTIONAL CONVENTION

Philadelphia, 1787

CONNECTICUT

Oliver Ellsworth
William S. Johnson
Roger Sherman

DELAWARE

Richard Bassett
Gunning Bedford, Jr.
Jacob Broom
John Dickinson
George Read

GEORGIA

Abraham Baldwin
William Few
William Houston
Nathaniel Pendleton
William Pierce
George Walton

MARYLAND

Daniel Carroll
Daniel Jenifer
James McHenry
Luther Martin
John Francis Mercer

MASSACHUSETTS

Francis Dana
Elbridge Gerry
Nathaniel Gorham
Rufus King
Caleb Strong

NEW HAMPSHIRE

John Langdon
John Pickering

NEW JERSEY

David Brearly
Abraham Clark
Jonathan Dayton
William C. Houston
William Livingston
John Neilson
William Paterson

NEW YORK

Alexander Hamilton
John Lansing, Jr.
Robert Yates

NORTH CAROLINA

William Blount
William R. Davie
Alexander Martin
Richard D. Spaight
Hugh Williamson

PENNSYLVANIA

George Clymer
Thomas Fitzsimons
Benjamin Franklin
Jared Ingersoll
Thomas Mifflin
Gouverneur Morris
Robert Morris
James Wilson

SOUTH CAROLINA

Pierce Butler
Charles Pinckney
Charles C. Pinckney
John Rutledge

VIRGINIA

John Blair
James Madison
Edmund Randolph
George Washington
George Wythe

THE CONTINENTAL CONGRESSES

(The First Continental Congress met in Philadelphia from 1774 to 1775 and the Second Continental Congress in various locations from 1775 to 1781. The Third Continental Congress, more commonly referred to as the Congress of the Confederation, met from 1781 to 1789.)

Presidents	*Elected*
Peyton Randolph, Virginia	Sept. 5, 1774
Henry Middleton, South Carolina	Oct. 22, 1774
Peyton Randolph, Virginia	May 10, 1775
John Hancock, Massachusetts	May 24, 1775
Henry Laurens, South Carolina	Nov. 1, 1777
John Jay, New York	Dec. 10, 1778
Samuel Huntington, Connecticut	Sept. 28, 1779
Thomas McKean, Delaware	July 10, 1781
John Hanson, Maryland	Nov. 5, 1781
Elias Boudinot, New Jersey	Nov. 5, 1781
Thomas Mifflin, Pennsylvania	Nov. 3, 1783
Richard Henry Lee, Virginia	Nov. 30, 1784
John Hancock, Massachusetts	Nov. 23, 1785
Nathaniel Gorham, Massachusetts	June 6, 1786
Arthur St. Clair, Pennsylvania	Feb. 2, 1787
Cyrus Griffin, Virginia	Jan. 22, 1788

DELEGATES

(Years indicate terms of service)

CONNECTICUT

Andrew Adams	1777-80, 1781-82
Joseph P. Cook	1784-88
Silas Deane	1774-76
Eliphalet Dyer	1774-79, 1780-83
Pierrepont Edwards	1787-88
Oliver Ellsworth	1777-84
William Hillhouse	1783-86
Titus Hosmer	1775-76, 1777-79
Benjamin Huntington	1780-84, 1787-88
Samuel Huntington	1776-84
William S. Johnson	1784-87
Richard Law	1778, 1783-84
Stephen M. Mitchell	1781-84, 1785-86, 1787-88
Jesse Root	1778-83
Roger Sherman	1774-84
Joseph Spencer	1778-79
Jedediah Strong	1782-84
Jonathan Sturges	1774-87
John Treadwell	1785-86
Joseph Trumbull	1774-75
James Wadsworth	1783-84, 1785-86
Jeremiah Wadsworth	1787-88
William Williams	1776-78, 1783-84
Oliver Wolcott	1775-78, 1780-84

DELAWARE

Gunning Bedford	1786-87
Gunning Bedford, Jr.	1783-85
John Dickinson	1776-77, 1779-80
Philemon Dickinson	1782-83
John Evans	1776-77
Dyre Kearney	1787-88
Eleazer McComb	1782-84
Thomas McKean	1774-76, 1778-83
Nathaniel Mitchell	1786-88
John Patten	1785-86
William Peery	1785-86
George Read	1774-77
Caesar Rodney	1774-76, 1777-78, 1782-84
Thomas Rodney	1781-83, 1785-87
James Sykes	1777-78
James Tilton	1783-85
Nicholas Van Dyke	1777-82
John Vining	1784-86
Samuel Wharton	1782-83

GEORGIA

Abraham Baldwin	1785-88
Nathan Brownson	1776-78
Archibald Bulloch	1776-78
Joseph Caly	1778-80
William Few	1780-82, 1785-88
William Gibbons	1784-86
Button Gwinnett	1776-77
John Habersham	1785-86
Lyman Hall	1775-77
John Houston	1775-77
William Houston	1784-87
Richard Howley	1780-81
Noble W. Jones	1775-76, 1781-83
Edward Langworthy	1777-79
William Pierce	1786-87
Edward Telfair	1777-79, 1780-83
George Walton	1776-79, 1780-81
Joseph Wood	1777-79
John J. Zubly	1775

MARYLAND

Robert Alexander	1775-77
William Carmichael	1778-80
Charles Carroll	1776-77
Charles Carroll of Carrollton	1776-77
Daniel Carroll	1780-84
Jeremiah T. Chase	1783-84
Samuel Chase	1774-78, 1784-85
Benjamin Contee	1787-88
James Forbes	1778-80
Uriah Forrest	1786-87
Robert Goldsborough	1774-75
John Hall	1775, 1783-84

John Hanson	1780-83
William Harrison, Jr.	1785-87
William Hemsley	1782-84
John Henry	1778-81, 1784-87
William Hindman	1784-87
John E. Howard	1787-88
Daniel Jenifer	1778-82
Thomas Johnson	1774-77
Thomas S. Lee	1783-84
Edward Lloyd	1783-84
James McHenry	1783-86
Luther Martin	1784-85
William Paca	1774-79
George Plater	1778-81
Richard Potts	1781-82
Nathaniel Ramsay	1785-87
Richard Ridgely	1785-86
John Rogers	1775-76
David Ross	1786-87
Benjamin Rumsey	1776-78
Gustavus Scott	1784-85
Joshua Seney	1787-88
William Smith	1777-78
Thomas Stone	1775-79, 1784-85
Matthew Tilghman	1774-77
Turbutt Wright	1781-82

MASSACHUSETTS

John Adams	1774-78
Samuel Adams	1774-82
Thomas Cushing	1774-76
Francis Dana	1776-78, 1784
Nathan Dane	1785-88
Elbridge Gerry	1776-85, 1782-85
Nathaniel Gorham	1782-83, 1785-87
John Hancock	1775-80, 1785-86
Stephen Higginson	1782-83
Samuel Holten	1778-80, 1782-83, 1784-85
Jonathan Jackson	1782
Rufus King	1784-87
James Lovell	1776-82
John Lowell	1782-83
Samuel Osgood	1780-84
Samuel A. Otis	1787-88
Robert Treat Paine	1774-78
George Partridge	1779-82, 1783-85
Theodore Sedgwick	1785-88
James Sullivan	1782
George Thacher	1787
Artemas Ward	1780-81

NEW HAMPSHIRE

Josiah Bartlett	1775-78
Jonathan Blanchard	1783-84, 1787
Nathaniel Folsom	1774-75, 1777-78, 1779-80
Abiel Foster	1783-85
George Frost	1777-79
John Taylor Gilman	1782-83
Nicholas Gilman	1768-89
John Langdon	1775-77, 1786-87
Woodbury Langdon	1779-80
Samuel Livermore	1780-83, 1785-86
Pierse Long	1784-86
Nathaniel Peabody	1779-80
John Sullivan	1774-75, 1780-81
Matthew Thornton	1776-78
John Wentworth, Jr.	1778-79
William Whipple	1776-79
Phillips White	1782-83
Paine Wingate	1787-88

NEW JERSEY

John Beatty	1783-85
Elias Boudinot	1777-78, 1781-83
William Burnet	1780-81
Lambert Cadwalader	1784-87
Abraham Clark	1776-78, 1779-83, 1786-89
Silas Condict	1781-84
John Cooper	1776
Stephen Crane	1774-76
Jonathan Dayton	1787-88
John De Hart	1774-75, 1776
Samuel Dick	1783-85
Jonathan Elmer	1776-78, 1781-84, 1787-88
John Fell	1778-80
Frederick Frelinghuysen	1778-79, 1782-83
John Hart	1776
Francis Hopkinson	1776
Josiah Hornblower	1785-86
William C. Houston 1779-82, 1784-85	083
James Kinsey	1774-75
William Livingston	1774-76
James Schureman	1786-87
Nathaniel Scudder	1777-79
Jonathan D. Sergeant	1776-77
Richard Smith	1774-76
John Stevens	1783-84
Charles Stewart	1784-85
Richard Stockton	1776
John Symmes	1785-86
John Witherspoon	1776-79, 1780-81, 1782

NEW YORK

John Alsop	1774-76
Egbert Benson	1784-85, 1786-88
Simon Boerum	1775
George Clinton	1775-77
Charles DeWitt	1783-85
James Duane	1774-84
William Duer	1777-78
William Floyd	1774-77, 1778-83
Leonard Ganesvoort	1787-88
David Ghelston	1788-89
Alexander Hamilton	1782-83, 1787-88
John Haring	1774-75, 1785-88
John Jay	1774-77, 1778-79
John Lansing, Jr.	1784-88
John Laurance	1785-86
Francis Lewis	1774-79
Ezra L'Hommedieu	1779-83, 1787-88
Philip Livingston	1774-78
Robert R. Livingston	1775-77, 1779-81
Walter Livingston	1784-85
Isaac Low	1774-75
Gouverneur Morris	1777-80
Lewis Morris	1775-77
Alexander McDougall	1781-82, 1784-85
Ephraim Paine	1784-85
Philip Pell	1788-89
Zephaniah Platt	1784-86
Philip Schuyler	1775-77, 1778-81
John Morin Scott	1780-83
Melancthon Smith	1785-88
Henry Wisner	1774-76
Abraham Yates	1787-88
Peter W. Yates	1785-87

NORTH CAROLINA

John B. Ashe	1787
Timothy Bloodworth	1786-87
William Blount	1782-83, 1786-87
Thomas Burke	1777-81
Robert Burton	1787-88
Richard Caswell	1774-76
William Cumming	1784
Cornelius Harnett	1777-80
Benjamin Hawkins	1781-84, 1786-87
Joseph Hewes	1774-77, 1779
Whitmil Hill	1778-81
William Hooper	1774-77
Samuel Johnston	1780-82
Allen Jones	1779-80
Willie Jones	1780-81
Abner Nash	1782-84, 1785-86
John Penn	1775-76, 1777-80

William Sharpe	1779-82
John Sitgreaves	1784-85
Richard D. Spaight	1783-85
John Swan	1787-88
James White	1786-88
John Williams	1778-79
Hugh Williamson	1782-85, 1787-88

PENNSYLVANIA

Andrew Allen	1775-76
John Armstrong	1778-80, 1787-88
Samuel J. Atlee	1778-82
John B. Bayard	1785-87
Edward Biddle	1774-76, 1778-79
William Bingham	1787-88
Matthew Clarkson	1785-86
William Clingan	1777-79
George Clymer	1776-78, 1780-83
Tench Coxe	1787-88
John Dickinson	1774-76
Thomas Fitzsimons	1782-83
Benjamin Franklin	1775-76
Joseph Galloway	1774-75
Joseph Gardner	1784-85
Edward Hand	1784-85
William Henry	1784-86
Charles Humphreys	1774-76
Jared Ingersoll	1780-81
William Irvine	1786-88
David Jackson	1785-86
James McClene	1779-80
Timothy Matlack	1780-81
Samuel Meredith	1787-88
Thomas Mifflin	1774-76, 1782-84
Joseph Montgomery	1783-84
Cadwalader Morris	1783-84
Robert Morris	1776-78
John Morton	1774-77
Frederick A.C. Muhlenberg	1778-80
Richard Peters, Jr.	1782-83
Charles Pettit	1785-87
Joseph Reed	1777-78
James R. Reid	1787-89
Samuel Rhoads	1774-75
Daniel Roberdeau	1777-79
George Ross	1774-77
Benjamin Rush	1776-77
Arthur St. Clair	1785-87
James Searle	1778-80
William Shippen	1778-80
James Smith	1776-78
Jonathan B. Smith	1777-78
Thomas Smith	1780-82
George Taylor	1776-77
Thomas Willing	1775-76
James Wilson	1775-76, 1782-83, 1785-87
Henry Wynkooop	1779-83

RHODE ISLAND

Jonathan Arnold	1782-84
Peleg Arnold	1787-89
John Collins	1778-83
Ezekiel Cornell	1780-83
William Ellery	1776-81, 1783-85
John Gardiner	1789
Sylvester Gardiner	1788-89
Jonathan J. Hazard	1787-89
Stephen Hopkins	1774-80
David Howell	1782-85
James Manning	1785-86
Henry Marchant	1777-80, 1783-84
Nathan Miller	1785-86
Daniel Mowry, Jr.	1780-82
James M. Varnum	1780-82, 1786-87
Samuel Ward	1774-76

SOUTH CAROLINA

Robert Barnwell	1788-89
Thomas Bee	1780-82
Richard Beresford	1783-85
John Bull	1784-87
Pierce Butler	1787-88
William H. Drayton	1778-79
Nicholas Eveleigh	1781-82
Christopher Gadsen	1774-76
John L. Gervais	1782-83
Thomas Heyward, Jr.	1776-78
Daniel Huger	1786-88
Richard Hutson	1778-79
Ralph Izard	1782-83
John Kean	1785-87
Francis Kinloch	1780-81
Henry Laurens	1777-80
Thomas Lynch, Sr.	1774-76
Thomas Lynch, Jr.	1776-77
John Mathews	1778-82
Arthur Middleton	1776-78, 1781-83
Henry Middleton	1774-76
Isaac Motte	1780-82
John Parker	1786-88
Charles Pinckney	1777-78, 1784-87
David Ramsay	1782-84, 1785-86
Jacob Read	1783-85
Edward Rutledge	1774-77
John Rutledge	1774-77, 1782-83
Paul Trapier	1777-78
Thomas T. Tucker	1787-88

VIRGINIA

Thomas Adams	1778-80
John Banister	1778-79
Richard Bland	1774-75
Theodorick Bland	1780-83
Carter Braxton	1775-76
John Brown	1787-88
Edward Carrington	1785-86
John Dawson	1788-89
William Fitzhugh	1779-80
William Fleming	1779-81
William Grayson	1784-87
Cyrus Griffin	1778-81, 1787-88
Samuel Hardy	1783-85
Benjamin Harrison	1774-78
John Harvie	1777-79
James Henry	1780-81
Patrick Henry	1774-76
Thomas Jefferson	1775-76, 1783-85
Joseph Jones	1777-78, 1780-83
Arthur Lee	1781-84
Francis Lightfoot Lee	1775-80
Henry Lee	1785-88
Richard Henry Lee	1774-80, 1784-87
James Madison	1780-83, 1786-88
James Mercer	1779-80
John F. Mercer	1782-85
James Monroe	1783-86
Thomas Nelson, Jr.	1775-77, 1779-80
Mann Page	1777
Edmund Pendleton	1774-75
Edmund Randolph	1779-82
Peyton Randolph	1774-75
Meriwether Smith	1778-82
George Washington	1774-75
George Wythe	1775-77

COLONIAL GOVERNORS

CONNECTICUT

1639 John Haynes
1640 Edward Hopkins
1641 John Haynes
1642 George Wyllys
1643 John Haynes
1644 Edward Hopkins
1645 John Haynes
1646 Edward Hopkins
1647 John Haynes
1648 Edward Hopkins
1649 John Haynes
1650 Edward Hopkins
1651 John Haynes
1652 Edward Hopkins
1653 John Haynes
1654 Edward Hopkins
1655 Thomas Welles
1656 John Webster
1657 John Winthrop, Jr.
1658 Thomas Welles
1659 John Winthrop, Jr.
1676 William Leete
1683 Robert Treat
1687 Edmund Andros
1689 Robert Treat
1698 Fitz-John Winthrop
1708 Gurdon Saltonstall
1725 Joseph Talcott
1741 Jonathan Law
1750 Roger Wolcott
1754 Thomas Fitch
1766 William Pitkin
1769 Jonathan Trumbull
1784 Matthew Griswold
1786 Samuel Huntington

DELAWARE

1776 John McKinly
1778 Caesar Rodney
1782 John Dickinson
1783 Nicholas Van Dyke
1786 Thomas Collins

GEORGIA

1733 James E. Oglethorpe
1743 William Stephens
1750 Henry Parker
1754 John Reynolds
1757 Henry Ellis
1760 James Wright
1776 Archibald Bulloch
1777 Button Gwinnett
1777 John A. Treutlen
1778 John Houston
1779 George Walton
1779 James Wright
1782 John Martin
1783 Lyman Hall
1784 John Houston
1785 Samuel Elbert
1786 Edward Telfair
1787 George Mathews
1788 George Handley

MARYLAND

1634 Leonard Calvert
1647 Thomas Green
1649 William Stone
1654 (Commissioners)
1657 Josias Fendall
1660 Philip Calvert
1661 Charles Calvert
1676 Thomas Notley
1680 Charles Calvert
1684 William Joseph
1688 (Protestant Associators)
1691 Lionel Copley
1694 Francis Nicholson
1699 Nathaniel Blackistone
1701 Thomas Tench
1703 John Seymour
1709 Edward Lloyd
1714 John Hart
1720 Charles Calvert
1727 Benedict L. Calvert
1731 Samuel Ogle
1732 Charles Calvert
1733 Samuel Ogle
1742 Thomas Bladen
1747 Samuel Ogle
1752 Benjamin Tasker
1753 Horatio Sharpe
1769 Robert Eden
1776 (Convention of the Council of Safety)
1777 Thomas Johnson
1779 Thomas S. Lee
1782 William Paca
1785 William Smallwood
1788 John E. Howard

MASSACHUSETTS

Plymouth Colony

1620 John Carver
1621 William Bradford
1633 Edward Winslow
1634 Thomas Prince
1635 William Bradford
1636 Edward Winslow
1637 William Bradford
1638 Thomas Prince
1639 William Bradford
1644 Edward Winslow
1645 William Bradford
1657 Thomas Prince
1673 Josiah Winslow
1681 Thomas Hinckley
1686 Edmund Andros
1689 Thomas Hinckley

Massachusetts Bay Colony

1629 John Endicott
1630 John Winthrop
1634 Thomas Dudley
1635 John Haynes
1636 Henry Vane
1637 John Winthrop
1640 Thomas Dudley
1641 Richard Bellingham
1642 John Winthrop
1644 John Endicott
1645 Thomas Dudley
1646 John Winthrop
1649 John Endicott
1650 Thomas Dudley
1651 John Endicott
1654 Richard Bellingham
1655 John Endicott
1665 Richard Bellingham
1673 John Leverett
1679 Simon Bradstreet
1686 Joseph Dudley
1687 Edmund Andros
1689 Simon Bradstreet
1692 William Phips
1694 William Stoughton
1699 Richard Coote
1700 William Stoughton
1701 (The Council)
1702 Joseph Dudley
1715 William Tailer (Acting)
1716 Samuel Shute
1723 William Dummer (Acting)
1728 William Burnet
1729 William Dummer (Acting)
1730 William Tailer
1730 Jonathan Belcher
1741 William Shirley
1749 Spencer Phipps
1753 William Shirley
1756 Spencer Phipps
1757 Thomas Pownall
1760 Francis Bernard
1769 Thomas Hutchinson
1774 Thomas Gage
1775 (The Council)

Commonwealth of Massachusetts

1780 John Hancock
1785 James Bowdoin
1787 John Hancock

NEW HAMPSHIRE

1679 John Cutts
1681 Richard Waldron
1682 Edward Cranfield
1685 Walter Barefoot
1686 Joseph Dudley
1687 Edmund Andros
1690 Simon Bradstreet
1692 Samuel Allen
1699 Richard Coote
1702 Joseph Dudley
1716 Samuel Shute
1728 William Burnet
1729 Jonathan Belcher
1741 Benning Wentworth
1767 John Wentworth
1775 Matthew Thornton
1767 Meshech Weare
1785 John Langdon
1786 John Sullivan
1788 John Langdon

NEW JERSEY

1702 Edward Hyde
1708 John Lovelace
1710 Robert Hunter
1720 William Burnet
1728 John Montgomerie
1731 Lewis Morris
1732 William Crosby
1736 John Hamilton
1738 Lewis Morris
1746 John Hamilton
1746 John Reading
1747 Jonathan Belcher
1757 John Reading
1758 Francis Bernard
1760 Thomas Boone
1761 Josiah Hardy
1763 William Franklin
1776 William Livingston

NEW YORK

New Amsterdam

1624 Cornelius J. Mey
1625 William Verhulst
1626 Peter Minuit
1633 Wouter Van Twiller
1638 William Kieft
1647 Peter Stuyvesant

New York

1664 Richard Nicolls
1668 Francis Lovelace
1673 Anthony Colve
1674 Edmund Andros
1683 Thomas Dongan
1688 Francis Nicholson
1689 Jacob Leisler
1691 Henry Slaughter
1691 Richard Ingoldsby
1692 Benjamin Fletcher
1698 Richard Coote
1702 Edward Hyde
1708 John Lovelace
1709 Richard Ingoldsby (Acting)
1710 Gerardus Beekman
1710 Robert Hunter
1719 Peter Schuyler (Acting)
1720 William Burnet
1728 John Montgomerie
1731 Rip Van Dam
1732 William Crosby
1736 George Clarke
1743 George Clinton
1753 Danvers Osborne
1753 James Delancey
1755 Charles Hardy
1760 Cadwallader Colden
1761 Robert Monckton
1761 Cadwallader Colden
1765 Henry Moore
1769 Cadwallader Colden
1770 John Murray
1771 William Tryon
1777 George Clinton

NORTH CAROLINA

1663 William Drummond
1667 Samuel Stephens
1670 Peter Carteret
1673 John Jenkins
1676 Thomas Eastchurch
1677 Thomas Miller
1677 John Culpeper
1678 Seth Sothell
1679 John Harvey
1679 John Jenkins
1682 Seth Sothell
1689 Philip Ludwell
1691 Thomas Jarvis
1694 John Archdale
1694 John Harvey
1699 Henderson Walker
1704 Robert Daniel
1705 Thomas Cary
1706 William Glover
1708 Thomas Cary
1710 Edward Hyde
1712 Thomas Pollock
1714 Charles Eden
1722 Thomas Pollock
1722 William Reed

1724 George Burrington
1725 Richard Everard
1731 George Burrington
1734 Gabriel Johnston
1752 Nathaniel Rice
1752 Matthew Rowan
1754 Arthur Dobbs
1765 William Tryon
1771 Josiah Martin
1776 Richard Caswell
1779 Abner Nash
1781 Thomas Burke
1782 Alexander Martin
1784 Richard Caswell
1787 Samuel Johnston

PENNSYLVANIA

1681 William Markham
1682 William Penn
1684 Thomas Lloyd
1688 (Five Commissioners)
1688 John Blackwell
1690 Thomas Lloyd
1691 William Markham
1693 Benjamin Fletcher
1695 William Markham
1699 William Penn
1701 Andrew Hamilton
1703 Edward Shippen
1704 John Evans
1709 Charles Gookin
1717 William Keith
1726 Patrick Gordon
1736 James Logan
1738 George Thomas
1747 Anthony Palmer
1748 James Hamilton
1754 Robert Hunter Morris
1756 William Denny
1759 James Hamilton
1763 John Penn
1771 Richard Penn
1773 John Penn
1776 Thomas Wharton
1778 George Ryan
1778 Joseph Reed
1781 William Moore
1782 John Dickinson
1785 Benjamin Franklin
1788 Thomas Mifflin

RHODE ISLAND

1640 William Coddington
1647 John Coggeshall
1648 Jeremy Clarke
1649 Roger Williams (Acting)
1649 John Smith
1650 Nicholas Easton
1651 William Coddington
1652 John Smith
1653 Gregory Dexter
1654 Nicholas Easton
1654 Roger Williams
1657 Benedict Arnold
1660 William Brenton
1662 Benedict Arnold
1666 William Brenton
1669 Benedict Arnold
1672 Nicholas Easton
1674 William Coddington
1676 Walter Clarke
1677 Benedict Arnold
1678 William Coddington
1678 John Cranston
1680 Peleg Sanford
1683 William Coddington, Jr.
1685 Henry Bull
1686 Walter Clarke
1686 (Charter Suspended)
1689 John Coggeshall, Jr.
1690 Henry Bull
1690 John Easton
1695 Caleb Carr
1696 Walter Clarke
1698 Samuel Cranston
1727 Joseph Jenckes
1732 William Wanton
1733 John Wanton
1740 Richard Ward
1743 William Greene
1745 Gideon Wanton
1746 William Greene
1747 Gideon Wanton
1748 William Greene
1755 Stephen Hopkins
1757 William Greene
1758 Stephen Hopkins
1762 Samuel Ward
1763 Stephen Hopkins
1765 Samuel Ward
1767 Stephen Hopkins
1768 Josias Lyndon
1769 Joseph Wanton
1775 Nicholas Cooke
1778 William Greene
1786 John Collins

SOUTH CAROLINA

1669 William Sayle
1672 John Yeamans
1674 Joseph West
1682 Joseph Morton
1684 Sir Richard Kyrle
1684 Robert Quarry
1685 Joseph West
1685 Joseph Morton
1686 James Colleton
1689 Thomas Smith
1690 John Sothell
1691 Philip Ludwell
1693 Thomas Smith
1694 Joseph Blake
1695 John Archdale
1696 Joseph Blake
1700 James Moore
1703 Nathaniel Johnson
1708 Edward Tynte
1709 Robert Gibbes
1712 Charles Craven
1716 Robert Daniel
1717 Robert Johnson
1719 James Moore
1721 Francis Nicholson
1725 Arthur Middleton
1731 Robert Johnson
1735 Thomas Broughton
1737 William Bull
1743 James Glen
1756 William H. Lyttleton
1760 William Bull
1761 Thomas Boone
1764 William Bull
1766 Charles G. Montagu
1768 William Bull
1768 Charles G. Montagu
1769 William Bull
1771 Charles G. Montagu
1773 William Bull
1775 William Campbell
1776 John Rutledge
1778 Rawlins Lowndes
1779 John Rutledge
1782 John Mathews
1783 Benjamin Guerrard
1785 William Moultrie
1787 Thomas Pinckney

VERMONT

1778 Thomas Chittenden
1789 Moses Robinson
1790 Thomas Chittenden

VIRGINIA

1607 Edward M. Wingfield
1607 John Ratcliffe
1608 John Smith
1609 George Percy
1610 Thomas Gates
1611 George Percy
1611 Thomas Dale
1611 Thomas Gates
1614 Thomas Dale
1616 George Yeardley
1617 Samuel Argall
1619 George Yeardley
1621 Francis Wyatt
1626 George Yeardley
1627 Francis West
1629 John Pott
1630 John Harvey
1635 John West
1636 John Harvey
1639 Francis Wyatt
1642 William Berkeley
1644 Richard Kemp
1645 William Berkeley
1652 Richard Bennett
1655 Edward Digges
1657 Sameul Matthews
1660 William Berkeley
1661 Francis Moryson
1662 William Berkeley
1677 Herbert Jeffreys
1678 Henry Chichley
1680 Thomas Colepepper
1683 Nicholas Spencer
1684 Francis Howard
1688 Nathaniel Bacon
1690 Francis Nicholson
1693 Edmund Andros
1698 Francis Nicholson
1705 Edward Nott
1706 Edmund Jennings
1710 Alexander Spotswood
1722 Hugh Drysdale
1726 Robert Carter
1727 William Gooch
1740 James Blair
1741 William Gooch
1749 John Robinson
1749 Thomas Lee
1750 Lewis Burwell
1751 Robert Dinwiddie
1758 John Blair
1758 Francis Fauquier
1768 John Blair
1768 Norborne Berkeley
1770 William Nelson
1771 John Murray
1776 Patrick Henry
1779 Thomas Jefferson
1781 Thomas Nelson, Jr.
1782 Benjamin Harrison
1784 Patrick Henry
1786 Edmund Randolph
1788 Beverly Randolph

COLONIAL CHIEF JUSTICES

CONNECTICUT

1711 Gurdon Saltonstall
1712 Nathan Gold
1713 William Pitkin
1714 Nathan Gold
1723 Peter Burr
1725 Jonathan Law
1741 Roger Wolcott
1750 Thomas Fitch
1754 William Pitkin
1766 Jonathan Trumbull
1769 Matthew Griswold
1784 Samuel Huntington
1785 Richard Law

DELAWARE

1776 William Killen

MARYLAND

1778 Benjamin Rumsey

MASSACHUSETTS

Massachusetts Bay Colony

1692 William Stoughton
1701 Waitsill Winthrop
1702 Isaac Addington
1708 Waitsill Winthrop
1718 Samuel Sewall
1729 Benjamin Lynde
1745 Paul Dudley
1753 Stephen Sewall
1761 Thomas Hutchinson
1769 Benjamin Lynde
1772 Peter Oliver
1775 John Adams
1777 William Cushing

Commonwealth of Massachusetts

1780 William Cushing

NEW JERSEY

1702 Roger Mompesson
1709 Thomas Gordon
1710 David Jamison
1723 William Trent
1724 Robert L. Hooper
1728 Thomas Farmer
1738 Robert Hunter Morris
1758 William Aynsley
1764 Charles Read
1764 Frederick Smyth
1777 Robert Morris
1779 David Brearley

NEW YORK

1691 Joseph Dudley
1692 William Smith
1700 Stephanus Van Cortlandt
1701 Abraham DePeyster
1701 William Attwood
1702 William Smith
1703 John Bridges
1704 Roger Mompesson
1715 Lewis Morris
1733 James Delancey
1761 Benjamin Pratt
1763 Daniel Horsmanden
1777 John Jay
1789 Richard Morris

PENNSYLVANIA

1778 Thomas McKean

RHODE ISLAND

1747 Gideon Cornell
1749 Joshua Babcock
1751 Stephen Hopkins
1755 Francis Willett
1755 Stephen Hopkins
1756 John Gardner
1761 Samuel Ward
1762 Jeremiah Niles
1763 Joshua Babcock
1764 John Cole
1765 Joseph Russell
1767 James Helm
1768 Joseph Russell
1769 James Helm
1770 Stephen Hopkins
1776 Metcalf Bowler
1777 William Greene
1778 Shearjashub Bourne
1781 Jabez Bowen
1781 Paul Mumford
1785 William Ellery
1786 Paul Mumford
1788 Othniel Gorton

SOUTH CAROLINA

1779 William H. Drayton

VERMONT

1778 Moses Robinson
1782 Paul Spooner
1784 Moses Robinson
1785 Nathaniel Chipman

VIRGINIA
(Presient, Court of Appeals)

1779 Edmund Pendleton

II

THE UNITED STATES GOVERNMENT: EXECUTIVE BRANCH

Presidents and Vice Presidents of the United States of America, Presidential and Vice Presidential candidates, and First Ladies.

PRESIDENTS OF THE UNITED STATES

		DATE OF BIRTH	POLITICS	INAUG.	STATE	RELIGION	DATE OF DEATH	PLACE OF BURIAL
1.	George Washington	Feb. 22, 1732	Fed.	1789	Va.	Episcopalian	Dec. 14, 1799	Mount Vernon, Va.
2.	John Adams	Oct. 30, 1735	Fed.	1797	Mass.	Unitarian	July 4, 1826	Quincy, Mass.
3.	Thomas Jefferson	Apr. 13, 1743	Dem-Rep	1801	Va.	Unitarian	July 4, 1826	Charlottesville, Va.
4.	James Madison	Mar. 16, 1751	Dem-Rep	1809	Va.	Episcopalian	June 28, 1836	Montpelier Station, Va.
5.	James Monroe	Apr. 28, 1758	Dem-Rep	1817	Va.	Episcopalian	June 4, 1831	Richmond, Va.
6.	John Quincy Adams	July 11, 1767	Dem-Rep	1825	Mass.	Unitarian	Feb. 23, 1848	Quincy, Mass.
7.	Andrew Jackson	Mar. 15, 1767	Dem.	1829	Tenn.	Presbyterian	June 8, 1845	Nashville, Tenn.
8.	Martin Van Buren	Dec. 5, 1782	Dem.	1837	N.Y.	Dutch Reformed	July 24, 1862	Kinderhook, N.Y.
9.	William Henry Harrison	Feb. 9, 1773	Whig	1841	Ohio	Episcopalian	Apr. 4, 1841	North Bend, Ohio
10.	John Tyler	Mar. 29, 1790	Whig	1841	Va.	Episcopalian	Jan. 18, 1862	Richmond, Va.
11.	James K. Polk	Nov. 1, 1795	Dem.	1845	Tenn.	Presbyterian	Jan. 15, 1849	Nashville, Tenn.
12.	Zachary Taylor	Nov. 24, 1784	Whig	1849	La.	Episcopalian	July 9, 1850	Louisville, Ky.
13.	Millard Fillmore	Jan. 7, 1800	Whig	1850	N.Y.	Episcopalian	Mar. 8, 1874	Buffalo, N.Y.
14.	Franklin Pierce	Nov. 23, 1804	Dem.	1853	N.H.	Episcopalian	Oct. 8, 1869	Concord, N.H.
15.	James Buchanan	Apr. 23, 1791	Dem.	1857	Pa.	Presbyterian	June 1, 1868	Lancaster, Pa.
16.	Abraham Lincoln	Feb. 12, 1809	Rep.	1861	Ill.	Unaffiliated	Apr. 15, 1865	Springfield, Ill.
17.	Andrew Johnson	Dec. 29, 1808	Dem.	1865	Tenn.	Methodist	July 31, 1875	Greenville, Tenn.
18.	Ulysses S. Grant	Apr. 27, 1822	Rep.	1869	Ohio	Methodist	July 23, 1885	New York, N.Y.
19.	Rutherford B. Hayes	Oct. 4, 1822	Rep.	1877	Ohio	Methodist	Jan. 17, 1893	Fremont, Ohio
20.	James A. Garfield	Nov. 19, 1831	Rep.	1881	Ohio	Disciples of Christ	Sept. 19, 1881	Cleveland, Ohio
21.	Chester A. Arthur	Oct. 5, 1830	Rep.	1881	N.Y.	Episcopalian	Nov. 18, 1886	Albany, N.Y.
22.	Grover Cleveland	Mar. 18, 1837	Dem.	1885	N.Y.	Presbyterian	June 24, 1908	Princeton, N.J.
23.	Benjamin Harrison	Aug. 20, 1833	Rep.	1889	Ind.	Presbyterian	Mar. 13, 1901	Indianapolis, Ind.
24.	Grover Cleveland	Mar. 18, 1837	Dem.	1893	N.Y.	Presbyterian	June 24, 1908	Princeton, N.J.
25.	William McKinley	Jan. 29, 1843	Rep.	1897	Ohio	Methodist	Sept. 14, 1901	Canton, Ohio
26.	Theodore Roosevelt	Oct. 27, 1858	Rep.	1901	N.Y.	Dutch Reformed	Jan. 6, 1919	Oyster Bay, N.Y.
27.	William Howard Taft	Sept. 15, 1857	Rep.	1909	Ohio	Unitarian	Mar. 8, 1930	Arlington, Va.
28.	Woodrow Wilson	Dec. 28, 1856	Dem.	1913	N.J.	Presbyterian	Feb. 3, 1924	Washington, D.C.
29.	Warren G. Harding	Nov. 2, 1865	Rep.	1921	Ohio	Presbyterian	Aug. 1, 1923	Marion, Ohio
30.	Calvin Coolidge	July 4, 1872	Rep.	1923	Mass.	Congregationalist	Jan. 5, 1933	Plymouth, Mass.
31.	Herbert Hoover	Aug. 10, 1874	Rep.	1929	Calif.	Society of Friends	Oct. 20, 1964	West Branch, Iowa
32	Franklin D. Roosevelt	Jan. 30, 1882	Dem.	1933	N.Y.	Episcopalian	Apr. 12, 1945	Hyde Park, N.Y.
33.	Harry S Truman	May 8, 1884	Dem.	1945	Mo.	Baptist	Dec. 26, 1972	Independence, Mo.
34.	Dwight D. Eisenhower	Oct. 14, 1890	Rep.	1953	Kansas	Presbyterian	Mar. 28, 1969	Abilene, Kansas
35.	John F. Kennedy	May 29, 1917	Dem.	1961	Mass.	Catholic	Nov. 22, 1963	Arlington, Va.
36.	Lyndon B. Johnson	Aug. 27, 1908	Dem.	1963	Texas	Disciples of Christ	Jan. 22, 1973	Johnson City, Texas
37.	Richard M. Nixon	Jan. 9, 1913	Rep.	1969	Calif.	Society of Friends		

VICE PRESIDENTS OF THE UNITED STATES

		DATE OF BIRTH	STATE	POLITICS	TERM	PRESIDENT	DATE OF DEATH
1.	John Adams	Oct. 30, 1735	Mass.	Fed.	1789-1797	Washington	July 4, 1826
2.	Thomas Jefferson	Apr. 13, 1743	Va.	Dem-Rep	1797-1801	Adams	July 4, 1826
3.	Aaron Burr	Feb. 6, 1756	N.Y.	Dem-Rep	1801-1805	Jefferson	Sept. 14, 1836
4.	George Clinton	July 26, 1739	N.Y.	Dem-Rep	1805-1812	Jefferson, Madison	Apr. 20, 1812
5.	Elbridge Gerry	July 17, 1744	Mass.	Dem-Rep	1813-1814	Madison	Nov. 23, 1814
6.	Daniel D. Tompkins	June 21, 1774	N.Y.	Dem-Rep	1817-1825	Monroe	June 11, 1825
7.	John C. Calhoun	Mar. 18, 1782	S.C.	Dem.	1825-1832	J.Q. Adams, Jackson	Mar. 31, 1850
8.	Martin Van Buren	Dec. 5, 1782	N.Y.	Dem.	1833-1837	Jackson	July 24, 1862
9.	Richard M. Johnson	Oct. 17, 1781	Ky.	Dem.	1837-1841	Van Buren	Nov. 19, 1850
10.	John Tyler	Mar. 29, 1790	Va.	Whig	1841	W.H. Harrison	Jan. 18, 1862
11.	George M. Dallas	July 10, 1792	Pa.	Dem.	1845-1849	Polk	Nov. 31, 1864
12.	Millard Fillmore	Jan. 7, 1800	N.Y.	Whig	1849-1850	Taylor	Mar. 8, 1874
13.	William R. King	Apr. 7, 1786	Ala.	Dem.	1853	Pierce	Apr. 18, 1853
14.	John C. Breckinridge	Jan. 21, 1821	Ky.	Dem.	1857-1816	Buchanan	May 17, 1875
15.	Hannibal Hamlin	Aug. 27, 1809	Maine	Rep.	1861-1865	Lincoln	July 4, 1891
16.	Andrew Johnson	Dec. 29, 1808	Tenn.	Dem.	1865	Lincoln	July 31, 1875
17.	Schuyler Colfax	Mar. 23, 1823	Ind.	Rep.	1869-1873	Grant	Jan. 13, 1885
18.	Henry Wilson	Feb. 16, 1812	Mass.	Rep.	1873-1875	Grant	Nov. 22, 1875
19.	William A. Wheeler	June 19, 1819	N.Y.	Rep.	1877-1881	Hayes	June 4, 1887
20.	Chester A. Arthur	Oct. 5, 1830	N.Y.	Rep.	1881	Garfield	Nov. 18, 1886
21.	Thomas A. Hendricks	Sept. 7, 1819	Ind.	Dem.	1885	Cleveland	Nov. 25, 1885
22.	Levi P. Morton	May 16, 1824	N.Y.	Rep.	1889-1893	B. Harrison	May 16, 1920
23.	Adlai E. Stevenson	Oct. 23, 1835	Ill.	Dem.	1893-1897	Cleveland	June 14, 1914
24.	Garret A. Hobart	June 3, 1844	N.J.	Rep.	1897-1899	McKinley	Nov. 21, 1899
25.	Theodore Roosevelt	Oct. 27, 1858	N.Y.	Rep.	1901	McKinley	Jan. 16, 1919
26.	Charles W. Fairbanks	May 11, 1852	Ind.	Rep.	1905-1909	T. Roosevelt	June 4, 1918
27	James S. Sherman	Oct. 24, 1855	N.Y.	Rep.	1909-1912	Taft	Oct. 30, 1912
28.	Thomas R. Marshall	Mar. 14, 1854	Ind.	Dem.	1913-1921	Wilson	June 1, 1925
29.	Calvin Coolidge	July 4, 1872	Mass.	Rep.	1921-1923	Harding	Jan. 5, 1933
30.	Charles G. Dawes	Aug. 27, 1865	Ill.	Rep.	1925-1929	Coolidge	Apr. 23, 1951
31.	Charles Curtis	Jan. 25, 1860	Kansas	Rep.	1929-1933	Hoover	Feb. 8, 1936
32.	John Nance Garner	Nov. 22, 1868	Texas	Dem.	1933-1941	F.D. Roosevelt	Nov. 7, 1967
33.	Henry A. Wallace	Oct. 7, 1888	Iowa	Dem.	1941-1945	F.D. Roosevelt	Nov. 18, 1965
34.	Harry S Truman	May 8, 1884	Mo.	Dem.	1945	F.D. Roosevelt	Dec. 26, 1972
35.	Alben W. Barkley	Nov. 24, 1877	Ky.	Dem.	1949-1953	Truman	Apr. 30, 1956
36.	Richard M. Nixon	Jan. 9, 1913	Calif.	Rep.	1953-1961	Eisenhower	
37.	Lyndon B. Johnson	Aug. 27, 1908	Texas	Dem.	1961-1963	Kennedy	Jan. 22, 1973
38.	Hubert H. Humphrey	May 27, 1911	Minn.	Dem.	1965-1969	L.B. Johnson	
39.	Spiro T. Agnew	Nov. 9, 1918	Md.	Rep.	1969	Nixon	

PRESIDENTIAL AND VICE PRESIDENTIAL CANDIDATES

CANDIDATES	PARTY	ELECTORAL VOTE	CANDIDATES	PARTY	ELECTORAL VOTE
	1789 Election			*1796 Election*	
George Washington		69	John Adams	Federalist	71
John Adams		34	Thomas Jefferson	Dem-Rep	68
John Jay		9	Thomas Pinckney	Federalist	59
Robert H. Harrison		6	Aaron Burr	Dem-Rep	30
John Rutledge		6	Samuel Adams		15
John Hancock		4	Oliver Ellsworth		11
George Clinton		3	George Clinton		7
Samuel Huntington		2	John Jay		5
John Milton		2	James Iredell		3
John Armstrong		1	John Henry		2
Benjamin Lincoln		1	Samuel Johnston		2
Edward Telfair		1	George Washington	Federalist	2
			Charles C. Pinckney		1
	1792 Election			*1800 Election*	
George Washington	Federalist	132	Thomas Jefferson	Dem-Rep	73
John Adams	Federalist	77	Aaron Burr	Dem-Rep	73
George Clinton	Anti-Federalist	50	John Adams	Federalist	65
Thomas Jefferson	Anti-Federalist	4	Charles C. Pinckney	Federalist	64
Aaron Burr	Anti-Federalist	1	John Jay	Federalist	1

Until 1804 each elector voted for two candidates for President. The one who received the largest number of votes was declared President, and the one who received the next largest number of votes was declared Vice President.

CANDIDATES	PARTY	ELECTORAL VOTE	CANDIDATES	PARTY	ELECTORAL VOTE
		1804 Election			
Thomas Jefferson	Dem-Rep	162	George Clinton	Dem-Rep	162
Charles C. Pinckney	Federalist	14	Rufus King	Federalist	14
		1808 Election			
James Madison	Dem-Rep	122	George Clinton	Dem-Rep	113
Charles C. Pinckney	Federalist	47	Rufus King	Federalist	47
George Clinton	Dem-Rep	6	John Langdon		9
			James Madison	Dem-Rep	3
			James Monroe	Dem-Rep	3
		1812 Election			
James Madison	Dem-Rep	128	Elbridge Gerry	Dem-Rep	131
De Witt Clinton	Federalist	89	Jared Ingersoll	Federalist	86
		1816 Election			
James Monroe	Dem-Rep	231	Daniel D. Tompkins	Dem-Rep	183
Rufus King	Federalist	34	John E. Howard	Federalist	22
			James Ross		5
			John Marshall	Federalist	4
			Robert G. Harper		3
		1820 Election			
James Monroe	Dem-Rep	231	Daniel D. Tompkins	Dem-Rep	218
John Quincy Adams	Dem-Rep	1	Richard Stockton		8
			Daniel Rodney		4
			Robert G. Harper		1
			Richard Rush		1

Candidate	Party	Votes	Vice-Presidential Candidate	Party	Votes
1824 Election					
Andrew Jackson		99	John C. Calhoun		182
John Quincy Adams		84	Nathan Sanford		30
William H. Crawford		41	Nathaniel Macon		24
Henry Clay		37	Andrew Jackson		13
			Martin Van Buren		9
			Henry Clay		2
1828 Election					
Andrew Jackson	Democrat	178	John C. Calhoun	Democrat	171
John Quincy Adams	Republican	83	Richard Rush	Republican	83
			William Smith		7
1832 Election					
Andrew Jackson	Democrat	219	Martin Van Buren	Democrat	189
Henry Clay	Republican	49	John Sergeant	Republican	49
John Floyd		11	William Wilkins		30
William Wirt	Anti-Masonic	7	Henry Lee		11
			Amos Ellmaker	Anti-Masonic	7
1836 Election					
Martin Van Buren	Democrat	170	Richard M. Johnson	Democrat	147
William Henry Harrison	Whig	73	Francis Granger	Whig	77
Hugh L. White	Whig	26	John Tyler	Whig	47
Daniel Webster	Whig	14	William Smith		23
Willie P. Mangum		11			
1840 Election					
William H. Harrison	Whig	234	John Tyler	Whig	234
Martin Van Buren	Democrat	60	Richard M. Johnson	Democrat	48
			Littleton W. Tazewell		11
			James K. Polk	Democrat	1
1844 Election					
James K. Polk	Democrat	170	George M. Dallas	Democrat	170
Henry Clay	Whig	105	Theodore Frelinghuysen	Republican	105
1848 Election					
Zachary Taylor	Whig	163	Millard Fillmore	Whig	163
Lewis Cass	Democrat	127	William O. Butler	Democrat	127
1852 Election					
Franklin Pierce	Democrat	254	William R. King	Democrat	254
Winfield Scott	Whig	42	William A. Graham	Whig	42
1856 Election					
James Buchanan	Democrat	174	John C. Breckinridge	Democrat	174
John C. Fremont	Republican	114	William L. Dayton	Republican	14
Millard Fillmore	American	8	Andrew J. Donelson	American	8
1860 Election					
Abraham Lincoln	Republican	180	Hannibal Hamlin	Republican	180
John C. Breckinridge	Democrat	72	Joseph Lane	Democrat	72
John Bell	Unionist	39	Edward Everett	Unionist	39
Stephen A. Douglas	Democrat	12	Herschel V. Johnson	Democrat	12
1864 Election					
Abraham Lincoln	Unionist	212	Andrew Johnson	Unionist	212
George B. McClellan	Democrat	21	George H. Pendleton	Democrat	21
1868 Election					
Ulysses S. Grant	Republican	214	Schuyler Colfax	Republican	214
Horatio Seymour	Democrat	80	Francis P. Blair, Jr.	Democrat	80

1872 Election

Presidential Candidate	Party	Electoral Votes	Vice-Presidential Candidate	Party	Electoral Votes
Ulysses S. Grant	Republican	286	Henry Wilson	Republican	286
Horace Greeley	Dem., Liberal	8	G. Gratz Brown	Dem., Liberal	47
Thomas A. Hendricks	Democrat	42	George W. Julian		5
B. Gratz Brown	Dem., Liberal	18	Alfred H. Colquitt		5
Charles J. Jenkins	Democrat	2	John M. Palmer		3
David Davis	Democrat	1	Thomas E. Bramlette		3
			Nathaniel P. Banks		1
			William S. Groesbeck		1
			Willis B. Machen		1

1876 Election

Presidential Candidate	Party	Electoral Votes	Vice-Presidential Candidate	Party	Electoral Votes
Rutherford B. Hayes	Republican	185	William A. Wheeler	Republican	185
Samuel J. Tilden	Democrat	184	Thomas A. Hendricks	Democrat	184
Peter Cooper	Greenbeck		Samuel F. Cary	Greenback	

1880 Election

Presidential Candidate	Party	Electoral Votes	Vice-Presidential Candidate	Party	Electoral Votes
James A. Garfield	Republican	214	Chester A. Arthur	Republican	214
Winfield S. Hancock	Democrat	155	William H. English	Democrat	155
James B. Weaver	Greenback		B.J. Chambers	Greenback	

1884 Election

Presidential Candidate	Party	Electoral Votes	Vice-Presidential Candidate	Party	Electoral Votes
Grover Cleveland	Democrat	219	Thomas A. Hendricks	Democrat	219
James G. Blaine	Republican	182	John A. Logan	Republican	182
Benjamin F. Butler	Greenback		A.M. West	Greenback	
John P. St. John	Prohibitionist		William Daniel	Prohibitionist	

1888 Election

Presidential Candidate	Party	Electoral Votes	Vice-Presidential Candidate	Party	Electoral Votes
Benjamin Harrison	Republican	233	Levi P. Morton	Republican	233
Grover Cleveland	Democrat	168	Allen Thurman	Democrat	168
Clinton B. Fisk	Prohibitionist		John A. Brooks	Prohibitionist	
Alson J. Streeter	Union-Labor		Charles E. Cunningham	Union-Labor	

1892 Election

Presidential Candidate	Party	Electoral Votes	Vice-Presidential Candidate	Party	Electoral Votes
Grover Cleveland	Democrat	277	Adlai E. Stevenson	Democrat	277
Benjamin Harrison	Republican	145	Whitelaw Reid	Republican	145
James B. Weaver	People's	22	James G. Field	People's	22
John Bidwell	Prohibitionist		James B. Cranfill	Prohibitionist	

1896 Election

Presidential Candidate	Party	Electoral Votes	Vice-Presidential Candidate	Party	Electoral Votes
William McKinley	Republican	271	Garret A. Hobart	Republican	271
William Jennings Bryan	Dem., People's	176	Arthur Sewall	Democrat	149
John M. Palmer	Democrat		Thomas E. Watson	People's	27
Joshua Levering	Prohibitionist		Simon B. Buckner	Democrat	
			Hale Johnson	Prohibitionist	

1900 Election

Presidential Candidate	Party	Electoral Votes	Vice-Presidential Candidate	Party	Electoral Votes
William McKinley	Republican	292	Theodore Roosevelt	Republican	292
William Jennings Bryan	Dem., People's	155	Adlai E. Stevenson	Democrat	155
John G. Wolley	Prohibitionist		Henry B. Metcalf	Prohibitionist	
Eugene V. Debs	Socialist		Job Harriman	Socialist	

1904 Election

Presidential Candidate	Party	Electoral Votes	Vice-Presidential Candidate	Party	Electoral Votes
Theodore Roosevelt	Republican	336	Charles W. Fairbanks	Republican	336
Alton B. Parker	Democrat	140	Henry G. Davis	Democrat	140
Eugene V. Debs	Socialist		Benjamin Hanford	Socialist	
Silas C. Swallow	Prohibitionist		George W. Carroll	Prohibitionist	
Thomas E. Watson	People's		Thomas H. Tibbles	People's	

1908 Election

Presidential Candidate	Party	Electoral Votes	Vice-Presidential Candidate	Party	Electoral Votes
William Howard Taft	Republican	321	James S. Sherman	Republican	321
William Jennings Bryan	Democrat	162	John W. Kern	Democrat	162
Eugene V. Debs	Socialist		Benjamin Hanford	Socialist	
Eugene W. Chafin	Prohibitionist		Aaron S. Watkins	Prohibitionist	

1912 Election

Woodrow Wilson	Democrat	435	Thomas R. Marshall	Democrat	435
Theodore Roosevelt	Progressive	88	Hiram W. Johnson	Progressive	88
William Howard Taft	Republican	8	Nicholas Murray Butler	Republican	8
Eugene V. Debs	Socialist		Emil Seidel	Socialist	
Eugene W. Chafin	Prohibitionist		Aaron S. Watkins	Prohibitionist	

1916 Election

Woodrow Wilson	Democrat	277	Thomas R. Marshall	Democrat	277
Charles Evans Hughes	Republican	254	Charles W. Fairbanks	Republican	254
A.L. Benson	Socialist		G.R. Kirkpatrick	Socialist	
J. Frank Hanly	Prohibitionist		Ira Landrith	Prohibitionist	

1920 Election

Warren G. Harding	Republican	404	Calvin Coolidge	Republican	404
James M. Cox	Democrat	127	Franklin D. Roosevelt	Democrat	127
Eugene V. Debs	Socialist		Seymour Stedman	Socialist	
P.P. Christensen	Farm-Labor		Max S. Hayes	Farm-Labor	
Aaron S. Watkins	Prohibitionist		D. Leigh Colvin	Prohibitionist	

1924 Election

Calvin Coolidge	Republican	382	Charles G. Dawes	Republican	382
John W. Davis	Democrat	136	Charles W. Bryan	Democrat	136
Robert M. La Follette	Progressive	13	Burton K. Wheeler	Progressive	13

1928 Election

Herbert Hoover	Republican	444	Charles Curtis	Republican	444
Alfred E. Smith	Democrat	87	Joseph T. Robinson	Democrat	87

1932 Election

Franklin D. Roosevelt	Democrat	472	John Nance Garner	Democrat	472
Herbert Hoover	Republican	59	Charles Curtis	Republican	59

1936 Election

Franklin D. Roosevelt	Democrat	523	John Nance Garner	Democrat	523
Alfred M. Landon	Republican	8	Frank Knox	Republican	8

1940 Election

Franklin D. Roosevelt	Democrat	449	Henry A. Wallace	Democrat	449
Wendell L. Willkie	Republican	82	Charles L. McNary	Republican	82

1944 Election

Franklin D. Roosevelt	Democrat	432	Harry S Truman	Democrat	432
Thomas E. Dewey	Republican	99	John W. Bricker	Republican	99

1948 Election

Harry S Truman	Democrat	303	Alben W. Barkley	Democrat	303
Thomas E. Dewey	Republican	189	Earl Warren	Republican	189
J. Strom Thurmond	States' Rights Dem.	39	Fielding L. Wright	States' Rights Dem.	39
Henry A. Wallace	Progressive		Glen Taylor	Progressive	

1952 Election

Dwight D. Eisenhower	Republican	442	Richard M. Nixon	Republican	442
Adlai E. Stevenson	Democrat	89	John J. Sparkman	Democrat	89

1956 Election

Dwight D. Eisenhower	Republican	457	Richard M. Nixon	Republican	457
Adlai E. Stevenson	Democrat	73	Estes Kefauver	Democrat	73
Walter B. Jones		1			

1960 Election

John F. Kennedy	Democrat	303	Lyndon B. Johnson	Democrat	303
Richard M. Nixon	Republican	219	Henry Cabot Lodge	Republican	219
Harry F. Byrd		15			

1964 Election

Lyndon B. Johnson	Democrat	486	Hubert J. Humphrey	Democrat	486
Barry M. Goldwater	Republican	52	William E. Miller	Republican	52

1968 Election

Richard M. Nixon	Republican	301	Spiro T. Agnew	Republican	301
Hubert H. Humphrey	Democrat	191	Edmund S. Muskie	Democrat	191
George C. Wallace			Curtis E. LeMay	Amer. Independent	46

1972 Election

Richard M. Nixon	Republican	521	Spiro T. Agnew	Republican	521
George S. McGovern	Democrat	14	R. Sargent Shriver	Democrat	14

FIRST LADIES

(The presidential first lady may be his wife or, if he is not married, any other woman he chooses to be the official hostess.)

1789-1797	Martha (Dandridge) Curtis, wife of George Washington
1797-1801	Abigail Smith, wife of John Adams
1801-1809	Martha (Wayles) Skelton, wife of Thomas Jefferson
1809-1817	Dolly [Dorothea] (Payne) Todd, wife of James Madison
1817-1825	Elizabeth Kortwright, wife of James Monroe
1825-1829	Louisa Catherine Johnson, wife of John Quincy Adams
1829-1837	Rachel (Donelson) Robards, wife of Andrew Jackson
1837-1841	Hanna Hoes, wife of Martin Van Buren
1841	Anna Tuthill Symmes, wife of William Henry Harrison
1841-1842	Letitia Christian, wife of John Tyler
1842-1844	Priscilla Cooper Tyler, daughter-in-law of John Tyler
1844-1845	Julia Gardiner, wife of John Tyler
1845-1849	Sarah Childress, wife of James Knox Polk
1849-1850	Margaret Mackall Smith, wife of Zachary Taylor
1850-1853	Abigail Powers, wife of Millard Fillmore
1853-1857	Janes Means Appleton, wife of Franklin Pierce
1857-1861	Harriet Lane, niece of James Buchanan
1861-1865	Mary Ann Todd, wife of Abraham Lincoln
1865-1869	Eliza McCardle, wife of Andrew Johnson
1869-1877	Julia Boggs Dent, wife of Ulysses S. Grant
1877-1881	Lucy Ware Webb, wife of Rutherford B. Hayes
1881-	Lucretia Randolph, wife of James A. Garfield
1881-1885	Ellen Lewis Herndon, wife of Chester A. Arthur
1885-1889	Frances Folsom, wife of Grover Cleveland
1889-1892	Caroline Lavinia Scott, wife of Benjamin Harrison
1892-1893	Mary Scott [Lord] Dimmock, wife of Benjamin Harrison
1893-1897	Frances Folsom, wife of Grover Cleveland
1897-1901	Ida Saxton, wife of William McKinley
1901-1909	Edith Kermit Carow, wife of Theodore Roosevelt
1909-1913	Helen Herron, wife of William Howard Taft
1913-1914	Ellen Louise Axson, wife of Woodrow Wilson
1914-1915	Helen Woodrow Bones, cousin of Woodrow Wilson
1915-1921	Edith Bolling Galt, wife of Woodrow Wilson
1921-1923	Florence (Kling) DeWolfe, wife of Warren G. Harding
1923-1929	Grace Goodhue, wife of Calvin Coolidge
1929-1933	Lou Henry, wife of Herbert C. Hoover
1933-1945	Eleanor Roosevelt, wife of Franklin Delano Roosevelt
1945-1953	Bess [Elizabeth Virginia] Wallace, wife of Harry S Truman
1953-1961	Mamie Geneva Doud, wife of Dwight David Eisenhower
1961-1963	Jacqueline Lee Bouvier, wife of John F. Kennedy
1963-1969	Lady Bird [Claudia Alta] Taylor, wife of Lyndon B. Johnson
1969-	Thelma Catherine Patricia Ryan, wife of Richard M. Nixon

CABINETS

A– Members listed by presidential term.

B– Members listed by departments. (First date indicates year department was established)

MEMBERS OF THE CABINET BY PRESIDENTIAL TERM

(Years in parentheses indicate tenure of officer; where no years are given, tenure coincides with Presidential term.)

1st PRESIDENTIAL TERM 1789-1793

President: George Washington
Vice President: John Adams

SECRETARY OF STATE	Thomas Jefferson (1790-1793)
SECRETARY OF THE TREASURY	Alexander Hamilton
SECRETARY OF WAR	Henry Knox
ATTORNEY GENERAL	Edmund Randolph (1790-1793)

2nd PRESIDENTIAL TERM 1793-1797

President: George Washington
Vice President: John Adams

SECRETARY OF STATE	Thomas Jefferson (1793-1794) Edmund Randolph (1794-1795) Timothy Pickering (1795-1797)
SECRETARY OF THE TREASURY	Alexander Hamilton (1793-1795) Oliver Wolcott, Jr. (1795-1797)
SECRETARY OF WAR	Henry Knox (1793-1795) Timothy Pickering (1795) James McHenry (1796-1797)
ATTORNEY GENERAL	Edmund Randolph (1793-1794) William Bradford (1794-1795) Charles Lee (1795-1797)

3rd PRESIDENTIAL TERM 1797-1801

President: John Adams
Vice President: Thomas Jefferson

SECRETARY OF STATE	Timothy Pickering (1797-1800) John Marshall (1800-1801)
SECRETARY OF THE TREASURY	Oliver Wolcott, Jr. (1797-1801) Samuel Dexter (1801)
SECRETARY OF WAR	James McHenry (1797-1800) Samuel Dexter (1800)
ATTORNEY GENERAL	Charles Lee
SECRETARY OF THE NAVY	Benjamin Stoddert (1798-1801)

4th PRESIDENTIAL TERM 1801-1805

President: Thomas Jefferson
Vice President: Aaron Burr

SECRETARY OF STATE	John Marshall (1801) James Madison (1801-1805)
SECRETARY OF THE TREASURY	Samuel Dexter (1801) Albert Gallatin (1801-1805)
SECRETARY OF WAR	Henry Dearborn
ATTORNEY GENERAL	Levi Lincoln
SECRETARY OF THE NAVY	Benjamin Stoddert (1801) Robert Smith (1801-1805)

5th PRESIDENTIAL TERM 1805-1809

President: Thomas Jefferson
Vice President: George Clinton

SECRETARY OF STATE	James Madison
SECRETARY OF THE TREASURY	Albert Gallatin
SECRETARY OF WAR	Henry Dearborn
ATTORNEY GENERAL	John Breckenridge (1805-1806) Caesar A. Rodney (1807-1809)
SECRETARY OF THE NAVY	Robert Smith

6th PRESIDENTIAL TERM 1809-1813

President: James Madison
Vice President: George Clinton (1809-1812)

SECRETARY OF STATE	Robert Smith (1809-1811) James Monroe (1811-1813)
SECRETARY OF THE TREASURY	Albert Gallatin
SECRETARY OF WAR	William Eustis (1809-1812) John Armstrong (1813)
ATTORNEY GENERAL	Caesar A. Rodney (1809-1811) William Pinkney (1811-1813)
SECRETARY OF THE NAVY	Robert Smith (1809) Paul Hamilton (1809-1812) William Jones (1813)

7th PRESIDENTIAL TERM 1813-1817

President: James Madison
Vice President: Eldridge Gerry (1813-1814)

SECRETARY OF STATE	James Monroe
SECRETARY OF THE TREASURY	Albert Gallatin (1813-1814) George W. Campbell (1814) Alexander J. Dallas (1814-1816) William H. Crawford (1816-1817)
SECRETARY OF WAR	John Armstrong (1813-1814) James Monroe (1814-1815) William H. Crawford (1815-1816)
ATTORNEY GENERAL	William Pinkney (1813-1814) Richard Rush (1814-1817)
SECRETARY OF THE NAVY	William Jones (1813-1814) Benjamin W. Crowninshield (1814-1817)

8th PRESIDENTIAL TERM 1817-1821

President: James Monroe
Vice President: Daniel D. Tompkins

SECRETARY OF STATE	John Quincy Adams
SECRETARY OF THE TREASURY	William H. Crawford
SECRETARY OF WAR	John C. Calhoun
ATTORNEY GENERAL	Richard Rush (1817) William Wirt (1817-1821)
SECRETARY OF THE NAVY	Benjamin W. Crowninshield (1817-1818) Smith Thompson (1818-1821)

9th PRESIDENTIAL TERM 1821-1825

President: James Monroe
Vice President: Daniel D. Tompkins

SECRETARY OF STATE	John Quincy Adams
SECRETARY OF THE TREASURY	William H. Crawford

SECRETARY OF WAR	John C. Calhoun
ATTORNEY GENERAL	William Wirt
SECRETARY OF THE NAVY	Smith Thompson (1821-1823) Samuel L. Southard (1823-1825)

10th PRESIDENTIAL TERM 1825-1829

President: John Quincy Adams
Vice President: John C. Calhoun

SECRETARY OF STATE	Henry Clay
SECRETARY OF THE TREASURY	Richard Rush
SECRETARY OF WAR	James Barbour (1825-1828) Peter B. Porter (1828-1829)
ATTORNEY GENERAL	William Wirt
SECRETARY OF THE NAVY	Samuel L. Southard

11th PRESIDENTIAL TERM 1829-1833

President: Andrew Jackson
Vice President: John C. Calhoun (1829-1832)

SECRETARY OF STATE	Martin Van Buren (1829-1831) Edward Livingston (1831-1833)
SECRETARY OF THE TREASURY	Samuel D. Ingham (1829-1831) Louis McLane (1831-1833)
SECRETARY OF WAR	John H. Eaton (1829-1831) Lewis Cass (1831-1833)
ATTORNEY GENERAL	John M. Berrien (1829-1831) Roger B. Taney (1831-1833)
POSTMASTER GENERAL	William T. Barry
SECRETARY OF THE NAVY	John Branch (1829-1831) Levi Woodbury (1831-1833)

12th PRESIDENTIAL TERM 1833-1837

President: Andrew Jackson
Vice President: Martin Van Buren

SECRETARY OF STATE	Edward Livingston (1833) Louis McLane (1833-1834) John Forsyth (1834-1837)
SECRETARY OF THE TREASURY	Louis McLane (1833) William Duane (1833) Roger B. Taney (1833-1834) Levi Woodbury (1834-1837)
SECRETARY OF WAR	Lewis Cass (1833-1836) Benjamin F. Butler (1836-1837)
ATTORNEY GENERAL	Roger B. Taney (1833) Benjamin F. Butler (1833-1837)
POSTMASTER GENERAL	William T. Barry (1833-1835) Amos Kendall (1835-1837)
SECRETARY OF THE NAVY	Levi Woodbury (1833-1834) Mahlon Dickerson (1834-1837)

13th PRESIDENTIAL TERM 1837-1841

President: Martin Van Buren
Vice President: Richard M. Johnson

SECRETARY OF STATE	John Forsyth
SECRETARY OF THE TREASURY	Levi Woodbury
SECRETARY OF WAR	Benjamin F. Butler (1837) Joel R. Poinsett (1837-1841)
ATTORNEY GENERAL	Benjamin F. Butler (1837-1838) Felix Grundy (1838-1840) Henry D. Gilpin (1840-1841)
POSTMASTER GENERAL	Amos Kendall (1837-1840) John M. Niles (1840-1841)
SECRETARY OF THE NAVY	Mahlon Dickerson (1837-1838) James K. Paulding (1838-1841)

14th PRESIDENTIAL TERM 1841-1845

President: William Henry Harrison (1841) John Tyler (1841-1845)
Vice President: John Tyler (1841)

SECRETARY OF STATE	Daniel Webster (1841-1843) Abel P. Upshur (1843-1844) John C. Calhoun (1844-1845)
SECRETARY OF THE TREASURY	Thomas Ewing (1841) Walter Forward (1841-1843) John C. Spencer (1843-1844) George M. Bibb (1844-1845)
SECRETARY OF WAR	John Bell (1841) John C. Spencer (1841-1843) James M. Porter (1843-1844) William Wilkins (1844-1845)
ATTORNEY GENERAL	John J. Crittenden (1841) Hugh S. Legare (1841-1843) John Nelson (1843-1845)
POSTMASTER GENERAL	Francis Granger (1841) Charles A. Wickliffe (1841-1845)
SECRETARY OF THE NAVY	George E. Badger (1841) Abel P. Upshur (1841-1843) David Henshaw (1843-1844) John Y. Mason (1844-1845)

15th PRESIDENTIAL TERM 1845-1849

President: James K. Polk
Vice President: George M. Dallas

SECRETARY OF STATE	John C. Calhoun (1845) James Buchanan (1845-1849)
SECRETARY OF THE TREASURY	George M. Bibb (1845) Robert J. Walker (1845-1849)
SECRETARY OF WAR	William Wilkins (1845) William L. Marcy (1845-1849)
ATTORNEY GENERAL	John Nelson (1845) John Y. Mason (1845-1846) Nathan Clifford (1846-1848) Isaac Toucey (1848-1849)
POSTMASTER GENERAL	Charles A. Wickliffe (1845) Cave Johnson (1845-1849)
SECRETARY OF THE NAVY	John Y. Mason (1845) George Bancroft (1845-1846) John Y. Mason (1846-1849)

16th PRESIDENTIAL TERM 1849-1853

President: Zachary Taylor (1849-1850) Millard Fillmore (1850-1853)
Vice President: Millard Fillmore (1849-1850)

SECRETARY OF STATE	James Buchanan (1848) John M. Clayton (1849-1850) Daniel Webster (1850-1852) Edward Everett (1852-1853)
SECRETARY OF THE TREASURY	Robert J. Walker (1849) William M. Meredith (1849-1850) Thomas Corwin (1850-1853)
SECRETARY OF WAR	William L. Marcy (1849) George W. Crawford (1849-1850) Charles M. Conrad (1850-1853)
ATTORNEY GENERAL	Isaac Toucey (1849) Reverdy Johnson (1849-1850) John J. Crittenden (1850-1853)
POSTMASTER GENERAL	Cave Johnson (1849) Jacob Collamer (1849-1850) Nathan K. Hall (1850-1852) Samuel D. Hubbard (1852-1853)
SECRETARY OF THE NAVY	John Y. Mason (1849) William B. Preston (1849-1850) William A. Graham (1850-1852) John P. Kennedy (1852-1853)
SECRETARY OF THE INTERIOR	Thomas Ewing (1849-1850) Thomas M.T. McKennan (1850) Alexander H.H. Stuart (1850-1853)

17th PRESIDENTIAL TERM 1853-1857

President: Franklin Pierce
Vice President: William R. King (1853)

SECRETARY OF STATE	William L. Marcy

SECRETARY OF THE TREASURY	Thomas Corwin (1853) James Guthrie (1853-1857)
SECRETARY OF WAR	Charles M. Conrad (1853) Jefferson Davis (1853-1857)
ATTORNEY GENERAL	John J. Crittenden (1853) Caleb Cushing (1853-1857)
POSTMASTER GENERAL	Samuel D. Hubbard (1853) James Campbell (1853-1857)
SECRETARY OF THE NAVY	John P. Kennedy (1853) James C. Dobbin (1853-1857)
SECRETARY OF THE INTERIOR	Alexander H.H. Stuart (1853) Robert McClelland (1853-1857)

18th PRESIDENTIAL TERM 1857-1861

President: James Buchanan
Vice President: John C. Breckinridge

SECRETARY OF STATE	William L. Marcy (1857) Lewis Cass (1857-1860) Jeremiah S. Black (1860-1861)
SECRETARY OF THE TREASURY	James Guthrie (1857) Howell Cobb (1857-1860) Philip F. Thomas (1860-1861) John A. Dix (1861)
SECRETARY OF WAR	John B. Floyd (1857-1861) Joseph Holt (1861)
ATTORNEY GENERAL	Caleb Cushing (1857) Jeremiah S. Black (1857-1860) Edwin M. Stanton (1860-1861)
POSTMASTER GENERAL	James Campbell (1857) Aaron V. Brown (1857-1859) Joseph Holt (1859-1860) Horatio King (1861)
SECRETARY OF THE NAVY	James C. Dobbin (1857) Isaac Toucey (1857-1861)
SECRETARY OF THE INTERIOR	Robert McClelland (1857) Jacob Thompson (1857-1861)

19th PRESIDENTIAL TERM 1861-1865

President: Abraham Lincoln
Vice President: Hannibal Hamlin

SECRETARY OF STATE	Jeremiah S. Black (1861) William H. Seward (1861-1865)
SECRETARY OF THE TREASURY	John A. Dix (1861) Salmon P. Chase (1861-1864) William P. Fessenden (1864-1865)
SECRETARY OF WAR	Joseph Holt (1861) Simon Cameron (1861-1862) Edwin M. Stanton (1862-1865)
ATTORNEY GENERAL	Edwin M. Stanton (1861) Edward Bates (1861-1864) James Speed (1864-1865)
POSTMASTER GENERAL	Horatio King (1861) Montgomery Blair (1861-1864) William Dennison (1864-1865)
SECRETARY OF THE NAVY	Isaac Toucey (1861) Gideon Welles (1861-1865)
SECRETARY OF THE INTERIOR	Caleb B. Smith (1861-1863) John P. Usher (1863-1865)

20th PRESIDENTIAL TERM 1865-1869

President: Abraham Lincoln (1865) Andrew Johnson (1865-1869)
Vice President: Andrew Johnson (1865)

SECRETARY OF STATE	William H. Seward
SECRETARY OF THE TREASURY	Hugh McCulloch
SECRETARY OF WAR	Edwin M. Stanton (1865-1868) John M. Schofield (1868-1869)
ATTORNEY GENERAL	James Speed (1865-1866) Henry Stanbery (1866-1868) William M. Evarts (1868-1869)
POSTMASTER GENERAL	William Dennison (1865-1866) Alexander W. Randall (1866-1869)
SECRETARY OF THE NAVY	Gideon Welles (1865-1869)
SECRETARY OF THE INTERIOR	John P. Usher (1865) James Harlan (1865-1866) Orville H. Browning (1866-1869)

21st PRESIDENTIAL TERM 1869-1873

President: Ulysses S. Grant
Vice President: Schuyler Colfax

SECRETARY OF STATE	William H. Seward (1869) Elihu B. Washburne (1869) Hamilton Fish (1869-1873)
SECRETARY OF THE TREASURY	Hugh McCulloch (1869) George S. Boutwell (1869-1873)
SECRETARY OF WAR	John M. Schoffield (1869) John A. Rawlins (1869) William W. Belknap (1869-1873)
ATTORNEY GENERAL	William M. Evarts (1869) Ebenezer R. Hoar (1869-1870) Amos T. Akerman (1870-1871) George H. Williams (1871-1873)
POSTMASTER GENERAL	John A.J. Creswell
SECRETARY OF THE NAVY	Adolph E. Borie (1869) George Robeson (1869-1873)
SECRETARY OF THE INTERIOR	Jacob D. Cox (1869-1870) Columbus Delano (1870-1873)

22nd PRESIDENTIAL TERM 1873-1877

President: Ulysses S. Grant
Vice President: Henry Wilson 1873-1875

SECRETARY OF STATE	Hamilton Fish
SECRETARY OF THE TREASURY	George S. Boutwell (1873-1874) Benjamin H. Bristow (1874-1876) Lot M. Morrill (1876-1877)
SECRETARY OF WAR	William W. Belknap (1873-1876) James D. Cameron (1876-1877)
ATTORNEY GENERAL	George H. Williams (1873-1875) Edward Pierrepont (1875-1876) Alphonso Taft (1876-1877)
POSTMASTER GENERAL	John A.J. Creswell (1873-1874) James W. Marshall (1874) Marshall Jewell (1874-1876) James N. Tyner (1876-1877)
SECRETARY OF THE NAVY	George M. Roseson
SECRETARY OF THE INTERIOR	Columbus Delano (1873-1875) Zachariah Chandler (1875-1877)

23rd PRESIDENTIAL TERM 1877-1881

President: Rutherford B. Hayes
Vice President: William A. Wheeler

SECRETARY OF STATE	Hamilton Fish (1877) William M. Evarts (1877-1881)
SECRETARY OF THE TREASURY	Lot M. Morrill (1877) John Sherman (1877-1881)
SECRETARY OF WAR	James D. Cameron (1877) George W. McCrary (1877-1879) Alexander Ramsey (1879-1881)
ATTORNEY GENERAL	Alphonso Taft (1877) Charles Devens (1877-1881)
POSTMASTER GENERAL	James N. Tyner (1877) David M. Key (1877-1880) Horace Maynard (1880-1881)
SECRETARY OF THE NAVY	George M. Robeson (1877) Richard W. Thompson (1877-1880) Nathan Goff, Jr. (1881)
SECRETARY OF THE INTERIOR	Zachariah Chandler (1877) Carl Schurz (1877-1881)

24th PRESIDENTIAL TERM 1881-1885

President: James A. Garfield (1881) Chester A. Arthur (1881-1885)
Vice President: Chester A. Arthur (1881)

SECRETARY OF STATE	William M. Evarts (1881) James G. Blaine (1881) Frederick T. Frelinghuysen (1881-1885)

SECRETARY OF THE TREASURY	William Windom (1881) Charles J. Folger (1881-1884) Walter Q. Gresham (1884) Hugh McCulloch (1884-1885)
SECRETARY OF WAR	Alexander Ramsey (1881) Robert T. Lincoln (1881-1885)
ATTORNEY GENERAL	Charles Devens (1881) Wayne McVeagh (1881) Benjamin Brewster (1881-1885)
POSTMASTER GENERAL	Horace Maynard (1881) Thomas L. James (1881) Timothy O. Howe (1881-1883) Walter Q. Gresham (1883-1884) Frank Hatton (1884-1885)
SECRETARY OF THE NAVY	Nathan Goff, Jr. (1881) William H. Hunt (1881-1882) William E. Chandler (1882-1885)
SECRETARY OF THE INTERIOR	Carl Schurz (1881) Samuel J. Kirkwood (1881-1882) Henry M. Teller (1882-1885)

25th PRESIDENTIAL TERM 1885-1889

President: Grover Cleveland
Vice President: Thomas A. Hendricks (1885)

SECRETARY OF STATE	Frederick T. Frelinghuysen (1885) Thomas F. Bayard (1885-1889)
SECRETARY OF THE TREASURY	Hugh McCulloch (1885) Daniel Manning (1885-1887) Charles S. Fairchild (1887-1889)
SECRETARY OF WAR	Robert T. Lincoln (1885) William C. Endicott (1885-1889)
ATTORNEY GENERAL	Benjamin H. Brewster (1885) Augustus H. Garland (1885-1889)
POSTMASTER GENERAL	Frank Hatton (1885) William F. Vilas (1885-1888) Don M. Dickinson (1888-1889)
SECRETARY OF THE NAVY	William E. Chandler (1885) William C. Whitney (1885-1889)
SECRETARY OF THE INTERIOR	Lucius Q.C. Lamar (1885-1888) William F. Vilas (1888-1889)
SECRETARY OF AGRICULTURE	Norman J. Colman (1889)

26th PRESIDENTIAL TERM 1889-1893

President: Benjamin Harrison
Vice President: Levi P. Morton

SECRETARY OF STATE	Thomas F. Bayard (1889) James G. Blaine (1889-1892) John W. Foster (1892-1893)
SECRETARY OF THE TREASURY	Charles S. Fairchild (1889) William Windom (1889-1891) Charles Foster (1891-1893)
SECRETARY OF WAR	William C. Endicott (1889) Redfield Proctor (1889-1891) Stephen B. Elkins (1891-1893)
ATTORNEY GENERAL	Augustus H. Garland (1889) William H.H. Miller (1889-1893)
POSTMASTER GENERAL	Don M. Dickinson (1889) John Wanamaker (1889-1893)
SECRETARY OF THE NAVY	William C. Whitney (1889) Benjamin F. Tracy (1889-1893)
SECRETARY OF THE INTERIOR	William F. Vilas (1889) John W. Noble (1889-1893)
SECRETARY OF AGRICULTURE	Norman J. Colman (1889) Jeremiah M. Rusk (1889-1893)

27th PRESIDENTIAL TERM 1893-1897

President: Grover Cleveland
Vice President: Adlai E. Stevenson

SECRETARY OF STATE	Walter Q. Gresham (1893-1895) Richard Olney (1895-1897)
SECRETARY OF THE TREASURY	Charles Foster (1893) John G. Carlisle (1893-1897)
SECRETARY OF WAR	Stephen B. Elkins (1893) Daniel S. Lamont (1893-1897)
ATTORNEY GENERAL	William H.H. Miller (1893) Richard Olney (1893-1895) Judson Harmon (1895-1897)

POSTMASTER GENERAL	John Wanamaker (1897) Wilson S. Bissell (1893-1895) William L. Wilson (1895-1897)
SECRETARY OF THE NAVY	Benjamin F. Tracy (1893) Hilary A. Herbert (1893-1897)
SECRETARY OF THE INTERIOR	John W. Noble (1893) Hoke Smith (1893-1896) David R. Francis (1897-1897)
SECRETARY OF AGRICULTURE	Jeremiah M. Rusk (1893) J. Sterling Morton (1893-1897)

28th PRESIDENTIAL TERM 1897-1901

President: William McKinley
Vice President: Garrett A. Hobart (1897-1899)

SECRETARY OF STATE	Richard Olney (1897) John Sherman (1897-1898) William R. Day (1898) John M. Hay (1898-1901)
SECRETARY OF THE TREASURY	John G. Carlisle (1897) Lyman J. Gage (1897-1901)
SECRETARY OF WAR	Daniel S. Lamont (1897) Russell A. Alger (1897-1899) Elihu Root (1899-1901)
ATTORNEY GENERAL	Judson Harmon (1897) Joseph McKenna (1897-1898) John W. Griggs (1898-1901)
POSTMASTER GENERAL	William L. Wilson (1897) James A. Gary (1897-1898) Charles E. Smith (1898-1901)
SECRETARY OF THE NAVY	Hilary A. Herbert (1897) John D. Long (1897-1901)
SECRETARY OF THE INTERIOR	David R. Francis (1897) Cornelius N. Bliss (1897-1898) Ethan A. Hitchcock (1898-1901)
SECRETARY OF AGRICULTURE	J. Sterling Morton (1897) James Wilson (1897-1901)

29th PRESIDENTIAL TERM 1901-1905

President: William McKinley (1901) Theodore Roosevelt (1901-1905)
Vice President: Theodore Roosevelt (1901)

SECRETARY OF STATE	John M. Hay (1901-1905)
SECRETARY OF THE TREASURY	Lyman J. Gage (1901-1902) Leslie M. Shaw (1902-1905)
SECRETARY OF WAR	Elihu Root (1901-1904) William Howard Taft (1904-1905)
ATTORNEY GENERAL	John W. Griggs (1901) Philander C. Knox (1901-1904) William H. Moody (1904-1905)
POSTMASTER GENERAL	Charles E. Smith (1901-1902) Henry C. Payne (1902-1904) Robert J. Wynne (1904-1905)
SECRETARY OF THE NAVY	John D. Long (1901-1902) William H. Moody (1902-1904) Paul Morton (1904-1905)
SECRETARY OF THE INTERIOR	Ethan A. Hitchcock
SECRETARY OF AGRICULTURE	James Wilson
SECRETARY OF COMMERCE AND LABOR	George B. Cortelyou (1903-1904) Victor H. Metcalf (1904-1905)

30th PRESIDENTIAL TERM 1905-1909

President: Theodore Roosevelt
Vice President: Charles W. Fairbanks

SECRETARY OF STATE	John M. Hay (1905) Elihu Root (1905-1909) Robert Bacon (1909)
SECRETARY OF THE TREASURY	Leslie M. Shaw (1905-1907) George B. Cortelyou (1907-1909)
SECRETARY OF WAR	William Howard Taft (1905-1908) Luke E. Wright (1908-1909)
ATTORNEY GENERAL	William H. Moody (1906) Charles J. Bonaparte (1906-1909)

POSTMASTER GENERAL — Robert J. Wynne (1905) George B. Cortelyou (1905-1907) George von L. Meyer (1907-1909)

SECRETARY OF THE NAVY — Paul Morton (1905) Charles J. Bonaparte (1905-1906) Victor H. Metcalk (1906-1908) Truman H. Newberry (1908-1909)

SECRETARY OF THE INTERIOR — Ethan A. Hitchcock (1905-1907) James R. Garfield (1907-1909)

SECRETARY OF AGRICULTURE — James Wilson

SECRETARY OF COMMERCE AND LABOR — Victor H. Metcalf (1905-1906) Oscar S. Straus (1906-1909)

31st PRESIDENTIAL TERM 1909-1913

President: William Howard Taft
Vice President: James S. Sherman (1909-1912)

SECRETARY OF STATE — Robert Bacon (1909) Philander C. Knox (1909-1913)

SECRETARY OF THE TREASURY — George B. Cortelyou (1909) Franklin MacVeagh (1909-1913)

SECRETARY OF WAR — Luke E. Wright (1909) Jacob M. Dickinson (1909-1911) Henry L. Stimson (1911-1913)

ATTORNEY GENERAL — Charles J. Bonaparte (1909) George W. Wickersham (1909-1913)

POSTMASTER GENERAL — George von L. Meyer (1909) Frank H. Hitchcock (1909-1913)

SECRETARY OF THE NAVY — Truman H. Newberry (1909) George von L. Meyer (1909-1913)

SECRETARY OF THE INTERIOR — James R. Garfield (1909) Richard A. Ballinger (1909-1911) Walter L. Fisher (1911-1913)

SECRETARY OF AGRICULTURE — James Wilson (1909-1913)

SECRETARY OF COMMERCE AND LABOR — Oscar S. Straus (1909) Charles Nagel (1909-1913)

32nd PRESIDENTIAL TERM 1913-1917

President: Woodrow Wilson
Vice President: Thomas R. Marshall

SECRETARY OF STATE — Philander C. Knox (1913) William Jennings Bryan (1913-1915) Robert Lansing (1915-1917)

SECRETARY OF THE TREASURY — Franklin MacVeagh (1913) Lindley M. Garrison (1913-1916) Newton D. Baker (1916-1917)

ATTORNEY GENERAL — George W. Wickersham (1913) James C. McReynolds (1913-1914) Thomas W. Gregory (1914-1917)

POSTMASTER GENERAL — Frank H. Hitchcock (1913) Albert S. Burleson (1913-1917)

SECRETARY OF THE NAVY — George von L. Meyer (1913) Josephus Daniels (1913-1917)

SECRETARY OF THE INTERIOR — Walter L. Fisher (1913) Franklin K. Lane (1913-1917)

SECRETARY OF AGRICULTURE — James Wilson (1913) David F. Houston (1913-1917)

SECRETARY OF COMMERCE — Charles Nagel (1913) William C. Redfield (1913-1917)

SECRETARY OF LABOR — Charles Nagel (1913) William B. Wilson (1913-1917)

33rd PRESIDENTIAL TERM 1917-1921

President: Woodrow Wilson
Vice President: Thomas R. Marshall

SECRETARY OF STATE — Robert Lansing (1917-1920) Bainbridge Colby (1920-1921)

SECRETARY OF THE TREASURY — William Gibbs McAdoo (1917-1918) Carter Glass (1918-1920) David F. Houston (1920-1921)

SECRETARY OF WAR	Newton D. Baker (1917-1921)
ATTORNEY GENERAL	Thomas W. Gregory (1917-1919) A. Mitchell Palmer (1919-1921)
POSTMASTER GENERAL	Albert S. Burleson
SECRETARY OF THE NAVY	Josephus Daniels
SECRETARY OF THE INTERIOR	Franklin K. Lane (1917-1920) John B. Payne (1920-1921)
SECRETARY OF AGRICULTURE	David F. Houston (1917-1920) Edwin T. Meredith (1920-1921)
SECRETARY OF COMMERCE	William C. Redfield (1917-1919) Joshua W. Alexander (1919-1921)
SECRETARY OF LABOR	William B. Wilson (1917-1921)

34th PRESIDENT TERM 1921-1925

President: Warren G. Harding (1921-1923) Calvin Coolidge (1923-1925)
Vice President: Calvin Coolidge (1921-1923)

SECRETARY OF STATE	Bainbridge Colby (1921) Charles Evans Hughes (1921-1925)
SECRETARY OF THE TREASURY	David F. Houston (1921) Andrew W. Mellon (1921-1925)
SECRETARY OF WAR	Newton D. Baker (1921) John W. Weeks (1921-1925)
ATTORNEY GENERAL	A. Mitchell Palmer (1921) Harry M. Daugherty (1921-1924) Harlan F. Stone (1924-1925)
POSTMASTER GENERAL	Albert S. Burleson (1921) Will H. Hays (1921-1922) Hubert Work (1922-1923) Harry S. New (1923-1925)
SECRETARY OF THE NAVY	Josephus Daniels (1921) Edwin Denby (1921-1924) Curtis D. Wilbur (1924-1925)
SECRETARY OF THE INTERIOR	John B. Payne (1921) Albert F. Gall (1921-1923) Hubert Work (1923-1925)
SECRETARY OF AGRICULTURE	Edwin T. Meredith (1921) Henry C. Wallace (1921-1924) Howard M. Gore (1924-1925)
SECRETARY OF COMMERCE	Joshua W. Alexander (1921) Herbert C. Hoover (1921-1925)
SECRETARY OF LABOR	William B. Wilson (1921) James J. Davis (1921-1925)

35th PRESIDENT TERM 1925-1929

President: Calvin Coolidge
Vice President: Charles G. Dawes

SECRETARY OF STATE	Charles Evans Hughes (1925) Frank B. Kellogg (1925-1929)
SECRETARY OF THE TREASURY	Andrew W. Mellon
SECRETARY OF WAR	John W. Weeks (1925) Dwight F. Davis (1925-1929)
ATTORNEY GENERAL	John G. Sargent
POSTMASTER GENERAL	Harry S. New
SECRETARY OF THE NAVY	Curtis D. Wilbur
SECRETARY OF THE INTERIOR	Hubert Work (1925-1928) Roy O. West (1929)
SECRETARY OF AGRICULTURE	Howard M. Gore (1925) William M. Hardine (1925-1929)
SECRETARY OF COMMERCE	Herbert C. Hoover (1925-1928) William F. Whiting (1928-1929)
SECRETARY OF LABOR	James J. Davis

36th PRESIDENTIAL TERM 1929-1933

President: Herbert Hoover
Vice President: Charles Curtis

SECRETARY OF STATE	Frank B. Kellogg (1929) Henry L. Stimson (1929-1933)
SECRETARY OF THE TREASURY	Andrew W. Mellon (1929-1932) Ogden L. Mills (1932-1933)
SECRETARY OF WAR	Dwight F. Davis (1929) James W. Good (1929) Patrick J. Hurley (1929-1933)
ATTORNEY GENERAL	John G. Sargent (1929) William D. Mitchell (1929-1933)
POSTMASTER GENERAL	Harry S. New (1929) Walter F. Brown (1929-1933)
SECRETARY OF THE NAVY	Curtis D. Wilbur (1929) Charles Francis Adams (1929-1933)
SECRETARY OF THE INTERIOR	Roy O. West (1929) Ray L. Wilbur (1929-1933)
SECRETARY OF AGRICULTURE	William M. Hardine (1929) Arthur M. Hyde (1929-1933)
SECRETARY OF COMMERCE	William F. Whiting (1929) Robert P. Lamont (1929-1932) Roy D. Chapman (1932-1933)
SECRETARY OF LABOR	James J. Davis (1929-1930) William N. Doak (1930-1933)

37th PRESIDENTIAL TERM 1933-1937

President: Franklin D. Roosevelt
Vice President: John Nance Garner

SECRETARY OF STATE	Cordell Hull
SECRETARY OF THE TREASURY	William H. Woodin (1933-1934) Henry Morgenthau, Jr. (1934-1937)
SECRETARY OF WAR	George H. Dern (1933-1936)
ATTORNEY GENERAL	Homer S. Cummings
POSTMASTER GENERAL	James A. Farley
SECRETARY OF THE NAVY	Claude A. Swanson
SECRETARY OF THE INTERIOR	Harold L. Ickes
SECRETARY OF AGRICULTURE	Henry Wallace
SECRETARY OF COMMERCE	Daniel C. Roper
SECRETARY OF LABOR	Frances Perkins

38th PRESIDENTIAL TERM 1937-1941

President: Franklin D. Roosevelt
Vice President: John Nance Garner

SECRETARY OF STATE	Cordell Hull
SECRETARY OF THE TREASURY	Henry Morgenthau, Jr.
SECRETARY OF WAR	Harry H. Woodring (1937-1940) Henry L. Stimson (1940-1941)
ATTORNEY GENERAL	Homer S. Cummings (1937-1939) Frank Murphy (1939-1940) Robert H. Jackson (1940-1941)
POSTMASTER GENERAL	James A. Farley (1937-1940) Frank C. Walker (1940-1941)
SECRETARY OF THE NAVY	Claude A. Swanson (1937-1939) Charles Edison (1940) Frank Knox (1940-1941)
SECRETARY OF THE INTERIOR	Harold L. Ickes
SECRETARY OF AGRICULTURE	Henry A. Wallace (1937-1940) Claude R. Wickard (1940-1941)

SECRETARY OF COMMERCE	Daniel C. Roper (1937-1938) Harry L. Hopkins (1939-1940) Jesse H. Jones (1940-1941)
SECRETARY OF LABOR	Frances Perkins

39th PRESIDENTIAL TERM 1941-1945

President: Franklin D. Roosevelt
Vice President: Henry A. Wallace

SECRETARY OF STATE	Cordell Hull (1941-1944) Edward R. Stettinius, Jr. (1944-1945)
SECRETARY OF THE TREASURY	Henry Morgenthau, Jr.
SECRETARY OF WAR	Henry L. Stimson
ATTORNEY GENERAL	Robert H. Jackson (1941) Francis Biddle (1941-1945)
POSTMASTER GENERAL	Frank C. Walker
SECRETARY OF THE NAVY	Frank Knox (1941-1944) James V. Forrestal (1944-1945)
SECRETARY OF THE INTERIOR	Harold L. Ickes
SECRETARY OF AGRICULTURE	Claude R. Wickard
SECRETARY OF COMMERCE	Jesse H. Jones
SECRETARY OF LABOR	Frances Perkins

40th PRESIDENTIAL TERM 1945-1949

President: Franklin D. Roosevelt (1945) Harry S Truman (1945-1949)
Vice President: Harry S Truman (1945)

SECRETARY OF STATE	Edward R. Stettinius, Jr. (1945) Hames F. Brynes (1945-1947) George C. Marshall (1947-1949)
SECRETARY OF DEFENSE	James V. Forrestal (1947-1949)
SECRETARY OF THE TREASURY	Henry Morgenthau, Jr. (1945) Fred M. Vinson (1945-1946) John W. Snyder (1946-1949)
SECRETARY OF WAR	Henry L. Stimson (1945) Robert P. Patterson (1945-1947) Kenneth C. Royall (1947)
ATTORNEY GENERAL	Francis Biddle (1945) Tom C. Clark (1945-1949)
POSTMASTER GENERAL	Frank C. Walker (1945) Robert E. Hannegan (1945-1947) Jesse M. Donaldson (1947-1949)
SECRETARY OF THE NAVY	James V. Forrestal (1945-1947)
SECRETARY OF THE INTERIOR	Harold L. Ickes (1945-1946) Julius A. Krug (1946-1949)
SECRETARY OF AGRICULTURE	Claude R. Wickard (1945) Clinton P. Anderson (1945-1948) Charles F. Brannan (1948-1949)
SECRETARY OF COMMERCE	Jesse H. Jones (1945) Henry A. Wallace (1945-1946) W. Averell Harriman (1947-1948) Charles Sawyer (1948-1949)
SECRETARY OF LABOR	Frances Perkins (1945) Lewis B. Schwellenbach (1945-1948) Maurice J. Tobin (1948-1949)

41st PRESIDENTIAL TERM (1949-1953)

President: Harry S Truman
Vice President: Alben W. Barkley

SECRETARY OF STATE	Dean G. Acheson
SECRETARY OF THE TREASURY	John W. Snyder
SECRETARY OF DEFENSE	James V. Forrestal (1949) Louis A. Johnson (1949-1950) George C. Marshall (1950-1951) Robert A. Lovett (1951-1953)

ATTORNEY GENERAL	Tom C. Clark (1949) J. Howard McGrath (1949-1952) James P. McGranery (1952-1953)
POSTMASTER GENERAL	Jesse M. Donaldson
SECRETARY OF THE INTERIOR	Julius A. Krug (1949) Oscar L. Chapman (1950-1953)
SECRETARY OF AGRICULTURE	Charles F. Brannan
SECRETARY OF COMMERCE	Charles Sawyer
SECRETARY OF LABOR	Maurice J. Tobin

42nd PRESIDENTIAL TERM 1953-1957

President: Dwight D. Eisenhower
Vice President: Richard M. Nixon

SECRETARY OF STATE	John Foster Dulles
SECRETARY OF THE TREASURY	George M. Humphrey
SECRETARY OF DEFENSE	Charles E. Wilson
ATTORNEY GENERAL	Herbert Brownell, Jr.
POSTMASTER GENERAL	Arthur E. Summerfield
SECRETARY OF THE INTERIOR	Douglas McKay (1953-1956) Frederick A. Seaton (1956-1957)
SECRETARY OF AGRICULTURE	Ezra Taft Benson
SECRETARY OF COMMERCE	Sinclair Weeks
SECRETARY OF LABOR	Martin P. Durkin (1953) James P. Mitchell (1954-1957)
SECRETARY OF HEALTH, EDUCATION, AND WELFARE	Oveta Culp Hobby (1953-1955) Marion B. Folsom (1955-1957)

43rd PRESIDENTIAL TERM 1957-1961

President: Dwight D. Eisenhower
Vice President: Richard M. Nixon

SECRETARY OF STATE	John Foster Dulles (1957-1959) Christian A. Herter (1959-1961)
SECRETARY OF THE TREASURY	George M. Humphrey (1957) Robert B. Anderson (1957-1961)
SECRETARY OF DEFENSE	Charles E. Wilson (1957) Neil H. McElroy (1957-1960) Thomas S. Gates, Jr. (1960-1961)
ATTORNEY GENERAL	Herbert Brownell, Jr. (1957) William P. Rogers (1958-1961)
POSTMASTER GENERAL	Arthur E. Summerfield
SECRETARY OF THE INTERIOR	Frederick A. Seaton
SECRETARY OF AGRICULTURE	Ezra Taft Benzon
SECRETARY OF COMMERCE	Sinclair Weeks (1957-1958) Lewis L. Strauss (1958-1959) Frederick H. Mueller (1959-1961)
SECRETARY OF LABOR	James P. Mitchell
SECRETARY OF HEALTH, EDUCATION, AND WELFARE	Marion B. Folsom (1957-1958) Arthur S. Flemming (1958-1961)

44th PRESIDENTIAL TERM 1961-1965

President: John F. Kennedy (1961-1963) Lyndon B. Johnson (1963-1965)
Vice President: Lyndon B. Johnson (1961-1963)

SECRETARY OF STATE	Dean Rusk
SECRETARY OF THE TREASURY	C. Douglas Dillon
SECRETARY OF DEFENSE	Robert S. McNamara

ATTORNEY GENERAL	Robert F. Kennedy
POSTMASTER GENERAL	J. Edward Day (1961-1963) John A. Gronouski (1963-1965)
SECRETARY OF THE INTERIOR	Stewart L. Udall
SECRETARY OF AGRICULTURE	Orville L. Freeman
SECRETARY OF COMMERCE	Luther H. Hodges
SECRETARY OF LABOR	Arthur J. Goldberg (1961-1962) W. Willard Wirtz (1962-1965)
SECRETARY OF HEALTH, EDUCATION, AND WELFARE	Abraham A. Ribicoff (1961-1962) Anthony J. Celebreeze (1962-1965)

45th PRESIDENTIAL TERM 1965-1969

President: Lyndon B. Johnson
Vice President: Hubert H. Humphrey

SECRETARY OF STATE	Dean Rusk
SECRETARY OF THE TREASURY	Henry H. Fowler (1965-1968) Joseph W. Barr (1968-1969)
SECRETARY OF DEFENSE	Robert S. McNamara (1965-1968) Clark M. Clifford (1968-1969)
ATTORNEY GENERAL	Nicholas de B. Katzenbach (1965-1967) Ramsey Clark (1967-1969)
POSTMASTER GENERAL	Lawrence F. O'Brien (1965-1968) M. Marvin Watson (1968-1969)
SECRETARY OF THE INTERIOR	Stewart L. Udall
SECRETARY OF AGRICULTURE	Orville L. Freeman
SECRETARY OF COMMERCE	John T. Connor (1965-1967) Alexander B. Trowbridge (1967-1968) Cyrus R. Smith (1968-1969)
SECRETARY OF LABOR	W. Willard Wirtz
SECRETARY OF HEALTH, EDUCATION, AND WELFARE	John W. Gardner (1965-1968) Wilbur J. Cohen (1968-1969)
SECRETARY OF HOUSING AND URBAN DEVELOPMENT	Robert C. Weaver (1966-1968) Robert C. Wood (1968-1969)
SECRETARY OF TRANSPORTATION	Alan S. Boyd (1966-1969)

46th PRESIDENTIAL TERM 1969-1973

President: Richard M. Nixon
Vice President: Spiro T. Agnew

SECRETARY OF STATE	William P. Rogers
SECRETARY OF THE TREASURY	David M. Kennedy (1969-1971) John B. Connally (1971-1972) George P. Shultz (1972-1973)
SECRETARY OF DEFENSE	Melvin R. Laird
ATTORNEY GENERAL	John N. Mitchell (1969-1972) Richard G. Kleindienst (1972-1973)
POSTMASTER GENERAL	Winton M. Blount (1969-1971)
SECRETARY OF THE INTERIOR	Walter J. Hickel (1969-1971) Rogers C.B. Morton (1971-1973)
SECRETARY OF AGRICULTURE	Clifford M. Hardin (1969-1971) Earl L. Butz (1971-1973)
SECRETARY OF COMMERCE	Maurice H. Stans (1969-1972) Peter G. Peterson (1972-1973)
SECRETARY OF LABOR	George P. Schultz (1969-1970) James D. Hodgson (1970-1973)
SECRETARY OF HEALTH, EDUCATION, AND WELFARE	Robert H. Finch (1969-1970) Elliot L. Richardson (1970-1973)
SECRETARY OF HOUSING AND URBAN DEVELOPMENT	George W. Romney
SECRETARY OF TRANSPORTATION	John A. Volpe

47th PRESIDENTIAL TERM 1973-1977

President: Richard M. Nixon
Vice President: Spiro T. Agnew

SECRETARY OF STATE	William P. Rogers
SECRETARY OF THE TREASURY	George P. Schultz
SECRETARY OF DEFENSE	Elliot L. Richardson
ATTORNEY GENERAL	Richard G. Kleindienst
SECRETARY OF THE INTERIOR	Rogers C.B. Morton
SECRETARY OF AGRICULTURE	Earl L. Butz
SECRETARY OF COMMERCE	Frederick B. Dent
SECRETARY OF LABOR	Peter J. Brennan
SECRETARY OF HEALTH, EDUCATION, AND WELFARE	Caspar W. Weinberger
SECRETARY OF HOUSING AND URBAN DEVELOPMENT	James T. Lynn
SECRETARY OF TRANSPORTATION	Claude S. Brinegar

MEMBERS OF THE CABINET BY DEPARTMENT

(First date indicates year department was established)

SECRETARIES OF STATE

NAME	YEARS IN OFFICE	STATE	PRESIDENTIAL TERMS
Thomas Jefferson	1790-1794	Virginia	Washington 1, 2
Edmund Randolph	1794-1795	Virginia	Washington 2
Timothy Pickering	1795-1800	Pensylvania	Washington 2, J. Adams
John Marshall	1800-1801	Virginia	J. Adams
James Madison	1801-1809	Virginia	Jefferson 1, 2
Robert Smith	1809-1811	Maryland	Madison 1
James Monroe	1811-1817	Virginia	Madison 1, 2
John Quincy Adams	1817-1825	Massachusetts	Monroe 1, 2
Henry Clay	1925-1829	Kentucky	J.Q. Adams
Martin Van Buren	1829-1831	New York	Jackson 1
Edward Livingston	1831-1833	Louisiana	Jackson 1, 2
Louis McLane	1833-1834	Delaware	Jackson 2
John Forsyth	1834-1841	Georgia	Jackson 2, Van Buren
Daniel Webster	1841-1843	Massachusetts	W.H. Harrison, Tyler
Abel P. Upshur	1843-1844	Massachusetts	Tyler
John C. Calhoun	1844-1845	Virginia	Tyler, Polk
James Buchanan	1845-1849	Pennsylvania	Polk, Taylor
John M. Clayton	1849-1850	Delaware	Taylor, Fillmore
Daniel Webster	1850-1852	Massachusetts	Fillmore
Edward Everett	1852-1853	Massachusetts	Fillmore
William L. Marcy	1853-1857	New York	Pierce, Buchanan
Lewis Cass	1857-1860	Michigan	Buchanan
Jeremiah S. Black	1860-1861	Pennsylvania	Buchanan, Lincoln 1
William H. Seward	1861-1869	New York	Lincoln 1, 2, A. Johnson, Grant 1
Elihu B. Washburne	1869	Illinois	Grant 1
Hamilton Fish	1869-1877	New York	Grant 1, 2, Hayes
William M. Evarts	1877-1881	New York	Hayes, Garfield
James G. Blaine	1881	Maine	Garfield, Arthur
Frederick T. Frelinghuysen	1881-1885	New Jersey	Arthur, Cleveland 1
Thomas F. Bayard	1885-1889	Delaware	Cleveland 1, B. Harrison
James G. Blaine	1889-1892	Maine	B. Harrison
John W. Foster	1892-1893	Indiana	B. Harrison
Walter Q. Gresham	1893-1895	Illinois	Cleveland 2
Richard Olney	1895-1897	Massachusetts	Cleveland 2, McKinley 1
John Sherman	1897-1898	Ohio	McKinley 1
William R. Day	1898	Ohio	McKinley 1
John M. Hay	1898-1905	District of Columbia	McKinley 1, 2, T. Roosevelt 1, 2
Elihu Root	1905-1909	New York	T. Roosevelt 2
Robert Bacon	1909	New York	T. Roosevelt 2, Taft
Philander C. Knox	1909-1913	Pennsylvania	Taft, Wilson 1
William Jennings Bryan	1913-1915	Nebraska	Wilson 1
Robert Lansing	1915-1920	New York	Wilson 1, 2
Bainbridge Colby	1920-1921	New York	Silson 2, Harding
Charles Evans Hughes	1921-1925	New York	Harding, Coolidge 1, 2
Frank B. Kellogg	1925-1929	Minnesota	Coolidge 2, Hoover
Henry L. Stimson	1929-1933	New York	Hoover
Cordell Hull	1933-1944	Tennessee	F.D. Roosevelt 1, 2, 3
Edward R. Stettinius, Jr.	1944-1945	Virginia	F.D. Roosevelt 3, 4, Truman 1
James F. Byrnes	1945-1947	South Carolina	Truman 1
George C. Marshall	1947-1949	Pennsylvania	Truman 1
Dean G. Acheson	1949-1953	Connecticut	Truman 2
John Foster Dulles	1953-1959	New York	Eisenhower 1, 2
Christian A. Herter	1959-1961	Massachusetts	Eisenhower 2
Dean Rusk	1961-1969	Georgia	Kennedy, L.B. Johnson 1, 2
William P. Rogers	1969-	New York	Nixon 1, 2

SECRETARIES OF THE TREASURY

NAME	YEARS IN OFFICE	STATE	PRESIDENTIAL TERMS
Alexander Hamilton	1789-1795	New York	Washington 1, 2
Oliver Wolcott, Jr.	1795-1801	Connecticut	Washington 2, J. Adams
Samuel Dexter	1801	Massachusetts	J. Adams, Jefferson 1
Albert Gallatin	1801-1814	Pennsylvania	Jefferson 1, 2, Madison 1, 2
George W. Campbell	1814	Tennessee	Madison 2
Alexander J. Dallas	1814-1816	Pennsylvania	Madison 2
William H. Crawford	1816-1825	Georgia	Madison 2, Monroe 1, 2
Richard Rush	1825-1828	Pennsylvania	J.Q. Adams
Samuel D. Ingham	1829-1831	Pennsylvania	Jackson 1
Louis McLane	1831-1833	Delaware	Jackson 1, 2
William J. Duane	1833	Pennsylvania	Jackson 2
Roger B. Taney	1833	Maryland	Jackson 2
Levi Woodbury	1834-1841	New Hampshire	Jackson 2, Van Buren
Thomas Ewing	1841	Ohio	W.H. Harrison, Tyler
Walter Forward	1841-1843	Pennsylvania	Tyler
John C. Spencer	1843-1844	New York	Tyler
George M. Bibb	1844-1845	Kentucky	Tyler, Polk
Robert J. Walker	1845-1849	Mississippi	Polk, Taylor
William M. Meredith	1849-1850	Pennsylvania	Taylor, Fillmore
Thomas Corwin	1850-1853	Ohio	Fillmore, Pierce
James Guthrie	1853-1857	Kentucky	Pierce, Buchanan
Howell Cobb	1857-1860	Georgia	Buchanan
Philip F. Thomas	1860-1861	Maryland	Buchanan
John A. Dix	1861	New York	Buchanan, Lincoln 1
Salmon P. Chase	1861-1864	Ohio	Lincoln 1
William P. Fessenden	1864-1865	Maine	Lincoln 1
Hugh McCulloch	1865-1869	Indiana	Lincoln 2, A. Johnson, Grant 1
George S. Boutwell	1869-1873	Massachusetts	Grant 1, 2
William A. Richardson	1873-1874	Massachusetts	Grant 2
Benjamin H. Bristow	1874-1876	Kentucky	Grant 2
Lot M. Morrill	1876-1877	Maine	Grant 2, Hayes
John Sherman	1877-1881	Ohio	Hayes
William Windom	1881	Minnesota	Garfield, Arthur
Charles J. Folger	1881-1884	New York	Arthur
Walter Q. Gresham	1884	Indiana	Arthur
Hugh McCulloch	1884-1885	Indiana	Arthur, Cleveland 1
Daniel Manning	1885-1887	New York	Cleveland
Charles S. Fairchild	1887-1889	New York	Cleveland 1, B. Harrison
William Windom	1889-1891	Minnesota	B. Harrison
Charles Foster	1891-1893	Ohio	B. Harrison, Cleveland 2
John G. Carlisle	1893-1897	Kentucky	Cleveland 2, McKinley 1
Lyman J. Gage	1897-1902	Illinois	McKinley 1, 2, T. Roosevelt 1
Leslie M. Shaw	1902-1907	Iowa	T. Roosevelt 1, 2
George B. Cortelyou	1907-1909	New York	T. Roosevelt 2, Taft
Franklin MacVeagh	1909-1913	Illinois	Taft, Wilson 1
William Gibbs McAdoo	1913-1918	New York	Wilson 1, 2
Carter Glass	1918-1920	Virginia	Wilson 2
David F. Houston	1920-1921	Missouri	Wilson 2, Harding
Andrew W. Mellon	1921-1932	Pennsylvania	Harding, Coolidge 1, 2, Hoover
Ogden L. Mills	1932-1933	New York	Hoover
WilliaM H. Woodin	1933-1934	New York	F.D. Roosevelt 1
Henry Morgenthau, Jr.	1934-1945	New York	F.D. Roosevelt 1, 2, 3, 4, Truman
Frederick (Fred) M. Vinson	1945-1946	Kentucky	Truman 1
John W. Snyder	1946-1953	Missouri	Truman 1, 2
George M. Humphrey	1953-1957	Ohio	Eisenhower 1, 2
Robert B. Anderson	1957-1961	Connecticut	Eisenhower 2
C. Douglas Dillon	1961-1965	New Jersey	Kennedy, L.B. Johnson 1
Joseph W. Barr	1968-1969	Indiana	L.B. Johnson 2
David M. Kennedy	1969-1971	Illinois	Nixon 1
John B. Connally	1971-1972	Texas	Nixon 1
George P. Schultz	1972-	Illinois	Nixon 1, 2

SECRETARIES OF WAR

NAME	YEARS IN OFFICE	STATE	PRESIDENTIAL TERMS
Henry Knox	1789-1795	Massachusetts	Washington 1, 2
Timothy Pickering	1795	Pennsylvania	Washington 2
James McHenry	1796-1800	Maryland	Washington 2, J. Adams
Samuel Dexter	1800-1801	Massachusetts	J. Adams
Henry Dearborn	1801-1809	Massachusetts	Jefferson 1, 2
William Eustis	1809-1812	Massachusetts	Madison 1
John Armstrong	1813-1814	New York	Madison 1, 2
James Monroe	1814-1815	Virginia	Madison 2
William H. Crawford	1815-1816	Georgia	Madison 2
John C. Calhoun	1817-1825	South Carolina	Monroe 1, 2
James Barbour	1825-1828	Virginia	J.Q. Adams
Peter B. Porter	1828-1829	New York	J.Q. Adams
John H. Eaton	1829-1831	Tennessee	Jackson 1
Lewis Cass	1831-1836	Ohio	Jackson 1, 2
Benjamin F. Butler	1837	New York	Jackson 2, Van buren
Joel R. Poinsett	1837-1841	South Carolina	Van Buren
John Bell	1841	Tennessee	W.H. Harrison, Tyler
John C. Spencer	1841-1843	New York	Tyler
James M. Porter	1843-1844	Pennsylvania	Tyler
William Wilkins	1844-1845	Pennsylvania	Tyler, Polk
William L. Marcy	1845-1849	New York	Polk, Taylor
George W. Crawford	1849-1850	Georgia	Taylor, Fillmore
Charles M. Conrad	1850-1853	Louisiana	Fillmore, Pierce
Jefferson Davis	1853-1857	Mississippi	Pierce
John B. Floyd	1857-1861	Virginia	Buchanan
Joseph Holt	1861	Kentucky	Buchanan, Lincoln 1
Simon Cameron	1861-1862	Pennsylvania	Lincoln 1
Edwin M. Stanton	1862-1868	Pennsylvania	Lincoln 1, 2, A. Johnson
John M. Schoefield	1868-1869	Illinois	Grant 1
William W. Belknap	1869-1876	Iowa	Grant 1, 2
Alphonso Taft	1876	Ohio	Grant 2
James D. Cameron	1876-1877	Pennsylvania	Grant 2, Hayes
George W. McCrary	1877-1879	Iowa	Hayes
Alexander Ramsey	1879-1881	Minnesota	Hayes, Garfield
Robert T. Lincoln	1881-1885	Illinois	Garfield, Arthur, Cleveland 1
William C. Endicott	1885-1889	Massachusetts	Garfield, Arthur, Cleveland 1
Redfield Proctor	1889-1891	Vermont	Cleveland 1, B. Harrison
Stephen B. Elkins	1891-1893	West Virginia	B. Harrison, Cleveland 2
Daniel S. Lamont	1893-1897	New York	Cleveland 2, McKinley 1
Russell A. Alger	1897-1899	Michigan	McKinley 1
Elihu Root	1899-1904	New York	McKinley 1, 2, T. Roosevelt 1
William Howard Taft	1904-1908	Ohio	T. Roosevelt 1, 2
Luke E. Wright	1908-1909	Tennessee	T. Roosevelt 2, Taft
Jacob M. Dickinson	1909-1911	Tennessee	Taft
Henry L. Stimson	1911-1913	New York	Taft, Wilson 1
Lindley M. Garrison	1913-1916	New Jersey	Wilson 1
Newton D. Baker	1916-1921	Ohio	Wilson 1, 2, Harding
John W. Weeks	1921-1925	Massachusetts	Harding, Coolidge 1, 2
Dwight F. Davis	1925-1929	Missouri	Coolidge 2, Hoover
James W. Good	1929	Illinois	Hoover
Patrick J. Hurley	1929-1933	Oklahoma	Hoover
George H. Dern	1933-1936	Utah	F.D. Roosevelt 1
Harry H. Woodring	1937-1940	Kansas	F.D. Roosevelt 2
Henry L. Stimson	1940-1945	New York	F.D. Roosevelt 2, 3, 4, Truman 1
Robert P. Patterson	1945-1947	New York	Truman 1
Kenneth C. Royall	1947	North Carolina	Truman 1

(Became part of the Department of Defense under the National Security Act of 1947)

ATTORNEYS GENERAL

NAME	YEARS IN OFFICE	STATE	PRESIDENTIAL TERMS
Edmund Randolph	1790-1794	Virginia	Washington 1, 2
William Bradford	1794-1795	Pennsylvania	Washington 2
Charles Lee	1795-1801	Virginia	Washington 2, J. Adams
Levi Lincoln	1801-1804	Massachusetts	Jefferson 1
John Breckenridge	1805-1806	Kentucky	Jefferson 2
Caesar A. Rodney	1807-1811	Delaware	Jefferson 2, Madison 1
William Pinkney	1811-1814	Maryland	Madison 1, 2
Richard Rush	1814-1817	Pennsylvania	Madison 2, Monroe 1
William Wirt	1817-1829	Virginia	Monroe 1, 2, J.Q. Adams
John M. Berrien	1829-1831	Georgia	Jackson 1
Roger B. Taney	1831-1833	Maryland	Jackson 1, 2
Benjamin F. Butler	1833-1838	New York	Jackson 2, Van Buren
Felix Grundy	1838-1840	Tennessee	Van Buren
Henry D. Gilpin	1840-1841	Pennsylvania	Van Buren
John J. Crittenden	1841	Kentucky	W.H. Harrison, Tyler
Hugh S. Legare	1841-1843	South Carolina	Tyler
John Nelson	1943-1845	Maryland	Tyler, Polk
John Y. Mason	1845-1846	Virginia	Polk
Nathan Clifford	1846-1848	Maine	Polk
Isaac Toucey	1848-1849	Connecticut	Polk, Taylor
Reverdy Johnson	1949-1850	Maryland	Taylor, Fillmore
John J. Crittenden	1850-1853	Kentucky	Filmore, Pierce
Caleb Cushing	1853-1857	Massachusetts	Pierce, Buchanan
Jeremiah S. Black	1857-1860	Pennsylvania	Buchanan
Edwin M. Stanton	1860-1861	Pennsylvania	Buchanan, Lincoln 1
Edward Bates	1861-1864	Missouri	Lincoln 1
James Speed	1864-1866	Kentucky	Lincoln 1, 2 A. Johnson
Henry Stanbery	1866-1868	Ohio	A. Johnson
William M. Evarts	1868-1869	New York	A. Johnson, Grant 1
Ebenezer R. Hoar	1869-1870	Massachusetts	Grant 1
Amos T. Akerman	1870-1871	Georgia	Grant 1
George H. Williams	1871-1875	Oregon	Grant 1, 2
Edwards Pierrespont	1875-1876	New York	Grant 2
Alphonso Taft	1876-1877	Ohio	Grant 2, Hayes
Charles Devens	1877-1881	Massachusetts	Hayes, Garfield
Wayne MacVeagh	1881	Pennsylvania	Garfield, Arthur
Benjamin H. Brewster	1881-1885	Pennsylvania	Arthur, Cleveland
Augustus H. Garland	1885-1889	Arkansas	Cleveland 1, B. Harrison
William H.H. Miller	1889-1893	Indiana	B. Harrison, Cleveland 2
Richard Olney	1893-1895	Massachusetts	Cleveland 2
Judson Harmon	1895-1897	California	McKinley 1
John W. Griggs	1898-1901	New Jersey	McKinley 1, 2
Philander C. Knox	1901-1904	Pennsylvania	McKinley 2, T. Roosevelt 1
William H. Moody	1904-1906	Massachusetts	T. Roosevelt 1, 2
Charles J. Bonaparte	1906-1909	Maryland	T. Roosevelt, Taft
George W. Wickersham	1909-1913	New York	Taft, Wilson 1
James C. McReynolds	1913-1914	Tennessee	Wilson 1
Thomas W. Gregory	1914-1919	Texas	Wilson 1, 2
A. Mitchell Palmer	1919-1921	Pennsylvania	Wilson 2, Harding
Harry M. Daugherty	1921-1924	Ohio	Harding, Coolidge 1
Harlan F. STone	1924-1925	New York	Coolidge 1
John G. Sargent	1925-1929	Vermont	Coolidge 2, Hoover
William D. Mitchell	1929-1933	Minnesota	Hoover
Homer S. Cummings	1933-1939	Connecticut	F.D. Roosevelt 1, 2
Frank Murphy	1939-1940	Michigan	F.D. Roosevelt 2
Robert H. Jackson	1940-1941	New York	F.D. Roosevelt 2, 3
Francis Biddle	1941-1945	Pennsylvania	F.D. Roosevelt 3, 4 Truman
Tom C. Clark	1945-1949	Texas	Truman 1, 2
J. Howard McGrath	1949-1952	Rhode Island	Truman 2
James P. McGranery	1952-1953	Pennsylvania	Truman 2
Herbert Brownell, Jr.	1953-1957	New York	Eisenhower 1, 2
William P. Rogers	1958-1961	New York	Eisenhower 2
Robert F. Kennedy	1961-1965	Massachusetts	Kennedy, L.B. Johnson 1
Nicholas de B. Katzenbach	1965-1967	New Jersey	L.B. Johnson 2
Ramsey Clark	1967-1969	Texas	L.B. Johnson 2
John N. Mitchell	1969-1972	New York	Nixon 1
Richard G. Kleindienst	1972-	Arizona	Nixon 1, 2

SECRETARIES OF THE NAVY

NAME	YEARS IN OFFICE	STATE	PRESIDENTIAL TERMS
Benjamin Stoddert	1798-1801	Maryland	J. Adams, Jefferson 1
Robert Smith	1801-1809	Maryland	Jefferson 1, 2, Madison 1
Paul Hamilton	1809-1812	South Carolina	Madison 1
William Jones	1813-1814	Pennsylvania	Madison 1, 2
Benjamin W. Crowninshield	1814-1818	Massachusetts	Madison 2, Monroe 1
Smith Thompson	1818-1823	New York	Monroe 1, 2
Samuel L. Southard	1823-1829	New Jersey	Monroe 2, J.Q. Adams
John Branch	1829-1831	North Carolina	Jackson 1
Levi Woodbury	1831-1834	New Hampshire	Jackson 1, 2
Mahlon Dickerson	1834-1838	New Jersey	Jackson 2, Van Buren
James K. Paulding	1838-1841	New York	Van Buren
George E. Badger	1841	North Carolina	W.H. Harrison, Tyler
Abel P. Upshur	1841-1843	Virginia	Tyler
David Henshaw	1843-1844	Massachusetts	Tyler
Thomas W. Gilmer	1844	Virginia	Tyler
John Y. Mason	1844-1845	Virginia	Tyler, Polk
George Bancroft	1845-1846	Massachusetts	Polk
John Y. Mason	1846-1849	Virginia	Polk, Taylor
William B. Preston	1849-1850	Virginia	Taylor, Fillmore
William A. Graham	1850-1852	North Carolina	Fillmore
John P. Kennedy	1852-1853	Maryland	Fillmore, Pierce
James C. Dobbin	1853-1857	North Carolina	Pierce, Buchanan
Isaac Toucey	1857-1861	Connecticut	Buchanan, Lincoln 1
Gideon Welles	1861-1869	Connecticut	Lincoln, 1, 2 A. Johnson
Adolph E. Borie	1869	Pennsylvania	Grant 1
George M. Robeson	1869-1877	New Jersey	Grant 1, 2 Hayes
Richard W. Thompson	1877-1880	Indiana	Hayes
Nathan Goff, Jr.	1881	West Virginia	Hayes, Garfield
William H. Hunt	1881-1882	Louisiana	Garfield, Arthur
William E. Chandler	1882-1885	New Hampshire	Arthur, Cleveland 1
William C. Whitney	1885-1889	New York	Cleveland 1, B. Harrison
Benjamin F. Tracy	1889-1893	New York	B. Harrison, Cleveland 2
Hilary A. Herbert	1893-1897	Alabama	Cleveland 2, McKinley 1
John D. Long	1897-1902	Massachusetts	McKinley 1, 2 T. Roosevelt
William H. Moody	1902-1904	Massachusetts	T. Roosevelt 1
Paul Morton	1904-1905	Illinois	T. Roosevelt 2
Charles J. Bonaparte	1905-1906	Maryland	T. Roosevelt 2
Victor H. Metcalf	1906-1908	California	T. Roosevelt 2
Truman H. Newberry	1908-1909	Michigan	T. Roosevelt 2, Taft
George von L. Meyer	1909-1913	Massachusetts	Taft, Wilson 1
Josephus Daniels	1913-1921	North Carolina	Wilson 1, 2, Harding
Edwin Denby	1921-1924	Michigan	Harding, Coolidge 1
Curtis D. Wilbur	1924-1929	California	Coolidge 1, 2, Hoover
Charles Francis Adams	1929-1933	Massachusetts	Hoover
Claude A. Swanson	1933-1939	Virginia	F.D. Roosevelt 1, 2
Charles Edison	1940	New Jersey	F.D. Roosevelt 2
Frank Knox	1940-1944	Illinois	F.D. Roosevelt 2, 3
James V. Forrestal	1944-1947	New York	F.D. Roosevelt 3, 4, Truman 1

(Became part of the Department of Defense under the National Security Act of 1947)

POSTMASTERS GENERAL

NAME	YEARS IN OFFICE	STATE	PRESIDENTIAL TERMS
William T. Barry	1829-1835	Kentucky	Jackson 1, 2
Amos Kendall	1835-1840	Kentucky	Jackson 2, Van Buren
John M. Niles	1840-1841	Connecticut	Van Buren
Francis Granger	1841	New York	W.H. Harrison, Tyler
Charles A. Wickliffe	1841-1845	Kentucky	Tyler, Polk
Cave Johnson	1845-1849	Tennessee	Polk, Taylor
Jacob Collamer	1849-1850	Vermont	Taylor, Fillmore
Nathan K. Hall	1850-1852	New York	Fillmore
Samuel D. Hubbard	1852-1853	Connecticut	Fillmore, Pierce
James Campbell	1853-1857	Pennsylvania	Pierce, Buchanan
Aaron V. Brown	1857-1859	Tennessee	Buchanan
Joseph Holt	1859-1861	Kentucky	Buchanan
Horatio King	1861	Maine	Buchanan, Lincoln 1
Montgomery Blair	1861-1864	District of Columbia	Lincoln 1
William Dennison	1864-1866	Ohio	Lincoln 1, 2, A. Johnson
Alexander W. Randall	1866-1869	Wisconsin	A. Johnson
John A.J. Creswell	1869-1874	Maryland	Grant 1, 2
James W. Marshall	1874	Virginia	Grant 2
Marshall Jewell	1874-1876	Connecticut	Grant 2
James N. Tyner	1876-1877	Indiana	Grant 2, Jayes
David M. Key	1877-1880	Tennessee	Hayes
Horace Maynard	1880-1881	Tennessee	Hayes, Garfield
Thomas L. James	1881	New York	Garfield, Arthur
Timothy O. Howe	1881-1883	Wisconsin	Arthur
Walter Q. Gresham	1883-1884	Indiana	Arthur
Frank Hatton	1884-1885	Iowa	Arthur, Cleveland 1
William F. Vilas	1885-1888	Wisconsin	Cleveland 1
Don M. Dickinson	1888-1889	Michigan	Cleveland 1, B. Harrison
John Wanamaker	1889-1893	Pennsylvania	B. Harrison, Cleveland 2
Wilson S. Bissell	1893-1895	New York	Cleveland 2
William L. Wilson	1895-1897	West Virginia	Cleveland 2, McKinley 1
James A. Gary	1897-1898	Maryland	McKinley 1
Charles E. Smith	1898-1902	Pennsylvania	McKinley 1, 2, T. Roosevelt 1
Henry C. Payne	1902-1904	Wisconsin	T. Roosevelt 1
Robert J. Wynne	1904-1905	Pennsylvania	T. Roosevelt 1, 2
George B. Cortelyou	1905-1907	New York	T. Roosevelt 2
George von L. Meyer	1907-1909	Massachusetts	T. Roosevelt 2, Taft
Frank H. Hitchcock	1909-1913	Massachusetts	Taft, Wilson 1
Albert S. Burleson	1913-1921	Texas	Wilson 1, 2, Harding
Will H. Hays	1921-1922	Indiana	Harding
Hubert Work	1922-1923	Colorado	Harding
Harry S. New	1923-1929	Indiana	Harding, Coolidge 1, 2, Hoover
Walter F. Brown	1929-1933	Ohio	Hoover
James A. Farley	1933-1940	New York	F.D. Roosevelt 1, 2
Frank C. Walker	1940-1945	Pennsylvania	F.D. Roosevelt 2, 3, 4, Truman 1
Robert E. Hannegan	1945-1947	Missouri	Truman 1
Jesse M. Donaldson	1947-1953	Missouri	Truman 1, 2
Arthur E. Summerfield	1953-1961	Michigan	Eisenhower 1, 2
J. Edward Day	1961-1963	Illinois	Kennedy
John A. Gronouski	1963-1965	Wisconsin	Kennedy, L.B. Johnson 1
Lawrence F. O'Brien	1965-1968	Massachusetts	L.B. Johnson 2
W. Marvin Watson	1968-1969	Texas	L.B. Johnson 2
Winton M. Blount	1969-1971	Alabama	Nixon 1

(Reorganized as an independent federal agency by Act of 1970)

SECRETARIES OF THE INTERIOR

NAME	YEARS IN OFFICE	STATE	PRESIDENTIAL TERMS
Thomas Ewing	1849-1850	Ohio	Taylor, Fillmore
Thomas M. T. McKennan	1850	Pennsylvania	Fillmore
Alexander H. H. Stuart	1850-1853	Virginia	Fillmore, Pierce
Robert McClelland	1853-1857	Michigan	Pierce, Buchanan
Jacob Thompson	1857-1861	Mississippi	Buchanan
Caleb B. Smith	1861-1863	Indiana	Lincoln 1
John P. Usher	1863-1865	Indiana	Lincoln 1, 2 A. Johnson
James Harlan	1865-1866	Iowa	A. Johnson
Orville H. Browning	1866-1869	Illinois	A. Johnson
Jacob D. Cox	1869-1870	Ohio	Grant 1
Columbus Delano	1870-1875	Ohio	Grant 1, 2
Zachariah Chandler	1875-1877	Michigan	Grant 2, Hayes
Carl Schurz	1877-1881	Missouri	Hayes, Garfield
Samuel J. Kirkwood	1881-1882	Iowa	Garfield, Arthur
Henry M. Teller	1882-1885	Colorado	Arthur
Lucius Q.C. Lamar	1885-1888	Mississippi	Cleveland 1
William F. Vilas	1888-1889	Wisconsin	Cleveland 1, B. Harrison
John W. Noble	1889-1893	Missouri	B. Harrison, Cleveland 2
Hoke Smith	1893-1896	Georgia	Cleveland 2
David R. Francis	1896-1897	Missouri	Cleveland 2, McKinley 1
Cornelius N. Bliss	1897-1898	New York	McKinley 1
Ethan A. Hitchcock	1898-1907	Missouri	McKinley 1, 2, T. Roosevelt 1, 2
James R. Garfield	1907-1909	Ohio	T. Roosevelt 2, Taft
Richard A. Ballinger	1909-1911	Washington	Taft
Walter L. Fisher	1911-1913	Illinois	Taft, Wilson 1
Franklin K. Lane	1913-1920	California	Wilson 1, 2
John B. Payne	1920-1921	Illinois	Wilson 2, Harding
Albert B. Fall	1921-1923	New Mexico	Harding
Hubert Work	1923-1928	Colorado	Harding, Coolidge, 1, 2
Roy O. West	1929	Illinois	Coolidge 2, Hoover
Ray L. Wilbur	1929-1933	California	Hoover
Harold L. Ickes	1933-1946	Iowa	F.D. Roosevelt 1, 2, 3, Truman 1
Julius A. Krug	1946-1949	Wisconsin	Truman 1, 2
Oscar L. Chapman	1950-1953	Colorado	Truman 2
Douglas McKay	1953-1956	Oregon	Eisenhower 1
Frederick A. Seaton	1956-1961	Nebraska	Eisenhower 1, 2
Stewart L. Udall	1961-1969	Arizona	Kennedy, L.B. Johnson 1, 2
Walter J. Hickel	1969-1970	Alaska	Nixon 1
Rogers C. B. Morton	1970-	Maryland	Nixon 1, 2

SECRETARIES OF AGRICULTURE

NAME	YEARS IN OFFICE	STATE	PRESIDENTIAL TERMS
Norman J. Colman	1889	Missouri	Cleveland 1, B. Harrison
Jeremiah M. Rusk	1889-1893	Wisconsin	B. Harrison, Cleveland
J. Sterling Morton	1893-1897	Nebraska	Cleveland 2, McKinley 1
James Wilson	1897-1913	Iowa	McKinley 1, 2, T. Roosevelt 1, 2 Taft, Wilson 1
David F. Houston	1913-1920	Missouri	Wilson 1, 2
Edwin T. Meredith	1920-1921	Iowa	Wilson 2, Harding
Henry C. Wallace	1921-1924	Iowa	Harding, Coolidge 1
Howard M. Gore	1924-1925	West Virginia	Coolidge 1, 2
William M. Jardine	1925-1929	Kansas	Coolidge 2, Hoover
Arthur M. Hyde	1929-1940	Iowa	F.D. Roosevelt 1, 2
Claude R. Wickard	1940-1945	Indiana	F.D. Roosevelt 2, 3, 4, Truman 1
Clinton P. Anderson	1945-1948	New Mexico	Truman 1
Charles F. Brannan	1948-1953	Colorado	Truman 1, 2
Ezra Taft Benson	1953-1961	Utah	Eisenhower 1, 2
Orville L. Freeman	1961-1969	Minnesota	Kennedy, L.B. Johnson 1, 2
Clifford M. Hardin	1969-1971	Indiana	Nixon 1
Earl L. Butz	1971-	Indiana	Nixon 1, 2

SECRETARIES OF COMMERCE AND LABOR

NAME	YEARS IN OFFICE	STATE	PRESIDENTIAL TERMS
George B. Cortelyou	1903-1904	New York	T. Roosevelt 1
Victor H. Metcalf	1904-1906	California	T. Roosevelt 1, 2
Oscar S. Straus	1906-1909	New York	T. Roosevelt 2, Taft
Charles Nagel	1909-1913	Missouri	Taft

(Became separate departments in 1913)

SECRETARIES OF LABOR

NAME	YEARS IN OFFICE	STATE	PRESIDENTIAL TERMS
William B. Wilson	1913-1921	Pennsylvania	Wilson 1, 2, Harding
James J. Davis	1921-1930	Pennsylvania	Harding, Coolidge 1, 2, Hoover
William N. Diak	1930-1933	Virginia	Hoover
Frances Perkins	1933-1945	New York	F.D. Roosevelt 1, 2, 3, 4, Truman
Lewis B. Schwellenbach	1945-1948	Washington	Truman 1
Maurice J. Tobin	1948-1953	Massachusetts	Truman 1, 2
Martin P. Durkin	1953	Illinois	Eisenhower 1
James P. Mitchell	1954-1961	New Jersey	Eisenhower 1, 2
Arthur J. Goldberg	1961-1962	Illinois	Kennedy
W. Willard Wirtz	1962-1969	Illinois	Kennedy, L.B. Johnson 1, 2
George P. Shultz	1969-1970	Illinois	Nixon 1
James D. Hodgson	1970-1973	California	Nixon 1
Peter J. Brennan	1973-		Nixon 2

SECRETARIES OF COMMERCE

NAME	YEARS IN OFFICE	STATE	PRESIDENTIAL TERMS
William C. Redfield	1913-1919	New York	Wilson 1, 2
Joshua W. Alexander	1919-1921	Missouri	Wilson 2, Harding
Herbert C. Hoover	1921-1928	California	Harding, Coolidge 1, 2
William F. Whiting	1928-1929	Massachusetts	Coolidge 2, Hoover
Robert P. Lamont	1929-1932	Illinois	Hoover
Roy D. Chapin	1932-1933	Michigan	Hoover
Daniel C. Roper	1933-1938	South Carolina	F.D. Roosevelt 1, 2
Harry L. Hopkins	1939-1940	New York	F.D. Roosevelt 2
Jesse H. Jones	1940-1945	Texas	F.D. Roosevelt 2, 3, 4
Henry A. Wallace	1945-1946	Iowa	F.D. Roosevelt 4, Truman 1
W. Averell Harriman	1947-1948	New York	Truman 1
Charles Sawyer	1948-1953	Ohio	Truman 1, 2
Sinclair Weeks	1953-1958	Massachusetts	Eisenhower 1, 2
Lewis L. Strauss	1958-1959	New York	Eisenhower 2
Frederick H. Mueller	1959-1961	Michigan	Eisenhower 2
Luther H. Hodges	1961-1965	North Carolina	Kennedy, L.B. Johnson 1
John T. Connor	1965-1967	New Jersey	L.B. Johnson 2
Alexander Trowbridge	1967-1968	New Jersey	L.B. Johnson 2
Cyrus R. Smith	1968-1969	New York	L.B. Johnson 2
Maurice H. Stans	1969-1972	Minnesota	Nixon 1
Peter G. Peterson	1972-1973	Illinois	Nixon 1
Frederick B. Dent	1973-	South Carolina	Nixon 2

SECRETARIES OF DEFENSE

(The Department of Defense was created in 1947 by consolidation of the Departments of the Navy and War into a single executive department. See Section VIII. The Military, for Secretaries of the Services.)

NAME	YEARS IN OFFICE	STATE	PRESIDENTIAL TERMS
James V. Forrestall	1947-1949	New York	Truman 1, 2
Louis A. Johnson	1949-1950	West Virginia	Truman 2
George C. Marshall	1950-1951	Pennsylvania	Truman 2
Robert A. Lovett	1951-1953	New York	Truman 2
Charles E. Wilson	1953-1957	Michigan	Eisenhower 1, 2
Neil H. McElroy	1957-1960	Ohio	Eisenhower 2
Thomas S. Gates, Jr.	1960-1961	Pennsylvania	Eisenhower 2
Robert S. McNamara	1961-1968	Michigan	Kennedy, L.B. Johnson 1, 2
Clark M. Clifford	1968-1969	Maryland	L.B. Johnson 2
Melvin R. Laird	1969-1973	Wisconsin	Nixon 1
Elliot L. Richardson	1973-	Massachusetts	Nixon 2

SECRETARIES OF HEALTH, EDUCATION, AND WELFARE

NAME	YEARS IN OFFICE	STATE	PRESIDENTIAL TERMS
Oveta Culp Hobby	1953-1955	Texas	Eisenhower 1
Marion B. Folsom	1955-1958	New York	Eisenhower 1, 2
Arthur S. Flemming	1958-1961	Ohio	Eisenhower 1
Abraham A. Ribicoff	1961-1962	Connecticut	Kennedy
Anthony J. Celebrezze	1962-1965	Ohio	Kennedy, L.B. Johnson 1
John W. Gardner	1965-1969	New York	L.B. Johnson
Wilbur J. Cohen	1968-1969	Michigan	L.B. Johnson 2
Robert H. Finch	1969-1970	California	Nixon 1
Elliot L. Richardson	1970-1973	Massachusetts	Nixon 1
Caspar W. Weinberger	1973-	California	Nixon 2

SECRETARIES OF HOUSING AND URBAN DEVELOPMENT

NAME	YEARS IN OFFICE	STATE	PRESIDENTIAL TERMS
Robert C. Weaver	1966-1968	Washington	L.B. Johnson 2
Robert C. Wood	1968-1969	Massachusetts	L.B. Johnson 2
George W. Romney	1969-1973	Michigan	Nixon 1
James T. Lynn	1973-	Ohio	Nixon 2

SECRETARIES OF TRANSPORTATION

NAME	YEARS IN OFFICE	STATE	PRESIDENTIAL TERMS
Alan S. Boyd	1966-1969	Florida	L.B. Johnson 2
John A. Volpe	1969-1973	Massachusetts	Nixon 1
Claude S. Brinegar	1973-	California	Nixon 2

IV

THE UNITED STATES GOVERNMENT:

LEGISLATIVE BRANCH

The members of the Senate and House of Representatives listed by Congresses.

1. The senior senator's name is placed first. When more than two names appear, the junior senator at the commencement of the congress is indicated by an extra space above his name.

2. The designation "r." followed by a month and year indicates the date that a congressman resigned, retired, or was removed from office.

3. The designation "d." following a congressman's name indicates the year of his death when in office.

4. The designation "ta." is used with dates to indicate the year(s) served by a temporary appointee.

5. The designation "s." is used when the year in which a congressman was seated is other than the first year of the congress.

As it was not uncommon for members of early congresses to be elected as non-partisan or independent candidates, political party designations often do not appear. They are indicated, however, when the member did have a party affiliation. Party symbols are as follows:

D	Democrat (Includes factions of the Democratic Party such as Union Democrats, Free-Soil Democrafts, and Jacksonian Democrats. Also includes Jeffersonian Republicans, the precursor of the Democratic Party.)
R	Republican (Includes Union Republicans)
F	Federalist
W	Whig
AF	Anti-Federalist
SRD	States Rights Democrat
SRW	States Rights Whig
NR	National Republican
FS	Free-Soiler
Un	Unionist
Null-D	Nullification Democrat
Amer	American
Con	Conservative
Lib	Liberal
Pop	Populist

FIRST CONGRESS

March 4, 1789 to March 3, 1791

President of The Senate: John Adams
President Pro Tempore of The Senate: John Langdon
Speaker of The House of Representatives: Frederick A. C. Muhlenberg

CONNECTICUT

Senators

Oliver Ellsworth (F)
William S. Johnson

Representatives

Benjamin Huntington
Roger Sherman
Jonathan Sturges (F)
Jonathan Trumbull (F)
Jeremiah Wadsworth (F)

DELAWARE

Senators

Richard Bassett (F)
George Read (F)

Representative

John Vining

GEORGIA

Senators

William Few (D)
James Gunn

Representatives

Abraham Baldwin (F)
James Jackson (D)
George Mathews

MARYLAND

Senators

John Henry (D)
Charles Carroll of Carrollton (F)

Representatives

Daniel Carroll (F)
Benjamin Contee
George Gale
Joshua Seney
William Smith (F)
Michael J. Stone

MASSACHUSETTS

Senators

Tristram Dalton
Caleb Strong (F)

Representatives

Fisher Ames (F)
Elbridge Gerry (AF)
Benjamin Goodhue (F)
Jonathan Grout (D)
George Leonard
George Partridge r. Aug. 1790
Theodore Sedgwick (F)
George Thacher (F)

NEW HAMPSHIRE

Senators

John Langdon (D)
Paine Wingate (F)

Representatives

Abiel Foster (F)
Nicholas Gilman (F)
Samuel Livermore

NEW JERSEY

Senators

Jonathan Elmer (F)

William Paterson (F) r. Nov. 1790
Philemon Dickinson s. 1790

Representatives

Elias Boudinot (F)
Lambert Cadwalader
James Schureman (F)
Thomas Sinnickson (F)

NEW YORK

Senators

Rufus King (F)
Philip Schuyler (F)

Representatives

Egbert Benson
William Floyd
John Hathorn (F)
John Laurance (F)
Peter Silvester
Jeremiah Van Rensselaer

NORTH CAROLINA

Senators

Benjamin Hawkins (F)
Samuel Johnston (F)

Representatives

John Ashe (F)
Timothy Bloodworth
John Sevier (D)
John Steele (F)
Hugh Williamson (F)

PENNSYLVANIA

Senators

William Maclay (D)
Robert Morris (F)

Representatives

George Clymer (F)
Thomas Fitzsimons (F)
Thomas Hartley (F)
Daniel Hiester (F)
Frederick A. C. Muhlenberg (F)
John Peter G. Muhlenberg (D)
Thomas Scott
Henry Wynkoop

RHODE ISLAND

Senators

Theodore Foster (Law & Order)
Joseph Stanton, Jr. (D)

Representative

Benjamin Bourn (F)

SOUTH CAROLINA

Senators

Pierce Butler (D)
Ralph Izard

Representatives

Aedanus Burke
Daniel Huger
William L. Smith (F)
Thomas Sumter (D)
Thomas T. Tucker (F)

VIRGINIA

Senators

William Grayson (AF)
d. Mar. 1790
John Walker s. 1790
James Monroe (D) s. 1790
Richard Henry Lee (AF)

Representatives

Theodorick Bland d. 1790
John Brown
Isaac Coles
William B. Giles (AF) s. 1790
Samuel Griffin
Richard Bland Lee (F)
James Madison (D)
Andrew Moore (F)
John Page (D)
Josiah Parker (AF)
Alexander White (F)

SECOND CONGRESS

March 4, 1791 to March 3, 1793

President of The Senate: John Adams
Presidents Pro Tempore of The Senate: Richard Henry Lee, John Langdon
Speaker of The House of Representatives: Jonathan Trumbull

CONNECTICUT

Senators

Oliver Ellsworth (F)

William S. Johnson r. Mar. 1791
Roger Sherman

Representatives

James Hillhouse (F)
Amasa Learned
Jonathan Sturges (F)
Jonathan Trumbull (F)
Jeremiah Wadsworth (F)

DELAWARE

Senators

Richard Bassett (F)
George Read (F)

Representative

John Vining

GEORGIA

Senators

William Few (D)
James Gunn

Representatives

Abraham Baldwin (F)
John Milledge s. 1792
Anthony Wayne r. 1792
Francis Willis

KENTUCKY

Senators

John Edwards
John Brown

Representatives

Alexander D. Orr
Christopher Greenup

MARYLAND

Senators

John Henry (D)

Charles Carroll of Carrollton (F)
r. Nov. 1792
Richard Potts (F) s. 1793

Representatives

William Hindman (F) s. 1793
Philip Key (F)
John F. Mercer (D) s. 1792
William Vans Murray (F)
William Pinkney r. Nov. 1791
Joshua Seney r. May 1792
Upton Sheredine (D)
Samuel Sterett (AF)

MASSACHUSETTS

Senators

Caleb Strong (F)
George Cabot (F)

Representatives

Fisher Ames (F)
Shearjashub Bourne
Elbridge Gerry (AF)
Benjamin Goodhue (F)
Theodore Sedgwick (F)
George Thacher (F)
Artemas Ward (F)

NEW HAMPSHIRE

Senators

John Langdon (D)
Paine Wingate (D)

Representatives

Nicholas Gilman (F)
Samuel Livermore
Jeremiah Smith (F)

NEW JERSEY

Senators

Philemon Dickinson
John Rutherfurd (F)

Representatives

Elias Boudinot (F)
Abraham Clark
Jonathan Dayton (F)
Aaron Kitchell (D)

NEW YORK

Senators

Rufus King (F)
Aaron Burr (D)

Representatives

Egbert Benson
James Gordon (F)
John Laurance (F)
Cornelius C. Schoonmaker
Peter Silvester
Thomas Tredwell

NORTH CAROLINA

Senators

Benjamin Hawkins (F)
Samuel Johnston (F)

Representatives

John Ashe (F)
William Grove (F)
Nathaniel Macon (D)
John Steele (F)
Hugh Williamson (F)

PENNSYLVANIA

Senator

Robert Morris (F)

Representatives

William Findley (D)
Thomas Fitzsimons (F)
Andrew Gregg (F)
Thomas Hartley (F)
Daniel Hiester (F)
Israel Jacobs
John W. Kittera (F)
Frederick A. C. Muhlenberg (F)

RHODE ISLAND

Senators

Theodore Foster (Law & Order)
Joseph Stanton, Jr. (D)

Representative

Benjamin Bourn (F)

SOUTH CAROLINA

Senators

Pierce Butler (D)
Ralph Izard

Representatives

Robert Barnwell (F)
Daniel Huger
William L. Smith (F)
Thomas Sumter (D)
Thomas T. Tucker (F)

VERMONT

Senators

Moses Robinson (D)
Stephen R. Bradley (D)

Representatives

Nathaniel Niles (D)
Israel Smith (D)

VIRGINIA

Senators

Richard Henry Lee (AF)
r. Oct. 1792
John Taylor (D)

James Monroe (D)

Representatives

John Brown
William B. Giles (AF)
Samuel Griffin
Richard Bland Lee (F)
James Madison (D)
Andrew Moore (F)
John Page (D)
Josiah Parker (AF)
Abraham B. Venable
Alexander White (F)

THIRD CONGRESS

March 4, 1793 to March 3, 1795

Presidents Pro Tempore of The Senate:	John Adams
President Pro Tempore of The Senate:	Ralph Izard, Henry Tazewell
Speaker of The House of Representatives:	Frederick A. C. Muhlenberg

CONNECTICUT

Senators

Oliver Ellsworth (F)

Roger Sherman d. July 1793
Stephen M. Mitchell (F)

Representatives

Joshua Coit (F)
James Hillhouse (F)
Amasa Learned
Zephaniah Swift (F)
Uriah Tracy (F)
Jonathan Trumbull (F)
Jeremiah Wadsworth (F)

DELAWARE

Senators

George Read (F) r. Sept. 1793
Henry Latimer s. 1795

John Vining

Representatives

Henry Latimer
John Patten

GEORGIA

Senators

James Gunn
James Jackson (D)

Representatives

Abraham Baldwin (F)
Thomas P. Carnes

KENTUCKY

Senators

John Edwards
John Brown

Representatives

Christopher Greenup
Alexander D. Orr

MARYLAND

Senators

John Henry (D)
Richard Potts (F)

Representatives

Gabriel Christie
George Dent (D)
Gabriel Duvall (D) s. 1794
Benjamin Edwards s. 1795
Uriah Forest r. Nov. 1794
William Hindman (F)
John F. Mercer r. Apr. 1794
William Vans Murray (F)
Samuel Smith (D)
Thomas Sprigg

MASSACHUSETTS

Senators

Caleb Strong (F)
George Cabot (F)

Representatives

Fisher Ames (F)
Shearjashub Bourne
David Cobb (F)
Peleg Coffin, Jr.
Henry Dearborn (D)
Samuel Dexter (F)
Dwight Foster (F)
Benjamin Goodhue (F)
Samuel Holten (AF)
William Lyman (D)
Theodore Sedgwick (F)
George Thacher (F)
Peleg Wadsworth
Artemas Ward (F)

NEW HAMPSHIRE

Senators

John Langdon (D)
Samuel Livermore

Representatives

Nicholas Gilman
John S. Sherburne
Jeremiah Smith (F)
Paine Wingate (F)

NEW JERSEY

Senators

John Rutherfurd (F)
Frederick Frelinghuysen (F)

Representatives

John Beatty
Elias Boudinot (F)
Lambert Cadwalader
Abraham Clark d. Sept. 1794
Jonathan Dayton (F)
Aaron Kitchell (D) s. 1795

NEW YORK

Senators

Rufus King (F)
Aaron Burr (D)

Representatives

Theodorus Bailey (D)
Ezekiel Gilbert
James Gordon (F)
Henry Glen
Silas Talbot (F)
Thomas Tredwell
John E. Van Alen (F)
Philip Van Cortlandt (D)
Peter Van Gaasbeck (AF)
John Watts

NORTH CAROLINA

Senators

Benjamin Hawkins (F)
Alexander Martin (F)

Representatives

Thomas Blount (D)
William J. Dawson
James Gillespie
William B. Grove (F)
Matthew Locke (D)
Joseph McDowell
Nathaniel Macon (D)
Alexander Mebane
Benjamin Williams
Joseph Winston

PENNSYLVANIA

Senators

Robert Morris (F)

Albert Gallatin (D) r. Feb. 1794
James Ross (F) s. 1794

Representatives

James Armstrong (F)
William Findley (D)
Thomas Fitzsimons (F)
Andrew Gregg (F)
Thomas Hartley (F)
Daniel Hiester (F)
William Irvine
John W. Kittera (F)
William Montgomery
Frederick A. C. Muhlenberg (F)
John Peter G. Muhlenberg (D)
Thomas Scott
John Smilie (D)

RHODE ISLAND

Senators

Theodore Foster (Law & Order)
William Bradford

Representatives

Benjamin Bourn (F)
Francis Malbone (F)

SOUTH CAROLINA

Senators

Pierce Butler (D)
Ralph Izard

Representatives

Lemuel Benton (D)
Alexander Gillon d. Oct. 1794
Robert G. Harper (F) s. 1795
John Hunter (F)
Andrew Pickens (D)
William L. Smith (F)
Richard Winn

VERMONT

Senators

Moses Robinson (D)
Stephen R. Bradley (D)

Representatives

Nathaniel Niles (D)
Israel Smith (D)

VIRGINIA

Senators

James Monroe (D) r. May 1794
Stevens T. Mason (D) s. 1795

John Taylor (D) r. May 1794
Henry Tazewell s. 1794

Representatives

Isaac Coles
Thomas Claiborne
William B. Giles (AF)
Samuel Griffin
George Hancock (D)
Carter B. Harrison
John Heath (D)
Richard Bland Lee (F)
James Madison (D)
Andrew Moore (F)
Joseph Neville
Anthony New (D)
John Nicholas (D)
John Page (D)
Josiah Parker (AF)
Francis Preston
Robert Rutherford
Abraham B. Venable
Francis Walker

FOURTH CONGRESS

March 4, 1795 to March 3, 1797

President of The Senate: John Adams
Presidents Pro Tempore of The Senate: Henry Tazewell, Samuel Livermore, William Bingham
Speaker of The House of Representatives: Jonathan Dayton

CONNECTICUT

Senators

Oliver Ellsworth (F) r. Mar. 1796
James Hillhouse (F) s. 1796

Jonathan Trumbull (F) r. June 1796
Uriah Tracy (F) s. 1796

Representatives

Joshua Coit (F)
Samuel W. Dana (F) s. 1797
James Davenport s. 1796
Chauncey Goodrich (F)
Roger Griswold (F)
James Hillhouse (F) r. 1796
Nathaniel Smith (F)
Zephaniah Swift (F)
Uriah Tracy (F) r. Oct. 1796

DELAWARE

Senators

John Vining
Henry Latimer

Representative

John Patten

GEORGIA

Senators

James Gunn

James Jackson (D) r. 1795
George Walton ta. 1795
Josiah Tattnall s. 1796

Representatives

Abraham Baldwin (F)
John Milledge

KENTUCKY

Senators

John Brown
Humphrey Marshall (F)

Representatives

Christopher Greenup
Alexander D. Orr

MARYLAND

Senators

John Henry (D)

Richard Potts (F) r. Oct. 1796
John E. Howard (F) s. 1796

Representatives

Gabriel Christie
Jeremiah Crabb (D) r. 1796
William Craik s. 1796
George Dent (D)
Gabriel Duvall (D) r. Mar. 1796
William Hindman (F)
William Vans Murray (F)
Samuel Smith (D)
Richard Sprigg, Jr. s. 1796
Thomas Sprigg

MASSACHUSETTS

Senators

Caleb Strong (F) r. June 1796
Theodore Sedgwick (F) s. 1796

George Cabot (F) r. June 1796
Benjamin Goodhue (F) s. 1796

Representatives

Fisher Ames (F)
Theophilus Bradbury (F)
Henry Dearborn (D)
Dwight Foster (F)
Nathaniel Freeman, Jr.
Benjamin Goodhue (F) r. June 1796
George Leonard
Samuel Lyman
William Lyman (D)
John Reed (F)
Theodore Sedgwick (F) r. June 1796
Samuel Sweall s. 1796
Thomson J. Skinner (D) s. 1797
George Thacher (F)
Joseph B. Varnum (AF)
Peleg Wadsworth

NEW HAMPSHIRE

Senators

John Langdon (D)
Samuel Livermore

Representatives

Abiel Foster (F)
Nicholas Gilman (F)
John S. Sherburne
Jeremiah Smith (F)

NEW JERSEY

Senators

John Rutherfurd (F)

Frederick Frelinghuysen (F) r. Nov. 1796
Richard Stockton (F) s. 1796

Representatives

Jonathan Dayton (F)
Thomas Henderson (F)
Aaron Kitchell (D)
Isaac Smith (F)
Mark Thomson (F)

NEW YORK

Senators

Rufus King (F) r. May 1796
John Laurance (F) s. 1796

Aaron Burr (D)

Representatives

Theodorus Bailey (D)
William Cooper (F)
Ezekiel Gilbert
Henry Glen
John Hathorn (F)
Jonathan N. Havens (D)
Edward Livingston (D)
John E. Van Alen (F)
Philip Van Cortlandt (D)
John Williams

NORTH CAROLINA

Senators

Alexander Martin (F)
Timothy Bloodworth

Representatives

Thomas Blount (D)
Nathan Bryan
Dempsey Burges
Jesse Franklin
James Gillespie
William B. Grove (F)
James Holland
Matthew Locke (D)
Nathaniel Macon (D)
William F. Strudwick s. 1796
Absalom Tatom r. June 1796

PENNSYLVANIA

Senators

James Ross (F)
William Bingham

Representatives

David Bard
George Ege s. 1796
William Findley (D)
Albert Gallatin (D)
Andrew Gregg (F)
Thomas Hartley (F)
Daniel Hiester (F) r. July 1796
John W. Kittera (F)
Samuel Maclay (F)
Frederick A. C. Muhlenberg (F)
John Richards
Samuel Sitgreaves (F)
John Swanwick (D)
Richard Thomas (F)

RHODE ISLAND

Senators

Theodore Foster (Law & Order)
William Bradford

Representatives

Benjamin Bourn (F) r. 1796
Francis Malbone (F)
Elisha R. Potter (F) s. 1796

SOUTH CAROLINA

Senators

Pierce Butler (D) r. Oct. 1796
John Hunter (F) s. 1797

Jacob Read (F)

Representatives

Lemuel Benton (D)
Samuel Earle
Wade Hampton (D)
Robert G. Harper (F)
William L. Smith (F)
Richard Winn

TENNESSEE

Senators

William Blount
William Cocke

Representative

Andrew Jackson (D)

VERMONT

Senators

Moses Robinson (D) r. Oct. 1796
Isaac Tichenor (F) s. 1796

Elijah Paine (F)

Representatives

Daniel Buck (F)
Israel Smith (D)

VIRGINIA

Senators

Henry Tazewell
Stevens T. Mason (D)

Representatives

Richard Brent
Samuel J. Cabell (D)
Thomas Claiborne
John Clopton (D)
Isaac Coles
William B. Giles (AF)
George Hancock (D)
Carter B. Harrison
John Heath
George Jackson
James Madison (D)
Andrew Moore (F)
Anthony New (D)
John Nicholas (D)
John Page (D)
Josiah Parker (AF)
Francis Preston
Robert Rutherford
Abraham B. Venable

FIFTH CONGRESS

March 4, 1797 to March 3, 1799

President of The Senate: Thomas Jefferson
Presidents Pro Tempore of The Senate: William Bradford
Jacob Read
Theodore Sedgwick
John Laurance
James Ross
Speaker of The House of Representatives: Jonathan Dayton

CONNECTICUT

Senators

James Hillhouse (F)
Uriah Tracy (F)

Representatives

John Allen (F)
Jonathan Brace (F) s. 1798
Joshua Coit (F) d. Sept. 1798
Samuel W. Dana (F)
James Davenport d. Aug. 1797
William Edmond
Chauncey Goodrich (F)
Roger Griswold (F)
Nathaniel Smith (F)

DELAWARE

Senators

John Vining r. Jan. 1798
Joshua Claton s. 1798 d. Aug. 1798
William H. Wells s. 1799

Henry Latimer

Representative

James A. Bayard, Sr. (F)

GEORGIA

Senators

James Gunn
Josiah Tattnall

Representatives

Abraham Baldwin (F)
John Milledge

KENTUCKY

Senators

John Brown
Humphrey Marshall (F)

Representatives

Thomas T. Davis
John Fowler

MARYLAND

Senators

John Henry (D) r. Dec. 1797
James Lloyd (D) s. 1798

John E. Howard (F)

Representatives

George Baer, Jr. (F)
William Craik
John Dennis (F)
George Dent (D)
William Hindman (F)
William Matthews
Samuel Smith
Richard Sprigg, Jr.

MASSACHUSETTS

Senators

Benjamin Goodhue (F)
Theodore Sedgwick (F)

Representatives

Bailey Bartlett (F)
Theophilus Bradbury (F) r. July 1797
Stephen Bullock (F)
Dwight Foster (F)
Nathaniel Freeman, Jr.
Samuel Lyman
Harrison G. Otis (F)
Isaac Parker
John Reed (F)
Samuel Sewall
William Shepard
Thomson J. Skinner (D)
George Thacher (F)
Joseph B. Varnum (AF)
Peleg Wadsworth

NEW HAMPSHIRE

Senators

John Langdon (D)
Samuel Livermore

Representatives

Abiel Foster (F)
Jonathan Freeman (F)
William Gordon
Jeremiah Smith (F) r. July 1797
Peleg Sprague

NEW JERSEY

Senators

John Rutherfurd (F) r. Nov. 1798
Franklin Davenport s. 1798

Richard Stockton (F)

Representatives

Jonathan Dayton (F)
James H. Imlay
James Schureman (F)
Thomas Sinnickson (F)
Mark Thomson (F)

NEW YORK

Senators

John Laurance (F)

Philip Schuyler (F) r. Jan. 1798
John S. Hobart s. 1798,
r. Apr. 1798
William North (F) ta. 1798
James Watson (D) s. 1798

Representatives

David Brooks
James Cochran
Lucas C. Elmendorf (D)
Henry Glen
Jonathan N. Havens (D)
Hezekiah L. Hosmer
Edward Livingston (D)
John E. Van Alen (F)
Philip Van Cortlandt (D)
John Williams

NORTH CAROLINA

Senators

Alexander Martin (F)
Timothy Bloodworth

Representatives

Thomas Blount (D)
Nathan Bryan d. June 1798
Dempsey Burges
James Gillespie
William B. Grove (F)
Matthew Locke (D)
Joseph McDowell
Nathaniel Macon (D)
Richard D. Spaight (D) s. 1798
Richard Stanford (D)
Robert Williams

PENNSYLVANIA

Senators

James Ross (F)
William Bingham

Representatives

David Bard
Robert Brown (D) s. 1798
John Chapman (F)
George Ege r. Oct. 1797
William Findley (D)
Albert Gallatin (D)
Andrew Gregg (F)
John A. Hanna (AF)
Thomas Hartley (F)
Joseph Hiester (F)
John W. Kittera (F)
Blair McClenachan
Samuel Sitgreaves (F) r. 1798
John Swanwick (D) d. Aug. 1798
Richard Thomas (F)
Robert Waln (F) s. 1798

RHODE ISLAND

Senators

Theodore Foster (Law & Order)

William Bradford r. Oct. 1797
Ray Greene

Representatives

Christopher G. Champlin
Elisha R. Potter (F) r. 1797
Thomas Tillinghast

SOUTH CAROLINA

Senators

Jacob Read (F)

John Hunter (F) r. Nov. 1798
Charles Pinckney (D) s. 1799

Representatives

Lemuel Benton (D)
Robert G. Harper (F)
Thomas Pinckney (F)
John Rutledge, Jr. (F)
William Smith (D)
William L. Smith (F) r. July 1797
Thomas Sumter (D)

TENNESSEE

Senators

William Blount r. July 1797
Joseph Anderson

William Cocke ta. 1797
Andrew Jackson (D) r. 1798
Daniel Smith (D) ta. 1798

Representative

William C. C. Claiborne

VERMONT

Senators

Elijah Paine (F)

Isaac Tichenor (F) r. Oct. 1797
Nathaniel Chipman (F)

Representatives

Matthew Lyon (AF)
Lewis R. Morris (F)

VIRGINIA

Senators

Henry Tazewell d. Jan. 1799
Stevens T. Mason (D)

Representatives

Richard Brent
Samuel J. Cabell (D)
Thomas Claiborne
Matthew Clay (D)
John Clopton (D)
John Dawson (D)
Joseph Eggleston s. 1798
Thomas Evans
William B. Giles (AF) r. Oct. 1798
Carter B. Harrison
David Holmes
Walter Jones (D)
James Machir
Daniel Morgan (F)
Anthony New (D)
John Nicholas (D)
Josiah Parker (AF)
Abram Trigg
John Trigg
Abraham B. Venable

SIXTH CONGRESS

March 4, 1799 to March 3, 1801

President of The Senate:	Thomas Jefferson
Presidents Pro Tempore of The Senate:	Samuel Livermore Uriah Tracy John E. Howard James Hillhouse
Speaker of The House of Representatives:	Theodore Sedgwick

CONNECTICUT

Senators

James Hillhouse (F)
Uriah Tracy (F)

Representatives

Jonathan Brace (F) r. 1800
Samuel W. Dana (F)
John Davenport (F)
William Edmond (F)
Chauncey Goodrich (R)
Elizur Goodrich (F)
Roger Griswold (F)
John C. Smith (F) s. 1800

DELAWARE

Senators

Henry Latimer r. Feb. 1801
Samuel White (F) s. 1801

William H. Wells

Representative

James A. Bayard, Sr. (F)

GEORGIA

Senators

James Gunn
Abraham Baldwin (F)

Representatives

James Jones (D)
Benjamin Taliaferro

KENTUCKY

Senators

John Brown
Humphrey Marshall (F)

Representatives

Thomas T. Davis
John Fowler

MARYLAND

Senators

John E. Howard (F)

James Lloyd (D) r. Dec. 1800
William Hindman (F) s. 1800

Representatives

George Baer, Jr. (F)
Gabriel Christie
William Craik
John Dennis (F)
George Dent (D)
Joseph H. Nicholson (D)
Samuel Smith (D)
John C. Thomas (F)

MASSACHUSETTS

Senators

Benjamin Goodhue (F)
r. Nov. 1800
Jonathan Mason (F) s. 1800

Samuel Dexter (F) r. May 1800
Dwight Foster (F) s. 1800

Representatives

Bailey Bartlett (F)
Phanuel Bishop
Dwight Foster (F) r. June 1800
Silas Lee (F)
Levi Lincoln (D)
Samuel Lyman r. Nov. 1800
Ebenezer Mattoon (F) s. 1801
Harrison G. Otis (F)
Nathan Read (F) s. 1800

John Reed (F)
Theodore Sedgwick (F)
Samuel Sewall r. Jan. 1800
William Shepard
George Thacher (F)
Joseph B. Varnum (AF)
Peleg Wadsworth
Lemuel Williams

NEW HAMPSHIRE

Senators

John Langdon (D)
Samuel Livermore

Representatives

Abiel Foster (F)
Jonathan Freeman (F)
William Gordon r. June 1800
James Sheafe (F)
Samuel Tenney s. 1800

NEW JERSEY

Senators

James Schureman (F)
r. Feb. 1801
Aaron Ogden (F) s. 1801

Jonathan Dayton (F)

Representatives

John Condit (D)
Franklin Davenport
James H. Imlay
Aaron Kitchell (D)
James Linn (D)

NEW YORK

Senators

John Laurance (F) r. Aug. 1800
John Armstrong s. 1801

James Watson (D) r. Mar. 1800
Gouverneur Morris (F) s. 1800

Representatives

Theodorus Bailey (D)
John Bird (D)
William Cooper (F)
Lucas C. Elmendorf (D)
Henry Glen
Jonathan N. Havens (D)
d. Oct. 1799
Edward Livingston (D)
Jonas Platt (F)
John Smith (D) s. 1800
John Thompson (D)
Philip Van Cortlandt (D)

NORTH CAROLINA

Senators

Timothy Bloodworth
Jesse Franklin (D)

Representatives

Willis Alston (D)
Joseph Dickson (F)
William B. Grove (F)
Archibald Henderson (F)
William H. Hill (F)
Nathaniel Macon (D)
Richard D. Spaight (D)
Richard Stanford (D)
David Stone (D)
Robert Williams

PENNSYLVANIA

Senators

James Ross (F)
William Bingham

Representatives

Robert Brown (D)
Albert Gallatin (D)
Andrew Gregg (F)
John A. Hanna (AF)
Thomas Hartley (F) d. Dec. 1800
Joseph Hiester (F)
John W. Kittera (F)
Michael Leib (D)
John Peter G. Muhlenberg (D)
John Smilie (D)
John Stewart (D) s. 1801
Richard Thomas (F)
Robert Waln (F)
Henry Woods

RHODE ISLAND

Senators

Theodore Foster (Law & Order)
Ray Greene

Representatives

John Brown (F)
Christopher G. Champlin

SOUTH CAROLINA

Senators

Jacob Read (F)
Charles Pinckney (D)

Representatives

Robert Harper (F)
Benjamin Huger
Abraham Nott (F)
Thomas Pinckney (F)
John Rutledge, Jr. (F)
Thomas Sumter (D)

TENNESSEE

Senators

Joseph Anderson
William Cocke

Representative

William C. C. Claiborne (D)

VERMONT

Senators

Elijah Paine (F)
Nathaniel Chipman (F)

Representatives

Matthew Lyon (AF)
Lewis R. Morris (F)

VIRGINIA

Senators

Stevens T. Mason (D)
Wilson C. Nicholas (D)

Representatives

Samuel J. Cabell (D)
Matthew Clay (D)
John Dawson (D)
Joseph Eggleston (D)
Thomas Evans
Samuel Goode
Edwin Gray
David Holmes
George Jackson
Henry Lee (F)
John Marshall (F) r. June 1800
Anthony New (D)
John Nicholas (D)
Robert Page (F)
Josiah Parker (AF)
Levin Powell (F)
John Randolph (SRD)
Littleton W. Tazewell (D) s. 1800
Abram Trigg
John Trigg

SEVENTH CONGRESS

March 4, 1801 to March 3, 1803

President of The Senate: Aaron Burr
Presidents Pro Tempore of The Senate: Abraham Baldwin
Stephen R. Bradley
Speaker of The House of Representatives: Nathaniel Macon

CONNECTICUT

Senators

James Hillhouse (F)
Uriah Tracy (F)

Representatives

Samuel W. Dana (F)
John Davenport (F)
Calvin Goddard (F)
Roger Griswold (F)
Elias Perkins (F)
John C. Smith (F)
Benjamin Tallmadge (F)

DELAWARE

Senators

William H. Wells
Samuel White (F)

Representative

James A. Bayard, Sr. (F)

GEORGIA

Senators

Abraham Baldwin (F)
James Jackson (D)

Representatives

Peter Early s. 1803
David Meriwether (D) s. 1802
John Milledge r. May 1802
Benjamin Taliaferro r. 1802

KENTUCKY

Senators

John Brown
John Breckinridge (D)

Representatives

Thomas T. Davis
John Fowler

MARYLAND

Senators

John E. Howard (F)

William Hindman (F) ta. 1801
Robert Wright (D)

Representatives

John Archer (D)
Walter Bowie (D) s. 1802
John Campbell (F)
John Dennis (F)
Daniel Hiester
Joseph H. Nicholson (D)
Thomas Plater
Samuel Smith (D)
Richard Sprigg, Jr. r. Feb. 1802

MASSACHUSETTS

Senators

Dwight Foster (F) r. Mar. 1803
Jonathan Mason (F)

Representatives

John Bacon (D)
Phanuel Bishop
Manasseh Cutler (F)
Richard Cutts (D)
William Eustis (D)
Seth Hastings (F) s. 1802
Silas Lee (F) r. Aug. 1801
Levi Lincoln (D) r. 1801
Ebenezer Mattoon (F)
Nathan Read (F)
William Shepard
Josiah Smith
Samuel Thatcher
Joseph B. Varnum (AF)
Peleg Wadsworth
Lemuel Williams

NEW HAMPSHIRE

Senators

Samuel Livermore r. June 1801
Simeon Olcott (F)

James Sheafe (F) r. Jan. 1802
William Plumer (F) s. 1802

Representatives

Abiel Foster (F)
Samuel Hunt s. 1802
Joseph Pierce r. 1802
Samuel Tenney
George B. Upham

NEW JERSEY

Senators

Jonathan Dayton (F)
Aaron Ogden (F)

Representatives

John Condit (D)
Ebenezer Elmer (D)
William Helms (D)
James Mott (D)
Henry Southard (D)

NEW YORK

Senators

Gouverneur Morris (F)

John Armstrong (D) r. Feb. 1802
De Witt Clinton (D) s. 1802

Representatives

Theodorus Bailey (D)
John Bird (D) r. July 1801
Lucas C. Elmendorf (D)
Samuel L. Mitchill (D)
Thomas Morris
John Smith (D)
David Thomas (D)
Thomas Tillotson r. Aug. 1801
Philip Van Cortlandt (D)
John P. Van Ness (D)
Killian K. Van Rensselaer (D)
Benjamin Walker (D)

NORTH CAROLINA

Senators

Jesse Franklin (D)
David Stone (D)

Representatives

Willis Alston (D)
William B. Grove (F)
Archibald Henderson (F)
William H. Hill (F)
James Holland (AF)
Charles Johnson d. 1802
Nathaniel Macon (D)
Richard Stanford (D)
John Stanly
Robert Williams
Thomas Wynns (F) s. 1802

PENNSYLVANIA

Senators

James Ross (F)

John Peter G. Muhlenberg (D) r. June 1801
George Logan (D)

Representatives

Thomas Boude (F)
Robert Brown (D)
Andrew Gregg (F)
John A. Hanna (AF)
Joseph Hemphill (F)
Joseph Hiester (F)
William Hoge (F)
William Jones (D)
Michael Leib (D)
John Smilie (D)
John Stewart (D)
Isaac Van Horne (D)
Henry Woods

RHODE ISLAND

Senators

Theodore Foster (Law & Order)

Ray Greene r. Mar. 1801
Christopher Ellery (D)

Representatives

Joseph Stanton, Jr. (D)
Thomas Tillinghast

SOUTH CAROLINA

Senators

Charles Pinckney (D) r. 1801
Thomas Sumter (D)

John E. Colhoun (D) d. Oct. 1802
Pierce Butler (D)

Representatives

William Butler (AF)
Benjamin Huger
Thomas Lowndes (F)
Thomas Moore
John Rutledge, Jr. (F)
Thomas Sumter (D) r. Dec. 1801
Richard Winn (D) s. 1803

TENNESSEE

Senators

Joseph Anderson
William Cocke

Representative

William Dickson

VERMONT

Senators

Elijah Paine (F) r. Sept. 1801
Stephen R. Bradley (D)

Nathaniel Chipman (F)

Representatives

Lewis R. Morris (F)
Israel Smith (D)

VIRGINIA

Senators

Stevens T. Mason (D)
Wilson C. Nicholas (D)

Representatives

Richard Brent
Samuel J. Cabell (D)
Thomas Claiborne
Matthew Clay (D)
John Clopton (D)
John Dawson (D)
William B. Giles (D)
Edwin Gray
David Holmes
George Jackson
Anthony New (D)
Thomas Newton, Jr. (D)
John Randolph (SDR)
John Smith
John Stratton
John Taliaferro (D)
Philip R. Thompson (D)
Abram Trigg
John Trigg

EIGHTH CONGRESS

March 4, 1803 to March 3, 1805

President of The Senate:	Aaron Burr
Presidents Pro Tempore of The Senate:	John Brown Jesse Franklin Joseph Anderson
Speaker of The House of Representatives:	Nathaniel Macon

CONNECTICUT

Senators

James Hillhouse (F)
Uriah Tracy (F)

Representatives

Simeon Baldwin (F)
Samuel W. Dana (F)
John Davenport (F)
Calvin Goodard (F)
Roger Griswold (F)
John C. Smith (F)
Benjamin Tallmadge (F)

DELAWARE

Senators

William H. Wells r. Nov. 1804
James A. Bayard, Sr. (F) s. 1805

Samuel White (F)

Representative

Caesar A. Rodney (D)

GEORGIA

Senators

Abraham Baldwin (F)
James Jackson (D)

Representatives

Joseph Bryan (D)
Peter Early
Samuel Hammond
David Meriwether (D)

KENTUCKY

Senators

John Brown
John Breckinridge (D)

Representatives

George M. Bedinger
John Boyle (D)
John Fowler
Matthew Lyon (AF)
Thomas Sandford (D)
Matthew Walton (D)

MARYLAND

Senators

Robert Wright (D)
Samuel Smith (D)

Representatives

John Archer (D)
Walter Bowie (D)
John Campbell (F)
John Dennis (F)
Daniel Hiester d. Mar. 1804
William McCreery
Nicholas R. Moore (D)
Roger Nelson (D) s. 1804
Joseph H. Nicholson (D)
Thomas Plater

MASSACHUSETTS

Senators

Timothy Pickering (F)
John Quincy Adams (F)

Representatives

Phanuel Bishop
Jacob Crowninshield (D)
Manasseh Cutler (F)
Richard Cutts (D)
Thomas Dwight (F)
William Eustis (D)
Seth Hastings (F)
Simon Larned s. 1804
Nahum Mitchell (F)
Ebenezer Seaver (D)
Thomson J. Skinner (D)
r. Aug. 1804
William Stedman (F)
Samuel Taggart (F)
Samuel Thatcher (D)
Joseph B. Varnum (AF)
Peleg Wadsworth
Lemuel Williams

NEW HAMPSHIRE

Senators

Simeon Olcott (F)
William Plumer (F)

Representatives

Silas Betton
Clifton Clagett
David Hough
Samuel Hunt
Samuel Tenney

NEW JERSEY

Senators

Jonathan Dayton (F)
John Condit (D)

Representatives

Adam Boyd (D)
Ebenezer Elmer (D)
William Helms (D)
James Mott (D)
James Sloan
Henry Southard (D)

NEW YORK

Senators

De Witt Clinton (D) r. Nov. 1803
John Armstrong ta. 1803-04
John Smith (D) s. 1804

Theodorus Bailey (D) r. 1804
Samuel L. Mitchill (D) s. 1804

Representatives

Isaac Bloom d. Apr. 1803
George Clinton, Jr. (D) s. 1805
Gaylord Griswold (F)
Josiah Hasbrouck
Henry W. Livingston
Andrew McCord
Samuel L. Mitchill (D)
r. Nov. 1804
Beriah Palmer
John Paterson
Oliver Phelps (D)
Samuel Riker s. 1804
Erastus Root (D)
Thomas Sammons (D)
Joshua Sands
John Smith (D) r. Feb. 1804
David Thomas (D)
George Tibbitts (F)
Philip Van Cortlandt (D)
Killian K. Van Rensselaer (D)
Daniel C. Verplanck (F)

NORTH CAROLINA

Senators

Jesse Franklin (D)
David Stone (D)

Representatives

Nathaniel Alexander
Willis Alston (D)
William Blackledge (D)
James Gillespie d. Jan. 1805
James Holland (AF)
William Kennedy (F)
Nathaniel Macon (D)
Samuel D. Purviance (F)
Richard Stanford (D)
Marmaduke Williams (D)
Joseph Winston (D)
Thomas Wynns (D

OHIO

Senators

John Smith (D)
Thomas Worthington (D)

Representative

Jeremiah Morrow

PENNSYLVANIA

Senators

George Logan (D)
Samuel Maclay

Representatives

Isaac Anderson (D)
David Bard
Robert Brown (D)
Joseph Clay
Frederick Conrad (D)
William Findley (D)
Andrew Gregg (F)
John A. Hanna (AF)
Joseph Hiester
John Hoge (D) s. 1804
William Hoge (F) r. Oct. 1804
Michael Leib (D)
John B. C. Lucas (D)
John Rea (D)
Jacob Richards (D)
John Smilie
John Stewart (D)
Isaac Van Horne (D)
John Whitehill

RHODE ISLAND

Senators

Christopher Ellery (D)

Benjamin Howland (D) s. 1804
Samuel J. Potter d. Oct. 1804

Representatives

Nehemiah Knight (AF)
Joseph Stanton, Jr. (D)

SOUTH CAROLINA

Senators

Thomas Sumter (D)

Pierce Butler r. Nov. 1804
John Gaillard (D) s. 1805

Representatives

William Butler (AF)
Levi Casey
John B. Earle
Wade Hampton (D)
Benjamin Huger
Thomas Lowndes (F)
Thomas Moore
Richard Winn (D)

TENNESSEE

Senators

Joseph Anderson
William Cocke

Representatives

George W. Campbell (D)
William Dickson
John Rhea (D)

VERMONT

Senators

Stephen R. Bradley (D)
Israel Smith (D)

Representatives

William Chamberlain (F)
Martin Chittenden
James Elliott (F)
Gideon Olin (D)

VIRGINIA

Senators

Stevens T. Mason (D)
d. May 1803
John Taylor (D) ta. 1803
Abraham B. Venable r. 1804
William B. Giles (D) s. 1804

Wilson C. Nicholas (D)
r. May 1804
Andrew Moore s. 1804

Representatives

Thomas Claiborne
Christopher Clark (D) s. 1804
Matthew Clay (D)
John Clopton (D)
John Dawson (D)
John W. Eppes (D)
Peterson Goodwyn (D)
Edwin Gray
Thomas Griffin
David Holmes (D)
John G. Jackson (D)
Walter Jones (D)
Joseph Lewis, Jr. (F)
Thomas Lewis r. Mar. 1804
Andrew Moore s. 1804;
r. Nov. 1804
Anthony New (D)
Thomas Newton, Jr. (D)
John Randolph (SRD)
Thomas M. Randolph (D)
John Smith (D)
James Stephenson (F)
Philip R. Thompson (D)
Abram Trigg
John Trigg d. June 1804
Alexander Wilson

NINTH CONGRESS

March 4, 1805 to March 3, 1807

President of The Senate:	George Clinton
President Pro Tempore of The Senate:	Samuel Smith
Speaker of The House of Representatives:	Nathaniel Macon

CONNECTICUT

Senators

James Hillhouse (F)
Uriah Tracy (F)

Representatives

Samuel W. Dana (F)
John Davenport (F)
Theodore Dwight (F) s. 1806
Jonathan O. Moseley (F)
Timothy Pitkin (F)
John C. Smith (F) r. 1806
Lewis B. Struges (F)
Benjamin Tallmadge (F)

DELAWARE

Senators

Samuel White (F)
James A. Bayard, Sr. (F)

Representative

James M. Broom (F)

GEORGIA

Senators

Abraham Baldwin (F)

James Jackson (D) d. Mar. 1806
John Milledge s. 1806

Representatives

William W. Bibb (D) s. 1807
Joseph Bryan (D) r. 1806
Peter Early
Cowles Mead r. Dec. 1805
David Meriwether (D)
Dennis Smelt s. 1806
Thomas Spalding r. 1806

KENTUCKY

Senators

John Breckinridge (D) r. Aug. 1805
John Adair (D) r. Nov. 1806
Henry Clay s. 1806

Buckner Thruston

Representatives

George M. Bedinger
John Boyle (D)
John Fowler
Matthew Lyon (AF)
Thomas Sandford (D)
Matthew Walton (D)

MARYLAND

Senators

Robert Wright (D) r. 1806
Philip Reed s. 1806

Samuel Smith (D)

Representatives

John Archer
John Campbell
Leonard Covington
Charles Goldsborough
Edward Lloyd s. 1806
William McCreery
Patrick Magruder
Nicholas R. Moore
Roger Nelson
Joseph H. Nicholson r. Mar. 1806

MASSACHUSETTS

Senators

Timothy Pickering (F)
John Quincy Adams (F)

Representatives

Joseph Barker (D)
Barnabas Bidwell
Phanuel Bishop
John Chandler
Orchard Cook
Jacob Crowninshield (D)
Richard Cutts (D)
William Ely (F)
Isaiah L. Green
Seth Hastings (F)
Jeremiah Nelson (F)
Josiah Quincy (F)
Ebenezer Seaver (D)
William Stedman (F)
Samuel Taggart (F)
Joseph B. Varnum (AF)
Peleg Wadsworth

NEW HAMPSHIRE

Senators

William Plumer (F)
Nicholas Gilman (D)

Representatives

Silas Betton
Caleb Ellis
David Hough
Samuel Tenney
Thomas W. Thompson

NEW JERSEY

Senators

John Condit (D)
Aaron Kitchell (D)

Representatives

Ezra Darby (D)
Ebenezer Elmer (D)
William Helms (D)
John Lambert (D)
James Sloan
Henry Southard (D)

NEW YORK

Senators

John Smith (D)
Samuel L. Mitchill (D)

Representatives

John Blake, Jr.
George Clinton, Jr. (D)
Silas Halsey (D)
Henry W. Livingston
Josiah Masters (D)
Gurdon S. Mumford (F)
John Russell
Peter Sailly (D)
Thomas Sammons (D)
Martin G. Schuneman (D)
David Thomas (D)
Uri Tracy (D)
Philip Van Cortlandt (D)
Killian K. Van Rensselaer (D)
Daniel C. Verplanck (F)
Eliphalet Wickes
Nathan Williams (D)

NORTH CAROLINA

Senators

David Stone r. Feb. 1807
James Turner

Representatives

Evan S. Alexander s. 1806
Nathaniel Alexander r. Nov. 1805
Willis Alston (D)
William Blackledge (D)
Thomas Blount (D)
James Holland (AF)
Thomas Kenan (D)
Duncan McFarlan
Nathaniel Macon (D)
Richard Stanford (D)
Marmaduke Williams (D)
Joseph Winston (D)
Thomas Wynns (F)

OHIO

Senators

John Smith (D)
Thomas Worthington (D)

Representative

Jeremiah Morrow (D)

PENNSYLVANIA

Senators

George Logan (D)
Samuel Maclay

Representatives

Isaac Anderson (D)
David Bard
Robert Brown (D)
Joseph Clay
Frederick Conrad (F)
William Findley (D)
Andrew Gregg (F)
John Hamilton (D)
John A. Hanna (AF) d. July 1805
James Kelly
Michael Leib (D) r. Feb. 1806
Christian Lower (D) d. Dec. 1806
John B. C. Lucas (D) r. 1805
John Porter s. 1806
John Pugh (D)
John Rea (D)
Jacob Richards (D)
John Smilie (D)
Samuel Smith s. 1805
John Whitehill
Robert Whitehill s. 1805

RHODE ISLAND

Senators

Benjamin Howland (D)
James Fenner (D)

Representatives

Nehemiah Knight (AF)
Joseph Stanton, Jr. (D)

SOUTH CAROLINA

Senators

Thomas Sumter (D)
John Gaillard (D)

Representatives

William Butler (AF)
Levi Casey d. Feb. 1807
Elias Earle (D)
Robert Marion
Thomas Moore
O'Brien Smith
David R. Williams (D)
Richard Winn

TENNESSEE

Senators

Joseph Anderson
Daniel Smith (D)

Representatives

George W. Campbell (D)
William Dickson
John Rhea (D)

VERMONT

Senators

Stephen R. Bradley (D)
Israel Smith (D)

Representatives

Martin Chittenden
James Elliott (F)
James Fisk (D)
Gideon Olin (D)

VIRGINIA

Senators

William B. Giles (D)
Andrew Moore

Representatives

Burwell Bassett
William A. Burwell (D) s. 1806
John Claiborne
Christopher Clark (D) r. July 1806
Matthew Clay (D)
John Clopton (D)
John Dawson (D)
John W. Eppes (D)
James M. Garnett (D)
Peterson Goodwyn (D)
Edwin Gray
David Holmes (D)
John G. Jackson (D)
Walter Jones (D)
Joseph Lewis, Jr. (F)
John Morrow
Thomas Newton, Jr. (D)
John Randolph (SRD)
Thomas M. Randolph (D)
John Smith
Philip R. Thompson (D)
Abram Trigg
Alexander Wilson

TENTH CONGRESS

March 4, 1807 to March 3, 1809

President of The Senate: George Clinton
Presidents Pro Tempore of The Senate: Samuel Smith
Stephen R. Bradley
John Milledge
Speaker of The House of Representatives: Joseph B. Varnum

CONNECTICUT

Senators

James Hillhouse (F)
Uriah Tracy (F) d. July 1807
Chauncey Goodrich (F)

Representatives

Epaphroditus Champion (F)
Samuel W. Dana (F)
John Davenport (F)
Jonathan O. Moseley (F)
Timothy Pitkin (F)
Lewis B. Sturges (F)
Benjamin Tallmadge (F)

DELAWARE

Senators

Samuel White (F)
James A. Bayard, Sr.

Representatives

James M. Broom (F) r. 1807
Nicholas Van Dyke (F)

GEORGIA

Senators

Abraham Baldwin (F)
d. Mar. 1807
George Jones ta. 1807
William H. Crawford

John Milledge

Representatives

William W. Bibb (D)
Howell Cobb
Dennis Smelt
George M. Troup

KENTUCKY

Senators

Buckner Thruston (D)
John Pope (D)

Representatives

John Boyle (D)
Joseph Desha (D)
Benjamin Howard
Richard M. Johnson
Matthew Lyon (AF)
John Rowan

MARYLAND

Senators

Samuel Smith (D)
Philip Reed

Representatives

John Campbell (F)
Charles Goldsborough (F)
Philip B. Key (F)
Edward Lloyd (D)
William McCreery
John Montgomery (D)
Nicholas R. Moore (D)
Roger Nelson (D)
Archibald Van Horne

MASSACHUSETTS

Senators

Timothy Pickering (F)

John Quincy Adams (F)
r. June 1808
James Lloyd (F) s. 1808

Representatives

Ezekiel Bacon (D)
Joseph Barker (D)
Barnabas Bidwell r. July 1807
John Chandler
Orchard Cook
Jacob Crowninshield (D)
d. Apr. 1808
Richard Cutts (D)
Josiah Dean
William Ely (F)
Isaiah L. Green
Daniel Ilsley
Edward S. Livermore (F)
Josiah Quincy
Ebenezer Seaver (D)
William Stedman (F)
Joseph Story s. 1808
Samuel Taggart (F)
Jabez Upham (F)
Joseph B. Varnum (AF)

NEW HAMPSHIRE

Senators

Nicholas Gilman (D)
Nahum Parker

Representatives

Peter Carleton
Daniel M. Durell
Francis Gardner
Jedediah K. Smith
Clement Storer

NEW JERSEY

Senators

John Condit
Aaron Kitchell

Representatives

Adam Boyd (D)
Ezra Darby (D) d. Jan. 1808
William Helms (D)
John Lambert (D)
Thomas Newbold (D)
James Sloan
Henry Southard (D)

NEW YORK

Senators

John Smith (D)
Samuel L. Mitchill (D)

Representatives

John Blake, Jr.
George Clinton, Jr. (D)
Barent Gardenier
John Harris
Reuben Humphrey
William Kirkpatrick (D)
Josiah Masters (D)
Gurdon S. Mumford (F)
Samuel Riker
John Russell
Peter Swart
David Thomas r. May 1808
John Thompson
James I. Van Alen
Philip Van Cortlandt (D)
Killian K. Van Rensselaer (D)
Daniel C. Verplanck (F)
Nathan Wilson s. 1808

NORTH CAROLINA

Senators

James Turner
Jesse Franklin

Representatives

Evan S. Alexander
Willis Alston (D)
William Blackledge (D)
Thomas Blount (D)
John Culpepper (F)
Meshack Franklin
James Holland (AF)
Thomas Kenan (D)
Nathaniel Macon (D)
Lemuel Sawyer
Richard Stanford (D)
Marmaduke Williams (D)

OHIO

Senators

John Smith (D) r. Apr. 1808
Return J. Meigs, Jr. s. 1809

Edward Tiffin r. Mar. 1809

Representative

Jeremiah Morrow (D)

PENNSYLVANIA

Senators

Samuel Maclay r. Jan. 1809
Michael Leib (D) s. 1809

Andrew Gregg (F)

Representatives

David Bard
Robert Brown (D)
Joseph Clay r. 1808
William Findley (D)
John Heister
William Hoge (F)
Robert Jenkins
James Kelly
William Milnor (F)
Daniel Montgomery, Jr. (D)
John Porter
John Pugh (D)
John Rea (D)
Jacob Richards (D)
Matthias Richards
Benjamin Say s. 1808
John Smilie (D)
Samuel Smith
Robert Whitehill

RHODE ISLAND

Senators

Benjamin Howland (D)

James Fenner (D) r. 1807
Elisha Mathewson (D) s. 1807

Representatives

Nehemiah Knight (AF)
d. June 1808
Richard Jackson, Jr. s. 1808
Isaac Wilbur

SOUTH CAROLINA

Senators

Thomas Sumter (D)
John Gaillard (D)

Representatives

Lemuel J. Alston
William Butler (AF)
Joseph Calhoun (D)
Robert Marion
Thomas Moore
John Taylor
David R. Williams (D)
Richard Winn (D)

TENNESSEE

Senators

Joseph Anderson
Daniel Smith (D)

Representatives

George W. Campbell (D)
John Rhea (D)
Jesse Wharton

VERMONT

Senators

Stephen R. Bradley (D)
Israel Smith (D) r. Oct. 1807
Jonathan Robinson

Representatives

Martin Chittenden
James Elliott (F)
James Fisk (D)
Samuel Shaw (D) s. 1808
James Witherell r. May 1808

VIRGINIA

Senators

William B. Giles (D)
Andrew Moore

Representatives

Burwell Bassett (D)
William A. Burwell (D)
John Claiborne d. Oct. 1808
Matthew Clay (D)
John Clopton (D)
John Dawson (D)
John W. Eppes (D)
James M. Garnett (D)
Thomas Gholson, Jr. s. 1808
Peterson Goodwyn (D)
Edwin Gray
David Holmes (D)
John G. Jackson (D)
Walter Jones (D)
Joseph Lewis, Jr. (F)
John Love (D)
John Morrow
Thomas Newton, Jr. (D)
Wilson C. Nicholas (D)
John Randolph
John Smith (D)
Abram Trigg
Alexander Wilson

ELEVENTH CONGRESS

March 4, 1809 to March 3, 1811

President of The Senate: George Clinton
Presidents Pro Tempore of The Senate: Andrew Gregg, John Gaillard, John Pope
Speaker of The House of Representatives: Joseph B. Varnum

CONNECTICUT

Senators

James Hillhouse (F) r. June 1810
Samuel W. Dana (F) s. 1810

Chauncey Goodrich (F)

Representatives

Epaphroditus Champion (F)
Samuel W. Dana (F) r. May 1810
John Davenport (F)
Ebenezer Huntington s. 1810
Jonathan O. Moseley (F)
Timothy Pitkin (F)
Lewis B. Sturges (F)
Benjamin Tallmadge (F)

DELAWARE

Senators

Samuel White (F) d. Nov. 1809
Outerbridge Horsey (F) s. 1810

James A. Bayard, Sr.

Representative

Nicholas Van Dyke (F)

GEORGIA

Senators

John Milledge r. Nov. 1809
Charles Tait

William H. Crawford

Representatives

William W. Bibb (D)
Howell Cobb
Dennis Smelt
George M. Troup

KENTUCKY

Senators

Buckner Thruston (D)
r. Dec. 1809
Henry Clay s. 1810

John Pope (D)

Representatives

William T. Barry (D) s. 1810
Henry Crist
Joseph Desha (D)
Benjamin Howard r. Apr. 1810
Richard M. Johnson (D)
Matthew Lyon (AF)
Samuel McKee (D)

MARYLAND

Senators

Samuel Smith (D)
Philip Reed

Representatives

John Brown (D) r. 1810
John Campbell
Charles Goldsborough (F)
Philip B. Key (F)
Alexander McKim (D)
John Montgomery (D)
Nicholas R. Moore (D)
Roger Nelson (D) r. May 1810
Samuel Ringgold s. 1810
Archibald Van Horne
Robert Wright (D) s. 1810

MASSACHUSETTS

Senators

Timothy Pickering (F)
James Lloyd (F)

Representatives

Joseph Allen (F) s. 1810
Ezekiel Bacon (D)
William Baylies (D) r. June 1809
Abijah Bigelow (F) s. 1810
Orchard Cook
Richard Cutts (D)
William Ely (F)
Barzillai Gannett (D)
Gideon Gardner (F)
Edward S. Livermore (F)
Benjamin Pickman, Jr.
Josiah Quincy
Ebenezer Seaver (D)
William Stedman (F) r. July 1809
Samuel Taggart (F)
Charles Turner, Jr.
Jabez Upham r. 1810
Joseph B. Varnum (AF)
Laban Wheaton
Ezekiel Whitman

NEW HAMPSHIRE

Senators

Nicholas Gilman (D)

Nahum Parker r. June 1810
Charles Cutts s. 1810

Representatives

Daniel Blaisdell (F)
John C. Chamberlain (F)
William Hale (F)
Nathaniel A. Haven (F)
James Wilson

NEW JERSEY

Senators

Aaron Kitchell (D) r. Mar. 1809
John Condit

John Lambert (D)

Representatives

Adam Boyd (D)
James Cox (D) d. Sept. 1810
William Helms (D)
Jacob Hufty (D)
Thomas Newbold (D)
John A. Scudder (D) s. 1810
Henry Southard

NEW YORK

Senators

John Smith (D)
Obadiah German (D)

Representatives

William Denning r. 1809
James Emott (F)
Jonathan Fisk (D)
Barent Gardenier
Thomas R. Gold (F)
Herman Knickerbocker (F)
Robert L. Livingston (F)
Vincent Mathews (F)
Samuel L. Mitchill (D)
Gurdon S. Mumford (F)
John Nicholson (D)
Peter B. Porter (D)
Erastus Root (D)
Ebenezer Sage (D)
Thomas Sammons (D)
John Thompson
Uri Tracy (D)
Killian K. Van Rensselaer (D)

NORTH CAROLINA

Senators

James Turner (D)
Jesse Franklin

Representatives

Willis Alston (D)
James Cochran (D)
Meshack Franklin
James Holland (AF)
Thomas Kenan (D)
William Kennedy (F)
Archibald McBryde (D)
Nathaniel Macon (D)
Joseph Pearson (F)
Lemuel Sawyer (D)
Richard Stanford
John Stanly

OHIO

Senators

Return J. Meigs, Jr. (D)
r. May 1810
Thomas Worthington (D) s. 1811

Stanley Griswold r. Jan. 1810
Alexander Campbell s. 1810

Representative

Jeremiah Morrow (D)

PENNSYLVANIA

Senators

Andrew Gregg (F)
Michael Leib (D)

Representatives

William Anderson (D)
David Bard
Robert Brown
William Crawford (D)
William Findley (D)
Daniel Hiester
Robert Jenkins
Aaron Lyle (D)
William Milnor (F)
John Porter
John Rea (D)
Matthias Richards
John Ross

Benjamin Say r. June 1809
Adam Seybert (D)
John Smilie
George Smith
Samuel Smith
Robert Whitehill

RHODE ISLAND

Senators

Elisha Mathewson (D)

Francis Malbone d. June 1809
Christopher G. Champlin s. 1810

Representatives

Richard Jackson, Jr. (F)
Elisha R. Potter (F)

SOUTH CAROLINA

Senators

Thomas Sumter (D) r. 1810
John Taylor s. 1810

John Gaillard (D)

Representatives

Lemuel J. Alston
William Butler
Joseph Calhoun
Langdon Cheves (D) s. 1811
Robert Marion r. Dec. 1810
Thomas Moore
John Taylor
Richard Winn (D)
Robert Witherspoon

TENNESSEE

Senators

Joseph Anderson

Daniel Smith r. Mar. 1809
Jenkin Whiteside

Representatives

Pleasant M. Miller
John Rhea (D)
Robert Weakley

VERMONT

Senators

Stephen R. Bradley
Jonathan Robinson

Representatives

William Chamberlain (F)
Martin Chittenden
Jonathan H. Hubbard (F)
Samuel Shaw (D)

VIRGINIA

Senators

William B. Giles (D)
Richard Brent

Representatives

Burwell Bassett (D)
James Breckinridge (F)
William A. Burwell (D)
Matthew Clay (D)
John Clopton (D)
John Dawson (D)
John W. Eppes (D)
David S. Garland s. 1810
Thomas Gholson, Jr.
Peterson Goodwyn (D)
Edwin Gray
John G. Jackson (D) r. Sept. 1810
Walter Jones (D)
Joseph Lewis, Jr. (F)
John Love (D)
William McKinley (D) s. 1810
Thomas Newton, Jr. (D)
Wilson C. Nicholas r. Nov. 1809
John Randolph (SRD)
John Roane (D)
Daniel Sheffey (F)
John Smith (D)
James Stephenson (F)
Jacob Swoope

TWELFTH CONGRESS

March 4, 1811 to March 3, 1813

President of The Senate:	George Clinton
President Pro Tempore of The Senate:	William H. Crawford
Speaker of The House of Representatives:	Henry Clay

CONNECTICUT

Senators

Chauncey Goodrich (F)
Samuel W. Dana (F)

Representatives

Epaphroditus Champion (F)
John Davenport (F)
Lyman Law (F)
Jonathan O. Moseley (F)
Timothy Pitkin (F)
Lewis B. Sturges (F)
Benjamin Tallmadge (F)

DELAWARE

Senators

James A. Bayard Sr. r. Mar. 1813
Outerbridge Horsey (F)

Representative

Henry M. Ridgeley (F)

GEORGIA

Senators

William H. Crawford
Charles Tait (D)

Representatives

William Barnett (SRD) s. 1812
William W. Bibb (D)
Howell Cobb r. 1812
Bolling Hall (D)
George M. Troup (D)

KENTUCKY

Senators

John Pope (D)
George M. Bibb

Representatives

Henry Clay
Joseph Desha (D)
Richard M. Johnson (D)
Samuel McKee (D)
Anthony New (D)
Stephen Ormsby (D)

LOUISIANA

Senators

Allan B. Magruder (D)

Thomas Posey ta. 1812
James Brown s. 1813

Representative

Thomas B. Robertson (D)

MARYLAND

Senators

Samuel Smith (D)
Philip Reed

Representatives

Stevenson Archer (D)
Charles Goldsborough (F)
Joseph Kent (F)
Philip B. Key (F)
Peter Little (D)
Alexander McKim (D)
John Montgomery (D)
r. Apr. 1811
Samuel Ringgold (D)
Philip Stuart (F)
Robert Wright (D)

MASSACHUSETTS

Senators

James Lloyd (F)
Joseph B. Varnum (AF)

Representatives

Ezekiel Bacon (D)
Abijah Bigelow (F)
Elijah Brigham (F)
Francis Carr (D) s. 1812
Richard Cutts (D)
William Ely (F)
Barzillai Gannett (D) r. 1812
Isaiah L. Green
Josiah Quincy (F)
William Reed (F)
William M. Richardson (F) s. 1812
Ebenezer Seaver (D)
Samuel Taggart (F)
Peleg Tallman
Charles Turner, Jr.
Joseph B. Varnum r. June 1811
Laban Wheaton
Leonard White
William Widgery

NEW HAMPSHIRE

Senators

Nicholas Gilman (D)
Charles Cutts

Representatives

Josiah Bartlett, Jr.
Samuel Dinsmoor (D)
Obed Hall (D)
John A. Harper (D)
George Sullivan

NEW JERSEY

Senators

John Lambert (D)
John Condit

Representatives

Adam Boyd (D)
Lewis Condict (AF)
Jacob Hufty (D)
George C. Maxwell
James Morgan (F)
Thomas Newbold (D)

NEW YORK

Senators

John Smith
Obadiah German (D)

Representatives

Daniel Avery (D)
Harmanus Bleecker (F)
Thomas B. Cooke (D)
James Emott (F)
Asa Fitch (F)
Thomas R. Gold (F)
Thomas P. Grosvenor (F) r. 1813
Robert L. Livingston (F)
r. May 1812
Arunah Metcalf (D)
Samuel L. Mitchill (D)
William Paulding, Jr. (D)
Benjamin Pond (D)
Peter B. Porter (D)
Ebenezer Sage (D)
Thomas Sammons (D)
Silas Stow
Uri Tracy (D)
Pierre Van Cortlandt, Jr.

NORTH CAROLINA

Senators

James Turner (D)
Jesse Franklin

Representatives

Willis Alston (D)
William Blackledge (D)
Thomas Blount (D) d. Feb. 1812

James Cochran
Meshack Franklin
William Kennedy (F) s. 1813
William R. King (D)
Archibald McBryde (D)
Nathaniel Macon (D)
Joseph Pearson (F)
Israel Pickens (D)
Lemuel Sawyer (D)
Richard Stanford

OHIO

Senators

Alexander Campbell
Thomas Worthington (D)

Representative

Jeremiah Morrow (D)

PENNSYLVANIA

Senators

Andrew Gregg
Michael Leib (D)

Representatives

William Anderson
David Bard
Robert Brown
William Crawford (D)
Roger Davis (D)
William Findley (D)
John M. Hyneman (D)
Abner Lacock (D)
Joseph Lefever (D)
Aaron Lyle (D)
James Milnor (F)
William Piper
Jonathan Roberts (F)
William Rodman (D)
Adam Seybert (D)
John Smilie d. Dec. 1812
George Smith
Robert Whitehill

RHODE ISLAND

Senators

Christopher G. Champlin
r. Oct. 1811
William Hunter (F)

Jeremiah B. Howell (F)

Representatives

Richard Jackson, Jr. (F)
Elisha R. Potter (F)

SOUTH CAROLINA

Senators

John Gaillard (D)
John Taylor (D)

Representatives

William Butler
John C. Calhoun (D)
Langdon Cheves
Elias Earle (D)
William Lowndes (D)
Thomas Moore
David R. Williams
Richard Winn

TENNESSEE

Senators

Joseph Anderson

Jenkin Whiteside r. Oct. 1811
George W. Campbell (D)

Representatives

Felix Grundy (D)
John Rhea (D)
John Sevier (D)

VERMONT

Senators

Stephen R. Bradley
Jonathan Robinson

Representatives

Martin Chittenden
James Fisk (D)
Samuel Shaw (D)
William Strong

VIRGINIA

Senators

William B. Giles (D)
Richard Brent

Representatives

John Baker (F)
Burwell Bassett (D)
James Breckinridge (F)
William A. Burwell (D)
Matthew Clay (D)
John Clopton (D)
John Dawson (D)
Thomas Gholson, Jr.
Peterson Goodwyn (D)
Edwin Gray
Aylett Hawes (D)
John P. Hungerford (D)
r. Nov. 1811
Joseph Lewis, Jr. (F)
William McCoy (D)
Hugh Nelson (D)
Thomas Newton, Jr. (D)
James Pleasants (D)
John Randolph (SRD)
John Roane (D)
Daniel Sheffey (F)
John Smith (D)
John Taliaferro (D)
Thomas Wilson

THIRTEENTH CONGRESS

March 4, 1813 to March 3, 1815

President of The Senate:	Elbridge Gerry
Presidents Pro Tempore of The Senate:	Joseph B. Varnum John Gaillard
Speakers of The House of Representatives:	Henry Clay Langdon Cheves

CONNECTICUT

Senators

Chauncey Goodrich (F)
r. May 1813
David Daggett

Samuel W. Dana (F)

Representatives

Ephaphroditus Champion (F)
John Davenport (F)
Lyman Law (F)
Jonathan O. Moseley (F)
Timothy Pitkin (F)
Lewis B. Sturges (F)
Benjamin Tallmadge (F)

DELAWARE

Senators

Outerbridge Horsey (F)
William H. Wells

Representatives

Thomas Cooper (F)
Henry M. Ridgeley (F)

GEORGIA

Senators

William H. Crawford r. Mar. 1813
William B. Bulloch (D) ta. 1813
William W. Bibb (D)

Charles Tait (D)

Representatives

William Barnett (SRD)
William W. Bibb (D) r. Nov. 1813
Alfred Cuthbert (D) s. 1814
John Forsyth (D)
Bolling Hall (D)
Thomas Telfair (D)
George M. Troup (D)

KENTUCKY

Senators

George M. Bibb r. Aug. 1814
George Walker r. 1814
William T. Barry (D) s. 1815

Jesse Bledsoe r. Dec. 1814
Isham Talbot s. 1815

Representatives

James Clark (D)
Henry Clay r. Jan. 1814
Joseph Desha (D)
William P. Duval (D)
Joseph H. Hawkins (F) s. 1814
Samuel Hopkins (D)
Richard M. Johnson (D)
Samuel McKee (D)
Thomas Montgomery (D)
Stephen Ormsby (D)
Solomon P. Sharp (D)

LOUISIANA

Senators

James Brown
Eligius Fromentin

Representative

Thomas B. Robertson (D)

MARYLAND

Senators

Samuel Smith (D)
Robert H. Goldsborough (F)

Representatives

Stevenson Archer (D)
Charles Goldsborough (F)
Alexander C. Hanson (F)
Joseph Kent (F)
Alexander McKim (D)
Nicholas R. Moore (D)
Samuel Ringgold (D)
Philip Stuart (F)
Robert Wright (D)

MASSACHUSETTS

Senators

James Lloyd (F) r. May 1813
Christopher Gore (F) s. May 1813

Joseph B. Varnum (AF)

Representatives

William Baylies
Abijah Bigelow (F)
George Bradbury (F)
Elijah Brigham (F)
Samuel Dana (D) s. 1814
Samuel Davis (F)

Daniel Dewey (W) r. Feb. 1814
Levi Hubbard (D)
John W. Hulbert (F) s. 1814
William Ely (F)
Cyrus King (F)
James Parker (D)
Timothy Pickering (F)
John Reed (F)
William Reed (F)
William M. Richardson (F) r. Apr. 1814
Nathaniel Ruggles (F)
Samuel Taggart (F)
Artemas Ward, Jr.
Laban Wheaton
John Wilson
Abiel Wood

NEW HAMPSHIRE

Senators

Nicholas Gilman (D) d. May 1814
Thomas W. Thompson s. 1814

Charles Cutts
Jeremiah Mason (F)

Representatives

Bradbury Cilley (F)
William Hale
Samuel Smith
Roger Vose (F)
Daniel Webster (F)
Jeduthun Wilcox (F)

NEW JERSEY

Senators

John Lambert (D)
John Condit

Representatives

Thomas Bines (D) s. 1814
Lewis Condict (AF)
William Coxe, Jr. (F)
Jacob Hufty (D) d. May 1814
James Schureman (F)
Richard Stockton
Thomas Ward (D)

NEW YORK

Senators

Obadiah German (D)
Rufus King

Representatives

Daniel Avery (D)
Egbert Benson r. Aug. 1813
John M. Bowers r. Dec. 1813
Alexander Boyd
Oliver C. Comstock (D)
Peter Denoyelles
Jonathan Fisk (F)
James Geddes
Thomas P. Grosvenor (F)
Abraham J. Hasbrouck (D)
Samuel M. Hopkins
Nathaniel W. Howell
William Irving (D) s. 1814
Moss Kent (F)
John Lefferts (D)
John Lovett (F)
Jacob Markell (F)
Morris S. Miller (F)
Hosea Moffitt (F)
Thomas J. Oakley (F)
Jothan Post, Jr. (F)
Ebenezer Sage (D)
Samuel Sherwood
Zebulon R. Shipherd (F)
William S. Smith
John W. Taylor (D)
Joel Thompson
Isaac Williams, Jr.
Elisha J. Winter

NORTH CAROLINA

Senators

James Turner
David Stone

Representatives

Willis Alston (D)
John Culpepper (F)
Peter Forney (D)
Meshack Franklin (D)
William Gaston (F)
William Kennedy (F)
William R. King (D)
Nathaniel Macon (D)
William H. Murfree (D)
Joseph Pearson (F)
Israel Pickens (D)
Richard Stanford
Bartlett Yancy

OHIO

Senators

Thomas Worthington (D) r. Dec. 1814
Joseph Kerr (D) s. 1814

Jeremiah Morrow (D)

Representatives

John Alexander (D)
Reasin Beall (W) r. June 1814
James Caldwell (D)
David Clendenin s. 1814
William Creighton, Jr. (D)
James Kilbourne (D)
John McLean (D)

PENNSYLVANIA

Senators

Michael Leib (D) r. Feb. 1814
Jonathan Roberts s. 1814

Abner Lacock (D)

Representatives

William Anderson
David Bard
Robert Brown
John Conard (D)
William Crawford (D)
Edward Crouch (D)
Roger Davis (D)
William Findley (D)
Hugh Glasgow
John Gloninger r. Aug. 1813
Isaac Griffin (D)
Samuel Henderson (F) s. 1814
John M. Hyneman (D) r. Aug. 1813
Charles J. Ingersoll (D)
Samuel D. Ingham (D)
Jared Irwin (D)
Aaron Lyle (D)
William Piper
John Rea (D)
Jonathan Roberts (D) r. Feb. 1814
Adam Seybert
Amos Slaymaker s. 1814
Isaac Smith
Adamson Tannehill
Daniel Udree (D)
James Whitehill r. Sept. 1814
Robert Whitehill d. Apr. 1813
Thomas Wilson (D)

RHODE ISLAND

Senators

Jeremiah B. Howell
William Hunter

Representatives

Richard Jackson, Jr. (F)
Elisha R. Potter (F)

SOUTH CAROLINA

Senators

John Gaillard (D)
John Taylor (D)

Representatives

John C. Calhoun (D)
John J. Chappell (D)
Langdon Cheves
Elias Earle (D)
David R. Evans (D)
Samuel Farrow (D)
Theodore Gourdin (D)
John Kershaw (D)
William Lowndes (D)

TENNESSEE

Senators

Joseph Anderson

George W. Campbell (D) r. Feb. 1814
Jesse Wharton s. 1814

Representatives

John H. Bowen (D)
Newton Cannon s. 1814
Felix Grundy (D) r. 1814
Thomas K. Harris (D)
Parry W. Humphreys (D)
John Rhea (D)
John Sevier (D)

VERMONT

Senators

Jonathan Robinson
Dudley Chase (D)

Representatives

William C. Bradley (D)
Ezra Butler (D)
James Fisk (D)
Charles Rich (D)
Richard Skinner
William Strong

VIRGINIA

Senators

William B. Giles (D) r. Mar. 1815

Richard Brent d. Dec. 1814
James Barbour s. 1815

Representatives

Philip P. Barbour (D) s. 1814
Thomas M. Bayly (D)
James Breckinridge (F)
William A. Burwell (D)
Hugh Caperton (F)
John Clopton (D)
John Dawson (D) d. Mar. 1814
John W. Eppes (D)
Thomas Gholson, Jr.
Peterson Goodwyn (D)
Aylett Hawes (D)
John P. Hungerford (D)
John G. Jackson (D)
James Johnson (D)
John Kerr (D)
Joseph Lewis, Jr. (F)
William McCoy (D)
Hugh Nelson (D)
Thomas Newton, Jr. (D)
James Pleasants (D)
John Roane (D)
Daniel Sheffey (F)
John Smith (D)
Francis White

FOURTEENTH CONGRESS

March 4, 1815 to March 3, 1817

President of The Senate: Vacant
President Pro Tempore of The Senate: John Gaillard
Speaker of The House of Representatives: Henry Clay

CONNECTICUT

Senators

Samuel W. Dana (F)
David Daggett (F)

Representatives

Epaphroditus Champion (F)
John Davenport (F)
Lyman Law (F)
Jonathan O. Moseley (F)
Timothy Pitkin (F)
Lewis B. Sturges (F)
Benjamin Tallmadge (F)

DELAWARE

Senators

Outerbridge Horsey (F)
William H. Wells

Representatives

Thomas Clayton (F)
Thomas Cooper (F)

GEORGIA

Senators

Charles Tait (D)

William W. Bibb (D) r. Nov. 1816
George M. Troup (SRD) s. 1816

Representatives

Zadock Cook s. 1817
Alfred Cuthbert (D) r. Nov. 1816
John Forsyth (D)
Bolling Hall (D)
Wilson Lumpkin (D)
Thomas Telfair (D)
Richard Wilde (D)

INDIANA

Senators

James Noble
Waller Taylor (D)

Representative

William Hendricks (D)

KENTUCKY

Senators

William T. Barry r. May 1816
Martin D. Hardin (D) s. 1816

Isham Talbot

Representatives

James Clark (D) r. 1816
Henry Clay
Joseph Desha (D)
Thomas Fletcher s. 1816
Benjamin Hardin (W)
Richard M. Johnson (D)
Samuel McKee (D)
Alney McLean
Stephen Ormsby (D)
Solomon P. Sharp (D)
Micah Taul (D)

LOUISIANA

Senators

James Brown
Eligius Fromentin

Representative

Thomas B. Robertson (D)

MARYLAND

Senators

Robert H. Goldsborough (F)

Robert G. Harper (F) r. Dec. 1816
Alexander C. Hanson (F) s. 1817

Representatives

Stevenson Archer (D)
George Baer, Jr.
Charles Goldsborough (F)
Alexander C. Hanson (F) r. 1816
John C. Herbert (F)
Peter Little (D) s. 1816
Nicholas R. Moore (D) r. 1815
George Peter (D) s. 1816
William Pinkney r. Apr. 1816
Samuel Smith (D) s. 1816
Philip Stuart (F)
Robert Wright (D)

MASSACHUSETTS

Senators

Joseph B. Varnum

Christopher Gore r. May 1816
Eli P. Ashmun s. 1816

Representatives

Benjamin Adams (F) s. 1816
William Baylies
George Bradbury (F)
Elijah Brigham (F) d. Feb. 1816
Benjamin Brown
James Carr
Samuel S. Conner
John W. Hulbert (F)
Cyrus King (F)
Elijah H. Mills (F)
Jeremiah Nelson (F)
Albion K. Parris (D)
Timothy Pickering (F)
John Reed (F)
Thomas Rice
Nathaniel Ruggles (F)
Asahel Stearns (F)
Solomon Strong (F)
Samuel Taggart (F)
Artemas Ward, Jr. (F)
Laban Wheaton (F)

NEW HAMPSHIRE

Senators

Jeremiah Mason (F)
Thomas W. Thompson

Representatives

Charles H. Atherton (F)
Bradbury Cilley (F)
William Hale (F)
Roger Vose (F)
Daniel Webster (F)
Jeduthun Wilcox (F)

NEW JERSEY

Senators

John Condit
James J. Wilson (D)

Representatives

Ezra Baker
Ephraim Bateman (D)
Benjamin Bennet
Lewis Condict (AF)
Henry Southard (D)
Thomas Ward (D)

NEW YORK

Senators

Rufus King (F)
Nathan Sanford (D)

Representatives

John Adams r. Dec. 1815
Asa Adgate (D)
Daniel Avery (D) s. 1816
Samuel R. Betts (D)
James Birdsall (D)
Victory Birdseye (W)
Micah Brooks
Daniel Cady (F)
Archibald S. Clarke s. 1816
Oliver C. Comstock (D)
Henry Crocheron (D)
Jonathan Fisk r. Mar. 1815
Thomas R. Gold (F)
Thomas P. Grosvenor (F)
Jabez D. Hammond (D)
William Irving (D)
Moss Kent (F)
John Lovett (F)
Hosea Moffitt (F)
Peter B. Porter (D) r. Jan. 1816
Erastus Root (D)
John Savage (D)
Abraham H. Schenck (D)
John W. Taylor (D)
Enos T. Throop (D) r. June 1816
George Townsend (D)
Jonathan Ward (D)
Peter H. Wendover (D)
James W. Wilkin (D)
Westel Willoughby, Jr. (D)
John B. Yates (D)

NORTH CAROLINA

Senators

James Turner r. Nov. 1816
Montfort Stokes (D) s. 1816

Nathaniel Macon (D)

Representatives

Joseph H. Bryan
James W. Clark (D)
John Culpepper (F)
Samuel Dickens s. 1816
Weldon N. Edwards (D) s. 1816
Daniel M. Forney
William Gaston (F)
Charles Hooks (D) s. 1816
William R. King (D) r. Nov. 1816
William C. Love (D)
Nathaniel Macon (D) r. Dec. 1815
William H. Murfree (D)
Israel Pickens (D)
Richard Stanford d. Apr. 1816
Lewis Williams
Bartlett Yancy

OHIO

Senators

Jeremiah Morrow (D)
Benjamin Ruggles (D)

Representatives

John Alexander (D)
James Caldwell (D)
David Clendenin
William Creighton, Jr. (D)
William Henry Harrison (W) s. 1816
James Kilbourne (D)
John McLean (D) r. 1816

PENNSYLVANIA

Senators

Abner Lacock (D)
Jonathan Roberts (D)

Representatives

David Bard d. Mar. 1815
Thomas Burnside s. 1816
William Crawford (D)
William Darlington (D)
Amos Ellmaker r. July 1815
William Findley (D)
Hugh Glasgow
Isaac Griffin (D)
John Hahn (D)
Joseph Hiester (F)
Joseph Hopkinson (F)
Samuel D. Ingham (D)
Jared Irwin (D)

Aaron Lyle (D)
William Maclay
William P. Maclay (D) s. 1816
William Milnor (F)
William Piper
John Ross
John Sergeant (F)
Thomas Smith (F)
James M. Wallace
John Whiteside (D)
Jonathan Williams d. May 1815
Thomas Wilson (D)
William Wilson

RHODE ISLAND

Senators

Jeremiah B. Howell (F)
William Hunter (F)

Representatives

John L. Boss, Jr.
James B. Mason (F)

SOUTH CAROLINA

Senators

John Gaillard (D)

John Taylor (D) r. Nov. 1816
William Smith (D) s. 1817

Representatives

John C. Calhoun (D)
John J. Chappell (D)
Benjamin Huger
William Lowndes (D)
William Mayrant r. Oct. 1816
Henry Middleton (D)
Stephen D. Miller (D) s. 1817
Thomas Moore
John Taylor
William Woodward

TENNESSEE

Senators

Jesse Wharton ta. 1815
John Williams

George W. Campbell

Representatives

William G. Blount (D) s. 1816
Newton Cannon (D)
Bennett H. Henderson
Samuel Powell
James B. Reynolds (D)
John Sevier (D) d. Sept. 1815
Isaac Thomas (D)

VERMONT

Senators

Dudley Chase (D)
Isaac Tichenor (F)

Representatives

Daniel Chipman (F) r. May 1816
Luther Jewett (F)
Chauncey Langdon (F)
Asa Lyon (F)
Charles Marsh (F)
John Noyes (F)

VIRGINIA

Senators

James Barbour (SRD)
Armistead T. Mason (D)

Representatives

Philip P. Barbour (D)
Burwell Bassett (D)
James Breckinridge (F)
William A. Burwell (D)
Matthew Clay d. May 1815
John Clopton (D) d. Sept. 1816
Peterson Goodwyn (D)
Thomas Gholson, Jr. d. July 1816
Aylett Hawes (D)
John P. Hungerford (D)
John G. Jackson (D)
James Johnson (D)
John Kerr (D) s. 1815
Joseph Lewis, Jr. (F)
William McCoy (D)
Hugh Nelson (D)
Thomas M. Nelson (D) s. 1816
Thomas Newton, Jr. (D)
James Pleasants (D)
John Randolph (SRD)
William H. Roane (D)
Daniel Sheffey (F)
Ballard Smith
Magnus Tate
Henry St. George Tucker
John Tyler (D) s. 1816

FIFTEENTH CONGRESS

March 4, 1817 to March 3, 1819

President of The Senate: Daniel D. Tompkins
Presidents Pro Tempore of The Senate: John Gaillard; James Barbour
Speaker of The House of Representatives: Henry Clay

CONNECTICUT

Senators

Samuel W. Dana (F)
David Daggert (F)

Representatives

Sylvester Gilbert s. 1818
Uriel Holmes (F) r. 1818
Ebenezer Huntington (W)
Jonathan O. Moseley (F)
Timothy Pitkin (F)
Samuel B. Sherwood (F)
Nathaniel Terry
Thomas S. Williams

DELAWARE

Senators

Outerbridge Horsey (F)
Nicholas Van Dyke (F)

Representatives

Willard Hall (D)
Louis McLane (D)

GEORGIA

Senators

Charles Tait

George M. Troup (SRD) r. Sept. 1818
John Forsyth (D) s. 1818

Representatives

Joel Abbot (D)
Thomas W. Cobb
Zadock Cook
Joel Crawford (D)
John Forsyth (D) r. Nov. 1818
Robert R. Reid (D) s. 1819
William Terrell (D)

ILLINOIS

Senators

Jesse B. Thomas s. 1818
Ninian Edwards (D) s. 1818

Representative

John McLean s. 1818

INDIANA

Senators

James Noble
Waller Taylor (D)

Representative

William Hendricks (D)

KENTUCKY

Senators

Isham Talbot
John J. Crittenden r. Mar. 1819

Representatives

Richard C. Anderson, Jr.
Henry Clay
Joseph Desha (D)
Richard M. Johnson (D)
Anthony New (D)
Tunstall Quarles (D)
George Robertson (W)
Thomas Speed
David Trimble (D)
David Walker

LOUISIANA

Senators

Eligius Fromentin

William C. C. Claiborne (D) d. Nov. 1817
Henry Johnson s. 1818

Representatives

Thomas Butler s. 1818
Thomas B. Robertson (D) r. Apr. 1818

MARYLAND

Senators

Robert H. Goldsborough (F)
Alexander C. Hanson (F)

Representatives

Thomas Bayly (D)
Thomas Culbreth (D)
John C. Herbert (F)
Peter Little (D)
George Peter (D)
Philip Reed
Samuel Ringgold (D)
Samuel Smith (D)
Philip Stuart (F)

MASSACHUSETTS

Senators

Eli P. Ashmun r. May 1818
Prentiss Mellen s. 1818

Harrison Gray Otis

Representatives

Benjamin Adams (F)
Samuel C. Allen
Walter Folger, Jr. (D)
Timothy Fuller (D)
Joshua Gage (D)
John Holmes (D)
Enoch Lincoln s. 1818
Jonathan Mason (F)
Elijah H. Mills (F)
Marcus Morton (D)
Jeremiah Nelson (F)
Benjamin Orr (F)
Albion K. Parris (D) r. Feb. 1818
Thomas Rice
Nathaniel Ruggles (F)
Zabdiel Sampson (D)
Henry Shaw (F)
Nathaniel Silsbee (D)
Solomon Strong (F)
Ezekiel Whitman
John Wilson

MISSISSIPPI

Senators

Walter Leake (D)
Thomas H. Williams

Representative

George Poindexter

NEW HAMPSHIRE

Senators

Jeremiah Mason (F) r. June 1817
Clement Storer

David L. Morril (D)

Representatives

Josiah Butler (D)
Clifton Clagett
Salma Hale (D)
Arthur Livermore (D)
John F. Parrott (D)
Nathaniel Upham (D)

NEW JERSEY

Senators

James J. Wilson (D)
Mahlon Dickerson (D)

Representatives

Ephraim Bateman (D)
Benjamin Bennet
Joseph Bloomfield (D)
Charles Kinsey
John Linn
Henry Southard (D)

NEW YORK

Senators

Rufus King (F)
Nathan Sanford (D)

Representatives

Oliver C. Comstock (D)
Daniel Cruger (D)
John P. Cushman
John R. Drake
Benjamin Ellicott (D)
Josiah Hasbrouck
John Herkimer (D)
Thomas H. Hubbard (D)
William Irving (D)
Dorrance Kirtland
Thomas Lawyer
David A. Ogden (F)
John Palmer (D)
James Porter (D)
John Savage (D)
Philip J. Schuyler
Tredwell Scudder
John C. Spencer
Henry R. Storrs (F)
James Tallmadge, Jr. (D)
John W. Taylor (D)
Caleb Tompkins
George Townsend (D)
Peter H. Wendover (D)
Rensselaer Westerlo (F)
James W. Wilkin (D)
Isaac Williams, Jr. (D)

NORTH CAROLINA

Senators

Nathaniel Macon (D)
Montfort Stokes (D)

Representatives

Joseph H. Bryan
William Davidson (F) s. 1818
Weldon N. Edwards (D)
Charles Fisher (D) s. 1819
Daniel M. Forney r. 1818
Thomas H. Hall (D)
George Mumford (D) d. Dec. 1818
James Owen (D)
Lemuel Sawyer (D)
Thomas Settle (D)
Jesse Slocumb (F)
James S. Smith (D)
James Stewart s. 1818
Felix Walker (D)
Lewis Williams

OHIO

Senators

Jeremiah Morrow (D)
Benjamin Ruggles (D)

Representatives

Levi Barber
Philemon Beecher (F)
John W. Campbell (D)
William Henry Harrison (W)
Samuel Herrick (D)
Peter Hitchcock

PENNSYLVANIA

Senators

Abner Lacock (D)
Jonathan Roberts (D)

Representatives

William Anderson
Henry Baldwin (F)
Andrew Boden
Isaac Darlington (F)
Joseph Hiester (F)
Joseph Hopkinson (F)
Jacob Hostetter (D) s. 1818
Samuel D. Ingham (D)
r. July 1818
William Maclay
William P. Maclay (D)
David Marchand
Robert Moore
Samuel Moore (D) s. 1818
John Murray
Alexander Ogle (D)
Thomas Patterson (D)
Levi Pawling (D)
John Ross r. Feb. 1818
Thomas J. Rogers (D) s. 1818
John Sergeant (F)
Adam Seybert (D)
Jacob Spangler r. Apr. 1818
Christian Tarr
James M. Wallace
John Whiteside (D)
William Wilson

RHODE ISLAND

Senators

William Hunter (F)
James Burrill, Jr.

Representatives

John L. Boss, Jr.
James B. Mason (F)

SOUTH CAROLINA

Senators

John Gaillard (D)
William Smith (D)

Representatives

Joseph Bellinger (D)
John C. Calhoun (D) r. Nov. 1817
Elias Earle (D)
James Ervin (D)
William Lowndes (D)
Henry Middleton (D)
Stephen D. Miller (D)
Wilson Nesbitt (D)
Eldred Simkins (D) s. 1818
Starling Tucker

TENNESSEE

Senators

George W. Campbell (D)
r. Apr. 1818
John H. Eaton (D) s. 1818

John Williams

Representatives

William G. Blount (D)
Thomas Claiborne (D)
Samuel Hogg (D)
Francis Jones
George W. L. Marr
John Rhea (D)

VERMONT

Senators

Dudley Chase (D) r. Nov. 1817
James Fisk (D) r. Jan. 1818
William A. Palmer (D) s. 1818

Isaac Tichenor (F)

Representatives

Heman Allen (D) r. Apr. 1818
Samuel C. Crafts
William Hunter (R)
Orsamus C. Merrill (D)
Charles Rich (D)
Mark Richards (D)

VIRGINIA

Senators

James Barbour (SRD)
John W. Eppes (D)

Representatives

Archibald Austin (D)
William Lee Ball (D)
Philip P. Barbour (D)
Burwell Bassett (D)
William A. Burwell (D)
Edward Colston (F)
John Floyd (D)
Robert S. Garnett (D)
Peterson Goodwyn d. Feb. 1818
James Johnson (D)
William J. Lewis (D)
William McCoy (D)
Charles F. Mercer (D)
Hugh Nelson (D)
Thomas M. Nelson (D)
Thomas Newton, Jr. (D)
John Pegram s. 1818
James Pindall (D)
James Pleasants (D)
Ballard Smith
Alexander Smyth
George F. Strother (D)
Henry St. George Tucker
John Tyler (D)

SIXTEENTH CONGRESS

March 4, 1819 to March 3, 1821

President of The Senate: Daniel D. Tompkins
Presidents Pro Tempore of The Senate: James Barbour
John Gaillard
Speakers of The House of Representatives: Henry Clay
John W. Taylor

ALABAMA

Senators

John W. Walker (D)
William R. King (D)

Representative

John Crowell

CONNECTICUT

Senators

Samuel W. Dana (F)
James Lanman (D)

Representatives

Henry W. Edwards (D)
Samuel A. Foote
Jonathan O. Moseley (F)
Elisha Phelps (D)
John Russ (D)
James Stevens (D)
Gideon Tomlinson (D)

DELAWARE

Senators

Outerbridge Horsey (F)
Nicholas Van Dyke (F)

Representatives

Willard Hall (D)
Louis McLane (D)

GEORGIA

Senators

John Elliott
Freeman Walker (D)

Representatives

Joel Abbot (D)
Thomas W. Cobb
Joel Crawford (D)
John A. Cuthbert (D)
Robert R. Reid (D)
William Terrell (D)

ILLINOIS

Senators

Jesse B. Thomas
Ninian Edwards (D)

Representative

Daniel P. Cook

INDIANA

Senators

James Nobel
Waller Taylor (D)

Representative

William Hendricks (D)

KENTUCKY

Senators

William Logan (D) r. May 1820
Isham Talbot s. 1820

Richard M. Johnson (D) s. 1820

Representatives

Richard C. Anderson, Jr.
William Brown
Henry Clay
Benjamin Hardin
Francis Johnson (D) s. 1820
Alney McLean
Thomas Metcalfe (D)
Thomas Montgomery (D) s. 1820
Tunstall Quarles (D) r. June 1820
George Robertson (W)
David Trimble (D)
David Walker d. Mar. 1820

LOUISIANA

Senators

Henry Johnson
James Brown

Representative

Thomas Butler

MAINE

Senators

John Chandler (D) s. 1820
John Holmes s. 1820

Representative

Joseph Dane (F) s. 1820

MARYLAND

Senators

Alexander C. Hanson (F)
d. Apr. 1819
William Pinkney s. 1820

Edward Lloyd (D)

Representatives

Stevenson Archer (D)
Thomas Bayly (D)
Thomas Culbreth (D)
Joseph Kent (D)
Peter Little (D)
Raphael Neale
Samuel Ringgold (D)
Samuel Smith (D)
Henry R. Warfield (F)

MASSACHUSETTS

Senators

Harrison Gray Otis (F)

Prentiss Mellen r. May 1820
Elijah H. Mills (F) s. 1820

Representatives

Benjamin Adams (F)
Samuel C. Allen
Joshua Cushman (D)
Edward Dowse (D) r. May 1820
William Eustis s. 1820
Walter Folger, Jr. (D)
Timothy Fuller (D)
Benjamin Gorham s. 1820
Mark L. Hill
Aaron Hobart (D) s. 1820
John Holmes (D) r. Mar. 1820
Jonas Kendall (F)
Martin Kinsley
Samuel Lathrop (F)
Enoch Lincoln
Jonathan Mason (F) r. May 1820
Marcus Morton (D)
Jeremiah Nelson (F)
James Parker (D)
Zabdiel Sampson (D) r. July 1820
Henry Shaw (F)
Nathaniel Silsbee (D)
Ezekiel Whitman

MISSISSIPPI

Senators

Walter Leake (D) r. May 1820
David Holmes (D) s. 1820

Thomas H. Williams (D)

Representative

Christopher Rankin (D)

NEW HAMPSHIRE

Senators

David L. Morril (D)
John F. Parrott (D)

Representatives

Joseph Buffum, Jr. (D)
Josiah Butler (D)
Clifton Clagett
Arthur Livermore (D)
William Plumer, Jr. (D)
Nathaniel Upham (D)

NEW JERSEY

Senators

James J. Wilson (D) r. Jan. 1821
Samuel L. Southard s. 1821

Mahlon Dickerson (D)

Representatives

Ephraim Bateman (D)
Joseph Bloomfield (D)
John Condit r. Nov. 1819
Charles Kinsey s. 1820
John Linn d. Jan. 1821
Bernard Smith
Henry Southard (D)

NEW YORK

Senators

Rufus King (F)
Nathan Sanford (D)

Representatives

Nathaniel Allen
Caleb Baker
Walter Case
Robert Clark (D)
Jacob H. De Witt (D)
John D. Dickinson (F)
John Fay (D)
William D. Ford (D)
Ezra C. Gross (D)
James Guyon, Jr. (F) s. 1820
Aaron Hackley, Jr.
George Hall (D)
Joseph S. Lyman
Henry Meigs (D)
Robert Monell (D)
Hermanus Peek
Nathaniel Pitcher (D)
Jonathan Richmond
Henry R. Storrs (F)
Randall S. Street
James Strong (F)
John W. Taylor (D)
Caleb Tompkins
Albert H. Tracy (D)
Solomon Van Rensselaer (F)
Peter H. Wendover (D)
Silas Wood (D)

NORTH CAROLINA

Senators

Nathaniel Macon (D)
Montfort Stokes (D)

Representatives

William S. Blackledge (D) s. 1821
Hutchins G. Burton
John Culpepper (F)
William Davidson (F)
Weldon N. Edwards (D)
Charles Fisher (D)
Thomas H. Hall (D)
Charles Hooks (D)
Lemuel Sawyer (D)
Thomas Settle (D)
Jesse Slocumb (F) d. Dec. 1820
James S. Smith (D)
Felix Walker (D)
Lewis Williams

OHIO

Senators

Benjamin Ruggles (D)
William A. Trimble

Representatives

Philemon Beecher (F)
Henry Brush
John W. Campbell (D)
Samuel Herrick (D)
Thomas R. Ross (D)
John Sloane (W)

PENNSYLVANIA

Senators

Jonathan Roberts
Walter Lowrie (D)

Representatives

Henry Baldwin (F)
Andrew Boden
William Darlington (D)
George Denison (D)
Samuel Edwards (F)
Thomas Forrest
David Fullerton r. May 1820
Samuel Gross (D)
Joseph Hemphill (F)
Jacob Hibshman
Joseph Hiester r. Dec. 1820
Jacob Hostetter (D)
Thomas G. McCullough s. 1820
William P. Maclay (D)
David Marchand
Robert Moore
Samuel Moore (D)
John Murray
Thomas Patterson (D)
Robert Philson
Thomas J. Rogers (D)
John Sergeant (F)
Christian Tarr
Daniel Udree (D) s. 1821
James M. Wallace

RHODE ISLAND

Senators

William Hunter (F)

James Burrill, Jr. d. Dec. 1820
Nehemiah R. Knight (AF) s. 1821

Representatives

Samuel Eddy (D)
Nathaniel Hazard (D)
d. Dec. 1820

SOUTH CAROLINA

Senators

John Gaillard (D)
William Smith (D)

Representatives

Joseph Brevard (W)
Elias Earle (D)
James Ervin (D)
William Lowndes (D)
John McCreary
James Overstreet
Charles Pinckney (D)
Eldred Simkins (D)
Startling Tucker

TENNESSEE

Senators

John Williams
John H. Eaton (D)

Representatives

Robert Allen (D)
Henry H. Bryan
Newton Cannon (D)
John Cocke
Francis Jones
John Rhea (D)

VERMONT

Senators

Isaac Tichenor (F)
William A. Palmer (D)

Representatives

Samuel C. Crafts
Rollin C. Mallary s. 1820
Ezra Meech (D)
Orsamus C. Merrill (D) r. Jan. 1820
Charles Rich (D)
Mark Richards (D)
William Strong

VIRGINIA

Senators

James Barbour (SR)

John W. Eppes r. Dec. 1819
James Pleasants (D)

Representatives

Mark Alexander (D)
William S. Archer s. 1820
William Lee Ball (D)
Philip P. Barbour (D)
William A. Burwell (D) d. Feb. 1821
John Floyd (D)
Robert S. GArnett (D)
John C. Gray s. 1820
Edward B. Jackson s. 1820
James Johnson (D) r. Feb. 1820
James Jones (D)
William McCoy (D)
Charles F. Mercer (D)
Thomas L. Moore s. 1820
Hugh Nelson (D)
Thomas Newton, Jr. (D)
Severn E. Parker
James Pindall (F) r. July 1820
James Pleasants (D) r. Dec. 1819
John Randolph (SRD)
Ballard Smith
Alexander Smyth
George F. Strother (D) r. Feb. 1820
George Tucker (D)
John Tyler (D)
Thomas Van Swearingen
Jared Williams (D)

SEVENTEENTH CONGRESS

March 9, 1821 to March 3, 1823

President of The Senate: Daniel D. Tompkins
President Pro Tempore of The Senate: John Gaillard
Speaker of The House of Representatives: Philip P. Barbour

ALABAMA

Senators

John W. Walker (D) r. Dec. 1822
William Kelly (D) s. 1823

William R. King (D)

Representative

Gabriel Moore

CONNECTICUT

Senators

James Lanman (D)
Elijah Boardman (D)

Representatives

Noyes Barber (D)
Daniel Burrows (D)
Henry W. Edwards (D)
John Russ (D)
Ansel Sterling
Ebenezer Stoddard
Gideon Tomlinson (D)

DELAWARE

Senators

Nicholas Van Dyke (F)
Caesar A. Rodney (D) s. 1822

Representatives

Louis McLane (D)
Caesar A. Rodney (D) r. Jan. 1822
Daniel Rodney (F) s. 1822

GEORGIA

Senators

John Elliott

Freeman Walker (D) r. Aug. 1821
Nicholas Ware

Representatives

Joel Abbott (D)
Alfred Cuthbert (D)
George R. Gilmer (D)
Robert R. Reid (D)
Edward F. Tattnall
Wiley Thompson (D)

ILLINOIS

Senators

Jesse B. Thomas
Ninian Edwards (D)

Representative

Daniel P. Cook

INDIANA

Senators

James Noble
Waller Taylor (D)

Representative

William Hendricks r. 1821
Jonathan Jennings s. 1822

KENTUCKY

Senators

Richard M. Johnson (D)
Isham Talbot

Representatives

James D. Breckinridge s. 1822
Wingfield Bullock d. Oct. 1821
Benjamin Hardin
Francis Johnson (D)
John T. Johnson (D)
Thomas Metcalfe (D)
Thomas Montgomery (D)
Anthony New (D)
George Robertson r. 1821
John S. Smith (D)
David Trimble (D)
Samuel H. Woodson

LOUISIANA

Senators

Henry Johnson
James Brown

Representative

Josiah S. Johnston (D)

MAINE

Senators

John Chandler (D)
John Holmes (D)

Representatives

Joshua Cushman (D)
Joseph Dane (F)
Mark Harris s. 1822
Ebenezer Herrick
Mark L. Hill
Enoch Lincoln
Ezekiel Whitman r. June 1822
William D. Williamson (D)

MARYLAND

Senators

Edward Lloyd (D)

William Pinkney d. Feb. 1822
Samuel Smith (D) s. 1822

Representatives

Thomas Bayly (D)
Jeremiah Cosden r. Mar. 1822
Joseph Kent (D)
Peter Little (D)
Isaac McKim (D) s. 1823
Raphael Neale
John Nelson (D)
Philip Reed s. 1822
Samuel Smith (D) r. Dec. 1822
Henry R. Warfield (F)
Robert Wright (D)

MASSACHUSETTS

Senators

Harrison Gray Otis (F) r. May 1822
James Lloyd (F) s. 1822

Elijah H. Mills (F)

Representatives

Samuel C. Allen
Gideon Barstow (D)
Francis Baylies
Lewis Bigelow
Henry W. Dwight
William Eustis (D)
Timothy Fuller (D)
Benjamin Gorham
Aaron Hobart (D)
Samuel Lathrop (F)
Jeremiah Nelson (F)
John Reed
Jonathan Russell (D)

MISSISSIPPI

Senators

Thomas H. Williams (D)
David Holmes (D)

Representative

Christopher Rankin (D)

MISSOURI

Senators

David Barton
Thomas H. Benton (D)

Representative

John Scott

NEW HAMPSHIRE

Senators

David L. Morril (D)
John F. Parrott (D)

Representatives

Josiah Butler (D)
Matthew Harvey (D)
Aaron Matson
William Plumer, Jr. (D)
Nathaniel Upham (D)
Thomas Whipple, Jr.

NEW JERSEY

Senators

Mahlon Dickerson (D)
Samuel L. Southard (D)

Representatives

Ephraim Bateman (D)
George Cassedy (D)
Lewis Condict (AF)
George Holcombe (D)
James Matlack
Samuel Swan

NEW YORK

Senators

Rufus King (F)
Martin Van Buren (D)

Representatives

Charles Borland, Jr.
Churchill C. Cambreleng (D)
Samuel Campbell
Cadwallader D. Colden (D)
Alfred Conkling
John D. Dickinson (F)
John Gebhard
James Hawkes
Thomas H. Hubbard (D)
Joseph Kirkland
Elisha Litchfield (D)
Richard McCarty (D)
John J. Morgan (D)
Walter Patterson
Jeremiah H. Pierson (F)
Nathaniel Pitcher (D)
William B. Rochester (D)
Charles H. Ruggles
Elijah Spencer (D)
Micah Sterling (F)
John W. Taylor
Albert H. Tracy (D)
Selah Tuthill d. Sept. 1821
Solomon Van Rensselaer (F) r. Jan. 1822
Stephen Van Rensselaer (F) s. 1822
William W. Van Wyck (D)
Reuben H. Walworth (D)
Silas Wood (D)
David Woodcock (D)

NORTH CAROLINA

Senators

Nathaniel Macon (D)
Montfort Stokes (D)

Representatives

William S. Blackledge (D)
Hutchins G. Burton
Henry W. Connor (D)
Josiah Crudup
Weldon N. Edwards (D)
Thomas H. Hall (D)
Charles Hooks (D)
John Long
Archibald McNeill
Romulus M. Saunders (D)
Lemuel Sawyer (D)
Felix Walker (D)
Lewis Williams

OHIO

Senators

Benjamin Ruggles (D)

William A. Trimble d. Dec. 1821
Ethan Allen Brown (D) s. 1822

Representatives

Levi Barber
John W. Campbell (D)
David Chambers
Thomas R. Ross (D)
John Sloane
Joseph Vance (D)

PENNSYLVANIA

Senators

Walter Lowrie (D)
William Findlay (D)

Representatives

Henry Baldwin (F) r. May 1822
John Brown
James Buchanan (F)
William Darlington (D)
George Denison (D)
Samuel Edwards (F)
Patrick Farrelly (D)
John Findlay (D)
Thomas Forrest s. 1822
Walter Forward (D) s. 1822
Samuel Gross (D)
Joseph Hemphill (F)
Samuel D. Ingham (D) s. 1822
James McSherry
William Milnor (F) r. May 1822
James S. Mitchell (D)
Samuel Moore (D) r. May 1822
Thomas Murray, Jr. (D)
Thomas Patterson (D)
John Phillips (F)
George Plumer (D)
Thomas J. Rogers (D)
John Sergeant (F)
Andrew Stewart
John Todd
Daniel Udree (D) s. 1822
Ludwig Worman (F) d. Oct. 1822

RHODE ISLAND

Senators

Nehemiah R. Knight (AF)
James DeWolf (D)

Representatives

Job Durfee (D)
Samuel Eddy (D)

SOUTH CAROLINA

Senators

John Gaillard (D)
William Smith (D)

Representatives

James Blair (D) r. May 1822
John Carter s. 1822
Joseph Gist (D)
Andrew R. Govan s. 1822
James Hamilton, Jr. (SRD) s. 1823
William Lowndes (D) r. May 1822
George McDuffie (D)
Thomas R. Mitchell
James Overstreet d. May 1822
Joel R. Poinsett (D)
Starling Tucker
John Wilson

TENNESSEE

Senators

John Williams (D)
John H. Eaton (D)

Representatives

Robert Allen (D)
Newton Cannon (D)
John Cocke
Francis Jones
John Rhea (D)

VERMONT

Senators

William A. Palmer (D)
Horatio Seymour (D)

Representatives

Samuel C. Crafts
Elias Keyes (R)
Rollin C. Mallary
John Mattocks
Charles Rich (D)
Phineas White (D)

VIRGINIA

Senators

James Barbour

James Pleasants (D) r. Dec. 1822
John Taylor (D) s. 1822

Representatives

Mark Alexander (D)
William S. Archer
William L. Ball (D)
Philip P. Barbour (D)
Burwell Bassett (D)
John Floyd (D)
Robert S. Garnett (D)
Edward B. Jackson (D)
James Jones (D)
Jabez Leftwich
William McCoy (D)
Charles F. Mercer (D)
Thomas L. Moore
Hugh Nelson (D) r. Jan. 1823
Thomas Newton, Jr. (D)
John Randolph (SRD)
Arthur Smith
William Smith
Alexander Smyth
James Stephenson (F) s. 1822
Andrew Stevenson (D)
George Tucker (D)
Thomas Van Swearingen d. Aug. 1822
Jared Williams (D)

EIGHTEENTH CONGRESS

March 4, 1823 to March 3, 1825

President of The Senate:	Daniel D. Tompkins
President Pro Tempore of The Senate:	John Gaillard
Speaker of The House of Representatives:	Henry Clay

ALABAMA

Senators

William R. King (D)
William Kelly (D)

Representatives

John McKee
Gabriel Moore
George W. Owen

CONNECTICUT

Senators

James Lanman (D)

Elijah Boardman (D) d. Oct. 1823
Henry W. Edwards (D)

Representatives

Noyes Barber (D)
Samuel A. Foote (AF)
Ansel Sterling
Ebenezer Stoddard
Gideon Tomlinson (D)
Lemuel Whitman (D)

DELAWARE

Senators

Nicholas Van Dyke (F)
Thomas Clayton s. 1824

Representative

Louis McLane (D)

GEORGIA

Senators

John Elliott

Nicholas Ware d. Sept. 1824
Thomas W. Cobb s. 1824

Representatives

Joel Abbot (D)
George Cary
Thomas W. Cobb r. Dec. 1824
Alfred Cuthbert (D)
John Forsyth (D)
Edward F. Tattnall
Wiley Thompson (D)
Richard H. Wilde (D)

ILLINOIS

Senators

Jesse B. Thomas

Ninian Edwards (D) r. Mar. 1824
John McLean (D) s. 1824

Representative

Daniel P. Cook

INDIANA

Senators

James Nobel
Waller Taylor (D)

Representatives

Jacob Call s. 1824
Jonathan Jennings (D)
William Prince d. Sept. 1824
John Test (D)

KENTUCKY

Senators

Richard M. Johnson (D)
Isham Talbot

Representatives

Richard A. Buckner (D)
Henry Clay
Robert P. Henry (D)
Francis Johnson (D)
John T. Johnson (D)
Robert P. Letcher (D)
Thomas Metcalfe (D)
Thomas P. Moore (D)
Philip Thompson
David Trimble (D)
David White
Charles A. Wickliffe (D)

LOUISIANA

Senators

Henry Johnson r. May 1824
Dominique Bouligny s. 1824

James Brown r. Dec. 1823
Josiah S. Johnston (D) s. 1824

Representatives

William L. Brent
Henry H. Gurley
Edward Livingston (D)

MAINE

Senators

John Chandler (D)
John Holmes (D)

Representatives

William Burleigh (D)
Joshua Cushman (D)
Ebenezer Herrick
David Kidder
Enoch Lincoln
Stephen Longfellow (F)
Jeremiah O'Brien (D)

MARYLAND

Senators

Edward Lloyd (D)
Samuel Smith (D)

Representatives

William Heyward, Jr. (D)
Joseph Kent (D)
John Lee (D)
Peter Little (D)
Isaac McKim (D)
George E. Mitchell (D)
Raphael Neale
John S. Spence (D)
Henry R. Warfield (F)

MASSACHUSETTS

Senators

Elijah H. Mills (F)
James Lloyd (F)

Representatives

Samuel C. Allen
John Bailey s. 1824
Francis Baylies
Benjamin W. Crowninshield (D)
Henry W. Dwight
Timothy Fuller (D)
Aaron Hobart (D)
Samuel Lathrop (F)
John Locke
Jeremiah Nelson (F)
John Reed
Jonas Sibley (D)
Daniel Webster (F)

MISSISSIPPI

Senators

Thomas H. Williams (D)
David Holmes (D)

Representative

Christopher Rankin (D)

MISSOURI

Senators

David Barton
Thomas H. Benton (D)

Representative

John Scott

NEW HAMPSHIRE

Senators

John F. Parrott (D)
Samuel Bell

Representatives

Ichabod Bartlett (D)
Matthew Harvey (D)
Arthur Livermore (D)
Aaron Matson
William Plumer, Jr. (D)
Thomas Whipple, Jr.

NEW JERSEY

Senators

Mahlon Dickerson (D)
Joseph McIlvaine (D)

Representatives

George Cassedy (D)
Lewis Condict (AF)
Daniel Garrison (D)
George Holcombe (D)
James Matlack
Samuel Swan

NEW YORK

Senators

Rufus King (F)
Martin Van Buren (D)

Representatives

Parmenio Adams s. 1824
John W. Cady
Churchill C. Cambreleng (D)
Lot Clark
Ela Collins (D)
Hector Craig (D)
Rowland Day (D)
Justin Dwinell
Lewis Eaton
Charles A. Foote (D)
Joel Frost
Moses Hayden
John Herkimer (D)
James L. Hogeboom
Lemuel Jenkins (D)
Samuel Lawrence (D)
Elisha Litchfield (D)
Henry C. Martindale (D)
Dudley Marvin (D)
John J. Morgan (D)
John Richards
Robert S. Rose
Peter Sharpe
Henry R. Storrs (F)
James Strong (F)
John W. Taylor (D)
Egbert Ten Eyck
Albert H. Tracy (D)
Jacob Tyson
Stephen Van Rensselaer (F)
William W. Van Wyck (D)
Isaac Williams, Jr. (D)
Isaac Wilson r. Jan. 1824
Silas Wood (D)

NORTH CAROLINA

Senators

Nathaniel Macon (D)
John Branch (D)

Representatives

Hutchins G. Burton r. Mar. 1824
Henry W. Connor (D)
John Culpepper (F)
Weldon N. Edwards (D)
Alfred M. Gatlin
Thomas H. Hall (D)
Charles Hooks (D)
John Long
Willie P. Mangum
George Outlaw (D) s. 1825
Romulus M. Saunders (D)
Richard D. Spaight, Jr. (D)
Robert B. Vance (D)
Lewis Williams

OHIO

Senators

Benjamin Ruggles (D)
Ethan Allen Brown (D)

Representatives

Mordecai Bartley
Philemon Beecher (F)
John W. Campbell (D)
James W. Gazlay (D)
Duncan McArthur (D)
William McLean
John Patterson (D)
Thomas R. Ross (D)
John Sloane
Joseph Vance (D)
Samuel F. Vinton
Elisha Whittlesey
William Wilson (D)
John C. Wright (D)

PENNSYLVANIA

Senators

Walter Lowrie (D)
William Findlay (D)

Representatives

James Allison, Jr.
Samuel Breck (F)
John Brown
James Buchanan (F)
Samuel Edwards (F)
William C. Ellis (F)
Patrick Farrelly (D)
John Findlay (D)
Walter Forward (D)
Robert Harris
Joseph Hemphill (F)
Samuel D. Ingham (D)
George Kremer
Samuel McKean (D)
Philip S. Markley (D)
Daniel H. Miller (D)
James S. Mitchell (D)
Thomas Patterson (D)
George Plumer (D)
Thomas J. Rogers r. Apr. 1824
Andrew Stewart
John Todd (D) r. 1824

Alexander Thomson s. 1824
Daniel Udree (D)
Isaac Wayne
Henry Wilson (D)
James Wilson
George Wolf (D) s. 1824

RHODE ISLAND

Senators

Nehemiah R. Knight (AF)
James DeWolf (D)

Representatives

Job Durfee (D)
Samuel Eddy (D)

SOUTH CAROLINA

Senators

John Gaillard (D)
Robert Y. Hayne (D)

Representatives

Robert B. Campbell
John Carter
Joseph Gist (D)
Andrew R. Govan
James Hamilton, Jr. (SRD)
George McDuffie (D)
Joel R. Poinsett (D)
Starling Tucker
John Wilson

TENNESSEE

Senators

John H. Eaton (D)
Andrew Jackson

Representatives

Adam R. Alexander (F)
Robert Allen (D)
John Blair (D)
John Cocke
Samuel Houston (D)
Jacob C. Isacks
James B. Reynolds (D)
James T. Sandford
James Standifer

VERMONT

Senators

William A. Palmer (D)
Horatio Seymour (D)

Representatives

William C. Bradley (D)
Daniel A. A. Buck (D)
Samuel C. Crafts
Rollin C. Mallary
Henry Olin (D) s. 1824
Charles Rich (D) d. Oct. 1824

VIRGINIA

Senators

James Barbour

John Taylor d. Aug. 1824
Littleton W. Tazewell (D) s. 1824

Representatives

Mark Alexander (D)
William S. Archer
William L. Ball (D) d. Feb. 1824
John S. Barbour (SRD)
Philip P. Barbour (SRD)
Burwell Bassett (D)
John Floyd (D)
Robert S. Garnett (D)
Joseph Johnson (D)
Jabez Leftwich
William McCoy (D)
Charles F. Mercer (D)
Thomas Newton, Jr. (D)
John Randolph (SRD)
William C. Rives (D)
Arthur Smith
William Smith
Alexander Smyth
James Stephenson (F)
Andrew Stevenson (D)
John Taliaferro (D) s. 1824
George Tucker (D)
Jared Williams (D)

NINETEENTH CONGRESS

March 4, 1825 to March 3, 1827

President of The Senate: John C. Calhoun
Presidents Pro Tempore of The Senate: John Gaillard, Nathaniel Macon
Speaker of The House of Representatives: John W. Taylor

ALABAMA

Senators

William R. King (D)

Henry H Chambers (D)
d. Jan. 1826
Israel Pickens (D) ta. 1826
John McKinley (D) s. 1826

Representatives

John McKee
Gabriel Moore
George W. Owen

CONNECTICUT

Senators

Henry W. Edwards (D)
Calvin Willey

Representatives

John Baldwin
Noyes Barber (D)
Ralph I. Ingersoll (D)
Orange Merwin
Elisha Phelps (D)
Gideon Tomlinson (D)

DELAWARE

Senators

Nicholas Van Dyke (F)
d. May 1826
Daniel Rodney (F) ta. 1826
Henry M. Ridgeley (F) s. 1827

Thomas Clayton

Representative

Louis McLane (D) r. 1825

GEORGIA

Senators

Thomas W. Cobb
John M. Berrien (D)

Representatives

George Cary
Alfred Cuthbert (D)
John Forsyth (D)
Charles E. Haynes (D)
James Meriwether
Edward F. Tattnall
Wiley Thompson (D)

ILLINOIS

Senators

Jesse B. Thomas
Elias K. Kane (D)

Representative

Daniel P. Cook

INDIANA

Senators

James Noble
William Hendricks (D)

Representatives

Ratliff Boon (D)
Jonathan Jennings (D)
John Test (D)

KENTUCKY

Senators

Richard M. Johnson (D)
John Rowan (D)

Representatives

Richard A. Buckner (AF)
James Clark (D)
John F. Henry s. 1826
Robert P. Henry (D) d. Aug. 1826
Francis Johnson (D)
James Johnson (D) d. Aug. 1826
Joseph Lecompte (D)
Robert P. Letcher (D)
Robert McHatton (D) s. 1826
Thomas Metcalfe (D)
Thomas P. Moore (D)
David Trimble (D)
Charles A. Wickliffe (D)
William S. Young (D)

LOUISIANA

Senators

Josiah S. Johnston (D)
Dominique Bouligny

Representatives

William L. Brent
Henry H. Gurley
Edward Livingston (D)

MAINE

Senators

John Chandler (D)
John Holmes (D)

Representatives

John Anderson (D)
William Burleigh (D)
Ebenezer Herrick
David Kidder
Enoch Lincoln r. Jan. 1826
Jeremiah O'Brien (D)
James W. Ripley (D) s. 1826
Peleg Sprague

MARYLAND

Senators

Edward Lloyd (D) r. Jan. 1826
Ezekiel F. Chambers s. 1826

Samuel Smith (D)

Representatives

John Barney (F)
Clement Dorsey
Joseph Kent (D) r. Jan. 1826
John L. Kerr
Peter Little (D)
Robert N. Martin (D)
George E. Mitchell (D)
George Peter (D)
John C. Weems (D) s. 1826
Thomas C. Worthington (D)

MASSACHUSETTS

Senators

Elijah H. Mills (F)

James Lloyd (F) r. Jan. 1826
Nathaniel Silsbee (D) s. 1826

Representatives

Samuel C. Allen
John Bailey
Francis Baylies
Benjamin W. Crowninshield (D)
John Davis (NR)
Henry W. Dwight
Edward Everett (MR)
Aaron Hobart (D)
Samuel Lathrop (F)
John Locke
John Reed
John Varnum (F)
Daniel Webster (F)

MISSISSIPPI

Senators

Thomas H. Williams (D)

David Holmes (R) r. Sept. 1825
Powhatan Ellis (D) ta. 1825
Thomas B. Reed (D) s. 1826

Representatives

William Haile s. 1826
Christopher Rankin (D) r. Mar. 1826

MISSOURI

Senators

David Barton
Thomas H. Benton (D)

Representative

John Scott

NEW HAMPSHIRE

Senators

Samuel Bell
Levi Woodbury

Representatives

Ichabod Bartlett (D)
Titus Brown
Nehemiah Eastman (D)
Jonathan Harvey
Joseph Healy (D)
Thomas Whipple, Jr.

NEW JERSEY

Senators

Mahlon Dickerson (D)

Joseph McIlvaine d. Aug. 1826
Ephraim Bateman (D) s. 1826

Representatives

George Cassedy (D)
Lewis Condict (AF)
Daniel Garrison (D)
George Holcombe (D)
Samuel Swan
Ebenezer Tucker

NEW YORK

Senators

Martin Van Buren (D)
Nathan Sanford (D) s. 1826

Representatives

Parmenio Adams
William G. Angel (D)
Henry Ashley
Luther Badger
Churchill C. Cambreleng (D)
William Dietz (D)
Nicoll Fosdick
Daniel G. Garnsey (D)
John Hallock, Jr. (D)
Abraham B. Hasbrouck (NR)
Moses Hayden
Michael Hoffman (D)
Daniel Hugunin, Jr.
Charles Humphrey (D)
Jeromus Johnson (D)
Charles Kellogg
William McManus
Henry Markell (D)
Henry C. Martindale
Dudley Marvin (D)
John Miller
Timothy H. Porter
Robert S. Rose
Henry H. Ross
Joshua Sands
Henry R. Storrs (F)
James Strong (F)
John W. Taylor (D)
Egbert Ten Eyck r. Dec. 1825
Stephen Van Rensselaer (F)
Gulian C. Verplanck (D)
Aaron Ward (D)
Bartow White
Elias Whitmore (D)
Silas Wood (D)

NORTH CAROLINA

Senators

Nathaniel Macon (D)
John Branch (D)

Representatives

Willis Alston (D)
Daniel L. Barringer (D) s. 1826
John H. Bryan
Samuel P. Carson (D)
Henry W. Connor (D)
Weldon N. Edwards (D)
Richard Hines (D)
Gabriel Holmes
John Long
Archibald McNeill
Willie P. Mangum r. Mar. 1826
Romulus M. Saunders (D)
Lemuel Sawyer (D)
Lewis Williams

OHIO

Senators

Benjamin Ruggles (D)
William Henry Harrison

Representatives

Mordecai Bartley (NR)
Philemon Beecher (F)
John W. Campbell (D)
James Findlay (D)
David Jennings r. May 1826
William McLean
Thomas Shannon (D) s. 1826
John Sloane
John Thomson (D)
Joseph Vance (D)
Samuel F. Vinton
Elisha Whittlesey
William Wilson (D)
John Woods
John C. Wright (D)

PENNSYLVANIA

Senators

William Findlay (D)
William Marks (D)

Representatives

William Addams (D)
James Allison, Jr. r. 1825
James Buchanan
Samuel Edwards (F)
Patrick Farrelly (D) d. Jan. 1826
John Findlay (D)
Chauncey Forward (D) s. 1826
Robert Harris
Joseph Hemphill (F) r. 1826
Samuel D. Ingham (D)
Thomas Kittera (F) s. 1826
Jacob Krebs (D) s. 1826
George Kremer
Joseph Lawrence
Samuel McKean (D)
Philip S. Markley (D)
Daniel H. Miller (D)
Charles Miner (F)
James S. Mitchell (D)
John Mitchell (D)
Robert Orr, Jr. (D)
George Plumer (D)
Thomas H. Sill s. 1826
James S. Stevenson
Andrew Stewart (D)
Alexander Thomson r. May 1826
Espy Van Horne (D)
Henry Wilson (D) d. Aug. 1826
James Wilson (D)
George Wolf (D)
John Wurts (NR)

RHODE ISLAND

Senators

Nehemiah R. Knight (AF)

James DeWolf r. Oct. 1825
Asher Robbins

Representatives

Tristam Burges (F)
Dutee J. Pearce (D)

SOUTH CAROLINA

Senators

John Gaillard (D) d. Feb. 1826
William Harper (D) s. 1826
William Smith (D) s. 1826

Robert Y. Hayne (D)

Representatives

John Carter
William Drayton (D)
Joseph Gist (D)
Andrew R. Govan
James Hamilton, Jr. (SRD)
George McDuffie (D)
Thomas R. Mitchell
Joel R. Poinsett (D) r. Mar. 1825
Starling Tucker
John Wilson

TENNESSEE

Senators

John H. Eaton (D)

Andrew Jackson r. Oct. 1825
Hugh L. White

Representatives

Adam R. Alexander (F)
Robert Allen (D)
John Blair (D)
John Cocke
Samuel Houston (D)
Jacob C. Isacks
John H. Marable (NR)
James C. Mitchell
James K. Polk (D)

VERMONT

Senators

Horatio Seymour (D)
Dudley Chase (D)

Representatives

William C. Bradley (D)
Rollin C. Mallary
John Mattocks
Ezra Meech (D)
George E. Wales

VIRGINIA

Senators

James Barbour r. Mar. 1825
John Randolph (SRD)

Littleton W. Tazewell (D)

Representatives

Mark Alexander (D)
William S. Archer
William Armstrong (D)
John S. Barbour (SRD)
Burwell Bassett (D)
Nathaniel H. Claiborne (F)
George W. Crump (D) s. 1826
Thomas Davenport (F)
Benjamin Estil
John Floyd (D)
Robert S. Garnett (D)
Joseph Johnson (D)
William McCoy (D)
Charles F. Mercer (D)
Thomas Newton, Jr. (D)
Alfred H. Powell
John Randolph (SRD) r. Dec. 1825
William C. Rives (D)
William Smith
Andrew Stevenson (D)
John Taliaferro (D)
Robert Taylor
James Trezvant

TWENTIETH CONGRESS

March 4, 1827 to March 3, 1829

President of The Senate:	John C. Calhoun
President Pro Tempore of The Senate:	Samuel Smith
Speaker of The House of Representatives:	Andrew Stevenson

ALABAMA

Senators

William R. King (D)
John McKinley (D)

Representatives

John McKee
Gabriel Moore
George W. Owen

CONNECTICUT

Senators

Calvin Willey (D)
Samuel A. Foote

Representatives

John Baldwin
Noyes Barber (D)
Ralph I. Ingersoll (D)
Orange Merwin
Elisha Phelps (D)
David Plant (NR)

DELAWARE

Senators

Henry M. Ridgeley (F)
Louis McLane (D)

Representative

Kensey Johns, Jr. (F)

GEORGIA

Senators

Thomas W. Cobb r. 1828
Oliver H. Prince s. 1828

John M. Berrien (D)

Representatives

John Floyd
John Forsyth (D) r. Nov. 1827
Tomlinson Fort (D)
George R. Gilmer
Charles E. Haynes (D)
Wilson Lumpkin (D)
Edward F. Tattnall r. 1827
Richard H. Wilde (D) s. 1828
Wiley Thompson (D)

ILLINOIS

Senators

Jesse B. Thomas
Elias K. Kane (D)

Representative

Joseph Duncan (D)

INDIANA

Senators

James Noble
William Hendricks (D)

Representatives

Thomas H. Blake
Jonathan Jennings (D)
Oliver H. Smith

KENTUCKY

Senators

Richard M. Johnson (D)
John Rowan (D)

Representatives

Richard A. Buckner (D)
John Chambers s. 1828
Thomas Chilton s. 1828
James Clark (D)
Henry Daniel (D)
Joseph Lecompte (D)
Robert P. Letcher
Chittenden Lyon (D)
Robert McHatton (D)
Thomas Metcalfe r. June 1828
Thomas P. Moore (D)
Charles A. Wickliffe (D)
Joel Yancey (D)
William S. Young (D)
d. Sept. 1827

LOUISIANA

Senators

Josiah S. Johnson (D)
Dominique Bouligny

Representatives

William L. Brent
Henry H. Gurley
Edward Livingston (D)

MAINE

Senators

John Chandler (D)

Albion K. Parris (D) r. Aug. 1828
John Holmes (D) s. 1829

Representatives

John Anderson (D)
Samuel Butman
Rufus McIntire (D)
Jeremiah O'Brien (D)
James W. Ripley (D)
Peleg Sprague
Joseph F. Wingate (D)

MARYLAND

Senators

Samuel Smith (D)
Ezekiel F. Chambers

Representatives

John Barney (F)
Clement Dorsey
Levin Gale
John L. Kerr
Peter Little (D)
Michael C. Sprigg (D)
George C. Washington
John C. Weems (D)
Ephraim K. Wilson (D)

MASSACHUSETTS

Senators

Nathaniel Silsbee (D)
Daniel Webster (F)

Representatives

Samuel C. Allen
John Bailey
Isaac C. Bates (D)
Benjamin W. Crowninshield (D)
John Davis (NR)
Henry W. Dwight
Edward Everett (NR)
Benjamin Gorham (D)
James L. Hodges
John Locke
John Reed
Joseph Richardson
John Varnum (F)

MISSISSIPPI

Senators

Thomas H. Williams (D)
Powhatan Ellis (D)

Representatives

William Haile r. Sept. 1828
Thomas Hinds s. 1828

MISSOURI

Senators

David Barton
Thomas H. Benton (D)

Representative

Edward Bates

NEW HAMPSHIRE

Senators

Samuel Bell
Levi Woodbury (D)

Representatives

David Barker, Jr.
Ichabod Bartlett (D)
Titus Brown
Jonathan Harvey
Joseph Healy (D)
Thomas Whipple, Jr.

NEW JERSEY

Senators

Ephraim Bateman (D) r. Jan. 1829
Mahlon Dickerson (D)

Representatives

Lewis Condict (AF)
George Holcombe (D) d. Jan. 1828
Isaac Pierson
James F. Randolph s. 1828
Thomas Sinnickson s. 1828
Samuel Swan
Hedge Thompson d. July 1828
Ebenezer Tucker

NEW YORK

Senators

Martin Van Buren (D)
r. Dec. 1829
Charles E. Dudley (D) s. 1829

Nathan Sanford (D)

Representatives

Daniel D. Barnard
George O. Belden (D)
Rudolph Bunner (D)
Churchill C. Cambreleng (D)
Samuel Chase (D)
John C. Clark (D)
John I. DeGraff (D)
John D. Dickinson
Jonas Earll, Jr. (D)
Daniel G. Garnsey (D)
Nathaniel Garrow (D)
John Hallock, Jr. (D)
Selah R. Hobbie (D)
Michael Hoffman (D)
Jeromus Johnson (D)
Richard Keese (D)
John Magee (D)
Henry Markell (D)
Henry C. Martindale
Dudley Marvin (D)
John Maynard
Thomas J. Oakley (D)
r. May 1828
Henry R. Storrs (F)
John G. Stower (D)
James Strong (F)
Thomas Taber (D) s. 1828
John W. Taylor (D)
Phineas L. Tracy
Stephen Van Rensselaer (F)
Gulian C. Verplanck (D)
Aaron Ward (D)
John J. Wood (D)
Silas Wood (D)
David Woodcock (D)
Silas Wright, Jr. (D) r. Feb. 1829

NORTH CAROLINA

Senators

Nathaniel Macon (D) r. Feb. 1828
James Iredell (D) s. 1828

John Branch (D)

Representatives

Willis Alston (D)
Daniel L. Barringer (D)
John H. Bryan
Samuel Carson (D)
Henry W. Connor (D)
John Culpepper (F)
Thomas H. Hall (D)
Gabriel Holmes
John Long (W)
Lemuel Sawyer (D)
Augustine H. Shepperd (D)
Daniel Turner (D)
Lewis Williams

OHIO

Senators

Benjamin Ruggles (D)

William Henry Harrison r. May 1828
Jacob Burnet (F) s. 1828

Representatives

Mordecai Bartley (NR)
Philemon Beecher (F)
William Creighton, Jr. r. 1828
John Davenport
James Findlay (D)
William McLean
Francis S. Muhlenberg (NR) s. 1828
William Russell (D)
John Sloane
William Stanbery (D)
Joseph Vance (D)
Samuel F. Vinton
Elisha Whittlesey
William Wilson (D) d. June 1827
John Woods
John C. Wright (D)

PENNSYLVANIA

Senators

William Marks (D)
Isaac D. Barnard (F)

Representatives

William Addams (D)
Samuel Anderson
Stephen Barlow (D)
James Buchanan (F)
Richard Coulter
Chauncey Forward (D)
Joseph Fry, Jr. (D)
Innis Green (D)
Samuel D. Ingham (D)
Adam King (D)
George Kremer
Joseph Lawrence
Samuel McKean (D)
Daniel H. Miller (D)
Charles Miner (F)
John Mitchell (D)
Robert Orr, Jr. (D)
William Ramsey (D)
John Sergeant (F)
John B. Sterigere (D)
James S. Stevenson
Andrew Stewart (D)
Joel B. Sutherland (D)
Espy Van Horne (D)
James Wilson (D)
George Wolf (D)

RHODE ISLAND

Senators

Nehemiah R. Knight (AF)
Asher Robbins

Representatives

Tristam Burges (F)
Dutee J. Pearce (D)

SOUTH CAROLINA

Senators

Robert Y. Hayne (D)
William Smith (D)

Representatives

John Carter
Warren R. Davis (SRD)
William Drayton (D)
James Hamilton, Jr. (SRD)
George McDuffie (D)
William D. Martin (D)
Thomas R. Mitchell
William T. Nuckolls
Starling Tucker

TENNESSEE

Senators

John H. Eaton (D)
Hugh L. White

Representatives

John Bell (D)
John Blair (D)
David Crockett (D)
Robert Desha
Jacob C. Isacks
Pryor Lea (D)
John H. Marable (NR)
James C. Mitchell
James K. Polk (D)

VERMONT

Senators

Horatio Seymour (D)
Dudley Chase (D)

Representatives

Daniel A. A. Buck (D)
Jonathan Hunt (NR)
Rollin C. Mallary
Benjamin Swift (F)
George E. Wales

VIRGINIA

Senators

Littleton W. Tazewell (D)
John Tyler (D)

Representatives

Mark Alexander (D)
Robert Allen (D)
William S. Archer
William Armstrong (D)
John S. Barbour (SRD)
Philip P. Barbour (D)
Burwell Bassett (D)
Nathaniel H. Claiborne
Thomas Davenport (F)
John Floyd (D)
Isaac Leffler
William McCoy (D)
Lewis Maxwell (NR)
Charles F. Mercer (D)
Thomas Newton, Jr. (D)
John Randolph (SRD)
William C. Rives
John Roane (D)
Alexander Smyth
Andrew Stevenson (D)
John Taliaferro (D)
James Trezvant

TWENTY-FIRST CONGRESS

March 4, 1829 to March 3, 1831

President of The Senate:	John C. Calhoun
President Pro Tempore of The Senate:	Samuel Smith
Speaker of The House of Representatives:	Andrew Stevenson

ALABAMA

Senators

William R. King (D)
John McKinley (D)

Representatives

Robert E. B. Baylor (D)
Clement Comer Clay (D)
Dixon H. Lewis (SRD)

CONNECTICUT

Senators

Calvin Willey (D)
Samuel A. Foote

Representatives

Noyes Barber (D)
William W. Ellsworth
Jabez W. Huntington
Ralph I. Ingersoll (D)
William L. Storrs
Ebenezer Young

DELAWARE

Senators

Louis McLane (D) r. Apr. 1829
Arnold Naudain s. 1830

John M. Clayton

Representative

Kensey Johns, Jr. (F)

GEORGIA

Senators

John M. Berrien (D) r. Mar. 1829
John Forsyth (D)
George M. Troup (SRD)

Representatives

Thomas F. Foster (D)
Charles E. Haynes (D)
Henry G. Lamar (D)
Wilson Lumpkin (D)
Wiley Thompson (D)
James M. Wayne (D)
Richard H. Wilde (D)

ILLINOIS

Senators

Elias K. Kane (D)

John McLean d. Oct. 1830
David J. Baker (D) s. 1830
John M. Robinson (D) s. 1831

Representative

Joseph Duncan (D)

INDIANA

Senators

James Noble d. Feb. 1831
William Hendricks (D)

Representatives

Ratliff Boon (D)
Jonathan Jennings (D)
John Test

KENTUCKY

Senators

John Rowan (D)
George M. Bibb

Representatives

Thomas Chilton
James Clark (D)
Nicholas D. Coleman (D)
Henry Daniel (D)
Nathan Gaither (D)
Richard M. Johnson (D)
John Kincaid (D)
Joseph Lecompte (D)
Robert P. Letcher
Chittenden Lyon (D)
Charles A. Wickliffe (D)
Joel Yancey (D)

LOUISIANA

Senators

Josiah S. Johnston (D)
Edward Livingston (D)

Representatives

Henry H. Gurley
Walter H. Overton (D)
Edward D. White

MAINE

Senators

John Holmes (D)
Peleg Sprague (NR)

Representatives

John Anderson (D)
Samuel Butman
George Evans
Cornelius Holland (D) s. 1830
Leonard Jarvis (D)
Rufus McIntire (D)
James W. Ripley (D) r. Mar. 1830
Joseph F. Wingate (D)

MARYLAND

Senators

Samuel Smith (D)
Ezekiel F. Chambers

Representatives

Elias Brown (W)
Clement Dorsey
Benjamin C. Howard (D)
George E. Mitchell (D)
Benedict J. Semmes (D)
Richard Spencer (D)
Michael C. Sprigg (D)
George C. Washington
Ephraim K. Wilson (D)

MASSACHUSETTS

Senators

Nathaniel Silsbee (D)
Daniel Webster

Representatives

John Bailey
Isaac C. Bates
Benjamin W. Crowninshield (D)
John Davis (NR)
Henry W. Dwight
Edward Everett (NR)
Benjamin Gorham
George Grennell, Jr.
James L. Hodges
Joseph G. Kendall
John Reed
Joseph Richardson
John Varnum

MISSISSIPPI

Senators

Powhatan Ellis (D)

Thomas B. Reed (D) d. Nov. 1820
Robert H. Adams (D)
d. Nov. 1830
George Poindexter s. 1830

Representative

Thomas Hinds (D)

MISSOURI

Senators

David Barton
Thomas H. Benton (D)

Representative

Spencer D. Pettis (D)

NEW HAMPSHIRE

Senators

Samuel Bell
Levi Woodbury (D)

Representatives

John Brodhead (D)
Thomas Chandler (D)
Joseph Hammons (D)
Jonathan Harvey
Henry Hubbard (D)
John W. Weeks

NEW JERSEY

Senators

Mahlon Dickerson (D)
Theodore Frelinghuysen (D)

Representatives

Lewis Condict (AF)
Richard M. Cooper
Thomas H. Hughes (W)
Isaac Pierson
James F. Randolph
Samuel Swan

NEW YORK

Senators

Nathan Sanford (D)
Charles E. Dudley (D)

Representatives

William G. Angel (D)
Benedict Arnold
Thomas Beekman
Abraham Bockee (D)
Peter I. Borst (D)
Churchill C. Cambreleng (D)
Timothy Childs
Henry B. Cowles
Hector Craig (D) r. July 1830
Jacob Crocheron (D)
Charles G. DeWitt (D)
John D. Dickinson
Samuel W. Eager (NR) s. 1830
Jonas Earll, Jr. (D)
Isaac Finch (D)
George Fisher r. Feb. 1830
Jehiel H. Halsey (D)
Joseph Hawkins (D)
Michael Hoffman (D)
Perkins King
James Lent (D)
John Magee (D)
Henry C. Martindale
Thomas Maxwell (D)
Robert Monell (D) r. Feb. 1831
Ebenezer F. Norton (D)
Gerhsom Powers (D)
Robert S. Rose
Jonah Sanford s. 1830
Ambrose Spencer
James Strong (F)
Henry R. Storrs
John W. Taylor (D)
Phineas L. Tracy
Gulian C. Verplanck (D)
Campbell P. White (D)

NORTH CAROLINA

Senators

John Branch (D) r. Mar. 1829
Bedford Brown (D)

James Iredell (D)

Representatives

Willis Alston (D)
Daniel L. Barringer (D)
Samuel P. Carson (D)
Henry W. Connor (D)
Edmund Deberry
Edward B. Dudley (NR)
Thomas H. Hall (D)
Robert Potter (D)
Abraham Rencher (NR)
William B. Shepard (NR)
Augustine H. Shepperd (D)
Jesse Speight
Lewis Williams

OHIO

Senators

Benjamin Ruggles (D)
Jacob Burnet (F)

Representatives

Mordecai Bartley
Joseph H. Crane
William Creighton, Jr. (D)
James Findlay (D)
William W. Irvin (D)
William Kennon, Sr. (D)
Humphrey H. Leavitt (D) s. 1830
William Russell (D)
James Shields (D)
William Stanbery (D)
John Thomson (D)
Joseph Vance (D)
Samuel F. Vinton
Elisha Whittlesey

PENNSYLVANIA

Senators

William Marks (D)
Isaac D. Barnard (F)

Representatives

James Buchanan (F)
Richard Coulter
Thomas H. Crawford (D)
Harmar Denny (Anti-Mason)
Joshua Evans, Jr. (D)
James Ford (D)
Chauncey Forward (D)
Joseph Fry, Jr. (D)
John Gilmore (D)
Innis Green (D)
Joseph Hemphill (D)
Peter Ihrie, Jr. (D)
Thomas Irwin (D)
Adam King (D)
George C. Leiper (D)
William McCreery (D)
Alem Marr (D)
Daniel H. Miller (D)
Henry A. P. Muhlenberg (D)
William Ramsey (D)
John Scott
Thomas H. Sill
Samuel A. Smith
Philander Stephens (D)
John B. Sterigere (D)
Joel B. Sutherland (D)

RHODE ISLAND

Senators

Nehemiah R. Knight (AF)
Asher Robbins

Representatives

Tristam Burges (F)
Dutee J. Pearce (D)

SOUTH CAROLINA

Senators

Robert Y. Hayne (D)
William Smith (D)

Representatives

Robert W. Barnwell (D)
James Blair (D)
John Campbell (SRW)
Warren R. Davis (SRD)
William Drayton (D)
George McDuffie (D)
William D. Martin (D)
William T. Nuckolls
Starling Tucker

TENNESSEE

Senators

John H. Eaton (D) r. Mar. 1829
Felix Grundy (D)

Hugh L. White (D)

Representatives

John Bell (D)
John Blair (D)
David Crockett (D)
Robert Desha
Jacob C. Isacks
Cave Johnson (D)
Pryor Lea (D)
James K. Polk (D)
James Standifer (W)

VERMONT

Senators

Horatio Seymour (D)
Dudley Chase (D)

Representatives

William Cahoon (Anti-Mason)
Horace Everett (W)
Jonathan Hunt (NR)
Rollin C. Mallary
Benjamin Swift (F)

VIRGINIA

Senators

Littleton W. Tazewell
John Tyler (D)

Representatives

Mark Alexander (D)
Robert Allen (D)
William S. Archer
William Armstrong (D)
John S. Barbour (SRD)
Philip P. Barbour (D) r. Oct. 1830
Thomas T. Bouldin (D)
Nathaniel H. Claiborne
Richard Coke, Jr. (D)
Robert Craig (D)
Thomas Davenport (F)
Philip Doddridge
Joseph Draper s. Dec. 1830
William F. Gordon (D)
s. Jan. 1830
George Loyall (D) s. 1830
William McCoy (D)
Lewis Maxwell (NR)
Charles F. Mercer (D)
Thomas Newton, Jr. (D)
r. Mar. 1830
John M. Patton (D) s. 1830
John Roane (D)
William C. Rives (D) r. 1829
Alexander Smyth d. Apr. 1830
Andrew Stevenson (D)
John Taliaferro (D)
James Trezvant

TWENTY-SECOND CONGRESS

March 4, 1831 to March 3, 1833

President of The Senate: John C. Calhoun
Presidents Pro Tempore of The Senate: Littleton W. Tazewell
Hugh L. White
Speaker of The House of Representatives: Andrew Stevenson

ALABAMA

Senators

William R. King (D)
Gabriel Moore

Representatives

Clement Comer Clay (D)
Dixon H. Lewis (SRD)
Samuel W. Mardis (D)

CONNECTICUT

Senators

Samuel A. Foote
Gideon Tomlinson

Representatives

Noyes Barber (D)
William W. Ellsworth
Jabez W. Huntington
Ralph I. Ingersoll (D)
William L. Storrs
Ebenezer Young

DELAWARE

Senators

John M. Clayton (W)
Arnold Naudain

Representative

John J. Mulligan (W)

GEORGIA

Senators

George M. Troup (SRD)
John Forsyth (D)

Representatives

Augustin S. Clayton (SRD)
s. 1832
Thomas F. Foster (D)
Henry G. Lamar (D)
Daniel Newnan (SRD)
Wiley Thompson (D)
James M. Wayne (D)
Richard H. Wilde (D)

ILLINOIS

Senators

Elias K. Kane (D)
John M. Robinson (D)

Representative

Joseph Duncan (D)

INDIANA

Senators

William Hendricks (D)

Robert Hanna
John Tipton (D) s. 1832

Representatives

Ratliff Boon (D)
John Carr (D)
Jonathan McCarty

KENTUCKY

Senators

George M. Bibb
Henry Clay (W)

Representatives

John Adair (D)
Chilton Allan (D)
Henry Daniel (D)
Nathan Gaither (D)
Albert G. Hawes (D)
Richard M. Johnson (D)
Joseph Lecompte (D)
Robert P. Letcher
Chittenden Lyon (D)
Thomas A. Marshall
Christopher Tompkins
Charles A. Wickliffe (D)

LOUISIANA

Senators

Josiah S. Johnson (D)

Edward Livingston (D)
r. May 1831
George A. Waggaman (NR)
s. 1832

Representatives

Henry A. Bullard
Philemon Thomas (D)
Edward D. White

MAINE

Senators

John Holmes (D)
Peleg Sprague (NR)

Representatives

John Anderson (D)
James Bates (D)
George Evans (NR)
Cornelius Holland (D)
Leonard Jarvis (D)
Edward Kavanagh (D)
Rufus McIntire (D)

MARYLAND

Senators

Samuel Smith (D)
Ezekiel F. Chambers

Representatives

Benjamin C. Howard (D)
Daniel Jenifer
John L. Kerr
George E. Mitchell (D)
d. June 1832
Benedict J. Semmes (D)
Charles S. Sewall s. 1832
John S. Spence (D)
Francis Thomas (D)
George C. Washington
John T. H. Worthington (D)

MASSACHUSETTS

Senators

Nathaniel Silsbee (D)
Daniel Webster

Representatives

John Quincy Adams
Nathan Appleton
Isaac C. Bates
George N. Briggs
Rufus Choate
John Davis (NR)
Henry A. S. Dearborn
Edward Everett (NR)
George Grennell, Jr.
James L. Hodges
Joseph G. Kendall
Jeremiah Nelson (F)
John Reed

MISSISSIPPI

Senators

Powhatan Ellis (D) r. July 1832
John Black s. 1832

George Poindexter

Representative

Franklin E. Plummer

MISSOURI

Senators

Thomas H. Benton (D)
Alexander Buckner

Representative

William H. Ashley

NEW HAMPSHIRE

Senators

Samuel Bell
Isaac Hill

Representatives

John Brodhead (D)
Thomas Chandler (D)
Joseph Hammons (D)
Joseph M. Harper (D)
Henry Hubbard (D)
John W. Weeks

NEW JERSEY

Senators

Mahlon Dickerson (D)
Theodore Frelinghuysen (D)

Representatives

Lewis Condict (AF)
Silas Condit (D)
Richard M. Cooper
Thomas H. Hughes (W)
James F. Randolph
Isaac Southard (D)

NEW YORK

Senators

Charles E. Dudley (D)

William L. Marcy (D) r. Jan. 1833
Silas Wright, Jr. (D) s. 1833

Representatives

William G. Angel (D)
William Babcock
Gamaliel H. Barstow (NR)
Samuel Beardsley (D)
John T. Bergen (D)
Joseph Bouck (D)
John C. Brodhead (C)
Churchill C. Cambreleng (D)
John A. Collier (D)
Bates Cooke (Anti-Mason)
Charles Dayan (D)
John Dickson
Ulysses F. Doubleday (D)
Michael Hoffman (D)
William Hogan (D)
Freeborn G. Jewett (D)
John King (D)
Gerrit Y. Lansing (D)
James Lent d. Feb. 1833
Edmund H. Pendleton

Job Pierson (D)
Nathaniel Pitcher (D)
Edward C. Reed (D)
Erastus Root (D)
Nathan Soule
John W. Taylor (D)
Phineas L. Tracy
Gulian C. Verplanck (D)
Aaron Ward (D)
Daniel Wardwell
Grattan H. Wheeler
Campbell P. White (D)
Frederick Whittlesey
Samuel J. Wilkin (D)

NORTH CAROLINA

Senators

Bedford Brown (D)
Willie P. Mangum (D)

Representatives

Daniel L. Barringer (D)
Lauchlin Bethune (D)
John Branch (D)
Samuel P. Carson (D)
Henry W. Connor (D)
Thomas H. Hall (D)
Micajah T. Hawkins (D)
James I. McKay (D)
Robert Potter (D)
Abraham Rencher (D)
William B. Shepard (NR)
Augustine H. Shepperd (D)
Jesse Speight
Lewis Williams

OHIO

Senators

Benjamin Ruggles (D)
Thomas Ewing

Representatives

Eleutheros Cooke
Thomas Corwin
Joseph H. Crane
William Creighton, Jr. (D)
James Findlay (D)
William W. Irvin (D)
William Kennon, Sr. (D)
Humphrey H. Leavitt (D)
William Russell (D)
William Stanbery (D)
John Thomson (D)
Joseph Vance (D)
Samuel F. Vinton
Elisha Whittlesey

PENNSYLVANIA

Senators

Isaac D. Barnard (F) r. Dec. 1831
George M. Dallas (D)

William Wilkins (D, Anti-Mason)

Representatives

Robert Allison
John Banks
John C. Bucher
George Burd
Richard Coulter (D)
Thomas H. Crawford (D)
Harmar Denny (Anti-Mason)
Lewis Dewart (D)
Joshua Evans, Jr. (D)
James Ford (D)
John Gilmore (D)
William Hiester
Henry Horn (D)
Peter Ihrie, Jr. (D)
Adam King (D)
Henry King (D)
Robert McCoy
Thomas M. T. McKennan
Joel K. Mann (D)
Henry A. P. Muhlenberg (D)
David Potts, Jr.
Samuel A. Smith
Philander Stephens (D)
Andrew Stewart (D)
Joel B. Sutherland (D)
John G. Watmough

RHODE ISLAND

Senators

Nehemiah R. Knight (AF)
Asher Robbins

Representatives

Tristam Burges (F)
Dutee J. Pearce (D)

SOUTH CAROLINA

Senators

Robert Y. Hayne (D) r. Dec. 1832
John C. Calhoun (D) s. 1833

Stephen D. Miller (D) r. Mar. 1833

Representatives

Robert W. Barnwell (D)
James Blair (D)
Warren R. Davis (SRD)
William Drayton (D)
John M. Felder (D)
John K. Griffin (SRW)
George McDuffie (D)
Thomas R. Mitchell
William T. Nuckolls

TENNESSEE

Senators

Hugh L. White (D)
Felix Grundy (D)

Representatives

Thomas D. Arnold
John Bell
John Blair (D)
William Fitzgerald (D)
William Hall (D)
Jacob C. Isacks
Cave Johnson (D)
James K. Polk (D)
James Standifer

VERMONT

Senators

Horatio Seymour (D)
Samuel Prentiss

Representatives

Heman Allen
William Cahoon (Anti-Mason)
Horace Everett
Hiland Hall s. 1833
Jonathan Hunt (NR) d. 1832
William Slade (W)

VIRGINIA

Senators

Littleton W. Tazewell r. July 1832
William C. Rives (D) s. 1833

John Tyler (D)

Representatives

Mark Alexander (D)
Robert Allen (D)
William S. Archer
William Armstrong (D)
John S. Barbour (SRD)
Thomas T. Bouldin (D)
Joseph W. Chinn (D)
Nathaniel H. Claiborne
Richard Coke, Jr. (D)
Robert Craig (D)
Thomas Davenport (F)
Philip Doddridge d. Nov. 1832
Joseph Draper s. 1832
William F. Gordon (D)
Joseph Johnson (D) s. 1833
Charles C. Johnston (SRD) d. June 1832
William McCoy (D)
John Y. Mason (D)
Lewis Maxwell (NR)
Charles F. Mercer (D)
Thomas Newton, Jr. (D)
John M. Patton (D)
John J. Roane (D)
Andrew Stevenson (D)

TWENTY-THIRD CONGRESS

March 4, 1833 to March 3, 1835

President of The Senate:	Martin Van Buren
Presidents Pro Tempore of The Senate:	Hugh L. White George Poindexter John Tyler
Speakers of The House of Representatives:	Andrew Stevenson John Bell

ALABAMA

Senators

William R. King (D)
Gabriel Moore

Representatives

Clement Comer Clay
Dixon H. Lewis (SRD)
John McKinley (D)
Samuel W. Mardis (D)
John Murphy (D)

CONNECTICUT

Senators

Gideon Tomlinson (D)
Nathan Smith (W)

Representatives

Noyes Barber (D)
William W. Ellsworth (W) r. July 1834
Samuel A. Foote (W) r. 1834
Jabez W. Huntington r. 1834
Phineas Miner (W) s. 1834
Joseph Trumbull (W) s. 1834
Samuel Tweedy (W)
Ebenezer Young

DELAWARE

Senators

John M. Clayton (W)
Arnold Naudain

Representative

John J. Milligan (W)

GEORGIA

Senators

George M. Troup r. Nov. 1833
John P. King (D)

John Forsyth (D) r. June 1834
Alfred Cuthbert (D) s. 1835

Representatives

Augustin S. Clayton (SRD)
John Coffee (D)
Thomas F. Foster (D)
Roger L. Gamble (W)
George R. Gilmer (D)
Seaborn Jones (D)
William Schley (D)
James M. Wayne (D) r. Jan. 1835
Richard H. Wilde (D)

ILLINOIS

Senators

Elias K. Kane (D)
John M. Robinson (D)

Representatives

Zadoc Casey (D)
Joseph Duncan (D) r. Sept. 1834
William L. May (D) s. 1834
John Reynolds (D) s. 1834
Charles Slade (D) d. July 1834

INDIANA

Senators

William Hendricks (D)
John Tipton (D)

Representatives

Ratliff Boon (D)
John Carr (D)
John Ewing (W)
Edward A. Hannegan (D)
George L. Kinnard (D)
Amos Lane (D)
Jonathan McCarty (W)

KENTUCKY

Senators

George M. Bibb
Henry Clay (W)

Representatives

Chilton Allan (D)
Martin Beaty (W)
Thomas Chilton (W)
Amos Davis (W)
Benjamin Hardin (W)
Albert G. Hawes (D)
Richard M. Johnson (D)
Robert P. Letcher (W) s. 1834
James Love
Chittenden Lyon (D)
Thomas A. Marshall (W)
Patrick H. Pope
Christopher Tompkins

LOUISIANA

Senators

Josiah S. Johnston (D)
d. May 1833
Alexander Porter (W) s. 1834

George A. Waggaman (D)

Representatives

Henry A. Bullard (W) r. Jan. 1834
Rice Garland (W) s. 1834
Henry Johnson (W) s. 1834
Philemon Thomas (D)
Edward D. White r. Nov. 1834

MAINE

Senators

Peleg Sprague (NR) r. Jan. 1834
John Ruggles (D) s. 1835

Ether Shepley (D)

Representatives

George Evans
Joseph Hall (D)
Leonard Jarvis (D)
Edward Kavanagh (D)
Rufus McIntire (D)
Moses Mason, Jr. (D)
Gorham Parks (D)
Francis O. J. Smith (D)

MARYLAND

Senators

Ezekiel F. Chambers (W) r. 1834
Robert H. Goldsborough (W)
s. 1835

Joseph Kent (NR)

Representatives

Richard B. Carmichael (D)
Littleton P. Dennis (W)
d. Apr. 1834
James P. Heath (D)
William Cost Johnson (W)
Isaac McKim (D)
John N. Steele (W) s. 1834
John T. Stoddert (D)
Francis Thomas (D)
James Turner (D)

MASSACHUSETTS

Senators

Nathaniel Silsbee (D)
Daniel Webster

Representatives

John Quincy Adams (W)
Isaac C. Bates
William Baylies
George N. Briggs (W)
Rufus Choate (W) r. June 1834
John Davis (NR) r. Jan. 1834
Edward Everett (NR)
Benjamin Gorham
George Grennell, Jr.
William Jackson (W)
Levi Lincoln s. Mar. 1835
Gayton P. Osgood (D)
Stephen C. Phillips (W) s. 1834
John Reed (W)

MISSISSIPPI

Senators

George Poindexter
John Black (W)

Representatives

Harry Cage
Franklin E. Plummer

MISSOURI

Senators

Thomas H. Benton (D)

Alexander Buckner d. June 1833
Lewis F. Linn (D)

Representatives

William H. Ashley (W)
John Bull (W)

NEW HAMPSHIRE

Senators

Samuel Bell
Isaac Hill (D)

Representatives

Benning M. Bean (D)
Robert Burns (D)
Joseph M. Harper (D)
Henry Hubbard (D)
Franklin Pierce (D)

NEW JERSEY

Senators

Theodore Frelinghuysen (D)
Samuel L. Southard (W)

Representatives

Philemon Dickerson (D)
Samuel Fowler (D)
Thomas Lee
James Parker (D)
Ferdinand S. Schenck (D)
William N. Shinn (D)

NEW YORK

Senators

Silas Wright, Jr. (D)
Nathaniel P. Tallmadge (D)

Representatives

John Adams (D)
Samuel Beardsley (D)
Abraham Bockee (D)
Charles Bodle
John W. Brown (D)
Churchill C. Cambreleng (D)
Samuel Clark (D)
John Craker (D)
John Cramer (D)
Rowland Day (D)
John Dickson (W)
Charles G. Ferris (D) s. 1834
Millard Fillmore (W)
Philo C. Fuller (W)
William K. Fuller (D)
Ranson H. Gillett (D)
Nicoll Halsey (D)
Gideon Hard (D)
Samuel G. Hathaway (D)
Abner Hazeltine (W)
Edward Howell (D)
Abel Huntington (D)
Noadiah Johnson (D)
Gerrit Y. Lansing (D)
Cornelius W. Lawrence (D)
r. May 1834
George W. Lay (W)
Charles McVean (D)
Abijah Mann, Jr. (D)
Henry C. Martindale
Henry Mitchell (D)
John J. Morgan (D) s. 1834
Sherman Page (D)
Job Pierson (D)
Dudley Selden (D) r. July 1834
William Taylor (D)
Joel Turrill (D)
Aaron Vanderpoel (D)
Isaac B. Van Houten (D)
Aaron Ward (D)
Daniel Wardwell
Reuben Whallon (D)
Campbell P. White (D)
Frederick Whittlesey

NORTH CAROLINA

Senators

Bedford Brown (D)
Willie P. Mangum (D)

Representatives

Daniel L. Barringer (D)
Jesse A. Bynum (D)
Henry W. Connor (D)
Edmund Deberry (W)
James Graham
Thomas H. Hall (D)
Micajah T. Hawkins (D)
James I. McKay (D)
Abraham Rencher (D)
William B. Shepard
Augustine H. Shepperd (D)
Jesse Speight
Lewis Williams

OHIO

Senators

Thomas Ewing (W)
Thomas Morris (D)

Representatives

William Allen (D)
James M. Bell (D)
John Chaney (D)
Thomas Corwin (W)
Joseph H. Crane (W)
Thomas L. Hamer (D)
Benjamin Jones (D)
Daniel Kilgore (D) s. 1834
Humphrey H. Leavitt (D)
r. July 1834
Robert T. Lytle (D) r. Mar. 1834
Jeremiah McLene (D)
Robert Mitchell (D)
William Patterson (D)
Jonathan Sloane (W)
David Spangler (W)
John Thomson (D)
Joseph Vance (D)
Samuel F. Vinton (W)
Taylor Webster (D)
Elisha Whittlesey

PENNSYLVANIA

Senators

William Wilkins (D) r. June 1834
James Buchanan (D) s. 1834

Samuel McKean (D)

Representatives

Joseph B. Anthony (D)
John Banks (W)
Charles A. Barnitz (W)
Andrew Beaumont (D)
Horace Binney (W)
George Burd
George Chambers (W)
William Clark (W)
Richard Coutler (D)
Edward Darlington (W)
Harmar Denny (Anti-Mason)
John Galbraith (D)
James Harper (D)
Samuel S. Harrison (D)
Joseph Henderson
William Hiester (W)
Henry King (D)
John Laporte
Thomas M. T. McKennan (W)
Joel K. Mann (D)
Jesse Miller (D)
Henry A. P. Muhlenberg (D)
David Potts, Jr. (W)
Robert Ramsey (W)

Andrew Stewart (D)
Joel B. Sutherland (D)
David D. Wagener (D)
John G. Watmough

RHODE ISLAND

Senators

Nehemiah R. Knight (AF)
Asher Robbins (W)

Representatives

Tristam Burges (F)
Dutee J. Pearce (D)

SOUTH CAROLINA

Senators

John C. Calhoun (D)
William C. Preston (Null)

Representatives

James Blair (D) d. Apr. 1834
Robert B. Campbell s.1834 (Null-D)
William K. Clowney (Null-D)
Warren R. Davis (SRD)
d. Jan. 1835
John M. Felder (D)
William J. Grayson (W)
John K. Griffin (SRW)
George McDuffie (D) r. 1834
Richard I. Manning (D) s. 1834
Francis W. Pickens (Null-D)
s. 1834
Henry L. Pinckney (D)

TENNESSEE

Senators

Hugh L. White (D)
Felix Grundy (D)

Representatives

John Bell (W)
John Blair (D)
Samuel Bunch (W)
David Crockett (W)
David W. Dickinson (D)
William C. Dunlap (D)
John B. Forester
William M. Inge (D)
Cave Johnson (D)
Luke Lea (D)
Balie Peyton (W)
James K. Polk (D)
James Standifer (W)

VERMONT

Senators

Samuel Prentiss (W)
Benjamin Swift (F)

Representatives

Heman Allen (W)
Benjamin F. Deming (W)
d. July 1834
Horace Everett (W)
Hiland Hall (W)
Henry F. Janes (W) s. 1834
William Slade (W)

VIRGINIA

Senators

John Tyler (W)

William C. Rives (D) r. Feb. 1834
Benjamin W. Leigh (W) s. 1834

Representatives

John J. Allen (W)
William S. Archer
James M. H. Beale (D)
James W. Bouldin (D) s. 1834
Thomas T. Bouldin (D)
d. Feb. 1834
Joseph W. Chinn (D)
Nathaniel H. Claiborne
Thomas Davenport (F)
John H. Fulton (W)
James H. Gholson (D)
William F. Gordon (D)
George Loyall (D)
Edward Lucas (D)
William McComas (W)
Samuel McDowell (W)
Samuel M. Moore (W)
John Y. Mason (D)
Charles F. Mercer (D)
John M. Patton (D)
John Randolph d. May 1833
John Robertson (W) s. 1834
Andrew Stevenson (D)
r. June 1834
William P. Taylor (W)
Edgar C. Wilson (W)
Henry A. Wise (D)

CONNECTICUT

Senators

Gideon Tomlinson (D)

Nathan Smith (W) d. Dec. 1835
John M. Niles (D)

Representatives

Elisha Haley (D)
Orrin Holt (D) s. 1836
Samuel Ingham (D)
Andrew T. Judson (D) r. July 1836
Lancelot Phelps (D)
Isaac Toucey (D)
Thomas T. Whittlesey (D) s. 1836
Zalmon Wildman (D) d. Dec. 1835

DELAWARE

Senators

John M. Clayton (W) r. Dec. 1836
Thomas Clayton (W) s. 1837

Arnold Naudain r. June 1836
Richard H. Bayard (W) s. 1836

Representative

John J. Milligan (W)

GEORGIA

Senators

John P. King (D)
Alfred Cuthbert (D)

Representatives

Julius C. Alford (SRW) s. 1837
Jesse F. Cleveland (D)
John Coffee (D) Sept. 1836
William C. Dawson (SRW) s. 1836
Thomas Glascock (D)
Seaton Grantland (Un)
Charles E. Haynes (D)
Hopkins Holsey (D)
Jabez Y. Jackson (D)
George W. Owens (Un)
John W. A. Sanford (D)
r. July 1835
William Schley (D) r. July 1835
James C. Terrell (D) r. July 1835
George W. B. Towns (D)
r. Sept. 1836

INDIANA

Senators

William Hendricks (D)
John Tipton (D)

Representatives

Ratliff Boon (D)
John Carr (D)
John W. Davis (D)
Edward A. Hannegan (D)
William Herod (W) s. 1837
George L. Kinnard (D)
d. Nov. 1836
Amos Lane (D)
Johnathan McCarty (W)

KENTUCKY

Senators

Henry Clay (W)
John J. Crittenden

Representatives

Chilton Allan (D)
Linn Boyd (D)
John Calhoon (W)
John Chambers (W)
Richard French (D)
William J. Graves (W)
Benjamin Hardin (W)
James Harlan (W)
Albert G. Hawes (D)
Richard M. Johnson (D)
John White (W)
Sherrod Williams (W)
Joseph R. Underwood (W)

TWENTY-FOURTH CONGRESS

March 4, 1835 to March 3, 1837

President of The Senate: Martin Van Buren
President Pro Tempore of The Senate: William R. King
Speaker of The House of Representatives: James K. Polk

ALABAMA

Senators

William R. King (D)
Gabriel Moore

Representatives

Reuben Chapman (D)
Joab Lawler (W)
Dixon H. Lewis (SRD)
Francis S. Lyon (W)
Joshua L. Martin (D)

ARKANSAS

Senators

William S. Fulton (D) s. 1836
Ambrose H. Sevier (D) s. 1836

Representative

Archibald Yell (D) s. 1836

ILLINOIS

Senators

Elias K. Kane (D) d. Dec. 1835
William L. D. Ewing (D) s. 1836

John M. Robinson (D)

Representatives

Zadoc Casey (D)
William L. May (D)
John Reynolds (D)

LOUISIANA

Senators

Alexander Porter (W) r. Jan. 1837
Alexander Mouton (D) s. 1837

Robert C. Nicholas (D) s. 1836

Representatives

Rice Garland (W)
Henry Johnson (W)
Eleazer W. Ripley (D)

MAINE

Senators

Ether Shepley (D) r. Mar. 1836
Judah Dana (D) s. 1836

John Ruggles (D)

Representatives

Jeremiah Bailey (S)
George Evans (W)
John Fairfield (D)
Joseph Hall (D)
Leonard Jarvis (D)
Moses Mason, Jr. (D)
Gorham Parks (D)
Francis O. J. Smith (D)

MARYLAND

Senators

Robert H. Goldsborough
John S. Spence (D)

Joseph Kent (NR)

Representatives

Benjamin C. Howard (D)
Daniel Jenifer (R)
Isaac McKim (D)
James A. Pearce (W)
John N. Steele (W)
Francis Thomas (D)
James Turner (D)
George C. Washington (W)

MASSACHUSETTS

Senators

Daniel Webster
John Davis (W)

Representatives

John Quincy Adams (W)
Nathaniel B. Borden (W)
George N. Briggs (W)
William B. Calhoun (W)
Caleb Cushing (W)
George Grennell, Jr.
Samuel Hoar
William Jackson (W)
Abbott Lawrence (W)
Levi Lincoln (W)
Stephen C. Phillips (W)
John Reed (W)

MISSISSIPPI

Senators

John Black (W)
Robert J. Walker (D)

Representatives

John F. H. Claiborne (D)
David Dickson (D) d. 1836
Samuel J. Gholson (D) s. 1837

MISSOURI

Senators

Thomas H. Benton (D)
Lewis F. Linn (D)

Representatives

William H. Ashley (W)
Albert G. Harrison (D)

NEW HAMPSHIRE

Senators

Isaac Hill (D) r. May 1836
John Page (D) s. 1836

Henry Hubbard (D)

Representatives

Benning M. Bean (D)
Robert Burns (D)
Samuel Cushman (D)
Franklin Pierce (D)
Joseph Weeks (D)

NEW JERSEY

Senators

Samuel L. Southard (W)
Garret D. Wall (D)

Representatives

William Chetwood (D) s. 1836
Philemon Dickerson (D)
r. Nov. 1836
Samuel Fowler (D)
Thomas Lee (D)
James Parker (D)
Ferdinand S. Schenck (D)
William N. Shinn (D)

NEW YORK

Senators

Silas Wright, Jr. (D)
Nathaniel P. Tallmadge (D)

Representatives

Samuel Barton (D)
Samuel Beardsley (D) r. Mar. 1836
Abraham Bockee (D)
Matthias J. Bovee (D)
John W. Brown (D)
Churchill C. Cambreleng (D)
Graham H. Chapin (D)
Timothy Childs (W)
John Cramer (D)
Ulysses F. Doubleday (D)
Valentine Efner (D)
Dudley Farlin (D)
Philo C. Fuller (W) r. Sept. 1836
William K. Fuller (D)
Ranson H. Gillet (D)
Francis Granger (W)
Gideon Hard (D)
Abner Hazeltine (W)
Hiram P. Hunt (W)
Abel Huntington (D)
Gerrit Y. Lansing (D)
George W. Lay (W)
Gideon Lee (D)
Joshua Lee (D)
Stephen B. Leonard (D)
Thomas C. Love (W)
John McKeon (D)
Abijah Mann, Jr. (D)
William Mason (D)
Rutger B. Miller (D) s. 1836
Ely Moore (D)
Sherman Page (D)
Joseph Reynolds (D)
David A. Russell (W)
William Seymour (D)
Nicholas Sickles (D)
William Taylor (D)
Joel Turrill (D)
Aaron Vanderpoel (D)
Aaron Ward (D)
Daniel Wardwell (NB)
John Young (W) s. 1836

NORTH CAROLINA

Senators

Beford Brown (D)

Willie P. Mangum (W)
r. Nov. 1836
Robert Strange (D) s. 1836

Representatives

Jesse A. Bynum (D)
Henry W. Connor (D)
Edmund Deberry (W)
James Graham s. 1836
Micajah T. Hawkins (D)
James I. McKay (D)
William Montgomery (D)
Ebenezer Pettigrew (W)
Abraham Rencher (D)
William B. Shepard (NR)
Augustine H. Shepperd (D)
Jesse Speight
Lewis Williams

OHIO

Senators

Thomas Ewing (W)
Thomas Morris (D)

Representatives

William K. Bond (W)
John Chaney (D)
Thomas Corwin (W)
Joseph H. Crane (W)
Thomas L. Hamer (D)
Elias Howell (W)
Benjamin Jones (D)
William Kennon, Sr. (D)
Daniel Kilgore (D)
Jeremiah McLene (D)
Samson Mason (W)
William Patterson (D)
Jonathan Sloane (W)
David Spangler (W)
Bellamy Storer (W)
John Thomson (D)
Samuel F. Vinton (W)
Taylor Webster (D)
Elisha Whittlesey (W)

PENNSYLVANIA

Senators

Samuel McKean (D)
James Buchanan (D)

Representatives

Joseph B. Anthony (D)
Michael W. Ash
John Banks (W) r. 1836
Andrew Beaumont (D)
James Black (D) s. 1836
Andrew Buchanan (D)
George Chambers (W)
William Clark (W)
Edward Darlington (W)
Harmar Denny (Anti-Mason)
Jacob Fry, Jr. (D)
John Galbraith (D)
James Harper (D)
Samuel S. Harrison (D)
Joseph Henderson
William Hiester (W)
Edward B. Hubley (D)
Joseph R. Ingersoll (W)
John Klingensmith, Jr. (D)
John Laporte
Henry Logan (D)
Thomas M. T. McKennan (W)
Job Mann (D)
Jesse Miller (D) r. Oct. 1836
Mathias Morris (W)
Henry A. P, Muhlenberg (D)
John J. Pearson (W) s. 1836
David Potts Jr. (W)
Joel B. Sutherland (D)
David D. Wagener

RHODE ISLAND

Senators

Nehemiah R. Knight (D)
Asher Robbins (W)

Representatives

Dutee J. Pearce (D)
William Sprague (W)

SOUTH CAROLINA

Senators

John C. Calhoun (D)
William C. Preston (Null-D)

Representatives

Robert B. Campbell (W)
Franklin H. Elmore (SRD) s. 1836
William J. Grayson (W)
John K. Griffin (SRW)
James H. Hammond, (SRD)
r. Feb. 1836
Richard I. Manning (D)
d. May 1836
Francis W. Pickens (Null-D)
Henry L. Pinckney (D)
John P. Richardson (SRD)
s. 1836
James Rogers (D)
Waddy Thompson, Jr. (W)

TENNESSEE

Senators

Hugh L. White (D)
Felix Grundy (D)

Representatives

John Bell (W)
Samuel Bunch (W)
William B. Carter (W)
William C. Dunlap (D)
John B. Forester
Adam Huntsman (D)
Cave Johnson (D)
Luke Lea (D)
Abram P. Maury (W)
Balie Peyton (W)
James K. Polk (D)
Ebenezer J. Shields (W)
James Standifer (W)

VERMONT

Senators

Samuel Prentiss (W)
Benjamin Swift (F)

Representatives

Heman Allen (W)
Horace Everett (W)
Hiland Hall (W)
Henry F. Janes (W)
William Slade (W)

VIRGINIA

Senators

John Tyler (W) r. Feb. 1836
William C. Rives (D) s. 1836

Benjamin W. Leigh (W)
r. July 1836
Richard E. Parker (D) s. 1836

Representatives

James M. H. Beale (D)
James W. Bouldin (D)
Nathaniel H. Claiborne

Walter Coles (D)
Robert Craig (D)
George C. Dromgoole (D)
James Garland (D)
George W. Hopkins (D)
Joseph Johnson (D)
John W. Jones (D)
George Loyall (D)
Edward Lucas (D)
William McComas (W)
John Y. Mason (D) r. Jan. 1837
Charles F. Mercer (D)
William S. Morgan (D)
John M. Patton (D)
John Roane
John Robertson (W)
John Taliaferro (W)
Henry A. Wise (D)

TWENTY-FIFTH CONGRESS

March 4, 1837 to March 3, 1839

President of The Senate: Richard M. Johnson
President Pro Tempore of The Senate: William R. King
Speaker of The House of Representatives: James K. Polk

ALABAMA

Senators

William R. King (D)
Clement Comer Clay (D)

Representatives

Reuben Chapman (D)
George W. Crabb (W) s. 1838
Joab Lawler (W) d. May 1838
Dixon H. Lewis (SRD)
Francis S. Lyon (W)
Joshua L. Martin (D)

ARKANSAS

Senators

William S. Fulton (D)
Ambrose H. Sevier (D)

Representative

Archibald Yell (D)

CONNECTICUT

Senators

John M. Niles (D)
Perry Smith (D)

Representatives

Elisha Haley (D)
Orrin Holt (D)
Samuel Ingham (D)
Lancelot Phelps (D)
Isaac Toucey (D)
Thomas T. Whittlesey

DELAWARE

Senators

Richard H. Bayard (W)
Thomas Clayton (W)

Representative

John J. Milligan (W)

GEORGIA

Senators

Alfred Cuthbert (D)

John P. King (D) r. Nov. 1837
Wilson Lumpkin (D)

Representatives

Jesse F. Cleveland (D)
William C. Dawson (SRW)
Thomas Glascock (D)
Seaton Grantland (UN)
Charles E. Haynes (D)
Hopkins Holsey (D)
Jabez Y. Jackson (D)
George W. Owens (UN)
George W. B. Towns (D)

ILLINOIS

Senators

John M. Robinson (D)
Richard M. Young (D)

Representatives

Zadoc Casey (D)
William L. May (D)
Adam W. Snyder (D)

INDIANA

Senators

John Tipton (D)
Oliver H. Smith (W)

Representatives

Ratliff Boon (D)
George H. Dunn (W)
John Ewing (W)
William Graham (W)
William Herod (W)
James Rariden (W)
Albert S. White (W)

KENTUCKY

Senators

Henry Clay (W)
John J. Crittenden

Representatives

John Calhoon (W)
John Chambers (W)
William J. Graves (W)
James Harlan (W)
Richard Hawes (W)
Richard H. Menifee (W)
John L. Murray (D)
John Pope (D)
Edward Rumsey (W)
William W. Southgate (W)
Joseph R. Underwood (W)
John White (W)
Sherrod Williams (W)

LOUISIANA

Senators

Robert C. Nicholas (D)
Alexander Mouton (D)

Representatives

Rice Garland (W)
Henry Johnson (W)
Eleazar W. Ripley (D)

MAINE

Senators

John Ruggles (D)
Reuel Williams (D)

Representatives

Hugh J. Anderson (D)
Timothy J. Carter (D)
(d. Mar. 1838)
Jonathan Cilley (D) d. Feb. 1838
Thomas Davee (D)
George Evans (W)
John Fairfield (D) r. Dec. 1838
Joseph C. Noyes (W)
Virgil D. Parris (SRD) s. 1838
Edward Robinson (W) s. 1838
Francis O. J. Smith (D)

MARYLAND

Senators

Joseph Kent (NR) d. Nov. 1837
William D. Merrick (W) s. 1838

John S. Spence (D)

Representatives

John Dennis (W)
Benjamin C. Howard (D)
Daniel Jenifer
William Cost Johnson (W)
John P. Kennedy (W) s. 1838
Isaac McKim (D) d. Apr. 1838
James A. Pearce (W)
Francis Thomas (D)
John T. H. Worthington (D)

MASSACHUSETTS

Senators

Daniel Webster (W)
John Davis (W)

Representatives

John Quincy Adams (W)
Nathaniel B. Borden (W)
George N. Briggs (W)
William B. Calhoun (W)
Caleb Cushing (W)
Richard Fletcher (W)
George Grennell, Jr.
William S. Hastings (D)
Levi Lincoln (W)
William Parmenter (D)
Stephen C. Phillips (W)
r. Sept. 1838
John Reed (W)
Leverett Saltonstall (W) s. 1838

MICHIGAN

Senators

Lucius Lyon (D)
John Norvell (D)

Representative

Isaac E. Crary (D)

MISSISSIPPI

Senators

John Black (W) r. Jan. 1838
James F. Trotter (D) ta. 1838
Thomas H. Williams (D) s. 1838

Robert J. Walker (D)

Representatives

John F. H. Claiborne (D)
Samuel J. Gholson (D)
Sergeant S. Prentiss (W) s. 1838
Thomas J. Word (W) s. 1838

MISSOURI

Senators

Thomas H. Benton (D)
Lewis F. Linn (D)

Representatives

Albert G. Harrison (D)
John Miller (D)

NEW HAMPSHIRE

Senators

Henry Hubbard (D)
Franklin Pierce (D)

Representatives

Charles G. Atherton (D)
Samuel Cushman (D)
James Farrington (D)
Joseph Weeks (D)
Jared W. Williams (D)

NEW JERSEY

Senators

Samuel L. Southward (W)
Garrett D. Wall (D)

Representatives

John B. Aycrigg (W)
William Halstead (W)
John P. B. Maxwell (W)
Joseph F. Randolph (W)
Charles C. Stratton (W)
Thomas Jones Yorke (W)

NEW YORK

Senators

Silas Wright, Jr. (D)
Nathaniel P. Tallmadge (D)

Representatives

John T. Andrews (D)
Cyrus Beers s. 1838
Bennett Bicknell (D)
Samuel Birdsall (D)
John C. Brodhead (D)
Isaac H. Bronson (D)
Andrew D. W. Bruyn (D) d. July 1838
Churchill C. Cambreleng (D)
Timothy Childs (W)
John C. Clark (D)
Edward Curtis (W)
John I. DeGraff (D)
John Edwards (D)
Millard Fillmore (W)
Henry A. Foster (D)
Albert Gallup (D)
Abraham P. Grant (D)
Hiram Gray (D)
J. Ogden Hoffman (W)
Thomas B. Jackson (D)
Nathaniel Jones (D)
Gouverneur Kemble (D)
Arphaxed Loomis (D)
Robert McClellan (D)
Richard P. Marvin (W)
Charles F. Mitchell (W)
Ely Moore (D)
William H. Noble (D)
John Palmer (D)
Amasa J. Parker (D)
William Patterson (W) d. Aug. 1838
Luther C. Peck (W)
Zadock Pratt (D)
John H. Prentiss (D)
Harvey Putnam (W) s. 1838
David A. Russell (W)
Mark H. Sibley (W)
James B. Spencer (D)
William Taylor (D)
Obadiah Titus (D)
Henry Vail (D)
Abraham Vanderveer (D)

NORTH CAROLINA

Senators

Bedford Brown (D)
Robert Strange (D)

Representatives

Jesse A. Bynum (D)
Henry W. Connor (D)
Edmund Deberry (W)
James Graham
Micajah T. Hawkins (D)
James I. McKay (D)
William Montgomery (D)
Abraham Rencher (D)
Samuel T. Sawyer (D)
Charles B. Shepard (D)
Augustine H. Shepperd (D)
Edward Stanly (W)
Lewis Williams

OHIO

Senators

Thomas Morris
William Allen (D)

Representatives

James Alexander, Jr. (D)
John W. Allen (W)
William K. Bond (W)
John Chaney (D)
Charles D. Coffin (W)
Thomas Corwin (W)
Alexander Duncan (W)
Joshua R. Giddings (W) s. 1838
Patrick G. Goode (W)
Thomas L. Hamer (D)
Alexander Harper (W)
William H. Hunter (D)
Daniel Kilgore (D) r. July 1838
Daniel P. Leadbetter (D)
Andrew W. Loomis (W) r. Oct. 1838
Samson Mason
Calvary Morris (W)
Joseph Ridgway (W)
Matthias Shepler (D)
Henry Swearingen (D) s. 1838
Taylor Webster (D)
Elisha Whittlesey (W) r. July 1838

PENNSYLVANIA

Senators

Samuel McKean (D)
James Buchanan (D)

Representatives

William Beatty (D)
Richard Biddle (W)
Andrew Buchanan (D)
Edward Darlington (Anti-Mason)
Edward Davies (W)
Jacob Fry, Jr. (D)
Robert H. Hammond (D)
Francis J. Harper (D) r. Mar. 1837
Thomas Henry (W)
Edward B. Hubley (D)
George M. Keim (D) s. 1838
John Klingensmith, Jr. (D)
Henry Logan (D)
Charles McClure (D)
Thomas M. T. McKennan (W)
Mathias Morris (W)
Samuel W. Morris (D)
Henry A. P. Muhlenberg (D) r. Feb. 1938
Charles Ogle (W)
Charles Naylor (W)
Lemuel Paynter (D)
David Petrikin (D)
Arnold Plumer (D)
William W. Potter (D)
David Potts, Jr. (W)
Luther Reily (D)
John Sergeant (F)
Daniel Sheffer (D)
George W. Toland (W)
David D. Wagener (D)

RHODE ISLAND

Senators

Nehemiah R. Knight (AF)
Asher Robbins (W)

Representatives

Robert B. Cranston (W)
Joseph L. Tillinghast (W)

SOUTH CAROLINA

Senators

John C. Calhoun (D)
William C. Preston (Null-D)

Representatives

John Campbell (SRD)
William K. Clowney (SRD)
Franklin H. Elmore (SRD)
John D. Griffin (SRW)
Hugh S. Legare
Francis W. Pickens (Null-D)
R. Barnwell Rhett (D)
John P. Richardson (SRD)
Waddy Thompson, Jr. (W)

TENNESSEE

Senators

Hugh L. White (D)

Felix Grundy (D) r. July 1838
Ephraim H. Foster (W) s. 1838

Representatives

John Bell (W)
William B. Campbell (W)
William B. Carter (W)
Richard Cheatham (W)
John W. Crockett (W)
Abraham McClellan (D)
Abram P. Maury (W)
James K. Polk (D)
Ebenezer J. Shields (W)
James Standifer (W) d. Aug. 1837
William Stone (W)
Hopkins L. Turney (D)
Christopher H. Williams (W)
Joseph L. Williams (W)

VERMONT

Senators

Samuel Prentiss (W)
Benjamin Swift (F)

Representatives

Heman Allen (W)
Horace Everett (W)
Isaac Fletcher (D)
Hiland Hall (W)
William Slade (W)

VIRGINIA

Senators

William C. Rives (D)

Richard E. Parker (D) r. Mar. 1837
William H. Roane (D) s. 1837

Representatives

Linn Banks (D) s. 1838
Andrew Beirne (D)
James W. Bouldin (D)
Walter Coles (D)
Robert Craig (D)
George C. Dromgoole (D)
James Garland (D)
George W. Hopkins (D)
Robert M. T. Hunter (D)
Joseph Johnson (D)
John W. Jones (D)
Francis Mallory (W)
James M. Mason (D)
Charles F. Mercer (D)
William S. Morgan (D)
John M. Patton (D) r. 1838
Isaac S. Pennybacker (D)
Francis E. Rives (D)
John Robertson (W)
Archibald Stuart (W)
John Taliaferro (W)
Henry A. Wise (W)

TWENTY-SIXTH CONGRESS

March 4, 1839 to March 3, 1841

President of The Senate: Richard M. Johnson
President Pro Tempore of The Senate: William R. King
Speaker of The House of Representatives: Robert M. T. Hunter

ALABAMA

Senators

William R. King (D)
Clement Comer Clay (D)

Representatives

Reuben Chapman (D)
George W. Crabb (W)
James Dellet (W)
David Hubbard (SRD)
Dixon H. Lewis (SRD)

ARKANSAS

Senators

William S. Fulton (D)
Ambrose H. Sevier (D)

Representative

Edward Cross (D)

CONNECTICUT

Senators

Perry Smith (D)

Thaddeus Betts (W) d. Apr. 1840
Jabez W. Huntington (W) s. 1840

Representatives

William W. Boardman (W) s. 1840
John H. Brockway (W)
Thomas B. Osborne (W)
Truman Smith (W)
William L. Storrs (W) r. June 1840
Joseph Trumbull (W)
Thomas W. Williams (W)

DELAWARE

Senators

Richard H. Bayard (W)
Thomas Clayton (W)

Representative

Thomas Robinson, Jr. (D)

GEORGIA

Senators

Alfred Cuthbert (D)
Wilson Lumpkin (D)

Representatives

Julius C. Alford (W)
Edward J. Black (SRW)
Walter T. Colquitt (SRW)
r. July 1840
Mark A. Cooper (SRW)
William C. Dawson (SRW)
Richard W. Habersham (D)
Hines Holt (W) s. 1841
Thomas B. King (W)
Eugenius A. Nisbet (W)
Lott Warren (W)

ILLINOIS

Senators

John M. Robinson (D)
Richard M. Young (D)

Representatives

Zadoc Casey (D)
John Reynolds (D)
John T. Stuart (W)

INDIANA

Senators

Oliver H. Smith (W)
Albert S. White (W)

Representatives

John Carr (D)
John W. Davis (D)
Tilgham A. Howard (D)
r. Aug. 1840
Henry S. Lane (W) s.Dec. 1840
George H. Proffit (W)
James Rariden (W)
Thomas Smith (D)
William W. Wick (D)

KENTUCKY

Senators

Henry Clay (W)
John J. Crittenden

Representatives

Simeon H. Anderson (W)
d. Aug. 1840
Landaff W. Andrews (W)
Linn Boyd (D)
William O. Butler (D)
Garrett Davis (W)
William J. Graves (W)
Willis Green (W)
Richard Hawes (W)
John Pope (D)
John B. Thompson (W) s. 1840
Philip Triplett (W)
John White (W)
Sherrod Williams (W)
Joseph R. Underwood (W)

LOUISIANA

Senators

Robert C. Nicholas (D)
Alexander Mouton (D)

Representatives

Thomas W. Chinn (W)
Rice Garland (W) r. July 1840
John Moore (W) s. 1840
Edward D. White (W)

MAINE

Senators

John Ruggles (D)
Reuel Williams (E)

Representatives

Hugh J. Anderson (D)
Nathan Clifford (D)
Thomas Davee (D)
George Evans (W)
Joshua A. Lowell (D)
Virgil D. Parris (SRD)
Benjamin Randall (W)
Albert Smith (D)

MARYLAND

Senators

John S. Spence (D) d. Oct. 1840
John L. Kerr (W) s. 1841

William D. Merrick (W)

Representatives

James Carroll (D)
John Dennis (W)
Solomon Hillen, Jr. (D)
Daniel Jenifer (R)
William Cost Johnson (W)
Francis Thomas (D)
Philip F. Thomas (D)
John T. H. Worthington (D)

MASSACHUSETTS

Senators

Daniel Webster (W) r. Feb. 1841
Rufus Choate (W) s. 1841

John Davis (W) r. Jan. 1841
Isaac C. Bates (W) s. 1841

Representatives

John Quincy Adams (W)
Osmyn Baker (W) s. 1840
George N. Briggs (W)
William B. Calhoun (W)
Caleb Cushing (W)
William S. Hastings (D)
Abbott Lawrence (W)
r. Sept. 1840
Levi Lincoln (W)
William Parmenter (D)
John Reed (W)
Leverett Saltonstall (W)
Henry Williams (D)
Robert C. Winthrop (W) s. 1840

MICHIGAN

Senators

John Norvell (D)
Augustus S. Porter (W)

Representative

Isaac E. Crary (D)

MISSISSIPPI

Senators

Robert J. Walker (D)
John Henderson (W)

Representatives

Albert G. Brown (D)
Jacob Thompson (D)

MISSOURI

Senators

Thomas H. Benton (D)
Lewis F. Linn (D)

Representatives

Albert G. Harrison (D)
d. Sept. 1839
John Jameson (D)
John Miller (D)

NEW HAMPSHIRE

Senators

Henry Hubbard (D)
Franklin Pierce (D)

Representatives

Charles G. Atherton (D)
Edmund Burke (D)
Ira A. Eastman (D)
Tristram Shaw
Jared W. Williams (D)

NEW JERSEY

Senators

Samuel L. Southard (W)
Garret D. Wall (D)

Representatives

William R. Cooper (D)
Philemon Dickerson (D)
Joseph Kille (D)
Joseph F. Randolph (W)
Daniel B. Ryall (D)
Peter D. Vroom (D)

NEW YORK

Senators

Silas Wright, Jr. (D)
Nathaniel P. Tallmadge (D)

Representatives

Judson Allen (D)
Daniel D. Barnard (W)
David P. Brewster (D)
Anson Brown (W)
d. June 1840
Thomas C. Chittenden (W)
John C. Clark (W)
Edward Curtis (W)
Amasa Dana (D)
James DeLa Montanya (D)
Nicholas B. Doe (W) s. 1840
Andrew W. Doig (D)
Nehemiah H. Earll (D)
John Ely (D)
Millard Fillmore (W)
John Fine (D)
John G. Floyd (D)
Seth M. Gates (W)
Francis Granger (W)
Moses H. Grinnell (W)
Augustus C. Hand (D)
Ogden J. Hoffman (W)
Hiram P. Hunt (W)
Thomas B. Jackson (D)
Charles Johnston (W)
Nathaniel Jones (D)
Gouverneur Kemble (D)
Thomas Kempshall (W)
Stephen B. Leonard (D)
Meredith Mallory (D)
Richard P. Marvin (W)
Charles F. Mitchell (W)
James Monroe (W)
Christopher Morgan (W)
Rufus Palen (W)
Luther C. Peck (W)
John H. Prentiss (D)
Edward Rogers (D)
David A. Russell (W)
Theron R. Strong (D)
Aaron Vanderpool (D)
Peter J. Wagner (W)

NORTH CAROLINA

Senators

Bedford Brown (D) r. Nov. 1840
Willie P. Mangum (W)

Robert Strange (D)
r. Nov. 1840
William A. Graham (W) s. 1840

Representatives

Jesse A. Bynum (D)
Henry W. Connor (D)
Edmund Deberry (W)
Charles Fisher (D)
James Craham
Micajah T. Hawkins (D)
John Hill (D)
James I. McKay (D)
William Montgomery (D)
Kenneth Rayner (W)
Charles B. Shepard (D)
Edward Stanly (W)
Lewis Williams

OHIO

Senators

William Allen (D)
Benjamin Tappan (D)

Representatives

John W. Allen (W)
William K. Bond (W)
Thomas Corwin (W) r. May 1840
William Doan (D)
Alexander Duncan (W)
Joshua R. Giddings (W)
Patrick G. Goode (W)
John Hastings (D)
Daniel P. Leadbetter (D)
Samson Mason (W)
William Medill (D)
Calvary Morris (W)
Jeremiah Morrow (W) s. 1840

Isaac Parrish (D)
Joseph Ridgway (W)
David A. Starkweather (D)
Henry Swearingen (D)
George Sweeny
Jonathan Taylor (D)
John B. Weller (D)

PENNSYLVANIA

Senators

James Buchanan (D)
Daniel Sturgeon (D) s. 1840

Representatives

William Beatty (D)
Richard Biddle (W) r. 1840
Henry M. Brackenridge (W) s. 1840
James Cooper (W)
Edward Davies (W)
John Davis (D)
John Edwards (W)
Joseph Fornance (D)
John Galbraith (D)
James Gerry (D)
Robert H. Hammond (D)
Thomas Henry (W)
Enos Hook (D)
Francis James (W)
George M. Keim (D)
Isaac Leet (D)
Charles McClure (D) s. 1840
George McCulloch (D)
Albert G. Marchand (D)
Samuel W. Morris
Charles Naylor (W)
Peter Newhard (D)
Charles Ogle (W)
Lemuel Paynter (D)
David Petrikin (D)
William S. Ramsey (D) d. Oct. 1840
John Sergeant (F)
William Simonton (W)
George W. Toland (W)
David D. Wagener (D)

RHODE ISLAND

Senators

Nehemiah R. Knight (D)
Nathan F. Dixon (W)

Representatives

Robert B. Cranston (W)
Joseph L. Tillinghast (W)

SOUTH CAROLINA

Senators

John C. Calhoun (D)
William C. Preston (Null-D)

Representatives

Sampson H. Butler (D)
John Campbell (SRD)
John K. Griffin (SRW)
Isaac E. Holmes (D)
Francis W. Pickens (Null-D)
R. Barnwell Rhett (D)
James Rogers (D)
Thomas D. Sumter (D)
Waddy Thompson, Jr. (W)

TENNESSEE

Senators

Hugh L. White (D) r. Jan. 1840
Alexander Anderson (D) s. 1840

Felix Grundy (D) d. Dec. 1840
Alfred O. P. Nicholson (D) s. 1841

Representatives

John Bell (W)
Julius W. Blackwell (D)
Aaron V. Brown (D)
William B. Campbell (W)
William B. Carter (W)
John W. Crockett (W)
Meredith P. Gentry (W)
Cave Johnson (D)
Abraham McClellan (D)
Harvey M. Watterson (D)
Christopher H. Williams (W)
Joseph L. Williams (S)
Hopkins L. Turney (D)

VERMONT

Senators

Samuel Prentiss (W)
Samuel S. Phelps (W)

Representatives

Horace Everett (W)
Isaac Fletcher (D)
Hiland Hall (W)
William Slade (W)
John Smith (D)

VIRGINIA

Senators

William H. Roane (D)
William C. Rives (D)

Representatives

Linn Banks (D)
Andrew Beirne (D)
John M. Botts (W)
Walter Coles (D)
Robert Craig (D)
George C. Dromgoole
James Garland (D)
William L. Goggin (W)
John Hill (W)
Joel Holleman (D) r. 1840
George W. Hopkins (D)
Robert M. T. Hunter (D)
Joseph Johnson (D)
John W. Jones (D)
William Lucas (D)
William M. McCarty (W) s. 1840
Francis Mallory (W) s. 1841
Charles F. Mercer (D) r. Dec. 1839
Francis E. Rives (D)
Green B. Samuels (D)
Lewis Steenrod (D)
John Taliaferro (W)
Henry W. Wise (W)

TWENTY-SEVENTH CONGRESS

March 4, 1841 to March 3, 1943

President of The Senate:	John Tyler
Presidents Pro Tempore of The Senate:	William R. King Samuel L. Southard Willie P. Mangum
Speaker of The House of Representatives:	John White

ALABAMA

Senators

William R. King (D)

Clement Comer Clay (D) r. Nov. 1841
Arthur P. Bagby (D)

Representatives

Reuben Chapman (D)
George S. Houston (D)
Dixon H. Lewis (SRD)
William W. Payne (D)
Benjamin G. Shields (W)

ARKANSAS

Senators

William S. Fulton (D)
Ambrose H. Sevier (D)

Representative

Edward Cross (D)

CONNECTICUT

Senators

Perry Smith (D)
Jabez W. Huntington (W)

Representatives

William W. Boardman (W)
John H. Brockway (W)
Thomas B. Osborne (W)
Truman Smith (W)
Joseph Trumbull (W)
Thomas W. Williams (W)

DELAWARE

Senators

Richard H. Bayard (W)
Thomas Clayton (W)

Representative

George B. Rodney (W)

GEORGIA

Senators

Alfred Cuthbert (D)
John M. Berrien (D)

Representatives

Julius C. Alford (W) r. 1841
Edward J. Black (SRW) s. 1842
Walter T. Colquitt (D) s. 1842
Mark A. Cooper (SRW) s. 1842
George W. Crawford (W)
William C. Dawson (SRW) r. Nov. 1841
Thomas F. Foster (D)
Roger L. Gamble (W)
Richard W. Habersham (D)
Thomas B. King (W)
James A. Meriwether (W)
Eugenius A. Nisbet (W) r. 1841
Lott Warren (W)

ILLINOIS

Senators

Richard M. Young (D)
Samuel McRoberts (D)

Representatives

Zadoc Casey (D)
John Reynolds (D)
John T. Stuart (W)

INDIANA

Senators

Oliver H. Smith (W)
Albert S. White (W)

Representatives

James H. Cravens (W)
Andrew Kennedy (D)
Henry S. Lane (W)
George H. Proffit (W)
Richard W. Thompson (W)
David Wallace (W)
Joseph L. White (W)

KENTUCKY

Senators

Henry Clay (W) r. Mar. 1842
John J. Crittenden (Un) s. 1842

James T. Morehead (W)

Representatives

Landaff W. Andrews (W)
Linn Boyd (D)
William O. Butler (D)
Garrett Davis (W)
Willis Green (W)
Thomas F. Marshall
Bryan Y. Owsley (W)
John Pope (D)
James C. Sprigg
John B. Thompson (W)
Philip Triplett (W)
Joseph R. Underwood (W)
John White (W)

LOUISIANA

Senators

Alexander Mouton (D) r. Mar. 1842
Charles M. Conrad (W) s. 1842

Alexander Barrow (W)

Representatives

John B. Dawson (D)
John Moore (W)
Edward D. White (W)

MAINE

Senators

Reuel Williams (D) r. Feb. 1843
John Fairfield (D) s. 1843

George Evans (W)

Representatives

Elisha H. Allen (W)
David Bronson (W)
Nathan Clifford (D)
William P. Fessenden (W)
Nathaniel S. Littlefield (D)
Joshua A. Lowell (D)
Alfred Marshall (D)
Benjamin Randall (W)

MARYLAND

Senators

William D. Merrick (W)
John L. Kerr (W)

Representatives

William Cost Johnson (W)
Isaac D. Jones (W)
John P. Kennedy (W)
John T. Mason (D)
James A. Pearce (W)
Alexander Randall (W)
Charles S. Sewall s. 1843
Augustus R. Sollers (W)
James W. Williams (D) d. Dec. 1842

MASSACHUSETTS

Senators

Isaac C. Bates (W)
Rufus Choate (W)

Representatives

John Quincy Adams (W)
Nathan Appleton (W) s. r. 1842
Osmyn Baker (W)
Nathaniel B. Borden (W)
George N. Briggs (W)
Barker Burnell (W)
William B. Calhoun (W)
Caleb Cushing (W)
William S. Hastings (D) d. June 1842
Charles Hudson (W)
William Parmenter (D)
Leverett Saltonstall (W)
Robert C. Winthrop (W)

MICHIGAN

Senators

Augustus S. Porter (W)
William Woodbridge (W, D)

Representative

Jacob M. Howard (W)

MISSISSIPPI

Senators

Robert J. Walker (D)
John Henderson (W)

Representatives

William M. Gwin (D)
Jacob Thompson (D)

MISSOURI

Senators

Thomas H. Benton (D)
Lewis F. Linn (D)

Representatives

John C. Edwards (D)
John Miller (D)

NEW HAMPSHIRE

Senators

Franklin Pierce (D) r. Feb. 1842
Leonard Wilcox s. 1842

Levi Woodbury (D)

Representatives

Charles G. Atherton (D)
Edmund Burke (D)
Ira A. Eastman (D)
John R. Reding (D)
Tristram Shaw

NEW JERSEY

Senators

Samuel L. Southard (W) d. June 1842
William L. Dayton (W) s. 1842

Jacob W. Miller (W)

Representatives

John B. Aycrigg (W)
William Halstead (W)
John P. B. Maxwell (W)
Joseph F. Randolph (W)
Charles C. Stratton (W)
Thomas Jones Yorke (W)

NEW YORK

Senators

Silas Wright, Jr. (D)
Nathaniel P. Tallmadge (D)

Representatives

Alfred Babcock (W)
Daniel D. Barnard (W)
Victory Birseye (W)
Bernard Blair (W)
Samuel S. Bowne (D)
David P. Brewster (D)
Timothy Childs (W)
Thomas C. Chittenden (W)
John C. Clark (W)
Staley N. Clarke (W)
James G. Clinton (D)
Richard D. Davis (D)
Andrew W. Doig (D)
Joseph Egbert (D)
Charles G. Ferris (D)
Millard Fillmore (W)
Charles A. Floyd (D)
John G. Floyd (D)
A. Lawrence Foster (W)
Seth M. Gates (W)
Samuel Gordon (D)
Francis Granger (W) r. Mar. 1841
John Greig (W)
Hiram P. Hunt (W)
Jacob Houck, Jr. (D)
Archibald L. Linn (W)
Robert McClellan (D)
John McKeon (D)
John Maynard (W)
Christopher Morgan (W)
William M. Oliver (D)
Samuel Partridge (D)
Lewis Riggs (D)
James I. Roosevelt (D)
John Sanford (D)
Thomas A. Tomlinson (W)
John Van Buren (D)
Henry B. Van Rensselaer (W)
Aaron Ward (D)
Fernando Wood (D)
John Young (W)

NORTH CAROLINA

Senators

Willie P. Mangum (W)
William A. Graham (W)

Representatives

Archibald H. Arrington (D)
Greene W. Caldwell (D)
John R. J. Daniel (D)
Edmund Deberry (W)
James Graham
James I. McKay (D)
Anderson Mitchell (W) s. 1842
Kenneth Rayner (W)
Abraham Rencher (D)
Romulus M. Saunders (D)
Augustine H. Shepperd (W)
Edward Stanly (W)
William H. Washington
Lewis Williams d. Feb. 1842

OHIO

Senators

William Allen (D)
Benjamin Tappan (D)

Representatives

Sherlock J. Andrews (W)
Benjamin S. Cowen (W)
Ezra Dean (D)
William Doan (D)
Joshua R. Giddings (W)
Patrick G. Goode (W)
John Hastings (D)
Samson Mason (W)
James Mathews (D)
Joshua Mathiot (W)
William Medill (D)
Calvary Morris (W)
Jeremiah Morrow (W)
Nathanel G. Pendleton (W)
Joseph Ridgway (W)
William Russell (W)
George Sweeny
Samuel Stokely (W)
John B. Weller (D)

PENNSYLVANIA

Senators

James Buchanan (D)
Daniel Sturgeon (D)

Representatives

Henry W. Beeson (D) s. 1841
Benjamin A. Bidlack (D)
Henry Black (W) d. Nov. 1841
Charles Brown (D)
Jeremiah Brown (W)
James Cooper (W)
Davis Dimock, Jr. (D) d. 1842
John Edwards (W)
Joseph Fornance (D)
James Gerry (D)
Amos Gustine (D)
Thomas Henry (W)
Enos Hook (D) r. Apr. 1842
Charles J. Ingersoll (D)
Joseph R. Ingersoll (W)
James Irvin (W)
William W. Irwin (W)
William Jack (D)
Francis James (W)
George M. Keim (D)
Joseph Lawrence (W) d. Apr. 1842
Thomas M. T. McKennan (W) s. 1842
Albert G. Marchand (D)
Peter Newhard (D)
Arnold Plumer (D)
Robert Ramsey (W)
Almon H. Read (D) s. 1842
James M. Russell (W) s. 1842
John Sergeant (F) r. Sept. 1841
William Simonton (W)
John Snyder
George W. Toland (W)
John Westbrook (D)

RHODE ISLAND

Senators

Nathan F. Dixon (W) d. Jan. 1842
William Sprague (W) s. 1842

James F. Simmons (W)

Representatives

Robert B. Cranston (W)
Joseph L. Tillinghast (W)

SOUTH CAROLINA

Senators

John C. Calhoun (D) r. Mar. 1843

William C. Preston (Null-D) r. Nov. 1842
George McDuffie (D) s. 1843

Representatives

Sampson H. Butler (D)
r. Sept. 1842
William Butler (W)
Patrick C. Caldwell (SRD)
John Campbell (SRD)
Isaac E. Holmes (D)
Francis W. Pickens (Null-D)
R. Barnwell Rhett (D)
James Rogers (D)
Thomas D. Sumter (D)
Samuel W. Trotti s. Dec. 1842

TENNESSEE

Senators

Alfred O. P. Nicholson (D)
r. Feb. 1842
Vacant

Representatives

Thomas D. Arnold (W)
Aaron V. Brown (D)
Milton Brown (W)
William B. Campbell (W)
Robert L. Caruthers (W)
Meredith P. Gentry (W)
Cave Johnson (D)
Abraham McClellan (D)
Hopkins L. Turney (D)
Harvey M. Watterson (D)
Christopher H. Williams (W)
Joseph L. Williams (W)

VERMONT

Senators

Samuel Prentiss (W) r. Apr. 1842
Samuel C. Crafts (W) s. 1842
Samuel S. Phelps (W)

Representatives

Horace Everett (W)
Hiland Hall (W)
John Mattocks (W)
William Slade (W)
Augustus Young (W)

VIRGINIA

Senators

William C. Rives (W)
William S. Archer (W)

Representatives

Linn Banks (D) r. Dec. 1841
Richard W. Bartin (W)
John M. Botts (W)
George B. Cary (D)
Walter Coles (D)
Thomas W. Gilmer (W)
William L. Goggin (W)
William O. Goode (D)
William A. Harris (D)
Samuel L. Hays (D)
George W. Hopkins (D)
Edmund W. Hubard (D)
Robert M. T. Hunter (D)
John W. Jones (D)
Francis Mallory (W)
Cuthbert Powell (W)
William Smith (D) s. 1841
Lewis Steenrod (D)
Alexander H. H. Stuart (W)
George W. Summers (W)
John Taliaferro (W)
Henry A. Wise (W)

TWENTY-EIGHTH CONGRESS

March 4, 1843 to March 3, 1845

President of The Senate: John Tyler
President Pro Tempore of The Senate: Willie P. Mangum
Speaker of The House of Representatives: John W. Jones

ALABAMA

Senators

William R. King (D) r. Apr. 1844
Dixon H. Lewis (D) s. 1844

Arthur P. Bagby (D)

Representatives

James E. Belser (D)
Reuben Chapman (D)
James Dellet (W)
George S. Houston (D)
Dixon H. Lewis (SRD) r. Apr. 1844
Felix G. McConnell (D)
William W. Payne (D)
William L. Yancey (D) s. 1844

ARKANSAS

Senators

William S. Fulton (D)
d. Aug. 1844
Chester Ashley (D) s. 1844

Ambros H. Sevier (D)

Representative

Edward Cross (D)

CONNECTICUT

Senators

Jabez W. Huntington (W)
John M. Niles (D)

Representatives

George S. Catlin (D)
Thomas H. Seymour (D)
Samuel Simons (D)
John Stewart (D)

DELAWARE

Senators

Richard H. Bayard (W)
Thomas Clayton (W)

Representative

George B. Rodney (W)

GEORGIA

Senators

John Berrien (W)
Walter T. Colquitt (D)

Representatives

Edward J. Black (SRW)
Absalom H. Chappell (SRW)
Duncan L. Clinch (W) s. 1844
Howell Cobb (D)
Mark A. Cooper (SRW)
r. June 1843
Hugh A. Haralson (D)
John B. Lamar (D) r. July 1843
John H. Lumpkin (D)
John Millen (D) d. Oct. 1943
Alexander H. Stephens (W)
Williams H. Stiles (D)

ILLINOIS

Senators

Samuel McRoberts (D)
d. Mar. 1843
James Semple (D) s. Dec. 1843

Sidney Breese (D)

Representatives

Stephen A. Douglas (D)
Orlando B. Fickin (D)
John J. Hardin (W)
Joseph P. Hoge (D)
John A. McClernand (D)
Robert Smith (D)
John Wentworth (D)

INDIANA

Senators

Albert S. White (W)
Edward A. Hannegan (D)

Representatives

William J. Brown (D)
John W. Davis (D)
Thomas J. Henley (D)
Andrew Kennedy (D)
Robert D. Owen (D)
John Pettit (D)
Samuel C. Sample (W)
Caleb B. Smith (W)
Thomas Smith (D)
Joseph A. Wright (D)

KENTUCKY

Senators

James T. Morehead (W)
John J. Crittenden

Representatives

Linn Boyd (D)
George A. Caldwell (D)
Garrett Davis (W)
Richard French (D)
Willis Green (W)
Henry Grider (W)
James W. Stone (D)
William P. Thomasson (W)
John W. Tibbatts (D)
John White (W)

LOUISIANA

Senators

Alexander Barrow (W)
Henry Johnson (W) s. 1844

Representatives

Pierre E. J. B. Bossier (D)
d. Apr. 1844
John B. Dawson (D)
Alcee L. La Branche (D)
Isaac E. Morse (D) s. 1844
John Slidell (SRD)

MAINE

Senators

George Evans (W)
John Fairfield (D)

Representatives

Shepard Cary (D) s. 1844
Robert P. Dunlap (D)
Hannibal Hamlin (D)
Joshua Herrick (D)
Freeman H. Morse (W)
Luther Severance (W)
Benjamin White (D) s. 1844

MARYLAND

Senators

William D. Merrick (W)
James A. Pearce (W)

Representatives

Francis Brengle (W)
John M. S. Causin (W)
John P. Kennedy (W)
Jacob A. Preston (W)
Thomas A. Spence (W)
John Wethered

MASSACHUSETTS

Senators

Isaac C. Bates (W)
Rufus Choate (W)

Representatives

Amos Abbott (W)
John Quincy Adams (W)
Osmyn Baker (W)
Barker Burnell (W) d. 1843
Joseph Grinnell (W)
Charles Hudson (W)
Daniel P. King (W)
William Parmenter (D)
Julius Rockwell (W)
Henry Williams (D)
Robert C. Winthrop (W)

MICHIGAN

Senators

Augustus S. Porter (W)
William Woodbridge (W,D)

Representatives

James B. Hunt (D)
Lucius Lyon (D)
Robert McClelland (D)

MISSISSIPPI

Senators

Robert J. Walker (D)
John Henderson (W)

Representatives

William H. Hammett (D)
Robert W. Roberts (D)
Jacob Thompson (D)
Tilghman M. Tucker (D)

MISSOURI

Senators

Thomas H. Benton (D)

Lewis F. Linn (D)
d. Oct. 1843
David R. Atchison (W)

Representatives

Gustavus M. Bower (D)
James B. Bowlin (D)
John Jameson (D)
James M. Hughes (D)
James H. Relfe (D)

NEW HAMPSHIRE

Senators

Levi Woodbury (D)
Charles G. Atherton (D)

Representatives

Edmund Burke (D)
John P. Hale (D)
Moses Norris, Jr. (D)
John R. Reding (D)

NEW JERSEY

Senators

Jacob W. Miller (W)
William L. Dayton (W)

Representatives

Lucius Q. C. Elmer (D)
Isaac G. Farlee
Littleton Kirkpatrick (D)
George Sykes (D)
William Wright (W)

NEW YORK

Senators

Silas Wright, Jr. (D)
r. Nov. 1844
Henry A. Foster (D) ta. 1844
John A. Dix (D) s. 1845

Nathaniel P. Tallmadge (D)
r. June 1844
Daniel S. Dickinson (D)
s. 1844

Representatives

Joseph H. Anderson (D)
Daniel D. Barnard (W)
Samuel Beardsley (D) r. Mar. 1844
Charles S. Benton (D)
Levi D. Carpenter (D) s. 1844
Charles H. Carroll (W)
Jeremiah E. Cary (D)
James G. Clinton (D)
Amasa Dana (D)
Richard D. Davis (D)
Chesselden Ellis (D)
Hamilton Fish (W)
Byram Green
William S. Hubbell (D)
Orville Hungerford (D)
Washington Hunt (W)
Preston King (D)
Moses G. Leonard (D)
William B. Maclay (D)
William A. Moseley (W)
Henry C. Murphy (D)
Thomas J. Patterson (W)
J. Phillips Phoenix (W)
Zadock Pratt (D)
Smith M. Purdy (D)
George Rathbun (D)
Orville Robinson (D)
Charles Rogers (W)
Jeremiah Russell (D)
David L. Seymour (D)
Albert Smith
Lemuel Stetson (D)
Selah B. Strong (D)
Asher Tyler (W)
Horace Wheaton (D)

NORTH CAROLINA

Senators

Willie P. Mangum (W)
William H. Haywood, Jr. (D)

Representatives

Archibald H. Arrington (D)
Daniel M. Barringer (W)
Thomas L. Clingman (W)
John R. J. Daniel (D)
Edmund Deberry (W)
James I. McKay (D)
Kenneth Rayner (W)
David S. Reid (D)
Romulus M. Saunders (D)

OHIO

Senators

William Allen (D)
Benjamin Tappan (D)

Representatives

Jacob Brinkerhoff (D)
Ezra Dean (D)
Alexander Duncan (W)
Elias Florence (W)
Joshua R. Giddings (W)
Edward S. Hamlin (W) s. 1844
Alexander Harper (W)
Perley B. Johnson (W)
William C. McCauslen (D)
Joseph J. McDowell (D)
James Mathews (D)
Heman A. Moore (D)
d. Apr. 1844
Joseph Morris (D)
Emery D. Potter (D)
Henry St. John (D)
Robert C. Schenck (W)
Alfred P. Stone (D) s. 1844
Daniel R. Tilden (W)
Joseph Vance (W)
John I. Vanmeter (W)
Samuel F. Vinton (W)
John B. Weller (D)

PENNSYLVANIA

Senators

James Buchanan (D)
Daniel Sturgeon (D)

Representatives

Benjamin A. Bidlack (D)
James Black (D)
Richard Brodhead (D)
Jeremiah Brown (W)
Joseph Buffington (D)
Cornelius Darragh (W)
s. 1844
John Dickey (W)
Henry D. Foster (D)
Henry Frick (W) d. Mar. 1844
George Fuller (D) s. 1844
Samuel Hays (D)
Charles J. Ingersoll (D)
Joseph R. Ingersoll (W)
James Irvin (W)
Michael H. Jenks (W)
Abraham R. McIlvaine (W)
Edward Joy Morris (W)
Henry Nes
James Pollock (W) s. 1844
Alexander Ramsey (W)
Almon H. Read (D) d. June 1844
Charles M. Reed (D)
John Ritter (D)
John T. Smith (D)
Andrew Stewart (W)
William Wilkins (D) r. Feb. 1844
Jacob S. Yost (D)

RHODE ISLAND

Senators

James F. Simmons (W)

William Sprague (W) r. Jan. 1844
John B. Francis (Law & Order)
s. 1844

Representatives

Henry Y. Cranston (W)
Elisha R. Potter, Jr. (W)

SOUTH CAROLINA

Senators

George McDuffie (D)
Daniel E. Huger (SRD)

Representatives

James A. Black (D)
Armistead Burt (D)
John Campbell (SRD)
Isaac E. Holmes (D)
R. Barnwell Rhett (D)
Richard F. Simpson (D)
Joseph A. Woodward (D)

TENNESSEE

Senators

Ephraim H. Foster (W)
Spencer Jarnagin (W)

Representatives

John B. Ashe (W)
Julius W. Blackwell (D)
Aaron V. Brown (D)
Milton Brown (W)
Alvan Cullom (D)
David W. Dickinson (W)
Andrew Johnson (D)
Cave Johnson (D)
George W. Jones (D)
Joseph H. Peyton (W)
William T. Senter (W)

VERMONT

Senators

Samuel S. Phelps (W)
William Upham (W)

Representatives

Jacob Collamer (W)
Paul Dillingham, Jr. (D)
Solomon Foot (W)
George F. Marsh (W)

VIRGINIA

Senators

William C. Rives (W)
William S. Archer (W)

Representatives

Archibald Atkinson (D)
Thomas H. Bayly (SRD) s. 1844
Augustus A. Chapman (D)
Samuel Chilton (W)
Walter Coles (D)
George C. Dromgoole (D)
Thomas W. Gilmer (W)
r. Feb. 1844
William L. Goggin (W) s. 1844
George W. Hopkins (D)
Edmund W. Hubard (D)
John W. Jones (D)
William Lucas (D)
Willoughby Newton (W)
Lewis Steenrod (D)
George W. Summers (W)
William Taylor (D)
Henry A. Wise (D) r. Feb. 1844

TWENTY-NINTH CONGRESS

March 4, 1845 to March 3, 1847

President of The Senate: George M. Dallas
Presidents Pro Tempore of The Senate: Ambrose H. Sevier
David R. Atchison

Speaker of The House of Representatives: John W. Davis

ALABAMA

Senators

Arthur P. Bagby (D)
Dixon H. Lewis (D)

Representatives

Franklin W. Bowdon (D)
s. 1846
Reuben Chapman (D)
James L. Cottrell (D)
s. 1846
Edmund S. Dargan (D)
Henry W. Hilliard (W)
George S. Houston (D)
Felix G. McConnell (D)
d. Sept. 1846
William W. Payne (D)
William L. Yancey (D)
r. Sept. 1846

ARKANSAS

Senators

Ambrose H. Sevier (D)
Chester Ashley (D)

Representatives

Thomas W. Newton (W) s. 1847
Archibald Yell (D) r. July 1846

CONNECTICUT

Senators

Jabez W. Huntington (W)
John M. Niles (D)

Representatives

James Dixon (W)
Samuel D. Hubbard (W)
John A. Rockwell (W)
Truman Smith (W)

DELAWARE

Senators

Thomas Clayton (W)
John M. Clayton (W)

Representative

John W. Houston

FLORIDA

Senators

David Levy Yulee
James D. Westcott, Jr. (D)

Representatives

William H. Brockenbrough (D)
s. 1846
Edward C. Cabell (W) r. Jan. 1846

GEORGIA

Senators

John M. Berrien (W)
Walter T. Colquitt (D)

Representatives

Howell Cobb (D)
Hugh A. Haralson (D)
Seaborn Jones (D)
Thomas B. King (W)
John H. Lumpkin (D)
Alexander H. Stephens (D)
Robert Toombs (SRD)
George W. B. Towns (D)
s. 1846

ILLINOIS

Senators

Sidney Breese (D)
James Semple (D)

Representatives

Edward D. Baker (W)
r. Dec. 1846
Stephen A. Douglas (D)
Orlando B. Ficklin (D)
John Henry (W) s. 1847
Joseph P. Hoge (D)
John A. McClernand (D)
Robert Smith (D)
John Wentworth (D)

INDIANA

Senators

Edward A. Hannegan (D)
Jesse D. Bright (D)

Representatives

Charles W. Cathcart (D)
John W. Davis (D)
Thomas J. Henley (D)
Andrew Kennedy (D)
Edward W. McGaughey (W)
Robert D. Owen (D)
John Pettit (D)
Caleb B. Smith (W)
Thomas Smith (D)
William W. Wick (D)

IOWA

Senators

Vacant

Representatives

S. Clinton Hastings (D) s. 1846
Shepherd Leffler (D) s. 1846

KENTUCKY

Senators

James T. Morehead (W)
John J. Crittenden

Representatives

Joshua F. Bell (W)
Linn Boyd (D)
Garrett Davis (W)
Henry Grider (W)
John H. McHenry (W)
John P. Martin (D)
William P. Thomasson (W)
John W. Tibbatts (D)
Andrew Trumbo (W)
Bryan R. Young (D)

LOUISIANA

Senators

Alexander Barrow (W) d. Dec. 1846
Pierre Soule s. 1847

Henry Johnson (W)

Representatives

John H. Harmanson (D)
Emile LaSere (D) s. 1846
Isaac E. Morse (D)
John Slidell (SRD) r. Nov. 1845
Bannon G. Thibodeaux

MAINE

Senators

George Evans (W)
John Fairfield (D)

Representatives

Robert P. Dunlap (D)
Hannibal Hamlin (D)
John D. McCrate (D)
Cullen Sawtelle (D)
John F. Scammon (D)
Luther Severance (W)
Hezekiah Williams (D)

MARYLAND

Senators

James A. Pearce (W)
Reverdy Johnson (W)

Representatives

John G. Chapman (W)
Albert Constable (D)
William F. Giles (D)
Thomas W. Ligon (D)
Edward H. C. Long (W)
Thomas J. Perry (D)

MASSACHUSETTS

Senators

Isaac C. Bates (W) d. Mar. 1845
John Davis (W) s. 1845

Daniel Webster (W)

Representatives

Amos Abbott (W)
John Quincy Adams (W)
George Ashmun (W)
Joseph Grinnell (W)
Artemas Hale (W)
Charles Hudson (W)
Daniel P. King (W)
Julius Rockwell (W)
Benjamin Thompson (W)
Robert C. Winthrop (W)

MICHIGAN

Senators

William Woodbridge (W,D)
Lewis Cass (D)

Representatives

John S. Chipman (D)
James B. Hunt (D)
Robert McClelland (D)

MISSISSIPPI

Senators

Robert J. Walker (D)
r. Mar. 1845
Joseph W. Chalmers (D) s. 1845

Jesse Speight (D)

Representatives

Stephen Adams (D)
Jefferson Davis (D) r. June 1846
Henry T. Ellett (D) s. 1847
Robert W. Roberts (D)
Jacob Thompson (D)

MISSOURI

Senators

Thomas H. Benton (D)
David R. Atchison (W)

Representatives

James B. Bowlin (D)
William McDaniel (D) s. 1846
Sterling Price (D) r. Aug. 1846
John S. Phelps (D)
James H. Relfe (D)
Leonard H. Sims (D)

NEW HAMPSHIRE

Senators

Levi Woodbury (D) r. Nov. 1845
Benning W. Jenness (D) ta. 1845
Joseph Cilley (D) s. 1846

Charles G. Atherton (D)

Representatives

James H. Johnson
Mace Moulton (D)
Moses Norris, Jr. (D)

NEW JERSEY

Senators

Jacob W. Miller (W)
William L. Dayton (W)

Representatives

Joseph E. Edsall (D)
James G. Hampton (W)
John Runk (W)
George Sykes (D) s. 1845
Samuel G. Wright
William Wright (W)

NEW YORK

Senators

Daniel S. Dickinson (D)
John A. Dix (D)

Representatives

Joseph H. Anderson (D)
Charles S. Benton (D)
William W. Campbell (Amer.)
Charles H. Carroll (D)
John F. Collin (D)
Erastus D. Culver (W)
John De Mott (D)
Samuel S. Ellsworth (D)
Charles Goodyear (D)
Samuel Gordon (D)
Martin Grover (D)
Richard P. Herrick (W)
d. June 1846
Elias B. Holmes (W)
William J. Hough (D)
Orville Hungerford (D)
Washington Hunt (W)
Timothy Jenkins (D)
Preston King (D)
John W. Lawrence (D)
Abner Lewis (W)
William B. Maclay (D)
William S. Miller
William A. Moseley (W)
Archibald C. Niven (D)
George Rathbun (D)
Thomas C. Ripley s. 1846
Joseph Russell (D)
Henry J. Seaman (Amer.)
Albert Smith (R)
Stephen Strong (D)
Horace Wheaton (D)
Hugh White
Bradford R. Wood (D)
Thomas M. Woodruff (D)
William W. Woodworth (D)

NORTH CAROLINA

Senators

Willie P. Mangum (W)
William H. Haywood, Jr. (D)
r. July 1846
George E. Badger (W) s. 1846

Representatives

Daniel M. Barringer (W)
Asa Biggs (D)
Henry S. Clark (D)
John R. J. Daniel (D)
James C. Dobbin (D)
Alfred Dockery (W)
James Graham (W)
James I. McKay (D)
David S. Reid (D)

OHIO

Senators

William Allen (D)
Thomas Corwin (W)

Representatives

Jacob Brinkerhoff (D)
John D. Cummins (D)
Francis A. Cunningham (D)
Columbus Delano (W)
James J. Faran (D)
George Fries (D)
Joshua R. Giddings (W)
Alexander Harper (W)
Joseph J. McDowell (D)
Joseph Morris (D)
Isaac Parrish (D)
Augustus L. Perrill (D)
Joseph M. Root (W)
William Sawyer (D)
Robert C. Schenck (W)
Henry St. John (D)
David A. Starkweather (D)
Allen G. Thurman (D)
Daniel R. Tilden (W)
Joseph Vance (W)
Samuel F. Vinton (W)

PENNSYLVANIA

Senators

James Buchanan (D) r. Mar. 1845
Simon Cameron (D) s. Mar. 1845

Daniel Sturgeon (D)

Representatives

James Black (D)
John Blanchard (W)
Richard Brodhead (D)
Joseph Buffington (W)
John H. Campbell (W)
Cornelius Darragh (W)
Jacob Erdman (D)
John H. Ewing (W)
Henry D. Foster (D)
William S. Garvin (D)
Charles J. Ingersoll (D)
Joseph R. Ingersoll (W)
Owen D. Leib (D)
Lewis C. Levin (Amer)
Moses McClean (D)
Abraham R. McIlvaine (W)
James Pollock (W)
Alexander Ramsey (W)
John Ritter (D)
Andrew Stewart (W)
John Strohm (W)
James Thompson (W)
David Wilmot (D)
Jacob S. Yost (D)

RHODE ISLAND

Senators

James F. Simmons (W)
Albert C. Greene (W)

Representatives

Lemuel H. Arnold (W)
Henry Y. Cranston (W)

SOUTH CAROLINA

Senators

George McDuffie (D) r. Aug. 1846
Andrew P. Butler (SRD) s. 1846

John C. Calhoun (D) s. 1846

Representatives

James A. Black (D)
Armidstead Burt (D)
Isaac E. Holmes (D)
R. Barnwell Rhett (D)
Richard F. Simpson (D)
Alexander D. Sims (D)
Joseph A. Woodward (D)

TENNESSEE

Senators

Spencer Jarnagin (W)
Hopkins L. Turney (D)

Representatives

Milton Brown (W)
Lucien B. Chase (D)
William M. Cocke (D)
John H. Crozier (W)
Alvan Cullom (D)
Edwin H. Ewing (W) s. 1846
Meredith P. Gentry (W)
Andrew Johnson (D)
George W. Jones (D)
Barclay Martin (D)
Joseph H. Peyton (W)
d. Nov. 1845
Frederick P. Stanton (D)

TEXAS

Senators

Sam Houston (D) s. 1846
Thomas J. Rusk (D) s. 1846

Representatives

David S. Kaufman (D) s. 1846
Timothy Pilsbury (D) s. 1846

VERMONT

Senators

Samuel S. Phelps (W)
William Upham (W)

Representatives

Jacob Collamer (W)
Paul Dillingham, Jr. (D)
Solomon Foot (W)
George P. Marsh (W)

VIRGINIA

Senators

William S. Archer (W)

Isaac S. Pennybacker (D)
d. Jan. 1847
James M. Mason (D) s. 1847

Representatives

Archibald Atkinson (D)
Thomas H. Bayly (SRD)
Henry Bedinger (D)
William G. Brown (D)
Augustus A. Chapman (D)
George C. Dromgoole (D)
George W. Hopkins (D)
Edmund W. Hubard (D)
Robert M. T. Hunter (D)
Joseph Johnson (D)
Shelton F. Leake (D)
James McDowell (D) s. 1846
John S. Pendleton (D)
James A. Seddon (D)
William Taylor (D) d. Jan. 1847
William M. Tredway (D)

THIRTIETH CONGRESS

March 4, 1847 to March 3, 1849

President of The Senate: George M. Dallas
President Pro Tempore of The Senate: David R. Atchison
Speaker of The House of Representatives: Robert C. Winthrop

ALABAMA

Senators

Arthur P. Bagby (D) r. June 1848
William R. King (D) s. 1848

Dixon H. Lewis (D) d. Oct. 1848
Benjamin Fitzpatrick (SRD)
s. 1848

Representatives

Franklin W. Bowdon (D)
Williamson R. W. Cobb (D)
John Gayle (W)
Sampson W. Harris (D)
Henry W. Hilliard (W)
George S. Houston (D)
Samuel W. Inge (D)

ARKANSAS

Senators

Ambrose H. Sevier (D)
r. Mar. 1848
Solon Borland (D) s. 1848

Chester Ashley (D) d. Apr. 1848
William K. Sebastian (D) s. 1848

Representative

Robert W. Johnson (D)

CONNECTICUT

Senators

Jabez W. Huntington (W)
d. Nov. 1847
Roger S. Baldwin (W) s. 1847

John M. Niles (D)

Representatives

James Dixon (W)
Samuel D. Hubbard (W)
John A. Rockwell (W)
Truman Smith (W)

DELAWARE

Senators

John M. Clayton (W)
r. Feb. 1849
John Wales s. 1849

Presley Spruance (W)

Representative

John W. Houston (W)

FLORIDA

Senators

David Levy Yulee
James D. Westcott, Jr. (D)

Representatives

Edward C. Cabell (W)

GEORGIA

Senators

Walter T. Colquitt (D)
r. Feb. 1848
Herschel V. Johnson (D) s. 1848

John M. Berrien (W)

Representatives

Howell Cobb (D)
Hugh A. Haralson (D)
Alfred Iverson (D)
John W. Jones (W)
Thomas B. King (W)
John H. Lumpkin (D)
Alexander H. Stephens (D)
Robert Toombs (SRD)

ILLINOIS

Senators

Sidney Breese (D)
Stephen A. Douglas (D)

Representatives

Orlando B. Ficklin (D)
Abraham Lincoln (W)
John A. McClernand (D)
William A. Richardson (D)
Robert Smith (D)
Thomas J. Turner (D)
John Wentworth (D)

INDIANA

Senators

Edward A. Hannegan (D)
Jesse D. Bright (D)

Representatives

Charles W. Cathcart (D)
George G. Dunn (W)
Elisha Embree (W)
Thomas J. Henley (D)
John Petit (D)
John L. Robinson (D)
William Rockhill (D)
Caleb B. Smith (W)
Richard W. Thompson (W)
William W. Wick (D)

IOWA

Senators

Augustus C. Dodge (D)
George W. Jones

Representatives

Shepherd Leffler (D)
William Thompson (D)

KENTUCKY

Senators

John J. Crittenden r. June 1848
Thomas Metcalfe (D) s. 1848

Joseph R. Underwood (W)

Representatives

Green Adams (W)
Linn Boyd (D)
Aylett Buckner (W)
Beverly L. Clarke (D)
W. Garnett Duncan (W)
Richard French (D)
John P. Gaines (W)
Charles S. Morehead (W)
Samuel O. Peyton (D)
John B. Thompson (W)

LOUISIANA

Senators

Henry Johnson (W)
Solomon W. Downs (D)

Representatives

John H. Harmanson (D)
Emile La Sere (D)
Isaac E. Morse (D)
Bannon G. Thibodeaux

MAINE

Senators

John Fairfield (D)
d. Dec. 1847
Wyman B. S. Moor (D) ta. 1848
Hannibal Hamlin (D) s. 1848

James W. Bradbury (D)

Representatives

Hiram Belcher (W)
Asa W. H. Clapp (D)
Franklin Clark (D)
David Hammons (D)
Ephraim K. Smart (D)
James S. Wiley (D)
Hezekiah Williams (D)

MARYLAND

Senators

James A. Pearce (W)
Reverdy Johnson (W)

Representatives

John G. Chapman (W)
John W. Crisfield (W)
Alexander Evans (W)
Thomas W. Ligon (D)
Robert M. McLane (D)
J. Dixon Roman (W)

MASSACHUSETTS

Senators

Daniel Webster (W)
John Davis (W)

Representatives

Amos Abbott (W)
John Quincy Adams (W)
d. Feb. 1848
George Ashmun (W)
Joseph Grinnell (W)
Artemas Hale (W)
Charles Hudson (W)
Daniel P. King (W)
Horace Mann (W) s. 1848
John G. Palfrey (W)
Julius Rockwell (W)
Robert C. Winthrop (W)

MICHIGAN

Senators

Lewis Cass (D) r. May 1848
Thomas Fitzgerald (D)
s. June 1848

Alpheus Felch (D)

Representatives

Kinsley S. Bingham (D)
Edward Bradley (D)
Robert McClelland (D)
Charles E. Stuart (D)

MISSISSIPPI

Senators

Jesse Speight (D) d. May 1847
Jefferson Davis (D) s. Aug. 1847

Henry S. Foote (Un)

Representatives

Albert G. Brown (D)
Winfield S. Featherston (D)
Jacob Thompson (D)
Patrick W. Tompkins (W)

MISSOURI

Senators

Thomas H. Benton (D)
David R. Atchison (W)

Representatives

James B. Bowlin (D)
James S. Green (D)
Willard P. Hall (D)
John Jameson (D)
John S. Phelps (D)

NEW HAMPSHIRE

Senators

Charles G. Atherton (D)
John P. Hale (Anti-Slavery)

Representatives

James H. Johnson
Charles H. Peaslee (D)
Amos Tuck
James Wilson (W)

NEW JERSEY

Senators

Jacob W. Miller (W)
William L. Dayton (W)

Representatives

Joseph E. Edsall (D)
Dudley S. Gregory (W)
James G. Hampton (W)
William A. Newell (W)
John Van Dyke (W)

NEW YORK

Senators

Daniel S. Dickinson (D)
John A. Dix (D)

Representatives

Ausburn Birdsall (D)
Esbon Blackmar (W) s. 1848
William Collins (D)
Harmon S. Conger (W)
William Duer (W)
Daniel Gott (W)
Horace Greeley (W) s. 1848
Nathan K. Hall (W)
John M. Holley (W)
d. Mar. 1848
Elias B. Holmes (W)
Washington Hunt (W)
David S. Jackson (D)
r. Apr. 1848
Timothy Jenkins (D)
Orlando Kellogg (W)
Sidney Lawrence (D)
William T. Lawrence (D)
Frederick W. Lord (W)
William B. Maclay (D)
Dudley Marvin (W)
Joseph Mullin
Henry C. Murphy (D)
William Nelson (W)
Henry Nicoll (D)
George Petrie
Harvey Putnam (W)
Gideon Reynolds (W)
Robert L. Rose (W)
David Rumsey, Jr. (W)
Daniel B. St. John (W)
Eliakim Sherrill (W)
Peter H. Silvester (W)
John I. Slingerland
George A. Starkweather (D)
Frederick A. Tallmadge (W)
Cornelius Warren (W)
Hugh White

NORTH CAROLINA

Senators

Willie P. Mangum (W)
George E. Badger (W)

Representatives

Daniel M. Barringer (W)
Nathaniel Boyden
Thomas L. Clingman (W)
John R. J. Daniel (D)
Richard S. Donnell (W)
James I. McKay (D)
David Outlaw (W)
Augustine H. Shepperd (W)
Abraham W. Venable (D)

OHIO

Senators

William Allen (D)
Thomas Corwin (W)

Representatives

Richard S. Canby (W)
John Crowell (W)
John D. Cummins (D)
Rodolphus Dickinson (D)
Daniel Duncan (W)
Thomas O. Edwards (W)
Nathan Evans (W)
James J. Faran (D)
David Fisher (W)
George Fries (D)
Joshua R. Giddings (W)
William Kennon, Jr. (D)
Samuel Lahm (D)
John K. Miller (D)
Jonathan D. Morris (D)
Thomas Ritchey (D)
Joseph M. Root (W)
William Sawyer (D)
Robert C. Schenck (W)
John L. Taylor (W)
Samuel F. Vinton (W)

PENNSYLVANIA

Senators

Daniel Sturgeon (D)
Simon Cameron (D)

Representatives

John Blanchard (W)
Jasper E. Brady (W)
Samuel A. Bridges (D) s. 1848
Richard Brodhead (D)
Charles Brown (D)
Chester P. Butler (W)
John Dickey (W)
George N. Eckert (W)
John W Farrelly (W)
John Freedley (W)
Moses Hampton (W)
John W. Hornbeck (W)
d. Jan. 1848
Charles J. Ingersoll (D)
Joseph R. Ingersoll (W)
Alexander Irvin (W)
Lewis C. Levin (Amer)
Abraham R. McIlvaine (W)
Job Mann (D)
Henry Nes
James Pollock (W)
Andrew Stewart (W)
John Strohm (W)
William Strong (D)
James Thompson (W)
David Wilmot (D)

RHODE ISLAND

Senators

Albert C. Greene (W)
John H. Clarke (W)

Representatives

Robert B. Cranston (W)
Benjamin B. Thurston (D)

SOUTH CAROLINA

Senators

John C. Calhoun (D)
Andrew P. Butler (SRD)

Representatives

James A. Black (D)
d. Apr. 1848
Armistead Burt (D)
Isaac E. Holmes (D)
John McQueen (D) s. 1849
R. Barnwell Rhett (D)
Richard F. Simpson (D)
Alexander D. Sims (D)
d. Nov. 1848
Daniel Wallace (W) s. 1848
Joseph A. Woodward (D)

TENNESSEE

Senators

Hopkins L. Turney (D)
John Bell (W)

Representatives

Washington Barrow (W)
Lucien B. Chase (D)
William M. Cocke (D)
John H. Crozier (W)
Meredith P. Gentry (W)
William T. Haskell (W)
Hugh L. W. Hill (D)
Andrew Johnson (D)
George W. Jones (D)
Frederick P. Stanton (D)
James H. Thomas (D)

TEXAS

Senators

Sam Houston (D)
Thomas J. Rusk (D)

Representatives

David S. Kaufman (D)
Timothy Pilsbury (D)

VERMONT

Senators

Samuel S. Phelps (W)
William Upham (W)

Representatives

Jacob Collamer (W)
William Henry (W)
George P. Marsh (W)
Lucius B. Peck (D)

VIRGINIA

Senators

James M. Mason (D)
Robert M. T. Hunter (D)

Representatives

Archibald Atkinson (D)
Thomas H. Bayly (SRD)
Richard L. T. Beale (D)
Henry Bedinger (D)
Thomas S. Bocock (D)
John M. Botts (W)
William G. Brown (D)
George C. Dromgoole (D)
d. Apr. 1847
Thomas S. Flournoy (W)
Andrew S. Fulton (W)
William L. Goggin (W)
James McDowell (D)
Richard K. Meade (D)
John S. Pendleton (W)
William B. Preston (W)
Robert A. Thompson (D)

WISCONSIN

Senators

Henry Dodge (D) s. 1848
Isaac P. Walker (D) s. 1848

Representatives

Mason C. Darling (D) s. 1848
William P. Lynde (D) s. 1848

THIRTY-FIRST CONGRESS

March 4, 1849 to March 3, 1851

President of The Senate: Millard Fillmore
Presidents Pro Tempore of The Senate: David R. Atchison
William R. King
Speaker of The House of Representatvies: Howell Cobb

ALABAMA

Senators

William R. King (D)

Benjamin Fitzpatrick (SRD)
r. Dec. 1849
Jeremiah Clemens (D)

Representatives

William J. Alston (W)
Franklin W. Bowdon (D)
Williamson R. W. Cobb (D)
Sampson W. Harris (D)
Henry W. Hilliard (W)
David Hubbard (SRD)
Samuel W. Inge (D)

ARKANSAS

Senators

Solon Borland (D)
William K. Sebastian (D)

Representative

Robert W. Johnson (D)

CALIFORNIA

Senators

William M. Gwin (D) s. 1850
John C. Fremont (D) s. 1850

Representatives

Edward Gilbert (D) s. 1850
George W. Wright s. 1850

CONNECTICUT

Senators

Roger S. Baldwin (W)
Truman Smith (W)

Representatives

Walter Booth (Free-Soiler)
Thomas B. Butler (W)
Chauncey F. Cleveland (D)
Loren P. Waldo (D)

DELAWARE

Senators

Presley Spruance (W)
John Wales

Representative

John W. Houston (W)

FLORIDA

Senators

David Levy Yulee (W)
Jackson Morton (W)

Representative

Edward C. Cabell (W)

GEORGIA

Senators

John M. Berrien (W)
William C. Dawson (SRW)

Representatives

Howell Cobb (D)
Thomas C. Hackett (D)
Hugh A. Haralson (D)
Joseph W. Jackson (D) s. 1850
Thomas B. King (W) r. 1850
Allen F. Owen (W)
Alexander H. Stephens (D)
Robert Toombs (SRD)
Marshall J. Wellborn (D)

ILLINOIS

Senators

Stephen A. Douglas (D)
James Shields (D)

Representatives

Edward D. Baker
William H. Bissell (D)
Thomas L. Harris (D)
John A. McClernand (D)
William A. Richardson (D)
John Wentworth (D)
Timothy R. Young (D)

INDIANA

Senators

Jesse D. Bright (D)
James Whitcomb (D)

Representatives

Nathaniel Albertson (D)
William J. Brown (D)
Cyrus L. Dunham (D)
Graham N. Fitch (D)
Willis A. Gorman (D)
Andrew J. Harlan (D)
George W. Julian (Free-Soiler)
Joseph E. McDonald (D)
Edward W. McGaughey (W)
John L. Robinson (D)

IOWA

Senators

Augustus C. Dodge (D)
George W. Jones (D)

Representatives

Shepherd Leffler (D)
Daniel F. Miller (W) s. 1850
William Thompson (D)
r. June 1850

KENTUCKY

Senators

Joseph R. Underwood (W)
Henry Clay (W)

Representatives

Daniel Breck (W)
Linn Boyd (D)
George A. Caldwell (D)
James L. Johnson (W)
Finis E. McLean (W)
Humphrey Marshall (W)
John C. Mason (D)
Charles S. Morehead (W)
Richard H. Stanton (D)
John B. Thompson (W)

LOUISIANA

Senators

Solomon W. Downs (D)
Pierre Soule (SRD)

Representatives

Henry A. Bullard (W) s. 1850
Charles M. Conrad (W)
r. Aug. 1850
John H. Harmanson (D)
d. Oct. 1850
Emile LaSere (D)
Isaac E. Morse (D)
Alexander G. Penn (D) s. 1850

MAINE

Senators

James W. Bradbury (D)
Hannibal Hamlin (D)

Representatives

Thomas J. D. Fuller (D)
Elbridge Gerry (D)
Rufus K. Goodenow (W)
Nathaniel S. Littlefield (D)
John Otis (W)
Cullen Sawtelle (D)
Charles Stetson (D)

MARYLAND

Senators

James A. Pearce (W)

Reverdy Johnson (W)
r. Mar. 1849
David Stewart (W) ta. 1849
Thomas G. Pratt (W) s. 1850

Representatives

Richard J. Bowie (W)
Alexander Evans (W)
William T. Hamilton (D)
Edward Hammond (D)
John B. Kerr (W)
Robert M. McLane (D)

MASSACHUSETTS

Senators

Daniel Webster (W) r. July 1850
Robert C. Winthrop (W) ta. 1850
Robert Rantoul, Jr. (D) s. 1851

John Davis (W)

Representatives

Charles Allen (Free-Soiler)
George Ashmun (W)
James H. Duncan (W)
Samuel A. Eliot (W) s. 1850
Orin Fowler (W)
Joseph Grinnell (W)
Daniel P. King (W)
d. July 1850
Horace Mann (W)
Julius Rockwell (W)
Robert C. Winthrop (W)
r. July 1850

MICHIGAN

Senators

Lewis Cass (D)
Alpheus Felch (D)

Representatives

Kinsley S. Bingham (D)
Alexander W. Buel (D)
William Sprague (W)

MISSISSIPPI

Senators

Henry S. Foote (Un)
Jefferson Davis (D)

Representatives

Albert G. Brown (D)
Winfield S. Featherston (D)
William McWillie (D)
Jacob Thompson (D)

MISSOURI

Senators

Thomas H. Benton (D)
David R. Atchison (W)

Representatives

William V. Bay (D)
James B. Bowlin (D)
James S. Green (D)
Willard P. Hall (D)
John S. Phelps (D)

NEW HAMPSHIRE

Senators

John P. Hale (Anti-Slavery)
Moses Norris, Jr. (D)

Representatives

Harry Hibbard (D)
George W. Morrison (D) s. 1850
Charles H. Peaslee (D)
Amos Tuck
James Wilson (W) r. Sept. 1850

NEW JERSEY

Senators

Jacob W. Miller (W)
William L. Dayton (W)

Representatives

Andrew K. Hay (W)
James G. King (W)
William A. Newell (W)
John Van Dyke (W)
Isaac Wildrick (D)

NEW YORK

Senators

Daniel S. Dickinson (D)
William H. Seward (W)

Representatives

Henry P. Alexander (W)
George R. Andrews (W)
Henry Bennett
David A. Bokee (W)
George Briggs (W)
James Brooks (W)
Lorenzo Burrows (W)
Charles E. Clarke (W)
Harmon S. Conger (W)
William Duer (W)
Daniel Gott (W)
Herman D. Gould (W)
Ransom Halloway (W)
William T. Jackson (W)
John A. King (W)
Preston King (D)
Thomas McKissock (W)
Orsamus B. Matteson (W)
William Nelson (W)
J. Phillips Phoenix (W)
Harvey Putnam (W)
Gideon Reynolds (W)
Elijah Risley (W)
Robert L. Rose (W)
David Rumsey, Jr. (W)
William A. Sackett (W)
Abraham M. Schermerhorn (W)
John L. Schoolcraft (W)
Peter H. Silvester (W)
Elbridge G. Spaulding (W)
John R. Thurman (W)
Walter Underhill (W)
Hiram Walden (D)
Hugh White

NORTH CAROLINA

Senators

Willie P. Mangum (W)
George E. Badger (W)

Representatives

William S. Ashe (D)
Joseph P. Caldwell (W)
Thomas L. Clingman (W)
John R. J. Daniel (D)
Edmund Deberry (W)
David Outlaw (W)
Augustine H. Shepperd (W)
Edward Stanly (W)
Abraham W. Venable (D)

OHIO

Senators

Thomas Corwin (W)
r. July 1850
Thomas Ewing (W) s. 1850

Salmon P. Chase (D)

Representatives

John Bell (W) s. 1851
Joseph Cable (D)
Lewis D. Campbell (W)
David K. Cartter (D)
Moses B. Corwin (W)
John Crowell (W)
Rodolphus Dickinson
d. Mar. 1849
David T. Disney (D)
Nathan Evans (W)
Joshua R. Giddings (W)
Moses Hoagland (D)
William F. Hunter (W)
John K. Miller (D)
Jonathan D. Morris (D)
Edson B. Olds (D)
Emery D. Potter (D)
Joseph M. Root (W)
Robert C. Schenck (W)
Charles Sweetser (D)
John L. Taylor (W)
Samuel F. Vinton (W)
William A. Whittlesey (D)
Amos E. Wood (D) d. Nov. 1850

PENNSYLVANIA

Senators

Daniel Sturgeon (D)
James Cooper (W)

Representatives

John Brisbin (W) s. 1851
Chester P. Butler (W)
d. Oct. 1850
Samuel Calvin (W)
Joseph Casey (W)
Joseph R. Chandler (W)
Joel B. Danner (D) s. 1850
Jesse C. Dickey (W)
Milo M. Dimmick (D)
John Freedley (W)
Alfred Gilmore (D)
Moses Hampton (W)
John W. Howe (W)
Lewis C. Levin (Amer)
James X. McLanahan (D)
Job Mann (D)
Henry D. Moore (W)

Henry Nes d. Sept. 1850
Andrew J. Ogle (W)
Charles W. Pitman (W)
Robert R. Reed (W)
John Robbins, Jr. (D)
Thomas Ross (D)
Thaddeus Stevens (W)
William Strong (D)
James Thompson (W)
David Wilmot (D)

RHODE ISLAND

Senators

Albert C. Greene (W)
John H. Clarke (W)

Representatives

Nathan F. Dixon (W)
George G. King (W)

SOUTH CAROLINA

Senators

John C. Calhoun (D) d. Mar. 1850
Franklin H. Elmore (D)
s. d. 1850
Robert W. Barnwell (D) ta. 1850
R. Barnwell Rhett (D) s. 1851

Andrew P. Butler (SRD)

Representatives

Armistead Burt (D)
William F. Colcock (D)
Isaac E. Holmes (D)
John McQueen (D)
James L. Orr (D)
Daniel Wallace (W)
Joseph A. Woodward (D)

TENNESSEE

Senators

Hopkins L. Turney (D)
John Bell (W)

Representatives

Josiah M. Anderson (W)
Andrew Ewing (D)
Meredith P. Gentry (W)
Isham G. Harris (W)
Andrew Johnson (D)
George W. Jones (D)
John H. Savage (D)
Frederick P. Stanton (D)
James H. Thomas (D)
Albert G. Watkins (W)
Christopher H. Williams (W)

TEXAS

Senators

Sam Houston (D)
Thomas J. Rusk (D)

Representatives

Volney E. Howard (D)
David S. Kaufman (D)
d. Jan. 1851

VERMONT

Senators

Samuel S. Phelps (W)
William Upham (W)

Representatives

William Hebard (W)
William Henry (W)
George P. Marsh (W) r. 1849
James Meacham (W)
Lucius B. Peck (D)

VIRGINIA

Senators

James M. Mason (D)
Robert M. T. Hunter (D)

Representatives

Thomas H. Averett (D)
Thomas H. Bayly (SRD)
James M. H. Beale (D)
Thomas S. Bocock (D)
Henry A. Edmundson (D)
Thomas S. Haymond (W)
Alexander R. Holladay (D)
James McDowell (D)
Fayette McMullen (D)
Richard K. Meade (D)
John S. Millson (D)
Jeremiah Morton (W)
Alexander Newman (D)
d. Sept. 1849
Richard Parker (D)
Paulus Powell (D)
James A. Seddon (D)

WISCONSIN

Senators

Henry Dodge (D)
Isaac P. Walker (D)

Representatives

Orsamus Cole (W)
James D. Doty (Free-Soiler)
Charles Durkee (Free-Soiler)

THIRTY-SECOND CONGRESS

March 4, 1851 to March 3, 1853

President of The Senate: Millard Fillmore
Presidents Pro Tempore of The Senate: William R. King
David R. Atchison
Speaker of The House of Representatives: Linn Boyd

ALABAMA

Senators

William R. King (D) r. Dec. 1852
Benjamin Fitzpatrick (SRD)
s. 1853

Jeremiah Clemens (D)

Representatives

James Abercrombie (W)
John Bragg (SRD)
Williamson R. W. Cobb (D)
Sampson W. Harris (D)
George W. Houston (D)
William R. Smith (W)
Alexander White (W)

ARKANSAS

Senators

William K. Sebastian (D)
Solon Borland (D)

Representative

Robert W. Johnson (D)

CALIFORNIA

Senators

William M. Gwin (D)
John B. Weller (D) s. 1852

Representatives

Joseph W. McCorkle (D)
Edward C. Marshall (D)

CONNECTICUT

Senators

Truman Smith (W)
Isaac Toucey (D) s. 1852

Representatives

Charles Chapman (W)
Chauncey F. Cleveland (D)
Colin M. Ingersoll (D)
Origen S. Seymour (D)

DELAWARE

Senators

Presley Spruance (W)
James A. Bayard (D)

Representative

George R. Riddle (D)

FLORIDA

Senators

Jackson Morton (W)
Stephen R. Mallory (D)

Representative

Edward C. Cabell (W)

GEORGIA

Senators

John M. Berrien (W)
r. May 1852
Robert M. Charlton s. 1852

William C. Dawson (SRW)

Representatives

David J. Bailey (SRD)
Elijah W. Chastain (D)
Junius Hillyer (D)
Joseph W. Jackson (D)
James Johnson (D)
Charles Murphey (D)
Alexander H. Stephens (D)
Robert Toombs (SRD)

ILLINOIS

Senators

Stephen A. Douglas (D)
James Shields (D)

Representatives

Willis Allen (D)
William H. Bissell (D)
Thompson Campbell (D)
Orlando B. Ficklin (D)
Richard S. Molony (D)
William A. Richardson (D)
Richard Yates (W)

INDIANA

Senators

Jesse D. Bright (D)

James Whitcomb (D)
d. Oct. 1852
Charles W. Cathcart (D)
ta. 1852
John Pettit (D) s. 1853

Representatives

Samuel Brenton (W)
John G. Davis (D)
Cyrus L. Dunham (D)
Graham N. Fitch (D)
Willis A. Gorman (D)
Thomas A. Hendricks (D)
James Lockhart (D)
Daniel Mace (D)
Samuel W. Parker (W)
John L. Robinson (D)

IOWA

Senators

Augustus C. Dodge (D)
George W. Jones (D)

Representatives

Lincoln Clark (D)
Bernhart Henn (D)

KENTUCKY

Senators

Joseph R. Underwood (W)

Henry Clay (W) d. June 1852
David Meriwether (D)
ta. 1852
Archibald Dixon (W) s. 1852

Representatives

John C. Breckinridge (D)
Linn Boyd (D)
Presley U. Ewing (W)
Benjamin E. Grey (W)
Humphrey Marshall (W)
r. Aug. 1852
John C. Mason (D)
William Preston (W) s. 1852
Richard H. Stanton (D)
James W. Stone (D)
William T. Ward (W)
Addison White (W)

LOUISIANA

Senators

Solomon W. Downs (D)
Pierre Soule (SRD)

Representatives

J. Aristide Landry (D)
John Moore (W)
Alexander G. Penn (D)
Louis St. Martin (D)

MAINE

Senators

James W. Bradbury (D)
Hannibal Hamlin (D)

Representatives

Charles Andrews (D)
d. Apr. 1852
John Appleton (D)
Thomas J. D. Fuller (D)
Robert Goodenow (W)
Moses Macdonald (D)
Isaac Reed (W) s. 1852
Ephraim K. Smart (D)
Israel Washburn, Jr. (W)

MARYLAND

Senators

James A. Pearce (W)
Thomas G. Pratt (W)

Representatives

Richard J. Bowie (W)
Joseph S. Cottman (W)
Alexander Evans (W)
William T. Hamilton (D)
Edward Hammond (D)
Thomas Yates Walsh (W)

MASSACHUSETTS

Senators

John Davis (W)
Charles Sumner (D)

Representatives

Charles Allen (Free-Soiler)
William Appleton (W)
George T. Davis (W)
James H. Duncan (W)
Francis B. Fay (W) s. 1852
Orin Fowler (W) d. Dec. 1852
John Z. Goodrich (W)
Edward P. Little (D) s. 1852
Horace Mann (W)
Robert Rantoul, Jr. (D)
d. Aug. 1852
Lorenzo Sabine (W) s. 1852
Zeno Scudder (W)
Benjamin Thompson (W)
d. Sept. 1852

MICHIGAN

Senators

Lewis Cass (D)
Alpheus Felch (D)

Representatives

James L. Conger (W)
Ebenezer J. Penniman (W)
Charles E. Stuart (D)

MISSISSIPPI

Senators

Henry S. Foote (Un) r. Jan. 1852
Walker Brooke (W) s. 1852

Jefferson Davis (D) r. Sept. 1851
John J. McRae (D) ta. 1852
Stephen Adams (D) s. 1852

Representatives

Albert G. Brown (D)
John D. Freeman (Un)
Benjamin D. Nabers (Un)
John A. Wilcox (W)

MISSOURI

Senators

David R. Atchison (W)
Henry S. Geyer (D)

Representatives

John F. Darby (W)
Willard P. Hall (D)
John G. Miller (W)
John S. Phelps (D)
Gilchrist Porter (W)

NEW HAMPSHIRE

Senators

John P. Hale (Anti-Slavery)
Moses Norris, Jr. (D)

Representatives

Harry Hibbard (D)
Charles H. Peaslee (D)
Jared Perkins (W)
Amos Tuck

NEW JERSEY

Senators

Jacob W. Miller (W)
Robert F. Stockton (D)

Representatives

George H. Brown (W)
Rodman M. Price (D)
Charles Skelton (D)
Nathan T. Stratton (D)
Isaac Wildrick (D)

NEW YORK

Senators

William H. Seward (W)
Hamilton Fish (W)

Representatives

Leander Babcock (D)
Henry Bennett (W)
Obadiah Bowne (W)
John H. Boyd (W)
George Briggs (W)
James Brooks (W)
Alexander H. Buell (D)
d. Jan. 1853
Lorenzo Burrows (W)
Gilbert Dean (D)
John G. Floyd (D)
Emanuel B. Hart (D)
Augustus P. Hascall (W)
Solomon G. Haven (W)
J. H. Hobart Haws (W)
Jerediah Horsford (W)
Thomas Y. Howe, Jr. (D)
Willard Ives (D)
Timothy Jenkins (D)
Daniel T. Jones (D)
Preston King (D)
Frederick S. Martin (W)
William Murray (D)
Reuben Robie (D)
Joseph Russell (D)
William A. Sackett (W)
Abraham M. Schermerhorn (W)
John L. Schoolcraft (W)
Marius Schoonmaker (W)
David L. Seymour (D)
William W. Snow (D)
Abraham P. Stephens
Josiah Sutherland (D)
Henry S. Walbridge (W)
John Wells (W)

NORTH CAROLINA

Senators

Willie P. Mangum (W)
George E. Badger (W)

Representatives

William S. Ashe (D)
Joseph P. Caldwell (W)
Thomas L. Clingman (W)
John R. J. Daniel (D)
Alfred Dockery (W)
James T. Morehead (W)
David Outlaw (W)
Edward Stanly (W)
Abraham W. Venable (D)

OHIO

Senators

Salmon P. Chase (D)
Benjamin F. Wade (W)

Representatives

Nelson Barrere (W)
Hiram Bell (W)
George H. Busby (D)
Joseph Cable (D)
Lewis D. Campbell (W)
David K. Cartter (D)
David T. Disney (D)
Alfred P. Edgerton (D)
James M. Gaylord
Joshua R. Giddings (W)
Frederick W. Green (D)
Alexander Harper (W)
William F. Hunter (W)
John Johnson
Eben Newton (W)
Edson B. Olds (D)
Benjamin Stanton (W)
Charles Sweetser (D)
John L. Taylor (W)
Norton S. Townshend (D)
John Welch (W)

PENNSYLVANIA

Senators

James Cooper (W)
Richard Brodhead (D)

Representatives

John Allison (W)
Thomas M. Bibighaus (W)
Joseph R. Chandler (W)
Carlton B. Curtis (D)
John L. Dawson (D)
Milo M. Dimmick (D)
Thomas B. Florence (D)
Henry M. Fuller (W)
James Gamble (D)
Alfred Gilmore (D)
Galusha A. Grow (D)
John W. Howe (W)
Thomas M. Howe (W)
J. Glancy Jones (D)
Joseph H. Kuhns (W)
William H. Kurtz (D)
James X. McLanahan (D)
John McNair (D)
Henry D. Moore (W)
John A. Morrison (D)
Andrew Parker (D)
John Robbins, Jr. (D)
Thomas Ross (D)
Thaddeus Stevens (W)

RHODE ISLAND

Senators

John H. Clarke (W)
Charles T. James (D)

Representatives

George G. King (W)
Benjamin B. Thurston (D)

SOUTH CAROLINA

Senators

Andrew P. Butler (SRD)

R. Barnwell Rhett (D)
r. May 1852
William F. DeSaussure (D) s. 1852

Representatives

William Aiken (D)
Armistead Burt (D)
William F. Colcock (D)
John McQueen (D)
James L. Orr (D)
Daniel Wallace (W)
Joseph A. Woodward (D)

TENNESSEE

Senators

John Bell (W)
James C. Jones (W)

Representatives

William M. Churchwell (D)
William Cullom (W)
Meredith P. Gentry (W)
Isham G.Harris (D)
Andrew Johnson (D)
George W. Jones (D)
William H. Polk (D)
John H. Savage (D)
Frederick P. Stanton (D)
Albert G. Watkins (W)
Christopher H. Williams (W)

TEXAS

Senators

Sam Houston (D)
Thomas J. Rusk (D)

Representatives

Volney E. Howard (D)
Richardson Scurry (D)

VERMONT

Senators

William Upham (W) d. Jan. 1853
Samuel S. Phelps (W) s. 1853

Solomon Foot

Representatives

Thomas Bartlett, Jr. (D)
William Hebard (W)
James Meacham (W)
Ahiman L. Miner (W)

VIRGINIA

Senators

James M. Mason (D)
Robert M. T. Hunter (D)

Representatives

Thomas H. Averett (D)
Thomas H. Bayly (SRD)
James M. H. Beale (D)
Thomas S. Bocock (D)
John S. Caskie (D)
Sherrard Clemens (D) s. 1852
Henry A. Edmundson (D)
Charles J. Faulkner
Alexander R. Holladay (D)
John Letcher (D)
Fayette McMullen (D)
Richard K. Meade (D)
John S. Millson (D)
Paulus Powell (D)
James F. Strother (W)
George W. Thompson (D)
r. July 1852

WISCONSIN

Senators

Henry Dodge (D)
Isaac P. Walker (D)

Representatives

James D. Doty (Free-Soiler)
Charles Durkee (Free-Soiler)
Ben C. Eastman (D)

THIRTY-THIRD CONGRESS

March 4, 1853 to March 3, 1855

President of The Senate: William R. King
Presidents Pro Tempore of The Senate: David R. Atchison
Lewis Cass
Jesse D. Bright
Speaker of The House of Representatives: Linn Boyd

ALABAMA

Senators

Benjamin Fitzpatrick (SRD)
Clement Claiborne Clay (D)

Representatives

James Abercrombie (W)
Williamson R. W. Cobb (D)
James F. Dowdell (SRD)
Sampson W. Harris (D)
George S. Houston (D)
Philip Phillips (D)
William R. Smith (W)

ARKANSAS

Senators

William K. Sebastian (D)

Solon Borland (D) r. Apr. 1853
Robert W. Johnson (D)
s. 1853

Representatives

Alfred B. Greenwood (D)
Edward A. Warren (D)

CALIFORNIA

Senators

William M. Gwin (D)
John B. Weller (D)

Representatives

Milton S. Latham (D)
James A. McDougall (D)

CONNECTICUT

Senators

Truman Smith (W) r. May 1854
Francis Gillette (W) s. 1854

Isaac Toucey (D)

Representatives

Nathan Belcher (D)
Colin M. Ingeroll (D)
James T.Pratt (D)
Origen S. Seymour (D)

DELAWARE

Senators

James A. Bayard (D)
John M. Clayton (W)

Representative

George R. Riddle (D)

FLORIDA

Senators

Jackson Morton (W)
Stephen R. Mallory (D)

Representative

Augustus E. Maxwell (D)

GEORGIA

Senators

William C. Dawson (SRW)
Robert Toombs (SRD)

Representatives

David J. Bailey (SRD)
Elijah W. Chastain (D)
Alfred H. Colquitt (D)
William B. W. Dent (D)
Junius Hillyer (D)
David A. Reese (W)
James L. Seward (D)
Alexander H. Stephens (D)

ILLINOIS

Senators

Stephen A. Douglas (D)
James Shields (D)

Representatives

James C. Allen (D)
Willis Allen (D)
William H. Bissell (D)
James Knox (W)
Jesse O. Norton
William A. Richardson (D)
Elihu B. Washburne (W)
John Wentworth (D)
Richard Yates (W)

INDIANA

Senators

Jesse D. Bright (D)
John Pettit (D)

Representatives

Ebenezer M. Chamberlain (D)
John G. Davis (D)
Cyrus L. Dunham (D)
Norman Eddy (D)
William H. English (D)
Andrew J. Harlan (D)
Thomas A. Hendricks (D)
James H. Lane (D)
Daniel Mace (D)
Smith Miller (D)
Samuel W. Parker (W)

IOWA

Senators

Augustus C. Dodge (D)
George W. Jones (D)

Representatives

John P. Cook (W)
Bernhart Henn (D)

KENTUCKY

Senators

Archibald Dixon (W)
John B. Thompson (W)

Representatives

Linn Boyd (D)
John C. Breckinridge (D)
Francis M. Bristow (W) s. 1854
James S. Chrisman (D)
Leander M. Cox (W)
John M. Elliott (D)
Presley U. Ewing (W)
d. Sept. 1854
Benjamin E. Grey (W)
Clement S. Hill (D)
William Preston (W)
Richard H. Stanton (D)

LOUISIANA

Senators

Pierre Soule (SRD) r 1853
John Slidell (SRD) s. 1853

Judah P. Benjamin (W)

Representatives

William Dunbar (D)
Theodore G. Hunt (W)
Roland Jones (D)
John Perkins, Jr. (D)

MAINE

Senators

Hannibal Hamlin (D)
William P. Fessenden (W) s. 1854

Representatives

Samuel P. Benson (W)
E. Wilder Farley (W)
Thomas J. D. Fuller (D)
Moses Macdonald (D)
Samuel Mayall (D)
Israel Washburn, Jr. (W)

MARYLAND

Senators

James A. Pearce (W)
Thomas G. Pratt (W)

Representatives

John R. Franklin (W)
William T. Hamilton (D)
Henry May (D)
Jacob Shower
Augustus R. Sollers (W)
Joshua Van Sant (D)

MASSACHUSETTS

Senators

Charles Sumner (D)

Edward Everett (R) r. June 1854
Julius Rockwell (R) ta. 1854
Henry Wilson (Free-Soiler) s. 1855

Representatives

William Appleton (W)
Nathaniel P. Banks (D)
Samuel L. Crocker (W)
Alexander De Witt (Amer)
Edward Dickinson (W)
J. Wiley Edmands (W)
Thomas D. Eliot s. 1854
John Z. Goodrich (W)
Zeno Scudder (W) r. Mar. 1854
Charles W. Upham (W)
Samuel H. Walley (W)
Tappan Wentworth (W)

MICHIGAN

Senators

Lewis Cass (D)
Charles E. Stuart (D)

Representatives

Samuel Clark (D)
David A. Noble (D)
Hestor L. Stevens (D)
David Stuart (D)

MISSISSIPPI

Senators

Stephen Adams (D)
Albert G. Brown (D) s. 1854

Representatives

William Barksdale (SRD)
William T. S. Barry (D)
Wiley P. Harris (D)
Otho R. Singleton (D)
Daniel B. Wright (D)

MISSOURI

Senators

David R. Atchison (W)
Henry S. Geyer (D)

Representatives

Thomas H. Benton (D)
Samuel Caruthers (W)
Alfred W. Lamb (D)
James J. Lindley (W)
John G. Miller (W)
Mordecai Oliver (W)
John S. Phelps (D)

NEW HAMPSHIRE

Senators

Moses Norris, Jr. (D) d. Jan. 1855
John S. Wells (D) s. 1855

Charles G. Atherton (D) d. Nov. 1853
Jared W. Williams (D) s. 1853

Representatives

Harry Hibbard (D)
George W. Kittredge (D)
George W. Morrison (D)

NEW JERSEY

Senators

John R. Thomson (D)
William Wright (D)

Representatives

Samuel Lilly (D)
Alexander C. M. Pennington (W)
Charles Skelton (D)
Nathan T. Stratton (D)
George Vail (D)

NEW YORK

Senators

William H. Seward (W)
Hamilton Fish (W)

Representatives

Henry Bennet (W)
Davis Carpenter (W)
George W. Chase (W)
Thomas W. Cumming (D)
Francis B. Cutting (D)
Gilbert Dean (D) r. July 1854
Reuben E. Fenton
Thomas T. Flagler (W)
Henry C. Goodwin s. 1854
George Hastings (D)
Solomon G. Haven (W)
Charles Hughes (D)
Daniel T. Jones (D)
Caleb Lyon (D)
Orsamus B. Matteson (W)
James Maurice (D)
Edwin B. Morgan (D)
William Murray (D)
Andrew Oliver (D)
Jared V. Peck (D)
Rufus W. Peckham (D)
Bishop Perkins (D)
Benjamin Pringle (W)
Peter Rowe (D)
Russell Sage (W)
George A. Simmons (W)
Gerrit Smith (Abolitionist) r. Aug. 1854
John J. Taylor (D)
Isaac Teller (D) s. 1854
William M. Tweed (D)
Hiram Walbridge (D)
William A. Walker (D)
Mike Walsh (D)
Theodore R. Westbrook (D)
John Wheeler (D)

NORTH CAROLINA

Senators

George E. Badger (W)
David S. Reid (D) s. 1854

Representatives

William S. Ashe (D)
Thomas L. Clingman (W)
F. Burton Craige (D)
John Kerr, Jr. (W)
Richard C. Puryear (W)
Sion H. Rogers (W)
Thomas Ruffin (D)
Henry M. Shaw (D)

OHIO

Senators

Salmon P. Chase (D)
Benjamin F. Wade (W)

Representatives

Edward Ball (W)
George Bliss (D)
Lewis D. Campbell (W)
Moses B. Corwin (W)
David T. Disney (D)
Alfred P. Edgerton (D)
Andrew Ellison (D)
Joshua R. Giddings (W)
Frederick W. Green (D)
Aaron Harlan (W)
John Scott Harrison (W)
Harvey H. Johnson (D)
William D. Lindsley (D)
Matthias H. Nichols (W)
Edson B. Olds (D)
Thomas Ritchey (D)
William R. Sapp (W)
Wilson Shannon (D)
Andrew Stuart (D)
John L. Taylor (W)
Edward Wade (W)

PENNSYLVANIA

Senators

James Cooper (W)
Richard Brodhead (D)

Representatives

Samuel A. Bridges (D)
Joseph R. Chandler (W)
Carlton B. Curtis (D)
John L. Dawson (D)
John Dick (W)
Augustus Drum (D)
William Everhart (W)
Thomas B. Florence (D)
James Gamble (D)
Galusha A. Grow (D)
Isaac E. Hiester (W)
Thomas M. Howe (W)
J. Glancy Jones (D) s. 1854
William H. Kurtz (D)
John McCulloch (W)
John McNair (D)
Ner Middleswarth (W)
Henry A. Muhlenberg (D) d. Jan. 1854
Asa Packer (D)
David Ritchie
John Robbins, Jr. (D)
Samuel L. Russell (W)
Christian M. Straub (D)
Michael C. Trout (D)
William H. Witte (D)
Hendrick B. Wright (D)

RHODE ISLAND

Senators

Charles T. James (D)
Philip Allen (D)

Representatives

Thomas Davis (D)
Benjamin B. Thurston (D)

SOUTH CAROLINA

Senators

Andrew P. Butler (SRD)
Josiah J. Evans (SRD)

Representatives

William Aiken (D)
William W. Boyce (SRD)
Preston S. Brooks (SRD)
Laurence M. Keitt (D)
John McQueen
James L. Orr (D)

TENNESSEE

Senators

John Bell (W)
James C. Jones (W)

Representatives

Robert M. Bugg (W)
William M. Churchwell (D)
William Cullom (W)
Emerson Etheridge (W)
George W. Jones (D)
Charles Ready (W)
Samuel A. Smith (D)
Frederick P. Stanton (D)
Nathaniel G. Taylor (W) s. 1854
Felix K. Zollicoffer (SRW)

TEXAS

Senators

Sam Houston (D)
Thomas J. Rusk (D)

Representatives

Peter H. Bell (D)
George W. Smyth

VERMONT

Senators

Solomon Foot

Samuel S. Phelps (W) r. Mar. 1854
Lawrence Brainerd (W) s. 1854

Representatives

James Meacham (W)
Alvah Sabin (W)
Andrew Tracy (W)

VIRGINIA

Senators

James M. Mason (D)
Robert M. T. Hunter (D)

Representatives

Thomas H. Bayly (SRD)
Thomas S. Bocock (D)
John S. Caskie (D)
Henry A. Edmundson (D)
Charles J. Faulkner
William O. Goode (D)
Zedekiah Kidwell (D)
John Letcher (D)
Charles S. Lewis (D) s. 1854
Fayette McMullen (D)
John S. Millson (D)
Paulus Powell (D)
William Smith (D)
John F. Snodgrass d. June 1854

WISCONSIN

Senators

Henry Dodge (D)
Isaac P. Walker (D)

Representatives

Ben C. Eastman (D)
John B. Macy (D)
Daniel Wells, Jr. (D)

FLORIDA

Senators

Stephen R. Mallory (D)
David Levy Yulee (D)

Representative

Augustus E. Maxwell (D)

GEORGIA

Senators

Robert Toombs (SRD)
Alfred Iverson (D)

Representatives

Martin J. Crawford (D)
Howell Cobb (D)
Nathaniel G. Foster (Amer)
John H. Lumpkin (D)
James L. Seward (D)
Alexander H. Stephens (D)
Robert P. Trippe (W)
Hiram Warner (D)

ILLINOIS

Senators

Stephen A. Douglas (D)
Lyman Trumbull (R)

Representatives

James C. Allen (D) s. 1856
Jacob C. Davis (D) s. 1856
Thomas L. Harris (D)
James Knox (W)
Samuel S. Marshall (D)
James L. D. Morrison (D) s. 1856
Jesse O. Norton
William A. Richardson (D) r. Aug. 1856
Elihu B. Washburne (W)
James H. Woodworth

INDIANA

Senators

Jesse D. Bright (D)
Graham N. Fitch (D) s. 1857

Representatives

Lucien Barbour (Free-Soiler)
Samuel Brenton (W)
Schuyler Colfax (R)
William Cumback
George G. Dunn
William H. English (D)
David P. Holloway (People's Party)
Daniel Mace (D)
Smith Miller (D)
John U. Pettit (R)
Harvey D. Scott

IOWA

Senators

George W. Jones (D)
James Harlan (W) s. 1857

Representatives

Augustus Hall (D)
James Thorington (W)

KENTUCKY

Senators

John B. Thompson (W)
John J. Crittenden (Un)

Representatives

Henry C. Burnett (D)
John P. Campbell, Jr. (Amer)
Leander M. Cox (Amer)
John M. Elliott (D)
Joshua H. Jewett (D)
Alexander K. Marshall (Amer)
Humphrey Marshall (Amer)
Samuel F. Swope (Amer)
Albert G. Talbott (D)
Warner L. Underwood (Amer)

LOUISIANA

Senators

Judah P. Benjamin (W)
John Slidell (SRD)

Representatives

Thomas G. Davidson (D)
George Eustis, Jr. (Amer)
John M. Sandidge (D)
Miles Taylor (D)

MAINE

Senators

Hannibal Hamlin (D) r. Jan. 1857
Amos Nourse s. 1857

William P. Fessenden (W)

Representatives

Samuel P. Benson
Thomas J. D. Fuller (D)
Ebenezer Knowlton
John J. Perry
Israel Washburn, Jr.
John M. Wood

MARYLAND

Senators

James A. Pearce (W)
Thomas G. Pratt (W)

Representatives

Thomas F. Bowie (D)
H. Winter Davis (Amer)
J. Morrison Harris (Amer)
Henry W. Hoffman (Amer)
James B. Ricaud (Amer)
James A. Stewart (D)

MASSACHUSETTS

Senators

Charles Sumner
Henry Wilson (Free-Soiler)

THIRTY-FOURTH CONGRESS

March 4, 1855 to March 3, 1857

President of The Senate:	Vacant
Presidents Pro Tempore of The Senate:	Jesse D. Bright
	Charles E. Stuart
	James M. Mason
Speaker of The House of Representatives:	Nathaniel P. Banks

ALABAMA

Senators

Clement Claiborne Clay (D)
Benjamin Fitzpatrick (SRD)

Representatives

Williamson R. W. Cobb (D)
James F. Dowdell (SRD)
Sampson W. Harris (D)
George S. Houston (D)
Eli S. Shorter (D)
William R. Smith (Amer)
Percy Walker (Amer)

ARKANSAS

Senators

William K. Sebastian (D)
Robert W. Johnson (D)

Representatives

Alfred B. Greenwood (SRD)
Albert Rust (D)

CALIFORNIA

Senators

John B. Weller (D)
William M. Gwin (D) s. 1857

Representatives

James W. Denver (D)
Philemon T. Herbert (D)

CONNECTICUT

Senators

Isaac Toucey (D)
Lafayette S. Foster (R)

Representatives

Ezra Clark, Jr. (Amer)
Sidney Dean (Amer)
William W. Welch (Amer)
John Woodruff (Amer)

DELAWARE

Senators

James A. Bayard (D)

John M. Clayton (W) d. Nov. 1856
Joseph P. Comegys (W) s. 1856
Martin W. Bates (D) s. 1857

Representative

Elisha D. Cullen (Amer)

Representatives

Nathaniel P. Banks (Amer)
James Buffinton (Amer)
Anson Burlingame (Amer)
Calvin C. Chaffee (Amer)
Linus B. Comins (Amer)
Timothy Davis (Amer)
William S. Damrell (Amer)
Alexander De Witt (Amer)
Robert B. Hall (Amer)
Chauncey L. Knapp (Amer)
Mark Trafton (Amer)

MICHIGAN

Senators

Lewis Cass (D)
Charles E. Stuart (D)

Representatives

William A. Howard
George W. Peck (D)
David S. Walbridge
Henry Waldron

MISSISSIPPI

Senators

Stephen Adams (D)
Albert G. Brown (D)

Representatives

William Barksdale (SRD)
Hendley S. Bennett (D)
William A. Lake (W)
John A. Quitman (D)
Daniel B. Wright (D)

MISSOURI

Senators

Henry S. Geyer (D)
James S. Green (D) s. 1857

Representatives

Thomas P. Akers (Amer)
s. 1856
Samuel Caruthers (W)
Luther M. Kennett (Amer)
James J. Lindley (W)
Mordecai Oliver (W)
John S. Phelps (D)
Gilchrist Porter (W)

NEW HAMPSHIRE

Senators

John P. Hale
James Bell (W)

Representatives

Aaron H. Cragin (Amer)
James Pike (Amer)
Mason W. Tappan (R)

NEW JERSEY

Senators

John R. Thompson (D)
William Wright (D)

Representatives

James Bishop (W)
Isaiah D. Clawson (W)
Alexander C. M. Pennington (W)
George R. Robbins (W)
George Vail (D)

NEW YORK

Senators

William H. Seward (R)
Hamilton Fish (W)

Representatives

Henry Bennett (W)
Bayard Clarke (Amer)
Samuel Dickson (W)
Edward Dodd (W)
Francis S. Edwards (Amer)
r. Feb. 1857
Thomas T. Flagler (W)
William A. Gilbert (W)
r. Feb. 1857
Amos P. Granger (W)
Solomon G. Haven (W)
Thomas R. Horton
Jonas A. Hughston (W)
John Kelly (D)
William H. Kelsey (W)
Rufus H. King (W)
Andrew Z. McCarty (W)
Orsamus B. Matteson (W)
r. Feb. 1857
Killian Miller (W)
Edwin B. Morgan (D)
Ambrose S. Murray
Andrew Oliver (D)
John M. Parker (W)
Guy R. Pelton (W)
Benjamin Pringle (W)
Russell Sage (W)
George A. Simmons (W)
Francis E. Spinner (D)
James S. T. Stranahan (W)
William W. Valk (Amer.)
Abram Wakeman (W)
John Wheeler (D)
Thomas R. Whitney (Amer)
John Williams (D)

NORTH CAROLINA

Senators

David S. Reid (D)
Asa Biggs (D)

Representatives

Lawrence O'B. Branch (D)
Thomas L. Clingman (W)
F. Burton Craige (D)
Robert T. Paine (Amer)
Richard C. Puryear (W)
Edwin G. Reade (Amer)
Thomas Ruffin (D)
Warren Winslow (D)

OHIO

Senators

Benjamin F. Wade (W)
George E. Pugh (D)

Representatives

Charles J. Albright
Edward Ball (W)
John A. Bingham
Philemon Bliss
Lewis D. Campbell (W)
Timothy C. Day
Jonas R. Emrie
Samuel Galloway
Joshua R. Giddings (W)
Aaron Harlan (W)
John Scott Harrison (W)
Valentine B. Horton (W)
Benjamin F. Leiter
Oscar F. Moore
Richard Mott
Matthias H. Nichols
William R. Sapp (W)
John Sherman
Benjamin Stanton (W)
Edward Wade (W)
Cooper K. Watson (Free-Soiler)

PENNSYLVANIA

Senators

Richard Brodhead (D)
William Bigler (D) s. 1856

Representatives

John Allison (W)
David Barclay (D)
Samuel C. Bradshaw (W)
Jacob Broom
John Cadwalader (D)
James H. Campbell (W)
John Covode (W)
John Dick
John R. Edie (W)
Thomas B. Florence (D)
Henry M. Fuller (W)
Galusha A. Grow (D)
John Hickman (D)
J. Glancy Jones (D)
Jonathan Knight (W)
John C. Kunkel (W)
William Millward (W)
Asa Packer (D)
John J. Pearce (W)
Samuel A. Purviance (W)
David Ritchie
Anthony E. Roberts (W)
David F. Robison (W)
Lemuel Todd
Job R. Tyson (W)

RHODE ISLAND

Senators

Charles T. James (D)
Philip Allen (D)

Representatives

Nathaniel B. Durfee (Amer)
Benjamin B. Thurston (D)

SOUTH CAROLINA

Senators

Andrew P. Butler (SRD)
Josiah J. Evans (SRD)

Representatives

William Aiken (D)
William W. Boyce (SRD)
Preston S. Brooks (SRD)
d. Jan. 1857
Laurence M. Keitt (D)
John McQueen (D)
James L. Orr (D)

TENNESSEE

Senators

John Bell (W)
James C. Jones (W)

Representatives

Emerson Etheridge (W)
George W. Jones (D)
Charles Ready (W)
Thomas Rivers (Amer)
John H. Savage
Samuel A. Smith (D)
William H. Sneed (Amer)
Albert G. Watkins (D)
John V. Wright (D)
Felix K. Zollicoffer (SRW)

TEXAS

Senators

Sam Houston (D)
Thomas J. Rusk (D)

Representatives

Lemuel D. Evans (Amer)
Peter H. Bell (D)

VERMONT

Senators

Solomon Foot (R)
Jacob Collamer (R)

Representatives

George T. Hodges
James Meacham (W) d. Aug. 1856
Justin S. Morrill (W)
Alvah Sabin (W)

VIRGINIA

Senators

James M. Mason (D)
Robert M. T. Hunter (D)

Representatives

Thomas H. Bayly (SRD)
d. June 1856
Thomas S. Bocock (D)
John S. Carlile (Amer.)
John S. Caskie (D)
Henry A. Edmundson (D)
Charles J. Faulkner
Muscoe R. H. Garnett (D)
s. 1856
William O. Goode (D)
Zedekiah Kidwell (D)
John Letcher (D)
Fayette McMullen (D)
John S. Millson (D)
Paulus Powell (D)
William Smith (D)

WISCONSIN

Senators

Henry Dodge (D)
Charles Durkee

Representatives

Charles Billingshurst
Cadwallader C. Washburn
Daniel Wells, Jr. (D)

THIRTY-FIFTH CONGRESS

March 4, 1857 to March 3, 1859

President of The Senate: John C. Breckinridge
Presidents Pro Tempore of The Senate: James M. Mason
Thomas J. Rusk
Benjamin Fitzpatrick
Speaker of The House of Representatives: James L. Orr

ALABAMA

Senators

Benjamin Fitzpatrick (SRD)
Clement Claiborne Clay (D)

Representatives

Williamson R. W. Cobb (D)
Jabez L. M. Curry (SRD)
James F. Dowdell (SRD)
George S. Houston (D)
Sydenham Moore (D)
Eli S. Shorter (D)
James A. Stallworth (D)

ARKANSAS

Senators

William K. Sebastian (D)
Robert W. Johnson (D)

Representatives

Alfred B. Greenwood (D)
Edward A. Warren (D)

CALIFORNIA

Senators

William M. Gwin (D)
David C. Broderick (D)

Representatives

Joseph C. McKibbin (D)
Charles L. Scott (D)

CONNECTICUT

Senators

Lafayette S. Foster (R)
James Dixon (R)

Representatives

Samuel Arnold (D)
William D. Bishop (D)
Ezra Clark, Jr. (R)
Sidney Dean (R)

DELAWARE

Senators

James A. Bayard (D)
Martin W. Bates (D)

Representative

William G. Whiteley (D)

FLORIDA

Senators

Stephen R. Mallory (D)
David Levy Yulee (D)

Representative

George S. Hawkins (D)

GEORGIA

Senators

Robert Toombs (SRD)
Alfred Iverson (D)

Representatives

Martin J. Crawford (D)
Lucius J. Gartrell (D)
Joshua Hill (Amer)
James Jackson (D)
James L. Seward (D)
Alexander H. Stephens (D)
Robert P. Trippe (W)
Augustus R. Wright (D)

ILLINOIS

Senators

Stephen A. Douglas (D)
Lyman Trumbull (R)

Representatives

John F. Farnsworth (R)
Thomas L. Harris (D)
d. Nov. 1858
Charles D. Hodges (D) s. 1859
William Kellogg (R)
Owen Lovejoy (R)
Samuel S. Marshall (D)
Isaac N. Morris (D)
Aaron Shaw (D)
Robert Smith (D)
Elihu B. Washburne (W)

INDIANA

Senators

Jesse D. Bright (D)
Graham N. Fitch (D)

Representatives

Samuel Brenton (W)
d. Mar. 1857
Charles Case (D)
Schuyler Colfax (R)
John G. Davis (D)
William H. English
James B. Foley (D)
James M. Gregg (D)
James Hughes (D)
David Kilgore (R)
James Lockhart (D)
d. Sept. 1857
William E. Niblack (D)
John U. Pettit (R)
James Wilson (R)

IOWA

Senators

George W. Jones (D)
James Harlan (R)

Representatives

Samuel R. Curtis (R)
Timothy Davis (W)

KENTUCKY

Senators

John B. Thompson (W)
John J. Crittenden (Un)

Representatives

Henry C. Burnett (D)
James B. Clay (D)
John M. Elliott (D)
Joshua H. Jewett (D)
Humphrey Marshall (Amer)
John C. Mason (D)
Samuel O. Peyton (D)
John W. Stevenson (D)
Albert G. Talbott (D)
Warner L. Underwood (Amer)

LOUISIANA

Senators

Judah P. Benjamin (W)
John Slidell (SRD)

Representatives

Thomas G. Davison (D)
George Eustis, Jr. (Amer)
John M. Sandidge (D)
Miles Taylor (D)

MAINE

Senators

William P. Fessenden (W)
Hannibal Hamlin (D)

Representatives

Nehemiah Abbott (R)
Stephen C. Foster (R)
Charles J. Gilman (R)
Freeman H. Morse (R)
Israel Washburn, Jr. (R)
John M. Wood (R)

MARYLAND

Senators

James A. Pearce (W)
Anthony Kennedy (Un.)

Representatives

Thomas F. Bowie (D)
H. Winter Davis (R)
J. Morrison Harris (Amer)
Jacob M. Kunkel (D)
James B. Ricaud (Amer)
James A. Stewart (D)

MASSACHUSETTS

Senators

Charles Sumner (R)
Henry Wilson (Free-Soiler)

Representatives

Nathaniel P. Banks (R)
r. Dec. 1857
James Buffinton (R)
Anson Burlingame (Amer)
Calvin C. Chaffee (Amer)
Linus B. Comins (R)
William S. Damrell (R)
Timothy Davis (R)
Henry L. Dawes
Daniel W. Gooch (R) s. 1858
Robert B. Hall (R)
Chauncey L. Knapp
Eli Thayer (R)

MICHIGAN

Senators

Charles E. Stuart (D)
Zachariah Chandler (R)

Representatives

William A. Howard (R)
DeWitt C. Leach (R)
David S. Walbridge (R)
Henry Waldron (R)

MINNESOTA

Senators

Henry M. Rice (D) s. 1858
James Shields s. 1858

Representatives

James M. Cavanaugh (D)
William W. Phelps (D)

MISSISSIPPI

Senators

Albert G. Brown (D)
Jefferson Davis (D)

Representatives

William Barksdale (SRD)
Reuben Davis (D)
Lucius Q. C. Lamar (D)
John J. McRae (SRD) s. 1858
John A. Quitman (D)
d. July 1858
Otho R. Singleton

MISSOURI

Senators

James S. Green (D)
Trusten Polk (D)

Representatives

Thomas L. Anderson (Amer)
Francis P. Blair, Jr. (Free-Soiler)
Samuel Caruthers (D)
John B. Clark (D)
James Craig (D)
John S. Phelps (D)
Samuel H. Woodson (Amer)

NEW HAMPSHIRE

Senators

James Bell (W) d. May 1857
Daniel Clark (R)

John P. Hale

Representatives

Aaron H. Cragin (R)
James Pike (Amer.)
Mason W. Tappan (R)

NEW JERSEY

Senators

John R. Thomson (D)
William Wright (D)

Representatives

Garnett B. Adrain (D)
Isaiah D. Clawson (W)
John Huyler (D)
George R. Robbins (W)
Jacob R. Wortendyke (D)

NEW YORK

Senators

William H. Seward (R)
Preston King (R)

Representatives

Samuel G. Andrews (R)
Thomas J. Barr (D) s. 1859
Henry Bennett (W)
Silas M. Burroughs (R)
Horace F. Clark (D)
Clark B. Cochrane (R)
John Cochrane (SRD)
Erastus Corning (D)
Edward Dodd (W)
Reuben E. Genton (R)
Henry C. Goodwin (R)
Amos P. Granger (W)
John B. Haskin (D)
Israel T. Hatch (D)
Charles B. Hoard (R)
John Kelly (D) r. Dec. 1858
William H. Kelsey (W)
William B. Maclay (D)
Orsamus B. Matteson (W)
Edwin B. Morgan (R)
Oliver A. Morse (R)
Ambrose S. Murray (R)
Abram B. Olin (R)
George W. Palmer (R)
John M. Parker (W)
Emory P. Pottle (R)
William F. Russell (D)
John A. Searing (D)
Judson W. Sherman (R)
Daniel E. Sickles (D)
Francis E. Spinner (R)
George Taylor (D)
John Thompson (R)
Elijah Ward (D)

NORTH CAROLINA

Senators

David S. Reid (D)

Asa Biggs (D) r. May 1858
Thomas L. Clingman (D)
s. 1858

Representatives

Lawrence O.B. Branch (D)
Thomas L. Clingman (W)
r. May 1858
F. Burton Craige (D)
John A. Gilmer (Amer)
Thomas Ruffin (D)
Alfred M. Scales (D)
Henry M. Shaw (D)
Zebulon B. Vance (D)
s. Dec. 1858
Warren Winslow (D)

OHIO

Senators

Benjamin F. Wade (R)
George E. Pugh (D)

Representatives

John A. Bingham (R)
Philemon Bliss (R)
Joseph Burns (D)
Lewis D. Campbell (W)
r. May 1858
Joseph R. Cockerill (D)
Samuel S. Cox (D)
Joshua R. Giddings (W)
William S. Groesbeck (D)
Lawrence W. Hall (D)
Aaron Harlan (W)
Valentine B. Horton (W)
William Lawrence (D)
Benjamin F. Leiter (R)
Joseph Miller (D)
Richard Mott (R)
Matthias H. Nichols (R)
George H. Pendleton (D)
John Sherman (R)
Benjamin Stanton (W)
Cydnor B. Tompkins (R)
Clement L. Vallandigham (D)
s. 1858
Edward Wade (R)

OREGON

Senators

Joseph Lane (D) s. 1859
Delazon Smith (D) s. 1859

Representative

La Fayette Grover (D) s. 1859

PENNSYLVANIA

Senators

William Bigler (D)
Simon Cameron (D)

Representatives

John A. Ahl (D)
Henry Chapman (D)
John Covode (R)
William L. Dewart (D)
John Dick (R)
William H. Dimmick (D)
John R. Edie (W)
Thomas B. Florence (D)
James L. Gillis (D)
Galusha A. Grow (R)
John Hickman (D)
J. Glancy Jones (D) r. Oct. 1858
Owen Jones (D)
William H. Keim (D) s. 1858
John C. Kunkel (W)
James Landy (D)
Paul Leidy (D)
William Montgomery (D)
Edward Joy Morris (W)
Henry M. Phillips (D)
Samuel A. Purviance (W)
Wilson Reilly (D)
David Ritchie (R)
Anthony E. Roberts (W)
William Stewart (R)
Allison White (D)

RHODE ISLAND

Senators

Philip Allen (D)
James F. Simmons

Representatives

William D. Brayton (R)
Nathaniel B. Durfee (R)

SOUTH CAROLINA

Senators

Andrew P. Butler (SRD)
d. May 1857
James H. Hammond (SRD) s. 1857

Josiah J. Evans (SRD) d. May 1858
Arthur P. Hayne (D) ta. 1858
James Chesnut, Jr. (SRD) s. 1859

Representatives

Milledge L. Bonham (SRD)
William W. Boyce (SRD)
Laurence M. Keitt (D)
W. Porcher Miles (D)
John McQueen (D)
James L. Orr (D)

TENNESSEE

Senators

John Bell (W)
Andrew Johnson (D)

Representatives

John D. C. Atkins (D)
William T. Avery (D)
George W. Jones (D)
Horace Maynard (Amer)
Charles Ready (W)
John H. Savage (D)
Samuel A. Smith (D)
Albert G. Watkins (D)
John V. Wright (D)
Felix K. Zollicoffer (SRW)

TEXAS

Senators

Sam Houston (D)

Thomas J. Rusk (D) d. July 1857
J. Pinckney Henderson ta. 1857
Matthias Ward (D) s. 1858

Representatives

Guy M. Bryan (D)
John H. Reagan (D)

VERMONT

Senators

Solomon Foot (R)
Jacob Collamer (R)

Representatives

Justin S. Morrill (W)
Homer E. Royce (R)
Eliakim P. Walton (R)

VIRGINIA

Senators

James M. Mason (D)
Robert M. T. Hunter (D)

Representatives

Thomas S. Bocock (D)
John S. Caskie (D)
Sherrard Clemens (D)
Henry A. Edmundson (D)
Charles J. Faulkner
Muscoe R. H. Garnett (D)
William O. Goode (D)
George W. Hopkins (D)
Albert G. Jenkins (D)
John Letcher (D)
John S. Millson (D)
Paulus Powell (D)
William Smith (D)

WISCONSIN

Senators

Charles Durkee (R)
James R. Doolittle (R)

Representatives

Charles Billinghurst (R)
John F. Potter (R)
Cadwallader C. Washburn (R)

THIRTY-SIXTH CONGRESS

March 4, 1859 to March 3, 1861

President of The Senate: John C. Breckinridge
Presidents Pro Tempore of The Senate: Benjamin Fitzpatrick
Jesse D. Bright
Solomon Foot
Speaker of The House of Representatives: William Pennington

ALABAMA

Senators

Benjamin Fitzpatrick (SRD)
Clement Claiborne Clay (D)

Representatives

David Clopton (SRD)
Williamson R. W. Cobb (D)
r. Jan. 1861
Jabez L. M. Curry (SRD)
George S. Houston (D)
Sydenham Moore (D)
James L. Pugh (D)
James A. Stallworth (D)

ARKANSAS

Senators

William K. Sebastian (D)
Robert W. Johnson (D)

Representatives

Thomas C. Hindman (D)
Albert Rust (D)

CALIFORNIA

Senators

William M. Gwin (D)

David C. Broderick (D)
d. Sept. 1859
Henry P. Haun (D) ta. 1859
Milton S. Latham (D) s. 1860

Representatives

John C. Burch (D)
Charles L. Scott (D)

CONNECTICUT

Senators

Lafayette S. Foster (R)
James Dixon (R)

Representatives

Alfred A. Burnham (R)
Orris S. Ferry (R)
Dwight Loomis (R)
John Woodruff (Amer)

DELAWARE

Senators

James A. Bayard (D)
Willard Saulsbury (D)

Representative

William G. Whitely (D)

FLORIDA

Senators

Stephen R. Mallory (D)
David Levy Yulee (D)

Representative

George S. Hawkins (D)

GEORGIA

Senators

Robert Toombs, (SRD)
r. Feb. 1861
Alfred Iverson (D) r. Jan. 1861

Representatives

Martin J. Crawford (D)
Lucius J. Gartrell (D)
Thomas Hardeman, Jr. (D)
Joshua Hill (Amer.)
r. Jan. 1861
James Jackson (D)
John J. Jones (D)
Peter E. Love (D)
John W. H. Underwood (D)

ILLINOIS

Senators

Stephen A. Douglas (D)
Lyman Trumbull (R)

Representatives

John F. Farnsworth (R)
Philip B. Fouke (D)
William Kellogg (R)
John A. Logan (D)
Owen Lovejoy (R)
John A. McClernand (D)
Isaac N. Morris (D)
James C. Robinson (D)
Elihu B. Washburne (W)

INDIANA

Senators

Jesse D. Bright (D)
Graham N. Fitch (D)

Representatives

Charles Case (D)
Schuyler Colfax (R)
John G. Davis (D)
William McK. Dunn (R)
William H. English (D)
William S. Holman (D)
David Kilgore (R)
William E. Niblack (D)
John U. Pettit (R)
Albert G. Porter (R)
James Wilson (R)

IOWA

Senators

James Harlan (F)
James W. Grimes (R)

Representatives

Samuel R. Curtis (R)
William Vandever (R)

KANSAS

Senators

Vacant
Vacant

Representative

Martin F. Conway (R)

KENTUCKY

Senators

John J. Crittenden (Un)
Lazarus W. Powell (D)

Representatives

Green Adams (Amer)
William C. Anderson (Amer)
Francis M. Bristow (W)
John Y. Brown (D)
Henry C. Burnett (D)
Robert Mallory (D)
Laban T. Moore (Amer)
Samuel O. Peyton (D)
William E. Simms (D)
John W. Stevenson (D)

LOUISIANA

Senators

Judah P. Benjamin (W)
John Slidell (SRD)

Representatives

John E. Bouligny (Amer)
Thomas G. Davidson (D)
John M. Landrum (D)
Miles Taylor (D)

MAINE

Senators

William P. Fessenden (W)

Hannibal Hamlin (D)
r. Jan. 1861
Lot M. Morrill (R) s. 1861

Representatives

Stephen Coburn (R) s. 1861
Stephen C. Foster (R)
Ezra B. French (R)
Freeman H. Morse (R)
John J. Perry (R)
Daniel E. Somes (R)
Israel Washburn, Jr. (R)
r. Jan. 1861

MARYLAND

Senators

James A. Pearce (W)
Anthony Kennedy (Un.)

Representatives

H. Winter Davis (R)
J. Morrison Harris (Amer)
George W. Hughes (D)
Jacob M. Kunkel (D)
James A. Stewart (D)
Edwin H. Webster (R)

MASSACHUSETTS

Senators

Charles Sumner (R)
Henry Wilson

Representatives

Charles Francis Adams (R)
John B. Alley (R)
James Buffinton (R)
Anson Burlingame (R)
Henry L. Dawes
Charles Delano (R)
Thomas D. Eliot (R)
Daniel W. Gooch (R)
Alexander H. Rice (R)
Eli Thayer (R)
Charles R. Train (R)

MICHIGAN

Senators

Zachariah Chandler (R)
Kinsley S. Bingham (R)

Representatives

George B. Cooper (D)
r. May 1860
William A. Howard (R) s. 1860
Francis W. Kellogg (R)
De Witt C. Leach (R)
Henry Waldron (R)

MINNESOTA

Senators

Henry M. Rice (D)
Morton S. Wilkinson (R)

Representatives

Cyrus Aldrich (R)
William Windom (R)

MISSISSIPPI

Senators

Albert G. Brown (D)
Jefferson Davis (D)

Representatives

William Barksdale (SRD)
Reuben Davis (D)
Lucius Q. C. Lamar (D)
r. Dec. 1860
John J. McRae (SRD)
Otho R. Singleton (D)

MISSOURI

Senators

James S. Green (D)
Trusten Polk (D)

Representatives

Thomas L. Anderson (D)
John R. Barret (D)
Francis P. Blair (Free-Soiler)
John B. Clark (D)
James Craig (D)
John W. Noell (D)
John S. Phelps (D)
Samuel H. Woodson (Amer)

NEW HAMPSHIRE

Senators

John P. Hale
Daniel Clark (R)

Representatives

Thomas M. Edwards (R)
Gilman Marston (R)
Mason W. Tappan (R)

NEW JERSEY

Senators

John R. Thomson (D)
John C. Ten Eyck (R)

Representatives

Garnett B. Adrain (D)
John T. Nixon (R)
William Pennington (W)
Jetur R. Riggs (D)
John L. N. Stratton (R)

NEW YORK

Senators

William H. Seward (R)
Preston King (R)

Representatives

Thomas J. Barr (D)
Charles L. Beale (R)
George Briggs (Amer)
Silas M. Burroughs (R)
d. June 1860
Martin Butterfield (R)
Luther C. Carter (R)
Horace F. Clark (D)
Clark B. Cochrane (R)
John Cochrane (SRD)
Roscoe Conkling
R. Holland Duell (R)
Alfred Ely (R)
Reuben E. Fenton (R)
Augustus Frank (R)
James H. Graham (R)
John B. Haskin (D)
Charles B. Hoard (R)
James Humphrey (R)
William Irvine (R)
William S. Kenyon (R)
M. Lindley Lee (R)
James B. McKean (R)
William B. Maclay (D)
Abram B. Olin (R)
George W. Palmer (R)
Emory B. Pottle (R)
Edwin R. Reynolds (R) s. 1860
John H. Reynolds (R)
Charles B. Sedgwick (R)
Daniel E. Sickles (D)
Elbridge G. Spaulding (Un)
Francis E. Spinner (R)
Charles H. Van Wyck (R)
Alfred Wells (R)

NORTH CAROLINA

Senators

Thomas L. Clingman (D)
Thomas Bragg (D)

Representatives

Lawrence O'B. Branch (D)
F. Burton Craige (D)
John A. Gilmer (Amer)
James M. Leach (W)
Thomas Ruffin (D)
William N. H. Smith (D)
Zebulon B. Vance (D)
Warren Winslow (D)

OHIO

Senators

Benjamin F. Wade (R)
George E. Pugh (D)

Representatives

William Allen (D)
James M. Ashley (R)
John A. Bingham (R)
Harrison G. O. Blake (R)
John Carey (R)
Thomas Corwin (R)
Samuel S. Cox (D)
Sidney Edgerton (R)
John A. Gurley (R)
William Helmick (R)
William Howard (D)
John Hutchins (R)
Charles D. Martin (D)
George H. Pendleton (D)
John Sherman (R)
Benjamin Stanton (R)
Thomas C. Theaker (R)
Cydnor B. Tompkins (R)
Carey A. Trimble (R)
Clement L. Vallandigham (D)
Edward Wade (R)

OREGON

Senators

Joseph Lane (D)
Edward D. Baker (R)

Representative

Lansing Stout (D)

PENNSYLVANIA

Senators

William Bigler (D)
Simon Cameron (D)

Representatives

Elijah Babbitt (Un)
Samuel S. Blair (R)
James H. Campbell (W)
John Covode (R)
William H. Dimmick (D)
Thomas B. Florence (D)
Galusha A. Grow (R)
James T. Hale (R)
Chapin Hall (R)
John Hickman (D)
Benjamin F. Junkin (R)
John W. Killinger (R)
Henry C. Longnecker (R)
Jacob K. McKenty (D) s. 1860
Robert McKnight (R)
Edward McPherson (R)
William Millward (W)
William Montgomery (D)
James K. Moorhead (R)
Edward Joy Morris (W)
John Schwartz (D)
d. June 1860
George W. Scranton (R)
Thaddeus Stevens (R)
William Stewart (R)
John P. Verree (R)
John Wood (R)

RHODE ISLAND

Senators

James F. Simmons (W)
Henry B. Anthony (R)

Representatives

Christopher Robinson (Amer.)
William D. Brayton (R)

SOUTH CAROLINA

Senators

James H. Hammond (SRD)
James Chesnut, Jr. (SRD)

Representatives

John D. Ashmore (D)
Milledge L. Bonham (SRD)
William W. Boyce (SRD)
Laurence M. Keitt (D)
W. Porcher Miles (D)
John McQueen (D)

TENNESSEE

Senators

Andrew Johnson (D)
Alfred O. P. Nicholson (D)
r. Mar. 1861

Representatives

William T. Avery (D)
Reese B. Brabson (D)
Emerson Etheridge (W)
Robert H. Hatton (Amer)
Horace Maynard (Amer)
Thomas A. R. Nelson (Un)
James M. Quarles (W)
William B. Stokes (W)
James H. Thomas (D)
John V. Wright (D)

TEXAS

Senators

Matthias Ward (D)
Louis T. Wigfall (D) s. 1859

John Hemphill (SRD)

Representatives

Andrew J. Hamilton (D)
John H. Reagan (D)

VERMONT

Senators

Solomon Foot (R)
Jacob Collamer (R)

Representatives

Justin S. Morrill (W)
Homer E. Royce (R)
Eliakim P. Walton (R)

VIRGINIA

Senators

James M. Mason (D)
Robert M. T. Hunter (D)

Representatives

Thomas S. Bocock (D)
Alexander R. Boteler (Amer)
Sherrard Clemens (D)
Daniel C. De Jarnette (D)
Henry A. Edmundson (D)
Muscoe R. H. Garnett (D)
William O. Goode (D)
d. July 1859
John T. Harris (D)
Albert G. Jenkins (D)
Shelton F. Leake (D)
Elbert S. Martin (Amer)
John S. Millson (D)
Roger A. Pryor (D)
William Smith (D)

WISCONSIN

Senators

Charles Durkee (R)
James R. Doolittle (R)

Representatives

Charles H. Larrabee (D)
John F. Potter (R)
Cadwallader C. Washburn (R)

THIRTY-SEVENTH CONGRESS

March 4, 1861 to March 3, 1863

President of The Senate: Hannibal Hamlin
President Pro Tempore of The Senate: Solomon Foot
Speaker of The House of Representatives: Galusha A. Grow

ALABAMA

Senators

Clement Claiborne Clay (D)
r. Mar. 1861
Vacant

Representative

Vacant

ARKANSAS

Senators

William K. Sebastian (D)
r. July 1861
Charles B. Mitchel (D)
r. July 1861

Representatives

Vacant

CALIFORNIA

Senators

Milton S. Latham (D)
James A. McDougall (D)

Representatives

Frederick F. Low (R)
Timothy G. Phelps (R)
Aaron A. Sargent (R)

CONNECTICUT

Senators

Lafayette S. Foster (R)
James Dixon (R)

Representatives

Alfred A. Burnham (R)
James E. English (D)
Dwight Loomis (R)
George C. Woodruff (D)

DELAWARE

Senators

James A. Bayard (D)
Willard Saulsbury (D)

Representative

George P. Fisher (R)

FLORIDA

Senators

Stephen R. Mallory (D)
r. Mar. 1861
Vacant

Representatives

Vacant

GEORGIA

Senators

Vacant

Representative

Vacant

ILLINOIS

Senators

Stephen A. Douglas (D)
d. June 1861
Orville H. Browning (R) ta. 1861
William A. Richardson (D)
s. 1863

Lyman Trumbull (R)

Representatives

William J. Allen (D) s. 1862
Isaac N. Arnold (R)
Philip B. Fouke (D)
William Kellogg (R)
Anthony L. Knapp (D)
John A. Logan (D)
r. Apr. 1862
Owen Lovejoy (R)
John A. McClernand (D)
r. Oct. 1861
William A. Richardson (D)
r. Jan. 1863
James C. Robinson (D)
Elihu B. Washburne (W)
Joseph A. Wright (D) s. 1862

INDIANA

Senators

Jesse D. Bright (D) r. Feb. 1862
David Turpie (D) ta. 1862
Joseph A. Wright (D) s. 1862

Henry S. Lane (R)

Representatives

Schuyler Colfax (R)
James A. Cravens (D)
William McK. Dunn (R)
William S. Holman (D)
George W. Julian (R)
John Law (D)
William Mitchell (R)
Albert G. Porter (R)
John P. C. Shanks (R)
Daniel W. Voorhees (D)
Albert S. White (R)

IOWA

Senators

James Harlan (R)
James W. Grimes (R)

Representatives

Samuel R. Curtis (R)
r. Aug. 1861
William Vandever (R)
James F. Wilson (R)

KANSAS

Senators

Samuel C. Pomeroy (R)
James H. Lane (R)

Representative

Martin F. Conway (R)

KENTUCKY

Senators

Lazarus W. Powell (R)
John C. Breckinridge (D)
r. Dec. 1861
Garrett Davis (W) s. 1861

Representatives

Henry C. Burnett (D)
r. Dec. 1861
Samuel L. Casey (R) s. 1862
John J. Crittenden (Un)
George W. Dunlap (Un)
Henry Grider (W)
Aaron Harding(Un)
James S. Jackson (Un)
r. Dec. 1861
Robert Mallory (D)
John W. Menzies (Un)
William H. Wadsworth (Un)
Charles A. Wickliffe (Un)
George H. Yeaman (Un) s. 1862

LOUISIANA

Senators

Judah P. Benjamin (W)
r. Mar. 1861
Vacant

Representatives

Benjamin F. Flanders (Un)
s. 1862
Michael Hahn (Un) s. 1863

MAINE

Senators

William P. Fessenden (W)
Lot M. Morrill (R)

Representatives

Thomas A. D. Fessenden (R)
s. 1862
Samuel C. Fessenden (R)
John N. Goodwin (R)
Anson P. Morrill (R)
Frederick A. Pike (R)
John H. Rice (R)
Charles W. Walton (R)
r. May 1862

MARYLAND

Senators

James A. Pearce (W)
d. Dec. 1862
Thomas H. Hicks (R) s. 1863

Anthony Kennedy (Un)

Representatives

Charles B. Calvert (D)
John W. Crisfield (Un)
Cornelius L. L. Leary (Un)
Henry May (D)
Francis Thomas (R)
Edwin H. Webster (R)

MASSACHUSETTS

Senators

Charles Sumner (R)
Henry Wilson

Representatives

Charles Francis Adams (R)
r. May 1861
John B. Alley (R)
William Appleton (W)
r. Sept. 1861
Goldsmith F. Bailey (R)
d. May 1862
James Buffinton (R)
Henry L. Dawes
Charles Delano (R)
Thomas D. Eliot (R)
Daniel W. Gooch (R)
Samuel Hooper (R)
Alexander H. Rice (R)
Benjamin F. Thomas (Un)
Charles R. Train
Amasa Walker (R) s. 1862

MICHIGAN

Senators

Zachariah Chandler (R)

Kinsley S. Bingham (R)
d. Oct. 1861
Jacob M. Howard (R) s. 1862

Representatives

Fernando C. Beaman (R)
Bradley F. Granger (D)
Francis W. Kellogg (R)
Rowland E. Trowbridge (R)

MINNESOTA

Senators

Henry M. Rice (D)
Morton S. Wilkinson (R)

Representatives

Cyrus Aldrich (R)
William Windom

MISSISSIPPI

Senators

Vacant

Representatives

Vacant

MISSOURI

Senators

Trusten Polk (D)
r. Jan. 1862
John B. Henderson (D)
s. 1862

Waldo P. Johnson (D)
r. Jan. 1862
Robert Wilson (Un) ta. 1862

Representatives

Francis P. Blair, Jr. (Free-Soiler) r. July 1862
John B. Clark (D) r. July 1861
William A. Hall (D) s. 1862
John W. Noell (D)
Elijah H. Norton (D)
John S. Phelps (D)
Thomas L. Price s. 1862
John W. Reid (D) r. Dec. 1862
James S. Rollins

NEW HAMPSHIRE

Senators

John P. Hale (R)
Daniel Clark (R)

Representatives

Thomas M. Edwards (R)
Gilman Marston (R)
Edward H. Rollins (R)

NEW JERSEY

Senators

John R. Thomson (D) d. Sept. 1862
Richard S. Field (R) ta. 1862
James W. Wall (D) s. 1863

John C. Ten Eyck (R)

Representatives

George T. Cobb (D)
John T. Nixon (R)
Nehemiah Perry (Un)
William G. Steele (D)
John L. N. Stratton (R)

NEW YORK

Senators

Preston King (R)
Ira Harris (R)

Representatives

Stephen Baker
Jacob P. Chamberlain (R)
Ambrose W. Clark (R)
Frederick A. Conkling (R)
Roscoe Conkling (R)
Erastus Corning (D)
Isaac C. Delaplaine
Alexander S. Diven (R)
R. Holland Duell (R)
Alfred Ely (R)
Reuben E. Fenton (R)
Richard Franchot (R)
Augustus Frank (R)
Edward Haight (D)
James E. Kerrigan (D)
William E. Lansing (R)
James B. McKean (R)
Moses F. Odell (D)
Abram B. Olin (R)
Theodore M. Pomeroy (R)
Charles B. Sedgwick (R)
Socrates N. Sherman (R)
Edward H. Smith (D)
Elbridge G. Spaulding (Un)
John B. Steele (D)
Burt Van Horn (R)
Robert B. Van Valkenburg (R)
Charles H. Van Wyck (R)
Chauncey Vibbard (D)
William Wall (R)
Elijah Ward (D)
William A. Wheeler (R)
Benjamin Wood (D)

NORTH CAROLINA

Senators

Thomas L. Clingman (D) r. Mar. 1861
Thomas Bragg (D) r. Mar. 1861

Representatives

Vacant

OHIO

Senators

Benjamin F. Wade (R)

Salmon P. Chase (D) r. Mar. 1861
John Sherman (R) s. 1861

Representatives

William Allen (D)
James M. Ashley (R)
John A. Bingham (R)
Harrison G. O. Blake (R)
Thomas Corwin (R) r. Mar. 1861
Samuel S. Cox (D)
William P. Cutler (R)
Sidney Edgerton (R)
John A. Gurley (R)
Richard A. Harrison (D) s. 1861
Valentine B. Horton (R)
John Hutchins (R)
James R. Morris (D)
Warren P. Noble (D)
Robert H. Nugen (D)
George H. Pendleton (D)
Albert G. Riddle (R)
Samuel Shellabarger (R)
John Sherman (R) r. Mar. 1861
Carey A. Trimble (R)
Clement L. Vallandigham (D)
Chilton A. White (D)
Samuel T. Worcester (R) s. 1861

OREGON

Senators

Edward D. Baker (R) d. Oct. 1861
Benjamin Stark (D) ta. 1862
Benjamin F. Harding (R) s. 1862

James W. Nesmith (D)

Representatives

George K. Shiel (D)
Andrew J. Thayer (D) r. July 1861

PENNSYLVANIA

Senators

Simon Cameron (R) r. Mar. 1861
David Wilmot (R) s. 1861

Edgar Cowan (R)

Representatives

Sydenham E. Ancona (D)
Elijah Babbitt (R)
Joseph Bailey (D)
Charles J. Biddle (D)
Samuel S. Blair (R)
James H. Campbell
Thomas B. Cooper (D) d. Apr. 1862
John Covode (R)
William M. Davis (R)
Galusha A. Grow (R)
James T. Hale (R)
John Hickman (R)
Philip Johnson (R)
William D. Kelley (R)
John W. Killinger (R)
Jesse Lazear (D)
William E. Lehman (D)
Robert McKnight (R)
Edward McPherson (R)
James K. Moorhead (R)
Edward J. Morris (W) r. June 1861
John Patton (R)
George W. Scranton (R) d. Mar. 1861
John D. Stiles (D) s. 1862
Thaddeus Stevens (R)
John P. Verree (R)
John W. Wallace (R)
Hendrick B. Wright (D)

RHODE ISLAND

Senators

James F. Simmons (W) r. Aug. 1862
Samuel G. Arnold (R) s. 1862

Henry B. Anthony (R)

Representatives

George H. Browne (D)
William P. Sheffield (R)

SOUTH CAROLINA

Senators

James Chesnut, Jr. (SRD) r. July 1861
Vacant

Representatives

Vacant

TENNESSEE

Senators

Andrew Johnson (D) r. Mar. 1862
Alfred O. P. Nicholson r. July 1861

Representatives

George W. Bridges (Un) s. 1863
Andrew J. Clements (Un) s. 1862
Horace Maynard (Amer)

TEXAS

Senators

John Hemphill (SRD) r. Mar. 1861
Louis Wigfall (D) r. Mar. 1861

Representatives

Vacant

VERMONT

Senators

Solomon Foot (R)
Jacob Collamer (R)

Representatives

Portus Baxter (R)
Justin S. Morrill (W)
Eliakim P. Walton (R)

VIRGINIA

Senators

James M. Mason (D) r. Mar. 1861
Waitman T. Willey

Robert M. T. Hunter r. Mar. 1861
John S. Carlile (Un)

Representatives

Jacob B. Blair (Un)
William G. Brown (Un)
John S. Carlile (Amer) r. July 1861
Lewis McKenzie Un) s. 1863
Joseph E. Segar (Un)
Charles H. Upton (R)
Kellian V. Whaley (R)

WISCONSIN

Senators

James R. Doolittle (R)
Timothy O. Howe (R)

Representatives

Luther Hanchett (R) d. Nov. 1862
Walter D. McIndoe (R) s. 1863
John F. Potter (R)
A. Scott Sloan (R)

THIRTY-EIGHTH CONGRESS

March 4, 1863 to March 3, 1865

President of The Senate: Hannibal Hamlin
Presidents Pro Tempore of The Senate: Solomon Foot, Daniel Clark
Speaker of The House of Representatives: Schuyler Colfax

ALABAMA

Senators

Vacant

Representatives

Vacant

ARKANSAS

Senators

Vacant

Representatives

Vacant

CALIFORNIA

Senators

James A. McDougall (D)
John Conness (D)

Representatives

Cornelius Cole (R)
William Higby (R)
Thomas B. Shannon (R)

CONNECTICUT

Senators

Lafayette S. Foster (R)
James Dixon (R)

Representatives

Augustus Brandegee (R)
Henry C. Deming (R)
James E. English (D)
John H. Hubbard (R)

DELAWARE

Senators

James A. Bayard (D)
r. Jan. 1864
George R. Riddle (D)
s. 1864

Willard Saulsbury (D)

Representative

Nathaniel B. Smithers (R)

FLORIDA

Senators

Vacant

Representatives

Vacant

GEORGIA

Senators

Vacant

Representatives

Vacant

ILLINOIS

Senators

Lyman Trumbull (R)
William A. Richardson (D)

Representatives

James C. Allen (D)
William J. Allen (D)
Isaac N. Arnold (R)
John R. Eden (D)
John F. Farnsworth (R)
Charles M. Harris (D)
Ebon C. Ingersoll (R) s. 1864
Anthony L. Knapp (D)
Owen Lovejoy (R) d. Mar. 1864
William R. Morrison (D)
Jesse O. Norton (R)
James C. Robinson (D)
Lewis W. Ross (D)
John T. Stuart (D)
Elihu B. Washburne (W)

INDIANA

Senators

Henry S. Lane (R)
Thomas A. Hendricks (D)

Representatives

Schuyler Colfax (R)
James A. Cravens (D)
Ebenezer Dumont (Un)
Joseph K. Edgerton (D)
Henry W. Harrington (D)
William S. Holman (D)
George W. Julian (R)
John Law (D)
James F. McDowell (D)
Godlove S. Orth (R)
Daniel W. Voorhees (D)

IOWA

Senators

James Harlan (R)
James W. Grimes (R)

Representatives

William B. Allison (R)
Josiah B. Grinnell (R)
Asahel W. Hubbard (R)
John A. Kasson (R)
Hiram Price (R)
James F. Wilson (R)

KANSAS

Senators

Samuel C. Pomeroy (R)
James H. Lane (R)

Representative

A. Carter Wilder

KENTUCKY

Senators

Lazarus W. Powell (D)
Garrett Davis (W)

Representatives

Lucien Anderson (Un)
Brutus J. Clay (Un)
Henry Grider (W)
Aaron Harding (Un)
Robert Mallory (D)
William H. Randall (R)
Green C. Smith
William H. Wadsworth (Un)
George H. Yeaman (Un)

LOUISIANA

Senators

Vacant

Representatives

Vacant

MAINE

Senators

William P. Fessenden (W)
r. July 1864
Nathan A. Farwell (R) s. 1864

Lot M. Morrill (R)

Representatives

James G. Blaine (R)
Sidney Perham (R)
Frederick A. Pike (R)
John H. Rice (R)
Lorenzo D. M. Sweat (D)

MARYLAND

Senators

Thomas H. Hicks (R)
d. Feb. 1865
Reverdy Johnson (D)

Representatives

John A. J. Creswell (R)
H. Winter Davis (Un.)
Benjamin G. Harris (D)
Francis Thomas (Un)
Edwin H. Webster (R)

MASSACHUSETTS

Senators

Charles Sumner (R)
Henry Wilson

Representatives

John B. Alley (R)
Oakes Ames (R)
John D. Baldwin (R)
George S. Boutwell (R)
Henry L. Dawes
Thomas D. Eliot (R)
Daniel W. Gooch (R)
Samuel Hooper (R)
Alexander H. Rice (R)
William B. Washburn (R)

MICHIGAN

Senators

Zachariah Chandler (R)
Jacob M. Howard (R)

Representatives

Augustus C. Baldwin (D)
Fernando C. Beaman (R)
John F. Driggs (R)
Francis W. Kellogg (R)
John W. Longyear (R)
Charles Upson (R)

MINNESOTA

Senators

Morton S.Wilkinson (R)
Alexander Ramsey (R)

Representatives

Ignatius Donnelly (R)
William Windom (R)

MISSISSIPPI

Senators

Vacant

Representative

Vacant

MISSOURI

Senators

John B. Henderson (D)

Robert Wilson (Un) r. 1863
B. Gratz Brown (D) s. 1863

Representatives

Francis P. Blair (Free-Soiler)
r. June 1864
Henry T. Blow (R)
Sempronius H. Boyd
(Emancipationist)
William A. H. Hall (D)
Austin A. King (D)
Samuel Knox (R) s. 1864
Benjamin F. Loan
(Emancipationist)
Joseph W. McClurg
(Emancipationist)
John W. Noell (D) d. Mar. 1863
James S. Rollins (Con)
John G. Scott (D)

NEVADA

Senators

William M. Stewart (R) s. 1865
James W. Nye (R) s. 1865

Representative

Henry G. Worthington (R) s. 1864

NEW HAMPSHIRE

Senators

John P. Hale (R)
Daniel Clark (R)

Representatives

Daniel Marcy (D)
James W. Patterson (R)
Edward H. Rollins (R)

NEW JERSEY

Senators

John C. Ten Eyck (R)
William Wright (D)

Representatives

George Middleton (D)
Nehemiah Perry (Un)
Andrew J. Rogers (D)
John F. Starr
William G. Steele (D)

NEW YORK

Senators

Ira Harris (R)
Edwin D. Morgan (R)

Representatives

James Brooks (D)
John W. Chanler (D)
Ambrose W. Clark (R)
Freeman Clarke (R)
Thomas T. Davis (Un)
Reuben E. Fenton (R)
r. Dec. 1864
Augustus Frank (R)
John Ganson (D)
John A. Griswold (D)
Anson Herrick (D)
Giles W. Hotchkiss (R)
Calvin T. Hulburd (R)
Martin Kalbfleisch (D)
Orlando Kellogg (R)
Francis Kernan (D)
De Witt C. Littlejohn (R)
James M. Marvin (Un)
Samuel F. Miller (R)
Daniel Morris (R)
Homer A. Nelson (D)
Moses F. Odell (D)
Theodore M. Pomeroy (R)
John V. L. Pruyn (D)
William Radford (D)
Henry G. Stebbins (D)
r. Oct. 1864
John B. Steele (D)
Dwight Townsend (D) s. 1864
Robert B. Van Valkenburg (R)
Elijah Ward (D)
Charles H. Winfield (D)
Benjamin Wood (D)
Fernando Wood (D)

NORTH CAROLINA

Senators

Vacant

Representatives

Vacant

OHIO

Senators

Benjamin F. Wade (R)
John Sherman (R)

Representatives

James M. Ashley (R)
George Bliss (D)
Samuel S. Cox (D)
Ephraim R. Eckley (R)
William E. Finck (D)
James A. Garfield (R)
Wells A. Hutchins (D)
William Johnston (D)
Francis C. Le Blond (D)
Alexander Long (D)
John F. McKinney (D)
James R. Morris (D)
Warren P. Noble (D)
John O'Neill (D)
George H. Pendleton (D)
Robert C. Schenck (R)
Rufus P. Spalding (D)
Chilton A. White (D)
Joseph W. White (D)

OREGON

Senators

James W. Nesmith (D)
Benjamin F. Harding (R)

Representative

John R. McBride (R)

PENNSYLVANIA

Senators

Edgar Cowan (R)
Charles R. Buckalew (D)

Representatives

Sydenham E. Ancona (D)
Joseph Bailey (D)
John M. Broomall (R)
Alexander H. Coffroth (D)
John L. Dawson (D)
Charles Dension (D)
James T. Hale (R)
Philip Johnson (R)
William D. Kelley (R)
Jesse Lazear (D)
Archibald McAllister (D)
William H. Miller (D)
James K. Moorhead (R)
Amos Myers (R)
Leonard Myers (R)
Charles O'Neill (R)
Samuel J. Randall (D)
Glenni W. Scofield (R)
Thaddeus Stevens (R)
John D. Stiles (D)
Myer Strouse (D)
M. Russell Thayer (R)
Henry W. Tracy (R)
Thomas Williams (R)

RHODE ISLAND

Senators

Henry B. Anthony (R)
William Sprague

Representatives

Nathan F. Dixon (R)
Thomas A. Jenckes (R)

SOUTH CAROLINA

Senators

Vacant

Representatives

Vacant

TENNESSEE

Senators

Vacant

Representatives

Vacant

TEXAS

Senators

Vacant

Representatives

Vacant

VERMONT

Senators

Solomon Foot (R)
Jacob Collamer (R)

Representatives

Portus Baxter (R)
Justin S. Morrill
Frederick E. Woodbridge (R)

VIRGINIA

Senators

John S. Carlile (Un)
Lemuel J. Bowden (R)
d. Jan. 1864

Representatives

Vacant

WEST VIRGINIA

Senators

Peter G. Van Winkle (Un)
Waitman T. Willey (R)

Representatives

Jacob B. Blair
William G. Brown (Un)
Kellian V. Whaley (R)

WISCONSIN

Senators

James R. Doolittle (R)
Timothy O. Howe (R)

Representatives

James S. Brown (D)
Amasa Cobb (R)
Charles A. Eldridge (D)
Walter D. McIndoe (R)
Ithamar C. Sloan (R)
Ezra Wheeler (D)

THIRTY-NINTH CONGRESS

March 4, 1865 to March 3, 1867

President of The Senate: Andrew Johnson
Presidents Pro Tempore of The Senate: Lafayette S. Foster
Benjamin F. Wade
Speaker of The House of Representatives: Schuyler Colfax

ALABAMA

Senators

Vacant

Representatives

Vacant

ARKANSAS

Senators

Vacant

Representatives

Vacant

CALIFORNIA

Senators

James A. McDougall (D)
John Conness (R)

Representatives

John Bidwell (Un)
William Higby (R)
Donald C. McRuer (R)

CONNECITICUT

Senators

Lafayette S. Foster (R)
James Dixon (R)

Representatives

Augustus Brandegee (R)
Henry C. Deming (R)
John H. Hubbard (R)
Samuel L. Warner (R)

DELAWARE

Senators

Willard Saulsbury (D)
George R. Riddle (D)

Representative

John A. Nicholson (D)

FLORIDA

Senators

Vacant

Representatives

Vacant

GEORGIA

Senators

Vacant

Representatives

Vacant

ILLINOIS

Senators

Lyman Trumbull (R)
Richard Yates (R)

Representatives

Jehu Baker (R)
Henry P. H. Bromwell (R)
Burton C. Cook (R)
Shelby M. Cullom (R)
John F. Farnsworth (R)
Abner C. Harding (R)
Ebon C. Ingeroll (R)
Andrew J. Kuykendall (R)
Samuel S. Marshall (D)
Samuel W. Moulton (D)
Lewis W. Ross (D)
Anthony Thornton (D)
Elihu B. Washburne (W)
John Wentworth (R)

INDIANA

Senators

Henry S. Lane (R)
Thomas A. Hendricks (D)

Representatives

Schuyler Colfax (R)
Joseph H. Defrees (R)
Ebenezer Dumont (Un)
John H. Farquhar (R)
Ralph Hill (R)
George W. Julian (R)
Michael C. Kerr (D)
William E. Niblack (D)
Godlove S. Orth (R)
Thomas N. Stillwell (R)
Daniel W. Voorhees (D) r. Feb. 1866
Henry D. Washburn (R) s. 1866

IOWA

Senators

James Harlan (R) r. May 1865
Samuel J. Kirkwood (R) s. 1866

James W. Grimes (R)

Representatives

William B. Allison (R)
Josiah B. Grinnell (R)
Asahel W. Hubbard (R)
John A. Kasson (R)
Hiram Price (R)
James F. Wilson (R)

KANSAS

Senators

Samuel C. Pomeroy (R)

James H. Lane (R) d. July 1866
Edmund G. Ross (R) s. 1866

Representative

Sidney Clarke (R)

KENTUCKY

Senators

Garrett Davis (W)
James Guthrie (D)

Representatives

Henry Grider (W) d. Sept. 1866
Aaron Harding (D)
Elijah Hise (D) s. 1866
Samuel McKee (R)
William H. Randall (R)
Burwell C. Ritter (Con)
Lovell H. Rousseau (R)
George S. Shanklin (D)
Green C. Smith (Un) r. 1866
Lawrence S. Trimble (D)
Andrew H. Ward s. 1866

LOUISIANA

Senators

Vacant

Representatives

Vacant

MAINE

Senators

Lot M. Morrill (R)
William P. Fessenden (W)

Representatives

James G. Blaine (R)
John Lynch (R)
Sidney Perham (R)
Frederick A. Pike (R)
John H. Rice (R)

MARYLAND

Senators

Reverdy Johnson (D)
John A. J. Creswell (R)

Representatives

Benjamin G. Harris (D)
Hiram McCullough (D)
Charles E. Phelps (Con)
Francis Thomas (R)
John L. Thomas, Jr. (R)
Edwin H. Webster r. July 1865

MASSACHUSETTS

Senators

Charles Sumner (R)
Henry Wilson

Representatives

John B. Alley (R)
Oakes Ames (R)
John D. Baldwin (R)
Nathaniel P. Banks (R)
George S. Boutwell (R)
Henry L. Dawes (R)
Thomas D. Eliot (R)
Samuel Hooper (R)
Alexander H. Rice (R)
William B. Washburn (R)

MICHIGAN

Senators

Zachariah Chandler (R)
Jacob M. Howard (R)

Representatives

Fernando C. Beaman (R)
John F. Driggs (R)
Thomas W. Ferry (R)
John W. Longyear (R)
Rowland E. Trowbridge (R)
Charles Upson (R)

MINNESOTA

Senators

Alexander Ramsey (R)
Daniel S. Norton (Con)

Representatives

Ignatius Donnelly (R)
William Windom (R)

MISSISSIPPI

Senators

Vacant

Representatives

Vacant

MISSOURI

Senators

John B. Henderson (D)
B. Gratz Brown (D)

Representatives

George W. Anderson (R)
John F. Benjamin (R)
Henry T. Blow (R)
John Hogan (D)
John R. Kelso (Radical)
Benjamin F. Loan (Emancipation)
Joseph W. McClurg (Radical)
Thomas E. Noel (D)
Robert T. Van Horn (R)

NEBRASKA

Senators

John M. Thayer (R) s. 1867
Thomas W. Tipton (R) s. 1867

Representative

Turner M. Marquette (R) s. 1867

NEVADA

Senators

William M. Stewart (R)
James W. Mye (R)

Representative

Delos R. Ashley (R)

NEW HAMPSHIRE

Senators

Daniel Clark (R) r. July 1866
George G. Fogg (R) s. 1866

Aaron H. Cragin (Amer)

Representatives

Gilman Marston (R)
James W. Patterson (R)
Edward H. Rollins (R)

NEW JERSEY

Senators

William Wright (D) d. Nov. 1866
Frederick T. Frelinghuysen (R) s. 1866

John P. Stockton (D) r. 1866
Alexander G. Cattell (R) s. 1866

Representatives

William A. Newell (R)
Andrew J. Rogers (D) r. Mar. 1866
Charles Sitgreaves (D)
John F. Starr (R)
Edwin R. V. Wright (D) s. 1866

NEW YORK

Senators

Ira Harris (R)
Edwin D. Morgan (R)

Representatives

Teunis G. Bergen (D)
James Brooks (D) r. Apr. 1866
John W. Chanler (D)
Roscoe Conkling (R) r. Mar. 1867
William A. Darling (R)
Thomas T. Davis (Un)
William E. Dodge (R) s. 1866
Charles Goodyear (D)
John A. Griswold (R)
Robert S. Hale (R) s. 1866
Roswell Hart (R)
Sidney T. Holmes (R)
Giles W. Hotchkiss (R)
Demas Hubbard, Jr. (R)

Edwin N. Hubbell (R)
Calvin T. Hulburd (R)
James Humphrey (R) d. June 1866
James M. Humphrey (D)
John W. Hunter s. 1866
Morgan Jones (D)
Orlando Kellogg (R)
d. Aug. 1865
John H. Ketcham (R)
Addison H. Laflin (R)
James M. Marvin (Un)
Daniel Morris (R)
Theodore M. Pomeroy (R)
William Radford (D)
Henry J. Raymond (R)
Stephen Taber (D)
Nelson Taylor (D)
Henry Van Aernam (R)
Burt Van Horn (R)
Hamilton Ward (R)
Charles H. Winfield (D)

NORTH CAROLINA

Senators

Vacant

Representatives

Vacant

OHIO

Senators

Benjamin F. Wade (R)
John Sherman (R)

Representatives

James M. Ashley (R)
John A. Bingham (R)
Ralph P. Buckland (R)
Hezekiah S. Bundy (R)
Reader W. Clarke (R)
Columbus Delano (R)
Ephraim R. Eckley (R)
Benjamin Eggleston (R)
William E. Finck (D)
James A. Garfield (R)
Rutherford B. Hayes (R)
James R. Hubbell (R)
William Lawrence (R)
Francis C. Le Blond (D)
Tobias A. Plants (R)
Robert C. Schenck (R)
Samuel Shellabarger (R)
Rufus P. Spalding (D)
Martin Welker (R)

OREGON

Senators

James W. Nesmith (D)
George H. Williams (R)

Representative

James H. Henderson (R)

PENNSYLVANIA

Senators

Edgar Cowan (R)
Charles R. Buckalew (D)

Representatives

Sydenham E. Ancona (D)
Abraham A. Barker (R)
Benjamin M. Boyer (D)
John M. Broomall (R)
Alexander H. Coffroth (D)
r. July 1866
Charles V. Culver
John L. Dawson (D)
Charles Denison (D)
Adam J. Glossbrenner (D)
Philip Johnson (R) d. Jan. 1867
William D. Kelley (R)
William H. Koontz (R) s. 1866
George V. Lawrence (W)
Ulysses Mercur (R)
George F. Miller (R)
James K. Moorhead (R)
Leonard Myers (R)
Charles O'Neill (R)
Samuel J. Randall (D)
Glenni W. Scofield (R)
Thaddeus Stevens (R)
Myer Strouse (D)
M. Russell Thayer (R)
Thomas Williams (R)
Stephen F. Wilson (R)

RHODE ISLAND

Senators

Henry B. Anthony (R)
William Sprague (R)

Representatives

Nathan F. Dixon (R)
Thomas A. Jenckes (R)

SOUTH CAROLINA

Senators

Vacant

Representatives

Vacant

TENNESSEE

Senators

Joseph S. Fowler (R) s. 1866
David T. Patterson (D) s. 1866

Representatives

Samuel M. Arnell (R) s. 1866
William B. Campbell (D) s. 1866
Edmund Cooper (Con) s. 1866
Isaac R. Hawkins (R) s. 1866
John W. Leftwich (D) s. 1866
Horace Maynard (R) s. 1866
William B. Stokes (R) s. 1866
Nathaniel G. Taylor s. 1866

TEXAS

Senators

Vacant

Representatives

Vacant

VERMONT

Senators

Solomon Foot (R) d. Mar. 1866
George F. Edmunds (R) s. 1866
Jacob Collamer (R) d. Nov. 1865
Luke P. Poland (R) s. 1865

Representatives

Portus Baxter (R)
Justin S. Morrill
Frederick E. Woodbridge (R)

VIRGINIA

Senators

Vacant

Representatives

Vacant

WEST VIRGINIA

Senators

Peter G. Van Winkle (Un)
Waitman T. Willey (R)

Representatives

Chester D. Hubbard (R)
George R. Latham (R)
Kellian V. Whaley (R)

WISCONSIN

Senators

James R. Dottlittle (R)
Timothy O. Howe (R)

Representatives

Amasa Cobb (R)
Charles A. Eldridge (D)
Walter D. McIndoe (R)
Halbert E. Paine (R)
Philetus Sawyer (R)
Ithamar C. Sloan (R)

FORTIETH CONGRESS

March 4, 1967 to March 3, 1869

President of The Senate:	Vacant
President Pro Tempore of The Senate:	Benjamin F. Wade
Speakers of The House of Representatives:	Schuyler Colfax
	Theodore M. Pomeroy

ALABAMA

Senators

George E. Spencer (R) s. 1868
Willard Warner (R) s. 1868

Representatives

Charles W. Buckley (R) s. 1868
John B. Callis (R) s. 1868
Thomas Haughey (R) s. 1868
Francis W. Kellogg (R) s. 1868
Benjamin W. Norris (R) s. 1868

ARKANSAS

Senators

Alexander McDonald (R) s. 1868
Benjamin F. Rice (R) s. 1868

Representatives

Thomas Boles (R) s. 1868
James T. Elliott (R) s. 1868
James Hinds (R) s. 1868
Logan H. Roots (R) s. 1868

CALIFORNIA

Senators

John Conness (R)
Cornelius Cole (R)

Representatives

Samuel B. Axtell (D) s. 1867
William Higby (R) s. 1867
James A. Johnson (D) s. 1867

CONNECTICUT

Senators

James Dixon (R)
Orris S. Ferry (R)

Representatives

William H. Barnum (D)
Julius Hotchkiss (R)
Richard D. Hubbard (D)
Henry H. Starkweather (R)

DELAWARE

Senators

George R. Riddle (D) d. Mar. 1867
James A. Bayard (D)

Willard Saulsbury (D)

Representative

John A. Nicholson (D)

FLORIDA

Senators

Thomas W. Osborn (R) s. 1868
Adonijah S. Welch (R) s. 1868

Representative

Charles M. Hamilton (R) s. 1868

GEORGIA

Senators

Vacant

Representatives

Joseph W. Clift (R) s. 1868
William P. Edwards (R) s. 1868
Samuel F. Gove (R) s. 1868
Charles H. Prince (R) s. 1868
Nelson Tift (D) s. 1868
Pierce M. B. Young (D) s. 1868

ILLINOIS

Senators

Lyman Trumbull (R)
Richard Yates (R)

Representatives

Jehu Baker (R)
Henry P. H. Bromwell (R)
Albert G. Burr (D)
Burton C. Cook (R)
Shelby M. Cullom (R)
John F. Farnsworth (R)
Abner C. Harding (R)
Ebon C. Ingersoll (R)
Norman B. Judd (R)
Samuel S. Marshall (D)
Green B. Raum (R)
Lewis W. Ross (D)
Elihu B. Washburne (W)

INDIANA

Senators

Thomas A. Hendricks (D)
Oliver H. P. T. Morton (R)

Representatives

John Coburn (R)
Schuyler Colfax (R)
William S. Holman (D)
Morton C. Hunter (R)
George W. Julian (R)
Michael C. Kerr (D)
William E. Niblack (D)
Godlove S. Orth (R)
John P. C. Shanks (R)
Henry D. Washburn (R)
William Williams (R)

IOWA

Senators

James W. Grimes (R)
James Harlan (R)

Representatives

William B. Allison (R)
Grenville M. Dodge (R)
Asahel W. Hubbard (R)
William Loughridge (R)
Hiram P. Rice (R)
James F. Wilson (R)

KANSAS

Senators

Samuel C. Pomeroy (R)
Edmund G. Ross (D)

Representative

Sidney Clarke (R)

KENTUCKY

Senators

Garrett Davis (W)

James Guthrie (D) r. Feb. 1868
Thomas C. McCreery (D) s. 1868

Representatives

George M. Adams (D)
James B. Beck (D)
Jacob S. Golladay (D)
Asa P. Grover (D)
Thomas L. Jones (D)
J. Proctor Knott (D)
Samuel McKee (R) s. 1868
Lawrence S. Trimble (D) s. 1868

LOUISIANA

Senators

John S. Harris (R) s. 1868
William P. Kellogg (R)

Representatives

W. Jasper Blackburn (R) s. 1868
James Mann (D) d. 1868
Joseph P. Newsham (R) s. 1868
J. Hale Sypher (R) s. 1868
Michel Vidal (R) s. 1868

MAINE

Senators

Lot M. Morrill (R)
William P. Fessenden (W)

Representatives

James G. Blaine (R)
John Lynch (R)
Sidney Perham (R)
John A. Peters (R)
Frederick A. Pike (R)

MARYLAND

Senators

Reverdy Johnson (D) r. July 1868
William P. Whyte (D) s. 1868

George Vickers (D) s. 1868

Representatives

Stevenson Archer (D)
Hiram McCullough (D)
Charles E. Phelps (Con)
Frederick Stone (D)
Francis Thomas (R)

MASSACHUSETTS

Senators

Charles Sumner (R)
Henry Wilson (Free-Soiler)

Representatives

Oakes Ames
John D. Baldwin (R)
Nathaniel P. Banks (R)
George S. Boutwell (R)
Benjamin F. Butler (R)
Henry L. Dawes
Thomas D. Eliot (R)
Samuel Hooper (R)
Ginery Twichell (R)
William B. Washburn (R)

MICHIGAN

Senators

Zachariah Chandler (R)
Jacob M. Howard (R)

Representatives

Fernando C. Beaman (R)
Austin Blair (R)
John F. Driggs (R)
Thomas W. Ferry (R)
Rowland E. Trowbridge (R)
Charles Upson (R)

MINNESOTA

Senators

Alexander Ramsey (R)
Daniel S. Norton (Con)

Representatives

William Windom (R)
Ignatius Donnelly (R)

MISSISSIPPI

Senators

Vacant

Representatives

Vacant

MISSOURI

Senators

John B. Henderson (D)
Charles D. Drake (R)

Representatives

George W. Anderson (R)
John F. Benjamin (R)
Joseph J. Gravely (R)
Joseph W. McClurg (Radical) r. 1868
Benjamin F. Loan (Radical)
James R. McCormick (D)
Carman A. Newcomb (R)
Thomas E. Noell (Radical) d. Oct. 1867
William A. Pile (R)
John H. Stover s. 1868
Robert T. Van Horn (R)

NEBRASKA

Senators

John M. Thayer (R)
Thomas W. Tipton (R)

Representative

John Taffe (R)

NEVADA

Senators

William M. Stewart (R)
James W. Nye (R)

Representative

Delos R. Ashley (R)

NEW HAMPSHIRE

Senators

Aaron H. Cragin (Amer)
James W. Patterson (R)

Representatives

Jacob Benton (R)
Jacob H. Ela (R)
Aaron F. Stevens (R)

NEW JERSEY

Senators

Alexander G. Cattell (R)
Frederick T. Frelinghuysen (R)

Representatives

Charles Haight (D)
George A. Halsey (R)
John Hill (R)
William Moore (R)
Charles Sitgreaves (D)

NEW YORK

Senators

Edwin D. Morgan (R)
Roscoe Conkling (R)

Representatives

Alexander H. Bailey (R)
Demas Barnes (D)
James Brooks (D)
John W. Chanler (D)
John C. Churchill (R)
Thomas Cornell (R)
Orange Ferriss (R)
William C. Fields (R)
John Fox (D)
John A. Griswold (R)
Calvin T. Hulburd (R)
James M. Humphrey (D)
William H. Kelsey (R)
John H. Ketcham (R)
Addison H. Laflin (R)
William S. Lincoln (R)
Dennis McCarthy (R)

James M. Marvin (Un)
John Morrissey (D)
Theodore M. Pomeroy (R)
John V. L. Pruyn (D)
William H. Robertson (R)
William E. Robinson (D)
Lewis Selye
Thomas E. Stewart
Stephen Taber (D)
Henry Van Aernam (R)
Burt Van Horn (R)
Charles H. Van Wyck (R)
Hamilton Ward (R)
Fernando Wood (D)

NORTH CAROLINA

Senators

Joseph C. Abbott (R) s. 1868
John Pool s. 1868

Representatives

Nathaniel Boyden (R) s. 1868
John T. Deweese (D) s. 1868
Oliver H. Dockery (R) s. 1868
John R. French (R) s. 1868
David Heaton (R) s. 1868
Alexander H. Jones (R) s. 1868
Israel G. Lash (R) s. 1868

OHIO

Senators

Benjamin F. Wade (R)
John Sherman (R)

Representatives

James M. Ashley (R)
John Beatty (R) s. 1868
John A. Bingham (R)
Ralph P. Buckland (R)
Samuel F. Cary (R)
Reader W. Clarke (R)
Columbus Delano (R) s. 1868
Ephraim R. Eckley (R)
Benjamin Eggleston (R)
James A. Garfield (R)
Cornelius S. Hamilton (R)
d. Dec. 1867
Rutherford B. Hayes (R)
r. July 1867
William Lawrence (R)
George W. Morgan (D) r. Jun. 1868
William Mungen (D)
Tobias A. Plants (R)
Robert C. Schenck (R)
Samuel Shellabarger (R)
Rufus P. Spalding (D)
Philadelph Van Trump (D)
Martin Welker (R)
John T. Wilson (R)

OREGON

Senators

George H. Williams (R)
Henry W. Corbett (R)

Representative

Rufus Mallory (R)

PENNSYLVANIA

Senators

Charles R. Buckalew (D)
Simon Cameron (R)

Representatives

Benjamin M. Boyer (D)
John M. Broomall (R)
Henry L. Cake (R)
John Covode (R)
Charles Denison (D) d. June 1867
Oliver J. Dickey (R) s. 1868
Darwin A. Finney (R) d. Aug. 1868
J. Lawrence Getz (D)
Adam J. Glossbrenner (D)
William D. Kelley (R)
William H. Koontz (R)
George V. Lawrence (W)
Ulysses Mercur (R)
George F. Miller (R)
James K. Moorhead
Daniel J. Morrell (R)
Leonard Myers (R)
Charles O'Neill (R)
S. Newton Pettis (R) s. 1868
Samuel J. Randall (D)
Glenni W. Scofield (R)
Thaddeus Stevens (R) d. Aug. 1868
Caleb N. Taylor (R)
Daniel M. Van Auken (D)
Thomas Williams (R)
Stephen F. Wilson (R)
George W. Woodward (D)

RHODE ISLAND

Senators

Henry B. Athony (R)
William Sprague (R)

Representatives

Thomas A. Jenckes (R)
Nathan F. Dixon (R)

SOUTH CAROLINA

Senators

Thomas J. Robertson (R) s. 1868
Frederick A. Sawyer (R) s. 1868

Representatives

Christopher C. Bowen (R) s. 1868
M. Simeon Corley (R) s. 1868
James H. Goss (R) s. 1868
B. Frank Whittemore (R) s. 1868

TENNESSEE

Senators

Joseph S. Fowler (R)
David T. Patterson (D)

Representatives

Samuel M. Arnell (R) s. 1868
Roderick R. Butler (R) s. 1868
Isaac R. Hawkins (R) s. 1868
Horace Maynard (R) s. 1868
James Mullins (R) s. 1868
David A. Nunn (R) s. 1868
William B. Stokes (R) s. 1868
John Trimble (R) s. 1868

TEXAS

Senators

Vacant

Representatives

Vacant

VERMONT

Senators

George F. Edmunds (R)
Justin S. Morrill (R)

Representatives

Luke P. Poland (R)
Worthington C. Smith (R)
Frederick E. Woodbridge (R)

VIRGINIA

Senators

Vacant

Representatives

Vacant

WEST VIRGINIA

Senators

Peter G. Van Winkle (Un)
Waitman T. Willey (R)

Representatives

Chester D. Hubbard (R)
Bethuel M. Kitchen (R)
Daniel H. Polsley (R)

WISCONSIN

Senators

James R. Doolittle (R)
Timothy O. Howe (R)

Representatives

Charles A. Eldredge (D)
Amasa Cobb (R)
Benjamin F. Hopkins (R)
Halbert E. Paine (R)
Philetus Sawyer (R)
Cadwallader C. Washburn (R)

FORTY-FIRST CONGRESS

March 4, 1869 to March 3, 1871

President of The Senate: Schuyler Colfax
President Pro Tempore of The Senate: Henry B. Anthony
Speaker of The House of Representatives: James G. Blaine

ALABAMA

Senators

George E. Spencer (R)
Willard Warner (R)

Representatives

Alfred E. Buck (R)
Charles W. Buckley (R)
Peter M. Dox (D)
Charles Hays (R)
Robert S. Heflin (R)
William C. Sherrod (D)

ARKANSAS

Senators

Alexander McDonald (R)
Benjamin F. Rice (R)

Representatives

Thomas Boles (R)
Anthony A. C. Rogers (D)
Logan H. Roots (R)

CALIFORNIA

Senators

Cornelius Cole (R)
Eugene Casserly (D)

Representatives

Samuel B. Axtell (D)
James A. Johnson (D)
Aaron A. Sargent (R)

CONNECTICUT

Senators

Orris S. Ferry (R)
William A. Buckingham (R)

Representatives

William H. Barnum (D)
Stephen W. Kellogg (R)
Henry H. Starkweather (R)
Julius L. Strong (R)

DELAWARE

Senators

Willard Saulsbury (D)
Thomas F. Bayard (D)

Representative

Benjamin T. Biggs (D)

FLORIDA

Senators

Thomas W. Osborn (R)
Abijah Gilbert (R)

Representative

Charles M. Hamilton (R)

GEORGIA

Senators

Joshua Hill (R) s. 1871
Homer V. M. Miller (D) s. 1871

Representatives

Marion Bethune (R) s. 1871
Stephen A. Corker (D) s. 1871
Jefferson F. Long (R) s. 1871
William W. Paine (D) s. 1871
William P. Price (D) s. 1871
Richard H. Whiteley (R) s. 1871
Pierce M. B. Young (D) s. 1871

ILLINOIS

Senators

Lyman Trumbull (R)
Richard Yates (R)

Representatives

Horatio C. Burchard (R)
Albert G. Burr (D)
Burton C. Cook (R)
John M. Crebs (D)
Shelby M. Cullom (R)
John F. Farnsworth (R)
John B. Hawley (R)
John B. Hay (R)
Ebon C. Ingersoll (R)
Norman B. Judd (R)
Thompson W. McNeely (D)
Samuel S. Marshall (D)
Jesse H. Moore (R)

INDIANA

Senators

Oliver H. P. T. Morton (R)
Daniel D. Pratt (R)

Representatives

John Coburn (R)
William S. Holman (R)
George W. Julian (R)
Michael C. Kerr (D)
William E. Niblack (D)
Godlove S. Orth (R)
Jasper Packard (R)
John P. C. Shanks (R)
James N. Tyner (R)
Daniel W. Voorhees (D)
William Williams (R)

IOWA

Senators

James W. Grimes (R) r. Dec. 1869
James B. Howell (R) s. 1870

James Harlan (R)

Representatives

William B. Allison (R)
William Loughridge (R)
George W. McCrary (R)
Frank W. Palmer (R)
Charles Pomeroy (R)
William Smyth (R) d. Sept. 1870
William P. Wolf (R) s. 1870

KANSAS

Senators

Samuel C. Pomeroy (R)
Edmund G. Ross (D)

Representative

Sidney Clarke (R)

KENTUCKY

Senators

Garrett Davis (D)
Thomas C. McCreery (D)

Representatives

George M. Adams (D)
James B. Beck (D)
Jacob S. Golladay (D) r. Feb. 1870
Thomas L. Jones (D)
J. Proctor Knott (D)
Joseph H. Lewis (D) s. 1870
John M. Rice (D)
William N. Sweeney (D)
Lawrence S. Trimble (D)
Boyd Winchester (D)

LOUISIANA

Senators

John S. Harris (R)
William P. Kellogg (R)

Representatives

Chester B. Darrall (R) s. 1870
Frank Morey (R) s. 1870
Joseph P. Newsham (R) s. 1870
Lionel A. Sheldon (R)
J. Hale Sypher (R) s. 1870

MAINE

Senators

William P. Fessenden d. Sept. 1869
Lot M. Morrill (R) s. Dec. 1869

Hannibal Hamlin (R)

Representatives

James G. Blaine (R)
Eugene Hale (R)
John Lynch (R)
Samuel P. Morrill (R)
John A. Peters (R)

MARYLAND

Senators

George Vickers (D)
William T. Hamilton (D)

Representatives

Stevenson Archer (D)
Samuel Hambleton (D)
Patrick Hamill (D)
Frederick Stone (D)
Thomas Swann (D)

MASSACHUSETTS

Senators

Charles Sumner (R)
Henry Wilson

Representatives

Oakes Ames (R)
Nathaniel P. Banks (R)
George S. Boutwell (R) r. Mar. 1869
George M. Brooks (R)
James Buffinton (R)
Benjamin F. Butler (R)
Henry L. Dawes
George F. Hoar (R)
Samuel Hooper (R)
Ginery Twichell (R)
William B. Wahsburn (R)

MICHIGAN

Senators

Zachariah Chandler (R)
Jacob M. Howard (R)

Representatives

Fernado C. Beaman (R)
Austin Blair (R)
Omar D. Conger (R)
Thomas W. Ferry (R)
Randolph Strickland (R)
William L. Stoughton (R)

MINNESOTA

Senators

Alexander Ramsey (R)

Daniel S. Norton (Con)
d. July 1870
William Windom (R) ta. 1870
Ozora P. Stearns (R) s. 1871

Representatives

Morton S. Wilkinson (R)
Eugene M. Wilson (D)

MISSISSIPPI

Senators

Hiram R. Revels (R) s. 1870
Adelbert Ames (R) s. 1870

Representatives

Henry W. Barry (R) s. 1870
George E. Harris (R) s. 1870
George C. McKee (R) s. 1870
Joseph L. Morphis (R) s. 1870
Legrand W. Perce (R) s. 1870

MISSOURI

Senators

Charles D. Drake (R) r. Dec. 1870
Daniel T. Jewett (R) ta. 1870
Francis P. Blair, Jr. (D) s. 1871

Carl Schurz (R)

Representatives

Joel F. Asper (R)
John F. Benjamin (R)
Sempronius H. Boyd
Samuel S. Burdett (R)
David P. Dyer (R)
Gustavus A. Finkelnburg (R)
James R. McCormick (D)
Robert T. Van Horn (R)
Erastus Wells (D)

NEBRASKA

Senators

John M. Thayer (R)
Thomas W. Tipton (D)

Representative

John Taffe (R)

NEVADA

Senators

William M. Stewart (R)
James W. Nye (R)

Representative

Thomas Fitch (R)

NEW HAMPSHIRE

Senators

Aaron H. Cragin (Amer)
James W. Patterson (R)

Representatives

Jacob Benton (R)
Jacob H. Ela (R)
Aaron F. Stevens (R)

NEW JERSEY

Senators

Alexander G. Catell (R)
John P. Stockton (D)

Representatives

John T. Bird (D)
Orestes Cleveland (D)
Charles Haight (D)
John Hill (R)
William Moore (R)

NEW YORK

Senators

Roscoe Conkling (R)
Reuben E. Fenton (R)

Representatives

Alexander H. Bailey (R)
David S. Bennett (R)
James Brooks (D)
Hervey C. Calkin (D)
John C. Churchill (R)
George W. Cowles (R)
Samuel S. Cox (D)
Noah Davis (R) r. July 1870
Orange Ferriss (R)
John Fisher (R)
John Fox (D)
George W. Greene (D) r. Feb. 1870
John A. Griswold (D)
Charles H. Holmes (R) s. 1870
Giles W. Hotchkiss (R)
William H. Kelsey (R)
John H. Ketcham (R)
Charles Knapp (R)
Addison H. Laflin (R)

Stephen L. Mayham (D)
Dennis McCarthy (R)
John Morrissey (D)
Clarkson N. Potter (D)
Henry A. Reeves (D)
Stephen Sanford (R)
John G. Schumaker (D)
Porter Sheldon (R)
Henry W. Slocum (D)
Adolphus H. Tanner (R)
Charles H. Van Wyck (R) s. 1870
Hamilton Ward (R)
William A. Wheeler (R)
Fernando Wood (D)

NORTH CAROLINA

Senators

Joseph C. Abbott (R)
John Pool

Representatives

Clinton L. Cobb (R)
John T. Deweese (D) r. Feb. 1870
Joseph Dixon (R) s. 1870
Oliver H. Dockery (R)
David Heaton (R) d. June 1870
Alexander H. Jones (R)
Israel G. Lash (R)
John Manning, Jr. (D) s. 1870
Francis E. Shober (D)

OHIO

Senators

John Sherman (R)
Allen G. Thurman (D)

Representatives

Jacob A. Ambler (R)
John Beatty (R)
John A. Bingham (R)
Edward F. Dickinson (D)
James A. Garfield (R)
Truman H. Hoag (D) d. Feb. 1870
William Lawrence (R)
Eliakim H. Moore (R)
George W. Morgan (D)
William Mungen (D)
Erasmus D. Peck (R) s. 1870
Robert C. Schenck (R)
r. Jan. 1871
John A. Smith (R)
Job E. Stevenson (R)
Peter W. Strader (D)
William H. Upson (R)
Philadelph Van Trump (D)
Martin Welker (R)
John T. Wilson (R)
James J. Winans (R)

OREGON

Senators

George H. Williams (R)
Henry W. Corbett (R)

Representative

Joseph S. Smith (D)

PENNSYLVANIA

Senators

Simon Cameron (R)
John Scott (R)

Representatives

William H. Armstrong (R)
Henry L. Cake (R)
John Cessna (R)
John Covode (R) s. 1870
d. Jan. 1871
Oliver J. Dickey (R)
Joseph B. Donley (R)
J. Lawrence Getz (D)
Calvin W. Gilfillan (R)
Richard J. Haldeman (D)
William D. Kelley (R)
Ulysses Mercur (R)
John Moffet (D) r. Apr. 1869
Daniel J. Morrell (R)
Leonard Myers (R)
James S. Negley (R)
Charles O'Neill (R)
John B. Packer (R)
Darwin Phelps (R)
Samuel J. Randall (D)
John R. Reading (R) r. Apr. 1870
Glenni W. Scofield (R)
John D. Stiles (D)
Caleb N. Taylor (R) s. 1870
Washington Townsend (R)
Daniel M. Van Auken (D)
George W. Woodward (D)

RHODE ISLAND

Senators

Henry B. Anthony (R)
William Sprague (R)

Representatives

Thomas A. Jenckes (R)
Nathan F. Fixon (R)

SOUTH CAROLINA

Senators

Thomas J. Robertson (R)
Frederick A. Sawyer (R)

Representatives

Christopher C. Bowen (R)
Solomon L. Hoge (R)
Joseph H. Rainey (R) s. 1870
Alexander S. Wallace (R) s. 1870
B. Frank Whittemore (R) r. Feb. 1870

TENNESSEE

Senators

Joseph S. Fowler (R)
William G. Brownlow (R)

Representatives

Samuel M. Arnell (R)
Roderick R. Butler (R)
Isaac R. Hawkins (R)
Horace Maynard (R)
William F. Prosser (R)
William J. Smith (R)
William B. Stokes (R)
Lewis Tillman (R)

TEXAS

Senators

Morgan C. Hamilton (R) s. 1870
James W. Flanagan (R) s. 1870

Representatives

William T. Clark (R) s. 1870
John C. Conner (D) s. 1870
Edward Degener (R) s. 1870
George W. Whitmore (R) s. 1870

VERMONT

Senators

George F. Edmunds (R)
Justin S. Morrill (R)

Representatives

Luke P. Poland (R)
Worthington C. Smith (R)
Charles W. Willard (R)

VIRGINIA

Senators

John W. Johnston (Con) s. 1870
John F. Lewis (R) s. 1870

Representatives

Richard S. Ayer (R) s. 1870
George W. Booker (Con) s. 1870
Richard T. W. Duke (Con) s. 1870
James King Gibson (D) s. 1870
Lewis McKenzie (Un) s. 1870
William Milnes, Jr. (Con) s. 1870
James H. Platt, Jr. (R) s. 1870
Charles H. Porter (R) s. 1870
Robert Ridgway (Con) d. 1870

WEST VIRGINIA

Senators

Waitman T. Willey (R)
Arthur I. Boreman (R)

Representatives

Isaac H. Duval (R)
James C. McGrew (R)
John S. Witcher (R)

WISCONSIN

Senators

Timothy O. Howe (R)
Matthew H. Carpenter (R)

Representatives

David Atwood (R) s. 1870
Amasa Cobb (R)
Charles A. Eldredge (D)
Benjamin F. Hopkins (R) d. 1870
Halbert E. Paine (R)
Philetus Sawyer (R)
Cadwallader C. Washburn (R)

FORTY-SECOND CONGRESS

March 4, 1871 to March 3, 1873

President of The Senate:	Schuyler Colfax
President Pro Tempore of The Senate:	Henry B. Anthony
Speaker of The House of Representatives:	James G. Blaine

ALABAMA

Senators

George E. Spencer (R)
George T. Goldthwaite (D)
s. 1872

Representatives

Charles W. Buckley (R)
Peter M. Dox (D)
William A. Handley s. 1872
Charles Hays (R)
Joseph H. Stloss (D)
Benjamin S. Turner (R)

ARKANSAS

Senators

Benjamin F. Rice (R)
Powell Clayton (R)

Representatives

Thomas Boles (R) s. 1872
John Edwards (R) r. Feb. 1872
James M. Hanks (D)
Oliver P. Snyder (R)

CALIFORNIA

Senators

Cornelius Cole (R)
Eugene Casserly (D)

Representatives

John M. Coghlan (R)
Sherman O. Houghton (R)
Aaron A. Sargent (R)

CONNECTICUT

Senators

Orris S. Ferry (R)
William A. Buckingham (R)

Representatives

William H. Barnum (D)
Joseph R. Hawley (R) s. Dec. 1872
Stephen W. Kellogg (R)
Henry H. Starkweather (R)
Julius L. Strong (R) d. Sept. 1872

DELAWARE

Senators

Thomas F. Bayard (D)
Eli Saulsbury (D)

Representative

Benjamin T. Biggs (D)

FLORIDA

Senators

Thomas W. Osborn (R)
Abijah Gilbert (R)

Representatives

Silas L. Niblack (D) s. 1873
Josiah T. Walls (R) r. Jan. 1873

GEORGIA

Senators

Joshua Hill (R)
Thomas M. Norwood (D)

Representatives

Erasmus W. Beck (D) s. 1872
John S. Bigby (R)
Dudley M. DuBose (D)
Archibald T. MacIntyre (D)
William P. Price (D)
Thomas J. Speer (R) d. Aug. 1872
Richard H. Whiteley (R)
Pierce M. B. Young

ILLINOIS

Senators

Lyman Trumbull (R)
John A. Logan (R)

Representatives

John L. Beveridge (R) r. Jan. 1873
Horatio C. Burchard (R)
Burton C. Cook (R) r. Aug. 1871
John M. Crebs (D)
John F. Farnsworth (R)
Charles B. Farwell (R)
John B. Hawley (R)
John B. Hay (R)
Thompson W. McNeeley (D)
Samuel S. Marshall (D)
Jesse H. Moore (D)
Edward Y. Rice (R)
James C. Robinson (D)
Henry Snapp (R)
Bradford N. Stevens (D)

INDIANA

Senators

Oliver H. P. T. Morton (R)
Daniel D. Pratt (D)

Representatives

John Coburn (R)
William S. Holman (D)
Michael C. Kerr (D)
Mahlon D. Manson (D)
William E. Niblack (D)
Jasper Packard (R)
John P. C. Shanks (R)
James N. Tyner (R)
Daniel W. Voorhees (D)
William Williams (R)
Jeremiah M. Wilson (R)

IOWA

Senators

James Harlan (R)
George G. Wright (R)

Representatives

Aylett R. Cotton (R)
William G. Donnan (R)
George W. McCrary (R)
Jackson Orr (R)
Frank W. Palmer (R)
Madison M. Walden (R)

KANSAS

Senators

Samuel C. Pomeroy (R)
Alexander Caldwell (R)

Representative

David P. Lowe (R)

KENTUCKY

Senators

Garrett Davis (D) d. Sept. 1872
Willis B. Machen (D) s. 1872

John W. Stevenson (D)

Representatives

George M. Adams (D)
William E. Arthur (D)
James B. Beck (D)
Edward Crossland (D)
Joseph H. Lewis (D)
Henry D. McHenry (D)
William B. Read (D)
John M. Rice (D)
Boyd Winchester (D)

LOUISIANA

Senators

William P. Kellogg (R)
r. Nov. 1872
J. Rodman West (R)

Representatives

Aleck Boarman (Lib) s. 1872
Chester B. Darrall (R)
James McCleery (D) d. Nov. 1871
Frank Morey (R)
Lionel A. Sheldon (R)
J. Hale Sypher (R)

MAINE

Senators

Hannibal Hamlin (R)
Lot M. Morrill (R)

Representatives

James G. Blaine (R)
William P. Frye (R)
Eugene Hale (R)
John Lynch (R)
John A. Peters (R)

MARYLAND

Senators

George Vickers (D)
William T. Hamilton (D)

Representatives

Stevenson Archer (D)
Samuel Hambleton (D)
William M. Merrick (D)
John Ritchie (D)
Thomas Swann (D)

MASSACHUSETTS

Senators

Charles Sumner (R)
Henry Wilson r. Mar. 1873

Representatives

Oakes Ames (R)
Nathaniel P. Banks (R)
George M. Brooks (R) r. May 1872
James Buffinton (R)
Benjamin F. Butler (R)
Alvah Crocker (R) s. 1872
Henry L. Dawes
Constantine C. Esty (R) s. 1872
George F. Hoar (R)
Samuel Hooper (R)
Ginery Twichell (R)
William B. Washburn (R)
r. Dec. 1871

MICHIGAN

Senators

Zachariah Chandler (R)
Thomas W. Ferry (R)

Representatives

Austin Blair (R)
Omar D. Conger (R)
Wilder D. Foster (R)
William L. Stoughton (R)
Jabez G. Sutherland (D)
Henry Waldron (R)

MINNESOTA

Senators

Alexander Ramsey (R)
William Windom (R)

Representatives

John T. Averill (R)
Mark H. Dunnell (R)

MISSISSIPPI

Senators

Adelbert Ames (R)
James L. Alcorn (R)

Representatives

Henry W. Barry (R)
George E. Harris (R)
George C. McKee (R)
Joseph L. Morphis (R
Legrand W. Perce (R)

MISSOURI

Senators

Carl Schurz (R)
Francis P. Blair, Jr. (D)

Representatives

James G. Blair (D)
Samuel S. Burdett (R)
Abram Comingo (D)
Gustavus A. Finkelnburg (R)
Harrison E. Havens (R)
Andrew King (D)
James R. McCormick (D)
Isaac C. Parker (R)
Erastus Wells (D)

NEBRASKA

Senators

Thomas W. Tipton (D)
Phineas W. Hitchcock (R)

Representative

John Taffee (R)

NEVADA

Senators

William M. Stewart (R)
James W. Nye (R)

Representative

Charles W. Kendall (D)

NEW HAMPSHIRE

Senators

Aaron H. Cragin (Amer)
James W. Patterson (R)

Representatives

Samuel N. Bell (D)
Ellery A. Hibbard (D)
Hosea W. Parker (D)

NEW JERSEY

Senators

John P. Stockton (D)
Frederick T. Frelinghuysen (R)

Representatives

John T. Bird (D)
Samuel C. Forker (D)
George A. Halsey (R)
John W. Hazelton (R)
John Hill (R)

NEW YORK

Senators

Roscoe Conkling (R)
Reuben E. Fenton (R)

Representatives

James Brooks (D)
John M. Carroll (D)
Freeman Clarke (R)
Samuel S. Cox (D)
R. Holland Duell (R)
Smith Ely, Jr. (D)
Milo Goodrich (R)
John H. Ketcham (R)
Thomas Kinsella (D)
William H. Lamport (R)
William E. Lansing (R)
Clinton L. Merriam (R)
Eli Perry (D)
Clarkson N. Potter (D)
Elizur H. Prindle (R)
Ellis H. Roberts (R)
William R. Roberts (D)
John Rogers (D)
Robert B. Roosevelt (D)
Charles St. John (R)
John E. Seeley (R)
Walter L. Sessions (R)
Henry W. Slocum (D)
H. Boardman Smith (R)
Dwight Townsend (D)
Joseph H. Tuthill (D)
Seth Wakeman (R)
Joseph M. Warren (D)
William A. Wheeler (R)
William Williams (D)
Fernando Wood (D)

NORTH CAROLINA

Senators

John Pool
Matt W. Ransom (D) s. 1872

Representatives

Clinton L. Cobb (R)
James C. Harper (Con)
James M. Leach (Con)
Sion H. Rogers (D) s. 1872
Francis E. Shober (D)
Charles R. Thomas (R)
Alfred M. Waddell (D)

OHIO

Senators

John Sherman (R)
Allen G. Thurman (D)

Representatives

Jacob A. Ambler (R)
John Beatty (R)
John A. Bingham (R)
Lewis D. Campbell (D)
Ozro J. Dodds (D) s. 1872
Charles Foster (R)
James A. Garfield (R)
Charles N. Lamison (D)
John F. McKinney (D)
James Monroe (R)
George W. Morgan (D)
Erasmus D. Peck (R)
Aaron F. Perry (R) r. 1872
Samuel Shellabarger
John A. Smith (R)
William P. Sprague (R)
Job E. Stevenson (R)
William H. Upson (R)
Philadelph Van Trump (D)
John T. Wilson (R)

OREGON

Senators

Henry W. Corbett (R)
James K. Kelly (D)

Representative

James H. Slater (D)

PENNSYLVANIA

Senators

Simon Cameron (R)
John Scott (R)

Representatives

Ephraim L. Acker (R)
Frank C. Bunnell s. 1873
John V. Creely (R)
Oliver J. Dickey (R)
Henry D. Foster (D)
J. Lawrence Getz (D)
Samuel Griffith (D)
Richard J. Haldeman (D)
Alfred C. Harmer (R)
William D. Kelley (R)
John W. Killinger (R)
William McClelland (D)
Ebenezer McJunkin (R)
Ulysses Mercur (R) r. Dec. 1872
Benjamin F. Meyers (D)
Leonard Myers (R)
James S. Negley (R)
John B. Packer (R)
Samuel J. Randall (D)
Glenni W. Scofield (R)
Henry Sherwood (D)
Lazarus D. Schoemaker (R)
R. Milton Speer (D)
John B. Storm (D)
Washington Townsend (R)

RHODE ISLAND

Senators

Henry B. Anthony (R)
William Sprague (R)

Representatives

Benjamin T. Eames (R)
James M. Pendleton (R)

SOUTH CAROLINA

Senators

Thomas J. Robertson (R)
Frederick A. Sawyer (R)

Representatives

Robert C. De Large (R)
r. Jan. 1873
Robert B. Elliott (R)
Joseph H. Rainey (R)
Alexander S. Wallace (R)

TENNESSEE

Senators

William G. Brownlow (R)
Henry Cooper (D)

Representatives

John M. Bright (D)
Roderick R. Butler (R)
Robert P. Caldwell (D)
Abraham E. Garrett
Edward I. Golladay (D)
Horace Maynard (R)
William W. Vaughan (D)
Washington C. Whitthorne (D)

TEXAS

Senators

Morgan C. Hamilton (R)
James W. Flanagan(R)

Representatives

William T. Clark (R) s. 1872
John C. Conner (D)
De Witt C. Giddings (D) s. 1872
John Hancock (D)
William S. Herndon (D)

VERMONT

Senators

George F. Edmunds (R)
Justin S. Morrill (R)

Representatives

Luke P. Poland (R)
Worthington C. Smith (R)
Charles W. Willard (R)

VIRGINIA

Senators

John W. Johnston (Con)
John F. Lewis (R)

Representatives

Elliott M. Braxton (D)
John Critcher (Con)
Richard T. W. Duke (Con)
John T. Harris (D)
James H. Platt, Jr. (R)
Charles H. Porter (R)
William H. H. Stowell (R)
William Terry (Con)

WEST VIRGINIA

Senators

Arthur I. Boreman (R)
Henry G. Davis (D)

Representatives

John J. Davis (D)
Frank Hereford (D)
James C. McGrew (R)

WISCONSIN

Senators

Timothy O. Howe (R)
Matthew H. Carpenter (R)

Representatives

J. Allen Barber (R)
Charles A. Eldredge (D)
Gerry W. Hazelton (R)
Alexander Mitchell (D)
Jeremiah M. Rusk (R)
Philetus Sawyer (R)

FORTY-THIRD CONGRESS

March 4, 1873 to March 3, 1875

President of The Senate: Henry Wilson
Presidents Pro Tempore of The Senate: Matthew H. Carpenter
Henry B. Anthony
Speaker of The House of Representatives: James G. Blaine

ALABAMA

Senators

George E. Spencer (R)
George T. Goldthwaite (D)

Representatives

Frederick G. Bromberg (D)
John H. Caldwell (D)
Charles Hays (R)
Charles Pelham (R)
James T. Rapier (R)
Joseph H. Sloss (D)
Thomas M. Gunter (D) s. 1874
Asa Hodges (R) s. 1874
Oliver P. Snyder (R)
William W. Wilshire (R) r. June 1874

ARKANSAS

Senators

Powell Clayton (R)
Stephen W. Dorsey (R)

Representatives

CALIFORNIA

Senators

Eugene Casserly (D) r. Nov. 1873
John S. Hager (D) s. 1874

Aaron A. Sargent (R)

Representatives

Charles Clayton (R)
Sherman O. Hougton (R)
John K. Luttrell (D)
Horace F. Page (R)

CONNECTICUT

Senators

Orris S. Ferry (R)

William A. Buckingham (R) d. 1875
William W. Eaton (D) s. 1875

Representatives

William H. Barnum (D)
Joseph R. Hawley (R)
Stephen W. Kellogg (R)
Henry H. Starkweather (R)

DELAWARE

Senators

Thomas F. Bayard (D)
Eli Saulsbury (D)

Representative

James R. Lofland (R)

FLORIDA

Senators

Abijah Gilbert (R)
Simon B. Conover (R)

Representatives

William J. Purman (R) r. Jan. 1875
Josiah T. Walls (R)

GEORGIA

Senators

Thomas M. Norwood (D)
John B. Gordon (D)

Representatives

Hiram P. Bell (D)
James H. Blount (D)
Philip Cook (D)
James C. Freeman (D)
Henry R. Harris (D)
Morgan Rawls (D) r. Mar. 1874
Andrew Sloan (R) s. 1874
Alexander H. Stephens (D) s. 1874
Richard H. Whiteley (R)
Pierce M. B. Young (D)

ILLINOIS

Senators

John A. Logan (R)
Richard J. Oglesby (R)

Representatives

Granville Barrere (R)
Horatio C. Burchard (R)
Joseph G. Cannon (R)
Bernard G. Caulfield (D) s. 1875
Isaac Clements (R)
Franklin Corwin (R)
John R. Eden (D)
Charles B. Farwell (R)
Greenbury L. Fort (R)
John B. Hawley (R)
Stephen A. Hurlbut (R)
Robert M. Knapp (D)
John McNulta (R)
Samuel S. Marshall (D)
James S. Martin (D)
William R. Morrison (D)
William H. Ray (R)
John B. Rice (D) d. 1874
James C. Robinson (D)
Jasper D. Ward (D)

INDIANA

Senators

Oliver H. P. T. Morton (R)
Daniel D. Pratt (R)

Representatives

Thomas J. Cason (D)
John Coburn (D)
William S. Holman (D)
Morton C. Hunter (R)
William E. Niblack (D)
Godlove S. Orth (R)
Jasper Packard (R)
John P. C. Shanks (R)
Henry B. Sayler (R)
James N. Tyner (R)
Jeremiah M. Wilson (R)
William Williams (R)
Simeon K. Wolfe (D)

IOWA

Senators

George G. Wright (R)
William B. Allison (R)

Representatives

Aylett R. Cotton (R)
William G. Donnan (R)
John A. Kasson (R)
William Loughridge (R)
George W. McCrary (R)
James W. McDill (R)
Henry O. Pratt (R)
Jackson Orr (R)
James Wilson (R)

KANSAS

Senators

Alexander Caldwell (R)
r. Mar. 1873
Robert Crozier (R) ta. 1873
James M. Harvey (R) s. 1874

John J. Ingalls (R)

Representatives

Stephen A. Cobb (R)
David P. Lowe (R)
William A. Phillips (R)

KENTUCKY

Senators

John W. Stevenson (D)
Thomas C. McCreery (D)

Representatives

George M. Adams (D)
William E. Arthur (D)
James B. Beck (D)
John Y. Brown (D)
Edward Crossland (D)
Milton J. Durham (D)
Charles W. Milliken (D)
William B. Read (D)
Elisha D. Standiford (D)
John D. Young (D)

LOUISIANA

Senators

J. Rodman West (R)
Vacant

Representatives

Chester B. Darrall (R)
Effingham Lawrence (D) s. 1875
Frank Morey (R)
Lionel A. Sheldon (R)
George A. Sheridan (Lib) s. 1875
George L. Smith (R)
J. Hale Sypher (R)

MAINE

Senators

Hannibal Hamlin (R)
Lot M. Morrill (R)

Representatives

James G. Blaine (R)
John H. Burleigh (R)
William P. Frye (R)
Eugene Hale (R)
Samuel Hersey (R) d. Feb. 1875

MARYLAND

Senators

William T. Hamilton (D)
George R. Dennis (D)

Representatives

William J. Albert (R)
Stevenson Archer (D)
Lloyd Lowndes, Jr. (R)
William J. O'Brien (D)
Thomas Swann (D)
Ephraim K. Wilson (D)

MASSACHUSETTS

Senators

Charles Sumner (R) d. Mar. 1874
William B. Washburn (R) s. 1874

George S. Boutwell (R)

Representatives

James Buffinton (R)
Benjamin F. Butler (R)
Alvah Crocker (R) d. Dec. 1874
Henry L. Dawes
Daniel W. Gooch (R)
Benjamin W. Harris (R)
Ebenezer R. Hoar (R)
George F. Hoar (R)
Samuel Hooper (R) d. Feb. 1875
Henry L. Pierce (R)
Charles A. Stevens
William Whiting (R) d. June 1873
John M. S. Williams (R)

MICHIGAN

Senators

Zachariah Chandler (R)
Thomas W. Ferry (R)

Representatives

Josiah W. Begole (R)
Nathan B. Bradley (R)
Julius C. Burrows (R)
Omar D. Conger (R)
Moses W. Field (R)
Jay A. Hubbell (R)
Henry Waldron (R)
George Willard (R)
William B. Williams (R)

MINNESOTA

Senators

Alexander Ramsey (R)
William Windom (R)

Representatives

John T. Averill (R)
Mark H. Dunnell (R)
Horace B. Strait (R)

MISSISSIPPI

Senators

Adelbert Ames (R) r. Jan. 1874
Henry R. Pease (R) s. 1874

James L. Alcorn (R)

Representatives

Henry W. Barry (R)
Albert R. Howe (R)
Lucius Q. C. Lamar (D)
John R. Lynch (R)
George C. McKee (R)
Jason Niles (R)

MISSOURI

Senators

Carl Schurz (R)
Lewis V. Bogy (D)

Representatives

Richard P. Bland (D)
Aylett H. Buckner (D)
John B. Clark, Jr. (D)
Abram Comingo (D)
Thomas T. Crittenden (D)
John M. Glover (D)
Robert A. Hatcher (D)
Harrison E. Havens (R)
Ira B. Hyde (R)
Isaac C. Parker (R)
Edwin O. Stanard (R)
William H. Stone (D)
Erastus Wells (D)

NEBRASKA

Senators

Thomas W. Tipton (D)
Phileas W. Hitchcock (R)

Representative

Lorenzo Crounse (R)

NEVADA

Senators

William M. Stewart (R)
John P. Jones (R)

Representative

Charles W. Kendall (D)

NEW HAMPSHIRE

Senators

Aaron H. Cragin (Amer)
Bainbridge Wadleigh (R)

Representatives

Hosea W. Parker (D)
Austin F. Pike (R)
William B. Small (R)

NEW JERSEY

Senators

John P. Stockton (D)
Frederick T. Frelinghuysen (R)

Representatives

Amos Clark, Jr. (R)
Samuel A. Dobbins (R)
Robert Hamilton (D)
John W. Hazelton (R)
William W. Phelps (R)
Isaac W. Scudder (R)
Marcus L. Ward (R)

NEW YORK

Senators

Roscoe Conkling (R)
Reuben E. Fenton (R)

Representatives

Lyman K. Bass (R)
James Brooks (D) d. Apr. 1873
Simeon B. Chittenden (R) s. 1874
Freeman Clarke (R)
Samuel S. Cox (D)
Thomas J. Creamer (D)
Philip S. Crooke (R)
David M. De Witt (D)
R. Holland Duell (R)
Robert S. Hale (R)
Henry H. Hathorn (R)
George G. Hoskins (R)
William H. Lamport (R)
William E. Lansing (R)
John D. Lawson (R)
Clinton MacDougall (R)
David B. Mellish (R) d. May 1874
Clinton L. Merriam (R)
Eli Perry (D)
Thomas C. Platt (R)
Clarkson N. Potter (D)
Ellis H. Roberts (R)
William R. Roberts (D)
Charles St. John (R)
Richard Schell (D) s. 1874
John G. Schumaker (D)
Henry J. Scudder (R)
Walter L. Sessions
James S. Smart (R)
H. Boardman Smith (R)
Lyman Tremain (R)
William A. Wheeler (R)
John O. Whitehouse (D)
David Wilber (R)
Fernando Wood (D)
Stewart L. Woodford (R) r. 1874

NORTH CAROLINA

Senators

Matt W. Ransom (D)
Augustus S. Merrimon

Representatives

Thomas S. Ashe (Con)
Clinton L. Cobb (R)
James M. Leach (Con)
William M. Robbins (D)
William A. Smith (R)
Charles R. Thomas (R)
Robert B. Vance (D)
Alfred M. Waddell (D)

OHIO

Senators

John Sherman
Allen G. Thurman (D)

Representatives

Henry B. Banning (D)
John Berry (D)
Hezekiah S. Bundy (R)
Lorenzo Danford (R)
William E. Finck (D) s. 1874
Charles Foster (R)
James A. Garfield (R)
Lewis B. Gunckel (R)
Hugh J. Jewett (D) r. June 1874
Charles N. Lamison (D)
William Lawrence (R)
James Monroe (R)
Lawrence T. Neal (D)
Richard C. Parsons (R)
James W. Robinson (R)
Milton Sayler (D)
Isaac R. Sherwood (R)
John Q. Smith (R)
Milton I. Southard (D)
William P. Sprague (R)
Laurin D. Woodworth (D)

OREGON

Senators

James K. Kelly (D)
John H. Mitchell (R)

Representatives

James W. Nesmith (D)
Joseph G. Wilson (R) d. July 1873

PENNSYLVANIA

Senators

Simon Cameron (R)
John Scott (R)

Representatives

Charles Albright (R)
James S. Biery (R)
John Cessna (R)
Hiester Clymer (D)
Carlton B. Curtis (R)
Alfred C. Harmer (R)
William D. Kelley (R)
John W. Killinger (D)
Ebenezer McJunkin (R)
r. Jan. 1875
John A. Magee (D)
William S. Moore (R)
Leonard Myers (R)
James S. Negley (R)
Charles O'Neill (R)
John B. Packer (R)
Samuel J. Randall (D)
Hiram L. Richmond (R)
Sobieski Ross (R)
Glenni W. Scofield (R)
Lazarus D. Shoemaker (R)
A. Herr Smith (R)
R. Milton Speer (D)
John B. Storm (D)
James D. Strawbridge (R)
Alexander W. Taylor (R)
John M. Thompson (R) s. 1875
Lemuel Todd (R)
Washington Townsend (R)

RHODE ISLAND

Senators

Henry B. Anthony (R)
William Sprague (R)

Representatives

Benjamin T. Eames (R)
James M. Pendleton (R)

SOUTH CAROLINA

Senators

Thomas J. Robertson (R)
John J. Patterson (R)

Representatives

Richard H. Cain (R)
Lewis C. Carpenter (R) s. 1874
Robert B. Elliott (R) r. Nov. 1874
Joseph H. Rainey (R)
Alonzo J. Ransier (R)
Alexander S. Wallace (R)

TENNESSEE

Senators

William G. Brownlow (R)
Henry Cooper (D)

Representatives

John D. C. Atlins (D)
John M. Bright (D)
Roderick R. Butler (R)
William Crutchfield (R)
Horace H. Harrison (R)
Barbour Lewis (R)
Horace Maynard (R)
David A. Nunn (R)
Jacob M. Thornburgh (R)
Washington C. Whitthorne (D)

TEXAS

Senators

Morgan C. Hamilton (R)
James W. Flanagan (R)

Representatives

De Witt C. Giddings (D)
John Hancock (D)
William S. Herndon (D)
William P. McLean (D)
Roger Q. Mills (D)
Asa H. Willie (D)

VERMONT

Senators

George F. Edmunds (R)
Justin S. Morrill (R)

Representatives

George W. Hendee (R)
Luke P. Poland (R)
Charles W. Willard (R)

VIRGINIA

Senators

John W. Johnston (Con)
John F. Lewis (R)

Representatives

Rees T. Bowen (Con)
Alexander M. Davis r. Mar. 1874
John T. Harris (D)
Eppa Hunton (D)
James H. Platt, Jr. (R)
James B. Sener (R)
J. Amber Smith (R)
William H. H. Stowell (R)
Christoper Y. Thomas (R) s. 1874
Thomas Whitehead (Con)

WEST VIRGINIA

Senators

Arthur I. Boreman (R)
Henry G. Davis (D)

Representatives

John J. Davis (D) s. 1874
John M. Hagans (R) s. 1874
Frank Hereford (D)

WISCONSIN

Senators

Timothy O. Howe (R)
Matthew H. Carpenter (R)

Representatives

J. Allen Barber (R)
Charles A. Eldredge (D)
Gerry W. Hazelton (R)
Alexander S. McDill (R)
Alexander Mitchell (R)
Jeremiah M. Rusk (R)
Philetus Sawyer (R)
Charles G. Williams (R)

FORTY-FOURTH CONGRESS

March 4, 1875 to March 3, 1877

President of The Senate: Henry Wilson
President Pro Tempore of The Senate: Thomas W. Ferry
Speakers of The House of Representatives: Michael C. Kerr
Samuel J. Randall

ALABAMA

Senators

George E. Spencer (R)
George T. Goldthwaite (D)

Representatives

Taul Bradford (D)
John H. Caldwell (D)
William H. Forney (D)
Jeremiah Haralson (R)
Charles Hays (R)
Goldsmith W. Hewitt (D)
Burwell B. Lewis (D)
Jeremiah N. Williams (D)

ARKANSAS

Senators

Powell Clayton (R)
Stephen W. Dorsey (R)

Representatives

Lucien C. Gause (D)
Thomas M. Gunter (D)
William F. Slemons (D)
William W. Wilshire (R)

CALIFORNIA

Senators

Aaron A. Sargent (R)
Newton Booth (Anti-Monopolist)

Representatives

John K. Luttrell (D)
Horace F. Page (R)
William A. Piper (D)
Peter D. Wigginton (D)

COLORADO

Senators

Jerome B. Chaffee (R) s. 1876
Henry M. Teller (R) s. 1876

Representative

James B. Belford (R) s. 1877

CONNECTICUT

Senators

Orris S. Ferry (R, D) d. Nov. 1875
James E. English (D) ta. 1875
William H. Barnum (D) s. 1876

William W. Eaton (D)

Representatives

William H. Barnum (D) r. May 1876
George M. Landers (D)
James Phelps (D)
Henry H. Starkweather (R) d. Jan. 1876
John T. Wait (R) s. 1876
Levi Warner (D) s. 1876

DELAWARE

Senators

Thomas F. Bayard (D)
Eli Saulsbury (D)

Representative

James Williams (D)

FLORIDA

Senators

Simon B. Conover (R)
Charles W. Jones (D)

Representatives

Jesse J. Finley (D) s. 1876
William J. Purman (R)
Josiah T. Walls (R) r. Apr. 1876

GEORGIA

Senators

Thomas M. Norwood (D)
John B. Gordon (D)

Representatives

James H. Blount (D)
Milton A. Candler (D)
Philip Cook (D)
William H. Felton (D)
Henry R. Harris (D)
Julian Hartridge (D)
Benjamin H. Hill (D)
William E. Smith (D)
Alexander H. Stephens (D)

ILLINOIS

Senators

John A. Logan (R)
Richard J. Oglesby (R)

Representatives

William B. Anderson (D)
John C. Bagby (R)
Horatio C. Burchard (R)
Alexander Campbell
Joseph G. Cannon (R)
Bernard G. Caulfield (D)
John R. Eden (D)
Charles B. Farwell (R) r. May 1876
Greenbury L. Fort (R)
Carter H. Harrison (D)
William Hartzell (D)
Thomas J. Henderson (R)
Stephen A. Hurlbut (R)
John V. Le Moyne (R) s. 1876
William R. Morrison (D)
William A. J. Sparks (D)
William M. Springer (D)
Adlai E. Stevenson (D)
Richard H. Whiting (R)
Scott Wike (D)

INDIANA

Senators

Oliver H. P. T. Morton (R)
Joseph E. McDonald (D)

Representatives

John H. Baker (R)
Nathan T. Carr (D) s. 1876
Thomas J. Cason (R)
James L. Evans (R)
Benoni S. Fuller (D)
Andrew H. Hamilton (D)
William S. Haymond (D)
William S. Holman (D)
Andrew Humphreys (D) s. 1876
Morton C. Hunter (R)
Michael C. Kerr (D) d. Aug. 1876
Franklin Landers (D)
Jeptha D. New (D)
Milton S. Robinson (R)
James D. Williams (D) r. Dec. 1876

IOWA

Senators

George G. Wright (R)
William B. Allison (R)

Representatives

Lucien L. Ainsworth (Anti-Monopolist)
John A. Kasson (R)
George W. McCrary (R)
James W. McDill (R)
S. Addison Oliver (R)
Henry O. Pratt (R)
Ezekiel S. Sampson (R)
John Q. Tufts (R)
James Wilson (R)

KANSAS

Senators

John J. Ingalls (R)
James M. Harvey (R)

Representatives

William R. Brown (R)
John R. Goodin (D)
William A. Phillips (R)

KENTUCKY

Senators

John W. Stevenson (D)
Thomas C. McCreery (D)

Representatives

Joseph C. S. Blackburn (D)
Andrew R. Boone (D)
John Y. Brown (D)
John B. Clarke (D)
Milton J. Durham (D)
Thomas L. Jones (D)
J. Proctor Knott (D)
Charles W. Milliken (D)
Edward Y. Parsons (D) d. July 1876
Henry Watterson (D) s. 1876
John D. White (R)

LOUISIANA

Senators

J. Rodman West (R)
James B. Eustis (D) s. 1876

Representatives

Chester B. Darrall (R)
E. John Ellis (D)
Randall L. Gibson (D)
William M. Levy (D)
Frank Morey (R) r. June 1876
Charles E. Nash (R)
William B. Spencer (D) s. 1876 r. Jan. 1877

MAINE

Senators

Hannibal Hamlin (R)

Lot M. Morrill (R) r. July 1876
James G. Blaine (R) s. 1876

Representatives

James G. Blaine (R) r. July 1876
John H. Burleigh (R)
Edwin Flye (R) s. 1876
William P. Frye (R)
Eugene Hale (R)
Harris M. Plaisted (R)

MARYLAND

Senators

George R. Dennis (D)
William P. Whyte (D)

Representatives

Eli J. Henkle (D)
William J. O'Brien (D)
Charles B. Roberts (D)
Thomas Swann (D)
Philip F. Thomas (D)
William Walsh (D)

MASSACHUSETTS

Senators

George S. Boutwell (R)
Henry L. Dawes (R)

Representatives

Josiah G. Abbott (D) s. 1876
Nathaniel P. Banks (R)
Chester W. Chapin (D)

William W. Crapo (R)
Rufus S. Frost (R) r. July 1876
Benjamin W. Harris (R)
George F. Hoar (R)
Henry L. Pierce (R)
Julius H. Seelye
John K. Tarbox (D)
Charles P. Thompson (D)
William W. Warren (D)

MICHIGAN

Senators

Thomas W. Ferry (R)
Isaac P. Christiancy (R)

Representatives

Nathan B. Bradley (R)
Omar D. Conger (R)
George H. Durand (D)
Jay A. Hubbell (R)
Allen Potter
Henry Waldron (R)
George Willard (R)
Alpheus S. Williams (D)
William B. Williams (R)

MINNESOTA

Senators

William Windom (R)
Samuel J. R. McMillan (R)

Representatives

Mark H. Dunnell (R)
William S. King (R)
Horace B. Strait (R)

MISSISSIPPI

Senators

James L. Alcorn (R)
Blanche K. Bruce (R)

Representatives

Charles E. Hooker (D)
Lucius Q. C. Lamar (D)
John R. Lynch (R)
Hernando D. Money (D)
Otho R. Singleton (D)
G. Wiley Wells (R)

MISSOURI

Senators

Lewis V. Bogy (D)
Francis M. Cockrell (D)

Representatives

Richard P. Bland (D)
Aylett H. Buckner (D)
John B. Clark, Jr. (D)
Rezin A. De Bolt (D)
Benjamin J. Franklin (D)
John M. Glover (D)
Robert A. Hatcher (D)
Edward C. Kehr (D)
Charles H. Morgan (D)
John F. Philips (D)
David Rea (D)
William H. Stone (D)
Erastus Wells (D)

NEBRASKA

Senators

Phineas W. Hitchock
Algernon S. Paddock (R)

Representative

Lorenzo Crounse (R)

NEVADA

Senators

John P. Jones (R)
William Sharon (R)

Representative

William Woodburn (R)

NEW HAMPSHIRE

Senators

Aaron H. Cragin (Amer)
Bainbridge Wadleigh (R)

Representatives

Samuel N. Bell (D)
Henry W. Blair (R)
Frank Jones (D)

NEW JERSEY

Senators

Frederick T. Frelinghuysen (R)
Theodore F. Randolph (D)

Representatives

Samuel A. Dobbins (R)
Augustus W. Cutler (D)
Robert Hamilton (D)
Augustus A. Hardenbergh (D)
Miles Ross (D)
Clement H. Sinnickson (R)
Frederick H. Teese (D)

NEW YORK

Senators

Roscoe Conkling (R)
Francis Kernan (D)

Representatives

Charles H. Adams (R)
George A. Bagley (R)
John H. Bagley, Jr. (D)
William H. Baker (R)
Lyman K. Bass (R)
George M. Beebe (D)
Archibald M. Bliss (D)
Simeon B. Chittendin (R)
Samuel S. Cox (D)
John M. Davy (R)
Smith Ely, Jr., (D) r. Dec. 1876
David Dudley Field (D) s. 1877
Henry H. Hathorn (R)
Abram S. Hewitt (D)
George G. Hoskins (R)
Elbridge G. Lapham (R)
Elias W. Leavenworth (R)
Scott Lord (D)
Clinton D. MacDougall (R)
Edwin R. Meade (D)
Henry B. Metcalfe (D)
Samuel F. Miller (R)
Nelson I. Norton (R)
N. Holmes Odell (D)
Thomas C. Platt (R)
John G. Schumaker (D)
Martin I. Townsend (R)
Charles C. B. Walker (D)
Elijah Ward (D)
William A. Wheeler (R)
John O. Whitehouse (D)
Andrew Williams (R)
Benjamin A. Willis
Fernando Wood (D)

NORTH CAROLINA

Senators

Matt W. Ransom (D)
Augustus S. Merrimon (D)

Representatives

Thomas S. Ashe (D)
Joseph J. Davis (D)
John A. Hyman (R)
William M. Robbins (D)
Alfred M. Scales (D)
Robert B. Vance (D)
Alfred M. Waddell (D)
Jesse J. Yeates (D)

OHIO

Senators

John Sherman (R)
Allen G. Thurman (D)

Representatives

Henry B. Banning (D)
Jacob P. Cowan
Lorenzo Danford (R)
Charles Foster (R)
James Garfield (R)
Frank H. Hurd (D)
William Lawrençe (R)
John A. McMahon (D)
James Monroe (R)
Lawrence T. Neal (D)
Henry B. Payne (D)
Earley F. Poppleton (D)
Americus V. Rice (D)
John S. Savage (D)
Milton Sayler (D)
Milton I. Southard (D)
John L. Vance (D)
Nelson H. Van Vorhes (R)
Ansel T. Walling (D)
Laurin D. Woodworth (R)

OREGON

Senators

James K. Kelly (D)
John H. Mitchell (R)

Representatives

George A. La Dow (D) d. May 1875
La Fayette Lane (D)

PENNSYLVANIA

Senators

Simon Cameron (R)
William A. Wallace (D)

Representatives

Hiester Clymer (D)
Alexander G. Cochran (D)
Francis D. Collins (D)
Albert G. Egbert (D)
Chapman Freeman (R)
James H. Hopkins (D)
George A. Jenks (D)
William D. Kelley (R)
Winthrop W. Ketchum (R) r. July 1876
Levi A. Mackey (D)
Levi Maish (D)
William Mutchler (D)
Charles O'Neill (R)
John B. Packer (R)
Joseph Powell (D)
Samuel J. Randall (D)
James B. Reilly (D)
John Reilly (D)
John Robbins (R)
Sobieski Ross (R)
James Sheakley (D)
A. Herr Smith (R)
William H. Stanton (D) s. 1876
William S. Stenger (D)
Washington Townsend (R)
Jacob Turney (D)
John W. Wallace (R)
Alan Wood, Jr. (R)

RHODE ISLAND

Senators

Henry B. Anthony (R)
Ambrose E. Burnside (R)

Representatives

Latimer W. Ballou (R)
Benjamin T. Eames (R)

SOUTH CAROLINA

Senators

Thomas J. Robertson (R)
John J. Patterson (R)

Representatives

Charles W. Buttz (R) s. 1877
Solomon L. Hoge (R)
Edmund W. M. Mackey (R) r. July 1876
Joseph H. Rainey (R)
Robert Smalls (R)
Alexander S. Wallace (R)

TENNESSEE

Senators

Henry Cooper (D)

Andrew Johnson (D) d. July 1875
David M. Key (D) ta. 1875
James E. Bailey (D) s. 1877

Representatives

John D. C. Atkins (D)
John M. Bright (D)
William P. Caldwell (D)
George G. Dibrell (D)
John F. House (D)
William McFarland (D)
Haywood Y. Riddle (D) s. 1876
Jacob M. Thornburgh (R)
Washington C. Whitthorne (D)
H. Casey Young (D)

TEXAS

Senators

Morgan C. Hamilton (R)
Samuel B. Maxey (D)

Representatives

David B. Culberson (D)
John Hancock (D)
Roger Q. Mills (D)
John H. Reagan (D)
Gustave Schleicher (D)
James W. Throckmorton (D)

VERMONT

Senators

George F. Edmunds (R)
Justin S. Morrill (R)

Representatives

Dudley C. Denison (R)
George W. Hendee (R)
Charles H. Joyce (R)

VIRGINIA

Senators

John W. Johnston (Con)
Robert E. Withers (Con)

Representatives

George C. Cabell (D)
Beverly B. Douglas (Con)
John Goode, Jr. (D)
John T. Harris (D)
Eppa Hunton (D)
William H. H. Stowell (R)
William Terry (Con)
John R. Tucker (D)
Gilbert C. Walker (Con)

WEST VIRGINIA

Senators

Henry G. Davis (D)

Allen T. Caperton (D) d. July 1876
Samuel Price ta. 1876
Frank Hereford (D) s. 1877

Representatives

Charles J. Faulkner (D)
Frank Hereford (D) r. Jan. 1877
Benjamin Wilson (D)

WISCONSIN

Senators

Timothy O. Howe (R)
Angus Cameron (R)

Representatives

Samuel D. Burchard (D)
Lucien B. Caswell (R)
George W. Cate
Alanson M. Kimball (R)
William P. Lynde (D)
Henry S. Magoon (R)
Jeremiah M. Rusk (R)
Charles G. Williams (R)

FORTY-FIFTH CONGRESS

March 4, 1877 to March 3, 1879

President of The Senate: William A. Wheeler
President Pro Tempore of The Senate: Thomas W. Ferry
Speaker of The House of Representatives: Samuel J. Randall

ALABAMA

Senators

George E. Spencer (R)
John T. Morgan (D)

Representatives

William H. Forney (D)
William W. Garth (D)
Hilary A. Herbert (D)
Goldsmith W. Hewitt (D)
James T. Jones (D)
Robert F. Ligon (D)
Charles M. Shelley (D)
Jeremiah N. Williams (D)

ARKANSAS

Senators

Stephen W. Dorsey (R)
Augustus H. Garland (D)

Representatives

Jordan E. Cravens (D)
Lucien C. Gause (D)
Thomas M. Gunter (D)
William F. Slemons (D)

CALIFORNIA

Senators

Aaron A. Sargent (R)
Newton Booth (Anti-Monopolist)

Representatives

Horace Davis (R)
John K. Luttrell (D)
Romualdo Pacheco (R) r. Feb. 1878
Horace F. Page (R)
Peter D. Wigginton (D) s. 1878

COLORADO

Senators

Jerome B. Chaffee (R)
Henry M. Teller (R)

Representatives

James B. Belford (R) r. Dec. 1877
Thomas M. Patterson (D)

CONNECTICUT

Senators

William W. Eaton (D)
William H. Barnum (D)

Representatives

George M. Landers (D)
James Phelps (D)
John T. Wait (R)
Levi Warner (D)

DELAWARE

Senators

Thomas F. Bayard (D)
Eli Saulsbury (D)

Representative

James Williams (D)

FLORIDA

Senators

Simon B. Conover (R)
Charles W. Jones (D)

Representatives

Horatio Bisbee, Jr. (R) r. Feb. 1879
Robert H. M. Davidson (D)
Jesse J. Finley (D) s. 1879

GEORGIA

Senators

John B. Gordon (D)
Benjamin H. Hill (D)

Representatives

Hiram P. Bell (D)
James H. Blount (D)
Milton A. Candler (D)
Philip Cook (D)
William H. Felton (D)
William B. Fleming (D) s. 1879
Henry R. Harris (D)
Julian Hartridge (D) d. Jan. 1879
William E. Smith (D)
Alexander H. Stephens

ILLINOIS

Senators

Richard J. Oglesby (R)
David Davis (R)

Representatives

William Aldrich (R)
Thomas A. Boyd (R)
Lorenzo Brentano (R)
Horatio C. Burchard (R)
Joseph G. Cannon (R)
John R. Eden (D)
Greenbury L. Fort (R)
Carter H. Harrison (D)
William Hartzell (D)
Philip C. Hayes (R)
Thomas J. Henderson (R)
Robert M. Knapp (D)
William Lathrop (R)
Benjamin F. Marsh (R)
William R. Morrison (D)
William A. J. Sparks (D)
William M. Springer (D)
Thomas F. Tipton (R)
Richard W. Townshend (D)

INDIANA

Senators

Oliver H. P. T. Morton (R) d. 1877
Daniel W. Voorhees (D)

Joseph E. McDonald (D)

Representatives

John H. Baker (R)
George A. Bicknell (D)
Thomas M. Browne (R)
William H. Calkins (R)
Thomas R. Cobb (D)
Benoni S. Fuller (D)
James L. Evans (R)
Andrew H. Hamilton (D)
John Hanna (R)
Morton C. Hunter (R)
Milton S. Robinson (R)
Leonidas Sexton (R)
Michael D. White (R)

IOWA

Senators

William B. Allison (R)
Samuel J. Kirkwood (R)

Representatives

Theodore W. Burdick (R)
Rush Clark (R)
Henry J. B. Cummings (R)
Nathaniel C. Deering (R)
S. Addison Oliver (R)
Hiram Price (R)
Ezekiel S. Sampson (R)
William F. Sapp (R)
Joseph C. Stone (R)

KANSAS

Senators

John J. Ingalls (R)
Preston B. Plumb (R)

Representatives

Dudley C. Haskell (R)
William A. Phillips (R)
Thomas Ryan (R)

KENTUCKY

Senators

Thomas C. McCreery (D)
James B. Beck (D)

Representatives

Joseph C. S. Blackburn (D)
Andrew R. Boone (D)
John W. Caldwell (D)
John G. Carlisle (D)
John B. Clarke (D)
Milton J. Durham (D)
J. Proctor Knott (D)
James A. McKenzie (D)
Thomas Turner (D)
Albert S. Willis (D)

LOUISIANA

Senators

William P. Kellogg (R)
James B. Eustis (D)

Representatives

Joseph H. Acklen (D) s. 1878
Chester B. Darrall (R) r. 1878
Joseph B. Elam (D)
E. John Ellis (D)
Randall L. Gibson (D)
John E. Leonard (R) d. 1878
Edward W. Robertson (D)
John S. Young (D) s. 1878

MAINE

Senators

Hannibal Hamlin (R)
James G. Blaine (R)

Representatives

William P. Frye (R)
Eugene Hale (R)
Stephen D. Lindsey (R)
Llewellyn Powers (R)
Thomas B. Reed (R)

MARYLAND

Senators

George R. Dennis (D)
William P. Whyte (D)

Representatives

Eli J. Henkle (D)
Daniel M. Henry (D)
William Kimmel (D)
Charles B. Roberts (D)
Thomas Swann (D)
William Walsh (D)

MASSACHUSETTS

Senators

Henry L. Dawes (R)
George F. Hoar (R)

Representatives

Nathaniel P. Banks (R)
Benjamin F. Butler (R)
William Claflin (R)
William W. Crapo (R)
Benjamin Dean (D) s. 1878
Walbridge A. Field (R) r. Mar. 1878
Benjamin W. Harris (R)
George B. Loring (R)
Leopold Morse (D)
Amasa Norcross (R)
William W. Rice (R)
George D. Robinson (R)

MICHIGAN

Senators

Thomas W. Ferry (R)
Isaac P. Christiancy (R)
r. Feb. 1879

Representatives

Mark S. Brewer (R)
Omar D. Conger (R)
Charles C. Ellsworth (R)
Jay A. Hubbell (R)
Edwin W. Keightley (R)
Jonas H. McGowan (R)
John W. Stone (R)
Alpheus S. Williams (D) d. 1878
Edwin Willits (R)

MINNESOTA

Senators

William Windom (R)
Samuel J. R. McMillan (R)

Representatives

Mark H. Dunnell (R)
Jacob H. Stewart (R)
Horace B. Strait (R)

MISSISSIPPI

Senators

Blanche K. Bruce (R)
Lucius Q. C. Lamar (D)

Representatives

James R. Chalmers (D)
Charles E. Hooker (D)
Vannoy H. Manning (D)
Hernando D. Money (D)
Henry L. Muldrow (D)
Otho R. Singleton (D)

MISSOURI

Senators

Lewis V. Bogy (D) d. Sept. 1877
David H. Armstrong (D) ta. 1877
James Shields (D) s. 1879

Francis M. Cockrell (D)

Representatives

Richard P. Bland (D)
Aylett H. Buckner (D)
John B. Clark, Jr. (D)
Nathan Cole (R)
Thomas T. Crittenden (D)
Benjamin J. Franklin (D)
John M. Glover (D)
Robert A. Hatcher (D)
Anthony Ittner (R)
Lyne S. Metcalfe (R)
Charles H. Morgan (D)
Henry M. Pollard (R)
David Rea (D)

NEBRASKA

Senators

Algernon S. Paddock (R)
Alvin Saunders (R)

Representative

Thomas J. Majors (R) s. 1878
Frank Welch (R) d. 1878

NEVADA

Senators

John P. Jones (R)
William Sharon (R)

Representative

Thomas Wren (R)

NEW HAMPSHIRE

Senators

Bainbridge Wadleigh (R)
Edward H. Rollins (R)

Representatives

Henry W. Blair (R)
James F. Briggs (R)
Frank Jones (D)

NEW JERSEY

Senators

Theodore F. Randolph (D)
John R. McPherson (D)

Representatives

Alvah A. Clark (D)
Augustus W. Cutler (D)
Augustus A. Hardenbergh (D)
Thomas B. Peddie (R)
John H. Pugh (R)
Miles Ross (D)
Clement H. Sinnickson (R)

NEW YORK

Senators

Roscoe Conkling (R)
Francis Kernan (D)

Representatives

William J. Bacon (R)
George A. Bagley (R)
John M. Bailey (R) s. 1878
William H. Baker (R)
George M. Beebe (D)
Charles B. Benedict (D)
Archibald M. Bliss (D)
Solomon Bundy (R)
John H. Camp (R)
Simeon B. Chittenden (R)
James W. Covert (D)
Samuel S. Cox (D)
Jeremiah W. Dwight (R)
Anthony Eickhoff (D)
E. Kirke Hart (D)
Abram S. Hewitt (D)
Frank Hiscock (R)
John N. Hungerford (R)
Amaziah B. James (R)
John H. Ketcham (R)
Elbridge G. Lapham (R)
Daniel N. Lockwood (R)
Anson G. McCook (R)
Stephen L. Mayham (D)
Nicholas Muller (D)
George W. Patterson (R)
Clarkson N. Potter (D)
Terence J. Quinn (D) d. June 1878
John H. Starin (R)
Martin I. Townsend (R)
William D. Veeder (D)
Andrew Williams (R)
Benjamin A. Willis (D)
Fernando Wood (D)

NORTH CAROLINA

Senators

Matt W. Ransom (D)
Augustus S. Merrimon (D)

Representatives

Curtis H. Brogden (R)
Joseph J. Davis (D)
William M. Robbins (D)
Alfred M. Scales (D)
Walter L. Steele (D)
Robert B. Vance (D)
Alfred M. Waddell (D)
Jesse J. Yeates (D)

OHIO

Senators

Stanley Matthews (R)
Allen G. Thurman (D)

Representatives

Henry B. Banning (D)
Jacob D. Cox (R)
Lorenzo Danford (R)
Henry L. Dickey (D)
Thomas Ewing (D)
Ebenezer B. Finley (D)
Charles Foster (R)
Mills Gardner (R)
James A. Garfield (R)
John S. Jones (R)
J. Warren Keifer (R)
William McKinley, Jr. (R)
John A. McMahon (D)
James Monroe (R)
Henry S. Neal (R)
Americus V. Rice (D)
Milton Sayler (D)
Milton I. Southard (D)
Amos Townsend (R)
Nelson H. Van Vorhes (R)

OREGON

Senators

John H. Mitchell (R)
La Fayette Grover (D)

Representative

Richard Williams (R)

PENNSYLVANIA

Senators

Simon Cameron (R) r. Mar. 1877
J. Donald Cameron (R) s. 1877

William A. Wallace (D)

Representatives

Thomas M. Bayne (R)
Samuel A. Bridges (D)
Jacob M. Campbell (R)
Hiester Clymer (D)
Francis D. Collins (D)
Russell Errett (R)
I. Newton Evans (R)
Chapman Freeman (R)
Alfred C. Harmer (R)
William D. Kelley (R)
John W. Killinger (R)
Levi A. Mackey (D)
Levi Maish (D)
John I. Mitchell (R)
Charles O'Neill (R)
Edward Overton, Jr. (R)
Samuel J. Randall (D)
James B. Reilly (D)
William S. Shallenberger (R)
A. Herr Smith (R)
William S. Stenger (D)
John M. Thompson (R)
Jacob Turney (D)
William Ward (R)
Lewis F. Watson (R)
Harry White (R)
Hendrick B. Wright (D)

RHODE ISLAND

Senators

Henry B. Anthony (R)
Ambrose E. Burnside (R)

Representatives

Latimer W. Ballou (R)
Benjamin T. Eames (R)

SOUTH CAROLINA

Senators

John J. Patterson (R)
Matthew C. Butler (D)

Representatives

D. Wyatt Aiken (D)
Richard H. Cain (D)
John H. Evins (D)
Joseph H. Rainey (R)
Robert Smalls (R)

TENNESSEE

Senators

James E. Bailey (D)
Isham G. Harris (D)

Representatives

John D. C. Atkins (D)
John M. Bright (D)
William P. Caldwell (D)
George G. Dibrell (D)
John F. House (D)
James H. Randolph (R)
Haywood Y. Riddle (D)
Jacob M. Thornburgh (R)
Washington C. Whitthorne (D)
H. Casey Young (D)

TEXAS

Senators

Samuel B. Maxey (D)
Richard Coke (D)

Representatives

David B. Culberson (D)
De Witt C. Giddings (D)
Roger Q. Mills (D)
John H. Reagan (D)
Gustave Schleicher (D)
d. Jan. 1879
James W. Throckmorton (D)

VERMONT

Senators

George F. Edmunds (R)
Justin S. Morrill (R)

Representatives

Dudley C. Denison (R)
George W. Hendee (R)
Charles H. Joyce (R)

VIRGINIA

Senators

John W. Johnston (Con)
Robert E. Withers (Con)

Representatives

Richard Lee T. Beale (D) s. 1879
George C. Cabell (D)
Beverly B. Douglas (D) d. 1878
John Goode, Jr. (Con)
John T. Harris (D)
Eppa Hunton (D)
Joseph Jorgensen (R)
Auburn L. Pridemore (D)
John R. Tucker (D)
Gilbert C. Walker (Con)

WEST VIRGINIA

Senators

Henry G. Davis (D)
Frank Hereford (D)

Representatives

John E. Kenna (D)
Benjamin F. Martin (D)
Benjamin Wilson (D)

WISCONSIN

Senators

Timothy O. Howe (R)
Angus Cameron (R)

Representatives

Gabriel Bouck (D)
Edward S. Bragg (D)
Lucien B. Caswell (R)
George C. Hazelton (R)
Herman L. Humphrey (R)
William P. Lynde (D)
Thaddeus C. Pound (R)
Charles G. Williams (R)

FORTY-SIXTH CONGRESS

March 4, 1879 to March 3, 1881

President of The Senate: William A. Wheeler
President Pro Tempore of The Senate: Allen G. Thurman
Speaker of The House of Representatives: Samuel J. Randall

ALABAMA

Senators

John T. Morgan (D)

George S. Houston (D) d. 1879
Luke Pryor (D) ta. 1880
James L. Pugh (D) s. 1880

Representatives

Newton N. Clements s. 1880
William H. Forney (D)
Hilary A. Herbert (D)
Thomas H. Herndon (D)
Burwell B. Lewis (D) r. Oct. 1880
William M. Lowe (D)
William J. Samford
Charles M. Shelley (D)
Thomas Williams (D)

ARKANSAS

Senators

Augustus H. Garland (D)
James D. Walker (D)

Representatives

Jordan E. Cravens (D)
Poindexter Dunn (D)
Thomas M. Gunter (D)
William F. Slemons (D)

CALIFORNIA

Senators

Newton Booth (Anti-Monopolist)
James T. Farley (R)

Representatives

Campbell P. Berry (R)
Horace Davis (R)
Romualdo Pacheco (R)
Horace F. Page (R)

COLORADO

Senators

Henry M. Teller (R)
Nathaniel P. Hill (R)

Representative

James B. Belford (R)

CONNECTICUT

Senators

William W. Eaton (D)
Orville H. Platt (R)

Representatives

Joseph R. Hawley (R)
Frederick Miles (R)
James Phelps (D)
John T. Wait (R)

DELAWARE

Senators

Thomas F. Bayard (D)
Eli Saulsbury (D)

Representative

Edward L. Martin (D)

FLORIDA

Senators

Charles W. Jones (D)
Wilkinson Call (D)

Representatives

Horatio Bisbee, Jr. (R) s. 1881
Robert H. M. Davidson (D)
Noble A. Hull (D) r. Jan. 1881

GEORGIA

Senators

Benjamin H. Hill (D)

John B. Gordon (D) r. May 1880
Joseph E. Brown (D) s. 1880

Representatives

James H. Blount (D)
Philip Cook (D)
William H. Felton (D)
Nathaniel J. Hammond (D)
John C. Nicholls (D)
Henry Persons (D)
William E. Smith (D)
Emory Speer (D)
Alexander H. Stephens (D)

ILLINOIS

Senators

David Davis (R)
John A. Logan (R)

Representatives

William Aldrich (R)
Hiram Barber, Jr. (R)
Thomas A. Boyd (R)
Joseph G. Cannon (R)
George R. Davis (R)
Albert P. Forsythe (R)

Greenbury L. Fort (R)
Robert M. A. Hawk (R)
Philip C. Hayes (R)
Thomas J. Henderson (R)
Benjamin F. Marsh (R)
William R. Morrison (D)
John C. Sherwin (R)
James W. Singleton (D)
William A. J. Sparks (D)
William M. Springer (D)
Adlai E. Stevenson (D)
John R. Thomas (R)
Richard W. Townshend (D)

INDIANA

Senators

Joseph E. McDonald (D)
Daniel W. Voorhees (D)

Representatives

John H. Baker (R)
George A. Bicknell (D)
Thomas M. Browne (R)
William H. Calkins (R)
Thomas R. Cobb (D)
Walpole G. Colerick (D)
Calvin Cowgill (R)
Gilbert De La Matyr (D)
William Heilman (R)
Abraham J. Hostetler (D)
William R. Myers (D)
Jeptha D. New (D)
Godlove S. Orth (R)

IOWA

Senators

William B. Allison (R)
Samuel J. Kirkwood (R)

Representatives

Cyrus C. Carpenter (R)
Rush Clark (R) d. Apr. 1879
Nathaniel C. Deering (R)
Edward H. Gillette (Greenback)
Moses A. McCoid (R)
Hiram Price (R)
William F. Sapp (R)
William G. Thompson (R)
Thomas Updegraff (R)
James B. Weaver (Greenback)

KANSAS

Senators

John J. Ingalls (R)
Preston B. Plumb (R)

Representatives

John A. Anderson (R)
Dudley C. Haskell (R)
Thomas Ryan (R)

KENTUCKY

Senators

James B. Beck (D)
John S. Williams (D)

Representatives

Joseph C. S. Blackburn (D)
John W. Caldwell (D)
John G. Carlisle (D)
J. Proctor Knott (D)
James A. McKenzie (D)
Elijah C. Phister (D)
Philip B. Thompson, Jr. (D)
Oscar Turner (D)
Thomas Turner (D)
Albert S. Willis (D)

LOUISIANA

Senators

William P. Kellogg (R)
Benjamin F. Jonas (D)

Representatives

Joseph H. Acklen (D)
Joseph B. Elam (D)
E. John Ellis (D)
Randall L. Gibson (D)
J. Floyd King (D)
Edward W. Robertson (D)

MAINE

Senators

Hannibal Hamlin (R)
James G. Blaine (R)

Representatives

William P. Frye (R)
George W. Ladd (Greenback, D)
Stephen D. Lindsey (R)
Thompson H. Murch (Greenback)
Thomas B. Reed (R)

MARYLAND

Senators

William P. Whyte (D)
James B. Groome (D)

Representatives

Eli J. Henkle (D)
Daniel M. Henry (D)
William Kimmel (D)
Robert M. McLane (D)
J. Fred C. Talbott (D)
Milton G. Urner (R)

MASSACHUSETTS

Senators

Henry L. Dawes (R)
George F. Hoar (R)

Representatives

Selwyn Z. Bowman (R)
William Claflin (R)
William W. Crapo (R)
Walbridge A. Field (R)
Benjamin W. Harris (R)
George B. Loring (R)
Leopold Morse (D)
Amasa Norcross (R)
William W. Rice (R)
George D. Robinson (R)
William A. Russell (R)

MICHIGAN

Senators

Thomas W. Ferry (R)

Zachariah Chandler (R) d. 1879
Henry P. Baldwin (R) s. 1879

Representatives

Mark S. Brewer (R)
Julius C. Burrows (R)
Omar D. Conger (R) r. Mar. 1879
Roswell G. Horr (R)
Jay A. Hubbell (R)
Jonas H. McGowan (R)
John S. Newberry (R)
John W. Stone (R)
Edwin Willits (R)

MINNESOTA

Senators

William Windom (R)
Samuel J. R. McMillan (R)

Representatives

Mark H. Dunnell (R)
Henry Poehler (D)
William D. Washburn (R)

MISSISSIPPI

Senators

Blanche K. Bruce (R)
Lucius Q. C. Lamar (D)

Representatives

James R. Chalmers (D)
Charles E. Hooker (D)
Vannoy H. Manning (D)
Hernando D. Money (D)
Henry L. Muldrow (D)
Otho R. Singleton (D)

MISSOURI

Senators

Francis M. Cockrell (D)
George G. Vest (D)

Representatives

Richard P. Bland (D)
Aylett H. Buckner (D)
Martin L. Clardy (D)
John B. Clark, Jr. (D)
Lowndes H. Davis (D)
Nicholas Ford (R)
Richard G. Frost (D)
William H. Hatch (D)
Alfred M. Lay (D) d. 1879
John F. Philips (D) s. 1880
Gideon F. Rothwell (D)
Samuel L. Sawyer (D)
James R. Waddill (D)
Erastus Wells (D)

NEBRASKA

Senators

Algernon S. Paddock (R)
Alvin Saunders (R)

Representatives

Edward K. Valentine (R)

NEVADA

Senators

John P. Jones (R)
William Sharon (R)

Representative

Rollin M. Daggett (R)

NEW HAMPSHIRE

Senators

Edward H. Rollins (R)

Charles H. Bell (R) ta. 1879
Henry W. Blair (R) s. 1879

Representatives

James F. Briggs (R)
Evarts W. Farr (D) d. Nov. 1880
Joshua G. Hall (R)
Ossian Ray (R) s. 1881

NEW JERSEY

Senators

Theodore F. Randolph (D)
John R. McPherson (D)

Representatives

John L. Blake (R)
Lewis A. Brigham (R)
Alvah A. Clark (D)
George M. Robeson (R)
Miles Ross (D)
Hezekiah B. Smith (D)
Charles H. Voorhis (R)

NEW YORK

Senators

Roscoe Conkling (R)
Francis Kernan (D)

Representatives

John M. Bailey (R)
Archibald M. Bliss (D)
John H. Camp (R)
Simeon B. Chittenden (R)
James W. Covert (D)
Samuel S. Cox (D)
Richard Crowley (R)
Jeremiah W. Dwight (R)
Edwin Einstein (R)
John W. Ferdon (R)
John Hammond (R)
Frank Hiscock (R)
Waldo Hutchins (D)
Amaziah B. James (R)
John H. Ketcham (R)
Elbridge G. Lapham (R)
William Lounsbery (D)
Anson G. McCook (R)
Joseph Mason (R)
Warner Miller (R)
Levi P. Morton (R)
Nicholas Muller (D)

James O'Brien (D)
Daniel O'Reilly (D)
Ray V. Pierce (R) r. 1880
Cyrus D. Prescott (R)
David P. Richardson (R)
Jonathan Scoville (D) s. 1880
John H. Starin (R)
Henry Van Aernam (R)
John Van Voorhis (R)
David Wilber (R)
Fernando Wood (D) d. Feb. 1881
Walter A. Wood (R)

NORTH CAROLINA

Senators

Matt W. Ransom (D)
Zebulon B. Vance (D)

Representatives

Robert F. Armfield (D)
Joseph J. Davis (D)
William H. Kitchin (D)
Joseph J. Martin (R) r. Jan. 1881
Daniel L. Russell (R)
Alfred M. Scales (D)
Walter L. Steele (D)
Robert B. Vance (D)
Jesse J. Yeates (D) s. 1881

OHIO

Senators

Allen G. Thurman (D)
George H. Pendleton (D)

Representatives

Gibson Atherton (D)
Benjamin Butterworth (R)
George L. Converse (D)
Henry L. Dickey (D)
Thomas Ewing (D)
Ebenezer B. Finley (D)
James A. Garfield (R) r. Nov. 1880
George W. Geddes (D)
William D. Hill (D)
Frank H. Hurd (D)
J. Warren Keifer (R)
Benjamin Le Fevre (D)
William McKinley, Jr. (R)
John A. McMahon (D)
James Monroe (R)
Henry S. Neal (R)
Ezra B. Taylor (R) s. 1880
Amos Townsend (R)
Jonathan T. Updegraff (R)
Adoniram J. Warner (D)
Thomas L. Young (R)

OREGON

Senators

La Fayette Grover (D)
James H. Slater (D)

Representative

John Whiteaker (D)

PENNSYLVANIA

Senators

William A. Wallace (D)
J. Donald Cameron (R)

Representatives

Reuben K. Bachman (D)
Thomas M. Bayne (R)
Frank E. Beltzhoover (D)
Henry H. Bingham (R)
Hiester Clymer (D)
Alexander H. Coffroth (D)
Samuel B. Dick (R)
Russell Errett (R)
Horatio G. Fisher (R)
William Godshalk (R)
Alfred C. Harmer (R)
William D. Kelley (R)
John W. Killinger (R)
Robert Klotz (D)
John I. Mitchell (R)
Charles O'Neill (R)
James H. Osmer (R)
Edward Overton, Jr. (R)
Samuel J. Randall (D)
John W. Ryon (D)
William S. Shallenberger (R)
A. Herr Smith (R)
William Ward (R)
Harry White (R)
Morgan R. Wise (D)
Hendrick B. Wright (D)
Seth H. Yocum (R)

RHODE ISLAND

Senators

Henry B. Anthony (R)
Ambrose E. Burnside (R)

Representatives

Nelson W. Aldrich (D)
Latimer W. Ballou (R)

SOUTH CAROLINA

Senators

Matthew C. Butler (D)
Wade Hampton (D)

Representatives

D. Wyatt Aiken (D)
John H. Evins (D)
Michael P. O'Connor (D)
John S. Richardson (D)
George D. Tillman (D)

TENNESSEE

Senators

James E. Bailey (D)
Isham G. Harris (D)

Representatives

John D. C. Atkins (D)
John M. Bright (D)
George G. Dibrell (D)
Leonidas C. Houk (R)
John F. House (D)
Benton McMillin (D)
Charles B. Simonton (D)
Robert L. Taylor (D)
Washington C. Whitthorne (D)
H. Casey Young (D)

TEXAS

Senators

Samuel B. Maxey (D)
Richard Coke (D)

Representatives

David B. Culberson (D)
George W. Jones (Greenback)
Roger Q. Mills (D)
John H. Reagan (D)
Christopher C. Upson (D)
Olin Wellborn (D)

VERMONT

Senators

George F. Edmunds (R)
Justin S. Morrill (R)

Representatives

Bradley Barlow (R)
Charles H. Joyce (R)
James M. Tyler (R)

VIRGINIA

Senators

John W. Jonston (C)
Robert E. Withers (C)

Representatives

Richard Lee T. Beale (D)
George C. Cabell (D)
John Goode, Jr. (D)
John T. Harris (D)
Eppa Hunton (D)
Joseph E. Johnston (D)
Joseph Jorgensen (R)
James B. Richmond (D)
John R. Tucker (D)

WEST VIRGINIA

Senators

Henry G. Davis (D)
Frank Hereford (D)

Representatives

John E. Kenna (D)
Benjamin F. Martin (D)
Benjamin Wilson (D)

WISCONSIN

Senators

Angus Cameron (R)
Matthew H. Carpenter (R) d. Feb. 1881

Representatives

Gabriel Bouck (D)
Edward S. Bragg (D)
Lucien B. Caswell (R)
Peter V. Deuster (D)
George C. Hazelton (R)
Herman L. Humprhrey (R)
Thaddeus C. Pound (R)
Charles G. Williams (R)

FORTY-SEVENTH CONGRESS

March 4, 1881 to March 3, 1883

President of The Senate:	Chester A. Arthur
Presidents Pro Tempore of The Senate:	Thomas F. Bayard David Davis George F. Edmunds
Speaker of The House of Representatives:	J. Warren Keifer

ALABAMA

Senators

John T. Morgan (D)
James L. Pugh (D)

Representatives

William H. Forney (D)
Hilary A. Herbert (D)
Thomas H. Herndon (D)
Goldsmith W. Hewitt (D)
William M. Lowe (D) d. 1882
William C. Oates (D)
Charles M. Shelley (D)
Joseph Wheeler (D)
Thomas Williams (D)

ARKANSAS

Senators

Augustus H. Garland (D)
James D. Walker (D)

Representatives

Poindexter Dunn (D)
Jordan E. Cravens (D)
Thomas M. Gunter (D)
James K. Jones (D)

CALIFORNIA

Senators

James T. Farley (R)
John F. Miller (R)

Representatives

Campbell P. Berry (R)
Romualdo Pacheco (R)
Horace F. Page (R)
William S. Rosecrans (D)

COLORADO

Senators

Henry M. Teller (R) r. Apr. 1882
George M. Chilcott (R) ta. 1882
Horace A. W. Tabor (R) s. 1883
Nathaniel P. Hill (R)

Representative

James B. Belford (R)

CONNECTICUT

Senators

Orville H. Platt (R)
Joseph R. Hawley (R)

Representatives

John R. Buck (R)
Frederick Miles (R)
James Phelps (D)
John T. Wait (R)

DELAWARE

Senators

Thomas F. Bayard (D)
Eli Saulsbury (D)

Representative

Edward L. Martin (D)

FLORIDA

Senators

Charles W. Jones (D)
Wilkinson Call (D)

Representatives

Horatio Bisbee, Jr. (R) s. 1882
Robert H. M. Davidson (D)
Jesse J. Finley (D) r. June 1882

GEORGIA

Senators

Benjamin H. Hill (D) d. 1882
M. Pope Barrow (D) s. 1882

Joseph E. Brown (D)

Representatives

George R. Black (D)
James H. Blount (D)
Hugh Buchanan (D)
Judson C. Clements (D)
Philip Cook (D)
Nathaniel J. Hammond (D)
Seaborn Reese (D) s. 1882
Emory Speer
Alexander H. Stephens (D)
r. Nov. 1882
Henry G. Turner (D)

ILLINOIS

Senators

David Davis (R)
John A. Logan (R)

Representatives

William Aldrich (R)
Joseph G. Cannon (R)
William Cullen (R)
George R. Davis (R)
Charles B. Farwell (R)
Robert M. A. Hawk (R)
d. June 1882
Thomas J. Henderson (R)
Robert R. Hitt (R) s. 1882
John H. Lewis (R)
Benjamin F. Marsh (R)
William R. Morrison (D)
Samuel W. Moulton (D)
Lewis E. Payson (R)
John C. Sherwin (R)
James W. Singleton (D)
Dietrich C. Smith (R)
William A. J. Sparks (D)
William M. Springer (D)
John R. Thomas (R)
Richard W. Townshend (D)

INDIANA

Senators

Daniel W. Voorhees (D)
Benjamin Harrison (R)

Representatives

Thomas M. Browne (R)
William H. Calkins (R)
Thomas R. Cobb (D)
Walpole G. Colerick (D)
Mark L. DeMotte (R)
Charles T. Doxey (R) s. 1883
William Heilman (R)
William S. Holman (D)
Courtland C. Matson (D)
Godlove S. Orth (R) d. Dec. 1882
Stanton J. Peelle (R)
Robert B. F. Pierce (R)
George W. Steele (R)
Strother M. Stockslager (D)

IOWA

Senators

William B. Allison (R)

Samuel J. Kirkwood (R)
r. Mar. 1881
James W. McDill (R) s. 1881

Representatives

Cyrus C. Carpenter (R)
Marsena E. Cutts (R)
Nathaniel C. Deering (R)
Sewall S. Farwell (R)
William P. Hepburn (R)
John A. Kasson (R)
Moses A. McCoid (R)
William G. Thompson (R)
Thomas Updegraff (R)

KANSAS

Senators

John J. Ingalls (R)
Preston B. Plumb (R)

Representatives

John A. Anderson (R)
Dudley C. Haskell (R)
Thomas Ryan (R)

KENTUCKY

Senators

James B. Beck (D)
John S. Williams (D)

Representatives

Joseph C. S. Blackburn (D)
John W. Caldwell (D)
John G. Carlisle (D)
J. Proctor Knott (D)
James A. McKenzie (D)
Elijah C. Phister (D)
Philip B. Thompson, Jr. (D)
Oscar Turner (D)
John D. White (R)
Albert S. Willis (D)

LOUISIANA

Senators

William P. Kellogg (R)
Benjamin F. Jonas (D)

Representatives

Newton C. Blanchard (D)
Chester B. Darrall (R)
E. John Ellis (D)
Randall L. Gibson (D)
J. Floyd King (D)
Edward W. Robertson (D)

MAINE

Senators

James G. Blaine (R) r. Mar. 1881
William P. Frye (R) s. 1881

Eugene Hale (R)

Representatives

Nelson Dingley, Jr. (R)
William P. Frye (R) r. Mar. 1881
George W. Ladd (Greenback, D)
Stephen D. Lindsey (R)
Thompson H. Murch (Greenback)
Thomas B. Reed (R)

MARYLAND

Senators

James B. Groome (D)
Arthur P. Gorman (D)

Representatives

Andrew G. Chapman (D)
George W. Covington (D)
Fetter S. Hoblitzell (D)
Robert M. McLane (D)
J. Fred C. Talbott (D)
Milton G. Urner (R)

MASSACHUSETTS

Senators

Henry L. Dawes (R)
George F. Hoar (R)

Representatives

Selwyn Z. Bowman (R)
John W. Candler (R)
William W. Crapo (R)
Benjamin W. Harris (R)
Leopold Morse (D)
Amasa Norcross (R)
Ambrose A. Ranney (R)
William W. Rice (R)
George D. Robinson (R)
William A. Russell (R)
Eben F. Stone (R)

MICHIGAN

Senators

Thomas W. Ferry (R)
Omar D. Conger (R)

Representatives

Julius C. Burrows (R)
Rosewell G. Horr (R)
Jay A. Hubbell (R)
Edward S. Lacey (R)
Henry W. Lord (R)
John T. Rich (R)
Oliver L. Spaulding (R)
George W. Webber (R)
Edwin Willits (R)

MINNESOTA

Senators

Samuel J. R. McMillan (R)

William Windom (R) r. Mar. 1881
Alonzo J. Edgerton (R) ta. 1881

Representatives

Mark H. Dunnell (R)
Horace B. Strait (R)
William D. Washburn (R)

MISSISSIPPI

Senators

Lucius Q. C. Lamar (D)
James Z. George (D)

Representatives

James R. Chalmers (D)
r. Apr. 1882
Charles E. Hooker (D)
John R. Lynch (R) s. 1882
Vannoy H. Manning (D)
Hernando D. Money (D)
Henry L. Muldrow (D)
Otho R. Singleton (D)

MISSOURI

Senators

Francis M. Cockrell (D)
George G. Vest (D)

Representatives

Thomas Allen (D) d. Apr. 1882
Richard P. Bland (D)
Aylett H. Buckner (D)
Joseph H. Burrows (Greenback)
Martin L. Clardy (D)
John B. Clark, Jr. (D)
Lowndes H. Davis (D)
Nicholas Ford (R)
Richard G. Frost (D)
William H. Hatch (D)
Ira S. Hazeltone (Greenback)
James H. McLean (R) s. 1882
Theron M. Rice (Greenback)
Robert T. Van Horn (R)

NEBRASKA

Senators

Alvin Saunders (R)
Charles H. Van Wyck (R)

Representative

Edward K. Valentine (R)

NEVADA

Senators

John P. Jones (R)
James G. Fair (D)

Representative

George W. Cassidy (D)

NEW HAMPSHIRE

Senators

Edward H. Rollins (R)
Henry W. Blair (R)

Representatives

James F. Briggs (R)
Joshua G. Hall (R)
Ossian Ray (R)

NEW JERSEY

Senators

John R. McPherson (D)
William J. Sewell (R)

Representatives

J. Hart Brewer (R)
Augustus A. Hardenbergh (D)
Henry S. Harris (D)
John Hill (R)
Phineas Jones (R)
George M. Robeson (R)
Miles Ross (D)

NEW YORK

Senators

Elbridge G. Lapham (R)
Warner Miller (R)

Representatives

Lewis Beach (D)
Perry Belmont (D)
Archibald M. Bliss (D)
John H. Camp (R)
Thomas Cornell (R)
Samuel S. Cox (D)
Richard Crowley (R)
P. Henry Dugro (D)
Jeremiah W. Dwight (R)
Roswell P. Flower (D)
John Hammond (R)
John Hardy (D)
Abram S. Hewitt (D)
Frank Hiscock (R)
Waldo Hutchins (D)
Ferris Jacobs (R)
John Ketcham (R)
Elbridge G. Lapham (R) r. 1881
Anson G. McCook (R)
Joseph Mason (R)
Warner Miller (R) r. July 1881
Levi P. Morton (R) r. Mar. 1881
Michael N. Nolan (D)
Abraham X. Parker (R)
Cyrus D. Prescott (R)
David P. Richardson (R)
William E. Robinson (D)
Jonathan Scoville (D)
Charles R. Skinner (R)
J. Hyatt Smith (R, D)
Henry Van Aernam (R)
John Van Voorhis (R)
James W. Wadsworth (R)
George West (R)
Benjamin Wood (D)
Walter A. Wood (R)

NORTH CAROLINA

Senators

Matt W. Ransom (D)
Zebulon B. Vance (D)

Representatives

Robert A. Armfield (D)
William R. Cox (D)
Clement Dowd (D)
Orlando Hubbs (R)
Louis C. Latham (D)
Alfred M. Scales (D)
John W. Shackelford (D) d. 1883
Robert B. Vance (D)

OHIO

Senators

George H. Pendleton (D)
John Sherman (R)

Representatives

Gibson Atherton (D)
Benjamin Butterworth (R)
George L. Converse (D)
Rufus R. Dawes (R)
George W. Geddes (D)
J. Warren Keifer (R)
John P. Leedom (D)
Benjamin Le Fevre (D)
Addison S. McClure (R)
William McKinley, Jr. (R)
Henry L. Morey (R)
Henry S. Neal (R)
John B. Rice (R)
James M. Ritchie (R)
James S. Robinson (R)
Emanuel Shultz (R)
Ezra B. Taylor (R)
Joseph D. Taylor (R) s. 1883
Amos Townsend (R)
Jonathan T. Updegraff (R) d. Nov. 1882
Thomas L. Young (R)

OREGON

Senators

La Fayette Grover (D)
James H. Slater (D)

Representative

Melvin C. George (R)

PENNSYLVANIA

Senators

J. Donald Cameron (R)
John I. Mitchell (R)

Representatives

Samuel F. Barr (R)
Thomas M. Bayne (R)
Frank E. Beltzhoover (D)
Henry H. Bingham (R)
Charles N. Brumm (Greenback, R)
Jacob M. Campbell (R)
Andrew G. Curtin (D)
Daniel Ermentrout (D)
Russell Errett (R)
Horatio G. Fisher (R)
William Godshalk (R)
Alfred C. Harmer (R)
Cornelius C. Jadwin (R)
William D. Kelley (R)
Robert Klotz (D)
Samuel H. Miller (R)
James Mosgrove (Greenback, D)
William Mutchler (D)
Charles O'Neill (R)
Samuel J. Randall (D)
Joseph A. Scranton (R)
William S. Shallenberger (R)
A. Herr Smith (R)
Robert J. C. Walker (R)
William Ward (R)
Lewis F. Watson (R)
Morgan R. Wise (D)

RHODE ISLAND

Senators

Henry B. Anthony (R)

Ambrose E. Burnside (R) d. Sept. 1881
Nelson W. Aldrich (R) s. 1881

Representatives

Nelson W. Aldrich (R) r. Oct. 1881
Jonathan Chace (R)
Henry J. Spooner (R)

SOUTH CAROLINA

Senators

Matthew C. Butler (D)
Wade Hampton (D)

Representatives

D. Wyatt Aiken (D)
Samuel Dibble (D) r. May 1882
John H. Evins (D)
Edmund W. M. Mackey (R) s. 1882
Michael P. O'Connor (D) d. Apr. 1881
John S. Richardson (D)
Robert Smalls (R) s. 1882
George D. Tillman (D) r. July 1882

TENNESSEE

Senators

Isham G. Harris (D)
Howell E. Jackson (D)

Representatives

John D. C. Atkins (D)
George G. Dibrell (D)
Leonidas C. Houk (R)
John F. House (D)
Benton McMillin (D)
William R. Moore (R)
Augustus H. Pettibone (R)
Charles B. Simonton (D)
Richard Warner (D)
Washington C. Whitthorne (D)

TEXAS

Senators

Samuel B. Maxey (D)
Richard Coke (D)

Representatives

David B. Culberson (D)
George W. Jones (Greenback)
Roger Q. Mills (D)
John H. Reagan (D)
Christopher C. Upson (D)
Olin Wellborn (D)

VERMONT

Senators

George F. Edmunds (R)
Justin S. Morrill (R)

Representatives

William W. Grout (R)
Charles H. Joyce (R)
James M. Tyler (R)

VIRGINIA

Senators

John W. Johnston
William Mahone (Readjuster)

Representatives

John S. Barbour (D)
George C. Cabell (D)
John F. Dezendorf (R)
Abram Fulkerson (Readjuster)
George T. Garrison (D)
Joseph Jorgensen (R)
John Paul (Readjuster)
John R. Tucker (D)
George D. Wise (D)

WEST VIRGINIA

Senators

Henry G. Davis (D)
Johnson N. Camden (D)

Representatives

John B. Hoge (D)
Benjamin Wilson (D)

WISCONSIN

Senators

Angus Cameron (R)
Philetus Sawyer (R)

Representatives

Edward S. Bragg (D)
Lucien B. Caswell (R)
Peter V. Deuster (D)
Richard W. Guenther (R)
George C. Hazelton (R)
Herman L. Humphrey (R)
Thaddeus C. Pound (R)
Charles G. Williams (R)

FORTY-EIGHTH CONGRESS

March 4, 1883 to March 3, 1885

President of The Senate:	None
President Pro Tempore of The Senate:	George F. Edmunds
Speaker of The House of Representatives:	John G. Carlisle

ALABAMA

Senators

John T. Morgan (D)
James L. Pugh (D)

Representatives

George H. Craig (R) s. 1885
William H. Forney (D)
Hilary A. Herbert (D)
Goldsmith W. Hewitt (D)
James T. Jones (D)
William C. Oates (D)
Luke Pryor (D)
Charles M. Shelley (D) r. Jan. 1885
Thomas Williams (D)

ARKANSAS

Senators

Augustus H. Garland (D)
James D. Walker (D)

Representatives

Clifton R. Breckinridge (D)
Poindexter Dunn (D)
James K. Jones (D) r. Feb. 1885
Samuel W. Peel (D)
John H. Rogers (D)

CALIFORNIA

Senators

James T. Farley (R)
John F. Miller (R)

Representatives

James H. Budd (D)
John R. Glascock (D)
Barclay Henley (D)
William S. Rosecrans (D)
Charles A. Sumner (D)
Pleasant B. Tully (D)

COLORADO

Senators

Nathaniel P. Hill (R)
Thomas M. Bowen (R)

Representative

James B. Belford (R)

CONNECTICUT

Senators

Orville H. Platt (R)
Joseph R. Hawley (R)

Representatives

William W. Eaton (D)
Charles L. Mitchell (D)
Edward W. Seymour (D)
John T. Wait (R)

DELAWARE

Senators

Thomas F. Bayard (D)
Eli Saulsbury (D)

Representative

Charles B. Lore (D)

FLORIDA

Senators

Charles W. Jones (D)
Wilkinson Call (D)

Representatives

Horatio Bisbee, Jr. (R)
Robert H. M. Davidson (D)

GEORGIA

Senators

Joseph E. Brown (D)
Alfred H. Colquitt (D)

Representatives

James H. Blount (D)
Hugh Buchanan (D)
Allen D. Candler (D)
Judson C. Clements (D)
Charles F. Crisp (D)
Nathaniel J. Hammond (D)
Thomas Hardeman (D)
John C. Nicholls (D)
Seaborn Reese (D)
Henry G. Turner (D)

ILLINOIS

Senators

John A. Logan (R)
Shelby M. Cullom (R)

Representatives

George E. Adams (R)
Joseph G. Cannon (R)
William Cullen (R)
George R. Davis (R)
Ransom W. Dunham (R)
Reuben Ellwood (R)
John F. Finerty (D)
Thomas J. Henderson (R)
Robert R. Hitt (R)
William R. Morrison (D)
Samuel W. Moulton (D)
William H. Neece (D)
Lewis E. Payson (R)
James M. Riggs (D)
Jonathan H. Rowell (R)
Aaron Shaw (D)
William M. Springer (D)
John R. Thomas (R)
Richard W. Townshend (D)
Nicholas E. Worthington (D)

INDIANA

Senators

Daniel W. Voorhees (D)
Benjamin Harrison (R)

Representatives

Thomas M. Browne (R)
William H. Calkins (R) r. Oct. 1884
Thomas R. Cobb (D)
William E. English (D) s. 1884
William S. Holman (D)
John J. Kleiner (D)
John E. Lamb (D)
Robert Lowry (D)
Courtland C. Matson (D)
Stanton J. Peelle (R) r. May 1884
Benjamin F. Shively (D) s. 1884
George W. Steele (R)
Strother M. Stockslager (D)
Thomas B. Ward (D)
Thomas J. Wood (D)

IOWA

Senators

William B. Allison (R)
James F. Wilson (R)

Representatives

John C. Cook (D)
Benjamin T. Frederick (D) s. 1885
David B. Henderson (R)
William P. Hepburn (R)
Adoniram J. Holmes (R)
John A. Kasson (R) r. July 1884
Moses A. McCoid (R)
Jeremiah H. Murphy (D)
William H. M. Pusey (D)
Hiram Y. Smith (R) s. 1884
Isaac S. Struble (R)
Luman H. Weller (D)
James Wilson (R) r. Mar. 1885

KANSAS

Senators

John J. Ingalls (R)
Preston B. Plumb (R)

Representatives

John A. Anderson (R)
Edward H. Funston (R) s. 1884
Lewis Hanback (R)
Dudley C. Haskell (R) d. Dec. 1883
Edmund N. Morrill (R)
Bishop W. Perkins (R)
Samuel R. Peters (R)
Thomas Ryan (R)

KENTUCKY

Senators

James B. Beck (D)
John S. Williams (D)

Representatives

Joseph C. S. Blackburn (D)
John G. Carlisle (D)
James F. Clay (D)
William W. Culbertson (R)
John E. Halsell (D)
Thomas A. Robertson (D)
Philip B. Thompson, Jr. (D)
Oscar Turner (D)
John D. White (R)
Albert S. Willis (D)
Frank L. Wolford (D)

LOUISIANA

Senators

Benjamin F. Jonas (D)
Randall L. Gibson (D)

Representatives

Newton C. Blanchard (D)
E. John Ellis (D)
Carleton Hunt (D)
William P. Kellogg (R)
J. Floyd King (D)
Edward T. Lewis (D)

MAINE

Senators

Eugene Hale (R)
William P. Frye (R)

Representatives

Charles A. Boutelle (R)
Nelson Dingley, Jr. (R)
Seth L. Milliken (R)
Thomas B. Reed (R)

MARYLAND

Senators

James B. Groome (D)
Arthur P. Gorman (D)

Representatives

George W. Covington (D)
John V. L. Findlay (D)
Fetter S. Hoblitzell (D)
Hart B. Holton (R)
Louis E. McComas (R)
J. Fred C. Talbott (D)

MASSACHUSETTS

Senators

Henry L. Dawes (R)
George F. Hoar (R)

Representatives

Patrick A. Collins (D)
Robert T. Davis (R)

John D. Long (R)
Henry B. Lovering (D)
Theodore Lyman
Leopold Morse (D)
Ambrose A. Ranney (R)
William W. Rice (R)
George D. Robinson (R)
r. Jan. 1884
Francis W. Rockwell (R)
s. Jan. 1884
William A. Russell (R)
Eben F. Stone (R)
William Whiting (R)

MICHIGAN

Senators

Omar D. Conger (R)
Thomas W. Palmer (R)

Representatives

Edward Breitung (R)
Ezra C. Carleton (D)
Byron M. Cutcheon (R)
Nathaniel B. Eldredge (D)
Herschel H. Hatch (R)
Roswell G. Horr (R)
Julius Houseman (D)
Edward S. Lacey (R)
William C. Maybury (D)
Edwin B. Winans (D)
George L. Yaple (Un)

MINNESOTA

Senators

Samuel J. R. McMillan (R)
Dwight M. Sabin (R)

Representatives

Knute Nelson (R)
Horace B. Strait (R)
James B. Wakefield (R)
William D. Washburn (R)
Milo White (R)

MISSISSIPPI

Senators

Lucius Q. C. Lamar (D)
James Z. George (D)

Representatives

Ethelbert Barksdale (D)
James R. Chalmers s. 1884
Elza Jeffords (R)
Hernando D. Money (D)
Henry L. Muldrow (D)
Otho R. Singleton (D)
Henry S. Van Eaton (D)

MISSOURI

Senators

Francis M. Cockrell (D)
George G. Vest (D)

Representatives

Armstead M. Alexander (D)
Richard P. Bland (D)
James O. Broadhead (D)
Aylett H. Buckner (D)
James N. Burnes (D)
Martin L. Clardy (D)
John Cosgrove (D)
Lowndes H. Davis (D)
Alexander M. Dockery (D)
Robert W. Fyan (D)
Alexander Graves (D)
William H. Hatch (D)
Charles H. Morgan (D)
John J. O'Neill (D)

NEBRASKA

Senators

Charles H. Van Wyck (R)
Charles F. Manderson (R)

Representatives

James Laird (R)
Edward K. Valentine (R)
Archibald J. Weaver (R)

NEVADA

Senators

John P. Jones (R)
James G. Fair (D)

Representative

George W. Cassidy (D)

NEW HAMPSHIRE

Senators

Henry W. Blair (R)
Austin F. Pike (R)

Representatives

Martin A. Haynes (R)
Ossian Ray (R)

NEW JERSEY

Senators

John R. McPherson (D)
William J. Sewell (R)

Representatives

J. Hart Brewer (D)
Thomas M. Ferrell (D)
William H. F. Fiedler (D)
Benjamin F. Howey (R)
John Kean (R)
William McAdoo (D)
William W. Phelps (R)

NEW YORK

Senators

Warner Miller (R)
Elbridge G. Lapham (R)

Representatives

John J. Adams (D)
John Arnot, Jr. (D)
John H. Bagley, Jr. (D)
Lewis Beach (D)
Perry Belmont (D)
Francis B. Brewer (R)
Henry G. Burleigh (R)
Felix Campbell (D)
Samuel S. Cox (D)
William Dorsheimer (D)
Halbert S. Greenleaf (D)
John Hardy (D)
Abram S. Hewitt (D)
Frank Hiscock (R)
Waldo Hutchins (D)
Darwin R. James (R)
Frederick A. Johnson
John H. Ketcham (R)
Stephen C. Millard (R)
Nicholas Muller (R)
Newton W. Nutting (R)
Abraham X. Parker (R)
Sereno E. Payne (R)
Orlando B. Potter (D)
George W. Ray (R)
William E. Robinson (D)
William F. Rogers (D)
Charles R. Skinner (R)
Henry W. Slocum (D)
John T. Spriggs (D)
Robert S. Stevens (D)
Thomas J. Van Alstyne (D)
James W. Wadsworth (R)
Edward Wemple (D)

NORTH CAROLINA

Senators

Matt W. Ransom (D)
Zebulon B. Vance (D)

Representatives

Risden T. Bennett (D)
William R. Cox (D)
Clement Dowd (D)
Wharton J. Green (D)
James E. O'Hara (R)
Walter F. Pool (R) d. Aug. 1883
James W. Reid (D) s. 1885
Alfred M. Scales (D) r. Dec. 1884
Thomas G. Skinner (D)
Tyre York (D)
Robert B. Vance (D)

OHIO

Senators

George H. Pendleton (D)
John Sherman (R)

Representatives

James E. Campbell (D) s. 1884
George L. Converse (D)
John F. Follett (D)
Martin A. Foran (D)
George W. Geddes (D)
Alphonso Hart (R)
William D. Hill (D)
Frank H. Hurd (D)
Isaac M. Jordan (D)
J. Warren Keifer (R)
Benjamin Le Fevre (D)
John W. McCormick (R)
William McKinley, Jr. (R)
r. May 1884
Henry L. Morey (R) r. June 1884
Robert M. Murray (D)
David R. Paige (D)
James S. Robinson (R) r. Jan. 1885
George E. Seney (D)
Ezra B. Taylor (R)
Joseph D. Taylor (R)
Jonathan H. Wallace (D) s. 1884
Adoniram J. Warner (D)
Beriah Wilkins (D)

OREGON

Senators

James H. Slater (D)
Joseph N. Dolph (R)

Representative

Melvin C. George (R)

PENNSYLVANIA

Senators

J. Donald Cameron (R)
John I. Mitchell (R)

Representatives

Louis E. Atkinson (R)
Samuel F. Barr (R)
Thomas M. Bayne (R)
Henry H. Bingham (R)
Charles E. Boyle (D)
Samuel M. Brainerd (R)
William W. Brown (R)
Charles N. Brumm (Greenback)
Jacob M. Campbell (R)
Daniel W. Connolly (D)
Andrew G. Curtin (D)
William A. Duncan (D)
d. Nov. 1884
Mortimer F. Elliott (D)
Daniel Ermentrout (D)
I. Newton Evans (R)
James B. Everhart (R)
Alfred C. Harmer (R)
James H. Hopkins (D)
William D. Kelley (R)
George V. Lawrence (R)
Samuel H. Miller (R)
William Mutchler (D)
Charles O'Neill (R)
John D. Patton (D)
George A. Post (D)
Samuel J. Randall (R)
A. Herr Smith (R)
John B. Storm (D)
John A. Swope (D) s. 1885

RHODE ISLAND

Senators

Henry B. Anthony (R)
d. Sept. 1884
William P. Sheffield (R) ta. 1884
Jonathan Chace (R) s. 1885

Nelson W. Aldrich (R)

Representatives

Jonathan Chace (R) r. Jan 1885
Nathan F. Dixon (R) s. 1885
Henry J. Spooner (R)

SOUTH CAROLINA

Senators

Matthew C. Butler (D)
Wade Hampton (D)

Representatives

D. Wyatt Aiken (D)
John Bratton (D) s. 1884
George W. Dargan (D)
Samuel Dibble (D)
John H. Evins (D) d. Oct. 1884
John J. Hemphill (D)
Edmund W. M. Mackey (R) d. Jan. 1884
Robert Smalls (R)
George D. Tillman (D)

TENNESSEE

Senators

Isham G. Harris (D)
Howell E. Jackson (D)

Representatives

John G. Ballentine (D)
Andrew J. Caldwell (D)
George G. Dibrell (D)
Leonidas C. Houk (R)
Benton McMillin (D)
Augustus H. Pettibone (R)
Rice A. Pierce (D)
John M. Taylor (D)
Richard Warner (D)
H. Casey Young (D)

TEXAS

Senators

Samuel B. Maxey (D)
Richard Coke (D)

Representatives

David B. Culberson (D)
John Hancock (D)
James H. Jones (D)
Samuel W. T. Lanham (D)
James F. Miller (D)
Roger Q. Mills (D)
Thomas P. Ochiltree
John H. Reagan (D)
Charles Stewart (D)
James W. Throckmorton (D)
Olin Wellborn (D)

VERMONT

Senators

George F. Edmunds (R)
Justin S. Morrill (R)

Representatives

Luke P. Poland (R)
John W. Stewart (R)

VIRGINIA

Senators

William Mahone (Readjuster)
Harrison H. Riddleberger (Readjuster)

Representatives

John S. Barbour (D)
Henry Bowen (Readjuster)
George C. Cabell (D)
George T. Garrison s. 1884
Benjamin S. Hooper (D)
Harry Libbey (R)
Robert M. Mayo (Readjuster) r. 1884
Charles T. O'Ferrall (D) s. 1884
John R. Tucker (D)
George D. Wise (D)
John S. Wise

WEST VIRGINIA

Senators

Johnson N. Camden (D)
John E. Kenna (D)

Representatives

Eustace Gibson (D)
Nathan Goff (R)
Charles P. Snyder (D)
William L. Wilson (D)

WISCONSIN

Senators

Angus Cameron (R)
Philetus Sawyer (R)

Representatives

Peter V. Deuster (D)
Richard W. Guenther (R)
Burr W. Jones (D)
William T. Price (R)
Joseph Rankin (D)
Isaac Stephenson (R)
Daniel H. Sumner (D)
John Winans (D)
Gilbert M. Woodward (D)

FORTY-NINTH CONGRESS

March 4, 1885 to March 3, 1887

President of The Senate: Thomas A. Hendricks
Presidents Pro Tempore of The Senate: John Sherman; John J. Ingalls
Speaker of The House of Representatives: John G. Carlisle

ALABAMA

Senators

John T. Morgan (D)
James L. Pugh (D)

Representatives

Alexander C. Davidson (D)
William H. Forney (D)
Hilary A. Herbert (D)
James T. Jones (D)
John M. Martin (D)
William C. Oates (D)
Thomas W. Sadler (D)
Joseph Wheeler (D)

ARKANSAS

Senators

Augustus H. Garland (D) r. Mar. 1885
James H. Berry (D) s. 1885

James K. Jones (D)

Representatives

Clifton R. Breckinridge (D)
Poindexter Dunn (D)
Thomas C. McRae (D)
Samuel W. Peel (D)
John H. Rogers (D)

CALIFORNIA

Senators

John F. Miller (R) d. Mar. 1886
George Hearst (D) ta. 1886
Abram P. Williams (R) s. 1886

Leland Stanford (R)

Representatives

Charles N. Felton (R)
Barclay Henley (D)
James A. Louttit (R)
Joseph McKenna (R)
Henry H. Markham (R)
William W. Morrow (R)

COLORADO

Senators

Thomas M. Bowen (R)
Henry M. Teller (R)

Representative

George G. Symes (R)

CONNECTICUT

Senators

Orville H. Platt (R)
Joseph R. Hawley (R)

Representatives

John R. Buck (R)
Charles L. Mitchell (D)
Edward W. Seymour (D)
John T. Wait (R)

DELAWARE

Senators

Thomas F. Bayard (D) r. Mar. 1885
George Gray (D) s. 1885

Eli Saulsbury (D)

Representative

Charles B. Lore (D)

FLORIDA

Senators

Charles W. Jones (D)
Wilkinson Call (D)

Representatives

Robert H. M. Davidson (D)
Charles Dougherty (D)

GEORGIA

Senators

Joseph E. Brown (D)
Alfred H. Colquitt (D)

Representatives

George T. Barnes (D)
James H. Blount (D)
Allen D. Candler (D)
Judson C. Clements (D)
Charles F. Crisp (D)
Nathaniel J. Hammond (D)
Henry R. Harris (D)
Thomas M. Norwood (D)
Seaborn Reese (D)
Henry G. Turner (D)

ILLINOIS

Senators

John A. Logan (R) d. Dec. 1886
Charles B. Farwell (R) s. Jan. 1887

Shelby M. Cullom (R)

Representatives

George E. Adams (R)
Joseph G. Cannon (R)
Ransom W. Dunham (R)
John R. Eden (D)

Reuben Ellwood (R) d. 1887
Thomas J. Henderson (R)
Robert R. Hitt (R)
Albert J. Hopkins (R)
Silas Z. Landes (D)
Frank Lawler (D)
William R. Morrison (D)
William H. Neece (D)
Lewis F. Payson (R)
Ralph Plumb (R)
James M. Riggs (D)
Jonathan H. Rowell (R)
William H. Springer (D)
John R. Thomas (R)
Richard W. Townshend (D)
James H. Ward (D)
Nicholas E. Worthington (D)

INDIANA

Senators

Daniel W. Voorhees (D)
Benjamin Harrison (R)

Representatives

Thomas M. Browne (R)
William D. Bynum (D)
Thomas R. Cobb (D)
George Ford (D)
William S. Holman (D)
Jonas G. Howard (D)
James T. Johnston (R)
John J. Kleiner (D)
Robert Lowry (D)
Courtland C. Matson (D)
William D. Owen (R)
George W. Steele (R)
Thomas B. Ward (D)

IOWA

Senators

William B. Allison (R)
James F. Wilson (R)

Representatives

Edwin H. Conger (R)
Benjamin T. Frederick (D)
William E. Fuller (R)
Benton J. Hall (D)
David B. Henderson (R)
William P. Hepburn (R)
Adoniram J. Holmes (R)
Joseph Lyman (R)
Jeremiah H. Murphy (D)
Isaac S. Struble (R)
James B. Weaver (Greenback)

KANSAS

Senators

John J. Ingalls (R)
Preston B. Plumb (R)

Representatives

John A. Anderson (R)
Edward H. Funston (R)
Lewis Hanback (R)
Edmund N. Morrill (R)
Bishop W. Perkins (R)
Samuel R. Peters (R)
Thomas Ryan (R)

KENTUCKY

Senators

James B. Beck (D)
Joseph C. S. Blackburn (D)

Representatives

William C. P. Breckinridge (D)
John G Carlisle (D)
John E. Halsell (D)
Polk Laffoon (D)
James B. McCreary (D)
Thomas A. Robertson (D)
William J. Stone (D)
William P. Taulbee (D)
William H. Wadsworth (R)
Albert S. Willis (D)
Frank L. Wolford (D)

LOUISIANA

Senators

Randall L. Gibson (D)
James B. Eustis (D)

Representatives

Newton C. Blanchard (D)
Edward J. Gay (D)
Michael Hahn (R) d. Mar. 1886
Alfred B. Irion (D)
J. Floyd King (D)
Louis St. Martin (D)
Nathaniel D. Wallace (D) s. 1886

MAINE

Senators

Eugene Hale (R)
William P. Frye (R)

Representatives

Charles A. Boutelle (R)
Nelson Dingley, Jr. (R)
Seth L. Miliken (R)
Thomas B. Reed (R)

MARYLAND

Senators

Arthur P. Gorman (D)
Ephraim K. Wilson (D)

Representatives

William H. Cole (D) d. July 1886
Barnes Compton (D)
John V. L. Dindlay (D)
Charles H. Gibson (D)
Louis E. McComas (R)
Harry W. Rusk (D) s. 1886
Frank T. Shaw (D)

MASSACHUSETTS

Senators

Henry L. Dawes (R)
George F. Hoar (R)

Representatives

Charles H. Allen (R)
Patrick A. Collins (D)
Robert T. Davis (R)
Frederick D. Ely (R)
Edward D. Hayden (R)
John D. Long (R)
Henry B. Lovering (D)
Ambrose A. Ranney (R)
William W. Rice (R)
Francis W. Rockwell (R)
Eben F. Stone (R)
William Whiting (R)

MICHIGAN

Senators

Omar D. Conger (R)
Thomas W. Palmer (R)

Representatives

Julius C. Burrows (R)
Ezra C. Carleton (D)
Charles C. Comstock (D)
Byron M. Cutcheon (R)
Nathaniel B. Eldredge (D)
Spencer O. Fisher (D)
William C. Maybury (D)
Seth C. Moffatt (R)
James O'Donnell (R)
Timothy E. Tarsney (D)
Edwin B. Winans (D)

MINNESOTA

Senators

Samuel J. R. McMillan (R)
Dwight M. Sabin (R)

Representatives

John B. Gilfillan (R)
Knute Nelson (R)
Horace B. Strait (R)
James B. Wakefield (R)
Milo White (R)

MISSISSIPPI

Senators

Lucius Q. C. Lamar (D)
r. Mar. 1885
Edward C. Walthall (D) s. 1885

James Z. George (D)

Representatives

John M.Allen (D)
Ethelbert Barksdale (D)
Frederick G. Barry (D)
Thomas C. Catchings (D)
James B. Morgan (D)
Otho R. Singleton (D)
Henry S. Van Eaton (D)

MISSOURI

Senators

Francis M. Cockrell (D)
George G. Vest (D)

Representatives

Richard P. Bland (D)
James N. Burnes (D)
Martin L. Clardy (D)
William Dawson (D)
Alexander M. Dockery (D)
John M. Glover (D)
John B. Hale (D)
William H. Hatch (D)
John T. Heard (D)
John E. Hutton (D)
John J. O'Neill (D)
William J. Stone (D)
William H. Wade (R)
William Warner (R)

NEBRASKA

Senators

Charles H. Van Wyck (R)
Charles F. Manderson (R)

Representatives

George W. E. Dorsey (R)
James Laird (R)
Archibald J. Weaver (R)

NEVADA

Senators

John P. Jones (R)
James G. Fair (D)

Representative

William Woodburn (R)

NEW HAMPSHIRE

Senators

Austin F. Pike (R) d. Oct. 1886
Person C. Cheney (R) s. 1886

Henry W. Blair (R)

Representatives

Martin A. Haynes (R)
Jacob H. Gallinger (R)

NEW JERSEY

Senators

John R. McPherson (D)
William J. Sewell (R)

Representatives

James Buchanan (R)
Robert S. Green (D) r. Jan. 1887
George Hires (R)
Herman Lehlbach (R)
William McAdoo (D)
William W. Phelps (R)
James N. Pidcock (D)

NEW YORK

Senators

Warner Miller (R)
William M. Evarts (R)

Representatives

John J. Adams (D)
John Arnot, Jr. (D) d. Nov. 1886
Henry Bacon (D) s. 1886

Charles S. Baker (R)
Lewis Beach (D) d. Aug. 1886
Perry Belmont (D)
Archibald M. Bliss (D)
Henry G. Burleigh (R)
Felix Campbell (D)
Timothy J. Campbell (D)
Ira Davenport (R)
Abraham Dowdney (D) d. Dec. 1886
John M. Farquhar (R)
Abram S. Hewitt (D) r. Dec. 1886
Frank Hiscock (R)
Darwin R. James (R)
Frederick A. Johnson
John H. Ketcham (R)
James G. Lindsley (R)
Peter P. Mahoney (D)
Truman A. Merriman (D)
Stephen C. Millard (R)
Nicholas Muller (D)
Abraham X. Parker (R)
Sereno E. Payne (R)
John S. Pindar (D)
Joseph Pulitzer (D) r. Apr. 1886
John G. Sawyer (R)
Walter L. Sessions (R)
William G. Stahlnecker (D)
John T. Spriggs (R)
John Swinburne (R)
Egbert L. Viele (D)
John B. Weber (R)
George West (R)

NORTH CAROLINA

Senators

Matt W. Ransom (D)
Zebulon B. Vance (D)

Representatives

Risden T. Bennett (D)
William H. H. Cowles (D)
William R. Cox (D)
Wharton J. Green (D)
John S. Henderson (D)
Thomas D. Johnston (D)
James E. O'Hara (R)
James W. Reid (D) r. Nov. 1886
Thomas G. Skinner (D)

OHIO

Senators

John Sherman (R)
Henry B. Payne (D)

Representatives

Charles M. Anderson (D)
Charles E. Brown (R)
Benjamin Butterworth (R)
James E. Campbell (D)
William C. Cooper (R)
William W. Ellsberry (D)
Martin A. Foran (D)
George W. Geddes (D)
Charles H. Grosvenor (R)
William D. Hill (D)
Benjamin Le Fevre (D)
John Little (R)
William McKinley, Jr. (R)
Joseph H. Outhwaite (D)
Jacob Romeis (R)
George E. Seney (D)
Ezra B. Taylor (R)
Isaac H. Taylor (R)
Albert C. Thompson (R)
Adoniram J. Warner (D)
Beriah Wilkins (D)

OREGON

Senators

Joseph N. Dolph (R)
John H. Mitchell (R)

Representative

Binger Hermann (R)

PENNSYLVANIA

Senators

J. Donald Cameron (R)
John I. Mitchell (R)

Representatives

Louis E. Atkinson (R)
Thomas M. Bayne (R)
Henry H. Bingham (R)
Franklin Bound (R)
Charles E. Boyle (D)
William W. Brown (R)
Charles N. Brumm (Greenback)
Frank C. Bunnell (R)
Jacob M. Campbell (R)
Andrew G. Curtin (D)
Daniel Ermentrout (D)
I. Newton Evans (R)
James B. Everhart (R)
George W. Fleeger (R)
Alfred C. Harmer (R)
John A. Hiestand (R)
Oscar L. Jackson (R)
William D. Kelley (R)
James S. Negley (R)
Charles O'Neill (R)
Edwin S. Osborne (R)
Samuel J. Randall (D)
William L. Scott (D)
Joseph A. Scranton (R)
William H. Sowden (D)
John B. Storm (D)
John A. Swope (D)
Alexander C. White (R)

RHODE ISLAND

Senators

Nelson W. Aldrich (R)
Jonathan Chace (R)

Representatives

Charles H. Page (D) s. 1887
William A. Pirce (R) r. Jan. 1887
Henry J. Spooner (R)

SOUTH CAROLINA

Senators

Matthew C. Butler (D)
Wade Hampton (D)

Representatives

D. Wyatt Aiken (D)
George W. Dargan (D)
Samuel Dibble (D)
John J. Hemphill (D)
William H. Perry (D)
Robert Smalls (R)
George D. Tillman (R)

TENNESSEE

Senators

Isham G. Harris (D)

Howell E. Jackson (D) r. Apr. 1886
Washington C. Whitthorne (D) s. 1886

Representatives

John G. Ballentine (D)
Andrew J. Caldwell (D)
Presley T. Glass (D)
Leonidas C. Houk (R)
Benton McMillin (D)
John R. Neal (D)
Augustus H. Pettibone (R)
James D. Richardson (D)
John M. Taylor (D)
Zachary Taylor (R)

TEXAS

Senators

Samuel B. Maxey (D)
Richard Coke (D)

Representatives

William H. Crain (D)
David B. Culberson (D)
James H. Jones (D)
Samuel W. T. Lanham (D)
James F. Miller (D)
Roger Q. Mills (D)
John H. Reagan (D)
Joseph D. Sayers (D)
Charles Stewart (D)
James W. Throckmorton (D)
Olin Wellborn (D)

VERMONT

Senators

George F. Edmunds (R)
Justin S. Morrill (R)

Representatives

William W. Grout (R)
John W. Stewart (R)

VIRGINIA

Senators

William Mahone (Readjuster)
Harrison H. Riddleberger (Readjuster)

Representatives

John S. Barbour (D)
James D. Brady (R)
George C. Cabell (D)
Thomas Croxton (D)
John W. Daniel (D)
Harry Libbey (R)
Charles T. O'Ferrall (D)
Connally F. Trigg (D)
John R. Tucker (D)
George D. Wise (D)

WEST VIRGINIA

Senators

Johnson N. Camden (D)
John E. Kenna (D)

Representatives

Eustace Gibson (D)
Nathan Goff (R)
Charles P. Snyder (D)
William L. Wilson (D)

WISCONSIN

Senators

Philetus Sawyer (R)
John C. Spooner (R)

Representatives

Edward S. Bragg (D)
Lucien B. Caswell (R)
Richard W. Guenther (R)
Thomas R. Hudd (D) s. 1886
Robert M. La Follette (R)
Hugh H. Price (R) s. 1887
William T. Price (R) d. Dec. 1886
Joseph Rankin (D) d. Jan. 1886
Isaac Stephenson (R)
Ormsby B. Thomas (R)
Isaac W. Van Schaick (R)

FIFTIETH CONGRESS

March 4, 1887 to March 3, 1889

President of The Senate:	Vacant
President Pro Tempore of The Senate:	John J. Ingalls
Speaker of The House of Representatives:	John G. Carlisle

ALABAMA

Senators

John T. Morgan (D)
James L. Pugh (D)

Representatives

John H. Bankhead (D)
James E. Cobb
Alexander C. Davidson (D)
William H. Forney (D)
Hilary A. Herbert (D)
James T. Jones (D)
William C. Oates (D)
Joseph Wheeler (D)

ARKANSAS

Senators

James K. Jones (D)
James H. Berry (D)

Representatives

Clifton R. Breckinridge (D)
Poindexter Dunn (D)
Thomas C. McRae (D)
Samuel W. Peel (D)
John H. Rogers (D)

CALIFORNIA

Senators

Leland Stanford (R)
George Hearst (D)

Representatives

Marion Biggs (D)
Charles N. Felton (R)
Joseph McKenna (R)
William W. Morrow (R)
Thomas L. Thompson (D)
William Vandever (R)

COLORADO

Senators

Thomas M. Bowen (R)
Henry M. Teller (R)

Representative

George G. Symes (R)

CONNECTICUT

Senators

Orville H. Platt (R)
Joseph R. Hawley (R)

Representatives

Carlos French (D)
Miles T. Granger (D)
Charles A. Russell (R)
Robert J. Vance (D)

DELAWARE

Senators

Eli Saulsbury (D)
George Gray (D)

Representative

John B. Penington (D)

FLORIDA

Senators

Wilkinson Call (D)
Samuel Pasco (D)

Representatives

Robert H. M. Davidson (D)
Charles Dougherty (D)

GEORGIA

Senators

Joseph E. Brown (D)
Alfred H. Colquitt (D)

Representatives

George T. Barnes (D)
James H. Blount (D)
Allen D. Candler (D)
Henry H. Carlton (D)
Judson C. Clements (D)
Charles F. Crisp (D)
Thomas W. Grimes (D)
Thomas M. Norwood (D)
John D. Stewart (D)
Henry G. Turner (D)

ILLINOIS

Senators

Shelby M. Cullom (R)
Charles B. Farwell (R)

Representatives

George E. Adams (R)
George A. Anderson (D)
Jehu Baker (R)
Joseph G. Cannon (R)
Ransom W. Dunham (R)
William H. Gest (R)
Thomas J. Henderson (R)
Robert R. Hitt (R)
Albert J. Hopkins (R)
Silas Z. Landes (D)
Edward Lane (D)
Frank Lawler (D)
William E. Mason (R)
Lewis E. Payson (R)
Ralph Plumb (R)
Philip S. Post (R)
Jonathan H. Rowell (R)
William M. Springer (D)
John R. Thomas (R)
Richard W. Townshend (D)

INDIANA

Senators

Daniel W. Voorhees (D)
David Turpie (D)

Representatives

Thomas M. Browne (R)
William D. Bynum (D)
Joseph B. Cheadle (R)
William S. Holman (D)
Alvin P. Hovey (R) r. Jan. 1889
Jonas G. Howard (D)
James T. Johnston (R)
Courtland C. Matson (D)
John H. O'Neall (D)
William D. Owen (R)
Francis B. Posey (R) s. 1889
Benjamin F. Shively (D)
George W. Steele (R)
James B. White

IOWA

Senators

William B. Allison (R)
James F. Wilson (R)

Representatives

Albert R. Anderson (R)
Edwin H. Conger (R0
William E. Fuller (R)
John H. Gear (R)
Walter I. Hayes (D)
David B. Henderson (R)
Adoniram J. Holmes (R)
Daniel Kerr (R)
Joseph Lyman (R)
Isaac S. Struble (R)
James B. Weaver (D.G. Labor.) *
* Democratic-Greenback Laborite

KANSAS

Senators

John J. Ingalls (R)
Preston B. Plumb (R)

Representatives

John A. Anderson (R)
Edward H. Funston (R)
Edmund N. Morrill (R)
Bishop W. Perkins (R)
Samuel R. Peters (R)
Thomas Ryan (R)
Erastus J. Turner (R)

KENTUCKY

Senators

James B. Beck (D)
Joseph C. S. Blackburn (D)

Representatives

William C. P. Breckinridge (D)
John G. Carlisle (D)
Asher G. Caruth (D)
Hugh F. Finley (R)
W. Godfrey Hunter (R)
Polk Laffoon (D)
James B. McCreary (D)
Alexander B. Montgomery (D)
William J. Stone (D)
William P. Taulbee (D)
George M. Thomas (R)

LOUISIANA

Senators

Randall L. Gibson (D)
James B. Eustis (D)

Representatives

Newton C. Blanchard (D)
Edward J. Gay (D)
Matthew D. Lagan (D)
Cherubusco Newton (D)
Samuel M. Robertson (D)
Theodore S. Wilkinson (D)

MAINE

Senators

Eugene Hale (R)
William P. Frye (R)

Representatives

Charles A. Boutelle (R)
Nelson Dingley, Jr. (R)
Seth L. Milliken (R)
Thomas B. Reed (R)

MARYLAND

Senators

Arthur P. Gorman (D)
Ephraim K. Wilson (D)

Representatives

Barnes Compton (D)
Charles H. Gibson (D)
Louis E. McComas (R)
Isidor Rayner (D)
Harry W. Rusk (D)
Frank T. Shaw (D)

MASSACHUSETTS

Senators

Henry L. Dawes (R)
George F. Hoar (R)

Representatives

Charles H. Allen (R)
Edward Burnett (D)
William Cogswell (R)
Patrick A. Collins (D)
Robert T. Davis (R)
Edward D. Hayden (R)
Henry Cabot Lodge (R)
John D. Long (R)
Leopold Morse (D)
Francis W. Rockwell (R)
John E. Russell (D)
William Whiting (R)

MICHIGAN

Senators

Thomas W. Palmer (R)
Francis B. Stockbridge (R)

Representatives

Edward P. Allen (R)
Mark S. Brewer (R)
Julius C. Burrows (R)
J. Logan Chipman (D)
Byron M. Cutcheon (R)
Spencer O. Fisher (D)
Melbourne H. Ford (D)
Seth C. Moffatt (R) d. Dec. 1887
James O'Donnell (R)
Henry W. Seymour (R) s. 1888
Timothy E. Tarsney (D)
Justin R. Whiting (Greenback, D)

MINNESOTA

Senators

Dwight M. Sabin (R)
Cushman K. Davis (R)

Representatives

John Lind (R)
John L. MacDonald (D)
Knute Nelson (R)
Edmund Rice (D)
Thomas Wilson (D)

MISSISSIPPI

Senators

James Z. George (D)
Edward C. Walthall (D)

Representatives

John M. Allen (D)
Chapman L. Anderson (D)
Frederick G. Barry (D)
Thomas C. Catchings (D)
Charles E. Hooker (D)
James B. Morgan (D)
Thomas R. Stockdale (D)

MISSOURI

Senators

Francis M. Cockrell (D)
George G. Vest (D)

Representatives

Richard P. Bland (D)
Charles F. Booher (D) s. 1889
James N. Burnes (D)
Martin L. Clardy (D)
Alexander M. Dockery (D)
John M. Glover (D)
William H. Hatch (D)
John T. Heard (D)
John E. Hutton (D)
Charles H. Mansur (D)
John J. O'Neill (D)
William J. Stone (D)
William H. Wade (R)
James P. Walker (D)
William Warner (R)

NEBRASKA

Senators

Charles F. Manderson (R)
Algernon S. Paddock (R)

Representatives

George W. E. Dorsey (R)
James Laird (R)
John A. McShane (D)

NEVADA

Senators

John P. Jones (R)
William M. Stewart (R)

Representative

William Woodburn (R)

NEW HAMPSHIRE

Senators

Henry W. Blair (R)
William E. Chandler (R)

Representatives

Jacob H. Gallinger (R)
Luther F. McKinney (D)

NEW JERSEY

Senators

John R. McPherson (D)
Rufus Blodgett (D)

Representatives

James Buchanan (R)
George Hires (R)
John Kean (R)
Herman Lehlbach (R)
William McAdoo (D)
William W. Phelps (R)
James N. Pidcock (D)

NEW YORK

Senators

William M. Evarts (R)
Frank Hiscock (R)

Representatives

Henry Bacon (D)
Charles S. Baker (R)
James J. Belden (R)
Perry Belmont (D) r. Dec. 1888
Archibald M. Bliss (D)
Lloyd S. Bryce (D)
Felix Campbell (D)
Timothy J. Campbell (D)
W. Bourke Cockran (D)
Samuel S. Cox (D)
Amos J. Cummings (D)
Ira Davenport (R)
Milton De Lano (R)
John M. Farquhar (R)
Ashbel P. Fitch (R)
Thomas S. Flood (R)
Edward W. Greenman (D)
Stephen T. Hopkins (R)
John H. Ketcham (R)
William G. Laidlaw (R)
Peter P. Mahoney (D)
Truman A. Merriman (D)
John H. Moffitt (R)
Newton W. Nutting (R)
Abraham X. Parker (R)
John G. Sawyer (R)
James S. Sherman (R)
Francis B. Spinola (D)
William G. Stahlnecker (D)
Charles Tracey (D)
John B. Weber (R)
George West (R)
Stephen V. White (R)
David Wilber (R)

NORTH CAROLINA

Senators

Matt W. Ransom (D)
Zebulon B. Vance (D)

Representatives

John M. Brower (R)
William H. H. Cowles (D)
John S. Henderson (D)
Thomas D. Johnston (D)
Louis C. Latham (D)
Charles W. McClammy (D)
John Nichols
Alfred Rowland (D)
Furnifold McL. Simmons (D)

OHIO

Senators

John Sherman (R)
Henry B. Payne (D)

Representatives

Melvin M. Boothman (R)
Charles E. Brown (R)
Benjamin Butterworth (R)
James E. Campbell (D)
William C. Cooper (R)
George W. Crouse (R)
Martin A. Foran (D)
Charles H. Grosvenor (R)
Robert P. Kennedy (R)
William McKinley, Jr. (R)
Joseph H. Outhwaite (D)
Jacob J. Pugsley (R)
Jacob Romeis (R)
George E. Seney (D)
Ezra B. Taylor (R)
Joseph D. Taylor (R)
Albert C. Thompson (R)
Charles P. Wickham (R)
Beriah Wilkins (D)
Elihu S. Williams (R)
Samuel S. Yoder (D)

OREGON

Senators

Joseph N. Dolph (R)
John H. Mitchell (R)

Representative

Binger Hermann (R)

PENNSYLVANIA

Senators

J. Donald Cameron (R)
Matthew S. Quay (R)

Representatives

Louis E. Atkinson (R)
Thomas M. Bayne (R)
Henry H. Bingham (R)
Franklin Bound (R)
Charles N. Brumm (Greenback)
Charles R. Buckalew (D)
Frank C. Bunnell (R)
John Dalzell (R)
Smedley Darlington (R)
Daniel Ermentrout (D)
Norman Hall (D)
Alfred C. Harmer (R)
John A. Hiestand (R)
Oscar L. Jackson (R)
William D. Kelley (R)
John Lynch (D)
Henry C. McCormick (R)
Welty McCullogh (R)
James T. Maffett (R)
Levi Maish (D)
Charles O'Neill (R)
Edwin S. Osborne (R)
John Patton (R)
Samuel J. Randall (D)
William L. Scott (D)
Edward Scull (R)
William H. Sowden (D)
Robert M. Yardley (R)

RHODE ISLAND

Senators

Nelson W. Aldrich (R)
Jonathan Chace (R)

Representatives

Warren O. Arnold (R)
Henry J. Spooner (R)

SOUTH CAROLINA

Senators

Matthew C. Butler (D)
Wade Hampton (D)

Representatives

James S. Cothran (D)
George W. Dargan (D)
Samuel Dibble (D)
William Elliott (D)
John J. Hemphill (D)
William H. Perry (D)
George D. Tillman (D)

TENNESSEE

Senators

Isham G. Harris (D)
William B. Bate (D)

Representatives

Roderick R. Butler (R)
Benjamin A. Enloe (D)
Presley T. Glass (D)
Leonidas C. Houk (R)
Benton McMillin (D)
John R. Neal (D)
James Phelan (D)
James D. Richardson (D)
Joseph E. Washington (D)
Washington C. Whitthorne (D)

TEXAS

Senators

Richard Coke (D)
John H. Reagan (D)

Representatives

Jo Abbott (D)
William H. Crain (D)
David B. Culberson (D)
Silas Hare (D)
Constantine B. Kilgore (D)
Samuel W. T. Lanham (D)
William H. Martin (D)
Roger Q. Mills (D)
Littleton W. Moore (D)
Joseph D. Sayers (D)
Charles Stewart (D)

VERMONT

Senators

George F. Edmunds (R)
Justin S. Morrill (R)

Representatives

William W. Grout (R)
John W. Stewart (R)

VIRGINIA

Senators

Harrison H. Riddleberger (Readjuster)
John W. Daniel (D)

Representatives

George E. Bowden (R)
Henry Bowen (R)

John R. Brown (R)
Thomas H. B. Browne (R)
William E. Gaines (R)
Samuel I. Hopkins (D)
William H. F. Lee (D)
Charles T. O'Ferrall (D)
George D. Wise (D)
Jacob Yost (R)

WEST VIRGINIA

Senators

John E. Kenna (D)
Charles J. Faulkner (D)

Representatives

Charles E. Hogg (D)
Nathan Goff (R)
Charles P. Snyder (D)
William L. Wilson (D)

WISCONSIN

Senators

Philetus Sawyer (R)
John C. Spooner (R)

Representatives

Lucien B. Caswell (R)
Charles B. Clark (R)
Richard W. Guenther (R)
Nils P. Haugen (R) s. 1888
Thomas R. Hudd (D)
Robert M. La Follette (R)
Henry Smith (People's Party)
Isaac Stephenson (R)
Ormsby B. Thomas (R)

FIFTY-FIRST CONGRESS

March 4, 1889 to March 3, 1891

President of The Senate: Levi P. Morton
Presidents Pro Tempore of The Senate: John J. Ingalls
Charles F. Manderson
Speaker of The House of Representatives: Thomas B. Reed

ALABAMA

Senators

John T. Morgan (D)
James L. Pugh (D)

Representatives

John H. Bankhead (D)
Richard H. Clarke (R)
James E. Cobb
William H. Forney (D)
Hilary A. Herbert (D)
John V. McDuffie (R) s. 1890
William C. Oates (D)
Louis W. Turpin (D) r. June 1890
Joseph Wheeler (D)

ARKANSAS

Senators

James K. Jones (D)
James H. Berry (D)

Representatives

Clifton R. Breckinridge (D)
William H. Cate (D) r. Mar. 1890
Lewis P. Featherstone (Laborite) s. 1890
Thomas C. McRae (D)
Samuel W. Peel (D)
John H. Rogers (D)

CALIFORNIA

Senators

Leland Stanford (R)
George Hearst (D)

Representatives

Marion Biggs (D)
Thomas J. Clunie (D)
John J. De Haven (R) r. Oct. 1890
Thomas J. Geary (D) s. 1890
Joseph McKenna (R)
William W. Morrow (R)
William Vandever (R)

COLORADO

Senators

Henry M. Teller (R)
Edward O. Wolcott (R)

Representative

Hosea Townsend (R)

CONNECTICUT

Senators

Orville H. Platt (R)
Joseph R. Hawley (R)

Representatives

Frederick Miles (R)
Charles A. Russell (R)
William E. Simonds (R)
Washington F. Willcox (D)

DELAWARE

Senators

George Gray (D)
Anthony Higgins (R)

Representative

John B. Penington (D)

FLORIDA

Senators

Wilkinson Call (D)
Samuel Pasco (D)

Representatives

Robert Bullock (D)
Robert H. M. Davidson (D)

GEORGIA

Senators

Joseph E. Brown (D)
Alfred H. Colquitt (D)

Representatives

George T. Barnes (D)
James H. Blount (D)
Allen D. Candler (D)
Henry H. Carlton (D)
Judson C. Clements (D)
Charles F. Crisp (D)
Thomas W. Grimes (D)
Rufus E. Lester (D)
John D. Stewart (D)
Henry G. Turner (D)

IDAHO

Senators

George L. Shoup (R) s. 1890
William J. McConnell (R) s. 1891

Representative

Willis Sweet (R) s. 1890

ILLINOIS

Senators

Shelby M. Cullom (R)
Charles B. Farwell (R)

Representatives

George E. Adams (R)
Joseph G. Cannon (R)
George W. Fithian (D)
William S. Forman (D)
William H. Gest (R)
Thomas J. Henderson (R)
Charles A. Hill (R)
Robert H. Hitt (R)
Albert J. Hopkins (R)
Edward Lane (D)
Frank Lawler (D)
William E. Mason (R)
Lewis E. Payson (R)
Philip S. Post (R)
Jonathan H. Rowell (R)
George W. Smith (R)
William M. Springer (D)
Abner Taylor (R)
Scott Wike (D)
James R. Williams (R)

INDIANA

Senators

Daniel W. Voorhees (D)
David Turpie (D)

Representatives

Elijah V. Brookshire (D)
Jason B. Brown (D)
Thomas M. Browne (R)
William D. Bynum (D)
Joseph B. Cheadle (R)
George W. Cooper (D)
William S. Holman (D)
Charles A. O. McClellan (D)
Augustus N. Martin (D)
John H. O'Neall (D)
William D. Owen (R)
William F. Parrett (D)
Benjamin F. Shively (D)

IOWA

Senators

William B. Allison (R)
James F. Wilson (R)

Representatives

Edwin H. Conger (R) r. Oct. 1890
Jonathan P. Dolliver (R)
James P. Flick (R)
John H. Gear (R)
Walter I. Hayes (D)
Edward R. Hays (R) s. 1890
David B. Henderson (R)
Daniel Kerr (R)
John F. Lacey (R)
Joseph R. Reed (R)
Isaac S. Struble (R)
Joseph H. Sweney (R)

KANSAS

Senators

John J. Ingalls (R)
Preston B. Plumb (R)

Representatives

John A. Anderson (R)
Edward H. Funston (R)
Harrison Kelley (R)
Edmund N. Morrill (R)
Samuel R. Peters (R)
Bishop W. Perkins (R)
Erastus J. Turner (R)

KENTUCKY

Senators

James B. Beck (D) d. May 1890
John G. Carlisle (D) s. 1890

Joseph C. S. Blackburn (D)

Representatives

William C. P. Breckinridge (D)
John G. Carlisle (D) r. May 1890
Asher G. Caruth (D)
William W. Dickerson (D) s. June 1890

William T. Ellis (D)
Hugh F. Finley (R)
Isaac H. Goodnight (D)
James B. McCreary (D)
Alexander B. Montgomery (D)
Thomas H. Paynter (D)
William J. Stone (D)
John H. Wilson (R)

LOUISIANA

Senators

Randall L. Gibson (D)
James B. Eustis (D)

Representatives

Newton C. Blanchard (D)
Charles J. Boatner (D)
Hamilton D. Coleman (R)
Andrew Price (D)
Samuel M. Robertson (D)
Theodore S. Wilkinson (D)

MAINE

Senators

Eugene Hale (R)
William P. Frye (R)

Representatives

Charles A. Boutelle (R)
Nelson Dingley, Jr. (R)
Seth L. Milliken (R)
Thomas B. Reed (R)

MARYLAND

Senators

Arthur P. Gorman (D)
Ephraim K. Wilson (D)
d. Feb. 1890

Representatives

Barnes Compton (D) r. Mar. 1890
Charles H. Gibson (D)
Louis E. McComas (R)
Sydney E. Mudd (R) s. 1890
Harry W. Rusk (D)
Henry Stockbridge (R)
Herman Stump (D)

MASSACHUSETTS

Senators

Henry L. Dawes (R)
George F. Hoar (R)

Representatives

John F. Andrew (D)
Nathaniel P. Banks (R)
John W. Candler (R)
William Cogswell (R)
Frederic T. Greenhalge (R)
Henry Cabot Lodge (R)
Elijah A. Morse (R)
Joseph H. O'Neil (D)
Charles S. Randall (R)
Francis W. Rockwell (R)
Joseph H. Walker (R)
Rodney Wallace (R)

MICHIGAN

Senators

Francis B. Stockbridge (R)
James McMillan (R)

Representatives

Edward P. Allen (R)
Charles E. Belknap (R)
Aaron T. Bliss (R)
Mark S. Brewer (R)
Julius C. Burrows (R)
J. Logan Chipman (D)
Byron M. Cutcheon (R)
James O'Donnell (R)
Samuel M. Stephenson (R)
Frank W. Wheeler (R)
Justin R. Whiting (D)

MINNESOTA

Senators

Cushman K. Davis (R)
William D. Washburn (R)

Representatives

Solomon G. Comstock (R)
Mark H. Dunnell (R)
Darwin S. Hall (R)
John Lind (R)
Samuel P. Snider (R)

MISSISSIPPI

Senators

James Z. George (D)
Edward C. Walthall (D)

Representatives

John M. Allen (D)
Chapman L. Anderson (D)
Thomas C. Catchings (D)
Charles E. Hooker (D)
Clarke Lewis (D)
James B. Morgan (D)
Thomas R. Stockdale (D)

MISSOURI

Senators

Francis M. Cockrell (D)
George G. Vest (D)

Representatives

Richard P. Bland (D)
Alexander M. Dockery (D)
Nathan Frank (R)
William H. Hatch (D)
John T. Heard (D)
William M. Kinsey (R)
Charles H. Mansur (D)
Frederick G. Niedringhaus (R)
Richard H. Norton (D)
William J. Stone (D)
John C. Tarsney (D)
William H. Wade (R)
James P. Walker (D) d. July 1890
Robert H. Whitelaw (D) s. 1890
Robert P. C. Wilson (D)

MONTANA

Senators

Thomas C. Power (R) s. 1890
Wilbur F. Sanders (R) s. 1890

Representative

Thomas H. Carter (R)

NEBRASKA

Senators

Charles F. Manderson (R)
Algernon S. Paddock (R)

Representatives

William J. Connell (R)
George W. E. Dorsey (R)
Gilbert L. Laws (R)

NEVADA

Senators

John P. Jones (R)
William M. Stewart (R)

Representative

Horace F. Bartine (R)

NEW HAMPSHIRE

Senators

Henry W. Blair (R)
William E. Chandler (R)

Representatives

Alonzo Nute (R)
Orren C. Moore (R)

NEW JERSEY

Senators

John R. McPherson (D)
Rufus Blodgett (D)

Representatives

Charles D. Beckwith (R)
Christopher A. Bergen (R)
James Buchanan (R)
Samuel Fowler (D)
Jacob A. Geissenhainer (D)
Herman Lehlbach (R)
William McAdoo (D)

NEW YORK

Senators

William M. Evarts (R)
Frank Hiscock (R)

Representatives

Charles S. Baker (R)
James J. Belden (R)
Felix Campbell (D)
John M. Clancy (D)
James W. Covert (D)
Amos J. Cummings (D)
Milton De Lano (R)
Edward J. Dunphy (D)
John M. Farquhar (R)
Ashbel P. Fitch (D)
Thomas S. Flood (R)
Roswell P. Flower (D)
John H. Ketcham (R)
Charles J. Knapp (R)
William G. Laidlaw (R)
Frederick Lansing (R)
John H. McCarthy (D)
r. Jan. 1891
Thomas F. Magner (D)
John H. Moffitt (R)
Sereno E. Payne (R)
John S. Pindar (D) s. 1890
John A. Quackenbush (R)
John Quinn (D)
John Raines (R)
John Sanford (R)
John G. Sawyer (R)
James S. Sherman (R)
Francis B. Spinola (D)
William G. Stahlnecker (D)
Moses D. Stivers (R)
Charles Tracey (D)
Charles H. Turner (D)
William C. Wallace (R)
David Wilber (R) d. Apr. 1890
John McC. Wiley (D)

NORTH CAROLINA

Senators

Matt W. Ransom (D)
Zebulon B. Vance (D)

Representatives

John M. Brower (R)
Benjamin H. Bunn (D)
Henry P. Cheatham (R)
William H. H. Cowles (D)
Hamilton G. Ewart (R)
John S. Henderson (D)
Charles W. McClammy (D)
Alfred Rowland (D)
Thomas G. Skinner (D)

NORTH DAKOTA

Senators

Lyman R. Casey (R)
Gilbert A. Pierce (R)

Representative

Henry C. Hansbrough (R)

OHIO

Senators

John Sherman (R)
Henry B. Payne (D)

Representatives

Melvin M. Boothman (R)
Thedore E. Burton (R)
Benjamin Butterworth (R)
John A. Caldwell (R)
William C. Cooper (R)
Charles H. Grosvenor (R)
William E. Haynes (D)
Robert P. Kennedy (R)

William McKinley, Jr. (R)
Henry L. Morey (R)
Joseph H. Outhwaite (D)
James W. Owens (D)
Jacob J. Pugsley (R)
George E. Seney (D)
Martin L. Smyser (R)
Ezra B. Taylor (R)
Joseph D. Taylor (R)
Albert C. Thompson (R)
Charles P. Wickham (D)
Elihu S. Williams (R)
Samuel S. Yoder (D)

OREGON

Senators

Joseph N. Dolph (R)
John H. Mitchell (R)

Representative

Binger Hermann (R)

PENNSYLVANIA

Senators

J. Donald Cameron (R)
Matthew S. Quay (R)

Representatives

Louis E. Atkinson (R)
Thomas M. Bayne (R)
Henry H. Bingham (R)
Marriott Broslus (R)
David B. Brunner (D)
Charles R. Buckalew (D)
Samuel A. Craig (R)
William C. Culbertson (R)
John Dalzell (R)
Smedley Darlington (R)
Alfred C. Harmer (R)
William D. Kelley (R) d. 1890
James Kerr (D)
Henry C. McCormick (R)
Levi Maish (D)
William Mutchler (D)
Charles O'Neill (R)
Edwin S. Osborne (R)
Samuel J. Randall (D) d. 1890
Joseph W. Ray (R)
James B. Reilly (D)
John E. Reyburn (R) s. 1890
John W. Rife (R)
Joseph A. Scranton (R)
Edward Scull (R)
Charles W. Stone (R) s. 1890
Charles C. Townsend (R)
Richard Vaux (R) s. 1890
Lewis F. Watson (R) d. Aug. 1890
Myron B. Wright (R)
Robert M. Yardley (R)

RHODE ISLAND

Senators

Nelson W. Aldrich (R)

Jonathan Chace (R) r. Apr. 1889
Nathan F. Dixon (R) s. 1889

Representatives

Warren O. Arnold (R)
Henry J. Spooner (R)

SOUTH CAROLINA

Senators

Matthew C. Butler (D)
Wade Hampton (D)

Representatives

James S. Cothran (D)
George W. Dargan (D)
Samuel Dibble (D)
William Elliott (D) r. Sept. 1890
John J. Hemphill (D)
Thomas E. Miller (R) s. 1890
William H. Perry (D)
George D. Tillman (D)

SOUTH DAKOTA

Senators

Richard F. Pettigrew (R)
Gideon C. Moody (R)

Representatives

Oscar S. Gifford (R)
John A. Pickler (R)

TENNESSEE

Senators

Isham G. Harris (D)
William B. Bate (D)

Representatives

Benjamin A. Enloe (D)
H. Clay Evans (R)
Leonidas C. Houk (R)
Benton McMillin (D)
James Phelan (D) d. Jan. 1891
Rice A. Pierce (D)
James D. Richardson (D)
Alfred A. Taylor (R)
Joseph E. Washington (D)
Washington C. Witthorne (D)

TEXAS

Senators

Richard Coke (D)
John H. Reagan (D)

Representatives

Jo Abbott (D)
William H. Crain (D)
David B. Culberson (D)
Silas Hare (D)
Constantine B. Kilgore (D)
Samuel W. T. Lanham (D)
William H. Martin (D)
Roger Q. Mills (D)
Littleton W. Moore (D)
Joseph D. Sayers (D)
Charles Stewart (D)

VERMONT

Senators

George F. Edmunds (R)
Justin S. Morrill (R)

Representatives

William W. Grout (R)
John W. Stewart (R)

VIRGINIA

Senators

John W. Daniel (D)
John S. Barbour (D)

Representatives

George E. Bowden (R)
Thomas H. B. Browne (R)
John A. Buchanan (D)
Paul C. Edmunds (D)
John M. Langston (R) s. 1890
William H. F. Lee (D)
Posey G. Lester (D)
Charles T. O'Ferrall (D)
Henry St. George Tucker (D)
Edward C. Venable (D) r. Sept. 1890
Edmund Waddill, Jr., (R) s. 1890
George D. Wise (R) r. Apr. 1890

WASHINGTON

Senators

John B. Allen (R)
Watson C. Squire (R)

Representative

John Wilson (R)

WEST VIRGINIA

Senators

John E. Kenna (D)
Charles J. Faulkner (D)

Representatives

John D. Alderson (D)
George W. Atkinson (R) s. 1890
J. Monroe Jackson (D)
r. Feb. 1890
John O. Pendleton (D)
r. Feb. 1890
Charles B. Smith (R) s. 1890
William L. Wilson (D)

WISCONSIN

Senators

Philetus Sawyer (R)
John C. Spooner (R)

Representatives

Charles Barwig (D)
George H. Brickner (D)
Lucien B. Caswell (R)
Charles B. Clark (R)
Nils P. Haugen (R)
Robert M. La Follette (R)
Myron H. McCord (D)
Ormsby B. Thomas (R)
Isaac W. Van Schaick (R)

WYOMING

Senators

Joseph M. Carey (R) s. 1890
Francis E. Warren (R) s. 1890

Representative

Clarence D. Clark (R) s. 1890

FIFTY-SECOND CONGRESS

March 4, 1891 to March 3, 1893

President of the Senate: Levi P. Morton
President Pro Tempore of The Senate: Charles F. Manderson
Speaker of The House of Representatives: Charles F. Crisp

ALABAMA

Senators

John T. Morgan (D)
James L. Pugh (D)

Representatives

John H. Bankhead (D)
Richard H. Clarke (R)
James E. Cobb
William H. Forney (D)
Hilary A. Herbert (D)
William C. Oates (D)
Louis W. Turpin (D)
Joseph Wheeler (D)

Representatives

Clifton R. Breckinridge (D)
William H. Cate (D)
Thomas C. McRae
Samuel W. Peel (D)
William L. Terry (D)

ARKANSAS

Senators

James K. Jones (D)
James H. Berry (D)

CALIFORNIA

Senators

Leland Stanford (R)
Charles N. Felton (R)

Representatives

William W. Bowers (R)
Anthony Caminetti (D)
John T. Cutting (R)
Thomas J. Geary (D)
Samuel G. Hilborn (R) s. 1892
Eugene F. Loud (R)
Joseph McKenna (R) r. Mar. 1892

COLORADO

Senators

Henry M. Teller (R)
Edward O. Wolcott (R)

Representative

Hosea Townsend (R)

CONNECTICUT

Senators

Orville H. Platt (R)
Joseph R. Hawley (R)

Representatives

Robert E. DeForest (D)
Charles A. Russell (R)
Lewis Sperry (D)
Washington F. Willcox (D)

DELAWARE

Senators

George Gray (D)
Anthony Higgins (R)

Representative

John W. Causey (D)

FLORIDA

Senators

Wilkinson Call (D)
Samuel Pasco (D)

Representatives

Robert Bullock (D)
Stephen R. Mallory (D)

GEORGIA

Senators

Alfred H. Colquitt (D)
John B. Gordon (D)

Representatives

James H. Blount (D)
Charles F. Crisp (D)
Robert W. Everett (D)
Thomas G. Lawson (D)
Rufus E. Lester (D)
Leonidas F. Livingston (D)
Charles L. Moses (D)
Henry G. Turner (D)
Thomas E. Watson (Pop)
Thomas E. Winn (D)

IDAHO

Senators

George L. Shoup (R)
Fred T. Dubois (R)

Representative

Willis Sweet (R)

ILLINOIS

Senators

Shelby M. Cullom (R)
John M. Palmer (D)

Representatives

Samuel T. Busey (D)
Benjamin T. Cable (D)
Allan C. Durborow, Jr. (D)
George W. Fithian (D)
William S. Forman (D)
Thomas J. Henderson (R)
Robert R. Hitt (R)
Albert J. Hopkins (R)
Edward Lane (D)
Lawrence E. McGann (D)
Walter C. Newberry (D)
Philip S. Post (R)
Owen Scott (D)
George W. Smith (R)
Herman W. Snow (D)
William M. Springer (D)
Lewis Steward (D)
Abner Taylor (R)
Scott Wike (D)
James R. Williams (D)

INDIANA

Senators

Daniel W. Voorhees (D)
David Turpie (D)

Representatives

John L. Bretz (D)
Elijah V. Brookshire (D)
Jason B. Brown (D)
William D. Bynum (D)
George W. Cooper (D)
William S. Holman (D)
Henry U. Johnson (R)
Charles A. O. McClellan (D)
Augustus N. Martin (D)
William F. Parrett (D)
David H. Patton (D)
Benjamin F. Shively (D)
Daniel W. Waugh (R)

IOWA

Senators

William B. Allison (R)
James F. Wilson (R)

Representatives

Thomas Bowman (D)
Walter H. Butler (D)
Jonathan P. Dolliver (R)
James P. Flick (R)
John T. Hamilton (D)
Walter I. Hayes (D)
David B. Henderson (R)
John A. T. Hull (R)
George D. Perkins (R)
John J. Seerley (D)
Frederick E. White (D)

KANSAS

Senators

Preston B. Plumb (R) d. 1892
Bishop W. Perkins (R) s. 1892

William A. Peffer (Pop)

Representatives

William Baker (People's Party)
Case Broderick (R)
Benjamin H. Clover
(Farmer's Alliance)
John Davis (People's Party)
Edward H. Funston (R)
John G. Otis (People's Party)
Jeremiah Simpson (Pop)

KENTUCKY

Senators

Joseph C. S. Blackburn (D)
John G. Carlisle (D) r. Feb. 1893

Representatives

William C. P. Breckinridge (D)
Asher G. Caruth (D)
William W. Dickerson (D)
William T. Ellis (D)
Isaac H. Goodnight (D)
John W. Kendall (D) d. Mar. 1892
Joseph M. Kendall (D) s. 1892
James B. McCreary (D)
Alexander B. Montgomery (D)
Thomas H. Paynter (D)
William J. Stone (D)
John H. Wilson (R)

LOUISIANA

Senators

Randall L. Gibson (D)
d. Dec. 1892
Donelson Caffery, (D) s. 1893

Edward D. White (D)

Representatives

Newton C. Blanchard (D)
Charles J. Boatner (D)
Matthew D. Lagan (D)
Adloph Meyer (D)
Andrew Price (D)
Samuel M. Robertson (D)

MAINE

Senators

Eugene Hale (R)
William P. Fyre (R)

Representatives

Charles A. Boutelle (R)
Nelson Dingley, Jr. (R)
Seth L. Milliken (R)
Thomas B. Reed (R)

MARYLAND

Senators

Arthur P. Gorman (D)
Charles H. Gibson (D)

Representatives

John B. Brown (D) s. 1892
Barnes Compton (D)
William M. McKaig (D)
Henry Page (D) r. Sept. 1892
Isidor Rayner (D)
Harry W. Rusk (D)
Herman Stump (D)

MASSACHUSETTS

Senators

Henry L. Dawes (R)
George F. Hoar (R)

Representatives

John F. Andrew (D)
William Cogswell (R)
Frederick S. Coolidge (D)
John C. Crosby (D)
Sherman Hoar (D)
Henry Cabot Lodge (R)
r. Mar. 1893
Elijah A. Morse (R)
Joseph H. O'Neil (D)
Charles S. Randall (R)
Moses T. Stevens (D)
Joseph H. Walker (R)
George F. Williams (D)

MICHIGAN

Senators

Francis B. Stockbridge (R)
James McMillan (R)

Representatives

Charles E. Belknap (R)
Julius C. Burrows (R)
J. Logan Chipman (D)
Melbourne H. Ford (D)
d. Apr. 1891
James S. Gorman (D)
James O'Donnell (R)
Samuel M. Stephenson (R)
Byron G. Stout (D)
Thomas A. E. Weadock (D)
Harrison H. Wheeler (R)
Justin R. Whiting (Greenback, D)
Henry M. Youmans (D)

MINNESOTA

Senators

Cushman K. Davis (R)
William D. Washburn (R)

Representatives

James N. Castle (D)
Osee M. Hall (D)
Kittel Halvorson
(Farmer's Alliance)
William H. Harries (D)
John Lind (R)

MISSISSIPPI

Senators

James Z. George (D)
Edward C. Walthall (D)

Representatives

John M. Allen (D)
Joseph H. Beeman (D)
Thomas C. Catchings (D)
Charles E. Hooker (D)
John C. Kyle (D)
Clarke Lewis (D)
Thomas R. Stockdale (D)

MISSOURI

Senators

Francis M. Cockrell (D)
George G. Vest (D)

Representatives

Marshall Arnold (D)
Richard P. Bland (D)
Samuel Byrns (D)
Seth W. Cobb (D)
David A. DeArmond (D)
Alexander M. Dockery (D)
Robert W. Fyan (D)
William H. Hatch (D)
John T. Heard (D)
Charles H. Mansur (D)
Richard H. Norton (D)
John J. O'Neill (D)
John C. Tarsney (D)
Robert P. C. Wilson (D)

MONTANA

Senators

Thomas C. Power (R)
Wilbur F. Sanders (R)

Representative

William W. Dixon (D)

NEBRASKA

Senators

Charles F. Manderson (R)
Algernon S. Paddock (R)

Representatives

William Jennings Bryan (D)
Omer M. Kem (Pop)
William A. McKeighan (D)

NEVADA

Senators

John P. Jones (R)
William M. Stewart (R)

Representative

Horace F. Bartine (R)

NEW HAMPSHIRE

Senators

William E. Chandler (R)
Jacob H. Gallinger (R)

Representatives

Warren F. Daniell (D)
Luther F. McKinney (D)

NEW JERSEY

Senators

John R. McPherson (D)
Rufus Blodgett (D)

Representatives

Christopher A. Bergen (R)
James Buchanan (R)
Cornelius A. Cadmus (D)
Thomas D. English (D)
Samuel Fowler (D)
Jacob A. Geissenhainer (D)
Edward F. McDonald (D)
d. Nov. 1892

NEW YORK

Senators

Frank Hiscock (R)
David B. Hill (D) s. 1892

Representatives

Henry Bacon (D)
James J. Belden (R)
Henry W. Bentley (D)
Thomas L. Bunting (D)
Timothy J. Campbell (D)
Alfred C. Chapin (D) r. Nov. 1892
John M. Clancy (D)
W. Bourke Cockran (D)
William J. Coombs (D)
James W. Covert (D)
Isaac N. Cox (D)
Amos J. Cummings (D)
Newton M. Curtis (R)
Edward J. Dunphy (D)
John R. Fellows (D)
Ashbel P. Fitch (D)
Halbert S. Greenleaf (D)
Warren B. Hooker (R)
John H. Ketcham (R)
Joseph J. Little (D)
Daniel N. Lockwood (D)
Thomas F. Magner (D)
Sereno E. Payne (R)
John A. Quackenbush (R)
John Raines (R)
George W. Ray (R)
Hosea H. Rockwell (D)
John Sanford (R)
William G. Stahlnecker (D)
Charles Tracey (D)
George Van Horn (D)
James W. Wadsworth (D)
J. De Witt Warner (D)
John M. Wever (R)

NORTH CAROLINA

Senators

Matt W. Ransom (D)
Zebulon B. Vance (D)

Representatives

Sydenham B. Alexander (D)
William A. B. Branch (D)
Benjamin H. Bunn (D)
Henry P. Cheatham (R)
William H. H. Cowles (D)
William T. Crawford (D)
Benjamin F. Grady (D)
John S. Henderson (D)
Archibald H. A. Williams (D)

NORTH DAKOTA

Senators

Lyman R. Casey (R)
Henry C. Hansbrough (R)

Representative

Martin N. Johnson (R)

OHIO

Senators

John Sherman (R)
Calvin S. Brice (D)

Representatives

John A. Caldwell (R)
Robert E. Doan (R)
Dennis D. Donovan (D)
James Irvine Dungan (D)
William H. Enochs (D)
Martin K. Gantz (D)
Darius D. Hare (D)
Michael D. Harter (D)
William E. Haynes (D)
George W. Houk (D)
Tom L. Johnson (D)
Fernando C. Layton (D)
Lewis P. Ohliger (D) s. 1892
Joseph H. Outhwaite (D)
James W. Owens (D)
John M. Pattison (D)
Albert J. Pearson (D)
Bellamy Storer (R)
Ezra B. Taylor (R)
Joseph D. Taylor (R)
Vincent A. Taylor (R)
John G. Warwick (D)

OREGON

Senators

Joseph N. Dolph (R)
John H. Mitchell (R)

Representative

Binger Hermann (R)

PENNSYLVANIA

Senators

J. Donald Cameron (R)
Matthew S. Quay (R)

Representatives

Lemuel Amerman (D)
Louis E. Atkinson (R)
Frank E. Beltzhoover (D)
Henry H. Bingham (R)
Marriott Brosius (R)
David B. Brunner (D)
Alexander K. Craig (D) d. 1892
John Dalzell (R)
Eugene P. Gillespie (D)
Matthew Griswold (R)
Edwin Hallowell (D)
Alfred C. Harmer (R)
Albert C. Hopkins (R)
George F. Huff (R)
George F. Kribbs (D)
William McAleer (D)
William Mutchler (D)
Charles O'Neill (R)
James B. Reilly (D)
John E. Reyburn (R)
John W. Rife (R)
John B. Robinson (R)
Edward Scull (R)
George W. Shonk (R)
William A. Sipe (D) s. 1892
Andrew Stewart (R) r. Feb. 1892
Charles W. Stone (R)
William A. Stone (R)
Simon P. Wolverton (D)
Myron B. Wright (R)

RHODE ISLAND

Senators

Nelson W. Aldrich (R)
Nathan F. Dixon (R)

Representatives

Oscar Lapham (D)
Charles H. Page (D)

SOUTH CAROLINA

Senators

Matthew C. Butler (D)
John L. M. Irby (D)

Representatives

William H. Brawley (D)
William Elliott (D)
John J. Hemphill (D)
George Johnstone (D)
John I. McLaurin (D) s. 1892
George W. Shell (D)
Eli T. Stackhouse (D) d. June 1892
George D. Tillman (D)

SOUTH DAKOTA

Senators

Richard F. Pettigrew (R)
James K. Kyle

Representatives

John R. Gamble (R) d. Aug. 1891
John L. Jolley (R)
John A. Pickler (R)

TENNESSEE

Senators

Isham G. Harris (D)
William B. Bate (D)

Representatives

Nicholas N. Cox (D)
Benjamin A. Enloe (D)
John C. Houk (R)
Benton McMillin (D)
Josiah Patterson (D)
Rice A. Pierce (D)
James D. Richardson (D)
Henry C. Snodgrass (D)
Alfred A. Taylor (R)
Joseph E. Washington (D)

TEXAS

Senators

Richard Coke (D)

John H. Reagan (D) r. 1891
Horace Chilton (D) ta. 1891
Roger Q. Mills (D) s. 1892

Representatives

Jo Abbott (D)
Edwin Le Roy Antony (D) s. 1892
Joseph W. Bailey (D)
William H. Crain (D)
David B. Culberson (D)
Constantine B. Kilgore (D)
Samuel W. T. Lanham (D)
John B. Long (D)
Roger Q. Mills (D) r. Mar. 1892
Littleton W. Moore (D)
Joseph D. Sayers (D)
Charles Stewart (D)

VERMONT

Senators

George F. Edmunds (R)
r. Nov. 1891
Redfield Proctor (R) s. 1891

Justin S. Morrill (R)

Representatives

William W. Grout (R)
H. Henry Powers (R)

VIRGINIA

Senators

John W. Daniel (D)

John S. Barbour (D) d. May 1892
Eppa Hunton (D) s. 1892

Representatives

John A. Buchanan (D)
Paul C. Edmunds (D)
James F. Epes (D)
William A. Jones (D)
John W. Lawson (D)
Posey G. Lester (D)
Elisha E. Meredith (D)
Charles T. O'Ferrall (D)
Henry St. George Tucker (D)
George D. Wise (D)

WASHINGTON

Senators

John B. Allen (R)
Watson C. Squire (R)

Representative

John L. Wilson (R)

WEST VIRGINIA

Senators

John E. Kenna (D) d. Jan. 1893
Johnson N. Camden (D) s. 1893

Charles J. Faulkner (D)

Representatives

John D. Alderson (D)
James Capehart (D)
John O. Pendleton (D)
William L. Wilson (D)

WISCONSIN

Senators

Philetus Sawyer (R)
William F. Vilas (D)

Representatives

Clinton Babbitt (D)
Charles Barwig (D)
George H. Brickner (D)
Allen R. Bushnell (D)
Frank P. Coburn (D)
Nils P. Haugen (R)
Thomas Lynch (D)
Lucas M. Miller (D)
John L. Mitchell (D)

WYOMING

Senators

Joseph M. Carey (R)
Francis E. Warren (R)

Representative

Clarence D. Clark (R)

FIFTY-THIRD CONGRESS

March 4, 1893 to March 3, 1895

President of The Senate: Adlai E. Stevenson
Presidents Pro Tempore of The Senate: Charles F. Manderson, Isham G. Harris, Matt W. Ransom
Speaker of The House of Representatives: Charles F. Crisp

ALABAMA

Senators

John T. Morgan (D)
James L. Pugh (D)

Representatives

John H. Bankhead (D)
Richard H. Clarke (D)
James E. Cobb
William H. Denson (D)
George P. Harrison (D) s. 1894
William C. Oates (D) r. Nov. 1894
Gaston A. Robbins (D)
Jesse F. Stallings (D)
Louis W. Turpin (D)
Joseph Wheeler (D)

ARKANSAS

Senators

James K. Jones (D)
James H. Berry (D)

Representatives

Clifton R. Breckinridge (D)
r. Aug. 1894
Hugh A. Dinsmore (D)
John S. Little (D) s. 1894
Philip D. McCulloch Jr. (D)
Thomas C. McRae (D)
Robert Neill (D)
William L. Terry (D)

CALIFORNIA

Senators

Leland Stanford (R) d. 1893
George C. Perkins (R) s. 1893

Stephen M. White (D)

Representatives

William W. Bowers (R)
Anthony Caminetti (D)
Marion Cannon (People's Party)
Warren B. English (D) s. 1894
Thomas J. Geary (D)
Samuel G. Hilborn (R)
r. Apr. 1894
Eugene F. Loud (R)
James G. Maguire (D)

COLORADO

Senators

Henry M. Teller (R)
Edward O. Wolcott (R)

Representatives

John C. Bell (D)
Lafayette Pence (D)

CONNECTICUT

Senators

Orville H. Platt (R)
Joseph R. Hawley (R)

Representatives

Robert E. DeForest (D)
James P. Pigott (D)
Charles A. Russell (R)
Lewis Sperry (D)

DELAWARE

Senators

George Gray (D)
Anthony Higgins (R)

Representative

John W. Causey (D)

FLORIDA

Senators

Wilkinson Call (D)
Samuel Pasco (D)

Representatives

Charles M. Cooper (D)
Stephen R. Mallory (D)

GEORGIA

Senators

Alfred H. Colquitt (D) d. Mar. 1894
Patrick Walsh (D) s. 1894

John B. Gordon (D)

Representatives

James C. C. Black (D)
Thomas B. Cabaniss (D)
Charles F. Crisp (D)
Thomas G. Lawson (D)
Rufus E. Lester (D)
Leonidas F. Livingston (D)
John W. Maddox (D)
Charles L. Moses (D)
Benjamin E. Russell (D)
Farish C. Tate (D)
Henry G. Turner (D)

IDAHO

Senators

George L. Shoup (R)
Fred T. Dubois (R)

Representative

Willis Sweet (R)

ILLINOIS

Senators

Shelby M. Cullom (R)
John M. Palmer (R)

Representatives

J. Frank Aldrich (R)
John C. Black (D) r. Jan. 1895
Joseph G. Cannon (R)
Robert A. Childs (R)
Allan C. Durborow, Jr. (D)
George W. Fithian (D)
William S. Forman (D)
Benjamin F. Funk (R)
Julius Golozier (D)
Thomas J. Henderson (R)
Robert R. Hitt (R)
Albert J. Hopkins (R)
Andrew J. Hunter (D)
Edward Lane (D)
John J. McDannold (D)
Lawrence E. McGann (D)
Benjamin F. Marsh (R)
Philip S. Post (R) d. Jan. 1895
George W. Smith (R)
William M. Springer (D)
Hamilton K. Wheeler (R)
James R. Williams (D)

INDIANA

Senators

Daniel W. Voorhees (D)
David Turpie (D)

Representatives

John L. Bretz (D)
Elijah V. Brookshire (D)
Jason B. Brown (D)
William D. Bynum (D)

Charles G. Conn (D)
George W. Cooper (D)
Thomas Hammond (D)
William S. Holman (D)
Henry U. Johnson (R)
William F. McNagny (D)
Augustus N. Martin (D)
Arthur H. Taylor (D)
Daniel W. Waugh (R)

IOWA

Senators

William B. Allison (R)
James F. Wilson (R)

Representatives

Robert G. Cousins (R)
Jonathan P. Dolliver (R)
John H. Gear (R)
Alva L. Hager (R)
Walter I. Hayes (D)
David B. Henderson (R)
William P. Hepburn (R)
John A. T. Hull (R)
John F. Lacey (R)
George D. Perkins (R)
Thomas Updegraff (R)

KANSAS

Senators

William A. Peffer (Pop)
John Martin (D)

Representatives

William Baker (People's Party)
Case Broderick (R)
Charles Curtis (R)
John Davis (People's Party)
Edward H. Funston r. Aug. 1894
William A. Harris (Pop)
Thomas J. Hudson (Progressive)
Horace L. Moore (D) s. 1894
Jeremiah Simpson (Progressive)

KENTUCKY

Senators

Joseph C. S. Blackburn (D)
William Lindsay (D)

Representatives

Silas Adams (R)
William M. Beckner (D) s. 1894
Albert S. Berry (D)
William C. P. Breckinridge (D)
Asher G. Caruth (D)
William T. Ellis (D)
Isaac H. Goodnight (D)
Marcus C. Lisle (D) d. July 1894
James B. McCreary (D)
Alexander B. Montgomery (D)
Thomas H. Paynter (D)
r. Jan. 1895
William J. Stone (D)

LOUISIANA

Senators

Edward D. White (D) r. Mar. 1894
Newton C. Blanchard (D) s. 1894

Donelson Caffery (D)

Representatives

Newton C. Blanchard (R)
r. Mar. 1894
Charles J. Boatner (D)
Robert C. Davey (D)
Adolph Meyer (D)
Henry W. Ogden (D) s. 1894
Andrew Price (D)
Samuel M. Robertson (D)

MAINE

Senators

Eugene Hale (R)
William P. Frye (R)

Representatives

Charles A. Boutelle (R)
Nelson Dingley, Jr. (R)
Seth L. Milliken (R)
Thomas B. Reed (R)

MARYLAND

Senators

Arthur P. Gorman (D)
Charles H. Gibson (D)

Representatives

Robert F. Bratton (D)
d. May 1894
Charles E. Coffin (R) s. 1894
Barnes Compton (D) r. May 1894
W. Laird Henry (D) s. 1894
William M. McKaig (D)
Isidor Rayner (D)
Harry W. Rusk (D)
J. Fred C. Talbott (D)

MASSACHUSETTS

Senators

George F. Hoar (R)
Henry Cabot Lodge (R)

Representatives

Lewis D. Apsley (R)
William Cogswell (R)
William F. Draper (R)
William Everett (D)
Frederick H. Gillett (R)
Samuel W. McCall (R)
Michael J. McEttrick (D)
Elijah A. Morse (R)
Joseph H. O'Neil (D)
Charles S. Randall (R)
Moses T. Stevens (D)
Joseph H. Walker (R)
Ashley B. Wright (R)

MICHIGAN

Senators

Francis B. Stockbridge (R)
d. Apr. 1894
John Patton, Jr. (R) ta. 1894
Julius C. Burrows (R) s. 1895

James McMillan (R)

Representatives

David D. Aitken (R)
John Avery (R)
Julius C. Burrows (R) r. 1895
J. Logan Chipman (D)
d. Aug. 1893
James S. Gorman (D)
Levi T. Griffin (D)
William S. Linton (D)
John W. Moon (R)
George F. Richardson (D)
Samuel M. Stephenson (R)
Henry F. Thomas (R)
Thomas A. E. Weadock (D)
Justin R. Whiting (Greenback)

MINNESOTA

Senators

Cushman K. Davis (R)
William D. Washburn (R)

Representatives

Melvin R. Baldwin (D)
Haldor E. Boen (People's Party)
Loren Fletcher (R)
Osee M. Hall (D)
Andrew R. Kiefer (R)
James T. McCleary (R)
James A. Tawney (R)

MISSISSIPPI

Senators

James Z. George (D)

Edward C. Walthall (D) r. Jan. 1894
Anselm J. McLaurin (D) s. 1894

Representatives

John M. Allen (D)
Thomas C. Catchings (D)
Charles E. Hooker (D)
John C. Kyle (D)
Hernando D. Money (D)
Thomas R. Stockdale (D)
John Sharp Williams (D)

MISSOURI

Senators

Francis M. Cockrell (D)
George G. Vest (D)

Representatives

Marshall Arnold (D)
Richard Bartholdt (R)
Richard P. Bland (D)
Daniel D. Burnes (D)
Champ Clark (D)
Seth W. Cobb (D)
David A. De Armond (D)
Alexander M. Dockery (D)
Robert W. Fyan (D)
Uriel S. Hall (D)
William H. Hatch (D)
John T. Heard (D)
Charles F. Joy (R) r. Apr. 1894
Charles H. Morgan (D)
John J. O'Neill (D) s. 1894
John C. Tarsney (D)

MONTANA

Senators

Thomas C. Power (R)
Lee Mantle (R)

Representative

Charles S. Hartman (R)

NEBRASKA

Senators

Charles F. Manderson (R)
William V. Allen (Pop)

Representatives

William Jennings Bryan (D)
Eugene J. Hainer (R)
Omer M. Kem (Pop)
William McKeighan
George D. Meiklejohn (R)
David H. Mercer (R)

NEVADA

Senators

John P. Jones (R)
William M. Stewart (R)

Representative

Francis G. Newlands (D)

NEW HAMPSHIRE

Senators

William E. Chandler (R)
Jacob H. Gallinger (R)

Representatives

Henry M. Baker (R)
Henry W. Blair (R)

NEW JERSEY

Senators

John R. McPherson (D)
James Smith, Jr. (D)

Representatives

Cornelius A. Cadmus (D)
Johnston Cornish (D)
John T. Dunn (D)
Thomas D. English (D)
George B. Fielder (D)
John J. Gardner (D)
Jacob A. Geissenhainer (D)
Henry C. Loudenslager (R)

NEW YORK

Senators

David B. Hill (D)
Edward Murphy, Jr. (D)

Representatives

Franklin Bartlett (D)
James J. Belden (R)
Timothy J. Campbell (D)
Charles A. Chickering (R)
John M. Clancy (D)
W. Bourke Cockran (D)

William J. Coombs (D)
James W. Covert (D)
Amos J. Cummings (D)
r. Nov. 1893
Newton M. Curtis (R)
Charles Daniels (R)
Edward J. Dunphy (D)
John R. Fellows (D) r. Dec. 1893
Ashbel P. Fitch (D) r. Dec. 1893
Charles W. Gillet (R)
John H. Graham (D)
Charles D. Haines (D)
Joseph C. Hendrix (D)
Warren B. Hooker (R)
Jacob Le Fever (R)
Daniel N. Lockwood (D)
Thomas F. Magner (D)
Francis Marvin (R)
Sereno E. Payne (R)
Lemuel E. Quigg (R) s. 1894
George W. Ray (R)
William Ryan (D)
Simon J. Schermerhorn (D)
James S. Sherman (R)
Daniel E. Sickles (D)
Isidor Straus (D) s. 1894
Charles Tracey (D)
John Van Voorhis (R)
James W. Wadsworth (R)
J. De Witt Warner (D)
John M. Wever (R)

NORTH CAROLINA

Senators

Matt W. Ransom (D)

Zebulon B. Vance (D)
d. Apr. 1894
Thomas J. Jarvis (D) ta. 1894
Jeter C. Pritchard (R) s. 1895

Representatives

Sydenham B. Alexander (D)
William H. Bower (D)
William A. B. Branch (D)
Benjamin H. Bunn (D)
William T. Crawford (D)
Benjamin F. Grady (D)
John S. Henderson (D)
Thomas Settle (R)
Frederick A. Woodard (D)

NORTH DAKOTA

Senators

Henry C. Hansbrough (R)
William N. Roach (D)

Representative

Martin N. Johnson (R)

OHIO

Senators

John Sherman (R)
Calvin S. Brice (D)

Representatives

Jacob H. Bromwell (R) s. 1894
Hezekiah S. Bundy (R)
John A. Caldwell (R) r. May 1894
Dennis D. Dovovan (D)
Charles H. Grosvenor (R)
Darius D. Hare (D)
Michael D. Harter (D)
George W. Houk (D) d. Feb. 1894
George W. Hulick (R)
George P. Ikirt (D)
Tom L. Johnson (D)
Fernando C. Layton (D)
Stephen A. Northway (R)
Joseph H. Outhwaite (D)
Albert J. Pearson (D)
James A. D. Richards (D)
Byron F. Ritchie (D)
Paul J. Sorg (D) s. 1894
Bellamy Storer (R)
Luther M. Strong (R)
Henry C. Van Voorhis (R)
William J. White (R)
George W. Wilson (R)

OREGON

Senators

Joseph N. Dolph (R)
John H. Mitchell (R)

Representatives

William R. Ellis (R)
Binger Hermann (R)

PENNSYLVANIA

Senators

J. Donald Cameron (R)
Matthew S. Quay (R)

Representatives

Robert Adams, Jr. (R) s. 1894
Frank E. Beltzhoover (D)
Henry H. Bingham (R)
Marriott Brosius (R)
John Dalzell (R)
Constantine J. Erdman (D)
Galusha A. Grow (R) s. 1894
Alfred C. Harmer (R)
Daniel B. Heiner (R)
Josiah D. Hicks (R)
William H. Hines (D)
Albert C. Hopkins (R)
Edwin J. Jorden (R) s. 1895
George F. Kribbs (D)
William Lilly (R) d. Dec. 1893
William McAleer (D)
Alexander McDowell (R)
Thaddeus M. Mahon (R)
Howard Mutchler (D)
Charles O'Neill (R) d. Nov. 1893
Thomas W. Phillips (R)
James B. Reilly (D)
John E. Reyburn (R)
John B. Robinson (R)
Joseph A. Scranton (R)
Joseph C. Sibley (D)
William A. Sipe (D)
Charles W. Stone (R)
William A. Stone (R)
Irving P. Wanger (R)
Simon P. Wolverton (D)
Ephraim M. Woomer (R)
Myron B. Wright (R) d. Nov. 1894

RHODE ISLAND

Senators

Nelson W. Aldrich (R)
Nathan F. Dixon (R)

Representatives

Oscar Lapham (D)
Charles H. Page (D)

SOUTH CAROLINA

Senators

Matthew C. Butler (D)
John L. M. Irby (D)

Representatives

William H. Brawley (D)
r. Feb. 1894
James F. Izlar (D) s. 1894
Asbury C. Latimer (D)
John L. McLaurin (D)
George W. Murray (R)
George W. Shell (D)
Thomas J. Strait (D)
W. Jasper Talbert (D)

SOUTH DAKOTA

Senators

Richard F. Pettigrew (R)
James H. Kyle

Representatives

William V. Lucas (R)
John A. Pickler (R)

TENNESSEE

Senators

Isham G. Harris (D)
William B. Bate (D)

Representatives

Nicholas N. Cox (D)
Benjamin A. Enloe (D)
John C. Houk (R)
James C. McDearmon (D)
Benton McMillin (D)
Josiah Patterson (D)
James D. Richardson (D)
Henry C. Snodgrass (D)
Alfred A. Taylor (R)
Joseph E. Washington (D)

TEXAS

Senators

Richard Coke (D)
Robert Q. Mills (D)

Representatives

Jo Abbott (D)
Joseph W. Bailey (D)
Charles K. Bell (D)
Jeremiah V. Cockrell (D)
Samuel B. Cooper (D)
William H. Crain (D)
David B. Culberson (D)
Walter Gresham (D)
Joseph C. Hutcheson (D)
Constantine B. Kilgore (D)
Thomas M. Paschal (D)
George C. Pendleton (D)
Joseph D. Sayers (D)

VERMONT

Senators

Justin S. Morrill (R)
Redfield Proctor (R)

Representatives

William W. Grout (R)
H. Henry Powers (R)

VIRGINIA

Senators

John W. Daniel (D)
Eppa Hunton (D)

Representatives

Paul C. Edmunds (D)
James F. Epes (D)
William A. Jones (D)
James W. Marshall (D)
Elisha E. Meredith (D)
Charles T. O'Ferrall (D)
r. Dec. 1893
Claude A. Swanson (D)
Henry St. George Tucker (D)
Smith S. Turner (D) s. 1894
D. Gardiner Tyler (D)
George D. Wise (D)

WASHINGTON

Senators

Watson C. Squire (R)
John L. Wilson (R) s. 1895

Representatives

William H. Doolittle (R)
John L. Wilson (R) r. Feb. 1895

WEST VIRGINIA

Senators

Charles J. Faulkner (D)
Johnson N. Camden (D)

Representatives

John D. Alderson (D)
James Capehart (D)
John O. Pendleton (D)
William L. Wilson (D)

WISCONSIN

Senators

William F. Vilas (D)
John L. Mitchell (D)

Representatives

Joseph W. Babcock (R)
Lyman E. Barnes (D)
Charles Barwig (D)
George H. Brickner (D)
Henry Allen Cooper (R)
Michael Griffin (R) s. 1894
Nils P. Haugen (R)
Thomas Lynch (D)
George B. Shaw (R) d. Aug. 1894
Peter J. Somers (D)
Owen A. Wells (D)

WYOMING

Senators

Joseph M. Carey (R)
Clarence D. Clark (R) s. 1895

Representative

Henry A. Coffeen (D)

FIFTY-FOURTH CONGRESS

March 4, 1895 to March 3, 1897

President of The Senate: Adlai E. Stevenson
President Pro Tempore of The Senate: William P. Frye
Speaker of The House of Representatives: Thomas B. Reed

ALABAMA

Senators

John T. Morgan (D)
James L. Pugh (D)

Representatives

Truman H. Aldrich (R) s. 1896
William F. Aldrich (R) s. 1896
John H. Bankhead (D)
Richard H. Clarke (D)
James E. Cobb r. Apr. 1896
Albert T. Goodwyn (D) s. 1896
George P. Harrison (D)
Milford W. Howard (Pop)
Gatson A. Robbins (D) r. Mar. 1896
Jesse F. Stallings (D)
Oscar W. Underwood (D) r. 1896
Joseph Wheeler (D)

ARKANSAS

Senators

James K. Jones (D)
James H. Berry (D)

Representatives

Hugh A. Dinsmore (D)
John S. Little (D)
Philip D. McCulloch, Jr. (D)
Thomas C. McRae (D)
Robert Neill (D)
William L. Terry (D)

CALIFORNIA

Senators

Stephen M. White (D)
George C. Perkins (R)

Representatives

John A. Barham (R)
William W. Bowers (R)
Samuel G. Hillborn (R)
Grove L. Johnson (R)
Eugene F. Loud (R)
James McLachlan (R)
James G. Maguire (D)

COLORADO

Senators

Henry M. Teller (R)
Edward O. Wolcott (R)

Representatives

John C. Bell (D)
John F. Shafroth (R)

CONNECTICUT

Senators

Orville H. Platt (R)
Joseph R. Hawley (R)

Representatives

E. Stevens Henry (R)
Ebenezer J. Hill (R)
Charles A. Russell (R)
Nehemiah D. Sperry (R)

DELAWARE

Senators

George Gray (D)
Richard R. Kenney (D) s. 1897

Representatives

Jonathan S. Willis (R)

FLORIDA

Senators

Wilkinson Call (D)
Samuel Pasco (D)

Representatives

Charles M. Cooper (D)
Stephen M. Sparkman (D)

GEORGIA

Senators

John B. Gordon (D)
Augustus O. Bacon (D)

Representatives

Charles L. Bartlett (D)
James C. C. Black (D)
Charles F. Crisp (D) d. Oct. 1896
Charles R. Crisp (D) s. 1896
Thomas G. Lawson (D)
Rufus E. Lester (D)
Leonidas F. Livingston (D)
John W. Maddox (D)
Charles L. Moses (D)
Benjamin E. Russell (D)
Farish C. Tate (D)
Henry G. Turner (D)

IDAHO

Senators

George L. Shoup (R)
Fred T. Dubois (R)

Representative

Edgar Wilson (R)

ILLINOIS

Senators

Shelby M. Cullom (R)
John McA. Palmer (D)

Representatives

J. Frank Aldrich (R)
Hugh R. Belknap (R)
Orlando Burrell (R)
Joseph G. Cannon (R)
James A. Connolly (R)
Edward D. Cooke (R)
Finis E. Downing (R) r. June 1896
George E. Foss (R)
Joseph V. Graff (R)
William F. L. Hadley (R)
Robert R. Hitt (R)
Albert J. Hopkins (R)
William Lorimer (R)
Lawrence E. McGann (D) r. Dec. 1895
Benjamin F. Marsh (R)
Everett J. Murphy (R)
George W. Prince (R)
Walter Reeves (R)
John I. Rinaker (R) s. 1896
George W. Smith (R)
Vespasian Warner (R)
George E. White (R)
Benson Wood (R)
Charles W. Woodman (R)

INDIANA

Senators

Daniel W. Voorhees (D)
David Turpie (D)

Representatives

George W. Faris (R)
J. Frank Hanly (R)
Alexander M. Hardy (R)
Jethro A. Hatch (R)
James A. Hemenway (R)
Charles L. Henry (R)
Henry U. Johnson (R)
Jacob D. Leighty (R)
Jesse Overstreet (R)
Lemuel W. Royse (R)
George W. Steele (R)
Robert J. Tracewell (R)
James E. Watson (R)

IOWA

Senators

William B. Allison (R)
John H. Gear (R)

Representatives

Samuel M. Clark (R)
Robert G. Cousins (R)
George M. Curtis (R)
Jonathan P. Dolliver (R)
Alva L. Hager (R)
David B. Henderson (R)
William P. Hepburn (R)
John A. T. Hull (R)
John F. Lacey (R)
George D. Perkins (R)
Thomas Updegraff (R)

KANSAS

Senators

William A. Peffer (Pop)
Lucien Baker (R)

Representatives

William Baker (People's Party)
Richard W. Blue (R)
Case Broderick (R)
William A. Calderhead (R)
Charles Curtis (R)
Snyder S. Kirkpatrick (R)
Chester I. Long (R)
Orrin L. Miller (R)

KENTUCKY

Senators

Joseph C. S. Blackburn (D)
William Lindsay (D)

Representatives

Albert S. Berry (D)
John D. Clardy (D)
David G. Colson (R)
Walter Evans (R)
John K. Hendrick (D)
Nathan T. Hopkins (R) s. 1897
W. Godfrey Hunter (R)
Joseph M. Kendall (D) r. Feb. 1897
John W. Lewis (R)
James B. McCreary (D)
William C. Owens (D)
Samuel J. Pugh

LOUISIANA

Senators

Donelson Caffery (D)
Newton C. Blanchard (D)

Representatives

Charles J. Boatner (D)
Charles F. Buck (D)
Adolph Meyer (D)
Henry W. Ogden (D)
Andrew Price (D)
Samuel M. Robertson (D)

MAINE

Senators

Eugene Hale (R)
William P. Frye (R)

Representatives

Charles A. Boutelle (R)
Nelson Dingley, Jr. (R)
Seth L. Milliken (R)
Thomas B. Reed (R)

MARYLAND

Senators

Arthur P. Gorman (D)
Charles H. Gibson (D)

Representatives

William B. Baker (R)
Charles E. Coffin (R)
John K. Cowen (D)
Joshua W. Miles (D)
Harry W. Rusk (D)
George L. Wellington (R)

MASSACHUSETTS

Senators

George F. Hoar (R)
Henry Cabot Lodge (R)

Representatives

Lewis D. Apsley (R)
Harrison H. Atwood (R)
William E. Barrett (R)
William F. Draper (R)
John F. Fitzgerald (D)
Frederick H. Gillett (R)
William S. Knox (R)
Samuel W. McCall (R)
William H. Moody (R)
Elijah A. Morse (R)
John Simpkins (R)
Joseph H. Walker (R)
Ashley B. Wright (R)

MICHIGAN

Senators

James McMillan (R)
Julius C. Burrows (R)

Representatives

David D. Aitken (R)
John Avery (R)
Roswell P. Bishop (R)
John B. Corliss (R)
Rousseau O. Crump (R)
William S. Linton (R)
Alfred Milnes (R)
William Alden Smith (R)
Horace G. Snover (R)
George Spalding (R)
Samuel M. Stephenson (R)
Henry F. Thomas (R)

MINNESOTA

Senators

Cushman K. Davis (R)
Knute Nelson (R)

Representatives

Frank M. Eddy (R)
Loren Fletcher (R)
Joel P. Heatwole (R)
Andrew R. Keifer (R)
James T. McCleary (R)
James A. Tawney (R)
Charles A. Towne (R)

MISSISSIPPI

Senators

James Z. George (D)
Edward C. Walthall (D)

Representatives

John M. Allen (D)
Thomas C. Catchings (D)
Walter McK. Denny (D)
John C. Kyle (D)
Hernando D. Money (D)
James G. Spencer (D)
John Sharp Williams (D)

MISSOURI

Senators

Francis M. Cockrell (D)
George G. Vest (D)

Representatives

Richard Bartholdt (R)
Charles G. Burton (R)
Charles N. Clark (R)
Seth W. Cobb (D)
George C. Crowther (R)
David A. De Armond (D)
Alexander M. Dockery (D)
Uriel S. Hall (D)
Joel D. Hubbard (R)
Charles F. Joy (R)
Norman A. Mozley (R)
John H. Raney (R)
John C. Tarsney (D) r. Feb. 1896
John P. Tracey (R)
William M. Treloar (R)
Robert T. Van Horn (R) s. 1896

MONTANA

Senators

Lee Mantle (R)
Thomas H. Carter (R)

Representative

Charles S. Hartman (R)

NEBRASKA

Senators

William V. Allen (Pop)
John M. Thurston (R)

Representatives

William E. Andrews (R)
Eugene J. Hainer (R)
Omer M. Kem (Pop)
George D. Meiklejohn (R)
David H. Mercer (R)
Jesse B. Strode (R)

NEVADA

Senators

John P. Jones (R)
William M. Stewart (R)

Representative

Francis G. Newlands (D)

NEW HAMPSHIRE

Senators

William E. Chandler (R)
Jacob H. Gallinger (R)

Representatives

Henry M. Baker (R)
Cyrus A. Sulloway (R)

NEW JERSEY

Senators

James Smith, Jr. (D)
William J. Sewell (R)

Representatives

Charles N. Fowler (R)
John J. Gardner (D)
Benjamin F. Howell (R)
Henry C. Loudenslager (R)
Thomas McEwan, Jr. (R)
Richard W. Parker (R)
Mahlon Pitney (R)
James F. Stewart (R)

NEW YORK

Senators

David B. Hill (D)
Edward Murphy, Jr. (D)

Representatives

Franklin Bartlett (D)
Charles G. Bennett (R)
Frank S. Black (R) r. Jan. 1897
Henry C. Brewster (R)
Charles A. Chickering (R)
Amos J. Cummings (D)
Newton M. Curtis (R)
Charles Daniels (R)
Benjamin L. Fairchild (R)
Israel F. Fischer (R)
Wallace T. Foote Jr. (R)
Charles W. Gillet (R)
Warren B. Hooker (R)
James R. Howe (R)
Dennis M. Hurley (R)
Jacob Le Fever (R)
Philip B. Low (R)
George B. McClellan (D)
Richard C. McCormick (R)
Rowland B. Mahany (R)
Henry Clay Miner (D)
John M. Mitchell (R) s. June 1896
Benjamin B. Odell Jr. (R)
Sereno E. Payne (R)
Theodore L. Poole (R)
Lemuel E. Quigg (R)
George W. Ray (R)
Richard C. Shannon (R)
James S. Sherman (R)
George N. Southwick (R)
William Sulzer (D)
James W. Wadsworth (R)
James J. Walsh (D) r. June 1896
David F. Wilber (R)
Francis H. Wilson (R)

NORTH CAROLINA

Senators

Jeter C. Pritchard (R)
Marion Butler (Pop)

Representatives

Romulus Z. Linney (R)
James A. Lockhart (D)
r. June 1896
Charles H. Martin (Pop) s. 1896
Richmond Pearson (R)
Thomas Settle (R)
John G. Shaw (D)
Alonzo C. Shuford (Pop)
Harry Skinner (Pop)
William F. Strowd (Pop)
Frederick A. Woodard (D)

NORTH DAKOTA

Senators

Henry C. Hansbroug (R)
William N. Roach (D)

Representative

Martin N. Johnson (R)

OHIO

Senators

John Sherman (D)
Clavin S. Brice (D)

Representatives

Clifton B. Beach (R)
Jacob H. Bromwell (R)
Theodore E. Burton (R)
Lorenzo Danford (R)
Francis B. De Witt (R)
Lucien J. Fenton (R)
Charles H. Grosvenor (R)
Stephen R. Harris (R)
George W. Hulick (R)
Winfield S. Kerr (R)
Fernando C. Layton (D)
Addison S. McClure (R)
Stephen A. Northway (R)
Paul J. Sorg (D)
James H. Southard (R)
Luther M. Strong (R)
Charles P. Taft (R)
Robert W. Tayler (R)
Henry C. Van Voorhis (R)
David K. Watson (R)
George W. Wilson (R)

OREGON

Senators

John H. Mitchell (R)
George W. McBride (R)

Representatives

William R. Ellis (R)
Binger Hermann (R)

PENNSYLVANIA

Senators

J. Donald Cameron (R)
Matthew S. Quay (R)

Representatives

Ernest F. Acheson (R)
Robert Adams, Jr. (R)
William C. Arnold (R)
Henry H. Bingham (R)
Marriott Brosius (R)
Charles N. Brumm (R)
James H. Codding (R)
John Dalzell (R)
Constantine J. Erdman (D)
Matthew Griswold (R)
Galusha A. Grow (R)
Frederick Halterman (R)
Alfred C. Harmer (R)
Joseph J. Hart (D)
Daniel B. Heiner (R)
Josiah D. Hicks (R)
George F. Huff (R)
Monroe H. Kulp (R)
John Leisenring (R)
Fred C. Leonard (R)
Thaddeus M. Mahon (R)
Thomas W. Phillips (R)
John E. Reyburn (R)

John B. Robinson (R)
Joseph A. Scranton (R)
James A. Stahle (R)
Charles W. Stone (R)
William A. Stone (R)
Irving P. Wanger (R)
Ephraim M. Woomer (R)

RHODE ISLAND

Senators

Nelson W. Aldrich (R)
George P. Wetmore (R)

Representatives

Warren O. Arnold (R)
Melville Bull (R)

SOUTH CAROLINA

Senators

John L. M. Irby (D)
Benjamin R. Tillman (D)

Representatives

William Elliott (D) r. June 1896
Asbury C. Latimer (D)
John L. McLaurin (D)
George W. Murray (R) s. 1896
J. William Stokes (D) s. 1896
Thomas J. Strait (Alliance D)
W. Jasper Talbert (D)
Stanyarne Wilson (D)

SOUTH DAKOTA

Senators

Richard F. Pettigrew (R)
James H. Kyle

Representatives

Robert J. Gamble (R)
John A. Pickler (R)

TENNESSEE

Senators

Isham G. Harris (D)
William B. Bate (D)

Representatives

William C. Anderson (R)
Foster V. Brown (R)
Nicholas N. Cox (D)
Henry R. Gibson (R)
John E. McCall (R)
James C. McDearmon (D)
Benton McMillin (D)
Josiah Patterson (D)
James D. Richardson (D)
Joseph E. Washington (D)

TEXAS

Senators

Roger Q. Mills (D)
Horace Chilton (D)

Representatives

Jo Abbott (D)
Joseph W. Bailey (D)
Charles K. Bell (D)
Jeremiah V. Cockrell (D)
Samuel L. Cooper (D)
William H. Crain (D) d. Feb. 1896
Miles Crowley (D)
David B. Culberson (D)
Joseph C. Hutcheson (D)
Rudolph Kleberg (D) s. 1896
George H. Noonan (R)
George C. Pendleton (D)
Joseph D. Sayers (D)
Charles H. Yoakum (D)

UTAH

Senators

Frank J. Cannon (R) s. 1896
Arthur Brown (R) s. 1896

Representative

Clarence E. Allen (R) s. 1896

VERMONT

Senators

Justin S. Morrill (R)
Redfield Proctor (R)

Representatives

William W. Grout (R)
H. Henry Powers (R)

VIRGINIA

Senators

John W. Daniel (D)
Thomas S. Martin (D)

Representatives

Tazewell Ellett (D)
William A. Jones (D)
William R. McKenney (D) r. May 1896
Elisha E. Meredith (D)
Peter J. Otey (D)
Claude A. Swanson (D)
Robert T. Thorp (R) s. 1896
Henry St. George Tucker (D)
Smith S. Turner (D)
D. Gardiner Tyler (D)
James A. Walker (R)

WASHINGTON

Senators

Watson C. Squire (R)
John L. Wilson (R)

Representatives

William H. Doolittle (R)
Samuel C. Hyde (R)

WEST VIRGINIA

Senators

Charles J. Faulkner (D)
Stephen B. Elkins (R)

Representatives

Alston G. Dayton (R)
Blackburn B. Dovener (R)
James H. Huling (R)
Warren Miller (R)

WISCONSIN

Senators

William F. Vilas (D)
John L. Mitchell (R)

Representatives

Joseph W. Babcock (R)
Samuel S. Barney (R)
Samuel A. Cook (R)
Henry A. Cooper (R)
Michael Griffin (R)
John J. Jenkins (R)
Edward S. Minor (R)
Theobald Otjen (R)
Edward Sauerhering (R)
Alexander Stewart (R)

WYOMING

Senators

Clarence D. Clark (R)
Francis E. Warren (R)

Representative

Frank W. Mondell (R)

FIFTY-FIFTH CONGRESS

March 4, 1897 to March 3, 1899

President of The Senate: Garret A. Hobart
President Pro Tempore of The Senate: William P. Frye
Speaker of The House of Representatives: Thomas B. Reed

ALABAMA

Senators

John T. Morgan (D)
Edmund W. Pettus (D)

Representatives

William F. Aldrich (R) s. 1898
John H. Bankhead (D)
Willis Brewer (D)
Henry D. Clayton (D)
Milford W. Howard (Pop)
Thomas S. Plowman (D) r. Feb. 1898
Jesse F. Stallings (D)
George W. Taylor (D)
Oscar W. Underwood (D)
Joseph Wheeler (D)

ARKANSAS

Senators

James K. Jones (D)
James H. Berry (D)

Representatives

Stephen Brundidge, Jr. (D)
Hugh A. Dinsmore (D)
John S. Little (D)
Philip D. McCulloch, Jr. (D)
Thomas C. McRae (D)
William L. Terry (D)

CALIFORNIA

Senators

Stephen M. White (D)
George C. Perkins (R)

Representatives

John A. Barham (R)
Charles A. Barlow (D)
Curtis H. Castle (D)
Marion De Vries (D)
Samuel G. Hilborn (R)
Eugene F. Loud (R)
James G. Maguire (D)

COLORADO

Senators

Henry M. Teller (R)
Edward O. Wolcott (R)

Representatives

John C. Bell (D)
John F. Shafroth (D)

CONNECTICUT

Senators

Orville H. Platt (R)
Joseph R. Hawley (R)

Representatives

E. Stevens Henry (R)
Ebenezer J. Hill (R)
Charles A. Russell (R)
Nehemiah D. Sperry (R)

DELAWARE

Senators

George Gray (D)
Richard R. Kenney (D)

Representative

Levin I. Handy (D)

FLORIDA

Senators

Samuel Pasco (D)
Stephen R. Mallory (D)

Representatives

Robert W. Davis (D)
Stephen M. Sparkman (D)

GEORGIA

Senators

Augustus O. Bacon (D)
Alexander S. Clay (D)

Representatives

William C. Adamson (D)
Charles L. Bartlett (D)
William G. Brantley (D)
William H. Fleming (D)
James M. Griggs (D)
William M. Howard (D)
Rufus E. Lester (D)
Elijah B. Lewis (D)
Leonidas F. Livingston (D)
John W. Maddox (D)
Farish C. Tate (D)

IDAHO

Senators

George L. Shoup (R)
Henry Heitfeld (D)

Representative

James Gunn (P)

ILLINOIS

Senators

Shelby M. Cullom (R)
William E. Mason (R)

Representatives

Jehu Baker (Fusion)
Hugh R. Belknap (R)
Henry S. Boutell (R)
James R. Campbell (D)
Joseph G. Cannon (R)
James A. Connolly (R)
Edward D. Cooke (R) d. June 1897
George E. Foss (R)
Joseph V. Graff (R)
William H. Hinrichsen (D)
Robert R. Hitt (R)
Albert J. Hopkins (R)
Andrew J. Hunter (D)
Thomas M. Jett (D)
William Lorimer (R)
James R. Mann (R)
Benjamin F. Marsh (R)
Daniel W. Mills (R)
George W. Prince (R)
Walter Reeves (R)
George W. Smith (R)
Vespasian Warner (R)
George E. White (R)

INDIANA

Senators

David Turpie (D)
Charles W. Fairbanks (R)

Representatives

Edgar D. Crumpacker (R)
George W. Faris (R)
Francis M. Griffith (D)
James A. Hemenway (R)
Charles L. Henry (R)
William S. Holman (D)
d. Apr. 1897
Henry U. Johnson (R)
Charles B. Landis (R)
Robert W. Miers (D)
Jesse Overstreet (R)
James M. Robinson (D)
Lemuel W. Royse (R)
George W. Steele (R)
William T. Zenor (D)

IOWA

Senators

William B. Allison (R)
John H. Gear (R)

Representatives

Samuel M. Clark (R)
Robert G. Cousins (R)
George M. Curtis (R)
Jonathan P. Dolliver (R)
Alva L. Hager (R)
David B. Henderson (R)
William P. Hepburn (R)
John A. T. Hull (R)
John F. Lacey (R)
George D. Perkins (R)
Thomas Updegraff (R)

KANSAS

Senators

Lucien Baker (R)
William A. Harris (D)

Representatives

Jeremiah D. Botkin (Fusion)
Case Broderick (R)
Charles Curtis (R)
Nelson B. McCormick (Pop)
Mason S. Peters (D)
Edwin R. Ridgely (People's)
Jeremiah Simpson (Pop)
William D. Vincent (Pop)

KENTUCKY

Senators

William Lindsay (D)
William J. DeBoe (R)

Representatives

Albert S. Berry (D)
John D. Clardy (D)
David G. Colson (R)
George M. Davison (R)
Walter Evans (R)
Thomas Y. Fitzpatrick (D)
Samuel J. Pugh (R)
John S. Rhea (D)
Evan E. Settle (D)
David H. Smith (D)
Charles K. Wheeler (D)

LOUISIANA

Senators

Donelson Caffery (D)
Samuel D. McEnery (D)

Representatives

Samuel T. Baird (D)
Robert F. Broussard (D)
Robert C. Davey (D)
Adolph Meyer (D)
Henry W. Ogden (D)
Samuel M. Robertson (D)

MAINE

Senators

Eugene Hale (R)
William P. Frye (R)

Representatives

Charles A. Boutelle (R)
Edwin C. Burleigh (R)
Nelson Dingley, Jr. (R)
d. Jan. 1899
Seth L. Milliken (R) d. Apr. 1897
Thomas B. Reed (R)

MARYLAND

Senators

Arthur P. Gorman (D)
George L. Wellington (D)

Representatives

William B. Baker (R)
Isaac A. Barber (R)
William S. Booze (R)
John McDonald (R)
William W. McIntire (R)
Sydney E. Mudd (R)

MASSACHUSETTS

Senators

George F. Hoar (R)
Henry Cabot Lodge (R)

Representatives

William E. Barrett (R)
Samuel J. Barrows (R)
John F. Fitzgerald (D)
Frederick H. Gillett (R)
William S. Greene (R) s. 1898
William S. Knox (R)
George P. Lawrence (R)
William C. Lovering (R)
Samuel W. McCall (R)
William H. Moody (R)
John Simpkins (R) d. Mar. 1898
Charles F. Sprague (R)
Joseph H. Walker (R)
George W. Weymouth (R)
Ashley B. Wright (R) d. Aug. 1897

MICHIGAN

Senators

James McMillan (R)
Julius C. Burrows (R)

Representatives

Roswell P. Bishop (R)
Ferdinand Brucker (D)
John B. Corliss (R)
Rousseau O. Crump (R)
Edward L. Hamilton (R)
William S. Mesick (R)
Carlos D. Shelden (R)
Samuel W. Smith (R)
William Alden Smith (R)
Horace G. Snover (R)
George Spalding (R)
Albert M. Todd

MINNESOTA

Senators

Cushman K. Davis (R)
Knute Nelson (R)

Representatives

Frank M. Eddy (R)
Loren Fletcher (R)
Joel P. Heatwole (R)
James T. McCleary (R)
R. Page W. Morris (R)
James A. Tawney (R)
Frederick C. Stevens (R)

MISSISSIPPI

Senators

James Z. George (D) d. Aug. 1897
Hernando D. Money (D) s. 1897

Edward C. Walthall (D)
d. Apr. 1898
William V. Sullivan (D) s. 1898

Representatives

John M. Allen (D)
Thomas C. Catchings (D)
Andrew F. Fox (D)
Patrick Henry (D)
William F. Love (D) d. Oct. 1898
Frank A. McLain (D) s. 1898
Thomas Spight (D) s. 1898
William V. Sullivan (D)
r. May 1898
John Sharp Williams (D)

MISSOURI

Senators

Francis M. Cockrell (D)
George G. Vest (D)

Representatives

Richard Bartholdt (R)
Maecenas E. Benton (D)
Richard P. Bland (D)
Robert N. Bodine (D)
Champ Clark (D)
Charles F. Cochran (D)
James Cooney (D)
William S. Cowherd (D)
David A. De Armond (D)
Alexander M. Dockery (D)
Charles F. Joy (R)
James T. Lloyd (D)
Charles E. Pearce (R)
Edward Robb (D)
Willard D. Vandiver (D)

MONTANA

Senators

Lee Mantle (R)
Thomas H. Carter (R)

Representative

Charles S. Hartman (R)

NEBRASKA

Senators

William V. Allen (Pop)
John M. Thurston (R)

Representatives

William L. Greene (Pop)
Samuel Maxwell (Fusion)
David H. Mercer (R)
William L. Stark (D)
Jesse B. Strode (R)
Roderick D. Sutherland (Pop)

NEVADA

Senators

John P. Jones (R)
William M. Stewart (R)

Representative

Francis G. Newlands (D)

NEW HAMPSHIRE

Senators

William E. Chandler (R)
Jacob H. Gallinger (R)

Representatives

Frank G. Clarke (R)
Cyrus A. Sulloway (R)

NEW JERSEY

Senators

James Smith Jr. (D)
William J. Sewell (R)

Representatives

Charles N. Fowler (R)
John J. Gardner (D)
Benjamin F. Howell (R)
Henry C. Loudenslager (R)
Thomas McEwan Jr. (R)
Richard W. Parker (R)
Mahlon Pitney (R) r. Jan. 1899
James F. Stewart (R)

NEW YORK

Senators

Edward Murphy, Jr. (D)
Thomas C. Platt (R)

Representatives

De Alva S. Alexander (R)
James J. Belden (R)
Joseph M. Belford (R)
Charles G. Bennett (R)
Thomas J. Bradley (D)
Henry C. Brewster (R)
Charles A. Chickering (R)
Aaron V. S. Cochrane (R)
Amos Cummings (D)
Edmund H. Driggs (D)
Israel F. Fischer (R)
Wallace T. Foote Jr. (R)
Charles W. Gillet (R)
Warren B. Hooker (R)
r. Nov. 1898
James R. Howe (R)
Denis M. Hurley (R) d. Feb. 1898
John H. Ketcham (R)
Lucius N. Littauer (R)
Philip B. Low (R)
George B. McClellan (D)
Rowland B. Mahany (R)
John M. Mitchell (R)
Benjamin B. Odell, Jr. (R)
Sereno E. Payne (R)
Lemuel E. Quigg (R)
George W. Ray (R)
Richard C. Shannon (R)
James S. Sherman (R)
George N. Southwick (R)
William Sulzer (D)
John H. G. Vehslage
James W. Wadsworth (R)
William L. Ward (R)
David F. Wilber (R)
Francis H. Wilson (R)
r. Sept. 1897

NORTH CAROLINA

Senators

Jeter C. Pritchard (R)
Marion Butler (Pop)

Representatives

John E. Fowler (Pop)
William W. Kitchin (D)
Romulus Z. Linney (R)
Charles H. Martin (Pop)
Richmond Pearson (R)
Alonzo C. Shuford (Pop)
Harry Skinner (Pop)
William F. Strowd (Pop)
George H. White (R)

NORTH DAKOTA

Senators

Henry C. Hansbrough (R)
William N. Roach (D)

Representative

Martin N. Johnson (R)

OHIO

Senators

Marcus A. Hanna (R)
Joseph B. Foraker (R)

Representatives

Clifton B. Beach (R)
John L. Brenner (D)
Jacob H. Bromwell (R)
Seth W. Brown (R)
Theodore E. Burton (R)
Lorenzo Danford (R)
Charles W. F. Dick (R) s. 1898
Lucien J. Fenton (R)
Charles H. Grosvenor (R)
Winfield S. Kerr (R)
John J. Lentz (D)
Archibald Lybrand (R)
John A. McDowell (D)
George A. Marshall (D)
David Meekison (D)
Stephen A. Northway (R)
d. Sept. 1898
James A. Norton (D)
William B. Shattuc (R)
James H. Southard (R)
Robert W. Tayler (R)
Henry C. Van Voorhis (R)
Walter L. Weaver (R)

OREGON

Senators

George W. McBride (R)
Joseph Simon (R) s. 1898

Representatives

William R. Ellis (R)
Thomas H. Tongue (R)

PENNSYLVANIA

Senators

Matthew S. Quay (R)
Boies Penrose (R)

Representatives

Ernest F. Acheson (R)
Robert Adams, Jr. (R)
William C. Arnold (R)
George J. Benner (D)
Henry H. Bingham (R)
Marriott Brosius (R)
Charles N. Brumm (R)
Thomas S. Butler (R)
James H. Codding (R)
William Connell (R)
John Dalzell (R)
Samuel A. Davenport (R)
Daniel Ermentrout (D)
William H. Graham (R) s. 1898
Galusha A. Grow (R)
Alfred C. Harmer (R)
Josiah D. Hicks (R)
William S. Kirkpatrick (R)
Monroe H. Kulp (R)
William McAleer (D)
Thaddeus M. Mahon (R)
Marlin E. Olmsted (R)
Horace B. Packer (R)
Edward E. Robbins (R)
Joseph B. Showalter (R)
Charles W. Stone (R)
William A. Stone (R) r. Nov. 1898
John C. Sturtevant (R)
Irving P. Wanger (R)
Morgan B. Williams (R)
James R. Young (R)

RHODE ISLAND

Senators

Nelson W. Aldrich (R)
George P. Wetmore (R)

Representatives

Melville Bull (R)
Adin B. Capron (R)

SOUTH CAROLINA

Senators

Benjamin R. Tillman (D)

Joseph H. Earle (D) d. May 1897
John L. McLaurin (D) s. 1897

Representatives

William Elliott (D)
Asbury C. Latimer (D)
John L. McLaurin (D) r. May 1897
James Norton (D)
J. William Stokes (D)
Thomas J. Strait (Alliance D)
W. Jasper Talbert (D)
Stanyarne Wilson (D)

SOUTH DAKOTA

Senators

Richard F. Pettigrew (R)
James H. Kyle

Representatives

John E. Kelley (D)
Freeman Knowles (Pop)

TENNESSEE

Senators

Isham G. Harris (D) d. July 1897
Thomas B. Turley (D) s. 1897

William B. Bate (D)

Representatives

Walter P. Brownlow (R)
Edward W. Carmack (D)
Nicholas N. Cox (D)
John W. Gaines (D)
Henry R. Gibson (R)
Benton McMillin (D) r. Jan. 1899
John A. Moon (D)
Rice A. Pierce (D)
James D. Richardson (D)
Thetus W. Sims (D)

TEXAS

Senators

Roger Q. Mills (D)
Horace Chilton (D)

Representatives

Joseph W. Bailey (D)
Thomas H. Ball (D)
Robert E. Burke (D)
Samuel B. Cooper (D)
John W. Cranford (D)
d. Mar. 1899
Reese C. De Graffenreid (D)
Robert B. Hawley (R)
Robert L. Henry (D)
Rudolph Kleberg (D)
Samuel W. T. Lanham (D)
Joseph D. Sayers (D) r. Jan. 1899
James L. Slayden (D)
John H. Stephens (D)

UTAH

Senators

Frank J. Cannon (R)
Joseph L. Rawlins (D)

Representative

William H. King (D)

VERMONT

Senators

Justin S. Morrill (R) d. Dec. 1898
Jonathan Ross (R) s. 1899

Redfield Proctor (R)

Representatives

William W. Grout (R)
H. Henry Powers (R)

VIRGINIA

Senators

John W. Daniel (D)
Thomas S. Martin (D)

Representatives

Sydney P. Epes (D) r. Mar. 1898
James Hay (D)
William A. Jones (D)
John Lamb (D)
Peter J. Otey (D)
John F. Rixey (D)
Claude A. Swanson (D)
Robert T. Thorp (R) s. 1898
James A. Walker (D)
Richard A. Wise (R) s. 1898
Jacob Yost (R)
William A. Young (D) r. Apr. 1898

WASHINGTON

Senators

John L. Wilson (R)
George Turner (Fusion)

Representatives

William C. Jones (R)
James Hamilton Lewis (D)

WEST VIRGINIA

Senators

Charles J. Faulkner (D)
Stephen B. Elkins (R)

Representatives

Alston G. Dayton (R)
Charles P. Dorr (R)
Blackburn B. Dovener (R)
Warren Miller (R)

WISCONSIN

Senators

John L. Mitchell (D)
John C. Spooner (R)

Representatives

Joseph W. Babcock (R)
Samuel S. Barney (R)
Henry Allen Cooper (R)
James H. Davidson (R)
Michael Griffin (R)
John J. Jenkins (R)
Edward S. Minor (R)
Theobald Otjen (R)
Edward Sauerhering (R)
Alexander Stewart (R)

WYOMING

Senators

Clarence D. Clark (R)
Francis E. Warren (R)

Representative

John E. Osborne (D)

FIFTY-SIXTH CONGRESS

March 4, 1899 to March 3, 1901

President of The Senate: Garret A. Hobart
President Pro Tempore of The Senate: William P. Frye
Speaker of The House of Representatives: David B. Henderson

ALABAMA

Senators

John T. Morgan (D)
Edmund W. Pettus (D)

Representatives

William F. Aldrich (R)
John H. Bankhead (D)
Willis Brewer (D)
John L. Burnett (D)
Henry D. Clayton (D)
William Richardson (D) s. 1900
Gaston A. Robbins (D) r. Mar. 1900
Jesse F. Stallings (D)
George W. Taylor (D)
Oscar W. Underwood (D)
Joseph Wheeler (D) r. Apr. 1900

ARKANSAS

Senators

James K. Jones (D)
James H. Berry (D)

Representatives

Stephen Brundidge Jr. (D)
Hugh A. Dinsmore (D)
John S. Little (D)
Philip D. McCulloch, Jr. (D)
Thomas C. McRae (D)
William L. Terry (D)

CALIFORNIA

Senators

George C. Perkins (R)
Thomas R. Bard (R)

Representatives

John A. Barham (R)
Marion De Vries (D) r. Aug. 1900
Julius Kahn (R)
Eugene F. Loud (R)
Victor H. Metcalf (R)
James C. Needham (R)
Russell J. Waters (R)
Samuel D. Woods (R) s. 1900

COLORADO

Senators

Henry M. Teller (R)
Edward O. Wolcott (R)

Representatives

John C. Bell (D)
John F. Shafroth (D)

CONNECTICUT

Senators

Orville H. Platt (R)
Joseph R. Hawley (R)

Representatives

E. Stevens Henry (R)
Ebenezer J. Hill (R)
Charles A. Russell (R)
Nehemiah D. Sperry (R)

DELAWARE

Senators

Richard R. Kenney (D)
Vacant

Representatives

John H. Hoffecker (R)
d. June 1900
Walter O. Hoffecker (R)

FLORIDA

Senators

Stephen R. Mallory (D)

Samuel Pasco (D) ta. 1899
James P. Taliaferro (D)
s. Dec. 1899

Representatives

Robert W. Davis (D)
Stephen M. Sparkman (D)

GEORGIA

Senators

Augustus O. Bacon (D)
Alexander S. Clay (D)

Representatives

William C. Adamson (D)
Charles L. Bartlett (D)
William G. Brantley (D)
William H. Fleming (D)
James M. Griggs (D)
William M. Howard (D)
Rufus E. Lester (D)
Elijah B. Lewis (D)
Leonidas F. Livingston (D)
John W. Maddox (R)
Farish C. Tate (D)

IDAHO

Senators

George L. Shoup (R)
Henry Heitfeld (Pop)

Representative

Edgar Wilson (R)

ILLINOIS

Senators

Shelby M. Cullom (R)
William E. Mason (R)

Representatives

Henry S. Boutell (R)
Ben F. Caldwell (D)
Joseph G. Cannon (R)
Joseph B. Crowley (D)
Thomas Cusack (D)
George E. Foss (R)
George P. Foster (D)
Joseph V. Graff (R)
Robert R. Hitt (R)
Albert J. Hopkins (R)
Thomas M. Jett (D)
William Lorimer (R)
James R. Mann (R)
Benjamin F. Marsh (R)
Edward T. Noonan (D)
George W. Prince (R)
Walter Reeves (R)
William A. Rodenberg (R)
George W. Smith (R)
Vespasian Warner (R)
James R. Williams (D)
William E. Williams (D)

INDIANA

Senators

Charles W. Fairbanks (R)
Albert J. Beveridge (R)

Representatives

Abraham L. Brick (R)
George W. Cromer (R)
Edgar D. Crumpacker (R)
George W. Faris (R)
Francis M. Griffith (D)
James A. Hemenway (R)
Charles B. Landis (R)
Robert W. Miers (D)
Jesse Overstreet (R)
James M. Robinson (D)
George W. Steele (R)
James E. Watson (R)
William T. Zenor (D)

IOWA

Senators

William B. Allison (R)

John H. Gear (R) d. July 1900
Jonathan P. Dolliver (R) s. 1900

Representatives

James P. Conner (R) s. 1900
Robert G. Cousins (R)
Jonathan P. Dolliver (R) r. Aug. 1900
Gilbert N. Haugen (R)
Thomas Hedge (R)
David B. Henderson (R)
William P Hepburn (R)
John A. T. Hull (R)
John F. Lacey (R)
Joseph R. Lane (R)
Smith McPherson (R) r. 1900
Walter I. Smith (R) s. 1900
Lot Thomas (R)

KANSAS

Senators

Lucien Baker (R)
William A. Harris (D)

Representatives

Willis J. Bailey (R)
Justin D. Browersock (R)
William A. Calderhead (R)
Charles Curtis (R)
Chester I. Long (R)
James M. Miller (R)
William A. Reeder (R)
Edwin R. Ridgely (D)

KENTUCKY

Senators

William Lindsay (D)
William J. DeBoe (R)

Representatives

Henry D. Allen (D)
Albert S. Berry (D)
Vincent S. Boreing (R)
Thomas Y. Fitzpatrick (D)
June W. Gayle (D)
George G. Gilbert (D)
Samuel J. Pugh (R)
John S. Rhea (D-P)
David H. Smith (D)
Oscar Turner (D)
Charles K. Wheeler (D)

LOUISIANA

Senators

Donelson Caffery (D)
Samuel D. McEnery (D)

Representatives

Phanor Breazeale (D)
Robert F. Broussard (D)
Robert C. Davey (D)
Adolph Meyer (D)
Joseph E. Ransdell (D)
Samuel M. Robertson (D)

MAINE

Senators

Eugene Hale (R)
William P. Frye (R)

Representatives

Amos L. Allen (R)
Charles A. Boutelle (R)
Edwin C. Burleigh (R)
Charles E. Littlefield (R)

MARYLAND

Senators

George L. Wellington (D)
Louis E. McComas (R)

Representatives

William B. Baker (R)
James W. Denny (D)
Josiah L. Kerr (R) s. 1900
Sydney E. Mudd (R)
George A. Pearre (R)
John Walter Smith (D) r. Jan. 1900
Frank C. Wachter (R)

MASSACHUSETTS

Senators

George F. Hoar (R)
Henry Cabot Lodge (R)

Representatives

John F. Fitzgerald (D)
Frederick H. Gillett (R)
William S. Greene (R)
William S. Knox (R)
George P. Lawrence (R)
William C. Lovering (R)
Samuel W. McCall (R)
William H. Moody (R)
Henry F. Naphen (D)
Ernest W. Roberts (R)
Charles F. Sprague (R)
John R. Thayer (D)
George W. Weymouth (R)

MICHIGAN

Senators

James McMillan (R)
Julius C. Burrows (R)

Representatives

Roswell P. Bishop (R)
John B. Corliss (R)
Rousseau O. Crump (R)
Joseph W. Fordney (R)
Washington Gardner (R)
Edward L. Hamilton (R)
William S. Mesick (R)
Carlos D. Shelden (R)
Henry C. Smith (R)
Samuel W. Smith (R)
William Alden Smith (R)
Edgar Weeks (R)

MINNESOTA

Senators

Cushman K. Davis (R) d. Nov. 1900
Charles A. Towne (D) ta. 1900
Moses E. Clapp (R) s. 1901

Knute Nelson (R)

Representatives

Frank M. Eddy (R)
Loren Fletcher (R)
Joel P. Heatwole (R)
James T. McCleary (R)
R. Page W. Morris (R)
Frederick C. Stevens (R)
James A. Tawney (R)

MISSISSIPPI

Senators

Hernando D. Money (D)
William V. Sullivan (D)

Representatives

John M. Allen (D)
Thomas C. Catchings (D)
Andrew F. Fox (D)
Patrick Henry (D)
Frank A. McLain (D)
Thomas Spight (D)
John Sharp Williams (D)

MISSOURI

Senators

Francis M. Cockrell (D)
George G. Vest (D)

Representatives

Richard Bartholdt (R)
Maecenas E. Benton (D)
Champ Clark (D)
Charles F. Cochran (D)
James Cooney (D)
William S. Cowherd (D)
David A. De Armond (D)
John Dougherty (D)
Charles F. Joy
James T. Lloyd (D)
Charles E. Pearce (R)
Edward Robb (D)
William W. Rucker (D)
Dorsey W. Shackleford (D)
Willard D. Vandiver (D)

MONTANA

Senators

Thomas H. Carter (R)
William A. Clark (D) r. May 1900

Representative

Albert J. Campbell (D)

NEBRASKA

Senators

John M. Thurston (R)
William V. Allen (Pop)

Representatives

Elmer J. Burkett (R)
David H. Mercer (R)
William Neville (Pop)
John S. Robinson (D)
William L. Stark (D)
Roderick D. Sutherland (Pop)

NEVADA

Senators

John P. Jones (R)
William M. Stewart (R)

Representative

Francis G. Newlands (D)

NEW HAMPSHIRE

Senators

William E. Chandler (R)
Jacob H. Gallinger (R)

Representatives

Frank G. Clarke (R) d. Jan. 1901
Cyrus A. Sulloway (R)

NEW JERSEY

Senators

William J. Sewell (R)
John Kean (R)

Representatives

William D. Daly (D) d. July 1900
Charles N. Fowler (R)
John J. Gardner (D)
Benjamin F. Howell (R)
Henry C. Loudenslager (R)
Allan L. McDermott (D) s. 1900
Richard W. Parker (R)
Joshua S. Salmon (D)
James F. Stewart (R)

NEW YORK

Senators

Thomas C. Platt (R)
Chauncey M. Depew (R)

Representatives

De Alva S. Alexander (R)
Thomas J. Bradley (D)
William A. Chanler (D)
Charles A. Chickering (R) d. Feb. 1900
Bertram T. Clayton (D)
Aaron V. S. Cochrane (R)
Amos J. Cummings (D)
Edmund H. Driggs (D)
Michael E. Driscoll (R)
Louis W. Emerson (R)
John J. Fitzgerald (D)
Charles W. Gillet (R)
Martin H. Glynn (D)
John H. Ketcham (R)
Jefferson M. Levy (D)
Lucius N. Littauer (R)
George B. McClellan (D)
Mitchell May (D)
Nicholas Muller (D)
James M. E. O'Grady (R)
Sereno E. Payne (R)
George W. Ray (R)
Daniel J. Riordan (D)
Jacob Ruppert, Jr. (D)
William H. Ryan (D)
Townsend Scudder (D)
Albert D. Shaw (R) s. 1900

James S. Sherman (R)
John K. Stewart (R)
William Sulzer (D)
Arthur S. Tompkins (R)
John Q. Underhill (D)
Edward B. Vreeland (R)
James W. Wadsworth (R)
Frank E. Wilson (D)

NORTH CAROLINA

Senators

Marion Butler (Pop)
Jeter C. Pritchard (R)

Representatives

John W. Atwater (Pop)
John D. Bellamy (D)
William T. Crawford (D) r. May 1900
William W. Kitchin (D)
Theodore F. Kluttz (D)
Romulus Z. Linney (R)
Richmond Pearson (R) s. 1900
John H. Small (D)
Charles R. Thomas (D)
George H. White (R)

NORTH DAKOTA

Senators

Henry C. Hansbrough (R)
Porter J. McCumber (R)

Representative

Burleigh F. Spalding (R)

OHIO

Senators

Joseph B. Foraker (R)
Marcus A. Hanna (R)

Representatives

John L. Brenner (D)
Jacob H. Bromwell (R)
Seth W. Brown (R)
Theodore E. Burton (R)
Charles W. F. Dick (R)
Joseph J. Gill (R)
Robert B. Gordon (D)
Charles H. Grosvenor (R)
Winfield S. Kerr (R)
John J. Lentz (D)
Archibald Lybrand (R)
John A. McDowell (D)
David Meekison (D)
Stephen Morgan (R)
James A. Norton (D)
Fremont O. Phillips (R)
William B. Shattuc (R)
James H. Southard (R)
Robert W. Tayler (R)
Henry C. Van Voorhis (R)
Walter L. Weaver (R)

OREGON

Senators

George W. McBride (R)
Joseph Simon (R)

Representatives

Malcolm A. Moody (R)
Thomas H. Tongue (R)

PENNSYLVANIA

Senators

Boies Penrose (R)
Matthew S. Quay (R)

Representatives

Ernest F. Acheson (R)
Robert Adams Jr. (R)
Laird H. Barber (D)
Henry H. Bingham (R)
Marriott Brosius (R)
Thomas S. Butler (R)
William Connell (R)
John Dalzell (R)
Samuel A. Davenport (R)
Stanley W. Davenport (D)
Athelston Gaston (D)
William H. Graham (R)
Henry D. Green (D)
Galusha A. Grow (R)
James K. P. Hall (D)
Alfred C. Harmer (R) d. Mar. 1900
Summers M. Jack (R)
William McAleer (D)
Thaddeus M. Mahon (R)
Edward de V. Morrell (R) s. 1900
Marlin E. Olmsted (R)
Horace B. Packer (R)
Rufus K. Polk (D)
James W. Ryan (D)
Joseph B. Showalter (R)
Joseph C. Sibley (D)
Joseph E. Thropp (R)
Irving P. Wanger (R)
Charles F. Wright (R)
James R. Young (R)
Edward Ziegler (D)

RHODE ISLAND

Senators

Nelson W. Aldrich (R)
George P. Wetmore (R)

Representatives

Melville Bull (R)
Adin B. Capron (R)

SOUTH CAROLINA

Senators

Benjamin R. Tillman (D)
John L. McLaurin (D)

Representatives

William Elliott (D)
David E. Finley (D)
Asbury C. Latimer (D)
James Norton (D)
J. William Stokes (D)
W. Jasper Talbert (D)
Stanyarne Wilson (D)

SOUTH DAKOTA

Senators

Richard F. Pettigrew (R)
James H. Kyle

Representatives

Charles H. Burke (R)
Robert J. Gamble (R)

TENNESSEE

Senators

William B. Bate (D)
Thomas B. Turley (D)

Representatives

Walter P. Brownlow (R)
Edward W. Carmack (D)
Nicholas N. Cox (D)
John W. Gaines (D)
Henry R. Gibson (R)
John A. Moon (D)
Rice A. Pierce (D)
James D. Richardson (D)
Thetus W. Sims (D)
Charles E. Snodgrass (D)

TEXAS

Senators

Horace Chilton (D)
Charles A. Culberson (D)

Representatives

Joseph W. Bailey (D)
Thomas H. Ball (D)
Robert E. Burke (D)
Albert S. Burleson (D)
Samuel B. Cooper (D)
Reese C. DeGraffenreid (D)
Robert B. Hawley (R)
Robert L. Henry (D)
Rudolph Kleberg (D)
Samuel W. T. Lanham (D)
John L. Sheppard (D)
James L. Slayden (D)
John H. Stephens (D)

UTAH

Senators

Joseph L. Rawlins (D)
Thomas Kearns (R) s. 1901

Representative

William H. King (D) s. 1900

VERMONT

Senators

Redfield Proctor (R)

Jonathan Ross (R) ta. 1899
William P. Dillingham (R) s. 1900

Representatives

William W. Grout (R)
H. Henry Powers (R)

VIRGINIA

Senators

John W. Daniel (D)
Thomas S. Martin (D)

Representatives

Sydney P. Epes (D) d. Mar. 1900
James Hay (D)
William A. Jones (D)
John Lamb (D)
Francis R. Lassiter (D) s. 1900
Peter J. Otey (D)
Julian M. Quarles (D)
William F. Rhea (D)
John F. Rixey (D)
Claude A. Swanson (D)
Richard A. Wise (R) d. 1900
William A. Young (D) r. Mar. 1900

WASHINGTON

Senators

George Turner (Fusion)
Addison G. Foster (R)

Representatives

Francis W. Cushman (R)
Wesley L. Jones (R)

WEST VIRGINIA

Senators

Stephen B. Elkins (R)
Nathan B. Scott (R)

Representatives

Alston G. Dayton (R)
Blackburn B. Dovener (R)
Romeo H. Freer (R)
David E. Johnston (D)

WISCONSIN

Senators

John C. Spooner (R)
Joseph V. Quarles (R)

Representatives

Joseph W. Babcock (R)
Samuel S. Barney (R)
Henry A. Cooper (R)
Herman B. Dahle (R)
James H. Davidson (R)
John J. Esch (R)
John J. Jenkins (R)
Edward S. Minor (R)
Theobald Otjen (R)
Alexander Stewart (R)

WYOMING

Senators

Clarence D. Clark (R)
Francis E. Warren (R)

Representative

Frank W. Mondell (R)

FIFTY-SEVENTH CONGRESS

March 4, 1901 to March 3, 1903

President of The Senate: Theodore Roosevelt
President Pro Tempore of The Senate: William P. Frye
Speaker of The House of Representatives: David B. Henderson

ALABAMA

Senators

John T. Morgan (D)
Edmund W. Pettus (D)

Representatives

John H. Bankhead (D)
Sydney J. Bowie (D)
John L. Burnett (D)
Henry D. Clayton (D)
William Richardson (D)
George W. Taylor (D)
Charles W. Thompson (D)
Oscar W. Underwood (D)
Ariosto A. Wiley (D)

ARKANSAS

Senators

James K. Jones (D)
James H. Berry (D)

Representatives

Stephen Brundidge, Jr. (D)
Hugh A. Dinsmore (D)
John S. Little (D)
Philip D. McCulloch, Jr. (D)
Thomas C. McRae (D)
Charles C. Reid (D)

CALIFORNIA

Senators

George C. Perkins (R)
Thomas R. Bard (R)

Representatives

Frank L. Coombs (R)
Julius Kahn (R)
Eugene F. Loud (R)
James McLachlan (R)
Victor H. Metcalf (R)
James C. Needham (R)
Samuel D. Woods (R)

COLORADO

Senators

Henry M. Teller (R)
Thomas M. Patterson (D)

Representatives

John C. Bell (D)
John F. Shafroth (D)

CONNECTICUT

Senators

Orville H. Platt (R)
Joseph R. Hawley (R)

Representatives

Frank B. Brandegee (R) s. 1902
E. Stevens Henry (R)
Ebenezer J. Hill (R)
Charles A. Russell (R)
d. Oct. 1902
Nehemiah D. Sperry (R)

DELAWARE

Senators

L. Heisler Ball (R) s. 1903
J. Frank Allee (R) s. 1903

Representative

L. Heisler Ball (R) r. March 1903

FLORIDA

Senators

Stephen R. Mallory (D)
James P. Taliaferro (D)

Representatives

Robert W. Davis (D)
Stephen M. Sparkman (D)

GEORGIA

Senators

Augustus O. Bacon (D)
Alexander S. Clay (D)

Representatives

William C. Adamson (D)
Charles L. Bartlett (D)
William G. Brantley (D)
William H. Fleming (D)
James M. Griggs (D)
William M. Howard (D)
Rufus E. Lester (D)
Elijah B. Lewis (D)
Leonidas F. Livingston (D)
John W. Maddox (D)
Farish C. Tate (D)

IDAHO

Senators

Henry Heitfeld (Pop)
Fred Dubois (R)

Representative

Thomas L. Glenn ((Pop)

ILLINOIS

Senators

Shelby M. Cullom (R)
William E. Mason (R)

Representatives

Henry S. Boutell (R)
Ben F. Caldwell (D)
Joseph G. Cannon (R)
Joseph B. Crowley (D)
John J. Feely (D)
George E. Foss (R)
George P. Foster (D)
Joseph V. Graff (R)
Robert R. Hitt (R)
Albert J. Hopkins (R)
Thomas M. Jett (D)
Frederick J. Kern (D)
James McAndrews (D)
William F. Mahoney (D)
James R. Mann (R)
J. Ross Mickey (D)
George W. Prince (R)
Walter Reeves (R)
Thomas J. Selby (D)
George W. Smith (R)
Vespasian Warner (R)
James R. Williams (D)

INDIANA

Senators

Charles W. Fairbanks (R)
Albert J. Beveridge (R)

Representatives

Abraham L. Brick (R)
George W. Cromer (R)
Edgar D. Crumpacker (R)
Francis M. Griffith (D)
James A. Hemenway (R)
Elias S. Holliday (R)
Charles B. Landis (R)
Robert W. Miers (D)
Jesse Overstreet (R)
James M. Robinson (D)
George W. Steele (R)
James E. Watson (R)
William T. Zenor (D)

IOWA

Senators

William B. Allison (R)
Jonathan P. Dolliver (R)

Representatives

James P. Conner (R)
Robert G. Cousins (R)
Gilbert N. Haugen (R)
Thomas Hedge (R)
David B. Henderson (R)
William P. Hepburn (R)
John A. T. Hull (R)
John F. Lacey (R)
John N. W. Rumple (R)
d. Jan. 1903
Walter I. Smith (R)
Lot Thomas (R)

KANSAS

Senators

William A. Harris (D)
Joseph R. Burton (R)

Representatives

Justin D. Bowersock (R)
William A. Calderhead (R)
Charles Curtis (R)
Alfred M. Jackson (D)
Chester I. Long (R)
James M. Miller (R)
William A. Reeder (R)

KENTUCKY

Senators

William J. Deboe (R)
Joseph C. S. Blackburn (D)

Representatives

Henry D. Allen (D)
Vincent Boreing (R)
George G. Gilbert (D)
Daniel L. Gooch (D)
Harvey S. Irwin (R)
James N. Kehoe (D)
J. McKenzie Moss (R) s. 1902
John S. Rhea (D, Pop)
David H. Smith (D)
South Trimble (D)
Charles K. Wheeler
James B. White (D)

LOUISIANA

Senators

Samuel D. McEnery (D)
Murphy J. Foster (D)

Representatives

Phanor Breazeale (D)
Robert F. Broussard (D)
Robert C. Davey (D)
Adolph Meyer (D)
Joseph E. Ransdell (D)
Samuel M. Robertson (D)

MAINE

Senators

Eugene Hale (R)
William P. Frye (R)

Representatives

Amos L. Allen (R)
Edwin C. Burleigh (R)
Charles E. Littlefield (R)
Llewellyn Powers (R)

MARYLAND

Senators

George L. Wellington (D)
Louis E. McComas (R)

Representatives

Albert A. Blakeney (R)
William H. Jackson (R)
Sydney E. Mudd (R)
George A. Pearre (R)
Charles R. Schirm (R)
Frank C. Wachter (R)

MASSACHUSETTS

Senators

George F. Hoar (R)
Henry Cabot Lodge (R)

Representatives

Joseph A. Conry (D)
Augustus P. Gardner (R) s. 1902
Frederick H. Gillett (R)
William S. Greene (R)
William S. Knox (R)
George P. Lawrence (R)
William C. Lovering (R)
Samuel W. McCall (R)
William H. Moody (R)
r. May 1902
Henry F. Naphen (D)
Samuel L. Powers (R)
Ernest W. Roberts (R)
John R. Thayer (D)
Charles Q. Tirrell (R)

MICHIGAN

Senators

James McMillan (R) d. Aug. 1902
Russell A. Alger (R) s. 1902

Julius C. Burrows (R)

Representatives

Henry H. Aplin (R)
Roswell P. Bishop (R)
John B. Corliss (R)
Archibald B. Darragh (R)
Joseph W. Fordney (R)
Washington Gardner (R)
Edward L. Hamilton (R)
Carlos D. Shelden (R)
Henry C. Smith (R)
Samuel W. Smith (R)
William Alden Smith (R)
Edgar Weeks (R)

MINNESOTA

Senators

Knute Nelson (R)
Moses E. Clapp (R) s. 1903

Representatives

Frank M. Eddy (R)
Loren Fletcher (R)
Joel P. Heatwole (R)
James T. McCleary (R)
R. Page W. Morris (R)
Frederick C. Stevens (R)
James A. Tawney (R)

MISSISSIPPI

Senators

Hernando D. Money (D)
Anselm J. McLaurin (D)

Representatives

Ezekiel S. Candler, Jr. (D)
Andrew F. Fox (D)
Patrick Henry (D)
Charles E. Hooker (D)
Frank A. McLain (D)
Thomas Spight (D)
John Sharp Williams (D)

MISSOURI

Senators

Francis M. Cockrell (D)
George G. Vest (D)

Representatives

Richard Bartholdt (R)
Maecenas E. Benton (D)
James J. Butler (D) s. 1902
Champ Clark (D)
Charles F. Cochran (D)
James Cooney (D)
William S. Cowherd (D)
David A. De Armond (D)
John Dougherty (D)
Charles F. Joy (R)
James T. Lloyd (D)
Edward Robb (D)
William W. Rucker (D)
Dorsey W. Shackleford (D)
Willard D. Vandiver (D)
George C. R. Wagoner (R) s. 1903

MONTANA

Senators

William A. Clark (D)
Paris Gibson (D)

Representative

Caldwell Edwards (D, Pop)

NEBRASKA

Senators

William V. Allen (Pop) r. 1901
Charles H. Dietrich (R) s. 1901

Joseph H. Millard (R)

Representatives

Elmer J. Burkett (D)
David H. Mercer (R)
William Neville (Pop)
John S. Robinson (D)
Ashton C. Shallenberger (D)
William L. Stark (D)

NEVADA

Senators

John P. Jones (R)
William M. Stewart (R)

Representative

Francis G. Newlands (D)

NEW HAMPSHIRE

Senators

Jacob H. Gallinger (R)
Henry E. Burnham (R)

Representatives

Frank D. Currier (R)
Cyrus A. Sulloway (R)

NEW JERSEY

Senators

William J. Sewell (R) d. Dec. 1901
John F. Dryden (R)

John Kean (R)

Representatives

De Witt C. Flanagan (D) s. 1903
Charles N. Fowler (R)
John J. Gardner (D)
Benjamin F. Howell (R)
Henry C. Loudenslager (R)
Allan L. McDermott (D)
Richard W. Parker (R)
Joshua S. Salmon (D) d. May 1902
James F. Stewart (R)

NEW YORK

Senators

Thomas C. Platt (R)
Chauncey M. Depew (R)

Representatives

De Alva S. Alexander (R)
Oliver H. P. Belmont (D)
Henry Bristow (R)
Thomas J. Creamer (D)
Amos J. Cummings (D)
d. May 1902
William H. Douglas (R)
William H. Draper (R)
Michael E. Driscoll (R)
John W. Dwight (R) s. 1902
Louis W. Emerson (R)
John J. Fitzgerald (D)
Charles W. Gillet (R)
Henry M. Goldfogle
Harry A. Hanbury (R)
John H. Ketcham (R)
Charles L. Knapp (R)
Montague Lessler (R) s. 1902
George H. Lindsay (D)
Lucius N. Littauer (R)
George B. McClellan (D)
Nicholas Muller (D) r. Dec. 1902
Sereno E. Payne (D)
James B. Perkins (R)
Cornelius A. Pugsley (D)
George W. Ray (R) r. Sept. 1902
Jacob Ruppert Jr. (D)
William H. Ryan (D)
James S. Sherman (R)
George N. Southwick (R)
John K. Stewart (R)
Frederic Storm (R)
William Sulzer (D)
Edward Swann (D) s. 1902
Arthur S. Tompkins (R)
Edward B. Vreeland (R)
James W. Wadsworth (R)
Frank E. Wilson (D)

NORTH CAROLINA

Senators

Jeter C. Pritchard (R)
Furnifold McL. Simmons (D)

Representatives

John D. Bellamy (D)
Edmond S. Blackburn (R)
Claude Kitchin (D)
William W. Kitchin (D)
Theodore F. Kluttz (D)
James M. Moody (R) d. Feb. 1903
Edward W. Pou (D)
John H. Small (D)
Charles R. Thomas (D)

NORTH DAKOTA

Senators

Henry C. Hansbrough (R)
Porter J. McCumber (R)

Representative

Thomas F. Marshall (R)

OHIO

Senators

Joseph B. Foraker (R)
Marcus A. Hanna (R)

Representatives

Jacob A. Beidler (R)
Jacob H. Bromwell (R)
Theodore E. Burton (R)
John W. Cassingham (D)
Charles W. F. Dick (R)
Joseph J. Gill (R)
Robert B. Gordon (D)
Charles H. Grosvenor (R)
Charles Q. Hildebrant (R)
Thomas B. Kyle (R)
Stephen Morgan (R)
Robert M. Nevin (R)
James A. Norton (D)
William B. Shattuc (R)
William W. Skiles (R)
John S. Snook (R)
James H. Southard (R)
Robert W. Tayler (R)
Emmett Tompkins (R)
Henry C. Van Voorhis (R)
William R. Warnock (R)

OREGON

Senators

Joseph Simon (R)
John H. Mitchell (R)

Representatives

Malcolm A. Moody (R)
Thomas H. Tongue (R)
d. Jan. 1903

PENNSYLVANIA

Senators

Boies Penrose (R)
Matthew S. Quay (R)

Representatives

Ernest F. Acheson (R)
Robert Adams Jr. (R)
Arthur L. Bates (R)
Alexander Billmeyer (D) s. 1902
Henry H. Bingham (R)
Henry Burk (R)

Thomas S. Butler (R)
Henry B. Cassel (R)
William Connell (R)
John Dalzell (R)
Elias Deemer (R)
Alvin Evans (R)
Robert H. Foerderer (R)
William H. Graham (R)
Henry D. Green (D)
Galusha A. Grow (R)
James K. P. Hall (D) r. Nov. 1902
Summers M. Jack (R)
Robert J. Lewis (R)
Thaddeus M. Mahon (R)
Edward de V. Morrell (R)
Howard Mutchler (D)
Martin E. Olmsted (R)
Henry W. Palmer (R)
George R. Patterson (R)
Rufus K. Polk (D) d. Mar. 1902
Joseph B. Showalter (R)
Joseph C. Sibley (R)
Irving P. Wanger (R)
Charles F. Wright (R)
James R. Young (R)

RHODE ISLAND

Senators

Nelson W. Aldrich (R)
George P. Wetmore (R)

Representatives

Melville Bull (R)
Adin B. Capron (R)

SOUTH CAROLINA

Senators

Benjamin R. Tillman (D)
John L. McLaurin (D)

Representatives

William Elliott (D)
David E. Finley (D)
Joseph T. Johnson (D)
Asbury C. Latimer (D)
Asbury F. Lever (D)
Robert B. Scarborough (D)
William J. Talbert (D)

SOUTH DAKOTA

Senators

James H. Kyle d. July 1901
Alfred B. Kittredge (R) s. 1901

Robert J. Gamble (R)

Representatives

Charles H. Burke (R)
Eben W. Martin (R)

TENNESSEE

Senators

William B. Bate (D)
Edward W. Carmack (D)

Representatives

Walter P. Brownlow (R)
John W. Gaines (D)
Henry R. Gibson (R)
John A. Moon (D)
Lemuel P. Padgett (D)
Malcolm R. Patterson (D)
Rice A. Pierce (D)
James D. Richardson (D)
Thetus W. Sims (D)
Charles E. Snodgrass (D)

TEXAS

Senators

Charles A. Culberson (D)
Joseph W. Bailey (D)

Representatives

Thomas H. Ball (D)
George F. Burgess (D)
Albert S. Burleson (D)
Samuel B. Cooper (D)
Reese C. De Graffenreid (D)
d. Aug. 1902
Robert L. Henry (D)
Rudolph Kleberg (D)
Samuel W. T. Lanham (D)
r. Jan. 1903
Choice B. Randell (D)
Gordon J. Russell (D) s. 1902
John L. Sheppard (D)
d. Oct. 1902
Morris Sheppard (D) s. 1902
James L. Slayden (D)
John H. Stephens (D)
Dudley G. Wooten (D)

UTAH

Senators

Joseph L. Rawlins (D)
Thomas Kearns (R)

Representative

George Sutherland (R)

VERMONT

Senators

Redfield Proctor (R)
William P. Dillingham (R)

Representatives

David J. Foster (R)
Kittredge Haskins (R)

VIRGINIA

Senators

John W. Daniel (D)
Thomas S. Martin (D)

Representatives

Henry D. Flood (D)
Carter Glass (D) s. 1902
James Hay (D)
William A. Jones (D)
John Lamb (D)
Francis R. Lassiter (D)
Harry L. Maynard (D)
Peter J. Otey (D) d. May 1902
William F. Rhea (D)
John F. Rixey (D)
Claude A. Swanson (D)

WASHINGTON

Senators

George Turner (Fusion)
Addison G. Foster (R)

Representatives

Francis W. Cushman (R)
Wesley L. Jones (R)

WEST VIRGINIA

Senators

Stephen B. Elkins (R)
Nathan B. Scott (R)

Representatives

Alston G. Dayton (R)
Blackburn B. Dovener (R)
Joseph H. Gaines (R)
James A. Hughes (R)

WISCONSIN

Senators

John C. Spooner (R)
Joseph V. Quarles (R)

Representatives

Joseph W. Babcock (R)
Samuel S. Barney (R)
Webster E. Brown (R)
Henry A. Cooper (R)
Herman B. Dahle (R)
James H. Davidson (R)
John J. Esch (R)
John J. Jenkins (R)
Edward S. Minor (R)
Theobald Otjen (R)

WYOMING

Senators

Clarence D. Clark (R)
Francis E. Warren (R)

Representative

Frank W. Mondell (R)

FIFTY-EIGHTH CONGRESS

March 4, 1903 to March 3, 1905

President of The Senate	Vacant
President Pro Tempore of The Senate:	William P. Frye
Speaker of The House of Representatives:	Joseph G. Cannon

ALABAMA

Senators

John T. Morgan (D)
Edmund W. Pettus (D)

Representatives

John H. Bankhead (D)
Sydney J. Bowie (D)
John L. Burnett (D)
Henry D. Clayton (D)
J. Thomas Heflin (D) s. 1904
William Richardson (D)
George W. Taylor (D)
Charles W. Thompson (D)
d. Mar. 1904
Oscar W. Underwood (D)
Ariosto A. Wiley (D)

ARKANSAS

Senators

James H. Berry (D)
James P. Clarke (D)

Representatives

Stephen Brundidge Jr. (D)
Hugh A. Dinsmore (D)
John S. Little (D)
Robert B. Macon (D)
Charles C. Reid (D)
Joseph T. Robinson (D)
Robert M. Wallace (D)

CALIFORNIA

Senators

George C. Perkins (R)
Thomas R. Bard (R)

Representatives

Theodore A. Bell (D)
Milton J. Daniels (R)
James N. Gillett (R)
Joseph R. Knowland (R) s. 1904
Edward J. Livernash
(Union Labor)
James McLachlan (R)
Victor H. Metcalf (R) r. July 1904
James C. Needham (R)
William J. Wynn (Union Labor)

COLORADO

Senators

Henry M. Teller (D)
Thomas M. Patterson (D)

Representatives

Robert W. Bonynge (R) s. 1904
Franklin E. Brooks (R)
Herschel M. Hogg (R)
John F. Shafroth (D) r. Feb. 1904

CONNECTICUT

Senators

Orville H. Platt (R)
Joseph R. Hawley (R)

Representatives

Frank B. Brandegee (R)
E. Stevens Henry (R)
Ebenezer J. Hill (R)
George L. Lilley (R)
Nehemiah D. Sperry (R)

DELAWARE

Senators

L. Heisler Ball (R)
J. Frank Allee (R)

Representative

Henry A. Houston (D)

FLORIDA

Senators

Stephen R. Mallory (D)
James P. Taliaferro (D)

Representatives

Robert W. Davis (D)
William B. Lamar (D)
Stephen M. Sparkman (D)

GEORGIA

Senators

Augustus O. Bacon (D)
Alexander S. Clay (D)

Representatives

William C. Adamson (D)
Charles L. Bartlett (D)
William G. Brantley (D)
James M. Griggs (D)
Thomas W. Hardwick (D)
William M. Howard (D)
Rufus E. Lester (D)
Elijah B. Lewis (D)
Leonidas F. Livingston (D)
John W. Maddox (D)
Farish C. Tate (D)

IDAHO

Senators

Fred T. Dubois (D)
Weldon B. Heyburn (R)

Representative

Burton L. French (R)

ILLINOIS

Senators

Shelby M. Cullom (R)
Albert J. Hopkins (R)

Representatives

Henry S. Boutell (R)
Ben F. Caldwell (D)
Joseph G. Cannon (R)
Joseph B. Crowley (D)
Martin Emerich (D)
George E. Foss (R)
George P. Foster (D)
Charles E. Fuller (R)
Joseph V. Graff (R)
Robert R. Hitt (R)
Philip Knopf (R)
William Lorimer (R)
James McAndrews (D)
William F. Mahoney (D)
d. Dec. 1904
James R. Mann (R)
Benjamin F. Marsh (R)
George W. Prince (R)
Henry T. Rainey (D)
William A. Rodenberg (R)
George W. Smith (R)
Howard M. Snapp (R)
John A. Sterling (R)
Vespasian Warner (R)
James R. Williams (D)
William W. Wilson (R)

INDIANA

Senators

Charles W. Fairbanks (R)
Albert J. Beveridge (R)

Representatives

Abraham L. Brick (R)
George W. Cromer (R)
Edgar D. Crumpacker (R)
Francis M. Griffith (D)
James A. Hemenway (R)
Elias S. Holliday (R)
Charles B. Landis (R)
Frederick Landis (R)
Robert W. Miers (D)
Jesse Overstreet (R)
James M. Robinson (D)
James E. Watson (R)
William T. Zenor (D)

IOWA

Senators

William B. Allison (R)
Jonathan P. Dolliver (R)

Representatives

Benjamin P. Birdsall (R)
James P. Conner (R)
Robert G. Cousins (R)
Gilbert N. Haugen (R)
Thomas Hedge (R)
William P. Hepburn (R)
John A. T. Hull (R)
John F. Lacey (R)
Walter I. Smith (R)
Lot Thomas (R)
Martin J. Wade (D)

KANSAS

Senators

Joseph R. Burton (R)
Chester I. Long (R)

Representatives

Justin D. Bowersock (R)
William A. Calderhead (R)
Philip P. Campbell (R)
Charles Curtis (R)
James M. Miller (R)
Victor Murdock (R)
William A. Reeder (R)
Charles F. Scott (R)

KENTUCKY

Senators

Joseph C. S. Blackburn (D)
James B. McCreary (D)

Representatives

George G. Gilbert (D)
Daniel L. Gooch (D)
Frank A. Hopkins (D)
W. Godfrey Hunter (R)
Ollie M. James (R)
James N. Kehoe (D)
John S. Rhea (D, Pop)
J. Swagar Sherley (D)
David H. Smith (D)
Augustus O. Stanley (D)
South Trimble (D)

LOUISIANA

Senators

Samuel D. McEnery (D)
Murphy J. Foster (D)

Representatives

Phanor Breazeale (D)
Robert F. Broussard (D)
Robert C. Davey (D)
Adolph Meyer (D)
Arsene P. Pujo (D)
Joseph E. Ransdell (D)
Samuel M. Robertson (D)

MAINE

Senators

Eugene Hale (R)
William P. Frye (R)

Representatives

Amos L. Allen (R)
Edwin C. Burleigh (R)
Charles E. Littlefield (R)
Llewellyn Powers (R)

MARYLAND

Senators

Louis E. McComas (R)
Arthur P. Gorman (D)

Representatives

James W. Denny (D)
William H. Jackson (R)
Sydney E. Mudd (R)
George A. Pearre (R)
J. Fred C. Talbott (D)
Frank C. Wachter (R)

MASSACHUSETTS

Senators

George F. Hoar (R) d. Sept. 1904
W. Murray Crane (R) s. 1904
Henry Cabot Lodge (R)

Representatives

Butler Ames (R)
Augustus P. Gardner (R)
Frederick H. Gillett (R)
William S. Greene (R)
John A. Keliher (D)
George P. Lawrence (R)
William C. Lovering (R)
Samuel W. McCall (R)
William S. McNary (D)
Samuel L. Powers (R)
Ernest W. Roberts (R)
John A. Sullivan (D)
John R. Thayer (D)
Charles Q. Tirrell (R)

MICHIGAN

Senators

Julius C. Burrows (R)
Russell A. Alger (R)

Representatives

Roswell P. Bishop (R)
Archibald B. Darragh (R)
Joseph W. Fordney (R)
Washington Gardner (R)
Edward L. Hamilton (R)
George A. Loud (R)
Alfred Lucking (D)
Henry McMorran (R)
Samuel W. Smith (R)
William Alden Smith (R)
Charles E. Townsend (R)
H. Olin Young (R)

MINNESOTA

Senators

Knute Nelson (R)
Moses E. Clapp (R)

Representatives

J. Adam Bede (R)
Clarence B. Buckman (R)
Charles R. Davis (R)
John Lind (D)
James T. McCleary (R)
Halvor Steenerson (R)
Frederick C. Stevens (R)
James A. Tawney (R)
Andrew J. Volstead (R)

MISSISSIPPI

Senators

Hernando D. Money (D)
Anselm J. McLaurin (D)

Representatives

Eaton J. Bowers (D)
Adam M. Byrd (D)
Ezekiel S. Candler, Jr. (D)
Wilson S. Hill (D)
Benjamin G. Humphreys (D)
Frank A. McLain (D)
Thomas Spight (D)
John Sharp Williams (D)

MISSOURI

Senators

Francis M. Cockrell (D)
William J. Stone (D)

Representatives

Richard Bartholdt (R)
Maecenas E. Benton (D)
James J. Butler (D)
Champ Clark (D)
Charles F. Cochran (D)
William S. Cowherd (D)
David A. De Armond (D)
John Dougherty (D)
Courtney W. Hamlin (D)
John T. Hunt (D)
J. Robert Lamar (D)
James T. Lloyd (D)
Edward Robb (D)
William W. Rucker (D)
Dorsey W. Shackleford (D)
Willard D. Vandiver (D)

MONTANA

Senators

William A. Clark (D)
Paris Gibson (D)

Representative

Joseph M. Dixon (R)

NEBRASKA

Senators

Charles H. Dietrich (R)
Joseph H. Millard (R)

Representatives

Elmer J. Burkett (D)
Edmund H. Hinshaw (R)
Gilbert M. Hitchcock (D)
Moses P. Kinkaid (R)
John J. McCarthy (R)
George W. Norris (R)

NEVADA

Senators

William M. Stewart (R)
Francis G. Newlands (D)

Representative

Clarence D. Van Duzer (D)

NEW HAMPSHIRE

Senators

Jacob H. Gallinger (R)
Henry E. Burnham (R)

Representatives

Frank D. Currier (R)
Cyrus A. Sulloway (R)

NEW JERSEY

Senators

John Kean (R)
John F. Dryden (R)

Representatives

Allan Benny (D)
Charles N. Fowler (R)
John J. Gardner (D)
Benjamin F. Howell (R)
William Hughes (D)
William M. Lanning (R) r. June 1904
Henry C. Loudenslager (R)
Allan L. McDermott (D)
Richard W. Parker (R)
William H. Wiley (R)
Ira W. Wood (R) s. 1904

NEW YORK

Senators

Thomas C. Platt (R)
Chauncey M. Depew (R)

Representatives

De Alva S. Alexander (R)
Robert Baker (D)
Edward M. Bassett (D)
Thomas W. Bradley (R)
W. Bourke Cockran (D) s. Mar. 1904
William H. Douglas (R)
William H. Draper (R)
Michael E. Driscoll (R)
Charles T. Dunwell (R)
John W. Dwight (R)
John J. Fitzgerald (D)
William H. Flack (R)
Charles W. Gillet (R)
Henry M. Goldfogle (D)
Joseph A. Goulden (D)
Francis B. Harrison (D)
William Randolph Hearst (D)
John H. Ketcham (R)
Charles L. Knapp (R)
George H. Lindsay (D)
Lucius N. Littauer (R)
George B. McClellan (D) r. Dec. 1903
Norton P. Otis (R) d. Feb. 1905
Sereno E. Payne (R)
James B. Perkins (R)
Ira E. Rider (D)
Jacob Ruppert Jr. (D)
William H. Ryan (D)
Townsend Scudder (D)
James S. Sherman (R)
Francis E. Shober (D)
George J. Smith (R)
George N. Southwick (R)
Timothy D. Sullivan (D)
William Sulzer (D)
Edward B. Vreeland (R)
James W. Wadsworth (R)
Frank E. Wilson (D)

NORTH CAROLINA

Senators

Furnifold McL. Simmons (D)
Lee S. Overman (D)

Representatives

James M. Gudger Jr. (D)
Claude Kitchin (D)
William W. Kitchin (D)
Theodore F. Kluttz (D)
Robert N. Page (D)
Gilbert B. Patterson (D)
Edward W. Pou (D)
John H. Small (D)
Charles R. Thomas (D)
Edwin Y. Webb (D)

NORTH DAKOTA

Senators

Henry C. Hansbrough (R)
Porter J. McCumber (R)

Representatives

Thomas F. Marshall (R)
Burleigh F. Spalding (R)

OHIO

Senators

Joseph B. Foraker (R)

Marcus A. Hanna (R) d. Feb. 1904
Charles W. F. Dick (R) s. 1904

Representatives

De Witt C. Badger (D)
Jacob A. Beidler (R)
Theodore E. Burton (R)
John W. Cassingham (D)
Charles W. F. Dick (R) r. Mar. 1904
Harvey C. Garber (D)
Herman P. Goebel (R)
Charles H. Grosvenor (R)
Charles Q. Hildebrant (R)
Amos H. Jackson (D)
James Kennedy (R)
Thomas B. Kyle (R)
Nicholas Longworth (R)
Stephen Morgan (R)
Robert M. Nevin (R)
William W. Skiles (R) d. Jan. 1904
John S. Snook (D)
James H. Southard (R)
William A. Thomas (R) s. 1904
Henry C. Van Voorhis (R)
William R. Warnock (R)
Amos R. Webber (R) s. 1904
Capell L. Weems (R)

OREGON

Senators

John H. Mitchell (R)
Charles W. Fulton (R)

Representatives

Binger Hermann (R)
John N. Williamson (R)

PENNSYLVANIA

Senators

Boies Penrose (R)

Matthew S. Quay (R) d. May 1904
Philander C. Knox (R) s. 1905

Representatives

Ernest F. Acheson (R)
Robert Adams, Jr. (R)
Arthur L. Bates (R)
Henry H. Bingham (R)
James W. Brown (R)
Henry Burk (R) d. Dec. 1903
Thomas S. Butler (R)
Henry B. Cassel (R)
George A. Castor (R) s. 1904
William Connell (R) s. 1904
Allen F. Cooper (R)
John Dalzell (R)
Elias Deemer (R)
Charles H. Dickerman (D)
Solomon R. Dresser (R)
Alvin Evans (R)
George Howell (R) r. Nov. 1903
George F. Huff (R)
Marcus C. L. Kline (D)
Daniel F. Lafean (R)
George D. McCreary (R)
Thaddeus M. Mahon (R)
Reuben O. Moon (R)
Edward de V. Morrell (R)
Marlin E. Olmsted (R)
Henry W. Palmer (R)
George R. Patterson (R)
Henry Kirke Porter
George Shiras (R)
Joseph H. Shull (D)
Joseph C. Sibley (R)
William O. Smith (R)
Irving P. Wanger (R)
Charles F. Wright (R)

RHODE ISLAND

Senators

Nelson W. Aldrich (R)
George P. Wetmore (R)

Representatives

Adin B. Capron (R)
Daniel L. D. Granger (D)

SOUTH CAROLINA

Senators

Benjamin R. Tillman (D)
Asbury C. Latimer (D)

Representatives

Wyatt Aiken (D)
George W. Croft (D) d. Mar. 1904
Theodore G. Croft (D) s. 1904
David E. Finley (D)
Joseph T. Johnson (D)
George S. Legare (D)
Asbury F. Lever (D)
Robert B. Scarborough (D)

SOUTH DAKOTA

Senators

Robert J. Gamble (R)
Alfred B. Kittredge (R)

Representatives

Charles H. Burke (R)
Eben W. Martin (R)

TENNESSEE

Senators

William B. Bate (D)
Edward W. Carmack (D)

Representatives

Walter P. Brownlow (R)
Morgan C. Fitzpatrick (D)

John W. Gaines (D)
Henry R. Gibson (R)
John A. Moon (D)
Lemuel P. Padgett (D)
Malcolm R. Patterson (D)
Rice A. Pierce (D)
James D. Richardson (D)
Thetus W. Sims (D)

TEXAS

Senators

Charles A. Culberson (D)
Joseph W. Bailey (D)

Representatives

Thomas H. Ball (D) r. Nov. 1903
Jack Beall (D)
George F. Burgess (D)
Albert S. Burleson (D)
Samuel B. Cooper (D)
Scott Field (D)
John Nance Garner (D)
Oscar W. Gillespie (D)
Alexander W. Gregg (D)
Robert L. Henry (D)
John M. Pickney (D)
Choice B. Randell (D)
Gordon J. Russell (D)
Morris Sheppard (D)
James L. Slayden (D)
William R. Smith (D)
John H. Stephens (D)

UTAH

Senators

Thomas Kearns (R)
Reed Smoot (R)

Representative

Joseph Howell (R)

VERMONT

Senators

Redfield Proctor (R)
William P. Dillingham (R)

Representatives

David J. Foster (R)
Kittredge Haskins (R)

VIRGINIA

Senators

John W. Daniel (D)
Thomas S. Martin (D)

Representatives

Henry D. Flood (D)
Carter Glass (D)
James Hay (D)
William A. Jones (D)
John Lamb (D)
Harry L. Maynard (D)
John F. Rixey (D)
Campbell Slemp (R)
Robert G. Southall (D)
Claude A. Swanson (D)

WASHINGTON

Senators

Addison G. Foster (R)
Levi Ankeny (R)

Representatives

Francis W. Cushman (R)
William E. Humphrey (R)
Wesley L. Jones (R)

WEST VIRGINIA

Senators

Stephen B. Elkins (R)
Nathan B. Scott (R)

Representatives

Alston G. Dayton (R)
Blackburn B. Dovener (R)
Joseph H. Gaines (R)
James A. Hughes (R)
Harry C. Woodyard (R)

WISCONSIN

Senators

John C. Spooner (R)
Joseph V. Quarles (R)

Representatives

Henry C. Adams (R)
Joseph W. Babcock (R)
Webster E. Brown (R)
Henry A. Cooper (R)
James H. Davidson (R)
John J. Esch (R)
John J. Jenkins (R)
Edward S. Minor (R)
Theobald Otjen (R)
William H. Stafford (R)
Charles H. Weisse (D)

WYOMING

Senators

Clarence D. Clark (R)
Francis E. Warren (R)

Representative

Frank W. Mondell (R)

FIFTY-NINTH CONGRESS

March 4, 1905 to March 3, 1907

President of The Senate:	Charles W. Fairbanks
President Pro Tempore of The Senate:	William P. Frye
Speaker of The House of Representatives:	Joseph G. Cannon

ALABAMA

Senators

John T. Morgan (D)
Edmund W. Pettus (D)

Representatives

John H. Bankhead (D)
Sydney J. Bowie (D)
John L. Burnett (D)
Henry D. Clayton (D)
J. Thomas Heflin (D)
William Richardson (D)
George W. Taylor (D)
Oscar W. Underwood (D)
Ariosto A. Wiley (D)

ARKANSAS

Senators

James H. Berry (D)
James P. Clarke (D)

Representatives

Stephen Brundidge, Jr. (D)
John C. Floyd (D)
John S. Little (D)
Robert B. Macon (D)
Charles C. Reid (D)
Joseph T. Robinson (D)
Robert M. Wallace (D)

CALIFORNIA

Senators

George C. Perkins (R)
Frank P. Flint (R)

Representatives

William F. Englebright (R) s. 1907
James N. Gillet r. Nov. 1906
Everis A. Hayes (R)
Julius Kahn (R)
Joseph R. Knowland (R)
Duncan E. McKinlay (R)
James McLachlan (R)
James C. Needham (R)
Sylvester C. Smith (R)

COLORADO

Senators

Henry M. Teller (D)
Thomas M. Patterson (D)

Represeniatives

Robert W. Bonynge (R)
Franklin E. Brooks (R)
Herschel M. Hogg (R)

CONNECTICUT

Senators

Orville H. Platt (R) d. Apr. 1905
Frank B. Brandegee (R) s. 1905

Morgan G. Bulkeley (R)

Representatives

E. Stevens Henry (R)
Edwin W. Higgins (R)
Ebenezer J. Hill (R)
George L. Lilley (R)
Nehemiah D. Sperry (R)

DELAWARE

Senators

J. Frank Allee (R)
Henry A. Du Pont (R) s. 1906

Representative

Hiram R. Burton (R)

FLORIDA

Senators

Stephen R. Mallory (D)
James P. Taliaferro (D)

Representatives

Frank Clark (R)
William B. Lamar (D)
Stephen M. Sparkman (D)

GEORGIA

Senators

Augustus O. Bacon (D)
Alexander S. Clay (D)

Representatives

William C. Adamson (D)
Charles L. Bartlett (D)
Thomas M. Bell (D)
William G. Brantley (D)
James M. Griggs (D)
Thomas W. Hardwick (D)
William M. Howard (D)
Gordon Lee (D)
Rufus E. Lester (D) d. June 1906
Elijah B. Lewis (D)
Leonidas F. Livingston (D)
James W. Overstreet (D) s. 1906

IDAHO

Senators

Fred T. Dubois (D)
Weldon B. Heyburn (R)

Representative

Burton L. French (R)

ILLINOIS

Senators

Shelby M. Cullom (R)
Albert J. Hopkins (R)

Representatives

Henry S. Boutell (R)
Joseph G. Cannon (R)
Pleasant T. Chapman (R)
Frank S. Dickson (R)
George E. Foss (R)
Charles E. Fuller (R)
Joseph V. Graff (R)
Robert R. Hitt (R) d. Sept. 1906
Philip Knopf (R)
William Lorimer (R)
Frank O. Lowden (R) s. 1906
Charles McGavin (R)
William B. McKinley (R)
James McKinney (R)
Martin B. Madden (R)
James R. Mann (R)
Anthony Michalek (R) s. 1906
George W. Prince (R)
Henry T. Rainey (R)
Zeno J. Rives (R)
William A. Rodenberg (R)
George W. Smith (R)
Howard M. Snapp (R)
John A. Sterling (R)
Charles S. Wharton (R)
William W. Wilson (R)

INDIANA

Senators

Albert J. Beveridge (R)
James A. Hemenway (R)

Representatives

Abraham L. Brick (R)
John C. Chaney (R)
George W. Cromer (R)
Edgar D. Crumpacker (R)
Lincoln Dixon (D)
John H. Foster (R)
Newton W. Gilbert (R)
r. Nov. 1906
Clarence C. Gilhams (R) s. 1906
Elias S. Holliday (R)
Charles B. Landis (R)
Frederick Landis (R)
Jesse Overstreet (R)
James E. Watson (R)
William T. Zenor (D)

IOWA

Senators

William B. Allison (R)
Jonathan P. Dolliver (R)

Representatives

Benjamin P. Birdsall (R)
James P. Conner (R)
Robert G. Cousins (R)
Albert F. Dawson (R)
Gilbert N. Haugen (R)
Thomas Hedge (R)
William P. Hepburn (R)
Elbert H. Hubbard (R)
John A. T. Hull (R)
John F. Lacey (R)
Walter I. Smith (R)

KANSAS

Senators

Joseph R. Burton (R) r. June 1906
Alfred W. Benson (R) ta. 1906
Charles Curtis (R) s. 1907

Chester I. Long (R)

Representatives

Justin D. Bowersock (R)
William A. Calderhead (R)
Philip P. Campbell (R)
Charles Curtis (R) r. Jan. 1907
James M. Miller (R)
Victor Murdock (R)
William A. Reeder (R)
Charles F. Scott (R)

KENTUCKY

Senators

Joseph C. S. Blackburn (D)
James B. McCreary (D)

Representatives

Joseph B. Bennett (R)
Don C. Edwards (R)
George G. Gilbert (D)
Frank A. Hopkins (D)
Ollie M. James (D)
James M. Richardson (D)
Joseph L. Rhinock (D)
J. Swagar Sherley (D)
David H. Smith (D)
Augustus O. Stanley (D)
South Trimble (D)

LOUISIANA

Senators

Samuel D. McEnery (D)
Murphy J. Foster (D)

Representatives

Robert F. Broussard (D)
Robert C. Davey (D)
Adolph Meyer (D)
Arsene P. Pujo (D)
Joseph E. Ransdell (D)
Samuel M. Robertson (D)
John T. Watkins (D)

MAINE

Senators

Eugene Hale (R)
William P. Frye (R)

Representatives

Amos L. Allen (R)
Edwin C. Burleigh (R)
Charles E. Littlefield (R)
Llewellyn Powers (R)

MARYLAND

Senators

Arthur P. Gorman (D)
d. June 1906
William P. Whyte (D) s. 1906

Isidor Rayner (D)

Representatives

John Gill, Jr. (D)
Sydney E. Mudd (R)
George A. Pearre (R)
Thomas A. Smith (D)
J. Fred C. Talbott (D)
Frank C. Wachter (R)

MASSACHUSETTS

Senators

Henry Cabot Lodge (R)
W. Murray Crane (R)

Representatives

Butler Ames (R)
Augustus P. Gardner (R)
Frederick H. Gillett (R)
William S. Greene (R)
Rockwood Hoar (R) d. Nov. 1906
John A. Keliher (D)
George P. Lawrence (R)
William C. Lovering (R)
Samuel W. McCall (R)
William S. McNary (D)
Ernest W. Roberts (R)
John A. Sullivan (D)
Charles Q. Tirrell (R)
Charles G. Washburn (R) s. 1907
John W. Weeks (R)

MICHIGAN

Senators

Julius C. Burrows (R)

Russell A. Alger (R) d. Jan. 1907
William Alden Smith (R) s. 1907

Representatives

Roswell P. Bishop (R)
Archibald B. Darragh (R)
Edwin Denby (R)
Joseph W. Fordney (R)
Washington Gardner (R)
Edward L. Hamilton (R)
George A. Loud (R)
Henry McMorran (R)
Samuel W. Smith (R)
William Alden Smith (R)
r. Feb. 1907
Charles E. Townsend (R)
H. Olin Young (R)

MINNESOTA

Senators

Knute Nelson (R)
Moses E. Clapp (R)

Representatives

J. Adam Bede (R)
Clarence B. Buckman (R)
Charles R. Davis (R)
Loren Fletcher (R)
James T. McCleary (R)
Halvor Steenerson (R)
Frederick C. Stevens (R)
James A. Tawney (R)
Andrew J. Volstead (R)

MISSISSIPPI

Senators

Hernando D. Money (D)
Anselm J. McLaurin (D)

Representatives

Eaton J. Bowers (D)
Adam M. Byrd (D)
Ezekiel S. Candler, Jr. (D)
Wilson S. Hill (D)
Benjamin G. Humphreys (D)
Frank A. McLain (D)
Thomas Spight (D)
John Sharp Williams (D)

MISSOURI

Senators

William J. Stone (D)
William Warner (R)

Representatives

Richard Bartholdt (R)
Champ Clark (D)
Harry M. Coudrey (R) s. 1906
David A. De Armond (D)
Edgar C. Ellis (R)
Frank B. Fulkerson (R)
John T. Hunt (D)
Frank B. Klepper (R)
James T. Lloyd (D)
Arthur P. Murphy (R)
Marion E. Rhodes (R)
William W. Rucker (D)
Dorsey W. Shackleford (D)
Cassius M. Shartel (R)
William T. Tyndall (R)
John Welborn (R)
Ernest E. Wood (D) r. June 1906

MONTANA

Senators

William A. Clark (D)
Thomas H. Carter (R)

Representative

Joseph M. Dixon (R)

NEBRASKA

Senators

Joseph H. Millard (R)
Elmer J. Burkett (R)

Representatives

Edmund H. Hinshaw (R)
John L. Kennedy (R)
Moses P. Kinkaid (R)
John J. McCarthy (R)
George W. Norris (R)
Ernest M. Pollard (R)

NEVADA

Senators

Francis G. Newlands (D)
George S. Nixon (R)

Representative

Clarence D. Van Duzer (D)

NEW HAMPSHIRE

Senators

Jacob H. Gallinger (R)
Henry E. Burnham (R)

Representatives

Frank D. Currier (R)
Cyrus A. Sulloway (R)

NEW JERSEY

Senators

John Kean (R)
John F. Dryden (R)

Representatives

Henry C. Allen (R)
Charles N. Fowler (R)
John J. Gardner (D)
Benjamin F. Howell (R)
Henry C. Loudenslager (R)
Allan L. McDermott (D)
Richard W. Parker (R)
Marshall Van Winkle (R)
William H. Wiley (R)
Ira W. Wood (R)

NEW YORK

Senators

Thomas C. Platt (R)
Chauncey M. Depew (R)

Representatives

De Alva S. Alexander (R)
John E. Andrus (R)
William S. Bennett (R)
Thomas W. Bradley (R)
William M. Calder (R)
W. Bourke Cockran (D)
William W. Cocks (R)
William H. Draper (R)
Michael E. Driscoll (R)
Charles T. Dunwell (R)
John W. Dwight (R)
J. Sloat Fassett (R)
John J. Fitzgerald (D)
William H. Flack (R) d. Feb. 1907
Henry M. Goldfogle (D)
Joseph A. Goulden (D)
William Randolph Hearst (D)
John H. Ketcham (R)
d. Nov. 1906
Charles L. Knapp (R)
Charles B. Law (R)
Frank J. Le Fevre (R)
George H. Lindsay (D)
Lucius N. Littauer (R)
J. Van Vechten Olcott (R)
Herbert Parsons (R)
Sereno E. Payne (R)
James B. Perkins (R)
Daniel B. Perkins (R)
Daniel J. Riordan (D) s. 1906
Jacob Ruppert, Jr. (D)
William H. Ryan (D)
James S. Sherman (R)
George N. Southwick (R)
Timothy D. Sullivan (D)
r. July 1906
William Sulzer (D)
Charles A. Towne (D)
Edward B. Vreeland (R)
James W. Wadsworth (R)
George E. Waldo (R)

NORTH CAROLINA

Senators

Furnifold McL. Simmons (D)
Lee S. Overman (D)

Representatives

Edmond Blackburn (D)
James M. Gudger Jr. (D)
Claude Kitchin (D)
William W. Kitchin (D)
Robert N. Page (D)
Gilbert B. Patterson (D)
Edward W. Pou (D)
John H. Small (D)
Charles R. Thomas (D)
Edwin Y. Webb (D)

NORTH DAKOTA

Senators

Henry C. Hansbrough (R)
Porter J. McCumber (R)

Representatives

Asle J. Gronna (R)
Thomas F. Marshall (R)

OHIO

Senators

Joseph B. Foraker (R)
Charles W. F. Dick (R)

Representatives

Henry T. Bannon (R)
Jacob A. Beidler (R)
Theodore E. Burton (R)
William W. Campbell (R)
Ralph D. Cole (R)
Beman G. Dawes (R)
Harvey C. Garber (D)
Herman P. Goebel (R)
Charles H. Grosvenor (R)
J. Warren Keifer (R)
James Kennedy (R)
Nicholas Longworth (R)
Grant E. Mouser (R)
Robert M. Nevin (R)
Thomas E. Scroggy (R)
Martin L. Smyser (R)
James H. Southard (R)
Edward L. Taylor, Jr. (R)
William A. Thomas (R)
Amos R. Webber (R)
Capell L. Weems (R)

OREGON

Senators

John H. Mitchell (R) d. Dec. 1905
John M. Gearin (D) ta. 1906
Frederick W. Mulkey (R) s. 1907

Charles W. Fulton (R)

Representative

Binger Hermann (R)

PENNSYLVANIA

Senators

Boies Penrose (R)
Philander C. Knox (R)

Representatives

Ernest F. Acheson (R)
Robert Adams, Jr. (R)
d. June 1906
Andrew J. Barchfeld (R)
Arthur L. Bates (R)
Henry H. Bingham (R)
Charles N. Brumm (R) s. 1906
James F. Burke (R)
Thomas S. Butler (R)
Henry B. Cassel (R)
George A. Castor (R) d. Feb. 1906
Allen F. Cooper (R)
Thomas H. Dale (R)
John Dalzell (R)
Elias Deemer (R)
Solomon R. Dresser (R)
William H. Graham (R)
George F. Huff (R)
Marcus C. L. Kline (D)
Daniel F. Lafean (R)
Mial E. Lilley (R)
George D. McCreary (R)
Thaddeus M. Mahon (R)
Reuben O. Moon (R)
J. Hampton Moore (R)
s. Dec. 1906
Edward de V. Morrell (R)
Marlin E. Olmsted (R)
Henry W. Palmer (R)
George R. Patterson (R)
d. March 1906
John E. Reyburn (R) s. 1906
John M. Reynolds (R)
Edmund W. Samuel (R)
Gustav A. Schneebeli (R)
Joseph C. Sibley (R)
William O. Smith (R)
Irving P. Wanger (R)

RHODE ISLAND

Senators

Nelson W. Aldrich (R)
George P. Wetmore (R)

Representatives

Adin B. Capron (R)
Daniel L. D. Granger (D)

SOUTH CAROLINA

Senators

Benjamin R. Tillman (D)
Asbury C. Latimer (D)

Representatives

Wyatt Aiken (D)
J. Edwin Ellerbe (D)
David E. Finley (D)
Joseph T. Johnson (D)
George S. Legare (D)
Asbury F. Lever (D)
James O. Patterson (D)

SOUTH DAKOTA

Senators

Robert J. Gamble (R)
Alfred B. Kittredge (R)

Representatives

Charles H. Burke (R)
Eben W. Martin (R)

TENNESSEE

Senators

James B. Frazier (D)
Edward W. Carmack (D)

Representatives

Walter P. Brownlow (R)
Mounce G. Butler (D)
Finis J. Garrett (D)
John W. Gaines (D)
Nathan W. Hale (R)
William C. Houston (D)
John A. Moon (D)
Lemuel P. Padgett (D)
Malcolm R. Patterson (D)
r. Nov. 1906
Thetus W. Sims (D)

TEXAS

Senators

Charles A. Culberson (D)
Joseph W. Bailey (D)

Representatives

Jack Beall (D)
Moses L. Broocks (D)
George F. Burgess (D)
Albert S. Burleson (D)
Scott Field (D)
John Nance Garner (D)
Oscar W. Gillespie (D)
Alexander W. Gregg (D)
Robert L. Henry (D)
John M. Moore (D)
Choice B. Randell (D)
Gordon J. Russell (D)
Morris Sheppard (D)
James L. Slayden (D)
William R. Smith (D)
John H. Stephens (D)

UTAH

Senators

Reed Smoot (R)
George Sutherland (R)

Representative

Joseph Howell (R)

VERMONT

Senators

Redfield Proctor (R)
William P. Dillingham (R)

Representatives

David J. Foster (R)
Kittredge Haskins (R)

VIRGINIA

Senators

John W. Daniel (D)
Thomas S. Martin (D)

Representatives

Henry D. Flood (D)
Carter Glass (D)
James Hay (D)
William A. Jones (D)
John Lamb (D)
Harry L. Maynard (D)
John F. Rixey (D) d. Feb. 1907
Edward W. Saunders (D) s. 1906
Campbell Slemp (R)
Robert G. Southall (D)
Claude A. Swanson (D) r. Jan. 1906

WASHINGTON

Senators

Levi Ankeny (R)
Samuel H. Piles (R)

Representatives

Francis W. Cushman (R)
William E. Humphrey (R)
Wesley L. Jones (R)

WEST VIRGINIA

Senators

Stephen B. Elkins (R)
Nathan B. Scott (R)

Representatives

Thomas B. Davis (D)
Alston G. Dayton (R) r. Mar. 1905
Blackburn B. Dovener (R)
Joseph H. Gaines (R)
James A. Hughes (R)
Harry C. Woodyard (R)

WISCONSIN

Senators

John C. Spooner (R)
Robert M. La Follette (R)

Representatives

Henry C. Adams (R) d. July 1906
Joseph W. Babcock (R)
Webster E. Brown (R)
Henry A. Cooper (R)
James H. Davidson (R)
John J. Esch (R)
John J. Jenkins (R)
Edward S. Minor (R)
John M. Nelson (R) s. 1906
Theobald Otjen (R)
William H. Stafford (R)
Charles H. Weisse (D)

WYOMING

Senators

Clarence D. Clark (R)
Francis E. Warren (R)

Representative

Frank W. Mondell (R)

SIXTIETH CONGRESS

March 4, 1907 to March 3, 1909

President of The Senate: Charles W. Fairbanks
President Pro Tempore of The Senate: William P. Frye
Speaker of The House of Representatives: Joseph G. Cannon

ALABAMA

Senators

John T. Morgan (D) d. June 1907
John H. Bankhead (D) s. 1907

Edmund W. Pettus (D) d. July 1907
Joseph F. Johnston (D)

Representatives

John L. Burnett (D)
Henry D. Clayton (D)
William B. Craig (D)
J. Thomas Heflin (D)
Richmond P. Hobson (D)
William Richardson (D)
George W. Taylor (D)
Oscar W. Underwood (D)
Ariosto A. Wiley (D) d. June 1908
Oliver C. Wiley (D) s. 1908

ARKANSAS

Senators

James P. Clarke (D)
Jeff Davis (D)

Representatives

Stephen Brundidge, Jr. (D)
William B. Cravens (D)
John C. Floyd (D)
Robert B. Macon (D)
Charles C. Reid (D)
Joseph T. Robinson (D)
Robert M. Wallace (D)

CALIFORNIA

Senators

George C. Perkins (R)
Frank P. Flint (R)

Representatives

William F. Englebright (R)
Everis A. Hayes (R)
Julius Kahn (R)
Joseph R. Knowland (R)
Duncan E. McKinlay (R)
James McLachlan (R)
James C. Needham (R)
Sylvester C. Smith (R)

COLORADO

Senators

Henry M. Teller (D)
Simon Guggenheim (R)

Representatives

Robert W. Bonynge (R)
George W. Cook (R)
Warren A. Haggott (R)

CONNECTICUT

Senators

Morgan G. Bulkeley (R)
Frank B. Brandegee (R)

Representatives

E. Stevens Henry (R)
Edwin W. Higgins (R)
Ebenezer J. Hill (R)
George L. Lilley (R)
Nehemiah D. Sperry (R)

DELAWARE

Senators

Henry A. Du Pont (R)
Harry A. Richardson (R)

Representative

Hiram R. Burton (R)

FLORIDA

Senators

Stephen R. Mallory (D) d. Dec. 1908
William J. Bryan (D) ta. 1908
William H. Milton (D) s. 1908

James P. Taliaferro (D)

Representatives

Frank Clark (D)
William B. Lamar (D)
Stephen M. Sparkman (D)

GEORGIA

Senators

Augustus O. Bacon (D)
Alexander S. Clay (D)

Representatives

William C. Adamson (D)
Charles L. Bartlett (D)
Thomas M. Bell (D)
William G. Brantley (D)
Charles G. Edwards (D)
James M. Griggs (D)
Thomas W. Hardwick (D)
William M. Howard (D)
Gordon Lee (D)
Elijah B. Lewis (D)
Leonidas F. Livingston (D)

IDAHO

Senators

Weldon B. Heyburn (R)
William E. Borah (R)

Representative

Burton L. French (R)

ILLINOIS

Senators

Shelby M. Cullom (R)
Albert J. Hopkins (R)

Representatives

Henry S. Boutell (R)
Ben Franklin Caldwell (D)
Joseph G. Cannon (R)
Pleasant T. Chapman (R)
George E. Foss (R)
Martin D. Foster (D)
Charles E. Fuller (R)
Joseph V. Graff (R)
Philip Knopf (R)
William Lorimer (R)
Frank O. Lowden (R)
James T. McDermott (D)
Charles McGavin (R)
William B. McKinley (R)
James McKinney (R)
Martin B. Madden (R)
James R. Mann (R)
George W. Prince (R)
Henry T. Rainey (D)
William A. Rodenberg (R)
Adolph J. Sabath (D)
Howard M. Snapp (R)
John A. Sterling (R)
Napoleon B. Thistlewood (R) s. 1908
William W. Wilson (R)

INDIANA

Senators

Albert J. Beveridge (R)
James A. Hemenway (R)

Representatives

John A. M. Adair (D)
Henry A. Barnhart (D) s. 1908
Abraham L. Brick (R) d. Apr. 1908
John C. Chaney (R)
William E. Cox (D)
Edgar D. Crumpacker (R)
Lincoln Dixon (D)
John H. Foster (R)
Clarence C. Gilhams (R)
Elias S. Holliday (R)
Charles B. Landis (R)
Jesse Overstreet (R)
George W. Rauch (D)
James E. Watson (R)

IOWA

Senators

William B. Allison (R)
d. Aug. 1908
Albert B. Cummins (R) s. 1908

Jonathan P. Dolliver (R)

Representatives

Benjamin P. Birdsall (R)
James P. Conner (R)
Robert G. Cousins (R)
Albert F. Dawson (R)
Daniel W. Hamilton (D)
Gilbert N. Haugen (R)
William P. Hepburn (R)
Elbert H. Hubbard (R)
John A. T. Hull (R)
Charles A. Kennedy (R)
Walter I. Smith (R)

KANSAS

Senators

Chester I. Long (R)
Charles Curtis (R)

Representatives

Daniel R. Anthony, Jr. (R)
William A. Calderhead (R)
Philip P. Campbell (R)
Edmond H. Madison (R)
James M. Miller (R)
Victor Murdock (R)
William A. Reeder (R)
Charles F. Scott (R)

KENTUCKY

Senators

James B. McCreary (D)
Thomas H. Paynter (D)

Representatives

Joseph B. Bennett (R)
Don C. Edwards (R)
Harvey Helm (D)
Addison D. James (R)
Ollie M. James (D)
Ben Johnson (D)
William P. Kimball (D)
John W. Langley (R)
Joseph L. Rhinock (D)
J. Swagar Sherley (D)
Augustus O. Stanley (D)

LOUISIANA

Senators

Samuel D. McEnery (D)
Murphy J. Foster (D)

Representatives

Robert F. Broussard (D)
Robert C. Davey (D) d. Dec. 1908
Albert Estopinal (D) s. 1908
George K. Favrot (D)
Adolph Meyer (D) d. Mar. 1908
Arsene P. Pujo (D)
Joseph E. Ransdell (D)
John T. Watkins (D)

MAINE

Senators

Eugene Hale (R)
William P. Frye (R)

Representatives

Amos L. Allen (R)
Edwin C. Burleigh (R)
Frank E. Guernsey (R) s. 1908
Charles E. Littlefield (R)
r. Sept. 1908
Llewellyn Powers (R) d. July 1908
John P. Swasey (R) s. 1908

MARYLAND

Senators

Isidor Rayner (D)

William P. Whyte (D) d. Mar. 1908
John Walter Smith (D) s. 1908

Representatives

John Gill, Jr. (D)
William H. Jackson (R)
Sydney E. Mudd (R)
George A. Pearre (R)
J. Fred C. Talbott (D)
Harry B. Wolf (D)

MASSACHUSETTS

Senators

Henry Cabot Lodge (R)
W. Murray Crane (R)

Representatives

Butler Ames (R)
Augustus P. Gardner (R)
Frederick H. Gillett (R)
William S. Greene (R)
John A. Keliher (D)
George P. Lawrence (R)
William C. Lovering (R)
Samuel W. McCall (R)
Joseph F. O'Connell (D)
Andrew J. Peters (D)
Ernest W. Roberts (R)
Charles Q. Tirrell (R)
Charles G. Washburn (R)
John W. Weeks (R)

MICHIGAN

Senators

Julius C. Burrows (R)
William Alden Smith (R)

Representatives

Archibald B. Darragh (R)
Edwin Denby (R)
Gerrit J. Diekema (R)
Joseph W. Fordney (R)
Washington Gardner (R)
Edward L. Hamilton (R)
George A. Loud (R)
James C. McLaughlin (R)
Henry McMorran (R)
Samuel W. Smith (R)
Charles E. Townsend (R)
H. Olin Young (R)

MINNESOTA

Senators

Knute Nelson (R)
Moses E. Clapp (R)

Representatives

J. Adam Bede (R)
Charles R. Davis (R)
Winfield S. Hammond (D)
Charles A. Lindbergh (R)
Frank M. Nye (R)
Halvor Steenerson (R)
Frederick C. Stevens (R)
James A. Tawney (R)
Andrew J. Volstead (R)

MISSISSIPPI

Senators

Hernando D. Money (D)
Anselm J. McLaurin (D)

Representatives

Eaton J. Bowers (D)
Adam M. Byrd (D)
Ezekiel S. Candler, Jr. (D)
Wilson S. Hill (D)
Benjamin G. Humphreys (D)
Frank A. McLain (D)
Thomas Spight (D)
John Sharp Williams (D)

MISSOURI

Senators

William J. Stone (D)
William Warner (R)

Representatives

Joshua W. Alexander (D)
Richard Bartholdt (R)
Charles F. Booher (D)
Henry S. Caulfield (R)
Champ Clark (D)
Harry M. Coudrey (R)
David A. De Armond (D)
Edgar C. Ellis (R)
Thomas Hackney (D)
Courtney W. Hamlin (D)
J. Robert Lamar (D)
James T. Lloyd (D)
William W. Rucker (D)
Joseph J. Russell (D)
Dorsey W. Shackleford (D)
Madison R. Smith (D)

MONTANA

Senators

Thomas H. Carter (R)
Joseph M. Dixon (R)

Representative

Charles N. Pray (R)

NEBRASKA

Senators

Elmer J. Burkett (R)
Norris Brown (R)

Representatives

John F. Boyd (R)
Edmund H. Hinshaw (R)
Gilbert M. Hitchcock (D)
Moses P. Kinkaid (R)
George W. Norris (R)
Ernest M. Pollard (R)

NEVADA

Senators

Francis G. Newlands (D)
George S. Nixon (R)

Representative

George A. Bartlett (D)

NEW HAMPSHIRE

Senators

Jacob H. Gallinger (R)
Henry E. Burnham (R)

Representatives

Frank D. Currier (R)
Cyrus A. Sulloway (R)

NEW JERSEY

Senators

John Kean (R)
Frank O. Briggs (R)

Representatives

Charles N. Fowler (R)
John J. Gardner (D)
James A. Hamill (D)
Benjamin F. Howell (R)
William Hughes (D)
Eugene W. Leake (D)
Henry C. Loudenslager (R)
Richard W. Parker (R)
Le Gage Pratt (D)
Ira W. Wood (R)

NEW YORK

Senators

Thomas C. Platt (R)
Chauncey M. Depew (R)

Representatives

De Alva S. Alexander (R)
John E. Andrus (R)
William S. Bennet (R)
Thomas W. Bradley (R)
William M. Calder (R)
W. Bourke Cockran (D)
William W. Cocks (R)
William H. Draper (R)
Michael E. Driscoll (R)
Charles T. Dunwell (R)
d. June 1908
Cyrus Durey (R)
John W. Dwight (R)
George W. Fairchild (R)
J. Sloat Fassett (R)
John J. Fitzgerald (D)
Otto G. Foelker (R) s. 1908

Charles V. Fornes (D)
Henry M. Goldfogle (D)
Joseph A. Goulden (D)
Francis B. Harrison (D)
Charles L. Knapp (R)
Charles B. Law (R)
George H. Lindsay (D)
Samuel McMillan (R)
George R. Malby (R)
J. Van Vechten Olcott (R)
Herbert Parsons (R)
Sereno E. Payne (R)
James B. Perkins (R)
Peter A. Porter (R,D)
Daniel J. Riordan (D)
William H. Ryan (D)
James S. Sherman (R)
George N. Southwick (R)
William Sulzer (D)
Edward B. Vreeland (R)
George E. Waldo (R)
William Willett, Jr. (D)

NORTH CAROLINA

Senators

Furnifold McL. Simmons (D)
Lee S. Overman (D)

Representatives

William T. Crawford (D)
Hannibal L. Godwin (D)
Richard N. Hackett (D)
Claude Kitchin (D)
William W. Kitchin (D)
r. Jan. 1909
Robert N. Page (D)
Edward W. Pou (D)
John H. Small (D)
Charles R.Thomas (D)
Edwin Y. Webb (D)

NORTH DAKOTA

Senators

Henry C. Hansbrough (R)
Porter J. McCumber (R)

Representatives

Asle J. Gronna (R)
Thomas F. Marshall (R)

OHIO

Senators

Joseph B. Foraker (R)
Charles W. F. Dick (R)

Representatives

Timothy T. Ansberry (D)
William A. Ashbrook (R)
Henry T. Bannon (R)
Theodore E. Burton (R)
Ralph D. Cole (R)
Beman G. Dawes (R)
Matthew R. Denver (D)
Albert Douglas (R)
Herman P. Goebel (R)
J. Eugene Harding (R)
L. Paul Howland (R)
J. Warren Keifer (R)
James Kennedy (R)
J. Ford Laning (R)
Nicholas Longworth (R)
Grant E. Mouser (R)
Isaac R. Sherwood (D)
Edward L. Taylor, Jr. (R)
William A. Thomas (R)
William E. Tou Velle (D)
Capell L. Weems (R)

OKLAHOMA

Senators

Thomas P. Gore (D)
Robert L. Owen (D)

Representatives

Charles D. Carter (D)
James S. Davenport (D)
Scott Ferris (D)
Elmer L. Fulton (D)
Bird S. McGuire (R)

OREGON

Senators

Charles W. Fulton (R)
Jonathan Bourne, Jr. (R)

Representatives

William R. Ellis (R)
Willis C. Hawley (R)

PENNSYLVANIA

Senators

Boies Penrose (R)
Philander C. Knox (R)

Representatives

Ernest F. Acheson (R)
Andrew J. Barchfeld (R)
Charles F. Barclay (R)
Arthur L. Bates (R)
Joseph G. Beale (R)
Henry H. Bingham (R)
J. Davis Brodhead (D)
Charles N. Brumm (R)
r. Jan. 1909
James F. Burke (R)
Thomas S. Butler (R)
Henry B. Cassel (R)
Joel Cook (R)
Allen F. Cooper (R)
John Dalzell (R)
Benjamin K. Focht (R)
William W. Foulkrod (R)
William H. Graham (R)
George F. Huff (R)
George W. Kipp (D)
Daniel F. Lafean (R)
John T. Lenahan (D)
George D. McCreary (R)
John G. McHenry (D)
Reuben O. Moon (R)
J. Hampton Moore (R)
Thomas D. Nicholls (D)
Marlin E. Olmsted (R)
John M. Reynolds (R)
John H. Rothermel (D)
Irving P. Wanger (R)
Nelson P. Wheeler (R)
William B. Wilson (D)

RHODE ISLAND

Senators

Nelson W. Aldrich (R)
George P. Wetmore (R)

Representatives

Adin B. Capron (R)
Daniel L. D. Granger (D)
d. Feb. 1909

SOUTH CAROLINA

Senators

Benjamin R. Tillman (D)

Asbury C. Latimer (D)
d. Feb. 1908
Frank B. Gary (D) s. 1908

Representatives

Wyatt Aiken (D)
J. Edwin Ellerbe (D)
David E. Finley (D)
Joseph T. Johnson (D)
George S. Legare (D)
Asbury F. Lever (D)
James O. Patterson (D)

SOUTH DAKOTA

Senators

Robert J. Gamble (R)
Alfred B. Kittredge (R)

Representatives

Philo Hall (R)
Eben W. Martin (R)
William H. Parker (R)

TENNESSEE

Senators

James B. Frazier (D)
Robert L. Taylor (D)

Representatives

Walter P. Brownlow (R)
John W. Gaines (D)
Finis J. Garrett (D)
George W. Gordon (D)
Nathan W. Hale (R)
William C. Houston (D)
Cordell Hull (D)
John A. Moon (D)
Lemuel P. Padgett (D)
Thetus W. Sims (D)

TEXAS

Senators

Charles A. Culberson (D)
Joseph W. Bailey (D)

Representatives

Jack Beall (D)
George F. Burgess (D)
Albert S. Burleson (D)
Samuel B. Cooper (D)
John Nance Garner (D)
Oscar W. Gillespie (D)
Alexander W. Gregg (D)
Rufus Hardy (D)
Robert L. Henry (D)
John M. Moore (D)
Choice B. Randell (D)
Gordon J. Russell (D)
Morris Sheppard (D)
James L. Slayden (D)
William R. Smith (D)
John H. Stephens (D)

UTAH

Senators

Reed Smoot (R)
George Sutherland (R)

Representative

Joseph Howell (R)

VERMONT

Senators

Redfield Proctor (R) d. Mar. 1908
John W. Stewart (R) ta. 1908
Carroll S. Page (R) s. 1908

William P. Dillingham (R)

Representatives

David J. Foster (R)
Kittredge Haskins (R)

VIRGINIA

Senators

John W. Daniel (D)
Thomas S. Martin (D)

Representatives

Charles C. Carlin (D)
Henry D. Flood (D)
Carter Glass (D)
James Hay (D)
William A. Jones (D)
John Lamb (D)
Francis R. Lassiter (D)
Harry L. Maynard (D)
Edward W. Saunders (D)
C. Bascom Slemp (R) s. 1908

WASHINGTON

Senators

Levi Ankeny (R)
Samuel H. Piles (R)

Representatives

Francis W. Cushman (R)
William E. Humphrey (R)
Wesley L. Jones (R)

WEST VIRGINIA

Senators

Stephen B. Elkins (R)
Nathan B.Scott (R)

Representatives

Joseph H. Gaines (R)
William P. Hubbard (R)
James A. Hughes (R)
George C. Sturgiss (R)
Harry C. Woodyard (R)

WISCONSIN

Senators

John C. Spooner (R) r. Apr. 1907
Isaac Stephenson (R) s. 1907

Robert M. La Follette (R)

Representatives

William J. Cary (R)
Henry A. Cooper (R)
James H. Davison (R)
John J. Esch (R)
John J. Jenkins (R)
Gustav Kustermann (R)
Elmer A. Morse (R)
James W. Murphy (D)
John M. Nelson (R)
William H. Stafford (R)
Charles H. Weisse (D)

WYOMING

Senators

Clarence D. Clark (R)
Francis E. Warren (R)

Representative

Frank W. Mondell (R)

SIXTY-FIRST CONGRESS

March 4, 1908 to March 3, 1911

President of The Senate:	James S. Sherman
President Pro Tempore of The Senate:	William P. Frye
Speaker of The House of Representatives:	Joseph G. Cannon

ALABAMA

Senators

John H. Bankhead (D)
Joseph F. Johnston (D)

Representatives

John L. Burnett (D)
Henry D. Clayton (D)
William B. Craig (D)
S. Hubert Dent, Jr. (D)
J. Thomas Heflin (D)
Richmond P. Hobson (D)
William Richardson (D)
George W. Taylor (D)
Oscar W. Underwood (D)

ARKANSAS

Senators

James P. Clarke (D)
Jeff Davis (D)

Representatives

William B. Cravens (D)
John C. Floyd (D)
Robert B. Macon (D)
William A. Oldfield (D)
Joseph T. Robinson (D)
Charles C. Reid (D)
Robert M. Wallace (D)

CALIFORNIA

Senators

George C. Perkins (R)
Frank P. Flint (R)

Representatives

William F. Englebright (R)
Everis A. Hayes (R)
Julius Kahn (R)
Joseph R. Knowland (R)
Duncan E. McKinlay (R)
James McLachlan (R)
James C. Needham (R)
Sylvester C. Smith (R)

COLORADO

Senators

Simon Guggenheim (R)
Charles J. Hughes, Jr. (D)
d. Jan. 1911

Representatives

John A. Martin (D)
Atterson W. Rucker (D)
Edward T. Taylor (D)

CONNECTICUT

Senators

Morgan G. Bulkeley (R)
Frank B. Brandegee (R)

Representatives

E. Stevens Henry (R)
Edwin W. Higgins (R)
Ebenezer J. Hill (R)
Nehemiah D. Sperry (R)
John Q. Tilson (R)

DELAWARE

Senators

Henry A. Du Pont (R)
Harry A. Richardson (R)

Representative

William H. Heald (R)

FLORIDA

Senators

James P. Taliaferro (D)
Duncan U. Fletcher (D)

Representatives

Frank Clark (D)
Dannitte H. Mays (D)
Stephen M. Sparkman (D)

GEORGIA

Senators

Augustus O. Bacon (D)

Alexander S. Clay (D)
d. Nov. 1910
Joseph M. Terrell (D) s. 1910

Representatives

William C. Adamson (D)
Charles L. Bartlett (D)
Thomas M. Bell (D)
William G. Brantley (D)
Charles G. Edwards (D)
James M. Griggs (D) d. Jan. 1910
Thomas W. Hardwick (D)
William M. Howard (D)
Dudley M. Hughes (D)
Gordon Lee (D)
Leonidas F. Livingston (D)
Seaborn A. Roddenbery (D)
s. 1910

IDAHO

Senators

Weldon B. Heyburn (R)
William E. Borah (R)

Representative

Thomas R. Hamer (R)

ILLINOIS

Senators

Shelby M. Cullom (R)
William Lorimer (R)

Representatives

Henry S. Boutell (R)
Joseph G. Cannon (R)
Pleasant T. Chapman (R)
George E. Foss (R)
Martin D. Foster (D)
Charles E. Fuller (R)
Thomas Gallagher (D)
Joseph V. Graff (R)
James M. Graham (D)
William Lorimer (R) r. June 1909
Frank O. Lowden (R)
Frederick Lundin (R)
James T. McDermott (D)
William B. McKinley (R)
James McKinney (R)
Martin B. Madden (R)
James R. Mann (R)
William J. Moxley (R)
r. June 1909
George W. Prince (R)
Henry T. Rainey (D)
William A. Rodenberg (R)
Adolph J. Sabath (D)
Howard M. Snapp (R)
John A. Sterling (R)
Napoleon B. Thistlewood (R)
William W. Wilson (R)

INDIANA

Senators

Albert J. Beveridge (R)
Benjamin F. Shively (D)

Representatives

John A. M. Adair (D)
William O. Barnard (R)
Henry A. Barnhart (D)
John W. Boehne (D)
Cyrus Cline (D)
William E. Cox (D)
Edgar D.Crumpacker (R)
William A. Cullop (D)
Lincoln Dixon (D)
Charles A. Korbly (D)
Martin A. Morrison (D)
Ralph W. Moss (D)
George W. Rauch (D)

IOWA

Senators

Johnathan P. Dolliver (R)
d. Oct. 1910
Lafayette Young (R) ta. 1910

Albert B. Cummins (R)

Representatives

Albert F. Dawson (R)
James W. Good (R)
Gilbert N. Haugen (R)
Elbert H. Hubbard (R)
John A. T. Hull (R)
William D. Jamieson (D)
Nathan E. Kendall (R)
Charles A. Kennedy (R)
Charles E. Pickett (R)
Walter I. Smith (R)
Frank P. Woods (R)

KANSAS

Senators

Charles Curtis (R)
Joseph L. Bristow (R)

Representatives

Daniel R. Anthony, Jr. (R)
William A. Calderhead (R)
Philip P. Campbell (R)
Edmond H. Madison (R)
James M. Miller (R)
Victor Murdock (R)
William A. Reeder (R)
Charles F. Scott (R)

KENTUCKY

Senators

Thomas H. Paynter (D)
William O. Bradley (R)

Representatives

Joseph B. Bennett (R)
James C. Cantrill (D)
Don C. Edwards (R)
Harvey Helm (D)
Ollie M. James (D)
Ben Johnson (D)

John W. Langley (R)
Joseph L. Rhinock (D)
J. Swagar Sherley (D)
Augustus O. Stanley (D)
Robert Y. Thomas, Jr. (D)

LOUISIANA

Senators

Samuel D. McEnery (D)
d. June 1910
John R. Thornton (D) s. 1910

Murphy J. Foster (D)

Representatives

Robert F. Broussard (D)
H. Garland Dupre (D) s. 1910
Albert Estopinal (D)
Samuel L. Gilmore (D)
d. July 1910
Arsene P. Pujo (D)
Joseph E. Ransdell (D)
John T. Watkins (D)
Robert C. Wickliffe (D)

MAINE

Senators

Eugene Hale (R)
William P. Frye (R)

Representatives

Amos L. Allen (R) d. Feb. 1911
Edwin C. Burleigh (R)
Frank E. Guernsey (R)
John P. Swasey (R)

MARYLAND

Senators

Isidor Rayner (D)
John Walter Smith (D)

Representatives

J. Harry Covington (D)
John Gill, Jr. (D)
John Kronmiller (R)
Sydney E. Mudd (R)
George A. Pearre (R)
J. Fred C. Talbott (D)

MASSACHUSETTS

Senators

Henry Cabot Lodge (R)
W. Murray Crane (R)

Representatives

Butler Ames (R)
Eugene N. Foss (D) s. 1910
Augustus P. Gardner (R)
Frederick H. Gillett (R)
William S. Greene (R)
John A. Keliher (D)
George P. Lawrence (R)
William C. Lovering (R)
d. Feb. 1910
Samuel W. McCall (R)
John J. Mitchell (D) s. 1910
Joseph F. O'Connell (D)
Andrew J. Peters (D)
Ernest W. Roberts (R)
Charles Q. Tirrell (R) d. July 1910

Charles G. Washburn (R)
John W. Weeks (R)

MICHIGAN

Senators

Julius C. Burrows (R)
William Alden Smith (R)

Representatives

Edwin Denby (R)
Gerrit J. Diekema (R)
Francis H. Dodds (R)
Joseph W. Fordney (R)
Washington Gardner (R)
Edward L. Hamilton (R)
George A. Loud (R)
James C. McLaughlin (R)
Henry McMorran (R)
Samuel W. Smith (R)
Charles E. Townsend (R)
H. Olin Young (R)

MINNESOTA

Senators

Knute Nelson (R)
Moses E. Clapp (R)

Representatives

Charles R. Davis (R)
Winfield S. Hammond (D)
Charles A. Lindbergh (R)
Clarence B. Miller (R)
Frank M. Nye (R)
Halvor Steenerson (R)
Frederick C. Stevens (R)
James A. Tawney (R)
Andrew J. Volstead (R)

MISSISSIPPI

Senators

Hernando D. Money (D)

Anselm J. McLaurin (D)
d. Dec. 1909
James Gordon (D) ta. 1910
Le Roy Percy (D) s. 1910

Representatives

Eaton J. Bowers (D)
Adam M. Byrd (D)
Ezekiel S. Candler, Jr. (D)
James W. Collier (D)
William A. Dickson (D)
Benjamin G. Humphreys (D)
Thomas U. Sisson (D)
Thomas Spight (D)

MISSOURI

Senators

William J. Stone (D)
William Warner (R)

Representatives

Joshua W. Alexander (D)
Richard Bartholdt (R)
Charles F. Booher (D)
William P. Borland (D)
Champ Clark (D)
Harry M. Coudrey (R)
Charles A. Crow (R)
David A. De Armond (D)
d. Nov. 1909

Clement C. Dickinson (D) s. 1910
Politte Elvins (R)
Patrick F. Gill (D)
Courtney W. Hamlin (D)
James T. Lloyd (D)
Charles H. Morgan (R)
Arthur P. Murphy (R)
William W. Rucker (D)
Dorsey W. Shackleford (D)

MONTANA

Senators

Thomas H. Carter (R)
Joseph M. Dixon (R)

Representative

Charles N. Pray (R)

NEBRASKA

Senators

Elmer J. Burkett (R)
Norris Brown (R)

Representatives

Edmund H. Hinshaw (R)
Gilbert M. Hitchcock (D)
Moses P. Kinkaid (R)
James P. Latta (D)
John A. Maguire (D)
George W. Norris (R)

NEVADA

Senators

Francis G. Newlands (D)
George S. Nixon (R)

Representative

George A. Bartlett (D)

NEW HAMPSHIRE

Senators

Jacob H. Gallinger (R)
Henry E. Burnham (R)

Representatives

Frank D. Currier (R)
Cyrus A. Sulloway (R)

NEW JERSEY

Senators

John Kean (R)
Frank O. Briggs (R)

Representatives

Charles N. Fowler (R)
John J. Gardner (D)
James A. Hamill (D)
Benjamin F. Howell (R)
William Hughes (D)
Eugene F. Kinkead (D)
Henry C. Loudenslager (R)
Richard W. Parker (R)
William H. Wiley (R)
Ira W. Wood (R)

NEW YORK

Senators

Chauncy M. Depew (R)
Elihu Root (R)

Representatives

De Alva S. Alexander (R)
John E. Andrus (R)
William S. Bennet (R)
Thomas W. Bradley (R)
William M. Calder (R)
William W. Cocks (R)
Michael F. Conry (D)
William H. Draper (R)
Daniel A. Driscoll (D)
Michael E. Driscoll (R)
Cyrus Durey (R)
John W. Dwight (R)
George W. Fairchild (R)
J. Sloat Fassett (R)
Hamilton Fish (R)
John J. Fitzgerald (D)
Otto G. Foelker (R)
Charles V. Fornes (D)
Henry M. Goldfogle (D)
Joseph A. Goulden (D)
Francis B. Harrison (D)
James S. Havens (D) s. 1910
Charles L. Knapp (R)
Charles B. Law (R)
George H. Lindsay (D)
George R. Malby (R)
Charles S. Millington (R)
J. Van Vechten Olcott (R)
Herbert Parsons (R)
Sereno E. Payne (R)
James B. Perkins (R)
d. Mar. 1910
Daniel J. Riordan (D)
James S. Simmons (R)
George N. Southwick (R)
William Sulzer (D)
Edward B. Vreeland (R)
William Willett, Jr. (D)
Richard Young (R)

NORTH CAROLINA

Senators

Furnifold McL. Simmons (D)
Lee S. Overman (D)

Representatives

Charles H. Cowles (R)
Hannibal L. Godwin (D)
John G. Grant (R)
Claude Kitchin (D)
John M. Morehead (R)
Robert N. Page (D)
Edward W. Pou (D)
John H. Small (D)
Charles R. Thomas (D)
Edwin Y. Webb (D)

NORTH DAKOTA

Senators

Porter J. McCumber (R)

Martin N. Johnson (R)
d. Oct. 1909
Fountain L. Thompson (D)
r. Jan. 1910
William E. Purcell (D) ta. 1910
Asle J. Gronna (R) s. 1911

Representatives

Asle J. Gronna (R) r. 1911
Louis B. Hanna (R)

OHIO

Senators

Charles W. F. Dick (R)
Theodore E. Burton (R)

Representatives

Carl C. Anderson (D)
Timothy T. Ansberry (D)
William A. Ashbrook (D)
James H. Cassidy (R)
Ralph D. Cole (R)
James M. Cox (D)
Matthew R. Denver (D)
Albert Douglas (R)
Herman P. Goebel (R)
David A. Hollingsworth (R)
L. Paul Howland (R)
Adna R. Johnson (R)
James Joyce (R)
J. Warren Keifer (R)
James Kennedy (R)
Nicholas Longworth (R)
William G. Sharp (D)
Isaac R. Sherwood (D)
Edward L. Taylor, Jr. (R)
William A. Thomas (R)
William E. Tou Velle (D)

OKLAHOMA

Senators

Thomas P. Gore (D)
Robert L. Owen (D)

Representatives

Charles D. Carter (D)
Charles E. Creager (R)
Scott Ferris (D)
Bird S. McGuire (R)
Dick T. Morgan (R)

OREGON

Senators

Jonathan Bourne, Jr. (R)
George E. Chamberlain (D)

Representatives

William R. Ellis (R)
Willis C. Hawley (R)

PENNSYLVANIA

Senators

Boies Penrose (R)
George T. Oliver (R)

Representatives

Andrew J. Barchfeld (R)
Charles F. Barclay (R)
Arthur L. Bates (R)
Henry H. Bingham (R)
James F. Burke (R)
Thomas S.Butler (R)
Joel Cook (R) d. Dec. 1910
Allen F. Cooper (R)
John Dalzell (R)
Benjamin K. Focht (R)
William W. Foulkrod (R)
d. Nov. 1910
Alfred B. Garner (R)
William H. Graham (R)
William W. Griest (R)
George F. Huff (R)
Daniel F. Lafean (R)
Jonathan N. Langham (R)
George D. McCreary (R)
John G. McHenry (D)
Reuben O. Moon (R)
J. Hampton Moore (R)
Thomas D. Nicholls (D)
Marlin E. Olmsted (R)
A. Mitchell Palmer (D)
Henry W. Palmer (R)
Charles C. Pratt (R)
John M. Reynolds (R)
John H. Rothermel (D)
John K. Tener (R)
Irving P. Wanger (R)
Nelson P. Wheeler (R)
William B. Wilson (D)

RHODE ISLAND

Senators

Nelson W. Aldrich (R)
George P. Wetmore (R)

Representatives

Adin B. Capron (R)
William P. Sheffield (R)

SOUTH CAROLINA

Senators

Benjamin R. Tillman (D)
Ellison D. Smith (D)

Representatives

Wyatt Aiken (D)
J. Edwin Ellerbe (D)
David E. Finley (D)
Joseph T. Johnson (D)
George S. Legare (D)
Asbury F. Lever (D)
James O. Patterson (D)

SOUTH DAKOTA

Senators

Robert J. Gamble (R)
Coe I. Crawford (R)

Representatives

Charles H. Burke (R)
Eben W. Martin (R)

TENNESSEE

Senators

James B. Frazier (D)
Robert L. Taylor (D)

Representatives

Richard W. Austin (R)
Walter P. Brownlow (R)
d. July 1910
Joseph W. Byrns (D)
Finis J. Garrett (D)
George W. Gordon (D)
William C. Houston (D)
Cordell Hull (D)
Zachary D. Massey (R) s. 1910
John A. Moon (D)
Lemuel P. Padgett (D)
Thetus W. Sims (D)

TEXAS

Senators

Charles A. Culberson (D)
Joseph W. Bailey (D)

Representatives

Jack Beall (D)
George F. Burgess (D)
Albert A. Burleson (D)
Martin Dies (D)
John Nance Garner (D)
Oscar W. Gillespie (D)
Alexander W. Gregg (D)
Rufus Hardy (D)
Robert L. Henry (D)
Robert M. Lively (D) s. 1910
John M. Moore (D)
Choice B. Randell (D)
Gordon J. Russell (D) r. June 1910
Morris Sheppard (D)
James L. Slayden (D)
William R. Smith (D)
John H. Stephens (D)

UTAH

Senators

Reed Smoot (R)
George Sutherland (R)

Representative

Joseph Howell (R)

VERMONT

Senators

William P. Dillingham (R)
Carroll S. Page (R)

Representatives

David J. Foster (R)
Frank Plumley (R)

VIRGINIA

Senators

John W. Daniel (D) d. June 1910
Claude A. Swanson (D) s. 1910

Thomas S. Martin (D)

Representatives

Charles C. Carlin (D)
Henry D. Flood (D)
Carter Glass (D)
James Hay (D)
William A. Jones (D)
John Lamb (D)
Francis R. Lassiter (D)
d. Oct. 1909
Harry L. Maynard (D)
Edward W. Saunders (D)
C. Bascom Slemp (R)
Robert Turnbull (D) s. 1910

WASHINGTON

Senators

Samuel H. Piles (R)
Wesley L. Jones (R)

Representatives

Francis W. Cushman (R)
d. July 1909
William E. Humphrey (R)
William W. McCredie (R)
Miles Poindexter (R)

WEST VIRGINIA

Senators

Stephen B. Elkins (R) d. Jan. 1911
Davis Elkins (R) ta. 1911
Clarence W. Watson (D) s. 1911

Nathan B. Scott (R)

Representatives

Joseph H. Gaines (R)
William P. Hubbard (R)
James A. Hughes (R)
George C. Sturgiss (R)
Harry C. Woodyard (R)

WISCONSIN

Senators

Robert M. La Follette (R)
Isaac Stephenson (R)

Representatives

William J. Cary (R)
Henry A. Cooper (R)
James H. Davidson (R)
John J. Esch (R)
Arthur W. Kopp (R)
Gustav Kustermann (R)
Irvine L. Lenroot (R)
Elmer A. Morse (R)
John M. Nelson (R)
William H. Stafford (R)
Charles H. Weisse (D)

WYOMING

Senators

Clarence D. Clark (R)
Francis E. Warren (R)

Representative

Frank W. Mondell (R)

SIXTY-SECOND CONGRESS

March 4, 1911 to March 3, 1913

President of The Senate: James S. Sherman
Presidents Pro Tempore of The Senate: William P. Frye
Charles Curtis
Augustus O. Bacon
Jacob H. Gallinger
Henry Cabot Lodge
Frank B. Brandegee
Speaker of The House of Representatives: Champ Clark

ALABAMA

Senators

John H. Bankhead (D)
Joseph F. Johnston (D)

Representatives

Fred L. Blackmon (D)
John L. Burnett (D)
Henry D. Clayton (D)
S. Hubert Dent, Jr. (D)
J. Thomas Heflin (D)
Richmond P. Hobson (D)
William Richardson (D)
George W. Taylor (D)
Oscar W. Underwood (D)

ARIZONA

Senators

Henry F. Ashurst (D) s. 1912
Marcus A. Smith (D) s. 1912

Representative

Carl Hayden (D) s. 1912

ARKANSAS

Senators

James P. Clarke (D)

Jeff Davis (D) d. Jan. 1913
John N. Heiskell (D) ta. 1913
William M. Kavanaugh (D) s. 1913

Representatives

William B. Cravens (D)
John C. Floyd (D)
William S. Goodwin (D)
Henderson M. Jacoway (D)
Robert B. Macon (D)
William A. Oldfield (D)
Joseph T. Robinson (D)
r. Jan. 1913
Samuel M. Taylor (D) s. 1913

CALIFORNIA

Senators

George C. Perkins (R)
John D. Works (R)

Representatives

Everis A. Hayes (R)
Julius Kahn (R)
William Kent (R)
Joseph R. Knowland (R)
James C. Needham (R)
John E. Raker (D)
Sylvester C. Smith (R) d. Jan. 1913
William D. Stephens (R)

COLORADO

Senators

Simon Guggenheim (R)
Charles S. Thomas (D) s. 1913

Representatives

John A. Martin (D)
Atterson W. Rucker (D)
Edward T. Taylor (D)

CONNECTICUT

Senators

Frank B. Brandegee (R)
George P. McLean (R)

Representatives

E. Stevens Henry (R)
Edwin W. Higgins (R)
Ebenezer J. Hill (R)
Thomas L. Reilly (D)
John Q. Tilson (R)

DELAWARE

Senators

Henry A. Du Pont (R)
Harry A. Richardson (R)

Representative

William H. Heald (R)

FLORIDA

Senators

Duncan U. Fletcher (D)
Nathan P. Bryan (D)

Representatives

Frank Clark (D)
Dannitte H. Mays (D)
Stephen M. Sparkman (D)

GEORGIA

Senators

Augustus O. Bacon (D)

Joseph M. Terrell (D) r. July 1911
Hoke Smith (D) s. 1911

Representatives

William C. Adamson (D)
Charles L. Bartlett (D)
Thomas M. Bell (D)
William G. Brantley (D)
Charles G. Edwards (D)
Thomas W. Hardwick (D)
William S. Howard (D)
Dudley M. Hughes (D)
Gordon Lee (D)
Seaborn A. Roddenbery (D)
Samuel J. Tribble (D)

IDAHO

Senators

Weldon B. Heyburn (R) d. Oct. 1911
Kirtland I. Perky (D) ta. 1912
James H. Brady (R) s. 1913

William E. Borah (R)

Representative

Burton L. French (R)

ILLINOIS

Senators

Shelby M. Cullom (R)
William Lorimer (R) r. July 1912

Representatives

Frank Buchanan (D)
Joseph G. Cannon (R)
Ira C. Copley (R)
Lynden Evans (D)
George E. Foss (R)
Martin D. Foster (D)
H. Robert Fowler (D)
Charles E. Fuller (R)
Thomas Gallagher (D)
James M. Graham (D)
James T. McDermott (D)
John C. McKenzie (R)
William B. McKinley (R)
James McKinney (R)
Martin B. Madden (R)
James R. Mann (R)
George W. Prince (R)
Henry T. Rainey (D)
William A. Rodenberg (R)
Adolph J. Sabath (D)
Edmund J. Stack (D)
John A. Sterling (R)
Claudius U. Stone (D)
Napoleon B. Thistlewood (R)
William W. Wilson (R)

INDIANA

Senators

Benjamin F. Shively (D)
John W. Kern (D)

Representatives

John A. M. Adair (D)
Henry A. Barnhart (D)
John W. Boehne (D)
Cyrus Cline (D)
William E. Cox (D)
Edgard D. Crumpacker (R)
William A. Cullop (D)
Lincoln Dixon(D)
Finly H. Gray (D)
Charles A. Korbly (D)
Martin A. Morrison (D)
Ralph W. Moss (D)
George W. Rauch (D)

IOWA

Senators

Albert B. Cummins (R)
William S. Kenyon (R)

Representatives

James W. Good (R)
William R. Green (R)
Gilbert N. Haugen (R)
Elbert H. Hubbard (R)
d. June 1912
Nathan E. Kendall (R)
Charles A. Kennedy (R)
Irvin S. Pepper (D)
Charles E. Pickett (R)
Solomon F. Prouty (R)
George C. Scott (R) s. 1912
Walter I. Smith (R) r. Mar. 1911
Horace M. Towner (R)
Frank P. Woods (R)

KANSAS

Senators

Charles Curtis (R)
Joseph L. Bristow (R)

Representatives

Daniel R. Anthony Jr. (R)
Philip P. Campbell (R)
Fred S. Jackson (R)
Edmond H. Madison (R)
d. Sept. 1911
Alexander C. Mitchell (R)
d. July 1911
Victor Murdock (R)
George A. Neeley (D) s. 1912
Rollin R. Rees (R)
Joseph Taggart (D)
Isaac D. Young (R)

KENTUCKY

Senators

Thomas H.Paynter (D)
William O. Bradley (R)

Representatives

James C. Cantrill (D)
William J. Fields (D)
Harvey Helm (D)
Ollie M. James (D)
Ben Johnson (D)
John W. Langley (R)
Caleb Powers (R)
Arthur B. Rouse (D)
J. Swagar Sherley (D)
Augustus O. Stanley (D)
Robert Y. Thomas, Jr. (D)

LOUISIANA

Senators

Murphy J. Foster (D)
John R. Thornton (D)

Representatives

Robert F. Broussard (D)
H. Garland Dupre (D)
Albert Estopinal (D)
Lewis L. Morgan (D) s. 1912
Arsene P. Pujo (D)
Joseph E. Ransdell (D)
John T. Watkins (D)
Robert C. Wickliffe (D)
d. June 1912

MAINE

Senators

William P. Frye (R) d. Aug. 1911
Obadiah Gardner (D) s. 1911

Charles F. Johnson (D)

Representatives

Samuel W. Gould (D)
Frank E. Guernsey (R)
Asher C. Hinds (R)
Daniel J. McGillicuddy (D)

MARYLAND

Senators

Isidor Rayner (D) d. Nov. 1912
William P. Jackson (R) ta. 1912

John Walter Smith (D)

Representatives

J. Harry Covington (D)
George Konig (D)
David J. Lewis (D)
J. Charles Linthicum (D)
Thomas Parran (R)
J. Fred C. Talbott (D)

MASSACHUSETTS

Senators

Henry Cabot Lodge (R)
W. Murray Crane (R)

Representatives

Butler Ames (R)
James M. Curley (D)
Augustus P. Gardner (R)
Frederick H. Gillett (R)
William S. Greene (R)
Robert O. Harris (R)
George P. Lawrence (R)
Samuel W. McCall (R)
William F. Murray (D)
Andrew J. Peters (D)
Ernest W. Roberts (R)
John A. Thayer (D)
John W. Weeks (R)
William H. Wilder (R)

MICHIGAN

Senators

William Alden Smith (R)
Charles E. Townsend (R)

Representatives

Francis H. Dodds (R)
Frank E. Doremus (D)
Joseph W. Fordney (R)
Edward L. Hamilton (R)
George A. Loud (R)
James C. McLaughlin (R)
Henry McMorran (R)
John M. C. Smith (R)
Samuel W. Smith (R)
Edwin F. Sweet (D)
William W. Wedemeyer (R)
d. Jan. 1913
H. Olin Young (R)

MINNESOTA

Senators

Knute Nelson (R)
Moses E. Clapp (R)

Representatives

Sydney Anderson (R)
Charles R. Davis (R)
Winfield S. Hammond (D)
Charles A. Lindbergh (R)
Clarence B. Miller (R)
Frank M. Nye (R)
Halvor Steenerson (R)
Frederick C. Stevens (R)
Andrew J. Volstead (R)

MISSISSIPPI

Senators

Le Roy Percy (D)
John Sharp Williams (D)

Representatives

Ezekiel S. Candler, Jr. (D)
James W. Collier (D)
William A. Dickson (D)
Pat Harrison (D)
Benjamin G. Humphreys (D)
Thomas U. Sisson (D)
Hubert D. Stephens (D)
Samuel A. Witherspoon (D)

MISSOURI

Senators

William J. Stone (D)
James A. Reed (D)

Representatives

Joshua W. Alexander (D)
Richard Bartholdt (R)
Charles F. Booher (D)
William P. Borland (D)
Theron E. Catlin (R) r. Aug. 1912
Champ Clark (D)
James A. Daugherty (D)
Clement C. Dickinson (D)
Leonidas C. Dyer (R)
Patrick F. Gill (D) s. 1912
Courtney H. Hamlin (D)
Walter L. Hensley (D)
James T. Lloyd (D)
Thomas L. Rubey (D)
William W. Rucker (D)
Joseph J. Russell (D)
Dorsey W. Shackleford (D)

MONTANA

Senators

Joseph M. Dixon (R)
Henry L. Myers (D)

Representative

Charles N. Pray (R)

NEBRASKA

Senators

Norris Brown (R)
Gilbert M. Hitchcock (D)

Representatives

Moses P. Kinkaid (R)
James P. Latta (D) d. Sept. 1911
Charles O. Lobeck (D)
John A. Maguire (D)
George W. Norris (R)
Charles H. Sloan (R)
Daniel V. Stephens (D)

NEVADA

Senators

Francis G. Newlands (D)

George S. Nixon (R) d. June 1912
William A. Massey (R) ta. 1912
Key Pittman (D) s. 1913

Representative

Edwin E. Roberts (R)

NEW HAMPSHIRE

Senators

Jacob H. Gallinger (R)
Henry E. Burnham (R)

Representatives

Frank D. Currier (R)
Cyrus A. Sulloway (R)

NEW JERSEY

Senators

Frank O. Briggs (R)
James E. Martine (D)

Representatives

William J. Browning (R)
John J. Gardner (D)
James A. Hamill (D)
Archibald C. Hart (D) s. 1912
William Hughes (D) r. Sept. 1912
Eugene F. Kinkead (D)
Henry C. Loudenslager (R)
d. Aug. 1911
Walter I. McCoy (D)
Thomas J. Scully (D)
Edward W. Townsend (D)
William E. Tuttle, Jr. (D)
Ira W. Wood (R)

NEW MEXICO

Senators

Thomas B. Catron (R) s. 1912
Albert B. Fall (R) s. 1912

Representatives

George Curry (R) s. 1912
Harvey B. Fergusson (D) s. 1912

NEW YORK

Senators

Elihu Root (R)
James A. O'Gorman (D)

Representatives

Theron Akin (R)
John E. Andrus (R)
Steven B. Ayres (D)
Thomas W. Bradley (R)
William M. Calder (R)
Richard E. Connell (D)
d. Oct. 1912
Michael F. Conry (D)
Henry G. Danforth (R)
Henry S. De Forest (R)
William H. Draper (R)
Daniel A. Driscoll (D)
Michael E. Driscoll (R)
John W. Dwight (R)
George W. Fairchild (R)
John J. Fitzgerald (D)
Charles V. Fornes (D)
Henry George Jr. (D)
Henry M. Goldfogle (D)
Francis B. Harrison (D)
John J. Kindred (D)
Jefferson M. Levy (D)
George H. Lindsay (D)
Martin W. Littleton (D)
James P. Maher (D)
George R. Malby (D) d. July 1912
Edwin A. Merritt, Jr. (R) s. 1912
Luther W. Mott (R)
Thomas G. Patten (D)
Sereno E. Payne (R)
William C. Redfield (D)
Daniel J. Riordan (D)
James S. Simmons (R)
Charles B. Smith (D)
William Sulzer (D) r. 1912
Charles A. Talcott (D)
Edwin S. Underhill (D)
Edward B. Vreeland (R)
Frank E. Wilson (D)

NORTH CAROLINA

Senators

Furnifold McL. Simmons (D)
Lee S. Overman (D)

Representatives

Robert L. Doughton (D)
John M. Faison (D)
Hannibal L. Godwin (D)
James M. Gudger, Jr. (D)
Claude Kitchin (D)
Robert N. Page (D)
Edward W. Pou (D)
John H. Small (D)
Charles M. Stedman (D)
Edwin Y. Webb (D)

NORTH DAKOTA

Senators

Porter J. McCumber (R)
Asle J. Gronna (R)

Representatives

Louis B. Hanna (R) r. Jan. 1913
Henry T. Helgesen (R)

OHIO

Senators

Theodore E. Burton (R)
Atlee Pomerene (D)

Representatives

Alfred G. Allen (D)
Carl C. Anderson (D) d. Oct. 1912
Timothy T. Ansberry (D)
William A. Ashbrook (D)
Ellsworth R. Bathrick (D)
Robert J. Bulkley (D)
Horatio C. Claypool (D)
James M. Cox (D) r. Jan. 1913
Matthew R. Denver (D)
William B. Francis (D)
J. Henry Goeke (D)
L. Paul Howland (R)
Nicholas Longworth (R)
James D. Post (D)
William G. Sharp (D)
Isaac R. Sherwood (D)
Robert M. Switzer (R)
Edward L. Taylor, Jr. (R)
John J. Whitacre (D)
George White (D)
Frank B. Willis (R)

OKLAHOMA

Senators

Thomas P. Gore (D)
Robert L. Owen (D)

Representatives

Charles D. Carter (D)
James S. Davenport (D)
Scott Ferris (D)
Bird S. McGuire (R)
Dick T. Morgan (R)

OREGON

Senators

Jonathan Bourne, Jr. (R)
George E. Chamberlain (D)

Representatives

Willis C. Hawley (R)
Abraham W. Lafferty (R)

PENNSYLVANIA

Senators

Boies Penrose (R)
George T. Oliver (R)

Representatives

William D. B. Ainey (R)
Andrew J. Barchfeld (R)
Arthur L. Bates (R)
Henry H. Bingham (R) d. Mar. 1912
Charles C. Bowman (R) r. Dec. 1912
James F. Burke (R)
Thomas S. Butler (R)
Thomas S. Crago (R)
John Dalzell (R)
Robert E. Diffenderfer (D)
Michael Donohoe (D)
John R. Farr (R)
Benjamin K. Focht (R)
Curtis H. Gregg (D)
William W. Griest (R)
Jesse L. Hartman (R)
George W. Kipp (D) d. July 1911
Daniel F. Lafean (R)
Jonathan N. Langham (R)
Robert E. Lee (D)
George D. McCreary (D)
John G. McHenry (D)
d. Dec. 1912
Charles Matthews (R)
Reuben O. Moon (R)
J. Hampton Moore (R)
Marlin E. Olmsted (R)
A. Mitchell Palmer (D)
Charles E. Patton (R)
Stephen G. Porter (R)
William S. Reyburn (R)
John H. Rothermel (D)
Peter M. Speer (R)
William S. Vare (R) s. 1912
William B. Wilson (D)

RHODE ISLAND

Senators

George P. Wetmore (R)
Henry F. Lippitt (R)

Representatives

George F. O'Shaunessy (D)
George H. Utter (R) d. Nov. 1912

SOUTH CAROLINA

Senators

Benjamin R. Tillman (D)
Ellison D. Smith (D)

Representatives

Wyatt Aiken (D)
James F. Byrnes (D)
J. Edwin Ellerbe (D)
David E. Finley (D)
Joseph T. Johnson (D)
George S. Legare (D) d. Jan. 1913
Asbury F. Lever (D)

SOUTH DAKOTA

Senators

Robert J. Gamble (R)
Coe I. Crawford (R)

Representatives

Charles H. Burke (R)
Eben W. Martin (R)

TENNESSEE

Senators

Robert L. Taylor (D) d. Mar. 1912
Newell Sanders (R) ta. 1912
William R. Webb (D) s. 1913
Luke Lea (D)

Representatives

Richard W. Austin (R)
Joseph W. Byrns (D)
Finis J. Garrett (D)
George W. Gordon (D)
d. Aug. 1911
William C. Houston (D)
Cordell Hull (D)
Kenneth D. McKellar (D)
John A. Moon (D)
Lemuel P. Padgett (D)
Sam R. Sells (R)
Thetus W. Sims (D)

TEXAS

Senators

Charles A. Culberson (D)

Joseph W. Bailey (D) r. Jan. 1913
Rienzi M. Johnston (D) ta. 1913
Morris Sheppard (D) s. 1913

Representatives

Jack Beall (D)
George F. Burgess (D)
Albert S. Burleson (D)
Oscar Callaway (D)
Martin Dies (D)
John Nance Garner (D)
Alexander W. Gregg (D)
Rufus Hardy (D)
Robert L. Henry (D)
John M. Moore (D)
Choice B. Randell (D)
Morris Sheppard (D) r. Feb. 1913
James L. Slayden (D)
William R. Smith (D)
John H. Stephens (D)
James Young (D)

UTAH

Senators

Reed Smoot (R)
George Sutherland (R)

Representative

Joseph Howell (R)

VERMONT

Senators

William P. Dillingham (R)
Carroll S. Page (R)

Representatives

David J. Foster (R) d. Mar. 1912
Frank L. Greene (R) s. 1912
Frank Plumley (R)

VIRGINIA

Senators

Thomas S. Martin (D)
Claude A. Swanson (D)

Representatives

Charles C. Carlin (D)
Henry D. Flood (D)
Carter Glass (D)
James Hay (D)
Edward E. Holland (D)
William A. Jones (D)
John Lamb (D)
Edward W. Saunders (D)
C. Bascom Slemp (R)
Robert Turnbull (D)

WASHINGTON

Senators

Wesley L. Jones (R)
Miles Poindexter (R)

Representatives

William E. Humphrey (R)
William L. La Follette (R)
Stanton Warburton (R)

WEST VIRGINIA

Senators

Clarence W. Watson (D)
William E. Chilton (D)

Representatives

William G. Brown, Jr. (D)
John W. Davis (D)
John M. Hamilton (D)
James A. Hughes (R)
Adam B. Littlepage (D)

WISCONSIN

Senators

Robert M. La Follette (R)
Isaac Stephenson (R)

Representatives

Victor L. Berger (Socialist)
Michael E. Burke (D)
William J. Cary (R)
Henry A. Cooper (R)
James H. Davidson (R)
John J. Esch (R)
Thomas F. Konop (D)
Arthur W. Kopp (R)
Irvine L. Lenroot (R)
Elmer A. Morse (R)
John M. Nelson (R)

WYOMING

Senators

Clarence D. Clark (R)
Francis E. Warren (R)

Representative

Frank W. Mondell (R)

SIXTY-THIRD CONGRESS

March 4, 1913 to March 3, 1915

President of The Senate: Thomas R. Marshall
President Pro Tempore of The Senate: James P. Clarke
Speaker of The House of Representatives: Champ Clark

ALABAMA

Senators

John H. Bankhead (D)

Joseph F. Johnston (D)
d. Aug. 1913
Frank S. White (D) s. 1914

Representatives

John W. Abercrombie (D)
Fred L. Blackmon (D)
John L. Burnett (D)
Henry D. Clayton (D)
r. May 1914
S. Hubert Dent, Jr. (D)
Christopher C. Harris (D) s. 1914
J. Thomas Heflin (D)
Richmond P. Hobson (D)
William O. Mulkey (D) s. 1914
William Richardson (D)
d. Mar. 1914
George W. Taylor (D)
Oscar W. Underwood (D)

ARIZONA

Senators

Henry F. Ashurst (D)
Marcus A. Smith (D)

Representative

Carl Hayden (D)

ARKANSAS

Senators

James P. Clarke (D)
Joseph T. Robinson (D)

Representatives

Thaddeus H. Caraway (D)
John C. Floyd (D)
William S. Goodwin (D)
Henderson M. Jacoway (D)
William A. Oldfield (D)
Samuel M. Taylor (D)
Otis Wingo (D)

CALIFORNIA

Senators

George C. Perkins (R)
John D. Works (R)

Representatives

Charles W. Bell (R)
Denver S. Church (D)
Charles F. Curry (R)
Everis A. Hayes (R)
Julius Kahn (R)
William Kettner (D)
William Kent
Joseph R. Knowland (R)
John I. Nolan (R)
John E. Raker (D)
William D. Stephens (R)

COLORADO

Senators

Charles S. Thomas (D)
John F. Shafroth (D)

Representatives

Edward Keating (D)
George J. Kindel (D)
Harry H. Seldomridge (D)
Edward T. Taylor (D)

CONNECTICUT

Senators

Frank B. Brandegee (R)
George P. McLean (R)

Representatives

Jeremiah Donovan (D)
William Kennedy (D)
Augustine Lonergan (D)
Bryan F. Mahan (D)
Thomas L. Reilly (D)

DELAWARE

Senators

Henry A. Du Pont (R)
Willard Saulsbury (D)

Representative

Franklin Brockson (D)

FLORIDA

Senators

Duncan U. Fletcher (D)
Nathan P. Bryan (D)

Representatives

Frank Clark (D)
Claude L'Engle (D)
Stephen M. Sparkman (D)
Emmett Wilson (D)

GEORGIA

Senators

Augustine O. Bacon (D)
d. Feb. 1914
William S. West (D) ta. 1914
Thomas W. Hardwick (D) s. 1914

Hoke Smith (D)

Representatives

William C. Adamson (D)
Charles L. Bartlett (D)
Thomas M. Bell (D)
Charles R. Crisp (D)
Charles G. Edwards (D)
Thomas W. Hardwick (D)
r. Nov. 1914
William S. Howard (D)
Dudley M. Hughes (D)
Gordon Lee (D)
Frank Park (D)
Seaborn A. Roddenbery (D)
d. Sept. 1913
Samuel J. Tribble (D)
Carl Vinson (D) s. 1914
John R. Walker (D)

IDAHO

Senators

William E. Borah (R)
James H. Brady (R)

Representatives

Burton L. French (R)
Addison T. Smith (R)

ILLINOIS

Senators

James H. Lewis (D)
Lawrence Y. Sherman (R)

Representatives

William N. Baltz (D)
Charles M. Borchers (D)
Fred A. Britten (R)
Frank Buchanan (D)
Ira C. Copley (R)
Louis FitzHenry (D)
Martin D. Foster (D)
H. Robert Fowler (D)
Thomas Gallagher (D)
George E. Gorman (D)
James M. Graham (D)
Robert P. Hill (D)
William H. Hinebaugh
(Progressive)
Stephen Hoxworth (D)
James McAndrews (D)
James T. McDermott (D) s. 1914
John C. McKenzie (R)
Martin B. Madden (R)
James R. Mann (R)
Frank T. O'Hair (D)
Henry T. Rainey (D)
Adolph J. Sabath (D)
Claudius U. Stone (D)
Lawrence B. Stringer (D)
Clyde H. Tavenner (D)
Charles M. Thomson (R)
William E. Williams (D)

INDIANA

Senators

Benjamin F. Shively (D)
John W. Kern (D)

Representatives

John A. M. Adair (D)
Henry A. Barnhart (D)
Cyrus Cline (D)
William E. Cox (D)
William A. Cullop (D)
Lincoln Dixon (D)
Finly H. Gray (D)
Charles A. Korbly (D)
Charles Lieb (D)
Martin A. Morrison (D)
Ralph W. Moss (D)
John B. Peterson (D)
George W. Rauch (D)

IOWA

Senators

Albert B. Cummins (R)
William S. Kenyon (R)

Representatives

Maurice Connolly (D)
James W. Good (R)
William R. Green (R)
Gilbert N. Haugen (R)
Charles A. Kennedy (R)
Sanford Kirkpatrick (D)
Irvin S. Pepper (D) d. Dec. 1913
Solomon F. Prouty (R)
George C. Scott (R)
Horace M. Towner (R)
Henry Vollmer (D) s. 1914
Frank P. Woods (R)

KANSAS

Senators

Joseph L. Bristow (R)
William H. Thompson (D)

Representatives

Daniel R. Anthony, Jr. (R)
Philip P. Campbell (R)
John R. Connelly (D)
Dudley Doolittle (D)
Guy T. Helvering (D)
Victor Murdock (R)
George A. Neeley (D)
Joseph Taggart (D)

KENTUCKY

Senators

William O. Bradley (R)
d. May 1914
Johnson N. Camden (D) s. 1914

Ollie M. James (D)

Representatives

Alben W. Barkley (D)
James C. Cantrill (D)
William J. Fields (D)
Harvey Helm (D)
Ben Johnson (D)
John W. Langley (R)
Caleb Powers (R)
Arthur B. Rouse (D)
J. Swagar Sherley (D)
Augustus O. Stanley (D)
Robert Y. Thomas, Jr. (D)

LOUISIANA

Senators

John R. Thornton (D)
Joseph E. Ransdell (D)

Representatives

James B. Aswell (D)
Robert F. Broussard (D)
H. Garland Dupre

J. Walter Elder (D)
Albert Estopinal (D)
Ladislas Lazaro (D)
Lewis L. Morgan (D)
John T. Watkins (D)

MAINE

Senators

Charles F. Johnson (D)
Edwin C. Burleigh (R)

Representatives

Forrest Goodwin (R) d. May 1913
Frank E. Guernsey (R)
Asher C. Hinds (R)
Daniel J. McGillicuddy (D)
John A. Peters (R)

MARYLAND

Senators

John Walter Smith (D)

William P. Jackson (R) r. 1914
Blair Lee (D) s. 1914

Representatives

Charles P. Coady (D)
J. Harry Covington (D) r. Sept. 1914
George Konig (D) d. May 1913
David J. Lewis (D)
J. Charles Linthicum (D)
Jesse D. Price (D) s. 1914
Frank O. Smith (D)
J. Fred C. Talbott (D)

MASSACHUSETTS

Senators

Henry Cabot Lodge (R)
John W. Weeks (R)

Representatives

James M. Curley (D) r. Feb. 1914
Frederick S. Deitrick (D)
James A. Gallivan (D) s. 1914
Augustus P. Gardner (R)
Frederick H. Gillett (R)
Edward Gilmore (D)
William S. Greene (R)
John J. Mitchell (D)
William F. Murray (D) r. Sept. 1914
Calvin D. Paige (R)
Andrew J. Peters (D) r. Aug. 1914
Michael F. Phelan (D)
Ernest W. Roberts (R)
John Jacob Rogers (R)
Thomas C. Thacher (D)
Allen T. Treadway (R)
William H. Wilder (R) d. Sept. 1913
Samuel E. Winslow (R)

MICHIGAN

Senators

William Alden Smith (R)
Charles E. Townsend (R)

Representatives

Samuel W. Beakes (D)
Louis C. Cramton (R)
Frank E. Doremus (D)
Joseph W. Fordney (R)
Edward L. Hamilton (R)
Patrick H. Kelley (R)
Francis O. Lindquist (R)
William J. MacDonald (Progressive)
James C. McLaughlin (R)
Carl E. Mapes (R)
John M. C. Smith (R)
Samuel W. Smith (R)
Roy O. Woodruff (R)
H. Olin Young (R) r. May 1913

MINNESOTA

Senators

Knute Nelson (R)
Moses E. Clapp (R)

Representatives

Sydney Anderson (R)
Charles R. Davis (R)
Winfield S. Hammond (D) r. 1915
Charles A. Lindbergh (R)
James Manahan (R)
Clarence B. Miller (R)
George R. Smith (R)
Halvor Steenerson (R)
Frederick C. Stevens (R)
Andrew J. Volstead (R)

MISSISSIPPI

Senators

John Sharp Williams (D)
James K. Vardaman (D)

Representatives

Ezekiel S. Candler, Jr. (D)
James W. Collier
Pat Harrison (D)
Benjamin G. Humphreys (D)
Percy E. Quin (D)
Thomas U. Sisson (D)
Hubert D. Stephens (D)
Samuel A. Witherspoon (D)

MISSOURI

Senators

William J. Stone (D)
James A. Reed (D)

Representatives

Joshua W. Alexander (D)
Richard Bartholdt (R)
Charles F. Booher (D)
William P. Borland (D)
Champ Clark (D)
Perl D. Decker (D)
Clement C. Dickinson (D)
Leonidas C. Dyer (R) r. June 1914
Michael J. Gill (D) s. 1914
Courtney W. Hamlin (D)
Walter L. Hensley (D)
William L. Igoe (D)
James T. Lloyd (D)
Thomas L. Rubey (D)
William W. Rucker (D)
Joseph J. Russell (D)
Dorsey W. Shackleford (D)

MONTANA

Senators

Henry L. Myers (D)
Thomas J. Walsh (D)

Representatives

John M. Evans (D)
Tom Stout (D)

NEBRASKA

Senators

Gilbert M. Hitchcock (D)
George W. Norris (R)

Representatives

Silas R. Barton (R)
Moses P. Kinkaid (R)
Charles O. Lobeck (D)
John A. Maguire (D)
Charles H. Sloan (R)
Daniel V. Stephens (D)

NEVADA

Senators

Francis G. Newlands (D)
Key Pittman (D)

Representative

Edwin E. Roberts (R)

NEW HAMPSHIRE

Senators

Jacob H. Gallinger (R)
Henry F. Hollis (D)

Representatives

Eugene E. Reed (D)
Raymond B. Stevens (D)

NEW JERSEY

Senators

James E. Martine (D)
William Hughes (D)

Representatives

J. Thompson Baker (D)
Robert G. Bremner (D) d. Feb. 1914
William J. Browning (R)
Dow H. Drukker (R) s. 1914
John J. Eagan (D)
James A. Hamill (D)
Archibald C. Hart (D)
Eugene F. Kinkead (D) r. Feb. 1915
Walter I. McCoy (D) r. Oct. 1914
Lewis J. Martin (D) d. May 1913
Richard W. Parker (R) s. 1914
Thomas J. Scully (D)
Edward W. Townsend (D)
William E. Tuttle, Jr. (D)
Allan B. Walsh (D)

NEW MEXICO

Senators

Thomas B. Catron (R)
Albert B. Fall (R)

Representative

Harvey B. Fergusson (D)

NEW YORK

Senators

Elihu Root (R)
James A. O'Gorman (D)

Representatives

Lathrop Brown (D)
Henry Bruckner (D)
William M. Calder (R)
Jacob A. Cantor (D)
John F. Carew (D)
Walter M. Chandler (Progressive)
John R. Clancy (D)
Michael F. Conry (D)
Harry H. Dale (D)
Henry G. Danforth (R)
Peter J. Dooling (D)
Daniel A. Driscoll (D)
Thomas B. Dunn (R)
George W. Fairchild (R)
John J. Fitzgerald (D)
Henry George, Jr. (D)
Robert H. Gittins (D)
Henry M. Goldfogle (D)
Joseph A. Goulden (D)
Daniel J. Griffin (D)
Charles M. Hamilton (R)
Francis B. Harrison (D) r. Sept. 1913
Jefferson M. Levy (D)
George W. Loft (D)
George McClellan (D)
James P. Maher (D)
Edwin A. Merritt, Jr. (R) d. Dec. 1914
Herman A. Metz (D)
Luther W. Mott (R)
James H. O'Brien (D)
Woodson R. Oglesby (D)
Denis O'Leary (D) r. Dec. 1914
James S. Parker (R)
Thomas G. Patten (D)
Sereno E. Payne (R) d. Dec. 1914
Edmund Platt (R)
Daniel J. Riordan (D)
Charles B. Smith (D)
Timothy D. Sullivan (D) d. Aug. 1913
Charles A. Talcott (D)
Benjamin I. Taylor (D)
Peter G. Ten Eyck (D)
Edwin S. Underhill (D)
Samuel Wallin (R)
Frank E. Wilson (D)

NORTH CAROLINA

Senators

Furnifold McL. Simmons (D)
Lee S. Overman (D)

Representatives

Robert L. Doughton (D)
John M. Faison (D)
Hannibal L. Godwin (D)
James M. Gudger, Jr. (D)
Claude Kitchin (D)
Robert N. Page (D)
Edward W. Pou (D)
John H. Small (D)
Charles M. Stedman (D)
Edwin Y. Webb (D)

NORTH DAKOTA

Senators

Porter J. McCumber (R)
Asle J. Gronna (R)

Representatives

Henry T. Helgesen (R)
Patrick D. Norton (R)
George M. Young (R)

OHIO

Senators

Theodore E. Burton (R)
Atlee Pomerene (D)

Representatives

Alfred G. Allen (D)
Timothy T. Ansberry (D) r. Jan. 1915
William A. Ashbrook (D)
Ellsworth R. Bathrick (D)
Stanley E. Bowdle (D)
Clement L. Brumbaugh (D)
Robert J. Bulkley (D)
Horatio C. Claypool (D)
Robert Crosser (D)
Simeon D. Fess (R)
William B. Francis (D)
Warren Gard (D)
J. Henry Goeke (D)
William Gordon (D)
John A. Key (D)
James D. Post (D)
William G. Sharp (D) r. July 1914
Isaac R. Sherwood (D)
Robert M. Switzer (R)
John J. Whitacre (D)
George White (D)
Frank B. Willis (R) r. Jan. 1915

OKLAHOMA

Senators

Thomas P. Gore (D)
Robert L. Owen (D)

Representatives

Charles D. Carter (D)
James S. Davenport (D)
Scott Ferris (D)
Bird S. McGuire (R)
Dick T. Morgan (R)
William H. Murray (D)
Joseph B. Thompson (D)
Claude Weaver (D)

OREGON

Senators

George E. Chamberlain (D)
Harry Lane (D)

Representatives

Willis C. Hawley (R)
Abraham W. Lafferty (R)
Nicholas J. Sinnott (R)

PENNSYLVANIA

Senators

Boies Penrose (R)
George T. Oliver (R)

Representatives

William D. B. Ainey (R)
Warren W. Bailey (D)
Andrew J. Barchfeld (R)
Andrew R. Brodbeck (D)
James F. Burke (R)
Thomas S. Butler (R)
Wooda N. Carr (D)
John J. Casey (D)
Frank L. Dershem (D)
Robert E. Diffenderfer (D)
Michael Donohoe (D)
George W. Edmonds (R)
John R. Farr (R)
George S. Graham (R)
William W. Griest (R)
Willis J. Hulings (Progressive)
Abraham L. Keister (R)
M. Clyde Kelly (R)
Edgar R. Kiess (R)
Aaron S. Kreider (R)
Jonathan N. Langham (R)
Robert E. Lee (D)
John V. Lesher (D)
Fred E. Lewis (R)
J. Washington Logue (D)
J. Hampton Moore (R)
John M. Morin (R)
A. Mitchell Palmer (D)
Charles E. Patton (R)
Stephen G. Porter (R)
John H. Rothermel (D)
Arthur R. Rupley (Progressive)
Milton W. Shreve (R)
Henry W. Temple (R)
William S. Vare (R)
Anderson H. Walters (R)

RHODE ISLAND

Senators

Henry F. Lippitt (R)
Le Baron B. Colt (R)

Representatives

Peter G. Gerry (D)
Ambrose Kennedy (R)
George F. O'Shaunessy (D)

SOUTH CAROLINA

Senators

Benjamin R. Tillman (D)
Ellison D. Smith (D)

Representatives

Wyatt Aiken (D)
James F. Byrnes (D)
David E. Finley (D)
Joseph T. Johnson (D)
Asbury F. Lever (D)
J. Willard Ragsdale (D)
Richard S. Whaley (D)

SOUTH DAKOTA

Senators

Coe I. Crawford (R)
Thomas Sterling (R)

Representatives

Charles H. Burke (R)
Charles H. Dillon (R)
Eben W. Martin (R)

TENNESSEE

Senators

Luke Lea (D)
John K. Shields (D)

Representatives

Richard W. Austin (R)
Joseph W. Byrns (D)
Finis J. Garrett (D)
William C. Houston (D)
Cordell Hull (D)
Kenneth D. McKellar (D)
John A. Moon (D)
Lemuel P. Padgett (D)
Sam R. Sells (R)
Thetus W. Sims (D)

TEXAS

Senators

Charles A. Culberson (D)
Morris Sheppard (D)

Representatives

Jack Beall (D)
James P. Buchanan (D)
George F. Burgess (D)
Albert S. Burleson (D) r. Mar. 1913
Oscar Callaway (D)
Martin Dies (D)
Joe H. Eagle (D)
John Nance Garner (D)
Daniel E. Garrett (D)
Alexander W. Gregg (D)
Rufus Hardy (D)
Robert L. Henry (D)
Sam Rayburn (D)
James L. Slayden (D)
William R. Smith (D)
John H. Stephens (D)
Hatton W. Sumners (D)
Horace W. Vaughan (D)
James Young (D)

UTAH

Senators

Reed Smoot (R)
George Sutherland (R)

Representatives

Joseph Howell (R)
Jacob Johnson (R)

VERMONT

Senators

William P. Dillingham (R)
Carroll S. Page (R)

Representatives

Frank L. Greene (R)
Frank Plumley (R)

VIRGINIA

Senators

Thomas S. Martin (D)
Claude A. Swanson (D)

Representatives

Charles C. Carlin (D)
Henry D. Flood (D)
Carter Glass (D)
James Hay (D)
Edward E. Holland (D)
William A. Jones (D)
Andrew J. Montague (D)
Edward W. Saunders (D)
C. Bascom Slemp (D)
Walter A. Watson (D)

WASHINGTON

Senators

Wesley L. Jones (R)
Miles Poindexter (R)

Representatives

James W. Bryan (R)
Jacob A. Falconer (Progressive)
William E. Humphrey (R)
Albert Johnson (R)
William L. La Follette (R)

WEST VIRGINIA

Senators

William E. Chilton (D)
Nathan Goff (R)

Representatives

Samuel B. Avis (R)
William G. Brown, Jr. (D)
John W. Davis (D) r. Aug. 1913
James A. Hughes (R)
Hunter H. Moss, Jr. (R)
Matthew M. Neely (D)
Howard Sutherland (R)

WISCONSIN

Senators

Robert M. La Follette (R)
Isaac Stephenson (R)

Representatives

Edward E. Browne (R)
Michael E. Burke (D)
William J. Cary (R)
Henry A. Cooper (R)
John J. Esch (R)
James A. Frear (R)
Thomas F. Konop (D)
Irvine L. Lenroot (R)
John M. Nelson (R)
Michael K. Reilly (D)
William H. Stafford (R)

WYOMING

Senators

Clarence D. Clark (R)
Francis E. Warren (R)

Representative

Frank W. Mondell (R)

SIXTY-FOURTH CONGRESS

March 4, 1915 to March 3, 1917

President of The Senate:	Thomas R. Marshall
Presidents Pro Tempore of The Senate:	James P. Clarke Willard Saulsbury
Speaker of The House of Representatives:	Champ Clark

ALABAMA

Senators

John H. Bankhead (D)
Oscar W. Underwood (D)

Representatives

John W. Abercrombie (D)
Edward B. Almon (D)
Fred L. Blackmon (D)
John L. Burnett (D)
S. Hubert Dent, Jr. (D)
Oscar L. Gray (D)
J. Thomas Heflin (D)
George Huddleston (D)
William B. Oliver (D)
Henry B. Steagall (D)

ARIZONA

Senators

Henry F. Ashurst (D)
Marcus A. Smith (D)

Representative

Carl Hayden (D)

ARKANSAS

Senators

James P. Clarke (D) d. Oct. 1916
William F. Kirby (D) s. 1916

Joseph T. Robinson (D)

Representatives

Thaddeus H. Caraway (D)
William S. Goodwin (D)
Henderson M. Jacoway (D)
William A. Oldfield (D)
Samuel M. Taylor (D)
John N. Tillman (D)
Otis Wingo (D)

CALIFORNIA

Senators

John D. Works (R)
James D. Phelan (D)

Representatives

H. Stanley Benedict (R) s. 1916
Denver S. Church (D)
Charles F. Curry (R)
John A. Elston (R)
Everis A. Hayes (R)
Julius Kahn (R)
William Kent
William Kettner (D)
John I. Nolan (R)
John E. Raker (D)
Charles H. Randall (D)
William D. Stephens (R)
r. July 1916

COLORADO

Senators

Charles S. Thomas (D)
John F. Shafroth (D)

Representatives

Benjamin C. Hilliard (D)
Edward Keating (D)
Edward T. Taylor (D)
Charles B. Timberlake (R)

CONNECTICUT

Senators

Frank B. Brandegee (R)
George P. McLean (R)

Representatives

Richard P. Freeman (R)
James P. Glynn (R)
Ebenezer J. Hill (R)
P. Davis Oakey (R)
John Q. Tilson (R)

DELAWARE

Senators

Henry A. Du Pont (R)
Willard Saulsbury (D)

Representative

Thomas W. Miller (R)

FLORIDA

Senators

Duncan U. Fletcher (D)
Nathan P. Bryan (D)

Representatives

Frank Clark (D)
William J. Sears (D)
Stephen M. Sparkman (D)
Emmett Wilson (D)

GEORGIA

Senators

Hoke Smith (D)
Thomas W. Hardwick (D)

Representatives

William C. Adamson (D)
Thomas M. Bell (D)
Charles R. Crisp (D)
Charles G. Edwards (D)
William S. Howard (D)
Dudley M. Hughes (D)
Gordon Lee (D)
Frank Park (D)
Tinsley W. Rucker (D) s. 1917
Samuel J. Tribble (D) d. Dec. 1916
Carl Vinson (D)
John R. Walker (D)
James W. Wise (D)

IDAHO

Senators

William E. Borah (R)
James H. Brady (R)

Representatives

Robert M. McCracken (R)
Addison T. Smith (R)

ILLINOIS

Senators

James H. Lewis (D)
Lawrence Y. Sherman (R)

Representatives

Fred A. Britten (R)
Frank Buchanan (D)
Joseph G. Cannon (R)
Burnett M. Chiperfield (R)
Ira C. Copley (R)
Edward E. Denison (R)
George E. Foss (R)
Martin D. Foster (D)
Charles E. Fuller (R)
Thomas Gallagher (D)
Edward J. King (R)
James McAndrews (D)
James T. McDermott (D)
John C. McKenzie (R)
William B. McKinley (R)
Martin B. Madden (R)
James R. Mann (R)
Henry T. Rainey (D)
William A. Rodenberg (R)
Adolph J. Sabath (D)
John A. Sterling (R)
Claudius U. Stone (D)
Clyde H. Tavenner (D)
Loren E. Wheeler (R)
Thomas S. Williams (R)
William E. Williams (D)
William W.Wilson (R)

INDIANA

Senators

Benjamin F. Shively (D)
d. Mar. 1916
Thomas Taggart (D) ta. 1916
James E. Watson (R) s. 1916

John W. Kern (D)

Representatives

John A. M. Adair (D)
Henry A. Barnhart (D)
Cyrus Cline (D)
William E. Cox (D)
William A. Cullop (D)
Lincoln Dixon (D)
Finly H. Gray (D)
Charles Lieb (D)
Merrill Moores (R)
Martin A. Morrison (D)
Ralph W. Moss (D)
George W. Rauch (D)
William R. Wood (R)

IOWA

Senators

Albert B. Cummins (R)
William S. Kenyon (R)

Representatives

Cassius C. Dowell (R)
James W. Good (R)
William R. Green (R)
Gilbert N. Haugen (R)
Harry E. Hull (R)
Charles A. Kennedy (R)
C. William Ramseyer (R)
Thomas J. Steele (D)
Burton E. Sweet (R)
Horace M. Towner (R)
Frank P. Woods (R)

KANSAS

Senators

William H. Thompson (D)
Charles Curtis (R)

Representatives

Daniel R. Anthony, Jr. (R)
William A. Ayres (D)
Philip P. Campbell (R)
John R. Connelly (D)
Dudley Doolittle (D)
Guy T. Helvering (D)
Jouett Shouse (D)
Joseph Taggart (D)

KENTUCKY

Senators

Ollie M. James (D)
Joseph C. W. Beckham (D)

Representatives

Alben W. Barkley (D)
James C. Cantrill (D)
William J. Fields (D)
Harvey Helm (D)
Ben Johnson (D)
David H. Kincheloe (D)
John W. Langley (R)
Caleb Powers (R)
Arthur B. Rouse (D)
J. Swagar Sherley (D)
Robert Y. Thomas, Jr. (D)

LOUISIANA

Senators

Joseph E. Ransdell (D)
Robert F. Broussard (D)

Representatives

James B. Aswell (D)
H. Garland Dupre (D)

Albert Estopinal (D)
Ladislas Lazaro (D)
Whitmell P. Martin (Progressive)
Lewis L. Morgan (D)
John T. Watkins (D)
Riley J. Wilson (D)

MAINE

Senators

Charles F. Johnson (D)

Edwin C. Burleigh (R)
d. June 1916
Bert M. Fernald (R) s. 1916

Representatives

Frank E. Guernsey (R)
Asher C. Hinds (R)
Daniel J. McGillicuddy (D)
John A. Peters (R)

MARYLAND

Senators

John Walter Smith (D)
Blair Lee (D)

Representatives

Charles P. Coady (D)
David J. Lewis (D)
J. Charles Linthicum (D)
Sydney E. Mudd (R)
Jesse D. Price (D)
J. Fred C. Talbott (D)

MASSACHUSETTS

Senators

Henry Cabot Lodge (R)
John W. Weeks (R)

Representatives

William H. Carter (R)
Frederick W. Dallinger (R)
James A. Gallivan (D)
Augustus P. Gardner (R)
Frederick H. Gillett (R)
William S. Greene (R)
Richard Olney (D)
Calvin D. Paige (R)
Michael F. Phelan (D)
Ernest W. Roberts (R)
John Jacob Rogers (R)
Peter F. Tague (D)
George H. Tinkham (R)
Allen T. Treadway (R)
Joseph Walsh (R)
Samuel E. Winslow (R)

MICHIGAN

Senators

William Alden Smith (R)
Charles E. Townsend (R)

Representatives

Samuel W. Beakes (D)
Louis C. Cramton (R)
Frank E. Doremus (D)
Joseph W. Fordney (R)
Edward L. Hamilton (R)
W. Frank James (R)
Patrick H. Kelley (R)
George A. Loud (R)
James C. McLaughlin (R)
Carl E. Mapes (R)
Charles A. Nichols (R)
Frank D. Scott (R)
John M. C. Smith (R)

MINNESOTA

Senators

Knute Nelson (R)
Moses E. Clapp (R)

Representatives

Sydney Anderson (R)
Charles R. Davis (R)
Franklin F. Ellsworth (R)
Charles A. Lindbergh (R)
Clarence B. Miller (R)
Thomas D. Schall (R)
George R. Smith (R)
Halvor Steenerson (R)
Carl C. Van Dyke (D)
Andrew J. Volstead (R)

MISSISSIPPI

Senators

John Sharp Williams (D)
James K. Vardaman (D)

Representatives

Ezekiel S. Candler, Jr. (D)
James W. Collier (D)
Pat Harrison (D)
Benjamin G. Humphreys (D)
Percy E. Quin (D)
Thomas U. Sisson (D)
Hubert D. Stephens (D)
William W. Venable (D) s. 1916
Samuel A. Witherspoon (D)
d. Nov. 1915

MISSOURI

Senators

William J. Stone (D)
James A. Reed (D)

Representatives

Joshua W. Alexander (D)
Charles F. Booher (D)
William P. Borland (D)
Champ Clark (D)
Perl D. Decker (D)
Clement C. Dickinson (D)
Leonidas C. Dyer (R)
Courtney W. Hamlin (D)
Walter L. Hensley (D)
William L. Igoe (D)
James T. Lloyd (D)
Jacob E. Meeker (R)
Thomas L. Rubey (D)
William L. Rucker (D)
Joseph J. Russell (D)
Dorsey W. Shackleford (D)

MONTANA

Senators

Henry L. Myers (D)
Thomas J. Walsh (D)

Representatives

John M. Evans (D)
Tom Stout (D)

NEBRASKA

Senators

Gilbert M. Hitchcock (D)
George W. Norris (R)

Representatives

Moses P. Kinkaid (R)
Charles O. Lobeck (D)
C. Frank Reavis (R)
Ashton C. Shallenberger (D)
Charles H. Sloan (R)
Daniel V. Stephens (D)

NEVADA

Senators

Francis G. Newlands (D)
Key Pittman (D)

Representative

Edwin E. Roberts (R)

NEW HAMPSHIRE

Senators

Jacob H. Gallinger (R)
Henry F. Hollis (D)

Representatives

Cyrus A. Sulloway (R)
Edward H. Wason (R)

NEW JERSEY

Senators

James E. Martine (D)
William Hughes (D)

Representatives

Isaac Bacharach (R)
William J. Browning (R)
John H. Capstick (R)
Dow H. Drukker (R)
John J. Eagan (D)
Edward W. Gray (R)
James A. Hamill (D)
Archibald C. Hart (D)
Elijah C. Hutchinson (R)
Frederick R. Lehlbach (R)
Richard W. Parker (R)
Thomas J. Scully (D)

NEW MEXICO

Senators

Thomas B. Catron (R)
Albert B. Fall (R)

Representative

Benigno C. Hernandez (R)

NEW YORK

Senators

James A. O'Gorman (D)
James W. Wadsworth, Jr. (R)

Representatives

William S. Bennet (R)
Henry Bruckner (D)
Charles P. Caldwell (D)
John F. Carew (D)
Walter M. Chandler (Progressive)
William B. Charles (R)
Michael F. Conry (D)
d. Mar. 1917
Harry H. Dale (D)
Henry G. Danforth (R)
S. Wallace Dempsey (R)
Peter J. Dooling (D)
Daniel A. Driscoll (D)
Thomas B. Dunn (R)
George W. Fairchild (R)
Michael F. Farley (D)
John J. Fitzgerald (D)
Joseph V. Flynn (D)
Norman J. Gould (R)
Joseph A. Goulden (D)
Daniel J. Griffin (D)
Charles M. Hamilton (R)
Reuben L. Haskell (R)
Frederick C. Hicks (R)
G. Murray Hulbert (D)
James W. Husted (R)
George W. Loft (D)
Meyer London (Socialist)
Walter W. Magee (R)
James P. Maher (D)
Luther W. Mott (R)
Woodson R. Oglesby (D)
James S. Parker (R)
Thomas G. Patten (D)
Edmund Platt (R)
Harry H. Pratt (R)
Daniel J. Riordan (D)
Frederick W. Rowe (R)
Rollin B. Sanford (R)
Isaac Siegel (R)
Charles B. Smith (D)
Bertrand H. Snell (R)
Homer P. Snyder (R)
Oscar W. Swift (R)
Charles B. Ward (R)

NORTH CAROLINA

Senators

Furnifold McL. Simmons (D)
Lee S. Overman (D)

Representatives

James J. Britt (R)
Robert L. Doughton (D)
Hannibal L. Godwin (D)
George E. Hood (D)
Claude Kitchin (D)
Robert N. Page (D)
Edward W. Pou (D)
John H. Small (D)
Charles M. Stedman (D)
Edwin Y. Webb (D)

NORTH DAKOTA

Senators

Porter J. McCumber (R)
Asle J. Gronna (R)

Representatives

Henry T. Helgesen (R)
Patrick D. Norton (R)
George M. Young (R)

OHIO

Senators

Atlee Pomerene (D)
Warren G. Harding (R)

Representatives

Alfred G. Allen (D)
William A. Ashbrook (D)
Clement L. Brumbaugh (D)
John G. Cooper (R)
Robert Crosser (D)
Henry I. Emerson (R)
Simeon D. Fess (R)
Warren Gard (D)
William Gordon (D)
David A. Hollingsworth (R)
Charles C. Kearns (R)
John A. Key (D)
Nicholas Longworth (R)
Roscoe C. McCulloch (R)
Nelson E. Matthews (R)
William C. Mooney (R)
Arthur W. Overmyer (D)
Edwin D. Ricketts (R)
J. Edward Russell (R)
Isaac R. Sherwood (D)
Robert M. Switzer (R)
Seward H. Williams (R)

OKLAHOMA

Senators

Thomas P. Gore (D)
Robert L. Owen (D)

Representatives

Charles D. Carter (D)
James S. Davenport (D)
Scott Ferris (D)
William W. Hastings (D)
James V. McClintic (D)
Dick T. Morgan (R)
William H. Murray (D)
Joseph B. Thompson (D)

OREGON

Senators

George E. Chamberlain (D)
Harry Lane (D)

Representatives

Willis C. Hawley (R)
Clifton N. McArthur (R)
Nicholas J. Sinnott (R)

PENNSYLVANIA

Senators

Boies Penrose (R)
George T. Oliver (R)

Representatives

Warren W. Bailey (D)
Andrew J. Barchfeld (R)
C. William Beales (R)
Thomas S. Butler (R)
John J. Casey (D)
William H. Coleman (R)
Peter E. Costello (R)
Thomas S. Crago (R)
George P. Darrow (R)
Arthur G. Dewalt (D)
George W. Edmonds (R)
John R. Farr (R)
Benjamin K. Focht (R)
Mahlon M. Garland (R)
George S. Graham (R)
William W. Griest (R)
Robert D. Heaton (R)
Robert F. Hopwood (R)
Abraham L. Keister (R)
Edgar R. Kiess (R)
Aaron S. Kreider (R)
Daniel F. Lafean (R)
John V. Lesher (D)
Michael Liebel, Jr. (D)
Louis T. McFadden (R)
Samuel H. Miller (R)
J. Hampton Moore (R)
John M. Morin (R)
S. Taylor North (R)
Stephen G. Porter (R)
Charles H. Rowland (R)
John R. K. Scott (R)
Henry J. Steele (D)
Henry W. Temple (R)
William S. Vare (R)
Henry W. Watson (R)

RHODE ISLAND

Senators

Henry F. Lippitt (R)
LeBaron B. Colt (R)

Representatives

Ambrose Kennedy (R)
George F. O'Shaunessy (D)
Walter R. Stiness (R)

SOUTH CAROLINA

Senators

Benjamin R. Tillman (D)
Ellison D. Smith (D)

Representatives

Wyatt Aiken (D)
James F. Byrnes (D)
David E. Finley (D) d. Jan. 1917
Joseph T. Johnson (D)
Asbury F. Lever (D)
Paul G. McCorkle (D) s. 1917
Samuel J. Nicholls (D)
J. Willard Ragsdale (D)
Richard S. Whaley (D)

SOUTH DAKOTA

Senators

Thomas Sterling (R)
Edwin S. Johnson (D)

Representatives

Charles H. Dillon (R)
Harry L. Gandy (D)
Royal C. Johnson (R)

TENNESSEE

Senators

Luke Lea (D)
John K. Shields (D)

Representatives

Richard W. Austin (R)
Joseph W. Byrns (D)
Finis J. Garrett (D)
William C. Houston (D)
Cordell Hull (D)
Kenneth D. McKellar (D)
John A. Moon (D)
Lemuel P. Padgett (D)
Sam R. Sells (R)
Thetus W. Sims (D)

TEXAS

Senators

Charles A. Culberson (D)
Morris Sheppard (D)

Representatives

Eugene Black (D)
James P. Buchanan (D)
George F. Burgess (D)
Oscar Callaway (D)
James H. Davis (D)
Martin Dies (D)
Joe H. Eagle (D)
John Nance Garner (D)
Alexander W. Gregg (D)
Rufus Hardy (D)
Robert L. Henry (D)
Jeff McLemore (D)
Sam Rayburn (D)
James L. Slayden (D)
William R. Smith (D)
John H. Stephens (D)
Hatton W. Sumners (D)
James Young (D)

UTAH

Senators

Reed Smoot (R)
George Sutherland (R)

Representatives

Joseph Howell (R)
James H. Mays (D)

VERMONT

Senators

William P. Dillingham (R)
Carroll S. Page (R)

Representatives

Porter H. Dale (R)
Frank L. Greene (R)

VIRGINIA

Senators

Thomas S. Martin (D)
Claude A. Swanson (D)

Representatives

Charles C. Carlin (D)
Henry D. Flood (D)
Carter Glass (D)
Thomas W. Harrison (D) s. 1916
James Hay (D) r. Oct. 1916
Edward E. Holland (D)
William A. Jones (D)
Andrew J. Montague (D)
Edward W. Saunders (D)
C. Bascom Slemp (D)
Walter A. Watson (D)

WASHINGTON

Senators

Wesley L. Jones (R)
Miles Poindexter (R)

Representatives

Clarence C. Dill (D)
Lindley H. Hadley (R)
William E. Humphrey (R)
Albert Johnson (R)
William L. La Follette (R)

WEST VIRGINIA

Senators

William E. Chilton (D)
Nathan Goff (R)

Representatives

George M. Bowers (R) s. 1916
William G. Brown, Jr. (D) d. Mar. 1916
Edward Cooper (R)
Adam B. Littlepage (D)
Hunter H. Moss, Jr. (R) d. July 1916
Matthew M. Neely (D)
Howard Sutherland (R)
Harry C. Woodyard (R) s. 1916

WISCONSIN

Senators

Robert M. La Follette (R)
Paul O. Husting (D)

Representatives

Edward E. Browne (R)
Michael E. Burke (D)
William J. Cary (R)
Henry A. Cooper (R)
John J. Esch (R)
James A. Frear (R)
Thomas F. Konop (D)
Irvine L. Lenroot (R)
John M. Nelson (R)
Michael K. Reilly (D)
William H. Stafford (R)

WYOMING

Senators

Clarence D. Clark (R)
Francis E. Warren (R)

Representative

Frank W. Mondell (R)

SIXTY-FIFTH CONGRESS

March 4, 1917 to March 3, 1919

President of The Senate: Thomas R. Marshall
President Pro Tempore of The Senate: Willard Saulsbury
Speaker of The House of Representatives: Champ Clark

ALABAMA

Senators

John H. Bankhead (D)
Oscar W. Underwood (D)

Representatives

Edward B. Almon (D)
William B. Bankhead (D)
Fred L. Backmon (D)
John L. Burnett (D)
S. Hubert Dent, Jr. (D)
Oscar L. Gray (D)
J. Thomas Heflin (D)
George Huddleston (D)
William B. Oliver (D)
Henry B. Steagall (D)

ARIZONA

Senators

Henry F. Ashurst (D)
Marcus A. Smith (D)

Representative

Carl Hayden (D)

ARKANSAS

Senators

Joseph T. Robinson (D)
William F. Kirby (D)

Representatives

Thaddeus H. Caraway (D)
William S. Goodwin (D)
Henderson M. Jacoway (D)
William A. Oldfield (D)
Samuel M. Taylor (D)
John N. Tillman (D)
Otis Wingo (D)

CALIFORNIA

Senators

James D. Phelan (D)
Hiram W. Johnson (R)

Representatives

Denver S. Church (D)
Charles F. Curry (R)
John A. Elston (R)
Everis A. Hayes (R)
Julius Kahn (R)
William Kettner (D)
Clarence F. Lea (D)
John I. Nolan (R)
Henry Z. Osborne (R)
John E. Raker (D)
Charles H. Randall (R)

COLORADO

Senators

Charles S. Thomas (D)
John F. Shafroth (D)

Representatives

Benjamin C. Hilliard (D)
Edward Keating (D)
Edward T. Taylor (D)
Charles B. Timberlake (R)

CONNECTICUT

Senators

Frank B. Brandegee (R)
George P. McLean (R)

Representatives

Richard P. Freeman (R)
James P. Glynn (R)
Ebenezer J. Hill (R)
d. Sept. 1917
Augustine Lonergan (D)
Schuyler Merritt (R) s. 1917
John Q. Tilson (R)

DELAWARE

Senators

Willard Saulsbury (D)
Josiah O. Wolcott (D)

Representative

Albert F. Polk (D)

FLORIDA

Senators

Duncan U. Fletcher (D)
Park Trammell (D)

Representatives

Frank Clark (D)
Herbert J. Drane (D)
J. Walter Kehoe (D)
William J. Sears (D)

GEORGIA

Senators

Hoke Smith (D)
Thomas W. Hardwick (D)

Representatives

William C. Adamson (D)
r. Dec. 1917
Thomas M. Bell (D)
Charles H. Brand (D)
Charles R. Crisp (D)
William S. Howard (D)
William W. Larsen (D)
Gordon Lee (D)
James W. Overstreet (D)
Frank Park (D)
Carl Vinson (D)
John R. Walker (D)
James W. Wise (D)
William C. Wright (D) s. 1918

IDAHO

Senators

William E. Borah (R)

James H. Brady (R) d. Jan. 1918
John F. Nugent (D) s. 1918

Representatives

Burton L. French (R)
Addison T. Smith (R)

ILLINOIS

Senators

James H. Lewis (D)
Lawrence Y. Sherman (R)

Representatives

Fred A. Britten (R)
Joseph G. Cannon (R)
Ira C. Copley (R)
Edward E. Denison (R)
George E. Foss (R)
Martin D. Foster (D)
Charles E. Fuller (R)
Thomas Gallagher (D)
William J. Graham (R)
Clifford Ireland (R)
Niels Juul (R)
Edward J. King (R)
James McAndrews (D)
Medill McCormick (R)
John C. McKenzie (R)
William B. McKinley (R)
Martin B. Madden (R)
James R. Mann (R)
Charles Martin (D) d. Oct. 1917
William E. Mason (R)
Henry T. Rainey (D)
John W. Rainey (D) s. 1918
William A. Rodenberg (R)
Adolph J. Sabath (D)
John A. Sterling (R) d. Oct. 1918
Loren E. Wheeler (R)
Thomas S. Williams (R)
William W. Wilson (R)

INDIANA

Senators

James E. Watson (R)
Harry S. New (R)

Representatives

Henry A. Barnhart (D)
Oscar E. Bland (R)
Daniel W. Comstock (R)
d. May 1917
William E. Cox (D)
George K. Denton (D)
Lincoln Dixon (D)
Richard N. Elliott (R)
Louis W. Fairfield (R)
Milton Kraus (R)
Merrill Moores (R)
Fred S. Purnell (R)
Everett Sanders (R)
Albert H. Vestal (R)
William R. Wood (R)

IOWA

Senators

Albert B. Cummins (R)
William S. Kenyon (R)

Representatives

Cassius C. Dowell (R)
William R. Green (R)
James W. Good (R)
Gilbert N. Haugen (R)
Harry E. Hull (R)
Charles A. Kennedy (R)
C. William Ramseyer (R)
George C. Scott (R)
Burton E. Sweet (R)
Horace M. Towner (R)
Frank P. Woods (R)

KANSAS

Senators

William H. Thompson (D)
Charles Curtis (R)

Representatives

Daniel R. Anthony, Jr. (R)
William A. Ayres (D)
Philip P. Campbell (R)
John R. Connelly (D)
Dudley Doolittle (D)
Guy T. Helvering (D)
Edward C. Little (R)
Jouett Shouse (D)

KENTUCKY

Senators

Ollie M. James (D) d. Aug. 1918
George B. Martin (D) s. 1918

John C. W. Beckham (D)

Representatives

Alben W. Barkley (D)
James C. Cantrill (D)
William J. Fields (D)
Harvey Helm (D)
Ben Johnson (D)
David H. Kincheloe (D)
John W. Langley (R)
Caleb Powers (R)
Arthur B. Rouse (D)
J. Swagar Sherley (D)
Robert Y. Thomas, Jr. (D)

LOUISIANA

Senators

Joseph E. Ransdell (D)

Robert F. Broussard (D)
d. Apr. 1918
Walter Guion (D) ta. 1918
Edward J. Gay (D) s. 1918

Representatives

James B. Aswell (D)
H. Garland Dupre (D)
Albert Estopinal (D)
Ladislas Lazaro (D)
Whitmell P. Martin (Progressive)
Jared Sanders (D)
John T. Watkins (D)
Riley J. Wilson (D)

MAINE

Senators

Bert M. Fernald (R)
Frederick Hale (R)

Representatives

Louis B. Goodall (R)
Ira G. Hersey (R)
John A. Peters (R)
Wallace H. White, Jr. (R)

MARYLAND

Senators

John Walter Smith (D)
Joseph I. France (R)

Representatives

Carville D. Benson (D) s. 1918
Charles P. Coady (D)
J. Charles Linthicum (D)
Sydney E. Mudd (R)
Jesse D. Price (D)
J. Fred C. Talbott (D)
d. Oct. 1918
Frederick N. Zihlman (R)

MASSACHUSETTS

Senators

Henry Cabot Lodge (R)
John W. Weeks (R)

Representatives

William H. Carter (R)
Frederick W. Dallinger (R)
Alvan T. Fuller (R)
James A. Gallivan (D)
Augustus P. Gardner (R)
r. May 1917
Frederick H. Gillett (R)
William S. Greene (R)
Willfred W. Lufkin (R)
Richard Olney (D)
Calvin D. Paige (R)
Michael F. Phelan (D)
John Jacob Rogers (R)
Peter F. Tague (D)
George H. Tinkham (R)
Allen T. Treadway (R)
Joseph Walsh (R)
Samuel E. Winslow (R)

MICHIGAN

Senators

William Alden Smith (R)
Charles E. Townsend (R)

Representatives

Mark R. Bacon (R) r. Dec. 1917
Samuel W. Beakes (D)
Louis C. Cramton (R)
Gilbert A. Currie (R)
Frank E. Doremus (D)
Joseph W. Fordney (R)
Edward L. Hamilton (R)
W. Frank James (R)
Patrick H. Kelley (R)
James C. McLaughlin (R)
Carl E. Mapes (R)
Charles A. Nichols (R)
Frank D. Scott (R)
John M. C. Smith (R)

MINNESOTA

Senators

Knute Nelson (R)
Frank B. Kellogg (R)

Representatives

Sydney Anderson (R)
Charles R. Davis (R)
Frank F. Ellsworth (R)
Harold Knutson (R)
Ernest Lundeen (R)
Clarence B. Miller (R)
Thomas D. Schall (R)
Halvor Steenerson (R)
Carl C. Van Dyke (D)
Andrew J. Volstead (R)

MISSISSIPPI

Senators

John Sharp Williams (D)
James K. Vardaman (D)

Representatives

Ezekiel S. Candler, Jr. (D)
James W. Collier (D)
Pat Harrison (D)
Benjamin G. Humphreys (D)
Percy E. Quin (D)
Thomas U. Sisson (D)
Hubert D. Stephens (D)
William W. Venable (D)

MISSOURI

Senators

William J. Stone (D)
d. Apr. 1918
Xenophon P. Wilfley (D) ta. 1918
Selden P. Spencer (R) s. 1918

James A. Reed (D)

Representatives

Joshua W. Alexander (D)
Charles F. Booher (D)
William P. Borland (D)
d. Feb. 1919
Champ Clark (D)
Perl D. Decker (D)
Clement C. Dickinson (D)
Leonidas C. Dyer (R)
Frederick Essen (R) s. Nov. 1918
Courtney W. Hamlin (D)
Walter L. Hensley (D)
William L. Igoe (D)
Jacob E. Meeker (R) d. Oct. 1918
Milton A. Romjue (D)
Thomas L. Rubey (D)
William W. Rucker (D)
Joseph J. Russell (D)
Dorsey W. Shackleford (D)

MONTANA

Senators

Henry L. Myers (D)
Thomas J. Walsh (D)

Representatives

John M. Evans (D)
Jeannette Rankin (R)

NEBRASKA

Senators

Gilbert M. Hitchcock (D)
George W. Norris (R)

Representatives

Moses P. Kinkaid (R)
Charles O. Lobeck (D)
C. Frank Reavis (R)
Ashton C. Shallenberger (D)
Charles H. Sloan (R)
Daniel V. Stephens (D)

NEVADA

Senators

Francis G. Newlands (D)
d. Dec. 1917
Charles B. Henderson (D) s. 1918

Key Pittman (D)

Representative

Edwin E. Roberts (R)

NEW HAMPSHIRE

Senators

Jacob H. Gallinger (R)
d. Aug. 1918
Irving W. Drew (R) ta. 1918
George H. Moses (R) s. 1918

Henry F. Hollis (D)

Representatives

Sherman E. Burroughs (R)
Cyrus A. Sulloway (R)
Edward H. Wason (R)

NEW JERSEY

Senators

William Hughes (D)
d. Mar. 1917
David Baird (R) s. 1918

Joseph S. Frelinghuysen (R)

Representatives

Isaac Bacharach (R)
William F. Birch (R) s. Nov. 1918
William J. Browning (R)
John H. Capstick (R)
d. Mar. 1918
Dow H. Drukker (R)
John J. Eagan (D)
Edward W. Gray (R)
James A. Hamill (D)
Elijah C. Hutchinson (R)
Frederick R. Lehlbach (R)
Richard W. Parker (R)
John R. Ramsey (R)
Thomas J. Scully (D)

NEW MEXICO

Senators

Albert B. Fall (R)
Andrieus A. Jones (D)

Representative

William B. Walton (D)

NEW YORK

Senators

James W. Wadsworth, Jr. (R)
William M. Calder (R)

Representatives

Henry Bruckner (D) r. Dec. 1917
Charles P. Caldwell (D)
John F. Carew (D)
Walter M. Chandler (Progressive)
William E. Cleary (D) s. 1918
Harry H. Dale (D)
John J. Delaney (D) s. 1918
S. Wallace Dempsey (R)
Jerome F. Donovan (D) s. 1918
Peter J. Dooling (D)
Thomas B. Dunn (R)
Benjamin L. Fairchild (R)
George W. Fairchild (R)
John J. Fitzgerald (D)
r. Dec. 1917
Joseph V. Flynn (D)
George B. Francis (R)
Norman J. Gould (R)
Anthony J. Griffin (D) s. 1918
Daniel J. Griffin (D) r. Dec. 1917
Charles M. Hamilton (R)
Reuben L. Haskell (R)
Frederick C. Hicks (R)
G. Murray Hulbert (D)
r. Jan. 1918
James W. Husted (R)
Fiorello H. LaGuardia (R)
Meyer London (Socialist)
George R. Lunn (D)
Walter W. Magee (R)
James P. Maher (R)
Luther W. Mott (R)
Daniel C. Oliver (D)
James S. Parker (R)
Edmund Platt (R)
Harry H. Pratt (R)
Daniel J. Riordan (D)
Frederick W. Rowe (R)
Archie D. Sanders (R)
Rollin B. Sanford (R)
Isaac Siegel (R)
Charles B. Smith (D)
Thomas F. Smith (D)
Bertrand H. Snell (R)
Homer P. Snyder (R)
Christopher D. Sullivan (D)
Oscar W. Swift (R)
William F. Waldo (R)
Charles B. Ward (R)

NORTH CAROLINA

Senators

Furnifold McL. Simmons (D)
Lee S. Overman (D)

Representatives

James J. Britt (D) s. 1919
Robert L. Doughton (D)
Hannibal L. Godwin (D)
George E. Hood (D)
Claude Kitchin (D)
Edward W. Pou (D)
Leonidas D. Robinson (D)
John H. Small (D)
Charles M. Stedman (D)
Zebulon Weaver (D)
Edwin Y. Webb (D)

NORTH DAKOTA

Senators

Porter J. McCumber (R)
Asle J. Groona (R)

Representatives

John M. Baer (R) s. 1917
Henry T. Helgesen (R)
d. Apr. 1917
Patrick D. Norton (R)
George M. Young (R)

OHIO

Senators

Atlee Pomerene (D)
Warren G. Harding (R)

Representatives

William A. Ashbrook (D)
Ellsworth R. Bathrick (D)
d. Dec. 1917
Clement L. Brumbaugh (D)
Horatio C. Claypool (D)
John G. Cooper (D)
Robert Crosser (D)
Martin L. Davey (D) s. 1918
Henry I. Emerson (R)
Simeon D. Fess (R)
Warren Gard (D)
William Gordon (D)
Victor Heintz (R)
David A. Hollingsworth (R)
Charles C. Kearns (R)
John A. Key (D)
Nicholas Longworth (R)
Roscoe G. McCulloch (R)
Arthur W. Overmyer (D)
Isaac R. Sherwood (D)
John S. Snook (D)
Robert M. Switzer (R)
Benjamin F. Welty (D)
George White (D)

OKLAHOMA

Senators

Thomas P. Gore (D)
Robert L. Owen (D)

Representatives

Charles D. Carter (D)
Thomas A. Chandler (R)
Scott Ferris (D)
William W. Hastings (D)
James V. McClintic (D)
Thomas D. McKeown (D)
Dick T. Morgan (R)
Joseph B. Thompson (D)

OREGON

Senators

George E. Chamberlain (D)

Harry Lane (D) d. May 1917
Charles L. McNary (R) s. 1918

Representatives

Willis C. Hawley (R)
Clifton N. McArthur (R)
Nicholas J. Sinnott (R)

PENNSYLVANIA

Senators

Boies Penrose (R)
Philander C. Knox (R)

Representatives

Earl H. Beshlin (D)
Andrew R. Brodbeck (D)
Thomas S. Butler (R)
Guy E. Campbell (D)
Henry A. Clark (R)
Peter E. Costello (R)
Thomas S. Crago (R)
George P. Darrow (R)
Arthur G. Dewalt (D)
George W. Edmonds (R)
John R. Farr (R)
Benjamin K. Focht (R)
Mahlon M. Garland (R)
George S. Graham (R)
William W. Griest (R)
Robert D. Heaton (R)
M. Clyde Kelly (R)
Edgar R. Kiess (R)
Aaron S. Kreider (R)
John V. Lesher (D)
Louis T. McFadden (R)
Joseph McLaughlin (R)
J. Hampton Moore (R)
John M. Morin (R)
Stephen G. Porter (R)
Edward E. Robbins (R)
d. Jan. 1919
John M. Rose (R)
Charles H. Rowland (R)
John R. K. Scott (R)
Henry J. Steele (D)
Bruce F. Sterling (D)
Nathan L. Strong (R)
Henry W. Temple (R)
Thomas W. Templeton (R)
William S. Vare (R)
Henry W. Watson (R)

RHODE ISLAND

Senators

LeBaron B. Colt (R)
Peter G. Gerry (D)

Representatives

Ambrose Kennedy (R)
George F. O'Shaunessy (D)
Walter R. Stiness (R)

SOUTH CAROLINA

Senators

Benjamin R. Tillman (D)
d. July 1918
Christie Benet (D) ta. 1918
William P. Pollock (D) s. 1918

Ellison D. Smith (D)

Representatives

James F. Byrnes (D)
Fred H. Dominick (D)
Asbury F. Lever (D)
Samuel J. Nicholls (D)
J. Willard Ragsdale (D)
William F. Stevenson (D)
Richard S. Whaley (D)

SOUTH DAKOTA

Senators

Thomas Sterling (R)
Edwin S. Johnson (D)

Representatives

Charles H. Dillon (R)
Harry L. Gandy (D)
Royal C. Johnson (R)

TENNESSEE

Senators

John K. Shields (D)
Kenneth D. McKellar (D)

Representatives

Richard W. Austin (R)
Joseph W. Byrns (D)
Hubert F. Fisher (D)
Finis J. Garrett (D)
William C. Houston (D)
Cordell Hull (D)
John A. Moon (D)
Lemuel P. Padgett (D)
Sam R. Sells (R)
Thetus W. Sims (D)

TEXAS

Senators

Charles A. Culberson (D)
Morris Sheppard (D)

Representatives

Eugene Black (D)
Thomas L. Blanton (D)
James P. Buchanan (D)
Tom T. Connally (D)
Martin Dies (D)
Joe H. Eagle (D)
John Nance Garner (D)
Daniel E. Garrett (D)
Alexander W. Gregg (D)
Rufus Hardy (D)
Marvin Jones (D)
A. Jeff McLemore (D)
Joseph J. Mansfield (D)
Sam Rayburn (D)
James L. Slayden (D)
Hatton W. Sumners (D)
James C. Wilson (D)
James Young (D)

UTAH

Senators

Reed Smoot (R)
William H. King (D)

Representatives

James H. Mays (D)
Milton H. Welling (D)

VERMONT

Senators

William P. Dillingham (R)
Carroll S. Page (R)

Representatives

Porter H. Dale (R)
Frank L. Greene (R)

VIRGINIA

Senators

Thomas S. Martin (D)
Claude A. Swanson (R)

Representatives

Schuyler Otis Bland (D) s. 1918
Charles C. Carlin (D)
Henry D. Flood (D)
Carter Glass (D) r. Dec. 1918
Thomas W. Harrison (D)
Edward E. Holland (D)
William A. Jones (D)
d. Apr. 1918
Andrew J. Montague (D)
Edward W. Saunders (D)
C. Bascom Slemp (D)
Walter A. Watson (D)
James P. Woods (D)

WASHINGTON

Senators

Wesley L. Jones (R)
Miles Poindexter (R)

Representatives

Clarence C. Dill (D)
Lindley H. Hadley (R)
Albert Johnson (R)
William L. LaFollette (R)
John F. Miller (R)

WEST VIRGINIA

Senators

Nathan Goff (R)
Howard Sutherland (R)

Representatives

George M. Bowers (R)
Edward Cooper (R)
Adam B. Littlepage (D)
Matthew M. Neely (D)
Stuart F. Reed (R)
Harry C. Woodyard (R)

WISCONSIN

Senators

Robert M. LaFollette (R)

Paul O. Husting (D) d. Oct. 1917
Irvine L. Lenroot (R) s. 1918

Representatives

Edward E. Browne (R)
William J. Cary (R)
David G. Classon (R)
Henry A. Cooper (R)
James H. Davidson
d. Aug. 1918
John J. Esch (R)
James A. Frear (R)
Florian Lampbert (R) s. 1918
Irvine L. Lenroot (R)
r. Apr. 1918
Adolphus P. Nelson (R) s. 1918
John M. Nelson (R)
William H. Stafford (R)
Edward Voigt (R)

WYOMING

Senators

Francis E. Warren (R)
John B. Kendrick (D)

Representative

Frank W. Mondell (R)

SIXTY-SIXTH CONGRESS

March 4, 1919 to March 3, 1921

President of The Senate:	Thomas R. Marshall
President Pro Tempore of The Senate:	Albert B. Cummins
Speaker of The House of Representatives:	Frederick H. Gillett

ALABAMA

Senators

John H. Bankhead (D) d. 1920
Braxton B. Comer (D) ta. 1920
J. Thomas Heflin (D) s. 1920

Oscar W. Underwood (D)

Representatives

Edward B. Almon (D)
William B. Bankhead (D)
Fred L. Blackmon (D)
William B. Bowling (D) s. 1920
S. Hubert Dent, Jr. (D)
J. Thomas Heflin (D)
r. Nov. 1920
George Huddleston (D)
John McDuffie (D)
William B. Oliver (D)
Lilius B. Rainey (D)
Henry B. Steagall (D)

ARIZONA

Senators

Henry F. Ashurst (D)
Marcus A. Smith (D)

Representative

Carl Hayden (D)

ARKANSAS

Senators

Joseph T. Robinson (D)
William F. Kirby (D)

Representatives

Thaddeus H. Caraway (D)
William S. Goodwin (D)
Henderson M. Jacoway (D)
William A. Oldfield (D)
Samuel M. Taylor (D)
John N. Tillman (D)
Otis Wingo (D)

CALIFORNIA

Senators

James D. Phelan (D)
Hiram W. Johnson (R)

Representatives

Henry E. Barbour (R)
Charles F. Curry (R)
John A. Elston (R)
Hugh S. Hersman (D)
Julius Kahn (R)
William Kettner (D)
Clarence F. Lea (D)
John I. Nolan (R)
Henry Z. Osborne (R)
John E. Raker (D)
Charles H. Randall (R)

COLORADO

Senators

Charles S. Thomas (D)
Lawrence C. Phipps (R)

Representatives

Guy U. Hardy (R)
Edward T. Taylor (D)
Charles B. Timberlake (R)
William N. Vaile

CONNECTICUT

Senators

Frank B. Brandegee (R)
George P. McLean (R)

Representatives

Richard P. Freeman (R)
James P. Glynn (R)
Augustine Lonergan (D)
Schuyler Merritt (R)
John Q. Tilson (R)

DELAWARE

Senators

Josiah O. Wolcott (D)
L. Heisler Ball (R)

Representative

Caleb R. Layton (R)

FLORIDA

Senators

Duncan U. Fletcher (D)
Park Trammell (D)

Representatives

Frank Clark (D)
Herbert J. Drane (D)
William J. Sears (D)
John H. Smithwick (D)

GEORGIA

Senators

Hoke Smith (D)
William J. Harris (D)

GEORGIA

Representatives

Thomas M. Bell (D)
Charles H. Brand (D)
Charles R. Crisp (D)
William C. Lankford (D)
William W. Larsen (D)
Gordon Lee (D)
James W. Overstreet (D)
Frank Park (D)
William D. Upshaw (D)
Carl Vinson (D)
James W. Wise (D)
William C. Wright (D)

IDAHO

Senators

William E. Borah (R)
John F. Nugent (D) r. Jan. 1921
Frank R. Gooding (R) s. 1921

Representatives

Burton L. French (R)
Addison T. Sith (R)

ILLINOIS

Senators

Lawrence Y. Sherman (R)
Medill McCormick (R)

Representatives

Fred A. Britten (R)
Edwin B. Brooks (R)
Joseph G. Cannon (R)
Carl R. Chindblom (R)
Ira C. Copley (R)
Edward E. Denison (R)
Charles E. Fuller (R)
Thomas Gallagher (D)
William J. Graham (R)
Clifford Ireland (R)
Niels Juul (R)
Edward J. King (R)
James McAndrews (D)
John C. McKenzie (R)
William B. McKinley (R)
Martin B. Madden (R)
James R. Mann (R)
William E. Mason (R)
John W. Rainey (D)
William A. Rodenberg (R)
Adolph J. Sabath (D)
Frank L. Smith (R)
Loren E. Wheeler (R)
Thomas S. Williams (R)
William W. Wilson (R)
Richard Yates (R)

INDIANA

Senators

James E. Watson (R)
Harry S. New (R)

Representatives

John S. Benham (R)
Oscar E. Bland (R)
James W. Dunbar (R)
Richard N. Elliott (R)
Louis W. Fairfield (R)
Andrew J. Hickey (R)
Milton Kraus (R)
Oscar R. Luhring (R)
Merrill Moores (R)
Fred S. Purnell (R)
Everett Sanders (R)
Albert H. Vestal (R)
William R. Wood (R)

IOWA

Senators

Albert B. Cummins (R)
William S. Kenyon (R)

Representatives

William D. Boies (R)
Lester J. Dickinson (R)
Cassius C. Dowell (R)
James W. Good (R)
William R. Green (R)
Gilbert N. Haugen (R)
Harry E. Hull (R)
Charles A. Kennedy (R)
C. William Ramseyer (R)
Burton E. Sweet (R)
Horace M. Towner (R)

KANSAS

Senators

Charles Curtis (R)
Arthur Capper (R)

Representatives

Daniel R. Anthony, Jr. (R)
William A. Ayres (D)
Philip P. Campbell (R)
Homer Hoch (R)
Edward C. Little (R)
James G. Strong (R)
Jasper N. Tincher (R)
Hays B. White (R)

KENTUCKY

Senators

John C. W. Beckham (D)
Augustus O. Stanley (D)

Representatives

Alben W. Barkley (D)
James C. Cantrill (D)
William J. Fields (D)
Ben Johnson (D)
David H. Kincheloe (D)
John W. Langley (R)
Charles F. Ogden (R)
John M. Robsion (R)
Arthur B. Rouse (D)
King Swope (R)
Robert Y. Thomas, Jr. (D)

LOUISIANA

Senators

Joseph E. Ransdell (D)
Edward J. Gay (D)

Representatives

James B. Aswell (D)
H. Garland Dupre (D)
Ladislas Lazaro (D)
Whitmell P. Martin (D)
James O'Connor (D)
Jared Y. Sanders (D)
John T. Watkins (D)
Riley J. Wilson (D)

MAINE

Senators

Bert M. Fernald (R)
Frederick Hale (R)

Representatives

Louis B. Goodall (R)
Ira G. Hersey (R)
John A. Peters (R)
Wallace H. White, Jr. (R)

MARYLAND

Senators

John Walter Smith (D)
Joseph I. France (R)

Representatives

William N. Andrews (R)
Carville D. Benson (D)
Charles P. Coady (D)
J. Charles Linthicum (D)
Sydney E. Mudd (R)
Frederick N. Zihlman (R)

MASSACHUSETTS

Senators

Henry Cabot Lodge (R)
David I. Walsh (D)

Representatives

Frederick W. Dallinger (R)
John F. Fitzgerald (D)
r. Oct. 1919
Alvan T. Fuller (R) r. Jan. 1921
James A. Gallivan (D)
Frederick H. Gillett (R)
William S. Greene (R)
Robert Luce (R)
Willfred W. Lufkin (R)
Richard Olney (D)
Calvin D. Paige (R)
Michael F. Phelan (D)
John Jacob Rogers (R)
Peter F. Tague (D)
George H. Tinkham (R)
Allen T. Treadway (R)
Joseph Walsh (R)
Samuel E. Winslow (R)

MICHIGAN

Senators

Charles E. Townsend (R)
Truman H. Newberry (R)

Representatives

Louis C. Cramton (R)
Gilbert A. Currie (R)
Frank E. Doremus (D)
Joseph W. Fordney (R)
Edward L. Hamilton (R)
W. Frank James (R)
Patrick H. Kelley (R)
James C. McLaughlin (R)
Clarence J. McLeod (R) s. 1920
Carl E. Mapes (R)
Earl C. Michener (R)
Charles A. Nichols (R)
d. Apr. 1920
Frank D. Scott (R)
John M. C. Smith (R)

MINNESOTA

Senators

Knute Nelson (R)
Frank B. Kellogg (R)

Representatives

Sydney Anderson (R)
William L. Carss
Charles R. Davis (R)
Franklin F. Ellsworth (R)
Oscar E. Keller (R)
Harold Knutson (R)
Walter H. Newton (R)
Thomas D. Schall (R)
Halvor Steenerson (R)
Carl C. Van Dyke (D)
d. May 1919
Andrew J. Volstead (R)

MISSISSIPPI

Senators

John Sharp Williams (D)
Pat Harrison (D)

Representatives

Ezekiel S. Candler, Jr. (D)
James W. Collier (D)
Benjamin G. Humphreys (D)
Paul B. Johnson (D)
Percy E. Quin (D)
Thomas U. Sisson (D)
Hubert D. Stephens (D)
William W. Venable (D)

MISSOURI

Senators

James A. Reed (D)
Selden P. Spencer (R)

Representatives

Joshua W. Alexander (D)
r. Dec. 1919
William T. Bland (D)
Charles F. Booher (D)
d. Jan. 1921
Champ Clark (D) d. Mar. 1921
Clement C. Dickinson (D)
Leonidas C. Dyer (R)
Edward D. Hays (R)
William L. Igoe (D)
Isaac V. McPherson (R)
Samuel C. Major (D)
Jacob L. Milligan (D) s. 1920
William L. Nelson (D)
Cleveland A. Newton (R)
Marion E. Rhodes (R)
Milton A. Romjue (D)
Thomas L. Rubey (D)
William W. Rucker (D)

MONTANA

Senators

Henry L. Myers (D)
Thomas J. Walsh (D)

Representatives

John M. Evans (D)
Carl W. Riddick (R)

NEBRASKA

Senators

Gilbert M. Hitchcock (D)
George W. Norris (R)

Representatives

William E. Andrews (R)
Robert E. Evans (R)
Albert W. Jefferis (R)
Moses P. Kinkaid (R)
Melvin O. McLaughlin (R)
C. Frank Reavis (R)

NEVADA

Senators

Key Pittman (D)
Charles B. Henderson (D)

Representative

Charles R. Evans (D)

NEW HAMPSHIRE

Senators

George H. Moses (R)
Henry W. Keyes (R)

Representatives

Sherman E. Burroughs (R)
Edward H. Wason (R)

NEW JERSEY

Senators

Joseph S. Frelinghuysen (R)
Walter E. Edge (R)

Representatives

Ernest R. Ackerman (R)
Isaac Bacharach (R)
William J. Browning (R)
d. Mar. 1920
John J. Eagan (D)
James A. Hamill (D)
Elijah C. Hutchinson (R)
Frederick R. Lehlbach (R)
Cornelius A. McGlennon (D)
Daniel F. Minahan (D)
Francis F. Patterson, Jr. (R)
s. 1920
Amos H. Radcliffe (R)
John R. Ramsey (R)
Thomas J. Scully (D)

NEW MEXICO

Senators

Albert B. Fall (R)
Andrieus A. Jones (D)

Representative

Benigno C. Hernandez (R)

NEW YORK

Senators

James W. Wadsworth, Jr. (R)
William M. Calder (R)

Representatives

Charles P. Caldwell (D)
John F. Carew (D)
William E. Cleary (D)
Frank Crowther (R)
Thomas H. Cullen (D)
S. Wallace Dempsey (R)
Jerome F. Donovan (D)
Peter J. Dooling (D)
Thomas B. Dunn (R)
Hamilton Fish, Jr. (R) s. Dec. 1920
James V. Ganly (D)
Henry M. Goldfogle (D)
Norman J. Gould (R)
Anthony J. Griffin (D)
Reuben L. Haskell (R) r. Dec. 1919
Frederick C. Hicks (R)
William H. Hill (R)
Alanson B. Houghton (R)
James W. Husted (R)
John B. Johnston (D)
Fiorello H. LaGuardia (R) r. Dec. 1919
John MacCrate (R) r. Dec. 1920
Clarence MacGregor (R)
Richard F. McKiniry (D)
Walter W. Magee (R)
James P. Maher (D)
James M. Mead (D)
Luther W. Mott (R)
David J. O'Connell (D)
James S. Parker (R)
Herbert Claiborne Pell (D)
Nathan D. Perlman (R) s. Dec. 1920
Edmund Platt (R) r. June 1920
Daniel A. Reed (R)
Daniel J. Riordan (D)
Joseph Rowan (D)
Frederick W. Rowe (R)
Archie D. Sanders (R)
Rollin B. Sanford (R)
Isaac Siegel (R)
Thomas F. Smith (D)
Bertrand H. Snell (R)
Homer P. Snyder (R)
Christopher D. Sullivan (D)
Lester D. Volk (R) s. 1920
Charles B. Ward (R)

NORTH CAROLINA

Senators

Furnifold M. Simmons (D)
Lee S. Overman (D)

Representatives

Samuel M. Brinson (D)
Robert L. Doughton (D)
Hannibal L. Godwin (D)
Clyde R. Hoey (D) s. 1920
Claude Kitchin (D)
Edward W. Pou (D)
Leonidas D. Robinson (D)
John H. Small (D)
Charles M. Stedman (D)
Zebulon Weaver (D)
Edwin Y. Webb (D) r. Nov. 1919

NORTH DAKOTA

Senators

Porter J. McCumber (R)
Asle J. Gronna (R)

Representatives

John M. Baer (R)
James H. Sinclair (R)
George M. Young (R)

OHIO

Senators

Atlee Pomerene (D)

Warren G. Harding (R) r. Jan. 1921
Frank B. Willis (R) s. 1921

Representatives

William A. Ashbrook (D)
John J. Babka (D)
James T. Begg (R)
Clement L. Brumbaugh (D)
R. Clint Cole (R)
John G. Cooper (R)
Martin L. Davey (D)
Henry I. Emerson (R)
Simeon D. Fess (R)
Israel M. Foster (R)
Warren Gard (D)
Charles C. Kearns (R)
Nicholas Longworth (R)
Roscoe C. McCulloch (R)
Charles A. Mooney (D)
C. Ellis Moore (R)
B. Frank Murphy (R)
Edwin D. Ricketts (R)
Isaac R. Sherwood (D)
Ambrose E. B. Stephens (R)
Charles J. Thompson (R)
Benjamin F. Welty (D)

OKLAHOMA

Senators

Thomas P. Gore (D)
Robert L. Owen (D)

Representatives

Charles D. Carter (D)
Scott Ferris (D)
John W. Harreld (R) s. 1919
William W. Hastings (D)
Everette B. Howard (D)
James V. McClintic (D)
Thomas D. McKeown (D)
Dick T. Morgan (R) d. June 1920
Charles Swindall (R) s. 1920
Joseph B. Thompson (D) d. Sept. 1919

OREGON

Senators

George E. Chamberlain (D)
Charles L. McNary (R)

Representatives

Willis C. Hawley (R)
Clifton N. McArthur (R)
Nicholas J. Sinnott (R)

PENNSYLVANIA

Senators

Boies Penrose (R)
Philander C. Knox (R)

Representatives

Edward S. Brooks (R)
William J. Burke (R)
Thomas S. Butler (R)
Guy E. Campbell (D)
John J. Casey (D)
Peter E. Costello (R)
Thomas S. Crago (R)
George P. Darrow (R)
Arthur G. Dewalt (D)
George W. Edmonds (R)
John R. Farr (R) s. 1921
Benjamin K. Focht (R)
Mahlon M. Garland (R) d. Nov. 1920
George S. Graham (R)
William W. Griest (R)
Willis J. Hulings (R)
Evan J. Jones (R)
M. Clyde Kelly (R)
Samuel A. Kendall (R)
Edgar R. Kiess (R)
Aaron S. Kreider (R)
John V. Lesher (D)
Louis T. McFadden (R)
Patrick McLane (D)
J. Hampton Moore (R) r. Jan. 1920
John M. Morin (R)
Stephen G. Porter (R)
Harry C. Ransley (R) s. 1920
John Reber (R)
John M. Rose (R)
Milton W. Shreve (R)
Henry J. Steele (D)
Nathan L. Strong (R)
Henry W. Temple (R)
William S. Vare (R)
Anderson H. Walters (R)
Henry W. Watson (R)
John H. Wilson (D) s. 1919

RHODE ISLAND

Senators

LeBaron B. Colt (R)
Peter G. Gerry (D)

Representatives

Clark Burdick (R)
Ambrose Kennedy (R)
Walter R. Stiness (R)

SOUTH CAROLINA

Senators

Ellison D. Smith (D)
Nathaniel B. Dial (D)

Representatives

James F. Byrnes (D)
Fred H. Dominick (D)
Asbury F. Lever (D) r. Aug. 1919
Edward C. Mann (D)
Samuel J. Nicholls (D)
J. Willard Ragsdale (D) d. July 1919
William F. Stevenson (D)
Philip H. Stoll (D) s. 1919
Richard S. Whaley (D)

SOUTH DAKOTA

Senators

Thomas Sterling (R)
Edwin S. Johnson (D)

Representatives

Charles A. Christopherson (R)
Harry L. Gandy (D)
Royal C. Johnson (R)

TENNESSEE

Senators

John K. Shields (D)
Kenneth D. McKellar (D)

Representatives

Joseph W. Byrns (D)
Ewin L. Davis (D)
Hubert F. Fisher (D)
Finis J. Garrett (D)
Cordell Hull (D)
John A. Moon (D)
Lemuel P. Padgett (D)
Sam R. Sells (R)
Thetus W. Sims (D)
J. Will Taylor (R)

TEXAS

Senators

Charles A. Culberson (D)
Morris Sheppard (D)

Representatives

Carlos Bee (D)
Eugene Black (D)
Thomas L. Blanton (D)
John C. Box (D)
Clay Stone Briggs (D)
James P. Buchanan (D)
Tom T. Connally (D)
Joe H. Eagle (D)
John Nance Garner (D)
Rufus Hardy (D)
Claude B. Hudspeth (D)
Marvin Jones (D)
Fritz G. Lanham (D)
Joseph J. Mansfield (D)
Lucian W. Parrish (D)
Sam Rayburn (D)
Hatton W. Sumners (D)
James Young (D)

UTAH

Senators

Reed Smoot (R)
William H. King (D)

Representatives

James H. Mays (D)
Milton H. Welling (D)

VERMONT

Senators

William P. Dillingham (R)
Carroll S. Page (R)

Representatives

Porter H. Dale (R)
Frank L. Greene (R)

VIRGINIA

Senators

Thomas S. Martin (D)
d. Nov. 1919
Carter Glass (D) s. 1920

Claude A. Swanson (D)

Representatives

Schuyler Otis Bland (D)
Patrick H. Drewry (D) s. 1920
Henry D. Flood (D)
Thomas W. Harrison (D)
Edward E. Holland (D)
Rorer A. James (D) s. 1920
Andrew J. Montague (D)
R. Walton Moore (D)
Edward W. Saunders (D)
r. Feb. 1920
C. Bascom Slemp (D)
Walter A. Watson (D)
d. Dec. 1919
James P. Woods (D)

WASHINGTON

Senators

Wesley L. Jones (R)
Miles Poindexter (R)

Representatives

Lindley H. Hadley (R)
Albert Johnson (R)
John F. Miller (R)
John W. Summers (R)
J. Stanley Webster (R)

WEST VIRGINIA

Senators

Howard Sutherland (R)
Davis Elkins (R)

Representatives

George M. Bowers (R)
Leonard S. Echols (R)
Wells Goodykoontz (R)
Matthew M. Neely (D)
Stuart F. Reed (R)
Harry C. Woodyard (R)

WISCONSIN

Senators

Robert M. La Follette (R)
Irvine L. Lenroot (R)

Representatives

Edward E. Browne (R)
David G. Classon (R)
John J. Esch (R)
James A. Frear (R)
John C. Kleczka (R)
Florian Lampert (R)
James G. Monahan (R)
Adolphus P. Nelson (R)
Clifford E. Randall (R)
Edward Voigt (R)

WYOMING

Senators

Francis E. Warren (R)
John B. Kendrick (D)

Representative

Frank W. Mondell (R)

SIXTY-SEVENTH CONGRESS

March 4, 1921 to March 3, 1923

President of the Senate:	Calvin Coolidge
President Pro Tempore of The Senate:	Albert B. Cummins
Speaker of The House of Representatives:	Frederick H. Gillett

ALABAMA

Senators

Oscar W. Underwood (D)
J. Thomas Heflin (D)

Representatives

Edward B. Almon (D)
William B. Bankhead (D)
William B. Bowling (D)
George Huddleston (D)
Lamar Jeffers (D)
John McDuffie (D)
William B. Oliver (D)
Lilius B. Rainey (D)
Henry B. Steagall (D)
John R. Tyson (D)

ARIZONA

Senators

Henry F. Ashurst (D)
Ralph H. Cameron (R)

Representative

Carl Hayden (D)

ARKANSAS

Senators

Joseph T. Robinson (D)
Thaddeus H. Caraway (D)

Representatives

William J. Driver (D)
Henderson M. Jacoway (D)
William A. Oldfield (D)
Tilman B. Parks (D)
Chester W. Taylor (D)
Samuel M. Taylor (D)
d. Sept. 1921
John N. Tillman (D)
Otis Wingo (D)

CALIFORNIA

Senators

Hiram W. Johnson (R)
Samuel M. Shortridge (R)

Representatives

Henry E. Barbour (R)
Charles F. Curry (R)
John A. Elston (R) d. Dec. 1921
Arthur M. Free (R)
Julius Kahn (R)
Clarence F. Lea (D,R)
Walter F. Lineberger (R)
James H. MacLafferty (R) s. 1922
Mae E. Nolan (R) s. 1923
John I. Nolan (R) d. Nov. 1922
Henry Z. Osborne (R)
d. Feb. 1923
John E. Raker (D)
Philip D. Swing (R)

COLORADO

Senators

Lawrence C. Phipps (R)
Samuel D. Nicholson (R)

Representatives

Guy U. Hardy (R)
Edward T. Taylor (D)
Charles B. Timberlake (R)
William N. Vaile (R)

CONNECTICUT

Senators

Frank B. Brandegee (R)
George P. McLean (R)

Representatives

E. Hart Fenn (R)
Richard P. Freeman (R)
James P. Glynn (R)
Schuyler Merritt (R)
John Q. Tilson (R)

DELAWARE

Senators

Josiah O. Wolcott (D) r. July 1921
T. Coleman Du Pont (R) ta. 1921
Thomas F. Bayard Jr. (D) s. 1922

L. Heisler Ball (R)

Representative

Caleb R. Layton (R)

FLORIDA

Senators

Duncan U. Fletcher (D)
Park Trammell (D)

Representatives

Frank Clark (D)
Herbert J. Drane (D)
William J. Sears (D)
John H. Smithwick (D)

GEORGIA

Senators

William J. Harris (D)

Thomas E. Watson (D)
d. Sept. 1922
Walter F. George (D) s. 1922

Representatives

Thomas M. Bell (D)
Charles H. Brand (D)
Charles R. Crisp (D)
William C. Lankford (D)
William W. Larsen (D)
Gordon Lee (D)
James W. Overstreet (D)
Frank Park (D)
William D. Upshaw (D)
Carl Vinson (D)
James W. Wise (D)
William C. Wright (D)

IDAHO

Senators

William E. Borah (R)
Frank R. Gooding (R)

Representatives

Burton L. French (R)
Addison T. Smith (R)

ILLINOIS

Senators

Medill McCormick (R)
William B. McKinley (R)

Representatives

Fred A. Britten (R)
Edwin B. Brooks (R)
Joseph G. Cannon (R)
Carl R. Chindblom (R)
Ira C. Copley (R)
Edward E. Denison (R)
Charles E. Fuller (R)
Frank H. Funk (R)
John J. Gorman (R)
William J. Graham (R)
Winnifred S. M. Huck (R) s. 1922
Clifford Ireland (R)
Edward J. King (R)
Stanley H. Kunz (D)
John C. McKenzie (R)
Martin B. Madden (R)
James R. Mann (R) d. Nov. 1922
William E. Mason (R)
d. June 1921
M. Alfred Michaelson (R)
Allen F. Moore (R)
John W. Rainey (D)
William A. Rodenberg (R)
Adolph J. Sabath (D)
Guy L. Shaw (R)
Elliott W. Sproul (R)
Loren E. Wheeler (R)
Thomas S. Williams (R)
Richard Yates (R)

INDIANA

Senators

James E. Watson (R)
Harry S. New (R)

Representatives

John S. Benham (R)
Oscar E. Bland (R)
James W. Dunbar (R)
Richard N. Elliott (R)
Louis W. Fairfield (R)
Andrew J. Hickey (R)
Milton Kraus (R)
Oscar R. Luhring (R)
Merrill Moores (R)
Fred S. Purnell (R)
Everett Sanders (R)
Albert H. Vestal (R)
William R. Wood (R)

IOWA

Senators

Albert B. Cummins (R)

William S. Kenyon (R)
r. Feb. 1922
Charles A. Rawson (R) ta. 1922
Smith W. Brookhart (R) s. 1922

Representatives

William D. Boies (R)
Cyrenus Cole (R)
Lester J. Dickinson (R)
Cassius C. Dowell (R)
James W. Good r. June 1921
William R. Green (R)
Gilbert N. Haugen (R)
Harry E. Hull (R)
William F. Kopp (R)
C. William Ramseyer (R)
Burton E. Sweet (R)
Horace M. Towner (R)

KANSAS

Senators

Charles Curtis (R)
Arthur Capper (R)

Representatives

Daniel R. Anthony, Jr. (R)
Richard E. Bird (R)
Philip P. Campbell (R)
Homer Hoch (R)
Edward C. Little (R)
James G. Strong (R)
Jasper N.Tincher (R)
Hays B. White (R)

KENTUCKY

Senators

Augustus O. Stanley (D)
Richard P. Ernst (R)

Representatives

Alben W. Barkley (D)
James C. Cantrill (D)
William J. Fields (D)
Ralph Gilbert (D)
Ben Johnson (D)
David H. Kincheloe (D)
John W. Langley (R)
Charles F. Ogden (R)
John M. Robsion (R)
Arthur B. Rouse (D)
Robert Y. Thomas, Jr. (D)

LOUISIANA

Senators

Joseph E. Ransdell (D)
Edwin S. Broussard (D)

Representatives

James B. Aswell (D)
H. Garland Dupre (D)
George K. Favrot (D)
Ladislas Lazaro (D)
Whitmell P. Martin (D)
James O'Connor (D)
John N. Sandlin (D)
Riley J. Wilson (D)

MAINE

Senators

Bert M. Fernald (R)
Frederick Hale (R)

Representatives

Carroll L. Beedy (R)
Ira G. Hersey (R)
John E. Nelson (R) s. 1922
John A. Peters (R) r. Jan. 1922
Wallace H. White, Jr. (R)

MARYLAND

Senators

Joseph I. France (R)
Ovington E. Weller (R)

Representatives

Albert A. Blakeney (R)
T. Alan Goldsborough (D)
John P. Hill (R)
J. Charles Linthicum (D)
Sydney E. Mudd (R)
Frederick N. Zihlman (R)

MASSACHUSETTS

Senators

Henry Cabot Lodge (R)
David I. Walsh (D)

Representatives

A. Piatt Andrew, Jr. (R)
Frederick W. Dallinger (R)
Louis A. Frothingham (R)
James A. Gallivan (D)
Charles L. Gifford (R) s. 1922
Frederick H. Gillett (R)
William S. Greene (R)
Robert Luce (R)
Willfred W. Lufkin (R)
r. June 1921
Robert S. Maloney (R)
Calvin D. Paige (R)
John Jacob Rogers (R)
Peter F. Tague (D)
George H. Tinkham (R)
Allen T. Treadway (R)
Charles L. Underhill (R)
Joseph Walsh (R) r. Aug. 1922
Samuel E. Winslow (R)

MICHIGAN

Senators

Charles E. Townsend (R)

Truman H. Newberry (R)
r. Nov. 1922
James Couzens (R) s. 1922

Representatives

Vincent M. Brennan (R)
George P. Codd (R)
Louis C. Cramton (R)
Joseph W. Fordney (R)
W. Frank James (R)
Patrick H. Kelley (R)
John C. Ketcham (R)
James C. McLaughlin (R)
Carl E. Mapes (R)
Earl C. Michener (R)
Frank D. Scott (R)
John M. C. Smith (R)
Roy O. Woodruff (R)

MINNESOTA

Senators

Knute Nelson (R)
Frank B. Kellogg (R)

Representatives

Sydney Anderson (R)
Frank Clague (R)
Charles R. Davis (R)

Oscar E. Keller (R)
Harold Knutson (R)
Oscar J. Larson (R)
Walter H. Newton (R)
Thomas D. Schall (R)
Halvor Steenerson (R)
Andrew J. Volstead (R)

MISSISSIPPI

Senators

John Sharp Williams (D)
Pat Harrison (D)

Representatives

James W. Collier (D)
Ross A. Collins (D)
Benjamin G. Humphreys (D)
Paul B. Johnson (D)
Bill G. Lowrey (D)
Percy E. Quin (D)
John E. Rankin (D)
Thomas U. Sission (D)

MISSOURI

Senators

James A. Reed (D)
Selden P. Spencer (R)

Representatives

William O. Atkeson (R)
Leonidas C. Dyer (R)
Edgar C. Ellis (R)
Charles L. Faust (R)
Harry B. Hawes (D)
Edward D. Hays (R)
Theodore W. Hukriede (R)
Henry F. Lawrence (R)
Isaac V. McPherson (R)
Frank C. Millspaugh (R)
r. Dec. 1922
Cleveland A. Newton (R)
Roscoe C. Patterson (R)
Marion E. Rhodes (R)
Sidney C. Roach (R)
William W. Rucker (D)
Samuel A. Shelton (R)

MONTANA

Senators

Henry L. Myers (D)
Thomas J. Walsh (D)

Representatives

Washington J. McCormick (R)
Carl W. Riddick (R)

NEBRASKA

Senators

Gilbert M. Hitchcock (D)
George W. Norris (R)

Representatives

William E. Andrews (R)
Robert E. Evans (R)
Augustin R. Humphrey (R)
s. 1922
Albert W. Jefferis (R)
Moses P. Kinkaid (R) d. July 1922
Melvin O. McLaughlin (R)
C. Frank Reavis (R) r. June 1922
Roy H. Thorpe (R) s. 1922

NEVADA

Senators

Key Pittman (D)
Tasker L. Oddie (R)

Representative

Samuel S. Arentz (R)

NEW HAMPSHIRE

Senators

George H. Moses (R)
Henry W. Keyes (R)

Representatives

Sherman E. Burroughs (R)
d. Jan. 1923
Edward H. Wason (R)

NEW JERSEY

Senators

Joseph S. Frelinghuysen (R)
Walter E. Edge (R)

Representatives

Ernest R. Ackerman (R)
T. Frank Appleby (R)
Isaac Bacharach (R)
Elijah C. Hutchinson (R)
Frederick R. Lehlbach (R)
Charles F. X. O'Brien (D)
Archibald E. Olpp (R)
Richard W. Parker (R)
Francis F. Patterson, Jr. (R)
Randolph Perkins (R)
Amos H. Radcliffe (R)
Herbert W. Taylor (R)

NEW MEXICO

Senators

Holm O. Bursum (R)
Andrieus A. Jones (D)

Representative

Nestor Montoya (R) d. Jan. 1923

NEW YORK

Senators

James W. Wadsworth, Jr. (R)
William M. Calder (R)

Representatives

Martin C. Ansorge (R)
Charles G. Bond (R)
John F. Carew (D)
Walter M. Chandler (R)
John D. Clarke (R)
W. Bourke Cockran (D)
d. Mar. 1923
Frank Crowther (R)
Thomas H. Cullen (D)
S. Wallace Dempsey (R)
Thomas B. Dunn (R)
Benjamin L. Fairchild (R)
Hamilton Fish, Jr. (R)
Norman J. Gould (R)
Anthony J. Griffin (D)
Lewis Henry (R) s. 1922
Frederick C. Hicks (R)
Michael J. Hogan (R)
Alanson B. Houghton (R)
r. Feb. 1922
James W. Husted (R)
John J. Kindred (D)
John Kissel (R)
Ardolph L. Kline (R)
Warren I. Lee (R)
Meyer London (Socialist)
Clarence MacGregor (R)
Walter W. Magee (R)
James M. Mead (D)
Ogden L. Mills (R)
Luther W. Mott (R)
James S. Parker (R)
Nathan D. Perlman (R)
Andrew N. Petersen (R)
Daniel A. Reed (R)
Daniel J. Riordan (D)
Albert B. Rossdale (R)
Thomas J. Ryan (R)
Archie D. Sanders (R)
Isaac Siegel (R)
Bertrand H. Snell (R)
Homer P. Snyder (R)
Christopher D. Sullivan (D)
Peter G. Ten Eyck (D)
Lester D. Volk (R)
Charles B. Ward (R)

NORTH CAROLINA

Senators

Furnifold M. Simmons (D)
Lee S. Overman (D)

Representatives

Charles L. Abernethy (D) s. 1922
Samuel M. Brinson (D)
d. Apr. 1922
Alfred L. Bulwinkle (D)
Robert L. Doughton (D)
William C. Hammer (D)
Claude Kitchin (D)
Homer L. Lyon (D)
Edward W. Pou (D)
Charles M. Stedman (D)
Hallett S. Ward (D)
Zebulon Weaver (D)

NORTH DAKOTA

Senators

Porter J. McCumber (R)
Edwin F. Ladd (R)

Representatives

Olger B. Burtness (R)
James H. Sinclair (R)
George M. Young (R)

OHIO

Senators

Atlee Pomerene (D)
Frank B. Willis (R)

Representatives

James T. Begg (R)
Theodore E. Burton (R)
John L. Cable (R)
William W. Chalmers (R)
R. Clint Cole (R)
John G. Cooper (R)
Simeon D. Fess (R)
Roy G. Fitzgerald (R)
Israel M. Foster (R)
Harry C. Gahn (R)
Joseph H. Himes (R)
Charles C. Kearns (R)
Charles L. Knight (R)
Nicholas Longworth (R)
C. Ellis Moore (R)
William M. Morgan (R)
B. Frank Murphy (R)
Miner G. Norton (R)
Edwin D. Ricketts (R)
John C. Speaks (R)
Ambrose E. B. Stephens (R)
Charles J. Thompson (R)

OKLAHOMA

Senators

Robert L. Owen (D)
John W. Harreld (R)

Representatives

Charles D. Carter (D)
Thomas A. Chandler (R)
Lorraine M. Gensman (R)
Manuel Herrick (R)
James V. McClintic (D)
Joseph C. Pringey (R)
Alice M. Robertson (R)
Fletcher B. Swank (D)

OREGON

Senators

Charles L. McNary (R)
Robert N. Stanfield (R)

Representatives

Willis C. Hawley (R)
Clinton N. McArthur (R)
Nicholas J. Sinnott (R)

PENNSYLVANIA

Senators

Boies Penrose (R) d. Dec. 1921
George Wharton Pepper (R) s. 1922

Philander C. Knox (R) d. Oct. 1921
William E. Crow (R) ta. 1921-22
David A. Reed (R) s. 1922

Representatives

Harris J. Bixler (R)
Edward S. Brooks (R)
William J. Burke (R)
Thomas S. Butler (R)
Guy E. Campbell (R)
Charles R. Connell (R) d. Sept. 1922
James J. Connolly (R)
Clarence D. Coughlin (R)
Thomas S. Crago (R)
George P. Darrow (R)
George W. Edmonds (R)
Benjamin K. Focht (R)
Fred B. Gernerd (R)
George S. Graham (R)
William W. Griest (R)
Evan J. Jones (R)
M. Clyde Kelly (R)
Samuel A. Kendall (R)
Edgar R. Kiess (R)
William H. Kirkpatrick (R)
I. Clinton Kline (R)
Aaron S. Kreider (R)
Louis T. McFadden (R)
Joseph McLaughlin (R)
John M. Morin (R)
Stephen G. Porter (R)
Harry C. Ransley (R)
John Reber (R)
John M. Rose (R)
Milton W. Shreve (R)
Nathan L. Strong (R)
Henry W. Temple (R)
William S. Vare (R)
Anderson H. Walters (R)
Henry W. Watson (R)
Adam M. Wyant (R)

RHODE ISLAND

Senators

LeBaron B. Colt (R)
Peter G. Gerry (D)

Representatives

Clark Burdick (R)
Ambrose Kennedy (R)
Walter R. Stiness (R)

SOUTH CAROLINA

Senators

Ellison D. Smith (D)
Nathaniel B. Dial (D)

Representatives

James F. Byrnes (D)
Fred H. Dominick (D)
Hampton P. Fulmer (D)
W. Turner Logan (D)
John J. McSwain (D)
William F. Stevenson (D)
Philip H. Stoll (D)

SOUTH DAKOTA

Senators

Thomas Sterling (R)
Peter Norbeck (R)

Representatives

Charles A. Christopherson (R)
Royal C. Johnson (R)
William Williamson (R)

TENNESSEE

Senators

John K. Shields (D)
Kenneth D. McKellar (D)

Representatives

Joseph E. Brown (R)
Joseph W. Byrns (D)
Wynne F. Clouse (R)
Ewin L. Davis (D)
Hubert F. Fisher (D)
Finis J. Garrett (D)
Lemuel P. Padgett (D) d. Aug. 1922
B. Carroll Reece (R)
Lon A. Scott (R)
J. Will Taylor (R)
Clarence W. Turner (D) s. 1922

TEXAS

Senators

Charles A. Culberson (D)
Morris Sheppard (D)

Representatives

Eugene Black (D)
Thomas L. Blanton (D)
John C. Box (D)
Clay S. Briggs (D)
James P. Buchanan (D)
Tom T. Connally (D)
John Nance Garner (D)
Daniel E. Garrett (D)
Rufus Hardy (D)
Claude B. Hudspeth (D)
Marvin Jones (D)
Fritz G. Lanham (D)
Joseph J. Mansfield (D)
Lucian W. Parrish (D) d. Mar. 1922
Sam Rayburn (D)
Morgan G. Sanders (D)
Hatton W. Sumners (D)
Guinn Williams (D) s. 1922
Harry M. Wurzbach (R)

UTAH

Senators

Reed Smoot (R)
William H. King (D)

Representatives

Don B. Colton (R)
Elmer O. Leatherwood (R)

VERMONT

Senators

William P. Dillingham (R)
Carroll S. Page (R)

Representatives

Porter H. Dale (R)
Frank L. Greene (R)

VIRGINIA

Senators

Claude A. Swanson (D)
Carter Glass (D)

Representatives

Schuyler Otis Bland (D)
Joseph T. Deal (D)
Patrick H. Drewry (D)
Henry D. Flood (D) d. Dec. 1921
Thomas W. Harrison (D) r. Dec. 1922
James M. Hooker (D)
Rorer A. James (D) d. Aug. 1921
R. Walton Moore (D)
Andrew J. Montague (D)
John Paul (R) s. 1922
C. Bascom Slemp (D)
Henry St. George Tucker (D) s. 1922
James P. Woods (D)

WASHINGTON

Senators

Wesley L. Jones (R)
Miles Poindexter (R)

Representatives

Lindley H. Hadley (R)
Albert Johnson (R)
John F. Miller (R)
John W. Summers (R)
J. Stanley Webster (R)

WEST VIRGINIA

Senators

Howard Sutherland (R)
Davis Elkins (R)

Representatives

George M. Bowers (R)
Leonard S. Echols (R)
Wells Goodykoontz (R)
Stuart F. Reed (R)
Benjamin L. Rosenbloom (R)
Harry C. Woodyard (R)

WISCONSIN

Senators

Robert M. La Follette (R)
Irvine L. Lenroot (R)

Representatives

Joseph D. Beck (R)
Edward E. Browne (R)
David G. Classon (R)
Henry A. Cooper (R)
James A. Frear (R)
John C. Kleczka (R)
Florian Lampert (R)
Adolphus P. Nelson (R)
John M. Nelson (R)
William H. Stafford (R)
Edward Voigt (R)

WYOMING

Senators

Francis E. Warren (R)
John B. Kendrick (D)

Representative

Frank W. Mondell (R)

SIXTY-EIGHTH CONGRESS

March 4, 1923 to March 3, 1925

President of The Senate: Calvin Coolidge
President Pro Tempore of The Senate: Albert B. Cummins
Speaker of The House of Representatives: Frederick H. Gillett

ALABAMA

Senators

Oscar W. Underwood (D)
J. Thomas Heflin (D)

Representatives

Miles C. Allgood (D)
Edward B. Almon (D)
William B. Bankhead (D)
William B. Bowling (D)
Lister Hill (D)
George Huddleston (D)
Lamar Jeffers (D)
John McDuffie (D)
William B. Oliver (D)
Henry B. Steagall (D)

ARIZONA

Senators

Henry F. Ashurst (D)
Ralph H. Cameron (R)

Representative

Carl Hayden (D)

ARKANSAS

Senators

Joseph T. Robinson (D)
Thaddeus H. Caraway (D)

Representatives

William J. Driver (D)
William A. Oldfield (D)
Tilman B. Parks (D)
Heartsill Ragon (D)
James B. Reed (D)
John N. Tillman (D)
Otis Wingo (D)

CALIFORNIA

Senators

Hiram W. Johnson (R)
Samuel M. Shortridge (R)

Representatives

Henry E. Barbour (R)
Charles F. Curry (R)
John D. Fredericks (R)
Arthur M. Free (R)
Clarence F. Lea (D,R)
Walter F. Lineberger (R)
James H. MacLafferty (R)
Mae E. Nolan (R)
John E. Raker (D)
Philip D. Swing (R)

COLORADO

Senators

Lawrence C. Phipps (R)

Samuel D. Nicholson (R)
d. Mar. 1923
Alva B. Adams (D) ta. 1923
Rice W. Means (R) s. 1924

Representatives

Guy U. Hardy (R)
Edward T. Taylor (D)
Charles B. Timberlake (R)
William N. Vaile (R)

CONNECTICUT

Senators

Frank B. Brandegee (R)
d. Oct. 1924
Hiram Bingham (R) s. 1925

George P. McLean (R)

Representatives

E. Hart Fenn (R)
Richard P. Freeman (R)
Schuyler Merritt (R)
Patrick B. O'Sullivan (D)
John Q. Tilson (R)

DELAWARE

Senators

L. Heisler Ball (R)
Thomas F. Bayard, Jr. (D)

Representative

William H. Boyce (D)

FLORIDA

Senators

Duncan U. Fletcher (D)
Park Trammell (D)

Representatives

Frank Clark (D)
Herbert J. Drane (D)
William J. Sears (D)
John H. Smithwick (D)

GEORGIA

Senators

William J. Harris (D)
Walter F. George (D)

Representatives

Thomas M. Bell (D)
Charles H. Brand (D)
Charles R. Crisp (D)
William C. Lankford (D)
William W. Larsen (D)
Gordon Lee (D)
R. Lee Moore (D)
Frank Park (D)
William D. Upshaw (D)
Carl Vinson (D)
William C. Wright (D)

IDAHO

Senators

William E. Borah (R)
Frank R. Gooding (R)

Representatives

Burton L. French (R)
Addison T. Smith (R)

ILLINOIS

Senators

Medill McCormick (R)
d. Feb. 1925
Charles S. Deneen (R) s. 1925

William B. McKinley (R)

Representatives

William W. Arnold (D)
Fred A. Britten (R)
James R. Buckley (D)
Carl R. Chindblom (R)
Edward E. Denison (R)
Thomas A. Doyle (D)
Charles E. Fuller (R)
Frank H. Funk (R)
William J. Graham (R)
r. June 1924
William P. Holaday (R)
Morton D. Hull (R)
William E. Hull (R)
Edward J. King (R)
Stanley H. Kunz (D)
John C. McKenzie (R)
Martin B. Madden (R)
J. Earl Major (D)
M. Alfred Michaelson (R)
Edward E. Miller (R)
Allen F. Moore (R)
Henry T. Rainey (D)
Henry R. Rathbone (R)
Frank R. Reid (R)
Adolph J. Sabath (D)

Elliott W. Sproul (R)
Thomas S. Williams (R)
Richard Yates (R)

INDIANA

Senators

James E. Watson (R)
Samuel M. Ralston (D)

Representatives

Harry C. Canfield (D)
Samuel E. Cook (D)
Richard N. Elliott (R)
Louis W. Fairfield (R)
Frank Gardner (D)
Arthur H. Greenwood (D)
Andrew J. Hickey (R)
Merrill Moores (R)
Fred S. Purnell (R)
Everett Sanders (R)
Albert H. Vestal (R)
William E. Wilson (D)
William R. Wood (R)

IOWA

Senators

Albert B. Cummins (R)
Smith W. Brookhart (R)

Representatives

William D. Boies (R)
Cyrenus Cole (R)
Lester J. Dickinson (R)
Cassius C. Dowell (R)
Hiram K. Evans (R)
William R. Green (R)
Gilbert N. Haugen (R)
Harry E. Hull (R)
William F. Kopp (R)
C. William Ramseyer (R)
Thomas J. B. Robinson (R)

KANSAS

Senators

Charles Curtis (R)
Arthur Capper (R)

Representatives

Daniel R. Anthony, Jr. (R)
William A. Ayres (D)
Ulysses S. Guyer (R) s. 1924
Homer Hoch (R)
Edward C. Little (R) d. June 1924
William H. Sproul (R)
James G. Strong (R)
Jasper N. Tincher (R)
Hays B. White (R)

KENTUCKY

Senators

Augustus O. Stanley (D)
Richard P. Ernst (R)

Representatives

Alben W. Barkley (D)
William J. Fields (D) r. Dec. 1923
Ralph Gilbert (D)
Ben Johnson (D)
David H. Kincheloe (D)
John W. Langley (R)
Joseph W. Morris (D)
John M. Robsion (R)
Arthur B. Rouse (D)
Maurice H. Thatcher (R)
Robert Y. Thomas, Jr. (D)
Fred M. Vinson (D) s. 1924

LOUISIANA

Senators

Joseph E. Ransdell (D)
Edwin S. Broussard (D)

Representatives

James B. Aswell (D)
H. Garland Dupre (D)
d. Feb. 1924
George K. Favrot (D)
Ladislas Lazaro (D)
Whitmell P. Martin (D)
James O'Connor (D)
John N. Sandlin (D)
J. Zach Spearing (D) s. 1924
Riley J. Wilson (D)

MAINE

Senators

Bert M. Fernald (R)
Frederick Hale (R)

Representatives

Carroll L. Beedy (R)
Ira G. Hersey (R)
John E. Nelson (R)
Wallace H. White, Jr. (R)

MARYLAND

Senators

Ovington E. Weller (R)
William Cabell Bruce (D)

Representatives

Stephen W. Gambrill (D) s. 1924
T. Alan Goldsborough (D)
John Philip Hill (R)
J. Charles Linthicum (D)
Sydney E. Mudd (R) d. Oct. 1924
Millard E. Tydings (D)
Frederick N. Zihlman (R)

MASSACHUSETTS

Senators

Henry Cabot Lodge (R)
d. Nov. 1924
William M. Butler (R) s. 1924

David I. Walsh (D)

Representatives

A. Piatt Andrew, Jr. (R)
William P. Connery, Jr. (D)
Frederick W. Dallinger (R)
Louis A. Frothingham (R)
James A. Gallivan (D)
Charles L. Gifford (R)
Frederick H. Gillett (R)
William S. Greene (R)
d. Sept. 1924
Robert M. Leach (R) s. 1924
Robert Luce (R)
Calvin D. Paige (R)
John Jacob Rogers (R)
Peter F. Tague (D)
George H. Tinkham (R)
Allen T. Treadway (R)
Charles L. Underhill (R)
Samuel E. Winslow (R)

MICHIGAN

Senators

James Couzens (R)
Woodbridge N. Ferris (D)

Representatives

Robert H. Clancy (D)
Louis C. Cramton (R)
Grant M. Hudson (R)
W. Frank James (R)
John C. Ketcham (R)
James C. McLaughlin (R)
Clarence J. McLeod (R)
Carl E. Mapes (R)
Earl C. Michener (R)
Frank D. Scott (R)
Bird J. Vincent (R)
Arthur B. Williams (R)
Roy O. Woodruff (R)

MINNESOTA

Senators

Magnus Johnson (Farm-Labor)
Henrik Shipstead (Farm-Labor)

Representatives

Sydney Anderson (R)
Frank Clague (R)
Charles R. Davis (R)
Oscar E. Keller (R)
Harold Knutson (R)
Ole J. Kvale (R)
Oscar J. Larson (R)
Walter H. Newton (R)
Thomas D. Schall (R)
Knud Wefald (Farm-Labor)

MISSISSIPPI

Senators

Pat Harrison (D)
Hubert D. Stephens (D)

Representatives

T. Jeff Busby (D)
James W. Collier (D)
Ross A. Collins (D)
William Y. Humphreys (D)
Bill G. Lowrey (D)
Percy E. Quin (D)
John E. Rankin (D)
T. Webber Wilson (D)

MISSOURI

Senators

James A. Reed (D)
Selden P. Spencer (R)

Representatives

Clarence Cannon (D)
Clement C. Dickinson (D)
Leonidas C. Dyer (R)
Charles L. Faust (R)
James F. Fulbright (D)
Harry B. Hawes (D)
Henry L. Jost (D)
Ralph F. Lozier (D)
Samuel C. Major (D)
Joe J. Manlove (R)
Jacob L. Milligan (D)
Cleveland A. Newton (R)
Sidney C. Roach (R)
Milton A. Romjue (D)
Thomas L. Rubey (D)
J. Scott Wolff (D)

MONTANA

Senators

Thomas J. Walsh (D)
Burton K. Wheeler (D)

Representatives

John M. Evans (D)
Scott Leavitt (R)

NEBRASKA

Senators

George W. Norris (R)
Robert B. Howell (R)

Representatives

Edgar Howard (D)
Melvin O. McLaughlin (R)
John H. Morehead (D)
Willis G. Sears (R)
Ashton C. Shallenberger (D)
Robert G. Simmons (R)

NEVADA

Senators

Key Pittman (D)
Tasker L. Oddie (R)

Representative

Charles L. Richards (D)

NEW HAMPSHIRE

Senators

George H. Moses (R)
Henry W. Keyes (R)

Representatives

William N. Rogers (D)
Edward H. Wason (R)

NEW JERSEY

Senators

Walter E. Edge (R)
Edward I. Edwards (D)

Representatives

Ernest R. Ackerman (R)
Isaac Bacharach (R)
Charles Browne (D)
John J. Eagan (D)
Elmer H. Geran (D)
Frederick R. Lehlbach (R)
Frank J. McNulty (D)
Daniel F. Minahan (D)
Charles F. X. O'Brien (D)
Francis F. Patterson, Jr. (R)
Randolph Perkins (R)
George N. Seger (R)

NEW MEXICO

Senators

Andrieus A. Jones (D)
Holm O. Bursum (R)

Representative

John Morrow (D)

NEW YORK

Senators

James W. Wadsworth, Jr. (R)
Royal S. Copeland (D)

Representatives

Robert L. Bacon (R)
Loring M. Black, Jr. (D)
Sol Bloom (D)
John J. Boylan (D)
John F. Carew (D)
Emanuel Celler (D)
John D. Clarke (R)
William E. Cleary (D)
Parker Corning (D)
Frank Crowther (R)
Thomas H. Cullen (D)
S. Wallace Dempsey (R)
Samuel Dickstein (D)

Benjamin L. Fairchild (R)
Hamilton Fish, Jr. (R)
Anthony J. Griffin (D)
Meyer Jacobstein (D)
John J. Kindred (D)
Fiorello H. LaGuardia (R)
George W. Lindsay (D)
Clarence MacGregor (R)
Walter W. Magee (R)
James M. Mead (D)
Odgen L. Mills (R)
David J. O'Connell (D)
John J. O'Connor (D)
Frank Oliver (D)
James S. Parker (R)
Nathan D. Perlman (R)
Anning S. Prall (D)
John F. Quayle (D)
Daniel A. Reed (R)
Archie D. Sanders (R)
Bertrand H. Snell (R)
Homer P. Snyder (R)
Gale H. Stalker (R)
Charles I. Stengle (D)
Christopher D. Sullivan (D)
Thaddeus C. Sweet (R)
John Taber (R)
J. Mayhew Wainwright (R)
Charles B. Ward (R)
Royal H. Weller (D)

NORTH CAROLINA

Senators

Furnifold M. Simmons (D)
Lee S. Overman (D)

Representatives

Charles L. Abernethy (D)
Alfred L. Bulwinkle (D)
Robert L. Doughton (D)
William C. Hammer (D)
John H. Kerr (D)
Homer L. Lyon (D)
Edward W. Pou (D)
Charles M. Stedman (D)
Hallett S. Ward (D)
Zebulon Weaver (D)

NORTH DAKOTA

Senators

Edwin F. Ladd (R)
Lynn J. Frazier (R)

Representatives

Olger B. Burtness (R)
Thomas Hall (D) s. 1924
James H. Sinclair (R)
George M. Young (R)
r. Sept. 1924

OHIO

Senators

Frank B. Willis (R)
Simeon D. Fess (R)

Representatives

James T. Begg (R)
Charles Brand (R)
Theodore E. Burton (R)
John L. Cable (R)
R. Clint Cole (R)
John G. Cooper (R)
Robert Crosser (D)
Martin L. Davey (D)
Roy G. Fitzgerald (R)
Israel M. Foster (R)
Charles C. Kearns (R)
Nicholas Longworth (R)
John McSweeney (D)
Charles A. Mooney (D)
C. Ellis Moore (R)
William M. Morgan (R)
B. Frank Murphy (R)
Isaac R. Sherwood (D)
John C. Speaks (R)
Ambrose E. B. Stephens (R)
Charles J. Thompson (R)
Mell G. Underwood (D)

OKLAHOMA

Senators

Robert L. Owen (D)
John W. Harreld (R)

Representatives

Charles D. Carter (D)
Milton C. Garber (R)
William W. Hastings (D)
Everette B. Howard (D)
James V. McClintic (D)
Thomas D. McKeown (D)
Fletcher B. Swank (D)
J. W. Elmer Thomas (D)

OREGON

Senators

Charles L. McNary (R)
Robert N. Stanfield (R)

Representatives

Willis C. Hawley (R)
Nicholas J. Sinnott (R)
Elton Watkins (D)

PENNSYLVANIA

Senators

George Wharton Pepper (R)
David A. Reed (R)

Representatives

Edward M. Beers (R)
Harris J. Bixler (R)
George F. Brumm (R)
Thomas S. Butler (R)
Guy E. Campbell (R)
John J. Casey (D)
James J. Connolly (R)
William M. Croll (D)
Herbert W. Cummings (D)
George P. Darrow (R)
George W. Edmonds (R)
Samuel F. Glatfelter (D)
George S. Graham (R)
William W. Griest (R)
M. Clyde Kelly (R)
Samuel A. Kendall (R)
Everett Kent (D)
Edgar R. Kiess (R)
J. Banks Kurtz (R)
Louis T. McFadden (R)
James M. Magee (R)
John M. Morin (R)
Thomas W. Phillips, Jr. (R)
Stephen G. Porter (R)
Harry C. Ransley (R)
Milton W. Shreve (R)
Frank C. Sites (D)
Nathan L. Strong (R)
William I. Swoope (R)
Henry W. Temple (R)
William S. Vare (R)
Laurence H. Watres (R)
Henry W. Watson (R)
George A. Welsh (R)
George M. Wertz (R)
Adam M. Wyant (R)

RHODE ISLAND

Senators

LeBaron B. Colt (R) d. Aug. 1924
Jesse H. Metcalf (R) s. 1924

Peter G. Gerry (D)

Representatives

Richard S. Aldrich (R)
Clark Burdick (R)
Jeremiah E. O'Connell (D)

SOUTH CAROLINA

Senators

Ellison D. Smith (D)
Nathaniel B. Dial (D)

Representatives

James F. Byrnes (D)
Fred H. Dominick (D)
Hampton P. Fulmer (D)
Allard H. Gasque (D)
W. Turner Logan (D)
John J. McSwain (D)
William F. Stevenson (D)

SOUTH DAKOTA

Senators

Thomas Sterling (R)
Peter Norbeck (R)

Representatives

Charles A. Christopherson (R)
Royal C. Johnson (R)
William Williamson (R)

TENNESSEE

Senators

John K. Shields (D)
Kenneth D. McKellar (D)

Representatives

Gordon Browning (D)
Joseph W. Byrns (D)
Ewin L. Davis (D)
Hubert F. Fisher (D)
Finis J. Garrett (D)
Cordell Hull (D)
Sam D. McReynolds (D)
B. Carroll Reece (R)
William C. Salmon (D)
J. Will Taylor (R)

TEXAS

Senators

Morris Sheppard (D)
Earle B. Mayfield (D)

Representatives

Eugene Black (D)
Thomas L. Blanton (D)
John C. Box (D)
Clay S. Briggs (D)
James P. Buchanan (R)
Tom T. Connally (D)
John Nance Garner (D)
Daniel E. Garrett (D)
Claude B. Hudspeth (D)
Luther A. Johnson (D)
Marvin Jones (D)
Fritz G. Lanham (D)
Joseph J. Mansfield (D)
Sam Rayburn (D)
Morgan G. Sanders (D)
Hatton W. Sumners (D)
Guinn Williams (D)
Harry M. Wurzbach (R)

UTAH

Senators

Reed Smoot (R)
William H. King (R)

Representatives

Don B. Colton (R)
Elmer O. Leatherwood (R)

VERMONT

Senators

Porter H. Dale (R)
Frank L. Greene (R)

Representatives

Frederick G. Fleetwood (R)
Ernest W. Gibson (R)

VIRGINIA

Senators

Claude A. Swanson (D)
Carter Glass (D)

Representatives

Schuyler Otis Bland (D)
Joseph T. Deal (D)
Patrick H. Drewry (D)
Thomas W. Harrison (D)
James M. Hooker (D)
Andrew J. Montague (D)
R. Walton Moore (D)
George C. Peery (D)
Henry St. George Tucker (D)
Clifton A. Woodrum (D)

WASHINGTON

Senators

Wesley L. Jones (R)
Clarence C. Dill (D)

Representatives

Lindley H. Hadley (R)
Samuel B. Hill (D)
Albert Johnson (R)
John F. Miller (R)
John W. Summers (R)

WEST VIRGINIA

Senators

Davis Elkins (R)
Matthew M. Neeley (D)

Representatives

Robert E. L. Allen (D)
George W. Johnson (D)
Thomas J. Lilly (D)
Stuart F. Reed (R)
Benjamin L. Rosenbloom (R)
J. Alfred Taylor (D)

WISCONSIN

Senators

Robert M. La Follette (R)
Irvine L. Lenroot (R)

Representatives

Joseph D. Beck (R)
Victor L. Berger (Socialist)
Edward E. Browne (R)
Henry A. Cooper (R)
James A. Frear (R)
Florian Lampert (R)
John M. Nelson (R)
Hubert H. Peavey (R)
John C. Schafer (R)
George J. Schneider (Progressive)
Edward Voigt (R)

WYOMING

Senators

Francis E. Warren (R)
John B. Kendrick (D)

Representative

Charles E. Winter (R)

SIXTY-NINTH CONGRESS

March 4, 1925 to March 3, 1927

President of The Senate:	Charles G. Dawes
Presidents Pro Tempore of The Senate:	Albert B. Cummins George H. Moses
Speaker of The House of Representatives:	Nicholas Longworth

ALABAMA

Senators

Oscar W. Underwood (D)
J. Thomas Heflin (D)

Representatives

Miles C. Allgood (D)
Edward B. Almon (D)
William B. Bankhead (D)
William B. Bowling (D)
Lister Hill (D)
George Huddleston (D)
Lamar Jeffers (D)
John McDuffie (D)
William B. Oliver (D)
Henry B. Steagall (D)

ARIZONA

Senators

Henry F. Ashurst (D)
Ralph H. Cameron (R)

Representative

Carl Hayden (D)

ARKANSAS

Senators

Joseph T. Robinson (D)
Thaddeus H. Caraway (D)

Representatives

William J. Driver (D)
William A. Oldfield (D)
Tilman B. Parks (D)
Heartsill Ragon (D)
James B. Reed (D)
John N. Tillman (D)
Otis Wingo (D)

CALIFORNIA

Senators

Hiram W. Johnson (R)
Samuel M. Shortridge (R)

Representatives

Henry E. Barbour (R)
Albert E. Carter (R)
Charles F. Curry (R)
Harry L. Englebright (R) s. 1926
Lawrence J. Flaherty (R)
d. June 1926
John D. Fredericks (R)
Arthur M. Free (R)
Florence Prag Kahn (R)
Clarence F. Lea (D, R)
Walter F. Lineberger (R)
Philip D. Swing (R)
Richard J. Welch (R) s. 1926

COLORADO

Senators

Lawrence C. Phipps (R)
Rice W. Means (R)

Representatives

Guy U. Hardy (R)
Edward T. Taylor (D)
Charles B. Timberlake (R)
William N. Vaile (R)

CONNECTICUT

Senators

George P. McLean (R)
Hiram Bingham (R)

Representatives

E. Hart Fenn (R)
Richard P. Freeman (R)
James P. Glynn (R)
Schuyler Merritt (R)
John Q. Tilson (R)

DELAWARE

Senators

Thomas F. Bayard, Jr. (D)
T. Coleman DuPont (R)

Representative

Robert G. Houston (R)

FLORIDA

Senators

Duncan U. Fletcher (D)
Park Trammell (D)

Representatives

Herbert J. Drane (D)
Robert A. Green (D)
William J. Sears (D)
John H. Smithwick (D)

GEORGIA

Senators

William J. Harris (D)
Walter F. George (D)

Representatives

Thomas M. Bell (D)
Charles H. Brand (D)
Edward E. Cox (D)
Charles R. Crisp (D)
Charles G. Edwards (D)
William C. Lankford (D)
William W. Larsen (D)
Gordon Lee (D)
Samuel Rutherford (D)
William D. Upshaw (D)
Carl Vinson (D)
William C. Wright (D)

IDAHO

Senators

William E. Borah (R)
Frank R. Gooding (R)

Representatives

Burton L. French (R)
Addison T. Smith (R)

ILLINOIS

Senators

William B. McKinley (R)
d. Dec. 1926
Charles S. Deneen (R)

Representatives

Charles Adkins (R)
John C. Allen (R)
William W. Arnold (D)
Fred A. Britten (R)

Carl R. Chindblom (R)
Edward E. Denison (R)
Thomas A. Doyle (D)
Charles E. Fuller (R)
d. June 1926
Frank H. Funk (R)
John J. Gorman (R)
William P. Holaday (R)
Morton D. Hull (R)
William E. Hull (R)
Edward M. Irwin (R)
William R. Johnson (R)
Edward J. King (R)
Stanley H. Kunz (D)
Martin B. Madden (R)
M. Alfred Michaelson (R)
Henry T. Rainey (D)
Henry R. Rathbone (R)
Frank R. Reid (R)
Adolph J. Sabath (D)
Elliott W. Sproul (R)
Loren E. Wheeler (R)
Thomas S. Williams (R)
Richard Yates (R)

INDIANA

Senators

James E. Watson (R)
Arthur R. Robinson (R)

Representatives

Harry C. Canfield (D)
Richard N. Elliott (R)
Frank Gardner (D)
Arthur H. Greenwood (D)
Albert R. Hall (R)
Andrew J. Hickey (R)
David Hogg (R)
Noble J. Johnson (R)
Fred S. Purnell (R)
Harry E. Rowbottom (R)
Ralph E. Updike (R)
Albert H. Vestal (R)
William R. Wood (R)

IOWA

Senators

Albert B. Cummins (R)
d. July 1926
David W. Stewart (R) s. 1926

Smith W. Brookhart (R)
r. Apr. 1926
Daniel F. Steck (D) s. 1926

Representatives

William D. Boies (R)
Cyrenus Cole (R)
Lester J. Dickinson (R)
Cassius C. Dowell (R)
William R. Green (R)
Gilbert N. Haugen (R)
William F. Kopp (R)
F. Dickinson Letts (R)
C. William Ramseyer (R)
Thomas J. B. Robinson (R)
Lloyd Thurston (R)

KANSAS

Senators

Charles Curtis (R)
Arthur Capper (R)

Representatives

Daniel R. Anthony, Jr. (R)
William A. Ayres (D)
Homer Hoch (R)
Chauncey B. Little (D)
William H. Sproul (R)
James G. Strong (R)
Jasper N. Tincher
Hays B. White (R)

KENTUCKY

Senators

Richard P. Ernst (R)
Frederic M. Sackett (R)

Representatives

Alben W. Barkley (D)
Virgil M. Chapman (D)
Ralph Gilbert (D)
Ben Johnson (D)
David H. Kincheloe (D)
Andrew J. Kirk (R)
John W. Moore (D)
John M. Robsion (R)
Arthur B. Rouse (D)
Maurice H. Thatcher (R)
Fred M. Vinson (D)

LOUISIANA

Senators

Joseph E. Ransdell (D)
Edwin S. Broussard (D)

Representatives

James B. Aswell (D)
Bolivar E. Kemp (D)
Ladislas Lazaro (D)
Whitmell P. Martin (D)
James O'Connor (D)
John N. Sandlin (D)
J. Zach Spearing (D)
Riley J. Wilson (D)

MAINE

Senators

Bert M. Fernald (R)
d. Aug. 1926
Arthur R. Gould (R) s. 1926
Frederick Hale (R)

Representatives

Carroll L. Beedy (R)
Ira G. Hersey (R)
John E. Nelson (R)
Wallace H. White, Jr. (R)

MARYLAND

Senators

Ovington E. Weller (R)
William Cabell Bruce (D)

Representatives

Stephen W. Gambrill (D)
T. Alan Goldsborough (D)
John P. Hill (R)
J. Charles Linthicum (D)
Millard E. Tydings (D)
Frederick N. Zihlman (R)

MASSACHUSETTS

Senators

William M. Butler (R)
David I. Walsh (D) s. 1926

Frederick H. Gillett (R)

Representatives

A. Piatt Andrew, Jr. (R)
Henry L. Bowles (R)
William P. Connery, Jr. (D)
Frederick W. Dallinger (D) s. 1926
John J. Douglass (D)
Frank H. Foss (R)
Louis A. Frothingham (R)
James A. Gallivan (D)
Charles L. Gifford (R)
Robert Luce (R)
Joseph W. Martin, Jr. (R)
Edith Nourse Rogers (R)
George R. Stobbs (R)
Harry I. Thayer (R) d. Mar. 1926
George H. Tinkham (R)
Allen T. Treadway (R)
Charles L. Underhill (R)

MICHIGAN

Senators

James Couzens (R)
Woodbridge N. Ferris (D)

Representatives

Louis C. Cramton (R)
Joseph L. Hooper (R)
Grant M. Hudson (R)
W. Frank James (R)
John C. Ketcham (R)
James C. McLaughlin (R)
Clarence J. McLeod (R)
Carl E. Mapes (R)
Earl C. Michener (R)
Frank D. Scott (R)
John B. Sosnowski (R)
Bird J. Vincent (R)
Roy O. Woodruff (R)

MINNESOTA

Senators

Henrik Shipstead (Farm-Labor)
Thomas D. Schall (R)

Representatives

August H. Andresen (R)
William L. Carss (Farm-Labor)
Frank Clague (R)
Allen J. Furlow (R)
Godfrey G. Goodwin (R)
Oscar E. Keller (R)
Harold Knutson (R)
Ole J. Kvale (Farm-Labor)
Walter H. Newton (R)
Knud Wefald (Farm-Labor)

MISSISSIPPI

Senators

Pat Harrison (D)
Hubert D. Stephens (D)

Representatives

T. Jeff Busby (D)
James W. Collier (D)
Ross A. Collins (D)
Bill G. Lowrey (D)
Percy E. Quin (D)
John E. Rankin (D)
William M. Whittington (D)
T. Webber Wilson (D)

MISSOURI

Senators

James A. Reed (D)

George H. Williams (R) ta. 1925
Harry B. Hawes (D) s. 1926

Representatives

Ralph E. Bailey (R)
Clarence Cannon (D)
John J. Cochran (D) s. 1926
Clement C. Dickinson (D)
Leonidas C. Dyer (R)
Edgar C. Ellis (R)
Charles L. Faust (R)
Harry B. Hawes (D) r. Oct. 1926
Charles E. Kiefner (R)
Ralph F. Lozier (D)
Samuel C. Major (R)
Joe J. Manlove (R)
Jacob L. Milligan (D)
William L. Nelson (D)
Cleveland A. Newton (R)
Milton A. Romjue (D)
Thomas L. Rubey (D)

MONTANA

Senators

Thomas J. Walsh (D)
Burton K. Wheeler (D)

Representatives

John M. Evans (D)
Scott Leavitt (R)

NEBRASKA

Senators

George W. Norris (R)
Robert B. Howell (R)

Representatives

Edgar Howard (D)
Melvin O. McLaughlin (R)
John H. Morehead (D)
Willis G. Sears (R)
Ashton C. Shallenberger (D)
Robert G. Simmons (R)

NEVADA

Senators

Key Pittman (D)
Tasker L. Oddie (R)

Representative

Samuel S. Arentz (R)

NEW HAMPSHIRE

Senators

George H. Moses (R)
Henry W. Keyes (R)

Representatives

Fletcher Hale (R)
Edward H. Wason (R)

NEW JERSEY

Senators

Walter E. Edge (R)
Edward I. Edwards (D)

Representatives

Ernest R. Ackerman (R)
Stewart H. Appleby (R)
Oscar L. Auf Der Heide (D)
Isaac Bacharach (R)
Charles A. Eaton (R)
Franklin W. Fort (R)
Frederick R. Lehlbach (R)
Mary T. Norton (D)
Francis F. Patterson, Jr. (R)
Randolph Perkins (R)
George N. Seger (R)
Herbert W. Taylor (R)

NEW MEXICO

Senators

Andrieus A. Jones (D)
Sam G. Bratton (D)

Representative

John Morrow (D)

NEW YORK

Senators

James W. Wadsworth, Jr. (R)
Royal S. Copeland (D)

Representatives

Robert L. Bacon (R)
Loring M. Black, Jr. (D)
Sol Bloom (D)
John J. Boylan (D)
John F. Carew (D)
Emanuel Celler (D)
William E. Cleary (D)
Parker Corning (D)
Frank Crowther (R)
Thomas H. Cullen (D)
Frederick M. Davenport (R)
S. Wallace Dempsey (R)
Samuel Dickstein (D)
Benjamin L. Fairchild (R)
Hamilton Fish, Jr. (R)
Anthony J. Griffin (D)
Meyer Jacobstein (D)
John J. Kindred (D)
Fiorello H. LaGuardia (Socialist)
George W. Lindsay (D)
Clarence MacGregor (R)
Walter W. Magee (R)
James M. Mead (D)
Ogden L. Mills (R)
David J. O'Connell (D)
John J. O'Connor (D)
Frank Oliver (D)
James S. Parker (R)
Nathan D. Perlman (R)
Anning S. Prall (D)
Harcourt J. Pratt (R)
John F. Quayle (D)
Daniel A. Reed (R)
Archie D. Sanders (R)
Bertrand H. Snell (R)
Andrew L. Somers (D)
Gale H. Stalker (R)
Christopher D. Sullivan (D)
Thaddeus C. Sweet (R)
John Taber (R)
Harold S. Tolley (R)
J. Mayhew Wainwright (R)
Royal H. Weller (D)

NORTH CAROLINA

Senators

Furnifold M. Simmons (D)
Lee S. Overman (D)

Representatives

Charles L. Abernethy (D)
Alfred L. Bulwinkle (D)
Robert L. Doughton (D)
William C. Hammer (D)
John H. Kerr (D)
Homer L. Lyon (D)
Edward W. Pou (D)
Charles M. Stedman (D)
Lindsay C. Warren (D)
Zebulon Weaver (D)

NORTH DAKOTA

Senators

Gerald P. Nye (R)
Lynn J. Frazier (R)

Representatives

Olger B. Burtness (R)
Thomas Hall (R)
James H. Sinclair (R)

OHIO

Senators

Frank B. Willis (R)
Simeon D. Fess (R)

Representatives

James T. Begg (R)
Charles Brand (R)
Theodore E. Burton (R)
William W. Chalmers (R)
John G. Cooper (R)
Robert Crosser (D)
Marin L. Davey (D)
Roy G. Fitzgerald (R)
William T. Fitzgerald (R)
Thomas B. Fletcher (D)
Thomas A. Jenkins (R)
Charles C. Kearns (R)
Nicholas Longworth (R)
John McSweeney (R)
Charles A. Mooney (D)
C. Ellis Moore (R)
William M. Morgan (R)
B. Frank Murphy (R)
John C. Speaks (R)
Ambrose E. B. Stephens
Charles J. Thompson (R)
Mell G. Underwood (D)

OKLAHOMA

Senators

John W. Harreld (R)
William B. Pine (R)

Representatives

Charles D. Carter (D)
Milton C. Garber (R)
William W. Hastings (D)
James V. McClintic (D)
Thomas D. McKeown (D)
Samuel J. Montgomery (R)
Fletcher B. Swank (D)
J. W. Elmer Thomas (D)

OREGON

Senators

Charles L. McNary (R)
Robert N. Stanfield (R)

Representatives

Maurice E. Crumpacker (R)
Willis C. Hawley (R)
Nicholas J. Sinnott (R)

PENNSYLVANIA

Senators

George Wharton Pepper (R)
David A. Reed (R)

Representatives

Edward M. Beers (R)
Harris J. Bixler (R)
George F. Brumm (R)
Thomas S. Butler (R)
Guy E. Campbell (R)
Edmund N. Carpenter (R)
James J. Connolly (R)
William R. Coyle (R)
George P. Darrow (R)
Charles J. Esterly (R)
Benjamin M. Golder (R)
George S. Graham (R)
William W. Griest (R)
M. Clyde Kelly (R)
Samuel A. Kendall (R)
Edgar R. Kiess (R)
J. Banks Kurtz (R)
Louis T. McFadden (R)
James M. Magee (R)
Frederick W. Magrady (R)
Franklin Menges (R)
John M. Morin (R)
Thomas W. Phillips, Jr. (R)
Stephen G. Porter (R)
Harry C. Ransley (R)
Milton W. Shreve (R)
Nathan L. Strong (R)
Joshua W. Swartz (R)
William I. Swoope (R)
Henry W. Temple (R)
William S. Vare (R)
Anderson H. Walters
Laurence H. Watres (R)
Henry W. Watson (R)
George A. Welsh (R)
Adam M. Wyant (R)

RHODE ISLAND

Senators

Peter G. Gerry (D)
Jesse H. Metcalf (R)

Representatives

Richard S. Aldrich (R)
Clark Burdick (R)
Jeremiah E. O'Connell (D)

SOUTH CAROLINA

Senators

Ellison D. Smith (D)
Coleman L. Blease (D)

Representatives

Fred H. Dominick (D)
Hampton P. Fulmer (D)
Allard H. Gasque (D)
Butler B. Hare (D)
Thomas S. McMillan (D)
John J. McSwain (D)
William F. Stevenson (D)

SOUTH DAKOTA

Senators

Peter Norbeck (R)
William H. McMaster (R)

Representatives

Charles A. Christopherson (R)
Royal C. Johnson (R)
William Williamson (R)

TENNESSEE

Senators

Kenneth D. McKellar (D)
Lawrence D. Tyson (D)

Representatives

Gordon Browning (D)
Joseph W. Byrns (D)
Ewin L. Davis (D)
Edward E. Eslick (D)
Hubert F. Fisher (D)
Finis J. Garrett (D)
Cordell Hull (D)
Sam D. McReynolds (D)
B. Carroll Reece (R)
J. Will Taylor (R)

TEXAS

Senators

Morris Sheppard (D)
Earle B. Mayfield (D)

Representatives

Eugene Black (D)
Thomas L. Blanton (D)
John C. Box (D)
Clay S. Briggs (D)
James P. Buchanan (D)
Tom T. Connally (D)
John Nance Garner (D)
Daniel E. Garrett (D)
Claude B. Hudspeth (D)
Luther A. Johnson (D)
Marvin Jones (D)
Fritz G. Lanham (D)
Joseph J. Mansfield (D)
Sam Rayburn (D)
Morgan G. Sanders (D)
Hatton W. Sumners (D)
Guinn Williams (D)
Harry M. Wurzbach (D)

UTAH

Senators

Reed Smoot (R)
William H. King (D)

Representatives

Don B. Colton (R)
Elmer O. Leatherwood (R)

VERMONT

Senators

Frank L. Greene (R)
Porter H. Dale (R)

Representatives

Elbert S. Brigham (R)
Ernest W. Gibson (R)

VIRGINIA

Senators

Claude A. Swanson (D)
Carter Glass (D)

Representatives

Schuyler Otis Bland (D)
Joseph T. Deal (D)
Patrick H. Drewry (D)
Thomas W. Harrison (D)
Andrew J. Montague (D)
R. Walton Moore (D)
George C. Peery (D)
Henry St. George Tucker (D)
Joseph Whitehead (D)
Clifton A. Woodrum (D)

WASHINGTON

Senators

Wesley L. Jones (R)
Clarence C. Dill (D)

Representatives

Lindley H. Hadley (R)
Samuel B. Hill (D)
Albert Johnson (R)
John F. Miller (R)
John W. Summers (R)

WEST VIRGINIA

Senators

Matthew M. Neely (D)
Guy D. Goff (R)

Representatives

Carl G. Bachmann (R)
Frank L. Bowman (R)
James F. Strother (R)
J. Alfred Taylor (D)
John M. Wolverton (R)
Harry C. Woodyard (R)

WISCONSIN

Senators

Robert M. LaFollette (R)
d. June 1925
Robert M. LaFollette, Jr.
(Progressive) s. 1925

Irvine L. Lenroot (R)

Representatives

Joseph D. Beck (R)
Victor L. Berger (Socialist)
Edward E. Browne (R)
Henry A. Cooper (R)
James A. Frear (R)
Hubert H. Peavey (R)
Florian Lampert (R)
John M. Nelson (R)
John C. Schafer (R)
George J. Schneider
(Progressive)
Edward Voigt (R)

WYOMING

Senators

Francis E. Warren (R)
John B. Kendrick (D)

Representative

Charles E. Winter (R)

SEVENTIETH CONGRESS

March 4, 1927 to March 3, 1929

President of The Senate: Charles G. Dawes
President Pro Tempore of The Senate: George H. Moses
Speaker of The House of Representatives: Nicholas Longworth

ALABAMA

Senators

J. Thomas Heflin (D)
Hugo L. Black (D)

Representatives

Miles C. Allgood (D)
Edward B. Almon (D)
William B. Bankhead (D)
William B. Bowling (D)
r. Aug. 1928
Lister Hill (D)
George Huddleston (D)
Lamar Jeffers (D)
John McDuffie (D)
William B. Oliver (D)
LaFayette L. Patterson (D) s. 1928
Henry B. Steagall (D)

ARIZONA

Senators

Henry F. Ashurst (D)
Carl Hayden (D)

Representative

Lewis W. Douglas (D)

ARKANSAS

Senators

Joseph T. Robinson (D)
Thaddeus H. Caraway (D)

Representatives

William J. Driver (D)
Pearl Peden Oldfield (D) s. 1929
William A. Oldfield (D)
d. Nov. 1928
Tilman B. Parks (D)
Heartsill Ragon (D)
James B. Reed (D)
John N. Tillman (D)
Otis R. Wingo (D)

CALIFORNIA

Senators

Hiram W. Johnson (R)
Samuel M. Shortridge (R)

Representatives

Henry E. Barbour (R)
Albert E. Carter (R)
Joe Crail (R)
Charles F. Curry (R)
Harry L. Englebright (R)
William E. Evans (R)
Arthur M. Free (R)
Florence Prag Kahn (R)
Clarence F. Lea (D, R)
Philip D. Swing (R)
Richard J. Welch (R)

COLORADO

Senators

Lawrence C. Phipps (R)
Charles W. Waterman (R)

Representatives

Guy U. Hardy (R)
Edward T. Taylor (D)
Charles B. Timberlake (R)
S. Harrison White (D)

CONNECTICUT

Senators

George P. McLean (R)
Hiram Bingham (R)

Representatives

E. Hart Fenn (R)
Richard P. Freeman (R)
James P. Glynn (R)
Schuyler Merritt (R)
John Q. Tilson (R)

DELAWARE

Senators

Thomas F. Bayard, Jr. (D)

T. Coleman DuPont (R)
r. Dec. 1928
Daniel O. Hastings (R) s. 1928

Representative

Robert G. Houston (R)

FLORIDA

Senators

Duncan U. Fletcher (D)
Park Trammell (D)

Representatives

Herbert J. Drane (D)
Robert A. Green (D)
William J. Sears (D)
Thomas A. Yon (D)

GEORGIA

Senators

William J. Harris (D)
Walter F. George (D)

Representatives

Thomas M. Bell (D)
Charles H. Brand (D)
Edward E. Cox (D)
Charles R. Crisp (D)
Charles G. Edwards (D)
William C. Lankford (D)
William W. Larsen (D)
Samuel Rutherford (D)
Leslie J. Steele (D)
Malcolm C. Tarver (D)
Carl Vinson (D)
William C. Wright (D)

IDAHO

Senators

William E. Borah (R)

Frank R. Gooding (R)
d. June 1928
John Thomas (R) s. 1928

Representatives

Burton L. French (R)
Addison T. Smith (R)

ILLINOIS

Senators

Charles S. Deneen (R)
Frank L. Smith (R)
r. Feb. 1928
Otis F. Glenn (R) s. 1928

Representatives

Charles Adkins (R)
John C. Allen (R)
William W. Arnold (D)
Fred A. Britten (R)
John T. Buckbee (R)
Carl R. Chindblom (R)
Edward E. Denison (R)
Thomas A. Doyle (D)
Homer W. Hall (R)
William P. Holaday (R)
Morton D. Hull (R)
William E. Hull (R)
James T. Igoe (D)
Edward M. Irwin (R)
William R. Johnson (R)
Edward J. King (R)
Stanley H. Kunz (D)
Martin B. Madden (R)
d. Apr. 1928
J. Earl Major (D)
M. Alfred Michaelson (R)
Henry T. Rainey (D)
Henry R. Rathbone (R)
d. July 1928
Frank R. Reid (R)
Adolph J. Sabath (D)
Elliott W. Sproul (R)
Thomas S. Williams (R)
Richard Yates (R)

INDIANA

Senators

James E. Watson (R)
Arthur R. Robinson (R)

Representatives

Harry C. Canfield (D)
Richard N. Elliott (R)
Frank Gardner (D)
Arthur H. Greenwood (R)
Albert R. Hall (R)
Andrew J. Hickey (R)
David Hogg (R)
Noble J. Johnson (R)
Fred S. Purnell (R)
Harry E. Rowbottom (R)
Ralph E. Updike (R)
Albert H. Vestal (R)
William R. Wood (R)

IOWA

Senators

Daniel F. Steck (D)
Smith W. Brookhart (D)

Representatives

William D. Boies (R)
Cyrenus Cole (R)
Lester J. Dickinson (R)
Cassius C. Dowell (R)
William R. Green (R) r. Mar. 1928
Gilbert N. Haugen (R)
William F. Kopp (R)
F. Dickinson Letts (R)
C. William Ramseyer (R)
Thomas J. B. Robinson (R)
Lloyd Thurston (R)
Earl W. Vincent (R) s. 1928

KANSAS

Senators

Charles Curtis (R) r. Mar. 1929
Arthur Capper (R)

Representatives

Daniel R. Anthony, Jr. (R)
William A. Ayres (D)
Homer Hoch (R)
Ulysses S. Guyer (R)
Clifford R. Hope (R)
William H. Sproul (R)
James G. Strong (R)
Hays B. White (R)

KENTUCKY

Senators

Frederic M. Sackett (R)
Alben W. Barkley (D)

Representatives

Virgil M. Chapman (D)
Ralph Gilbert (D)
William V. Gregory (D)
David H. Kincheloe (D)
Katherine Langley (R)
Henry D. Moorman (D)
John W. Moore (D)
John M. Robsion (R)
Maurice H. Thatcher (R)
Fred M. Vinson (D)
Orie S. Ware (D)

LOUISIANA

Senators

Joseph E. Ransdell (D)
Edwin S. Broussard (D)

Representatives

James B. Aswell (D)
Rene L. DeRouen (D)
Bolivar E. Kemp (D)
Whitmell P. Martin (D)
James O'Connor (D)
John N. Sandlin (D)
J. Zach Spearing (D)
Riley J. Wilson (D)

MAINE

Senators

Frederick Hale (R)
Arthur R. Gould (R)

Representatives

Carroll L. Beedy (R)
Ira G. Hersey (R)
John E. Nelson (R)
Wallace H. White, Jr. (R)

MARYLAND

Senators

William Cabell Bruce (D)
Millard E. Tydings (D)

Representatives

William P. Cole, Jr. (D)
Stephen W. Gambrill (D)
T. Alan Goldsborough (D)
J. Charles Linthicum (D)
Vincent L. Palmisano (D)
Frederick N. Zihlman (R)

MASSACHUSETTS

Senators

Frederick H. Gillett (R)
David I. Walsh (D)

Representatives

A. Piatt Andrew, Jr. (R)
Henry L. Bowles (R)
William P. Connery, Jr. (D)
Frederick W. Dallinger (D)
John J. Douglass (D)
Frank H. Foss (R)
Louis A. Frothingham (R)
d. Aug. 1928
James A. Gallivan (D)
d. Apr. 1928
Charles L. Gifford (D)
Robert Luce (R)
John W. McCormack (D) s. 1928
Joseph W. Martin, Jr. (R)
Edith Nourse Rogers (R)
George R. Stobbs (R)
George H. Tinkham (R)
Allen T. Treadway (R)
Charles L. Underhill (R)
Richard B. Wigglesworth (R)
s. 1928

MICHIGAN

Senators

James Couzens (R)

Woodbridge N. Ferris (D)
d. Mar. 1928
Arthur H. Vandenberg (R) s. 1928

Representatives

Frank P. Bohn (R)
Robert H. Clancy (D)
Louis C. Cramton (R)
Joseph L. Hooper (R)
Grant M. Hudson (R)
W. Frank James (R)
John C. Ketcham (R)
James C. McLaughlin (R)
Clarence J. McLeod (R)
Carl E. Mapes (R)
Earl C. Michener (R)
Bird J. Vincent (R)
Roy O. Woodruff (R)

MINNESOTA

Senators

Henrik Shipstead (Farm-Labor)
Thomas D. Schall (R)

Representatives

August H. Andresen (R)
William L. Carss (Farm-Labor)
Frank Clague (R)
Allen J. Furlow (R)
Godfrey G. Goodwin (R)
Harold Knutson (R)
Ole J. Kvale (Farm-Labor)
Melvin J. Maas (R)
Walter H. Newton (R)
Conrad G. Selvig (R)

MISSISSIPPI

Senators

Pat Harrison (D)
Hubert D. Stephens (D)

Representatives

T. Jeff Busby (D)
James W. Collier (D)
Ross A. Collins (D)

Bill G. Lowrey (D)
Percy E. Quin (D)
John E. Rankin (D)
William M. Whittington (D)
T. Webber Wilson (D)

MISSOURI

Senators

James A. Reed (D)
Harry B. Hawes (D)

Representatives

Clarence Cannon (D)
John J. Cochran (D)
George H. Combs (D)
Clement C. Dickinson (D)
Leonidas C. Dyer (R)
Charles L. Faust (R) d. Dec. 1928
James F. Fulbright (D)
David W. Hopkins (R) s. 1929
Ralph F. Lozier (D)
Samuel C. Major (D)
Joe J. Manlove (R)
Jacob L. Milligan (D)
William L. Nelson (D)
Henry F. Niedringhaus (R)
Milton A. Romjue (D)
Thomas L. Rubey (D)
d. Nov. 1928
Clyde Williams (D)

MONTANA

Senators

Thomas J. Walsh (D)
Burton K. Wheeler (D)

Representatives

John M. Evans (D)
Scott Leavitt (R)

NEBRASKA

Senators

George W. Norris (R)
Robert B. Howell (R)

Representatives

Edgar Howard (D)
John H. Morehead (D)
John N. Norton (D)
Willis G. Sears (R)
Ashton C. Shallenberger (D)
Robert G. Simmons (R)

NEVADA

Senators

Key Pittman (D)
Tasker L. Oddie (R)

Representative

Samuel S. Arentz (R)

NEW HAMPSHIRE

Senators

George H. Moses (R)
Henry W. Keyes (R)

Representatives

Fletcher Hale (R)
Edward H. Wason (R)

NEW JERSEY

Senators

Walter E. Edge (R)
Edward I. Edwards (D)

Representatives

Ernest R. Ackerman (R)
Oscar L. Auf Der Heide (D)
Isaac Bacharach (R)
Charles A. Eaton (R)
Franklin W. Fort (R)
Harold G. Hoffman (R)
Frederick R. Lehlbach (R)
Paul J. Moore (D)
Mary T. Norton (D)
Randolph Perkins (R)
George N. Seger (R)
Charles A. Wolverton (R)

NEW MEXICO

Senators

Andrieus A. Jones (D)
d. Dec. 1927
Bronson M. Cutting (R) ta. 1928
Octaviano A. Larrazolo (R)
s. 1928

Sam G. Bratton (D)

Representative

John Morrow (D)

NEW YORK

Senators

Royal S. Copeland (D)
Robert F. Wagner (D)

Representatives

Robert L. Bacon (R)
Loring M. Black, Jr. (D)
Sol Bloom (D)
John J. Boylan (D)
John F. Carew (D)
Patrick J. Carley (D)
Emanuel Celler (D)
John D. Clarke (R)
William W. Cohen (D)
Parker Corning (D)
Frank Crowther (R)
Francis D. Culkin (R) s. 1928
Thomas H. Cullen (D)
Frederick M. Davenport (R)
S. Wallace Dempsey (R)
Samuel Dickstein (D)
Hamilton Fish, Jr. (R)
James M. Fitzpatrick (D)
Anthony J. Griffin (D)
Clarence E. Hancock (R)
Meyer Jacobstein (D)
John J. Kindred (D)
Fiorello H. LaGuardia (R)
George W. Lindsay (D)
Clarence MacGregor (R)
r. Dec. 1928
James M. Mead (D)
David J. O'Connell (D)
John J. O'Connor (D)
Frank Oliver (D)
James S. Parker (R)
Anning S. Prall (D)
Harcourt J. Pratt (R)
John F. Quayle (D)
Daniel A. Reed (R)
Archie D. Sanders (R)
William I. Sirovich (D)
Bertrand H. Snell (R)
Andrew L. Somers (D)
Gale H. Stalker (R)
Christopher D. Sullivan (D)
Thaddeus C. Sweet (R)
d. May 1928
John Taber (R)
J. Mayhew Wainwright (R)
Royal H. Weller (D) d. Mar. 1929

NORTH CAROLINA

Senators

Furnifold M. Simmons (D)
Lee S. Overman (D)

Representatives

Charles L. Abernethy (D)
Alfred L. Bulwinkle (D)
Robert L. Doughton (D)
William C. Hammer (D)
John H. Kerr (D)
Homer L. Lyon (D)
Edward W. Pou (D)
Charles M. Stedman (D)
Lindsay C. Warren (D)
Zebulon Weaver (D)

NORTH DAKOTA

Senators

Lynn Frazier (R)
Gerald P. Nye (R)

Representatives

Olger B. Burtness (R)
Thomas Hall (R)
James H. Sinclair (R)

OHIO

Senators

Frank B. Willis (R) d. Mar. 1928
Cyrus Locher (D) ta. 1928
Theodore E. Burton (R) s. 1928
Simeon D. Fess (R)

Representatives

James T. Begg (R)
Charles Brand (R)
Theodore E. Burton (R)
r. Dec. 1928
William W. Chalmers (R)
John G. Cooper (R)
Robert Crosser (D)
Martin L. Davey (D)
Roy G. Fitzgerald (R)
William T. Fitzgerald (R)
Thomas B. Fletcher (D)
Thomas A. Jenkins (R)
Charles C. Kearns (R)
Nicholas Longworth (R)
John McSweeney (D)
Charles A. Mooney (D)
C. Ellis Moore (R)
William M. Morgan (R)
B. Frank Murphy (R)
John C. Speaks (R)
Charles Tatgenhorst, Jr. (R)
Charles J. Thompson (R)
Mell G. Underwood (D)

OKLAHOMA

Senators

William B. Pine (R)
J. W. Elmer Thomas (D)

Representatives

Wilburn Cartwright (D)
Milton C. Garber (R)
William W. Hastings (D)
Everett B. Howard (D)
Jed Johnson (D)
James V. McClintic (D)
Thomas D. McKeown (D)
Fletcher B. Swank (D)

OREGON

Senators

Charles L. McNary (R)
Frederick Steiwer (R)

Representatives

Robert R. Butler (R) s. 1928
Willis C. Hawley (R)
Franklin F. Korell (R)
Nicholas J. Sinnott (R)
r. May 1928

PENNSYLVANIA

Senators

David A. Reed (R)
William S. Vare (R)

Representatives

James M. Beck (R)
Edward M. Beers (R)
Robert G. Bushong (R)
Thomas S. Butler (R)
d. May 1928
Guy E. Campbell (R)
John J. Casey (D)
J. Mitchell Chase (R)

Thomas C. Cochran (R)
James J. Connolly (R)
George P. Darrow (R)
Isaac H. Doutrich (R)
Harry A. Estep (R)
Benjamin M. Golder (R)
George S. Graham (R)
William W. Griest (R)
M. Clyde Kelly (R)
Samuel A. Kendall (R)
Everett Kent (D)
Edgar R. Kiess (R)
J. Banks Kurtz (R)
J. Russell Leech (R)
Louis T. McFadden (R)
Frederick W. Magrady (R)
Franklin Menges (R)
John M. Morin (R)
Cyrus M. Palmer (R)
Stephen G. Porter (R)
Harry C. Ransley (R)
Milton W. Shreve (R)
Nathan L. Strong (R)
J. Howard Swick (R)
Henry W. Temple (R)
Laurence H. Watres (R)
Henry W. Watson (R)
George A. Welsh (R)
James Wolfenden (R) s. 1928
Adam M. Wyant (R)

RHODE ISLAND

Senators

Peter G. Gerry (D)
Jesse H. Metcalf (R)

Representatives

Richard S. Aldrich (R)
Clark Burdick (R)
Louis Monast (R)

SOUTH CAROLINA

Senators

Ellison D. Smith (D)
Coleman L. Blease (D)

Representatives

Fred H. Dominick (D)
Hampton P. Fulmer (D)
Allard H. Gasque (D)
Butler B. Hare (D)
Thomas S. McMillan (D)
John J. McSwain (D)
William F. Stevenson (D)

SOUTH DAKOTA

Senators

Peter Norbeck (R)
William H. McMaster (R)

Representatives

Charles A. Christopherson (R)
Royal C. Johnson (R)
William Williamson (R)

TENNESSEE

Senators

Kenneth D. McKellar (D)
Lawrence D. Tyson (D)

Representatives

Gordon Browning (D)
Joseph W. Byrns (D)
Ewin L. Davis (D)
Edward E. Eslick (D)
Hubert F. Fisher (D)
Finis J. Garrett (D)
Cordell Hull (D)
Sam D. McReynolds (D)
B. Carroll Reece (R)
J. Will Taylor (R)

TEXAS

Senators

Morris Sheppard (D)
Earle B. Mayfield (D)

Representatives

Eugene Black (D)
Thomas L. Blanton (D)
John C. Box (D)
Clay S. Briggs (D)
James P. Buchanan (D)
Tom T. Connally (D)
John Nance Garner (D)
Daniel E. Garrett (D)
Claude B. Hudspeth (D)
Luther A. Johnson (D)
Marvin Jones (D)
Fritz G. Lanham (D)
Joseph J. Mansfield (D)
Sam Rayburn (D)
Morgan G. Sanders (D)
Hatton W. Sumners (D)
Guinn Williams (D)
Harry M. Wurzbach (D)

UTAH

Senators

Reed Smoot (R)
William H. King (D)

Representatives

Don B. Colton (R)
Elmer O. Leatherwood (R)

VERMONT

Senators

Frank L. Greene (R)
Porter H. Dale (R)

Representatives

Elbert S. Brigham (R)
Ernest W. Gibson (R)

VIRGINIA

Senators

Claude A. Swanson (D)
Carter Glass (D)

Representatives

Schuyler Otis Bland (D)
Joseph T. Deal (D)
Patrick H. Drewry (D)
Thomas W. Harrison (D)
Andrew J. Montague (D)
R. Walton Moore (D)
George C. Peery (D)
Henry St. George Tucker (D)
Joseph Whitehead (D)
Clifton A. Woodrum (D)

WASHINGTON

Senators

Wesley L. Jones (R)
Clarence C. Dill (D)

Representatives

Lindley H. Hadley (R)
Samuel B. Hill (D)
Albert Johnson (R)
John F. Miller (R)
John W. Summers (R)

WEST VIRGINIA

Senators

Matthew M. Neely (D)
Guy D. Goff (R)

Representatives

Carl G. Bachmann (R)
Frank L. Bowman (R)

Edward T. England (R)
James A. Hughes (R)
William S. O'Brien (D)
James F. Strother (R)

WISCONSIN

Senators

Robert M. LaFollette, Jr. (Progressive)
John J. Blaine (R)

Representatives

Victor L. Berger (Socialist)
Joseph D. Beck (R)
Edward E. Browne (R)
Henry A. Cooper (R)
James A. Frear (R)
Charles A. Kading (R)
Florian Lampert (R)
John M. Nelson (R)
Hubert H. Peavey (R)
John C. Schafer (R)
George J. Schneider (Progressive)

WYOMING

Senators

Francis E. Warren (R)
John B. Kendrick (D)

Representative

Charles E. Winter (R)

SEVENTY-FIRST CONGRESS

March 4, 1929 to March 3, 1931

President of The Senate:	Charles Curtis
President Pro Tempore of The Senate:	George H. Moses
Speaker of The House of Representatives:	Nicholas Longworth

ALABAMA

Senators

J. Thomas Heflin (D)
Hugo L. Black (D)

Representatives

Miles C. Allgood (D)
Edward B. Almon (D)
William B. Bankhead (D)
Lister Hill (D)
George Huddleston (D)
Lamar Jeffers (D)
John McDuffie (D)
William B. Oliver (D)
LaFayette L. Patterson (D)
Henry B. Steagall (D)

ARIZONA

Senators

Henry F. Ashurst (D)
Carl Hayden (D)

Representative

Lewis W. Douglas (D)

ARKANSAS

Senators

Joseph T. Robinson (D)
Thaddeus H. Caraway (D)

Representatives

William J. Driver (D)
Claude A. Fuller (D)
David D. Glover (D)
Pearl Peden Oldfield (D)
Tilman B. Parks (D)
Heartsill Ragon (D)
Effiegene (Locke) Wingo (D) s. 1930
Otis Wingo (D) d. Oct. 1930

CALIFORNIA

Senators

Hiram W. Johnson (R)
Samuel M. Shortridge (R)

Representatives

Henry E. Barbour (R)
Albert E. Carter (R)
Joe Crail (R)
Charles F. Curry (R) d. Oct. 1930
Harry L. Englebright (R)
William E. Evans (R)
Arthur M. Free (R)
Florence Prag Kahn (R)
Clarence F. Lea (D, R)
Philip D. Swing (R)
Richard J. Welch (R)

COLORADO

Senators

Lawrence C. Phipps (R)
Charles W. Waterman (R)

Representatives

William R. Eaton (R)
Guy U. Hardy (R)
Edward T. Taylor (D)
Charles B. Timberlake (R)

CONNECTICUT

Senators

Hiram Bingham (R)
Frederic C. Walcott (R)

Representatives

E. Hart Fenn (R)
Richard P. Freeman (R)
James P. Glynn (R) d. Mar. 1930
Edward W. Goss (R) s. 1930
Schuyler Merritt (R)
John Q. Tilson (R)

DELAWARE

Senators

Daniel O. Hastings (R)
John G. Townsend, Jr. (R)

Representative

Robert G. Houston (R)

FLORIDA

Senators

Duncan U. Fletcher (D)
Park Trammell (D)

Representatives

Herbert J. Drane (D)
Robert A. Green (D)
Ruth Bryan Owen (D)
Thomas A. Yon (D)

GEORGIA

Senators

William J. Harris (D)
Walter F. George (D)

Representatives

Thomas M. Bell (D)
Charles H. Brand (D)
Edward E. Cox (D)
Charles R. Crisp (D)
Charles G. Edwards (D)
William C. Lankford (D)
William W. Larsen (D)
Robert C. Ramspeck (D)
Samuel Rutherford (D)
Leslie J. Steele (D) d. July 1929
Malcolm C. Tarver (D)
Carl Vinson (D)
William C. Wright (D)

IDAHO

Senators

William E. Borah (R)
John Thomas (R)

Representatives

Burton L. French (R)
Addison T. Smith (R)

ILLINOIS

Senators

Charles S. Deneen (R)
Otis F. Glenn (R)

Representatives

Charles Adkins (R)
John C. Allen (R)
William W. Arnold (D)
Fred A. Britten (R)
John T. Buckbee (R)
Carl R. Chindblom (R)
Burnett M. Chiperfield (R) s. 1930
Edward E. Denison (R)
Oscar DePriest (R)
Thomas A. Doyle (D)
Homer W. Hall (R)
William P. Holaday (R)
Morton D. Hull (R)
William E. Hull (R)
James T. Igoe (D)
Edward M. Irwin (R)
William R. Johnson (R)
Stanley H. Kunz (D)
Ruth H. McCormick (R)
M. Alfred Michaelson (R)
Claude V. Parsons (D) s. 1930
Henry T. Rainey (D)
Frank M. Ramey (R)
Frank R. Reid (R)
Adolph J. Sabath (D)
Elliott W. Sproul (R)
Thomas S. Williams (R) r. Nov. 1929
Richard Yates (R)

INDIANA

Senators

James E. Watson (R)
Arthur R. Robinson (R)

Representatives

Harry C. Canfield (D)
James W. Dunbar (R)
Richard N. Elliott (R)
Arthur H. Greenwood (D)
Albert R. Hall (R)
Andrew J. Hickey (R)
David Hogg (R)
Noble J. Johnson (R)
Louis L. Ludlow (D)
Fred S. Purnell (R)
Harry E. Rowbottom (R)
Albert H. Vestal (R)
William R. Wood (R)

IOWA

Senators

Daniel F. Steck (D)
Smith W. Brookhart (R)

Representatives

Ed H. Campbell (R)
Cyrenus Cole (R)
Lester J. Dickinson (R)
Cassius C. Dowell (R)
Gilbert N. Haugen (R)
William F. Kopp (R)
F. Dickinson Letts (R)
C. William Ramseyer (R)
Thomas J. B. Robinson (R)
Charles E. Swanson (R)
Lloyd Thurston (R)

KANSAS

Senators

Arthur Capper (R)

Henry J. Allen (R) ta. 1929
George McGill (D) s. 1930

Representatives

William A. Ayres (D)
Ulysses S. Guyer (R)
Homer Hoch (R)
Clifford R. Hope (R)
William P. Lambertson (R)
Charles I. Sparks (R)
William H. Sproul (R)
James G. Strong (R)

KENTUCKY

Senators

Frederic M. Sackett (R) r. Jan. 1930
John M. Robsion (R) ta. 1930
Ben M. Williamson (D) s. 1930

Alben W. Barkley (D)

Representatives

Robert E. Lee Blackburn (R)
John D. Craddock (R)
John L. Dorsey, Jr. (D) s. 1930
Charles Finley (R) s. 1930
William V. Gregory (D)
Elva R. Kendall (R)
David H. Kincheloe (D) r. Oct. 1930
Katherine Langley (R)
John W. Moore (D)
J. Lincoln Newhall (R)
John M. Robsion (R) r. Jan. 1930
Maurice H. Thatcher (R)
Lewis L. Walker (R)

LOUISIANA

Senators

Joseph E. Ransdell (D)
Edwin S. Broussard (D)

Representatives

James B. Aswell (D)
Rene L. DeRouen (D)
Bolivar E. Kemp (D)
Numa F. Montet (D)
James O'Connor (D)
John N. Sandlin (D)
J. Zach Spearing (D)
Riley J. Wilson (D)

MAINE

Senators

Frederick Hale (R)
Arthur R. Gould (R)

Representatives

Carroll L. Beedy (R)
John E. Nelson (R)
Donald F. Snow (R)
Wallace H. White, Jr. (R)

MARYLAND

Senators

Millard E. Tydings (D)
Phillips Lee Goldsborough (R)

Representatives

Linwood L. Clark (R)
Stephen W. Gambrill (D)
T. Alan Goldsborough (D)
J. Charles Linthicum (D)
Vincent L. Palmisano (D)
Frederick N. Zihlman (R)

MASSACHUSETTS

Senators

Frederick H. Gillett (R)
David I. Walsh (D)

Representatives

A. Piatt Andrew, Jr. (R)
William P. Connery, Jr. (D)
Frederick W. Dallinger (D)
John J. Douglass (D)
Frank H. Foss (R)
Charles L. Gifford (R)
William J. Granfield (D) s. 1930
William K. Kaynor (R) d. Dec. 1929
Robert Luce (R)
John W. McCormack (D)
Joseph W. Martin, Jr. (R)
Edith Nourse Rogers (R)
George R. Stobbs (R)
George H. Tinkham (R)
Allen T. Treadway (R)
Charles L. Underhill (R)
Richard B. Wigglesworth (R)

MICHIGAN

Senators

James Couzens (R)
Arthur H. Vandenberg (R)

Representatives

Frank P. Bohn (R)
Robert H. Clancy (D)
Louis C. Cramton (R)
Joseph L. Hooper (R)
Grant M. Hudson (R)
W. Frank James (R)
John C. Ketcham (R)
James C. McLaughlin (R)
Clarence J. McLeod (R)
Carl E. Mapes (R)
Earl C. Michener (R)
Bird J. Vincent (R)
Roy O. Woodruff (R)

MINNESOTA

Senators

Henrik Shipstead (Farm-Labor)
Thomas D. Schall (R)

Representatives

August H. Andresen (R)
Victor Christgau (R)
Frank Clague (R)
Godfrey G. Goodwin (R)
Harold Knutson (R)
Ole J. Kvale (Farm-Labor) d. Sept. 1929
Melvin J. Maas (R)
Walter H. Newton (R) r. June 1929
William I. Nolan (R)
William A. Pittenger (R)
Conrad G. Selvig (R)

MISSISSIPPI

Senators

Pat Harrison (D)
Hubert D. Stephens (D)

Representatives

T. Jefferson Busby (D)
James W. Collier (D)
Ross A. Collins (D)
Wall Doxey (D)
Robert S. Hall (D)
Percy E. Quin (D)
John E. Rankin (D)
William M. Whittington (D)

MISSOURI

Senators

Harry B. Hawes (D)
Roscoe C. Patterson (R)

Representatives

Clarence Cannon (D)
John J. Cochran (D)
Leonidas C. Dyer (R)
Edgar C. Ellis (R)
Thomas J. Halsey (R)
David W. Hopkins (R)
Rowland L. Johnston (R)
Charles E. Kiefner (R)
Ralph F. Lozier (D)
Joe J. Manlove (R)
Jacob L. Milligan (D)
William L. Nelson (D)
Henry F. Niedringhaus (R)
John W. Palmer (R)
Milton A. Romjue (D)
Dewey Short (R)

MONTANA

Senators

Thomas J. Walsh (D)
Burton K. Wheeler (D)

Representatives

John M. Evans (D)
Scott Leavitt (R)

NEBRASKA

Senators

George W. Norris (R)
Robert B. Howell (R)

Representatives

Edgar Howard (D)
Fred G. Johnson (R)
John H. Morehead (D)
Willis G. Sears (R)
Robert G. Simmons (R)
Charles H. Sloan (R)

NEVADA

Senators

Key Pittman (D)
Tasker L. Oddie (R)

Representative

Samuel S. Arentz (R)

NEW HAMPSHIRE

Senators

George H. Moses (R)
Henry W. Keyes (R)

Representatives

Fletcher Hale (R)
Edward H. Wason (R)

NEW JERSEY

Senators

Walter E. Edge (R) r. Nov. 1929
David Baird, Jr. (R) ta. 1929
Dwight W. Morrow (R) s. 1930

Hamilton F. Kean (R)

Representatives

Ernest R. Ackerman (R)
Oscar L. Auf Der Heide (D)
Isaac Bacharach (R)
Charles A. Eaton (R)
Franklin W. Fort (R)
Fred A. Hartley, Jr. (R)
Harold G. Hoffman (R)
Frederick R. Lehlbach (R)
Mary T. Norton (D)
Randolph Perkins (R)
George N. Seger (R)
Charles A. Wolverton (R)

NEW MEXICO

Senators

Sam G. Bratton (D)
Bronson M. Cutting (R)

Representative

Albert G. Simms (R)

NEW YORK

Senators

Royal S. Copeland (D)
Robert F. Wagner (D)

Representatives

Robert L. Bacon (R)
Loring M. Black, Jr. (D)
Sol Bloom (D)
John J. Boylan (D)
William F. Brunner (D)
John F. Carew (D) r. Dec. 1929
Patrick J. Carley (D)
Emanuel Celler (D)
John D. Clarke (R)
Edmund F. Cooke (R)
Parker Corning (D)
Frank Crowther (R)
Francis D. Culkin (R)
Thomas H. Cullen (D)
Frederick M. Davenport (R)
W. Wallace Dempsey (R)
Samuel Dickstein (D)
Hamilton Fish, Jr. (R)
James M. Fitzpatrick (D)
Joseph A. Gavagan (D)
Anthony J. Griffin (D)
Clarence E. Hancock (R)
Martin J. Kennedy (D) s. 1930
Fiorello H. LaGuardia (R)
George W. Lindsay (D)
James M. Mead (D)
David J. O'Connell (D) d. Dec. 1930
John J. O'Connor (D)
Frank Oliver (D)
James S. Parker (R)
Anning S. Prall (D)
Harcourt J. Pratt (R)
Ruth S. B. Pratt (R)
John F. Quayle (D) d. Nov. 1930
Daniel A. Reed (R)
Archie D. Sanders (R)
William I. Sirovich (D)
Bertrand H. Snell (R)
Andrew L. Somers (D)
Gale H. Stalker (R)
Christopher D. Sullivan (D)
John Taber (R)
J. Mayhew Wainwright (R)
James L. Whitley (R)

NORTH CAROLINA

Senators

Furnifold M. Simmons (D)

Lee S. Overman (D) d. Dec. 1930
Cameron A. Morrison (D) s. 1930

Representatives

Charles L. Abernethy (D)
J. Bayard Clark (D)
Robert L. Doughton (D)
William C. Hammer (D) d. Sept. 1930
Franklin W. Hancock, Jr. (D) s. 1930
Hinton James (D) s. 1930
Charles A. Jonas (R)
John H. Kerr (D)
Edward W. Pou (D)
George M. Pritchard (R)
Charles M. Stedman (D) d. Sept. 1930
Lindsay C. Warren (D)

NORTH DAKOTA

Senators

Lynn J. Frazier (R)
Gerald P. Nye (R)

Representatives

Olger B. Burtness (R)
Thomas Hall (R)
James H. Sinclair (R)

OHIO

Senators

Simeon D. Fess (R)

Theodore E. Burton (R) d. Oct. 1929
Roscoe C. McCulloch (R) ta. 1929
Robert J. Bulkley (D) s. 1930

Representatives

Joseph E. Baird (R)
Chester C. Bolton (R)
Charles Brand (R)
John L. Cable (R)
William W. Chalmers (R)
John G. Cooper (R)
Robert Crosser (D)
Roy G. Fitzgerald (R)
William E. Hess (R)
Thomas A. Jenkins (R)
Charles C. Kearns (R)
Nicholas Longworth (R)
Charles B. McClintock (R)
Charles A. Mooney (D)
C. Ellis Moore (R)
William M. Morgan (R)
Grant E. Mouser, Jr. (R)
B. Frank Murphy (R)
Francis Seiberling (R)
John C. Speaks (R)
Charles J. Thompson (R)
Mell G. Underwood (R)

OKLAHOMA

Senators

William B. Pine (R)
J. W. Elmer Thomas (D)

Representatives

Wilburn Cartwright (D)
Milton C. Garber (R)
William W. Hastings (D)
Jed Johnson (D)
James V. McClintic (D)
Thomas D. McKeown (D)
Charles O'Connor (R)
Ulysses S. Stone (R)

OREGON

Senators

Charles L. McNary (R)
Frederick Steiwer (R)

Representatives

Robert R. Butler (R)
Willis C. Hawley (R)
Franklin F. Korell (R)

PENNSYLVANIA

Senators

David A. Reed (R)

Joseph R. Grundy (R) ta. 1929
James J. Davis (R) s. 1930

Representatives

James M. Beck (R)
Edward M. Beers (R)
George F. Brumm (R)
Guy E. Campbell (R)
John J. Casey (D) d. May 1929
J. Mitchell Chase (R)
Thomas C. Cochran (R)
James J. Connolly (R)
William R. Coyle (R)
George P. Darrow (R)
Isaac H. Doutrich (R)
Edmund F. Erk (R) s. 1930
Harry A. Estep (R)
Charles J. Esterly (R)
Benjamin Golder (R)
George S. Graham (R)
William W. Griest (R)
d. Dec. 1929
M. Clyde Kelly (R)
Samuel A. Kendall (R)
Edgar R. Kiess (R) d. July 1930
J. Roland Kinzer (R) s. 1930
J. Banks Kurtz (R)
J. Russell Leech (R)
Louis T. McFadden (R)
Frederick W. Magrady (R)
Franklin Menges (R)
Stephen G. Porter (R)
d. June 1930
Harry C. Ransley (R)
Robert F. Rich (R) s. 1930
Milton W. Shreve (R)
Nathan L. Strong (R)
Patrick J. Sullivan (R)
J. Howard Swick (R)
Henry W. Temple (R)
C. Murray Turpin (R)
Laurence H. Watres (R)
Henry W. Watson (R)
George A. Welsh (R)
James Wolfenden (R)
Adam M. Wyant (R)

RHODE ISLAND

Senators

Jesse H. Metcalf (R)
Felix Hebert (R)

Representatives

Richard S. Aldrich (R)
Clark Burdick (R)
Francis B. Condon (D) s. 1930
Jeremiah E. O'Connell (D)
r. May 1930

SOUTH CAROLINA

Senators

Ellison D. Smith (D)
Coleman L. Blease (D)

Representatives

Fred H. Dominick (D)
Hampton P. Fulmer (D)
Allard H. Gasque (D)
Butler B. Hare (D)
Thomas S. McMillan (D)
John J. McSwain (D)
William F. Stevenson (D)

SOUTH DAKOTA

Senators

Peter Norbeck (R)
William H. McMaster (R)

Representatives

Charles A. Christopherson (R)
Royal C. Johnson (R)
William Williamson (R)

TENNESSEE

Senators

Kenneth D. McKellar (D)

Lawrence D. Tyson (D)
d. Aug. 1929
William E. Brock (D) s. 1929

Representatives

Gordon Browning (D)
Joseph W. Byrns (D)
Jere Cooper (D)
Ewin L. Davis (D)
Edward E. Eslick (D)
Hubert F. Fisher (D)
Cordell Hull (D)
Sam D. McReynolds (D)
B. Carroll Reece (R)
J. Will Taylor (R)

TEXAS

Senators

Morris Sheppard (D)
Tom T. Connally (D)

Representatives

John C. Box (D)
Clay Stone Briggs (D)
Thomas L. Blanton (D)
James P. Buchanan (D)
Oliver H. Cross (D)
John Nance Garner (D)
Daniel E. Garrett (D)
Claude B. Hudspeth (D)
Luther A. Johnson (D)
Marvin Jones (D)
Fritz G. Lanham (D)
Robert Q. Lee (D) d. Apr. 1930
Augustus McCloskey (D)
r. Feb. 1930
Joseph J. Mansfield (D)
Wright Patman (D)
Sam Rayburn (D)
Morgan G. Sanders (D)
Hatton W. Sumners (D)
Guinn Williams (D)
Harry M. Wurzbach (D)

UTAH

Senators

Reed Smoot (R)
William H. King (D)

Representatives

Don B. Colton (R)
Elmer O. Leatherwood (R)
d. Dec. 1929
Frederick C. Loofbourow (R)
s. 1930

VERMONT

Senators

Frank L. Greene (R) d. Dec. 1930
Frank C. Partridge (R)
ta. Jan. 1931

Porter H. Dale (R)

Representatives

Elbert S. Brigham (R)
Ernest W. Gibson (R)

VIRGINIA

Senators

Claude A. Swanson (D)
Carter Glass (D)

Representatives

Schuyler Otis Bland (D)
Patrick H. Drewry (D)
Jacob A. Garber (R)
Menalcus Lankford (R)
Andrew J. Montague (D)
R. Walton Moore (D)
Joseph C. Shaffer (R)
Henry St. George Tucker (D)
Joseph Whitehead (D)
Clifton A. Woodrum (D)

WASHINGTON

Senators

Wesley L. Jones (R)
Clarence C. Dill (D)

Representatives

Lindley H. Hadley (R)
Samuel B. Hill (D)
Albert Johnson (R)
John F. Miller (R)
John W. Summers (R)

WEST VIRGINIA

Senators

Guy D. Goff (R)
Henry D. Hatfield (R)

Representatives

Carl G. Bachmann (R)
Frank L. Bowman (R)
Robert L. Hogg (R) s. 1930
James A. Hughes (R)
d. Mar. 1930
Hugh I. Shott (R)
Joe L. Smith (D)
John M. Wolverton (R)

WISCONSIN

Senators

Robert M. LaFollette, Jr.
(Progressive)
John J. Blaine (R)

Representatives

Edward E. Browne (R)
Henry A. Cooper (R) d. Mar. 1931
James A. Frear (R)
Merlin Hull (R)
Charles A. Kading (R)
Florian Lampert (R) d. July 1930
John M. Nelson (R)
Hubert H. Peavey (R)
Michael K. Reilly (D) s. 1930
John C. Schafer (R)
George J. Schneider (Progressive)
William H. Stafford (R)

WYOMING

Senators

Francis E. Warren (R)
d. Nov. 1929
Patrick J. Sullivan (R) ta. 1929
Robert D. Carey (R) s. 1930

John B. Kendrick (D)

Representative

Vincent M. Carter (R)

CONNECTICUT

Senators

Hiram Bingham (R)
Frederic C. Walcott (R)

Representatives

Richard P. Freeman (R)
Edward W. Goss (R)
Augustine Lonergan (D)
William L. Tierney (D)
John Q. Tilson (R) r. Dec. 1932

DELAWARE

Senators

Daniel O. Hastings (R)
John G. Townsend, Jr. (R)

Representative

Robert G. Houston (R)

FLORIDA

Senators

Duncan U. Fletcher (D)
Park Trammell (D)

Representatives

Herbert J. Drane (D)
Robert A. Green (D)
Ruth Bryan Owen (D)
Thomas A. Yon (D)

GEORGIA

Senators

William J. Harris (D)
d. Apr. 1932
John S. Cohen (D) ta. 1932
Richard B. Russell (D) s. 1933

Walter F. George (D)

Representatives

Charles H. Brand (D)
Bryant T. Castellow (D) s. 1932
Edward E. Cox (D)
Charles R. Crisp (D) r. Oct. 1932
William C. Lankford (D)
William W. Larsen (D)
W. Carlton Mobley (D)
s. Mar. 1932
Homer C. Parker (D)
Robert C. Ramspeck (D)
Samuel Rutherford (D)
d. Feb. 1932
Malcolm C. Tarver (D)
Carl Vinson (D)
John S. Wood (D)
William C. Wright (D)

IDAHO

Senators

William E. Borah (R)
John Thomas (R)

Representatives

Burton L. French (R)
Addison T. Smith (R)

ILLINOIS

Senators

Otis F. Glenn (R)
J. Hamilton Lewis (D)

Representatives

Charles Adkins (R)
John C. Allen (R)
William W. Arnold (D)
Harry P. Beam (D)
Fred A. Britten (R)
John T. Buckbee (R)
Carl R. Chindblom (R)
Burnett M. Chiperfield (R)
Oscar DePriest (R)
William Dieterich (D)
Peter C. Granata (R)
r. Apr. 1932
Homer W. Hall (R)
William P. Holaday (R)
Morton D. Hull (R)
William E. Hull (R)
James T. Igoe (D)
William R. Johnson (R)
Charles A. Karch (D)
d. Nov. 1932
Kent E. Keller (D)
Edward A. Kelly (D)
Stanley H. Kunz (D) s. 1932
J. Earl Major (D)
Claude V. Parsons (D)
Henry T. Rainey (D)
Frank R. Reid (R)
Adolph J. Sabath (D)
Leonard W. Schuetz (D)
Richard Yates (R)

INDIANA

Senators

James E. Watson (R)
Arthur R. Robinson (R)

Representatives

John W. Boehne, Jr. (D)
Harry C. Canfield (D)
Eugene B. Crowe (D)
Courtland C. Gillen (D)
Arthur H. Greenwood (D)
Glenn Griswold (D)
David Hogg (R)
William H. Larrabee (D)
Louis L. Ludlow (D)
Samuel B. Pettengill (D)
Fred S. Purnell (R)
Albert H. Vestal (R)
d. Apr. 1932
William R. Wood (R)

IOWA

Senators

Smith W. Brookhart (R)
Lester J. Dickinson (R)

SEVENTY-SECOND CONGRESS

March 4, 1931 to March 3, 1933

President of The Senate: Charles Curtis
President Pro Tempore of The Senate: George H. Moses
Speaker of The House of Representatives: John Nance Garner

ALABAMA

Senators

Hugo L. Black (D)
John H. Bankhead 2d (D)

Representatives

Miles C. Allgood (D)
Edward B. Almon (D)
William B. Bankhead (D)
Lister Hill (D)
George Huddleston (D)
Lamar Jeffers (D)
John McDuffie (D)
William B. Oliver (D)
LaFayette L. Patterson (D)
Henry B. Steagall (D)

ARIZONA

Senators

Henry F. Ashurst (D)
Carl Hayden (D)

Representative

Lewis W. Douglas (D)

ARKANSAS

Senators

Joseph T. Robinson (D)

Thaddeus H. Caraway (D)
d. Oct. 1931
Hattie W. Caraway (D) s. 1931

Representatives

William J. Driver (D)
Claude A. Fuller (D)
David D. Glover (D)
John E. Miller (D)
Tilman B. Parks (D)
Heartsill Ragon (D)
Effiegene (Locke) Wingo (D)

CALIFORNIA

Senators

Hiram W. Johnson (R)
Samuel M. Shortridge (R)

Representatives

Henry E. Barbour (R)
Albert E. Carter (R)
Joe Crail (R)
Charles F. Curry, Jr. (R)
Harry L. Englebright (R)
William E. Evans (R)
Arthur M. Free (R)
Florence Prag Kahn (R)
Clarence F. Lea (D, R)
Philip D. Swing (R)
Richard J. Welch (R)

COLORADO

Senators

Charles W. Waterman (R)
d. Aug. 1932
Walter Walker (D) ta. 1932
Karl C. Schuyler (R) s. 1932
Edward P. Costigan (D)

Representatives

William R. Eaton (R)
Guy U. Hardy (R)
Edward T. Taylor (D)
Charles B. Timberlake (R)

Representatives

Ed H. Campbell (R)
Cyrenus Cole (R)
Cassius C.Dowell (R)
Fred C. Gilchrist (R)
Gilbert N. Haugen (R)
Bernhard M. Jacobsen (D)
William F. Kopp (R)
C. William Ramseyer (R)
Thomas J. B. Robinson (R)
Charles E. Swanson (R)
Lloyd Thurston (R)

KANSAS

Senators

Arthur Capper (R)
George McGill (D)

Representatives

William A. Ayres (D)
Ulysses S. Guyer (R)
Homer Hoch (R)
Clifford R. Hope (R)
William P. Lambertson (R)
Harold C. McGugin (R)
Charles I. Sparks (R)
James G. Strong (R)

KENTUCKY

Senators

Alben W. Barkley (D)
Marvel M. Logan (D)

Representatives

Cap R. Garden (D)
Glover H. Cary (D)
Virgil M. Chapman (D)
Charles Finley (R)
Ralph Gilbert (D)
William V. Gregory (D)
Andrew J. May (D)
John W. Moore (D)
Brent Spence (D)
Maurice H. Thatcher (R)
Fred M. Vinson (D)

LOUISIANA

Senators

Edwin S. Broussard (D)
Huey P. Long (D) s. 1932

Representatives

Rene L. DeRouen (D)
Joachim O. Fernandez (D)
Bolivar E. Kemp (D)
Paul H. Maloney (D)
Numa F. Montet (D)
John H. Overton (D)
John N. Sandlin (D)
Riley J. Wilson (D)

MAINE

Senators

Frederick Hale (R)
Wallace H. White, Jr. (R)

Representatives

Carroll L. Beedy (R)
John E. Nelson (R)
Donald B. Patridge (R)
Donald F. Snow (R)

MARYLAND

Senators

Millard E. Tydings (D)
Phillips Lee Goldsborough (R)

Representatives

William P. Cole, Jr. (D)
Stephen W. Gambrill (D)
T. Alan Goldsborough (D)
Ambrose J. Kennedy (D) s. 1932
David J. Lewis (D)
J. Charles Linthicum (D)
d. Oct. 1932
Vincent L. Palmisano (D)

MASSACHUSETTS

Senators

David I. Walsh (D)
Marcus A. Coolidge (D)

Representatives

A. Piatt Andrew, Jr. (R)
William P. Connery, Jr. (D)
Frederick W. Dallinger (D)
r. Oct. 1932
John J. Douglass (D)
Frank H. Foss (R)
Charles L. Gifford (R)
William J. Granfield (D)
Pehr G. Holmes (R)
Robert Luce (R)
John W. McCormack (D)
Joseph W. Martin, Jr. (R)
Edith Nourse Rogers (R)
George H. Tinkham (R)
Allen T. Treadway (R)
Charles L. Underhill (R)
Richard B. Wigglesworth (R)

MICHIGAN

Senators

James Couzens (R)
Arthur H. Vandenberg (R)

Representatives

Frank P. Bohn (R)
Robert H. Clancy (D)
Michael J. Hart (D)
Joseph L. Hooper (R)
W. Frank James (R)
John C. Ketcham (R)
James C. McLaughlin (R)
d. Nov. 1932
Clarence J. McLeod (R)
Carl E. Mapes (R)
Earl C. Michener (R)
Seymour H. Person (R)
Jesse P. Wolcott (R)
Roy O. Woodruff (R)

MINNESOTA

Senators

Henrik Shipstead (Farm-Labor)
Thomas D. Schall (R)

Representatives

August H. Andresen (R)
Victor Christgau (R)
Frank Clague (R)
Godfrey G. Goodwin (R)
d. Feb. 1933
Harold Knutson (R)
Paul J. Kvale (Farm-Labor)
Melvin J. Maas (R)
William I. Nolan (R)
William A. Pittenger (R)
Conrad G. Selvig (R)

MISSISSIPPI

Senators

Pat Harrison (D)
Hubert D. Stephens (D)

Representatives

T. Jeff Busby (D)
James W. Collier (D)
Ross A. Collins (D)
Wall Doxey (D)
Lawrence R. Ellzey (D) s. 1932
Robert S. Hall (D)
Percy E. Quin (D) d. Feb. 1932
John E. Rankin (D)
William M. Whittington (D)

MISSOURI

Senators

Harry B. Hawes (D) r. Feb. 1933
Bennett Champ Clark (D) s. 1933

Roscoe C. Patterson (R)

Representatives

William E. Barton (D)
Clarence Cannon (D)
John J. Cochran (D)
Clement C. Dickinson (D)
Leonidas C. Dyer (R)
James F. Fulbright (D)
David W. Hopkins (R)
Robert D. Johnson (D)
Ralph F. Lozier (D)
Joe J. Manlove (R)
Jacob L. Milligan (D)
William L. Nelson (D)
Henry F. Niedringhaus (R)
Milton A. Romjue (D)
Joseph B. Shannon (D)
Clyde Williams (D)

MONTANA

Senators

Thomas J. Walsh (D) d. Mar. 1933
Burton K. Wheeler (D)

Representatives

John M. Evans (D)
Scott Leavitt (R)

NEBRASKA

Senators

George W. Norris (R)
Robert B. Howell (R)

Representatives

H. Malcolm Baldrige (R)
Edgar Howard (D)
John H. Morehead (D)
John N. Norton (D)
Ashton C. Shallenberger (D)
Robert G. Simmons (R)

NEVADA

Senators

Key Pittman (D)
Tasker L. Oddie (R)

Representative

Samuel S. Arentz (R)

NEW HAMPSHIRE

Senators

George H. Moses (R)
Henry W. Keyes (R)

Representatives

William N. Rogers (D) s. 1932
Edward H. Wason (R)

NEW JERSEY

Senators

Hamilton F. Kean (R)
Dwight W. Morrow (R)
d. Oct. 1931
W. Warren Barbour (R) s. 1931

Representatives

Oscar L. Auf Der Heide (D)
Isaac Bacharach (R)
Peter A. Cavicchia (R)
Charles A. Eaton (R)
Fred A. Hartley, Jr. (R)
Frederick P. Lehlbach (R)
Mary T. Norton (D)
Randolph Perkins (R)
George N. Seger (R)
Percy H. Stewart (D)
William H. Sutphin (D)
Charles A. Wolverton (R)

NEW MEXICO

Senators

Sam G. Bratton (D)
Bronson M. Cutting (R)

Representative

Dennis Chavez (D)

NEW YORK

Senators

Royal S. Copeland (D)
Robert F. Wagner (D)

Representatives

Walter G. Andrews (R)
Robert L. Bacon (R)
Loring M. Black, Jr. (D)
Sol Bloom (D)
John J. Boylan (D)
William F. Brunner (D)
Patrick J. Carley (D)
Emanuel Celler (D)
John D. Clarke (R)
Edmund F. Cooke (R)
Parker Corning (D)
Frank Crowther (R)
Francis D. Culkin (R)
Thomas H. Cullen (D)
Frederick M. Davenport (R)
John J. Delaney (D)
Samuel Dickstein (D)
Hamilton Fish, Jr. (R)
James M. Fitzpatrick (D)
Joseph A. Gavagan (D)
Anthony J. Griffin (D)
Clarence E. Hancock (R)
Martin J. Kennedy (D)
Fiorello H. LaGuardia (R)
George W. Lindsay (D)
James M. Mead (D)
Charles D. Millard (R)
John J. O'Connor (D)
Frank Oliver (D)
James S. Parker (R)
Anning S. Prall (D)
Harcourt J. Pratt (R)
Ruth S. B. Pratt (R)
Daniel A. Reed (R)
Stephen A. Rudd (D)
Archie D. Sanders (R)
William I. Sirovich (D)
Bertrand H. Snell (R)
Andrew L. Somers (D)
Gale H. Stalker (R)
Christopher D. Sullivan (D)
John Taber (R)
James L. Whitley (R)

NORTH CAROLINA

Senators

Cameron A. Morrison (D)
ta. 1931
Robert R. Reynolds (D)
s. 1932
Jesiah W. Bailey (D)

Representatives

Charles L. Abernethy (D)
Alfred L. Bulwinkle (D)
J. Bayard Clark (D)
Robert L. Doughton (D)
Franklin W. Hancock, Jr. (D)
John H. Kerr (D)
J. Walter Lambeth (D)
Edward W. Pou (D)
Lindsay C. Warren (D)
Zebulon Weaver (D)

NORTH DAKOTA

Senators

Lynn J. Frazier (R)
Gerald P. Nye (R)

Representatives

Olger B. Burtness (R)
Thomas Hall (R)
James H. Sinclair (R)

OHIO

Senators

Simeon D. Fess (R)
Robert J. Bulkley (D)

Representatives

Chester C. Bolton (R)
Charles Brand (R)
John L. Cable (R)
John G. Cooper (R)
Robert Crosser (D)
William L. Fiesinger (D)
Byron B. Harlan (D)
William E. Hess (R)
John B. Hollister (R)
Thomas A. Jenkins (R)
Frank C. Kniffin (D)
Arthur P. Lamneck (D)
Charles B. McClintock (R)
C. Ellis Moore (R)
Grant E. Mouser, Jr. (R)
B. Frank Murphy (R)
James G. Polk (D)
Francis Seiberling (R)
Martin L. Sweeney (D)
Mell G. Underwood (D)
Charles West (D)
Wilbur M. White (R)

OKLAHOMA

Senators

J. W. Elmer Thomas (D)
Thomas P. Gore (D)

Representatives

Wilburn Cartwright (D)
Wesley E. Disney (D)
Milton C. Garber (R)
William W. Hastings (D)
Jed Johnson (D)
James V. McClintic (D)
Thomas D. McKeown (D)
Fletcher B. Swank (D)

OREGON

Senators

Charles L. McNary (R)
Frederick Steiwer (R)

Representatives

Robert R. Butler (R)
d. Jan. 1933
Willis C. Hawley (R)
Charles H. Martin (D)

PENNSYLVANIA

Senators

David A. Reed (R)
James J. Davis (R)

Representatives

James M. Beck (R)
Edward M. Beers (R) d. Apr. 1932
Joseph F. Biddle (R)
s. Dec. 1932
Patrick J. Boland (D)
George F. Brumm (R)
Guy E. Campbell (R)
J. Mitchell Chase (R)
Thomas C. Cochran (R)
James J. Connolly (R)
William R. Coyle (R)
George P. Darrow (R)
Robert L. Davis (R) s. 1932
Isaac H. Doutrich (R)
Edmund F. Erk (R)
Harry A. Estep (R)
Benjamin M. Golder (R)
Harry L. Haines (D)
M. Clyde Kelly (R)
Samuel A. Kendall (R)
d. Jan. 1933
J. Roland Kinzer (R)
J. Banks Kurtz (R)
J. Russell Leech (R) r. Jan. 1932
Norton L. Lichtenwalner (D)
Louis T. McFadden (R)
Frederick W. Magrady (R)
Harry C. Ransley (R)
Robert F. Rich (R)
Milton W. Shreve (R)
Edward L. Stokes (R)
Nathan L. Strong (R)
Howard W. Stull (R) s. 1932
Patrick J. Sullivan (R)
J. Howard Swick (R)
Henry W. Temple (R)
C. Murray Turpin (R)
Henry W. Watson (R)
George A. Welsh (R) r. May 1932
James Wolfenden (R)
Adam M. Wyant (R)

RHODE ISLAND

Senators

Jesse H. Metcalf (R)
Felix Hebert (R)

Representatives

Richard S. Aldrich (R)
Clark Burdick (R)
Francis B. Condon (D)

SOUTH CAROLINA

Senators

Ellison D. Smith (D)
James F. Byrnes (D)

Representatives

Fred H. Dominick (D)
Hampton P. Fulmer (D)
Allard H. Gasque (D)
Butler B. Hare (D)
Thomas S. McMillan (D)
John J. McSwain (D)
William F. Stevenson (D)

SOUTH DAKOTA

Senators

Peter Norbeck (R)
William J. Bulow (D)

Representatives

Charles A. Christopherson (R)
Royal C. Johnson (R)
William Williamson (R)

TENNESSEE

Senators

Kenneth D. McKellar (D)
Cordell Hull (D)

Representatives

Gordon Browning (D)
Joseph W. Byrns (D)
Jere Cooper (D)
Edward H. Crump (D)
Ewin L. Davis (D)
Edward E. Eslick (D)
d. June 1932
Willa M. B. Eslick (D) s. 1932
Oscar B. Lovette (R)
Sam D. McReynolds (D)
John R. Mitchell (D)
J. Will Taylor (R)

TEXAS

Senators

Morris Sheppard (D)
Tom T. Connally (D)

Representatives

Thomas L. Blanton (D)
Clay Stone Briggs (D)
James P. Buchanan (D)
Oliver H. Cross (D)
Martin Dies, Jr. (D)
Joe H. Eagle (D) s. 1933
John Nance Garner (D)
Daniel E. Garrett (D)
d. Dec. 1932
Luther A. Johnson (D)
Marvin Jones (D)
Richard M. Kleberg (D) s. 1931
Fritz G. Lanham (D)
Joseph J. Mansfield (D)
Wright Patman (D)

Sam Rayburn (D)
Morgan G. Sanders (D)
Hatton W. Sumners (D)
R. Ewing Thomason (D)
Guinn Williams (D)

UTAH

Senators

Reed Smoot (R)
William H. King (D)

Representatives

Don B. Colton (R)
Frederick C. Loofbourow (R)

VERMONT

Senators

Porter H. Dale (R)

Frank C. Partridge (R) ta. 1931
Warren R. Austin (R) s. 1931

Representatives

Ernest W. Gibson (R)
John E. Weeks (R)

VIRGINIA

Senators

Claude A. Swanson (D)
Carter Glass (D)

Representatives

Schuyler Otis Bland (D)
Thomas G. Burch (D)
Patrick H. Drewry (D)
John W. Fishburne (D)
John W. Flannagan, Jr. (D)
Joel W. Flood s. 1932
Menalcus Lankford (R)
Andrew J. Montague (D)
Howard W. Smith (D)
Henry St. George Tucker (D)
d. July 1932
Clifton A. Woodrum (D)

WASHINGTON

Senators

Wesley L. Jones (R)
d. Nov. 1932
Elijah S. Grammer (R) s. 1932

Clarence C. Dill (D)

Representatives

Lindley H. Hadley (R)
Samuel B. Hill (D)
Ralph A. Horr (R)
Albert Johnson (R)
John W. Summers (R)

WEST VIRGINIA

Senators

Henry D. Hatfield (R)
Matthew M. Neely (D)

Representatives

Carl G. Bachmann (R)
Frank L. Bowman (R)
Robert L. Hogg (R)
Lynn S. Hornor (D)
Hugh I. Shott (R)
Joe L. Smith (D)

WISCONSIN

Senators

Robert M. LaFollette, Jr. (R)
John J. Blaine (R)

Representatives

Thomas R. Amlie (R)
Gerald J. Boileau (R)
James A. Frear (R)
Charles A. Kading (R)
John M. Nelson (R)
Hubert H. Peavey (R)
Michael K. Reilly (D)
John C. Shafer (R)
George J. Schneider (Progressive)
William H. Stafford (R)
Gardner R. Withrow (R)

WYOMING

Senators

John B. Kendrick (D)
Robert D. Carey (R)

Representative

Vincent M. Carter (R)

SEVENTY-THIRD CONGRESS

March 4, 1933 to January 3, 1935

President of The Senate: John Nance Garner
President Pro Tempore of The Senate: Key Pittman
Speaker of The House of Representatives: Henry T. Rainey

ALABAMA

Senators

Hugo L. Black (D)
John H. Bankhead 2d (D)

Representatives

Miles C. Allgood (D)
Edward B. Almon (D)
d. June 1933
William B. Bankhead (D)
Archibald H. Carmichael (D)
s. 1934
Lister Hill (R)
George Huddleston (D)
Lamar Jeffers (D)
John McDuffie (D)
William B. Oliver (D)
Henry B. Steagall (D)

ARIZONA

Senators

Henry F. Ashurst (D)
Carl Hayden (D)

Representative

Isabella S. Greenway (D)
s. 1934

ARKANSAS

Senators

Joseph T. Robinson (D)
Hattie W. Caraway (D)

Representatives

William B. Cravens (D)
William J. Driver (D)
Claude A. Fuller (D)
David D. Glover (D)
John E. Miller (D)
Tilman B. Parks (D)
Heartsill Ragon (D)
r. June 1933
David D. Terry (D) s. 1934

CALIFORNIA

Senators

Hiram W. Johnson (R)
William Gibbs McAdoo (D)

Representatives

Frank H. Buck (D)
John H.Burke (D)
George Burnham (D)
Albert E. Carter (R)
Denver S. Church (D)
Charles J. Colden (D)
Samuel L. Collins (R)
John F. Dockweiler (D)
Ralph R. Eltse (R)
Harry L. Englebright (R)
William E. Evans (R)
Thomas F. Ford (D)
John H. Hoeppel (D)
Florence Prag Kahn (R)
Charles Kramer (D)
Clarence F. Lea (D, R)
John J. McGrath (D)
Henry E. Stubbs (D)
William I. Traeger (R)
Richard J. Welch (R)

COLORADO

Senators

Edward P. Costigan (D)
Alva B. Adams (D)

Representatives

Fred Cummings (D)
Lawrence Lewis (D)
John A. Martin (D)
Edward T. Taylor (D)

CONNECTICUT

Senators

Frederic C. Walcott (R)
Augustine Lonergan (D)

Representatives

Charles M. Bakewell (R)
Edward W. Goss (R)
William L. Higgins (R)
Herman P. Kopplemann (D)
Francis T. Maloney (D)
Schuyler Merritt (R)

DELAWARE

Senators

Daniel O. Hastings (R)
John G. Townsend, Jr. (R)

Representative

Wilbur L. Adams (D)

FLORIDA

Senators

Duncan U. Fletcher (D)
Park Trammell (D)

Representatives

Millard F. Caldwell (D)
Robert A. Green (D)
J. Hardin Peterson (D)
William J. Sears (D)
J. Mark Wilcox (D)

GEORGIA

Senators

Walter F. George (D)
Richard B. Russell (D)

Representatives

Charles H. Brand (D)
d. May 1933
Paul Brown (D) s. 1934
Bryant T. Castellow (D)
Edward E. Cox (D)
Braswell D. Deen (D)
Emmett M. Owen (D)
Homer C. Parker (D)
Robert C. Ramspeck (D)
Malcolm C. Tarver (D)
Carl Vinson (D)
John S. Wood (D)

IDAHO

Senators

William E. Borah (R)
James P. Pope (D)

Representatives

Thomas C. Coffin (D)
d. June 1934
Compton I. White (D)

ILLINOIS

Senators

H. Hamilton Lewis (D)
William H. Dieterich (D)

Representatives

J. Leroy Adair (D)
Leo E. Allen (R)
William W. Arnold (D)
Harry P. Beam (D)
Martin A. Brennan (D)
Fred A. Britten (R)
John T. Buckbee (R)
Oscar DePriest (R)
Everett M. Dirksen (R)
Donald C. Dobbins (D)
Frank Gillespie (D)
Kent E. Keller (D)
Edward A. Kelly (D)
Leo Kocialkowski (D)
J. Earl Major (D) r. Oct. 1933
James A. Meeks (D)
Patrick H. Moynihan (R)
Walter Nesbit (D)
Thomas J. O'Brien (D)
Claude V. Parsons (D)
Henry T. Rainey (D) d. Aug. 1934
Frank R. Reid (R)
Adolph J. Sabath (D)
Edwin M. Schaefer (D)
Leonard W. Schuetz (D)
James J. Simpson, Jr. (R)
Chester C. Thompson (D)

INDIANA

Senators

Arthur R. Robinson (R)
Frederick Van Nuys (D)

Representatives

John W. Boehne, Jr. (D)
Eugene B. Crowe (D)
George R. Durgan (D)
James I. Farley (D)
Finley H. Gray (D)
Arthur H. Greenwood (D)
Glenn Griswold (D)
Virginia Ellis Jenckes (D)
William H. Larrabee (D)
Louis L. Ludlow (D)
Samuel B. Pettengill (D)
William T. Schulte (D)

IOWA

Senators

Lester J. Dickinson (R)
Richard L. Murphy (D)

Representatives

Fred Biermann (D)
Cassius C. Dowell (R)
Edward C. Eicher (D)
Fred C. Gilchrist (R)
Guy M. Gillette (D)
Bernhard M. Jacobsen (D)
Lloyd Thurston (R)
Otha D. Wearin (D)
Albert C. Willford (D)

KANSAS

Senators

Arthur Capper (R)
George McGill (D)

Representatives

William A. Ayres (D)
r. Aug. 1934
William R. Carpenter (D)
Ulysses S. Guyer (R)
Clifford R. Hope (R)
William P. Lambertson (R)
Kathryn O'Loughlin McCarthy (D)
Harold McGugin (R)

KENTUCKY

Senators

Alben W. Barkley (D)
Marvel M. Logan (D)

Representatives

John Y. Brown (D)
Cap R. Carden (D)
Glover H. Cary (D)
Virgil M. Chapman (D)
William V. Gregory (D)
Finley Hamilton (D)
Andrew J. May (D)
Brent Spence (D)
Fred M. Vinson (D)

LOUISIANA

Senators

Huey P. Long (D)
John H. Overton (D)

Representatives

Cleveland Dear (D)
Rene L. DeRouen (D)
Joachim O. Fernandez (D)
Bolivar E. Kemp (D)
d. June 1933
Paul H. Maloney (D)
Numa F. Montet (D)
Jared Y. Sanders, Jr. (D)
s. 1934
John N. Sandlin (D)
Riley J. Wilson (D)

MAINE

Senators

Frederick Hale (R)
Wallace H. White, Jr. (R)

Representatives

Carroll L. Beedy (R)
Edward C. Moran, Jr. (R)
John G. Utterback (D)

MARYLAND

Senators

Millard E. Tydings (D)
Phillips Lee Goldsborough (R)

Representatives

William P. Cole, Jr. (D)
Stephen W. Gambrill (D)
T. Alan Goldsborough (D)
Ambrose J. Kennedy (D)
David J. Lewis (D)
Vincent L. Palmisano (D)

MASSACHUSETTS

Senators

David I. Walsh (D)
Marcus A. Coolidge (D)

Representatives

A. Piatt Andrew, Jr. (R)
William P. Connery, Jr. (D)
John J. Douglass (D)
Frank H. Foss (R)
Charles L. Gifford (R)
William J. Granfield (D)
Arthur D. Healey (D)
Pehr G. Holmes (R)
Robert Luce (R)
John W. McCormack (D)
Joseph W. Martin, Jr. (R)
Edith Nourse Rogers (R)
George H. Tinkham (R)
Allen T. Treadway (R)
Richard B. Wigglesworth (R)

MICHIGAN

Senators

James Couzens (R)
Arthur H. Vandenberg (R)

Representatives

Prentiss M. Brown (R)
Claude E. Cady (D)
John D. Dingell (D)
George A. Dondero (R)
George E. Foulkes (D)
Michael J. Hart (D)
Joseph L. Hooper (R)
d. Feb. 1934
W. Frank James (R)
John C. Lehr (D)
John Lesinski (D)
Clarence J. McLeod (R)
Carl E. Mapes (R)
Harry W. Musselwhite (D)
George G. Sadowski (D)
Carl M. Weideman (D)
Jesse P. Wolcott (R)
Roy O. Woodruff (R)

MINNESOTA

Senators

Henrik Shipstead (Farm-Labor)
Thomas D. Schall (R)

Representatives

Henry Arens (Farm-Labor)
Ray P. Chase (R)
Theodore Christianson (R)
Einar Hoidale (D)
Magnus Johnson (Farm-Labor)
Harold Knutson (R)
Paul J. Kvale (Farm-Labor)
Ernest Lundeen (Farm-Labor)
Francis H. Shoemaker
(Farm-Labor)

MISSISSIPPI

Senators

Pat Harrison (D)
Hubert D. Stephens (D)

Representatives

T. Jeff Busby (D)
Wall Doxey (D)
Lawrence R. Ellzey (D)
Ross A. Collins (D)
William M. Colmer (D)
John E. Rankin (D)
William M. Whittington (D)

MISSOURI

Senators

Roscoe C. Patterson (R)
Bennett Champ Clark (D)

Representatives

Clarence Cannon (D)
James R. Claiborne (D)
John J. Cochran (D)
Clement C. Dickinson (D)
Richard M. Duncan (D)
Frank H. Lee (D)
Ralph F. Lozier (D)
Jacob L. Milligan (D)
Milton A. Romjue (D)
James E. Ruffin (D)
Joseph B. Shannon (D)
Clyde Williams (D)
Reuben T. Wood (D)

MONTANA

Senators

Burton K. Wheeler (D)

John E. Erickson (D) ta. 1933-34
James E. Murray (D) s. 1935

Representatives

Roy E. Ayers (D)
Joseph P. Monaghan (D)

NEBRASKA

Senators

George W. Norris (R)

Robert B. Howell (R)
d. Mar. 1933
William H. Thompson ta. 1933-34
Richard C. Hunter (D) s. 1934

Representatives

Edward R. Burke (D)
Terry M. Carpenter (D)
Edgar Howard (D)
John M. Morehead (D)
Ashton C. Shallenberger (D)

NEVADA

Senators

Key Pittman (D)
Patrick A. McCarran (D)

Representative

James G. Scrugham (D)

NEW HAMPSHIRE

Senators

Henry W. Keyes (R)
Fred H. Brown (D)

Representatives

William N. Rogers (D)
Charles W. Tobey (R)

NEW JERSEY

Senators

Hamilton F. Kean (R)
W. Warren Barbour (R)

Representatives

Oscar L. Auf Der Heide (D)
Isaac Bacharach (R)
Peter A. Cavicchia (R)
Charles A. Eaton (R)
Fred A. Hartley, Jr. (R)
Edward A. Kenney (D)
Frederick R. Lehlbach (R)
Donald H. McLean (R)
Mary T. Norton (D)
Randolph Perkins (R)
D. Lane Powers (R)
George N. Seger (R)
William H. Sutphin (D)
Charles A. Wolverton (R)

NEW MEXICO

Senators

Sam G. Bratton (D)
r. June 1933
Carl A. Hatch (D) s. 1934
Bronson M. Cutting (R)

Representative

Dennis Chavez (D)

NEW YORK

Senators

Royal S. Copeland (D)
Robert F. Wagner (D)

Representatives

Walter G. Andrews (R)
Robert L. Bacon (R)
Alfred F. Beiter (D)
Loring M. Black, Jr. (D)
Sol Bloom (D)
John J. Boylan (D)
William F. Brunner (D)
Patrick J. Carley (D)
Emanuel Celler (D)
John D. Clarke (R) d. 1934
Marian W. Clarke (R) s. 1934
Parker Corning (D)
Frank Crowther (R)
Francis D. Culkin (R)
Thomas Cullen (D)
John J. Delaney (D)
Samuel Dickstein (D)
Hamilton Fish, Jr. (R)
John Fitzgibbons (D)
James M. Fitzpatrick (D)
Joseph A. Gavagan (D)
Philip A. Goodwin (R)
Anthony J. Griffin (D)
Clarence E. Hancock (R)
Martin J. Kennedy (D)
James J. Lanzetta (D)
George W. Lindsay (D)
James M. Mead (D)
Charles D. Millard (R)
John J. O'Connor (D)
Frank Oliver (D) r. June 1934
James S. Parker (R)
d. Dec. 1933
Theodore A. Peyser (D)
Anning S. Prall (D)
Daniel A. Reed (R)
Stephen A. Rudd (D)
William I. Sirovich (D)
Fred J. Sisson (D)
Bertrand H. Snell (R)
Andrew L. Somers (D)
Gale H. Stalker (R)
Elmer E. Studley (D)
Christopher D. Sullivan (D)
John Taber (R)
William D. Thomas (R) s. 1934
James W. Wadsworth, Jr. (R)
James L. Whitley (R)

NORTH CAROLINA

Senators

Josiah W. Bailey (D)
Robert R. Reynolds (D)

Representatives

Charles Abernethy (D)
Alfred L. Bulwinkle (D)
J. Bayard Clark (D)
Harold D. Cooley (D) s. 1934
Robert L. Doughton (D)
Franklin W. Hancock, Jr. (D)
John H. Kerr (D)
J. Walter Lambeth (D)
Edward W. Pou (D)
d. Apr. 1934
William B. Umstead (D)
Lindsay C. Warren (D)
Zebulon Weaver (D)

NORTH DAKOTA

Senators

Lynn J. Frazier (R)
Gerald P. Nye (R)

Representatives

William Lemke (R)
James H. Sinclair (R)

OHIO

Senators

Simeon D. Fess (R)
Robert J. Bulkley (D)

Representatives

Chester C. Bolton (R)
John G. Cooper (R)
Robert Crosser (D)
Warren J. Duffey (D)
William L. Fiesinger (D)
Thomas B. Fletcher (D)
Byron B. Harlan (D)
Dow W. Harter (D)
William E. Hess (R)
John B. Hollister (R)
Lawrence E. Imhoff (D)
Thomas A. Jenkins (R)
Frank L. Kloeb (D)
Frank C. Kniffin (D)
Arthur P. Lamneck (D)
Leroy T. Marshall (R)
James G. Polk (D)
Robert T. Secrest (D)
Martin L. Sweeney (D)
William R. Thom (D)
Charles V. Truax (D)
Mell G. Underwood (D)
Charles West (D)
Stephen M. Young (D)

OKLAHOMA

Senators

J. W. Elmer Thomas (D)
Thomas P. Gore (D)

Representatives

Wilburn Cartwright (D)
Wesley E. Disney (D)
William W. Hastings (D)
Jed Johnson (D)
James V. McClintic (D)
Thomas D. McKeown (D)
Ernest W. Marland (D)
Will Rogers (D)
Fletcher B. Swank (D)

OREGON

Senators

Charles L. McNary (R)
Frederick Steiwer (R)

Representatives

Charles H. Martin (D)
James W. Mott (R)
Walter M. Pierce (D)

PENNSYLVANIA

Senators

David A. Reed (R)
James J. Davis (R)

Representatives

James M. Beck (R) r. Sept. 1934
William M. Berlin (D)
Patrick J. Boland (D)
J. Twing Brooks (D)
George F. Brumm (R)
d. May 1934
Thomas C. Cochran (R)
James J. Connolly (R)
Charles N. Crosby (D)
George P. Darrow (R)
J. William Ditter (R)
Isaac H. Doutrich (R)
Matthew A. Dunn (D)
George W. Edmonds (R)
Henry Ellenbogen (D)
Charles I. Faddis (D)
Benjamin K. Focht (R)
Oliver W. Frey (D) s. 1934
Harry L. Haines (D)
M. Clyde Kelly (R)
J. Roland Kinzer (R)
J. Banks Kurtz (R)
Louis T. McFadden (R)
Michael J. Muldowney (R)
Harry C. Ransley (R)
Robert F. Rich (R)
William E. Richardson (D)
J. Buell Snyder (D)
Edward L. Stokes (R)
Nathan L. Strong (R)
J. Howard Swick (R)
C. Murray Turpin (R)
Alfred M. Waldron (R)
Francis E. Walter (D)
Henry W. Watson (R)
d. Aug. 1933
James Wolfenden (R)

RHODE ISLAND

Senators

Jesse H. Metcalf (R)
Felix Hebert (R)

Representatives

Francis B. Condon (D)
John M. O'Connell (D)

SOUTH CAROLINA

Senators

Ellison D. Smith (D)
James F. Byrnes (D)

Representatives

Hampton P. Fulmer (D)
Allard H. Gasque (D)
Thomas S. McMillan (D)
John J. McSwain (D)
James P. Richards (D)
John C. Taylor (D)

SOUTH DAKOTA

Senators

Peter Norbeck (R)
William J. Bulow (D)

Representatives

Fred H. Hildebrandt (D)
Theodore B. Werner (D)

TENNESSEE

Senators

Kenneth D. McKellar (D)
Nathan L. Bachman (D)

Representatives

Gordon Browning (D)
Joseph W. Byrns (D)
Jere Cooper (D)
Edward H. Crump (D)
Sam D. McReynolds (D)
John R. Mitchell (D)
B. Carroll Reece (R)
J. Will Taylor (R)
Clarence W. Turner (D)

TEXAS

Senators

Morris Sheppard (D)
Tom T. Connally (D)

Representatives

Joseph W. Bailey, Jr. (D)
Thomas L. Blanton (D)
Clay Stone Briggs (D)
James P. Bucahanan (D)
Oliver H. Cross (D)
Martin Dies, Jr. (D)
Joe H. Eagle (D)
Luther A. Johnson (D)
Marvin Jones (D)
Richard M. Kleberg (D)
Fritz G. Lanham (D)
William D. McFarlane (D)
Joseph J. Mansfield (D)
Wright Patman (D)
Sam Rayburn (D)
Morgan G. Sanders (D)
Sterling P. Strong
Hatton W. Sumners (D)
George B. Terrell (D)
R. Ewing Thomason (D)
Clark W. Thompson (D)
Milton H. West (D)

UTAH

Senators

William H. King (D)
Elbert D. Thomas (D)

Representatives

Abe Murdock (D)
J. W. Robinson (D)

VERMONT

Senators

Porter H. Dale
d. Oct. 1933 (R)
Ernest W. Gibson s. 1934

Warren R. Austin (R)

Representatives

Ernest W. Gibson (R)
r. Oct. 1933
Charles A. Plumley (R) s. 1934

VIRGINIA

Senators

Carter Glass (D)
Harry F. Byrd (D)

Representatives

Schuyler Otis Bland (D)
Thomas G. Burch (D)
Colgate W. Darden, Jr. (D)
Patrick H. Drewry (D)
John W. Flannagan, Jr. (D)
Andrew J. Montague (D)
A. Willis Robertson (D)
Howard W. Smith (D)
Clifton A. Woodrum (D)

WASHINGTON

Senators

Clarence C. Dill (D)
Homer T. Bone (D)

Representatives

Knute Hill (D)
Samuel B. Hill (D)
Wesley Lloyd (D)
Martin F. Smith (D)
Monrad C. Wallgren (D)
Marion A. Zioncheck (D)

WEST VIRGINIA

Senators

Henry D. Hatfield (R)
Matthew M. Neely (D)

Representatives

Andrew Edmiston (D) s. 1934
Lynn S. Hornor (D)
d. Sept. 1933
George W. Johnson (D)
John Kee (D)
Robert L. Ramsay (D)
Jennings Randolph (D)
Joe L. Smith (D)

WISCONSIN

Senators

Robert M. La Follette, Jr.
(Progressive)
F. Ryan Duffy (D)

Representatives

George W. Blanchard (R)
Gerald J. Boileau (R)
Raymond J. Cannon (D)
James A. Frear (R)
Charles W. Henney (D)
James F. Hughes (D)
Thomas O'Malley (D)
Hubert H. Peavey (R)
Michael K. Reilly (D)
Gardner R. Withrow (R)

WYOMING

Senators

John B. Kendrick (D)
d. Nov. 1933
Joseph C. O'Mahoney (D) s. 1934

Robert D. Carey (R)

Representative

Vincent M. Carter (R)

SEVENTY-FOURTH CONGRESS

January 3, 1935 to January 3, 1937

President of The Senate	John Nance Garner
President Pro Tempore of The Senate	Key Pittman
Speakers of The House of Representatives	Joseph W. Byrns William B. Bankhead

ALABAMA

Senators

Hugo L. Black (D)
John H. Bankhead 2d (D)

Representatives

William B. Bankhead (D)
Frank W. Boykin (D)
Archibald H. Carmichael (D)
Lister Hill (D)
Sam Hobbs (D)
George Huddleston (D)
John McDuffie (D)
r. Mar. 1935
William B. Oliver (D)
Joe Starnes (D)
Henry B. Steagall (D)

ARIZONA

Senators

Henry F. Ashurst (D)
Carl Hayden (D)

Representative

Isabella S. Greenway (D)

ARKANSAS

Senators

Joseph T. Robinson (D)
Hattie W. Caraway (D)

Representatives

William B. Cravens (D)
William J. Driver (D)
Claude A. Fuller (D)
John L. McClellan (D)
John E. Miller (D)
Tilman B. Parks (D)
David D. Terry (D)

CALIFORNIA

Senators

Hiram W. Johnson (R)
William Gibbs McAdoo (D)

Representatives

Frank H. Buck (D)
George Burnham (R)
Albert E. Carter (R)
Charles J. Colden (D)
Samuel L. Collins (R)
John M. Costello (D)
John F. Dockweiler (D)
Harry L. Englebright (R)
Thomas F. Ford (D)
Bertrand W. Gearhart (R)
John H. Hoeppel (D)
Florence Prag Kahn (R)
Charles Kramer (D)
Clarence F. Lea (D,R)
John J. McGrath (D)
John S. McGroarty (D)
Bryon N. Scott (D)
Henry E. Stubbs (D)
John H. Tolan (D)
Richard J. Welch (R)

COLORADO

Senators

Edward P. Costigan (D)
Alva B. Adams (D)

Representatives

Fred Cummings (D)
Lawrence Lewis (D)
John A. Martin (D)
Edward T. Taylor (D)

CONNECTICUT

Senators

Augustine Lonergan (D)
Francis T. Maloney (D)

Representatives

William M. Citron (D)
William L. Higgins (R)
Herman P. Kopplemann (D)
Schuyler Merritt (R)
James A. Shanley (D)
J. Joseph Smith (D)

DELAWARE

Senators

Daniel O. Hastings (R)
John G. Townsend, Jr. (R)

Representative

John G. Stewart (R)

FLORIDA

Senators

Duncan U. Fletcher (D)
d. June 1936
William L. Hill (D)
ta. July 1936
Claude D. Pepper (D) s. 1937
Park Trammell (D)
d. May 1936

Scott Loftin (D) ta. May 1936
Charles O. Andrews (D)
s. 1937

Representatives

Millard F. Caldwell (D)
Robert A. Green (D)
J. Hardin Peterson (D)
William J. Sears (D)
J. Mark Wilcox (D)

GEORGIA

Senators

Walter F. George (D)
Richard B. Russell (D)

Representatives

Paul Brown (D)
Bryant T. Castellow (D)
Edward E. Cox (D)
Braswell D. Deen (D)
Emmett M. Owen (D)
Hugh Peterson (D)
Robert Ramspeck (D)
Malcolm C. Tarver (D)
Carl Vinson (D)
B. Frank Whelchel (D)

IDAHO

Senators

William E. Borah (R)
James P. Pope (D)

Representatives

D. Worth Clark (D)
Compton I. White (D)

ILLINOIS

Senators

J. Hamilton Lewis (D)
William H. Dieterich (D)

Representatives

J. Leroy Adair (D)
Leo E. Allen (R)
Leslie C. Arends (R)
William W. Arnold (D)
r. Sept. 1935
Harry P. Beam (D)
Martin A. Brennan (D)
John T. Buckbee (R)
d. Apr. 1936
Ralph E. Church (R)
Everett M. Dirksen (R)
Donald C. Dobbins (D)
Michael L. Igoe (D)
r. June 1935
Kent E. Keller (D)
Edward A. Kelly (D)
Leo Kocialkowski (D)
Scott W. Lucas (D)
James McAndrews (D)
Raymond S. McKeough (D)
Harry H. Mason (D)
James A. Meeks (D)
Arthur W. Mitchell (D)
Thomas J. O'Brien (D)
Claude V. Parsons (D)
Chauncey W. Reed (R)
Adolph J. Sabath (D)
Edwin M. Schaefer (D)
Leonard W. Schuetz (D)
Chester C. Thompson (D)

INDIANA

Senators

Frederick Van Nuys (D)
Sherman Minton (D)

Representatives

John W. Boehne, Jr. (D)
Eugene B. Crowe (D)
James I. Farley (D)
Finly H. Gray (D)
Arthur H. Greenwood (D)
Glenn Griswold (D)
Charles A. Halleck (R)
Virginia E. Jenckes (D)
William H. Larrabee (D)
Louis Ludlow (D)
Samuel B. Pettengill (D)
William T. Schulte (D)

IOWA

Senators

Lester J. Dickinson (R)

Richard L. Murphy (D)
d. July 1936
Guy M. Gillette (D) s. 1936

Representatives

Fred Biermann (D)
Edward C. Eicher (D)
Fred C. Gilchrist (R)
Guy M. Gillettee (D)
r. Nov. 1936
John W. Gwynne (R)
Bernhard M. Jacobsen (D)
d. June 1936
Lloyd Thurston (R)
Hubert Utterback (D)
Otha D. Wearin (D)

KANSAS

Senators

Arthur Capper (R)
George McGill (D)

Representatives

Frank Carlson (R)
William R. Carpenter (D)
Ulysses Guyer (R)
Clifford R. Hope (R)
John M. Houston (D)
William P. Lambertson (R)
Edward W. Patterson (D)

KENTUCKY

Senators

Alben W. Barkley (D)
Marvel M. Logan (D)

Representatives

Cap R. Carden (D)
d. June 1935
Glover H. Cary (D)
d. Dec. 1936
Virgil M. Chapman (D)
Edward W. Creal (D)
s. Oct. 1936
William V. Gregory (D)
Andrew J. May (D)
Emmet O'Neal (D)
John M. Robsion (R)
Brent Spence (D)
Fred M. Vinson (D)

LOUISIANA

Senators

Huey P. Long (D)
d. Sept. 1935
Rose McConnell Long (D)
s. 1936

John H. Overton (D)

Representatives

Cleveland Dear (D)
Rene L. DeRouen (D)
Joachim O. Fernandez (D)
Paul H. Maloney (D)
Numa F. Montet (D)
Jared Y. Sanders, Jr. (D)
John N. Sandlin (D)
Riley J. Wilson (D)

MAINE

Senators

Frederick Hale (R)
Wallace H. White, Jr. (R)

Representatives

Ralph O. Brewster (R)
Simon M. Hamlin (D)
Edward C. Moran, Jr. (R)

MARYLAND

Senators

Millard E. Tydings (D)

George L. Radcliffe (D)

Representatives

William P. Cole, Jr. (D)
Stephen W. Gambrill (D)
T. Alan Goldsborough (D)
Ambrose J. Kennedy (D)
David J. Lewis (D)
Vincent L. Palmisano (D)

MASSACHUSETTS

Senators

David I. Walsh (D)
Marcus A. Coolidge (D)

Representatives

A. Piatt Andrew, Jr. (R)
d. June 1936
Joseph E. Casey (D)
William P. Connery, Jr. (D)
Charles L. Gifford (R)
William J. Granfield (D)
Arthur D. Healey (D)
John P. Higgins (D)
Pehr G. Holmes (R)
John W. McCormack (D)
Joseph W. Martin, Jr. (R)
Edith Nourse Rogers (R)
Richard M. Russell (D)
George H. Tinkham (R)
Allen T. Treadway (R)
Richard B. Wigglesworth (R)

MICHIGAN

Senators

James Couzens (R)
d. Oct. 1936
Prentiss M. Brown (D)
ta. Nov. 1936

Arthur H. Vandenberg (R)

Representatives

William W. Blackney (R)
Prentiss M. Brown (D)
r. Nov. 1936
Fred L. Crawford (R)
John D. Dingell (D)
George A. Dondero (R)
Albert J. Engel (R)
Clare E. Hoffman (R)
Frank E. Hook (D)
Henry M. Kimball (R)
d. Oct. 1935
John Lesinski (D)
Clarence J. McLeod (R)
Verner W. Main (R) s. 1936
Carl E. Mapes (R)
Earl C. Michener (R)
Louis C. Rabaut (D)
George G. Sadowski (D)
Jesse P. Wolcott (R)
Roy O. Woodruff (R)

MINNESOTA

Senators

Henrik Shipstead (Farm-Labor)

Thomas D. Schall (R)
d. Dec. 1935
Elmer A. Benson (Farm-Labor)
ta. Jan. 1936
Guy V. Howard (R) s. 1936

Representatives

August H. Andresen (R)
Richard T. Buckler (Farm-Labor)
Theodore Christianson (R)
Harold Knutson (R)
Paul J. Kvale (Farm-Labor)
Ernest Lundeen (Farm-Labor)
Melvin J. Maas (R)
William A. Pittenger (R)
Elmer J. Ryan (D)

MISSISSIPPI

Senators

Pat Harrison (D)
Theodore G. Bilbo (D)

Representatives

William M. Colmer (D)
Wall Doxey (D)
Aubert C. Dunn (D)
Aaron L. Ford (D)
Dan R. McGehee (D)
John E. Rankin (D)
William M. Whittington (D)

MISSOURI

Senators

Bennett Champ Clark (D)
Harry S Truman (D)

Representatives

C. Jasper Bell (D)
Clarence Cannon (D)
James R. Claiborne (D)
John J. Cochran (D)
Richard M. Duncan (D)
Thomas C. Hennings, Jr. (D)
William L. Nelson (D)
Milton A. Romjue (D)
Joseph B. Shannon (D)
Dewey Short (R)
Clyde Williams (D)
Reuben T. Wood (D)
Orville Zimmerman (D)

MONTANA

Senators

Burton K. Wheeler (D)
James E. Murray (D)

Representatives

Roy E. Ayers (D)
Joseph P. Monaghan (D)

NEBRASKA

Senators

George W. Norris (R)
Edward R. Burke (D)

Representatives

Charles G. Binderup (D)
Harry B. Coffee (D)
Henry C. Luckey (D)
Charles F. McLaughlin (D)
Karl Stefan (R)

NEVADA

Senators

Key Pittman (D)
Patrick A. McCarran (D)

Representative

James G. Scrugham (D)

NEW HAMPSHIRE

Senators

Henry W. Keyes (R)
Fred H. Brown (D)

Representatives

William N. Rogers (D)
Charles W. Tobey (R)

NEW JERSEY

Senators

W. Warren Barbour (R)
A. Harry Moore (D)

Representatives

Isaac Bacharach (R)
Peter A. Cavicchia (R)
Charles A. Eaton (R)
Edward J. Hart (D)
Fred A. Hartley, Jr. (R)
Edward A. Kenney (D)
Frederick R. Lehlbach (R)
Donald H. McLean (R)
Mary T. Norton (D)
Randolph Perkins (R)
d. May 1936
D. Lane Powers (R)
George N. Seger (R)
William H. Sutphin (D)
Charles A. Wolverton (R)

NEW MEXICO

Senators

Bronson M. Cutting (R)
d. May 1935
Dennis Chavez (D)

Carl A. Hatch (D)

Representative

John J. Dempsey (D)

NEW YORK

Senators

Royal S. Copeland (D)
Robert F. Wagner (D)

Representatives

Walter G. Andrews (R)
Robert L. Bacon (R)
William B. Barry (D) s. 1936
Alfred F. Beiter (D)
Sol Bloom (D)
John J. Boylan (D)
William F. Brunner (D)
r. Sept. 1935
Charles A. Buckley (D)
Emanuel Celler (D)
W. Sterling Cole (R)
Parker Corning (D)
Frank Crowther (R)
Francis D. Culkin (R)
Thomas H. Cullen (D)
Edward W. Curley (D) s. 1936
John J. Delaney (D)
Samuel Dickstein (D)
James P. B. Duffy (D)
Marcellus H. Evans (D)
Hamilton Fish, Jr. (R)
James M. Fitzpatrick (D)
Joseph A. Gavagan (D)
Philip A. Goodwin (R)
Anthony J. Griffin (D)
d. Jan. 1935
Clarence E. Hancock (R)
Martin J. Kennedy (D)
Bert Lord (R)
Vito Marcantonio (R)
James M. Mead (D)
Matthew J. Merritt (D)
Charles D. Millard (R)
John J. O'Connor (D)
Caroline O'Day (D)
James A. O'Leary (D)
Theodore A. Peyser (D)
Joseph L. Pfeifer (D)
Daniel A. Reed (R)
Stephen A. Rudd (D)
d. Mar. 1936
William I. Sirovich (D)
Fred J. Sisson (D)
Bertrand H. Snell (R)
Andrew L. Somers (D)
Christopher D. Sullivan (D)
John Taber (R)
William D. Thomas (R)
d. May 1936
Richard J. Tonry (D)
James W. Wadsworth, Jr. (R)

NORTH CAROLINA

Senators

Josiah W. Bailey (D)
Robert R. Reynolds (D)

Representatives

Graham A. Barden (D)
Alfred L. Bulwinkle (D)
J. Bayard Clark (D)
Harold D. Cooley (D)
Robert L. Doughton (D)
Franklin W. Hancock, Jr. (D)
John H. Kerr (D)
J. Walter Lambeth (D)
William B. Umstead (D)
Lindsay C. Warren (D)
Zebulon Weaver (D)

NORTH DAKOTA

Senators

Lynn J. Frazier (R)
Gerald P. Nye (R)

Representatives

Usher L. Burdick (R)
William Lemke (R)

OHIO

Senators

Robert J. Bulkley (D)
A. Victor Donahey (D)

Representatives

William A. Ashbrook (D)
Chester C. Bolton (R)
John G. Cooper (R)
Robert Crosser (D)
Warren J. Duffey (D) d. July 1936
Daniel S. Earhart (D) s. 1936
William L. Fiesinger (D)
Thomas B. Fletcher (D)
Peter F. Hammond (D) s. 1936
Byron B. Harlan (D)
Dow W. Harter (D)
William E. Hess (R)
John B. Hollister (R)
Lawrence E. Imhoff (D)
Thomas A. Jenkins (R)
Frank L. Kloef (D)
Frank C. Kniffin (D)
Arthur P. Lamneck (D)
Leroy T. Marshall (R)
James G. Polk (D)
Robert T. Secrest (D)
Martin L. Sweeney (D)
William R. Thom (D)
Charles V. Truax (D)
d. Aug. 1935
Mell G. Underwood (D)
r. Apr. 1936
Stephen M. Young (D)

OKLAHOMA

Senators

J. W. Elmer Thomas (D)
Thomas P. Gore (D)

Representatives

Wilburn Cartwright (D)
Wesley E. Disney (D)
Phil Ferguson (D)
P. L. Gassaway (D)
Jed Johnson (D)
Josh Lee (D)
Sam C. Massingale (D)
Jack Nichols (D)
Will Rogers (D)

OREGON

Senators

Charles L. McNary (R)
Frederick Steiwer (R)

Representatives

William A. Ekwall (R)
James W. Mott (R)
Walter M. Pierce (D)

PENNSYLVANIA

Senators

James J. Davis (R)
Joseph F. Guffey (D)

Representatives

William M. Berlin (D)
Patrick J. Boland (D)
J. Twing Brooks (D)
Charles N. Crosby (D)
J. Burrwood Daly (D)
George P. Darrow (R)
C. Elmer Dietrich (D)
J. William Ditter (R)
Frank J. G. Dorsey (D)
Isaac H. Doutrich (R)
D. J. Driscoll (D)
Matthew A. Dunn (D)
Charles R. Eckert (D)
Henry Ellenbogen (D)
Charles I. Faddis (D)
Clare G. Fenerty (R)
Benjamin K. Focht (R)
Oliver W. Frey (D)
James H. Gildea (D)
Don Gingery (D)
Joseph Gray (D)
Harry L. Haines (D)
J. Roland Kinzer (R)
Theodore L. Moritz (D)
James L. Quinn (D)
Harry C. Ransley (R)
Robert F. Rich (R)
William E. Richardson (D)
J. Buell Snyder (D)
Michael J. Stack (D)
C. Murray Turpin (R)
Francis E. Walter (D)
William H. Wilson (R)
James Wolfenden (R)

RHODE ISLAND

Senators

Jesse H. Metcalf (R)
Peter G. Gerry (D)

Representatives

Francis B. Condon (D)
r. Jan. 1935
John M. O'Connell (D)
Charles F. Risk (R)

SOUTH CAROLINA

Senators

Ellison D. Smith (D)
James F. Byrnes (D)

Representatives

Hampton P. Fulmer (D)
Allard H. Gasque (D)
Thomas S. McMillan (D)
John J. McSwain (D)
d. Aug. 1936
G. Heyward Mahon, Jr. (D)
s. 1936
James P. Richards (D)
John C. Taylor (D)

SOUTH DAKOTA

Senators

Peter Norbeck (R)
d. Dec. 1936
Herbert E. Hitchcock (D)
ta. Jan. 1937

William J. Bulow (D)

Representatives

Fred H. Hildebrandt (D)
Theodore B. Werner (D)

TENNESSEE

Senators

Kenneth D. McKellar (D)
Nathan L. Bachman (D)

Representatives

Joseph W. Byrns (D)
d. June 1936
Walter Chandler (D)
Jere Cooper (D)
Sam D. McReynolds (D)
John R. Mitchell (D)
Herron Pearson (D)
B. Carroll Reece (R)
J. Will Taylor (R)
Clarence W. Turner (D)

TEXAS

Senators

Morris Sheppard (D)
Tom T. Connally (D)

Representatives

Thomas L. Blanton (D)
James P. Buchanan (D)
Oliver H. Cross (D)
Martin Dies, Jr. (D)
Joe H. Eagle (D)
Luther A. Johnson (D)
Marvin Jones (D)
Richard M. Kleberg (D)
Fritz G. Lanham (D)
William D. McFarlane (D)
George H. Mahon (D)
Joseph J. Mansfield (D)
Maury Maverick (D)
Wright Patman (D)
Nat Patton (D)
Sam Rayburn (D)
Morgan G. Sanders (D)
Charles L. South (D)
Hatton W. Sumners (D)
R. Ewing Thomason (D)
Milton H. West (D)

UTAH

Senators

William H. King (D)
Elbert D. Thomas (D)

Representatives

Abe Murdock (D)
J. W. Robinson (D)

VERMONT

Senators

Warren R. Austin (R)
Ernest W. Gibson (R)

Representative

Charles A. Plumley (R)

VIRGINIA

Senators

Carter Glass (D)
Harry F. Byrd (D)

Representatives

Schuyler Otis Bland (D)
Thomas G. Burch (D)
Colgate W. Darden, Jr. (D)
Patrick H. Drewry (D)
John W. Flannagan, Jr. (D)
Andrew J. Montague (D)
A. Willis Robertson (D)
Howard W. Smith (D)
Clifton A. Woodrum (D)

WASHINGTON

Senators

Homer T. Bone (D)
Lewis B.Schwellenbach (D)

Representatives

Knute Hill (D)
Samuel B. Hill (D)
r. June 1936
Wesley Lloyd (D)
d. Jan. 1936
Martin F. Smith (D)
Monrad C. Wallgren (D)
Marion A. Zioncheck (D)
d. Aug. 1936

WEST VIRGINIA

Senators

Matthew M. Neely (D)
Rush D. Holt (D)

Representatives

Andrew Edmiston (D)
George W. Johnson (D)
John Kee (D)
Robert L. Ramsay (D)
Jennings Randolph (D)
Joe L. Smith (D)

WISCONSIN

Senators

Robert M. La Follette, Jr.
(Progressive)
F. Ryan Duffy (D)

Representatives

Thomas R. Amlie (Progressive)
Gerald J. Boileau (R)
Raymond J. Cannon (D)
Bernard J. Gehrmann (Progressive)
Merlin Hull (Progressive)
Thomas O'Malley (D)
Michael K. Reilly (D)
Harry Sauthoff (Progressive)
George J. Schneider (Progressive)
Gardner R. Withrow (Progressive)

WYOMING

Senators

Robert D. Carey (R)
Joseph C. O'Mahoney (D)

Representative

Paul R. Greever (D)

SEVENTY-FIFTH CONGRESS

January 3, 1937 to January 3, 1939

President of The Senate: John Nance Garner
President Pro Tempore of The Senate: Key Pittman
Speaker of The House of Representatives: William B. Bankhead

ALABAMA

Senators

Hugo L. Black (D)
r. Aug. 1937
Dixie Bibb Graves (D)
ta. 1937
Lister Hill (D) s. 1938

John H. Bankhead 2nd (D)

Representatives

William B. Bankhead (D)
Frank W. Boykin (D)
George M. Grant (D) s. 1938
Lister Hill (D) r. Jan. 1938
Sam Hobbs (D)
Pete Jarman (D)
Luther Patrick (D)
John J. Sparkman (D)
Joe Starnes (D)
Henry B. Steagall (D)

ARIZONA

Senators

Henry F. Ashurst (D)
Carl Hayden (D)

Representative

John R. Murdock (D)

ARKANSAS

Senators

Joseph T. Robinson (D)
d. July 1937
John E. Miller (D)

Hattie W. Caraway (D)

Representatives

William B. Cravens (D)
William J. Driver (D)
Claude A. Fuller (D)
Wade H. Kitchens (D)
John L. McClellan (D)
John E. Miller (D)
r. Nov. 1937
David D. Terry (D)

CALIFORNIA

Senators

Hiram W. Johnson (R)

William Gibbs McAdoo (D)
r. Nov. 1938
Thomas M. Storke (D) s. 1938

Representatives

Frank H. Buck (D)
Albert E. Carter (R)
Charles J. Colden (D) d. Apr. 1938
John M. Costello (D)
John F. Dockweiler (D)
Alfred J. Elliott (D)
Harry L. Englebright (R)
Thomas F. Ford (D)
Bertrand W. Gearhart (R)
Franck R. Havenner (Progressive)
Edouard V. M. Izac (D)
Charles Kramer (D)
Clarence F. Lea (D,R)
John J. McGrath (D)
John S. McGroarty (D)
Byron N. Scott (D)
Harry R. Sheppard (D)
Henry E. Stubbs (D)
d. Feb. 1937
John H. Tolan (D)
H. Jerry Voorhis (D)
Richard J. Welch (R)

COLORADO

Senators

Alva B. Adams (D)
Edwin C. Johnson (D)

Representatives

Fred Cummings (D)
Lawrence Lewis (D)
John A. Martin (D)
Edward T. Taylor (D)

CONNECTICUT

Senators

Augustine Lonergan (D)
Francis T. Maloney (D)

Representatives

William M. Citron (D)
William J. Fitzgerald (D)
Herman P. Kopplemann (D)
Alfred N. Phillips, Jr. (D)
James A. Shanley (D)
J. Joseph Smith (D)

DELAWARE

Senators

John G. Townsend, Jr. (R)
James H. Hughes (D)

Representative

William F. Allen (D)

FLORIDA

Senators

Charles O. Andrews (D)
Claude D. Pepper (D)

Representatives

Millard F. Caldwell (D)
Robert A. Green (D)
Joe Hendricks (D)
J. Hardin Peterson (D)
J. Mark Wilcox (D)

GEORGIA

Senators

Walter F. George (D)
Richard B. Russell (D)

Representatives

Paul Brown (D)
Edward E. Cox (D)
Braswell D. Deen (D)
Emmet M. Owen (D)
Stephen Pace (D)
Hugh Peterson (D)
Robert Ramspeck (D)
Malcolm C. Tarver (D)
Carl Vinson (D)
B. Frank Whelchel (D)

IDAHO

Senators

William E. Borah (R)
James P. Pope (D)

Representatives

D. Worth Clark (D)
Compton I. White (D)

ILLINOIS

Senators

J. Hamilton Lewis (D)
William H. Dieterich (D)

Representatives

Leo E. Allen (R)
Leslie C. Arends (R)
Laurence F. Arnold (D)
Harry P. Beam (D)
Lewis L. Boyer (D)
Edwin V. Champion (D)
Ralph E. Church (R)
Everett M. Dirksen (R)
Frank W. Fries (D)
Kent E. Keller (D)
Edward A. Kelly (D)
Leo Kocialkowski (D)
Lewis M. Long (D)
Scott W. Lucas (D)
James McAndrews (D)
Raymond S. McKeough (D)
Noah M. Mason(R)
James A. Meeks (D)
Arthur W. Mitchell (D)
Thomas J. O'Brien (D)
Claude V. Parsons (D)
Chauncey W. Reed (R)
Hugh M. Rigney (D)
Adolph J. Sabath (D)
Edwin M. Schaefer (D)
Leonard W. Schuetz (D)
Chester C. Thompson (D)

INDIANA

Senators

Frederick Van Nuys (D)
Sherman Minton (D)

Representatives

John W. Boehne, Jr. (D)
Eugene B. Crowe (D)
James I. Farley (D)
Finly H. Gray (D)
Arthur H. Greenwood (D)
Glenn Griswold (D)
Charles A. Halleck (R)
Virginia Ellis Jenckes (D)
William H. Larrabee (D)
Louis Ludlow (D)
Samuel B. Pettengill (D)
William T. Schulte (D)

IOWA

Senators

Guy M. Gillette (D)
Clyde L. Herring (D)

Representatives

Fred Biermann (D)
Cassius C. Dowell (R)
Edward C. Eicher (D)
r. Dec. 1938
Fred C. Gilchrist (R)
John W. Gwynne (R)
Vincent F. Harrington (D)
William S. Jacobsen (D)
Lloyd Thurston (R)
Otha D. Wearin (D)

KANSAS

Senators

Arthur Capper (R)
George McGill (D)

Representatives

Frank Carlson (R)
Ulysses S. Guyer (R)
Clifford R. Hope (R)
John M. Houston (D)
William P. Lambertson (R)
Edward W. Patterson (D)
Edward H. Rees (R)

KENTUCKY

Senators

Alben W. Barkley (D)
Marvel M. Logan (D)

Representatives

Joe B. Bates (D) s. 1938
Virgil M. Chapman (D)
Edward W. Creal (D)

Noble J. Gregory (D)
Andrew J. May (D)
Emmet O'Neal (D)
John M. Robsion (R)
Brent Spence (D)
Beverly M. Vincent (D)
Fred M. Vinson (D)
r. May 1938

LOUISIANA

Senators

John H. Overton (D)
Allen J. Ellender (D)

Representatives

A. Leonard Allen (D)
Overton Brooks (D)
Rene L. De Rouen (D)
Joachim O. Fernandez (D)
John K. Griffith (D)
Paul H. Maloney (D)
Newt V. Mills (D)
Robert L. Mouton (D)

MAINE

Senators

Frederick Hale (R)
Wallace H. White, Jr. (R)

Representatives

Ralph O. Brewster (R)
James C. Oliver (R)
Clyde H. Smith (R)

MARYLAND

Senators

Millard E. Tydings (D)
George L. Radcliffe (D)

Representatives

William P. Cole, Jr. (D)
Stephen W. Gambrill (D)
T. Alan Goldsborough (D)
Ambrose J. Kennedy (D)
David J. Lewis (D)
Vincent L. Palmisano (D)

MASSACHUSETTS

Senators

David I. Walsh (D)
Henry Cabot Lodge, Jr. (R)

Representatives

George J. Bates (R)
Joseph E. Casey (D)
Charles R. Clason (R)
Lawrence J. Connery (D)
William P. Connery, Jr. (D)
d. June 1937
Thomas A. Flaherty (D) s. 1938
Charles L. Gifford (R)
Arthur D. Healey (D)
John P. Higgins (D)
r. Sept. 1937
Pehr G. Holmes (R)
Robert Luce (R)
John W. McCormack (D)
Joseph W. Martin, Jr. (R)
Edith Nourse Rogers (R)
George H. Tinkham (R)
Allen T. Treadway (R)
Richard B. Wigglesworth (R)

MICHIGAN

Senators

Arthur H. Vandenberg (R)
Prentiss M. Brown (D)

Representatives

Fred L. Crawford (R)
John D. Dingell (D)
George A. Dondero (R)
Albert J. Engel (R)
Clare E. Hoffman (R)
Frank E. Hook (D)
John Lesinski (D)
John Luecke (D)
Carl E. Mapes (R)
Earl C. Michener (R)
George D. O'Brien (D)
Louis C. Rabaut (D)
George G. Sadowski (D)
Paul W. Shafer (R)
Andrew J. Transue (D)
Jesse P. Wolcott (R)
Roy O. Woodruff (R)

MINNESOTA

Senators

Henrik Shipstead (Farm-Labor)
Ernest Lundeen (Farm-Labor)

Representatives

August H. Andresen (R)
John T. Bernard (Farm-Labor)
Richard T. Buckler (Farm-Labor)
Dewey W. Johnson (Farm-Labor)
Harold Knutson (R)
Paul K. Kvale (Farm-Labor)
Melvin J. Maas (R)
Elmer J. Ryan (D)
Henry G. Teigan (Farm-Labor)

MISSISSIPPI

Senators

Pat Harrison (D)
Theodore G. Bilbo (D)

Representatives

Ross A. Collins (D)
William M. Colmer (D)
Wall Doxey (D)
Aaron L. Ford (D)
Dan R. McGehee (D)
John E. Rankin (D)
William M. Whittington (D)

MISSOURI

Senators

Bennett Champ Clark (D)
Harry S Truman (D)

Representatives

C. Arthur Anderson (D)
C. Jasper Bell (D)
Clarence Cannon (D)
John J. Cochran (D)
Richard M. Duncan (D)
Thomas C. Hennings, Jr. (D)
William L. Nelson (D)
Milton A. Romjue (D)
Joseph B. Shannon (D)
Dewey Short (R)
Clyde Williams (D)
Reuben T. Wood (D)
Orville Zimmerman (D)

MONTANA

Senators

Burton K. Wheeler (D)
James E. Murray (D)

Representatives

Jerry J. O'Connell (D)
James F. O'Connor (D)

NEBRASKA

Senators

George W. Norris (R)
Edward R. Burke (D)

Representatives

Charles G. Binderup (D)
Harry B. Coffee (D)
Henry C. Luckey (D)
Charles F. McLaughlin (D)
Karl Stefan (R)

NEVADA

Senators

Key Pittman (D)
Patrick A. McCarran (D)

Representative

James G. Scrugham (D)

NEW HAMPSHIRE

Senators

Fred H. Brown (D)
H. Styles Bridges (R)

Representatives

Arthur B. Jenks (R)
r. June 1938
Alsphonse Roy (D) s. 1938
Charles W. Tobey (R)

NEW JERSEY

Senators

A. Harry Moore (D)
r. Jan. 1938
John Milton (D)
ta. 1938
W. Warren Barbour (R) s. 1939

William H. Smathers (D)

Representatives

Charles A. Eaton (R)
Edward J. Hart (D)
Fred A. Hartley, Jr. (R)
Edward A. Kenney (D)
Donald H. McLean (R)
Mary T. Norton (D)
Edward L. O'Neill (D)
D. Lane Powers (R)
George N. Seger (R)
William H. Sutphin (D)
J. Parnell Thomas (R)
Frank W. Towey, Jr. (D)
Elmer H. Wene (D)
Charles A. Wolverton (R)

NEW MEXICO

Senators

Carl A. Hatch (D)
Dennis Chavez (D)

Representative

John J. Dempsey (D)

NEW YORK

Senators

Royal S. Copeland (D)
James M. Mead (D) s. 1939

Robert F. Wagner (D)

Representatives

Walter G. Andrews (R)
Robert L. Bacon (R)
d. Sept. 1938
William B. Barry (D)
Bruce Barton (R)
Alfred F. Beiter (D)
Sol Bloom (D)
John J. Boylan (D)
d. Oct. 1938
Charles A. Buckley (D)
William T. Byrne (D)
Emanuel Celler (D)
E. Harold Cluett (R)
W. Sterling Cole (R)
Frank Crowther (R)
Francis D. Culkin (R)
Thomas H. Cullen (D)
Edward W. Curley (D)
John J. Delaney (D)
Samuel Dickstein (D)
Fred J. Douglas (R)
Marcellus H. Evans (D)
Hamilton Fish, Jr. (R)
James M. Fitzpatrick (D)
Ralph A. Gamble (R)
Joseph A. Gavagan (D)
Philip A. Goodwin (R)
d. June 1937
Clarence E. Hancock (R)
George B. Kelly (D)
Martin J. Kennedy (D)
Eugene J. Keogh (D)
James J. Lanzetta (D)

Bert Lord (R)
James M. Mead (D)
r. Dec. 1938
Matthew J. Merritt (D)
Charles D. Millard (R)
r. Sept. 1937
John J. O'Connor (D)
Caroline O'Day (D)
James A. O'Leary (D)
Donald L. O'Toole (D)
Theodore A. Peyser (D)
d. Aug. 1937
Joseph L. Pfeifer (D)
Daniel A. Reed (R)
Lewis K. Rockefeller (R)
William I. Sirovich (D)
Bertrand H. Snell (R)
Andrew L. Somers (D)
Christopher D. Sullivan (D)
John Taber (R)
James W. Wadsworth, Jr. (R)

NORTH CAROLINA

Senators

Josiah W. Bailey (D)
Robert R. Reynolds (D)

Representatives

Graham A. Barden (D)
Alfred L. Bulwinkle (D)
J. Bayard Clark (D)
Harold D. Cooley (D)
Robert L. Doughton (D)
Franklin W. Hancock, Jr. (D)
John H. Kerr (D)
J. Walter Lambeth (D)
William B. Umstead (D)
Lindsay C. Warren (D)
Zebulon Weaver (D)

NORTH DAKOTA

Senators

Lynn J. Frazier (R)
Gerald P. Nye (R)

Representatives

Usher L. Burdick (R)
William Lemke (R)

OHIO

Senators

Robert J. Bulkley (D)
A. Victor Donahey (D)

Representatives

Walter H. Albaugh (R) s. 1938
Arthur W. Aleshire (D)
William A. Ashbrook (D)
Herbert S. Bigelow (D)
Harold K. Claypool (D)
Robert Crosser (D)
Joseph A. Dixon (D)
Anthony A. Fleger (D)
Thomas B. Fletcher (D)
Byron B. Harlan (D)
Dow W. Harter (D)
John F. Hunter (D)
Lawrence E. Imhoff (D)
Thomas A. Jenkins (R)
Michael J. Kirwan (D)
Frank L. Kloeb (D)
r. Aug. 1937
Frank C. Kniffin (D)
Arthur P. Lamneck (D)
John McSweeney (D)
Harold G. Mosier (D)
James G. Polk (D)
Robert T. Secrest (D)
Martin L. Sweeney (D)
William R. Thom (D)
Dudley A. White (R)

OKLAHOMA

Senators

J. W. Elmer Thomas (D)
Josh Lee (D)

Representatives

Lyle H. Boren (D)
Wilburn Cartwright (D)
Wesley E. Disney (D)
Phil Ferguson (D)
Robert P. Hill (D)
d. Oct. 1937
Jed Johnson (D)
Sam C. Massingale (D)
Jack Nichols (D)
Will Rogers (D)
Gomer Smith (D) s. 1938

OREGON

Senators

Charles L. McNary (R)

Frederick Steiwer (R)
r. Jan. 1938
Alfred E. Reames (D)
ta. 1938
Alexander G. Barry (R)
s. 1938

Representatives

Nan Wood Honeyman (D)
James W. Mott (R)
Walter M. Pierce (D)

PENNSYLVANIA

Senators

James J. Davis (R)
Joseph F. Guffey (D)

Representatives

Robert G. Allen (D)
Patrick J. Boland (D)
Michael J. Bradley (D)
Charles N. Crosby (D)
J. Burrwood Daly (D)
George P. Darrow (R)
Peter J. DeMuth (D)
J. William Ditter (R)
Frank J. G. Dorsey (D)
Ira W. Drew (D)
Matthew A. Dunn (D)
Herman P. Eberharter (D)
Charles R. Eckert (D)
Henry Ellenbogen (D)
r. Jan. 1938
Charles I. Faddis (D)
J. Harold Flannery (D)
Benjamin K. Focht (R)
d. March. 1937
Oliver W. Frey (D)
James H. Gildea (D)
Don Gingery (D)
Joseph Gray (D)
Harry L. Haines (D)
Benjamin Jarrett (R)
J. Roland Kinzer (R)
James P. McGranery (D)
Guy L. Moser (D)
James L. Quinn (D)
Robert F. Rich (R)
Albert G. Rutherford (R)
Leon Sacks (D)
Richard M. Simpson (R)
J. Buell Snyder (D)
Michael J. Stack (D)
Guy J. Swope (D)
Francis E. Walter (D)
James Wolfenden (R)

RHODE ISLAND

Senators

Peter G. Gerry (D)
Theodore F. Green (D)

Representatives

Aime J. Forand (D)
John M. O'Connell (D)

SOUTH CAROLINA

Senators

Ellison D. Smith (D)
James F. Byrnes (D)

Representatives

Hampton P. Fulmer (D)
Allard H. Gasque (D)
d. June 1938
Bessie H. Gasque (D) s. 1938
Thomas S. McMillan (D)
G. Heyward Mahon, Jr. (D)
James P. Richards (D)
John C. Taylor (D)

SOUTH DAKOTA

Senators

William J. Bulow (D)

Herbert E. Hitchcock (D)
ta. 1938
Gladys Pyle (R) s. 1938

Representatives

Francis H. Case (R)
Fred H. Hildebrandt (D)

TENNESSEE

Senators

Kenneth D. McKellar (D)

Nathan L. Bachman (D)
d. Apr. 1937
George L. Berry (D)
ta. 1937-1938
A. Tom Stewart (D) s. 1938

Representatives

Richard M. Atkinson (D)
Walter Chandler (D)
Jere Cooper (D)
Sam D. McReynolds (D)
John R. Mitchell (D)
Herron C. Pearson (D)
B. Carroll Reece (R)
J. Will Taylor (R)
Clarence W. Turner (D)

TEXAS

Senators

Morris Sheppard (D)
Tom T. Connally (D)

Representatives

James P. Buchanan (D)
d. Feb. 1937
Martin Dies, Jr. (D)
Clyde L. Garrett (D)
Luther A. Johnson (D)
Lyndon B. Johnson (D)
Marvin Jones (D)
Richard M. Kleberg (D)
Fritz G. Lanham (D)
William D. McFarlane (D)
George H. Mahon (D)
Joseph J. Mansfield (D)
Maury Maverick (D)
Wright Patman (D)
Nat Patton (D)
William R. Poage (D)
Sam Rayburn (D)
Morgan G. Sanders (D)
Charles L. South (D)
Hatton W. Sumners (D)
Albert Thomas (D)
R. Ewing Thomason (D)
Milton H. West (D)

UTAH

Senators

William H. King (D)
Elbert D. Thomas (D)

Representatives

Abe Murdock (D)
J. W. Robinson (D)

VERMONT

Senators

Warren R. Austin (R)
Ernest W. Gibson (R)

Representatives

Charles A. Plumley (R)

VIRGINIA

Senators

Carter Glass (D)
Harry F. Byrd (D)

Representatives

Schuyler Otis Bland (D)
Thomas G. Burch (D)
Patrick H. Drewry (D)
Norman R. Hamilton (D)
John W. Flannagan, Jr. (D)
Andrew J. Montague (D)
d. Jan. 1937
A. Willis Robertson (D)
Dave E. Satterfield, Jr. (D)
s. 1937
Howard W. Smith (D)
Clifton A. Woodrum (D)

WASHINGTON

Senators

Homer T. Bone (D)
Lewis B. Schwellenbach (D)

Representatives

John M. Coffee (D)
Knute Hill (D)
Charles H. Leavy (D)
Warren G. Magnuson (D)
Martin F. Smith (D)
Monrad C. Wallgren (D)

WEST VIRGINIA

Senators

Matthew M. Neely (D)
Rush D. Holt (D)

Representatives

Andrew Edmiston (D)
George W. Johnson (D)
John Kee (D)
Robert L. Ramsay (D)
Jennings Randolph (D)
Joe L. Smith (D)

WISCONSIN

Senators

Robert M. La Follette, Jr.
(Progressive)
F. Ryan Duffy (D)

Representatives

Thomas R. Amlie (Progressive)
Gerald J. Boileau (R)
Raymond J. Cannon (D)
Bernard J. Gehrmann (Progressive)
Merlin Hull (Progressive)
Thomas O'Malley (D)
Michael K. Reilly (D)
Harry Sauthoff (Progressive)
George J. Schneider (Progressive)
Gardner R. Withrow (Progressive)

WYOMING

Senators

Joseph C. O'Mahoney (D)
H. H. Schwartz (D)

Representative

Paul R. Greever (D)

SEVENTY-SIXTH CONGRESS

January 3, 1939 to January 3, 1941

President of The Senate:	John Nance Garner
President Pro Tempore of The Senate:	Key Pittman William King
Speakers of The House of Representatives:	William B. Bankhead Sam Rayburn

ALABAMA

Senators

John H. Bankhead 2d (D)
Lister Hill (D)

Representatives

William B. Bankhead (D)
d. Sept. 1940
Frank W. Boykin (D)
George M. Grant (D)
Sam Hobbs (D)
Pete Jarman (D)
Luther Patrick (D)
Joe Starnes (D)
John J. Sparkman (D)
Henry B. Steagall (D)
Zadoc L. Weatherford (D)
s. 1940

ARIZONA

Senators

Henry F. Ashurst (D)
Carl Hayden (D)

Representative

John R. Murdock (D)

ARKANSAS

Senators

Hattie W. Caraway (D)
John E. Miller (D)

Representatives

Fadjo Cravens (D)
William B. Cravens (D)
d. Jan. 1939
Clyde T. Ellis (D)
Ezekiel C. Gathings (D)
Wade H. Kitchens (D)
Wilbur D. Mills (D)
William F. Norrell (D)
David D. Terry (D)

CALIFORNIA

Senators

Hiram W. Johnson (R)
Sheridan Downey (D)

Representatives

John Z. Anderson (R)
Frank H. Buck (D)
Albert E. Carter (R)
John M. Costello (D)
Thomas M. Eaton (R)
d. Sept. 1939
Alfred J. Elliott (D)
Harry L. Englebright (R)
Leland M. Ford (R)
Thomas F. Ford (D)
Bertrand W. Gearhart (R)
Lee E. Geyer (D)
Franck R. Havenner (D)
Carl Hinshaw (R)
Edouard V. M. Izac (D)
Charles Kramer (D)
Clarence F. Lea (D)
Harry R. Sheppard (D, R)
John H. Tolan (D)
H. Jerry Voorhis (D)
Richard J. Welch (R)

COLORADO

Senators

Alva B. Adams (D)
Edwin C. Johnson (D)

Representatives

William E. Burney (D) s. 1940
Fred Cummings (D)
Lawrence Lewis (D)
John A. Martin (D)
d. Sept. 1939
Edward T. Taylor (D)

CONNECTICUT

Senators

Francis T. Maloney (D)
John A. Danaher (R)

Representatives

Albert E. Austin (R)
Thomas R. Ball (R)
William J. Miller (R)
Boleslaus J. Monkiewicz (R)
James A. Shanley (D)
J. Joseph Smith (D)

DELAWARE

Senators

John G. Townsend, Jr. (R)
James H. Hughes (D)

Representative

George S. Williams (R)

FLORIDA

Senators

Charles O. Andrews (D)
Claude D. Pepper (R)

Representatives

Millard F. Caldwell (D)
Arthur P. Cannon (D)
Robert A. Green (D)
Joe Hendricks (D)
J. Hardin Peterson (D)

GEORGIA

Senators

Walter F. George (D)
Richard B. Russell (D)

Representatives

Paul Brown (D)
A. Sidney Camp (D)
Edward E. Cox (D)
Florence R. Gibbs (D)
s. 1940
W. Benjamin Gibbs (D)
d. Aug. 1940
Emmett M. Owen (D)
d. June 1939
Stephen Pace (D)
Hugh Peterson (D)
Robert Ramspeck (D)
Malcolm C. Tarver (D)
Carl Vinson (D)
B. Frank Whelchel (D)

IDAHO

Senators

William E. Borah (R)
d. Jan. 1940
John Thomas (R) s. 1940

D. Worth Clark (D)

Representatives

Henry C. Dworshak (R)
Compton I. White (D)

ILLINOIS

Senators

J. Hamilton Lewis (D)
d. Apr. 1939
James M. Slattery (D)
ta. 1939-1940
C. Wayland Brooks (R)
s. 1940

Scott W. Lucas (D)

Representatives

Leo E. Allen (R)
Leslie C. Arends (R)
Laurence F. Arnold (D)
James M. Barnes (D)
Harry P. Beam (D)

Robert B. Chiperfield (R)
Ralph E. Church (R)
Everett M. Dirksen (R)
Frank W. Fries (D)
Anton J. Johnson (R)
Kent E. Keller (D)
Edward A. Kelly (D)
Leo Kocialkowski (D)
James McAndrews (D)
Raymond S. McKeough (D)
Anton F. Maciejewski (D)
John C. Martin (D)
Noah M. Mason (R)
Arthur W. Mitchell (D)
Claude V. Parsons (D)
Chauncey W. Reed (R)
Adolph J. Sabath (D)
Edwin M. Schaefer (D)
Leonard W. Schuetz (D)
Thomas V. Smith (D)
Jessie Sumner (R)
William H. Wheat (R)

INDIANA

Senators

Frederick Van Nuys (D)
Sherman Minton (D)

Representatives

John W. Boehne, Jr. (D)
Eugene B. Crowe (D)
George W. Gillie (R)
Robert A. Grant (R)
Charles A. Halleck (R)
Forest A. Harness (R)
Noble J. Johnson (R)
Gerald W. Landis (R)
William H. Larrabee (D)
Louis Ludlow (D)
William T. Schulte (D)
Raymond S. Springer (R)

IOWA

Senators

Guy M. Gillette (D)
Clyde L. Herring (D)

Representatives

Cassius C. Dowell (R)
d. Feb. 1940
Fred C. Gilchrist (R)
Robert K. Goodwin (R) s. 1940
John W. Gwynne (R)
Vincent F. Harrington (D)
William S. Jacobsen (D)
Ben F. Jensen (R)
Karl M. LeCompte (R)
Thomas E. Martin (R)
Henry O. Talle (R)

KANSAS

Senators

Arthur Capper (R)
Clyde M. Reed (R)

Representatives

Frank Carlson (R)
Ulysses S. Guyer (R)
Clifford R. Hope (R)
John M. Houston (D)
William P. Lambertson (R)
Edward H. Rees (R)
Thomas D. Winter (R)

KENTUCKY

Senators

Alben W. Barkley (D)

Marvel M. Logan (D)
d. Oct. 1939
Albert B. Chandler (D)

Representatives

Joe B. Bates (D)
Virgil M. Chapman (D)
Edward W. Creal (D)
Noble J. Gregory (D)
Andrew J. May (D)
Emmet O'Neal (D)
John M. Robsion (R)
Brent Spence (D)
Beverly M. Vincent (D)

LOUISIANA

Senators

John H. Overton (D)
Allen J. Ellender (D)

Representatives

A. Leonard Allen (D)
Overton Brooks (D)
Rene L. De Rouen (D)
Joachim O. Fernandez (D)
John K. Griffith (D)
Paul H. Maloney (D)
r. Dec. 1940
Newt V. Mills (D)
Robert L. Mouton (D)

MAINE

Senators

Frederick Hale (R)
Wallace H. White,Jr. (R)

Representatives

Ralph O. Brewster (R)
James C. Oliver (R)
Clyde H. Smith (R)
d. Apr. 1940
Margaret Chase Smith (R)
s. 1940

MARYLAND

Senators

Millard E. Tydings (D)
George L. Radcliffe (D)

Representatives

William D. Byron (D)
William P. Cole, Jr. (D)
Thomas D'Alesandro, Jr. (D)
T. Alan Goldsborough (D)
r. Apr. 1939
Ambrose J. Kennedy (D)
Lansdale G. Sasscer (D)
David J. Ward (D)

MASSACHUSETTS

Senators

David I. Walsh (D)
Henry Cabot Lodge, Jr. (R)

Representatives

George J. Bates (R)
Joseph E. Casey (D)
Charles R. Clason (R)
Lawrence J. Connery (D)
Thomas A. Flaherty (D)
Charles L. Gifford (R)
Arthur D. Healey (D)
Pehr G. Holmes (R)
Robert Luce (R)
John W. McCormack (D)
Joseph W. Martin, Jr. (R)
Edith Nourse Rogers (R)
George H. Tinkham (R)
Allen T. Treadway (R)
Richard B. Wigglesworth (R)

MICHIGAN

Senators

Arthur H. Vandenberg (R)
Prentiss M. Brown (D)

Representatives

William W. Blackney (R)
Frederick V. Bradley (R)
Fred L. Crawford (R)
John D. Dingell (D)
George A. Dondero (R)
Albert J. Engel (R)
Clare E. Hoffman (R)
Frank E. Hook (D)
Bartel J. Jonkman (R)
s. 1940
John Lesinski (D)
Clarence J. McLeod
Carl E. Mapes (R)
d. Apr. 1939
Earl C. Michener (R)
Louis C. Rabaut (D)
Paul W. Shafer (R)
Rudolph G. Tenerowicz (D)
Jesse P. Wolcott (R)
Roy O. Woodruff (R)

MINNESOTA

Senators

Henrik Shipstead (R)
Ernest Lundeen (Farm-Labor)
d. Aug. 1940
Joseph H. Ball s. 1940

Representatives

John G. Alexander (R)
H. Carl Andersen (R)
August H. Andresen (R)
Richard T. Buckler (Farm-Labor)
Harold Knutson (R)
Melvin J. Maas (R)
William A. Pittenger (R)
Elmer J. Ryan (D)
Oscar Youngdahl (R)

MISSISSIPPI

Senators

Pat Harrison (D)
Theodore G. Bilbo (D)

Representatives

Ross A. Collins (D)
William M. Colmer (D)
Wall Doxey (D)
Aaron L. Ford (D)
Dan R. McGehee (D)
John E. Rankin (D)
William M. Whittington (D)

MISSOURI

Senators

Bennett Champ Clark (D)
Harry S Truman (D)

Representatives

C. Arthur Anderson (D)
C. Jasper Bell (D)
Clarence Cannon (D)
John J. Cochran (D)
Richard M. Duncan (D)
Thomas C. Hennings, Jr. (D)
r. Dec. 1940
William L. Nelson (D)
Milton A. Romjue (D)
Joseph B. Shannon (D)
Dewey Short (R)
Clyde Williams (D)
Reuben T. Wood (D)
Orville Zimmerman (D)

MONTANA

Senators

Burton K. Wheeler (D)
James E. Murray (D)

Representatives

James F. O'Connor
Jacob Thorkelson (R)

NEBRASKA

Senators

George W. Norris (R)
Edward R. Burke (D)

Representatives

Harry B. Coffee (D)
Carl T. Curtis (R)
George H. Heinke (R)
d. Jan. 1940
Charles F. McLaughlin (D)
Karl Stefan (R)
John H. Sweet (R) s. 1940

NEVADA

Senators

Key Pittman (D)
 d. Nov. 1940
Berkeley L. Bunker (D)
 s. 1940

Patrick A. McCarran (D)

Representative

James G. Scrugham (D)

NEW HAMPSHIRE

Senators

H. Styles Bridges (R)
Charles W. Tobey (R)

Representatives

Arthur B. Jenks (R)
Foster Stearns (R)

NEW JERSEY

Senators

William H. Smathers (D)
W.Warren Barbour (R)

Representatives

Charles A. Eaton (R)
Edward J. Hart (D)
Fred A. Hartley, Jr. (R)
Walter S. Jeffries (R)
Robert W. Kean (R)
Donald H. McLean (R)
Mary T. Norton (D)
Frank C. Osmers, Jr. (R)
D. Lane Powers (R)
George N. Seger (R)
 d. Aug. 1940
William H. Sutphin (D)
J. Parnell Thomas (R)
Albert L. Vreeland (R)
Charles A. Wolverton (R)

NEW MEXICO

Senators

Carl A. Hatch (D)
Dennis Chavez (D)

Representative

John J. Dempsey (D)

NEW YORK

Senators

Robert F. Wagner (D)
James M. Mead (D)

Representatives

Walter G. Andrews (R)
William B. Barry (D)
Bruce Barton (R)
Sol Bloom (D)
Charles A. Buckley (D)
William T. Byrne (D)
Emanuel Celler (D)
E. Harold Cluett (R)
W. Sterling Cole (R)
Frank Crowther (R)
Francis D. Culkin (R)
Thomas H. Cullen (D)
Edward W. Curley (D)
 d. Jan. 1940
John J. Delaney (D)
Samuel Dickstein (D)
Fred J. Douglas (R)
M. Michael Edelstein (D) s. 1940
Marcellus H. Evans (D)
James H. Fay (D)
Hamilton Fish, Jr. (R)
James M. Fitzpatrick (D)
Ralph A. Gamble (R)
Joseph A. Gavagan (D)
Edwin A. Hall (R) s. 1940
Leonard W. Hall (R)
Clarence E. Hancock (R)
J. Francis Harter (R)
Martin J. Kennedy (D)
Michael J. Kennedy (D)
Eugene J. Keogh (D)
Clarence E. Kilburn (R) s. 1940
Bert Lord (R) d. May 1939
Walter A. Lynch (D) s. 1940
Vito Marcantonio
 (Amer. Labor)
Matthew J. Merritt (D)
Joseph J. O'Brien (R)
Caroline O'Day (D)
James A. O'Leary (D)
Donald L. O'Toole (D)
Wallace E. Pierce (R)
 d. Jan. 1940
Joseph L. Pfeifer (D)
Daniel A. Reed (R)
Lewis K. Rockefeller (R)
Pius L. Schwert (D)
William I Sirovich (D)
 d. Dec. 1939
Andrew L. Somers (D)
Christopher D. Sullivan (D)
John Taber (R)
James W. Wadsworth, Jr. (R)

NORTH CAROLINA

Senators

Josiah W. Bailey (D)
Robert R. Reynolds (D)

Representatives

Graham A. Barden (D)
Herbert C. Bonner (D) s. 1940
Alfred L. Bulwinkle (D)
William O. Burgin (D)
J. Bayard Clark (D)
Harold D. Cooley (D)
Robert L. Doughton (D)
Carl T. Durham (D)
Alonzo D. Folger (D)
John H. Kerr (D)
Lindsay C. Warren (D)
 r. Oct. 1940
Zebulon Weaver (D)

NORTH DAKOTA

Senators

Lynn J. Frazier (R)
Gerald P. Nye (R)

Representatives

Usher L. Burdick (R)
William Lemke (R)

OHIO

Senators

A. Victor Donahey (D)
Robert A. Taft (R)

Representatives

William A. Ashbrook (D)
 d. Jan. 1940
George H. Bender (R)
Chester C. Bolton (R)
 d. Oct. 1939
Frances P. Bolton (R) s. 1940
Clarence J. Brown (R)
Harold K. Claypool (D)
Cliff Clevenger (R)
Robert Crosser (D)
Charles H. Elston (R)
Dow W. Harter (D)
William E. Hess (R)
John F. Hunter (D)
Thomas A. Jenkins (R)
Robert F. Jones (R)
Michael J. Kirwan (D)
Earl R. Lewis (R)
J. Harry McGregor (R)
 s. 1940
Lycurgus L. Marshall (R)
James G. Polk (D)
Harry N. Routzohn (R)
James Seccombe (R)
Robert T. Secrest (D)
Frederick C. Smith (R)
Martin L. Sweeney (D)
John M. Vorys (R)
Dudley A. White (R)

OKLAHOMA

Senators

J. W. Elmer Thomas (D)
Josh Lee (D)

Representatives

Lyle H. Boren (D)
Wilburn Cartwright (D)
Wesley E. Disney (D)
Phil Ferguson (D)
Jed Johnson (D)
Sam C. Massingale (D)
A. S. Mike Monroney (D)
Jack Nichols (D)
Will Rogers (D)

OREGON

Senators

Charles L. McNary (R)
Rufus C. Holman (R)

Representatives

Homer D. Angell (R)
James W. Mott (R)
Walter M. Pierce (D)

PENNSYLVANIA

Senators

James J. Davis (R)
Joseph F. Guffey (D)

Representatives

Robert G. Allen (D)
Patrick J. Boland (D)
Michael J. Bradley (D)
Robert J. Corbett (R)
J. Burrwood Daly (D)
 d. Mar. 1939
George P. Darrow (R)
J. William Ditter (R)
Matthew A. Dunn (D)
Herman P. Eberharter (D)
Charles I. Faddis (D)
Ivor D. Fenton (R)
J. Harold Flannery (D)
Fred C. Gartner (R)
Charles L. Gerlach (R)
Louis E. Graham (R)
Chester H. Gross (R)
Benjamin Jarrett (R)
J. Roland Kinzer (R)
John C. Kunkel (R)
Joseph A. McArdle (D)
John R. McDowell (R)
James P. McGranery (D)
Guy L. Moser (D)
Francis J. Myers (D)
Robert F. Rich (R)
Robert L. Rodgers (R)
Albert G. Rutherford (R)
Leon Sacks (D)
John E. Sheridan (D) s. 1940
Richard M. Simpson (R)
J. Buell Snyder (D)
Harve Tibbott (R)
James E. Van Zandt (R)
Francis E. Walter (D)
James Wolfenden (R)

RHODE ISLAND

Senators

Peter G. Gerry (D)
Theodore F. Green (D)

Representatives

Charles F. Risk (R)
Harry Sandager (R)

SOUTH CAROLINA

Senators

Ellison D. Smith (D)
James F. Byrnes (D)

Representatives

Joseph R. Bryson (D)
Hampton P. Fulmer (D)
Butler B. Hare (D)
Clara Gooding McMillan (D)
 s. 1940
John L. McMillan (D)
Thomas S. McMillan (D)
 d. Sept. 1939
James P. Richards (D)

SOUTH DAKOTA

Senators

William J. Bulow (D)
J. Chandler Gurney (R)

Representatives

Francis H. Case (R)
Karl E. Mundt (R)

TENNESSEE

Senators

Kenneth D. McKellar (D)
A. Tom Stewart (D)

Representatives

Joseph W. Byrns, Jr. (D)
Walter Chandler (D)
r. Jan. 1940
Jere Cooper (D)
Wirt Courtney (D)
Clifford Davis (D) s. 1940
Albert A. Gore (D)
John Jennings, Jr. (R) s. 1940
Estes Kefauver (D)
Sam D. McReynolds (D)
d. July 1939
Herron Pearson (D)
B. Carroll Reece (R)
J. Will Taylor (R)
d. Nov. 1939
Clarence W. Turner (D)
d. Mar. 1939

TEXAS

Senators

Morris Sheppard (D)
Tom T. Connally (D)

Representatives

Lindley Beckworth (D)
Martin Dies, Jr. (D)
Clyde L. Garrett (D)
Ed Gossett (D)
Luther A. Johnson (D)
Lyndon B. Johnson (D)
Marvin Jones (D) r. Nov. 1940
Paul J. Kilday (D)
Richard M. Kleberg (D)
Fritz G. Lanham (D)
George H. Mahon (D)
Joseph J. Mansfield (D)
Wright Patman (D)
Nat Patton (D)
William R. Poage (D)
Sam Rayburn (D)
Charles L. South (D)
Hatton W. Sumners (D)
Albert Thomas (D)
R. Ewing Thomason (D)
Milton H. West (D)

UTAH

Senators

William H. King (D)
Elbert D. Thomas (D)

Representatives

Abe Murdock (D)
J. W. Robinson (D)

VERMONT

Senators

Warren R. Austin (R)

Ernest W. Gibson (R)
d. June 1940
Ernest W. Gibson, Jr. (R)
s. 1940

Representative

Charles A. Plumley (R)

VIRGINIA

Senators

Carter Glass (D)
Harry F. Byrd (D)

Representatives

Schuyler Otis Bland (D)
Thomas G. Burch (D)
Colgate W. Darden, Jr. (D)
Patrick H. Drewry (D)
John W. Flannagan, Jr. (D)
A. Willis Robertson (D)
Dave E. Satterfield, Jr. (D)
Howard W. Smith (D)
Clifton A. Woodrum (D)

WASHINGTON

Senators

Homer T. Bone (D)

Lewis B. Schwellenbach (D)
r. Dec. 1940
Monrad C. Wallgren (D) s. 1940

Representatives

John M. Coffee (D)
Knute Hill (D)
Charles H. Leavy (D)
Warren G. Magnuson (D)
Martin F. Smith (D)
Monrad C. Wallgren (D)
r. Dec. 1940

WEST VIRGINIA

Senators

Matthew M. Neely (D)
Rush D. Holt (D)

Representatives

Andrew Edmiston (D)
George W. Johnson (D)
John Kee (D)
Jennings Randolph (D)
Andrew C. Schiffler (R)
Joe L. Smith (D)

WISCONSIN

Senators

Robert M. La Follette, Jr.
(Progressive)
Alexander Wiley (R)

Representatives

Stephen Bolles (R)
Bernard J. Gehrmann
(Progressive)
Harry W. Griswold (R)
d. July 1939
Charles Hawks, Jr. (R)
Merlin Hull (R)
Joshua L. Johns (R)
Frank B. Keefe (R)
Reid F. Murray (R)
John C. Schafer (R)
Lewis D. Thill (R)

WYOMING

Senators

Joseph C. O'Mahoney (D)
H. H. Schwartz (D)

Representative

Frank O. Horton (R)

SEVENTY-SEVENTH CONGRESS

January 3, 1941 to January 3, 1943

Presidents of The Senate:	John Nance Garner Henry A. Wallace
Presidents Pro Tempore of The Senate:	Pat Harrison Carter Glass
Speaker of The House of Representatives:	Sam Rayburn

ALABAMA

Senators

John H. Bankhead 2d (D)
Lister Hill (D)

Representatives

Walter W. Bankhead (D)
r. Feb. 1941
Frank W. Boykin (D)
George M. Grant (D)
Sam Hobbs (D)
Pete Jarman (D)
Carter Manasco (D)
Luther Patrick (D)
John J. Sparkman (D)
Joe Starnes (D)
Henry B. Steagall (D)

ARIZONA

Senators

Carl Hayden (D)
Ernest W. McFarland (D)

Representative

John R. Murdock (D)

ARKANSAS

Senators

Hattie W. Caraway (D)

John E. Miller (D) r. Mar. 1941
George L. Spencer (D)

Representatives

Fadjo Cravens (D)
Clyde T. Ellis (D)
Ezekiel C. Gathings (D)
Oren Harris (D)
Wilbur D. Mills (D)
William F. Norrell (D)
David D. Terry (D)

CALIFORNIA

Senators

Hiram W. Johnson (R)
Sheridan Downey (D)

Representatives

John Z. Anderson (R)
Frank H. Buck (D) d. Sept. 1942
Albert E. Carter (R)
John M. Costello (D)
Alfred J. Elliott (D)
Harry L. Englebright (R)
Leland M. Ford (R)
Thomas F. Ford (D)
Bertrand W. Gearhart (R)
Lee E. Geyer (D) d. Oct. 1941
Carl Hinshaw (R)
Edouard V. M. Izac (D)
Ward Johnson (R)
Cecil R. King (D) s. 1942
Charles Kramer (D)
Clarence F. Lea (D, R)
Thomas Rolph (R)
Harry R. Sheppard (D)
John H. Tolan (D)
H. Jerry Voorhis (D)
Richard J. Welch (R)

COLORADO

Senators

Alva B. Adams (D) d. Dec. 1941
Eugene D. Millikin (R) s. 1942

Edwin C. Johnson (D)

Representatives

J. Edgar Chenoweth (D)
William S. Hill (R)
Lawrence Lewis (D)
Robert F. Rockwell (R)
Edward T. Taylor (D)
d. Sept. 1941

CONNECTICUT

Senators

Francis T. Maloney (D)
John A. Danaher (R)

Representatives

Le Roy D. Downs (D)
William J. Fitzgerald (D)
Herman P. Kopplemann (D)
Lucien J. Maciora (D)
James A. Shanley (D)
J. Joseph Smith (D) r. Nov. 1942
Joseph E. Talbot (R) s. 1942

DELAWARE

Senators

James H. Hughes (D)
James M. Tunnell (D)

Representative

Philip A. Traynor (D)

FLORIDA

Senators

Charles O. Andrews (D)
Claude D. Pepper (D)

Representatives

Arthur P. Cannon (D)
Robert A. Green (D)
Joe Hendricks (D)
J. Hardin Peterson (D)
Robert L. F. Sikes (D)

GEORGIA

Senators

Walter F. George (D)
Richard B. Russell (D)

Representatives

Paul Brown (D)
A. Sidney Camp (D)
Edward E. Cox (D)
John S. Gibson (D)
Stephen Pace (D)
Hugh Peterson (D)
Robert Ramspeck (D)
Malcolm C. Tarver (D)
Carl Vinson (D)
B. Frank Whelchel (D)

IDAHO

Senators

D. Worth Clark (D)
John Thomas (R)

Representatives

Henry C. Dworshak (R)
Compton I. White (D)

ILLINOIS

Senators

Scott W. Lucas (D)
C. Wayland Brooks (R)

Representatives

Leo E. Allen (R)
Leslie C. Arends (R)
Laurence F. Arnold (D)
James M. Barnes (D)
Harry P. Beam (D) r. Dec. 1942
Cecil W. Bishop (R)
Robert B. Chiperfield (R)
Stephen A. Day (R)
Charles S. Dewey (R)
Everett M. Dirksen (R)
James V. Heidinger (R)
Evan Howell (R)
Anton J. Johnson (R)
Edward A. Kelly (D)
Leo Kocialkowski (D)
Raymond S. McKeough (D)
Anton F. Maciejewski (D)
r. Dec. 1942
Noah M. Mason (R)
Arthur W. Mitchell (D)
George A. Paddock (R)
Chauncey W. Reed (R)
Adolph J. Sabath (D)
Edwin M. Schaefer (D)
Leonard W. Schuetz (D)
William G. Stratton (R)
Jessie Sumner (R)
William H. Wheat (R)

INDIANA

Senators

Frederick Van Nuys (D)
Raymond E. Willis (R)

Representatives

John W. Boehne, Jr. (D)
George W. Gillie (R)
Robert A. Grant (R)
Charles A. Halleck (R)
Forest A. Harness (R)
Noble J. Johnson (R)
Gerald W. Landis (R)
William H. Larrabee (D)
Louis Ludlow (D)
William T. Schulte (D)
Raymond S. Springer (R)
Earl Wilson (R)

IOWA

Senators

Guy M. Gillette (D)
Clyde L. Herring (D)

Representatives

Paul Cunningham (R)
Fred C. Gilchrist (R)
John W. Gwynne (R)
Vincent F. Harrington (D)
r. Sept. 1942
William S. Jacobsen (D)
Ben F. Jensen (R)
Karl M. LeCompte (R)
Thomas E. Martin (R)
Harry E. Narey (R) s. 1942
Henry O. Talle (R)

KANSAS

Senators

Arthur Capper (R)
Clyde M. Reed (R)

Representatives

Frank Carlson (R)
Ulysses S. Guyer (R)
Clifford R. Hope (R)
John M. Houston (D)
William P. Lambertson (R)
Edward H. Rees (R)
Thomas D. Winter (R)

KENTUCKY

Senators

Alben W. Barkley (D)
Albert B. Chandler (D)

Representatives

Joe B. Bates (D)
Virgil M. Chapman (D)
Edward W. Creal (D)
Noble J. Gregory (D)
Andrew J. May (D)
Emmet O'Neal (D)
John M. Robsion (R)
Brent Spence (D)
Beverly M. Vincent (D)

LOUISIANA

Senators

John H. Overton (D)
Allen J. Ellender (D)

Representatives

A. Leonard Allen (D)
T. Hale Boggs (D)
Overton Brooks (D)
James Domengeaux (D)
F. Edward Hebert (D)
Newt V. Mills (D)
Vance Plauche (D)
Jared Y. Sanders, Jr. (D)

MAINE

Senators

Wallace H. White, Jr. (R)
Ralph O. Brewster (R)

Representatives

Frank Fellows (R)
James C. Oliver (R)
Margaret Chase Smith (R)

MARYLAND

Senators

Millard E. Tydings (D)
George L. Radcliffe (D)

Representatives

Katharine E. Byron (D)
William D. Byron (D) d. Feb. 1941
William P. Cole, Jr. (D)
r. Oct. 1942
Thomas D'Alesandro, Jr. (D)
John A. Meyer (D)
Lansdale G. Sasscer (D)
David J. Ward (D)

MASSACHUSETTS

Senators

David I. Walsh (D)
Henry Cabot Lodge, Jr. (R)

Representatives

George J. Bates (R)
Joseph E. Casey (R)
Charles R. Clason (R)
Lawrence J. Connery (D)
d. Oct. 1941
Thomas H. Eliot (D)
Thomas A. Flaherty (D)
Charles L. Gifford (R)
Arthur D. Healey (D) r. Aug. 1942
Pehr G. Holmes (R)
Thomas J. Lane (D) s. 1942
John W. McCormack (D)
Joseph W. Martin, Jr. (R)
Edith Nourse Rogers (R)
George H. Tinkham (R)
Allen T. Treadway (R)
Richard B. Wigglesworth (R)

MICHIGAN

Senators

Arthur H. Vandenberg (R)
Prentiss M. Brown (D)

Representatives

William W. Blackney (R)
Frederick V. Bradley (R)
Fred L. Crawford (R)
John D. Dingell (D)
George A. Dondero (R)
Albert J. Engel (R)
Clare E. Hoffman (R)
Frank E. Hook (D)
Bartel J. Jonkman (R)
John Lesinski (D)
Earl C. Michener (R)
George D. O'Brien (D)
Louis C. Rabaut (D)
Paul W. Shafer (R)
Rudolph G. Tenerowicz (D)
Jesse P. Wolcott (R)
Roy O. Woodruff (R)

MINNESOTA

Senators

Henrik Shipstead (R)

Joseph H. Ball (R) ta. 1941-1942
Arthur E. Nelson (R) s. 1942

Representatives

H. Carl Andersen (R)
August H. Andresen (R)
Richard T. Buckler (Farm-Labor)
Richard P. Gale (R)
Harold Knutson (R)
Melvin J. Maas (R)
Joseph P. O'Hara (R)
William A. Pittenger (R)
Oscar Youngdahl (R)

MISSISSIPPI

Senators

Pat Harrison (D) d. June 1941
James O. Eastland (D) ta. 1941
Wall Doxey (D)

Theodore G. Bilbo (D)

Representatives

Ross A. Collins (D)
William M. Colmer (D)
Wall Doxey (D) r. Sept. 1941
Aaron L. Ford (D)
Dan R. McGehee (D)
John E. Rankin (D)
Jamie L. Whitten (D)
William Whittington (D)

MISSOURI

Senators

Bennett Champ Clark (D)
Harry S Truman (D)

Representatives

C. Jasper Bell (D)
Philip A. Bennett (R) d. Dec. 1942
Clarence Cannon (D)
John J. Cochran (D)
Richard M. Duncan (D)
William L. Nelson (D)
Walter C. Ploeser (R)
Milton A. Romjue (D)
Joseph B. Shannon (D)
Dewey Short (R)
John B. Sullivan (D)
Clyde Williams (D)
Orville Zimmerman (D)

MONTANA

Senators

Burton K. Wheeler (D)
James E. Murray (D)

Representatives

James F. O'Connor (D)
Jeannette Rankin (R)

NEBRASKA

Senators

George W. Norris (R)
Hugh A. Butler (R)

Representatives

Harry B. Coffee (D)
Oren S. Copeland (R)
Carl T. Curtis (R)
Charles F. McLaughlin (D)
Karl Stefan (R)

NEVADA

Senators

Patrick A. McCarran (D)

Berkeley L. Bunker (R)
ta. 1941-1942
James G. Scrugham (D) s. 1942

Representative

James G. Scrugham (D)

NEW HAMPSHIRE

Senators

H. Styles Bridges (R)
Charles W. Tobey (R)

Representatives

Arthur B. Jenks (R)
Foster Stearns (R)

NEW JERSEY

Senators

William H. Smathers (D)
W. Warren Barbour (R)

Representatives

Gordon Canfield (R)
Charles A. Eaton (R)
Edward J. Hart (D)
Fred A. Hartley, Jr. (R)
Robert W. Kean (R)
Donald H. McLean (R)
Mary T. Norton (D)
Frank C. Osmers, Jr. (R)
D. Lane Powers (R)
William H. Sutphin (D)
J. Parnell Thomas (R)
Albert L. Vreeland (R)
Elmer H. Wene (D)
Charles A. Wolverton (R)

NEW MEXICO

Senators

Carl A. Hatch (D)
Dennis Chavez (D)

Representative

Clinton P. Anderson (D)

NEW YORK

Senators

Robert F. Wagner (D)
James M. Mead (D)

Representatives

Walter G. Andrews (R)
William B. Barry (D)
Joseph C. Baldwin (R)
Alfred F. Beiter (D)
Sol Bloom (D)
Charles A. Buckley (D)
John C. Butler (R)
William T. Byrne (D)
Louis J. Capozzoli (D)
Emanuel Celler (D)
E. Harold Cluett (R)
W. Sterling Cole (R)
Frank Crowther (R)
Francis D. Culkin (R)
Thomas H. Cullen (D)
John J. Delaney (D)
Samuel Dickstein (D)
Fred J. Douglas (R)
M. Michael Edelstein (D)
d. June 1941
Hamilton Fish, Jr. (R)
James M. Fitzpatrick (D)
Ralph A. Gamble (R)
Joseph A. Gavagan (D)
Edwin A. Hall (R)
Leonard W. Hall (R)
Clarence E. Hancock (R)
James J. Heffernan (D)
Martin J. Kennedy (D)
Michael J. Kennedy (D)
Eugene J. Keogh (D)
Clarence E. Kilburn (R)
Arthur G. Klein (D)
Walter A. Lynch (D)
Vito Marcantonio (Amer. Labor)
Matthew J. Merritt (D)
Joseph J. O'Brien (R)
Caroline O. Day (D)
James A. O'Leary (D)
Donald L. O'Toole (D)
Joseph L. Pfeifer (D)
William T. Pheiffer (R)
Daniel A. Reed (R)
Lewis K. Rockefeller (R)
Pius L. Schwert (D) d. Mar. 1941
Kenneth F. Simpson (R)
d. Jan. 1941
Andrew L. Somers (D)
John Taber (R)
James W. Wadsworth, Jr. (R)

NORTH CAROLINA

Senators

Josiah W. Bailey (D)
Robert R. Reynolds (D)

Representatives

Graham A. Barden (D)
Herbert C. Bonner (D)
Alfred L. Bulwinkle (D)
William O. Burgin (D)
J. Bayard Clark (D)
Harold D. Cooley (D)
Robert L. Doughton (D)
Carl T. Durham (D)
Alonzo D. Folger (D)
d. Apr. 1941
John H. Folger (D)
John H. Kerr (D)
Zebulon Weaver (D)

NORTH DAKOTA

Senators

Gerald P. Nye (R)
William Langer (R)

Representatives

Usher L. Burdick (R)
Charles R. Robertson (R)

OHIO

Senators

Robert A. Taft (R)
Harold H. Burton (R)

Representatives

Albert D. Baumhart, Jr. (R)
r. Sept. 1942
George H. Bender (R)
Frances P. Bolton (R)
Clarence J. Brown (R)
Cliff Clevenger (R)
Harold K. Claypool (D)
Robert Crosser (D)
Jacob E. Davis (D)
Charles H. Elston (R)
Dow W. Harter (D)
William E. Hess (R)
Greg J. Holbrock (D)
John F. Hunter (D)
Lawrence E. Imhoff (D)
Thomas A. Jenkins (R)
Robert F. Jones (R)
Michael J. Kirwan (D)
J. Harry McGregor (R)
Robert T. Secrest (D)
r. Aug. 1942
Frederick C. Smith (R)
Martin L. Sweeney (D)
William R. Thom (D)
John M. Vorys (R)
Stephen M. Young (D)

OKLAHOMA

Senators

J. W. Elmer Thomas (D)
Josh Lee (D)

Representatives

Lyle H. Boren (D)
Wilburn Cartwright (D)
Wesley E. Disney (D)
Jed Johnson (D)
Sam C. Massingale (D)
d. Jan. 1941
A. S. Mike Monroney (D)
Jack Nichols (D)
Ross Rizley (R)
Will Rogers (D)
Victor Wickersham (D)

OREGON

Senators

Charles L. McNary (R)
Rufus C. Holman (R)

Representatives

Homer D. Angell (R)
James W. Mott (R)
Walter M. Pierce (D)

PENNSYLVANIA

Senators

James J. Davis (R)
Joseph F. Guffey (D)

Representatives

Michael J. Bradley (D)
Patrick J. Boland (D)
d. May 1942
Veronica Boland (D)
J. William Ditter (R)
Herman P. Eberharter (D)
Charles I. Faddis (D)
r. Dec. 1942
Ivor D. Fenton (R)
J. Harold Flannery (D)
r. Jan. 1942
Charles L. Gerlach (R)
Wilson D. Gillette (R)
s. 1941
Louis E. Graham (R)
Harry L. Haines (D)
Elmer J. Holland (D)
s. 1942
Benjamin Jarrett (R)
Augustine B. Kelley (D)
J. Roland Kinzer (R)
John C. Kunkel (R)
Joseph A. McArdle (D)
r. Jan. 1942
James P. McGranery (D)
Thomas B. Miller (R)
s. 1942
Guy L. Moser (D)
Francis J. Myers (D)
Robert F. Rich (R)
Robert L. Rodgers (R)
Albert G. Rutherford (R)
d. Aug. 1941
Leon Sacks (D)
Thomas E. Scanlon (D)
Hugh D. Scott, Jr. (R)
John E. Sheridan (D)
Richard M. Simpson (R)
Francis R. Smith (D)
J. Buell Snyder (D)
Harve Tibbott (R)
James E. Van Zandt (R)
Francis E. Walter (D)
Samuel A. Weiss (D)
James A. Wright (D)
James Wolfenden (R)

RHODE ISLAND

Senators

Peter G. Gerry (D)
Theodore F. Green (D)

Representatives

John E. Fogarty (D)
Aime J. Forand (D)

SOUTH CAROLINA

Senators

Ellison D. Smith (D)

James F. Byrnes (D) r. July 1941
Roger C. Peace (D) ta. 1941
Burnet R. Maybank (D)

Representatives

Joseph R. Bryson (D)
Hampton P. Fulmer (D)
Butler B. Hare (D)
John L. McMillan (D)
James P. Richards (D)
L. Mendel Rivers (D)

SOUTH DAKOTA

Senators

William J. Bulow (D)
J. Chandler Gurney (R)

Representatives

Francis H. Case (R)
Karl E. Mundt (R)

TENNESSEE

Senators

Kenneth D. McKellar (D)
A. Tom Stewart (D)

Representatives

Jere Cooper (D)
Wirt Courtney (D)
Clifford Davis (D)
Albert A. Gore (D)
John Jennings, Jr. (R)
Estes Kefauver (D)
Herron Pearson (D)
J. Percy Priest (D)
B. Carroll Reece (R)

TEXAS

Senators

Morris Shepard (D) d. Apr. 1941
W. Lee O'Daniel (D)

Tom T. Connally (D)

Representatives

Lindley Beckworth (D)
Martin Dies, Jr. (D)
Ed Gossett (D)
Luther A. Johnson (D)
Lyndon B. Johnson (D)
Paul J. Kilday (D)
Richard M. Kleberg (D)
Fritz G. Lanham (D)
George H. Mahon (D)
Joseph J. Mansfield (D)
Wright Patman (D)
Nat Patton (D)
William R. Poage (D)
Sam Rayburn (D)
Sam M. Russell (D)
Charles L. South (D)
Hatton W. Sumners (D)
Albert Thomas (D)
R. Ewing Thomason (D)
Milton H. West (D)
Eugene Worley (D)

UTAH

Senators

Elbert D. Thomas (D)
Abe Murdock (D)

Representatives

Walter K. Granger (D)
J. W. Robinson (D)

VERMONT

Senators

Warren R. Austin (R)
George D. Aiken (R)

Representative

Charles A. Plumley (R)

VIRGINIA

Senators

Carter Glass (D)
Harry F. Byrd (D)

Representatives

Schuyler Otis Bland (D)
Thomas G. Burch (D)
Colgate W. Darden, Jr. (D)
r. Mar. 1941
Patrick H. Drewry (D)
John W. Flannagan, Jr. (D)
Winder R. Harris (D)
A. Willis Robertson (D)
Dave E. Satterfield, Jr. (D)
Howard W. Smith (D)
Clifton A. Woodrum (D)

WASHINGTON

Senators

Homer T. Bone (D)
Monrad C. Wallgren (D)

Representatives

John M. Coffee (D)
Knute Hill (D)
Henry M. Jackson (D)
Charles H. Leavy (D)
r. Aug. 1942
Warren G. Mangnuson (D)
Martin F. Smith (D)

WEST VIRGINIA

Senators

Matthew M. Neely (D)
r. Jan. 1941
Joseph Rosier (D) ta. 1941
Hugh I. Shott (R) s. 1942

Harley M. Kilgore (D)

Representatives

Andrew Edmiston (D)
George W. Johnson (D)
John Kee (D)
Robert L. Ramsay (D)
Jennings Randolph (D)
Joe L. Smith (D)

WISCONSIN

Senators

Robert M. La Follette, Jr.
(Progressive)
Alexander Wiley (R)

Representatives

Stephen Bolles (R) d. July 1941
Bernard J. Gehrmann (Progressive)
Merlin Hull (R)
Joshua L. Johns (R)
Frank B. Keefe (R)
Reid F. Murray (R)
Harry Sauthoff (Progressive)
Lawrence H. Smith (R)
William H. Stevenson (R)
Lewis D. Thill (R)
Thaddeus F. B. Wasielewski (D)

WYOMING

Senators

Joseph C. O'Mahoney (D)
H. H. Schwartz (D)

Representative

John J. McIntyre (D)

SEVENTY-EIGHTH CONGRESS

January 3, 1943 to January 3, 1945

President of The Senate:	Henry A. Wallace
President Pro Tempore of The Senate:	Cater Glass
Speaker of The House of Representatives:	Sam Rayburn

ALABAMA

Senators

John H. Bankhead 2d (D)
Lister Hill (D)

Representatives

George W. Andrews (D) s. 1944
Frank W. Boykin (D)
George M. Grant (D)
Sam Hobbs (D)
Pete Jarman (D)
Carter Manasco (D)
John P. Newsome (D)
John J. Sparkman (D)
Joe Starnes (D)
Henry B. Steagall (D)
d. Nov. 1943

ARIZONA

Senators

Carl Hayden (D)
Ernest W. McFarland (D)

Representatives

Richard F. Harless (D)
John R. Murdock (D)

ARKANSAS

Senators

Hattie W. Caraway (D)
John L. McClellan (D)

Representatives

Fadjo Cravens (D)
J. William Fulbright (D)
Ezekiel C. Gathings (D)
Oren Harris (D)
Brooks Hays (D)
Wilbur D. Mills (D)
William F. Norrell (D)

CALIFORNIA

Senators

Hiram W. Johnson (R)
Sheridan Downey (D)

Representatives

John Z. Anderson (R)
Albert E. Carter (R)
John M. Costello (D)
Alfred J. Elliott (D)
Clair Engle (D)
Harry L. Englebright (R)
Thomas F. Ford (D)
Bertrand W. Gearhart (R)
Carl Hinshaw (R)
Chet Holifield (D)
Edouard V. M. Izac (D)
Leroy Johnson (R)
Ward Johnson (R)
Cecil R. King (D)
Clarence F. Lea (D,R)
George E. Outland (D)
John Phillips (R)
Norris Poulson (R)
Will Rogers, Jr. (D)
Thomas Rolph (R)
Harry R. Sheppard (D)
John H. Tolan (D)
H. Jerry Voorhis (D)
Richard J. Welch (R)

COLORADO

Senators

Edwin C. Johnson (D)
Eugene D. Millikin (R)

Representatives

J. Edgar Chenoweth (D)
Dean M. Gillespie (R)
William S. Hill (R)
Lawrence Lewis (D)
Robert F. Rockwell (R)

CONNECTICUT

Senators

Francis T. Maloney (D)
John A. Danaher (R)

Representatives

Ranulf Compton (R)
Clare Boothe Luce (R)
John D. McWilliams (R)
William J. Miller (R)
Boleslaus J. Monkiewicz (R)
Joseph E. Talbot (R)

DELAWARE

Senators

James M. Tunnell (D)
C. Douglass Buck (R)

Representative

Earle D. Willey (R)

FLORIDA

Senators

Charles O. Andrews (D)
Claude D. Pepper (D)

Representatives

Arthur P. Cannon (D)
Robert A. Green (D)
Joe Hendricks (D)
J. Hardin Peterson (D)
Emory H. Price (D)
Robert L. F. Sikes (D)

GEORGIA

Senators

Walter F. George (D)
Richard B. Russell (D)

Representatives

Paul Brown (D)
A. Sidney Camp (D)
Edward E. Cox (D)
John S. Gibson (D)
Stephen Pace (D)
Hugh Peterson (D)
Robert Ramspeck (D)
Malcolm C. Tarver (D)
Carl Vinson (D)
B. Frank Whelchel (D)

IDAHO

Senators

D. Worth Clark (D)
John Thomas (R)

Representatives

Henry C. Dworshak (R)
Compton I. White (D)

ILLINOIS

Senators

Scott W. Lucas (D)
C. Wayland Brooks (R)

Representatives

Leo E. Allen (R)
Leslie C. Arends (R)
Cecil W. Bishop (R)
Fred E. Busbey (R)
Robert B. Chiperfield (R)
Ralph E. Church (R)
William L. Dawson (D)
Stephen A. Day (R)
Charles S. Dewey (R)
Everett M. Dirksen (R)
Martin Gorski (D)
Thomas S. Gordon (D)
James V. Heidinger (R)
Evan Howell (R)
Anton J. Johnson (R)
Calvin D. Johnson (R)
Rolla C. McMillen (R) s. 1944
Noah M. Mason (R)
Thomas J. O'Brien (D)
Chauncey W. Reed (R)
William A. Rowan (D)
Adolph J. Sabath (D)
Leonard W. Schuetz (D)
d. Feb. 1944
Sidney E. Simpson (R)
Jessie Sumner (R)
Charles W. Vursell (R)
William H. Wheat (R)
d. Jan. 1944

INDIANA

Senators

Frederick Van Nuys (D)
d. Jan. 1944
Samuel D. Jackson (D) ta. 1944
William E. Jenner (R) s. 1944

Raymond E. Willis (R)

Representatives

George W. Gillie (R)
Robert A. Grant (R)
Charles A. Halleck (R)
Forest A. Harness (R)
Noble J. Johnson (R)
Charles M. La Follette (R)
Gerald W. Landis (R)
Louis Ludlow (D)
Ray J. Madden (D)
Earl Wilson (R)
Raymond S. Springer (R)

IOWA

Senators

Guy M. Gillette (D)
George A. Wilson (R)

Representatives

Paul Cunningham (R)
Fred C. Gilchrist (R)
John W. Gwynne (R)
Charles B. Hoeven (R)
Ben F. Jensen (R)
Karl M. LeCompte (R)
Thomas E. Martin (R)
Henry O. Talle (R)

KANSAS

Senators

Arthur Capper (R)
Clyde M. Reed (R)

Representatives

Frank Carlson (R)
Ulysses S. Guyer (R) d. June 1943
Clifford R. Hope (R)
William P. Lambertson (R)
Edward H. Rees (R)
Errett P. Scrivner (R)
Thomas D. Winter (R)

KENTUCKY

Senators

Alben W. Barkley (D)
Albert B. Chandler (D)

Representatives

Joe B. Bates (D)
Chester O. Carrier (R)
Virgil M. Chapman (D)
Edward W. Creal (D) d. Oct. 1943
Noble J. Gregory (D)
Andrew J. May (D)
Emmet O'Neal (D)
John M. Robsion (R)
Brent Spence (D)
Beverly M. Vincent (D)

LOUISIANA

Senators

John H. Overton (D)
Allen J. Ellender (D)

Representatives

A. Leonard Allen (D)
Overton Brooks (D)
James Domengeaux (D)
r. Apr. 1944
F. Edward Hebert (D)
Henry D. Larcade, Jr. (D)
Charles E. McKenzie (D)
Paul H. Maloney (D)
James H. Morrison (D)

MAINE

Senators

Wallace H. White, Jr. (R)
Ralph O. Brewster (R)

Representatives

Frank Fellows (R)
Robert Hale (R)
Margaret Chase Smith (R)

MARYLAND

Senators

Millard E. Tydings (D)
George L. Radcliffe (D)

Representatives

H. Streett Baldwin (D)
J. Glenn Beall (R)
Thomas D'Alesandro, Jr. (D)
Daniel Ellison (R)
Lansdale G. Sasscer (D)
David J. Ward (D)

MASSACHUSETTS

Senators

David I. Walsh (D)

Henry Cabot Lodge, Jr. (R)
r. Feb. 1944
Sinclair Weeks (R) s. 1944

Representatives

George J. Bates (R)
Charles R. Clason (R)
James M. Curley (D)
Charles L. Gifford (R)
Angier L. Goodwin (R)
Christian A. Herter (R)
Pehr G. Holmes (R)
Thomas J. Lane (D)
John W. McCormack (D)
Joseph W. Martin, Jr. (R)
Philip J. Philbin (D)
Edith Nourse Rogers (R)
Allen T. Treadway (R)
Richard B. Wigglesworth (R)

MICHIGAN

Senators

Arthur H. Vandenberg (R)
Homer Ferguson (R)

Representatives

John B. Bennett (R)
William W. Blackney (R)
Frederick V. Bradley (R)
Fred L. Crawford (R)
John D. Dingell (D)
George A. Dondero (R)
Albert J. Engel (R)
Clare E. Hoffman (R)
Bartel J. Jonkman (R)
John Lesinski (D)
Earl C. Michener (R)
George D. O'Brien (D)
Louis C. Rabaut (D)
George G. Sadowski (D)
Paul W. Shafer (R)
Jesse P. Wolcott (R)
Roy O. Woodruff (R)

MINNESOTA

Senators

Henrik Shipstead (R)
Joseph H. Ball (R)

Representatives

H. Carl Andersen (R)
August H. Andresen (R)
Richard P. Gale (R)
Harold C. Hagen (Farm-Labor)
Walter H. Judd (R)
Harold Knutson (R)
Melvin J. Maas (R)
Joseph P. O'Hara (R)
William A. Pittenger (R)

MISSISSIPPI

Senators

Theodore G. Bilbo (D)
James O. Eastland (D)

Representatives

Thomas G. Abernethy (D)
William M. Colmer (D)
Dan R. McGehee (D)
John E. Rankin (D)
W. Arthur Winstead (D)
Jamie L. Whitten (D)
William M. Whittington (D)

MISSOURI

Senators

Bennett Champ Clark (D)
Harry S Truman (D)

Representatives

Samuel W. Arnold (R)
C. Jasper Bell (D)
Marion T. Bennett (R)
Clarence Cannon (D)
John J. Cochran (D)
William C. Cole (R)
William P. Elmer (R)
Louis E. Miller (R)
Walter C. Ploeser (R)
Max Schwabe (R)
Dewey Short (R)
Roger C. Slaughter (D)
Orville Zimmerman (D)

MONTANA

Senators

Burton K. Wheeler (D)
James E. Murray (D)

Representatives

Mike Mansfield (D)
James F. O'Connor (D)

NEBRASKA

Senators

Hugh A. Butler (R)
Kenneth S. Wherry (R)

Representatives

Howard H. Buffett (R)
Carl T. Curtis (R)
Arthur L. Miller (R)
Karl Stefan (R)

NEVADA

Senators

Patrick A. McCarran (D)
James G. Scrugham (D)

Representative

Maurice J. Sullivan (D)

NEW HAMPSHIRE

Senators

H. Styles Bridges (R)
Charles W. Tobey (R)

Representatives

Chester E. Merrow (R)
Foster Stearns (R)

NEW JERSEY

Senators

W. Warren Barbour (R)
d. Nov. 1943
Arthur Walsh (D) ta. 1943-1944
H. Alexander Smith (R) s. 1944

Albert W. Hawkes (R)

Representatives

James C. Auchincloss (R)
Gordon Canfield (R)
Charles A. Eaton (R)
Edward J. Hart (D)
Fred A. Hartley, Jr. (R)
Robert W. Kean (R)
Donald H. McLean (R)
Mary T. Norton (D)
D. Lane Powers (R)
Frank L. Sundstrom (R)
J. Parnell Thomas (R)
Harry L. Towe (R)
Elmer H. Wene (D)
Charles A. Wolverton (R)

NEW MEXICO

Senators

Carl A. Hatch (D)
Dennis Chavez (D)

Representatives

Clinton P. Anderson (D)
Antonio M. Fernandez (D)

NEW YORK

Senators

Robert F. Wagner (D)
James M. Mead (D)

Representatives

Walter G. Andrews (R)
Joseph C. Baldwin (R)
William B. Barry (D)
Sol Bloom (D)
Ellsworth B. Buck (R) s. 1944
Charles A. Buckley (D)
Thomas F. Burchill (D)
John C. Butler (R)
William T. Byrne (D)
Emanuel Celler (D)
Louis J. Capozzoli (D)
W. Sterling Cole (R)
Francis D. Culkin (R)
d. Aug. 1943
Thomas H. Cullen (D)
d. Mar. 1944
John J. Delaney (D)
Samuel Dickstein (D)
Fred J. Douglas (R)
James H. Fay (D)
Hamilton Fish, Jr. (R)
James M. Fitzpatrick (D)
Hadwen C. Fuller (R) s. 1943
Ralph A. Gamble (R)
Joseph A. Gavagan (D)
r. Dec. 1943
Edwin A. Hall (R)
Leonard W. Hall (R)
Clarence E. Hancock (R)
James J. Heffernan (D)
Bernard W. Kearney (R)
Martin J. Kennedy (D)
Eugene J. Keogh (D)
Clarence E. Kilburn (R)
Arthur G. Klein (D)
Jay LeFevre (R)
Walter A. Lynch (D)
Vito Marcantonio (Amer. Labor)
Matthew J. Merritt (D)
Joseph Mruk (R)
Joseph J. O'Brien (R)
James A. O'Leary (D)
d. Mar. 1944
Donald L. O'Toole (D)
Joseph L. Pfeifer (D)
Daniel A. Reed (R)

John J. Rooney (D) s. 1944
Andrew L. Somers (D)
Winifred C. Stanley (R)
John Taber (R)
Dean P. Taylor (R)
James H. Torrens (D)
s. 1944
James W. Wadsworth, Jr. (R)

NORTH CAROLINA

Senators

Josiah W. Bailey (D)
Robert R. Reynolds (D)

Representatives

Graham A. Barden (D)
Herbert C. Bonner (D)
Alfred L. Bulwinkle (D)
William O. Burgin (D)
J. Bayard Clark (D)
Harold D. Cooley (D)
Robert L. Doughton (D)
Carl T. Durham (D)
John H. Folger (D)
John H. Kerr (D)
Cameron Morrison (D)
Zebulon Weaver (D)

NORTH DAKOTA

Senators

Gerald P. Nye (R)
William Langer (R)

Representatives

Usher L. Burdick (R)
William Lemke (R)

OHIO

Senators

Robert A. Taft (R)
Harold H. Burton (R)

Representatives

George H. Bender (R)
Frances P. Bolton (R)
Walter E. Brehm (R)
Clarence J. Brown (R)
Henderson H. Carson (R)
Cliff Clevenger (R)
Robert Crosser (D)
Charles H. Elston (R)
Michael A. Feighan (D)
Percy W. Griffiths (R)
William E. Hess (R)
Harry P. Jeffrey (R)
Thomas A. Jenkins (R)
Robert F. Jones (R)
Michael J. Kirwan (D)
Earl R. Lewis (R)
Edward O. McCowen (R)
J. Harry McGregor (R)
Homer A. Ramey (R)
Ed Rowe (R)
Frederick C. Smith (R)
John M. Vorys (R)
Alvin F. Weichel (R)

OKLAHOMA

Senators

J. W. Elmer Thomas (D)
Edward H. Moore (R)

Representatives

Lyle H. Boren (D)
Wesley E. Disney (D)
Jed Johnson (D)
A. S. Mike Monroney (D)
Jack Nichols (D) r. July 1943
Ross Rizley (R)
Paul Stewart (D)
William G. Stigler (D) s. 1944
Victor Wickersham (D)

OREGON

Senators

Charles L. McNary (R)
d. Feb. 1944
Guy Cordon (R) s. 1944

Rufus C. Holman (R)

Representatives

Homer D. Angell (R)
Harris Ellsworth (R)
James W. Mott (R)
Lowell Stockman (R)

PENNSYLVANIA

Senators

James J. Davis (R)
Joseph F. Guffey (D)

Representatives

Michael J. Bradley (D)
D. Emmert Brumbaugh (R)
J. William Ditter (R)
d. Nov. 1943
Herman P. Eberharter (D)
Ivor D. Fenton (R)
Grant Furlong (D)
James Gallagher (R)
Leon H. Gavin (R)
Charles L. Gerlach (R)
Wilson D. Gillette (R)
Louis E. Graham (R)
Chester H. Gross (R)
Daniel K. Hoch (D)
Augustine B. Kelley (D)
J. Roland Kinzer (R)
John C. Kunkel (R)
Samuel K. McConnell (R)
s. 1944
James P. McGranery (D)
r. Nov. 1943
Thomas B. Miller (R)
John W. Murphy (D)
Francis J. Myers (D)
C. Frederick Pracht (R)
Joseph M. Pratt (R) s. 1944
Robert L. Rodgers (R)
Thomas E. Scanlon (D)
Hugh D. Scott, Jr. (R)
John E. Sheridan (D)
Richard M. Simpson (R)
J. Buell Snyder (D)
Harve Tibbott (R)

William I. Troutman (R)
r. Jan. 1945
James E. Van Zandt (R)
r. Sept. 1943
Francis E. Walter (D)
Samuel A. Weiss (D)
James Wolfenden (R)
James A. Wright (D)

RHODE ISLAND

Senators

Peter G. Gerry (D)
Theodore F. Green (D)

Representatives

John E. Fogarty (D)
r. Dec. 1944
Aime J. Forand (D)

SOUTH CAROLINA

Senators

Ellison D. Smith (D)
d. Nov. 1944
Wilton E. Hall (D)
s. 1944

Burnet R. Maybank (D)

Representatives

Joseph R. Bryson (D)
Hampton P. Fulmer (D)
d. Oct. 1944
Willa L. Fulmer (D) s. 1944
Butler B. Hare (D)
John L. McMillan (D)
James P. Richards (D)
L. Mendel Rivers (D)

SOUTH DAKOTA

Senators

J. Chandler Gurney (R)
Harlan J. Bushfield (R)

Representatives

Francis H. Case (R)
Karl E. Mundt (R)

TENNESSEE

Senators

Kenneth D. McKellar (D)
A. Tom Stewart (D)

Representatives

Jere Cooper (D)
Wirt Courtney (D)
Clifford Davis (D)
Albert A. Gore (D)
John Jennings, Jr. (R)
Estes Kefauver (D)
Jim Nance McCord (D)
Thomas J. Murray (D)
J. Percy Priest (D)
B. Carroll Reece (R)

TEXAS

Senators

Tom T. Connally (D)
W. Lee O'Daniel (D)

Representatives

Lindley Beckworth (D)
Martin Dies, Jr. (D)
O. Clark Fisher (D)
Ed Gossett (D)
Luther A. Johnson (D)
Lyndon B. Johnson (D)
Paul J. Kilday (D)
Richard M. Kleberg (D)
Fritz G. Lanham (D)
George H. Mahon (D)
Joseph J. Mansfield (D)
Wright Patman (D)
Nat Patton (D)
William R. Poage (D)
Sam Rayburn (D)
Sam M. Russell (D)
Hatton W. Sumners (D)
Albert Thomas (D)
R. Ewing Thomason (D)
Milton H. West (D)
Eugene Worley (D)

UTAH

Senators

Elbert D. Thomas (D)
Abe Murdock (D)

Representatives

Walter K. Granger (D)
J. W. Robinson (D)

VERMONT

Senators

Warren R. Austin (R)
George D. Aiken (R)

Representative

Charles A. Plumley (R)

VIRGINIA

Senators

Carter Glass (D)
Harry F. Byrd (D)

Representatives

Schuyler Otis Bland (D)
Thomas G. Burch (D)
Ralph H. Daughton (D)
Patrick H. Drewry (D)
John W. Flannagan, Jr. (D)
Winder R. Harris (D)
A. Willis Robertson (D)
Dave E. Satterfield, Jr. (D)
Howard W. Smith (D)
Clifton A. Woodrum (D)

WASHINGTON

Senators

Homer T. Bone (D)
Warren G. Magnuson (D)

Monrad C. Wallgren (D)

Representatives

John M. Coffee (D)
Hal Holmes (R)
Walter F.Horan (R)
Henry M. Jackson (D)
Warren G. Magnuson (D)
Fred Norman (R)

WEST VIRGINIA

Senators

Harley M. Kilgore (D)
Chapman Revercomb (R)

Representatives

Hubert S. Ellis (R)
John Kee (D)
Jennings Randolph (D)
Edward G. Rohrbough (R)
Andrew C. Schiffler (R)
Joe L. Smith (D)

WISCONSIN

Senators

Robert M. La Follette, Jr. (Progressive)
Alexander Wiley (R)

Representatives

LaVern R. Dilweg (D)
Merlin Hull (R)
Frank B. Keefe (R)
Howard J. McMurray (D)
Reid F. Murray (R)
Alvin E. O'Konski (R)
Harry Sauthoff (Progressive)
Lawrence H. Smith (R)
William H. Stevenson (R)
Thaddeus F. B. Wasielewski (D)

WYOMING

Senators

Joseph C. O'Mahoney (D)
Edward V. Robertson (R)

Representative

Frank A. Barrett (R)

SEVENTY-NINTH CONGRESS

January 3, 1945 to January 3, 1947

President of The Senate: Harry S Truman
President Pro Tempore of The Senate: Kenneth McKellar
Speaker of The House of Representatives: Sam Rayburn

ALABAMA

Senators

John H. Bankhead 2d (D) d. Nov. 1946
George R. Swift ta. 1946
John J. Sparkman (D) s. 1946

Lister Hill (D)

Representatives

George W. Andrews (D)
Frank W. Boykin (D)
George M. Grant (D)
Sam Hobbs (D)
Pete Jarman (D)
Carter Manasco (D)
Luther Patrick (D)
Albert Rains (D)
John J. Sparkman (D) r. Nov. 1946

ARIZONA

Senators

Carl Hayden (D)
Ernest W. McFarland (D)

Representatives

Richard F. Harless (D)
John R. Murdock (D)

ARKANSAS

Senators

John L. McClellan (D)
J. William Fulbright (D)

Representatives

Fadjo Cravens (D)
Ezekiel C. Gathings (D)
Oren Harris (D)
Brooks Hays (D)
Wilbur D. Mills (D)
William F. Norrell (D)
James W. Trimble (D)

CALIFORNIA

Senators

Hiram W. Johnson (R) d. Aug. 1945
William F. Knowland (R)

Sheridan Downey (D)

Representatives

John Z. Anderson (R)
Helen Gahagan Douglas (D)
Clyde G. Doyle (D)
Alfred J. Elliott (D)
Clair Engle (D)
Bertrand W. Gearhart (R)
Franck R. Havenner (D)
Ned R. Healy (D)
Carl Hinshaw (R)
Chet Holifield (D)
Edouard V. M. Izac (D)
Leroy Johnson (R)
Cecil R. King (D)
Clarence F. Lea (D,R)
Gordon L. McDonough (R)
George P. Miller (D)
George E. Outland (D)
Ellis E. Patterson (D)
John Phillips (R)
Harry R. Sheppard (D)
John H. Tolan (D)
H. Jerry Voorhis (D)
Richard J. Welch (R)

COLORADO

Senators

Edwin C. Johnson (D)
Eugene D. Millikin (R)

Representatives

J. Edgar Chenoweth (D)
Dean M. Gillespie (R)
William S. Hill (R)
Robert F. Rockwell (R)

CONNECTICUT

Senators

Francis T. Maloney (D) d. Jan. 1945
Thomas C. Hart (R)

Brien McMahon (D)

Representatives

James P. Geelan (D)
Herman P. Kopplemann (D)
Clare Boothe Luce (R)
Joseph F. Ryter (D)
Joseph E. Talbot (R)
Chase Going Woodhouse (D)

DELAWARE

Senators

James M. Tunnell (D)
C. Douglass Buck (R)

Representative

Philip A. Traynor (D)

FLORIDA

Senators

Charles O. Andrews (D) d. Sept. 1946
Spessard L. Holland (D) s. 1946

Claude D. Pepper (D)

Representatives

Arthur P. Cannon (D)
Joe Hendricks (D)
J. Hardin Peterson (D)
Emory H. Price (D)
Dwight L. Rogers (D)
Robert L. F. Sikes (D)

GEORGIA

Senators

Walter F. George (D)
Richard B. Russell (D)

Representatives

Paul Brown (D)
A. Sidney Camp (D)
Edward E. Cox (D)
Helen Douglas Mankin (D) s. 1946
John S. Gibson (D)
Stephen Pace (D)
Hugh Peterson (D)
Robert Ramspeck (D) r. Dec. 1945
Malcolm C. Tarver (D)
Carl Vinson (D)
John S. Wood (D)

IDAHO

Senators

John Thomas (R) d. Nov. 1945
Charles C. Gossett (D) ta. 1945

Glen H. Taylor (D)

Representatives

Henry C. Dworshak (R)
Compton I. White (D)

ILLINOIS

Senators

Scott W. Lucas (D)
C. Wayland Brooks (R)

Representatives

Leo E. Allen (R)
Leslie C. Arends (R)
Cecil W. Bishop (R)
Robert B. Chiperfield (R)
Ralph E. Church (R)
Roy Clippinger (R)
William L. Dawson (D)
Everett M. Dirksen (R)
Emily Taft Douglas (D)
Thomas S. Gordon (D)
Martin Gorski (D)
James V. Heidinger (R)
Evan Howell (R)
Anton J. Johnson (R)
Edward A. Kelly (D)
William W. Link (D)
Rolla C. McMillen (R)
Noah M. Mason (R)
Thomas J. O'Brien (D)
Melvin Price (D)
Chauncey W. Reed (R)
Alexander J. Resa (D)
William A. Rowan (D)
Adolph J. Sabath (D)
Sidney E. Simpson (R)
Jessie Sumner (R)
Charles W. Vursell (R)

INDIANA

Senators

Raymond E. Willis (R)
Homer E. Capehart (R)

Representatives

George W. Gillie (R)
Robert A. Grant (R)
Charles A. Halleck (R)
Forest A. Harness (R)
Noble J. Johnson (R)
Charles M. La Follette (R)
Gerald W. Landis (R)
Louis Ludlow (D)
Ray J. Madden (D)
Raymond S. Springer (R)
Earl Wilson (R)

IOWA

Senators

George A. Wilson (R)
Bourke B. Hickenlooper (R)

Representatives

Paul Cunningham (R)
James I. Dolliver (R)
John W. Gwynne (R)
Charles B. Hoeven (R)
Ben F. Jensen (R)
Karl M. LeCompte (R)
Thomas E. Martin (R)
Henry O. Talle (R)

KANSAS

Senators

Arthur Capper (R)
Clyde M. Reed (R)

Representatives

Frank Carlson (R)
Albert M. Cole (R)
Clifford R. Hope (R)
Edward H. Rees (R)
Errett P. Scrivner (R)
Thomas D. Winter (R)

KENTUCKY

Senators

Alben W. Barkley (D)

Albert B. Chandler (D)
r. Nov. 1945
William A. Stanfill (R)
ta. 1945-1946

Representatives

Joe B. Bates (D)
Virgil M. Chapman (D)
Frank L. Chelf (D)
Earle C. Clements (D)
Noble J. Gregory (D)
Andrew J. May (D)
Emmet O'Neal (D)
John M. Robsion (R)
Brent Spence (D)

LOUISIANA

Senators

John H. Overton (D)
Allen J. Ellender (D)

Representatives

A. Leonard Allen (D)
Overton Brooks (D)
James Domengeaux (D)
F. Edward Hebert
Henry D. Larcade, Jr. (D)
Charles E. McKenzie (D)
Paul H. Maloney (D)
James H. Morrison (D)

MAINE

Senators

Wallace H. White, Jr. (R)
Ralph O. Brewster (R)

Representatives

Frank Fellows (R)
Robert Hale (R)
Margaret Chase Smith (R)

MARYLAND

Senators

Millard E. Tydings (D)
George L. Radcliffe (D)

Representatives

H. Streett Baldwin (D)
J. Glenn Beall (R)
Thomas D'Alesandro, Jr. (D)
George H. Fallon (D)
Dudley G. Roe (D)
Lansdale G. Sasscer (D)

MASSACHUSETTS

Senators

David I. Walsh (D)
Leverett Saltonstall (R)

Representatives

George J. Bates (R)
Charles R. Clason (R)
James M. Curley (D)
Charles L. Gifford (R)
Angier L. Goodwin (R)
Christian A. Herter (R)
John W. Heselton (R)
Pehr G. Holmes (R)
Thomas J. Lane (D)
John W. McCormack (D)
Joseph W. Martin, Jr. (R)
Philip J. Philbin (D)
Edith Nourse Rogers (R)
Richard B. Wigglesworth (R)

MICHIGAN

Senators

Arthur H. Vandenberg (R)
Homer Ferguson (R)

Representatives

William W. Blackney (R)
Frederick V. Bradley (R)
Fred L. Crawford (R)
John D. Dingell (D)
George A. Dondero (R)
Albert J. Engel (R)
Clare E. Hoffman (R)
Frank E. Hook (D)
Bartel J. Jonkman (R)
John Lesinski (D)
Earl C. Michener (R)
George D. O'Brien (D)
Louis C. Rabaut (D)
George G. Sadowski (D)
Paul W. Shafer (R)
Jesse P. Wolcott (R)
Roy O. Woodruff (R)

MINNESOTA

Senators

Henrik Shipstead (R)
Joseph H. Ball (R)

Representatives

H. Carl Andersen (R)
August H. Andresen (R)
William J. Gallagher (D)
d. Aug. 1946
Harold C. Hagen (R)
Walter H. Judd (R)
Harold Knutson (R)
Joseph P. O'Hara (R)
William A. Pittenger (R)
Frank T. Starkey (D)

MISSISSIPPI

Senators

Theodore G. Bilbo (D)
James O. Eastland (D)

Representatives

Thomas G. Abernethy (D)
William M. Colmer (D)
Dan R. McGehee (D)
John E. Rankin (D)
Jamie L. Whitten (D)
William M. Whittington (D)
W. Arthur Winstead (D)

MISSOURI

Senators

Harry S Truman (D)
r. Jan. 1945
Frank P. Briggs (D)

Forrest C. Donnell (R)

Representatives

Samuel W. Arnold (R)
C. Jasper Bell (D)
Marion T. Bennett (R)
Clarence Cannon (D)
Albert S. J. Carnahan (D)
John J. Cochran (D)
William C. Cole (R)
Walter C. Ploeser (R)
Max Schwabe (R)
Dewey Short (R)
Roger C. Slaughter (D)
John B. Sullivan (D)
Orville Zimmerman (D)

MONTANA

Senators

Burton K. Wheeler (D)
James E. Murray (D)

Representatives

Wesley A. D'Ewart (R)
Mike Mansfield (D)
James F. O'Connor (D)
d. Jan. 1945

NEBRASKA

Senators

Hugh A. Butler (R)
Kenneth S. Wherry (R)

Representatives

Howard H. Buffett (R)
Carl T. Curtis (R)
Arthur L. Miller (R)
Karl Stefan (R)

NEVADA

Senators

Patrick A. McCarran (D)

James G. Scrugham (D)
d. June 1945
Edward P. Carville (D)

Representative

Berkeley L. Bunker (D)

NEW HAMPSHIRE

Senators

H. Styles Bridges (R)
Charles W. Tobey (R)

Representatives

Sherman Adams (R)
Chester E. Merrow (R)

NEW JERSEY

Senators

Albert W. Hawkes (R)
H. Alexander Smith (R)

Representatives

James C. Auchincloss (R)
Gordon Canfield (R)
Clifford P. Case (R)
Charles A. Eaton (R)
T. Millet Hand (R)
Edward J. Hart (D)
Fred A. Hartley, Jr. (R)
Robert W. Kean (R)
Frank A. Mathews, Jr. (R)
Mary T. Norton (D)
D. Lane Powers (R)
r. Aug. 1945
Frank L. Sundstrom (R)
J. Parnell Thomas (R)
Harry L. Towe (R)
Charles A. Wolverton (R)

NEW MEXICO

Senators

Carl A. Hatch (D)
Dennis Chavez (D)

Representatives

Clinton P. Anderson (D)
Antonio M. Fernandez (D)

NEW YORK

Senators

Robert F. Wagner (D)
James M. Mead (D)

Representatives

Walter G. Andrews (R)
Joseph C. Baldwin (R)
William B. Barry (D)
d. Oct. 1946
Augustus W. Bennet (R)
Sol Bloom (D)
Ellsworth B. Buck (R)
Charles A. Buckley (D)
John C. Butler (R)
William T. Byrne (D)
Emanuel Celler (D)
W. Sterling Cole (R)
James J. Delaney (D)
John J. Delaney (D)
Samuel Dickstein (D)
r. Dec. 1945
Edward J. Elsaesser (R)
Hadwen C. Fuller (R)
Ralph A. Gamble (R)
Ralph W. Gwinn (R)
Edwin A. Hall (R)
Leonard W. Hall (R)
Clarence E. Hancock (R)
James J. Heffernan (D)
Bernard W. Kearney (R)
Eugene J. Keogh (D)
Clarence E. Kilburn (R)
Arthur G. Klein (D) s. 1946
Henry J. Latham (R)
Jay LeFevre (R)
Walter A. Lynch (D)
Vito Marcantonio (Amer. Labor)
Donald L. O'Toole (D)
Joseph L. Pfeifer (D)
Adam Clayton Powell, Jr. (D)
Peter A. Quinn (D)
Benjamin J. Rabin (D)
Leo F. Rayfiel (D)
Daniel A. Reed (R)
James A. Roe (D)
George F. Rogers (D)
John J. Rooney (D)
Edgar A. Sharp (R)
Andrew L. Somers (D)
John Taber (R)
Dean P. Taylor (R)
James H. Torrens (D)
James W. Wadsworth, Jr. (R)

NORTH CAROLINA

Senators

Josiah W. Bailey (D)
d. Dec. 1946
Clyde R. Hoey (D)

Representatives

Graham A. Barden (D)
Herbert C. Bonner (D)
Alfred L. Bulwinkle (D)
William O. Burgin (D)
d. Apr. 1946
J. Bayard Clark (D)
Harold D. Cooley (D)
Robert L. Doughton (D)
Carl T. Durham (D)
John H. Folger (D)
Joe W. Ervin (D)
d. Dec. 1945
Sam J. Ervin, Jr. (D)
s. 1946
John H. Kerr (D)
Eliza Jane Pratt (D)
s. 1946
Zebulon Weaver (D)

NORTH DAKOTA

Senators

William Langer (R)

John Moses (D) d. Mar. 1945
Milton R. Young (R)

Representatives

William Lemke (R)
Charles R. Robertson (R)

OHIO

Senators

Robert A. Taft (R)

Harold H. Burton (R)
r. Sept. 1945
James W. Huffman (D)
ta. 1945-1946
Kingsley A. Taft (R)
s. 1946

Representatives

George H. Bender (R)
Frances P. Bolton (R)
Walter E. Brehm (R)
Clarence J. Brown (R)
Cliff Clevenger (R)
Robert Crosser (D)
Charles H. Elston (R)
Michael A. Feighan (D)
Edward J. Gardner (D)
Percy W. Griffiths (R)
William E. Hess (R)
Walter B. Huber (D)
Thomas A. Jenkins (R)
Robert F. Jones (R)
Michael J. Kirwan (D)
Earl R. Lewis (R)
Edward O. McCowen (R)
J. Harry McGregor (R)
Homer A. Ramey (R)
Frederick C. Smith (R)
William R. Thom (D)
John M. Vorys (R)
Alvin F. Weichel (R)

OKLAHOMA

Senators

J. W. Elmer Thomas (D)
Edward H. Moore (R)

Representatives

Lyle H. Boren (D)
Jed Johnson (D)
A. S. Mike Monroney (D)
Ross Rizley (R)
George B. Schwabe (R)
Paul Stewart (D)
William G. Stigler (D)
Victor Wickersham (D)

OREGON

Senators

Guy Gordon (R)
Wayne L. Morse (R)

Representatives

Homer D. Angell (R)
Harris Ellsworth (R)
James W. Mott (R)
A. Walter Norblad, Jr. (R)
Lowell Stockman (R)

PENNSYLVANIA

Senators

Joseph F. Guffey (D)
Francis J. Myers (D)

Representatives

William A. Barrett (D)
Michael J. Bradley (D)
D. Emmert Brumbaugh (R)
Frank Buchanan (D) s. 1946
Howard E. Campbell (R)
Robert J. Corbett (R)
Herman P. Eberharter (D)
Ivor D. Fenton (R)
Daniel J. Flood (D)
James G. Fulton (R)
Leon H. Gavin (R)
Charles L. Gerlach (R)
Wilson D. Gillette (R)
Louis E. Graham (R)
William T. Granahan (D)
William J. Green, Jr. (D)
Chester H. Gross (R)
Daniel K. Hoch (D)
Carl H. Hoffman (R) s. 1946
Augustine B. Kelley (D)
J. Roland Kinzer (R)
John C. Kunkel (R)
Samuel K. McConnell, Jr. (R)
Herbert J. McGlinchey (D)
Thomas E. Morgan (D)
John W. Murphy (D) r. July 1946
Robert F. Rich (R)
Robert L. Rodgers (R)
John E. Sheridan (D)
Richard M. Simpson (R)
J. Buell Snyder (D) d. Feb. 1946
Harve Tibbott (R)
Francis E. Walter (D)
Samuel A. Weiss (D) r. Jan. 1946
James Wolfenden (R)

RHODE ISLAND

Senators

Peter G. Gerry (D)
Theodore F. Green (D)

Representatives

John E. Fogarty (D)
Aime J. Forand (D)

SOUTH CAROLINA

Senators

Burnet R. Maybank (D)
Olin D. Johnston (D)

Representatives

Joseph R. Bryson (D)
Butler B. Hare (D)
John L. McMillan (D)
James P. Richards (D)
John J. Riley (D)
L. Mendel Rivers (D)

SOUTH DAKOTA

Senators

J. Chandler Gurney (R)
Harlan J. Bushfield (R)

Representatives

Francis H. Case (R)
Karl E. Mundt (R)

TENNESSEE

Senators

Kenneth D. McKellar (D)
A. Tom Stewart (D)

Representatives

Jere Cooper (D)
Wirt Courtney (D)
Clifford Davis (D)
Harold H. Earthman (D)
Albert A. Gore (D)
John Jennings, Jr. (R)
Estes Kefauver (D)
Thomas J. Murray (D)
J. Percy Priest (D)
B. Carroll Reece (R)

TEXAS

Senators

Tom T. Connally (D)
W. Lee O'Daniel (D)

Representatives

Lindley Beckworth (D)
Jesse M. Combs (D)
O. Clark Fisher (D)
Ed Gossett (D)
Luther A. Johnson (D)
r. July 1946
Lyndon B. Johnson (D)
Paul J. Kilday (D)
Fritz G. Lanham (D)
John E. Lyle, Jr. (D)
George H. Mahon (D)
Joseph J. Mansfield (D)
Wright Patman (D)
Tom Pickett (D)

William R. Poage (D)
Sam Rayburn (D)
Sam M. Russell (D)
Hatton W. Sumners (D)
Albert Thomas (D)
R. Ewing Thomason (D)
Milton H. West (D)
Eugene Worley (D)

UTAH

Senators

Elbert D. Thomas (D)
Abe Murdock (E)

Representatives

Walter K. Granger (D)
J. W. Robinson (D)

VERMONT

Senators

Warren R. Austin (R)
r. Aug. 1945
Ralph E. Flanders (R) ta. 1946
George D. Aiken (R)

Representative

Charles A. Plumley (R)

VIRGINIA

Senators

Carter Glass (D) d. May 1946
Thomas G. Burch (D) ta. 1946

Harry F. Byrd (D)

Representatives

J. Lindsay Almond, Jr. (D)
s. 1946
Schuyler Otis Bland (D)
Thomas G. Burch (D) r. May 1946
Ralph H. Daughton (D)
Patrick H. Drewry (D)
John W. Flannagan, Jr. (D)
J. Vaughan Gary s. 1945 (D)
A. Willis Robertson (D)
r. Nov. 1946
Dave E. Satterfield, Jr. (D)
r. Nov. 1945
Howard W. Smith (D)
Clifton A. Woodrum (D) r. 1945

WASHINGTON

Senators

Warren G. Magnuson (D)
Hugh B. Mitchell (D) s. 1945

Representatives

John M. Coffee (D)
Hugh DeLacy (D)
Hal Holmes (R)
Walter F. Horan (R)
Henry M. Jackson (D)
Charles R. Savage (D)

WEST VIRGINIA

Senators

Harley M. Kilgore (D)
Chapman Revercomb (R)

Representatives

Cleveland M. Bailey (D)
Hubert S. Ellis (R)
Erland H. Hedrick (D)
John Kee (D)
Matthew M. Neeley (D)
Jennings Randolph (D)

WISCONSIN

Senators

Robert M. La Follette, Jr.
(Progressive)
Alexander Wiley (R)

Representatives

Andrew J. Biemiller (D)
John W. Byrnes (R)
Robert K. Henry (R)
d. Nov. 1946
Merlin Hull (R)
Frank B. Keefe (R)
Reid F. Murray (R)
Alvin E. O'Konski (R)
Lawrence H. Smith (R)
William H. Stevenson (R)
Thaddeus F. B. Wasielewski (D)

WYOMING

Senators

Joseph C. O'Mahoney (D)
Edward V. Robertson (R)

Representative

Frank A. Barrett (R)

EIGHTIETH CONGRESS

January 3, 1947 to January 3, 1949

President of The Senate:	None
President Pro Tempore of The Senate:	Arthur H. Vandenberg
Speaker of The House of Representatives:	Joseph W. Martin, Jr.

ALABAMA

Senators

Lister Hill (D)
John J. Sparkman (D)

Representatives

George W. Andrews (D)
Laurie C. Battle (D)
Frank W. Boykin (D)
George M. Grant (D)
Sam Hobbs (D)
Pete Jarman (D)
Robert E. Jones, Jr. (D)
Carter Manasco (D)
Albert Rains (D)

ARIZONA

Senators

Carl Hayden (D)
Ernest W. McFarland (D)

Representatives

Richard F. Harless (D)
John R. Murdock (D)

ARKANSAS

Senators

John L. McClellan (D)
J. William Fulbright (D)

Representatives

Fadjo Cravens (D)
Ezekiel C. Gathings (D)
Oren Harris (D)
Brooks Hays (D)
Wilbur D. Mills (D)
William F. Norrell (D)
James W. Trimble (D)

CALIFORNIA

Senators

Sheridan Downey (D)
William F. Knowland (R)

Representatives

John J. Allen, Jr. (R)
John Z. Anderson (R)
Willis W. Bradley (R)
Ernest K. Bramblett (R)
Helen Gahagan Douglas (D)
Alfred J. Elliott (D)
Clair Engle (D)
Charles K. Fletcher (R)
Bertrand W. Gearhart (R)
Franck R. Havenner (D)
Carl Hinshaw (R)
Chet Holifield (D)
Donald L. Jackson (R)
Leroy Johnson (R)
Cecil R. King (D)
Clarence F. Lea (D,R)
Gordon L. McDonough (R)
George P. Miller (D)
Richard M. Nixon (R)
John Phillips (R)
Norris Poulson (R)
Harry R. Sheppard (D)
Richard J. Welch (R)

COLORADO

Senators

Edwin C. Johnson (D)
Eugene D. Millikin (R)

Representatives

John A. Carroll (D)
J. Edgar Chenoweth (D)
William S. Hill (R)
Robert F. Rockwell (R)

CONNECTICUT

Senators

Brien McMahon (D)
Raymond E. Baldwin (R)

Representatives

Ellsworth B. Foote (R)
John Davis Lodge (R)
William J. Miller (R)
James T. Patterson (R)
Antoni N. Sadlak (R)
Horace Seely-Brown, Jr. (R)

DELAWARE

Senators

C. Douglass Buck (R)
John J. Williams (R)

Representative

J. Caleb Boggs (R)

FLORIDA

Senators

Claude D. Pepper (D)
Spessard L. Holland (D)

Representatives

Joe Hendricks (D)
J. Hardin Peterson (D)
Emory H. Price (D)
Dwight L. Rogers (D)
Robert L. F. Sikes (D)
George A. Smathers (D)

GEORGIA

Senators

Walter F. George (D)
Richard B. Russell (D)

Representatives

Paul Brown (D)
A. Sidney Camp (D)
Edward E. Cox (D)
James C. Davis (D)
Henderson L. Lanham (D)
Stephen Pace (D)
Prince H. Preston, Jr. (D)
Carl Vinson (D)
William M. Wheeler (D)
John S. Wood (D)

IDAHO

Senators

Glen H. Taylor (D)
Henry C. Dworshak (R)

Representatives

Abe McGregor Goff (R)
John C. Sanborn (R)

ILLINOIS

Senators

Scott W. Lucas (D)
C. Wayland Brooks (R)

Representatives

Leo E. Allen (R)
Leslie C. Arends (R)
Cecil W. Bishop (R)
Fred E. Busbey (R)
Robert B. Chiperfield (R)
Ralph E. Church (R)
Roy Clippinger (R)
William L. Dawson (D)
Everett M. Dirksen (R)
Thomas S. Gordon (D)
Martin Gorski (D)
Evan Howell (R) r. Oct. 1947
Edward H. Jenison (R)
Anton J. Johnson (R)
Rolla C. McMillen (R)
Noah M. Mason (R)
Thomas J. O'Brien (D)
Thomas L. Owens (R)
d. June 1948
Melvin Price (D)
Chauncey W. Reed (R)
Adolph J. Sabath (D)
Sidney E. Simpson (R)
William G. Stratton (R)
Robert J. Twyman (R)
Richard B. Vail (R)
Charles W. Vursell (R)

INDIANA

Senators

Homer E. Capehart (R)
William E. Jenner (R)

Representatives

George W. Gillie (R)
Robert A. Grant (R)
Charles A. Halleck (R)
Forest A. Harness (R)
Ralph Harvey (R)
Noble J. Johnson (R) r. July 1948
Gerald W. Landis (R)
Louis Ludlow (D)
Ray J. Madden (D)
Edward A. Mitchell (R)
Raymond S. Springer (R)
d. Aug. 1947
Earl Wilson (R)

IOWA

Senators

George A. Wilson (R)
Bourke B. Hickenlooper (R)

Representatives

Paul Cunningham (R)
James I. Dolliver (R)
John W. Gwynne (R)
Charles B. Hoeven (R)
Ben F. Jensen (R)
Karl M. LeCompte (R)
Thomas E. Martin (R)
Henry O. Talle (R)

KANSAS

Senators

Arthur Capper (R)
Clyde M. Reed (R)

Representatives

Albert M. Cole (R)
Clifford R. Hope (R)
Herbert A. Meyer (R)
Edward H. Rees (R)
Errett P. Scrivner (R)
Wint Smith (R)

KENTUCKY

Senators

Alben W. Barkley (D)
John Sherman Cooper (R)

Representatives

Joe B. Bates (D)
Virgil M. Chapman (D)
Frank L. Chelf (D)
Earle C. Clements (D) r. Jan. 1948
Noble J. Gregory (D)
William Lewis (R) s. 1948
W. Howes Meade (R)
Thruston B. Morton (R)
John M. Robsion (R) d. Feb. 1948
Brent Spence (D)
John A. Whitaker (R) s. 1948

LOUISIANA

Senators

John H. Overton (D) d. May 1948
William C. Feazel (D) ta. 1948

Russell B. Long (D) s. 1948
Allen J. Ellender (D)

Representatives

A. Leonard Allen (D)
T. Hale Boggs (D)
Overton Brooks (D)
James Domengeaux (D)
F. Edward Hebert (D)
Henry D. Larcade, Jr. (D)
James H. Morrison (D)
Otto E. Passman (D)

MAINE

Senators

Wallace H. White, Jr. (R)
Ralph O. Brewster (R)

Representatives

Frank Fellows (R)
Robert Hale (R)
Margaret Chase Smith (R)

MARYLAND

Senators

Millard E. Tydings (D)
Herbert R. O'Connor (D)

Representatives

J. Glenn Beall (R)
Thomas D'Alesandro, Jr. (D)
r. May 1947
George H. Fallon (R)
Edward A. Garmatz (D)
Hugh A. Meade (D)
Edward T. Miller (R)
Lansdale G. Sasscer (D)

MASSACHUSETTS

Senators

Leverett Saltonstall (R)
Henry Cabot Lodge, Jr. (R)

Representatives

George J. Bates (R)
Charles R. Clason (R)
Harold D. Donohue (D)
Charles L. Gifford (R)
d. Aug. 1947
Angier L. Goodwin (R)
Christian A. Herter (R)
John W. Heselton (R)
John F. Kennedy (D)
Thomas J. Lane (D)
John W. McCormack (D)
Joseph W. Martin, Jr. (R)
Donald W. Nicholson (R)
Philip J. Philbin (D)
Edith Nourse Rogers (R)
Richard B. Wigglesworth (R)

MICHIGAN

Senators

Arthur H. Vandenberg (R)
Homer Ferguson (R)

Representatives

John B. Bennett (R)
William W. Blackney (R)
Frederick V. Bradley (R)
d. May 1947
Howard A. Coffin (R)
Fred L. Crawford (R)
John D. Dingell (D)
George A. Dondero (R)
Albert J. Engel (R)
Clare E. Hoffman (R)
Bartel J. Jonkman (R)
John Lesinski (D)
Earl C. Michener (R)
Charles E. Potter (R)
George G. Sadowski (D)
Paul W. Shafer (R)
Jesse P. Wolcott (R)
Roy O. Woodruff (R)
Harold F. Youngblood (R)

MINNESOTA

Senators

Joseph H. Ball (R)
Edward J. Thye (R)

Representatives

H. Carl Andersen (R)
August H. Andresen (R)
John A. Blatnik (D)
Edward J. Devitt (R)
Harold C. Hagen (R)
Walter H. Judd (R)
Harold Knutson (R)
George E. MacKinnon (R)
Joseph P. O'Hara (R)

MISSISSIPPI

Senators

Theodore G. Bilbo (D)
d. Aug. 1947
John C. Stennis (D)

James O. Eastland (D)

Representatives

Thomas G. Abernethy (D)
William M. Colmer (D)
John E. Rankin (D)
Jamie L. Whitten (D)
William M. Whittington (D)
John Bell Williams (D)
W. Arthur Winstead (D)

MISSOURI

Senators

Forrest C. Donnell (R)
James P. Kem (R)

Representatives

Samuel W. Arnold (R)
Claude I. Bakewell (R)
Parke M. Banta (R)
C. Jasper Bell (D)
Marion T. Bennett (R)
Clarence Cannon (D)
William C. Cole (R)
Paul C. Jones (D) s. 1948

Frank M. Karsten (D)
Walter C. Ploeser (R)
Albert L. Reeves, Jr. (R)
Max Schwabe (R)
Dewey Short (R)
Orville Zimmerman (D)
d. Apr. 1948

MONTANA

Senators

James E. Murray (D)
Zales N. Ecton (R)

Representatives

Wesley A. D'Ewart (R)
Mike Mansfield (D)

NEBRASKA

Senators

Hugh A. Butler (R)
Kenneth S. Wherry (R)

Representatives

Howard H. Buffett (R)
Carl T. Curtis (R)
Arthur L. Miller (R)
Karl Stefan (R)

NEVADA

Senators

Patrick A. McCarran (D)
George W. Malone (R)

Representative

Charles H. Russell (R)

NEW HAMPSHIRE

Senators

H. Styles Bridges (R)
Charles W. Tobey (R)

Representatives

Norris Cotton (R)
Chester E. Merrow (R)

NEW JERSEY

Senators

Albert W. Hawkes (R)
H. Alexander Smith (R)

Representatives

James C. Auchincloss (R)
Gordon Canfield (R)
Clifford P. Case (R)
Charles A. Eaton (R)
T. Millet Hand (R)
Edward J. Hart (D)
Fred A. Hartley, Jr. (R)
Robert W. Kean (R)
Frank A. Mathews, Jr. (R)
Mary T. Norton (D)
Frank L. Sundstrom (R)
J. Parnell Thomas (R)
Harry L. Towe (R)
Charles A. Wolverton (R)

NEW MEXICO

Senators

Carl A. Hatch (D)
Dennis Chavez (D)

Representatives

Antonio M. Fernandez (D)
Georgia L. Lusk (D)

NEW YORK

Senators

Robert F. Wagner (D)
Irving M. Ives (R)

Representatives

Walter G. Andrews (R)
Sol Bloom (D)
Ellsworth B. Buck (R)
Charles A. Buckley (D)
John C. Butler (R)
William T. Byrne (D)
Emanuel Celler (D)
W. Sterling Cole (R)
Frederic R. Coudert, Jr. (R)
John J. Delaney (D) d. Nov. 1948
Edward J. Elsaesser (R)
Hadwen C. Fuller (R)
Ralph A. Gamble (R)
Ralph W. Gwinn (R)
Edwin A. Hall (R)
Leonard W. Hall (R)
James J. Heffernan (D)
Leo Isacson (Amer. Labor)
s. 1948
Jacob K. Javits (R)
Bernard W. Kearney (R)
Kenneth B. Keating (R)
Eugene J. Keogh (D)
Clarence E. Kilburn (R)
Arthur G. Klein (D)
Henry J. Latham (R)
Jay LeFevre (R)
Walter A. Lynch (D)
Gregory McMahon (R)
W. Kingsland Macy (R)
Vito Marcantonio (Amer. Labor)
Abraham J. Multer (D)
Robert J. Nodar, Jr. (R)
Donald L. O'Toole (D)
Joseph L. Pfeifer (D)
David M. Potts (R)
Adam Clayton Powell, Jr. (D)
Benjamin J. Rabin (D)
r. Dec. 1947
Leo F. Rayfiel (D) r. Sept. 1947
Daniel A. Reed (R)
R. Walter Riehlman (R)
John J. Rooney (D)
Robert T. Ross (R)
Katherine St. George (R)
Andrew L. Somers (D)
John Taber (R)
Dean P. Taylor (R)
James W. Wadsworth, Jr. (R)

NORTH CAROLINA

Senators

Clyde R. Hoey (D)

William B. Umstead (D)
ta. 1947-1948
J. Melville Broughton (D) s. 1948

Representatives

Graham A. Barden (D)
Herbert C. Bonner (D)
Alfred L. Bulwinkle (D)
J. Bayard Clark (D)
Harold D. Cooley (D)
Charles B. Deane (D)
Robert L. Doughton (D)
Carl T. Durham (D)
John H. Folger (D)
Hamilton C. Jones (D)
John H. Kerr (D)
Monroe M. Redden (D)

NORTH DAKOTA

Senators

William Langer (R)
Milton R. Young (R)

Representatives

William Lemke (R)
Charles R. Robertson (R)

OHIO

Senators

Robert A. Taft (R)
John W. Bricker (R)

Representatives

George H. Bender (R)
Frances P. Bolton (R)
Walter E. Brehm (R)
Clarence J. Brown (R)
Raymond H. Burke (R)
Henderson H. Carson (R)
Cliff Clevenger (R)
Robert Crosser (D)
Charles H. Elston (R)
Michael A. Feighan (D)
William E. Hess (R)
Walter B. Huber (D)
Percy W. Griffiths (R)
Thomas A. Jenkins (R)
Robert F. Jones (R) r. Sept. 1947
Michael J. Kirwan (D)
Earl R. Lewis (R)
Edward O. McCowen (R)
William M. McCulloch (R)
J. Harry McGregor (R)
Homer A. Ramey (R)
Frederick C. Smith (R)
John M. Vorys (R)
Alvin F. Weichel (R)

OKLAHOMA

Senators

J. W. Elmer Thomas (D)
Edward H. Moore (R)

Representatives

Carl Albert (D)
Glen D. Johnson (D)
A. S. Mike Monroney (D)
Toby Morris (D)
Preston E. Peden (D)
Ross Rizley (R)
George B.Schwabe (R)
William G. Stigler (D)

OREGON

Senators

Guy Cordon (R)
Wayne L. Morse (R)

Representatives

Homer D. Angell (R)
Harris Ellsworth (R)
A. Walter Norblad, Jr. (R)
Lowell Stockman (R)

PENNSYLVANIA

Senators

Francis J. Myers (D)
Edward Martin (R)

Representatives

Frank Buchanan (D)
E. Wallace Chadwick (R)
Robert J. Corbett (R)
William J. Crow (R)
Paul B. Dague (R)
Herman P. Eberharter (D)
Ivor D. Fenton (R)
James G. Fulton (R)
James Gallagher (R)
Leon H. Gavin (R)
Charles L. Gerlach (R)
d. May 1947
Wilson D. Gillette (R)
Louis E. Graham (R)
Chester H. Gross (R)
Mitchell Jenkins (R)
Carroll D. Kearns (R)
Augustine B. Kelley (D)
John C. Kunkel (R)
Franklin H. Lichtenwalter (R)
Samuel K. McConnell, Jr. (R)
John R. McDowell (R)
Robert N. McGarvey (R)
Franklin J. Maloney (R)
Thomas E. Morgan (D)
Frederick A. Muhlenberg (R)
Robert F. Rich (R)
George W. Sarbacher, Jr. (R)
James P. Scoblick (R)
Hardie Scott (R)
Hugh D. Scott, Jr. (R)
Richard M. Simpson (R)
Harve Tibbott (R)
James E. Van Zandt (R)
Francis E. Walter (D)

RHODE ISLAND

Senators

Theodore F. Green (D)
J. Howard McGrath (D)

Representatives

John E. Fogarty (D)
Aime J. Forand (D)

SOUTH CAROLINA

Senators

Burnet R. Maybank (D)
Olin D. Johnston (D)

Representatives

Joseph R. Bryson (D)
W. J. Bryan Dorn (D)
John L. McMillan (D)
James P. Richards (D)
John J. Riley (D)
L. Mendel Rivers (D)

SOUTH DAKOTA

Senators

J. Chandler Gurney (R)
Harlan J. Bushfield (R)
d. Sept. 1948

Karl E. Mundt (R) s. 1948

Representatives

Francis H. Case (R)
Karl E. Mundt (R) r. Dec. 1948

TENNESSEE

Senators

Kenneth D. McKellar (D)
A. Tom Stewart (D)

Representatives

Jere Cooper (D)
Wirt Courtney (D)
Clifford Davis (D)
Joe L. Evins (D)
Albert A. Gore (D)
John Jennings, Jr. (R)
Estes Kefauver (D)
Thomas J. Murray (D)
Dayton E. Phillips (R)
J. Percy Priest (D)

TEXAS

Senators

Tom T. Connally (D)
W. Lee O'Daniel (D)

Representatives

Lindley Beckworth (D)
Lloyd M. Bentsen, Jr. (D) s. 1948
Omar T. Burleson (D)
Jesse M. Combs (D)
O. Clark Fisher (D)
Ed Gossett (D)
Lyndon B. Johnson (D)
Paul J. Kilday (D)
Wingate H. Lucas (D)
John E. Lyle, Jr. (D)
George H. Mahon (D)
Joseph J. Mansfield (D)
d. July 1947
Wright Patman (D)
Tom Pickett (D)
William R. Poage (D)
Sam Rayburn (D)
Kenneth M. Regan (D)
Olin E. Teague (D)
Albert Thomas (D)
R. Ewing Thomason (D)
r. July 1947
Clark W. Thompson (D)
Milton H. West (D) d. Oct. 1948
J. Frank Wilson (D)
Eugene Worley (D)

UTAH

Senators

Elbert D. Thomas (D)
Arthur V. Watkins (R)

Representatives

William A. Dawson (R)
Walter K. Granger (D)

VERMONT

Senators

George D. Aiken (R)
Ralph E. Flanders (R)

Representative

Charles A. Plumley (R)

VIRGINIA

Senators

Harry F. Byrd (D)
A. Willis Robertson (D)

Representatives

Watkins M. Abbitt (D) s. 1948
J. Lindsay Almond, Jr. (D)
r. Apr. 1948
Schuyler Otis Bland (D)
Clarence G. Burton (D) s. 1948
Patrick H. Drewry (D)
d. Dec. 1947
John W. Flannagan, Jr. (D)
J. Vaughan Gary (D)
Porter Hardy, Jr. (D)
Burr P. Harrison (D)
Howard W. Smith (D)
Thomas B. Stanley (D)

WASHINGTON

Senators

Warren G. Magnuson (D)
Harry P. Cain (R)

Representatives

Hal Holmes (R)
Walter F. Horan (R)
Henry M. Jackson (D)
Homer R. Jones (R)
Russell V. Mack (R)
Fred B. Norman (R) d. Apr. 1947
Thor C. Tollefson (R)

WEST VIRGINIA

Senators

Harley M. Kilgore (D)
Chapman Revercomb (R)

Representatives

Hubert S. Ellis (R)
Erland H. Hedrick (D)
John Kee (D)
Francis J. Love (R)
Edward G. Rohrbough (R)
Melvin C. Snyder (R)

WISCONSIN

Senators

Alexander Wiley (R)
Joseph R. McCarthy (R)

Representatives

John C. Brophy (R)
John W. Byrnes (R)
Glenn R. Davis (R)
Merlin Hull (R)
Frank B. Keefe (R)
Charles J. Kersten (R)
Reid F. Murray (R)
Alvin E. O'Konski (R)
Lawrence H. Smith (R)
William H. Stevenson (R)

WYOMING

Senators

Joseph C. O'Mahoney (D)
Edward V. Robertson (R)

Representative

Frank A. Barrett (R)

EIGHTY-FIRST CONGRESS

January 3, 1949 to January 3, 1951

President of The Senate: Alben W. Barkley
President Pro Tempore of The Senate: Kenneth D. McKellar
Speaker of The House of Representatives: Sam Rayburn

ALABAMA

Senators

Lister Hill (D)
John J. Sparkman (D)

Representatives

George W. Andrews (D)
Laurie C. Battle (D)
Frank W. Boykin (D)
Edward deGraffenried (D)
Carl A. Elliott (D)
George M. Grant (D)
Sam Hobbs (D)
Robert E. Jones, Jr. (D)
Albert Rains (D)

ARIZONA

Senators

Carl Hayden (D)
Ernest W. McFarland (D)

Representatives

John R. Murdock (D)
Harold A. Patten (D)

ARKANSAS

Senators

John L. McClellan (D)
J. William Fulbright (D)

Representatives

Ezekiel C. Gathings (D)
Oren Harris (D)
Brooks Hays (D)
Wilbur D. Mills (D)
William F. Norrell (D)
Boyd Tackett (D)
James W. Trimble (D)

CALIFORNIA

Senators

Sheridan Downey (D)
r. Nov. 1950
Richard M. Nixon (R) s. 1950

William F. Knowland (R)

Representatives

John J. Allen Jr. (R)
John Z. Anderson (R)
Ernest K. Bramblett (R)
Helen Gahagan Douglas (D)
Clyde G. Doyle (D)
Clair Engle (D)
Franck R. Havenner (D)
Carl Hinshaw (R)
Chet Holifield (D)
Donald L. Jackson (R)
Leroy Johnson (R)
Cecil R. King (D)
Gordon L. McDonough (R)
Clinton D. McKinnon (D)
George P. Miller (D)
Richard M. Nixon (R)
r. Nov. 1950

John Phillips (R)
Norris Poulson (R)
Hubert B. Scudder (R)
John F. Shelley (D) s. 1950
Harry R. Sheppard (D)
Richard J. Welch (R) d. Sept. 1949
Thomas H. Werdel (R)
Cecil F. White (D)

COLORADO

Senators

Edwin C. Johnson (D)
Eugene D. Millikin (R)

Representatives

Wayne N. Aspinall (D)
John A. Carroll (D)
William S. Hill (R)
John H. Marsalis (D)

CONNECTICUT

Senators

Brien McMahon (D)

Raymond E. Baldwin (R)
r. Dec. 1949
William Benton (D) s. 1950

Representatives

John Davis Lodge (R)
John A. McGuire (D)
James T. Patterson (R)
Abraham A. Ribicoff (D)
Antoni N. Sadlak (R)
Chase Going Woodhouse (D)

DELAWARE

Senators

John J. Williams (R)
J. Allen Frear, Jr. (D)

Representative

J. Caleb Boggs (R)

FLORIDA

Senators

Claude D. Pepper (D)
Spessard L. Holland (D)

Representatives

Charles E. Bennett (D)
Albert S. Herlong, Jr. (D)
J. Hardin Peterson (D)
Dwight L. Rogers (D)
Robert L. F. Sikes (D)
George A. Smathers (D)

GEORGIA

Senators

Walter F. George (D)
Richard B. Russell (D)

Representatives

Paul Brown (D)
A. Sidney Camp (D)
Edward E. Cox (D)
James C. Davis (D)
Henderson L. Lanham (D)
Stephen Pace (D)
Prince H. Preston, Jr. (D)
Carl Vinson (D)
William M. Wheeler (D)
John S. Wood (D)

IDAHO

Senators

Glen H. Taylor (D)

Bert H. Miller (D) d. Oct. 1949
Henry C. Dworshak (R)

Representatives

John C. Sanborn (R)
Compton I. White (D)

ILLINOIS

Senators

Scott W. Lucas (D)
Paul H. Douglas (D)

Representatives

Leo E. Allen (R)
Leslie C. Arends (R)
Cecil W. Bishop (R)
James V. Buckley (D)
Chester A. Chesney (D)
Robert B. Chiperfield (R)
Ralph E. Church (R) d. Mar. 1950
William L. Dawson (D)
Thomas S. Gordon (D)
Martin Gorski (D) d. Dec. 1949
Richard W. Hoffman (R)
Edward H. Jenison (R)
Edgar A. Jonas (R)
Neil J. Linehan (D)
Rolla C. McMillen (R)
Peter F. Mack, Jr. (D)
Noah M. Mason (R)
Thomas J. O'Brien (D)
Barratt O'Hara (D)
Melvin Price (D)
Chauncey W. Reed (R)
Adolph J. Sabath (D)
Sidney E. Simpson (R)
Harold H. Velde (R)
Charles W. Vursell (R)
Sidney R. Yates (D)

INDIANA

Senators

Homer E. Capehart (R)
William E. Jenner (R)

Representatives

Thurman C. Crook (D)
Winfield K. Denton (D)
Charles A. Halleck (R)
Cecil M. Harden (R)
Ralph Harvey (R)
Andrew Jacobs, Sr. (D)
Edward H. Kruse, Jr. (D)
Ray J. Madden (D)
James E. Noland (D)
John R. Walsh (D)
Earl Wilson (R)

IOWA

Senators

Bourke B. Hickenlooper (R)
Guy M. Gillette (D)

Representatives

Paul Cunningham (R)
James I. Dolliver (R)
Harold R. Gross (R)
Charles B. Hoeven (R)
Ben F. Jensen (R)
Karl M. LeCompte (R)
Thomas E. Martin (R)
Henry O. Talle (R)

KANSAS

Senators

Clyde M. Reed (R) d. Nov. 1949
Harry Darby (R) ta. 1950
Frank Carlson (R) s. 1950

Andrew F. Schoeppel (R)

Representatives

Albert M. Cole (R)
Myron V. George (R) s. 1950
Clifford R. Hope (R)
Herbert A. Meyer (R) d. Oct. 1950
Edward H. Rees (R)
Errett P. Scrivner (R)
Wint Smith (R)

KENTUCKY

Senators

Alben W. Barkley (D) r. Jan. 1949
Garrett L. Withers (D) ta. 1949
Earle C. Clements (D) s. 1950

Virgil M. Chapman (D)

Representatives

Joe B. Bates (D)
Frank L. Chelf (D)
James S. Golden (R)
Noble J. Gregory (D)
Thruston B. Morton (R)
Carl D. Perkins (D)
Brent Spence (D)
Thomas R. Underwood (D)
John A. Whitaker (D)

LOUISIANA

Senators

Allen J. Ellender, Sr. (D)
Russell B. Long (D)

Representatives

A. Leonard Allen (D)
T. Hale Boggs (D)
Overton Brooks (D)
F. Edward Hebert (D)
Henry D. Larcade, Jr. (D)
James H. Morrison (D)
Otto E. Passman (D)
Edwin E. Willis (D)

MAINE

Senators

Ralph O. Brewster (R)
Margaret Chase Smith (R)

Representatives

Frank Fellows (R)
Robert Hale (R)
Charles P. Nelson (R)

MARYLAND

Senators

Millard E. Tydings (D)
Herbert R. O'Conor (D)

Representatives

J. Glenn Beall (R)
William P. Bolton (D)
George H. Fallon (D)
Edward A. Garmatz (D)
Edward T. Miller (R)
Lansdale G. Sasscer (D)

MASSACHUSETTS

Senators

Leverett Saltonstall (R)
Henry Cabot Lodge, Jr. (R)

Representatives

George J. Bates (R) d. Nov. 1949
William H. Bates (R) s. 1950
Harold D. Donohue (D)
Foster Furcolo (D)
Angier L. Goodwin (R)
Christian A. Herter (R)
John W. Heselton (R)
John F. Kennedy (D)
Thomas J. Lane (D)
John W. McCormack (D)
Joseph W. Martin, Jr. (R)
Donald W. Nicholson (R)
Philip J. Philbin (D)
Edith Nourse Rogers (R)
Richard B. Wigglesworth (R)

MICHIGAN

Senators

Arthur H. Vandenberg (R)
Homer Ferguson (R)

Representatives

John B. Bennett (R)
William W. Blackney (R)
Fred L. Crawford (R)
John D. Dingell (D)
George A. Dondero (R)
Albert J. Engel (R)
Gerald R. Ford, Jr. (R)
Clare E. Hoffman (R)
John Lesinski (D) d. May 1950
Earl C. Michener (R)
George D. O'Brien (D)
Charles E. Potter (R)
Louis C. Rabaut (D)
George G. Sadowski (D)
Paul W. Shafer (R)
Jesse P. Wolcott (R)
Roy O. Woodruff (R)

MINNESOTA

Senators

Edward J. Thye (R)
Hubert H. Humphrey (D)

Representatives

H. Carl Andersen (R)
August H. Andresen (R)
John A. Blatnik (D)
Harold C. Hagen (R)
Walter H. Judd (R)
Eugene J. McCarthy (D)
Fred Marshall (D)
Joseph P. O'Hara (R)
Roy W. Wier (D)

MISSISSIPPI

Senators

James O. Eastland (D)
John C. Stennis (D)

Representatives

Thomas G. Abernethy (D)
William M. Colmer (D)
John E. Rankin (D)
Jamie L. Whitten (D)
William M. Whittington (D)
John Bell Williams (D)
W. Arthur Winstead (D)

MISSOURI

Senators

Forrest C. Donnell (R)
James P. Kem (R)

Representatives

Richard W. Bolling (D)
Clarence Cannon (D)
Albert S. J. Carnahan (D)
George H. Christopher (D)
Theodore L. Irving (D)
Paul C. Jones (D)
Raymond W. Karst (D)
Frank M. Karsten (D)
Clare Magee (D)
Morgan M. Moulder (D)
Dewey Short (R)
John B. Sullivan (D)
Philip J. Welch (D)

MONTANA

Senators

James E. Murray (D)
Zales N. Ecton (R)

Representatives

Wesley A. D'Ewart (R)
Mike Mansfield (D)

NEBRASKA

Senators

Hugh A. Butler (R)
Kenneth S. Wherry (R)

Representatives

Carl T. Curtis (R)
Arthur L. Miller (R)
Eugene D. O'Sullivan (D)
Karl Stefan (R)

NEVADA

Senators

Patrick A. McCarran (D)
George W. Malone (R)

Representative

Walter S. Baring (D)

NEW HAMPSHIRE

Senators

H. Styles Bridges (R)
Charles W. Tobey (R)

Representatives

Norris Cotton (R)
Chester E. Merrow (R)

NEW JERSEY

Senators

H. Alexander Smith (R)
Robert C. Hendrickson (R)

Representatives

Hugh J. Addonizio (D)
James C. Auchincloss (R)
Gordon Canfield (R)
Clifford P. Case (R)
Charles A. Eaton (R)
T. Millet Hand (R)
Edward J. Hart (D)
Charles R. Howell (D)
Robert W. Kean (R)
Mary T. Norton (D)
Peter W. Rodino, Jr. (D)
J. Parnell Thomas (R) r. Jan. 1950
Harry L. Towe (R)
William B. Widnall (R) s. 1950
Charles A. Wolverton (R)

NEW MEXICO

Senators

Dennis Chavez (D)
Clinton P. Anderson (D)

Representatives

Antonio M. Fernandez (D)
John E. Miles (D)

NEW YORK

Senators

Robert F. Wagner (D)
r. June 1949
John Foster Dulles (R) ta. 1950
Herbert H. Lehman (D) s. 1950

Irving M. Ives (R)

Representatives

Sol Bloom (D) d. Mar. 1949
Charles A. Buckley (D)
William T. Byrne (D)
Emanuel Celler (D)
L. Gary Clemente (D)
W. Sterling Cole (R)
Frederic R. Coudert, Jr. (R)
John C. Davies (D)
James J. Delaney (D)
Isidore Dollinger (D)
Ralph A. Gamble (R)
Chester C. Gorski (D)
Ralph W. Gwinn (R)
Edwin A. Hall (R)
Leonard W. Hall (R)
James J. Heffernan (D)
Louis B. Heller (D)
Jacob K. Javits (R)
Bernard W. Kearney (R)
Kenneth B. Keating (R)
Edna F. Kelly (D) s. 1950
Eugene J. Keogh (D)
Clarence E. Kilburn (D)
Arthur G. Klein (D)
Henry J. Latham (R)
Jay LeFevre (R)
Walter A. Lynch (D)
Christopher C. McGrath (D)
W. Kingsland Macy (R)
Vito Marcantonio (Amer. Labor)
Abraham J. Multer (D)
James J. Murphy (D)
Donald L. O'Toole (D)
Joseph L. Pfeifer (R)
William L. Pfeiffer (R)
Adam Clayton Powell, Jr. (D)
T. Vincent Quinn (D)
Daniel A. Reed (R)
R. Walter Riehlman (R)
John J. Rooney (D)
Franklin D. Roosevelt, Jr. (D)
Katherine St. George (R)
Andrew L. Somers (D)
d. Apr. 1949
John Taber (R)
Anthony F. Tauriello (D)
Dean P. Taylor (R)
James W. Wadsworth, Jr. (R)

NORTH CAROLINA

Senators

Clyde R. Hoey (D)

J. Melville Broughton (D)
d. Mar. 1949
Frank P. Graham (D) ta. 1949-50
Willis Smith (D) s. 1950

Representatives

Graham A. Barden (D)
Herbert C. Bonner (D)
Alfred L. Bulwinkle (D)
d. Aug. 1950
F. Ertel Carlyle (D)
Richard T. Chatham (D)
Harold D. Cooley (D)
Charles B. Deane (D)
Robert L. Doughton (D)
Carl T. Durham (D)
John H. Kerr (D)
Hamilton C. Jones (D)
Woodrow W. Jones (D) s. 1950
Monroe M. Redden (D)

NORTH DAKOTA

Senators

William Langer (R)
Milton R. Young (R)

Representatives

Usher L. Burdick (R)
William Lemke (R) d. May 1950

OHIO

Senators

Robert A. Taft (R)
John W. Bricker (R)

Representatives

Frances P. Bolton (R)
Edward F. Breen (D)
Walter E. Brehm (R)
Clarence J. Brown (R)
Thomas H. Burke (D)
Cliff Clevenger (R)
Robert Crosser (D)
Charles H. Elston (R)
Michael A. Feighan (D)
Wayne L. Hays (D)
Walter B. Huber (D)
Thomas A. Jenkins (R)
Michael J. Kirwan (D)
William M. McCulloch (R)
J. Harry McGregor (R)
John McSweeney (D)
James G. Polk (D)
Robert T. Secrest (D)
Frederick C. Smith (R)
John M. Vorys (R)
Earl T. Wagner (D)
Alvin F. Weichel (R)
Stephen M. Young (D)

OKLAHOMA

Senators

J. W. Elmer Thomas (D)
Robert S. Kerr (D)

Representatives

Carl Albert (D)
William F. Gilmer (D)
A. S. Mike Monroney (D)
Toby Morris (D)
Thomas J. Steed (D)
William G. Stigler (D)
Victor E. Wickersham (D)
George H. Wilson (D)

OREGON

Senators

Guy Cordon (R)
Wayne L. Morse (R)

Representatives

Homer D. Angell (R)
Harris Ellsworth (R)
A. Walter Norblad, Jr. (R)
Lowell Stockman (R)

PENNSYLVANIA

Senators

Francis J. Myers (D)
Edward Martin (R)

Representatives

William A. Barrett (D)
Frank Buchanan (D)
Anthony Cavalcante (D)
Earl Chudoff (D)
Robert L. Coffey, Jr. (D)
Robert J. Corbett (R)
Paul B. Dague (R)
Harry J. Davenport (D)
Herman P. Eberharter (D)
Ivor D. Fenton (R)
Daniel J. Flood (D)
James G. Fulton (R)
Leon H. Gavin (R)
Wilson D. Gillette (R)
Louis E. Graham (R)
William T. Granahan (D)
William J. Green, Jr. (R)
Benjamin F. James (R)
Carroll D. Kearns (R)
Augustine B. Kelley (D)
John C. Kunkel (R)
Franklin H. Lichtenwalter (R)
James F. Lind (D)
Samuel K. McConnell, Jr. (R)
Thomas E. Morgan (D)
Harry P. O'Neill (D)
George M. Rhodes (D)
Robert F. Rich (R)
John P. Saylor (R)
Hardie Scott (D)
Hugh D. Scott, Jr. (D)
Richard M. Simpson (R)
James E. Van Zandt (R)
Francis E. Walter (D)

RHODE ISLAND

Senators

Theodore F. Green (D)

J. Howard McGrath (D)
r. Aug. 1949
Edward L. Leahy (D) ta. 1949-50
John O. Pastore (D) s. 1950

Representatives

John E. Fogarty (D)
Aime J. Forand (D)

SOUTH CAROLINA

Senators

Burnet R. Maybank (D)
Olin D. Johnston (D)

Representatives

Joseph R. Bryson (D)
James B. Hare (D)
John L. McMillan (D)
James P. Richards (D)
L. Mendel Rivers (D)
Hugo S. Sims, Jr. (D)

SOUTH DAKOTA

Senators

J. Chandler Gurney (R)
Karl E. Mundt (R)

Representatives

Francis H. Case (R)
Harold O. Lovre (R)

TENNESSEE

Senators

Kenneth D. McKellar (D)
Estes Kefauver (D)

Representatives

Jere Cooper (D)
Clifford Davis (D)
Joseph L. Evins (D)
James B. Frazier, Jr. (D)
Albert A. Gore (D)
John Jennings, Jr. (R)
Thomas J. Murray (D)
Dayton E. Phillips (R)
J. Percy Priest (D)
James P. Sutton (D)

TEXAS

Senators

Tom T. Connally (D)
Lyndon B. Johnson (D)

Representatives

Lindley Beckworth (D)
Lloyd M. Bentsen, Jr. (D)
Omar T. Burleson (D)
Jesse M. Combs (D)
O. Clark Fisher (D)
Ed Gossett (D)
Ben H. Guill (D) s. 1950
Paul J. Kilday (D)
Wingate H. Lucas (D)
John E. Lyle, Jr. (D)
George H. Mahon (D)
Wright Patman (D)
Tom Pickett (D)
William R. Poage (D)
Sam Rayburn (D)

Kenneth M. Regan (D)
Olin E. Teague (D)
Albert Thomas (D)
Clark W. Thompson (D)
W. Homer Thornberry (D)
J. Frank Wilson (D)
Eugene Worley (D) r. Apr. 1950

UTAH

Senators

Elbert D. Thomas (D)
Arthur V. Watkins (R)

Representatives

Reva Z. B. Bosone (D)
Walter K. Granger (D)

VERMONT

Senators

George D. Aiken (R)
Ralph E. Flanders (R)

Representative

Charles A. Plumley (R)

VIRGINIA

Senators

Harry F. Byrd (D)
A. Willis Robertson (D)

Representatives

Watkins M. Abbitt (D)
Schuyler Otis Bland (D)
d. Feb. 1950
Clarence G. Burton (D)
Thomas B. Fugate (D)
J. Vaughan Gary (D)
Porter Hardy, Jr. (D)
Burr P. Harrison (D)
Edward J. Robeson, Jr. (D)
s. 1950
Howard W. Smith (D)
Thomas B. Stanley (D)

WASHINGTON

Senators

Warren G. Magnuson (D)
Harry P. Cain (D)

Representatives

Hal Holmes (R)
Walter F. Horan (R)
Henry M. Jackson (D)
Russell V. Mack (R)
Hugh B. Mitchell (D)
Thor C. Tollefson (R)

WEST VIRGINIA

Senators

Harley M. Kilgore (D)
Matthew M. Neely

Representatives

Cleveland M. Bailey (D)
Maurice G. Burnside (D)
Erland H. Hedrick (D)
John Kee (D)
Robert L. Ramsay (D)
Harley O. Staggers (D)

WISCONSIN

Senators

Alexander Wiley (R)
Joseph R. McCarthy (R)

Representatives

Andrew J. Biemiller (D)
John W. Byrnes (R)
Glenn R. Davis (R)
Merlin Hull (R)
Frank B. Keefe (R)
Reid F. Murray (R)
Alvin E. O'Konski (R)
Lawrence H. Smith (R)
Gardner R. Withrow (R)
Clement J. Zablocki (D)

WYOMING

Senators

Joseph C. O'Mahoney (D)
Lester C. Hunt (D)

Representative

Frank A. Barrett (R)

EIGHTY-SECOND CONGRESS

January 3, 1951 to January 3, 1953

President of The Senate: Alben W. Barkley
President Pro Tempore of The Senate: Kenneth D. McKellar
Speaker of The House of Representatives: Sam Rayburn

ALABAMA

Senators

Lister Hill (D)
John J. Sparkman (D)

Representatives

George W. Andrews (D)
Laurie C. Battle (D)
Frank W. Boykin (D)
Edward de Graffenried (D)
Carl A. Elliott (D)
George M. Grant (D)
Robert E. Jones, Jr. (D)
Albert Rains (D)
Kenneth A. Roberts (D)

ARIZONA

Senators

Carl Hayden (D)
Ernest W. McFarland (D)

Representatives

John R. Murdock (D)
Harold A. Patten (D)

ARKANSAS

Senators

John L. McClellan (D)
J. William Fulbright (D)

Representatives

Ezekiel C. Gathings (D)
Oren Harris (D)
Brooks Hays (D)
Wilbur D. Mills (D)
William F. Norrell (D)
Boyd Tackett (D)
James W. Trimble (D)

CALIFORNIA

Senators

William F. Knowland (R)
Richard M. Nixon (R)

Representatives

John J. Allen, Jr. (R)
John Z. Anderson (R)
Ernest K. Bramblett (R)
Clyde G. Doyle (D)
Clair Engle (D)
Franck R. Havenner (D)
Patrick J. Hillings (R)
Carl Hinshaw (R)
Chet Holifield (D)
Allan O. Hunter (R)
Donald L. Jackson (R)
Leroy Johnson (R)
Cecil R. King (D)
Gordon L. McDonough (R)
Clinton D. McKinnon (D)
George P. Miller (D)
John Phillips (R)
Norris Poulson (R)
Hubert B. Scudder (R)
John F. Shelley (D)
Harry R. Sheppard (D)
Thomas H. Werdel (R)
Samuel W. Yorty (D)

COLORADO

Senators

Edwin C. Johnson (D)
Eugene D. Millikin (R)

Representatives

Wayne N. Aspinall (D)
J. Edgar Chenoweth (R)
William S. Hill (R)
Byron G. Rogers (D)

CONNECTICUT

Senators

Brien McMahon (D) d. July 1952
William Benton (D)

Representatives

John A. McGuire (D)
Albert P. Morano (R)
James T. Patterson (R)
Abraham A. Ribicoff (D)
Antoni N. Sadlak (R)
Horace Seely-Brown, Jr. (R)

DELAWARE

Senators

John J. Williams (R)
J. Allen Frear, Jr. (D)

Representative

J. Caleb Boggs (R)

FLORIDA

Senators

Spessard L. Holland (D)
George A. Smathers (D)

Representatives

Charles E. Bennett (D)
Albert S. Herlong, Jr. (D)
William C. Lantaff (D)
Chester B. McMullen (D)
Dwight L. Rogers (D)
Robert L. F. Sikes (D)

GEORGIA

Senators

Walter F. George (D)
Richard B. Russell (D)

Representatives

Paul Brown (D)
A. Sidney Camp (D)
Edward E. Cox (D) d. Dec. 1952
James C. Davis (D)
Elijah L. Forrester (D)
Henderson L. Lanham (D)
Prince H. Preston, Jr. (D)
Carl Vinson (D)
William M. Wheeler (D)
John S. Wood (D)

IDAHO

Senators

Henry C. Dworshak (R)
Herman Welker (R)

Representatives

Hamer H. Budge (R)
John T. Wood (R)

ILLINOIS

Senators

Paul H. Douglas (D)
Everett M. Dirksen (D)

Representatives

Leo E. Allen (R)
Leslie C. Arends (R)
Cecil W. Bishop (R)
Fred E. Busbey (R)
Robert B. Chiperfield (R)
Marguerite Stitt Church (R)
William L. Dawson (D)
Thomas S. Gordon (D)
Richard W. Hoffman (R)
Edward H. Jenison (R)
Edgar A. Jonas (R)
John C. Kluczynski (D)
William E. McVey (R)
Peter F. Mack, Jr. (D)
Noah M. Mason (R)
Thomas J. O'Brien (D)
Melvin Price (D)
Chauncey W. Reed (R)
Adolph J. Sabath (D)
d. Nov. 1952
Timothy P. Sheehan (R)
Sidney E. Simpson (R)
William L. Springer (R)
Richard B. Vail (R)
Harold H. Velde (R)
Charles W. Vursell (R)
Sidney Yates (D)

INDIANA

Senators

Homer E. Capehart (R)
William E. Jenner (R)

Representatives

E. Ross Adair (R)
William G. Bray (R)
John V. Beamer (R)
Charles B. Brownson (R)
Shepard J. Crumpacker, Jr. (R)
Winfield K. Denton (D)
Charles A. Halleck (R)
Cecil M. Harden (R)
Ralph Harvey (R)
Ray J. Madden (D)
Earl Wilson (R)

IOWA

Senators

Bourke B. Hickenlooper (R)
Guy M. Gillette (D)

Representatives

Paul Cunningham (R)
James I. Dolliver (R)
Harold R. Gross (R)
Charles B. Hoeven (R)
Ben F. Jensen (R)
Karl M. LeCompte (R)
Thomas E. Martin (R)
Henry O. Talle (R)

KANSAS

Senators

Andrew F. Schoeppel (R)
Frank Carlson (R)

Representatives

Albert M. Cole (R)
Myron V. George (R)
Clifford R. Hope (R)
Edward H. Rees (R)
Errett P. Scrivner (R)
Wint Smith (R)

KENTUCKY

Senators

Virgil M. Chapman (D)
d. Mar. 1951
Thomas R. Underwood (D)

Earle C. Clements (D)

Representatives

Joe B. Bates (D)
Frank L. Chelf (D)
Noble J. Gregory (D)
James S. Golden (R)
Thruston B. Morton (R)
Carl D. Perkins (D)
Brent Spence (D)
Thomas R. Underwood (D)
r. Mar. 1951
John C. Watts (D)
John A. Whitaker (D)
d. Dec. 1951

LOUISIANA

Senators

Allen J. Ellender, Sr. (D)
Russell B. Long (D)

Representatives

A. Leonard Allen (D)
T. Hale Boggs (D)
Overton Brooks (D)
F. Edward Hebert (D)
Henry D. Larcade, Jr. (D)
James H. Morrison (D)
Otto E. Passman (D)
Edwin E. Willis (D)

MAINE

Senators

Ralph O. Brewster (R)
Margaret Chase Smith (R)

Representatives

Frank Fellows (R) d. Aug. 1951
Robert Hale (R)
Clifford G. McIntire (R) s. 1952
Charles P. Nelson (R)

MARYLAND

Senators

Herbert R. O'Conor (D)
John Marshall Butler (R)

Representatives

J. Glenn Beall (R)
James P. S. Devereux (R)
George H. Fallon (D)
Edward A. Garmatz (D)
Edward T. Miller (R)
Lansdale G. Sasscer (D)

MASSACHUSETTS

Senators

Leverett Saltonstall (R)
Henry Cabot Lodge, Jr. (R)

Representatives

William H. Bates (R)
Harold D. Donohue (D)
Foster Furcolo (D) r. Sept. 1952
Angier L. Goodwin (R)

Christian A. Herter (R)
John W. Heselton (R)
John F. Kennedy (D)
Thomas J. Lane (D)
John W. McCormack (D)
Joseph W. Martin, Jr. (R)
Donald W. Nicholson (R)
Philip J. Philbin (D)
Edith Nourse Rogers (R)
Richard B. Wigglesworth (R)

MICHIGAN

Senators

Arthur H. Vandenberg (R)
d. Apr. 1951
Arthur Blair Moody (D)

Homer Ferguson (R)

Representatives

John B. Bennett (R)
William W. Blackney (R)
Fred L. Crawford (R)
John D. Dingell (D)
George A. Dondero (R)
Gerald R. Ford, Jr. (R)
Clare E. Hoffman (R)
John Lesinski, Jr. (D)
Thaddeus M. Machrowicz (D)
George Meader (R)
George D. O'Brien (D)
Charles E. Potter (R) r. Nov. 1952
Louis C. Rabaut (D)
Paul W. Shafer (R)
Ruth Thompson (R)
Jesse P. Wolcott (R)
Roy O. Woodruff (R)

MINNESOTA

Senators

Edward J. Thye (R)
Hubert H. Humphrey (D)

Representatives

H. Carl Andersen (R)
August H. Andresen (R)
John A. Blatnik (D)
Harold C. Hagen (R)
Walter H. Judd (R)
Eugene J. McCarthy (D)
Fred Marshall
Joseph P. O'Hara (R)
Roy W. Wier (D)

MISSISSIPPI

Senators

James O. Eastland (D)
John C. Stennis (D)

Representatives

Thomas G. Abernethy (D)
William M. Colmer (D)
John E. Rankin (D)
Frank E. Smith (D)
Jamie L. Whitten (D)
John Bell Williams (D)
W. Arthur Winstead (D)

MISSOURI

Senators

James P. Kem (R)
Thomas C. Hennings, Jr. (D)

Representatives

Orland K. Armstrong (R)
Claude I. Bakewell (R)
Richard W. Bolling (D)
Clarence Cannon (D)
Albert S. J. Carnahan (D)
Thomas B. Curtis (R)
Theodore L. Irving (D)
Paul C. Jones (D)
Frank M. Karsten (D)
Clare Magee (D)
Morgan M. Moulder (D)
Dewey Short (R)
John B. Sullivan (D) d. Jan. 1951
Philip J. Welch (D)

MONTANA

Senators

James E. Murray (D)
Zales N. Ecton (R)

Representatives

Wesley A. D'Ewart (R)
Mike Mansfield (D)

NEBRASKA

Senators

Hugh A. Butler (R)

Kenneth S. Wherry (R)
d. Nov. 1951
Frederick A. Seaton (R) s. 1952

Representatives

Howard H. Buffett (R)
Carl T. Curtis (R)
Robert D. Harrison (R) s. 1952
Arthur L. Miller (R)
Karl Stefan (R) d. Oct. 1951

NEVADA

Senators

Patrick A. McCarran (D)
George W. Malone (R)

Representative

Walter S. Baring (D)

NEW HAMPSHIRE

Senators

H. Styles Bridges (R)
Charles W. Tobey (R)

Representatives

Norris Cotton (R)
Chester E. Merrow (R)

NEW JERSEY

Senators

H. Alexander Smith (R)
Robert C. Hendrickson (R)

Representatives

Hugh J. Addonizio (D)
James C. Auchincloss (R)
Gordon Canfield (R)
Clifford P. Case (R)
Charles A. Eaton (R)
T. Millet Hand (R)
Edward J. Hart (D)
Charles R. Howell (D)
Robert W. Kean (R)
Frank C. Osmers, Jr. (R) s. 1952
Peter W. Rodino, Jr. (D)
Alfred D. Sieminski (D)
Harry L. Towe (R) r. Sept. 1951
William B. Widnall (R)
Charles A. Wolverton (R)

NEW MEXICO

Senators

Dennis Chavez (D)
Clinton P. Anderson (D)

Representatives

John J. Dempsey (D)
Antonio M. Fernandez (D)

NEW YORK

Senators

Irving M. Ives (R)
Herbert H. Lehman (D)

Representatives

Victor L. Anfuso (D)
Charles A. Buckley (D)
John C. Butler (R)
William T. Byrne (D) d. Jan. 1952
Emanuel Celler (D)
L. Gary Clemente (D)
W. Sterling Cole (R)
Frederic R. Coudert, Jr. (R)
James J. Delaney (D)
Isidore Dollinger (D)
James G. Donovan, (D,R,L)
Sidney A. Fine (D)
Ralph A. Gamble (R)
Ernest Greenwood (D)
Ralph W. Gwinn (R)
Edwin A. Hall (R)
Leonard W. Hall (R)
James J. Heffernan (D)
Louis B. Heller (D)
Jacob K. Javits (R)
Bernard W. Kearney (R)
Kenneth B. Keating (R)
Edna F. Kelly (D)
Eugene J. Keogh (D)
Clarence E. Kilburn (R)
Arthur G. Klein (D)
Henry J. Latham (R)
Christopher C. McGrath (D)
William E. Miller (R)
Abraham J. Multer (D)
James J. Murphy (D)
Leo W. O'Brien (D) s. 1952
Donald L. O'Toole (D)
Harold C. Ostertag (R)
Adam Clayton Powell, Jr. (D)
T. Vincent Quinn (D)
r. Dec. 1951
Edmund P. Radwan (R)
Daniel A. Reed (R)
R. Walter Riehlman (R)
John J. Rooney (D)
Franklin D. Roosevelt, Jr. (D)
Robert T. Ross (R) s. 1952
Katharine St. George (R)
John Taber (R)
Dean P. Taylor (R)
J. Ernest Wharton (R)
William R. Williams (R)

NORTH CAROLINA

Senators

Clyde R. Hoey (D)
Willis Smith (D)

Representatives

Graham A. Barden (D)
Herbert C. Bonner (D)
F. Ertel Carlyle (D)
Richard T. Chatham (D)
Harold D. Cooley (D)
Charles B. Deane (D)
Robert L. Doughton (D)
Carl T. Durham (D)
Hamilton C. Jones (D)
Woodrow W. Jones (D)
John H. Kerr (D)
Monroe M. Redden (D)

NORTH DAKOTA

Senators

William Langer (R)
Milton R. Young (R)

Representatives

Fred G. Aandahl (R)
Usher L. Burdick (R)

OHIO

Senators

Robert A. Taft (R)
John W. Bricker (R)

Representatives

William H. Ayres (R)
George H. Bender (R)
Jackson E. Betts (R)
Frances P. Bolton (R)
Frank T. Bow (R)
Edward F. Breen (D) r. Oct. 1951
Walter E. Brehm (R)
Clarence J. Brown (R)
Cliff Clevenger (R)
Robert Crosser (D)
Charles H. Elston (R)
Michael A. Feighan (D)
Wayne L. Hays (D)
William E. Hess (R)
Thomas A. Jenkins (R)
Michael J. Kirwan (D)
J. Harry McGregor (R)

William M. McCulloch (R)
James G. Polk (D)
Henry F. Reams
Paul F. Scheneck (R) s. 1952
Robert T. Secrest (D)
John M. Vorys (R)
Alvin F. Weichel (R)

OKLAHOMA

Senators

Robert S. Kerr (D)
A. S. Mike Monroney (D)

Representatives

Carl Albert (D)
Page H. Belcher (R)
John Jarman (D)
Toby Morris (D)
George B. Schwabe (R) d. Apr. 1952
Thomas J. Steed (D)
William G. Stigler (D) d. Aug. 1952
Victor E. Wickersham (D)

OREGON

Senators

Guy Gordon (R)
Wayne L. Morse (R)

Representatives

Homer D. Angell (R)
Harris Ellsworth (R)
A. Walter Norblad, Jr. (R)
Lowell Stockman (R)

PENNSYLVANIA

Senators

Edward Martin (D)
James H. Duff (R)

Representatives

William A. Barrett (D)
Frank B. Buchanan (D) d. Apr. 1951
Vera D. Buchanan (D)
Alvin R. Bush (R)
Joseph L. Carrigg (R) s. 1952
Robert J. Corbett (D)
Earl Chudoff (D)
Paul B. Dague (R)
Harmar J. Denny, Jr. (D)
Herman P. Eberharter (D)
Ivor D. Fenton (R)
Daniel J. Flood (D)
James G. Fulton (R)
Leon H. Gavin (R)
Wilson D. Gillette (R) d. Aug. 1951
Louis E. Graham (R)
William T. Granahan (D)
William J. Green, Jr. (D)
Benjamin F. James (R)
Carroll D. Kearns (R)
Augustine B. Kelley (D)
Karl C. King (R) s. 1952
James F. Lind (D)
Samuel K. McConnell, Jr. (R)
Thomas E. Morgan (D)
Walter M. Mumma (R)
Harry P. O'Neill (D)
George M. Rhodes (D)
John P. Saylor (R)
Hardie Scott (R)
Hugh D. Scott, Jr. (R)
Richard M. Simpson (R)
Edward L. Sittler, Jr. (R)
James E. Van Zandt (R)
Albert C. Vaughn (R) d. Sept. 1951
Francis E. Walter (D)

RHODE ISLAND

Senators

Theodore F. Green (D)
John O. Pastore (D)

Representatives

John E. Fogarty (D)
Aime J. Forand (D)

SOUTH CAROLINA

Senators

Burnet R. Maybank (D)
Olin D. Johnston (D)

Representatives

Joseph R. Bryson (D)
W. J. Bryan Dorn (D)
John L. McMillan (D)
James P. Richards (D)
John J. Riley (D)
L. Mendel Rivers (D)

SOUTH DAKOTA

Senators

Karl E. Mundt (R)
Francis H. Case (R)

Representatives

Ellis Y. Berry (R)
Harold O. Lovre (R)

TENNESSEE

Senators

Kenneth D. McKellar (D)
Estes Kefauver (D)

Representatives

Howard H. Baker (R)
Jere Cooper (D)
Clifford Davis (D)
Joseph L. Evins (D)
James B. Frazier, Jr. (D)
Albert A. Gore (D)
Thomas J. Murray (D)
J. Percy Priest (D)
B. Carroll Reece (R)
James P. Sutton (D)

TEXAS

Senators

Tom T. Connally (D)
Lyndon B. Johnson (D)

Representatives

Lindley Beckworth (D)
Lloyd M. Bentsen, Jr. (D)
Omar T. Burleson (D)
Jesse M. Combs (D)
O. Clark Fisher (D)
Ed Gossett (D) r. July 1951
Frank N. Ikard (D)
Paul J. Kilday (D)
Wingate H. Lucas (D)
John E. Lyle, Jr. (D)
George H. Mahon (D)
Wright Patman (D)
Tom Pickett (D) r. June 1952
William R. Poage (D)
Sam Rayburn (D)
Kenneth M. Regan (D)
Walter E. Rogers (D)
Olin E. Teague (D)
Albert Thomas (D)
Clark W. Thompson (D)
W. Homer Thornberry (D)
J. Frank Wilson (D)

UTAH

Senators

Arthur V. Watkins (R)
Wallace F. Bennett (R)

Representatives

Reva Z. B. Bosone (D)
Walter K. Granger (D)

VERMONT

Senators

George D. Aiken (R)
Ralph E. Flanders (R)

Representative

Winston L. Prouty (R)

VIRGINIA

Senators

Harry F. Byrd (D)
A. Willis Robertson (D)

Representatives

Watkins M. Abbitt (D)
Clarence G. Burton (D)
Thomas B. Fugate (D)
J. Vaughan Gary (D)
Porter Hardy, Jr. (D)
Burr P. Harrison (D)
Edward J. Robeson, Jr. (D)
Howard W. Smith (D)
Thomas B. Stanley (D)

WASHINGTON

Senators

Warren G. Magnuson (D)
Harry P. Cain (D)

Representatives

Hal Holmes (R)
Walter F. Horan (R)
Henry M. Jackson (D)
Russell V. Mack (R)
Hugh B. Mitchell (D)
Thor C. Tollefson (R)

WEST VIRGINIA

Senators

Harley M. Kilgore (D)
Matthew M. Neely (D)

Representatives

Cleveland M. Bailey (D)
Maurice G. Burnside (D)
Erland H. Hedrick (D)
John Kee (D) d. May 1951
Maude Elizabeth Kee (D)
Robert L. Ramsay (D)
Harley O. Staggers (D)

WISCONSIN

Senators

Alexander Wiley (R)
Joseph R. McCarthy (R)

Representatives

John W. Byrnes (R)
Glenn R. Davis (R)
Merlin Hull (R)
Charles J. Kersten (R)
Reid F. Murray (R) d. Apr. 1952
Alvin E. O'Konski (R)
William K. Van Pelt (R)
Lawrence H. Smith (R)
Gardner R. Withrow (R)
Clement J. Zablocki (D)

WYOMING

Senators

Joseph C. O'Mahoney (D)
Lester C. Hunt (D)

Representative

William H. Harrison (R)

EIGHTY-THIRD CONGRESS

January 3, 1953 to January 3, 1955

President of The Senate:	Richard M. Nixon
President Pro Tempore of The Senate:	H. Styles Bridges
Speaker of The House of Representatives:	Joseph W. Martin, Jr.

ALABAMA

Senators

Lister Hill (D)
John J. Sparkman (D)

Representatives

George W. Andrews (D)
Laurie C. Battle (D)
Frank W. Boykin (D)
Carl A. Elliott (D)
George M. Grant (D)
Robert E. Jones, Jr. (D)
Albert Rains (D)
Kenneth A. Roberts (D)
Armistead I. Selden, Jr. (D)

ARIZONA

Senators

Carl Hayden (D)
Barry M. Goldwater (D)

Representatives

Harold A. Patten (D)
John J. Rhodes (R)

ARKANSAS

Senators

John L. McClellan (D)
J. William Fulbright (D)

Representatives

Ezekiel C. Gathings (D)
Oren Harris (D)
Brooks Hays (D)
Wilbur D. Mills (D)
William F. Norell (D)
James W. Trimble (D)

CALIFORNIA

Senators

William F. Knowland (R)
Thomas H. Kuchel (R)

Representatives

John J. Allen, Jr. (R)
Ernest K. Bramblett (R)
Robert L. Condon (D)
Clyde G. Doyle (D)
Clair Engle (D)
Charles S. Gubser (R)
Harlan F. Hagen (D)
Edgar W. Hiestand (R)
Patrick J. Hillings (R)
Carl Hinshaw (R)
Chet Holifield (D)
Joseph F. Holt (R)
Craig Hosmer (R)
Allan O. Hunter (R)
Donald L. Jackson (R)
Leroy Johnson (R)
Cecil R. King (D)
Glenard P. Lipscomb (R) s. 1954
Gordon L. McDonough (R)
William S. Mailliard (R)
George P. Miller (D)
John E. Moss, Jr. (D)
John Phillips (R)
Norris Poulson (R) r. June 1953
Hubert B. Scudder (R)
John F. Shelley (D)
Harry R. Sheppard (D)
James B. Utt (R)
Robert C. Wilson (R)
Samuel W. Yorty (D)
J. Arthur Younger (R)

COLORADO

Senators

Edwin C. Johnson (D)
Eugene D. Millikin (R)

Representatives

Wayne N. Aspinall (D)
J. Edgar Chenoweth (R)
William S. Hill (R)
Byron G. Rogers (R)

CONNECTICUT

Senators

Prescott S. Bush (R)
William A. Purtell (R)

Representatives

Albert W. Cretella (R)
Thomas J. Dodd (D)
Albert P. Morano (R)
James T. Patterson (R)
Antoni N. Sadlak (R)
Horace Seely-Brown, Jr. (R)

DELAWARE

Senators

John J. Williams (R)
J. Allen Frear, Jr. (D)

Representative

Herbert B. Warburton (R)

FLORIDA

Senators

Spessard L. Holland (D)
George A. Smathers (D)

Representatives

Charles E. Bennett (D)
Courtney W. Campbell (D)
James A. Haley (D)
Albert S. Herlong, Jr. (D)
William C. Lantaff (D)
Donald R. Matthews (D)
Dwight L. Rogers (D) d. Dec. 1954
Robert L. F. Sikes (D)

GEORGIA

Senators

Walter F. George (D)
Richard B. Russell (D)

Representatives

Paul Brown (D)
A. Sidney Camp (D) d. July 1954
James C. Davis (D)
Elijah L. Forrester (D)
Phillip M. Landrum (D)
Henderson L. Lanham (D)
John L. Pilcher (D)
Prince H. Preston, Jr. (D)
Carl Vinson (D)
William M. Wheeler (D)

IDAHO

Senators

Henry C. Dworshak (R)
Herman Welker (R)

Representatives

Hamer H. Budge (R)
Gracie B. Pfost (D)

ILLINOIS

Senators

Paul H. Douglas (D)
Everett M. Dirksen (R)

Representatives

Leo E. Allen (R)
Leslie C. Arends (R)
Cecil W. Bishop (R)
Fred E. Busbey (R)
Robert B. Chiperfield (R)
Marguerite Stitt Church (R)
William L. Dawson (D)
Thomas S. Gordon (D)
Richard W. Hoffman (R)
Edgar A. Jonas (R)
John C. Kluczynski (D)
William E. McVey (R)
Peter F. Mack, Jr. (D)
Noah M. Mason (R)
Thomas J. O'Brien (D)
Barratt O'Hara (D)
Melvin Price (D)
Chauncey W. Reed (R)
Timothy P. Sheehan (R)
Sidney E. Simpson (R)
William L. Springer (R)
Harold H. Velde (R)
Charles W. Vursell (R)
Sidney R. Yates (D)

INDIANA

Senators

Homer E. Capehart (R)
William E. Jenner (R)

Representatives

E. Ross Adair (R)
John V. Beamer (R)
William G. Bray (R)
Charles B. Brownson (R)
Shepard J. Crumpacker, Jr. (R)
Charles A. Halleck (R)
Cecil M. Harden (R)
Ralph Harvey (R)
Ray J. Madden (D)
D. Bailey Merrill (R)
Earl Wilson (R)

IOWA

Senators

Bourke B. Hickenlooper (R)
Guy M. Gillette (D)

Representatives

Paul Cunningham (R)
James I. Dolliver (R)
Harold R. Gross (R)
Charles B. Hoeven (R)
Ben F. Jensen (R)
Karl M. LeCompte (R)
Thomas E. Martin (R)
Henry O. Talle (R)

KANSAS

Senators

Andrew F. Schoeppel (R)
Frank Carlson (R)

Representatives

Myron V. George (R)
Clifford R. Hope (R)
Howard S. Miller (D)
Edward H. Rees (R)
Errett P. Scrivner (R)
Wint Smith (R)

KENTUCKY

Senators

Earle C. Clements (D)
John Sherman Cooper (R)

Representatives

Frank L. Chelf (D)
James S. Golden (R)
Noble J. Gregory (D)
William H. Natcher (D) s. 1954
Carl D. Perkins (D)
John M. Robsion, Jr. (R)
Brent Spence (D)
John C. Watts (D)
Garrett L. Withers (D)
d. April 1953

LOUISIANA

Senators

Allen J. Ellender, Sr. (D)
Russell B. Long (D)

Representatives

T. Hale Boggs (D)
Overton Brooks (D)
F. Edward Hebert (D)
George S. Long (D)
James H. Morrison (D)
Otto E. Passman (D)
T. Ashton Thompson (D)
Edwin E. Willis (D)

MAINE

Senators

Margaret Chase Smith (R)
Frederick G. Payne (R)

Representatives

Robert Hale (R)
Clifford G. McIntire (R)
Charles P. Nelson (R)

MARYLAND

Senators

John Marshall Butler (R)
J. Glenn Beall (R)

Representatives

James P. S. Devereux (R)
George H. Fallon (D)
Samuel N. Friedel (D)
Edward A. Garmatz (D)
DeWitt S. Hyde (R)
Edward T. Miller (R)
Frank Small, Jr. (R)

MASSACHUSETTS

Senators

Leverett Saltonstall (R)
John F. Kennedy (D)

Representatives

William H. Bates (R)
Edward P. Boland (D)
Laurence Curtis (R)
Harold D. Donohue (D)
Angier L. Goodwin (R)
John W. Heselton (R)
Thomas J. Lane (D)
John W. McCormack (D)
Joseph W. Martin, Jr. (R)
Donald W. Nicholson (R)
Thomas P. O'Neill, Jr. (D)
Philip J. Philbin (D)
Edith Nourse Rogers (R)
Richard B. Wigglesworth (R)

MICHIGAN

Senators

Homer Ferguson (R)
Charles E. Potter (R)

Representatives

John B. Bennett (R)
Alvin M. Bentley (R)
Elford A. Cederberg (R)
Kit F. Clardy (R)
John D. Dingell (D)
George A. Dondero (R)
Gerald R. Ford, Jr. (R)
Clare E. Hoffman (R)
Victor A. Knox (R)
John Lesinski, Jr. (D)
Thaddeus M. Machrowicz (D)
George Meader (R)
Charles G. Oakman (R)
George D. O'Brien (D)
Louis C. Rabaut (D)
Paul W. Shafer (R) d. Aug. 1954
Ruth Thompson (R)
Jesse P. Wolcott (R)

MINNESOTA

Senators

Edward J. Thye (R)
Hubert H. Humphrey (D)

Representatives

H. Carl Andersen (R)
August H. Andresen (R)
John A. Blatnik (D)
Harold C. Hagen (R)
Walter H. Judd (R)
Eugene J. McCarthy (D)
Fred Marshall (D)
Joseph P. O'Hara (R)
Roy W. Wier (D)

MISSISSIPPI

Senators

James O. Eastland (D)
John C. Stennis (D)

Representatives

Thomas G. Abernethy (D)
William M. Colmer (D)
Frank E. Smith (D)
Jamie L. Whitten (D)
John Bell Williams (D)
W. Arthur Winstead (D)

MISSOURI

Senators

Thomas C. Hennings, Jr. (D)
Stuart Symington (D)

Representatives

Richard W. Bolling (D)
Clarence Cannon (D)
Albert S. J. Carnahan (D)
William C. Cole (R)
Thomas B. Curtis (R)
Jeffrey P. Hillelson (D)
Paul C. Jones (D)
Frank M. Karsten (D)
Morgan M. Moulder (D)
Dewey Short (R)
Leonor Kretzer Sullivan (D)

MONTANA

Senators

James E. Murray (D)
Mike Mansfield (D)

Representatives

Wesley A. D'Ewart (R)
Lee Metcalf (D)

NEBRASKA

Senators

Hugh A. Butler (R) d. July 1954
Sam W. Reynolds (R) ta. 1954
Roman L. Hruska (R) s. 1954

Dwight P. Griswold (R)
d. Apr. 1954
Eva K. Bowring (R) ta. 1954
Hazel H. Abel (R) s. 1954,
r. Dec. 1954

Representatives

Carl T. Curtis (R)
Robert D. Harrison (R)
Roman L. Hruska (R)
r. Nov. 1954
Arthur L. Miller (R)

NEVADA

Senators

Patrick A. McCarran (D)
d. Sept. 1954
Ernest S. Brown (R) ta. 1954
Alan H. Bible (D) s. 1954

George W. Malone (R)

Representative

Clifton Young (R)

NEW HAMPSHIRE

Senators

H. Styles Bridges (R)

Charles W. Tobey (R)
d. July 1953
Robert W. Upton (R) ta. 1954
Norris Cotton (R) s. 1954

Representatives

Norris Cotton (R) r. Nov. 1954
Chester E. Merrow (R)

NEW JERSEY

Senators

H. Alexander Smith (R)
Robert C. Hendrickson (R)

Representatives

Hugh J. Addonizio (D)
James C. Auchincloss (R)
Gordon Canfield (R)
Clifford P. Case (R) r. Aug. 1953
Peter H. B. Frelinghuysen, Jr. (R)
T. Millet Hand (R)
Edward J. Hart (D)
Charles R. Howell (D)
Robert W. Kean (R)
Frank C. Osmers, Jr. (R)
Peter W. Rodino, Jr. (D)
Alfred D. Sieminski (D)
William B. Widnall (R)
Harrison A. Williams, Jr. (D)
s. 1954
Charles A. Wolverton (R)

NEW MEXICO

Senators

Dennis Chavez (D)
Clinton P. Anderson (D)

Representatives

John J. Dempsey (D)
Antonio M. Fernandez (D)

NEW YORK

Senators

Irving M. Ives (R)
Herbert H. Lehman (D)

Representatives

Frank J. Becker (R)
Albert H. Bosch (R)
Charles A. Buckley (D)
Emanuel Celler (D)
W. Sterling Cole (R)
Frederic R. Coudert, Jr. (R)
James J. Delaney (D)
Steven B. Derounian (R)
Isidore Dollinger (D)
James G. Donovan (D)
Francis E. Dorn (R)
Sidney A. Fine (D)
Paul A. Fino (R)
Ralph A. Gamble (R)
Ralph W. Gwinn (R)
Louis B. Heller (D) r. July 1954
Lester Holtzman (D)
Jacob K. Javits (R)
Bernard W. Kearney (R)
Kenneth B. Keating (R)
Edna F. Kelly (D)
Eugene J. Keogh (D)
Clarence E. Kilburn (R)
Arthur G. Klein (D)
Henry J. Latham (R)
William E. Miller (R)
Abraham J. Multer (D)
Leo W. O'Brien (D)
Harold C. Ostertag (R)
John R. Pillion (R)
Adam Clayton Powell, Jr. (D)
Edmund P. Radwan (R)
John H. Ray (R)
Daniel A. Reed (R)
R. Walter Riehlman (R)
John J. Rooney (D)
Franklin D. Roosevelt, Jr. (D)
Katharine St. George (R)
John Taber (R)
Dean P. Taylor (R)
Stuyvesant Wainwright 2d (R)
J. Ernest Wharton (R)
William R. Williams (R)

NORTH CAROLINA

Senators

Clyde R. Hoey (D) d. May 1954
Sam J. Ervin, Jr. (D) s. 1954

Willis Smith (D) d. June 1953
Alton A. Lennon (D)ta. 1953
W. Kerr Scott (D) s. 1954

Representatives

Hugh Q. Alexander (D)
Graham A. Barden (D)
Herbert C. Bonner (D)
F. Ertel Carlyle (D)
Richard T. Chatham (D)
Harold D. Cooley (D)
Charles B. Deane (D)
Carl T. Durham (D)
Lawrence H. Fountain (D)
Charles R. Jonas (R)
Woodrow W. Jones (D)
George A. Shuford (D)

NORTH DAKOTA

Senators

William Langer (R)
Milton R. Young (R)

Representatives

Usher L. Burdick (R)
Otto Krueger (R)

OHIO

Senators

Robert A. Taft (R) d. July 1953
Thomas A. Burke (D) ta. 1954

John W. Bricker (R)

Representatives

William H. Ayers (R)
George H. Bender (R) r. Dec. 1954
Jackson E. Betts (R)
Frances P. Bolton (R)
Oliver P. Bolton (R)
Frank T. Bow (R)
Clarence J. Brown (R)
Cliff Clevenger (R)
Robert Crosser (D)
Michael A. Feighan (D)
Wayne L. Hays (D)
William E. Hess (R)
Thomas A. Jenkins (R)
Michael J. Kirwan (D)
William M. McCulloch (R)
J. Harry McGregor (R)
James G. Polk (D)
Henry F. Reams (I)
Paul F. Schenck (R)
Gordon H. Scherer (R)
Robert T. Secrest (D)
r. Sept. 1954
John M. Vorys (R)
Alvin F. Weichel (R)

OKLAHOMA

Senators

Robert S. Kerr (D)
A. S. Mike Monroney (D)

Representatives

Carl Albert (D)
Page H. Belcher (R)
Edmond Emondson (D)
John Jarman (D)
Thomas J. Steed (D)
Victor E. Wickersham (D)

OREGON

Senators

Guy Cordon (R)
Wayne L. Morse (R)

Representatives

Homer D. Angell (R)
Samuel H. Coon (R)
Harris Ellsworth (R)
A. Walter Norblad, Jr. (R)

PENNSYLVANIA

Senators

Edward Martin (D)
James H. Duff (R)

Representatives

William A. Barrett (D)
Edward J. Bonin (R)
Vera D. Buchanan (D)
Alvin R. Bush (R)
James A. Byrne (D)
Joseph L. Carrigg (R)
Earl Chudoff (D)
Robert J. Corbett (R)
Paul B. Dague (R)
Herman P. Eberharter (D)
Ivor D. Fenton (R)
James G. Fulton (R)
Leon H. Gavin (R)
Louis E. Graham (R)
William T. Granahan (D)
William J. Green, Jr. (D)
Benjamin F. James (R)
Carroll D. Kearns (R)
Augustine B. Kelly (D)
Karl C. King (R)
Samuel K. McConnell, Jr. (R)
Thomas E. Morgan (D)
Walter M. Mumma (R)
George M. Rhodes (D)
John P. Saylor (R)
Hugh D. Scott, Jr. (D)
Richard M. Simpson (R)
S. Walter Stauffer (R)
James E. Van Zandt (R)
Francis E. Walter (D)

RHODE ISLAND

Senators

Theodore F. Green (D)
John O. Pastore (D)

Representatives

John E. Fogarty (D)
Aime J. Forand (D)

SOUTH CAROLINA

Senators

Burnet R. Maybanks (D)
d. Sept. 1954
Charles E. Daniel (D) s. 1954

Olin D. Johnston (D)

Representatives

Robert T. Ashmore (D)
Joseph R. Bryson (D) d. Mar. 1953
W. J. Bryan Dorn (D)
John L. McMillan (D)
James P. Richards (D)
John J. Riley (D)
L. Mendel Rivers (D)

SOUTH DAKOTA

Senators

Karl E. Mundt (R)
Francis H. Case (R)

Representatives

Ellis Y. Berry (R)
Harold O. Lovre (R)

TENNESSEE

Senators

Estes Kefauver (D)
Albert A. Gore (D)

Representatives

Howard H. Baker (R)
Jere Cooper (D)
Clifford Davis (D)
Joseph L. Evins (D)
James B. Frazier, Jr. (D)
Thomas J. Murray (D)
J. Percy Priest (D)
B. Carroll Reece (R)
James P. Sutton (D)

TEXAS

Senators

Lyndon B. Johnson (D)
M. Price Daniel (D)

Representatives

Lloyd M. Bentsen, Jr. (D)
Jack B. Brooks (D)
Omar T. Burleson (D)
Martin Dies, Jr. (D)
John V. Dowdy (D)
O. Clark Fisher (D)
Brady P. Gentry (D)
Frank N. Ikard (D)
Paul J. Kilday (D)
Wingate H. Lucas (D)
John E. Lyle, Jr. (D)
George H. Mahon (D)
Wright Patman (D)
William R. Poage (D)
Sam Rayburn (D)
Kenneth M. Regan (D)
Walter E. Rogers (D)
Olin E. Teague (D)
Albert Thomas (D)
Clark W. Thompson (D)
W. Homer Thornberry (D)
J. Frank Wilson (D)

UTAH

Senators

Arthur V. Watkins (R)
Wallace F. Bennett (R)

Representatives

William A. Dawson (R)
Douglas R. Stringfellow (R)

VERMONT

Senators

George D. Aiken (R)
Ralph E. Flanders (R)

Representative

Winston L. Prouty (R)

VIRGINIA

Senators

Harry F. Byrd (D)
A. Willis Robertson (D)

Representatives

Watkins M. Abbitt (D)
Joel T. Broyhill (R)
J. Vaughan Gary (D)
Porter Hardy, Jr. (D)
Burr P. Harrison (D)
Richard H. Poff (R)
Edward J. Robeson, Jr. (D)
Howard W. Smith (D)
Thomas B. Stanley (D)
r. Feb. 1953
William M. Tuck (D)
William C. Wampler (R)

WASHINGTON

Senators

Warren G. Magnuson (D)
Henry M. Jackson (D)

Representatives

Hal Holmes (R)
Walter F. Horan (R)
Russell V. Mack (R)
Donald H. Magnuson (D)
Thomas M. Pelly (R)
Thor C. Tollefson (R)
Alfred J. Westland (R)

WEST VIRGINIA

Senators

Harley M. Kilgore (D)
Matthew M. Neely (D)

Representatives

Cleveland M. Bailey (D)
Robert C. Byrd (D)
Maude Elizabeth Kee (D)
Robert H. Mollohan (D)
William E. Neal (R)
Harley O. Staggers (D)

WISCONSIN

Senators

Alexander Wiley (R)
Joseph R. McCarthy (R)

Representatives

John W. Byrnes (R)
Glenn R. Davis (R)
Merlin Hull (R) d. May 1953
Lester R. Johnson (D) s. 1954
Charles J. Kersten (R)
Melvin R. Laird (R)
Alvin E. O'Konski (R)
Lawrence H. Smith (R)
William K. Van Pelt (R)
Gardner R. Withrow (R)
Clement J. Zablocki (D)

WYOMING

Senators

Lester C. Hunt (D) d. June 1954
Edward D. Crippa (R) ta. 1954
Joseph C. O'Mahoney (D) s. 1954

Frank A. Barrett (R)

Representative

William H. Harrison (R)

EIGHTY-FOURTH CONGRESS

January 3, 1955 to January 3, 1957

President of The Senate: Richard M. Nixon
President Pro Tempore of The Senate: Walter F. George
Speaker of The House of Representatives: Sam Rayburn

ALABAMA

Senators

Lister Hill (D)
John J. Sparkman (D)

Representatives

George W. Andrews (D)
Frank W. Boykin (D)
Carl A. Elliott (D)
George M. Grant (D)
George Huddleston, Jr. (D)
Robert E. Jones, Jr. (D)
Albert Rains (D)
Kenneth A. Roberts (D)
Armistead I. Selden, Jr. (D)

ARIZONA

Senators

Carl Hayden (D)
Barry M. Goldwater (D)

Representatives

John J. Rhodes (R)
Stewart L. Udall (D)

ARKANSAS

Senators

John L. McClellan (D)
J. William Fulbright (D)

Representatives

Ezekiel C. Gathings (D)
Oren Harris (D)
Brooks Hays (D)
Wilbur D. Mills (D)
William F. Norrell (D)
James W. Trimble (D)

CALIFORNIA

Senators

William F. Knowland (R)
Thomas H. Kuchel (R)

Representatives

John J. Allen, Jr. (R)
John F. Baldwin, Jr. (R)
Clyde G. Doyle (D)
Clair Engle (D)
Charles S. Gubser (R)
Harlan F. Hagen (D)
Patrick J. Hillings (R)
Edgar W. Hiestand (R)
Carl Hinshaw (R)
Chet Holifield (D)
Joseph F. Holt (R)
Craig Hosmer (R)
Donald L. Jackson (R)
Leroy Johnson (R)
Cecil R. King (D)
Glenard P. Lipscomb (R)
Gordon L. McDonough (R)
William S. Mailliard (R)
George P. Miller (D)
John E. Moss, Jr. (D)
John Phillips (R)
James Roosevelt (D)
Hubert B. Scudder (R)
John F. Shelley (D)
Harry R. Sheppard (D)
Bernice F. Sisk (D)
Charles M. Teague (R)
James B. Utt (R)
Robert C. Wilson (R)
J. Arthur Younger (R)

COLORADO

Senators

Eugene D. Millikin (R)
Gordon L. Allott (R)

Representatives

Wayne N. Aspinall (D)
J. Edgar Chenoweth (R)
William S. Hill (R)
Byron G. Rogers (D)

CONNECTICUT

Senators

Prescott S. Bush (R)
William A. Purtell (R)

Representatives

Albert W. Cretella (R)
Thomas J. Dodd (D)
Albert P. Morano (R)
James T. Patterson (R)
Antoni N. Sadlak (R)
Horace Seely-Brown, Jr. (R)

DELAWARE

Senators

John J. Williams (R)
J. Allen Frear, Jr. (D)

Representative

Harris B. McDowell, Jr. (D)

FLORIDA

Senators

Spessard L. Holland (D)
George A. Smathers (D)

Representatives

Charles E. Bennett (D)
William C. Cramer (R)
Dante B. Fascell (D)
James A. Haley (D)
Albert S. Herlong, Jr. (D)
Donald R. Matthews (D)
Paul G. Rogers (D)
Robert L. F. Sikes (D)

GEORGIA

Senators

Walter F. George (D)
Richard B. Russell (D)

Representatives

Iris F. Blitch (D)
Paul Brown (D)
James C. Davis (D)
Elijah L. Forrester (D)
John J. Flynt, Jr. (D)
Phillip M. Landrum (D)
Henderson L. Lanham (D)
John L. Pilcher (D)
Prince H. Preston, Jr. (D)
Carl Vinson (D)

IDAHO

Senators

Henry C. Dworshak (R)
Herman Welker (R)

Representatives

Hamer H. Budge (R)
Gracie B. Pfost (D)

ILLINOIS

Senators

Paul H. Douglas (D)
Everett M. Dirksen (R)

Representatives

Leo E. Allen (R)
Leslie C. Arends (R)
James B. Bowler (D)
Charles A. Boyle (D)
Robert B. Chiperfield (R)
Marguerite Stitt Church (R)
William L. Dawson (D)
Thomas S. Gordon (D)
Kenneth J. Gray (D)
Richard W. Hoffman (R)
John C. Kluczynski (D)
William E. McVey (R)
Peter F. Mack, Jr. (R)
Noah M. Mason (R)
James C. Murray (D)
Thomas J. O'Brien (D)
Barratt O'Hara (D)
Melvin Price (D)
Chauncey W. Reed (R)
d. Feb. 1956
Timothy P. Sheehan (R)
Sidney E. Simpson (R)
William L. Springer (R)
Harold H. Velde (R)
Charles W. Vursell (R)
Sidney R. Yates (D)

INDIANA

Senators

Homer E. Capehart (R)
William E. Jenner (R)

Representatives

E. Ross Adair (R)
John V. Beamer (R)
William G. Bray (R)
Charles B. Brownson (R)
Shepard J. Crumpacker, Jr. (R)
Winfield K. Denton (D)
Charles A. Halleck (R)
Cecil M. Harden (R)
Ralph Harvey (R)
Ray J. Madden (D)
Earl Wilson (R)

IOWA

Senators

Bourke B. Hickenlooper (R)
Thomas E. Martin (R)

Representatives

Paul Cunningham (R)
James I. Dolliver (R)
Harold R. Gross (R)
Charles B. Hoeven (R)
Ben F. Jensen (R)
Karl M. LeCompte (R)
Frederick D. Schwengel (R)
Henry O. Talle (R)

KANSAS

Senators

Andrew F. Schoeppel (R)
Frank Carlson (R)

Representatives

William H. Avery (R)
Myron V. George (R)
Clifford R. Hope (R)
Edward H. Rees (R)
Errett P. Scrivner (R)
Wint Smith (R)

KENTUCKY

Senators

Earle C. Clements (D)

Alben W. Barkley (D)
d. Apr. 1956
Robert Humphreys (D) ta. 1956
John Sherman Cooper (R)
s. 1957

Representatives

Frank L. Chelf (D)
Noble J. Gregory (D)
William H. Natcher (D)
Carl D. Perkins (D)
John M. Robsion, Jr. (R)
Eugene Siler (R)
Brent Spence (D)
John C. Watts (D)

LOUISIANA

Senators

Allen J. Ellender, Sr. (D)
Russell B. Long (D)

Representatives

T. Hale Boggs (D)
Overton Brooks (D)
F. Edward Hebert (D)
George S. Long (D)
James H. Morrison (D)
Otto E. Passman (D)
T. Ashton Thompson (D)
Edwin E. Willis (D)

MAINE

Senators

Margaret Chase Smith (R)
Frederick G. Payne (R)

Representatives

Robert Hale (R)
Clifford G. McIntire (R)
Charles P. Nelson (R)

MARYLAND

Senators

John Marshall Butler (R)
J. Glenn Beall (R)

Representatives

James P. S. Devereux (R)
George H. Fallon (D)
Samuel N. Friedel (D)
Edward A. Garmatz (D)
DeWitt S. Hyde (R)
Richard E. Lankford (D)
Edward T. Miller (R)

MASSACHUSETTS

Senators

Leverett Saltonstall (R)
John F. Kennedy (D)

Representatives

William H. Bates (R)
Edward P. Boland (D)
Laurence Curtis (R)
Harold D. Donohue (D)
John W. Heselton (R)
Thomas J. Lane (D)
John W. McCormack (D)
Torbert H. Macdonald (D)
Joseph W. Martin, Jr. (R)
Donald W. Nicholson (R)
Thomas P. O'Neill, Jr. (D)
Philip J. Philbin (D)
Edith Nourse Rogers (R)
Richard B. Wigglesworth (R)

MICHIGAN

Senators

Charles E. Potter (R)
Patrick V. McNamara (D)

Representatives

John B. Bennett (R)
Alvin M. Bentley (R)
Elford A. Cederberg (R)
Charles C. Diggs, Jr. (D)
John D. Dingell (D) d. Sept. 1955
John D. Dingell, Jr. (D) s. 1956
George A. Dondero (R)
Gerald R. Ford, Jr. (R)
Martha W. Griffiths (R)
Don Hayworth (D)
Clare E. Hoffman (R)
August E. Johansen (R)
Victor A. Knox (R)
John Lesinski, Jr. (D)
Thaddeus M. Machrowicz (D)
George Meader (R)
Louis C. Rabaut (D)
Ruth Thompson (R)
Jesse P. Wolcott (R)

MINNESOTA

Senators

Edward J. Thye (R)
Hubert H. Humphrey (D)

Representatives

H. Carl Andersen (R)
August H. Andresen (R)
John A. Blatnik (D)
Walter H. Judd (R)
Coya G. Knutson (R)
Eugene J. McCarthy (D)
Fred Marshall (D)
Joseph P. O'Hara (R)
Roy W. Wier (D)

MISSISSIPPI

Senators

James O. Eastland (D)
John C. Stennis (D)

Representatives

Thomas G. Abernethy (D)
William M. Colmer (D)
Frank E. Smith (D)
Jamie L. Whitten (D)
John Bell Williams (D)
W. Arthur Winstead (D)

MISSOURI

Senators

Thomas C. Hennings, Jr. (D)
Stuart Symington (D)

Representatives

Richard W. Bolling (D)
Clarence Cannon (D)
Albert S. J. Carnahan (D)
George H. Christopher (D)
Thomas B. Curtis (R)
William R. Hull, Jr. (D)
Paul C. Jones (D)
Frank M. Karsten (D)
Morgan M. Moulder (D)
Dewey Short (R)
Leonor Kretzer Sullivan (D)

MONTANA

Senators

James E. Murray (D)
Mike Mansfield (D)

Representatives

Orvin B. Fjare (R)
Lee Metcalf (D)

NEBRASKA

Senators

Roman L. Hruska (R)
Carl T. Curtis (R)

Representatives

Jackson B. Chase (R)
Robert D. Harrison (R)
Arthur L. Miller (R)
Phillip H. Weaver (R)

NEVADA

Senators

George W. Malone (R)
Alan H. Bible (D)

Representative

Clifton Young (R)

NEW HAMPSHIRE

Senators

H. Styles Bridges (R)
Norris Cotton (R)

Representatives

Perkins Bass (R)
Chester E. Merrow (R)

NEW JERSEY

Senators

H. Alexander Smith (R)
Clifford B. Case (R)

Representatives

Hugh Addonizio (D)
James C. Auchincloss (R)
Gordon Canfield (R)
Peter H. B. Frelinghuysen, Jr. (R)
T. Millet Hand (R) d. Dec. 1956
Robert W. Kean (R)
Frank C. Osmers, Jr. (R)
Peter W. Rodino, Jr. (D)
Alfred D. Sieminski (D)
Frank Thompson, Jr. (D)
T. James Tumulty (D)
William B. Widnall (R)
Harrison A. Williams, Jr. (D)
Charles A. Wolverton (R)

NEW MEXICO

Senators

Dennis Chavez (D)
Clinton P. Anderson (D)

Representatives

John J. Dempsey (D)
Antonio M. Fernandez (D)
d. Nov. 1956

NEW YORK

Senators

Irving M. Ives (R)
Herbert H. Lehman (D)

Representatives

Victor L. Anfuso (D)
Frank J. Becker (R)
Albert H. Bosch (R)
Charles A. Buckley (D)
Emanuel Celler (D)
W. Sterling Cole (R)
Frederic R. Coudert, Jr. (R)
Irwin D. Davidson (D)
James J. Delaney (D)
Steven B. Derounian (R)
Isidore Dollinger (D)
James G. Donovan (D)
Francis E. Dorn (R)
Sidney A. Fine (D) r. Jan. 1956
Paul A. Fino (R)
Ralph A. Gamble (R)
Ralph W. Gwinn (R)
James C. Healey (D) s. 1956
Lester Holtzman (D)
Bernard W. Kearney (R)
Kenneth B. Keating (R)
Edna F. Kelly (D)
Eugene J. Keogh (D)
Clarence E. Kilburn (R)
Arthur G. Klein (D)
Henry J. Latham (R)

William E. Miller (R)
Abraham J. Multer (D)
Leo W. O'Brien (D)
Harold C. Ostertag (R)
John R. Pillion (R)
Adam Clayton Powell, Jr.
Edmund P. Radwan (R)
John H. Ray (R)
Daniel A. Reed (R)
R. Walter Riehlman (R)
John J. Rooney (D)
Katharine St. George (R)
John Taber (R)
Dean P. Taylor (R)
Stuyvesant Wainwright (R)
J. Ernest Wharton (R)
William R. Williams (R)
Herbert Zelenko (D)

NORTH CAROLINA

Senators

Sam J. Ervin, Jr. (D)
W. Kerr Scott (D)

Representatives

Hugh Q. Alexander (D)
Graham A. Barden (D)
Herbert C. Bonner (D)
F. Ertel Carlyle (D)
Richard T. Chatham (D)
Harold D. Cooley (D)
Charles B. Deane (D)
Carl T. Durham (D)
Lawrence H. Fountain (D)
Charles R. Jonas (R)
Woodrow W. Jones (D)
George A. Shuford (D)

NORTH DAKOTA

Senators

William Langer (R)
Milton R. Young (R)

Representatives

Usher L. Burdick (R)
Otto Krueger (R)

OHIO

Senators

John W. Bricker (R)
George H. Bender (R)

Representatives

Thomas L. Ashley (D)
William H. Ayres (R)
Albert D. Baumhart, Jr. (R)
Jackson E. Betts (R)
Frances P. Bolton (R)
Oliver P. Bolton (R)
Frank T. Bow (R)
Clarence J. Brown (R)
Cliff Clevenger (R)
Michael A. Feighan (D)
Wayne L. Hays (D)
John E. Henderson (R)
William E. Hess (R)
Thomas A. Jenkins (R)
Michael J. Kirwan (D)
William M. McCulloch (R)
J. Harry McGregor (R)
William E. Minshall (R)
James G. Polk (D)
Paul F. Schenck (R)
Gordon H. Scherer (R)
Charles A. Vanik (D)
John M. Vorys (R)

OKLAHOMA

Senators

Robert S. Kerr (D)
A. S. Mike Monroney (D)

Representatives

Carl Albert (D)
Page H. Belcher (R)
Edmond Edmondson (D)
John Jarman (D)
Thomas J. Steed (D)
Victor E. Wickersham (D)

OREGON

Senators

Wayne L. Morse (D)
Richard L. Neuberger (D)

Representatives

Samuel H. Coon (R)
Harris Ellsworth (R)
Edith S. Green (D)
A. Walter Norblad (R)

PENNSYLVANIA

Senators

Edward Martin (D)
James H. Duff (R)

Representatives

William A. Barrett (D)
Vera D. Buchanan (D)
d. Nov. 1955
Alvin R. Bush (R)
James A. Byrne (D)
Joseph L. Carrigg (R)
Earl Chudoff (D)
Frank M. Clark (D)
Robert J. Corbett (R)
Paul B. Dague (R)
Herman P. Eberharter (D)
Ivor D. Fenton (R)
Daniel J. Flood (D)
James G. Fulton (R)
Leon H. Gavin (R)
William T. Granahan (D)
d. May 1956
William J. Green, Jr. (D)
Elmer J. Holland (D) s. 1956
Benjamin F. James (R)
Carroll D. Kearns (R)
Augustine B. Kelley (D)
Karl C. King (R)
Samuel K. McConnell, Jr. (R)
Thomas E. Morgan (D)
Walter E. Mumma (R)
James M. Quigley (D)
George M. Rhodes (D)
John P. Saylor (R)
Hugh D. Scott, Jr. (R)
Richard M. Simpson (R)
James E. VanZandt (R)
Francis E. Walter (D)

RHODE ISLAND

Senators

Theodore F. Green (D)
John O. Pastore (D)

Representatives

John E. Fogarty (D)
Aime J. Forand (D)

SOUTH CAROLINA

Senators

Olin D. Johnston (D)

J. Strom Thurmond (D)
r. Apr. 1956
Thomas A. Woffard (D) s. 1956

Representatives

Robert T. Ashmore (D)
W. J. Bryan Dorn (D)
John L. McMillan (D)
James P. Richards (D)
John J. Riley (D)
L. Mendel Rivers (D)

SOUTH DAKOTA

Senators

Karl E. Mundt (R)
Francis H. Case (R)

Representatives

Ellis Y. Berry (R)
Harold O. Lovre (R)

TENNESSEE

Senators

Estes Kefauver (D)
Albert A. Gore (D)

Representatives

Howard H. Baker (R)
Ross Bass (D)
Jere Cooper (D)
Clifford Davis (D)
Joseph L. Evins (D)
James B. Frazier, Jr. (D)
Thomas J. Murray (D)
J. Percy Priest (D) d. Oct. 1956
B. Carroll Reece (R)

TEXAS

Senators

Lyndon B. Johnson (D)
M. Price Daniel (D)

Representatives

Bruce R. Alger (R)
John J. Bell (D)
Jack B. Brooks (D)
Omar T. Burleson (D)
Martin Dies, Jr. (D)
John V. Dowdy (D)
O. Clark Fisher (D)
Brady P. Gentry (D)
Frank N. Ikard (D)
Paul J. Kilday (D)
Joe M. Kilgore (D)
George H. Mahon (D)
Wright Patman (D)
William R. Poage (D)
Sam Rayburn (D)
Walter E. Rogers (D)
J. T. Rutherford (D)
Olin E. Teague (D)
Albert Thomas
Clark W. Thompson (D)
W. Homer Thornberry (D)
James C. Wright, Jr. (D)

UTAH

Senators

Arthur V. Watkins (R)
Wallace F. Bennett (R)

Representatives

William A. Dawson (R)
Henry A. Dixon (R)

VERMONT

Senators

George D. Aiken (R)
Ralph E. Flanders (R)

Representative

Winston L. Prouty (R)

VIRGINIA

Senators

Harry F. Byrd (D)
A. Willis Robertson (D)

Representatives

Watkins M. Abbitt (D)
Joel T. Broyhill (R)
J. Vaughan Gary (D)
Porter Hardy, Jr. (D)
Burr P. Harrison (D)
William P. Jennings (D)
Richard H. Poff (R)
Edward J. Robeson, Jr. (D)
Howard W. Smith (D)
William M. Tuck (D)

WASHINGTON

Senators

Warren G. Magnuson (D)
Henry M. Jackson (D)

Representatives

Hal Holmes (R)
Walter F. Horan (R)
Russell V. Mack (R)
Donald H. Magnuson (D)
Thomas M. Pelly (R)
Thor C. Tollefson (R)
Alfred J. Westland (R)

WEST VIRGINIA

Senators

Harley M. Kilgore (D)
d. Feb. 1956
William R. Laird 3rd (D) ta. 1956
Chapman Revercomb (R) s. 1957

Matthew M. Neely (D)

Representatives

Cleveland M. Bailey (D)
Maurice B. Burnside (D)
Robert C. Byrd (D)
Maude Elizabeth Kee (D)
Robert H. Mollohan (D)
Harley O. Staggers (D)

WISCONSIN

Senators

Alexander Wiley (R)
Joseph R. McCarthy (R)

Representatives

John W. Byrnes (R)
Glenn R. Davis (R)
Lester R. Johnson (D)
Melvin R. Laird (R)
Alvin E. O'Konski (R)
Henry S. Reuss (D)
Lawrence H. Smith (R)
William K. VanPelt (R)
Gardner R. Withrow (R)
Clement J. Zablocki (D)

WYOMING

Senators

Frank A. Barrett (R)
Joseph C. O'Mahoney (D)

Representative

E. Keith Thomson (R)

EIGHTY-FIFTH CONGRESS

January 3, 1957 to January 3, 1959

President of The Senate: Richard M. Nixon
President Pro Tempore of The Senate: Carl Hayden
Speaker of The House of Representatives: Sam Rayburn

ALABAMA

Senators

Lister Hill (D)
John J. Sparkman (D)

Representatives

George W. Andrews (D)
Frank W. Boykin (D)
Carl A. Elliott (D)
George M. Grant (D)
George Huddleston, Jr. (D)
Robert E. Jones, Jr. (D)
Albert Rains (D)
Kenneth A. Roberts (D)
Armistead I. Selden, Jr. (D)

ARIZONA

Senators

Carl Hayden (D)
Barry M. Goldwater (R)

Representatives

John J. Rhodes (R)
Stewart L. Udall (D)

ARKANSAS

Senators

John L. McClellan (D)
J. William Fulbright (D)

Representatives

Ezekiel C. Gathings (D)
Oren Harris (D)
Brooks Hays (D)
Wilbur D. Mills (D)
William F. Norrell (D)
James W. Trimble (D)

CALIFORNIA

Senators

William F. Knowland (R)
Thomas H. Kuchel (R)

Representatives

John J. Allen, Jr. (R)
John F. Baldwin, Jr. (R)
Clyde G. Doyle (D)
Clair Engle (D)
Charles S. Gubser (R)
Harlan F. Hagen (D)
Edgar W. Hiestand (R)
Patrick J. Hillings (R)
Chet Holifield (D)
Joseph F. Holt (R)
Craig Hosmer (R)
Donald L. Jackson (R)
Cecil R. King (D)
Glenard P. Lipscomb (R)
Gordon L. McDonough (R)
John J. McFall (D)
William S. Mailliard (R)
George P. Miller (D)
John E. Moss, Jr. (D)
James Roosevelt (D)
Dalip S. Saund (D)
Hubert B. Scudder (R)
John F. Shelley (D)
Harry R. Sheppard (D)
Bernice F. Sisk (D)
H. Allen Smith (R)
Charles M. Teague (R)
James B. Utt (R)
Robert C. Wilson (R)
J. Arthur Younger (R)

COLORADO

Senators

Gordon L. Allott (R)
John A. Carroll (D)

Representatives

Wayne N. Aspinall (D)
J. Edgar Chenoweth (R)
William S. Hill (R)
Byron G. Rogers (D)

CONNECTICUT

Senators

Prescott S. Bush (R)
William A. Purtell (R)

Representatives

Albert W. Cretella (R)
Edwin H. May, Jr. (D)
Albert P. Morano (R)
James T. Patterson (R)
Antoni N. Sadlak (R)
Horace Seely-Brown, Jr. (R)

DELAWARE

Senators

John J. Williams (R)
J. Allen Frear, Jr. (D)

Representative

Harry G. Haskell, Jr. (R)

FLORIDA

Senators

Spessard L. Holland (D)
George A. Smathers (D)

Representatives

Charles E. Bennett (D)
William C. Cramer (R)
Dante B. Fascell (D)
James A. Haley (D)
Albert S. Herlong, Jr. (D)
Donald R. Matthews (D)
Paul G. Rogers (D)
Robert L. F. Sikes (D)

GEORGIA

Senators

Richard B. Russell (D)
Herman E. Talmadge (D)

Representatives

Iris F. Blitch (D)
Paul Brown (D)
James C. Davis (D)
John James Flynt, Jr. (D)
Elijah L. Forrester (D)
Phillip M. Landrum (D)
Henderson L. Lanham (D)
d. Nov. 1957
Harlan E. Mitchell (D) s. 1958
John L. Pilcher (D)
Prince H. Preston, Jr. (D)
Carl Vinson (D)

IDAHO

Senators

Henry C. Dworshak (R)
Frank Church (D)

Representatives

Hamer H. Budge (R)
Gracie B. Pfost (D)

ILLINOIS

Senators

Paul H. Douglas (D)
Everett M. Dirksen (R)

Representatives

Leo E. Allen (R)
Leslie C. Arends (R)
James B. Bowler (D) d. July 1957
Charles A. Boyle (D)
Emmet F. Byrne (R)
Robert B. Chiperfield (R)
Marguerite Stitt Church (R)
Harold R. Collier (R)
William L. Dawson (D)
Kenneth J. Gray (D)
Thomas S. Gordon (D)
Russell W. Keeney (R)
d. Jan. 1958
John C. Kluczynski (D)
Roland V. Libonati (D) s. 1958
William E. McVey (R)
d. Aug. 1958
Peter F. Mack, Jr. (D)
Noah M. Mason (R)
Robert H. Michel (R)
Melvin Price (D)
Thomas J. O'Brien (D)
Barratt O'Hara (D)
Timothy P. Sheehan (R)
Sidney E. Simpson (R)
d. Oct. 1958
William L. Springer (R)
Charles W. Vursell (R)
Sidney R. Yates (D)

INDIANA

Senators

Homer E. Capehart (R)
William E. Jenner (R)

Representatives

E. Ross Adair (R)
John V. Beamer (R)

William G. Bray (R)
Charles B. Brownson (R)
Winfield K. Denton (D)
Charles A. Halleck (R)
Cecil M. Harden (R)
Ralph Harvey (R)
Ray J. Madden (D)
F. Jay Nimtz (R)
Earl Wilson (R)

IOWA

Senators

Bourke B. Hickenlooper (R)
Thomas E. Martin (R)

Representatives

Merwin Coad (D)
Paul Cunningham (R)
Harold R. Gross (R)
Charles B. Hoeven (R)
Ben F. Jensen (R)
Karl M. LeCompte (R)
Frederick D. Schwengel (R)
Henry O. Talle (R)

KANSAS

Senators

Andrew F. Schoeppel (R)
Frank Carlson (R)

Representatives

William H. Avery (R)
J. Floyd Breeding (D)
Myron V. George (R)
Edward H. Rees (R)
Errett P. Scrivner (R)
Wint Smith (R)

KENTUCKY

Senators

John Sherman Cooper (R)
Thruston B. Morton (R)

Representatives

Frank L. Chelf (D)
Nobel J. Gregory (D)
William H. Natcher (D)
Carl D. Perkins (D)
John M. Robsion, Jr. (R)
Eugene Siler (R)
Brent Spence (D)
John C. Watts (D)

LOUISIANA

Senators

Allen J. Ellender (D)
Russell B. Long (D)

Representatives

T. Hale Boggs (D)
Overton Brooks (D)
F. Edward Hebert (D)
George S. Long (D) d. Mar. 1958
James H. Morrison (D)
Otto E. Passman (D)
T. Ashton Thompson (D)
Edwin E. Willis (D)

MAINE

Senators

Margaret Chase Smith (R)
Frederick G. Payne (R)

Representatives

Frank M. Coffin (R)
Robert Hale (R)
Clifford G. McIntire (R)

MARYLAND

Senators

John Marshall Butler (R)
J. Glenn Beall (R)

Representatives

James P. S. Devereux (R)
George H. Fallon (D)
Samuel N. Friedel (D)
Edward A. Garmatz (D)
DeWitt S. Hyde (R)
Richard E. Lankford (D)
Edward T. Miller (R)

MASSACHUSETTS

Senators

Leverett Saltonstall (R)
John F. Kennedy (D)

Representatives

William H. Bates (R)
Edward P. Boland (D)
Laurence Curtis (R)
Harold D. Donohue (D)
John W. Heselton (R)
Thomas J. Lane (D)
John W. McCormack (D)
Torbert H. Macdonald (D)
Joseph W. Martin, Jr. (R)
Donald W. Nicholson (R)
Thomas P. O'Neill, Jr. (D)
Philip J. Philbin (D)
Edith Nourse Rogers (R)
Richard B. Wigglesworth (R)
r. Nov. 1958

MICHIGAN

Senators

Charles E. Potter (R)
Patrick V. McNamara (D)

Representatives

John B. Bennett (R)
Alvin M. Bentley (R)
William S. Broomfield (R)
Elford A. Cederberg (R)
Charles E. Chamberlain (R)
Charles C. Diggs, Jr. (D)
John D. Dingell, Jr. (D)
Gerald R. Ford, Jr. (R)
Robert P. Griffin (R)
Martha W. Griffiths (R)
Clare E. Hoffman (R)
August E. Johansen (R)
Victor A. Knox (R)
John Lesinski, Jr. (D)
Robert J. McIntosh (R)
Thaddeus M. Machrowicz (D)
George Meader (R)
Louis C. Rabaut (D)

MINNESOTA

Senators

Edward J. Thye (R)
Hubert H. Humphrey (D)

Representatives

H. Carl Andersen (R)
August H. Andresen (R)
d. Jan. 1958
John A. Blatnik (D)
Walter H. Judd (R)
Coya G. Knutson (R)
Eugene J. McCarthy (D)
Fred Marshall (D)
Joseph P. O'Hara (R)
Albert H. Quie (R) s. 1958
Roy W. Wier (D)

MISSISSIPPI

Senators

James O. Eastland (D)
John C. Stennis (D)

Representatives

Thomas G. Abernethy (D)
William M. Colmer (D)
Frank E. Smith (D)
Jamie L. Whitten (D)
John Bell Williams (D)
W. Arthur Winstead (D)

MISSOURI

Senators

Thomas C. Hennings, Jr. (D)
Stuart Symington (D)

Representatives

Richard W. Bolling (D)
Charles H. Brown (D)
Clarence Cannon (D)
Albert S. J. Carnahan (D)
George H. Christopher (D)
Thomas B. Curtis (R)
William R. Hull, Jr. (D)
Paul C. Jones (D)
Frank M. Karsten (D)
Morgan M. Moulder (D)
Leonor Kretzer Sullivan (D)

MONTANA

Senators

James E. Murray (D)
Mike Mansfield (D)

Representatives

LeRoy H. Anderson (D)
Lee Metcalf (D)

NEBRASKA

Senators

Roman L. Hruska (R)
Carl T. Curtis (R)

Representatives

Glenn C. Cunningham (R)
Robert D. Harrison (R)
Arthur L. Miller (R)
Phillip H. Weaver (R)

NEVADA

Senators

George W. Malone (R)
Alan H. Bible (D)

Representative

Walter S. Baring (D)

NEW HAMPSHIRE

Senators

H. Styles Bridges (R)
Norris Cotton (R)

Representatives

Perkins Bass (R)
Chester E. Merrow (R)

NEW JERSEY

Senators

H. Alexander Smith (R)
Clifford P. Case (R)

Representatives

Hugh J. Addonizio (D)
James C. Auchincloss (R)
Gordon Canfield (R)
Vincent J. Dellay (R)
Florence P. Dwyer (R)
Peter H. B. Frelinghuysen, Jr. (R)
Milton W. Glenn (R) s. 1958
Robert W. Kean (R)
Frank C. Osmers, Jr. (R)
Peter W. Rodino, Jr. (D)
Alfred D. Sieminski (D)
Frank Thompson, Jr. (D)
William B. Widnall (R)
Charles A. Wolverton (R)

NEW MEXICO

Senators

Dennis Chavez (D)
Clinton P. Anderson (D)

Representatives

John J. Dempsey (R) d. Mar. 1958
Joseph M. Montoya (D) s. 1957

NEW YORK

Senators

Irving M. Ives (R)
Jacob K. Javits (R)

Representatives

Victor L. Anfuso (D)
Frank J. Becker (R)
Albert H. Bosch (R)
Charles A. Buckley (D)
Emanuel Celler (D)
W. Sterling Cole (R)
r. Dec. 1957
Frederic R. Coudert, Jr. (R)
James J. Delaney (D)
Steven B. Derounian (R)
Isidore Dollinger (D)
Edwin B. Dooley (R)
Francis E. Dorn (R)
Leonard Farbstein (D)
Paul A. Fino (R)
Ralph W. Gwinn (R)
James C. Healey (D)
Lester Holtzman (D)
Bernard W. Kearney (R)
Kenneth B. Keating (R)
Edna F. Kelly (D)
Eugene J. Keogh (D)
Clarence E. Kilburn (R)
Henry J. Latham (R)
William E. Miller (R)
Abraham J. Multer (D)
Leo W. O'Brien (D)
Harold C. Ostertag (R)
John R. Pillion (R)
Adam Clayton Powell, Jr. (D)
Edmund P. Radwan (R)
John H. Ray (R)
Daniel A. Reed (R)
R. Walter Riehlman (R)
Howard W. Robison (R) s. 1958
John J. Rooney (D)
Katharine St. George (R)
Alfred E. Santangelo (D)
John Taber (R)
Dean P. Taylor (R)
Ludwig Teller (D)
Stuyvesant Wainwright (R)
J. Ernest Wharton (R)
William R. Williams (R)
Herbert Zelenko (D)

NORTH CAROLINA

Senators

Sam J. Ervin, Jr. (D)

W. Kerr Scott (D) d. Apr. 1958
B. Everett Jordan (D) s. 1958

Representatives

Hugh Q. Alexander (D)
Graham A. Barden (D)
Herbert C. Booner (D)
Harold D. Cooley (D)
Carl T. Durham (D)
Lawrence H. Fountain (D)
Charles R. Jonas (R)
A. Paul Kitchin (D)
Alton A. Lennon (D)
Ralph J. Scott (D)
George A. Shuford (D)
Basil L. Whitener (D)

NORTH DAKOTA

Senators

William Langer (R)
Milton R. Young (R)

Representatives

Usher L. Burdick (R)
Otto Krueger (R)

OHIO

Senators

John W. Bricker (R)
Frank J. Lausche (D)

Representatives

William H. Ayres (R)
Thomas L. Ashley (D)
Albert D. Baumhart, Jr. (R)
Jackson E. Betts (R)
Frances P. Bolton (R)
Frank T. Bow (R)
Clarence J. Brown (R)
Cliff Clevenger (R)
David S. Dennison (R)
Michael A. Feighan (D)
Wayne L. Hays (D)
John E. Henderson (R)
William E. Hess (R)
Thomas A. Jenkins (R)
Michael J. Kirwan (D)
William M. McCulloch (R)
J. Harry McGregor (R)
d. Oct. 1958
William E. Minshall (R)
James G. Polk (D)
Paul F. Schenck (R)
Gordon H. Scherer (R)
Charles A. Vanik (D)
John M. Vorys (R)

OKLAHOMA

Senators

Robert S. Kerr (D)
A. S. Mike Monroney (D)

Representatives

Carl Albert (D)
Page H. Belcher (R)
Edmond Edmondson (D)
John Jarman (D)
Toby Morris (D)
Thomas J. Steed (D)

OREGON

Senators

Wayne L. Morse (D)
Richard L. Neuberger (D)

Representatives

Edith Green (D)
A. Walter Norblad (R)
Charles O. Porter (D)
Albert C. Ullman (D)

PENNSYLVANIA

Senators

Edward Martin (D)
Joseph S. Clark (D)

Representatives

William A. Barrett (D)
Alvin R. Bush (R)
James A. Byrne (D)
Joseph L. Carrigg (R)
Earl Chudoff (D) r. Jan. 1958
Frank M. Clark (D)
Robert J. Corbett (R)
Willard S. Curtin (R)
Paul B. Dague (R)
John H. Dent (D) s. 1958
Herman P. Eberharter (D)
d. Sept. 1958
Ivor D. Fenton (R)
Daniel J. Flood (D)
James G. Fulton (R)
Leon H. Gavin (R)
Kathryn E. Granahan (D)
William J. Green, Jr. (D)
Elmer J. Holland (D)
Benjamin F. James (R)
Carroll D. Kearns (R)
Augustine B. Kelley (D)
d. Nov. 1957
John A. Lafore, Jr. (R) s. 1958
Samuel K. McConnell, Jr. (R)
r. Sept. 1957
Thomas E. Morgan (D)
Walter M. Mumma (R)
Robert N. C. Nix (D) s. 1958
George M. Rhodes (D)
John P. Saylor (R)
Hugh D. Scott, Jr. (R)
Richard M. Simpson (R)
S. Walter Stauffer (R)
James E. VanZandt (R)
Francis E. Walter (D)

RHODE ISLAND

Senators

Theodore F. Green (D)
John O. Pastore (D)

Representatives

John E. Fogarty (D)
Aime J. Forand (D)

SOUTH CAROLINA

Senators

Olin D. Johnston (D)
J. Strom Thurmond (D)

Representatives

Robert T. Ashmore (D)
W.J. Bryan Dorn (D)
Robert W. Hemphill (D)
John L. McMillan (D)
John J. Riley (D)
L. Mendel Rivers (D)

SOUTH DAKOTA

Senators

Karl E. Mundt (R)
Francis H. Case (R)

Representatives

Ellis Y. Berry (R)
George S. McGovern (D)

TENNESSEE

Senators

Estes Kefauver (D)
Albert A. Gore (D)

Representatives

Howard H. Baker (R)
Ross Bass (D)
Jere Cooper (D) d. Dec. 1957
Clifford Davis (D)
Robert A. Everett (D) s. 1958
Joseph L. Evins (D)
James B. Frazier, Jr. (D)
J. Carlton Loser (D)
Thomas J. Murray (D)
B. Carroll Reece (R)

TEXAS

Senators

Lyndon B. Johnson (D)

M. Price Daniel (D)
r. Jan. 1957
William A. Blakley (D) ta. 1957
Ralph W. Yarborough (D)

Representatives

Bruce R. Alger (R)
Lindley G. Beckworth (D)
Jack B. Brooks (D)
Omar T. Burleson (D)
Martin Dies, Jr. (D)
John V. Dowdy (D)
O. Clark Fisher (D)
Frank N. Ikard (D)
Paul J. Kilday (D)
Joe M. Kilgore (D)
George H. Mahon (D)
Wright Patman (D)
William R. Poage (D)
Sam Rayburn (D)
Walter E. Rogers (D)
J. T. Rutherford (D)
Olin E. Teague (D)
Albert Thomas (D)
Clark W. Thompson (D)
W. Homer Thornberry (D)
James C. Wright, Jr. (D)
John A. Young (D)

UTAH

Senators

Arthur V. Watkins (R)
Wallace F. Bennett (R)

Representatives

William A. Dawson (R)
Henry A. Dixon (R)

VERMONT

Senators

George D. Aiken (R)
Ralph E. Flanders (R)

Representative

Winston L. Prouty (R)

VIRGINIA

Senators

Harry F. Byrd (D)
A. Willis Robertson (D)

Representatives

Watkins M. Abbitt (D)
Joel T. Broyhill (D)
J. Vaughan Gary (D)
Porter Hardy, Jr. (D)
Burr P. Harrison (D)
William P. Jennings (D)
Richard H. Poff (R)
Edward J. Robeson, Jr. (D)
Howard W. Smith (D)
William M. Tuck (D)

WASHINGTON

Senators

Warren G. Magnuson (D)
Henry M. Jackson (D)

Representatives

Hal Holmes (R)
Walter F. Horan (R)
Russell V. Mack (R)
Donald H. Magnuson (D)
Thomas M. Pelly (R)
Thor C. Tollefson (R)
Alfred J. Westland (R)

WEST VIRGINIA

Senators

Matthew M. Neely (D)
d. Jan. 1958
John D. Hoblitzell, Jr. (R)
ta. 1958
Jennings Randolph (D) s. 1959

Chapman Revercomb (R)

Representatives

Cleveland M. Bailey (D)
Robert C. Byrd (D)
Maude Elizabeth Kee (D)
Arch A. Moore, Jr. (R)
William E. Neal (R)
Harley O. Staggers (D)

WISCONSIN

Senators

Alexander Wiley (R)

Joseph R. McCarthy (R)
d. May 1957
William Proxmire (D)

Representatives

John W. Byrnes (R)
Lester R. Johnson (D)
Melvin R. Laird (R)
Alvin E. O'Konski (R)
Henry S. Reuss (D)
Lawrence H. Smith (R)
d. Jan. 1958
Donald E. Tewes (R)
William K. VanPelt (R)
Gardner R. Withrow (R)
Clement J. Zablocki (D)

WYOMING

Senators

Frank A. Barrett (R)
Joseph C. O'Mahoney (D)

Representative

E. Keith Thomson (R)

EIGHTY-SIXTH CONGRESS

January 3, 1959 to January 3, 1961

President of The Senate:	Richard M. Nixon
President Pro Tempore of The Senate:	Carl Hayden
Speaker of The House of Representatives:	Sam Rayburn

ALABAMA

Senators

Lister Hill (D)
John J. Sparkman (D)

Representatives

George W. Andrews (D)
Frank W. Boykin (D)
Carl A. Elliott (D)
George M. Grant (D)
George Huddleston, Jr. (D)
Robert E. Jones, Jr. (D)
Albert Rains (D)
Kenneth A. Roberts (D)
Armistead I. Selden, Jr. (D)

ALASKA

Senators

Edward L. Bartlett (D)
Ernest Gruening (D)

Representative

Ralph J. Rivers (D)

ARIZONA

Senators

Carl Hayden (D)
Barry M. Goldwater (R)

Representatives

John J. Rhodes (D)
Steward L. Udall (D)

ARKANSAS

Senators

John L. McClellan (D)
J. William Fulbright (D)

Representatives

T. Dale Alford (D)
Ezekiel C. Gathings (D)
Oren Harris (D)
Wilbur D. Mills (D)
William F. Norrell (D)
James W. Trimble (D)

CALIFORNIA

Senators

Thomas H. Kuchel (R)
Clair Engle (D)

Representatives

John F. Baldwin, Jr. (R)
Jeffery Cohelan (D)
Clyde G. Doyle (D)
Charles S. Gubser (R)
Harlan F. Hagen (D)
Edgar W. Hiestand (R)
Chet Holifield (D)
Joseph F. Holt (R)
Craig Hosmer (R)
Donald L. Jackson (R)
Harold T. Johnson (D)
George A. Kasem (D)
Cecil R. King (D)
Glenard P. Lipscomb (R)
Gordon L. McDonough (R)
John J. McFall (D)
William S. Mailliard (R)
Clement W. Miller (D)
George P. Miller (D)
John E. Moss, Jr. (D)
James Roosevelt (D)
Dalip S. Saund (D)
John F. Shelley (D)
Harry R. Sheppard (D)
Bernice F. Sisk (D)
H. Allen Smith (R)
Charles M. Teague (R)
James B. Utt (R)
Robert C. Wilson (R)
J. Arthur Younger (R)

COLORADO

Senators

Gordon L. Allott (R)
John A. Carroll (D)

Representatives

Wayne N. Aspinall (D)
J. Edgar Chenoweth (R)
Byron L. Johnson (D)
Byron G. Rogers (D)

CONNECTICUT

Senators

Prescott S. Bush (R)
Thomas J. Dodd (D)

Representatives

Chester B. Bowles (D)
Emilio Q. Daddario (D)
Robert N. Giaimo (D)
Donald J. Irwin (D)
Frank Kowalski (D)
John S. Monagan (D)

DELAWARE

Senators

John J. Williams (R)
J. Allen Frear, Jr. (D)

Representative

Harris B. McDowell, Jr. (D)

FLORIDA

Senators

Spessard L. Holland (D)
George A. Smathers (D)

Representatives

Charles E. Bennett (D)
William C. Cramer (R)
Dante B. Fascell (D)
James A. Haley (D)
Albert S. Herlong, Jr. (D)
Donald R. Matthews (D)
Paul G. Rogers (D)
Robert L. F. Sikes (D)

GEORGIA

Senators

Richard B. Russell (D)
Herman E. Talmadge (D)

Representatives

Iris F. Blitch (D)
Paul Brown (D)
James C. Davis (D)
John J. Flynt, Jr. (D)
Elijah L. Forrester (D)
Phillip M. Landrum (D)
Harlan E. Mitchell (D)
John L. Pilcher (D)
Prince H. Preston, Jr. (D)
Carl Vinson (D)

HAWAII

Senators

Hiram L. Fong (R)
Oren E. Long (D)

Representative

Daniel K. Inouye (D)

IDAHO

Senators

Henry C. Dworshak (R)
Frank Church (D)

Representatives

Hamer H. Budge (R)
Gracie B. Pfost (D)

ILLINOIS

Senators

Paul H. Douglas (D)
Everett M. Dirksen (R)

Representatives

Leo E. Allen (R)
Leslie C. Arends (R)
Charles A. Boyle (D)
d. Nov. 1959
Robert B. Chiperfield (R)
Marguerite Stitt Church (R)
Harold R. Collier (R)
William L. Dawson (D)
Edward J. Derwinski (R)
Kenneth J. Gray (D)
Elmer J. Hoffman (R)
John C. Kluczynski (D)
Roland V. Libonati (D)
Peter F. Mack, Jr. (D)
Noah M. Mason (R)
Robert H. Michel (R)
William T. Murphy (D)
Thomas J. O'Brien (D)
Barratt O'Hara (D)
Melvin Price (D)
Roman C. Pucinski (D)
Daniel D. Rostenkowski (D)
George E. Shipley (D)
Edna Oakes Simpson (R)
William L. Springer (R)
Sidney R. Yates (D)

INDIANA

Senators

Homer E. Capehart (R)
Vance Hartke (D)

Representatives

E. Ross Adair (R)
Joseph W. Barr (D)
John Brademas (D)
William G. Bray (R)
Winfield K. Denton (D)
Charles A. Halleck (R)
Randall S. Harmon (D)
Earl L. Hogan (D)
Ray J. Madden (D)
J. Edward Roush (D)
Fred Wampler (D)

IOWA

Senators

Bourke B. Hickenlooper (R)
Thomas E. Martin (R)

Representatives

Steven V. Carter (D) d. Nov. 1959
Merwin Coad (D)
Harold R. Gross (R)
Charles B. Hoeven (R)
Ben F. Jensen (R)
John H. Kyl (R) s. 1960
Frederick D. Schwengel (R)
Neal Smith (D)
Leonard G. Wolf (D)

KANSAS

Senators

Andrew F. Schoeppel (R)
Frank Carlson (R)

Representatives

William H. Avery (R)
J. Floyd Breeding (D)
Newell A. George (D)
Denver D. Hargis (D)
Edward H. Rees (R)
Wint Smith (R)

KENTUCKY

Senators

John Sherman Cooper (R)
Thruston B. Morton (R)

Representatives

Frank W. Burke (D)
Frank L. Chelf (D)
William H. Natcher (D)
Carl D. Perkins (D)
Eugene Siler (R)
Brent Spence (D)
Frank A. Stubblefield (D)
John C. Watts (D)

LOUISIANA

Senators

Allen J. Ellender (D)
Russell B. Long (D)

Representatives

T. Hale Boggs (D)
Overton Brooks (D)
F. Edward Hebert (D)
Harold B. McSween (D)
James H. Morrison (D)
Otto E. Passman (D)
T. Ashton Thompson (D)
Edwin E. Willis (D)

MAINE

Senators

Margaret Chase Smith (R)
Edmund S. Muskie (D)

Representatives

Frank M. Coffin (R)
Clifford G. McIntire (R)
James C. Oliver (D)

MARYLAND

Senators

John Marshall Butler (R)
J. Glenn Beall (R)

Representatives

Daniel B. Brewster (D)
George H. Fallon (D)
Edward A. Garmatz (D)
John R. Foley (D)
Samuel N. Friedel (D)
Thomas F. Johnson (D)
Richard E. Lankford (D)

MASSACHUSETTS

Senators

Leverett Saltonstall (R)
John F. Kennedy (D) r. Dec. 1960

Representatives

William H. Bates (R)
Edward P. Boland (D)
James A. Burke (D)
Silvio O. Conte (R)
Laurence Curtis (R)
Harold D. Donohue (D)
Hastings Keith (R)
Thomas J. Lane (D)
John W. McCormack (D)
Torbert H. Macdonald (D)
Joseph W. Martin, Jr. (R)
Thomas P. O'Neill, Jr. (D)
Philip J. Philbin (D)
Edith Nourse Rogers (R)
d. Sept. 1960

MICHIGAN

Senators

Patrick V. McNamara (D)
Philip A. Hart (D)

Representatives

John B. Bennett (R)
Alvin M. Bentley (R)
William S. Broomfield (R)
Elford A. Cederberg (R)
Charles E. Chamberlain (R)
Charles C. Diggs, Jr. (D)
John D. Dingell, Jr. (D)
Gerald R. Ford, Jr. (R)
Robert P. Griffin (R)
Martha W. Griffiths (R)
Clare E. Hoffman (R)
August E. Johansen (R)
Victor A. Knox (R)
John Lesinski, Jr. (D)
Thaddeus M. Machrowicz (D)
George Meader (R)
James G. O'Hara (D)
Louis C. Rabaut (D)

MINNESOTA

Senators

Hubert H. Humphrey (D)
Eugene J. McCarthy (D)

Representatives

H. Carl Andersen (R)
John A. Blatnik (D)
Walter H. Judd (R)
Joseph E. Karth (D)
Odin Langen (R)
Fred Marshall (D)
Ancher Nelsen (R)
Albert H. Quie (R)
Roy W. Wier (D)

MISSISSIPPI

Senators

James O. Eastland (D)
John C. Stennis (D)

Representatives

Thomas G. Abernethy (D)
William M. Colmer (D)
Frank E. Smith (D)
Jamie L. Whitten (D)
John Bell Williams (D)
W. Arthur Winstead (D)

MISSOURI

Senators

Thomas C. Hennings, Jr. (D)
d. Sept. 1960
Edward V. Long (D) s. 1960

Stuart Symington (D)

Representatives

Richard W. Bolling (D)
Charles H. Brown (D)
Clarence Cannon (D)
Albert S. J. Carnahan (D)
George H. Christopher (D)
d. Jan. 1959
Thomas B. Curtis (R)
William R. Hull, Jr. (D)
Paul C. Jones (D)
Frank M. Karsten (D)
Morgan M. Moulder (D)
William J. Randall (D)
Leonor Kretzer Sullivan (D)

MONTANA

Senators

James E. Murray (D)
Mike Mansfield (D)

Representatives

LeRoy H. Anderson (D)
Lee Metcalf (D)

NEBRASKA

Senators

Roman L. Hruska (R)
Carl T. Curtis (R)

Representatives

Lawrence Brock (D)
Glenn C. Cunningham (R)
Donald F. McGinley (D)
Phillip H. Weaver (R)

NEVADA

Senators

Alan H. Bible (D)
Howard W. Cannon (D)

Representative

Walter S. Baring (D)

NEW HAMPSHIRE

Senators

H. Styles Bridges (R)
Norris Cotton (R)

Representatives

Perkins Bass (R)
Chester E. Merrow (R)

NEW JERSEY

Senators

Clifford P. Case (R)
Harrison A. Williams, Jr. (D)

Representatives

Hugh J. Addonizio (D)
James C. Auchincloss (R)
William T. Cahill (R)
Gordon Canfield (R)
Dominick V. Daniels (D)
Florence P. Dwyer (R)
Peter H. B. Frelinghuysen, Jr. (R)
Cornelius E. Gallagher (D)
Milton W. Glenn (R)
Frank C. Osmers, Jr. (R)
Peter W. Rodino, Jr. (D)
Frank Thompson, Jr. (D)
George M. Wallhauser (R)
William B. Widnall (R)

NEW MEXICO

Senators

Dennis Chavez (D)
Clinton P. Anderson (D)

Representatives

Joseph M. Montoya (D)
Thomas G. Morris (D)

NEW YORK

Senators

Jacob K. Javits (R)
Kenneth B. Keating (R)

Representatives

Victor L. Anfuso (D)
Robert R. Barry (R)
Frank J. Becker (R)
Albert H. Bosch (R)
Charles A. Buckley (D)
Emanuel Celler (D)
James J. Delaney (D)
Steven B. Derounian (R)
Isidore Dollinger (D)
r. Dec. 1959
Edwin B. Dooley (R)
Francis E. Dorn (R)
Thaddeus J. Dulski (D)
Leonard Farbstein (D)
Paul A. Fino (R)
Jacob H. Gilbert (D) s. 1960
Charles E. Goodell (R)
Seymour Halpern (R)
James C. Healey (D)
Lester Holtzman (D)
Edna F. Kelly (D)
Eugene J. Keogh (D)
Clarence E. Kilburn (R)
John V. Kindsay (R)
William E. Miller (R)
Abraham J. Multer (D)
Leo W. O'Brien (D)
Harold C. Ostertag (R)
John R. Pillion (R)
Alexander Pirnie (R)
Adam Clayton Powell, Jr. (D)
John H. Ray (R)
Daniel A. Reed (R) d. Feb. 1959
R. Walter Riehlman (R)
Howard W. Robison (R)
John J. Rooney (D)
Katharine St. George (R)
Alfred E. Santangelo (D)
Samuel S. Stratton (D)
John Taber (R)
Dean P. Taylor (R)
Ludwig Teller (D)
Stuyvesant Wainwright (R)
Jessica McCullough Weis (R)
J. Ernest Wharton (R)
Herbert Zelenko (D)

NORTH CAROLINA

Senators

Sam J. Ervin, Jr. (D)
B. Everett Jordan (D)

Representatives

Hugh Q. Alexander (D)
Graham A. Barden (D)
Herbert C. Bonner (D)
Harold D. Cooley (D)
Carl T. Durham (D)
Lawrence H. Fountain (D)
David M. Hall (D) d. Jan. 1960
Charles R. Jonas (R)
A. Paul Kitchin (D)
Alton A. Lennon (D)
Ralph J. Scott (D)
Roy A. Taylor (D) s. 1960
Basil L. Whitener (D)

NORTH DAKOTA

Senators

William Langer (R) d. Nov. 1959
C. Norman Brunsdale (R)
ta. 1960
Quentin N. Burdick (D) s. 1960

Milton R. Young (R)

Representatives

Quentin N. Burdick (D)
r. Aug. 1960
Don L. Short (R)

OHIO

Senators

Frank J. Lausche (D)
Stephen M. Young (D)

Representatives

Thomas L. Ashley (D)
William H. Ayres (R)
Albert D. Baumhart, Jr. (R)
Jackson E. Betts (R)
Frances P. Bolton (R)
Frank T. Bow (R)
Clarence J. Brown (R)
Robert E. Cook (D)
Samuel L. Devine (R)
Michael A. Feighan (D)
Wayne L. Hays (D)
John E. Henderson (R)
William E. Hess (R)
Michael J. Kirwan (D)
Delbert L. Latta (R)
Robert W. Levering (D)
William M. McCulloch (R)
William E. Minshall (R)
Walter H. Moeller (D)
James G. Polk (D) d. Apr. 1959
Paul F. Schenck (R)
Gordon H. Scherer (R)
Charles A. Vanik (D)

OKLAHOMA

Senators

Robert S. Kerr (D)
A. S. Mike Monroney (D)

Representatives

Carl Albert (D)
Page H. Belcher (R)
Edmond Edmondson (D)
John Jarman (D)
Toby Morris (D)
Thomas J. Steed (D)

OREGON

Senators

Wayne L. Morse (D)

Richard L. Neuberger (D)
d. Mar. 1960
Hall S. Lusk (D) ta. 1960

Representatives

Edith S. Green (D)
A. Walter Norblad (R)
Charles O. Porter (D)
Albert C. Ullman (D)

PENNSYLVANIA

Senators

Joseph S. Clark (D)
Hugh D. Scott, Jr. (R)

Representatives

William A. Barrett (D)
Alvin R. Bush (R) d. Nov. 1959
James A. Byrne (D)
Frank M. Clark (D)
Robert J. Corbett (R)
Willard S. Curtin (R)
Paul B. Dague (R)
John H. Dent (D)
Douglas H. Elliott (R)
s. 1960, d. June 1960
Ivor D. Fenton (R)
Daniel J. Flood (D)
James G. Fulton (R)
Leon H. Gavin (R)
Kathryn E. Granahan (D)
William J. Green, Jr. (D)
Elmer J. Holland (D)
Carroll D. Kearns (R)
John A. Lafore, Jr. (R)
William H. Milliken, Jr. (R)
William S. Moorhead (D)
Thomas E. Morgan (D)
Walter M. Mumma (R)
Robert N. C. Nix (D)
Stanley A. Prokop (D)
James M. Quigley (D)
George M. Rhodes (D)
John P. Saylor (R)
Herman T. Schneebeli (R) s. 1960
Richard M. Simpson (R)
d. Jan. 1960
Herman Toll (D)
James E. VanZandt (R)
Francis E. Walter (D)

RHODE ISLAND

Senators

Theodore F. Green (D)
John O. Pastore (D)

Representatives

John E. Fogarty (D)
Aime J. Forand (D)

SOUTH CAROLINA

Senators

Olin D. Johnston (D)
J. Strom Thurmond (D)

Representatives

Robert T. Ashmore (D)
W. J. Bryan Dorn (D)
Robert W. Hemphill (D)
John L. McMillan (D)
John J. Riley (D)
L. Mendel Rivers (D)

SOUTH DAKOTA

Senators

Karl E. Mundt (R)
Francis H. Case (R)

Representatives

Ellis Y. Berry (R)
George S. McGovern (D)

TENNESSEE

Senators

Estes Kefauver (D)
Albert A. Gore (D)

Representatives

Howard H. Baker (R)
Ross Bass (D)
Clifford Davis (D)

Robert A. Everett (D)
Joseph L. Evins (D)
James B. Frazier, Jr. (D)
J. Carlton Loser (D)
Thomas J. Murray (D)
B. Carroll Reece (R)

TEXAS

Senators

Lyndon B. Johnson (D)
Ralph W. Yarborough (D)

Representatives

Bruce R. Alger (R)
Lindley G. Beckworth (D)
Jack B. Brooks (D)
Omar T. Burleson (D)
Robert R. Casey (D)
John V. Dowdy (D)
O. Clark Fisher (D)
Frank N. Ikard (D)
Paul J. Kilday (D)
Joe M. Kilgore (D)
George H. Mahon (D)
Wright Patman (D)
William R. Poage (D)
Sam Rayburn (D)
Walter E. Rogers (D)
J. T. Rutherford (D)
Olin E. Teague (D)
Albert Thomas (D)
Clark W. Thompson (D)
W. Honer Thornberry (D)
James C. Wright, Jr. (D)
John A. Young (D)

UTAH

Senators

Wallace F. Bennett (R)
Frank E. Moss (D)

Representatives

Henry Aldous Dixon (R)
David S. King (D)

VERMONT

Senators

George D. Aiken (R)
Winston L. Prouty (R)

Representatives

William H. Meyer (D)

VIRGINIA

Senators

Harry F. Byrd (D)
A. Willis Robertson (D)

Representatives

Watkins M. Abbitt (D)
Joel T. Broyhill (D)
Thomas N. Downing (D)
J. Vaughan Gary (D)
Porter Hardy, Jr. (D)
Burr P. Harrison (D)
William P. Jennings (D)
Richard H. Poff (R)
Howard W. Smith (D)
William M. Tuck (D)

WASHINGTON

Senators

Warren G. Magnuson (D)
Henry M. Jackson (D)

Representatives

Walter F. Horan (R)
Russell V. Mack (R) d. Mar. 1960
Donald H. Magnuson (D)
Catherine D. May (R)
Thomas M. Pelly (R)
Thor C. Tollefson (R)
Alfred J. Westland (R)

WEST VIRGINIA

Senators

Jennings Randolph (D)
Robert C. Byrd (D)

Representatives

Cleveland M. Bailey (D)
Kenneth Hechler (D)
Maude Elizabeth Kee (D)
Arch A. Moore, Jr. (R)
John M. Slack, Jr. (D)
Harley O. Staggers (D)

WISCONSIN

Senators

Alexander Wiley (R)
William Proxmire (D)

Representatives

John W. Byrnes (R)
Gerald T. Flynn (D)
Lester R. Johnson (D)
Robert W. Kastenmeier (D)
Melvin R. Laird (R)
Alvin E. O'Konski (R)
Henry S. Reuss (D)
William K. VanPelt (R)
Gardner R. Withrow (R)
Clement J. Zablocki (D)

WYOMING

Senators

Joseph C. O'Mahoney (D)
Gale W. McGee (D)

Representative

E. Keith Thomson (R)
d. Nov. 1960

EIGHTY-SEVENTH CONGRESS

January 3, 1961 to January 3, 1963

Presidents of The Senate: Richard M. Nixon; Lyndon B. Johnson
President Pro Tempore of The Senate: Carl Hayden
Speakers of The House of Representatives: Sam Rayburn; John W. McCormack

ALABAMA

Senators

Lister Hill (D)
John J. Sparkman (D)

Representatives

George W. Andrews (D)
Frank W. Boykin (D)
Carl Elliott (D)
George M. Grant (D)
George Huddleston, Jr. (D)
Robert E. Jones, Jr . (D)
Albert Rains (D)
Kenneth A. Roberts (D)
Armistead I. Selden, Jr. (D)

ALASKA

Senators

Edward L. Bartlett (D)
Ernest Gruening (D)

Representative

Ralph J. Rivers (D)

ARIZONA

Senators

Carl Hayden (D)
Barry M. Goldwater (R)

Representatives

John J. Rhodes (R)
Morris K. Udall (D)

ARKANSAS

Senators

John L. McClellan (D)
J. W. Fulbright (D)

Representatives

T. Dale Alford (D)
Ezekiel C. Gathings (D)
Oren Harris (D)
Wilbur D. Mills (D)
Catherine D. Norrell (D)
James W. Trimble (D)

CALIFORNIA

Senators

Thomas H. Kuchel (R)
Clair Engle (D)

Representatives

John F. Baldwin, Jr. (R)
Alphonzo Bell (R)
Jeffery Cohelan (D)
James C. Corman (D)
Clyde G. Doyle (D)
Charles S. Gubser (R)
Harlan F. Hagen (D)
Edgar W. Hiestand (R)
Chet Holifield (D)
Craig Hosmer (R)
Harold T. Johnson (D)
Cecil R. King (D)
Glenard P. Lipscomb (R)
Gordon L. McDonough (R)
John J. McFall (D)
William S. Mailliard (R)
Clement W. Miller (D)
d. Oct. 1962
George P. Miller (D)
John E. Moss, Jr. (D)
James Roosevelt (D)
John H. Rousselot (R)
Dalie S. Saund (D)
John F. Shelley (D)
Harry R. Sheppard (D)
Bernice F. Sisk (D)
H. Allen Smith (R)
Charles M. Teague (R)
James B. Utt (R)
Robert C. Wilson (R)
J. Arthur Younger (R)

COLORADO

Senators

Gordon L. Allott (R)
John A. Carroll (D)

Representatives

Wayne N. Aspinall (D)
J. Edgar Chenoweth (R)
Peter H. Dominick (R)
Byron G. Rogers (D)

CONNECTICUT

Senators

Prescott Bush (R)
Thomas J. Dodd (D)

Representatives

Emilio Q. Daddario (D)
Robert N. Giaimo (D)
Frank Kowalski (D)
John S. Monagan (D)
Horace Seely-Brown, Jr. (R)
Abner W. Sibal (R)

DELAWARE

Senators

John J. Williams (R)
J. Caleb Boggs (R)

Representative

Harris B. McDowell, Jr. (D)

FLORIDA

Senators

Spessard L. Holland (D)
George A. Smathers (D)

Representatives

Charles E. Bennett (D)
William C. Cramer (R)
Dante B. Fascell (D)
James A. Haley (D)
Albert S. Herlong, Jr. (D)
Donald R. Matthews (D)
Paul G. Rogers (D)
Robert L. F. Sikes (D)

GEORGIA

Senators

Richard B. Russell (D)
Herman E. Talmadge (D)

Representatives

Iris F. Blitch (D)
James C. Davis (D)
John W. Davis (D)
John J. Flynt, Jr. (D)
Elijah L. Forrester (D)
G. Elliott Hagan (D)
Phillip M. Landrum (D)
John L. Pilcher (D)
Robert G. Stephens (D)
Carl Vinson (D)

HAWAII

Senators

Hiram L. Fong (R)
Oren E. Long (D)

Representative

Daniel K. Inouye

IDAHO

Senators

Henry C. Dworshak (R)
d. July 1962
Len B. Jordan (R) s. 1962

Frank Church (D)

Representatives

Ralph R. Harding (D)
Gracie Pfost (D)

ILLINOIS

Senators

Paul H. Douglas (D)
Everett M. Dirksen (R)

Representatives

John B. Anderson (R)
Leslie C. Arends (R)
Robert B. Chiperfield (R)
Marguerite Stitt Church (R)
Harold R. Collier (R)
William L. Dawson (D)
Edward J. Derwinski (R)
Paul Findley (R)
Edward R. Finnegan (D)
Kenneth J. Gray (D)
Elmer J. Hoffman (R)
John C. Kluczynski (D)
Roland V. Libonati (D)
Peter F. Mack, Jr. (D)
Noah M. Mason (R)
Robert H. Michel (R)
William T. Murphy (D)
Thomas J. O'Brien (D)
Barratt O'Hara (D)
Melvin Price (D)
Roman C. Pucinski (D)
Dan Rostenkowski (D)
George E. Shipley (D)
William L. Springer (R)
Sidney R. Yates (D)

INDIANA

Senators

Homer E. Capehart (R)
Vance Hartke (D)

Representatives

E. Ross Adair (R)
John Brademas (D)
William G. Bray (R)
Donald C. Bruce (R)
Winfield K. Denton (D)
Charles A. Halleck (R)
Ralph Harvey (R)
Ray J. Madden (D)
Richard L. Roudebush (R)
J. Edward Roush (D)
Earl Wilson (R)

IOWA

Senators

Bourke B. Hickenlooper (R)
Jack R. Miller (R)

Representatives

James E. Bromwell (R)
Merwin Coad (D)
Harold R. Gross (R)
Charles B. Hoeven (R)
Ben F. Jensen (R)
John H. Kyl (R)
Frederick D. Schwengel (R)
Neal Smith (D)

KANSAS

Senators

Andrew F. Schoeppel (R)
d. Jan. 1962
James B. Pearson (R) s. 1962

Frank Carlson (R)

Representatives

William H. Avery (R)
J. Floyd Breeding (D)
Bob Dole (R)
Robert F. Ellsworth (R)
Walter L. McVey (R)
Garner E. Shriver (R)

KENTUCKY

Senators

John Sherman Cooper (R)
Thruston B. Morton (R)

Representatives

Frank W. Burke (D)
Frank Chelf (D)
William H. Natcher (D)
Carl D. Perkins (D)
Eugene Siler (R)
Brent Spence (D)
Frank A. Stubblefield (D)
John C. Watts (D)

LOUISIANA

Senators

Allen J. Ellender (D)
Russell B. Long (D)

Representatives

T. Hale Boggs (D)
Overton Brooks (D) d. Sept. 1961
F. Edward Hebert (D)
Harold B. McSween (D)
James H. Morrison (D)
Otto E. Passman (D)
T. Ashton Thompson (D)
Joe D. Waggonner, Jr. (R)
s. 1962
Edwin E. Willis (D)

MAINE

Senators

Margaret Chase Smith (R)
Edmund S. Muskie (D)

Representatives

Peter A. Garland (R)
Clifford G. McIntire (R)
Stanley R. Tupper (R)

MARYLAND

Senators

John Marshall Butler (R)
J. Glenn Beall (R)

Representatives

Daniel B. Brewster (D)
George H. Fallon (D)
Samuel N. Friedel (D)
Edward A. Garmatz (D)
Thomas F. Johnson (D)
Richard E. Lankford (D)
Charles McC.Mathias, Jr. (R)

MASSACHUSETTS

Senators

Leverett Saltonstall (R)

Benjamin A. Smith 2d (D) ta. 1961
Edward M. Kennedy (D) s. 1962

Representatives

William H. Bates (R)
Edward P. Boland (D)
James A. Burke (D)
Silvio O. Conte (R)
Laurence Curtis (R)
Harold D. Donohue (D)
Hastings Keith (R)
Thomas J. Lane (D)
John W. McCormack (D)
Torbert H. Macdonald (D)
Joseph W. Martin, Jr. (R)
F. Bradford Morse (R)
Thomas P. O'Neill, Jr. (D)
Philip J. Philbin (D)

MICHIGAN

Senators

Patrick V. McNamara (D)
Philip A. Hart (D)

Representatives

John B. Bennett (R)
William S. Broomfield (R)
Elford A. Cederberg (R)
Charles E. Chamberlain (R)
Charles C. Diggs, Jr. (D)
John D. Dingell (D)
Gerald R. Ford, Jr. (R)
Robert P. Griffin (R)
Martha W. Griffiths (D)
James Harvey (R)
Clare E. Hoffman (R)
August E. Johansen (R)
Victor A. Knox (R)
John Lesinski (D)
Thaddeus M. Machrowicz (D)
r. Sept. 1961
George Meader (R)
Lucien N. Nedzi (D) s. 1962
James G. O'Hara (D)
Louis C. Rabaut (D) d. Nov. 1961
Harold M. Ryan (D) s. 1962

MINNESOTA

Senators

Hubert H. Humphrey (D)
Eugene J. McCarthy (D)

Representatives

H. Carl Andersen (R)
John A. Blatnik (D)
Walter H. Judd (R)
Joseph E. Karth (D)
Odin Langen (R)
Clark MacGregor (R)
Fred Marshall (D)
Ancher Nelsen (R)
Albert H. Quie (R)

MISSISSIPPI

Senators

James O. Eastland (D)
John C. Stennis (D)

Representatives

Thomas G. Abernethy (D)
William M. Colmer (D)
Frank E. Smith (D) r. Nov. 1962
Jamie L. Whitten (D)
John Bell Williams (D)
W. Arthur Winstead (D)

MISSOURI

Senators

Stuart Symington (D)
Edward V. Long (D)

Representatives

Richard W. Bolling (D)
Clarence Cannon (D)
Thomas B. Curtis (R)
Durward G. Hall (R)
William R. Hull, Jr. (D)
Richard H. Ichord (D)
Paul C. Jones (D)
Frank M. Karsten (D)
Leonor Kretzer Sullivan (D)
Morgan M. Moulder (D)
William J. Randall (D)

MONTANA

Senators

Mike Mansfield (D)
Lee Metcalf (D)

Representatives

James F. Battin (R)
Arnold Olsen (D)

NEBRASKA

Senators

Roman L. Hruska (R)
Carl T. Curtis (R)

Representatives

Ralph F. Beermann (R)
Glenn C. Cunningham (R)
David T. Martin (R)
Philip H. Weaver (R)

NEVADA

Senators

Alan Bible (D)
Howard W. Cannon (D)

Representative

Walter S. Baring (D)

NEW HAMPSHIRE

Senators

Styles Bridges (R) d. Nov. 1961
Maurice J. Murphy, Jr. (R)
ta. 1962

Norris Cotton (R)

Representatives

Perkins Bass (R)
Chester E. Merrow (R)

NEW JERSEY

Senators

Clifford P. Case (R)
Harrison A. Williams, Jr. (D)

Representatives

Hugh J. Addonizio (D)
r. June 1962
James C. Auchincloss (R)
William T. Cahill (R)
Dominick V. Daniels (D)
Florence P. Dwyer (R)
Peter H. B. Frelinghuysen, Jr. (R)
Cornelius E. Gallagher (D)
Milton W. Glenn (R)
Charles S. Joelson (D)
Frank C. Osmers, Jr. (R)
Peter W. Rodino, Jr. (D)
Frank Thompson, Jr. (D)
George M. Wallhauser (R)
William D. Widnall (R)

NEW MEXICO

Senators

Dennis Chavez (D) d. Nov. 1962
Clinton P. Anderson (D)

Representatives

Joseph M. Montoya (D)
Thomas G. Morris (D)

NEW YORK

Senators

Jacob K. Javits (R)
Kenneth B. Keating (R)

Representatives

Joseph P. Addabbo (D)
Victor L. Anfuso (D)
Robert R. Barry (R)
Frank J. Becker (R)
Charles A. Buckley (D)
Hugh L. Carey (D)
Emanuel Celler (D)
James J. Delaney (D)
Steven B. Derounian (R)
Edwin B. Dooley (R)
Thaddeus J. Dulski (D)
Leonard Farbstein (D)
Paul A. Fino (R)
Jacob H. Gilbert (D)
Charles E. Goodell (R)
Seymour Halpern (R)
James C. Healey (D)
Lester Holtzman (D) r. Dec. 1961
Edna F. Kelly (D)
Eugene J. Keogh (D)
Clarence E. Kilburn (R)
Carleton J. King (R)
John V. Lindsay (R)
William E. Miller (R)
Abraham J. Multer (D)
Leo W. O'Brien (D)
Harold C. Ostertag (R)
Otis G. Pike (D)
John R. Pillion (R)
Alexander Pirnie (R)
Adam Clayton Powell (D)
John H. Ray (R)
R. Walter Riehlman (R)
Howard W. Robison (R)
John J. Rooney (D)
Benjamin S. Rosenthal (D)
s. 1962
William F. Ryan (D)
Katharine St. George (R)
Alfred E. Santangelo (D)
Samuel S. Stratton (D)
John Taber (R)
Jessica McCullough Weis (R)
J. Ernest Wharton (R)
Herbert Zelenko (D)

NORTH CAROLINA

Senators

Sam J. Ervin, Jr. (D)
B. Everett Jordan (D)

Representatives

Hugh Q. Alexander (D)
Herbert C. Bonner (D)
Harold D. Cooley (D)
Lawrence H. Fountain (D)
David N. Henderson (D)
Charles R. Jonas (R)
A. Paul Kitchin (D)
Horace R. Kornegay (D)
Alton A. Lennon (D)
Ralph J. Scott (D)
Roy A. Taylor (D)
Basil L. Whitener (D)

NORTH DAKOTA

Senators

Milton R. Young (R)
Quentin N. Burdick (D)

Representatives

Hjalmar C. Nygaard (R)
Don L. Short (R)

OHIO

Senators

Frank J. Lausche (D)
Stephen M. Young (D)

Representatives

John M. Ashbrook (R)
Thomas L. Ashley (D)
William H. Ayres (R)
Jackson E. Betts (R)
Frances P. Bolton (R)
Frank T. Bow (R)
Clarence J. Brown (R)
Donald D. Clancy (R)
Robert E. Cook (D) r. Dec. 1962
Samuel L. Devine (R)
Michael A. Feighan (D)
William H. Harsha, Jr. (R)
Wayne L. Hays (D)
Michael J. Kirwan (D)
Delbert L. Latta (R)
William M. McCulloch (R)
William E. Minshall, Jr. (R)
Walter H. Moeller (D)
Tom V. Moorehead (R)
Charles A. Mosher (R)
Paul F. Schenck (R)
Gordon H. Scherer (R)
Charles A. Vanik (D)

OKLAHOMA

Senators

Robert S. Kerr (D) d. Jan. 1963
A. S. Mike Monroney (D)

Representatives

Carl Albert (D)
Page Belcher (R)
Edmond Edmondson (R)
John Jarman (D)
Thomas J. Steed (D)
Victor Wickersham (D)

OREGON

Senators

Wayne L. Morse (D)
Maurine B. Neuberger (D)

Representatives

Edwin R. Durno (R)
Edith Green (D)
A. Walter Norblad, Jr. (R)
Al Ullman (D)

PENNSYLVANIA

Senators

Joseph S. Clark (D)
Hugh Scott (R)

Representatives

William A. Barrett (D)
James A. Byrne (D)
Frank M. Clark (D)
Robert J. Corbett (R)
Willard S. Curtin (R)
Paul B. Dague (R)
John H. Dent (D)
Ivor D. Fenton (R)
Daniel J. Flood (D)
James G. Fulton (R)
Leon H. Gavin (R)
George A. Goodling (R)
Kathryn E. Granahan (D)
William J. Green, Jr. (D)
Elmer J. Holland (D)
Carroll D. Kearns (R)
John C. Kunkel (R)
William H. Milliken, Jr. (R)
William S. Moorhead (D)
Thomas E. Morgan (D)
Robert N. C. Nix (D)
George M. Rhodes (D)
John P. Saylor (R)
Herman T. Schneebeli (R)
Richard S. Schweiker (R)
William W. Scranton (R)
Herman Toll (D)
Francis E. Walter (D)
J. Irving Whalley (R)
James E. Van Zandt (R)

RHODE ISLAND

Senators

John O. Pastore (D)
Claiborne Pell (D)

Representatives

John E. Fogarty (D)
Fernand J. St. Germain (D)

SOUTH CAROLINA

Senators

Olin D. Johnston (D)
J. Strom Thurmond (D)

Representatives

Robert T. Ashmore (D)
W. J. Bryan Dorn (D)
Robert W. Hemphill (D)
John L. McMillan (D)
John J. Riley (D) d. Jan. 1962
Corinne B. Riley (D) s. 1962
L. Mendel Rivers (D)

SOUTH DAKOTA

Senators

Karl E. Mundt (R)

Francis Case (R) d. June 1962
Joseph H. Bottum (R) s. 1962

Representatives

Ellis Y. Berry (R)
Benjamin Reifel (R)

TENNESSEE

Senators

Estes Kefauver (D)
Albert A. Gore (D)

Representatives

Howard H. Baker (R)
Ross Bass (D)
Clifford Davis (D)
Robert A. Everett (D)
Joe L. Evins (D)
James B. Frazier, Jr. (D)
J. Carlton Loser (D)
Thomas J. Murray (D)
B. Carroll Reece (R) d. Mar. 1961
Louise G. Reece (R)

TEXAS

Senators

Ralph W. Yarborough (D)

William A. Blakley (D) ta. 1961
John G. Tower (R)

Representatives

Bruce R. Alger (R)
Lindley G. Beckworth (D)
Jack B. Brooks (D)
Omar Burleson (D)
Robert R. Casey (D)
John Dowdy (D)
O. Clark Fisher (D)
Henry B. Gonzalez (D) s. 1962
Frank Ikard (D) r. Dec. 1961
Paul J. Kilday (D) r. Sept. 1961
Joe M. Kilgore (D)
George H. Mahon (D)
Wright Patman (D)
William R. Poage (D)
Graham Purcell, Jr. (D) s. 1962
Sam Rayburn (D) d. Nov. 1961
H. Ray Roberts (D) s. 1962
Walter E. Rogers (D)
J. T. Rutherford (D)
Olin E. Teague (D)
Albert Thomas (D)
Clark W. Thompson (D)
W. Homer Thornberry (D)
James C. Wright, Jr. (D)
John A. Young (D)

UTAH

Senators

Wallace F. Bennett (R)
Frank E. Moss (D)

Representatives

David S. King (D)
M. Blaine Peterson (D)

VERMONT

Senators

George D. Aiken (R)
Winston L. Prouty (R)

Representative

Robert T. Stafford (R)

VIRGINIA

Senators

Hary F. Byrd (D)
A. Willis Robertson (D)

Representatives

Watkins M. Abbitt (D)
Joel T. Broyhill (R)
Thomas N. Downing (D)
J. Vaughan Gary (D)
Porter Hardy, Jr. (D)
Burr P. Harrison (D)
William P. Jennings (D)
Richard H. Poff (R)
Howard W. Smith (D)
William M. Tuck (D)

WASHINGTON

Senators

Warren G. Magnuson (D)
Henry M. Jackson

Representatives

Julia Butler Hansen (D)
Walter F. Horan (R)
Donald H. Magnuson (D)
Catherine D. May (R)
Thomas M. Pelly (R)
Thor C. Tollefson (R)
Alfred J. Westland (R)

WEST VIRGINIA

Senators

Jennings Randolph (D)
Robert C. Byrd (D)

Representatives

Cleveland M. Bailey (D)
Kenneth Hechler (D)
Maude Elizabeth Kee (D)
Arch A. Moore, Jr. (R)
John M. Slack, Jr. (D)
Harley O. Staggers (D)

WISCONSIN

Senators

Alexander Wiley (R)
William Proxmire (D)

Representatives

John W. Byrnes (R)
Lester R. Johnson (D)
Robert W. Kastenmeier (D)
Melvin R. Laird (R)
Alvin E. O'Konski (R)
Henry S. Reuss (D)
Henry C. Schadeberg (R)
Vernon W. Thomson (R)
William K. Van Pelt (R)
Clement J. Zablocki (D)

WYOMING

Senators

Gale W. McGee (D)
John J. Hickey (D)

Representative

William H. Harrison (R)

EIGHTY-EIGHTH CONGRESS

January 3, 1963 to January 3, 1965

President of The Senate: Lyndon B. Johnson
President Pro Tempore of The Senate: Carl Hayden
Speaker of The House of Representatives: John W. McCormack

ALABAMA

Senators

Lister Hill (D)
John J. Sparkman (D)

Representatives

George W. Andrews (D)
Carl Elliott (D)
George M. Grant (D)
George Huddleston, Jr. (D)
Robert E. Jones, Jr. (D)
Albert Rains (D)
Kenneth A. Roberts (D)
Armistead I. Selden, Jr. (D)

ALASKA

Senators

Edward L. Bartlett (D)
Ernest Gruening (D)

Representative

Ralph J. Rivers (D)

ARIZONA

Senators

Carl Hayden (D)
Barry M. Goldwater (R)

Representatives

John J. Rhodes (R)
George F. Senner, Jr. (D)
Morris K. Udall (D)

ARKANSAS

Senators

John L. McClellan (D)
J. W. Fulbright (D)

Representatives

Eziekel C. Gathings (D)
Oren Harris (D)
Wilbur D. Mills (D)
James W. Trimble (D)

CALIFORNIA

Senators

Thomas H. Kuchel (R)

Clair Engle (D) d. July 1964
Pierre Salinger (D) ta. 1964

Representatives

John F. Baldwin, Jr. (R)
Alphonzo Bell (R)
George E. Brown, Jr. (D)
Everett G. Burkhalter (D)

Phillip Burton (D) s. 1964
Ronald B. Cameron (D)
Don H. Clausen (R)
Del Clawson (R) s. 1963
Jeffery Cohelan (D)
James C. Corman (D)
Clyde G. Doyle (D) d. Mar. 1963
Don Edwards (D)
Charles S. Gubser (R)
Harlan F. Hagen (D)
Richard T. Hanna (D)
Augustus F. Hawkins (D)
Chet Holifield (D)
Craig Hosmer (R)
Harold T. Johnson (D)
Cecil R. King (D)
Robert L. Leggett (D)
Glenard P. Lipscomb (R)
John J. McFall (D)
William S. Mailliard (R)
Pat M. Martin (R)
George P. Miller (D)
John E. Moss, Jr. (D)
James Roosevelt (D)
Edward R. Roybal (D)
John F. Shelley (D)
r. Jan. 1964
Harry R. Sheppard (D)
Bernice F. Sisk (D)
H. Allen Smith (R)
Burt L. Talcott (R)
Charles M. Teague (R)
James B. Utt (R)
Lionel Van Derrlin (D)
Charles H. Wilson (D)
Robert C. Wilson (R)
J. Arthur Younger (R)

COLORADO

Senators

Gordon L. Allott (R)
Peter H. Dominick (R)

Representatives

Wayne N. Aspinall (D)
Donald G. Brotzman (R)
J. Edgar Chenoweth (R)
Byron G. Rogers (D)

CONNECTICUT

Senators

Thomas J. Dodd (D)
Abraham A. Ribicoff (D)

Representatives

Emilio Q. Daddario (D)
Robert N. Giaimo (D)
Bernard F. Grabowski (D)
John S. Monagan (D)
William L. St. Onge (D)
Abner W. Sibal (R)

DELAWARE

Senators

John J. Williams (R)
J. Caleb Boggs (R)

Representative

Harris B. McDowell, Jr. (D)

FLORIDA

Senators

Spessard L. Holland (D)
George A. Smathers (D)

Representatives

Charles E. Bennett (D)
William C. Cramer (R)
Dante B. Fascell (D)
Don Fuqua (D)
Sam M. Gibbons (D)
Edward J. Gurney (R)
James A. Haley (D)
Albert S. Herlong, Jr. (D)
Donald R. Matthews (D)
Claude D. Pepper (D)
Paul G. Rogers (D)
Robert L. F. Sikes (D)

GEORGIA

Senators

Richard B. Russell (D)
Herman E. Talmadge (D)

Representatives

John W. Davis (D)
John J. Flynt, Jr. (D)
E. L. Forrester (D)
G. Elliott Hagan (D)
Phillip M. Landrum (D)
John L. Pilcher (D)
Robert G. Stephens, Jr. (D)
J. Russell Tuten (D)
Carl Vinson (D)
Charles L. Weltner (R)

HAWAII

Senators

Hiram L. Fong (R)
Daniel K. Inouye (D)

Representatives

Thomas P. Gill (D)
Spark M. Matsunaga (R)

IDAHO

Senators

Frank Church (D)
Len B. Jordan (R)

Representatives

Ralph R. Harding (D)
Compton I. White, Jr. (D)

ILLINOIS

Senators

Paul H. Douglas (D)
Everett M. Dirksen (R)

Representatives

John B. Anderson (R)
Leslie C. Arends (R)
Harold R. Collier (R)
William L. Dawson (D)
Edward J. Derwinski (R)
Paul Findley (R)
Edward R. Finnegan (D) r. Dec. 1964
Kenneth J. Gray (D)
Elmer J. Hoffman (R)
John C. Kluczynski (D)
d. Apr. 1964
Roland V. Libonati (D)
Robert McClory (R)
Robert T. McLoskey (R)
Robert H. Michel (R)
William T. Murphy (D)
Thomas J. O'Brien (D)
Barratt O'Hara (D)
Melvin Price (D)
Roman C. Pucinski (D)
Charlotte T. Reid (R)
Daniel Rostenkowski (D)
Donald Rumsfeld (R)
George E. Shipley (D)
William L. Springer (R)

INDIANA

Senators

Vance Hartke (D)
Birch Bayh (D)

Representatives

E. Ross Adair (R)
William G. Bray (R)
John Brademas (D)
Donald C. Bruce (R)
Winfield K. Denton (D)
Charles A. Halleck (R)
Ralph Harvey (R)
Ray J. Madden (D)
Richard L. Roudebush (R)
J. Edward Roush (D)
Earl Wilson (R)

IOWA

Senators

Bourke B. Hickenlooper (R)
Jack R. Miller (R)

Representatives

James E. Bromwell (R)
Harold R. Gross (R)
Charles B. Hoeven (R)
Ben F. Jensen (R)
John H. Kyl (R)
Frederick D. Schwengel (R)
Neal Smith (D)

KANSAS

Senators

Frank Carlson (R)
James B. Pearson (R)

Representatives

William H. Avery (R)
Robert J. Dole (R)
Robert F. Ellsworth (R)
Garner E. Shriver (R)
Joe Skubitz (R)

KENTUCKY

Senators

John Sherman Cooper (R)
Thruston B. Morton (R)

Representatives

Frank L. Chelf (D)
William H. Natcher (D)
Carl D. Perkins (D)
Eugene Siler (R)
M. G. (Gene) Snyder (R)
Frank A. Subblefield (D)
John C. Watts (D)

LOUISIANA

Senators

Allen J. Ellender (D)
Russell B. Long (D)

Representatives

T. Hale Boggs (D)
F. Edward Hebert (D)
Gillis W. Long (D)
James H. Morrison (D)
Otto E. Passman (D)
T. Ashton Thompson (D)
Joe D. Waggonner, Jr. (D)
Edwin E. Willis (D)

MAINE

Senators

Margaret Chase Smith (R)
Edmund S. Muskie (D)

Representatives

Clifford C. McIntire (R)
Stanley R. Tupper (R)

MARYLAND

Senators

J. Glenn Beall (R)
Daniel B. Brewster (D)

Representatives

George H. Fallon (D)
Samuel N. Friedel (D)
Edward A. Garmatz (D)
Richard E. Lankford (D)
Clarence D. Long (D)
Charles McC. Mathias, Jr. (R)
Rogers C. B. Morton (R)
Carlton R. Sickles (D)

MASSACHUSETTS

Senators

Leverett Saltonstall (R)
Edward M. Kennedy (D)

Representatives

William H. Bates (R)
Edward P. Boland (D)

James A. Burke (D)
Silvio O. Conte (R)
Harold D. Donohue (D)
Hastings Keith (R)
John W. McCormack (D)
Torbert H. Macdonald (D)
Joseph W. Martin, Jr. (R)
F. Bradford Morse (R)
Thomas P. O'Neill, Jr. (D)
Philip J. Philbin (D)

MICHIGAN

Senators

Patrick V. McNamara (D)
Philip A. Hart (D)

Representatives

John B. Bennett (R)
d. Aug. 1964
William S. Broomfield (R)
Elford A. Cederberg (R)
Charles E. Chamberlain (R)
Charles C. Diggs, Jr. (D)
John D. Dingell, Jr. (D)
Gerald R. Ford, Jr. (R)
Robert P. Griffin (R)
Martha W. Griffiths (D)
James Harvey (R)
Edward Hutchinson (R)
August E. Johansen (R)
Victor A. Knox (R)
John Lesinski (D)
George Meader (R)
Lucien N. Nedzi (D)
James G. O'Hara (D)
Harold M. Ryan (D)
Neil Staebler (D)

MINNESOTA

Senators

Hubert H. Humphrey (D)
Eugene J. McCarthy (D)

Representatives

John A. Blatnik (D)
Donald M. Fraser (D)
Joseph E. Karth (D)
Odin Langen (R)
Clark MacGregor (R)
Ancher Nelsen (R)
Alec G. Olson (D)
Albert H. Quie (R)

MISSISSIPPI

Senators

James O. Eastland (D)
John C. Stennis (D)

Representatives

Thomas G. Abernethy (D)
William M. Colmer (D)
Jamie L. Whitten (D)
John Bell Williams (D)
W. Arthur Winstead (D)

MISSOURI

Senators

Stuart Symington (D)
Edward V. Long (D)

Representatives

Richard W. Bolling (D)
Clarence Cannon (D) d. May 1964
Thomas B. Curtis (R)
Durward G. Hall (R)
William R. Hull, Jr. (D)
William L. Hungate (D) s. 1964
Richard H. Ichord (D)
Paul C. Jones (D)
Frank M. Karsten (D)
William J. Randall (D)
Leonor Kretzer Sullivan (D)

MONTANA

Senators

Mike Mansfield (D)
Lee Metcalf (F)

Representatives

James F. Battin (R)
Arnold Olsen (D)

NEBRASKA

Senators

Roman L. Hruska (R)
Carl T. Curtis (R)

Representatives

Ralph F. Beermann (R)
Glenn C. Cunningham (R)
David T. Martin (R)

NEVADA

Senators

Alan Bible (D)
Howard W. Cannon (D)

Representative

Walter S. Baring (D)

NEW HAMPSHIRE

Senators

Norris Cotton (R)
Thomas J. McIntyre (D)

Representatives

James C. Cleveland (D)
Louis C. Wyman (R)

NEW JERSEY

Senators

Clifford P. Case (R)
Harrison A. Williams, Jr. (D)

Representatives

James C. Auchincloss (R)
William T. Cahill (R)
Dominick V. Daniels (D)
Florence P. Dwyer (R)
Peter H. B. Frelinghuysen, Jr. (R)
Cornelius E. Gallagher (D)
Milton W. Glenn (R)
Charles S. Joelson (D)
Joseph G. Minish (D)
Frank C. Osmers, Jr. (R)
Edward J. Patten (D)
Peter W. Rodino, Jr. (D)
Frank Thompson, Jr. (D)
George M. Wallhauser (R)
William B. Widnall (R)

NEW MEXICO

Senators

Clinton P. Anderson (D)
Edwin L. Mechem (R)

Representatives

Joseph M. Montoya (D)
r. Nov. 1964
Thomas G. Morris (D)

NEW YORK

Senators

Jacob K. Javits (R)
Kenneth B. Keating (R)

Representatives

Joseph P. Addabbo (R)
Robert R. Barry (R)
Frank J. Becker (R)
Charles A. Buckley (D)
Hugh L. Carey (D)
Emanuel Celler (D)
James J. Delaney (D)
Steven B. Derounian (R)
Thaddeus J. Dulski (D)
Leonard Farbstein (D)
Paul A. Fino (R)
Jacob H. Gilbert (D)
Charles E. Goodell (R)
James R. Grover, Jr. (R)
Seymour Halpern (R)
James C. Healey (D)
Frank J. Horton (R)
Edna F. Kelly (D)
Eugene J. Keogh (D)
Clarence E. Kilburn (R)
Carleton J. King (R)
John V. Lindsay (R)
William E. Miller (R)
Abraham J. Multer (D)
John M. Murphy (D)
Leo W. O'Brien (D)
Harold C. Ostertag (R)
Otis G. Pike (D)
John R. Pillion (R)
Alexander Pirnie (R)
Adam Clayton Powell (D)
Ogden R. Reid (R)
R. Walter Riehlman (R)
Howard W. Robison (R)
John J. Rooney (D)
Benjamin S. Rosenthal (D)
William F. Ryan (D)
Katharine St. George (R)
Samuel S. Stratton (D)
J. Ernest Wharton (R)
John W. Wydler (R)

NORTH CAROLINA

Senators

Sam J. Ervin, Jr. (D)
B. Everett Jordan (D)

Representatives

Herbert C. Bonner (D)
James T. Broyhill (R)
Harold D. Cooley (D)
L. H. Fountain (D)
David N. Henderson (D)
Charles R. Jonas (R)
Horace R. Kornegay (D)
Alton A. Lennon (D)
Ralph J. Scott (D)
Roy A. Taylor (D)
Basil L. Whitener (D)

NORTH DAKOTA

Senators

Milton R. Young (R)
Quentin N. Burdick (D)

Representatives

Mark Andrews (R)
Hjalmar C. Nygaard (R)
d. July 1963
Don L. Short (R)

OHIO

Senators

Frank J. Lausche (D)
Stephen M. Young (D)

Representatives

Homer E. Abele (R)
John M. Ashbrook (R)
Thomas L. Ashley (D)
William H. Ayres (R)
Jackson E. Betts (R)
Frances P. Bolton (R)
Oliver P. Bolton (R)
Frank T. Bow (R)
Clarence J. Brown (R)
Donald D. Clancy (R)
Samuel L. Divine (R)
Michael A. Feighan (D)
William H. Harsha, Jr. (R)
Wayne L. Hays (D)
Michael J. Kirwan (D)
Delbert L. Latta (R)
William M. McCulloch (R)
William E. Minshall (R)
Charles A. Mosher (R)
Carl W. Rich (R)
Paul F. Schenck (R)
Robert T. Secrest (D)
Robert Taft, Jr. (R)
Charles A. Vanik (D)

OKLAHOMA

Senators

A.S. Mike Monroney (D)

J. Howard Edmondson (D) ta. 1963
Fred R. Harris (D) s. 1964

Representatives

Carl Albert (D)
Page H. Belcher (R)
Edmond Edmondson (D)
John Jarman (D)
Thomas J. Steed (D)
Victor Wickersham (D)

OREGON

Senators

Wayne Morse (D)
Maurine B. Neuberger (D)

Representatives

Robert B. Duncan (D)
Edith Green (D)
A. Walter Norblad (R)
d. Sept. 1964
Al Ullman (D)

PENNSYLVANIA

Senators

Joseph S. Clark (D)
Hugh Scott (R)

Representatives

William A. Barrett (D)
James A. Byrne (D)
Frank M. Clark (D)
Robert J. Corbett (R)
Willard S. Curtin (R)
Paul B. Dague (R)
John H. Dent (D)
Daniel J. Flood (R)
James G. Fulton (R)
Leon H. Gavin (R)
d. Sept. 1963
George A. Goodling (R)
William J. Green (D) s. 1964
William J. Green, Jr. (D)
d. Dec. 1963
Elmer J. Holland (D)
Albert W. Johnson
John C. Kunkel (R)
Joseph M. McDade (R)
William H. Milliken (R)
William S. Moorhead (D)
Thomas E. Morgan (D)
Robert N. C. Nix (D)
George M. Rhodes (D)
Fred B. Rooney (D)
John P. Saylor (R)
Herman T. Schneebeli (R)
Richard S. Schweiker (R)
Herman Toll (D)
Francis E. Walter (D)
d. May 1963
James D. Weaver (R)
J. Irving Whalley (R)

RHODE ISLAND

Senators

John O. Pastore (D)
Claiborne Pell (D)

Representatives

John E. Fogarty (D)
Fernand J. St. Germain (D)

SOUTH CAROLINA

Senators

Olin D. Johnston (D)
J. Strom Thurmond (D)

Representatives

Robert T. Ashmore (D)
W. J. Bryan Dorn (D)
Robert W. Hemphill (D)
r. May 1964
John L. McMillan (D)
L. Mendel Rivers (D)
Albert W. Watson (D)

SOUTH DAKOTA

Senators

Karl E. Mundt (R)
George McGovern (D)

Representatives

Ellis Y. Berry (R)
Benjamin Reifel (R)

TENNESSEE

Senators

Estes Kefauver (D)
d. Aug. 1963
Herbert S. Walters (D) ta. 1963

Albert Gore (D)

Representatives

Howard H. Baker (R)
d. Jan. 1964
Irene Bailey Baker (R) s. 1964
Ross Bass (D)
William E. Brock 3d (R)
Clifford Davis (D)
Robert A. Everett (D)
Joe L. Evins (D)
Richard H. Fulton (D)
Thomas J. Murray (D)
James H. Quillen (R)

TEXAS

Senators

Ralph W. Yarborough (D)
John G. Tower (R)

Representatives

Bruce R. Alger (R)
Lindley G. Beckworth (D)
Jack B. Brooks (D)
Omar Burleson (D)
Robert R. Casey (D)
John V. Dowdy (D)
O. Clark Fisher (D)
Edgar F. Forman (R)
Henry B. Gonzalez (D)
Joe M. Kilgore (D)
George H. Mahon (D)
Wright Patman (D)
J. J. Pickle (D)
William R. Poage (D)
Joe R. Pool (D)
Graham Purcell (D)
H. Ray Roberts (D)
Walter E. Rogers (D)
Olin E. Teague (D)
Albert Thomas (D)
Clark W. Thompson (D)
W. Homer Thornberry (D)
r. Dec. 1963
James C. Wright, Jr. (D)
John A. Young (D)

UTAH

Senators

Wallace F. Bennett (R)
Frank E. Moss (D)

Representatives

Laurence J. Burton (R)
Sherman P. Lloyd (R)

VERMONT

Senators

George D. Aiken (R)
Winston L. Prouty (R)

Representative

Robert T. Stafford (R)

VIRGINIA

Senators

Harry F. Byrd (D)
A. Willis Robertson (D)

Representatives

Watkins M. Abbitt (D)
Joel T. Broyhill (R)
Thomas N. Downing (D)
J. Vaughan Gary (D)
Porter Hardy, Jr. (D)
William P. Jennings (D)
John O. Marsh, Jr. (D)
Richard H. Poff (R)
Howard W. Smith (D)
William M. Tuck (D)

WASHINGTON

Senators

Warren G. Magnuson (D)
Henry M. Jackson (D)

Representatives

Julia Butler Hansen (D)
Walter F. Horan (R)
Catherine May (R)
Thomas M. Pelly (R)
Bill Stinson (R)
Thor C. Tollefson (R)
Alfred J. Westland (R)

WEST VIRGINIA

Senators

Jennings Randolph (D)
Robert C. Byrd (D)

Representatives

Kenneth Hechler (D)
Maude Elizabeth Kee (D)
Arch A. Moore, Jr. (R)
John M. Slack, Jr. (D)
Harley O. Staggers (D)

WISCONSIN

Senators

William Proxmire (D)
Gaylord A. Nelson (D)

Representatives

John W. Byrnes (R)
Lester R. Johnson (D)
Robert W. Kastenmeier (D)
Melvin R. Laird (R)
Alvin E. O'Konski (R)
Henry S. Reuss (D)
Henry C. Schadeberg (R)
Vernon W. Thomson (R)
William K. VanPelt (R)
Clement J. Zablocki (D)

WYOMING

Senators

Gale W. McGee (D)
Milward L. Simpson (R)

Representative

William H. Harrison (R)

EIGHTY-NINTH CONGRESS

January 3, 1965 to January 3, 1967

President of The Senate: Hubert H. Humphrey
President Pro Tempore of The Senate: Carl Hayden
Speaker of The House of Representatives: John W. McCormack

ALABAMA

Senators

Lister Hill (D)
John J. Sparkman (D)

Representatives

George W. Andrews (D)
Glenn Andrews (R)
John H. Buchanan, Jr. (R)
William L. Dickinson (R)
Jack Edwards (R)
Robert E. Jones, Jr. (D)
James D. Martin (R)
Armistead I. Selden, Jr. (D)

ALASKA

Senators

Edward L. Bartlett (D)
Ernest Gruening (D)

Representative

Ralph J. Rivers (D)

ARIZONA

Senators

Carl Hayden (D)
Paul J. Fannin (R)

Representatives

John J. Rhodes (R)
George F. Senner, Jr. (D)
Morris K. Udall (D)

ARKANSAS

Senators

John L. McClellan (D)
J. W. Fulbright (D)

Representatives

Ezekiel C. Gathings (D)
Oren Harris (D) r. Feb. 1966
Wilbur D. Mills (D)
James W. Trimble (D)

CALIFORNIA

Senators

Thomas H. Kuchel (R)
George L. Murphy (R)

Representatives

John F. Baldwin, Jr. (R)
d. Mar. 1966
Alphonzo Bell (R)
George E. Brown, Jr. (D)
Phillip Burton (D)
Ronald B. Cameron (D)
Don H. Clausen (R)
Del Clawson (R)
Jeffery Cohelan (D)
James C. Corman (D)
Ken W. Dyal (D)
Don Edwards (D)
Charles S. Gubser (R)
Harlan F. Hagen (D)
Richard T. Hanna (D)
Augustus F. Hawkins (D)
Chet Holifield (D)
Craig Hosmer (R)
Harold T. Johnson (D)
Cecil R. King (D)
Robert L. Leggett (D)
Glenard P. Lipscomb (R)
John J. McFall (D)
William S. Mailliard (R)
George P. Miller (D)
John E. Moss, Jr. (D)
Thomas M. Rees (D) s. 1966
Ed Reinecke (R)
James Roosevelt (D)
r. Sept. 1965
Edward R. Roybal (D)
Bernice F. Sisk (D)
H. Allen Smith (R)
Burt L. Talcott (R)
Charles M. Teague (R)
John V. Tunney (D)
James B. Utt (R)
Lionel Van Deerlin (D)
Jerome R. Waldie (D) s. 1966
Charles H. Wilson (D)
Robert C. Wilson (R)
J. Arthur Younger (R)

COLORADO

Senators

Gordon L Allott (R)
Peter H. Dominick (R)

Representatives

Wayne N. Aspinall (D)
Frank E. Evans (D)
Roy H. McVicker (D)
Byron G. Rogers (D)

CONNECTICUT

Senators

Thomas J. Dodd (D)
Abraham A. Ribicoff (D)

Representatives

Emilio Q. Daddario (D)
Robert N. Giaimo (D)
Bernard F. Grabowski (D)
Donald J. Irwin (D)
John S. Monagan (D)
William L. St. Onge (D)

DELAWARE

Senators

John J. Williams (R)
J. Caleb Boggs (R)

Representative

Harris B. McDowell, Jr. (D)

FLORIDA

Senators

Spessard L. Holland (D)
George A. Smathers (D)

Representatives

Charles E. Bennett (D)
William C. Cramer (R)
Dante B. Fascell (D)
Don Fuqua (D)
Sam M. Gibbons (D)
Edward J. Gurney (R)
James A. Haley (D)
Albert S. Herlong, Jr. (D)
Donald R. Matthews (D)
Claude D. Pepper (D)
Paul G. Rogers (D)
Robert L. F. Sikes (D)

GEORGIA

Senators

Richard B. Russell (D)
Herman E. Talmadge (D)

Representatives

Howard H. Callaway (R)
John W. Davis (D)
John J. Flynt, Jr. (D)
G. Elliott Hagan (D)
Phillip M. Landrum (D)
James A. Mackay (D)
Maston O'Neal, Jr. (D)
Robert G. Stephens, Jr. (R)
J. Russell Tuten (D)
Charles L. Weltner (D)

HAWAII

Senators

Hiram L. Fong (R)
Daniel K. Inouye (D)

Representatives

Spark M. Matsunaga (D)
Patsy T. Mink (D)

IDAHO

Senators

Frank Church (D)
Len B. Jordan (R)

Representatives

George V. Hansen (R)
Compton I. White, Jr. (D)

ILLINOIS

Senators

Paul H. Douglas (D)
Everett M. Dirksen (R)

Representatives

John B. Anderson (R)
Frank Annunzio (D)
Leslie C. Arends (R)
Harold R. Collier (R)
William L. Dawson (R)
Edward J. Derwinski (R)
John N. Erlenborn (R)
Paul Findley (R)
Kenneth J. Gray (D)
John C. Kluczynski (D)
Robert McClory (R)
Robert H. Michel (R)
William T. Murphy (D)
Barratt O'Hara (D)
Melvin Price (D)
Roman C. Pucinski (R)
Charlotte T. Reid (R)
Daniel J. Ronan (D)
Dan Rostenkowski (D)
Donald Rumsfeld (R)
Gale Schisler (D)
George E. Shipley (D)
William L. Springer (R)
Sidney R. Yates (D)

INDIANA

Senators

Vance Hartke (D)
Birch Bayh (D)

Representatives

E. Ross Adair (R)
John Brademas (D)
William G. Bray (R)
Winfield K. Denton (D)
Charles A. Halleck (R)
Lee H. Hamilton (D)
Ralph Harvey (R)
Andrew Jacobs, Jr. (D)
Ray J. Madden (D)
Richard L. Roudebush (R)
J. Edward Roush (D)

IOWA

Senators

Bourke B. Hickenlooper (R)
Jack R. Miller (R)

Representatives

Bert A. Bandstra (D)
John C. Culver (D)
Stanley L. Greigg (D)
Harold R. Gross (R)
John R. Hansen (D)
John R. Schmidhauser (D)
Neal Smith (D)

KANSAS

Senators

Frank Carlson (R)
James B. Pearson (R)

Representatives

Robert J. Dole (R)
Robert F. Ellsworth (R)
Chester L. Mize (R)
Garner E. Shriver (R)
Joe Skubitz (R)

KENTUCKY

Senators

John Sherman Cooper (R)
Thruston B. Morton (R)

Representatives

Tim Lee Carter (R)
Frank L. Chelf (D)
Charles P. Farnsley (D)
William H. Natcher (D)
Carl D. Perkins (D)
Frank A. Stubblefield (D)
John C. Watts (D)

LOUISIANA

Senators

Allen J. Ellender (D)
Russell B. Long (D)

Representatives

T. Hale Boggs (D)
Edwin W. Edwards (D) s. 1965
F. Edward Hebert (D)
Speedy O. Long (D)
James H. Morrison (D)
Otto E. Passman (D)
T. Ashton Thompson (D)
d. July 1965
Joe D. Waggonner, Jr. (D)
Edwin E. Willis (D)

MAINE

Senators

Margaret Chase Smith (R)
Edmund S. Muskie (D)

Representatives

William D. Hathaway (D)
Stanley R. Tupper (R)

MARYLAND

Senators

Daniel B. Brewster (D)
Joseph D. Tydings (D)

Representatives

George H. Fallon (D)
Samuel N. Friedel (D)
Edward A. Garmatz (D)
Clarence D. Long (D)
Rogers C. B. Morton (R)
Hervey G. Machen (D)
Charles M. Mathias, Jr. (R)
Carlton R. Sickles (D)

MASSACHUSETTS

Senators

Leverett Saltonstall (R)
Edward M. Kennedy (D)

Representatives

William H. Bates (R)
Edward P. Boland (D)
James A. Burke (D)
Silvio O. Conte (R)
Harold D. Donohue (D)
Hastings Keith (R)
John W. McCormack (D)
Torbert H. Macdonald (D)
Joseph W. Martin, Jr. (R)
F. Bradford Morse (R)
Thomas P. O'Neill, Jr. (D)
Philip J. Philbin (D)

MICHIGAN

Senators

Patrick V. McNamasra (D)
d. Apr. 1966
Robert P. Griffin (R) s. 1966

Philip A. Hart (D)

Representatives

William S. Broomfield (R)
Elford A. Cederberg (R)
Charles E. Chamberlain (R)
Raymond F. Clevenger (D)
John Conyers, Jr. (D)
Charles C. Diggs, Jr. (R)
John D. Dingell, Jr. (D)
Billie S. Farnum (D)
Gerald R. Ford (R)
William D. Ford (D)
Robert P. Griffin (R)
r. May 1966
Martha W. Griffiths (D)
James Harvey (R)
Edward Hutchinson (R)
John C. Mackie (D)
Lucien N. Nedzi (D)
James G. O'Hara (D)
Paul H. Todd, Jr. (D)
Weston E. Vivian (D)

MINNESOTA

Senators

Eugene J. McCarthy (D)
Walter F. Mondale (D)

Representatives

John A. Blatnik (D)
Donald M. Fraser (D)
Joseph E. Karth (D)
Odin Langen (R)
Clark MacGregor (R)
Ancher Nelsen (R)
Alec G. Olson (D)
Albert H. Quie (R)

MISSISSIPPI

Senators

James O. Eastland (D)
John C. Stennis (D)

Representatives

Thomas G. Abernethy (D)
William M. Colmer (D)
Prentiss Walker (R)
Jamie L. Whitten (D)
John Bell Williams (D)

MISSOURI

Senators

Stuart Symington (D)
Edward V. Long (D)

Representatives

Richard W. Bolling (D)
Thomas B. Curtis (R)
Durward G. Hall (R)
William R. Hull, Jr. (D)
William L. Hungate (D)
Richard H. Ichord (D)
Paul C. Jones (D)
Frank M. Karsten (D)
William J. Randall (D)
Leonor Kretzer Sullivan (D)

MONTANA

Senators

Mike Mansfield (D)
Lee Metcalf (D)

Representatives

James F. Battin (R)
Arnold Olsen (D)

NEBRASKA

Senators

Roman L. Hurska (R)
Carl T. Curtis (R)

Representatives

Clair A. Callan (D)
Glenn C. Cunningham (R)
David T. Martin (R)

NEVADA

Senators

Alan Bible (D)
Howard W. Cannon (D)

Representative

Walter S. Baring (D)

NEW HAMPSHIRE

Senators

Norris Cotton (R)
Thomas J. McIntyre (D)

Representatives

James C. Cleveland (R)
J. Oliva Huot (D)

NEW JERSEY

Senators

Clifford P. Case (R)
Harrison A. Williams, Jr. (D)

Representatives

William T. Cahill (R)
Dominick V. Daniels (D)
Florence P. Dwyer (R)
Peter H. B. Frelinghuysen, Jr. (R)
Cornelius E. Gallagher (D)
Henry Helstoski (D)
James J. Howard (D)
Charles S. Joelson (D)
Paul J. Krebs (D)
Thomas C. McGrath, Jr. (D)
Joseph G. Minish (D)
Edward J. Patten (D)
Peter W. Rodino, Jr. (D)
Frank Thompson, Jr. (D)
William B. Widnall (R)

NEWMEXICO

Senators

Clinton P. Anderson (D)
Joseph M. Montoya (D)

Representatives

Thomas G. Morris (D)
E. S. Johnny Walker (D)

NEW YORK

Senators

Jacob K. Javits (R)
Robert F. Kennedy (D)

Representatives

Joseph P. Addabbo (D)
Jonathan B. Bingham (D)
Hugh L. Carey (D)
Emanuel Celler (D)
Barber B. Conable, Jr. (R)
James J. Delaney (D)
John G. Dow (D)
Thaddeus J. Dulski (D)
Leonard Farbstein (D)
Paul A. Fino (R)
Jacob H. Gilbert (D)
Charles E. Goodell (R)
James R. Grover, Jr. (R)
Seymour Halpern (R)

James M. Hanley (D)
Frank J. Horton (R)
Edna F. Kelly (D)
Eugene J. Keogh (D)
Carleton J. King (R)
Theodore Kupferman (R) s. 1966
John V. Lindsay (R)
r. Dec. 1965
Richard D. McCarthy (D)
Robert C. McEwen (R)
Abraham J. Multer (D)
John M. Murphy (D)
Leo W. O'Brien (D)
Richard L. Ottinger (D)
Otis G. Pike (D)
Alexander Pirnie (R)
Adam Clayton Powell (D)
Ogden R. Reid (R)
Joseph Y. Resnick (D)
Howard W. Robison (R)
John J. Rooney (D)
Benjamin S. Rosenthal (D)
William F. Ryan (D)
James H. Scheuer (D)
Henry P. Smith 3d (R)
Samuel S. Stratton (D)
Herbert Tenzer (D)
Lester L. Wolff (D)
John W. Wydler (R)

NORTH CAROLINA

Senators

Sam J. Ervin, Jr. (D)
B. Everett Jordan (D)

Representatives

Herbert C. Bonner (D)
d. Nov. 1965
James T. Broyhill (R)
Harold D. Cooley (D)
Lawrence H. Fountain (D)
David N. Henderson (D)
Charles R. Jonas (R)
Walter B. Jones (D) s. 1966
Horace R. Kornegay (D)
Alton A. Lennon (D)
Ralph J. Scott (D)
Roy A. Taylor (D)
Basil L. Whitener (D)

NORTH DAKOTA

Senators

Milton R. Young (R)
Quentin N. Burdick (D)

Representatives

Mark Andrews (R)
Rolland Redlin (D)

OHIO

Senators

Frank J. Lausche (D)
Stephen M. Young (D)

Representatives

John M. Ashbrook (R)
Thomas L. Ashley (D)
William H. Ayres (R)
Jackson E. Betts (R)
Frances P. Bolton (R)
Frank T. Bow (R)
Clarence J. Brown (R)
d. Aug. 1965
Clarence J. Brown, Jr. (R)
s. 1966
Donald D. Clancy (R)
Samuel L. Devine (R)
Michael A. Feighan (D)
John J. Gilligan (D)
William H. Harsha, Jr. (R)
Wayne L. Hays (D)
Michael J. Kirwan (D)
Delbert L. Latta (R)
Rodney M. Love (D)
William M. McCulloch (R)
William E. Minshall (R)
Walter H. Moeller (D)
Charles A. Mosher (R)
Robert T. Secrest (D)
J. William Stanton (R)
Robert E. Sweeney (D)
Charles A. Vanik (D)

OKLAHOMA

Senators

A. S. Mike Monroney (D)
Fred R. Harris (D)

Representatives

Carl Albert (D)
Page H. Belcher (R)
Edmond Edmondson (D)
John Jarman (D)
Jed Johnson, Jr. (D)
Thomas J. Steed (D)

OREGON

Senators

Wayne Morse (D)
Maurine B. Neuberger (D)

Representatives

Robert B. Duncan (D)
Edith Green (D)
Wendell Wyatt (R)
Albert C. Ullman (D)

PENNSYLVANIA

Senators

Joseph S. Clark (D)
Hugh Scott (R)

Representatives

William A. Barrett (D)
James A. Byrne (D)
Frank M. Clark (D)
Robert J. Corbett (R)
N. Neiman Craley, Jr. (D)
Willard S. Curtin (R)
Paul B. Dague (R)
John H. Dent (D)
Daniel J. Flood (D)
James G. Fulton (R)
William J. Green (D)
Elmer J. Holland (D)
Albert W. Johnson (R)
John C. Kunkel (R)
Joseph M. McDade (R)
William S. Moorhead (D)
Thomas E. Morgan (D)
Robert N. C. Nix (D)
George M. Rhodes (D)
Fred B. Rooney (D)
John P. Saylor (R)
Herman T. Schneebeli (R)
Richard S. Schweiker (R)
Herman Toll (D)
Joseph P. Vigorito (D)
G. Robert Watkins (R)
J. Irving Whalley (R)

RHODE ISLAND

Senators

John O. Pastore (D)
Claiborne Pell (D)

Representatives

John E. Fogarty (D)
Fernand J. St. Germain (D)

SOUTH CAROLINA

Senators

Olin D. Johnston (D)
d. Apr. 1965
Donald S. Russell (D) s. 1965

J. Strom Thurmond (R)

Representatives

Robert T. Ashmore (D)
W. J. Bryan Dorn (D)
Tom S. Gettys (D)
John L. McMillan (D)
L. Mendel Rivers (D)
Albert W. Watson (R) r. 1965

SOUTH DAKOTA

Senators

Karl E. Mundt (R)
George McGovern (D)

Representatives

Ellis Y. Berry (R)
Benjamin Reifel (R)

TENNESSEE

Senators

Albert A. Gore (D)
Ross Bass (D)

Representatives

William R. Anderson (D)
William E. Brock 3d (R)
John J. Duncan (R)
Robert A. Everett (D)
Joe L. Evins (D)
Richard H. Fulton (D)
George W. Grider (D)
Thomas J. Murray (D)
James H. Quillen (R)

TEXAS

Senators

Ralph W. Yarborough (D)
John G. Tower (R)

Representatives

Lindley G. Beckworth (D)
Jack B. Brooks (D)
Omar T. Burleson (D)
Earle Cabell (D)
Robert R. Casey (D)
Eligio de la Garza 2d (D)
John V. Dowdy (D)
O. Clark Fisher (D)
Henry B. Gonzalez (D)
George H. Mahon (D)
Wright Patman (D)
J. J. Pickle (D)
William R. Poage (D)
Joe R. Pool (D)
Graham Purcell (D)
H. Ray Roberts (D)
Walter E. Rogers (D)
Olin E. Teague (D)
Albert Thomas (D) d. 1965
Lera Thomas (D) s. 1966
Clark W. Thompson (D)
Richard C. White (D)
James C. Wright, Jr. (D)
John A. Young (D)

UTAH

Senators

Wallace F. Bennett (R)
Frank E. Moss (D)

Representatives

Laurence J. Burton (R)
David S. King (D)

VERMONT

Senators

George D. Aiken (R)
Winston L. Prouty (R)

Representative

Robert T. Stafford (R)

VIRGINIA

Senators

Harry F. Byrd (D) r. Nov. 1965
Harry F. Byrd, Jr. (D)

A. Willis Robertson (D)

Representatives

Watkins M. Abbitt (D)
Joel T. Broyhill (R)
Thomas N. Downing (D)
Porter Hardy, Jr. (D)
William P. Jennings (D)
John O. Marsh, Jr. (D)
Richard H. Poff (R)
David E. Satterfield 3d (D)
Howard W. Smith (D)
William M. Tuck (D)

WASHINGTON

Senators

Warren G. Magnuson (D)
Henry M. Jackson (D)

Representatives

Brock Adams (D)
Thomas S. Foley (D)
Julia Butler Hansen
Floyd V. Hicks (D)
Catherine May (R)
Lloyd Meeds (D)
Thomas M. Pelly (R)

WEST VIRGINIA

Senators

Jennings Randolph (D)
Robert C. Byrd (D)

Representatives

Kenneth Hechler (D)
James Kee (D)
Arch A. Moore, Jr. (R)
John M. Slack, Jr. (D)
Harley O. Staggers (D)

WISCONSIN

Senators

William Proxmire (D)
Gaylord A. Nelson (D)

Representatives

John W. Byrnes (R)
Glenn R. Davis (R)
Robert W. Kastenmeier (D)
Melvin R. Laird (R)
Alvin E. O'Konski (R)
John A. Race (D)
Henry S. Reuss (D)
Lynn E. Stalbaum (D)
Vernon W. Thomson (R)
Clement J. Zablocki (D)

WYOMING

Senators

Gale W. McGee (D)
Milward L. Simpson (R)

Representative

Teno Roncalio (D)

NINETIETH CONGRESS

January 3, 1967 to January 3, 1969

President of The Senate: Hubert H. Humphrey
President Pro Tempore of The Senate: Carl Hayden
Speaker of The House of Representatives: John W. McCormack

ALABAMA

Senators

Lister Hill (D)
John J. Sparkman (D)

Representatives

George W. Andrews (D)
Tom Bevill (D)
John H. Buchanan, Jr. (R)
William L. Dickinson (R)
Jack Edwards (R)
Robert E. Jones, Jr. (D)
William Nichols (D)
Armistead I. Selden, Jr. (D)

ALASKA

Senators

dward L. Bartlett (D)
d. Dec. 1968
rnest Gruening (D)

Representative

oward W. Pollock (R)

ARIZONA

Senators

rl Hayden (D)
l J. Fannin (R)

Representatives

John J. Rhodes (R)
Sam Steiger (R)
Morris K. Udall (D)

ARKANSAS

Senators

John L. McClellan (D)
J. W. Fulbright (D)

Representatives

Eziekel C. Gathings (D)
John P. Hammerschmidt (R)
Wilbur D. Mills (D)
David H. Pryor (D)

CALIFORNIA

Senators

Thomas H. Kuchel (R)
George Murphy (R)

Representatives

Alphonzo Bell (R)
George E. Brown, Jr. (D)
Phillip Burton (D)
Don H. Clausen (R)
Del Clawson (R)
Jeffery Cohelan (D)
James C. Corman (D)
Don Edwards (D)
Charles S. Gubser (R)
Richard T. Hanna (D)
Augustus F. Hawkins (D)
Chet Holifield (D)
Craig Hosmer (R)
Harold T. Johnson (D)
Cecil R. King (D)
Robert L. Leggett (D)
Glenard P. Lipscomb (R)
Paul N. McCloskey, Jr. (R)
John J. McFall (D)
William S. Mailliard (R)
Robert B. Mathias (R)
George P. Miller (D)
John E. Moss, Jr. (D)
Jerry L. Pettis (R)
Thomas M. Rees (D)
Ed Reinecke (R)
Edward R. Roybal (D)
Bernice F. Sisk (D)
H. Allen Smith (R)
Burt L. Talcott (R)
Charles M. Teague (R)
John V. Tunney (D)
James B. Utt (R)
Lionel Van Deerlin (D)
Jerome R. Waldie (D)
Charles E. Wiggins (R)
Charles H. Wilson (D)
Robert C. Wilson (R)
J. Arthur Younger (R)
d. June 1967

COLORADO

Senators

Gordon L. Allott (R)
Peter H. Dominick (R)

Representatives

Wayne N. Aspinall (D)
Donald G. Brotzman (R)
Frank E. Evans (D)
Byron G. Rogers (D)

CONNECTICUT

Senators

Thomas J. Dodd (D)
Abraham A. Ribicoff (D)

Representatives

Emilio Q. Daddario (D)
Robert N. Giaimo (D)
Donald J. Irwin (D)
Thomas J. Meskill (R)
John S. Monagan (D)
William L. St. Onge (D)

DELAWARE

Senators

John J. Williams (R)
J. Caleb Boggs (R)

Representative

William V. Roth, Jr. (R)

FLORIDA

Senators

Spessard L. Holland (D)
George A. Smathers (D)

Representatives

Charles E. Bennett (D)
J. Herbert Burke (R)
William C. Cramer (R)
Dante B. Fascell (D)
Don Fuqua (D)
Sam M. Gibbons (D)
Edward J. Gurney (R)
James A. Haley (D)
Albert S. Herlong, Jr. (D)
Claude D. Pepper (D)
Paul G. Rogers (D)
Robert L. F. Sikes (D)

GEORGIA

Senators

Richard B. Russell (D)
Herman E. Talmadge (D)

Representatives

Benjamin B. Blackburn (R)
Jack Brinkley (D)
John W. Davis (D)
John J. Flynt, Jr. (D)
G. Elliott Hagan (D)
Phillip M. Landrum (D)
Maston O'Neal (D)
Robert G. Stephens, Jr. (D)
Williamson S. Stuckey, Jr. (D)
Fletcher Thompson (R)

HAWAII

Senators

Hiram L. Fong (R)
Daniel K. Inouye (D)

Representatives

Spark M. Matsunaga (D)
Patsy T. Mink (D)

IDAHO

Senators

Frank Church (D)
Len B. Jordan (R)

Representatives

George V. F. Hansen (R)
James A. McClure (R)

ILLINOIS

Senators

Everett M. Dirksen (R)
Charles H. Percy (R)

Representatives

John B. Anderson (R)
Frank Annunzio (D)

Leslie C. Arends (R)
Harold R. Collier (R)
William L. Dawson (D)
Edward J. Derwinski (R)
John N. Erlenborn (D)
Paul Findley (R)
Kenneth J. Gray (D)
John C. Kluczynski (D)
Robert McClory (R)
Robert H. Michel (R)
William T. Murphy (D)
Barratt O'Hara (D)
Melvin Price (D)
Roman C. Pucinski (D)
Thomas F. Railsback (R)
Charlotte T. Reid (R)
Daniel J. Ronan (D)
Dan Rostenkowski (D)
Donald Rumsfeld (R)
George E. Shipley (D)
William L. Springer (R)
Sidney R. Yates (D)

INDIANA

Senators

Vance Hartke (D)
Birch Bayh (D)

Representatives

E. Ross Adair (R)
John Brademas (D)
William G. Bray (R)
Charles A. Halleck (R)
Lee H. Hamilton (D)
Andrew Jacobs, Jr. (D)
Ray J. Madden (D)
John T. Myers (R)
Richard L. Roudebush (R)
J. Edward Roush (D)
Roger H. Zion (R)

IOWA

Senators

Bourke B. Hickenlooper (R)
Jack R. Miller (R)

Representatives

John C. Culver (D)
Harold R. Gross (R)
John H. Kyl (R)
Wiley Mayne (R)
William J. Scherle (R)
Fred Schwengel (R)
Neal Smith (D)

KANSAS

Senators

Frank Carlson (R)
James B. Pearson (R)

Representatives

Robert J. Dole (R)
Chester L. Mize (R)
Garner E. Shriver (R)
Joe Skubitz (R)
Larry Winn, Jr. (R)

KENTUCKY

Senators

John Sherman Cooper (R)
Thruston B. Morton (R)

Representatives

Tim Lee Carter (R)
William O. Cowger (R)
William H. Natcher (D)
Carl D. Perkins (D)
M. G. (Gene) Snyder (R)
Frank A. Stubblefield (D)
John C. Watts (D)

LOUISIANA

Senators

Allen J. Ellender (D)
Russell B. Long (D)

Representatives

T. Hale Boggs (D)
Edwin W. Edwards (D)
F. Edward Hebert (D)
Speedy O. Long (D)
Otto E. Passman (D)
John R. Rarick (D)
Joe D. Waggonner, Jr. (D)
Edwin E. Willis (D)

MAINE

Senators

Margaret Chase Smith (R)
Edmund S. Muskie (D)

Representatives

William D. Hathaway (D)
Peter N. Kyros (D)

MARYLAND

Senators

Daniel B. Brewster (D)
Joseph D. Tydings (D)

Representatives

George H. Fallon (D)
Samuel N. Friedel (D)
Edward A. Garmatz (D)
Gilbert Gude (R)
Clarence D. Long (D)
Hervey G. Machen (D)
Charles McC. Mathias, Jr. (R)
Rogers C. B. Morton (R)

MASSACHUSETTS

Senators

Edward M. Kennedy (D)
Edward W. Brooke (R)

Representatives

William H. Bates (R)
Edward P. Boland (D)
James A. Burke (D)
Silvio O. Conte (R)
Harold D. Donohue (D)
Margaret M. Heckler (R)
Hastings Keith (R)
John W. McCormack (D)
Torbert H. Macdonald (D)
F. Bradford Morse (R)
Thomas P. O'Neill, Jr. (D)
Philip J. Philbin (D)

MICHIGAN

Senators

Philip A. Hart (D)
Robert P. Griffin (R)

Representatives

William S. Broomfield (R)
Garry E. Brown (R)
Elford A. Cederberg (R)
Charles E. Chamberlain (R)
John Conyers, Jr. (D)
Charles C. Diggs, Jr. (D)
John D. Dingell, Jr. (D)
Marvin L. Esch (R)
Gerald R. Ford, Jr. (R)
William D. Ford (D)
Martha W. Griffiths (D)
James Harvey (R)
Edward Hutchinson (R)
Jack H. McDonald (R)
Lucien N. Nedzi (D)
James G. O'Hara (D)
Donald W. Riegle, Jr. (R)
Phillip E. Ruppe (R)
Guy Vander Jagt (R)

MINNESOTA

Senators

Eugene J. McCarthy (D)
Walter F. Mondale (D)

Representatives

John A. Blatnik (D)
Donald M. Fraser (D)
Joseph E. Karth (D)
Odin Langen (R)
Clark MacGregor (R)
Ancher Nelsen (R)
Albert H. Quie (R)
John M. Zwach (R)

MISSISSIPPI

Senators

James O. Eastland (D)
John C. Stennis (D)

Representatives

Thomas G. Abernethy (D)
William M. Colmer (D)
Charles H. Griffin (D) s. 1968
Gillespie V. Montgomery (D)
Jamie L. Whitten (D)
John Bell Williams (D)
r. Jan. 1968

MISSOURI

Senators

Stuart Symington (D)
Edward V. Long (D)

Representatives

Richard W. Bolling (D)
Thomas B. Curtis (R)
Durward G. Hall (R)
William R. Hull, Jr. (D)
William L. Hungate (D)
Richard H. Ichord (D)
Paul C. Jones (D)
Frank M. Karsten (D)
William J. Randall (D)
Leonor Kretzer Sullivan (D)

MONTANA

Senators

Mike Mansfield (D)
Lee Matcalf (D)

Representatives

James F. Battin (R)
Arnold Olsen (D)

NEBRASKA

Senators

Roman L. Hruska (R)
Carl T. Curtis (R)

Representatives

Glenn C. Cunningham (R)
Robert V. Denney (R)
David T. Martin (R)

NEVADA

Senators

Alan Bible (D)
Howard W. Cannon (D)

Representative

Walter S. Baring (D)

NEW HAMPSHIRE

Senators

Norris Cotton (R)
Thomas J. McIntyre (D)

Representatives

James C. Cleveland (R)
Louis C. Wyman (R)

NEW JERSEY

Senators

Clifford P. Case (R)
Harrison A. Williams, Jr. (D)

Representatives

William T. Cahill (R)
Dominick V. Daniels (D)
Florence P. Dwyer (R)
Peter H. B. Frelinghuysen, Jr. (R)
Cornelius E. Gallagher (D)

Henry Helstoski (D)
James J. Howard (D)
John E. Hunt (R)
Charles S. Joelson (D)
Joseph G. Minish (D)
Edward J. Patten (D)
Peter W. Rodino, Jr. (D)
Charles W. Sandman, Jr. (R)
Frank Thompson, Jr. (D)
William B. Widnall (R)

NEW MEXICO

Senators

Clinton P. Anderson (D)
Joseph M. Montoya (D)

Representatives

Thomas G. Morris (D)
E. S. Johnny Walker (D)

NEW YORK

Senators

Jacob K. Javits (R)

Robert F. Kennedy (D)
d. June 1968
Charles E. Goodell (R) s. 1968

Representatives

Joseph P. Addabbo (D)
Jonathan B. Bingham (D)
Frank J. Brasco (D)
Daniel E. Button (R)
Hugh L. Carey (D)
Emanuel Celler (D)
Barber B. Conable, Jr. (R)
James J. Delaney (D)
John G. Dow (D)
Thaddeus J. Dulski (D)
Leonard Farbstein (D)
Paul A. Fino (R)
Jacob H. Gilbert (D)
Charles E. Goodell (R)
James R. Grover, Jr. (R)
Seymour Halpern (R)
James M. Hanley (D)
Frank J. Horton (R)
Edna F. Kelly (D)
Carleton J. King (R)
Theodore R. Kupferman (R)
Richard D. McCarthy (D)
Robert C. McEwen (R)
Abraham J. Multer (D)
r. Dec. 1967
John M. Murphy (D)
Richard L. Ottinger (D)
Otis G. Pike (D)
Alexander Pirnie (R)
Bertram L. Podell (D) s. 1968
Adam Clayton Powell (D)
Ogden R. Reid (R)
Joseph Y. Resnick (D)
Howard W. Robison (R)
John J. Rooney (D)
Benjamin S. Rosenthal (D)
William F. Ryan (D)
James H. Scheuer (D)
Henry P. Smith 3d (R)
Samuel S. Stratton (D)
Herbert Tenzer (D)
Lester L. Wolff (D)
John W. Wydler (R)

NORTH CAROLINA

Senators

Sam J. Ervin, Jr. (D)
B. Everett Jordan (D)

Representatives

James T. Broyhill (R)
Lawrence H. Fountain (D)
Nick Galifianakis (D)
James C. Gardner (R)
David N. Henderson (D)
Charles R. Jonas (R)
Walter B. Jones (D)
Horace R. Kornegay (D)
Alton A. Lennon (D)
Roy A. Taylor (D)
Basil L. Whitener (D)

NORTH DAKOTA

Senators

Milton R. Young (R)
Quentin N. Burdick (D)

Representatives

Mark Andrews (R)
Thomas S. Kleppe (R)

OHIO

Senators

Frank J. Lausche (D)
Stephen M. Young (D)

Representatives

John M. Ashbrook (R)
Thomas L. Ashley (D)
William H. Ayres (R)
Jackson E. Betts (R)
Frances P. Bolton (R)
Frank T. Bow (R)
Clarence J. Brown, Jr. (R)
Donald D. Clancy (R)
Samuel L. Devine (R)
Michael A. Feighan (D)
William H. Harsha, Jr. (R)
Wayne L. Hays (D)
Michael J. Kirwan (D)
Delbert L. Latta (R)
Donald E. Lukens (R)
William M. McCulloch (R)
Clarence E. Miller (R)
William E. Minshall (R)
Charles A. Mosher (R)
J. William Stanton (R)
Robert Taft, Jr. (R)
Charles A. Vanik (D)
Charles W. Whalen, Jr. (R)
Chalmers P. Wylie (R)

OKLAHOMA

Senators

A. S. Mike Monroney (D)
Fred R. Harris (D)

Representatives

Carl Albert (D)
Page H. Belcher (R)
Edmond Edmondson (D)
John Jarman (D)
James V. Smith (R)
Thomas J. Steed (D)

OREGON

Senators

Wayne Morse (D)
Mark O. Hatfield (R)

Representatives

John R. Dellenback (R)
Edith Green (D)
Albert C. Ullman (D)
Wendell Wyatt (R)

PENNSYLVANIA

Senators

Joseph S. Clark (D)
Hugh Scott (R)

Representatives

William A. Barrett (D)
Edward G. Biester, Jr. (R)
James A. Byrne (D)
Frank M. Clark (D)
Robert J. Corbett (R)
John H. Dent (D)
Joshua Eilberg (D)
Edwin D. Eshleman (R)
Daniel J. Flood (D)
James G. Fulton (R)
George A. Goodling (R)
William J. Green (D)
Elmer J. Holland (D)
d. Aug. 1968
Albert W. Johnson (R)
Joseph M. McDade (R)
William S. Moorhead (D)
Thomas E. Morgan (D)
Robert N. C. Nix (R)
George M. Rhodes (D)
Fred B. Rooney (D)
John P. Saylor (R)
Herman T. Schneebeli (R)
Richard S. Schweiker (R)
Joseph P. Vigorito (D)
G. Robert Watkins (R)
J. Irving Whalley (R)
Lawrence G. Williams (R)

RHODE ISLAND

Senators

John O. Pastore (D)
Claiborne Pell (D)

Representatives

Fernand J. St. Germain (D)
Robert O. Tiernan (D)

SOUTH CAROLINA

Senators

J. Strom Thurmond (R)
Ernest F. Hollings (D)

Representatives

Robert T. Ashmore (D)
W. J. Bryan Dorn (D)
Tom S. Gettys (D)
John L. McMillan (D)
L. Mendel Rivers (D)
Albert W. Watson (R)

SOUTH DAKOTA

Senators

Karl E. Mundt (R)
George S. McGovern (D)

Representatives

Ellis Y. Berry (R)
Benjamin Reifel (R)

TENNESSEE

Senators

Albert Gore (D)
Howard H. Baker, Jr. (R)

Representatives

William R. Anderson (D)
L. Ray Blanton (D)
William E. Brock 3d (R)
John J. Duncan (R)
Robert A. Everett (D)
Joe L. Evins (D)
Richard H. Fulton (D)
Dan H. Kuykendall (R)
James H. Quillen (R)

TEXAS

Senators

Ralph W. Yarborough (D)
John G. Tower (R)

Representatives

Jack B. Brooks (D)
Omar T. Burleson (D)
George Bush (R)
Earle Cabell (D)
Robert R. Casey (D)
James M. Collins (D) s. 1968
Eligio de la Garza 2d (D)
John V. Dowdy (D)
Robert C. Eckhardt (D)
O. Clark Fisher (D)
Henry B. Gonzalez (D)
Abraham Kazen, Jr. (D)
George H. Mahon (D)
Wright Patman (D)
J. J. Pickle (D)
William R. Poage (D)
Joe R. Pool (D) d. July 1968
Robert D. Price (R)
Graham Purcell (D)
H. Ray Roberts (D)
Olin E. Teague (D)
Richard C. White (D)
James C. Wright, Jr. (D)
John A. Young (D)

UTAH

Senators

Wallace F. Bennett (R)
Frank E. Moss (D)

Representatives

Laurence J. Burton (R)
Sherman P. Lloyd (R)

VERMONT

Senators

George D. Aiken (R)
Winston L. Prouty (R)

Representative

Robert T. Stafford (R)

VIRGINIA

Senators

Harry F. Byrd, Jr. (D)
William B. Spong, Jr. (D)

Representatives

Watkins M. Abbitt (D)
Joel T. Broyhill (R)
Thomas N. Downing (D)
Porter Hardy, Jr. (D)
John O. Marsh, Jr. (D)
Richard H. Poff (R)
David E. Satterfield 3d (D)
William L. Scott (R)
William M. Tuck (D)
William C. Wampler (R)

WASHINGTON

Senators

Warren G. Magnuson (D)
Henry M. Jackson (D)

Representatives

Brock Adams (D)
Thomas S. Foley (D)
Julia Butler Hansen (D)
Floyd V. Hicks (D)
Catherine May (R)
Lloyd Meeds (D)
Thomas M. Pelly (R)

WEST VIRGINIA

Senators

Jennings Randolph (D)
Robert C. Byrd (D)

Representatives

Kenneth Hechler (D)
James Kee (D)
Arch A. Moore, Jr. (R)
John M. Slack, Jr. (D)
Harley O. Staggers (D)

WISCONSIN

Senators

William Proxmire (D)
Gaylord A. Nelson (D)

Representatives

John W. Byrnes (R)
Glenn R. Davis (R)
Robert W. Kastenmeier (R)
Melvin R. Laird (R)
Alvin E. O'Konski (R)
Henry S. Reuss (D)
Henry C. Schadeberg (R)
William A. Steiger (R)
Vernon W. Thomson (R)
Clement J. Zablocki (D)

WYOMING

Senators

Gale W. McGee (D)
Clifford P. Hansen (R)

Representative

William H. Harrison

NINETY-FIRST CONGRESS

January 3, 1969 to January 3, 1971

President of The Senate: Spiro T. Agnew
President Pro Tempore of The Senate: Richard B. Russell
Speaker of The House of Representatives: John W. McCormack

ALABAMA

Senators

John J. Sparkman (D)
James B. Allen (D)

Representatives

George W. Andrews (D)
Tom Bevill (D)
John H. Buchanan, Jr. (R)
William L. Dickinson (R)
Jack Edwards (R)
Walter Flowers (D)
Robert E. Jones, Jr. (D)
William Nichols (D)

ALASKA

Senators

Ted Stevens (R)
Mike Gravel (D)

Representative

Howard W. Pollock (R)

ARIZONA

Senators

Paul J. Fannin (R)
Barry M. Goldwater (R)

Representatives

John J. Rhodes (R)
Sam Steiger (R)
Morris K. Udall (D)

ARKANSAS

Senators

John L. McClellan (D)
J. W. Fulbright (D)

Representatives

Bill Alexander (D)
John P. Hammerschmidt (R)
Wilbur D. Mills (D)
David H. Pryor (D)

CALIFORNIA

Senators

George Murphy (R)
Alan Cranston (D)

Representatives

Glenn M. Anderson (D)
Alphonzo Bell (R)
George E. Brown, Jr. (D)
Phillip Burton (D)
Don H. Clausen (R)
Del Clawson (R)
Jeffery Cohelan (D)
James C. Corman (D)
Don Edwards (D)
Barry Goldwater, Jr. (R)
Charles S. Gubser (R)
Richard T. Hanna (D)
Augustus F. Hawkins (D)
Chet Holifield (D)
Craig Hosmer (R)
Harold T. Johnson (D)
Robert L. Leggett (D)
Glenard P. Lipscomb (R)
d. Feb. 1970
Paul N. McCloskey, Jr. (R)
John J. McFall (D)
William S. Mailliard (R)
Robert B. Mathias (R)
George P. Miller (D)
John E. Moss, Jr. (D)
Jerry L. Pettis (R)
Thomas M. Rees (D)
John H. Rousselot (R) s. 1970
Edward R. Roybal (D)
John G. Schmitz (R) s. 1970
Bernice F. Sisk (D)
H. Allen Smith (R)
Burt L. Talcott (R)
Charles M. Teague (R)
John V. Tunney (D)
James B. Utt (R) d. Mar. 1970
Lionel Van Deerlin (D)
Jerome R. Waldie (D)
Charles E. Wiggins (R)
Charles H. Wilson (D)
Robert C. Wilson (R)

COLORADO

Senators

Gordon L. Allott (R)
Peter H. Dominick (R)

Representatives

Wayne N. Aspinall (D)
Donald G. Brotzman (R)
Frank E. Evans (D)
Byron G. Rogers (D)

CONNECTICUT

Senators

Thomas J. Dodd (D)
Abraham A. Ribicoff (D)

Representatives

Emilio Q. Daddario (D)
Robert N. Giaimo (D)
Thomas J. Meskill (R)
John S. Monagan (D)
William L. St. Onge (D)
d. May 1970
Robert H. Steele (R) s. 1970
Lowell P. Weicker, Jr. (R)

DELAWARE

Senators

John J. Williams (R)
J. Caleb Boggs (R)

Representative

William V. Roth, Jr. (R)

FLORIDA

Senators

Spessard L. Holland (D)
Edward J. Gurney (R)

Representatives

Charles E. Bennett (D)
J. Herbert Burke (R)
Bill Chappell, Jr. (D)
William C. Cramer (R)
Dante B. Fascell (D)
Louis Frey, Jr. (R)
Don Fuqua (D)
Sam M. Gibbons (D)
James A. Haley (D)
Claude D. Pepper (D)
Paul G. Rogers (D)
Robert L. F. Sikes (D)

GEORGIA

Senators

Richard B. Russell (D)
Herman E. Talmadge (D)

Representatives

Benjamin B. Blackburn (R)
Jack Brinkley (D)

John W. Davis (D)
John J. Flynt, Jr. (D)
G. Elliott Hagan (D)
Phillip M. Landrum (D)
Maston O'Neal (D)
Robert G. Stephens, Jr. (D)
William S. Stuckey, Jr. (D)
Fletcher Thompson (R)

HAWAII

Senators

Hiram L. Fong (R)
Daniel K. Inouye (D)

Representatives

Spark M. Matsunaga (D)
Patsy T. Mink (D)

IDAHO

Senators

Frank Church (D)
Len B. Jordan (R)

Representatives

Orval Hansen (R)
James A. McClure (R)

ILLINOIS

Senators

Everett M. Dirksen (R)
d. Sept. 1969
Ralph T. Smith (R) ta. 1969
Adlai E. Stevenson 3d (D)
s. 1970

Charles H. Percy (R)

Representatives

John B. Anderson (R)
Frank Annunzio (D)
Leslie C. Arends (R)
Harold R. Collier (R)
George W. Collins (D) s. 1970
Philip M. Crane (R)
William L. Dawson (D)
d. Sept. 1970
Edward J. Derwinski (R)
John N. Erlenborn (R)
Paul Findley (R)
Kenneth J. Gray (D)
John C. Kluczynski (D)
Robert McClory (R)
Robert H. Michel (R)
Abner J. Mikva (D)
William T. Murphy (D)
Melvin Price (D)
Roman C. Pucinski (D)
Thomas F. Railsback (R)
Charlotte T. Reid (R)
Daniel J. Ronan (D) d. Aug. 1969
Dan Rostenkowski (D)
Donald Rumsfeld (R) r. May 1969
George E. Shipley (D)
William L. Springer (R)
Sidney R. Yates (D)

INDIANA

Senators

Vance Hartke (D)
Birch Bayh (D)

Representatives

E. Ross Adair (R)
John Brademas (D)
William G. Bray (R)
David W. Dennis (R)
Lee H. Hamilton (D)
Andrew Jacobs, Jr. (D)
Earl F. Landgrebe (R)
Ray J. Madden (D)
John T. Myers (R)
Richard L. Roudebush (R)
Roger H. Zion (R)

IOWA

Senators

Jack R. Miller (R)
Harold E. Hughes (D)

Representatives

John C. Culver (D)
Harold R. Gross (R)
John H. Kyl (R)
Wiley Mayne (R)
William J. Scherle (R)
Fred Schwengel (R)
Neal Smith (D)

KANSAS

Senators

James B. Pearson (R)
Robert J. Dole (R)

Representatives

Chester L. Mize (R)
Keith G. Sebelius (R)
Garner E. Shriver (R)
Joe Skubitz (R)
Larry Winn, Jr. (R)

KENTUCKY

Senators

John Sherman Cooper (R)
Marlow W. Cook (R)

Representatives

Tim Lee Carter (R)
William O. Cowger (R)
William H. Natcher (D)
Carl D. Perkins (D)
M. G. (Gene) Snyder (R)
Frank A. Stubblefield (D)
John C. Watts (D)

LOUISIANA

Senators

Allen J. Ellender (D)
Russell B. Long (D)

Representatives

T. Hale Boggs (D)
Patrick T. Caffery (D)
Edwin W. Edwards (D)
F. Edward Hebert (D)
Speedy O. Long (D)
Otto E. Passman (D)
John R. Rarick (D)
Joe D. Waggoner, Jr. (D)

MAINE

Senators

Margaret Chase Smith (R)
Edmund S. Muskie (D)

Representatives

William D. Hathaway (D)
Peter N. Kyros (D)

MARYLAND

Senators

Joseph D. Tydings (D)
Charles McC. Mathias, Jr. (D)

Representatives

J. Glenn Beall, Jr. (R)
George H. Fallon (D)
Samuel N. Friedel (D)
Edward A. Garmatz (R)
Gilbert Gude (R)
Lawrence J. Hogan (R)
Clarence D. Long (D)
Rogers C. B. Morton (R)

MASSACHUSETTS

Senators

Edward M. Kennedy (D)
Edward W. Brooke (R)

Representatives

William H. Bates (R) d. June 1969
Edward P. Boland (D)
James A. Burke (D)
Silvio O. Conte (R)
Harold D. Donohue (D)
Michael J. Harrington (D) s. 1969
Margaret M. Heckler (R)
Hastings Keith (R)
John W. McCormack (D)
Torbert H. Macdonald (D)
F. Bradford Morse (R)
Thomas P. O'Neill, Jr. (D)
Philip J. Philbin (D)

MICHIGAN

Senators

Philip A. Hart (D)
Robert P. Griffin (R)

Representatives

William S. Broomfield (R)
Garry E. Brown (R)
Elford A. Cederberg (R)
Charles E. Chamberlain (R)
John Conyers, Jr. (D)
Charles C. Diggs, Jr. (D)
John D. Dingell, Jr. (D)
Marvin L. Esch (R)
Gerald R. Ford, Jr. (R)
William D. Ford (D)
Martha W. Griffiths (D)
James Harvey (R)
Edward Hutchinson (R)
Jack H. McDonald (R)
Lucien N. Nedzi (D)
James G. O'Hara (D)
Donald W. Riegle, Jr. (R)
Philip E. Ruppe (R)
Guy Vander Jagt (R)

MINNESOTA

Senators

Eugene J. McCarthy (D)
Walter F. Mondale (D)

Representatives

John A. Blatnik (D)
Donald M. Fraser (D)
Joseph E. Karth (D)
Odin Langen (R)
Clark MacGregor (R)
Ancher Nelsen (R)
Albert H. Quie (R)
John M. Zwach (R)

MISSISSIPPI

Senators

James O. Eastland (D)
John C. Stennis (D)

Representatives

Thomas G. Abernethy (D)
William M. Colmer (D)
Charles H. Griffin (D)
Gillespie V. Montgomery (D)
Jamie L. Whitten (D)

MISSOURI

Senators

Stuart Symington (D)
Thomas F. Eagleton (D)

Representatives

Richard W. Bolling (D)
Bill D. Burlison (D)
William L. Clay (D)
Durward G. Hall (R)
William R. Hull, Jr. (D)
William L. Hungate (D)
Richard H. Ichord (D)
William J. Randall (D)
Leonor Kretzer Sullivan (D)
James W. Symington (D)

MONTANA

Senators

Mike Mansfield (D)
Lee Metcalf (D)

Representatives

James F. Battin (R) r. Feb. 1969
John Melcher (D)
Arnold Olsen (D)

NEBRASKA

Senators

Roman L. Hruska (R)
Carl T. Curtis (R)

Representatives

Glenn C. Cunningham (R)
Robert V. Denney (R)
David T. Martin (R)

NEVADA

Senators

Alan Bible (D)
Howard W. Cannon (D)

Representative

Walter S. Baring (D)

NEW HAMPSHIRE

Senators

Norris Cotton (R)
Thomas J. McIntyre (D)

Representatives

James C. Cleveland (R)
Louis C. Wyman (R)

NEW JERSEY

Senators

Clifford P. Case (R)
Harrison A. Williams, Jr. (D)

Representatives

William T. Cahill (R)
r. Jan. 1970
Dominick V. Daniels (D)
Florence P. Dwyer (R)
Edwin B. Forsythe (R) s. 1970
Peter H. B. Frelinghuysen, Jr. (R)
Cornelius E. Gallagher (D)
Henry Helstoski (D)
James J. Howard (D)
John E. Hunt (R)
Charles S. Joelson (D)
r. Sept. 1969
Joseph G. Minish (D)
Edward J. Patten (D)
Peter W. Rodino, Jr. (D)
Robert A. Roe (D)
Charles W. Sandman, Jr. (D)
William B. Widnall (R)

NEW MEXICO

Senators

Clinton P. Anderson (D)
Joseph M. Montoya (D)

Representatives

Edgar F. Foreman (R)
Manuel Lujan, Jr. (R)

NEW YORK

Senators

Jacob K. Javits (R)
Charles E. Goodell (R)

Representatives

Joseph P. Addabbo (D)
Mario Biaggi (D)
Jonathan B. Bingham (D)
Frank J. Brasco (D)
Daniel E. Button (R)
Hugh L. Carey (D)
Emanuel Celler (D)
Shirley Chisholm (D)
Barber B. Conable, Jr. (R)
James J. Delaney (D)
Thaddeus J. Dulski (D)
Leonard Farbstein (D)
Hamilton Fish, Jr. (R)
Jacob H. Gilbert (D)
James R. Grover, Jr. (R)
Seymour Halpern (R)
James M. Hanley (D)
James F. Hastings (R)
Frank J. Horton (R)
Carleton J. King (R)
Edward I. Koch (D)
Allard K. Lowenstein (D)
Richard D. McCarthy (D)
Robert C. McEwen (R)
Martin B. McKneally (R)
John M. Murphy (D)
Richard L. Ottinger (D)
Otis G. Pike (D)
Alexander Pirnie (R)
Bertram L. Podell (D)
Adam Clayton Powell (D)
Ogden R. Reid (R)
Howard W. Robison (R)
John J. Rooney (D)
Benjamin S. Rosenthal (D)
William F. Ryan (D)
James H. Scheuer (D)
Henry P. Smith 3d (R)
Samuel S. Stratton (D)
Lester L. Wolff (D)
John W. Wydler (R)

NORTH CAROLINA

Senators

Sam J. Ervin, Jr. (D)
B. Everett Jordan (D)

Representatives

James T. Broyhill (R)
Lawrence H. Fountain (D)
Nick Galifianakis (D)
David N. Henderson (D)
Charles R. Jonas (R)
Walter B. Jones (D)
Alton A. Lennon (D)
Wilmer D. Mizell (R)
Richardson Preyer (D)
Earl B. Ruth (R)
Roy A. Taylor (D)

NORTH DAKOTA

Senators

Milton R. Young (R)
Quentin N. Burdick (D)

Representatives

Mark Andrews (R)
Thomas S. Kleppe (R)

OHIO

Senators

Stephen M. Young (D)
William B. Saxbe (R)

Representatives

John M. Ashbrook (R)
Thomas L. Ashley (D)
William H. Ayres (R)
Jackson E. Betts (R)
Frank T. Bow (R)
Clarence J. Brown, Jr. (R)
Charles J. Carney (D) s. 1970
Donald D. Clancy (R)
Samuel L. Devine (R)
Michael A. Feighan (R)
William H. Harsha, Jr. (R)
Wayne L Hays (D)
Michael J. Kirwan (D)
d. July 1970
Delbert L. Latta (R)
Donald E. Lukens (R)
William M. McCulloch (R)
Clarence E. Miller (R)
William E. Minshall (R)
Charles A. Mosher (R)
J. William Stanton (R)
Louis Stokes (D)
Robert Taft, Jr. (R)
Charles E. Vanik (D)
Charles W. Whalen, Jr. (R)
Chalmers P. Wylie (R)

OKLAHOMA

Senators

Fred R. Harris (D)
Henry L. Bellmon (R)

Representatives

Carl Albert (D)
Page H. Belcher (R)
John N. Camp (R)
Edmond Edmondson (D)
John Jarman (D)
Thomas J. Steed (D)

OREGON

Senators

Mark O. Hatfield (R)
Robert W. Packwood (R)

Representatives

John R. Dellenback (R)
Edith Green (D)
Albert C. Ullman (D)
Wendell Wyatt (R)

PENNSYLVANIA

Senators

Hugh Scott (R)
Richard S. Schweiker (R)

Representatives

William A. Barrett (D)
Edward G. Biester, Jr. (R)
James A. Byrne (D)
Frank M. Clark (D)
Robert J. Corbett (R)
R. Lawrence Coughlin (R)
John H. Dent (D)
Joshua Eilberg (D)
Edwin D. Eshleman (R)
Daniel J. Flood (D)
James G. Fulton (R)
Joseph M. Gaydos (D)
George A. Goodling (R)
William J. Green (D)
Albert W. Johnson (R)
Joseph M. McDade (R)
William S. Moorhead (D)
Thomas E. Morgan (D)
Robert N. C. Nix (D)
Fred B. Rooney (D)
John P. Saylor (R)
Herman T. Schneebeli (R)
Joseph P. Vigorito (D)
John H. Ware 3d (R) s. 1970
G. Robert Watkins (R)
d. Aug. 1970
J. Irving Whalley (R)
Lawrence G. Williams (R)
Gus Yatron (D)

RHODE ISLAND

Senators

John O. Pastore (D)
Claiborne Pell (D)

Representatives

Fernand J. St. Germain (D)
Robert O. Tiernan (D)

SOUTH CAROLINA

Senators

J. Strom Thurmond (R)
Ernest H. Hollings (D)

Representatives

W. J. Bryan Dorn (D)
Tom S. Gettys (D)
John L. McMillan (D)
James R. Mann (D)
L. Mendel Rivers (D) d. Dec. 1970
Albert W. Watson (R)

SOUTH DAKOTA

Senators

Karl E. Mundt (R)
George McGovern (D)

Representatives

Ellis Y. Berry (R)
Benjamin Reifel (R)

TENNESSEE

Senators

Albert Gore (D)
Howard H. Baker, Jr. (R)

Representatives

William R. Anderson (D)
L. Ray Blanton (D)
William E. Brock 3d (R)
John J. Duncan (R)
Joe L. Evins (D)
Richard H. Fulton (D)
Ed Jones (D)
Dan H. Kuykendall (R)
James H. Quillen (R)

TEXAS

Senators

Ralph W. Yarborough (D)
John G Tower (R)

Representatives

Jack B. Brooks (D)
Omar T. Burleson (D)
George Bush (R)
Earle Cabell (D)
Robert R. Casey (D)
James M. Collins (R)
Eligio de la Garza 2d (D)
John V. Dowdy (D)
Robert C. Eckhardt (D)
O. Clark Fisher (D)
Henry B. Gonzalez (D)
Abraham Kazen, Jr. (D)
George H. Mahon (D)
Wright Patman (D)
J. J. Pickle (D)
William R. Poage (D)
Robert D. Price (R)
Graham Purcell (D)
H. Ray Roberts (D)
Olin E. Teague (D)
Richard C. White (D)
James C. Wright, Jr. (D)
John A. Young (D)

UTAH

Senators

Wallace F. Bennett (R)
Frank E. Moss (R)

Representatives

Laurence J. Burton (R)
Sherman P. Lloyd (R)

VERMONT

Senators

George D. Aiken (R)
Winston L. Prouty (R)

Representative

Robert T. Stafford (R)

VIRGINIA

Senators

Harry F. Byrd, Jr. (D)
William B. Spong, Jr. (D)

Representatives

Watkins M. Abbitt (D)
Joel T. Broyhill (R)
W. C. (Dan) Daniel (D)
Thomas N. Downing (D)
John O. Marsh, Jr. (D)
Richard H. Poff (R)
David E. Satterfield 3d (D)
William L. Scott (R)
William C. Wampler (R)
G. William Whitehurst (R)

WASHINGTON

Senators

Warren G. Magnuson (D)
Henry M. Jackson (D)

Representatives

Brock Adams (D)
Thomas S. Foley (D)
Julia Butler Hansen (D)
Floyd V. Hicks (D)
Catherine May (R)
Lloyd Meeds (D)
Thomas M. Pelly (R)

WEST VIRGINIA

Senators

Jennings Randolph (D)
Robert C. Byrd (D)

Representatives

Kenneth Hechler (D)
James Kee (D)
Robert H. Mollohan (D)
John M. Slack, Jr. (D)
Harley O. Staggers (D)

WISCONSIN

Senators

William Proxmire (D)
Gaylord Nelson (D)

Representatives

John W. Byrnes (R)
Glenn R. Davis (R)
Robert W. Kastenmeier (D)
David R. Obey (D)
Alvin E. O'Konski (R)
Henry S. Reuss (D)
Henry C. Schadeberg (R)
William A. Steiger (R)
Vernon W. Thomson (R)
Clement J. Zablocki (D)

WYOMING

Senators

Gale W. McGee (D)
Clifford P. Hansen (R)

Representative

John Wold (R)

NINETY-SECOND CONGRESS

January 3, 1971 to January 3, 1973

President of The Senate: Spiro T. Agnew
President Pro Tempore of The Senate: Allen J. Ellender
Speaker of The House of Representatives: Carl Albert

ALABAMA

Senators

John J. Sparkman (D)
James B. Allen (D)

Representatives

Elizabeth Andrews (D)
s. Apr. 1972
George Andrews (D) d. 1972
Tom Bevill (D)
John H. Buchanan, Jr. (R)
William L. Dickinson (R)
Jack Edwards (R)
Walter Flowers (D)
Robert E. Jones (D)
William Nichols (D)

ALASKA

Senators

Ted Stevens (R)
Mike Gravel (D)

Representative

Nick Begich (D)

ARIZONA

Senators

Paul J. Fannin (R)
Barry M. Goldwater (R)

Representatives

John J. Rhodes (R)
Sam Steiger (R)
Morris K. Udall (D)

ARKANSAS

Senators

John L. McClellan (D)
J. William Fulbright (D)

Representatives

Bill Alexander, Jr. (D)
John P. Hammerschmidt (R)
Wilbur D. Mills (D)
David H. Pryor (D)

CALIFORNIA

Senators

Alan Cranston (D)
John V. Tunney (D)

Representatives

Glenn M. Anderson (D)
Alphonzo Bell (R)
Phillip Burton (D)
Don H. Clausen (R)
Del M. Clawson (R)
James C. Corman (D)
George E. Danielson (D)
Ronald V. Dellums (D)
Don Edwards (D)
Barry M. Goldwater, Jr. (R)
Charles S. Gubser (R)
Richard T. Hanna (D)
Augustus F. Hawkins (D)
Chet Holifield (D)
Craig Hosmer (R)
Harold T. Johnson (D)
Robert L. Leggett (D)
Paul N. McCloskey, Jr. (R)
John J. McFall (D)
William S. Mailliard (R)
Robert B. Mathias (R)
George P. Miller (D)
John E. Moss (D)
Jerry L. Pettis (R)
Thomas M. Rees (D)
John H. Rousselot (R)
Edward R. Roybal (D)
John G. Schmitz (R)
Bernice F. Sisk (D)
H. Allen Smith (R)
Burt L. Talcott (R)
Charles M. Teague (R)
Lionel Van Deerlin (D)
Victor V. Veysey (R)
Jerome R. Waldie (D)
Robert C. Wilson (R)
Charles H. Wilson (D)
Charles E. Wiggins (R)

COLORADO

Senators

Gordon L. Allott (R)
Peter H. Dominick (R)

Representatives

Wayne N. Aspinall (D)
Donald G. Brotzman (R)
Frank E. Evans (D)
James D. McKevitt (R)

CONNECTICUT

Senators

Abraham A. Ribicoff (D)
Lowell P. Weicker, Jr. (R)

Representatives

William R. Cotter (D)
Robert N. Giaimo (D)
Ella T. Grasso (D)
Stewart B. McKinney (R)
John S. Monagan (D)
Robert H. Steele (R)

DELAWARE

Senators

J. Caleb Boggs (R)
William V. Roth, Jr. (R)

Representative

Pierre S. duPont 4th (R)

FLORIDA

Senators

Edward J. Gurney (R)
Lawton M. Chiles, Jr. (D)

Representatives

Charles E. Bennett (D)
J. Herbert Burke (R)
William V. Chappell, Jr. (D)
Dante B. Fascell (D)
Louis Frey, Jr. (R)
Don Fuqua (D)
Sam M. Gibbons (D)
James A. Haley (D)
Claude D. Pepper (D)
Paul G. Rogers (D)
Robert L. F. Sikes (D)
C. W. Bill Young (R)

GEORGIA

Senators

Herman E. Talmadge (D)
David H. Gambrell (D)

Representatives

Ben B. Blackburn (R)
Jack T. Brinkley (D)
John W. Davis (D)
John J. Flynt, Jr. (D)
G. Elliott Hagan (D)
Phil M. Landrum (D)
M. Dawson Mathis (D)
Robert G. Stephens, Jr. (D)
William S. Stuckey, Jr.
Fletcher Thompson (R)

HAWAII

Senators

Hiram L. Fong (R)
Daniel K. Inouye (D)

Representatives

Spark M. Matsunaga (D)
Patsy T. Mink (D)

IDAHO

Senators

Frank Church (D)
Len B. Jordan (R)

Representatives

Orval Hansen (R)
James A. McClure (R)

ILLINOIS

Senators

Charles H. Percy (R)
Adlai E. Stevenson 3d (D)

Representatives

John B. Anderson (R)
Frank Annunzio (D)
Leslie C. Arends (R)
Harold R. Collier (R)
George W. Collins (D)
Philip M. Crane (R)
Edward J. Derwinski (R)
John N. Erlenborn (R)
Paul Findley (R)
Kenneth J. Gray (D)
John C. Kluczynski (D)
Robert McClory (R)
Ralph H. Metcalfe (D)
Robert H. Michel (R)
Abner J. Mikva (D)
Morgan F. Murphy (D)
C. Melvin Price (D)
Roman C. Pucinski (D)
Thomas F. Railsback (R)
Charlotte T. Reid (R) r. Oct. 1971
Dan Rostenkowski (D)
George E. Shipley (D)
William L. Springer (R)
Sidney R. Yates

INDIANA

Senators

Vance Hartke (D)
Birch Bayh (D)

Representatives

John Brademas (D)
William G. Bray (R)
David W. Dennis (R)
Lee H. Hamilton (D)
Elwood H. Hillis (R)
Andrew Jacobs, Jr. (D)
Earl F. Landgrebe (R)
Ray J. Madden (D)
John T. Myers (R)
J. Edward Roush (D)
Roger H. Zion (R)

IOWA

Senators

Jack R. Miller (R)
Harold E. Hughes (D)

Representatives

John C. Culver (D)
Harold R. Gross (R)
John H. Kyl (R)
Wiley Mayne (R)
William J. Scherle (R)
Fred Schwengel (R)
Neal Smith (D)

KANSAS

Senators

James B. Pearson (R)
Robert J. Dole (R)

Representatives

William R. Roy (D)
Keith G. Sebelius (R)
Garner E. Shriver (R)
Joe Skubitz (R)
Larry Winn, Jr. (R)

KENTUCKY

Senators

John Sherman Cooper (R)
Marlow W. Cook (R)

Representatives

Tim Lee Carter (R)
William O. Cowger (R)
d. Oct. 1971
William P. Curlin, Jr. (D)
Romano L. Mazzoli (D)
William H. Natcher (D)
Carl D. Perkins (D)
M. Gene Snyder (R)
Frank A. Stubblefield (D)
John C. Watts (D) d. Sept. 1971

LOUISIANA

Senators

Allen J. Ellender (D) d. July 1972
Russell B. Long (D)

Representatives

T. Hale Boggs (D)
Patrick T. Caffery (D)
Edwin W. Edwards (D)
F. Edward Hebert (D)
Speedy O. Long (D)
Otto E. Passman (D)
John R. Rarick (D)
Joe D. Waggonner, Jr. (D)

MAINE

Senators

Margaret Chase Smith (R)
Edmund S. Muskie (D)

Representatives

William D. Hathaway (D)
Peter N. Kyros (D)

MARYLAND

Senators

Charles McC. Mathias, Jr. (R)
J. Glenn Beall, Jr. (R)

Representatives

Goodloe E. Byron (D)
Edward A. Garmatz (D)
Gilbert Gude (R)
Lawrence J. Hogan (R)
Clarence D. Long (D)
William O. Mills (R)
Parren J. Mitchell (D)
Paul S. Sarbanes (D)

MASSACHUSETTS

Senators

Edward M. Kennedy (D)
Edward W. Brooke (R)

Representatives

James A. Burke (D)
Edward P. Boland (D)
Silvio O. Conte (R)
Harold D. Donohue (D)
Robert F. Drinan (D)
Michael J. Harrington (D)
Margaret M. Heckler (R)
Louise Day Hicks (D)
Hastings Keith (R)
Torbert H. Macdonald (D)
F. Bradford Morse (R)
Thomas P. O'Neill, Jr. (D)

MICHIGAN

Senators

Philip A. Hart (D)
Robert P. Griffin (R)

Representatives

William S. Broomfield (R)
Garry E. Brown (R)
Elford A. Cederberg (R)
Charles E. Chamberlain (R)
John Conyers, Jr. (D)
Charles C. Diggs, Jr. (D)
John D. Dingell (D)
Marvin L. Esch (R)
Gerald R. Ford (D)
William D. Ford (D)
Martha W. Griffiths (D)
James Harvey (R)
Edward Hutchinson (R)
Jack H. McDonald (R)
Lucien N. Nedzi (D)
James G. O'Hara (D)
Donald W. Riegle, Jr. (R)
Philip E. Ruppe (R)
Guy Vander Jagt (R)

MINNESOTA

Senators

Walter F. Mondale (D)
Hubert H. Humphrey (D)

Representatives

Bob Bergland (D)
John A. Blatnik (D)
Donald M. Fraser (D)
Bill Frenzel (R)
Joseph E. Karth (D)
Ancher Nelsen (R)
Albert H. Quie (R)
John M. Zwach (R)

MISSISSIPPI

Senators

James O. Eastland (D)
John C. Stennis (D)

Representatives

Thomas G. Abernethy (D)
William M. Colmer (D)
Charles H. Griffin (D)
Gillespie V. Montgomery (D)
Jamie L. Whitten (D)

MISSOURI

Senators

Stuart Symington (D)
Thomas F. Eagleton (D)

Representatives

Richard Bolling (D)
Bill D. Burlison (D)
William L. Clay (D)
Durward G. Hall (R)
W. R. Hull, Jr. (D)
William L. Hungate (D)
Richard H. Ichord (D)
William J. Randall (R)
Leonor Kretzer Sullivan (D)
James W. Symington (D)

MONTANA

Senators

Mike Mansfield (D)
Lee Metcalf (D)

Representatives

John Melcher (D)
Richard G. Shoup (R)

NEBRASKA

Senators

Roman L. Hruska (R)
Carl T. Curtis (R)

Representatives

John Y. McCollister (R)
David T. Martin (R)
Charles Thone (R)

NEVADA

Senators

Alan Bible (D)
Howard W. Cannon (D)

Representative

Walter S. Baring (D)

NEW HAMPSHIRE

Senators

Norris Cotton (R)
Thomas J. McIntyre (D)

Representatives

James C. Cleveland (R)
Louis C. Wyman (R)

NEW JERSEY

Senators

Clifford P. Case (R)
Harrison A. Williams, Jr. (D)

Representatives

Dominick V. Daniels (D)
Florence P. Dwyer (R)
Edwin B. Forsythe (R)
Peter H. B. Frelinghuysen (R)
Cornelius E. Gallagher (D)
Henry Helstoski (D)
James J. Howard (D)
John E. Hunt (R)
Joseph G. Minish (D)
Edward J. Patten (D)
Peter W. Rodino, Jr. (D)
Robert A. Roe (D)
Charles W. Sandman, Jr. (R)
Frank Thompson, Jr. (D)
William B. Widnall (R)

NEW MEXICO

Senators

Clinton P. Anderson (D)
Joseph M. Montoya (D)

Representatives

Manuel Lujan, Jr. (R)
Harold Runnels (D)

NEW YORK

Senators

Jacob K. Javits (R)
James L. Buckley (Con-R)

Representatives

Bella S. Abzug (D)
Joseph P. Addabbo (D)
Herman Badillo (D)
Mario Biaggi (D)
Jonathan B. Bingham (D)
Frank J. Brasco (D)
Hugh L. Carey (D)
Emanuel Celler (D)
Shirley Chisholm (D)
Barber B. Conable, Jr. (R)
James J. Delaney (D)
John G. Dow (D)
Thaddeus J. Dulski (D)
Hamilton Fish, Jr. (R)
James R. Grover, Jr. (R)
Seymour Halpern (R)
James M. Hanley (D)
James F. Hastings (R)
Frank Horton (R)
Jack F. Kemp (R)
Carleton J. King (R)
Edward I. Koch (D)
Norman F. Lent (R)
Robert C. McEwen (R)
John M. Murphy (D)
Peter A. Peyser (R)
Otis G. Pike (D)
Alexander Pirnie (R)
Bertram L. Podell (D)
Charles B. Rangel (D)
Ogden R. Reid (R)
Howard W. Robison (R)
John J. Rooney (D)
Benjamin S. Rosenthal (D)
William F. Ryan (D) d. Sept. 1972
James H. Scheuer (D)
Henry P. Smith 3d (R)
Samuel S. Stratton (D)
John H. Terry (R)
Lester L. Wolff (D)
John W. Wydler (R)

NORTH CAROLINA

Senators

Sam J. Ervin, Jr. (D)
B. Everett Jordan (D)

Representatives

James T. Broyhill (R)
Lawrence H. Fountain (D)
Nick Galifianakis (D)
David N. Henderson (D)
Charles R. Jonas (R)
Walter B. Jones (D)
Alton A. Lennon (D)
Wilmer D. Mizell (R)
L. Richardson Preyer (D)
Earl B. Ruth (R)
Roy A. Taylor (D)

NORTH DAKOTA

Senators

Milton R. Young (R)
Quentin N. Burdick (D)

Representatives

Mark Andrews (R)
Arthur A. Link (D)

OHIO

Senators

William B. Saxbe (R)
Robert Taft, Jr. (R)

Representatives

John M. Ashbrook (R)
Thomas L. Ashley (D)
Jackson E. Betts (R)
Frank T. Bow (R)
Clarence J. Brown, Jr. (R)
Charles J. Carney (D)
Donald D. Clancy (R)
Samuel L. Devine (R)
William H. Harsha, Jr. (R)
Wayne L. Hays (D)
William J. Keating (R)
Delbert L. Latta (R)
William M. McCulloch (R)
Clarence E. Miller (R)
William E. Minshall (R)
Charles A. Mosher (R)
Walter E. Powell (R)
John F. Seiberling (D)
J. William Stanton (R)
James V. Stanton (D)
Louis Stokes (D)
Charles A. Vanik (D)
Charles W. Whalen, Jr. (R)
Chalmers P. Wylie (R)

OKLAHOMA

Senators

Fred R. Harris (D)
Henry L. Bellman (R)

Representatives

Carl Albert (D)
Page H. Belcher (R)
John N. Camp (R)
Edmond Edmondson (D)
John Jarman (D)
Thomas J. Steed (D)

OREGON

Senators

Mark O. Hatfield (R)
Robert Packwood (R)

Representatives

John Dellenbach (R)
Edith Green (D)
Al Ullman (D)
Wendel Wyatt (R)

PENNSYLVANIA

Senators

Hugh Scott (R)
Richard S. Schweiker (R)

Representatives

William A. Barrett (D)
Edward G. Biester, Jr. (R)
James A. Byrne (D)
Frank M. Clark (D)
Robert J. Corbett (R) d. Apr. 1971
R. Lawrence Coughlin (R)
John H. Dent (D)
Joshua Eilberg (D)
Edwin D. Eshleman (R)
Daniel J. Flood (D)
James G. Fulton (R) d. Oct. 1971
Joseph M. Gaydos (D)
George A. Goodling (R)
William J. Green (D)
H. John Heinz 3d (R)
Albert W. Johnson (R)
Joseph M. McDade (R)
William S. Moorhead (D)
Thomas E. Morgan (D)
Robert N. C. Nix (D)
Fred B. Rooney (D)
John P. Saylor (R)
Herman T. Schneebeli (R)
Joseph P. Vigorito (D)
John J. Ware 3d (R)
J. Irving Whalley (R)
Lawrence G. Williams (R)
Gus Yatron (D)

RHODE ISLAND

Senators

John O. Pastore (D)
Claiborne Pell (D)

Representatives

Fernand J. St. Germain (D)
Robert O. Tiernan (D)

SOUTH CAROLINA

Senators

J. Strom Thurmond (R)
Ernest F. Hollings (D)

Representatives

Mendel J. Davis (D)
W. J. Bryan Dorn (D)
Tom S. Gettys (D)
John L. McMillan (D)
James R. Mann (D)
Floyd D. Spence (R)

SOUTH DAKOTA

Senators

Karl E. Mundt (R)
George McGovern (D)

Representatives

James G. Abourezk (D)
Frank E. Denholm (D)

TENNESSEE

Senators

Howard H. Baker, Jr. (R)
William E. Brock 3d (R)

Representatives

William R. Anderson (D)
LaMar Baker (R)
L. Ray Blanton (D)
John J. Duncan (R)
Joe L. Evins (D)
Richard H. Fulton (D)
Ed Jones (D)
Dan H. Kuykendall (R)
James H. Quillen (R)

TEXAS

Senators

John G. Tower (R)
Lloyd M. Bentsen, Jr. (D)

Representatives

Bill Archer (D)
Jack B. Brooks (D)
Omar T. Burleson (D)
Earle Cabell (D)
Robert R. Casey (D)
James M. Collins (R)
Eligo de la Garza 2d (D)
John V. Dowdy (D)
Robert C. Eckhardt (E)
O. Clark Fisher (D)
Henry B. Gonzalez (D)
Abraham Kazen, Jr. (D)
George H. Mahon (D)
Wright Patman (D)
J. J. Pickle (D)
William R. Poage (D)
Robert D. Price (R)
Graham Purcell (D)
Ray Roberts (R)
Olin E. Teague (D)
Richard C. White (D)
James C. Wright, Jr. (D)
John Young (D)

UTAH

Senators

Wallace F. Bennett (R)
Frank E. Moss (D)

Representatives

Sherman P. Lloyd (R)
K. Gunn McKay (D)

VERMONT

Senators

George D. Aiken (R)

Winston L. Prouty (R)
d. Sept. 1971
Robert T. Stafford (R)

Representative

Robert T. Stafford (R)
r. Sept. 1971

VIRGINIA

Senators

Harry F. Byrd, Jr. (Independent)
William B. Spong, Jr. (D)

Representatives

Watkins M. Abbitt (D)
Joel T. Broyhill (R)
W. C. (Dan) Daniel (D)
Thomas N. Downing (D)
Richard H. Poff (R)
J. Kenneth Robinson (R)
David E. Satterfield 3d (D)
William L. Scott (R)
William C. Wampler (R)
G. William Whitehurst (R)

WASHINGTON

Senators

Warren G. Magnuson (D)
Henry M. Jackson (D)

Representatives

Brock Adams (D)
Thomas S. Foley (D)
Julia Butler Hansen (D)
Floyd V. Hicks (D)
Mike McCormack (D)
Lloyd Meeds (D)
Thomas M. Pelly (R)

WEST VIRGINIA

Senators

Jennings Randolph (D)
Robert C. Byrd (D)

Representatives

Kenneth Hechler (D)
James Kee (D)
Robert H. Mollohan (D)
John M. Slack, Jr. (D)
Harley O. Staggers (D)

WISCONSIN

Senators

William Proxmire (D)
Gaylord Nelson (D)

Representatives

Les Aspin (D)
John W. Byrnes (R)
Glenn R. Davis (R)
Robert W. Kastenmeier (D)
David R. Obey (D)
Alvin E. O'Konski (R)
Henry S. Reuss (D)
William A. Steiger (R)
Vernon W. Thomson (R)
Clement J. Zablocki (D)

WYOMING

Senators

Gale W. McGee (D)
Clifford P. Hansen (R)

Representative

Teno Roncalio (D)

NINETY-THIRD CONGRESS

January 3, 1973 to January 3, 1975

President of The Senate: Spiro T. Agnew
Speaker of The House of Representatives: Carl Albert

ALABAMA

Senators

John J. Sparkman (D)
James B. Allen (D)

Representatives

Tom Bevill (D)
John H. Buchanan, Jr. (R)
William L. Dickinson (R)
Jack Edwards (D)
Walter Flowers (D)
Robert E. Jones (D)
William Nichols (D)

ALASKA

Senators

Ted Stevens (R)
Mike Gravel (D)

Representative

Vacant

ARIZONA

Senators

Paul J. Fannin (R)
Barry M. Goldwater (R)

Representatives

John B. Conlan (R)
John J. Rhodes (R)
Sam Steiger (R)
Morris K. Udall (D)

ARKANSAS

Senators

John L. McClellan (D)
J. William Fulbright (D)

Representatives

William V. Alexander, Jr. (D)
John P. Hammerschmidt (R)
Wilbur D. Mills (D)
Ray Thornton (D)

CALIFORNIA

Senators

Alan Cranston (D)
John V. Tunney (D)

Representatives

Glenn M. Anderson (D)
Alphonzo Bell (R)
George E. Brown, Jr. (D)
Clair W. Burgener (R)
Yvonne Braithwaite Burke (D)
Phillip Burton (D)
Don H. Clausen (R)
Del M. Clawson (R)
James C. Corman (D)
George E. Danielson (D)
Ronald V. Dellums (D)
Don Edwards (D)
Barry M. Goldwater, Jr. (R)
Charles S. Gubser (R)
Richard T. Hanna (D)
Augustus F. Hawkins (D)
Andrew J. Hinshaw (R)
Chet Holifield (D)
Craig Hosmer (R)
Harold T. Johnson (D)
William M. Ketchum (R)
Robert L. Leggett (D)
Paul N. McCloskey, Jr. (R)
John J. McFall (D)
William S. Mailliard (R)
Robert B. Mathias (R)
Carlos J. Moorhead (R)
John E. Moss (D)
Jerry L. Pettis (R)
Thomas M. Rees (D)
John H. Rousselot (R)
Edward R. Roybal (D)
Leo J. Ryan (D)
B.F. Sisk (D)
Fortney H. Stark (D)
Burt L. Talcott (R)

Charles M. Teague (R)
Lionel Van Deerlin (D)
Victor V. Veysey (R)
Jerome R. Waldie (D)
Charles E. Wiggins (R)
Charles H. Wilson (D)
Robert C. Wilson (R)

COLORADO

Senators

Peter H. Dominick (R)
Floyd K. Haskell (D)

Representatives

William L. Armstrong (R)
Donald G. Brotzman (R)
Frank E. Evans (D)
James P. Johnson (R)
Patricia Schroeder (D)

CONNECTICUT

Senators

Abraham A. Ribicoff (D)
Lowell P. Weicker, Jr. (R)

Representatives

William R. Cotter (D)
Robert N. Giaimo (D)
Ella T. Grasso (D)
Stewart B. McKinney (R)
Ronald A. Sarasin (R)
Robert H. Steele (R)

DELAWARE

Senators

William V. Roth, Jr. (R)
Joseph R. Biden, Jr. (D)

Representative

Pierre S. duPont 4th (R)

FLORIDA

Senators

Edward J. Gurney (R)
Lawton M. Chiles, Jr. (D)

Representatives

L. A. Bafalis (R)
Charles E. Bennett (D)
J. Herbert Burke (R)
William V. Chappell, Jr. (D)
Dante B. Fascell (D)
Louis Frey, Jr. (R)
Don Fuqua (D)
Sam M. Gibbons (D)
William D. Gunter, Jr. (D)
James Haley (D)
William Lehman (D)
Claude D. Pepper (D)
Paul G. Rogers (D)
Robert L. F. Sikes (D)
C. W. (Bill) Young (R)

GEORGIA

Senators

Herman E. Talmadge (D)
Sam Nunn (D)

Representatives

Ben B. Blackburn (R)
Jack T. Brinkley (D)
John W. Davis (D)
Ronald B. Ginn (D)
John J. Flynt, Jr. (D)
Phil M. Landrum (D)
M. Dawson Mathis (D)
Robert G. Stephens, Jr. (D)
William S. Stuckey, Jr. (D)
Andrew Young (D)

HAWAII

Senators

Hiram L. Fong (R)
Daniel K. Inouye (D)

Representatives

Spark M. Matsunaga (D)
Patsy T. Mink (D)

IDAHO

Senators

Frank Church (D)
James A. McClure (R)

Representatives

Orval Hansen (R)
Steven D. Symms (R)

ILLINOIS

Senators

Charles H. Percy (R)
Adlai E. Stevenson 3d (D)

Representatives

John B. Anderson (R)
Frank Annunzio (D)
Leslie C. Arends (R)
Harold R. Collier (R)
George W. Collins (D)
Philip M. Crane (R)
Edward J. Derwinski (R)
John N. Erlenborn (R)
Paul Findley (R)
Kenneth J. Gray (D)
Robert P. Hanrahan (R)
John C. Kluczynski (D)
Robert McClory (R)
Edward R. Madigan (R)
Ralph H. Metcalfe (D)
Robert H. Michel (R)
Morgan F. Murphy (D)
George M. O'Brien (R)
C. Melvin Price (D)
Thomas F. Railsback (R)
Dan Rostenkowski (D)
George E. Shipley (D)
Sidney R. Yates (D)
Samuel H. Young (R)

INDIANA

Senators

Vance Hartke (D)
Birch Bayh (D)

Representatives

John Brademas (D)
William G. Bray (R)
David W. Dennis (R)
Lee H. Hamilton (D)
Elwood H. Hillis (R)
William H. Hudnut 3d (R)
Earl F. Landgrebe (R)
Ray J. Madden (D)
John T. Myers (R)
J. Edward Roush (D)
Roger H. Zion (R)

IOWA

Senators

Harold E. Hughes (D)
Richard Clark (D)

Representatives

John C. Culver (D)
Harold R. Gross (R)
Wiley Mayne (R)
Edward Mezvinsky (D)
William J. Scherle (R)
Neal Smith (D)

KANSAS

Senators

James B. Pearson (R)
Robert J. Dole (R)

Representatives

William R. Roy (D)
Keith G. Sebelius (R)
Garner E. Shriver (R)
Joe Skubitz (R)
Larry Winn, Jr. (R)

KENTUCKY

Senators

Marlow W. Cook (R)
Walter Huddleston (R)

Representatives

John B. Breckinridge (D)
Tim Lee Carter (R)
Romano L. Mazzoli (D)
William H. Natcher (D)
Carl D. Perkins (D)
M. Gene Snyder (R)
Frank A. Stubblefield (D)

LOUISIANA

Senators

Russell B. Long (D)
J. Bennett Johnston, Jr. (D)

Representatives

John B. Breaux (D)
F. Edward Hebert (D)
Gillis W. Long (D)
Otto E. Passman (D)
John R. Rarick (D)
David C. Treen (R)
Joe D. Waggonner, Jr. (D)

MAINE

Senators

Edmund S. Muskie (D)
William B. Hathaway (D)

Representatives

William S. Cohen (R)
Peter N. Kyros (D)

MARYLAND

Senators

Charles McC. Mathias, Jr. (R)
J. Glenn Beall, Jr. (R)

Representatives

Goodloe E. Bryon (D)
Gilbert Gude (R)
Lawrence J. Hogan (R)
Marjorie S. Holt (R)
Clarence D. Long (D)
William O. Mills (R)
Parren J. Mitchell (D)
Paul S. Sarbanes (D)

MASSACHUSETTS

Senators

Edward M. Kennedy (D)
Edward W. Brooke (R)

Representatives

James A. Burke (D)
Edward P. Boland (D)
Silvio O. Conte (R)
Paul W. Cronin (R)
Harold D. Donohue (D)
Robert F. Drinan (D)
Michael J. Harrington (D)
Margaret M. Heckler (R)
Torbert H. Macdonald (D)
John J. Moakley
Thomas P. O'Neill, Jr. (D)
Gerry E. Studds (D)

MICHIGAN

Senators

Philip A. Hart (D)
Robert P. Griffin (R)

Representatives

William S. Broomfield (R)
Garry E. Brown (R)
Elford A. Cederberg (R)
Charles E. Chamberlain (R)
John Conyers, Jr. (D)
Charles C. Diggs, Jr. (D)
John D. Dingell (D)

Marvin L. Esch (R)
Gerald R. Ford (D)
William D. Ford (D)
Martha W. Griffiths (D)
James Harvey (R)
Robert J. Huber (R)
Edward Hutchinson (R)
Lucien N. Nedzi (D)
James G. O'Hara (D)
Donald W. Riegle, Jr. (R)
Philip E. Ruppe (R)
Guy Vander Jagt (R)

MINNESOTA

Senators

Walter F. Mondale (D)
Hubert H. Humphrey (D)

Representatives

Bob Bergland (D)
John A. Blatnik (D)
Donald M. Fraser (D)
Bill Frenzel (R)
Joseph E. Karth (D)
Ancher Nelsen (R)
Albert H. Quie (R)
John M. Zwach (R)

MISSISSIPPI

Senators

James O. Eastland (D)
John C. Stennis (D)

Representatives

David R. Bowen
Thad Cochran (R)
Trent Lott (R)
Gillespie V. Montgomery (D)
Jamie L. Whitten (D)

MISSOURI

Senators

Stuart Symington (D)
Thomas F. Eagleton (D)

Representatives

Richard Bolling (D)
Bill D. Burlison (D)
William L. Clay (D)
William L. Hungate (D)
Richard H. Ichord (D)
Jerry Litton (D)
William J. Randall (R)
Leonor Kretzer Sullivan (D)
James W. Symington (D)
Gene Taylor (R)

MONTANA

Senators

Mike Mansfield (D)
Lee Metcalf (D)

Representatives

John Melcher (D)
Richard G. Shoup (R)

NEBRASKA

Senators

Roman L. Hruska (R)
Carl T. Curtis (R)

Representatives

John Y. McCollister (R)
David T. Martin (R)
Charles Thone (R)

NEVADA

Senators

Alan Bible (D)
Howard W. Cannon (D)

Representative

David Powell (R)

NEW HAMPSHIRE

Senators

Norris Cotton (R)
Thomas J. McIntyre (D)

Representatives

James C. Cleveland (R)
Louis C. Wyman (R)

NEW JERSEY

Senators

Clifford P. Case (R)
Harrison A. Williams, Jr. (D)

Representatives

Dominick V. Daniels (D)
Edwin B. Forsythe (R)
Peter H. B. Frelinghuysen (R)
Henry Helstoski (D)
James J. Howard (D)
John E. Hunt (R)
Joseph J. Maraziti (R)
Joseph G. Minish (D)
Edward J. Patten (D)
Matthew J. Rinaldo (R)
Peter W. Rodino, Jr. (D)
Robert A. Roe (D)
Charles W. Sandman, Jr. (R)
Frank Thompson, Jr. (D)
William B. Widnall (R)

NEW MEXICO

Senators

Joseph M. Montoya (D)
Peter V. Domenici (R)

Representatives

Manuel Lujan, Jr. (R)
Harold Runnels (D)

NEW YORK

Senators

Jacob K. Javits (R)
James L. Buckley (Con-R)

Representatives

Bella S. Abzug (D)
Joseph P. Addabbo (D)
Herman Badillo (D)
Mario Biaggi (D)
Jonathan B. Bingham (D)
Frank J. Brasco (D)
Hugh L. Carey (D)
Shirley Chisholm (D)
Barber B. Conable, Jr. (R)
James J. Delaney (D)
Thaddeus J. Dulski (D)
Hamilton Fish, Jr. (R)
Benjamin A. Gilman (R)
James R. Grover, Jr. (R)
James M. Hanley (D)
James F. Hastings (R)
Elizabeth Holtzman (D)
Frank J. Horton (R)
Jack F. Kemp (R)
Carleton J. King (R)
Edward I. Koch (D)
Norman F. Lent (R)
Robert C. McEwen (R)
Donald J. Mitchell (R)
John M. Murphy (D)
Peter A. Peyser (R)
Otis G. Pike (D)
Bertram L. Podell (D)
Charles B. Rangel (D)
Ogden R. Reid (D)
Howard W. Robison (R)
Angelo D. Roncallo (R)
John J. Rooney (D)
Benjamin S. Rosenthal (D)
Henry P. Smith 3d (R)
Samuel S. Stratton (D)
William F. Walsh (R)
Lester L. Wolff (D)
John W. Wydler (R)

NORTH CAROLINA

Senators

Sam J. Ervin, Jr. (D)
Jesse A. Helms (R)

Representatives

Ike F. Andrews (D)
James T. Broyhill (R)
L. H. Fountain (D)
David N. Henderson (D)
Walter B. Jones (D)
James G. Martin (R)
Wilmer D. Mizell (R)
L. Richardson Preyer (D)
Charles G. Rose 3d (D)
Earl B. Ruth (R)
Roy A. Taylor (D)

NORTH DAKOTA

Senators

Milton R. Young (R)
Quentin N. Burdick (D)

Representative

Mark Andrews (R)

OHIO

Senators

William B. Saxbe (R)
Robert Taft, Jr. (R)

Representatives

John M. Ashbrook (R)
Thomas L. Ashley (D)
Clarence J. Brown (R)
Charles J. Carney (D)
Donald D. Clancy (R)
Samuel L. Devine (R)
Tennyson Guyer (R)
William H. Harsha, Jr. (R)
Wayne L. Hays (D)
William J. Keating (R)
Delbert L. Latta (R)
Clarence E. Miller (R)
William E. Minshall (R)
Charles A. Mosher (R)
Walter E. Powell (R)
Ralph S. Regula (R)
John F. Seiberling (D)
J. William Stanton (R)
James V. Stanton (D)
Louis Stokes (D)
Charles A. Vanik (D)
Charles W. Whalen, Jr. (R)
Chalmers P. Wylie (R)

OKLAHOMA

Senators

Henry L. Bellmon (R)
Dewey F. Bartlett (R)

Representatives

Carl Albert (D)
John N. Camp (R)
John Jarman (D)
James R. Jones (D)
Clem R. McSpadden (D)
Tom Steed (D)

OREGON

Senators

Mark O. Hatfield (R)
Robert W. Packwood (R)

Representatives

John Dellenback (R)
Edith Green (D)
Al Ullman (D)
Wendell Wyatt (R)

PENNSYLVANIA

Senators

Hugh Scott (R)
Richard S. Schweiker (R)

Representatives

William A. Barrett (D)
Edward G. Biester, Jr. (R)
Frank M. Clark (D)
R. Lawrence Coughlin (R)
John H. Dent (D)

Joshua Eilberg (D)
Edwin D. Eshleman (R)
Daniel J. Flood (D)
Joseph M. Gaydos (D)
George A. Goodling (R)
William J. Green (D)
H. John Heinz 3d (R)
Albert W. Johnson (R)
Joseph M. McDade (R)
William S. Moorhead (D)
Thomas E. Morgan (D)
Robert N. C. Nix (D)
Fred B. Rooney (D)
John P. Saylor (R)
Herman T. Schneebeli (R)
E. G. Shuster (R)
Joseph P. Vigorito (D)
John H. Ware (R)
Lawrence G. Williams (R)
Gus Yatron (D)

RHODE ISLAND

Senators

John O. Pastore (D)
Claiborne Pell (D)

Representatives

Fernand J. St. Germain (D)
Robert O. Tiernan (D)

SOUTH CAROLINA

Senators

J. Strom Thurmond (R)
Ernest F. Hollings (D)

Representatives

Mendel J. Davis (D)
W. J. Bryan Dorn (D)
Tom S. Gettys (D)
James R. Mann (D)
Floyd D. Spence (R)
Edward L. Young (R)

SOUTH DAKOTA

Senators

James G. Abourezk (D)
George McGovern (D)

Representatives

James Abdnor (R)
Frank E. Denholm (D)

TENNESSEE

Senators

Howard H. Baker, Jr. (R)
William E. Brock 3d (R)

Representatives

LaMar Baker (R)
Robin L. Beard, Jr. (R)
John J. Duncan (R)
Joe L. Evins (D)
Richard H. Fulton (D)
Ed Jones (D)
Dan H. Kuykendall (R)
James H. Quillen (R)

TEXAS

Senators

John G. Tower (R)
Lloyd M. Bentsen, Jr. (D)

Representatives

Bill Archer (R)
Jack B. Brooks (D)
Omar T. Burleson (D)
Robert R. Casey (D)
James M. Collins (R)
Eligio de la Garza 2d (D)
Robert C. Eckhardt (D)
O. Clark Fisher (D)
Henry B. Gonzalez (D)
Barbara Jordan (D)
Abraham Kazen, Jr. (D)
George H. Mahon (D)
Dale Milford (D)
Wright Patman (D)
J. J. Pickle (D)
William R. Poage (D)
Robert D. Price (R)
Ray Roberts (D)
Alan Steelman (R)
Olin E. Teague (D)
Richard C. White (D)
Charles Wilson (D)
James C. Wright, Jr. (D)
John Young (D)

UTAH

Senators

Wallace F. Bennett (R)
Frank E. Moss (D)

Representatives

K. Gunn McKay (D)
D. Wayne Owens (D)

VERMONT

Senators

George D. Aiken (R)
Robert T. Stafford (R)

Representative

Richard W. Mallary (R)

VIRGINIA

Senators

Harry F. Byrd, Jr.
William L. Scott (R)

Representatives

Joel T. Broyhill (R)
M. Caldwell Butler (R)
Robert W. Daniel, Jr. (R)
W. C. (Dan) Daniel (D)
Thomas N. Downing (D)
Stanford E. Parris (R)
J. Kenneth Robinson (R)
David E. Satterfield 3d (D)
William C. Wampler (R)
G. William Whitehurst (R)

WASHINGTON

Senators

Warren G. Magnuson (D)
Henry M. Jackson (D)

Representatives

Brock Adams (D)
Thomas S. Foley (D)
Julia Butler Hansen (D)
John Hempelmann (D)
Floyd V. Hicks (D)
Mike McCormack (D)
Lloyd Meeds (D)

WEST VIRGINIA

Senators

Jennings Randolph (D)
Robert C. Byrd (D)

Representatives

Kenneth Hechler (D)
Robert H. Mollohan (D)
John Slack (D)
Harley O. Staggers (D)

WISCONSIN

Senators

William Proxmire (D)
Gaylord Nelson (D)

Representatives

Les Aspin (D)
Glenn R. Davis (R)
Harold V. Froehlich (R)
Robert W. Kastenmeier (D)
David R. Obey (D)
Henry S. Reuss (D)
William A. Steiger (R)
Vernon W. Thomson (R)
Clement J. Zablocki (D)

WYOMING

Senators

Gale W. McGee (D)
Clifford P. Hansen (R)

Representative

Teno Roncalio (D)

V

THE UNITED STATES GOVERNMENT: JUDICIAL BRANCH

A. Justices of the Supreme Court of the United States.

B. Justices of the Circuit Courts of Appeals and other high courts judges.

JUSTICES OF THE SUPREME COURT

Year	*Presidents*	*Associate Justices*	*Chief Justices*
1789	Washington	John Rutledge (until 1791)	John Jay (until 1795)
1789		William Cushing (until 1810)	
1789		James Wilson (until 1798)	
1789		John Blair (until 1796)	
1790		James Iredell (until 1799)	
1791		Thomas Johnson (until 1793)	
1793		William Paterson (until 1806)	
1795			John Rutledge (until 1795)
1796		Samuel Chase (until 1811)	Oliver Ellsworth (until 1800)
1797	J. Adams		
1789		Bushrod Washington (until 1829)	
1799		Alfred Moore (until 1804)	
1801			John Marshall (until 1835)
1801	Jefferson		
1804		William Johnson (until 1834)	
1806		Henry B. Livingston (until 1823)	
1807		Thomas Todd (until 1826)	
1809	Madison		
1811		Gabriel Duval (until 1836)	
1811		Joseph Story (until 1845)	
1817	Monroe		
1823		Smith Thompson (until 1843)	
1825	J.W. Adams		
1826		Robert Trimble (until 1828)	
1829	Jackson	John McLean (until 1861)	
1830		Henry Baldwin (until 1844)	
1835		James M. Wayne (until 1867)	
1836		Philip P.Barbour (until 1841)	Roger B. Taney (until 1864)
1837		John Catron (until 1865)	
1837	Van Buren	John McKinley (until 1852)	
1841		Peter V. Daniel (until 1860)	
1841	W.H. Harrison		
1841	Tyler		
1845		Samuel Nelson (until 1872)	
1845	Polk	Levi Woodbury (until 1851)	
1846		Robert C. Grier (until 1870)	
1849	Taylor		
1850	Fillmore		
1851		Benajmin R. Curtis (until 1857)	
1853	Pierce	John A. Campbell (until 1861)	
1857	Buchanan		
1858		Nathan Clifford (until 1881)	
1861	Lincoln		
1862		Noah H. Swayne (until 1881)	
1862		Samuel F. Miller (until 1890)	
1862		David Davis (until 1877)	
1863		Stephen J. Field (until 1897)	
1864			Salmon P. Chase (until 1873)
1865	Johnson		
1869	Grant		
1870		William Strong (until 1880)	
1870		Joseph P. Bradley (until 1892)	
1872		Ward Hunt (until 1882)	
1874			Morrison R. Waite (until 1888)
1877	Hayes	John M. Harlan (until 1911)	
1880		William B. Woods (until 1887)	
1881	Garfield	Stanley Matthews (until 1889)	
1881	Arthur	Horace Gray (until 1902)	
1882		Samuel Blatchford (until 1893)	
1885	Cleveland		
1888		Lucius Q. C. Lamar (until 1893)	Melville W. Fuller (until 1910)
1889	Harrison	David J. Brewer (until 1910)	
1890		Henry B. Brown (until 1906)	
1892		George Shiras, Jr. (until 1903)	
1893		Howell E. Jackson (until 1895)	
1893	Cleveland		
1894		Edward D. White (until 1910)	
1895		Rufus W. Peckham (until 1909)	
1897	McKinley		
1898		Joseph McKenna (until 1925)	
1901	T. Roosevelt		
1902		Oliver Wendell Holmes (until 1932)	
1903		William R. Day (until 1922)	
1906		William H. Moody (until 1910)	
1909	Taft		

Year	*Presidents*	*Associate Justices*	*Chief Justices*
1910		Horace H. Lurton (until 1914)	Edward D. White (until 1921)
1910		Charles Evans Hughes (until 1916)	
1910		Willis Van Devanter (until 1937)	
1910		Joseph R. Lamar (until 1916)	
1912		Mahlon Pitney (until 1922)	
1913	Wilson		
1914		James C. McReynolds (until 1941)	
1916		Louis D. Brandeis (until 1939)	
1916		John H. Clarke (until 1922)	
1921	Harding		William Howard Taft (until 1930)
1922		George Sutherland (until 1938)	
1922		Pierce Butler (until 1939)	
1923		Edward T. Sanford (until 1930)	
1923	Coolidge		
1925		Harlan F. Stone (until 1941)	
1929	Hoover		
1930		Owen J. Roberts (until 1945)	Charles Evans Hughes (until 1941)
1932	F.D. Roosevelt	Benjamin N. Cardozo (until 1938)	
1937		Hugo L. Black (until 1971)	
1938		Stanley F. Reed (until 1957)	
1939		Felix Frankfurter (until 1962)	
1939		William O. Douglas	
1940		Frank Murphy (until 1949)	
1941		James F. Byrnes (until 1942)	Harlan F. Stone (until 1946)
1941		Robert H. Jackson (until 1954)	
1943		Wiley B. Rutledge (until 1949)	
1945	Truman	Harold H. Burton (until 1958)	
1946			Fred M. Vinson (until 1953)
1949		Tom C. Clark (until 1967)	
1949		Sherman Minton (until 1956)	
1953	Eisenhower		Earl Warren (until 1969)
1955		John Marshall Harlan (until 1971)	
1956		William J. Brennan, Jr.	
1957		Charles E. Whittaker (until 1962)	
1959		Potter Stewart	
1961	Kennedy		
1962		Byron R. White	
1962		Arthur J. Goldberg (until 1965)	
1963	L. B. Johnson		
1965		Abe Fortas (until 1969)	
1967		Thurgood Marshall	
1969	Nixon		Warren E. Burger
1970		Harry A. Blackmun	
1971		Lewis F. Powell, Jr.	
1971		William H. Rehnquist	

U.S. COURT OF APPEALS FOR THE FIRST CIRCUIT
Boston, Massachusetts

1891-1913	LeBaron B. Colt
1892-1917	William L. Putnam
1905-1911	Francis C. Lowell
1911-1912	William Schofield
1912-1918	Frederic Dodge
1913-1939	George H. Bingham
1917-1929	Charles F. Johnson
1918-1931	George W. Anderson
1929-1940	Scott Wilson
1932-1939	James M. Morton, Jr.
1939-1959	Calvert Magruder
1940-1950	John C. Mahoney
1941-1964	Peter Woodbury
1951-1965	John P. Hartigan
1959-	Bailey Aldrich
1965-	Edward M. McEntee
1965-	Frank M. Coffin

U.S. COURT OF APPEALS FOR THE SECOND CIRCUIT
New York, New York

1882-1906	William J. Wallace
1888-1915	E. Henry LaCombe
1892-1902	Nathaniel Shipman
1902-1907	William K. Townsend
1902-1917	Alfred C. Coxe
1908-1923	Henry G. Ward
1908-1913	Walter C. Noyes
1913-1927	Henry W. Rogers
1916-1927	Charles M. Hough
1916-1939	Martin T. Manton
1921-1924	Julius M. Mayer
1924-1961	Learned Hand
1924-1939	Julian W. Mack
1926-	Thomas W. Swan
1927-1953	Augustus N. Hand
1929-1969	Harrie Brigham Chase
1939-1964	Charles E. Clark
1939-1940	Robert P. Patterson
1941-1957	Jerome N. Frank
1951-	Harold R. Medina
1953-1964	Carroll C. Hincks
1954-1955	John M. Harlan
1955-	J. Edward Lumbard
1955-	Sterry R. Waterman
1957-	Leonard P. Moore
1959-	Henry J. Friendly
1960-	J. Joseph Smith
1961-	Irving R. Kaufman
1961-1965	Thurgood Marshall
1961-	Paul R. Hayes
1964-	Robert P. Anderson
1966-	Wilfred Feinberg
1971-	Walter T. Mansfield
1971-	James L. Oakes
1971-	William H. Mulligan
1971-	William H. Timbers

U.S. COURT OF APPEALS FOR THE THIRD CIRCUIT
Philadelphia, Pennsylvania

1869-1891	William McKennan
1891-1906	Marcus W. Acheson
1892-1909	George M. Dallas
1899-1914	George Gray
1906-1938	Joseph Buffington
1909-1912	William M. Lanning
1911-1913	Robert W. Archbald
1912-1919	John B. McPherson
1914-1941	Victor B. Woolley
1919-1920	Thomas G. Haight
1920-1941	John W. Davis
1931-1938	Joseph W. Thompson
1937-	John Biggs, Jr.
1938-	Albert B. Maris
1938-1943	William Clark
1939-1940	Francis Biddle
1939-1944	Charles A. Jones
1940-	Herbert F. Goodrich
1943-	Gerald McLaughlin
1945-1949	John J. O'Connell
1946-	Harry E. Kalodner
1949-	William H. Hastie
1950-	Austin L. Staley
1959-1961	Philip Forman
1961-1966	J. Cullen Ganey
1961-1968	William F. Smith
1964-1971	Abraham L. Freedman
1966-	Collins J. Seitz
1967-	Francis L. Van Dusen
1968-	Ruggero J. Aldisert
1968-1970	David Stahl
1969-	John J. Gibbons
1969-	Arlin M. Adams
1970-	Max Rosenn

U.S. COURT OF APPEALS FOR THE FOURTH CIRCUIT
Richmond, Virginia

1892-1913	Nathan Goff
1893-1904	Charles H. Simonton
1904-1921	Jeter C. Pritchard
1910-1923	Martin A. Knapp
1913-1925	Charles A. Woods
1921-1931	Edmund Waddill, Jr.
1922-1927	John C. Rose
1925–1958	John J. Parker
1927-1939	Elliott Northcott
1931-1955	Morris A. Soper
1939-1956	Armistead M. Dobie
1956-	Simon E. Sobeloff
1957-	Clement F. Haynsworth, Jr.
1959-	Herbert S. Boreman
1961-	Albert V. Gryan
1961-1967	J. Spencer Bell
1966-	Harrison L. Winter
1966-	J. Braxton Craven, Jr.
1967-	John D. Butzner, Jr.
1971-	Donald S. Russell

U.S. COURT OF APPEALS FOR THE FIFTH CIRCUIT
New Orleans, Louisiana

1891-1919	Don A. Pardee
1892-1916	Andrew P. McCormick
1899-1914	David D. Shelby
1914-1936	Richard W. Walker
1917-1919	Robert L. Batts
1920-1935	Nathan P. Bryan
1920-1925	Alexander C. King
1925-1942	Rufus E. Foster
1931-1949	Samuel H. Sibley
1931-1971	Joseph C. Hutcheson, Jr.
1936-1961	Edwin R. Holmes
1939-1951	Leon P. McCord
1944-1951	Curtis L. Waller
1944-1949	Elmo P. Lee, Sr.
1949-1966	Wayne G. Borah
1949-1956	Robert L. Russell
1951-1955	Louie W. Strum
1951-	Richard T. Rives
1955-	Elbert P. Tuttle
1956-1963	Ben F. Cameron
1956-	Warren L. Jones
1956-	John R. Brown
1958-	John M. Wisdom
1962-	Walter P. Gewin
1961-	Griffin B. Bell
1966-	Homer Thornberry
1967-	James P. Coleman
1967-	Irving L. Goldberg
1967-	Robert A. Ainsworth, Jr.
1967-	John C. Godbold
1967-	David W. Dyer
1968-	Bryan Simpson
1968-1969	Claude F. Clayton
1969-	Lewis R. Morgan
1969-1970	G. Harrold Carswell
1970-	Charles Clark
1970-	Joe Ingraham
1971-	Paul H. Roney

U.S. COURT OF APPEALS FOR THE SIXTH CIRCUIT
Cincinnati, Ohio

1891-1893	Howell E. Jackson
1892-1900	William Howard Talf
1893-1909	Horace H. Lurton
1899-1903	William R. Day
1900-1911	Henry F. Severns
1903-1909	John K. Richards
1909-1919	John W. Warrington
1910-1930	Loyal E. Knappen
1911-1931	Arthur C. Denison
1919-1928	Maurice H. Donahue
1925-1938	Charles H. Morrman
1928-1951	Xenophon Hicks
1928-1933	Smith Hickenlooper
1932-1958	Charles C. Simons
1934-1959	Florence E. Allen
1938-	Elwood Hamilton
1939-	Herschel W. Arant
1940-1962	John D. Martin
1941-	Thomas F. McAllister

1945-1965 Shackelford Miller, Jr.
1954-1958 Potter Stewart
1959- Lester L. Cecil
1959- Paul C. Weick
1960- Clifford O'Sullivan
1963- Harry Phillips
1963- George Edwards
1965- Anthony J. Celebrezze
1966- John W. Peck
1966- Wade H. McCree, Jr.
1967-1970 Bert T. Combs
1969- Henry L. Brooks
1970- William E. Miller
1971- W. Wallace Kent

U.S. COURT OF APPEALS
FOR THE SEVENTH CIRCUIT
Chicago, Illinois

1891-1893 Walter Q. Gresham
1892-1901 William A. Woods
1893-1905 James G. Jenkins
1895-1898 John W. Showalter
1899-1911 Peter S. Grosscup
1902-1924 Francis E. Baker
1905-1918 Christian C. Kohlsaat
1905-1915 William H. Seaman
1915-1936 Samuel Alschuler
1916-1948 Evan A. Evans
1919-1930 George T. Page
1925-1929 Albert B. Anderson
1929-1948 William M. Sparks
1933-1935 Louis FitzHenry
1937-1956 J. Earl Major
1937-1941 Walter E. TReanor
1939-1952 Otto Kerner
1941-1949 Sherman Minton
1949-1966 F. Ryan Duffy
1949-1959 Philip J. Finnegan
1949-1958 Walter C. Lindley
1949-1957 H. Nathan Swaim
1954-1968 Elmer J. Schnackenberg
1957-1969 John S. Hastings
1957-1959 W. Lynn Parkinson
1958-1967 Win G. Knoch
1959-1970 Lathan Castle
1961- Roger J. Kiley
1961- Luther M. Swygert
1966- Thomas E. Fairchild
1966- Walter J. Cummings
1968- Otto Kerner
1970- Wilbur F. Pell, Jr.
1970- John P. Stevens
1971- Robert A. Sprecher

U.S. COURT OF APPEALS
FOR THE EIGHTH CIRCUIT
St. Louis, Missouri

1891-1903 Henry C. Caldwell
1892-1928 Walter H. Sanborn
1894-1905 Amos M. Thayer
1903-1910 Willis VanDevanter
1903-1921 William C. Hook
1905-1916 Elmer B. Adams
1911-1922 John E. Carland
1911-1922 Walter I. Smith
1916-1947 Kimbrough Stone
1921-1929 Robert E. Lewis
1922-1933 William S. Kenyon
1925-1931 Wilbur F. Booth
1925-1933 Arba S. Van Valkenburgh
1928-1933 John H. Cotteral
1929-1960 Archibald K. Gardner
1932-1959 John B. Sanborn
1933-1961 Joseph W. Woodrough
1935-1936 Charles B. Faris
1935-1954 Seth Thomas
1940-1965 Harvey M. Johnsen
1942-1953 Walter G. Riddick
1947-1955 John C. Collet
1954-1968 Charles J. Vogel
1954-1971 Martin D. Van Oosterhout
1956-1957 Charles E. Whittaker
1958- Marion C. Matthes
1961-1965 Albert A. Ridge
1963- Pat Mehaffy
1965- Floyd R. Gibson
1966- Doland P. Lay
1966- Gerald W. Heaney
1968- Myron H. Bright
1971- Donald R. Ross

U.S. COURT OF APPEALS
FOR THE NINTH CIRCUIT
San Francisco, California

1891 Lorenzo Sawyer
1892-1896 Joseph McKenna
1892-1931 William B. Gilbert
1895-1925 Erskine M. Ross
1897-1923 William W. Morrow
1911-1928 William H. Hunt
1923-1936 Frank H. Rudkin
1925-1926 Wallace McCamant
1927-1930 Frank S. Dietrich
1929-1945 Curtis D. Wilbur
1931-1934 William H. Sawtelle
1933-1948 Francis A. Garrecht
1935-1957 William Denman
1935-1953 Clifton Mathews
1935-1943 Bert E. Haney
1937-1965 Albert Lee Stephens
1937-1962 William Healy
1944-1956 Homer T. Bone
1945-1956 William E. Orr
1949-1969 Walter L. Pope
1954-1958 Dal M. Lemmon
1954-1959 James A. Fee
1954- Richard H. Chambers
1956- Stanley N. Barnes
1956- Frederick G. Hamley
1958- Oliver D. Hamlin
1958- Gilbert H. Jertberg
1959- Charles M. Merrill
1959- M. Oliver Koelsch
1961- James R. Browning
1961- Ben C. Duniway
1964- Walter Ely
1967- James M. Carter
1968- Shirley M. Hufstedler
1969- Eugene A. Wright
1969- John F. Kilkenny
1969- Ozell M. Trask
1971- Herbert Y. C. Choy

U.S. COURT OF APPEALS
FOR THE TENTH CIRCUIT
Denver, Colorado

1929-1940 Robert E. Lewis
1929-1933 John H. Cotteral
1929- Orie L. Phillips
1929-1937 George T. McDermott
1933-1963 Sam G. Bratton
1937-1939 Robert Lee Williams
1939- Walter Huxman
1940- Alfred P. Murrah
1949- John C. Pickett
1956- David T. Lewis
1957- Jean S. Breitenstein
1961- Delmas C. Hill
1962- Oliver Seth
1966-1970 John J. Hickey
1968- William J. Holloway, Jr.
1970- Robert H. McWilliams
1971- James E. Barrett
1971- William E. Doyle

U.S. COURT OF APPEALS
FOR THE
DISTRICT OF COLUMBIA

1919-1937 Josiah A. Van Orsdel
1919-1938 Charles H. Robb
1919-1924 Constantine J. Smyth
1923-1927 James F. Smith
1923-1929 Orion M. Barber
1923-1938 George E. Martin
1924-1929 Charles S. Hatfield
1924-1929 Oscar E. Bland
1925-1929 William J. Graham
1928-1929 Finis J. Garrett
1932-1935 William Hitz
1932-1948 D. Lawrence Grover
1936-1955 Harold M. Stephens
1937-1945 Justin Miller
1938-1943 Fred M. Vinson
1938-1969 Henry W. Edgerton
1940-1945 Wiley B. Rutledge, Jr.
1944-1945 Thurman W. Arnold
1946-1954 Bennett C. Clark
1946-1965 Wilbur K. Miller
1946-1971 E. Barrett Prettyman
1948-1953 James M. Proctor
1949- David L. Bazelon
1949- George T. Washington
1951- Charles Fahy
1953- John A. Danaher
1954- Walter M. Bastian
1957-1970 Warren E. Burger
1963- J. Skelly Wright
1964- Carl McGowan
1966- Edward A. Tamm
1966- Harold Leventhal
1968- Spottswood W. Robinson III
1970- George E. MacKinnon
1970- Roger Robb
1970- Malcolm R. Wilkey

U.S. COURT OF CUSTOMS
AND PATENT APPEALS

1910-1920 Robert M. Montgomery
1910-1911 William H. Hunt
1910-1928 Orion M. Barber
1910-1922 Marion DeVries
1910-1928 James F. Smith
1911-1924 George E. Martin
1923-1947 Oscar E. Bland
1923-1950 Charles S. Hatfield
1924-1927 William J. Graham
1929-1955 Finis J. Garrett

1929-1944 Irvine L. Lenroot
1937-1952 Joseph R. Jackson
1944-1962 Ambrose O'Connell
1948-1959 Noble J. Johnson
1950- Eugene Worley
1952-1957 William P. Cole, Jr.
1956- Giles S. Rich
1958-1966 I. Jack Martin
1959-1968 Arthur M. Smith
1962- J. Lindsay Almond, Jr.
1968- Philip E. Baldwin
1969- Donald E. Lane

U.S. COURT OF CLAIMS

1855-1858 John J. Gilchrist
1855-1859 Isaac N. Blackford
1855-1861 George P. Scarburgh
1858-1877 Edward G. Loring
1860-1865 James Hughes
1861-1870 Joseph Casey
1863-1868 David Wilmot
1863-1878 Ebenezer Peck
1865-1896 Charles C. Nott
1868-1874 Samuel Milligan
1870-1885 Charles D. Drake
1874-1896 William A. Richardson
1877-1881 J.C. Bancroft Davis
1878-1881 William H. Hunt
1881-1892 Glenni W. Scofield
1882-1883 J.C. Bancroft Davis
1883-1905 Lawrence Weldon
1885-1902 John Davis
1892-1913 Stanton J. Peelle
1896-1906 Charles C. Nott
1897-1915 Charles B. Howry
1903-1905 Francis M. Wright
1905-1939 Fenton W. Booth
1905-1916 George W. Atkinson
1906-1919 Samuel S. Barney
1913-1928 Edward K. Campbell
1915-1926 George E. Downey
1916-1928 James Hay
1919-1930 Samuel J. Graham
1926-1929 McKenzie Moss
1928-1940 William R. Green
1928-1958 Benjamin H. Littleton
1930-1947 Richard S. Whaley
1939-1964 Samuel Whitaker
1940-1964 Marvin Jones
1941-1961 J. Warren Madden
1947-1953 Evan Howell
1954- Don N. Laramore
1960- James R. Durfee
1962- Oscar H. Davis
1964- Wilson Cowen
1964- Linton M. Collins
1966- Byron Skelton
1966- Philip Nichols, Jr.

U.S. CUSTOMS COURT

1926-1932 Israel F. Fischer
1926-1927 William B. Howell
1926-1930 Byron S. Waite
1926-1939 Charles M. McClelland
1926-1939 Jerry B. Sullivan
1926-1942 George S. Brown
1926-1928 William C. Adamson
1926-1931 George E. Weller
1926-1932 George M. Young
1928-1955 Genevieve R. Cline
1928-1949 William J. Tilson
1931-1948 David H. Kincheloe
1931-1941 Walter H. Evans
1932-1942 Frederick W. Dallinger
1933-1946 William J. Keefe
1940-1944 Thomas J. Walker
1940-1969 Webster J. Oliver
1942-1952 William P. Cole
1942-1957 William A. Ekwall
1943- Charles D. Lawrence
1945-1962 Irvin C. Mollison
1947-1963 Jed Johnson
1948- Paul P. Rao
1949- Morgan Ford
1954- David J. Wilson
1955- Mary H. Donlon
1957- Scovel Richardson
1964-1966 Philip Nichols, Jr.
1965- Frederick Landis
1966- James L. Watson
1967-1968 Lindley Beckworth
1967- Herbert N. Maletz
1968- Samuel M. Rosenstein
1968- Bernard Newman
1968- Edward D. Re
1971- Nils A. Boe

U.S. EMERGENCY COURT OF APPEALS

1943-1962 Albert B. Maris
1943-1962 Calvert Magruder
1943-1958 Bolitha J. Laws
1945-1962 Thomas F. McAllister
1944-1958 Walter C. Lindley

VI

STATES OF THE UNION

Governors, United States senators, and state chief justices arranged chronologically by state.

ALABAMA

	Governors	*United States Senators*			*Chief Justices*	
1819	William W. Bibb	John W. Walker	1819	William R. King		1819
1820	Thomas Bibb		1820		Clement Comer Clay	1820
1821	Israel Pickens		1821			1821
1822			1822			1822
1823		William Kelly	1823		Abner Lipscomb	1823
1824			1824			1824
1825	John Murphy	Henry H. Chambers	1825			1825
1826		Israel Pickens	1826			1826
1826		John McKinley	1826			1826
1827			1827			1827
1828			1828			1828
1829	Gabriel Moore		1829			1829
1830			1830			1830
1831	Samuel B. Moore	Gabriel Moore	1831			1831
1831	John Gayle		1831			1831
1832			1832			1832
1833			1833			1833
1834			1834			1834
1835	Clement Comer Clay		1835		Reuben Saffold	1835
1836			1836		Henry Hitchcock	1836
1837	Arthur P. Bagby	Clement Comer Clay	1837		Arthur F. Hopkins	1837
1837			1837		Henry W. Collier	1837
1838			1838			1838
1839			1839			1839
1840			1840			1840
1841	Benjamin Fitzpatrick	Arthur P. Bagby	1841			1841
1842			1842			1842
1843			1843			1843
1844			1844	Dixon H. Lewis		1844
1845	Joshua L. Martin		1845			1845
1846			1846			1846
1847	Reuben Chapman		1847			1847
1848		William R. King	1848	Benjamin Fitzpatrick		1848
1849	Henry W. Collier		1849	Jeremiah Clemens	Edmund S. Dargan	1849
1850			1850			1850
1851			1851			1851
1852			1852		William P. Chilton	1852
1853	John A. Winston	Benjamin Fitzpatrick	1853	Clement Claiborne Clay		1853
1854			1854			1854
1855			1855			1855
1856			1856		George Goldthwaite	1856
1857	Andrew B. Moore		1857		Samuel F. Rice	1857
1858			1858			1858
1859			1859		Abram J. Walker	1859
1860			1860			1860
1861	John G. Shorter	*Vacant*	1861	*Vacant*		1861
1862			1862			1862
1863	Thomas H. Watts		1863			1863
1864			1864			1864
1865	Lewis E. Parsons		1865		Elijah W. Peck	1865
1865	Robert M. Patton		1865			1865
1866			1866			1866
1867			1867			1867
1868	William H. Smith	George E. Spencer	1868	Willard Warner		1868
1869			1869			1869
1870	Robert B. Lindsay		1870			1870
1871			1871			1871
1872	David P. Lewis		1872	George T. Goldthwaite		1972
1873			1873		Thomas M. Peters	1873
1874	George S. Houston		1874		Robert C. Brickell	1874
1875			1875			1875
1876			1876			1876
1877			1877	John T. Morgan		1877
1878	Rufus W. Cobb		1878			1878
1879		George S. Houston	1879			1879
1880		Luke Pryor	1880			1880
1880		James L. Pugh	1880			1880
1881			1881			1881
1882	Edward A. O'Neal		1882			1882
1883			1883			1883
1884			1884		George W. Stone	1884
1885			1885			1885
1886	Thomas Seay		1886			1886
1887			1887			1887

ALABAMA – Continued

	Governors	*United States Senators*			*Chief Justices*	
1888			1888			1888
1889			1889			1889
1890	Thomas G. Jones		1890			1890
1891			1891			1891
1892			1892			1892
1893			1893			1893
1894	William C. Oates		1894		Robert C. Brickell	1894
1895			1895			1895
1896	Joseph F. Johnston		1896			1896
1897		Edmund W. Pettus	1897			1897
1898			1898		Thomas N. McClellan	1898
1899			1899			1899
1900	William J. Samford		1900			1900
1901			1901			1901
1902			1902			1902
1903	William D. Jelks		1903			1903
1904			1904			1904
1905			1905			1905
1906			1906		Samuel D. Weakley	1906
1907	Braxton B. Comer	Joseph F. Johnston	1907	John H. Bankhead	John R. Tyson	1907
1908			1908			1908
1909			1909		James R. Dowdell	1909
1910			1910			1910
1911	Emmet O'Neal		1911			1911
1912			1912			1912
1913			1913			1913
1914		Frank S. White	1914		John C. Anderson	1914
1915	Charles Henderson	Oscar W. Underwood	1915			1915
1916			1916			1916
1917			1917			1917
1918			1918			1918
1919	Thomas E. Kilby		1919			1919
1920			1920	Braxton B. Comer		1920
1920			1920	J. Thomas Heflin		1920
1921			1921			1921
1922			1922			1922
1923	William W. Brandon		1923			1923
1924			1924			1924
1925			1925			1925
1926			1926			1926
1927	David Bibb Graves	Hugo L. Black	1927			1927
1928			1928			1928
1929			1929			1929
1930			1930			1930
1931	Benjamin M. Miller		1931	John H. Bankhead II		1931
1932			1932			1932
1933			1933			1933
1934			1934			1934
1935	David Bibb Graves		1935			1935
1936			1936			1936
1937		Dixie Bibb Graves	1937			1937
1938		Lister Hill	1938			1938
1939	Frank M. Dixon		1939			1939
1940			1940		Lucien D. Gardner	1940
1941			1941			1941
1942			1942			1942
1943	Chauncey Sparks		1943			1943
1944			1944			1944
1945			1945			1945
1946			1946	George R. Swift		1946
1947	James E. Folsom		1947	John J. Sparkman		1947
1948			1948			1948
1949			1949			1949
1950			1950			1950
1951	Gordon Persons		1951		J. Ed Livingston	1951
1952			1952			1952
1953			1953			1953
1954			1954			1954
1955	James E. Folsom		1955			1955
1956			1956			1956
1957			1957			1957
1958			1958			1958
1959	John M. Patterson		1959			1959
1960			1960			1960

ALABAMA–Continued

	Governors	*United States Senators*			*Chief Justices*	
1961			1961			1961
1962			1962			1962
1963	George C. Wallace		1963			1963
1964			1964			1964
1965			1965			1965
1966			1966			1966
1967	Lurleen B. Wallace		1967			1967
1968	Albert P. Brewer		1968			1968
1969		James B. Allen	1969			1969
1970			1970			1970
1971	George C. Wallace		1971		Howell T. Heflin	1971
1972			1972			1972
1973			1973			1973

ALASKA

	Governors	*United States Senators*			*Chief Justices*	
1959	William A. Egan	Edward L. Bartlett	1959	Ernest Gruening	Buell A. Nesbett	1959
1960			1960			1960
1961			1961			1961
1962			1962			1962
1963			1963			1963
1964			1964			1964
1965			1965			1965
1966			1966			1966
1967	Walter J. Hickel		1967			1967
1968			1968			1968
1969	Keith J. Miller	Theodore F. Stevens	1969	Mike (Maurice R.) Gravel		1969
1970			1970		George F. Boney	1970
1971	William A. Egan		1971			1971
1972			1972		Jay A. Rabinowitz	1972
1973			1973			1973

ARIZONA

	Governors	*United States Senators*			*Chief Justices*	
1912	George W. P. Hunt	Henry F. Ashurst	1912	Marcus A. Smith	*Justices of the Supreme Court serve on a rotating basis as Chief Presiding Judge*	1912
1913			1913			1913
1914			1914			1914
1915			1915			1915
1916			1916			1916
1917			1917			1917
1918			1918			1918
1919	Thomas E. Campbell		1919			1919
1920			1920			1920
1921			1921	Ralph H. Cameron		1921
1922			1922			1922
1923	George W. P. Hunt		1923			1923
1924			1924			1924
1925			1925			1925
1926			1926			1926
1927			1927	Carl T. Hayden		1927
1928			1928			1928
1929	John C. Phillips		1929			1929
1930			1930			1930
1931	George W. P. Hunt		1931			1931
1932			1932			1932
1933	Benjamin B. Moeur		1933			1933
1934			1934			1934
1935			1935			1935
1936	R. C. Stanford		1936			1936
1937			1937			1937
1938	R. T. Jones		1938			1938
1939			1939			1939
1940	Sidney P. Osborn		1940			1940
1941		Ernest W. McFarland	1941			1941
1942			1942			1942
1943			1943			1943
1944			1944			1944
1945			1945			1945
1946			1946			1946
1947			1947			1947
1948	Dan E. Garvey		1948			1948
1949			1949			1949
1950	Howard Pyle		1950			1950
1951			1951			1951
1952			1952			1952
1953		Barry M. Goldwater	1953			1953
1954	Ernest W. McFarland		1954			1954
1955			1955			1955
1956			1956			1956
1957			1957			1957
1958	Paul J. Fannin		1958			1958
1959			1959			1959
1960			1960			1960
1961			1961			1961
1962			1962			1962
1963			1963			1963
1964	Samuel P. Goddard		1964			1964
1965		Paul J. Fannin	1965			1965
1966	Jack Williams		1966			1966
1967			1967			1967
1968			1968			1968
1969			1969	Barry M. Goldwater		1969
1970			1970			1970
1971			1971			1971
1972			1972			1972
1973			1973			1973

ARKANSAS

	Governors	*United States Senators*			*Chief Justice*	
1836	James S. Conway	William S. Fulton	1836	Ambrose H. Sevier	Daniel Ringo	1836
1837			1837			1837
1838			1838			1838
1839			1839			1839
1840	Archibald Yell		1840			1840
1841			1841			1841
1842			1842			1842
1843			1843			1843
1844	Samuel Adams (Acting)	Chester Ashley	1844			1844
1844	Thomas S. Drew		1844			1844
1845			1845		Thomas Johnson	1845
1846			1846			1846
1847			1847			1847
1848		William K. Sebastian	1848	Solon Borland		1848
1849	Richard C. Byrd (Acting)		1849			1849
1849	John S. Roane		1849			1849
1850			1850			1850
1851	John R. Hampton (Acting)		1851			1851
1852	Elias N. Conway		1852			1852
1853			1853	Robert W. Johnson	George C. Watkins	1853
1854			1854			1854
1855			1855		Elbert H. English	1855
1856			1856			1856
1857			1857			1857
1858			1858			1858
1859			1859			1859
1860	Henry M. Rector		1860			1860
1861		*Vacant*	1861	Charles B. Mitchel		1861
1862	Thomas Fletcher (Acting)		1862	*Vacant*		1862
1862	Harris Flanagin		1862			1862
1863			1863			1863
1864	Isaac Murphy		1864		Elisha Baxter	1864
1865			1865			1865
1866			1866		David Walker	1866
1867			1867			1867
1868	Powell Clayton	Alexander McDonald	1868	Benjamin F. Rice	William W. Wilshire	1868
1869			1869			1869
1870			1870			1870
1871	Ozro A. Hadley (Acting)	Powell Clayton	1871		John McClure	1871
1872			1872			1872
1873	Elisha Baxter		1873	Stephen W. Dorsey		1873
1874	Augustus H. Garland		1874		Elbert H. English	1874
1875			1875			1875
1876			1876			1876
1877	William R. Miller	Augustus H. Garland	1877			1877
1878			1878			1878
1879			1879	James D. Walker		1879
1880			1880			1880
1881	Thomas J. Churchill		1881			1881
1882			1882			1882
1883	James H. Berry		1883			1883
1884			1884		Sterling R. Cockrill	1884
1885	Simon P. Hughes	James H. Berry	1885	James K. Jones		1885
1886			1886			1886
1887			1887			1887
1888			1888			1888
1889	James P. Eagle		1889			1889
1890			1890			1890
1891			1891			1891
1892	William M. Fishback		1892		Henry G. Bunn	1892
1893	Clay Sloan (Acting)		1893			1893
1894			1894			1894
1895	James P. Clarke		1895			1895
1896			1896			1896
1897	Daniel W. Jones		1897			1897
1898			1898			1898
1899			1899			1899
1900			1900			1900
1901	Jeff Davis		1901			1901
1902			1902			1902
1903			1903	James P. Clarke		1903
1904			1904		Joseph M. Hill	1904
1905			1905			1905
1906			1906			1906
1907	John S. Little	Jeff Davis	1907			1907
1907	Xenophon Pindall		1907			1907
1908			1908			1908
1909	George W. Donaghey		1909		Edgar A. McCulloch	1909
1910			1910			1910

ARKANSAS – Continued

	Governors	*United States Senators*		*United States Senators*	*Chief Justices*	
1911			1911			1911
1912			1912			1912
1913	Joseph T. Robinson	Joseph T. Robinson	1913			1913
1913	George W. Hays		1913			1913
1914			1914			1914
1915			1915			1915
1916			1916	William F. Kirby		1916
1917	Charles H. Brough		1917			1917
1918			1918			1918
1919			1919			1919
1920			1920			1920
1921	Thomas C. McRae		1921	Thaddeus H. Caraway		1921
1922			1922			1922
1923			1923			1923
1924			1924			1924
1925	Thomas J. Terral		1925			1925
1926			1926			1926
1927	John E. Martineau		1927		Jesse C. Hart	1927
1928	Harvey Parnell		1928			1928
1929			1929			1929
1930			1930			1930
1931			1931			1931
1932			1932	Hattie W. Caraway	C. E. Johnson	1932
1933	J. Marion Futrell		1933			1933
1934			1934			1934
1935			1935			1935
1936			1936			1936
1937	Carl E. Bailey	John E. Miller	1937		Griffin Smith	1937
1938			1938			1938
1939			1939			1939
1940			1940			1940
1941	Homer M. Adkins	George L. Spencer	1941			1941
1942			1942			1942
1943		John C. McClellan	1943			1943
1944			1944			1944
1945	Ben Laney		1945	J. William Fulbright		1945
1946			1946			1946
1947			1947			1947
1948			1948			1948
1949	Sid McMath		1949			1949
1950			1950			1950
1951			1951			1951
1952			1952			1952
1953	Francis Cherry		1953			1953
1954			1954			1954
1955	Orville Faubus		1955		Lee Seamster	1955
1956			1956			1956
1957			1957		Carleton Harris	1957
1958			1958			1958
1959			1959			1959
1960			1960			1960
1961			1961			1961
1962			1962			1962
1963			1963			1963
1964			1964			1964
1965			1965			1965
1966			1966			1966
1967	Winthrop Rockefeller		1967			1967
1968			1968			1968
1969			1969			1969
1970			1970			1970
1971	Dale Bumpers		1971			1971
1972			1972			1972
1973			1973			1973

CALIFORNIA

	Governors	*United States Senators*			*Chief Justice*	
1849	Peter H. Burnett		1849		S. Clinton Hastings	1849
1850		William M. Gwin	1850	John C. Fremont		1850
1851	John McDougall		1851			1851
1852	John Bigler		1852	John B. Weller	Henry A. Lyons	1852
1853			1853		Hugh C. Murray	1853
1854			1854			1854
1855		*Vacant*	1855			1855
1856	James N. Johnson		1856			1856
1857		William M. Gwin	1857	David C. Broderick	David S. Terry	1857
1858	John B. Weller		1858			1858
1859			1859	Henry P. Haun	Stephen J. Field	1859
1860	Milton S. Latham		1860	Milton S. Latham		1860
1860	John G. Downey		1860			1860
1861		James A. McDougall	1861			1861
1862	Leland Stanford		1862			1862
1863	Frederick F. Low		1863	John Conness	Edwin B. Crocker	1863
1864			1864		Silas W. Sanderson	1864
1865			1865			1865
1866			1866			1866
1867	Henry H. Haight	Cornelius Cole	1867			1867
1868			1868			1868
1869			1869	Eugene Casserly		1869
1870			1870		Jackson Temple	1870
1871	Newton Booth		1871			1871
1872			1872		Addison C. Niles	1872
1873		Aaron A. Sargent	1873	John S. Hager		1873
1874			1874			1874
1875	Romualdo Pacheco		1875	Newton Booth		1875
1875	William Irwin		1875			1875
1876			1876			1876
1877			1877			1877
1878			1878			1878
1879		James T. Farley	1879			1879
1880	George C. Perkins		1880		Robert F. Morrison	1880
1881			1881	John F. Miller		1881
1882			1882			1882
1883	George Stoneman		1883			1883
1884			1884			1884
1885		Leland Stanford	1885			1885
1886			1886	George Hearst		1886
1886			1886	Abram P. Williams		1886
1887	Washington Bartlett		1887	George Hearst	Niles Searls	1887
1887	Robert W. Waterman		1887			1887
1888			1888		William H. Beatty	1888
1889			1889			1889
1890			1890			1890
1891	Henry H. Markham		1891	Charles N. Felton		1891
1892			1892			1892
1893		George C. Perkins	1893	Stephen M. White		1893
1894			1894			1894
1895	James H. Budd		1895			1895
1896			1896			1896
1897			1897			1897
1898			1898			1898
1899	Henry T. Gage		1899			1899
1900			1900	Thomas R. Bard		1900
1901			1901			1901
1902			1902			1902
1903	George C. Pardee		1903			1903
1904			1904			1904
1905			1905	Frank P. Flint		1905
1906			1906			1906
1907	James N. Gillett		1907			1907
1908			1908			1908
1909			1909			1909
1910			1910			1910
1911	Hiram W. Johnson		1911	John D. Works		1911
1912			1912			1912
1913			1913			1913
1914			1914		Matt I. Sullivan	1914
1915		James D. Phelan	1915		Frank M. Angellotti	1915
1916			1916			1916
1917	William D. Stephens		1917	Hiram W. Johnson		1917

CALIFORNIA – Continued

	Governors	*United States Senators*			*Chief Justices*	
1918			1918			1918
1919			1919			1919
1920			1920			1920
1921		Samuel M. Shortridge	1921		Lucien Shaw	1921
1922			1922			1922
1923	Friend W. Richardson		1923		Curtis D. Wilbur	1923
1924			1924		Louis W. Myers	1924
1925			1925			1925
1926			1926		William H. Waste	1926
1927	Clement C. Young		1927			1927
1928			1928			1928
1929			1929			1929
1930			1930			1930
1931	James Rolph, Jr.		1931			1931
1932			1932			1932
1933		William Gibbs McAdoo	1933			1933
1934	Frank F. Merriam		1934			1934
1935			1935			1935
1936			1936			1936
1937			1937			1937
1938		Thomas M. Storke	1938			1938
1939	Culbert L. Olson	Sheridan Downey	1939			1939
1940			1940		Phil S. Gibson	1940
1941			1941			1941
1942			1942			1942
1943	Earl Warren		1943			1943
1944			1944			1944
1945			1945	William F. Knowland		1945
1946			1946			1946
1947			1947			1948
1949			1949			1949
1950		Richard M. Nixon	1950			1950
1951			1951			1951
1952			1952			1952
1953	Goodwin J. Knight	Thomas H. Kuchel	1953			1953
1954			1954			1954
1955			1955			1955
1956			1956			1956
1957			1957			1957
1958			1958			1958
1959	Edmund G. Brown		1959	Clair Engle		1959
1960			1960			1960
1961			1961			1961
1962			1962			1962
1963			1963			1963
1964			1964	Pierre Salinger	Roger J. Traynor	1964
1965			1965	George Murphy		1965
1966			1966			1966
1967	Ronald Reagan		1967			1967
1968			1968			1968
1969		Alan Cranston	1969			1969
1970			1970		Donald R. Wright	1970
1971			1971	John V. Tunney		1971
1972			1972			1972
1973			1973			1973

COLORADO

	Governors	*United States Senators*			*Chief Justice*	
1876	John L. Routt	Jerome B. Chaffee	1876	Henry M. Teller	Moses Hallett	1876
1877			1877		Henry C. Thatcher	1877
1878			1878			1878
1879	Frederick W. Pitkin	Nathaniel P. Hill	1879			1879
1880			1880		Samuel H. Elbert	1880
1881			1881			1881
1882			1882	George M. Chilcott		1882
1883	James B. Grant		1883	Horace A. W. Tabor	William E. Beck	1883
1883			1883	Thomas A. Bowen		1883
1884			1884			1884
1885	Benjamin H. Eaton	Henry M. Teller	1885			1885
1886			1886			1886
1887	Alva Adams		1887			1887
1888			1888			1888
1889	Job A. Cooper		1889	Edward O. Wolcott	Joseph C. Helm	1889
1890			1890			1890
1891	John L. Routt		1891			1891
1892			1892			1892
1893	Davis H. Waite		1893		Charles D. Hayt	1893
1884			1894			1894
1895	Albert W. McIntire		1895			1895
1896			1896			1896
1897	Alva Adams		1897			1897
1898			1898		John Campbell	1898
1899	Charles S. Thomas		1899			1899
1900			1900			1900
1901	James B. Orman		1901	Thomas M. Patterson		1901
1902			1902			1902
1903	James H. Peabody		1903			1903
1904			1904		William H. Gabbert	1904
1905	Alva Adams		1905			1905
1905	James H. Peabody		1905			1905
1905	Jesse F. McDonald		1905			1905
1906			1906			1906
1907	Henry A. Buchtel		1907	Simon Guggenheim	Robert W. Steele	1907
1908			1908			1908
1909	John F. Shafroth	Charles J. Hughes, Jr.	1909			1909
1910			1910		John Campbell	1910
1911		*Vacant*	1911			1911
1912			1912			1912
1913	Elias M. Ammons	John F. Shafroth	1913	Charles S. Thomas	George W. Musser	1913
1914			1914			1914
1915	George A. Carlson		1915		William H. Gabbert	1915
1916			1916		S. Harrison White	1916
1917	Julius C. Gunter		1917			1917
1918			1918		William A. Hill	1918
1919	Oliver H. Shoup	Lawrence C. Phipps	1919		James A. Garrigues	1919
1920			1920			1920
1921			1921	Samuel D. Nicholson	Tully Scott	1921
1911			1922			1922
1923	William E. Sweet		1923	Alva B. Adams	James H. Teller	1923
1924			1924	Rice W. Means		1924
1925	Clarence J. Morley		1925		George W. Allen	1925
1926			1926			1926
1927	William H. Adams		1927	Charles W. Waterman	Haslett P. Burke	1927
1928			1928		John H. Dennison	1928
1929			1929		Greeley W. Whitford	1929
1930			1930			1930
1931		Edward P. Costigan	1931		John T. Adams	1931
1932			1932	Karl C. Schuyler		1932
1933	Edwin C. Johnson		1933	Alva B. Adams		1933
1934			1934			1934
1935			1935		Charles C. Butler	1935
1936			1936		John Campbell	1936
1937	Ray H. Talbot	Edwin C. Johnson	1937		Haslett P. Burke	1937
1937	Teller Ammons		1937			1937

COLORADO—Continued

	Governors	*United States Senators*		*Chief Justices*
1938				
1939	Ralph L. Carr			Benjamin C. Hilliard
1940				Francis E. Bouck
1941				John C. Young
1942			Eugene D. Millikin	
1943	John C. Vivian			
1944				
1945				Norris C. Bakke
1946				William L. Knous
1947	William L. Knous			Haslett P. Burke
1948				
1949				Benjamin C. Hilliard
1950	Walter W. Johnson			
1951	Dan Thornton			William S. Jackson
1952				Mortimer Stone
1953				
1954				
1955	Edwin C. Johnson	Gordon L. Allott		Wilbur M. Alter
1956				
1957	Stephen L. R. McNichols		John A. Carroll	O. Otto Moore
1958				E. V. Holland
1959				Francis J. Knauss
1960				Leonard B. Sutton
1961				Frank H. Hall
1962				Edward C. Day
1963	John A. Love		Peter H. Dominick	Albert T. Frantz
1964				Robert H. McWilliams
1965				Edward E. Pringle
1966				Leonard B. Sutton
1967				O. Otto Moore
1968				
1969				Robert H. McWilliams
1970				Edward E. Pringle
1971				
1972				
1973		Floyd K. Haskell		

CONNECTICUT

	Governors	*United States Senators*			*Chief Justices*	
1789	Samuel Huntington	Oliver Ellsworth	1789	William S. Johnson	Eliphalet Dyer	1789
1790			1790			1790
1791			1791	Roger Sherman		1791
1792			1792			1792
1793			1793	Stephen M. Mitchell	Andrew Adams	1793
1794			1794			1794
1795			1795	Jonathan Trumbull		1795
1796	Oliver Wolcott	James Hillhouse	1796	Uriah Tracy		1796
1797	Jonathan Trumbull 2nd		1797			1797
1798			1798		Jesse Root	1798
1799			1799			1799
1800			1800			1800
1801			1801			1801
1802			1802			1802
1803			1803			1803
1804			1804			1804
1805			1805			1805
1806			1806			1806
1807			1807	Chauncey Goodrich	Stephen M. Mitchell	1807
1808			1808			1808
1809	John Treadwell		1809			1809
1810		Samuel W. Dana	1810			1810
1811	Roger Griswold		1811			1811
1812			1812			1812
1813	John C. Smith		1813	David Daggett		1813
1814			1814		Tapping Reeve	1814
1815			1815		Zephaniah Swift	1815
1816			1816			1816
1817	Oliver Wolcott, Jr.		1817			1817
1818			1818			1818
1819			1819	James Lanman	Stephen T. Hosmer	1819
1820			1820			1820
1821		Elijah Boardman	1821			1821
1822			1822			1822
1823		Henry W. Edwards	1823			1823
1824			1824			1824
1825			1825	Calvin Willey		1825
1826			1826			1826
1827	Gideon Tomlinson	Samuel A. Foote	1827			1827
1828			1828			1828
1829			1829			1829
1830			1830			1830
1831	John S. Peters		1831	Gideon Tomlinson		1831
1832			1832			1832
1833	Henry W. Edwards	Nathan Smith	1833		David Daggett	1833
1834	Samuel A. Foote		1834		Thomas S. Williams	1834
1835	Henry W. Edwards	John M. Niles	1835			1835
1836			1836			1836
1837			1837	Perry Smith		1837
1838	William W. Ellsworth		1838			1838
1839		Thaddeus Betts	1839			1839
1840		Jabez W. Huntington	1840			1840
1841			1841			1841
1842	Chauncey F. Cleveland		1842			1842
1843			1843	John M. Niles		1843
1844	Roger S. Baldwin		1844			1844
1845			1845			1845
1846	Isaac Toucey		1846			1846
1847	Clark Bissell	Roger S. Baldwin	1847		Samuel Church	1847
1848			1848			1848
1849	Joseph Trumbull		1849	Truman Smith		1849
1850	Thomas H. Seymour		1850			1850
1851			1851			1851
1852		Isaac Toucey	1852			1852
1853	Charles H. Pond		1853			1853
1854	Henry Dutton		1854	Francis Gillette	Henry M. Waite	1854
1855	William T. Minor		1855	Lafayette S. Foster		1855
1856			1856			1856
1857	Alexander H. Holley	James Dixon	1857		William L. Storrs	1857

CONNECTICUT–Continued

	Governors	*United States Senators*			*Chief Justices*	
1858	William A. Buckingham		1858			1858
1859			1859			1859
1860			1860			1860
1861			1861		Joel Hinman	1861
1862			1862			1862
1863			1863			1863
1864			1864			1864
1865			1865			1865
1866	Joseph R. Hawley		1866			1866
1867	James E. English		1867	Orris S. Ferry		1867
1868			1868			1868
1869	Marshall Jewell	William A. Buckingham	1869			1869
1870	James E. English		1870		Thomas B. Butler	1870
1871	Marshall Jewell		1871			1871
1872			1872			1872
1873	Charles R. Ingersoll		1873		Origen S. Seymour	1873
1874			1874		John D. Park	1874
1875		William W. Eaton	1875	James E. English		1875
1876			1876	William H. Barnum		1876
1877	Richard D. Hubbard		1877			1877
1878			1878			1878
1879	Charles B. Andrews		1879	Orville H. Platt		1879
1880			1880			1880
1881	Hobart B. Bigelow	Joseph R. Hawley	1881			1881
1882			1882			1882
1883	Thomas M. Waller		1883			1883
1884			1884			1884
1885	Henry B. Harrison		1885			1885
1886			1886			1886
1887	Phineas C. Lounsbury		1887			1887
1888			1888			1888
1889	Morgan G. Bulkeley		1889		Charles B. Andrews	1889
1890			1890			1890
1891			1891			1891
1892			1892			1892
1893	Luzon B. Morris		1893			1893
1894			1894			1894
1895	Owen V. Coffin		1895			1895
1896			1896			1896
1897	Lorrin A. Cooke		1897			1897
1898			1898			1898
1899	George E. Lounsbury		1899			1899
1900			1900			1900
1901	George P. McLean		1901		David Torrance	1901
1902			1902			1902
1903	Abiram Chamberlain		1903			1903
1904			1904			1904
1905	Henry Roberts	Morgan G. Bulkeley	1905	Frank B. Brandegee		1905
1906			1906			1906
1907	Rollins S. Woodruff		1907		Simeon E. Baldwin	1907
1908			1908			1908
1909	George L. Lilley		1909			1909
1909	Frank B. Weeks		1909			1909
1910			1910		Frederick B. Hall	1910
1911	Simeon E. Baldwin	George P. McLean	1911			1911
1912			1912			1912
1913			1913		Samuel O. Prentice	1913
1914			1914			1914
1915	Marcus H. Holcomb		1915			1915
1916			1916			1916
1917			1917			1917
1918			1918			1918
1919			1919			1919
1920			1920		George W. Wheeler	1920
1921	Everett J. Lake		1921			1921
1922			1922			1922
1923	Charles A. Templeton		1923			1923

CONNECTICUT—Continued

	Governors	*United States Senators*			*Chief Justices*	
1924			1924	Hiram Bingham		1924
1925	John H. Trumbull		1925			1925
1926			1926			1926
1927			1927			1927
1928			1928			1928
1929		Frederic C. Walcott	1929			1929
1930			1930		William M. Maltbie	1930
1931	Wilbur L. Cross		1931			1931
1932			1932			1932
1933			1933	Augustine Lonergan		1933
1934			1934			1934
1935		Francis T. Maloney	1935			1935
1936			1936			1936
1937			1937			1937
1938			1938			1938
1939	Raymond E. Baldwin	John A. Danaher	1939			1939
1940			1940			1940
1941	Robert E. Hurley		1941			1941
1942			1942			1942
1943	Raymond E. Baldwin		1943			1943
1944			1944			1944
1945		J. Brien McMahon	1945	Thomas C. Hart		1945
1946	Wilbert Snow		1946	Raymond E. Baldwin		1946
1947	James L. McConaughy		1947			1947
1948	James C. Shannon		1948			1948
1949	Chester Bowles		1949	William Benton		1949
1950			1950		Allyn M. Brown	1950
1951	John D. Lodge		1951			1951
1952		William A. Purtell	1952			1952
1953		Prescott Bush	1953	William A. Purtell	Ernest A. Inglis	1953
1954			1954			1954
1955	Abraham Ribicoff		1955			1955
1956			1956			1956
1957			1957		Patrick B. O'Sullivan	1957
1957			1957		Kenneth Wynne	1957
1958			1958		Edward J. Daly	1958
1959			1959	Thomas J. Dodd	Raymond E. Baldwin	1959
1960			1960			1960
1961	John Dempsey		1961			1961
1962			1962			1962
1963		Abraham Ribicoff	1963		John H. King	1963
1964			1964			1964
1965			1965			1965
1966			1966			1966
1967			1967			1967
1968			1968			1968
1969			1969			1969
1970			1970	Lowell P. Weicker, Jr.	Howard W. Alcorn	1970
1971	Thomas Meskill		1971			1971
1972			1972			1972
1973			1973			1973

DELAWARE

	Governors	*United States Senators*			*Chief Justices* *(Chancellors until 1951)*	
1789	Joshua Clayton	Richard Bassett	1789	George Read		1789
1790			1790			1790
1791			1791			1791
1792			1792			1792
1793		John Vining	1793	*Vacant*	William Killen	1793
1794			1794			1794
1795			1795	Henry Latimer		1795
1796	Gunning Bedford		1796			1796
1797	Daniel Rogers (Acting)		1797			1797
1798		Joshua Clayton	1798			1798
1799	Richard Bassett	William H. Wells	1799			1799
1800			1800			1800
1801	James Sykes (Acting)		1801	Samuel White	Nicholas Ridgely	1801
1802	David Hall		1802			1802
1803			1803			1803
1804		James A. Bayard, Sr.	1804			1804
1805	Nathaniel Mitchell		1805			1805
1806			1806			1806
1807			1807			1807
1808	George Truitt		1808			1808
1809			1809			1809
1810			1810	Outerbridge Horsey		1810
1811	Joseph Haslet		1811			1811
1812			1812			1812
1813		William H. Wells	1813			1813
1814	Daniel Rodney		1814			1814
1815			1815			1815
1816			1816			1816
1817	John Clark	Nicholas Van Dyke	1817			1817
1818			1818			1818
1819			1819			1819
1820	Jacob Stout (Acting)		1820			1820
1821	John Collins		1821			1821
1822	Caleb Rodney (Acting)		1822	Caesar A. Rodney		1822
1823	Joseph Haslet		1823			1823
1824	Samuel Paynter		1824	Thomas Clayton		1824
1825			1825			1825
1826		Daniel Rodney	1826			1826
1827	Charles Polk	Henry M. Ridgely	1827	Louis McLane		1827
1828			1828			1828
1829			1829	John M. Clayton		1829
1830	David Hazzard	Arnold Naudain	1830		Kensey Johns	1830
1831			1831			1831
1832			1832		Kensey Johns, Jr.	1832
1833	Caleb P. Bennett		1833			1833
1834			1834			1834
1835			1835			1835
1836	Charles Polk (Acting)	Richard H. Bayard	1836			1836
1837	Cornelius P. Comegys		1837	Thomas Clayton		1837
1838			1838			1838
1839		*Vacant*	1839			1839
1840			1840			1840
1841	William B. Cooper	Richard H. Bayard	1841			1841
1842			1842			1842
1843			1843			1843
1844			1844			1844
1845	Thomas Stockton	John M. Clayton	1845			1845
1846	William Temple (Acting)		1846			1846
1847	William Tharp		1847	Presley Spruance		1847
1848			1848			1848
1849		John Wales	1849			1849
1850			1850			1850
1851	William H. H. Ross	James A. Bayard, Jr.	1851			1851
1852			1852			1852
1853			1853	John M. Clayton		1853
1854			1854			1854
1855	Peter F. Causey		1855			1855
1856			1856	Joseph P. Comegys		1856

DELAWARE–Continued

	Governors	*United States Senators*			*Chief Justices*	
1857			1857	Martin W. Bates	Samuel M. Harrington	1857
1858			1858			1858
1859	William Burton		1859	Willard Saulsbury, Sr.		1859
1860			1860			1860
1861			1861			1861
1862			1862			1862
1863	William Cannon		1863			1863
1864		George R. Riddle	1864			1864
1865	Gove Saulsbury		1865		Daniel M. Bates	1865
1866			1866			1866
1867		James A. Bayard, Jr.	1867			1867
1868			1868			1868
1869		Thomas F. Bayard	1869			1869
1870			1870			1870
1871	James Ponder		1871	Eli Saulsbury		1871
1872			1872			1872
1873			1873		Willard Saulsbury	1873
1874			1874			1874
1875	John P. Cochran		1875			1875
1876			1876			1876
1877			1877			1877
1878			1878			1878
1879	John W. Hall		1879			1879
1880			1880			1880
1881			1881			1881
1882			1882			1882
1883	Charles C. Stockley		1883			1883
1884			1884			1884
1885		George Gray	1885			1885
1886			1886			1886
1887	Benjamin T. Biggs		1887			1887
1888			1888			1888
1889			1889	Anthony Higgins		1889
1890			1890			1890
1891	Robert J. Reynolds		1891			1891
1892			1892		James L. Wolcott	1892
1893			1893			1893
1894			1894			1894
1895	Joshua H. Marvil		1895	*Vacant*	John R. Nicholson	1895
1896			1896			1896
1897	Elbe W. Tunnell		1897	Richard R. Kenney		1897
1898			1898			1898
1899		*Vacant*	1899			1899
1900			1900			1900
1901	John Hunn		1901	*Vacant*		1901
1902			1902			1902
1903		L. Heisler Ball	1903	J. Frank Allee		1903
1904			1904			1904
1905	Preston Lea	Henry A. duPont	1905			1905
1906			1906			1906
1907			1907	Harry A. Richardson		1907
1908			1908			1908
1909	Simeon S. Pennewill		1909		Charles M. Curtis	1909
1910			1910			1910
1911			1911			1911
1912			1912			1912
1913	Charles R. Miller		1913	Willard Saulsbury, Jr.		1913
1914			1914			1914
1915			1915			1915
1916			1916			1916
1917	John G. Townsend, Jr.	Josiah O. Wolcott	1917			1917
1918			1918			1918
1919			1919	L. Heisler Ball		1919
1920			1920			1920
1921	William D. Denney	T. Coleman duPont	1921		Josiah O. Wolcott	1921
1922		Thomas F. Bayard, Jr.	1922			1922
1923			1923			1923

DELAWARE—Continued

Year	*Governors*	*United States Senators*	*United States Senators*	*Chief Justices*
1924				
1925	Robert P. Robinson		T. Coleman duPont	
1926				
1927				
1928			Daniel O. Hastings	
1929	C. Douglass Buck	John G. Townsend, Jr.		
1930				
1931				
1932				
1933				
1934				
1935				
1936				
1937	Richard C. McMullen		James H. Hughes	
1938				William W. Harrington
1939				
1940				
1941	Walter W. Bacon	James M. Tunnell		
1942				
1943			C. Douglass Buck	
1944				
1945				
1946				
1947		John J. Williams		
1948				
1949	Elbert N. Carvel		J. Allen Frear, Jr.	
1950				Daniel F. Wolcott
1951				Clarence A. Southerland
1952				
1953	J. Caleb Boggs			
1954				
1955				
1956				
1957				
1958				
1959				
1960	David P. Buckson			
1961	Elbert N. Carvel		J. Caleb Boggs	
1962				
1963				Charles L. Terry, Jr.
1964				Daniel F. Wolcott
1965	Charles L. Terry, Jr.			
1966				
1967				
1968				
1969	Russell W. Peterson			
1970				
1971		William V. Roth, Jr.		
1972				
1973	Sherman W. Tribbitt		Joseph R. Biden, Jr.	

FLORIDA

	Governors	United States Senators		United States Senators	Chief Justices	
1845	William D. Moseley	David Levy Yulee	1845	James D. Westcott, Jr.		1845
1846			1846		Thomas Douglas	1846
1847			1847			1847
1848			1848			1848
1849	Thomas Brown		1849	Jackson Morton		1849
1850			1850			1850
1851		Stephen R. Mallory	1851		Walker Anderson	1851
1852			1852			1852
1853	James E. Broome		1853		Benjamin D. Wright	1853
1854			1854		Thomas Baltzell	1854
1855			1855	David Levy Yulee		1855
1856			1856			1856
1857	Madison S. Perry		1857			1857
1858			1858			1858
1859			1859			1859
1860			1860		Charles H. Dupont	1860
1861	John Milton	*Vacant*	1861	*Vacant*		1861
1862			1862			1862
1863			1863			1863
1864			1864			1864
1865	William Marvin		1865			1865
1866	David S. Walker		1866			1866
1867			1867			1867
1868	Harrison Reed	Thomas W. Osborn	1868	Adonijah S. Welch	Edwin M. Randall	1868
1869			1869	Abijah Gilbert		1869
1870			1870			1870
1871			1871			1871
1872			1872			1872
1873	Ossian B. Hart	Simon B. Conover	1873			1873
1874	Marcellus L. Stearns		1874			1874
1875			1875	Charles W. Jones		1875
1876			1876			1876
1877	George F. Drew		1877			1877
1878			1878			1878
1879		Wilkinson Call	1879			1879
1880			1880			1880
1881	WilliaM D. Bloxham		1881			1881
1882			1882			1882
1883			1883			1883
1884			1884			1884
1885	Edward A. Perry		1885		George G. McWhorter	1885
1886			1886			1886
1887			1887	Samuel Pasco	Augustus E. Maxwell	1887
1888			1888			1888
1889	Francis P. Fleming		1889		George P. Raney	1889
1890			1890			1890
1891			1891			1891
1892			1892			1892
1893	Henry L. Mitchell		1893			1893
1894			1894		Benjamin S. Liddon	1894
1895			1895		Milton H. Mabry	1895
1896			1896			1896
1897	William D. Bloxham	Stephen R. Mallory, Jr.	1897		Robert F. Taylor	1897
1898			1898			1898
1899			1899	James P. Taliaferro		1899
1900			1900			1900
1901	William S. Jennings		1901			1901
1902			1902			1902
1903			1903			1903
1904			1904			1904
1905	Napoleon B. Broward		1905		Thomas M. Shackleford	1905
1906			1906			1906
1907		William J. Bryan	1907			1907
1908		William H. Milton	1908			1908
1909	Albert W. Gilchrist	Duncan U. Fletcher	1909		James B. Whitfield	1909
1910			1910			1910
1911			1911	Nathan P. Bryan	*Hereafter justices of*	1911
1912			1912		*Supreme Court serve*	1912
1913	Park Trammell		1913		*on a rotating basis*	1913
1914			1914		*as Chief Presiding Judge*	1914
1915			1915			1915
1916			1916			1916
1917	Sidney J. Catts		1917	Park Trammell		1917
1918			1918			1918
1919			1919			1919
1920			1920			1920

FLORIDA–Continued

Governors

Year	Governor
1921	Cary A. Hardee
1922	
1923	
1924	
1925	John W. Martin
1926	
1927	
1928	
1929	Doyle E. Carlton
1930	
1931	
1932	
1933	David Scholtz
1934	
1935	
1936	
1936	
1937	Fred P. Cone
1938	
1939	
1940	
1941	Spessard L. Holland
1942	
1943	
1944	
1945	Millard F. Caldwell
1946	
1947	
1948	
1949	Fuller Warren
1950	
1951	
1952	
1953	Dan McCarty
1953	Charley E. Johns
1954	
1955	Leroy Collins
1956	
1957	
1958	
1959	
1960	
1961	Farris Bryant
1962	
1963	
1964	
1965	Haydon Burns
1966	
1967	Claude R. Kirk
1968	
1969	
1970	
1971	Reubin Askew
1972	
1973	

United States Senators

Senator	Year	Senator
	1921	
	1922	
	1923	
	1924	
	1925	
	1926	
	1927	
	1928	
	1929	
	1930	
	1931	
	1932	
	1933	
	1934	
	1935	
William L. Hill	1936	Scott M. Loftin
Claude D. Pepper	1936	Charles O. Andrews
	1937	
	1938	
	1939	
	1940	
	1941	
	1942	
	1943	
	1944	
	1945	
	1946	Spessard L. Holland
	1947	
	1948	
	1949	
	1950	
George A. Smathers	1951	
	1952	
	1953	
	1953	
	1954	
	1955	
	1956	
	1957	
	1958	
	1959	
	1960	
	1961	
	1962	
	1963	
	1964	
	1965	
	1966	
	1967	
	1968	
Edward J. Gurney	1969	
	1970	
	1971	Lawton M. Chiles, Jr.
	1972	
	1973	

Chief Justices

Chief Justice	Year
	1921
	1922
	1923
	1924
	1925
	1926
	1927
	1928
	1929
	1930
	1931
	1932
	1933
	1934
	1935
	1936
	1936
	1937
	1938
	1939
	1940
	1941
	1942
	1943
	1944
	1945
	1946
	1947
	1948
	1949
	1950
	1951
	1952
	1953
	1953
	1954
	1955
	1956
	1957
	1958
	1959
	1960
	1961
	1962
	1963
	1964
	1965
	1966
	1967
	1968
	1969
	1970
	1971
	1972
	1973

GEORGIA

	Governors	*United States Senators*			*Chief Justices*	
1789	George Walton	William Few	1789	James Gunn		1789
1789	Edward Telfair		1789			1789
1792			1792			1792
1793	George Mathews	James Jackson	1793			1793
1794			1794			1794
1795		George Walton	1795			1795
1796	Jared Irwin	Josiah Tattnall	1796			1796
1797			1797			1797
1798	James Jackson		1798			1798
1799		Abraham Baldwin	1799			1799
1800			1800			1800
1801	David Emanuel		1801	James Jackson		1801
1801	Josiah Tattnall		1801			1801
1802	John Milledge		1802			1802
1803			1803			1803
1804			1804			1804
1805			1805			1805
1806	Jared Irwin		1806	John Milledge		1806
1807		George Jones	1807			1807
1807		William H. Crawford	1807		*The Office of Chief Justice was created in 1866*	1807
1808			1808			1808
1809	David B. Mitchell		1809	Charles Tait		1809
1810			1810			1810
1811			1811			1811
1812			1812			1812
1813	Peter Early	William B. Bulloch	1813			1813
1813		William W. Bibb	1813			1813
1814			1814			1814
1815	David B. Mitchell		1815			1815
1816		George M. Troup	1816			1816
1817	William Rabun		1817			1817
1818		John Forsyth	1818			1818
1819	John Clark	Freeman Walker	1819	John Elliott		1819
1820			1820			1820
1821		Nicholas Ware	1821			1821
1822			1822			1822
1823	George M. Troup		1823			1823
1824		Thomas W. Cobb	1824			1824
1825			1825	John M. Berrien		1825
1826			1826			1826
1827	John Forsyth		1827			1827
1828		Oliver H. Prince	1828			1828
1829	George R. Gilmer	George M. Troup	1829	John Forsyth		1829
1830			1830			1830
1831	Wilson Lumpkin		1831			1831
1832			1832			1832
1833		John P. King	1833			1833
1834			1834			1834
1835	William Schley		1835	Alfred Cuthbert		1835
1836			1836			1836
1837	George R. Gilmer	Wilson Lumpkin	1837			1837
1838			1838			1838
1839	Charles J. McDonald		1839			1839
1840			1840			1840
1841		John M. Berrien	1841			1841
1842			1842			1842
1843	George W. Crawford		1843	Walter T. Colquitt		1843
1844			1844			1844
1845			1845			1845
1846			1846			1846
1847	George W. Towns		1847			1847
1848			1848	Herschel V. Johnson		1848
1849			1849	William C. Dawson		1849
1850			1850			1850
1851	Howell Cobb		1851			1851
1852		Robert M. Charlton	1852			1852
1853	Herschel V. Johnson	Robert Toombs	1853			1853
1854			1854			1854

GEORGIA–Continued

	Governors	*United States Senators*			*Chief Justices*	
1855			1855	Alfred Iverson		1855
1856			1856			1856
1857	Joseph E. Brown		1857			1857
1858			1858			1858
1859			1859			1859
1860			1860			1860
1861		*Vacant*	1861	*Vacant*		1861
1862			1862			1862
1863			1863			1863
1864			1864			1864
1865	James Johnson		1865			1865
1865	Charles J. Jenkins		1865			1865
1866			1866		Joseph H. Lumpkin	1866
1867			1867		Hiram Warner	1867
1868	Thomas H. Ruger		1868		Joseph E. Brown	1868
1868	Rufus B. Bullock		1868			1868
1869			1869			1869
1871	Benjamin Conley	Joshua Hill	1871	Homer V. M. Willer	Osborne A. Lochrane	1871
1871			1871	Thomas M. Norwood		1871
1872	Joseph M. Smith		1872		Hiram Warner	1872
1873		John B. Gordon	1873			1873
1874			1874			1874
1875			1875			1875
1876			1876			1876
1877	Alfred H. Colquitt		1877	Benjamin H. Hill		1877
1878			1878			1878
1879			1879			1879
1880		Joseph E. Brown	1880		James Jackson	1880
1881			1881			1881
1882	Alexander H. Stephens		1882	M. Pope Barrow		1882
1883	Henry D. McDaniel		1883	Alfred H. Colquitt		1883
1884			1884			1884
1885			1885			1885
1886	John B. Gordon		1886			1886
1887			1887		Logan E. Bleckley	1887
1888			1888			1888
1889			1889			1889
1890	William J. Northen		1890			1890
1891		John B. Gordon	1891			1891
1892			1892			1892
1893			1893			1893
1894	William Y. Atkinson		1894	Patrick Walsh	Thomas J. Simmons	1894
1895			1895	Augustus O. Bacon		1895
1896			1896			1896
1897		Alexander S. Clay	1897			1897
1898	Allen D. Candler		1898			1898
1899			1899			1899
1900			1900			1900
1901			1901			1901
1902	Joseph M. Terrell		1902			1902
1903			1903			1903
1904			1904			1904
1905			1905		William H. Fish	1905
1906			1906			1906
1907	Hoke Smith		1907			1907
1908			1908			1908
1909	Joseph M. Brown		1909			1909
1910		Joseph M. Terrell	1910			1910
1911	Hoke Smith	Hoke Smith	1911			1911
1912	Joseph M. Brown		1912			1912
1913	John M. Slaton		1913			1913
1914			1914	William S. West		1914
1914			1914	Thomas W. Hardwick		1914
1915	Nathaniel E. Harris		1915			1915
1916			1916			1916
1917	Hugh M. Dorsey		1917			1917

GEORGIA–Continued

	Governors	*United States Senators*			*Chief Justices*	
1918			1918			1918
1919			1919	William J. Harris		1919
1920			1920			1920
1921	Thomas W. Hardwick	Thomas E. Watson	1921			1921
1922		Walter F. George	1922			1922
1923	Clifford Walker		1923		Richard B. Russell	1923
1924			1924			1924
1925			1925			1925
1926			1926			1926
1927	Lamartine G. Hardman		1927			1927
1928			1928			1928
1929			1929			1929
1930			1930			1930
1931	Richard B. Russell		1931			1931
1932			1932	John S. Cohen		1932
1933	Eugene Talmadge		1933	Richard B. Russell, Jr.		1933
1934			1934			1934
1935			1935			1935
1936			1936			1936
1937	Eurith D. Rivers		1937			1937
1938			1938		Charles S. Reid	1938
1939			1939			1939
1940			1940			1940
1941	Eugene Talmadge		1941			1941
1942			1942			1942
1943	Ellis G. Arnall		1943		Reason C. Bell	1943
1944			1944			1944
1945			1945			1945
1946			1946			1946
1947	Melvin E. Thompson		1947		William F. Jenkins	1947
1948	Herman E. Talmadge		1948		William H. Duckworth	1948
1949			1949			1949
1950			1950			1950
1951			1951			1951
1952			1952			1952
1953			1953			1953
1954			1954			1954
1955	S. Marvin Griffin		1955			1955
1956			1956			1956
1957		Herman E. Talmadge	1957			1957
1958			1958			1958
1959	Samuel E. Vandiver, Jr.		1959			1959
1960			1960			1960
1961			1961			1961
1962			1962			1962
1963	Carl E. Sanders		1963			1963
1964			1964			1964
1965			1965			1965
1966			1966			1966
1967	Lester Maddox		1967			1967
1968			1968			1968
1969			1969		Bond Almand	1969
1970			1970			1970
1971	James Earl Carter		1971	David H. Gambrell		1971
1972			1972			1972
1973			1973	Sam Nunn		1973

HAWAII

	Governors	*United States Senators*			*Chief Justices*	
1959	William F. Quinn	Hiram L. Fong	1959	Oren E. Long	Wilfred C. Tsukiyama	1959
1960			1960			1960
1961			1961			1961
1962	John A. Burns		1962			1962
1963			1963	Daniel K. Inouye		1963
1964			1964			1964
1965			1965			1965
1966			1966		William S. Richardson	1966
1967			1967			1967
1968			1968			1968
1969			1969			1969
1970			1970			1970
1971			1971			1971
1972			1972			1972
1973			1973			1973

IDAHO

	Governors	*United States Senators*			*Chief Justices*	
1890	George L. Shoup		1890			1890
1890	Norman B. Willey	George L. Shoup	1890	William J. McConnell		1890
1891			1891	Fred T. Dubois		1891
1892			1892			1892
1893	William J. McConnell		1893			1893
1894			1894			1894
1895			1895			1895
1896			1896			1896
1897	Frank Steunenberg		1897	Henry Heitfeld		1897
1898			1898			1898
1899			1899			1899
1900			1900			1900
1901	Frank W. Hunt	Fred T. Dubois	1901			1901
1902			1902			1902
1903	John T. Morrison		1903	Weldon B. Heyburn		1903
1904			1904			1904
1905	Frank R. Gooding		1905			1905
1906			1906			1906
1907		William E. Borah	1907			1907
1908			1908			1908
1909	James H. Brady		1909			1909
1910			1910			1910
1911	James H. Hawley		1911			1911
1912			1912	Kirtland I. Perky		1912
1913	John M. Haines		1913	James H. Brady	*Justices of the Supreme Court serve on a rotating basis as Chief Presiding Judge*	1913
1914			1914			1914
1915	Moses Alexander		1915			1915
1916			1916			1916
1917			1917			1917
1918			1918	John F. Nugent		1918

IDAHO—Continued

	Governors	*United States Senators*			*Chief Justices*	
1919	David W. Davis		1919			1919
1920			1920			1920
1921			1921	Frank R. Gooding		1921
1922			1922			1922
1923	Charles C. Moore		1923			1923
1924			1924			1924
1925			1925			1925
1926			1926			1926
1927	H. Clarence Baldridge		1927			1927
1928			1928	John Thomas		1928
1929			1929			1929
1930			1930			1930
1931	C. Ben Ross		1931			1931
1932			1932			1932
1933			1933	James P. Pope		1933
1934			1934			1934
1935			1935			1935
1936			1936			1936
1937	Barzilla W. Clark		1937			1937
1938			1938			1938
1939	C. A. Bottolfsen		1939	D. Worth Clark		1939
1940		John Thomas	1940			1940
1941	Charles A. Clark		1941			1941
1942			1942			1942
1943	C. A. Bottolfsen		1943			1943
1944			1944			1944
1945	Charles C. Gossett	Charles C. Gossett	1945	Glen H. Taylor		1945
1946			1946			1946
1947	C. A. Robins	Henry C. Dworshak	1947			1947
1948			1948			1948
1949		Bert H. Miller	1949			1949
1949		Henry C. Dworshak	1949			1949
1950			1950			1950
1951	Len B. Jordan		1951	Herman Welker		1951
1952			1952			1952
1953			1953			1953
1954			1954			1954
1955	Robert E. Smylie		1955			1955
1956			1956			1956
1957			1957	Frank F. Church		1957
1958			1958			1958
1959			1959			1959
1960			1960			1960
1961			1961			1961
1962			1962			1962
1963		Len B. Jordan	1963			1963
1964			1964			1964
1965			1965			1965
1966			1966			1966
1967	Don Samuelson		1967			1967
1968			1968			1968
1969			1969			1969
1970			1970			1970
1971	Cecil D. Andrus		1971			1971
1972			1972			1972
1973		James A. McClure	1973			1973

ILLINOIS

Year	*Governors*	*United States Senators*	Year	*United States Senators*	*Chief Justices*	Year
1819			1819			1819
1820			1820			1820
1821			1821			1821
1822	Edward Coles		1822		Thomas Reynolds	1822
1823			1823			1823
1824			1824	John McLean		1824
1825			1825	Elias K. Kane	William Wilson	1825
1826	Ninian Edwards		1826			1826
1827			1827			1827
1828			1828			1828
1829		John McLean	1829			1829
1830	John Reynolds	David J. Baker	1830			1830
1830		John M. Robinson	1830			1830
1831			1831			1831
1832			1832			1832
1833			1833			1833
1834	Joseph Duncan		1834			1834
1835			1835	William L. D. Ewing		1835
1836			1836			1836
1837			1837	Richard M. Young		1837
1838	Thomas Carlin		1838			1838
1839			1839			1839
1840			1840			1840
1841		Samuel McRoberts	1841			1841
1842	Thomas Ford		1842			1842
1843		James Semple	1843	Sidney Breese		1843
1844			1844			1844
1845			1845			1845
1846	Augustus C. French		1846			1846
1847		Stephen A. Douglas	1847			1847
1848			1848		Samuel H. Treat	1848
1849			1849	James Shields		1849
1850			1850			1850
1851			1851			1851
1852			1852			1852
1853	Joel A. Matteson		1853			1853
1854			1854			1854
1855			1855	Lyman Trumbull	Onias C. Skinner	1855
1856			1856		Walter B. Scates	1856
1857	William H. Bissell		1857		Sidney Breese	1857
1858			1858		John D. Caton	1858
1859			1859			1859
1860	John Wood (Acting)		1860			1860
1861	Richard Yates	Orville H. Browning	1861			1861
1862			1862			1862
1863		William A. Richardson	1863			1863
1864			1864		Pinkney H. Walker	1864
1865	Richard J. Oglesby	Richard Yates	1865			1865
1866			1866			1866
1867			1867		Sidney Breese	1867
1868			1868			1868
1869	John M. Palmer		1869			1869
1870			1870		Charles B. Lawrence	1870
1871		John A. Logan	1871			1871
1872			1872			1872
1873	Richard J. Oglesby		1873	Richard J. Oglesby		1873
1873	John L. Beveridge		1873		*Since 1873 justices of the Supreme Court have served on a rotating basis as a Chief Presiding Judge*	1873
1874			1874			1874
1875			1875			1875
1876			1876			1876
1877	Shelby M. Cullom	David Davis	1877			1877
1878			1878			1878
1879			1879	John A. Logan		1879
1880			1880			1880
1881			1881			1881
1882			1882			1882
1883	John M. Hamilton	Shelby M. Cullom	1883			1883
1884			1884			1884
1885	Richard J. Oglesby		1885			1885
1886			1886			1886
1887			1887	Charles B. Farwell		1887
1888			1888			1888
1889	Joseph W. Fifer		1889			1889
1890			1890			1890
1891			1891	John M. Palmer		1891
1892			1892			1892
1893	John P. Altgeld		1893			1893
1894			1894			1894
1895			1895			1895
1896			1896			1896
1897	John R. Tanner		1897	William E. Mason		1897
1898			1898			1898
1899			1899			1899
1900			1900			1900
1901	Richard Yates		1901			1901
1902			1902			1902
1903			1903	Albert J. Hopkins		1903
1904			1904			1904

ILLINOIS–Continued

	Governors	*United States Senators*			*Chief Justices*	
1905	Charles S. Deneen		1905			1905
1906			1906			1906
1907			1907			1907
1908			1908			1908
1909			1909	William Lorimer		1909
1910			1910			1910
1911			1911			1911
1912			1912	*Vacant*		1912
1913	Edward F. Dunne	J. Hamilton Lewis	1913	Lawrence Y. Sherman		1913
1914			1914			1914
1915			1915			1915
1916			1916			1916
1917	Frank O. Lowden		1917			1917
1918			1918			1918
1919		Medill McCormick	1919			1919
1920			1920			1920
1921	Len Small		1921	William B. McKinley		1921
1922			1922			1922
1923			1923			1923
1924			1924			1924
1925		Charles S. Deneen	1925			1925
1926			1926	*Vacant*		1926
1927			1927			1927
1928			1928	Otis F. Glenn		1928
1929	Louis L. Emmerson		1929			1929
1930			1930			1930
1931		J. Hamilton Lewis	1931			1931
1932			1932			1932
1933	Henry Horner		1933	William H. Dieterich		1933
1934			1934			1934
1935			1935			1935
1936			1936			1936
1937			1937			1937
1938			1938			1938
1939		James M. Slattery	1939	Scott W. Lucas		1939
1940	John H. Stelle	C. Wayland Brooks	1940			1940
1941	Dwight H. Green		1941			1941
1942			1942			1942
1943			1943			1943
1944			1944			1944
1945			1945			1945
1946			1946			1946
1947			1947			1947
1948			1948			1948
1949	Adlai E. Stevenson	Paul H. Douglas	1949			1949
1950			1950			1950
1951			1951	Everett M. Dirksen		1951
1952			1952			1952
1953	William G. Stratton		1953			1953
1954			1954			1954
1955			1955			1955
1956			1956			1956
1957			1957			1957
1958			1958			1958
1959			1959			1959
1960			1960			1960
1961	Otto Kerner		1961			1961
1962			1962			1962
1963			1963			1963
1964			1964			1964
1965			1965			1965
1966			1966			1966
1967		Charles H. Percy	1967			1967
1968	Samuel H. Shapiro		1968			1968
1969	Richard B. Ogilvie		1969	Ralph T. Smith		1969
1970			1970			1970
1971			1971	Adlai E. Stevenson III		1971
1972			1972			1972
1973	Daniel Walker		1973			1973

INDIANA

	Governors	*United States Senators*			*Chief Justices*	
1816	Jonathan Jennings	James Noble	1816	Waller Taylor		1816
1817			1817			1817
1818			1818			1818
1819			1819			1819
1820			1820			1820
1821			1821			1821
1822	Ratliff Boon		1822			1822
1822	William Hendricks		1822			1822
1823			1823			1823
1824			1824			1824
1825	James B. Ray		1825	William Hendricks		1825
1826			1826			1826
1827			1827			1827
1828			1828			1828
1829			1829			1829
1830			1830			1890
1831	Noah Noble	Robert Hanna	1831			1831
1832		John Tipton	1832			1832
1833			1833			1833
1834			1834			1834
1835			1835			1835
1836			1836			1836
1837	David Wallace		1837	Oliver H. Smith	*Justices of the Supreme Court serve on a rotating basis as Chief Presiding Judge*	1837
1838			1838			1838
1839		Albert S. White	1839			1839
1840	Samuel Bigger		1840			1840
1841			1841			1841
1842			1842			1842
1843	James Whitcomb		1843	Edward A. Hannegan		1843
1844			1844			1844
1845		Jesse D. Bright	1845			1845
1846			1846			1846
1847			1847			1847
1848	Paris C. Dunning		1848			1848
1849	Joseph A. Wright		1849	James Whitcomb		1849
1850			1850			1850
1851			1851			1851
1852			1852	Charles W. Cathcart		1852
1853			1853	John Pettit		1853
1854			1854			1854
1855			1855			1855
1850			1856	*Vacant*		1856
1857	Ashbel P. Willard		1857	Graham N. Fitch		1857
1858			1858			1858
1859			1859			1859
1860	Abram A. Hammond		1860			1860
1861	Henry S. Lane		1861	Henry S. Lane		1861
1861	Oliver H.P.T. Morton		1861			1861
1862		Joseph A. Wright	1862			1862
1863		David Turpie	1863			1863
1863		Thomas A. Hendricks	1863			1863
1864			1864			1864
1865			1865			1865
1866			1866			1866
1867	Conrad Baker		1867	Oliver H.P.T. Morton		1867
1868			1868			1868
1869		Daniel D. Pratt	1869			1869
1870			1870			1870
1871			1871			1871
1872			1872			1872
1873	Thomas A. Hendricks		1873			1873
1874			1874			1874
1875		Joseph E. McDonald	1875			1875
1876			1876			1876
1877	James D. Williams		1877	Daniel W. Voorhees		1877
1878			1878			1878
1879			1879			1879
1880	Isaac P. Gray		1880			1880
1881	Albert G. Porter	Benjamin Harrison	1881			1881
1882			1882			1882
1883			1883			1883
1884			1884			1884
1885	Isaac P. Gray		1885			1885
1886			1886			1886
1887		David Turpie	1887			1887
1888			1888			1888
1889	Alvin P. Hovey		1889			1889
1890			1890			1890
1891	Ira J. Chase		1891			1891
1892			1892			1892
1893	Claude Matthews		1893			1893
1894			1894			1894
1895			1895			1895
1896			1896			1896
1897	James A. Mount		1897	Charles W. Fairbanks		1897
1898			1898			1898
1899		Albert J. Beveridge	1899			1899
1900			1900			1900
1901	Winfield T. Durbin		1901			1901

INDIANA–Continued

	Governors	*United States Senators*			*Chief Justices*	
1902			1902			1902
1903			1903			1903
1904			1904			1904
1905	J. Frank Hanly		1905	James A. Hemenway		1905
1906			1906			1906
1907			1907			1907
1908			1908			1908
1909	Thomas R. Marshall		1909	Benjamin F. Shively		1909
1910			1910			1910
1911		John W. Kern	1911			1911
1912			1912			1912
1913	Samuel M. Ralston		1913			1913
1914			1914			1914
1915			1915			1915
1916			1916	Thomas Taggart		1916
1916			1916	James E. Watson		1916
1917	James P. Goodrich	Harry S. New	1917			1917
1918			1918			1918
1919			1919			1919
1920			1920			1920
1921	Warren T. McCray		1921			1921
1922			1922			1922
1923		Samuel M. Ralston	1923			1923
1924	Emmet F. Branch		1924			1924
1925	Ed Jackson	Arthur R. Robinson	1925			1925
1926			1926			1926
1927			1927			1927
1928			1928			1928
1929	Harry G. Leslie		1929			1929
1930			1930			1930
1931			1931			1931
1932			1932			1932
1933	Paul V. McNutt		1933	Frederick Van Nuys		1933
1934			1934			1934
1935		Sherman Minton	1935			1935
1936			1936			1936
1937	H. Clifford Townsend		1937			1937
1938			1938			1938
1939			1939			1939
1940			1940			1940
1941	Henry F. Schricker	Raymond E. Willis	1941			1941
1942			1942			1942
1943			1943			1943
1944			1944	Samuel D. Jackson		1944
1944			1944	William E. Jenner		1944
1945	Ralph E. Gates		1945	Homer E. Capehart		1945
1946			1946			1946
1947		William E. Jenner	1947			1947
1948			1948			1948
1949	Henry F. Schricker		1949			1949
1950			1950			1950
1951			1951			1951
1952			1952			1952
1953	George Craig		1953			1953
1954			1954			1954
1955			1955			1955
1956			1956			1956
1957	Harold W. Handley		1957			1957
1958			1958			1958
1959		Vance Hartke	1959			1959
1960			1960			1960
1961	Matthew E. Welsh		1961			1961
1962			1962			1962
1963			1963	Birch Bayh		1963
1964			1964			1964
1965	Roger D. Branigin		1965			1965
1966			1966			1966
1967			1967			1967
1968			1968			1968
1969	Edgar Whitcomb		1969			1969
1970			1970			1970
1971			1971			1971
1972			1972			1972
1973	Otis R. Bowen		1973			1973

IOWA

Year	*Governors*	*United States Senators*	Year	*United States Senators*	*Chief Justices*	Year
1846	Ansel Briggs	*Vacant*	1846	*Vacant*		1846
1847			1847			1847
1848		Augustus C. Dodge	1848	George W. Jones		1848
1849			1849			1849
1850	Stephen Hempstead		1850			1850
1851			1851			1851
1852			1852			1852
1853			1853			1853
1854	James W. Grimes		1854			1854
1855		*Vacant*	1855	*Vacant*		1855
1856			1856			1856
1857		James Harlan	1857			1857
1858	Ralph P. Lowe		1858			1858
1859			1859	James W. Grimes		1859
1860	Samuel J. Kirkwood		1860			1860
1861			1861			1861
1862			1862			1862
1863			1863			1863
1864	William M. Stone		1864			1864
1865			1865		*Justices of the Supreme*	1865
1866		Samuel J. Kirkwood	1866		*Court serve on a rotating*	1866
1867		James Harlan	1867		*basis as Chief Presiding*	1867
1868	Samuel Merrill		1868		*Judge*	1868
1869			1869			1869
1870			1870	James B. Howell		1870
1871			1871	George G. Wright		1871
1872	Cyrus C. Carpenter		1872			1872
1873		William B. Allison	1873			1873
1874			1874			1874
1875			1875			1875
1876	Samuel J. Kirkwood		1876			1876
1877	Joshua G. Newbold		1877	Samuel J. Kirkwood		1877
1878	John H. Gear		1878			1878
1879			1879			1879
1880			1880			1880
1881			1881	James W. McDill		1881
1882	Buren R. Sherman		1882			1882
1883			1883	James F. Wilson		1883
1884			1884			1884
1885			1885			1885
1886	William Larrabee		1886			1886
1887			1887			1887
1888			1888			1888
1889			1889			1889
1890	Horace Boies		1890			1890
1891			1891			1891
1892			1892			1892
1893			1893			1893
1894	Frank D. Jackson		1894			1894
1895			1895	John H. Gear		1895
1896	Francis M. Drake		1896			1896
1897			1897			1897
1898	Leslie M. Shaw		1898			1898
1899			1899			1899
1900			1900	Jonathan P. Dolliver		1900
1901			1901			1901
1902	Albert B. Cummins		1902			1902
1903			1903			1903
1904			1904			1904
1905			1905			1905
1906			1906			1906
1907			1907			1907
1908		Albert B. Cummins	1908			1908
1909	Beryl F. Carroll		1909			1909
1910			1910	Lafayette Young		1910
1911			1911	William S. Kenyon		1911
1912			1912			1912
1913	George W. Clarke		1913			1913
1914			1914			1914
1915			1915			1915
1916			1916			1916
1917	William L. Harding		1917			1917
1918			1918			1918
1919			1919			1919
1920			1920			1920

IOWA–Continued

	Governors	*United States Senators*			*Chief Justices*	
1921	Nathan E. Kendall		1921			1921
1922			1922	Charles A. Rawson		1922
1922			1922	Smith W. Brookhart		1922
1923			1923			1923
1924			1924			1924
1925	John Hammill		1925			1925
1926		David W. Stewart	1926	Daniel F. Steck		1926
1927		Smith W. Brookhart	1927			1927
1928			1928			1928
1929			1929			1929
1930			1930			1930
1931	Dan W. Turner		1931	Lester J. Dickinson		1931
1932			1932			1932
1933	Clyde L. Herring	Richard L. Murphy	1933			1933
1934			1934			1934
1935			1935			1935
1936		Guy M. Gillette	1936			1936
1937	Nelson G. Kraschel		1937	Clyde L. Herring		1937
1938			1938			1938
1939	George A. Wilson		1939			1939
1940			1940			1940
1941			1941			1941
1942			1942			1942
1943	Bourke B. Hickenlooper		1943	George A. Wilson		1943
1944			1944			1944
1945	Robert D. Blue	Bourke B. Hickenlooper	1945			1945
1946			1946			1946
1947			1947			1947
1948			1948			1948
1949	William S. Beardsley		1949	Guy M. Gillette		1949
1950			1950			1950
1951			1951			1951
1952			1952			1952
1953			1953			1953
1954	Leo Elthon		1954			1954
1955	Leo A. Hoegh		1955	Thomas E. Martin		1955
1956			1956			1956
1957	Herschel C. Loveless		1957			1957
1958			1958			1958
1959			1959			1959
1960			1960			1960
1961	Norman A. Erbe		1961	Jack R. Miller		1961
1962			1962			1962
1963	Harold E. Hughes		1963			1963
1964			1964			1964
1965			1965			1965
1966			1966			1966
1967			1967			1967
1968			1968			1968
1969	Robert D. Fulton (Acting)	Harold E. Hughes	1969			1969
1969	Robert D. Ray		1969			1969
1970			1970			1970
1971			1971			1971
1972			1972			1972
1973			1973	Richard Clark		1973

KANSAS

	Governors	*United States Senators*			*Chief Justices*	
1861	Charles Robinson	Samuel C. Pomeroy	1861	James H. Lane	Thomas Ewing	1861
1862			1862		Nelson Cobb	1862
1863	Thomas Carney		1863			1863
1864			1864		Robert Crozier	1864
1865	Samuel J. Crawford		1865			1865
1866			1866	Edmund G. Ross		1866
1867			1867		Samuel A. Kingman	1867
1868	Nehemiah Greene		1868			1868
1869	James M. Harvey		1869			1869
1870			1870			1870
1871			1871	Alexander Caldwell		1871
1872			1872			1872
1873	Thomas A. Osborn	John J. Ingalls	1873	Robert Crozier		1873
1874			1874	James M. Harvey		1874
1875			1875			1875
1876			1876			1876
1877	George T. Anthony		1877	Preston B. Plumb	Albert H. Horton	1877
1878			1878			1878
1879	John P. St. John		1879			1879
1880			1880			1880
1881			1881			1881
1882			1882			1882
1883	George W. Glick		1883			1883
1884			1884			1884
1885	John A. Martin		1885			1885
1886			1886			1887
1887			1887			1887
1888			1888			1888
1889	Lyman U. Humphrey		1889			1889
1890			1890			1890
1891		William A. Peffer	1891			1891
1892			1892	Bishop W. Perkins		1892
1893	Lorenzo D. Lewelling		1893	John A. Martin		1893
1894			1894			1894
1895	Edmund N. Morill		1895	Lucien Baker	David Martin	1895
1896			1896			1896
1897	John W. Leedy	William A. Harris	1897		Frank Doster	1897
1898			1898			1898
1899	William E. Stanley		1899			1899
1900			1900			1900
1901			1901	Joseph R. Burton		1901
1902			1902			1902
1903	Willis J. Bailey	Chester I. Long	1903		William A. Johnston	1903
1904			1904			1904
1905	Edward W. Hoch		1905			1905
1906			1906	Alfred W. Benson		1906
1907			1907	Charles Curtis		1907
1908			1908			1908
1909	Walter R. Stubbs	Joseph L. Bristow	1909			1909
1910			1910			1910
1911			1911			1911
1912			1912			1912
1913	George H. Hodges		1913	William H. Thompson		1913
1914			1914			1914
1915	Arthur Capper		1915	Charles Curtis		1915
1916			1916			1916
1917			1917			1917
1918			1918			1918
1919	Henry J. Allen	Arthur Capper	1919			1919
1920			1920			1920
1921			1921			1921
1922			1922			1922
1923	Jonathan M. Davis		1923			1923
1924			1924			1924
1925	Ben S. Paulen		1925			1925
1926			1926			1926
1927			1927			1927
1928			1928			1928
1929	Clyde M. Reed		1929	Henry J. Allen		1929

KANSAS–Continued

	Governors	*United States Senators*			*Chief Justices*	
1930			1930	George McGill		1930
1931	Harry H. Woodring		1931			1931
1932			1932			1932
1933	Alf M. Landon		1933			1933
1934			1934			1934
1935			1935		Rousseau A Burch	1935
1936			1936			1936
1937	Walter A. Huxman		1937		John S. Dawson	1937
1938			1938			1938
1939	Payne H. Ratner	Clyde M. Reed	1939			1939
1940			1940			1940
1941			1941			1941
1942			1942			1942
1943	Andrew F. Schoeppel		1943			1943
1944			1944			1944
1945			1945		William W. Harvey	1945
1946			1946			1946
1947	Frank Carlson		1947			1947
1948			1948			1948
1949		Harry Darby	1949	Andrew F. Schoeppel		1949
1950	Frank L. Hagaman	Frank Carlson	1950			1950
1951	Edward F. Arn		1951			1951
1952			1952			1952
1953			1953			1953
1954			1954			1954
1955	Fred Hall		1955			1955
1956			1956		William A. Smith	1956
1957	John McCuish		1957		Walter G. Thiele	1957
1957	George Docking		1957		Jay S. Parker	1957
1958			1958			1958
1959			1959			1959
1960			1960			1960
1961	John Anderson, Jr.		1961			1961
1962			1962			1962
1963			1963	James B. Pearson		1963
1964			1964			1964
1965	William H. Avery		1965			1965
1966			1966		Robert T. Price	1966
1967	Robert B. Docking		1967			1967
1968			1968			1968
1969		Robert J. Dole	1969			1969
1970			1970			1970
1971			1971			1971
1972			1972			1972
1973			1973			1973

KENTUCKY

	Governors	*United States Senators*			*Chief Justices*	
1792			1792		Harry Innes	1792
1792	Isaac Shelby	John Edwards	1792	John Brown	George Muter	1792
1793			1793			1793
1794			1794			1794
1795		Humphrey Marshall	1795			1795
1796	James Garrard		1796			1796
1797			1797			1797
1798			1798			1798
1799			1799			1799
1800			1800			1800
1801		John Breckinridge	1801			1801
1802			1802			1802
1803			1803			1803
1804	Christopher Greenup		1804			1804
1805		John Adair	1805	Buckner Thruston		1805
1806		Henry Clay	1806		Thomas Todd	1806
1807		John Pope	1807		Felix Grundy	1807
1808	Charles Scott		1808		Ninian Edwards	1808
1809			1809		George M. Bibb	1809
1810			1810	Henry Clay	John Boyle	1810
1811			1811	George M. Bibb		1811
1812	Isaac Shelby		1812			1812
1813		Jesse Bledsoe	1813			1813
1814		George Walker	1814	William T. Barry		1814
1815		Isham Talbot	1815			1815
1816	George Madison		1816	Martin D. Hardin		1816
1816	Gabriel Slaughter		1816			1816
1817			1817	John J. Crittenden		1817
1818			1818			1818
1819		William Logan	1819	Richard M. Johnson		1819
1820	John Adair	Isham Talbot	1820			1820
1821			1821			1821
1822			1822			1822
1823			1823			1823
1824	Joseph Desha		1824			1824
1825		John Rowan	1825			1825
1826			1826			1826
1827			1827		George M. Bibb	1827
1828	Thomas Metcalfe		1828			1828
1829			1829	George M. Bibb	George Robertson	1829
1830			1830			1830
1831		Henry Clay	1831			1831
1832	John Breathitt		1832			1832
1833			1833			1833
1834	James T. Morehead		1834			1834
1835			1835	John J. Crittenden		1835
1836	James Clark		1836			1836
1837			1837			1837
1838			1838			1838
1839	Charles A. Wickliffe		1839			1839
1840	Robert P. Letcher		1840			1840
1841			1841	James T. Morehead		1841
1842		John J. Crittenden	1842			1842
1843			1843		Ephraim M. Ewing	1843
1844	William Owsley		1844			1844
1845			1845			1845
1846			1846			1846
1847		Joseph R. Underwood	1847		Thomas A. Marshall	1847
1848	John J. Crittenden		1848	Thomas Metcalfe		1848
1849			1849	Henry Clay		1849
1850	John L. Helm		1850			1850
1851	Lazarus W. Powell		1851			1851
1852			1852	Archibald Dixon	*After 1852 members of*	1852
1853		John B. Thompson	1853		*the Court of Appeals*	1853
1854			1854		*served on a rotating*	1854
1855	Charles S. Morehead		1855	John J. Crittenden	*basis as Chief Presiding*	1855
1856			1856		*Judge*	1856
1857			1857			1857
1858			1858			1858

KENTUCKY–Continued

	Governors	*United States Senators*			*Chief Justices*	
1859	Beriah Magoffin	Lazarus W. Powell	1859			1859
1860			1860			1860
1861			1861	John C. Breckinridge		1861
1861			1861	Garrett Davis		1861
1862	James F. Robinson		1862			1862
1863	Thomas E. Bramlette		1863			1863
1864			1864			1864
1865		James Guthrie	1865			1865
1866			1866			1866
1867	John L. Helm		1867			1867
1867	John W. Stevenson		1867			1867
1868		Thomas C. McCreery	1868			1868
1869			1869			1869
1870			1870			1870
1871	Preston H. Leslie	John W. Stevenson	1871			1871
1872			1872	Willis B. Machen		1872
1873			1873	Thomas C. McCreery		1873
1874			1874			1874
1875	James B. McCreary		1875			1875
1876			1876			1876
1877		James B. Beck	1877			1877
1878			1878			1878
1879	Luke P. Blackburn		1879	John S. Williams		1879
1880			1880			1880
1881			1881			1881
1882			1882			1882
1883	J. Proctor Knott		1883			1883
1884			1884			1884
1885			1885	Joseph C. S. Blackburn		1885
1886			1886			1886
1887	Simon B. Buckner		1887			1887
1888			1888			1888
1889			1889			1889
1890		John G. Carlisle	1890			1890
1891	John Y. Brown		1891			1891
1892			1892			1892
1893		William Lindsay	1893			1893
1894			1894			1894
1895	William O. Bradley		1895			1895
1896			1896			1896
1897			1897	William J. Deboe		1897
1898			1898			1898
1899	William S. Taylor		1899			1899
1900	William Goebel		1900			1900
1900	John C.W. Beckham		1900			1900
1901		Joseph C.S. Blackburn	1901			1901
1902			1902			1902
1903			1903	James B. McCreary		1903
1904			1904			1904
1905			1905			1905
1906			1906			1906
1907	Augustus E. Willson	Thomas H. Paynter	1907			1907
1908			1908			1908
1909			1909	William O. Bradley		1909
1910			1910			1910
1911	James B. McCreary		1911			1911
1912			1912			1912
1913		Ollie M. James	1913			1913
1914			1914	Johnson N. Camden, Jr.		1914
1915	Augustus O. Stanley		1915	John C.W. Beckham		1915
1916			1916			1916
1917			1917			1917
1918		George B. Martin	1918			1918
1919	James D. Black	Augustus O. Stanley	1919			1919
1919	Edwin P. Morrow		1919			1919
1920			1920			1920
1921			1921	Richard P. Ernst		1921
1922			1922			1922

KENTUCKY–Continued

	Governors	*United States Senators*			*Chief Justices*	
1923	William J. Fields		1923			1923
1924			1924			1924
1925		Frederic M. Sackett	1925			1925
1926			1926			1926
1927	Flem D. Sampson		1927	Alben W. Barkley		1927
1928			1928			1928
1929			1929			1929
1930		John M. Robsion	1930			1930
1930		Ben M. Williamson	1930			1930
1931	Ruby Laffoon	Marvel M. Logan	1931			1931
1932			1932			1932
1933			1933			1933
1934			1934			1934
1935	Albert B. Chandler		1935			1935
1936			1936			1936
1937			1937			1937
1938			1938			1938
1939	Keen Johnson	Albert B. Chandler	1939			1939
1940			1940			1940
1941			1941			1941
1942			1942			1942
1943	Simeon S. Willis		1943			1943
1944			1944			1944
1945		William A. Stanfill	1945			1945
1946		John Sherman Cooper	1946			1946
1947	Earle C. Clements		1947			1947
1948			1948			1948
1949		Virgil M. Chapman	1949	Garrett L. Withers		1949
1950	Lawrence W. Wetherby		1950	Earle C. Clements		1950
1951		Thomas R. Underwood	1951			1951
1952		John Sherman Cooper	1952			1952
1953			1953			1953
1954			1954			1954
1955	Albert B. Chandler	Alben W. Barkley	1955			1955
1956		Robert Humphreys	1956			1956
1956		John Sherman Cooper	1956			1956
1957			1957	Thruston B. Morton		1957
1958			1958			1958
1959	Bert T. Combs		1959			1959
1960			1960			1960
1961			1961			1961
1962			1962			1962
1963	Edward T. Breathitt		1963			1963
1964			1964			1964
1965			1965			1965
1966			1966			1966
1967	Louis B. Nunn		1967			1967
1968			1968			1968
1969			1969	Marlow W. Cook		1969
1970			1970			1970
1971			1971			1971
1972			1972			1972
1973		Walter Huddleston	1973			1973

LOUISIANA

	Governors	*United States Senators*			*Chief Justices*	
1812	William C.C. Claiborne	Allen B. Magruder	1812	Thomas Posey		1812
1813		Eligius Fromentin	1813	James Brown	George Mathews	1813
1814			1814			1814
1815			1815			1815
1816	Jacques P. Villere		1816			1816
1817			1817	William C.C. Claiborne		1817
1818			1818	Henry Johnson		1818
1819		James Brown	1819			1819
1820	Thomas B. Robertson		1820			1820
1821			1821			1821
1822			1822			1822
1823			1823			1823
1824	Henry Johnson	Josiah S. Johnston	1824	Dominique Bouligny		1824
1825			1825			1825
1826			1826			1826
1827			1827			1827
1828	Pierre Derbigny		1828			1828
1829	Armand Beauvais		1829	Edward Livingston		1829
1830	Jacques Dupre		1830			1830
1831	Andre B. Roman		1831	George A. Waggaman		1831
1832			1832			1832
1833		Alexander Porter	1833			1833
1834			1834			1834
1835	Edward D. White		1835	*Vacant*		1895
1836			1836	Robert C. Nicholas	Francois X. Martin	1836
1837		Alexander Mouton	1837			1837
1838			1838			1838
1839	Andre B. Roman		1839			1839
1840			1840			1840
1841			1841	Alexander Barrow		1841
1842		Charles M. Conrad	1842			1842
1843	Alexander Mouton		1843	*Vacant*		1843
1844			1844	Henry Johnson		1844
1845			1845			1845
1846	Isaac Johnson		1846		George Eustis	1846
1847			1847	Pierre Soule		1847
1847			1847	Solomon W. Downs		1847
1848			1848			1848
1849		Pierre Soule	1849			1849
1850	Joseph M. Walker		1850			1850
1851			1851			1851
1852			1852			1852
1853	Paul O. Hebert	John Slidell	1853	Judah P. Benjamin	Thomas Slidell	1853
1854			1854			1854
1855			1855		Edwin T. Merrick	1855
1856	Robert C. Wickliffe		1856			1856
1857			1857			1857
1858			1858			1858
1859			1859			1859
1860	Thomas O. Moore		1860			1860
1861		*Vacant*	1861	*Vacant*		1801
1862	George F. Shepley		1862			1862
1863			1863			1863
1864	Henry W. Allen		1864			1804
1864	Michael Hahn		1864			1864
1865	James M. Wells		1865		William B. Hyman	1865
1866			1866			1866
1867	Benjamin F. Flanders		1867			1867
1868	Joshua Baker		1868			1868
1868	Henry C. Warmoth	John S. Harris	1868	William P. Kellogg	John T. Ludeling	1868
1869			1869			1869
1870			1870			1870
1871		J. Rodman West	1871			1871
1872	P.B.S. Pinchback (Acting)		1872	*Vacant*		1872
1873	William P. Kellogg		1879			1873
1874			1874			1874
1875			1875			1875

LOUISIANA–Continued

	Governors	*United States Senators*		*United States Senators*	*Chief Justices*	
1876			1876	James B. Eustis		1876
1877	Francis T. Nicholls	William P. Kellogg	1877		Thomas C. Manning	1877
1878			1878			1878
1879			1879	Benjamin F. Jonas		1879
1880	Louis A. Wiltz		1880		Edward E. Bermudez	1880
1881	Samuel D. McEnery		1881			1881
1882			1882			1882
1883		Randall L. Gibson	1883			1883
1884			1884			1884
1885			1885	James B. Eustis		1885
1886			1886			1886
1887			1887			1887
1888	Francis T. Nicholls		1888			1888
1889			1889			1889
1890			1890			1890
1891			1891	Edward D. White		1891
1892	Murphy J. Foster	Donelson Caffery	1892		Francis T. Nicholls	1892
1893			1893			1893
1894			1894	Newton C. Blanchard		1894
1895			1895			1895
1896			1896			1896
1897			1897	Samuel D. McEnery		1897
1898			1898			1898
1899			1899			1899
1900	William W. Heard		1900			1900
1901		Murphy J. Foster	1901			1901
1902			1902			1902
1903			1903			1903
1904	Newton C. Blanchard		1904		Joseph A. Breaux	1904
1905			1905			1905
1906			1906			1906
1907			1907			1907
1908	Jared Y. Sanders		1908			1908
1909			1909			1909
1910			1910	John R. Thornton		1910
1911			1911			1911
1912	Luther E. Hall		1912			1912
1913		Joseph E. Ransdell	1913			1913
1914			1914		Frank A. Monroe	1914
1915			1915	Robert F. Broussard		1915
1916	Ruffin G. Pleasant		1916			1916
1917			1917			1917
1918			1918	Walter Guion		1918
1918			1918	Edward J. Gay		1918
1919			1919			1919
1920	John M. Parker		1920			1920
1921			1921	Edwin S. Broussard		1921
1922			1922		Olivier O. Provosty	1922
1922			1922		Charles A. O'Neill	1922
1923			1923			1923
1924	Henry L. Fuqua		1924			1924
1925			1925			1925
1926	Oramel H. Simpson		1926			1926
1927			1927			1927
1928	Huey P. Long		1928			1928
1929			1929			1929
1930			1930			1930
1931		*Vacant*	1931			1931
1932	Oscar K. Allen	Huey P. Long	1932			1932
1933			1933	John H. Overton		1933
1934			1934			1934
1935		*Vacant*	1935			1935
1936	James A. Noe	Rose McConnell Long	1936			1936
1936	Richard W. Leche		1936			1936
1937		Allen J. Ellender	1937			1937
1938			1938			1938
1939	Earl K. Long		1939			1939

LOUISIANA–Continued

	Governors	*United States Senators*			*Chief Justices*	
1940	Sam Houston Jones		1940			1940
1941			1941			1941
1942			1942			1942
1943			1943			1943
1944	James H. Davis		1944			1944
1945			1945			1945
1946			1946			1946
1947			1947			1947
1948	Earl K. Long		1948	William C. Feazel		1948
1948			1948	Russell B. Long		1948
1949			1949		John B. Fournet	1949
1950			1950			1950
1951			1951			1951
1952	Robert F. Kennon		1952			1952
1953			1953			1953
1954			1954			1954
1955			1955			1955
1956	Earl K. Long		1956			1956
1957			1957			1957
1958			1958			1958
1959			1959			1959
1960	James H. Davis		1960			1960
1961			1961			1961
1962			1962			1962
1963			1963			1963
1964	John J. McKeithen		1964			1964
1965			1965			1965
1966			1966			1966
1967			1967			1967
1968			1968			1968
1969			1969			1969
1970			1970		Joe B. Hamiter	1970
1971			1971		E. Howard McCaleb	1971
1972	Edwin W. Edwards		1972			1972
1973		J. Bennett Johnston, Jr.	1973			1973

MAINE

	Governors	*United States Senators*			*Chief Justices*	
1820	William King	John Chandler	1820	John Holmes	Prentis Mellen	1820
1821	William D. Williamson		1821			1821
1822	Albion K. Parris		1822			1822
1823			1823			1823
1824			1824			1824
1825			1825			1825
1826			1826			1826
1827	Enoch Lincoln		1827	Albion K. Parris		1827
1828			1828	*Vacant*		1828
1829	Nathan Cutler	Peleg Sprague	1829	John Holmes		1829
1830	Jonathan G. Hunton		1830			1830
1831	Samuel E. Smith		1831			1831
1832			1832			1832
1833			1833	Ether Shepley		1833
1834	Robert P. Dunlap		1834		Nathan Weston	1834
1835		John Ruggles	1835			1835
1836			1836	Judah Dana		1836
1837			1837	Reuel Williams		1837
1838	Edward Kent		1838			1838
1839	John Fairfield		1839			1839
1840	Edward Kent		1840			1840
1841	John Fairfield	George Evans	1841		Ezekiel Whitman	1841
1842			1842			1842
1843	Edward Kavanagh		1843	John Fairfield		1843
1844	Hugh H. Anderson		1844			1844
1845			1845			1845
1846			1846			1846
1847	John W. Dana	James W. Bradbury	1847			1847
1848			1848	Wyman B.S. Moor	Ether Shepley	1848
1848			1848	Hannibal Hamlin		1848
1849			1849			1849
1850	John Hubbard		1850			1850
1851			1851			1851
1852			1852			1852
1853	William G. Crosby	*Vacant*	1853			1853
1854		William P. Fessenden	1854			1854
1855	Anson P. Morrill		1855		John S. Tenney	1855
1856	Samuel Wells		1856			1856
1857	Hannibal Hamlin		1857	Amos Nourse		1857
1857	Joseph H. Williams		1857	Hannibal Hamlin		1857
1858	Lot M. Morrill		1858			1858
1859			1859			1859
1860			1860			1860
1861	Israel Washburn, Jr.		1861	Lot M. Morrill		1861
1862			1862		John Appleton	1862
1863	Abner Coburn		1863			1863
1864	Samuel Cony	Nathan A. Farwell	1864			1864
1865		William P. Fessenden	1865			1865
1866			1866			1866
1867	Joshua L. Chamberlain		1867			1867
1868			1868			1868
1869		Lot M. Morrill	1869	Hannibal Hamlin		1869
1870			1870			1870
1871	Sidney Perham		1871			1871
1872			1872			1872
1873			1873			1873
1874	Nelson Dingley, Jr.		1874			1874
1875			1875			1875
1876	Seldon Connor	James G. Blaine	1876			1876
1877			1877			1877
1878			1878			1878
1879	Alonzo Garcelon		1879			1879
1880	Daniel F. Davis		1880			1880
1881	Harris M. Plaisted	William P. Frye	1881	Eugene Hale		1881
1882			1882			1882
1883	Frederick Robie		1883		John A. Peters	1883
1884			1884			1884
1885			1885			1885
1886			1886			1886
1887	Joseph R. Bodwell		1887			1887
1887	Sebastian S. Marble		1887			1887
1888			1888			1888
1889	Edwin C. Burleigh		1889			1889
1890			1890			1890
1891			1891			1891
1892			1892			1892
1893	Henry B. Cleaves		1893			1893
1894			1894			1894
1895			1895			1895
1896			1896			1896
1897	Llewellyn Powers		1897			1897
1898			1898			1898
1899			1899			1899
1900			1900		Andrew P. Wiswell	1900
1901	John F. Hill		1901			1901
1902			1902			1902
1903			1903			1903
1904			1904			1904

MAINE–Continued

Year	*Governors*	*United States Senators*	Year	*United States Senators*	*Chief Justices*	Year
1905	William T. Cobb		1905			1905
1906			1906		Lucilius A. Emery	1906
1907			1907			1907
1908			1908			1908
1909	Bert M. Fernald		1909			1909
1910			1910			1910
1911	Frederick W. Plaisted	Obadiah Gardner	1911	Charles F. Johnson	William P. Whitehouse	1911
1912			1912			1912
1913	William T. Haines	Edwin C. Burleigh	1913		Albert R. Savage	1913
1914			1914			1914
1915	Oakley C. Curtis		1915			1915
1916		Bert M. Fernald	1916			1916
1917	Carl E. Milliken		1917	Frederick Hale	Leslie C. Cornish	1917
1918			1918			1918
1919			1919			1919
1920			1920			1920
1921	Frederick H. Parkhurst		1921			1921
1921	Percival P. Baxter		1921			1921
1922			1922			1922
1923			1923			1923
1924			1924			1924
1925	Ralph O. Brewster		1925		Scott Wilson	1925
1926		Arthur R. Gould	1926			1926
1927			1927			1927
1928			1928			1928
1929	William T. Gardiner		1929		Luere B. Deasy	1929
1930			1930		William R. Pattangall	1930
1931		Wallace H. White, Jr.	1931			1931
1932			1932			1932
1933	Louis J. Brann		1933			1933
1934			1934			1934
1935			1935		Charles J. Dunn	1935
1936			1936			1936
1937	Lewis O. Barrows		1937			1937
1938			1938			1938
1939			1939		Charles P. Barnes	1939
1940			1940		Guy H. Sturgis	1940
1941	Sumner Sewall		1941	Ralph O. Brewster		1941
1942			1942			1942
1943			1943			1943
1944			1944			1944
1945	Horace A. Hildreth		1945			1945
1946			1946			1946
1947			1947			1947
1948			1948			1948
1949	Frederick G. Payne	Margaret Chase Smith	1949		Harold H. Murchie	1949
1950			1950			1950
1951			1951			1951
1952	Burton M. Cross		1952	Frederick G. Payne		1952
1953			1953		Edward F. Merrill	1953
1954			1954		Raymond Fellows	1954
1955	Edmund S. Muskie		1955			1955
1956			1956			1956
1957			1957		Robert B. Williamson	1957
1958			1958			1958
1959	Robert N. Haskell		1959	Edmund S. Muskie		1959
1959	Clinton A. Clauson		1959			1959
1960	John H. Reed		1960			1960
1961			1961			1961
1962			1962			1962
1963			1963			1963
1964			1964			1964
1965			1965			1965
1966			1966			1966
1967	Kenneth M. Curtis		1967			1967
1968			1968			1968
1969			1969			1969
1970			1970		Armand A. Dufresne, Jr.	1970
1971			1971			1971
1972			1972			1972
1973		William D. Hathaway	1973			1973

MARYLAND

	Governors	*United States Senators*			*Chief Justices*	
1789	John E. Howard	Charles Carroll	1789	John Henry	Benjamin Rumsey	1789
1790			1790			1790
1791	George Plater		1791			1791
1792	Thomas S. Lee		1792			1792
1793		Richard Potts	1793			1793
1794	John H. Stone		1794			1794
1795			1795			1795
1796		John E. Howard	1796			1796
1797	John Henry		1797	James Lloyd		1797
1798	Benjamin Ogle		1798			1798
1799			1799			1799
1800			1800	William Hindman		1800
1801	John F. Mercer		1801	Robert Wright		1801
1802			1802			1802
1803	Robert Bowie	Samuel Smith	1803			1803
1804			1804			1804
1805			1805			1805
1806	Robert Wright		1806	Philip Reed	Jeremiah T. Chase	1806
1807			1807			1807
1808			1808			1808
1809	Edward Lloyd		1809			1809
1810			1810			1810
1811	Robert Bowie		1811			1811
1812	Levin Winder		1812			1812
1813			1813	Robert H. Goldsborough		1813
1814			1814			1814
1815	Charles C. Ridgely	*Vacant*	1815			1815
1816		Robert G. Harper	1816			1816
1816		Alexander C. Hanson	1816			1816
1817			1817			1817
1818	Charles Goldsborough		1818			1818
1819	Samuel Sprigg	William Pinkney	1819	*Vacant*		1819
1819			1819	Edward Lloyd		1819
1820			1820			1820
1821			1821			1821
1822	Samuel Stevens, Jr.	Samuel Smith	1822			1822
1823			1823			1823
1824			1824			1824
1825			1825		John Buchanan	1825
1826	Joseph Kent		1826	Ezekiel F. Chambers		1826
1827			1827			1827
1828	Daniel Martin		1828			1828
1829	Thomas K. Carroll		1829			1829
1830	Daniel Martin		1830			1830
1831	George Howard		1831			1831
1832			1832			1832
1833	James Thomas	Joseph Kent	1833			1833
1834			1834			1834
1835	Thomas W. Veazey		1835	Robert H. Goldsborough		1835
1836			1836	John S. Spence		1836
1837			1837			1837
1838	William Grason	William D. Merrick	1838			1838
1839			1839			1839
1840			1840			1840
1841	Francis Thomas		1841	John L. Kerr		1841
1842			1842			1842
1843			1843	James A. Pearce		1843
1844	Thomas G. Pratt		1844		Stevenson Archer	1844
1845		Reverdy Johnson	1845			1845
1846			1846			1846
1847	Philip F. Thomas		1847			1847
1828			1848		Thomas B. Dorsey	1848
1849		David Stewart	1849			1849
1850	Enoch L. Lowe	Thomas G. Pratt	1850			1850
1851			1851		John C. Le Grand	1851
1852			1852			1852
1853			1853			1853
1854	Thomas W. Ligon		1854			1854

MARYLAND–Continued

	Governors	*United States Senators*			*Chief Justices*	
1855			1855			1855
1856			1856			1856
1857		Anthony Kennedy	1857			1857
1858	Thomas H. Hicks		1858			1858
1859			1859			1859
1860			1860			1860
1861			1861		Richard J. Bowie	1861
1862	Augustus W. Bradford		1862	Thomas H. Hicks		1862
1863		Reverdy Johnson	1863			1863
1864			1864			1864
1865	Thomas Swann		1865	John A.J. Creswell		1865
1866			1866			1866
1867			1867	*Vacant*	James L. Bartol	1867
1868		William P. Whyte	1868	George Vickers		1868
1869	Oden Bowie	William T. Hamilton	1869			1869
1870			1870			1870
1871			1871			1871
1872	William P. Whyte		1872			1872
1873			1873	George R. Dennis		1873
1874	James B. Groome		1874			1874
1875		William P. Whyte	1875			1875
1876	John L. Carroll		1876			1876
1877			1877			1877
1878			1878			1878
1879			1879	James B. Groome		1879
1880	William T. Hamilton		1880			1880
1881		Arthur P. Gorman	1881			1881
1882			1882			1882
1883			1883		Richard H. Alvey	1883
1884	Robert M. McLane		1884			1884
1885	Henry Lloyd		1885	Ephraim K. Wilson		1885
1886			1886			1886
1887			1887			1887
1888	Elihu E. Jackson		1888			1888
1889			1889			1889
1890			1890			1890
1891			1891	Charles H. Gibson		1891
1892	Frank Brown		1892			1892
1893			1893		John M. Robinson	1893
1894			1894			1894
1895			1895			1895
1896	Lloyd Lowndes		1896		James McSherry	1896
1897			1897	George L. Wellington		1897
1898			1898			1898
1899		Louis E. McComas	1899			1899
1900	John W. Smith		1900			1900
1901			1901			1901
1902			1902			1902
1903			1903	Arthur P. Gorman		1903
1904	Edwin Warfield		1904			1904
1905		Isidor Rayner	1905			1905
1906			1906	William P. Whyte		1906
1907			1907		A. Hunter Boyd	1907
1908	Austin L. Crothers		1908	John W. Smith		1908
1909			1909			1909
1910			1910			1910
1911			1911			1911
1912	Phillips L. Goldsborough	William P. Jackson	1912			1912
1913			1913			1913
1914		Blair Lee	1914			1914
1915			1915			1915
1916	Emerson C. Harrington		1916			1916
1917		Joseph I. France	1917			1917
1918			1918			1918
1919			1919			1919
1920	Albert C. Ritchie		1920			1920
1921			1921	Ovington E. Weller		1921
1922			1922			1922

MARYLAND–Continued

	Governors	*United States Senators*			*Chief Justices*	
1923		William Cabell Bruce	1923			1923
1924			1924		Carroll T. Bond	1924
1925			1925			1925
1926			1926			1926
1927			1927	Millard E. Tydings		1927
1928			1928			1928
1929		Phillips L. Goldsborough	1928			1929
1930			1930			1930
1931			1931			1931
1932			1932			1932
1933			1933			1933
1934			1934			1934
1935	Harry W. Nice	George L. Radcliffe	1935			1935
1936			1936			1936
1937			1937			1937
1938			1938			1938
1939	Herbert R. O'Conor		1939			1939
1940			1940			1940
1941			1941			1941
1942			1942			1942
1943			1943		D. Lindley Stoan	1943
1944			1944		Ogle Marbury	1944
1945			1945			1945
1946			1946			1946
1947	William P. Lane, Jr.	Herbert R. O'Conor	1947			1947
1948			1948			1948
1949			1949			1949
1950			1950			1950
1951	Theodore R. McKeldin		1951	John M. Butler		1951
1952			1952		Charles Markell	1952
1952			1952		Simon E. Sobeloff	1952
1953		J. Glenn Beall	1953			1953
1954			1954		Frederick W. Brune	1954
1955			1955			1955
1956			1956			1956
1957			1957			1957
1958			1958			1958
1959	J. Millard Tawes		1959			1959
1960			1960			1960
1961			1961			1961
1962			1962			1962
1963			1963	Daniel B. Brewster		1963
1964			1964		William L. Henderson	1964
1964			1964		Stedman Prescott	1964
1965		Joseph D. Tydings	1965			1965
1966			1966		Hall Hammond	1966
1967	Spiro T. Agnew		1967			1967
1968			1968			1968
1969	Marvin Mandel		1969	Charles M.C. Mathias		1969
1970			1970			1970
1971		J. Glenn Beall, Jr.	1971			1971
1972			1972			1972
1973			1973			1973

MASSACHUSETTS

	Governors	*United States Senators*			*Chief Justices*	
1789	John Hancock	Tristam Dalton	1789	Caleb Strong	Nathaniel P. Sargeant	1789
1790			1790			1790
1791		George Cabot	1791		Francis Dana	1791
1792			1792			1792
1793			1793			1793
1794	Samuel Adams		1794			1794
1795			1795			1795
1796		Benjamin Goodhue	1796	Theodore Sedgwick		1796
1797	Increase Sumner		1797			1797
1798			1798			1798
1799			1799	Samuel Dexter		1799
1800	Caleb Strong	Jonathan Mason	1800	Dwight Foster		1800
1801			1801			1801
1802			1802			1802
1803		John Quincy Adams	1803	Timothy Pickering		1803
1804			1804			1804
1805			1805			1805
1806			1806		Theophilus Parsons	1806
1807	James Sullivan		1807			1807
1808		James Lloyd	1808			1808
1809	Christopher Gore		1809			1809
1810	Elbridge Gerry		1810			1810
1811			1811	Joseph B. Varnum		1811
1812	Caleb Strong		1812			1812
1813		Christopher Gore	1813		Samuel Sewall	1813
1814			1814		Isaac Parker	1814
1815			1815			1815
1816	John Brooks	Eli P. Ashmun	1816			1816
1817			1817	Harrison G. Otis		1817
1818		Prentiss Mellen	1818			1818
1819			1819			1819
1820		Elijah H. Mills	1820			1820
1821			1821			1821
1822			1822	James Lloyd		1822
1823	William Eustis		1823			1823
1824			1824			1824
1825	Levi Lincoln		1825			1825
1826			1826	Nathaniel Silsbee		1826
1827		Daniel Webster	1827			1827
1828			1828			1828
1829			1829			1829
1830			1830		Lemuel Shaw	1830
1831			1831			1831
1832			1832			1832
1833			1833			1833
1834	John Davis		1834			1834
1835			1835	John Davis		1835
1836	Edward Everett		1836			1836
1837			1837			1837
1838			1838			1838
1839			1839			1839
1840	Marcus Morton		1840			1840
1841	John Davis	Rufus Choate	1841	Isaac C. Bates		1841
1842			1842			1842
1843	Marcus Morton		1843			1843
1844	George N. Briggs		1844			1844
1845		Daniel Webster	1845	John Davis		1845
1846			1846			1846
1847			1847			1847
1848			1848			1848
1849			1849			1849
1850		Robert C. Winthrop	1850			1850
1851	George S. Boutwell	Robert Rantoul, Jr.	1851			1851
1851		Charles Sumner	1851			1851
1852			1852			1852
1853	John H. Clifford		1853	Edward Everett		1853
1854	Emory Washburn		1854	Julius Rockwell		1854
1855	Henry J. Gardner		1855	Henry Wilson		1855

MASSACHUSETTS–Continued

	Governors	*United States Senators*			*Chief Justices*	
1856			1856			1856
1857			1857			1857
1858	Nathaniel P. Banks		1858			1858
1859			1859			1859
1860			1800		George T. Bigelow	1860
1861	John A. Andrew		1861			1861
1862			1862			1862
1863			1863			1863
1864			1864			1864
1865			1865			1865
1866	Alexander H. Bullock		1866			1866
1867			1867			1867
1868			1868		Reuben A. Chapman	1868
1869	William Claflin		1869			1869
1870			1870			1870
1871			1871			1871
1872	William B. Washburn		1872			1872
1873			1873	George S. Boutwell	Horace Gray	1873
1874		William B. Washburn	1874			1874
1875	William Gaston	Henry L. Dawes	1875			1875
1876	Alexander H. Rice		1876			1876
1877			1877	George F. Hoar		1877
1878			1878			1878
1879	Thomas Talbot		1879			1879
1880	John D. Long		1880			1880
1881			1881			1881
1882			1882		Marcus Morton	1882
1883	Benjamin F. Butler		1883			1889
1884	George D. Robinson		1884			1884
1885			1885			1885
1886			1886			1886
1887	Oliver Ames		1887			1887
1888			1888			1888
1889			1889			1889
1890	John Q.A. Brackett		1890		Walbridge A. Field	1890
1891	William E. Russell		1891			1891
1892			1892			1892
1893		Henry Cabot Lodge	1893			1893
1894	Frederic T. Greenhalge		1894			1894
1895			1895			1895
1896	Roger Wolcott		1896			1896
1897			1897			1897
1898			1898			1898
1899			1899		Oliver Wendell Holmes	1899
1900	Winthrop M. Crane		1900			1900
1901			1901			1901
1902			1902			1902
1903	John L. Bates		1903		Marcus P. Knowlton	1903
1904			1904	Winthrop M. Crane		1904
1905	William L. Douglas		1905			1905
1906	Curtis Guild, Jr.		1906			1906
1907			1907			1907
1908			1908			1908
1909	Eben S. Draper		1909			1909
1910			1910			1910
1911	Eugene N. Foss		1911		Arthur P. Rugg	1911
1912			1912			1912
1913			1913	John W. Weeks		1913
1914	David I. Walsh		1914			1914
1915			1915			1915
1916	Samuel W. McCall		1916			1916
1917			1917			1917
1918			1918			1918
1919	Calvin Coolidge		1919	David I. Walsh		1919
1920			1920			1920
1921	Channing H. Cox		1921			1921
1922			1922			1922
1923			1923			1923

MASSACHUSETTS–Continued

	Governors	*United States Senators*			*Chief Justices*	
1924		William M. Butler	1924			1924
1925	Alvan T. Fuller		1925	Frederick H. Gillett		1925
1926		David I. Walsh	1926			1926
1927			1927			1927
1928			1928			1928
1929	Frank G. Allen		1929			1929
1930			1930			1930
1931	Joseph B. Ely		1931	Marcus A. Coolidge		1931
1932			1932			1932
1933			1933			1933
1934			1934			1934
1935	James M. Curley		1935			1935
1936			1936			1936
1937	Charles F. Hurley		1937	Henry Cabot Lodge, Jr.		1937
1938			1938		Fred T. Field	1938
1939	Leverett Saltonstall		1939			1939
1940			1940			1940
1941			1941			1941
1942			1942			1942
1943			1943			1943
1944			1944	Sinclair Weeks		1944
1945	Maurice J. Tobin		1945	Leverett Saltonstall		1945
1946			1946			1946
1947	Robert F. Bradford	Henry Cabot Lodge, Jr.	1947		Stanley E. Qua	1947
1948			1948			1948
1949	Paul A. Dever		1949			1949
1950			1950			1950
1951			1951			1951
1952			1952			1952
1953	Christian A. Herter	John F. Kennedy	1953			1953
1954			1954			1954
1955			1955			1955
1956			1956		Raymond S. Wilkins	1956
1957	Foster Furcolo		1957			1957
1958			1958			1958
1959			1959			1959
1960			1960			1960
1961	John A. Volpe	Benjamin A. Smith	1961			1961
1962			1962			1962
1963	Endicott Peabody	Edward M. Kennedy	1963			1963
1964			1964			1964
1965	John A. Volpe		1965			1965
1966			1966			1966
1967			1967	Edward W. Brooke		1967
1968			1968			1968
1969			1969			1969
1970	Francis W. Sargent		1970		G. Joseph Tauro	1970
1971			1971			1971
1972			1972			1972
1973			1973			1973

MICHIGAN

	Governors	*United States Senators*			*Chief Justices*	
1837	Stevens T. Mason	Lucius Lyon	1837	John Norvell		1837
1838			1838			1838
1839		*Vacant*	1839			1839
1840	William Woodbridge	Augustus S. Porter	1840			1840
1841	James W. Gordon		1841	William Woodbridge		1841
1842	John S. Barry		1842			1822
1843			1843			1843
1844			1844			1844
1845		Lewis Cass	1845			1845
1846	Alpheus Felch		1846			1846
1847	William L. Greenly		1847	Alpheus Felch		1847
1848	Epaphroditus Ransom	Thomas Fitzgerald	1848			1848
1849		Lewis Cass	1849			1849
1850	John S. Barry		1850			1850
1851			1851			1851
1852	Robert McClelland		1852			1852
1853	Andrew Parsons		1853	Charles E. Stuart		1853
1854			1854			1854
1855	Kinsley S. Bingham		1855			1855
1856			1856			1856
1857		Zachariah Chandler	1857			1857
1858			1858			1858
1859	Moses Wisner		1859	Kinsley S. Bingham	*Justices of the Supreme Court serve on a rotating basis as Chief Presiding Judge*	1859
1860			1860			1860
1861	Austin Blair		1861			1861
1862			1862	Jacob M. Howard		1862
1863			1863			1863
1864			1864			1864
1865	Henry H. Crapo		1865			1865
1866			1866			1866
1867			1867			1867
1868			1808			1868
1869	Henry P. Baldwin		1869			1869
1870			1870			1870
1871			1871	Thomas W. Ferry		1871
1872			1872			1872
1873	John J. Bagley		1873			1873
1874			1874			1874
1875		Isaac P. Chrstiancy	1875			1875
1876			1876			1876
1877	Charles M. Croswell		1877			1877
1878			1878			1878
1879		Zachariah Chandler	1879			1879
1879		Henry P. Baldwin	1879			1879
1880			1880			1880
1881	David H. Jerome	Omar D. Conger	1881			1881
1882			1882			1882
1883	Josiah W. Begole		1883	Thomas W. Palmer		1883
1884			1884			1884
1885	Russell A. Alger		1885			1885
1886			1886			1886
1887	Cyrus G. Luce	Francis B. Stockbridge	1887			1887
1888			1888			1888
1889			1889	James McMillan		1889
1890			1890			1890
1891	Edwin B. Winans		1891			1891
1892			1892			1892
1893	John T. Rich		1893			1893
1894		John Patton, Jr.	1894			1894
1895		Julius C. Burrows	1895			1895
1896			1896			1896
1897	Hazen S. Pingree		1897			1897
1898			1898			1898
1899			1899			1899
1900			1900			1900
1901	Aaron T. Bliss		1901			1901
1902			1902	Russell A. Alger		1902
1903			1903			1903
1904			1904			1904
1905	Frederick M. Warner		1905			1905
1906			1906			1906
1907			1907	William S. Smith		1907
1908			1908			1908
1909			1909			1909
1910			1910			1910
1911	Chase S. Osborn	Charles E. Townsend	1911			1911
1912			1912			1912
1913	Woodbridge N. Ferris		1913			1913
1914			1914			1914
1915			1915			1915
1916			1916			1916
1917	Albert E. Sleeper		1917			1917
1918			1918			1918
1919			1919	Truman H. Newberry		1919
1920			1920			1920
1921	Alexander J. Groesbeck		1921			1921
1922		James Couzens	1922			1922

MICHIGAN–Continued

	Governors	*United States Senators*			*Chief Justices*	
1923		Woodbridge N. Ferris	1923			1923
1924			1924			1924
1925			1925			1925
1926			1926			1926
1927	Fred W. Green		1927			1927
1928		Arthur H. Vandenberg	1928			1928
1929			1929			1929
1930			1930			1930
1931	Wilber M. Brucker		1931			1931
1932			1932			1932
1933	William A. Comstock		1933			1933
1934			1934			1934
1935	Frank D. Fitzgerald		1935			1935
1936			1936	Prentis M. Brown		1936
1937	Frank D. Murphy		1937			1937
1938			1938			1938
1939	Frank D. Fitzgerald		1939			1939
1939	Lauren D. Dickinson		1939			1939
1940			1940			1940
1941	Murray D. Van Wagoner		1941			1941
1942			1942			1942
1943	Harry F. Kelly		1943	Homer Ferguson		1943
1944			1944			1944
1945			1945			1945
1946			1946			1946
1947	Kim Sigler		1947			1947
1948			1948			1948
1949	G. Mennen Williams		1949			1949
1950			1950			1950
1951		Arthur E.B. Moody	1951			1951
1952		Charles E. Potter	1952			1952
1953			1953			1953
1954			1954			1954
1955			1955	Patrick V. McNamara		1955
1950			1956			1956
1957			1957			1957
1958			1958			1958
1959		Philip A. Hart	1959			1959
1960			1960			1960
1961	John B. Swainson		1961			1961
1962			1962			1962
1963	George Romney		1963			1963
1964			1964			1964
1965			1965			1965
1966			1966			1966
1967			1967	Robert P. Griffin		1967
1968			1968			1968
1969	William G. Milliken		1969			1969
1970			1970			1970
1971			1971			1971
1972			1972			1972
1973			1973			1973

MINNESOTA

	Governors	*United States Senators*			*Chief Justices*	
1858	Henry J. Sibley	Henry M. Rice	1858	James Shields	Lafayette Emmett	1858
1859			1859	Morton S. Wilkinson		1859
1860	Alexander Ramsey		1860			1860
1861			1861			1861
1862			1862			1862
1863	H. A. Swift	Alexander Ramsey	1863			1863
1864	Stephen Miller		1864			1864
1865			1865	Daniel S. Norton	Thomas Wilson	1865
1866	William R. Marshall		1866			1866
1867			1867			1867
1868			1868			1868
1869			1869		James Gilfillan	1869
1870	Horace Austin		1870	William Windom	Christopher G. Ripley	1870
1871			1871	Ozora P. Stearns		1871
1871			1871	William Windom		1871
1872			1872			1872
1873			1873			1873
1874	Cushman K. Davis		1874		Samuel J.R. McMillan	1874
1875		Samuel J.R. McMillan	1875		James Gilfillan	1875
1876	John S. Pillsbury		1876			1876
1877			1877			1877
1878			1878			1878
1879			1879			1879
1880			1880			1880
1881			1881	Alonzo J. Edgerton		1881
1881			1881	William Windom		1881
1882	Lucius F. Hubbard		1882			1882
1883			1883	Dwight M. Sabin		1883
1884			1884			1884
1885			1885			1885
1886			1886			1886
1887	Andrew R. McGill	Cushman K. Davis	1887			1887
1888			1888			1888
1889	William R. Merriam		1889	William D. Washburn		1889
1890			1890			1890
1891			1891			1891
1892			1892			1892
1893	Knute Nelson		1893			1893
1894			1894			1894
1895	David M. Clough		1895	Knute Nelson	Charles N. Start	1895
1896			1896			1896
1897			1897			1897
1898			1898			1898
1899	John Lind		1899			1899
1900		Charles A. Towne	1900			1900
1901	Samuel R. Van Sant	Moses E. Clapp	1901			1901
1902			1902			1902
1903			1903			1903
1904			1904			1904
1905	John A. Johnson		1905			1905
1906			1906			1906
1907			1907			1907
1908			1908			1908
1909	Adolph O. Eberhart		1909			1909
1910			1910			1910
1911			1911			1911
1912			1912			1912
1913			1912		Calvin L. Brown	1913
1914			1914			1914
1915	Winfield S. Hammond		1915			1915
1915	Joseph A.A. Burnquist		1915			1915
1916			1916			1916
1917		Frank B. Kellogg	1917			1917
1918			1918			1918
1919			1919			1919
1920			1920			1920
1921	Jacob A.O. Preus		1921			1921
1922			1922			1922

MINNESOTA–Continued

	Governors	*United States Senators*			*Chief Justices*	
1923		Henrik Shipstead	1923	Magnus Johnson	Samuel B. Wilson	1923
1924			1924			1924
1925	Theodore Christianson		1925	Thomas D. Schall		1925
1926			1926			1926
1927			1927			1927
1928			1928			1928
1929			1929			1929
1930			1930			1930
1931	Floyd B. Olson		1931			1931
1932			1932			1932
1933			1933		John P. Devaney	1933
1934			1934			1934
1935			1935	Elmer A. Benson		1935
1936	Hjalmar Peterson		1936	Guy V. Howard		1936
1937	Elmer A. Benson		1937	Ernest Lundeen	Henry M. Gallagher	1937
1938			1938			1938
1939	Harold E. Stassen		1939			1939
1940			1940	Joseph H. Ball		1940
1941			1941			1941
1942			1942	Arthur E. Nelson		1942
1943	Edward J. Thye		1943	Joseph H. Ball		1943
1944			1944		Charles Loring	1944
1945			1945			1945
1946			1946			1946
1947	Luther W. Youngdahl	Edward J. Thye	1947			1947
1948			1948			1948
1949			1949	Hubert H. Humphrey		1949
1950			1950			1950
1951	C. Elmer Anderson		1951			1951
1952			1952			1952
1953			1953		Roger L. Dell	1953
1954			1954			1954
1955	Orville L. Freeman		1955			1955
1956			1956			1956
1957			1957			1957
1958			1958			1958
1959		Eugene J. McCarthy	1959			1959
1960			1960			1960
1961	Elmer L. Andersen		1961			1961
1962			1962		Oscar R. Knutson	1962
1963	Karl F. Rolvaag		1963			1963
1964			1964			1964
1965			1965	Walter F. Mondale		1965
1966			1966			1966
1967	Harold LeVander		1967			1967
1968			1968			1968
1969			1969			1969
1970			1970			1970
1971	Wendell R. Anderson	Hubert H. Humphrey	1971			1971
1972			1972			1972
1973			1973			1973

MISSISSIPPI

Year	*Governors*	*United States Senators*	Year	*United States Senators*	*Chief Justices*	Year
1817	David Holmes	Walter Leake	1817	Thomas H. Williams		1817
1818			1818			1818
1819			1819			1819
1820	George Poindexter	David Holmes	1820			1820
1821			1821			1821
1822	Walter Leake		1822			1822
1823			1823			1823
1824			1824			1824
1825	Gerard Brandon (Acting)	Powhatan Ellis	1825			1825
1826	David Holmes	Thomas B. Reed	1826			1826
1827	Gerard C. Brandon	Powhatan Ellis	1827			1827
1828			1828			1828
1829			1829	Thomas B. Reed		1829
1830			1830	Robert H. Adams		1830
1830			1830	George Poindexter		1830
1831			1831			1831
1832	Abram M. Scott	John Black	1832			1832
1833	Hiram G. Runnels		1833		William L. Sharkey	1833
1834			1834			1834
1835	John A. Quitman (Acting)		1835	Robert J. Walker		1835
1836	Charles Lynch		1836			1836
1837			1837			1837
1838	Alexander G. McNutt	James F. Trotter	1838			1838
1838		Thomas H. Williams	1838			1838
1839		John Henderson	1839			1839
1840			1840			1840
1841			1841			1841
1842	Tilghman M. Tucker		1842			1842
1843			1843			1843
1844	Albert G. Brown		1844			1844
1845		Jesse Speight	1845	Joseph W. Chalmers		1845
1846			1846			1846
1847		Jefferson Davis	1847	Henry S. Foote		1847
1848	Joseph W. Matthews		1848			1848
1849			1849			1849
1850	John A. Quitman		1850			1850
1851	John I. Guion	John J. McRae	1851		Cotesworth P. Smith	1851
1851	James Whitfield		1851			1851
1852	Henry S. Foote	Stephen Adams	1852	Walker Brooke		1852
1853			1853	*Vacant*		1853
1854	John J. Pettus		1854	Albert G. Brown		1854
1854	John J. McRae		1854			1854
1855			1855			1855
1856			1856			1856
1857	William McWillie	Jefferson Davis	1857			1857
1858			1858			1858
1859	John J. Pettus		1859			1859
1860			1860			1860
1861		*Vacant*	1861	*Vacant*		1861
1862			1862			1862
1863	Charles Clark		1863			1863
1864			1864		Alexander H. Handy	1864
1865	Benjamin G. Humphreys	*Vacant*	1865	*Vacant*		1865
1866			1866			1866
1867			1867			1867
1868	Adelbert Ames		1868		Thomas G. Shackleford	1868
1869			1869			1869
1870	James L. Alcorn	Hiram R. Revels	1870	Adelbert Ames	Ephraim G. Peyton	1870
1871	Ridgley C. Powers (Acting)	James L. Alcorn	1871			1871
1872			1872			1872
1873			1873			1873
1874	Adelbert Ames		1874	Henry R. Pease		1874
1875			1875	Blanche K. Bruce		1875
1876	John M. Stone (Acting)		1876		Horatio F. Simrall	1876
1877		Lucius Q.C. Lamar	1877			1877
1878			1878		James Z. George	1878

MISSISSIPPI–Continued

	Governors	*United States Senators*			*Chief Justices*	
1879			1879			1879
1880			1880		Josiah A.P. Campbell	1880
1881			1881	James Z. George		1881
1882	Robert Lowry		1882			1882
1883			1883			1883
1884			1884			1884
1885		Edward C. Walthall	1885			1885
1886			1886			1886
1887			1887			1887
1888			1888			1888
1889			1889			1889
1890	John M. Stone		1890			1890
1891			1891			1891
1892			1892			1892
1893			1893			1893
1894		Anselm J. McLaurin	1894		Tim E. Cooper	1894
1895		Edward C. Walthall	1895			1895
1896	Anselm J. McLaurin		1896		Thomas H. Woods	1896
1897			1897	Hernando D. Money		1897
1898		William V. Sullivan	1898			1898
1899			1899			1899
1900	Andrew H. Longino		1900		Albert H. Whitfield	1900
1901		Anselm J. McLaurin	1901			1901
1902			1902			1902
1903			1903			1903
1904	James K. Vardaman		1904			1904
1905			1905			1905
1906			1906			1906
1907			1907			1907
1908	Edmund F. Noel		1908			1908
1909		James Gordon	1909			1909
1910		Le Roy Percy	1910		Robert B. Mayes	1910
1911			1911	John S. Williams		1911
1912	Earl L. Brewer		1912		Sydney Smith	1912
1913		James K. Vardaman	1913			1913
1914			1914			1914
1915			1915			1915
1916	Theodore G. Bilbo		1916			1916
1917			1917			1917
1918			1918			1918
1919		Byron P. Harrison	1919			1919
1920	Lee M. Russell		1920			1920
1921			1921			1921
1922			1922			1922
1923			1923	Hubert D. Stephens		1923
1924	Henry L. Whitfield		1924			1924
1925			1925			1925
1926			1926			1926
1927	Dennis Murphree		1927			1927
1928	Theodore G. Bilbo		1928			1928
1929			1929			1929
1930			1930			1930
1931			1931			1931
1932	Martin S. Conner		1932			1932
1933			1933			1933
1934			1934			1934
1935			1935	Theodore G. Bilbo		1935
1936	Hugh White		1936			1936
1937			1937			1937
1938			1938			1938
1939			1939			1939
1940	Paul B. Johnson		1940			1940
1941		James O. Eastland	1941			1941

MISSISSIPPI–Continued

	Governors	*United States Senators*			*Chief Justices*	
1941		Wall Doxey	1941			1941
1942			1942			1942
1943	Dennis Murphree	James O. Eastland	1943			1943
1944	Thomas L. Bailey		1944			1944
1945			1945			1945
1946	Fielding L. Wright		1946			1946
1947			1947	John C. Stennis		1947
1948			1948		Virgil Griffith	1948
1949			1949		Harvey McGehee	1949
1950			1950			1950
1951			1951			1951
1952	Hugh L. White		1952			1952
1953			1953			1953
1954			1954			1954
1955			1955			1955
1956	James P. Coleman		1956			1956
1957			1957			1957
1958			1958			1958
1959			1959			1959
1960	Ross R. Barnett		1960			1960
1961			1961			1961
1962			1962			1962
1963			1963			1963
1964	Paul B. Johnson		1964		Percy M. Lee	1964
1965			1965			1965
1966			1966		William N. Ethridge, Jr.	1966
1967			1967			1967
1968	John Bell Williams		1968			1968
1969			1969			1969
1970			1970			1970
1971			1971			1971
1972	William L. Waller		1972			1972
1973			1973			1973

MISSOURI

	Governors	*United States Senators*			*Chief Justices*	
1821	Alexander McNair	David Barton	1821	Thomas H. Benton	Matthias McGirk	1821
1822			1822			1822
1823			1823			1823
1824	Frederick Bates		1824			1824
1825			1825			1825
1826	John Miller		1826			1826
1827			1827			1827
1828			1828			1828
1829			1829			1829
1830			1830			1830
1831		Alexander Buckner	1831			1831
1832	Daniel Dunklin		1832			1832
1833		Lewis F. Linn	1833			1833
1834			1834			1834
1835			1835			1835
1836	Lilburn W. Boggs		1836			1836
1837			1837			1837
1838			1838			1838
1839			1839			1839
1840	Thomas Reynolds		1840		George Tompkins	1840
1841			1841			1841
1842			1842			1842
1843		David R. Atchison	1843			1843
1844	John C. Edwards		1844			1844
1845			1845		William B. Napton	1845
1846			1846			1846
1847			1847			1847
1848	Austin A. King		1848			1848
1849			1849			1849
1850			1850			1850
1851			1851	Henry S. Geyer	Hamilton R. Gamble	1851
1852			1852			1852
1853	Sterling Price		1853			1853
1854			1854		William Scott	1854
1855		*Vacant*	1855			1855
1856			1856			1856
1857	Trusten Polk	James S. Green	1857	Trusten Polk		1857
1857	Hancock Jackson		1857			1857
1857	Robert M. Stewart		1857			1857
1858			1858			1858
1859			1859			1859
1860			1860			1860
1861	Claiborne F. Jackson	Waldo P. Johnson	1861			1861
1861	Hamilton R. Gamble		1861			1861
1862		Robert Wilson	1862	John B. Henderson	Barton Bates	1862
1863		B. Gratz Brown	1863			1863
1864	Willard P. Hall (Acting)		1864			1864
1865	Thomas C. Fletcher		1865		David Wagner	1865
1866			1866			1866
1867		Charles D. Drake	1867			1867
1868			1868			1868
1869	Joseph W. McClurg		1869	Carl Schurz		1869
1870		Daniel T. Jewett	1870			1870
1871	B. Gratz Brown	Francis P. Blair, Jr.	1871			1871
1872			1872			1872
1873	Silas Woodson	Lewis V. Bogy	1873			1873
1874			1874			1874
1875	Charles H. Hardin		1875	Francis M. Cockrell		1875
1876			1876		Thomas A. Sherwood	1876
1877	John S. Phelps	David H. Armstrong	1877			1877
1878			1878			1878
1879		James Shields	1879			1879
1879		George G. Vest	1879			1879
1880			1880			1880
1881	Thomas T. Crittenden		1881			1881
1882			1882			1882
1883			1883		Warwick Hough	1883
1884			1884			1884
1885	John S. Marmaduke		1885		John W. Henry	1885
1886			1886			1886
1887	Allen P. Morehouse		1887		Elijah H. Norton	1887
1888			1888			1888
1889	David R. Francis		1889		Robert D. Ray	1889
1890			1890			1890
1891			1891		Thomas A. Sherwood	1891
1892			1892			1892
1893	William J. Stone		1893		Francis M. Black	1893
1894			1894			1894
1895			1895			1895
1896			1896			1896
1897	Lon V. Stephens		1897		Shepard Barclay	1897
1898			1898		James B. Gantt	1898
1899			1899			1899
1900			1900			1900
1901	Alexander M. Dockery		1901		Gavon D. Burgess	1901
1902			1902			1902
1903		William J. Stone	1903		Waltour M. Robinson	1903
1904			1904			1904
1905	Joseph W. Folk		1905	William Warner	Theodore Brace	1905
1906			1906			1906

MISSOURI–Continued

	Governors	*United States Senators*			*Chief Justices*	
1907			1907		James B. Gantt	1907
1908			1908			1908
1909	Herbert S. Hadley		1909		Leroy B. Valliant	1909
1910			1910			1910
1911			1911	James A. Reed		1911
1912			1912			1912
1913	Elliott W. Major		1913		Henry Lamm	1913
1914			1914			1914
1915			1915		Archelaus M. Woodson	1915
1916			1916		Waller W. Graves	1916
1917	Frederick D. Gardner		1917			1917
1918		Xenophon P. Wilfley	1918		Henry W. Bond	1918
1918		Seldon P. Spencer	1918			1918
1919			1919		Robert F. Walker	1919
1920			1920			1920
1921	Arthur M. Hyde		1921			1921
1922			1922		James T. Blair	1922
1922			1922		Archelaus M. Woodson	1922
1923			1923		*Hereafter justices of*	1923
1924			1924		*the Supreme Court*	1924
1925	Sam A. Baker	George H. Williams	1925		*serve on a rotating*	1925
1926		Harry B. Hawes	1926		*basis as Chief*	1926
1927			1927		*Presiding Judge*	1927
1928			1928			1928
1929	Henry S. Caulfield		1929	Roscoe C. Patterson		1929
1930			1930			1930
1931			1931			1931
1932			1932			1932
1933	Guy B. Park	Bennett Champ Clark	1933			1933
1934			1934			1934
1935			1935	Harry S Truman		1935
1936			1936			1936
1937	Lloyd Crow Stark		1937			1937
1938			1938			1938
1939			1939			1939
1940			1940			1940
1941	Forrest C. Donnell		1941			1941
1942			1942			1942
1943			1943			1943
1944			1944			1944
1945	Phil M. Donnelly	Forest C. Donnell	1945	Frank P. Briggs		1945
1946			1946			1946
1947			1947	James P. Kem		1947
1948			1948			1948
1949	Forrest Smith		1949			1949
1950			1950			1950
1951		Thomas C. Hennings, Jr.	1951			1951
1952			1952			1952
1953	Phil M. Donnelly		1953	W. Stuart Symington		1953
1954			1954			1954
1955			1955			1955
1956			1956			1956
1957	James T. Blair, Jr.		1957			1957
1958			1958			1958
1959			1959			1959
1960		Edward V. Long	1960			1960
1961	John M. Dalton		1961			1961
1962			1962			1962
1963			1963			1963
1964			1964			1964
1965	Warren E. Hearnes		1965			1965
1966			1966			1966
1967			1967			1967
1968			1968			1968
1969		Thomas F. Eagleton	1969			1969
1970			1970			1970
1971			1971			1971
1972			1972			1972
1973	Christopher S. Bond		1973			1973

MONTANA

	Governors	*United States Senators*			*Chief Justices*	
1889	Joseph K. Toole		1889		Henry N. Blake	1889
1890		Thomas C. Power	1890	Wilbur F. Sanders		1890
1891			1891			1891
1892			1892			1892
1893	John E. Rickards		1893	*Vacant*	William Y. Pemberton	1893
1894			1894			1894
1895		Thomas H. Carter	1895	Lee Mantle		1895
1896			1896			1896
1897	Robert B. Smith		1897			1897
1898			1898		Theodore Brantly	1898
1899			1899	William A. Clark		1899
1900			1900	*Vacant*		1900
1901	Joseph K. Toole	william A. Clark	1901	Paris Gibson		1901
1902			1902			1902
1903			1903			1903
1904			1904			1904
1905			1905	Thomas H. Carter		1905
1906			1906			1906
1907		Joseph M. Dixon	1907			1907
1908	Edwin L. Norris		1908			1908
1909			1909			1909
1910			1910			1910
1911			1911	Henry L. Myers		1911
1912			1912			1912
1913	Samuel V. Stewart	Thomas J. Walsh	1913			1913
1914			1914			1914
1915			1915			1915
1916			1916			1916
1917			1917			1917
1918			1918			1918
1919			1919			1919
1920			1920			1920
1921	Joseph M. Dixon		1921			1921
1922			1922		Llewllyn L. Callaway	1922
1923			1923	Burton K. Wheeler		1923
1924			1924			1924
1925	John E. Erickson		1925			1925
1926			1926			1926
1927			1927			1927
1928			1928			1928
1929			1929			1929
1930			1930			1930
1931			1931			1931
1932			1932			1932
1933	Frank H. Cooney	John E. Erickson	1933			1933
1934		James E. Murray	1934			1934
1935	Elmer Holt		1935		W.B. Sands	1935
1936			1936			1936
1937	Roy E. Ayers		1937			1937
1938			1938		O.F. Goddard	1938
1939			1939		Howard A. Johnson	1939
1940			1940			1940
1941	Sam C. Ford		1941			1941
1942			1942			1942
1943			1943			1943
1944			1944			1944
1945			1945			1945
1946			1946		Carl Lindquist	1946
1947			1947	Zales N. Ecton	Hugh Adair	1947
1948			1948			1948
1949	John W. Bonner		1949			1949
1950			1950			1950
1951			1951			1951
1952			1952			1952
1953	J. Hugo Aronson		1953	Mike Mansfield		1953
1954			1954			1954

MONTANA–Continued

	Governors	*United States Senators*			*Chief Justices*	
1955				1955		1955
1956				1956		1956
1957				1957	James T. Harrison	1957
1958				1958		1958
1959				1959		1959
1960				1960		1960
1961	Donald G. Nutter	Lee Metcalf		1961		1961
1962	Tim Babcock			1962		1962
1963				1963		1963
1964				1964		1964
1965				1965		1965
1966				1966		1966
1967				1967		1967
1968				1968		1968
1969	Forrest H. Anderson			1969		1969
1970				1970		1970
1971				1971		1971
1972				1972		1972
1973	Thomas L. Judge			1973		1973

NEBRASKA

	Governors	*United States Senators*			*Chief Justices*	
1867	David Butler	John M. Thayer	1867	Thomas W. Tipton	Oliver P. Mason	1867
1868			1868			1868
1869			1869			1869
1870			1870			1870
1871	William H. James	Phineas W. Hitchcock	1871			1871
1872			1872			1872
1873	Robert W. Furnas		1873		George B. Lake	1873
1874			1874			1874
1875	Silas Garber		1875	Algernon S. Paddock		1875
1876			1876			1876
1877		Alvin Saunders	1877			1877
1878			1878		Daniel Gantt	1878
1878			1878		Samuel Maxwell	1878
1879	Albinus Nance		1879			1879
1880			1880			1880
1881			1881	Charles H. Van Wyck		1881
1882			1882		George B. Lake	1882
1883	James W. Dawes	Charles F. Manderson	1883			1883
1884			1884		Amasa Cobb	1884
1885			1885			1885
1886			1886		Samuel Maxwell	1886
1887	John M. Thayer		1887	Algernon S. Paddock		1887
1888			1888		Manoah B. Reese	1888
1889			1889			1889
1890			1890		Amasa Cobb	1890
1891	James E. Boyd		1891			1891
1891	John M. Thayer		1891			1891
1892	James E. Boyd		1892		Samuel Maxwell	1892
1893	Lorenzo Crounse		1893	William V. Allen		1893
1894			1894		Theophilus L. Norval	1894
1895	Silas A. Holcomb	John M. Thurston	1895			1895
1896			1896		A.M. Post	1896
1897			1897			1897
1898			1898		T.O.C. Harrison	1898
1899	William A. Poynter		1899	Monroe L. Hayward		1899
1899			1899	William V. Allen		1899
1900			1900		Theophilus L. Norval	1900
1901	Charles H. Dietrich	Joseph H. Millard	1901	Charles H. Dietrich		1901
1901	Ezra P. Savage		1901			1901
1902			1902		John L. Sullivan	1902
1903	John H. Mickey		1903			1903
1904			1904		Silas A. Holcomb	1904
1905			1905	Elmer J. Burkett		1905
1906			1906		Samuel H. Sedgwick	1906
1907	George L. Sheldon	Norris Brown	1907			1907
1908			1908		John B. Barnes	1908
1908			1908		Manoah B. Reese	1908
1909	Ashton C. Shallenberger		1909			1909
1910			1910			1910
1911	Chester H. Aldrich		1911	Gilbert M. Hitchcock		1911
1912			1912			1912
1913	John H. Morehead	George W. Norris	1913			1913
1914			1914			1914
1915			1915		Conrad Hollenbeck	1915
1915			1915		Jacob Fawcett	1915
1915			1915		Andrew M. Morrissey	1915
1916			1916			1916
1917	Keith Neville		1917			1917
1918			1918			1918
1919	Samuel R. McKelvie		1919			1919
1920			1920			1920
1921			1921			1921
1922			1922			1922
1923	Charles W. Bryan		1923	Robert B. Howell		1923
1924			1924			1924
1925	Adam McMullen		1925			1925
1926			1926			1926
1927			1927		Charles A. Goss	1927
1928			1928			1928

NEBRASKA—Continued

	Governors	*United States Senators*			*Chief Justices*	
1929	Arthur J. Weaver		1929			1929
1930			1930			1930
1931	Charles W. Bryan		1931			1931
1932			1932			1932
1933			1933	William H. Thompson		1933
1934			1934	Richard C. Hunter		1934
1935	Robert L. Cochran		1935	Edward R. Burke		1935
1936			1936			1936
1937			1937			1937
1938			1938			1938
1939			1939		Robert G. Simmons	1939
1940			1940			1940
1941	Dwight Griswold		1941	Hugh A. Butler		1941
1942			1942			1942
1943		Kenneth S. Wherry	1943			1943
1944			1944			1944
1945			1945			1945
1946			1946			1946
1947	Val Peterson		1947			1947
1948			1948			1948
1949			1949			1949
1950			1950			1950
1951		Frederick A. Seaton	1951			1951
1952		Dwight P. Griswold	1952			1952
1953	Robert B. Crosby		1953			1953
1954		Eva K. Bowring	1954	Sam W. Reynolds		1954
1954		Hazel H. Abel	1954	Roman L. Hruska		1954
1955	Victor E. Anderson	Carl T. Curtis	1955			1955
1956			1956			1956
1957			1957			1957
1958			1958			1958
1959	Ralph G. Brooks		1959			1959
1960	Dwight W. Burney		1960			1960
1961	Frank B. Morrison		1961			1961
1962			1962			1962
1963			1963		Paul W. White	1963
1964			1964			1964
1965			1965			1965
1966			1966			1966
1967	Norbert T. Tiemann		1967			1967
1968			1968			1968
1969			1969			1969
1970			1970			1970
1971	J. James Exon		1971			1971
1972			1972			1972
1973			1973			1973

NEVADA

	Governors	*United States Senators*			*Chief Justices*	
1864	Henry G. Blasdel	William M. Stewart	1864	James W. Nye		1864
1865			1865			1865
1866			1866			1866
1867			1867			1867
1868			1868			1868
1869			1869			1869
1870			1870			1870
1871	Lewis R. Bradley		1871			1871
1872			1872			1872
1873			1873	John P. Jones		1873
1874			1874			1874
1875		William Sharon	1875			1875
1876			1876			1876
1877			1877			1877
1878			1878			1878
1879	John H. Kinkead		1879			1879
1880			1880			1880
1881		James G. Fair	1881			1881
1882			1882			1882
1883	Jewett W. Adams		1883			1883
1884			1884		*Justices of the Supreme Court serve on a rotating basis as Chief Presiding Judge*	1884
1885			1885			1885
1886			1886			1886
1887	Charles C. Stevenson	William M. Stewart	1887			1887
1888			1888			1888
1889			1889			1889
1890	Frank Bell		1890			1890
1891	Roswell K. Colcord		1891			1891
1892			1892			1892
1893			1893			1893
1894			1894			1894
1895	John S. Jones		1895			1895
1896	Reinhold Sadler		1896			1896
1897			1897			1897
1898			1898			1898
1899			1899			1899
1900			1900			1900
1901			1901			1901
1902			1902			1902
1903	John Sparks		1903	Francis G. Newlands		1903
1904			1904			1904
1905		George S. Nixon	1905			1905
1906			1906			1906
1907			1907			1907
1908	Denver S. Dickerson		1908			1908
1909			1909			1909
1910			1910			1910
1911	Tasker L. Oddie		1911			1911
1912		William A. Massey	1912			1912
1913		Key Pittman	1913			1913
1914			1914			1914
1915	Emmet D. Boyle		1915			1915
1916			1916			1916
1917			1917			1917
1918			1918	Charles B. Henderson		1918
1919			1919			1919
1920			1920			1920
1921			1921	Tasker L. Oddie		1921
1922			1922			1922
1923	James G. Scrugham		1923			1923
1924			1924			1924
1925			1925			1925
1926			1926			1926
1927	Frederick B. Balzar		1927			1927
1928			1928			1928
1929			1929			1929
1930			1930			1930
1931			1931			1931

NEVADA–Continued

	Governors		*United States Senators*			*Chief Justices*	
1932				1932			1932
1933				1933	Patrick A. McCarran		1933
1934	Morley Griswold			1934			1934
1935	Richard Kirman			1935			1935
1936				1936			1936
1937				1937			1937
1938				1938			1938
1939	Edward P. Carville			1939			1939
1940			Berkeley L. Bunker	1940			1940
1941				1941			1941
1942			James G. Scrugham	1942			1942
1943				1943			1943
1944				1944			1944
1945			Edward P. Carville	1945			1945
1946	Vail M. Pittman			1946			1946
1947			George W. Malone	1947			1947
1948				1948			1948
1949				1949			1949
1950				1950			1950
1951	Charles H. Russell			1951			1951
1952				1952			1952
1953				1953			1953
1954				1954	Ernest Brown		1954
1954				1954	Alan H. Bible		1954
1955				1955			1955
1956				1956			1956
1957				1957			1957
1958				1958			1958
1959	Grant Sawyer		Howard W. Cannon	1959			1959
1960				1960			1960
1961				1961			1961
1962				1962			1962
1963				1963			1963
1964				1964			1964
1965				1965			1965
1966				1966			1966
1967	Paul Laxalt			1967			1967
1968				1968			1968
1969				1969			1969
1970				1970			1970
1971	Mike O'Callaghan			1971			1971
1972				1972			1972
1973				1973			1973

NEW HAMPSHIRE

	Governors	*United States Senators*			*Chief Justices*	
1789	John Sullivan	John Langdon	1789	Paine Wingate	Josiah Bartlett	1789
1790	Josiah Bartlett		1790		John Pickering	1790
1791			1791			1791
1792			1792			1792
1793			1793	Samuel Livermore		1793
1794	John T. Gilman		1794			1794
1795			1795		Simeon Olcott	1795
1796			1796			1796
1797			1797			1797
1798			1798			1798
1799			1799			1799
1800			1800			1800
1801		James Sheafe	1801	Simeon Olcott		1801
1802		William Plumer	1802		Jeremiah Smith	1802
1803			1803			1803
1804			1804			1804
1805	John Langdon		1805	Nicholas Gilman		1805
1806			1806			1806
1807		Nahum Parker	1807			1807
1808			1808			1808
1809	Jeremiah Smith		1809		Arthur Livermore	1809
1810	John Langdon	Charles Cutts	1810			1810
1811			1811			1811
1812	William Plumer		1812			1812
1813	John T. Gilman	Jeremiah Mason	1813		Jeremiah Smith	1813
1814			1814	Thomas W. Thompson		1814
1815			1815			1815
1816	William Plumer		1816		William M. Richardson	1816
1817		Clement Storer	1817	David L. Morril		1817
1818			1818			1818
1819	Samuel Bell	John F. Parrott	1819			1819
1820			1820			1820
1821			1821			1821
1822			1822			1822
1823	Levi Woodbury		1823	Samuel Bell		1823
1824	David L. Morrill		1824			1824
1825		Levi Woodbury	1825			1825
1826			1826			1826
1827	Benjamin Pierce		1827			1827
1828	John Bell		1828			1828
1829	Benjamin Pierce		1829			1829
1830	Matthew Harvey		1830			1830
1831	Samuel Dinsmoor	Isaac Hill	1831			1831
1832			1832			1832
1833			1833			1833
1834	William Badger		1834			1834
1835			1835	Henry Hubbard		1835
1836	Isaac Hill	John Page	1836			1836
1837		Franklin Pierce	1837			1837
1838			1838		Joel Parker	1838
1839	John Page		1839			1839
1840			1840			1840
1841			1841	Levi Woodbury		1841
1842	Henry Hubbard	Leonard Wilcox	1842			1842
1843		Charles G. Atherton	1843			1843
1844	John H. Steele		1844			1844
1845			1845	Benning W. Jenness		1845
1846	Anthony Colby		1846	Joseph Cilley		1846
1847	Jared W. Williams		1847	John P. Hale		1847
1848			1848		John J. Gilchrist	1848
1849	Samuel Dinsmoor	Moses Norris, Jr.	1849			1849
1850			1850			1850
1851			1851			1851
1852	Noah Martin		1852			1852
1853			1853	Jared W. Williams		1853
1854	Nathaniel B. Baker		1854			1854
1855	Ralph Metcalf	John S. Wells	1855	John P. Hale	Andrew S. Woods	1855
1855		James Bell	1855		Ira Perley	1855

NEW HAMPSHIRE–Continued

	Governors	*United States Senators*			*Chief Justices*	
1856			1856			1856
1857	William Haile	Daniel Clark	1857			1857
1858			1858			1858
1859	Ichabod Goodwin		1859		Samuel Bell	1859
1860			1860			1860
1861	Nathaniel S. Berry		1861			1861
1862			1862			1862
1863	Joseph A. Gilmore		1863			1863
1864			1864		Ira Perley	1864
1865	Frederick Smyth		1865	Aaron H. Cragin		1865
1866		George G. Fogg	1866			1866
1867	Walter Harriman	James W. Patterson	1867			1867
1868			1868			1868
1869	Onslow Stearns		1869		Henry A. Bellows	1869
1870			1870			1870
1871	James A. Weston		1871			1871
1872	Ezekiel A. Straw		1872			1872
1873		Bainbridge Wadleigh	1873		Jonathan E. Sargent	1873
1874	James A. Weston		1874		Edmund L. Cushing	1874
1875	Person C. Cheney		1875			1875
1876			1876		Charles Doe	1876
1877	Benjamin F. Prescott		1877	Edward H. Rollins		1877
1878			1878			1878
1879	Natt Head	Charles H. Bell	1879			1879
1879		Henry W. Blair	1879			1879
1880			1880			1880
1881	Charles H. Bell		1881			1881
1882			1882			1882
1883	Samuel W. Hale		1883	Austin F. Pike		1883
1884			1884			1884
1885	Moody Currier		1885			1885
1886			1886	Person C. Cheney		1886
1887	Charles H. Sawyer		1887	William E. Chandler		1887
1888			1888			1888
1889	David H. Goodell		1889	Gillman Marston		1889
1889			1889	William E. Chandler		1889
1890			1890			1890
1891	Hiram A. Tuttle	Jacob H. Gallinger	1891			1891
1892			1892			1892
1893	John B. Smith		1893			1893
1894			1894			1894
1895	Charles A. Busiel		1895			1895
1896			1896		Alonzo P. Carpenter	1896
1897	George A. Ramsdell		1897			1897
1898			1898		Lewis W. Clark	1898
1898			1898		Isaac N. Blodgett	1898
1899	Frank W. Rollins		1899			1899
1900			1900			1900
1901	Chester B. Jordan		1901	Henry E. Burnham		1901
1902			1902		Frank N. Parsons	1902
1903	Nahum J. Bachelder		1903			1903
1904			1904			1904
1905	John McLane		1905			1905
1906			1906			1906
1907	Charles M. Floyd		1907			1907
1908			1908			1908
1909	Henry B. Quinby		1909			1909
1910			1910			1910
1911	Robert P. Bass		1911			1911
1912			1912			1912
1913	Samuel D. Felker		1913	Henry F. Hollis		1913
1914			1914			1914
1915	Rolland H. Spaulding		1915			1915
1916			1916			1916
1917	Henry W. Keyes		1917			1917
1918		Irving W. Drew	1918			1918
1918		George H. Moses	1918			1918
1919	John H. Bartlett		1919	Henry W. Keyes		1919

NEW HAMPSHIRE–Continued

	Governors	*United States Senators*			*Chief Justices*	
1920			1920			1920
1921	Albert O. Brown		1921			1921
1922			1922			1922
1923	Fred H. Brown		1923			1923
1924			1924		Robert J. Peaslee	1924
1925	John G. Winant		1925			1925
1926			1926			1926
1927	Huntley N. Spaulding		1927			1927
1928			1928			1928
1929	Charles W. Tobey		1929			1929
1930			1930			1930
1931	John G. Winant		1931			1931
1932			1932			1932
1933		Fred H. Brown	1933			1933
1934			1934		John E. Allen	1934
1935	H. Styles Bridges		1935			1935
1936			1936			1936
1937	Francis P. Murphy		1937	H. Styles Bridges		1937
1938			1938			1938
1939		Charles W. Tobey	1939			1939
1940			1940			1940
1941	Robert O. Blood		1941			1941
1942			1942			1942
1943			1943		Thomas L. Marble	1943
1944			1944			1944
1945	Charles M. Dale		1945			1945
1946			1946		Oliver W. Branch	1946
1947			1947			1947
1948			1948			1948
1949	Sherman Adams		1949		Francis W. Johnston	1949
1950			1950			1950
1951			1951			1951
1952			1952		Frank R. Kenison	1952
1953	Hugh Gregg	Robert W. Upton	1953			1953
1954		Norris Cotton	1954			1954
1955	Lane Dwinell		1955			1955
1956			1956			1956
1957			1957			1957
1958			1958			1958
1959	Wesley Powell		1959			1959
1960			1960			1960
1961			1961			1961
1962			1962	Maurice J. Murphy, Jr.		1962
1963	John W. King		1963	Thomas J. McIntyre		1963
1964			1964			1964
1965			1965			1965
1966			1966			1966
1967			1967			1967
1968			1968			1968
1969	Walter Peterson		1969			1969
1970			1970			1970
1971			1971			1971
1972			1972			1972
1973	Meldrim Thomson, Jr.		1973			1973

NEW JERSEY

	Governors	*United States Senators*			*Chief Justices*	
1789	William Livingston	Jonathan Elmer	1789	William Paterson	James Kinsey	1789
1790	William Paterson		1790	Philemon Dickinson		1790
1791		John Rutherfurd	1791			1791
1792			1792			1792
1793	Richard Howell		1793	Frederick Frelinghuysen		1793
1794			1794			1794
1795			1795			1795
1796			1796	Richard Stockton		1796
1797			1797			1797
1798		Franklin Davenport	1798			1798
1799		James Schureman	1799	Jonathan Dayton		1799
1800			1800			1800
1801	Joseph Bloomfield	Aaron Ogden	1801			1801
1802	John Lambert (Acting)		1802			1802
1803	Joseph Bloomfield	John Condit	1803		Andrew Kirkpatrick	1803
1804			1804			1804
1805			1805	Aaron Kitchell		1805
1806			1806			1806
1807			1807			1807
1808			1808			1808
1809		John Lambert	1809	John Condit		1809
1810			1810			1810
1811			1811			1811
1812	Aaron Ogden		1812			1812
1813	William S. Pennington		1813			1813
1814			1814			1814
1815	Mahlon Dickerson	James J. Wilson	1815			1815
1816			1816			1816
1817	Isaac H. Williamson		1817	Mahlon Dickerson		1817
1818			1818			1818
1819			1819			1819
1820			1820			1820
1821		Samuel L. Southard	1821			1821
1822			1822			1822
1823		Joseph McIlvaine	1823			1823
1824			1824		Charles Ewing	1824
1825			1825			1825
1826		Ephraim Bateman	1826			1826
1827			1827			1827
1828			1828			1828
1829	Peter D. Vroom	Mahlon Dickerson	1829	Theodore Frelinghuysen		1829
1830			1830			1830
1831			1831			1831
1832	Samuel L. Southard		1832		Joseph C. Hornblower	1832
1833	Elias P. Seeley	Samuel L. Southard	1833			1833
1833	Peter D. Vroom		1833			1893
1834			1834			1834
1835			1835	Garret D. Wall		1835
1836	Philemon Dickerson		1836			1836
1837	William Pennington		1837			1837
1838			1838			1838
1839			1839			1839
1840			1840			1840
1841			1841	Jacob W. Miller		1841
1842		William L. Dayton	1842			1842
1843	Daniel Haines		1843			1843
1844	Charles C. Stratton		1844			1844
1845			1845			1845
1846			1846		Henry W. Green	1846
1847			1847			1847
1848	Daniel Haines		1848			1848
1849			1849			1849
1850			1850			1850
1851	George F. Fort	Robert F. Stockton	1851			1851
1852			1852			1852
1853		John R. Thomson	1853	William Wright		1853
1854	Rodman M. Price		1854			1854
1855			1855			1855

NEW JERSEY–Continued

	Governors	*United States Senators*			*Chief Justices*	
1856			1856			1856
1857	William A. Newell		1857			1857
1858			1858			1858
1859			1859	John C. Ten Eyck		1859
1860	Charles S. Olden		1860			1860
1861			1861		Edward W. Whelpley	1861
1862		Richard S. Field	1862			1862
1863	Joel Parker	James W. Wall	1863			1863
1863		William Wright	1863			1863
1864			1864		Mercer Beasley	1864
1865			1865	John P. Stockton		1865
1866	Marcus L. Ward	Frederick T. Frelinghuysen	1866	Alexander G. Cattell		1866
1867			1867			1867
1868			1868			1868
1869	Theodore F. Randolph	John P. Stockton	1869			1869
1870			1870			1870
1871			1871	Frederick T. Frelinghuysen		1871
1872	Joel Parker		1872			1872
1873			1873			1873
1874			1874			1874
1875	Joseph D. Bedle	Theodore F. Randolph	1875			1875
1876			1876			1876
1877			1877	John R. McPherson		1877
1878	George B. McClellan		1878			1878
1879			1879			1879
1880			1880			1880
1881	George C. Ludlow	William J. Sewell	1881			1881
1882			1882			1882
1883			1883			1883
1884	Leon Abbett		1882			1884
1885			1885			1885
1886			1886			1886
1887	Robert S. Green	Rufus Blodgett	1887			1887
1888			1888			1888
1889			1889			1889
1890	Leon Abbett		1890			1890
1891			1891			1891
1892			1892			1892
1893	George T. Werts	James Smith, Jr.	1893			1893
1894			1894			1894
1895			1895	William J. Sewell		1895
1896	John W. Griggs		1896			1896
1897			1897		William J. Magie	1897
1898	David O. Watkins		1898			1898
1899	Foster M. Voorhees	John Kean	1899			1899
1900			1900		David A. Depue	1900
1901			1901		William S. Gummere	1901
1902	Franklin Murphy		1902	John F. Dryden		1902
1903			1903			1903
1904			1904			1904
1905	Edward C. Stokes		1905			1905
1906			1906			1906
1907			1907	Frank O. Briggs		1907
1908	John F. Fort		1908			1908
1909			1909			1909
1910			1910			1910
1911	Woodrow Wilson	James E. Martine	1911			1911
1912			1912			1912
1913	Leon Taylor (Acting)		1913	William Hughes		1913
1914	James F. Fielder		1914			1914
1915			1915			1915
1916			1916			1916
1917	Walter E. Edge	Joseph S. Frelinghuysen	1917			1917
1918			1918	David Baird		1918
1919	William N. Runyon (Acting)		1919	Walter E. Edge		1919
1920	Edward I. Edwards		1920			1920
1921			1921			1921
1922			1922			1922

NEW JERSEY–Continued

	Governors	*United States Senators*			*Chief Justices*	
1923	George S. Silzer	Edward I. Edwards	1923			1923
1924			1924			1924
1925			1925			1925
1926	A. Harry Moore		1926			1920
1927			1927			1927
1928			1928			1928
1929	Morgan F. Larson	Hamilton F. Kean	1929	David Baird, Jr.		1929
1930			1930	Dwight W. Morrow		1930
1931			1931	W. Warren Barbour		1931
1932	A. Harry Moore		1932			1932
1933			1933		Thomas J. Brogan	1933
1934			1934			1934
1935	Harold G. Hoffman	A. Harry Moore	1935			1935
1936			1936			1936
1937			1937	William H. Smathers		1937
1938	A. Harry Moore	John Milton	1938			1938
1938		W. Warren Barbour	1938			1938
1939			1939			1939
1940			1940			1940
1941	Charles Edison		1941			1941
1942			1942			1942
1943		Arthur Walsh	1943	Albert W. Hawkes		1943
1944	Walter E. Edge	H. Alexander Smith	1944			1944
1945			1945			1945
1946			1946		Clarence E. Case	1946
1947	Alfred E. Driscoll		1947			1947
1948			1948		Arthur T. Vanderbilt	1948
1949			1949	Robert C. Hendrickson		1949
1950			1950			1950
1951			1951			1951
1952			1952			1952
1953			1953			1953
1954	Robert B. Meyner		1954			1954
1955			1955	Clifford P. Case		1955
1956			1956			1956
1957			1957		Joseph T. Weintraub	1957
1958			1958			1958
1959		Harrison A. Williams, Jr.	1959			1959
1960			1960			1960
1961			1961			1961
1962	Richard J. Hughes		1962			1962
1963			1963			1963
1964			1964			1964
1965			1965			1965
1966			1966			1966
1967			1967			1967
1968			1968			1968
1969			1969			1969
1970	William T. Cahill		1970			1970
1971			1971			1971
1972			1972			1972
1973			1973			1973

NEW MEXICO

	Governors	*United States Senators*			*Chief Justices*	
1912	William C. McDonald	Thomas B. Catron	1912	Albert B. Fall		1912
1913			1913			1913
1914			1914			1914
1915			1915			1915
1916			1916			1916
1917	Ezequiel C. DeBaca	Andrieus A. Jones	1917			1917
1917	Washington E. Lindsey		1917			1917
1918			1918			1918
1919	Octaviano A. Larrazolo		1919			1919
1920			1920			1920
1921	Merritt C. Mechem		1921	Holm O. Bursum		1921
1922			1922			1922
1923	James F. Hinkle		1923			1923
1924			1924			1924
1925	Arthur T. Hannett		1925	Sam G. Bratton		1925
1926			1926			1926
1927	Richard C. Dillon	Bronson M. Cutting	1927			1927
1928		Octaviano A. Larrazolo	1928			1928
1929		Bronson M. Cutting	1929			1929
1930			1930			1930
1931	Arthur Seligman		1931			1931
1932			1932			1932
1933	Andy W. Hockenhull		1933	Carl A. Hatch	*Justices of the Supreme Court serve on a rotating basis as Chief Presiding Judge*	1933
1934			1934			1934
1935	Clyde Tingley	Dennis Chavez	1935			1935
1936			1936			1936
1937			1937			1937
1938			1938			1938
1939	John E. Miles		1939			1939
1940			1940			1940
1941			1941			1941
1942			1942			1942
1943	John J. Dempsey		1943			1943
1944			1944			1944
1945			1945			1945
1946			1946			1946
1947	Thomas J. Mabry		1947			1947
1948			1948			1948
1949			1949	Clinton P. Anderson		1949
1950			1950			1950
1951	Edwin L. Mechem		1951			1951
1952			1952			1952
1953			1953			1953
1954			1954			1954
1955	John F. Simms		1955			1955
1956			1956			1956
1957	Edwin L. Mechem		1957			1957
1958			1958			1958
1959	John Burroughs		1959			1959
1960			1960			1960
1961	Edwin L. Mechem		1961			1961
1962	Tom Bolack		1962			1962
1963	Jack M. Campbell	Edwin L. Mechem	1963			1963
1964			1964			1964
1965		Joseph M. Montoya	1965			1965
1966			1966			1966
1967	David F. Cargo		1967			1967
1968			1968			1968
1969			1969			1969
1970			1970			1970
1971	Bruce King		1971			1971
1972			1972			1972
1973			1973	Peter V. Domenici		1973

NEW YORK

	Governors	*United States Senators*			*Chief Justices*	
1789	George Clinton	Rufus King	1789	Philip J. Schuyler	Richard Morris	1789
1790			1790		Robert Yates	1790
1791			1791	Aaron Burr		1791
1792			1792			1792
1793			1793			1793
1794			1794			1794
1795	John Jay		1795			1795
1796		John Laurance	1796			1796
1797			1797	Philip J. Schuyler		1797
1798			1798	John S. Hobart	John Lansing, Jr.	1798
1798			1798	William North		1798
1798			1798	James Watson		1798
1799			1799			1799
1800		John Armstrong	1800	Gouverneur Morris		1800
1801	George Clinton		1801		Morgan Lewis	1801
1802		De Witt Clinton	1802			1802
1803		John Armstrong	1803	Theodorus Bailey		1803
1804	Morgan Lewis	John Smith	1804	Samuel L. Mitchill	James Kent	1804
1805			1805			1805
1806			1806			1806
1807	Daniel D. Tompkins		1807			1807
1808			1808			1808
1809			1809	Obadiah German		1809
1810			1810			1810
1811			1811			1811
1812			1812			1812
1813		Rufus King	1813			1813
1814			1814		Smith Thompson	1814
1815			1815	Nathan Sanford		1815
1816			1816			1816
1817	John Taylor		1817			1817
1817	DeWitt Clinton		1817			1817
1818			1818			1818
1819			1819		Ambrose Spencer	1819
1820			1820			1820
1821			1821	Martin Van Buren		1821
1822			1822			1822
1823	Joseph C. Yates		1823		John Savage	1823
1824			1824			1824
1825	DeWitt Clinton	*Vacant*	1825			1825
1826		Nathan Sanford	1826			1826
1827			1827			1827
1828	Nathaniel Pitcher		1828			1828
1829	Martin Van Buren		1829	Charles E. Dudley		1829
1829	Enos T. Throop		1829			1829
1830			1830			1830
1831		William L. Marcy	1831			1831
1832			1832			1832
1833	William L. Marcy	Silas Wright, Jr.	1833	Nathaniel P. Tallmadge		1833
1834			1834			1834
1835			1835			1835
1836			1836			1836
1837			1837		Samuel Nelson	1837
1838			1838			1838
1839	William H. Seward		1839			1839
1840			1840			1840
1841			1841			1841
1842			1842			1842
1843	William C. Bouck		1843			1843
1844		Henry A. Foster	1844	Daniel S. Dickinson		1844
1845	Silas Wright, Jr.	John A. Dix	1845		Greene C. Bronson	1845
1846			1846			1846
1847	John Young		1847		Samuel Beardsley	1847
1847			1847		Freeborn G. Jewett	1847
1848			1848			1848
1849	Hamilton Fish	William H. Seward	1849			1849
1850			1850		Greene C. Bronson	1850
1851	Washington Hunt		1851	Hamilton Fish	Charles H. Ruggles	1851

NEW YORK–Continued

	Governors	*United States Senators*			*Chief Justices*	
1852			1852			1852
1853	Horatio Seymour		1853			1853
1854			1854		Addison Gardiner	1854
1855	Myron H. Clark		1855			1855
1856			1856		Hiram Denio	1856
1857	John A. King		1857	Preston King		1857
1858			1858		Alexander S. Johnson	1858
1859	Edwin D. Morgan		1859			1859
1860			1860		George F. Comstock	1860
1861		Ira Harris	1861			1801
1862			1862		Samuel L. Selden	1862
1862			1862		Hiram Denio	1862
1863	Horatio Seymour		1863	Edwin D. Morgan		1863
1864			1864			1864
1865	Reuben E. Fenton		1865			1865
1866			1866		Henry E. Davies	1866
1867		Roscoe Conkling	1867			1867
1868			1868		Ward Hunt	1868
1869	John T. Hoffman		1869	Reuben E. Fenton		1869
1870			1870		Robert Earl	1870
1870			1870		Sanford E. Church	1870
1871			1871			1871
1872			1872			1872
1873	John A. Dix		1873			1873
1874			1874			1874
1875	Samuel J. Tilden		1875	Francis Kernan		1875
1876			1876			1876
1877	Lucius Robinson		1877			1877
1878			1878			1878
1879			1879			1879
1880	Alonzo B. Cornell		1880		Charles J. Folger	1880
1881		Elbridge G. Lapham	1881	Thomas C. Platt	Charles Andrews	1881
1881			1881	Warner Miller		1881
1882			1882		William C. Ruger	1882
1883	Grover Cleveland		1883			1883
1884			1884			1884
1885	David B. Hill	William M. Evarts	1885			1885
1886			1886			1886
1887			1887	Frank Hiscock		1887
1888			1888			1888
1889			1889			1889
1890			1890			1890
1891			1891			1891
1892	Roswell P. Flower	David B. Hill	1892		Robert Earl	1892
1893			1893	Edward Murphy, Jr.		1893
1894			1894			1894
1895	Levi P. Morton		1895			1895
1896			1896			1896
1897	Frank S. Black	Thomas C. Platt	1897		Alton B. Parker	1897
1898			1898			1898
1899	Theodore Roosevelt		1899	Chauncey M. Depew		1899
1900			1900			1900
1901	Benjamin B. Odell, Jr.		1901			1901
1902			1902			1902
1903			1903			1903
1904			1904		Edgar M. Cullen	1904
1905	Frank W. Higgins		1905			1905
1906			1906			1906
1907	Charles Evans Hughes		1907			1907
1908			1908			1908
1909		Elihu Root	1909			1909
1910	Horace White		1910			1910
1911	John Alden Dix		1911	James A. O'Gorman		1911
1912			1912			1912
1913	William Sulzer		1913		Willard Bartlett	1913
1914	Martin H. Glynn		1914			1914
1915	Charles S. Whitman	James W. Wadsworth, Jr.	1915			1915
1916			1916			1916

NEW YORK–Continued

Year	*Governors*	*United States Senators*		*Chief Justices*
1917			William M. Calder	Frank H. Hiscock
1918				
1919	Alfred E. Smith			
1920				
1921	Nathan L. Miller			
1922				
1923	Alfred E. Smith		Royal S. Copeland	
1924				
1925				
1926				Benjamin N. Cardozo
1927		Robert F. Wagner, Sr.		
1928				
1929	Franklin D. Roosevelt			
1930				
1931				
1932				Cuthbert W. Pound
1933	Herbert H. Lehman			
1934				
1935				Frederick E. Crane
1936				
1937				
1938			*Vacant*	
1939			James M. Mead	Irving Lehman
1940				
1941				
1942	Charles Poletti			
1943	Thomas E. Dewey			
1944				
1945				John A. Loughran
1946				
1947			Irving M. Ives	
1948				
1949		John Foster Dulles		
1949		Herbert H. Lehman		
1950				
1951				
1952				
1953				Edmund H. Lewis
1954				Albert Conway
1955	W. Averell Harriman			
1956				
1957		Jacob K. Javits		
1958				
1959	Nelson Rockefeller		Kenneth B. Keating	Charles S. Desmond
1960				
1961				
1962				
1963				
1964				
1965			Robert F. Kennedy	
1966				Stanley Fuld
1967				
1968			Charles E. Goodell	
1969				
1970				
1971			James L. Buckley	
1972				
1973				

NORTH CAROLINA

	Governors	*United States Senators*			*Chief Justices*	
1789	Alexander Martin	Benjamin Hawkins	1789	Samuel Johnston		1789
1790			1790			1790
1791			1791			1791
1792	Richard D. Spaight		1792			1792
1793			1793	Alexander Martin		1793
1794			1794			1794
1795	Samuel Ashe	Timothy Bloodworth	1795			1795
1796			1796			1796
1797			1797			1797
1798	William R. Davie		1798			1798
1799	Benjamin Williams		1799	Jesse Franklin		1799
1800			1800			1800
1801		David Stone	1801			1801
1802	James Turner		1802			1802
1803			1803			1803
1804			1804			1804
1805	Nathaniel Alexander		1805	James Turner		1805
1806			1806			1806
1807	Benjamin Williams	Jesse Franklin	1807			1807
1808	David Stone		1808			1808
1809			1809		John L. Taylor	1809
1810	Benjamin Smith		1810			1810
1811	William Hawkins		1811			1811
1812			1812			1812
1813		David Stone	1813			1813
1814	William Miller		1814			1814
1815		Nathaniel Macon	1815			1815
1816			1816	Montfort Stokes		1816
1817	John Branch		1817			1817
1818			1818			1818
1819			1819			1819
1820	Jesse Franklin		1820			1820
1821	Gabriel Holmes		1821			1821
1822			1822			1822
1823		John Branch	1823			1823
1824	Hutchings G. Burton		1824			1824
1825			1825			1825
1826			1826			1826
1827	James Iredell, Jr.		1827			1827
1828	John Owen	James Iredell	1828			1828
1829			1829	Bedford Brown	Leonard Henderson	1829
1830	Montfort Stokes		1830			1830
1831		Willie P. Mangum	1831			1831
1832	David L. Swain		1832			1832
1833			1833		Thomas Ruffin	1833
1834			1834			1834
1835	Richard D. Spaight		1835			1835
1836	Edward B. Dudley	Robert Strange	1836			1836
1837			1837			1837
1838			1838			1838
1839			1839			1839
1840		William A. Graham	1840	Willie P. Mangum		1840
1841	John M. Morehead		1841			1841
1842			1842			1842
1843		William H. Haywood, Jr.	1843			1843
1844			1844			1844
1845	William A. Graham		1845			1845
1846		George E. Badger	1846			1846
1847			1847			1847
1848			1848			1848
1849	Charles Manly		1849			1849
1850			1850			1850
1851	David S. Reid		1851			1851
1852			1852		Frederick Nash	1852
1853			1853	*Vacant*		1853
1854	Warren Winslow (Acting)		1854	David S. Reid		1854
1855	Thomas Bragg	Asa Biggs	1855			1855
1856			1856			1856

NORTH CAROLINA–Continued

	Governors	*United States Senators*			*Chief Justices*	
1857			1857			1857
1858		Thomas L. Clingman	1858		Richmond M. Pearson	1858
1859	John W. Ellis		1859	Thomas Bragg		1859
1860			1860			1860
1861	Henry T. Clark	*Vacant*	1861	*Vacant*		1861
1862	Zebulon B. Vance		1802			1862
1863			1863			1863
1864			1864			1864
1865	Jonathan Worth		1865			1865
1866			1866			1866
1867			1867			1867
1868	William W. Holden	Joseph C. Abbott	1868	John Pool		1868
1869			1869			1869
1870			1870			1870
1871	Tod R. Caldwell		1871			1871
1872		Matt W. Ransom	1872			1872
1873			1873	Augustus S. Merrimon		1873
1874	Curtis H. Brogden		1874			1874
1875			1875			1875
1876			1876			1876
1877	Zebulon B. Vance		1877			1877
1878			1878		William N.H. Smith	1878
1879	Thomas J. Jarvis		1879	Zebulon B. Vance		1879
1880			1880			1880
1881			1881			1881
1882			1882			1882
1883			1883			1883
1884			1884			1884
1885	Alfred M. Scales		1885			1885
1886			1886			1886
1887			1887			1887
1888			1888			1888
1889	Daniel G. Fowle		1889		Augustus S. Merrimon	1889
1890			1890			1890
1891	Thomas M. Holt		1891			1891
1892			1892		James E. Shepherd	1892
1893	Elias Carr		1893			1893
1894			1894	Thomas J. Jarvis		1894
1895		Marion Butler	1895	Jeter C. Pritchard	William T. Faircloth	1895
1896			1896			1896
1897	Daniel L. Russell		1897			1897
1898			1898			1898
1899			1899			1899
1900			1900			1900
1901	Charles B. Aycock	Furnifold M. Simmons	1901		David M. Furches	1901
1902			1902			1902
1903			1903	Lee S. Overman	Walter Clark	1903
1904			1904			1904
1905	Robert B. Glenn		1905			1905
1906			1906			1906
1907			1907			1907
1908			1908			1908
1909	William W. Kitchin		1909			1909
1910			1910			1910
1911			1911			1911
1912			1912			1912
1913	Locke Craig		1913			1913
1914			1914			1914
1915			1915			1915
1916			1916			1916
1917	Thomas W. Bickett		1917			1917
1918			1918			1918
1919			1919			1919
1920			1920			1920
1921	Cameron Morrison		1921			1921
1922			1922			1922
1923			1923			1923
1924			1924		William A. Hoke	1924

NORTH CAROLINA–Continued

	Governors	*United States Senators*			*Chief Justices*	
1925	Angus W. McLean		1925		Walter P. Stacy	1925
1926			1926			1926
1927			1927			1927
1928			1928			1928
1929	O. Max Gardner		1929			1929
1930			1930	Cameron Morrison		1930
1931		Josiah W. Bailey	1931			1931
1932			1932	Robert R. Reynolds		1932
1933	John C.B. Ehringhaus		1933			1933
1934			1934			1934
1935			1935			1935
1936			1936			1936
1937	Clyde R. Hoey		1937			1937
1938			1938			1938
1939			1939			1939
1940			1940			1940
1941	J. Melville Broughton		1941			1941
1942			1942			1942
1943			1943			1943
1944			1944			1944
1945	R. Gregg Cherry		1945	Clyde R. Hoey		1945
1946		William B. Umstead	1946			1946
1947			1947			1947
1948		J. Melville Broughton	1948			1948
1949	W. Kerr Scott	Frank P. Graham	1949			1949
1950		Willis Smith	1950			1950
1951			1951		William A. Devin	1951
1952			1952			1952
1953	William B. Umstead	Alton A. Lennon	1953			1953
1954	Luther H. Hodges	W. Kerr Scott	1954	Samuel J. Ervin, Jr.	M.V. Barnhill	1954
1955			1955			1955
1956			1956		J. Wallace Winborne	1956
1957			1957			1957
1958		B. Everett Jordan	1958			1958
1959			1959			1959
1960			1960			1960
1961	Terry Sanford		1961			1961
1962			1962		Emery B. Denny	1962
1963			1963			1963
1964			1964			1964
1965	Daniel K. Moore		1965			1965
1966			1966		R. Hunt Parker	1966
1967			1967			1967
1968			1968			1968
1969	Robert W. Scott		1969			1969
1970			1970			1970
1971			1971			1971
1972			1972			1972
1973	James E. Holshouser	Jesse A. Helms	1973	Jesse A. Helms		1973

NORTH DAKOTA

	Governors	*United States Senators*			*Chief Justices*	
1889	John Miller	Lyman R. Casey	1889	Gilbert A. Pierce	*Justices of the Supreme Court serve on a rotating basis as Chief Presiding Judge*	1889
1890			1890			1890
1891	Andrew H. Burke		1891			1891
1892			1982			1892
1893	Eli C. D. Shortridge	William N. Roach	1893			1893
1894			1894			1894
1895	Roger Allen		1895			1895
1896			1896			1896
1897	Frank A. Briggs		1897			1897
1898	Joseph M. Devine		1898			1898
1899	Frederick B. Fancher	Porter J. McCumber	1899			1899
1900			1900			1900
1901	Frank White		1901			1901
1902			1902			1902
1903			1903			1903
1904			1904			1904
1905	Elmore Y. Sarles		1905			1905
1906			1906			1906
1907	John Burke		1907			1907
1908			1908			1908
1909			1909	Martin N. Johnson		1909
1909			1909	Fountain L. Thompson		1909
1910			1910	William E. Purcell		1910
1911			1911	Asle J. Gronna		1911
1912			1912			1912
1913	Louis B. Hanna		1913			1913
1914			1914			1914
1915			1915			1915
1916			1916			1916
1917	Lynn J. Frazier		1917			1917
1918			1918			1918
1919			1919			1919
1920			1920			1920
1921	Ragnvald A. Nestos		1921	Edwin F. Ladd		1921
1921			1921			1921
1922			1922			1922
1923		Lynn J. Frazier	1923			1923
1924			1924			1924
1925	Arthur G. Sorlie		1925	Gerald P. Nye		1925
1926			1926			1926
1927			1927			1927
1928	Walter Maddock		1928			1928
1929	George F. Shafer		1929			1929
1930			1930			1930
1931			1931			1931
1932			1932			1932
1933	William Langer		1933			1933
1934	Ole H. Olson		1934			1934
1935	Thomas H. Moodie		1935			1935
1935	Walter Welford		1935			1935
1936			1936			1936
1937	William Langer		1937			1937
1938			1938			1938
1939	John Moses		1939			1939
1940			1940			1940
1941		William Langer	1941			1941
1942			1942			1942
1943			1943			1943
1944			1944			1944
1945	Fred Aandahl		1945	John Moses		1945
1945			1945	Milton R. Young		1945
1946			1946			1946
1947			1947			1947
1948			1948			1948
1949			1949			1949
1950			1950			1950

NORTH DAKOTA—Continued

	Governors	*United States Senators*		*Chief Justices*	
1951	C. Norman Brunsdale		1951		1951
1952			1952		1952
1953			1953		1953
1954			1954		1954
1955			1955		1955
1956			1956		1956
1957	John E. Davis		1957		1957
1958			1958		1958
1959		C. Norman Brunsdale	1959		1959
1960		Quentin N. Burdick	1960		1960
1961	William L. Guy		1961		1961
1962			1962		1962
1963			1963		1963
1964			1964		1964
1965			1965		1965
1966			1966		1966
1967			1967		1967
1968			1968		1968
1969			1969		1969
1970			1970		1970
1971			1971		1971
1972			1972		1972
1973	Arthur A. Link		1973		1973

OHIO

	Governors	*United States Senators*			*Chief Justices*	
1803	Edward Tiffin	John Smith	1803	Thomas Worthington	Samuel Huntington	1803
1804			1804			1804
1805			1805			1805
1806			1806			1806
1807	Thomas Kirker		1807	Edward Tiffin		1807
1808	Samuel Huntington	Return J. Meigs, Jr.	1808		William Sprigg	1808
1809			1809	Stanley Griswold		1809
1809			1809	Alexander Campbell		1809
1810	Return J. Meigs, Jr.	Thomas Worthington	1810		Thomas Scott	1810
1811			1811			1811
1812			1812			1812
1813			1813	Jeremiah Morrow		1813
1814	Othneil Looker (Acting)	Joseph Kerr	1814			1814
1814	Thomas Worthington		1814			1814
1815		Benjamin Ruggles	1815		Ethan A. Brown	1815
1816			1816			1816
1817			1817			1817
1818	Ethan A. Brown		1818		Jessup N. Couch	1818
1819			1819	William A. Trimble		1819
1820			1820			1820
1821			1821		Calvin Pease	1821
1822	Jeremiah Morrow		1822	Ethan A. Brown		1822
1823			1823			1823
1824			1824			1824
1825			1825	William Henry Harrison		1825
1826	Allen Trimble		1826			1826
1827			1827			1827
1828			1828	Jacob Burnet		1828
1829			1829		Peter Hitchcock	1829
1830	Duncan McArthur		1830			1830
1831			1831	Thomas Ewing		1831
1832	Robert Lucas		1832			1832
1833		Thomas Morris	1833		Joshua Collett	1833
1834			1834			1834
1835			1835		Ebenezer Lane	1835
1836	Joseph Vance		1836			1836
1837			1837	William Allen		1837
1838	Wilson Shannon		1838			1838
1839		Benjamin Tappan	1839			1839
1840	Thomas Corwin		1840			1840
1841			1841			1841
1842	Wilson Shannon		1842			1842
1843			1843			1843
1844	Thomas W. Bartley (Acting)		1844			1844
1845	Mordecai Bartley	Thomas Corwin	1845		Reuben Wood	1845
1846	William Bebb		1846			1846
1847			1847		Matthew Birchard	1847
1848			1848		Peter Hitchcock	1848
1849	Seabury Ford		1849	Salmon P. Chase		1849
1850	Reuben Wood	Thomas Ewing	1850			1850
1851		Benjamin F. Wade	1851			1851
1852			1852		William B. Caldwell	1852
1853	William Medill		1853			1853
1854			1854			1854
1855			1855	George E. Pugh	Rufus P. Ranney	1855
1856	Salmon P. Chase		1856			1856
1857			1857		Thomas W. Bartley	1857
1858			1858		Joseph R. Swan	1858
1859			1859		Jacob Brinkerhoff	1859
1860	William Dennison		1860			1860
1861			1861	Salmon P. Chase		1861
1861			1861	John Sherman		1861
1862	David Tod		1862			1862
1863			1863			1863
1864	John Brough		1864			1864
1865			1865			1865
1866	Jacob D. Cox		1866			1866

OHIO–Continued

	Governors	*United States Senators*			*Chief Justices*	
1867			1867			1867
1868	Rutherford B. Hayes		1868			1868
1869		Allen G. Thurman	1869			1869
1870			1870			1870
1871			1871		Josiah Scott	1871
1872	Edward F. Noyes		1872		John Welch	1872
1873			1873		William White	1873
1874	William Allen		1874		Luther Day	1874
1875			1875		George Rex	1875
1876	Rutherford B. Hayes		1876			1876
1877	Thomas L. Young		1877	Stanley Matthews	John Welch	1877
1878	Richard M. Bishop		1878		William White	1878
1879			1879	George H. Pendleton	William J. Gilmore	1879
1880	Charles Foster		1880		George W. McIlvaine	1880
1881		John Sherman	1881		Washington W. Boynton	1881
1882			1882		John W. Okey	1882
1883			1883		William White	1883
1884	George Hoadly		1884		Selwyn N. Owen	1884
1885			1885	Henry B. Payne	George W. McIlvaine	1885
1886	Joseph B. Foraker		1886		Selwyn N. Owen	1886
1887			1887			1887
1888			1888			1888
1889			1889		Thaddeus A. Minshall	1889
1890	James E. Campbell		1890			1890
1891			1891	Calvin S. Brice	Marshall J. Williams	1891
1892	William McKinley		1892		William T. Spear	1892
1893			1893		Joseph P. Bradbury	1893
1894			1894		Franklin Dickman	1894
1895			1895		Thaddeus A. Minshall	1895
1896	Asa S. Bushnell		1896		Marshall J. Williams	1896
1897		Marcus A. Hanna	1897	Joseph B. Foraker	Jacob Burket	1897
1898			1898		William T. Spear	1898
1899			1899		Joseph P. Bradbury	1899
1900	George K. Nash		1900		John A. Shauck	1900
1901			1901		Thaddeus A. Minshall	1901
1902			1902		Jacob Burket	1902
1903			1903			1903
1904	Myron T. Herrick	Charles W. F. Dick	1904			1904
1905			1905		William Z. Davis	1905
1906	John M. Pattison		1906		John A. Shauck	1906
1906	Andrew L. Harris		1906			1906
1907			1907			1907
1908			1908		James L. Price	1908
1909	Judson Harmon		1909	Theodore E. Burton	William B. Crew	1909
1910			1910		Augustus N. Summers	1910
1911		Atlee Pomerene	1911		William T. Spear	1911
1912			1912		William Z. Davis	1912
1913	James M. Cox		1913		John A. Shauck	1913
1913			1913		Hugh L. Nichols	1913
1914			1914			1914
1915	Frank B. Willis		1915	Warren G. Harding		1915
1916			1916			1916
1917	James M. Cox		1917			1917
1918			1918			1918
1919			1919			1919
1920			1920			1920
1921	Harry L. Davis		1921	Frank B. Willis	Carrington T. Marshall	1921
1922			1922			1922
1923	A. Victor Donahey	Simeon D. Fess	1923			1923
1924			1924			1924
1925			1925			1925
1926			1926			1926
1927			1927			1927
1928			1928	Cyrus Locher		1928
1928			1928	Theodore E. Burton		1928
1929	Myers Y. Cooper		1929	Roscoe C. McCulloch		1929
1930			1930	Robert J. Bulkley		1930
1931	George White		1931			1931

OHIO–Continued

Year	*Governors*	*United States Senators*	*United States Senators*	*Chief Justices*
1932				
1933				Carl V. Weygandt
1934				
1935	Martin L. Davey	A. Victor Donahey		
1936				
1937				
1938				
1939	John W. Bricker		Robert A. Taft	
1940				
1941		Harold H. Burton		
1942				
1943				
1944				
1945	Frank J. Lausche	James W. Huffman		
1946		Kingsley A. Taft		
1947	Thomas J. Herbert	John W. Bricker		
1948				
1949	Frank J. Lausche			
1950				
1951				
1952				
1953			Thomas A. Burke	
1954			George H. Bender	
1955				
1956				
1957	C. William O'Neill		Frank J. Lausche	
1958				
1959	Michael V. DiSalle	Stephen M. Young		
1960				
1961				
1962				
1963	James A. Rhodes			Kingsley A. Taft
1964				
1965				
1966				
1967				
1968				
1969			William B. Saxbe	
1970				C. William O'Neill
1971	John J. Gilligan			
1972				
1973				

OKLAHOMA

Governors

Year	Governor
1907	Charles N. Haskell
1908	
1909	
1910	
1911	Lee Cruce
1912	
1913	
1914	
1915	Robert L. Williams
1916	
1917	
1918	
1919	James B. A. Robertson
1919	
1920	
1921	
1922	
1923	James C. Walton
1923	Martin E. Trapp
1924	
1925	
1926	
1927	Henry S. Johnston
1928	
1929	William J. Holloway
1930	
1931	William H. Murray
1932	
1933	
1934	
1935	Ernest W. Marland
1936	
1937	
1938	
1939	Leon C. Phillips
1940	
1941	
1942	
1943	Robert S. Kerr
1944	
1945	
1946	
1947	Roy J. Turner
1948	
1949	
1950	
1951	Johnston Murray
1952	
1953	
1954	
1955	Raymond S. Gary
1956	
1957	
1958	
1959	J. Howard Edmondson
1960	
1961	
1962	
1963	Henry Bellmon
1964	
1965	
1966	
1967	Dewey F. Bartlett
1968	
1969	
1970	
1971	David Hall
1972	
1973	

United States Senators

Senator	Year	Senator
Thomas P. Gore	1907	Robert L. Owen
	1908	
	1909	
	1910	
	1911	
	1912	
	1913	
	1914	
	1915	
	1916	
	1917	
	1918	
1919		Summers Hardy
	1919	
	1920	
John W. Harreld	1921	
	1922	
	1923	
	1923	
	1924	
	1925	William B. Pine
	1926	
J. W. Elmer Thomas	1927	
	1928	
	1929	
	1930	Thomas P. Gore
	1931	
	1932	
	1933	
	1934	
	1935	
	1936	
	1937	Josh Lee
	1938	
	1939	
	1940	
	1941	
	1942	
	1943	Edward H. Moore
	1944	
	1945	
	1946	
	1947	
	1948	
	1949	Robert S. Kerr
	1950	
A. S. Mike Monroney	1951	
	1952	
	1953	
	1954	
	1955	
	1956	
	1957	
	1958	
	1959	
	1960	
	1961	
	1962	
	1963	J. Howard Edmondson
	1964	
	1965	Fred R. Harris
	1966	
	1967	
	1968	
Henry L. Bellmon	1969	
	1970	
	1971	
	1972	
	1973	

Chief Justices

Chief Justice	Year
Robert L. Williams	1907
	1908
Matthew J. Kane	1909
Jesse J. Dunn	1910
John B. Turner	1911
	1912
Samuel W. Hayes	1913
Matthew J. Kane	1914
	1915
	1916
John F. Sharp	1917
	1918
1919	
Thomas H. Owen	1919
Robert M. Rainey	1920
John B. Harrison	1921
	1922
John H. Pitchford	1923
John T. Johnson	1923
Neal E. McNeill	1924
George M. Nicholson	1925
	1926
Fred P. Branson	1927
	1928
Charles W. Mason	1929
	1930
E. F. Lester	1931
	1932
Fletcher Riley	1933
	1934
Edwin R. McNeill	1935
	1936
Monroe Osborn	1937
	1938
Wayne W. Bayless	1939
	1940
Earl Welch	1941
	1942
N. S. Corn	1943
	1944
Thomas L. Gibson	1945
	1946
Thurman S. Hurst	1947
	1948
Denver N. Davison	1949
	1950
Ben Arnold	1951
	1952
Harry L. S. Halley	1953
	1954
N. B. Johnson	1955
	1956
Earl Welch	1957
	1958
Denver M. Davison	1959
	1960
Ben T. Williams	1961
	1962
W. H. Blackbird	1963
	1964
Harry L. S. Halley	1965
	1966
Floyd L. Jackson	1967
	1968
Pat Irwin	1969
	1970
William A. Berry	1971
	1972
	1973

OREGON

	Governors	United States Senators			Chief Justices	
1859	John Whiteaker	Joseph Lane	1859	Delazon Smith	*Justices of the Supreme Court serve on a rotating basis as Chief Presiding Judge*	1859
1860			1860	Edward D. Baker		1860
1861		James W. Nesmith	1861	Benjamin Stark		1861
1862	Addison C. Gibbs		1862	Benjamin F. Harding		1862
1863			1863			1863
1864			1864			1864
1865			1865	George H. Williams		1865
1866	George L. Woods		1866			1866
1867		Henry W. Corbett	1867			1867
1868			1868			1868
1869			1869			1869
1870	LaFayette Grover		1870			1870
1871			1871	James K. Kelly		1871
1872			1872			1872
1873		John H. Mitchell	1873			1873
1874			1874			1874
1875			1875			1875
1876			1876			1876
1877	Stephen F. Chadwick		1877	LaFayette Grover		1877
1878	William W. Thayer		1878			1878
1879		James H. Slater	1879			1879
1880			1880			1880
1881			1881			1881
1882	Zenas F. Moody		1882			1882
1883			1883	Joseph N. Dolph		1883
1884			1884			1884
1885		*Vacant*	1885			1885
1885		John H. Mitchell	1885			1885
1886			1886			1886
1887	Sylvester Pennoyer		1887			1887
1888			1888			1888
1889			1889			1889
1890			1890			1890
1891			1891			1891
1892			1892			1892
1893			1893			1893
1894			1894			1894
1895	William P. Lord		1895	George W. McBride		1895
1896			1896			1896
1897		*Vacant*	1897			1897
1898		Joseph Simon	1898			1898
1899	Theodore T. Geer		1899			1899
1900			1900			1900
1901			1901	John H. Mitchell		1901
1902			1902			1902
1903	George E. Chamberlain	Charles W. Fulton	1903			1903
1904			1904			1904
1905			1905	John M. Gearin		1905
1906			1906			1906
1907			1907	Frederick W. Mulkey		1907
1907			1907	Jonathan Bourne, Jr.		1907
1908			1908			1908
1909	Frank W. Benson	George E. Chamberlain	1909			1909
1910	Jay R. Bowerman (Acting)		1910			1910
1911	Oswald West		1911			1911
1912			1912			1912
1913			1913	Harry Lane		1913
1914			1914			1914
1915	James Withycombe		1915			1915
1916			1916			1916
1917			1917	Charles L. McNary		1917
1918			1918			1918
1919	Ben W. Olcott		1919			1919
1920			1920			1920
1921		Robert N. Stanfield	1921			1921
1922			1922			1922
1923	Walter M. Pierce		1923			1923
1924			1924			1924

OREGON–Continued

Year	*Governors*	*United States Senators*	*United States Senators*	*Chief Justices*
1925				
1926				
1927	Isaac L. Patterson	Frederick Steiwer		
1928				
1929	Albin W. Norblad			
1930				
1931	Julius Meier			
1932				
1933				
1934				
1935	Charles H. Martin			
1936				
1937				
1938		Alfred E. Reames		
1939	Charles A. Sprague	Rufus C. Holman		
1940				
1941				
1942				
1943	Earl Snell			
1944			Guy Cordon	
1945		Wayne L. Morse		
1946				
1947	John H. Hall			
1948				
1949	Douglas McKay			
1950				
1951				
1952	Paul L. Patterson			
1953				
1954				
1955			Richard L. Neuberger	
1956	Elmo Smith			
1957	Robert D. Holmes			
1958				
1959	Mark O. Hatfield			
1960			Hall S. Lusk	
1961			Maurine B. Neuberger	
1962				
1963				
1964				
1965				
1966				
1967	Tom McCall		Mark O. Hatfield	
1968				
1969		Robert W. Packwood		
1970				
1971				
1972				
1973				

PENNSYLVANIA

	Governors	*United States Senators*			*Chief Justices*	
1789	Thomas Mifflin	William Maclay	1789	Robert Morris	Thomas McKean	1789
1790			1790			1790
1791		*Vacant*	1791			1791
1792			1792			1792
1793		Albert Gallatin	1793			1793
1794		James Ross	1794			1794
1795			1795	William Bingham		1795
1796			1796			1796
1797			1797			1797
1798			1798			1798
1799	Thomas McKean		1799		Edward Shippen	1799
1800			1800			1800
1801			1801	John Peter G. Muhlenberg		1801
1801			1801	George Logan		1801
1802			1802			1802
1803		Samuel Maclay	1803			1803
1804			1804			1804
1805			1805			1805
1806			1806		William Tilghman	1806
1807			1807	Andrew Gregg		1807
1808	Simon Synder		1808			1808
1809		Michael Leib	1809			1809
1810			1810			1810
1811			1811			1811
1812			1812			1812
1813			1813	Abner Lacock		1813
1814		Jonathan Roberts	1814			1814
1815			1815			1815
1816			1816			1816
1817	William Findlay		1817			1817
1818			1818			1818
1819			1819	Walter Lowrie		1819
1820	Joseph Hiester		1820			1820
1821		William Findlay	1821			1821
1822			1822			1822
1823	John A. Schulze		1823			1823
1824			1824			1824
1825			1825	William Marks		1825
1826			1826			1826
1827		Isaac D. Barnard	1827		John B. Gibson	1827
1828			1828			1828
1829	George Wolf		1829			1829
1830			1830			1830
1831		George M. Dallas	1831	William Wilkins		1831
1832			1832			1832
1833		Samuel McKean	1833			1833
1834			1834	James Buchanan		1834
1835	Joseph Ritner		1835			1835
1836			1836			1836
1837			1837			1837
1838			1898			1838
1839	David R. Porter	*Vacant*	1839			1839
1820		Daniel Sturgeon	1840			1840
1841			1841			1841
1842			1842			1842
1843			1843			1843
1844			1844			1844
1845	Francis R. Shunk		1845	Simon Cameron		1845
1846			1846			1846
1847			1847			1847
1848	William F. Johnston		1848			1848
1849			1849	James Cooper		1849
1850			1850			1850
1851		Richard Brodhead	1851		Jeremiah S. Black	1851
1852	William Bigler		1852			1852
1853			1853			1853
1854			1854		Ellis Lewis	1854
1855	James Pollock		1855	*Vacant*		1855
1856			1856	William Bigler		1856

PENNSYLVANIA–Continued

	Governors	*United States Senators*			*Chief Justices*	
1857		Simon Cameron	1857		Walter H. Lowrie	1857
1858	William F. Packer		1858			1858
1859			1859			1859
1860			1860			1860
1861	Andrew G. Curtin	David Wilmot	1861	Edgar Cowan		1861
1862			1862			1862
1863		Charles R. Buckalew	1863		George W. Woodward	1863
1864			1864			1804
1865			1865			1865
1866			1866			1806
1867	John W. Geary		1867	Simon Cameron	James Thompson	1867
1868			1868			1868
1869		John Scott	1869			.1869
1870			1870			1870
1871			1871			1871
1872			1872		John M. Read	1872
1873	John F. Hartranft		1873		Daniel Agnew	1873
1874			1874			1874
1875		William A. Wallace	1875			1875
1876			1876			1876
1877			1877	J. Donald Cameron		1877
1878			1878			1878
1879	Henrv M. Hoyt		1879		George Sharswood	1879
1880			1880			1880
1881		John I. Mitchell	1881			1881
1882			1882			1882
1883	Robert E. Pattison		1883		Ulysses Mercur	1883
1884			1884			1884
1885			1885			1885
1886			1886			1886
1887	James A. Beaver	Matthew S. Quay	1887		Isaac G. Gordon	1887
1888			1888			1888
1889			1889		Edward M. Paxson	1889
1890			1890			1890
1891	Robert E. Pattison		1891			1891
1892			1892			1892
1893			1893		James P. Sterett	1893
1894			1894			1894
1895	Daniel H. Hastings		1895			1895
1896			1896			1896
1897			1897	Boies Penrose		1897
1898			1898			1898
1899	William A. Stone	*Vacant*	1899		Henry Green	1899
1900			1900		J. Brewster McCollum	1900
1901		Matthew S. Quay	1901			1901
1902			1902			1902
1903	Samuel W. Pennypacker		1903		James T. Mitchell	1903
1904		Philander C. Knox	1904			1904
1905			1905			1905
1906			1906			1906
1907	Edwin S. Stuart		1907			1907
1908			1908			1908
1909		George T. Oliver	1909			1909
1910			1910		D. Newlin Fell	1910
1911	John K. Tener		1911			1911
1912			1912			1912
1913			1913			1913
1914			1914			1914
1915	Martin G. Brumbaugh		1915		J. Hay Brown	1915
1916			1916			1916
1917		Philander C. Knox	1917			1917
1918			1918			1918
1919	William C. Sproul		1919			1919
1920			1920			1920
1921		William E. Crow	1921		Robert Von Moschzisker	1921
1922		David A. Reed	1922	George W. Pepper		1922

PENNSYLVANIA–Continued

	Governors		*United States Senators*		*Chief Justices*	
1923	Gifford Pinchot	1923				1923
1924		1924				1924
1925		1925				1925
1926		1926				1926
1927	John S. Fischer	1927		William S. Vare		1927
1928		1928				1928
1929		1929		Joseph R. Grundy		1929
1930		1930		James J. Davis	Robert S. Frazer	1930
1931	Gifford Pinchot	1931				1931
1932		1932				1932
1933		1933				1933
1934		1934				1934
1935	George H. Earle	1935	Joseph F. Guffey			1935
1936		1936			John W. Kephart	1936
1937		1937				1937
1938		1938				1938
1939	Arthur H. James	1939				1939
1940		1940			William I. Schaffer	1940
1941		1941				1941
1942		1942				1942
1943	Edward Martin	1943			George Maxey	1943
1944		1944				1944
1945		1945		Francis J. Myers		1945
1946		1946				1946
1947		1947	Edward Martin			1947
1947	James H. Duff	1947				1947
1948		1948				1948
1949		1949				1949
1950		1950			James B. Drew	1950
1951	John S. Fine	1951		James H. Duff		1951
1952		1952			Horace Stern	1952
1953		1953				1953
1954		1954				1954
1955	George M. Leader	1955				1955
1956		1950			Charles A. Jones	1956
1957		1957		Joseph S. Clark		1957
1958		1958				1958
1959	David L. Lawrence	1959	Hugh D. Scott, Jr.			1959
1960		1960				1960
1961		1961			John C. Bell, Jr.	1961
1962		1962				1962
1963	William W. Scranton	1963				1963
1964		1964				1964
1965		1965				1965
1966		1966				1966
1967	Raymond P. Shafer	1967				1967
1968		1968				1968
1969		1969		Richard S. Schweiker		1969
1970		1970				1970
1971	Milton J. Shapp	1971				1971
1972		1972				1972
1973		1973				1973

RHODE ISLAND

	Governors	*United States Senators*			*Chief Justices*	
1789	John Collins		1789		Othniel Gorton	1789
1790	Arthur Fenner	Theodore Foster	1790	Joseph Stanton, Jr.	Daniel Owen	1790
1791			1791			1791
1792			1792			1792
1793			1793	William Bradford		1793
1794			1794			1794
1795			1795		Peleg Arnold	1795
1796			1796			1796
1797			1797	Ray Greene		1797
1798			1798			1798
1799			1799			1799
1800			1800			1800
1801			1801	Christopher Ellery		1801
1802			1802			1802
1803		Samuel J. Potter	1803			1803
1804		Benjamin Howland	1804			1804
1805	Henry Smith (Acting)		1805	James Fenner		1805
1806	Isaac Wilbour (Acting)		1806			1806
1807	James Fenner		1807	Elisha Mathewson		1807
1808			1808			1808
1809		Francis Malbone	1809		Thomas Arnold	1809
1809		Christopher G. Champlin	1809			1809
1810			1810		Peleg Arnold	1810
1811	William Jones	William Hunter	1811	Jeremiah B. Howell		1811
1812			1812		Daniel Lyman	1812
1813			1813			1813
1814			1814			1814
1815			1815			1815
1816			1816		James Burrill, Jr.	1816
1817	Nehemiah R. Knight		1817	James Burrill, Jr.	Tristam Burges	1817
1818			1818		James Fenner	1818
1819			1819		Isaac Wilbour	1819
1820			1820			1820
1821	William C. Gibbs	James De Wolf	1821	Nehemiah R. Knight		1821
1822			1822			1822
1823			1823			1823
1824	James Fenner		1824			1824
1825		Asher Robbins	1825			1825
1826			1826			1826
1827			1827		Samuel Eddy	1827
1828			1828			1828
1829			1829			1829
1830			1830			1830
1831	Lemuel H. Arnold		1831			1831
1832			1832			1832
1833	John B. Francis		1833			1833
1834			1834			1834
1835			1835		Job Durfee	1835
1836			1836			1836
1837			1837			1837
1838	William Sprague		1838			1838
1839	Samuel W. King	Nathan F. Dixon	1839			1839
1840			1840			1840
1841			1841	James F. Simmons		1841
1842		William Sprague	1842			1842
1843	James Fenner		1843			1843
1844		John B. Francis	1844			1844
1845	Charles Jackson	Albert C. Greene	1845			1845
1846	Byron Diman		1846			1846
1847	Elisha Harris		1847	John H. Clarke		1847
1848			1848		Richard W. Greene	1848
1849	Henry B. Anthony		1849			1849
1850			1850			1850
1851	Philip Allen	Charles T. James	1851			1851
1852			1852			1852
1853	Francis M. Dimond		1853	Philip Allen		1853
1854	William W. Hoppin		1854		William R. Staples	1854
1855			1855			1855

RHODE ISLAND–Continued

	Governors	*United States Senators*			*Chief Justices*	
1856			1856		Samuel Ames	1856
1857	Elisha Dyer	James F. Simmons	1857			1857
1858			1858			1858
1859	Thomas G. Turner		1859	Henry B. Anthony		1859
1860	William Sprague		1860			1860
1861			1861			1861
1862		Samuel G. Arnold	1862			1862
1863	James Y. Smith	William Sprague	1863			1863
1864			1864			1864
1865			1865			1865
1866	Ambrose E. Burnside		1866		Charles S. Bradley	1866
1867			1867			1867
1868			1868		George A. Brayton	1868
1869	Seth Padelford		1869			1869
1870			1870			1870
1871			1871			1871
1872			1872			1872
1873	Henry Howard		1873			1873
1874			1874			1874
1875	Henry Lippitt	Ambrose E. Burnside	1875		Thomas Durfee	1875
1876			1876			1876
1877	Charles C. Van Zandt		1877			1877
1878			1878			1878
1879			1879			1879
1880	Alfred H. Littlefield		1880			1880
1881		Nelson W. Aldrich	1881			1881
1882			1882			1882
1883	Augustus O. Bourn		1883			1883
1884			1884	William P. Sheffield		1884
1885	George P. Wetmore		1885	Jonathan Chace		1885
1880			1886			1886
1887	John W. Davis		1887			1887
1888	Royal C. Taft		1888			1888
1889	Herbert W. Ladd		1889	Nathan F. Dixon		1889
1890	John W. Davis		1890			1890
1891	Herbert W. Ladd		1891		Charles Matteson	1891
1892	Daniel R. Brown		1892			1892
1893			1893			1893
1894			1894			1894
1895	Charles W. Lippitt		1895	George P. Wetmore		1895
1896			1896			1896
1897	Elisha Dyer		1897			1897
1898			1898			1898
1899			1899			1899
1900	William Gregory		1900		John H. Stiness	1900
1901	Charles D. Kimball		1901			1901
1902			1902			1902
1903	Lucius F. C. Garvin		1903		Pardon E. Tillinghast	1903
1904			1904			1904
1905	George H. Utter		1905		William W. Douglas	1905
1906			1906			1906
1907	James H. Higgins		1907	*Vacant*		1907
1908			1908	George P. Wetmore		1908
1909	Aram J. Pothier		1909		Edward C. Dubois	1909
1910			1910			1910
1911		Henry F. Lippitt	1911			1911
1912			1912			1912
1913			1913	LeBaron B. Colt	Clarke H. Johnson	1913
1914			1914			1914
1915	R. Livingston Beeckman		1915			1915
1916			1916			1916
1917		Peter G. Gerry	1917		Christopher F. Parkhurst	1917
1918			1918			1918
1919			1919			1919
1920			1920		William H. Sweetland	1920
1921	Emery J. San Souci		1921			1921
1922			1922			1922
1923	William S. Flynn		1923			1923

RHODE ISLAND—Continued

	Governors	*United States Senators*			*Chief Justices*	
1924			1924	Jesse H. Metcalf		1924
1925	Aram J. Pothier		1925			1925
1926			1926			1926
1927			1927			1927
1928	Norman S. Case		1928			1928
1929		Felix E. Hebert	1929		Charles F. Stearns	1929
1930			1930			1930
1931			1931			1931
1932			1932			1932
1933	Theodore F. Green		1933			1933
1934			1934			1934
1935		Peter G. Gerry	1935		Edmund W. Flynn	1935
1936			1936			1936
1937	Robert E. Quinn		1937	Theodore F. Green		1937
1938			1938			1938
1939	William H. Vanderbilt		1939			1939
1940			1940			1940
1941	J. Howard McGrath		1941			1941
1942			1942			1942
1943			1943			1943
1944			1944			1944
1945	John O. Pastore		1945			1945
1946			1946			1946
1947		J. Howard McGrath	1947			1947
1948			1948			1948
1949		Edward L. Leahy	1949			1949
1950	John S. McKiernan	John O. Pastore	1950			1950
1951	Dennis J. Roberts		1951			1951
1952			1952			1952
1953			1953			1953
1954			1954			1954
1955			1955			1955
1956			1956			1956
1957			1957			1957
1958			1958		Francis B. Condon	1958
1959	Christopher Del Sesto		1959			1959
1960			1960			1960
1961	John A. Notte, Jr.		1961	Claiborne Pell		1961
1962			1962			1962
1963	John H. Chafee		1963			1963
1964			1964			1964
1965			1965			1965
1966			1966		Thomas H. Roberts	1966
1967			1967			1967
1968			1968			1968
1969	Frank Licht		1969			1969
1970			1970			1970
1971			1971			1971
1972			1972			1972
1973	Philip W. Noel		1973			1973

SOUTH CAROLINA

	Governors	*United States Senators*			*Chief Justices*	
1789	Charles Pinckney	Pierce Butler	1789	Ralpy Izard	William H. Drayton	1789
1790			1790			1790
1791			1791		John Rutledge	1791
1792	Arnoldus Vanderhorst		1792			1792
1793			1793			1793
1794	William Moultrie		1794			1794
1795			1795	Jacob Read		1795
1796	Charles Pinckney	John Hunter	1796			1796
1797			1797			1797
1798	Edward Rutledge	Charles Pinckney	1798			1798
1799			1799			1799
1800	John Drayton		1800			1800
1801		Thomas Sumter	1801	John E. Colhoun		1801
1802	James R. Richardson		1802	Pierce Butler		1802
1803			1803			1803
1804	Paul Hamilton		1804	John Gaillard		1804
1805			1805		*There were no Chief Justices of South Carolina from 1795 to 1860.*	1805
1806	Charles Pinckney		1806			1806
1807			1807			1807
1808	John Drayton		1808			1808
1809			1809			1809
1810	Henry Middleton	John Taylor	1810			1810
1811			1811			1811
1812	Joseph Alston		1812			1812
1813			1813			1813
1814	David R. Williams		1814			1814
1815			1815			1815
1816	Andrew Pickens	William Smith	1816			1816
1817			1817			1817
1818	John Geddes		1818			1818
1819			1819			1819
1820	Thomas Bennett		1820			1820
1821			1821			1821
1822	John L. Wilson		1822			1822
1823		Robert Y. Hayne	1823			1823
1824	Richard I. Manning		1824			1824
1825			1825			1825
1826	John Taylor		1826	William Harper		1826
1826			1826	William Smith		1826
1827			1827			1827
1828	Stephen D. Miller		1828			1828
1829			1829			1829
1830	James Hamilton		1830			1830
1831			1831	Stephen D. Miller		1831
1832	Robert Y. Hayne	John C. Calhoun	1832			1832
1833			1833	William C. Preston		1833
1834	George McDuffie		1834			1834
1835			1835			1835
1836	Pierce M. Butler		1836			1836
1837			1837			1837
1838	Patrick Noble		1838			1838
1839			1839			1839
1840	John P. Richardson		1840			1840
1841			1841			1841
1842	James H. Hammond		1842	George McDuffie		1842
1843		Daniel E. Huger	1843			1843
1844	William Aiken		1844			1844
1845		John C. Calhoun	1845			1845
1846	David Johnson		1846	Andrew P. Butler		1846
1847			1847			1847
1848	Whitemarsh B. Seabrook		1848			1848
1849			1849			1849
1850	John H. Means	Franklin H. Elmore	1850			1850
1850		Robert W. Barnwell	1850			1850
1850		R. Barnwell Rhett	1850			1850
1851			1851			1851
1852	John L. Manning	William F. De Saussure	1852			1852

SOUTH CAROLINA–Continued

	Governors	*United States Senators*			*Chief Justices*	
1853		Josiah J. Evans	1853			1853
1854	James H. Adams		1854			1854
1855			1855			1855
1856	Robert F.W. Allston		1856			1856
1857			1857	James H. Hammond		1857
1858	William H. Gist	Arthur P. Hayne	1858			1858
1858		James Chestnut, Jr.	1858			1858
1859			1859			1859
1860	Francis W. Pickens	*Vacant*	1860	*Vacant*	John B. O'Neall	1860
1861			1861			1861
1862	Milledge L. Bonham		1862			1862
1863			1863			1863
1864	Andrew G. Magrath		1864			1864
1865	Benjamin F. Perry		1865		Benjamin F. Dunkin	1865
1866	James L. Orr		1866			1866
1867			1867			1867
1868	Robert K. Scott	Thomas J. Robertson	1868	Frederick A. Sawyer		1868
1869			1869			1869
1870			1870			1870
1871			1871			1871
1872	Franklin J. Moses		1872			1872
1873			1873	John J. Patterson		1873
1874	Daniel H. Chamberlain		1874			1874
1875			1875			1875
1876	Wade Hampton		1876			1876
1877		Matthew C. Butler	1877		Ammiel J. Willard	1877
1878	William D. Simpson		1878			1878
1879			1879	Wade Hampton	William D. Simpson	1879
1880	Thomas B. Jeter		1880			1880
1880	Johnson Hagood		1880			1880
1881			1881			1881
1882	Hugh S. Thompson		1882			1882
1883			1883			1883
1884			1884			1884
1885			1885			1885
1886	John C. Sheppard		1886			1886
1886	John P. Richardson		1886			1886
1887			1887			1887
1888			1888			1888
1889			1889			1889
1890	Benjamin R. Tillman		1890			1890
1891			1891	John L.M. Irby		1891
1892			1892			1892
1893			1893			1893
1894	John G. Evans		1894			1894
1895		Benjamin R. Tillman	1895			1895
1896	William H. Ellerbe		1896			1896
1897			1897	Joseph H. Earle		1897
1897			1897	John L. McLaurin		1897
1898			1898			1898
1899	Miles B. McSweeney		1899		Henry McIver	1899
1900			1900			1900
1901			1901			1901
1902			1902			1902
1903	Duncan C. Heyward		1903	Asbury C. Latimer	Young J. Pope	1903
1904			1904			1904
1905			1905			1905
1906			1906			1906
1907	Martin F. Ansel		1907			1907
1908			1908	Frank B. Gary		1908
1909			1909	Ellison D. Smith	Ira B. Jones	1909
1910			1910			1910
1911	Coleman L. Blease		1911			1911
1912			1912		Eugene B. Gary	1912
1913			1913			1913
1914			1914			1914
1915	Richard I. Manning		1915			1915
1916			1916			1916
1917			1917			1917

SOUTH CAROLINA–Continued

	Governors	*United States Senators*			*Chief Justices*	
1918		Christie Benet	1918			1918
1918		William P. Pollock	1918			1918
1919	Robert A. Cooper	Nathaniel B. Dial	1919			1919
1920			1920			1920
1921			1921			1921
1922			1922			1922
1923	Thomas G. McLeod		1923			1923
1924			1924			1924
1925		Coleman L. Blease	1925			1925
1926			1926		Richard C. Watts	1926
1927	John G. Richards		1927			1927
1928			1928			1928
1929			1929			1929
1930			1930			1930
1931	Irbra C. Blackwood	James F. Byrnes	1931		Euguene S. Blease	1931
1932			1932			1932
1933			1933			1933
1934			1934			1934
1935	Olin D. Johnston		1935		John G. Stabler	1935
1936			1936			1936
1937			1937			1937
1938			1938			1938
1939	Burnet R. Maybank		1939			1939
1940			1940		Milledge Bonham	1940
1941	J.E. Harley	Roger C. Peace	1941			1941
1941		Burnet R. Maybank	1941			1941
1942	R.M. Jefferies		1942			1942
1943	Olin D. Johnston		1943			1943
1944			1944	Wilton E. Hall	D. Gordon Baker	1944
1945	Ransome J. Williams		1945	Olin D. Johnston		1945
1946			1946			1946
1947	J. Strom Thurmond		1947			1947
1948			1948			1948
1949			1949			1949
1950			1950			1950
1951	James F. Byrnes		1951			1951
1952			1952			1952
1953			1953			1953
1954		Charles E. Daniel	1954			1954
1955	George Bell Timmerman, Jr.	J. Strom Thurmond	1955			1955
1956		Thomas A. Wofford	1956		Taylor H. Stukes	1956
1957		J. Strom Thurmond	1957			1957
1958			1958			1958
1959	Ernest F. Hollings		1959			1959
1960			1960			1960
1961			1961		Claude A. Taylor	1961
1962			1962			1962
1963	Donald S. Russell		1963			1963
1964			1964			1964
1965	Robert E. McNair		1965	Donald S. Russell		1965
1966			1966		Joseph R. Moss	1966
1967			1967	Ernest F. Hollings		1968
1969			1969			1969
1970			1970			1970
1971	John C. West		1971			1971
1972			1972			1972
1973			1973			1973

SOUTH DAKOTA

	Governors	*United States Senators*			*Chief Justices*	
1889	Arthur C. Mellette	Richard F. Pettigrew	1889	Gideon C. Moody		1889
1890			1890			1890
1891			1891	James H. Kyle		1891
1892			1892			1892
1893	Charles H. Sheldon		1893			1893
1894			1894			1894
1895			1895			1895
1896			1896			1896
1897	Andrew E. Lee		1897			1897
1898			1898			1898
1899			1899			1899
1900			1900			1900
1901	Charles N. Herreid	Robert J. Gamble	1901	Alfred B. Kittredge		1901
1902			1902			1902
1903			1903			1903
1904			1904			1904
1905	Samuel H. Elrod		1905			1905
1906			1906			1906
1907	Corie I. Crawford		1907			1907
1908			1908			1908
1909	Robert S. Vessey		1909	Coe I. Crawford	*Justices of the Supreme Court serve on a rotating basis as Chief Presiding Judge*	1909
1910			1910			1910
1911			1911			1911
1912			1912			1912
1913	Frank M. Byrne	Thomas Sterling	1913			1913
1914			1914			1914
1915			1915	Edwin S. Johnson		1915
1916			1916			1916
1917	Peter Norbeck		1917			1917
1918			1918			1918
1919			1919			1919
1920			1920			1920
1921	William H. McMaster		1921	Peter Norbeck		1921
1922			1922			1922
1923			1923			1923
1924			1924			1924
1925	Carl Gunderson	William H. McMaster	1925			1925
1926			1926			1926
1927	William J. Bulow		1927			1927
1928			1928			1928
1929			1929			1929
1930			1930			1930
1931	Warren E. Green	William J. Bulow	1931			1931
1932			1932			1932
1933	Tom Berry		1933			1933
1934			1934			1934
1935			1935			1935
1936			1936			1936
1937	Leslie Jensen		1937	Herbert E. Hitchcock		1937
1938			1938	Gladys Pyle		1938
1939	Harlan J. Bushfield		1939	J. Chandler Gurney		1939
1940			1940			1940
1941			1941			1941
1942			1942			1942
1943	M. Q. Sharpe	Harlan J. Bushfield	1943			1943
1944			1944			1944
1945			1945			1945
1946			1946			1946
1947	George T. Mickelson	Karl E. Mundt	1947			1947
1948			1948			1948
1949			1949			1949
1950			1950			1950
1951	Sigurd Anderson		1951	Francis H. Case		1951
1952			1952			1952
1953			1953			1953
1954			1954			1954

SOUTH DAKOTA–Continued

	Governors	*United States Senators*			*Chief Justices*	
1955	Joe Foss		1955			1955
1956			1956			1956
1957			1957			1957
1958			1958			1958
1959	Ralph Herseth		1959			1959
1960			1960			1960
1961	Archie Gubbrud		1961			1961
1962			1962	Joseph J. Bottum		1962
1963			1963	George S. McGovern		1963
1964			1964			1964
1965	Nils A. Boe		1965			1965
1966			1966			1966
1967			1967			1967
1968			1968			1968
1969	Frank L. Farrar		1969			1969
1970			1970			1970
1971	Richard F. Kneip		1971			1971
1972			1972			1972
1973		James Abourezk	1973			1973

TENNESSEE

Year	*Governors*	*United States Senators*	Year	*United States Senators*	*Chief Justices*	Year
1796	John Sevier	William Blount	1796	William Cocke		1796
1797		Joseph Anderson	1797	Andrew Jackson		1797
1798			1798	Daniel Smith		1798
1799			1799	William Cocke		1799
1800			1800			1800
1801	Archibald Roane		1801			1801
1802			1802			1802
1803	John Sevier		1803			1803
1804			1804			1804
1805			1805	Daniel Smith		1805
1806			1806			1806
1807			1807			1807
1808			1808			1808
1809	Willie Blount		1809	Jenkin Whiteside		1809
1810			1810			1810
1811			1811	George W. Campbell		1811
1812			1812			1812
1813			1813			1813
1814			1814	Jesse Wharton		1814
1815	Joseph McMinn	George W. Campbell	1815	John Williams		1815
1816			1816			1816
1817			1817			1817
1818		John H. Eaton	1818			1818
1819			1819			1819
1820			1820			1820
1821	William Carroll		1821			1821
1822			1822			1822
1823			1823	Andrew Jackson		1823
1824			1824			1824
1825			1825	Hugh L. White		1825
1826			1826			1826
1827	Samuel Houston		1827			1827
1828			1828			1828
1829	William Hall	Felix Grundy	1829			1829
1829	William Carroll		1829			1829
1830			1830			1830
1831			1831		John Catron	1831
1832			1832			1832
1833			1833			1833
1834			1834			1834
1835	Newton Cannon		1835		*There were no Chief*	1835
1836			1836		*Justices of Tennessee*	1836
1837			1837		*between 1835 and 1870*	1837
1838		Ephraim H. Foster	1838			1838
1839	James K. Polk		1839			1839
1839		Felix Grundy	1839			1839
1840		Alfred O. P. Nicholson	1840	Alexander Anderson		1840
1841	James C. Jones		1841	*Vacant*		1841
1842			1842			1842
1843		Ephraim H. Foster	1843	Spencer Jarnagin		1843
1844			1844			1844
1845	Aaron V. Brown	Hopkins L. Turney	1845			1845
1846			1846			1846
1847	Neil S. Brown		1847	John Bell		1847
1848			1848			1848
1849	William Trousdale		1849			1849
1850			1850			1850
1851	William B. Campbell	James C. Jones	1851			1851
1852			1852			1852
1853	Andrew Johnson		1853			1853
1854			1854			1854
1855			1855			1855
1856			1856			1856
1857	Isham G. Harris	Andrew Johnson	1857			1857
1858			1858			1858
1859			1859	Alfred O. P. Nicholson		1859
1860			1860			1860
1861			1861			1861
1862	Andrew Johnson		1862			1862

TENNESSEE—Continued

	Governors	*United States Senators*			*Chief Justices*	
1863		*Vacant*	1863	*Vacant*		1863
1864			1864			1864
1865	William G. Brownlow		1865			1865
1866		Joseph S. Fowler	1866	David T. Patterson		1866
1867			1867			1867
1868			1868			1868
1869	DeWitt C. Senter		1869	William G. Brownlow		1869
1870			1870		Alfred O. P. Nicholson	1870
1871	John C. Brown	Henry Cooper	1871			1871
1872			1872			1872
1873			1873			1873
1874			1874			1874
1875	James D. Porter		1875	Andrew Johnson		1875
1875			1875	David M. Key		1875
1876			1876		James W. Deaderick	1876
1877		Isham G. Harris	1877	James E. Bailey		1877
1878			1878			1878
1879	Albert S. Marks		1879			1879
1880			1880			1880
1881	Alvin Hawkins		1881	Howell E. Jackson		1881
1882			1882			1882
1883	William B. Bate		1883			1883
1884			1884			1884
1885			1885			1885
1886			1886	Washington C. Whitthorne	Peter Turney	1886
1887	Robert L. Taylor		1887	William B. Bate		1887
1888			1888			1888
1889			1889			1889
1890			1890			1890
1891	John P. Buchanan		1891			1891
1892			1892			1892
1893	Peter Turney		1893		Horace W. Lurton	1893
1893			1893		Benjamin J. Lea	1893
1894			1894		David L. Snodgrass	1894
1895			1895			1895
1896			1896			1896
1897	Robert L. Taylor	Thomas B. Turley	1897			1897
1898			1898			1898
1899	Benton McMillin		1899			1899
1900			1900			1900
1901		Edward W. Carmack	1901			1901
1902			1902		William D. Beard	1902
1903	James B. Frazier		1903			1903
1904			1904			1904
1905	John I. Cox		1905	James B. Frazier		1905
1906			1906			1906
1907	Malcolm R. Petterson	Robert L. Taylor	1907			1907
1908			1908			1908
1909			1909			1909
1910			1910		John K. Shields	1910
1911	Ben W. Hooper		1911	Luke Lea		1911
1912		Newell Sanders	1912			1912
1913		William R. Webb	1913		Matt M. Neil	1913
1913		John K. Shields	1913			1913
1914			1914			1914
1915	Thomas C. Rye		1915			1915
1916			1916			1916
1917			1917	Kenneth D. McKellar		1917
1918			1918		Dick L. Lansden	1918
1919	Albert H. Roberts		1919			1919
1920			1920			1920
1921	Alfred A. Taylor		1921			1921
1922			1922			1922
1923	Austin Peay		1923		Grafton Green	1923
1924			1924			1924
1925		Lawrence D. Tyson	1925			1925
1926			1926			1926
1927	Henry H. Horton		1927			1927

TENNESSEE—Continued

	Governors	*United States Senators*			*Chief Justices*	
1928			1928			1928
1929		William E. Brock	1929			1929
1930			1930			1930
1931		Cordell Hull	1931			1931
1932			1932			1932
1933	Hill McAlister	Nathan L. Bachman	1933			1933
1934			1934			1934
1935			1935			1935
1936			1936			1936
1937	Gordon Browning	George L. Berry	1937			1937
1938		*Vacant*	1938			1938
1939	Prentice Cooper	A. Tom Stewart	1939			1939
1940			1940			1940
1941			1941			1941
1942			1942			1942
1943			1943			1943
1944			1944			1944
1945	Jim McCord		1945			1945
1946			1946			1946
1947			1947		Alex W. Chambliss	1947
1947			1947		A. B. Neil	1947
1948			1948			1948
1949	Gordon Browning	Estes Kefauver	1949			1949
1950			1950			1950
1951			1951			1951
1952			1952			1952
1953	Frank Clement		1953	Albert A. Gore		1953
1954			1954			1954
1955			1955			1955
1956			1956			1956
1957			1957			1957
1958			1958			1958
1959	Buford Ellington		1959			1959
1960			1960		Alan M. Prewitt	1960
1961			1961			1961
1962			1962			1962
1963	Frank Clement		1693		Hamilton S. Burnett	1963
1964		Herbert S. Walters	1964			1964
1964		Ross Bass	1964			1964
1965			1965			1965
1967	Buford Ellington	Howard H. Baker, Jr.	1967			1967
1968			1968			1968
1969			1969		Ross W. Dyer	1969
1970			1970			1970
1971	Winfield Dunn		1971	William E. Brock III		1971
1972			1972			1972
1973			1973			1973

TEXAS

	Governors	*United States Senators*			*Chief Justices*	
1846	James P. Henderson	Sam Houston	1846	Thomas J. Rusk	John Hemphill	1846
1847	George T. Wood		1847			1847
1848			1848			1848
1849	Peter H. Bell		1849			1849
1850			1850			1850
1851			1851			1851
1852			1852			1852
1853	J. W. Henderson (Acting)		1853			1853
1853	Elisha M. Pease		1853			1853
1854			1854			1854
1855			1855			1855
1856			1856			1856
1857	Hardin R. Runnels		1857	James P. Henderson		1857
1858			1858	Matthias Ward	Royal T. Wheeler	1858
1859	Sam Houston	John Hemphill	1859	Louis T. Wigfall		1859
1860			1860			1860
1861	Edward Clark (Acting)	*Vacant*	1861	*Vacant*		1861
1861	Francis R. Lubbock		1861			1861
1862			1862			1862
1863	Pendleton Murrah		1863			1863
1864			1864		Oran M. Roberts	1864
1865	Andrew J. Hamilton		1865			1865
1866	James W. Throckmorton		1866		George F. Moore	1866
1867	Elisha M. Pease		1867		Amos Morrill	1867
1868			1868			1868
1869			1869			1869
1870	Edmund J. Davis	Morgan C. Hamilton	1870	James W. Flanagan	Lemuel D. Evans	1870
1871			1871			1871
1872			1872			1872
1873			1873		Wesley Ogden	1873
1874	Richard Coke		1874		Oran M. Roberts	1874
1875			1875	Samuel B. Maxey		1875
1876	Richard B. Hubbard		1876			1876
1877		Richard Coke	1877			1877
1878			1878		George F. Moore	1878
1879	Oran M. Roberts		1879			1879
1880			1880			1880
1881			1881		Robert S. Gould	1881
1882			1882		Asa H. Willie	1882
1883	John Ireland		1883			1883
1884			1884			1884
1885			1885			1885
1886			1886			1886
1887	Lawrence S. Ross		1887	John H. Reagan		1887
1888			1888		John W. Stayton	1888
1889			1889			1889
1890			1890			1890
1891	James S. Hogg		1891	Horace Chilton		1891
1892			1892	Roger Q. Mills		1892
1893			1893			1893
1894			1894		Reuben R. Gaines	1894
1895	Charles A. Culberson	Horace Chilton	1895			1895
1896			1896			1896
1897			1897			1897
1898			1898			1898
1899	Joseph D. Sayers		1899	Charles A. Culberson		1899
1900			1900			1900
1901		Joseph W. Bailey	1901			1901
1902			1902			1902
1903	Samuel W. T. Lanham		1903			1903
1904			1904			1904
1905			1905			1905
1906			1906			1906
1907	Thomas M. Campbell		1907			1907
1908			1908			1908
1909			1909			1909
1910			1910			1910
1911	Oscar B. Colquitt		1911		Thomas J. Brown	1911
1912			1912			1912
1913		Rienzi M. Johnston	1913			1913
1913		Morris Sheppard	1913			1913
1914			1914			1914
1915	James E. Ferguson		1915		Nelson Phillips	1915
1916			1916			1916
1917	William P. Hobby		1917			1917
1918			1918			1918

TEXAS–Continued

	Governors	*United States Senators*		*United States Senators*	*Chief Justices*	
1919			1919			1919
1920			1920			1920
1921	Pat M. Neff		1921		Calvin M. Cureton	1921
1922			1922			1922
1923			1923	Earle B. Mayfield		1923
1924			1924			1924
1925	Miriam A. Ferguson		1925			1925
1926			1926			1926
1927	Dan Moody		1927			1927
1928			1928			1928
1929			1929	Tom T. Connally		1929
1930			1930			1930
1931	Ross S. Sterling		1931			1931
1932			1932			1932
1933	Miriam A. Ferguson		1933			1933
1934			1934			1934
1935	James V. Allred		1935			1935
1936			1936			1936
1937			1937			1937
1938			1938			1938
1939	W. Lee O'Daniel		1939			1939
1940			1940		W. F. Moore	1940
1941	Coke R. Stevenson	W. Lee O'Daniel	1941		James P. Alexander	1941
1942			1942			1942
1943			1943			1943
1944			1944			1944
1945			1945			1945
1946			1946			1946
1947	Beauford H. Jester		1947			1947
1948			1948		J. E. Hickman	1948
1949	Allan Shivers	Lyndon B. Johnson	1949			1949
1950			1950			1950
1951			1951			1951
1952			1952			1952
1953			1953	M. Price Daniel		1953
1954			1954			1954
1955			1955			1955
1956			1956			1956
1957	M. Price Daniel		1957	William A. Blakley		1957
1957			1957	Ralph W. Yarborough		1957
1958			1958			1958
1959			1959			1959
1960			1960			1960
1961		William A. Blakley	1961		Robert W. Calvert	1961
1961		John G. Tower	1961			1961
1962			1962			1962
1963	John B. Connally		1963			1963
1964			1964			1964
1965			1965			1965
1966			1966			1966
1967			1967			1967
1968			1968			1968
1969	Preston Smith		1969			1969
1970			1970			1970
1971			1971			1971
1972			1972			1972
1973	Adolph Briscoe		1973			1973

UTAH

	Governors	*United States Senators*			*Chief Justices*	
1896	Heber M. Wells	Frank J. Cannon	1896	Arthur Brown	*Justices of the Supreme Court serve on a rotating basis as Chief Presiding Judge*	1896
1897			1897	Joseph L. Rawlins		1897
1898			1898			1898
1899		*Vacant*	1899			1899
1900			1900			1900
1901		Thomas Kearns	1901			1901
1902			1902			1902
1903			1903	Reed Smoot		1903
1904			1904			1904
1905	John C. Cutler	George Sutherland	1905			1905
1906			1906			1906
1907			1907			1907
1908			1908			1908
1909	William Spry		1909			1909
1910			1910			1910
1911			1911			1911
1912			1912			1912
1913			1913			1913
1914			1914			1914
1915			1915			1915
1916			1916			1916
1917	Simon Bamberger	William H. King	1917			1917
1918			1918			1918
1919			1919			1919
1920			1920			1920
1921	Charles R. Mabey		1921			1921
1922			1922			1922
1923			1923			1923
1924			1924			1924
1925	George H. Dern		1925			1925
1926			1926			1926
1927			1927			1927
1928			1928			1928
1929			1929			1929
1930			1930			1930
1931			1931			1931
1932			1932			1932
1933	Henry H. Blood		1933	Elbert D. Thomas		1933
1934			1934			1934
1935			1935			1935
1936			1936			1936
1937			1937			1937
1938			1938			1938
1939			1939			1939
1940			1940			1940
1941	Herbert B. Maw	Abe Murdock	1941			1941
1942			1942			1942
1943			1943			1943
1944			1944			1944
1945			1945			1945
1946			1946			1946
1947		Arthur V. Watkins	1947			1947
1948			1948			1948
1949	J. Bracken Lee		1949			1949
1950			1950			1950
1951			1951	Wallace F. Bennett		1951
1952			1952			1952
1953			1953			1953
1954			1954			1954
1955			1955			1955
1956			1956			1956
1957	George D. Clyde		1957			1957
1958			1958			1958
1959		Frank E. Moss	1959			1959
1960			1960			1960
1961			1961			1961
1962			1962			1962
1963			1963			1963
1964			1964			1964
1965	Calvin L. Rampton		1965			1965
1966			1966			1966
1967			1967			1967
1968			1968			1968
1969			1969			1969
1970			1970			1970
1971			1971			1971
1972			1972			1972
1973			1973			1973

VERMONT

	Governors	*United States Senators*			*Chief Justices*	
1791	Thomas Chittenden	Moses Robinson	1791	Stephen R. Bradley	Samuel Knight	1791
1792			1792			1792
1793			1793			1793
1794			1794		Isaac Tichenor	1794
1795			1795	Elijah Paine		1795
1796		Isaac Tichenor	1796		Nathaniel Chipman	1796
1797	Paul Brigham	Nathaniel Chipman	1797		Israel Smith	1797
1797	Isaac Tichenor		1797			1797
1798			1798		Enoch Woodbridge	1798
1799			1799			1799
1800			1800			1800
1801			1801	Stephen R. Bradley	Jonathan Robinson	1801
1802			1802			1802
1803		Israel Smith	1803			1803
1804			1804			1804
1805			1805			1805
1806			1806			1806
1807	Israel Smith	Jonathan Robinson	1807		Royall Tyler	1807
1808	Isaac Tichenor		1808			1808
1809	Jonas Galusha		1809			1809
1810			1810			1810
1811			1811			1811
1812			1812			1812
1813	Martin Chittenden		1813	Dudley Chase	Nathaniel Chipman	1813
1814			1814			1814
1815	Jonas Galusha	Isaac Tichenor	1815		Asa Aldis	1815
1816			1816			1816
1817			1817	James Fisk	Dudley Chase	1817
1818			1818	William A. Palmer		1818
1819			1819			1819
1820	Richard Skinner		1820			1820
1821		Horatio Seymour	1821		Cornelius P. Van Ness	1821
1822			1822			1822
1823	Cornelius P. Van Ness		1823		Richard Skinner	1823
1824			1824			1824
1825			1825	Dudley Chase		1825
1826	Ezra Butler		1826			1826
1827			1827			1827
1828	Samuel C. Crafts		1828			1828
1829			1829		Samuel Prentiss	1829
1830			1830		Titus Hutchinson	1830
1831	William A. Palmer		1831	Samuel Prentiss		1831
1832			1832			1832
1833		Benjamin Swift	1833		Charles K. Williams	1833
1834			1834			1834
1835	Silas H. Jenison		1835			1835
1836			1836			1836
1837			1837			1837
1838			1838			1838
1839		Samuel S. Phelps	1839			1839
1840			1840			1840
1841	Charles Paine		1841			1841
1842			1842	Samuel C. Crafts		1842
1843	John Mattocks		1843	William Upham		1843
1844	William Slade		1844			1844
1845			1845			1845
1846	Horace Eaton		1846		Stephen Royce	1846
1847			1847			1847
1848			1848			1848
1849	Carlos Coolidge		1849			1849
1850	Charles K. Williams		1850			1850
1851		Solomon Foot	1851			1851
1852	Erastus Fairbanks		1852		Isaac F. Redfield	1852
1853	John S. Robinson		1853	Samuel S. Phelps		1853
1854	Stephen Royce		1854	Lawrence Brainerd		1854
1855			1855	Jacob Collamer		1855
1856	Ryland Fletcher		1856			1856
1857			1857			1857

VERMONT–Continued

	Governors	*United States Senators*			*Chief Justices*	
1858	Hiland Hall		1858			1858
1859			1859			1859
1860	Erastus Fairbanks		1800		Luke P. Poland	1860
1860	Hiland Hall		1860			1860
1861	Frederick Holbrook		1801			1861
1862			1862			1862
1863	John G. Smith		1863			1863
1864			1864			1864
1865	Paul Dillingham, Jr.		1865	Luke P. Poland	John Pierpoint	1865
1866		George F. Edmunds	1866			1866
1867	John B. Page		1867	Justin S. Morrill		1867
1868			1868			1868
1869	Peter T. Washburn		1869			1869
1870	George W. Hendee		1870			1870
1870	John W. Stewart		1870			1870
1871			1871			1871
1872	Julius Converse		1872			1872
1873			1873			1873
1874	Asahel Peck		1874			1874
1875			1875			1875
1876	Horace Fairbanks		1870			1876
1877			1877			1877
1878	Redfield Proctor		1878			1878
1879			1879			1879
1880	Roswell Farnham		1880			1880
1881			1881			1881
1882	John L. Barstow		1882		Homer E. Royce	1882
1883			1883			1883
1884	Samuel E. Pingree		1884			1884
1885			1885			1885
1886	Ebenezer J. Ormsbee		1886			1886
1887			1887			1887
1888	William P. Dillingham		1888			1888
1889			1889			1889
1890	Carroll S. Page		1890		Jonathan Ross	1890
1891		Redfield Proctor	1891			1891
1892	Levi K. Fuller		1892			1892
1893			1893			1893
1894	Urban A. Woodbury		1894			1894
1895			1895			1895
1896	Josiah Grout		1896			1896
1897			1897			1897
1898	Edward C. Smith		1898		Russell S. Taft	1898
1899			1899	Jonathan Ross		1899
1900	William W. Stickney		1900	William P. Dillingham		1900
1901			1901			1901
1902	John G. McCullough		1902		John W. Rowell	1902
1903			1903			1903
1904	Charles J. Bell		1904			1904
1905			1905			1905
1906	Fletcher D. Proctor		1906			1906
1907			1907			1907
1908	George H. Prouty	John W. Stewart	1908			1908
1908		Carroll S. Page	1908			1908
1909			1909			1909
1910	John A. Mead		1910			1910
1911			1911			1911
1912	Allen M. Fletcher		1912			1912
1913			1913		George M. Powers	1913
1914			1914			1914
1915	Charles W. Gates		1915		Loveland Munson	1915
1916			1916			1916
1917	Horace F. Graham		1917		John H. Watson	1917
1918			1918			1918
1919	Percival W. Clement		1919			1919
1920			1920			1920
1921	James Hartness		1921			1921
1922			1922			1922

VERMONT–Continued

	Governors	*United States Senators*		*United States Senators*	*Chief Justices*	
1923	Redfield Proctor	Frank L. Greene	1923	Porter H. Dale		1923
1924			1924			1924
1925	Franklin S. Billings		1925			1925
1926			1926			1926
1927	John E. Weeks		1927			1927
1928			1928			1928
1929			1929		George M. Powers	1929
1930		Frank C. Partridge	1930			1930
1931	Stanley C. Wilson	Warren R. Austin	1931			1931
1932			1932			1932
1933			1933	Ernest W. Gibson		1933
1934			1934			1934
1935	Charles M. Smith		1935			1935
1936			1936			1936
1937	George D. Aiken		1937			1937
1938			1938		Sherman R. Moulton	1938
1939			1939			1939
1940			1940	Ernest W. Gibson, Jr.		1940
1941	William H. Wills		1941	George D. Aiken		1941
1942			1942			1942
1943			1943			1943
1944			1944			1944
1945	Mortimer R. Proctor		1945			1945
1946		Ralph E. Flanders	1946			1946
1947	Ernest W. Gibson, Jr.		1947			1947
1948			1948			1948
1949			1949		John C. Sherburne	1949
1950	Harold J. Arthur		1950			1950
1951	Lee E. Emerson		1951			1951
1952			1952			1952
1953			1953			1953
1954			1954			1954
1955	Joseph B. Johnson		1955		Olin M. Jeffords	1955
1956			1956			1956
1957			1957			1957
1958			1958		Walter H. Cleary	1958
1959	Robert T. Stafford	Winston L. Prouty	1959		Benjamin N. Hulburd	1959
1960			1960			1960
1961	F. Ray Keyser, Jr.		1961			1961
1962			1962			1962
1963	Philip H. Hoff		1963		James S. Holden	1963
1964			1964			1964
1965			1965			1965
1966			1966			1966
1967			1967			1967
1968			1968			1968
1969	Deane C. Davis		1969			1969
1970			1970			1970
1971			1971			1971
1972			1972			1972
1973	Thomas Salmon		1973			1973

VIRGINIA

	Governors	*United States Senators*			*Chief Justices*	
1788			1788		Edmund Pendleton	1788
1789	Beverly Randolph	William Grayson	1789	Richard Henry Lee		1789
1790		John Walker	1790			1790
1790		James Monroe	1790			1790
1791	Henry Lee		1791			1791
1792			1792	John Taylor		1792
1793			1793			1793
1794	Robert Brooke	Stevens T. Mason	1794	Henry Tazewell		1794
1795			1795			1795
1796	James Wood		1796			1796
1797			1797			1797
1798			1798			1798
1799	James Monroe		1799	Wilson C. Nicholas		1799
1800			1800			1800
1801			1801			1801
1802	John Page		1802			1802
1803		John Taylor	1803			1803
1803		Abraham B. Venable	1803			1803
1804		William B. Giles	1804	Andrew Moore	Peter Lyons	1804
1805	William H. Cabell		1805			1805
1806			1806			1806
1807			1807			1807
1808	John Tyler		1808			1808
1809			1809	Richard Brent		1809
1810			1810		William F. Fleming	1810
1811	James Monroe		1811			1811
1811	George W. Smith		1811			1811
1812	James Barbour		1812			1812
1813			1813			1813
1814	Wilson C. Nicholas		1814			1814
1815			1815	James Barbour		1815
1816	James P. Preston	Armistead T. Mason	1816			1816
1817		John W. Eppes	1817			1817
1818			1818			1818
1819	Thomas M. Randolph	James Pleasants	1819			1819
1820			1820			1820
1821			1821			1821
1822	James Pleasants	John Taylor	1822			1822
1823			1823			1823
1824		Littleton W. Tazewell	1824		Francis T. Brooke	1824
1825	John Tyler		1825	John Randolph		1825
1826			1820			1826
1827	William B. Giles		1827	John Tyler		1827
1828			1828			1828
1829			1829			1829
1830	John Floyd		1830			1830
1831			1831		Henry St. George Tucker	1831
1832		William C. Rives	1832			1832
1833			1833			1893
1834	Littleton W. Tazewell	Benjamin W. Leigh	1834			1834
1835			1835			1895
1836	Wyndham Robertson	Richard E. Parker	1836	William C. Rives		1836
1837	David Campbell	William H. Roane	1837			1837
1898			1838			1838
1839			1839			1839
1840	Thomas W. Gilmer		1840			1840
1841	John Rutherford	William S. Archer	1841			1821
1842	John M. Gregory		1842		William H. Cabell	1842
1843	James McDowell		1843			1843
1844			1844			1844
1845			1845	Isaac S. Pennybacker		1845
1846	William Smith		1846			1846
1847		Robert M. T. Hunter	1847	James M. Mason		1847
1848			1828			1848
1849	John B. Floyd		1849			1849
1850			1850			1850
1851			1851			1851
1852	Joseph Johnson		1852		John J. Allen	1852

VIRGINIA–Continued

	Governors	*United States Senators*			*Chief Justices*	
1853			1853			1853
1854			1854			1854
1855			1855			1855
1856	Henry A. Wise		1856			1856
1857			1857			1857
1858			1858			1858
1859			1859			1859
1860	John Letcher		1860			1860
1861		John S. Carlile	1861	Waitman T. Willey		1861
1862			1862			1862
1863			1863	Lemuel J. Bowden		1863
1864	William Smith		1864			1864
1865	Francis H. Pierpont	*Vacant*	1865	*Vacant*		1865
1866			1866		Richard C. L. Moncure	1866
1867			1867			1867
1868	Henry H. Wells		1868			1868
1869	Gilbert C. Walker		1869			1869
1870		John W. Johnston	1870	John F. Lewis		1870
1871			1871			1871
1872			1872			1872
1873			1873			1873
1874	James L. Kemper		1874			1874
1875			1875	Robert E. Withers		1875
1876			1876			1876
1877			1877			1877
1878	Frederick W. M. Holliday		1878			1878
1879			1879			1879
1880			1880			1880
1881			1881	William Mahone		1881
1882	William E. Cameron		1882		Lunsford L. Lewis	1882
1883		Harrison H. Riddleberger	1883			1883
1884			1884			1884
1885			1885			1885
1886	Fitzhugh Lee		1886			1886
1887			1887	John W. Daniel		1887
1888			1888			1888
1889		John S. Barbour	1889			1889
1890	Philip W. McKinney		1890			1890
1891			1891			1891
1892		Eppa Hunton	1892			1892
1893			1893			1893
1894	Charles T. O'Ferrall		1894		James Keith	1894
1895		Thomas S. Martin	1895			1895
1896			1896			1896
1897			1897			1897
1898	J. Hoge Tyler		1898			1898
1899			1899			1899
1900			1900			1900
1901			1901			1901
1902	Andrew J. Montague		1902			1902
1903			1903			1903
1904			1904			1904
1905			1905			1905
1906	Claude A. Swanson		1906			1906
1907			1907			1907
1908			1908			1908
1909			1909			1909
1910	William H. Mann		1910	Claude A. Swanson		1910
1911			1911			1911
1912			1912			1912
1913			1913			1913
1914	Henry C. Stuart		1914			1914
1915			1915			1915
1916			1916		Richard H. Cardwell	1916
1916			1916		George M. Harrison	1916
1917			1917		Stafford G. White	1917
1918	Westmoreland Davis		1918			1918
1919			1919			1919

VIRGINIA—Continued

	Governors	*United States Senators*			*Chief Justices*	
1920		Carter Glass	1920		Joseph L. Kelly	1920
1921			1921			1921
1922	E. Lee Trinkle		1922			1922
1923			1923			1923
1924			1924		Frederick W. Sims	1924
1925			1925		Robert R. Prentis	1925
1926	Harry F. Byrd		1926			1926
1927			1927			1927
1928			1928			1928
1929			1929			1929
1930	John G. Pollard		1930			1930
1931			1931		Preston W. Campbell	1931
1932			1932			1932
1933			1933	Harry F. Byrd		1933
1934	George C. Peery		1934			1934
1935			1935			1935
1936			1936			1936
1937			1937			1937
1938	James H. Price		1938			1938
1939			1939			1939
1940			1940			1940
1941			1941			1941
1942	Colgate W. Darden, Jr.		1942			1942
1943			1943			1943
1944			1944			1944
1945			1945			1945
1946	William M. Tuck	Thomas G. Burch	1946		Henry W. Holt	1946
1947		A. Willis Robertson	1947		Edward W. Hudgins	1947
1948			1948			1948
1949			1949			1949
1950	John S. Battle		1950			1950
1951			1951			1951
1952			1952			1952
1953			1953			1953
1954	Thomas B. Stanley		1954			1954
1955			1955			1955
1956			1956			1950
1957			1957			1957
1958	J. Lindsay Almond, Jr.		1958		John W. Eggleston	1958
1959			1959			1959
1960			1960			1960
1961			1961			1961
1962	Albertis S. Harrison, Jr.		1962			1962
1963			1963			1963
1964			1964			1964
1965			1965	Harry F. Byrd, Jr.		1965
1966	Mille E. Godwin, Jr.		1966			1966
1967		William B. Spong, Jr.	1967			1967
1968			1968			1968
1969			1969		Harold F. Snead	1969
1970	Linwood Holton		1970			1970
1971			1971			1971
1972			1972			1972
1973		William L. Scott	1973			1973

WASHINGTON

Year	*Governors*	*United States Senators*		*Chief Justices*
1889	Elisha P. Ferry	John B. Allen	Watson C. Squire	Thomas J. Anders
1890				
1891				
1892				
1893	John H. McGraw	*Vacant*		Ralph O. Dunbar
1894				
1895		John L. Wilson		John P. Hoyt
1896				
1897	John R. Rogers		George Turner	Elmon Scott
1898				
1899		Addison G. Foster		Merritt J. Gordon
1900				Ralph O. Dunbar
1901	Henry McBride			James B. Reavis
1902				
1903			Levi Ankeny	Mark A. Fullerton
1904				
1905	Albert E. Mead	Samuel H. Piles		Wallace Mount
1906				
1907				Hiram E. Hadley
1908				
1909	Samuel G. Cosgrove		Wesley L. Jones	Frank H. Rudkin
1909	Marion E. Hay			
1910				
1911		Miles Poindexter		Ralph O. Dunbar
1912				
1913	Ernest Lister			Herman D. Crow
1914				
1915				George E. Morris
1916				
1917				Overton G. Ellis
1918				John F. Main
1919	Louis F. Hart			Stephen J. Chadwick
1920				
1921				Emmett N. Parker
1922				
1923		Clarence C. Dill		John F. Main
1924				
1925	Roland H. Hartley			Warren W. Tolman
1926				John F. Main
1927				Kenneth Mackintosh
1928				Mark A. Fullerton
1929				John R. Mitchell
1930				
1931				Warren W. Tolman
1932			Elijah S. Grammer	
1933	Clarence D. Martin		Homer T. Bone	Walter B. Beals
1934				
1935		Lewis B. Schwellenbach		William J. Millard
1936				
1937				William J. Steinert
1938				
1939				Bruce Blake
1940		Monrad C. Wallgren		
1941	Arthur B. Langlie			John S. Robinson
1942				
1943				George B. Simpson
1944			Warren G. Magnuson	
1945	Monrad C. Wallgren	Hugh B. Mitchell		Walter B. Beals
1946				Samuel M. Driver
1946		Harry P. Cain		
1947				Joseph A. Mallery
1948				
1949	Arthur B. Langlie			Clyde G. Jeffers
1949				George B. Simpson
1950				
1951				E. W. Schwellenbach

WASHINGTON–Continued

Year	*Governors*	*United States Senators*	*Chief Justices*
1952			
1953		Henry M. Jackson	Thomas E. Grady
1954			
1955			Frederick G. Hamley
1956			
1957	Albert D. Rosellini		Matthew W. Hill
1958			
1959			Frank P. Weaver
1960			
1961			Robert C. Finley
1962			
1963			Richard B. Ott
1964			
1965	Daniel J. Evans		Hugh J. Rosellini
1966			
1967			Robert C. Finley
1968			
1969			Robert T. Hunter
1970			
1971			Orris L. Hamilton
1972			
1973			

WEST VIRGINIA

	Governors	*United States Senators*			*Chief Justices*	
1863	Arthur I. Boreman	Peter G. Van Winkle	1863	Waitman T. Willey	*Justices of the Supreme Court serve on a rotating basis as Chief Presiding Judge*	1863
1864			1864			1864
1865			1865			1865
1866			1866			1866
1867			1867			1867
1868			1868			1868
1869	Daniel D. T. Farnsworth	Arthur I. Boreman	1869			1869
1869	William E. Stevenson		1869			1869
1870			1870			1870
1871	John J. Jacob		1871	Henry G. Davis		1871
1872			1872			1872
1873			1873			1873
1874			1874			1874
1875		Allen T. Caperton	1875			1875
1876		Samuel Price	1876			1876
1877	Henry M. Mathews	Frank Hereford	1877			1877
1878			1878			1878
1879			1879			1879
1880			1880			1880
1881	Jacob B. Jackson	Johnson N. Camden	1881			1881
1882			1882			1882
1883			1883	John E. Kenna		1883
1884			1884			1884
1885	Emanuel W. Wilson		1885			1885
1886			1886			1886
1887		Charles J. Faulkner	1887			1887
1888			1888			1888
1889			1889			1889
1890	Aretas B. Fleming		1890			1890
1891			1891			1891
1892			1892			1892
1893	William A. MacCorkle		1893	Johnson N. Camden		1893
1894			1894			1894
1895			1895	Stephen B. Elkins		1895
1896			1896			1896
1897	George W. Atkinson		1897			1897
1898			1898			1898
1899		Nathan B. Scott	1899			1899
1900			1900			1900
1901	Albert B. White		1901			1901
1902			1902			1902
1903			1903			1903
1904			1904			1904
1905	William M. O. Dawson		1905			1905
1906			1906			1906
1907			1907			1907
1908			1908			1908
1909	William E. Glasscock		1909			1909
1910			1910			1910
1911		William E. Chilton	1911	Davis Elkins		1911
1911			1911	Clarence W. Watson		1911
1912			1912			1912
1913	Henry D. Hatfield		1913	Nathan Goff		1913
1914			1914			1914
1915			1915			1915
1916			1916			1916
1917	John J. Cornwell	Howard Sutherland	1917			1917
1918			1918			1918
1919			1919	Davis Elkins		1919
1920			1920			1920
1921	Ephraim F. Morgan		1921			1921
1922			1922			1922
1923		Matthew M. Neely	1923			1923
1924			1924			1924
1925	Howard M. Gore		1925	Guy D. Goff		1925
1926			1926			1926
1927			1927			1927
1928			1928			1928

WEST VIRGINIA—Continued

Year	*Governors*	*United States Senators*	Year	*United States Senators*	*Chief Justices*	Year
1929	William G. Conley	Henry Hatfield	1929			1929
1930			1930			1930
1931			1931	Matthew M. Neely		1931
1932			1932			1932
1933	Herman G. Kump		1933			1933
1934			1934			1934
1935		Rush D. Holt	1935			1935
1936			1936			1936
1937	Homer A. Holt		1937			1937
1938			1938			1938
1939			1939			1939
1940			1940			1940
1941	Matthew M. Neely	Joseph Rosier	1941	Harley M. Kilgore		1941
1942		Hugh Ike Shott	1942			1942
1943		Chapman Revercomb	1943			1943
1944			1944			1944
1945	Clarence W. Meadows		1945			1945
1946			1946			1946
1948			1948			1948
1949	Okey L. Patteson	Matthew M. Neely	1949			1949
1950			1950			1950
1951			1951			1951
1952			1952			1952
1953	William C. Marland		1953			1953
1954			1954			1954
1955			1955			1955
1956			1956	William R. Laird		1956
1957	Cecil Underwood		1957	Chapman Revercomb		1957
1958		John D. Hoblitzell, Jr.	1958			1958
1959		Jennings Randolph	1959	Robert C. Byrd		1959
1960			1960			1960
1961	William W. Barron		1961			1961
1962			1962			1962
1963			1963			1963
1964			1964			1964
1965	Hulett C. Smith		1965			1965
1966			1966			1966
1967			1967			1967
1968			1968			1968
1969	Arch A. Moore, Jr.		1969			1969
1970			1970			1970
1971			1971			1971
1972			1972			1972
1973			1973			1973

WISCONSIN

	Governors	*United States Senators*			*Chief Justices*	
1848	Nelson Dewey	Henry Dodge	1848	Isaac P. Walker	Alexander W. Stow	1848
1849			1849			1849
1850			1850			1850
1851			1851			1851
1852	Leonard J. Farwell		1852			1852
1853			1853		Edward V. Whiton	1853
1854	William A. Barstow		1854			1854
1855			1855	Charles Durkee		1855
1856	Arthur MacArthur		1856			1856
1856	Coles Bashford		1856			1856
1857		James R. Doolittle	1857			1857
1858	Alexander W. Randall		1858			1858
1859			1859		Luther S. Dixon	1859
1860			1860			1860
1861			1861	Timothy O. Howe		1861
1862	Louis P. Harvey		1862			1862
1862	Edward Salomon		1862			1862
1863			1863			1863
1864	James T. Lewis		1864			1864
1865			1865			1865
1866	Lucius Fairchild		1866			1866
1867			1867			1867
1868			1868			1868
1869		Matthew H. Carpenter	1869			1869
1870			1870			1870
1871			1871			1871
1872	Cadwallader Washburn		1872			1872
1873			1873			1873
1874	William R. Taylor		1874		Edward G. Ryan	1874
1875		Angus Cameron	1875			1875
1876	Harrison Ludington		1876			1876
1877			1877			1877
1878	William E. Smith		1878			1878
1879			1879	Matthew H. Carpenter		1879
1880			1880		Orsamus Cole	1880
1881		Philetus Sawyer	1881	Angus Cameron		1881
1882	Jeremiah M. Rusk		1882			1882
1883			1883			1883
1884			1884			1884
1885			1885	John C. Spooner		1885
1886			1886			1886
1887			1887			1887
1888			1888			1888
1889	William D. Hoard		1889			1889
1890			1890			1890
1891	George W. Peck		1891	William F. Vilas		1891
1892			1892		William P. Lyon	1892
1893		John L. Mitchell	1893			1893
1894			1894		Harlow S. Orton	1894
1895	William H. Upham		1895		John P. Cassoday	1895
1896			1896			1896
1897	Edward Scofield		1897	John C. Spooner		1897
1898			1898			1898
1899		Joseph V. Quarles	1899			1899
1900			1900			1900
1901	Robert M. LaFollette		1901			1901
1902			1902			1902
1903			1903			1903
1904			1904			1904
1905	James O. Davidson		1905			1905
1906		Robert M. LaFollette	1906			1906
1907			1907	Isaac Stephenson	John B. Winslow	1907
1908			1908			1908
1909			1909			1909
1910			1910			1910
1911	Francis E. McGovern		1911			1911
1912			1912			1912
1913			1913			1913
1914			1914			1914
1915	Emanuel L. Philipp		1915	Paul O. Husting		1915
1916			1916			1916
1917			1917			1917
1918			1918	Irvine L. Lenroot		1918
1919			1919			1919
1920			1920		Robert C. Siebecker	1920
1921	John J. Blaine		1921			1921

WISCONSIN–Continued

	Governors	*United States Senators*			*Chief Justices*	
1922			1922		Aad J. Vinje	1922
1923			1923			1923
1924			1924			1924
1925		Robert M. LaFollette, Jr.	1925			1925
1926			1926			1926
1927	Fred R. Zimmerman		1927	John G. Blaine		1927
1928			1928			1928
1929	Walter J. Kohler		1929		Marvin B. Rosenberry	1929
1930			1930			1930
1931	Philip F. LaFollette		1931			1931
1932			1932			1932
1933	Albert G. Schmedeman		1933	F. Ryan Duffy		1933
1934			1934			1934
1935	Philip F. LaFollette		1935			1935
1936			1936			1936
1937			1937			1937
1938			1938			1938
1939	Julius P. Heil		1939	Alexander Wiley		1939
1940			1940			1940
1941			1941			1941
1942			1942			1942
1943	Walter S. Goodland		1943			1943
1944			1944			1944
1945			1945			1945
1946			1946			1946
1947	Oscar Rennebohm	Joseph R. McCarthy	1947			1947
1948			1948			1948
1949			1949			1949
1950			1950		Oscar M. Fritz	1950
1951	Walter J. Kohler, Jr.		1951			1951
1952			1952			1952
1953			1953			1953
1954			1954		Edward T. Fairchild	1954
1955			1955			1955
1956			1956			1956
1957	Vernon W. Thomson	William Proxmire	1957		John E. Martin	1957
1958			1958			1958
1959	Gaylord A. Nelson		1959			1959
1960			1960			1960
1961			1961	Gaylord A. Nelson		1961
1962			1962		Grover L. Broadfoot	1962
1962			1962		Timothy Brown	1962
1963	John W. Reynolds		1963			1963
1964			1964		George R. Currie	1964
1965	Warren P. Knowles		1965			1965
1966			1966			1966
1967			1967			1967
1968			1968		E. Harold Hallows	1968
1969			1969			1969
1970			1970			1970
1971	Patrick J. Lucey		1971			1971
1972			1972			1972
1973			1973			1973

WYOMING

	Governors	*United States Senators*			*Chief Justices*	
1890	Francis E. Warren	Joseph M. Carey	1890	Francis E. Warren	Willis Van Devanter	1890
1890	Amos W. Barber		1890		Herman V. S. Groesbeck	1890
1891			1891			1891
1892			1892			1892
1893	John E. Osborne		1893	*Vacant*		1893
1894			1894			1894
1895	William A. Richards	Francis E. Warren	1895	Clarence D. Clark		1895
1896			1896			1896
1897			1897		Asbury B. Conway	1897
1897			1897		Charles N. Potter	1897
1898			1898			1898
1899	DeForest Richards		1899			1899
1900			1900			1900
1901			1901			1901
1902			1902			1902
1903	Fenimore Chatterton		1903		Samuel T. Corn	1903
1904			1904			1904
1905	Bryant B. Brooks		1905		Jesse Knight	1905
1905			1905		Charles N. Potter	1905
1906			1906			1906
1907			1907			1907
1908			1908			1908
1909			1909			1909
1910			1910			1910
1911	Joseph M. Carey		1911		Cyrus Beard	1911
1912			1912			1912
1913			1913		Richard H. Scott	1913
1914			1914			1914
1915	John B. Kendrick		1915		Charles N. Potter	1915
1916			1916			1916
1917	Frank L. Houx		1917	John B. Kendrick		1917
1918			1918			1918
1919	Robert D. Carey		1919		Cyrus Beard	1919
1920			1920		Charles N. Potter	1920
1921			1921			1921
1922			1922			1922
1923	William B. Ross		1923			1923
1924	Frank Lucas		1924			1924
1925	Nellie T. Ross		1925			1925
1926			1926			1926
1927	Frank C. Emerson		1927		Fred H. Blume	1927
1928			1928			1928
1929		Patrick J. Sullivan	1929			1929
1930		Robert D. Carey	1930			1930
1931	Alonzo M. Clark		1931		Ralph Kimball	1931
1932			1932			1932
1933	Leslie A. Miller		1933			1933
1934			1934	Joseph C. O'Mahoney		1934
1935			1935			1935
1936			1936			1936
1937		Harry H. Schwartz	1937		Fred H. Blume	1937
1938			1938			1938
1939	Nels H. Smith		1939		William A. Riner	1939
1940			1940			1940
1941			1941			1941
1942			1942			1942
1943	Lester C. Hunt	Edward V. Robertson	1943		Ralph Kimball	1943
1944			1944			1944
1945			1945		Fred H. Blume	1945
1946			1946			1946
1947			1947		William A. Riner	1947
1948			1948			1948
1949	Arthur G. Crane (Acting)	Lester C. Hunt	1949			1949
1950			1950			1950
1951	Frank A. Barrett		1951		Ralph Kimball	1951
1952			1952			1952

WYOMING—Continued

Year	*Governors*	*United States Senators*		*Chief Justices*
1953	C. J. Rogers (Acting)		Frank A. Barrett	Fred H. Blume
1954		Edward D. Crippa		
1954		Joseph C. O'Mahoney		
1955	Milward L. Simpson			William A. Riner
1956				
1957				Fred H. Blume
1958				
1959	John J. Hickey		Gale W. McGee	
1960				
1961	Jack R. Gage	John J. Hickey		
1962				
1963	Clifford P. Hansen	Milward L. Simpson		Glenn Parker
1964				
1965				
1966				
1967	Stanley K. Hathaway	Clifford P. Hansen		Harry S. Harnsberger
1968				
1969				Norman B. Gray
1970				
1971				John J. McIntyre
1972				
1973				

VII

THE CONFEDERACY

The leaders of the government, members of the Congresses, and military commanders of the Confederate States of America, 1861-1865.

PRESIDENT

1861-1865	Jefferson Davis

VICE PRESIDENT

1861-1865	Alexander H. Stephens

SECRETARY OF STATE

1861	Robert Toombs
1861-62	Robert M. T. Hunter
1862	William M. Browne (Acting)
1862-65	Judah P. Benjamin

ATTORNEY GENERAL

1861	Judah P. Benjamin
1861	Thomas Bragg
1862-63	Thomas H. Watts
1863-64	Wade Keyes (Acting)
1864-65	George Davis

SECRETARY OF THE TREASURY

1861-64	Christopher G. Memminger
1864-65	George A. Trenholm

SECRETARY OF THE NAVY

1861-65	Stephen R. Mallory

POSTMASTER GENERAL

1861-65	John H. Reagan

SECRETARY OF WAR

1861	Leroy P. Walker
1861-62	Judah P. Benjamin
1862	George W. Randolph
1865-65	James A. Seddon
1865	John C. Breckinridge

THE CONSTITUTIONAL CONVENTION

Montgomery, Alabama, February 4-9, 1861

President: Howell Cobb, Georgia

Secretary: Johnson J. Hooper, Alabama

DELEGATES

ALABAMA

William P. Chilton
Jabez L. M. Curry
Thomas M. Fearn
S. L. Hale
Johnson J. Hooper
David P. Lewis
Colin J. McRae
John G. Shorter
Robert H. Smith
Richard W. Walker

FLORIDA

J. Patton Anderson
Jackson Morton
James B. Owens

GEORGIA

Frank S. Barton
Howell Cobb
Thomas R. R. Cobb
Martin J. Crawford
Benjamin H. Hill
August Kenan
Eugenius A. Nisbet
Alexander Stephens
Robert Toombs
August R. Wright

LOUISIANA

Charles M. Conrad
A. DeCluet
Duncan F. Kenner
Henry Marshall
John Perkins, Jr.
Edward Sparrow

MISSISSIPPI

William T. Barry
Walker Brooks
Josiah A. P. Campbell
A. M. Clayton
Wiley P. Harris
James T. Harrison
W. T. Wilson

SOUTH CAROLINA

Robert W. Barnwell
W. W. Boyce
James Chestnut
Christopher G. Memminger
William P. Miles
L. M. Reitt
Robert B. Rhett
Thomas J. Withers

PROVISIONAL CONGRESS

Montgomery, Alabama
February 4, 1861 to February 17, 1862

DELEGATES

ALABAMA

William P. Dhilton
Jabez L. M. Curry
Nicholas Davis
Thomas Fearn
Stephen F. Hale
David P. Lewis
Colin J. McRae
Cornelius Robinson
John Gill Shorter
Robert H. Smith
Richard W. Walker

ARKANSAS

August H. Garland
Robert W. Johnson
Albert Rust
Hugh F. Thomason
W. W. Watkins

FLORIDA

J. Patton Anderson
Jackson Morton
James Owens
John P. Sanderson
George T. Ward

GEORGIA

Nathan Bass
Francis S. Bartow
Howell Cobb
Thomas R. R. Cobb
Martin J. Crawford
Thomas M. Foreman
Augustus H. Kenan
Eugenius A. Nisbet
Alexander H. Stephens
Robert Toombs
Augustus H. Wright

KENTUCKY

Henry C. Burnett
Theodore L. Burnett
John M. Elliott
George W. Ewing
L. H. Ford
George B. Hodge
Thomas Johnson
Thomas Monroe
John J. Thomas
Daniel P. White

LOUISIANA

Alexander D. Clouet
Charles M. Conrad
Duncan F. Kenner
Henry Marshall
John Perkins, Jr.

MISSISSIPPI

William S. Barry
Alexander B. Bradford
Walker Brooke
J. A. P. Campbell
Alexander M. Clayton
Wiley P. Harris
James T. Harrison
John A. Orr
William S. Wilson

MISSOURI

Casper W. Bell
John B. Clark
Aaron H. Conrow
Thomas A. Harris
Robert L. Y. Peyton
George G. Vest

NORTH CAROLINA

W. W. Avery
Burton Craige
George Davis
A. T. Davidson
Thomas D. McDowell
John P. Morehead
R. C. Puryear
Thomas Ruffin
W. N. H. Smith
A. W. Venable

SOUTH CAROLINA

Robert W. Barnwell
William W. Boyce
James Chesnut, Jr.
Lawrence M. Keitt
Charles G. Memminger
W. Porcher Miles
James L. Orr
R. Barnwell Rhett, Sr.
Thomas J. Withers

TENNESSEE

John D. C. Atkins
Robert L. Caruthers
David M. Currin
W. H. DeWitt
John F. House
Thomas M. Jones

TEXAS

John Gregg
John Hemphill
William B. Ochiltree
William S. Oldham
John H. Reagan
Thomas N. Waul
Louis T. Wigfall

VIRGINIA

Thomas S. Bocock
Alexander R. Boteler
John W. Brockenbrough
Robert M. T. Hunter
Robert Johnson
W. H. MacFarland
James M. Mason
Walter Preston
William B. Preston
Roger A. Pryor
William C. Rives
Charles W. Russell
Robert E. Scott
James A. Seddon
Waller R. Staples
John Tyler

FIRST CONGRESS

Montgomery, Alabama
February 18, 1862 to February 17, 1864

ALABAMA

Senators

Clement Claiborne Clay
Robert Jemison, Jr.
William L. Yancey

Representatives

William P. Chilton
David Clopton
Jabez L. M. Curry
E. S. Dargan
Thomas J. Foster
Francis L. Lyon
James L. Pugh
John P. Ralls
William R. Smith

ARKANSAS

Senators

Robert W. Johnson
Charles B. Mitchell

Representatives

Felix I. Batson
Augustus H. Garland
Thomas B. Hanly
Grandison D. Royston

FLORIDA

Senators

Augustus E. Maxwell
James M. Baker

Representatives

James B. Dawkins
Robert B. Hilton
John M. Martin

GEORGIA

Senators

Benjamin H. Hill
Herschel V. Johnson
John W. Lewis

Representatives

William W. Clark
Lucius J. Gartrell
Julian Hartridge
Hines Holt
Porter Ingram
Augustus H. Kenan
David W. Lewis
Charles J. Munnerlyn
Hardy Strickland
Robert P. Trippe
Augustus R. Wright

KENTUCKY

Senators

Henry C. Burnett
William E. Simms

Representatives

Robert J. Breckinridge
Horatio W. Bruce
John W. Crockett
John M. Elliott
George W. Ewing
Willis B. Machen
James W. Moore

LOUISIANA

Senators

Thomas J. Semmes
Edward Sparrow

Representatives

Ely M. Bruce
Theodore L. Burnett
James S. Chrisman
George B. Hodge

MISSISSIPPI

Senators

Albert G. Brown
James Phelan

Representatives

Ethelbert Barksdale
Henry C. Chambers
J. W. Clapp
Reuben Davis
William D. Holder
John J. McRae
Otho R. Singleton
Israel Welsh

MISSOURI

Senators

John B. Clark
Waldo P. Johnson
Robert L. Y. Peyton

Representatives

Casper W. Bell
Aaron H. Conrow
William M. Cook
Thomas W. Freeman
Thomas A. Harris
George C. Vest

NORTH CAROLINA

Senators

George Davis
William T. Dortch
Edwin G. Reade

Representatives

Archibald H. Arrington
Thomas S. Ashe
Robert R. Bridgers
A. T. Davidson
Burgess S. Gaither
Owen R. Kenan
William Lander
J. R. McLean
W. N. H. Smith

SOUTH CAROLINA

Senators

Robert W. Barnwell
James L. Orr

Representatives

Lewis M. Ayer
Milledge L. Bonham
William W. Boyce
James Farrow
John McQueen
W. Porcher Miles
William D. Simpson

TENNESSEE

Senators

Landon C. Haynes
Gustavus A. Henry

Representatives

John D. C. Atkins
David M. Currin
Henry S. Foote
E. L. Gardenhier
Meredith P. Gentry
Joseph B. Heiskell
George W. Jones
Thomas Menees
William G. Swan
William H. Tibbs
John V. Wright

TEXAS

Senators

William S. Oldham
Louis T. Wigfall

Representatives

M. D. Graham
Peter W. Gray
Caleb C. Herbert
Frank B. Sexton
John A. Wilcox

VIRGINIA

Senators

Allen T. Caperton
Robert M. T. Hunter
William B. Preston

Representatives

John B. Baldwin
Thomas S. Bocock
Alexander R. Boteler
John R. Chambliss
Charles F. Collier
Daniel C. De Jarnette
David Funsten
Muscoe R. Garnett
John Goode, Jr.
James P. Holcombe
Albert G. Jenkins
Robert Johnson
James Lyons
Samuel A. Miller
Walter Preston
Roger A. Pryor
Charles W. Russell
William Smith
Waller R. Staples

SECOND CONGRESS

Richmond, Virginia, May 2, 1864 to March 18, 1865

ALABAMA

Senators

Robert Jemison, Jr.
Richard W. Walker

Representatives

William P. Chilton
David Clopton
M. H. Cruikshank
James S. Dickinson
Thomas J. Foster
Francis S. Lyon
James L. Pugh
William R. Smith

ARKANSAS

Senators

Augustus H. Garland
Robert W. Johnson
Charles B. Mitchell

Representatives

Felix I. Batson
David W. Carroll
Augustus H. Garland
Rufus H. Garland
Thomas B. Hanley

FLORIDA

Senators

James E. Baker
Augustus E. Maxwell

Representatives

Robert B. Hilton
S. St. George Rogers

GEORGIA

Senators

Benjamin H. Hill
Herschel V. Johnson

Representatives

Warren Akin
Clifford Anderson
Hiram P. Bell
Mark H. Blandford
Joseph H. Echols
Julian Hartridge
George N. Lester
John T. Shewmake
James M. Smith
William E. Smith

KENTUCKY

Senators

Henry C. Burnett
William E. Simms

Representatives

Benjamin F. Bradley
Ely M. Bruce
Horatio W. Bruce
Theodore L. Burnett
James S. Chrisman
John M. Elliott
George W. Ewing
Willis B. Machen
Humphrey Marshall
James W. Moore
Henry E. Read
George W. Triplett

LOUISIANA

Senators

Thomas J. Semmes
Edward Sparrow

Representatives

Charles M. Conrad
Lucien J. Dupre
Henry Gray
Benjamin L. Hodge
Duncan F. Kenner
John Perkins, Jr.
Charles J. Villere

MISSISSIPPI

Senators

Albert G. Brown
John W. C. Watson

Representatives

Ethelbert Barksdale
Henry C. Chambers
William D. Holder
John T. Lampkin
John A. Orr
Otho R. Singleton
Israel Welsh

MISSOURI

Senators

Waldo P. Johnson
George G. Vest

Representatives

John B. Clark
Aaron H. Conrow
Robert A. Hatcher
R. L. Norton
Thomas L. Snead
George G. Vest
Peter S. Wilkes

NORTH CAROLINA

Senators

William A. Graham
William T. Dortch

Representatives

Robert R. Bridgers
Thomas C. Fuller
Burgess S. Gaither
John A. Gilmer
James M. Leach
James T. Leach
George W. Logan
James G. Ramsey
W. N. H. Smith
Josiah Turner

SOUTH CAROLINA

Senators

Robert W. Barnwell
James L. Orr

Representatives

Lewis M. Ayer
William W. Boyce
James Farrow
W. Porcher Miles
William D. Simpson
James H. Witherspoon

TENNESSEE

Senators

Landon C. Haynes
Gustavus A. Henry

Representatives

John D. C. Atkins
Michael W. Cluskey
Arthur S. Colyar
David M. Currin
Henry S. Foote
Joseph B. Heiskell
Edwin A. Keeble
James McCallum
Thomas Menees
John P. Murray
William G. Swan
John V. Wright

TEXAS

Senators

William S. Oldham
Louis T. Wigfall

Representatives

John R. Baylor
A. M. Branch
Stephen H. Darden
Caleb C. Herbert
Simpson H. Morgan
Frank B. Sexton

VIRGINIA

Senators

Allen T. Caperton
Robert M. T. Hunter

Representatives

John B. Baldwin
Thomas S. Bocock
Daniel C. De Jarnette
David Funsten
Thomas S. Gholson
John Goode, Jr.
Frederick W. M. Holliday
Robert Johnston
Fayette McMullen
Samuel A. Miller
Robert L. Montague
William C. Rives
Charles W. Russell
Waller R. Staples
Robert L. Whitfield
William C. Wickham

CONFEDERATE BATTLEFIELD COMMANDERS

FIRST BATTLE OF BULL RUN, or MANASSAS

21 July 1861

Army of The Shenandoah	Joseph E. Johnston
Army of The Potomac	Pierre G. T. Beauregard

BATTLE OF SHILOH

6-7 April 1862

Army of The Mississippi	Albert S. Johnston
I Corps	Leonidas Polk
First Division	Charles Clark
	Alexander P. Stewart
Second Division	Benhamin F. Cheatham
II Corps	Braxton Bragg
First Division	Daniel Ruggles
Second Division	Jones M. Withers
III Corps	William J. Hardee
Reserve Corps	John C. Breckinridge

BATTLE OF SEVEN PINES, or FAIR OAKS

31 May – 1 June 1862

Army of Northern Virginia	Joseph E. Johnston
	Robert E. Lee
Right Wing	James Longstreet
Longstreet's Division	Richard H. Anderson
Hill's Division	Daniel H. Hill
Huger's Division	Benjamin Huger
Left Wing	Gustavus W. Smith
Smith's Division	William H. C. Whiting

SEVEN DAYS' BATTLES

25 June – 1 July 1862

Army of Northern Virginia	Robert E. Lee
Jackson's Corps	Thomas J. ("Stonewall") Jackson
Whiting's Division	William H. C. Whiting
Third Division	Richard S. Ewell
Hill's Division	Daniel H. Hill
Magruder's Corps	John B. Magruder
Jones' Division	David R. Jones
McLaws' Division	Lafayette McLaws
Longstreet Corps	James Longstreet
Hill's Division	Ambrose P. Hill
Holmes' Division	Theophilus H. Holmes
Cavalry	James E. B. ("Jeb") Stuart
Reserve Artillery	William N. Pendleton

SECOND BATTLE OF BULL RUN, or MANASSAS

29-30 August 1862

Army of Northern Virginia	Robert E. Lee
Right Wing	James Longstreet
Anderson's Division	Richard H. Anderson
Jones' Division	David R. Jones
Wilcox's Division	Cadmus M. Wilcox
Hood's Division	John B. Hood
Kemper's Division	James L. Kemper
Left Wing	Thomas J. ("Stonewall") Jackson
First Division	William B. Taliaferro
Second (Light) Division	Ambrose P. Hill
Third Division	Richard S. Ewell
Cavalry Division	James E. B. ("Jeb") Stuart

BATTLE OF ANTIETAM

17 Sept. 1862

Army of Northern Virginia	Robert E. Lee
Longstreet's Corps	James Longstreet
McLaws' Division	Lafayette McLaws
Anderson's Division	Richard H. Anderson
Jones' Division	David R. Jones
Walker's Division	John C. Walker
Hood's Division	John B. Hood
Jackson's Corps	Thomas J. ("Stonewall") Jackson
Ewell's Division	A. R. Lawton
Light Division	Ambrose P. Hill
Jackson's Division	John R. Jones
Hill's Division	Daniel H. Hill
Cavalry	James E. B. ("Jeb") Stuart
Reserve Artillery	William N. Pendleton

BATTLE OF CORINTH

3-4 Oct. 1862

Army of West Tennessee	Earl Van Dorn
Price's Corps	Sterling Price
First Division	Louis Hebert
Maury's Division	Dabney H. Maury
District of The Mississippi	
First Division	Mansfield Lovell

BATTLE OF FREDERICKSBURG

13 Dec. 1862

Army of Northern Virginia	Robert E. Lee
I Corps	James Longstreet
McLaws' Division	Lafayette McLaws
Anderson's Division	Richard H. Anderson
Pickett's Division	George E. Pickett
Hood's Division	John B. Hood
Ransom's Division	Robert Ransom
II Corps	Thomas J. ("Stonewall") Jackson
Hill's Division	Daniel H. Hill
Light Division	Ambrose P. Hill
Ewell's Division	Jubal A. Early
Jackson's Division	William B. Taliaferro
Reserve Artillery	William N. Pendleton
Cavalry	James E. B. ("Jeb") Stuart

BATTLE OF STONES RIVER, or MURFREESBORO

31 Dec. 1862 – 2 Jan. 1863

Army of Tennessee	Braxton Bragg
Polk's Corps	Leonidas Polk
First Division	Benjamin F. Cheatham

Second Division	Jones M. Withers
Hardee's Corps	William J. Hardee
First Division	John C. Breckinridge
Second Division	Patrick R. Cleburne
McCown's Division	John P. McCown
Cavalry	Joseph Wheller

BATTLE OF CHANCELLORSVILLE

2-4 May 1863

Army of Northern Virginia	Robert E. Lee
I Corps	James Longstreet
McLaws' Division	Lafayette McLaws
Anderson's Division	Richard H. Anderson
II Corps	Thomas J. ("Stonewall") Jackson
Light Division	Ambrose P. Hill
D. H. Hill's Division	Robert E. Rodes
	S. D. Ramseur
Early's Division	Jubal A. Early
Trimble's Division	R. E. Colston
Cavalry	James E. B. ("Jeb") Stuart

VICKSBURG CAMPAIGN

1 May – 4 July 1863

Commanders	John C. Pemberton
	Joseph E. Johnston
First Division	William W. Loring
Stevenson's Division	Carter L. Stevenson
Forney's Division	John H. Forney
Smith's Division	Martin L. Smith
Bowen's Division	John S. Bowen

BATTLE OF GETTYSBURG

1-3 July 1863

Army of Northern Virginia	Robert E. Lee
I Corps	James Longstreet
McLaws' Division	Lafayette McLaws
Pickett's Division	George E. Pickett
Hood's Division	John B. Hood
II Corps	Richard S. Ewell
Early's Division	Jubal A. Early
Johnson's Division	Edward Johnson
Rodes' Division	Robert E. Rodes
III Corps	Ambrose P. Hill
Anderson's Division	Richard H. Anderson
Heth's Division	Henry Heth
Pender's Division	William D. Pender
Cavalry	James E. B. ("Jeb") Stuart

BATTLE OF CHICKAMAUGA

19-20 Sept. 1863

Army of Tennessee	Braxton Bragg
Right Wing (Polk's Corps)	Leonidas Polk
Cheatham's Division	Benjamin F. Cheatham
Hindman's Division	Thomas C. Hindman
Hill's Corps	Daniel H. Hill
Cleburne's Division	Patrick R. Cleburne
Breckinridge's Division	John C. Breckinridge
Reserve Corps	William H. T. Walker
Walker's Division	States R. Gist
Liddell's Division	St. John R. Liddell
Left Wing	James Longstreet
Buckner's Corps	Simon B. Buckner
Stewart's Division	Alexander P. Stewart
Preston's Division	William Preston
Johnson's Division	Bushrod R. Johnson
Longstreet's Corps	John B. Hood
McLaws' Division	Lafayette McLaws
Hood's Division	John B. Hood
Wheeler's Cavalry Corps	Joseph Wheeler
Wharton's Division	John A. Wharton
Martin's Division	Will T. Martin
Forrest's Corps	Nathan B. Forrest
Armstrong's Division	Frank C. Armstrong
Pegram's Division	John Pegram

BATTLE OF CHATTANOOGA

23-25 Nov. 1863

Commander	Braxton Bragg
Hardee's Corps	WilliaM J. Hardee
Cheatham's Division	John K. Jackson
Stevenson's Division	Carter L. Stevenson
Cleburne's Division	Patrick R. Cleburne
Walker's Division	States R. Gist
Breckinridge's Corps	John C. Breckinridge
Hindman's Division	J. Patton Anderson
Breckinridge's Division	William B. Bate
Stewart's Division	Alexander P. Stewart

BATTLE OF THE WILDERNESS AND SPOTTSYLVANIA COURT HOUSE

5-21 May 1864

Army of Northern Virginia	Robert E. Lee
I Corps	James Longstreet
	Richard H. Anderson
Kershaw's Division	Joseph B. Kershaw
Field's Division	Charles W. Field
Artillery	Edward P. Alexander
II Corps	Richard S. Ewell
	Jubal A. Early
Early's Division	Jubal E. Early
Johnson's Division	Edward Johnson
Rode's Division	Robert E. Rodes
Artillery	Armistead L. Long
III Corps	Ambrose P. Hill
Anderson's Division	Richard H. Anderson
Heth's Division	Henry Heth
Wilcox's Division	Cadmus M. Wilcox
Artillery	R. Lindsay Walker
Cavalry Corps	James E. B. ("Jeb") Stuart
Hampton's Division	Wade Hampton
Fitz-Lee's Division	Fitzhugh Lee
W. H. F. Lee's Division	William H. F. Lee

ATLANTA CAMPAIGN

3 May – 8 Sept. 1864

Army of Tennessee	Joseph E. Johnston
	John B. Hood
Cheatham's Division	Benjamin F. Cheatham
Cleburne's Division	Patrick R. Cleburne
	Mark B. Lowrey
Walker's Division	William H. T. Walker
Bate's Division	William B. Bate
	John C. Brown
Hood's Corps	John B. Hood
	Carter L. Stevenson
	Benjamin F. Cheatham
	Stephen D. Lee

Hindman's Division	Thomas C. Hindman
Stevenson's Division	Carter L. Stevenson
Stewart's Division	Alexander P. Stewart
Cavalry Corps	Joseph Wheeler
Martin's Division	Will T. Martin
Kelly's Division	John H. Kelly
Humes' Division	William Y. C. Humes
Roddey's Command	Philip D. Roddey
Army of The Mississippi	
Polk's Corps	Leonidas Polk
	William W. Loring
	Alexander P. Stewart
	Benjamin F. Cheatham
Loring's Division	William W. Loring
	Winfield S. Featherstone
French's Division	S. G. French
Cantey's Division	James Cantey
	Edward C. Walthall
Cavalry Division	William H. Jackson
Georgia Militia	
First Division	G. A. Smith

BATTLE OF NASHVILLE

15-16 Dec. 1864

Army of Tennessee	John B. Hood
Lee's Corps	Stephen D. Lee
Johnson's Division	Edward Johnson
Stevenson's Division	Carter L. Stevenson
Clayton's Division	Henry D. Clayton
Stewart's Corps	Alexander P. Stewart
Loring's Division	William W. Loring
French's Division	Samuel G. French
Walthall's Division	Edward C. Walthall
Cheatham's Corps	Benjamin F. Cheatham
Brown's Division	John C. Brown
Cleburne's Division	J. A. Smith
Bate's Division	William B. Bate
Cavalry Division	James R. Chalmers

CAMPAIGN OF THE CAROLINAS

Feb.–Mar. 1865

Army of Tennessee	Joseph E. Johnson
Hardee's Corps	William J. Hardee
Hoke's Division	R. F. Hoke
Cheatham's Division	Benjamin F. Cheatham
Stewart's Corps	Alexander P. Stewart
Loring's Division	William W. Loring
Anderson's Division	J. Patton Anderson
Walthall's Division	Edward C. Walthall
Lee's Corps	Stephen D. Lee
Hill's Division	D. H. Hill
Stevenson's Division	Carter L. Stevenson
Cavalry	Wade Hampton

CONFEDERATE NAVAL COMMANDERS

CHARLESTON SQUADRON

1862	Duncan N. Ingraham
1863	John R. Tucker

GALVESTON SQUADRON

1861	William N. Hunter
1863	Joseph N. Barney

JAMES RIVER SQUADRON

1861	Samuel Barron
1861	William F. Lynch
1862	Franklin Buchanan
1862	Josiah Tatnall
1862	Samuel Barron
1863	French Forrest
1864	John K. Mitchell
1865	Raphael Semmes

MISSISSIPPI RIVER SQUADRON

1861	Lawrence Rousseau
1861	George N. Hollins
1862	John K. Mitchell
1862	William F. Lynch

MOBILE SQUADRON

1862	Victor M. Randolph
1862	Franklin Buchanan
1864	Ebenezer Farrand

NORTH CAROLINA SQUADRON

1862	William F. Lynch
1864	Robert F. Pinkney

RED RIVER SQUADRON

1863	Thomas R. Brent
1863	Jonathan H. Carter

SAVANNAH RIVER SQUADRON

1861	Josiah Tatnall
1863	Richard L. Page
1863	William A. Webb
1863	William W. Hunter

NAVAL FORCES IN EUROPE

1862-64	Samuel Barron

VIII

THE MILITARY

The Armed Forces of the United States:

- Deputy Secretaries of Defense
- Secretaries of the Services since 1947
- Joint Chiefs of Staff
- United States Army
- Army Commanders during Wartime
- United States Navy
- United States Air Force
- Colleges of the Armed Forces

DEPUTY SECRETARIES OF DEFENSE

See CABINET – Section III – for Secretaries of Defense

1949 Stephen T. Early
1950 Robert A. Lovett
1951 William C. Foster
1953 Roger M. Kyes
1953 Robert B. Anderson
1955 Reuben B. Robertson, Jr.
1957 Donald A. Quarles
1959 Thomas S. Gates, Jr.
1959 James H. Douglas, Jr.
1961 Roswell L. Gilpatric
1964 Cyrus R. Vance
1967 Paul H. Nitze
1969 David Packard
1972 Kenneth Rush
1973 William P. Clements, Jr.

SECRETARIES OF THE U.S. ARMY, NAVY, AND AIR FORCE

Not members of the cabinet

Army

1947 Kenneth C. Royall
1949 Gordon Gray
1950 Frank Pace, Jr.
1953 Robert T. Stevens
1955 Wilbur M. Brucker
1961 Elvis J. Stahr, Jr.
1962 Cyrus R. Vance
1964 Stephen Ailes
1965 Stanley R. Resor
1971 Robert F. Froehlke

Navy

1947 John L. Sullivan
1949 Francis P. Matthews
1951 Dan A. Kimball
1953 Robert B. Anderson
1954 Charles S. Thomas
1957 Thomas S. Gates, Jr.
1958 William B. Franke
1958 John B. Connally, Jr.
1961 Fred Korth
1963 Paul H. Nitze
1967 Paul R. Ignatius
1969 John H. Chaffee
1972 John W. Warner

Air Force

1947 W. Stuart Symington
1950 Thomas K. Finletter
1953 Harold E. Talbot
1955 Donald A. Quarles
1957 James H. Douglas, Jr.
1959 Dudley C. Sharpe
1961 Eugene M. Zuckert
1965 Harold Brown
1969 Robert C. Seamens, Jr.

CHAIRMEN, JOINT CHIEFS OF STAFF

Chiefs of Staff listed separately under respective services

Aug. 1949 Omar N. Bradley
Aug. 1953 Arthur W. Radford
Aug. 1957 Nathan F. Twining
Oct. 1960 Lyman L. Lemnitzer
Oct. 1962 Maxwell D. Taylor
July 1964 Earle G. Wheeler
July 1970 Thomas H. Moorer

Joint Staff, Joint Chiefs of Staff

Directors

1947 Alfred M. Gruenther
1949 Arthur C. Davis
1951 Charles P. Cabell
1953 Frank F. Everest
1954 Lemuel Mathewson
1956 Bernard L. Austin
1958 Oliver S. Picher
1960 Earle G. Wheeler
1962 Herbert D. Riley
1964 David A. Burchinal
1966 Andrew J. Goodpaster
1967 Berton E. Spivy, Jr.
1968 Nels C. Johnson
1970 John W. Vogt, Jr.

UNITED STATES ARMY

Chiefs of Staff

Before 1903 known as commanders of the Army

June	1775	George Washington
Dec.	1783	Henry Knox
June	1784	John Doughty
Aug.	1784	Josiah Harmer
Mar.	1791	Arthur St. Clair
Apr.	1792	Anthony Wayne
Dec.	1796	James Wilkinson
July	1798	George Washington
Dec.	1799	Alexander Hamilton
June	1800	James Wilkinson
Jan.	1812	Henry Dearborn
June	1815	Jacob Brown
May	1828	Alexander Macomb
July	1841	Winfield Scott
Nov.	1816	George B. McClellan
July	1862	Henry W. Halleck
Mar.	1864	Ulysses S. Grant
Mar.	1869	William T. Sherman
Nov.	1883	Philip H. Sheridan
Aug.	1888	John M. Schofield
Oct.	1895	Nelson A. Miles
Aug.	1903	Samuel B. M. Young
Jan.	1904	Adna R. Chaffee
Jan.	1906	John C. Bates
Apr.	1906	J. Franklin Bell
Apr.	1910	Leonard Wood
Apr.	1914	William W. Witherspoon
Nov.	1914	Hugh L. Scott
Sept.	1917	Tasker H. Bliss
May	1918	Peyton C. March
July	1921	John J. Pershing
Sept.	1924	John L. Hines
Nov.	1926	Charles P. Summerall
Nov.	1930	Douglas MacArthur
Oct.	1935	Malin Craig
Sept.	1939	George C. Marshall
Nov.	1945	Dwight D. Eisenhower
Feb.	1948	Omar N. Bradley
Aug.	1949	J. Lawton Collins
Aug.	1953	Matthew B. Ridgway
June	1955	Maxwell D. Taylor
July	1959	Lyman L. Lemnitzer
Sept.	1960	George H. Decker
Oct.	1962	Earle G. Wheeler
July	1964	Harold K. Johnson
July	1968	William C. Westmoreland
June	1972	**Creighton W. Abrams, Jr.**

United States Army General Staff

Deputy Chiefs of Staff for Personnel

Prior to 1956 known as G1 – Personnel and Administration

Sept.	1921	James H. McRae
Sept.	1922	Charles H. Martin
May	1925	Campbell King
May	1929	Albert J. Bowley
Oct.	1931	Andrew Moses
Nov.	1935	Harry E. Knight
Sept.	1937	Lorenzo D. Gasser
Oct.	1939	William E. Shedd
Feb.	1941	Wade H. Haislip
Jan.	1942	John H. Hilldring
July	1942	Donald Wilson
Sept.	1942	Miller G. White
Aug.	1944	Stephen G. Henry
Oct.	1945	Willard S. Paul
Jan.	1949	Edward H. Brooks
June	1951	Clovis E. Byers (Acting)
July	1951	Anthony C. McAuliffe
Mar.	1953	Robert N. Young
Apr.	1955	Donald P. Booth
Jan.	1956	Walter L. Weibel
Dec.	1956	Donald P. Booth
Mar.	1958	James F. Collins
Mar.	1961	Russell L. Vittrup
May	1963	James L. Richardson, Jr.
July	1965	James K. Woolnough
June	1967	Albert O. Connor
Aug.	1969	Walter J. Kerwin, Jr.

Assistant Chiefs of Staff For Intelligence

Prior to 1956 known as G-2 – Intelligence

May	1917	Ralph H. Van Deman
June	1918	Marlborough Churchill
Sept.	1920	Dennis E. Nolan
Sept.	1921	Stuart Heintzelman
Nov.	1922	William K. Naylor
July	1924	James H. Reeves
May	1927	Stanley H. Ford
Jan.	1931	Alfred T. Smith
Feb.	1935	Harry E. Knight
Nov.	1935	Francis H. Lincoln
July	1937	E. R. Warner McCabe
Apr.	1940	Sherman Miles
Feb.	1942	Raymond E. Lee
May	1942	George V. Strong
Feb.	1944	Clayton Bissell
Jan.	1946	Hoyt S. Vandenberg
June	1946	Stephen J. Chamberlin
Nov.	1948	Stafford L. Irwin
Sept.	1950	Alexander R. Bolling
Sept.	1952	Richard C. Partridge
Nov.	1953	Arthur G. Trudeau
Aug.	1955	Ridgely Gaither
July	1956	Robert A. Schow
Oct.	1958	John M. Willens
Oct.	1961	Alvah R. Fitch
Dec.	1963	Edgar C. Doleman
Aug.	1965	John J. Davis
Nov.	1966	William P. Yarborough
May	1971	Phillip B. Davidson, Jr.

Deputy Chiefs of Staff for Military Operations

From 1921 to 1949 known as Chiefs of Plans and Operations Division – G-3; from 1949 to 1955 G-3 was known as Deputy Chief of Staff/Operations

Sept.	1921	Briant H. Wells
Dec.	1923	Stuart Heintzelman
July	1924	Leroy Eltinge
July	1925	Harry A. Smith
Sept.	1927	George S. Simonds
Sept.	1931	Joseph P. Tracy
Sept.	1932	Charles E. Kilbourne
Mar.	1935	Stanley D. Embick
May	1936	Walter Krueger
July	1938	George C. Marshall
Oct.	1938	George V. Strong
Dec.	1940	Leonard T. Gerow
Feb.	1942	Dwight D. Eisenhower
June	1942	Thomas T. Handy
Oct.	1944	John E. Hull
June	1946	Lauris Norstad
Oct.	1947	Albert C. Wedemeyer
Nov.	1948	Ray T. Maddocks
1949-1953		*See Organization and Training*
Oct.	1955	Clyde D. Eddelman
May	1958	James E. Moore
Oct.	1959	John C. Oakes
Jan.	1961	Barksdale Hamlett
Mar.	1962	Edwin H. J. Carns
May	1962	Theodore W. Parker
May	1963	Harold K. Johnson
July	1964	Bruce Palmer, Jr.
Apr.	1965	Vernon P. Mock
Aug.	1966	Harry J. Lemley, Jr.
Aug.	1969	Richard D. Stilwell

Chiefs of Organization and Training – G-3

After 1949 known as Deputy Chiefs of Staff/Operations

Sept.	1921	William Lassiter
Dec.	1923	Hugh A. Drum
Apr.	1926	Malin Craig
Apr.	1927	Frank Parker
July	1929	Edward L. King
Feb.	1932	Edgar T. Collins
July	1933	John H. Hughes
Apr.	1937	George P. Tyner
Mar.	1938	R. M. Beck
Aug.	1939	F. M. Andrews
Nov.	1940	Harry L. Twaddle
Apr.	1941	Harry J. Malony

Apr. 1941 Harry L. Twaddle
Mar. 1942 Harold R. Bull
May 1942 Idwal H. Edwards
May 1943 Ray E. Porter
Feb. 1945 Idwal H. Edwards
July 1946 Charles P. Hall
Nov. 1948 Harold R. Bull
May 1949 Clift Andrus
Mar. 1950 Charles L. Bolte
Feb. 1951 Maxwell D. Taylor
Sept. 1951 Reuben E. Jenkins
Sept. 1952 Clyde D. Eddleman
Mar. 1954 James M. Gavin
Mar. 1955 Paul D. Adams
July 1955 Paul D. Harkins

For Oct. 1955 to present see Deputy Chiefs of Staff for Military Operations

Deputy Chiefs of Staff For Logistics

Prior to 1955 known as G-4 – Logistics

Dec. 1917 George W. Goethals
Feb. 1918 P. E. Pierce
Apr. 1918 George W. Goethals
Mar. 1919 George W. Burr
Sept. 1920 William M. Wright
Sept. 1921 William D. Connor
Nov. 1922 Stuart Heintzelman
Dec. 1923 Dennis E. Nolan
Dec. 1924 Fox Conner
Mar. 1926 Briant H. Wells
May 1927 E. E. Booth
Jan. 1931 R. E. Callan
Feb. 1935 C. S. Lincoln
June 1956 George R. Spalding
Apr. 1937 George P. Tyner
Aug. 1940 Eugene Reybold (Acting)
Nov. 1941 Brehon B. Somervell
Mar. 1942 Raymond G. Moses
Sept. 1943 Russell L. Maxwell
Mar. 1946 Stanley L. Scott (Acting)
June 1946 LeRoy Lutes
Jan. 1948 Henry S. Aurand
Mar. 1949 Thomas B. Larkin
Mar. 1953 Williston B. Palmer
Apr. 1955 Carter B. Magruder
June 1959 Robert W. Colglazier, Jr.
July 1964 Lawrence J. Lincoln, Jr.
June 1967 Jean E. Engler
Sept. 1969 Joseph M. Heiser, Jr.
Sept. 1970 Verne L. Bowers

Chiefs of Research and Development

1956 James M. Gavin
1958 Arthur G. Trudeau
1962 Dwight E. Beach
1963 William W. Dick, Jr.
1966 Austin W. Betts
1969 W. C. Gribble, Jr.

Directors, Women's Army Corps

1943 Oveta Culp Hobby
1945 Westray Battle Boyce
1947 Mary A. Hallaren
1953 Irene O. Galloway
1957 Mary L. Milligan
1962 Emily C. Gorman
1966 Elizabeth B. Hoisington

United States Army Special Staff

Adjutants General

June 1775 Horatio Gates
June 1776 Joseph Reed
Jan. 1777 Arthur St. Clair (Acting)
Feb. 1777 George Weedon (Acting)
Apr. 1777 Morgan Connor
June 1777 Timothy Pickering
Jan. 1778 Alexander Scammel
Jan. 1781 Edward Hand
Nov. 1783 William North
Oct. 1787 Ebenezer Denny (Acting)
Nov. 1790 John Pratt
Sept. 1791 Winthrop Sargent
Nov. 1791 Ebenezer Denny (Acting)
Mar. 1792 Henry DeButts (Acting)
Feb. 1793 Michael Rudolph (Acting)
July 1793 Edward Butler (Acting)
May 1794 John Mills (Acting)
Feb. 1796 Jonathan Haskell (Acting)
Aug. 1796 Edward Butler (Acting)
Feb. 1797 Thomas H. Cushing (Acting)
July 1798 William North
June 1800 Thomas H. Cushing
Apr. 1807 A. Y. Nicholl
Apr. 1812 Alexander Macomb
July 1812 Thomas H. Cushing
Mar. 1813 Zebulon M. Pike
May 1814 William H. Winder
Nov. 1814 Daniel Parker
Aug. 1821 James Gadsden
May 1822 C. J. Nourse (Acting)
Mar. 1825 Roger Jones
July 1852 Samuel Cooper
Mar. 1861 Lorenzo Thomas
Feb. 1869 E. D. Townsend
June 1880 R. C. Drum
June 1889 J. C. Kelton
Nov. 1893 G. D. Ruggles
Sept. 1897 Samuel Breck
Feb. 1898 Henry C. Corbin
Apr. 1904 Fred C. Ainsworth
Feb. 1912 William P. Hall
Aug. 1912 George Andrews
Aug. 1914 Henry P. McCain
Sept. 1918 Peter C. Harris
Sept. 1922 Robert C. Davis
July 1927 Lutz Wahl
Dec. 1928 Charles H. Bridges
Feb. 1933 James F. McKinley
Nov. 1935 Edgar T. Conley
May 1938 Emory S. Adams
Mar. 1942 James A. Ulio
July 1945 Edward F. Witsell (Acting)
Feb. 1946 Edward F. Witsell
July 1951 William E. Bergin (Acting)
July 1951 William E. Bergin
June 1954 John A. Klein
Jan. 1957 Herbert M. Jones
Nov. 1958 Robert V. Lee
Oct. 1961 Joe C. Lambert
July 1966 Kenneth J. Wickham
Sept. 1970 Verne L. Bowers

Commanders, Army Air Corps

Reorganized as separate service in 1947

1918 Charles T. Menoher
1921 Mason M. Patrick
1927 James E. Fechet
1931 Benjamin D. Foulois
1935 Oscar Westover
1938 Henry H. Arnold

Chiefs of Artillery

Reorganized as Coast Artillery in 1908

Feb. 1903 Wallace F. Randolph
Jan. 1904 John P. Story
June 1905 Samuel M. Mills
Oct. 1906 Arthur Murray

Chiefs of Cavalry

July 1920 Williard A. Holbrook
July 1924 Malin Craig
Mar. 1926 Herbert B. Crosby
Mar. 1930 Guy V. Henry
Mar. 1934 Leon B. Kromer
Mar. 1938 John K. Herr *to March 1942*

Chiefs of Chaplains

1920 John T. Axton
1927 Edmund P. Easterbrook
1929 Julian E. Yates
1933 Alva J. Brasted
1937 William R. Arnold
1945 Luther D. Miller
1949 Roy H. Parker
1952 Ivan L. Bennett
1954 Patrick J. Ryan
1958 Frank A. Tobey
1962 Charles E. Brown, Jr.
1967 Francis L. Sampson
1971 Gerhardt W. Hyatt

Chiefs of Chemical Corps

Prior to 1946 known as Chemical Warfare Service

July 1918 William L. Sibert
July 1920 Amos A. Fries
Mar. 1929 Harry L. Gilchrist

May 1933 Claude E. Brigham
May 1937 Walter C. Baker
May 1941 William N. Porter
Nov. 1945 Alden H. Waitt
Oct. 1949 Anthony C. McAuliffe
June 1951 Egbert F. Bullene
May 1954 William M. Creasy
Sept. 1958 Marshall Stubbs
to July 1962

Chiefs of Coast Artillery

July 1908 Arthur Murray
Mar. 1911 Erasmus M. Weaver
May 1918 Frank W. Coe
Mar. 1926 Andrew Hero, Jr.
Mar. 1930 John W. Gulick
Mar. 1934 William F. Hase
Jan. 1935 Harry L. Steele
Apr. 1936 Archibald H. Sutherland
Apr. 1940 Joseph A. Green
to March 1942

Chiefs of Engineers

June 1775 Richard Gridley
Aug. 1776 Rufus Putnam
July 1777 L. L. Duportail
Feb. 1795 Stephen Rochefontaine
May 1798 Henry Burbeck
July 1802 Jonathan Williams
July 1812 Joseph G. Swift
Nov. 1818 W. K. Armistead
June 1821 Alexander Macomb
May 1828 Charles Gratiat
Dec. 1838 J. G. Totten
Apr. 1864 Richard Delafield
Aug. 1866 A. A. Humphries
June 1879 Horatio G. Wright
Mar. 1884 John Newton
Oct. 1886 J. C. Duane
July 1888 T. L. Casey
May 1895 William P. Craighill
Feb. 1897 John M. Wilson
May 1901 L. Gillespie
Jan. 1904 Alexander Mackenzie
July 1908 William L. Marshall
June 1910 William H. Bixby
Aug. 1913 William T. Rossell
Oct. 1913 Dan C. Kingman
Mar. 1916 William M. Black
Jan. 1920 Lansing H. Beach
June 1924 Harry Taylor
June 1926 Edgar Jadwin
Oct. 1929 Lytle Brown
Oct. 1933 Edward M. Markham
Oct. 1937 Julian L. Schley
Oct. 1941 Eugene Reybold
Oct. 1945 Raymond A. Wheeler
Mar. 1949 Lewis A. Pick
Mar. 1953 Samuel D. Sturgis, Jr.
Oct. 1956 E. C. Itschner
Mar. 1961 Keith R. Barney (Acting)
May 1961 Walter K. Wilson, Jr.
June 1965 William F. Cassidy
Aug. 1969 Frederick J. Clarke

Chiefs of Field Artillery

July 1920 William J. Snow
Dec. 1927 Fred T. Austin
Mar. 1930 Harry G. Bishop
Mar. 1934 Upton Birnie, Jr.
Mar. 1938 Robert M. Danford
to March 1942

Chiefs of Infantry

July 1920 Charles S. Farnsworth
Mar. 1925 Robert H. Allen
Mar. 1929 Stephen O. Fuqua
May 1933 Edward Croft
May 1937 George A. Lynch
May 1941 Courtney H. Hodges
to March 1942

Inspectors General

Dec. 1777 Thomas Conway
May 1778 F. W. A. von Steuben
Apr. 1784 William North
Mar. 1792 Henry DeButts
Feb. 1793 Michael Rudolph
July 1793 Edward Butler
May 1794 John Mills
Feb. 1796 Jonathan Haskell
Aug. 1796 Edward Butler
Feb. 1797 Thomas H. Cushing
July 1798 Alexander Hamilton
June 1800 Thomas H. Cushing
Apr. 1807 Abimael Y. Nicoll
July 1812 Alexander Smyth
Mar. 1813 Zebulon M. Pike
May 1814 William H. Winder
Nov. 1814 Daniel Parker
June 1821 John E. Wood
June 1841 George Croghan
Jan. 1849 Sylvester Churchill
Aug. 1861 Randolph B. Marcy
Jan. 1881 Delos B. Sacket
Mar. 1885 Nelson H. Davis
Sept. 1885 Absolom Baird
Aug. 1888 Roger Jones
Jan. 1889 Joseph C. Breckinridge
Apr. 1903 Peter D. Vroom
Apr. 1903 George H. Burton
Oct. 1906 Ernest A. Garlington
Feb. 1917 John L. Chamberlain
Nov. 1912 Eli A. Helmick
Sept. 1927 William C. Rivers
Jan. 1930 Hugh A. Drum
Dec. 1931 John F. Preston
Dec. 1935 Walter L. Reed
Dec. 1939 Virgil L. Peterson
July 1945 Daniel I. Sultan
Jan. 1947 Ira T. Wyche
July 1948 Louis A. Craig
June 1952 Daniel Noce
Nov. 1954 Wayne C. Zimmerman
Feb. 1956 David A. D. Ogden
Nov. 1957 Albert Pierson
July 1959 Edward H. McDaniel
Nov. 1963 Hiram D. Ives
Oct. 1965 James A. Richardson III
Nov. 1966 William C. Garrison
Aug. 1968 William A. Enemark

Judge Advocates General

July 1775 William Tudor
Apr. 1777 John Lawrence
Oct. 1782 Thomas Edwards
July 1794 Campbell Smith
Mar. 1849 John F. Lee
Sept. 1862 Joseph Holt
Dec. 1875 William M. Dunn
Feb. 1881 David G. Swain
Jan. 1895 G. Norman Lieber
May 1901 George B. Davis
Feb. 1911 Enoch H. Crowder
Feb. 1923 Walter A. Bethel
Nov. 1924 John A. Hull
Nov. 1928 Edward A. Kreger
Mar. 1931 Blanton Winship
Dec. 1933 Arthur W. Brown
Dec. 1937 Allen W. Gullion
Dec. 1941 Myron C. Cramer
Dec. 1945 Thomas H. Green
Jan. 1950 Ernest M. Brannon
Jan. 1954 Eugene M. Caffey
Jan. 1957 George W. Hickman, Jr.
Dec. 1960 Charles T. Decker
Feb. 1964 Robert H. McCaw
June 1967 Kenneth J. Hodson
July 1971 George S. Prugh

Chiefs of National Guard Bureau

Prior to 1933 known as Militia Bureau

1908 Erasmus M. Weaver
1911 Robert K. Evans
1912 Albert L. Mills
1916 William A. Mann
1917 Jessie M. Carter
1918 John W. Heavey (Acting)
1919 Jessie M. Carter
1921 George C. Rickards
1925 Creed C. Hammond
1929 Ernest R. Redmond (Acting)
1929 William G. Everson
1931 George E. Leach
1935 Herold J. Weiler (Acting)
1936 John F. Williams (Acting)
1936 Albert H. Blanding
1940 John F. Williams
1946 Butler B. Miltonberger
1947 Kenneth F. Cramer
1950 Raymond H. Fleming
1953 Earl T. Ricks
1953 Edgar C. Erickson
1959 Donald W. McGowan
1964 Winston P. Wilson
1972 Francis F. Greenlief

Chiefs of Ordnance

July 1812 Decius Wadsworth
June 1821 George Bomford
Mar. 1848 George Talcott
July 1851 Henry K. Craig
Apr. 1861 James W. Ripley
Sept. 1863 George D. Ramsay
Sept. 1864 Alexander B. Dyer
June 1874 Stephen V. Benet
June 1891 Daniel W. Flagler
Apr. 1899 Adelbert R. Buffington
Nov. 1901 William Crozier
July 1918 Clarence C. Williams
June 1930 Samuel Hof
June 1934 William H. Tschappat
June 1938 Charles M. Wesson
June 1942 Levin H. Campbell
June 1946 Everett S. Hughes
Nov. 1949 Elbert L. Ford
Nov. 1953 Emerson L. Cummings
Feb. 1958 John H. Hinrichs
May 1962 Horace F. Bigelow
to July 1962

Provost Marshals General

July	1941	Allen W. Gullion
June	1944	Archer L. Lerch
Dec.	1945	Blackshear M. Bryan
Apr.	1948	Edwin P. Parker, Jr.
Feb.	1953	William H. Maglin
Nov.	1957	Haydon L. Boatner
Oct.	1960	Ralph J. Butchers
June	1964	Carl C. Turner
July	1970	Lloyd B. Ramsey

Quartermasters General

Aug.	1775	Thomas Mifflin
June	1776	Stephen Moylan
Sept.	1776	Thomas Mifflin
Mar.	1778	Nathaniel Greene
Aug.	1780	Timothy Pickering
Mar.	1791	Samuel Hodgson
Apr.	1792	James O'Hara
June	1796	John Wilkins, Jr.
Apr.	1812	Morgan Lewis
Mar.	1813	Robert Swartwout
Apr.	1816	James Mullaney and George Gibson
May	1818	Thomas S. Jesup
June	1860	Joseph E. Johnston
May	1861	Montgomery C. Meigs
Feb.	1882	Daniel H. Rucker
Feb.	1882	Rufus Ingalls
July	1883	Samuel B. Holabird
June	1890	Richard N. Batchelder
Aug.	1896	Charles G. Sawtelle
Feb.	1897	George H. Weeks
Feb.	1898	Marshall I. Ludington
Apr.	1903	Charles F. Humphrey
July	1907	James B. Aleshire
Sept.	1916	Henry G. Sharpe
July	1918	Harry L. Rogers
Aug.	1922	William H. Hart
Jan.	1926	B. Franklin Cheatham
Feb.	1930	John L. DeWitt
Feb.	1934	Louis H. Bash
Apr.	1936	Henry Gibbins
Apr.	1940	Edmund B. Gregory
Feb.	1946	Thomas B. Larkin
Mar.	1949	Herman Feldman
Oct.	1951	George A. Horkan
Feb.	1954	Kester L. Hastings
June	1957	Andrew T. McNamara
June	1961	Webster Anderson *to July 1962*

Chiefs, U.S. Army Reserve

Mar.	1927	David L. Stone
July	1930	Charles D. Herron
July	1935	Edwin S. Hartshorn
Sept.	1938	Charles F. Thompson
June	1940	John H. Hester
June	1941	Frank E. Lowe
Sept.	1942	Edward W. Smith
Oct.	1945	Edward S. Bres
June	1948	Wendell Westover
Nov.	1949	George E. Butler (Acting)
Jan.	1950	James B. Cress
Aug.	1950	George E. Butler (Acting)
Feb.	1951	Hugh M. Milton II
Nov.	1953	Philip F. Lindeman
Aug.	1957	Ralph A. Palladino
July	1959	Frederick M. Warren
Aug.	1963	William J. Sutton
June	1970	J. Milnor Roberts, Jr.

Chief Signal Officers

June	1860	Albert J. Myer
Oct.	1863	William J. L. Nicodemus
Dec.	1864	Albert J. Myer
Dec.	1880	William B. Hazen
Mar.	1887	Adolphus W. Greely
Feb.	1906	James Allen
Mar.	1913	George P. Scriven
Feb.	1917	George O. Squier
Jan.	1924	Charles M. Saltzman
Jan.	1928	George S. Gibbs
July	1931	Irving J. Carr
Jan.	1935	James B. Allison
Oct.	1937	Joseph O. Mauborgne
Oct.	1941	Dawson Olmstead
July	1943	Harry C. Ingles
Apr.	1947	Spencer B. Akin
May	1951	George I. Back
May	1955	James D. O'Connell
Apr.	1959	Ralph T. Nelson
June	1962	Earle F. Cook
June	1963	David P. Gibbs *to July 1966*

Surgeons General

July	1775	Benjamin Church
Oct.	1775	John Morgan
Apr.	1777	William Shippen, Jr.
Jan.	1781	John Cochran
July	1798	James Craik
June	1813	James Tilton
Apr.	1818	Joseph Lovell
Nov.	1836	Thomas Lawson
May	1861	Clement A. Finley
Apr.	1862	William A. Hammond
Aug.	1864	Joseph K. Barnes
July	1882	Charles H. Crane
Nov.	1883	Robert Murray
Nov.	1886	John Moore
Aug.	1890	Jedediah H. Baxter
Dec.	1890	Charles Sutherland
May	1893	George M. Sternberg
June	1902	William H. Forwood
Sept.	1902	Robert M. O'Reilly
Jan.	1909	George H. Torney
Jan.	1914	William C. Gorgas
Oct.	1918	Merritte W. Ireland
June	1931	Robert U. Patterson
June	1935	Charles R. Reynolds
June	1939	James C. Magee
June	1943	Norman T. Kirk
June	1947	Raymond W. Bliss
June	1951	George E. Armstrong
June	1955	Silas B. Hays
May	1959	Leonard D. Heaton
Oct.	1969	Hal B. Jennings, Jr.

UNITED STATES ARMY

Major Field Commanders

Commanders, Army Ground Forces

Mar. 1942 Lesley J. McNair
July 1944 Ben Lear
Jan. 1945 Joseph W. Stilwell
July 1945 Jacob L. Devers
to March 1948

Commander Generals, Continental Army Command

Feb. 1955 John E. Dahlquist
Mar. 1956 Willard G. Wyman
Aug. 1958 Bruce C. Clarke
Sept. 1960 Herbert B. Powell
Jan. 1963 John K. Waters
Feb. 1964 Hugh Harris
Feb. 1965 Paul L. Freeman, Jr.
June 1967 James K. Woolnough
Nov. 1970 Ralph E. Haines, Jr.

Commanders-In-Chief, U.S. Army, Europe

May 1945 Dwight D. Eisenhower
Nov. 1945 George S. Patton, Jr.
Nov. 1945 Joseph T. McNarney
Mar. 1947 Lucius D. Clay
May 1949 Clarence R. Huebner
Sept. 1949 Thomas T. Handy
Aug. 1952 Manton S. Eddy
Apr. 1953 Charles L. Bolte
Sept. 1953 William M. Hoge
Feb. 1955 Anthony C. McAuliffe
May 1956 Henry I. Hodes
Mar. 1959 Clyde D. Eddleman
Oct. 1960 Bruce C. Clarke
Apr. 1962 Paul L. Freeman, Jr.
Feb. 1965 Andrew P. O'Meara
May 1967 James H. Polk
May 1971 Michael S. Davison
1972 Andrew J. Goodpaster

Commanders, Supreme Headquarters Allied Powers in Europe (SHAPE)

Feb. 1951 Dwight D. Eisenhower
May 1952 Matthew B. Ridgway
Aug. 1953 Alfred M. Gruenther
Nov. 1956 Lauris Norstad
Dec. 1962 Lyman L. Lemnitzer
to 1969

Commanders-In-Chief, United Nations Command

July 1950 Douglas MacArthur
Apr. 1951 Matthew B. Ridgway
May 1952 Mark W. Clark
Oct. 1953 John E. Hull
Apr. 1955 Maxwell D. Taylor
June 1955 Lyman L. Lemnitzer
July 1957 George H. Decker
June 1959 Carter B. Magruder
June 1961 Guy S. Meloy, Jr.
July 1963 Hamilton H. Howze
June 1965 Dwight E. Beach
Aug. 1966 Charles H. Bonesteel, Jr.
to 1969

Commanders-In-Chief, U.S. Army, Pacific

1909 W. S. Schuyler
1911 M. M. Macomb
1913 Frederick Funston
1914 M.M. Macomb
1914 N. H. Carter
1915 John P. Wisser
1916 Robert K. Evans
1916 Frederick S. Strong
1917 Charles G. Treat
1917 John P. Wisser
1918 Augustus P. Blocksom
1918 J. W. Heard
1919 J. C. Hodges, Jr.
1919 Charles G. Morton
Aug. 1921 Charles P. Summerall
Aug. 1924 Charles T. Menoher
Jan. 1925 Edward M. Lewis
Aug. 1927 William R. Smith
Jan. 1928 Fox Conner
Aug. 1930 Edwin B. Winans
Oct. 1930 William Lassiter
Sept. 1931 Briant H. Wells
Sept. 1934 Halstead Dorey
Mar. 1935 Hugh A. Drum
July 1937 Andrew Moses
Mar. 1938 Charles D. Herron
Feb. 1941 Walter Short
Dec. 1941 Delos C. Emmons
June 1943 Robert C. Richardson
Mar. 1946 George F. Moore
July 1946 John E. Hull
Feb. 1949 Floyd L. Parks
Apr. 1949 Henry S. Aurand
Sept. 1952 John W. O'Daniel
June 1954 Clark L. Ruffner
Dec. 1954 Bruce C. Clarke
July 1956 Blackshear M. Bryan
July 1957 Isaac D. White
Apr. 1961 Carter B. Magruder
Apr. 1962 James F. Collins
Feb. 1964 John K. Waters
Aug. 1966 Dwight E. Beach
Oct. 1970 William B. Rosson

Commanders-in-Chief, U.S. Army Forces in Far East

July 1941 Douglas MacArthur
Mar. 1951 Matthew B. Ridgway
May 1952 Mark W. Clark
Oct. 1953 John E. Hull
Dec. 1954 Maxwell D. Taylor
Mar. 1955 Lyman L. Lemnitzer
July 1955 Isaac D. White
to June 1957

Commanding Generals, Combat Developments Command

June 1962 John P. Daley
Aug. 1963 Dwight E. Beach
May 1965 Ben Harrell
June 1967 Harry W. O. Kinnard
Jan. 1970 George I. Forsythe
Oct. 1970 John Norton

Commanders-in-Chief, U.S. Readiness Command

Formerly Strike Command

Oct. 1961 Paul D. Adams
Oct. 1966 Theodore J. Conway
Aug. 1969 John L. Throckmorton

Commanding Generals, Air Defense Command

Apr. 1957 Stanley R. Mickelson
Oct. 1957 Charles E. Hart
July 1960 Robert J. Wood
Aug. 1962 William W. Dick, Jr.
Aug. 1963 Charles B. Duff
July 1966 Robert Hackett
Apr. 1971 Richard T. Cassidy

UNITED STATES ARMY
Commanders

First Army

July 1918 John J. Pershing
Oct. 1918 Hunter Liggett
to April 1919
Nov. 1938 Hugh A. Drum
Jan. 1944 Omar N. Bradley
Aug. 1944 Courtney H. Hodges
Feb. 1949 Roscoe B. Woodruff
Mar. 1949 Walter Bedell Smith
Nov. 1950 Willis D. Crittenberger
Jan. 1953 Withers A. Burress
Dec. 1954 Thomas W. Herren
Aug. 1957 Blackshear M. Bryan
Feb. 1960 Edward J. O'Neill
Mar. 1962 Garrison H. Davidson
Apr. 1964 Robert W. Porter, Jr.
Feb. 1965 Thomas W. Dunn
Dec. 1965 William F. Train
May 1967 Jonathan O. Seaman
Mar. 1971 Claire E. Hutchin

Second Army

Oct. 1918 Robert L. Bullard
to April 1919
Oct. 1940 Ben Lear
Apr. 1943 Lloyd R. Fredendall
Apr. 1946 William H. Simpson
Sept. 1946 Albert C. Wedemeyer
Oct. 1947 John T. Lewis
Jan. 1948 Leonard T. Gerow
Aug. 1950 James A. Van Fleet
June 1951 Edward H. Brooks
Sept. 1953 Floyd L. Parks
Apr. 1956 Charles E. Hart
Oct. 1957 George W. Read, Jr.
July 1960 Ridgely Gaither
Apr. 1962 John S. Upham, Jr.
June 1964 William F. Train

Second U. S. Army merged with First U. S. Army, Jan. 1966

Third Army

Nov. 1918 Joseph T. Dickman
to July 1919
Oct. 1936 George Van Horne Moseley
Oct. 1939 Stanley D. Embick
Oct. 1940 Herbert J. Brees
May 1941 Walter Krueger
Feb. 1943 Courtney H. Hodges
Jan. 1944 George S. Patton, Jr.
Oct. 1945 Lucien K. Truscott, Jr.
Apr. 1946 Geoffrey Keyes
Jan. 1947 Ernest N. Harmon
Mar. 1947 Oscar W. Griswold
Apr. 1947 Edward H. Brooks
June 1947 Alvan C. Gillem, Jr.
Sept. 1950 John R. Hodge
May 1952 William A. Beiderlinden
Aug. 1952 Alexander R. Bolling
Aug. 1955 Thomas F. Hickey
May 1958 Clark L. Ruffner
Feb. 1960 Herbert B. Powell
Oct. 1960 Paul D. Adams
Oct. 1961 Thomas J. H. Trapnell
Nov. 1962 Hamilton H. Howze (Acting)
Dec. 1962 Albert Watson II
July 1964 Charles W. G. Rich
June 1965 Louis W. Truman
July 1967 John L. Throckmorton
Aug. 1969 Albert O. Connor
1972 Melvin Zais

Fourth Army

Aug. 1932 Johnson Hagood
Oct. 1936 George S. Simonds
May 1938 Albert J. Bowley
Dec. 1939 John H. DeWitt
Oct. 1943 William H. Simpson
Apr. 1944 John P. Lucas
July 1945 Alexander M. Patch, Jr.
Oct. 1945 John P. Lucas
June 1946 Jonathan M. Wainwright
Sept. 1947 Thomas T. Handy
Aug. 1949 Andrew D. Bruce
Oct. 1949 LeRoy Lutes
Feb. 1952 Hobart R. Gay
Feb. 1952 William M. Hoge
Mar. 1953 John E. Dahlquist
June 1953 Haydon L. Boatner
Sept. 1953 Isaac D. White
June 1955 Samuel T. Williams
Oct. 1955 John H. Collier
Oct. 1958 Guy S. Meloy, Jr.
Sept. 1959 Edward T. Williams
Feb. 1961 Donald P. Booth
Feb. 1962 Paul H. Jark
July 1964 Robert W. Colglazier, Jr.
Jan. 1966 Thomas W. Dunn
Jan. 1967 Lawrence J. Lincoln, Jr.
July 1968 Harry H. Critz
to July 1971

Fifth Army

Jan. 1943 Mark W. Clark
Dec. 1944 Lucien K. Truscott, Jr.
June 1946 Walton H. Walker
Oct. 1948 Stephen J. Chamberlin
Jan. 1952 Albert C. Smith
July 1952 William B. Kean
Oct. 1954 Hobart R. Gay
Aug. 1955 Philip D. Ginder
Nov. 1955 William H. Arnold
Jan. 1961 Emerson L. Cummings
May 1962 John K. Waters
Jan. 1963 Charles G. Dodge
Mar. 1966 John H. Michaelis
June 1969 Vernon P. Mock
Sept. 1970 G. V. Underwood, Jr.
Sept. 1971 Patrick F. Cassidy

Sixth Army

Feb. 1943 Walter Krueger
Mar. 1946 Joseph W. Stilwell
Oct. 1946 George P. Hays
June 1947 Mark W. Clark
Oct. 1949 Albert C. Wedemeyer
Aug. 1951 Joseph M. Swing
Mar. 1954 Willard G. Wyman
July 1955 Robert N. Young
Oct. 1957 Lemuel Mathewson
Jan. 1958 Robert L. Howze
Mar. 1958 Charles D. Palmer
Aug. 1959 Robert N. Cannon
Aug. 1961 John T. Ryan, Jr.
July 1963 Frederic J. Brown
July 1965 James T. Richardson, Jr.
June 1967 Ben Harrell
June 1968 Stanley R. Larsen
June 1971 Alexander D. Surles, Jr.

Seventh Army

July 1943 George S. Patton, Jr.
Jan. 1944 Mark W. Clark
Mar. 1944 Alexander M. Patch, Jr.
June 1945 Wade H. Haislip
Sept. 1945 Geoffrey Keyes
June 1946 Oscar W. Griswald
Jan. 1951 Manton S. Eddy
Sept. 1952 Charles L. Bolte
Mar. 1953 William M. Hoge
Oct. 1953 Anthony C. McAuliffe
Jan. 1955 Henry I. Hodes
Apr. 1956 Bruce C. Clarke
June 1958 Clyde D. Eddleman
Mar. 1959 Francis W. Farrell
June 1960 Garrison H. Davidson
Mar. 1962 John C. Oakes
Dec. 1962 Hugh P. Harris
Feb. 1964 William W. Quinn
Feb. 1966 Theodore J. Conway
to Oct. 1966

Eighth Army

Sept. 1944 Robert L. Eichelberger
Sept. 1948 Walton H. Walker
Dec. 1950 Matthew B. Ridgway
Apr. 1951 James A. Van Fleet
Feb. 1953 Maxwell D. Taylor
Mar. 1955 Lyman L. Lemnitzer
June 1955 Thomas F. Hickey (Acting)
July 1955 Isaac D. White
July 1957 George H. Decker
July 1959 Carter B. Magruder
Aug. 1961 Guy S. Meloy, Jr.
Aug. 1963 Hamilton H. Howze
July 1965 Dwight E. Beach
Sept. 1966 Charles H. Bonesteel III
to Sept. 1969

ARMY COMMANDERS DURING WARTIME

Revolutionary War

War of 1812

Civil War

Union Army Commanders
Union Battlefield Commanders
Confederate Army Commanders
(See Section VII – The Confederacy)
Confederate Battlefield Commanders
(See Section VII – The Confederacy)

First World War

Second World War

Army Group Commanders
Field Commanders
Commanders, Army Air Forces
Corps Commanders
Division Commanders

Revolutionary War

Commander-in-Chief

George Washington

Commanding Generals

John Armstrong
Benedict Arnold
John Ashe
George Rogers Clark
George Clinton
James Clinton
Thomas Conway
Philemon Dickinson
David Forman
John Glover
Nathaniel Greene
John Hancock
Edward Hand
William Heath
Nicholas Herkimer
Robert Howe
Isaac Huger
William Irvine
Henry Knox
Robert Lawson
Charles Lee
Benjamin Lincoln
Solomon Lovell
Alexander McDougall
Lauchlin McIntosh
Francis Marion
William Maxwell
Thomas Mifflin
Richard Montgomery
Daniel Morgan
Peter Muhlenberg
Francis Nash
John Nixon
Samuel Parsons
John Patterson
Earl Hugh Percy
Andrew Pickens
Timothy Pickering
Seth Pomeroy
Enoch Poor
Israel Putnam
Griffith Rutherford
Arthur St. Clair
Philip Schuyler
Charles Scott
Gold Silliman
William Smallwood
Joseph Spencer
Adam Stephen
John Sullivan
Jethro Sumner
Thomas Sumter
John Thomas
Robert van Renssalaer
James Varnum
Artemas Ward
David Waterbury, Jr.
Anthony Wayne
George Wheedon
Andrew Williamson
William Woodford
David Wooster

War of 1812

Commanding Generals

Isaac Brock
Jacob Brown
Henry Dearborn
Wade Hampton
William Henry Harrison
William Hull
Andrew Jackson
Zebulon Pike
Winfield Scott
Alexander Smyth
Stephen Van Renssalaer
James Wilkinson

Civil War

UNION ARMY COMMANDERS

Generals-in-Chief of the Armies

Apr. 1861 – Nov. 1861
Winfield Scott
Nov. 1861 – Mar. 1862
George B. McClellan
July 1862 – Mar. 1864
Henry W. Halleck
Mar. 1864 – Apr. 1865
Ulysses S. Grant

Army of the Potomac

Aug. 1861 George B. McClellan
Nov. 1862 Ambrose E. Burnside
Jan. 1863 Joseph Hooker
June 1863 George G. Meade

Army of the Ohio

Nov. 1861 Don Carlos Buell
Aug. 1862 Horatio G. Wright
Mar. 1863 Ambrose E. Burnside
Dec. 1863 John G. Foster
Feb. 1864 John M. Schofield

Army of the Southwest

Dec. 1861 Samuel R. Curtis
Sept. 1862 Eugene A. Carr
Oct. 1862 Willis A. Gorman

Army of the Mississippi

Feb. 1862 John Pope
June 1862 William S. Rosecrans

Army of the Mountain Department

Mar. 1862 John C. Fremont
to June 1862

Army of the Cumberland

Oct. 1862 William S. Rosecrans
Oct. 1863 George H. Thomas

Army of the Frontier

Oct. 1862 John M. Schofield
Mar. 1863 Francis J. Herron

Army of the Tennessee

Oct. 1862 Ulysses S. Grant
Oct. 1863 William T. Sherman
Mar. 1864 James B. McPherson
July 1864 Oliver O. Howard

Army of the James

Nov. 1862 Benjamin F. Butler
to Dec. 1864

Army of West Virginia

June 1863 B. F. Kelley
Mar. 1864 Franz Sigal
May 1864 David Hunter
Aug. 1864 George Crook

Army of the Shenandoah

Aug. 1864 Philip H. Sheridan
Feb. 1865 Alfred T. A. Torbert

Army of Georgia

Nov. 1864 Henry W. Slocum

Union Battlefield Commanders

FIRST BATTLE OF BULL RUN, or MANASSAS
21 JULY 1861

Commander	Irvin McDowell
First Division	Daniel Tyler
Second Division	David Hunter
Third Division	Samuel P. Heintzelman
Fourth Division	Theodore Runyon
Fifth Division	D. S. Miles

BATTLE OF SHILOH
6-7 APRIL 1862

Army of the Tennessee	Ulysses S. Grant
First Division	John A. McClernand
Second Division	William H. L. Wallace
Third Division	Lew Wallace
Fourth Division	Stephen A. Hurlbut
Fifth Division	William T. Sherman
Sixth Division	Benjamin M. Prentiss
Army of the Ohio	Don Carlos Buell
Second Division	Alexander M. McCook
Fourth Division	William Nelson
Fifth Division	Thomas L. Crittenden
Sixth Division	Thomas J. Wood

BATTLE OF SEVEN PINES, or FAIR OAKS
31 MAY-JUNE 1862

Army of the Potomac	George B. McClellan
II Corps	Edwin V. Sumner
First Division	Israel B. Richardson
Second Division	John Sedgwick
III Corps	Samuel P. Heintzelman
Second Division	Joseph Hooker
Third Division	Philip Kearny
IV Corps	Erasmus D. Keyes
First Division	Darius N. Couch
Second Division	Silas Casey

SEVEN DAYS' BATTLES
25 JUNE-1 JULY 1862

Army of the Potoma	George B. McClellan
II Corps	Edwin V. Sumner
First Division	Israel B. Richardson
Second Division	John Sedgwick
III Corps	Samuel P. Heintzelman
Second Division	Joseph Hooker
Third Division	Philip Kearny
IV Corps	Erasmus D. Keyes
First Division	Darius N. Couch
Second Division	John J. Peck
V Corps	Fitz-John Porter
First Division	George W. Morell
Second Division	George Sykes
Third Division	George A. McCall
VI Corps	William B. Franklin
First Division	Henry W. Slocum
Second Division	William F. Smith

SECOND BATTLE OF BULL RUN, or MANASSAS
29-30 AUG. 1862

Army of Virginia	John Pope
I Corps	Franz Sigel
First Division	Robert C. Schenck
Second Division	Adolph von Steinwehr
Third Division	Carl Schurz
II Corps	Nathaniel P. Banks
First Division	Alpheus S. Williams
Second Division	George S. Greene
III Corps	Irvin McDowell
First Division	Rufus King, Abner Doubleday
Second Division	James B. Ricketts
Reynolds Division	John F. Reynolds
Reserve Corps	Samuel D. Sturgis
Army of the Potomac	George B. McClellan
III Corps	Samuel P. Heintzelman
First Division	Philip Kearny
Second Division	Joseph Hooker
V Corps	Fitz-John Porter
First Division	George W. Morell
Second Division	George Stykes
IX Corps	Jesse L. Reno
First Division	Isaac I. Stevens
	Benjamin C. Christ

BATTLE OF ANTIETAM
17 SEPT. 1862

Army of the Potomac	George B. McClellan
I Corps	Joseph Hooker
First Division	Abner Doubleday
Second Division	James B. Ricketts
Third Division	George G. Meade
II Corps	Edwin V. Sumner
First Division	Israel B. Richardson
Second Division	John Sedgwick
Third Division	William H. French
IV Corps	
First Division	Darius N. Couch
V Corps	Fitz-John Porter
Second Division	George Sykes
VI Corps	William B. Franklin
First Division	Henry W. Slocum
Second Division	William F. Smith
IX Corps	Ambrose E. Burnside
First Division	Orlando B. Willcox
Second Division	Samuel D. Sturgis
Third Division	Isaac P. Rodman
Kanawha Division	Jacob D. Cox

BATTLE OF CORINTH
3-4 OCT. 1862

Army of the Mississippi	William S. Rosecrans
Second Division	David S. Stanley
Third Division	Charles S. Hamilton
Cavalry	John K. Mizner
District of West Tennessee	
Second Division	Thomas A. Davies
Sixth Division	Thomas J. McKean

BATTLE OF FREDERICKSBURG
13 Dec. 1862

Army of the Potomac	Ambrose E. Burnside
I Corps	Joseph Hooker
First Division	Abner Doubleday
Second Division	James B. Ricketts
Third Division	George G. Meade
II Corps	Edwin V. Sumner
First Division	Israel B. Richardson
Second Division	John Sedgwick
Third Division	William H. French

IV Corps	
First Division	Darius N. Couch
V Corps	Fitz-John Porter
First Division	George W. Morell
Second Division	George Sykes
VI Corps	William B. Franklin
First Division	Henry W. Slocum
Second Division	William F. Smith
IX Corps	Ambrose E. Burnside
First Division	Orlando B. Willcox
Second Division	Samuel D. Sturgis
Third Division	Isaac P. Rodman
Kanawha Division	Jacob D. Cox
Right Grand Division	Edwin V. Sumner
II Corps	Darius N. Couch
First Division	Winfield S. Hancock
Second Division	Oliver O. Howard
Third Division	William H. French
IX Corps	Orlando B. Willcox
First Division	William W. Burns
Second Division	Samuel D. Sturgis
Third Division	George W. Getty
Cavalry Division	Alfred Pleasanton
Center Grand Division	Joseph Hooker
III Corps	George Stoneman
First Division	D. B. Binney
Second Division	Daniel E. Sickles
Third Division	Amiel W. Whipple
V Corps	Daniel Butterfield
First Division	Charles Griffin
Second Division	George Sykes
Third Division	Andrew A. Humphreys
Left Grand Division	William B. Franklin
I Corps	John F. Reynolds
First Division	Abner Doubleday
Second Division	John Gibbon
Third Division	George G. Meade
VI Corps	William F. Smith
First Division	William T. H. Brooks
Second Division	Albion P. Howe
Third Division	John Newton

BATTLE OF STONES RIVER, or MURFREESBORO
31 Dec. 1862-2 Jan. 1863

Army of the Cumberland	William S. Rosecrans
Right Wing	Alexander M. McCook
First Division	Jefferson C. Davis
Second Division	Richard W. Johnson
Third Division	Philip H. Sheridan
Center Wing	George H. Thomas
First Division	Lovell H. Rousseau
Second Division	James S. Negley
Third Division	M. B. Walker
Left Wing	Thomas L. Crittenden
First Division	Thomas J. Wood
Second Division	John M. Palmer
Third Division	H. P. Van Cleve
Cavalry	David S. Stanley
Cavalry Division	John Kennett

BATTLE OF CHANCELLORSVILLE
2-4 MAY 1863

Army of the Potomac	Joseph Hooker
I Corps	John F. Reynolds
First Division	James S. Wadsworth
Second Division	John C. Robinson
Third Division	Abner Doubleday
II Corps	Darius N. Couch
First Division	Winfield S. Hancock
Second Division	John Gibbon
Third Division	William H. French
III Corps	Daniel E. Sickles
First Division	David B. Birney
Second Division	Hiram G. Berry, Joseph B. Carr
Third Division	Amiel W. Whipple, Charles K. Graham
V Corps	George G. Meade
First Division	Charles Griffin
Second Division	George Sykes
VI Corps	John Sedgwick
First Division	William T. H. Brooks
Second Division	Albion P. Howe
Third Division	John Newton
Light Division	Hiram Burnham
XI Corps	Oliver O. Howard
First Division	Charles Devens
Second Division	Adolph von Steinwehr
Third Division	Carl Schurz
XII Corps	Henry W. Slocum
First Division	Alpheus S. Williams
Second Division	John W. Geary
Cavalry Corps	George Stoneman
First Division	Alfred Pleasanton
Second Division	William W. Averell
Third Division	David M. Gregg

VICKSBURG CAMPAIGN
1 MAY-4 JULY 1863

Army of the Tennessee	Ulysses S. Grant
IX Corps	John G. Parke
First Division	Thomas Welsh
Second Division	Robert B. Potter
XIII Corps	John A. McClernand, Edward O. C. Ord
Ninth Division	Peter J. Osterhaus
Tenth Division	Andrew J. Smith
Twelfth Division	Alvin P. Hovey
Fourteenth Division	Eugene A. Carr
XV Corps	William T. Sherman
First Division	Frederick Steele
Second Division	Francis P. Blair, Jr.
Third Division	James M. Tuttle
XVI Corps	Cadwallader C. Washburn
First Division	William S. Smith
Fourth Division	J. C. Lauman
Provisional Division	Nathan Kimball
XVII Corps	James B. McPherson
Third Division	John A. Logan
Sixth Division	John McArthur
Seventh Division	Marcellus M. Crocker, J. F. Quimby, John E. Smith
Herron's Division	Francis J. Herron

BATTLE OF GETTYSBURG
1-3 JULY 1863

Army of the Potomac	
I Corps	George G. Meade, John F. Reynolds, Abner Doubleday, John Newton
First Division	James S. Wadsworth
Second Division	John C. Robinson
Third Division	T. A. Rowley
II Corps	Winfield S. Hancock, John Gibbon
First Division	John C. Caldwell
Second Division	John Gibbon
Third Division	Alexander Hayes
III Corps	Daniel E. Sickles
First Division	David B. Birney
Second Division	Andrew A. Humphreys
V Corps	George Sykes
First Division	James Barnes
Second Division	Romeyn B. Ayres
Third Division	Samuel W. Crawford
VI Corps	John Sedgwick
First Division	Horatio G. Wright
Second Division	Albion P. Howe
Third Division	John Newton

XI Corps	Oliver O. Howard
First Division	Francis C. Barlow
Second Division	Adolph von Steinwehr
Third Division	Carl Schurz
XII Corps	Henry W. Slocum
First Division	Alpheus S. Williams
Second Division	John W. Geary
Cavalry Corps	Alfred Pleasanton
First Division	John Buford
Second Division	David M. Gregg
Thrid Division	Judson Kilpatrick

BATTLE OF CHICKAMAUGA
19-20 SEPT. 1863

Army of the Cumberland	William S. Rosecrans
XIV Corps	George H. Thomas
First Division	Absolom Baird
Second Division	James S. Negley
Third Division	John M. Brannan
Fourth Division	Joseph J. Reynolds
XX Corps	Alexander M. McCook
First Division	Jefferson C. Davis
Second Division	Richard W. Johnson
Third Division	Philip H. Sheridan
XXI Corps	Thomas L. Crittenden
First Division	Thomas J. Wood
Second Division	John M. Palmer
Third Division	H. P. Van Cleve
Reserve Corps	Gordon Granger
First Division	James B. Steedman
Cavalry Corps	Robert B. Mitchell
First Division	Edward M. McCook
Second Division	George Crook

BATTLE OF CHATTANOOGA
23-25 NOV. 1863

Union Forces	Ulysses S. Grant
Army of the Cumberland	George H. Thomas
IV Corps	Gordon Granger
First Division	Charles Cruft
Second Division	Philip H. Sheridan
Third Division	Thomas J. Wood
XIV Corps	John M. Palmer
First Division	Richard W. Johnson
Second Division	Jefferson C. Davis
Third Division	Absolom Baird
Army of the Tennessee	William T. Sherman
XV Corps	Francis P. Blair, Jr.
First Division	Peter J. Osterhaus
Second Division	Mathew C. Smith
Fourth Division	Hugh Ewing
XVII Corps	John E. Smith
Second Division	John E. Smith
XI Corps	Oliver O. Howard
Second Division	Adolph von Steinwehr
Third Division	Carl Schurz
XII Corps	Joseph Hooker

BATTLES OF WILDERNESS and
SPOTTSYLVANIA COURT HOUSE
5-21 May 1864

Union Forces	Ulysses S. Grant
Army of the Potomac	George G. Meade
II Corps	Winfield S. Hancock
First Division	Francis C. Barlow
Second Division	John Gibbon
Third Division	David B. Birney
Fourth Division	Gerhsom Mott
V Corps	Gouverneur K. Warren
First Division	Charles Griffin
Second Division	John C. Robinson
Third Division	Samuel W. Crawford
Fourth Division	James S. Wadsworth
VI Corps	John Sedgwick
First Division	Horatio G. Wright
Second Division	George W. Getty
Third Division	James B. Ricketts
IX Corps	Ambrose E. Burnside
First Division	Thomas G. Stevenson
Second Division	Robert B. Potter
Third Division	Oralndo B. Willcox
Fourth Division	Edward Ferrero
Cavalry Corps	Philip H. Sheridan
First Division	Alfred T. A. Torbert
Second Division	David M. Gregg
Third Division	James H. Wilson

ATLANTA CAMPAIGN
3 May-8 Sept. 1864

Union Forces	William T. Sherman
Army of the Cumberland	George H. Thomas
IV Corps	Oliver O. Howard, David S. Stanley
First Division	David S. Stanley, William Grose, Nathan Kimball
Second Division	John Newton
Third Division	Thomas J. Wood
XIV Corps	John M. Palmer, Richard W. Johnson, Jefferson C. Davis
First Division	Richard W. Johnson, John H. King, William P. Carlin
Second Division	Jefferson C. Davis, J. D. Morgan
Third Division	Absolom Baird
XX Corps	Joseph Hooker, Alpheus S. Williams, Henry W. Slocum
First Division	Alpheus S. Williams, J. F. Knipe
Second Division	John W: Geary
Third Division	Daniel Butterfield
Cavalry Corps	W. D. Elliott
First Division	Edward M. McCook
Second Division	Kenner Garrard
Third Division	Judson Kilpatrick
Army of the Tennessee	James B. McPherson, John A. Logan, Oliver O. Howard
XV Corps	John A. Logan, Martin L. Smith
First Division	Peter J. Osterhaus, C. R. Woods
Second Division	Martin L. Smith, J. M. J. Lightburn, William B. Hazen
Fourth Division	William Harrow
XVI Corps	Grenville M. Dodge Thomas E. G. Ransom
Second Division	Thomas W. Sweeney, Elliott W. Rice, John M. Corse
Fourth Division	James C. Veatch, John W. Fuller, Thomas E. G. Ransom
XVII Corps	Francis P. Blair, Jr.
Third Division	Mortimer D. Leggett, C. R. Woods
Fourth Division	Walter Q. Gresham, William Hall, G. A. Smith
Army of the Ohio	John M. Schofield
XXIII Corps	John M. Schofield
First Division	Alvin P. Hovey
Third Division	Jacob D. Cox
Cavalry Division	George Stoneman

BATTLE OF NASHVILLE
15-16 Dec. 1864

Union Forces	George H. Thomas
IV Corps	Thomas J. Wood
First Division	Nathan Kimball
Second Division	Washington L. Elliott
Third Division	Samuel Beatty
XXIII Corps	John M. Schofield
Second Division	Darius N. Couch
Third Division	Jacob D. Cox
Garrison of Nashville	John F. Miller
Cavalry Corps	James H. Wilson
Fifth Division	Edward Hatch
Sixth Division	Richard W. Johnson
Seventh Division	J. F. Knipe

CAMPAIGN OF THE CAROLINAS
FEB.-MAR. 1865

Army of the Tennessee	Oliver O. Howard
XV Corps	John A. Logan
First Division	Charles R. Woods
Second Division	William B. Hazen
Third Division	John E. Smith
Fourth Division	John M. Course
XVII Corps	Francis P. Blair, Jr.
First Division	Joseph A. Mower, Manning F. Force
Third Division	Mortimer D. Leggett
Fourth Division	Giles A. Smith
Army of Georgia	Henry W. Slocum
XIV Corps	Jefferson C. Davis
First Division	William P. Carlin, George P. Buell
Second Division	James D. Morgan
Third Division	Absalom Baird
XX Corps	Alpheus S. Williams
First Division	Nathaniel J. Jackson
Second Division	Alpheus S. Williams, John W. Geary
Third Division	William T. Ward
Cavalry Corps	
Third Division	Judson Kilpatrick
Army of the Ohio	John M. Schofield
X Corps	Alfred H. Terry
First Division	Henry W. Birge
Second Division	Adelbert Ames
Third Division	Charles J. Paine
XXIII Corps	Jacob D. Cox
First Division	Thomas H. Ruger
Second Division	Nathaniel C. McLean, Orlando H. Moore, Joseph A. Cooper
Third Division	James W. Reilly, Samuel P. Carter

First World War
COMMANDERS

American Expeditionary Forces

1917-1918	John J. Pershing

I Corps

Jan. 1918	Hunter Liggett
Oct. 1918	Joseph T. Dickman
Nov. 1918	William M. Wright

II Corps

June 1918	George W. Read

III Corps

June 1918	William M. Wright
July 1918	Robert L. Bullard
Oct. 1918	John L. Hines

IV Corps

Aug. 1918	Joseph T. Dickman
Oct. 1918	Charles H. Muir

V Corps

July 1917	William M. Wright
Aug. 1918	George H. Cameron
Oct. 1918	Charles P. Summerall

VI Corps

Aug. 1918	Omar Bundy
Oct. 1918	Charles T. Ballou
Nov. 1918	Charles T. Menoher

VII Corps

Aug. 1918	William M. Wright
Sept. 1918	Omar Bundy
Nov. 1918	William G. Haan

VIII Corps

Nov. 1918	Henry T. Allen

IX Corps

Nov. 1918	Adelbert Cronkhite

Northeastern Department

May 1917	Clarence R. Edwards
Sept. 1917	John A. Johnston
May 1918	John W. Ruckman
July 1918	William Crozier
Dec. 1918	Clarence R. Edwards

Eastern Department

Apr. 1917	Leonard Wood
May 1917	J. Franklin Bell
Aug. 1917	Eli D. Hoyle
Jan. 1918	William A. Mann
Aug. 1918	J. Franklin Bell
Jan. 1919	Thomas H. Barry
Oct. 1919	Robert L. Bullard

Southeastern Department

May 1917	Leonard Wood
Aug. 1917	William P. Duvall
Jan. 1918	William L. Sibert
June 1918	Henry G. Sharpe

Central Department

Apr. 1917	Thomas H. Barry
Aug. 1917	William H. Carter
Mar. 1918	Thomas H. Barry
Jan. 1919	Leonard Wood

Southern Department

Apr. 1917	John J. Pershing
Aug. 1917	John W. Ruckman
May 1918	Williard A. Holbrook
Sept. 1918	De Rosey C. Cabell
Aug. 1919	Joseph T. Dickman

Western Department

Apr. 1917	J. Franklin Bell
May 1917	Hunter Liggett
Sept. 1917	Arthur Murray
May 1918	Charles G. Treat
June 1918	John F. Morrison
July 1919	Hunter Liggett

Panama Canal Department

July 1917	Edward H. Plummer
Aug. 1917	Adelbert Cronkhite
Feb. 1918	Richard M. Blatchford
Apr. 1919	Chase W. Kennedy

Philippine Department

Apr. 1917	Charles J. Bailey
Aug. 1918	Henry A. Greene
Feb. 1919	Francis H. French

Hawaiian Department

Apr. 1917	Frederick S. Strong
Sept. 1917	John P. Wisser
May 1918	Augustus P. Blocksom
Mar. 1919	Henry C. Hodges, Jr.
July 1919	Charles G. Morton

Second World War

ARMY GROUP COMMANDERS

(Army commanders listed earlier in this Section)

1st Army Group

Oct. 1943-July 1944 Omar N. Bradley

6th Army Group

Aug. 1944-June 1945 Jacob L. Devers

12th Army Group

July 1944-July 1945 Omar N. Bradley

15th Army Group

Dec. 1944-July 1945 Mark W. Clark

FIELD COMMANDERS

Airborne Command

Mar. 1942 William C. Lee
Aug. 1942 Elbridge G. Chapman
Nov. 1943 Les Donovan
Jan. 1944 Josiah T. Dalbey
Sept. 1945 Anthony C. McAuliffe
to June 1946

Allied Expeditionary Force, Supreme Headquarters (SHAEF)

Feb. 1944 Dwight D. Eisenhower
to July 1945

Antiaircraft Command

Mar. 1942 Joseph A. Green
Oct. 1944 Frank C. McConnell
Feb. 1945 George R. Meyer
to Oct. 1945

Armored Force

Aug. 1941 Jacob L. Devers
May 1943 Alvan C. Gillem, Jr.
Dec. 1943 Charles L. Scott
to Oct. 1945

Army Ground Forces

Mar. 1942 Leslie J. McNair
July 1944 Ben Lear
Jan. 1945 Joseph W. Stilwell
July 1945 Jacob L. Devers
to Dec. 1947

Caribbean Defense Command

Sept. 1941 F. M. Andrews
Nov. 1942 G. H. Brett

Central Defense Command

July 1941 Ben Lear
July 1943 Lloyd R. Fredendall
to Jan. 1944

Central Pacific Area

Aug. 1943 Robert C. Richardson, Jr.
to March 1946

China Theater

Oct. 1944 Albert C. Wedemeyer
to May 1946

China-Burma-India

See also India-Burma Theater

Mar. 1942 Joseph W. Stilwell
Apr. 1943 Raymond A. Wheeler
June 1943 Joseph W. Stilwell
to Oct. 1944

Eastern Defense Command

Dec. 1941 Hugh A. Drum
Oct. 1943 George Grunert
Aug. 1945 Kennet P. Lord
to Feb. 1946

European Theater of Operations

June 1942 Dwight D. Eisenhower
Feb. 1943 William S. Key
May 1943 Jacob L. Devers
Jan. 1944 Dwight D. Eisenhower
to Nov. 1945

Far East

July 1941 Douglas MacArthur
Mar. 1942 Jonathan Wainwright
to June 1942

General Headquarters, U. S. Army (GHQ)

July 1940 George C. Marshall
to March 1942

India-Burma Theater

See also China-Burma-India

Oct. 1944 Daniel I. Sultan
June 1945 Raymond A. Wheeler
Sept. 1945 Thomas A. Terry
to Feb. 1946

Mediterranean Theater of Operations

Nov. 1944 Joseph T. McNarney
Dec. 1945 John C. H. Lee
to Sept. 1947

Middle East Forces

June 1942 Russell L. Maxwell
Nov. 1942 Frank L. Andrews
Jan. 1943 Lewis H. Brereton
Sept. 1943 Ralph Royce
Mar. 1944 Benjamin F. Giles
to Mar. 1945

Military District of Washington

May 1942 John T. Lewis
Sept. 1944 Charles F. Thompson

North African Theater of Operations

Feb. 1943 Dwight D. Eisenhower
Jan. 1944 Jacob L. Devers
to Oct. 1944

Pacific Theater of Operations

Apr. 1942 Douglas MacArthur
to Dec. 1946

Persian Gulf Command

Oct. 1942 Donald H. Connolly
Dec. 1944 Donald P. Booth
Aug. 1945 George A. M. Anderson
to Oct. 1945

South Atlantic Forces

Nov. 1942 Robert L. Walsh
May 1944 Ralph Wooten
to Oct. 1945

Southern Defense Command

May 1941 Walter Krueger
Feb. 1943 Courtney H. Hodges
Jan. 1944 Henry C. Pratt
to Oct. 1944

Western Defense Command

Mar. 1941 John L. DeWitt
Sept. 1943 Delos C. Emmons
June 1944 Charles H. Bonesteel
Dec. 1944 Henry C. Pratt
to Nov. 1945

COMMANDERS, ARMY AIR FORCES

First Air Force

Dec. 1941 Arnold N. Krogstad
Mar. 1942 Follett Bradley
July 1942 James E. Chaney
Apr. 1943 Ralph Royce
Sept. 1943 Frank O. Hunter
July 1944 Caleb V. Haynes
Sept. 1944 Frank O. Hunter
Oct. 1945 Robert W. Douglass, Jr.

Second Air Force

Dec. 1941 John B. Brooks
Feb. 1942 Frederick L. Martin
May 1942 Robert Olds
Feb. 1943 Davenport Johnson
July 1953 Eugene Eubank
Sept. 1943 St. Clair Streett
Jan. 1944 Uzal G. Ent
Oct. 1944 Robert B. Williams

Third Air Force

Oct. 1941 Walter H. Frank
June 1942 Carlyle H. Wash
Dec. 1942 St. Clair Streett
Sept. 1943 Westside T. Larson
May 1945 Thomas W. Blackburn
July 1945 Lewis H. Brereton

Fourth Air Force

Jan. 1941 Jacob E. Fickel
Apr. 1942 George C. Kenney
July 1942 Barney M. Giles
Mar. 1943 William E. Kepner
July 1944 James E. Parker
May 1945 Edward M. Morris
July 1945 Willis H. Hale

Fifth Air Force

Nov. 1941 Lewis H. Brereton
Feb. 1942 George H. Brett
Sept. 1942 George C. Kenney
June 1944 Ennis C. Whitehead

Sixth Air Force

Sept. 1941 Davenport Johnson
Nov. 1942 Hubert R. Harmon
Nov. 1943 Ralph H. Wooten
May 1944 Edgar P. Sorenson
Sept. 1944 William O. Butler
July 1945 Earl H. DeFord

Seventh Air Force

Dec. 1941 Clarence L. Tinker
June 1942 Willis H. Hale
Apr. 1944 Robert W. Douglass, Jr.
June 1945 Thomas D. White

Eighth Air Force

Jan. 1942 Asa N. Duncan
May 1942 Carl A. Spaatz
Dec. 1942 Ira C. Eaker
Jan. 1944 James H. Doolittle
Sept. 1945 Earle E. Partridge

Ninth Air Force

June 1942 Lewis H. Brereton
Aug. 1944 Hoyt S. Vandenberg
May 1945 Otto P. Weyland
Aug. 1945 William E. Kepner

Tenth Air Force

Mar. 1942 Lewis H. Brereton
June 1942 Earl L. Naiden
Aug. 1942 Clayton L. Bissell
Aug. 1943 Howard C. Davidson
Aug. 1945 Albert F. Hegenberger

Eleventh Air Force

Mar. 1942 William O. Butler
Sept. 1943 Davenport Johnson
July 1945 John B. Brooks
Nov. 1945 Edmund C. Lynch

Thirteenth Air Force

Jan. 1943 Nathan F. Twining
Jan. 1944 Hubert R. Harmon
June 1944 St. Clair Streett
Feb. 1945 Paul B. Wurtsmith

Fourteenth Air Force

Mar. 1943 Claire L. Chennault
Aug. 1945 Charles B. Stone

Fifteenth Air Force

Nov. 1943 James H. Doolittle
Jan. 1944 Nathan F. Twining
May 1945 James A. Mollison

Twentieth Air Force

Apr. 1944 Henry A. Arnold
Aug. 1945 Nathan F. Twining
Oct. 1945 James E. Parker

CORPS COMMANDERS

I Corps

Oct. 1940 Charles F. Thompson
June 1942 Robert L. Eichelberger
Aug. 1944 Innis P. Swift

II Corps

Aug. 1941 Lloyd R. Fredendall
July 1942 Mark W. Clark
Oct. 1942 Lloyd R. Fredendall
Mar. 1943 George S. Patton, Jr.
Apr. 1943 Omar N. Bradley
Sept. 1943 Geoffrey Keyes

III Corps

July 1941 Joseph W. Stilwell
Dec. 1941 Walter K. Wilson
Apr. 1942 John P. Lucas
June 1943 Harold R. Bull
Oct. 1943 John Milikin
Mar. 1945 James A. Van Fleet

IV Corps

Oct. 1941 Jay L. Benedict
July 1942 Oscar W. Griswold
Apr. 1943 Alexander M. Patch, Jr.
Mar. 1944 Willis D. Crittenberger

V Corps

Jan. 1942 William S. Key
May 1942 Russell P. Hartle
July 1943 Leonard T. Gerow
Jan. 1945 Clarence R. Huebner

VI Corps

Dec. 1941 George Grunert
Apr. 1942 Ernest J. Dawley
Sept. 1943 John P. Lucas
Feb. 1944 Lucien K. Truscott, Jr.
Oct. 1944 Edward H. Brooks
June 1945 William H. H. Morris, Jr.

VII Corps

Aug. 1941 Robert C. Richardson, Jr.
May 1943 Roscoe B. Woodruff
Mar. 1944 J. Lawton Collins
Aug. 1945 Alvan C. Gillem, Jr.

VIII Corps

Dec. 1943 Emil F. Reinhardt
Mar. 1944 Troy H. Middleton

IX Corps

Oct. 1940 Kenyon A. Joyce
Apr. 1942 Charles H. White
Mar. 1944 Emil F. Reinhardt
Sept. 1944 Charles W. Ryder

X Corps

May 1942 Courtney H. Hodges
Mar. 1943 Jonathan W. Anderson
Aug. 1944 Franklin C. Sibert

XI Corps

June 1942 Lloyd R. Fredendall
Oct. 1942 Charles P. Hall

XII Corps

Sept. 1942 William H. Simpson
Oct. 1943 Gilbert R. Cook
Aug. 1944 Manton S. Eddy
Apr. 1945 Stafford L. Irwin

XIII Corps

Dec. 1942 Emil F. Reinhardt
Dec. 1943 Alvan C. Gillem, Jr.

XIV Corps

Jan. 1943 Alexander M. Patch, Jr.
Apr. 1943 Oscar W. Griswold

XV Corps

Feb. 1943 Wade H. Haislip
June 1945 Walter M. Robertson

XVI Corps

Jan. 1944 John B. Anderson

XVIII Corps.

Oct. 1943 William H. H. Morris, Jr.
Sept. 1944 Matthew B. Ridgway

XIX Corps

Oct. 1943 Willis D. Crittenberger
Mar. 1944 Charles H. Corlett
Nov. 1944 Raymond S. McLain

XX Corps

Oct. 1943 Walton H. Walker
May 1945 Louis A. Craig

XXI Corps

Dec. 1943 Frank W. Milburn

XXII Corps

Jan. 1944 Henry Terrell, Jr.
Jan. 1945 Ernest N. Harmon

XXIII Corps

Jan. 1944 Louis A. Craig
Sept. 1944 James I. Muir
Dec. 1944 Jesmond Balmer
Feb. 1945 James A. Van Fleet
Mar. 1945 Hugh J. Gaffey

XXIV Corps

Apr. 1944 John R. Hodge

XXXVI Corps

July 1944 Jonathan W. Anderson
Jan. 1945 Charles H. Corlett

I Armored Corps

Apr. 1941 Charles L. Scott
Jan. 1942 George S. Patton, Jr.
to July 1943

III Armored Corps

Sept. 1942 Willis D. Crittenberger
to Oct. 1943

IV Armored Corps

Sept. 1942 Walton H. Walker
to Oct. 1943

DIVISION COMMANDERS

1st Infantry Division

Feb. 1941 Donald Cubbison
Aug. 1942 Terry Allen
July 1943 Clarence R. Huebner
Dec. 1944 Clift Andrus

2nd Infantry Division

Nov. 1941 John C. H. Lee
May 1942 Walter M. Robertson
June 1945 William K. Harrison, Jr.

3rd Infantry Division

Sept. 1941 John P. Lucas
Mar. 1942 Jonathan W. Anderson
Mar. 1943 Lucian K. Truscott, Jr.
Feb. 1944 John W. O'Daniel
July 1945 William R. Schmidt

4th Infantry Division

Dec. 1941 Terry Allen
Jan. 1942 Fred C. Wallace
July 1942 Raymond O. Barton
Dec. 1944 Harold W. Blakeley

5th Infantry Division

Aug. 1941 Cortlandt Parker
June 1943 Stafford L. Irwin
Apr. 1945 Albert E. Brown

6th Infantry Division

Jan. 1941 Clarence S. Ridley
Sept. 1942 Durward S. Wilson
Oct. 1942 Franklin C. Sibert
Aug. 1944 Edwin D. Patrick
Mar. 1945 Charles E. Hurdis

7th Infantry Division

Aug. 1941 Charles H. White
Oct. 1942 Albert E. Brown
May 1943 Eugene M. Landrum
July 1943 Archibald V. Arnold
Sept. 1943 Charles H. Corlett
Feb. 1944 Archibald V. Arnold

8th Infantry Division

Apr. 1941 James P. Marley
Aug. 1942 Paul E. Peabody
Feb. 1943 William C. McMahon
July 1944 Donald A. Stroh
Dec. 1944 William G. Weaver
Feb. 1945 Bryant E. Moore

9th Infantry Division

Aug. 1941 Rene E. D. Hoyle
Aug. 1942 Manton S. Eddy
Aug. 1944 Louis A. Craig
May 1945 Jesse A. Ladd

10th Infantry Division

Nov. 1944 George P. Hays

23rd Infantry Division

May 1942 Alexander M. Patch, Jr.
Jan. 1943 Edmund B. Sebree
May 1943 John R. Hodge
Apr. 1944 Robert B. McClure
Nov. 1944 William H. Arnold

24th Infantry Division

Oct. 1941 Durward S. Wilson
Aug. 1942 Frederick A. Irving
Nov. 1944 Roscoe B. Woodruff

25th Infantry Division

Oct. 1941 Maxwell Murray
May 1942 L. Lawton Collins
Jan. 1944 Charles L. Mullins, Jr.

26th Infantry Division

Jan. 1940 Robert W. Eckfeldt
Aug. 1943 Willard S. Paul
June 1945 Harlan N. Hartness
July 1945 Stanley E. Reinhart

27th Infantry Division

Nov. 1941 Ralph M. Pennell
Nov. 1942 Ralph C. Smith
June 1944 George W. Griner, Jr.

28th Infantry Division

Jan. 1942 J. Garsche Ord
June 1942 Omar N. Bradley
Jan. 1943 Lloyd D. Brown
Aug. 1944 Norman D. Cota

29th Infantry Division

Feb. 1942 Leonard T. Gerow
July 1943 Charles H. Gerhardt

30th Infantry Division

Dec. 1940 Henry D. Russell
May 1942 William H. Simpson
Sept. 1942 Leland S. Hobbs

31st Infantry Division

Nov. 1940 John C. Persons
Sept. 1944 Clarence A. Martin

32nd Infantry Division

Feb. 1942 Edwin F. Harding
Dec. 1942 Frayne Baker
Mar. 1943 William H. Gill

33rd Infantry Division

Mar. 1941 Samuel T. Lawton
May 1942 Frank C. Mahin
Aug. 1942 John Millikin
Oct. 1943 Percy W. Clarkson

34th Infantry Division

Aug. 1941 Russell P. Hartle
May 1942 Charles W. Ryder
July 1944 Charles L. Bolte

35th Infantry Division

Oct. 1941 William H. Simpson
May 1942 Maxwell Murray
Jan. 1943 Paul W. Baade

36th Infantry Division

Sept. 1941 Fred L. Walker
July 1944 John E. Dahlquist

37th Infantry Division

Dec. 1940 Robert S. Beightler

38th Infantry Division

Apr. 1941 Daniel I. Sultan
Apr. 1942 Henry L. L. Jones
Feb. 1945 William C. Chase

40th Infantry Division

Sept. 1941 Ernest J. Dawley
Apr. 1942 Rapp Brush
July 1945 Donald J. Myers

41st Infantry Division

Dec. 1941 Horace H. Fuller
June 1944 Jens A. Doe

42nd Infantry Division

July 1943 Henry J. Collins

43rd Infantry Division

Aug. 1941 John H. Hester
Aug. 1943 Leonard F. Wing

44th Infantry Division

Aug. 1941 James I. Muir
Aug. 1944 Robert L. Spragins
Jan. 1945 William F. Dean

45th Infantry Division

Sept. 1940 William S. Key
Oct. 1942 Troy H. Middleton
Dec. 1943 William W. Eagles
Dec. 1944 Robert T. Frederick

63rd Infantry Division

June 1943 Louis E. Hibbs

65th Infantry Division

Aug. 1943 Stanley E. Reinhart

66th Infantry Division

Apr. 1943 Herman F. Kramer

69th Infantry Division

May 1943 Charles L. Bolte
Sept. 1944 Emil F. Reinhardt

70th Infantry Division

June 1943 John E. Dahlquist
July 1944 Allison J. Barnett
July 1945 Thomas W. Herren

71st Infantry Division

July 1943 Robert L. Spragins
Oct. 1944 Eugene M. Landrum
Nov. 1944 Willard G. Wyman

75th Infantry Division

Apr. 1943 Willard S. Paul
Aug. 1943 Fay B. Prickett
Jan. 1945 Ray E. Porter
June 1945 Arthur A. White

76th Infantry Division

June 1942 Emil F. Reinhardt
Dec. 1942 William R. Schmidt
Aug. 1945 Henry C. Evans

77th Infantry Division

Mar. 1942 Robert L. Eichelberger
June 1942 Roscoe B. Woodruff
May 1943 Andrew D. Bruce

78th Infantry Division

1942 Edwin P. Parker, Jr.

79th Infantry Division

June 1942 Ira T. Wyche
May 1945 LeRoy H. Watson

80th Infantry Division

July 1942 Joseph D. Patch
Mar. 1943 Horace L. McBride

81st Infantry Division

June 1942 Gustave H. Franke
Aug. 1942 Paul J. Mueller

83rd Infantry Division

Aug. 1942 Frank W. Milburn
Jan. 1944 Robert C. Macon

84th Infantry Division

June 1944 Alexander R. Bolling

85th Infantry Division

May 1942 Wade H. Haislip
Feb. 1943 John B. Coulter

86th Infantry Division

Dec. 1942 Alexander E. Anderson
Jan. 1943 Harris M. Melasky

87th Infantry Division

Dec. 1942 Percy W. Clarkson
Oct. 1943 Eugene M. Landrum
Apr. 1944 Frank L. Culin, Jr.

88th Infantry Division

July 1942 John E. Sloan
Sept. 1944 Paul W. Kendall
July 1945 James C. Fry

89th Infantry Division

July 1942 William H. Gill
Feb. 1943 Thomas D. Finley

90th Infantry Division

Mar. 1942 Henry Terrell, Jr.
Jan. 1944 Jay W. Mackelvie
July 1944 Eugene M. Landrum
Aug. 1944 Raymond S. McLain
Oct. 1944 James A. Van Fleet
Feb. 1945 Lowell W. Rooks
Mar. 1945 Herbert L. Earnest

91st Infantry Division

Aug. 1942 Charles H. Gerhardt
July 1943 William G. Livesay

92nd Infantry Division

Oct. 1942 Edward M. Almond
Aug. 1945 John E. Weed

93rd Infantry Division

May 1942 Charles P. Hall
Oct. 1942 Fred W. Miller
May 1943 Raymond G. Lehman
Aug. 1944 Harry H. Johnson

94th Infantry Division

Sept. 1942 Harry J. Maloney
June 1945 Louis J. Fortier
Aug. 1945 Allison J. Barnett

95th Infantry Division

July 1942 Harry L. Twaddle

96th Infantry Division

Aug. 1942 James L. Bradley

97th Infantry Division

Feb. 1943 Louis A. Craig
Jan. 1944 Milton B. Halsey

98th Infantry Division

Sept. 1942 Paul L. Ransom
Nov. 1943 George W. Griner, Jr.
July 1944 Ralph C. Smith
Nov. 1944 Arthur M. Harper

99th Infantry Division

Nov. 1942 Thompson Lawrence
July 1943 Walter F. Lauer
Aug. 1945 Frederick H. Black

100th Infantry Division

Nov. 1942 Withers A. Burress

102nd Infantry Division

Sept. 1942 John B. Anderson
Jan. 1944 Frank A. Keating

103rd Infantry Division

Nov. 1942 Charles C. Haffner, Jr.
Jan. 1945 Anthony C. McAuliffe
Aug. 1945 John N. Robinson

104th Infantry Division

June 1942 Gilbert R. Cook
Oct. 1943 Terry Allen

106th Infantry Division

Mar. 1943 Alan W. Jones
Dec. 1944 Herbert T. Perrin
Feb. 1945 Donald A. Stroh
Aug. 1945 Francis A. Woolfley

Americal Infantry Division

May 1942 Alexander M. Patch, Jr.
Jan. 1943 Edmund B. Sebree
May 1943 John R. Hodge
Apr. 1944 Robert McClure
Nov. 1944 William H. Arnold

1st Armored Division

July 1940 Bruce Magruder
Mar. 1942 Orlando Ward
Apr. 1943 Ernest N. Harmon
July 1944 Vernon E. Prichard

2nd Armored Division

July 1940 George S. Patton, Jr.
Feb. 1942 Willis D. Crittenberger
July 1942 Ernest N. Harmon
May 1943 Hugh J. Gaffey
Apr. 1944 Edward H. Brooks
Sept. 1944 Ernest N. Harmon
Jan. 1945 Isaac D. White
May 1945 John H. Collier
Aug. 1945 John M. Devine

3rd Armored Division

Apr. 1941 Alvan C. Gillem, Jr.
Jan. 1942 Walton H. Walker
Aug. 1942 Leroy H. Watson
Aug. 1944 Maurice Rose
Mar. 1945 Doyle O. Hickey
June 1945 Truman E. Boudinot
July 1945 Robert W. Grow

4th Armored Division

Apr. 1941 Henry W. Baird
May 1942 J. S. Wood
Dec. 1944 Hugh J. Gaffey
Mar. 1945 William M. Hoge
June 1945 Bruce C. Clarke
July 1945 W. Lyn Roberts

5th Armored Division

Oct. 1941 Jack W. Heard
Mar. 1943 Lunsford E. Oliver
June 1945 Morrill Ross

6th Armored Division

Feb. 1942 William H. H. Morris, Jr.
May 1943 Robert W. Grow
Apr. 1945 George W. Read, Jr.

7th Armored Division

Mar. 1942 Lindsay M. Silvester
Nov. 1944 Robert W. Hasbrouck

8th Armored Division

Apr. 1942 William M. Grimes
Oct. 1944 John M. Devine
Aug. 1945 Charles F. Colson

9th Armored Division

June 1942 Geoffrey Keyes
Oct. 1942 John W. Leonard

10th Armored Division

July 1942 Paul W. Newgarden
July 1944 William H. H. Morris, Jr.
May 1945 Fay B. Prickett

11th Armored Division

Aug. 1942 Edward H. Brooks
Mar. 1944 Charles S. Kilburn
Mar. 1945 Holmes E. Dager

12th Armored Division

Sept. 1942 Carlos Brewer
Aug. 1944 Douglass T. Greene
Sept. 1944 Roderick R. Allen
July 1945 Willard A. Holbrook, Jr.

13th Armored Division

Oct. 1942 John B. Wogan
Apr. 1945 John Millikin

14th Armored Division

Nov. 1942 Vernon E. Prichard
July 1944 Albert C. Smith

16th Armored Division

July 1943 Douglass T. Greene
Sept. 1944 John L. Pierce

20th Armored Division

Feb. 1943 Stephen G. Henry
Oct. 1943 Roderick R. Allen
Sept. 1944 Orlando Ward
Aug. 1945 John W. Leonard

11th Airborne Division

Feb. 1943 Joseph M. Swing

13th Airborne Division

Aug. 1943 George W. Griner
Nov. 1943 Elbridge G. Chapman, Jr.

17th Airborne Division

April 1943 William M. Miley

82nd Airborne Division

Mar. 1942 Omar N. Bradley
June 1942 Matthew B. Ridgway
Aug. 1944 James M. Gavin

101st Airborne Division

Aug. 1942 William C. Lee
Mar. 1944 Maxwell D. Taylor

1st Cavalry Division

Apr. 1941 Innis P. Swift
Aug. 1944 Verne D. Mudge
Feb. 1945 Hugh F. T. Hoffman

10th Mountain Division

July 1943 Lloyd E. Jones
Nov. 1944 George P. Hays

UNITED STATES AIR FORCE

Chiefs of Staff

Sept. 1947 Carl A. Spaatz
Apr. 1948 Hoyt S. Vandenberg
June 1953 Nathan F. Twining
July 1957 Thomas D. White
June 1961 Curtis E. LeMay
Feb. 1965 John P. McConnell
Aug. 1969 John D. Ryan

Vice Chiefs of Staff

1947 Hoyt S. Vandenberg
1948 Muir S. Fairchild
1950 Lauris Norstad (Acting)
1950 Nathan F. Twining
1953 Thomas D. White
1957 Curtis E. LeMay
1961 Frederic H. Smith, Jr.
1962 William F. McKee
1964 John P. McConnell
1965 William H. Blanchard
1966 Bruce K. Holloway
1968 John D. Ryan
1969 John C. Meyer
1972 Horace M. Wade

Logistics Commanders

1947 Joseph T. McNarney
1949 Benjamin W. Chidlaw
1951 Edwin W. Rawlings
1959 Samuel E. Anderson
1961 William F. McKee
1962 Mark E. Bradley, Jr.
1965 Kenneth B. Hobson
1967 Thomas P. Gerrity
1968 Jack G. Merrell

Military Airlift Commanders

1948 Laurence S. Kuter
1951 Joseph Smith
1958 William H. Tunner
1960 Joe W. Kelly
1964 Howell M. Estes, Jr.
1969 Jack J. Catton

Strategic Air Commanders

1946 George C. Kenney
1948 Curtis E. LeMay
1957 Thomas S. Power
1964 John D. Ryan
1967 Joseph J. Nazzaro
1968 Bruce K. Holloway
1972 John C. Meyer

Systems Commanders

Prior to 1961 the Systems Command was known as the Air Research Development Command

1950 David M. Schlatter
1951 Earle E. Partridge
1953 Donald R. Putt
1954 Thomas S. Power
1957 Samuel E. Anderson
1959 John W. Sessums, Jr.
1959 Bernard A. Schreiver
1966 James Ferguson
1970 George S. Brown

Tactical Air Commanders

1946 Elwood R. Quesada
1948 Robert M. Lee
1950 Glenn D. Barcus
1951 John K. Cannon
1954 Otto P. Weyland
1959 Frank F. Everest
1961 Walter C. Sweeney, Jr.
1965 Gabriel P. Disosway
1968 William W. Momyer

Commanders-in-Chief, North American Air Defense Command

1957 Earle E. Partridge
1959 Laurence S. Kuter
1962 John K. Gerhart
1965 Dean C. Strother
1966 Raymond J. Reeves
1969 Seth J. McKee

Commanders, Pacific Air Forces

1946 Ennis C. Whitehead
1949 George E. Stratemeyer
1951 Otto P. Weyland
1954 Earle E. Partridge
1955 Laurence S. Kuter
1959 Emmett O'Donnell, Jr.
1963 Jacob E. Smart
1964 Hunter Harris
1967 John D. Ryan
1968 Joseph J. Nazzaro
1971 Lucius D. Clay, Jr.

Commanders, U. S. Air Forces in Europe

1947 Curtis E. LeMay
1948 John K. Cannon
1950 Lauris Norstad
1953 William H. Tunner
1957 Frank F. Everest
1959 Frederic H. Smith, Jr.
1961 Truman H. Landon
1963 Gabriel P. Disosway
1965 Bruce K. Holloway
1966 Maurice A. Preston
1968 Horace M. Wade
1969 Joseph R. Holzapple
1971 David C. Jones

UNITED STATES NAVY

Chiefs of Naval Operations

May 1915 William Benson
Nov. 1919 Robert E. Coontz
July 1923 Edward W. Eberle
Nov. 1927 Charles F. Hughes
Sept. 1930 William V. Pratt
July 1933 William H. Standley
Jan. 1937 William D. Leahy
Aug. 1939 Harold R. Stark
Mar. 1942 Ernest J. King
Dec. 1945 Chester W. Nimitz
Dec. 1947 Louis E. Denfeld
Nov. 1949 Forest P. Sherman
Aug. 1951 William M. Fechteler
Aug. 1953 Robert B. Carney
Aug. 1955 Arleigh A. Burke
Aug. 1961 George W. Anderson, Jr.
Aug. 1963 David L. McDonald
Aug. 1967 Thomas H. Moorer
July 1970 Elmo R. Zumwalt, Jr.

Commanders in Chief, Pacific (CINPAC)

1949 Arthur W. Radford
1953 Felix B. Stump
1958 Harry D. Felt
1964 Ulysses S. G. Sharp
1968 John S. McCain, Jr.
1972 Noel Gayler

Commanders, U. S. Naval Forces in Europe

Includes predecessor commands

1940 Robert L. Ghormley
1942 Harold R. Stark
1945 H. Kent Hewitt
1946 Richard L. Connolly
1950 Robert B. Carney
1952 Jerauld Wright
1954 John H. Cassady
1956 Walter F. Boone
1958 James L. Holloway, Jr.
1959 Robert L. Dennison
1960 Harold P. Smith
1963 Charles D. Griffin
1965 John S. Thach
1967 John S. McCain, Jr.
1968 Waldemar F. Wendt
1971 William F. Bringle

Assistant Chiefs of Naval Operations (Intelligence)

Formerly known as Office of Naval Intelligence

1915 James Oliver
1917 Roger Welles
1919 Albert P. Niblack
1921 Luke McNamee
1923 Henry H. Hough
1925 W. W. Galbraith
1926 A. J. Hepburn
1928 A. W. Johnson
1930 H. A. Baldridge
1931 Hayne Ellis
1934 W. D. Puleston
1937 Ralston S. Holmes
1939 W. S. Anderson
1941 Alan G. Kirk
1941 T. S. Wilkinson
1943 H. C. Train
1944 R. E. Schuirmann
1945 Hewlett Thebaud
1946 T. B. Inglis
1949 Felix Johnson
1952 Richard F. Stout
1953 Carl Espe
1956 Lawrence H. Frost
1961 V. L. Lowrance
1963 R. L. Taylor
1967 Eugene B. Fluckey
1968 Frederick J. Harlfinger
1971 Earl F. Rectanus

U. S. Navy Judge Advocates General

1880 William B. Remey
1892 Samuel C. Lemly
1904 Samuel W. B. Diehl
1907 Edward H. Campbell
1909 Robert L. Russell
1913 Ridley McLean
1917 William C. Watts
1918 George R. Clark
1921 Julian L. Latimer
1925 Edward H. Campbell
1929 David F. Seller
1931 Orrin G. Murfin
1934 Claude C. Block
1936 Gilbert J. Rowcliff
1938 Walter B. Woodson
1943 Thomas L. Gatch
1945 Oswald S. Colcough
1948 George L. Russell
1952 Ira H. Nunn
1956 Chester Ward
1960 W. C. Mott
1964 W. A. Hearn
1968 Joseph B. McDevitt

U. S. Navy Surgeons General

1869 William M. Wood
1871 J. M. Foltz
1872 Joseph C. Palmer
1873 Joseph Beale
1877 William Grier
1878 J. Winthrop Taylor
1879 P. S. Wales
1884 Francis M. Gunnell
1888 J. M. Browne
1893 J. R. Tryon
1897 William K. Van Reyper
1902 Presley M. Rixley
1910 Charles F. Stokes
1914 W. C. Braisted
1920 E. R. Stitt
1928 C. E. Riggs
1933 Percival S. Rossiter
1938 Ross T. McIntyre
1946 Clifford A. Swanson
1951 Herbert L. Pugh
1955 Bartholomew W. Hogan
1961 Edward C. Kenney
1965 R. B. Brown
1969 George M. Davis

U.S. Marine Corps

Commandants

1798 William S. Burrows
1804 Franklin Wharton
1819 Anthony Gale
1820 Archibald Henderson
1859 John Harris
1864 Jacob Zeilin
1876 Charles G. McCawley
1891 Charles Heywood
1903 George F. Elliott
1911 William P. Biddle
1914 George Barnett
1920 John A. Lejeune
1929 Wendell C. Neville
1930 Ben H. Fuller
1934 John H. Russell
1936 Thomas Holcomb
1944 Alexander A. Vandegrift
1948 Clifton B. Cates
1952 Lemuel C. Shepherd
1956 Randolph M. Pate
1960 David M. Shoup
1964 Wallace M. Greene, Jr.
1968 Leonard F. Chapman, Jr.
1972 Richard E. Cushman, Jr.

Naval Commanders

(Through the Civil War)

REVOLUTIONARY WAR

Commander-in-Chief

Esek Hopkins

Commodores

John P. Hazlewood
John Paul Jones
Dudley Saltonstall

WAR OF 1812

Commodores

Isaac Chauncey
Stephen Decatur
Thomas Macdonough
Oliver H. Perry
David Porter

CIVIL WAR

Gunboat Squadron, Western Waters

1861 George W. Rodgers
1861 Andrew H. Foote
1862 Charles H. Davis

Mississippi Squadron

1862 David D. Porter
1864 Samuel P. Lee

North Atlantic Blockading Squadron

1861 Silas H. Strigham
1861 Louis M. Goldsborough
1862 Samuel P. Lee
1864 David D. Porter

South Atlantic Blockading Squadron

1861 Samuel F. DuPont
1863 John A. Dahlgren

West Gulf Blockading Squadron

1862 David G. Farragut
1864 James S. Palmer
1865 Henry K. Thatcher

West Indies Squadron

1862 Charles Wilkes
1863 James L. Lardner

United States Navy Fleet Commanders

Pacific Fleet

1941 Husband E. Kimmell
1942 Chester W. Nimitz
1945 Raymond A. Spruance
1946 John H. Towers
1947 Louis E. Denfeld
1948 Dewitt C. Ramsey
1949 Arthur W. Radford
1953 Felix B. Stump
1958 Herbert G. Hopwood
1960 John H. Sides
1963 Ulysses S. G. Sharp
1964 Thomas H. Moorer
1965 Roy L. Johnson
1967 John J. Hyland
1970 Bernard A. Clarey

Atlantic Fleet

Feb. 1941 Ernest J. King
Dec. 1941 Royal E. Ingersoll
Nov. 1944 Jonas H. Ingram
Sept. 1946 Marc A. Mitscher
Feb. 1947 William H. P. Blandy
Feb. 1950 William M. Fechteler
Aug. 1951 Lynde D. McCormick
Apr. 1954 Jerauld Wright
Feb. 1960 Robert L. Dennison
Apr. 1963 Harold P. Smith
Apr. 1965 Thomas H. Moorer
June 1967 Ephraim P. Holmes
Sept. 1970 Charles K. Duncan

First Fleet

Aug. 1943 Raymond A. Spruance
Nov. 1945 John H. Towers
Jan. 1946 Frederick C. Sherman
Sept. 1946 Alfred E. Montgomery
Aug. 1947 George D. Murray
Aug. 1948 Laurence T. Du Bose
Jan. 1949 Gerald F. Bogan
July 1951 Ralph A. Ofstie
July 1952 Joseph J. Clark
Oct. 1952 Harold M. Martin
Sept. 1953 William K. Phillips
Aug. 1955 Herbert G. Hopwood
June 1956 Robert L. Dennison
Aug. 1958 Ruthven E. Libby
Apr. 1960 Ulysses S. G. Sharp
July 1960 Charles L. Melson
May 1962 Robert T. S. Keith
Dec. 1963 Paul D. Stroop
Jan. 1964 Ephraim P. Holmes
July 1964 Lawson P. Ramage
July 1966 Bernard F. Roeder
Sept. 1969 Isaac C. Kidd, Jr.
Aug. 1970 Raymond E. Peet
Aug. 1972 James F. Calvert

Second Fleet

Mar. 1946 Marc A. Mitscher
Aug. 1946 Joseph A. E. Hindman
Mar. 1947 Arthur W. Radford
Feb. 1948 Donald B. Duncan
June 1950 Robert B. Carney
Sept. 1950 Matthias B. Gardner
Apr. 1951 Felix B. Stump
June 1953 Thomas S. Combs
Apr. 1954 Edmund T. Wooldridge
June 1955 Charles Wellborn, Jr.
July 1957 Robert B. Pirie
May 1958 Bernard L. Austin
Mar. 1959 William R. Smedberg III
Jan. 1960 Harold T. Deutermann
Feb. 1961 Claude V. Ricketts
Dec. 1972 John G. Finneran
Sept. 1961 John M. Taylor
Oct. 1962 Alfred G. Ward
Aug. 1963 Charles B. Martell
Apr. 1964 Kleber S. Masterson
Aug. 1966 Bernard A. Clarey
May 1967 Charles K. Duncan
Apr. 1968 Benedict J. Semmes, Jr.
Sept. 1970 Gerald E. Miller

Sixth Fleet

June 1946 Bernard H. Bieri
Feb. 1948 Forrest P. Sherman
Nov. 1949 John J. Ballentine
Mar. 1951 Matthias B. Gardner
May 1952 John H. Cassady
Mar. 1954 Thomas S. Combs
Mar. 1955 Ralph A. Ofstie
Apr. 1956 Harry D. Felt
Aug. 1956 Charles R. Brown
Sept. 1958 Clarence E. Ekstrom
Sept. 1959 George W. Anderson, Jr.
July 1961 David L. McDonald
Mar. 1963 William E. Gentner, Jr.
June 1964 William E. Ellis
May 1966 Frederick L. Ashworth
Apr. 1967 William I. Martin
Aug. 1968 David C. Richardson
Aug. 1970 Issac C. Kidd, Jr.
Dec. 1972 Daniel J. Murphy

Seventh Fleet

1942 Herbert F. Leary
1942 Arthur S. Carpender
1943 Thomas C. Kinkaid
1946 Charles M. Cooke, Jr.
1948 Oscar C. Badger
1949 Russell S. Berkey
1950 Arthur D. Struble
1951 Harold M. Martin
1952 Joseph J. Clark
1953 Alfred M. Pride
1955 Stuart H. Ingersoll
1957 Wallace M. Beakeley
1958 Frederick N. Kivette
1960 Charles D. Griffin
1961 William A. Schoech
1962 Thomas H. Moorer
1964 Roy L. Johnson
1965 Paul P. Blackburn, Jr.
1965 John J. Hyland
1967 Walter F. Bringle
1970 Maurice F. Weisner
1972 James L. Holloway III

United States Navy Bureau Chiefs

Naval Air Systems Command

Known as the Bureau of Aeronautics until 1959 when it combined with the Bureau of Ordnance to form the Bureau of Naval Weapons. Present Command was established in 1966.

1921 William A. Moffett
1933 Ernest J. King
1936 A. B. Cook
1939 J. H. Towers
1942 J. S. McCain
1943 De Witt C. Ramsey
1945 H. B. Sallada
1947 Alfred M. Pride
1951 Thomas S. Combs
1953 Appolo Soucer
1955 James S. Russell
1957 Robert E. Dixon
1959 Paul D. Stroop
1962 K. S. Masterson
1964 Wellington T. Hines
1964 Allen M. Shinn
1966 Robert L. Townsend
1969 T. J. Walker
1971 T. R. McClellan

Bureau of Engineering

In 1940 combined with the Bureau of Construction and Repair to become the Bureau of Ships.

1862 Benjamin F. Isherwood
1870 J. W. King
1874 W. W. Wood
1878 W. H. Shock

1884 Charles H. Loring
1888 George W. Melville
1903 C. W. Rae
1908 John K. Barton
1909 Hutch I. Cone
1913 Robert S. Griffin
1921 John K. Robison
1925 John Halligan, Jr.
1928 H. E. Yarnell
1931 Samuel M. Robinson
1935 H. G. Bowen
1939 Samuel M. Robinson

Bureau of Naval Personnel

Known as the Bureau of Navigation until 1942

1862 Charles Henry Davis
1865 Percival Drayton
David D. Porter
T. A. Jenkins
1869 James Alden
1871 Daniel Ammen
1878 William D. Whiting
1881 John D. G. Walker
1889 Francis M. Ramsay
1897 A. S. Crowninshield
1902 Henry Clay Taylor
1904 George A. Converse
1907 Willard H. Brownson
1908 John E. Pillsbury
1909 William P. Potter,
R. F. Nicholson
1912 Philip Andrews
1913 Victor Blue
1916 Leigh C. Palmer
1918 Victor Blue
1919 Thomas Washington
1923 Andrew T. Long
1924 William R. Shoemaker
1927 Richard H. Leigh
1930 Frank B. Upham
1933 William D. Leahy
1935 Adolphus Andrews
1938 James O. Richardson
1939 Chester W. Nimitz
1941 Randall Jacobs
1945 Louis E. Denfeld
1947 Thomas L. Sprague
1949 John W. Roper
1951 Laurance T. Debose
1953 James L. Holloway, Jr.
1958 H. Page Smith
1960 William R. Smedberg
1964 B. J. Semmes, Jr.

Naval Facilities Engineering Command

Until 1966 known as the Bureau of Yards and Docks

1842 Lewis Warrington
1846 Joseph Smith
1869 Daniel Ammen
1871 C. R. P. Rodgers
1874 John Howell
1878 Richard L. Law
1881 Edward T. Nichols
1885 David B. Harmony
1889 George B. White
1890 Norman H. Farquhar
1894 Edmund O. Matthews
1898 Mordecai T. Endicott
1907 R. C. Hollyday
1912 Homer R. Stanford
1916 Frederic R. Harris
1918 Charles W. Parks
1921 Luther E. Gregory
1929 Archibald L. Parsons
1933 Norman M. Smith
1937 Ben Moreell
1945 John J. Manning
1949 Joseph F. Jelley, Jr.
1953 John R. Perry
1955 Robert H. Meade
1959 Eugene J. Peltier
1962 P. Corradi
1965 A. C. Husband
1970 W. M. Enger

Office of Naval Material

1942 Samuel M. Robinson
1946 Ben Moreell
1947 Edward L. Cochrane
1948 Arthur C. Miles
1950 E. D. Foster
1951 Albert G. Noble
1952 Charles W. Fox
1954 John Gingrich
1955 M. L. Royar
1956 Edward W. Clexton
1962 G. F. Beardsley
1963 William A. Schoech
1965 Ignatius J. Galantin
1970 Jackson D. Arnold
1971 H. C. Kidd, Jr.

Naval Ordnance Systems Command

Known as the Bureau of Ordnance until 1960 when it combined with Bureau of Aeronautics to form the Bureau of Naval Weapons. Present command was established in 1966.

1842 William M. Crane
1846 Lewis Warrington
1851 Charles Morris
1856 Duncan N. Ingraham
1860 George A. Magruder
1861 Andrew A. Harwood
1862 John A. Dahlgren
1863 Henry Augustus Wise
1868 John A. Dahlgren
1869 Augustus Ludlow Case
1873 William N. Jeffers
1881 Montgomery Sicard
1890 William M. Folger
1893 William T. Sampson
1897 Charles O'Neil
1904 George A. Converse,
Newton E. Mason
1911 Nathan C. Twining
1913 Joseph Strauss
1916 Ralph Earle
1920 Charles B. McVay, Jr.
1923 Claude C. Bloch
1927 William D. Leahy
1931 Edgar B. Larimer
1934 Harold R. Stark
1937 William R. Furlong
1941 William H. P. Blandy
1943 George F. Hussey, Jr.
1947 Albert G. Noble
1950 Malcolm F. Schoeppel
1954 Frederic S. Withington
1958 Paul D. Stroop
1966 Arthur R. Gralla
1970 M. W. Woods

Naval Ship Systems Command

Known as the Bureau of Construction and Repairs until it united in 1940 with the Bureau of Engineering to become the Bureau of Ships; title changed to present name in 1966.

1842 David Conner
1843 Beverly Kennon
1844 Charles Morris
1847 Charles W. Skinner
1852 William B. Shubrick
1853 Samuel Hartt,
John Lenthall
1872 Isaiah Hanscom
1878 J. W. Easby
1882 Theodore D. Wilson
1894 Philip Hichborn
1901 F. T. Bowles
1903 W. L. Capps
1910 Richard M. Watt
1914 David W. Taylor
1922 John D. Beuret
1929 George H. Rock
1933 Emory S. Land
1937 William G. DuBose
1939 Alexander H. Van Keuren
1940 Samuel M. Robinson
1942 Alexander H. Van Keuren,
Edward L. Cochrane
1946 Earle W. Mills
1949 David H. Clark
1951 Homer N. Wallin
1953 Wilson D. Leggett, Jr.
1955 Albert G. Mumma
1959 Ralph K. James
1963 William A. Brockett
1966 Edward J. Fahy
1970 N. Sonenshein

COLLEGES OF THE ARMED FORCES

See Section XII – Higher Education for commandants of Service Academies

Armed Forces Staff College

Commandants

Aug. 1946 Delos C. Emmons
June 1948 John L. Hall, Jr.
July 1951 Andrew D. Bruce
July 1954 David M. Schlatter
July 1957 Charles Wellborn, Jr.
Mar. 1960 Thomas J. Sands
May 1960 John S. Upham, Jr.
Apr. 1962 Robert Wienecke
July 1963 J. Stanley Holtoner
June 1965 Lawrence R. Daspit
Oct. 1967 Frank W. Norris

Army War College

Presidents

July 1902 Samuel B. M. Young
Aug. 1903 Tasker H. Bliss
June 1905 W. W. Wotherspoon (Acting)
Dec. 1905 Thomas H. Barry
Feb. 1907 W. W. Wotherspoon (Acting)
Oct. 1907 W. W. Wotherspoon
June 1909 Tasker H. Bliss
Dec. 1909 W. W. Wotherspoon
Feb. 1912 Albert L. Mills
Sept. 1912 William Crozier
July 1913 Hunter Liggett
Apr. 1914 M. M. Macomb
Feb. 1917 Joseph E. Kuhn
June 1919 James W. McAndrew
July 1921 E. F. McGlachlin, Jr.
July 1923 Hanson E. Ely
Dec. 1927 William D. Connor
May 1932 George S. Simonds
Feb. 1935 Malin Craig
Oct. 1935 Walter S. Grant
June 1937 John L. DeWitt
Dec. 1939 Philip B. Peyton
Apr. 1950 Joseph M. Swing
Aug. 1951 Edward M. Almond
Dec. 1952 Verdi B. Barnes (Acting)
Apr. 1953 James E. Moore
Feb. 1955 Thomas W. Dunn (Acting)
May 1955 Clyde D. Eddleman
Oct. 1955 Max S. Johnson
Mar. 1959 William P. Ennis, Jr.
July 1960 Thomas W. Dunn
Apr. 1962 William F. Train
June 1964 Eugene A. Salet
Sept. 1967 William J. McCaffrey

U. S. Army National War College

Commandants

1947-1949 Harry W. Hill
1949-1952 Harold R. Bull
1953-1955 Howard A. Craig
1956-1958 Edmund F. Wooldridge
1959-1961 Thomas L. Harrold
1961-1964 Francis H. Griswold
1964-1967 Fitzhugh Lee
1967-1970 Andrew J. Goodpaster
1970- John E. Kelly

Army Command and General Staff College

Commandants

Nov. 1881 Elwell S. Otil
June 1885 Thomas H. Ruger
May 1886 Alexander M. McCook
Aug. 1890 Edwin F. Townsend
Oct. 1894 Hamilton S. Hawkins
Sept. 1902 C. W. Miner
July 1903 J. Franklin Bell
Aug. 1906 C. B. Hall
Apr. 1908 John F. Morrison (Acting)
Aug. 1908 Frederick Funston
Jan. 1911 R. D. Potts
Feb. 1913 William P. Burnham (Acting)
Sept. 1914 Henry A. Greene
Aug. 1916 Eben Swift
Nov. 1916 James W. McAndrew
July 1917 William A. Shunk
July 1919 Charles H. Muir
Aug. 1920 Lucius R. Holbrook
Sept. 1920 Hugh A. Drum
Aug. 1921 Hanson E. Ely
July 1923 Harry A. Smith
July 1925 Edward L. King
July 1929 Stuart Heintzelman
Feb. 1935 Herbert J. Brees
June 1936 Charles M. Bundel
Apr. 1939 Lesley J. McNair
Oct. 1940 Edmund L. Gruber
June 1941 Horace H. Fuller
Mar. 1942 Karl Truesdell
Nov. 1945 Leonard T. Gerow
Jan. 1948 Manton S. Eddy
July 1950 Harlan N. Hartness (Acting)
Oct. 1950 Horace L. McBride
Mar. 1952 Henry I. Hodes
Mar. 1954 Charles E. Beauchamp (Acting)
July 1954 Garrison H. Davidson
July 1956 Lionel C. McGarr
July 1960 Harold K. Johnson
Feb. 1963 Harry J. Lemley, Jr.
Aug. 1966 Michael S. Davison

U. S. Army Industrial College of the Armed Forces

1924 Harley B. Ferguson
1928 William P. Wooten
1929 Irving J. Carr
1930 William A. McCain
1934 Harry B. Jordan
1938 Francis H. Miles, Jr.
1940 John E. Lewis
1941 Frank Whitehead
1944 Donald Armstrong
1946 Edward B. McKinley
1948 Arthur W. Vanaman
1952 Wesley M. Hague
1955 Robert P. Hollis
1957 George W. Mundy
1961 Rufus E. Rose
1964 August Schomburg
1967 Leighton I. Davis

Naval War College

Presidents

1884 Stephen B. Luce
1886 Alfred T. Mahan
1889 Casper F. Goodrich
1892 Alfred T. Mahan
1893 Henry C. Taylor
1896 Casper F. Goodrich
1898 Charles H. Stockton
1900 French E. Chadwick
1903 Charles S. Sperry
1906 John P. Merrell
1909 Raymond P. Rodgers
1911 William L. Rodgers
1913 Austin M. Knight
1917 William S. Sims
1922 Clarence S. Williams
1925 William V. Pratt
1927 Joel R. P. Pringle
1930 Harris Lanning
1933 Luke McNamee
1934 Edward C. Kalbfus
1937 Charles P. Snyder
1939 Edward C. Kalbfus
1942 William S. Pye
1946 Raymond A. Spruance
1948 Allen E. Smith (Acting)
1948 Donald B. Beary
1950 Richard L. Connolly
1953 Thomas H. Robbins, Jr.
1954 Lynde D. McCormick
1956 Thomas H. Robbins, Jr.
1957 Stuart H. Ingersoll
1960 Bernard L. Austin
1964 Charles L. Melson
1966 John T. Hayward
1968 Richard C. Colbert
1971 Benedict J. Semmes, Jr.

IX

THE FOREIGN SERVICE

A complete listing of diplomatic representatives heading United States delegations to foreign countries from 1790.

Note: The office ENVOY EXTRAORDINARY AND MINISTER PLENIPOTENTIARY is abbreviated EEMP throughout this Section.

ALGERIA

Ambassadors

1962-1965 William J. Porter
1965-1967 John D. Jernigan

(Embassy closed 1967)

ARGENTINA

Minister Plenipotentiary

1823-1824 Caesar A. Rodney

Charges d'Affaires

1825-1831 John M. Forbes
1932-1843 Francis Baylies
1944-1846 William Brent, Jr.
1846-1851 William A. Harris
1851-1854 John S. Pendleton

Ministers

1854-1858 James A. Peden
1858-1859 Benjamin C. Yancey
1859-1861 John F. Cushman
1861-1862 Robert M. Palmer
1862-1866 Robert C. Kirk
1866-1868 Alexander Asboth
1868-1869 Henry G. Worthington
1869-1871 Robert C. Kirk
1872-1874 Julius White
1874-1885 Thomas O. Osborn
1885-1887 Bayless W. Hanna

EEMP

1887-1889 Bayless W. Hanna
1889-1894 John R. G. Pitkin
1894-1899 William I. Buchanan
1899-1903 William P. Lord
1903-1904 John Barrett
1904-1907 Arthur M. Beaupre
1907-1909 Spencer F. Eddy
1909-1911 Charles H. Sherrill
1911 John R. Carter
1911-1914 John W. Garrett

Ambassadors

1914-1921 Frederic J. Stimson
1921-1924 John W. Riddle
1924-1927 Peter A. Jay
1927-1933 Robert W. Bliss
1933-1939 Alexander W. Weddell
1939-1944 Norman Armour
1945 Spruille Braden
1946-1947 George S. Messersmith
1947-1949 James M. Bruce
1949-1950 Stanton Griffis
1951-1952 Ellsworth Bunker
1952-1956 Albert F. Nufer
1956-1960 Willard L. Beaulac
1960-1961 Roy R. Rubottom, Jr.
1962-1964 Robert McClintock
1964-1967 Edwin M. Martin
1968-1969 Carter L. Burgess
1969- John Davis Lodge

ABYSSINIA

(See Ethiopia for later representation)

Minister

1908-1909 Hoffman Philip
1909-1911 Vacant

(Legation closed 1911)

AFGHANISTAN

EEMP

1935-1936 William H. Hornibrook
1937-1940 Vacant
1940-1942 Louis G. Dreyfus, Jr.
1942-1945 Cornelius Van H. Engert
1945-1948 Ely E. Palmer

Ambassadors

1948-1949 Ely E. Palmer
1949-1951 Louis G. Dreyfus, Jr.
1951-1952 George R. Merrell
1952-1956 Angus Ward
1956-1959 Sheldon T. Mills
1959-1962 Henry A. Bryoade
1962-1965 John M. Steeves
1965- Robert G. Neumann

ALBANIA

EEMP

1922-1925 Ulysses Grant-Smith
1925-1929 Charles C. Hart
1930-1933 Herman Bernstein
1933-1934 Post Wheeler
1935-1939 Hugh G. Grant

(Legation closed 1939)

AUSTRALIA

EEMP

1940-1941 Clarence E. Hauss
1941-1946 Nelson T. Johnson

Ambassadors

1946-1948 Robert Butler
1948-1949 Myron M. Cowen
1949-1953 Peter Jarman
1953-1956 Amos J. Peasley
1956 Douglas M. Moffat
1957-1961 William J. Sebald
1962-1964 William C. Battle
1965-1968 Edward A. Clark
1968-1969 William H. Crook
1969- Walter L. Rice

AUSTRIA

(Austria-Hungary 1868-1919; see also Hungary)

EEMP

1838-1840 Henry A. P. Muhlenberg
1841-1845 Daniel Jenifer

Charges d'Affaires

1845-1849 William H. Stiles
1849-1850 James W. Webb
1850-1852 Charles J. McCurdy
1852-1853 Thomas M. Foote
1853-1854 Henry R. Jackson

Ministers

1854-1858 Henry R. Jackson
1858-1861 J. Glancy Jones

EEMP

1861-1867 J. Lothrop Motley
1868-1869 Henry M. Watts
1869-1875 John Jay
1875-1876 Godlove S. Orth
1876-1877 Edward F. Beale
1877-1882 John A. Kasson
1882-1884 Alphonso Taft
1884-1885 John M. Francis
1887-1889 Alexander R. Lawton
1889-1893 Frederick D. Grant
1893-1897 Bartlett Tripp
1897-1899 Charlemagne Tower
1899-1901 Addison C. Harris
1901-1902 Robert S. McCormick

Ambassadors

1902-1906 Bellamy Storer
1906-1909 Charles S. Francis
1909-1913 Richard C. Kerens
1913-1917 Frederic C. Penfield

(Embassy closed 1917-1919)

Commissioners

1919-1920 Albert Halstead
1920-1921 Arthur H. Frazier

Charge d'Affaires

1921-1922 Arthur H. Frazier

EEMP

1922-1930 Albert H. Washburn
1930-1933 Gilchrist B. Stockton
1933-1934 George H. Earle
1934-1937 George S. Messersmith
1937-1938 Grenville T. Emmet

(Legation closed 1939-1946)

1946-1950 John G. Erhardt
1950-1952 Walter J. Donnelly

Ambassadors

1952-1957 Llewellyn E. Thompson
1957-1962 H. Freeman Matthews
1962-1967 James W. Riddleberger
1967-1969 Douglas MacArthur II
1969- John P. Humes

BARBADOS

Charge d'Affaires

1965-1967 George Dolgin

Ambassadors

1967-1969 Frederic R. Mann
1969- Eileen R. Donovan

BELGIUM

Charges d'Affaires

1832-1836 Hugh S. Legare
1837-1842 Virgil Maxcy
1842-1844 Henry W. Hillhard
1844-1851 Thomas C. Clemson
1850-1853 Richard H. Bayard
1853-1854 John J. Seibels

Ministers

1854-1856 John J. Seibels
1858-1861 Elisha Y. Fair
1861-1869 Henry S. Sanford
1869-1875 J. Russel Jones
1876-1877 Ayres P. Merrill
1878-1880 William C. Goodloe
1880-1882 James O. Putnam
1882-1885 Nicholas Fish
1885-1888 Lambert Tree

EEMP

1888-1889 John G. Parkhurst
1889-1893 Edwin E. Terrell
1893-1897 James S. Ewing
1897-1899 Bellamy Storer
1899-1905 Lawrence Townsend
1905-1909 Henry L. Wilson
1909-1911 Charles P. Bryan
1911-1912 Larz Anderson
1912-1913 Theodore Marburg
1913-1922 Brand Whitlock

Ambassadcrs

1922-1924 Henry P. Fletcher
1924-1927 William Phillips
1927-1933 Hugh S. Gibson
1933-1937 Dave H. Morris
1937-1938 Hugh S. Gibson
1938-1940 Joseph E. Davies
1940 John Cudahy
1941-1943 Anthony J. Drexel Biddle, Jr.
1944-1945 Charles Sawyer
1946-1949 Alan G. Kirk
1949-1952 Robert D. Murphy
1952-1953 Myron M. Cowen
1953-1957 Frederick M. Alger, Jr.
1957-1959 John C. Folger
1959-1961 William A. M. Burden
1961-1965 Douglas MacArthur II
1965-1969 Ridgway B. Knight
1969-1972 John S. D. Eisenhower
1972- Robert Strausz-Hupe

BOLIVIA

Charges d'Affaires

1848-1849 John Appleton
1849-1851 Alexander K. McClung
1852-1853 Horace H. Miller

Ministers

1853-1858 John W. Dana
1859-1861 John C. Smith, Jr.
1861-1863 David K. Cartter
1863-1867 Allen A. Hall
1868-1869 John W. Caldwell
1869-1873 Leopold Markbreit
1873-1874 John T. Croxton
1874-1877 Robert M. Reynolds
1878-1880 S. Newton Pettis
1880-1882 Charles Adams
1882-1883 George Maney
1883-1885 Richard Gibbs
1885-1887 William A. Seay
1887-1890 S. S. Carlisle

EEMP

1890-1892 Thomas H. Anderson
1892-1894 Frederick J. Grant
1894-1897 Thomas Moonlight
1897-1902 George Herbert Bridgman
1902-1908 William B. Sorsby
1908-1910 James F. Stutesman
1910-1913 Horace G. Knowles
1913-1918 John D. O'Rear
1919-1921 S. Abbot Maginnis
1921-1928 Jesse S. Cottrell
1928-1929 David E. Kaufman
1929-1930 Evan E. Young
1930-1933 Edward F. Feely
1933-1936 Fay A. Des Portes
1936-1937 R. Henry Norweb
1937-1939 Robert G. Caldwell
1939-1941 Douglas Jenkins

Ambassadors

1942-1944 Pierre de L. Boal
1944-1946 Walter Thurston
1946-1949 Joseph Flack
1949-1951 Irving Florman
1951-1954 Edward J. Sparks
1954-1957 Gerald A. Drew
1957-1959 Philip W. Bonsal
1959-1961 Carl W. Strom
1961-1963 Ben S. Stephansky
1963-1968 Douglas Henderson
1968-1969 Raul H. Castro
1969- Ernest V. Siracusa

BOTSWANA

Ambassador

1971- Charles J. Nelson

BRAZIL

Charges d'Affaires

1825-1827 Condy Raquet
1827-1830 William Tudor
1830-1834 Ethan A. Brown
1834-1841 William Hunter

EEMP

1841-1843 William Hunter
1843-1844 George H. Proffit
1844-1847 Henry A. Wise
1847-1851 David Tod
1851-1853 Robert C. Schenck
1853-1857 William Trousdale
1857-1861 Richard K. Meade
1861-1869 James W. Webb
1869-1871 Henry T. Blow
1871-1877 James R. Partridge
1877-1881 Henry W. Hilliard
1881-1885 Thomas A. Osborn
1885-1890 Thomas J. Jarvis
1890-1893 Edwin H. Conger
1893-1898 Thomas L. Thompson
1898-1902 Charles P. Bryan
1902-1905 David E. Thompson

Ambassadors

1905-1907 Lloyd C. Griscom
1907-1912 Irving B. Dudley
1912-1933 Edwin V. Morgan
1933-1937 Hugh S. Gibson
1937-1944 Jefferson Caffery
1945-1946 Adolf A. Berle, Jr.
1946-1948 William D. Pawley
1948-1953 Herschel V. Johnson
1953-1955 James S. Kemper
1955-1956 James C. Dunn
1956-1959 Ellis O. Briggs
1959-1961 John M. Cabot
1961-1966 Lincoln Gordon
1966-1969 John W. Tuthill
1969-1970 C. Burke Elbrick
1971- William M. Rountree

BULGARIA

Agents

1901-1903 Charles M. Dickinson
1903-1907 John B. Jackson
1907-1909 Horace G. Knowles
1909 John R. Carter

EEMP

1910 John R. Carter
1911 John B. Jackson
1913-1919 Charles J. Vopicka
1921-1928 Charles S. Wilson
1928-1929 H. F. Arthur Schoenfeld
1930-1933 Henry W. Shoemaker
1933-1937 Frederick A. Sterling
1937-1939 Ray Atherton
1940-1941 George H. Earle

(Legation closed 1941-1947)

1947-1950 Donald R. Heath

(Legation closed 1950-1960)

1960-1962 Edward Page, Jr.
1962-1965 Eugenie Anderson
1965-1966 Nathaniel Davis

Ambassadors

1966-1970 John McSweeney
1970- Horace G. Torbert, Jr.

BURMA

Ambassadors

1947-1949 J. Klahr Huddle
1950-1952 David McK. Key
1952-1954 William J. Sebald
1955-1957 Joseph C. Satterthwaite
1957-1959 Walter P. McConaughy
1959-1961 William P. Snow
1961-1963 John S. Everton
1963-1968 Henry A. Byroade
1968-1972 Arthur W. Hummel, Jr.
1972- Edwin W. Martin

BURUNDI

EEMP

1962-1966 Donald A. Dumont

Ambassadors

1968-1969 George W. Renchard
1969-1972 Thomas P. Melady
1972- Robert L. Yost

CAMBODIA

EEMP

1950-1952 Donald R. Heath

Ambassadors

1952 Donald R. Heath
1952-1956 Robert McClintock
1956-1959 Carl W. Strom
1959-1962 William C. Trimble
1962-1964 Philip D. Sprouse
1964-1965 Randolph A. Kidder

(Embassy closed 1956-1969)

Charges d'Affaires

1969-1970 Lloyd M. Rives
1970- Emery C. Swank

CAMEROON

Ambassadors

1960-1966 Leland Barrows
1967-1969 Robert L. Payton
1969-1972 Lewis Hoffacker
1972- C. Robert Moore

CANADA

EEMP

1927-1929 William Phillips
1930-1932 Hanford MacNider
1933-1935 Warren D. Robbins
1935-1937 Norman Armour
1939 Daniel C. Roper
1940 James H. R. Cromwell
1940-1943 Jay Pierrepont Moffat
1943 Ray Atherton

Ambassadors

1944-1948 Ray Atherton
1948-1950 Laurence A. Steinhardt
1950-1952 Stanley Woodward
1953-1956 R. Douglas Stuart
1956-1958 Livingston T. Merchant
1958-1960 Richard B. Wigglesworth
1961-1962 Livingston T. Merchant
1962-1968 W. Walton Butterworth
1968-1969 Harold F. Linder
1969- Adolph W. Schmidt

CENTRAL AFRICAN REPUBLIC

Ambassadors

1960-1961 W. Wendell Blancke
1961-1963 John H. Burns
1963-1967 Claude G. Ross
1967-1970 Geoffrey W. Lewis
1970- Melvin L. Manfull

FEDERATION OF CENTRAL AMERICA

Charges d'Affaires

1825-1826 John Williams
1827-1828 William B. Rochester
1833-1839 Charles G. DeWitt

Special Diplomatic Agents

1839-1840 John L. Stephens
1841-1842 William S. Murphy

CEYLON

Ambassadors

1948-1949 Felix Cole
1949-1953 Joseph C. Satterthwaite
1953-1957 Philip K. Crowe
1957-1958 Maxwell H. Gluck
1958-1959 Lampton Berry
1959-1961 Bernard A. Gufler
1961-1964 Frances E. Willis
1964-1967 Cecil B. Lyon
1967-1970 Andrew V. Corry
1970-1972 Robert Strausz-Hupe
1972- Christopher Van Hollen

CHAD

Ambassadors

1960-1961 W. Wendell Blancke
1961-1962 John A. Calhoun
1963-1967 Brewster H. Morris
1967-1969 Sheldon B. Vance
1969- Terence A. Todman

CHILE

Minister Plenipotentiary

1823-1827 Heman Allen

Charges d'Affaires

1828-1829 Samuel Larned
1830-1833 John Hamm
1834-1842 Richard Pollard
1842-1844 John S. Pendleton
1844-1847 William Crump
1847-1849 Seth Barton

EEMP

1849-1853 Balie Peyton
1854-1857 David A. Starkweather
1857-1861 John Bigler
1861-1866 Thomas H. Nelson
1866-1870 Judson Kilpatrick
1870-1873 Joseph P. Root
1873-1877 Cornelius A. Logan
1877-1882 Thomas A. Osborn
1882-1885 Cornelius A. Logan
1885-1889 William R. Roberts
1889-1893 Patrick Egan
1893-1894 James D. Porter
1894-1897 Edward H. Strobel
1897-1905 Henry L. Wilson
1905-1909 John Hicks
1909-1916 Henry P. Fletcher

Ambassadors

1916-1921 Joseph H. Shea
1921-1928 William M. Collier
1928-1933 William S. Culbertson
1933-1935 Hal H. Sevier
1935-1938 Hoffman Philip
1938-1939 Norman Armour
1939-1953 Claude G. Bowers
1953-1956 Willard L. Beaulac
1956-1958 Cecil B. Lyon
1958-1961 Walter Howe
1961 Robert F. Woodward
1961-1964 Charles W. Cole
1964-1967 Ralph A. Dungan
1967-1972 Edward M. Korry
1972- Nathaniel Davis

CHINA

Commissioners

1843-1845 Caleb Cushing
1846-1847 Alexander H. Everett
1848-1850 John W. Davis
1851-1852 Thomas A. R. Nelson
1852-1854 Humphrey Marshall
1854-1857 Robert M. McLane

EEMP

1857-1858 William B. Reed
1858-1860 John E. Ward
1861-1867 Anson Burlingame
1868-1869 J. Ross Browne
1869-1874 Frederick F. Low
1874-1876 Benjamin P. Avery
1876-1880 George F. Seward
1880-1882 James B. Angell
1882-1885 J. Russel Young
1885-1898 Charles Denby
1898-1905 Edwin H. Conger
1905-1909 William W. Rockhill
1909-1913 William J. Calhoun
1913-1919 Paul S. Reinsch
1920-1921 Charles R. Crane
1921-1924 Jacob G. Schurman
1925-1929 John Van A. MacMurray
1929-1935 Nelson T. Johnson

Ambassadors

1935-1941 Nelson T. Johnson
1941-1944 Clarence E. Gauss
1944-1945 Patrick J. Hurley
1946-1950 J. Leighton Stuart

Minister
(to China on Taiwan)

1950-1953 Karl L. Rankin

Ambassadors
(to China on Taiwan)

1953-1957 Karl L. Rankin
1958-1962 Everett F. Drumwright
1962-1963 Alan G. Kirk
1963-1966 Jerauld Wright
1966- Walter P. McConaughy

COLOMBIA

Ministers Plenipotentiary

1823-1826 Richard C. Anderson, Jr.
1826-1829 William Henry Harrison
1829-1833 Thomas P. Moore

Charges d'Affaires

1833-1837 Robert B. McAfee
1837-1842 James Semple
1842-1844 William M. Blackford
1845-1849 Benjamin A. Bidlack
1849-1850 Thomas M. Foote
1851-1853 Yelverton P. King
1853-1854 James S. Green

Ministers

1854-1857 James B. Bowlin
1859-1861 George W. Jones
1861-1867 Allan A. Burton
1867-1869 Peter J. Sullivan

1869-1872 Stephen A. Hurlbut
1873-1876 William L. Scruggs
1878-1882 Ernst Dichman
1882-1886 William L. Scruggs

EEMP

1886-1889 Dabney H. Maury
1889-1893 John T. Abbott
1893-1897 Luther F. McKinney
1897-1903 Charles B. Hart
1903-1904 Arthur M. Beaupre
1904-1905 William W. Russell
1905-1907 John Barrett
1907-1909 Thomas C. Dawson
1909-1911 Elliott Northcott
1911-1913 James T. DuBois
1913-1916 Thaddeus A. Thomson
1917-1922 Hoffman Philip
1922-1928 Samuel H. Piles
1928-1933 Jefferson Caffery
1933-1934 Sheldon Whitehouse
1934-1937 William Dawson
1938-1939 Spruille Braden

Ambassadors

1939-1942 Spruille Braden
1942-1944 Arthur Bliss Lane
1944-1947 John C. Wiley
1947-1951 Willard L. Beaulac
1951-1953 Capus M. Waynick
1953-1955 Rudolf E. Schoenfeld
1955-1957 Philip W. Bonsal
1957-1959 John M. Cabot
1959-1961 Dempster McIntosh
1961-1964 Fulton Freeman
1964-1966 Covey T. Oliver
1966-1969 Reynold E. Carlson
1969-1970 Jack H. Vaughn
1970- Leonard J. Saccio

DEMOCRATIC REPUBLIC OF THE CONGO (Kinshasa)

Ambassadors

1960-1961 Clare H. Timberlake
1961-1964 Edmund A. Gullion
1964-1967 G. McMurtie Godley
1967-1969 Robert H. McBride
1969- Sheldon B. Vance

PEOPLE'S REPUBLIC OF THE CONGO (Brazzaville)

Ambassadors

1960-1964 W. Wendell Blancke
1964-1965 Henry L. Koren

(Embassy closed 1965)

COSTA RICA

Special Envoy

1852 Robert M. Walsh

EEMP

1853-1854 Solon Borland

Ministers

1858-1859 Mirabeau B. Lamar
1859-1861 Alexander Dimitry
1861-1867 Charles N. Riotte
1867-1868 Albert G. Lawrence
1868-1873 Jacob B. Blair
1873-1879 George Williamson
1879-1882 Cornelius A. Logan

EEMP

1882-1891 Henry C. Hall
1891-1893 Richard C. Shannon
1893-1897 Lewis Baker
1897-1911 William M. Merry
1911-1913 Lewis Einstein
1913-1919 Edward J. Hale
1922-1929 Roy T. Davis
1929-1930 H. F. Arthur Schoenfeld
1930-1933 Charles C. Eberhardt
1933-1937 Leo R. Sack
1937-1941 William H. Hornibrook
1941-1942 Arthur Bliss Lane
1942-1943 Robert M. Scotten

Ambassadors

1943-1944 Fay A. Des Portes
1944-1947 Hallett Johnson
1947 Walter J. Donnelly
1947-1949 Nathaniel Davis
1949-1950 Joseph Flack
1951-1953 Philip B. Fleming
1953-1954 Robert C. Hill
1954-1958 Robert F. Woodward
1958-1961 Whiting Willauer
1961-1967 Raymond Telles
1967-1969 Clarence A. Boonstra
1970-1972 Walter C. Ploeser
1972- Viron P. Baky

CUBA

EEMP

1902-1905 Herbert G. Squiers
1905-1909 Edwin V. Morgan
1909-1911 John B. Jackson
1911-1913 Arthur M. Beaupre
1913-1919 William E. Gonzales
1919-1922 Boaz W. Long

Ambassadors

1923-1927 Enoch H. Crowder
1927-1929 Noble B. Judah
1929-1933 Harry F. Guggenheim
1933-1934 Sumner Welles
1934-1937 Jefferson Caffery
1937-1940 J. Butler Wright
1940-1941 George S. Messersmith
1941-1945 Spruille Braden
1945-1948 R. Henry Norweb
1948-1951 Robert Butler
1951-1953 Willard L. Beaulac
1953-1957 Arthur Gardner
1957-1959 Earl E. T. Smith
1959-1960 Philip W. Bonsal

(Embassy closed 1961)

CYPRUS

Ambassadors

1960-1964 Fraser Wilkins
1964-1969 Taylor G. Belcher
1969- David H. Popper

CZECHOSLOVAKIA

EEMP

1919-1921 Richard Crane
1921-1930 Lewis Einstein
1930-1932 Abraham C. Ratshesky
1933-1934 Francis White
1934-1937 J. Butler Wright
1937-1939 Wilbur J. Carr

(Legation closed 1939; in London 1941-1945)

1941-1943 Anthony J. Drexel Biddle, Jr.

Ambassadors

1943-1944 Anthony J. Drexel Biddle, Jr.
1944-1948 Laurence A. Steinhardt
1948-1949 Joseph E. Jacobs
1949-1952 Ellis O. Briggs
1952-1953 George Wadsworth
1953-1958 U. Alexis Johnson
1958-1960 John M. Allison
1960-1961 Christian M. Ravndal
1961-1962 Edward T. Wailes
1962-1966 Outerbridge Horsey
1966-1969 Jacob D. Beam
1969-1972 Malcolm Toon
1972- Albert W. Sherer, Jr.

DAHOMEY

Ambassadors

1960-1961 R. Borden Reams
1961-1964 Robinson McIlvaine
1964-1969 Clinton E. Knox
1969-1972 Matthew J. Lorram, Jr.
1972- Robert Anderson

DENMARK

Special Minister

1811-1812 George W. Irving

Charges d'Affaires

1827-1835 Henry Wheaton
1835-1841 Jonathan F. Woodside
1841-1842 Isaac Rand Jackson
1843-1847 William W. Irwin
1847-1849 Robert P. Flennikan
1849-1851 Walter Forward
1852-1853 Miller Grieve
1853-1854 Henry Bedinger

Ministers

1854-1858 Henry Bedinger
1858-1861 James M. Buchanan
1861-1865 Bradford R. Wood

1865-1870 George H. Yeaman
1870-1876 M. J. Cramer
1882-1883 J. P. Wickersham
1883-1885 Wickham Hoffman
1885-1890 Rasmus B. Anderson

EEMP

1890-1893 Clark E. Carr
1893-1897 John E. Risley
1897-1905 Laurits S. Swenson
1905-1907 Thomas J. O'Brien
1907-1918 Maurice F. Egan
1919-1921 Norman Hapgood
1921-1926 John D. Prince
1926-1930 H. Percival Dodge
1930-1931 Ralph H. Booth
1931-1933 Frederick W. B. Coleman
1933-1936 Ruth Bryan Owen
1937-1939 Alvin M. Owsley
1939-1945 Ray Atherton
1945-1946 Michael B. Davis
1946-1947 Josiah Marvel, Jr.

Ambassadors

1947-1949 Josiah Marvel, Jr.
1949-1952 Eugenie Anderson
1953-1957 Robert D. Coe
1957-1961 Val Peterson
1961-1964 William M. Blair, Jr.
1964-1968 Katharine E. White
1968-1969 Angier Biddle Duke
1969-1972 Guilford Dudley, Jr.

DOMINICAN REPUBLIC
(Santo Domingo 1883-1895)

Charges d'Affaires

1883-1885 John M. Langston
1885-1891 John E. W. Thompson
1891-1893 John S. Durgan
1893-1897 Henry M. Smythe
1897-1904 William F. Powell

Ministers

1904-1907 Thomas C. Dawson
1907-1909 Fenton R. McCreery
1909-1910 Horace G. Knowles
1910-1913 William W. Russell

EEMP

1913-1915 James M. Sullivan
1915-1925 William W. Russell
1925-1929 Evan E. Young
1929-1931 Charles B. Curtis
1931-1937 H. F. Arthur Schoenfeld
1937-1940 R. Henry Norweb
1940-1942 Robert M. Scotten
1942-1943 Avra M. Warren

Ambassadors

1943-1944 Avra M. Warren
1944-1945 Ellis O. Briggs
1945-1946 Joseph M. McGurk
1946-1948 George H. Butler
1948-1952 Ralph H. Ackerman
1952-1953 Phelps Phelps
1953-1957 William T. Pheiffer
1957-1960 Joseph S. Farland
1962-1964 John Bartlow Martin
1964-1966 W. Tapley Bennett, Jr.
1966-1969 John H. Crimmins
1969- Francis E. Meloy, Jr.

ECUADOR

Special Agent

1844 Delazon Smith

Charges d'Affaires

1848-1849 Vanbrugh Livingston
1849-1850 John T. Van Allen
1850-1853 Courtland Cushing
1853-1854 Philo White

Ministers

1854-1858 Philo White
1858-1861 Charles R. Buckalew
1861-1866 Frederick Hassaurek
1866-1867 William T. Coggeshall
1869-1875 E. Rumsey Wing
1875-1892 Christian Willweber

EEMP

1892-1893 Rowland B. Mahany
1895-1897 James D. Tillman
1897-1905 Archibald J. Sampson
1905-1907 Joseph W. J. Lee
1907-1911 Williams C. Fox
1911-1912 Evan E. Young
1913-1922 Charles S. Hartman
1922-1930 Gerard A. Bading
1930-1934 William Dawson
1934-1938 Antonio C. Gonzalez
1938-1942 Boaz W. Long

Ambassadors

1942-1943 Boaz W. Long
1943-1947 Robert M. Scotten
1947-1950 John F. Simmons
1951-1953 Paul C. Daniels
1954-1956 Sheldon T. Mills
1956-1960 Christian Ravndal
1960-1965 Maurice M. Bernbaum
1965-1968 Wymberley D. Coerr
1968-1970 Edson O. Sessions
1970- Findley Burns, Jr.

EGYPT
(See United Arab Republic for later representation)

Agents

1893-1897 Frederic C. Penfield
1897-1899 Thomas S. Harrison
1899-1903 John G. Long
1903-1905 John W. Riddle
1905-1909 Lewis M. Iddings
1909-1913 Peter A. Jay
1913-1916 Olney Arnold
1917-1921 Hampson Gary
1921-1922 J. Morton Howell

EEMP

1922-1927 J. Morton Howell
1928-1930 Franklin M. Gunther
1930-1933 William M. Jardine
1933-1941 Bert Fish
1941-1944 Alexander C. Kirk
1944-1946 S. Pinkney Tuck

Ambassadors

1946-1948 S. Pinkney Tuck
1948-1949 Stanton Griffis
1949-1955 Jefferson Caffery
1955-1956 Henry A. Bryoade
1956-1958 Raymond A. Hare

EL SALVADOR
(See Salvador for earlier representation)

EEMP

1929-1931 Warren D. Robbins
1931-1933 Charles B. Curtis
1934-1937 Frank P. Corrigan
1937-1942 Robert Frazer
1942-1943 Walter Thurston

Ambassadors

1943-1944 Walter Thurston
1944-1947 John F. Simmons
1947-1949 Albert F. Nufer
1949-1952 George P. Shaw
1952-1953 Angier Biddle Duke
1953-1954 Michael J. McDermott
1954-1955 Robert C. Hill
1955-1957 Thomas C. Mann
1957-1961 Thorsten V. Kalijarvi
1961-1964 Murat W. Williams
1964-1968 Raul H. Castro
1968-1972 Henry C. Catto, Jr.

EQUATORIAL GUINEA

Ambassadors

1968-1969 Albert W. Sherer, Jr.
1969- Lewis Hoffacker

ESTONIA

EEMP

1922-1931 Frederick W. B. Coleman
1931-1933 Robert P. Skinner
1933-1936 John Van A. MacMurray
1936-1937 Arthur Bliss Lane
1937-1938 Frederick A. Sterling
1938-1941 John C. Wiley

(Legation closed 1941)

ETHIOPIA
(See Abyssinia for earlier representation)

Ministers

1927-1934 Addison E. Southard
1936-1937 Cornelius Van H. Engert

(Legation closed 1937-1943)

1943-1944 John K. Caldwell

EEMP

1844-1945 John K. Caldwell
1945-1947 Felix Cole
1947-1949 George R. Merrell

Ambassadors

1949-1951 George R. Merrell
1951-1952 J. Rives Childs
1953-1957 Joseph Simonson
1957-1960 Don C. Bliss
1960-1963 Arthur L. Richards
1963-1966 Edward M. Korry
1966-1967 Robert Donhauser
1967-1971 William O. Hall
1971- E. Ross Adair

FINLAND

EEMP

1921-1924 Charles L. Kagey
1925 John B. Stetson, Jr.
1925-1930 Alfred J. Pearson
1930-1933 Edward E. Brodie
1933-1937 Edward Albright
1937-1944 H. F. Arthur Schoenfeld
1945-1947 Maxwell M. Hamilton
1947-1950 Avra M. Warren
1950-1952 John M. Cabot
1952-1955 Jack McFall

Ambassadors

1955-1959 John D. Hickerson
1959-1960 Edson O. Sessions
1961-1963 Bernard A. Gufler
1963-1964 Carl T. Rowan
1964-1969 Tyler Thompson
1969- Val Peterson

FRANCE

Charge d'Affaires

1790-1792 William Short

Ministers Plenipotentiary

1792-1794 Gouverneur Morris
1794-1796 James Monroe

EEMP

1797-1798 Elbridge Gerry
1799-1800 Oliver Ellsworth
William V. Murray
William R. Davie
1801-1804 Robert B. Livingston
1804-1810 James Monroe

Ministers Plenipotentiary

1810-1811 Jonathan Russell
1811-1812 Joel Barlow
1813-1815 William H. Crawford

EEMP

1815-1823 Albert Gallatin
1823-1829 James Brown
1829-1832 William C. Rives

Charge d'Affaires

1833 Leavitt Harris

EEMP

1833-1835 Edward Livingston
1836-1842 Lewis Call
1844-1846 William R. King
1847-1849 Richard Rush
1849-1853 William C. Rives
1853-1859 John Y. Mason
1860-1861 Charles J. Faulkner
1861-1864 William L. Dayton
1865-1866 John Bigelow
1866-1869 John A. Dix
1869-1877 Elihu B. Washburne
1877-1881 Edward F. Noyes
1881-1885 Levi P. Morton
1885-1892 Robert M. McLane
1892-1893 T. Jefferson Coolidge

Ambassadors

1893-1897 James B. Eustis
1897-1905 Robert S. McCormick
1906-1909 Henry White
1909-1912 Robert Bacon
1912-1914 Myron T. Herrick
1914-1919 William G. Sharp
1919-1921 Hugh C. Wallace
1921-1929 Myron T. Herrick
1929-1933 Walter E. Edge
1933-1936 Jesse I. Straus
1936-1940 William C. Bullitt
1940-1942 William D. Leahy

(Embassy closed 1942-1944)

1944-1949 Jefferson Caffery
1949-1952 David K. E. Bruce
1952-1953 James C. Dunn
1953-1957 C. Douglas Dillon
1957-1961 Amory Houghton
1961-1962 James M. Gavin
1962-1968 Charles S. Bohlen
1968-1970 R. Sargent Shriver, Jr.
1970- Arthur K. Watson

GABON

Ambassadors

1960-1961 W. Wendell Blancke
1961-1965 Charles F. Darlington
1965-1969 David M. Bane
1969-1971 Richard Funkhouser
1971- John A. McKesson III

GAMBIA

Ambassadors

1965-1966 Mercer Cook
1966-1967 William R. Rivkin
1967-1971 L. Dean Brown
1971- G. Edward Clark

GERMANY
(See also Prussia)

EEMP

1871-1874 George Bancroft
1875-1876 J. C. Bancroft Davis
1879-1882 Andrew D. White
1882-1884 Aaron A. Sargent
1884-1885 John A. Kasson
1885-1889 George H. Pendleton
1889-1893 William W. Phelps
1893-1894 Theodore Runyon

Ambassadors

1894-1896 Theodore Runyon
1896-1897 Edwin F. Uhl
1897-1902 Andrew D. White
1902-1908 Charlemagne Tower
1908-1911 David Hill
1911-1913 John G. A. Leishman
1913-1917 James W. Gerard

(Embassy closed 1917-1922)

1922-1925 Alanson B. Houghton
1925-1930 Jacob G. Shurman
1930-1933 Frederick M. Sackett, Jr.
1933-1938 William E. Dodd
1938-1939 Hugh R. Wilson
1939-1941 Vacant

(Embassy closed 1941-1949)

U.S. Political Adviser

1945-1949 Robert D. Murphy

U.S. High Commissioners
(to Federal Republic of Germany)

1949-1952 John J. McCloy
1952-1953 Walter J. Donnelly
1953-1955 James B. Conant

Ambassadors

1955-1957 James B. Conant
1957-1959 David K. E. Bruce
1959-1963 Walter C. Dowling
1963-1968 George C. McGhee
1968-1969 Henry Cabot Lodge
1969-1972 Kenneth Rush
1972- Martin J. Hillenbrand

GHANA

Charge d'Affaires

1957 Donald W. Lamm

Ambassadors

1957-1960 Wilson C. Flake
1960-1962 Francis H. Russell
1962-1965 William P. Mahoney, Jr.
1966-1968 Franklin H. Williams
1968-1971 Thomas W. McElhiney
1971- Fred L. Hadsel

GREAT BRITAIN

Minister Plenipotentiary

1792-1796 Thomas Pinckney

Envoy Extraordinary

1794-1795 John Jay

Ministers Plenipotentiary

1796-1803 Rufus King
1803-1807 James Monroe
1806-1811 William Pinkney

Commissioners

1806-1807 James Monroe
1806-1811 William Pinkney

Charge d'Affaires

1811-1812 Jonathan Russell

(Relations suspended 1812-1814)

Ministers Plenipotentiary and Envoys

1814 John Quincy Adams
James A. Bayard
Henry Clay
Jonathan Russell
Albert Gallatin

EEMP

1815-1817 John Quincy Adams
1817-1825 Richard Rush
1825-1826 Rufus King
1826-1827 Albert Gallatin
1828-1829 James Barbour
1829-1831 Louis McLane
1831-1832 Martin Van Buren

Charge d'Affaires

1832-1836 Aaron Vail

EEMP

1836-1841 Andrew Stevenson
1841-1845 Edward Everett
1845-1846 Louis McLane
1846-1849 George Bancroft
1849-1852 Abbott Lawrence
1852-1853 Joseph R. Ingersoll
1853-1856 James Buchanan
1856-1861 George M. Dallas
1861-1868 Charles Francis Adams
1868-1869 Reverdy Johnson
1869-1870 J. Lothrop Motley
1870-1876 Robert C. Schenck
1876-1877 Edwards Pierrepont
1877-1879 John S. Welsh
1880-1885 James Russell Lowell
1885-1889 Edward J. Phelps
1889-1893 Robert T. Lincoln

Ambassadors

1893-1897 Thomas F. Bayard
1897-1899 John Hay
1899-1905 Joseph H. Choate
1905-1913 Whitelaw Reid
1913-1918 Walter H. Page
1918-1921 John W. Davis
1921-1923 George Harvey
1923-1925 Frank B. Kellogg
1925-1929 Alanson B. Houghton
1929-1932 Charles G. Dawes
1932-1933 Andrew W. Mellon
1933-1938 Robert W. Bingham
1938-1940 Joseph P. Kennedy
1941-1946 John G. Winant
1946 W. Averell Harriman
1947-1950 Lewis W. Douglas
1950-1953 Walter S. Gifford
1953-1957 Winthrop W. Aldrich
1957-1961 John Hay Whitney
1961-1969 David K. E. Bruce
1969- Walter H. Annenberg

GREECE

Ministers

1868-1871 Charles K. Tuckerman
1871-1873 John M. Francis
1873-1882 John M. Read, Jr.
1882-1885 Eugene Schuyler
1885-1892 J. Walker Fearn
1892-1893 Truxtun Beale

EEMP

1893-1897 Eben Alexander
1897-1899 William W. Rockhill
1899-1900 Arthur S. Hardy
1900-1902 Charles S. Francis
1902-1907 John B. Jackson
1907-1909 Richmond Pearson
1909-1912 George H. Moses
1912-1913 Jacob G. Schurman
1914-1921 Garrett Droppers
1924-1926 Irwin B. Laughlin
1926-1931 Robert P. Skinner
1933-1941 Lincoln MacVeagh
1941-1942 Anthony J. Drexel Biddle, Jr.

Ambassadors

1942-1943 Anthony J. Drexel Biddle, Jr.
1943 Alexander C. Kirk
1943-1948 Lincoln MacVeagh
1948-1950 Henry F. Grady
1950-1953 John E. Peurifoy
1953-1956 Cavendish W. Cannon
1956-1957 George V. Allen
1958-1959 James W. Riddleberger
1959-1961 Ellis O. Briggs
1961-1965 Henry R. Labouisse
1965-1969 Phillips Talbot
1969- Henry J. Tasca

GUATEMALA

Charges d'Affaires

1848-1849 Elijah Hise
1849-1850 E. George Squier

Ministers

1853-1854 Solon Borland
1854-1858 John L. Marling
1858-1860 Beverly L. Clarke
1861-1864 Elisha O. Crosby
1865-1869 FitzHenry Warren
1869-1872 Silas A. Hudson
1873-1879 George Williamson
1879-1882 Cornelius A. Logan

EEMP

1882-1891 Henry C. Hall
1891-1893 Romualdo Pacheco
1893-1896 Pierce M. B. Young
1896-1897 Macgrane Coxe
1897-1902 W. Godfrey Hunter
1902-1907 Leslie Combs
1907-1908 Joseph W. J. Lee
1908-1909 William Heimke
1909-1910 William F. Sands
1910-1913 R. S. Reynolds Hitt
1913-1919 William H. Leavell
1919-1921 Benton McMillin
1921-1922 Roy T. Davis
1922-1929 Arthur H. Geissler
1929-1933 Sheldon Whitehouse
1933-1936 Matthew E. Hanna
1936-1943 Fay A. Des Portes
1943-1945 Boaz W. Long
1945-1948 Edwin J. Kyle
1948-1951 Richard C. Patterson, Jr.
1951-1953 Rudolf E. Schoenfeld
1953-1954 John E. Peurifoy
1954-1955 Norman Armour
1955-1958 Edward J. Sparks
1958-1959 Lester D. Mallory
1959-1961 John J. Muccio
1961-1965 John O. Bell
1965-1967 John G. Mein
1967-1968 Max V. Krebs
1968-1972 Nathaniel Davis
1972- William G. Bowdler

GUINEA

Ambassadors

1959-1961 John H. Morrow
1961-1963 William Attwood
1963-1966 James I. Loeb
1966-1969 Robinson McIlvaine
1970-1972 Albert W. Sherer, Jr.
1972- Terrence A. Todman

GUYANA

Ambassadors

1964-1969 Delmar R. Carlson
1969- Spencer M. King

HAITI

Commissioners

1862-1865 Benjamin F. Whidden
1865-1866 H. E. Peck

Ministers

1866-1867 H. E. Peck
1868-1869 Gideon H. Hollister
1869-1877 Ebenezer D. Bassett
1877-1885 John M. Langston
1885-1891 John E. W. Thompson
1891-1893 John S. Durham
1893-1897 Henry M. Smythe

EEMP

1897-1905 William F. Powell
1905-1913 Henry W. Furniss
1913-1914 Madison R. Smith
1914-1925 Arthur Bailly-Blanchard
1930-1932 Dana G. Munro
1932-1935 Norman Armour
1935-1937 George A. Gordon
1937-1940 Ferdinand L. Mayer
1940-1943 John C. White

Ambassadors

1943-1944 John C. White
1944-1946 Orme Wilson
1946-1948 Harold H. Tittmann, Jr.
1948-1951 William E. De Courcy
1951-1953 Howard K. Travers
1953-1957 Roy T. Davis
1957-1960 Gerald A. Drew
1960-1961 Robert Newbegin
1961-1963 Raymond L. Thurston
1963-1967 Benson E. L. Timmons III
1967-1969 Claude G. Ross
1969- Clinton E. Knox

HAWAIIAN ISLANDS

Commissioners

1843-1846 George Brown
1846-1849 Anthony Ten Eyck
1849 Charles Eames
1850-1853 Luther Severence
1853-1858 David L. Gregg
1958-1861 James W. Borden
1861-1863 Thomas J. Dryer

Ministers

1863-1866 James McBride
1866-1868 Edward M. McCook
1869-1877 Henry A. Pierce
1877 James M. Comly
1877-1885 Rollin M. Daggett
1885-1890 George W. Merrill

EEMP

1890-1893 John L. Stevens
1893 James H. Blount
1893-1896 Albert S. Willis
1897 Harold M. Sewall

HONDURAS

EEMP

1853-1854 Solon Borland

Ministers

1858-1860 Beverly L. Clarke
1862-1863 James R. Partridge
1863-1866 Thomas H. Clay
1866-1869 Richard H. Rousseau
1869-1873 Henry Baxter
1873-1879 George Williamson
1879-1882 Cornelius A. Logan

EEMP

1882-1891 Henry C. Hall
1891-1893 Romualdo Pacheco
1893-1896 Pierce M. B. Young
1896-1897 Macgrane Coxe
1897-1902 W. Godfrey Hunter
1902-1907 Leslie Combs
1907-1908 H. Percival Dodge
1908-1909 William B. Sorsby
1909-1911 Fenton R. McCreery
1911-1913 Charles D. White
1913-1918 John Ewing
1918-1921 T. Sambola Jones
1921-1925 Franklin E. Morales
1925-1929 George T. Summerlin
1929-1934 Julius G. Lay
1935-1937 Leo J. Keena
1937-1943 John D. Erwin

Ambassadors

1943-1947 John D. Erwin
1947 Paul C. Daniels
1947-1950 Herbert S. Bursley
1951-1954 John D. Erwin
1954-1958 Whiting Willauer
1958-1960 Robert Newbegin
1960-1965 Charles R. Burrows
1965-1969 Joseph J. Jova
1969- Hewson A. Ryan

HUNGARY

EEMP

1922-1927 Theodore Brentano
1927-1930 J. Butler Wright
1930-1933 Nicholas Roosevelt
1933-1941 John F. Montgomery
1941 Herbert Claiborne Pell

(Legation closed 1941-1945)

1945-1947 H. F. Arthur Schoenfeld
1947-1949 Selden Chapin
1949-1951 Nathaniel P. Davis
1951-1956 Christian M. Ravndal
1956-1957 Edward T. Wailes
1957-1967 Vacant

Ambassadors

1967-1969 Martin J. Hillenbrand
1969- Alfred Puhan

ICELAND

EEMP

1941-1942 Lincoln MacVeagh
1942-1944 Leland B. Morris
1944-1946 Louis G. Dreyfus, Jr.
1948-1949 Richard P. Butrick
1949-1954 Edward B. Lawson
1954-1955 John J. Muccio

Ambassadors

1955-1959 John J. Muccio
1960-1961 Tyler Thompson
1961-1967 James K. Penfield
1967-1969 Karl F. Rolvaag
1969-1972 Luther J. Replogle
1972- Frederick Irving

INDIA

Charge d'Affaires

1946-1947 George R. Merrell

Ambassadors

1947-1948 Henry F. Grady
1948-1951 Loy W. Henderson
1951-1953 Chester Bowles
1953-1955 George V. Allen
1955-1956 John Sherman Cooper
1956-1961 Ellsworth Bunker
1961-1963 John Kenneth Galbraith
1963-1969 Chester Bowles
1969-1972 Kenneth B. Keating
1972- Daniel P. Moynihan

INDONESIA

Ambassadors

1949-1953 H. Merle Cochran
1953-1957 Hugh S. Cumming, Jr.
1957-1958 John M. Allison
1958-1965 Howard P. Jones
1965-1969 Marshall Green
1969- Francis J. Galbraith

IRAN

(See Persia for earlier representation)

EEMP

1935-1936 William H. Hornibrook
1936-1939 Vacant
1939-1944 Louis G. Dreyfus, Jr.

Ambassadors

1944-1945 Leland B. Morris
1945-1946 Wallace Murray
1946-1948 George V. Allen
1948-1950 John C. Wiley
1950-1951 Henry F. Grady
1951-1955 Loy W. Henderson
1955-1958 Selden Chapin
1959-1961 Edward T. Wailes
1961-1965 Julius C. Holmes
1965-1969 Armin H. Meyer
1969-1972 Douglas MacArthur II
1972- Joseph S. Farland

IRAQ

Charge d'Affaires

1931-1932 Alexander K. Sloan

Ministers

1932-1942 Paul Knabenshue
1942-1943 Thomas M. Wilson

EEMP

1943-1945 Loy W. Henderson
1946 Lowell C. Pinkerton

Ambassadors

1946-1948 George Wadsworth
1948-1952 Edward S. Crocker II
1952-1954 Burton Y. Berry
1954-1958 Waldemar J. Gallman
1958-1962 John D. Jernegan
1963-1967 Robert C. Strong

(Embassy closed 1967)

IRELAND

(Irish Free State 1927-1937)

EEMP

1927-1933 Frederick A. Sterling
1933-1934 W. W. McDowell
1935-1937 Alvin M. Owsley
1937-1940 John Cudahy
1940-1947 David Gray
1947-1950 George A. Garrett

Ambassadors

1950-1951 George A. Garrett
1951-1953 Francis P. Matthews
1953-1957 William Howard Taft III
1957-1961 Scott McLeod
1961-1962 Edward G. Stockdale
1962-1964 Matthew H. McCloskey
1965-1968 Raymond R. Guest
1968-1969 Leo J. Sheridan
1969- John D. J. Moore

ISRAEL

Ambassadors

1948-1951 James G. McDonald
1951-1954 Monnett B. Davis
1954-1959 Edward B. Lawson
1959-1961 Ogden R. Reid
1961- Walworth Barbour

ITALY

(See Papal States, Sardinia, Sicily for earlier representation)

EEMP

1861-1882 George P. Marsh
1882-1885 William W. Astor
1885-1889 John B. Stallo
1889-1892 Albert G. Porter
1892-1893 William Potter

Ambassadors

1893-1897 Wayne MacVeagh
1897-1900 William F. Draker
1900-1905 George V. L. Mayer
1905-1906 Henry White
1906-1909 Lloyd C. Griscom
1909-1911 John G. A. Leishman
1911-1913 Thomas J. O'Brien
1913-1919 Thomas N. Page
1921-1924 Richard W. Child
1924-1929 Henry P. Fletcher
1929-1933 John W. Garrett
1933-1936 Breckinridge Long
1936-1941 William Phillips

(Embassy closed 1941-1944)

1944-1946 Alexander C. Kirk
1946-1952 William C. Dunn
1952-1953 Ellsworth Bunker
1953-1956 Clare Booth Luce
1956-1960 James D. Zellerbach
1961-1968 G. Frederick Reinhardt
1968-1969 H. Gardner Ackley
1969-1972 Graham A. Martin
1972- John A. Volpe

IVORY COAST

Ambassadors

1960-1962 R. Borden Reams
1962-1965 James W. Wine
1965-1969 George A. Morgan
1969- John F. Root

JAMAICA

Ambassadors

1962-1964 William C. Doherty
1965-1967 Wilson T. M. Beale, Jr.
1967-1969 Walter N. Tobriner
1969- Vincent deRoulet

JAPAN

Commissioner General

1855-1859 Townsend Harris

Ministers

1862-1865 Robert H. Pruyn
1866-1869 Robert B. Van Valkenburgh
1869-1870 Charles E. DeLong

EEMP

1870-1873 Charles E. DeLong
1873-1885 John A. Bingham
1885-1892 Richard B. Hubbard
1892-1893 Frank L. Coombs
1893-1897 Edwin Dun
1897-1902 Alfred E. Buck
1902-1906 Lloyd C. Griscom

Ambassadors

1906-1907 Luke E. Wright
1907-1911 Thomas J. O'Brien
1911-1913 Charles P. Bryan
1913-1917 George W. Guthrie
1917-1921 Roland S. Morris
1921-1923 Charles B. Warren
1923-1924 Cyrus E. Woods
1924-1925 Edgar A. Bancroft
1925-1929 Charles MacVeagh
1929-1930 William R. Castle, Jr.
1930-1932 W. Cameron Forbes
1932-1941 Joseph C. Grew

(Embassy closed 1941-1945)

Political Advisor

1945-1952 William J. Sebald

Ambassadors

1952-1953 Robert D. Murphy
1953-1956 John M. Allison
1956-1961 Douglas MacArthur II
1961-1966 Edwin O. Reischauer
1966-1969 U. Alexis Johnson
1969-1972 Armin H. Meyer
1972- Robert S. Ingersoll

JORDAN

EEMP

1950-1952 Gerald A. Drew
1952 Joseph C. Green

Ambassadors

1952-1953 Joseph C. Green
1953-1958 Lester deWitt Mallory
1959-1961 Sheldon T. Mills
1961-1964 William B. Macomber, Jr.
1964-1966 Robert G. Barnes
1966-1967 Findley Burns, Jr.
1967-1970 Harrison M. Symmes
1970- L. Dean Brown

KENYA

Ambassadors

1964-1966 William Attwood
1966-1969 Glenn W. Ferguson
1969- Robinson McIlvaine

KOREA

(See South Korea for later representation)

EEMP

1883-1885 Lucius H. Foote

Ministers

1887-1890 Hugh A. Dinsmore
1890-1894 Augustine Heard
1894-1897 John M. B. Sill
1897-1905 Horace N. Allen

EEMP

1905 Edwin V. Morgan

(Annexed by Japan 1905-1945)

KUWAIT

Ambassadors

1961-1963 Parker T. Hart
1963-1969 Howard R. Cottam
1969-1972 John P. Walsh
1972- William A. Stoltzfus, Jr.

LAOS

EEMP

1950-1954 Donald R. Heath
1954-1955 Charles W. Yost

Ambassadors

1955-1956 Charles W. Yost
1956-1958 J. Graham Parsons
1958-1960 Horace H. Smith
1960-1962 Winthrop G. Brown
1962-1964 Leonard Unger
1964-1969 William H. Sullivan
1969- G. McMurtrie Godley

LATVIA

EEMP

1922-1931 Frederick W. B. Coleman
1931-1933 Robert P. Skinner
1933-1936 John Van A. MacMurray
1936-1937 Arthur Bliss Lane
1937-1938 Frederick A. Sterling
1938-1941 John C. Wiley

(Legation closed 1941)

LEBANON

Diplomatic Agent

1942-1944 George Wadsworth

EEMP

1944-1946 George Wadsworth
1946-1951 Lowell C. Pinkerton
1951-1953 Harold B. Minor

Ambassadors

1951-1953 Harold B. Minor
1953-1954 Raymond A. Hare
1955-1957 Donald R. Heath
1957-1961 Robert M. McClintock
1961-1965 Armin H. Meyer
1965-1971 Dwight J. Porter
1971- William B. Buffum

LESOTHO

Ambassador

1971- Charles J. Nelson

LIBERIA

Commissioner

1863-1866 Abraham Hanson

Ministers

1866-1870 Jahn Seys
1871-1878 J. Milton Turner
1878-1885 John H. Smyth
1888-1892 Ezekiel Smith
1892-1893 William D. McCoy
1895-1898 William H. Heard
1898-1902 Owen L. W. Smith
1902-1903 J. R. A. Crossland
1903-1910 Ernest Lyon
1910-1913 William D. Crum
1913-1914 George W. Buckner
1915-1917 James L. Curtis
1918-1921 Joseph L. Johnson
1921-1926 Solomon P. Hood
1927-1929 William T. Francis
1930-1933 Charles E. Mitchell

EEMP

1935-1946 Lester A. Walton
1946-1948 Raphael O. Lanier
1948-1949 Edward R. Dudley

Ambassadors

1949-1953 Edward R. Dudley
1953-1955 Jesse D. Locker
1955-1959 Richard Lee Jones
1959-1962 Elbert G. Mathews
1962-1965 Charles E. Rhetts
1965-1969 Ben H. Brown, Jr.
1969- Samuel Z. Westerfield, Jr.

LIBYAN AFRICAN REPUBLIC

(Known as Libya prior to 1972)

EEMP

1952-1954 Henry S. Villard

Ambassadors

1954-1958 John L. Tappin
1958-1963 J. Wesley Jones
1963-1965 E. Allen Lightner
1965-1969 David D. Newsom
1969- Joseph Palmer II

LITHUANIA

EEMP

1922-1931 Frederick W. B. Coleman
1931-1933 Robert B. Skinner
1933-1936 John Van A. MacMurray
1936-1937 Arthur Bliss Lane
1937-1940 Owen J. C. Norem

(Legation closed 1941)

LUXEMBOURG

EEMP

1903-1905 Stanford Newel
1905-1908 David J. Hill
1908-1911 Arthur M. Beaupre
1911-1913 Lloyd Bryce
1913-1917 Henry Van Dyke
1917-1919 John W. Garrett
1920-1922 William Phillips
1923-1924 Henry P. Fletcher
1924-1927 William Phillips
1927-1933 Hugh S. Gibson
1933-1937 Dave H. Morris
1937-1938 Hugh S. Gibson
1938-1940 Joseph E. Davies
1940 John Cudahy
1941-1943 Jay Pierrepont Moffat
1943-1944 Ray Atherton

Charge d'Affaires

1944 Rudolph E. Schoenfeld

Ambassador

1944-1945 Charles Sawyer

EEMP

1946-1949 Alan G. Kirk
1949-1953 Perle Mesta
1953-1957 Wiley T. Buchanan, Jr.
1957-1960 Vinton Chapin

Ambassadors

1960-1961 A. Burke Summers
1961-1962 James W. Wine
1962-1965 William R. Rivkin
1965-1967 Patricia R. Harris
1967-1969 George J. Feldman
1969- Kingdon Gould, Jr.

MADAGASCAR

(See Malagasy for earlier representation)

Ambassador

1970-1972 Anthony D. Marshall
1972- Joseph A. Mendenhall

MALAGASY

(See Madagascar for later representation)

Ambassadors

1960-1962 Frederic P. Bartlett
1962-1966 C. Vaughan Ferguson
1967-1969 David S. King

MALAWI

Ambassadors

1964-1966 Sam P. Gilstrap
1966-1970 Marshall P. Jones
1970- William C. Burdett

MALAYSIA

(Malaya 1957-1963)

1957-1961 Homer M. Byington, Jr.
1961-1964 Charles F. Baldwin
1964-1969 James K. Bell
1969- Jack W. Lydman

MALDIVE ISLANDS

Ambassadors

1969-1970 Andrew V. Corry
1970-1972 Robert Strausz-Hupe

MALI

Ambassadors

1960-1961 Thomas K. Wright
1961-1964 William J. Handley
1965-1968 C. Robert Moore
1968-1971 G. Edward Clark
1971- Robert O. Blake

MALTA

Ambassadors

1965-1967 George J. Feldman
1967-1969 Hugh H. Smythe
1969-1972 John C. Pritzlaff, Jr.
1972- John I. Getz

MAURITANIA

Ambassadors

1960-1961 Henry S. Villard
1961-1964 Philip M. Kaiser
1965-1967 Geoffrey W. Lewis

(Embassy closed 1967-1970)

1970-1971 Vacant

MAURITIUS

Ambassadors

1968-1969 David S. King
1970- William D. Brewer

MEXICO

EEMP

1825-1829 Joel R. Poinsett

Charges d'Affaires

1829-1836 Anthony Butler
1836 Powhatan Ellis

(Legation closed 1836-1839)

EEMP

1839-1842 Powhatan Ellis
1842-1844 Waddy Thompson, Jr.
1844-1845 Wilson Shannon

(Legation closed 1845-1847)

Commissioner

1847-1848 Nicholas P. Trist

EEMP

1848 Ambrose H. Sevier
1848-1849 Nathan Clifford
1849-1852 Robert P. Latcher
1852-1853 Alfred Conkling
1853-1856 James Godsden
1856-1858 John Forsyth
1859-1860 Robert M. McLane
1860-1861 John B. Weller
1861-1864 Thomas Corwin
1864-1868 Vacant
1868-1869 William S. Rosecrans
1869-1873 Thomas H. Nelson
1873-1880 John W. Foster
1880-1886 P. H. Morgan
1886-1887 Thomas C. Manning
1888-1889 Edward S. Bragg
1889-1893 Thomas Ryan
1893-1895 Isaac P. Gray
1895-1897 Matt W. Ransom
1897-1898 Powell Clayton

Ambassadors

1898-1905 Powell Clayton
1905-1906 Edwin H. Conger
1906-1909 David E. Thompson
1909-1912 Henry L. Wilson
1912-1916 Vacant
1916-1921 Henry P. Fletcher
1921-1923 Vacant
1924 Charles B. Warren
1924-1927 James R. Sheffield
1927-1930 Dwight W. Morrow
1930-1933 J. Reuben Clark, Jr.
1933-1941 Josephus Daniels
1941-1946 George S. Messersmith
1946-1950 Walter Thurston
1950-1953 William O'Dwyer
1953-1957 Francis White
1957-1960 Robert C. Hill
1961-1964 Thomas C. Mann
1964-1969 Fulton Freeman
1969- Robert H. McBride

MONTENEGRO

(See Yugoslavia for later representation)

EEMP

1905-1907 John B. Jackson
1907-1909 Richmond Pearson
1909-1912 George H. Moses
1912-1913 Jacob G. Schurman
1914-1920 Garrett Droppers

MOROCCO

EEMP

1905-1909 Samuel R. Gummere
1909-1910 H. Percival Dodge
1910-1912 Fred W. Carpenter
1912-1917 Vacant

Agents

1917-1922 Maxwell Blake
1922-1924 Joseph M. Denning

Diplomatic Agents

1925-1940 Maxwell Blake
1940-1941 John C. White
1941-1945 Vacant
1945-1947 Paul H. Alling
1947-1951 Edwin A. Plitt
1951-1953 John Carter Vincent
1953-1955 Joseph C. Satterthwaite
1955-1956 Julius C. Holmes

Charge d'Affaires

1956 William J. Porter

Ambassadors

1956-1958 Cavendish W. Cannon
1958-1961 Charles W. Yost
1961-1962 Philip W. Bonsal
1962-1964 John H. Ferguson
1965-1969 Henry J. Tasca
1970- Stuart W. Rockwell

NEPAL

EEMP

1948-1951 Loy W. Henderson

Ambassadors

1951-1953 Chester Bowles
1953-1955 George V. Allen
1955-1959 John Sherman Cooper
1956-1959 Ellsworth Bunker
1959-1966 Henry E. Stebbins
1966- Carol C. Laise

NETHERLANDS

Ministers

1792-1794 William Short
1794-1797 John Quincy Adams
1797-1801 William V. Murray

EEMP

1814-1818 William Eustis

Charges d'Affaires

1818-1824 Alexander H. Everett
1825-1829 Christopher Hughes, Jr.

EEMP

1829-1831 William P. Preble

Charges d'Affaires

1831-1839 Auguste Davezac
1839-1842 Harmanus Bleecker
1842-1845 Christopher Hughes
1845-1850 Auguste Davezac
1850-1853 George Folsom
1853-1854 August Belmont

Ministers

1854-1857 August Belmont
1857-1861 Henry C. Murphy
1861-1866 James S. Pike
1866-1870 Hugh Ewing
1870-1875 Charles T. Gorham
1875-1876 Francis B. Stockbridge
1876-1882 James Birney
1882-1885 William L. Dayton, Jr.
1885-1888 Isaac Bell, Jr.

EEMP

1888-1889 Robert B. Roosevelt
1889-1893 Samuel R. Thayer
1893-1897 William E. Quinby
1897-1905 Stanford Newel
1905-1908 David J. Hill
1908-1911 Arthur M. Beaupre
1911-1913 Lloyd Bryce
1913-1917 Henry Van Dyke
1917-1919 John W. Garrett
1920-1922 William Phillips
1923-1929 Richard M. Tobin
1929-1931 Gerrit J. Diekema
1931-1934 Laurits S. Swenson
1934-1937 Grenville T. Emmet
1937-1941 George A. Gordon
1941-1942 Anthony J. Drexel Biddle, Jr.

Ambassadors

1942-1943 Anthony J. Drexel Biddle, Jr.
1944-1947 Stanley K. Hornbeck
1947-1949 Herman B. Baruch
1949-1953 Selden Chapin
1953-1957 H. Freeman Matthews
1957-1961 Philip Young
1961-1964 John S. Rice
1965-1969 William R. Tyler
1969- J. William Middendorf II

NEW ZEALAND

EEMP

1942-1943 Patrick J. Hurley
1943 William C. Burdett
1944-1945 Kenneth S. Patton
1945-1947 Avra M. Warren

Ambassadors

1947-1955 Robert M. Scotten
1955-1956 Robert C. Hendrickson
1957-1960 Francis H. Russell
1961-1963 Anthony B. Akers
1963-1967 Herbert B. Powell
1967-1969 John F. Henning
1969- Kenneth Franzheim II

NICARAGUA

Charge d'Affaires

1851-1853 John B. Kerr

Ministers

1854-1856 John H. Wheeler
1858-1859 Mirabeau B. Lamar
1859-1861 Alexander Dimitry
1861-1862 Andrew B. Dickinson
1862-1863 Thomas H. Clay
1863-1869 Andrew B. Dickinson
1869-1873 Charles N. Riotte
1873-1879 George Williamson
1879-1882 Cornelius A. Logan

EEMP

1882-1891 Henry C. Hall
1891-1893 Richard C. Shannon
1893-1897 Lewis Bader
1897-1908 William L. Merry
1908-1909 John G. Coolidge
1909-1911 Vacant
1911 Elliott Northcott
1911-1913 George T. Weitzel
1913-1921 Benjamin L. Jefferson
1921-1925 John E. Ramer
1925-1929 Charles C. Eberhardt
1929-1933 Matthew E. Hanna
1933-1936 Arthur Bliss Lane
1936-1938 Boaz W. Long
1938-1941 Meredith Nicholson
1941-1942 Pierre de L. Boal
1942-1943 James B. Stewart

Ambassadors

1943-1945 James B. Stewart
1945-1947 Fletcher Warren
1948-1949 George P. Shaw
1949-1951 Capus M. Waynick
1951-1961 Thomas E. Whelan
1961-1967 Aaron S. Brown
1967-1970 Kennedy M. Crockett
1970- Turner B. Shelton

NIGER

Ambassadors

1960-1961 R. Borden Reams
1961-1964 Mercer Cook
1964-1968 Robert J. Ryan
1968-1969 Samuel C. Adams, Jr.
1970- Roswell D. McClelland

NIGERIA

Ambassadors

1960-1964 Joseph Palmer II
1964-1969 Elbert G. Mathews
1969-1972 William C. Trueheart
1972- John E. Reinhardt

NORWAY

(See Sweden for earlier representation)

EEMP

1906-1911 Herbert H. D. Peirce
1911-1913 Laurits S. Swenson
1913-1921 Albert G. Schmedeman
1921-1930 Laurits S. Swenson
1930-1935 Hoffman Philip
1935-1937 Anthony J. Drexel Biddle, Jr.
1937-1941 Florence Jaffray Harriman
1941-1942 Anthony J. Drexel Biddle, Jr.

Ambassadors

1942-1943 Anthony J. Drexel Biddle, Jr.
1944-1946 Lithgow Osborne
1946-1953 Charles U. Bay
1953-1957 L. Corrin Strong
1957-1961 Frances E. Willis
1961-1964 Clifton R. Wharton
1964-1969 Margaret J. Tibbetts
1969- Philip K. Crowe

PAKISTAN

Ambassadors

1947-1949 Paul H. Alling
1949 H. Merle Cochran
1949-1953 Avra M. Warren
1953-1957 Horace A. Hildreth
1957-1959 James M. Langley
1959-1962 William M. Rountree
1962-1966 Walter P. McConaughy
1966-1967 Eugene M. Locke
1967-1969 Benjamin H. Olgeert, Jr.
1969-1972 Joseph S. Farland

PANAMA

EEMP

1903-1904 William L. Buchanan
1904-1905 John Barrett
1905-1906 Chares E. Magoon
1906-1909 Herbert G. Squiers
1909-1910 R. S. Reynolds Hitt
1910-1911 Thomas C. Dawson
1911-1913 H. Percival Dodge
1913-1921 William J. Price
1921-1929 John G. South
1929-1933 Roy T. Davis
1933-1934 Antonio C. Gonzalez
1934-1937 George T. Summerlin
1937-1939 Frank P. Corrigan

Ambassadors

1939-1941 William Dawson
1941-1943 Edwin C. Wilson
1944-1945 Avra M. Warren
1945-1948 Frank T. Hines
1948-1951 Monnett B. Davis
1951-1953 John C. Wiley
1953-1955 Selden Chapin
1955-1960 Julian F. Harrington
1960-1963 Joseph S. Farland
1964-1965 Jack H. Vaughn
1965-1969 Charles W. Adair, Jr.
1969-1972 Robert M. Sayre
1972- Frank T. Bow

PAPAL STATES

(See Italy for later representation)

Charges d'Affaires

1848 J. L. Martin
1848-1854 Lewis Cass, Jr.

Ministers

1854-1858 Lewis Cass, Jr.
1858-1861 John P. Stockton
1861-1862 Alexander W. Randall
1862-1863 Richard M. Blatchford
1863-1867 Rufus King

PARAGUAY

Commissioners

1858-1859 James B. Bowlin
1858-1859 Charles A. Washburn

Ministers

1863-1868 Charles A. Washburn
1868-1869 Martin T. McMahon
1870-1873 John L. Stevens
1874-1876 John C. Caldwell

Charges d'Affaires

1876-1882 John C. Caldwell
1882-1885 William Williams
1885-1890 John E. Bacon

EEMP

1890-1894 George Maney
1894-1897 Granville Stuart
1897-1905 William R. Finch
1905-1909 Edward C. O'Brien
1909-1911 Edwin V. Morgan
1911-1914 Nicolay A. Grevstad
1914-1922 Daniel F. Mooney
1922-1924 William J. O'Toole
1925-1929 George L. Kreeck
1929-1933 Post Wheeler
1933-1935 Meredith Nicholson
1935-1941 Findley B. Howard
1941-1942 Wesley Frost

Ambassadors

1942-1944 Wesley Frost
1944-1947 Willard L. Beaulac
1947-1950 Fletcher Warren
1950-1952 Howard H. Tewksbury
1952-1954 George P. Shaw
1954-1957 Arthur A. Ageton
1957-1959 Walter C. Ploeser
1959-1960 Harry F. Stimpson, Jr.
1961-1967 William P. Snow
1967-1969 Benigno C. Hernandez
1969-1972 J. Raymond Ylitalo
1972- George W. Landau

PERSIA

(See Iran for later representation)

Ministers

1883-1886 S. C. W. Benjamin
1886-1892 E. Spencer Pratt

1892-1893 Watson R. Sperry
1893-1897 Alexander McDonald
1897-1899 Arthur S. Hardy
1899-1901 Herbert W. Bowen
1901-1902 Lloyd C. Griscom
1902-1905 Richmond Pearson

EEMP

1905-1907 Richmond Pearson
1907-1909 John B. Jackson
1909-1914 Charles W. Russell
1914-1921 John L. Caldwell
1921-1924 Joseph S. Kornfeld
1925-1929 Hoffman Philip
1929-1933 Charles C. Hart
1933-1935 William H. Hornibrook

PERU

Charges d'Affaires

1826-1828 James Cooley
1828-1837 Samuel Larned
1836-1838 James B. Thornton
1838-1845 J. C. Pickett
1844-1845 John A. Bryan
1845-1847 Albert G. Jewett
1847-1853 John Randolph Clay

EEMP

1853-1860 John Randolph Clay
1861-1865 Christopher Robinson
1865-1870 Alvin P. Hovey
1871-1872 Thomas Settle
1872-1875 Francis Thomas
1875-1879 Richard Gibbs
1879-1882 Isaac B. Christiancy
1883-1885 Seth L. Phelps
1885-1889 Charles W. Buck
1889-1893 John Hicks
1893-1897 James A. McKenzie
1897-1906 Irving B. Dudley
1906-1911 Leslie Combs
1911-1913 H. Clay Howard
1913-1919 Benton McMillin

Ambassadors

1919-1921 William E. Gonzales
1923-1928 Miles Poindexter
1928-1930 Alexander P. Moore
1930-1937 Fred M. Dearing
1937-1939 Laurence A. Steinhardt
1940-1944 R. Henry Norweb
1944-1945 John Campbell White
1945-1946 William D. Pawley
1946-1948 Prentice Cooper
1948-1955 Harold H. Tittmann, Jr.
1955-1956 Ellis O. Briggs
1956-1960 Theodore C. Achilles
1960-1961 Selden Chapin
1961-1962 James Loeb
1962-1969 J. Wesley Jones
1969- Taylor G. Belcher

PHILIPPINES

Ambassadors

1946-1947 Paul V. McNutt
1947-1949 Emmet O'Neal
1949-1951 Myron M. Cowen
1952-1955 Raymond A. Spruance
1955-1956 Homer Ferguson
1956 Albert F. Nufer
1957-1959 Charles E. Bohlen
1959-1961 John D. Hickerson
1961-1964 William E. Stevenson
1964-1967 William M. Blair, Jr.
1968-1969 G. Mennen Williams
1969- Henry A. Byroade

POLAND

EEMP

1919-1924 Hugh S. Gibson
1924-1925 Alfred J. Pearson
1925-1930 John B. Stetson, Jr.

Ambassadors

1930-1932 John N. Willys
1932-1933 F. Lammot Belin
1933-1937 John Cudahy
1937-1943 Anthony J. Drexel Biddle, Jr.
1944-1947 Arthur Bliss Lane
1947-1948 Stanton Griffis
1948-1950 Waldemar J. Gallman
1950-1955 Joseph Flack
1955-1957 Joseph E. Jacobs
1957-1962 Jacob D. Beam
1962-1965 John M. Cabot
1965-1968 John A. Gronouski
1968- Walter J. Stoessel, Jr.

PORTUGAL

Ministers Plenipotentiary

1791-1797 David Humphreys
1797-1801 William L. Smith
1801-1809 Vacant
1809-1819 Thomas Sumter, Jr.
1819-1820 John Graham
1822-1824 Henry Dearborn

Charges d'Affaires

1825-1834 Thomas L. L. Brent
1835-1841 Edward Kavanagh
1841-1844 Washington Barrow
1843-1847 Abraham Rencher
1847-1849 George W. Hopkins
1849-1850 John B. Clay
1850-1854 Charles B. Haddock

Ministers

1854-1858 John L. O'Sullivan
1858-1861 George W. Morgan
1861-1869 James E. Harvey
1869 Samuel Shellabarger
1870-1874 Charles H. Lewis
1874-1882 Benjamin Moran
1882-1884 John M. Francis
1884-1885 Lewis Richmond
1885-1890 E. P. C. Lewis
1890-1893 George S. Batcheller
1893 Gilbert A. Pierce

EEMP

1893-1897 George W. Caruth
1897-1899 Lawrence Townsend
1899-1901 John N. Irwin
1901-1903 Francis B. Loomis
1903-1909 Charles P. Bryan
1909-1911 Henry T. Gage
1911 Edwin V. Morgan
1912-1913 Cyrus E. Woods
1913-1922 Thomas H. Birch
1922-1929 Fred M. Dearing
1929-1933 John G. South
1933-1937 Robert G. Caldwell
1937-1941 Herbert Claiborne Pell
1941-1943 Bert Fish
1943-1945 R. Henry Norweb

Ambassadors

1945-1947 Herman B. Baruch
1947-1948 John C. Wiley
1948-1952 Lincoln MacVeagh
1952-1953 Cavendish W. Cannon
1953-1954 M. Robert Guggenheim
1955-1958 James C. H. Bonbright
1958-1963 C. Burke Elbrick
1963-1966 George W. Anderson, Jr.
1966-1969 W. Tapley Bennett, Jr.
1969- Ridgway B. Knight

PRUSSIA

Ministers Plenipotentiary

1797-1801 John Quincy Adams

Charge d'Affaires

1835-1837 Henry Wheaton

EEMP

1846-1849 Andrew J. Donelson
1849-1850 Edward A. Hannegan
1850-1853 Daniel D. Barnard
1853-1857 Peter D. Vroom
1857-1861 Joseph A. Wright
1861-1865 Norman B. Judd
1865-1867 Joseph A. Wright
1867-1871 George Bancroft

RUMANIA

Ministers

1882-1885 Eugene Schuyler
1885-1889 J. Walker Fearn
1889-1892 A. Landon Snowden
1892-1893 Truxtun Beale

EEMP

1893-1897 Eben Alexander
1897-1899 William W. Rockhill
1899-1900 Arthur S. Hardy
1900-1902 Charles S. Francis
1902-1905 John B. Jackson
1905-1907 John W. Riddle
1907-1909 Horace G. Knowles
1909-1911 John R. Carter
1911-1913 John B. Jackson
1913-1921 Charles J. Vopicka
1921-1925 Peter A. Jay
1925-1928 William S. Culbertson
1928-1933 Charles S. Wilson
1933-1935 Alvin M. Owsley
1935-1937 Leland Harrison
1937-1941 Franklin M. Gunther

(Legation closed 1941-1947)

1947-1951 Rudolf E. Schoenfeld
1953-1955 Harold Shantz
1955-1958 Robert H. Thayer
1958-1961 Clifton R. Wharton
1961-1965 William A. Crawford

Ambassadors

1965-1969 Richard H. Davis
1969- Leonard C. Meeker

RUSSIA
(See U.S.S.R. for later representation)

Minister Plenipotentiary

1809-1814 John Quincy Adams

Charge d'Affaires

1814-1817 Leavitt Harris

EEMP

1816-1818 William Pinkney
1818-1820 George W. Campbell
1820-1830 Henry Middleton
1830 John Randolph
1832-1833 James Buchanan
1834-1835 William Wilkins

Charge d'Affaires

1836-1837 John Randolph Clay

EEMP

1837-1839 George M. Sallas
1840-1841 Churchill C. Cambreleng
1841-1846 Charles S. Todd
1846-1848 Ralph J. Ingersoll
1848-1849 Arthur P. Bagby
1850-1853 Neil S. Brown
1853-1858 Thomas H. Seymour
1858-1860 Francis W. Pickens
1860-1861 John Appleton
1861-1862 Cassius M. Clay
1862 Simon Cameron
1863-1869 Cassius M. Clay
1869-1872 Andrew G. Curtin
1872-1873 James L. Orr
1873-1875 Marshall Jewell
1875-1877 George H. Boker
1877-1879 E. W. Stoughton
1880-1882 John W. Foster
1882-1884 William H. Hunt
1884-1885 Alphonso Taft
1885-1888 George V. N. Lothrop
1888-1892 Lambert Tree
1892-1894 Andrew D. White
1894-1897 Clifton R. Breckinridge
1897-1899 Ethan A. Hitchcock

Ambassadors

1899-1902 Charlemagne Tower
1902-1905 Robert S. McCormick
1905-1906 George V. L. Meyer
1906-1909 John W. Riddle
1909-1911 William W. Rockhill
1911-1913 Curtis Gould
1914-1916 George T. Marye
1916-1921 David R. Francis

RWANDA

Ambassadors

1963-1966 Charles D. Withers
1966-1972 Leo G. Cyr
1972- Robert F. Corrigan

SALVADOR
(See El Salvador for later representation)

EEMP

1853-1854 Solon Borland

Ministers

1863-1866 James R. Partridge
1866-1869 Alpheus S. Williams
1869-1871 Alfred T. A. Torbert
1871-1873 Thomas Biddle
1873-1879 George Williamson
1879-1882 Cornelius A. Logan

EEMP

1882-1891 Henry C. Hall
1891-1893 Richard C. Shannon
1893-1897 Lewis Baker
1897-1906 William L. Merry
1907-1909 H. Percival Dodge
1909-1914 William Heimke
1914-1919 Boaz W. Long
1921-1925 Montgomery Schuyler
1926-1928 Jefferson Caffery
1928-1929 Warren D. Robbins

SARDINIA

Charges d'Affaires

1840-1841 H. Gold Rogers
1841-1843 Ambrose Baber
1843-1848 Robert Wickliffe, Jr.
1848-1850 Nathaniel Niles
1850-1853 William B. Kinney
1853 John M. Daniel

Ministers

1854-1861 John M. Daniel

SAUDI ARABIA

EEMP

1939-1941 Bert Fish
1941-1943 Alexander C. Kirk
1943-1944 James S. Moose, Jr.
1944-1946 William A. Eddy
1946-1949 J. Rives Childs

Ambassadors

1949-1950 J. Rives Childs
1950-1953 Raymond A. Hare
1953-1957 George Wadswroth
1957-1961 Donald R. Heath
1961-1966 Parker T. Hart
1966-1971 Herman F. Eilts
1971- Nicholas G. Thacher

SENEGAL

Ambassadors

1960-1961 Henry S. Villard
1961-1964 Philip M. Kaiser
1964-1966 Mercer Cook
1966-1967 William R. Rivkin
1967-1971 L. Dean Brown
1971- G. Edward Clark

SERBIA
(See Yugoslavia for later representation)

Ministers

1882-1885 Eugene Schuyler
1885-1890 J. Walker Fearn
1890-1893 Truxtun Beale

EEMP

1893-1897 Eben Alexander
1897-1899 William W. Rockhill
1899-1900 Arthur S. Hardy
1900-1902 Charles S. Francis
1902-1905 John B. Jackson
1905-1907 John W. Riddle
1907-1909 Horace G. Knowles
1909-1911 John R. Carter
1911-1913 John B. Jackson
1913-1919 Charles J. Vopicka
1919-1926 H. Percival Dodge
1926-1929 John D. Prince

SIAM
(See Thailand for later representation)

Ministers

1882-1886 J. A. Halderman
1886-1890 Jacob T. Child
1890-1894 Sempronius H. Boyd
1894-1898 John Barrett
1898-1903 Hamilton King

EEMP

1903-1912 Hamilton King
1912-1913 Fred W. Carpenter
1915-1916 William H. Hornibrook
1917-1918 George P. Ingersoll
1921-1925 Edward E. Brodie
1925-1926 William W. Russell
1927-1930 Harold O. Mackenzie
1930-1933 David E. Kaufman
1933-1937 James M. Baker

SICILY
(See Italy for later representation)

Minister Plenipotentiary

1816 William Pinkney

Charges d'Affaires

1831-1832 John Nelson
1838-1842 Enos T. Throop
1841-1845 William Boulware
1845-1847 William H. Polk
1848-1850 John Rowan
1849 Thomas W. Chinn
1850-1853 Edward J. Morris
1953-1854 Robert D. Owen

Ministers

1854-1858 Robert D. Owen
1858-1860 Joseph R. Chandler

SIERRA LEONE

Ambassadors

1961-1963 A. S. J. Carnahan
1964-1967 Andrew V. Corry
1967-1972 Robert G. Miner
1972- Clinton L. Olson

SINGAPORE

Ambassadors

1966-1969 Francis J. Galbraith
1969-1972 Charles T. Cross
1972- Edward M. Krouk

SOMALIA

Ambassadors

1960-1962 Andrew G. Lynch
1962-1965 Horace G. Torbert, Jr.
1965-1968 Raymond L. Thurston
1969-1971 Fred L. Hadsel
1972- Matthew Looram

REPUBLIC OF SOUTH AFRICA

(See Union of South Africa for earlier representation)

Ambassadors

1961-1965 Joseph C. Satterthwaite
1965-1970 William M. Rountree
1970- John G. Hurd

SOUTH KOREA

(See Korea for earlier representation)

Ambassadors

1949-1952 John J. Muccio
1952-1955 Ellis O. Briggs
1955 William S. B. Lacy
1956-1959 Walter C. Dowling
1959-1961 Walter P. McConaughy
1961-1964 Samuel D. Berger
1964-1967 Winthrop G. Brown
1967- William J. Porter

SOUTHERN YEMEN

Charge d'Affaires

1967-1969 William Eagleton, Jr.

(Embassy closed 1969)

SPAIN

Charge d'Affaires

1790-1794 William Carmichael

Minister

1794-1795 William Short

Envoy Extraordinary

1794-1795 Thomas Pinckney

Ministers Plenipotentiary

1796-1801 David Humphreys
1801-1805 Charles Pinckney
1805-1808 James Bowdoin
1808-1814 Vacant
1814-1819 George W. Erving
1819-1823 John Forsyth
1823-1825 Hugh Nelson

EEMP

1825-1829 Alexander H. Everett
1829-1836 Cornelius P. Van Ness
1836-1840 John H. Eaton

Charge d'Affaires

1840-1842 Aaron Vail

EEMP

1842-1846 Washington Irving
1846-1849 Romulus M. Saunders
1849-1853 Daniel M. Barringer
1853-1855 Pierre Soule
1855-1858 Augustus C. Dodge
1858-1861 William Preston
1861-1862 Carl Schurz
1862-1864 Gustavus Koerner
1865-1869 John P. Hale
1869-1873 Daniel E. Sickles
1874-1877 Caleb Cushing
1877-1880 James Russell Lowell
1880-1881 Lucius Fairchild
1881-1883 Hannibal Hamlin
1883-1885 John W. Foster
1885-1888 Jabez L. M. Curry
1888-1892 Perry Belmont
1892-1893 A. Landon Snowden
1893-1897 Hannis Taylor
1897-1898 Stewart L. Woodford
1899-1902 Bellamy Storer
1902-1905 Arthur S. Hardy
1905-1909 William M. Collier
1909-1913 Henry C. Ide

Ambassadors

1913-1921 Joseph E. Willard
1921-1923 Cyrus E. Woods
1923-1925 Alexander P. Moore
1925-1929 Ogden H. Hammond
1929-1933 Irwin B. Laughlin
1933-1939 Claude G. Bowers
1939-1942 Alexander W. Weddell
1942-1944 Carlton J. H. Hayes
1944-1945 Norman Armour
1945-1951 Vacant
1951-1952 Stanton Griffis
1952-1953 Lincoln MacVeagh
1953-1955 James C. Dunn
1955-1961 John Davis Lodge
1961 Anthony J. Drexel Biddle, Jr.
1962-1965 Robert F. Woodward
1965-1968 Angier Biddle Duke
1968-1969 Robert F. Wagner
1969-1972 Robert C. Hill
1972- Horacio Rivero

SUDAN

Ambassadors

1956-1958 Lowell C. Pinkerton
1958-1962 James S. Moose, Jr.
1962-1965 William M. Rountree
1965-1967 William H. Weatherby

(Embassy closed 1967)

SWAZILAND

1972- Charles J. Nelson

SWEDEN

(Sweden and Norway 1797-1905)

Commissioner

1798 John Quincy Adams

Minister Plenipotentiary

1814-1818 Jonathan Russell

Charges d'Affaires

1819-1825 Christopher Hughes
1826-1830 John J. Appleton
1830-1841 Christopher Hughes
1842-1845 George W. Lay
1845-1849 Henry W. Ellsworth
1849-1854 Francis Schroeder

Ministers

1854-1857 Francis Schroeder
1857-1861 Benjamin F. Angel
1861-1864 Jacob S. Haldeman
1864-1867 James H. Campbell
1867-1869 Joseph J. Bartlett
1869-1877 Christopher C. Andrews
1877-1883 John L. Stevens
1883-1885 William W. Thomas, Jr.
1885-1889 Rufus Magee

EEMP

1889-1894 William W. Thomas, Jr.
1894-1897 Thomas B. Ferguson
1897-1905 William W. Thomas, Jr.
1905-1914 Charles H. Graves
1914-1923 Ira N. Morris
1923-1927 Robert W. Bliss
1927-1929 Leland Harrison
1930-1933 John M. Morehead
1933-1937 Laurence A. Steinhardt
1937-1938 Fred M. Dearing
1938-1941 Frederick A. Sterling
1941-1946 Herschel V. Johnson
1946-1947 Louis G. Dreyfus, Jr.

Ambassadors

1947-1950 H. Freeman Matthews
1951-1954 W. Walton Butterworth
1954-1957 John M. Cabot
1957-1958 Francis White
1958-1961 James C. H. Bonbright
1961-1967 J. Graham Parsons
1967-1969 William W. Heath
1970-1972 Jerome H. Holland

SWITZERLAND

Ministers

1853-1861 Theodore S. Fay
1861-1865 George G. Fogg
1865-1869 George Harrington
1869-1876 Horace Rublee

Charges d'Affaires

1876-1877 Horace Rublee
1877-1882 Nicholas Fish

Ministers

1882-1885 Michael J. Cramer
1885-1890 Boyd Winchester

EEMP

1890-1892 John D. Washburn, Jr.
1892-1893 Person C. Cheney
1893-1895 James O. Broadhead
1895-1897 John L. Peak
1897-1900 John G. A. Leishman
1900-1902 Arthur S. Hardy
1903-1905 David J. Hill
1905-1909 Brutus J. Clay
1909-1911 Laurits S. Swenson
1911-1913 Henry S. Bortell
1913-1921 Pleasant A. Stovall
1921-1924 Joseph C. Grew
1924-1927 Hugh S. Gibson
1927-1937 Hugh R. Wilson
1937-1947 Leland Harrison
1947-1951 John Carter Vincent
1951-1953 Richard C. Patterson
1953 Frances E. Willis

Ambassadors

1953-1957 Frances E. Willis
1957-1961 Henry J. Taylor
1961-1963 Robert M. McKinney
1963-1966 W. True Davis, Jr.
1966-1969 John S. Hayes
1969- Shelby Davis

SYRIA
(Syrian Arab Republic 1958-1967)

EEMP

1942-1946 George Wadsworth
1947 Pul Alling
1947-1950 James H. Keeley, Jr.
1950-1952 Cavendish W. Cannon

Ambassadors

1952-1957 James S. Moose, Jr.
1957-1958 Charles W. Yost
1958-1961 Vacant
1961-1965 Ridgway B. Knight
1965-1967 Hugh H. Smythe

(Embassy closed 1967)

TANZANIA
(Tanganyika 1962-1964)

Ambassadors

1962-1965 William Leonhart
1965-1969 John H. Burns
1969-1972 Claude G. Ross
1972- W. Beverly Carter, Jr.

REPUBLIC OF TEXAS

Charges d'Affaires

1837-1840 Alcee La Branche
1841-1843 George H. Hood
1841-1843 Joseph Eve
1843-1844 William S. Murphy
1844 Tilghman A. Howard
1844-1845 Andrew J. Donelson

THAILAND
(See Siam for earlier representation)

EEMP

1939-1940 Edwin L. Neville
1940-1941 Hugh G. Grant
1941-1942 Willys R. Peck

(Legation closed 1942-1946)

1946 Edwin F. Stanton

Ambassadors

1947-1953 Edwin F. Stanton
1953-1954 William J. Donovan
1954-1955 John E. Peurifoy
1955-1958 Max W. Bishop
1958-1961 U. Alexis Johnson
1961-1963 Kenneth T. Young
1963-1967 Graham A. Martin
1967- Leonard Unger

TOGO

Ambassadors

1960-1961 Leland Barrows
1961-1964 Leon B. Poullada
1964-1967 William Witman II
1967-1971 Albert W. Sherer, Jr.
1971- Dwight Dickinson

TRINIDAD AND TOBAGO

Ambassadors

1962-1967 Robert G. Miner
1967-1969 William A. Costello
1969-1972 J. Fife Symington, Jr.
1972- Anthony D. Marshall

TUNISIA

Ambassadors

1956-1959 G. Lewis Jones
1959-1962 Walter N. Walmsley, Jr.
1962-1969 Francis H. Russell
1969-1972 John A. Calhoun
1972- Talcott W. Seelye

TURKEY

Charge d'Affaires

1831-1839 David Porter

Ministers

1839-1843 David Porter
1843-1849 Dabney S. Carr
1849-1853 George P. Marsh
1853-1857 Carroll Spence
1858-1861 James Williams
1861-1870 Edward J. Morris
1870-1871 Wayne MacVeagh
1871-1875 George H. Boker
1875-1880 Horace Maynard
1880-1882 James Longstreet

EEMP

1882-1885 Lew Wallace
1887-1889 Oscar S. Straus
1889-1892 Solomon Hirsch
1892-1893 David P. Thompson
1893-1897 Alexander W. Terrell
1897-1898 James B. Angell
1898-1900 Oscar S. Straus
1900-1906 John G. A. Leishman

Ambassadors

1906-1909 John G. A. Leishman
1909-1911 Oscar S. Straus
1911-1913 William W. Rockhill
1913-1916 Henry Morgenthau
1916-1917 Abram I. Elkus
1927-1932 Joseph C. Grew
1932-1933 Charles H. Sherrill
1933-1936 Robert P. Skinner
1936-1942 John Van A. MacMurray
1942-1944 Laurence A. Steinhardt
1945-1948 Edwin C. Wilson
1948-1951 George Wadsworth
1951-1953 George C. McGhee
1953-1956 Avra M. Warren
1956-1960 Fletcher Warren
1961-1965 Raymond A. Hare
1965-1968 Parker T. Hart
1968-1969 Robert W. Komer
1969- William J. Handley

UGANDA

Ambassadors

1963-1966 Olcott H. Deming
1966-1969 Henry E. Stebbins
1970-1972 Clarence C. Ferguson, Jr.
1972- Thomas P. Melady

UNION OF SOUTH AFRICA
(See Republic of South Africa for later representation)

Minister

1929-1937 Ralph J. Totten

EEMP

1937-1942 Leo J. Keena
1942-1943 Lincoln MacVeagh
1944-1948 Thomas Holcomb
1948-1949 North Winship

Ambassadors

1949-1950 North Winship
1950-1951 John G. Erhardt
1951-1954 Waldemar J. Gallman
1954-1956 Edward T. Wailes
1956-1959 Henry A. Myronde
1959-1961 Philip K. Crowe

UNION OF SOVIET SOCIALIST REPUBLICS
(See Russia for earlier representation)

Ambassadors

1933-1936 William C. Bullitt
1936-1938 Joseph E. Davies
1939-1942 Laurence A. Steinhardt
1942-1943 William H. Standley
1943-1946 W. Averell Harriman
1946-1949 Walter Bedell Smith
1949-1952 Alan G. Kirk
1952-1953 George F. Kennan
1953-1957 Charles E. Bohlen
1957-1962 Llewellyn E. Thompson
1962-1967 Foy D. Kohler
1967-1969 Llewellyn E. Thompson
1969- Jacob D. Beam

UNITED ARAB REPUBLIC
(See Egypt, Syria for earlier representation)

Ambassadors

1958-1960 Raymond A. Hare
1960-1961 G. Frederick Reinhardt
1961-1964 John S. Badeau
1964-1967 Lucius D. Battle
1967-1971 Richard H. Nolte

UPPER VOLTA

Ambassadors

1960-1961 R. Borden Reams
1961-1966 Thomas S. Estes
1966-1969 Elliott P. Skinner
1969-1972 William E. Schaufele, Jr.
1972- Donald B. Easum

URUGUAY

Ministers

1867-1868 Alexander Asboth
1869-1870 Henry G. Worthington
1869-1870 Robert C. Kirk
1870-1873 John L. Stevens
1874-1876 John C. Caldwell

Charges d'Affaires

1876-1882 John C. Caldwell
1882-1885 William Williams
1885-1890 John E. Bacon

EEMP

1890-1894 George Maney
1894-1897 Granville Stuart
1897-1905 William R. Finch
1905-1909 Edward C. O'Brien
1909-1911 Edwin V. Morgan
1911-1915 Nicolay A. Grevstad
1915-1921 Robert E. Jeffrey
1922-1925 Hoffman Philip
1925-1929 Ulysses Grant-Smith
1929-1930 Leland Harrison
1930-1934 J. Butler Wright
1934-1937 Julius G. Lay
1937-1939 William Dawson
1939-1941 Edwin C. Wilson

Ambassadors

1941-1946 William Dawson
1946-1947 Joseph F. McGurk
1947-1949 Ellis O. Briggs
1949-1951 Christian M. Ravndal
1951-1953 Edward L. Roddan
1953-1956 Dempster McIntosh
1956-1958 Jefferson Patterson
1958-1961 Robert F. Woodward
1961-1962 Edward J. Sparks
1962-1965 Wymberley D. Coerr
1965-1967 Henry A. Hoyt
1968-1969 Robert M. Sayre
1969- Charles W. Adair, Jr.

VENEZUELA

Charges d'Affaires

1835-1840 John G. A. Williamson
1841-1844 Allen A. Hall
1844-1845 Vespasian Ellis
1845-1850 Benjamin G. Shields
1850-1853 Isaac N. Steele
1854 Charles Eames

Ministers

1854-1858 Charles Eames
1858-1861 Edward A. Turpin
1861-1862 Henry T. Blow
1862-1866 Erastus D. Culver
1866-1867 James Wilson
1867-1868 Thomas N. Stilwell
1869-1870 James R. Partridge
1870-1874 William A. Pile
1874-1878 Thomas Russell
1878-1885 Jehu Baker
1885-1889 Charles L. Scott

EEMP

1889-1893 William L. Scruggs
1893-1894 Frank C. Partridge
1894-1895 Seneca Haselton
1895-1897 Allen Thomas
1897-1901 Francis B. Loomis
1901-1905 Herbert W.Bowen
1905-1909 William W. Russell
1910-1911 John W. Garrett
1911-1913 Elliott Northcott
1913-1921 Preston McGoodwin
1921-1929 Willis C. Cook
1929-1934 George T. Summerlin
1935-1938 Meredith Nicholson
1938-1939 Antonio C. Gonzales

Ambassadors

1939-1947 Frank P. Corrigan
1947-1950 Walter J. Donnelly
1950-1951 Norman Armour
1951-1956 Fletcher Warren
1956-1957 Dempster McIntosh
1958-1961 Edward J. Sparks
1961-1962 Teodoro Moscoso
1962-1964 C. Allan Stewart
1965-1969 Maurice M. Bernbaum
1970- Robert McClintock

VIETNAM
(Republic of Vietnam after 1954)

Charge d'Affaires

1949-1950 Edmund A. Gullion

EEMP

1950-1952 Donald R. Heath

Ambassadors

1952-1955 Donald R. Heath
1955-1957 G. Frederick Reinhardt
1957-1961 Elbridge Durbrow
1961-1963 Frederick E. Nolting, Jr.
1963-1964 Henry Cabot Lodge
1964-1965 Maxwell D. Taylor
1965-1967 Henry Cabot Lodge
1967- Ellsworth Bunker

WESTERN SAMOA

Ambassador

1971- Kenneth Franzheim II

YEMEN
(See also Southern Yemen)

EEMP

1946-1950 J. Rives Childs
1950-1953 Raymond A. Hare
1953-1957 George Wadsworth
1957-1959 Donald R. Heath
1959-1960 Raymond A. Hare
1960-1961 G. Frederick Reinhardt
1961-1963 Parker T. Hart
1963-1967 Vacant

(Embassy closed 1967)

YUGOSLAVIA
(See Montenegro, Serbia)

EEMP

1929-1933 John D. Prince
1933-1937 Charles S. Wilson
1937-1941 Arthur Bliss Lane
1941-1942 Anthony J. Drexel Biddle, Jr.

Ambassadors

1942-1943 Anthony J. Drexel Biddle, Jr.
1943-1944 Lincoln MacVeagh
1944-1947 Richard C. Patterson, Jr.
1947-1949 Cavendish W. Cannon
1949-1953 George V. Allen
1953-1957 James W. Riddleberger
1957-1961 Karl L. Rankin
1961-1963 George F. Kennan
1964-1969 C. Burke Elbrick
1969-1972 William Leonhart
1972- Malcolm Toon

ZAMBIA

Ambassadors

1965-1969 Robert C. Good
1969-1972 Oliver L. Troxel, Jr.
1972- Jean M. Wilkowski

THE FEDERAL SERVICES

Chiefs of bureaus and agencies of the United States government.

AGENCY FOR INTERNATIONAL DEVELOPMENT

(and predecessor agencies)

ECONOMIC COOPERATION ADMINISTRATION

Administrators

1948 Paul G. Hoffman
1950 William C. Foster

TECHNICAL COOPERATION ADMINISTRATION

Administrators

1950 Henry G. Bennett
1952 Stanley Andrews

MUTUAL SECURITY AGENCY

Directors

1951 W. Averell Harriman
1953 Harold E. Stassen

FOREIGN OPERATIONS ADMINISTRATION

Director

1953 Harold E. Stassen

INTERNATIONAL COOPERATION ADMINISTRATION

Directors

1955 John B. Hollister
1957 James H. Smith, Jr.
1959 James W. Riddleberger
1961 Henry R. Labouisse

AGENCY FOR INTERNATIONAL DEVELOPMENT

Administrators

1961 Fowler Hamilton
1962 David E. Bell
1966 William S. Gaud
1969 John A. Hannah

ATOMIC ENERGY COMMISION

Chairmen

1946 David E. Lilienthal
1950 Sumner T. Pike (Acting)
1950 Gordon Dean
1953 Lewis L. Strauss
1958 John A. McCone
1961 Glenn T. Seaborg
1971 James R. Schlesinger

BUREAU OF CUSTOMS

Commissioners

1927 Ernest W. Camp
1929 Francis X. A. Eble
1933 James H. Moyle
1939 Basil Harris
1940 William R. Johnson
1949 Frank Dow
1954 Ralph Kelly
1961 Philip Nichols, Jr.
1965 Lester Johnson
1969 Myles J. Ambrose

CENTRAL INTELLIGENCE AGENCY

Directors

1947 Roscoe H. Millenkoetter
1950 Walter Bedell Smith
1953 Allen Dulles
1961 John A. McCone
1965 William A. Radford
1966 Richard M. Helms

EXPORT-IMPORT BANK OF THE UNITED STATES

Presidents

1934 George N. Peek
1935 Jesse H. Jones
1936 Warren L. Pierson
1945 Wayne C. Taylor
1946 William McChesney Martin, Jr.
1949 Herbert E. Gaston
1953 Glen E. Edgerton
1955 Samuel C. Waugh
1961 Harold F. Linder
1969 Henry Kearns

FEDERAL COMMUNICATIONS COMMISSION

Chairmen

1934 Eugene O. Sykes
1935 Anning S. Prall
1937 Frank R. McNinch
1939 James L. Fly
1944 Paul A. Porter
1946 Charles R. Denny
1947 Wayne Coy
1952 Paul A. Walker
1953 Rosel H. Hyde
1954 George C. McConnaughey
1957 John C. Doerfer
1960 Frederick W. Ford
1961 Newton N. Minow
1963 E. William Henry
1966 Rosel H. Hyde
1969 Dean Burch

FEDERAL HOME LOAN BANK BOARD

Chairmen

1932 Franklin W. Fort
1933 William F. Stevenson
1933 John H. Fahey
1947 William K. Divers
1953 Walter W. McAllister
1956 Albert J. Robertson
1961 Joseph P. McMurray
1963 John E. Horne
1968 Robert L. Rand (Acting)
1969 Preston Martin

FEDERAL MARITIME COMMISSION

1961 James L. Pimper (Acting)
1961 Thomas E. Stakem, Jr.
1963 John Harllee
1969 Helen Delich Bentley

FEDERAL MEDIATION AND CONCILIATION SERVICE

(Prior to 1947 known as the U.S. Conciliation Service)

Directors

1917 Hugh L. Kerwin
1937 John R. Steelman
1944 Howard T. Colvin (Acting)
1945 Edgar L. Warren
1947 Cyrus S. Ching
1952 David L. Cole
1953 Clyde M. Mills (Acting)
1953 Whitley P. McCoy
1955 Joseph F. Finnegan
1961 William E. Sinkin
1969 J. Curtis Counts

FEDERAL POWER COMMISSION

Chairmen

1930 George O. Smith
1933 Frank R. McNinch
1939 Clyde L. Seavey
1940 Leland Olds
1944 Basil Manly
1945 Leland Olds
1947 Nelson Lee Smith
1950 Mon C. Wallgren
1952 Thomas C. Buchanan
1953 Jerome K. Kuykendall
1961 Joseph C. Swidler
1966 Lee C. White
1969 John N. Nassikas

FEDERAL RESERVE SYSTEM

Chairmen

1914 Charles S. Hamlin
1916 W. P. G. Harding
1923 Daniel R. Crissinger
1927 Roy A. Young
1930 Eugene Meyer
1933 Eugene R. Black
1934 Marriner S. Eccles
1948 Thomas B. McCabe
1951 William McChesney Martin, Jr.
1970 Arthur F. Burns

GEOLOGICAL SURVEY

Directors

1879 Clarence King
1881 John W. Powell
1894 Charles D. Walcott
1907 George O. Smith
1931 Walter C. Mendenhall
1943 William E. Wrather
1956 Thomas B. Nolan
1965 William T. Pecora
1971 Vincent E. McKelvey

GOVERNMENT PRINTING OFFICE

Public Printers

1861 John D. Defrees
1866 Cornelius Wendell
1867 John D. Defrees
1869 Almon M. Clapp
1877 John D. Defrees
1882 Sterling P. Rounds
1886 Thomas B. Benedict
1889 Frank W. Palmer
1894 Thomas B. Benedict
1897 Frank W. Palmer
1905 Charles A. Stillings
1908 Samuel B. Donnelly
1913 Cornelius Ford
1921 George H. Carter
1934 Augustus E. Geigengack
1948 John J. Deviny
1953 Raymond Blattenberger
1961 James L. Harrison
1971 Adolphus N. Spence II

IMMIGRATION AND NATURALIZATION SERVICE

Formed in 1933 by consolidation of the Bureau of Immigration and Bureau of Naturalization.

Commissioners

1933 Daniel W. MacCormack
1937 James L. Houghteling
1940 Lemuel B. Schofield
1942 Earl G. Harrison
1945 Ugo Carusi
1947 Watson B. Miller
1951 Argyle R. Mackey
1954 Joseph M. Swing
1962 Raymond F. Farrell

INTERNAL REVENUE SERVICE

Commissioners

1862 George S. Boutwell
1863 Joseph J. Lewis
1865 William Orton
1865 Edward A. Rollins
1869 Columbus Delano
1871 Alfred Pleasonton
1871 John W. Douglass
1875 Daniel D. Pratt
1876 Green B. Raum
1883 Walter Evans
1885 Joseph S. Miller
1889 John W. Mason
1893 Joseph S. Miller
1896 W. St. John Forman
1898 Nathan B. Scott
1899 George W. Wilson
1900 John W. Yerkes
1907 John G. Capers
1909 Royal E. Cabell
1913 William H. Osborn
1917 Daniel C. Roper
1920 William M. Williams
1921 David H. Blair
1929 Robert H. Lucas
1930 David Burnet
1933 Guy T. Helevering
1943 Robert E. Hannegan
1944 Joseph D. Nunan, Jr.
1947 George J. Schoeneman
1951 John B. Dunlap
1953 T. Coleman Andrews
1955 Russell C. Harrington
1958 Dana Latham
1961 Mortimer M. Caplin
1965 Sheldon S. Cohen
1969 Randolph W. Thrower
1971 Johnnie M. Walters

LIBRARY OF CONGRESS

Librarians

1802 John James Beckley
1807 Patrick Magruder
1815 George Watterston
1829 John S. Meehan
1861 John G. Stephenson
1864 Ainsworth R. Spofford
1897 John R. Young
1899 Herbert Putnam
1939 Archibald MacLeish
1945 Luther H. Evans
1954 Lawrence Q. Mumford

NATIONAL AERONAUTICS AND SPACE ADMINISTRATION

Administrators

1958 T. Keith Glennan
1961 James E. Webb
1968 Thomas O. Paine
1971 James C. Fletcher

NATIONAL MEDIATION BOARD

Chairmen

1934 William M. Leiserson
1936 James W. Carmalt
1937 Otto S. Beyer
1939 George A. Cook
1941 David J. Lewis
1942 William M. Leiserson
1944 Harry H. Schwartz
1946 Frank P. Douglass
1948 Francis A. O'Neill, Jr.
1950 John Thad Scott, Jr.
1951 Leverett Edwards
1952 Francis A. O'Neill, Jr.
1955 Leverett Edwards
1956 Robert O. Boyd
1957 Francis A. O'Neill, Jr.
1958 Leverett Edwards
1959 Robert O. Boyd
1960 Francis A. O'Neill, Jr.
1961 Leverett Edwards
1963 Francis A. O'Neill, Jr.
1964 Howard G. Gamser
1965 Leverett Edwards
1966 Francis A. O'Neill, Jr.
1967 Howard G. Gamser
1968 Leverett Edwards
1969 Francis A. O'Neill, Jr.
1970 George S. Ives

NATIONAL PARK SERVICE

Directors

1921 Stephen T. Mather
1929 Horace M. Albright
1933 Arno Cammerer
1940 Newton B. Drury
1951 Arthur E. Demaray
1951 Conrad L. Wirth
1964 George B. Hartzog, Jr.

NATIONAL SCIENCE FOUNDATION

Directors

1951 Alan T. Waterman
1963 Leland J. Haworth
1969 William D. McElroy
1972 H. Guyford Stever

NATIONAL SECURITY AGENCY

Directors

1951 Ralph J. Canine
1956 John A. Samford
1960 Laurence H. Frost
1962 Gordon A. Blake
1965 Marshall S. Carter
1969 Noel Gayler

OFFICE OF ECONOMIC OPPORTUNITY

Directors

1964 Sargent Shriver
1968 R. Bertrand Harding (Acting)
1969 Donald Rumsfeld
1970 Frank Carlucci
1971 Phillip Sanchez

OFFICE OF EDUCATION

Commissioners

1867 Henry Barnard
1870 John Eaton
1886 N.H.R. Dawson
1889 William T. Harris
1906 Elmer E. Brown
1911 Philander P. Claxton
1921 John J. Tigert
1929 William J. Cooper
1933 George F. Zook
1934 John W. Studebaker
1949 Earl J. McGrath
1953 Lee M. Thurston
1953 Samuel M. Brownell
1956 Lawrence G. Derthick
1961 Sterling M. McMurrin
1962 Francis Keppel
1966 Harold Howe II

OFFICE OF MANAGEMENT AND BUDGET

(Prior to 1970 known as the Bureau of the Budget)

Directors

1921 Charles G. Dawes
1922 Herbert M. Lord
1929 J. Clawson Roop
1933 Lewis W. Douglas
1934 Daniel W. Bell
1939 Harold D. Smith
1946 James E. Webb
1949 Frank Pace
1950 Frederick J. Lawton
1953 Joseph M. Dodge
1954 Rowland R. Hughes
1956 Percival F. Brundage
1958 Maurice H. Stans
1961 David E. Bell
1962 Kermit Gordon
1965 Charles L. Schultze
1968 Charles J. Zwick
1969 Robert P. Mayo
1970 George P. Schultz

OFFICE OF THE TREASURY

Treasurers

1775 Michael Hillegas
1789 Samuel Meredith
1801 Thomas T. Tucker
1828 Wilbur Clark
1829 John Campbell
1839 William Selden
1850 John Sloan
1853 Samuel Casey
1860 William C. Price
1861 F.E. Spinner
1875 John C. New
1876 A.U. Wyman
1877 James Gilfillan
1883 A.U. Wyman
1885 Conrad N. Jordan
1887 James W. Hyatt
1889 J.N. Huston
1891 Enos H. Nebecker
1893 D.N. Morgan
1897 Ellis H. Roberts
1905 Charles H. Treat
1909 Lee McClung
1912 Carmi A. Thompson
1913 John Burke
1921 Frank White
1928 H.T. Tate
1929 W.O. Woods
1933 W.A. Julian
1949 Georgia Neese Clark
1953 Ivy Baker Priest
1961 Elizabeth Rudel Smith
1963 Kathryn O'Hay Granahan
1966 William T. Howell (Acting)
1969 Dorothy Andrews Kabis
1971 Romana Acosta Banuelos

PATENT OFFICE

Commissioners

1836 Henry L. Ellsworth
1845 Edmund Burke
1849 Thomas Ewbank
1852 Silas H. Hodges
1853 Charles Mason
1857 Joseph Holt
1859 William D. Bishop
1860 Philip F. Thomas
1861 David P. Holloway
1865 Thomas C. Theaker
1868 Elisha Foote
1869 Samuel S. Fisher
1871 Mortimer D. Leggett
1875 John M. Thacher
1875 Robert H. Duell
1877 Ellis Spear
1878 Halbert E. Paine
1880 Edgar M. Marble
1883 Benjamin Butterworth
1885 Martin V.B. Montgomery
1887 Benton J. Hall
1889 Charles E. Mitchell
1891 William E. Simonds
1893 John S. Seymour
1897 Benjamin Butterworth
1898 Charles H. Duell
1901 Frederick I. Allen
1907 Edward B. Moore
1913 Thomas Ewing
1917 James T. Newton
1920 Robert F. Whitehead
1921 Thomas E. Robertson
1933 Conway P. Coe
1945 Casper W. Ooms
1947 Lawrence C. Kingsland
1949 John A. Marzall
1953 Robert C. Watson
1961 David L. Ladd
1964 Edward J. Brenner
1969 William E. Schuyler, Jr.
1971 Robert Gottschalk

PUBLIC HEALTH SERVICE

Surgeons General

1871 John M. Woodworth
1879 John B. Hammond
1891 Walter Wyman
1912 Rupert Blue
1920 Hugh S. Cumming
1936 Thomas Parran
1948 Leonard A. Scheele
1956 Leroy E. Burney
1961 Luther L. Terry
1965 William H. Stewart
1969 Jesse L. Steinfeld

SECURITIES AND EXCHANGE COMMISSION

Chairmen

1934 Joseph P. Kennedy
1935 James M. Landis
1937 William O. Douglas
1939 Jerome N. Frank
1941 Edward C. Eicher
1942 Ganson Purcell
1946 James J. Caffrey
1948 Edmond M. Hanrahan
1949 Harry A. McDonald
1952 Donald C. Cook
1953 Ralph H. Demmler
1955 J. Sinclair Armstrong
1957 Edward N. Gadsby
1961 William L. Cary
1964 Manuel F. Cohen
1969 Hamer H. Budge
1971 William J. Casey

SELECTIVE SERVICE SYSTEM

Directors

1940 Clarence A. Dykstra
1941 Lewis B. Hershey
1970 Curtis W. Tarr

SMALL BUSINESS ADMINISTRATION

Administrators

1953 William D. Mitchell
1954 Wendell B. Barnes
1959 Philip McCallum
1961 John E. Horne
1963 Eugene P. Foley
1966 Bernard L. Boutin
1967 Robert C. Moot
1968 Howard J. Samuels
1969 Hilary J. Sandoval, Jr.
1971 Thomas S. Kleppe

SOCIAL SECURITY ADMINISTRATION

(Established as the Social Security Board which was abolished in 1946 and later replaced by present agency.)

Chairmen

1935 John G. Winant
1937 Arthur J. Altmeyer

Commissioners

1946 Arthur J. Altmeyer
1953 John W. Tramburg
1954 Charles I. Schottland
1959 William L. Mitchell
1962 Robert M. Ball

TENNESSEE VALLEY AUTHORITY

Chairmen

1933 Arthur E. Morgan
1938 Harcourt A. Morgan
1941 David E. Lilienthal
1946 Gordon R. Clapp
1954 Herbert D. Vogel
1962 Aubrey J. Wagner

UNITED STATES CIVIL SERVICE COMMISSION

Presidents

1883 Dorman B. Eaton
1885 Alfred P. Edgerton
1886 Charles Lyman
1893 John R. Proctor
1904 John C. Black
1906 John A. McIlhenny
1919 Martin A. Morrison
1921 John H. Bartlett
1923 William C. Deming
1930 Thomas E. Campbell
1933 Harry B. Mitchell

Chairmen

1949 Harry B. Mitchell
1951 Robert Ramspeck
1953 Philip Young
1957 Harris Ellsworth
1959 Roger W. Jones
1961 John W. Macy, Jr.
1969 Robert E. Hampton

UNITED STATES COAST GUARD

Commandants

1915 Ellsworth P. Bertholf
1919 William E. Reynolds
1924 Frederick C. Billard
1932 Harry G. Hamlet
1936 Russell R. Waesche
1946 Joseph F. Farley
1950 Merlin O'Neill
1954 Alfred C. Richmond
1962 Edwin J. Roland
1966 Willard J. Smith
1970 Chester R. Bender

UNITED STATES INFORMATION AGENCY

Directors

1953 Theodore Streibert
1956 Arthur Larson
1957 George V. Allen
1961 Edward R. Murrow
1964 Carl Rowan
1965 Leonard H. Marks
1969 Frank Shakespeare

UNITED STATES POSTAL SERVICE

(Temporarily established as a branch of the Treasury Department in 1789 although the Postmaster General was not made a Cabinet member until 1829. The Post Office Department was reorganized as an independent federal agency in 1970.)

Postmasters General

1789 Samuel Osgood
1791 Timothy Pickering
1795 Joseph Habersham
1801 Gideon Granger
1814 Return J. Meigs, Jr.
1823 John McLean

(See Cabinet section (III) for Postmasters General from 1829 to 1970.)

1971 Edwin T. Klassen

UNITED STATES TARIFF COMMISSION

Chairmen

1917 Frank W. Taussig
1920 Thomas W. Page
1922 Thomas O. Marvin
1930 Edgar B. Brossard
1930 Henry P. Fletcher
1931 Robert L. O'Brien
1937 Raymond B. Stevens
1942 Oscar B. Ryder
1953 Edgar B. Brossard
1959 Joseph E. Talbot
1961 Ben Dorfman
1966 Paul Kaplowitz
1967 Stanley D. Metzger
1969 Glenn W. Sutton
1971 Chester L. Mize
1971 Catherine Bedell

XI

LOCAL GOVERNMENT

A listing of mayors and other chief executives of 75 cities selected on the basis of being state capitals, of having populations in excess of 500,000, or of having been among the 10 most populous in any census from 1800.

ALBANY, NEW YORK

1686 Pieter Schuyler
1694 Johannes Abeel
1695 Evert Bancker
1696 Dirck Ten Broeck
1698 Hendrick Hansen
1699 Pieter Van Brugh
1700 Johannes Bleecker
1701 Johannes Bleecker, Jr.
1702 Albert J. Ryckman
1703 Johannes Schuyler
1706 David Schuyler
1707 Evert Bancker
1709 Johannes Abeel
1710 Robert Livingston, Jr.
1719 Myndert Schuyler
1721 Pieter Van Brugh
1723 Myndert Schuyler
1725 Johannes Cuyler
1726 Rutger Bleecker
1729 Johannes De Peyster
1731 Johannes Hansen
1732 Johannes De Peyster
1733 Edward Holland
1741 Johannes Schuyler
1742 Cornelis Cuyler
1746 Dirck Ten Broeck
1748 Jacob C. Ten Eyck
1750 Robert Sanders
1754 Johannes Hansen
1756 Sybrant G. Van Schaick
1761 Volckert P. Douw
1770 Abraham C. Cuyler
1778 John Barclay
1779 Abraham Ten Broeck
1783 Johannes Beeckman
1786 John Lansing, Jr.
1789 Abraham Yates
1796 Abraham Ten Broeck
1799 Philip S. Van Rensselaer
1816 Elisha Jenkins
1819 Philip S. Van Rensselaer
1821 Charles E. Dudley
1824 Ambrose Spencer
1826 James Stevenson
1828 Charles E. Dudley
1829 John Townsend
1831 Francis Bloodgood
1832 John Townsend
1833 Francis Bloodgood
1834 Erastus Corning
1837 Teunis Van Vechten
1838 Jared L. Rathbone
1841 Teunis Van Vechten
1842 Barent P. Staats
1843 Friend Humphrey
1845 John K. Paige
1846 William Parmelee
1848 John Taylor
1849 Friend Humphrey
1850 Franklin Townsend
1851 Eli Perry
1854 William Parmelee
1855 Charles W. Godard
1856 Eli Perry
1860 George H. Thacher
1862 Eli Perry
1866 George H. Thacher
1868 Charles E. Bleecker
1870 George H. Thacher
1874 John G. Burch
1875 Edmund L. Judson
1876 A. Bleecker Banks
1878 Michael N. Nolan
1883 John Swinburne
1884 A. Bleecker Banks
1886 John B. Thacher
1888 Edward A. Maher
1890 James M. Manning
1894 Oren E. Wilson
1896 John B. Thacher
1898 Thomas J. Van Alstyne
1900 James H. Blessing
1902 Charles H. Gaus
1909 Henry F. Snyder
1910 James B. McEwan
1914 Joseph W. Stevens
1918 James R. Watt
1922 William S. Hackett
1926 John B. Thacher II
1941 Herman F. Hoogkamp
1942 Erastus Corning II

ANNAPOLIS, MARYLAND

1708 Amos Garrett
1720 Thomas Larkin
1721 Benjamin Tasker
1722 Vachel Denton
1726 Benjamin Tasker
1727 Vachel Denton
1749 John Ross
1753 Michael McNamar
1754 Benjamin Tasker
1755 John Brice
1756 Benjamin Tasker
1757 John Bullen
1758 John Ross
1759 George Stewart
1760 Michael McNamar
1761 Stephen Bordley
1762 John Brice
1763 George Stewart
1764 Daniel Dulany
1765 John Ross
1766 Walter Dulany
1767 Upton Scott
1768 Allen Quynn
1780 John Brice
1781 John Bullen
1782 James Brice
1783 Jeremiah T. Chase
1784 Nicholas Carroll
1785 Robert Couden
1786 Allen Quynn
1788 James Brice
1789 John Bullen
1790 Nicholas Carroll
1791 Robert Couden
1792 Allen Quynn
1793 John Bullen
1794 James Williams
1795 William Pinkney
1800 John Davidson
1801 James Williams
1802 Allen Quynn
1803 Samuel Ridout
1804 John Johnson
1805 James Williams
1806 Samuel Ridout
1807 Burton Whetcroft
1808 John Kelly
1809 Burton Whetcroft
1810 John Johnson
1811 Nicholas Brewer
1812 Gideon White
1813 John Randall
1814 Nicholas Brewer
1815 John Randall
1816 Nicholas Brewer
1817 John Randall
1818 Nicholas Brewer
1819 Lewis Duvall
1823 James Boyle
1825 Richard Harwood
1828 Dennis Claude
1837 John Miller
1840 Alexander C. Magruder
1843 Richard Swann
1848 Abram Claude
1851 Brice T. B. Worthington
1852 Richard R. Goodwin
1853 Dennis Claude
1855 Nicholas Brewer, Jr.
1856 Richard Swann
1858 Joseph Brown
1859 William Harwood
1860 John R. Magruder
1864 Solomon Phillips
1865 Richard R. Goodwin
1866 Richard Swann
1867 Abram Claude
1869 Augustus Gassway
1870 John T. E. Hyde
1871 James Munroe
1875 Arthur W. Wells
1877 James H. Brown
1879 Thomas E. Martin
1883 Abram Claude
1889 James H. Brown
1893 John H. Thomas
1897 Richard Green
1899 Edwin A. Seidewitz
1901 Charles A. Dubois
1903 Samuel Jones
1905 John DeP. Douw
1907 Gordon H. Claude
1909 James F. Strange
1919 John J. Levy
1921 Samuel Jones
1923 Charles W. Smith
1925 Allen B. Howard
1927 Charles W. Smith
1929 Walter E. Quenstedt
1935 Louis N. Phipps
1939 George W. Haley
1941 William U. McCready
1949 Roscoe C. Rowe
1952 Arthur G. Ellington
1961 Joseph H. Griscom, Sr.
1965 Roger W. Moyer

ATLANTA, GEORGIA

1848 Moses W. Formwalt
1849 Benjamin F. Bomar
1850 Willis Buell
1851 Jonathan Norcross
1852 Thomas F. Gibbs
1853 John F. Mims
William Markham
1854 William M. Butt
1855 Allison Nelson
John Glen
1856 William Ezzard
1858 Luther J. Glenn
1860 William Ezzard
1861 Jard I. Whitaker
Thomas F. Lowe
1862 James M. Calhoun
1866 James E. Williams
1869 William H. Hulsey
1870 William Ezzard
1871 Dennis F. Hammond
1872 John H. James
1873 Cicero C. Hammock
1874 S. B. Spencer
1875 Cicero C. Hammock
1877 Nedom L. Angier
1879 William L. Calhoun
1881 James W. English
1883 John B. Goodwin
1885 George Hillyer
1887 John T. Cooper
1889 John T. Glenn
1891 William A. Hemphill
1893 John B. Goodwin
1895 Porter King
1897 Charles A. Collier
1899 James G. Woodward
1901 Livingston Mims
1903 Evan P. Howell
1905 James G. Woodward
1907 W. R. Joyner
1909 Robert F. Maddox
1911 Courtland S. Winn
1913 James G. Woodward
1917 Asa G. Candler
1919 James L. Key
1923 Walter A. Sims
1927 Isaac N. Ragsdale
1931 James L. Key
1937 William B. Hartsfield
1941 Roy LeCraw
1943 William B. Hartsfield
1962 Ivan Allen, Jr.
1970 Sam Massell

AUGUSTA, MAINE

1850 Alfred Redington
1852 John A. Pettingill
1854 Samuel Cony
1855 Joseph W. Patterson
1856 Albert M. Dole
1857 James W. North
1861 Sylvanus Caldwell
1863 William T. Johnson
1864 Sylvanus Caldwell
1865 Joseph W. Patterson
1866 Sylvanus Caldwell
1867 Joseph W. Patterson
1868 Daniel Williams
1869 Samuel Titcomb
1871 Joseph J. Eveleth
1874 James W. North
1875 Daniel Cony
1876 Charles E. Nash
1880 Peleg O. Vickery
1883 Alden W. Philbrook
1884 Seth C. Whitehouse
1885 George E. Weeks
1886 George E. Macomber
1889 Samuel W. Lane
1891 John W. Chase
1893 Moses R. Leighton
1894 Charles A. Milliken
1896 Winfield S. Choate
1898 J. Manchester Haynes
1899 Samuel W. Lane
1901 Lendall Titcomb
1903 Gustavus A. Robertson
1905 Charles S. Hichborn
1906 Frederick W. Plaisted
1909 Treby Johnson
1910 Frederick W. Plaisted
1911 Reuel J. Noyes
1913 Elmer E. Newbert
1915 Blaine S. Viles
1917 Willis E. Swift
1919 Burleigh Martin
1921 Sanford L. Fogg
1923 Ernest L. McLean
1929 Robert A. Cony
1934 Frederick G. Payne
1941 Sanford L. Fogg, Jr.

1943 Levi T. Williams
1945 Sanford L. Fogg, Jr.
1947 Charles P. Nelson
1949 Richard B. Sanborn
1953 Brooks Brown, Jr.
1957 H. Lloyd Carey
1960 Sylvio J. Gilbert
1969 Anthony Violette
1971 Stanley E. Sproul

AUSTIN, TEXAS

1839 Edwin N. Waller
1851 S. G. Haynie
1852 George J. Durham
1853 Thomas W. Ward
1854 John S. Ford
1855 J. T. Cleveland
1856 E. R. Peck
1857 Thomas E. Sneed
1858 B. F. Carter
1860 James W. Smith
1863 S. G. Haynie
1865 Thomas W. Ward
1866 W. H. Carr
1867 Leander Brown
1871 John W. Glenn
1872 T. B. Wheeler
1877 J. C. De Gress
1880 L. M. Crooker
1881 W. A. Saylor
1884 J. W. Robertson
1887 Joseph Nalle
1889 John McDonald
1895 Lewis Hancock
1897 John D. McCall
1901 R. E. White
1905 W. D. Shelley
1907 F. M. Maddox
1909 A. P. Woolridge
1919 W. D. Yett
1926 P. W. McFadden
1933 Tom Miller
1949 Taylor Glass
1951 W. S. Drake, Jr.
1953 C. A. McAden
1955 Tom Miller
1961 Lester E. Palmer
1967 Harry Akin
1969 Travis LaRue
1971 Roy Butler

BALTIMORE, MARYLAND

1797 James Calhoun
1804 Thorowgood Smith
1808 Edward Johnson
1814 Vacant
1816 George Stiles
1819 Edward Johnson
1820 John Montgomery
1822 Edward Johnson
1824 John Montgomery
1826 Jacob Small
1831 William Steuart
1832 Jesse Hunt
1835 Samuel Smith
1838 Sheppard Leakin
1840 Samuel Brady
1842 Solomon Hillen, Jr.
1843 James O. Law
1844 Jacob G. Davies
1848 Elijah Stansbury
1850 J. Hanson Jerome
1852 John S. Hollins
1854 Samuel Hinks
1856 Thomas Swann
1860 George W. Brown
1861 John C. Blackburn
1862 John L. Chapman
1867 Robert T. Banks
1871 Joshua Vansant
1875 F. C. Latrobe
1877 George P. Kane
1878 F. C. Latrobe
1881 William P. Whyte
1883 F. C. Latrobe
1885 James Hodges
1887 F. C. Latrobe
1889 Robert C. Davidson
1891 F. C. Latrobe
1895 Alcaeus Hooper
1897 William T. Malster
1899 Thomas G. Hayes
1903 Robert M. McLane
1904 E. Clay Timanus
1907 J. Barry Mahool
1911 James H. Preston
1919 William F. Broening
1923 Howard W. Jackson
1927 William F. Broening
1931 Howard W. Jackson
1943 Theodore R. McKeldin
1947 Thomas D'Alesandro, Jr.
1959 J. Harold Grady
1962 Philip H. Goodman
1963 Theodore R. McKeldin
1967 Thomas J. D'Alesandro III
1972 William D. Schaefer

BATON ROUGE, LOUISIANA

1850 John R. Dufrocq
1855 Joseph Monget
1857 Edward Cousinard
1859 James E. Elam
1862 B. F. Bryan
1865 Jordan Holt
James E. Elam
1869 O. P. Skolfield
1870 James E. Elam
1872 Henry Schorten
James E. Elam
1873 Henry Schorten
1876 Leon Justremski
1882 J. C. Charrotte
1883 William S. Booth
1884 G. L. Vay
1888 B. F. Bryan
1890 G. L. Vay
1894 B. F. Bryan
1896 John J. Wax
1898 Robert A. Hart
1902 Robert L. Pruyn
1903 W. H. Bynum
1910 Jules Roux
1913 Alex Grouchy, Jr.
1922 Turner Bynum
1923 W. H. Bynum
1941 Fred S. LeBlanc
1944 Powers Higginbottom
1953 Jesse L. Webb, Jr.
1956 Mrs. Jesse L. Webb, Jr.
1957 John Christian
1965 Woodrow W. Dumas

BISMARCK, NORTH DAKOTA

1885 I. P. Hunt
1887 William A. Bentley
1890 I. P. Baker
1891 William A. Bentley
1892 Edward S. Allen
1894 A. N. Leslie
1896 Edward G. Patterson
1901 W. H. Webb, Jr.
1905 F. R. Smythe
1909 E. A. Williams
1913 A. W. Lucas
1921 A. P. Lenhart
1937 Obert Olson
1939 Neil Churchill
1947 A. P. Lenhart
1950 Tom Kleppe
1954 Evan Lips
1964 E. V. Lahr

BOISE, IDAHO

1867 H. E. Prickett
1868 Thos. B. Hart
1869 Charles Himrod
1872 Geo. H. Twitchell
1874 John Lemp
1876 T. E. Logan
1879 Charles Himrod
1880 Cy Jacobs
1881 C. P. Bilderback
1883 J. A. Pinney
1885 Sol Hasbrook
1886 J. W. Huston
1887 Peter J. Pefley
1889 J. A. Pinney
1892 Peter Sonna
1895 W. E. Pierce
1897 Moses Alexander
1899 J. H. Richards
1901 M. Alexander
1903 James H. Hawley
1906 J. A. Pinney
1907 John M. Haines
1909 J. T. Pence
1911 Harry K. Fritchman
1912 Arthur Hodges
1915 Jeremiah W. Robinson
1916 S. H. Hays
1919 Ern G. Eagleson
1921 Eugene B. Sherman
1925 Ern G. Eagleson
1927 Walter F. Hansen
1929 J. P. Pope
1931 Ross Cady
1933 J. J. McCue
1935 Byron E. Hyatt
1936 J. L. Edlefsen
1939 James L. Straight
1941 H. Westerman Whillock
1942 Austin A. Walker
1945 Sam S. Griffin
1946 H. Westerman Whillock
1947 Potter P. Howard
1951 Russell E. Edlefsen
1959 Robert Day
1961 Eugene W. Shellworth
1965 Jay S. Amyx

BOSTON, MASSACHUSETTS

1822 John Phillips
1823 Josiah Quincy
1829 Harrison G. Otis
1832 Charles Wells
1834 Theodore Lyman, Jr.
1836 Samuel T. Armstrong
1837 Samuel A. Eliot
1840 Jonathan Chapman
1843 Martin Brimmer
1845 Thomas A. Davis
1846 Josiah Quincy, Jr.
1849 John P. Bigelow
1852 Benjamin Seaver
1854 Jerome V. C. Smith
1856 Alexander H. Rice
1858 Frederic W. Lincoln, Jr.
1861 Joseph M. Wightman
1863 Frederic W. Lincoln, Jr.
1867 Otis Norcross
1868 Nathaniel B. Shurtleff
1871 William Gaston
1873 Henry L. Pierce
Leonard R. Cutter
1874 Samuel C. Cobb
1877 Frederick O. Prince
1878 Henry L. Pierce
1879 Frederick O. Prince
1882 Samuel A. Green
1883 Albert Palmer
1884 Augustus P. Martin
1885 Hugh O'Brien
1889 Thomas N. Hart
1891 Nathan Matthews, Jr.
1895 Edwin U. Curtis
1896 Josiah Quincy
1900 Thomas N. Hart
1902 Patrick A. Collins
1905 Daniel A. Whelton
1906 John F. Fitzgerald
1908 George A. Hibbard
1910 John F. Fitzgerald
1914 James M. Curley
1918 Andrew J. Peters
1922 James M. Curley
1926 Malcolm E. Nichols
1930 James M. Curley
1934 Frederick W. Mansfield
1938 Maurice J. Tobin
1945 John E. Kerrigan
1946 James M. Curley
1947 John B. Hynes
1960 John F. Collins
1968 Kevin H. White

BUFFALO, NEW YORK

1832 Ebenezer Johnson
1833 Major A. Andrews
1834 Ebenezer Johnson
1835 Hiram Pratt
1836 Samuel Wilkeson
1837 Josiah Trowbridge
Pierre A. Barker
1838 Ebenezer Walden
1839 Hiram Pratt
1840 Sheldon Thompson
1841 Isaac R. Harrington
1842 George W. Clinton
1843 Joseph G. Masten
1844 William Ketchum
1845 Joseph G. Masten

1846 Solomon G. Haven
1847 Elbridge G. Spaulding
1848 Orlando Allen
1849 Hiram Barton
1850 Henry K. Smith
1851 James Wadsworth
1852 Hiram Barton
1853 Eli Cook
1856 Frederick Stephens
1858 Timothy T. Lockwood
1860 Franklin A. Alberger
1862 William G. Fargo
1866 Chandler J. Wells
1870 Alexander Brush
1874 Louis P. Dayton
1876 Philip Becker
1878 Solomon Scheu
1880 Alexander Brush
1882 Grover Cleveland
Marcus M. Drake
Harmon S. Cutting
1883 John B. Manning
1884 Jonathan Scoville
1886 Philip Becker
1890 Charles F. Bishop
1895 Edgar B. Jewett
1898 Conrad Diehl
1902 Erastus C. Knight
1906 James N. Adam
1910 Louis P. Fuhrmann
1918 George S. Buck
1922 Frank X. Schwab
1930 Charles E. Roesch
1934 George J. Zimmerman
1938 Thomas L. Holling
1942 Joseph J. Kelly
1946 Bernard J. Dowd
1950 Joseph Mruk
1954 Steven Pankow
1958 Frank A. Sedita
1962 Chester W. Kowal
1966 Frank A. Sedita

CHARLESTON, SOUTH CAROLINA

Intendants

1783 Richard Hutson
Arnoldus Vander Horst
1786 John F. Grimke
1788 Rawlins Lowndes
1789 Thomas Jones
1790 Arnoldus Vander Horst
1792 John Huger
1794 John B. Holmes
1795 John Edwards
1797 Henry W. deSaussure
1799 Thomas Roper
1801 John Ward
1802 David Deas
1803 John Drayton
1804 Thomas Winstanley
1805 Charles B. Cochran
1806 John Dawson, Jr.
1808 Benjamin Boyd
William Rouse
1810 Thomas McCalla
1812 Thomas Bennett
1813 Thomas Rhett Smith
1815 Elias Horry
1817 John Geddes
1819 Daniel Stevens
1820 Elias Horry
1821 James Hamilton, Jr.
1823 John Geddes
1824 Samuel Prioleau
1825 Joseph Johnson
1827 John Gadsden
1829 Henry L. Pinckney
1830 James R. Pringle
1831 Henry L. Pinckney
1833 Edward W. North

Mayors

1836 Robert W. Hayne
1837 Henry L. Pinckney
1840 Jacob F. Mintzing
1842 John Schnierle
1846 T. Leger Hutchinson
1850 John Schnierle
1852 T. Leger Hutchinson
1855 W. Porcher Miles
1857 Charles Macbeth
1865 Peter C. Gaillard
1868 Gilbert Pillsbury
1871 John A. Wagener
1873 G. I. Cunningham
1877 W. W. Sale
1879 William A. Courtenay
1887 George D. Bryan
1891 John F. Ficken
1895 J. Adger Smyth
1903 R. Goodwin Rhett
1911 John P. Grace
1915 Tristram T. Hyde
1919 John P. Grace
1923 Thomas P. Stoney
1931 Burnet R. Maybank
1938 Henry W. Lockwood
1944 E. Edward Wehman, Jr.
1947 William M. Morrison
1959 J. Palmer Gaillard, Jr.

CHARLESTON, WEST VIRGINIA

1861 Jacob Goshorn
1865 John A. Truslow
1867 George Ritter
1869 John Williams
1870 J. W. Wingfield
1871 H. C. Dickinson
John P. Hale
1872 John Williams
1873 C. P. Synder
1875 John C. Ruby
1877 C. J. Botkin
1881 R. R. Delaney
1883 J. D. Baines
1885 J. H. Huling
1887 Joseph L. Fry
1891 J. B. Pemberton
1893 E. W. Staunton
1895 J. A. de Gruyter
1899 W. Herman Smith
1900 John B. Floyd
1901 George S. Morgan
1903 C. E. Rudesill
1905 John A. Jarrett
1907 James A. Holley
1913 J. F. Bedell
1914 O. A. Petty
1915 George E. Breece
1917 G. A. MacQueen
1918 R. L. Walker
1919 Grant P. Hall
1923 William W. Wertz
1931 R. P. Devan
1935 D. Boone Dawson
1947 R. Carl Andrews
1951 J. T. Copenhaver
1959 John A. Shanklin
1967 Elmer H. Dodson
1971 John G. Hutchinson

CHEYENNE, WYOMING

Mayors

1867 H. M. Hook
1868 L. Murrin
1869 W. M. Slaughter

City Council Presidents

1869 J. H. Martin
1871 Jervis Joslin
1872 M. Sloan
1873 M. V. Boughten
1874 George Cassels
1875 J. C. Whipple
1876 L. R. Bresnahen
1877 Dwight Fisk

Mayors

1878 L. R. Bresnahen
1880 F. E. Addoms
1881 J. M. Carey
1885 F. E. Warren
1885 A. H. Reel
1887 C. W. Riner
1891 L. R. Bresnahen
1893 Edward F. Stahle
1895 Samuel Merrill
1897 W. R. Schnitger
1901 J. L. Murray
1903 M. P. Keefe
1904 D. W. Gill
1907 P. S. Cook
1911 L. R. Bresnahen
1913 D. W. Gill
1914 R. N. Lafountaine
1918 Edward W. Stone
1920 Ed R. Taylor
1924 Archie Allison
1926 C. W. Riner
1930 Cal Holliday
1932 J. F. Weybrecht
1934 Archie Allison
1940 Ed Warren
1944 Ira L. Hanna
Bruce S. Jones
1946 John J. McInerney
1948 Ben Nelson
1951 Ed Warren
1952 R. E. Cheever
1954 Val S. Christensen
1958 Worth Story
1962 Bill Nation
1966 Herbert Kingham
1968 George R. Cox
1969 Floyd Holland

CHICAGO, ILLINOIS

1837 William B. Ogden
1838 Buckner S. Morris
1839 Benjamin W. Raymond
1840 Alexander Loyd
1841 Francis C. Sherman
1842 Benjamin W. Raymond
1843 Augustus Garrett
1844 Alson S. Sherman
1845 Augustus Garrett
1846 John P. Chapin
1847 James Curtiss
1848 James H. Woodworth
1850 James Curtiss
1851 Walter S. Gurnee
1853 Charles M. Gray
1854 Isaac L. Milliken
1855 Levi D. Boone
1856 Thomas Dyer
1857 John Wentworth
1858 John C. Haines
1860 John Wentworth
1861 Julian S. Rumsey
1862 Francis C. Sherman
1865 John B. Rice
1869 Roswell B. Mason
1871 Joseph Medill
1873 Harvey D. Colvin
1876 Monroe Heath
1879 Carter H. Harrison, Sr.
1887 John A. Roche
1889 De Witt C. Cregier
1891 Hempstead Washburne
1893 Carter H. Harrison, Sr.
George B. Swift
John P. Hopkins
1895 George B. Swift
1897 Carter H. Harrison, Jr.
1905 Edward F. Dunne
1907 Fred A. Busse
1911 Carter H. Harrison, Jr.
1915 William H. Thompson
1923 William E. Dever
1927 William H. Thompson
1931 Anton J. Cermak
1933 Frank J. Corr (Acting)
Edward J. Kelly
1947 Martin H. Kennelly
1955 Richard J. Daley

CINCINNATI, OHIO

1815 William Corry
1819 Isaac G. Burnet
1831 Elisha Hotchkiss
1833 Samuel W. Davies
1843 Henry E. Spencer
1851 Mark P. Taylor
1853 David T. Snelbaker
1855 James J. Faran
1857 Nicholas W. Thomas
1859 Richard M. Bishop
1861 George Hatch
1863 Leonard A. Harris
1867 Charles F. Wilstach
1869 John F. Torrence
1871 S. S. Davis
1873 George W. C. Johnston
1877 Robert M. Moore
1879 Charles Jacob
1881 William Means
1883 Thomas J. Stephens
1885 Amor Smith, Jr.

1889 John B. Mosby
1894 John A. Caldwell
1897 Gustav Tafel
1900 Julius Fleischman
1906 Edward J. Dempsey
1908 Leopold Markbreit
1909 John Galvin
1910 Louis Schwab
1912 Henry T. Hunt
1914 Frederick S. Spiegel
1916 George Puchta
1918 John Galvin
1922 George P. Carrel
1926 Murray Seasongood
1930 Russell Wilson
1938 James G. Stewart
1947 Carl W. Rich
1948 Albert D. Cash
1951 Carl W. Rich
1953 Edward N. Waldvogel
1954 Dorothy N. Dolbey
Carl W. Rich
1955 Charles P. Taft
1957 Donald D. Clancy
1960 Walton Bachrach
1967 Eugene P. Ruehlmann
1971 Thomas Luken

CLEVELAND, OHIO

Mayors

1836 John W. Willey
1838 Joshua Mills
1840 Nicholas Dohrstader
1841 John W. Allen
1842 Joshua Mills
1843 Nelson Haywood
1844 Samuel Starkweather
1846 George Hoadley
1847 Joshua Hadley
1848 Lorenzo A. Kelsey
1849 Flavel Bingham
1850 William Case
1852 Abner C. Brownell
1855 William B. Castle
1857 Samuel Starkweather
1859 George B. Senter
1861 Edward S. Flint
1863 Irving U. Masters
1865 Herman A. Chapin
1867 Stephen Buher
1871 F. W. Pelton
1873 Charles W. Otis
1875 Nathan F. Payne
1877 William G. Rose
1879 P. R. Herrick
1883 John H. Farley
1885 George W. Gardner
1887 Brenton D. Babcock
1889 George W. Gardner
1891 William G. Rose
1893 Robert Blee
1895 Robert E. McKisson
1899 John H. Farley
1901 Tom L. Johnson
1910 Herman Baehr
1912 Newton D. Baker
1916 Harry L. Davis
1920 William S. FitzGerald
1921 Fred Kohler

City Managers

1923 William R. Hopkins
1930 Daniel E. Morgan

Mayors

1931 Harold H. Burton
1932 Ray T. Miller
1933 Harry L. Davis
1935 Harold H. Burton
1940 Edward Blythin
1941 Frank Lausche
1945 Thomas Burke
1953 Anthony Celebrezze
1962 Ralph S. Locher
1967 Carl B. Stokes
1972 Ralph J. Perk

COLUMBIA, SOUTH CAROLINA

Intendants

1806 John Taylor
1807 Abraham Nott
Claiborne Clifton
1808 John Hooker
Daniel Faust
1809 Simon Taylor
1810 Robert Stark
1811 Simon Taylor
1812 Daniel Faust
1815 William E. Hayne
1816 James Gregg
1817 Daniel Morgan
1818 James T. Goodwyn
1822 David J. McCord
1823 James T. Goodwyn
1824 David J. McCord
1825 James T. Goodwyn
1826 William F. deSaussure
1828 E. H. Maxcy
1830 William C. Preston
1831 William C. Clifton
1832 E. H. Maxcy
1833 M. H. DeLeon
1836 John Bryce
1839 R. W. Gibbes
1841 Benjamin T. Elmore
R. H. Goodwin
1842 William M. Myers
1845 William B. Stanley
1846 Joel Stevenson
1847 Edward Sill
1850 Henry Lyons
1851 A. H. Gladden
1853 William Maybin

Mayors

1855 Edward J. Arthur
1857 James D. Tradewell
1859 Allen J. Green
1861 John H. Boatwright
1863 Thomas J. Goodwyn
1865 James G. Gibbes
1866 Theodore Start
1868 John McKenzie
1870 John Alexander
1876 John Agnew
1878 W. B. Stanley
1880 R. O'Neale
1882 John T. Rhett
1890 F. W. McMaster
1892 W. C. Fisher
1894 W. McB. Sloan
1898 T. J. Lipscomb
1900 F. S. Earle
1904 T. H. Gibbes
1908 W. S. Reamer
1910 W. H. Gibbes
1914 L. A. Griffith
1918 R. J. Blalock
1922 W. A. Coleman
1926 L. B. Owens
1941 Fred D. Marshall
1946 Frank C. Owens
1950 J. Macfie Anderson
1954 J. Clarence Dreher, Jr.
1958 Lester L. Bates
1970 John T. Campbell

COLUMBUS, OHIO

1816 Jarvis Pike
1818 John Kerr
1820 Eli C. King
1823 John Longhenry
1824 William T. Martin
1827 James Robinson
1828 William Long
1833 Philo H. Olmstead
1834 John Brooks
1836 Warren Jenkins
1838 Philo H. Olmstead
1840 John G. Miller
1842 Abraham J. McDowell
1843 Smithson E. Wright
1845 Alexander Patton
1846 A. S. Decker
1847 Alexander Patton
1850 Lorenzo English
1861 Wray Thomas
1865 James G. Bull
1869 George W. Meeker
1871 James G. Bull
1875 John H. Heitman
1879 G. G. Collins
1881 George S. Peters
1883 Charles C. Walcutt
1887 Philip H. Bruck
1891 George J. Karb
1895 Cotton H. Allen
1897 Samuel L. Black
1899 Samuel J. Schwartz
1901 John H. Hinkle
1903 Robert H. Jeffrey
1906 DeWitt C. Badger
1908 Charles A. Bond
1910 George S. Marshall
1912 George J. Karb
1920 James J. Thomas
1932 Henry W. Worley
1936 Myron B. Gessaman
1940 Floyd F. Green
1944 James A. Rhodes
1953 Robert T. Ostreicher
1954 Maynard E. Sensenbrenner
1960 W. Ralston Westlake
1964 Maynard E. Sensenbrenner

CONCORD, NEW HAMPSHIRE

1853 Joseph Low
1855 Rufus Clements
1956 John Abbott
1859 Moses T. Willard
1861 Moses Humphrey
1863 Benjamin F. Gale
1865 Moses Humphrey
1866 John Abbott
1868 Lyman D. Stevens
1870 Abraham G. Jones
1872 John Kimball
1876 George A. Pillsbury
1878 Horace A. Brown
1880 George A. Cummings
1883 Edgar H. Woodman
1887 John E. Robertson
1889 Stillman Humphrey
1891 Henry W. Clapp
1893 Parsons B. Cogswell
1895 Henry Robinson
1897 Albert B. Woodworth
1899 Nathaniel Martin
1901 Harry G. Sargent
1903 Charles R. Corning
1909 Charles J. French
1916 Nathaniel W. Hobbs
1918 Charles J. French
1920 Henry E. Chamberlin
1924 Willis H. Flint
1926 Fred N. Marden
1928 Olin H. Chase
Robert W. Brown
1934 John W. Storrs
1942 Charles J. McKee
1946 Charles C. Davie
1948 Charles J. McKee
1950 Shelby Walker
1954 Herbert W. Rainie
1958 Charles P. Johnson
1962 Charles C. Davie
1966 J. Herbert Quinn
1967 William P. Gove
1968 John E. Henchey
(City Manager)
1970 Malcolm McLane

DALLAS, TEXAS

1856 Samuel B. Pryor
1857 John M. Crockett
1858 Isaac Naylor
A. D. Rice
1859 John M. Crockett
1860 J. L. Smith
1861 Thomas E. Sherwood
1862 John W. Lane
1868 Benjamin Long
1870 Henry S. Ervay
1872 Benjamin Long
1875 W. L. Cabell
1876 John D. Kerfoot
1877 W. L. Cabell
1879 J. M. Thurman
1881 John Stone
1883 W. L. Cabell
1885 John Henry Brown
1887 W. C. Conner
1895 F. P. Holland
1897 Bryan T. Barry
1898 John H. Traylor
1900 Benjamin E. Cabell
1904 Bryan T. Barry
1906 Curtis P. Smith
1907 S. J. Hay
1911 W. M. Holland
1915 Henry D. Lindsley
1917 Joe E. Lawther
1919 Frank W. Wozencraft
1921 Sawnie R. Aldredge

1923 L. Blaylock
1927 R. E. Burt
1929 J. Waddy Tate
1931 T. L. Bradford
1933 Charles E. Turner
1935 George Sergeant
1937 George A. Sprague
1939 Woodall Rogers
1947 J. R. Temple
1949 Wallace H. Savage
1951 J. B. Adoue, Jr.
1953 R. L. Thornton
1961 Earle Cabell
1964 Erik Jonsson
1971 Wes Wise

DENVER, COLORADO

1859 John C. Moore
1861 Charles A. Cook
1863 Amos Steck
1864 Hiram J. Brendlinger
1865 George T. Clark
1866 Milton M. DeLano
1868 William M. Clayton
1869 Baxter B. Stiles
1871 John Harper
1872 Joseph E. Bates
1873 Francis M. Case
1874 William J. Barker
1876 Richard G. Buckingham
1877 Baxter B. Stiles
1878 Richard Sopris
1881 Robert Morris
1883 John L. Routt
1885 Joseph E. Bates
1887 William S. Lee
1889 Wolfe Londoner
1891 Platt Rogers
1893 Marion D. Van Horn
1895 Thomas S. McMurry
1899 Henry V. Johnson
1901 Robert R. Wright
1904 Robert W. Speer
1912 Henry J. Arnold
1913 James M. Perkins
1915 William H. Sharpley
1916 Robert W. Speer
1918 William F. R. Mills
1919 Dewey C. Bailey
1923 Benjamin F. Stapleton
1931 George D. Begole
1935 Benjamin F. Stapleton
1947 James Q. Newton
1955 Will F. Nicholson
1959 Richard Y. Batterton
1963 Thomas G. Currigan
1969 William H. McNichols, Jr.

DES MOINES, IOWA

1852 Thompson Bird
1853 B. Luce
1854 L. P. Sherman
1855 B. Granger
1856 W. DeFord
1857 C. W. Nash
W. H. McHenry
1858 H. E. Lamereaux
1859 R. L. Tidrick
1860 P. H. W. Latshaw
1861 Ira Cook
W. S. Barnes
1862 Thomas Cavenaugh
1863 W. H. Leas
1865 G. W. Cleveland
1868 S. F. Spofford
1869 J. H. Hatch
1871 Martin Tuttle
1872 J. P. Foster
1873 G. H. Turner
1874 A. Newton
1876 G. H. Turner
1877 George Sneer
1880 W. H. Merritt
1878 George Sneer
1882 P. V. Carey
1886 J. H. Phillips
1888 W. L. Carpenter
1890 J. H. Campbell
1892 C. C. Lane
1894 Isaac L. Hillis
1896 John MacVicar
1900 J. J. Hartenbower
1902 J. M. Brenton
1904 George W. Mattern
1908 A. J. Mathis
1910 James R. Hanna
1916 John MacVicar
1918 Thomas Fairweather
1920 H. H. Barton
1922 C. M. Garver
1926 Fred H. Hunter
1928 John MacVicar
E. H. Muloch
1930 Parker L. Crouch
1932 Dwight N. Lewis
1936 Joseph E. Allen
1938 Dwight N. Lewis
Mark L. Conkling
1942 John MacVicar, Jr.
1948 Heck Ross
1950 A. B. Chambers
1952 Allan W. Denny
1954 Joseph Van Dresser
1956 Ray Mills
1958 Charles F. Iles
1960 Reinhold O. Carlson
1962 Charles F. Iles
1966 George C. Whitmer
1968 Thomas N. Urban, Jr.

DETROIT, MICHIGAN

1824 John R. Williams
1826 Henry J. Hunt
Jonathon Kearsley
1827 John Biddle
1829 Jonathon Kearsley
1830 John R. Williams
1831 Marshall Chapin
1832 Levi Cook
1833 Marshall Chapin
1834 C. C. Trowbridge
Andrew Mack
1835 Levi Cook
1837 Henry Howard
1838 Augustus A. Porter
1839 De Garmo Jones
1840 Zina Pitcher
1842 Douglas Houghton
1843 Zina Pitcher
1844 John R. Williams
1847 James A. Van Dyke
1848 Frederick Buhl
1849 Charles Howard
1850 John LaDue
1851 Zachariah Chandler
1852 John H. Harmon
1854 Oliver M. Hyde
1855 Henry Ledyard
1856 Oliver M. Hyde
1858 John Patton
1860 Christian H. Buhl
1862 William C. Duncan
1864 Kirkland C. Barker
1866 Merrill I. Mills
1868 William W. Wheaton
1872 Hugh Moffat
1876 Alexander Lewis
1878 George C. Langdon
1880 William G. Thompson
1884 S. B. Grummond
1886 M. H. Chamberlain
1888 John Pridgeon, Jr.
1890 H. S. Pingree
1897 William Richert
William C. Maybury
1905 George P. Codd
1907 William B. Thompson
1909 Philip Breitmeyer
1911 William B. Thompson
1913 Oscar B. Marx
1919 James Couzens
1922 John C. Lodge
1923 Frank E. Doremus
1924 Joseph A. Martin
John C. Lodge
John W. Smith
1928 John C. Lodge
1930 Charles Bowles
Frank Murphy
1933 Frank Couzens
1938 Richard W. Reading
1940 Edward J. Jeffries, Jr.
1948 Eugene I. Van Antwerp
1950 Albert E. Cobo
1957 Louis C. Miriani
1962 Jerome P. Cavanagh
1970 Roman S. Gribbs

FRANKFORT, KENTUCKY

1849 Phillip Swigert
1868 S. I. M. Major
1871 E. H. Taylor, Jr.
1877 William S. Chinn
1879 S. I. M. Major
1881 E. H. Taylor, Jr.
1891 Louis Mangan
1892 Richard Tobin
1894 Ira Julian
1898 W. S. Dehoney
1902 J. S. Darnell
1906 E. E. Hume
1910 James Polsgrove
1914 Joseph Rupert
1918 W. S. Rosson
1922 D. D. Smith
1926 C. T. Coleman
1930 T. E. Kenny
1934 C. T. Coleman
1938 D. D. Smith
1942 C. T. Coleman
1946 A. C. Jones
1950 C. T. Coleman
1954 Robert C. Yount
1958 John Gerard
1960 Paul Judd
1962 J. W. Flynn
1967 Farnham F. Dudgeon (Acting)
1968 Frank W. Sower

HARRISBURG, PENNSYLVANIA

1860 William H. Hepner
1863 Augustus L. Roumfort
1866 Oliver Edwards
1869 William W. Hayes
1870 George B. Cole
1871 William K. Verbeke
1873 Jacob D. Boas
1875 John D. Patterson
1881 John C. Herman
1883 Simon C. Wilson
1886 Samuel W. Fleming
1887 John A. Fritchey
1893 Maurice C. Eby
1896 John D. Patterson
1899 John A. Fritchey
1902 Vance C. McCormick
1905 Edward Z. Gross
1908 Ezra S. Meals
1912 John K. Royal
1916 Ezra S. Meals
1917 William L. Gorgas
Charles A. Miller
William L. Gorgas
J. William Bowman
Daniel L. Keister
1920 George A. Hoverter
1936 John A. F. Hall
1940 Howard E. Milliken
1948 Claude R. Robins
1956 Nolan F. Ziegler
1963 Daniel J. Barry
1964 William K. McBride
1968 Albert H. Straub
1970 Harold A. Swanson

HARTFORD, CONNECTICUT

1784 Thomas Seymour
1812 Chauncey Goodrich
1815 Jonathan Brace
1824 Nathaniel Terry
1831 Thomas S. Williams
1835 Henry L. Ellsworth
Jared Griswold
Jeremy Hoadley
1836 Henry Hudson
1840 Thomas K. Brace
1843 Amos M. Collins
1847 Philip Ripley
1851 Ebenezer Flower
1853 William J. Hamersley
1854 Henry C. Deming
1858 Timothy M. Allyn
1860 Henry C. Deming
1862 Charles Benton
William J. Hamersley

1864 Allyn S. Stillman
1866 Charles R. Chapman
1872 Henry C. Robinson
1874 Joseph H. Sprague
1878 George G. Sumner
1880 Morgan G. Bulkeley
1888 John G. Root
1890 Henry C. Dwight
1892 William W. Hyde
1894 Leverett Brainard
1896 Miles B. Preston
1900 Alexander Harbison
1902 Ignatius A. Sullivan
1904 William F. Henney
1908 Edward W. Hooker
1910 Edward L. Smith
1912 Louis R. Cheney
1914 Joseph H. Lawler
1916 Frank A. Hagarty
1918 Richard J. Kinsella
1920 Newton C. Brainard
1922 Richard J. Kinsella
1924 Norman C. Stevens
1928 Walter E. Batterson
1931 William J. Rankin
1933 Joseph W. Beach
1935 John A. Pilgard
Thomas J. Spellacy
1943 Dennis P. O'Connor
William H. Mortensen
1945 Cornelius A. Moylan
1947 Edward N. Allen
1948 Cyril Coleman
1951 Joseph V. Cronin
1953 Dominick J. DeLucco
1955 Joseph V. Cronin
1957 James H. Kinsella
1960 Dominick J. DeLucco
1961 William E. Glynn
1965 George B. Kinsella
1967 Antonina P. Uccello
1971 George A. Athanson

HELENA, MONTANA

1881 John Kinna
1882 E. W. Knight
1883 T. H. Kleinschmidt
1884 W. B. Hundley
1885 James Sullivan
1886 T. H. Kleinschmidt
1887 W. L. Steele
1888 T. P. Fuller
1891 Donald Bradford
1892 T. H. Kleinschmidt
1893 John C. Curtin
1894 E. D. Weed
1895 W. L. Steele
1898 J. D. Edwards
1904 R. R. Purcell
1906 F. S. P. Lindsay
1908 J. D. Edwards
1911 Edward Horsky
1912 R. R. Purcell
1914 Lincoln Working
1916 R. R. Purcell
1918 John Dryburgh
1922 Percy Witmer
1930 George P. Arnold
1932 C. J. Bausch
1936 A. J. Roberts
1940 John J. Haytin
1946 J. R. Wine, Jr.
1950 J. R. Kaiserman

1953 Otto L. Brackman
1960 Wanna F. Thompson
1962 Robert E. Johnson
1964 John W. Schroeder
1966 David A. Lewis
1968 Darryl A. Lee
David A. Lewis

HONOLULU, HAWAII

1909 Joseph J. Fern
1915 John C. Lane
1917 Joseph J. Fern
1920 John H. Wilson
1927 Charles N. Arnold
1929 John H. Wilson
1931 George Fred Wright
1938 Charles S. Crane
1941 Lester Petrie
1947 John H. Wilson
1955 Neal S. Blaisdell
1969 Frank F. Fasi

HOUSTON, TEXAS

1838 Francis Moore, Jr.
1839 G. W. Lively
1840 Charles Bigelow
1841 John D. Andrews
1843 Francis Moore, Jr.
1844 Horace Baldwin
1845 W. W. Swain
1846 James Bailey
1847 Benjamin P. Buckner
1849 Francis Moore, Jr.
1853 Nathan Fuller
1855 James H. Stevens
1857 Cornelius Ennis
1858 Alexander McGowan
1859 William H. King
1860 Thomas Whitmarsh
1861 W. J. Hutchins
1862 T. W. House, Sr.
1863 William Andrews
1866 Horace D. Taylor
1867 Alexander McGowan
1868 Joseph R. Morris
1870 Timothy H. Scanlan
1874 James T. D. Wilson
1875 I. C. Lord
1877 James T. D. Wilson
1879 Andrew J. Burke
1880 William R. Baker
1886 Daniel C. Smith
1890 Henry Scheriffus
1892 John T. Browne
1896 Baldwin Rice
1898 Samuel H. Brashear
1901 John D. Woolford
1902 O. T. Holt
1904 Andrew L. Jackson
1905 H. Baldwin Rice
1913 Ben Campbell
1917 Joseph J. Pastoriza
J. C. Hutcheson, Jr.

1918 A. E. Amerman
1921 Oscar Holcombe
1929 Walter E. Monteith
1933 Oscar Holcombe
1937 R. H. Fonville
1939 Oscar Holcombe
1941 Neal C. Pickett
1943 Otis Massey
1947 Oscar Holcombe
1953 Roy Hofheinz
1956 Oscar Holcombe
1958 Lewis Cutrer
1964 Louie Welch

INDIANAPOLIS, INDIANA

1847 Samuel Henderson
1849 Horatio C. Newcomb
1851 Caleb Scudder
1854 James McCready
1856 Henry F. West
Charles G. Covlin
William J. Wallace
1858 Samuel D. Maxwell
1863 John Caven
1867 Daniel McCauley
1873 James L. Mitchell
1875 John Caven
1881 Daniel W. Grubbs
1884 John L. McMaster
1886 Caleb S. Denny
1890 Thomas L. Sullivan
1893 Caleb S. Denny
1895 Thomas Taggart
1901 Charles A. Bookwalter
1903 John W. Holtzman
1906 Charles A. Bookwalter
1910 Samuel L. Shank
1913 Harry R. Wallace
1914 Joseph E. Bell
1918 Charles W. Jewett
1922 Samuel L. Shank
1926 John L. Duvall
1927 L. Ert Slack
1930 Reginald H. Sullivan
1935 John W. Kern, Jr.
1937 Walter C. Boetcher
1939 Reginald H. Sullivan
1943 Robert Tyndall
1947 George L. Denny
1948 Al G. Feeney
1950 Phillip L. Bayt, Jr .
1951 Christian J. Emhardt
1952 Alex M. Clark
1956 Phillip L. Bayt, Jr.
1959 Charles Boswell
1962 Albert Losche
1964 John J. Barton
1968 Richard G. Lugar

JACKSON, MISSISSIPPI

1834 Thomas H. Dickson
1835 S. P. Baley
1837 John P. Oldham
1842 James H. Boyd
1844 John P. Oldham
1852 William H. Taylor
1854 Richard Fletcher

1855 James H. Boyd
1859 W. A. Purdom
1860 Richard C. Kerr
1862 Charles H. Manship
1864 D. N. Barrows
1868 Thomas H. Norton
James Biddle
James P. Sessions
1869 Rhesa Hatcher
Joseph C. Crane
F. A. Field
A. Way Kelly
E. W. Cabaniss
1870 Oliver Clifton
1871 Rhesa Hatcher
1872 Marion Smith
1874 John McGill
1888 William Henry
1893 L. F. Chiles
1895 Oliver Clifton
1897 Ramsey Wharton
1899 H. M. Taylor
W. M. Morrison
W. H. Reber
1901 William Hemingway
1905 Ramsey Wharton
1908 William Hamilton
1909 A. C. Crowder
1913 S. J. Taylor
1917 Walter Scott
1945 Leland Speed
1949 Allen C. Thompson
1969 Russell C. Davis

JACKSONVILLE, FLORIDA

1865 Halstead H. Hoeg
1866 Holmes Steele
1867 John Clark
1868 Edward Hopkins
1870 Peter Jones
1873 J. C. Greeley
1874 Peter Jones
1876 Luther McConihe
1877 W. Stokes Boyd
1878 Luther McConihe
1879 Peter Jones
1880 J. Ramsey Dey
1881 Morris A. Dzialynski
1883 W. McLaws Dancy
1885 M. C. Rice
1886 Patrick McQuaid
1887 J. Q. Burbridge
C. B. Smith
1889 Patrick McQuaid
1891 Henry Robinson
1893 Duncan U. Fletcher
1895 William M. Bostwick
1897 Raymond D. Knight
1899 J. E. T. Bowden
1901 Duncan U. Fletcher
1903 George M. Nolan
1906 William H. Baker
1907 William H. Sebring
1909 William S. Jordan
1913 Van C. Swearingen
1915 J. E. T. Bowden
1916 John W. Martin
1923 John T. Alsop, Jr.
1937 George C. Blume
1941 John T. Alsop, Jr.
1945 C. Frank Whitehead
1949 Haydon Burns
1965 Louis Ritter
1967 Hans Tanzler, Jr.

JEFFERSON CITY, MISSOURI

1839 Thomas L. Price
1841 John F. Hogle
1843 E. L. Edwards
1844 Jefferson T. Rogers
1846 Calvin Gunn
1847 Jefferson T. Rogers
1850 A. P. Dorris
1851 Jason Harrison
1854 Alfred Sanford
1855 Jefferson T. Rogers
1858 J. B. Gardenhire
1859 Jefferson T. Rogers
1861 H. Clay Ewing
1862 Bernard Bruns
1864 M. M. Flesh
1865 Andrew Gundellinger
1866 Sylvester W. Cox
1868 Jonathan Grimshaw
1869 Ellwood Kirby
1870 Frank Schmidt
1872 J. H. Bodine
1873 Charles F. McCarty
1874 Fred Fischer
1876 Phil E. Chappell
1877 James E. Carter
1879 A. M. Davison
1881 Sylvester W. Cox
1883 Joseph R. Edwards
1884 Fred H. Binder
1885 John G. Riddler
1888 Ashley W. Ewing
1889 Phillip Ott
1891 Arthur P. Grimshaw
1895 Edwin Silver
1899 Arthur P. Grimshaw
1901 A. C. Shoup
1903 J. P. Porth
1905 H. J. Wallau
1909 John F. Heinrichs
1911 C. W. Thomas
1917 Frank Chapman
1919 Louis S. Rephlo
1921 Paul C. Hunt
1923 C. W. Thomas
1928 Earl W. Jenkins
1931 Henry C. Asel
1933 Means R. Ray
1937 Jesse N. Owens
1947 James T. Blair, Jr.
1949 Robert E. Dorr
1950 Lawrence Lutkewitte
1951 Arthur W. Ellis
1959 C. Forrest Whaley
1963 John G. Christy

JUNEAU, ALASKA

1900 A. K. Delaney
1901 George F. Forrest
1902 O. H. Adsit
1903 P. H. Adsit
1904 George F. Forrest
1905 John F. Maloney
1906 H. T. Tripp
1907 George F. Forrest
1908 Emery Valentine
1912 Harry Bishop
1913 Charles W. Carter
1914 John Reck
1916 B. D. Stewart
1917 Emery Valentine
1919 E. L. Gray
1920 R. E. Robertson
1923 I. Goldstein
1925 J. J. Connors
1927 Thomas B. Judson
1933 I. Goldstein
1937 Thomas B. Judson
1938 Harry I. Lucas
1944 A. B. Hayes
1945 Ernest Parsons
1946 Waino Hendrickson
1953 Bert F. McDowell
1955 M. L. MacSpadden
1959 Lauris S. Parker
1961 A. W. Boddy
Wayne Johnson
1962 Lauris S. Parker
1967 Timothy O'Day
1968 Joseph L. George
1969 Joseph A. McLean

KANSAS CITY, MISSOURI

1853 William S. Gregory
1854 Johnston Lykins
1855 John Johnson
Milton J. Payne
1860 George M. B. Haughs
1861 Robert T. Van Horn
1862 Milton J. Payne
1863 William Bonnifield
1864 Robert T. Van Horn
1865 Patrick Shannon
1866 Alexander L. Harris
1867 Edward H. Allen
1868 Alexander L. Harris
1869 Francis R. Long
1870 Elijah M. McGee
1871 William Warner
1872 Robert H. Hunt
1873 Edward L. Martin
1874 Smith D. Woods
1875 Turner A. Gill
1876 James W. L. Slavens
1878 George M. Shelley
1880 Charles A. Chace
1881 Daniel A. Frink
1882 Thomas B. Bullene
1883 James Gibson
1884 Leander J. Talbott
1885 John W. Moore
1886 Henry C. Kumpf
1889 Joseph J. Davenport
1890 Benjamin Holmes
1892 William S. Cowherd
1894 Webster Davis
1896 James M. Jones
1900 James A. Reed
1904 Jay H. Neff
1906 Henry M. Beardsley
1908 Thomas T. Crittenden, Jr.
1910 Darius A. Brown
1912 Henry L. Jost
1916 George H. Edwards
1918 James Cowgill
1922 Samuel B. Strother
Frank H. Cromwell
1924 Albert I. Beach
1930 Bryce B. Smith
1939 Charles S. Keith
1940 John B. Gage
1946 William E. Kemp
1955 H. Roe Bartle
1963 Ilus W. Davis
1971 Charles B. Wheeler, Jr.

LANSING, MICHIGAN

1859 Hiram H. Smith
1860 John A. Kerr
1861 William H. Chapman
1863 Ira H. Bartholomew
1866 William H. Haze
1867 George W. Peck
1868 Cyrus Hewitt
1870 Solomon W. Wright
1871 John Robson
1872 John S. Tooker
1874 Daniel W. Buck
1876 John S. Tooker
1877 Orlando M. Barnes
1878 Joseph E. Warner
1879 William H. Van Buren
1881 John Robson
1882 Orlando F. Barnes
1884 William Donovan
1886 Daniel W. Buck
1887 Jacob F. Shultz
1888 John Crotty
1889 James M. Turner
1890 Frank B. Johnson
1892 A. O. Bement
1894 Alroy A. Wilbur
1895 James M. Turner
1896 Russell C. Ostrander
1897 Charles J. Davis
1900 James F. Hammell
1904 Hugh Lyons
1908 John S. Bennett
1912 J. G. Reutter
1918 Jacob W. Ferle
1920 Benjamin A. Kyes
1922 Jacob W. Ferle
Silas S. Main
1923 Alfred H. Doughty
1927 Laird J. Troyer
1931 Peter F. Gray
1933 Max A. Templeton
1941 Arthur E. Stoppel
Sam S. Hughes
1943 Ralph W. Crego
1961 Willard I. Bowerman, Jr.
1965 Max E. Murninghan
1969 Gerald W. Graves

LINCOLN, NEBRASKA

1871 W. F. Chapin
1872 E. E. Brown
1873 Robert D. Silver, Jr.
1874 Samuel W. Little
1875 Amasa Cobb
1876 Robert D. Silver, Jr.
1877 H. W. Hardy
1879 Seth P. Galey
1880 John B. Wright
1882 John Doolittle
1883 Robert E. Moore
1885 C. C. Burr
1887 Andrew J. Sawyer
1889 Robert B. Graham
1891 A. H. Weir
1895 Frank A. Graham
1899 H. J. Winnett
1903 George A. Adams
1905 Frances W. Brown
1909 Don L. Love
1911 A. H. Armstrong
1913 Frank C. Zehrung
1915 Charles W. Bryan
1917 John E. Miller
1921 Frank C. Zehrung
1927 Verne Hedge
1929 Don L. Love
1931 Frank C. Zehrung
1933 Fenton B. Fleming
1935 Charles W. Bryan
1937 Oren S. Copeland
1940 R. E. Campbell
1941 Richard O. Johnson
1943 Lloyd Marti
1947 Clarence G. Miles
1950 Victor E. Anderson
1953 Clark Jeary
1956 Bennett S. Martin
1959 Bartlett E. Boyles
1963 D. L. Tyrrell
Dean H. Petersen
1965 Sam Schwartzkopf

LITTLE ROCK, ARKANSAS

1835 James Pitcher
1838 Jesse Brown
1840 S. H. Webb
1842 John Widgery
1844 William Brown, Sr.
1845 Lambert J. Reardon
1847 R. L. Dodge
1848 S. H. Webb
1849 Roswell Beebe
1850 D. J. Baldwin
1851 John E. Knight
1852 A. J. Hutt
1854 Thomas D. Merrick
1855 C. P. Bertrand
1857 W. E. Ashley
1859 Gordon N. Peay
1861 William E. Ashley
1863 Vacant
1866 J. J. McAlmont
1867 J. W. Hopkins
1868 John Wassell
1869 A. K. Hartman
1871 J. G. Botsford
Robert F. Catterson
1873 Frederick Kramer
1875 John G. Fletcher
1881 Frederick Kramer
1887 William G. Whipple
1891 H. L. Fletcher
1893 M. G. Hall
1895 James A. Woodson
1900 W. R. Duley
1903 W. E. Lenon
1908 John H. Hollis
1911 Charles E. Taylor
1919 Ben D. Brickhouse
1925 Charles E. Moyer
1929 Pat L. Robinson
1931 Horace A. Knowlton
1935 Richard E. Overman
1939 J. V. Satterfield, Jr.
1941 Charles E. Moyer

1945 Dan T. Sprick
1947 Sam M. Wassell
1952 Pratt C. Remmell
1956 Woodrow W. Mann
1958 Werner C. Knoop
1963 Byron R. Morse
1965 Harold Henson
1967 Martin Borchert
1969 Haco Boyd
1971 George Wimberly

LOS ANGELES, CALIFORNIA

1850 Alpheus P. Hodges
1851 Benjamin D. Wilson
1852 John G. Nichols
1853 Antonio F. Coronel
1854 Stephen C. Foster
1855 Thomas Foster
1856 Stephen C. Foster
John G. Nichols
1859 Damien Marchessault
1860 Henry Mellus
1861 Damien Marchessault
1865 Jose Mascarel
1866 Cristobal Aguilar
1868 Joel H. Turner
1871 Cristobal Aguilar
1872 James R. Toberman
1874 Prudent Beaudry
1876 Frederick A. MacDougall
1878 James R. Toberman
1882 Cameron E. Thom
1884 Edward F. Spence
1886 William H. Workman
1888 John Bryson
1889 Henry T. Hazard
1892 Thomas E. Rowan
1894 Frank Rader
1896 Meredith P. Snyder
1898 Fred Eaton
1900 Meredith P. Snyder
1904 Owen C. McAleer
1906 Arthur C. Harper
1909 William D. Stephens
George Alexander
1913 Henry R. Rose
1915 Charles E. Sebastian
1916 Frederick T. Woodman
1919 Meredith P. Snyder
1921 George E. Cryer
1929 John C. Porter
1933 Frank L. Shaw
1938 Fletcher Bowron
1953 Norris Poulson
1961 Sam Yorty

LOUISVILLE, KENTUCKY

1828 John C. Bucklin
1834 John Joves
1837 Frederick A. Kaye
1841 D. L. Beatty
1844 Frederick A. Kaye
1847 William F. Vance
1850 John M. Delph
1853 James S. Speed
1855 John Barbee
1857 W. S. Pilcher
1859 T. H. Crawford
1861 John M. Delph
1863 William Kaye
1865 Phil Tomppert
James S. Lithgow
1867 Phil Tomppert
1869 J. H. Bunce
1870 John G. Baxter
1873 Charles D. Jacob
1879 John G. Baxter
1882 Charles D. Jacob
1885 P. Barker Reed
1888 Charles D. Jacob
1890 William L. Lyons (protem)
1891 Henry S. Tyler
1896 Goerge D. Todd
1897 Charles P. Weaver
1901 Charles F. Grainger
1905 Paul C. Barth
1907 Robert W. Bingham
James F. Grinstead
1909 W. O. Head
1913 John H. Buschmeyer
1917 George W. Smith
1921 Huston Quinn
1925 Arthur A. Will
1927 Joseph T. O'Neal
William S. Harrison
1933 Neville Miller
1937 Joseph D. Scholtz
1941 Wilson W. Wyatt
1946 E. Leland Taylor
1948 Charles P. Farnsley
1953 Andrew Broaddus
1957 Bruce Hoblitzell
1961 William O. Cowger
1965 Kenneth A. Schmied
1969 Frank W. Burke

MADISON, WISCONSIN

1856 Jairus C. Fairchild
1857 Augustus A. Bird
1858 George B. Smith
1861 Levi B. Vilas
1862 William T. Leitch
1865 Elisha W. Keyes
1867 Alden S. Sanborn
1868 David Atwood
1869 Andrew Proudfit
1871 J. B. Bowen
1872 James L. Hill
1873 J. C. Gregory
1874 Silas U. Pinney
1876 John N. Jones
1877 Harlow S. Orton
1878 George B. Smith
1879 John R. Baltzell
1880 Philip L. Spooner, Jr.
1881 James Conklin
1884 Breese J. Stevens
1885 H. N. Moulton
1887 James Conklin
1888 M. R. Doyton
1890 Robert M. Bashford
1891 William H. Rogers
1893 John Corscot
1895 Jabe Alford
1896 Albert A. Dye
1897 Mathew J. Hoven
1898 Charles E. Whelan
1899 Mathew J. Hoven
1901 Storm Bull
1902 John W. Groves
1904 W. D. Curtis
1906 Joseph C. Schubert
1912 John B. Heim
1914 A. H. Kayser
1916 George C. Sayle
1920 I. Milo Kittleson
1926 A. G. Schmedeman
1932 James R. Law
1943 F. Halsey Kraege
1947 Leonard C. Howell
(City Manager)
1951 George J. Forster
1955 A. W. Bareis
1956 Ivan A. Nestingen
1961 Harold E. Hanson
Henry E. Reynolds
1965 Otto Festge
1969 William D. Dyke

MEMPHIS, TENNESSEE

1827 M. B. Winchester
1829 Isaac Rawlings
1831 Seth Wheatley
1832 Robert Lawrence
1833 Isaac Rawlings
1836 Enoch Banks
1837 John H. Morgan
1838 Enoch Banks
1839 Thomas Dixon
1841 William Spickernagle
1842 E. Hickman
1845 Jesse J. Finley
1846 E. Hickman
1847 Enoch Banks
1848 G. B. Locke
1849 E. Hickman
1852 A. B. Taylor
1855 A. H. Douglass
1856 T. B. Carroll
1857 R. D. Baugh
1861 John Park
1864 Thomas H. Harris (Acting)
C. Richards (Acting)
1865 John Park
1866 William O. Lofland
1868 John W. Leftwich
1869 John Johnson
1873 John Logue
1875 John R. Flippin
1879 D. T. Porter
1881 John Overton, Jr.
1883 D. P. Hadden
1891 W. D. Bethell
1893 W. L. Clapp
1898 J. J. Williams
1906 James H. Malone
1910 Edward H. Crump
1915 George C. Love
1916 T. C. Ashcroft
1917 H. H. Litty
1918 F. L. Monteverde
1920 Rowlett Paine
1928 Watkins Overton
1939 Edward H. Crump
1940 Walter Chandler
1946 Sylvanus Polk
1947 James J. Pleasants, Jr.
1949 Watkins Overton
1953 F. T. Tobey
1955 Walter Chandler
1956 Edmund Orgill
1960 Henry Loeb III
1963 Claude A. Armour
1964 William B. Ingram, Jr.
1968 Jenry Loeb III

MILWAUKEE, WISCONSIN

1846 Solomon Juneau
1847 H. N. Wells
1848 Byron Kilbourn
1849 Don A. J. Upham
1851 George H. Walker
1852 Hans Crocker
1853 George H. Walker
1854 Byron Kilbourn
1855 James B. Cross
1858 William A. Prentiss
1859 Herman L. Page
1860 William P. Lynde
1861 James S. Brown
1862 Horace Chase
1863 Edward O'Neill
1864 Abner Kirby
1865 John J. Tallmadge
1867 Edward O'Neill
1870 Joseph Phillips
1871 Harrison Ludington
1872 David G. Hooker
1873 Harrison Ludington
1876 A. A. R. Butler
1878 John Black
1880 Thomas H. Brown
1882 John M. Stowell
1884 Emil Wallber
1888 Thomas H. Brown
1890 George W. Peck
P. J. Somers
1893 John C. Koch
1896 William G. Rauschenberger
1898 David S. Rose
1906 Sherburn M. Becker
1908 David S. Rose
1910 Emil Seidel
1912 Gerhard A. Bading
1916 Daniel W. Hoan
1940 Carl F. Zeidler
1942 John L. Bohn
1948 Frank P. Zeidler
1960 Henry W. Maier

MINNEAPOLIS, MINNESOTA

1855 H. T. Welles
1856 Alvarin Allen
1857 William W. Wales
1858 Orrin Curtis
1860 R. B. Graves
1861 O. C. Merriman
1863 E. S. Brown
1864 O. C. Merriman
1865 William W. Wales
1867 Dorilus Morrison
O. C. Merriman
1868 Winthrop Young
Hugh Harrison
1869 Dorilus Morrison
O. C. Merriman
William W. McNair

1870 Eli B. Ames
1871 E. S. Brown
1872 Eugene M. Wilson
1873 G. A. Brackett
1874 Eugene M. Wilson
1875 O. C. Merriman
1876 A. A. Ames
1877 John DeLaittre
1878 A. C. Rand
1882 A. A. Ames
1884 George A. Pillsbury
1886 A. A. Ames
1887 E. C. Babb
1890 Phillip B. Winston
1892 William H. Eustis
1894 Robert Pratt
1898 James Gray
1900 A. A. Ames
1902 J. C. Haynes
1904 D. P. Jones
1906 J. C. Haynes
1912 Wallace G. Nye
1916 Thomas Van Lear
1918 J. E. Meyers
1921 George E. Leach
1929 William F. Kunze
1931 William A. Anderson
1933 A. G. Bainbridge
1935 Thomas E. Latimer
1937 George E. Leach
1941 Marvin L. Kline
1945 Hubert H. Humphrey, Jr.
1948 Eric G. Hoyer
1957 P. Kenneth Peterson
1961 Arthur Naftalin
1968 Charles Stenvig

MONTGOMERY, ALABAMA

1819 William Graham
1821 W. E. Benson
1824 John Gindrat
1825 William Cook
1826 John Edmondson
1827 Francis McGehee
Andrew Dexter
1828 William Sayre
F. Bugbee
1829 John Edmondson
1830 William Sayre
1831 B. Gordon
1832 J. Wyman
1833 John Lambert
Isaac Tinker
1834 M. B. Tatum
1835 John H. Thorington
1836 F. Bugbee
1837 G. D. Shortridge
1838 J. Hutchinson
Samuel D. Holt
1839 Jack Thorington
1841 Hardy Herbert
1842 Perez Coleman
1847 Nimrod E. Benson
1848 Edwin B. Harris
1850 Robert T. Davis
1851 Thomas Welch
1852 Samuel D. Holt
1853 Charles R. Hansford
1860 Andrew J. Noble
1862 J. T. Johnson
1864 Walter L. Coleman
1868 Thomas O. Glasscock
1870 H. E. Faber
1876 M. L. Moses
1881 J. B. Gaston
1885 W. S. Reese
1890 Edward A. Graham
1891 John H. Crommelin
1895 John H. Clisby
1900 E. B. Joseph
1903 Thomas H. Carr
1905 C. P. McIntyre
W. M. Teague
1909 Gaston Gunter
1910 W. A. Gunter
1915 W. T. Robertson
1920 W. A. Gunter
1940 Cyrus B. Brown
1944 David E. Dunn
1946 John L. Goodwyn
1951 W. A. Gayle
1960 Earl D. James

MONTPELIER, VERMONT

1895 George W. Wing
1896 George O. Stratton
1897 George H. Guernsey
1898 John H. Senter
1900 Joseph G. Brown
1902 James M. Boutwell
1903 Frank M. Corry
1906 James S. Haley
1908 Frank R. Dawley
1911 Smith S. Ballard
1912 James B. Estee
1914 James M. Boutwell
1917 Frank W. Mitchell
1919 Harry C. Shurtleff
1921 George L. Blanchard
1922 Dean K. Lillie
1924 George L. Edson
1926 Edward H. Deavitt
1930 Riley C. Bowers
1933 William L. McKee
1934 Perry H. Merrill
1935 James F. Ewing
1936 William H. Dyer
1938 Birney L. Hall
1939 William F. Corry
1945 Harry R. Sheridan
1947 Daughly Gould
1949 Anson F. Barber
1956 Edward F. Knapp
1959 Elbert B. Colburn
1963 Manuel Canas, Jr.
1966 Willard R. Strong

NASHVILLE, TENNESSEE

1806 Joseph Coleman
1809 Benjamin J. Bradford
1811 William Tait
1814 Joseph T. Elliston
1817 Stephen Cantrell, Jr.
1818 Felix Robertson
1819 Thomas Crutcher
1820 James Condon
1821 John P. Endin
1822 Robert B. Currey
1824 Randal McGavock
1825 Wilkins Tennehill
1827 Felix Robertson
1829 William Armstrong
1833 John M. Bass
1834 John P. Erwin
1835 William Nichol
1837 Henry Hollinsworth
1839 Charles C. Trahue
1841 Samuel V. D. Stout
1842 Thomas B. Coleman
1843 Powhattan W. Maxey
1845 John Hugh Smith
1846 John A. Goodlett
1847 Alexander Anderson
1849 John M. Lea
1850 John Hugh Smith
1853 Williamson H. Horn
1854 Robert B. Castleman
1856 Andrew Anderson
1857 John A. McEwen
1858 Randal W. McGavock
1859 S. N. Hollinsworth
1860 Richard B. Cheatham
1862 John Hugh Smith
1865 W. Matt Brown
1867 A. E. Alden
1869 Kindred J. Morris
1872 Thomas A. Kercheval
1874 Morton B. Howell
1875 Thomas A. Kercheval
1883 C. Hooper Phillips
1885 Thomas A. Kercheval
1887 C. P. McCarver
1890 William Litterer
1891 George B. Guild
1895 William McCarthy
1897 R. H. Dudley
1899 J. M. Head
1903 A. S. Williams
1905 T. O. Morris
1907 James S. Brown
1909 Hilary E. Howse
1915 Robert Ewing
1917 William Gupton
1921 Felix Z. Wilson
1922 Percy Sharpe
1923 Hilary E. Howse
1938 Thomas L. Cummings
1951 Ben West
1963 Beverly Briley

NEW ORLEANS, LOUISIANA

Mayors

1803 Etienne De Bore
1804 James Pitot
1805 John Watkins
1807 James J. Mather
1812 Charles Trudeau (Acting)
Nicholas Girod
1815 August McCarty
1820 Joseph Roffignoc
1828 Denis Prieur
1838 Paul Bertus (Acting)
Charles Benois
1840 William Freret
1844 Joseph E. Montegut
1846 Abdil D. Crossman
1854 John L. Lewis
1856 Charles M. Waterman
1858 Gerald Stith
1860 John T. Monroe

Military Mayors

1862 George F. Shepley
Godfrey Weitzel
Jonas H. French
Godfrey Weitzel
Hanry C. Deming
1863 James F. Miller
1864 Stephen Hoyt
1865 Hugh Kennedy
Samuel M. Quincy
Hugh Kennedy
1866 George Clark
John T. Monroe
1867 Edward Heath
1868 John R. Conway
1870 Benjamin F. Flanders
1872 Louis A. Wiltz
1874 Charles J. Leeds
1876 Edward Pilsbury

Mayors

1878 Isaac W. Patton
1880 Joseph A. Shakspeare
1882 W. J. Behan
1884 J. Valsin Guillotte
1888 Joseph A. Shakspeare
1892 John Fitzpatrick
1896 Walter C. Flower
1900 Paul Capdeville
1904 Martin Behrman
1920 Andrew J. McShane
1926 Arthur J. O'Keefe
1929 T. Semmes Walmsley
1936 Robert S. Maestri
1946 deLesseps S. Morrison
1961 Victor H. Schiro
1970 Moon Landrieu

NEW YORK CITY

1665 Thomas Willett
1666 Thomas Delavall
1667 Thomas Willett
1668 Cornelius Steenwyck
1671 Thomas Delavall
1672 Matthias Nicolls
1673 John Lawrence
1675 William Dervall
1676 Nicholas De Meyer
1677 Stephanus Van Cortlandt
1678 Thomas Delavall
1679 Francis Rombouts
1680 William Dyre
1682 Cornelius Steenwyck
1684 Gabriel Minvielle
1685 Nicholas Bayard
1686 Stephanus Van Cortlandt
1689 Peter Delanoy
1691 John Lawrence
1692 Abraham De Peyster
1694 Charles Lodwick
1695 William Merritt
1698 Johannes De Peyster
1699 David Provoost
1700 Isaac De Reimer
1701 Thomas Noell
1702 Philip French
1703 William Peartree
1707 Ebenezer Wilson

1710 Jacobus Van Cortlandt
1711 Caleb Heathcote
1714 John Johnston
1719 Jacobus Van Cortlandt
1720 Robert Walters
1725 Johannes Jansen
1726 Robert Lurting
1735 Paul Richard
1739 John Cruger
1744 Stephen Bayard
1747 Edward Holland
1757 John Cruger, Jr.
1766 Whitehead Hicks
1776 David Matthews
1784 James Duane
1789 Richard Varick
1801 Edward Livingston
1803 De Witt Clinton
1807 Marinus Willett
1808 De Witt Clinton
1810 Jacob Radcliff
1811 De Witt Clinton
1815 John Ferguson
Jacob Radcliff
1818 Cadwallader D. Colden
1821 Stephen Allen
1825 William Paulding
1826 Philip Hone
1827 William Paulding
1829 Walter Bowne
1833 Gideon Lee
1834 Cornelius V. Lawrence
1837 Aaron Clark
1839 Isaac L. Varian
1841 Robert H. Morris
1844 James Harper
1845 William F. Havemeyer
1846 Andrew H. Mickle
1847 William V. Brady
1848 William F. Havemeyer
1849 Caleb S. Woodhull
1851 Ambrose C. Kingsland
1853 Jacob A. Westervelt
1855 Fernando Wood
1858 Daniel F. Tiemann
1860 Fernando Wood
1862 George Opdyke
1864 C. Godfrey Gunther
1866 John T. Hoffman
1868 T. Coman (Acting)
1869 A. Oakey Hall
1873 William F. Havemeyer
1874 S. B. H. Vance (Acting)
1875 William H. Wickham
1877 Smith Ely
1879 Edward Cooper
1881 William R. Grace
1883 Franklin Edson
1885 William R. Grace
1887 Abram S. Hewitt
1889 Hugh J. Grant
1893 Thomas F. Gilroy
1895 William L. Strong
1898 Robert A. Van Wyck
1902 Seth Low
1904 George B. McClellan
1910 William J. Gaynor
1913 Ardolph L. Kline
1914 John P. Mitchel
1918 John F. Hylan
1926 James J. Walker
1932 Joseph V. McKee
1933 John P. O'Brien
1934 Fiorello H. La Guardia
1946 William O'Dwyer
1950 Vincent R. Impellitteri
1954 Robert F. Wagner
1966 John V. Lindsay

NORFOLK, VIRGINIA

1898 C. Brooks Johnston
1901 Nathaniel Beaman
1902 E. G. Riddick
1912 Wyndham R. Mayo
1918 Albert L. Roper
1924 S. Heth Tyler
1931 E. Jeff Robertson
1932 Philip H. Mason
1933 S. L. Slover
1934 W. R. L. Taylor
1938 John A. Gurkin
1940 Joseph D. Wood
1944 James W. Reed
1946 R. D. Cooke
1949 Pretlow Darden
1950 W. F. Duckworth
1962 Roy B. Martin, Jr.

OKLAHOMA CITY, OKLAHOMA

1890 W. J. Gault
1892 O. A. Mitscher
1894 Nelson Button
1896 C. G. Jones
1897 J. P. Allen
1899 Lee Van Winkle
1901 C. G. Jones
1903 Lee Van Winkle
1905 J. F. Messenbaugh
1907 Henry M. Scales
1910 Dan V. Lackey
1911 Whit M. Grant
1915 Ed Overholser
1918 Byron D. Shear
1919 J. C. Walton
1923 Mike Donnelly
1925 O. A. Cargill
1927 Walter C. Dean
1931 C. J. Blinn
1933 Tom E. McGee
1935 John Frank Martin
1939 R. A. Hefner
1947 Allen Street
1959 James H. Norick
1963 Jack S. Wilkes
1964 George H. Shirk
1967 James H. Norick
1971 Patience Latting

OLYMPIA, WASHINGTON

1873 W. W. Miller
1874 I. C. Ellis
1875 T. F. McElroy
1876 J. C. Horr
1877 John P. Judson
1878 E. N. Quinette
1880 George A. Barnes
1881 E. T. Young
1882 N. Ostrander
1884 J. S. Dobbins
1885 A. A. Phillips
1886 A. H. Chambers
1889 J. F. Gowey
1891 J. C. Horr
1892 R. G. O'Brien
1893 J. W. Robinson
1894 C. B. Mann
1896 Charles H. Ayer
1897 John Byrne
1898 George B. Lane
1899 C. S. Reinhart
1902 C. J. Lord
1904 H. G. Richardson
1905 P. H. Carlyon
1907 Thomas McLarty
1908 W. A. Hagemeyer
1909 Mitchell Harris
1912 W. L. Bridgford
1913 G. A. Mottman
1917 Jesse T. Mills
1921 C. H. Bowen
1923 George W. Draham
1925 James C. Johnson
1929 George G. Mills
1932 E. N. Steele
1934 F. B. Longaker
1941 J. T. Trullinger
1947 Ernest Mallory
1950 Ralph A. Swanson
1953 Amanda B. Smith
1960 Neil R. McKay
1969 Thomas Allen

PHILADELPHIA, PENNSYLVANIA

1691 Humphrey Morrey
1701 Edward Shippen
1703 Anthony Morris
1704 Griffith Jones
1705 Joseph Wilcox
1706 Nathan Stanbury
1707 Thomas Masters
1709 Richard Hill
1710 William Carter
1711 Samuel Preston
1712 Jonathan Dickinson
1713 George Roch
1714 Richard Hill
1717 Jonathan Dickinson
1719 William Fishbourn
1722 James Logan
1723 Clement Plumsted
1724 Isaac Norris
1725 William Hudson
1726 Charles Read
1728 Thomas Lawrence
1729 Thomas Griffiths
1731 Samuel Hasell
1733 Thomas Griffiths
1734 Thomas Lawrence
1735 William Allen
1736 Clement Plumsted
1737 Thomas Griffiths
1738 Anthony Morris
1739 Edward Roberts
1740 Samuel Hasell
1741 Clement Plumsted
1742 William Till
1743 Benjamin Shoemaker
1744 Edward Shippen
1745 James Hamilton
1746 William Atwood
1748 Charles Willing
1749 Thomas Lawrence
1750 William Plumsted
1751 Robert Strettell
1752 Benjamin Shoemaker
1753 Thomas Lawrence
1754 Charles Willing
1755 William Plumsted
1756 Atwood Shute
1758 Thomas Lawrence
1759 John Stamper
1760 Benjamin Shoemaker
1761 Jacob Duche
1762 Henry Harrison
1763 Thomas Willing
1764 Thomas Lawrence
1765 John Lawrence
1767 Isaac Jones
1769 Samuel Shoemaker
1771 John Gibson
1773 William Fisher
1774 Samuel Rhoads
1775 Samuel Powel
1790 Samuel Miles
1791 John Barclay
1792 Matthew Clarkson
1796 Hillary Baker
1798 Robert Wharton
1800 John Inskeep
1801 Matthew Lawlor
1804 John Inskeep
1806 Robert Wharton
1808 John Barker
1810 Robert Wharton
1811 Michael Keppelle
1812 John Barker
1813 John Geyer
1814 Robert Wharton
1819 James N. Barker
1820 Robert Wharton
1824 Joseph Watson
1828 George M. Dallas
1829 Benjamin W. Richards
1832 John Swift
1838 Isaac Roach
1839 John Swift
1841 John M. Scott
1844 Peter McCall
1845 John Swift
1849 Joel Jones
1850 Charles Gilpin
1853 Robert T. Conrad
1856 Richard Vaux
1858 Alexander Henry
1866 Morton McMichael
1869 Daniel M. Fox
1872 William S. Stokley
1881 Samuel G. King
1884 William B. Smith
1887 Edwin H. Fitler
1891 Edwin S. Stuart
1895 Charles F. Warwick
1899 Samuel H. Ashbridge
1903 John Weaver
1907 John E. Reyburn
1911 R. Blankenburg
1916 Thomas B. Smith
1920 J. Hampton Moore
1924 W. Freeland Kendrick
1928 Harry A. Mackey
1932 J. Hampton Moore
1936 S. Davis Wilson
1939 George Connell (Acting)
1940 Robert E. Lamberton
1941 Bernard Samuel
1952 Joseph S. Clark
1956 Richardson Dilworth
1962 James H. J. Tate
1971 Frank L. Rizzo

PHOENIX, ARIZONA

1881 John T. Alsop
1882 Francis T. Shaw
1883 De Forest Porter
1884 George F. Coats
1885 E. Ganz
1886 De Forest Porter
1888 A. Leonard Meyer
1889 George F. Coats
1890 T. N. E. McGlasson
1891 Joseph Campbell
1893 P. J. Cole
1894 J. O. Monihan
1895 R. S. Rossin
R. Allyn Lewis
1896 F. B. Moss
J. D. Monihan
1897 J. C. Adams
1898 C. J. Dyer
1899 E. Ganz
1901 Walter Talbot
1903 Walter Bennett
1904 John T. Dunlop
1905 F. B. Moss
1906 R. H. Greene (Acting)
L. W. Coggins (Acting)
1909 Lloyd B. Christy
1914 George U. Young
1916 Peter Corpstein
1920 Willis H. Plunkett
1922 L. L. Harmon
1923 Louis B. Whitney
1925 Frank A. Jefferson
1928 F. J. Paddock
1930 Franklin D. Lane
1932 F. J. Paddock
1934 Joseph S. Jenckes
1936 John H. Udall
1938 Walter J. Thalheimer
1940 Reed Shupe
1942 Newell Stewart
1944 J. R. Fleming
1946 Ray Busey
1948 Nicholas Udall
1952 Hohen Foster
1954 Frank Murphy
1956 Jack Williams
1960 Sam Mardian
1964 Milton H. Graham
1970 John D. Driggs

PIERRE, SOUTH DAKOTA

1883 Henry Blakeley
1885 P. F. McClure
1887 A. W. Johnston
1890 B. J. Templeton
1892 Louis Kehr
1894 James H. Owen
1896 J. E. Mallery
1898 Louis B. Albright
1902 A. W. Ewert
1906 Louis B. Albright
1908 L. B. Wadleigh
1909 G. H. Jaynes
1910 J. E. Mallery
1911 L. L. Stephens
1915 William Borst
1918 Joseph B. Binder
1924 J. E. Hipple
1939 Godfrey M. Roberts, Sr. (Acting)
1940 John B. Griffin
1955 A. E. Munck
1958 John B. Griffin
1965 Godfrey M. Roberts, Jr.
1970 Clint Gregory

PITTSBURGH, PENNSYLVANIA

1816 Ebenezer Denny
1817 John Darragh
1825 J. M. Snowden
1828 M. M. Murray
1830 M. B. Laurie
1832 Samuel Pettigrew
1836 J. R. McClintock
1839 William Little
1840 William W. Irwin
1841 James Thompson
1842 Alexander Hay
1845 W. J. Howard
1846 William Kerr
1847 Gabriel Adams
1849 John Herron
1850 Joseph Barker
1851 J. B. Guthrie
1853 R. M. Rittle
1854 R. E. Voltz
1856 William Bingham
1857 H. A. Weaver
1860 George Wilson
1862 B. C. Sawyer
1864 James Lawyer
1866 W. S. McCarthy
1868 James Blackmore
1869 Gerard M. Brush
1875 William C. McCarthy
1878 Walter Lidwell
1881 Robert W. Lyons
1884 Andrew Fulton
1887 William McCallim
1890 H. J. Gourley
1893 Bernard McKenna
1896 Henry P. Ford
1899 William J. Diehl
1901 J. O. Brown
A. M. Brown
1903 W. G. Hays
1906 George W. Guthrie
1909 William A. Magee
1914 Joseph G. Armstrong
1918 E. G. Babcock
1922 William A. Magee
1926 Charles H. Kline
1933 John S. Herron
1934 William McNair
1936 Cornelius Scully
1946 David L. Lawrence
1959 Thomas J. Gallagher
Joseph M. Barr
1970 Peter F. Flaherty

PROVIDENCE, RHODE ISLAND

1832 Samuel W. Bridgham
1841 Thomas M. Burgess
1852 Amos C. Barstow
1853 Walter R. Danforth
1854 Edward P. Knowles
1855 James Y. Smith
1857 William M. Rodman
1859 Jabez C. Knight
1864 Thomas A. Doyle
1869 George L. Clarke
1870 Thomas A. Doyle
1881 William S. Hayward
1884 Thomas A. Doyle
1886 Gilbert F. Robbins
1889 Henry R. Barker
1891 Charles S. Smith
1892 William K. Potter
1894 Frank F. Olney
1896 Edwin D. McGuinness
1898 William C. Baker
1901 Daniel L. D. Granger
1903 Augustus S. Miller
1906 Elisha Dyer
1907 Patrick J. McCarthy
1909 Henry Fletcher
1913 Joseph H. Gainer
1927 James E. Dunne
1939 John F. Collins
1941 Dennis J. Roberts
1951 Walter H. Reynolds
1964 Joseph A. Doorley, Jr.

RALEIGH, NORTH CAROLINA

1880 B. C. Manly
1882 William H. Dodd
1887 Al A. Thompson
1891 Thomas Badger
1895 William M. Russ
1899 A. M. Powell
1903 James I. Johnson
1909 J. S. Wynne
1911 James I. Johnson
1921 T. B. Eldridge
1923 E. E. Culbreth
1931 George A. Iseley
1939 Graham H. Andrews
1947 P. D. Snipes
1951 James E. Briggs
1953 Fred B. Wheeler
1957 W. G. Enloe
1963 James W. Reid
1965 Travis H. Tomlinson
1969 Seby B. Jones

RENO, NEVADA

1931 Arnold A. Millard
1939 M. E. Norton
1941 C. B. Austin
1945 George Lind
1947 R. M. Elston
1949 Caro Pendergraft
1951 Wilbur H. Stodieck
1955 Turner Houston
1959 Harley W. Carter
1960 Turner Houston
1961 Al Autrand
1963 James Y. Robertson
1969 Eugene M. Scrivner

RICHMOND, VIRGINIA

1782 William Foushee
1783 John Beckley
1784 Robert Mitchell
1785 John Harvie
1786 William Pennock
1787 Richard Adams, Sr.
1788 John Beckley
1789 Alexander McRoberts
1790 Robert Boyd
George Nicholas
1791 John Barrett
1792 Robert Mitchell
1793 John Barrett
1794 Robert Mitchell
1795 Andrew Dunscomb
1796 Robert Mitchell
1797 James McClurg
1798 John Barrett
1799 George Nicholas
1800 James McClurg
1801 William Richardson
1802 John Foster
1803 James McClurg
1804 Robert Mitchell
1805 William DuVal
1806 Edward Carrington
1810 David Bullock
1811 Benjamin Tate
1812 Thomas Wilson
1813 Robert Greenhow
1814 Thomas Wilson
1815 Robert Gamble
1816 Thomas Wilson
1817 William H. Fitzwhylson
1818 Thomas Wilson
1819 John Adams
1826 Joseph Tate
1839 Francis Worker
1840 William Lambert
1852 Samuel Pulliam
1853 Joseph Mayo
1865 David J. Saunders
1866 Joseph Mayo
1868 George Chahoon
Joseph Mayo
1870 Vacant
1871 A. M. Keiley
1876 William C. Carrington
1888 J. Taylor Ellyson
1894 Richard M. Taylor
1904 Carlton McCarthy
1908 David C. Richardson
1912 George Ainslie
1924 J. Fulmer Bright
1940 Gordon B. Ambler
1944 William C. Herbert
1946 Horace H. Edwards
1948 W. Stirling King
1950 T. Nelson Parker
1952 Edward E. Haddock
1954 Thomas P. Bryan, Jr.
1956 F. Henry Garber
1958 A. Scott Anderson
1960 Claude W. Woodward
1962 Eleanor P. Sheppard
1964 Morrill M. Crowe
1968 Phil J. Bagley, Jr.
1970 Thomas J. Bliley, Jr.

SACRAMENTO, CALIFORNIA

1849 A. M. Winn
1850 Hardin Bigelow
Horace Smith
1851 James R. Hardenberg
1852 C. I. Hutchinson
1853 James R. Hardenberg
1854 R. P. Johnson
1855 James L. English
1856 B. B. Redding
1857 J. P. Dyer
1858 H. L. Nichols
1859 W. Shattuck
1863 C. H. Swift
1872 Christopher Green
1878 Jabez Turner
1881 John Q. Brown
1887 Eugene J. Gregory
1889 W. D. Comstock
1893 B. U. Steinman
1896 C. H. Hubbard
1898 William Land
1900 George H. Clark
1904 W. J. Hassett
1906 M. R. Beard
1908 Clinton I. White
1910 M. R. Beard
1912 M. J. Burke
1915 G. C. Simmons
1917 D. W. Carmichael
1919 John Q. Brown
1920 Charles A. Bliss
1921 Albert Alkus
1926 A. E. Goddard
1928 R. E. Conley
1929 Martin I. Welsh
1930 C. H. S. Bidwell
1934 Thomas P. Scollan
1935 Arthur D. Ferguson
1938 Tom B. Monk
1946 George L. Klumpp
1948 Belle Cooledge
1950 Bert E. Geisreiter
1952 Leslie E. Wood
1953 W. A. Hicks
1954 H. H. Hendren
1956 Clarence L. Azevedo
1960 James B. McKinney
1966 Walter Christensen
1968 Richard H. Marriott

ST. LOUIS, MISSOURI

1823 William C. Lane
1829 Daniel D. Page
1833 John W. Johnston
1835 John F. Darby
1837 William C. Lane
1840 John F. Darby
1841 John D. Daggett
1842 George Maguire
1843 John M. Wimer
1844 Bernard Pratte
1846 Peter G. Camden
1847 Bryan Mullanphy
1848 John M. Krum
1849 James G. Barry
1850 Luther M. Kennett
1853 John How
1855 Washington King
1856 John How
1857 John M. Wimer
1858 Oliver D. Filley
1861 Daniel G. Taylor
1863 Chauncey I. Filley
1864 James S. Thomas
1869 Nathan Cole
1871 Joseph Brown
1875 Arthur B. Barret
James H. Britton
1876 Henry Overstolz
1881 William L. Ewing
1885 David R. Francis
1889 Edward A. Noonan
1893 Cyrus P. Walbridge
1897 Henry Ziegenhein
1901 Rolla Wells
1909 Frederick Kreismann
1913 Henry W. Kiel
1925 Victor J. Miller
1933 Bernard F. Dickmann
1941 William D. Becker
1943 Aloys P. Kaufmann
1949 Joseph M. Darst
1953 Raymond R. Tucker
1965 Alfonso J. Cervantes

ST. PAUL, MINNESOTA

1850 Thomas R. Potts
1851 Robert Kennedy
1852 Bushrod W. Lott
1854 David Olmsted
1855 Alexander Ramsey
1856 George L. Becker
1857 John B. Brisbin
1858 Norman W. Kittson
1859 Daniel A. Robertson
1860 John S. Prince
1863 John E. Warren
1864 Jacob H. Stewart
1865 John S. Prince
1867 George L. Otis
1868 Jacob H. Stewart
1869 James T. Maxfield
1870 William Lee
1872 Jacob H. Stewart
1875 James T. Maxfield
1878 William Dawson
1881 Edmund Rice
1883 Christopher D. O'Brien
1885 Edmund Rice
1887 Robert A. Smith
1892 Frederick P. Wright
1894 Robert A. Smith
1896 Frank B. Doran
1898 Andrew R. Kiefer
1900 Robert A. Smith
1908 Daniel W. Lawler
1910 Herbert P. Keller
1914 Winn Powers
1916 Vivian R. Irvin
1918 Laurence C. Hodgson
1922 Arthur E. Nelson
1926 Laurence C. Hodgson
1930 Gerhard J. Bundlie
1932 William Mahoney
1934 Mark H. Gehan
1938 William H. Fallon
1940 John J. McDonough
1948 Edward K. Delaney
1952 John E. Daubney
1954 Joseph E. Dillon
1960 George J. Vavoulis
1966 Thomas R. Byrne
1970 Charles P. McCarty

SALEM, MASSACHUSETTS

1836 Leverett Saltonstall
1838 Stephen C. Phillips
1842 Stephen P. Webb
1845 Joseph S. Cabot
1849 Nathaniel Silsbee, Jr.
1851 David Pingree
1852 Charles W. Upham
1853 Asahel Huntington
1854 Joseph Andrews
1856 William S. Messervy
1858 Nathaniel Silsbee, Jr.
1860 Stephen P. Webb
1863 Stephen G. Wheatland
1865 Joseph B. Osgood
1866 David Roberts
1868 William Cogswell
1870 Nathaniel Brown
1872 Samuel Calley
1873 William Cogswell
1875 Henry L. Williams
1877 Henry K. Oliver
1881 Samuel Calley
1883 William M. Hill
1885 Arthur L. Huntington
1886 John M. Raymond
1890 Robert S. Rantoul
1894 James H. Turner
1898 David P. Waters
1899 James H. Turner
1900 David M. Little
1901 John F. Hurley
1903 Joseph N. Peterson
1906 Thomas C. Pinnock
1908 John F. Hurley
1910 Arthur F. Howard
1911 Rufus D. Adams
1913 John F. Hurley
1915 Matthias J. O'Keefe
1916 Henry P. Benson
1918 Denis J. Sullivan
1924 George J. Bates
1938 Edward A. Coffey
1948 Joseph B. Harrington
1950 Francis X. Collins
1970 Samuel E. Zoll

SALEM, OREGON

1857 Wiley Kenyon
1861 Lucien Heath
1862 E. N. Cooke
1863 H. M. Thatcher
1864 John H. Moores
1865 J. Q. Wilson
1866 John H. Moores
1869 L. S. Scott
1871 J. W. Smith
1872 Daniel Payton
1873 A. J. Monroe
1874 John G. Wright
1877 T. M. Gatch
1879 G. W. Gray
1880 T. B. Wait
1881 J. W. Crawford
1883 Andrew Kelly
1885 W. W. Skinner
1887 William M. Ramsey
1888 J. J. Murphy
1889 George Williams
1891 P. H. D'Arcy
1893 Claude Gatch
1897 J. A. Richardson
1899 Charles P. Bishop
1904 F. W. Waters
1907 G. F. Rodgers
1911 Louis Lachmund
1913 J. C. Siegmund
1914 B. L. Steeves
1915 H. O. White
1917 Walter Keyes
1919 C. E. Albin
1920 O. J. Wilson
1921 G. E. Halvorsen
1923 J. B. Giesy
1927 T. A. Livesley
1931 P. M. Gregory
1933 Douglas McKay
1935 V. E. Kuhn
1939 W. W. Chadwick
1943 I. M. Doughton
1947 Robert L. Elfstrom
1951 Alfred W. Loucks
1954 Robert White
1959 Russell F. Bonesteele
1963 Willard C. Marshall
1965 Vern W. Miller

SALT LAKE CITY, UTAH

1851 Jedediah M. Grant
1857 Abraham O. Smoot
1866 Daniel H. Wells
1876 Feramorz Little
1882 William Jennings
1884 James Sharp
1886 Francis Armstrong
1890 George M. Scott
1892 Robert N. Baskin
1896 James Glendinning
1898 John Clark
1900 Ezra Thompson
1904 Richard P. Morris
1906 Ezra Thompson
1907 John S. Bransford
1912 Samuel C. Park
1916 William M. Ferry
1920 E. A. Bock
Charles C. Neslen
1928 John F. Bowman
1932 Louis Marcus
1936 E. B. Erwin
1938 John M. Wallace
1940 Ab. Jenkins
1944 Earl J. Glade
1956 Adiel F. Stewart
1960 J. Bracken Lee

SAN ANTONIO, TEXAS

1837 John W. Smith
1838 Antonio Menchaca
1839 S. A. Maverick
1840 John W. Smith
1841 Juan N. Sequin
Francis Gilbeau (Acting)
1842 John W. Smith
1844 Edward Dwyer
1847 S. S. Smith
1848 Charles F. King

1849 J. M. Devine
1851 J. S. McDonald
1852 C. F. King
1853 J. M. Devine
1854 John M. Carolan
1855 James R. Sweet
1856 J. M. Devine
1857 J. H. Beck (Acting)
A. A. Lockwood
1858 James R. Sweet
1862 S. A. Maverick
1863 P. S. Buquor
1865 J. H. Lyons
1867 W. C. A. Thielepape
1872 S. G. Newton
F. Giraud
1875 James H. French
1885 Bryan Callaghan
1892 A. I. Lockwood
1893 George Paschal
1894 Henry Elmendorf
1897 Bryan Callaghan
1899 Marshall Hicks
1903 John S. Campbell
1905 Bryan Callaghan
1912 A. H. Jones
1913 Clinton G. Brown
1917 Sam C. Bell
1921 O. B. Black
1923 John W. Tobin
1927 C. M. Chambers
1933 C. K. Quin
1939 Maury Maverick
1941 C. K. Quin
1943 Gus B. Mauerman
1947 Alfred Callaghan
1949 A. C. White
1952 Sam B. Steves
1953 A. C. White
1954 R. L. Lester
R. N. White, Sr.
1955 J. Edwin Kuykendall
1961 Walter W. McAllister
1971 John Gatti

SAN DIEGO, CALIFORNIA

1850 Joshua H. Bean
1851 David B. Kurtz
1852 George P. Tebbetts
1887 W. J. Hunsaker
1889 Douglas Gunn
1891 Matthew Sherman
1893 William H. Carlson
1897 D. C. Reed
1899 Edwin M. Capps
1901 Frank P. Frary
1905 John L. Sehon
1907 John F. Forward, Jr.
1909 Grant Conard
1911 James E. Wadham
1913 Charles F. O'Neall
1915 Edwin M. Capps
1917 Louis J. Wilde
1921 John L. Bacon
1927 Harry C. Clark
1931 Walter W. Austin
1932 John F. Forward, Jr.
1934 Rutherford B. Irones
1935 Percy J. Benbough
1942 Howard B. Bard
1943 Harley E. Knox
1951 John D. Butler
1955 Charles C. Dail
1963 Frank E. Curran

SAN FRANCISCO, CALIFORNIA

Alcaldes

1846 Washington A. Bartlett
1847 G. Hyde Bryant
1848 J. Townsend
T. M. Leavenworth
1849 John W. Geary

Mayors

1850 John W. Geary
1851 Charles J. Brenham
1852 Steven R. Harris
1853 Cornelius K. Garrison
1854 Stephen P. Webb
1855 James Van Ness
1856 Ephriam W. Burr
1859 Henry F. Teschemacher
1863 Henry P. Coon
1867 Frank McCoppin
1869 Thomas H. Selby
1871 William Alvord
1873 James Otis
1875 George Hewston
Andrew J. Bryant
1879 Isaac S. Kalloch
1881 Maurice C. Blake
1883 Washington Bartlett
1887 Edward B. Pond
1891 George H. Sanderson
1893 Levi R. Ellert
1895 Adolph Sutro
1897 James D. Phelan
1902 Eugene E. Schmitz
1907 Charles Boxton
Edward R. Taylor
1910 Patrick H. McCarthy
1912 James Rolph, Jr.
1931 Angelo J. Rossi
1944 Roger D. Lapham
1948 Elmer E. Robinson
1956 George Christopher
1964 John F. Shelley
1968 Joseph L. Alioto

SANTA FE, NEW MEXICO

1891 William T. Thornton
1892 Manuel Valdez
1893 R. E. Twitchell
1894 J. H. Sloan
1895 Charles F. Easley
1896 Pedro Delgado
1897 Charles A. Spiess
1898 J. R. Hudson
1899 J. H. Sloan
1901 Amado Chaves
1902 I. Sparks
1904 A. R. Gibson
1906 Thomas B. Catron
1908 Jose D. Sena
1910 Arthur Seligman
1912 Celso Lopez
1914 William G. Sargent
1918 E. P. Davies
1920 T. Z. Winter
1922 Charles C. Closson
1924 Nathan Jaffa
1926 Edward L. Safford
1928 James C. McConnery
1932 David Chavez, Jr.
1934 William Barker
1936 Frank Andrews
1938 Alfredo Ortiz
1942 Manuel Lujan
1948 Frank S. Ortiz
1952 H. Paul Huss
1956 Leo T. Murphy
1962 Pat Hollis
1965 George A. Gonzales

SEATTLE, WASHINGTON

1869 Henry A. Atkins
1871 John T. Jordan
1872 Corliss P. Stone
1873 Moses R. Maddocks
John Collins
1874 Henry L. Yesler
1875 Bailey Gatzert
1876 Gideon A. Weed
1878 Beriah Brown
1879 Orange Jacobs
1880 L. P. Smith
1882 Henry G. Struve
1884 John Leary
1885 Henry L. Yesler
1886 William H. Shoudy
1887 Thomas T. Minor
1888 Robert Moran
1890 Harry White
1891 George W. Hall
1892 James T. Ronald
1894 Byron Phelps
1896 Frank D. Black
W. D. Wood
1897 Thomas D. Humes
1904 Richard A. Ballinger
1906 William H. Moore
1908 John F. Miller
1910 Hiram C. Gill
1911 George W. Dilling
1912 George F. Cotterill
1914 Hiram C. Gill
1918 Ole Hanson
1919 C. B. Fitzgerald
1920 Hugh M. Caldwell
1922 Edwin J. Brown
1926 Bertha K. Landes
1928 Frank E. Edwards
1931 Robert H. Harlin
1932 John F. Dore
1934 Charles L. Smith
1936 John F. Dore
1938 Arthur B. Langlie
1941 John E. Carroll
Earl Milliken
1942 William F. Devin
1952 Allan Pomeroy
1956 Gordon S. Clinton
1964 J. D. Braman
1969 Floyd C. Miller
Wesley C. Uhlman

SPRINGFIELD, ILLINOIS

1840 Banjamin S. Clements
1841 William L. May
1842 Daniel B. Campbell
1843 Daniel B. Hill
1844 Andrew McCromick
1845 James C. Conkling
1846 Eli Cook
1849 John Calhoun
1852 William Lavely
1853 Josiah Francis
1854 William H. Herndon
1855 John Cook
1856 John W. Priest
1859 William Jayne
1860 Goyn A. Sutton
1861 George L. Huntington
1863 John W. Smith
1864 John S. Vredenburgh
1865 John J. Dennis
1866 John S. Bradford
1867 Norman M. Broadwell
1868 William E. Shutt
1869 Norman M. Broadwell
1870 John W. Priest
1871 John W. Smith
1873 Charles E. Hay
1874 Obed Lewis
1875 Charles E. Hay
1876 William Jayne
1878 John A. Vincent
1879 R. L. McGuire
1880 Horace C. Irwin
1881 John McCreery
1882 A. N. J. Crook
1883 John McCreery
1885 James M. Garland
1887 Charles E. Hay
1891 Rheuna D. Lawrence
1894 Frank Kramer
1896 Marion U. Woodruff
1898 Loren E. Wheeler
1901 John L. Phillips
1903 Harry H. Devereux
1907 David S. Griffiths
Roy R. Reece
1909 John S. Schnepp
1915 Charles T. Baumann
1923 Samuel Bullard
1926 J. Emil Smith
1930 Hal M. Smith
1931 John W. Kapp, Jr.
1947 Harry Eielson
1951 John E. MacWherter
1955 Nelson O. Howarth
1959 Lester E. Collins
1963 Nelson O. Howarth
1971 William C. Telford

TALLAHASSEE, FLORIDA

1826 Charles Haire
1827 David Ochiltree
1828 John Y. Gary
1830 Leslie A. Thompson
1831 Charles Austin
1832 Leslie A. Thompson
1834 Robert J. Hackley
1835 William Wilson
Charles Haire
William Hilliard
1836 John Rea
1837 William P. Gorman
1838 William Hilliard
1839 R. F. Ker
1840 Leslie A. Thompson
1841 Francis Epps
1845 James A. Berthelot
1846 Simon Towle

1847 James Kirksey
1848 F. H. Flagg
1849 Thomas J. Perkins
1850 D. P. Hogue
1852 David S. Walker
1853 Richard Hayward
1854 Thomas Hayward
1856 Francis Epps
1858 D. P. Hogue
1861 P. T. Pearce
1866 Francis Epps
1867 D. P. Hogue
1869 T. P. Tatum
1871 C. E. Dyke
1872 C. H. Edwards
1875 David S. Walker, Jr.
1876 Samuel Walker
1877 Jesse T. Bernard
1878 David S. Walker, Jr.
1880 Henry Bernreuter
1881 Edward Lewis
1882 John W. Nash
1883 Edward Lewis
1884 Charles C. Pearce
1886 George W. Walker
1887 A. J. Fish
1888 R. B. Gorman
1890 R. B. Carpenter
1895 Jesse T. Bernard
1897 R. A. Shino
1898 R. B. Gorman
1903 William L. Moor
1905 John W. Henderson
1906 F. C. Gilmore
1907 W. M. McIntosh, Jr.
1908 F. C. Gilmore
1909 Francis B. Winthrop
1910 D. M. Lowry
1918 J. R. McDaniel
1919 Guyte P. McCord
1922 A. P. McCaskill
1923 Guyte P. McCord
B. A. Meginniss
1928 W. Theodore Proctor
1930 G. E. Lewis
1931 Frank D. Moor
W. Theo Proctor
W. L. Marshall
1934 J. L. Fain
1935 L. A. Wesson
1936 H. J. Yaeger
1937 L. A. Wesson
1938 J. R. Jinks
1939 S. A. Wahnish
1940 F. C. Moor
S. A. Wahnish
1941 Charles S. Ausley
1942 Jack W. Simmons
1943 A. R. Richardson
1944 Charles S. Ausley
1945 Ralph E. Proctor
1946 Fred S. Winterle
1947 George I. Martin
1948 Fred N. Lowry
1949 Robert C. Parker
1951 W. H. Cates
1952 B. A. Ragsdale
1953 William T. Mayo
1954 H. G. Easterwood
H. C. Summitt
1955 J. T. Williams
1956 Fred S. Winterle
John Y. Humphress
1957 J. W. Cordell
1958 Davis H. Atkinson
1959 Hugh E. Williams, Jr.
1960 George Taff
1961 J. W. Cordell
1962 Davis H. Atkinson
1963 Sam E. Teague, Jr.
1964 Hugh E. Williams, Jr.
1965 George S. Taff
1966 W. H. Cates
John A. Rudd, Sr.
1967 Gene Berkowitz
Spurgeon Camp
1968 W. H. Cates
George S. Taff
1969 Lee A. Everhart
1970 Spurgeon Camp
Gene Berkowitz
1972 Arvah B. Hopkins

TOPEKA, KANSAS

1858 Loring Farnsworth
1859 Lorenzo Dow
Cyrus K. Holliday
1860 Hiram W. Farnsworth
1861 Harris F. Otis
1862 N. W. Cox
1863 J. F. Cummings
1864 Samuel H. Fletcher
1865 W. W. Ross
1866 Ross Burns
1867 Cyrus K. Holliday
1868 Orin T. Welch
1869 Cyrus K. Holliday
1870 J. B. McAfee
1871 Orin T. Welch
1873 Henry Bartling
1875 Thomas J. Anderson
1877 W. H. Case
1881 Joseph C. Wilson
1883 Bradford Miller
1885 Rosswell T. Cofran
1887 D. C. Metsker
1889 Rosswell T. Cofran
1893 D. C. Jones
W. Harrison
1895 Charles A. Fellows
1899 Charles J. Drew
1901 J. W. F. Hughes
1902 Albert Parker
1903 W. S. Bergundthal
1905 W. H. Davis
1907 William Green
1910 J. B. Billard
1913 Rosswell T. Cofran
1915 Jay E. House
1919 Herbert J. Corwine
1923 Earl Akers
1925 James E. Thomas
1927 W. O. Rigby
1931 Omar B. Ketchum
1935 Herbert G. Barrett
1939 John F. Scott
1941 Frank J. Warren
1951 Kenneth W. Wilke
1953 George G. Schnellbacher
1959 E. J. Camp
1963 Hal W. Gerlach
1965 Charles W. Wright, Jr.
1969 Gene C. Martin
1971 William B. McCormick

TRENTON, NEW JERSEY

1792 Moore Furman
1794 Aaron D. Woodruff
1797 James Ewing
1803 Joshua Wright
1806 Stacy Potts
1814 Robert McNealy
1832 Charles Burroughs
1847 Samuel R. Hamilton
1849 William C. Howell
1850 William Napton
1852 John R. Tucker
1854 William Napton
1855 William P. Sherman
John R. Tucker
1856 Joseph Wood
1859 Franklin S. Mills
1861 William R. McKean
1863 Franklin S. Mills
1867 Alfred Reed
1868 William Napton
1871 John Briest
1875 Wesley Creveling
1877 Daniel R. Bodine
1879 William Rice
1881 Garret D. W. Vroom
1884 Richard A. Donnelly
1886 John Woolverton
1887 Frank A. Magowan
1889 Anthony A. Skirm
1891 Daniel J. Bechtel
1893 Joseph B. Shaw
1895 Emory N. Yard
1897 Welling G. Sickel
1899 Frank O. Briggs
1902 Frank S. Katzenbach, Jr.
1906 Frederick W. Gnichtel
1908 Walter Madden
1911 Frederick W. Donnelly
1932 George B. LaBarre
1935 William J. Connor
1939 Leo J. Rogers
Edward W. Lee
1941 John A. Hartmann
1943 Andrew J. Duch
1947 Donal J. Connolly
1959 Arthur J. Holland
1966 Carmen J. Armenti
1970 Arthur J. Holland

WASHINGTON, D. C.

Mayors

1802 Robert Brent
1812 Daniel Rapine
1813 James Blake
1817 Benjamin G. Orr
1819 Samuel N. Smallwood
1822 Thomas Carberry
1824 Samuel N. Smallwood
Roger C. Weightman
1827 Joseph Gales, Jr.
1830 John P. Van Ness
1834 William A. Bradley
1836 Peter Force
1840 William W. Seaton
1850 Walter Lenox
1852 John W. Maury
1854 John T. Towers
1856 William B. Magruder
1858 James G. Berrett
1861 Richard Wallach
1868 Sayles J. Bowen
1870 Matthew G. Emery
1871 Vacant

Presidents of the Board of Commissioners

1878 Seth L. Phelps
1879 Josiah Dent
1882 Joseph R. West
1885 James B. Edmonds
1886 William B. Webb
1889 John W. Douglass
1893 John W. Ross
1898 John B. Wright
1900 Henry B. F. Macfarland
1910 C. Hugo Rudolph
1913 Oliver P. Newman
1917 Louis Brownlow
1920 Charles W. Kutz (Acting)
John T. Hendrick
1921 C. Hugo Rudolph
1926 Proctor L. Dougherty
1930 Luther H. Reichelderfer
1933 Melvin C. Hazen
1941 John R. Young
1952 F. Joseph Donohue
1953 Samuel Spencer
1956 Robert E. McLaughlin
1961 Walter N. Tobriner

Commissioners (Mayors)

1967 Walter E. Washington

XII

HIGHER EDUCATION

Included in this listing are the chief executives of 300 leading colleges and universities of the United States. The first year for each entry represents the year in which the school became a degree-granting, four-year institution and not necessarily the year of its founding. In some instances the president was named to that post in a year earlier than that of the initial entry; this occurs when the institution was elevated to four year status during the president's term of office. Unless otherwise specified the chief executive has the title of president.

ADELPHI UNIVERSITY
Garden City, New York

Adelphi College until 1963

1896 Charles H. Levermore
1912 S. Parkes Cadman (Acting)
1915 Frank D. Blodgett
1937 Paul D. Eddy
1965 Arthur W. Brown
1967 Robert G. Olmsted (Acting)
1969 Charles Vevier
1972 Timothy W. Costello

UNIVERSITY OF AKRON
Akron, Ohio

Buchtel College until 1913
Municipal University of Akron until 1926

1872 S. H. McCollester
1878 E. L. Rexford
1880 Orello Cone
1896 Charles M. Knight (Acting)
1897 Ira A. Priest
1901 A. B. Church
1913 Parke R. Kolbe
1925 George F. Zook
1933 Hezzleton E. Simmons
1951 Norman P. Auburn
1971 Dominic J. Guzzetta

UNIVERSITY OF ALABAMA
Tuscaloosa, Alabama

1831 Alva Woods
1837 Basil Manly
1855 Landon C. Garland
1866 Vacant
1871 Nathaniel T. Lupton
1874 Carlos G. Smith
1878 Josiah Gorgas
1879 William S. Wyman (Acting)
1880 B. B. Lewis
1885 William S. Wyman (Acting)
1886 Henry D. Clayton
1890 Richard C. Jones
1897 James K. Powers
1901 William S. Wyman
1902 John W. Abercrombie
1911 William B. Saffold
1912 George H. Denny
1937 Richard C. Foster
1941 George H. Denny
1942 Raymond R. Paty
1947 Ralph E. Adams (Acting)
1948 John M. Gallalee
1953 Lee Bidgood (Acting)
1953 Oliver C. Carmichael
1957 James H. Newman (Acting)
1958 Frank A. Rose
1969 F. David Mathews
1969 Joseph Volker (Birmingham)
1969 Benjamin B. Graves (Huntsville)

ALBION COLLEGE
Albion, Michigan

1861 Thomas H. Sinex
1864 George B. Jocelyn
1870 William B. Silber
1871 J. L. G. McKeown
1871 George B. Jocelyn
1877 Lewis R. Fiske
1898 John P. Ashley
1902 Samuel Dickie
1921 John W. Laird
1924 John L. Seaton
1945 William W. Whitehouse
1960 Louis W. Norris
1970 Bernard T. Lomas

ALBRIGHT COLLEGE
Reading, Pennsylvania

Central Pennsylvania College until 1902

1887 Aaron Gobble
1902 James D. Woodring
1908 Clellan A. Bowman (Acting)
1909 John F. Dunlap
1915 L. Clarence Hunt
1923 Clellan A. Bowman
1928 Warren F. Teel
1932 J. Warren Klein
1938 Harry V. Masters
1965 Arthur L. Schultz

ALFRED UNIVERSITY
Alfred, New York

1857 William C. Kenyon
1867 Jonathan M. Allen
1892 Alpheus B. Kenyon (Acting)
1893 Arthur E. Main
1895 Boothe C. Davis
1933 Paul E. Titsworth
1933 John N. Norwood
1945 Jack E. Walters
1948 Miles E. Drake
1967 Leland W. Miles

ALLEGHENY COLLEGE
Meadville, Pennsylvania

1815 Timothy Alden
1833 Martin Ruter
1837 Homer J. Clark
1947 John Barker
1860 George Loomis
1874 Jonathan Hamnett (Acting)
1875 Lucius Bugbee
1882 Jonathan Hamnett (Acting)
1883 David H. Wheeler
1888 Wilbur G. Williams
1889 David H. Wheeler
1893 William H. Crawford
1920 Fred W. Hixson
1924 Clarence F. Ross (Acting)
1926 James A. Beebe
1930 Clarence F. Ross (Acting)
1931 William P. Tolley
1942 John R. Schultz
1947 Chester A. Darling (Acting)
1948 Louis T. Benezet
1955 Lawrence L. Pelletier

THE AMERICAN UNIVERSITY
Washington, D. C.

Chancellors

1891 John F. Hurst
1902 Charles C. McCabe
1906 Wilbur L. Davidson (in charge)
1907 Franklin Hamilton
1922 Lucius C. Clark
1933 Edwin H. Hughes (Acting)
1934 Joseph M. M. Gray

Presidents

1940 E. W. Engel (Acting)
1941 Paul F. Douglass
1951 James J. Robbins (Acting)
1952 Hurst R. Anderson
1968 George H. Williams

AMHERST COLLEGE
Amherst, Massachusetts

1821 Zephaniah S. Moore
1823 Heman Humphrey
1845 Edward Hitchcock
1854 William A. Stearns
1876 Julius H. Seelye
1890 Merrill E. Gates
1899 George Harris
1912 Alexander Meiklejohn
1924 George D. Olds
1927 Arthur S. Pease
1932 Stanley King
1946 Charles W. Cole
1960 Calvin H. Plimpton
1971 John W. Ward

ANTIOCH COLLEGE
Yellow Springs, Ohio

1853 Horace Mann
1860 Thomas Hill
1862 Austin Craig
1862 John B. Weston (Acting)
1866 George W. Hosmer
1872 Edward Orton
1873 Samuel C. Derby (Acting)
1876 John B. Weston (Acting)
1882 Orin J. Wait
1883 Daniel A. Long
1899 William A. Bell
1902 Franklin Hooper (Acting)
1906 Simeon D. Fess
1917 George D. Black (Acting)
1919 William M. Dawson (Acting)
1921 Arthur E. Morgan
1935 Algo D. Henderson
1948 Douglas McGregor
1954 Samuel B. Gould
1959 James P. Dixon, Jr.

UNIVERSITY OF ARIZONA
Tucson, Arizona

1893 Theodore B. Comstock
1895 Howard Billman
1897 Millard M. Parker
1901 Frank Y. Adams
1903 Kendric C. Babcock
1910 Andrew E. Douglass
1911 Arthur H. Wilde
1914 Rufus B. von KleinSmid
1922 Francis C. Lockwood
1922 Cloyd H. Marvin
1927 Byron Cummings
1928 Homer L. Shantz
1936 Paul S. Burgess
1937 Alfred Atkinson
1947 James B. McCormick
1951 Richard A. Harvill
1972 John P. Schaefer

ARIZONA STATE UNIVERSITY
Tempe, Arizona

1925 Arthur J. Matthews
1930 Ralph W. Swetman
1933 Grady Gammage
1959 Harold D. Richardson (Acting)
1960 G. Homer Durham
1969 Harry K. Newburn
1971 John W. Schwada

UNIVERSITY OF ARKANSAS
Fayetteville, Arkansas

Arkansas Industrial University until 1899

1871 Noah P. Gates
1873 Albert W. Bishop
1875 Noah P. Gates
1877 Daniel H. Hill
1884 George M. Edgar
1887 Edward H. Murfee
1894 John L. Buchanan
1902 Henry S. Hartzog
1905 John N. Tillman
1913 John C. Futrall
1939 J. William Fulbright
1941 Arthur M. Harding
1947 Lewis W. Jones
1951 Joe E. Covington
1952 John T. Caldwell
1959 Storm H. Whaley
1960 David W. Mullins

AUBURN UNIVERSITY
Auburn, Alabama

East Alabama Male College until 1899

1858 William J. Sasmett
1866 James F. Dowdell
1872 Isaac T. Tichenor
1882 William L. Broun
1883 David F. Boyd
1884 William L. Broun

1902 Charles C. Thach
1919 Bennett B. Ross (Acting)
1920 Spright Dowell
1928 Bradford Knapp
1932 John J. Wilmore
Bolling H. Crenshaw
Luther N. Duncan
1935 Luther N. Duncan
1947 Ralph B. Draughon
1965 Harry M. Philpott

BAKER UNIVERSITY
Baldwin City, Kansas

1858 Werter R. Davis
1862 George W. Paddock
1864 Leonard L. Hartman
1865 John W. Locke
1866 John W. Horner
1867 Elial J. Rice
1869 John A. Simpson
1870 Patterson McNutt
1871 Robert L. Harford
1873 Samuel S. Weatherby
1874 Joseph J. Denison
1879 William H. Sweet
1886 Hillary A. Gobin
1890 William A. Quayle
1894 Lemuel H. Murlin
1911 Wilbur N. Mason
1917 Samuel A. Lough
1921 Osmon G. Markham
1922 Wallace B. Fleming
1936 Nelson P. Horn
1956 William J. Scarborough
1966 James E. Doty

BALL STATE UNIVERSITY
Muncie, Indiana

Ball State Teachers College until 1965

1927 Lemuel A. Pittenger
1943 W. E. Wagoner (Acting)
1945 John R. Emens
1968 John J. Pruis

BARD COLLEGE
Annandale, New York

St. Stephens College until 1934

1860 George F. Seymour
1861 Thomas Richey
1863 Robert B. Fairbairn
1899 Lawrence T. Cole
1904 Thomas R. Harris
1909 William C. Rodgers
1919 Bernard I. Bell
1933 Donald G. Tewksbury
1938 Harold Mestre
1940 Harold Gray
1948 Edward C. Fuller
1950 James H. Case, Jr.
1960 Reamer Kline

BARNARD COLLEGE
New York City

Deans

1894 Emily James (Smith) Putnam
1901 Laura Drake Gill
1907 Vacant
1911 Virginia Crocheron Gildersleeve

Presidents

1947 Millicent Carey McIntosh
1962 Rosemary (Park) Anastos
1967 Martha E. Peterson

BERNARD M. BARUCH COLLEGE OF THE CITY UNIVERSITY OF NEW YORK

1968 Samuel F. Thomas (Acting)
1969 Robert C. Weaver
1970 Jerome B. Cohen (Acting)
1971 Clyde J. Wingfield

BATES COLLEGE
Lewiston, Maine

1863 Oren B. Cheney
1894 George C. Chase
1920 Clifton D. Gray
1944 Charles F. Phillips
1967 Thomas H. Reynolds

BAYLOR UNIVERSITY
Waco, Texas

1845 Henry L. Graves
1851 Rufus C. Burleson
1861 George W. Baines
1863 William C. Crane
1885 Reddin Andrews
1886 Rufus C. Burleson
1897 Vacant
1899 Oscar H. Cooper
1902 Samuel P. Brooks
1932 Pat M. Neff
1948 William R. White
1961 Abner V. McCall

BELOIT COLLEGE
Beloit, Wisconsin

1850 Aaron L. Chapin
1886 Edward D. Eaton
1917 Melvin A. Brannon
1923 Edward D. Eaton (Acting)
1924 W. Irving Maurer
1942 W. Bradley Tyrell (Acting)
1944 Carey Croneis
1954 Harold S. Wood (Acting)
1954 Miller Upton

BENNINGTON COLLEGE
Bennington, Vermont

1928 Robert D. Leigh
1941 Lewis W. Jones
1947 Frederick Burkhardt
1957 William C. Fels
1965 Edward J. Bloustein
1971 Gail T. Parker

BEREA COLLEGE
Berea, Kentucky

1853 John G. Fee
1869 Edward Fairchild
1892 William G. Frost
1920 William J. Hutchins
1939 Francis S. Hutchins
1967 Willis D. Weatherford

BETHANY COLLEGE
Bethany, West Virginia

1840 Alexander Campbell
1866 William K. Pendleton
1887 W. H. Woolery
1889 Archibald McLean
1891 Hugh McDiarmid
1897 B. C. Hagerman
1899 J. M. Kershey
1901 Thomas E. Cramblet
1919 Cloyd Goodnight
1933 Joseph A. Serena
1934 W. H. Cramblet
1953 Perry E. Gresham

BOSTON COLLEGE
Chestnut Hill, Massachusetts

1863 John Bapst
1869 Robert W. Brady
1870 Robert B. Fulton
1880 Jeremiah O'Connor
1884 Edward V. Boursaud
1887 Thomas H. Stack
1887 Nicholas Russo
1888 Robert B. Fulton
1891 Edward I. Devitt
1894 Timothy Brosnahan
1898 W. J. Reid Mullan
1903 William F. Gannon
1907 Thomas I. Gasson
1914 Charles W. Lyons
1919 William Devlin
1925 James H. Dolan
1932 Louis Gallagher
1937 William J. McGarry
1939 William J. Murphy
1945 William J. Keleher
1951 Joseph R. N. Maxwell
1958 Michael P. Walsh
1968 W. Seavey Joyce
1972 T. Donald Moran

BOSTON UNIVERSITY
Boston, Massachusetts

1873 William F. Warren
1903 William E. Huntington
1911 Lemuel H. Murlin
1925 W. F. Anderson
1926 Daniel L. Marsh
1951 Harold C. Case
1967 Arland F. Christ-Janer
1970 John R. Silber

BOWDOIN COLLEGE
Brunswick, Maine

1802 Joseph McKeen
1807 Jesse Appleton
1820 William Allen
1839 Leonard Woods
1867 Samuel Harris
1871 Joshua L. Chamberlain
1885 William D. Hyde
1918 Kenneth C. M. Sills
1952 James S. Coles
1968 Athern P. Daggett (Acting)
1969 Roger Howell, Jr.

BOWLING GREEN STATE UNIVERSITY

Bowling Green State Normal College until 1929
Bowling Green State College until 1935

1912 Homer B. Williams
1937 Roy E. Offenhauer
1939 Frank J. Prout
1951 Ralph W. McDonald
1961 Ralph G. Harshman
1963 William T. Jerome III
1970 Hollis A. Moore

BRADLEY UNIVERSITY
Peoria, Illinois

Bradley Polytechnic Institute until 1946

1897 William R. Harper
1906 Theodore C. Burgess
1925 Charles T. Wyckoff (Acting)
1925 Frederick R. Hamilton
1946 David B. Owen
1952 A. G. Haussler (Acting)
1954 Harold P. Rodes
1960 A. G. Haussler (Acting)
1961 T. W. Van Arsdale, Jr.

BRANDEIS UNIVERSITY
Waltham, Massachusetts

1948 Abram B. Sachar
1968 Morris B. Abram
1970 Charles I. Schottland
1971 Marver H. Bernstein

UNIVERSITY OF BRIDGEPORT
Bridgeport, Connecticut

Junior College of Connecticut until 1947

1946 James H. Halsey
1962 Henry W. Littlefield
1971 Thurston E. Manning

BRIGHAM YOUNG UNIVERSITY
Provo, Utah

Brigham Young Academy until 1903

1904 George H. Brimhall
1921 Franklin S. Harris
1945 Howard S. McDonald
1951 Ernest L. Wilkinson
1972 Dallin H. Oaks

BROOKLYN COLLEGE OF THE CITY UNIVERSITY OF NEW YORK

Brooklyn College until 1961

1930 William A. Boylan
1939 Harry D. Gideonse
1966 Francis P. Kilcoyne
1968 Harold C. Syrett
1969 John W. Kneller

BROWN UNIVERSITY
Providence, Rhode Island

Rhode Island College until 1804

1765 James Manning
1792 Jonathan Maxcy
1802 Asa Messer
1827 Francis Wayland
1855 Barnas Sears
1868 Alexis Caswell
1872 Ezekiel G. Robinson
1889 Elisha B. Andrews
1899 William H. P. Faunce
1929 Clarence A. Barbour
1937 Henry M. Wriston
1955 Barnaby C. Keeney
1966 Ray L. Heffner
1969 Merton P. Stoltz (Acting)
1970 Donald F. Hornig

BRYN MAWR COLLEGE
Bryn Mawr, Pennsylvania

1885 James E. Rhoads
1894 M. Carey Thomas
1922 Marion Edwards Park
1944 Katherine E. McBride
1970 Harris L. Wofford, Jr.

BUCKNELL UNIVERSITY
Lewisburg, Pennsylvania

The University at Lewisburg until 1886

1851 Howard Malcolm
1858 Justin R. Loomis
1879 David J. Hill
1889 John H. Harris
1919 Emory W. Hunt
1931 Homer P. Rainey
1935 Arnaud C. Marts (Acting)
1945 Herbert L. Spencer
1949 Horace A. Hildreth
1954 Merle M. Odgers
1964 Charles H. Watts II

BUTLER UNIVERSITY
Indianapolis, Indiana

1855 John Young
1858 Samuel Hoshour
1861 Allen R. Benton
1868 Otis R. Burgess
1870 W. F. Black
1873 Otis R. Burgess
1881 Harvey W. Everest
1885 Allen R. Benton
1891 Scot Butler
1904 Winfred E. Garrison
1906 Scot Butler
1907 Thomas Carr Howe
1920 James W. Putnam
1921 Robert J. Aley
1931 Walter S. Athearn
1933 James W. Putnam
1939 Daniel S. Robinson
1942 Maurice O. Ross
1963 Alexander E. Jones

UNIVERSITY OF CALIFORNIA
Berkeley, California

Presidents since 1952 have presided over the statewide university system and the chancellors over the Berkeley campus.

1868 John Le Conte (Acting)
1870 Henry Durant
1872 Daniel C. Gilman
1875 John Le Conte
1881 William T. Reid
1885 Edward S. Holden
1888 Horace Davis
1890 Martin Kellogg
1899 Benjamin I. Wheeler
1919 David P. Barrows
1923 William W.Campbell
1930 Robert G. Sproul
1958 Clark Kerr
1967 Henry R. Wellman (Acting)
1968 Charles J. Hitch

Chancellors

1952 Clark Kerr
1958 Glenn T. Seaborg
1961 Edward W. Strong
1965 Roger Heyns
1970 Albert W. Bowker

CALIFORNIA INSTITUTE OF TECHNOLOGY
Pasadena, California

Throop Polytechnic Institute until 1912
Throop College of Technology until 1919

1891 Charles H. Keyes
1897 Walter A. Edwards
1908 James A. B. Scherer
1921 Robert A. Millikan (Chairman of the Executive Council)
1946 Lee A. DuBridge
1969 Harold Brown

CALIFORNIA STATE COLLEGE, LONG BEACH
Long Beach, California

Long Beach State College from 1950 to 1964

1949 P. Victor Peterson
1959 Henry Magnusen (Interim)
1959 Carl W. McIntosh
1969 Donald Simonsen (Acting)
1970 Stephen Horn

CANISIUS COLLEGE
Buffalo, New York

1870 William Becker
1872 Henry Behrens
1876 John B. Lessmann
1877 Martin Port
1883 Theodore Van Rossum
1888 J. Ulric Heinzle
1891 John I. Zahm
1897 James A. Rockliff
1898 John B. Theis
1901 Aloysius J. Pfeil
1905 Augustine A. Miller
1913 George J. Krim
1919 Michael J. Ahern
1923 Peter Cusick
1929 Rudolph J. Eichhorn
1934 James P. Sweeney
1937 Francis A. O'Malley
1941 Timothy J. Coughlin
1947 Raymond W. Schouten
1952 Philip E. Dobson
1959 James J. McGinley
1966 James M. Demske

CAPITAL UNIVERSITY
Columbus, Ohio

1850 W. M. Reynolds
1854 C. Spielmann
1857 William F. Lehmann
1881 M. Loy
1890 C. H. Schuette
1894 William F. Stellhorn
1900 L. H. Schuh
1913 Otto Mees
1946 Harold L. Yochum
1969 Thomas H. Langevin

CARLETON COLLEGE
Northfield, Minnesota

1870 James W. Strong
1903 William H. Sallmon
1909 Donald J. Cowling
1945 Laurence M. Gould
1962 John W. Nason
1970 Howard R. Swearer

CARNEGIE-MELLON UNIVERSITY
Pittsburgh, Pennsylvania

Carnegie Institute of Technology until 1967

1912 Arthur A. Hamerschlag
1923 Thomas S. Baker
1936 Robert E. Doherty
1950 John C. Warner
1965 H. Guyford Stever
1972 Edward Schatz (Acting)

CARROLL COLLEGE
Waukesha, Wisconsin

1850 John A. Savage
1863 Rensellaer B. Hammond
1864 William Alexander
1866 Walter L. Rankin
1871 Vacant
1893 Walter L. Rankin
1903 Wilbur O. Carrier
1918 Herbert P. Houghton
1921 William A. Ganfield
1940 Gerrit T. Vander Lught
1946 Nelson V. Russell
1952 Robert D. Steele
1967 John T. Middaugh
1971 Robert V. Cramer

CARSON-NEWMAN COLLEGE
Jefferson City, Tennessee

1851 William Rogers
1851 R. R. Bryan
1853 Samuel Anderson
1857 Matt Hillsman
1859 N. B. Goforth
1866 R. R. Bryan
1869 Jesse Baker
1870 N. B. Goforth
1882 B. O. Manard
1883 S. W. Tindell
1888 W. A. Montgomery
1892 J. T. Henderson
1903 M. D. Jeffries
1912 J. M. Burnett
1917 W. L. Gentry
1920 Oscar E. Sams
1927 James T. Warren
1948 Daniel H. Fite
1968 John A. Fincher

CASE WESTERN RESERVE UNIVERSITY
Cleveland, Ohio

Created in 1967 from the merger of Case Institute of Technology with Western Reserve University.

1967 Robert W. Morse
1971 Louis A. Toepfer

CATHOLIC UNIVERSITY OF AMERICA
Washington, D.C.

1887 John J. Keane
1896 Thomas J. Conaty
1908 Denis J. O'Connell
1909 Thomas J. Shahan
1928 James H. Ryan
1936 Joseph M. Corrigan
1943 Patrick J. McCormick
1953 Bryan J. McEntegart
1957 William J. McDonald
1967 John P. Whalen
1968 Nivard Scheel
1969 Clarence C. Walton

UNIVERSITY OF CHICAGO
Chicago, Illinois

1891 William R. Harper
1906 Harry P. Judson
1923 Ernest D. Burton
1925 Max Mason
1928 Frederic C. Woodward (Acting)
1929 Robert M. Hutchins
1951 Lawrence A. Kimpton
1960 R. W. Harrison (Acting)
1961 George W. Beadle
1968 Edward H. Levi

UNIVERSITY OF CINCINNATI

Cincinnati College until 1870

1819 Elijah Slack
1822 Philander Chase
1823 Elijah Slack (Acting)
1836 William H. McGuffey
1839 Thomas J. Biggs
1845 Vacant
1873 George H. Harper
1877 Thomas Vickers
1884 Henry T. Eddy (Acting)
1885 Jacob D. Cox
1889 Henry T. Eddy
1891 Vacant
1899 Howard Ayers
1904 Joseph E. Harry (Acting)
1904 Charles W. Dabney
1920 Frederick C. Hicks
1928 Herman Schneider
1932 Raymond Walters
1955 Walter C. Langsam
1972 Warren G. Bennis

THE CITY COLLEGE OF THE CITY UNIVERSITY OF NEW YORK

City College of New York until 1961

1848 Horace Webster
1869 Alexander Webb
1902 Alfred G. Compton (Acting)
1903 John H. Finley
1913 Adolph Werner (Acting)
1915 Sidney E. Mezes
1927 Frederick B. Robinson
1938 Nelson P. Mead (Acting)
1941 Harry N. Wright
1952 Buell G. Gallagher
1961 Harry N. Rivlin (Acting)
1962 Buell G. Gallagher
1969 Joseph J. Copeland (Acting)
1970 Robert E. Marshak

CLEMSON UNIVERSITY
Clemson, South Carolina

Clemson Agricultural College of South Carolina until 1964

1890 H. A. Strode
1893 Edwin B. Craighead
1897 Henry S. Hartzog
1902 Patrick H. Mell
1910 Walter M. Riggs
1924 S. B. Earle (Acting)
1925 Enoch W. Sikes
1940 R. F. Poole
1958 Robert C. Edwards

COLBY COLLEGE
Waterville, Maine

Maine Literary and Theological Institution until 1821
Waterville College until 1867
Colby University until 1899

1818 Jeremiah Chaplin
1933 Rufus Babcock
1836 Robert E. Pattison
1839 George W. Keely (Acting)
1841 Eliphaz Fay
1843 David N. Sheldon
1854 Robert E. Pattison
1857 James T. Champlin
1873 Henry E. Robins
1882 George D. B. Pepper
1889 Albion W. Small
1892 Benaiah L. Whitman
1896 Nathaniel Butler, Jr.
1901 Charles L. White
1908 Arthur J. Roberts
1929 Franklin W. Johnson
1942 Julius S. Bixler
1960 Robert E. L. Strider II

COLGATE UNIVERSITY
Hamilton, New York

Madison University from 1846 to 1890

1851 Stephen W. Taylor
1856 George W. Eaton
1868 Ebenezer Dodge
1890 Vacant
1895 George W. Smith
1897 William H. Crawshaw (Acting)
1899 George E. Merrill
1909 Elmer B. Bryan
1922 George B. Cutten
1942 Everett N. Case
1963 Vincent M. Barnett, Jr.
1969 Thomas A. Bartlett

COLORADO UNIVERSITY
Boulder, Colorado

1877 Joseph A. Sewall
1887 Horace M. Hale
1892 James H. Baker
1914 Livingston Farrand
1919 George Norlin
1939 Robert L. Stearns
1953 Ward Darley
1956 James Q. Newton
1963 Joseph R. Smiley
1969 Eugene H. Wilson
1969 Frederick P. Thieme

COLORADO STATE UNIVERSITY
Fort Collins, Colorado

State Agricultural College of Colorado until 1935. Colorado State College of Agriculture and Mechanic Arts until 1944. Colorado Agricultural and Mechanical College until 1957.

1879 Elijah E. Edwards
1882 Charles L. Ingersoll
1892 Alston Ellis
1899 Barton O. Aylesworth
1909 Charles A. Lory
1940 Roy M. Green
1948 Isaac E. Newsom
1949 William E. Morgan
1969 Adrian R. Chamberlain

COLUMBIA UNIVERSITY
New York, New York

King's College until 1784
Columbia College until 1912

1754 Samuel Johnson
1763 Myles Cooper
1775 Benjamin Moore (Acting)
1781 Vacant
1787 William S. Johnson
1801 Charles H. Wharton
1801 Benjamin Moore
1811 William Harris
1829 William A. Duer
1842 Nathaniel F. Moore
1849 Charles King
1864 Frederick A. P. Barnard
1890 Seth Low
1902 Nicholas Murray Butler
1945 Frank D. Fackenthal (Acting)
1948 Dwight D. Eisenhower
1953 Grayson Kirk
1968 Andrew W. Cordier
1970 William J. McGill

UNIVERSITY OF CONNECTICUT

Connecticut Agricultural College from 1899 to 1933
Connecticut State College until 1939

1898 George W. Flint
1901 Rufus W. Stimson
1908 Edwin O. Smith (Acting)
1908 Charles L. Beach
1928 Charles B. Gentry
1929 George A. Works
1930 Charles C. McCracken
1935 Charles B. Gentry (Acting)
1935 Albert N. Jorgensen
1962 Homer D. Babbidge, Jr.

CORNELL COLLEGE
Mount Vernon, Iowa

1857 Richard W. Keeler
1859 Samuel M. Fellows
1863 William F. King
1908 James E. Harlan
1914 Hamline H. Freer (Acting)
1915 Charles W. Flint
1922 William S. Ebersole (Acting)
1923 Harlan Updegraff
1927 Herbert J. Burgstahler
1939 John B. Magee
1943 Russell D. Cole
1960 Arland F. Christ-Janer
1967 Samuel E. Stumpf

CORNELL UNIVERSITY
Ithaca, New York

1865 Andrew D. White
1885 Charles K. Adams
1892 Jacob G. Schurman
1921 Livingston Farrand
1937 Edmund E. Day
1949 Cornelis W. deKiewiet (Acting)
1951 Theodore P. Wright (Acting)
1951 Deane W. Malott
1963 James A. Perkins
1969 Dale R. Corson

CREIGHTON UNIVERSITY
Omaha, Nebraska

1878 Romanus A. Shaffel
1880 Thomas H. Miles
1883 Joseph Zealand
1884 Hugh M. Finnegan
1885 Michael P. Dowling
1889 Thomas S. Fitzgerald
1891 James F. X. Hoeffer
1895 John N. X. Pahls
1908 Eugene A. Magevney
1914 Francis X. McMenamy
1919 John F. McCormick
1925 William J. Grace
1928 William H. Agnew
1931 Patrick J. Mahan
1937 Joseph P. Zuercher
1943 Thomas S. Bowdern
1945 William H. McCabe
1950 Carl M. Reinert
1962 Henry W. Linn
1969 C. J. Schneider (Acting)
1970 Joseph J. Labaj

DARTMOUTH COLLEGE
Hanover, New Hampshire

1769 Eleazar Wheelock
1779 John Wheelock
1815 Franics Brown
1820 Daniel Dana
1821 Bennett T. Tyler
1828 Nathan Lord
1863 Asa D. Smith
1877 Samuel C. Bartlett
1893 William J. Tucker
1909 Ernest F. Nichols
1916 Ernest M. Hopkins
1945 John S. Dickey
1970 John G. Kemeny

DAVIDSON COLLEGE
Davidson, North Carolina

1836 Robert H. Morrison
1841 Samuel Williamson
1855 Drury Lacy
1860 John L. Kirkpatrick
1866 George W. McPhail
1871 John R. Blake (Chairman of Faculty)
1877 Andrew D. Hepburn
1885 Luther McKinnon
1887 William J. Martin (Acting)
1888 John B. Shearer
1901 Henry L. Smith
1912 William J. Martin
1929 William L. Lingle
1941 John R. Cunningham
1957 Clarence J. Pietenpol (Acting)
1958 David G. Martin
1968 Frontis W. Johnston (Acting)
1968 Samuel R. Spencer, Jr.

UNIVERSITY OF DAYTON
Dayton, Ohio

St. Mary's College from 1912 to 1920

1912 Bernard P. O'Reilly
1918 Joseph Tetzlaff
1923 Bernard P. O'Reilly
1932 Walter S. Tredtin
1938 John A. Elbert
1944 George J. Renneker
1953 Andrew L. Seebold
1959 Raymond A. Roesch

UNIVERSITY OF DELAWARE
Newark, Delaware

Newark College until 1843
Delaware College until 1921

1834 Eliphalet W. Gilbert
1835 Richard S. Mason
1840 Eliphalet W. Gilbert
1847 James P. Wilson
1850 William A. Norton
1850 Matthew Meigs
1851 Walter S. F. Graham
1854 Daniel Kirkwood
1856 Ellis J. Newlin
1859 Vacant
1870 William H. Purnell
1885 John H. Caldwell
1888 Lewis P. Bush (Acting)
1888 Albert N. Raub
1896 George A. Harter
1914 Samuel C. Mitchell
1920 Walter Hullihen
1944 Wilbur O. Sypherd
1946 William S. Carlson
1950 John A. Perkins
1967 John W. Shirley (Acting)
1968 Edward A. Trabant

DENISON UNIVERSITY
Granville, Ohio

Granville College from 1845 to 1856

1846 Silas Bailey
1852 John Pratt (Acting)
1853 Jeremiah Hall
1863 Samson Talbot
1873 Fletcher O. Marsh (Acting)
1875 Elisha B. Andrews
1879 Alfred Owen
1886 Nathan S. Burton (Acting)
1887 Galusha Anderson
1890 Daniel B. Purinton
1901 Emory W. Hunt
1912 Richard S. Colwell (Acting)
1913 Clark W. Chamberlain
1925 Bunyan Spencer (Acting)
1927 Avery A. Shaw
1940 Kenneth I. Brown
1950 Cyril F. Richards (Acting)
1951 A. Blair Knapp
1968 Parker E. Lichtenstein (Acting)
1969 Joel P. Smith

UNIVERSITY OF DENVER
Denver, Colorado

1880 David H. Moore
1890 William F. McDowell
1899 Henry A. Buchtel
1922 Heber R. Harper
1928 Frederick M. Hunter
1935 David S. Duncan
1941 Caleb F. Gates, Jr.
1943 Ben M. Cherrington
1946 Caleb F. Gates, Jr.
1948 James F. Price
1948 Alfred C. Nelson
1949 Albert C. Jacobs
1953 Chester M. Alter
1967 Maurice B. Mitchell

DePAUL UNIVERSITY
Chicago, Illinois

St. Vincent's College until 1907

1898 Peter V. Byrne
1909 John J. Martin
1910 Francis X. McCabe
1920 Thomas F. Levan
1930 Francis V. Corcoran
1935 Michael J. O'Connell
1944 Comerford J. O'Malley
1964 John R. Cortelyou

DePAUW UNIVERSITY
Greencastle, Indiana

Indiana Asbury University until 1884

1937 Cyrus Nutt (Acting)
1839 Matthew Simpson
1848 William C. Larrabee (Acting)
1849 Lucien W. Berry
1854 Daniel Curry
1857 Cyrus Nutt (Acting)
1858 Thomas Bowman
1872 Reuben Andrus
1875 Alexander Martin
1889 John P. D. John
1895 Hillary A. Gobin
1903 Edwin H. Hughes
1909 Francis J. McConnell
1912 George R. Grose
1924 Henry B. Longden (Acting)
1925 Lemuel H. Murlin
1928 G. Bromley Oxnam
1936 Clyde E. Wildman
1951 Russell J. Humbert
1962 Glenn W. Thompson (Acting)
1963 William E. Kerstetter

UNIVERSITY OF DETROIT
Detroit, Michigan

1877 John B. Miege
1880 James J. Walshe
1885 John P. Frieden
1889 Michael P. Dowling
1893 Henry A. Schaapman
1897 James D. Foley
1902 Louis Kellinger
1907 Richard D. Slevin
1911 William F. Dooley
1915 William T. Doran
1921 John P. Nichols
1932 Albert H. Poetker
1939 Charles H. Cloud
1944 William J. Millor
1949 Celestin J. Steiner
1960 Laurence V. Britt
1966 Malcolm Carron

DICKINSON COLLEGE
Carlisle, Pennsylvania

1784 Charles Nisbet
1804 Robert Davidson
1809 Jeremiah Atwater
1815 John McKnight
1816 College Closed
1821 John M. Mason
1824 William Neill
1830 Samuel B. How
1831 College Closed
1833 John P. Durbin
1845 Robert Emory
1848 Jesse T. Peck
1852 Charles Collins
1860 Herman M. Johnson
1868 Robert L. Dashiell
1872 James A. McCauley
1889 George E. Reed
1911 Eugene A. Noble
1914 James H. Morgan
1928 Mervin G. Filler
1931 James H. Morgan
1932 Karl T. Waugh
1933 James H. Morgan
1934 Fred P. Corson
1944 Cornelius W. Prettyman
1946 William W. Edel
1959 Gilbert Malcolm
1961 Howard L. Rubendall

DRAKE UNIVERSITY
Des Moines, Iowa

1881 George T. Carpenter
1894 Barton O. Aylesworth
1897 William B. Craig
1902 H. McClelland Bell
1918 Arthur Holmes
1922 Daniel W. Morehouse
1941 Henry G. Harmon
1966 Paul F. Sharp
1972 Wilbur C. Miller

DREXEL UNIVERSITY
Philadelphia, Pennsylvania

Drexel Institute of Art, Science and Industry until 1936
Drexel Institute of Technology until 1970

1892 James MacAlister
1913 Hollis Godfrey
1922 Kenneth G. Matheson
1932 Parke R. Kolbe
1942 George P. Rea
1944 Robert C. Disque (Acting)
1945 James Creese
1963 W. W. Hagerty

DUKE UNIVERSITY
Durham, North Carolina

Normal College until 1859; Trinity College until 1924.

1851 Braxton Craven
1883 Marquis L. Wood
1884 Vacant
1887 John F. Crowell
1894 John C. Kilgo
1910 William P. Few
1941 Robert L. Flowers
1948 Arthur H. Edens
1960 Julian D. Hart
1963 Douglas M. Knight
1969 Barnes Woodhall (Chancellor pro tem)
1970 Terry Sanford

DUQUESNE UNIVERSITY
Pittsburgh, Pennsylvania

Pittsburgh Catholic College of the Holy Ghost until 1911

1878 Joseph Graf (Acting)
1879 W. Power
1885 John Willms
1886 John T. Murphy
1899 Martin A. Hehir
1931 J. Joseph Callahan
1940 Raymond V. Kirk
1946 Francis P. Smith
1950 Vernon F. Gallagher
1959 Henry J. McAnulty

EARLHAM COLLEGE
Richmond, Indiana

1867 Barnabas C. Hobbs
1968 Joseph Moore
1883 William P. Pinkham (Acting)
1884 Joseph J. Mills
1903 Robert L. Kelly
1917 David M. Edwards
1929 William C. Dennis
1946 Thomas E. Jones
1958 Landrum R. Bolling

ELMIRA COLLEGE
Elmira, New York

1856 Augustus W. Cowles
1889 Wilson Phraner (Acting)
1890 Charles Van Norden
1893 Rufus S. Green
1896 A. Cameron MacKenzie
1915 John B. Shaw
1918 Frederick Lent
1935 W. S. A. Pott
1949 Lewis Eldred
1954 J. Ralph Murray

EMORY UNIVERSITY
Atlanta, Georgia

Emory College (Oxford, Ga.) until 1915

1837 Ignatius A. Few
1840 Augustus B. Longstreet
1848 George F. Pierce
1854 Alexander Means
1855 James R. Thomas
1867 Luther M. Smith
1871 Osborn L. Smith
1875 Atticus G. Haygood
1884 Isaac S. Hopkins
1888 Warren A. Candler
1898 Charles E. Dowman
1902 James E. Dickey
1915 Warren A. Candler (Chancellor)
1920 Harvey W. Cox
1942 Goodrich C. White
1957 S. Walter Martin
1963 Sanford S. Atwood

EMORY AND HENRY COLLEGE
Emory, Virginia

1838 Charles Collins
1852 E. E. Wiley
1879 John L. Buchanan
1880 David Sullins
1885 E. Embry Hoss
1885 Thomas W. Jordan
1888 R. W. Jones
1889 James Atkins
1893 R. G. Waterhouse
1910 C. C. Weaver
1920 J. Stewart French
1922 James N. Hillman
1941 Foye G. Gibson
1956 Earl G. Hunt, Jr.
1964 Daniel G. Leidig (Acting)
1965 William C. Finch
1970 C. Glenn Mingledorff

FAIRLEIGH DICKINSON UNIVERSITY
Rutherford, New Jersey

1942 Peter Sammartino
1969 J. O. Fuller

UNIVERSITY OF FLORIDA
Gainesville, Florida

1904 Andrew Sledd
1909 Albert A. Murphree
1928 John J. Tigert
1947 J. Hillis Miller
1953 John S. Allen (Acting)
1955 J. Wayne Reitz
1967 Stephen C. O'Connell

FLORIDA AGRICULTURAL AND MECHANICAL UNIVERSITY

1901 N. B. Young
1923 W. H. A. Howard
1924 J. R. E. Lee
1944 J. B. Bragg (Acting)
1944 W. H. Gray, Jr.
1949 H. Manning Efferson (Acting)
1950 George W. Gore
1969 Benjamin L. Perry, Jr.

FLORIDA STATE UNIVERSITY
Tallahassee, Florida

Florida State College from 1901 to 1905
Florida State College for Women until 1947

1897 Albert A. Murphree
1909 Edward Conradi
1941 Doak S. Campbell
1957 Robert M. Strozier
1960 Gordon W. Blackwell
1965 John E. Champion
1969 J. Stanley Marshall

FORDHAM UNIVERSITY
Bronx, New York

St. John's College until 1905

1841 John McCloskey
1843 John Harley
1844 James R. Bayley
1946 Augustus J. Thebaud
1851 John Larkin
1854 Remigius I. Tellier
1859 Augustus J. Thebaud
1863 Edward Doucet
1865 William Moylan
1868 Joseph Shea
1874 F. William Gockeln
1882 Patrick F. Dealy
1885 Thomas J. Campbell
1888 John Scully
1891 Thomas Gannon
1896 Thomas J. Campbell
1900 George A. Petit
1904 John J. Collins
1906 Daniel J. Quinn
1911 Thomas J. McCluskey
1915 Joseph A. Mulry
1919 Edward P. Tivnan
1924 William J. Duane
1930 Aloysius J. Hogan
1936 Robert I. Gannon
1949 Laurence J. McGinley
1963 Vincent T. O'Keefe
1965 Leo P. McLaughlin
1969 Michael P. Walsh
1972 James C. Finley

FRANKLIN AND MARSHALL COLLEGE
Lancaster, Pennsylvania

Marshall College until 1852

1836 Frederick A. Rauch
1841 John W. Nevin
1855 Emanuel V. Gerhart
1866 John W. Nevin
1877 Thomas G. Apple
1889 John S. Stahr
1909 Henry H. Apple
1935 John A. Schaeffer
1941 H. M. J. Klein (Acting)
1941 Theodore A. Distler
1955 William W. Hall
1956 Frederick deW. Bolman, Jr.
1962 Anthony R. Appel
1962 G. Wyane Glick (Acting)
1963 Keith Spalding

FRESNO STATE COLLEGE
Fresno, California

Fresno State Normal School until 1921
Fresno State Teachers College until 1935

1911 Charles L. McLane
1927 Frank W. Thomas
1948 Arnold E. Joyal
1964 Frederick W. Ness
1969 Karl L. Falk (Acting)
1970 Norman A. Baxter

FURMAN UNIVERSITY
Greenville, South Carolina

1859 James C. Furman
1881 Charles Manly
1897 Andrew P. Montague
1903 Edwin McN. Poteat
1919 William J. McGlothlin
1933 Bennette E. Geer
1939 John P. Plyler
1964 Gordon W. Blackwell

THE GEORGE WASHINGTON UNIVERSITY

Columbian College until 1873
Columbian University until 1904

1821 William Straughton
1827 Stephen Chapin
1843 Joel S. Bacon
1854 Joseph G. S. Binney
1859 George W. Samson
1871 James C. Welling
1894 S. H. Greene
1895 Benaiah L. Whitman
1900 S. H. Greene
1902 Charles W. Needham
1910 Charles H. Stockton
1918 William M. Collier
1921 Howard L. Hodgkins
1923 William L. Lewis
1927 Cloyd H. Marvin
1959 Oswald S. Colclough (Acting)
1961 Thomas H. Carroll
1964 Oswald S. Colclough (Acting)
1965 Lloyd H. Elliott

GEORGETOWN UNIVERSITY

Georgetown College until 1815

1791 Robert Plunkett
1793 Robert Molyneux
1796 Louis G. du Bourg
1798 Leonard Neal
1806 Robert Molyneux
1808 Francis Neale
1809 William Matthews
1809 Francis Neale
1812 John A. Grassi
1817 Benedict J. Fenwick
1817 Anthony Kohlmann
1820 Enoch Fenwick
1822 Benedict J. Fenwick
1825 Stephen J. Dubuisson
1826 William Feiner
1829 John W. Beschter
1829 Thomas F. Mulledy
1837 William McSherry
1840 Joseph A. Lopez
1840 James Ryder
1845 Samuel Mulledy
1845 Thomas F. Mulledy
1848 James Ryder
1851 Charles H. Stonestreet
1852 Bernard A. Maguire
1858 John Early
1866 Bernard A. Maguire
1870 John Early
1873 Patrick F. Healy
1882 James A. Doonan
1888 J. Havens Richards
1898 John D. Whitney
1901 Jerome Daugherty
1905 David H. Buel
1908 Joseph J. Himmel
1912 Alphonsus J. Donlon
1918 John B. Creeden
1924 Charles W. Lyons
1928 W. Coleman Nevils
1935 Arthur A. O'Leary
1942 Lawrence C. Gorman
1949 Hunter Guthrie
1952 Edward B. Bunn
1964 Gerard J. Campbell
1969 Edwin A. Quain (Acting)
1969 Robert J. Henle

THE UNIVERSITY OF GEORGIA
Athens, Georgia

1801 Josiah Meigs
1811 John Brown
1816 Robert Finley
1817 Vacant
1819 Moses Waddel
1829 Alonzo Church
1860 Andrew A. Lipscomb

Chancellors

1874 Henry H. Tucker
1878 Patrick H. Mell
1888 William E. Boggs
1899 Walter B. Hill
1906 David C. Barrow
1926 Charles M. Snelling

Presidents

1932 Steadman V. Sanford
1935 Harmon W. Caldwell
1948 Johnathan C. Rogers
1950 Omer C. Aderhold
1967 Fred C. Davison

GEORGIA INSTITUTE OF TECHNOLOGY
Atlanta, Georgia

Georgia School of Technology until 1948

1888 Isaac S. Hopkins
1896 Lyman Hall
1905 Kenneth G. Matheson
1922 Nathan P. Pratt (Acting)
1922 Marion L. Brittain
1944 Blake R. Van Leer
1956 Paul Weber (Acting)
1957 Edwin D. Harrison
1969 Vernon D. Crawford
1969 Arthur G. Hansen
1972 Joseph M. Pettit

GEORGIA STATE UNIVERSITY
Atlanta, Georgia

Georgia State College of Business Administration from 1955 to 1961
Georgia State College until 1969

1955 George M. Sparks
1957 Noah Langdale, Jr.

GETTYSBURG COLLEGE
Gettysburg, Pennsylvania

Pennsylvania College of Gettysburg until 1921

1832 Samuel S. Shmucker
1934 Charles P. Krauth
1850 Henry L. Baugher
1868 Milton Valentine
1884 Harvey W. McKnight
1904 Samuel G.Hefelbower
1910 William A. Granville
1923 Henry W. A. Hanson
1952 Walter C. Langsam
1956 Willard S. Paul
1961 C. Arnold Hanson

GOUCHER COLLEGE
Towson, Maryland

Woman's College of Baltimore until 1910

1886 William H. Hopkins
1890 John F. Goucher
1908 Eugene A. Noble
1913 William W. Guth
1930 David A. Robertson
1948 Otto F. Kraushaar
1967 Marvin B. Perry, Jr.

GRINNELL COLLEGE
Grinnell, Iowa

Iowa College until 1909

1863 George F. Magoun
1884 Samuel J. Buck (Acting)
1887 George A. Gates
1900 John H. T. Main (Acting)
1902 Dan F. Bradley
1906 John H. T. Main
1931 John S. Nollen
1940 Samuel N. Stevens
1954 Rupert A. Hawk (Acting)
1955 Howard R. Bowen
1964 James H. Struss (Acting)
1965 Glenn Leggett

HAMILTON COLLEGE
Clinton, New York

1812 Azel Backus
1817 Henry Davis
1833 Sereno E. Dwight
1835 Joseph Penney
1839 Simeon North
1858 Samuel W. Fisher
1866 Samuel G. Brown
1881 Henry Darling
1892 Melancthon W. Stryker
1917 Frederick C. Ferry
1938 William H. Cowley
1945 David Worcester
1947 Thomas B. Rudd
1949 Robert W. McEwen
1967 John W. Chandler

HAMLINE UNIVERSITY
St. Paul, Minnesota

1854 Jabez Brooks
1857 Benjamin Crary
1880 David C. John
1883 George H. Bridgman
1912 Samuel F. Kerfoot
1927 Alfred F. Hughes
1932 Henry L. Osborn (Acting)
1934 Charles N. Pace
1948 Hurst R. Anderson
1952 Walter C. Coffey (Acting)
1953 Paul H. Giddens
1968 Richard P. Bailey

HAMPDEN-SYDNEY COLLEGE
Hampden-Sydney, Virginia

1775 S. Stanhope Smith
1779 John B. Smith
1789 Drury Lacy
1797 Archibald Alexander
1807 William S. Reid (Acting)
1807 Moses Hoge
1821 Jonathan P. Cushing
1835 George A. Baxter (Acting)
1835 Daniel L. Carroll
1838 William Maxwell
1845 Patrick J. Sparrow
1848 Lewis W. Green
1856 Charles Martin (Acting)
1857 John M. P. Atkinson
1883 Richard McIlwaine
1904 William H. Whiting, Jr. (Acting)
1905 James G. McAllister
1908 Henry T. Graham
1917 Ashton W. McWhorter (Acting)
1919 Joseph D. Eggleston
1939 Edgar G. Gammon
1955 Joseph C. Robert
1960 Thomas E. Gilmer
1963 W. Taylor Reveley

HARDIN-SIMMONS UNIVERSITY
Abilene, Texas

Simmons College until 1925
Simmons University until 1934

1892 W. C. Friley
1894 George O. Thatcher
1898 O. C. Pope
1901 J. C. Hairfield
1902 Oscar H. Cooper
1909 Jefferson D. Sandefer
1940 Lucian Q. Campbell (Acting)
1940 William R. White
1943 Rupert N. Richardson
1953 Evan A. Reiff
1962 George L. Graham (Acting)
1963 James H. Landis
1966 Elwin L. Skiles

HARVARD UNIVERSITY
Cambridge, Massachusetts

1640 Henry Dunster
1654 Charles Chauncy
1672 Leonard Hoar
1675 Urian Oakes
1682 John Rogers
1685 Increase Mather
1708 John Leverett
1725 Benjamin Wadsworth
1737 Edward Holyoke
1770 Samuel Locke
1774 Samuel Langdon
1781 Joseph Willard
1806 Samuel Webber
1810 John T. Kirkland
1829 Josiah Quincy
1846 Edward Everett
1849 Jared Sparks
1853 James Walker
1860 Cornelius C. Felton
1862 Thomas Hill
1869 Charles W. Eliot
1909 A. Lawrence Lowell
1933 James B. Conant
1953 Nathan M. Pusey
1971 Derek C. Bok

HAVERFORD COLLEGE
Haverford, Pennsylvania

1857 Joseph G. Harlan
1857 Vacant
1863 Samuel J. Gummere
1874 Thomas Chase
1887 Isaac Sharpless
1917 William W. Comfort
1940 Felix M. Morley
1946 Gilbert F. White
1957 Hugh Borton
1967 John R. Coleman

UNIVERSITY OF HAWAII
Honolulu, Hawaii

College of Agriculture and Mechanic Arts until 1911
College of Hawaii until 1920

1907 Willia T. Pope (Acting)
1908 John W. Gilmore
1913 John S. Donaghho (Acting)
1914 Arthur L. Dean
1927 David L. Crawford
1941 Arthur R. Keller (Acting)
1942 Gregg M. Sinclair
1955 Paul S. Bachman
1957 Willard Wilson (Acting)
1958 Laurence H. Snyder
1963 Thomas H. Hamilton
1968 Robert W. Hiatt (Acting)
1969 Harlan Cleveland

HEIDELBERG COLLEGE
Tiffin, Ohio

1851 Emanuel V. Gerhart
1855 Moses Kieffer
1863 G. W. Aughinbaugh
1866 George W. Williard
1890 John A. Peters
1902 Charles E. Miller
1937 Clarence E. Josephson
1945 Nevin C. Harner
1948 William T. Wickham
1969 Leslie H. Fishel, Jr.

HIRAM COLLEGE
Hiram, Ohio

1867 Silas E. Shepard
1868 John M. Atwater
1870 Burke A. Hinsdale
1882 Bailey S. Dean (Acting)
1883 George H. Laughlin
1887 Colman Bancroft (Acting)
1888 Ely V. Zollars
1902 James A. Beattie
1903 Edmund B. Wakefield (Acting)
1905 C. C. Rowlinson
1907 Miner L. Bates
1930 Kenneth I. Brown
1940 Paul H. Fall
1957 Paul F. Sharp
1964 James N. Primm
1965 Wendell G. Johnson (Acting)
1967 Elmer Jagow

HOBART AND WILLIAM SMITH COLLEGES
Geneva, New York

Geneva College until 1852
Hobart Free College until 1860
William Smith College founded 1908

1826 Jasper Adams
1828 Richard S. Mason
1835 Benjamin Hale
1858 Abner Jackson
1867 James K. Stone
1869 James Rankine
1871 Maunsell Van Renssalaer
1876 William S. Perry
1876 Robert G. Hinsdale
1884 Eliphalet N. Potter
1897 Robert E. Jones
1902 Langdon C. Stewardson
1913 Lyman P. Powell
1919 Murray Bartlett
1936 William A. Eddy
1942 John M. Potter
1947 Walter H. Durfee
1948 Alan W. Brown
1956 Horace N. Hubbs
1956 Louis M. Hirshson
1966 Albert E. Holland
1968 Beverley D. Causey, Jr.
1970 Allan A. Kuusisto

HOFSTRA UNIVERSITY
Hempstead, New York

1937 Truesdale P. Calkins
1942 Howard Brower (Acting)
1944 John C. Adams
1964 Clifford L. Lord
1972 James Marshall

COLLEGE OF THE HOLY CROSS
Worcester, Massachusetts

1848 John Early
1851 Anthony F. Ciampi
1854 Peter J. Blenkinsop
1857 Anthony F. Ciampi
1861 James Clark
1867 Robert W. Brady
1869 Anthony F. Ciampi
1872 Joseph B. O'Hagan
1878 Edward D. Boone
1883 Robert W. Brady
1887 Samuel Cahill
1889 Michael O'Kane
1893 Edward A. McGurk
1895 John F. Lehy
1901 Joseph F. Hanselman
1906 Thomas E. Murphy
1911 Joseph N. Dinand
1918 James J. Carlin
1924 Joseph N. Dinand
1927 John M. Fox
1933 Francis J. Dolan
1939 Joseph R. N. Maxwell
1945 William J. Healy
1948 John A. O'Brien
1954 William A. Donaghy
1960 Raymond J. Swords
1970 John E. Brooks

UNIVERSITY OF HOUSTON
Houston, Texas

1927 Edison E. Oberholtzer
1950 W. W. Kemmerer
1953 C. F. McElhinney (Acting)
1954 A. D. Bruce
1956 Clanton W. Williams
1961 Philip G. Hoffman

HOWARD UNIVERSITY
Washington, D.C.

1867 Charles B. Boynton
1967 Byron Sunderland
1969 Oliver O. Howard
1873 John M. Langston (Acting)
1875 F. W. Fairfield (Acting)
1875 Edward P. Smith
1876 F. W. Fairfield (Acting)
1877 William M. Patton
1890 Jeremiah Rankin
1903 Teunis S. Hamlin (Acting)
1903 John Gordon
1906 F. W. Fairfield (Acting)
1906 Wilbur Thirkfield
1912 Stephen M. Newman
1918 J. Stanley Durkee
1926 Mordecai W. Johnson
1960 James M. Nabrit, Jr.
1965 Stanton L. Wormley (Acting)
1969 James E. Cheek

HUNTER COLLEGE OF THE CITY UNIVERSITY OF NEW YORK

Normal College of the City of New York until 1914
Hunter College until 1961

1870 Thomas Hunter
1906 Joseph A. Gillet (Acting)
1908 George S. Davis
1929 James Kieran
1933 Eugene Colligan
1940 George N. Shuster
1960 John J. Meng
1966 Mary L. Gambrell
1967 Douglas Maynard (Acting)
1967 Robert D. Cross
1969 F. Joachim Weyl (Acting)
1970 Jacqueline G. Wexler

UNIVERSITY OF IDAHO
Moscow, Idaho

1892 Franklin B. Gault
1898 Joseph P. Blanton
1900 James A. MacLean
1914 Melvin A. Brannon
1917 Earnest H. Lindly
1920 Alfred H. Upham
1928 Frederick J. Kelly
1930 Mervin G. Neale
1937 Harrison C. Dale
1946 Jesse E. Buchanan
1954 Donald R. Theophilus
1965 Ernest W. Hartung

UNIVERSITY OF ILLINOIS
Urbana, Illinois

1867 John M. Gregory
1880 Selim H. Peabody
1891 Thomas J. Burrill (Acting)
1894 Andrew S. Draper
1904 Edmund J. James
1920 David Kinley
1930 Harry W. Chase
1933 Arthur H. Daniels (Acting)
1934 Arthur C. Willard
1946 George D. Stoddard
1953 Lloyd Morey
1955 David D. Henry
1971 John E. Corbally, Jr.

ILLINOIS STATE UNIVERSITY
Normal, Illinois

Illinois State Normal University until 1963

1907 David Felmley
1930 Harry A. Brown
1933 Raymond W. Fairchild
1956 Robert G. Bone
1967 Samuel E. Braden
1970 F. R. Geigle (Acting)
1971 David K. Berlo

ILLINOIS WESLEYAN UNIVERSITY
Bloomington, Illinois

1855 Clinton W. Sears
1857 Oliver S. Munsell
1873 Samuel J. Fallows
1875 William H. H. Adams
1888 William H. Wilder
1898 Edgar M. Smith
1905 Francis G. Barnes
1908 Theodore Kemp
1922 William J. Davidson
1932 Harry W. McPherson
1937 Wiley G. Brooks
1939 William E. Shaw
1947 Merrill J. Holmes
1958 Lloyd M. Bertholf
1968 Robert C. Eckley

INDIANA UNIVERSITY
Bloomington, Indiana

Indiana College until 1838

1829 Andrew Wylie
1852 Alfred Ryors
1853 William M. Daily
1859 John H. Lathrop
1860 Cyrus Nutt
1875 Lemuel Moss
1885 David S. Jordan
1891 John M. Coulter
1893 Joseph Swain
1902 William L. Bryan
1937 Herman B. Wells
1962 Elvis J. Stahr, Jr.
1968 Joseph L. Sutton
1971 John W. Ryan

INDIANA STATE UNIVERSITY
Terre Haute, Indiana

Indiana State Normal School until 1929
Indiana State Teachers College until 1961
Indiana State College until 1965

1908 William W. Parsons
1921 Linnaeus Hines
1933 Lemuel A. Pittenger (Acting)
1934 Ralph W. Tirey
1953 Raleigh W. Holmstedt
1965 Alan C. Rankin

UNIVERSITY OF IOWA
Iowa City, Iowa

1855 Amos Dean
1859 Silas Totten
1862 Oliver Spencer
1867 Nathan R. Leonard (pro tem)
1868 James Black
1871 George Thacher
1877 Christian W. Slagle (Acting)
1878 Josiah L. Pickard
1887 Charles A. Schaeffer
1898 Amos N. Currier (Acting)
1899 George E. MacLean
1911 John G. Bowman
1914 Thomas H. MacBride
1916 Walter A. Jessup
1934 Eugene A. Gilmore
1940 Virgil M. Hancher
1964 Howard R. Bowen
1969 Willard L. Boyd

IOWA STATE UNIVERSITY
Ames, Iowa

Iowa Agricultural until 1898
Iowa State College of Agriculture and Mechanic Arts until 1958

1868 A. S. Welsh
1883 S. A. Knapp
1885 Leigh Hunt
1886 W. I. Chamberlain
1891 W. M. Beardshear
1903 A. B. Storms
1912 Raymond A. Pearson
1927 Raymond M. Hughes
1936 Charles E. Friley
1953 James H. Hilton
1965 W. Robert Parks

JOHN CARROLL UNIVERSITY
Cleveland, Ohio

St. Ignatius College until 1923

1886 John B. Neustich
1888 Henry Knappenmeyer
1893 Joseph Le Halle
1897 Godfrey V. Schulte
1902 John I. Zahm
1907 George J. Pickel
1910 John B. Furay
1915 William B. Sommerhauser
1919 Thomas J. Smith
1925 Murtha A. Boylan
1928 Benedict J. Rodman
1937 George J. Pickel (pro tem)
1938 William G. Magee
1938 Edmund C. Horne
1942 Thomas J. Donnelly
1946 Frederick E. Welfle
1956 Hugh E. Dunn
1967 Joseph O. Schell
1970 Henry F. Birkenhauer

THE JOHNS HOPKINS UNIVERSITY
Baltimore, Maryland

1875 Daniel C. Gilman
1901 Ira Remsen
1914 Frank J. Goodnow
1929 Joseph S. Ames
1935 Isaiah Bowman
1949 Detlev W. Bronk
1953 Lowell Reed
1956 Milton S. Eisenhower
1967 Lincoln Gordon
1971 Milton S. Eisenhower
1972 Steven Muller

KALAMAZOO COLLEGE
Kalamazoo, Michigan

1843 J. A. B. Stone
1864 John M. Gregory
1867 Daniel Putnam (Interim)
1868 Silas Bailey (Acting)
1868 Kendall Brooks
1883 Thedore Nelson (Acting)
1884 Kendall Brooks
1887 Monson A. Willcox
1891 Theodore Nelson
1892 A. Gaylord Slocum
1912 Herbert L. Stetson
1922 Allan Hoben
1935 Charles T. Goodsell
1936 Stewart G. Cole
1938 Paul Thompson
1948 Allen B. Stowe (Interim)
1949 John S. Everton
1953 Harold T. Smith (Interim)
1953 Weimer K. Hicks

THE UNIVERSITY OF KANSAS

1865 Robert W. Oliver
1867 John Fraser
1875 James Marvin
1883 Joshua A. Lippincott
1889 W. C. Spangler (Acting)
1890 Francis H. Snow
1901 W. C. Spangler (Acting)
1902 Frank Strong
1920 Ernest H. Lindley
1939 Deane W. Malott
1951 John H. Nelson (Acting)
1951 Franklin D. Murphy
1960 W. Clarke Wescoe
1969 James R. Surface (Acting)
1969 E. Lawrence Chalmers, Jr.

KANSAS STATE UNIVERSITY
Manhattan, Kansas

Kansas State Agricultural College until 1931

1863 Joseph Denison
1873 John A. Anderson
1879 George T. Fairchild
1897 Thomas E. Will
1899 Ernest R. Nichols
1909 Henry J. Waters
1918 William M. Jardine
1925 Francis D. Farrell
1943 Milton S. Eisenhower
1950 James A. McCain

KENT STATE UNIVERSITY
Kent, Ohio

Kent State College from 1929 to 1935.

1928 James O. Engleman
1938 Karl C. Leebrick
1943 Raymond M. Clark (Acting)
1944 George A. Bowman
1963 Robert I. White
1971 Glenn A. Olds

UNIVERSITY OF KENTUCKY
Lexington, Kentucky

Agricultural and Mechanical College of Kentucky until 1908

1865 John B. Bowman (Regent)
1866 John A. Williams (Presiding Officer)
1868 Joseph D. Pickett (Presiding Officer)
1869 James K. Patterson
1910 Henry S. Barker
1917 Frank L. McVey
1940 Thomas P. Cooper (Acting)
1941 Herman L. Donovan
1956 Frank G. Dickey
1963 John W. Oswald
1968 Albert D. Kirwan
1969 Otis A. Singletary

KENYON COLLEGE
Gambier, Ohio

1824 Philander Chase
1831 Charles P. McIlvaine
1840 David B. Douglass
1844 Samuel Fuller (Acting)
1845 Sherlock A. Bronson
1851 Thomas M. Smith
1854 Lorin Andrews
1861 Benjamin S. Lange (Acting)
1863 Charles Short
1867 James K. Stone
1868 Eli T. Tappan
1874 Edward C. Benson (Acting)
1876 William B. Bodine
1890 Theodore Sterling
1896 William F. Peirce
1937 Gordon K. Chalmers
1956 Frank E. Bailey (Acting)
1957 F. Edward Lund
1968 William G. Caples

KNOX COLLEGE
Galesburg, Illinois

Knox Manual Labor College until 1857

1841 Hiram H. Kellogg
1845 Jonathan Blanchard
1858 Harvey Curtis
1863 William S. Curtis
1868 John P. Gulliver
1874 Newton Bateman
1892 John H. Finley
1900 Thomas McClelland
1918 James L. McConaughy
1925 Albert Britt
1936 Carter Davidson
1947 Lyndon O. Brown
1949 Sharvy G. Umbeck

LAFAYETTE COLLEGE
Easton, Pennsylvania

1832 George Junkin
1841 John W. Yeomans
1844 George Junkin
1849 Charles W. Nassau
1850 Daniel V. McLean
1857 George W. McPhail
1863 William C. Cattell
1883 James H. M. Knox
1890 Traill Green (Acting)
1891 Ethelbert D. Warfield
1914 William S. Kirkpatrick (Acting)
1915 John H. MacCracken
1926 Donald B. Prentice (Acting)
1927 William M. Lewis
1945 Ralph C. Hutchison
1957 Guy Snavely (Interim)
1958 K. Roald Bergethon

LAWRENCE UNIVERSITY
Appleton, Wisconsin

Lawrence University of Wisconsin until 1913
Lawrence College of Wisconsin until 1964

1853 Edward Cooke
1859 Russell Z. Mason
1865 George McK. Steele
1879 Elias D. Huntley
1883 Bradford P. Raymond
1889 Charles W. Gallagher
1893 L. Wesley Underwood (Acting)
1894 Samuel Plantz
1924 Wilson S. Naylor (Acting)
1925 Henry M. Wriston
1937 Thomas N. Barrows
1943 Ralph J. Watts (Acting)
1944 Nathan M. Pusey
1954 Douglas M. Knight
1963 Curtis W. Tarr
1969 Thomas S. Smith

LEHIGH UNIVERSITY
Bethlehem, Pennsylvania

1866 Henry Coppee
1875 John McD. Leavitt
1880 Robert A. Lamberton
1895 Thomas M. Drown
1905 Henry S. Drinker
1920 Vacant
1922 Charles R. Richards
1935 Clement C. Williams
1944 Vacant
1946 Martin D. Whitaker
1960 Harvey A. Neville
1964 Willard D. Lewis

LEWIS AND CLARK COLLEGE
Portland, Oregon

Albany College until 1942

1867 William J. Monteith
1868 Henry Bushnell
1869 Edward R. Geary
1871 Royal K. Warren
1876 Howard W. Stratton
1878 David B. Rice
1879 Elbert N. Condit
1885 Joseph C. Wyckoff
1886 Earl T. Lockhard
1886 Edwin J. Thompson
1887 Elbert N. Condit
1894 Frederick G. Young
1895 Wallace H. Lee
1905 Harry M. Crooks
1915 Wallace H. Lee (Acting)
1920 Alfred M. Williams
1922 Raymond J. Baker (Acting)
1923 Clarence W. Green
1929 Thomas W. Bibb
1938 Clarence W. Greene
1941 Benjamin A. Thaxter (Acting)
1942 Morgan S. Odell
1960 John R. Howard

THE LOUISIANA STATE UNIVERSITY
Baton Rouge, Louisiana

Louisiana State Seminary of Learning until 1870

1859 William T. Sherman
1861 (Seminary Closed)
1865 David F. Boyd
1880 William P. Johnston
1883 James W. Nicholson
1884 David F. Boyd
1887 James W. Nicholson
1896 Thomas D. Boyd
1927 Thomas W. Atkinson
1930 James M. Smith
1939 Paul M. Hebert (Acting)
1941 Campbell B. Hodges
1944 William B. Hatcher
1947 Fred C. Frey (Acting)
1947 Harold W. Stoke
1951 Troy H. Middleton
1962 John A. Hunter

UNIVERSITY OF LOUISVILLE
Louisville, Kentucky

1914 Y. A. Ford
1926 George Colvin
1928 John L. Patterson (Acting)
1929 Raymond A. Kent
1943 Einar W. Jacobsen
1946 Frederick W. Stamm (Acting)
1947 John W. Taylor
1950 Eli H. Brown 3d (Acting)
1951 Philip Davidson
1968 Woodrow M. Strickler

LOYOLA UNIVERSITY OF CHICAGO
Chicago, Illinois

Saint Ignatius College until 1909
Loyola University until 1970

1870 Arnold Damen
1872 Ferdinand Coosemans
1874 John De Blieck
1877 Thomas Miles
1880 Thomas O'Neill
1884 Joseph Zealand
1887 Edward A. Higgins
1891 Thomas Fitzgerald
1894 James F. X. Hoeffer
1898 John Pahls
1900 Henry Dumbach
1908 Alexander J. Burrowes
1912 John Mathery
1915 John Furay
1921 William Agnew
1927 Robert Kelley
1933 Samuel K. Wilson
1942 Joseph Egan
1945 James T. Hussey
1955 James F. Maguire
1970 Raymond C. Baumhart

MACALESTER COLLEGE
Saint Paul, Minnesota

1874 Edward D. Neill
1884 Thomas A. McCurdy
1890 David J. Burrell
1892 Adam W. Ringland
1894 James Wallace
1907 Thomas M. Hodgman
1918 Elmer A. Bess
1924 John C. Acheson
1939 Charles J. Turck
1958 Harvey M. Rice
1968 Arthur S. Flemming
1972 James A. Robinson

UNIVERSITY OF MAINE
Orono, Maine

Maine State College of Agriculture and the Mechanic Arts until 1897

1867 Merritt C. Fernald
1871 Charles F. Allen
1879 Merritt C. Fernald
1893 Abram W. Harris
1902 George E. Fellows
1910 Robert J. Aley
1922 Clarence C. Little
1925 Harold S. Boardman
1934 Arthur A. Hauck
1958 Charles E. Crossland (Acting)
1958 Lloyd H. Elliott
1965 H. Edwin Young
1968 Winthrop C. Libby
1972 Donald McNeil (Chancellor)

MANHATTAN COLLEGE
Bronx, New York

1863 Patrick Murphy
1873 Paulian Fanning
1879 Anthony Byrnes
1886 Justin McMahon
1890 Anthony Byrnes
1894 Justin McMahon
1900 B. Charles Foley
1902 E. Jerome Daley
1904 Arnold E. Saunders
1907 B. Peter Tracey
1909 E. Jerome Daley
1912 Arnold E. Saunders
1918 Apelles J. Scanlon
1921 Cantidius T. Fitzsimmons
1927 Cornelius M. Hession
1932 Adelphus P. McKenzie
1938 Alexius V. Lally
1944 Bonaventure T. McGinty
1953 Augustine P. Nelan
1962 Gregory Nugent

MARIETTA COLLEGE
Marietta, Ohio

1835 Joel H. Linsley
1846 Henry Smith
1855 Israel W. Andrews
1885 John Eaton
1892 John W. Simpson
1896 Joseph H. Chamberlain (Acting)
1900 Alfred T. Perry
1912 Joseph Manley (Acting)
1913 George W. Hinman
1918 Jesse V. McMillan (Acting)
1919 Edward S. Parsons
1937 Harry K. Eversull
1942 Draper T. Schoonover
1945 William A. Shimer
1947 Vacant
1948 William B. Irvine
1963 Frank E. Duddy, Jr.

MARQUETTE UNIVERSITY
Milwaukee, Wiconsin

Marquette College until 1907

1881 Joseph Rigge
1882 Isidor Boudreaux
1884 Thomas S. Fitzgerald
1887 Stanislaus P. Lalumiere
1889 Joseph Grimmelsman
1891 Rudolph J. Meyer
1893 Leopold Bushart
1898 William B. Rogers
1900 Alexander J. Burrowes
1908 James McCabe
1911 Joseph Grimmelsman
1915 Herbert C. Noonan
1922 Albert C. Fox
1928 William M. Magee
1936 Raphael C. McCarthy
1944 Peter A. Brooks
1948 Edward J. O'Donnell
1962 William F. Kelley
1965 John P. Raynor

UNIVERSITY OF MARYLAND
College Park, Maryland

1813 Robert Smith
1815 James Kemp
1826 Roger B. Taney
1839 Ashton Alexander
1850 John P. Kennedy
1870 Severn T. Wallis
1894 Bernard Carter
1912 Henry Stockbridge, Jr. (Acting)

1913 Thomas B. Fell
1920 Albert F. Woods
1926 Raymond A. Pearson
1935 Harry C. Byrd
1954 Wilson H. Elkins

UNIVERSITY OF MASSACHUSETTS

Amherst, Massachusetts

Massachusetts Agricultural College until 1931
Massachusetts State Collegyuntil 1947

1866 Paul A. Chadbourne
1867 William S. Clark
1879 Charles L. Flint
1880 Levi Stockbridge
1882 Paul A. Chadbourne
1883 James C. Greenough
1886 Henry H. Goodell
1905 William P. Brooks (Acting)
1906 Kenyon L. Butterfield
1924 Edward M. Lewis
1927 Roscoe W. Thatcher
1933 Hugh P. Baker
1947 Ralph A. Van Meter
1954 Jean Paul Mather
1960 John W. Lederle
1970 Robert Wood

BOSTON CAMPUS – *Chancellors*

1964 John W. Ryan
1968 Francis L. Broderick

MASSACHUSETTS INSTITUTE OF TECHNOLOGY

Cambridge, Massachusetts

1862 William B. Rogers
1870 John D. Runkle
1879 William B. Rogers
1881 Francis A. Walker
1897 James M. Crafts
1900 Henry S. Pritchett
1907 Arthur A. Noyes (Acting)
1909 Richard C. Maclaurin
1921 Ernest F. Nichols
1923 Samuel W. Stratton
1930 Karl T. Compton
1949 James R. Killian, Jr.
1959 Julius A. Stratton
1966 Howard W. Johnson
1971 Jerome B. Weisner

MEMPHIS STATE UNIVERSITY

Memphis, Tennessee

West Tennessee State Teachers College from 1929 to 1941
Memphis State College until 1957

1924 John W. Brister
1939 Richard Jones
1943 Jennings B. Sanders
1946 J. Millard Smith
1960 Cecil C. Humphreys

MERCER UNIVERSITY

Macon, Georgia

1833 B. M. Sanders
1839 Otis Smith
1844 John L. Dagg
1854 N. M. Crawford
1866 Henry H. Tucker
1871 A. J. Battle
1890 G. A. Nunnally
1893 J. B. Gambrell
1896 P. D. Pollock
1905 Charles L. Smith
1906 Samuel Y. Jameson
1914 William L. Pickard
1918 Rufus W. Weaver
1928 Spright Dowell
1953 George B. Connell
1959 Spright Dowell (Interim)
1960 Rufus C. Harris

UNIVERSITY OF MIAMI

Coral Gables, Florida

1926 Bowman F. Ashe
1953 Jay F. W. Pearson
1962 Henry K. Stanford

MIAMI UNIVERSITY

Oxford, Ohio

1824 Robert H. Bishop
1841 George Junkin
1845 Erasmus D. McMaster
1849 William C. Anderson
1854 John W. Hall
1866 Robert L. Stanton
1871 Andrew D. Hepburn
1873 (University closed)
1885 Robert W. McFarland
1888 Ethelbert D. Warfield
1891 William O. Thompson
1899 David S. Tappan
1902 Guy P. Benton
1911 Raymond M. Hughes
1928 Alfred H. Upham
1946 Ernest H. Hahne
1953 John D. Millett
1965 Phillip R. Shriver

UNIVERSITY OF MICHIGAN

Ann Arbor, Michigan

1852 Henry P. Tappan
1863 Erastus O. Haven
1869 Henry S. Frieze (Acting)
1871 James B. Angell
1909 Harry B. Hutchins
1920 Marion L. Burton
1925 Clarence C. Little
1929 Alexander G. Ruthven
1951 Harlan H. Hatcher
1968 Robben W. Fleming

MICHIGAN STATE UNIVERSITY

East Lansing, Michigan

State Agricultural College until 1909
Michigan Agricultural College until 1925
Michigan State College of Agriculture and Applied Science until 1955
Michigan State University of Agriculture and Applied Science until 1964

1857 Joseph R. Williams
1859 Lewis R. Fisk
1862 Theophilus C. Abbot
1885 Edwin Willits
1889 Oscar Clute
1893 Lewis G. Gorton
1896 Jonathan L. Snyder
1915 Frank S. Kedzie
1921 David Friday
1924 Kenyon L. Butterfield
1928 Robert S. Shaw
1941 John A. Hannah
1969 Walter Adams
1970 Clifton R. Wharton, Jr.

MIDDLEBURY COLLEGE

Middlebury, Vermont

1800 Jeremiah Atwater
1809 Henry Davis
1818 Joshua Bates
1840 Benjamin Labaree
1866 Harvey D. Kitchel
1873 Vacant
1875 Calvin B. Hulbert
1880 Cyrus Hamlin
1885 Ezra Brainerd
1908 John M. Thomas
1921 Paul D. Moody
1943 Samuel S. Stratton
1963 James I. Armstrong

MILLS COLLEGE

Oakland, California

Mills Seminary until 1877
Mills Seminary-College until 1885

1865 Cyrus T. Mills
1885 Homer B. Sprague
1887 C. S. Stratton
1890 Susan T. Mills
1909 Luella C. Carson
1914 Hettie B. Ege (Acting)
1916 Aurelia H. Reinhardt
1943 Lynn T. White, Jr.
1958 Mary W. Bennett (Acting)
1959 Charles E. Rothwell
1967 Robert J. Wert

UNIVERSITY OF MINNESOTA

Minneapolis, Minnesota

1869 William W. Folwell
1884 Cyrus Northrop
1911 George E. Vincent
1917 Marion L. Burton
1920 Lotus D. Coffman
1938 Guy S. Ford
1941 Walter C. Coffey
1945 James L. Morrill
1960 Owen M. Wilson
1967 Malcolm Moos

THE UNIVERSITY OF MISSISSIPPI

University, Mississippi

Chancellors

1848 George F. Holmes
1849 Albert T. Bledsoe (Acting)
1849 Augustus B. Longstreet
1856 Frederick A. P. Barnard
1860 William D. Moore (Acting)
1865 John N. Waddell
1874 John J. Wheat (Acting)
1874 Alexander P. Stewart
1886 Edward Mayes
1891 Robert B. Fulton
1906 Alfred Hume (Acting)
1907 Andrew A. Kincannon
1914 Joseph N. Powers
1924 Alfred Hume
1930 Joseph N. Powers
1930 Christopher Longest (Acting)
1932 Alfred Hume
1935 Alfred B. Butts
1942 Alfred Hume (Acting)
1946 John D. Williams
1968 Porter L. Fortune, Jr.

MISSISSIPPI STATE UNIVERSITY

State College, Mississippi

A & M College until 1932
Mississippi State College until 1958

1880 Stephen D. Lee
1899 John M. Stone
1900 John C. Hardy
1912 George R. Hightower
1916 William H. Smith
1920 David C. Hull
1925 Buz M. Walker
1930 Hugh Critz
1934 George D. Humphrey
1945 Fred T. Mitchell
1953 Benjamin F. Hilbun
1960 Dean W. Colvard
1966 William L. Giles

UNIVERSITY OF MISSOURI

Columbia, Missouri

1841 John H. Lathrop
1849 William W. Hudson (Acting)
1850 James Shannon
1856 William W. Hudson

1859 George H. Matthews (Chairman)
1860 Benjamin B. Minor
1862 John H. Lathrop (Chairman)
1866 Daniel Read
1876 Samuel S. Laws
1889 Michael M. Fisher (Chairman)
1891 Richard H. Jesse
1908 Albert R. Hill
1921 John C. Jones
1923 Isidor Loeb (Acting)
1923 Stratton D. Brooks
1930 Walter Williams
1935 Frederick A. Middlebush
1954 Elmer Ellis
1966 John C. Weaver
1970 C. Brice Ratchford (Interim)

UNIVERSITY OF MONTANA
Missoula, Montana

University of Montana until 1913
State University of Montana until 1935
Montana State University until 1965

1895 Oscar J. Craig
1908 Clyde A. Duniway
1912 Edwin B. Craighead
1915 Frederick C. Scheuch (Acting)
1917 Edward O. Sisson
1921 Charles H. Clapp
1935 Frederick C. Scheuch (Acting)
1936 George F. Simmons
1941 Ernest O. Melby
1945 James A. McCain
1950 R. H. Jesse (Acting)
1951 Carl McFarland
1958 Gordon B. Castle (Acting)
1959 Harry K. Newburn
1963 Robert Johns
1966 Robert T. Pantzer

MONTANA STATE UNIVERSITY
Bozeman, Montana

Agricultural College of the State of Montana until 1911
Montana State College until 1965

1893 Augustus M. Ryon
1895 James Reid
1904 James M. Hamilton
1919 Alfred Atkinson
1937 August L. Strand
1942 William M. Cobleigh (Acting)
1943 Roland R. Renne
1963 Leon H. Johnson
1969 William A. Johnstone (Acting)
1970 Carl W. McIntosh

MORAVIAN COLLEGE
Bethlehem, Pennsylvania

Moravian College and Theological Seminary until merger in 1954 with Moravian College for Women

1864 Lewis L. Kampmann
1865 R. H. Huebner
1867 Edmund A. deSchweinitz
1885 Augustus Schultze
1918 John T. Hamilton
1928 William Schwarze
1944 Raymond S. Haupert
1969 Herman E. Collier, Jr.

MOREHOUSE COLLEGE
Atlanta, Georgia

1871 Joseph T. Robert
1884 David F. Estes
1885 Samuel Graves
1900 George Sale
1906 John Hope
1930 Samuel H. Archer
1937 Charles D. Hubert
1940 Benjamin E. Mays
1967 Hugh M. Gloster

MOUNT HOLYOKE COLLEGE
South Hadley, Massachusetts

1888 Elizabeth Blanchard (Acting)
1889 Louis F. Cowles (Acting)
1890 Elizabeth Storrs Mead
1901 Mary E. Wolley
1937 Rosewell G. Ham
1957 Richard G. Gettell
1968 Meribeth E. Cameron (Acting)
1969 David B. Truman

MUHLENBERG COLLEGE
Allentown, Pennsylvania

1867 Frederick A. Muhlenberg
1877 Benjamin Stadtler
1885 Theodore L. Seip
1904 John A. W. Haas
1937 Levering Tyson
1953 J. Conrad Seegers
1961 Erling N. Jensen
1969 John H. Morey

MUSKINGUM COLLEGE
New Concord, Ohio

1837 Benjamin Waddle
1838 Samuel Wilson
1846 David A. Wallace
1848 John Milligan
1849 Samuel G. Irvine
1851 Samuel McArthur
1855 Benjamin Waddle
1861 L. B. Shryock
1865 David Paul
1879 Frank M. Spencer
1887 John D. Irons
1893 Jesse Johnson
1904 John K. Montgomery
1932 Robert N. Montgomery
1962 Glenn M. McConagha
1965 Harry S. Manley
1972 William P. Miller

UNIVERSITY OF NEBRASKA
Lincoln, Nebraska

1871 Allen R. Benton
1876 Edmund B. Fairfield
1882 Henry E. Hitchcock (Acting)
1884 James I. Mannatt
1889 Charles E. Bessey (Acting)
1891 James H. Canfield
1895 George E. McLean
1899 Charles E. Bessey (Acting)
1900 Elisha B. Andrews
1908 Samuel Avery
1927 Edgar A. Burnett
1938 Chauncey S. Boucher
1946 Reuben G. Gustavson
1953 John K. Selleck (Acting)
1954 Clifford M. Hardin
1969 Merk Hobson (Acting)
1970 Durward B. Varner
1972 James H. Zumberge

THE UNIVERSITY OF NEBRASKA AT OMAHA
Omaha, Nebraska

The University of Omaha until 1930
The Municipal University of Omaha until 1968

1908 Daniel E. Jenkins
1917 Karl F. Whetstone
1926 Walter G. James
1928 Ernest Emery
1931 Walter G. James
1931 William E. Sealock
1935 Rowland Haynes
1948 P. Milo Bail
1965 Leland Traywick
1966 Kirk E. Naylor

THE UNIVERSITY OF NEVADA
Reno, Nevada

1887 LeRoy D. Brown
1890 Stephen A. Jones
1894 Joseph E. Stubbs
1914 Archer W. Hendrick
1917 Walter E. Clark
1939 Leon W. Hartman
1944 John O. Moseley
1950 Malcolm A. Love
1952 Minard W. Stout
1958 Charles J. Armstrong
1968 N. Edd Miller

UNIVERSITY OF NEW HAMPSHIRE
Durham, New Hampshire

New Hampshire College of Agriculture and Mechanic Arts until 1923

1891 Lyman D. Stevens
1893 Charles S. Murkland
1903 Charles H. Pettee (Acting)
1903 William D. Gibbs
1912 Charles H. Pettee (Acting)
1912 Edward T. Fairchild
1917 Charles H. Pettee (Acting)
1917 Ralph D. Hetzel
1927 Edward M. Lewis
1936 Roy D. Hunter (Acting)
1937 Fred Engelhardt
1944 Roy D. Hunter (Acting)
1944 Harold W. Stoke
1948 Arthur S. Adams
1950 Robert F. Chandler, Jr.
1954 Edward D. Eddy, Jr. (Acting)
1955 Eldon L. Johnson
1962 John F. Reed (Acting)
1962 Jere A. Chase (Acting)
1963 John W. McConnell
1972 Thomas Bonner

UNIVERSITY OF NEW MEXICO
Albuquerque, New Mexico

1892 Elias S. Stover
1897 Clarence L. Herrick
1901 William G. Tight
1909 Edward M. Gray
1912 David R. Boyd
1919 David S. Hill
1927 James F. Zimmerman
1945 John P. Wernette
1948 Thomas L. Popejoy
1968 Ferrell Heady

NEW MEXICO STATE UNIVERSITY
Las Cruces, New Mexico

Las Cruces College until 1889
New Mexico College of Agriculture and Mechanic Arts until 1960

1888 Hiram Hadley
1894 Samuel P. McCrea
1896 Cornelius T. Jordan
1899 Frederic W. Sanders
1901 Luther Foster
1908 Winfred E. Garrison
1913 George E. Ladd
1917 Austin D. Crile
1920 Robert W. Clothier
1921 Harry L. Kent
1935 Hugh M. Gardner (Acting)
1936 Ray Fife
1938 Hugh M. Milton II
1941 John W. Branson (Acting)
1946 Hugh M. Milton II
1947 John R. Nichols
1949 John W. Branson
1955 Roger B. Corbett
1970 Gerald W. Thomas

THE CITY UNIVERSITY OF NEW YORK
New York City

Chancellors

1961 John R. Everett
1963 Albert H. Bowker
1971 Robert J. Kibbee

(See also Bernard M. Baruch College; Brooklyn College; City College; Hunter College; Queens College)

STATE UNIVERSITY OF NEW YORK

1949 Alvia C. Eurich
1952 Charles Garside (Acting)
1952 William S. Carlson
1959 Thomas H. Hamilton

Chancellors

1964 Samuel B. Gould
1970 Ernest L. Boyer

STATE UNIVERSITY OF NEW YORK AT ALBANY

1889 William J. Milne
1915 Abram R. Brubacher
1939 John M. Sayles
1947 Milton G. Nelson (Acting)
1949 Evan R. Collins
1969 Allan A. Kuusisto
1970 Louis T. Benezet

STATE UNIVERSITY OF NEW YORK AT BUFFALO

University of Buffalo until 1962

Chancellors

1846 Millard Fillmore
1882 Orsamus H. Marshall
1885 E. Carleton Sprague
1895 James O. Putnam
1902 Wilson S. Bissell
1905 Charles P. Norton
1922 Samuel P. Capen
1950 T. Raymond McConnell
1954 Clifford C. Furnas

Presidents

1962 Clifford C. Furnas
1966 Martin Meyerson
1970 Robert L. Ketter

NEW YORK UNIVERSITY
New York, New York

The University of the City of New York until 1896

Chancellors

1831 James M. Mathews
1839 Theodore Frelinghuysen
1850 Vacant
1853 Isaac Ferris
1870 Howard Crosby
1882 John Hall
1891 Henry M. MacCracken
1911 Elmer E. Brown
1933 Harry W. Chase
1951 James L. Madden (Acting)
1952 Henry T. Heald

Presidents

1956 Carroll V. Newsom
1962 James M. Hester

NEWARK STATE COLLEGE
Union, New Jersey

Newark State Teachers College from 1935 to 1958

1877 William N. Barringer
1896 Charles B. Gilbert
1897 William S. Willis
1928 Bertha R. Kain
1929 M. Ernest Townsend
1940 Roy L. Shaffer
1944 John B. Dougall
1950 Eugene G. Wilkins
1970 Nathan Weiss

NIAGARA UNIVERSITY
Niagara, New York

Seminary of Our Lady of the Angels until 1883

1856 John J. Lynch
1859 John O'Reilly
1862 Thomas J. Smith
1863 Robert E. Rice
1878 Patrick V. Kavanagh
1894 Patrick S. McHale
1901 William F. Likly
1906 Perry J. Conroy
1908 Edward J. Walsh
1912 Michael A. Drennan
1917 William F. Likly
1919 Willian E. Katzenberger
1927 Francis J. Dodd
1929 John J. O'Byrne
1932 Joseph M. Noonan
1947 Francis L. Meade
1957 Vincent T. Swords
1964 Joseph T. Cahill
1965 Kenneth F. Slattery

THE UNIVERSITY OF NORTH CAROLINA
Chapel Hill, North Carolina

1804 Joseph Caldwell
1812 Robert H. Chapman
1817 Joseph Caldwell
1835 David L. Swain
1868 Solomon S. Pool
1876 Kemp P. Battle
1891 George T. Winston
1896 Edwin A. Alderman
1900 Francis P. Venable
1914 Edward K. Graham
1919 Harry W. Chase
1930 Frank P. Graham
1959 Gordon Gray
1966 William C. Friday

UNIVERSITY OF NORTH CAROLINA AT GREENSBORO

State Normal and Industrial College until 1919
North Carolina College for Women until 1932
Women's College of the University of North Carolina until 1963

1892 Charles D. McIver
1906 Julius I. Foust

Chancellors

1934 Walter C. Jackson
1950 Edward K. Graham
1956 W. W. Pierson, Jr. (Acting)
1957 Gordon W. Blackwell
1961 Otis Singletary
1966 James S. Ferguson

UNIVERSITY OF NORTH CAROLINA AT RALEIGH

North Carolina State University until 1968

1889 Alexander Q. Holladay
1899 George T. Winston
1908 Daniel H. Hall
1916 Wallace C. Riddick
1923 Eugene C. Brooks

Chancellors

1934 John W. Harrelson
1953 Carey H. Bostian
1959 John T. Caldwell

UNIVERSITY OF NORTH DAKOTA
Grand Forks, North Dakota

1884 William M. Blackburn
1885 Henry Montgomery (Acting)
1887 Homer B. Sprague
1891 Webster Merrifield
1909 Frank L. McVey
1918 Thomas F. Kane
1933 John C. West
1954 George W. Starcher
1971 Thomas J. Clifford

NORTH DAKOTA STATE UNIVERSITY OF AGRICULTURE AND APPLIED SCIENCE
Fargo, North Dakota

North Dakota Agricultural College until 1960

1890 H. E. Stockbridge
1893 J. B. Power (Acting)
1895 J. H. Worst
1916 E. F. Ladd
1921 E. S. Keene (Acting)
1921 John L. Coulter
1929 A. E. Minard (Acting)
1929 J. H. Shepperd
1937 J. C. West (Acting)
1939 F. L. Eversull
1946 J. H. Longwell
1948 Fred S. Hultz
1961 Arlon G. Hazen (Acting)
1962 H. R. Albrecht
1968 L. D. Loftsgard

NORTH TEXAS STATE UNIVERSITY
Denton, Texas

North Texas State Teachers College from 1923 to 1949
North Texas State College until 1961

1923 Robert L. Marquis
1934 W. Joseph McConnell
1951 James C. Matthews
1968 John J. Kamerick
1970 John L. Carter, Jr. (Acting)
1972 C. C. Nolen

NORTHEASTERN UNIVERSITY
Boston, Massachusetts

1940 Carl S. Ell
1959 Asa S. Knowles

NORTHERN ILLINOIS UNIVERSITY
DeKalb, Illinois

Northern Illinois State Teachers College from 1921 to 1955

Northern Illinois State College until 1957

1921 J. Stanley Brown
1927 J. Clifton Brown
1929 Karl L. Adams
1949 Leslie A. Holmes
1967 Rhoten A. Smith

UNIVERSITY OF NORTHERN IOWA
Cedar Falls, Iowa

Iowa State Teachers College from 1909 to 1961
State College of Iowa from 1961 to 1967

1903 Homer H. Seerley
1928 Orval R. Latham
1940 Malcolm Price
1950 James W. Maucker
1970 John J. Kamerick

NORTHWESTERN UNIVERSITY
Evanston, Illinois

1853 Clark T. Hinman
1854 Henry S. Noyes
1856 Randolph S. Foster
1860 Henry S. Noyes
1867 David H. Wheeler
1869 Erastus O. Haven
1872 Charles H. Fowler
1876 Oliver Marcy
1881 Joseph Cummings
1890 Henry W. Rogers
1900 Daniel Bonbright
1902 Edmund J. James
1904 Thomas F. Holgate
1906 Abram W. Harris
1916 Thomas F. Holgate
1919 Lynn H. Hough
1920 Walter D. Scott
1939 Franklyn B. Snyder
1949 J. Roscoe Miller
1970 Robert H. Strotz

NORWICH UNIVERSITY
Northfield, Vermont

1819 Alden Partridge
1844 Truman B. Ransom
1847 James D. Butler
1848 Henry S. Wheaton
1850 Edward Bourns
1867 Thomas W. Walker
1869 Roger S. Howard
1871 Malcolm Douglass
1875 Josiah Swett
1876 Charles A. Curtis
1880 Charles H. Lewis
1896 Allen D. Brown
1904 Charles H. Spooner
1915 Ira L. Reeves
1920 Charles A. Plumley
1934 Porter H. Adams
1940 John M. Thomas
1944 Homer L. Dodge
1950 Ernest N. Harmon
1965 Barksdale Hamlett

UNIVERSITY OF NOTRE DAME
South Bend, Indiana

1842 Edward F. Sorin
1865 Patrick Dillon
1866 William Corby
1872 August Lemmonier
1874 Patrick Colovin
1877 William Corby
1881 Thomas E. Walsh
1893 Andrew Morrissey
1905 John W. Cavanaugh
1919 James A. Burns
1922 Matthew J. Walsh
1928 Charles L. O'Donnell
1934 John F. O'Hara
1940 J. Hugh O'Donnell
1946 John J. Cavanaugh
1952 Theodore M. Hesburgh

OBERLIN COLLEGE
Oberlin, Ohio

1835 Asa Mahan
1849 Charles G. Finney (Acting)
1850 John Morgan (Acting)
1851 Charles G. Finney
1866 James H. Fairchild
1889 Henry M. Tenney (Acting)
1891 William G. Ballantine
1896 James H. Fairchild (Acting)
1899 John H. Barrows
1902 Henry C. King
1909 Henry M. Tenney
1911 Henry C. King
1918 Edward I. Bosworth
1920 Henry C. King
1927 Ernest H. Wilkins
1946 William E. Stevenson
1960 Robert K. Carr
1972 Robert Fuller

OCCIDENTAL COLLEGE
Los Angeles, California

1887 Samuel H. Weller
1891 J. Melville McPherron
1894 Elbert N. Condit
1896 James W. Parkhill
1897 Guy W. Wadsworth
1905 William S. Young (Acting)
1906 John W. Baer
1916 Thomas G. Burt (Acting)
1917 Silas Evans
1920 Thomas G. Burt (Acting)
1921 Remsen Bird
1946 Arthur G. Coons
1965 Richard C. Gilman

OGLETHORPE UNIVERSITY
Atlanta, Georgia

1836 Carlyle P. Beman
1841 Samuel K. Talmage
1869 William M. Cunningham
1870 David Wills
1913 Thornwell Jacobs
1944 Philip Weltner
1953 James W. Bunting
1956 Donald R. Wilson
1958 Donald C. Agnew
1965 Paul R. Beall
1967 Paul K. Vonk

OHIO UNIVERSITY
Athens, Ohio

1809 Jacob Lindly
1822 James Irvine
1824 Robert G. Wilson
1839 William H. McGuffey
1843 (University Closed)
1848 Alfred Ryors
1852 Solomon Howard
1872 William H. Scott
1883 Charles W. Super
1896 Isaac Crook
1899 Charles W. Super
1901 Alston Ellis
1920 Edwin W. Chubb (Acting)
1921 Elmer B. Bryan
1934 Edwin W. Chubb (Acting)
1935 Herman G. James
1943 Walter S. Gamertsfelder
1945 John C. Baker
1961 Vernon R. Alden
1969 Claude R. Sowle

THE OHIO STATE UNIVERSITY
Columbus, Ohio

Ohio Agricultural and Mechanical College until 1878

1873 Edward Orton
1881 Walter Q. Scott
1883 William H. Scott
1895 James H. Canfield
1899 William O. Thompson
1926 George W. Rightmire
1938 William McPherson (Acting)
1940 Howard L. Bevis
1956 Novice G. Fawcett
1972 Harold L. Enarson

THE UNIVERSITY OF OKLAHOMA
Norman, Oklahoma

1892 David R. Boyd
1908 Arthur G. Evans
1911 Julien C. Monnet
1912 Stratton D. Brooks
1923 James S. Buchanan
1925 William B. Bizzell
1941 Joseph A. Brandt
1944 George L. Cross
1968 John H. Hollomon
1970 Peter K. McCarter (Interim)
1971 Paul F. Sharp

OKLAHOMA STATE UNIVERSITY
Stillwater, Oklahoma

Oklahoma A & M College until 1957

1891 R. J. Barker
1894 Henry E. Alvord
1895 Edmund D. Murdaugh
1895 George E. Morrow
1899 Angelo C. Scott
1908 James H. Connell
1914 Lowry L. Lewis
1915 James W. Cantwell
1921 James B. Eskridge
1923 George Wilson
1923 Richard G. Tyler
1923 Bradford Knapp
1928 Clarence H. McElroy
1928 Henry G. Bennett
1952 Oliver S. Willham
1966 Robert B. Kamm

UNIVERSITY OF OREGON
Eugene, Oregon

1876 John W. Johnson
1893 Charles H. Chapman
1899 Frank Strong
1902 Prince L. Campbell
1926 Arnold B. Hall
1932 Vacant
1934 Clarence V. Boyer
1938 Donald M. Erb
1944 Orlando J. Hollis (Acting)
1945 Harry K. Newburn
1953 Victor P. Morris (Acting)
1954 O. Meredith Wilson
1960 William C. Jones (Acting)
1961 Arthur S. Flemming
1968 Charles E. Johnson (Acting)
1969 N. Ray Hawk (Acting)
1969 Robert D. Clark

OREGON STATE UNIVERSITY
Corvallis, Oregon

Agricultural College of the State of Oregon until 1929
Oregon State Agricultural College until 1953
Oregon State College until 1961

1865 W. A. Finley
1872 B. L. Arnold
1892 John D. Letcher
1892 John M. Bloss
1896 H. B. Miller
1897 Thomas M. Gatch
1907 William J. Kerr
1932 George W. Peavy
1940 Frank L. Ballard
1941 Francois A. Gilfillan
1942 August L. Strand

1961 James H. Jensen
1969 Roy A. Young
1970 Robert W. MacVicar

UNIVERSITY OF THE PACIFIC

Stockton, California

College of the Pacific from 1911 to 1961

1852 Edward Bannister
1854 M. C. Briggs
1856 William J. Maclay
1857 A. S. Gibbons
1859 Edward Bannister
1867 Thomas H. Sinex
1872 A. S. Gibbons
1877 C. S. Stratton
1887 A. C. Hirst
1891 Isaac Crook
1893 W. C. Sawyer (Acting)
1894 J. N. Beard
1896 Eli McClish
1906 M. S. Cross (Acting)
1908 William W. Guth
1913 B. J. Morris
1914 John L. Seaton
1919 Tully C. Knoles
1946 Robert E. Burns
1972 Stanley McCaffrey

WILLIAM PATERSON COLLEGE OF NEW JERSEY

Wayne, New Jersey

Paterson State Teachers College from 1937 to 1954
Paterson State College from 1954 to 1971

1937 Clair S. Wightman
1954 Marion E. Shea
1966 Michael B. Gilligan (Acting)
1967 James J. Forcina (Acting)
1968 James K. Olsen

UNIVERSITY OF PENNSYLVANIA

Philadelphia, Pennsylvania

College of Philadelphia until 1779

Provosts

1754 William Smith
1779 John Ewing
1802 Vacant
1806 John Mc Dowell
1810 John Andrews
1813 Frederick Beasley
1828 William H. DeLancey
1834 John Ludlow
1854 Henry Vethake
1860 Daniel R. Goodwin
1868 Charles J. Stille
1881 William Pepper
1894 Charles C. Harrison
1910 Edgar F. Smith
1921 Josiah H. Penniman

Presidents

1930 Thomas S. Gates
1944 George W. McClelland
1948 Harold E. Stassen
1953 Gaylord P. Harnwell
1970 Martin Meyerson

THE PENNSYLVANIA STATE UNIVERSITY

University Park, Pennsylvania

Agricultural College of Pennsylvania until 1874
The Pennsylvania State College until 1953

1864 William H. Allen
1866 John Fraser
1868 Thomas H. Burrowes
1871 James Calder
1880 Joseph Shortlidge
1881 James Y. McKee (Acting)
1882 George W. Atherton
1906 James A. Beaver (Acting)
1908 Edwin E. Sparks
1920 Vacant
1921 John M. Thomas
1926 Vacant
1927 Ralph D. Hetzel
1947 James Milholland (Acting)
1950 Milton S. Eisenhower
1956 Eric A. Walker
1970 John W. Oswald

UNIVERSITY OF PITTSBURGH

Pittsburgh, Pennsylvania

Western University of Pennsylvania until 1908

1819 Robert Bruce
1835 Gilbert Morgan
1836 Robert Bruce
1843 Heman Dyer
1849 David H. Riddle (Acting)
1855 John F. McLaren
1858 George Woods
1880 Milton B. Goff (Acting)
1881 Henry M. MacCracken
1884 Milton B. Goff
1891 William J. Holland
1901 John A. Brashear (Acting)
1904 Samuel B. McCormick
1921 John G. Bowman
1945 Rufus H. Fitzgerald
1955 Charles B. Nutting (Acting)
1956 Edward H. Litchfield
1965 Stanton H. Crawford (Acting)
1966 David H. Kurtzman
1967 Wesley W. Posvar

POLYTECHNIC INSTITUTE OF BROOKLYN

Brooklyn, New York

1889 David H. Cochran
1899 Henry S. Snow (Interim)
1904 Fred W. Atkinson
1925 Parke Rexford Kolbe
1932 Charles E. Potts (Interim)
1933 Henry S. Rogers
1957 Ernst Weber
1969 Benjamin Adler (Interim)
1971 Arthur Grad

POMONA COLLEGE

Claremont, California

1890 Cyrus G. Baldwin
1897 Franklin L. Ferguson
1901 George A. Gates
1910 James A. Blaisdell
1928 Charles K. Edmunds
1941 E. Wilson Lyon
1969 J. David Alexander

PRATT INSTITUTE

Brooklyn, New York

1937 Charles Pratt
1953 Francis H. Horn
1957 Robert Oxnam
1961 Richard H. Heindel
1967 William P. Maddox (Acting)
1968 James B. Donovan
1970 Henry Saltzman
1972 Richardson Pratt, Jr.

PRINCETON UNIVERSITY

Princeton, New Jersey

Known originally as the College of New Jersey

1747 Jonathan Dickinson
1747 Aaron Burr
1757 Jonathan Edwards
1759 Samuel Davies
1761 Samuel Finley
1768 John Witherspoon
1795 S. Stanhope Smith
1812 Ashbel Green
1823 James Carnahan
1854 John Maclean
1868 James McCosh
1888 Francis L. Patton
1902 Woodrow Wilson
1912 John G. Hibben
1933 Harold W. Dodds
1957 Robert F. Goheen
1971 William C. Bowen

PURDUE UNIVERSITY

Lafayette, Indiana

1872 Richard Owen
1874 Abram C. Shortridge
1876 Emerson E. White
1883 James H. Smart
1900 Winthrop E. Stone
1922 Edward C. Elliott
1946 Frederick L. Hovde
1972 Arthur G. Hansen

QUEENS COLLEGE OF THE CITY UNIVERSITY OF NEW YORK

Flushing, New York

Queens College until 1961

1937 Paul Klapper
1947 Margaret V. Kiely (Acting)
1949 John J. Theobald
1956 Thomas V. Garvey (Provost)
1958 Harold W. Stoke
1965 Joseph P. McMurray
1971 Joseph S. Murphy

RADCLIFFE COLLEGE

Cambridge, Massachusetts

1882 Elizabeth C. Agassiz
1903 LeBaron R. Briggs
1923 Ada L. Comstock
1943 Wilbur K. Jordan
1960 Mary I. Bunting
1972 Matina S. Horner

RANDOLPH-MACON COLLEGE

Ashland, Virginia

1833 Stephen Olin
1837 Landon C. Garland
1846 William A. Smith
1866 Thomas C. Johnson
1868 James A. Duncan
1877 William W. Bennett
1886 William W. Smith
1897 John A. Kern
1899 William G. Starr
1902 Robert E. Blackwell
1938 Samuel C. Hatcher (Acting)
1939 Jesse E. Morland
1967 Luther W. White III

UNIVERSITY OF RHODE ISLAND

Kingston, Rhode Island

Rhode Island College of Agriculture and Mechanic Arts until 1909
Rhode Island State College until 1951

1892 John H. Washburn
1902 Homer J. Wheeler (Acting)
1903 Kenyon L. Butterfield
1906 Howard Edwards
1930 John Barlow (Acting)
1931 Raymond G. Bressler
1940 John Barlow (Acting)
1941 Carl R. Woodward
1958 Francis H. Horn
1967 F. Don James (Acting)
1968 Werner A. Baum

RICE UNIVERSITY
Houston, Texas

Rice Institute until 1960

1912 Edgar O. Lovett
1946 William V. Houston
1960 Carey Croneis (Acting)
1961 Kenneth S. Pitzer
1968 Frank E. Vandiver (Acting)
1970 Norman Hackerman

UNIVERSITY OF RICHMOND
Richmond, Virginia

Richmond College until 1920

1840 Robert Ryland
1866 Tiberius G. Hones
1869 Bennett Puryear (Chairman)
1885 H. H. Harris (Chairman)
1889 Bennett Puryear (Chairman)
1895 F. W. Boatwright
1946 George M. Modlin
1971 E. Bruce Heilman

ROANOKE COLLEGE
Salem, Virginia

1853 David F. Bittle
1877 Thomas W. Dosh
1878 Julius D. Dreher
1904 John A. Morehead
1920 Charles J. Smith
1949 Henry S. Oberly
1963 Perry F. Kendig

UNIVERSITY OF ROCHESTER
Rochester, New York

Chancellor

1850 Ira Harris

Presidents

1853 Martin B. Anderson
1890 David J. Hall
1896 Samuel A. Lattimore
1898 Henry F. Burton (Acting)
1900 Rush Rhees
1935 Alan Valentine
1951 Cornelis W. deKiewiet
1962 W. Allen Wallis

Chancellor

1970 W. Allen Wallis

ROCHESTER INSTITUTE OF TECHNOLOGY
Rochester, New York

1953 Mark Ellingson
1969 Paul A. Miller

ROLLINS COLLEGE
Winter Park, Florida

1885 Edward Payson Hooker
1892 John H. Ford (Acting)
1893 Charles G. Fairchild
1895 John H. Ford (Acting)
1896 George M. Ward
1902 William F. Blackman
1916 George M. Ward (Acting)
1917 Calvin H. French
1919 George M. Ward (Acting)
1923 Robert J. Sprague
1924 William C. Weir
1925 Hamilton Holt
1949 Paul A. Wagner
1951 Hugh F. McKean
1969 Jack B. Critchfield

RUTGERS–THE STATE UNIVERSITY
New Brunswick, New Jersey

Queens College until 1825
Rutgers College until 1924
Rutgers University until 1956

1785 Jacob R. Hardenbergh
1791 William Linn
1794 Ira Condict
1810 John H. Livingston
1825 Philip Milledoler
1840 Abraham B. Hasbrouck
1850 Theodore Frelinghuysen
1863 William H. Campbell
1882 Merrill E. Gates
1891 Austin Scott
1906 William H. S. Demarest
1925 John M. Thomas
1930 Philip M. Brett
1932 Robert C. Clothier
1951 Lewis W. Jones
1959 Mason W. Gross
1971 Edward J. Bloustein

SACRAMENTO STATE COLLEGE
Sacramento, California

1947 Guy A. West
1965 F. Blair Mayne (Acting)
1965 Stephen L. Walker (Acting)
1966 Robert Johns
1969 Otto Butz (Acting)
1970 Bernard L. Hyink
1972 Glenn S. Dumke (Chancellor)

ST. BONAVENTURE UNIVERSITY
St. Bonaventure, New York

1874 Charles Vissani
1877 Leo DaSaracena
1880 Theophilus Pospisilik
1886 Joseph Butler
1911 Fidelis Reynolds
1916 Alexander Hickey
1920 Thomas Plassmann
1949 Juvenal Lalor
1955 Brian Lhota
1961 Francis W. Kearney
1967 Reginald Redlon

ST. JOHN'S COLLEGE
Annapolis, Maryland

1790 John McDowell
1807 Bethel Judd
1812 John McDowell
1820 Henry L. Davis
1824 William Rafferty
1831 Hector Humphreys
1857 Cleland K. Nelson
1861 (College Closed)
1866 Henry Barnard
1867 James C. Welling
1870 James M. Garnett
1880 John M. Leavitt
1884 William H. Hopkins
1886 Thomas Fell
1923 Enoch B. Garey
1929 Vacant
1931 Douglas H. Gordon
1934 Amos W. W. Woodcock
1937 Stringfellow Barr
1947 John S. Kieffer
1949 Richard D. Weigle

ST. JOHN'S UNIVERSITY
Jamaica, New York

1870 John T. Landry
1875 Patrick M. O'Regan
1877 Andrew J. Meyer
1882 Jeremiah A. Hartnett
1897 James J. Sullivan
1901 Patrick S. McHale
1906 John W. Moore
1925 John J. Cloonan
1931 Thomas F. Ryan
1935 Edward J. Walsh
1942 William J. Mahoney
1947 John A. Flynn
1961 Edward J. Burke
1965 Joseph T. Cahill

ST. JOSEPH'S COLLEGE
Philadelphia, Pennsylvania

1851 Felix Barbelin
1856 James Ryder
1857 James A. Ward
1860 Felix Barbelin
1868 Burchard Villiger
1893 Patrick J. Dooley
1896 William F. Clark
1900 Cornelius Gillespie
1907 Dean T. O'Sullivan
1908 Cornelius Gillespie
1909 Charles W. Lyons
1914 Charles Davey
1917 Redmond J. Walsh
1920 Patrick F. O'Gorman
1921 Albert G. Brown
1927 William T. Tallon
1933 Thomas J. Higgins
1939 Thomas J. Love
1944 John J. Long
1950 Edward G. Jacklin
1956 J. Joseph Bluett
1962 William F. Maloney
1968 Terrence Toland

THE ST. LAWRENCE UNIVERSITY
Canton, New York

St. Lawrence College until 1899

1859 John S. Lee
1868 Richmond Fisk
1872 Absalom G. Gaines
1889 Alpheus B. Hervey
1894 Vacant
1896 John C. Lee
1899 Almon Gunnison
1914 Vacant
1916 Frank A. Gallup
1919 Richard E. Sykes
1935 Laurens H. Seelye
1940 Millard H. Jencks
1945 Eugene G. Bewkes
1963 Foster S. Brown
1969 Frank P. Piskor

SAINT LOUIS UNIVERSITY
St. Louis, Missouri

1818 Francis Niel
1824 Edmond Saulnier
1828 Charles F. Van Quickenborne
1829 Peter J. Verhaegen
1836 John A. Elet
1840 James O. Van deVelde
1843 George A. Carrell
1847 John B. Druyts
1854 John S. Verdin
1859 Ferdinand Coosemans
1862 Thomas O'Neill
1868 Francis F. Stuntebeck
1871 Joseph Zealand
1874 Leopold Bushart
1877 Joseph E. Keller
1881 Rudolph J. Meyer
1885 Henry Moeller
1889 Edward J. Gleeson
1891 Joseph Grimmelsman
1898 James F. X. Hoeffer
1900 William B. Rogers
1907 Francis B. O'Boyle
1908 John P. Frieden
1912 Alexander J. Burrowes
1913 Bernard J. Otting
1920 William F. Robison
1922 Michael J. O'Connor
1924 Charles H. Cloud
1930 Robert S. Johnston
1936 Harry B. Crimmins
1942 Robert Kelley
1943 Patrick J. Holloran
1949 Paul C. Reinert

SAN DIEGO STATE COLLEGE
San Diego, California

San Diego State Teachers College from 1925 to 1935

1925 Edward L. Hardy
1935 Walter R. Hepner
1952 Malcolm A. Love
1972 Donald Walker (Acting)

SAN FERNANDO VALLEY STATE COLLEGE
Northridge, California

1958 Ralph Prator
1968 Paul B. Blomgren (Acting)
1969 Malcolm O. Sillars (Acting)
1969 James W. Cleary

UNIVERSITY OF SAN FRANCISCO
San Francisco, California

St. Ignatius College until 1930

1855 Anthony Maraschi
1862 Nicholas Congiato
1865 Burchard Villiger
1866 Nicholas Congiato
1869 Joseph Bayma
1873 Aloysius Masnata
1876 John Pinasco
1880 Robert E. Kenna
1883 Joseph Sasia
1887 Henry Imoda
1893 Edward Allen
1896 John P. Frieden
1908 Joseph Saisa
1911 Albert Trivelli
1915 Patrick Foote
1919 Pius Moore
1925 Edward Whelan
1932 William Lonergan
1934 Harold Ring
1938 William Dunne
1954 John F. X. Connolly
1963 Charles Dullea
1969 Albert R. Jonsen

SAN FRANCISCO STATE COLLEGE
San Francisco, California

1899 Frederick L. Burk
1924 Archibald B. Anderson
1927 Alexander C. Roberts
1945 J. Paul Leonard
1957 Glenn S. Dumke
1961 Frank Fenton (Acting)
1962 Paul Dodd
1966 John Summerskill
1968 S. I. Hayakawa

SAN JOSE STATE COLLEGE
San Jose, California

San Jose State Teachers College from 1921 to 1935

1921 William W. Kemp
1923 Alexander R. Heron (Acting)
1923 Edwin R. Snyder
1925 Herman F. Minssen (Acting)
1925 Thomas W. MacQuarrie
1952 John T. Wahlquist
1964 Robert D. Clark
1969 Hobert W. Burns (Acting)
1970 John H. Bunzel

THE UNIVERSITY OF SANTA CLARA
Santa Clara, California

Santa Clara College until 1912

1851 John Nobili
1856 Nicholas Congiato
1857 Felix Cicaterri
1861 Burchard Villiger
1865 Aloysius Masnata
1868 Aloysius Varsi
1876 Aloysius Brunengo
1880 John Pinasco
1883 Robert E. Kenna
1888 John Pinasco
1893 Joseph W. Riordan
1899 Robert E. Kenna
1905 Richard A. Gleeson
1910 James P. Morrissey
1913 Walter F. Thornton
1918 Timothy L. Murphy
1921 Zacheus J. Maher
1926 Cornelius J. McCoy
1932 James J. Lyons
1935 Louis C. Rudolph
1940 Charles J. Walsh
1945 William C. Gianera
1951 Herman J. Hauck
1958 Patrick A. Donohoe
1968 Thomas D. Terry

SARAH LAWRENCE COLLEGE
Bronxville, New York

1928 Marion Coats
1929 Constance Warren
1945 Harold Taylor
1959 Harrison Tweed
1960 Paul Ward
1965 Esther Raushenbush
1969 Charles DeCarlo

SIMMONS COLLEGE
Boston, Massachusetts

1902 Henry Lefavour
1933 Bancroft Beatley
1955 William E. Park
1970 William J. Holmes, Jr.

SKIDMORE COLLEGE
Saratoga Springs, New York

1912 Charles H. Keyes
1925 Henry T. Moore
1957 Val H. Wilson
1965 Joseph C. Palamountain, Jr.

SMITH COLLEGE
Northampton, Massachusetts

1873 Laurenus Seelye
1910 Marion L. Burton
1917 William A. Neilson
1939 Elizabeth Morrow (Acting)
1940 Herbert J. Davis
1949 Benjamin F. Wright
1959 Thomas C. Mendenhall

THE UNIVERSITY OF THE SOUTH
Sewanee, Tennessee

1867 Charles T. Quintard
1872 Josiah Gorgas
1878 John B. Elliott (Acting)
1879 Telfair Hodgson
1890 Thomas F. Gailor
1893 Benjamin L. Wiggins
1909 William B. Hall
1914 Albion W. Knight
1922 Benjamin F. Finney
1938 Alexander Guerry
1948 George M. Baker (Acting)
1949 Cordes B. Green
1951 Edward McCrady

UNIVERSITY OF SOUTH CAROLINA
Charleston, South Carolina

1805 Jonathan Maxcy
1821 Thomas Cooper
1833 Vacant
1835 Robert W. Barnwell
1842 Robert Henry
1846 William C. Preston
1851 James H. Thornwell
1856 Charles F. McCay
1858 Augustus B. Longstreet
1862 (University Closed)
1865 Robert W. Barnwell (Chairman)
1873 Vacant
1880 W. Porcher Miles
1882 John M. McBryde
1891 James Woodrow
1897 Frank C. Woodward
1902 Benjamin M. Sloan
1909 Samuel C. Mitchell
1914 William S. Currell
1922 William D. Melton
1927 Davison M. Douglas
1932 Leonard T. Baker
1935 James R. McKissick
1945 Norman M. Smith
1952 Donald S. Russell
1957 Robert L. Sumwalt
1962 Thomas F. Jones

UNIVERSITY OF SOUTH DAKOTA
Vermillion, South Dakota

1882 Ephraim M. Epstein
1883 John W. Simonds
1885 John W. Herrick
1887 Edward Olson
1890 Howard B. Grose
1891 Joseph W. Mauck
1899 Garrett Droppers
1906 Benjamin F. Gault
1914 Robert L. Slagle
1929 Herman G. James
1935 I. D. Weeks
1966 Edward Q. Moulton
1968 Richard L. Bowen

UNIVERSITY OF SOUTH FLORIDA
Tampa, Florida

1957 John S. Allen
1970 Harris W. Dean (Acting)
1971 M. Cecil Mackey

UNIVERSITY OF SOUTHERN CALIFORNIA
Los Angeles, California

1880 Marion M. Bovard
1892 Joseph P. Widney
1895 George W. White
1903 George F. Bovard
1921 Rufus B. von KleinSmid
1947 Fred D. Fagg, Jr.
1958 Norman Topping
1970 John R. Hubbard

SOUTHERN ILLINOIS UNIVERSITY
Carbondale, Illinois

1874 Robert Allyn
1892 John Hull (Regent)
1893 Harvey W. Everest
1897 Daniel B. Parkinson
1913 Henry W. Shyrock
1935 Roscoe Pulliam
1944 Bruce W. Merwin (Interim)
1945 Chester F. Lay
1948 Delyte W. Morris

Chancellor

1970 Robert Layer

SOUTHERN METHODIST UNIVERSITY
Dallas, Texas

1911 Robert S. Hyer
1920 Hiram A. Boaz
1923 Charles C. Selecman
1939 Umphrey Lee
1954 Willis M. Tate
1972 Paul Hardin

STANFORD UNIVERSITY
Stanford, California

1891 David S. Jordan
1913 John C. Branner

1915 Ray L. Wilbur
1943 Donald B. Tresidder
1949 J. E. Wallace Sterling
1968 Kenneth S. Pitzer
1970 Richard W. Lyman

STEPHENS COLLEGE
Columbia, Missouri

1870 E. S. Dulin
1877 R. P. Rider
1883 T. W. Barrett
1894 Sam F. Taylor
1904 J. R. Pentuff
1905 W. B. Peeler
1910 H. N. Quisenberry
1912 James M. Wood
1947 Homer P. Rainey
1952 Thomas A. Spragens
1958 Seymour A. Smith

STETSON UNIVERSITY
DeLand, Florida

1885 John F. Forbes
1904 Lincoln Hulley
1934 William S. Allen
1948 J. Ollie Edmunds
1967 Paul F. Geren
1970 John E. Johns

SUSQUEHANNA UNIVERSITY
Selinsgrove, Pennsylvania

1893 Franlin P. Manhart
1895 Jonathan R. Dimm
1899 Charles W. Heisler
1902 George W. Enders
1904 John B. Focht
1905 Charles T. Aikens
1928 G. Morris Smith
1959 Gustave W. Weber

SWARTHMORE COLLEGE
Swarthmore, Pennsylvania

1864 Edward Parrish
1872 Edward H. Magill
1890 William H. Appleton
1891 Charles DeGarmo
1898 William W. Birdsall
1902 Joseph Swain
1921 Frank Aydelotte
1940 John W. Nason
1953 Courtney C. Smith
1969 Robert D. Cross
1972 Theodore W. Friend 3d

SYRACUSE UNIVERSITY
Syracuse, New York

1873 Alexander Winchell
1874 Erastus O. Haven
1881 Charles N. Sims
1894 James R. Day
1922 Charles W. Flint
1936 William P. Graham
1942 William P. Tolley
1969 John E. Corbally, Jr.

Chancellor

1971 Melvin A. Eggers

TEMPLE UNIVERSITY
Philadelphia, Pennsylvania

1891 Russell H. Conwell
1925 Charles E. Beury
1941 Robert L. Johnson
1959 Millard E. Gladfelter
1967 Paul R. Anderson

THE UNIVERSITY OF TENNESSEE
Knoxville, Tennessee

Blount College until 1809
East Tennessee College until 1840
East Tennessee University until 1879

1794 Samuel Carrick
1809 (College Closed)
1820 David A. Sherman
1825 James McBath
1827 Charles Coffin
1833 James H. Piper
1834 Joseph Estabrook
1850 William B. Reese
1853 George Cooke
1858 W. D. Carnes
1860 J. J. Ridley
1862 (University Closed)
1865 Thomas W. Humes
1883 Vacant
1887 Charles W. Dabney
1904 Brown Ayres
1919 Harcourt A. Morgan
1934 James D. Hoskins
1946 C. E. Brehm
1959 Andrew D. Holt
1970 Edward J. Boling
1972 Archie R. Dykes

UNIVERSITY OF TEXAS
Austin, Texas

1895 Leslie Waggener (Interim)
1896 George T. Winston
1899 William L. Prather
1905 David F. Houston
1908 Sidney E. Mezes
1914 William J. Battle (Interim)
1916 Robert E. Vinson
1923 William S. Sutton (Interim)
1924 Walter M. W. Splawn
1927 Harry Y. Benedict
1937 John W. Calhoun (Interim)
1939 Homer P. Rainey
1944 Theophilus S. Painter
1952 James C. Dolley
1953 Logan Wilson
1960 Harry H. Ransom
1961 Joseph R. Smiley
1963 Vacant
1967 Norman Hackerman
1970 Bryce Jorden (Interim)

Chancellor

1971 Charles LeMaistre

TEXAS A AND M UNIVERSITY
College Station, Texas

1876 Thomas S. Gathright
1879 John G. James
1883 James R. Cole
1883 Hardaway H. Dinwiddie
1888 Louis M. McInnis
1890 William L. Bringhurst
1891 Lawrence S. Ross
1898 Roger H. Whitlock
1898 Lafayette L. Foster
1901 Roger H. Whitlock
1902 David F. Houston
1905 Henry H. Harrington
1908 Robert T. Milner
1913 Charles Puryear (Acting)
1914 William B. Bizzell
1925 Thomas O. Walton
1943 Frank C. Bolton (Acting)
1944 Gibb Gilchrist
1948 Frank C. Bolton
1950 Marion T. Harrington
1953 David H. Morgan
1956 David W. Williams (Acting)
1957 Marion T. Harrington
1959 James E. Rudder
1970 Alvin R. Luedecke (Acting)
1970 Jack K. Williams

TEXAS CHRISTIAN UNIVERSITY
Fort Worth, Texas

Add-Ran College until 1889
Add-Ran Christian University until 1902

1873 Addison Clark
1899 Vacant
1902 Ely V. Zollars
1906 Clinton Lockhart
1911 Frederick D. Kershner
1916 Edward M. Waits
1941 McGruder E. Sadler
1965 James M. Moudy

TEXAS TECH UNIVERSITY
Lubbock, Texas

1925 Paul W. Horn
1932 Bradford Knapp
1938 Clifford B. Jones
1944 William M. Whyburn
1948 Dossie M. Wiggins
1952 Edward N. Jones
1959 Robert C. Goodwin
1966 Grover E. Murray

UNIVERSITY OF TOLEDO
Toledo, Ohio

Toledo University until 1921
The University of the City of Toledo until 1947

1909 Jerome H. Raymond
1910 Charles A. Cockayne
1914 A. Monroe Stowe
1925 John W. Dowd
1926 Ernest A. Smith
1926 Lee W. MacKinnon (Acting)
1928 Henry J. Doermann
1932 Lee W. MacKinnon (Acting)
1933 Philip C. Nash
1947 Raymond L. Carter (Acting)
1947 Wilbur W. White
1951 Asa S. Knowles
1958 William S. Carlson

TRANSYLVANIA UNIVERSITY
Lexington, Kentucky

1794 Harry Toulmin
1796 James Moore
1804 James Blythe
1818 Horace Holley
1828 Alva Woods
1833 Benjamin O. Peers
1835 Thomas W. Coit
1838 Louis Marshall
1840 Robert Davidson
1842 Hanry B. Bascom
1849 James B. Dodd
1856 Lewis W. Green
1857 *University Closed*
1865 John B. Bowman
1878 Henry H. White
1880 Charles L. Loos
1897 Reuben L. Cave
1900 Alexander R. Milligan
1901 Burris A. Jenkins
1906 Thomas B. Macartney
1908 Richard H. Crossfield
1921 Thomas B. Macartney
1922 Andrew D. Harmon
1928 Thomas B. Macartney
1929 Elmer G. Campbell
1930 Arthur Braden
1938 Richard H. Crossfield
1939 Raymond F. McLain
1943 Leland A. Brown
1946 Raymond F. McLain
1951 Frank A. Rose
1957 Irvin E. Lunger

TRINITY COLLEGE
Hartford, Connecticut

Washington College until 1845

1824 Thomas C. Brownell
1831 Nathaniel S. Wheaton
1837 Silas Totten
1848 John Williams
1853 Daniel R. Goodwin
1860 Samuel Eliot
1864 John B. Kerfott
1866 John Brocklesby (Acting)
1867 Abner Jackson
1874 Thomas R. Pynchon
1883 George W. Smith
1904 Flavel S. Luther
1915 Henry A. Perkins (Acting)
1920 Remsen B. Ogilby
1943 Arthur H. Hughes (Acting)
1945 G. Keith Funston

1951 Arthur H. Hughes (Acting)
1953 Albert C. Jacobs
1968 Theodore D. Lockwood

TRINITY UNIVERSITY
San Antonio, Texas

1882 S. T. Anderson
1883 B. G. McLeskey
1886 Luther A. Johnson
1888 J. L. Dickens
1890 B. D. Cockrill
1896 Vacant
1901 Jesse Anderson
1902 L. C. Kirkes
1904 Archelaus F. Turner
1907 Samuel L. Hornbeak
1921 John H. Burma
1934 Raymond H. Leach
1937 Frank L. Wear
1942 Monroe G. Everett
1950 Marion B. Thomas (Interim)
1951 James W. Laurie
1970 Duncan Wimpress

TUFTS UNIVERSITY
Medford, Massachusetts

Tufts College until 1955

1853 Hosea Ballou II
1861 John P. Marshall (Acting)
1862 Alonzo A. Miner
1875 Elmer H. Capen
1905 Frederick W. Hamilton
1912 William L. Hooper (Acting)
1914 Hermon C. Bumpus
1919 John A. Cousens
1937 George S. Miller (Acting)
1938 Leonard Carmichael
1953 Nils Y. Wessell
1966 Leonard C. Mead (Acting)
1967 Burton C. Hallowell

TULANE UNIVERSITY
New Orleans, Louisiana

Medical College of Louisiana until 1847
University of Louisiana until 1884

1834 Thomas Hunt
1847 Francis L. Hawks
1850 Theodore H. McCaleb
1863 University closed
1865 Thomas Hunt
1867 Randell Hunt
1884 William P. Johnston
1889 William O. Rogers (Acting)
1900 Edwin A. Alderman
1904 Edwin B. Craighead
1912 Robert Sharp
1918 Albert B. Dinwiddie
1935 Douglas S. Anderson (Acting)
1936 Robert L. Menuet (Acting)
1937 Rufus C. Harris
1960 Herbert E. Longenecker

THE UNIVERSITY OF TULSA
Tulsa, Oklahoma

1920 James M. Gordon
1924 Franklin G. Dill (Acting)
1927 John D. Finlayson (Chancellor)
1934 Ralph L. Langenheim (Acting)
1935 Clarence I. Pontius
1958 Ben G. Henneke
1967 Eugene L. Swearingen
1968 Joseph P. Twyman

TUSCULUM COLLEGE
Greeneville, Tennessee

Tusculum and Greeneville College from 1868 to 1912

1868 Stephenson Doak
1882 Jeremiah Moore
1901 Samuel A. Coile
1907 Charles O. Gray
1931 Charles A. Anderson
1942 John McSween
1944 Jere A. Moore (Acting)
1946 George K. Davies
1950 Leslie K. Patton (Acting)
1951 Raymond C. Rankin
1965 Douglas G. Trout
1968 Charles J. Ping (Acting)
1969 Andrew N. Cothran

TUSKEGEE UNIVERSITY
Tuskegee Institute, Alabama

Tuskegee Normal and Industrial Institute until 1937

1881 Booker T. Washington
1916 Robert R. Moton
1936 Frederick D. Patterson
1953 Luther H. Foster

UNION COLLEGE AND UNIVERSITY
Schenectady, New York

1795 John B. Smith
1799 Jonathan Edwards
1801 Jonathan Maxcy
1804 Eliphalet Nott
1866 Laurens P. Hickok
1869 Charles A. Aiken
1871 Eliphalet N. Potter
1884 Judson Landon (Interim)
1888 Harrison E. Webster
1894 Andrew Van V. Raymond
1907 George Alexander
1909 Charles A. Richmond
1929 Frank P. Day
1933 Edward Ellery (Acting)
1934 Dixon R. Fox
1945 Benjamin P. Whitaker (Acting)
1946 Carter Davidson
1965 Harold C. Martin

UNITED STATES AIR FORCE ACADEMY
Colorado Springs, Colorado

1954 Hubert R. Harmon
1956 James E. Briggs
1959 William S. Stone
1962 Robert H. Warren
1965 Thomas S. Moorman
1970 Albert P. Clark

UNITED STATES COAST GUARD ACADEMY
New London, Connecticut

1877 J. A. Henriques
1883 L. G. Shepard
1887 D. B. Hodgson
1894 J. W. Congdon
1895 O. C. Hamlet
1898 D. A. Hall
1902 W. E. Reynolds
1908 J. E. Reinburg
1910 W. V. E. Jacobs
1914 Frederick C. Billard
1918 T. G. Crapster
1919 B. L. Reed
1919 W. V. E. Jacobs
1923 H. D. Hinckley
1928 Harry G. Hamlet
1932 R. Ridgley, Jr.
1935 E. D. Jones
1940 James Pine
1947 Wilfred N. Derby
1950 A. G. Hall
1954 R. J. Mauerman
1957 F. A. Leamy
1960 S. H. Evans
1962 W. J. Smith
1965 Chester R. Bender
1967 A. B. Engel
1970 J. F. Thompson

UNITED STATES MILITARY ACADEMY
West Point, New York

1802 Jonathan Williams
1803 Vacant
1805 Jonathan Williams
1812 Joseph G. Swift
1815 Alden Partridge
1817 Sylvanus Thayer
1833 Rene E. DeRussy
1838 Richard Delafield
1845 Henry Brewerton
1852 Robert E. Lee
1855 John G. Barnard
1856 Richard Delafield
1861 Pierre G. T. Beauregard
1861 Richard Delafield
1861 Alexander H. Bowman
1864 Zealous B. Tower
1864 George W. Cullum
1866 Thomas G. Pitcher
1871 Thomas H. Ruger
1876 John M. Schofield
1881 Oliver O. Howard
1882 Wesley Merritt
1887 John G. Parke
1889 John M. Wilson
1893 Oswald H. Ernst
1898 Albert L. Mills
1906 Hugh L. Scott
1910 Thomas H. Barry
1912 Clarence P. Townsley
1916 John Biddle
1917 Samuel E. Tillman
1919 Douglas MacArthur
1922 Fred W. Sladen
1926 Merch B. Stewart
1927 Edwin B. Winans
1928 William R. Smith
1932 William D. Connor
1938 Jay L. Benedict
1940 Robert I. Eichelberger
1942 Frances B. Wilby
1945 Maxwell D. Taylor
1949 Bryant E. Moore
1951 Frederick A. Irving
1954 Blackshear M. Bryan
1956 Garrison H. Davidson
1960 William C. Westmoreland
1963 James B. Lampert
1966 Donald V. Bennett
1968 Samuel W. Koster
1970 William V. Knowlton

UNITED STATES NAVAL ACADEMY
Annapolis, Maryland

1845 Franklin Buchanan
1847 George P. Upshur
1850 C. K. Stribling
1853 Louis M. Goldsborough
1857 George S. Blake
1865 David D. Porter
1869 John L. Worden
1874 C. R. P. Rodgers
1878 F. A. Parker
1879 George B. Balch
1881 C. R. P. Rodgers
1881 Francis M. Ramsay
1886 W. T. Sampson
1890 Robert L. Phythian
1894 Philip H. Cooper
1898 F. V. McNair
1900 Richard Wainwright
1902 Willard H. Brownson
1905 James H. Sands
1907 Charles J. Badger
1909 John M. Bowyer
1911 John H. Gibbons
1914 William F. Fullam
1915 Edward W. Eberle
1919 Archibald H. Scales
1921 Henry B. Wilson
1925 Louis M. Nulton
1928 Samuel S. Robison
1931 Thomas C. Hart
1934 David F. Sellers
1938 Wilson Brown
1941 Russell Willson
1942 John R. Beardall
1945 Aubrey W. Fitch
1947 James L. Holloway, Jr.
1950 Harry W. Hill
1952 C. Turner Joy
1954 Walter F. Boone
1956 William R. Smedberg III
1958 Charles L. Melson
1960 John F. Davidson
1962 C. C. Kirkpatrick
1964 Charles S. Minter, Jr.
1965 Draper L. Kauffman
1968 Lawrence Heyworth, Jr.
1968 James Calvert
1972 William P. Mack

UNIVERSITY OF UTAH
Salt Lake City, Utah

1894 James E. Talmage
1897 Joseph R. Kingsbury
1916 John A. Widsoe
1921 George Thomas
1941 LeRoy E. Cowles
1946 A. Ray Olpin
1964 James C. Fletcher

VALPARAISO UNIVERSITY
Valparaiso, Indiana

Northern Indiana Normal School until 1900; Valparaiso College until 1907

1873 Henry B. Brown
1912 Oliver P. Kinsey (Acting)
1919 Henry K. Brown
1920 Daniel R. Hodgdon
1921 John E. Roessler
1922 Milo J. Bowman
1923 Horace M. Evans
1926 John C. Baur
1926 William H. T. Dau
1930 Oscar C. Kreinheder
1939 Walter G. Friedrich (Acting)
1940 Otto P. Kretzmann
1968 A. G. Huegli

VANDERBILT UNIVERSITY
Nashville, Tennessee

1875 Landon C. Garland
1893 James H. Kirkland
1937 Oliver C. Carmichael
1946 Harvie Branscomb
1963 Alexander Heard

VASSAR COLLEGE
Poughkeepsie, New York

1861 Milo P. Jewett
1864 John H. Raymond
1878 Samuel L. Caldwell
1885 J. Ryland Kendrick (Acting)
1886 James M. Taylor
1915 Henry N. MacCracken
1946 Sarah G. Blanding
1964 Alan Simpson

UNIVERSITY OF VERMONT
Burlington, Vermont

1800 Daniel C. Sanders
1815 Samuel Austin
1821 Daniel Haskel
1825 Willard Preston
1826 James Marsh
1833 John Wheeler
1849 Worthington Smith
1855 Calvin Pease
1862 Joseph Torrey
1866 James B. Angell
1871 Matthew H. Buckham
1911 Guy P. Benton
1920 Guy W. Bailey
1941 John S. Millis
1950 William S. Carlson
1952 Carl W. Borgmann
1958 John T. Fey
1965 Shannon McCune
1966 Lyman S. Rowell
1970 Edward C. Andrews, Jr.

VILLANOVA UNIVERSITY
Villanova, Pennsylvania

1843 John P. O'Dwyer
1847 William Harnett
1848 John P. O'Dwyer
1850 William Harnett
1851 Patrick E. Moriarty
1855 William Harnett
1857 *University Closed*
1865 Ambrose Mullen
1869 Patrick Stanton
1872 Thomas Galberry
1876 Thomas Middleton
1878 John Fedigan
1880 Joseph Coleman
1886 Francis Sheeran
1890 Christopher McEvoy
1894 Francis McShane
1895 Lawrence Delurey
1910 Edward G. Dohan
1917 James Dean
1920 Francis A. Driscoll
1924 Joseph A. Hickey
1925 Mortimer A. Sullivan
1926 James H. Griffin
1932 Edward V. Stanford
1944 Francis X. N. McGuire
1954 James A. Donnellon
1959 John A. Klekotka
1965 Joseph A. Flaherty
1967 Robert J. Welsh

UNIVERSITY OF VIRGINIA
Charlottesville, Virginia

1825 George Tucker
1826 Robley Dunglison
1827 John T. Lomax
1828 George Tucker
1828 Robley Dunglison
1830 Robert M. Patterson
1832 George Tucker
1833 Charles Bonnycastle
1835 John A. G. Davis
1837 Gessner Harrison
1839 John A. G. Davis
1840 Gessner Harrison
1842 Henry St. George Tucker
1844 William B. Rogers
1845 Edward H. Courteney
1846 James L. Cabell
1847 Gessner Harrison
1854 Socrates Maupin
1870 Charles S. Venable
1873 James F. Harrison
1886 Charles S. Venable
1888 William M. Thornton
1896 Paul B. Barringer
1904 Edwin A. Alderman
1931 John L. Newcomb
1947 Colgate W. Darden, Jr.
1959 Edgar F. Shannon, Jr.

VIRGINIA MILITARY INSTITUTE
Lexington, Virginia

1839 Francis H. Smith
1890 Scott Shipp
1907 Edward W. Nichols
1924 William H. Cocke
1929 John A. LeJeune
1937 Charles E. Kilbourne
1946 Richard J. Marshall
1952 William H. Milton, Jr.
1960 George R. E. Shell
1972 Richard Irby

VIRGINIA POLYTECHNIC INSTITUTE AND STATE UNIVERSITY
Blacksburg, Virginia

Virginia Agricultural and Mechanical College until 1896
Virginia Agricultural and Mechanical College and Polytechnic Institute until 1944
Virginia Polytechnic Institute until 1970

1872 Charles L. C. Minor
1880 John L. Buchanan
1882 Thomas N. Conrad
1886 Lunsford L. Lomax
1891 John M. McBryde
1907 Paul B. Barringer
1913 Joseph D. Eggleston
1919 Julian A. Burruss
1945 John R. Hutcheson
1947 Walter S. Newman
1962 Thomas M. Hahn, Jr.

WABASH COLLEGE
Crawfordsville, Indiana

1834 Elihu W. Baldwin
1841 Charles White
1862 Joseph F. Futtle
1892 George S. Burroughs
1899 William P. Kane
1907 George L. Mackintosh
1926 Louis B. Hopkins
1941 Frank H. Sparks
1955 Byron K. Trippet
1966 Paul W. Cook, Jr.
1969 Thaddeus Seymour

WAKE FOREST UNIVERSITY
Winston-Salem, North Carolina

Wake Forest College until 1967

1834 Samuel Wait
1845 William Hooper
1849 John B. White
1854 Washington M. Wingate
1879 Thomas H. Pritchard
1882 Vacant
1884 Charles E. Taylor
1905 William L. Poteat
1927 Francis P. Gaines
1930 Thurman D. Kitchin
1950 Harold W. Tribble
1967 James R. Scales

WASHBURN UNIVERSITY OF TOPEKA
Topeka, Kansas

Washburn College until 1942
Washburn Municipal University of Topeka until 1952

1869 H. Q. Butterfield
1871 Peter MacVicar
1896 George M. Herrick
1902 Norman Plass
1909 Frank K. Sanders
1915 Parley P. Womer
1931 Philip C. King
1942 Bryan S. Stoffer
1961 Harold E. Sponberg
1965 John W. Henderson

UNIVERSITY OF WASHINGTON
Seattle, Washington

1861 Asa S. Mercer
1863 William E. Barnard
1866 George F. Whitworth
1867 *(University Closed)*
1869 John H. Hall
1872 Eugene K. Hill
1874 University closed
1874 George F. Whitworth
1876 *(University Closed)*
1877 Alexander J. Anderson
1882 Leonard J. Powell
1887 Thomas M. Gatch
1895 Mark W. Harrington
1897 William F. Edwards
1897 Charles F. Reeves (Acting)
1898 Frank P. Graves
1902 Thomas F. Kane
1914 Henry Landes (Acting)
1915 Henry Suzzallo
1926 David Thomson (Acting)
1927 Matthew L. Spencer
1933 Hugh Winkenwerder (Acting)
1934 Lee P. Sieg
1946 Raymond B. Allen
1952 H. P. Everest (Acting)
1952 Henry Schmitz
1958 Charles E. Odegaard

WASHINGTON UNIVERSITY
St. Louis, Missouri

1858 Joseph G. Hoyt
1862 William Chauvenet
1869 Benjamin Tweed (Acting)
1870 William G. Eliot
1887 Marshall S. Snow (Acting)
1891 Winfield S. Chaplin (Acting)
1907 Marshall S. Snow (Acting)
1908 David F. Houston
1913 Frederic A. Hall
1923 Herbert S. Hadley

1927 George R. Throop
1944 Harry B. Wallace (Acting)
1945 Arthur H. Compton
1953 Ethan A. H. Shepley
1961 Carl Tolman
1962 Thomas H. Eliot
1971 William H. Danforth

WASHINGTON AND JEFFERSON COLLEGE
Washington, Pennsylvania

Jefferson College merged with Washington College in 1866 to form Washington and Jefferson College.

JEFFERSON COLLEGE

1802 John Watson
1803 James Dunlap
1812 Andrew Wylie
1817 William McMillan
1822 Matthew Brown
1845 Robert J. Breckinridge
1847 Alexander B. Brown
1857 Joseph Alden
1862 David H. Riddle

WASHINGTON COLLEGE

1806 Matthew Brown
1817 Andrew Wylie
1828 Vacant
1830 David Elliot
1831 Davic McConaughy
1850 James Clark
1852 James I. Brownson (pro tem)
1853 John W. Scott

WASHINGTON AND JEFFERSON COLLEGE

1866 Jonathan Edwards
1869 Samuel J. Wilson (pro tem)
1870 James I. Brownson
1870 George P. Hays
1882 James D. Moffat
1915 Frederick W. Hinitt
1915 Vacant
1918 William E. Slemmons (pro tem)
1919 Samuel C. Black
1922 Simon S. Baker
1932 Ralph C. Hutchison
1946 James H. Case, Jr.
1950 Boyd C. Patterson
1970 Howard J. Burnett

WASHINGTON AND LEE UNIVERSITY
Lexington, Virginia

Liberty Hall Academy from 1782 to 1798
Washington Academy until 1813
Washington College until 1871

1782 William Graham
1797 Samuel L. Campbell
1799 George A. Baxter
1830 Louis Marshall
1834 Henry Vethake
1836 Henry Ruffner
1848 George Junkin
1865 Robert E. Lee
1871 George W. C. Lee
1897 William L. Wilson
1900 Henry St. George Tucker (Acting)
1901 George H. Denny
1911 Henry D. Campbell (Acting)
John L. Campbell (Acting)
1912 Henry L. Smith
1930 Robert H. Tucker (Acting)
1930 Francis P. Gaines
1959 Fred C. Cole
1967 William W. Pusey III (Acting)
1968 Robert E. R. Huntley

WASHINGTON STATE UNIVERSITY
Pullman, Washington

Washington State Agricultural College and School of Science until 1892
Agricultural College, Experiment Station, and School of Science until 1905
State College of Washington until 1959

1891 George X. Lilley
1892 John W. Heston
1893 Enoch A. Bryan
1916 Ernest O. Holland
1945 Wilson M. Compton
1951 William A. Pearl (Acting)
1952 C. Clement French
1966 Wallis Beasley (Acting)
1967 W. Glen Terrell, Jr.

WAYNE STATE UNIVERSITY
Detroit, Michigan

Wayne University until 1956

1933 Frank Cody
1942 Warren Bow
1945 David Henry
1952 Clarence Hilberry
1965 William R. Keast
1972 George Cullen (Acting)

WAYNESBURG COLLEGE
Waynesburg, Pennsylvania

1849 Joshua Loughran
1855 Jonathan P. Weethee
1858 John C. Flenniken (Acting)
1859 Alfred B. Miller
1899 J. W. McKay (Acting)
1900 Archelaus E. Turner
1904 Alvin F. Lewis
1905 J. F. Bucher
1908 William M. Hudson
1911 Henry Patton (Acting)
1912 Ezra F. Baker
1915 Herbert P. Houghton
1918 J. W. McKay
1921 Paul R. Stewart
1963 Bennett M. Rich

WELLESLEY COLLEGE
Wellesley, Massachusetts

1875 Ada Howard
1881 Alice Freeman
1887 Helen Shafer
1894 Julia Irvine
1899 Caroline Hazard
1911 Ellen F. Pendleton
1936 Mildred M. Horton
1949 Margaret Clapp
1966 Ruth M. Adams
1972 Barbara W. Newell

WELLS COLLEGE
Aurora, New York

1868 William W. Howard
1869 S. Irenaeus Prime
1873 Thomas C. Strong
1875 Edward S. Frisbee
1894 William E. Waters
1900 Jasper W. Freley (Acting)
1904 George M. Ward
1912 Thomas J. Preston, Jr.
1912 Robert Zabriskie (Acting)
1913 Kerr D. Macmillan
1936 William E. Weld
1946 Richard L. Greene
1950 Jerome H. Bentley
1951 Louis J. Long
1969 John D. Wilson

WESLEYAN UNIVERSITY
Middletown, Connecticut

1831 Wilbur Fisk
1839 Stephen Olin
1841 Nathan Bangs
1842 Stephan Olin
1852 Augustus W. Smith
1857 Joseph Cummings
1875 Cyrus D. Foss
1880 John W. Beach
1887 John M. Van Vleck (Acting)
1889 Bradford P. Raymond
1909 William A. Shanklin
1923 Leroy A. Howland (Acting)
1925 James L. McConaughy
1943 Victor L. Butterfield
1967 Edwin D. Etherington
1970 Colin G. Campbell

WEST VIRGINIA UNIVERSITY
Morgantown, West Virginia

1867 Alexander Martin
1875 John W. Scott (Acting)
1877 John R. Thompson
1881 Daniel B. Purinton (Acting)
1882 William L. Wilson
1883 Vacant
1885 Eli M. Turner
1893 Powell B. Reynolds (Acting)
1895 James L. Goodnight
1897 Robert A. Armstrong (Acting)
1897 Jerome H. Raymond
1901 Powell B. Reynolds (Acting)
1901 Daniel B. Purinton
1911 Alexander R. Whitehill (Acting)
1911 Thomas E. Hodges
1914 Frank B. Trotter
1928 John R. Turner
1935 Robert A. Armstrong (Acting)
1935 Chauncey S. Boucher
1938 Charles E. Lawall
1945 Charles T. Neff, Jr. (Acting)
1946 Irvin Stewart
1958 Clyde Colson (Acting)
1959 Elvis J. Stahr, Jr.
1962 Paul A. Miller
1966 Harry B. Heflin (Acting)
1967 James G. Harlow

WESTERN MICHIGAN UNIVERSITY
Kalamazoo, Michigan

Western State Normal School until 1927
Western State Teachers College until 1941
Western Michigan College of Education until 1955

1903 Dwight B. Waldo
1936 Paul V. Sangren
1961 James W. Miller

WESTERN RESERVE UNIVERSITY
Cleveland, Ohio

Merged in 1967 with Case Institute of Technology to form Case Western Reserve University.

1830 Charles B. Storrs
1834 George E. Pierce
1855 Henry L. Hitchcock
1871 Carroll Cutler
1887 Hiram C. Haydn
1890 Charles F. Thwing
1921 James D. Williamson (Acting)
1923 Robert E. Vinson
1933 Winfred G. Leutner
1949 John S. Millis

WESTMINSTER COLLEGE
Fulton, Missouri

1855 Samuel S. Laws
1864 John Montgomery
1865 Michael M. Fisher (Acting)
1868 Nathan L. Rice
1874 Michael M. Fisher (Acting)
1877 Charles C. Hersman
1887 William H. Marquess
1894 Edward C. Gordon
1897 John J. Rice (Acting)
1899 John H. MacCracken
1903 John J. Rice (Acting)

1904 David R. Kerr
1911 Charles B. Boving
1914 John J. Rice (Acting)
1915 Elmer E. Reed
1926 Marion E. Melvin
1933 Franc L. McCluer
1947 William W. Hall
1955 Robert L. D. Davidson

WICHITA STATE UNIVERSITY
Wichita, Kansas

Fairmont College from 1895 to 1926
Municipal University of Wichita until 1964

1895 N. J. Morrison
1908 Henry E. Thayer
1915 Walter H. Rollins
1926 John D. Finlayson
1928 H. W. Foght
1934 W. M. Jardine
1949 Harry F. Corbin
1963 Emory Lindquist
1968 Clark D. Ahlberg

WILBERFORCE UNIVERSITY
Wilberforce, Ohio

1856 M. P. Gaddis
1857 James K. Parker
1858 Richard S. Rust
1863 D. A. Payne
1876 Benjamin F. Lee
1884 S. T. Mitchell
1900 J. H. Jones
1908 W. S. Scarborough
1920 J. A. Gregg
1924 G. H. Jones
1932 Charles H. Wesley
1932 R. R. Wright, Jr.
1936 D. Ormonde Walker
1941 R. R. Wright, Jr.
1942 Charles H. Wesley
1947 Charles L. Hill
1956 Rembert Stokes

WILLAMETTE UNIVERSITY
Salem, Oregon

1853 Francis S. Hoyt
1860 Thomas M. Gatch
1865 Joseph H. Wythe
1867 Luther T. Woodward
1868 Nelson Rounds
1870 Thomas M. Gatch
1879 Charles E. Lambert
1880 Thomas Van Scoy
1891 George Whitaker
1893 Willis C. Hawley
1902 John Coleman
1907 Fletcher Homan
1914 George H. Alden (Acting)
1915 Carl G. Doney
1934 Bruce R. Baxter
1941 Carl S. Knopf
1942 George H. Smith
1969 Roger J. Fritz

THE COLLEGE OF WILLIAM AND MARY
Williamsburg, Virginia

1693 James Clair
1743 William Dawson
1752 William Stith
1755 Thomas Dawson
1761 William Yates
1764 James Horrocks
1771 John Camm
1777 James Madison
1812 John Bracken
1814 John A. Smith
1826 William H. Wilmer
1827 Adam Empie
1836 Thomas R. Dew
1847 Robert Saunders
1848 Benjamin S. Ewell
1849 John Johns
1854 Benjamin S. Ewell
1888 Lyon G. Tyler
1919 Julian A. C. Chandler
1934 John S. Bryan
1942 John E. Pomfret
1951 Alvin D. Chandler
1960 Davis Y. Paschall
1971 Thomas A. Graves

WILLIAM JEWELL COLLEGE
Liberty, Missouri

1853 Robert S. Thomas
1857 William Thompson
1868 Thomas Rambaut
1873 William R. Rothwell
1883 James G. Clark
1892 John P. Greene
1920 David J. Evans
1923 H. C. Wayman
1928 John F. Herget
1942 H. I. Hester (Interim)
1943 Walter P. Binns
1962 Minetry L. Jones (Interim)
1962 H. Guy Moore
1968 B. G. Olson (Interim)
1969 E. W. Holzapfel
1970 Thomas S. Field

WILLIAMS COLLEGE
Williamstown, Massachusetts

1793 Ebenezer Fitch
1815 Zephaniah S. Moore
1821 Edward D. Griffin
1836 Mark Hopkins
1872 Paul A. Chadbourne
1881 Franklin Carter
1901 John H. Hewitt (Acting)
1902 Henry Hopkins
1908 Harry A. Garfield
1934 Tyler Dennett
1937 James P. Baxter III
1961 John E. Sawyer

UNIVERSITY OF WISCONSIN
Madison, Wisconsin

1849 John H. Lathrop
1859 Henry Barnard
1861 John W. Sterling
1867 Paul A. Chadbourne
1871 John Twombly
1874 John Bascom
1887 Thomas C. Chamberlin
1892 Charles K. Adams
1901 Edward A. Birge (Acting)
1903 Charles R. Van Hise
1918 Edward A. Birge
1925 Glenn Frank
1937 George C. Sellery (Acting)
1937 Clarence A. Dykstra
1945 Edwin B. Fred
1958 Conrad A. Elvehjem
1962 Fred H. Harrington
1970 Robert L. Clodius
1971 John C. Weaver

MILWAUKEE CAMPUS

1956 J. Martin Klotsche (Chancellor)

WISCONSIN STATE UNIVERSITY
Eau Claire, Wisconsin

The individual campuses of the Wisconsin state university system originated as normal schools and in 1927 became separate four year teachers colleges. Each became a branch of the state university in 1964.

EAU CALIRE

1927 Harvey A. Schofield
1941 W. R. Davies
1959 Leonard Haas

LA CROSSE

1927 George M. Snodgrass
1939 Rexford S. Mitchell
1966 Samuel G. Gates
1971 Kenneth E. Lindner

PLATTEVILLE

1927 Asa M. Royce
1944 Chester O. Newlun
1958 Bjarne R. Ullsvik

RIVER FALLS

1927 Jesse H. Ames
1946 Eugene H. Kleinpell
1967 Richard J. Delorit (Interim)
1968 George R. Field

STEVENS POINT

1927 Robert D. Baldwin
1930 Frank S. Hyer
1938 Phillip H. Falk
1939 Ernest T. Smith
1940 William C. Hansen
1962 James H. Albertson
1967 Lee S. Dreyfus

SUPERIOR

1927 Arthur D. S. Gillett
1931 Jin D. Hill
1964 Karl W. Meyer

WHITEWATER

1927 Frank S. Hyer
1930 Claude M. Yoder
1946 Robert C. Williams
1962 Walker D. Wyman
1967 Cord O. Wells (Acting)
1967 William L. Carter

WITTENBERG UNIVERSITY
Springfield, Ohio

Wittenberg College until 1959

1845 Ezra Keller
1848 Michael Diehl (Acting)
1849 Samuel Sprecher
1874 John B. Helwig
1882 Samuel A. Ort
1900 John M. Ruthrauff
1902 Samuel A. Ort
1903 Charles G. Heckert
1920 Rees E. Tulloss
1949 Clarence C. Stoughton
1963 John N. Stauffer
1969 G. Kenneth Andeen

WOFFORD COLLEGE
Spartansburg, South Carolina

1854 William M. Wightman
1859 Albert M. Shipp
1875 James H. Carlisle
1902 Henry N. Snyder
1942 Walter K. Greene
1951 Clarence C. Norton (Acting)
1952 Francis P. Gaines
1957 Philip S. Covington (Acting)
1958 Charles F. Marsh
1968 Paul Hardin III

THE COLLEGE OF WOOSTER
Wooster, Ohio

University of Wooster until 1914

1870 Willis Lord
1873 Archibald A. E. Taylor
1883 Sylvester F. Scoval
1899 Louis E. Holden
1915 John Campbell White
1919 Charles F. Wishart
1944 Howard F. Lowry
1967 J. Garber Drushal

WORCESTER POLYTECHNIC INSTITUTE
Worcester, Massachusetts

1868 Charles O. Thompson
1883 Homer T. Fuller
1894 Thomas C. Mendenhall
1901 Edmund A. Engler
1911 Levi L. Conant (Acting)
1913 Ira N. Hollis

1925 Ralph Earle
1939 Francis W. Roys (Acting)
1939 Wat Tyler Cluverius
1952 Francis W. Roys (Acting)
1953 Alvin E. Cormeny
1954 Francis W. Roys (Acting)
1955 Arthur B. Bronwell
1962 Harry P. Storke
1969 George W. Hazzard

THE UNIVERSITY OF WYOMING

Laramie, Wyoming

1887 John W. Hoyt
1891 Albinus A. Johnson
1896 Frank P. Graves
1898 Elmer E. Smiley
1903 Charles W. Lewis
1904 Frederick M. Tisdel
1912 Clyde A. Duniway
1917 Aven Nelson
1922 Arthur G. Crane
1942 James L. Morrill
1945 John A. Hill (Acting)
1945 George D. Humphrey
1964 John T. Fey
1966 John E. King, Jr.
1967 H. T. Person
1968 William D. Carlson

XAVIER UNIVERSITY

Cincinnati, Ohio

1831 James I. Mullon
1834 John B. Purcell
1840 John A. Elet
1847 J. E. Blox
1848 John DeBlieck
1851 George A. Carrell
1853 Isidor Boudreaux
1856 M. Oakley
1861 John Schultz
1865 W. H. Hill
1869 Thomas O'Neil
1871 Leopold Bushart
1874 Edward A. Higgins
1878 Thomas O'Neil
1879 Rudolph J. Meyer
1881 John I. Coghlan
1884 Henry Moeller
1885 Edward A. Higgins
1887 Henry Schapman
1893 Alexander J. Burrowes
1896 Michael J. O'Connor
1900 Albert A. Dierckes
1907 Joseph Grimmelsman
1911 Francis Heiermann
1916 James McCabe
1922 Hubert F. Brockman
1930 Hugo F. Sloctemyer
1934 Dennis F. Burns
1940 Celestin J. Steiner
1949 James F. Maguire
1955 Paul L. O'Connor

YALE UNIVERSITY

New Haven, Connecticut

The Collegiate School until 1718
Yale College until 1872

1701 Abraham Pierson (Rector)
1707 Samuel Andrew (Rector)
1719 Timothy Cutler (Rector)
1722 Vacant
1726 Elisha Williams (Rector)
1740 Thomas Clap
1766 Naphtali Daggett (pro tem)
1778 Ezra Stiles
1795 Timothy Dwight
1817 Jeremiah Day
1846 Theodore D. Woolsey
1871 Noah Porter
1886 Timothy Dwight
1899 Arthur T. Hadley
1921 James R. Angell
1937 Charles Seymour
1950 A. Whitney Griswold
1963 Kingman Brewster, Jr.

XIII

AMERICAN FOUNDATIONS

Presidents of 100 leading foundations, trusts, and funds.

Allen-Bradley Foundation, Inc.

1942 Harry L. Bradley
1955 Louis Quarles
1967 Arloe W. Paul
1970 I. Andrew Rader

Allstate Foundation

1952 Calvin Fentress, Jr.
1957 Judson B. Branch

American Can Company Foundation

1960 R. J. Sund
1965 W. C. Stolk
1966 W. F. May

American Metal Climax Foundation, Inc.

1956 Arthur H. Bunker
1958 Thomas W. Childs
1959 Ian K. MacGregor
1964 Frank X. White
1966 Donald J. Donahue
1968 John F. Frawley
1969 Roger C. Sonnemann

M. D. Anderson Foundation

1936 M. D. Anderson
1939 W. B. Bates
1949 John H. Freeman

M. C. Annenberg Foundation

1944 Walter H. Annenberg

Vincent Astor Foundation

1949 Vincent Astor
1960 Mrs. Vincent Astor

Mary Reynolds Babcock Foundation, Inc.

1953 Charles H. Babcock
1968 Katharine B. Mountcastle

George F. Baker Trust

1942 Sheridan A. Logan
1966 G. S. Newell

Mary Louise Curtis Bok Foundation

1932 Mary Louise Curtis Bok
1969 Cary W. Bok

Brown Foundation, Inc.

1951 Herman Brown
1962 George R. Brown

Callaway Foundation, Inc.

1943 Fuller E. Callaway, Jr.
1949 Willis E. Howard
1952 Arthur B. Edge, Jr.
1970 Horace B. Thom

Carnegie Corporation of New York

1920 James R. Angell
1921 Henry S. Pritchett
1923 Frederick P. Keppel
1941 Walter A. Jessup
1945 Devereux C. Josephs
1948 Charles Dollard
1955 John W. Gardner
1967 Alan Pifer

Amon G. Carter Foundation

1945 Amon G. Carter
1955 Amon G. Carter, Jr.

Allis Chalmers Foundation, Inc.

1951 W. A. Roberts
1955 R. S. Stevenson
1969 David C. Scott

Chartor Foundation

1953 Aaron J. Farfel

Chrysler Corporation Fund

1953 Howard J. Pridmore
1953 George W. Troost
1956 Frank W. Misch
1967 Tom Killefer

Clark Foundation

1931 Edward S. Clark
1934 Stephen C. Clark
1960 Charles E. Main
1963 Stephen C. Clark, Jr.

Robert Sterling Clark Foundation, Inc.

1953 Robert Sterling Clark
1959 Francine J. M. Clark
1962 Hugo Kohlmann
1966 Eugene W. Goodwillie

Commonwealth Fund

1918 Edward S. Harkness
1940 Malcolm P. Aldrich
1963 James Newton

S. H. Cowell Foundation

1956 Max Thelen
1970 Max Thelen, Jr.

Crown Zellerbach Foundation

1952 James D. Zellerbach
1963 Richard G. Shephard

Cummins Engine Foundation

1954 J. Irwin Miller
1970 R. B. Stoner

Danforth Foundation

1951 Kenneth I. Brown
1961 Merrimon Cuninggim

Henry L. And Grace Doherty Charitable Foundation, Inc.

1947 Grace Doherty
1949 Helen Lee Wessel Lassen
1965 Walter L. Brown

Duke Endowment

1925 George V. Allen
1960 Thomas L. Perkins

El Pomar Foundation

1937 Spencer Penrose
1939 Julie V. L. Penrose
1956 Charles L. Tutt
1961 William T. Tutt

Esso Education Foundation

1955 Claude L. Alexander
1959 George M. Buckingham
1970 F. deW. Bolman

Samuel S. Fels Fund

1936 Samuel S. Fels
1950 Jerome J. Rothschild
1956 Lewis M. Stevens
1963 Nochem S. Winnet

First National City Bank Foundation

1967 Carl W. Desch

Ford Foundation

1936 Edsel Ford
1943 Henry Ford II
1950 Paul G. Hoffman
1953 H. Rowan Gaither, Jr.
1956 Henry T. Heald
1966 McGeorge Bundy

Charles A. Frueauff Foundation, Inc.

1950 Harry D. Frueauff
1959 Lena R. Frueauff
1968 Harry D. Frueauff, Jr.

General Foods Fund, Inc.

1953 William M. Robbins
1956 L. E. Waterbury
1960 A. F. Watters
1961 L. F. Genz

Grant Foundation, Inc.

1936 William T. Grant
1947 Perrin C. Galpin
1955 John G. Byler
1965 Douglas D. Bond

John Simon Guggenheim Memorial Foundation

1925 Simon Guggenheim
1942 Olga H. Guggenheim
1961 Henry A. Moe
1963 Gordon N. Ray

Solomon R. Guggenheim Foundation

1937 to 1949 Solomon R. Guggenheim
1957 to 1969 Harry F. Guggenheim

Haas Community Fund

1945 Otto Haas
1960 John C. Haas

Charles Hayden Foundation

1937 J. Willard Hayden
1955 Edgar A. Doubleday
1968 William T. Wachenfeld

M. S. Hershey Foundation

1936 M. S. Hershey
1945 P. A. Staples
1957 C. Paul Witmer
1960 James E. Bobb

Houston Endowment Inc.

1953 John T. Jones, Jr.
1964 J. H. Creekmore

The Lillia Babbitt Hyde Foundation

1924 Lillia Babbitt Hyde
1939 Charles C. Harris
1959 Robert W. Parsons
1969 Robert W. Parsons, Jr.

Inland Steel-Ryerson Foundation, Inc.

1945 Edward L. Ryerson
1956 Leigh B. Block
1965 Lemuel B. Hunter
1969 Robert J. Greenebaum

W. Alton Jones Foundation, Inc.

1944 W. Alton Jones
1962 Nettie M. Jones

Kalamazoo Foundation

1926 W. H. Upjohn
1929 A. B. Connable
1934 D. S. Gilmore

W. K. Kellogg Foundation

1930 A. C. Selmon
1930 Wendell L. Smith
1933 Stuart Pritchard
1940 George B. Darling
1943 Emory W. Morris
1970 Russell G. Mawby

Joseph P. Kennedy Jr. Foundation

1945 Edward J. O'Leary
1946 John F. Kennedy
1953 Robert F. Kennedy
1961 Edward M. Kennedy

Charles F. Kettering Foundation

1927 Charles F. Kettering
1942 Eugene W. Kettering
1967 Richard D. Lombard
1971 Robert G. Chollar

Samuel H. Kress Foundation

1929 Samuel H. Kress
1955 Rush H. Kress
1963 Franklin D. Murphy

Kresge Foundation

1924 Paul W. Voorhies
1952 Stanley S. Kresge
1966 William H. Baldwin

Albert and Mary Lasker Foundation

1942 Albert Lasker
1952 Mary Lasker

Lilly Endowment, Inc.

1938 Josiah K. Lilly
1948 Josiah K. Lilly, Jr.
1966 Eli Lilly

Lincoln Foundation, Inc.

1947 John C. Lincoln
1959 David C. Lincoln

John and Mary R. Markle Foundation

1927 John Markle
1933 J. Pierpont Morgan
1943 Thomas W. Lamont
1948 George Whitney
1960 John M. Russell
1969 Lloyd N. Morrisett

A. W. Mellon Educational and Charitable Trust

1950 Donald D. Shepard
Administrative trustee
from 1930
1954 Adolph W. Schmidt
1965 Theodore L. Hazlett, Jr.

Andrew W. Mellon Foundation

(Avalon Foundation before 1969)

1954 G. Lauder Greenway
1958 Thomas Parran
1961 Charles S. Hamilton, Jr.

Eugene and Agnes E. Meyer Foundation

1950 Davidson Sommers
1970 Charles A. Horsky

Charles Stewart Mott Foundation

1926 Charles Stewart Mott
1965 C. S. Harding Mott

National Cash Register Foundation

1953 Stanley C. Allyn
1962 Robert S. Oelman

Nemours Foundation

1936 Mrs. Alfred I. duPont
1970 Edward Ball

New York Community Trust

1923 Ralph Hayes
1967 Herbert B. West

New York Foundation

1909 Morris Loeb
1912 Alfred M. Heinsheimer
1930 Felix M. Warburg
1937 David M. Heyman
1967 D. John Heyman

Edward John Noble Foundation

1940 Edward John Noble
1958 Alger B. Chapman

Jessie Smith Noyes Foundation, Inc.

1947 Charles F. Noyes
1969 Edith N. Muma

Old Dominion Foundation

(Merged into Andrew W. Mellon Foundation in 1969)

1941 Donald D. Shepard
1946 Paul Mellon
1956 Ernest Brooks, Jr.

Olin Foundation, Inc.

1938 Franklin W. Olin
1951 Charles L. Horn

Gustavus and Louise Pfeiffer Research Foundation

1942 Marvin R. Thompson
1945 Gustavus A. Pfeiffer
1951 Elmer H. Bobst

PPG Industries Foundation

1951 H. B. Higgins
1955 David G. Hill
1966 R. F. Barker
1967 J. A. Neubauer

Procter & Gamble Fund

1954 Kelly Y. Siddall
1961 Dean P. Fite

Public Welfare Foundation, Inc.

1951 Claudia H. Marsh

Reader's Digest Foundation

1938 DeWitt Wallace
1970 Paul W. Thompson

Research Corporation

1915 Elon H. Hooker
1922 Arthur H. Hamerschlag
1927 Howard A. Poillon
1946 Joseph W. Barker
1957 J. William Hinkley
1967 James S. Coles

Resources for the Future, Inc.

1952 Horace M. Albright
1953 Reuben G. Gustavson
1959 Joseph L. Fisher

Smith Richardson Foundation, Inc.

1968 H. Smith Richardson, Jr.
1969 John W. Red, Jr.

Fannie E. Rippel Foundation

1953 Julius A. Rippel

Rockefeller Foundation

1913 John D. Rockefeller, Jr.
1917 George E. Vincent
1929 Max Mason
1936 Raymond B. Fosdick
1948 Chester I. Barnard
1952 Dean Rusk
1961 J. George Harrar
1971 John H. Knowles

Rockefeller Brothers Fund

1940 Arthur W. Packard
1951 Dana S. Creel

Rogoff Foundation

1938 Julius M. Rogoff
1966 Fannie Rogoff

Rosenberg Foundation

1956 Richard E. Guggenheim
1957 Roy Sorenson
1961 Eleanor Anderson
1964 Ben C. Duniway
1965 Frederic B. Whitman
1968 Ben C. Duniway
1971 Mrs. Allan E. Charles

S & H Foundation, Inc.

1962 William S. Beinecke

Russell Sage Foundation

1907 John M. Glen
1931 Shelby M. Harrison
1947 Ralph G. Hurlin *(Acting)*
1948 Donald Young
General directors before 1964
1964 Orville G. Brim, Jr.

Sarah Mellon Scaife Foundation, Inc.

1941 Alan M. Scaife
1958 James M. Bovard

Scriven Foundation, Inc.

1937 Walter C. Flanders
1950 W. Beach Day
1961 Charles J. Nourse
1967 Paul S. Kerr

Sears-Roebuck Foundation

1941 Robert E. Wood
1954 T. B. Houser
1957 J. C. Worthy
1961 James T. Griffin
1966 William F. McCurdy

Alfred P. Sloan Foundation

1934 Alfred P. Sloan, Jr.
1962 Everett Case
1968 Nils Y. Wessell

Elliott White Springs Foundation, Inc.

1942 Elliott White Springs
1959 H. William Close

W. Clement & Jessie V. Stone Foundation

1958 W. Clement Stone
1970 Donna S. Bradshaw

Aaron Straus & Lillie Straus Foundation Inc.

1926 Aaron Straus
1958 S. Meyer Barnett

Taconic Foundation, Inc.

1958 Stephen R. Currier
1967 John G. Simon

Teagle Foundation, Inc.

1944 Walter C. Teagle
1962 Frank E. Mott

Timken Foundation of Canton

1934 Henry H. Timken
1942 Edith K. Timken
1948 Henry H. Timken, Jr.
1968 W. R. Timken

Turrell Fund

1935 Herbert Turrell
1947 Margaret Turrell
1948 Leon H. Johnston
1961 S. Whitney Landon

Twentieth Century Fund

1919 Edward A. Filene
1938 John H. Fahey
Chairman of the Board after 1951
1951 Adolf A. Berle, Jr.
1971 James Rowe

United States Steel Foundation, Inc.

1953 Clifford F. Hood
1959 Leslie B. Worthington
1967 Edwin H. Gott
1969 Edgar B. Speer

William Volker Fund

1932 William Volker
1944 Harold W. Luhnow

Western Electric Fund

1953 F. W. Bierworth
1954 A. B. Goetze
1956 T. E. Shea
1957 A. P. Clow
1960 Robert D. Lilley
1962 H. G. Mehlhouse
1965 P. E. Hogin
1966 W. G. Chaffee

Westinghouse Electric Fund

1953 Dale McFeatters
1960 Howard S. Kaltenborn

Whitehall Foundation, Inc.

1953 James A. Moffett, II
1967 J. Wright Rumbough, Jr.

Amherst H. Wilder Foundation

1910 Victor M. Watkins
1921 Charles L. Spencer
1941 Frederic R. Bigelow
1947 George W. Morgan
1957 Roger B. Shepard
1961 Julian B. Baird

Woodrow Wilson National Fellowship Foundation

1958 Hugh S. Taylor
1969 Hans Rosenhaupt

Gustav Wurzweiler Foundation, Inc.

1969 Max Gruenewald
1971 Joseph H. Lookstein

XIV

ART AND SCIENCE COLLECTIONS

A listing of directors of principal museums and art galleries in the United States.

THE AKRON ART INSTITUTE
Akron, Ohio

1924 Wilbur Peat
1929 Theodore H. Pond
1931 Vacant
1945 Charles Val Clear
1949 George D. Culler
1954 Leroy Flint
1965 Paul Binai (Acting)
1966 Forrest Selvig
1968 Leroy Flint (Acting)
1969 Orrel Thompson

THE ALBANY INSTITUTE OF HISTORY AND ART
Albany, New York

1923 R. Loring Dunn
1940 John Davis Hatch, Jr.
1948 Robert C. Wheeler
1956 Janet R. MacFarlane
1966 Norman S. Rice

ALBRIGHT-KNOX ART GALLERY
Buffalo, New York

1905 Charles M. Kurtz
1909 Cornelia B. Sage (Acting)
1910 Cornelia B. Sage Quinton
1924 William M. Hekking
1931 Gordon B. Washburn
1942 Andrew C. Ritchie
1949 Edgar C. Schenck
1955 Gordon M. Smith

ALLEN MEMORIAL ART MUSEUM Oberlin College
Oberlin, Ohio

1917 Clarence Ward
1941 Charles Parkhurst
1962 John R. Spencer

LYMAN ALLYN MUSEUM
New London, Connecticut

1932 Winslow Ames
1942 William Douglass
1950 Edgar deN. Mayhew

AMERICAN MUSEUM OF NATURAL HISTORY
New York City

1869 Albert S. Bickmore
1884 Morris K. Jessup
1902 Hermon C. Bumpus
1910 Charles H. Townsend (Acting)
1911 Frederic A. Lucas
1924 George H. Sherwood
1935 Roy Chapman Andrews
1942 Albert E. Parr
1959 James A. Oliver
1969 Thomas D. Nicholson

ARIZONA STATE MUSEUM
Tucson, Arizona

1893 Herbert Brown
1914 John J. Thornber
1915 Byron Cummings
1938 Emil W. Haury
1964 Raymond H. Thompson

ARNOT ART MUSEUM
Elmira, New York

1913 Jeannette Murdock Diven
1943 Ernfred Anderson
1961 Dorotha McClurkin Masters
1964 J. R. von Reinhold-Jameson
1965 Mary-Ellen Earl

ART GALLERY UNIVERSITY OF NOTRE DAME
Notre Dame, Indiana

Wightman Gallery until 1952

1925 Gregory Gerrer
1934 Maurice Goldblatt
1955 Anthony J. Lauck

THE ART INSTITUTE OF CHICAGO
Chicago, Illinois

1879 William M. R. French
1914 Newton H. Carpenter
1916 George W. Eggers (Pro Tem)
1921 Robert B. Harshe
1938 Potter Palmer (Pro Tem)
1938 Daniel C. Rich
1958 John Maxon
1965 Charles C. Cunningham
1972 E. Lawrence Chalmers, Jr.

THE BALTIMORE MUSEUM OF ART
Baltimore, Maryland

1923 Florence N. Levy
1927 Meyric C. Rogers
1929 Roland J. McKinney
1937 (Administrative Committee)
1939 Leslie Cheek, Jr.
1942 Adelym D. Breeskin
1962 Charles Parkhurst
1971 William V. Elder III (Acting)
1972 Thomas Freudenheim

THE BENNINGTON MUSEUM
Bennington, Vermont

Bennington Historical Museum and Art Gallery until 1953

1928 John Spargo
1954 Richard C. Barrett

BERNICE P. BISHOP MUSEUM
Honolulu, Hawaii

1898 William T. Brigham
1920 Herbert E. Gregory
1936 Peter H. Buck
1951 Vacant
1953 Alexander Spoehr
1962 Roland W. Force

BOWDOIN COLLEGE MUSEUM OF ART
Brunswick, Maine

1914 Henry Johnson
1918 Charles T. Burnett
1921 Henry E. Andrews
1939 Philip C. Beam
1964 Marvin S. Sadik
1967 Richard V. West

THE BROOKLYN MUSEUM
Brooklyn, New York

1899 Franklin W. Hooper
1914 William H. Fox
1934 Philip N. Youtz
1938 Laurance P. Roberts
1943 Albert N. Henrickson (Acting)
1943 Mrs. Laurance P. Roberts
1946 Charles Nagel
1955 Edgar C. Schenck
1960 Thomas S. Buechner
1971 Duncan F. Cameron

BROOKS MEMORIAL ART GALLERY
Memphis, Tennessee

1916 Florence McIntyre
1922 Valerie Farrington
1933 Louise Bennett Clark
1962 Robert L. Shalkop
1964 Robert J. McKnight

BUFFALO MUSEUM OF SCIENCE
Buffalo, New York

1866 Charles Linden
1873 Augustus R. Grote
1880 Charles Linden
1883 Julius Pohlman
1890 William C. Barrett
1892 Frederick K. Mixer
1900 Elizabeth J. Letson
1909 William L. Bryant
1926 Charles J. Fish
1934 Carlos E. Cummings
1951 Fred T. Hall
1970 Virginia L. Cummings

BUTLER INSTITUTE OF AMERICAN ART
Youngstown, Ohio

Butler Art Institute until 1954

1919 Margaret Evans
1935 Joseph G. Butler

CALIFORNIA ACADEMY OF SCIENCES
San Francisco, California

1868 Robert E. C. Stearns
1868 Henry G. Bloomer
1875 Albert Kellogg
1876 W. G. W. Harford
1887 J. G. Cooper
1892 J. Z. Davis
1897 Charles A. Keeler
1902 Leverett M. Loomis
1913 Gulian P. Rixford
1914 Barton W. Evermann
1932 Carl E. Grunsky (Acting)
1934 Frank M. MacFarland (Acting)
1938 Robert C. Miller
1963 George E. Lindsay

CALIFORNIA PALACE OF THE LEGION OF HONOR
San Francisco, California

1924 Cornelia B. Sage Quinton
1931 Lloyd Rollins
1933 Walter Heil
1940 Thomas C. Howe
1968 Ian McKibbin White

CARNEGIE INSTITUTE, CARNEGIE MUSEUM
Pittsburgh, Pennsylvania

1896 Frank H. Gerrodette
1898 William J. Holland
1922 Douglas Stewart
1926 Andrey Avinoff
1946 O. E. Jennings
1949 Wallace Richards
1954 M. Graham Netting

CARNEGIE INSTITUTE MUSEUM OF ART
Pittsburgh, Pennsylvania

The Department of Fine Arts, Carnegie Institute until 1963

1896 John W. Beatty
1922 Homer Saint-Gaudens
1950 Gordon B. Washburn
1963 Gustave von Groschwitz
1968 Leon A. Arkus

THE CHICAGO ACADEMY OF SCIENCES
Chicago, Illinois

Secretaries

1879 Selim H. Peabody
1892 William K. Higley
1905 Frank C. Baker
1907 Charles S. Raddin
1908 Wallace W. Atwood
1918 Charles F. Hills
1926 Nathan S. Davis III

Directors

1928 Alfred M. Bailey
1937 Howard K. Gloyd
1958 William J. Beecher

CINCINNATI ART MUSEUM
Cincinnati, Ohio

1881 Alfred T. Goshorn
1902 Joseph H. Gest
1929 Walter H. Siple
1945 Philip R. Adams

CITY ART MUSEUM OF ST. LOUIS
St. Louis, Missouri

1909 Halsey C. Ives
1911 R. A. Holland
1922 Samuel L. Sherer
1928 Charles P. Davis
1929 Meyric C. Rogers
1939 James B. Musick
1940 Perry T. Rathbone
1955 Charles Nagel
1964 Charles E. Buckley

CLEVELAND HEALTH MUSEUM AND EDUCATION CENTER
Cleveland, Ohio

1939 Bruno Gebhard
1965 John J. Beeston
1968 Lowell F. Bernard

THE CLEVELAND MUSEUM OF ART
Cleveland, Ohio

1913 Frederic A. Whiting
1930 William M. Milliken
1958 Sherman E. Lee

UNIVERSITY OF COLORADO MUSEUM
Boulder, Colorado

1902 Junius Henderson
1933 Hugo G. Rodeck

COLORADO SPRINGS FINE ARTS CENTER
Colorado Springs, Colorado

1935 Stanley Lothrop
1939 Paul Parker
1945 Mitchell A. Wilder
1953 James Byrnes
1955 Fred S. Bartlett

COLUMBUS GALLERY OF FINE ARTS
Columbus, Ohio

1931 Karl S. Bolander
1934 Philip R. Adams
1946 Lee H.B. Malone
1953 Mahonri S. Young

THE CORCORAN GALLERY OF ART
Washington, D. C.

1873 William MacLeod
1889 F. Sinclair Barbarin
1900 Frederick B. McGuire
1915 C. Powell Minnigerode
1947 Hermann W. Williams, Jr.
1968 James Harithas
1970 Walter Hopps

E. B. CROCKER ART GALLERY
Sacramento, California

1885 William Jackson
1936 Harry N. Pratt
1944 Frederick P. Vickery
1950 Don R. Birrell
1954 Ernest Van Harlingen
1958 Frank W. Kent
1969 John A. Mahey

THE CURRIER GALLERY OF ART
Manchester, New Hampshire

1929 Maud Briggs Knowlton
1946 Gordon M. Smith
1955 Charles E. Buckley
1965 William F. Hutton
1968 David S. Brooke

DALLAS MUSEUM OF FINE ARTS
Dallas, Texas

1935 Richard F. Howard
1943 Jerry Bywaters
1964 Merrill C. Rueppel

DALLAS MUSEUM OF NATURAL HISTORY
Dallas, Texas

1935 Fredric W. Miller
1964 Hal P. Kirby

THE DAYTON ART INSTITUTE
Dayton, Ohio

1921 Herman Sachs
1922 Theodore H. Pond
1929 Siegfried R. Weng
1950 Esther I. Seaver
1956 Mrs. Alvin Raffel
1957 Thomas C. Colt, Jr.

DELAWARE ART MUSEUM
Wilmington, Delaware

Delaware Art Center until 1970

1938 Constance Moore
1957 Bruce St. John

M. H. de YOUNG MEMORIAL MUSEUM
San Francisco, California

Curators

1895 C. P. Wilcomb
1905 John W. Rogers
1908 Albert E. Gray
1910 George Barron
1917 William Altmann
1917 Charles Penez
1922 George Barron

Directors

1931 Lloyd Rollins
1933 Walter Heil
1961 Richard S. Rheem
1963 Jack R. McGregor
1970 Ian McKibbin White

DENVER ART MUSEUM
Denver, Colorado

1919 Reginald R. Poland
1921 George W. Eggers
1927 Arnold Ronnebeck
1929 Samuel Heavenrich
1931 Anne Evans (Acting)
1931 Cyril Kay-Scott
1936 Donald J. Bear
1941 Frederick Douglas
1942 Charles Bayly, Jr. (Acting)
1944 Otto Karl Bach

DENVER MUSEUM OF NATURAL HISTORY
Denver, Colorado

1910 Jessie D. Figgins
1936 Alfred M. Bailey
1970 Roy E. Coy

THE HENRY FRANCIS du PONT WINTERTHUR MUSEUM
Winterthur, Delaware

1951 Joseph Downs
1954 Charles F. Montgomery
1962 Edgar P. Richardson
1966 Charles van Ravenswaay

GEORGE EASTMAN HOUSE
Rochester, New York

1949 Oscar N. Solbert
1959 Beaumont Newhall

ESSEX INSTITUTE

Formed in 1848 through merger of Essex Historical Society and Essex County Natural History Society.

Presidents

1848 Daniel A. White
1861 Asahel Huntington
1865 Francis Peabody
1868 Henry Wheatland
1893 Edmund B. Wilson
1895 Robert S. Rantoul
1905 Francis H. Appleton
1916 William C. Endicott
1926 Alden P. White
1934 William C. Endicott
1937 Stephen W. Phillips
1956 W. Hammond Bowden
1961 Albert Goodhue

Directors

1945 Russell L. Jackson
1953 Bessom Smith Harris (Acting)
1954 Walter M. Merrill
1959 Huldah M. Smith (Acting)
1959 Dean A. Fales, Jr.
1967 David B. Little

WILLIAM A. FARNSWORTH LIBRARY AND ART MUSEUM
Rockland, Maine

1948 James M. Brown III
1951 Wendell S. Hadlock

FIELD MUSEUM OF NATURAL HISTORY
Chicago, Illinois

Columbian Museum until 1894
Field Columbian Museum until 1905
Field Museum of Natural History until 1943
Chicago Natural History Museum until 1966

1893 Frederick J. V. Skiff
1921 David C. Davies
1928 Stephen C. Simms
1937 Clifford C. Gregg
1942 Orr Goodson (Acting)
1945 Clifford C. Gregg
1962 E. Leland Webber

FINE ARTS GALLERY OF SAN DIEGO
San Diego, California

1926 Reginald R. Poland
1950 Thomas B. Robertson
1955 Warren W. Beach
1969 Henry G. Gardiner

ROBERT HULL FLEMING MUSEUM
Burlington, Vermont

1931 Henry F. Perkins
1945 Horace B. Eldred
1954 Alan Gowans
1956 Thomas McCormick
1958 Richard Janson

THE FLORIDA STATE MUSEUM
Gainesville, Florida

1917 Thompson Van Hyning
1946 Nile C. Schaffer (Acting)
1952 Arnold B. Grobman
1961 J. C. Dickinson

FOGG ART MUSEUM
Cambridge, Massachusetts

1896 Charles H. Moore
1909 Edward W. Forbes
1944 Arthur Pope (Acting)
1948 John Coolidge
1968 Agnes Mongan

THE FOLGER SHAKESPEARE LIBRARY
Washington, D. C.

1930 William A. Slade
1934 Joseph Q. Adams
1946 James G. McManaway (Acting)
1948 Louis B. Wright
1968 Philip A. Knachel (Acting)
1969 O. B. Hardison, Jr.

FREER GALLERY OF ART
Washington, D. C.

1920 John E. Lodge
1943 Archibald G. Wenley
1962 John A. Pope

THE FRICK COLLECTION
New York City

1931 Frederick M. Clapp
1951 Franklin M. Biebel
1964 Harry D. M. Grier

ISABELLA STEWART GARDNER MUSEUM
Boston, Massachusetts

1900 Isabella Stewart Gardner
1924 Morris Carter
1955 George L. Stout
1970 Rollin van N. Hadley

GUGGENHEIM MUSEUM
New York City

Museum of Non-Objective Art until 1953

1947 Hilla Rebay
1952 James Johnson Sweeney
1961 Thomas Messmer

HONOLULU ACADEMY OF ARTS
Honolulu, Hawaii

1924 Frank M. Moore
1927 Catharine E. B. Cox (Acting)
1929 Kathrine McLane (Acting)
1935 Edgar C. Schenck
1947 Robert P. Griffing, Jr.
1963 James W. Foster, Jr.

HOPKINS CENTER ART GALLERIES
Hanover, New Hampshire

1930 Churchill P. Lathrop
1967 Truman H. Brackett, Jr.

HUDSON RIVER MUSEUM
Yonkers, New York

Yonkers Museum of Sciences and Arts until 1948

1925 William N. Berkeley
1937 H. Armour Smith
1953 Thomas W. Voter
1969 Donald M. Halley, Jr.

HENRY E. HUNTINGTON LIBRARY AND ART GALLERY
San Marino, California

1927 Max Farrand
1941 (Executive Committee)
1948 J. E. Wallace Sterling
1949 (Executive Committee)
1951 John E. Pomfret
1966 James Thorpe

INDIANAPOLIS MUSEUM OF ART
Indianapolis, Indiana

John Herron Art Institute until 1962
Herron Museum of Art until 1968

1905 William H. Fox
1910 Vacant
1912 Frederic A. Whiting
1914 Harold H. Brown
1919 Vacant
1923 J. Arthur Maclean
1926 Vacant
1929 Wilbur D. Peat
1965 Carl J. Weinhardt, Jr.

THE JEWISH MUSEUM
New York City

1931 Paul Romanoff
1943 Alexander Marx
1947 Stephen Kayser
1962 Alan Solomon
1964 Hans van Weeren-Griek
1965 Sam Hunter
1968 Karl Katz
1971 Vacant

JOSLYN ART MUSEUM
Omaha, Nebraska

1931 Paul Grumman
1946 Eugene Kingman
1969 Richard N. Gregg

LAYTON ART GALLERY
Milwaukee, Wisconsin

Merged with the Milwaukee Art Institute in 1957 to form the Milwaukee Art Center.

1888 Edwin C. Eldridge
1902 George Raab
1922 Charlotte Partridge
1953 LaVera Pohl
1955 Edward H. Dwight

LONG BEACH MUSEUM OF ART
Long Beach, California

Municipal Art Center until 1957

1951 Samuel W. Heavenrich
1956 Edwin Castagna (Acting)
1956 Jerome Donson
1961 Frederick Black
1965 Jason D. Wong

LOS ANGELES COUNTY MUSEUM OF ART
Los Angeles, California

1961 Richard F. Brown
1966 Kenneth Donahue

THE ROBERT H. LOWIE MUSEUM OF ANTHROPOLOGY
Berkeley, California

1903 Frederic W. Putnam
1908 Alfred L. Kroeber
1947 Edward W. Gifford
1955 George M. Foster (Acting)
1957 William Bascom

MEAD ART BUILDING, AMHERST COLLEGE
Amherst, Massachusetts

1950 Charles H. Morgan
1969 Frank A. Trapp

THE METROPOLITAN MUSEUM OF ART
New York City

1879 Louis Palma di Cesnola
1905 Caspar P. Clarke
1910 Edward Robinson
1932 Herbert E. Winlock
1940 Francis Henry Taylor
1955 James J. Rorimer
1967 Thomas P. F. Hoving

MILWAUKEE ART CENTER
Milwaukee, Wisconsin

Milwaukee Art Society until 1916; Milwaukee Art Institute until 1957, when it merged with Layton Art Gallery to form Milwaukee Art Center. In 1953 director of Milwaukee Art Institute became director also of Layton Art Gallery.

1913 Dudley C. Watson
1925 John E. D. Trask
1926 Alfred G. Pelikan
1940 Marion Burnham
1941 Burton Cumming
1943 Mary Francis Coan
1946 Burton Cumming
1951 LaVera Pohl
1955 Edward H. Dwight
1963 Tracy Atkinson

MILWAUKEE PUBLIC MUSEUM
Milwaukee, Wisconsin

1883 Carl Doerflinger
1887 William M. Wheeler
1890 Henry Nehrling
1900 Henry L. Ward
1920 Samuel A. Barrett
1940 Ira Edwards
1943 Will C. McKern
1958 Albert M. Fuller (Acting)
1959 Stephan F. deBorhegyi
1960 Wallace N. MacBriar, Jr. (Acting)
1970 M. Kenneth Starr

THE MINT MUSEUM OF ART
Charlotte, North Carolina

1936 Mrs. Lewis C. Burwell
1945 Joseph Hutchinson
1951 Bruce St. John
1955 Mrs. Dayrell Kortheuer (Acting)
1958 Robert W. Schlageter
1966 Herbert Cohen
1967 Russell Hicken
1968 Herbert Cohen (Acting)
1969 Cleve K. Scarbrough

THE MONTCLAIR ART MUSEUM
Montclair, New Jersey

1919 Katherine Innes
1929 Marion Haviland
1932 Mary Cooke Swartwout
1953 Kathryn E. Gamble

MONTGOMERY MUSEUM OF FINE ARTS
Montgomery, Alabama

Private museum 1930-1959

1959 Donald A. Winer
1962 Elizabeth Metcalf (Acting)
1963 Paul Chatelain
1968 David W. Chase

THE PIERPONT MORGAN LIBRARY
New York City

1905 Belle Da Costa Greene
1948 Frederick B. Adams, Jr.
1969 Charles A. Ryskamp

MUSEUM OF THE AMERICAN INDIAN HEYE FOUNDATION
New York City

1916 George G. Heye
1957 Edwin K. Burnett
1960 Frederick J. Dockstader

MUSEUM OF ART MUNSON-WILLIAMS-PROCTOR INSTITUTE
Utica, New York

1937 Arthur Derbyshire
1943 Vacant
1947 Harris K. Prior
1951 Mahonri S. Young
1953 Harris K. Prior
1957 Richard B. McLanthan
1962 Edward H. Dwight

MUSEUM OF FINE ARTS
Boston, Massachusetts

1876 Charles G. Loring
1902 Edward Robinson
1907 Arthur Fairbanks
1925 Edward J. Holmes
1934 George H. Edgell
1955 Perry T. Rathbone

MUSEUM OF FINE ARTS
Houston, Texas

1924 James Chillman, Jr.
1953 Lee H. B. Malone
1959 James Chillman, Jr.
1961 James Johnson Sweeney
1969 Philippe de Montebello

THE MUSEUM OF MODERN ART
New York City

1929 Alfred H. Barr, Jr.
1949 Rene d'Harnoncourt
1968 Bates Lowry
1970 John B. Hightower
1972 Richard Oldenburg

MUSEUM OF SCIENCE AND HAYDEN PLANETARIUM
Boston, Massachusetts

New England Museum of Natural History until 1950

1864 Samuel H. Scudder
1870 Alpheus Hyatt
1903 Charles W. Johnson
1917 Edward Wigglesworth
1939 Bradford Washburn

MUSEUM OF SCIENCE AND INDUSTRY
Chicago, Illinois

1928 Waldemar Kaempffert
1931 John R. Van Pelt (Acting)
1931 Otto T. Kreusser
1937 Philip Fox
1940 Lenox R. Lohr
1950 Daniel M. MacMaster

MUSEUM OF THE CITY OF NEW YORK
New York City

1926 Hardinge Scholle
1951 John W. Myer
1958 K. Ross Toole
1960 Ralph R. Miller
1970 Joseph V. Noble

NATIONAL AIR AND SPACE MUSEUM
Washington, D. C.

1958 P. S. Hopkins
1965 S. Paul Johnston
1970 Frank A. Taylor (Acting)
1971 David Challinor (Acting)

NATIONAL COLLECTION OF FINE ARTS
Washington, D. C.

1920 William H. Holmes
1935 Ruel P. Tolman
1948 Thomas M. Beggs
1964 David W. Scott
1969 Robert Tyler Davis (Acting)
1970 Joshua C. Taylor

NATIONAL GALLERY OF ART
Washington, D. C.

1941 David E. Finley
1956 John Walker
1969 J. Carter Brown

NATIONAL MUSEUM OF HISTORY AND TECHNOLOGY
Washington, D. C.

1958 Frank A. Taylor
1964 John C. Ewers
1966 Robert P. Multhauf
1969 Daniel J. Boorstin

NATIONAL MUSEUM OF NATURAL HISTORY
Washington, D. C.

1958 A. C. Smith
1962 T. Dale Stewart
1965 Richard S. Cowan
1972 Porter M. Kier

NATIONAL PORTRAIT GALLERY
Washington, D. C.

1964 Charles Nagel
1969 Marvin S. Sadik

NATURAL HISTORY MUSEUM OF LOS ANGELES COUNTY
Los Angeles, California

Museum of History, Science and Art until 1928
Los Angeles Museum of History, Science and Art until 1938
Los Angeles County Museum of History, Science and Art until 1961
Los Angeles County Museum until 1965
Los Angeles County Museum of Natural History until 1970

1911 Frank S. Daggett
1920 Howard Robertson (Acting)
1921 William A. Bryan
1939 Roland J. McKinney
1946 James H. Breasted, Jr.
1951 C. F. Gehring (Acting)
1952 Jean Delacour
1960 C. F. Gehring (Acting)
1961 Herbert Friedmann
1970 Giles W. Mead

NEVILLE PUBLIC MUSEUM
Green Bay, Wisconsin

1927 Arthur C. Neville
1929 Theodore Brown
1933 Henry L. Ward
1941 Earl Wright
1952 Ellis Burcaw
1958 James L. Quinn

NEW JERSEY STATE MUSEUM
Trenton, New Jersey

1890 Helen Perry
1918 Kathryn Greywacz
1963 Kenneth W. Prescott

THE NEW BRITAIN MUSEUM OF AMERICAN ART
New Britain, Connecticut

1937 Sanford Low
1965 Charles B. Ferguson

MUSEUM OF NEW MEXICO
Santa Fe, New Mexico

1909 Edgar L. Hewett
1947 Paul A. F. Walter (Acting)
1947 Sylvanus G. Morley
1948 Boaz W. Long
1956 Wayne L. Mauzy (Acting)
1959 Bruce T. Ellis (Acting)
1960 K. Ross Toole
1962 James T. Forrest
1964 Delmar M. Kolb
1969 George Ewing (Acting)
1969 Carlos R. Nagel

NEW YORK STATE MUSEUM AND SCIENCE SERVICE
Albany, New York

New York State Museum of Natural History until 1904
New York State Museum until 1945

1870 James Hall
1894 Frederick J. H. Merrill
1904 John Clarke
1926 Charles C. Adams
1943 Carl Guthe (Assistant Commissioner)
1953 William Fenton (Assistant Commissioner)
1967 John G. Broughton (Assistant Commissioner)
1971 Carroll Lindsay (Museum services)
Hugo Jamnback (Science services)

THE OAKLAND MUSEUM
Oakland, California

1964 James M. Brown III
1968 J. S. Holliday
1970 John E. Peetz

THE OHIO HISTORICAL SOCIETY
Columbus, Ohio

Curators

1894 Warren K. Moorehead
1897 Clarence Loveberry
1898 William C. Mills

Directors

1921 William C. Mills
1928 Henry C. Shetrone
1947 Erwin C. Zepp
1965 Daniel R. Porter III

UNIVERSITY OF OREGON MUSEUM OF ART
Eugene, Oregon

1929 Gertrude Bass Warner
1951 Mabel Klockars Garner (Acting)
1953 Paul S. Dull
1953 Wallace S. Baldinger
1960 James F. Colley (Acting)
1970 Richard C. Paulin (Acting)

THE ORIENTAL INSTITUTE
Chicago, Illinois

1919 James H. Breasted
1936 John A. Wilson
1946 Thorkild P. R. Jacobsen
1950 Carl H. Kraeling
1960 John A. Wilson
1961 Emery T. Filbey
1962 Robert McCormick Adams
1968 George R. Hughes

PEABODY MUSEUM OF ARCHAEOLOGY AND ETHNOLOGY
Cambridge, Massachusetts

1866 Jeffries Wyman
1874 Asa Gray
1875 Frederic W. Putnam
1915 Charles C. Willoughby
1928 Edward Reynolds
1932 Donald Scott
1948 John O. Brew
1967 Stephen Williams

PEABODY MUSEUM OF NATURAL HISTORY
New Haven, Connecticut

1866 Othniel C. Marsh
1900 Charles S. Beecher
1904 Charles Schuchert
1922 Richard S. Lull
1938 Albert E. Parr
1943 Carl O. Dunbar
1959 S. Dillon Ripley
1964 Alfred W. Crompton
1970 Charles G. Sibley

PEABODY MUSEUM OF SALEM
Salem, Massachusetts

The museum of the Salem East India Marine Society until 1867
Peabody Academy of Science until 1915

Superintendents

1820 Seth Bass
1825 Malthus A. Ward
1831 George Osborne
1835 Charles G. Page
1837 Henry Wheatland
1848 George D. Phippen
1855 Vacant
1957 Thomas Saul

Directors

1867 Frederic W. Putnam
1876 Alpheus S. Packard
1880 Edward S. Morse
1916 Lawrence W. Jenkins
1950 Ernest S. Dodge

THE PEALE MUSEUM
Baltimore, Maryland

1931 Raphael Semmes
1933 Macgill James
1940 Richard C. Medford
1945 Jean Heimer (Acting)
1946 Wilbur H. Hunter

THE PENNSYLVANIA ACADEMY OF THE FINE ARTS
Philadelphia, Pennsylvania

Secretaries

1805 Charles Chauncey
1805 William S. Biddle
1807 Nicholas Biddle
1813 William Smith
1817 Francis Hopkinson
1842 J. G. Morris
1843 R. Rundle Smith
1844 John Rutherford
1846 John T. Lewis
1856 John Sartain
1859 John T. Lewis
1868 John Sartain
1877 George Corliss
1891 J. D. Woodward
1892 Harrison S. Morris
1905 John E. D. Trask
1913 John A. Myers
1938 Joseph T. Fraser, Jr.

Directors

1946 Joseph T. Fraser, Jr.
1969 William B. Stevens
1970 Henry H. Hotz, Jr. (Acting)

PHILADELPHIA MUSEUM OF ART
Philadelphia, Pennsylvania

Pennsylvania Museum of Art until 1938

1876 William P. Pepper
1879 William W. Justice
1880 Vacant
1893 Balton Dorr
1899 William P. Pepper
1907 Edwin A. Barber
1917 Langdon Warner
1923 Samuel W. Woodhouse, Jr. (Acting)
1925 Fiske Kimball
1955 Henri Marceau
1965 Evan H. Turner

PHOENIX ART MUSEUM
Phoenix, Arizona

1957 Forest M. Hinkhouse
1967 Hugh T. Broadley
1970 Goldthwaite H. Dorr III

PORTLAND ART MUSEUM
Portland, Oregon

1909 Anna Belle Crocker (Curator)
1936 Frederick A. Sweet
1939 Robert Tyler Davis
1948 Thomas C. Colt, Jr.
1957 Max W. Sullivan
1960 Francis J. Newton

THE ART MUSEUM PRINCETON UNIVERSITY
Princeton, New Jersey

1882 Allan Marquand
1922 Frank J. Mather, Jr.
1947 Ernest T. DeWald
1960 Patrick J. Kelleher
1972 David Steadman

JOHN AND MABLE RINGLING MUSEUM OF ART
Sarasota, Florida

1946 A. Everett Austin, Jr.
1958 Kenneth Donahue
1965 Curtis G. Coley

ROCHESTER MUSEUM AND SCIENCE CENTER
Rochester, New York

1924 Arthur C. Parker
1946 W. Stephen Thomas
1969 Alan R. Mahl
1970 Charles F. Hayes III

ABBY ALDRICH ROCKEFELLER FOLK ART COLLECTION
Williamsburg, Virginia

1957 Mitchell Wilder
1958 Lucius D. Battle
1961 Mary Black
1964 Bruce Etchison
1966 Peter A. G. Brown
1971 Graham S. Hood

SAN FRANCISCO MUSEUM OF ART
San Francisco, California

1935 Grace L. McCann Morley
1960 George D. Culler
1964 Clifford Peterson (Acting)
1966 Gerald Nordland

SANTA BARBARA MUSEUM OF ART
Santa Barbara, California

1939 Donald J. Bear
1952 Ala Story
1957 James W. Foster, Jr.
1966 Thomas W. Leavitt
1968 Goldthwaite H. Dorr III
1970 Paul C. Mills

SANTA BARBARA MUSEUM OF NATURAL HISTORY
Santa Barbara, California

1916 William L. Dawson
1923 Ralph Hoffmann
1932 Harold Sidebotham
1933 Paul M. Rea
1936 Nora K. Morres (Acting)
1937 Arthur S. Coggeshall
1958 Nora K. Morres (Acting)
1959 V. L. Vanderhoff
1963 Nora K. Morres (Acting)
1965 Frederick H. Pough
1966 Nora K. Morres (Acting)
1969 Lawrence J. Pinter

SEATTLE ART MUSEUM
Seattle, Washington

1928 John Davis Hatch, Jr.
1930 Richard E. Fuller

SMITH COLLEGE MUSEUM OF ART
Northampton, Massachusetts

1920 Alfred V. Churchill
1932 Jere Abbott
1946 Frederick C. Hartt (Acting)
1947 Edgar Schenck
1949 Henry-Russell Hitchcock
1955 Robert O. Parks
1962 Charles Chetham

SMITHSONIAN INSTITUTION
Washington, D. C.

Secretaries

1846 Joseph Henry
1878 Spencer F. Baird
1887 Samuel P. Langley
1907 Charles D. Walcott
1928 Charles G. Abbot
1945 Alexander Wetmore
1953 Leonard Carmichael
1964 S. Dillon Ripley

See also:

Freer Gallery
National Air and Space Museum
National Collection of Fine Arts
National Museum of History and Technology
National Museum of Natural History
National Portrait Gallery
United States National Museum

THE J. B. SPEED ART MUSEUM
Louisville, Kentucky

1927 Hattie B. Speed
1942 Catherine Grey (Acting)
1946 Paul S. Harris
1962 Addison F. Page

STATEN ISLAND MUSEUM
Staten Island, New York

1907 Charles L. Pollard (Curator-in-Chief)
1913 Arthur Hollick
1919 Charles W. Leng
1941 Roswell S. Coles
1951 James L. Whitehead
1962 George O. Pratt, Jr.

THE TAFT MUSEUM
Cincinnati, Ohio

1932 Walter H. Siple
1945 Philip R. Adams
1952 Katherine Hanna

THE TOLEDO MUSEUM OF ART
Toledo, Ohio

1903 George W. Stevens
1927 Blake-More Godwin
1959 Otto Wittmann

UNITED STATES NATIONAL MUSEUM
Washington, D. C.

Reorganized in 1958 to form the National Museum of History and Technology and the National Museum of Natural History.

1850 Spencer F. Baird
1878 G. Brown Goode
1896 Charles D. Walcott
1898 Richard Rathbun
1918 William deC. Ravenel
1925 Alexander Wetmore
1948 A. Remington Kellogg

UNIVERSITY OF NEBRASKA GALLERIES
Lincoln, Nebraska

1912 Paul Grumman
1931 Dwight Kirsch
1950 Duard Laging
1953 Norman Geske

VALENTINE MUSEUM
Richmond, Virginia

1930 Helen G. McCormack
1942 Mrs. Robert W. Claiborne
1956 Edward M. Davis
1963 Leslie D. Carter (Acting)
1966 Robert B. Mayo

VIRGINIA MUSEUM OF FINE ARTS
Richmond, Virginia

1936 Thomas C. Colt, Jr.
1941 Mrs. John Garland Pollard
Beatrice von Keller
1945 Thomas C. Colt, Jr.
1948 Leslie Cheek, Jr.
1969 James M. Brown III

WADSWORTH ATHENEUM
Hartford, Connecticut

1911 Frank B. Gay
1927 A. Everett Austin, Jr.
1946 Charles C. Cunningham
1966 James Elliott

THE WALTERS ART GALLERY
Baltimore, Maryland

1933 C. Morgan Marshall
1946 Edward S. King
1966 Richard H. Randall

WHITNEY MUSEUM OF AMERICAN ART
New York City

1931 Juliana Force
1948 Hermon More
1958 Lloyd Goodrich
1968 John I. H. Baur

WILLIAMS COLLEGE MUSEUM OF ART
Williamstown, Massachusetts

1926 Karl E. Weston
1948 S. Lane Faison, Jr.

WORCESTER ART MUSEUM
Worcester, Massachusetts

1908 Philip Gentner
1917 Frederick Pratt (Acting)
1918 Raymond Henniker-Heaton
1926 George W. Eggers
1931 Francis Henry Taylor
1940 Charles H. Sawyer
1943 Perry Cott (Acting)
1947 George L. Stout
1955 Francis Henry Taylor
1958 Daniel C. Rich
1970 Richard S. Teitz

YALE UNIVERSITY ART GALLERY
New Haven, Connecticut

1869 John F. Weir
1913 William S. Kendall
1922 Everett V. Meeks
1941 John Marshall Phillips (Acting)
1942 Emerson Tuttle (Acting)
1945 Theodore Sizer
1946 John Marshall Phillips
1953 Lamont Moore
1957 Andrew C. Ritchie
1971 Alan Shestack

RELIGION IN AMERICA

The Protestant Episcopal Church in the United States of America

a) Bishops by order of succession
b) Bishops by diocese

The Roman Catholic Church in America

a) Cardinals
b) Archibishops by archdiocese
c) Bishops by diocese

The United Methodist Church

The United Presbyterian Church in the United States of America

a) Moderators of the Presbyterian Church in the U.S.A.
b) Moderators of the United Presbyterian Church of North America
c) Moderators of the United Presbyterian Church in the U.S.A.

The United Church of Christ

The American Baptist Convention

The Southern Baptist Convention

The Christian Church (Disciples of Christ)

The Church of Christ, Scientist

The Church of Jesus Christ of Latter-Day Saints (Mormon)

The Lutheran Churches

Union of American Hebrew Congregations

Union of Orthodox Jewish Congregations of America

Founders of Religious Sects, Societies, and Movements in the United States

THE PROTESTANT EPISCOPAL CHURCH IN THE UNITED STATES OF AMERICA

Succession of Bishops

Succession	*Date of Consecration*	*Name*	*Diocese*
1	1784	Samuel Seabury	Connecticut
2	1787	William White	Pennsylvania
3	1787	Samuel Provoost	New York
4	1790	James Madison	Virginia
5	1792	John T. Claggett	Maryland
6	1795	Robert Smith	South Carolina
7	1797	Edward Bass	Massachusetts
8	1797	Abraham Jarvis	Connecticut
9	1801	Benjamin Moore	New York, coadjutor; bishop, 1815
10	1804	Samuel Parker	Massachusetts
11	1811	John H. Hobart	New York, coadjutor; bishop, 1816
12	1811	Alexander V. Griswold	Eastern Diocese
13	1812	Theodore Dehon	South Carolina
14	1814	Richard C. Moore	Virginia
15	1814	James Kemp	Maryland, suffragan; bishop, 1816
16	1815	John Croes	New Jersey
17	1818	Nathaniel Bowen	South Carolina
18	1819	Philander Chase	Ohio; Illinois, 1835
19	1819	Thomas C. Brownell	Connecticut
20	1823	John S. Ravenscroft	North Carolina
21	1827	Henry U. Onderdonk	Pennsylvania, assistant; bishop, 1836
22	1829	William Meade	Virginia, coadjutor; bishop, 1841
23	1830	William M. Stone	Maryland
24	1830	Benjamin T. Onderdonk	New York
25	1831	Levi S. Ives	North Carolina
26	1832	John H. Hopkins	Vermont
27	1832	Benjamin B. Smith	Kentucky
28	1832	Charles P. McIlvaine	Ohio
29	1832	George W. Doane	New Jersey
30	1834	James H. Otey	Tennessee
31	1835	Jackson Kemper	Missouri and Indiana; Wisconsin, 1859
32	1836	Samuel A. McCoskry	Michigan
33	1838	Leonidas Polk	Arkansas, missionary; Louisiana, 1841
34	1839	William H. DeLancey	Western New York
35	1840	Christopher E. Gadsden	South Carolina
36	1840	William R. Whittingham	Maryland
37	1841	Stephen Elliott	Georgia
38	1841	Alfred Lee	Delaware
39	1842	John Johns	Virginia, assistant; bishop, 1862
40	1842	Manton Eastburn	Massachusetts, coadjutor; bishop, 1843
41	1843	John P. K. Henshaw	Rhode Island
42	1844	Carlton Chase	New Hampshire
43	1844	Nicholas H. Cobbs	Alabama
44	1844	Cicero S. Hawks	Missouri
45	1844	William J. Boone	Amoy (China), missionary
46	1844	George W. Freeman	Arkansas and the Southwest, missionary
47	1844	Horatio Southgate	Constantinople, missionary

PROTESTANT EPISCOPAL BISHOPS – SUCCESSION

48	1845	Alonzo Potter	Pennsylvania
49	1847	George Burgess	Maine
50	1849	George Upfold	Indiana
51	1850	William M. Green	Mississippi
52	1851	John Payne	Africa, missionary
53	1851	Francis H. Rutledge	Florida
54	1851	John Williams	Connecticut, coadjutor; bishop, 1865
55	1851	Henry J. Whitehouse	Illinois, coadjutor; bishop, 1852
56	1852	Jonathan M. Wainwright	New York, provisional
57	1853	Thomas F. Davis	South Carolina
58	1853	Thomas Atkinson	North Carolina
59	1853	William I. Kip	California, missionary; bishop, 1857
60	1854	Thomas F. Scott	Oregon and Washington territory, missionary
61	1854	Henry W. Lee	Iowa
62	1854	Horatio Potter	New York, provisional; bishop, 1861
63	1854	Thomas M. Clark	Rhode Island
64	1858	Samuel Bowman	Pennsylvania, assistant
65	1859	Alexander Gregg	Texas
66	1859	William H. Odenheimer	New Jersey; Northern New Jersey, 1874
67	1859	Gregory T. Bedell	Ohio, coadjutor; bishop, 1873
68	1859	Henry B. Whipple	Minnesota
69	1859	Henry C. Lay	Southwest, missionary; Arkansas, missionary; Easton, 1869
70	1860	Joseph C. Talbot	Northwest, missionary; Indiana, coadjutor, 1865; bishop, 1872
71	1862	William B. Stevens	Pennsylvania, coadjutor; bishop, 1865
72	1862	Richard H. Wilmer	Alabama
73	1864	Thomas H. Vail	Kansas
74	1865	Arthur C. Coxe	Western New York, coadjutor; bishop, 1865
75	1865	Charles T. Quintard	Tennessee
76	1865	Robert H. Clarkson	Nebraska, missionary; bishop, 1870
77	1865	George M. Randall	Colorado and adjacent territory, missionary
78	1866	John B. Kerfoot	Pittsburgh
79	1866	Channing M. Williams	China and Japan, missionary; Yedo, 1874
80	1866	Joseph P. B. Wilmer	Louisiana
81	1866	George D. Cummins	Kentucky, assistant
82	1866	William E. Armitage	Wisconsin, coadjutor; bishop, 1870
83	1867	Henry A. Neely	Maine
84	1867	Daniel S. Tuttle	Montana, Idaho and Utah, missionary; Missouri, 1886
85	1867	John F. Young	Florida
86	1868	John W. Beckwith	Georgia
87	1868	Francis McN. Whittle	Virginia, coadjutor; bishop, 1876
88	1868	William H. A. Bissell	Vermont
89	1868	Charles F. Robertson	Missouri
90	1868	Benjamin W. Morris 2d	Oregon and Washington territory; Oregon, missionary, 1880; bishop, 1889
91	1869	Abram N. Littlejohn	Long Island
92	1869	William C. Doane	Albany
93	1869	Frederic D. Huntington	Central New York
94	1869	Ozi W. Whitaker	Nevada and Arizona, missionary; Nevada, 1874; Pennsylvania, coadjutor, 1886; bishop, 1887

PROTESTANT EPISCOPAL BISHOPS – SUCCESSION

95	1870	Henry N. Pierce	Arkansas, missionary; bishop, 1871
96	1870	William W. Niles	New Hampshire
97	1870	William Pinkney	Maryland, coadjutor; bishop, 1879
98	1871	William B. W. Howe	South Carolina
99	1871	Mark A. deW. Howe	Central Pennsylvania
100	1873	William H. Hare	Niobrara, missionary
101	1873	John G. Auer	Cape Palmas (Africa), missionary
102	1873	Benjamin H. Paddock	Massachusetts
103	1873	Theodore B. Lyman	New York, coadjutor; bishop, 1881
104	1873	John F. Spalding	Colorado, missionary; bishop, 1887
105	1874	Edward R. Welles	Wisconsin
106	1874	Robert W. B. Elliott	West Texas, missionary
107	1874	John H. D. Wingfield	Northern California, missionary
108	1874	Alexander C. Garrett	Northern Texas, missionary; Dallas, 1895
109	1875	William F. Adams	New Mexico and Arizona, missionary; Easton, 1887
110	1875	Thomas U. Dudley	Kentucky, coadjutor; bishop, 1884
111	1875	John Scarborough	New Jersey
112	1875	George DeN. Gillespie	Western Michigan
113	1875	Thomas A. Jaggar	Southern Ohio
114	1875	William E. McLaren	Illinois; Chicago, 1883
115	1875	J. H. Hobart Brown	Fond du Lac
116	1876	William S. Perry	Iowa
117	1877	Charles C. Penick	Cape Palmas, missionary
118	1877	Samuel I. J. Schereschewsky	Shanghai, missionary
119	1878	Alexander Burgess	Quincy
120	1878	George W. Peterkin	West Virginia
121	1878	George F. Seymour	Springfield
122	1879	Samuel S. Harris	Michigan
123	1880	Thomas A. Starkey	Northern New Jersey
124	1880	John N. Galleher	Louisiana
125	1880	George K. Dunlop	New Mexico and Arizona, missionary
126	1880	Leigh R. Brewer	Montana, missionary; bishop, 1904
127	1880	John A. Paddock	Washington territory, missionary; Olympia, missionary, 1892
128	1882	Cortlandt Whitehead	Pittsburgh
129	1883	Hugh M. Thompson	Mississippi, coadjutor; bishop, 1887
130	1883	David B. Knickerbacker	Indiana
131	1883	Henry C. Potter	New York, coadjutor; bishop, 1887
132	1883	Alfred M. Randolph	Virginia, coadjutor; bishop, Southern Virginia, 1892
133	1883	William D. Walker	North Dakota, missionary; Western New York, bishop, 1897
134	1884	Alfred A. Watson	East Carolina
135	1884	William J. Boone	Shanghai, missionary
136	1884	Nelson S. Rulison	Central Pennsylvania, coadjutor; bishop, 1895
137	1885	William Paret	Maryland
138	1885	George Worthington	Nebraska
139	1885	Samuel D. Ferguson	Liberia, missionary
140	1886	Edwin G. Weed	Florida
141	1886	Mahlon N. Gilbert	Minnesota, coadjutor
142	1887	Elisha S. Thomas	Kansas, coadjutor; bishop, 1889
143	1887	Ethelbert Talbot	Wyoming and Idaho, missionary; transferred to Central Pennsylvania, 1897; Bethlehem, 1908

PROTESTANT EPISCOPAL BISHOPS – SUCCESSION

144	1888	James S. Johnston	West Texas, missionary; bishop, 1904
145	1888	Abiel Leonard III	Nevada and Utah; Salt Lake, missionary, 1898
146	1888	Leighton Coleman	Delaware
147	1889	John M. Kendrick	New Mexico and Arizona, missionary; Arizona, 1892
148	1889	Boyd Vincent	Southern Ohio, coadjutor; bishop, 1904
149	1889	Cyrus F. Knight	Milwaukee
150	1889	Charles C. Grafton	Fond du Lac
151	1889	William A. Leonard	Ohio
152	1889	Thomas F. Davies	Michigan
153	1890	Anson R. Graves	The Platte, missionary; Kearney, missionary, 1907
154	1890	William F. Nichols	California, coadjutor; bishop, 1893
155	1890	Edward R. Atwill	West Missouri; Kansas City, 1904
156	1891	Henry M. Jackson	Alabama, coadjutor
157	1891	Davis Sessums	Louisiana, coadjutor; bishop, 1891
158	1891	Phillips Brooks	Massachusetts
159	1891	Isaac L. Nicholson	Milwaukee
160	1892	Cleland K. Nelson	Georgia; Atlanta, 1907
161	1892	Charles R. Hale	Springfield, coadjutor
162	1892	George H. Kinsolving	Texas, coadjutor; bishop, 1893
163	1892	Lemuel H. Wells	Spokane, missionary
164	1892	William C. Gray	South Florida, missionary
165	1893	Francis K. Brooke	Oklahoma, missionary
166	1893	William M. Barker	Western Colorado, missionary; Olympia, 1894; bishop, 1894
167	1893	John McKim	North Tokyo, missionary
168	1893	Frederick R. Graves	Shanghai, missionary
169	1893	Ellison Capers	South Carolina, coadjutor; bishop, 1894
170	1893	Thomas F. Gailor	Tennessee, coadjutor; bishop, 1898
171	1893	William Lawrence	Massachusetts
172	1893	Joseph B. Cheshire, Jr.	North Carolina, coadjutor; bishop, 1893
173	1894	Arthur C. A. Hall	Vermont
174	1894	John B. Newton	Virginia, coadjutor
175	1895	John H. White	Indiana; Michigan City, 1899
176	1895	Frank R. Millspaugh	Kansas
177	1895	Peter T. Rowe	Alaska, missionary
178	1896	Lewis W. Burton	Lexington
179	1896	Joseph H. Johnson	Los Angeles
180	1896	Henry Y. Satterlee	Washington
181	1896	Gershom M. Williams	Marquette
182	1897	James D. Morrison	Duluth, missionary
183	1897	Chauncey B. Brewster	Connecticut, coadjutor; bishop, 1899
184	1897	Robert A. Gibson	Virginia, coadjutor; bishop, 1902
185	1898	William N. McVickar	Rhode Island, coadjutor; bishop, 1903
186	1898	William M. Brown	Arkansas, coadjutor; bishop, 1899
187	1898	Junius M. Horner	Asheville, missionary; Western North Carolina, 1922
	1899	Lucien L. Kinsolving	Southern Brazil, missionary, 1907
188	1899	William H. Moreland	Sacramento, missionary
189	1899	Samuel C. Edsall	North Dakota, missionary; Minnesota, bishop, 1901
190	1899	Theodore N. Morrison	Iowa
191	1899	James B. Funsten	Boise, missionary; Wyoming, 1907; Idaho, 1907
192	1899	Joseph M. Francis	Indiana

PROTESTANT EPISCOPAL BISHOPS – SUCCESSION

193	1899	Arthur L. Williams	Nebraska, coadjutor; bishop, 1908
194	1899	William L. Gravatt	West Virginia, coadjutor; bishop, 1916
195	1900	Sidney C. Partridge	Kyoto, missionary; West Missouri, 1911
196	1900	Robert Codman	Maine
197	1900	Charles P. Anderson	Chicago, coadjutor; bishop, 1905
198	1900	Robert W. Barnwell	Alabama
199	1900	Reginald H. Weller	Fond du Lac, coadjutor; bishop, 1912
200	1901	Frederick W. Taylor	Quincy
201	1901	Cameron Mann	North Dakota, missionary; South Florida, missionary, 1913; bishop, 1922
202	1901	Charles H. Brent	Philippines, missionary; Western New York, bishop, 1918
203	1902	Frederick W. Keator	Olympia, missionary
204	1902	Frederick Burgess	Long Island
205	1902	James A. Ingle	Hankow, missionary
206	1902	Alexander H. Vinton	Western Massachusetts
207	1902	Charles S. Olmsted	Colorado
208	1902	Alexander Mackay-Smith	Pennsylvania, coadjutor; bishop, 1911
209	1902	James H. VanBuren	Puerto Rico, missionary
210	1902	Henry B. Restarick	Honolulu
211	1902	Charles T. Olmsted	Central New York, coadjutor; bishop, 1904
212	1902	Charles M. Beckwith	Alabama
213	1903	Sheldon M. Griswold	Salina, missionary; Chicago, suffragan, 1917; bishop, 1930
214	1903	Theodore DuB. Bratton	Mississippi
215	1903	Edwin S. Lines	Newark
216	1904	M. Edward Fawcett	Quincy
217	1904	David H. Greer	New York, coadjutor; bishop, 1908
218	1904	Richard H. Nelson	Albany, coadjutor; bishop, 1913
219	1904	Edward W. Osborne	Springfield, coadjutor; bishop, 1906
220	1904	Robert Strange	East Carolina, coadjutor; bishop, 1905
221	1904	Logan H. Roots	Hankow, missionary
222	1904	Franklin S. Spalding	Salt Lake, missionary (Western Colorado, 1904-07)
223	1904	Henry D. Aves	Mexico, missionary
224	1904	Albion W. Knight	Cuba, missionary; New Jersey, coadjutor, 1923
225	1905	Charles E. Woodcock	Kentucky
226	1905	James H. Darlington	Harrisburg
227	1905	Frederick F. Johnson	South Dakota, assistant; missionary, 1910; Missouri, coadjutor, 1911; bishop, 1923
228	1906	Charles D. Williams	Michigan
229	1906	Edward M. Parker	New Hampshire, coadjutor; bishop, 1914
230	1906	John N. McCormick	Western Michigan, coadjutor; bishop, 1909
231	1906	William W. Webb	Milwaukee, coadjutor; bishop, 1906
232	1906	Charles Scadding	Oregon
233	1906	Beverly D. Tucker	Southern Virginia, coadjutor; bishop, 1918
234	1907	William A. Guerry	South Carolina, coadjutor; bishop, 1908
235	1907	Robert L. Paddock	Eastern Oregon, missionary
236	1907	Edward J. Knight	Western Colorado, missionary
237	1908	Henry D. Robinson	Nevada, missionary
238	1908	Frederick F. Reese	Georgia
239	1908	Frederick J. Kinsman	Delaware
240	1909	Alfred Harding	Washington, D.C.
241	1909	Nathaniel S. Thomas	Wyoming, missionary

PROTESTANT EPISCOPAL BISHOPS – SUCCESSION

242	1909	Benjamin Brewster	Western Colorado, missionary; Maine, bishop, 1916
243	1909	John G. Murray	Maryland, coadjutor; bishop, 1911
244	1909	Arthur S. Lloyd	Virginia, coadjutor; New York, suffragan, 1921
245	1910	George A. Beecher	Kearney, missionary
246	1910	Edward A. Temple	North Texas, missionary
247	1911	James DeWolf Perry	Rhode Island
248	1911	Julius W. Atwood	Arizona, missionary
249	1911	Theodore P. Thurston	Eastern Oklahoma, missionary; combined Eastern Oklahoma and Oklahoma, 1919
250	1911	Louis C. Sanford	San Joaquin, missionary
251	1911	Charles S. Burch	New York, suffragan; bishop, 1919
252	1911	Rogers Israel	Erie
253	1911	James R. Winchester	Arkansas, coadjutor; bishop, 1912
254	1911	Thomas F. Davies	Western Massachusetts
255	1911	Philip M. Rhinelander	Pennsylvania, coadjutor; bishop, 1911
256	1911	Thomas J. Garland	Pennsylvania, suffragan; bishop, 1924
257	1911	William E. Toll	Chicago, suffragan
258	1912	Henry St. G. Tucker	Kyoto, missionary; Virginia, coadjutor, 1926; bishop, 1927
259	1912	Daniel T. Huntington	Anking, missionary
260	1912	George Biller, Jr.	South Dakota, missionary
261	1912	Harry S. Longley	Iowa, suffragan; coadjutor, 1917; bishop, 1929
262	1912	Frank A. McElwain	Minnesota, suffragan; bishop, 1917
263	1913	William F. Weeks	Vermont, coadjutor
264	1913	Theodore I. Reese	Southern Ohio, coadjutor; bishop, 1929
265	1913	Samuel G. Babcock	Massachusetts, suffragan
266	1913	Charles B. Colmore	Puerto Rico, missionary
267	1914	John P. Tyler	North Dakota, missionary
268	1914	Frank DuMoulin	Ohio, coadjutor
269	1914	Frederick B. Howden	New Mexico, missionary
270	1914	William T. Capers	West Texas, coadjutor; bishop, 1916
271	1914	William C. Brown	Virginia, coadjutor; bishop, 1919
272	1914	William F. Faber	Montana, coadjutor; bishop, 1916
273	1914	George C. Hunting	Nevada, missionary
274	1914	Paul Jones	Utah, missionary
275	1915	Thomas C. Darst	East Carolina
276	1915	Walter T. Sumner	Oregon
277	1915	Hiram R. Hulse	Cuba, missionary
278	1915	Paul Matthews	New Jersey
279	1915	Herman Page	Spokane, missionary; Michigan, 1923
280	1915	George Y. Bliss	Vermont, coadjutor
281	1915	Charles Fiske	Central New York, coadjutor; bishop, 1924
282	1915	Wilson R. Stearly	Newark, suffragan; coadjutor, 1917; bishop, 1927
283	1915	E. Campion Acheson	Connecticut, suffragan; coadjutor, 1926; bishop, 1928
284	1916	James Wise	Kansas, coadjutor; bishop, 1916
285	1916	Hugh L. Burleson	South Dakota, missionary
286	1917	Irving P. Johnson	Colorado, coadjutor; bishop, 1918
287	1917	Frank H. Touret	Western Colorado, missionary; Idaho, 1919
288	1917	Granville H. Sherwood	Springfield
289	1917	Edwin W. Saphore	Arkansas, suffragan; bishop, 1935
290	1917	Arthur C. Thomson	Southern Virginia, suffragan; coadjutor, 1919; bishop, 1930

PROTESTANT EPISCOPAL BISHOPS – SUCCESSION

291	1917	Harry T. Moore	Dallas, coadjutor; bishop, 1924
292	1917	Henry J. Mikell	Atlanta
293	1918	William P. Remington	South Dakota, suffragan; Eastern Oregon, missionary, 1922
294	1918	John C. Sage	Salina, missionary
295	1918	Robert LeR. Harris	Marquette, coadjutor; bishop, 1919
296	1918	Edward T. Denby	Arkansas and Province of the Southwest, suffragan
297	1918	Clinton S. Quin	Texas, coadjutor; bishop, 1928
298	1918	Henry B. Delany	North Carolina, suffragan
299	1919	William M. Green	Mississippi, coadjutor; bishop, 1938
300	1919	Ernest V. Shayler	Nebraska
301	1919	Troy Beatty	Tennessee, coadjutor
302	1919	Edward L. Parsons	California, coadjutor; bishop, 1924
303	1919	Walter H. Overs	Liberia, missionary
304	1920	James C. Morris	Canal Zone, missionary; Louisiana, bishop, 1930
305	1920	Gouverneur F. Mosher	Philippine Islands, missionary
306	1920	Robert C. Jett	Southwestern, Virginia
307	1920	Arthur W. Moulton	Utah
308	1920	George W. Davenport	Easton
309	1920	William B. Stevens	Los Angeles, coadjutor; bishop, 1928
310	1920	David L. Ferris	Western New York, suffragan; coadjutor, 1924; bishop, 1929; Rochester, 1931
311	1920	Philip Cook	Delaware
312	1920	Herbert H. H. Fox	Montana, suffragan; coadjutor, 1925; bishop, 1934
313	1920	Granville G. Bennett	Duluth, coadjutor; bishop, 1922; Rhode Island, suffragan, 1939; bishop, 1946
314	1921	Robert H. Mize	Salina, missionary
315	1921	Kirkman G. Finlay	South Carolina, coadjutor; Upper South Carolina, bishop, 1922
316	1921	William T. Manning	New York
317	1921	Fred Ingley	Colorado, coadjutor; bishop, 1938
318	1921	Theophilus M. Gardiner	Liberia, suffragan
319	1921	John D. LaMothe	Honolulu, missionary
320	1921	John C. Ward	Erie
321	1921	Herbert Shipman	New York, suffragan
322	1922	Edwin A. Penick	North Carolina, coadjutor; bishop, 1932
323	1922	James M. Maxon	Tennessee, coadjutor; bishop, 1935
324	1922	William C. McDowell	Alabama, coadjutor; bishop, 1928
325	1922	George A. Oldham	Albany, coadjutor; bishop, 1929
326	1922	Charles L. Slattery	Massachusetts, coadjutor; bishop, 1927
327	1922	William B. Roberts	South Dakota, suffragan; bishop, 1931
328	1923	Harry R. Carson	Haiti, missionary
329	1923	Alexander Mann	Pittsburgh
330	1923	James E. Freeman	Washington, D.C.
331	1923	Robert E. L. Strider	West Virginia, coadjutor; bishop, 1939
332	1923	Frank W. Sterrett	Bethlehem, coadjutor; bishop, 1928
333	1924	Charles S. Reifsnider	North Tokyo, suffragan; missionary, 1935
334	1924	Edward M. Cross	Spokane, missionary
335	1924	John C. White	Springfield
336	1924	Edward H. Coley	Central New York, suffragan; bishop, 1936
337	1924	Frank A. Juhan	Florida

PROTESTANT EPISCOPAL BISHOPS – SUCCESSION

338	1925	Eugene C. Seaman	North Texas, missionary
339	1925	Samuel B. Booth	Vermont, coadjutor; bishop, 1930
340	1925	Alfred A. Gilman	Hankow, suffragan; bishop, 1937
341	1925	Warren L. Rogers	Ohio, coadjutor; bishop, 1930
342	1925	Campbell Gray	Northern Indiana
343	1925	Benjamin F. P. Ivins	Milwaukee, coadjutor; bishop, 1933
344	1925	Simeon A. Huston	Olympia
345	1925	John D. Wing	South Florida, coadjutor; bishop, 1932
346	1925	Ernest M. Stires	Long Island
347	1925	Robert E. Campbell	Liberia, missionary
348	1925	William M. M. Thomas	Southern Brazil, suffragan; missionary, 1928
349	1925	Middleton S. Barnwell	Idaho, missionary; Georgia, coadjutor, 1935; bishop, 1937
350	1926	Walter Mitchell	Arizona, missionary
351	1926	Frank W. Creighton	Mexico, missionary; Long Island, suffragan, 1933; Michigan, coadjutor; bishop, 1939
352	1926	Shirley H. Nichols	Kyoto, missionary; Salina, 1943
353	1926	John T. Dallas	New Hampshire
354	1926	Edward T. Helfenstein	Maryland, coadjutor; bishop, 1929
355	1927	Thomas Casady	Oklahoma, missionary
356	1928	Albert S. Thomas	South Carolina
357	1928	Norman S. Binsted	Tohuku, missionary; Philippines, bishop, 1942
358	1929	Thomas Jenkins	Nevada, missionary
359	1929	John I. B. Larned	Long Island, suffragan
360	1929	Frank E. Wilson	Eau Claire
361	1929	Henry P. A. Abbott	Lexington
362	1929	Francis M. Taitt	Pennsylvania, coadjutor; bishop, 1931
363	1929	Harwood Sturtevant	Fond du Lac, coadjutor; bishop, 1933
364	1929	Elmer N. Schmuck	Wyoming, missionary
365	1930	Cameron J. Davis	Western New York, coadjutor; bishop, 1931
366	1930	Samuel H. Littell	Honolulu, missionary
367	1930	Hayward S. Ablewhite	Marquette
368	1930	Henry W. Hobson	Southern Ohio, coadjutor; bishop, 1931
369	1930	William Scarlett	Missouri, coadjutor; bishop, 1933
370	1930	Robert B. Gooden	Los Angeles, suffragan
371	1930	George C. Stewart	Chicago, coadjutor; bishop, 1930
372	1930	Henry K. Sherrill	Massachusetts
373	1930	Frederick D. Goodwin	Virginia, coadjutor; bishop, 1944
374	1930	Charles K. Gilbert	New York, suffragan; bishop, 1947
375	1930	Robert M. Spencer	Western Missouri
376	1930	Benjamin T. Kemerer	Duluth, coadjutor; bishop, 1933; Minnesota, suffragan, 1944
377	1931	Hunter Wyatt-Brown	Harrisburg
378	1931	Stephen E. Keeler	Minnesota, coadjutor; bishop, 1944
379	1931	John B. Bentley	Alaska, suffragan; bishop, 1943
380	1931	Efrain Salinas y Velasco	Mexico, suffragan; missionary, 1934
381	1931	Frederick G. Budlong	Connecticut, coadjutor; bishop, 1934
382	1931	Frederick B. Bartlett	North Dakota, missionary; Idaho, missionary, 1936
383	1932	Benjamin M. Washburn	Newark, coadjutor; bishop, 1935
384	1932	Ralph E. Urban	New Jersey, suffragan
385	1933	A. W. Noel Porter	Sacramento, coadjutor; bishop, 1933
386	1934	Robert E. Gribbin	Western North Carolina
387	1934	John W. Nichols	Shanghai, suffragan

PROTESTANT EPISCOPAL BISHOPS – SUCCESSION

388	1936	Theodore R. Ludlow	Newark, suffragan
389	1936	Benjamin D. Dagwell	Oregon
390	1936	Leopold Kroll	Liberia, missionary
391	1936	Vedder VanDyck	Vermont
392	1936	Bartel H. Reinheimer	Rochester, coadjutor; bishop, 1938
393	1936	Charles Clingman	Kentucky
394	1936	Lewis B. Whittemore	Western Michigan, coadjutor; bishop, 1937
395	1936	Wallace J. Gardner	New Jersey, coadjutor
396	1936	William L. Essex	Quincy
397	1936	Winfred H. Ziegler	Wyoming
398	1937	William A. Lawrence	Western Massachusetts
399	1937	Harry Beal	Panama and Canal Zone
400	1937	Douglass H. Atwill	North Dakota
401	1937	Goodrich R. Fenner	Kansas, coadjutor; bishop, 1939
402	1937	William P. Roberts	Shanghai
403	1938	Robert F. Wilner	Philippines, suffragan
404	1938	Raymond A. Heron	Massachusetts, suffragan
405	1938	William A. Brown	Southern Virginia
406	1938	Charles C. J. Carpenter	Alabama
407	1938	Edmund P. Dandridge	Tennessee, coadjutor; bishop, 1947
408	1938	Henry D. Phillips	Southwestern Virginia
409	1938	Beverley D. Tucker	Ohio
410	1938	Malcolm E. Peabody	Central New York, coadjutor; bishop, 1942
411	1938	Karl M. Block	California, coadjutor; bishop, 1941
412	1938	Richard B. Mitchell	Arkansas
413	1939	Richard A. Kirchhoffer	Indianapolis
414	1939	Arthur R. McKinstry	Delaware
415	1939	A. H. Blankingship	Cuba
416	1939	Spence Burton	Haiti, suffragan; Nassau, bishop, 1942
417	1939	John J. Gravatt	Upper South Carolina
418	1939	William McClelland	Easton
419	1939	Henry H. Daniels	Montana
420	1939	Edwin J. Randall	Chicago, suffragan
421	1940	Howard R. Brinker	Nebraska
422	1940	Athalicio T. Pithan	Southern Brazil, suffragan; bishop, 1950
423	1940	John L. Jackson	Louisiana
424	1940	Walter H. Gray	Connecticut, coadjutor; bishop, 1951
425	1940	Lloyd R. Craighill	Anking
426	1941	Wallace E. Conkling	Chicago
427	1941	Oliver L. Loring	Maine
428	1941	Noble C. Powell	Maryland, coadjutor; bishop, 1944
429	1942	James M. Stoney	New Mexico and Southwest Texas, missionary, 1942; bishop, 1954
430	1942	Frank A. Rhea	Idaho
431	1942	James P. DeWolfe	Long Island
432	1942	William F. Lewis	Nevada, Olympia, 1960
433	1942	Wiley R. Mason	Virginia, suffragan
434	1942	John M. Walker	Atlanta
435	1942	Oliver J. Hart	Pennsylvania, coadjutor; bishop, 1943
436	1942	Herman R. Page	Northern Michigan
437	1943	Duncan M. Gray	Mississippi
438	1943	John T. Heistand	Harrisburg

PROTESTANT EPISCOPAL BISHOPS – SUCCESSION

439	1943	Edward P. Wroth	Erie
440	1943	Everett H. Jones	West Texas
441	1943	Charles A. Voegeli	Haiti
442	1944	Charles F. Boynton	Puerto Rico, coadjutor; bishop, 1947
443	1944	Sumner F. D. Walters	San Joaquin
444	1944	Harry S. Kennedy	Honolulu; Taiwan, 1960
445	1944	Austin Pardue	Pittsburgh
446	1944	Angus Dun	Washington, D.C.
447	1944	Thomas N. Carruthers	South Carolina
448	1944	Elwood L. Haines	Iowa
449	1944	William W. Horstick	Eau Claire
450	1944	James R. Mallett	Northern Indiana
451	1945	Bravid W. Harris	Liberia
452	1945	Conrad H. Gesner	South Dakota, suffragan; bishop, 1954
453	1945	Donald B. Aldrich	Michigan, coadjutor
454	1945	Reginald H. Gooden	Panama Canal Zone
455	1945	Henry I. Louttit	South Florida, suffragan; bishop, 1951
456	1945	Arthur B. Kinsvoling II	Arizona, missionary; bishop, 1959
457	1945	Frederick L. Barry	Albany, coadjutor; bishop, 1949
458	1945	Charles A. Mason	Dallas
459	1945	Alfred L. Banyard	New Jersey, suffragan; bishop, 1955
460	1945	Thomas H. Wright	East Carolina
461	1945	John E. Hines	Texas, coadjutor; bishop, 1955
462	1945	William R. Moody	Lexington
463	1946	Richard S. M. Emrich	Michigan
464	1946	Harold E. Sawyer	Erie
465	1946	Lane W. Barton	Eastern Oregon
466	1946	George H. Quarterman	Northwest Texas
467	1946	Stephen C. Clark	Utah
468	1947	Norman B. Nash	Massachusetts
469	1947	Stephen F. Bayne, Jr.	Olympia
470	1947	Harold L. Bowen	Colorado, coadjutor; bishop, 1949
471	1947	Richard T. Loring, Jr.	Springfield
472	1947	Horace W. B. Donegan	New York City, suffragan, 1947; bishop, 1950
473	1948	George P. Gunn	Southern Virginia, coadjutor, 1948; bishop, 1950
474	1948	Charles F. Hall	New Hampshire
475	1948	Louis C. Melcher	Southern Brazil, suffragan; bishop, 1944
476	1948	James W. Hunter	Wyoming
477	1948	Francis E. I. Bloy	Los Angeles
478	1948	Lauriston L. Scaife	Western New York
479	1948	William J. Gordon, Jr.	Alaska
480	1948	Russell S. Hubbard	Michigan, suffragan; Spokane, bishop, 1954
481	1948	Charles A. Clough	Springfield
482	1948	Theodore N. Barth	Tennessee, coadjutor; bishop, 1953
483	1948	Matthew G. Henry	Western North Carolina
484	1948	Edward H. West	Florida, coadjutor; bishop, 1956
485	1948	Walter M. Higley	Central New York, suffragan
486	1949	Jonathan G. Sherman	Long Island, suffragan; bishop, 1966
487	1949	Donald J. Campbell	Los Angeles, suffragan
488	1949	Girault M. Jones	Louisiana

PROTESTANT EPISCOPAL BISHOPS – SUCCESSION

489	1949	Randolph R. Claiborne, Jr.	Alabama, suffragan; Atlanta, bishop, 1953
490	1949	Robert F. Gibson, Jr.	Virginia, suffragan; bishop, 1961
491	1949	Joseph G. Armstrong	Pennsylvania, suffragan; coadjutor, 1960; bishop, 1963
492	1949	Charles L. Street	Chicago, suffragan
493	1949	Allen J. Miller	Easton
494	1949	Nelson M. Burroughs	Ohio, coadjutor; bishop, 1952
496	1950	Dudley S. Stark	Rochester
497	1950	Edward R. Welles	West Missouri
498	1950	Gordon V. Smith	Iowa
499	1950	Wilburn C. Campbell	West Virginia, coadjutor; bishop, 1955
500	1950	G. Francis Burrill	Dallas, suffragan; Chicago, bishop, 1954
501	1950	Henry H. Shires	California, suffragan
502	1951	Richard H. Baker	North Carolina, coadjutor; bishop, 1959
503	1951	Arthur C. Lichtenberger	Missouri, coadjutor; bishop, 1952
504	1951	Robert M. Hatch	Connecticut, suffragan; Western Massachusetts, 1957
505	1951	Richard S. Watson	Utah
506	1951	A. Ervine Swift	Puerto Rico; South Florida, suffragan, 1969
507	1951	Richard R. Emery	North Dakota
508	1951	David E. Richards	Albany, suffragan
509	1951	Martin J. Bram	South Florida, suffragan
510	1951	Chilton Powell	Oklahoma
511	1952	John B. Walthour	Atlanta
512	1952	Donald H. V. Hallock	Milwaukee
513	1952	Hamilton H. Kellogg	Minnesota, coadjutor; bishop, 1956
514	1952	William Crittenden	Erie
515	1952	Iveson B. Noland	Louisiana
516	1953	Lyman C. Ogilby	Philippines, suffragan; bishop, 1957; South Dakota, coadjutor, 1967
517	1953	John S. Higgins	Rhode Island, coadjutor; bishop, 1955
518	1953	Frederick J. Warnecke	Bethlehem
519	1953	William H. Brady	Fond du Lac, coadjutor; bishop, 1956
520	1953	Leland Stark	Newark, coadjutor; bishop, 1958
521	1953	George M. Murray	Alabama, suffragan; bishop, 1968
522	1953	Dudley B. McNeil	Western Michigan
523	1953	William S. Thomas	Pittsburgh, suffragan
524	1953	Clarence A. Cole	Upper South Carolina
525	1953	Charles J. Kinsolving III	New Mexico and Southwest Texas, coadjutor, 1953; bishop, 1956
526	1953	J. Brooke Mosley	Delaware, coadjutor; bishop, 1955
527	1954	Charles G. Marmion	Kentucky
528	1954	William H. Marmion	Southwestern Virginia
529	1954	Joseph M. Harte	Dallas, suffragan; Arizona, bishop, 1962
530	1954	Joseph S. Minnis	Colorado
531	1954	Archie H. Crowley	Michigan, suffragan
532	1954	Albert R. Stuart	Georgia
533	1954	Anson P. Stokes, Jr.	Massachusetts, coadjutor; bishop, 1966
534	1955	John VanderHorst	Tennessee, suffragan; bishop, 1961
535	1955	Harry L. Doll	Maryland, suffragan; coadjutor, 1958; bishop, 1963
536	1955	Richard E. Dicus	West Texas, suffragan
537	1955	Frederick P. Goddard	Texas, suffragan

PROTESTANT EPISCOPAL BISHOPS – SUCCESSION

538	1955	Robert R. Brown	Arkansas, coadjutor; bishop, 1956
539	1956	Arnold M. Lewis	Salina
540	1956	James W. F. Carman	Oregon, coadjutor; bishop, 1958
541	1956	Earl M. Honaman	Harrisburg
543	1956	Edward C. Turner	Kansas, coadjutor; bishop, 1959
544	1956	James P. Clements	Texas, suffragan
545	1956	William F. Moses	South Florida, suffragan
546	1956	Chandler W. Sterling	Montana, coadjutor; bishop, 1957
547	1956	Frederic C. Lawrence	Massachusetts, suffragan
548	1957	Norman L. Foote	Idaho
549	1957	John P. Craine	Indianapolis, 1959
550	1957	Clarence R. Haden	Sacramento, coadjutor; bishop, 1958
552	1958	Philip F. McNairy	Minnesota, coadjutor
553	1958	John H. Esquirol	Connecticut, suffragan; bishop, 1969
554	1958	Daniel Corrigan	Colorado, suffragan
555	1958	James A. Pike	California
556	1958	David S. Rose	Southern Virginia, suffragan
557	1958	Francis W. Lickfield	Quincy
558	1958	Donald Macadie	Newark, suffragan
559	1958	Roger W. Blanchard	Southern Ohio, coadjutor; bishop, 1959
560	1959	Edmund K. Sherrill	Central Brazil
561	1959	Allen W. Brown	Albany, suffragan; bishop, 1961
563	1959	George L. Cadigan	Missouri
564	1959	William F. Creighton	Washington, D.C., suffragan; bishop, 1962
565	1960	C. Richard Millard	California, suffragan
566	1960	William G. Wright	Nevada
567	1960	Charles E. Bennison	Western Michigan
568	1960	Paul A. Kellogg	Dominican Republic
569	1960	James S. Wetmore	New York, suffragan
570	1960	Ivol I. Curtis	Los Angeles, suffragan; Olympia, 1964
571	1960	Samuel B. Chilton	Virginia, suffragan
572	1960	Thomas A. Fraser, Jr.	North Carolina, coadjutor; bishop, 1965
573	1960	Robert L. DeWitt	Michigan, suffragan, Pennsylvania, 1964
574	1960	Edwin B. Thayer	Colorado
575	1961	Gray Temple	South Carolina
576	1961	Harvey D. Butterfield	Vermont
577	1961	Russell T. Rauscher	Nebraska, coadjutor; bishop, 1962
578	1961	Charles P. Gilson	Honolulu, suffragan
580	1961	Dillard H. Brown, Jr.	Liberia
581	1961	John M. Allin	Mississippi, suffragan; bishop, 1966
582	1961	Joseph W. Hutchens	Connecticut, suffragan
583	1961	James L. Duncan	South Florida, suffragan
584	1961	William L. Hargrave	South Florida
585	1962	Charles W. MacLean	Long Island, suffragan
586	1962	William F. Sanders	Tennessee, coadjutor
587	1962	James W. Montgomery	Chicago, suffragan; coadjutor, 1965
588	1962	Albert A. Chambers	Springfield
589	1962	Theodore H. McCrea	Dallas, suffragan
590	1962	John M. Burgess	Massachusetts, suffragan
591	1963	Edward G. Longid	Philippines

PROTESTANT EPISCOPAL BISHOPS – SUCCESSION

592	1963	Charles B. Persell, Jr.	Albany, suffragan
593	1963	Cedric Earl Mills	Panama Canal Zone
594	1963	George W. Barrett	Rochester
595	1963	Frederick W. Putman, Jr.	Oklahoma, suffragan
596	1963	Walter C. Klein	Northern Indiana
597	1963	John A. Pinckney	Upper South Carolina
598	1964	Paul Moore, Jr.	Washington, suffragan; New York, suffragan, 1970; bishop, 1972
601	1964	George E. Rath	Newark, suffragan
602	1964	Ned Cole, Jr.	Central New York
603	1964	David B. Reed	Colombia
604	1964	Scott Field Bailey	Texas, suffragan
605	1964	C. Kilmer Myers	Michigan, suffragan; California, bishop, 1966
606	1964	Robert C. Rusack	Los Angeles, suffragan
607	1964	George R. Selway	Northern Michigan
608	1964	Francisco Reus-Froylan	Puerto Rico
610	1965	George T. Masuda	North Dakota
611	1965	James M. Richardson	Texas
612	1965	Hal R. Gross	Oregon, suffragan
613	1966	William Davidson	Western Kansas
614	1966	Albert W. Van Duzer	New Jersey, suffragan
615	1966	William F. Gates, Jr.	Tennessee, suffragan
616	1966	William P. Barnds	Dallas, suffragan
617	1966	Dean T. Stevenson	Harrisburg
618	1966	Robert B. Hall	Virginia, coadjutor
619	1966	George A. Taylor	Easton
620	1967	Richard B. Martin	Long Island, suffragan
621	1967	John H. Burt	Ohio, suffragan; bishop, 1968
622	1967	William M. Moore	North Carolina, suffragan
623	1967	John R. Wyatt	Spokane
624	1967	Robert R. Spears	West Missouri, suffragan; Rochester, 1970
625	1967	Milton L. Wood	Atlanta, suffragan
626	1967	Christopher Keller, Jr.	Arkansas, coadjutor
627	1967	William C. Frey	Guatemala
628	1967	Edward McNair	Northern California, suffragan
629	1967	Edwin L. Hanchett	Honolulu
630	1968	Edmond Browning	Okinawa
631	1968	Robert Appleyard	Pittsburgh
632	1968	Harold Robinson	Western New York, coadjutor
633	1968	Harold C. Gosnell	West Texas
634	1968	Jackson Gilliam	Montana
635	1968	Victor M. Rivera	San Joaquin
636	1968	Huntley A. Elebash	East Carolina, suffragan
637	1968	Frederick B. Wolfe	Maine
638	1968	William H. Mead	Delaware
639	1968	David K. Leighton	Maryland, coadjutor
640	1969	George Haynsworth	Nicaragua
643	1969	William B. Spofford, Jr.	Eastern Oregon
644	1969	David R. Thornberry	Wyoming
645	1969	Stanley H. Atkins	Eau Claire, coadjutor
646	1969	George P. Reeves	Georgia, coadjutor
647	1970	Philip A. Smith	Virginia, suffragan

PROTESTANT EPISCOPAL BISHOPS – SUCCESSION

648	1970	William Folwell	Florida
649	1970	Addison Hosea	Lexington
650	1970	A. Donald Davies	Dallas
651	1970	Walter H. Jones	South Dakota
652	1970	George Browne	Liberia
653	1970	Alexander D. Stewart	Western Massachusetts
654	1970	Lloyd E. Gressle	Bethlehem
656	1971	Clarence Hobgood	Suffragan, Armed Forces
658	1971	Furman C. Stough	Alabama
659	1971	John M. Krumm	Southern Ohio
661	1971	Robert P. Varley	Nebraska, coadjutor
662	1971	Arthur A. Vogel	West Missouri, coadjutor
663	1971	Willis R. Henton	N.W. Texas, coadjutor
664	1971	John T. Walker	Washington, suffragan
665	1971	E. Otis Charles	Utah
666	1971	Frederick H. Belder	Rhode Island, coadjutor
667	1971	H. Coleman McGehee, Jr.	Michigan, coadjutor
668	1971	Morgan Porteus	Connecticut, suffragan
669	1971	Bennett J. Sims	Atlanta

PROTESTANT EPISCOPAL BISHOPS BY DIOCESE

Alabama

1844 Nicholas H. Cobbs
1862 Richard H. Wilmer
1900 Robert W. Barnwell
1902 Charles M. Beckwith
1928 William G. McDowell
1938 Charles C. J. Carpenter
1968 George M. Murray
1971 Furman C. Stough

Alaska

1895 Peter T. Rowe
1943 John B. Bentley
1948 William J. Gordon, Jr.

Albany, N.Y.

1869 William C. Doane
1913 Richard H. Nelson
1929 George A. Oldham
1949 Frederick L. Barry
1961 Allen W. Brown

Arizona

1869 Ozi W. Whitaker
1875 William F. Adams
1880 George K. Dunlop
1892 John M. Kendrick
1911 Julius W. Atwood
1926 Walter Mitchell
1945 Arthur B. Kinsolving II
1962 Joseph M. Harte

Arkansas

1838 Leonidas Polk
1844 George W. Freeman
1859 Henry C. Lay
1871 Henry N. Pierce
1899 William M. Brown
1912 James R. Winchester
1935 Edwin W. Saphore
1938 Richard B. Mitchell
1956 Robert R. Brown

Asheville, North Carolina

See Western North Carolina

Atlanta, Georgia

1907 Cleland K. Nelson
1917 Henry J. Mikell
1942 John M. Walker
1952 John B. Walthour
1953 Randolph R. Claiborne, Jr.
1972 Bennett J. Sims

Bethlehem, Pennsylvania

Diocese of Central Pennsylvania until 1908

1871 Mark A. DeW. Howe
1895 Nelson S. Rulison
1897 Ethelbert Talbot
1928 Frank W. Sterrett
1953 Frederick J. Warnecke
1971 Lloyd E. Gressle

California

1857 William I. Kip
1893 William F. Nichols
1924 Edward L. Parsons
1941 Karl M. Block
1958 James A. Pike
1966 C. Kilmer Myers

Central New York

1869 Frederic D. Huntington
1904 Charles T. Olmsted
1924 Charles Fiske
1936 Edward H. Coley
1942 Malcolm E. Peabody
1964 Ned Cole, Jr.

Central Pennsylvania

See Bethlehem

Chicago, Illinois

Diocese of Illinois until 1883

1835 Philander Chase
1852 Henry J. Whitehouse
1875 William E. McLaren
1905 Charles P. Anderson
1930 Sheldon M. Griswold
1930 George C. Stewart
1941 Wallace E. Conkling
1954 Francis G. Burrill

Colorado

1865 George M. Randall
1873 John F. Spalding
1902 Charles S. Olmsted
1918 Irving P. Johnson
1938 Fred Ingley
1949 Harold L. Bowen
1955 Joseph S. Minnis
1960 Edwin B. Thayer

Connecticut

1784 Samuel Seabury
1797 Abraham Jarvis
1819 Thomas C. Brownell
1865 John Williams
1899 Chauncey B. Brewster
1928 E. Campion Acheson
1934 Frederick G. Budlong
1951 Walter H. Gray
1969 John H. Esquirol

Dallas, Texas

Diocese of Northern Texas until 1895

1874 Alexander C. Garrett
1924 Harry T. Moore
1945 Charles A. Mason
1970 A. Donald Davies

Delaware

1841 Alfred Lee
1888 Leighton Coleman
1908 Frederick J. Kinsman
1920 Philip Cook
1939 Arthur R. McKinstry
1955 J. Brooke Mosley
1968 William H. Mead

Duluth, Minnesota

Reunited with Minnesota in 1944

1897 James D. Morrison
1922 Granville G. Bennett
1933 Benjamin T. Kemerer

East Carolina

1884 Alfred A. Watson
1905 Robert Strange
1915 Thomas C. Darst
1945 Thomas H. Wright

Eastern Diocese

Included present states of Maine, New Hampshire, Vermont, Massachusetts and Rhode Island; discontinued in 1843

1811 Alexander V. Griswold

Eastern Oklahoma

Reunited with Oklahoma in 1919

1911 Theodore P. Thurston

Eastern Oregon

1907 Robert L. Paddock
1922 William P. Remington
1946 Lane W. Barton
1969 William B. Spofford, Jr.

Easton, Pennsylvania

1869 Henry C. Lay
1887 William F. Adams
1920 George W. Davenport
1939 William McClelland
1949 Allen J. Miller
1966 George A. Taylor

Eau Claire, Wisconsin

1929 Frank E. Wilson
1944 William W. Horstick

Erie, Pennsylvania

1911 Rogers Israel
1921 John C. Ward
1943 Edward P. Wroth
1946 Harold E. Sawyer
1952 William Crittenden

Florida

1851 Francis H. Rutledge
1867 John F. Young
1886 Edwin G. Weed
1924 Frank A. Juhan
1956 Edward H. West
1970 William H. Folwell

Fond du Lac, Wisconsin

1875 J. H. Hobart Brown
1889 Charles C. Grafton
1912 Reginald H. Weller
1933 Harwood Sturtevant
1956 William H. Brady

Georgia

1841 Stephen Elliott
1868 John W. Beckwith
1892 Cleland K. Nelson
1908 Frederick F. Reese
1937 Middleton S. Barnwell
1954 Albert R. Stuart

Harrisburg, Pennsylvania

1905 James H. Darlington
1931 Hunter Wyatt-Brown
1943 John T. Heistand
1956 Earl M. Honaman
1966 Dean T. Stevenson

Honolulu, Hawaii

1902 Henry B. Restarick
1921 John D. LaMothe
1930 Samuel H. Littell
1944 Harry S. Kennedy
1967 Edwin L. Hanchett

Idaho

1867 Daniel S. Tuttle
1887 Ethelbert Talbot
1899 James B. Funsten
1919 Frank H. Touret
1925 Middleton S. Barnwell
1936 Frederick B. Bartlett
1942 Frank A. Rhea
1957 Norman L. Foote

Illinois

See Chicago

Indiana

See Indianapolis

PROTESTANT EPISCOPAL BISHOPS – DIOCESE

Indianapolis, Indiana
Diocese of Indiana until 1902

1835 Jackson Kemper
1849 George Upfold
1872 Joseph C. Talbot
1883 David B. Knickerbacker
1895 John H. White
1899 Joseph M. Francis
1939 Richard A. Kirchhoffer
1959 John P. Craine

Iowa

1854 Henry W. Lee
1876 William S. Perry
1899 Theodore N. Morrison
1929 Harry S. Longley
1944 Elwood L. Haines
1950 Gordon V. Smith

Kansas

1864 Thomas H. Vail
1889 Elisha S. Thomas
1895 Frank R. Millspaugh
1916 James Wise
1939 Goodrich R. Fenner
1959 Edward C. Turner

Kansas City, Missouri

See West Missouri

Kearney, Nebraska

See Western Nebraska

Kentucky

1832 Benjamin B. Smith
1884 Thomas U. Dudley
1905 Charles E. Woodcock
1936 Charles Clingman
1954 Charles G. Marmion

Lexington, Kentucky

1896 Lewis W. Burton
1929 Henry P. A. Abbott
1945 William R. Moody
1970 Addison Hosea

Long Island

1869 Abram N. Littlejohn
1902 Fredrick Burgess
1925 Ernest M. Stires
1942 James P. DeWolfe
1966 Jonathan G. Sherman

Los Angeles, California

1896 Joseph H. Johnson
1928 William B. Stevens
1948 Francis E. I. Bloy

Louisiana

1841 Leonida Polk
1866 Joseph P. B. Wilmer
1880 John N. Galleher
1891 Davis Sessums
1930 James C. Morris
1940 John L. Jackson
1949 Girault M. Jones
1952 Iveson B. Noland

Maine
Part of Eastern Diocese 1811-1843

1847 George Burgess
1867 Henry A. Neely
1900 Robert Codman
1916 Benjamin Brewster
1941 Oliver L. Loring
1968 Frederick B. Wolfe

Marquette

See Northern Michigan

Maryland

1792 John T. Claggett
1816 James Kemp
1830 William M. Stone
1840 William B. Whittingham
1879 William Pinkney
1885 William Paret
1911 John G. Murray
1929 Edward T. Helfenstein
1944 Noble C. Powell
1963 Harry L. Doll

Massachusetts

1797 Edward Bass
1804 Samuel Parker
1811 See Eastern Diocese
1843 Manton Eastburn
1873 Benjamin H. Paddock
1891 Phillips Brooks
1893 William Lawrence
1927 Charles L. Slattery
1930 Henry K. Sherrill
1947 Norman B. Nash
1966 Anson B. Stokes

Michigan

1836 Samuel A. McCoskry
1879 Samuel S. Harris
1889 Thomas F. Davies
1906 Charles D. Williams
1923 Herman Page
1939 Frank W. Creighton
1946 Richard S. M. Emrich

Michigan City, Indiana

See Northern Indiana

Milwaukee, Wisconsin
Diocese of Wisconsin until 1884

1859 Jackson Kemper
1870 William E. Armitage
1874 Edward R. Welles
1889 Cyrus F. Knight
1891 Isaac L. Nicholson
1906 William W. Webb
1933 Benjamin F. P. Ivins
1952 Donald H. V. Hallock

Minnesota

1859 Henry B. Whipple
1901 Samuel C. Edsall
1917 Frank A. McElwain
1944 Stephen E. Keeler
1956 Hamilton H. Kellogg

Mississippi

1850 William M. Green
1887 Hugh M. Thompson
1903 Theodore DuB. Bratton
1938 William M. Green
1943 Duncan M. Gray
1966 John M. Allin

Missouri

1835 Jackson Kemper
1844 Cicero S. Hawks
1868 Charles F. Robertson
1886 Daniel S. Tuttle
1923 Frederick F. Johnson
1933 William Scarlett
1952 Arthur C. Lichtenberger
1959 George L. Cadigan

Montana

1867 Daniel S. Tuttle
1880 Leigh R. Brewer
1916 William F. Faber
1934 Herbert H. H. Fox
1939 Henry H. Daniels
1957 Chandler W. Sterling
1968 Jackson E. Gilliam

Nebraska

1870 Robert H. Clarkson
1885 George Worthington
1908 Arthur L. Williams
1919 Ernest V. Shayler
1940 Howard R. Brinker
1962 Russell T. Rauscher

Nevada
Diocese divided between Sacramento (Northern California) and Salt Lake (Utah) from 1898 to 1907

1874 Ozi W. Whitaker
1888 Abiel Leonard III
1908 Henry D. Robinson
1914 George C. Hunting
1929 Thomas Jenkins
1942 William F. Lewis
1960 William G. Wright

New Hampshire
Part of Eastern Diocese 1811-1843

1844 Carlton Chase
1870 William W. Niles
1914 Edward M. Parker
1926 John T. Dallas
1948 Charles F. Hall

New Jersey

1815 John Croes
1832 George W. Doane
1859 William H. Odenheimer
1875 John Scarborough
1915 Paul Matthews
1937 Wallace J. Gardner
1955 Alfred L. Banyard

New Mexico and Southwest Texas

1880 George K. Dunlop
1889 John M. Kendrick
1914 Frederick B. Howden
1942 James M. Stoney
1956 Charles J. Kinsolving III

New York

1787 Samuel Provoost
1815 Benjamin Moore
1816 John H. Hobart
1830 Benjamin T. Onderdonk
1952 Jonathan M. Wainwright (provisional)
1854 Horatio Potter
1881 Theodore B. Lyman
1887 Henry C. Potter
1908 David H. Greer
1919 Charles S. Burch
1921 William T. Manning
1947 Charles K. Gilbert
1950 Horace W. B. Donegan
1972 Paul Moore, Jr.

PROTESTANT EPISCOPAL BISHOPS – DIOCESE

Newark, New Jersey

Diocese of Northern New Jersey until 1886

1874 William H. Odenheimer
1880 Thomas A. Starkey
1903 Edwin S. Lines
1927 Wilson R. Stearly
1935 Benjamin M. Washburn
1958 Leland Stark

Niobrara

See South Dakota

North Carolina

1823 John S. Ravenscroft
1831 Levi S. Ives
1853 Thomas Atkinson
1893 Joseph B. Cheshire, Jr.
1932 Edwin A. Penick
1959 Richard H. Baker
1965 Thomas A. Fraser, Jr.

North Dakota

1883 William D. Walker
1899 Samuel C. Edsall
1901 Cameron Mann
1914 John P. Tyler
1931 Frederick B. Bartlett
1937 Douglass H. Atwill
1951 Richard R. Emery
1965 George T. Masuda

North Texas

See Northwest Texas

Northern California

Known as Sacramento until 1961

1874 John H. D. Wingfield
1899 William H. Moreland
1933 A. W. Noel Porter
1958 Clarence R. Haden

Northern Indiana

Diocese of Michigan City until 1925

1899 John H. White
1925 Campbell Gray
1944 James R. Mallett
1963 Walter C. Klein

Northern Michigan

Known as Marquette until 1937

1896 Gershom M. Williams
1919 Robert LeR. Harris
1930 Hayward S. Ablewhite
1942 Herman R. Page
1964 George R. Selway

Northern New Jersey

See Newark

Northern Texas

See Dallas

Northwest

Diocese discontinued in 1865

1860 Joseph C. Talbot

Northwest Texas

Name changed from North Texas in 1958

1910 Edward A. Temple
1925 Eugene C. Seaman
1946 George H. Quarterman

Ohio

1819 Philander Chase
1832 Charles P. McIlvaine
1873 Gregory T. Bedell
1889 William A. Leonard
1930 Warren L. Rogers
1938 Beverley D. Tucker
1952 Nelson M. Burroughs
1968 John H. Burt

Oklahoma

1893 Francis K. Brooke
1919 Theodore P. Thurston
1927 Thomas Casady
1951 Chilton Powell

Olympia, Washington

Diocese of Oregon and Washington Territory until 1880; Washington Territory until 1892

1854 Thomas F. Scott
1868 Benjamin W. Morris
1880 John A. Paddock
1894 William M. Barker
1902 Frederick W. Keator
1925 Simeon A. Huston
1947 Stephen F. Bayne, Jr.
1960 William F. Lewis
1964 Ivol I. Curtis

Oregon

Diocese of Oregon and Washington Territory until 1880

1854 Thomas F. Scott
1889 Benjamin W. Morris 2d
1906 Charles Scadding
1915 Walter T. Sumner
1936 Benjamin D. Dagwell
1958 James F. W. Carman

Oregon and Washington Territory

See Olympia, Oregon

Panama and The Canal Zone

1920 James C. Morris
1930 Vacant
1937 Harry Beal
1945 Reginald H. Gooden

Pennsylvania

1787 William White
1836 Henry U. Onderdonk
1845 Alonzo Potter
1865 William B. Stevens
1887 Ozi W. Whitaker
1911 Alexander Mackay-Smith
1911 Philip M. Rhinelander
1924 Thomas J. Garland
1931 Francis M. Taitt
1943 Oliver J. Hart
1963 Joseph G. Armstrong
1964 Robert L. DeWitt

Philippines

1901 Charles H. Brent
1920 Gouverneur F. Mosher
1942 Norman S. Binsted
1957 Lyman C. Ogilby

Pittsburgh, Pennsylvania

1866 John B. Kerfoot
1882 Cortlandt Whitehead
1923 Alexander Mann
1944 Austin Pardue
1968 Robert Appleyard

The Platt

See Western Nebraska

Puerto Rico

1902 James H. VanBuren
1913 Charles B. Colmore
1947 Charles F. Boynton
1951 A. Ervine Smith
1965 Francisco Reus-Froylan

Quincy, Illinois

1878 Alexander Burgess
1901 Frederick W. Taylor
1904 M. Edward Fawcett
1936 William L. Essex
1958 Francis W. Lickfield

Rhode Island

See Connecticut, Massachusetts, Eastern Diocese for earlier bishops

1843 John P. K. Henshaw
1854 Thomas M. Clark
1903 William N. McVicker
1911 James DeWolf Perry
1946 Granville G. Bennett
1955 John S. Higgins

Rochester, New York

1931 David L. Ferris
1938 Bartel H. Reinheimer
1950 Dudley S. Stark
1963 George W. Barrett
1970 Robert B. Spears

Sacramento

See Northern California

Salina

See Western Kansas

San Joaquin, California

1911 Louis C. Sanford
1944 Sumner F. D. Walters
1968 Victor M. Rivera

South Carolina

1795 Robert Smith
1812 Theodore Dehon
1818 Nathaniel Bowen
1840 Christopher E. Gadsden
1853 Thomas F. Davis
1871 William B. W. Howe
1894 Ellison Capers
1908 William A. Guerry
1928 Albert S. Thomas
1944 Thomas N. Carruthers
1961 Gray Temple

South Dakota

Diocese of Niobrara until 1883

1873 William H. Hare
1910 Frederick F. Johnson
1912 George Biller, Jr.
1916 Hugh L. Burleson
1931 William B. Roberts
1954 Conrad H. Gesner
1970 Walter H. Jones

South Florida

1892 William C. Gray
1913 Cameron Mann
1932 John D. Wing
1951 Henry I. Louttit
1961 William L. Hargrave

PROTESTANT EPISCOPAL BISHOPS – DIOCESE

Southern Ohio

1875 Thomas A Jaggar
1904 Boyd Vincent
1929 Theodore I. Reese
1931 Henry W. Hobson
1959 Roger W. Blanchard
1971 John M. Krumm

Southern Virginia

1892 Alfred M. Randolph
1918 Beverly D. Tucker
1930 Arthur C. Thomson
1938 William A. Brown
1950 George P. Gunn

Southwest

Included present states of Arkansas, New Mexico, Arizona and the Indian Territory; discontinued in 1865

1859 Henry C. Lay

Southwestern Virginia

1920 Robert C. Jett
1938 Henry D. Phillips
1954 William H. Marmion

Spokane, Washington

1892 Lemuel H. Wells
1915 Herman Page
1924 Edward M. Cross
1954 Russell S. Hubbard
1967 John R. Wyatt

Springfield, Illinois

1878 George F. Seymour
1906 Edward W. Osborne
1917 Granville H. Sherwood
1924 John C. White
1947 Richard T. Loring, Jr.
1948 Charles A. Clough
1962 Albert A. Chambers

Tennessee

1834 James H. Otey
1865 Charles T. Quintard
1898 Thomas F. Gailor
1935 James M. Maxon
1947 Edmund P. Dendridge
1953 Theodore N. Barth
1961 John VanderHorst

Texas

1859 Alexander Gregg
1893 George H. Kinsolving
1928 Clinton S. Quin
1955 John E. Hines
1965 James M. Richardson

Upper South Carolina

1922 Kirkman G. Finlay
1939 John J. Gravatt
1953 Clarence A. Cole
1963 John A. Pinckney

Utah

Diocese of Utah from 1867, and then apparently disçontinued; Diocese of Salt Lake from 1898 to 1907

1867 Daniel S. Tuttle
1888 Abiel Leonard III
1904 Franklin S. Spalding
1914 Paul Jones
1920 Arthur W. Moulton
1946 Stephen C. Clark
1951 Richard S. Watson
1971 E. Otis Charles

Vermont

See Eastern Diocese for period 1811-1832

1832 John H. Hopkins
1868 William H. A. Bissell
1894 Arthur C. A. Hall
1930 Samuel B. Booth
1936 Vedder Van Dyck
1961 Harvey D. Butterfield

Virginia

1790 James Madison
1814 Richard C. Moore
1841 William Meade
1862 John Johns
1876 Francis McN. Whittle
1902 Robert A. Gibson
1919 William C. Brown
1927 Henry St. G. Tucker
1944 Frederick D. Goodwin
1961 Robert F. Gibson, Jr.

Washington, D.C.

1896 Henry Y. Satterlee
1909 Alfred Harding
1923 James E. Freeman
1944 Angus Dun
1962 William F. Creighton

Washington Territory

See Olympia

West Missouri

Diocese of Kansas City from 1904 to 1911

1890 Edward R. Atwill
1911 Sidney C. Partridge
1930 Robert N. Spencer
1950 Edward R. Welles

West Texas

1874 Robert W. B. Elliott
1904 James S. Johnston
1916 William T. Capers
1943 Everett H. Jones
1968 Harold C. Gosnell

West Virginia

1878 George W. Peterkin
1916 William L. Gravatt
1939 Robert E. L. Strider
1955 Wilburn C. Campbell

Western Colorado

Reunited with Colorado in 1919

1893 William M. Barker
1895 Abiel Leonard III
1904 Franklin S. Spalding
1907 Edward J. Knight
1909 Benjamin Brewster
1917 Frank H. Touret

Western Kansas

Known as Salina until 1960

1903 Sheldon M. Griswold
1918 John C. Sage
1921 Robert H. Mize
1943 Shirley H. Nichols
1956 Arnold M. Lewis
1966 William Davidson

Western Massachusetts

1902 Alexander H. Vinton
1911 Thomas F. Davies
1937 William A. Lawrence
1957 Robert M. Hatch
1970 Alexander D. Stewart

Western Michigan

1875 George DeN. Gillespie
1909 John N. McCormick
1937 Lewis B. Wittemore
1953 Dudley B. McNeil
1960 Charles E. Bennison

Western Nebraska

Diocese of The Platt 1889-1898; Laramie 1898-1908; Kearney 1908-1913; reunited with Nebraska 1946

1890 Anson R. Graves
1910 George A. Beecher

Western New York

1839 William H. DeLancey
1865 Arthur C. Coxe
1897 William D. Walker
1918 Charles H. Brent
1929 David L. Ferris
1931 Cameron J. Davis
1948 Lauriston L. Scaife

Western North Carolina

Diocese of Asheville until 1922

1898 Junius M. Horner
1934 Robert E. Gribbin
1948 Matthew G. Henry

Wisconsin

See Milwaukee

Wyoming

1887 Ethelbert Talbot
1907 James B. Funsten
1909 Nathaniel S. Thomas
1929 Elmer N. Schmuck
1936 Winfred H. Zigler
1948 James W. Hunter
1969 David R. Thornberry

THE ROMAN CATHOLIC CHURCH IN AMERICA

Cardinals

Year	*Name*	*City*
1875	John McCloskey	New York
1886	James Gibbons	Baltimore
1911	John M. Farley	New York
1911	William H. O'Connell	Boston
1921	Dennis J. Dougherty	Philadelphia
1924	George W. Mundelein	Chicago
1924	Patrick J. Hayes	New York
1946	John J. Glennon	St. Louis
1946	Samuel A. Stritch	Chicago
1946	Edward A. Mooney	Detroit
1946	Francis J. Spellman	New York
1953	James McIntyre	Los Angeles
1958	Richard J. Cushing	Boston
1958	John F. O'Hara	Philadelphia
1959	Aloisius J. Muench	Fargo
1959	Albert G. Meyer	Chicago
1961	Joseph Ritter	St. Louis
1965	Lawrence Shehan	Baltimore
1967	Francis Brennan	(Roman Curial Official)
1967	Patrick O'Boyle	Washington
1967	John J. Krol	Philadelphia
1967	John P. Cody	Chicago
1969	John F. Dearden	Detroit
1969	John J. Carberry	St. Louis
1969	Terence J. Cooke	New York
1969	John J. Wright	(Roman Curial Official)

Roman Catholic Archbishops by Archdiocese

First inauguration date also indicates year Archdiocese was created

Anchorage, Alaska

1966 Joseph T. Ryan

Atlanta, Georgia

1962 Paul J. Hallinan
1968 Thomas A. Donnellan

Baltimore, Maryland

1808 John Carroll
1815 Leonard Neale
1817 Ambrose Marechal
1828 James Whitfield
1834 Samuel Eccleston
1851 Francis P. Kenrick
1864 Martin J. Spalding
1872 James R. Bayley
1877 James Gibbons
1921 Michael J. Curley
1947 Francis P. Keough
1961 Lawrence Shehan

Boston, Massachusetts

1875 John J. Williams
1907 William H. O'Connell
1944 Richard J. Cushing
1970 Humberto S. Medeiros

Chicago, Illinois

1880 Patrick A. Feehan
1903 James E. Quigley
1915 George W. Mundelein
1939 Samuel A. Stritch
1958 Albert G. Meyer
1965 John P. Cody

Cincinnati, Ohio

1850 John B. Purcell
1883 William H. Elder
1904 Henry Moeller
1925 John T. McNicholas
1950 Karl J. Alter
1969 Paul F. Leibold

Denver, Colorado

1941 Urban J. Vehr
1967 James V. Casey

Detroit, Michigan

1937 Edward A. Mooney
1958 John F. Dearden

Dubuque, Iowa

1893 John Hennessy
1900 John J. Keane
1911 James J. Keane
1930 Francis J. Beckman
1946 Henry P. Rohlman
1954 Leo Binz

Hartford, Connecticut

1953 Henry J. O'Brien
1969 John F. Whealon

Indianapolis, Indiana

1944 Joseph E. Ritter
1946 Paul C. Schulte
1970 George J. Biskup

Kansas City, Kansas

1952 Edward J. Hunkeler
1969 Ignatius J. Strecker

Los Angeles, California

1936 John J. Cantwell
1948 James McIntyre
1970 Timothy Manning

Louisville, Kentucky

1937 John A. Floersh
1967 Thomas J. McDonough

Miami, Florida

1958 Coleman F. Carroll

Milwaukee, Wisconsin

1875 John M. Henni
1881 Michael Heiss
1891 Frederick F. X. Katzer
1903 Sebastian G. Messmer
1930 Samuel A. Stritch
1940 Moses E. Kiley
1953 Albert G. Meyer
1959 William E. Cousins

Newark, New Jersey

1937 Thomas J. Walsh
1953 Thomas A. Boland

ROMAN CATHOLIC ARCHBISHOPS BY ARCHDIOCESE

New Orleans, Louisiana

1850 Anthony Blanc
1861 Jean Marie Odin
1870 Napoleon J. Perche
1883 Francis X. Leray
1888 Francis A. Janssens
1897 Placide L. Chapelle
1906 James H. Blenk
1918 John W. Shaw
1935 Joseph F. Rummel
1964 John P. Cody
1965 Philip M. Hannan

New York, New York

1850 John J. Hughes
1864 John McCloskey
1885 Michael A. Corrigan
1902 John M. Farley
1919 Patrick J. Hayes
1939 Francis J. Spellman
1965 John J. Maguire
1968 Terence J. Cooke

Omaha, Nebraska

1945 James H. Ryan
1948 Gerald T. Bergan
1969 Daniel E. Sheehan

Philadephia, Pennsylvania

1875 James F. B. Wood
1884 Patrick J. Ryan
1911 Edmond F. Predergast
1918 Dennis J. Dougherty
1951 John F. O'Hara
1961 John J. Krol

Portland, Oregon

1846 Francis N. Blanchet
1880 Charles J. Seghers
1885 William H. Gross
1889 Alexander Christie
1926 Edward D. Howard
1966 Robert J. Dwyer

St. Louis, Missouri

1847 Perer R. Kenrick
1895 John J. Kain
1903 John J. Glennon
1945 Joseph Ritter
1968 John J. Carberry

St. Paul, Minnesota

1888 John Ireland
1919 John Dowling
1931 John G. Murray
1956 William O. Brady
1962 Leo Binz
1967 Leo C. Byrne

San Antonio, Texas

1926 Jerome Drossaerts
1941 Robert E. Lucey
1969 Francis J. Furey

San Francisco, California

1853 Joseph S. Alemany
1884 Patrick W. Riordan
1915 Edward J. Hanna
1935 John Mitty
1962 Joseph T. McGucken

Santa Fe, New Mexico

1875 John B. Lamy
1885 John B. Salpointe
1894 Placide L. Chapelle
1899 Peter Bourgade
1909 John B. Pitaval
1919 Albert T. Daeger
1933 Rudolph A. Gerken
1943 Edwin V. Byrne
1964 James P. Davis

Seattle, Washington

1951 Thomas A. Connolly

Washington, D.C.

1939 Michael J. Curley
1948 Patrick O'Boyle

ROMAN CATHOLIC BISHOPS BY DIOCESE

First date indicates year in which diocese was created unless otherwise specified

Albany, New York

1847 John McCloskey
1865 John J. Conroy
1877 Francis McNeirny
1894 Thomas M. A. Burke
1915 Thomas F. Cusack
1919 Edmund F. Gibbons
1954 William A. Scully
1969 Edwin B. Broderick

Alexandria, Louisiana

Diocese of Natchitoches 1853-1910

1853 Augustus M. Martin
1877 Francis X. Leray
1885 Anthony Durier
1904 Cornelius Van de Ven
1933 Daniel F. Desmond
1946 Charles P. Greco

Allentown, Pennsylvania

1961 Joseph McShea

Altoona-Johnstown, Pennsylvania

Diocese of Altoona until 1957

1901 Eugene A. Garvey
1920 John J. McCort
1936 Richard T. Guilfoyle
1958 Howard J. Carroll
1960 J. Carroll McCormick
1966 James J. Hogan

Amarillo, Texas

1927 Rudolph A. Gerken
1934 Robert E. Lucey
1941 Laurence J. Fitzsimmons
1958 John L. Morkovsky
1963 Lawrence M. De Falco

Atlanta, Georgia

Part of Savannah-Atlanta 1937-1956; raised to archdiocese 1962

1956 Francis E. Hyland
1962 Paul J. Hallinan

Austin, Texas

1947 Louis J. Reicher

Baker, Oregon

1903 Charles J. O'Reilly
1918 Joseph F. McGrath
1950 Francis P. Leipzig

Baltimore, Maryland

Raised to archdiocese 1808

1789 John Carroll

Baton Rouge, Louisiana

1961 Robert E. Tracy

Beaumont, Texas

1966 Vincent M. Harris

Belleville, Illinois

1888 John Janssen
1913 Henry Althoff
1947 Albert R. Zuroweste

Birmingham, Alabama

See Mobile for earlier bishops

1969 Joseph G. Vath

Bismarck, North Dakota

1910 Vincent Wehrle
1940 Vincent J. Ryan
1952 Lambert A. Hoch
1957 Hilary B. Hacker

Boise, Idaho

1893 Alphonse J. Glorieux
1918 Daniel M. Gorman
1928 Edward J. Kelly
1956 James J. Byrne
1962 Sylvester W. Treinen

Boston, Massachusetts

Raised to archdiocese 1875

1808 John L. de Cheverus
1825 Benedict J. Fenwick
1846 John J. Williams

Bridgeport, Connecticut

1953 Lawrence J. Shehan
1961 Walter W. Curtis

Brooklyn, New York

1853 John Loughlin
1892 Charles E. McDonnell
1921 Thomas E. Molloy
1957 Bryan J. McEntegart
1968 Francis J. Mugavaro

Buffalo, New York

1847 John Timon
1868 Stephen V. Ryan
1897 James E. Quigley
1903 Charles H. Colton
1915 Dennis J. Dougherty
1919 William Turner
1937 John A. Duffy
1944 John F. O'Hara
1952 Joseph A. Burke
1963 James A. McNulty

Burlington, Vermont

1853 Louis J. DeGoesbriand
1892 John S. Michaud
1910 Joseph J. Rice
1938 Matthew F. Brady
1945 Edward F. Ryan
1957 Robert F. Joyce

Camden, New Jersey

1937 Bartholomew J. Eustace
1957 Justin J. McCarthy
1960 Celestine J. Damiano
1968 George H. Guilfoyle

Charleston, South Carolina

1820 John England
1843 Ignatius A. Reynolds
1857 Patrick N. Lynch
1883 Henry P. Northrop
1916 William T. Russell
1927 Emmet M. Walsh
1950 John J. Russell
1958 Paul J. Hallinan
1962 Francis F. Reh
1964 Ernest L. Unterkoefler

Cheyenne, Wyoming

1887 Maurice F. Burke
1896 Thomas M. Lenihan
1902 James J. Keane
1912 Patrick A. McGovern
1951 Hubert M. Newell

Chicago, Illinois

Raised to archdiocese 1880

1843 William Quarter
1848 James O. Van de Velde
1854 Anthony O'Regan
1858 James Duggan

Cincinnati, Ohio

Raised to archdiocese 1850

1822 Edward Fenwick
1833 John B. Purcell

Cleveland, Ohio

1847 Amadeus Rappe
1872 Richard Gilmour
1891 Ignatius F. Horstmann
1909 John P. Farrelly
1921 Joseph Schrembs
1945 Edward F. Hoban
1966 Clarence G. Issenmann

Columbus, Ohio

1868 Sylvester H. Rosecrans
1880 John A. Watterson
1900 Henry Moeller
1904 James J. Hartley
1944 Michael J. Ready
1957 Clarence G. Issenmann
1965 John J. Carberry
1968 Clarence E. Elwell

Corpus Christi, Texas

1913 Paul J. Nussbaum
1921 Emmanuel B. Ledvina
1949 Mariano S. Garriga
1965 Thomas J. Drury

Covington, Kentucky

1853 George A. Carrell
1870 Augustus M. Toebbe
1885 Camillus P. Maes
1916 Ferdinand Brossart
1923 Francis W. Howard
1945 William T. Mulloy
1960 Richard H. Ackerman

Crookston, Minnesota

1910 Timothy Corbett
1938 John H. Peschges
1945 Francis J. Schenk
1960 Laurence A. Glenn
1970 Kenneth J. Povich

Dallas, Texas

Dallas – Fort Worth 1953-1969

1891 Thomas F. Brennan
1893 Edward J. Dunne
1911 Joseph P. Lynch
1954 Thomas K. Gorman
1969 Thomas Tschoepe

Davenport, Iowa

1881 John McMullen
1884 Henry Cosgrove
1906 James Davis
1927 Henry P. Rohlman
1944 Ralph L. Hayes
1966 Gerald F. O'Keefe

ROMAN CATHOLIC BISHOPS BY DIOCESE

Denver, Colorado

Raised to archdiocese 1941

1887 Joseph P. Macheboeuf
1889 Nicholas C. Matz
1917 John H. Tihen
1931 Urban J. Vehr

Des Moines, Iowa

1912 Austin Dowling
1919 Thomas W. Drumm
1934 Gerald T. Bergan
1948 Edward C. Daly
1965 George J. Biskup
1968 Maurice J. Dingman

Detroit, Michigan

Raised to archdiocese 1937

1833 Frederick Rese
1841 Peter P. Lefevre (coadjutor)
1870 Caspar H. Borgess
1888 John S. Foley
1918 Michael J. Gallagher

Dodge City, Kansas

1951 John B. Franz
1960 Marion F. Frost

Dubuque, Iowa

Raised to archdiocese 1893

1837 Peter J. M. Loras
1858 Timothy C. Smyth
1866 John Hennessy

Duluth, Minnesota

1889 James McGolrick
1918 John T. McNicholas
1926 Thomas A. Welch
1960 Francis J. Schenk
1969 Paul F. Anderson

El Paso, Texas

1915 Anthony J. Schuler
1942 Sidney M. Metzger

Erie, Pennsylvania

1853 Michael O'Connor
1854 Josue M. Young
1869 Tobias Mullen
1899 John E. Fitzmaurice
1920 John M. Gannon
1966 John F. Whealon
1969 Alfred M. Watson

Evansville, Indiana

1944 Henry J. Grimmelsman
1966 Paul F. Leibold
1969 Francis R. Shea

Fairbanks, Alaska

1962 Francis D. Gleeson
1968 Robert L. Whelan

Fall River, Massachusetts

1904 William Stang
1907 Daniel F. Feehan
1934 James E. Cassidy
1951 James L. Connolly

Fargo, North Dakota

Diocese of Jamestown until 1897

1889 John Shanley
1909 James O'Reilly
1935 Aloisius J. Muench
1960 Leo F. Dworchak
1970 Justin A. Driscoll

Fort Wayne-South Bend, Indiana

Diocese of Fort Wayne until 1960

1857 John H. Luers
1872 Joseph Dwenger
1893 Joseph Rademacher
1900 Herman J. Alerding
1925 John F. Noll
1957 Leo A. Pursley

Fort Worth, Texas

Dallas-Fort Worth 1953-1969

1969 John J. Cassata

Fresno, California

1967 Timothy Manning
1969 Hugh A. Donohue

Gallup, New Mexico

1940 Bernard T. Espelage
1969 Jerome J. Hastrich

Galveston-Houston, Texas

Diocese of Galveston until 1959

1847 Jean Marie Odin
1862 Claude M. Dubuis
1892 Nicholas A. Gallagher
1918 Christopher E. Byrne
1950 Wendelin J. Nold

Gary, Indiana

1956 Andrew G. Grutka

Grand Island, Nebraska

Diocese of Kearney until 1917

1913 James A. Duffy
1932 Stanislaus V. Bona
1945 Edward J. Hunkeler
1951 John L. Paschang

Grand Rapids, Michigan

1883 Henry J. Richter
1916 Michael J. Gallagher
1919 Edward D. Kelly
1926 Joseph G. Pinten
1941 Joseph C. Plagens
1943 Francis J. Haas
1954 Allen J. Babcock
1969 Joseph Breitenbeck

Great Falls, Montana

1904 Mathias C. Lenihan
1930 Edwin V. O'Hara
1939 William J. Condon
1968 Eldon B. Schuster

Green Bay, Wisconsin

1868 Joseph Melcher
1875 Francis X. Krautbauer
1886 Frederick X. Katzer
1892 Sebastian G. Messmer
1904 Joseph J. Fox
1915 Paul P. Rhode
1945 Stanislaus V. Bona
1968 Aloysius J. Wycislo

Greensburg, Pennsylvania

1951 Hugh L. Lamb
1960 William G. Connare

Harrisburg, Pennsylvania

1868 Jeremiah F. Shanahan
1888 Thomas McGovern
1899 John W. Shanahan
1916 Philip R. McDevitt
1935 George L. Leech

Hartford, Connecticut

Raised to archdiocese 1953

1843 William Tyler
1850 Bernard O'Reilly
1859 Francis P. MacFarland
1876 Thomas Galberry
1879 Laurence S. McMahon
1894 Michael Tierney
1910 John J. Nilan
1934 Maurice F. McAuliffe
1945 Henry J. O'Brien

Helena, Montana

1884 John B. Brondel
1904 John P. Carroll
1927 George J. Finnegan
1933 Ralph L. Hayes
1936 Joseph M. Gilmore
1962 Raymond G. Hunthausen

Honolulu, Hawaii

1941 James J. Sweeney
1968 John J. Scanlan

Indianapolis, Indiana

Diocese of Vincennes until 1898; raised to archdiocese 1944

1834 Simon G. Brute de Remur
1839 Celestine de la Hailandiere
1847 John S. Bazin
1849 James M. de Saint-Palais
1878 Francis S. Chatard
1918 Joseph Chartrand
1934 Joseph E. Ritter

Jefferson City, Missouri

1956 Joseph M. Marling
1969 Michael F. McAuliffe

Joliet, Illinois

1948 Martin D. McNamara
1966 Romeo Blanchette

Juneau, Alaska

1951 Dermot O'Flanagan
1970 Francis D. Hurley (auxiliary)

Kansas City, Kansas

Diocese of Leavenworth until 1891; Kansas City in Kansas 1891-1897; Leavenworth 1897-1947; raised to archdiocese 1952

1877 Michael L. Fink
1904 Thomas F. Lillis
1910 John Ward
1929 Francis Johannes
1937 Paul C. Schulte
1944 George J. Donnelly
1951 Edward J. Hunkeler

Kansas City-Saint Joseph, Missouri

Diocese of Kansas City until 1956; see also diocese of St. Joseph

1880 John J. Hogan
1913 Thomas F. Lillis
1938 Edwin V. O'Hara
1956 John P. Cody
1961 Charles H. Helmsing

ROMAN CATHOLIC BISHOPS BY DIOCESE

LaCrosse, Wisconsin

1868 Michael Heiss
1881 Kilian C. Flasch
1892 James Schwebach
1921 Alexander J. McGavick
1948 John P. Treacey
1965 Frederick W. Freking

Lafayette, Indiana

1944 John G. Bennett
1957 John J. Carberry
1965 Raymond J. Gallagher

Lafayette, Louisiana

1918 Jules B. Jeanmard
1956 Maurice Schexnayder

Lansing, Michigan

1937 Joseph H. Albers
1965 Alexander M. Zaleski

Leavenworth, Kansas

See Kansas City, Kansas

Lincoln, Nebraska

1887 Thomas Bonacum
1911 John H. Tihen
1918 Charles J. O'Reilly
1924 Francis J. Beckman
1930 Louis B. Kucera
1957 James V. Casey
1967 Glennon P. Flavin

Little Rock, Arkansas

1843 Andrew Byrne
1866 Edward Fitzgerald
1907 John B. Morris
1946 Albert L. Fletcher

Los Angeles, California

Diocese of the Two Californias until 1850; Monterey 1850-1859; Monterey-Los Angeles 1859-1922; Los Angeles-San Diego 1922-1936; raised to archdiocese 1936

1840 Francisco Garcia Diego y Moreno
1850 Joseph S. Alemany
1854 Thaddeus Amat
1878 Francis Mora
1896 George T. Montgomery
1903 Thomas J. Conaty
1917 John J. Cantwell

Louisville, Kentucky

Diocese of Bardstown until 1841; raised to archdiocese 1937

1808 Benedict J. Flaget
1819 John B. M. David
1833 Benedict J. Flaget
1850 Martin J. Spalding
1865 Peter J. Lavialle
1868 William G. McCloskey
1910 Denis O'Donaghue
1924 John A. Floersh

Madison, Wisconsin

1946 William P. O'Connor
1967 Cletus F. O'Donnell

Manchester, New Hampshire

1884 Denis M. Bradley
1904 John B. Delaney
1907 George A. Guertin
1932 John B. Peterson
1944 Matthew F. Brady
1960 Ernest J. Primeau

Marquette, Michigan

Diocese of Sainte-Marie until 1865; Sault Sainte-Marie and Marquette 1865-1937

1857 Frederic Baraga
1869 Ignatius Mrak
1879 John Vertin
1899 Frederick Eis
1922 Paul N. Nussbaum
1935 Joseph C. Plagens
1941 Francis J. Magner
1947 Thomas L. Noa
1968 Charles A. Salatka

Miami, Florida

Raised to archdiocese 1968

1958 Coleman F. Carroll

Milwaukee, Wisconsin

Raised to archdiocese 1875

1843 John M. Henni

Mobile, Alabama

Diocese of Mobile-Birmingham 1954-1969

1829 Michael Portier
1859 John Quinlan
1884 Dominic Manucy
1885 Jeremiah O'Sullivan
1897 Edward P. Allen
1927 Thomas J. Toolen
1969 John L. May

Monterey in California

Monterey-Fresno until 1967; see Los Angeles for earlier bishops

1922 John J. Cantwell (apostolic administrator)
1924 John B. MacGinley
1933 Philip G. Scher
1953 Aloysius J. Willinger
1967 Harry A. Clinch

Nashville, Tennessee

1837 Richard P. Miles
1859 James Whelan
1865 Patrick A. Feehan
1883 Joseph Rademacher
1894 Thomas S. Byrne
1924 Alphonse J. Smith
1936 William L. Adrian
1969 Joseph A. Durwick

Natchez-Jackson, Mississippi

1840 John J. Chanche
1853 James O. Van de Velde
1857 William H. Elder
1881 Francis A. Janssens
1889 Thomas Heslin
1911 John E. Gunn
1924 Richard O. Gerow
1967 Joseph B. Brunini

New Orleans, Louisiana

Diocese of Louisiana and The Two Floridas 1793-1826; raised to archdiocese 1850

1827 Joseph Rosati (apostolic administrator)
1829 Leo R. De Neckere
1835 Anthony Blanc

New Ulm, Minnesota

1958 Alphonse J. Schladweiler

New York, New York

Raised to archdiocese 1850

1808 Richard L. Concanen
1814 John Connolly
1926 John Dubois
1842 John J. Hughes

Newark, New Jersey

Raised to archdiocese 1937

1853 James R. Bayley
1873 Michael A. Corrigan
1881 Winand M. Wigger
1901 John J. O'Connor
1928 Thomas J. Walsh

Norwich, Connecticut

1953 Bernard J. Flanagan
1960 Vincent J. Hines

Oakland, California

1962 Floyd L. Begin

Ogdensburg, New York

1872 Edgar P. Wadhams
1892 Henry Gabriels
1921 Joseph H. Conroy
1939 Francis J. Monaghan
1943 Bryan J. McEntegart
1954 Walter P. Kellenberg
1957 James J. Navagh
1962 Leo R. Smith
1964 Thomas A. Donnellan
1968 Stanislaus Brzana

Oklahoma City and Tulsa, Oklahoma

Diocese of Oklahoma until 1930

1905 Theophile Meerschaert
1924 Francis C. Kelley
1948 Eugene J. McGuinness
1958 Victor J. Reed

Omaha, Nebraska

Raised to archdiocese 1945

1885 James O'Connor
1891 Richard Scannell
1916 Jeremiah J. Harty
1926 Francis J. Beckman (apostolic administrator)
1928 Joseph F. Rummell
1935 James H. Ryan

Orlando, Florida

1968 William Borders

Owensboro, Kentucky

1937 Francis R. Cotton
1961 Henry J. Soenneker

Paterson, New Jersey

1937 Thomas H. McLaughlin
1947 Thomas A. Boland
1953 James A. McNulty
1963 James J. Navagh
1966 Lawrence B. Casey

Peoria, Illinois

Erected 1875

1876 John L. Spalding
1909 Edmund M. Dunne
1930 Joseph H. Schlarman
1952 William E. Cousins
1959 John B. Franz

ROMAN CATHOLIC BISHOPS BY DIOCESE

Philadelphia, Pennsylvania

Raised to archdiocese 1875

1808 Michael F. Egan
1819 Henry Conwell
1942 Francis P. Kenrick
1852 John N. Neumann
1860 James F. B. Wood

Phoeniz, Arizona

1969 Edward A. McCarthy

Pittsburgh, Pennsylvania

1843 Michael O'Connor
1860 Michael Domenec
1876 John Tuigg
1889 Richard Phelan
1904 John F. R. Canevin
1921 Hugh C. Boyle
1950 John F. Dearden
1959 John J. Wright
1969 Vincent M. Leonard

Portland, Maine

Erected 1853

1855 David W. Bacon
1875 James A. Healy
1901 William H. O'Connell
1906 Louis S. Walsh
1925 John G. Murray
1932 Joseph E. McCarthy
1955 Daniel J. Feeney
1969 Peter L. Gerety

Providence, Rhode Island

1872 Thomas F. Henricken
1887 Matthew Harkins
1921 William A. Hickey
1934 Francis P. Keough
1948 Russell J. McVinney

Pueblo, Colorado

1941 Joseph C. Willging
1959 Charles A. Buswell

Raleigh, North Carolina

Erected 1924

1925 William J. Hafey
1937 Eugene J. McGuinness
1945 Vincent S. Waters

Rapid City, South Dakota

Diocese of Lead until 1930

1902 John N. Stariha
1910 Joseph F. Busch
1916 John J. Lawler
1948 William T. McCarty
1969 Harold J. Dimmerling

Reno, Nevada

1931 Thomas K. Gorman
1952 Robert J. Dwyer
1967 Joseph Green

Richmond, Virginia

1820 Patrick Kelly
1822 Ambrose Marechal (apostolic administrator)
1828 James Whitfield (apostolic administrator)
1834 Samuel Eccleston (apostolic administrator)
1841 Richard V. Whelan
1850 John McGill
1872 James Gibbons
1878 John J. Keane
1889 Augustine Van de Vyver
1912 Denis J. O'Connell
1926 Andrew J. Brennan
1945 Peter L. Ireton
1958 John J. Russell

Rochester, New York

1868 Bernard J. McQuaid
1909 Thomas F. Hickey
1929 John F. O'Hern
1933 Edward A. Mooney
1937 James E. Kearney
1966 Fulton J. Sheen
1969 Joseph L. Hogan

Rockford, Illinois

1908 Peter J. Muldoon
1928 Edward F. Hoban
1943 John J. Boylan
1953 Raymond P. Hillinger
1956 Loras T. Lane
1968 Arthur J. O'Neill

Rockville Centre, New York

1957 Walter P. Kellenberg

Sacramento, California

Diocese of Grass Valley until 1886

1868 Eugene O'Connell
1884 Patrick Manogue
1896 Thomas L. Grace
1922 Patrcik J. Keane
1929 Robert J. Armstrong
1957 Joseph T. McGucken
1962 Alden J. Bell

Saginaw, Michigan

1938 William F. Murphy
1950 Stephen S. Woznicki
1969 Francis F. Reh

St. Augustine, Florida

1870 Augustine Verot
1877 John Moore
1902 William J. Kenny
1914 Michael J. Curley
1922 Patrick J. Barry
1940 Joseph P. Hurley
1968 Paul F. Tanner

St. Cloud, Minnesota

1889 Otto Zardetti
1894 Martin Marty
1897 James Trobec
1915 Joseph F. Busch
1953 Peter W. Bartholome
1968 George H. Speltz

St. Joseph, Missouri

Kansas City-St. Joseph after 1956

1868 John J. Hogan
1893 Maurice F. Burke
1923 Francis Gilfillan
1933 Charles H. LeBlond

St. Louis, Missouri

Raised to archdiocese 1847

1826 Joseph Rosati
1843 Peter R. Kenrick

St. Paul, Minnesota

Raised to archdiocese 1888

1850 Joseph Cretin
1859 Thomas L. Grace
1884 John Ireland

St. Petersburg, Florida

1968 Charles McLaughlin

Salina, Kansas

Diocese of Concordia until 1944

1887 Richard Scannell
1891 John J. Hennessey (apostolic administrator)
1898 John F. Cunningham
1919 Francis J. Tief
1938 Frank A. Thill
1957 Frederick W. Freking
1965 Cyril J. Vogel

Salt Lake City, Utah

Diocese of Salt Lake until 1951

1891 Lawrence Scanlan
1915 Joseph S. Glass
1926 John J. Mitty
1932 James E. Kearney
1937 Juane G. Hunt
1960 J. Lennox Federal

San Angelo, Texas

1961 Thomas J. Drury
1966 Thomas Tschoepe
1969 Stephen A. Leven

San Antonio, Texas

Raised to archdiocese 1926

1874 Anthony D. Pellicer
1881 John C. Neraz
1895 John A. Forest
1911 John W. Shaw
1918 Jerome Drossaerts

San Diego, California

1936 Charles F. Buddy
1966 Francis J. Furey
1969 Leo T. Maher

Santa Fe, New Mexico

Raised to archdiocese 1875

1853 John B. Lamy

Santa Rosa, California

1962 Leo T. Maher
1969 Mark J. Hurley

Savannah, Georgia

Diocese of Savannah-Atlanta 1937-1956

1850 Francis X. Gartland
1954 John Barry
1861 Augustin Verot
1870 Ignatius Persico
1873 William H. Gross
1886 Thomas A. Becker
1900 Benjamin J. Keiley
1922 Michael J. Keyes
1935 Gerald P. O'Hara
1960 Thomas J. McDonough
1967 Gerald L. Frey

Scranton, Pennsylvania

1868 William O'Hara
1899 Michael J. Hoban
1928 Thomas C. O'Reilly
1938 William J. Hafey
1954 Jerome D. Hannan
1966 J. Carroll McCormick

Seattle, Washington

Diocese of Nesqually until 1907; raised to archdiocese 1951

1850 Augustine M. A. Blanchet
1879 Aegidius Junger
1896 Edward J. O'Dea
1933 Gerald Shaughnessy
1950 Thomas A. Connolly

ROMAN CATHOLIC BISHOPS BY DIOCESE

Sioux City, Iowa

1902 Philip J. Garrigan
1920 Edmond Heelan
1948 Joseph M. Mueller
1970 Frank Greteman

Sioux Falls, South Dakota

1889 Martin Marty
1896 Thomas O'Gorman
1922 Bernard J. Mahoney
1939 William O. Brady
1956 Lambert A. Hoch

Spokane, Washington

Erected 1913

1914 Augustine F. Schinner
1927 Charles D. White
1955 Bernard J. Topel

Springfield, Illinois

Diocese of Quincy until 1857; Alton until 1923

1853 Peter R. Kenrick (apostolic administrator)
1855 Anthony O'Regan (apostolic administrator)
1857 Henry D. Juncker
1870 Peter J. Baltes
1888 James Ryan
1924 James A. Griffin
1949 William A. O'Connor

Springfield, Massachusetts

1870 Patrick T. O'Reilly
1892 Thomas D. Beaven
1921 Thomas M. O'Leary
1950 Christopher J. Weldon

Springfield-Cape Girardeau, Missouri

1956 Charles Helmsing
1962 Ignatius J. Strecker
1970 William Baum

Steubenville, Ohio

Erected 1944

1945 John K. Mussio

Stockton, California

1962 Hugh A. Donohoe
1969 Merlin J. Guilfoyle

Superior, Wisconsin

1905 Augustine F. Schinner
1913 Joseph M. Koudelka
1922 Joseph G. Pinten
1926 Theodore M. Reverman
1942 William P. O'Connor
1946 Albert G. Meyer
1954 Joseph Annabring
1960 George A. Hammes

Syracuse, New York

1886 Patrick A. Ludden
1912 John Grimes
1923 Daniel J. Curley
1933 James A. Duffy
1937 Walter A. Foery
1970 David F. Cunningham

Toledo, Ohio

Erected 1910

1911 Joseph Schrembs
1921 Samuel A. Stritch
1931 Karl J. Alter
1950 George J. Rehring
1967 John A. Donovan

Trenton, New Jersey

1881 Michael J. O'Farrell
1894 James A. McFaul
1918 Thomas J. Walsh
1928 John J. McMahon
1934 Moses E. Kiley
1940 William A. Griffin
1950 George W. Ahr

Tucson, Arizona

1897 Peter Bourgade
1900 Henry Granjon
1923 Daniel J. Gercke
1960 Francis J. Green

Wheeling, West Virginia

1850 Richard V. Whelan
1875 John J. Kain
1894 Patrick J. Donahue
1922 John J. Swint
1962 Joseph H. Hodges

Wichita, Kansas

Erected 1887

1888 John J. Hennessy
1921 Augustus J. Schwertner
1940 Christian H. Winkelmann
1947 Mark K. Carroll
1967 David M. Maloney

Wilmington, Delaware

1868 Thomas A. Becker
1886 Alfred A. Curtis
1897 John J. Monaghan
1925 Edmond J. Fitzmaurice
1960 Michael Hyle
1968 Thomas Mardaga

Winona, Minnesota

1889 Joseph B. Cotter
1910 Patrick R. Heffron
1928 Francis M. Kelly
1949 Edward A. Fitzgerald
1969 Loras J. Watters

Worcester, Massachusetts

1950 John J. Wright
1959 Bernard J. Flanagan

Yakima, Washington

1951 Joseph P. Dougherty
1969 Cornelius M. Power

Youngstown, Ohio

1943 James A. McFadden
1952 Emmet M. Walsh
1968 James W. Malone

THE UNITED METHODIST CHURCH

The Methodist Church was originally known as the Methodist Episcopal Church in America but in 1844 split into two separate churches – the Methodist Episcopal Church and the Methodist Episcopal Church, South. These churches were reunited in 1939 along with The Methodist Protestant Church to form The Methodist Church.

The United Methodist Church came into being in 1968 as a union of The Methodist Church and The Evangelical United Brethren Church. See further notes below.

Bishops of the Methodist Episcopal Church

1800 Richard Whatcoat
1808 William McKendree
1816 Enoch George
1816 Robert R. Roberts
1824 Elijah Hedding
1824 Joshua Soule
1832 James O. Andrew
1832 John Emory
1836 Thomas A. Morris
1836 Beverly Waugh
1841 Henry Kumler, Jr.
1844 Leonidas L. Hamline
1844 Edmund S. Janes
1845 William Hanby
1852 Edward R. Ames
1852 Osmon C. Baker
1852 Levi Scott
1852 Matthew Simpson
1858 Francis Burns
1864 Davis W. Clark
1864 Calvin Kingsley
1864 Edward Thomson
1866 John W. Roberts
1872 Edward G. Andrews
1872 Thomas Bowman
1872 Randolph S. Foster
1872 William L. Harris
1872 Gilbert Haven
1872 Stephen M. Merrill
1872 Jesse T. Peck
1872 Isaac W. Wiley
1880 Cyrus D. Foss
1880 Erastus O. Haven
1880 John F. Hurst
1880 Henry W. Warren
1884 Charles H. Fowler
1884 Willard F. Mallalieu
1884 William X. Ninde
1884 William Taylor
1884 John M. Walden
1888 Daniel A. Goodsell
1888 Isaac W. Joyce
1888 John P. Newman
1888 James M. Thoburn
1888 John H. Vincent
1890 Oscar P. Fitzgerald
1896 Earl Cranston
1896 Charles C. McCabe
1900 John W. Hamilton
1900 David H. Moore
1900 Edwin W. Parker
1900 Frank W. Warne
1902 Henry Hartzler
1904 James W. Bashford
1904 Joseph F. Berry
1904 William Burt
1904 Merriman C. Harris
1904 William F. McDowell
1904 Thomas B. Neely
1904 William F. Oldham
1904 John E. Robinson
1904 Isaiah B. Scott
1904 Henry Spellmeyer
1904 Luther B. Wilson
1908 William F. Anderson
1908 Frank M. Bristol
1908 Edwin H. Hughes
1908 Wilson S. Lewis
1908 Robert McIntyre
1908 John L. Nuelson
1908 William A. Quayle
1908 Charles W. Smith
1912 Richard J. Cooke
1912 William P. Eveland
1912 Theodore S. Henderson
1912 Frederick D. Leete
1912 Naphtali Luccock
1912 Francis J. McConnell
1912 John W. Robinson
1912 William O. Shepard
1912 Homer C. Stuntz
1912 Wilbur P. Thirkield
1916 Alexander P. Camphor
1916 Franklin Hamilton
1916 Matthew S. Hughes
1916 Eben S. Johnson
1916 Adna W. Leonard
1916 Charles B. Mitchell
1916 Thomas Nicholson
1916 Herbert Welch
1920 George H. Bickley
1920 Lauriss J. Birney
1920 Edgar Blake
1920 Charles W. Burns
1920 Matthew W. Clair
1920 Frederick B. Fisher
1920 Robert E. Jones
1920 Frederick T. Keeney
1920 Charles E. Locke
1920 Charles L. Mead
1920 Ernest G. Richardson
1920 H. Lester Smith
1920 Ernest L. Waldorf
1924 Brenton T. Badley
1924 Wallace E. Brown
1924 George R. Grose
1924 Titus Lowe
1924 George A. Miller
1928 James C. Baker
1928 Edwin F. Lee
1928 Raymond J. Wade
1930 John Gowdy
1930 Chi P'ing Wang
1932 Ralph S. Cushman
1932 J. Ralph Magee
1936 Charles W. Flint
1936 Wilbur E. Hammaker
1936 G. Bromley Oxnam
1936 J. Waskom Pickett
1936 Alexander P. Shaw
1936 John M. Springer
1937 Ralph A. Ward
1938 John L. Decell
1938 Ivan Lee Holt
1938 William C. Martin
1938 William W. Peele
1938 Clare Purcell
1938 Charles C. Selecman
1938 William T. Watkins
1939 John C. Broomfield
1939 James H. Straughn

Bishops of the Methodist Episcopal Church, South

1846 William Capers
1846 Robert Paine
1854 John Early
1854 Hubbard R. Kavanaugh
1854 George F. Pierce
1866 David S. Doggett
1866 Enoch M. Marvin
1866 Holland N. McTyeire
1866 William M. Wightman
1870 John C. Keener
1882 John C. Granbery
1882 Robert K. Hargrove
1882 Linus Parker
1882 Alpheus W. Wilson
1886 William W. Duncan
1886 Charles B. Galloway
1886 Eugene R. Hendrix
1886 Joseph S. Key
1888 James N. Fitzgerald
1890 Atticus G. Haygood
1898 Warren A. Candler
1898 Henry C. Morrison
1902 E. Embree Hoss
1902 A. Coke Smith
1906 James Atkins
1906 John J. Tigert
1906 Seth Ward
1910 Collins Denny
1910 John C. Kilgo
1910 Walter R. Lambuth
1910 James H. McCoy
1910 Edwin D. Mouzon
1910 William B. Murrah
1918 William N. Ainsworth
1918 James Cannon, Jr.
1918 Urban V. W. Darlington
1918 Horace M. DuBose
1918 John F. McMurry
1918 John M. Moore
1922 William B. Beauchamp
1922 Hiram A. Boaz
1922 James E. Dickey
1922 Hoyt M. Dobbs
1922 Sam R. Hay
1930 Paul B. Kern
1930 Arthur J. Moore
1930 A. Frank Smith

The Methodist Protestant Church

There were no bishops of the Methodist Protestant Church from its organization in 1828 until 1939, when Bishops John C. Broomfield and James H. Straughn were elected to represent their church at the union from which The Methodist Church was formed.

Bishops of The Methodist Church

1940 Bruce R. Baxter
1940 William A. C. Hughes
1940 Lorenzo H. King
1941 Carleton Lacy
1941 Clement D. Rockey
1941 Newell S. Booth
1944 Charles W. Brashares
1944 Robert N. Brooks
1944 Fred P. Corson
1944 Paul N. Garber

1944 Schuyler E. Garth
1944 Costen J. Harrell
1944 Lewis O. Hartman
1944 Edward W. Kelly
1944 Willis J. King
1944 W. Earl Ledden
1944 Paul E. Martin
1944 W. Angie Smith
1944 Arthur F. Wesley
1948 J. W. E. Bowen
1948 Dana Dawson
1948 Gerald H. Kennedy
1948 John W. Lord
1948 H. Clifford Northcott
1948 Glenn R. Phillips
1948 Richard C. Raines
1948 Marshall R. Reed
1948 Roy H. Short
1948 Donald H. Tippett
1948 Hazen G. Werner
1948 Lloyd C. Wicke
1949 Sante Uberto Barbieri
1950 Raymond L. Archer
1952 John W. Branscomb
1952 Matthew W. Clair, Jr.
1952 D. Stanley Coors
1952 F. Gerald Ensley
1952 A. Raymond Grant
1952 Edgar A. Love
1952 Frederick B. Newell
1952 Edwin E. Voigt
1952 H. Bascom Watts
1956 Hobart B. Amstutz
1956 Ralph E. Dodge
1956 Eugene M. Frank
1956 Nolan B. Harmon
1956 Bachman G. Hodge
1956 Prince A. Taylor, Jr.
1958 Paul M. Herrick
1960 Ralph T. Alton
1960 Kenneth W. Copeland
1960 Paul V. Galloway
1960 Edwin R. Garrison
1960 Charles F. Golden
1960 Walter C. Gum
1960 Paul Hardin, Jr.
1960 Marquis L. Harris
1960 James W. Henley
1960 Fred G. Holloway
1960 James K. Mathews
1960 W. Vernon Middleton
1960 Noah W. Moore, Jr.
1960 T. Otto Nall
1960 Everett W. Palmer
1960 W. Kenneth Pope
1960 O. Eugene Slater
1960 B. Foster Stockwell
1960 Aubrey G. Walton
1960 W. Ralph Ward
1964 H. Ellis Finger, Jr.
1964 W. Kenneth Goodson
1964 Earl G. Hunt, Jr.
1964 Francis E. Kearns
1964 Dwight H. Loder
1964 Robert F. Lundy
1964 Edward J. Pendergrass
1964 Thomas M. Pryer
1964 W. McFerrin Stowe
1964 R. Marvin Stuart
1964 James S. Thomas
1964 Lance Webb
1967 L. Scott Allen

The union of The Methodist Church and the Evangelical United Brethren Church took place in 1968 and resulted in the creation of The United Methodist Church. The Evangelical United Brethren Church had been formed in 1946 from a consolidation of the Church of the United Brethren in Christ with the Evangelical Church.

Bishops of the Church of the United Brethren in Christ

1800 Martin Boehm
1800 Philip W. Otterbein
1800 Christian Newcomer
1817 Andrew Zeller
1821 Joseph Hoffman
1825 Henry Kumler
1833 William Brown
1833 Samuel Heistand
1837 Jacob Erb
1841 John Coons
1845 Jacob Glossbrenner
1845 John Russell
1849 David Edwards
1853 Lewis Davis
1861 Jacob Markwood
1861 Daniel Shuck
1865 Jonathan Weaver
1869 John Dickson
1877 Nicholas Castle
1877 Milton Wright
1881 Ezekiel Kephart
1885 Daniel Flickinger
1889 James Hott
1893 Job Mills
1902 George Mathews
1905 William Bell
1905 Thomas Carter
1905 William Weekley
1913 Henry H. Fout
1913 Alfred T. Howard
1913 Cyrus J. Kephart
1917 William Washinger
1921 Arthur Clippinger
1925 Arthur Statton
1926 John S. Stamm
1929 Grant D. Batdorf
1929 Ira D. Warner
1941 Fred L. Dennis
1945 J. Balmer Showers

Bishops of the Evangelical Church (Methodist)

1807 Jacob Albright
1839 John Seybert
1843 Joseph Long
1859 William Orwig
1863 John Esher
1871 Reuben Yeakel
1875 Thomas Bowman
1875 Rudolph Dubs
1891 Sylvanus Breyfogel
1891 William Horn
1896 Joseph C. Hartzell
1902 William Heil
1907 Samuel Spreng
1910 William Fouke
1910 Uriah Swengel

Bishops of the Evangelical United Brethren Church

1950 David T. Gregory
1954 Lyle L. Baughman
1954 Harold R. Heininger
1954 Reuben H. Mueller
1957 J. Gordon Howard
1957 Paul E. V. Shannon
1958 H. W. Kaebnick
1958 W. Maynard Sparks
1960 Paul W. Milhouse
1968 Paul A. Washburn

The United Methodist Church was formed in 1968 after a merger between The Methodist Church and the Evangelical United Brethren Church.

Bishops of The United Methodist Church

1968 Arthur J. Armstrong
1968 William R. Cannon
1968 Alsie H. Carleton
1968 Roy C. Nichols
1968 D. Frederick Wertz

THE UNITED PRESBYTERIAN CHURCH IN THE UNITED STATES OF AMERICA

Created by the union in 1958 of the Presbyterian Church in the United States of American and the United Presbyterian Church of North America

Moderators of the Presbyterian Church in the United States of America

From 1838 to 1870 the church was divided between the Old School and the New School factions; moderators of both are listed in this table.

1789 John Witherspoon
1789 John Rodgers
1790 Robert Smith
1791 John Woodhull
1792 John King
1793 James Latta
1794 Alexander McWhorter
1795 John McKnight
1796 Robert Davidson
1797 William M. Tennent
1798 John B. Smith
1799 S. Stanhope Smith
1800 Joseph Clark
1801 Nathaniel Irwin
1802 Azel Roe
1803 James Hall
1804 James F. Armstrong
1805 James Richards
1806 Samuel Miller
1807 Archibald Alexander
1808 Philip Milledoler
1809 Drury Lacy
1810 John B. Romeyn
1811 Eliphalet Nott
1812 Andre Flinn
1813 Samuel Blachford
1814 James Inglis
1815 William Neill
1816 James Blythe
1817 Jonas Coe
1818 Jacob J. Janeway
1819 John H. Rice
1820 John McDowell
1821 William Hill
1822 Obadiah Jennings
1823 John Chester
1824 Ashbel Green
1825 Stephen N. Rowan
1826 Thomas McAuley
1827 Francis Herron
1828 Ezra S. Ely
1829 Benjamin H. Rice
1830 Ezra Fisk
1831 Nathan S. S. Beman
1832 James Hoge
1833 William A. McDowell
1834 Philip Lindsley
1835 William W. Phillips
1836 John Witherspoon
1837 David Elliott
1838 William S. Plumer
Samuel Fisher
1839 Joshua L. Wilson
Baxter Dickinson
1840 William M. Engles
William Wisner
1841 Robert J. Breckenridge
1842 John T. Edgar
1843 Gardiner Spring
Ansel D. Eddy
1844 George Junkin
1845 John M. Krebs
1846 Charles Hodge
Samuel H. Cox
1847 James H. Thornwell
1848 Alexander T. McGill
1849 Nicholas Murray
Philip C. Hay
1850 Aaron W. Leland
David H. Riddle
1851 Edward P. Humphrey
Albert Barnes
1852 John C. Lord
William Adams
1853 John C. Young
Diarca H. Allen
1854 Henry A. Boardman
Thomas H. Skinner
1855 Nathan L. Rice
William C. Wisner
1856 Francis McFarland
Laurens P. Hickok
1857 Cortlandt Van Rensselaer
Samuel W. Fisher
1858 William A. Scott
Matthew L. P. Thompson
1859 William L. Breckenridge
Robert W. Patterson
1860 John W. Yeomans
Thornton A. Mills
1861 J. Chester Backus
Jonathan B. Condit
1862 Charles C. Beatty
George Duffield
1863 John H. Morrison
Henry B. Smith
1864 James Wood
Thomas Brainerd
1865 John C. Lowrie
James B. Shaw
1866 Robert L. Stanton
Samuel M. Hopkins
1867 Phineas D. Gurley
Henry A. Nelson
1868 George W. Musgrave
Jonathan F. Stearns
1869 M. W. Jocobus
Philemon H. Fowler
1870 J. Trumbull Backus
1871 Zephaniah M. Humphrey
1872 Samuel J. Niccolls
1873 Howard Crosby
1874 Samuel J. Wilson
1875 Edward D. Morris
1876 Henry J. Van Dyke
1877 James Eells
1878 Francis L. Patton
1879 Henry H. Jessup
1880 William M. Paxton
1881 Henry Darling
1882 Herrick Johnson
1883 Edwin F. Hatfield
1884 George P. Hays
1885 Elijah R. Craven
1886 David C. Marquis
1887 Joseph T. Smith
1888 Charles L. Thompson
1889 William C. Roberts
1890 William E. Moore
1891 W. Henry Green
1892 William C. Young
1893 Willis G. Craig
1894 S. A. Mutchmore
1895 Robert R. Booth
1896 John L. Withrow
1897 Sheldon Jackson
1898 Wallace Radcliffe
1899 Robert F. Sample
1900 Charles A. Dickey
1901 Henry C. Minton
1902 Henry Van Dyke
1903 Robert F. Coyle
1904 J. Addison Henry
1905 James D. Moffat
1906 Hunter Corbett
1907 William H. Roberts
1908 Baxter P. Fullerton
1909 James M. Barkley
1910 Charles Little
1911 John F. Carson
1912 Mark A. Matthews
1913 John T. Stone
1914 Maitland Alexander
1915 J. Ross Stevenson
1916 John A. Marquis
1917 J. Wilbur Chapman
1918 J. Frank Smith
1919 John W. Baer
1920 Samuel S. Palmer
1921 Henry C. Swearingen
1922 Calvin C. Hays
1923 Charles F. Wishart
1924 Clarence E. Macartney
1925 Charles R. Erdman
1926 William O. Thompson
1927 Robert E. Speer
1928 Hugh K. Walker
1929 Cleland B. McAfee
1930 Hugh T. Kerr
1931 Lewis S. Mudge
1932 Charles W. Kerr
1933 John McDowell
1934 William C. Covert
1935 Joseph A. Vance
1936 Henry B. Master
1937 William H. Foulkes
1938 Charles W. Welch
1939 Sam Higginbottom
1940 William L. Young
1941 Herbert B. Smith
1942 Stuart N. Hutchison
1943 Henry S. Coffin
1944 Roy E. Vale
1945 William B. Lampe
1946 Frederick W. Evans
1947 Wilbur LaRoe, Jr.
1948 Jesse H. Baird
1949 Clifford E. Barbour
1950 Hugh I. Evans
1951 H. Ray Anderson
1952 Hermann N. Morse
1953 John A. Mackay
1954 Ralph W. Lloyd
1955 Paul S. Wright
1956 David W. Proffitt
1957 Harold R. Martin
1958 Harold R. Martin

Moderators of the United Presbyterian Church of North America

1858 John T. Pressly
1859 Peter Bullions
1860 Joseph Clokey
1861 R. D. Harper
1862 J. T. Cooper
1863 A. Young
1864 D. A. Wallace
1865 John B. Clark
1866 David R. Kerr
1867 John B. Dales
1868 James Harper
1869 R. A. Browne
1870 T. S. Kendall
1871 R. A. McAyeal
1872 John S. Easton
1873 John Y. Scouller
1874 John G. Brown
1875 W. W. Barr
1876 James Brown
1877 Robert B. Ewing
1878 S. G. Irvine
1879 William Bruce
1880 E. T. Jeffers
1881 David W. Carson
1882 David Paul
1883 W. H. McMillan
1884 William H. French
1885 William Johnston
1886 John T. Brownlee
1887 Matthew M. Gibson
1888 William T. Meloy
1889 E. S. McKitrick
1890 Andrew Watson
1891 Thomas J. Kennedy
1892 David MacDill
1893 James Bruce
1894 John A. Wilson
1895 J. B. McMichael
1896 James White
1897 Thomas H. Hanna
1898 R. G. Ferguson
1899 William J. Robinson
1900 James P. Sankey
1901 J. A. Thompson
1902 James C. Wilson
1903 James P. Cowan
1904 James W. Witherspoon
1905 William C. Williamson
1906 J. K. McClurkin
1907 William T. Campbell
1908 James G. Carson
1909 D. A. McClenahan
1910 James D. Rankin
1911 John C. Scouller
1912 Hugh H. Bell
1913 R. M. Russell
1914 Joseph Kyle
1915 T. H. McMichael
1916 W. B. Smiley
1917 W. E. McCulloch
1918 W. M. Anderson
1919 James T. McCrory
1920 F. M. Spencer
1921 A. F. Kirkpatrick
1922 J. Kelly Giffen
1923 W. R. Sawhill
1924 Charles H. Robinson
1925 W. I. Wishart
1926 R. A. Hutchison
1927 M. G. Kyle
1928 William A. Spalding
1929 John McNaugher
1930 T. C. Atchison
1931 J. K. Montgomery
1932 Charles S. Cleland
1933 W. B. Anderson
1934 J. Alvin Orr
1935 E. C. McCown
1936 Robert W. Thompson
1937 A. R. Robinson
1938 Ralph Atkinson
1939 H. Walton Mitchell
1940 Homer B. Henderson
1941 R. L. Lanning
1942 Thomas C. Pollock
1943 W. Bruce Wilson
1944 James H. Grier
1945 James M. Ferguson
1946 Lytle R. Free
1947 Samuel A. Fulton
1948 Albert H. Baldinger
1949 Tim J. Campbell
1950 J. Lowrie Anderson
1951 W. Kyle George
1952 James L. Kelso
1953 Samuel C. Weir
1954 Albert E. Kelly
1955 George A. Long
1956 Robert W. Gibson
1957 Robert N. Montgomery
1958 Robert N. Montgomery

Moderators of the United Presbyterian Church in the United States of America

1958 Theophilus M. Taylor
1959 Arthur L. Miller
1960 Herman L. Turner
1961 Paul D. McKelvey
1962 Marshal L. Scott
1963 Silas G. Kessler
1964 Edler G. Hawkins
1965 William P. Thompson
1966 Ganse Little
1967 Eugene Smathers
1968 John C. Smith
1969 George E. Sweazey
1970 William R. Laws, Jr.
1971 Mrs. Ralph M. Stair

THE UNITED CHURCH OF CHRIST

The United Church of Christ was founded in 1957 through a merger of the Evangelical and Reformed Church with the Congregational Christian Church. The Evangelical and Reformed Church had been the result of a merger in 1934 of the Evangelical Synod of North America with the Reformed Church in the U.S. The Congregational Christian Church was founded in 1930 by a merger of the Congregational Church with the American Christian Church.

Moderators of the Congregational Christian Church

1931 Carl S. Patton
Frank G. Coffin
1936 Jay T. Stocking
John V. Sees
1938 Roger W. Babson
1940 Oscar E. Maurer
1942 William E. Sweet
John V. Sees
1944 Ferdinand Q. Blanchard
1946 Ronald Bridges
1948 Albert W. Palmer
1949 Helen Kenyon
1952 Vere V. Loper
1954 Robert Cashman
1956 Albert B. Coe
1958 George B. Hastings

Presidents of the Evangelical and Reformed Church

1934 George W. Richards
1939 Louis W. Goebel
1954 James E. Wagner

The United Church of Christ

Presidents

1957 Fred Hoskins
1957 James E. Wagner
1961 Ben Herbster
1969 Robert V. Moss

Moderators

1957 Louis W. Goebel
1957 George B. Hastings
1959 Frances Kapitzky
1959 Ray E. Phillips
1961 Mrs. George E. Kahlenberg
1961 Ernst Press
1963 Donald Webber
1965 Gerhard W. Grauer
1967 Hollis F. Price
1969 Gibson I. Daniels
1969 Richard C. Pfeiffer

AMERICAN BAPTIST CONVENTION

Northern Baptist Convention until 1950

Presidents

1907 Charles Evans Hughes
1908 Harry P. Judson
1910 Emory W. Hunt
1912 Henry Bond
1914 Edward S. Clinch
1915 Shailer Mathews
1916 Clarence A. Barbour
1917 George W. Coleman
1918 Francis W. Ayer
1919 D. C. Shull
1920 Ernest L. Tustin
1921 Helen Barrett Montgomery
1922 Frederick E. Taylor
1923 Corwin S. Shank
1924 Carl E. Milliken
1925 Edward H. Rhoades, Jr.
1926 J. Whitcomb Brougher
1927 William C. Coleman
1928 Arthur M. Harris
1929 Alton L. Miller
1930 Albert W. Beaven
1931 Mattison B. Jones
1932 C. Oscar Johnson
1933 William S. Abernethy
1934 Avery A. Shaw
1935 James H. Franklin
1936 Herbert B. Clark
1937 Earle V. Pierce
1938 Arthur J. Hudson
1939 Elmir A. Fridell
1940 E. J. Millington
1941 William A. Elliott
1942 Joseph C. Robbins
1944 Mrs. Leslie E. Swain
1946 Edwin T. Dahlberg
1948 Sandford Fleming
1949 Mrs. Howard G. Colwell
1950 Edward H. Pruden
1951 Kenneth S. Latourette
1952 John A. Dawson
1953 Winfield Edson
1954 V. Carney Hargroves
1955 Frank A. Nelson
1956 Harry L. Dillin
1957 Clarence W. Cranford
1958 Mrs. Maurice B. Hodge
1959 Herbert Gezork
1960 C. Stanton Gallup
1961 Warner R. Cole
1962 Benjamin P. Browne
1963 Harold E. Stassen
1964 J. Lester Harnish
1965 Robert G. Torbet
1966 Carl W. Tiller
1967 L. Doward McBain
1968 C. G. Rutenber
1969 Thomas Kilgore, Jr.
1970 Roger L. Fredrikson
1971 Marcus Rohlfs

SOUTHERN BAPTIST CONVENTION

Presidents

1845 William B. Johnson
1851 R. B. C. Howell
1859 Richard Fuller
1863 Patrick H. Mell
1872 James P. Boyce
1880 Patrick H. Mell
1888 James P. Boyce
1889 Jonathan Haralson
1899 William J. Northen
1902 James P. Eagle
1905 E. W. Stephens
1908 Joshua Levering
1911 Edwin C. Dargan
1914 Lansing Burrows
1917 J. B. Gambrell
1921 Edgar Y. Mullins
1924 George W. McDaniel
1927 George W. Truett
1930 William J. McGlothlin
1933 Frederick F. Brown
1934 Monroe E. Dodd
1936 John R. Sampey
1939 Lee R. Scarborough
1941 William W. Hamilton
1944 Pat M. Neff
1947 Louie D. Newton
1949 Robert G. Lee
1952 J. D. Grey
1954 James W. Storer
1956 Casper C. Warren
1958 Brooks Hays
1960 Ramsey Pollard
1962 Herschel H. Hobbs
1964 K. Owen White
1965 W. Wayne Dehoney
1967 H. Franklin Paschall
1969 W. A. Criswell

THE LUTHERAN CHURCHES

The Lutheran Church – Missouri Synod

Presidents

1847 C. F. W. Walther
1850 F. C. D. Wyneken
1864 C. F. W. Walther
1878 H. C. Schwan
1899 Franz Pieper
1911 F. Pfotenhauer
1935 J. W. Behnken
1962 Oliver R. Harms
1969 J. A. O. Preus

United Lutheran Church

Formed in 1918 as a result of a merger involving the separate branches of The Evangelical Lutheran Church.

Presidents

1918 Frederick H. Knubel
1945 Franklin C. Fry

Lutheran Church in America

Formed in 1962 from the consolidation of the Augustana Evangelical Lutheran Church, the Finnish Evangelical Lutheran Church of America, the American Evangelical Lutheran Church, and the United Lutheran Church.

Presidents

1962 Franklin C. Fry
1968 Robert J. Marshall

American Lutheran Church

Formed in 1930 by the merger of the Buffalo, Iowa, and Ohio Synods.

Presidents

1930 C. C. Hein
1937 Emanuel Poppen
1950 Henry F. Schuh
1961 Fredrik A. Schiotz
1971 Kent S. Knutson

CHRISTIAN CHURCH (DISCIPLES OF CHRIST)

Presidents

1849 D. S. Burnet
1850 Alexander Campbell
1867 D. S. Burnet
1868 Richard M. Bishop
1875 Isaac Errett
1877 William K. Pendleton
1878 A. I. Hobbs
1879 W. H. Hopson
1880 Thomas P. Haley
1881 Robert Moffett
1882 B. B. Tyler
1883 D. R. Dungan
1884 A. G. Thomas
1885 L. L. Carpenter
1886 Francis M. Drake
1887 Charles L. Loos
1888 James H. Garrison
1889 Nathaniel S. Haynes
1890 T. M. Phillips
1891 D. R. Ewing
1892 A. M. Atkinson
1893 George Darsie
1894 J. W. Allen
1895 Jabez Hall
1896 J. M. Hardin
1897 M. M. Davis
1898 F. D. Power
1899 W. R. Richardson
1900 W. K. Homan
1901 I. J. Spencer
1902 H. O. Breeden
1903 A. B. Philputt
1904 Zachary T. Sweeney
1905 E. I. Powell
1906 S. M. Copper
1907 George H. Coombs
1908 R. A. Long
1909 Charles S. Medbury
1910 Peter Ainslie
1911 Harry D. Smith
1912 C. M. Chilton
1913 Fred A. Henry
1914 Hill M. Bell
1915 Walter M. White
1916 William F. Richardson
1917 Jesse N. Haymaker
1919 Edgar D. Jones
1920 Raphael H. Miller
1921 George A. Miller
1922 Stephen E. Fisher
1923 T. W. Grafton
1924 Abram E. Cory
1925 Jacob H. Goldner
1926 Andrew D. Harmon
1928 Edward S. Jouett
1929 Harry H. Rogers
1930 Robert A. Long
1931 L. D. Anderson
1932 Homer W. Carpenter
1933 George A. Campbell
1934 William F. Rothenburger
1935 Daniel W. Morehouse
1936 L. N. D. Wells
1937 Alonzo W. Fortune
1938 Frederick D. Kershner
1939 Roger T. Nooe
1941 Harry B. McCormick
1942 William A. Shullenberger
1944 Clarence E. Lemmon
1946 McGruder E. Sadler
1947 Hampton Adams
1948 Roy C. Snodgrass
1949 Frank E. Davison
1950 John A. Tate
1952 Marvin O. Sansbury
1953 Howard T. Wood
1954 Cleveland Kleihauer
1956 Riley B. Montgomery
1957 John Rogers
1958 Cranville T. Walker
1959 John Paul Pack
1960 Loren E. Lair
1961 Perry E. Gresham
1962 Leslie R. Smith
1963 Robert W. Burns
1964 W. A. Welsh
1966 Stephen J. England
1967 Forrest L. Richeson

Moderators

1968 Ronald E. Osborn
1969 Myron C. Cole
1971 James M. Moudy

THE CHURCH OF CHRIST, SCIENTIST

Presidents

1892 E. J. Foster Eddy
1895 Edward P. Bates
1896 Septimus J. Hanna
1898 Albert A. Metcalf
1899 William P. McKenzie
1900 Edward P. Bates
1901 John B. Willis
1902 John W. Reeder
1903 Irving C. Tomlinson
1903 Edward P. Bates
1904 Alfred Farlow
1905 Hermann S. Hering
1906 William P. McKenzie
1906 Willis F. Gross
1907 Eugene H. Greene
1908 John Blish
1909 William P. McKenzie
1910 William D. Baldwin
1911 Clifford P. Smith
1912 James A. Neal
1912 Bliss Knapp
1913 Frederick Dixon
1914 John C. Lathrop
1915 Edward A. Merritt
1916 Calvin A. Frye
1917 William P. McKenzie
1917 William D. McCrackan
1918 Francis J. Fluno
1919 John W. Doorly
1920 Willard P. Emery
1921 Irving C. Tomlinson
1922 Albert F. Gilmore
1923 Charles E. Heitman
1924 Torrance Parker
1925 David N. McKee
1926 Archie E. Van Ostrand
1927 Ella W. Hoag
1928 Frank C. Colby
1929 William W. Davis
1930 Duncan Sinclair
1931 Robert E. Buffum
1932 Ralph O. Brewster
1933 Mary G. Ewing
1934 John M. Brewer
1935 A. Harry Bacon
1936 Frank C. Colby
1936 Elizabeth Tomlinson
1937 Clifford P. Smith
1938 Ralph H. Knapp
1939 George Shaw Cook
1940 Margaret M. G. Matters
1941 John R. Dunn
1942 Elisabeth Norwood
1943 Daisette D. S. McKenzie
1944 Paul S. Seeley
1945 Myrtle Holm Smith
1946 Luther P. Cudworth
1947 Helen Chaffee Elwell
1948 Harry C. Browne
1949 Emma C. Shipman
1950 Walter S. Cross
1951 Lora C. Rathvon
1952 Robert E. Key
1953 Grace F. Cudworth
1954 William R. Knox
1955 Gertrude W. Eiseman
1956 Clifford A. Woodard
1957 Mabel E. Lucas
1958 Leonard T. Carney
1959 Kathryn F. Cook
1960 Arthur W. Eckman
1961 Mary L. G. Nay
1962 Ralph E. Wagers
1963 Helen Wood Bauman
1964 Edward Froderman
1965 Frances S. Wells
1966 Erwin D. Canham
1967 Beatrice T. Pittman
1968 Gordon V. Comer
1969 L. Ivimy Gwalter
1970 Clem W. Collins
1971 Elizabeth Glass Barlow

THE CHURCH OF JESUS CHRIST OF LATTER-DAY SAINTS (MORMON)

Presidents

1832 Joseph Smith
1847 Brigham Young
1880 John Taylor
1889 Wilford Woodruff
1898 Lorenzo Snow
1901 Joseph F. Smith
1918 Heber J. Grant
1945 George A. Smith
1951 David O. McKay
1970 Joseph Fielding Smith

UNION OF ORTHODOX JEWISH CONGREGATIONS OF AMERICA

Presidents

1898 H. Pereira Mendes
1913 Bernard Drachman
1918 Charles H. Shapiro
1920 Julius J. Dukas
1924 Herbert S. Goldstein
1933 William Weiss
1942 Samuel Nirenstein
1949 William B. Herlands
1951 Max Etra
1954 Moses I. Feuerstein
1966 Joseph Karasick

UNION OF AMERICAN HEBREW CONGREGATIONS

Presidents

1873 Morris Loth
1889 Julius Freiberg
1903 Samuel Woolner
1907 Louis J. Goodman
1911 J. Walter Freiberg
1921 Charles Shohl
1925 Ludwig Vogelstein
1934 Jacob W. Mack
1937 Robert P. Goldman
1943 Adolph Rosenberg
1946 Maurice Eisendrath
1973 Alex Schindler

FOUNDERS OF RELIGIOUS SECTS, SOCIETIES, AND MOVEMENTS IN THE UNITED STATES

Title	*Year Founded*	*Founder*
Abyssinian Baptist Church	1809	Thomas Paul
Adventists (Millerites)	1831	William Miller
African Methodist Episcopal Church	1816	Richard Allen
African Orthodox Church	1921	George A. McGuire
Allenites	1774	Henry Allen
Amana Society	1855	Christian Metz
Apostolic Faith	1907	Florence L. Crawford
Black Muslims	1930	Wallace D. Fard
Brethren in Christ (See Christadelphians)		
Brotherhood of the New Life	1861	Thomas L. Harris
Campbellites (See Disciples of Christ)		
Christadelphians	1847	John Thomas
Christian Catholic Church	1893	John A. Dowie
Christian and Missionary Alliance	1881	A. B. Simpson
Christians	1793	James O'Kelly
Church of Christ (Holiness)	1894	C. P. Jones
Church of Christ, Scientist	1879	Mary Baker Eddy
Church of God	1830	John Winebrenner
Disciples of Christ	1827	Alexander Campbell
Dunkards (See German Baptist Brethren)		
Ebenezer Society (See Amana Society)		
Ethical Culture Society	1876	Felix Adler
First Century Christian Fellowship	1921	Frank N. D. Buchman
Freewill Baptists	1780	Benjamin Randall
German Baptist Brethren	1728	Johann C. Beissel
Harmonists	1803	George Rapp
Hicksites	1827	Elias Hicks
Hopedale Community (See Practical Christian Republic)		
House of David	1903	Benjamin Purnell
Independent Christian Universalists	1779	John Murray
Jehovah's Witnesses	1884	Charles T. Russell
Mellannial Church (See Shakers)		
Millerites (See Adventists)		
Moravian Church in the United States	1742	Nicholas Zinzendorf; Augustus G. Spangenberg
Nothingarians	1636	Samuel Gorton
Oneida Community	1848	John H. Noyes
Osgoodites	1848	Jacob Osgood
Oxford Movement (See First Century Christian Fellowship)		
Peace Mission	1915	George Baker (Father Divine)
Peoples Liberal Church	1917	Henry Frank
Perfectionists (See Society of Bible Communists)		
Pillar of Fire Church	1901	Alma B. White
Practical Christian Republic	1842	Adin Ballou
Quakers (See Society of Friends)		
Reformed Mennonites	1912	John Herr
River Brethren	1776	Jacob Engel
Salvation Army	1878	Ballington Booth; Maud Booth
Sandemanians	1765	Robert Sandeman

Separatist Society of Zoar	1817	Joseph M. Bimeler
Shakers	1774	Ann Lee
Society of Bible Communists	1836	John H. Noyes
Society of Friends	1647	George Fox
Spiritualists	1848	Margaret Fox; Kate Fox
Theosophical Society	1875	Helena P. H. Blavatsky
Thomasites (See Christadelphians)		
Unitarian Church	1787	James Freeman
Unity Movement	1914	Charles Fillmore
Universal Brotherhood and Theosophical Society	1897	Katherine Tingley
Universalists	1774	John Murray
Volunteers of America	1896	Ballington Booth; Maud Booth
Wesleyan Methodist Church	1843	Orange Scott
Winebrennians (See Church of God)		
Zoarites (See Separatist Society of Zoar)		

XVI

COMMERCE AND INDUSTRY

A listing of presidents, board chairmen, and/or chief executive officers of 160 corporations, banks, insurance companies, and public utilities in the United States with assets or sales in excess of $1 billion.

The asterisk designates chief executive officer when that post is not specified.

Aetna Life & Casualty

Presidents

1850 Eliphalet A. Bulkeley
1872 Thomas O. Enders
1879 Morgan G. Bulkeley
1922 Morgan B. Brainard
1957 Henry S. Beers
1963 Olcott D. Smith

Board Chairmen

1962 Henry S. Beers
1963 Olcott D. Smith*

Aluminum Company of America (ALCOA)

Presidents

1888 Alfred E. Hunt
1899 Richard B. Mellon
1910 Arthur V. Davis
1928 Roy A. Hunt
1951 I. W. Wilson
1957 Frank L. Magee
1960 Lawrence Litchfield, Jr.
1963 John D. Harper*
1970 W. H. Krome George

Board Chairmen

1928 Arthur V. Davis
1957 I. W. Wilson
1960 Frank L. Magee*
1963 Lawrence Litchfield, Jr.*
1966 Frederick J. Close
1970 John D. Harper

American Airlines Inc.

Presidents

1934 L. D. Seymour
1935 C. R. Smith*
1964 Marion Sadler
1968 George A. Spater*

American Brands, Inc.

Formerly known as the American Tobacco Company.

Presidents

1904 James B. Duke
1912 Percival S. Hill
1925 George W. Hill
1946 Vincent Riggio
1950 Paul M. Hahn
1963 Robert B. Walker
1969 Robert K. Heimann

Board Chairman

1965 Robert B. Walker

American Cyanamid Company

Presidents

1907 Frank S. Washburn*
1922 William B. Bell*
1951 Raymond C. Gaugler*
1952 Kenneth C. Towe*
1957 Wilbur G. Malcolm*
1961 Kenneth H. Klipstein
1965 John Allegaert*
1967 Clifford D. Siverd*
1972 James G. Affleck

Board Chairmen

1957 Kenneth C. Towe
1958 Thomas L. Perkins
1961 Wilbur G. Malcolm*
1967 John Allegaert
1972 Clifford D. Siverd

American Electric Power Company

Presidents

1906 Willard C. Humstone
1907 Henry L. Doherty
1910 R. E. Breed
1923 George N. Tidd
1947 Philip Sporn
1961 Donald C. Cook

American Metal Climax, Inc.

Formed in 1957 from the merger of the American Metal Company, Ltd. and the Climax Molybdenum Company.

Presidents

1957 Hans A. Vogelstein
1959 Walter Hochschild
1960 Frank Coolbaugh
1966 Ian K. MacGregor
1969 Donald J. Donahue

Board Chairmen

1957 Arthur H. Bunker
1960 Walter Hochschild
1965 Frank Coolbaugh
1969 Ian K. MacGregor

American Motors Corporation

Presidents

1916 Charles W. Nash
1932 Earl H. McCarty
1936 George W. Mason
1954 George W. Romney
1962 Roy Abernathy
1967 William V. Luneburg

Board Chairmen

1916 James J. Storrow
1926 Charles W. Nash
1948 George W. Mason
1954 George W. Romney
1962 Richard E. Cross
1966 Robert B. Evans
1967 Roy D. Chapin, Jr.

American National Insurance Company

Presidents

1905 William L. Moody, Jr.*
1955 Mary Moody Northern*
1961 William L. Vogler*
1962 R. A. Furbush
1969 Phil B. Noah*
1971 Glendon E. Johnson

Board Chairmen

1962 William L. Vogler*
1969 R. A. Furbush
1969 Phil B. Noah

American Telephone & Telegraph Company (AT & T)

Presidents

1885 Theodore N. Vail
1887 John E. Hudson
1900 Alexander Cochrane
1901 Frederick P. Fish
1907 Theodore N. Vail
1919 Harry B. Thayer
1925 Walter S. Gifford
1948 Leroy A. Wilson
1951 Cleo F. Craig
1956 Frederick R. Kappel
1961 Eugene J. McNeely
1965 Hakon I. Romnes
1967 Ben S. Gilmer
1970 Hakon I. Romnes
1972 Robert D. Lilley

Board Chairmen

1919 Theodore N. Vail
1956 Cleo F. Craig
1961 Frederick R. Kappel*
1967 Hakon I. Romnes*
1972 John D. deButts

The Anaconda Company

Presidents

1895 James B. A. Haggin
1899 Marcus Daly
1901 William Scanlon
1905 John D. Ryan
1909 Benjamin B. Thayer
1915 John D. Ryan
1918 Cornelius F. Kelly
1940 James R. Hobbins
1949 William H. Hoover
1952 Robert E. Dwyer
1956 Clyde E. Weed
1958 Charles M. Brinckerhoff
1965 C. Jay Parkinson
1969 John G. Hall
1971 John B. M. Place*

Board Chairmen

1919 John D. Ryan
1940 Cornelius F. Kelly
1955 Roy H. Glover
1958 Clyde E. Weed
1969 C. Jay Parkinson
1971 John B. M. Place*

Armco Steel Corporation

Name changed in 1947 from the American Rolling Mill Co.

Presidents

1900 George M. Verity*
1930 Charles R. Hook*
1948 W. W. Sebald*
1956 Ralph L. Gray*
1960 Logan T. Johnston*
1965 C. William Verity, Jr.*

Armour and Company

Presidents

1878 Philip D. Armour
1900 J. Ogden Armour
1923 F. Edson White
1931 T. George Lee
1935 Robert H. Cabell
1939 George A. Eastwood
1947 Frederick W. Specht
1957 William Wood Prince
1961 Edward W. Wilson
1965 Edward J. McAdams
1968 Charles R. Orem
1971 Jess Nicks

Board Chairmen

1923 J. Ogden Armour
1934 Frederick H. Prince
1947 George A. Eastwood
1952 Frederick W. Specht
1961 William Wood Prince*
1970 Gerald H. Trautman*

Atchison, Topeka and Santa Fe Railway Company

Presidents

1895 Edward P. Ripley
1920 William B. Storey
1933 Samuel T. Bledsoe
1939 Edward J. Engel
1944 Fred G. Gurley
1957 Ernest S. Marsh
1967 John S. Reed*

Board Chairmen

1916 to 1918 Walter D. Hines
1920 Edward. P. Ripley
1957 to 1958 Fred G. Gurley*
1967 to 1968 Ernest S. Marsh*

Atlantic Richfield Company

Prior to merger with the Richfield Oil Corporation in 1966 was known as the Atlantic Refining Company. Sinclair Oil Corporation was merged into present company in 1969.

Presidents

1951 Robert H. Colley
1952 Henderson Supplee, Jr.
1964 Thornton F. Bradshaw

Board Chairmen

1952 Robert H. Colley
1964 Henderson Supplee, Jr.*
1965 Robert O. Anderson*

Avco Corporation

Presidents

1929 Graham B. Grosvenor
1930 Frederic G. Coburn
1932 Lucius B. Manning
1937 Victor Emanuel
1945 Irving B. Babcock
1948 Victor Emanuel
1957 Raymond A. Rich
1958 Kendrick R. Wilson, Jr.
1960 James R. Kerr

Board Chairmen

1929 W. Averell Harriman
1932 Erritt L. Cord
1936 Lucius B. Manning
1945 Victor Emanuel
1960 Kendrick R. Wilson, Jr.

Chief Executive Officers

1929 W. Averell Harriman
1932 Erritt L. Cord
1934 Lucius B. Manning
1937 Victor Emanuel
1960 Kendrick R. Wilson, Jr.
1969 James R. Kerr

Bank of America

Name changed in 1930 from Bank of Italy.

Presidents

1904 Antonio Chichizola
1905 Lorenzo Scatena
1915 A. P. Giannini
1924 James A. Bacigalupi
1929 Arnold J. Mount
1932 William F. Morrish
1934 A. P. Giannini
1936 Lawrence M. Giannini
1952 C. F. Wente
1954 S. Clark Beise
1963 R. A. Peterson
1970 A. W. Clausen

The Bank of New York

Merged in 1922 with the New York Life Insurance and Trust Company and in 1966 with the Empire Trust Co.

Presidents

1784 Alexander McDougall
1785 Jeremiah Wadsworth
1786 Isaac Roosevelt
1791 Gulian Verplanck
1799 Nicholas Gouverneur
1802 Herman LeRoy
1804 Matthew Clarkson, Jr.
1825 Charles Wilkes
1832 Cornelius Heyer
1843 John Oothout
1858 Anthony P. Halsey
1863 Charles P. Leverich
1876 Charles M. Fry
1892 E. S. Mason
1901 Herbert L. Griggs
1922 Edwin G. Merrill
1931 John C. Traphagan
1948 Albert C. Simmonds
1963 Samuel H. Wooley*
1971 Elliott Averett

Board Chairmen

1948 Albert C. Simmonds*
1968 Samuel H. Wooley*

Bankers Trust Company

Presidents

1902 Edmund C. Converse
1914 Benjamin Strong
1914 Seward Prosser
1923 A. A. Tilney
1929 Henry J. Cochran
1931 S. Sloan Colt
1957 William H. Moore
1971 Lewis A. Lapham

Board Chairmen

1956 S. Sloan Colt
1957 William H. Moore

Bethlehem Steel Corporation

Presidents

1905 Charles M. Schwab
1916 Eugene G. Grace
1945 Arthur B. Homer
1960 Edmund F. Martin
1963 Stewart J. Cort
1970 Lewis W. Foy

Board Chairmen

1905 Charles M. Schwab
1945 Eugene G. Grace
1960 Arthur B. Homer
1964 Edmund F. Martin
1970 Stewart J. Cort

The Boeing Company

Presidents

1916 William E. Boeing*
1922 E. N. Gott*
1925 William E. Boeing*
1926 P. G. Johnson*
1933 C. L. Egtvedt*
1939 P. G. Johnson*
1945 William M. Allen*
1969 Thornton A. Wilson
1972 Malcolm T. Stamper

Borg-Warner Corporation

Presidents

1928 George W. Borg
1929 Charles S. Davis
1950 Roy C. Ingersoll
1956 Robert S. Ingersoll
1961 Lester G. Porter
1968 James F. Bere

Board Chairmen

1928 Charles S. Davis
1929 George W. Borg
1950 Charles S. Davis
1955 Roy C. Ingersoll
1961 Robert S. Ingersoll
1972 James F. Bere

Burlington Industries, Inc.

Formerly Burlington Mills Corp.

Presidents

1937 J. Spencer Love
1947 John C. Cowan, Jr.
1954 J. Spencer Love
1955 Herman D. Ruhm, Jr.
1957 J. Spencer Love
1962 Charles F. Myers, Jr.*
1968 Ely R. Callaway, Jr.

Board Chairmen

1947 J. Spencer Love
1962 Henry E. Rauch
1968 Charles F. Myers, Jr.*

Burlington Northern Inc.

See also Chicago, Burlington & Quincy Railroad Co., Great Northern Railway Company, & Northern Pacific Railway Company.

Presidents

1970 Louis W. Menk
1971 Robert W. Downing

Board Chairmen

1970 John M. Budd*
1971 Louis W. Menk*

Campbell Soup Company

Presidents

1892 Joseph Campbell
1894 Arthur Dorrance
1914 John T. Dorrance
1930 Arthur C. Dorrance
1946 James McGowan, Jr.
1953 William B. Murphy

Board Chairmen

1914 Arthur Dorrance
1930 George M. Dorrance
1953 James McGowan, Jr.
1956 Oliver G. Willits
1962 John T. Dorrance, Jr.

Carnation Company

Presidents

1899 Elbridge A. Stuart
1932 Elbridge H. Stuart
1957 Alfred M. Ghormley
1963 H. Everett Olson

Board Chairmen

1932 Elbridge A. Stuart
1957 Elbridge H. Stuart
1971 H. Everett Olson

Caterpillar Tractor Co.

Presidents

1925 Raymond C. Force*
1930 B. C. Heacock*
1941 Louis B. Neumiller*
1954 Harmon S. Eberhard
1962 William Blackie
1966 William H. Franklin

Board Chairmen

1954 Louis B. Neumiller*
1962 Harmon S. Eberhard*
1966 William Blackie*

Celanese Corporation

Presidents

1918 Camille Dreyfus
1945 Harold Blancke
1960 K. C. Loughlin
1961 Harold Blancke
1965 John W. Brooks

Chief Executive Officer

1968 John W. Brooks

The Chase Manhattan Bank

Created from the merger in 1955 of the Chase National Bank with the Bank of the Manhattan Company.

Presidents

1955 J. Stewart Baker
1956 George Champion*
1961 David Rockefeller*
1968 Herbert P. Patterson
1972 Willard C. Butcher

Board Chairmen

1955 John J. McCloy
1961 George Champion*
1968 David Rockefeller*

Presidents (Bank of the Manhattan Co.)

1799 Daniel Ludlow
1808 Henry Remsen
1825 John C. Costar
1829 Maltby Galston
1840 Johnathan Thompson
1847 Caleb O. Halsted
1860 James M. Morrison
1879 John S. Harberger
1880 William Henry Smith
1884 DeWitt C. Hays
1893 Stephen Baker
1927 J. Stewart Baker
1929 Park A. Rowley
1932 F. Abbot Goodhue
1948 Lawrence Marshall

Presidents (Chase National Bank)

1877 Samuel C. Thompson
1884 John Thompson
1886 Henry W. Cannon
1904 A. Barton Hepburn
1911 Albert H. Wiggin
1926 John McHugh
1928 Robert L. Clarkson
1929 Charles S. McCain
1930 Winthrop W. Aldrich
1934 H. Donald Campbell
1946 Arthur W. McCain
1949 Percy J. Ebbott

Chemical Bank

New York Chemical Manufacturing Company 1824-1844
Chemical Bank 1844-1865
The Chemical National Bank 1865-1929
Chemical Bank & Trust Company 1929-1954
Chemical Corn Exchange Bank 1954-1959
Chemical Bank New York Trust Company 1959-1969

Presidents

1824 Balthazar P. Melick
1831 John Mason
1839 Isaac Jones
1844 John Quentin Jones
1878 George G. Williams
1903 William H. Porter
1910 Joseph B. Martindale
1917 Herbert K. Twitchell
1920 Percy H. Johnston
1935 Frank K. Houston
1946 N. Baxter Jackson
1947 Harold H. Helm
1956 Isaac B. Grainger
1960 William S. Renchard
1966 Howard W. McCall, Jr.

Board Chairmen

1920 Herbert K. Twitchell
1929 John W. Platten
1930 Percy H. Johnston*
1946 Frank K. Houston*
1947 N. Baxter Jackson*
1956 Harold H. Helm*
1966 William S. Renchard*

Chicago, Burlington & Quincy Railroad Co.

Merged into Burlington Northern Inc., 1970.

Presidents

1857 John Van Nortwick
1865 James F. Joy
1871 James M. Walker
1876 Robert Harris
1878 John M. Forbes
1881 Charles E. Perkins
1901 George B. Harris
1910 Darius Miller
1914 Hale Holden
1918 Charles E. Perkins, Jr.
1920 Hale Holden
1929 Frederick E. Williamson
1932 Ralph Budd
1949 Harry C. Murphy
1965 Louis W. Menk
1966 William J. Quinn

Cities Service Company

Presidents

1910 Henry L. Doherty*
1940 W. Alton Jones*
1953 Burl S. Watson*
1959 J. Edward Warren
1966 Charles S. Mitchell*
1968 J. Edgar Heston

Board Chairmen

1953 W. Alton Jones*
1959 Burl S. Watson*
1966 John L. Burns*
1968 Charles S. Mitchell*
1972 Robert V. Sellers*

The Cleveland Trust Company

Presidents

1895 John G. W. Cowles*
1903 Calvary Morris*
1908 F. H. Goff
1923 Harris Creech
1941 George Gund*
1962 George F. Karch*
1969 Everett W. Smith

Board Chairmen

1903 John G. W. Cowles
1908 Calvary Morris*
1941 I. F. Freiberger
1962 George Gund
1966 George F. Karch*

Chief Executive Officers

1933 Charles Y. Freeman
1961 Willis Gale
1964 Morgan F. Murphy

The Coca-Cola Company

Presidents

1892 Asa G. Candler
1916 Charles H. Candler
1919 Samuel C. Dobbs
1920 Charles H. Candler
1923 Robert W. Woodruff
1939 A. A. Acklin
1945 Robert W. Woodruff
1946 William J. Hobbs
1952 H. Burke Nicholson
1955 William E. Robinson
1958 Lee Talley
1962 J. Paul Austin

Board Chairmen

1919 Charles H. Candler
1920 William C. Bradley
1939 Robert W. Woodruff
1942 Harrison Jones
1952 Robert W. Woodruff
1955 H. Burke Nicholson
1958 William E. Robinson*
1961 Lee Talley*
1970 J. Paul Austin*

Commonwealth Edison Company

Presidents

1907 Samuel Insull
1930 Edward J. Doyle
1951 Willis Gale
1953 John W. Evers
1959 J. Harris Wood
1964 Thomas G. Ayers

Board Chairmen

1930 Samuel Insull
1932 James Simpson
1939 Charles Y. Freeman
1953 Willis Gale
1961 J. Harris Ward

Connecticut Mutual Life Insurance Company

Presidents

1846 Eliphalet A. Bulkeley
1848 James Goodwin
1866 Guy R. Phelps
1869 James Goodwin
1878 Jacob L. Greene
1905 John M. Taylor
1918 Henry S. Robinson
1926 James L. Loomis
1945 Peter M. Fraser
1955 George F. B. Smith
1956 Charles J. Zimmerman*
1967 Edward B. Bates*

Consolidated Edison Company of New York, Inc.

Name changed from Consolidated Gas Company of New York in 1936.

Presidents

1884 Charles Roome
1886 James W. Smith
1894 Harrison E. Gawtry
1909 George B. Cortelyou
1935 Frank W. Smith
1937 Ralph H. Tapscott
1949 Hudson R. Searing
1955 Harland C. Forbes
1957 Charles E. Eble
1966 John V. Cleary
1969 Louis H. Roddis, Jr.

Board Chairmen

1905 Harrison E. Gawtry
1932 Floyd L. Carlisle
1949 Ralph H. Tapscott
1955 Hudson R. Searing
1957 Harland C. Forbes
1966 Charles E. Eble
1967 Charles F. Luce

Consumers Power Company

Presidents

1910 William A. Foote
1915 Bernard C. Cobb
1932 T. A. Kenney
1941 Justin R. Whiting
1951 Daniel E. Karn
1960 James H. Campbell

Board Chairmen

1930 Bernard C. Cobb
1934 Wendell L. Willkie
1940 Justin R. Whiting
1960 Alphonse H. Aymond

Continental Illinois National Bank

Merchants' Savings, Loan and Trust Company until 1923; Illinois Merchants' Trust Company until 1930.

Presidents

1857 John H. Dunham
1862 Henry Farnham
1863 Solomon A. Smith
1879 John Tyrrell
1884 John W. Doane
1898 Orson Smith
1916 Edmund D. Hulbert
1923 John J. Mitchell
1927 Eugene M. Stevens
1932 James R. Leavell
1948 Carl Birdsall
1956 David M. Kennedy
1959 Richard Aishton
1960 Tilden Cummings

Board Chairmen

1930 Arthur Reynolds
1932 Stanley Field
1934 Walter J. Cummings, Sr.
1959 David M. Kennedy
1969 Donald M. Graham

Continental Oil Company

Presidents

1929 Dan Moran
1947 Leonard F. McCollum
1964 Andrew W. Tarkington
1969 John G. McLean

Board Chairmen

1929 Edward T. Wilson
1946 James J. Cosgrove
1963 Charles A. Perlitz, Jr.
1964 Leonard F. McCollum

Crocker-Citizens National Bank

From 1893 to 1956 known as Crocker First National; from 1956 to 1963 Crocker-Anglo National.

Presidents

1893 William H. Crocker
1936 W. W. Crocker
1950 Jerd F. Sullivan, Jr.
1956 Paul A. Hoover
1962 Emmett G. Solomon*
1968 Joseph F. Hogan
1970 Leslie C. Peacock

Board Chairmen

1936 William H. Crocker
1937 James K. Moffitt
1950 W. W. Crocker
1963 Paul A. Hoover
1968 Emmett G. Solomon*

Deere & Company

Presidents

1869 John Deere
1886 Charles H. Deere
1907 William Butterworth
1928 Charles Deere Wiman
1942 Burton F. Peek
1944 Charles Deere Wiman
1955 William A. Hewitt
1964 Ellwood F. Curtis

The Detroit Edison Company

Presidents

1903 Charles W. Wetmore
1912 Alex Dow
1940 Alfred C. Marshall
1944 James W. Parker
1951 Walker L. Cisler
1964 Donald F. Kigar
1967 Edwin O. George
1970 William G. Meese

Board Chairmen

1944 Prentiss M. Brown*
1964 Walker L. Cisler*

The Dow Chemical Company

Presidents

1897 Albert E. Convers
1918 Herbert Dow
1930 Willard H. Dow
1949 Leland I. Doan
1962 Herbert D. Doan
1971 C. B. Branch

Board Chairmen

1962 Leland I. Doan
1971 C. B. Branch

Duke Power Company

Name changed from Wateree Electric Company in 1924.

Presidents

1917 James B. Duke
1925 George G. Allen
1949 Edward C. Marshall
1953 Norman A. Cocke
1959 William B. McGuire
1971 Carl Horn, Jr.

Board Chairmen

1949 George G. Allen
1957 William S. O. Robinson, Jr.
1961 Thomas L. Perkins

E. I. du Pont de Nemours & Company

Presidents

1802 Eleuthere Irenne du Pont
1834 Antoine Bidermann
1837 Alfred Victor du Pont
1850 Henry du Pont
1889 Eugene du Pont
1902 T. Coleman du Pont
1915 Pierre S. du Pont
1919 Irenee du Pont
1926 Lammot du Pont
1940 Walter S. Carpenter, Jr.
1948 Crawford H. Greenewalt
1962 Lammot du Pont Copland
1967 Charles B. McCoy

Eastern Air Lines Inc.

Presidents

1938 Edward V. Rickenbacker
1953 Thomas F. Armstrong
1959 Malcolm M. MacIntyre
1963 Floyd D. Hall
1970 Samuel I. Higginbottom

Board Chairmen

1953 Edward V. Rickenbacker
1967 Floyd D. Hall

Eastman Kodak Company

Presidents

1884 Henry A. Strong
1919 George Eastman
1925 William G. Stuber
1934 Frank W. Lovejoy
1941 Thomas J. Hargrave
1952 Albert K. Chapman
1960 William S. Vaughn*
1967 Louis K. Eilers
1970 Gerald B. Zornow
1972 Walter A. Fallon

Board Chairmen

1925 George Eastman
1934 William G. Stuber
1941 Frank W. Lovejoy
1945 Perry Wilcox
1952 Thomas J. Hargrave
1962 Albert K. Chapman
1967 William S. Vaughn*
1970 Louis K. Eilers*
1972 Gerald B. Zornow

The Equitable Life Assurance Society of the United States

Presidents

1859 William C. Alexander
1874 Henry B. Hyde
1899 James W. Alexander
1905 Paul Morton
1911 William A. Day
1927 Thomas I. Parkinson
1953 Ray D. Murphy
1957 James F. Oates, Jr.*
1967 J. Henry Smith*
1972 Coy G. Ecklund

Board Chairmen

1958 James F. Oates, Jr.*
1969 J. Henry Smith*
1971 Davidson Sommers
1972 J. Henry Smith

FMC Corporation

Presidents

1929 John D. Crummey
1940 Paul L. Davies
1956 Ernest Hart
1960 James M. Hait
1966 Jack M. Pope

Board Chairmen

1929 William C. Anderson
1940 John D. Crummey
1956 Paul L. Davies
1966 James M. Hait
1971 Benjamin C. Carter

The Fidelity Bank

Presidents

1926 Henry G. Brengle
1938 Marshall M. Morgan
1948 Stanley W. Cousley
1950 Howard C. Peterson*
1961 Carl K. Dellmuth
1971 Samuel H. Ballam, Jr.

Board Chairman

1961 Howard C. Peterson*

The First National Bank of Chicago

Presidents

1863 Edmun Aiken
1867 Samuel M. Nickerson
1891 Lyman J. Gage
1897 Samuel M. Nickerson
1900 James B. Forgan
1916 Frank O. Wetmore
1925 Melvin A. Traylor
1934 Edward E. Brown
1945 Bentley G. McCloud
1950 Homer J. Livingston
1960 Gaylord Freeman

1962 Herbert V. Prochnow
1967 Edward F. Blettner
1969 John E. Drick

Board Chairmen

1916 James B. Forgan
1925 Frank O. Wetmore
1945 Edward E. Brown
1960 Homer J. Livingston
1969 Gaylord Freeman

Chief Executive Officers

1900 James B. Forgan
1916 Frank O. Wetmore
1930 Melvin A. Traylor
1940 Edward E. Brown
1955 Homer J. Livingston
1969 Gaylord Freeman

First National City Bank

Presidents

1812 Samuel Osgood
1813 William Few
1817 Peter Stagg
1825 Thomas L. Smith
1827 Isaac Wright
1832 Thomas Bloodgood
1843 Gorham A. Worth
1856 Moses Taylor
1882 Percy R. Pyne
1891 James Stillman
1909 F. A. Vanderlip
1919 James A. Stillman
1921 Charles E. Mitchell
1929 Gordon S. Rentschler
1940 William G. Brady, Jr.
1948 Howard C. Sheperd
1952 James S. Rockefeller
1959 George S. Moore
1967 Walter B. Wriston
1970 William I. Spencer

Board Chairmen

1909 James Stillman
1918 James A. Stillman
1921 Eric P. Swenson
1929 Charles E. Mitchell
1933 James H. Perkins
1940 Gordon S. Rentschler
1948 William G. Brady, Jr.
1952 Howard C. Sheperd
1959 James S. Rockefeller
1967 George S. Moore
1970 Walter B. Wriston

The First Pennsylvania Banking and Trust Company

Presidents

1809 Joseph Ball
1812 James Paul
1813 Samuel Hodgdon
1814 Samuel Yorke
1816 Condy Raguet
1819 Jacob Sperry
1822 Robert U. Patterson
1826 William Boyd
1827 Thomas Astley
1837 Hyman Gratz
1857 Charles Dutilh
1873 Lindley Smyth
1893 Henry N. Paul
1899 C. S. W. Packard
1934 C. S. Newhall
1938 William F. Kurtz
1952 William L. Day
1955 William F. Kelly
1965 William B. Walker
1968 John R. Bunting

Board Chairmen

1952 William F. Kurtz
1955 William L. Day

Ford Motor Company

Presidents

1903 John S. Gray
1906 Henry Ford
1919 Edsel Ford
1943 Henry Ford
1945 Henry Ford II
1960 Robert S. McNamara
1961 John Dykstra
1963 Arjay Miller
1968 Simon E. Knudsen
1969 Lee A. Iacocca

Board Chairman

1960 Henry Ford II

General Dynamics Corporation

Presidents

1952 John Jay Hopkins
1957 Frank Pace, Jr.
1959 Earl D. Johnson
1962 Roger Lewis*
1971 Hilliard W. Page

Board Chairmen

1952 John Jay Hopkins
1959 Frank Pace, Jr.
1962 Roger Lewis
1970 David S. Lewis*

General Foods Corporation

Known as Postum Cereal Inc. before 1930.

Presidents

1924 Colby M. Chester
1935 Clarence Francis
1943 Austin S. Igleheart
1954 Charles G. Mortimer
1959 Wayne C. Marks
1962 C. W. Cook
1966 Arthur E. Larkin, Jr.
1972 James L. Ferguson

Board Chairmen

1923 Edward F. Hutton*
1935 Colby M. Chester*
1943 Clarence Francis*
1954 Austin S. Igleheart*
1959 Charles G. Mortimer*
1966 C. W. Cook*

General Mills, Inc.

Presidents

1928 James F. Bell
1934 Donald D. Davis
1943 Harry A. Bullis
1948 Leslie N. Perrin
1952 Charles H. Bell
1961 Edwin W. Rawlings
1967 James P. McFarland
1969 James A. Summer

Board Chairmen

1934 James F. Bell
1948 Harry A. Bullis
1959 Gerald S. Kennedy
1961 Charles H. Bell
1967 Edwin W. Rawlings
1969 James P. McFarland*

General Motors Corporation

Presidents

1916 Benoni Lockwood*
1917 W. C. Durant*
1920 Pierre S. duPont*
1923 Alfred P. Sloan, Jr.*
1937 William S. Knudsen
1940 Charles E. Wilson*
1953 Harlow H. Curtice*
1958 John F. Gordon
1965 James M. Roche
1967 Edward N. Cole

Board Chairmen

1917 Pierre S. du Pont
1929 Lammot du Pont
1937 Alfred P. Sloan, Jr.
1956 Albert Bradley
1958 Frederic G. Donner*
1967 James M. Roche*
1972 Richard Gerstenberg

Getty Oil Company

Prior to 1956 known as the Pacific Western Oil Corp. Acquired the Tidewater Oil Company in 1967.

Presidents

1929 William C. McDuffie
1932 H. P. Grimm
1937 William G. Skelly
1947 D. T. Staples
1948 J. Paul Getty*

Girard Bank

Presidents

1939 James E. Gowen
1948 Geoffrey S. Smith
1959 George H. Brown, Jr.
1966 Stephen S. Gardner
1971 William B. Eagleson, Jr.

Board Chairmen

1948 James E. Gowen
1951 David E. Williams
1954 James E. Gowen
1959 Geoffrey S. Smith
1966 George H. Brown, Jr.
1971 Stephen S. Gardner

The B. F. Goodrich Company

Presidents

1880 B. F. Goodrich
1888 G. T. Perkins
1907 Bertram G. Work
1927 Harry Hough
1928 James D. Tew
1937 Samuel B. Robertson
1939 John L. Collyer
1954 William S. Richardson
1957 Jefferson W. Keener
1967 Harry B. Warner

Board Chairmen

1880 B. F. Goodrich*
1886 G. T. Perkins*
1912 F. A. Hardy
1920 Bertram G. Work*
1927 Daivid M. Goodrich*
1950 John L. Collyer*
1967 Jefferson W. Keener*

The Goodyear Tire & Rubber Company

Presidents

1898 D. E. Holl
1899 R. C. Penfield
1903 L. C. Miles
1906 Frank A. Seiberling
1921 E. G. Wilmer
1923 G. M. Stadelman
1926 Paul W. Litchfield
1940 Edwin J. Thomas
1958 Russell DeYoung
1971 Victor Holt, Jr.
1972 Charles J. Pilliod, Jr.

Board Chairmen

1930 P. W. Litchfield*
1958 E. J. Thomas*
1964 Russell DeYoung*

Great Northern Railway Company

Presidents

1888 James J. Hill
1907 Louis W. Hill

1912 Carl R. Gray
1914 Louis W. Hill
1919 Ralph Budd
1932 William P. Kenney
1939 Frank J. Gavin
1951 John M. Budd

Gulf Oil Corporation

Presidents

1901 James M. Guffey
1907 Andrew W. Mellon
1908 W. L. Mellon
1931 J. Frank Drake
1948 Sidney A. Swensrud
1953 William K. Whiteford*
1960 Ernest D. Brockett, Jr.
1965 Bob R. Dorsey

Board Chairmen

1960 William K. Whiteford*
1965 Ernest D. Brockett, Jr.*
1971 Bob R. Dorsey

Honeywell, Inc.

Presidents

1927 Mark C. Honeywell*
1933 Harold W. Sweatt*
1952 Paul B. Wishart*
1960 James H. Binger*
1964 Stephen F. Keating*

Illinois Central Gulf Railroad (IC Industries)

Illinois Central merged with Gulf Mobile and Ohio in 1971.

Presidents

1851 Robert Schuyler
1853 William P. Burrall
1854 John N. A. Griswold
1855 William H. Osborn
1865 John M. Douglas
1871 John Newell
1874 Wilson G. Hunt
1875 John M. Douglas
1877 William K. Ackerman
1883 James C. Clarke
1887 Stuyvesant Fish
1906 James T. Hanrahan
1911 Charles H. Markham
1918 Charles A. Peabody
1919 Charles H. Markham
1926 Lawrence A. Downs
1938 John L. Beven
1945 Wayne A. Johnston
1966 William B. Johnson
1969 Alan S. Boyd

Board Chairmen

1926 Charles H. Markham
1938 Lawrence A. Downs
1966 Wayne A. Johnston
1969 William B. Johnson*
1972 Glenn P. Brock

Inland Steel Company

Presidents

1893 Joseph E. Porter
1898 George H. Jones
1906 Charles Hart
1908 Alexis W. Thompson
1919 Philip D. Block
1941 Wilfred Sykes
1949 Clarence B. Randall
1953 Joseph L. Block
1959 John F. Smith, Jr.
1966 Frederick G. Jaicks

Board Chairmen

1906 Alexis W. Thompson
1919 Leigh E. Block
1940 Edward L. Ryerson
1953 Clarence B. Randall
1959 Joseph L. Block*
1967 Philip D. Block, Jr.*

International Business Machines Corporation (IBM)

Before 1923 known as Computer-Tabulating-Recording Co.

Presidents

1915 Thomas J. Watson
1949 John G. Phillips
1951 Thomas J. Watson, Jr.
1961 Albert L. Williams
1966 T. Vincent Learson
1971 Frank T. Cary

Board Chairmen

1915 George W. Fairchild
1949 Thomas J. Watson
1961 Thomas J. Watson, Jr.
1971 T. Vincent Learson
1972 Frank T. Cary

International Harvester Company

Presidents

1902 Cyrus H. McCormick
1918 Harold F. McCormick
1922 Alexander Legge
1929 Herbert F. Perkins
1931 Alexander Legge
1933 Addis E. McKinstry
1935 Sydney G. McAllister
1941 Fowler McCormick
1946 John L. McCaffrey
1956 Peter V. Moulder
1957 Frank W. Jenks
1962 Harry O. Bercher
1968 Brooks McCormick

Board Chairmen

1904 Charles Deering
1918 Cyrus H. McCormick
1935 Harold F. McCormick
1941 Judson F. Stone
1946 Fowler McCormick
1956 John L. McCaffrey
1968 Harry O. Bercher

John Hancock Mutual Life Insurance Company

Presidents

1862 George P. Sanger
1873 Lafayette A. Lyon
1874 George Thornton
1879 Samuel Atherton
1879 Stephen H. Rhodes
1909 Roland O. Lamb
1921 Walton L. Crocker
1936 Guy W. Cox
1945 Paul F. Clark
1957 Byron K. Elliott
1965 Clyde F. Gay
1966 Robert E. Slater
1970 Frank B. Maher

Board Chairmen

1945 Guy W. Cox
1948 Paul F. Clark*
1963 Byron K. Elliott*
1969 Robert E. Slater*
1970 Gerhard D. Bleicken*

Johnson & Johnson

Presidents

1888 Robert W. Johnson
1910 James W. Johnson
1932 Robert W. Johnson
1938 A. R. Clapham
1942 F. A. Cosgrove (Acting)
1943 George F. Smith
1961 Robert W. Johnson, Jr.
1965 Gustav O. Lienhard
1970 Richard B. Sellars

Board Chairmen

1938 Robert W. Johnson
1963 P. B. Hoffmann*

Kaiser Aluminum & Chemical Corporation

Known as the Permanente Metals Corporation before 1949.

Presidents

1941 Henry J. Kaiser
1959 Donald A. Rhoades
1963 Thomas J. Ready, Jr.
1971 Cornell C. Maier

Board Chairman

1970 Edgar F. Kaiser
1971 Thomas J. Ready, Jr.
1972 Cornell C. Maier

Kennecott Copper Corporation

Presidents

1915 Stephen Birch*
1933 E. T. Stannard*
1950 Charles R. Cox*
1961 Frank R. Milliken*

Kimberly-Clark Corporation

Presidents

1872 John A. Kimberly
1928 Frank J. Sensenbrenner
1942 Cola G. Parker
1953 John R. Kimberly
1959 William R. Kellett
1964 John R. Kimberly
1967 Guy M. Minard
1970 Darwin E. Smith
1972 Harry J. Sheerin

Board Chairmen

1942 Frank J. Sensenbrenner
1953 Cola G. Parker
1955 John R. Kimberly
1970 Guy M. Minard
1972 Darwin E. Smith

Kraftco Corporation

Formerly National Dairy Products Corporation.

Presidents

1923 Thomas H. McInnerney
1941 Leroy A. Van Bomel
1952 E. E. Stewart
1959 J. Huber Wetenhall
1965 Gordon Edwards
1968 W. O. Beers

Board Chairmen

1924 Edward E. Rieck
1925 Loton Horton
1941 Thomas H. McInnerney
1952 Leroy A. Van Bomel
1957 E. E. Stewart
1965 J. Huber Wetenhall
1968 Gordon Edwards

Chief Executive Officers

1941 Thomas H. McInnerney
1942 Leroy A. Van Bomel
1952 E. E. Stewart
1961 J. Huber Wetenhall
1966 Gordon Edwards

Lockheed Aircraft Corporation

Presidents

1932 Lloyd Stearman
1934 Robert E. Gross
1956 Courtlandt S. Gross
1961 Daniel J. Haughton
1967 A. C. Kotchian

Board Chairmen

1933 Robert E. Gross
1961 Courtlandt S. Gross
1967 Daniel J. Haughton

Louisville & Nashville Railroad Company

Presidents

1851 Levin L. Shreve
1854 John L. Helm

1860 James Guthrie
1868 Russell Houston
1868 Horatio D. Newcomb
1874 Thomas Martin
1875 Elisha D. Standiford
1880 Horatio D. Newcomb
1880 Edward Green
1881 Christopher C. Baldwin
1884 Jacob S. Rogers
1884 Milton H. Smith
1886 Eckstein Norton
1891 Milton H. Smith
1921 Wible L. Mapother
1926 Whitefoord R. Cole
1934 James B. Hill
1950 John E. Tilford
1959 William H. Kendall

1891 August Belmont
1903 Henry Walters
1931 Lyman Delano
1944 Frederick B. Adams
1948 A. L. M. Wiggins

McDonnell Douglas Corporation

McDonnell Aircraft merged with Douglas Aircraft in 1967.

Presidents

1939 James S. McDonnell
1962 David S. Lewis
1970 James S. McDonnell

Board Chairman

1939 James S. McDonnell*

Manufacturers National Bank of Detroit

Presidents

1933 John Ballantyne
1938 Henry H. Sanger
1943 Charles A. Kanter
1949 William A. Mayberry
1959 Arthur J. Fushman
1963 Roland A. Mewhort
1969 Dean E. Richardson

Board Chairmen

1943 Henry H. Sanger
1949 Charles A. Kanter
1959 William A. Mayberry
1969 Roland A. Mewhort

Marathon Oil Company

Presidents

1887 H. M. Ernst*
1889 William P. Fleming*
1892 John D. Archbold*
1911 James C. Donnell*
1927 Otto D. Donnell*
1948 James C. Donnell II*

Marine Midland Banks, Inc.

Presidents

1929 George F. Rand*
1942 Charles H. Diefendorf*
1955 Baldwin Maull
1966 J. Fred Schoellkopf IV
1970 Charles A. Winding
1972 Crocker Nevin

Board Chairmen

1955 Charles H. Diefendorf*
1966 Baldwin Maull*
1968 J. Fred Schoellkopf IV*
1970 Charles A. Winding*
1972 John S. Lawson*

Massachusetts Mutual Life Insurance Company

Presidents

1851 Caleb Rice
1873 Ephraim W. Bond
1886 Martin V. B. Edgerly
1895 John A. Hall
1908 William W. McClench
1928 William H. Sargeant
1936 Bertrand J. Perry
1945 Alexander T. Maclean
1950 Leland J. Kalmbach
1962 Charles H. Schaaff
1968 James R. Martin*

The Mead Corporation

Presidents

1930 George H. Mead
1942 Sydney Ferguson
1948 C. R. Van de Carr, Jr.
1952 H. E. Whitaker
1957 Donald F. Morris
1963 George H. Pringle
1968 James W. McSwiney*

Board Chairmen

1937 George H. Mead
1948 Sydney Ferguson
1957 to 1968 H. E. Whitaker*

Metropolitan Life Insurance Company

Presidents

1868 James R. Dow
1871 Joseph F. Knapp
1891 John R. Hegeman
1919 Haley Fiske
1929 Frederick H. Ecker
1936 Leroy A. Lincoln
1951 Charles G. Taylor, Jr.*
1953 Frederic W. Ecker*
1959 Cecil J. North
1963 Gilbert W. Fitzhugh*
1966 Charles A. Siegfried
1969 Richard R. Shinn

Board Chairmen

1936 Frederick H. Ecker
1951 Leroy A. Lincoln
1959 Frederic W. Ecker*
1966 Gilbert W. Fitzhugh*

Minnesota Mining and Manufacturing Company (3M)

Presidents

1902 Henry S. Bryan*
1905 Edgar B. Ober*
1906 Lucius P. Ordway*
1909 Edgar B. Ober*
1929 William L. McKnight*
1949 Richard P. Carlton*
1953 Herbert P. Buetow*
1963 Bert S. Cross*
1966 Harry Heltzer
1970 Raymond H. Herzog

Board Chairmen

1949 William L. McKnight
1966 Bert S. Cross*
1970 Harry Heltzer*

Missouri Pacific Railroad Company

Presidents

1876 Cornelius K. Garrison
1879 Jay Gould
1892 George J. Gould
1911 B. F. Bush
1917 John G. Drew
1917 B. F. Bush
1918 Harry Brouner
1920 B. F. Bush
1923 L. W. Baldwin
1946 Paul J. Neff
1956 R. L. Dearmont
1961 Downing B. Jenks

Monsanto Company

Presidents

1901 John F. Queeny
1919 Gaston DuBois
1923 John F. Queeny
1928 Edgar Monsanto Queeny
1943 Charles Belknap
1945 William McN. Rand
1951 Charles A. Thomas
1960 Charles H. Sommer
1968 Edward J. Bock
1972 Charles H. Sommer
1972 John W. Hanley

Board Chairmen

1939 Edgar Monsanto Queeny
1960 Charles A. Thomas
1965 Edward A. O'Neal, Jr.
1968 Charles H. Sommer

The Mutual Life Insurance Company of New York (MONY)

Presidents

1842 Morris Robinson
1849 Joseph B. Collins
1853 Frederick S. Winston
1885 Richard A. McCurdy
1905 Charles Peabody
1927 David F. Houston
1940 Lewis W. Douglas
1947 Alex E. Patterson
1948 Louis W. Dawson
1959 Roger Hull
1967 J. McCall Hughes

Board Chairmen

1950 Lewis W. Douglas
1959 Louis W. Dawson
1967 Roger Hull

The National Bank of Commerce of Seattle

Presidents

1906 Manson F. Backus
1932 Andrew Price
1948 Maxwell Carlson
1971 T. Robert Faragher*

The National Cash Register Company (NCR)

Presidents

1884 John H. Patterson*
1921 Frederick B. Patterson*
1935 Edward A. Deeds
1940 Stanley C. Allyn
1957 Robert S. Oelman
1964 R. Stanley Laing

Board Chairmen

1931 Edward A. Deeds*
1957 Stanley C. Allyn*
1961 Robert S. Oelman*

National Life Insurance Company

Presidents

1849 William C. Kittredge
1851 Julius Y. Dewey
1877 Charles Dewey
1901 James C. Houghton
1902 Joseph A. DeBoer
1916 Fred A. Howland
1937 Elbert S. Brigham
1948 Ernest M. Hopkins
1950 Deane C. Davis
1966 John T. Fey

Board Chairmen

1937 Fred A. Howland
1950 Ernest M. Hopkins
1965 Deane C. Davis
1969 Robert S. Gillette

New England Mutual Life Insurance Company

Presidents

1843 Willard Phillips
1865 Benjamin F. Stevens
1908 Alfred D. Foster
1924 Daniel F. Appel
1929 George W. Smith
1951 O. Kelley Anderson
1966 Abram T. Collier

Board Chairmen

1924 Alfred D. Foster
1932 George W. Smith
1964 O. Kelley Anderson

Niagara Mohawk Power Corporation

Presidents

1937 John L. Haley
1950 Earle J. Machold
1968 James A. O'Neill

Board Chairmen

1937 Alfred H. Schoellkopf
1941 H. Edmund Machold

North American Rockwell

Known as North American Aviation prior to the merger in 1967 with the Rockwell-Standard Corp.

Presidents

1928 Clement M. Keys
1931 Thomas A. Morgan
1934 James H. Kindelberger
1948 John L. Atwood
1970 Robert Anderson

Board Chairmen

1928 Clement M. Keys
1931 Harold E. Talbot
1932 George N. Armsby
1933 Ernest R. Breech
1942 Henry H. Hogan
1948 James H. Kindelberger
1962 John L. Atwood
1967 Willard F. Rockwell, Jr.

Northern Natural Gas Company

Presidents

1930 William Chamberlain
1933 Louis E. Fischer
1936 F. H. Brooks
1939 Burt R. Bay
1950 John F. Merriam
1960 Willis A. Strauss

Board Chairmen

1930 Clement Studebaker, Jr.
1933 William Chamberlain
1936 Charles S. McCain
1938 J. D. Mortimer
1960 John F. Merriam
1966 Willis A. Strauss

Northern Pacific Railway Company

Merged into Burlington Northern Inc., 1970.

Presidents

1896 Edwin W. Winter
1897 Charles S. Mellen
1903 Howard Elliott
1913 Jule M. Hannaford
1918 Howard Elliott
1920 Jule M. Hannaford
1920 Charles Donnelly
1939 C. E. Denney
1951 Robert S. MacFarlane*
1966 Louis W. Menk

Board Chairman

1966 Robert S. MacFarlane*

The Northern Trust Company

Presidents

1889 Byron L. Smith
1914 Solomon A. Smith
1963 Douglas R. Fuller

Board Chairmen

1914 Solomon A. Smith
1963 Edward Byron Smith

The Northwestern Mutual Life Insurance Company

Presidents

1858 Joseph A. Sleeper*
1858 Henry W. Collins*
1859 Samuel S. Daggett*
1869 Lester Sexton*
1869 John H. Van Dyke*
1874 Henry L. Palmer*
1908 George C. Markham*
1919 William D. Van Dyke*
1932 Michael J. Cleary*
1947 Edmund Fitzgerald*
1958 Donald C. Slichter*
1965 Robert E. Dineen
1968 Francis E. Ferguson

Board Chairmen

1958 Edmund Fitzgerald
1965 Donald C. Slichter*
1968 Robert E. Dineen*

Occidental Petroleum Corporation

Presidents

1956 Dave E. Harris
1957 Armand Hammer*
1968 Thomas F. Willers
1970 William Bellano
1972 Armand Hammer

Board Chairmen

1968 Armand Hammer*

Olin Corporation

Presidents

1954 Thomas S. Nichols
1957 Stanley deJ. Osborne
1963 N. Harvey Collison
1965 Gordon Grand
1972 James F. Towey

Board Chairmen

1954 John M. Olin
1957 Thomas S. Nichols
1963 Stanley deJ. Osborne
1964 N. Harvey Collison
1966 Gordon Grand
1967 G. Keith Funston

Owens-Illinois, Inc.

Presidents

1925 W. H. Boshart
1930 W. E. Levis
1941 J. P. Levis
1950 C. R. Megowen
1961 R. H. Mulford
1968 Edwin D. Dodd

Board Chairmen

1925 William S. Walbridge*
1928 William Ford*
1941 W. E. Levis*
1950 J. P. Levis*
1968 R. H. Mulford*

PPG Industries, Inc.

Formerly known as Pittsburgh Plate Glass Co.

Presidents

1883 Edward Ford
1898 John Pitcairn
1905 William L. Clause
1916 C. W. Brown
1928 Harry S. Wherrett
1941 Robert L. Clause
1944 Harry B. Higgins
1955 David G. Hill
1966 Robinson F. Barker
1968 Joseph A. Neubauer

Board Chairmen

1898 John Pitcairn
1916 William L. Clause
1931 Clarence M. Brown
1955 Harry B. Higgins
1957 E. T. Asplundh
1966 David G. Hill
1968 Robinson F. Barker

Pacific Lighting Corporation

Presidents

1886 James M. Livingston
1898 C. O. G. Miller
1940 Robert W. Miller
1956 Robert A. Hornby
1968 Paul A. Miller

Board Chairmen

1940 to 1952 C. O. G. Miller
1956 to 1967 Robert W. Miller

Pan American World Airways

Presidents

1927 Juan T. Trippe*
1964 Harold E. Gray
1969 Najeeb E. Halaby
1971 William T. Seawell

Board Chairmen

1931 Cornelius V. Whitney
1964 Juan T. Trippe*
1968 Harold E. Gray*
1969 Najeeb E. Halaby*
1972 William T. Seawell*

Penn Mutual Life Insurance Company

Presidents

1847 Daniel L. Miller
1862 James Traquair
1870 Samuel C. Huey
1886 Edward M. Needles
1897 Harry F. West
1906 George K. Johnson
1922 William A. Law
1936 William H. Kingsley
1939 John A. Stevenson*
1949 Malcolm Adam*
1961 Charles R. Tyson*
1971 Frank K. Tarbox

Board Chairmen

1939 William H. Kingsley
1949 William A. Bodine
1961 Malcolm Adam
1971 Charles R. Tyson

J. C. Penney Company, Inc.

Presidents

1913 James C. Penney*
1917 Earl C. Sams*
1946 Albert W. Hughes*
1958 William M. Batten*
1964 Ray H. Jordan
1968 Cecil L. Wright

Board Chairmen

1917 James C. Penney
1946 Earl C. Sams
1950 James C. Penney
1958 Albert W. Hughes
1964 William M. Batten*

Pennzoil United, Inc.

Formed in 1968 from the consolidation of Pennzoil Company and United Gas Corp. Pennzoil was known as the South Penn Oil Company before additional mergers in 1963.

Presidents

1911 Joseph Seep
1919 L. W. Young, Jr.
1932 P. H. Curry
1942 Noel Robinson
1944 George J. Hanks
1953 R. W. Grunert
1955 George J. Hanks
1957 John E. Selden
1962 J. Hugh Liedtke
1967 William C. Liedtke, Jr.

Chief Executive Officers

1955 George J. Hanks
1957 John E. Selden
1962 J. Hugh Liedtke

Phelps Dodge Corporation

Presidents

1909 James Douglas
1917 Walter Douglas
1930 Louis S. Cates
1954 Robert G. Page
1966 George B. Munroe

Board Chairmen

1917 James Douglas
1924 Cleveland H. Dodge
1954 Louis S. Cates
1966 Robert G. Page

Chief Executive Officers

1930 Louis S. Cates
1954 Robert G. Page
1969 George B. Munroe

Philadelphia Electric Company

Chief Executive Officers

1902 Joseph B. McCall
1924 W. H. Johnson
1928 Arthur W. Thompson
1929 John E. Zimmerman
1938 William H. Taylor
1940 John E. Zimmerman
1943 Horace P. Liversidge
1955 Roy G. Rincliffe
1970 Robert F. Gilkeson

The Philadelphia National Bank

Presidents

1803 George Clymer
1813 David Lenox
1818 John Read
1842 Samuel F. Smith
1852 Thomas Robins
1879 Benjamin B. Comegys
1900 N. Parker Shortridge
1907 Levi L. Rue
1926 Joseph Wayne, Jr.
1941 Evan Randolph
1947 Frederick A. Potts
1964 G. Morris Dorrance, Jr.

Board Chairmen

1907 N. Parker Shortridge
1926 Levi L. Rue
1941 Joseph Wayne, Jr.
1947 J. William Hardt
1964 Frederick A. Potts
1969 John McDowell
1970 G. Morris Dorrance, Jr.

Phillips Petroleum Company

Presidents

1917 Frank Phillips
1938 K. S. Adams
1951 Paul Endacott
1962 Stanley Learned
1967 W. W. Keeler
1968 John M. Houchin
1971 W. F. Martin

Board Chairmen

1938 Frank Phillips
1951 K. S. Adams
1968 W. W. Keeler

The Phoenix Insurance Company

Presidents

1854 Nathaniel H. Morgan
1855 Simeon L. Loomis
1863 Henry Kellogg
1891 D. W. C. Skilton
1913 Edward Milligan
1937 George C. Long, Jr.
1951 John A. North
1961 Jack D. Taylor

Phoenix Mutual Life Insurance Company

Presidents

1851 Barzillai Hudson
1852 Benjamin E. Hale
1853 Edson Fessenden
1875 Aaron C. Goodman
1889 Jonathan B. Bunce
1904 John M. Holcombe
1924 Archibald A. Welch
1935 Arthur M. Collens
1948 Benjamin L. Holland
1961 Lyndes B. Stone
1971 Robert J. Jackson

The Procter & Gamble Company

Presidents

1890 William A. Procter
1907 William C. Procter
1930 Richard R. Deupree
1948 Neil H. McElroy
1957 Howard J. Morgens
1971 Edward G. Harness

Board Chairmen

1930 William C. Procter
1948 Richard R. Deupree
1959 Neil H. McElroy
1972 Howard J. Morgens

Provident Mutual Life Insurance Company of Philadelphia

Presidents

1865 Samuel R. Shipley
1905 Asa S. Wing
1931 M. Albert Linton
1953 Thomas A. Bradshaw
1969 Edward L. Stanley

The Prudential Insurance Company of America

Presidents

1875 Allen L. Bassett
1879 Noah F. Blanchard
1881 John F. Dryden
1912 Forrest F. Dryden
1922 Edward D. Duffield
1938 Franklin D'Olier
1946 Carrol M. Shanks
1961 Louis R. Menagh
1962 Orville E. Beal
1969 Donald S. MacNaughton
1970 Kenneth C. Foster

Board Chairman

1970 Donald S. MacNaughton*

Public Service Electric and Gas Company

Presidents

1924 Thomas N. McCarter
1939 Edmund W. Wakelee
1945 George H. Blake
1954 Donald C. Luce
1965 Edwin H. Snyder
1968 Edward R. Eberle
1972 Robert I. Smith

Chief Executive Officers

1924 Thomas N. McCarter
1945 George H. Blake
1954 Lyle McDonald
1958 Donald C. Luce
1965 Watson F. Tait, Jr.
1968 Edwin H. Snyder
1971 Edward R. Eberle

Radio Corporation of America (RCA)

Presidents

1919 Edward J. Nally*
1923 James G. Harbord*
1930 David Sarnoff
1949 Frank M. Folsom
1957 John L. Burns
1961 Elmer W. Engstrom
1966 Robert W. Sarnoff
1972 Anthony L. Conrad

Board Chairmen

1919 Owen D. Young
1930 James G. Harbord
1947 David Sarnoff*
1966 Elmer W. Engstrom*
1970 Robert W. Sarnoff*

Ralston Purina Company

Presidents

1896 William H. Danforth
1932 Donald Danforth
1956 Raymond E. Rowland
1964 R. Hal Dean

Board Chairmen

1932 William H. Danforth
1956 Donald Danforth
1963 Raymond E. Rowland*
1968 R. Hal Dean*

Raytheon Company

Presidents

1948 Charles F. Adams*
1964 Thomas L. Phillips*

Board Chairman

1964 Charles F. Adams

Reynolds Metals Company

Formerly Reynolds Aluminum Co.

Presidents

1928 Richard S. Reynolds, Sr.*
1948 Richard S. Reynolds, Jr.
1963 Joseph H. McConnell

Board Chairmen

1948 to 1955 Richard S. Reynolds, Sr.*
1963 Richard S. Reynolds, Jr.*

R. J. Reynolds Tobacco Company

Became a subsidiary of R. J. Reynolds Industries in 1970.

Presidents

1911 Richard J. Reynolds
1918 William N. Reynolds
1924 Bowman Gray
1931 S. Clay Williams
1934 James A. Gray
1946 James W. Glenn
1948 John C. Whitaker
1952 Edward A. Darr
1957 Bowman Gray, Jr.
1959 F. G. Carter
1960 Alexander H. Galloway
1970 William S. Smith, Jr.

Board Chairmen

1924 William N. Reynolds
1931 Bowman Gray
1935 S. Clay Williams
1949 James A. Gray
1952 John C. Whitaker
1959 Bowman Gray, Jr.
1969 Alexander H. Galloway
1970 Colin Stokes

St. Regis Paper Company

Presidents

1899 George E. Dodge
1901 George W. Knowlton, Jr.
1908 Gordon H. P. Gould
1916 Floyd L. Carlisle
1934 Roy K. Furguson
1957 William R. Adams
1971 William E. Caldwell

Board Chairman

1971 William R. Adams*
1972 George J. Kneeland

Scott Paper Company

Presidents

1900 Arthur H. Scott
1927 Thomas B. McCabe*
1962 Harrison F. Dunning
1968 Charles D. Dickey, Jr.
1971 G. Willing Pepper

Board Chairmen

1962 Thomas B. McCabe
1968 Harrison F. Dunning*
1971 Charles D. Dickey, Jr.

Joseph E. Seagram & Sons, Inc.

Presidents

1933 Julius Kessler
1933 George V. Reilly
1933 W. B. Cleland
1943 Frank R. Schwengel
1957 Edgar M. Bronfman
1971 John Yogman

Sears, Roebuck and Company

Presidents

1886 Richard W. Sears
1908 Julius Rosenwald*
1924 Charles M. Kittle
1928 Robert E. Wood*
1939 Thomas J. Carney
1942 Arthur S. Barrows
1946 Fowler B. McConnell*
1958 Charles H. Kellstadt*
1960 Crowdus Baker
1968 Arthur M. Wood

Board Chairmen

1924 Julius Rosenwald*
1932 Lessing Rosenwald*
1939 Robert E. Wood*
1954 Theodore V. Houser*
1958 Fowler B. McConnell*
1960 Charles H. Kellstadt*
1962 Austin T. Cushman*
1967 Gordon M. Metcalf*

The Signal Companies, Inc.

Presidents

1928 Samuel B. Mosher*
1958 Russell H. Green
1964 Forrest N. Shumway*

Southern California Edison Company

Presidents

1909 John B. Miller*
1918 William A. Brackenridge
1920 John B. Miller*
1928 Russell H. Ballard
1932 George C. Ward
1933 Harry J. Bauer*
1945 William C. Mullendore*
1954 Harold Quinton*
1959 Jack K. Horton*
1968 Thomas M. McDaniel, Jr.

Board Chairmen

1918 John B. Miller*
1932 Harry J. Bauer*
1959 Harold Quinton*
1968 Jack K. Horton*

Southern Pacific Transportation Company

Presidents

1884 Frank H. Davis
1884 William E. Brown
1885 Leland Stanford
1890 Collis P. Huntington
1900 Charles M. Hays
1901 Edward H. Harriman
1909 Robert S. Lovett
1911 William Sproule
1918 Julius Kruttschnitt
1920 William Sproule
1929 Paul Shoup
1932 A. D. McDonald
1941 Armand T. Mercier
1952 Donald J. Russell
1964 Benjamin F. Biaggini

Board Chairmen

1900 Charles H. Tweed
1929 Henry W. deForest
1932 Hale Holden
1964 Donald J. Russell

Southern Railway System

Presidents

1894 Samuel Spencer
1906 W. W. Finley
1913 Fairfax Harrison
1937 Ernest E. Norris
1952 Harry A. DeButts
1962 D. William Brosnan
1967 W. Graham Claytor, Jr.

Sperry Rand Corporation

Formed in 1955 through the consolidation of the Sperry Corporation and Remington Rand, Inc.

Presidents

1955 Harry F. Vickers*
1965 J. Frank Forster
1971 Jean P. Lyet

Board Chairmen

1965 Harry F. Vickers*
1967 J. Frank Forster*

Standard Oil Company (Ohio)

Presidents

1870 John D. Rockefeller
1900 Ambrose M. McGregor
1901 Frank Q. Barstow
1908 Henry M. Tilford
1911 Walter C. Teagle
1911 A. Palmer Coombe
1928 Wallace T. Holliday
1949 Clyde T. Foster
1957 Charles E. Spahr
1970 Alton W. Whitehouse, Jr.

Board Chairmen

1949 Wallace T. Holliday
1950 Armstrong A. Stambaugh
1956 Clyde T. Foster
1970 Charles E. Spahr

Standard Oil Company of California

Presidents

1926 Kenneth R. Kingsbury
1937 William H. Berg
1940 Henry D. Collier
1945 R. Gwin Follis
1948 Theodore S. Petersen
1961 Otto N. Miller
1966 J. E. Gosline
1969 H. J. Haynes

Board Chairmen

1945 Henry D. Collier
1949 R. Gwin Follis
1966 Otto N. Miller

Standard Oil Company (Indiana)

Presidents

1911 William P. Cowan
1918 Lauren J. Drake
1918 William M. Burton
1927 Edward G. Seubert*
1945 Alonzo W. Peake
1955 Frank O. Prior
1958 John E. Swearingen
1965 Robert C. Gunness

Board Chairmen

1918 Robert W. Stewart*
1945 Robert E. Wilson*
1958 Frank O. Prior*
1965 John E. Swearingen*

Standard Oil Company (New Jersey)

Presidents

1882 Henry M. Flagler
1883 James McGee
1885 Paul Babcock, Jr.
1892 Henry M. Flagler
1899 John D. Rockefeller
1911 John D. Archbold
1916 Alfred C. Bedford
1917 Walter C. Teagle
1937 William S. Farish
1943 Ralph W. Gallagher
1944 Eugene Holman
1954 Monroe J. Rathbone
1963 Michael L. Haider
1965 J. Kenneth Jamieson
1969 Milo M. Brisco
1972 Clifton C. Garvin, Jr.

Board Chairmen

1917 Alfred C. Bedford
1925 George H. Jones
1933 William S. Farish
1937 Walter C. Teagle
1942 Ralph W. Gallagher
1946 Frank W. Abrams
1954 Eugene Holman
1960 Leo D. Welch
1963 M. J. Rathbone
1965 M. L. Haider
1969 J. Kenneth Jamieson

State Mutual Life Assurance Company of America

Presidents

1845 John Davis
1854 Isaac Davis
1882 Philip L. Moen
1883 A. George Bullock
1910 Burton H. Wright
1927 Chandler Bullock
1942 George A. White
1951 H. Ladd Plumley
1968 Robert A. Miller
1969 W. Douglas Bell

Board Chairman

1960 H. Ladd Plumley

Sun Oil Company

Presidents

1901 Joseph N. Pew
1912 J. Howard Pew
1947 Robert G. Dunlop
1970 H. Robert Sharbaugh

Board Chairmen

1947 Joseph N. Pew, Jr.
1963 J. Howard Pew
1970 Robert G. Dunlop

Swift & Company

Presidents

1885 Gustavus F. Swift, Sr.
1903 Louis F. Swift
1931 Gustavus F. Swift, Jr.
1937 John Holmes
1955 Porter M. Jarvis
1964 Robert W. Reneker

Board Chairmen

1931 Louis F. Swift
1937 Gustavus F. Swift, Jr.
1955 John Holmes
1964 Porter M. Jarvis

Texaco Inc.

Presidents

1902 Joseph S. Gullinan
1913 Elgood C. Lufkin
1920 Amos L. Beaty
1926 Ralph C. Holmes
1933 W. S. S. Rodgers
1944 Harry T. Klein
1952 J. S. Leach
1953 Augustus C. Long
1956 J. W. Foley
1964 J. Howard Rambin, Jr.
1965 Marion J. Epley, Jr.
1970 Maurice F. Granville
1971 John K. McKinley

Board Chairmen

1920 Elgood C. Lufkin
1926 Amos L. Beaty
1933 Ralph C. Holmes
1933 Charles B. Ames
1935 Torkild Rieber
1944 W. S. S. Rodgers
1953 J. S. Leach
1956 Augustus C. Long
1965 J. Howard Rambin, Jr.
1970 Marion J. Epley, Jr.
1971 Maurice F. Granville

Chief Executive Officer

1965 Augustus C. Long

Textron Inc.

Name changed from Franklin Rayon Corp. in 1939 and from Atlantic Rayon Corp. in 1944.

Presidents

1928 Eugene S. Graves
1930 William A. Traver
1936 Royal Little
1953 Robert L. Huffines, Jr.
1955 Royal Little
1956 Rupert C. Thompson, Jr.
1960 G. William Miller*

Board Chairmen

1928 Eliot Farley
1930 William A. Traver
1936 Eliot Farley
1953 Royal Little
1960 Rupert C. Thompson, Jr.

Chief Executive Officers

1955 to 1957 Joseph B. Ely
1955 to 1961 Royal Little
1969 to 1970 George W. Miller

Trans World Airlines, Inc. (TWA)

Presidents

1930 H. M. Hanshue
1931 Richard W. Robbins
1934 Jack Frye
1947 LaMotte T. Cohu
1949 Ralph S. Damon
1956 Carter L. Burgess
1958 Charles S. Thomas
1961 Charles C. Tillinghast, Jr.
1969 F. C. Wiser, Jr.

Board Chairman

1969 Charles C. Tillinghast, Jr.*

Transcontinental Gas Pipe Line Corporation

Presidents

1946 Claude A. Williams
1953 Tom P. Walker
1957 E. Clyde McGraw
1967 James B. Henderson

Board Chairmen

1957 Tom P. Walker
1967 E. Clyde McGraw

Travelers Insurance Companies

Merged with Phoenix Insurance Co. in 1966. See also Phoenix Insurance Co.

Presidents

1864 James G. Batterson
1901 Sylvester C. Dunham
1915 Louis F. Butler
1929 L. Edmund Zacher
1945 Jesse W. Randall
1952 J. Doyle DeWitt
1964 Sterling T. Tooker
1969 Roger C. Wilkins
1971 Morrison H. Beach

Board Chairmen

1945 Francis W. Cole*
1964 J. Doyle DeWitt*
1971 Roger C. Wilkins*

U. S. Industries, Inc.

Prior to 1954 known as Pressed Steel Car Co.

Presidents

1902 Frank N. Hoffstot
1934 W. A. Bonitz
1937 J. F. MacEnulty
1946 Ernest Murphy
1948 John I. Snyder
1966 I. John Billera
1970 Charles E. Selecman

Board Chairmen

1934 Lester N. Selig
1946 J. F. MacEnulty
1947 John I. Snyder
1966 I. John Billera

U. S. Plywood-Champion Papers Inc.

Presidents

1937 Lawrence Ottinger
1952 S. W. Antoville*
1964 Gene C. Brewer*
1967 Karl R. Bendetsen*
1972 Thomas F. Willers

Union Carbide Corporation

Presidents

1917 George O. Knapp
1925 Jesse J. Ricks
1941 Benjamin O'Shea
1944 Fred H. Haggerson
1952 Morse G. Dial
1958 Howard S. Bunn
1960 Birny Mason, Jr.
1966 Kenneth Rush
1969 F. Perry Wilson
1971 William S. Sneath

Board Chairmen

1951 Fred H. Haggerson
1958 Morse G. Dial
1966 Birny Mason, Jr.
1971 F. Perry Wilson

Union Electric Company

Presidents

1902 Julius S. Walsh*
1905 John I. Beggs*
1907 W. V. N. Powelson*
1909 Charles W. Wetmore*
1910 Alten S. Miller*
1911 J. D. Mortimer*
1920 Louis H. Egan*
1939 William McClellan*
1941 James W. McAfee*
1966 Charles J. Dougherty*

Board Chairmen

1941 William McClellan
1954 Ralph E. Moody
1966 James W. McAfee

Union Oil Company of California

Presidents

1890 Thomas R. Bard*
1894 D. T. Perkins*
1894 Lyman Stewart*
1914 William L. Stewart*
1930 Leonard P. St. Clair*
1938 Reese H. Taylor*
1956 Albert C. Rubel
1960 Dudley Tower
1962 Albert C. Rubel*
1964 Fred L. Hartley*

Board Chairmen

1956 Reese H. Taylor*
1962 William L. Stewart, Jr.
1964 Albert C. Rubel

Union Pacific Railroad Company

Presidents

1862 William B. Ogden
1863 John A. Dix
1866 Oliver Ames
1871 Thomas A. Scott
1872 Horace Clark
1873 John Duff
1874 Sidney Dillon
1884 Charles Francis Adams
1890 Sidney Dillon
1892 S. H. H. Clark
1897 Winslow S. Pierce (Acting)
1897 Horace G. Burt
1904 Edward H. Harriman
1909 Robert S. Lovett
1911 A. L. Mohler
1916 Edgar E. Calvin
1918 Charles B. Seger
1919 Robert S. Lovett
1920 Carl R. Gray
1937 William M. Jeffers
1946 George F. Ashby
1949 A. E. Stoddard
1965 Edd H. Bailey
1971 John C. Kenefick

Board Chairmen

1897 Winslow S. Pierce
1898 Edward H. Harriman
1909 Robert S. Lovett
1932 W. Averell Harriman
1946 E. Roland Harriman
1969 Frank E. Barnett*

Uniroyal, Inc.

United States Rubber Co. until 1967.

Presidents

1892 W. L. Trenholm
1892 Robert D. Evans
1893 Joseph Banigan
1896 Robert D. Evans
1897 Frederick M. Shepard
1901 Samuel P. Colt
1918 Charles P. Seger
1929 Francis B. Davis, Jr.
1942 Herbert E. Smith
1949 Harry E. Humphreys, Jr.
1957 John W. McGovern
1960 George R. Vila

Board Chairmen

1918 Samuel P. Colt
1921 Charles B. Seger
1929 Francis B. Davis, Jr.
1949 Herbert E. Smith*
1951 Harry E. Humphreys, Jr.*
1965 George R. Vila*

United Aircraft Corporation

Presidents

1934 Donald L. Brown*
1939 Eugene E. Wilson*
1943 H. Mansfield Horner*
1955 William P. Gwinn
1967 Arthur E. Smith
1971 Harry J. Gray

Board Chairmen

1935 Frederick B. Rentschler
1955 H. Mansfield Horner*
1967 William P. Gwinn
1972 Arthur E. Smith

United States National Bank of Oregon

Presidents

1891 Donald Macleay
1895 Tyler Woodward
1902 John C. Ainsworth
1931 Paul S. Dick
1945 Edward C. Sammons
1960 Edward J. Kolar
1966 LeRoy B. Staver
1971 Earl L. Dresler

Board Chairmen

1960 Edward C. Sammons*
1966 Edward J. Kolar*
1971 LeRoy B. Staver*

United States Steel Corporation

Presidents

1901 Charles M. Schwab
1903 William E. Corey
1911 James A. Farrell
1932 William A. Irvin
1938 Benjamin F. Fairless
1953 Clifford F. Hood
1959 Walter F. Munford
1959 Leslie B. Worthington
1967 Edwin H. Gott
1969 Edgar B. Speer

Board Chairmen

1903 Elbert H. Gary
1927 J. Pierpont Morgan, Jr.
1932 Myron C. Taylor
1938 Edward R. Stettinius, Jr.
1940 Irving S. Olds
1952 Benjamin F. Fairless
1955 Roger M. Blough
1969 Edwin H. Gott

Chief Executive Officers

1910 Elbert H. Gary
1927 James A. Farrell
1932 Myron C. Taylor
1952 Benjamin F. Fairless
1955 Roger M. Blough
1969 Edwin H. Gott

United Utilities, Incorporated

Presidents

1938 Harry S. Berlin
1939 Ralph W. Dockstader
1940 Alden L. Hart
1959 Carl A. Scupin
1964 Paul H. Henson

Virginia Electric and Power Company

Presidents

1909 William Northrop
1912 Thomas S. Wheelwright
1925 Luke C. Bradley
1927 William E. Wood
1929 J. Frank McLaughlin
1929 Jack G. Holtzclaw
1956 Erwin H. Will
1958 Alfred H. McDowell, Jr.
1967 John M. McGurn
1970 T. Justin Moore, Jr.

Wells Fargo Bank

Presidents

1960 Ransom M. Cook*
1964 H. Stephens Chase*
1966 Richard P. Cooley*

Board Chairmen

1960 I. W. Hellman
1964 Ransom M. Cook
1966 H. Stephens Chase
1968 Ernest C. Arbuckle

Western Electric Company, Inc.

Presidents

1872 Anson Stager
1885 William A. S. Smoot
1886 Enos M. Barton
1908 Harry B. Thayer
1919 Charles G. DuBois
1926 Edgar S. Bloom
1940 Clarence G. Stoll
1947 Stanley Bracken
1954 Frederick R. Kappel
1956 Arthur B. Goetze
1959 Haakon I. Romnes
1964 Paul A. Gorman
1969 Harvey G. Melhouse
1971 Donald E. Procknow

Board Chairman

1971 Harvey G. Melhouse*

Westinghouse Electric Corporation

Presidents

1886 George Westinghouse, Jr.*
1910 Edwin F. Atkins
1911 Edwin M. Herr
1929 Frank A. Merrick
1938 George H. Bucher
1946 Gwilym A. Price*
1958 Mark W. Cresap, Jr.*
1963 Donald C. Burnham*

Board Chairmen

1891 Brayton Ives
1909 Robert Mather*
1912 Guy E. Tripp*
1927 Paul D. Cravath
1929 Andrew W. Robertson*
1955 Gwilym A. Price*
1969 Donald C. Burnham*

XVII

ORGANIZED LABOR

Presidents of 60 leading unions and guilds in the United States.

Actors Equity Association

1913 Francis Wilson
1920 John Emerson
1928 Frank Gilmore
1938 Arthur Byron
1940 Bert Lytell
1946 Clarence Derwent
1952 Ralph Bellamy
1964 Frederick O'Neal

Allied Industrial Workers of America

1935 F. J. Dillon
1936 Homer Martin
1940 Irvan Cary
1943 Lester Washburn
1954 George Grisham
1954 Earl Heaton
1957 Carl W. Griepentrog
1970 Gilbert Jewell

Aluminum Workers International Union

1953 Eddie R. Stahl
1967 Henry S. Olsen

Amalgamated Clothing Workers of America

1914 Sidney Hillman
1946 Jacob S. Potofsky

Amalgamated Meat Cutters and Butcher Workmen

1897 George Byer
1898 Michael Donnelly
1905 Howard W. Potter
1909 John E. Carney
1910 John F. Hart
1921 C. J. Hayes
1923 Patrick E. Gorman
1942 Earl W. Jimerson
1959 Thomas J. Lloyd

Amalgamated Transit Union

1892 William Law
1893 W. D. Mahon
1946 A. L. Spradling
1959 John M. Elliott

American Federation of Government Employees

1932 John A. Shaw
1933 E. Claude Babcock
1936 Charles I. Stengle
1939 Cecil E. Custer
1939 James B. Burns
1948 James G. Yaden
1950 Henry Ihler
1951 James A. Campbell
1962 John F. Griner

American Federation of Musicians

1896 Owen Miller
1900 Joseph N. Weber
1940 James C. Petrillo
1958 Herman Kenin
1970 Hal C. Davis

American Federation of Teachers

1916 Charles B. Stillman
1923 Florence Rood
1925 Mary C. Barker
1931 Henry R. Linville
1934 Raymond E. Lowry
1936 Jerome C. Davis
1939 George S. Counts
1942 John M. Fewkes
1943 Joseph F. Landis
1948 John M. Eklund
1952 Carl J. Megel
1964 Charles Cogen
1968 David Selden

American Federation of Television and Radio Artists

1937 Eddie Cantor
1940 Lawrence Tibbett
1946 Kenneth Carpenter
1948 Clayton Collyer
1950 Knox Manning
1952 Alan Bunce
1954 Frank Nelson
1957 Clayton Collyer
1959 Virginia Payne
1961 Art Gilmore
1963 Vicki Vola
1965 Tyler McVey
1967 Mel Brandt
1970 Bill Baldwin

American Newspaper Guild

1933 Heywood Broun
1940 Kenneth G. Crawford
1940 Donal M. Sullivan
1941 Milton Murray
1947 Harry Martin
1953 Joseph F. Collis
1959 Arthur Rosenstock
1967 James B. Woods
1969 Charles A. Perlik, Jr.

Bricklayers, Masons and Plasterers, International Union of America

1865 John A. White
1867 John S. Frost
1869 Samuel Gaul
1870 John O'Keefe
1871 Meredith Moore
1872 James T. Kirby
1874 Stephen A. Carr
1875 Lewis Carpenter
1877 Charles H. Rihl
1878 Lewis Carpenter
1879 Thomas R. Gockel
1881 E. J. O'Rourk
1882 Henry O. Cole
1884 John Pearson
1885 Thomas R. Gockel
1886 Alex Darragh
1890 Alfred J. McDonald
1891 John Heartz
1894 William Klein
1901 George P. Gubbins
1904 William J. Bowers
1928 George T. Thornton
1936 Harry C. Bates
1960 John J. Murphy
1966 Thomas F. Murphy

Brotherhood of Locomotive Engineers

1863 W. D. Robinson
1864 Charles Wilson
1874 P. M. Arthur
1903 A. B. Youngson
1903 Warren S. Stone
1924 William B. Prenter
1925 Alvanley Johnston
1950 J. P. Shields
1953 Guy L. Brown
1960 Roy E. Davidson
1964 Perry S. Heath
1969 C. J. Coughlin

Brotherhood of Maintenance of Way Employes

1887 John T. Wilson
1908 A. B. Lowe
1914 T. H. Gerrey
1914 A. E. Barker
1920 E. F. Grable
1922 F. H. Fljozdal
1940 Elmer E. Milliman
1947 T. C. Carroll
1958 H. C. Crotty

Brotherhood of Railroad Signalmen

1908 Philip Weller
1908 John Bindscheattel
1909 M. J. Hooper
1910 J. A. Martin
1913 W. J. Pettit
1917 D. W. Helt
1934 A. E. Lyon
1945 Jesse Clark
1967 C. J. Chamberlain

Brotherhood of Railroad Trainmen

Became part of the United Transportation Union in 1969.

1883 J. E. Grimes
1885 S. E. Wilkinson
1895 P. H. Morrissey
1909 William G. Lee
1928 A. F. Whitney
1949 W. P. Kennedy
1960 Charles Luna

Glass Bottle Blowers Association of the United States and Canada

1876 Samuel Simpson
1880 Louis Arrington
1894 Joseph D. Troth
1896 Denis A. Hayes
1917 John A. Voll
1924 James Maloney
1946 Lee W. Minton
1971 Newton W. Black

Industrial Union of Marine and Shipbuilding Workers of America

1933 John Green
1951 John J. Grogan
1968 Andrew A. Pettis

International Association of Bridge, Structural and Ornamental Iron Workers

1896 Edward J. Ryan
1899 John T. Butler
1901 Frank Buchanan
1905 Frank M. Ryan
1914 James E. McClory
1918 P. J. Morrin
1948 John H. Lyons, Sr.
1961 John H. Lyons, Jr.

International Association of Machinists and Aerospace Workers

1888 Thomas W. Talbot
1890 J. J. Creamer
1892 John O'Day
1893 James O'Connell
1911 William H. Johnston
1926 A. O. Wharton
1939 Harvey W. Brown
1949 A. J. Hayes
1965 P. L. Siemiller
1969 Floyd E. Smith

International Brotherhood of Electrical Workers

1891 Henry Miller
1893 Quinn Jansen
1894 H. W. Sherman
1897 J. A. Maloney
1899 Thomas Wheeler
1901 W. A. Jackson
1903 F. J. McNulty
1919 J. P. Noonan
1929 H. H. Broach
1933 D. W. Tracy
1940 Edward J. Brown
1947 D. W. Tracy
1954 J. Scott Milne
1955 Gordon M. Freeman
1968 Charles H. Pillard

International Brotherhood of Painters and Allied Trades

1887 Joseph Harrold
1888 George A. Thompson
1892 James W. McKinney
1894 John M. Welter
1894 James H. Sullivan
1896 Michael P. Carrick
1897 Robert H. Siekmann
1898 Fred Kneeland
1899 William DeVaux
1901 Joseph Bahlhorn
1909 George F. Hedrick
1928 John M. Finan
1929 Lawrence P. Lindelof
1952 Lawrence M. Raftery
1965 S. Frank Raftery

International Brotherhood of Paper Makers

(Became part of United Papermakers and Paperworkers in 1957)
1902 George Mackey
1905 Jeremiah T. Carey
1924 Matthew H. Parker
1926 William R. Smith
1930 Matthew J. Burns
1940 Arthur Huggins
1944 Matthew J. Burns
1948 Paul L. Phillips

International Brotherhood of Pottery & Allied Workers

1890 Harry Layden
1892 A. S. Hughes
1912 Edward Menge
1921 John T. Wood
1927 James M. Duffy
1953 Frank Hull
1956 E. L. Wheatley
1969 Lester H. Null, Sr.

International Brotherhood of Pulp, Sulphite and Paper Mill Workers

1906 James E. Fitzgerald
1909 John H. Malin
1917 John P. Burke
1965 William H. Burnell
1965 Joseph P. Tonelli

International Brotherhood of Teamsters, Chauffeurs, Warehousemen & Helpers of America

1899 John Callahan
1900 Jasper Clark
1902 N. W. Evans
1902 Albert Young
1903 Cornelius P. Shea
1907 Daniel J. Tobin
1952 David Beck
1957 James R. Hoffa
1971 Frank Fitzsimmons

International Ladies' Garment Workers Union

1900 Herman Grossman
1903 Benjamin Schlesinger
1904 James McCauley
1905 Herman Grossman
1907 Mortimer Julian
1908 Charles Jacobson
1908 Abraham Rosenberg
1914 Benjamin Schlesinger
1923 Salvatore Ninfo
1923 Morris Sigman
1928 Benjamin Schlesinger
1931 Salvatore Ninfo
1932 David Dubinsky
1966 Louis Stulberg

International Longshoremen's Association

1895 Daniel J. Keefe
1909 T. V. O'Connor
1921 Anthony Chlopek
1927 Joseph P. Ryan
1953 William V. Bradley
1964 Thomas W. Gleason

International Longshoremen's & Warehousemen's Union

1938 Harry Bridges

International Molders and Allied Workers Union

1859 William C. Rea
1860 Isaac J. Neall
1861 Norman Van Alstyne
1863 William H. Sylvis
1869 F. J. Meyers
1870 William Saffin
1879 P. F. Fitzpatrick
1890 Martin Fox
1903 Joseph F. Valentine
1924 M. J. Keough
1932 Lawrence O'Keefe
1939 Harry Stevenson
1948 Chester A. Sample
1960 William A. Lazzerini

International Typographical Union

1850 J. W. Peregoy
1851 J. L. Gibbons
1852 J. S. Nafew
1853 Gerard Stith
1854 Lewis Graham
1855 Charles F. Town
1856 M. C. Brown
1857 William Cuddy
1858 R. C. Smith
1860 J. M. Farquhar
1863 Eugene Valette
1864 A. M. Carver
1865 Robert E. Craig
1866 John H. Oberly
1868 Robert McKechnie
1869 Isaac D. George
1870 W. J. Hammond
1873 W. R. McLean
1874 William H. Bodwell
1875 Walter W. Bell
1876 John McVicar
1877 D. R. Streeter
1878 John Armstrong
1879 Samuel Haldeman
1880 William P. Atkinson
1881 George Clark
1883 M. L. Crawford
1884 R. H. Witter
1886 William Aimison
1888 E. T. Plank
1891 W. B. Prescott
1899 Samuel B. Donnelly
1901 James M. Lynch
1914 James M. Duncan
1915 M. G. Scott
1921 John McParland
1923 Charles P. Howard
1925 James M. Lynch
1927 Charles P. Howard
1938 C. M. Baker
1944 Woodruff Randolph
1958 Elmer Brown
1968 John J. Pilch

International Union of Electrical, Radio and Machine Workers

1949 James B. Carey
1965 Paul Jennings

International Union of Operating Engineers

1896 C. J. DeLong
1897 Frank Bowker
1898 Frank Pfohl
1898 S. L. Bennett
1899 P. A. Peregrine
1900 Frank B. Monaghan
1901 George Lighthall
1903 Patrick McMahon
1904 John E. Bruner
1905 Matt Comerford
1916 Milton Snelling
1921 Arthur M. Huddell
1931 John Possehl
1940 William E. Maloney
1958 Joseph J. Delaney
1962 Hunter P. Wharton

International Woodworkers of America

1937 Harold Pritchett
1940 O. M. Orton
1941 Worth Lowery
1943 Claude Ballard
1944 J. E. Fadling
1951 A. F. Hartung
1967 Ronald F. Roley

National Association of Postal Supervisors

1908 L. E. Palmer
1910 George A. Gasman
1911 Ernest Green
1916 William Sansom
1917 J. J. Fields
1921 V. C. Burke
1922 H. M. Tittle
1924 Peter Wiggle
1925 Harry Folger
1930 W. Bruce Luna
1931 M. F. O'Connell
1933 Herschel Ressler
1937 M. F. Fitzpatrick
1941 John J. Lane
1946 John McMahon
1950 M. C. Nave
1958 Fred J. O'Dwyer
1970 Donald N. Ledbetter

National Federation of Federal Employees

1917 H. M. McLarin
1918 Luther C. Steward
1955 Michael E. Markwood
1957 Vaux Owen
1964 Nathan T. Wolkomir

National Maritime Union of America

1937 Joseph E. Curran

Office & Professional Employees International Union

1945 Paul Hutchings
1953 Howard Coughlin

Retail, Wholesale and Department Store Union

1937 Samuel Wolchok
1948 Irving M. Simon
1954 Max Greenberg

The Screen Actors Guild

1933 Ralph Morgan
1933 Eddie Cantor
1935 Robert Montgomery
1938 Ralph Morgan
1940 Edward Arnold
1942 James Cagney
1944 George Murphy
1946 Robert Montgomery
1947 Ronald Reagan
1952 Walter Pidgeon
1957 Leon Ames
1958 Howard Keel
1959 Ronald Reagan
1960 George Chandler
1963 Dana Andrews
1965 Charlton Heston
1971 John Gavin

The Seafarers International Union of North America

1938 Harry Lundeberg
1957 Paul Hall

Service Employees International Union

1940 William L. McFetridge
1960 David Sullivan
1971 George Hardy

Textile Workers Union of America

1939 Emil Rieve
1956 William Pollock

Tobacco Workers International Union

1895 John Fischer
1908 A. McAndrews
1921 W. R. Walden
1925 E. Lewis Evans
1940 W. Warren Smith
1943 Radford G. Powell
1944 John O'Hare
1968 Howard W. Vogt
1970 Rene Rondou

Transport Workers Union of America

1934 Michael J. Quill
1966 Matthew Guinan

United Association of Journeyman and Apprentices of the Plumbing and Pipe Fitting Industry of the United States and Canada

1889 Patrick J. Quinlan
1891 John A. Lee
1892 Patrick H. Gleason
1893 John A. Lee
1894 M. J. Moran
1896 William P. Redmond
1896 Thomas H. O'Brien
1897 John S. Kelley
1900 William M. Merrick
1906 John R. Alpine
1919 John Coefield
1940 George Masterton
1943 Martin P. Durkin
1955 Peter T. Schoemann

International Union, United Automobile, Aerospace & Agricultural Implement Workers of America-UAW

1935 Francis J. Dillon
1936 Homer Martin
1939 R. J. Thomas
1946 Walter P. Reuther
1970 Leonard Woodcock

United Brotherhood of Carpenters and Joiners of America

1881 Gabriel Edmonston
1882 John D. Allen
1883 J. P. McGinley
1884 Joseph P. Billingsley
1886 William J. Shields
1888 D. P. Rowland
1890 W. H. Kliver
1892 Henry H. Trenor
1894 Charles B. Owens
1896 Harry Lloyd
1898 John Williams
1899 William D. Huber
1913 James Kirby
1915 William L. Hutcheson
1952 Maurice A. Hutcheson
1972 William Sidell

United Electrical, Radio and Machine Workers of America

1936 James B. Carey
1941 Albert J. Fitzgerald

United Federation of Postal Clerks

1906 Edward B. Goltra
1910 Oscar F. Nelson
1913 George Pfeiffer
1915 Arthur Honewell
1917 Gilbert E. Hyatt
1923 Leo E. George
1956 J. Cline House
1960 Elroy C. Hallbeck
1969 Francis S. Filbey

United Hatters, Cap and Millinery Workers International Union

1934 Michael F. Greene
1936 Max Zaritsky
1950 Alex Rose

United Papermakers and Paperworkers

1957 Paul L. Phillips
1968 Harry D. Sayre

United Rubber, Cork, Linoleum and Plastic Workers of America

1935 Sherman H. Dalrymple
1945 L. S. Buckmaster
1960 George Burdon
1966 Peter Bommarito

United Shoe Workers of America

1937 Powers Hapgood
1939 Frank McGrath
1947 Raymond Swansen
1948 Rocco Francheschini
1949 William Thornton
1952 Russell J. Taylor
1956 George O. Fecteau

United Steelworkers of America

1942 Philip Murray
1952 David J. McDonald
1965 I. W. Abel

United Transportation Union

1969 Charles Luna

Upholsterers' International Union of North America

1882 William Gratz
1884 Frank Kreis
1892 Anton J. Engel
1907 James H. Hatch
1921 William Kohn
1931 James H. Hatch
1937 Sal B. Hoffman

Utility Workers Union of America

1945 Joseph A. Fisher
1960 William J. Pachler
1970 William R. Munger

XVIII

NATIONAL ASSOCIATIONS

A listing of presidents of national learned, scientific, technical, professional, and fraternal organizations in the United States.

Academy of Motion Picture Arts and Sciences

1927 Douglas Fairbanks
1929 William DeMille
1931 M. C. Levee
1932 Conrad Nagel
1933 J. Theodore Reed
1934 Frank Lloyd
1935 Frank Capra
1939 Walter Wanger
1941 Bette Davis
1941 Walter Wanger
1945 Jean Hersholt
1949 Charles Brackett
1955 George Seaton
1958 George Stevens
1959 Bejamin B. Kahane
1960 Valentine Davies
1961 Wendell Corey
1963 Arthur Freed
1967 Gregory Peck
1971 Daniel Taradash

Academy of Natural Sciences

1812 Gerard Troost
1817 William Maclure
1840 William Hembel
1849 Samuel G. Morton
1851 George Ord
1858 Isac Lea
1863 Thomas B. Wilson
1864 Robert Bridges
1865 Isaac Hays
1869 William S. W. Ruschenberger
1881 Joseph Leidy
1891 Isaac J. Wistar
1895 Samuel G. Dixon
1918 John Cadwalader
1922 Richard A. F. Penrose
1926 T. Chalkley Palmer
1928 Effingham B. Morris
1937 Charles M. B. Cadwalader
1951 M. Albert Linton
1962 George R. Clark
1963 John W. Bodine

The American Academy of Arts and Letters

1908 William Dean Howells
1920 William Milligan Sloane
1928 Nicholas Murray Butler
1941 Walter Damrosch
1948 Paul Manship
1953 Archibald MacLeish
1956 Mark Van Doren
1959 Douglas Moore
1962 Lewis Mumford
1965 Allan Nevins
1968 George F. Kennan
1971 Aaron Copland

American Academy of Arts and Sciences

1780 James Bowdoin
1791 John Adams
1814 Edward A. Holyoke
1820 John Quincy Adams
1829 Nathaniel Bowditch
1838 James Jackson
1839 John Pickering
1846 Jacob Bigelow
1863 Asa Gray
1873 Charles Francis Adams
1880 Joseph Lovering
1892 Josiah P. Cooke
1894 Alexander Agassiz
1903 William W. Goodwin
1908 John Trowbridge
1915 Henry P. Walcott
1917 Charles P. Bowditch
1919 Theodore W. Richards
1921 George F. Moore
1924 Theodore Lyman
1927 Edwin B. Wilson
1931 Jeremiah D. M. Ford
1933 George H. Parker
1935 Roscoe Pound
1937 Dugald C. Jackson
1939 Harlow Shapley
1944 Howard Mumford Jones
1951 Edwin H. Land
1954 John E. Burchard
1957 Kirtley F. Mather
1961 Hudson Hoagland
1964 Paul A. Freund
1967 Talcott Parsons
1971 Harvey Brooks

The American Academy of Political and Social Science

1890 Edmund J. James
1901 Samuel M. Lindsay
1902 Leo S. Rowe
1930 Ernest M. Patterson
1953 James C. Charlesworth

American Anthropological Association

1947 Clyde Kluckhohn
1948 Harry L. Shapiro
1949 A. Irving Hallowell
1950 Ralph L. Beals
1951 William W. Howells
1952 Wendell C. Bennett
1953 Fred Eggan
1954 John O. Brew
1955 George P. Murdock
1956 Emil W. Haury
1957 E. Adamson Hoebel
1958 Harry Hoijer
1959 Sol Tax
1960 Margaret Mead
1961 Gordon R. Willey
1962 Sherwood L. Washburn
1963 Marvin K. Opler
1964 Leslie A. White
1965 Alexander Spoehr
1966 John P. Gillin
1967 Frederica de Laguna
1968 Irving Rouse
1969 Cora Du Bois
1970 George M. Foster, Jr.
1971 Charles Wagley
1972 Anthony F. C. Wallace

American Antiquarian Society

1812 Isaiah Thomas
1831 Thomas L. Winthrop
1841 Edward Everett
1853 John Davis
1854 Stephen Salisbury
1884 George F. Hoar
1887 Stephen Salisbury, Jr.
1906 Edward E. Hale
1907 Waldo Lincoln
1927 Charles L. Nichols
1929 Calvin Coolidge
1933 Arthur P. Rugg
1938 Samuel Eliot Morison
1952 Thomas W. Streeter
1955 Clarence S. Brigham
1959 Carleton R. Richmond
1964 Clifton W. Barrett

American Association for the Advancement of Science

1848 William B. Rogers (Acting)
1848 William C. Redfield
1850 Alexander D. Bache
1851 Louis Agassiz
1852 Benjamin Peirce
1854 James D. Dana
1855 John Torrey
1856 James Hall
1857 J. W. Bailey
1857 Alexis Caswell
1858 Jeffries Wyman
1859 Stephen Alexander
1860 Isaac Lea
1866 Frederick A. P. Barnard
1867 J. S. Newberry
1868 Benjamin A. Gould
1869 J. W. Foster
1870 William Chauvenet
1870 T. Sterry Hunt
1871 Asa Gray
1872 J. Lawrence Smith
1873 Joseph Lovering
1874 John L. LeConte
1875 Julius L. Hilgard
1876 William B. Rogers
1877 Simon Newcomb
1878 O. C. Marsh
1879 George F. Barker
1880 Lewis H. Morgan
1881 George J. Brush
1882 J. William Dawson
1883 Charles A. Young
1884 J. P. Lesley
1885 H. A. Newton
1886 Edward S. Morse
1887 S. P. Langley
1888 J. W. Powell
1889 T. C. Mendenhall
1890 George L. Goodale
1891 Albert B. Prescott
1892 Joseph LeConte
1893 William Harkness
1894 Daniel G. Brinton
1895 Edward W. Morley
1896 Edward D. Cope
1896 Theodore Gill
1897 Wolcott Gibbs
1897 W. J. McGee
1898 F. W. Putnam
1899 Edward Orton
1899 Marcus Benjamin
1899 Grove K. Gilbert
1900 R. S. Woodward
1901 Charles S. Minot
1902 Asaph Hall
1902 Ira Remsen
1903 Carroll D. Wright
1904 William G. Farlow
1905 C. M. Woodward
1906 William H. Welch
1907 E. L. Nichols
1908 Thomas C. Chamberlin
1909 David S. Jordan
1910 A. A. Michelson
1911 Charles E. Bessey
1912 E. C. Pickering
1913 Edmund B. Wilson
1914 Charles W. Eliot
1915 William W. Campbell
1916 Charles R. Van Hise
1917 Theodore W. Richards
1918 John M. Coulter
1919 Simon Flexner
1920 Leland O. Howard
1921 Eliakim H. Moore
1922 J. Playfair McMurrich
1923 Charles D. Walcott
1924 J. McKeen Cattell
1925 Michael I. Pupin
1926 Liberty Hyde Bailey
1927 Arthur A. Noyes
1928 Henry F. Osborn
1929 Robert A. Millikan
1930 Thomas H. Morgan
1931 Franz Boas
1932 John J. Abel
1933 Henry N. Russell
1934 Edward L. Thorndike
1935 Karl T. Compton
1936 Edwin G. Conklin
1937 George D. Birkhoff
1938 Wesley C. Mitchell
1939 Walter B. Cannon
1940 Albert F. Blakeslee
1941 Irving Langmuir
1942 Arthur H. Compton
1943 Isaiah Bowman
1944 Anton J. Carlson
1946 Charles F. Kettering
1946 James B. Conant
1947 Harlow Shapley
1948 Edmund W. Sinnott
1949 Elvin C. Stakman
1950 Roger Adams
1951 Kirtley F. Mather
1952 Detlev W. Bronk
1953 Edward U. Condon
1954 Warren Weaver
1955 George W. Beadle
1956 Paul B. Sears
1957 Laurence H. Snyder
1958 Wallace R. Brode
1959 Paul E. Klopsteg

1960 Chauncey D. Leake
1961 Thomas Park
1962 Paul M. Gross
1963 Alan T. Waterman
1964 Laurence M. Gould
1965 Henry Eyring
1966 Alfred S. Romer
1967 Don K. Price
1968 Walter Orr Roberts
1969 H. Bentley Glass
1970 Athelstan Spilhaus
1971 Mina Rees
1972 Glenn T. Seaborg

The American Association of Petroleum Geologists

1917 J. Elmer Thomas
1918 Alexander Deussen
1919 I. C. White
1920 Wallace E. Pratt
1921 George C. Matson
1922 William E. Wrather
1923 Max W. Ball
1924 James H. Gardner
1925 E. L. DeGolyer
1926 Alex W. McCoy
1927 George C. Gester
1928 R. S. McFarland
1929 J. Y. Snyder
1930 Sidney Powers
1931 L. P. Garrett
1932 Frederic H. Lahee
1933 Frank R. Clark
1934 William B. Heroy
1935 A. I. Levorsen
1936 Ralph D. Reed
1937 Herbert B. Fuqua
1938 Donald C. Barton
1939 Henry A. Ley
1940 Luther C. Snider
1941 Edgar W. Owen
1942 Fritz L. Aurin
1943 Rodger Denison
1944 Ira H. Cram
1945 Monroe G. Cheney
1946 Earl B. Noble
1947 C. E. Dobbin
1948 Paul Weaver
1949 C. W. Tomlinson
1950 Clarence L. Moody
1951 Frank A. Morgan
1952 Morgan J. Davis, Sr.
1953 John E. Adams
1954 Ed. A. Koester
1955 G. Moses Knebel
1956 Theodore A. Link
1957 Graham B. Moody
1958 George S. Buchanan
1959 Lewis G. Weeks
1960 Ben H. Parker
1961 Mason L. Hill
1962 Robert E. Rettger
1963 John C. Sproule
1964 Grover E. Murray
1965 Orlo E. Childs
1966 Michel T. Halbouty
1967 J. Ben Carsey
1968 Frank B. Conselman
1969 Kenneth H. Crandall

American Association of University Professors

1915 John Dewey
1916 John H. Wigmore
1917 Frank Thilly
1918 John M. Coulter
1919 A. O. Lovejoy
1920 Edward Capps
1921 Vernon L. Kellogg

1921 E. R. A. Seligman
1922 J. V. Denney
1924 A. O. Leuschner
1926 W. T. Semple
1928 Henry Crew
1930 W. B. Munro
1932 Walter C. Cook
1934 S. A. Mitchell
1936 Anton J. Carlson
1938 Mark H. Ingraham
1940 Frederick S. Deibler
1942 W. T. Laprade
1944 Quincy Wrights
1946 Edward C. Kirkland
1948 Ralph H. Lutz
1950 Richard H. Shryock
1952 Fred B. Millett
1954 William E. Britton
1956 Helen C. White
1958 H. Bentley Glass
1960 Ralph F. Fuchs
1962 Fritz Machlup
1964 David Fellman
1966 Clark Byse
1968 Ralph S. Brown
1970 Sanford N. Kadish
1972 Walter Adams

American Astronautical Society

1953 Hans Behm
1955 Norman V. Petersen
1957 Ross Fleisig
1959 George Arthur
1961 Alfred M. Mayo
1963 William O. Whitson
1964 George W. Morgenthaler
1966 Lewis Larmore
1968 Eugene B. Konecci
1969 Paul Dergarabedian
1971 Paul B. Richards

American Astronomical Society

1899 Simon Newcomb
1905 Edward C. Pickering
1919 Frank Schlesinger
1922 William W. Campbell
1925 George C. Comstock
1928 Ernest W. Brown
1931 Walter S. Adams
1934 Henry N. Russell
1937 Robert G. Aitken
1940 Joel Stebbins
1943 Harlow Shapley
1946 Otto Struve
1949 Alfred H. Joy
1952 Robert R. McMath
1954 Donald H. Menzel
1956 Paul Merrill
1958 G. M. Clemence
1960 Lyman Spitzer, Jr.
1962 C. S. Beals
1964 Leo Goldberg
1967 A. E. Whitvord
1969 Martin Schwarzschild
1972 Bart J. Bok

The American Bankers Association

1875 Charles B. Hall
1878 Alex Mitchell
1881 George S. Coe
1883 Lyman J. Gage
1886 Logan C. Murray
1888 Charles Parsons
1890 Morton McMichael
1892 William H. Rhawn
1893 M. M. White
1894 John J. P. Odell
1895 Eugene H. Pullen
1896 Robert J. Lowry
1897 Joseph C. Hendrix
1898 George H. Russel
1899 Walker Hill
1900 Alvah Trowbridge
1901 Myron T. Herrick
1902 Caldwell Hardy
1904 E. F. Swinney
1905 John L. Hamilton
1906 G. S. Whitson
1907 J. D. Powers
1908 George M. Reynolds
1909 Lewis E. Pierson
1910 F. O. Watts
1911 William Livingstone
1912 Charles H. Huttig
1913 Arthur Reynolds
1914 William A. Law
1915 James K. Lynch
1916 P. W. Goebell
1917 Charles A. Hinsch
1918 Robert F. Maddox
1919 Richard S. Hawes
1920 John S. Drum
1921 Thomas B. McAdams
1922 John H. Puelicher
1923 Walter W. Head
1924 William E. Knox
1925 Oscar Wells
1926 Melvin A. Traylor
1927 Thomas R. Preston
1928 Craig B. Hazlewood
1929 John G. Lonsdale
1930 Rome C. Stephenson
1931 Harry J. Haas
1932 Francis H. Sisson
1933 Francis M. Law
1934 Rudolph S. Hecht
1935 Robert V. Fleming
1936 Tom K. Smith
1937 Orval W. Adams
1938 Philip A. Benson
1939 Robert M. Hanes
1940 P. D. Houston
1941 H. W. Koeneke
1942 W. L. Hemingway
1943 A. L. M. Wiggins
1944 W. Randolph Burgess
1945 Frank C. Rathje
1946 C. W. Bailey
1947 Joseph M. Dodge
1948 Evans Woollen, Jr.
1949 F. Raymond Peterson
1950 James E. Shelton
1951 C. Francis Cocke
1952 W. Harold Brenton
1953 Everett D. Reese
1954 Homer J. Livingston
1955 Fred F. Florence
1956 Erle Cocke, Sr.
1957 J. C. Welman
1958 Lee P. Miller
1959 John W. Remington
1960 Carl A. Bimson
1961 Sam M. Fleming
1962 M. Monroe Kimbrel
1963 William F. Kelly
1964 Reno Odlin
1965 Archie K. Davis
1966 Jack T. Conn
1967 J. Howard Laeri
1968 Willis W. Alexander
1969 Nat S. Rogers
1970 George H. Gustafson
1971 Clifford C. Sommer
1972 Allen P. Stults

American Bar Association

1878 James O. Broadhead
1879 Benjamin H. Bristow
1880 Edward J. Phelps
1881 Clarkson N. Potter
1882 Alexander R. Lawton
1883 Cortlandt Parker
1884 John W. Stevenson
1885 William Allen Butler
1886 Thomas J. Semmes
1887 George G. Wright
1888 David Dudley Field
1889 Henry Hitchcock
1890 Simeon E. Baldwin
1891 John F. Dillon
1892 John Randolph Tucker
1893 Thomas M. Cooley
1894 James C. Carter
1895 Moorfield Storey
1896 James M. Woolworth
1897 William Wirt Howe
1898 Joseph H. Choate
1899 Charles F. Manderson
1900 Edmund Wetmore
1901 U. M. Rose
1902 Francis Rawle
1903 James Hagerman
1904 Henry St. George Tucker
1905 George R. Peck
1906 Alton B. Parker
1907 Jacob M. Dickinson
1908 Frederick W. Lehmann
1909 Charles F. Libby
1910 Edgar H. Farrar
1911 Stephen S. Gregory
1912 Frank B. Kellogg
1913 William H. Taft
1914 Peter W. Meldrim
1915 Elihu Root
1916 George Sutherland
1917 Walter George Smith
1918 George T. Page
1919 Hampton L. Carson

1920 William A. Blount
1921 Cordenio A. Severance
1922 John W. Davis
1923 R. E. L. Saner
1924 Charles E. Hughes
1925 Chester I. Long
1926 Charles S. Whitman
1927 Silas H. Strawn
1928 Gurney E. Newlin
1929 Henry Upson Sims
1930 Josiah Marvel
1930 Charles A. Boston
1931 Guy A. Thompson
1932 Clarence E. Martin
1933 Earle W. Evans
1934 Scott M. Loftin
1935 William L. Ransom
1936 Frederick H. Stinchfield
1937 Arthur T. Vanderbilt
1938 Frank J. Hogan
1939 Charles A. Beardsley
1940 Jacob M. Lashly
1941 Walter P. Armstrong
1942 George M. Morris
1943 Joseph W. Henderson
1944 David A. Simmons
1945 Willis Smith
1946 Carl B. Rix
1947 Tappan Gregory
1948 Frank E. Holman
1949 Harold J. Gallagher
1950 Cody Fowler
1951 Howard L. Barkdull
1952 Robert G. Storey
1953 William J. Jameson
1954 Loyd Wright
1955 E. Smythe Gambrell
1956 David F. Maxwell
1957 Charles S. Rhyne
1958 Ross L. Malone
1959 John D. Randall
1960 Whitney North Seymour
1961 John C. Satterfield
1962 Sylvester C. Smith, Jr.
1963 Walter E. Craig
1964 Lewis F. Powell, Jr.
1965 Edward W. Kuhn
1966 Orison S. Marden
1967 Earl F. Morris
1968 William T. Gossett
1969 Bernard G. Segal
1970 Edward L. Wright
1971 Leon Jaworski
1972 Robert W. Meserve

American Bible Society

1816 Elias Boudinot
1821 John Jay
1828 Richard Varick
1831 John Cotton Smith
1846 Theodore Frelinghuysen
1862 Luther Bradish
1864 James Lenox
1872 William H. Allen
1881 S. Wells Williams
1884 Frederick T. Frelinghuysen
1885 Enoch L. Fancher
1903 Daniel Coit Gilman
1909 Theophilus A. Brouwer
1911 James Wood
1919 Churchill H. Cutting
1924 E. Francis Hyde
1931 J. Frederick Talcott
1934 John T. Manson

1944 Daniel Burke
1962 Everett Smith
1967 Edmund F. Wagner

American Cancer Society, Inc.

1913 George C. Clark
1919 Charles A. Powers
1923 Edward Reynolds
1925 Howard C. Taylor
1930 Jonathan M. Wainwright
1932 George H. Bigelow
1934 Burton T. Simpson
1936 Robert B. Greenough
1937 Frederick F. Russell
1938 John J. Morton, Jr.
1942 Herman C. Pitts
1944 Frank E. Adair
1947 Edwin P. Lehman
1948 Clifford C. Nesselrode
1949 Alton Ochsner
1950 Guy Aud
1951 Charles C. Lund
1952 Harry M. Nelson
1953 Alfred M. Popma
1954 Howard C. Taylor, Jr.
1955 George V. Brindley
1956 David A. Wood
1957 Lowell T. Coggeshall
1958 Eugene P. Pendergrass
1959 Warren H. Cole
1960 John W. Cline
1961 Thomas Carlile
1962 Isidor S. Ravdin
1963 Wendell G. Scott
1964 Murray M. Copeland
1965 Leonard W. Larson
1966 Ashbel C. Williams
1967 Roger A. Harvey
1968 Sidney Farber
1969 Jonathan E. Rhoads
1970 H. Marvin Pollard
1971 A. Hamblin Letton

American Chemical Society

1876 John W. Draper
1877 J. Lawrence Smith
1878 Samuel W. Johnson
1879 T. Sterry Hunt
1880 Frederick A. Genth
1881 Charles F. Chandler
1882 John W. Mallet
1883 James C. Booth
1886 Albert B. Prescott
1887 Charles A. Goessmann
1888 T. Sterry Hunt
1889 Charles F. Chandler
1890 Henry B. Nason
1891 George F. Barker
1892 George C. Caldwell
1893 Harvey W. Wiley
1895 Edgar F. Smith
1896 Charles B. Dudley
1898 Charles E. Munroe
1899 Edward W. Morley
1900 William McMurtrie
1901 Frank W. Clarke
1902 Ira Remsen
1903 John H. Long
1904 Arthur A. Noyes
1905 Francis P. Venable
1906 William F. Hillebrand
1907 Marston T. Bogert
1909 Willis R. Whitney
1910 Wilder D. Bancroft
1911 Alexander Smith
1912 Arthur D. Little
1914 Theodore W. Richards
1915 Charles H. Herty
1917 Julius Stieglitz
1918 William H. Nichols
1920 William A. Noyes
1921 Edgar F. Smith
1923 Edward C. Franklin
1924 Leo H. Baekeland
1925 James F. Norris
1927 George D. Rosengarten
1928 Samuel W. Parr
1929 Irving Langmuir
1930 William McPherson
1931 Moses Gomberg
1932 L. V. Redman
1933 Arthur B. Lamb
1934 Charles L. Reese
1935 Roger Adams
1936 Edward Bartow
1937 Edward R. Weidlein
1938 Frank C. Whitmore
1939 Charles A. Kraus
1940 Samuel C. Lind
1941 William Lloyd Evans
1942 Harry N. Holmes
1943 Per K. Frolich
1944 Thomas Midgley, Jr.
1945 Carl S. Marvel
1946 Bradley Dewey
1947 W. Albert Noyes, Jr.
1948 Charles A. Thomas
1949 Linus Pauling
1950 Ernest H. Volwiler
1951 N. Howell Furman
1952 Edgar C. Britton
1953 Farrington Daniels
1954 Harry L. Fisher
1955 Joel H. Hildebrand
1956 J. C. Warner
1957 Roger J. Williams
1958 C. F. Rassweiler
1959 John C. Bailar, Jr.
1960 Albert L. Elder
1961 Arthur C. Cope
1962 Karl Folkers
1963 Henry Eyring
1964 Maurice H. Arveson
1965 Charles C. Price
1966 William J. Sparks
1967 Charles G. Overberger
1968 Robert W. Cairns
1969 Wallace R. Brode
1970 Byron Riegel
1971 Melvin Calvin

American College of Surgeons

1913 John M. T. Finney
1916 George W. Crile
1918 William J. Mayo (to 1920)
1921 John B. Deaver
1922 Harvey Cushing
1923 Albert J. Ochsner
1924 Charles H. Mayo
1925 Rudolph Matas (to 1926)
1927 George D. Stewart
1928 Franklin H. Martin
1929 Merritte W. Ireland
1930 C. Jeff Miller
1931 Allen B. Kanavel
1932 J. Bentley Squier
1933 William D. Haggard
1934 Robert B. Greenough
1935 Donald C. Balfour
1936 Eugene H. Pool
1937 Frederic A. Besley
1938 Howard C. Naffziger
1939 George P. Muller
1940 Evarts A. Graham
1942 *(Vacant)*
1946 Irvin W. Abell
1947 Arthur W. Allen
1948 Dallas B. Phemister
1949 Frederick A. Coller
1950 Henry W. Cave
1951 Alton Ochsner
1952 Harold L. Foss
1953 Fred W. Rankin
1954 Frank Glenn
1954 Alfred Blalock
1955 Warren H. Cole
1956 Daniel C. Elkin
1957 William L. Estes, Jr. (to 1958)
1959 Owen H. Wangensteen
1960 I. S. Ravdin
1961 Robert M. Zollinger
1962 Loyal Davis
1963 J. Englebert Dunphy
1964 James T. Priestley
1965 Howard A. Patterson (to 1966)
1967 Reed M. Nesbit
1968 Preston A. Wade
1969 Joel Baker
1970 Howard Mahorner
1971 Jonathan E. Rhoads

American College of Trial Lawyers

1950 Emil Gumpert
1951 C. Ray Robinson
1952 Cody Fowler
1953 E. D. Bronson
1954 Cody Fowler
1955 Wayne E. Stichter
1956 Jesse E. Nichols
1957 Lewis C. Ryan
1958 Albert E. Jenner, Jr.
1959 Samuel P. Sears
1960 Lon Hocker
1961 Leon Jaworski
1962 Grant B. Cooper
1963 Whitney North Seymour
1964 Bernard G. Segal
1965 Edward L. Wright
1966 Frank G. Raichle
1967 Joseph A. Ball
1968 Robert W. Meserve
1969 Lewis F. Powell, Jr.
1970 Barnabas F. Sears
1971 Hicks Epton

The American Correctional Association

1945 Sanford Bates
1946 E. R. Cass
1947 Blanche La Du
1948 Austin H. MacCormick
1949 James V. Bennett
1950 Richard A. McGee

1951 Garrett Heyns
1952 W. Frank Smyth
1953 John C. Burke
1954 Joseph E. Ragen
1955 Walter M. Wallack
1956 Kenyon J. Scudder
1957 Myrl E. Alexander
1958 E. Preston Sharp
1959 Roberts J. Wright
1960 Gervaise Brinkman
1961 Sanger B. Powers
1962 Arthur T. Prasse
1963 Peter P. Lejins
1964 Harry C. Tinsley
1965 Harold V. Langlois
1966 Walter Dunbar
1967 Parker L. Hancock
1968 Ellis C. MacDougall
1969 George Beto
1970 Louie L. Wainwright
1971 Maurice H. Sigler

American Council of Learned Societies

1919 Waldo Leland (Director)
1946 Richard H. Shryock (Acting Director)
1947 Cornelius Kruse (Exec. Director)
1948 Charles Odegaard (Exec. Director)
1953 Mortimer Graves (Exec. Director)
1957 Frederick Burkhardt

American Dental Association

1859 William W. Allport
1860 William H. Atkinson
1862 George Watt
1863 William H. Allen
1864 John H. McQuillen
1865 Christopher W. Spalding
1866 Chauncey P. Fitch
1867 Ambrose Lawrence
1868 Jonathan Taft
1869 Homer Judd
1870 William H. Morgan
1871 George H. Cushing
1872 Phineas G. C. Hunt
1873 Thomas L. Buckingham
1874 Mason S. Dean
1875 Aaron L. Northrop
1876 George W. Keely
1877 Frederick H. Rehwinkel
1878 Henry J. McKellops
1879 Luther D. Shepard
1880 Cyrus N. Pierce
1881 H. A. Smith
1882 William H. Goddard
1883 Edwin T. Darby
1884 John N. Crouse
1885 William C. Barrett
1886 William W. Allport
1887 Frank Abbott
1888 Charles R. Butler
1889 Matthew W. Foster
1890 Allison W. Harlan
1891 William W. Walker
1892 John D. Patterson
1894 James Y. Crawford
1896 James Truman
1897 Thomas Fillerbrown
1898 Harvey J. Burkhart
1899 B. Holly Smith
1900 Greene V. Black
1901 James A. Libbey
1902 Llewellyn G. Noel
1903 Charles C. Chittenden
1904 Waldo E. Boardman
1905 Mark F. Finley
1906 Adelbert H. Peck
1907 William Carr
1908 Vines E. Turner
1909 Burton L. Thorpe
1910 Edmund S. Gaylord
1911 Arthur R. Melendy
1912 Frank O. Hetrick
1913 Homer C. Brown
1914 Donald M. Gallie
1915 Thomas P. Hinman
1916 Lafayette L. Barber
1917 William H. G. Logan
1918 Clement V. Vignes
1919 John V. Conzett
1920 H. Edmund Friesell
1921 Thomas B. Hartzell
1922 John P. Buckley
1923 William A. Giffen
1924 Charles N. Johnson
1925 Sheppard W. Foster
1926 Henry L. Banzhaf
1927 Roscoe H. Volland
1928 Percy R. Howe
1929 Robert B. Bogle
1930 Robert T. Oliver
1931 Martin Dewey
1932 George W. Dittmar
1933 Arthur C. Wherry
1934 Frank M. Casto
1935 George Ben W. Winter
1936 Leroy M. S. Miner
1937 C. Willard Camalier
1938 Marcus L. Ward
1939 Arthur H. Merritt
1940 Wilfred H. Robinson
1941 Oren A. Oliver
1942 J. Ben Robinson
1943 Charles R. Wells
1944 Walter H. Scherer
1946 Sterling V. Mead
1947 Harvey B. Washburn
1948 Clyde E. Minges
1949 Philip E. Adams
1950 Harold W. Oppice
1951 LeRoy M. Ennis
1952 Otto W. Brandhorst
1953 Leslie M. Fitzgerald
1954 Daniel F. Lynch
1955 Bernerd C. Kingsbury
1956 Harry Lyons
1957 William R. Alstadt
1958 Percy T. Phillips
1959 Paul H. Jeserich
1960 Charles H. Patton
1961 John R. Abel
1962 Gerald D. Timmons
1963 James P. Hollers
1964 Fritz A. Pierson
1965 Maynard K. Hine
1966 William A. Garrett
1967 Floyd D. Ostrander
1968 Hubert A. McGuirl
1969 Harry M. Klenda
1970 John M. Deines
1971 Carl A. Laughlin

The American Dialect Society

1890 F. J. Child
1891 James M. Hart
1893 James M. Garnett
1894 Edward S. Sheldon
1896 Charles H. Grandgent
1897 G. L. Kittredge
1898 O. F. Emerson
1899 Lewis F. Mott
1901 George Hempl
1906 Oliver F. Emerson
1910 Raymond Weeks
1911 Calvin Thomas
1913 William E. Mead
1916 James W. Bright
1946 Kemp Malone
1947 Atcheson L. Hench
1949 Allen W. Read
1951 E. H. Criswell
1953 James B. McMillan
1956 Levette J. Davidson
1958 Frederic G. Cassidy
1960 Thomas Pyles
1962 Albert H. Marckwardt
1964 Allan F. Hubbell
1965 Einar Haugen
1967 Raven I. McDavid
1969 David W. Maurer
1971 Harold B. Allen

American Economic Association

1886 Francis A. Walker
1893 Charles F. Dunbar
1894 John B. Clark
1896 Henry C. Adams
1898 Arthur T. Hadley
1900 Richard T. Ely
1902 Edwin R. A. Seligman
1904 Frank W. Taussig
1906 Jeremiah W. Jenks
1908 Simon N. Patten
1909 Davis R. Dewey
1910 Edmund J. James
1911 Henry W. Farnam
1912 Frank A. Fetter
1913 David Kinley
1914 John H. Gray
1915 Walter F. Willcox
1916 Thomas N. Carver
1917 John R. Commons
1918 Irving Fisher
1919 Henry B. Gardner
1920 Herbert J. Davenport
1921 Jacob H. Hollander
1922 Henry R. Seager
1923 Carl C. Plehn
1924 Wesley C. Mitchell
1925 Allyn A. Young
1926 Edwin W. Kemmerer
1927 Thomas S. Adams
1928 Fred M. Taylor
1929 Edwin F. Gay
1930 Matthew B. Hammond
1931 Ernest L. Bogart
1932 George E. Barnett
1933 William Z. Ripley
1934 Harry A. Millis
1935 John M. Clark
1936 Alvin S. Johnson
1937 Oliver M. W. Sprague
1938 Alvin H. Hansen
1939 Jacob Viner
1940 Frederick C. Mills
1941 Sumner H. Slichter
1942 Edwin G. Nourse
1943 Albert B. Wolfe
1944 Joseph S. Davis
1945 I. L. Sharfman
1946 Emanuel A. Goldenweiser
1947 Paul H. Douglas
1948 Joseph A. Schumpeter
1949 Howard S. Ellis
1950 Frank H. Knight
1951 John H. Williams
1953 Calvin B. Hoover
1954 Simon Kuznets
1955 John D. Black
1956 Edwin E. Witte
1957 Morris A. Copeland
1958 George W. Stocking
1959 Arthur F. Burns
1960 Theodore W. Schultz
1961 Paul A. Samuelson
1962 Edward S. Mason
1963 Gottfried Haberler
1964 George J. Stigler
1965 Joseph J. Spengler
1966 Fritz Machlup
1967 Milton Friedman
1968 Kenneth E. Boulding
1969 Wassily Leontief
1970 James Tobin
1971 John Kenneth Galbraith
1972 Kenneth J. Arrow

American Geographical Society

1852 George Bancroft
1854 Francis L. Hawks
1861 Henry Grinnell
1864 Charles P. Daly
1900 Seth Low
1903 Robert E. Peary
1907 Archer M. Huntington
1916 John Greenough
1925 John H. Finley
1934 Roland L. Redmond
1947 Richard U. Light
1957 Walter A. Wood
1967 Serge A. Korff

American Geophysical Union

1920 William Bowie
1922 Louis A. Bauer
1924 Harry F. Reid
1926 H. S. Washington
1929 William Bowie
1932 W. J. Humphreys
1935 N. H. Heck
1938 Richard M. Field

1941 W. C. Lowdermilk
1944 Leason H. Adams
1947 O. E. Meinzer
1948 W. H. Bucher
1953 James B. Macelwane
1956 Maurice Ewing
1959 L. V. Berkner
1961 Thomas F. Malone
1964 George P. Woollard
1966 William C. Ackerman
1968 Helmut E. Landsberg
1970 Homer E. Newell

American Heart Association

1924 Lewis A. Connor
1925 Joseph Sailor
1927 James B. Herrick
1929 William H. Robey
1931 Robert H. Halsey
1933 Stewart R. Roberts
1935 John Wyckoff
1937 William J. Kerr
1939 William D. Stroud
1941 Paul D. White
1943 Roy W. Scott
1946 Howard West
1947 Arlie R. Barnes
1948 Tinsley R. Harrison
1949 H. M. Marvin
1950 Howard B. Sprague
1951 Louis N. Katz
1952 Irving S. Wright
1953 Robert L. King
1954 E. Cowles Andrus
1955 Irvine H. Page
1956 Edgar V. Allen
1957 Robert W. Wilkins
1958 Francis L. Chamberlain
1959 A. Carlton Ernestene
1960 Oglesby Paul
1961 J. Scott Butterworth
1962 James W. Warren
1963 John J. Sampson
1964 Carleton B. Chapman
1965 Helen B. Taussig
1966 Lewis E. January
1967 Jesse E. Edwards
1968 Walter B. Frommeyer, Jr.
1969 W. Proctor Harvey
1971 William Glenn
1972 J. Willis Hurst

American Historical Association

1884 Andrew D. White
1885 George Bancroft
1886 Justin Winsor
1887 William F. Poole
1888 Charles K. Adams
1889 John Jay
1890 William W. Henry
1891 James B. Angell
1893 Henry Adams
1895 George F. Hoar
1896 Richard S. Storrs
1897 James Schouler
1898 George P. Fisher
1899 James F. Rhodes
1900 Edward Eggleston
1901 Charles Francis Adams
1902 Alfred T. Mahan
1903 Henry C. Lea
1904 Goldwin Smith
1905 John B. McMaster
1906 Simeon E. Baldwin
1907 J. Franklin Jameson
1908 George B. Adams
1909 Albert B. Hart
1910 Frederick J. Turner
1911 William M. Sloane
1912 Theodore Roosevelt
1913 William A. Dunning
1914 Andrew C. McLaughlin
1915 H. Morse Stephens
1916 George L. Burr
1917 Worthington C. Ford
1918 William R. Thayer
1920 Edward Channing
1922 Charles H. Haskins
1923 Edward P. Cheyney
1924 Woodrow Wilson
1925 Charles M. Andrews
1926 Dana C. Munro
1927 Henry O. Taylor
1928 James H. Breasted
1929 James H. Robinson
1930 Evarts B. Greene
1931 Carl L. Becker
1932 Herbert E. Bolton
1933 Charles A. Beard
1934 William E. Dodd
1936 Charles McIlwain
1937 Guy S. Ford
1938 Laurence M. Larson
1938 Frederic L. Paxson
1939 William S. Ferguson
1940 Max Farrand
1941 James W. Thompson
1942 Arthur M. Schlesinger, Sr.
1943 Nellie Neilson
1944 William L. Westermann
1945 Carlton J. H. Hayes
1946 Sidney B. Fay
1947 Thomas J. Wertenbaker
1948 Kenneth S. Latourette
1949 Conyers Read
1950 Samuel Eliot Morison
1951 Robert L. Schuyler
1952 James G. Randall
1953 Louis Gottschalk
1954 Merle Curti
1955 Lynn Thorndike
1956 Dexter Perkins
1957 William Langer
1958 Walter P. Webb
1959 Allan Nevins
1960 Bernadotte E. Schmitt
1961 Samuel F. Bemis
1962 Carl Bridenbaugh
1963 Crane Brinton
1964 Julian P. Boyd
1965 Frederic C. Lane
1966 Roy F. Nichols
1967 Hajo Holborn
1968 John K. Fairbank
1969 C. Vann Woodward
1970 Robert R. Palmer
1971 David M. Potter
1971 Joseph R. Strayer (Acting)
1972 Thomas G. Cochran

American Institute of Aeronautics and Astronautics

1963 William H. Pickering
1964 Courtland D. Perkins
1965 Richard E. Horner
1966 Raymond L. Bisplinghoff
1967 Harold T. Luskin
1968 Floyd L. Thompson
1969 Robert C. Seamans, Jr.
1969 Ronald Smelt
1970 Martin Goland
1971 Allen E. Puckett

The American Institute of Architects

1857 Richard Upjohn
1877 Thomas U. Walter
1888 Richard M. Hunt
1892 Edward H. Kendall
1894 Daniel H. Burnham
1896 George B. Post
1899 Henry Van Brunt
1900 Robert S. Peabody
1902 Charles F. McKim
1904 William S. Eames
1906 Frank Miles Day
1908 Cass Gilbert
1910 Irving K. Pond
1912 Walter Cook
1913 R. Clipston Sturgis
1915 John L. Mauran
1918 Thomas R. Kimball
1920 Henry H. Kendall
1922 William B. Faville
1924 Dan Everett Waid
1926 Milton B. Medary
1928 C. Herrick Hammond
1930 Robert D. Kohn
1932 Ernest J. Russell
1935 Stephen F. Voorhees
1937 Charles D. Maginnis
1939 Edwin Bergstrom
1941 R. H. Shreve
1943 Raymond J. Ashton
1945 James R. Edmunds, Jr.
1947 Douglas W. Orr
1949 Ralph Walker
1951 Glenn Stanton
1953 Clair W. Ditchy
1955 George B. Cummings
1956 Leon Chatelain, Jr.
1958 John N. Richards
1960 Philip Will, Jr.
1962 Henry L. Wright
1963 J. Roy Carroll, Jr.
1964 Art hur G. Odell, Jr.
1965 Morris Ketchum, Jr.
1966 Charles M. Nes, Jr.
1967 Robert L. Durham
1968 George E. Kassabaum
1969 Rex W. Allen
1970 Robert F. Hastings
1971 Max O. Urbahn

American Institute of Certified Public Accountants

1949 J. Harold Stewart
1950 T. Coleman Andrews
1951 J. William Hope
1952 Jay A. Phillips
1953 Arthur B. Foye
1954 Maurice H. Stans
1955 John H. Zebley, Jr.
1956 Marquis G. Eaton
1957 Alvin R. Jennings
1958 Louis H. Penney
1959 J. S. Seidman
1960 Louis H. Pilie
1961 John W. Queenan
1962 Robert E. Witschey
1963 Clifford V. Heimbucher
1964 Thomas D. Flynn
1965 Robert M. Trueblood
1966 Hilliard R. Giffen
1967 Marvin L. Stone
1968 Ralph E. Kent
1969 Louis M. Kessler
1970 Marshall S. Armstrong
1971 Walter T. Oliphant

American Institute of Chemists

1923 Horace G. Byers
1924 M. L. Crossley
1926 Treat B. Johnson
1928 Frederick E. Breithut
1932 Henry G. Knight
1934 M. L. Crossley
1936 Maximilian Toch
1938 Robert J. Moore
1940 Harry L. Fisher
1942 Gustav Egloff
1946 Foster D. Snell
1948 Lawrence Flett
1952 Lincoln T. Work
1954 Donald B. Keyes
1955 Ray P. Dinsmore
1956 John H. Nair
1957 Henry B. Hass
1958 Emil Ott
1959 Wayne E. Kuhn
1960 Milton Harris
1961 Johan Bjorksten
1962 C. Harold Fisher
1963 W. George Parks
1964 W. E. Hanford
1965 Lloyd H. Reyerson
1966 John L. Hickson
1967 Emmett B. Carmichael
1969 Emerson Venable
1971 David W. Young

American Institute of Mining, Metallurgical, and Petroleum Engineers

1932 Scott Turner
1941 John R. Suman
1943 Champion H. Mathewson
1947 Clyde Williams
1950 Donald H. McLaughlin
1951 Willis M. Peirce
1952 Michael L. Haider
1953 Andrew Fletcher
1954 Leo F. Reinartz
1956 Carl E. Reistle, Jr.
1957 Grover J. Holt
1958 Augustus B. Kinzel
1959 Howard C. Pyle
1961 Ronald R. McNaughton
1962 Lloyd E. Elkins
1964 Karl L. Fetters
1965 Thomas C. Frick
1966 William B. Stephenson
1967 Walter R. Hibbard, Jr.
1968 John R. McMillan
1969 James Boyd
1970 John C. Kennear, Jr.
1971 John S. Bell

American Iron and Steel Institute

1908 Elbert H. Gary
1927 Charles M. Schwab
1932 Robert P. Lamont
1934 Eugene G. Grace
1937 Tom M. Girdler
1939 E. T. Weir
1940 Walter S. Tower
1955 Benjamin F. Fairless
1962 Max D. Howell
1963 John P. Roche

American Judicature Society

1914 Harry Olson (Chairman)
1929 Charles Evans Hughes
1930 Newton D. Baker
1938 Frank E. Atwood
1938 Arthur T. Vanderbilt
1940 David A. Simmons
1944 Merrill E. Otis
1944 George E. Brand
1953 Albert J. Harno
1956 William J. Jameson
1958 Albert E. Jenner, Jr.
1960 Cecil E. Burney
1962 Sterry R. Waterman
1964 Henry L. Woolfenden
1966 Herbert Brownell
1968 Gerald C. Snyder
1970 Robert H. Hall

The American Law Institute

1923 George W. Wickersham
1935 George Wharton Pepper
1947 Harrison Tweed
1961 Norris Darrell

The American Legion

National Commanders

1919 Franklin D'Olier
1920 Frederick W. Galbraith, Jr.
1921 John G. Emery
1921 Hanford MacNider
1922 Alvin M. Owsley
1923 John R. Quinn
1924 James A. Drain
1925 John R. McQuigg
1926 Howard P. Savage
1927 Edward P. Spafford
1928 Paul V. McNutt
1929 O. L. Bodenhamer
1930 Ralph T. O'Neill
1931 Henry L. Stevens, Jr.
1932 Louis A. Johnson
1933 Edward A. Hayes
1934 Frank N. Belgrano
1935 Ray Murphy
1936 Harry W. Colmery
1937 Daniel J. Doherty
1938 Stephen F. Chadwick
1939 Raymond J. Kelly
1940 Milo J. Warner
1941 Lynn U. Stambaugh
1942 Roane Waring
1943 Warren H. Atherton
1944 Edward N. Scheiberling
1945 John Stelle
1946 Paul H. Griffith
1947 James F. O'Neil
1948 S. Perry Brown
1949 George N. Craig
1950 Erle Cocke, Jr.
1951 Donald R. Wilson
1952 Lewis K. Gough
1953 Arthur J. Connell
1954 Seaborn P. Collins
1955 J. Addington Wagner
1956 W. C. Daniel
1957 John S. Gleason, Jr.
1958 Preston J. Moore
1959 Martin M. McKneally
1960 William R. Burke
1961 Charles L. Bacon
1962 James E. Powers
1963 Daniel F. Foley
1964 Donald E. Johnson
1965 L. Eldon James
1966 John E. Davis
1967 William E. Galbraith
1968 William C. Doyle
1969 J. Milton Patrick
1970 Alfred P. Chamie
1971 John H. Geiger

American Library Association

1876 Justin Winsor
1885 William F. Poole
1887 Charles A. Cutter
1889 Frederick M. Crunden
1890 Melvil Dewey
1891 Samuel S. Green
1891 William I. Fletcher
1892 Melvil Dewey
1893 Josephus N. Larned
1894 Henry M. Utley
1895 John C. Dana
1896 William H. Brett
1897 Justin Winsor
1898 Herbert Putnam
1898 William C. Lane
1899 Reuben G. Thwaites
1900 Henry J. Carr
1901 John S. Billings
1902 James K. Hosmer
1903 Herbert Putnam
1904 Ernest C. Richardson
1905 Frank P. Hill
1906 Clement W. Andrews
1907 Arthur E. Bostwick
1908 Charles H. Gould
1909 Nathaniel D. C. Hodges
1910 James I. Wyer
1911 Theresa West Elmendorf
1912 Henry E. Legler
1913 Edwin H. Anderson
1914 Hiller C. Wellman
1915 Mary W. Plummer
1916 Walter L. Brown
1917 Thomas L. Montgomery
1918 William W. Bishop
1919 Chalmers Hadley
1920 Alice S. Tyler
1921 Azariah S. Root
1922 George B. Utley
1923 Judson T. Jennings
1924 Herman H. B. Meyer
1925 Charles F. D. Belder
1926 George H. Locke
1927 Carl B. Roden
1928 Linda A. Eastman
1929 Andrew Keogh
1930 Adam Strohm
1931 Josephine A. Rathbone
1932 Harry M. Lydenberg
1933 Gratia A. Countryman
1934 Charles H. Compton
1935 Louis R. Wilson
1936 Malcolm G. Wyer
1937 Harrison W. Craver
1938 Milton J. Ferguson
1939 Ralph Munn
1940 Essae M. Culver
1941 Charles H. Brown
1942 Keyes D. Metcalf
1943 Althea H. Warren
1944 Carl Vitz
1945 Ralph A. Ulveling
1946 Mary U. Rothrock
1947 Paul N. Rice
1948 Errett W. McDiarmid
1949 Milton E. Lord
1950 Clarence R. Graham
1951 Loleta Dawson Fyan
1952 Robert B. Downs
1953 Flora B. Ludington
1954 Lewis Q. Mumford
1955 John S. Richards
1956 Ralph R. Shaw
1957 Lucile M. Morsch
1958 Emerson Greenaway
1959 Benjamin E. Powell
1960 Frances L. Spain
1961 Florrinell F. Morton
1962 James E. Bryan
1963 Frederick H. Wagman
1964 Edwin Castagna
1965 Robert Vosper
1966 Mary V. Gaver
1967 Foster E. Mohrhardt
1968 Roger McDonough
1969 William S. Dix

American Management Association

1923 Sam A. Lewisohn
1926 Frank L. Sweetser
1928 Cyrus S. Ching
1930 William J. Graham
1934 Malcolm C. Rorty
1936 Alvin E. Dodd
1948 Lawrence A. Appley
1968 Alexander B. Trowbridge
1970 Don G. Mitchell

American Marketing Association

1936 Frank R. Coutant
1938 Fred E. Clark
1939 N. H. Engle
1940 Donald R. G. Cowan
1941 Howard T. Hovde
1942 Vergil D. Reed
1943 Albert Haring
1944 Howard W. Green
1945 Donald M. Hobart
1946 Lyman Hill
1947 Ross M. Cunningham
1948 Wroe Alderson
1949 Harvey W. Huegy
1950 Everett P. Smith
1951 George H. Brown
1952 Gordon A. Hughes
1953 Neil H. Borden
1954 Thomas G. MacGowan
1955 Ira D. Anderson
1956 Charles W. Smith
1957 D. Maynard Phelps
1958 Wendell R. Smith
1959 Reavis Cox
1960 William F. O'Dell
1961 Albert W. Frey
1962 Donald R. Longman
1963 William R. Davidson
1964 Edwin H. Sonnecken
1965 Schuyler F. Otteson
1966 Robert J. Lavidge
1967 Robert J. Holloway
1968 Victor P. Buell
1969 Robert Ferber
1970 Elmer Lotshaw

American Mathematical Society

1889 John H. Van Amringe
1891 Emory McClintock
1895 G. W. Hill
1897 Simon Newcomb
1899 Robert S. Woodward
1901 Eliakim H. Moore
1903 Thomas S. Fiske
1905 William F. Osgood
1907 Henry S. White
1909 Maxime Bocher
1911 Henry B. Fine
1913 Edward B. Van Vleck
1915 Ernest W. Brown
1917 Leonard E. Dickson
1919 Frank Morley
1921 Gilbert A. Bliss
1923 Oswald Veblen
1925 George D. Birkhoff
1927 Virgil Snyder
1929 Earle R. Hedrick
1931 Luther P. Eisenhart
1933 Arthur B. Coble
1935 Solomon Lefschetz
1937 Robert L. Moore
1939 Griffith C. Evans
1941 Marston Morse
1943 Marshall H. Stone
1945 Theophil H. Hildebrandt
1947 Einar Hille
1949 Joseph L. Walsh
1951 John von Neumann
1953 Gordon T. Whyburn
1955 Raymond L. Wilder
1957 Richard D. Brauer
1959 Edward J. McShane
1961 Deane Montgomery
1963 Joseph L. Doob
1965 A. Adrian Albert
1967 Charles B. Morrey, Jr.
1969 Oscar Zariski
1971 Nathan Jacobson

American Medical Association

1847 Nathaniel Chapman
1848 Alexander H. Stevens
1849 John C. Warren
1850 Reuben D. Mussey
1851 James Moultrie
1852 Beverley R. Wellford
1853 Jonathan Knight
1854 Charles A. Pope
1855 George B. Wood
1856 Zina Pitcher
1857 Paul F. Eve
1858 Harvey Lindsly
1859 Henry Miller
1860 Eli Ives
1863 Alden March
1864 Nathan S. Davis
1866 D. Humphreys Storer
1867 Henry F. Askew
1868 Samuel D. Gross
1869 William O. Baldwin
1870 George Mendenhall
1871 Alfred Stille
1872 David W. Yandell
1873 Thomas M. Logan
1874 Joseph M. Toner
1875 William K. Bowling
1876 J. Marion Sims
1877 Henry I. Bowditch
1878 Tobias G. Richardson
1879 Theophilus Parvin
1880 Lewis A. Sayre
1881 John T. Hodgen
1882 Joseph J. Woodward
1883 John L. Atlee
1884 Austin Flint, Sr.
1885 Henry F. Campbell
1886 William Brodie
1887 Elisha H. Gregory
1888 Alexander Y. P. Garnett
1889 William W. Dawson
1890 Edward M. Moore
1891 William T. Briggs
1892 Henry O. Marcy
1893 Hunter McGuire
1894 James F. Hibberd
1895 Donald MacLean
1896 R. Beverly Cole
1897 Nicholas Senn
1898 George M. Sternberg
1899 Joseph M. Mathews
1900 William W. Keen
1901 Charles A. L. Reed
1902 John W. Wyeth
1903 Frank Billings
1904 John H. Musser.
1905 Lewis S. McMurty
1906 William J. Mayo
1907 Joseph D. Bryant
1908 Herbert L. Burrell
1909 William C. Gorgas
1910 William H. Welch
1911 John B. Murphy
1912 Abraham Jacobi
1913 John A. Witherspoon
1914 Victor C. Vaughan
1915 William L. Rodman
1916 Rupert Blue
1917 Charles H. Mayo
1918 Arthur D. Bevan
1919 Alexander Lambert
1920 William C. Braisted
1921 Hubert Work
1922 George E. Schweinitz
1923 Ray L. Wilbur
1924 William A. Pusey
1925 William D. Haggard
1926 Wendell C. Phillips
1927 Jabez N. Jackson
1928 William S. Thayer
1929 Malcolm L. Harris
1930 William G. Morgan
1931 E. Starr Judd
1932 Edward H. Cary
1933 Dean D. Lewis
1934 Walter L. Bierring
1935 James S. McLester
1936 James T. Mason
1936 Charles G. Heyd
1937 John H. J. Upham
1938 Irvin W. Abell
1939 Rock Sleyster
1940 Nathan B. Van Etten
1941 Frank H. Lahey
1942 Fred W. Rankin
1943 James E. Paullin
1944 Herman L. Kretschmer
1945 Roger I. Lee
1946 Harrison H. Shoulders
1947 Edward L. Bortz
1948 R. L. Sensenich
1949 Ernest E. Irons
1950 Elmer L. Henderson
1951 John W. Cline
1952 Louis H. Bauer
1953 Edward J. McCormick
1954 Walter B. Martin
1955 Elmer Hess
1956 Dwight H. Murray
1957 David B. Allman
1958 Gunnar Gundersen
1959 Louis M. Orr
1960 E. Vincent Askey
1961 Leonard W. Larson
1962 George M. Fister
1963 Edward R. Annis
1964 Norman A. Welch
1964 Donovan F. Wood
1965 James Z. Appel
1966 Charles L. Hudson
1967 Milford O. Rouse
1968 Dwight L. Wilbur
1969 Gerald D. Dorman
1970 Walter C. Bornemeier
1971 Wesley W. Hall
1972 C. A. Hoffman

The American National Red Cross

1881 Clara Barton
1904 William K. Van Reypen
1906 Robert M. O'Reilly
1906 George W. Davis
1915 William Howard Taft
1919 Livingston Farrand
1921 John Barton Payne
1935 Cary T. Grayson
1938 Norman H. Davis
1944 Basil O'Connor
1949 George C. Marshall
1950 E. Roland Harriman
1954 Ellsworth Bunker
1957 Alfred M. Gruenther
1964 James F. Collins
1970 George M. Elsey

American Neurological Association

1880 Frank T. Miles
1881 Roberts Bartholow
1882 William A. Hammond
1883 Robert T. Edes
1884 Isaac Ott
1885 Burt G. Wilder
1886 Charles K. Mills
1887 Landon C. Gray
1888 James J. Putnam
1889 Edouard C. Seguin
1890 Edward C. Spitzka
1891 Wharton Sinkler
1892 Charles L. Dana
1893 Henry M. Lyman
1894 Bernard Sachs
1895 Philip C. Knapp
1896 Francis X. Dercum
1897 Moses A. Starr
1898 Graeme M. Hammond
1899 James H. Lloyd
1900 Edward D. Fisher
1901 George L. Walton
1902 Joseph Collins
1903 James W. Putmam
1904 Frank R. Fry
1905 William G. Spiller
1906 Henry R. Stedman
1907 Hugh T. Patrick
1908 Charles W. Burr
1909 S. Weir Mitchell
1910 Morton Prince
1911 Henry M. Thomas
1912 William N. Bullard
1913 Pearce Bailey
1914 Henry Hun
1915 George W. Jacoby
1916 Lewellys F. Barker
1917 Edward W. Taylor
1918 Theodore H. Weisenburg
1919 James McBride
1920 J. Ramsey Hunt
1921 Sidney I. Schwab
1922 Adolf Meyer
1923 Harvey Cushing
1924 Charles K. Mills
1925 Frederick Peterson
1926 Frederick Tilney
1927 Peter Bassoe
1928 Charles L. Dana
1929 Charles H. Frazier
1930 Smith E. Jelliffe
1931 James B. Ayer
1932 Bernard Sachs
1933 Daniel J. McCarthy
1934 Israel Strauss
1936 Albert M. Barrett
1937 Henry H. Donaldson
1938 Charles A. Elsberg
1939 Williams B. Cadwalader
1940 Foster Kennedy
1941 H. Douglas Singer
1941 Harry Solomon
1942 Lewis J. Pollock
1943 Ernest Sachs
1944 Edwin G. Zabriskie
1945 Walter F. Schaller
1947 Henry A. Riley
1948 George Wilson
1949 Stanley Cobb
1950 Henry W. Woltman
1952 S. Bernard Wortis
1953 Hans H. F. Reese
1954 Roland P. Mackay
1955 Percival Bailey
1956 Johannes M. Nielsen
1957 H. Houston Merritt
1958 Israel S. Wechsler
1959 Bernard J. Alpers
1960 Dered E. Denny-Brown
1961 Harold G. Wolff
1962 James L. O'Leary
1963 Charles D. Aring
1964 Richard B. Richter
1965 Russell N. DeJong
1966 A. Earl Walker
1967 Raymond D. Adams
1968 Adolph L. Sahs
1969 Augustus S. Rose
1970 Melvin D. Yahr
1971 A. B. Baker

American Nuclear Society

1956 C. Rogers McCullough
1957 Leland J. Haworth
1958 Chauncey Starr
1959 Alvin M. Weinberg
1960 Miles C. Leverett
1961 William B. Lewis
1962 Manson Benedict
1963 Clarke Williams
1964 William E. Shoupp
1965 Norman Hilberry
1966 Sidney Siegel
1967 Raemer Schreiber
1968 Karl P. Cohen
1969 Louis H. Roddis, Jr.
1970 N. Joseph Palladino
1971 John W. Landis

The American Ornithologists' Union

1883 Joel A. Allen
1890 Daniel G. Elliot
1892 Elliott Coues
1895 William Brewster
1898 Robert Ridgway
1900 C. Hart Merriam
1903 Charles B. Cory
1905 Charles F. Batchelder
1908 Edward W. Nelson
1911 Frank M. Chapman
1914 Albert K. Fisher
1917 John H. Sage
1920 Witmer Stone
1923 Jonathan Dwight
1926 Alexander Wetmore
1929 Joseph Grinnell
1932 James H. Fleming
1935 Arthur C. Bent
1937 Herbert Friedmann
1939 James P. Chapin
1942 James L. Peters
1945 Hoyes Lloyd
1948 Robert C. Murphy
1950 Josselyn Van Tyne
1953 Alden H. Miller
1956 Ernst Mayr
1959 George H. Lowery, Jr.
1962 Austin L. Rand
1964 Dean Amadon
1966 Harold F. Mayfield
1968 John W. Aldrich
1971 Robert W. Storer

American Peace Society

1837 William Ladd
1841 Samuel E. Coues
1846 Theodore Frelinghuysen
1847 Anson G. Phelps
1848 William Jay
1859 Francis Wayland
1861 Howard Malcolm
1873 Edward S. Tobey
1891 Robert Treat Paine
1911 Theodore E. Burton
1916 George W. Kirchwey
1917 James L. Slayden
1920 Andrew J. Montague
1923 Theodore E. Burton
1929 William Fortune
1930 John J. Esch
1938 Mark L. Bristol
1940 Philip M. Brown
1946 Amos J. Peaslee
1949 Ulysses S. Grant III
1959 Charles W. Lowry
1962 Paul M. A. Linebarger
1964 Charles J. Zinn
1966 Donald Armstrong
1967 Claude E. Hawley
1969 Evron M. Kirkpatrick

American Petroleum Institute

1919 T. A. O'Donnell
1925 J. Edgar Pew
1926 William S. Farish
1927 Edward W. Clark
1929 Edwin B. Reeser
1932 Amos L. Beaty
1933 Charles B. Ames
1934 Axtell J. Byles
1942 William R. Boyd, Jr.
1950 Frank M. Porter
1963 Frank N. Ikard

American Pharmaceutical Association

1936 George D. Beal
1937 E. N. Gathercoal
1938 J. Leon Lascoff
1939 Andrew G. DuMez
1940 Charles H. Evans
1941 B. V. Christensen
1942 Roy B. Cook
1943 Ivor Griffith
1944 George A. Moulton
1946 Earl R. Serles
1947 Sylvester H. Dretzka
1948 Ernest Little
1949 Glenn L. Jenkins
1950 Henry H. Gregg
1951 Don E. Francke
1952 R. Q. Richards
1953 F. Royce Franzoni
1954 Newell W. Stewart
1955 John B. Heinz
1956 John A. McCartney
1957 Joseph B. Burt
1958 Louis J. Fischl
1959 Howard C. Newton
1960 Ronald V. Robertson
1961 J. Warren Landsdowne
1962 George F. Archambault
1963 Robert J. Gillespie
1964 J. Curtis Nottingham
1965 Grover C. Bowles
1966 Linwood F. Tice
1967 George W. Grider
1968 Max W. Eggleston
1969 William B. Hennessey
1970 William R. Whitten
1971 Lloyd M. Parks

American Philological Association

1869 William D. Whitney
1870 Howard Crosby
1871 William W. Goodwin
1872 Asahel C. Kendrick
1873 Francis A. March
1874 James H. Trumbull
1875 Albert Harkness
1876 Samuel S. Haldeman
1877 Basil L. Gildersleeve
1878 Jotham B. Sewall
1879 Crawford H. Toy
1880 Lewis R. Packard
1881 Frederic D. Allen
1882 Milton W. Humphreys
1883 Martin L. D'Ooge
1884 William W. Goodwin
1885 Tracy Peck
1886 Augustus C. Merriam
1887 Isaac H. Hall
1888 Thomas D. Seymour
1889 Charles R. Lanman
1890 Julius Sachs
1891 Samuel Hart
1892 William G. Hale
1893 James M. Garnett
1894 John H. Wright
1895 Francis A. March
1896 Bernadotte Perrin
1897 Minton Warren
1898 Clement L. Smith
1899 Abby Leach
1900 Samuel B. Platner
1901 Andrew F. West
1902 Charles F. Smith
1903 George Hempl
1904 Herbert W. Smyth
1905 Elmer T. Merrill
1906 Francis W. Kelsey
1907 Charles E. Bennett
1908 Basil L. Gildersleeve
1909 Paul Shorey
1910 John C. Rolfe
1911 Thomas D. Goodell
1912 Harold N. Fowler
1913 Edward Capps
1914 Edward P. Morris
1915 Carl D. Buck
1916 Frank G. Moore
1917 Frank F. Abbott
1918 John A. Scott
1919 Clifford H. Moore
1920 Walton B. McDaniel
1921 Francis G. Allinson
1922 Edward K. Rand
1923 Samuel E. Bassett
1926 Frank C. Babbitt
1927 Clarence P. Bill
1928 Tenney Frank
1929 Charles B. Gulick
1930 Henry W. Prescott
1931 Ivan M. Linforth
1932 Campbell Bonner
1933 Elizabeth H. Haight
1934 Berthold L. Ullman
1935 George L. Hendrickson
1936 Henry A. Sanders
1937 William A. Oldfather
1938 Austin M. Harmon
1939 Arthur S. Pease
1940 George M. Calhoun
1941 Lily R. Taylor
1942 Marbury B. Ogle
1943 John G. Winter
1944 George D. Hadzsits
1945 Levi A. Post
1946 Norman W. DeWitt
1947 Cornelia C. Coulter
1948 William H. Alexander
1949 Lucius R. Shero
1950 William C. Greene
1951 Jakob A. O. Larsen
1952 Benjamin D. Meritt
1954 Harry Caplan
1955 George E. Duckworth
1956 Charles B. Welles
1957 Gertrude E. Smith
1960 Robert S. Rogers
1961 Inez S. Ryberg
1962 Howard Comfort
1963 Gerald F. Else
1964 Dorothy M. Robathan
1965 John L. Heller
1966 Phillip H. DeLacy
1967 Frederick M. Combellack
1968 Herbert Bloch
1970 Malcolm F. McGregor
1971 Edward T. Salmon
1972 Agnes K. L. Michels

American Philosophical Society

1769 Benjamin Franklin
1791 David Rittenhouse
1797 Thomas Jefferson
1815 Caspar Wistar
1819 Robert Patterson
1825 William Tilghman
1828 Peter S. Du Ponceau
1845 Robert M. Patterson
1846 Nathaniel Chapman
1849 Robert M. Patterson
1853 Franklin Bache
1855 Alexander D. Bache
1857 John K. Kane
1859 George B. Wood
1880 Frederick Fraley
1902 Isaac J. Wistar
1903 Edgar F. Smith
1908 William W. Keen
1918 William B. Scott
1925 Charles D. Walcott
1927 Francis X. Dercum
1931 Henry N. Russell
1932 Roland S. Morris
1942 Edwin G. Conklin
1945 Thomas S. Gates
1948 Edwin G. Conklin
1952 Owen J. Roberts
1956 William J. Robbins
1959 Henry A. Moe
1970 Leonard Carmichael

The American Physical Society

1899 Henry A. Rowland
1901 Albert A. Michelson
1903 Arthur G. Webster
1905 Carl Barus
1907 Edward L. Nichols
1909 Henry Crew
1911 William F. Magie
1913 B. O. Pierce
1914 Ernest Merritt
1916 Robert A. Millikan
1918 Henry A. Bumstead
1919 Joseph S. Ames
1921 Theodore Lyman
1923 Charles E. Mendenhall
1925 Dayton C. Miller
1927 Karl T. Compton
1929 Henry G. Gale
1933 Paul D. Foote
1934 Arthur H. Compton
1935 Robert W. Wood
1936 Floyd K. Richtmyer
1937 Harrison M. Randall
1938 Lyman J. Briggs
1939 John T. Tate
1940 John Zeleny
1941 George B. Pegram
1941 George W. Stewart
1942 Percy W. Bridgman
1943 Albert W. Hull
1944 Arthur J. Dempster
1945 Harvey Fletcher
1946 Edward U. Condon
1947 Lee A. DuBridge
1948 J. Robert Oppenheimer
1949 Francis W. Loomis
1950 Isidor I. Rabi
1951 Charles C. Lauritsen
1952 John H. Van Vleck
1953 Enrico Fermi
1954 Hans A. Bethe
1955 Raymond T. Birge
1956 Eugene P. Wigner
1957 Henry D. Smyth
1958 Jesse W. Beams
1959 George E. Uhlenbeck
1960 Victor F. Weisskopf
1961 Frederick Seitz
1962 William V. Houston
1963 John H. Williams
1964 Robert F. Bacher
1965 Felix Bloch
1966 John A. Wheeler
1967 Charles H. Townes
1968 John Bardeen
1969 Luis W. Alvarez
1970 Edward M. Purcell
1971 Robert Serber

The American Physiological Society

1888 Henry P. Bowditch
1889 S. Weir Mitchell
1891 Henry P. Bowditch
1896 Russell H. Chittenden
1905 William H. Howell
1911 Samuel J. Meltzer
1914 Walter B. Cannon
1917 Frederick S. Lee
1919 Warren P. Lombard
1923 Anton J. Carlson
1926 E. Joseph Erlanger

1930 Walter J. Meek
1933 Arno B. Luckhardt
1935 Clarence W. Greene
1936 Frank C. Mann
1938 Walter E. Garrey
1940 Andrew C. Ivy
1942 Phillip Bard
1946 Wallace O. Fenn
1948 Maurice B. Visscher
1949 Carl J. Wiggers
1950 David B. Dill
1951 Ralph W. Gerard
1952 Eugene M. Landis
1953 Edward F. Adolph
1954 Hiram E. Essex
1955 William F. Hamilton
1956 Alan C. Burton
1957 Louis N. Katz
1958 Hallowell Davis
1959 Robert F. Pitts
1960 Julius H. Comroe, Jr.
1961 Horace W. Davenport
1962 Hymen S. Mayerson
1963 Herman Rahn
1964 John R. Pappenheimer
1965 John M. Brookhart
1966 Robert E. Forster
1967 Robert W. Berliner
1968 Loren D. Carlson
1969 C. Ladd Prosser
1970 A. Clifford Barger
1971 John R. Brobeck

The American Political Science Association

1904 Frank J. Goodnow
1906 Albert Shaw
1907 Frederick N. Judson
1908 James Bryce
1909 A. Lawrence Lowell
1910 Woodrow Wilson
1911 Simeon E. Baldwin
1912 Albert B. Hart
1913 Westel W. Willoughby
1914 John B. Moore
1915 Ernest Freund
1916 Jesse Macy
1917 Munroe Smith
1918 Henry J. Ford
1920 Paul S. Reinsch
1921 Leo S. Rowe
1922 William A. Dunning
1923 Harry A. Garfield
1924 James W. Garner
1925 Charles E. Merriam
1926 Charles A. Beard
1927 William B. Munro
1928 Jesse S. Reeves
1929 John A. Fairlie
1930 Benjamin F. Shambaugh
1931 Edward S. Corwin
1932 W. F. Willoughby
1933 Isidor Loeb
1934 Walter J. Shepard
1935 Francis W. Coker
1936 Arthur N. Holcombe
1937 Thomas R. Powell
1938 Clarence A. Dykstra
1939 Charles G. Haines
1940 Robert C. Brooks
1941 Frederic A. Ogg
1942 William Anderson
1943 Robert E. Cushman
1944 Leonard D. White
1945 John M. Gaus
1946 Walter F. Dodd
1947 Arthur W. Macmahon
1948 Henry R. Spencer
1949 Quincy Wright
1950 James K. Pollock
1951 Peter H. Odegard
1952 Luther Gulick
1953 Pendleton Herring
1954 Ralph J. Bunche
1955 Charles McKinley
1956 Harold D. Lasswell
1957 E. E. Schattschneider
1958 V. O. Key, Jr.
1959 R. Taylor Cole
1960 Carl B. Swisher
1961 Emmette S. Redford
1962 Charles S. Hyneman
1963 Carl J. Friedrich
1964 C. Herman Pritchett
1965 David B. Truman
1966 Gabriel A. Almond
1967 Robert A. Dahl
1968 Merle Fainsod
1969 David Easton
1970 Karl W. Deutsch
1971 Robert E. Lane

American Psychiatric Association

1844 Samuel B. Woodward
1848 William McClay Awl
1851 Luther V. Bell
1855 Isaac Ray
1859 Andrew McFarland
1862 Thomas S. Kirkbride
1870 John S. Butler
1873 Charles H. Nichols
1879 Clement A. Walker
1882 John H. Callender
1883 John P. Gray
1884 Pliny Earle
1885 Orpheus Everts
1886 H. A. Buttolph
1887 Eugene Grissom
1888 John P. Chapin
1889 W. W. Godding
1890 H. P. Stearns (to 1891)
1892 J. B. Andrews
1893 John Curwen
1894 Edward Cowles
1895 Richard Dewey
1896 Theophilus O. Powell (to 1897)
1898 Henry M. Hurd
1899 Joseph G. Rogers
1900 Peter M. Wise
1901 Robert J. Preston
1902 G. Alder Blumer
1903 A. E. Macdonald (to 1904)
1905 C. B. Burr
1906 Charles G. Hill
1907 Charles P. Bancroft
1908 Arthur F. Kilbourne
1909 William F. Drewry
1910 Charles W. Pilgrim
1911 Hubert Work
1912 James T. Searcy
1913 Carlos F. MacDonald
1914 Samuel E. Smith
1915 Edward N. Brush
1916 Charles G. Wagner (to 1917)
1918 Elmer E. Southard
1919 Henry C. Eyman
1920 Owen Copp
1921 Albert M. Barrett
1922 Henry W. Mitchell
1923 Thomas W. Salmon
1924 William A. White
1925 C. Floyd Haviland
1926 George M. Kline
1927 Adolf Meyer
1928 Samuel T. Orton
1929 Earl D. Bond (to 1930)
1931 William L. Russell
1932 James V. May
1933 George H. Kirby
1934 C. Fred Williams
1935 Clarence O. Cheney
1936 C. Macfie Campbell
1937 Ross M. Chapman
1938 Richard H. Hutchings
1939 William C. Sandy
1940 George H. Stevenson
1941 James K. Hall
1942 Arthur H. Ruggles
1943 Edward A. Strecker
1944 Karl M. Bowman
1946 Samuel W. Hamilton
1947 Winfred Overholser
1948 William C. Menninger
1949 George S. Stevenson
1950 John C. Whitehorn
1951 Leo H. Bartemeier (to 1952)
1953 Kenneth E. Appel
1954 Arthur P. Noyes
1955 R. Finley Gayle, Jr.
1956 Francis J. Braceland
1957 Harry C. Solomon
1958 Francis J. Gerty
1959 William Malamud
1960 Robert H. Felix
1961 Walter E. Barton
1962 C. H. Hardin Branch
1963 Jack R. Ewalt
1964 Daniel Blain
1965 Howard P. Rome
1966 Harvey J. Tompkins
1967 Henry W. Brosin
1968 Lawrence C. Kolb
1969 Raymond W. Waggoner
1970 Robert S. Garber
1971 Ewald W. Busse

American Psychological Association

1892 Granville S. Hall
1893 George T. Ladd
1894 William James
1895 J. McKeen Cattell
1896 George S. Fullerton
1897 James M. Baldwin
1898 H. Muensterberg
1899 John Dewey
1900 Joseph Jastrow
1901 Josiah Royce
1902 Edmund C. Sanford
1903 William L. Bryan
1904 William James
1905 Mary W. Calkins
1906 James R. Angell
1907 Henry R. Marshall
1908 George M. Stratton
1909 Charles H. Judd
1910 Walter B. Pillsbury
1911 Carl E. Seashore
1912 Edward L. Thorndike
1913 Howard C. Warren
1914 Robert S. Woodworth
1915 John B. Watson
1916 Raymond Dodge
1917 Robert M. Yerkes
1918 John W. Baird
1919 Walter D. Scott
1920 Shepherd I. Franz
1921 Margaret F. Washburn
1922 Knight Dunlap
1923 Lewis M. Terman
1924 Granville S. Hall
1925 Madison Bentley
1926 Harvey A. Carr
1927 Harry L. Hollingworth
1928 Edwin G. Boring
1929 Karl S. Lashley
1930 Herbert S. Langfeld
1931 Walter S. Hunter
1932 Walter R. Miles
1933 Louis L. Thurstone
1934 Joseph Peterson
1935 Albert T. Poffenberger
1936 Clark L. Hull
1937 Edward C. Tolman
1938 John F. Dashiell
1939 Gordon W. Allport
1940 Leonard Carmichael
1941 Herbert Woodrow
1942 Calvin P. Stone
1943 John E. Anderson
1944 Gardner Murphy
1945 Edwin R. Guthrie
1946 Henry E. Garrett
1947 Carl R. Rogers
1948 Donald G. Marquis
1949 Ernest R. Hilgard
1950 J. Paul Guilford
1951 Robert R. Sears
1952 Joseph M. Hunt
1953 Laurence F. Shaffer
1954 Orral H. Mowrer
1955 Everett L. Kelly
1956 Theodore M. Newcomb
1957 Lee J. Cronbach
1958 Harry F. Harlow
1959 Wolfgang Köhler
1960 Donald O. Hebb
1961 Neal E. Miller
1962 Paul E. Meehl
1963 Charles E. Osgood
1964 Quinn McNemar
1965 Jerome S. Bruner
1966 Nicholas Hobbs
1967 Gardner Lindzey
1968 Abraham H. Maslow
1969 George A. Miller
1970 George W. Albee
1971 Kenneth B. Clark

American Public Health Association

1872 Stephen Smith
1875 Joseph M. Toner
1876 Edwin M. Snow
1877 John Henry Rauch
1878 Elisha Harris
1879 James L. Cabell
1880 John Shaw Billings
1881 Charles B. White

1882 Robert C. Kedzie
1883 Ezra M. Hunt
1884 Albert L. Gihon
1885 James E. Reeves
1886 Henry P. Walcott
1887 George M. Sternberg
1888 Charles N. Hewitt
1889 Hosmer A. Johnson
1890 Henry B. Baker
1892 Felix Formento
1893 Samuel H. Durgin
1895 William Bailey
1897 Henry B. Horlbeck
1898 Charles A. Lindsey
1899 Henry Mitchell
1901 Benjamin Lee
1902 Henry D. Holton
1903 Walter Wyman
1905 Frank F. Wesbrook
1906 Franklin C. Robinson
1908 Richard H. Lewis
1909 Gardner T. Swarts
1910 Charles O. Probst
1912 John N. Hurty
1913 Rudolph Hering
1914 William C. Woodward
1915 William T. Sedgwick
1916 John F. Anderson
1917 William A. Evans
1919 L.K. Frankel
1920 Watson S. Rankin
1921 Mazyck P. Ravenel
1922 Allan J. McLaughlin
1923 Ernest C. Levy
1924 William H. Park
1925 Henry F. Vaughan
1926 Charles-Edward A. Winslow
1927 Charles V. Chapin
1928 Herman H. Bundesen
1929 George W. Fuller
1930 Albert J. Chesley
1931 Hugh S. Cumming
1932 Louis I. Dublin
1933 John A. Ferrell
1934 Haven Emerson
1935 Eugene L. Bishop
1936 Walter H. Brown
1937 Thomas Parran
1938 Arthur T. McCormack
1939 Abel Wolman
1940 Edward S. Godfrey, Jr.
1941 W. S. Leathers
1942 John L. Rice
1943 Allen W. Freeman
1944 Felix J. Underwood
1945 John J. Sippy
1947 Harry S. Mustard
1948 Martha M. Eliot
1949 Charles F. Wilinsky
1950 Lowell J. Reed
1951 William P. Shepard
1952 Gaylord W. Anderson
1953 Wilton L. Halverson
1954 Hugh R. Leavell
1955 Herman E. Hilleboe
1956 Ira V. Hiscock
1957 John W. Knutson
1958 Roy J. Morton
1959 Leona Baumgartner
1960 Malcolm H. Merrill
1961 Marion Sheahan
1962 Charles G. King
1963 John W. R. Norton
1964 John D. Porterfield
1965 Dwight F. Metzler
1966 Ernest L. Stebbins
1967 Milton Terris
1968 John J. Hanlon
1969 Lester Breslow
1970 Paul B. Cornely

American Society for Metals

1920 Albert E. White
1921 Frank P. Gilligan
1922 Tillman D. Lynch
1923 George K. Burgess
1924 William S. Bidle
1925 Robert M. Bird
1926 J. Fletcher Harper
1927 Fredrick G. Hughes
1928 Zay Jeffries
1929 Robert G. Guthrie
1930 James M. Watson
1931 Alex. H. D'Arcambal
1932 William B. Coleman
1933 William H. Phillips
1934 Benjamin F. Shepherd
1935 Robert S. Archer
1936 Edgar C. Bain
1937 George B. Waterhouse
1938 William P. Woodside
1939 James P. Gill
1940 Oscar E. Harder
1941 Bradley Stoughton
1942 Herbert J. French
1943 Marcus A. Grossman
1944 Kent. R. Van Horn
1945 Charles H. Herty, Jr.
1946 A. L. Boegehold
1947 Francis B. Foley
1948 Harold K. Work
1949 Arthur E. Focke
1950 Walter E. Jominy
1951 John Chipman
1952 Ralph L. Wilson
1953 James B. Austin
1954 George A. Roberts
1955 Adolph O. Schaefer
1956 Donald S. Clark
1957 G. M. Young
1958 Clarence H. Lorig
1959 Walter Crafts
1960 William Pennington
1961 Carl E. Swartz
1962 Robert Raudebaugh
1963 Merrill A. Scheil
1964 John A. Fellows
1965 Stewart G. Fletcher
1966 John Convey
1967 Earl Parker
1968 Carl Samans
1969 Morris Cohen
1970 Thomas E. Leontis
1971 N. E. Promisel

American Society of Civil Engineers

1853 James Laurie
1868 James P. Kirkwood
1869 William J. McAlpine
1870 Alfred Craven
1872 Horatio Allen
1874 Julius W. Adams
1876 George S. Greene
1878 Ellis S. Chesbrough
1879 William M. Roberts
1880 Albert Fink
1881 James B. Francis
1882 Ashbel Welch
1883 Charles Paine
1884 Don Juan Whittemore
1885 Frederic Graff
1886 Henry Flad
1887 William E. Worthen
1888 Thomas C. Keefer
1889 Max J. Becker
1890 William P. Shinn
1891 Octave Chanute
1892 Mendes Cohen
1893 William Metcalf
1894 William P. Craighill
1895 George S. Morison
1896 Thomas C. Clarke
1897 Benjamin M. Harrod
1898 Alphonse Fteley
1899 Desmond FitzGerald
1900 John F. Wallace
1901 John J. R. Croes
1902 Robert Moore
1903 Alfred Noble
1904 Charles Hermany
1905 Charles C. Schneider
1906 Frederic P. Stearns
1907 George H. Benzenberg
1908 Charles Macdonald
1909 Onward Bates
1910 John A. Bensel
1911 Mordecai T. Endicott
1912 John A. Ockerson
1913 George F. Swain
1914 Hunter McDonald
1915 Charles D. Marx
1916 Elmer L. Corthell
1916 Clemens Herschel
1917 George H. Pegram
1918 Arthur N. Talbot
1919 Fayette S. Curtis
1920 Arthur P. Davis
1921 George S. Webster
1922 John R. Freeman
1923 Charles F. Loweth
1924 Carl E. Grunsky
1925 Robert Ridgway
1926 George S. Davison
1927 John F. Stevens
1928 Lincoln Bush
1929 Anson Marston
1930 John F. Coleman
1931 Francis L. Stuart
1932 Herbert S. Crocker
1933 Alonzo J. Hammond
1934 Harrison P. Eddy
1935 Arthur S. Tuttle
1936 Daniel W. Mead
1937 Louis C. Hill
1938 Henry E. Riggs
1939 Donald H. Sawyer
1940 John P. Hogan
1941 Frederick H. Fowler
1942 Ernest B. Black
1943 Ezra B. Whitman
1944 Malcolm Pirnie
1945 John C. Stevens
1946 Wesley W. Horner
1947 Edgar M. Hastings
1948 Richard E. Dougherty
1949 Franklin Thomas
1950 Ernest E. Howard
1951 Gail A. Hathaway
1952 Carlton S. Proctor
1953 Walter L. Huber
1954 Daniel V. Terrell
1955 William R. Glidden
1956 Enoch R. Needles
1957 Mason G. Lockwood
1958 Louis R. Howson
1959 Francis S. Friel
1960 Frank A. Marston
1961 Glenn W. Holcomb
1962 George B. Earnest
1963 Edmund Friedman
1964 Waldo G. Bowman
1965 Wallace L. Chadwick
1966 William J. Hedley
1967 Earle T. Andrews
1968 Richard H. Tatlow
1969 Frank H. Newnam, Jr.
1970 Thomas M. Niles
1971 Samuel Baxter
1972 Oscar Bray

The American Society of Clinical Pathologists

1922 Philip Hillkowitz
1923 William C. MacCarty
1924 John A. Kolmer
1925 Frederic E. Sondern
1926 William G. Exton
1927 Arthur H. Sanford
1928 Frank W. Hartman
1929 James H. Black
1930 Kenneth M. Lynch
1931 Harry J. Corper
1932 Walter M. Simpson
1933 Alvin G. Foord
1934 Frederick H. Lamb
1935 Foster M. Johns
1935 Robert A. Kilduffe
1936 Roy R. Kracke
1937 Carl W. Maynard
1938 Thomas B. Magath
1939 Leonard W. Larson
1940 Armin V. St. George
1941 John L. Lattimore
1942 Harry Goldblatt
1943 Walter S. Thomas
1944 Frank W. Konzelmann
1946 Stanley P. Reimann
1947 Theodore J. Curphey
1948 Osborne A. Brines
1949 James B. McNaught
1950 F. William Sunderman
1951 Israel Davidsohn
1952 Henry F. Hunt
1953 John R. Schenken
1954 Frank B. Queen
1955 Emma S. Moss
1956 John L. Goforth
1957 Harry P. Smith
1958 Edward L. Burns
1959 John J. Clemmer
1960 John J. Andujar
1961 Merlin L. Trumbull
1961 Richard E. Palmer
1962 Harold D. Palmer
1963 Robert W. Coon
1964 William O. Russell
1965 Albert L. McQuown
1966 Lall G. Montgomery
1967 Rosser L. Mainwaring
1968 Thomas M. Peery
1969 Clyde G. Culbertson
1970 Elmer R. Jennings
1971 William D. Dolan
1972 Jack M. Layton

American Society of Composers, Authors and Publishers (ASCAP)

1914 George Maxwell
1925 Gene Buck
1942 Deems Taylor
1948 Fred E. Ahlert
1950 Otto A. Harbach
1953 Stanley Adams
1956 Paul Cunningham
1959 Stanley Adams

The American Society of International Law

1907 Elihu Root
1925 Charles Evans Hughes
1930 James B. Scott
1940 Cordell Hull
1943 Frederic R. Coudert
1946 Charles C. Hyde
1950 Manley O. Hudson
1953 Edwin D. Dickinson
1954 Charles G. Fenwick
1955 Philip C. Jessup
1956 Quincy Wright
1957 Lester H. Woolsey
1958 Robert R. Wilson
1959 Myres S. McDougal
1960 Herbert W. Briggs
1961 Charles E. Martin
1962 Arthur H. Dean
1963 Hardy C. Dillard
1964 James N. Hyde
1965 Brunson MacChesney
1967 John R. Stevenson
1969 Oscar Schachter
1971 Harold D. Lasswell

The American Society of Landscape Architects

1899 John C. Olmsted
1902 Samuel Parsons, Jr.
1903 Nathan F. Barrett
1904 John C. Olmsted
1906 Samuel Parsons, Jr.
1908 Frederick L. Olmsted, Jr.
1910 Charles N. Lowrie
1912 Harold A. Caparn
1913 Ossian C. Simonds
1914 Warren H. Manning
1915 James S. Pray
1919 Frederick L. Olmsted, Jr.
1923 James L. Greenleaf
1927 Arthur A. Shurcliff
1931 Henry V. Hubbard
1935 Albert D. Taylor
1941 S. Herbert Hare
1945 Markley Stevenson
1949 Gilmore D. Clarke
1951 Lawrence G. Linnard
1953 Leon Zach
1957 Norman T. Newton
1961 John I. Rogers
1963 John O. Simonds
1965 Hubert B. Owens
1967 Theodore Osmundson
1969 Campbell E. Miller
1971 Raymond L. Freeman

The American Society of Mechanical Engineers

1880 Robert H. Thurston
1883 Erasmus D. Leavitt
1884 John E. Sweet
1885 Josephus F. Holloway
1886 Coleman Sellers
1887 George H. Babcock
1888 Horace See
1889 Henry R. Towne
1890 Oberlin Smith
1891 Robert W. Hunt
1892 Charles H. Loring
1893 Eckley B. Coxe
1895 E. F. C. Davies
1895 Charles E. Billings
1896 John Fritz
1897 Worcester R. Warner
1898 Charles W. Hunt
1899 George W. Melville
1900 Charles H. Morgan
1901 Samuel T. Wellman
1902 Edwin Reynolds
1903 James M. Dodge
1904 Ambrose Swasey
1905 John R. Freeman
1906 Frederick W. Taylor
1907 Frederick R. Hutton
1908 Minard L. Holman
1909 Jesse M. Smith
1910 George Westinghouse
1911 E. D. Meier
1912 Alex C. Humphreys
1913 William F. Goss
1914 James Hartness
1915 John A. Brashear
1916 D. S. Jacobus
1917 Ira N. Hollis
1918 Charles T. Main
1919 Mortimer E. Cooley
1920 Fred J. Miller
1921 Edwin S. Carman
1922 Dexter S. Kimball
1923 John L. Harrington
1924 Fred R. Low
1925 William F. Durand
1926 William L. Abbott
1927 Charles M. Schwab
1928 Alex Dow
1929 Elmer A. Sperry
1930 Charles Piez
1931 Roy V. Wright
1932 Conrad N. Lauer
1933 A. A. Potter
1934 Paul Doty
1935 Ralph E. Flanders
1936 William L. Batt
1937 James H. Herron
1938 Harvey N. Davis
1939 Alexander G. Christie
1940 Warren H. McBryde
1941 William A. Hanley
1942 James W. Parker
1943 Harold V. Coes
1944 Robert M. Gates
1945 Alex D. Bailey
1946 D. Robert Yarnall
1947 Eugene W. O'Brien
1948 Ervin G. Bailey
1949 James M. Todd
1950 James D. Cunningham
1951 J. Calvin Brown
1952 R. J. S. Pigott
1953 Frederick S. Blackall, Jr.
1954 Lewis K. Sillcox
1955 David W. R. Morgan
1956 Joseph W. Barker
1957 William F. Ryan
1958 James N. Landis
1959 Glenn B. Warren
1960 Walker L. Cisler
1961 William H. Byrne
1962 Clifford H. Shumaker
1963 Ronald B. Smith
1964 Elmer O. Bergman
1965 Henry N. Muller
1966 James H. Harlow
1967 Louis N. Rowley
1968 George F. Habach
1969 Donald E. Marlowe
1970 Allen F. Rhodes
1971 Kenneth Roe

American Society of Newspaper Editors

1922 Casper S. Yost
1926 Erie C. Hopwood
1928 Walter M. Harrison
1930 Fred F. Shedd
1933 Paul Bellamy
1934 Grove Patterson
1936 Marvin H. Creager
1937 A. H. Kirchhofer
1938 William A. White
1939 Donald J. Sterling
1940 Tom Wallace
1941 Dwight Marvin
1942 W. S. Gilmore
1943 Roy A. Roberts
1944 John S. Knight
1946 Wilbur Forrest
1947 N. R. Howard
1948 Erwin D. Canham
1949 B. M. McKelway
1950 Dwight Young
1951 Alexander F. Jones
1952 Wright Bryan
1953 Basil L. Walters
1954 James S. Pope
1955 Kenneth MacDonald
1956 Jenkin L. Jones
1957 Virginius Dabney
1958 George W. Healy, Jr.
1959 J. R. Wiggins
1960 Turner Catledge
1961 Felix R. McKnight
1962 Lee Hills
1963 Herbert Brucker
1964 Miles H. Wolff
1965 Vermont C. Royster
1966 Robert C. Notson
1967 Michael J. Ogden
1968 Vincent S. Jones
1969 Norman E. Isaacs
1970 Newbold Noyes

American Society of Zoologists

1914 Clarence E. McClung
1915 William A. Locy
1916 David H. Tennent
1917 M. M. Metcalf
1918 George Lefevre
1919 C. M. Child
1920 Gilman A. Drew
1921 C. A. Kofoid
1922 H. H. Wilder
1923 M. F. Guyer
1924 Ross G. Harrison
1925 Charles R. Stockard
1926 Samuel O. Mast
1927 S. J. Holmes
1928 Caswell Grave
1929 Charles B. Davenport
1930 Herbert V. Neal
1931 Fernandus Payne
1932 W. C. Curtis
1933 Charles Zeleny
1934 A. H. Sturtevant
1935 R. W. Hegner
1936 W. C. Allee
1937 F. L. Hisaw
1938 M. H. Jacobs
1939 J. T. Patterson
1940 Wesley R. Coe
1941 R. E. Coker
1942 L. L. Woodruff
1943 T. S. Painter
1944 Sewall Wright
1945 A. S. Pearse
1946 D. E. Minnich
1947 J. H. Bodine
1948 C. G. Hartman
1949 Robert Chambers
1950 Alfred S. Romer
1951 D. M. Whitaker
1952 Franz Schrader
1953 E. Newton Harvey
1954 J. Walter Wilson
1955 Viktor Hamburger
1956 Tracy M. Sonneborn
1957 Elmer G. Butler
1958 H. Burr Steinbach
1959 Victor C. Twitty
1960 Emil Witschi
1961 C. Ladd Prosser
1962 Curt Stern
1963 Theodosius Dobzhansky
1964 George G. Simpson
1965 Theodore H. Bullock
1966 Clifford Grobstein
1967 Howard A. Bern
1968 Vincent G. Dethier
1969 Clement L. Markert
1970 James D. Ebert
1971 Arthur D. Hasler
1972 John O. Corliss

American Sociological Association

1906 Lester F. Ward
1908 William G. Sumner
1910 Franklin H. Giddings
1912 Albion W. Small
1914 Edward A. Ross
1916 George E. Vincent
1917 George E. Howard
1918 Charles H. Cooley
1919 Frank W. Blackmar
1920 James W. Dealey
1921 Edward C. Hayes
1922 James P. Lichtenberger
1923 Ulysses G. Weatherly
1924 Charles A. Ellwood
1925 Robert E. Park
1926 John L. Gillin
1927 William I. Thomas
1928 John M. Gillette
1929 Willaim F. Ogburn
1930 Howard W. Odum
1931 Emory S. Bogardus
1932 Luther L. Bernard
1933 Edward B. Reuter
1934 Ernest W. Burgess
1935 F. Stuart Chapin
1936 Henry P. Fairchild
1937 Ellsworth Faris
1938 Frank H. Hankins
1939 Edwin H. Sutherland
1940 Robert M. MacIver
1941 Stuart A. Queen
1942 Dwight Sanderson
1943 George A. Lundberg
1944 Rupert B. Vance
1945 Kimball Young
1946 Carl C. Taylor
1947 Louis Wirth
1948 E. Franklin Fraizer
1949 Talcott Parsons
1950 Leonard S. Cottrell, Jr.
1951 Robert C. Angell
1952 Dorothy S. Thomas
1953 Samuel A. Stouffer
1954 Florian Znaniecki

1955 Donald Young
1956 Herbert Blumer
1957 Robert K. Merton
1958 Robin M. Williams, Jr.
1959 Kingley Davis
1960 Howard Becker
1961 Robert E.L. Faris
1962 Paul Fl Lazarsfeld
1963 Everett C. Hughes
1964 George C. Homans
1965 Pitirim A. Sorokin
1966 Wilbert E. Moore
1967 Charles P. Loomis
1968 Philip M. Hauser
1969 Arnold M. Rose
1969 Ralph H. Turner
1970 Reinhard Bendix
1971 William H. Sewell
1972 William J. Goode

American Watercolor Society

1866 Samuel Colman
1870 William Hart
1872 James D. Smillie
1878 Thomas W. Wood
1887 J. G. Brown
1905 James C. Nicoll
1910 Alex T. Van Laer
1914 William S. Robinson
1920 Eliot Clark
1923 John W. Dunsmore
1930 George P. Ennis
1936 Hobart Nichols
1938 Roy Brown
1949 Frederic Whitaker
1956 William A. Smith
1957 Hans A. Walleen
1959 Mario Cooper

Archaeological Institute of America

1883 Charles E. Norton
1890 Seth Low
1897 John W. White
1904 Thomas D. Seymour
1908 Francis W. Kelsey
1913 Harry L. Wilson
1914 F. W. Shipley
1918 James C. Egbert
1922 Ralph V. D. Magoffin
1932 Louis E. Lord
1936 William B. Dinsmoor
1946 Sterling Dow
1949 Hugh Hencken
1952 Kenneth J. Conant
1953 Henry T. Rowell
1957 George E. Mylonas
1961 Jotham Johnson
1965 Margaret Thompson
1969 Rodney S. Young

The Authors League of America

1913 Winston Churchill
1917 Rex Beach
1921 Jesse L. Williams
1922 Ellis P. Butler
1924 George B. McCutcheon
1926 Owen Davis
1928 Arthur Train
1929 Arthur Richman
1931 Inez Haynes Irwin
1933 Marc Connelly
1939 Elmer Davis
1941 Howard Lindsay
1943 Russel Crouse
1945 Elmer Rice
1947 Oscar Hammerstein II
1951 Rex Stout
1955 Moss Hart
1961 Rex Stout
1969 Jerome Weidman

Benevolent and Protective Order of Elks (BPOE)

Grand Exalted Rulers

1871 George J. Green
1871 Charles T. White
1872 Joseph C. Pinckney
1874 James W. Powell
1875 Henry P. O'Neil
1876 Frank Girard
1878 George R. Maguire
1879 Charles E. Davies
1879 Louis C. Waehner
1880 Thomas E. Garrett
1882 John J. Tindale
1883 Edwin A. Perry
1884 Henry S. Sanderson
1885 Daniel A. Kelly
1886 William E. English
1887 Hamilton E. Leach
1889 Simon Quinlin
1891 Edwin B. Hay
1893 Astley Apperly
1894 Edwin B. Hay
1895 William G. Meyers
1896 Meade D. Detweiler
1898 John Galvin
1899 B. M. Allen
1900 Jerome B. Fisher
1901 Charles E. Pickett
1902 George P. Cronk
1903 Joseph T. Fanning
1904 William J. O'Brien, Jr.
1905 Robert W. Brown
1906 Henry A. Melvin
1907 John K. Tener
1908 Rush L. Holland
1909 J. U. Sammis
1910 August Herrmann
1911 John P. Sullivan
1912 Thomas B. Mills
1913 Edward Leach
1914 Raymond Benjamin
1915 James R. Nicholson
1916 Edward Rightor
1917 Fred Harper
1918 Bruce A. Campbell
1919 Frank L. Rain
1920 William M. Abbott
1921 W. W. Mountain
1922 J. E. Masters
1923 James G. McFarland
1924 John G. Price
1925 William H. Atwell
1926 Charles H. Grakelow
1927 John F. Malley
1928 Murray Hulbert
1929 Walter P. Andrews
1930 Lawrence H. Rupp
1931 John R. Coen
1932 Floyd E. Thompson
1933 Walter F. Meier
1934 Michael F. Shannon
1935 James T. Hallinan
1936 David Sholtz
1937 Charles S. Hart
1938 Edward J. McCormick
1939 Henry C. Warner
1940 Joseph G. Buch
1941 John S. McClelland
1942 E. Mark Sullivan
1943 Frank J. Lonergan
1944 Robert S. Barrett
1945 Wade H. Kepner
1946 Charles E. Broughton
1947 L. A. Lewis
1948 George I. Hall
1949 Emmett T. Anderson
1950 Joseph B. Kyle
1951 Howard R. Davis
1952 Sam Stern
1953 Earl E. James
1954 William J. Jernick
1955 John L. Walker
1956 Fred L. Bohn
1957 H. L. Blackledge
1958 H. R. Wisely
1959 W. S. Hawkins
1960 John E. Fenton
1961 William A. Wall
1962 Lee A. Donaldson
1963 Ronald J. Dunn
1964 Robert G. Pruitt
1965 R. Leonard Bush
1966 Raymond C. Dobson
1967 Robert E. Boney
1968 Edward W. McCabe
1969 Frank Hise
1970 Glenn L. Miller
1971 E. Gene Fournace

Botanical Society of America

1907 George F. Atkinson
1908 William F. Ganong
1909 Roland Thaxter
1910 Erwin F. Smith
1911 William G. Farlow
1912 Lewis R. Jones
1913 Douglas H. Campbell
1914 Albert S. Hitchcock
1915 John M. Coulter
1916 Robert A. Harper
1917 F. C. Newcombe
1918 William Trelease
1919 Joseph C. Arthur
1920 Nathaniel L. Britton
1921 Charles E. Allen
1922 Henry C. Cowles
1923 Benjamin M. Duggar
1924 William Crocker
1925 Jacob R. Schramm
1926 Liberty Hyde Bailey
1927 H. H. Bartlett
1928 A. H. R. Buller
1929 Margaret C. Ferguson
1930 L. W. Sharp
1931 C. J. Chamberlain
1932 G. J. Peirce
1933 E. J. Kraus
1934 E. D. Merrill
1935 Aven Nelson
1936 C. Stuart Gager
1937 Edmund W. Sinnott
1938 Art hur J. Eames
1939 Karl M. Wiegand
1940 Edgar N. Transeau
1941 John T. Buchholz
1942 Merritt L. Fernald
1943 William J. Robbins
1944 Gilbert M. Smith
1945 I. W. Bailey
1946 Neil E. Stevens
1947 Ralph E. Cleland
1948 Henry A. Gleason
1949 Ivey F. Lewis
1950 Albert F. Blakeslee
1951 Katherine Esau
1952 Edgar Anderson
1953 Ralph H. Wetmore
1954 Adriance S. Foster
1955 Oswald Tippo
1956 Harriet B. Creighton
1957 George S. Avery, Jr.
1958 Frits W. Went
1959 William C. Steere
1960 Kenneth V. Thimann
1961 Vernon I. Cheadle
1962 G. Ledyard Stebbins, Jr.
1963 Constantine J. Alexopoulos
1964 Paul J. Kramer
1965 Aaron J. Sharp
1966 Harold C. Bold
1967 Ralph Emerson
1968 Arthur Galston
1969 Harlan P. Banks
1970 Lincoln Constance
1971 Richard C. Starr
1972 Charles Heimsch

Boy Scouts of America

1910 Colin H. Livingstone
1925 James J. Storrow
1926 Milton A. McRae
1926 Walter W. Head
1931 Mortimer L. Schiff
1946 Amory Houghton
1951 John M. Schiff
1956 Kenneth K. Bechtel
1959 Ellsworth H. Augustus
1964 Thomas J. Watson, Jr.
1968 Irving J. Feist

Chamber of Commerce of the United States

1912 Harry A. Wheeler
1914 John H. Fahey
1916 R. G. Rhett
1918 Harry A. Wheeler
1919 Homer L. Ferguson
1920 Joseph H. Defrees

1922 Julius H. Barnes
1924 Richard F. Grant
1925 John W. O'Leary
1927 Lewis E. Pierson
1928 William Butterworth
1931 Silas H. Strawn
1932 Henry I. Harriman
1935 Harper Sibley
1937 George H. Davis
1939 W. Gibson Carey, Jr.
1940 James S. Kemper
1941 Albert W. Hawkes
1942 Eric A. Johnston
1946 William K. Jackson
1947 Earl O. Shreve
1949 Herman W. Steinkraus
1950 Otto A. Seyferth
1951 Dechard A. Hulcy
1952 Laurence F. Lee
1953 Richard L. Bowditch
1954 Clem D. Johnston
1955 A. Boyd Campbell
1956 John C. Coleman
1957 Philip M. Talbott
1958 William A. McDonnell
1959 Erwin D. Canham
1960 Arthur H. Motley
1961 Richard Wagner
1962 H. Ladd Plumley
1963 Edwin P. Neilan
1964 Walter F. Carey
1965 Robert P. Gerholz
1966 M. A. Wright
1967 Allan Shivers
1968 Winton M. Blount
1969 Jenkin L. Jones
1970 F. Ritter Shumway
1971 Archie K. Davis

Directors Guild of America
(Formerly Screen Directors Guild)

1936 King Vidor
1938 Frank Capra
1941 George Stevens
1943 Mark Sandrich
1944 John Cromwell
1946 George Stevens
1948 George Marshall
1950 Joseph L. Mankiewicz
1951 George Sidney
1959 Frank Capra
1961 George Sidney
1967 Delbert Mann
1971 Robert Wise

Ecological Society of America

1916 V. E. Shelford
1917 Ellsworth Huntington
1918 Henry C. Cowles
1919 Barrington Moore
1921 Stephen A. Forbes
1922 Forest Shreve
1923 Charles C. Adams
1924 E. N. Transeau
1925 A. S. Pearse
1926 J. W. Harshberger
1927 Chancey Juday
1928 H. L. Shantz
1929 W. C. Allee
1930 J. E. Weaver
1931 A. O. Feese
1932 G. E. Nichols
1933 E. B. Powers
1934 George D. Fuller
1935 Walter P. Taylor
1936 William S. Cooper
1937 R. E. Coker
1938 H. C. Hanson
1939 Charles T. Vorhies
1940 Francis Ramaley
1941 Alfred E. Emerson
1942 C. F. Korstian
1943 Orlando Park
1944 Robert F. Griggs
1945 Alfred C. Redfield
1946 John M. Aikman
1947 Aldo Leopold
1948 Paul B. Sears
1949 Z. P. Metcalf
1950 E. Lucy Braun
1951 S. Charles Kendeigh
1952 Frank C. Gates
1953 Lee R. Dice
1954 John E. Potzger
1955 W. J. Hamilton, Jr.
1956 Henry J. Oosting
1957 W. A. Dreyer
1958 Stanley A. Cain
1959 Thomas Park
1960 Charles E. Olmsted
1961 Arthur D. Hasler
1962 Murray F. Buell
1963 W. Frank Blair
1964 John F. Reed
1965 Eugene P. Odum
1966 Bostwick H. Ketchum
1967 Rexford Daubenmire
1968 LaMont C. Cole
1969 John E. Cantlon
1970 Edward S. Deevey
1971 S. I. Auerbach
1972 Robert B. Platt

The Electrochemical Society

1902 Joseph W. Richards
1904 Henry S. Carhart
1905 Wilder D. Bancroft
1906 Carl Hering
1907 Charles F. Burgess
1908 Edward G. Acheson
1909 Leo H. Baekeland
1910 William H. Walker
1911 Willis R. Whitney
1913 Eugene F. Roeber
1914 Frank A. Lidbury
1915 Lawrence Addicks
1916 Francis A. J. Fitzgerald
1917 Colin G. Fink
1918 Frank J. Tone
1919 Wilder D. Bancroft
1920 Walter S. Landis
1921 Acheson Smith
1922 Carl G. Schluederberg
1923 Arthur T. Hinckley
1924 Howard C. Parmelee
1925 Frederick M. Becket
1926 William Blum
1927 Samuel C. Lind
1928 Paul J. Kruesi
1929 Francis C. Frary
1930 Louis Kahlenberg
1931 Bradley Stoughton
1933 John Johnston
1934 Hiram S. Lukens
1935 James H. Critchett
1936 Duncan A. MacInnes
1937 William G. Harvey
1938 Robert L. Baldwin
1939 H. Jermain Creighton
1940 Frank C. Mathers
1941 Raymond R. Ridgway
1942 Edwin M. Baker
1943 Robert M. Burns
1944 Sidney D. Kirkpatrick
1945 William R. Veazey
1946 William C. Moore
1947 George W. Heise
1948 James A. Lee
1949 Albert L. Ferguson
1950 Charles L. Faust
1951 Ralph M. Hunter
1952 John C. Warner
1953 Robert J. Mackay
1954 Marvin J. Udy
1955 Herbert H. Uhlig
1956 Hans Thurnauer
1957 Norman Hackerman
1958 Sherlock Swann, Jr.
1959 William C. Gardiner
1960 Ralph A. Schaefer
1961 Henry B. Linford
1962 Francis L. LaQue
1963 Walter J. Hamer
1964 Lyle I. Gilbertson
1965 Ernest B. Yeager
1966 Harold J. Read
1967 Harry C. Gatos
1968 Ivor E. Campbell
1969 N. Corey Cahoon
1970 Charles W. Tobias

English-Speaking Union of the United States

1921 William Howard Taft
1930 John W. Davis
1938 James R. Angell
1946 Lewis W. Douglas
1947 William V. Griffin
1957 Arthur A. Houghton, Jr.
1959 J. W. F. Treadwell (Acting)
1961 Charles E. Saltzman
1966 Archbold Van Beuren

The Franklin Institute

1824 James Ronaldson
1842 Samuel V. Merrick
1855 John C. Cresson
1864 William Sellers
1867 J. Vaughan Merrick
1870 Coleman Sellers
1875 Robert E. Rogers
1879 William P. Tatham
1886 Charles H. Banes
1887 Joseph M. Wilson
1897 John Birkinbine
1907 Walton Clark
1924 William C. L. Eglin
1929 Nathan Haywood
1937 Philip C. Staples
1941 Charles S. Redding
1946 Richard T. Nalle
1952 S. Wyman Rolph
1958 Wynn L. LePage
1967 Athelstan F. Spilhaus
1970 Bowen C. Dees

General Society of Colonial Wars

Governers General

1893 Frederic J. de Peyster
1905 Arthur J. C. Sowdon
1911 Howland Pell
1915 Richard M. Cadwalader
1918 William W. Ladd
1927 Henry G. Sanford
1929 Louis R. Cheney
1930 George de B. Keim
1936 Francis R. Stoddard
1939 Robert M. Boyd, Jr.
1942 Edwin O. Lewis
1945 Alexander G. Brown, Jr.
1948 Philip L. Poe
1951 Daniel M. Bates
1953 Harry P. Cross
1954 Walter M. Pratt
1957 Branton H. Henderson
1960 Robert W. Groves
1963 Anastasio C. M. Azoy
1965 Nathaniel C. Hale
1969 Asa E. Phillips, Jr.

General Society of Mayflower Descendants

Governors General

1897 Henry E. Howland
1903 Charles Francis Adams
1903 Samuel B. Capen
1909 Howland Davis
1912 Thomas S. Hopkins
1915 Leonard Wood
1921 John P. Tilden
1924 Addison P. Munroe
1930 Robert M. Boyd
1933 Burnham S. Colburn
1939 Francis R. Stoddard
1942 Frederick A. Van Fleet
1948 Walter M. Pratt
1954 Waldo M. Allen
1960 Lewis E. Neff
1963 Tilbee D. Gray II
1966 Norman J. Greene
1969 Lee D. Van Antwerp

Geological Society of America

1889 James Hall
1890 James D. Dana
1891 Alexander Winchell
1892 Grove K. Gilbert
1893 J. William Dawson
1894 Thomas C. Chamberlin
1895 N. S. Shaler
1896 Joseph Le Conte
1897 Edward Orton
1898 John V. Stevenson
1899 Benjamin K. Emerson
1900 G. M. Dawson
1901 Charles D. Walcott
1902 Newton H. Winchell
1903 S. F. Emmons
1904 John C. Branner
1905 Raphael Pumpelly
1906 Israel C. Russell
1907 C. R. Van Hise
1908 Samuel Calvin
1909 Grove K. Gilbert
1910 Arnold Hague

1911 William M. Davis
1912 H. L. Fairchild
1913 Eugene A. Smith
1914 George F. Becker
1915 Arthur P. Coleman
1916 John M. Clarke
1917 Frank D. Adams
1918 Whitman Cross
1919 J. C. Merriam
1920 Israel C. White
1921 James F. Kemp
1922 Charles Schuchert
1923 David White
1924 Waldemar Lindgren
1925 William B. Scott
1926 Andrew C. Lawson
1927 Arthur Keith
1928 Bailey Willis
1929 Heinrich Ries
1930 R.A.F. Penrose, Jr.
1931 Alfred C. Lane
1932 Reginald A. Daly
1933 C. K. Leith
1934 W. H. Collins
1935 Nevin M. Fenneman
1936 W. C. Mendenhall
1937 Charles Palache
1938 Arthur L. Day
1939 T. Wayland Vaughan
1940 Eliot Blackwelder
1941 Charles P. Berkey
1942 Douglas Johnson
1943 E. L. Bruce
1944 Adeolph Knopf
1945 Edward W. Berry
1946 Norman L. Bowen
1947 A. I. Levorsen
1948 James Gilluly
1949 Chest R. Longwell
1950 William W. Rubey
1951 Chester Stock
1952 Thomas S. Lovering
1953 Wendell P. Woodring
1954 Ernst Cloos
1955 Walter H. Bucher
1956 George S. Hume
1957 Richard J. Russell
1958 Raymond C. Moore
1959 Marland P. Billings
1960 Hollis D. Hedberg
1961 Thomas B. Nolan
1962 M. King Hubbert
1963 Harry H. Hess
1964 Francis Birch
1965 Wilmot H. Bradley
1966 Robert F. Legget
1967 Konrad B. Krauskopf
1968 Ian Campbell
1969 Morgan J. Davis
1970 John Rodgers
1971 Richard E. Jahns
1972 Luna B. Leopold

Girl Scouts of the United States of America

1915 Mrs. Juliette Low
1920 Mrs. Arthur O. Choate
1922 Mrs. Herbert Hoover
1925 Dean Sarah Louise Arnold
1928 Mrs. William H. Hoffman
1930 Mrs. Frederick Edey
1935 Mrs. Herbert Hoover
1937 Mrs. Fredereick H. Brooke
1939 Mrs. Harvey S. Mudd
1941 Mrs. Alan H. Means
1946 Mrs. C. Vaughan Ferguson
1951 Mrs. Roy F. Layton
1957 Mrs. Charles U. Culmer
1963 Mrs. Holton R. Price, Jr.
1969 Mrs. Douglas H. MacNeil

The Institute of Electrical and Electronics Engineers, Inc.

Prior to 1963 known as the Association of Electrical and Electronic Engineers)

1934 J. Allen Johnson
1935 E. B. Meyer
1936 A. M. MacCutcheon
1937 W. H. Harrison
1938 John C. Parker
1939 F. Malcolm Farmer
1940 R. W. Sorensen
1941 David C. Prince
1942 Harold S. Osborne
1943 Nevin E. Funk
1944 C. A. Powel
1945 W. E. Wickenden
1946 J. Elmer Housley
1947 B. D. Hull
1948 Everett S. Lee
1949 James F. Fairman
1950 Titus G. LeClair
1951 F. O. McMillan
1952 Donald A. Quarles
1953 Elgin B. Robertson
1954 A. C. Monteith
1955 M. D. Hooven
1956 M. S. Coover
1957 W. J. Barrett
1958 L. F. Hickernell
1959 J. H. Foote
1960 C. H. Linder
1961 W. H. Chase
1962 B. R. Teare, Jr.
1963 Ernst Weber
1964 Clarence H. Linder
1965 Bernard M. Oliver
1966 William G. Shepherd
1967 Walter K. MacAdam
1968 Seymour W. Herwald
1969 F. Karl Willenbrock
1970 J. V. N. Granger
1971 James H. Mulligan, Jr.
1972 Robert H. Tanner

The Izaak Walton League of America

1922 Will H. Dilg
1925 Charles W. Folds
1926 Jacob M. Dickinson
1927 Henry B. Ward
1931 Preston Bradley
1935 George W. Wood
1938 Otto C. Doering
1940 Tappan Gregory
1942 Ivar Hennings
1944 Paul Clement
1946 Tom Wallace
1948 Walter Frye
1950 William B. Holton
1952 John W. Tobin
1953 William H. H. Wertz
1955 L. H. Dunten
1956 William H. Pringle
1958 Robert C. O'Hair
1959 George F. Jackson
1960 Alden J. Erskine
1962 L. C. "Jack" Binford
1963 Burt G. Brickner
1965 Reynolds T. Harnsberger
1967 J. Justin Rogers
1968 Raymond A. Haik
1970 Roy B. Crockett

Kiwanis International

1916 George F. Hixson
1918 Perry S. Patterson (to 1919)
1920 J. Mercer Barnett
1921 Harry E. Karr (to 1922)
1923 Edmund F. Arras
1924 Victor M. Johnson
1925 John H. Moss
1926 Ralph A. Amerman
1927 Henry C. Heinz
1928 O. Sam Cummings
1929 Horace W. McDavid
1930 Raymond M. Crossman
1931 William O. Harris
1932 Carl E. Endicott
1933 Joshua L. Johns
1934 William J. Carrington
1935 Harper Gatton
1936 A. Copeland Callen (to 1937)
1938 H. G. Hatfield
1939 Bennett O. Knudson
1940 Mark A. Smith
1941 Charles S. Donley (to 1942)
1943 Donald B. Rice
1944 Ben Dean
1945 Hamilton Holt
1946 J. N. Emerson
1947 Charles W. Armstrong
1948 J. Belmont Mosser
1949 J. Hugh Jackson (to 1950)
1951 Claude B. Hellmann
1952 Walter J. L. Ray
1953 Donald T. Forsythe
1954 Don E. Engdahl
1955 J. A. Raney
1956 Reed C. Culp
1957 H. Park Arnold (to 1958)
1959 Albert J. Tully
1960 J. O. Tally, Jr.
1961 I. R. Witthuhn
1962 Merle H. Tucker
1963 Charles A. Swain
1964 Edward B. Moylan, Jr.
1965 Edward C. Keefe
1966 R. Glenn Reed, Jr.
1967 James M. Moler
1968 Harold M. Heimbaugh
1969 Robert F. Weber
1970 T. R. Johnson
1971 Wes H. Bartlett

Knights of Pythias

Supreme Chancellors

1868 Samuel Reed
1872 Henry C. Berry
1874 Stillman S. Davis
1878 David B. Woodruff
1880 George W. Lindsay
1882 John P. Linton
1884 John Van Valkenberg
1886 Howard Douglass
1888 William Ward
1890 George B. Shaw
1892 William B. Blackwell
1894 Walter B. Ritchie
1896 Philip T. Colgrove
1898 Thomas G. Sample
1900 Ogden H. Fethers
1902 Tracy R. Bangs
1904 Charles E. Shiveley
1906 Charles A. Barnes
1908 Henry P. Brown
1910 George M. Hanson
1912 Thomas J. Carling
1914 Brig S. Young
1916 John J. Brown
1918 Charles S. Davis
1920 William Ladew
1922 George C. Cabell
1924 John Ballantyne
1926 Richard S. Witte
1928 Alva S. Lumpkin
1930 Leslie E. Crouch
1932 James Dunn, Jr.
1934 Reno S. Harp
1936 Fred H. Jones
1938 E. Lee Stapp
1940 Roy O. Garber
1942 John Lee Smith
1944 Charles J. Schuck
1946 Willard M. Kent
1948 Fred Ratliff
1950 Earle N. Genzberger
1952 Sheldon M. Roper
1954 Peter S. Ford
1956 ARchie B. Jackson
1958 William H. Pierce
1960 Leonard M. Eisenberg
1962 Joseph B. Hacker
1964 James C. Bayley
1966 Otto E. Nobis
1968 Otto R. Shuman

Lions International

1917 W. P. Woods
1918 L. H. Lewis
1919 Jesse Robinson
1920 C. C. Reid
1921 Ewen W. Cameron
1922 Ed. S. Vaught
1923 John S. Noel (to 1924)
1925 Benjamin F. Jones
1926 William A. Westfall
1927 Irving L. Camp
1928 Ben A. Ruffin
1929 Ray L. Riley
1930 Earle W. Hodges
1931 Julien C. Hyer
1932 Charles H. Hatton
1933 Roderick Beddow
1934 Vincent C. Hascall
1935 Richard J. Osenbaugh
1936 Edwin R. Kingsley
1937 Frank V. Birch
1938 Walter F. Dexter
1939 Alexander T. Wells
1940 Karl M. Sorrick
1941 George R. Jordan
1942 Edward H. Paine
1943 E. G. Gill
1944 D. A. Skeen (to 1945)
1946 Clifford D. Pierce
1947 Fred W. Smith
1948 Eugene S. Briggs

1949 Walter C. Fisher
1950 Herb C. Petry, Jr.
1951 Harold P. Nutter
1952 Edgar M. Elbert
1953 S. A. Dodge
1954 Monroe L. Nute (to 1955)
1956 John L. Stickley
1957 Edward G. Barry
1958 Dudley L. Simms
1959 Clarence L. Sturm
1960 Finis E. Davis (to 1961)
1962 Curtis D. Lovill
1963 Aubrey D. Green
1964 Claude M. DeVorss
1965 Walter H. Campbell
1966 Edward M. Lindsey (to 1967)
1968 David A. Evans
1969 W. R. Bryan
1970 Robert D. McCullough
1971 Robert J. Uplinger

Loyal Order of Moose

Governors

1904 Abner C. Jones
1905 Morey M. Dunlap
1906 O. W. Edmunds
1907 Curtis H. Gregg
1908 Ewing B. Marshall
1909 John D. O'Brien
1910 Edmund E. Tanner
1911 Arthur H. Jones
1912 Ralph W. E. Donges
1913 Walter E. Dorn
1914 Mahlon M. Garland
1915 Edward J. Henning
1916 Hyman D. Davis
1917 John W. Ford
1918 Charles A. A. McGee
1919 William F. Broening
1920 Darius A. Brown
1921 James F. Griffin
1922 J. Willis Pierson
1923 Frank J. Monahan
1924 Willard A. Markle
1925 J. Albert Cassedy
1926 Norman G. Heyd
1927 Ethelred M. Stafford
1928 Wallace A. McGowan
1929 Albert H. Ladner, Jr.
1930 Rodney H. Brandon
1931 Frederick N. Zihlman
1932 Henry W. Busch
1933 Albert J. Sartori
1934 William E. Buehler
1935 Walter S. Ruff
1936 William A. Anderson
1937 William J. Egan
1938 Roy H. Williams
1939 Bert W. Johnson
1940 Francis J. Clohessy
1941 Matthew M. Neely
1942 Frank J. LaBell
1943 Mark R. Gray
1944 George E. Gwilliam
1945 Charles W. Bowers
1946 Leo W. Ryan
1947 F. Roy Yoke
1948 Walter Gibson
1949 Willis E. Donley
1950 Oliver S. Twist
1951 James M. Ballard
1952 Fritchof T. Sallness
1953 Willard D. Campbell
1954 Ray V. Gibbens
1955 Paul E. McCarville
1956 George W. Young
1957 Ralph A. Villani
1958 Henry F. Wallenwein
1959 Louis K. Thaler
1960 Clayton J. Crooks
1961 H. C. Byrd
1962 Gordon Jeffery
1963 Robert H. Mollohan
1964 Thomas J. Griffin
1965 Elmer E. Harter
1966 Harold D. Ross
1967 George R. Reilly
1969 Cecil Webster
1969 Carl A. Weis
1970 Howard Kline
1971 Edward C. Boyle

The Mediaeval Academy of America

1926 Edward K. Rand
1926 Charles H. Haskins
1927 Edward K. Rand
1929 John M. Manly
1930 Dana B. Munro
1933 Ralph A. Cram
1936 Charles H. Beeson
1939 Jeremiah D. M. Ford
1942 John S. P. Tatlock
1945 George R. Coffman
1948 Fred N. Robinson
1951 William E. Lunt
1954 Austin P. Evans
1957 Ernest H. Wilkins
1960 Berthold L. Ullman
1963 Albert C. Baugh
1966 Joseph R. Strayer
1969 Hamilton M. Smyser

Modern Language Association of America

1884 Franklin Carter
1887 James Russell Lowell
1892 Francis A. March
1894 A. Marshall Elliott
1895 James M. Hart
1896 Calvin Thomas
1897 Albert S. Cook
1898 Alcee Fortier
1899 Hans C. C. von Jagemann
1900 Thomas R. Price
1901 Edward S. Sheldon
1902 James W. Bright
1903 George Hempl
1904 George Lyman Kittredge
1905 Francis B. Gummere
1906 Henry A. Todd
1907 Fred N. Scott
1908 Frederick M. Warren
1909 Marion D. Learned
1910 Brander Matthews
1911 Lewis F. Mott
1912 Charles H. Grandgent
1913 Alexander R. Hohlfeld
1914 Felix E. Schelling
1915 Jefferson B. Fletcher
1916 James D. Bruce
1917 Kuno Francke
1918 Edward C. Armstrong
1920 John M. Manly
1921 William G. Howard
1922 Raymond Weeks
1923 Oliver F. Emerson
1924 William A. Neilson
1925 Hermann Collitz
1926 T. Atkinson Jenkins
1927 Ashley H. Thorndike
1928 Hugo K. Schilling
1929 William A. Nitze
1930 Frederick Tupper
1931 George O. Curme
1932 C. Carroll Marden
1933 John L. Lowes
1934 James T. Hatfield
1935 Colbert Searles
1936 Carleton Brown
1937 Eduard Prokosch
1938 John S. P. Tatlock
1939 H. Carrington Lancaster
1940 Karl Young
1941 John A. Walz
1942 Frederick M. Padelford
1943 Rudolph Schevill
1944 Robert H. Fife
1945 Fred N. Robinson
1946 Ernest H. Wilkins
1947 T. Moody Campbell
1948 Percy W. Long
1949 George W. Sherburn
1950 S. Griswold Morley
1951 Archer Taylor
1952 Albert C. Baugh
1953 Hayward Keniston
1954 LeRoy S. Kimball
1955 Louise Paund
1956 Gilbert Chinard
1957 Tyalor Starck
1958 James H. Hanford
1959 William R. Parker
1960 Henri M. Peyre
1961 Henry W. Nordmeyer
1962 Kemp Malone
1963 Marjorie Nicolson
1964 Morris Bishop
1965 Howard M. Jones
1966 Hermann J. Weigand
1967 George W. Stone, Jr.
1968 Otis W. Green
1969 Henry N. Smith
1970 Maynard Mack
1971 Louis Kamps
1972 Stuart P. Atkins

Motion Picture Association of America

1922 Will H. Hays
1945 Eric Johnston
1963 Ralph D. Hetzel (Acting)
1966 Jack Valenti

National Academy of Design

1826 Samuel F. B. Morse
1845 Asher B. Durand
1861 Samuel F. B. Morse
1862 Daniel Huntington
1870 Henry P. Gray
1871 William Page
1873 J. Q. A. Ward
1874 Worthington Whittredge
1877 Daniel Huntington
1890 Thomas W. Wood
1900 Frederick Dielman
1909 John W. Alexander
1915 J. Alden Weir
1917 Herbert Adams
1920 Edwin H. Blashfield
1926 Cass Gilbert
1933 Harry W. Watrous
1934 Jonas Lie
1939 Hobart Nichols
1949 DeWitt M. Lockman
1950 Lawrence G. White
1956 Eliot Clark
1959 John F. Harbeson
1962 Edgar I. Williams
1966 Alfred E. Poor

The National Academy of Television Arts and Sciences

1957 Ed Sullivan
1958 Harry S. Ackerman
1959 Walter Cronkite
1960 Harry S. Ackerman
1961 Robert F. Lewine
1963 Mort Werner
1964 Rod Serling
1966 Royal E. Blakeman
1968 Seymour Berns
1970 Robert F. Lewine

National Aeronautic Association

1922 Howard E. Coffin
1923 Frederick B. Patterson
1924 Godfrey L. Cabot
1926 Porter H. Adams
1928 Hiram Bingham
1934 William Gibbs McAdoo
1936 Charles F. Horner
1940 Gill R. Wilson
1944 William R. Enyart
1946 L. Welch Pogue
1947 Arthur I. Boreman
1948 Louis E. Leverone
1951 Donald D. Webster
1951 Joseph T. Geuting, Jr.
1952 Harry K. Coffey
1954 Thomas G. Lanphier, Jr.
1960 Jacqueline Cochran
1962 Martin M. Decker
1963 William A. Ong
1965 Edward C. Sweeny
1966 James F. Nields
1968 Frederick B. Lee
1970 A. S. "Mike" Monroney

National Association of Accountants

1919 J. Lee Nicholson
1920 William M. Lybrand
1922 J. P. Jordan
1924 William S. Kemp
1925 Clinton H. Scovell
1926 C. M. Finney
1927 Charles R. Stevenson
1928 Frank L. Sweetser

1929 Addison Boren
1930 Walter S. Gee
1930 V. W. Collins
1931 Thomas H. Sanders
1932 Harry A. Bullis
1933 Arthur H. Carter
1934 Eric A. Camman
1935 Grant R. Lohnes
1936 F. Richmond Fletcher
1937 William F. Marsh
1938 J. Hugh Jackson
1939 C. Howard Knapp
1940 Victor H. Stempf
1941 Harry E. Howell
1942 Wyman P. Fiske
1943 John H. DeVitt
1944 Martin A. Moore
1945 Frank Klein
1946 William J. Carter
1947 Mason Smith
1948 Clinton W. Bennett
1949 Logan Monroe
1950 William B. McCloskey
1951 Herman A. Papenfoth
1952 J. Brooks Heckert
1953 I. Wayne Keller
1954 Alexander J. Lindsay
1955 Charles R. Israel
1956 Philip J. Warner
1957 Harold W. Scott
1958 John B. Inglis
1959 Leslie I. Asher
1960 George A. Hewitt
1961 Donald G. Eder
1962 John B. Bachofer
1963 Merwin P. Cass
1964 Colin A. Stillwagen
1965 Joseph L. Brumit
1966 Firman H. Hass
1967 Thomas L. Morison
1968 James E. Meredith, Jr.
1969 Grant U. Meyers
1970 Ettore Barbatelli
1971 Julius E. Underwood

National Association for the Advancement of Colored People (NAACP)

Presidents

1909 Storey Moorfield
1930 Joel E. Spingarn
1939 Arthur B. Spingarn
1966 Kivie Kaplan

Executive Secretaries

1909 Frances Blascoer
1917 Royal Nash
1918 John Shillady
1920 James Weldon Johnson
1929 Walter White
1955 Roy Wilkins

National Association of Broadcasters

1923 Eugene F. McDonald, Jr.
1925 Frank W. Elliot
1926 Earle C. Anthony
1928 William S. Hedges
1930 Walter J. Damm
1931 Harry Shaw
1932 Alfred J. McCosker
1934 J. Truman Ward
1935 Leo J. Fitzpatrick
1936 Charles W. Myers
1937 John Elmer
1938 Mark Ethridge
1938 Neville Miller
1944 J. Harold Ryan
1945 Justin Miller
1951 Harold E. Fellows
1961 LeRoy Collins
1965 Vincent T. Wasilewski

National Association of Manufacturers (NAM)

1895 Thomas Dolan
1896 Theodore C. Search
1902 D. M. Parry
1906 J. W. Van Cleave
1909 John Kirby, Jr.
1913 George Pope
1918 Steven Mason
1921 John E. Edgerton
1932 Robert L. Lund
1934 C. L. Bardo
1936 C. W. Chester
1937 W. B. Warner
1938 Charles R. Hook
1939 Howard Coonley
1940 H. W. Prentis, Jr.
1941 W. D. Fuller
1942 W. P. Witherow
1943 F. C. Crawford
1944 R. M. Gaylord
1945 Ira Mosher
1946 R. R. Wason
1947 Earl Bunting
1948 Morris Sayre
1949 W. F. Bennett
1950 C. A. Putnam
1951 William H. Ruffin
1952 William J. Grede
1953 Charles R. Sligh, Jr.
1954 H. C. McClellan
1955 G. H. Riter III
1956 C. G. Parker
1957 Ernest G. Swiger
1958 Milton C. Lightner
1959 Stanley C. Hope
1960 R. F. Bannow
1961 John W. McGovern
1962 Donald J. Hardenbrook
1963 W. P. Gullander

The National Conference of Christians and Jews

1928 Everett R. Clinchy
1958 Lewis W. Jones
1965 Sterling W. Brown

National Education Association

1939 Amy Hinrichs
1942 A. Cline Flora
1944 Frank L. Schlagle
1946 Pearl Wanamaker
1947 Glenn E. Snow
1948 Mabel Studebaker
1949 Andrew D. Holt
1950 Corma A. Mowrey
1951 J. Cloyd Miller
1952 Sarah C. Caldwell
1953 William A. Early
1954 Waurine Walker
1955 John L. Buford
1956 Martha A. Shull
1957 Lyman V. Ginger
1958 Ruth S. Wright
1959 Walter W. Eshelman
1960 Clarice Kline
1961 Ewald Turner
1962 Hazel B. Nielson
1963 Robert H. Wyatt
1964 Lois V. Edinger
1965 Richard D. Batchelder
1966 Irvamae Applegate
1967 Braulio Alonso
1968 Libby Koontz
1969 George D. Fischer
1970 Helen Bain
1971 Donald E. Morrison
1972 Catharine Barrett

National Geographic Society

1888 Gardiner G. Hubbard
1898 Alexander Graham Bell
1904 W. J. McGee
1904 Grove K. Gilbert (Acting)
1905 Willis L. Moore
1910 Henry Gannett
1915 O. H. Tittmann
1919 John E. Pillsbury
1920 Gilbert H. Grosvenor
1954 John O. La Gorce
1957 Melville B. Grosvenor
1967 Melvin M. Payne

National Grange

1868 William Saunders
1874 D. W. Adams
1876 John T. Jones
1878 S. E. Adams
1880 J. J. Woodman
1886 Put Darden
1888 James Draper
1889 J. H. Brigham
1898 Aaron Jones
1906 N. J. Bachelder
1912 Oliver Wilson
1920 S. J. Lowell
1924 L. J. Taber
1942 A. S. Goss
1950 Henry Sherwood
1951 Herschel D. Newsom
1969 John W. Scott

National Health Council

1921 Livingston Farrand
1923 L. K. Frankel
1927 William F. Snow
1934 Theodore Roosevelt
1936 Donald B. Armstrong
1938 Ira V. Hiscock
1940 Kendall Emerson
1942 George S. Stevenson
1944 Eleanor Brown Merrill
1946 Philip R. Mather
1950 Ernest L. Stebbins
1952 Mrs. Oswald B. Lord
1953 Robin C. Buerki
1953 A. W. Dent
1955 Hugh R. Leavell
1956 Leona Baumgartner
1957 Basil O'Connor
1958 Norvin C. Kiefer
1959 Ruth B. Freeman
1960 James E. Perkins
1961 James H. Sterner
1962 George Bugbee
1963 Rome A. Betts
1964 Edwin L. Crosby
1965 George James
1966 John W. Knutson
1967 J. Douglas Colman
1968 Leroy E. Burney
1969 Margaret B. Dolan
1970 Hollis S. Ingraham
1971 Richard P. McGrail

National Institute of Arts and Letters

1899 Charles D. Warner
1901 William Dean Howells
1904 Edmund C. Stedman
1906 William M. Sloane
1909 Henry Van Dyke
1911 John W. Alexander
1912 Brander Matthews
1914 Edwin H. Blashfield
1916 Augustus Thomas
1918 Cass Gilbert
1920 Robert Grant
1923 Maurice F. Egan
1924 John C. Van Dyke
1925 Arthur T. Hadley
1927 Walter Damrosch
1929 William Lyon Phelps
1931 Wilbur L. Cross
1936 Walter Damrosch
1941 Arthur Train
1945 Douglas Moore
1953 Marc Connelly
1956 Malcolm Cowley
1959 Glenway Wescott
1962 Malcolm Cowley
1965 George F. Kennan
1968 Allen Tate
1969 William Maxwell
1972 Jacques Barzun

National Institute of Social Sciences

1912 Hamilton W. Mabie
1916 Nicholas Murray Butler

1917 Irving Fisher
1918 Emory R. Johnson
1922 Austin B. Fletcher
1923 Helen Hartley Jenkins
1924 Chester S. Lord
1926 William C. Redfield
1932 C. Stuart Gager
1935 Henry Fletcher
1937 William E. Hall
1942 Colby M. Chester
1945 Clarence G. Michalis
1950 Hugh Bullock
1953 Walter Hoving
1956 Frank Pace, Jr.
1959 Arthur K. Watson
1962 Frank Pace, Jr.

National Municipal League

1894 James C. Carter
1903 Charles J. Bonaparte
1910 William D. Foulke
1915 Lawson Purdy
1919 Charles Evans Hughes
1921 Henry M. Waite
1923 Frank L. Polk
1927 Richard S. Childs
1931 Murray Seasongood
1934 Harold W. Dodds
1937 Clarence A. Dykstra
1940 John G. Winant
1946 Charles Edison
1950 Henry Bruere
1953 George H. Gallup
1957 Cecil Morgan
1960 William Collins
1963 Alfred E. Driscoll
1970 William W. Scranton

National Sculpture Society

1893 J.Q.A. Ward
1905 Daniel Chester French
1906 Karl Bitter
1908 Herbert Adams
1910 Hermon A. MacNeil
1912 Herbert Adams
1914 Karl Bitter
1915 Herbert Adams
1917 Paul W. Bartlett
1919 F. G. R. Roth
1920 Robert Aitken
1922 Hermon A. MacNeil
1924 James E. Fraser
1927 Chester Beach
1928 Adolph A. Weinman
1931 Charles Keck
1934 John Gregory
1939 Paul Manship
1942 Edmond Amateis
1944 Cecil Howard
1944 Paul Manship (Acting)
1945 Donald De Lue
1948 Sidney Waugh
1950 Karl H. Gruppe
1951 Wheeler Williams
1954 Leo Friedlander
1957 Adlai S. Hardin
1960 C. Paul Jennewein
1963 Adolph Block
1965 Herbert L. Kammerer
1967 Frank Eliscu
1970 Michael Lantz

National Society Daughters of The American Revolution

Presidents General

1890 Mrs. Benjamin Harrison
1893 Mrs. Adlai E. Stevenson
1895 Mrs. John W. Foster
1896 Mrs. Adlai E. Stevenson
1898 Mrs. Daniel Manning
1901 Mrs. Charles W. Fairbanks
1905 Mrs. Donald McLean
1909 Mrs. Matthew T. Scott
1913 Mrs. William Cumming Story
1917 Mrs. George Thacher Guernsey
1920 Mrs. George Maynard Minor
1923 Mrs. Anthony Wayne Cook
1926 Mrs. Grace L. H. Brosseau
1929 Mrs. Lowell Fletcher Hobart
1932 Mrs. Russell W. Magna
1935 Mrs. William A. Becker
1938 Mrs. Henry M. Robert, Jr.
1941 Mrs. William H. Pouch
1944 Mrs. Julius Y. Talmadge
1947 Mrs. Roscoe C. O'Byrne
1950 Mrs. James B. Patton
1953 Gertrude S. Carraway
1956 Mrs. Frederic A. Groves
1959 Mrs. Ashmead White
1962 Mrs. Robert V. H. Duncan
1965 Mrs. William H. Sullivan, Jr.
1968 Mrs. Erwin F. Seimes
1971 Mrs. Donald Spicer

The National Society of the Sons of the American Revolution

Presidents General

1889 Lucius P. Deming
1890 William S. Webb
1892 Horace Porter
1897 Edwin S. Barrett
1899 Franklin Murphy
1900 J. C. Breckinridge
1901 Walter S. Logan
1902 Edwin Warfield
1903 Edwin S. Greeley
1904 James D. Hancock
1905 Francis H. Appleton
1906 Cornelius A. Pugsley
1907 Nelson A. McClary
1908 Henry Stockbridge
1909 Morris B. Beardsley
1910 William A. Marble
1911 Moses G. Parker
1912 James M. Richardson
1913 R. C. Ballard Thruston
1915 Newell B. Woodworth
1916 Elmer M. Wentworth
1918 Louis A. Ames
1919 Chancellor L. Jenks
1920 James H. Preston
1921 Wallace McCamant
1922 W. I. L. Adams
1923 Arthur P. Sumner
1924 Harrison L. Lewis
1925 Harvey F. Remington
1926 Wilbert H. Barrett
1927 Ernest E. Rogers
1928 Ganson Depew
1929 Howard C. Rowley
1930 Josiah A. Van Orsdel
1931 Benjamin N. Johnson
1932 Frederick W. Millspaugh
1933 Arthur M. McCrillis
1935 Henry F. Baker
1936 Messmore Kendall
1940 Loren E. Souers
1941 G. Ridgely Sappington
1942 Sterling F. Mutz
1943 Smith L. Multer
1946 Allen L. Oliver
1947 A. Herbert Foreman
1948 Charles B. Shaler
1948 Ben H. Powell, III
1949 John W. Finger
1950 Wallace C. Hall
1952 Ray O. Edwards
1953 Arthur A. de la Houssaye
1954 Milton M. Lory
1955 Edgar Williamson, Jr.
1956 Eugene P. Carver, Jr.
1957 George E. Tarbox, Jr.
1958 Walter A. Wentworth
1959 Charles A. Jones
1960 Herschel S. Murphy
1961 Horace Y. Kitchell
1962 Charles A. Anderson
1963 Robert L. Sonfield
1964 Harry T. Burn
1965 Howard E. Coe
1966 Kenneth G. Smith
1967 Len Y. Smith
1968 Walter G. Sterling
1969 James B. Gardiner
1970 Walter R. Martin
1971 Eugene C. McGuire

National Urban League

Executive Directors

1910 George E. Haynes
1917 Eugene K. Jones
1941 Lester B. Granger
1961 Whitney M. Young, Jr.
1971 Vernon E. Jordan, Jr.

National Wildlife Federation

1936 Jay N. Darling
1938 David A. Aylward
1950 Claude D. Kelley
1961 Paul A. Herbert
1963 Ross Leffler
1964 Louis D. McGregor
1967 Donald J. Zinn
1970 James H. Shaeffer

Nobles of the Mystic Shrine (Shriners)

Imperial Potentates

1876 Walter M. Fleming
1886 Sam Briggs
1892 William B. Melish
1893 Thomas J. Hudson
1894 William B. Melish
1895 Charles L. Field
1896 Harrison Dingman
1897 Albert B. McGaffey
1898 Ethelbert F. Allen
1899 John H. Atwood
1900 Lou B. Winsor
1901 Philip C. Shaffer
1902 Henry C. Akin
1903 George H. Green
1904 George L. Brown
1905 Henry A. Collins
1906 Alvah P. Clayton
1907 Frank C. Roundy
1908 Edwin I. Alderman
1909 George L. Street
1910 Fred A. Hines
1911 John F. Treat
1912 William J. Cunningham
1913 William W. Irwin
1914 Frederick R. Smith
1915 J. Putnam Stevens
1916 Henry F. Niedringhaus
1917 Charles E. Ovenshire
1918 Elias J. Jacoby
1919 W. Freeland Kendrick
1920 Ellis L. Garretson
1921 Ernest A. Cutts
1922 James S. McCandless
1923 Conrad V. Dykeman
1924 James E. Chandler
1925 James C. Burger
1926 David W. Crosland
1927 Clarence M. Dunbar
1928 Frank C. Jones
1929 Leo V. Youngworth
1930 Esten A. Fletcher
1931 Thomas J. Houston
1932 Earl C. Mills
1933 John N. Sebrell
1934 Dana S. Williams
1935 Leonard P. Steuart
1936 Hugh M. Caldwell
1936 Clyde I. Webster
1937 Walter S. Sugden
1938 A. A. D. Rahn
1939 Walter D. Cline
1940 George F. Olendorf
1941 Thomas C. Law
1942 Albert H. Fiebach
1943 Morley E. Mackenzie
1944 Alfred G. Arvold
1945 William H. Woodfield, Jr.
1946 George H. Rowe
1947 Karl R. Hammers
1948 Galloway Calhoun
1949 Harold Lloyd
1950 Hubert M. Poteat
1951 Robert G. Wilson, Jr.
1952 Harvey A. Beffa
1953 Remmie L. Arnold
1954 Frank S. Land
1955 Walter C. Guy
1956 Gerald D. Crary
1957 Thomas W. Melham
1958 George E. Stringfellow
1959 Clayton F. Andrews
1960 George A. Mattison, Jr.
1961 Marshall M. Porter
1962 George M. Klepper
1963 Harold C. Close
1964 O. Carlyle Brock
1965 Barney W. Collins
1966 Orville F. Rush
1967 Thomas F. Seay
1968 Chester A. Hogan
1969 J. Worth Baker

Optical Society of America

1916 P. G. Nutting
1918 F. E. Wright
1920 F. K. Richtmyer
1921 J. P. C. Southall
1922 L. T. Troland
1924 H. E. Ives
1926 W. E. Forsythe
1928 I. G. Priest
1930 L. A. Jones
1932 E. C. Crittenden
1933 W. B. Rayton
1935 Arthur C. Hardy
1937 R. C. Gibbs
1939 K. S. Gibson
1941 A. G. Worthing
1943 A. H. Pfund
1945 G. R. Harrison
1947 Rudolf Kingslake
1949 William F. Meggers
1951 Brian O'Brien
1953 Deane B. Judd
1955 Ralph A. Sawyer
1958 Irvine C. Gardner
1959 John Strong
1960 James G. Baker
1961 Wallace R. Brode
1962 David L. MacAdam
1963 Stanley S. Ballard
1964 Richard C. Lord
1965 S. Q. Duntley
1966 Van Zandt Williams
1967 John A. Sanderson
1968 A. Francis Turner
1969 Karl G. Kessler
1970 W. Lewis Hyde

Pilgrim Society

1820 Joshua Thomas
1821 John Watson
1826 Alden Bradford
1841 Nathaniel M. David
1845 Charles H. Warren
1853 Richard Warren
1862 Edward Everett
1865 Edward S. Tobey
1872 William T. Davis
1879 Thomas Russell
1887 John Davis Long
1895 Arthur Lord
1925 Howland Davis
1930 William R. Hedge
1943 Ellis W. Brewster
1965 Horace C. Weston
1970 Ralph C. Weaver

The Poetry Society of America

1910 Edward J. Wheeler
1920 Witter Bynner
1922 John Erskine
1924 Charles W. Stork
1925 Arthur Guiterman
1927 Curtis H. Page
1929 William Griffith
1932 Harold T. Pulsifer
1933 Leonora Speyer
1935 Henry G. Leach
1938 Padraic Colum
1940 A. M. Sullivan
1943 Alfred Kreymborg
1945 J. Donald Adams
1947 Carl Carmer
1949 Robert Hillyer
1950 A. M. Sullivan
1952 Robert Hillyer
1954 George N. Shuster
1955 Edward Davison
1957 Clarence R. Decker
1961 Cecil Hemley
1963 Richard V. Lindabury
1963 Loyd Haberly
1969 Charles Angoff

Rotary International

1910 Paul P. Harris
1912 Glenn C. Mead
1913 Russell F. Greiner
1914 Frank L. Mulholland
1915 Allen D. Albert
1916 Arch C. Klumph
1918 John Poole
1919 Albert S. Adams
1920 Estes Snedecor
1922 Raymond M. Mavens
1923 Guy Gundaker
1924 Everett W. Hill
1925 Donald A. Adams
1926 Harry H. Rogers
1927 Arthur H. Sapp
1929 M. Eugene Newsom
1930 Almon E. Roth
1932 Clinton P. Anderson
1934 Robert S. Lee Hill
1935 Edward R. Johnson
1936 Will R. Manier, Jr.
1938 George C. Hager
1939 Walter D. Head
1941 Tom J. Davis
1943 Charles L. Wheeler
1944 Richard H. Wells
1946 Richard C. Hedke
1947 S. Kendrick Guernsey
1949 Percy Hodgson
1951 Frank E. Spain
1952 H. J. Brunnier
1954 Herbert J. Taylor
1955 A. Z. Baker
1957 Charles G. Tennent
1958 Clifford A. Randall
1960 J. Edd McLaughlin
1961 Joseph A. Abey
1963 Carl P. Miller
1964 Charles W. Pettengill
1966 Richard L. Evans
1967 Luther H. Hodges
1969 James F. Conway
1970 William E. Walk, Jr.
1972 Ernst G. Breitholtz

The Society of the Cincinnati

Presidents General

1783 George Washington
1800 Alexander Hamilton
1805 Charles C. Pinckney
1825 Thomas Pinckney
1829 Aaron Ogden
1839 Morgan Lewis
1844 William Popham
1848 Henry A. S. Dearborn
1854 Hamilton Fish
1896 William Wayne
1902 Winslow Warren
1932 John C. Daves
1939 Bryce Metcalf
1950 Isaac A. Pennypacker
1950 Edgar E. Hume
1952 John F. R. Scott
1953 Richard H. Wilmer
1956 Catesby Jones
1959 Blanchard Randall
1962 Francis W. Hatch
1965 Charles W. Lippitt
1968 Frank A. Chisholm

Society of Motion Picture and Television Engineers

1916 C. Francis Jenkins
1919 H. A. Campe
1922 Lawrence C. Porter
1924 Lloyd A. Jones
1926 Willard B. Cook
1929 Lawrence C. Porter
1930 John I. Crabtree
1932 Alfred N. Goldsmith
1934 Homer G. Tasker
1937 Sidney K. Wolf
1939 E. Allan Williford
1941 Emery Huse
1943 Herbert Griffin
1945 Donald E. Hyndman
1947 Loren L. Ryder
1949 Earl I. Sponable
1951 Peter Mole
1953 Herbert Barnett
1955 John G. Frayne
1957 Barton Kreuzer
1959 Norwood L. Simmons
1961 John W. Servies
1963 Reid H. Ray
1965 Ethan M. Stifle
1967 G. Carleton Hunt
1969 Deane R. White
1971 Wilton R. Holm

Veterans of Foreign Wars of the United States

1913 Rice W. Means
1914 Thomas Crago
1915 Gus E. Hartung
1916 Albert Rabing
1917 William E. Ralston
1918 F. Warner Karling
1920 Robert G. Woodside
1922 Tillinghast Huston
1923 Lloyd M. Brett
1924 John H. Dunn
1925 Fred Stover
1926 Theodore Stitt
1927 Frank T. Strayer
1928 Eugene P. Carver
1929 Hezekiah N. Duff
1930 Paul C. Wolman
1931 Darold D. DeCoe
1932 Robert E. Coontz
1933 James E. VanZandt
1936 Bernard W. Kearney
1937 Scott P. Squyers
1938 Eugene I. Van Antwerp
1939 Otis N. Brown
1940 Joseph C. Menendez
1941 Max Singer
1942 Robert T. Merrill
1943 Carl J. Schoeninger
1944 Jean A. Brunner
1945 Joseph M. Stack
1946 Louis E. Starr
1947 Ray H. Brannaman
1948 Lyall T. Beggs
1949 Clyde A. Lewis
1950 Charles C. Ralls
1951 Frank C. Hilton
1952 James W. Cothran
1953 Wayne E. Richards
1954 Merton B. Tice
1955 Timothy J. Murphy
1956 Cooper T. Holt
1957 Richard L. Roudebush
1958 John W. Mahan
1959 Louis G. Feldmann
1960 Ted C. Connell
1961 Robert E. Hansen
1962 Byron B. Gentry
1963 Joseph J. Lombardo
1964 John A. Jenkins
1965 Andy Borg
1966 Leslie M. Fry
1967 Joseph A. Scerra
1968 Richard Homan
1969 Ray Gallagher
1970 Herbert R. Rainwater
1971 Joseph L. Vicites

XIX

LAUREATES

A listing of Americans who have been recognized for outstanding achievements in the arts, sciences, and the humanities and for contributions to the betterment of mankind.

– Pulitzer Prize Winners

– Recipients of other noteworthy prizes

PULITZER PRIZE WINNERS

Names are listed alphabetically by year

1917

Name	Category
Maude Howe Elliott	Biography
Florence Howe Hall	Biography
Laura E. Richards	Biography
Herbert Bayard Swope	General reporting

1918

Name	Category
William Cabell Bruce	Biography
Minna Lewinson and Harry Beetle Hough	Newspaper history award
Harold A. Littledale	General reporting
Ernest Poole	Fiction
James Ford Rhodes	History
Sara Teasdale	Poetry (Poetry Society award)
Jesse Lynch Williams	Drama

1919

Name	Category
Henry Adams	Autobiography
Carl Sandburg	Poetry (Poetry Society award)
Booth Tarkington	Fiction
Margaret Widdemer	Poetry (Poetry Society award)

1920

Name	Category
Albert J. Beveridge	Biography
John J. Leary, Jr.	General reporting
Harvey E. Newbranch	Editorial writing
Eugene O'Neill	Drama
Justin H. Smith	History

1921

Name	Category
Edward Bok	Autobiography
Zona Gale	Drama
Burton J. Hendrick	History
Louis Seibold	General reporting
William S. Sims	History
Edith Wharton	Fiction

1922

Name	Category
James Truslow Adams	History
Hamlin Garland	Biography
Rollin Kirby	Cartoon
Frank M. O'Brien	Editorial writing
Eugene O'Neill	Drama
Edwin Arlington Robinson	Poetry
Kirke L. Simpson	General reporting
Booth Tarkington	Fiction

1923

Name	Category
Willa Cather	Fiction
Owen Davis	Drama
Burton J. Hendrick	Biography
Alva Johnston	General reporting
Edna St. Vincent Millay	Poetry
Charles Warren	History
William Allen White	Editorial writing

1924

Name	Category
Frank I. Cobb	Editorial writing
Jay N. Darling	Cartoon
Robert Frost	Poetry
Charles H. McIlwain	History
Hatcher Hughes	Drama
Magner White	General reporting
Margaret Wilson	Fiction

1925

Name	Category
Edna Ferber	Fiction
Alvin H. Goldstein	General reporting
Sidney Howard	Drama
Mark A. DeWolfe Howe	Biography
Rollin Kirby	Cartoon
James W. Mulroy	General reporting
Frederic L. Paxson	History
Michael I. Pupin	Autobiography
Edwin Arlington Robinson	Poetry

1926

Name	Category
Edward Channing	History
Harvey Cushing	Biography
Daniel R. Fitzpatrick	Cartoon
George Kelly	Drama
Edward M. Kingsbury	Editorial writing
Sinclair Lewis	Fiction
Amy Lowell	Poetry
William B. Miller	General reporting

1927

Name	Category
Samuel F. Bemis	History
Louis Bromfield	Fiction
F. Lauriston Bullard	Editorial writing
Paul Green	Drama
Nelson Harding	Cartoon
Emory Holloway	Biography
John T. Rogers	General reporting
Leonora Speyer	Poetry

1928

Name	Category
Grover C. Hall	Editorial writing
Nelson Harding	Cartoon
Eugene O'Neill	Drama
Vernon L. Parrington	History
Edwin Arlington Robinson	Poetry
Charles E. Russell	Biography
Thornton Wilder	Fiction

1929

Name	Category
Paul Y. Anderson	General reporting
Stephen Vincent Benet	Poetry
Burton J. Hendrick	Biography
Louis I. Jaffe	Editorial writing
Rollin Kirby	Cartoon
Paul Scott Mowrer	General Correspondence
Julia Peterkin	Fiction
Elmer L. Rice	Drama
Fred A. Shannon	History

1930

Name	Category
Conrad Aiken	Poetry
Marc Connelly	Drama
Marquis James	Biography
Oliver LaFarge	Fiction
Charles R. Macauley	Cartoon
Russell D. Owen	General reporting
Leland Stowe	General correspondence
Claude H. Van Tyne	History

1931

Name	Category
Margaret Ayer Barnes	Fiction
Edmund Duffy	Cartoon
Robert Frost	Poetry
Susan Glaspell	Drama
Henry James	Biography
H. R. Knickerbocker	General correspondence
A. B. MacDonald	General reporting
Charles S. Ryckman	Editorial writing
Bernadotte E. Schmitt	History

PULITZER PRIZE WINNERS

1932

Pearl S. Buck	Fiction
George Dillon	Poetry
Walter Duranty	General correspondence
Ira Gershwin	Drama
George S. Kaufman	Drama
John T. McCutcheon	Cartoon
D. D. Martin	General reporting
John J. Pershing	History
J. S. Pooler	General reporting
Henry F. Pringle	Biography
W. C. Richards	General reporting
Charles G. Ross	General correspondence
Morrie Ryskind	Drama
F. D. Webb	General reporting

1933

Maxwell Anderson	Drama
Francis A. Jamieson	General reporting
Archibald MacLeish	Poetry
Edgar Ansel Mowrer	General correspondence
Allan Nevins	Biography
T. S. Stribling	Fiction
Harold M. Talburt	Cartoon
Frederick Jackson Turner	History

1934

Herbert Agar	History
Frederick T. Birchall	General correspondence
Royce Brier	General reporting
E. P. Chase	Editorial writing
Tyler Dennett	Biography
Edmund Duffy	Cartoon
Robert Hillyer	Poetry
Sidney Kingsley	Drama
Caroline Miller	Fiction

1935

Zoe Akins	Drama
Charles McLean Andrews	History
Douglas Southall Freeman	Biography
Josephine Winslow Johnson	Fiction
Arthur Krock	General correspondence
Ross A. Lewis	Cartoon
William H. Taylor	General reporting
Audrey Wurdemann	Poetry

1936

Wilfred C. Barber	General correspondence
Robert P. Tristram Coffin	Poetry
H. L. Davis	Fiction
Lauren D. Lyman	General reporting
Andrew C. McLaughlin	History
Felix Morley	Editorial writing
George B. Parker	Editorial writing
Ralph B. Perry	Biography
Robert E. Sherwood	Drama

1937

Clarence D. Batchelor	Cartoon
Howard W. Blakeslee	General reporting
Van Wyck Brooks	History
David Dietz	General reporting
Robert Frost	Poetry
Moss Hart	Drama
George S. Kaufman	Drama
Gobind Behari Lal	General reporting
William L. Laurence	General reporting
Anne O'Hare McCormick	General correspondence
Margaret Mitchell	Fiction
Allan Nevins	Biography
John J. O'Neill	General reporting
John W. Owens	Editorial writing

1938

Paul H. Buck	History
Marquis James	Biography
Arthur Krock	General correspondence
John P. Marquand	Fiction
Odell Shepard	Biography
Vaughn Shoemaker	Cartoon
Raymond Sprigle	General reporting
W. W. Waymack	Editorial writing
Thornton Wilder	Drama
Marya Zaturenska	Poetry

1939

Ronald G. Callvert	Editorial writing
John Gould Fletcher	Poetry
Louis P. Lochner	General correspondence
Frank Luther Mott	History
Marjorie Kinnan Rawlings	Fiction
Robert E. Sherwood	Drama
Thomas L. Stokes	General reporting
Carl Van Doren	Biography
Charles G. Werner	Cartoon

1940

Ray S. Baker	Biography
Edmund Duffy	Cartoon
S. Burton Heath	General reporting
Bart Howard	Editorial writing
Carl Sandburg	History
William Saroyan	Drama (declined)
John Steinbeck	Fiction
Otto D. Tolischus	General correspondence
Mark Van Doren	Poetry

1941

Leonard Bacon	Poetry
Jacob Burck	Cartoon
Marcus Lee Hanson	History
Reuben Maury	Editorial writing
Westbrook Pegler	General reporting
Robert E. Sherwood	Drama
Loa Elizabeth Winslow	Biography

1942

Laurence E. Allen	International telegraphic reporting
William Rose Benet	Poetry
Herbert L. Block	Cartoon
Milton Brooks	News photography
Stanton Delaplane	General reporting
Ellen Glasgow	Fiction
Margaret Leech	History
Geoffrey Parsons	Editorial writing
Carlos P. Romulo	General correspondence
Louis Stark	National telegraphic reporting
Forrest Wilson	Biography

1943

Hanson W. Baldwin	General correspondence
Jay N. Darling	Cartoon
Esther Forbes	History
Robert Frost	Poetry
Samuel Eliot Morison	Biography
Frank Noel	News photography
William Schuman	Music
Forrest W. Seymour	Editorial writing
Upton Sinclair	Fiction
George Weller	General reporting
Thornton Wilder	Drama
Ira Wolpert	International telegraphic reporting

PULITZER PRIZE WINNERS

1944

Stephen Vincent Benet	Poetry
Clifford K. Berryman	Cartoon
Earle L. Bunker	News photography
Merle Curti	History
Daniel De Luce	International telegraphic reporting
Frank Filan	News photography
Martin Flavin	Fiction
Dewey L. Fleming	National telegraphic reporting
Oscar Hammerstein II	Special citation
Howard Hanson	Music
Henry J. Haskell	Editorial writing
Carleton Mabee	Biography
Byron Price	Newspaper and radio codes
Ernest T. (Ernie) Pyle	General correspondence
Richard Rodgers	Special citation
Paul Schoenstein	General reporting
William Allen White	Special citation

1945

Stephen Bonsal	History
Harold V. Boyle	General correspondence
Mary Chase	Drama
Aaron Copland	Music
John Hersey	Fiction
Jack S. McDowell	General reporting
William Mauldin	Cartoon
Russell B. Nye	Biography
George W. Potter	Editorial writing
James Reston	National telegraphic reporting
Joe Rosenthal	News photography
Karl Shapiro	Poetry
Mark S. Watson	International telegraphic reporting

1946

Homer W. Bigart	International telegraphic reporting
Hodding Carter, Jr.	Editorial writing
Arnaldo Cortesi	General correspondence
Russell Crouse	Drama
Edward A. Harris	National telegraphic reporting
William L. Laurence	General reporting
Howard Lindsay	Drama
Bruce A. Russell	Cartoon
Arthur M. Schlesinger, Jr.	History
Leo Sowerby	Music
Linnie Marsh Wolfe	Biography

1947

Brooks Atkinson	General correspondence
James P. Baxter III	History
Edward T. Folliard	National telegraphic reporting
Eddy Gilmore	International telegraphic reporting
William H. Grimes	Editorial writing
Arnold Hardy	News photography
Charles Ives	Music
Robert Lowell	Poetry
Vaughn Shoemaker	Cartoon
Robert Penn Warren	Fiction
William Allen White	Autobiography
Frederick Woltman	General reporting

1948

Bert Andrews	National reporting
W. H. Auden	Poetry
Margaret Clapp	Biography
Frank Cushing	News photography
Virginius Dabney	Editorial writing
Bernard DeVoto	History
Frank D. Fackenthal	Special citation
Nat S. Finney	National reporting
Reuben L. Goldberg	Cartoon
George E. Goodwin	General reporting
James A. Michener	Fiction
Walter Piston	Music
Paul W. Ward	International correspondence
Tennessee Williams	Drama

1949

James Gould Cozzens	Fiction
John H. Crider	Editorial writing
Price Day	International correspondence
Herbert Elliston	Editorial writing
Nathaniel Fein	News photography
Malcolm Johnson	General reporting
Arthur Miller	Drama
Roy F. Nichols	History
Lute Pease	Cartoon
Robert E. Sherwood	Biography
Virgil Thompson	Music
C. P. Trussel	National reporting
Peter Viereck	Poetry

1950

Samuel F. Bemis	Biography
Meyer Berger	General reporting
James T. Berryman	Cartoon
Gwendolyn Brooks	Poetry
Bill Crouch	News photography
A. B. Guthrie, Jr.	Fiction
Edwin O. Guthman	National reporting
Oscar Hammerstein II	Drama
Oliver W. Larkin	History
Joshua Logan	Drama
Gian-Carlo Menotti	Music
Richard Rodgers	Drama
Carl M. Saunders	Editorial writing
Edmund Stevens	International correspondence

1951

Keyes Beech	International correspondence
Homer W. Bigart	International correspondence
R. Carlyle Buley	History
Margaret Louise Coit	Biography
Max Desfor	News photography
William H. Fitzpatrick	Editorial writing
Marguerite Higgins	International correspondence
Reginald W. Manning	Cartoon
Edward S. Montgomery	General reporting
Douglas Moore	Music
Relman Morin	International correspondence
Conrad Richter	Fiction
Carl Sandburg	Poetry
Fred Sparks	International correspondence
Cyrus L. Sulzberger	Special citation
Don Whitehead	International correspondence

1952

George de Carvalho	General reporting
Oscar Handlin	History
John M. Hightower	International correspondence
Max Kase	Special citation
Joseph Kramm	Drama
Gail Kubick	Music
Louis LaCoss	Editorial writing
Anthony Leviero	National reporting
Marianne Moore	Poetry
Fred L. Packer	Cartoon
Merlo J. Pusey	Biography
John Robinson	News photography
Don Ultany	News photography
Herman Wouk	Fiction

PULITZER PRIZE WINNERS

1953

Name	Category
George Dangerfield	History
William M. Gallagher	News photography
Ernest Hemingway	Fiction
William Inge	Drama
Edward D. Kuekes	Cartoon
Archibald MacLeish	Poetry
Donald J. Mays	Biography
Edward J. Mowery	Local reporting
Vermont C. Royster	Editorial writing
Austin Wehrwein	International correspondence
Don Whitehead	National reporting

1954

Name	Category
Herbert L. Block	Cartoon
Bruce Catton	History
Charles A. Lindbergh	Autobiography
Jim C. Lucas	International correspondence
Alvin S. McCoy	Local reporting
Don Murray	Editorial writing
John Patrick	Drama
Quincy Porter	Music
Theodore Roethke	Poetry
Mrs. Walter M. Schau	News photography
Richard Wilson	National reporting

1955

Name	Category
Mrs. Caro Brown	Local reporting
William Faulkner	Fiction
Daniel R. Fitzpatrick	Cartoon
John L. Gaunt, Jr.	News photography
Paul Horgan	History
Royce Howes	Editorial writing
Anthony Lewis	National reporting
Gian-Carlo Menotti	Music
Harrison E. Salisbury	International correspondence
Wallace Stevens	Poetry
Roland K. Towery	Local reporting
William S. White	Biography
Tennessee Williams	Drama

1956

Name	Category
Charles L. Bartlett	National reporting
Elizabeth Bishop	Poetry
Frank Coniff	International correspondence
Arthur Daley	Local reporting
Frances Goodrich	Drama
Albert Hackett	Drama
Talbot F. Hamlin	Biography
William Randolph Hearst, Jr.	International correspondence
Lee Hills	Local reporting, against deadline
Richard Hofstadter	History
MacKinlay Kantor	Fiction
Kingsbury Smith	International correspondence
Lauren K. Soth	Editorial writing
Ernest Toch	Music
Robert York	Cartoon

1957

Name	Category
Buford Boone	Editorial writing
Norman Dello Joio	Music
Russell Jones	International correspondence
George F. Kennan	History
John F. Kennedy	Biography
William Lambert	Local reporting
Tom Little	Cartoon
Eugene O'Neill	Drama
James Reston	National reporting
Kenneth Roberts	Nonfiction
Harry A. Trask	News photography
Wallace Turner	Local reporting
Richard Wilbur	Poetry

1958

Name	Category
James Agee	Fiction
Harry S. Ashmore	Editorial writing
Mary Wells Ashworth	Biography
Samuel Barber	Music
William C. Beall	News photography
George Beveridge	Local reporting
John A. Carroll	Biography
Douglas Southall Freeman	Biography
Ketti Frings	Drama
Bray Hammond	History
Walter Lippmann	Special citation
Clark R. Mollenhoff	National reporting
Relman Morin	National reporting
Bruce M. Shanks	Cartoon
Robert Penn Warren	Poetry

1959

Name	Category
John H. Brislin	Local reporting
Stanley Kunitz	Poetry
John La Montaine	Music
Ralph McGill	Editorial writing
Archibald MacLeish	Drama
Joseph Martin	International correspondence
William Mauldin	Cartoon
Philip Santora	International correspondence
Jean Schneider	History
William Seaman	News photography
Robert Lewis Taylor	Fiction
Howard Van Smith	National reporting
Arthur Walworth	Biography
Mary Lou Werner	Local reporting, against deadline
Leonard D. White	History

1960

Name	Category
George Abbott	Drama
Jerry Bock	Drama
Elliott Carter	Music
Lenoir Chambers	Editorial writing
Allen Drury	Fiction
Sheldon Harnick	Drama
Margaret Leech	History
Andrew Lopez	News photography
Garrett Mattingly	Nonfiction
Samuel Eliot Morison	Biography
Jack Nelson	Local reporting, against deadline
Miriam Ottenberg	Local reporting
A. M. Rosenthal	International correspondence
W. D. Snodgrass	Poetry
Vana Trimble	National reporting
Jerome Weidman	Drama

1961

Name	Category
Edward R. Cony	National reporting
Sanche de Gramont	Local reporting, against deadline
David Donald	Biography
William J. Dorvillier	Editorial writing
Herbert Feis	History
Lyman Heinzerling	International correspondence
Harper Lee	Fiction
Phyllis McGinley	Poetry
Edgar May	Local reporting
Tad Mosel	Drama
Carey Orr	Cartoon
Walter Piston	Music

PULITZER PRIZE WINNERS

1962

George Bliss	Local reporting
Abe Burrows	Drama
Nathan G. Caldwell	National reporting
Alan Dugan	Poetry
Lawrence H. Gipson	History
Gene S. Graham	National reporting
Walter Lippmann	International correspondence
Frank Loesser	Drama
Robert D. Mullins	Local reporting, against deadline
Edwin O'Connor	Fiction
Thomas M. Storke	Editorial writing
Edmund S. Valtman	Cartoon
Paul Vathis	News photography
Robert Ward	Music
Theodore H. White	Nonfiction

1963

Samuel Barber	Music
Leon Edel	Biography
William Faulkner	Fiction
Sylvan Fox	Local reporting, against deadline
Constance McLaughlin Green	History
Oscar O. Griffin, Jr.	Local reporting
Ira B. Harkey, Jr.	Editorial writing
Hall Hendrix	International correspondence
Anthony Lewis	National reporting
William Longgood	Local reporting, against deadline
Frank Miller	Cartoon
Hector Rondon	News photography
Anthony Shannon	Local reporting, against deadline
Barbara W. Tuchman	Nonfiction
William Carlos Williams	Poetry

1964

Walter J. Bates	Biography
Malcolm W. Browne	International correspondence
Paul Conrad	Cartoon
Albert V. Gaudiosi	Local reporting
David Halberstam	International correspondence
Richard Hofstadter	Nonfiction
Robert Hill Jackson	News photography
James V. Magee	Local reporting
Frederick A. Meyer	Local reporting
Norman C. Miller	Local reporting, against deadline
Sumner Chilton Powell	History
Louis Simpson	Poetry
Hazel Brannan Smith	Editorial writing
Merriman Smith	National reporting

1965

John Berryman	Poetry
Frank D. Gilroy	Drama
Gene Goltz	Local reporting
Shirley Ann Grau	Fiction
John R. Harrison	Editorial writing
Howard Mumford Jones	Nonfiction
Louis M. Kohlmeier	National reporting
J. A. Livingston	International correspondence
Melvin H. Ruder	Local reporting, against deadline
Ernest Samuels	Biography
Irwin Unger	History

1966

Peter Arnett	International correspondence
Leslie Bassett	Music
John A. Frasca	Local reporting
Haynes Johnson	National reporting
Robert Lasch	Editorial writing
Perry Miller	History
Katherine Ann Porter	Fiction
Arthur M. Schlesinger, Jr.	Biography
Edwin W. Teale	Nonfiction
Don Wright	Cartoon

1967

Edward Albee	Drama
Robert V. Cox	Local reporting, against deadline
David B. Davis	Nonfiction
William H. Goetzmann	History
R. John Hughes	International correspondence
Justin Kaplan	Biography
Monroe W. Karmin	National reporting
Leon Kirchner	Music
Bernard Malamud	Fiction
Gene Miller	Local reporting
Patrick B. Oliphant	Cartoon
Eugene Patterson	Editorial writing
Stanley W. Penn	National reporting
Anne Sexton	Poetry
Jack R. Thornell	News photography

1968

Bernard Bailyn	History
George Crumb	Music
Ariel Durant	Nonfiction
Will Durant	Nonfiction
Alfred Friendly	International correspondence
Anthony Hecht	Poetry
Howard James	National reporting
Nathan K. Katz	National reporting
George F. Kennan	Autobiography
John S. Knight	Editorial writing
J. Anthony Lukas	Local reporting
Eugene Gray Payne	Cartoon
William Styron	Fiction

1969

Edward T. Adams	News photography
Robert Cahn	National reporting
Albert L. Delugach	Local reporting
Rene J. Dubos	Nonfiction
John Fetterman	Local reporting, against deadline
John Fischetti	Cartoon
Paul Greenberg	Editorial writing
Karel Husa	Music
Leonard W. Levy	History
Norman Mailer	Nonfiction
M. Scott Momaday	Fiction
George Oppen	Poetry
Benjamin L. Reid	Biography
Howard Sackler	Drama
Moneta Sleet, Jr.	News photography
William Tuohy	International correspondence
Denny Walsh	Local reporting

1970

Dean G. Acheson	History
Marquis Childs	Commentary
Thomas F. Darcy	Cartoons
William J. Eaton	National reporting
Erik H. Erikson	Nonfiction
Thomas Fitzpatrick	Local reporting, general
Philip L. Geyelin	Editorial writing
Charles Gordone	Drama
Seymour M. Hersh	International reporting
Richard Howard	Poetry
Ada Louise Huxtable	Criticism
Dallas Kinney	Feature photography
Harold E. Martin	Local reporting, special
Jean Stafford	Fiction
Steve Starr	Spot news photography
T. Harry Williams	Biography
Charles W. Wuorinen	Music

PULITZER PRIZE WINNERS

1971

James MacGregor Burns	History
William A. Caldwell	Commentary
Paul Conrad	Editorial cartooning
Mario Davidovsky	Music
Horace G. Davis, Jr.	Editorial writing
Jack Dykinga	Feature photography
John Paul Filo	Spot news photography
Lucinda Franks	National reporting
Jimmie Lee Hoagland	International reporting
William H. Jones	Local reporting, special
William S. Merwin	Poetry
Thomas Powers	National reporting
Harold C. Schonberg	Criticism
Lawrance R. Thompson	Biography
John Toland	General nonfiction
Paul Zindel	Drama

1972

Jack Anderson	National reporting
Richard Cooper	Local reporting
Carl N. Degler	History
Ann Desantis	Special local reporting
Jacob Druckman	Music
Horst Fass	Spot news photography
Peter R. Kann	International reporting
David Kennerly	Feature photography
Stephen A. Kurkjian	Special local reporting
Michael Laurent	Spot news photography
Joseph P. Lash	Biography
Timothy Leland	Special local reporting
John Machacek	General local reporting
Jeffrey K. Macnelly	Editorial cartooning
Gerard M. O'Neill	Special local reporting
Frank Peters, Jr.	Music criticism
Mike Royko	Commentary
Wallace E. Stegner	Fiction
John Strohmeyer	Editorial writing
Barbara W. Tuchman	General nonfiction
James Wright	Poetry

Academy of American Poets Fellowship

Awarded to recognize distinguished poetic achievement.

1937 Edwin Markham
1946 Edgar Lee Masters
1947 Ridgely Torrence
1948 Percy Mackaye
1950 E. E. Cummings
1952 Padraic Colum
1953 Robert Frost
1954 Louise Townsend Nicholl
1955 Rolfe Humphries
1956 William Carlos Williams
1957 Conrad Aiken
1958 Robinson Jeffers
1959 Louis Bogan
Leonie Adams
1960 Jesse Stuart
1961 Horace Gregory
1962 John Crowe Ransom
1963 Ezra Pound
Allen Tate
1964 Elizabeth Bishop
1965 Marianne Moore
1966 Archibald MacLeish
John Berryman
1967 Mark Van Doren
1968 Stanley Kunitz
1969 Richard Eberhart
Anthony Hecht
1970 Howard Nemiroff
1971 James Wright

Edward Goodrich Acheson Medal and Prize

Awarded every second year by The Electrochemical Society, Inc., for a distinguished contribution to any of the branches fostered by the society.

1929 Edward G. Acheson
1931 Edwin F. Northrup
1933 Colin G. Fink
1935 Frank J. Tone
1937 Frederick M. Becket
1939 Francis C. Frary
1942 Charles F. Burgess
1944 William Blum
1948 Duncan A. MacInnes
1950 George W. Vinal
1952 John W. Marden
1954 George W. Heise
1956 Robert M. Burns
1958 William J. Kroll
1960 Henry B. Linford
1962 Charles L. Faust
1964 Earl A. Gulbransen
1966 Warren C. Vosburgh
1968 Francis L. LaQue

Benjamin Altman Prize

Awarded annually by the National Academy of Design to recognize achievement in painting in oil.

Figure Painting

1915 Charles W. Hawthorne
1916 Lawton Parker
1917 Daniel Garber
1918 Victor Higgins
1919 Charles C. Curran
1921 Walter Ufer
Ernest L. Blumenschein
1922 Leon Kroll
1923 Louis Betts
1924 Childe Hassam
1926 Karl Anderson
Wayman Adams
1927 Lilian Wescott Hale
1928 J. W. Schlaikjer
1929 Harry W. Watrous
1930 Gifford Beal
1931 Eugene Higgins
1932 Leon Kroll
1935 Jean MacLane
1936 Sidney E. Dickinson
1937 Charles S. Duncan
1939 Abram Poole
1940 Abram Poole
1941 Randall Davey
1942 Eugene Higgins
1943 Paul Clemens
1944 Ivan Albright
1945 Greta Matson
Guy Pene Du Bois
1947 Philip Guston
1948 John Carroll
1949 Fletcher Martin
1951 Robert Philipp
1952 Marion Greenwood
1953 Fred Nagler
1954 John Carroll
1955 Isabel Bishop
1956 Morton Roberts
1957 Nancy Ellen Craig
1958 Ben Kamihira
1959 Joseph Hirsch
1960 Ann Eshner
1961 Jules Kirschenbaum
1962 Ben Kamihira
1963 John W. Reilly
1964 Edward Melcarth
1966 Joseph Hirsch
1967 Isabel Bishop
1968 Barbara Adrian
1969 Burton Silverman
1971 Alice Neel
1972 Gregorio Prestopino

Landscape Painting

1916 Charles Rosen
1917 Charles H. Davis
1918 Paul Dougherty
1919 Edward W. Redfield
1920 W. Elmer Schofield
1921 Ernest Lawson
1922 Daniel Garber
1923 Paul King
1924 William L. Lathrop
1925 Hobart Nichols
1926 Childe Hassam
1927 Daniel Garber
1928 Ernest Lawson
1929 William S. Robinson
1930 Theodore Van Soelen
1931 Aldro T. Hibbard
1932 Victor Higgins
1933 W. Granville-Smith
1934 Hobart Nichols
1935 Leon Kroll
1937 Sidney Laufman
1938 Frank Mechau
1940 Chauncey F. Ryder
1941 John F. Folinsbee
1942 Zsissly
1943 Antonio P. Martino
1944 Carl Gaertner
1945 James W. Kerr
Guy Pene Du Bois
1950 John F. Folinsbee
1951 Francis Speight
1952 Carl Gaertner
1953 Walter Stuempfig
1954 William Thon
1955 Furman J. Finck
1956 Ethel Magafan
1957 Edward Betts
1958 Francis Speight
1959 Edward Betts
1960 Seymour Reminick
1961 William Thon
1962 Paul Sample
1963 Karl Knaths
1964 Zsissly
1965 Karl Knaths
1966 Edward Betts
1967 William Thon
1968 Ida Oganoff
1969 Paul W. Zimmerman
1970 Richard Mayhew
1971 Anne Poor
1972 John Hultberg

American Academy of Arts and Letters Gold Medal

Awarded to an American citizen, not a member of the academy of National Institute of Arts and Letters, to recognize special distinction in literature, art, or music. Discontinued in order to avoid confusion with the Gold Medal of the Institute, which is presented in the name of the academy.

1915 Charles W. Eliot
1923 Mariana Griswold
Van Rensselaer
1925 Cecilia Beaux
1929 Edith Wharton
1930 Anna Hyatt Huntington
1942 Ernest Bloch
1948 Bruce Rogers

American Academy of Arts and Letters Award of Merit Medal

Presented annually to an outstanding person in America, not a member of the institute, representing the following arts: painting, sculpture, novel, poetry, and drama.

1942 Charles E. Burchfield
1944 Theodore Dreiser
1945 W. H. Auden
1947 Andrew Wyeth
1948 Donal Hord
1951 Sidney Kingsley
1952 Rico Lebrun
1953 Ivan Mestrovic
1954 Ernest Hemingway
1957 Raphael Soyer
1960 Hilda Doolittle
1961 Clifford Odets
1962 Charles Sheeler
1963 Chaim Gross
1964 John O'Hara
1967 John E. Heliker
1968 Joseph Cornell
1969 Vladimir Nabokov
1970 Reed H. Whittemore
1971 Clyfford Still

American Bar Association Medal

Awarded to a member of the bar in the United States who has rendered conspicuous service to the cause of American jurisprudence.

1929 Samuel Williston
1930 Elihu Root
1931 Oliver Wendell Holmes
1932 John H. Wigmore
1934 George W. Wickersham
1938 Herbert Harley
1939 Edgar B. Tolman
1940 Roscoe Pound
1941 George Wharton Pepper
1942 Charles Evans Hughes
1943 John J. Parker
1944 Hatton W. Sumners
1946 Carl McFarland
1947 William L. Ransom
1948 Arthur T. Vanderbilt
1950 Orie L. Phillips
1951 Reginald H. Smith
1952 Harrison Tweed
1953 Frank E. Holman
1954 George M. Morris
1956 Robert G. Storey
1957 William C. Mason
1958 E. Smythe Gambrell
1959 Grenville Clark
1960 William A. Schnader
1961 Jacob M. Lashly
1962 Tom C. Clark
1963 Felix Frankfurter
1964 Henry S. Drinker
1965 Edmund M. Morgan
1966 Charles S. Rhyne
1967 Roger J. Traynor
1968 J. Edward Lumbard
1969 Walter V. Schaefer
1970 Frank J. Haymond
1971 Whitney North Seymour
1972 Harold J. Gallagher

American Heart Association Research Achievement Award

Conferred annually to recognize outstanding achievement in the field of cardiovascular research.

1953 Paul Dudley White
1954 Albert Szent-Gyorgyi
1955 Carl J. Wiggers
1956 Louis N. Katz
1957 Isaac Starr
1958 Irvine H. Page
1959 Robert E. Gross
1960 Karl P. Link
Edgar V. Allen
Irving S. Wright
1961 Charles H. Rammelkamp, Jr.
1962 Maurice B. Visscher
1963 Donald E. Gregg
1964 Rebecca C. Lancefield
1965 John H. Gibbon, Jr.
1966 Harry Goldblatt
1967 Wallace O. Fenn
1968 Julius H. Comroe, Jr.
1969 Otto Krayer

American Institute of Architects Fine Arts Medal

Awarded annually to honor distinguished achievement in the fine arts, including painting, sculpture, music, and literature.

1921 Paul Manship
1923 Arthur F. Mathews
1925 John Singer Sargent
1926 Leopold Stokowski
1927 Lee Lawrie
1928 H. Siddons Mowbray
1930 Adolph A. Weinman
1931 Frederick L. Olmsted
1934 James H. Breasted
1936 Robert Edmond Jones
1944 John Taylor Arms
1947 Samuel Chamberlain
1948 John Marin
1949 Louis C. Rosenberg
1950 Edward Steichen
1951 Thomas Church
1952 Marshall M. Fredericks
1953 Donal Hord
1954 Julian H. Harris
1955 Ivan Mestrovic
1956 M. Hidreth Meiere
1957 Mark Tobey
1958 Viktor Schreckengost
1959 Kenneth Hedrich
1960 Thomas Hart Benton
1961 Alexander Calder
1962 Stuart Davis
1963 Isamu Noguchi
1965 Roberto B. Marx
1966 Ben Shahn
1967 Constantino Nivola
1968 Gyorgy Kepes
1970 Richard Lippald
1971 Anthony Smith
1972 George Rickey

American Institute of Architects Gold Medal

Awarded from time to time to honor distinguished achievement in architecture.

1909 Charles F. McKim
1911 George B. Post
1923 Henry Bacon
1925 Bertram G. Goodhue
1927 Howard V. Shaw
1929 Milton B. Medary
1938 Paul P. Cret
1944 Louis H. Sullivan
1947 Eliel Saarinen
1948 Charles D. Maginnis
1949 Frank Lloyd Wright
1951 Bernard R. Maybeck
1953 William A. Delano
1956 Clarence S. Stein
1957 Ralph Walker
Louis Skidmore
1958 John W. Root
1959 Walter Gropius
1960 Ludwig Mies van der Rohe
1962 Eero Saarinen
1967 Wallace K. Harrison
1968 Marcel Breuer
1969 William W. Wurster
1970 R. Buckminster Fuller

American Institute of Chemists Gold Medal

Awarded annually to recognize achievement of outstanding service to the science of chemistry or to the profession of chemistry in America.

1926 William Blum
1927 Lafayette B. Mendel
1929 Francis P. Garvan and
Mrs. Francis P. Garvan
1930 George Eastman
1931 Andrew W. Mellon and
Richard B. Mellon
1932 Charles H. Herty
1933 Henry C. Sherman
1934 James B. Conant
1936 Marston T. Bogert
1937 James F. Norris
1938 Frederick G. Cottrell
1940 Gustav Egloff
1941 Henry G. Knight
1942 William L. Evans
1943 Walter S. Landis
1944 Willard H. Dow
1945 John W. Thomas
1946 Robert P. Russell
1947 M. L. Crossley
1948 Charles A. Thomas
1949 Warren K. Lewis
1950 Walter J. Murphy
1951 Harry N. Holmes
1952 Fred J. Emmerich
1953 J. C. Warner
1954 William J. Sparks
1955 Carl S. Marvel
1956 Raymond Stevens
1957 Roy C. Newton
1958 Lawrence Flett
1959 Crawford H. Greenewalt
1960 Ernest H. Volwiler
1961 Alden H. Emery
1962 W. George Parks
1963 Ralph Connor
1964 Roger Adams
1965 Edwin Cox
1966 John H. Nair
1967 Wayne E. Kuhn
1968 Orville E. May
1969 Henry B. Hass
1970 Willard F. Libby

American Medical Association Distinguished Service Award

Presented annually to recognize outstanding service in the science and art of medicine.

1938 Rudolph Matas
1939 James B. Herrick
1940 Chevalier Jackson
1941 James Ewing
1942 Ludvig Hektoen
1943 Elliott P. Joslin
1944 George Dock
1945 George R. Minot
1946 Anton J. Carlson
1947 Henry A. Christian
1948 Isaac A. Abt
1949 Seale Harris
1950 Evarts A. Graham
1951 Allen C. Whipple
1952 Paul Dudley White
1953 Alfred Blalock
1954 W. Wayne Babcock
1955 Donald C. Balfour
1956 Walter L. Bierring
1957 Tom D. Spies
1958 Frank H. Krusen
1959 Michael E. De Bakey
1960 Charles Doan
1961 Walter H. Judd
1962 Russell L. Cecil
1963 Lester R. Dragstedt
1964 Irvine H. Page
1965 Tinsley R. Harrison
1966 Warren H. Cole
1967 Alton Ochsner
1968 Owen H. Wangensteen
1969 Jay Arnold Bargen
1970 Henry L. Bockus
1971 Milton Helpern

American Petroleum Institute Gold Medal for Distinguished Achievement

Awarded from time to time to recognize contributions to the arts and sciences, particularly befitting the petroleum industry.

1946 Henry Ford
1947 William M. Burton
1948 Charles F. Kettering
1949 J. Howard Pew
1950 Walter C. Teagle
1951 Ernest O. Thompson
1953 Otto D. Donnell
1954 Wallace E. Pratt
1956 J. Frank Drake
1957 Warren K. Lewis
1958 W. S. S. Rodgers
1960 Eugene Holman
1965 M. J. Rathbone
1966 Albert C. Rubel
1967 Alfred Jacobsen
1968 R. Gwin Follis
1969 Hugo A. Anderson
John E. Warren
1971 Michael L. Haider

American Psychiatric Association Distinguished Service Award

Presented annually to honor meritorious service to American psychiatry.

1965 Karl Menninger
1966 Franklin Ebaugh, Sr.
1967 Howard Potter
1968 Lister Hill
1969 Nolan D. C. Lewis
1970 Lauren H. Smith

American Society for Metals Gold Medal

Awarded to recognize outstanding metallurgical knowledge, versatility in the application of science to the metal industry, and the ability to diagnose and solve diversified metallurgical problems.

1943 Zay Jeffries
1945 Earle C. Smith
1947 Champion H. Mathewson
1948 Francis C. Frary
1949 Edgar C. Bain
1951 Paul D. Merica
1952 Robert F. Mehl
1953 George Sachs
1955 A. L. Boegehold
1956 William H. Eisenman
1957 John Chipman
1958 Albert J. Phillips
1959 Matthew A. Hunter
1960 John B. Johnson
1961 Cyril S. Smith
1962 Clarence H. Lorig
1963 Francis B. Foley
1964 Walter Crafts
1965 Joseph D. Hanawalt
1966 Carl E. Swartz
1967 William J. Kroll
1968 Morris Cohen

American Society of Mechanical Engineers Medal

Awarded annually for distinguished service in engineering and science. May be presented for service in science having possible application in engineering.

1921 Hjalmar G. Carlson
1922 Frederick A. Halsey
1923 John R. Freeman
1926 Robert A. Millikan
1927 Wilfred Lewis
1928 Julian Kennedy
1930 William L. Emmet
1931 Albert Kingsbury
1933 Ambrose Swasey
1934 Willis H. Carrier
1935 Charles T. Main
1936 Edward Bausch
1937 Edward P. Bullard, Jr.
1938 Stephen J. Pigott
1939 James E. Gleason
1940 Charles F. Kettering
1941 Theodore von Karman
1942 Ervin G. Bailey
1943 Lewis K. Sillcox
1944 Edward G. Budd
1945 William F. Durand
1946 Morris E. Leeds
1947 Paul W. Kiefer
1948 Frederick G. Keyes
1949 Fred L. Dornbrook
1950 Harvey C. Knowles
1951 Glenn B. Warren
1952 Nevin E. Funk
1953 Crosby Field
1954 E. Burnley Powell
1955 Granville M. Read
1956 Harry F. Vickers
1957 L. M. K. Boelter

1958 Wilbur H. Armacost
1959 Martin Frisch
1960 C. Richard Soderberg
1962 Philip Sporn
1963 Igor I. Sikorsky
1964 Alan Howard
1965 Johannes M. Burgers
1967 Mayo D. Hersey
1968 Samuel C. Collins
1969 Lloyd H. Donnell
1970 Robert R. Gilruth
1971 Horace S. Beattie

American Watercolor Society Gold Medal of Honor

Awarded for the best watercolor painting shown in the society's annual exhibition.

1948 Ogen Pleissner
1949 John Taylor
1950 Leonard Cutrow
1951 Walter Biggs
1952 Andrew Wyeth
1953 Donald Teague
1954 Ted Kautzky
1955 Emerton Heitland
1956 Ogden Pleissner
1957 William A. Smith
1958 Maurice Logan
1959 Morton Roberts
1960 Morton Grossman
1961 Roy Mason
1962 Claus Hoie
1963 Doris White
1964 Donald Teague
1965 William A. Smith
1966 Chen Chi
1967 Avel de Knight
1968 Hugh Gumpel
1969 Tom Nicholas

Archaeological Institute of America Gold Medal

Awarded annually to recognize distinguished achievement by a professional archaeologist.

1965 Carl W. Blegen
1966 Hetty Goldman
1967 William F. Albright
1968 Gisela M. A. Richter
1969 Oscar T. Broneer
1970 Rys Carpenter
1971 William B. Dinsmoor

Arches of Science Award

Presented annually by the Pacific Science Center, Seattle, Wash., to honor those who have contributed notably to man's deeper understanding of the fundamental meaning of scientific activity.

1965 Warren Weaver
1966 Rene J. Dubos
1967 James B. Conant
1968 Glenn T. Seaborg
1969 Gerard Piel

Architectural League of New York Gold Medal of Honor

Awarded to recognize work of high quality in architectural design and several related fields.

Architecture

1916 Cass Gilbert
1917 John Russell Pope
1918 Benjamin W. Morris
1921 Charles Z. Klauder
1923 Dwight J. Baum
1925 Arthur L. Harmon
1926 John M. Howells and Raymond M. Hood
1927 Ralph T. Walker
1928 Paul P. Cret
1929 William P. Barney
1931 Eliel Saarinen
William F. Lamb
1933 Henry R. Shepley
Thomas H. Ellett
1950 Philip L. Goodwin
Edward Durrell Stone
1951 Jean B. Fletcher
Norman Fletcher
Walter Gropius
Sarah Harkness
John Harkness
Robert S. McMillan
Louis A. McMillan
Benjamin Thompson
1952 Edward D. Stone
Karl J. Holzinger
1954 Carl Koch
1956 Leo Lionni and Giorgio Cavaglieri
1960 Ludwig Mies van der Rohe and Philip Johnson

Engineering

1953 William H. Dietrick and Matthew Nowicki
1954 Thomas C. Kavanagh and Camilo Piccone
1955 Emil H. Praeger

Mural Decoration

1909 John LaFarge
1910 Kenyon Cox
1911 Edwin H. Blashfield
1912 Charles Y. Turner
1914 Barry Faulkner
1916 Violet Oakley
1917 Maxfield Parrish
1920 Arthur Crisp
Eugene Savage
1922 Ezra Winter
1923 Edward Simmons
1925 Arthur Covey
1926 George Davidson
1927 J. Monroe Hewlett
1928 Hildreth Meiere
1929 Eugene Savage
1930 Boardman Robinson
1931 John Norton
1932 D. Putnam Brinley
1933 Thomas Hart Benton
1936 James M. Newell
1937 Howard Cook
1951 Dean Cornwell
1951 Sante Graziani
1953 George Harding
1954 Allyn Cox
1956 Fred Conway

Sculpture

1909 John Q. A. Ward
1911 A. Philmister Proctor
1912 Daniel Chester French
1913 Adolph A. Weinman
1914 Karl Bitter
1915 Robert Aitken
1916 Herbert Adams
1917 Hermon A. MacNeil
1918 Paul W. Bartlett
1921 John Gregory
1922 Leo Lentelli
1923 Edward McCartan
1924 Chester Beach
1925 James E. Fraser
1926 Charles Keck
1927 C. Paul Jennewein
1929 Ulric Ellerhusen
1931 Lee Lawrie
1932 A. Stirling Calder
1933 Leo Friedlander
1951 Donald De Lue
1954 Cecil Howard
1955 Ernest Morenon
1956 Marshall M. Fredericks
1958 Jean de Marco
1960 Alexander Calder
1965 Isamu Noguchi

The Audubon Medal

Awarded from time to time by the National Audubon Society to honor distinguished service to the conservation of natural resources.

1947 Hugh H. Bennett
1949 Ira N. Gabrielson
1950 John D. Rockefeller, Jr.
1952 Louis Bromfield
1955 Walt Disney
1956 Ludlow Griscom
1959 Olaus J. Murie
1960 Jay N. Darling
1961 Clarence Cottam
1962 William O. Douglas
1963 Rachel Carson
1964 Laurance S. Rockefeller
1966 A. Starker Leopold
1967 Stewart L. Udall
1968 Fairfield Osborn
1969 Horace M. Albright
1971 Roger Tory Peterson

The Bancroft Prize

Awarded by Columbia University to honor distinguished published works in the categories of American history, including biography, American diplomacy, and the international relations of the United States.

1948 Allan Nevins
Bernard DeVoto
1949 Robert E. Sherwood
Samuel Eliot Morison
1950 Lawrence H. Gipson
Herbert E. Bolton
1951 Arthur N. Holcombe
Henry N. Smith
1952 Merlo J. Pusey
C. Vann Woodward
1953 George Dangerfield
Eric F. Goldman
1954 Clinton Rossiter
William L. Langer and S. Everett Gleason
1955 Paul Horgan
Leonard D. White
1956 Elizabeth Stevenson
James G. Randall and Richard N. Current
1957 George F. Kennan
Arthur S. Link
1958 Arthur M. Schlesinger, Jr.
Frank Luther Mott
1959 Ernest Samuels
Daniel J. Boorstin
1960 Robert R. Palmer
Margaret Leech
1961 Merrill D. Peterson
Arthur S. Link
1962 Lawrence A. Cremin
Felix Gilbert
Martin B. Duberman
1963 Page Smith
Roberta Wohlstetter
John G. Stoessinger
1964 William E. Leuchtenburg
John L. Thomas
Paul Seabury
1965 Bradford Perkins
William B. Willcox
Dorothy Borg
1966 Richard B. Morris
Theodore W. Friend III
1967 William W. Freehling
Charles Sellers
James S. Young
1968 Henry A. Bullock
Richard L. Bushman
Bernard Bailyn
1969 Winthrop Jordan
N. Gordon Levin, Jr.
Rexford Guy Tugwell
1970 Charles C. Sellers
Gordon S. Wood
Dan T. Carter
1971 Erik Barnouw
David M. Kennedy
Joseph F. Wall
1972 Carl M. Degler
Robert Middlekauff
Samuel Eliot Morrison

Barnard Medal

Awarded by Columbia University on the recommendation of the National Academy of Sciences to honor outstanding achievement during a five-year period in the form of a notable discovery in physical or astronomical science or a novel application of science to purposes beneficial to the human race.

1920 Albert Einstein
1935 Edwin P. Hubble
1950 Enrico Fermi
1955 Merle A. Tuve
1960 Isidor I. Rabi
1965 William A. Fowler

Bollingen Prize

Awarded biennially (originally each year) by the Yale University Library to recognize distinguished achievement by an American poet.

1949 Wallace Stevens
1950 John Crowe Ransom
1951 Marianne Moore
1952 Archibald MacLeish
William Carlos Williams
1953 W. H. Auden
1954 Leonie Adams
Louise Bogan
1955 Conrad Aiken
1956 Allen Tate
1957 E. E. Cummings
1958 Theodore Roethke
1959 Delmore Schwartz
1960 Yvor Winters
1961 John Hall Wheelock
Richard Eberhart
1962 Robert Frost
1964 Horace Gregory
1966 Robert Penn Warren
1968 John Berryman
Karl Shapiro
1970 Richard Wilbur
Mona Van Duyn
1972 James Merrill

The Borden Award

Presented annually by the American Academy of Pediatrics for contributions in the areas of nutrition and development of infants and children.

1944 Harry H. Gordon and
S. Z. Levine
1945 Edwards A. Park
1946 James L. Gamble
1947 Grover F. Powers
1948 Dorothy Andersen
1949 Alfred Washburn
1950 Josef Warkany
1951 Daniel C. Darrow
1952 Julius Hess
1953 Lawson Wilkins
1954 Paul Gyorgy
1955 L. Emmett Holt, Jr.
1956 A. Ashley Weech
1957 Arild E. Hansen
1958 Charles D. May
1959 Harold C. Stuart
1960 Harold E. Harrison
1961 Clement A. Smith
1962 Nathan B. Talbot
1963 David Gitlin
1964 Gilbert Forbes
1965 Joseph Dancis
1966 Samuel J. Fomon
1967 Donald B. Cheek
1968 Bruce Mackler
1969 Norman Kretchmer
1970 Albert Dorfman

Brandeis University Creative Arts Award

Presented annually to recognize outstanding artistic contributions by artists in several fields for a life-time of distinguished achievement.

Theatre Arts

1957 Hallie Flanagan Davis
1958 Stark Young
1959 George Kelly
1960 Thornton Wilder
1961 Lillian Hellman
1962 S. N. Behrman
1963 Jo Mielziner
1964 Cheryl Crawford
1965 Tennessee Williams
1966 Eva Le Gallienne
1967 Jerome Robbins
1968 Richard Rodgers
1969 Boris Aronson
1970 Arthur Miller
1972 Alfred Lunt
Lynn Fontanne

Literature

1957 William Carlos Williams
1958 John Crowe Ransom
1959 Hilda Doolittle
1960 Yvor Winters
1961 Allen Tate
1962 Louise Bogan
1963 Marianne Moore
1964 Vladimir Nabokov
1965 Stanley Kunitz
1966 Eudora Welty
1967 Conrad Aiken
1968 Lionel Trilling
1969 Leonie Adams
1970 Isaac Bashevis Singer

Fine Arts

1957 Stuart Davis
1959 Edwin Dickinson
1960 Naum Gabo
1961 Karl Knaths
1962 Alexander Calder
1963 Georgia O'Keefe
1964 David Smith
1965 Mark Rothko
1966 Isamu Noguchi
1967 Ludwig Mies van der Rohe
1968 Joseph Cornell
1969 Jose de Rivera
1970 Barnett Newman
1971 Claes Oldenburg
Louise Nevelson
1972 Louis I. Kahn

Music

1957 William Schuman
1958 Roger Sessions
1959 Ernest Bloch
1960 Aaron Copland
1961 Wallingford Riegger
1962 Edgard Varese
1963 Walter Piston
1964 Carl Ruggles
1965 Elliott Carter
1966 Stefan Wolpe
1967 Ross Lee Finney
1968 Virgil Thomson
1969 Ernst Krenek
1970 Milton Babbitt
1971 Earl Kim
1972 John Harbison

Commission Award for Notable Achievement

1964 R. Buckminster Fuller
1965 Alfred H. Barr, Jr.
1966 Meyer Schapiro
1967 Kenneth Burke
1968 Martha Graham
1969 Lewis Mumford
1970 Lloyd Goodrich
1971 George Balanchine
1972 I. A. Richards

Film

1971 Bruce Baille

Poetry

1971 Richard Wilbur
James Wright

Dance

1972 Merce Cunningham

Brewster Memorial Award

Presented annually (originally every two years) by the American Ornithologists' Union to the author of an important work relating to the birds of the Western Hemisphere.

1921 Robert Ridgway
1923 Arthur C. Bent
1925 W. E. Clyde Todd and
M. A. Carriker, Jr.
1927 John C. Phillips
1931 Florence Merriam Bailey
1933 Frank M. Chapman
1935 Herbert L. Stoddard
1937 Robert C. Murphy
1938 Thomas S. Roberts
1939 Witmer Stone
1940 James Lee Peters
1941 Donald E. Dickey and
Adrian J. Van Rossem
1942 Margaret Morse Nice
1943 Alden H. Miller
1944 Roger Tory Peterson
1950 Alexander Skutch
1951 S. Charles Kendeigh
1952 John T. Zimmer
1953 Hildegarde Howard
1954 James Bond
1956 George H. Lowery, Jr.
1957 Robert Porter Allen
1958 Arlie W. Schorger
1959 Alexander Wetmore
1960 Donald S. Farner
1961 Harold F. Mayfield
1962 Albert Wolfson
1963 Ralph S. Palmer
1964 Herbert Friedmann
1965 Ernst Mayr
1966 George A. Batholomew, Jr.
1967 W. E. Clyde Todd
1968 Wesley E. Lanyon

Bronfman Prize

Awarded annually by the American Public Health Association in recognition of meritorious achievement leading directly to improved health for large numbers of people.

1961 James E. Perkins
James Watt
1962 Theodore F. Hatch
Charles E. Smith
1963 Harold D. Chope
Marion B. Folsom
Herman E. Hillboe
1964 Robert H. Felix
Malcolm E. Merrill
George E. Moore
1965 Guillermo Arbona
Alexander D. Langmuir
George James
1966 Bernard G. Greenberg
Emmett M. Hall
1967 Wilbur J. Cohen
Forrest E. Linder
Myron E. Wegman
1968 Moises Behar
James L. Goddard
Abraham L. Lilienfeld
1969 William Haddon, Jr.
Edwin H. Lennette
1970 Karl Evarg
Alan Guttmacher
Edmund S. Muskie
1971 Ruth Freeman
John F. Brotherston
James H. Steele
Herman E. Hilleboe

Franklin L. Burr Prize for Science

Awarded by the National Geographic Society to leaders of the Society's expeditions and to researchers to recognize meritorious work in the field of geographic science.

1933 Albert W. Stevens
1936 Albert W. Stevens
Orvil A. Anderson
Randolph P. Williams
1938 William M. Mann and
Mrs. William M. Mann
1939 Bradford Washburn
Matthew W. Stirling
1941 Matthew W. Stirling
Mrs. Matthew W. Stirling

1944 Alexander Wetmore
1945 Thomas A. Jaggar
Lyman J. Briggs
1947 George Van Biesbroeck
1948 Edward A. Halbach,
Francis J. Heyden,
Carl W. Miller,
Charles H. Smiley, and
George Van Biesbroeck
Arthur A. Allen
1950 Frank M. Setzler
1952 Harold E. Edgerton
1953 George Van Biesbroeck
1954 Lyman J. Briggs
1955 Neil M. Judd
Mrs. Robert E. Peary
Marie Peary Stafford
1956 Robert F. Griggs
1957 Matthew W. Stirling
1959 Carl F. Miller
1962 Lyman J. Briggs
1963 Donald B. MacMillan
Neil M. Judd
Barry C. Bishop
1965 Bradford Washburn
Norman G. Dyhrenfurth
1967 Maynard M. Miller

Burroughs Medal

Awarded at intervals by the John Burroughs Memorial Association, Inc., to the author of a distinguished book in the field of nature writing.

1926 William Beebe
1927 Ernest Thompson Seton
1929 Frank M. Chapman
1930 Archibald Rutledge
1933 Oliver P. Medsger
1934 W. W. Christman
1936 Charles C. Gorst
1938 Robert C. Murphy
1939 T. Gilbert Pearson
1940 Arthur C. Bent
1941 Louis J. Halle, Jr.
1943 Edwin W. Teale
1945 Rutherford Platt
1946 Francis Lee Jaques and
Mrs. Francis Lee Jaques
1948 Theodora Stanwell-Fletcher
1949 Allan D. Cruickshank and
Mrs. Allan D. Cruickshank
1950 Roger Tory Peterson
1952 Rachel Carson
1953 Gilbert Klingel
1954 Joseph Wood Krutch
1955 Wallace B. Grange
1956 Guy Murchie
1957 Archie Carr
1958 Robert Porter Allen
1960 John Kieran
1961 Loren Eiseley
1962 George M. Sutton
1963 Adolph Murie
1964 John Hay
1965 Paul Brooks
1966 Louis Darling
1967 Charlton Ogburn
1968 Hal Borland
1969 Louise de Kiriline Lawrence
1970 Victor B. Scheffer
1971 John K. Terres
1972 Robert Arbib

Butler Medal

Awarded by Columbia University to honor a distinguished contribution made during a five-year period to philosophy or to educational theory, practice, or administration.

1925 Edward L. Thorndike
1930 Alfred North Whitehead
1935 John Dewey
1945 George Santayana
1950 Clarence I. Lewis
1965 Rudolf Carnap
1970 Willard V. Quine

Capezio Dance Award

Presented annually by Capezio, Inc., to focus attention on meritorious work in the field of dancing.

1952 Zachary Solov
1953 Lincoln Kirstein
1954 Doris Humphrey
1955 Louis Horst
1956 Genevieve Oswald
1957 Ted Shawn
1958 Alexandra Danilova
1959 Sol Hurok
1960 Martha Graham
1961 Ruth St. Denis
1962 Barbara Karinska
1963 Donald McKayle
1964 Jose Limon
1965 Maria Tallchief
1966 Agnes DeMille
1967 Paul Taylor
1968 Lucia Chase
1969 John Martin
1970 William Kolodney
1971 Gladys Laubin
Reginald Laubin

W. A. Clark Prize

Awarded biennially by the Corcoran Gallery of Art to recognize achievement in oil painting by living American artists.

First Prize

1907 Willard L. Metcalf
1908 Edward W. Redfield
1910 Edmund C. Tarbell
1912 Childe Hassam
1914 J. Alden Weir
1916 Arthur B. Davies
1919 Frank W. Benson
1921 Daniel Garber
1923 George Bellows
1926 Charles W. Hawthorne
1928 Bernard Karfiol
1930 Maurice Sterne
1932 George Luks
1935 Eugene Speicher
1937 Edward Hopper
1939 Franklin C. Watkins
1941 John E. Heliker
1943 Henry Mattson
1945 Reginald Marsh
1947 Sigmund Menkes
1949 Eric Isenburger
1951 Raphael Soyer
1953 Abraham Rattner
1955 John Hultberg
1957 Loren MacIver
1959 Walter Plate
1961 Lee Gatch
1963 Jack Tworkov
1965 Robert Rauschenberg
1967 Jules Olitski

Second Prize

1907 Frank W. Benson
1908 Joseph DeCamp
1910 Gari Melchers
1912 Daniel Garber
1914 Charles H. Woodbury
1916 Ernest Lawson
1919 Charles H. Davis
1921 Burtis Baker
1923 Charles W. Hawthorne
1926 W. Elmer Schofield
1928 Eugene Speicher
1930 Gifford Beal
1932 John R. Grabach
1935 F. C. Frieseke
1937 Guy Pene DuBois
1939 Robert Philipp
1941 Fred Nagler
1943 Aaron Bohrod
1945 Zsissly
1947 Walter Stuempfig
1949 Fred Conway
1951 Philip Evergood
1953 Hobson Pittman
1955 Ivan Albright
1957 Fritz Glarner
1959 Jack Levine
1961 Ben Kamihira
1963 Lee Bontecou
1965 Richard Pousette-Dart
1967 Paul Jenkins

Thomas B. Clarke Prize

Awarded by the National Academy of Design to recognize outstanding figure composition painted in oil.

1884 Charles F. Ulrich
1885 Francis C. Jones
1886 Walter Satterlee
1887 Thomas W. Dewing
1888 H. Siddons Mowbray
1889 Irving R. Wiles
1890 Edmund C. Tarbell
1891 Frank W. Benson
1892 William S. Harper
1893 Charles C. Curran
1894 Harry W. Watrous
1895 Henry O. Walker
1896 Robert Reid
1898 Abbott H. Thayer
1899 Edward H. Potthast
1900 Charles Schreyvogel
1901 William F. Kline
1902 Eliott Daingerfield
1903 Lydia Amanda Sewell
1904 Harry M. Walcott
1905 Childe Hassam
1906 Hugo Ballin
1907 Henry Prellwitz
1908 Robert D. Gauley
1909 Lydia F. Emmet
1910 Frederick J. Waugh
1911 Charles W. Hawthorne
1912 Charles Bittinger
1913 Gifford Beal
1914 Ivan G. Olinsky
1915 Richard E. Miller
1916 Frederic E. Church
1917 Max Bohm
1918 Walter Ufer
1919 Jerome Myers
1920 James Hopkins
1921 Leon Kroll
1922 Gertrude Fiske
1923 Eugene F. Savage
1924 Clifford Addams
1925 Gertrude Fiske
1926 Will Foster
1927 John E. Costigan
1928 Alice K. Stoddard
1929 Ettore Caser
1930 Ernest Trubach
1931 Gordon Samstag
1932 Robert Brackman
1933 Jerry Farnsworth
1934 Gerald Leake
1935 Maurice Sterne
1936 Franklin Robbins
1937 Reginald Marsh
1938 Randall Davey
1940 Hugo Ballin
1941 Dan Lutz
1942 Douglas W. Gorsline
1944 Robert Philipp
1945 Eugene Higgins
Raphael Soyer
1947 Louis DiValentin
1948 Raphael Soyer
1949 Eugene Berman
1950 Hazel J. Teyral
1951 Lee Jackson
1952 Doris Rosenthal
1953 Sigmund Menkes
1954 Fletcher Martin
1955 Thomas Yerxa
1956 Adolf Konrad
1957 Morton Roberts
1958 Robert Sivard
1959 Hughie Lee-Smith
1960 Werner Groshans
1961 Aaron Shikler
1962 David Levine
1963 Thomas Yerxa
1964 Moses Soyer
1965 Philip B. White
1966 Bruce Currie
1967 Jack Henderson
1968 Philip B. White
1969 Edward Melcarth
1970 Philip B. White

Robert J. Collier Trophy

Presented annually by the National Aeronautic Association for the greatest achievement in aviation in America, the value of which has been demonstrated by astral use during the preceding year.

1911 Glenn H. Curtiss
1912 Glenn H. Curtiss
1913 Orville Wright
1914 Elmer A. Sperry

1915 W. Sterling Burgess
1916 Elmer A. Sperry
1921 Grover Loening
1925 S. Albert Reed
1926 E. L. Hoffman
1927 Charles L. Lawrence
1930 Harold Pitcairn
1932 Glenn L. Martin
1933 Frank W. Caldwell
1934 Albert F. Hegenberger
1935 Donald Douglas
1938 Howard Hughes
1940 Sanford Moss
1942 Henry H. Arnold
1943 Luis de Florez
1944 Carl A. Spaatz
1945 Luis W. Alvarez
1946 Lewis A. Rodert
1947 John Stack, Lawrence D. Bell, and Charles E. Yeager
1949 William P. Lear
1951 John Stack
1952 Leonard S. Hobbs
1953 James H. Kindelberger
Edward H. Heinemann
1954 Richard T. Whitcomb
1955 William M. Allen
Nathan F. Twining
1956 Charles J. McCarthy
James S. Russell
1957 Edward P. Curtis
1958 Clarence L. Johnson
Neil Burgess
Gerhard Neumann
Howard C. Johnson
Walter W. Irwin
1960 William F. Raborn
1961 Robert M. White, Joseph A. Walker, A. S. Crossfield, and Forrest Petersen
1962 M. Scott Carpenter, L. Gordon Cooper, John H. Glenn, Jr., Virgil I. Grissom, Walter M. Schirra, Jr., Alan B. Sheppard, Jr., and Donald K. Slayton
1963 Clarence L. Johnson
1964 Curtis E. LeMay
1965 James E. Webb
Hugh L. Dryden
1966 James S. McDonnell
1967 Lawrence A. Hyland
1968 Frank Borman, James A. Lovell, Jr., and William A. Anders
1969 Neil A. Armstrong, Edwin E. Aldrin, Jr., and Michael Collins
1970 William M. Allen
1971 David R. Scott
James B. Irwin
Alfred M. Worden
Robert R. Gilruth

Elliott Cresson Medal

Awarded by The Franklin Institute to recognize notable discoveries or original research in the arts or sciences, invention or improvement of a useful machine, and new processes or combinations of materials in manufacture.

1875 William G. A. Bonwill
Benjamin C. Tilghman
Joseph Zentmayer
1877 Plimmon H. Dudley
1878 Henry Bower
Williams F. Goodwin
1881 W. Woodnut Griscom
1886 Patrick B. Delany
Thaddeus S. C. Lowe
Robert H. Ramsay
1887 Charles F. Albert
Eugene H. Cowles and Alfred H. Cowles
1889 Edward A. Cowper and T. Hart Robertson
Ottmar Mergenthaler
G. F. Simonds
1890 James B. Hammond
1891 Stockton Bates, Edwin Shaw, and G. M. von Culin
James H. Bevington
Bradley A. Fiske
1892 Philip H. Holmes
Henry M. Howe
1893 Clifford H. Batchellor
Frederic E. Ives
George E. Marks
1894 Nikola Tesla
1895 Henry M. Howe
J. Peckover
Lester A. Pelton
1896 Patrick B. Delany
Tolbert Lanston
1897 Hamilton Y. Castner
Elisha Gray
1898 Wilbur O. Atwater and Edward B. Rosa
Clemens Herschel
Thomas Corscaden
Charles F. Jenkins
1900 Louis E. Levy
1901 John S. Forbes and A. G. Waterhouse
Lewis M. Haupt
1902 Charles E. Acker
Fred W. Taylor and Maunsel White
1903 Guilliam H. Clamer
Joseph L. Ferrell
Frank J. Sprague
Wilson L. Gill
1904 James M. Dodge
Louis E. Levy
Alexander E. Outerbridge, Jr.
John C. Parker
1905 Michael I. Pupin
1906 William J. Hammer
1907 J. Allen Heany
Ferdinand Philips
Edward R. Taylor
1908 Romeyn B. Hough
1909 James Gayley
George O. Squier
Walter V. Turner
H. A. Wise Wood
1910 John A. Brashear
Peter C. Hewitt
John Fritz
Edward Weston
Harvey W. Wiley
1912 Alexander Graham Bell
Albert A. Michelson
Edward W. Morley
Alfred Noble
Samuel W. Stratton
Elihu Thomson
1913 Emile Berliner
Emil Fischer
Isham Randolph
Albert Sauveur
Charles P. Steinmetz
1914 Karl P. G. Linde
Edgar F. Smith
Orville Wright
1915 Michael J. Owens
1916 Byron E. Eldred
1917 Edwin F. Northrup
1918 Isaac N. Lewis
1920 William L. Emmet
1923 Lee de Forest
Raymond D. Johnson
Albert Kingsbury
1925 Francis Hodgkinson
1926 George E. Hale
Charles S. Hastings
1927 Dayton C. Miller
Edward L. Nichols
1928 Gustaf W. Elmen
Henry Ford
Vladimir Karapetoff
Charles L. Lawrance
1929 Chevalier Jackson
Elmer A. Sperry
1930 Norman R. Gibson
Irving E. Moultrop
1931 Clinton J. Davisson and Lester H. Germer
Theodore Lyman
1932 Percy W. Bridgman
Charles L. Fortescue
John B. Whitehead
1934 Stuart Ballantine
1936 George O. Curme, Jr.
Robert J. Van de Graaff
1937 Carl D. Anderson
William Bowie
William F. Giauque
Ernest O. Lawrence
1938 Edwin H. Land
1939 George A. Campbell
John R. Carson
1940 Frederick M. Becket
Robert R. Williams
1942 Claude S. Hudson
Isidor I. Rabi
1943 Charles M. Allen
1944 Roger Adams
1945 Stanford C. Hooper
Lewis F. Moody
1946 Gladeon M. Barnes
1948 Edwin H. Colpitts
1952 Edward C. Molina
H. Birchard Taylor
1953 William Blum
George R. Harrison
William F. Meggers
1957 Willard F. Libby
Reginald J. S. Pigott
1958 Joseph C. Patrick
Stephen P. Timoshenko
1959 John H. Hammond, Jr.
Henry C. Harrison
Irving Wolff
1960 Hugh L. Dryden
Arpad L. Nadai
William F. G. Swann
1961 Donald A. Glaser
Reinhold Rudenberg
James A. Van Allen
1962 Wernher von Braun
James G. Baker
1963 Grote Reber
1964 Waldo L. Semon
Robert R. Wilson
1965 Donald D. Van Slyke
1966 Everitt P. Blizard
Herman F. Mark
1969 Henry Eyring
Peter C. Goldmark
1970 Walter H. Zinn
1971 Paul J. Flory
John H. Van Vleck
1972 William P. Lear
Brian D. Josephson

Cullum Geographical Medal

Awarded from time to time by the American Geographical Society to honor those who distinguish themselves by geographical discoveries or in the advancement of geographical science.

1896 Robert E. Peary
1901 Thomas C. Mendenhall
1902 A. Donaldson Smith
1906 Robert Bell
1908 William M. Davis
1914 Ellen C. Semple
1917 George W. Goethals
1918 Frederick H. Newell
1919 Henry Fairfield Osborn
1925 Harvey C. Hayes
1930 Curtis F. Marbut
1931 Mark Jefferson
1935 Douglas Johnson
1938 Louise Arner Boyd
1940 Robert Cushman Murphy
1948 Hugh H. Bennett
1956 J. Russell Smith
1958 Charles W. Thornthwaite
1959 Albert P. Crary
1961 William M. Ewing
1962 Richard J. Russell
1963 Rachel L. Carson
1964 John Leighly
1965 Kirtley F. Mather
1968 Luna B. Leopold
1969 Neil A. Armstrong
Edwin E. Aldrin, Jr.
Michael Collins

Charles P. Daly Medal

Awarded intermittently by the American Geographical Society to explorers, writers, and men of science who have contributed to the advancement of geographical knowledge.

1902 Robert E. Peary
1908 George Davidson
1909 William W. Rockhill
Charles Chaille-Long
1910 Grove K. Gilbert
1913 Alfred H. Brooks
1918 Vilhjalmur Stefansson
1920 George O. Smith
1922 Adolphus W. Greely
Ernest de K. Leffingwell
1924 Claude H. Birdseye
1925 Robert A. Bartlett
David L. Brainard

1930 Nelson H. Darton
1935 Roy Chapman Andrews
1939 Herbert J. Fleure
1940 Carl O. Sauer
1954 John K. Wright
1959 Richard Hartshorne
1962 Osborn M. Miller
1965 William S. Cooper
1967 Marston Bates
1969 Paul B. Sears
William O. Field
1971 Gilbert F. White

Melvil Dewey Award

Awarded annually by the American Library Association to honor creative professional achievement in the fields of library management, training, cataloging, classification, and the tools and techniques of librarianship.

1953 Ralph R. Shaw
1954 Herman H. Fussler
1955 Maurice F. Tauber
1956 Norah A. MacColl
1957 Wyllis E. Wright
1958 Janet S. Dickson
1959 Benjamin A. Custer
1960 Harriet E. Howe
1961 Julia C. Pressey
1962 Leon Carnovsky
1963 Frank B. Rogers
1964 John W. Cronin
1965 Bertha M. Frick
1966 Lucile Morsch
1967 Walter H. Kaiser
1968 Jesse H. Shera
1969 William S. Dix

James Douglas Gold Medal

Awarded annually by the American Institute of Mining, Metallurgical and Petroleum Engineers to recognize achievement in nonferrous metallurgy.

1923 Frederick Laist
1924 Charles W. Merrill
1925 William H. Bassett
1926 John M. Callow
1927 Zay Jeffries
1928 Selwyn G. Blalock
1929 Paul D. Merica
1930 John V. Dorr
1931 William H. Peirce
1932 Champion H. Mathewson
1933 James O. Elton
1935 George C. Stone
1938 Harry W. Hardinge
1940 Louis D. Ricketts
1942 Arthur S. Dwight
1945 Robert F. Mehl
1949 William Wraith
1950 Francis C. Frary
1954 William J. Kroll
1955 E. L. Oliver
1956 Charles R. Kuzell
1957 R. B. Caples
1958 J. R. Gordon
1959 Clyde Williams
1960 Augustus B. Kinzel
1961 Frank H. Spedding
1963 Cyril S. Smith
1964 T. D. Jones
1965 Frank A. Forward
1966 Albert J. Phillips
1967 Walter R. Hibbard, Jr.
1968 Paul Queneau
1969 S. W. K. Morgan
1970 Reinhardt Schuhmann, Jr.

Lucy Wharton Drexel Medal

Awarded by the University of Pennsylvania to honor a notable archaeological excavation or publication by an English-speaking scholar.

1902 Frederic W. Putnam
1910 Howard C. Butler
1958 Alfred V. Kidder
1962 J. Eric S. Thompson
1966 Richard S. MacNeish

Edison Medal

Awarded annually by the Institute of Electrical and Electronic Engineers to recognize a career of meritorious achievement in electrical science, electrical engineering, or the electrical arts.

1909 Elihu Thomson
1910 Frank J. Sprague
1911 George Westinghouse
1912 William Stanley
1913 Charles F. Brush
1914 Alexander Graham Bell
1916 Nikola Tesla
1917 John J. Carty
1918 Benjamin G. Lamme
1919 William L. Emmet
1920 Michael I. Pupin
1921 Cummings C. Chesney
1922 Robert A. Millikan
1923 John W. Lieb
1924 John W. Howell
1925 Harris J. Ryan
1927 William D. Coolidge
1928 Frank B. Jewett
1929 Charles F. Scott
1930 Frank Conrad
1931 E. Wilbur Rice, Jr.
1932 Bancroft Gherardi
1933 Arthur E. Kennelly
1934 Willis R. Whitney
1935 Willis B. Stillwell
1936 Alex Dow
1937 Gano S. Dunn
1938 Dugald C. Jackson
1939 Philip Torchio
1940 George A. Campbell
1941 John B. Whitehead
1942 Edwin H. Armstrong
1943 Vannevar Bush
1944 E. F. W. Alexanderson
1945 Philip Sporn
1946 Lee deForest
1947 Joseph Slepian
1948 Morris E. Leeds
1949 Karl B. McEachron
1950 Otto B. Blackwell
1951 Charles F. Wagner
1952 Vladimir K. Zworykin
1953 John F. Peters
1954 Oliver E. Buckley
1956 Comfort A. Adams
1957 John K. Hodnette
1958 Charles F. Kettering
1959 James F. Fairman
1960 Harold S. Osborne
1961 William B. Kouwenhoven
1962 Alexander C. Monteith
1963 John R. Pierce
1965 Walker L. Cisler
1966 Wilmer L. Barrow
1967 George H. Brown
1968 Charles F. Avila
1969 Hendrik W. Bode
1970 Howard H. Aiken
1971 William H. Pickering

Albert Einstein Commemorative Award

Presented annually (at first intermittently) by the Albert Einstein College of Medicine of Yeshiva University to honor outstanding contributions in various fields of human endeavor.

1956 Carl Sandburg
Herbert H. Lehman
John von Neumann
Stanley Cobb
1957 John Hay Whitney
Edward R. Murrow
Paul Muni
Samuel Levine
1958 Marion B. Folsom
Archibald MacLeish
George W. Beadle
Marian Anderson
Selman Waksman
1960 Jacob Blaustein
Leonard Bernstein
Richard P. Feynman
1962 Arthur J. Goldberg
Leo Szilard
1967 Andrew Wyeth
James Michener
1968 Harry Eagle
James Reston
Robert C. Weaver
Jack D. Weiler
1969 Marshall W. Nirenberg
Joseph I. Lubin
John W. Gardner
1970 Charles Frost
Salvador Luria
Zero Mostel
R. Sargent Shriver
1971 Julius Axelrod
Luis A. Ferre
Danny Kaye
Paul A. Samuelson
Harry Belafonte
1972 W. Averell Harriman
George Wald
Max M. Fisher
Norman Rockwell

Einstein Medal and Award

Presented by the Institute for Advanced Study, Princeton, N.J., to honor contributions to knowledge in the mathematical and physical sciences.

1951 Julian Schwinger
Kurt Godel
1954 Richard P. Feynman
1958 Edward Teller
1959 Willard F. Libby
1960 Leo Szilard
1961 Luis W. Alvarez
1962 Shields Warren
1965 John A. Wheeler
1967 Marshall N. Rosenbluth
1972 Eugene P. Wigner

Benjamin F. Fairless Award

Presented annually by the American Institute of Mining, Metallurgical and Petroleum Engineers to honor achievement in iron and steel production and ferrous metallurgy.

1955 Stewart J. Cort
1956 Stephen M. Jenks
1957 Leo F. Reinartz
1958 Hjalmar W. Johnson
1959 James L. Mauthe
1960 Charles M. White
1961 Thomas E. Millsop
1962 Harold M. Griffith
1963 John Chipman
1964 Thomas L. Joseph
1965 Edward J. Hanley
1966 Robert Durrer
1967 Alexander L. Feild
1968 Herbert W. Graham
1969 James B. Austin
1970 Edmund F. Martin

Enrico Fermi Award

Presented annually by the U.S. Atomic Energy Commission to recognize outstanding scientific or technical achievement related to the development, use, or control of nuclear energy.

1954 Enrico Fermi
1956 John von Neumann
1957 Ernest O. Lawrence
1958 Eugene P. Wigner
1959 Glenn T. Seaborg
1961 Hans A. Bethe
1962 Edward Teller
1963 J. Robert Oppenheimer
1964 Hyman G. Rickover
1968 John A. Wheeler
1969 Walter H. Zinn
1970 Norris E. Bradbury
1971 Stafford L. Warren
Shields Warren
1972 Manson Benedict

Henry Johnson Fisher Award

Presented annually by the Magazine Publishers Association, Inc., to honor outstanding achievement in magazine publishing.

1964 DeWitt Wallace
1965 Henry R. Luce
1966 Richard E. Berlin
1967 Edward Weeks
1968 Arnold Gingrich
1969 Albert L. Cole
1970 Roy E. Larsen
Maurice R. Robinson
1971 Gibson McCabe
1972 John H. Johnson

The Franklin Medal

Awarded annually by The Franklin Institute to honor physical scientists or technologists who have notably advanced a knowledge of physical science or its application.

1915 Thomas A. Edison
1916 John J. Carty
Theodore W. Richards
1917 David W. Taylor
1918 Thomas C. Mendenhall
1919 George O. Squier
1921 Frank J. Sprague
1922 Ralph Modjeski
1923 Albert A. Michelson
1924 Edward Weston
1925 Elihu Thomson
1926 Samuel Rea
1927 George E. Hale
1928 Charles F. Brush
1929 Emile Berliner
1930 John F. Stevens
1931 Willis R. Whitney
1932 Ambrose Swasey
1933 Orville Wright
1934 Henry N. Russell
Irving Langmuir
1935 Albert Einstein
1936 Frank B. Jewett
Charles F. Kettering
1937 Robert A. Millikan
1938 William F. Durand
Charles A. Kraus
1939 Edwin P. Hubble
Albert Sauveur
1940 Leo H. Baekeland
Arthur H. Compton
1941 Edwin H. Armstrong
1942 Jerome C. Hunsaker
Paul D. Merica
1943 George W. Pierce
Harold C. Urey
1944 William D. Coolidge
1945 Harlow Shapley
1946 Henry C. Sherman
1947 Enrico Fermi
1948 Wendell M. Stanley
Theodore von Karman
1950 Eugene P. Wigner
1953 William F. Gibbs
1954 C. E. Kenneth Mees
1957 Hugh S. Taylor
1958 Donald W. Douglas
1959 Hans A. Bethe
1960 Roger Adams
1961 Detlev W. Bronk
1963 Glenn T. Seaborg
1964 Gregory Breit
1965 Frederick Seitz
1966 Britton Chance
1967 Murray Gell-Mann
1968 Marshall W. Nirenberg
1969 John A. Wheeler
1970 Wolfgang K. H. Panofsky
1972 George B. Kistiakowsky

Freedom Award

An award presented by Freedom House for outstanding contributions to the cause of human liberty.

1943 Walter Lippmann
1944 Sumner Welles
1945 Dwight D. Eisenhower
1946 Bernard M. Baruch
1947 George C. Marshall
1948 Arthur H. Vandenberg
1949 Lucius D. Clay
David E. Lilienthal
1950 Dean G. Acheson
1951 Paul G. Hoffman
1952 James B. Conant
Matthew B. Ridgway
1954 Edward R. Murrow
1963 Medgar W. Evers
1965 Harry S Truman
1966 Lyndon B. Johnson
1967 Roy Wilkins
1969 Earl Warren
1970 Edmund S. Muskie

John Fritz Medal

Presented annually by the John Fritz Medal Board of Award for notable scientific or industrial achievement in the field of pure or applied science. Sponsored by the American Society of Civil Engineers; American Institute of Electrical and Electronics Engineers; and Institute of Mining, Metallurgical and Petroleum Engineers; American Society of Mechanical Engineers; American Institute of Chemical Engineers.

1902 John Fritz
1906 George Westinghouse
1907 Alexander Graham Bell
1908 Thomas A. Edison
1909 Charles T. Porter
1912 Robert W. Hunt
1914 John E. Sweet
1915 James Douglas
1916 Elihu Thomson
1917 Henry M. Howe
1918 J. Waldo Smith
1919 George W. Goethals
1920 Orville Wright
1924 Ambrose Swasey
1925 John F. Stevens
1926 Edward D. Adams
1927 Elmer A. Sperry
1928 John J. Carty
1929 Herbert Hoover
1930 Ralph Modjeski
1931 David W. Taylor
1932 Michael I. Pupin
1933 Daniel C. Jackling
1934 John R. Freeman
1935 Frank J. Sprague
1936 William F. Durand
1937 Arthur N. Talbot
1938 Paul D. Merica
1939 Frank B. Jewett
1940 Clarence F. Hirshfeld
1941 Ralph Budd
1942 E. L. DeGolyer
1943 Willis R. Whitney
1944 Charles F. Kettering
1945 John L. Savage
1946 Zay Jeffries
1947 Lewis W. Chubb
1948 Theodore von Karman
1949 Charles M. Allen
1950 Walter H. Aldridge
1951 Vannevar Bush
1952 Ervin G. Bailey
1953 Benjamin F. Fairless
1954 William E. Wrather
1955 Harry A. Winne
1956 Philip Sporn
1957 Ben Moreell
1958 John R. Suman
1959 Mervin J. Kelly
1960 Gwilym A. Price
1961 Stephen D. Bechtel
1962 Crawford H. Greenewalt
1963 Hugh L. Dryden
1964 Lucius D. Clay
1965 Frederick R. Kappel
1966 Warren K. Lewis
1967 Walker L. Cisler
1968 Igor I. Sikorsky
1969 Michael L. Haider
1970 Glenn B. Warren
1971 Patrick E. Haggerty
1972 William Webster
1973 Lyman D. Wilbur

Gary Memorial Medal

Awarded from time to time by the American Iron and Steel Institute for outstanding contributions to the iron and steel industry.

1929 James A. Farrell
1930 Charles M. Schwab
1931 William J. Filbert
1932 Julian Kennedy
1933 Willis L. King
1934 Eugene G. Grace
1935 John B. Tytus
1944 Quincy Bent
1949 Benjamin F. Fairless
1951 Edward L. Ryerson
1952 Walter S. Tower
1954 Elton Hoyt II
1955 Tom M. Girdler
Charles R. Hook
Ernest T. Weir
1961 Charles M. White
1964 Arthur B. Homer
1965 Thomas F. Patton
1967 Leslie B. Worthington
1968 Roger M. Blough
1969 Edmund F. Martin

Willard Gibbs Medal

Awarded annually by the Chicago Section of the American Chemical Society to honor eminent work in and original contributions to pure or applied chemistry.

1912 Theodore W. Richards
1913 Leo H. Baekeland
1914 Ira Remsen
1915 Arthur A. Noyes
1916 Willis R. Whitney
1917 Edward W. Morley
1918 William M. Burton
1919 William A. Noyes
1920 Frederick G. Cottrell
1923 Julius Stieglitz
1924 Gilbert N. Lewis
1925 Moses Gomberg
1927 John J. Abel
1928 William D. Harkins
1929 Claude S. Hudson
1930 Irving Langmuir
1931 Phoebus A. Levene
1932 Edward C. Franklin
1934 Harold C. Urey
1935 Charles A. Kraus
1936 Roger Adams
1937 Herbert N. McCoy
1938 Robert R. Williams
1939 Donald D. Van Slyke
1940 Vladimir Ipatieff
1941 Edward A. Doisy
1942 Thomas Midgely, Jr.
1943 Conrad A. Elvehjem
1944 George O. Curme, Jr.
1945 Frank C. Whitmore
1946 Linus Pauling
1947 Wendell M. Stanley
1948 Carl F. Cori
1949 Peter J. W. Debye
1950 Carl S. Marvel
1951 William F. Giauque
1952 William C. Rose
1953 Joel H. Hildebrand
1954 Elmer K. Bolton
1955 Farrington Daniels
1956 Vincent du Vigneaud
1957 W. Albert Noyes, Jr.
1958 Willard F. Libby
1959 Hermann I. Schlesinger
1960 George B. Kistiakowsky
1961 Louis P. Hammett
1962 Lars Onsager
1963 Paul D. Bartlett
1964 Izaak M. Kolthoff
1965 Robert S. Mulliken
1966 Glenn T. Seaborg
1967 Robert B. Woodward
1968 Henry Eyring
1970 Frank H. Westheimer

Goddard Award

Presented annually by the American Institute of Aeronautics and Astronautics for notable contributions to the engineering science of propulsion or energy.

1966 Hans J. P. von Ohain
A. Wade Blackman
George D. Lewis
1967 Robert O. Bullock
Irving A. Johnsen
Seymour Lieblein
1968 Donald C. Berkey
Ernest C. Simpson
James E. Worsham
1969 Perry W. Pratt
1970 Gerhard Neumann
1972 Howard Shumacher
Bryan Brimelow
Gary Tlourde

Daniel Guggenheim Medal

Awarded annually by the Daniel Guggenheim Medal Board of Award for outstanding contributions to the promotion of aeronautics, the medal is sponsored by the American Society of Mechanical Engineers, Society of Automotive Engineers, and American Institute of Aeronautics and Astronautics.

1929 Orville Wright
1933 Jerome C. Hunsaker
1934 William E. Boeing
1935 William F. Durand
1936 George W. Lewis
1939 Donald W. Douglas
1940 Glenn L. Martin
1941 Juan T. Trippe
1942 James H. Doolittle
1944 Lawrence D. Bell
1945 Theodore P. Wright
1947 Lester D. Gardner
1948 Leroy R. Grumman
1949 Edward P. Warner
1950 Hugh L. Dryden
1951 Igor I. Sikorsky
1953 Charles A. Lindbergh
1955 Theodore Von Karman
1956 Frederick B. Rentschler
1957 Arthur E. Raymond
1958 William Littlewood
1960 Grover Loening
1961 Jerome F. Lederer
1962 James H. Kindelberger
1963 James S. McDonnell
1964 Robert H. Goddard
1966 Charles S. Draper
1967 George S. Schairer
1968 H. Mansfield Horner
1969 H. Julian Allen
1972 William C. Mentzer

Hayden Memorial Geological Award

Awarded every three years (at first annually) by the Academy of Natural Sciences of Philadelphia for the best publication, exploration, discovery or research in the sciences of geology or paleontology.

1890 James Hall
1891 Edward D. Cope
1905 Charles D. Walcott
1908 John M. Clark
1911 John C. Branner
1914 Henry Fairfield Osborn
1917 William M. Davis
1920 Thomas C. Chamberlin
1926 William B. Scott
1929 Charles Schuchert
1932 Reginald A. Daly
1935 Andrew C. Lawson
1941 Amadeus W. Grabau
1944 Joseph A. Cushman
1950 George G. Simpson
1953 Norman L. Bowen
1956 Raymond C. Moore
1959 Carl O. Dunbar
1962 Alfred S. Romer
1965 Norman D. Newell
1968 Elso S. Barghoorn

Hall of Fame For Great Americans

Administered by New York University, the hall of fame honors notable Americans of the past whose achievements in various fields of endeavor have been of outstanding inspiration. Elections to the hall are held every five years.

1900

John Adams
John James Audubon
Henry Ward Beecher
William Ellery Channing
Henry Clay
Peter Cooper
Jonathan Edwards
Ralph Waldo Emerson
David G. Farragut
Benjamin Franklin
Robert Fulton
Ulysses S. Grant
Asa Gray
Nathaniel Hawthorne
Washington Irving
Thomas Jefferson
James Kent
Robert E. Lee
Abraham Lincoln
Henry Wadsworth Longfellow
Horace Mann
John Marshall
Samuel F. B. Morse
George Peabody
Joseph Story
Gilbert Stuart
George Washington
Daniel Webster
Eli Whitney

1905

John Quincy Adams
James Russell Lowell
Mary Lyon
James Madison
Maria Mitchell
William T. Sherman
John Greenleaf Whittier
Emma Willard

1910

George Bancroft
Phillips Brooks
William Cullen Bryant
James Fenimore Cooper
Oliver Wendell Holmes
Andrew Jackson
John Lothrop Motley
Edgar Allan Poe
Harriet Beecher Stowe
Frances E. Willard

1915

Louis Agassiz
Daniel Boone
Rufus Choate
Charlotte S. Cushman
Alexander Hamilton
Joseph Henry
Mark Hopkins
Elias Howe
Francis Parkman

1920

Samuel L. Clemens
James Buchanan Eads
Patrick Henry
William T. G. Morton
Alice Freeman Palmer
Augustus Saint-Gaudens
Roger Williams

1925

Edwin Booth
John Paul Jones

1930

Matthew F. Maury
James Monroe
James A. McNeill Whistler
Walt Whitman

1935

Grover Cleveland
Simon Newcomb
William Penn

1940

Stephen Collins Foster

1945

Sidney Lanier
Thomas Paine
Walter Reed
Booker T. Washington

1950

Susan B. Anthony
Alexander Graham Bell
Josiah W. Gibbs
William C. Gorgas
Theodore Roosevelt
Woodrow Wilson

1955

Thomas "Stonewall" Jackson
George Westinghouse
Wilbur Wright

1960

Thomas A. Edison
Edward A. MacDowell
Henry David Thoreau

1965

Jane Addams
Oliver Wendell Holmes, Jr.
Sylvanus Thayer
Orville Wright

1970

Lillian D. Wald
Albert A. Michelson

Louis W. Hill Space Transportation Award

Presented annually by the American Institute of Aeronautics and Astronautics to honor significant contributions to the art and science of space flight.

1958 Robert H. Goddard
1959 James A. Van Allen
1960 Samuel K. Hoffman
Thomas F. Dixon
1961 Robert R. Gilruth
1962 Charles S. Draper
1963 Robert J. Parks
Jack M. James
1964 Hugh L. Dryden
1965 Wernher von Braun
1966 W. Randolph Lovelace II
1967 Abe Silverstein
1968 William H. Pickering
1969 George M. Low
1970 Christopher C. Kraft, Jr.
1971 Hubertus Strughold

Sidney Hillman Foundation Award For Meritorious Public Service

Presented from time to time to outstanding figures in public life who have devoted themselves to community welfare.

1949 Frank P. Graham
1950 Oscar R. Ewing
1951 Herbert H. Lehman
1952 William O. Douglas
1953 Harry S Truman
1954 Bernard J. Sheil
1955 Wayne L. Morse
1956 Eleanor Roosevelt
1957 Paul H. Douglas
1958 Robert M. Hutchins
1966 Martin Luther King, Jr.
George C. Higgins
Jacob Weinstein
1968 W. Willard Wirtz

Lester H. Hofheimer Prize

Awarded annually by the American Psychiatric Association to recognize outstanding research accomplishment in psychiatry and mental hygiene.

1949 Benjamin Pasamanick
1951 Jurgen Ruesch
1952 Robert Arnot
Beatrice Talbot
Milton Greenblatt
1953 Thomas H. Holmes and
Helen Goodell,
Stewart Wolf,
and Harold G. Wolff
1955 Philip F. D. Seitz
1956 John Money
Joan G. Hampson
and John L. Hampson
1957 Christoph M. Heinicke

1958 James Olds
1959 Irving L. Janis
1960 Albert J. Stunkard
1961 Seymour Levine
1962 Ogden R. Lindsley
Joseph D. Matarazzo
1963 Howard E. Freeman
Ozzie G. Simmons
Jerome Kagan
Howard A. Moss
1964 William C. Dement
1965 Jack H. Mendelson
1966 Lyman C. Wynne
Margaret Thaler Singer
1967 Benjamin Pasamanick
Simon Dinitz
Frank Scarpitti
1968 Robert Coles
1969 Jonathan O. Cole
Gerald L. Klerman
Solomon C. Goldberg
1970 Arnold M. Ludwig
Jerome Levine
Louis H. Stark

Holley Medal

Awarded from time to time by the American Society of Mechanical Engineers to honor an act of genius in engineering that has accomplished a great and timely public benefit.

1924 Hjalmar G. Carlson
1928 Elmer A. Sperry
1934 Irving Langmuir
1936 Henry Ford
1937 Frederick G. Cottrell
1938 Francis Hodgkinson
1939 Carl E. Johansson
1940 Edwin H. Armstrong
1941 John C. Garand
1942 Ernest O. Lawrence
1943 Vannevar Bush
1944 Carl L. Norden
1945 Sanford A. Moss
1946 Norman R. Gibson
1947 Raymond D. Johnson
1948 Edwin H. Land
1950 Charles G. Curtis
1951 George R. Fink
1952 Sanford L. Cluett
1953 Philip M. McKenna
1954 Walter A. Shewhart
1955 George J. Hood
1957 Charles S. Draper
1959 Maurice J. Fletcher
1961 Thomas E. Moon
1963 William Schockley
1968 Chester F. Carlson
1969 Willis J. Whitfield

Hoover Medal

Awarded to honor distinguished public service by an engineer. Administered by a board of award representing The American Society of Mechanical Engineers, American Society of Civil Engineers, Institute of Electrical and Electronics Engineers, and American Institute of Mining, Metallurgical and Petroleum Engineers.

1930 Herbert Hoover
1936 Ambrose Swasey
1938 John F. Stevens
1940 Gano S. Dunn
1941 D. Robert Yarnall
1942 Gerard Swope
1944 Ralph E. Flanders
1945 William Henry Harrison
1946 Vannevar Bush
1948 Malcolm Pirnie
1949 Frank B. Jewett
1950 Karl T. Compton
1951 William L. Batt
1952 Clarence D. Howe
1954 Alfred P. Sloan, Jr.
1955 Charles F. Kettering
1956 Herbert Hoover, Jr.
1957 Scott Turner
1958 Raymond A. Wheeler
1959 Henry T. Heald
1960 Dwight D. Eisenhower
1961 Mervin J. Kelly
1962 Walker L. Cisler
1963 James R. Killian, Jr.
1964 John A. McCone
1966 Lillian M. Gilbreth
1967 Lucius D. Clay
1969 Edgar F. Kaiser
1971 Luis A. Ferre

Howells Medal

Awarded once every five years by the American Academy of Arts and Letters to recognize the most distinguished work of American fiction published during that period.

1925 Mary E. Wilkins Freeman
1930 Willa Cather
1935 Pearl S. Buck
1940 Ellen Glasgow
1945 Booth Tarkington
1950 William Faulkner
1955 Eudora Welty
1960 James Gould Cozzens
1965 John Cheever
1970 William Styron

Hubbard Medal

Presented from time to time by the National Geographic Society to recognize distinction in geographic research, exploration, and discovery.

1906 Robert E. Peary
1909 Robert A. Bartlett
Grove K. Gilbert
1919 Vilhjalmur Stefansson
1926 Richard E. Byrd, Jr.
1927 Charles A. Lindbergh
1931 Roy Chapman Andrews
1934 Anne Morrow Lindbergh
1935 Albert W. Stevens
Orvil A. Anderson
1936 Lincoln Ellsworth
1945 Henry H. Arnold
1953 Donald B. MacMillan
1958 Paul A. Siple
1962 John H. Glenn, Jr.
1967 Juan T. Trippe
1969 Frank Borman
James A. Lovell, Jr.
William A. Anders
1970 Neil A. Armstrong
Edwin E. Aldrin, Jr.
Michael Collins

Charles Evans Hughes Award

Presented annually by the National Conference of Christians and Jews to recognize courageous leadership in governmental service.

1965 LeRoy Collins
Nelson A. Rockefeller
Edmund G. Brown
George Romney
1966 Dwight D. Eisenhower
1967 Harry S Truman
Edward W. Brooke
Paul H. Douglas
1968 Lewis L. Strauss
John W. Gardner
1969 Ivan Allen, Jr.
Earl Warren
1970 Constance Baker Motley
Theodore M. Hesburgh
1971 Lucius D. Clay
Tom C. Clark
Walter E. Washington
1972 Jerome H. Holland

Institute of Electrical and Electronics Engineers Medal of Honor

Awarded for outstanding achievement in engineering science and technology.

1917 Edwin H. Armstrong
1919 E. F. W. Alexanderson
1921 Reginald A. Fessenden
1922 Lee deForest
1924 Michael I. Pupin
1926 Greenleaf W. Pickard
1927 Louis W. Austin
1928 Jonathan Zenneck
1929 George W. Pierce
1930 P. O. Pedersen
1932 Arthur E. Kennelly
1933 John A. Fleming
1934 Stanford C. Hooper
1936 George A. Campbell
1937 Melville Eastham
1938 John H. Dellinger
1940 Lloyd Espenscheid
1941 Alfred N. Goldsmith
1942 A. H. Taylor
1944 Haraden Pratt
1945 Harold H. Beverage
1949 Ralph Bown
1950 Frederick E. Terman
1951 Vladimir K. Zworykin
1954 William L. Everitt
1955 Harald T. Friis
1957 Julius A. Stratton
1958 Albert W. Hull
1959 E. Leon Chaffee
1960 Harry Nyquist
1961 Ernst A. Guillemin
1962 Edward V. Appleton
1963 John H. Hammond, Jr.
George C. Southworth
1964 Harold A. Wheeler
1966 Claude E. Shannon
1967 Charles H. Townes
1968 Gordon K. Teal
1969 Edward L. Ginzton
1971 John Bardeen
1972 Jay W. Forrester

Joseph S. Isidor Medal

Awarded by the National Academy of Design to recognize achievement in figure painting composition.

1907 Hugo Ballin
1908 Sergeant Kendall
1909 Frederick B. Williams
1910 Kenyon Cox
1911 E. Irving Couse
1912 Ernest L. Blumenschein
1913 Francis C. Jones
1914 Charles W. Hawthorne
1915 Charles W. Hawthorne
1916 George Bellows
1917 Alice Kent Stoddard
1918 Adolphe W. Blondheim
1919 Ralph McLellan
1921 Howard E. Smith
George L. Nelson
1923 Marie Danforth Page
1924 Eugene F. Savage
1926 F. Martin Hennings
Walter Ufer
1927 Sergeant Kendall
1928 Robert Spencer
1929 Edmund C. Tarbell
1930 John W. Benson
1931 Leopold Seyffert
1932 Paul Sample
1935 Andrew Winter
1936 Jerry Farnsworth
1937 Gerald Leake
1938 Jerome Myers
1940 Herbert M. Stoops
1941 Louis Betts
1953 Colleen Browning
1954 Lou Sardella
1955 Gladys Rockmore Davis
1956 Philip Reisman
1957 Isabel Bishop
1958 John Fenton
1961 Umberto Romano
1962 Leon Kroll
1963 Joseph Floch
1965 William Rose
1967 Burton Silverman
1969 Seymour Pearlstein
1970 Robert Vickrey

Thomas Jefferson Memorial Foundation Medal in Architecture

Awarded by the University of Virginia to honor distinguished achievement in architecture.

1966 Ludwig Mies van der Rohe
1968 Marcel Breuer
1969 John Ely Burchard

E. Mead Johnson Award

Presented by the American Academy of Pediatrics for outstanding research work in the fields of special interest to the academy.

1940 Robert E. Gross
Lee E. Farr
1941 Rene J. Dubos
Albert B. Sabin
1942 David Bodian
and Howard A. Howe
Harold E. Harrison
and Helen C. Harrison
1943 Hattie E. Alexander
Philip Levine
1944 Fuller Albright
Joseph Warkany
Horace L. Hodes
1946 Paul A. Harper
1947 Helen B. Taussig
Louis K. Diamond
1948 Wolf W. Zuelzer
Benjamin M. Spock
Nathan B. Talbot
1949 Henry L. Barnett
1950 Charles D. May
and Harry Shwachman
Gertrude Henle
and Werner Henle
1951 William M. Wallace
Victor A. Najjar
1952 Seymour S. Cohen
Orvar Swenson and
Edward B. D. Newhauser
1953 Frederick C. Robbins
and Thomas H. Weller
Margaret H. D. Smith
1954 Robert E. Cooke
Vincent C. Kelley
1955 Robert A. Good
1956 David Gitlin
Arnall Patz
1957 Alfred M. Bongiovanni
and Walter R. Eberlein
1958 William A. Silverman
Norman Kretchmer
1959 C. Henry Kempe
Barton Childs
1960 Robert A. Aldrich
Irving Schulman
1961 Lytt I. Gardner
Donald E. Pickering
1962 Park S. Gerald
Robert L. Vernier
1963 D. Carleton Gajdusek
Richard T. Smith
1964 Robert M. Chanock
Abraham M. Rudolph
1965 David Y. Hsia
L. Stanley James
1966 William H. Tooley
Robert W. Winters
1967 Henry N. Kirkman, Jr.
Harry M. Meyer, Jr.
and Paul D. Parkman
1968 Mary Ellen Avery
1969 Frederick C. Battaglia
Gerard P. Odell
1970 Joseph A. Bellanti
Myron Winick

The Elisha Kent Kane Gold Medal

Awarded from time to time by the Geographical Society of Philadelphia for outstanding geographical research.

1901 A. Donaldson Smith
1902 Robert E. Peary
1903 Angelo Heilprin
1905 William B. Scott
1911 George W. Melville
1912 William M. Davis
1915 Ellsworth Huntington
1916 William C. Farabee
1918 Vilhjalmur Stefansson
1920 A. Hamilton Rice
1922 Douglas W. Johnson
1926 Richard E. Byrd, Jr.
1928 Roy Chapman Andrews
1933 Owen Lattimore
1936 Lincoln Ellsworth
1959 William R. Anderson
1962 John H. Glenn, Jr.
1964 Norman G. Dyhrenfurth
1965 Edwin A. Link
1966 Finn Ronne
1968 M. Scott Carpenter

Joseph P. Kennedy International Award in Mental Retardation

Presented every two years by the Joseph P. Kennedy, Jr. Foundation to honor outstanding achievement in research, service, and leadership in the field of mental retardation.

1962 Samuel A. Kirk
1964 Grover F. Powers
Lister Hill
John E. Fogarty
Bert T. Combs
1966 Louis K. Diamond
Fred H. Allen, Jr.
Alexander S. Wiener
Philip Levine
1968 Harold M. Skeels
Marie P. Skodak
Robert E. Cooke
Harvey A. Stevens

The Laetare Medal

Presented annually by the University of Notre Dame to an American Catholic to recognize achievement in the fields of art, science, literature, law, medicine, philosophy, philanthropy, and statesmanship.

1883 John G. Shea
1884 Patrick C. Keeley
1885 Eliza A. Starr
1886 John Newton
1887 Edward Preuss
1888 Patrick V. Hickey
1889 Anna H. Dorsey
1890 William J. Onahan
1891 Daniel Dougherty
1892 Henry F. Brownson
1893 Patrick Donohue
1894 Augustine Daly
1895 Mary A. Sadlier
1896 William S. Rosecrans
1897 Thomas A. Emmet
1898 Timothy E. Howard
1899 Mary G. Caldwell
1900 John A. Creighton
1901 W. Bourke Cockran
1902 John B. Murphy
1903 Charles J. Bonaparte
1904 Richard C. Kerens
1905 Thomas B. Fitzpatrick
1906 Francis J. Quinlan
1907 Katherine E. Conway
1908 James C. Monaghan
1909 Frances C. F. Tiernan
1910 Maurice F. Egan
1911 Agnes Repplier
1912 Thomas M. Mulry
1913 Charles G. Herbermann
1914 Edward D. White
1915 Mary V. Merrick
1916 James J. Walsh
1917 William S. Benson
1918 Joseph Scott
1919 George L. Duval
1920 Lawrence F. Flick
1921 Elizabeth Nourse
1922 Charles R. Neill
1923 Walter G. Smith
1924 Charles D. Maginnis
1925 Albert F. Zahm
1926 Edward N. Hurley
1927 Margaret Anglin
1928 John J. Spaulding
1929 Alfred E. Smith
1930 Frederick P. Kenkel
1931 James J. Phelan
1932 Stephen J. Maher
1933 John McCormack
1934 Genevieve G. Brady
1935 Francis H. Spearman
1936 Richard Reid
1937 Jeremiah D. M. Ford
1938 Irvin W. Abell
1939 Josephine Van Dyke
Brownson
1940 Hugh A. Drum
1941 William T. Walsh
1942 Helen C. White
1943 Thomas F. Woodlock
1944 Anne O'Hare McCormick
1945 G. Howland Shaw
1946 Carlton J. H. Hayes
1947 William Cabell Bruce
1948 Frank C. Walker
1949 Irene Dunne
1950 J. Lawton Collins
1951 John H. Phelan
1952 Thomas E. Murray
1953 I. A. O'Shaughnessy
1954 Jefferson Caffery
1955 George Meany
1956 Alfred M. Gruenther
1957 Clare Booth Luce
1958 Frank M. Folsom
1959 Robert D. Murphy
1960 George M. Shuster
1961 John F. Kennedy
1962 Francis J. Braceland
1963 George W. Anderson, Jr.
1964 Phyllis McGinley
1965 Frederick D. Rossini
1966 Patrick F. Crowley and
Mrs. Patrick F. Crowley
1967 J. Peter Grace
1968 R. Sargent Shriver
1969 William J. Brennan, Jr.
1970 William B. Walsh
1971 Walter F. Kerr
and Jean Kerr
1972 Dorothy Day

Lamme Medal

Awarded annually by the Institute of Electrical and Electronic Engineers to recognize meritorious achievement in the development of electrical or electronic apparatus or systems.

1928 Allan B. Field
1929 Rudolf E. Hellmund
1930 William J. Foster
1931 Giuseppe Faccioli
1932 Edward Weston
1933 Lewis B. Stillwell
1934 Henry E. Warren
1935 Vannevar Bush
1936 Frank Conrad
1937 Robert E. Doherty
1938 Marion A. Savage
1939 Norman W. Storer
1940 Comfort A. Adams
1941 Forrest E. Ricketts
1942 Joseph Slepian
1943 A. H. Kehoe
1944 S. H. Mortensen
1945 David C. Prince
1946 John B. MacNeill
1947 Aleck M. MacCutcheon
1948 Vladimir K. Zworykin
1949 C. M. Laffoon
1950 Donald I. Bohn
1951 Arthur E. Silver
1952 I. F. Kinnard
1953 F. A. Cowan
1954 A. M. deBellis
1955 Clinton R. Hanna
1956 Harold H. Beverage
1957 Harold S. Black
1958 Philip L. Alger
Sterling Beckwith
1959 L. A. Kilgore
1960 John G. Trump
1961 Charles Concordia
1962 E. L. Harder
1963 Loyal V. Bewley
1965 A. Uno Lamm
1967 Warren P. Mason
1968 Nathan Cohn
1969 James D. Cobine
1970 Harry F. Olson
1971 Winthrop M. Leeds
1972 Robert H. Park

Albert Lasker Medical Research Awards

Presented by the Albert and Mary Lasker Foundation (originally through the American Public Health Association) to honor those who have made significant contributions to basic or clinical research in disabling and fatal diseases.

Basic Research

1946 Carl F. Cori
1947 Oswald T. Avery
Thomas Francis, Jr.
Homer W. Smith

1948 Vincent du Vigneaud
Selman A. Waksman
Rene J. Dubos
1949 Andre F. Cournand
William S. Tillett
1950 George W. Beadle
1951 Karl F. Meyer
1953 Michael Heidelberger
George Wald
1954 Edwin P. Astwood
John F. Enders
1955 Karl P. Link
1956 Karl Meyer
Francis O. Schmitt
1958 Peyton Rous
Theodore Puck
Alfred D. Hershey
1959 Albert H. Coons
Jules Freund
1960 James D. Watson
James V. Neel
James Hillier
1962 Choh H. Li
1963 Lyman C. Craig
1964 Renato Dulbecco
Harry Rubin
1965 Robert W. Holley
1966 George E. Palade
1967 Bernard B. Brodie
1968 Marshall W. Nirenberg
1969 H. Gobind Khorana
William F. Windle
Bruce Merrifield
1970 Robert A. Good
Earl W. Sutherland, Jr.
1971 Seymour Benzer
Charles Yanofsky

Clinical Research

1946 John F. Mahoney
1949 Max Theiler
1951 Catherine MacFarlane
William G. Lennox
Frederic A. Gibbs
1952 Conrad A. Elvehjem
Frederick S. McKay
H. Trendley Dean
1954 Alfred Blalock
Helen B. Taussig
Robert E. Gross
1955 C. Walton Lillehei
Herbert E. Warden
Richard L. Varco
Edward H. Robitzek
Irving Selikoff
Walsh McDermott
Carl Muschenheim
1956 Jonas E. Salk
V. Everett Kinsey
Arnall Patz
1957 Nathan S. Kline
Robert H. Noce
Heinz E. Lehmann
1958 Robert W. Wilkins
1959 John H. Dingle
Gilbert Dalldorf
1962 Joseph Smadel
1963 Michael E. De Bakey
Charles B. Huggins
1964 Nathan S. Kline
1965 Albert B. Sabin
1966 Sidney Farber
1967 Robert A. Phillips
1968 John H. Gibbin, Jr.
1969 George C. Cotzias
1971 Edward D. Fries

The Leidy Medal

Awarded every three years by the Academy of Natural Sciences of Philadelphia for the best publication, exploration, discovery, or research in the natural sciences.

1925 Herbert S. Jennings
1928 Henry A. Pilsbry
1931 William M. Wheeler, Jr.
1934 Gerrit S. Miller, Jr.
1937 Edwin Linton
1940 Merritt L. Fernald
1943 Chancey Juday
1946 Ernst Mayr
1949 Warren P. Spencer
1952 G. Evelyn Hutchinson
1955 Herbert Friedmann
1958 H. B. Hungerford
1961 Robert E. Snodgrass
1964 Carl L. Hubbs
1967 Donn E. Rosen

Joseph W. Lippincott Award

Presented annually by the American Library Association to honor noteworthy service in the profession of librarianship.

1938 Mary U. Rothrock
1939 Herbert Putnam
1948 Carl H. Milam
1949 Harry M. Lydenberg
1950 Halsey W. Wilson
1951 Helen Haines
1952 Carl Vitz
1953 Marian C. Manley
1954 Jack Dalton
1955 Emerson Greenway
1956 Ralph A. Ulveling
1957 Flora B. Ludington
1958 Carleton B. Joeckel
1959 Essae M. Culver
1960 Verner W. Clapp
1961 Joseph L. Wheeler
1962 David H. Clift
1963 Frances W. Henne
1964 Robert B. Downs
1965 Frances C. Sayers
1966 Keyes D. Metcalf
1967 Edmon Low
1968 Lucile Nix
1969 Germaine Krettek

Loines Award for Poetry

Presented periodically by the National Institute of Arts and Letters as administrators of the Russell Loines Memorial Fund to recognize distinguished poetic achievements.

1931 Robert Frost
1942 Horace Gregory
1948 William Carlos Williams
1951 John Crowe Ransom
1960 Abbie Huston Evans
1962 I. A. Richards
1964 John Berryman
1966 William Meredith
1968 Anthony Hecht
1970 Robert Hayden

Edward Longstreth Medal

Awarded by The Franklin Institute to recognize notable inventions or meritorious improvements and developments in machines and mechanical processes.

1891 Wallace H. Dodge
Albert J. Pitkin
Henry W. Roby
W. George Schemerhorn
John J. White
1892 Alexander C. Chenoweth
J. R. Jones
J. E. Roeder
1893 W. G. Adams
and John S. Forbes
Frederick B. Hill
William M. Mackay
1894 Christian H. Baush
Victor G. Bloede
W. H. Bristol
William H. Clark
and Frank W. Collins
W. R. DeVoe
E. Ivins
A. Langstaff Johnston
John F. Lewis
and William F. Mattes
Max E. Schmidt
and Joseph Sieber
1895 E. G. Bates
Walter L. Cheney
W. S. Cooper
Charles Goodyear
C. C. Taintor
1896 William T. Armstrong
and Jacob D. Cox
G. Kroll
George Lodge
1897 Angelo Heilprin
E. B. Marsh
H. C. Regan, Jr.
G. M. Richards
1898 Thomas B. Doolittle
W. B. Hollingshead
1899 Harold P. Brown
and Thomas A. Edison
Frederick Frick
G. C. Henning
W. Lewis
1900 Charles Deshler
and Edwin J. McAllister
C. N. Fay,
Z. G. Sholes,
and H. Hochklassen
Henry Goldman
Horace G. Hoadley,
Eugene C. Lewis,
and Henry D. Williams
Milton O. Reeves
C. L. Riker
William H. Tucker
1901 Russell Bonnell
and Henry J. Schmitt
Arthur Kitson
1902 Willis J. Roussel
1903 Bion J. Arnold
Henry H. Cummings
Henry F. Eberhardt
and Frederick L. Ulrich
Frederic E. Ives
W. F. C. Morsell
J. W. von Pittler
Edward W. Scripture
William L. Schellenbach
C. C. Wentworth
1904 C. W. Draper
Henry J. Seitz
H. M. Shaw
1905 John E. Alexander
John J. Carty
Michael Miley
and Henry M. Miley
1906 W. I. Follett
George H. Meeker
Charles B. Weidlog
Henry E. Wetherill
1907 Herbert F. Ives
1908 G. Breed
Allerton S. Cushman
1909 Charles A. Bennett
J. A. Pearce Christfield
J. H. Granberry
B. F. Teal
1910 B. D. Reese
Kenneth Rushton
1911 Joseph S. Hepburn
E. P. Hyde
Morton G. Lloyd
Walter V. Turner
Charles Roper
1912 Charles Baskerville
Edwin M. Chance
E. Lathrop
and Oswald Schreiner
Edwin F. Northrup
C. G. Thomas
1913 Cleveland Abbe
E. Leon Chaffee
Harry C. Jones
Isaac N. Knapp
John S. Stone
1914 Herbert T. Herr
Hiram H. Hirsch
W. J. Humphreys
J. M. Rusby
George A. Wheeler
1915 Herbert E. Ives
Will G. Lenker
Max von Recklinghausen
Carrington C. Tutwiler
Charles D. Young
1916 Carleton Ellis
George W. Fuller
George F. Stradling
Benjamin G. Waggner
1917 F. H. Achard,
Arthur E. Kennelly,
and A. S. Dana
John T. Austin
John D. Ball
Christopher A. Becker
Max Levy
Dayton C. Miller
George A. Rankin
Albert Ringland
and Frank Schoenfuss
1918 H. Jemain Creighton
Levi T. Edwards
John H. Taussig
and Charles F. Zeek
John B. Whitehead
1919 Herbert E. Ives,
Edwin P. Kingsbury,
and Enoch Karrer
John W. Ledoux
Richard B. Moore
Frederick J. Schlink

Joshua J. Skinner
Homer C. Snook
1920 Bert H. Hite
William W. Kemp
and William H. Van Horn
Gottdank L. Kothny
and Robert Suczek
Morris E. Leeds
Matthew Luckiesh
1921 Leason H. Adams
and E. D. Williamson
William B. Eddison
James Hartness
Thomas W. Hicks
Jacob M. Spitzglass
1922 Edward J. Brandt
Samuel T. Freas
Joseph F. Keller
A. Herman Pfund
Martin F. Tierman
and Charles F. Wallace
1923 Harry S. Parks
1924 William S. Elliott
Thomas C. McBride
Milton R. Sheen
William F. Zimmermann
1925 Thomas M. Chance
William E. Hoke
Daniel H. Meloche
Thomas Midgley, Jr.
Carl P. Nachod
1926 Alonzo G. Kinyon
1927 Harry W. Hardinge
Wilfred Lewis
James F. Smathers
1928 Frank N. Speller
Warren P. Valentine
1929 Edward G. Herbert
Adolph W. Machlet
John F. Peters
1930 Ervin G. Bailey
Charles N. Weyl
1933 Howard L. Ingersoll
Dunlap J. McAdam, Jr.
1934 William E. Sykes
1935 Edmond Bruce
Howard D. Colman
and Burt A. Peterson
Peter Davey
Karl B. McEachron
1936 Alfred V. deForest
and William R. Hoke
Elmer A. Sperry, Jr.
1937 Emile M. Chamot
Richard T. Erban
John S. Haug
Herbert L. Whittemore
1938 Clarence W. Balke
Frederick Hellweg
and Paul Sollenberger
Frederick C. Langenberg
and Norman F. S. Russell
1939 Arthur C. Hardy
Jesse E. Stareck
John D. Strong
Robley C. Williams
1940 Leopold Godowsky, Jr.
and Leopold Mannes
Games Slayter
Richard L. Templin
Maxwell M. Upson
1941 Benjamin J. Wilson
1942 Ralph E. Flanders
and Ernest V. Flanders
Charles M. Kearns
1943 Robert G. De La Mater
and William Schwemlein
1944 Frank B. Allen
Edward E. Simmons, Jr.
J. Stogdell Stokes
1945 Sanford L. Cluett
1947 Samuel Berman
Harold J. W. Fay
1948 Nicholas F. Arone
and Edwin H. Brink
Raleigh J. Wise
1949 William H. Millspaugh
Arthur M. Young
1951 Howard O. McMahon
1953 Chester F. Carlson
1955 Richard Y. Case
1956 Floyd A. Firestone
1957 John B. Johnson
1958 Price C. McLemore
George S. Crampton
1959 David M. Potter
Jacob Rabinow
1960 W. Edward Chamberlain
John W. Coltman
Frederick A. Keidel
Moulton B. Taylor
1961 Robert L. Alcorn, Jr.,
Eugene C. Clark,
and Henry A. Weyer
Josiah L. Merrill, Jr.
1962 Felix Zandman
Albert L. Genter
Walter O. Snelling
Carlos B. Mirick
and Matthew H. Schrenk
1963 Herman Epstein
Norman M. Imbertson
Reinout P. Kroon
and Stewart Way
1964 P. R. Bell
Bolton L. Corson
Ernest Wildhaber
1966 Frederick D. Braddon
1967 Raymond C. Goertz
1968 Henry C. Theuerer
1969 Carl J. Frosch
Jean A. Hoerni
1970 Darrell H. Harting
1971 Harold G. Mead
1972 Samuel A. Ruben

Elijah Parish Lovejoy Award

Awarded annually by Colby College to a newsman who has made an outstanding contribution to the nation's journalistic a-chievement.

1952 James S. Pope
1953 Irving Dilliard
1954 James R. Wiggins
1955 Charles A. Sprague
1956 Arthur Hays Sulzberger
1957 Buford Boone
1958 John N. Heiskell
1959 Clark R. Mollenhoff
1960 Ralph McGill
1961 Bernard Kilgore
1962 Thomas M. Storke
1963 Louis M. Lyons
1964 John Hay Whitney
1965 Colbert A. McKnight
1966 Otis Chandler
1967 Edwin A. Lahey
1968 Carl T. Rowan
1969 John S. Knight
1971 Erwin D. Canham

Anthony F. Lucas Gold Medal

Awarded annually by the American Institute of Mining, Metallurgical and Petroleum Engineers to honor achievement in improving the technique and practice of finding and producing petroleum.

1937 J. Edgar Pew
1938 Henry L. Doherty
1940 E. L. DeGolyer
1941 Conrad Schlumberger
Marcel Schlumberger
1943 John R. Suman
1944 Charles Van O. Millikan
1946 James O. Lewis
1947 William N. Lacey
1948 Wallace E. Pratt
1950 William E. Wrather
1953 Morris Muskat
1954 Bruce H. Sage
1956 Stuart E. Buckley
1957 J. E. Brantly
1958 Carl E. Reistle, Jr.
1959 John T. Hayward
1960 Albert C. Rubel
1961 Edwin O. Bennett
1962 John E. Elliott
1963 Lyon F. Terry
1964 William Hurst
1965 Ralph D. Wyckoff
1966 Lloyd E. Elkins
1967 John E. Sherborne
1968 Antonius F. van Everdingen
1969 C. J. Coberly
1970 Henri G. Doll

National Book Award

Presented annually by the National Book Committee to honor the authors of books in several categories considered the most distinguished works published by American citizens during the preceding year.

1950

Nelson Algren	Fiction
Ralph L. Rusk	Nonfiction
William Carlos Williams	Poetry

1951

William Faulkner	Fiction
Newton Arvin	Nonfiction
Wallace Stevens	Poetry

1952

James Jones	Fiction
Rachel Carson	Nonfiction
Marianne Moore	Poetry

1953

Ralph Ellison	Fiction
Bernard DeVoto	Nonfiction
Archibald MacLeish	Poetry

1954

Saul Bellow	Fiction
Bruce Catton	Nonfiction
Conrad Aiken	Poetry

1955

William Faulkner	Fiction
Joseph Wood Krutch	Nonfiction
Wallace Stevens	Poetry

1956

John O'Hara	Fiction
Herbert Kubly	Nonfiction
W. H. Auden	Poetry

1957

Wright Morris	Fiction
George F. Kennan	Nonfiction
Richard Wilbur	Poetry

1958

John Cheever	Fiction
Catherine Drinker Bowen	Nonfiction
Robert Penn Warren	Poetry

1959

Bernard Malamud	Fiction
J. Christopher Herold	Nonfiction
Theodore Roethke	Poetry

1960

Philip Roth	Fiction
Richard Ellmann	Nonfiction
Robert Lowell	Poetry

1961

Conrad Richter	Fiction
William L. Shirer	Nonfiction
Randall Jarrell	Poetry

1962

Walker Percy	Fiction
Lewis Mumford	Nonfiction
Alan Dugan	Poetry

1963

J. F. Powers	Fiction
Leon Edel	Nonfiction
William Stafford	Poetry

1964

John Updike	Fiction
John Crowe Ransom	Poetry
Aileen Ward	Arts and Letters
William H. McNeill	History and Biography
Christopher Tunnard and Boris Pushkarev	Science, Philosophy, and Religion

1965

Saul Bellow	Fiction
Theodore Roethke	Poetry
Eleanor Clark	Arts and Letters
Louis Fischer	History and Biography
Norbert Wiener	Science, Philosophy, and Religion

1966

Katherine Anne Porter	Fiction
James Dickey	Poetry
Janet Flanner	Arts and Letters
Arthur M. Schlesinger, Jr.	History and Biography

1967

Bernard Malamud	Fiction
James Merrill	Poetry
Justin Kaplan	Arts and Letters
Peter Gay	History and Biography
Oscar Lewis	Science, Philosophy, and Religion
Gregory Rabassa	Translation
Willard Trask	Translation

1968

Thornton Wilder	Fiction
Robert Bly	Poetry
William Troy	Arts and Letters
George F. Kennan	History and Biography
Jonathan Kozol	Science, Philosophy, and Religion
Howard Hong and Edna Hong	Translation

1969

Jerzy Kosinski	Fiction
John Berryman	Poetry
Norman Mailer	Arts and Letters
Winthrop Jordan	History and Biography
Robert J. Lifton	The Sciences
William Weaver	Translation
Meindert Dejong	Children's Literature

1970

Joyce Carol Oates	Fiction
Elizabeth Bishop	Poetry
Lillian Hellman	Arts and Letters
T. Harry Williams	History and Biography
Erik H. Erikson	Philosophy and Religion
Ralph Manheim	Translation
Isaac Bashevis Singer	Children's Literature

1971

Saul Bellow	Fiction
Mona Van Duyn	Poetry
James McGregor Burns	History and Biography
Francis Steegmuller	Arts and Letters
Frank Jones and Edward G. Seidensticker	Translation
Raymond P. Stearns	Science
Lloyd Alexander	Children's Books

1972

Charles Rosen	Arts and Letters
Joseph P. Lash	Biography
Donald Barthelme	Children's Books
Stewart Brand	Contemporary Affairs
Flannery O'Connor	Fiction
Allan Nevins	History
Martin E. Marty	Philosophy and Religion
Howard Moss and Frank O'Hara	Poetry
George L. Small	The Sciences
Austryn Wainhouse	Translation

National Council on the Arts Distinguished Service Award

Presented annually by the Library Programs Division to recognize life-long contributions to American letters.

1967 Kenneth Patchen
1968 John Berryman
Louise Bogan
Malcolm Cowley
John Crowe Ransom
Yvor Winters
1969 Kenneth Burke
Reed Whittemore

National Institute of Arts and Letters Award for Distinguished Service to the Arts

Presented from time to time to an American citizen, not a member of the Institute, who has made outstanding contributions to the arts.

1941 Robert Moses
1944 Samuel S. McClure
1949 Mrs. Edward MacDowell
1952 Mrs. Simon Guggenheim
1954 J. William Fulbright
1955 Henry A. Moe
1957 Francis Henry Taylor
1958 Lincoln Kirstein
1959 Elizabeth Ames
1962 Paul Mellon
1963 Marie L. Bullock
1965 Frances Steloff
1968 Alfred H. Barr, Jr.
1969 Leopold Stokowski

The National Institute of Arts and Letters Gold Medal

Awarded by the Institute in the name of the American Academy of Arts and Letters to recognize achievement in the arts based on the entire work of the recipient.

1909 Augustus Saint-Gaudens
1910 James Ford Rhodes
1911 James Whitcomb Riley
1912 W. Rutherford Mead
1913 Augustus Thomas
1914 John Singer Sargent
1915 William Dean Howells
1916 John Burroughs
1917 Daniel Chester French
1918 William R. Thayer
1919 Charles M. Loeffler
1921 Cass Gilbert
1922 Eugene O'Neill
1923 Edwin H. Blashfield
1924 Edith Wharton
1925 William C. Brownell
1926 Herbert Adams
1927 William M. Sloane
1928 George W. Chadwick
1929 Edwin Arlington Robinson
1930 Charles Adams Platt
1931 William Gillette
1932 Gari Melchers
1933 Booth Tarkington
1935 Agnes Repplier
1936 George G. Barnard
1937 Charles McLean Andrews
1938 Walter Damrosch
1939 Robert Frost
1940 William Adams Delano
1941 Robert E. Sherwood
1942 Cecilia Beaux
1943 Stephen Vincent Benet
1944 Willa Cather
1945 Paul Manship
1946 Van Wyck Brooks
1947 John Alden Carpenter
1948 Charles A. Beard
1949 Frederick Law Olmsted
1950 John Sloan
Henry L. Mencken
1951 James E. Fraser
Igor Stravinsky
1952 Thornton Wilder
Carl Sandburg
1953 Marianne Moore
Frank Lloyd Wright
1954 Maxwell Anderson
Reginald Marsh
1955 Edward Hopper
Ivan Mestrovic
1956 Aaron Copland
1957 John Dos Passos
Allan Nevins
1958 Conrad Aiken
Henry R. Shepley
1959 Arthur Miller
George Grosz
1960 Charles E. Burchfield
E. B. White
1961 William Zorach
Roger Sessions
1962 William Faulkner
Samuel Eliot Morison
1963 William Carlos Williams
Ludwig Mies van der Rohe
1964 Lillian Hellman
Ben Shahn
1965 Andrew Wyeth
Walter Lippmann
1966 Virgil Thomson
1967 Katherine Anne Porter
Arthur Schlesinger, Jr.
1968 R. Buckminster Fuller
W. H. Auden
1969 Tennessee Williams
Leonard Baskin
1970 Georgia O'Keefe
Lewis Mumford
1971 Alexander Calder
Elliott Carter
1972 Eudora Welty
Henry Steele Commager

National Institute of Social Sciences Gold Medal

Awarded annually for outstanding contributions in the form of distinguished service to humanity.

1913 Archer M. Huntington
Samuel L. Parrish
William Howard Taft
1914 Charles W. Eliot
George W. Goethals
Abraham Jacobi
Henry F. Osborn
1915 Luther Burbank
Andrew Carnegie
1916 Robert Bacon
Helen Hartley Jenkins
Adolph Lewisohn
1917 George W. Crile
William C. Gorgas
John P. Mitchell
Michael I. Pupin
1918 Henry P. Davison
Herbert C. Hoover
William J. Mayo
1919 Samuel Gompers
William H. Welch
1920 Alexis Carrel
H. Holbrook Curtis
Harry P. Judson
1921 Charles F. Chandler
Calvin Coolidge
Cleveland H. Dodge
1923 Charles B. Davenport
Emory R. Johnson
John D. Rockefeller, Sr.
1924 Walter Hampden
Charles Evans Hughes
Mrs. C. Lorillard Spencer
1925 Mary W. Harriman
William H. Park
Elihu Root
1926 S. Parkes Cadman
Clarence H. Mackay
Stephen T. Mather
Mary Schenck Woolman
1927 George Pierce Baker
Walter Damrosch
Harry Emerson Fosdick
Adolph S. Ochs
1928 Liberty Hyde Bailey
Robert W. deForest
Willis R. Whitney
1929 Valeria Langeloth
Rose Livingston
John D. Rockefeller, Jr.
James T. Shotwell
Daniel Willard
1930 Anna B. Gallup
George R. Minot
William Lyon Phelps
Nathan Straus
1931 Grace Abbott
Richard C. Cabot
Grace Goodhue Coolidge
Frank B. Kellogg
1932 Edward E. Allen
James H. Post
William C. Redfield
Gerard Swope
1933 Newton D. Baker
Clifford W. Beers
Evangeline Booth
1934 Eleanor Robson Belmont
Walter B. Cannon
Samuel Seabury
1935 Cornelius N. Bliss
Harvey Cushing
Carter Glass
George E. Vincent
1936 Nicholas Murray Butler
Dorothy H. Eustis
William E. Hall
J. Pierpont Morgan
1937 James R. Angell
Mrs. Edward W. Bok
J. Edgar Hoover
Wesley C. Mitchell
1938 John W. Davis
Walter S. Gifford
Dorothy Thompson
1939 Martha Berry
William C. Osborn
George Wharton Pepper
1940 Carrie Chapman Catt
James E. West
Wendell L. Wilkie
1941 Norman H. Davis
Mrs. J. Borden Harriman
Alfred E. Smith
1942 Rufus B. von KleinSmid
Anne O'Hare McCormick
Donald M. Nelson
1943 Edwin G. Conklin
Mildred H. McAffee
Juan T. Trippe
1944 Bernard Baruch
Mrs. Henry Pomeroy Davison
James G. K. McClure
1945 Vannevar Bush
Mrs. John H. Hammond
William M. Lewis
1946 Virginia Crocheron Gildersleeve
Robert Moses
Edward R. Stettinius, Jr.
1947 Katherine F. Lenroot
Edward Johnson
Thomas J. Watson, Sr.
1948 Georgiana F. Sibley
Basil O'Connor
Warren R. Austin
1949 Lilian M. Gilbreth
Alfred P. Sloan, Jr.
George C. Marshall
1950 Henry Bruere
Sarah G. Blanding
1951 Bayard F. Pope
Paul G. Hoffman
John Foster Dulles
Lewis W. Douglas
Douglas MacArthur
1952 Harold R. Medina
Helen Keller
Robert A. Lovett
John J. McCloy
1953 E. Roland Harriman
Oveta Culp Hobby
Charles F. Kettering
1954 Howard A. Rusk
Mrs. Lytle Hull
Walter Bedell Smith
1955 Samuel D. Leidesdorf
Elizabeth Luce Moore
Henry Cabot Lodge, Jr.
1956 Clarence G. Michalis
Mary Pilsbury Lord
Henry T. Heald
1957 William F. Graham, Jr.
Clare Booth Luce
Alfred M. Gruenther
1958 Marion Anderson
James R. Killian, Jr.
Robert B. Anderson
Herbert Hoover
1959 Helen Hayes
Laurance S. Rockefeller
Jonas E. Salk
1960 Rudolf Bing
Gilbert Darlington
Millicent C. McIntosh
Grayson L. Kirk
1961 Mary L. Bullock
Karl Menninger
William C. Menninger
Edward Durrell Stone
1962 Mary I. Bunting
Ralph J. Bunche
John W. Gardner

Lucius D. Clay
1963 Arthur H. Dean
Katherine E. McBride
Nathan M. Pusey
Frank Stanton
1964 Margaret Chase Smith
Dean Rusk
Frederick R. Kappel
Bob Hope
1965 Dorothy B. Chandler
James A. Perkins
Maxwell D. Taylor
1966 Lady Bird Johnson
Francis Cardinal Spellman
David Sarnoff
G. Keith Funston
Danny Kaye
1967 John D. Rockefeller, 3rd
Nelson A. Rockefeller
Laurance S. Rockefeller
Winthrop Rockefeller
David Rockefeller
1968 Anne Morrow Lindbergh
Ralph W. Sockman
Eugene R. Black
Charles A. Lindbergh
1969 Frank Borman
Theodore M. Hesburgh
1970 William P. Rogers
Katharine Graham
Lauris Norstad
Eric Severeid
1971 Joan Ganz Cooney
Arthur K. Watson
Thomas J. Watson, Jr.

National Medal For Literature

Conferred annually by the National Book Committee under an endowment of the Guinzburg Fund on a living American writer to honor his total contribution to American letters.

1965 Thornton Wilder
1966 Edmund Wilson
1967 W. H. Auden
1968 Marianne Moore
1969 Conrad Aiken
1970 Robert Penn Warren
1971 E. B. White
1972 Lewis Mumford

National Medal of Science

Presented annually by the president of the United States for outstanding achievement in science.

1962 Theodore von Karman
1963 Luis W. Alvarez
Vannevar Bush
John R. Pierce
Cornelis B. Van Niel
Norbert Wiener
1964 Roger Adams
Othmar H. Ammann
Theodosius Dobzhansky
Charles S. Draper
Solomon Lefschetz
Neal E. Miller
Marston Morse
Marshall W. Nirenberg
Julian Schwinger
Harold C. Urey
Robert B. Woodward
1965 John Bardeen
Peter J. W. Debye
Hugh L. Dryden
Clarence L. Johnson
Leon M. Lederman
Warren K. Lewis
Francis P. Rous
William W. Rubey
George G. Simpson
Donald D. Van Slyke
Oscar Zariski
1966 Jacob Bjerknes
Subrahmanyan Chandrasekhar
Henry Eyring
Edward F. Knipling
Fritz A. Lipmann
John W. Milnor
William C. Rose
Claude E. Shannon
John H. Van Vleck
Sewall Wright
Vladimir K. Zworykin
1967 Jesse W. Beams
Francis Birch
Gregory Breit
Paul J. Cohen
Kenneth S. Cole
Louis P. Hammett
Harry F. Harlow
Michael Heidelberger
George B. Kistiakowsky
Edwin H. Land
Igor I. Sikorsky
Alfred H. Sturtevant
1968 Horace A. Barker
Paul D. Bartlett
Bernard B. Brodie
Detlev W. Bronk
J. Presper Eckert
Herbert Friedman
Jay L. Lush
Nathan M. Newmark
Jerzy Neyman
Lars Onsager
Burrhus F. Skinner
Eugene P. Wigner
1969 Herbert C. Brown
William Feller
Robert J. Huebner
Jack S. Kilby
Ernst Mayr
Wolfgang Panofsky
1970 Richard D. Brauer
Robert H. Dicke
Barbara McClintock
George E. Mueller
Albert Sabin
Allan R. Sandage
John C. Slater
John A. Wheeler
Saul Winstein

William H. Nichols Medal

Awarded by the New York Section of the American Chemical Society to recognize outstanding original research in chemistry.

1903 Edward B. Vorhees
1905 Charles L. Parsons
1906 Marston T. Bogert
1907 Howard B. Bishop
1908 William H. Walker
1909 William A. Noyes
Henry C. P. Weber
1910 Leo H. Baekeland
Charles W. Easley
1911 Martin A. Rosanoff
1912 Charles James
1914 Moses Gomberg
1915 Irving Langmuir
1916 Claude S. Hudson
1918 Treat B. Johnson
1920 Irving Langmuir
1921 Gilbert N. Lewis
1923 Thomas Midgley, Jr.
1924 Charles A. Kraus
1925 Edward C. Franklin
1926 Samuel C. Lind
1927 Roger Adams
1928 Hugh S. Taylor
1929 William L. Evans
1930 Samuel E. Sheppard
1931 John A. Wilson
1932 James B. Conant
1934 Henry C. Sherman
1935 Julius A. Nieuwland
1936 William M. Clark
1937 Frank C. Whitmore
1938 Phoebus A. Levene
1939 Joel H. Hildebrand
1940 John M. Nelson
1941 Linus Pauling
1942 Duncan A. MacInnes
1943 Arthur B. Lamb
1944 Carl S. Marvel
1945 Vincent du Vigneaud
1946 Wendell M. Stanley
1947 George B. Kistiakowsky
1948 Glenn T. Seaborg
1949 Izaak M. Kolthoff
1950 Oskar Wintersteiner
1951 Henry Eyring
1952 Frank H. Spedding
1953 Reynold C. Fuson
1954 Charles P. Smyth
1955 Wendell M. Latimer
1956 Robert B. Woodward
1957 Louis P. Hammett
1958 Melvin Calvin
1959 Herbert C. Brown
1960 Herman F. Mark
1961 Peter J. W. Debye
1962 Paul J. Flory
1963 Louis F. Fieser
1964 Arthur C. Cope
1965 Herbert E. Carter
1966 Frederick D. Rossini
1967 Karl Folkers
1968 William S. Johnson
1969 Marshall W. Nirenberg
1970 Britton Chance

American Nobel Prize Winners

The asterisk (*) denotes sharing of the award with a person not an American citizen.

1906

Theodore Roosevelt — Peace

1907

Albert A. Michelson — Physics

1912

Elihu Root — Peace
Alexis Carrel — Physiology and Medicine

1914

Theodore W. Richards — Chemistry

1919

Woodrow Wilson — Peace

1921

Albert Einstein — Physics

1922

Otto F. Meyerhof* — Physiology and Medicine

1923

Robert A. Millikan — Physics

1925

Charles G. Dawes* — Peace

1927

Arthur H. Compton — Physics

1929

Frank B. Kellogg — Peace

1930

Karl Landsteiner — Physiology and Medicine
Sinclair Lewis — Literature

1931

Jane Addams and Nicholas Murray Butler — Peace

1932

Irving Langmuir — Chemistry

1933

Thomas H. Morgan — Physiology and Medicine

1934

George R. Minot* — Physiology and Medicine
William P. Murphy* — Physiology and Medicine
Harold C. Urey — Chemistry
George H. Whipple* — Physiology and Medicine

1936

Carl D. Anderson* — Physics
Peter J. W. Debye — Chemistry
Victor F. Hess* — Physics
Otto Loewi* — Physiology and Medicine
Eugene O'Neill — Literature

1937

Clinton J. Davisson* — Physics
Albert von Szent-Gyorgyi — Physiology and Medicine

1938

Pearl S. Buck — Literature
Enrico Fermi — Physics

1939

Ernest O. Lawrence — Physics

1943

Edward A. Doisy* — Physiology and Medicine
Otto Stern — Physics

1944

E. Joseph Erlanger* — Physiology and Medicine
Herbert S. Gasser* — Physiology and Medicine
Isidor I. Rabi — Physics

1945

Cordell Hull — Peace
Wolfgang Pauli — Physics

1946

Emily Balch* and John R. Mott* — Peace
Percy W. Bridgman — Physics
Hermann J. Muller — Physiology and Medicine
John H. Northrop, Wendell M. Stanley, and James B. Sumner — Chemistry

1947

Gerty T. Cori and Carl F. Cori — Physiology and Medicine

1949

William Faulkner — Literature
William F. Giauque — Chemistry

1950

Ralph J. Bunche — Peace
Philip S. Hench and Edward C. Kendall — Physiology and Medicine

1951

Edwin M. McMillan and Glenn T. Seaborg — Chemistry
Max Theiler — Physiology and Medicine

Year	Laureate	Prize
1952	Felix Bloch and Edward M. Purcell	Physics
	Selman A. Waksman	Physiology and Medicine
1953	Fritz A. Lipmann*	Physiology and Medicine
	George C. Marshall	Peace
1954	John F. Enders*	Physiology and Medicine
	Ernest Hemingway	Literature
	Linus C. Pauling	Chemistry
	Frederick C. Robbins and Thomas H. Weller	Physiology and Medicine
1955	Vincent du Vigneaud	Chemistry
	Polykarp Kusch and Willis E. Lamb, Jr.	Physics
1956	John Bardeen and Walter H. Brattain	Physics
	Andre F. Cournand and D. W. Richards	Physiology and Medicine
	William B. Shockley*	Physics
1957	Tsung-Dao Lee and Chen Ning Yang	Physics
1958	George W. Beadle, Joshua Lederberg, and Edward L. Tatum	Physiology and Medicine
1959	Owen Chamberlain*	Physics
	Arthur Kornberg and Servero Ochoa	Physiology and Medicine
	Emilio G. Segre*	Physics
1960	Donald A. Glaser	Physics
	Willard F. Libby	Chemistry
1961	Melvin Calvin	Chemistry
	Robert Hofstadter*	Physics
	George von Bekesy	Physiology and Medicine
1962	Linus Pauling	Peace
	John Steinbeck	Literature
	James D. Watson*	Physiology and Medicine
1963	Maria Goeppert-Mayer and Eugene P. Wigner	Physics
1964	Konrad E. Bloch*	Physiology and Medicine
	Martin Luther King. Jr.	Peace
	Charles H. Townes*	Physics
1965	Richard P. Feynman and Julian S. Schwinger	Physics
	Robert B. Woodward	Chemistry
1966	Charles B. Huggins and Francis P. Rous	Physiology and Medicine
	Robert S. Mulliken	Chemistry
1967	Hans A. Bethe	Physics
	Haldan K. Hartline and George Wald	Physiology and Medicine
1968	Luis W. Alvarez	Physics
	Robert W. Holley, F. Gobind Khorana, and Marshall W. Nirenberg	Physiology and Medicine
	Lars Onsager	Chemistry
1969	Max Delbruck, Alfred D. Hershey, and Salvador E. Luria	Physiology and Medicine
	Murray Gell-Mann	Physics
1970	Julius Axelrod*	Physiology and Medicine
	Norman E. Borlaug	Peace
	Paul A. Samuelson	Economics
1971	Earl W. Sutherland, Jr.	Physiology and Medicine
	Simon Kuznets	Economics
1972	Gerald M. Edelman	Physiology and Medicine
	Christian B. Anfinsen, Stanford Moore, and William H. Stein	Chemistry
	John Bardeen, Leon N. Cooper, and John R. Schrieffer	Physics
	Kenneth J. Arrow	Economics

The Passano Award

Presented annually by the Passano Foundation to an American citizen who has made an outstanding contribution to the advancement of medical science, particularly for work having a clinical application.

1945 Edwin J. Cohn
1946 Ernest W. Goodpasture
1947 Selman A. Waksman
1948 Helen B. Taussig
Alfred Blalock
1949 Oswald T. Avery
1950 Edward C. Kendall
Philip S. Hench
1951 Philip Levine
Alexander S. Wiener
1952 Herbert M. Evans
1953 John F. Enders
1954 Homer W. Smith
1955 Vincent du Vigneaud
1956 George N. Papanicolaou
1957 William M. Clark
1958 George W. Corner
1959 Stanhope Bayne-Jones
1960 Rene J. Dubos
1961 Owen H. Wangensteen
1962 Albert H. Coons
1963 Horace W. Magoun
1964 Keith R. Porter
George E. Palade
1965 Charles B. Huggins
1966 John T. Edsall
1967 Irvine H. Page
1968 John E. Howard
1969 George H. Hitchings
1970 Paul C. Zamecnik

Pennsylvania Academy of The Fine Arts Gold Medal of Honor

Awarded from time to time to American painters and sculptors in recognition of high achievement in their profession, or to those who have given eminent service in the cause of art or the Academy.

1893 D. Ridgeway Knight
1894 Alexander Harrison
1895 William M. Chase
1896 Winslow Homer
1898 Edwin A. Abbey
Cecilia Beaux
1899 Charles Grafly
1901 Henry J. Thouron
1902 James A. McNeill Whistler
1903 John Singer Sargent
1904 John W. Alexander
1905 William T. Richards
Violet Oakley
1906 Horatio Walker
1907 Edward W. Redfield
1908 Edmund C. Tarbell
1909 Thomas P. Anschutz
1911 Willard L. Metcalf
1914 Mary Cassatt
1915 Edward H. Coates
1916 J. Alden Weir
1918 John McClure Hamilton
1919 Hugh H. Breckenridge
1920 Childe Hassam
1926 Frank W. Benson
1929 Daniel Garber
1939 C. Paul Jennewein
1949 Alfred G. B. Steel
Franklin C. Watkins
1953 Walker Hancock
George Harding
1955 Joseph T. Fraser, Jr.
William C. Mason
1959 John F. Lewis, Jr.
1961 Francis Speight
1966 Andrew Wyeth

Penrose Medal

Awarded annually by the Geological Society of America to honor achievement marking a decided advance in the science of geology.

1927 Thomas C. Chamberlin
1931 William M. Davis
1932 Edward O. Ulrich
1933 Waldemar Lindgren
1934 Charles Schuchert
1935 Reginald A. Daly
1938 Andrew C. Lawson
1939 William B. Scott
1940 Nelson H. Darton
1941 Norman L. Bowen
1942 Charles K. Leith
1944 Bailey Willis
1946 T. Wayland Vaughan
1947 Arthur L. Day
1949 Wendell P. Woodring
1952 George G. Simpson
1953 Esper S. Larsen, Jr.
1954 Arthur F. Buddington
1958 James Gilluly
1959 Adolph Knopf
1960 Walter H. Bucher
1962 Alfred S. Romer
1963 William W. Rubey
1964 Donnel F. Hewett
1965 Philip B. King
1966 Harry H. Hess
1969 Francis Birch

Pittsburgh International Prizes

Selections made by a jury of award from entries in the Pittsburgh International Exhibition of Contemporary Painting and Sculpture (formerly the Carnegie Institute International Exhibition).

First Prize

1898 Dwight W. Tryon
1899 Cecilia Beaux
1901 Alfred Maurer
1903 Frank W. Benson
1904 W. Elmer Schofield
1908 Thomas W. Dewing
1909 Edmund C. Tarbell
1911 John W. Alexander
1914 Edward W. Redfield
1920 Abbott H. Thayer
1921 Ernest Lawson
1922 George W. Bellows
1923 Arthur B. Davies
1931 Franklin C. Watkins
1934 Peter Blume
1936 Leon Kroll
1939 Alexander Brook
1959 Alexander Calder
1961 Mark Tobey
1964 Ellsworth Kelly
1967 Josef Albers

Second Prize

1898 Childe Hassam
1899 Frank W. Benson
1900 Ben Foster
1901 Ellen W. Ahrens
1903 Bryson Burroughs
1904 Edmund C. Tarbell
1905 Edward W. Redfield
1907 Thomas Eakins
1910 Karl Anderson
1912 Paul Dougherty
1921 Howard Giles
1923 Eugene Speicher
1929 William J. Glackens
1930 Alexander Brook
1933 John S. Curry
1935 Charles E. Burchfield
1939 Yasuo Kuniyoshi
1950 Lyonel Feininger
1961 Jules Olitski
George Sugarman

Third Prize

1896 Cecilia Beaux
1897 J. Alden Weir
1900 William S. Kendall
1901 Edmund C. Tarbell
1903 William L. Lathrop
1904 Howard G. Cushing
1905 Childe Hassam
1908 Emil Carlsen
1909 Bruce Crane
1910 Edward F. Rook
1913 Gifford Beal
1914 George W. Bellows
1920 Walter Ufer
1921 Eugene Speicher
1924 Daniel Garber
1925 Charles W. Hawthorne
1926 Robert Spencer
1927 Andrew Dasburg
1928 Glenn O. Coleman
1933 Henry V. Poor
1934 Sidney Laufman
1935 Henry E. Mattson
1938 Arnold Blanch
1950 Priscilla Roberts
1961 Adolph Gottlieb

George Polk Memorial Award

Awarded by the Overseas Press Club for best reporting in any medium requiring exceptional courage and enterprise in other countries.

1948 Homer Bigart
1949 Wayne Richardson
1950 Marguerite Higgins
1951 William Oatis
1952 Homer Bigart
1954 Robert Capa
1955 Gene Symonds
1956 Russell Jones
1957 Herbert Matthews
1958 Joseph Taylor
1960 Henry Taylor
Lionel Durant
1961 Dickey Chapelle
1962 Dana Adams Schmidt
1963 Richard Tregaskis
1964 George Clay
1965 Morley Safer
1966 Ron Nessen
1967 Eric Pace
1968 Peter Rehak
1969 Horst Faas
Peter Arnett
1970 John Laurence
Keith Kay
James Clevenger
Russ Bensley
Ernest Leiser
1971 Nicholas W. Stroh

Howard N. Potts Medal

Awarded by The Franklin Institute to honor distinguished work in science or the arts, important development of previous basic discoveries, and inventions or products of superior excellence or utilizing important principles.

1911 William W. Coblentz
1912 William A. Bone
1913 James A. Bizzell
and T. L. Lyon
1914 Ralph Modjeski
1915 W. J. Humphreys
1917 Ulric Dahlgren
1918 Alexander Gray
Arthur B. Kennelly
1919 Reynold Janney and
Harvey D. Williams
Clarence P. Landreth
1920 Wendell A. Barker
Edward P. Bullard, Jr.
1921 Elmer V. McCollum
1922 E. G. Coker
Charles R. Downs
and J. M. Weiss
Richard B. Moore
1923 Albert W. Hull
1924 John A. Anderson
William Gaertner
1925 Charles T. R. Wilson
1926 William D. Coolidge
1927 George E. Beggs
Marion Eppley
1928 Eugene C. Sullivan
and William C. Taylor
Oscar G. Thurlow
1933 Igor I. Sikorsky
1934 Ernst G. Fischer
1937 John C. Hostetter
1938 Lars O. Grondahl
1939 Newcomb K. Chaney
H. Jermain Creighton
1941 Harold E. Edgerton
1942 Jesse W. Beams
Harcourt C. Drake
1943 Paul R. Heyl

1945 Edwin A. Link
1946 Ira S. Bowen
Sanford A. Moss
1947 Robert H. Kent
Vladimir K. Zworykin
1948 David B. Parkinson
and Clarence A. Lovell
Eugene J. Houdry
1949 John W. Mauchly
and J. Presper Eckert
Clinton R. Hanna
1950 Merle A. Tuve
1951 Clifford M. Foust
1956 Edwin H. Land
1958 William N. Goodwin, Jr.
Emanuel Rosenberg
1959 George W. Morey
1960 Charles S. Draper
1962 Wilbur H. Goss
1964 Erwin H. Mueller
1966 Robert Kunin
1967 John L. Moll
1969 Albert Ghiorso
Charles P. Ginsburg
1971 William D. McElroy

Sidney Powers Memorial Medal

Presented by the American Association of Petroleum Geologists in recognition of distinguished contributions to and achievements in the field of special interest to the association.

1945 Wallace E. Pratt
1947 Alexander Deussen
1948 A. I. Levorsen
1950 E. L. DeGolyer
1952 K. C. Heald
1953 Frederic H. Lahee
1956 William E. Wrather
1957 J. P. D. Hull
1958 Paul Weaver
1959 Raymond C. Moore
1960 Henry V. Howe
1961 Clarence L. Moody
1962 Lewis G. Weeks
1963 Hollis D. Hedberg
1964 Edgar W. Owen
1965 Victor E. Monnett
1966 William B. Heroy
1967 Carey Croneis
1968 Maurice Ewing
1969 Ira H. Cram
1970 Frank R. Clark

Presidential Medal of Freedom

Known as the Medal of Freedom before 1963 and awarded by the President of the United States to recognize meritorious contributions to the country's security or national interest, to world peace, or to cultural or other significant public or private endeavors.

1946 George L. Howe
Gordon T. Jackson
Richard Mazzarini
Dennis Puleston
Chen Sun
William M. Wheeler, Jr.
1955 Robert B. Anderson
1956 John Von Neumann
1957 Charles E. Wilson
1958 Lewis L. Strauss
1959 John Foster Dulles
Neil H. McElroy
Donald A. Quarles
1961 James H. Douglas, Jr.
Thomas S. Gates, Jr.
Gordon Gray
Christian A. Herter
George B. Kistiakowsky
1963 Marian Anderson
Ralph J. Bunche
Ellsworth Bunker
Genevieve Caulfield
James B. Conant
John F. Enders
Felix Frankfurter
Karl Holton
John F. Kennedy
Robert J. Kiphuth
Edwin H. Land
Herbert H. Lehman
Robert A. Lovett
John J. McCloy
J. Clifford MacDonald
George Meany
Alexander Meiklejohn
Luis Munoz-Marin
Clarence B. Randall
Rudolph Serkin
Edward Steichen
George W. Taylor
Ludwig Mies van der Rohe
Alan T. Waterman
Mark S. Watson
Annie D. Wauneka
E. B. White
Thornton N. Wilder
Edmund Wilson
Andrew Wyeth
1964 Dean G. Acheson
Detlev W. Bronk
Aaron Copland
Willem deKooning
Walt Disney
J. Frank Dobie
Lena F. Edwards
Lynn Fontanne
John W. Gardner
Theodore M. Hesburgh
Clarence L. Johnson
Frederick R. Kappel
Helen Keller
John L. Lewis
Walter Lippmann
Alfred Lunt
Ralph McGill
Samuel Eliot Morison
Lewis Mumford
Edward R. Murrow
Reinhold Niebuhr
Leontyne Price
A. Philip Randolph
Carl Sandburg
John Steinbeck
Helen B. Taussig
Carl Vinson
Thomas J. Watson, Jr.
Paul Dudley White
1968 Ellsworth Bunker
Robert W. Komer
Eugene M. Locke
Robert S. McNamara
James E. Webb
1969 Edwin E. Aldrin, Jr.
Neil A. Armstrong
Eugene R. Black
McGeorge Bundy
Clark M. Clifford
Michael Collins
Michael E. DeBakey
David Dubinsky
Edward (Duke) Ellington
Ralph Ellison
Henry Ford II
W. Averell Harriman
Bob Hope
Edgar F. Kaiser
Mary Lasker
John W. Macy, Jr.
Gregory Peck
Laurance S. Rockefeller
Walt W. Rostow
Dean Rusk
Merriman Smith
Cyrus R. Vance
William S. White
Roy Wilkins
Whitney M. Young, Jr.
1970 Earl C. Behrens
Edward T. Folliard
Fred W. Haise, Jr.
William M. Henry
Arthur Krock
David Lawrence
George G. Lincoln
James A. Lovell, Jr.
Raymond Moley
Eugene Ormandy
Adela Rogers St. Johns
John L. Swigert, Jr.
1971 Samuel Goldwyn
1972 John Paul Vann

Priestly Medal

Awarded annually (originally every three years) by the American Chemical Society to honor distinguished service to chemistry.

1923 Ira Remsen
1926 Edgar F. Smith
1929 Francis P. Garvan
1932 Charles L. Parsons
1935 William A. Noyes
1938 Marston T. Bogert
1941 Thomas Midgley, Jr.
1944 James B. Conant
1946 Roger Adams
1947 Warren K. Lewis
1948 Edward R. Weidlein
1949 Arthur B. Lamb
1950 Charles A. Kraus
1951 E. J. Crane
1952 Samuel C. Lind
1953 Robert Robinson
1954 W. Albert Noyes, Jr.
1955 Charles A. Thomas
1956 Carl S. Marvel
1957 Farrington Daniels
1958 Ernest H. Volwiler
1959 Hermann I. Schlesinger
1960 Wallace R. Brode
1961 Louis P. Hammett
1962 Joel H. Hildebrand
1963 Peter J. W. Debye
1964 John C. Bailar, Jr.
1965 William J. Sparks
1966 William O. Baker
1967 Ralph Connor
1968 William G. Young
1969 Kenneth S. Pitzer
1970 Max Tishler
1971 Frederick D. Rossini

Isaac Ray Award

Presented by the American Psychiatric Association for outstanding contributions to forensic phychiatry or to the psychiatric aspects of jurisprudence.

1952 Winfred Overholser
1953 Gregory Zilboorg
1954 John Biggs, Jr.
1955 Henry Weihofen
1956 Philip Q. Roche
1957 Manfred S. Guttmacher
1960 David L. Bazelon
1961 Sheldon Glueck
1962 Karl Menninger
1963 Morris Ploscowe
1964 Justine Wise Polier
1968 Bernard Diamond

Sylvanus Albert Reed Award

Presented annually by the American Institute of Aeronautics and Astronautics to honor a contribution to aeronautical engineering design or the aeronautical sciences whose influence is apparent on the development of practical aeronautics.

1934 C. G. Rossby
H. G. Willett
1935 Frank W. Caldwell
1936 Edward S. Taylor
1937 Eastman N. Jacobs
1938 Alfred V. de Forest
1939 George J. Mead
1940 Hugh L. Dryden
1941 Theodore von Karman
1942 Igor I. Sikorsky
1943 Sanford A. Moss
1944 Fred E. Weick
1945 Charles S. Draper
1946 Robert T. Jones
1947 Galen B. Schubauer
Harold K. Skromstad
1948 George W. Brady
1949 George S. Schairer
1950 Robert R. Gilruth
1951 Edward H. Heinemann
1952 John Stack
1953 Ernest G. Stout
1954 Clark B. Millikan
1955 H. Julian Allen
1956 Clarence L. Johnson
1957 Raymond L. Bisplinghoff
1958 Victor E. Carbonera
1959 Karel J. Bossart
1960 John W. Becker
1961 Alfred J. Eggers, Jr.
1962 Walter C. Williams
1964 Abe Silverstein
1965 Arthur E. Raymond
1966 Clarence L. Johnson
1967 Adolph Busemann
1968 William H. Cook
1969 Rene H. Miller
1970 Richard T. Whitcomb
1971 Ira G. Hedrick
1972 Max M. Munk

Remington Honor Medal

Awarded by the American Pharaceutical Association (New York Chapter) for distinguished service to pharmacy in the preceding year or for outstanding achievement during a longer period of activity.

1919 James H. Beal
1920 John Uri Lloyd
1922 Henry V. Arny
1923 Henry H. Rusby
1924 George M. Beringer
1925 Henry M. Whelpley
1926 H. A. B. Dunning
1928 Charles H. LaWall
1929 Wilbur L. Scoville
1930 Edward Kremers
1931 Ernest F. Cook
1932 Eugene G. Eberle
1933 Evander F. Kelly
1935 Samuel L. Hilton
1936 Edmund N. Gathercoal
1937 J. Leon Lascoff
1938 Henry C. Christensen
1940 Robert L. Swain
1941 George D. Beal
1942 Josiah K. Lilly
1943 Robert P. Fischelis
1944 H. Evert Kendig
1945 Joseph Rosin
1947 Rufus A. Lyman
1948 Andrew G. DuMez
1949 Ernest Little
1950 Edwin L. Newcomb
1951 Hugo H. Schaefer
1952 Patrick H. Costello
1953 Hugh C. Muldoon
1955 Roy B. Cook
1956 Frank W. Moudry
1957 W. Paul Briggs
1958 Eli Lilly
1959 Justin L. Powers
1960 Ivor Griffith
1962 Harry J. Anslinger
1963 Glenn L. Jenkins
1964 Robert A. Hardt
1965 K. K. Chen
1967 William S. Apple
1969 George F. Archambault
1970 Don E. Francke
1971 Linwood F. Tice
1972 Glenn Sonnedecker

Theodore William Richards Medal

Awarded biennially by the Northeastern Section of the American Chemical Society for conspicuous achievement in the field of pure chemistry.

1930 Theodore W. Richards
1932 Arthur A. Noyes
1934 Gregory P. Baxter
1936 Charles A. Kraus
1938 Gilbert A. Lewis
1940 Claude S. Hudson
1942 Frederik G. Keyes
1946 Roger Adams
1947 Linus Pauling
1948 Edwin J. Cohn
1950 John G. Kirkwood
1952 Morris S. Kharasch
1954 George Scatchard
1956 Melvin Calvin
1958 Robert B. Woodward
1960 Robert S. Mulliken
1962 Saul Winstein
1964 Lars Onsager
1966 Paul D. Bartlett
1968 George B. Kistiakowsky

Theodore Roosevelt Distinguished Service Medal

Awarded annually by the Theodore Roosevelt Association for notable contributions in the following domains: public and international law, industrial peace, American literature, outdoor life, national defense, international affairs, administration of public office, conservation of natural resources, advancement of social justice, expression of the pioneer virtues, distinguished public service by a private citizen, and leadership of youth and the development of the American character.

1923 Louisa L. Schuyler
Henry Fairfield Osborn
Leonard Wood
1924 Oliver Wendell Holmes
Charles W. Eliot
Elihu Root
1925 Gifford Pinchot
George B. Grinnell
Martha Berry
1926 Daniel C. Beard
William S. Sims
Albert J. Beveridge
1927 John B. Moore
Herbert Hoover
John J. Pershing
1928 Charles Evans Hughes
Frank M. Chapman
Charles A. Lindbergh
1929 Herbert Putnam
Owen Wister
Owen D. Young
1930 Richard E. Byrd
William Green
Hastings H. Hart
1931 Hamlin Garland
Benjamin N. Cardozo
C. Hart Merriam
1932 Robert A. Millikan
1933 Stephen Vincent Benet
1934 William Allen White
Samuel Seabury
1935 William H. Park
1936 Helen Keller
Anne Sullivan Macy
1937 James H. Dillard
1938 Carter Glass
Robert Moses
1939 George Washington Carver
Frank R. McCoy
Carl Sandburg
1940 Grenville Clark
Homer Folks
Chester H. Rowell
1942 Rufus M. Jones
Henry L. Stimson
Booth Tarkington
1943 Eleanor Robson Belmont
Jay N. Darling
Joseph C. Grew
1945 Vannevar Bush
Cordell Hull
George C. Marshall
1946 Irving Berlin
Dwight D. Eisenhower
William F. Halsey
Douglas MacArthur
Chester N. Nimitz
1947 Omar N. Bradley
Learned Hand
Jeremiah Milbank
Arthur Hays Sulzberger
1948 James B. Conant
Millicent C. McIntosh
Arthur H. Vandenberg
1949 Lucius D. Clay
David Hinshaw
J. Edgar Hoover
1950 Warren R. Austin
Bernard M. Baruch
Anne O'Hare McCormick
1951 Frederick M. Davenport
Lewis W. Douglas
Frank C. Laubach
1952 John Foster Dulles
Fairfield Osborn
1953 William Beebe
Van Wyck Brooks
1954 Ralph J. Bunche
Robert Frost
DeWitt Wallace
Mrs. DeWitt Wallace
1955 Arthur H. Compton
Thomas E. Dewey
1956 Herman Hagedorn
Samuel Eliot Morison
Clarence B. Randall
1957 David E. Finley
Helen Rogers Reid
1958 Alfred M. Gruenther
Hyman G. Rickover
1959 Horace M. Albright
Henry Cabot Lodge
1960 Irving S. Olds
Don Walsh
Theodore Roosevelt, Jr.
1961 Erwin D. Canham
John J. McCloy
Alan B. Shepard, Jr.
1962 Arthur H. Dean
John H. Glenn, Jr.
Stanley M. Isaacs
1963 Laurance S. Rockefeller
1964 Louis K. Diamond
Gilbert H. Grosvenor
Harry L. Shapiro
1965 Richard K. Mellon
Robert D. Murphy
Conrad L. Wirth
1966 Wallace K. Harrison
Henry Viscardi, Jr.
1967 Arthur Kantrowitz
William B. Walsh
Roy Wilkins

Richard and Hinda Rosenthal Foundation Awards

I Administered by the National Institute of Arts and Letters and presented to the author of a novel published during the preceding 12 months that is judged to be a considerable literary achievement.

1957 Elizabeth Spencer
1958 Bernard Malamud
1959 Frederick Buechner
1960 John Updike
1961 John H. Knowles
1962 Paule Marshall
1963 William M. Kelley
1964 Ivan Gold
1965 Thomas Berger
1966 Tom Cole
1967 Thomas Pynchon
1968 Joyce Carol Oates
1969 Frederick Exley
1970 Jonathan Strong
1971 Donald Perlis

II Administered by the National Institute of Arts and Letters and presented to a young American painter of distinction.

1960 Ann Steinbrocker
1961 Zubel Kachadoorian
1962 Robert Andrew Parker
1963 Karen Arden
1964 Gregory Gillespie
1965 Marcia Marcus
1966 Howard Hack
1967 Robert D'Arista
1968 Elizabeth Osborn
1969 Nicholas Sperakis

Rumford Prize

Awarded by the American Academy of Arts and Sciences to recognize important discoveries or useful improvements in the fields of heat or light.

1839 Robert Hare
1862 John Ericsson
1865 Daniel Treadwell
1866 Alvan Clark
1869 George H. Corliss
1871 Joseph Harrison, Jr.
1873 Lewis M. Rutherfurd
1875 John W. Draper
1880 Josiah W. Gibbs
1883 Henry A. Rowland
1886 Samuel P. Langley
1888 Albert A. Michelson
1891 Edward C. Pickering
1895 Thomas A. Edison
1898 James E. Keeler
1899 Charles F. Brush
1900 Carl Barus
1901 Elihu Thomson

1902 George E. Hale
1904 Ernest F. Nichols
1907 Edward G. Acheson
1909 Robert W. Wood
1910 Charles G. Curtis
1911 James M. Crafts
1912 Frederic E. Ives
1913 Joel Stebbins
1914 William D. Coolidge
1915 Charles G. Abbot
1917 Percy W. Bridgman
1918 Theodore Lyman
1920 Irving Langmuir
1925 Henry N. Russell
1926 Arthur H. Compton
1928 Edward L. Nichols
1931 Karl T. Compton
1933 Harlow Shapley
1937 William W. Coblentz
1939 George R. Harrison
1941 Vladimir K. Zworykin
1943 C. E. Kenneth Mees
1945 Edwin H. Land
1947 Edmund N. Harvey
1949 Ira S. Bowen
1951 Herbert E. Ives
1953 Enrico Fermi
Willis E. Lamb, Jr.
Lars Onsager
1955 James Franck
1957 Subrahmanyan Chandrasekhar
1959 George Wald
1961 Charles H. Townes
1963 Hans A. Bethe
1965 Samuel C. Collins
William D. McElroy
1967 Robert H. Dicke
Cornelis B. Van Niel
1968 Maarten Schmidt

Saltus Gold Medal For Merit

Awarded by the National Academy of Design to recognize outstanding achievement in painting or sculpture.

1908 Edmund C. Tarbell
1909 George de F. Brush
1910 Douglas Volk
1911 John C. Johansen
1912 Bruce Crane
1913 Gardner Symons
1914 Cecilia Beaux
1915 Abbot H. Thayer
1916 Emil Carlsen
1917 Charles S. Chapman
1918 Joseph T. Pearson, Jr.
1919 Malcolm Parcell
1920 Anna V. Hyatt
1921 Charles H. Davis
1922 Anna V. Hyatt
1923 Eugene F. Savage
1924 Laura G. Fraser
1925 John E. Costigan
1926 Attilio Piccirilli
1927 Edward W. Redfield
1928 Laura G. Fraser
1929 Carl Rungius
1930 Ernest Lawson
1931 Louis Betts
1933 Ruth Nickerson
1934 Harry W. Watrous
1935 Childe Hassam
1936 Jonas Lie
1937 Arthur Lee
1938 Jonas Lie
1940 Charles S. Chapman
1941 Robert Brackman
1942 C. Paul Jennewein
1943 Kenneth H. Miller
1944 Jon Corbino
1945 Stanley Crane
1946 Adlai S. Hardin
1947 Jean de Marco
1948 Gifford Beal
1949 Ben Stahl
1950 Alexander Brook
1951 Charles Hopkinson
1952 Karl H. Gruppe
1953 Hobson Pittman
1954 Everett G. Du Pen
1955 Stephen Etnier
1956 Andrew Winter
1957 Raphael Soyer
1958 Lenard Kester
1959 Umberto Romano
1960 Katharine L. Weems
1961 Aaron Bohrod
1962 John Koch
1963 Paul Manship
1964 Antonio P. Martino
1965 Alan Price
1966 Leon Kroll
1967 Joseph Floch
1968 George Bobritzky
1969 Chen Chi
1970 Gertrude K. Lathrop

Margaret Sanger Award

Presented annually by Planned Parenthood – World Population to honor distinguished service in promoting the course of family planning and in advancing social justice.

1966 William H. Draper, Jr.
Carl G. Hartman
Martin Luther King. Jr.
Lyndon B. Johnson
1967 John D. Rockefeller III
1968 Ernest Gruening
1970 Joseph Tidings
1971 Louis Hellman
1972 Alan F. Guttmacher

William Lawrence Saunders Gold Medal

Awarded annually by the American Institute of Mining, Metallurgical and Petroleum Engineers to recognize achievement in the mining of metals, coal, and other nonmetallic minerals.

1927 David W. Brunton
1928 Herbert Hoover
1929 Hohn Hays Hammond
1930 Daniel C. Jackling
1931 Francis W. Maclennan
1932 F. W. Bradley
1933 Walter H. Aldridge
1934 Pope Yeatman
1935 James MacNaughton
1936 Clinton H. Crane
1937 Erskine Ramsay
1939 Louis S. Cates
1941 Herman C. Bellinger
1944 George B. Harrington
1946 Fred Searls, Jr.
1947 LeRoy Salsich
1949 Stanly A. Easton
1950 Howard N. Eavenson
1951 Clyde E. Weed
1954 Simeon S. Clarke
1956 Louis Buchman
1958 W. J. Coulter
1959 John B. Knaebel
1960 Robert J. Linney
1961 Marcus D. Banghart
1962 Joseph H. Reid
1963 Edward I. Renouard
1964 Walter C. Lawson
1965 Francis Cameron
1966 Wesley P. Goss
1967 Ralph D. Parker
1968 Charles M. Brinckerhoff
1970 Elmer A. Jones

Sedgwick Memorial Medal

Awarded annually by the American Public Health Association to honor distinguished service over a long period of time in areas of special interest to the association.

1929 Charles V. Chapin
1930 Theobald Smith
1931 George W. McCoy
1932 William H. Park
1933 Milton J. Rosenau
1934 Edwin O. Jordan
1935 Haven Emerson
1936 Frederick F. Russell
1938 Wade H. Frost
1939 Thomas Parran
1940 Hans Zinsser
1941 Charles Armstrong
1942 Charles Edward Winslow
1943 James S. Simmons
1944 Ernest W. Goodpasture
1946 Karl F. Meyer
1947 Reginald M. Atwater
1948 Abel Wolman
1949 Henry F. Vaughan
1950 Rolla E. Dyer
1951 Edward S. Godfrey, Jr.
1952 Kenneth F. Maxcy
1953 Carl E. Buck
1954 Wilson G. Smillie
1955 Albert J. Chesley
1956 Frederick W. Jackson
1957 Lowell J. Reed
1958 Martha M. Eliot
1959 Louis I. Dublin
1960 Fred T. Foard
1961 Frank G. Boudreau
1962 Ira V. Hiscock
1963 Gaylord W. Anderson
1964 Leona Baumgartner
1965 Willimina R. Walsh
1966 Fred L. Soper
1967 George Baehr
1968 Herman E. Hilleboe
1969 Marion W. Sheahan
1970 Hugh R. Leavell
1971 Margaret G. Arnstein
1972 Paul B. Cornely

Shelley Memorial Award

Presented annually by the Poetry Society of America to a living American poet selected on the basis of genius and need.

1929 Conrad Aiken
1930 Lizette W. Reese
1931 Archibald MacLeish
1932 Stephen Vincent Benet
1933 Lola Ridge
Frances Frost
1934 Lola Ridge
Marya Zaturemska
1935 Josephine Miles
1936 Charlotte Wilder
Ben Belitt
1937 Lincoln Fitzel
1938 Robert Francis
Harry Brown
1939 Herbert Bruncken
Winfield T. Scott
1940 Marianne Moore
1941 Ridgely Torrence
1942 Robert Penn Warren
Percy MacKaye
1943 Edgar Lee Masters
1944 E. E. Cummings
1945 Karl Shapiro
1946 Rolfe Humphries
1947 Janet Lewis
1948 John Berryman
1949 Louis Kent
1950 Jeremy Ingalls
1951 Richard Eberhart
1952 Elizabeth Bishop
1953 Kenneth Patchen
1954 Leonie Adams
1955 Robert Fitzgerald
1956 George Abbe
1957 Kenneth Rexroth
1958 Jose Garcia Villa
1959 Delmore Schwartz
1960 Robinson Jeffers
1961 Theodore Roethke
1962 Eric Barker
1963 William Stafford
1964 Ruth Stone
1965 David Ignatow
1966 Anne Sexton
1967 May Swenson
1968 Ann Stanford
1969 X. J. Kennedy
Mary Oliver
1970 Louise Townsend Nicholl
Adrienne Rich
1971 Galway Kinnell

Elmer A. Sperry Award

An award presented under the joint sponsorship of several engineering societies in recognition of a distinguished engineering contribution which has advanced the art of transportation.

1955 William F. Gibbs
1956 Donald W. Douglas
1957 Harold L. Hamilton
Richard M. Dilworth
Eugene W. Kettering
1960 Frederick D. Braddon
1961 Robert G. Letourneau
1962 Lloyd J. Hibbard
1963 Earl A. Thompson
1964 Igor I. Sikorsky
Michael E. Gluhareff

1965 Maynard L. Pennell
Richard L. Rouzie
John E. Steiner
William H. Cook
Richards L. Loesch, Jr.
1967 Edward R. Dye
Hugh DeHaven
Robert A. Wolf
1969 Douglas C. MacMillan
M. Nielsen
Edward L. Teale, Jr.

Spingarn Medal

Awarded annually by the National Association for the Advancement of Colored People to recognize the highest achievement by an American Negro in the many fields of human endeavor.

1915 Ernest E. Just
1916 Charles Young
1917 Harry T. Burleigh
1918 William S. Braithwaite
1919 Archibald H. Grimke
1920 William E. B. DuBois
1921 Charles S. Gilpin
1922 Mary B. Talbert
1923 George Washington Carver
1924 Roland Hayes
1925 James Weldon Johnson
1926 Carter G. Woodson
1927 Anthony Overton
1928 Charles W. Chesnutt
1929 Mordecai W. Johnson
1930 Henry A. Hunt
1931 Richard B. Harrison
1932 Robert R. Moton
1933 Max Yergan
1934 William T. B. Williams
1935 Mary McLeod Bethune
1936 John Hope
1937 Walter White
1939 Marian Anderson
1940 Louis T. Wright
1941 Richard Wright
1942 A. Philip Randolph
1943 WilliaM H. Hastie
1944 Charles R. Drew
1945 Paul Robeson
1946 Thurgood Marshall
1947 Percy L. Julian
1948 Channing H. Tobias
1949 Ralph J. Bunche
1950 Charles H. Houston
1951 Mabel Keaton Staupers
1952 Harry T. Moore
1953 Paul R. Williams
1954 Theodore K. Lawless
1955 Carl Murphy
1956 Jack R. Robinson
1957 Martin Luther King, Jr.
1958 Daisy Bates
1959 Edward (Duke) Ellington
1960 Langston Hughes
1961 Kenneth B. Clark
1962 Robert C. Weaver
1963 Medgar W. Evers
1964 Roy Wilkins
1965 Leontyne Price
1966 John H. Johnson
1967 Edward W. Brooke
1968 Sammy Davis, Jr.
1969 Clarence M. Mitchell, Jr.
1970 Leon Sullivan
1971 Gordon Parks

Spirit of St. Louis Medal

Awarded from time to time by the American Society of Mechanical Engineers to recognize meritorious service in the advancement of aeronautics.

1929 Daniel Guggenheim
1932 Paul Litchfield
1935 Will Rogers
1938 James H. Doolittle
1941 John E. Younger
1944 George W. Lewis
1947 John K. Northrop
1950 Reinout P. Kroon
1954 Arthur E. Raymond
1955 Ralph S. Damon
1958 George S. Schairer
1961 Samuel K. Hoffman
1962 Robert H. Widmer
1963 Frederick C. Crawford
1964 Robert R. Gilruth
1965 William H. Pickering
1966 Christopher C. Craft
1967 Ira G. Hedrick
1968 George S. Moore
1969 G. Merritt Preston
1970 Clarence L. Johnson
1971 Ralph L. Creel
1972 Neil A. Armstrong

David W. Taylor Medal

Awarded by the Society of Naval Architects and Marine Engineers for notable achievement in the areas of special interest to the society.

1936 David W. Taylor
1938 William L. Emmett
1939 Hugo P. Frear
1940 John F. Metten
1942 Samuel M. Robinson
1943 William Hovgaard
1945 Edward L. Cochrane
1946 William F. Gibbs
1947 David Arnott
1948 Earle W. Mills
1949 George G. Sharp
1950 Harold E. Saunders
1951 C. Richard Waller
1953 John E. Burkhardt
1954 Edwin L. Stewart
1955 Kenneth S. M. Davidson
1956 Andrew I. McKee
1957 David P. Brown
1958 John C. Niedermair
1959 Olin J. Stephens
1960 Glenn B. Warren
1961 Mark L. Ireland, Jr.
1962 Charles D. Wheelock
1963 Arthur R. Gatewood
1964 Henry A. Schade
1965 John P. Comstock
1966 Richard B. Couch
1967 Wilson D. Leggett, Jr.
1968 Matthew G. Forrest
1969 Douglas C. MacMillan

Viking Fund Medal

Awarded from time to time (originally each year) by the Wenner-Gren Foundation for Anthropological Research for notable achievement in anthropology and archaeology.

General Anthropology

1946 Alfred L. Kroeber
1947 Robert H. Lowie
1948 John R. Swanton
1949 George P. Murdock
1950 Clyde K. Kluckhohn
1951 Ralph Linton
1952 Julian H. Steward
1953 Melville J. Herskovits
1954 Robert Redfield
1955 A. Irving Hallowell
1956 Fred Eggan
1957 Margaret Mead
1959 Leslie A. White
1960 Leslie Spier
1961 Sol Tax

Archaeology

1946 Alfred V. Kidder
1947 John O. Brew
1948 Alex D. Krieger
1949 Hallum L. Movius, Jr.
1950 Emil W. Haury
1951 Frank H. H. Roberts, Jr.
1953 Gordon R. Willey
1954 William D. Strong
1955 J. Eric S. Thompson
1956 Junius B. Bird
1957 James B. Griffin
1958 Jesse D. Jennings
1959 Irving B. Rouse
1960 S. K. Lothrop

Physical Anthropology

1946 Franz Weidenreich
1947 Ernest A. Hooton
1948 Adolph H. Schultz
1949 William K. Gregory
1950 Wilton M. Krogman
1951 Carleton S. Coon
1952 William L. Straus, Jr.
1953 T. Dale Stewart
1954 William W. Howells
1956 Mildred Trotter
1959 William Greulich
1960 Sherwood L. Washburn

Marjorie Peabody Waite Award

Presented annually by the National Institute of Arts and Letters to an older person for continuing achievement and integrity in his art and given in rotation to an artist, a composer, and a writer.

1956 Fred Nagler
1957 Theodore Ward Chanler
1958 Dorothy Parker
1959 Leon Hartl
1960 Louise Talma
1961 Edward McSorley
1962 Abraham Walkowitz
1963 Richard Donovan
1964 Dawn Powell
1965 Paul Burlin
1966 Harry Partch
1967 Stringfellow Barr
1968 Abraham Harriton
1969 Herbert Elwell
1970 Ramon Guthrie
1971 Ben Benn
1972 Vittorio Rieti

John Price Wetherill Medal

Awarded by the Franklin Institute for discovery or invention in the physical sciences or for new and important combinations of principles or methods already known.

1926 Frank Twyman
1927 Carl Akeley
1928 Albert S. Howell
Frank E. Ross
1929 Gustave Fast
William H. Mason
1930 Charles S. Chrisman
William N. Jennings
1931 Thomas T. Gray
Arthur J. Mason
Henry M. Sutton,
Walter L. Steele,
and Edwin G. Steele
Edward C. Wente
1932 Halvor O. Hem
Frank Wenner
1933 Henry S. Hulbert,
Francis C. McMath,
and Robert R. McMath
1934 E. Newton Harvey and
Alfred L. Loomis
1935 Francis F. Lucas
Robert Naumberg
James E. Shrader
Louis B. Tuckerman
Henry E. Warren
1936 Albert L. Marsh
1939 William A. Hyde
1940 Laurens Hammond
Edward E. Kleinschmidt
Howard L. Krum
1941 Harold S. Black
1943 Robert H. Leach
1944 Willem F. Westendorp
Richard C. du Pont
1946 Lewis A. Rodert
1947 Kenneth S. M. Davidson
1948 Wendell F. Hess
1949 Edgar C. Bain
Thomas L. Fawick
Harlan D. Fowler
1950 Kenneth C. D. Hickman
Donald W. Kerst
Russell H. Varian
and Sigurd F. Varian
1951 Samuel C. Collins
Reid B. Gray
Gaylord W. Penney
1952 Harrison P. Hood
and Martin E. Nordberg
Albert J. Williams, Jr.

1953 Robert H. Dalton
and S. Donald Stookey
1954 William D. Buckingham
Clarence N. Hickman
Edwin T. Lorig
1955 Rene A. Higonnet
and Louis M. Moyroud
1957 Warren W. Carpenter
1959 Robert B. Aitchison
Clarence Zener
1960 Walter Juda
Victor Vacquier
1961 Albert E. Hitchcock and
Percy W. Zimmerman
1962 S. Donald Stookey
Chien-Shiung Wu
Ernest Ambler
Raymond W. Hayward
Dale D. Hoppes
Ralph P. Hudson
1963 Daryl M. Chapin,
Calvin S. Fuller,
and Gerald L. Pearson
1964 Howard H. Aiken
Bernd T. Matthias
and John K. Hulm
John E. Kunzler
1965 Wendell F. Moore
John H. Reynolds
Frederick D. Rossini
Eugene Merle Shoemaker
and Edward Ching-Te
Chao
Fred N. Spiess
1966 Howard G. Rogers
1967 Ernest O. Wollan
1968 Nathan Cohn
1969 George R. Cowan,
John J. Douglass, and
Arnold H. Holtzman
1970 Paul D. Bartlett
1972 Otto H. Schmitt

Woodrow Wilson Award

Awarded annually by Princeton University to an outstanding alumnus.

1957 Norman Armour
1958 Allen O. Whipple
1959 Charles L. House
1960 Bayard Dodge
1961 Raymond B. Fosdick
1962 C. Tyler Wood
1963 Adlai E. Stevenson
1964 Henry D. Smyth
1965 Nicholas deB. Katzenbach
1966 William F. Ballard
1967 Eugene Carson Blake
1968 James H. Cleveland
1969 Walsh McDermott
1970 John B. Oakes
1971 George B. Schultz
1972 Ralph Nader

Wright Brothers Memorial Trophy

Awarded annually by the National Aeronautic Association to honor public service of enduring value to aviation in the United States.

1948 William F. Durand
1949 Charles A. Lindbergh
1950 Grover Loening
1951 Jerome C. Hunsaker
1952 James H. Doolittle
1953 Carl Hinshaw
1954 Theodore Von Karman
1955 Hugh L. Dryden
1956 Edward P. Warher
1957 Stuart Symington
1958 John F. Victory
1959 William P. MacCracken, Jr.
1960 Frederick C. Crawford
1961 A. S. Mike Monroney
1962 John Stack
1963 Donald W. Douglas
1964 Harry F. Guggenheim
1965 Jerome F. Lederer
1966 Juan T. Trippe
1967 Igor I. Sikorski
1968 Warren G. Magnuson
1969 William M. Allen
1970 Howard W. Cannon

INDEX

AANDAHL, Fred G. 230, 350
ABBEE
  Cleveland 600
  George 610
ABBETT, Leon 341*
ABBEY, Edwin A. 607
ABBITT, Watkins M. 225, 228, 231, 234, 237, 241, 244, 247, 250, 253, 257, 260, 263
ABBOT
  Charles G. 502, 610
  Theophilus C. 475
ABBOTT
  Amos 87, 89, 91
  Frank 566
  Frank F. 570
  George 586
  Grace 603
  Henry P.A. 512, 520
  Jere 502
  Jo 133, 136, 139, 141, 144
  Joel 66, 68, 69, 71
  John 452*
  John T. 426
  Joseph C. 111, 113, 348
  Josiah G. 118
  Nehemiah 100
  William L. 573
  William M. 574
ABDNOR, James 266
ABEEL, Johannes 449*
ABEGG, Martin G. 466
ABEL
  Hazel H. 233, 334
  I.W. 559
  John J. 563, 596
  John R. 566
ABELE, Homer E. 249
ABELL, Irwin W. 565, 569, 599
ABERCROMBIE
  James 94, 96
  John W. 167, 170, 465
ABERNATHY, Roy 543
ABERNETHY
  Charles L. 181, 185, 188, 191, 194, 198, 201
  Thomas G. 217, 220, 223, 227, 230, 233, 236, 239, 242, 246, 249, 252, 255, 258, 262
  William S. 534
ABEY, Joseph A. 580
ABLEWHITE, Hayward W. 512, 521
ABOUREZK, James G. 263, 266, 368
ABRAMS
  Creighton W., Jr. 400
  Frank W. 553
ABT, Isaac A. 590
ABZUG, Bella S. 262, 265
ACHARD, F.H. 600
ACHESON
  Dean G. 34, 38, 587, 596, 608
  E. Campion 510, 519
  Edward G. 575, 589, 610
  Ernest F. 143, 146, 149, 151, 154, 157, 160
  John C. 474
  Marcus W. 271
ACHILLES, Theodore C. 435
ACKER
  Charles E. 594
  Ephraim L. 115
ACKERMAN
  Ernest R. 177, 181, 184, 188, 191, 194
  Harry S. 577*
  Ralph H. 427
  Richard 525
  William C. 567
  William K. 548
ACKLEN, Joseph H. 121, 123
ACKLEY, H. Gardner 431
ACKLIN, A.A. 545
ACREE, Vernon D. 443
ADAIR
  Charles W., Jr. 434, 439
  E. Ross 229, 232, 235, 238, 242, 245, 248, 251, 255, 258, 428
  Frank E. 565
  Hugh 331
  J. Leroy 200, 203
  John 59, 77, 308*
  John A.M. 158, 161, 164, 167, 170
ADAM
  James N. 451
  Malcolm 550, 551
ADAMS
  Albert S. 580
  Alva 285*
  Alva B. 183, 199, 203, 206, 209, 212, 285*
  Andrew 4, 5, 287
  Arlin M. 271
  Arthur S. 476
  Benjamin 65, 66, 68
  Brock 254, 257, 260, 263, 266
  Charles 424
  Charles C. 501, 575
  Charles F. 552*
  Charles Francis 554
  Charles Francis (b. 1807) 102, 104, 429, 563
  Charles Francis (b. 1866) 33, 42, 567, 575
  Charles H. 119
  Charles K. 468, 486, 567
  Comfort A. 595, 599
  D.W. 578
  Donald A. 580
  Edward D. 596
  Edward T. 587
  Elmer B. 272
  Emory S. 401
  Frank D. 576
  Frank Y. 465
  Frederick B. 549
  Frederick B., Jr. 500
  Gabriel 459
  George A. 455
  George B. 567
  George E. 127, 129, 132, 134
  George M. 110, 112, 114, 116
  Green 91, 102
  Hampton 536
  Henry 567, 583
  Henry C. 566
  Henry Cullen 155, 158
  Herbert 577, 579*, 591, 603
  J.C. 459
  J. Donald 580
  James H. 365
  James Truslow 583
  Jasper 472
  Jewett W. 335
  John (Mass.) 3, 6, 10, 13, 14, 15*, 51*, 52, 53, 563, 597
  John (N.Y.) 65, 79
  John (Va.) 459
  John C. (Educator) 472
  John C. (Mayor) 459
  John E. 564
  John J. 128, 130
  John Quincy 13, 15, 16*, 24*, 38, 57, 59, 60, 77, 79, 81, 82, 84, 86, 87, 89, 91, 319, 429*, 433, 435, 436, 437, 563, 597
  John T. 285
  Joseph Q. 499
  Julius W. 572
  K.S. 551*
  Leason H. 601
  Leonie 589, 592
  Orval W. 564
  Parmenio 71, 73
  Paul D. 401, 404, 405
  Philip E. 566
  Philip R. 498*, 502
  Porter H. 478, 577
  Ralph E. 465
  Raymond D. 569
  Richard, Sr. 459
  Robert, Jr. 141, 143, 146, 149, 151, 154, 157
  Robert H. 76, 326
  Robert McCormick 501
  Roger 563, 565, 590, 594, 596, 604, 608, 609
  Rufus D. 460
  Ruth M. 485
  S.E. 578
  Samuel 3, 4*, 6, 15, 319
  Samuel (Ark.) 281
  Samuel C., Jr. 434
  Sherman 220, 339
  Silas 140
  Stanley 572*
  Stephen 89, 95, 97, 99, 326
  Thomas 4, 7
  Thomas S. 566
  W.G. 600
  W.I.L. 579
  Walter 475
  Walter S. 564
  Wayman 589
  Wilbur L. 199
  William 532
  William F. 507, 519
  William H. 285
  William H.H. 473
  William R. 552
ADAMSON, William C. 145, 147, 150, 153, 155, 158, 161, 164, 167, 170, 173, 273
ADDABBO, Joseph P. 246, 249, 252, 256, 259, 262, 265
ADDAMS
  Clifford 593
  Jane 597, 605
  William 73, 75
ADDICKS, Lawrence 575
ADDINGTON, Isaac 10
ADDOMS, F.E. 451
ADDONIZIO, Hugh J. 227, 230, 233, 236, 239, 243, 246
ADERHOLD, Omer C. 472
ADGATE, Asa 65
ADKINS,
  Charles 186, 190, 193, 196
  Homer M. 282
ADLER
  Benjamin 479
  Felix 538
ADOLPH, Edward F. 571
ADOUE, J.B., Jr. 453
ADRAIN, Garnett B. 101, 103
ADRIAN
  Barbara 589
  William L. 527
ADSIT
  O.H. 455
  P.H. 455
AFFLECK, James G. 543
AGAR, Herbert 584
AGASSIZ
  Alexander 563
  Elizabeth C. 479
  Louis 563, 597
AGEE, James 586
AGETON, Arthur A. 434
AGNEW
  Daniel 359
  Donald C. 478
  John 452
  Spiro T. 14, 19, 257, 260, 263, 318
  William H. 469, 474
AGUILAR, Cristobal 456*
AHERN, Michael J. 469
AHL, John A. 101
AHLBERG, Clark D. 486
AHLERT, Fred E. 572
AHR, George W. 529
AHRENS, Ellen W. 607
AIKEN
  Charles A. 483
  Conrad 583, 589, 592*, 602, 603, 604, 610
  D. Wyatt 122, 124, 126, 129, 131
  Edmun 546
  George D. 215, 218, 222, 225, 228, 231, 234, 237, 240, 244, 247, 250, 253, 257, 260, 263, 266, 377*
  Howard H. 594, 610
  William 96, 97, 99, 364
  Wyatt 154, 157, 160, 163, 166, 169, 172
AIKENS, Charles T. 482
AIKMAN, John M. 575
AILES, Stephen 399
AIMISON, William 558
AINEY, William D.B. 166, 169
AINSLIE
  George 459
  Peter 536
AINSWORTH
  Fred C. 401
  John C. 554
  Lucien L. 118
  Robert A., Jr. 271
  William N. 530
AISHTON, Richard 546
AITCHISON, Robert B. 612
AITKEN
  David D. 140, 143
  Robert 579, 591
  Robert G. 564
AKELEY, Carl 611
AKERMAN, Amos T. 28, 41
AKERS
  Anthony B. 433
  Earl 462
  Thomas P. 99
AKIN
  Harry 450
  Henry C. 579
  Spencer B. 403
  Theron 165
  Warren 343
AKINS, Zoe 584
ALBAUGH, Walter H. 208
ALBEE
  Edward 587
  George W. 571
ALBERGER, Franklin A. 451
ALBERS
  Josef 607
  Joseph H. 527
ALBERT
  A. Adrian 568
  Allen D. 580
  Carl 224, 227, 231, 234, 237, 240, 243, 246, 250, 253, 256, 259, 260, 262, 263, 265
  Charles F. 597
  William J. 116
ALBERTSON
  James H. 486
  Nathaniel 93
ALBIN, C.E. 460
ALBRECHT, H.R. 477
ALBRIGHT
  Charles 117
  Charles J. 99
  Edward 428
  Fuller 599
  Horace M. 444, 492, 591, 609
  Ivan 589, 593
  Jacob 531
  Louis B. 459*
  William F. 591
ALCORN
  Howard W. 289
  James L. 114, 116, 119, 326*
  Robert L., Jr. 601
ALDEN
  A.E. 457
  George H. 486
  James 418
  John 3
  Joseph 485
  Timothy 465
  Vernon R. 478
ALDERMAN
  Edwin A. 477, 483, 484
  Edwin I. 579
ALDERSON
  John D. 136, 139, 141
  Wroe 568
ALDIS, Asa 375
ALDISERT, Ruggero L. 271
ALDREDGE, Sawnie R. 452
ALDRICH
  Bailey 271
  Chester H. 333
  Cyrus 102, 104
  Donald B. 514
  J. Frank 139, 142
  John W. 569
  Malcolm P. 491
  Nelson W. 124, 126, 128, 131, 133, 136, 138, 141, 144, 146, 149, 151, 154, 157, 160, 163, 362
  Richard S. 185, 188, 192, 195, 198
  Robert A. 599
  Truman H. 142
  William 120, 122, 125
  William F. 142, 144, 147
  Winthrop W. 429, 545
ALDRIDGE, Walter H. 596, 610
ALDRIN, Edwin E., Jr. 596*, 598, 610
ALEMANY, Joseph S. 524, 527
ALERDING, Herman J. 526
ALESHIRE
  Arthur W. 208
  James B. 403
ALEXANDER
  Adam R. 72, 73
  Archibald 471, 532
  Armstead M. 128
  Ashton 474
  Bill 257, 260, 263
  Claude L. 491
  De Alva S. 146, 148, 151, 154, 157, 159, 162
  Eben 429, 435, 436
  Edward P. 395
  Evan S. 59, 60
  George (educator) 483
  George (mayor) 456
  Hattie E. 599
  Henry P. 93
  Hugh Q. 234, 237, 240, 243, 246
  J. David 479
  James, Jr. 83
  James P. 269, 373
  James W. 546

John 64, 65
John (mayor) 452
John E. 600
John G. 210
John W. 577, 578, 607*
Joshua W. 32*, 46, 159, 162, 165, 168, 171, 174, 177
Lloyd 602
Maitland 532
Mark 69, 70, 72, 73, 75, 77, 78
Moses 298, 450*
Myrl E. 566
Nathaniel 58, 59, 347
Robert 5
Stephen 563
Sydenham B. 138, 141
William 467
William C. 546
William H. 570
Willis W. 564
ALEXANDERSON, E.F.W. 595, 598
ALEXOPOULOS, Constantine J. 574
ALEY, Robert J. 467, 474
ALFORD
Jabe 456
Julius C. 80, 84, 85
T. Dale 241, 244
ALFRED, James V. 373
ALGER
Bruce R. 237, 240, 244, 247, 250
Frederick M., Jr. 424
Philip L. 599
Russell A. 30, 40, 151, 153, 156, 322*
ALGREN, Nelson 602
ALIOTO, Joseph L. 461
ALKUS, Albert 460
ALLAN, Chilton 77, 79, 80
ALLEE
J. Frank 150, 153, 155, 291
W.C. 573, 575
ALLEGAERT, J. 543*
ALLEN
A. Leonard 207, 210, 213, 217, 220, 223, 226, 229
Alfred G. 166, 169, 172
Alvarin 456
Amos L. 148, 150, 153, 156, 159, 162
Andrew 7
Arthur A. 593
Arthur W. 565
B.M. 574
Charles 93, 95
Charles E. 574
Charles F. 474
Charles H. 130, 132
Charles M. 594, 596
Clarence E. 144
Cotton H. 452
Diarca H. 532
Edgar V. 567, 589
Edward 481
Edward E. 603
Edward H. 455
Edward N. 454
Edward P. 527
Edward P. (Mich.) 132, 135
Edward S. 450
Elisha H. 86
Ethelbert F. 579
Florence E. 271
Frank B. 601
Frank G. 321
Fred H., Jr. 599
Frederic D. 570
Frederick I. 444
George G. 546*
George V. 429, 430*, 433, 439, 445, 491
George W. 285
H. Julian 597, 608
Harold B. 566
Heman 67, 78, 80, 81, 83, 425
Henry 538
Henry C. 157
Henry D. 148, 150
Henry J. 193, 306*
Henry T. 410
Henry W. 311
Horace N. 431
Horatio 572
Ivan, Jr. 449, 598
J.P. 458
J.W. 536
James 403
James B. 257, 260, 263, 279
James C. 96, 98, 106
Joel A. 569
John 54
John B. 136, 139, 381
John C. 186, 190, 193, 196
John D. 559
John E. 339
John J., Jr. 222, 225, 229, 232, 235, 238
John J. 80, 378
John M. 130, 132, 135, 137, 140, 143, 145, 148
John S. 470, 481
John W. 83, 84, 452
Jonathan M. 465
Joseph 61
Joseph E. 453
Judson 84
L. Scott 531
Laurence E. 584
Leo E. 200, 203, 206, 209, 213, 216, 219, 223, 226, 229, 232, 235, 238, 242
Nathaniel 68
Orlando 451
Oscar K. 312
Phillip 97, 99, 101, 361*
Raymond B. 484
Rex W. 567
Richard 538
Robert (Tenn.) 69, 70, 72, 73
Robert 75, 77, 78
Robert E.L. 186
Robert G. 208, 211
Robert H. 402
Robert Porter 592, 593
Roderick R. 415*
Roger 350
Samuel 8
Samuel C. 66, 68, 69, 71, 72, 74
Stephen 458
Terry M. 413*, 414
Thomas (Mo.) 125
Thomas (Wash.) 458
Waldo M. 575
William (b. 1803) 79, 83, 84, 86, 88, 90
William (b. 1827) 92, 103, 105, 352, 353
William (mayor) 458
William (educator) 466
William F. 206
William H. 479, 565
William H. (dentist) 566
William J. 104, 106
William M. 544, 594*, 612
William S. 482
William V. 140, 143, 146, 148, 151, 333*
Willis 94, 96
ALLERTON, Isaac 3
ALLEY, John B. 102, 104, 106, 108
ALLGOOD, Miles C. 183, 186, 189, 192, 196, 199
ALLIN
John M. 516, 520
Roger 350
ALLING, Paul H. 433, 434, 438
ALLINSON, Francis G. 570
ALLISON
Archie 451*
James, Jr. 71, 73
James B. 403
John 95, 99
John M. 426, 430, 431
Robert 78
William B. 106, 108, 110, 112, 116, 118, 120, 123, 125, 127, 130, 132, 134, 137, 140, 142, 145, 147, 150, 153, 156, 159, 304
ALLMAN, David B. 569
ALLOTT, Gordon L. 235, 238, 241, 244, 248, 251, 254, 257, 260, 286
ALLPORT
Gordon W. 571
William W. 566*
ALLRED, James 373
ALLSTON, Robert F.W. 365
ALLYN
Robert 481
Stanley C. 492, 549*
Timothy M. 453
ALMAND, Bond 297
ALMON, Edward B. 170, 173, 176, 179, 183, 186, 189, 192, 196, 199
ALMOND
Edward M. 414, 419
Gabriel A. 571
J. Lindsay, Jr. 222, 225, 273, 380
ALONSO, Braulio 578
ALPERS, Bernard J. 569
ALPINE, John R. 559
ALSCHULER, Samuel 272
ALSOP
John 6
John T. 459
John T., Jr. 454*
ALSTADT, William R. 566
ALSTON
Joseph 364
Lemuel J. 60, 62
William J. 92
Willis 56, 57, 58, 59, 60, 61, 62, 64, 73, 75, 76
ALTER
Chester M. 469
Karl J. 523, 529
Wilbur M. 286
ALTGELD, John P. 300
ALTHOFF, Henry 525
ALTMANN, William 498
ALTMEYER, Arthur J. 445
ALTON, Ralph T. 531
ALVAREZ, Luis W. 570, 594, 595, 604, 606
ALVEY, Richard H. 317
ALVORD
Henry E. 478
William 461
AMADON, Dean 569
AMAT, Thaddeus 527
AMATEIS, Edmond 579
AMBLER
Gordon B. 459
Ernest 612
Jacob A. 113, 115
AMBROSE, Myles J. 443
AMERMAN
A.E. 454
Lemuel 138
Ralph A. 576
AMES
A.A. 457*
Adelbert 112, 114, 116, 326*, 410
Butler 153, 156, 159, 162, 165
Charles B. 553, 570
Edward R. 530
Eli B. 457
Elizabeth 603
Fisher 51, 52*, 53
Jesse H. 486
Joseph S. 473, 570
Leon 559
Louis A. 579
Oakes 106, 108, 110, 112, 114
Oliver (b. 1807) 554
Oliver (b. 1831) 320
Samuel 362
Winslow 497
AMLIE, Thomas R. 199, 205, 209
AMMANN, Othmar H. 604
AMMEN, Daniel 418*
AMMONS
Elias M. 285
Teller 285
AMSTUTZ, Hobart B. 531
AMY, Jay S. 450
ANASTOS, Rosemary (Park)-466
ANCONA, Sydenham E. 105, 107, 109
ANDEEN, G. Kenneth 486
ANDERS
Thomas J. 381
William A. 594, 598
ANDERSEN
Dorothy 592
Elmer L. 325
H. Carl 210, 214, 217, 220, 223, 227, 230, 233, 236, 239, 242, 245
ANDERSON
A. Scott 459
Albert B. 272
Albert R. 132
Alexander 85, 369, 457
Alexander E. 414
Alexander J. 484
Andrew 457
Archibald B. 481
C. Arthur 207, 210
C. Elmer 325
Carl C. 163, 166
Carl D. 594, 605
Chapman L. 132, 135
Charles A. 579
Charles A. (educator) 483
Charles M. 131
Charles P. 509, 519
Clifford 393
Clinton P. 34, 45, 214, 217, 221, 227, 230, 233, 236, 239, 243, 246, 249, 252, 256, 259, 262, 343, 580
Douglas S. 483
Edgar 574
Edwin H. 568
Eleanor 492
Emmett T. 574
Ernfred 497
Eugenie 424, 427
Forrest H. 332
Galusha 469
Gaylord W. 572
George A. 132
George A.M. 411
George W. 271
George W., Jr. 416, 417, 435, 599
George Washington 108, 110
Glenn M. 257, 260, 263
H. Ray 532
Howe 452
Hugh J. 82, 84, 314
Hugo A. 590
Hurst R. 465, 471
Ira D. 568
Isaac 58, 59
J. Lowrie 533
J. Macfie 452
J. Patton 391, 392, 395, 396
Jack 588
Jesse 483
John 72, 74, 76, 77
John, Jr. 307
John A. 607
John A. (Rep.) 123, 125, 127, 130, 132, 134, 473
John B. (Ill.) 245, 248, 251, 254, 258, 261, 264, 412, 414
John C. 278
John E. 571
John F. 572
John Z. 209, 212, 216, 219, 222, 225, 229
Jonathan W. 412, 413*
Joseph 55, 56, 57*, 58, 59, 60, 62, 63, 64, 369
Joseph H. 88, 90
Josia M. 94
Karl 589, 607
L.D. 536
Larz 424
LeRoy H. 239, 242
Lucian 106
M.D. 491
Marian 595, 603, 608, 611
Martin B. 480
Maxwell 584, 603
O. Kelley 550*
Orvil A. 592, 598
Paul F. 526
Paul R. 482
Paul Y. 583
Rasmus B. 427
Richard C., Jr. 66, 68, 425
Richard H. 394*, 395*
Robert 426, 550
Robert B. 35, 39, 399*, 603, 608
Robert O. 544
Robert P. 271
S.T. 483
Samuel 467
Samuel (Pa.) 75
Samuel E. 415*
Sigurd 367
Simeon H. 84
Sydney 165, 168, 171, 174, 177, 180, 184
Thomas H. 424
Thomas J. 462
Thomas L. 100, 103
Victor E. 334, 455
W.B. 533
W.F. 466
W.M. 533
W.S. 416
Walker 293
Webster 403
Wendell R. 325
William 571
William (Pa.) 61, 63, 64, 67
William A. 577
William A. (mayor) 457
William B. 118
William C. (educator) 475
William C. (executive) 546
William C. (b. 1826) 102
William C. (b. 1853) 144
William F. 530
William R. 253, 256, 260, 263, 599

ANDRESEN, August H. 187, 190, 194, 197, 204, 207, 210, 214, 217, 220, 223, 227, 230, 233, 236, 239, 242, 245
ANDREW
Abram P., Jr. 180, 184, 187, 190, 194, 197, 200, 203
James O. 530
John A. 320
John F. 135, 137
Samuel 487
ANDREWS
A. 450
Adolphus 418
Bert 585
Charles (Maine) 95
Charles 345
Charles B. 288*
Charles McLean 567, 584, 603
Charles O. 203, 206, 209, 213, 216, 219, 294
Christopher C. 437
Clayton F. 579
Clement W. 568
Dana 559
Earle T. 572
Edward C., Jr. 484
Edward G. 530
Elisha B. 467, 469, 476
F.M. 400, 411
Frank 461
Frank L. 411
George 401
George R. 93
George W. 216, 219, 222, 225, 228, 232, 235, 238, 241, 244, 247, 251, 254, 257, 260, 263
Glenn 251
Graham H. 459
Henry E. 497
Ike F. 265
Israel W. 474
J.B. 571
John 479
John D. 454
John T. 83
Joseph 460
Landaff W. 84, 85
Lorin 473
Mark 249, 253, 256, 259, 262, 265
Philip 418
R. Carl 451
Reddin 466
Roy Chapman 497, 595, 598, 599
Samuel G. 101
Sherlock J. 86
Stanley 443
T. Coleman 444, 567
Walter G. 198, 201, 204, 207, 211, 214, 217, 221, 224
Walter P. 574
William 454
William E. 143, 177, 187
William N. 177
ANDROS, Edmund 8*, 9
ANDRUS
Cecil D. 299
Clift 401, 413
E. Cowles 567
John E. 157, 159, 162, 165
Reuben 469
ANDUJAR, John J. 572
ANFINSEN, Christian B. 606
ANFUSO, Victor L. 230, 236, 240, 243, 246
ANGEL
Benjamin F. 437
William G. 73, 76, 77
ANGELL
Homer D. 211, 215, 218, 221, 224, 227, 231, 234
James B. 425, 438, 475, 484, 567
James R. 487, 491, 571, 575, 603
Robert C. 573
ANGELLOTTI, Frank M. 283
ANGIER, Nedon L. 449
ANGLIN, Margaret 599
ANGOFF, Charles 580
ANKENY, Levi 155, 158, 160, 381
ANNABRING, Joseph 529
ANNENBERG, Walter H. 429, 491
ANNIS, Edward R. 569
ANNUNZIO, Frank 251, 254, 258, 261, 264
ANSBERRY, Timothy T. 160, 163, 166, 169
ANSCHUTZ, Thomas P. 607
ANSEL, Martin F. 365
ANSLINGER, Harry J. 609
ANSORGE, Martin C. 181
ANTHONY
Daniel R., Jr. 159, 161, 164, 167, 170, 173, 177, 180, 183, 187, 190
Earle C. 578
George T. 306
Henry B. 103, 105, 107, 109, 111*, 113*, 115*, 117, 119, 122, 124, 126, 128, 361, 362
Joseph B. 79, 81, 362
Susan B. 597
ANTONY, Edwin L. 139
ANTOVILLE, S.W. 553*
APLIN, Henry H. 151
APPEL
Anthony R. 470
Daniel F. 550
James Z. 569
Kenneth E. 571
APPERLY, Astley 574
APPLE
Henry H. 470
Thomas G. 470
William S. 609
APPLEBY
Stewart H. 188
T. Frank 181
APPLEGATE, Irvamae 578
APPLETON
Edward V. 598
Francis H. 498, 579
Jane Means 20
Jesse 466
John (b. 1804) 314
John (b. 1815) 95, 314, 424, 436
John J. 437
Nathan 77, 86
William 95, 97, 104
William H. 482
APPLEY, Lawrence A. 568
APPLEYARD, Robert 517, 521
APSLEY, Louis Dewart 140, 143
ARANT, Herschel W. 271
ARBIB, Robert 593
ARBONA, Guillermo 592
ARBUCKLE, Ernest C. 554
ARCHAMBAULT, George F. 570, 609
ARCHBALD, Robert W. 271
ARCHBOLD, John D. 549, 553
ARCHDALE, John 8, 9
ARCHER
Bill (W.R.) 263, 266
John 56, 57, 58, 59
Raymond L. 531
Robert S. 572
Samuel H. 476
Stevenson 62, 63, 65, 68, 316
Stevenson (b. 1827) 110, 112, 114, 116
William S. 69, 70, 72, 73, 75, 77, 78, 80, 87, 88, 90, 378
ARDEN, Karen 609
ARENDS, Leslie C. 203, 206, 209, 213, 216, 219, 223, 226, 229, 232, 235, 238, 242, 245, 248, 251, 255, 258, 261, 264
ARENS, Henry 200
ARENTZ, Samuel S. 181, 188, 191, 194, 197
ARGALL, Samuel 9
ARING, Charles D. 569
ARKUS, Leon A. 498
ARMACOST, Wilbur H. 591
ARMENTI, Carmen J. 462
ARMFIELD, Robert F. 124, 126
ARMITAGE, William E. 506, 520
ARMISTEAD, W.K. 402
ARMOUR
Claude A. 456
J. Ogden 543*
Norman 423, 425*, 429*, 437, 439, 612
Philip D. 543
ARMS, John Taylor 590
ARMSBY, George N. 550
ARMSTRONG
A.H. 455
Arthur J. 531
Charles (b. 1886) 610
Charles J. (b. 1911) 476
Charles W. 576
David H. 121, 319
Donald 419, 570
Donald B. 578
Edward C. 577
Edwin H. 595, 596, 598*
Francis 460
Frank C. 395
George E. 403
J. Sinclair 445
James 53
James F. 532
James I. 475
John (b. 1717) 7, 406
John (b. 1755) 15, 24*, 40, 56, 57, 58, 344*
John (b. 1830) 558
Joseph G. (mayor) 459
Joseph G. (bishop) 515, 521
Marshall S. 567
Neil A. 594*, 598, 608, 611
Orland K. 230
Robert A. 485*
Robert J. 528
Samuel T. 450
Thomas F. 546
Walter P. 565
William (Tenn.) 457
William (Va.) 73, 75, 77, 78
William H. 113
William L. 264
William T. 600
ARN, Edward F. 307
ARNALL, Ellis G. 297
ARNELL, Samuel M. 109, 111, 113
ARNETT, Peter 587, 607
ARNOLD
Archibald V. 413
B.L. 478
Ben 355
Benedict (b. 1615) 9*
Benedict (b. 1780) 76, 406
Bion J. 600
Charles N. 454
Edward 559
George P. 454
H. Park 576
Henry A. 412
Henry H. 401, 594
Henry J. 453
Henry N. 598
Isaac N. 104, 106
Jackson D. 418
Jonathan 7
Laurence F. 206, 209, 213
Lemuel H. 90, 361
Marshall 138, 140
Olney 427
Peleg 7, 361*
Remmie L. 579
Samuel 100
Samuel G. 105, 362
Samuel W. 217, 220, 223
Sarah Louise 576
Thomas 361
Thomas D. 78, 87
Thurman W. 272
Warren O. 133, 136, 144
William C. 143, 146
William H. 405, 413, 414
William R. 401
William W. 183, 186, 190, 193, 196, 200, 203
ARNOT
John, Jr. 128, 130
Robert 597
ARNOTT, David 611
ARNSTEIN, Margaret G. 610
ARNY, Henry V. 609
ARONE, Nicholas F. 601
ARONSON
Boris 592
J. Hugo 331
ARRAS, Edmund F. 576
ARRINGTON
Archibald H. 86, 88, 392
Louis 557
ARROW, Kenneth 566, 606
ARTHUR
Chester A. 13, 14, 17, 124
Edward J. 452
George 564
Harold J. 377
Joseph C. 574
William E. 114, 116
ARVESON, Maurice H. 565
ARVIN, Newton 602
ARVOLD, Alfred G. 579
ASBOTH, Alexander 423, 439
ASEL, Henry C. 455
ASH
Michael W. 81
Roy L. 444
ASHBRIDGE, Samuel H. 458
ASHBROOK
John M. 246, 249, 253, 256, 259, 262, 265
William A. 160, 163, 166, 169, 172, 175, 178, 204, 208, 211
ASHBY, G.F. 554
ASHCROFT, T.C. 456
ASHE
Bowman F. 475
John B. (b. 1748) 6, 51, 52, 406
John B. (b. 1810) 88
Samuel 347
Thomas S. 117, 119, 392
William S. 93, 95, 97
ASHER, Leslie I. 578
ASHLEY
Chester 87, 89, 90, 281
Delos R. 108, 110
Henry 73
James M. 103, 105, 107, 109, 111
John P. 465
Thomas L. 237, 240, 243, 246, 249, 253, 256, 259, 262, 265
William E. 455*
William H. 77, 79, 81
ASHMORE
Harry S. 269
John D. 103
Robert T. 103, 234, 237, 240, 243, 247, 250, 253, 256
ASHMUN
Eli P. 65, 66, 319
George 89, 91, 93
ASHURST, Henry F. 164, 167, 170, 173, 176, 179, 183, 186, 189, 192, 196, 199, 202, 206, 209, 280
ASHTON, Raymond J. 567
ASHWORTH
Frederick L. 417
Mary Wells 269
ASKEW
Henry F. 569
Reubin 294
ASKEY, E. Vincent 569
ASPER, Joel F. 112
ASPIN, Les 263, 266
ASPINALL, Wayne N. 226, 229, 232, 235, 238, 241, 244, 248, 251, 254, 257, 260
ASPLUNDH, E.T. 550
ASTLEY, Thomas 547
ASTOR
Vincent 491
Mrs. Vincent 491
William W. 431
ASTWOOD, Frank P. 600
ASWELL, James B. 167, 170, 174, 177, 180, 184, 187, 190, 193
ATCHISON
David R. 88, 89*, 90, 91, 92, 93, 94, 95, 96, 97, 329
T.C. 533
ATHANSON, George A. 454
ATHEARN, Walter S. 467
ATHERTON
Charles G. 82, 86, 88, 89, 91, 97, 337
Charles H. 65
George W. 479
Gibson 124, 126
Ray 424, 425*, 427, 432
Samuel 548
Warren H. 568
ATKESON, William O. 181
ATKINS
Edwin F. 554
Henry A. 461
James 470, 530
John D.C. 101, 117, 120, 122, 124, 126, 392, 393*
Stanley 517, 519
Stuart P. 577
ATKINSON
A.M. 536
Alfred 465, 476
Archibald 88, 90, 92
Brooks 585
Davis H. 462
Fred W. 479
George F. 574
George W. 136, 383, 497
John M.P. 471
Louis E. 128, 131, 133, 136, 138

Ralph 533
Richard M. 208
Theodore 3
Thomas 506, 521
Thomas W. 474
Tracy 499
William H. 566
William P. 558
William Y. 296
ATLEE
John L. 569
Samuel J. 7
ATTWOOD
William (diplomat) 429, 431
ATWATER
Jeremiah 469, 475
John M. 472
John W. 149
Reginald M. 610
Wilbur O. 594
William H. 574
ATWELL, William H. 574
ATWILL
Douglass H. 513, 521
Edward R. 508, 522
ATWOOD
David 113, 456
Frank E. 568
Harrison H. 143
John H. 579
John L. 550
Julius W. 510, 519
Sanford S. 470
Wallace W. 498
William 458
AUBURN, Norman P. 465
AUCHINCLOSS, James C. 217, 220, 224, 227, 230, 233, 236, 239, 243, 246, 249
AUD, Guy 565
AUDEN, W.H. 585, 589, 592, 602, 603, 604
AUDUBON, John James 597
AUER, John G. 507
AUERBACH, S.I. 575
AUF DER HEIDE, OSCAR L. 188, 191, 194, 197, 201
AUGHINBAUGH, G.W. 472
AUGUSTUS, Ellsworth H. 574
AURAND, Henry S. 401, 404
AURIN, Fritz L. 564
AUSLEY, Charles S. 462*
AUSTIN
A. Everett, Jr. 501, 502
Albert E. 209
Archibald 67
Bernard L. 399, 417, 419
C.B. 459
Charles 461
Fred T. 402
Horace 324
J. Paul 545*
James B. 572, 595
John T. 600
Louis W. 598
Richard W. 163, 166, 169, 172, 175
Samuel 484
Walter W. 461
Warren R. 199, 202, 205, 208, 212, 215, 218, 222, 377, 603, 609
AUTRAND, Al 459
AVERELL, William W. 408
AVERETT
Elliott 544
Thomas H. 94, 96
AVERILL, John T. 114, 116
AVERY
Benjamin P. 425
Daniel 62, 64, 65
George S., Jr. 574
John 140, 143
Mary Ellen 599
Oswald T. 599, 607
Samuel 476
W.W. 392
William H. 236, 239, 242, 245, 248, 307
William T. 101, 103
AVES, Henry D. 509
AVILA, Charles F. 595
AVINOFF, Andrey 497
AVIS, Samuel B. 169
AWL, William McC. 571
AXELROD, Julius 595, 606
AXSON, Ellen Louise 20
AXTELL, Samuel B. 109, 111
AXTON, John T. 401
AYCOCK, Charles B. 348
AYCRIGG, John B. 82, 86
AYDELOTTE, Frank 482
AYER
Charles H. 458
Francis W. 534
James B. 569
Lewis M. 393*
Richard 113
AYERS
Howard 468
Roy E. 201, 204, 331
Steven B. 165
Thomas G. 545
AYLESWORTH, Barton O. 468, 469
AYLWARD, David A. 579
AYMOND, Alphonse H. 546
AYNSLEY, William 10
AYRES
Brown 482
Romeyn B. 408
William A. 170, 173, 177, 183, 187, 190, 193, 197, 200
William H. 230, 234, 237, 240, 243, 246, 249, 253, 256, 259
AZEVEDO, Clarence L. 460
AZOY, Anastasio C.M. 575

B

BAADE, Paul W. 413
BABB, E.C. 457
BABBIDGE, Homer D., Jr. 468
BABBITT
Clinton 139
Elijah 103, 105
Frank C. 570
Milton 592
BABCOCK
Alfred 86
Allen J. 526
Brenton D. 452
Charles H. 491
E. Claude 557
E.G. 459
George H. 573
Irving B. 544
Joseph W. 141, 144, 147, 149, 152, 155, 158
Joshua 10*
Kendric C. 465
Leander 95
Paul, Jr. 553
Rufus 468
Samuel G. 510
Tim 332
W. Wayne 590
William 77
BABER, Ambrose 436
BABKA, John J. 178
BABSON, Roger W. 534
BACH, Otto Karl 498
BACHARACH, Isaac 171, 174, 177, 181, 184, 188, 191, 194, 197, 201, 204
BACHE
Alexander D. 563, 570
Franklin 570
BACHELDER, Nahum J. 338, 578
BACHER, Robert F. 570
BACHMAN
Nathan L. 202, 205, 208, 371
Paul S. 472
Reuben K. 124
BACHMANN, Carl G. 189, 192, 195, 199
BACHOFER, John B. 578
BACHRACH, Walton 452
BACIGALUPI, James A. 544
BACK, George I. 403
BACKUS
Azel 471
J. Chester 532
J. Trumbull 532
Manson F. 549
BACON
A. Harry 536
Augustus O. 142, 145, 147, 150, 153, 155, 158, 161, 164*, 167, 296
Charles L. 568
David W. 528
Ezekiel 60, 61, 62
Henry (N.Y.) 130, 133, 138
Henry 590
Joel S. 471
John 56
John E. 434, 439
John L. 461
Leonard 584
Mark R. 174
Nathaniel 9
Robert 30, 31, 38, 428, 603
Robert L. 184, 188, 191, 194, 198, 201, 204, 207
Walter W. 292
William J. 121
BADEAU, John S. 439
BADER, Lewis 434
BADGER
Charles J. 483
DeWitt C. 154, 452
George E. 26, 42, 90, 91, 93, 95, 97, 347
Luther 73
Oscar C. 417
Thomas 459
William 337
BADILLO, Herman 262, 265
BADING, Gerhard A. 427, 456
BADLEY, Brenton T. 530
BADSKEY, Lorin J. 576
BAEHR
George 610
Herman 452
BAEKELAND, Leo H. 565, 575, 596*, 604
BAER
George, Jr. 54, 55, 65
John M. 175, 178
John W. 478, 532
BAFALIS, L.A. 264
BAGBY
Arthur P. 85, 87, 89, 90, 277*, 436
John C. 118
BAGLEY
George A. 119, 121
John H., Jr. 119, 128
John J. 322
Phil J., Jr. 459
BAHLHORN, Joseph 558
BAIL, P. Milo 476
BAILAR, John C., Jr. 565, 608
BAILEY
Alex D. 573
Alexander H. 110, 112
Alfred M. 498
C.W. 564
Carl E. 282
Charles J. 410
Cleveland M. 222, 228, 231, 234, 238, 241, 244, 247
David J. 94, 96
Dewey C. 453
E.H. 554
Ervin G. 573, 590, 596, 601
Florence Merriam 592
Frank E. 473
Goldsmith F. 104
Guy W. 484
I.W. 574
J.W. 563
James 454
James E. 119, 122, 124, 370
Jeremiah 80
John 70, 72, 74, 76
John M. 121, 123
Joseph 105, 107
Joseph W. 139, 141, 144, 146, 149, 152, 155, 157, 160, 163, 166, 372
Joseph W., Jr. 202
Josiah W. 198, 201, 204, 208, 211, 214, 218, 221, 349
Liberty Hyde 563, 574, 603
Pearce 569
Percival 569
Ralph E. 187
Richard P. 471
Scott F. 517
Silas 469, 473
Theodorus 53, 54, 56, 57, 58, 344
Thomas L. 328
Warren W. 169, 172
William 572
Willis J. 148, 306
BAILLE, Bruce 592
BAILLY-BLANCHARD, Arthur 429
BAILYN, Bernard 587, 591
BAIN
Edgar C. 572, 590, 611
Helen 578
BAINBRIDGE, A.G. 457
BAINES
George W. 466
J.D. 451
BAIRD
Absolom 402, 409*, 410
David 174, 341
David, Jr. 194, 342
Henry W. 415
Jesse H. 532
John W. 571
Joseph E. 195
Julian B. 493
Samuel 145
Spencer F. 502*
BAKER
A.B. 569
A.Z. 580
Burtis 593
C.M. 558
Caleb 68
Charles S. 131, 133, 135
Conrad 302
Crowdus 552
D. Gordon 366
David J. 75, 300
Edward D. 89, 92, 103, 105, 356
Edwin M. 575
Ezra 65
Ezra F. 485
Francis E. 272
Frank C. 498
Frayne 413
George (Father Devine) 538
George M. 481
George Pierce 603
Henry B. 572
Henry F. 579
Henry M. 140, 143
Hillary 458
Howard H. 231, 234, 237, 240, 243, 247, 250
Howard H., Jr. 256, 259, 263, 266, 371
Hugh P. 475
I.P. 450
Irene Bailey 250
J. Stewart 545*
J. Thompson 168
J. Worth 579
James 392, 393
James C. 530
James G. 580, 594
James H. 468
James M. 436
Jehu 108, 110, 132, 145, 439
Jesse 467
Joel 565
John 63
John C. 478
John H. 118, 120, 123
Joshua 311
LaMar 263, 266
Leonard T. 481
Lewis 426, 436
Lucien 142, 145, 148, 306
Nathaniel B. 337
Newton D. 31, 32, 40, 452, 568, 603
Osmon C. 530
Osmyn 84, 86, 87
Ray S. 584
Raymond J. 474
Richard H. 515, 521
Robert 154
Sam A. 330
Simon S. 485
Stephen (N.Y.) 105
Stephen 545
Thomas S. 467
Walter C. 402
William 137, 140, 142
William B. 142, 145, 148
William C. 459
William H. (N.Y.) 119, 121
William H. (Fla.) 454
William O. 608
William R. 454
BAKEWELL
Charles M. 199
Claude I. 223, 230
BAKKE, Norris C. 286
BALANCHINE, George 592
BALCH
Emily 605
George B. 483
BALDINGER
Albert H. 533
Wallace S. 501
BALDRIDGE
H.A. 416
H. Clarence 299
BALDRIGE, H. Malcolm 197
BALDWIN
Abraham 4, 5, 51, 52, 53, 54, 55, 56, 57, 58, 60, 295
Augustus C. 106
Bill 557
Charles F. 432
Christopher C. 549
Cyrus G. 479

D.J. 455
Elihu W. 484
Hanson W. 584
H. Strett 217, 220
Henry 67, 68, 70, 269
Henry P. 123, 322*
Horace 454
James M. 571
John 72, 74
John B. 393*
John D. 106, 108, 110
John F., Jr. 235, 238, 241, 244, 247, 251
Joseph C. 214, 217, 221
L.W. 549
Melvin R. 140
Philip E. 272
Raymond E. 222, 226, 289*
Robert D. 486
Robert L. 575
Roger S. 90, 92, 287*
Simeon 57
Simeon E. (b. 1840) 288*, 564, 567, 571
William D. 536
William H. 492
William O. 569
BALEY, S.P. 454
BALFOUR, Donald C. 565, 590
BALKE, Clarence W. 601
BALL
Edward 492
Edward (Ohio) 97, 99
John D. 600
Joseph 547
Joseph A. 565
Joseph H. 210, 213, 217, 220, 223, 325*
L. Heisler 150*, 153, 176, 179, 183, 291*
Max W. 564
Robert M. 445
Thomas H. 146, 149, 152, 155
Thomas R. 209
William L. 67, 69, 70, 72
BALLAM, Samuel H., Jr. 546
BALLANTINE
Stuart 594
William G. 478
BALLANTYNE, John 549, 576
BALLARD
Claude 558
Frank L. 478
James M. 577
Russell H. 552
Smith S. 457
Stanley S. 580
William F. 612
BALLENTINE
John G. 129, 131
John J. 417
BALLIN, Hugo 593, 598
BALLINGER, Richard A. (b. 1858) 31, 44, 461
BALLOU
Adin 538
Charles T. 410
Hosea II 483
Latimer W. 119, 122, 124
BALMER, Jesmond 413
BALTES, Peter J. 529
BALTZ, William N. 167
BALTZELL
John R. 456
Thomas 293
BALZAR, Frederick B. 335
BAMBERGER, Simon 374
BANCKER, Evert 449
BANCROFT
Charles P. 571
Colman 472
Edgar A. 431
George 26, 42, 428, 429, 435, 566, 567, 597
Wilder D. 565, 575*
BANDSTRA, Bert A. 252
BANE, David M. 428
BANES, Charles H. 575
BANGHART, Marcus D. 610
BANGS
Nathan 485
Tracy R. 576
BANIGAN, Joseph 554
BANISTER, John 4, 7
BANKHEAD
John H. 131, 134, 136, 139, 142, 144, 147, 150, 152, 155, 158, 161, 164, 167, 170, 173, 176, 278
John H., 2d 196, 199, 202, 206, 209, 212, 216, 219, 278
Walter W. 212
William B. 173, 176, 179, 183, 186, 189, 192, 196, 199, 202*, 206*, 209*, 212
BANKS
A. Bleecker 449*
Enoch 456*
Harlan P. 574
John 78, 79, 81
Linn 83, 85, 87
Nathaniel P. 17, 97, 98, 99, 100, 108, 110, 112, 114, 118, 121, 135, 320, 407
Robert T. 450
BANNING, Henry B. 117, 119, 121
BANNISTER, Edward 479
BANNON, Henry T. 157, 160
BANNOW, R.F. 578
BANTA, Parke M. 223
BANUELOS, Romana Acosta 444
BANYARD, Alfred L. 514, 520
BANZHAF, Henry L. 566
BAPST, John 466
BARAGA, Frederic 527
BARBARIN, F. Sinclair 498
BARBATELLI, Ettore 578
BARBELIN, Felix 480*
BARBEE, John 456
BARBER
Amos W. 387
Anson F. 457
Edwin A. 387
Hiram, Jr. 122
Isaac A. 145
J. Allen 115, 117
Lafayette L. 566
Laird H. 149
Levi 67, 70
Noyes 69, 70, 72, 74, 75, 77, 78
Wilfred C. 584, 586, 587
BARBIERI, Sante Uberto 531
BARBOUR
Clarence A. 467, 534
Clifford E. 532
Henry E. 176, 179, 183, 186, 189, 193, 196
James 25, 40, 64, 66*, 67*, 69, 70, 72, 73, 378*, 429
John S. 72, 73, 75, 77, 78, 126, 129, 131, 136, 139, 379
Lucien 98
Philip P. 64, 66, 67, 69*, 70, 72, 75, 77, 269
W. Warren 197, 201, 204, 207, 211, 214, 217, 342*
Walworth 431
BARCHFELD, Andrew J. 157, 160, 163, 166, 169, 172
BARCLAY
Charles F. 160, 163
David 99
John 449, 458
Shepard 329
BARCUS, Glenn D. 415
BARD
David 54, 55, 58, 59, 60, 61, 63, 64, 65
Howard B. 461
Phillip 571
Thomas R. 147, 150, 152, 283, 554
BARDEEN, John 570, 598, 604, 606
BARDEN, Graham A. 204, 208, 211, 214, 218, 221, 224, 227, 230, 234, 237, 240, 243
BARDO, C.L. 578
BAREFOOT, Walter 8
BAREIS, A.W. 456
BARGEN, J. Arnold 590
BARGER, A. Clifford 571
BARGHOORN, Elso S. 597
BARHAM, John A. 142, 144, 147
BARING, Walter S. 227, 230, 239, 243, 246, 249, 252, 255, 259, 262
BARKDULL, Howard L. 565
BARKER
A.E. 557
Abraham A. 109
David, Jr. 74
Eric 271
George F. 563, 565
Henry R. 459
Henry S. 473
Horace A. 604
James N. 458
John 458, 465
Joseph (Mass.) 59, 60
Joseph 459
Joseph W. 492, 573
Kirkland C. 453
Lewellys F. 569
Mary C. 557
Pierre A. 450
Robinson F. 492, 550*
R.J. 478
Wendell A. 607
William 461
William J. 453
William M. 508, 521, 522
BARKLEY
Alben W. 14, 18, 167, 170, 173, 177, 180, 184, 187, 190, 193, 197, 200, 203, 206, 210, 213, 216, 220, 223, 225, 226, 228, 236, 310*
James M. 532
BARKSDALE
Ethelbert 128, 130, 392, 393
William 97, 99, 100, 102
BARLOW
Bradley 124
Charles A. 144
Elizabeth Glass 536
Francis C. 409*
Joel 428
John 479
Stephen 75
BARNARD
Chester I. 492
Daniel D. 74, 84, 86, 88, 435
Frederick A.P. 468, 475, 563
George G. 603
Henry 444, 480, 486
Isaac D. 75, 76, 78, 358
John G. 483
William E. 484
William O. 161
BARNDS, William Paul 517
BARNES
Abraham 3
Albert 532
Arlie R. 567
Charles A. 576
Charles P. 315
Demas 110
Francis G. 473
George A. 458
George T. 129, 132, 134
Gladeon M. 594
James 408
James M. 209, 213
John B. 333
Joseph K. 403
Julius H. 575
Lyman E. 141
Margaret Ayer 583
Orlando F. 455*
Robert G. 431
Stanley N. 272
Verdi B. 419
W.S. 453
Wendell B. 445
BARNETT
Allison J. 414
Frank E. 554
George 416
George E. 566
Henry L. 599
Herbert 580
J. Mercer 576
Ross R. 328
S. Meyer 493
Vincent M., Jr. 468
William 62, 63
BARNEY
John 72, 74
Joseph N. 396
Keith R. 402
Samuel S. 144, 147, 149, 152, 273
William P. 591
BARNHART, Henry A. 158, 161, 164, 167, 170, 173
BARNHILL, M.V. 349
BARNITZ, Charles A. 79
BARNOUW, Erik 591
BARNUM, William H. 109, 111, 113, 116, 118, 120, 288
BARNWELL, Middleton S. 512, 519*
Robert (b. 1761) 7, 52, 94
Robert W. 509, 519
Robert W. (S.C.) 76, 78, 364, 391, 392, 393*, 481*, 519
BARR
Alfred H., Jr. 500, 592, 603
Joseph M. 459
Joseph W. 36, 39, 242
Samuel F. 126, 128
Stringfellow 480, 611
Thomas J. 101, 103
W.W. 533
BARRERE
Granville 116
Nelson 95
BARRET, John R. 103
BARRETT
Albert M. 569, 571
Catharine 578
Clifton W. 563
Edwin S. 579
Frank A. 219, 222, 225, 228, 235, 238, 241, 387, 388
George W. 517, 521
Herbert G. 462
James E. 272
John (diplomat) 423, 426, 434, 436
John (mayor) 459*
Nathan F. 573
Richard C. 497
Robert S. 574
Samuel A. 500
W.J. 576
Wilbert H. 579
William A. 221, 228, 231, 234, 237, 240, 243, 246, 250, 253, 256, 259, 262, 265
William C. 497, 566
William E. 143, 145
BARRINGER
Daniel L. 73, 75, 76, 78, 79
Daniel M. 88, 90, 91, 437
Paul B. 484*
William N. 477
BARRON
George 498*
Samuel 396*
William W. 384
BARROW
Alexander 86, 87, 89, 311
David C. 471
Lewis O. 315
M. Pope 125, 296
Washington 92, 435
Wilmer L. 595
BARROWS
Arthur S. 552
D.N. 454
David P. 467
John H. 478
Leland 425, 438
Lewis O. 315
Samuel J. 145
Thomas N. 474
BARRY
Alexander G. 208
Bryan T. 452
Daniel J. 453
Edward G. 577
Frederick G. 130, 132
Frederick L. 514, 519
Henry W. 112, 114, 116
James G. 460
John 528
John S. 322*
Patrick 528
Robert R. 243, 246, 249
Thomas H. 410*, 419, 483
William B. 204, 207, 211, 214, 217, 221
William T. (Ky.) 25*, 43, 61, 63, 65, 308
William T. (Miss.) 97, 391, 392
BARSTOW
Amos C. 459
Frank Q. 552
Gamaliel H. 77
Gideon 69
John L. 376
William A. 385
BARTEMEIER, Leo H. 571
BARTH
Paul C. 456
Theodore N. 514, 522
BARTHELME, Donald 602
BARTHOLDT, Richard 140, 143, 145, 148, 151, 154, 156, 159, 162, 165, 168
BARTHOLOME, Peter 528
BARTHOLOMEW
George A., Jr. 592
Ira H. 455
BARTHOLOW, Roberts 569

BARTIN, Richard W. 87
BARTINE, Horace F. 135, 138
BARTLE, H. Roe 455
BARTLETT
Bailey 54, 55
Charles L. (b. 1853) 142, 145, 147, 150, 153, 155, 158, 161, 164, 167
Charles L. (b. 1921) 586
Dewey F. 265, 355
Edward L. 241, 244, 247, 251, 254, 279
Franklin 140, 143
Fred S. 498
Frederic P. 432
Frederick B. 512, 519, 521
George A. 159, 162
H.H. 574
Ichabold 71, 73, 74
John H. 338, 445
Joseph J. 437
Josiah 3, 4*, 6, 337*
Josiah, Jr. 62
Murray 472
Paul D. 596, 604, 609, 612
Paul W. 579, 591
Robert A. 594, 598
Samuel C. 469
Thomas, Jr. 96
Thomas A. 468
Washington 293, 461
Wes H. 576
Willard 345
BARTLEY
Mordecai 71, 73, 75, 76, 352
Thomas W. 352*
BARTLING, Henry 462
BARTOL, James L. 317
BARTON
Bruce 207, 211
Clara 569
David 69, 71, 73, 74, 76, 329
Donald C. 564
Enos M. 554
Frank S. 391
H.H. 453
Hiram 451
John J. 454
John K. 418
Lane W. 514, 519
Raymond O. 413
Samuel 81
Seth 425
Silas R. 168
Walter E. 571
William E. 197
BARTOW
Edward 565
Francis S. 392
BARUCH
Bernard M. 596, 603, 609
Herman B. 433, 435
BARUS, Carl 570, 609
BARWIG, Charles 136, 139, 141
BARZUN, Jacques 578
BASCOM
Henry B. 482
John 486
William 499
BASH, Louis H. 403
BASHFORD
Coles 385
James W. 530
Robert M. 456
BASKERVILLE, Charles 600
BASKIN
Leonard 603
Robert N. 460
BASS
Edward 505, 520
John M. 457
Lyman K. 117, 119
Nathan 392
Perkins 236, 239, 243, 246
Robert P. 338
Ross 237, 240, 243, 247, 250, 253, 371
Seth 501
BASSETT
Allen L. 551
Burwell 59, 61, 62, 63, 66, 67, 70, 72, 73, 75
Ebenezer D. 429
Edward M. 154
Leslie 587
Richard 51*, 290*
Samuel E. 570
William H. 595
BASTIAN, Walter M. 272
BATCHELDER
Charles F. 569
Richard D. 578
Richard N. 403
BATCHELLER, George S. 435
BATCHELLOR, Clifford H. 594
BATCHELOR, Clarence D. 584
BATDORF, Grant D. 531
BATE, William B. 133, 136, 138, 141, 144, 146, 149, 152, 154, 157, 370*, 395*, 396
BATEMAN
Ephraim 65, 67, 68, 70, 73, 74, 340
Newton 473
BATES
Arthur L. 151, 154, 157, 160, 163, 166
Barton 329
Daniel M. (b. 1821) 291
Daniel M. (b. 1876) 575
Edward 27, 41, 74
Edward B. 545
Edward P. 536*
Daisy 611
E.G. 600
Edward 27, 41, 74
Frederick 329
George J. 207, 210, 213, 217, 220, 223, 226, 460
Harry C. 557
Isaac C. 74, 76, 77, 79, 84, 86, 87, 89, 319
James 77
Joe B. 206, 210, 213, 216, 220, 223, 226, 229
John C. 400
John L. 320
Joseph E. 453
Joshua 475
Lester L. 452
Marston 595
Martin W. 98, 100, 291
Miner L. 472
Onward 572
Sanford 565
Stockton 594
W.B. 491
Walter Jackson 587
William H. 226, 229, 233, 236, 239, 242, 245, 248, 252, 255, 258
BATHRICK, Elsworth R. 166, 169, 175
BATSON, Felix I. 392, 393
BATT, William L. 573, 598
BATTAGLIA, Frederick C. 599
BATTEN, William M. 551
BATTERSON
James G. 553
Walter E. 454
BATTERTON, Richard Y. 453
BATTIN, James F. 246, 249, 252, 255, 258
BATTLE
A.J. 475
John J. 326
John S. 380
Laurie C. 222, 225, 228, 232
Kemp P. 477
Lucius D. 439, 502
William C. 423
William J. 482
BATTS, Robert L. 271
BAUER
Harry J. 552
Louis A. 566
Louis H. 569
BAUGH
Albert C. 577*
R.D. 456
BAUGHER, Henry L. 471
BAUGHMAN, Lyle L. 531
BAUM
Dwight J. 591
Werner A. 479
William 529
BAUMAN, Helen Wood 536
BAUMANN, Charles T. 461
BAUMGARTNER, Leona 572, 578, 610
BAUMHART
Albert D., Jr. 214, 237, 240, 243
Raymond C. 474
BAUR
John C. 484
John I.H. 502
BAUSCH, Edward 590
BAUSH, Christian H. 600
BAXTER
Bruce R. 486, 530
Elisha 281*
George A. 471, 485
Gregory P. 609
Henry 430
James P. III 486, 585
Jedediah H. 403
John G. 456
Norman A. 470
Percival P. 315
Portus 105, 107, 109
Samuel 572
BAY
Burt R. 550
Charles U. 434
William V. 93
BAYARD
James A. 54, 55, 56, 57, 58, 60, 61, 62, 290, 429
James A., Jr. 94, 96, 98, 100, 102, 104, 106, 109, 290
John B. 7
Nicholas 457
Richard H. 80, 82, 83, 85, 87, 290*, 423
Stephen 458
Thomas F. 29, 38, 111, 114, 116, 118, 120, 122, 124, 125, 127, 291, 429
Thomas F., Jr. 179, 183, 186, 189, 291
William 3
BAYH, Birch 248, 251, 255, 258, 261, 264, 303
BAYLESS, Wayne W. 355
BAYLEY
James C. 576
James R. 470, 523, 527
BAYLIES
Francis 69, 71, 72, 423
William 61, 63, 65, 79
BAYLOR
John R. 393
Robert E. 75
BAYLY
Charles, Jr. 498
Thomas 66, 68, 69
Thomas H. 88, 90, 92, 94, 96, 98, 99
Thomas M. 64
BAYMA, Joseph 481
BAYNE
Stephen F., Jr. 514, 521
Thomas M. 122, 124, 126, 128, 131, 133, 136
BAYNE-JONES, Stanhope 607
BAYT, Phillip L., Jr. 454
BAZELON, David L. 272, 608
BAZIN, John S. 526
BEACH
Albert I. 455
Charles L. 468
Chester 579, 591
Clifton B. 143, 146
Dwight E. 401, 404*, 405
John W. 485
Joseph W. 454
Lansing H. 402
Lewis 126, 128, 131
Morrison H. 553
Rex 574
Warren W. 499
BEADLE, George W. 468, 563, 595, 600, 606
BEAKELEY, Wallace M. 417
BEAKES, Samuel W. 168, 171, 174
BEAL
George D. 570, 609
Gifford 589, 593, 607, 610
Harry 513, 521
James H. 609
Orville E. 551
BEALE
Charles L. 103
Edward F. 423
James M.H. 80, 81, 94, 96
Joseph 416
Joseph G. 160
Richard L.T. 92, 122, 124
Truxtun 429, 435, 436
Wilson T.M., Jr. 431
BEALES, C. William 172
BEALL
J. Glenn 217, 220, 223, 226, 229, 233, 236, 239, 242, 245, 248, 318
J. Glenn, Jr. 258, 261, 264, 318
James A. 155, 157, 160, 163, 166, 169
Paul R. 478
Reasin 64
William C. 586
BEALS
C.S. 564
Ralph L. 563
Walter B. 381*
BEAM
Harry P. 196, 200, 203, 206, 209, 213
Jacob D. 426, 435, 439
Philip C. 497
BEAMAN
Nathaniel 458
Fernado C. 104, 106, 108, 110, 112
BEAMER,
John V. 229, 232, 235, 238
BEAMS, Jesse W. 570, 604, 607
BEAN
Benning M. 79, 81
Joshua H. 461
BEAR, Donald J. 498, 502
BEARD
Charles A. 567, 571, 603
Cyrus 387
Daniel C. 609
J.N. 479
M.R. 460
Robin L., Jr. 266
William D. 370
BEARDALL, John R. 483
BEARDSHEAR, W.M. 473
BEARDSLEY
Charles A. 565
G.F. 418
Henry M. 455
Morris B. 579
Samuel 77, 79, 81, 88, 344
William S. 305
BEARY, Donald B. 419
BEASLEY
Frederick 479
Mercer 341
Wallis 485
BEATLEY, Bancroft 481
BEATTIE
Horace S. 591
James A. 472
BEATTY
Charles C. 532
D.L. 456
John (N.J.) 6, 53
John (Ohio) 111, 113, 115
John W. 498
Samuel 410
Troy 511
William 83, 85
William H. 283
BEATY
Amos L. 553*, 570
Martin 79
BEAUCHAMP
Charles E. 419
William B. 530
BEAUDRY, Prudent 456
BEAULAC, Willard L. 423, 425, 426*, 434
BEAUMONT, Andrew 79, 81
BEAUPRE, Arthur M. 423, 426*, 432, 433
BEAUREGARD, Pierre G.T. 394, 483
BEAUVAIS, Armand 311
BEAUX, Cecilia 589, 603, 607*, 610
BEAVEN, Albert W. 534
BEAVER, James A. 359, 479
BEBB, William 352
BECHTEL
Daniel J. 462
Kenneth K. 574
Stephen D. 596
BECK
David 558
Erasmus 114
George W. 456
James B. 110, 112, 114, 116, 120, 123, 125, 127, 130, 132, 134, 309
James M. 191, 195, 198, 201
Joseph D. 182, 186, 189, 192
R.M. 400
William E. 285
BECKER
Carl L. 567
Christopher A. 600
Frank J. 233, 236, 240, 243, 246, 249
George F. 576
George L. 460
Howard 574
John W. 608
Max J. 572
Philip 451*
Sherburn M. 456
Thomas A. 528, 529
William 467
Mrs. William A. 579
William D. 460
BECKET, Frederick M. 575,

589, 594
BECKHAM, John C.W. 170, 173, 177, 309*
BECKLEY
John 459*
John James 444
BECKMAN, Francis J. 523, 527*
BECKNER, William M. 140
BECKWITH
Charles D. 135
Charles M. 509, 519
John W. 506, 519
Sterling 599
BECKWORTH, Lindley G. 212, 215, 218, 221, 225, 228, 231, 240, 244, 247, 250, 253, 273
BEDDOW, Roderick 576
BEDE, J. Adam 153, 156, 159
BEDELL
Catherine 445
Gregory T. 506, 521
J.F. 451
BEDFORD
Alfred C. 553
Gunning 5, 290
Gunning, Jr. 4, 5
BEDINGER
George M. 57, 59
Henry 90, 92, 426*
BEDLE, Joseph D. 341
BEE
Carlos 179
Thomas 7
BEEBE
George M. 119, 121
James A. 465
Roswell 455
William 593, 609
BEECH, Keyes 585
BEECHER
Charles S. 501
George A. 510, 522
Henry Ward 597
Philemon 67, 68, 71, 73, 75
William J. 498
BEECKMAN
Johannes 449
R. Livingston 362
BEEDY, Carroll L. 180, 184, 187, 190, 193, 197, 200
BEEKMAN
Gerardus 8
Thomas 76
BEEMAN, Joseph H. 137
BEERMANN, Ralph F. 246, 249
BEERS
Clifford W. 603
Cyrus 83
Edward M. 185, 188, 191, 195, 198
Henry S. 543*
W.O. 548
BEESON
Charles H. 577
Henry W. 86
BEESTON, John J. 498
BEFFA, Harvey A. 579
BEGG, James T. 178, 181, 185, 188, 191
BEGGS
George E. 607
John I. 553
Lyall T. 580
Thomas M. 500
BEGICH, Nick J. 260, 263
BEGIN, Floyd L. 527
BEGOLE
George D. 453
Josiah W. 116, 322
BEHAN, W.J. 457
BEHAR, Moises 592
BEHM, Hans 564
BEHNKEN, J.W. 535
BEHR, Urban J. 523
BEHRENS
Earl C. 608
Henry 467
BEHRMAN
Martin 457
S.N. 592
BEIDERLINDEN, William A.- 405
BEIDLER, Jacob A. 151, 154, 157
BEIGHTLER, Robert S. 413
BEIRNE, Andrew 83, 85
BEINECKE, William S. 492
BEISE, S. Clark 544
BEISSEL, Johann C. 538
BEITER, Alfred F. 201, 204, 207, 214
BELAFONTE, Harry 595
BELCHER
Hiram 91
Jonathan 8*
Nathan 96
Page H. 231, 234, 237, 240, 243, 246, 250, 253, 256, 259, 262
Taylor G. 426, 435
BELDEN
Frederick H. 521
George O. 74
James J. 133, 135, 138, 140, 146
BELDER
Charles F.D. 568
Frederick H. 518
BELFORD
James B. 118, 120, 122, 125, 127
Joseph M. 146
BELGRANO, Frank N. 568
BELI, Hill M. 536
BELIN, F. Lammot 435
BELITT, Ben 610
BELKNAP
Charles 549
Charles E. 135, 137
Hugh R. 142, 145
William W. 28*, 40
BELL
Alden J. 528
Alexander Graham 578, 594, 595, 596, 597
Alphonzo 244, 247, 251, 254, 257, 260, 263
Bernard I. 466
C. Jasper 204, 207, 210, 214, 217, 220, 223
Casper W. 392*
Charles H. (b. 1907) 547*
Charles H. (b. 1823) 123, 338*
Charles J. 376
Charles K. 141, 144
Charles W. 167
Daniel W. 444
David E. 443, 444
Frank 335
Griffin B. 271
H. McClelland 469
Hiram 95, 116
Hiram P. 120, 393
Hugh H. 533
Isaac, Jr. 433
J. Franklin 400, 410*, 419
J. Spencer 271
James 99, 101, 337
James F. 547*
James K. 432
James M. 79
John (N.H.) 337
John (Ohio) 93
John (Tenn.) 16, 26, 40, 75, 76, 78*, 80, 81, 83, 85, 92, 94, 96, 97, 99, 101, 369
John C. 139, 142, 144, 147, 150
John C., Jr. 360*
John J. 237
John O. 429
John S. 567
Joseph E. 454
Joshua F. 89
Lawrence D. 594, 597
Luther V. 571
P.R. 601
Peter H. 98, 99, 372
Reason C. 297
Robert 594
Sam C. 461
Samuel 71, 73, 74, 76, 77, 79, 337*, 338
Samuel N. 114, 119
Theodore A. 152
Thomas M. 155, 158, 161, 164, 167, 170, 173, 176, 180, 183, 186, 190, 193,
W. Douglas 553
Walter W. 558
William 531
William A. 465
William B. 543
BELLAMY
John D. 149, 151
Paul 573
Ralph 557
BELLANTI, Joseph A. 599
BELLANO, William 550
BELLINGER
Herman C. 610
Joseph 67
BELLINGHAM, Richard 8*
BELLMON, Henry L. 259, 262 265, 355*
BELLOW, Saul 602*
BELLOWS
George 593, 598, 607*
Henry A. 338
BELMONT
August (b. 1816) 433*
August (b. 1853) 549
Eleanor Robson 603, 609
Oliver H.P. 151
Perry 126, 128, 131, 133, 437
BELSER, James E. 87
BELTZHOOVER, Frank E.- 124, 126, 138, 141
BEMAN
Carlyle P. 478
Nathan S.S. 532
BEMENT, A.O. 455
BEMIS, Samuel F. 567, 583, 585
BENBOUGH, Percy J. 461
BENDER
Chester R. 445, 483
George H. 211, 214, 218, 221, 224, 230, 234, 237, 354
BENDETSEN, Karl R. 553
BENDIX, Reinhard 574
BENEDICT
Charles B. 121
Harry Y. 482
Henry S. 170
Jay L. 412, 483
Manson 569, 595
Thomas B. 443*
BENET
Christie 175, 366
Stephen V. 402
Stephen Vincent 583, 585, 603, 609, 610
William Rose 584
BENEZET, Louis T. 465, 477
BENHAM, John S. 176, 180
BENJAMIN
John F. 108, 110, 112
Judah P. 96, 98, 100, 102, 104, 311, 391*
Marcus 563
Raymond 574
S.C.W. 434
BENN, Ben 611
BENNER, George J. 146
BENNET
Augustus W. 221
Benjamin 65, 67
William S. 171
BENNETT
Caleb P. 290
Charles A. 600
Charles E. (b. 1882) 570
Charles E. (b. 1910) 226, 229, 232, 235, 238, 241, 245, 248, 251, 254, 257, 261, 264
Charles G. 143, 146
Clinton W. 578
David S. 112
Donald V. 483
Edwin O. 601
Granville G. (b. 1882) 511, 519, 521
Hendley S. 99
Henry 93, 95, 97, 99, 101
Henry G. 443, 478
Hugh H. 591, 594
Ivan L. 401
James J. 481
James V. 565
John B. 217, 223, 226, 230, 233, 236, 239, 242, 245, 249
John G. 527
John S. 455
Joseph B. 156, 159, 161
Marion T. 217, 220, 223
Mary W. 475
Philip A. 214
Richard 9
Risden T. 128, 131
S.L. 558
Thomas 364, 451
W.F. 578
W. Tapley, Jr. 427, 435
Wallace F. 231, 234, 237, 240, 244, 247, 250, 253, 256, 260, 263, 266, 374
Walter 459
Wendell C. 563
William S. 157, 159, 162
William W. 479
BENNIS, Warren G. 468
BENNISON, Charles E. 516, 522
BENNY, Allan 154
BENOIS, Charles 457
BENSEL, John A. 572
BENSLEY, Russ 607
BENSON
A.L. 18
Alfred W. 156, 306
Carville D. 174, 177
Edward C. 473
Egbert 6, 51, 52, 64
Elmer A. 204, 325*
Ezra Taft 35*, 45
Frank W. (b. 1858) 356
Frank W. (b. 1862) 593*, 607*
Henry P. 460
John W. 598
Nimrod E. 457
Philip A. 564
Samuel P. 97, 98
W.E. 457
William 416
William S. 599
BENT
Arthur C. 592, 593, 569
Quincy 596
BENTLEY
Alvin M. 233, 236, 239, 242
Helen Delich 443
Henry W. 138
Jerome H. 485
John B. 512, 519
Madison 571
William A. 450*
BENTON
Allen R. 467*, 476
Charles 453
Charles S. 88, 90
Guy P. 475, 484
Jacob 110, 112
Lemuel 53, 54, 55
Maecenas E. 145, 148, 151, 154
Thomas H. (b. 1782) 69, 71, 73, 74, 76, 77, 79, 81, 82, 84, 86, 88, 89, 91, 93, 97, 329
Thomas Hart (b. 1889) 590, 591
William 226, 229, 289
BENTSEN, Lloyd M., Jr. 225, 228, 231, 234, 263, 266
BENZENBERG, George H. 572
BENZER, Seymour 600
BERCHER, Harry O. 548*
BERE James F. 544
BERESFORD, John Bull 7
BERG, W.H. 552
BERGAN, Gerald T. 524, 526
BERGEN
Christopher A. 135, 138
John T. 77
Teunis G. 108
BERGER
Meyer 585
Samuel D. 437
Thomas 609
Victor L. 166, 186, 189, 192
BERGETHON, K. Roald 474
BERGIN, William E. 401*
BERGLAND, Robert 261, 265
BERGMAN, Elmer O. 573
BERGSTROM, Edwin 567
BERGUNDTHAL, W.S. 462
BERINGER, George M. 609
BERKELEY
Norborne 9
William 9*
William N. 499
BERKEY
Charles P. 576
Donald C. 596
Russell S. 417
BERKNER, L.V. 567
BERKOWITZ, Gene 462*
BERLE, Adolf A., Jr. 424, 493
BERLIN
Harry S. 554
Irving 609
Richard E. 596
William M. 201, 205
BERLINER
Emile 594, 596
Robert W. 571
BERLO, David K. 472
BERMAN
Eugene 593
Samuel 601
BERMUDEZ, Edward E. 312
BERN, Howard A. 573
BERNARD
Francis 8*
Jesse T. 462*
John T. 207
Lowell F. 498
Luther L. 573

BERNBAUM, Maurice M. 427, 439
BERNREUTER, Henry 462
BERNS, Seymour 577
BERNSTEIN
Herman 423
Leonard 595
Marver H. 466
BERRET, James G. 462
BERRIEN, John M. 25, 41, 72, 74, 75, 85, 87, 89, 91, 92, 94, 295
BERRY
Albert S. 140, 142, 145, 148
Burton Y. 430
Campbell P. 122, 124
Edward W. 576
Ellis Y. 231, 234, 237, 240, 243, 247, 250, 253, 256, 259
George L. 208, 371
Henry C. 576
Hiram G. 408
James H. 129, 131, 134, 136, 139, 142, 144, 147, 150, 152, 155, 281*
John 117
Joseph F. 530
Lampton 425
Lucien W. 469
Martha 603, 609
Nathaniel S. 338
Tom 367
William A. 355
BERRYMAN
Clifford K. 585
James T. 585
John 587, 589, 592, 600, 602, 603, 610
BERTHELOT, James A. 461
BERTHOLF
Ellsworth P. 445
Lloyd M. 473
BERTRAND, C.P. 455
BERTUS, Paul 457
BESCHTER, John W. 471
BESHLIN, Earl H. 175
BESLEY, Frederic A. 565
BESS, Elmer A. 474
BESSEY, Charles E. 476*, 563
BETHE, Hans A. 570, 595, 596, 606, 610
BETHEL, Walter A. 402
BETHELL, W.D. 456
BETHUNE
Lauchin 78
Marion 112
Mary McLeod 611
BETO, George 566
BETTON, Silas 58, 59
BETTS
Austin W. 401
Edward 589*
Jackson E. 230, 234, 237, 240, 243, 246, 249, 253, 256, 259, 262
Louis 589, 598, 610
Rome A. 578
Samuel R. 65
Thaddeus 83, 287
BEURET, John D. 418
BEURY, Charles E. 482
BEVAN
Arthur D. 569
Thomas D. 529
BEVEN, John L. 548
BEVERAGE, Howard H. 598, 599
BEVERIDGE
Albert J. 147, 150, 153, 156, 158, 161, 302, 583, 609
George 586
John L. 114
BEVILL, Tom 254, 257, 260, 263
BEVINGTON, James H. 594
BEVIS, Howard L. 478
BEWKES, Eugene G. 480
BEWLEY, Loyal V. 599
BEYER, Otto S. 444
BIAGGI, Mario 259, 262, 265
BIAGGINI, Benjamin F. 552
BIBB
George 26, 39, 62, 63, 75, 77, 79, 308*
Thomas 277
Thomas W. 474
William W. 59, 60, 61, 62, 63, 65, 277, 295
BIBIGHAUS, Thomas M. 95
BIBLE, Alan H. 233, 236, 239, 242, 246, 249, 252, 255, 259, 262, 265, 266
BICKETT, Thomas W. 348
BICKLEY, George H. 530
BICKMORE, Albert S. 497
BICKNELL
Bennet 83
George A. 120, 123
BIDDLE
Anthony J. Drexel, Jr. 424, 426*, 429*, 433*, 434*, 435, 437, 439*
Charles J. 105
Edward 7
Francis 34*, 41, 271
James 454
John (mayor) 453
John (soldier) 483
Joseph F. 198
Nicholas 501
Richard 83, 85
Thomas 436
William P. 416
William S. 501
BIDEN, Joseph R., Jr. 264, 292
BIDERMANN, Antoine 546
BIDGOOD, Lee 465
BIDLACK, Benjamin A. 86, 88, 425
BIDLE, William S. 572
BIDWELL
Barnabas 59, 60
C.H.S. 460
John 17, 107
Joseph R. 314
BIEBEL, Franklin M. 499
BIEMILLER, Andrew J. 222, 228
BIERI, Bernard H. 417
BIERMANN, Fred 200, 203, 206
BIERRING, Walter L. 569, 590
BIERWORTH, F.W. 493
BIERY, James S. 117
BIESTER, Edward G., Jr. 256, 259, 262, 265
BIGART, Homer 585*, 607
BIGBY, John S. 114
BIGELOW
Abijah 61, 62, 63
Charles 454
Frederic R. 493
George H. 565
George T. 320
Hardin 460
Herbert S. 208
Hobart B. 288
Horace F. 402
Jacob 563
John 428
John P. 450
Lewis 69
BIGGER, Samuel 302
BIGGS
Asa 90, 99, 101, 347
Benjamin T. 111, 114, 291
John, Jr. 271, 608
Marion 132, 134
Thomas J. 468
Walter 591
BIGLER
John 283, 425
William 99, 101, 103, 358*
BILBO, Theodore G. 204, 207, 210, 214, 217, 220, 223, 327*
BILDERBACK, C.P. 450
BILL, Clarence P. 570
BILLARD
Frederick C. 445, 483
J.B. 462
BILLER, George, Jr. 510, 521
BILLERA, I. John 553
BILLINGHURST, Charles 99, 101
BILLINGS
Charles E. 573
Frank 569
Franklin S. 377
John S. 568
John Shaw 571
Marland P. 576
BILLINGSLEY, Joseph P. 559
BILLINGTON, John 3
BILLMAN, Howard 465
BILLMEYER, Alexander 151
BIMELER, Joseph M. 538
BIMSON, Carl A. 564
BINAI, Paul 497
BINDER
Fred H. 455
Joseph B. 459
BINDERUP, Charles G. 204, 207
BINDSCHEATTEL, John 557
BINES, Thomas 64
BINFORD, L.C. "Jack" 576
BING, Rudolf 603
BINGER, J.H. 548
BINGHAM
Flavel 452
George H. 271
Henry H. 124, 126, 128, 131, 133, 136, 138, 141, 143, 146, 149, 151, 154, 157, 160, 163, 166
Hiram 183, 186, 189, 193, 196, 289, 577
John A. 99, 101, 103, 105, 109, 111, 113, 115, 431
Jonathan B. 252, 256, 259, 262, 265
Kingsley S. 91, 93, 102, 104, 322*
Robert W. 429, 456
William (Congressman) 7, 53, 54, 55, 56, 358
William (Mayor) 459
BINNEY
D.B. 408
Horace 79
Joseph G.S. 471
BINNS, Walter P. 486
BINSTED, Norman S. 512, 521
BINZ, Leo 523, 524
BIRCH
Francis 576, 604, 607
Frank V. 576
Stephen 548
Thomas H. 435
William F. 174
BIRCHALL, Frederick T. 584
BIRCHARD, Matthew 352
BIRD
Augustus A. 456
John 56, 57
John T. 112, 114
Junius B. 611
Remsen 478
Richard E. 180
Robert M. 572
Thompson 453
BIRDSALL
Ausburn 91
Benjamin P. 153, 156, 159
Carl 546
James 65
Samuel 83
William W. 482
BIRDSEYE
Claude H. 594
Victory 65, 86
BIRGE
Edward A. 486
Henry W. 410
Raymond T. 570
BIRKENHAUER, Henry F. 473
BIRKHOFF, George D. 563, 568
BIRKINBINE, John 575
BIRNEY
David B. 408*, 409
James 433
Lauriss J. 530
BIRNIE, Upton, Jr. 402
BIRRELL, Don R. 498
BISBEE, Horatio, Jr. 120, 122, 125, 127
BISHOP
Albert W. 465
Barry C. 593
Cecil W. 213, 216, 219, 223, 226, 229, 232
Charles F. 451
Charles P. 460
Elizabeth 586, 589, 602, 610
Eugene L. 572
Harry 455
Harry G. 402
Howard B. 604
Isabel 589*, 598
James 99
Max W. 538
Phanuel 55, 56, 58, 59
Morris 577
Richard M. 353, 451, 536
Robert H. 475
Roswell P. 143, 145, 148, 151, 153, 156
William D. 100, 444
William W. 568
BISKUP, George J. 523, 526
BISPLINGHOFF, Raymond L. 567, 608
BISSELL
Clark 287
Clayton L. 400, 412
William H. 92, 94, 96, 300
William H.A. 506, 522
Wilson S. 30, 43, 477
BITTER, Karl 579, 591
BITTINGER, Charles 593
BITTLE, David F. 480
BIXBY, William H. 402
BIXLER
Harris J. 182, 185, 188
Julius S. 468
BIZZELL
James A. 607
William B. 478, 482
BJERKNES, Jacob 604
BJORKSTEN, Johan, 567
BLACK
Edward J. 84, 85, 87
Ernest B. 572
Eugene 172, 175, 179, 182, 185, 189, 192
Eugene R. 443, 604, 608
Francis M. 329
Frank D. 461
Frank S. 143, 345
Frederick 499
Frederick H. 414
George D. 465
George R. 125
Greene V. 566
Harold S. 599, 611
Henry 86
Hugo L. 189, 192, 196, 199, 202, 206, 270, 278
James (Iowa) 473
James (Pa.) 81, 88, 90
James A. 88, 90, 92
James C.C. 139, 142
James D. 309
James H. 572
Jeremiah S. 27*, 38, 41, 358
John (Wis.) 456
John (Miss.) 77, 79, 81, 82, 326
John C. 139, 445
John D. 566
Loring M., Jr. 184, 188, 191, 194, 198, 201
Mary 502
Newton W. 557
O.B. 461
Samuel C. 485
Samuel L. 452
W.F. 467
William M. 402
BLACKALL, Frederick S., Jr. 573
BLACKBIRD, W.H. 355
BLACKBURN
Benjamin B. 254, 257, 261, 264
E. Spencer 157
John C. 450
Joseph C.S. 118, 121, 123, 125, 127, 130, 132, 134, 137, 140, 142, 150, 153, 156, 309*
Luke P. 309
Paul P., Jr. 417
Robert E. Lee 193
Thomas W. 412
William M. 477
BLACKFORD
Isaac N. 273
William M. 425
BLACKIE, William 544
BLACKISTONE, Nathaniel 8
BLACKLEDGE
H.L. 574
William 58, 59, 60, 62
William S. 68, 70
BLACKMAN
A. Wade 596
William F. 480
BLACKMAR
Esbon 91
Frank W. 573
BLACKMON, Fred L. 164, 167, 170, 173, 176
BLACKMORE, James 459
BLACKMUN, Harry A. 270
BLACKNEY, William W. 204, 210, 213, 217, 220, 223, 226, 230
BLACKWELDER, Eliot 576
BLACKWELL
Gordon T. 470*, 477
John 9
Julius W. 85, 88
Otto B. 595
Robert E. 479
William B. 576
BLACKWOOD, Ibra C. 366
BLADEN, Thomas 8
BLAIN, Daniel 571
BLAINE
James G. 17, 28, 29, 38*, 106, 108, 110, 111, 112, 113, 114, 115, 116, 118,

121, 123, 125, 314
John J. 192, 195, 199, 385, 386
BLAIR
Austin 110, 112, 114, 322
Bernard 86
David H. 444
Francis P., Jr. 16, 100, 103, 105, 106, 112, 114, 329, 408, 409*, 410
Henry W. 119, 121, 123, 126, 128, 130, 133, 135, 140, 338
Jacob B. 105, 107, 426
James (Ga.) 9
James (S.C.) 70, 76, 78, 80
James G. 114
James T. 330
James T., Jr. 330, 455
John (b. 1689) 9*
John (b. 1732) 4, 269
John (b. 1790) 72, 73, 75, 76, 78, 80
Montgomery 27, 43
Samuel S. 103, 105
W. Frank 575
William M., Jr. 427, 435
BLAISDELL
Daniel 61
James A. 479
Neal S. 454
BLAKE
Bruce 381
Edgar 530
Eugene Carson 612
George H. 551
George S. 483
Gordon A. 444
Harrison G. 103, 105
Henry N. 331
James 462
John, Jr. 59, 60
John L. 123
John R. 469
Joseph 9*
Maurice C. 461
Maxwell 433*
Robert O. 432
Thomas H. 74
BLAKELEY
Harold W. 413
Henry 459
BLAKEMAN, Royal E. 577
BLAKENEY, Albert A. 150, 180
BLAKESLEE,
Albert F. 563, 574
Howard W. 584
BLAKLEY, William A. 240, 247, 373*
BLALOCK
Alfred 565, 590, 600, 607
R.J. 452
Selwyn G. 595
BLANC, Anthony 524, 527
BLANCH, Arnold 607
BLANCHARD
Elizabeth 476
Ferdinand Q. 534
George L. 457
George W. 202
Jonathan (b. 1738) 6
Jonathan (b. 1811) 473
John 90, 92
Newton C. 125, 127, 130, 132, 135, 137, 140, 142, 312*
Noah F. 551
Roger W. 515, 522
William H. 415
BLANCHET
Augustine M.A. 528
Francis N. 524
BLANCHETTE, Romeo 526
BLANCKE
Harold 544
W. Wendell 425*, 426, 428
BLAND
Oscar E. 173, 176, 180, 272*
Richard 7
Richard P. 116, 119, 121, 123, 125, 128, 130, 133, 135, 138, 140, 145
Schuyler Otis 175, 179, 182, 186, 189, 192, 195, 199, 202, 205, 209, 212, 215, 218, 222, 225, 228
Theodorick 7, 51
William T. 177
BLANDFORD, Mark H. 393
BLANDING
Albert H. 402
Sarah G. 484, 603
BLANDY, William H.P. 417, 418
BLANKENBURG, R. 458
BLANKINGSHIP, A.H. 513
BLANTON
Joseph P. 472
L. Ray 256, 260, 263, 266
Thomas L. 175, 179, 182, 185, 189, 192, 195, 198, 202, 205
BLASCOER, Frances 578
BLASDEL, Henry G. 335
BLASHFIELD, Edwin H. 577, 579, 591, 603
BLATCHFORD
Richard M. 410, 434
Samuel (b. 1750) 532
Samuel (b. 1820) 269
BLATNIK, John A. 223, 227, 230, 233, 236, 239, 242, 245, 249, 252, 255, 258, 261, 265
BLATTENBERGER, Raymond 443
BLAUSTEIN, Jacob 595
BLAVATSKY, Helena P.H. 538
BLAYLOCK, L. 453
BLEASE
Coleman L. 188, 192, 195, 365, 366
Eugene S. 366
BLECKLEY, Logan E. 296
BLEDSOE
Albert T. 543
Jesse 63, 308
Samuel T. 543
BLEE, Robert 452
BLEECKER
Harmanus 62, 433
Jan Jansen 449
Johannes, Jr. 449
Rutger 449
BLEEKER, Charles E. 449
BLEGEN, Carl W. 591
BLEICKEN, Gerhard D. 548
BLENK, James H. 524
BLENKINSOP, Peter J. 472
BLESSING, James H. 449
BLETTNER, Edward F. 547
BLILEY, Thomas J., Jr. 459
BLINN, C.J. 458
BLISH, John 536
BLISS
Aaron T. 135, 322
Archibald M. 119, 121, 123, 126, 131, 133
Charles A. 460
Cornelius N. (b. 1833) 30, 44
Cornelius N. (b. 1874) 603
Don C. 428
George 97, 107
George W. 587
George Y. 510
Gilbert A. 568
Philemon 99, 101
Raymond W. 403
Robert W. 423, 437
Tasker H. 400, 419*
BLITCH, Iris F. 235, 238, 241, 245
BLIZARD, Everitt P. 594
BLOCH
Claude C. 416, 418
Ernest 589, 592
Felix 570, 606
Herbert 570
Konrad E. 606
BLOCK
Adolph 579
Herbert L. 584, 586
Joseph L. 548*
Karl M. 513, 519
Leigh B. 492
Leigh E. 548
Philip D. 548
Philip D., Jr. 548
BLOCKSOM, Augustus P. 404, 410
BLODGETT
Frank D. 465
Isaac N. 338
Rufus 133, 135, 138, 341
BLOEDE, Victor G. 600
BLOMGREN, Paul B. 481
BLONDHEIM, Adolphe W. 598
BLOOD
Henry H. 374
Robert O. 339
BLOODGOOD
Francis 449*
Thomas 547
BLOODWORTH, Timothy 6, 51, 54, 55, 56, 347
BLOOM
Edgar S. 554
Isaac 58
Sol 184, 188, 191, 194, 198, 201, 204, 207, 211, 214, 217, 221, 224, 227
BLOOMER, Henry G. 497
BLOOMFIELD, Joseph 67, 68, 340
BLOSS, John M. 478
BLOUGH, Roger M. 554*, 596
BLOUNT
James H. 116, 118, 120, 122, 125, 127, 129, 132, 134, 137, 430
Thomas 53, 54, 55, 59, 60, 62
William 4, 6, 54, 55, 369
William A. 565
William G. 66, 67
Willie 369
Winton M. 36, 43, 575
BLOUSTEIN, Edward J. 466, 480
BLOW, Henry T. 106, 108, 424, 439
BLOX, J.E. 487
BLOXHAM, William D. 293*
BLOY, Francis E.I. 514, 520
BLUE
Richard W. 142
Robert D. 305
Rupert 445, 569
Victor 418*
BLUETT, J. Joseph 480
BLUM, William 575, 589, 590, 594
BLUME
Fred H. 387*, 388*
George C. 454
Peter 607
BLUMENSCHEIN, Ernest L. 589, 598
BLUMER
G. Alder 571
Herbert 574
BLY, Robert 602
BLYTHE, James 482, 532
BLYTHIN, Edward 452
BOAL, Pierre de L. 424, 434
BOARDMAN
Elijah 69, 70, 287
Harold S. 474
Henry A. 532
Waldo E. 566
William W. 83, 85
BOARMAN, Aleck 114
BOAS
Franz 563
Jacob D. 453
BOATNER
Charles J. 135, 137, 140, 142
Haydon L. 403, 405
BOATWRIGHT
F.W. 480
John H. 452
BOAZ, Hiram A. 481, 530
BOBB, James E. 491
BOBRITZKY, George 610
BOBST, Elmer H. 492
BOCHER, Maxime 568
BOCK
E.A. 460
Edward J. 549
Jerry 586
BOCKEE, Abraham 76, 79, 81
BOCKUS, Henry L. 590
BOCOCK, Thomas S. 92, 94, 96, 98, 99, 101, 103, 392, 393*
BODDY, A.W. 455
BODE, Hendrik W. 595
BODEN, Andrew 67, 68
BODENHAMER, O.L. 568
BODIAN, David 599
BODINE
Daniel R. 462
J.H. (mayor) 455
J.H. (zoologist) 573
John W. 563
Robert N. 145
William A. 551
William B. 473
BODLE, Charles 79
BODWELL
Joseph R. 314
William H. 558
BOE, Nils A. 273, 368
BOEGEHOLD, A.L. 572, 590
BOEHM, Martin 543
BOEHNE
John W. 161, 164
John W., Jr. 196, 200, 203, 206, 210, 213
BOEING, William E. 544*, 597
BOELTER, L.M.K. 590
BOEN, Haldor E. 140
BOERUM, Simon 6
BOETCHER, Walter C. 454
BOGAN
Gerald F. 417
Louise 589, 592*, 603
BOGARDUS, Emory S. 573
BOGART, Ernest L. 566
BOGERT, Marston T. 565, 590, 604, 608
BOGGS
J. Caleb 222, 226, 229, 245, 248, 251, 254, 257, 261, 292*
Lilburn W. 329
T. Hale 213, 223, 226, 229, 233, 236, 239, 242, 245, 248, 252, 255, 258, 261
William E. 471
BOGLE, Robert B. 566
BOGY, Lewis 116, 119, 121, 329
BOHLEN, Charles E. 428, 435, 439
BOHM, Max 593
BOHN
Donald I. 599
Frank P. 190, 197
Fred L. 574
John L. 456
BOHROD, Aaron 593, 610
BOIES
Horace 304
William D. 176, 180, 183, 187, 190
BOILEAU, Gerald J. 199, 202, 205, 209
BOJES, Horace 304
BOK
Bart J. 564
Cary W. 491
Derek C. 472
Edward 583
Mrs. Edward W. (Mary Louise Curtis Bok) 441, 491, 603
BOKEE, David A. 93
BOKER, George H. 436, 438
BOLACK, Tom 343
BOLAND
Edward P. 233, 236, 239, 242, 245, 248, 252, 255, 258, 261, 264
Patrick J. 198, 201, 205, 208, 211, 215
Thomas A. 523, 527
Veronica G. 215
BOLANDER, Karl S. 498
BOLD, Harold C. 574
BOLES, Thomas 109, 111, 113
BOLING, Edward J. 482
BOLLES, Stephen 212, 215
BOLLING
Alexander R. 400, 405, 414
Landrum R. 470
Richard W. 227, 230, 233, 236, 239, 242, 246, 249, 252, 255, 258, 262, 265
BOLMAN, Frederick deW., Jr. 470, 491
BOLTE, Charles L. 401, 404, 405, 413, 414
BOLTON
Chester C. 195, 198, 201, 204, 211
Elmer K. 596
Frances P. 211, 214, 218, 221, 224, 227, 230, 234, 237, 240, 243, 246, 249, 253, 256
Frank C. 482*
Herbert E. 567, 591
Oliver P. 234, 237, 249
William P. 226
BOMAR, Benjamin F. 449
BOMFORD, George 402
BOMMARITO, Peter 559
BONA, Stanislaus V. 526*
BONACUM, Thomas 527
BONAPARTE, Charles J. 30, 31*, 41, 42, 579, 599
BONBRIGHT
Daniel 478
James C.H. 435, 437
BOND
Carroll T. 318
Charles A. 452
Charles G. 181
Christopher S. 330
Douglas D. 491
Earl D. 571
Ephraim W. 549
Henry 534

  Henry W. 330
  James 592
  Shadrach 300
  William K. 81, 83, 84
BONE
  Homer T. 202, 205, 209, 212, 215, 219, 272, 381
  Robert G. 472
  William A. 607
BONES, Helen Woodrow 20
BONESTEEL
  Charles H. (b. 1885) 411
  Charles H., 3d 404, 405
  Russell F. 460
BONEY
  George F. 279
  Robert E. 574
BONGIOVANNI, Alfred M. 599
BONHAM
  Milledge 366
  Milledge L. 101, 103, 365, 393
BONIN, Edward J. 234
BONITZ, W.A. 553
BONNELL, Russell 600
BONNER
  Campbell 570
  Herbert C. 211, 214, 218, 221, 224, 227, 230, 234, 237, 240, 243, 246, 249, 253
  John W. 331
  Thomas 476
BONNIFIELD, William 455
BONNYCASTLE, Charles 484
BONSAL
  Philip W. 424, 426*, 433
  Stephen 585
BONTECOU, Lee 593
BONWILL, William G.A. 594
BONYNGE, Robert W. 152, 155, 158
BOOHER, Charles F. 133, 159, 162, 165, 168, 171, 174, 177
BOOKER, George W. 113
BOOKWALTER, Charles A. 454
BOON
  Ratliffe (b. 1781) 302
  Ratliffe (b. 1871) 72, 75, 77, 79, 80, 82
BOONE
  Andrew R. 118, 121
  Buford 586, 601
  Daniel 597
  Edward D. 472
  Levi D. 451
  Thomas 8, 9
  Walter F. 416, 483
  William J. 505, 507
BOONSTRA, Clarence A. 426
BOORSTIN, Daniel J. 500, 591
BOOTH
  Ballington 538, 539
  Donald P. 400, 405, 411
  E.E. 401
  Edwin 597
  Evangeline 603
  Fenton W. 273
  James C. 565
  Maud 538, 539
  Newell S. 530
  Newton 118, 120, 122, 283*
  Ralph H. 427
  Robert R. 532
  Samuel B. 512, 522
  Walter 92
  Wilbur F. 272
  William S. 450
BOOTHMAN, Melvin M. 133, 135
BOOZE, William S. 145
BORAH
  Wayne G. 271
  William E. 158, 161, 164, 167, 170, 173, 176, 180, 183, 186, 190, 193, 196, 200, 203, 206, 209
BORCHERS, Charles M. 167
BORCHERT, Martin 456
BORDEN
  James W. 430
  Joseph 3
  Nathaniel B. 81, 82, 86
  Neil H. 568
BORDERS, William 527
BORDLEY, Stephen 449
BOREING, Vincent 148, 150
BOREMAN
  Arthur I. 577
  Arthur I. (sen.) 113, 115, 117, 383*
  Herbert S. 271
BOREN
  Addison 578
  Lyle H. 208, 211, 214, 218, 221
BORG
  Andy 580
  Dorothy 591
  George W. 544*
BORGESS, Caspar H. 526
BORGMANN, Carl W. 484
BORIE, Adolph E. 28, 42
BORING, Edwin G. 571
BORLAND
  Charles, Jr. 70
  Hal 593
  Solon 90, 92, 94, 96, 281, 426, 429, 430, 436
  William P. 162, 165, 168, 171, 174
BORLAUG, Norman E. 606
BORMAN, Frank ,594, 598, 604
BORNEMEIER, Walter C. 569
BORST
  Peter I. 76
  William 459
BORTELL, Henry S. 438
BORTON, Hugh 472
BORTZ, Edward L. 569
BOSCH, Albert H. 233, 236, 240, 243
BOSHART, W.H. 550
BOSONE, Reva Z.B. 228, 231
BOSS, John L. 66, 67
BOSSART, Karel J. 608
BOSSIER, Pierre E.J.B. 87
BOSTIAN, Cary H. 477
BOSTON, Charles A. 565
BOSTWICK
  Arthur E. 568
  William M. 454
BOSWELL, Charles 454
BOSWORTH, Edward I. 478
BOTELER, Alexander R. 103, 392, 393
BOTKIN
  C.J. 451
  Jeremiah D. 145
BOTTOLFSEN, C.A. 299
BOTTS, JOHN M. 85, 87, 92
BOTTUM, Joseph H. 247, 368
BOUCHER, Chauncey S. 476, 485
BOUCK
  Francis E. 286
  Gabriel 122, 124
  Joseph 77
  William C. 344
BOUDE, Thomas 57
BOUDINOT
  Elias 5, 6, 51, 52, 53, 565
  Truman E. 415
BOUDREAU, Frank G. 610
BOUDREAUX, Isidor 474, 487
BOUGHTEN, M.V. 451
BOULDIN
  James W. 80, 81, 83
  Thomas T. 77, 78, 80
BOULDING, Kenneth E. 566
BOULIGNY
  Dominique 71, 72, 74, 311
  John E. 102
BOULWARE, William 436
BOUND, Franklin 131, 133
BOURGADE, Peter 524, 529
BOURN
  Augustus O. 362
  Benjamin 51, 52, 53, 54
BOURNE
  Jonathan, Jr. 160, 163, 166, 356
  Sherjashub 10, 52*
BOURNS, Edward 478
BOURSAUD, Edward V. 466
BOUTELL, Henry S. 145, 147, 150, 153, 156, 158, 161
BOUTELLE, Charles A. 127, 130, 132, 135, 137, 140, 142, 145, 148
BOUTIN, Bernard L. 445
BOUTWELL
  George S. 28*, 39, 106, 108, 110, 112, 114, 116, 118, 319, 320, 444
  James M. 457*
BOUVIER, Jacqueline Lee 20
BOVARD
  George F. 481
  James M. 493
  Marion M. 481
BOVEE, Matthias J. 81
BOVING, Charles B. 486
BOW
  Frank T. 230, 234, 237, 240, 243, 246, 249, 253, 256, 259, 262, 434
  Warren 485
BOWDEN
  George E. 133, 136
  J.E.T. 454
  Lemuel J. 107
  W. Hammond 498
BOWDERN, Thomas S. 469
BOWDITCH
  Charles P. 563
  Henry I. 569
  Henry P. 570*
  Nathaniel 563
  Richard L. 575
BOWDLE, Stanley E. 169
BOWDLER, William G. 427, 429
BOWDOIN, James 8, 437, 563
BOWDON, Franklin W. 89, 90, 92
BOWEN
  C.H. 458
  Catherine Drinker 602
  Christopher C. 111, 113
  David R. 265
  H.G. 418
  Harold L. 514, 519
  Henry 129, 133
  Herbert W. 435, 439
  Howard R. 471, 473
  Ira S. 608, 610
  J.B. 456
  J.W.E. 531
  Jabez 10
  John H. 64
  John S. 395
  Nathaniel 505, 521
  Norman L. 576, 597, 607
  Otis R. 303
  Rees T. 117
  Richard L. 481
  Sayles J. 462
  Thomas M. 127, 129, 132, 285
  William C. 479
BOWER
  Gustavus M. 88
  Henry 594
  William H. 141
BOWERMAN
  Jay R. 356
  Willard I. 455
BOWERS
  Charles W. 577
  Claude G. 425, 437
  Eaton J. 153, 156, 159, 162
  George M. 172, 175, 179, 182
  John M. 64
  Riley C. 457
  Verne L. 401
  William J. 557
  William W. 136, 139, 142
BOWERSOCK, Justin D. 150, 153, 156
BOWIE
  Oden 317
  Robert 316*
  Richard J. 93, 95, 317
  Sydney J. 150, 152, 155
  Thomas F. 98, 100
  Walter 56, 57
  William 566*, 594
BOWKER
  Albert H. 467, 477
  Frank 558
BOWLER
  James B. 235, 238
  Metcalf 3, 10
BOWLES
  Charles 453
  Chester B. 241, 289, 430*, 433
  F.T. 418
  Grover C. 570
  Henry L. 187, 190
BOWLEY, Albert J. 400, 405
BOWLIN, James B. 88, 89, 91, 93, 425, 434
BOWLING
  William B. 176, 179, 183, 186, 189
  William K. 569
BOWMAN
  Alexander H. 483
  Charles C. 166
  Clellan A. 465
  Frank L. 189, 192, 195, 199
  George A. 473
  Isaiah 473, 563
  J. William 453
  John B. 473, 482
  John F. 460
  John G. 473, 479
  Karl M. 571
  Milo J. 484
  Samuel 506
  Selwyn Z. 123, 125
  Thomas (b. 1817) 469, 530
  Thomas (b. 1836) 531
  Thomas (b. 1848) 137
  Waldo G. 572
BOWN, Ralph 598
BOWNE
  Obadiah 95
  Samuel O. 86
  Walter 458
BOWRING, Eva K. 233, 334
BOWRON, Fletcher 456
BOWYER, John M. 483
BOX, John C. 179, 182, 185, 189, 192, 195
BOXTON, Charles 461
BOYCE
  James P. 534
  Westray Battle 401
  William H. 183
  William W. 97, 99, 101, 103, 391, 392, 393*
BOYD
  A. Hunter 317
  Adam 58, 60, 61, 62
  Alan S. 36, 47, 548
  Alexander 64
  Benjamin 451
  David F. 465, 474*
  David R. 476, 478
  Haco 456
  James 567
  James E. 333*
  James H. 454
  John F. 159
  John H. 95
  Julian P. 567
  Linn 80, 84, 85, 87, 89, 91, 93, 94, 95, 96*
  Louise Arner 594
  Robert 459
  Robert M. 575*
  Robert O. 444*
  Sempronius H. 106, 112, 436
  Thomas A. 120, 122
  Thomas D. 474
  W. Stokes 454
  Willard L. 473
  William 547
  William R., Jr. 570
BOYDEN, Nathaniel 91, 111
BOYER
  Benjamin M. 109, 111
  Clarence V. 478
  Ernest L. 477
  Lewis L. 206
BOYKIN, Frank W. 202, 206, 209, 212, 216, 219, 222, 225, 228, 232, 235, 238, 241, 244
BOYLAN
  John J. (Rep.) 184, 188, 191, 194, 198, 201, 204, 207
  John J. (bishop) 528
  Murtha A. 473
  William A. 467
BOYLE
  Charles A. 235, 238, 242
  Charles E. 128, 131
  Edward C. 577
  Emmet D. 335
  Harold V. 585
  Hugh C. 528
  James 449
  John 57, 59, 60, 308
BOYLES, Bartlett E. 455
BOYNTON
  Charles B. 472
  Charles F. 514, 521
  Washington W. 353
BRABSON, Reese B. 103
BRACE
  Jonathan 54, 55, 453
  Theodore 329
  Thomas K. 453
BRACELAND, Francis J. 571, 599
BRACKEN
  John 486
  Stanley 554
BRACKENBRIDGE
  Henry M. 85
  William A. 552
BRACKETT
  Charles 563
  G.A. 457
  John Q.A. 320
  Truman H., Jr. 499
BRADBURY
  George 63, 65

James W. 91, 93, 95, 314
Joseph P. 353*
Norris E. 595
Theophilus 53, 54
BRADDON, Frederick D. 601, 610
BRADEMAS, John 242, 245, 248, 251, 255, 258, 261, 264
BRADEN
Arthur 482
Samuel E. 472
Spruille 423, 426*
BRADFORD
Alden 580
Alexander, B. 392
Augustus, W. 317
Benjamin J. 457
Donald 454
John S. 461
Robert F. 321
T.L. 453
Taul 118
William 3, 8*, 23, 41, 53, 54*, 55, 361
BRADISH, Luther 565
BRADLEY
Albert 547
Benjamin F. 393
Charles S. 362
Dan F. 471
Denis M. 527
Edward 91
F.W. 610
Follett 411
Frederick V. 210, 213, 217, 220, 223
Harry L. 491
James L. 414
Joseph P. 269
Lewis R. 335
Luke C. 554
Mark E., Jr. 415
Michael J. 208, 211, 215, 218, 221
Nathan B. 116, 119
Omar N. 399, 400, 405, 411*, 412, 413, 415, 609
Preston 576
Stephen R. 52, 53, 56, 57, 58, 59, 60, 61, 62, 63, 375*
Thomas J. 146
Thomas W. 148, 154, 157, 159, 162, 165
William A. 462
William C. 545
William C. (Rep.) 64, 72, 73
William O. 161, 164, 167, 309*
William V. 558
Willis W. 222
Wilmot H. 576
BRADSHAW
Donna S. 493
Samuel C. 99
Thomas A. 551
Thornton F. 544
BRADSTREET, Simon 8*
BRADY
Genevieve G. 599
George W. 608
James D. 131
James H. 164, 167, 170, 173, 298*
Jasper E. 92
Matthew F. 525, 527
Robert W. 466, 472*
Samuel 450
William G. 547*
William H. 515, 519
William O. 524, 529
William T. 578
William V. 458
BRAGG
Braxton 394*, 395*
Edward S. 122, 124, 126, 131, 433
J.B. 470
John 94
Thomas 103, 105, 347, 348, 391
BRAINARD
David L. 594
Leverett 454
Morgan B. 543
Newton C. 454
BRAINERD
Ezra 475
Lawrence 98, 375
Samuel M. 128
Thomas 532
BRAISTED
W.G. 416
William C. 569
BRAITHWAITE, William S. 611
BRAM, Martin J. 515
BRAMAN, J.D. 461
BRAMBLETT, Ernest K. 222, 225, 229, 232
BRAMLETTE, Thomas E. 17, 309
BRANCH
A.M. 393
C.B. 546
C.H. Hardin 571
Emmet F. 303
John 25, 42, 71, 73, 74, 76, 78, 347
Judson B. 491
Lawrence O. 99, 101, 103
Oliver W. 339
William A.B. 138, 141
BRAND
Charles 185, 188, 191, 195, 198
Charles H. 173, 176, 180, 183, 186, 190, 193, 196, 200
George E. 568
Stewart 602
BRANDEGEE
Augustus 106, 107
Frank B. 150, 153, 155, 158, 161, 164*, 170, 173, 176, 179, 183, 288
BRANDEIS, Louis D. 270
BRANDHORST, Otto W. 566
BRANDON
Gerard C. 326
Rodney H. 577
William W. 278
BRANDT
Edward J. 601
Joseph A. 478
Mel 557
BRANIGIN, Roger D. 303
BRANN, Louis J. 315
BRANNAMAN, Ray H. 580
BRANNAN
Charles F. 34, 35, 45
John M. 409
BRANNER, John C. 481, 575, 597
BRANNON
Ernest M. 402
Melvin A. 466, 472
BRANSCOMB
Harvie 484
John W. 531
BRANSFORD, John S. 460
BRANSON
Fred P. 355
John W. 476*
BRANTLEY, William G. 145, 147, 150, 153, 155, 158, 161, 164
BRANTLY
J.E. 601
Theodore 331
BRASCO, Frank J. 256, 259, 262, 265
BRASHARES, Charles W. 530
BRASHEAR
John A. 479, 573, 594
Samuel H. 454
BRASSART, Ferdinand 525
BRASTED, Alva J. 401
BRATTAIN, Walter H. 606
BRATTON
John 129
Robert F. 140
Sam G. 188, 191, 194, 198, 201, 272, 343
Theodore DuB. 509, 520
BRAUER, Richard D. 568, 604
BRAUN, E. Lucy 575
BRAWLEY, William H. 138, 141
BRAXTON
Carter 3, 7
Elliot M. 115
BRAY
Oscar 572
William G. 229, 232, 235, 239, 242, 245, 248, 251, 255, 258, 261, 264
BRAYTON
George A. 362
William D. 101, 103
BREARLEY, David 4, 10
BREASTED
James H. 501, 567, 590
James H., Jr. 500
BREATHITT
Edward T. 310
John 308
BREAUX
John B. 264
Joseph A. 312
BREAZEALE, Phanor 148, 150, 153
BRECK
Daniel 93
Samuel (b. 1771) 71
Samuel (b. 1831) 401
BRECKENRIDGE, Hugh H. 607
BRECKINRIDGE
Clifton R. 127, 129, 131, 134, 136, 139, 436
J.C. 579
James 62, 63, 64, 66
James D. 69
John 23, 41, 56, 57, 59, 308
John B. 264
John C. 14, 16*, 95, 96, 100, 102, 104, 309, 391, 394, 395*
Joseph C. 402
Robert J. 392, 485, 532
William C.P. 130, 132, 134, 137, 140
William L. 532
BREECE, George E. 451
BREECH, Ernest R. 550
BREED
G. 600
R.E. 543
BREEDEN, H.O. 536
BREEN, Edward F. 227, 230
BREES, Herbert J. 405, 419
BREESE, Sidney 87, 89, 91, 300
BREESKIN, Adelyn D. 497
BREHM
C.E. 482
Walter E. 218, 221, 224, 227, 230
BREIT, Gregory 596, 604
BREITENBACK, Joseph 526
BREITENSTEIN, Jean S. 272
BREITHOLTZ, Ernest G. 580
BREITHUT, Frederick E. 567
BREITMEYER, Philip 453
BREITUNG, Edward 128
BREMNER, Robert G. 168
BRENDLINGER, Hiram J. 453
BRENGLE
Francis 87
Henry G. 546
BRENHAM, C.J. 461
BRENNAN
Andrew J. 528
Francis 523
Martin A. 200, 203
Peter J. 37, 46
Thomas F. 525
Vincent M. 180
William J., Jr. 270, 599
BRENNER
Edward J. 444
John L. 146, 149
BRENT
Charles H. 509, 522, 521
Richard 54, 55, 57, 62, 63, 64, 378
Robert 462
Thomas L.L. 435
Thomas R. 396
William, Jr. 423
William L. 71, 72, 74
BRENTANO
Lorenzo 120
Theodore 430
BRENTON
J.M. 453
Samuel 94, 98, 100
W. Harold 564
William 9*
BRERETON, Lewis H. 411, 412*
BRES, Edward S. 403
BRESLOW, Lester 572
BRESNAHEN, L.R. 451*
BRESSLER, Raymond G. 479
BRESTER, William 569
BRETT
George H. 411, 412
Lloyd M. 580
Philip M. 480
William H. 568
BRETZ, John L. 137, 139
BREUER, Marcel 590, 598
BREVARD, Joseph 69
BREW, John O. 501, 563, 611
BREWER
Albert P. 279
Carlos 415
David J. 269
Earl L. 327
Francis B. 128
Gene C. 553
J. Hart 126, 128
John M. 536
Leigh R. 507, 520
Mark S. 121, 123, 132, 135
Nicholas 449*
Nicholas, Jr. 449
William D. 432
Willis 144, 147
BREWERTON, Henry 483
BREWSTER
Albert 279
Benjamin 510, 520
Benjamin H. 29*, 41
Chauncey B. 508, 519, 522
Daniel B. 242, 245, 248, 252, 255, 318
David P. 84, 86
Ellis W. 580
Henry C. 143, 146
Kingman, Jr. 487
Ralph O. 203, 207, 210, 213, 217, 220, 223, 226, 229, 315*, 536
William 3
BREYFOGEL, Sylvanus 531
BRICE
Calvin S. 138, 141, 143, 353
James 449*
John 449*
BRICK, Abraham L. 147, 150, 153, 156, 158
BRICKELL, Robert C. 277, 278
BRICKER, John W. 18, 224, 227, 230, 234, 237, 240, 354*
BRICKHOUSE, Ben D. 455
BRICKNER
Burt G. 576
George H. 136, 139, 141
BRIDENBAUGH, Carl 567
BRIDGERS, Robert R. 392, 393
BRIDGES
Charles H. 401
George W. 105
H. Styles 207, 211, 214, 217, 220, 224, 227, 230, 232, 233*, 236, 239, 243, 246, 339*
Harry 558
John 10
Robert 563
Ronald 534
Samuel A. 92, 97, 122
BRIDGFORD, W.L. 458
BRIDGHAM, Samuel W. 459
BRIDGMAN
George H. (b. 1841) 471
George H. (b. 1853) 424
Percy W. 570, 594, 605, 610
BRIER, Royce 584
BRIEST, John 461
BRIGGS
Ansel 304
Clay Stone 179, 182, 185, 189, 192, 195, 198, 202
Ellis O. 424, 426, 427, 429, 435, 437, 439
Eugene S. 576
Frank A. 350
Frank O. 159, 162, 165, 341, 462
Frank P. 220, 330
George 93, 95, 103
George N. 77, 79, 81, 82, 84, 86, 319
Herbert W. 573
James E. (mayor) 459
James E. (USAF) 483
James F. 121, 123, 126
Le Baron R. 479
Lyman J. 570, 593*
M.C. 479
Sam 579
W. Paul 609
William T. 569
BRIGHAM
Clarence S. 563
Claude E. 402
Elbert S. 189, 192, 195, 549
Elijah 62, 63, 65
J.H. 578
Lewis A. 123
Paul 375
William T. 497
BRIGHT
J. Fulmer 459
James W. 566, 577
Jesse D. 89, 91, 93, 94, 96*, 98*, 100, 102*, 104, 302
John M. 115, 117, 120, 122, 124

Myron H. 272
BRILEY, Beverly 457
BRIM, Orville G. 493
BRIMELOW, Bryan 596
BRIMHALL, George H. 467
BRIMMER, Martin 450
BRINEGAR, Claude S. 37, 47
BRINCKEROFF, Charles M. 543, 610
BRINDLEY, George V. 565
BRINES, Osborne A. 572
BRINGHURST, William L. 482
BRINGLE, William F. 416, 417
BRINK, Edwin H. 601
BRINKER, Howard R. 513, 520
BRINKERHOFF
Henry R. 88
Jacob 88, 90, 352
BRINKLEY, Jack T. 254, 257, 261, 264
BRINKMAN, Gervaise 566
BRINLEY, D. Putnam 591
BRINSON, Samuel M. 178, 181
BRINTON
Crane 567
Daniel G. 563
BRISBIN
John 93
John B. 460
BRISCO, M.M. 553
BRISCOE, Adolph 373
BRISLIN, John H. 586
BRISTER, John W. 475
BRISTOL
Frank M. 530
W.H. 600
BRISTOW
Benjamin H. 28, 39, 564
Francis M. 96, 102
Henry 151
Joseph L. 161, 164, 167, 306
BRITT
Albert 473
James J. 171, 175
Laurence V. 469
BRITTAIN, Marion L. 471
BRITTEN, Fred A. 167, 170, 173, 176, 180, 183, 186, 190, 193, 196, 200
BRITTERIDGE, Richard 3
BRITTON
Edgar C. 565
James H. 460
Nathaniel L. 574
William E. 564
BROACH, H.H. 558
BROADDUS, Andrew 456
BROADFOOT, Grover L. 386
BROADHEAD, James O. 128, 438, 564
BROADLEY, Hugh T. 501
BROADWELL, Norman M. 461
BROBECK, John R. 571
BROCK
Glenn P. 548
Isaac 406
Lawrence 242
O. Carlyle 579
William E. 195, 371
William E., 3d 250, 253, 256, 260, 263, 266, 371
BROCKENBROUGH
John W. 392
William H. 89
BROCKETT
E.D. 548*
William A. 418
BROCKLESBY, John 482
BROCKMAN, Hubert F. 487
BROCKSON, Franklin 167
BROCKWAY, John H. 83, 85
BRODBECK, Andrew R. 169, 175
BRODE, Wallace R. 563, 565, 580, 608
BRODERICK
Case 137, 140, 142, 145
David C. 100, 102, 283
Edwin B. 525
Francis L. 475
BRODHEAD
J. Davis 160
John 76, 77
John C. 77, 83
Richard 88, 90, 92, 95, 97, 99, 358
BRODIE
Bernard B. 600, 604
Edward E. 428, 436
William 569
BROENING, William F. 450, 591
BROGAN, Thomas J. 342
BROGDEN, Curtis H. 121, 348
BROMBERG, Frederick G. 115
BROMFIELD, Louis 583, 591
BROMWELL
Henry P.H. 108, 110
Jacob H. 141, 143, 146, 149, 151
James E. 245, 248
BRONDEL, John B. 526
BRONEER, Oscar T. 591
BRONFMAN, Edgar M. 552
BRONK, Detlev W. 473, 563, 596, 604, 608
BRONSON
David 86
E.D. 565
Greene C. 344*
Isaac H. 83
Sherlock A. 473
BRONWELL, Arthur B. 487
BROOCKS, Moses L. 157
BROOK, Alexander 607*, 610
BROOKE
David S. 498
Edward W. 255, 258, 261, 264, 321, 598, 611
Francis K. 508, 521
Francis T. 378
Mrs. Frederick H. 576
Robert 378
Walker 95, 326, 391, 392
BROOKHART
John M. 571
Smith W. 180, 183, 187, 190, 193, 196, 305*
BROOKS
Alfred H. 594
Bryant B. 387
C. Wayland 209, 213, 216, 219, 223, 301
David 55
Edward H. 400, 405*, 412, 415*
Edward S. 178, 182
Edwin B. 176, 180
Ernest, Jr. 492
Eugene C. 477
F.H. 550
Franklin E. 152, 155
George M. 112, 114
Gwendolyn 585
Harvey 563
Henry L. 272
J. Twing 201, 205
Jabez 471
Jack B. 234, 237, 240, 244, 247, 250, 253, 256, 260, 263, 266
James 93, 95, 107, 108, 110, 112, 115, 117
John (gov.) 319
John (mayor) 452
John A. 17
John B. 411, 412
John E. 472
John W. 544*
Kendall 473*
Micah 65
Milton 584
Overton 207, 210, 213, 217, 220, 223, 226, 229, 233, 236, 239, 242, 245
Paul 593
Peter A. 474
Phillips 508, 520, 597
Preston S. 97, 99
Ralph G. 334
Robert C. 571
Robert N. 530
Samuel P. 466
Stratton D. 476, 478
Van Wyck 584, 603, 609
Wiley G. 473
William P. 475
William T.H. 408*
BROOKSHIRE, Elijah V. 134, 137, 139
BROOM
Jacob (b. 1752) 4
Jacob (b. 1808) 99
BROOMALL, John M. 107, 109, 111
BROOME
James E. 293
James M. 58, 60
BROOMFIELD
John C. 530
William S. 239, 242, 245, 249, 252, 255, 258, 261, 264
BROPHY, John C. 225
BROSIN, Henry W. 571
BROSIUS, Marriott 136, 138, 141, 143, 146, 149
BROSNAHAN, Timothy 466
BROSNAN, D. William 552
BROSSARD, Edgar B. 445
BROSSEAU, Grace L.H. 579
BROTHERSTON, John H.F. 592
BROTZMAN, Donald G. 248, 254, 257, 260, 264
BROUGH
Charles H. 282
John 352
BROUGHER, J. Whitcomb 534
BROUGHTON
Charles E. 574
J. Melville 224, 227, 349*
John G. 501
Thomas 9
BROUN
Heywood 557
William L. 465*
BROUNER, Harry 549
BROUSSARD
E.S. 180, 184, 187, 190, 193, 197, 312
Robert F. 145, 148, 150, 153, 156, 159, 162, 165, 167, 170, 173, 312
BROUWER, Theophilus A. 565
BROWARD, Napoleon B. 293
BROWER
Howard 472
John M. 133, 135
BROWERSOCK, Justin D. 148
BROWN
A.M. 543
Aaron S. 434
Aaron V. 27, 43, 85, 87, 88, 369
Alan W. 472
Albert E. 413*
Albert G. (Rep.) 84, 91, 93, 95, 97, 99, 100, 102, 326*, 392, 393
Albert G. 480
Albert O. 339
Alexander B. 485
Alexander G., Jr. 575
Allan D. 478
Allen W. 516, 519
Allyn M. 289
Anson 84
Arthur 144, 374
Arthur W. (gen.) 402
Arthur W. 465
B. Gratz 17*, 106, 108, 329
Bedford 76, 78, 79, 81, 83, 84, 347
Ben H., Jr. 432
Benjamin 65
Beriah 461
Brooks, Jr. 450
C.W. 550
Calvin L. 324
Carleton 577
Mrs. Caro 586
Charles 86, 92
Charles E. 131, 133
Charles E., Jr. 401
Charles H. (b. 1875) 568
Charles H. (b. 1920) 239, 242
Charles R. 417
Clarence J. 211, 214, 218, 221, 224, 227, 230, 234, 237, 240, 243, 246, 249, 253
Clarence J., Jr. 253, 256, 259, 262, 265
Clarence W. 550
Clinton G. 461
Cyrus B. 457
Daniel R. 362
Darius A. 455, 577
David P. 611
Dillard H., Jr. 543
Donald L. 554
E.E. 455
E.S. 456, 457
Edmund G. 284, 298
Edward E. 546, 547*
Edward J. 558
Edwin J. 461
Eli H., 3d 474
Elias 76
Elmer 558
Elmer E. 444, 477
Ernest S. 233, 336
Ernest W. 564, 568
Ethan A. 70, 71, 352*, 424
Foster S. 480
Foster V. 144
Frances W. 455
Francis 469
Fred H. 201, 204, 207, 339*
Frederic J. 405
Frederick F. 534
Garry E. 255, 258, 261, 264
George 430
George E., Jr. 247, 251, 254, 257, 260, 263
George H. (b. 1810) 95
George H. (b. 1908) 595
George H. (b. 1910) 568
George H., Jr. 547*
George L. 579
George R. 491
George S. (b. 1871) 273
George S. (b. 1918) 415
George W. 578
George W. (mayor) 450
Guy L. 557
Harold 399, 467
Harold H. 499
Harold P. 600
Harry 610
Harry A. 472
Harvey W. 557
Henry B. 484
Henry B. (judge) 269
Henry K. 484
Henry P. 576
Herbert 497
Herbert C. 604*
Herman 491
Homer C. 566
Horace A. 452
J. Calvin 573
J. Carter 500
J. Clifton 478
J.G. 574
J.H. Hobart 507, 519
J. Hay 359
J.O. 543
J. Stanley 478
Jacob 400, 406
James 533
James (sen.) 62, 63, 65, 68, 69, 71, 311*, 428
James H. 449
James M., 3d 498, 501, 502
James S. (mayor) 457
James S. (rep.) 107, 456
James W. 154
Jason B. 134, 137, 139
Jeremiah 86, 88
Jesse 455
John (b. 1736) 56
John (b. 1750) 61
John (b. 1757) 7, 51, 52, 53, 54, 55, 56, 57*, 308
John (b. 1763) 471
John (b. 1772) 70, 71
John B. 137
John C. 370, 395, 396
John G. 533
John Henry 452
John J. 576
John Q. 480*
John R. (b. 1842) 134
John R. (b. 1909) 271
John W. 79, 81
John Y. (b. 1835) 102, 116, 118, 309
John Y. (b. 1900) 200
Joseph (Md.) 449
Joseph (Mo.) 460
Joseph E. (sen.) 122, 125, 127, 129, 132, 134, 296*
Joseph E. (Rep.) 182
Joseph G. 457
Joseph M. 296*
Kenneth I. 469, 472, 491
L. Dean 428, 431, 436
Lathrop 168
Leander 450
Leland A. 482
LeRoy D. 476
Lloyd D. 413
Lyndon O. 473
Lytle 402
M.C. 558
Matthew 485*
Milton 87, 88, 90
Nathaniel 460
Neil S. 369, 436
Norris 159, 162, 165, 333
Otis N. 580
Paul 200, 203, 206, 209, 213, 216, 219, 223, 226, 229, 232, 235, 238, 241
Peter 3
Peter A.G. 502
Philip M. 570
Prentiss M. 200, 203, 204, 207, 210, 213, 323, 546

R.B. 416
Ralph S. 564
Richard F. 499
Robert 55, 56, 57, 58, 59, 60, 61, 63 64
Robert R. 516, 519
Robert W. 574
Robert W. (mayor) 452
Roy 574
S. Perry 568
Samuel G. 471
Seth W. 146, 149
Sterling W. 578
Theodore 500
Thomas 293
Thomas H. 456*
Thomas J. 372
Timothy 386
Titus 73, 74
W. Matt 457
Wallace E. 530
Walter F. 33, 43
Walter H. 572
Walter L. (b. 1861) 568
Walter L. (b. 1903) 491
Webster E. 152, 155, 158
William 531
William (Ky.) 68
William, Sr. 455
William A. 513, 522
William C. 510, 522
William E. 552
William G. 90, 92, 105, 107
William G., Jr. 166, 169, 172
William J. 87, 93
William M. 508, 519
William R. 118
William W. 128, 131
Wilson 483
Winthrop G. 431, 437

BROWNE
Benjamin P. 534
Charles 184
Edward E. 169, 172, 176, 179, 182, 186, 189, 192, 196
George 518
George H. 105
Harry C. 536
J.M. 416
J. Ross 425
John T. 454
Malcolm W. 587
R.A. 533
Thomas H.B. 134, 136
Thomas M. 120, 123, 125, 127, 130, 132, 134
William M. 391

BROWNELL
Abner C. 452
Herbert, Jr. 35*, 41, 568
Samuel M. 444
Thomas C. 482, 505, 519
William C. 603

BROWNING
Colleen 598
Edmund 517
Gordon 185, 189, 192, 195, 198, 202, 371*
James R. 272
Orville H. 27, 44, 104, 300
William J. 165, 168, 171, 174, 177

BROWNLEE, John T. 533

BROWNLOW
Louis 462
Walter P. 146, 149, 152, 154, 157, 160, 163
William G. 113, 115, 117, 370*

BROWNSON
Charles B. 229, 232, 235, 239
Henry F. 599
James I. 485*
Josephine Van Dyke 599
Nathan 5
Willard H. 418, 483

BROYHILL
James T. 249, 253, 256, 259, 262, 265
Joel T. 234, 237, 241, 244, 247, 250, 257, 260, 263, 266

BRUBACHER, Abram R. 477

BRUCE
A.D. 472
Andrew D. 405, 414, 419
Blanche K. 119, 121, 123, 326
Donald C. 245, 248
E.L. 576
Edmond 601
Ely M. 392, 393
Horatio W. 393

James 533
James D. 577
James M. 423
Robert 479
William 533
William Cabell 184, 187, 190, 318, 583, 599

BRUCK, Philip H. 452

BRUCKER
Ferdinand 145
Herbert 573
Wilber M. 323, 399

BRUCKNER, Henry 168, 171, 174

BRUERE, Henry 579, 603

BRUMBAUGH
Clement L. 169, 172, 175, 178
D. Emmert 218, 221
Martin G. 359

BRUMIT, Joseph L. 578

BRUMM
Charles N. 126, 128, 131, 133, 143, 146, 157, 160
George F. 185, 188, 198, 201

BRUNCKEN, Herbert 610
BRUNDAGE, Percival F. 444
BRUNDIDGE, Stephen, Jr. 144, 147, 150, 152, 155, 158
BRUNE, Frederick W. 318
BRUNENGO, Aloysius 481

BRUNER
Jerome S. 571
John E. 558

BRUNINI, Joseph B. 527

BRUNNER
David B. 136, 138
Jean A. 580
William F. 194, 198, 201, 204

BRUNNIER, H.J. 580
BRUNS, Bernard 455
BRUNSDALE, C. Norman 243, 351*
BRUNTON, David W. 610

BRUSH
Alexander 451
Edward N. 571
George de F. 610
George J. 563
Gerard M. 459
Henry 68
Rapp 413

BRUYN, Andrew D.W. 83

BRYAN
Albert V. 271
B.F. 450*
Blackshear M. 403, 404, 405, 483
Charles P. 424*, 431, 435
Charles W. 18, 333, 334, 455*
Elmer B. 468, 478
Enoch A. 485
George 3
George D. 451
Guy M. 101
Henry H. 69
Henry S. 549
James E. 568
James W. 169
John A. 435
John H. 73, 75
John S. 486
Joseph 57, 59
Joseph H. 65, 67
Nathan 54, 55
Nathan P. 164, 167, 170, 271, 293
R.R. 467*
Thomas P., Jr. 459
W.R. 577
William A. 500
William J. 158, 293
William Jennings 17*, 31, 38, 138, 140
William L. 473, 571
Wright 573

BRYANT
Andrew J. 461
Farris 294
G. Hyde 461
Joseph D. 569
William Cullen 597
William L. 497

BRYCE
James 571
John 452
Lloyd S. 133, 432, 433

BRYSON
John 456
Joseph R. 211, 215, 218, 221, 225, 228, 231, 234

BRZANA, Stanislaus 527

BUCH, Joseph C. 574

BUCHANAN
Andrew 81, 83
Frank (b. 1862) 164, 167, 170, 557
Frank (b. 1902) 221, 224, 228, 231
Franklin 396*, 483
George S. 564
Hugh 125, 127
James (b. 1791) 13, 16, 26*, 38, 70, 71, 73, 75, 76, 79, 81, 83, 85, 86, 88, 90, 358, 429, 436
James (b. 1839) 130, 133, 135, 138
James M. 426
James P. 169, 172, 175, 179, 182, 185, 189, 192, 195, 198, 202, 205, 208
James S. 478
Jesse E. 472
John 316
John A. 136, 139
John H., Jr. 251, 254, 257, 260, 263
John L. 465, 470, 484
John P. 370
Thomas C. 443
Vera D. 231, 234, 237
Wiley T., Jr. 432
William L. 423, 434

BUCHER
George H. 554
J.F. 485
John C. 78
Walter H. 567, 576, 607

BUCHMAN
Frank N.D. 538
Louis 610

BUCHOLZ, John T. 574
BUCHTEL, Henry A. 285, 469

BUCK
Alfred E. 111, 431
C. Douglass 216, 219, 222, 292*
Carl D. 570, 610
Charles F. 142
Charles W. 435
Daniel 54
Daniel A. 72, 75
Daniel W. 455*
Ellsworth B. 217, 221, 224
Frank H. 199, 202, 206, 209, 212
Gene 572
George S. 451
John R. 125, 129
Paul H. 584
Pearl S. 584, 598, 605
Peter H. 497
Samuel J. 471

BUCKALEW, Charles R. 107, 109, 111, 133, 136, 359, 427
BUCKBEE John T. 190, 193, 196, 200, 203
BUCKHAM, Matthew H. 484

BUCKINGHAM
George M. 491
Richard G. 453
Thomas L. 566
William A. 111, 113, 116, 288*
William D. 612

BUCKLAND, Ralph P. 109, 111
BUCKLER, Richard T. 204, 207, 210, 214

BUCKLEY
Charles A. 204, 207, 211, 214, 217, 221, 224, 227, 230, 233, 236, 240, 243, 246, 249
Charles E. 498*
Charles W. 109, 111, 113
James L. 262, 265, 346
James R. 183
James V. 226
John P. 566
Oliver E. 595
Stuart E. 601

BUCKLIN, John C. 456
BUCKMAN, Clarence B. 154, 156
BUCKMASTER, L.S. 559

BUCKNER
Alexander 77, 79, 329
Aylette 91
Aylett H. 91, 116, 119, 121, 123, 125, 128
Benjamin P. 454
George W. 432
Richard A. 71, 72, 74
Simon B. 17, 309, 395

BUCKSON, David P. 292

BUDD
Edward G. 590
James H. 127, 283
John M. 544, 548
Ralph 545, 548, 596

BUDDINGTON, Arthur F. 607
BUDDY, Charles F. 528
BUDGE, Hamer H. 229, 232, 235, 238, 242, 445
BUDLONG, Frederick G. 512, 519

BUECHNER
Frederick 609
Thomas S. 497

BUEHLER, William E. 577

BUEL
Alexander W. 93
David H. 471

BUELL
Alexander H. 95
Don Carlos 406, 407
George P. 410
Murray F. 575
Victor P. 568
Willis 449

BUERKI, Robin C. 578
BUETOW, Herbert P. 549
BUFFETT, Howard H. 217, 220, 224, 230

BUFFINGTON
Adelbert R. 402
James 99, 100, 102, 104, 112, 114, 116
Joseph (b. 1803) 88, 90
Joseph (b. 1855) 271

BUFFINTON, James (See Buffington)

BUFFUM
Joseph, Jr. 68
Robert E. 536
William B. 432

BUFORD
John 409
John L. 578

BUGBEE
F. 457*
George 578
Lucius 465

BUGG, Robert M. 97
BUHER, Stephen 452
BUHL, Christian H. 453*
BULEY, R. Carlyle 585

BULKELEY
Eliphalet A. 543*, 545
Morgan G. 155, 158, 161, 288*, 454

BULKLEY, Robert J. 166, 169, 194, 198, 201, 204, 208, 353

BULL
Harold R. 401*, 412, 419
Henry 9*
James G. 453*
John (Mo.) 79
John (S.C.) 7
Melville 144, 146, 149, 152
Storm 456
William 9*

BULLARD
Edward P., Jr. 590, 607
F. Lauriston 583
Henry A. 77, 79, 93
Robert L. 405, 410*
Samuel 461
William N. 569

BULLEN, John 449*

BULLENE
Egbert F. 402
Thomas B. 455

BULLER, A.H.R. 574
BULLIONS, Peter 533
BULLIS, Harry A. 547*, 578
BULLITT, William C. 428, 439

BULLOCH
Archibald 5, 8
William B. 63, 295

BULLOCK
A. George 553
Alexander H. 320
Chandler 553
David 459
Henry A. 591
Hugh 579
Marie L. 603
Robert 134, 137
Robert O. 596
Rufus B. 296
Stephen 54
Theodore H. 573
Wingfield 69

BULOW, William J. 198, 202, 205, 208, 212, 215, 367*
BULWINKLE, Alfred L. 181, 185, 188, 191, 198, 201, 204, 208, 211, 214, 218, 221, 224, 227

BUMPERS, Dale 282
BUMPUS, Hermon C. 483, 497
BUMSTEAD, Henry A. 570
BUNCE
Alan 557
J.H. 456
Jonathan B. 551
BUNCH, Samuel 80, 81
BUNCHE, Ralph J. 571, 603, 605, 608, 611
BUNDEL, Charles M. 419
BUNDESEN, Herman H. 572
BUNDLIE, Gerhard J. 460
BUNDY
Hezekiah S. 109, 117, 141
McGeorge 491, 608
Omar 410*
Solomon 121
BUNKER
Arthur H. 491, 543
Berkeley L. 211, 214, 220, 336
Earle L. 585
Ellsworth 423, 430, 431, 433, 439, 569, 608*
BUNN
Benjamin H. 135, 138, 141
Edward B. 471
Henry G. 281
Howard S. 553
BUNNELL, Frank C. 115, 131, 133
BUNNER, Rudolph 74
BUNTING
Earl 578
James W. 478
John R. 547
Mary I. 479, 603
Thomas L. 138
BUNZEL, John H. 481
BUQUOR, P.S. 461
BURALL, William P. 548
BURBANK, Luther 603
BURBECK, Henry 402
BURBRIDGE, J.Q. 454
BURCAW, Ellis 500
BURCH
Charles S. 510, 520
Dean 443
John C. 102
John G. 449
Rousseau A. 307
Thomas G. 199, 202, 205, 209, 212, 215, 218, 222*, 380
BURCHARD
Horatio C. 112, 114, 116, 118, 120
John E. 563, 598
Samuel D. 120
BURCHFIELD, Charles E. 589, 603, 607
BURCHILL, Thomas F. 217
BURCHINAL, David A. 399
BURCK, Jacob 584
BURD, George 78, 79
BURDEN, William A.M. 424
BURDETT
Samuel S. 112, 114
William C. 432, 433
BURDICK
Clark 178, 182, 185, 188, 192, 195, 198
Quentin N. 243*, 246, 249, 253, 256, 259, 262, 265, 351
Theodore W. 120
Usher L. 204, 208, 211, 214, 218, 227, 230, 234, 237, 240
BURDON, George 559
BURGENER, Clair W. 263
BURGER
James C. 579
Warren E. 270, 272
BURGERS, Johannes M. 591
BURGES
Dempsey 54, 55
George F. 152, 155, 157, 160, 163, 166, 169, 172
Tristam 73, 75, 76, 78, 80, 361
BURGESS
Alexander 507, 521
Carter L. 423, 553
Charles F. 575, 589
Ernest W. 573
Gavon D. 329
Frederick 509, 520
George 506, 520
George K. 572
John M. 516, 520
Neil 594
Otis R. 467
Paul S. 465
Theodore C. 466
Thomas M. 459
W. Randolph 564
W. Sterling 594
BURGIN, William O. 211, 214, 218, 221
BURGSTAHLER, Herbert J. 468
BURK
Frederick L. 481
Henry 151, 154
BURKE
Aedanus 51
Andrew H. 350
Andrew J. 454
Arleigh A. 416
Charles H. 149, 152, 154, 157, 163, 166, 169
Daniel 565
Edmund 84, 86, 88, 444
Edward J. 480
Edward R. 201, 204, 207, 210, 334
Frank W. 242, 245, 456
Glendy 457
Haslett P. 285*, 286
J. Herbert 254, 257, 261, 264
James A. 242, 245, 249, 252, 255, 258, 261, 264
James F. 157, 160, 163, 166, 169
John 350, 444
John C. 566
John H. 199
John P. 558
Joseph A. 525
Kenneth 592, 603
M.J. 460
Maurice F. 525, 528
Michael E. 166, 169, 172
Raymond H. 224
Robert E. 146, 149
Thomas 6, 9
Thomas A. 234, 354, 452
Thomas H. 227
Thomas M.A. 525
V.C. 558
William J. 178, 182
William R. 568
Yvonne Braithwaite 263
BURKET, Jacob 353*
BURKETT, Elmer J. 148, 151, 154, 156, 159, 162, 333
BURKHALTER, Everett G. 247
BURKHARDT
Frederick 466, 566
John E. 611
BURKHART, Harvey J. 566
BURLEIGH
Edwin C. 145, 148, 150, 153, 156, 159, 162, 168, 171, 314, 315
Harry T. 611
Henry G. 128, 131
John H. 116, 118
William 71, 72
BURLESON
Albert S. 31, 32*, 43, 149, 152, 155, 157, 160, 163, 166, 169
Hugh L. 510, 521
Omar T. 225, 228, 231, 234, 237, 240, 244, 247, 250, 253, 256, 260, 263, 266
Rufus C. 466*
BURLIN, Paul 611
BURLINGAME, Anson 99, 100, 102, 425
BURLISON, Bill D. 258, 262, 265
BURMA, John H. 483
BURN, Harry T. 579
BURNELL
Barker 86, 87
William H. 558
BURNES
Daniel D. 140
James J. 128, 130, 133
BURNET
D.S. 536*
David 444
Isaac G. 451
Jacob 75, 76, 352
William (b. 1688) 8
William (b. 1730) 6
BURNETT
Charles T. 497
Edgar A. 476
Edward 132
Edwin K. 500
Hamilton S. 371
Henry C. 98, 100, 102, 104, 392*, 393
Howard J. 485
J.M. 467
John L. 147, 150, 152, 155, 158, 161, 164, 167, 170, 173
Peter H. 283
Theodore L. 392, 393
BURNEY
Cecil E. 568
Dwight W. 334
Leroy E. 445, 578
William E. 209
BURNHAM
Alfred A. 102, 104
Daniel H. 567
Donald C. 554*
George 199, 202
Henry E. 151, 154, 157, 159, 162, 165, 338
Hiram 408
Marion 499
William P. 419
BURNQUIST, Joseph A.A. 324
BURNS
Arthur F. 443, 566
Charles W. 530
Dennis F. 487
Edward L. 572
Findley, Jr. 427, 431
Francis 530
Haydon 294, 454
Hobert W. 481
James A. 478
James B. 557
James McGregor 588, 602
John A. 298
John H. 425, 438
John L. 545, 551
Joseph 101
Matthew J. 558*
Robert 79, 81
Robert E. 479
Robert M. 575, 589
Robert W. 536
Ross 462
William W. 408
BURNSIDE
Ambrose E. 119, 122, 124, 126, 362*, 406*, 407*, 408, 409
Maurice G. 228, 231
Thomas 65
BURR
Aaron 14, 15*, 52, 53, 54, 56, 57, 344, 479
Albert G. 110, 112
C.B. 571
C.C. 455
Charles W. 569
Ephraim W. 461
George L. 567
George W. 401
Peter 10
BURRELL
David J. 474
Herbert L. 569
Orlando 142
BURRESS, Withers A. 405, 414
BURRILL
G. Francis 515, 519
James, Jr. 67, 68, 361*
Thomas J. 472
BURRINGTON, George 9
BURROUGHS
Bryson 607
Charles 462
George S. 484
John 603
John (gov.) 343
Nelson M. 515, 521
Sherman E. 174, 177, 181
Silas M. 101, 103
BURROWES
Alexander J. 474*, 480, 487
Thomas H. 479
BURROWS
Abe 587
Charles R. 430
Daniel 69
Joseph H. 125
Julius C. 116, 123, 125, 130, 132, 135, 137, 140, 143, 145, 148, 151, 153, 156, 159, 162, 322
Lansing 534
Lorenzo 93, 95
William W. 416
BURRUSS, Julian A. 484
BURSLEY, Herbert S. 430
BURSUM, Holm O. 181, 184, 343
BURT
Armistead 88, 90, 92, 94, 96
H.G. 554
John H. 517, 521
Joseph B. 570
R.E. 453
Thomas G. 478*
William 530
BURTNESS, Olger B. 181, 185, 188, 191, 194, 198
BURTON
Alan C. 571
Allan A. 425
Charles G. 143
Clarence G. 225, 228, 231
Ernest D. 468
George H. 402
Harold H. 214, 218, 221, 270, 354, 452
Henry F. 480
Hiram R. 155, 158
Hutchins G. 68, 70, 71, 347
Joseph R. 150, 153, 156, 306
Laurence J. 250, 253, 257, 260
Lewis W. 508, 520
Marion L. 475, 481
Nathan S. 469
Phillip 248, 251, 254, 257, 260, 263
Robert 6
Spence 513
Theodore E. 135, 143, 146, 149, 151, 154, 157, 160, 163, 166, 169, 181, 185, 188, 191, 194, 353*, 570*
William 291
William M. 552, 590, 596
BURWELL
Lewis 9
Mrs. Lewis C. 500
William A. 59, 61, 62, 63, 64, 66, 67, 69
BUSBEY, Fred E. 216, 223, 229, 232
BUSBY
George H. 95
T. Jefferson 184, 187, 190, 194, 197, 200
BUSCH
Henry W. 577
Joseph F. 528*
BUSCHMEYER, John H. 456
BUSEMANN, Adolph 608
BUSEY
Ray 459
Samuel T. 137
BUSH
Alvin R. 231, 234, 237, 240, 243
B.F. 549
George 256, 260
Lewis P. 469
Lincoln 572
Prescott S. 232, 235, 238, 241, 244, 289
R. Leonard 574
Vannevar 595, 596, 598*, 599, 603, 604, 609
BUSHART, Leopold 474, 480, 487
BUSHFIELD, Harlan J. 218, 221, 225, 367*
BUSHMAN, Richard L. 591
BUSHNELL
Allen R. 139
Asa S. 353
Henry 474
BUSHONG, Robert G. 191
BUSIEL, Charles A. 338
BUSSE
Ewald W. 571
Fred A. 451
BUSWELL, Charles A. 528
BUTCHER, Willard C. 545
BUTCHERS, Ralph J. 403
BUTLER
A.A.R. 456
Andrew P. 90, 92, 94, 96, 97, 99, 101, 364
Anthony 433
Benjamin F. (b. 1795) 25*, 40, 41, 406
Benjamin F. (b. 1818) 17, 110, 112, 114, 116, 121, 320
Charles C. 285
Charles R. 566
Chester P. 92, 93
David 333
Edward 401*, 402
Ellis P. 574
Elmer G. 573
Ezra 64, 375
George E. 403*

George H. 427
Howard C. 595
Hugh A. 214, 217, 220, 224, 227, 230, 233, 334
James D. 478
James J. 151, 154
John C. 214, 217, 221, 224, 230
John D. 461
John M. 229, 233, 236, 239, 242, 245, 318
John S. 571
John T. 557
Joseph 480
Joseph G. 497
Josiah 67, 68, 70
Louis F. 553
M. Caldwell 266
Marion 143, 146, 149, 348
Matthew C. 122, 124, 126, 128, 131, 133, 136, 138, 141, 365
Mounce G. 157
Nathaniel, Jr. 468
Nicholas Murray 18, 468, 563, 578, 603, 605
Pierce (b. 1744) 4, 51, 52, 53, 54, 57, 58, 364*
Pierce (b. 1866) 270
Pierce M. 364
Robert 423, 426
Robert R. 191, 195, 198
Roderick R. 111, 113, 115, 117, 133
Roy 450
Sampson H. 85, 87
Scot 467
Thomas 66, 68
Thomas B. 92, 288
Thomas S. 146, 149, 152, 154, 157, 160, 163, 166, 169, 172, 175, 178, 182, 185, 188, 191
Walter H. 137
William 57, 58, 59, 60, 62, 63, 87
William A. 564
William M. 184, 187, 321
William O. (b. 1791) 16, 84, 85
William O. (b. 1895) 412*
BUTMAN, Samuel 74, 76
BUTRICK, Richard P. 430
BUTT, William M. 449
BUTTERFIELD
Daniel 408, 409
H.Q. 484
Harvey D. 516, 522
Kenyon L. 475*, 479
Martin 103
Victor L. 485
BUTTERWORTH
Benjamin 124, 126, 131, 133, 135, 444*
J. Scott 567
W. Walton 425, 437
William 546, 575
BUTTOLPH, H.A. 571
BUTTON
Daniel E. 256, 259
Nelson 458
BUTTS, Alfred B. 475
BUTTZ, Charles W. 119
BUTZ
Earl L. 36, 37, 45
Otto 480
BUTZNER, John D., Jr. 271
BYER, George 557
BYERS
Clovis E. 400
Horace G. 567
BYINGTON, Homer M., Jr. 432
BYLER, John G. 491
BYLES, Axtell J. 570
BYNNER, Witter 580
BYNUM
Jesse A. 79, 81, 83, 84
Turner 450
W.H. 450*
William D. 130, 132, 134, 137, 139
BYRD
Adam M. 153, 156, 159, 162
H.C. 577
Harry C. 475
Harry F. 18, 202, 205, 208, 212, 215, 218, 222, 225, 228, 231, 234, 237, 241, 244, 247, 250, 253, 380*
Harry F., Jr. 253, 257, 260, 263, 266, 380
Richard C. 281
Richard E. 598, 599, 609
Robert C. 234, 238, 241, 244, 247, 250, 254, 257, 260, 263, 266, 384
BYRNE
Andrew 527
Christopher E. 526
Edwin V. 524
Emmet F. 238
Frank H. 367
James A. 234, 237, 240, 243, 246, 250, 253, 256, 259, 262
James J. 523, 525
John 458
Leo C. 524
Peter V. 469
Thomas R. 460
Thomas S. 527
William H. 573
William T. 207, 211, 214, 217, 221, 224, 227, 230
BYRNES
Anthony 474*
James 498
James F. 34, 38, 166, 169, 172, 175, 178, 182, 185, 198, 202, 205, 208, 211, 215, 270, 366*
John W. 222, 225, 228, 231, 235, 238, 241, 244, 247, 250, 254, 257, 260, 263
BYRNS
Joseph W. 163, 166, 169, 172, 175, 178, 182, 185, 189, 192, 195, 198, 202, 205, 206, 212
Joseph W., Jr. 212
BYROADE, Henry A. 423, 424, 427, 435, 439
BYRON
Arthur 557
Goodloe E. 261, 264
Katharine E. 213
William D. 210, 213
BYSE, Clark 564
BYWATERS, Jerry 498

C

CABANISS, Thomas B. 139
CABELL
Benjamin E. 452
Charles P. 399
Earle 253, 256, 260, 263, 453
Edward C. 89, 91, 92, 94
George C. 576
George C. 120, 122, 124, 126, 129, 131
De Rosey C. 410
James L. 484, 571
Robert H. 543
Royal E. 444
Samuel J. 54, 55, 56, 57
W.L. 452*
William H. 378*
CABLE
Benjamin T. 137
John L. 181, 185, 195, 198
Joseph 93, 95
CABOT
George 52*, 53, 319
Godfrey L. 577
John M. 424, 426, 428, 435, 437
Joseph S. 460
Richard C. 603
CADIGAN, George L. 516, 520
CADMAN, S. Parkes 465, 603
CADMUS, Cornelius A. 138, 140
CADWALADER
Charles M.B. 563
John 563
John (Pa.) 99
Lambert 6, 51, 53
Richard M. 575
William B. 569
CADY
Claude E. 200
Daniel 65
John W. 71
Ross 450
CAFFERY
Donelson 137, 140, 142, 145, 148, 312
Jefferson 424, 426*, 427, 428, 436, 599
Patrick T. 258, 261, 264
CAFFEY, Eugene M. 402
CAFFREY, James J. 445
CAGE, Harry 79
CAGNEY, James 559
CAHILL
Joseph T. 477, 480
Samuel 472
William T. 243, 246, 249, 252, 255, 259, 342
CAHN, Robert 587
CAHOON
N. Corey 575
William 76, 78
CAIN
Harry P. 225, 228, 231, 381
Richard H. 117, 122
Stanley A. 575
CAIRNS, Robert W. 565
CAKE, Henry L. 111, 113
CALDER
A. Stirling 591
Alexander 590, 591, 592, 603, 607
James 479
William M. 157, 159, 162, 165, 168, 174, 178, 181, 346
CALDERHEAD, William A. 142, 148, 150, 153, 156, 159, 161
CALDWELL
Alexander 114, 116, 306
Andrew J. 129, 131
Ben F. 147, 150, 153, 158
Charles P. 171, 174, 178
Frank W. 594, 608
George A. 87, 93
George C. 565
Greene W. 86
Harmon W. 471
Henry C. 272
Hugh M. 461, 579
James 64, 65
John A. 135, 138, 141, 452
John C. 408, 434*, 439*
John H. 115, 118, 469
John K. 427
John L. 435
John T. 465, 477
John W. 121, 123, 125, 424
Joseph 477*
Joseph P. 93, 95
Mary G. 599
Millard F. 200, 203, 206, 209, 294
Nathan G. 587
Patrick C. 87
Robert G. 424, 435
Robert P. 115
Samuel L. 484
Sarah C. 578
Sylvanus 449*
Tod R. 348
William A. 588
William B. 352
William E. 552
William P. 120, 122
CALHOON, John 80, 82
CALHOUN
Galloway 579
George M. 570
James 450
James M. 449
John 461
John A. 425, 438
John C. 14, 16*, 24, 25*, 26*, 38, 40, 63, 64, 66, 67, 72, 74, 75, 77, 78, 80, 81, 83, 85, 86, 90, 92, 94, 364*
John W. 482
Joseph 60, 62
William B. 81, 82, 84, 86
William J. 425
William L. 449
CALKIN, Hervey C. 112
CALKINS
Mary W. 571
Truesdale P. 472
William H. 120, 123, 125, 127
CALL
Jacob 71
Lewis 428
Wilkinson 122, 125, 127, 129, 132, 134, 137, 139, 142, 293
CALLAGHAN
Alfred 461
Bryan 461*
CALLAHAN
J. Joseph 470
John 558
CALLAN
Clair 252
R.E. 401
CALLAWAY
Ely R., Jr. 544
Fuller E., Jr. 491
Howard H. 251
Llewellyn L. 331
Oscar 166, 169, 172
CALLEN, A. Copeland 576
CALLENDER, John H. 571
CALLEY, Samuel 460*
CALLIS, John B. 109
CALLOW, John M. 595
CALLVERT, Ronald G. 584
CALVERT
Benedict L. 8
Charles 8*
Charles B. 104
James F. 417, 483
Leonard 8
Philip 8
Robert W. 373
CALVIN
Edgar E. 554
Melvin 565, 604, 606, 609
Samuel (b. 1811) 93
Samuel (b. 1840) 575
CAMALIER, C. Willard 566
CAMBRELENG, Churchill C. 70, 71, 73, 74, 76, 77, 79, 81, 83, 436
CAMDEN
Johnson N. 126, 129, 131, 139, 141, 383*
Johnson N., Jr. 167, 309
Peter G. 460
CAMERON
Angus 120, 122, 124, 126, 129, 385*
Ben F. 271
Duncan F. 497
Ewen W. 576
Francis 610
George H. 410
J. Donald 28*, 40, 122, 124, 126, 128, 131, 133, 136, 138, 141, 143, 359
Meribeth E. 476
Ralph H. 179, 183, 186, 280
Ronald B. 249, 251
Simon 27, 40, 90, 92, 101, 103, 105, 111, 113, 115, 117, 119, 122, 358, 359*, 436
William E. 379
CAMINETTI, Anthony 136, 139
CAMM, John 486
CAMMAN, Eric A. 578
CAMMERER, Arno 444
CAMP
A. Sidney 209, 213, 216, 219, 223, 226, 229, 232
E.J. 462
Ernest W. 443
Irving L. 576
John H. 121, 123, 126
John N. 259, 262, 265
Spurgeon 462
CAMPBELL
A. Boyd 575
Albert J. 148
Alexander (b. 1779) 61, 63, 352
Alexander (b. 1786) 466, 536, 538
Alexander (b. 1814) 118
Ben 454
Bruce A. 574
C. Macfie 571
Colin G. 485
Courtney W. 232
Daniel B. 461
David 378
Doak S. 470
Donald J. 514
Douglas H. 574
Ed H. 193
Edward H. 416*
Edward K. 273
Elmer G. 482
Felix 128, 131, 133, 135
George A. (Engr.) 594, 595, 598
George A. 536
George W. 24, 39, 58, 59, 60, 63, 64, 66, 67, 369*, 436
Gerard J. 471
Guy E. 175, 178, 182, 185, 188, 191, 195, 198
H. Donald 545
Henry D. 485
Henry F. 569
Howard E. 221
Ian 576
Ivor E. 575
J.A.P. 392
J.H. 453
Jack M. 343
Jacob M. 122, 126, 128, 131
James 27*, 43

James A. 557
James E. 128, 131, 133, 353
James H. (b. 1820) 99, 103, 105, 437
James H. (b. 1910) 545
James R. 145
John (S.C.) 76, 83, 85, 87, 88
John (Colo.) 285*
John (Md.) 56, 57, 59, 60, 61
John 444
John A. 269
John H. 90
John L. 485
John P., Jr. 98
John S. 461
John T. 452
John W. 67, 68, 70, 71, 73
Joseph 544
Joseph (mayor) 459
Josiah A.P. 327, 391
Levin H. 402
Lewis D. 93, 95, 97, 99, 101, 115
Lucian Q. 471
Philip P. 153, 156, 159, 161, 164, 167, 170, 173, 177, 180
Preston W. 380
Prince L. 478
R.E. 455
Robert B. 72, 80, 81
Robert E. 512
Samuel 70
Samuel L. 485
T. Moody 577
Thomas E. 280, 445
Thomas J. 470*
Thomas M. 372
Thompson 94
Tim J. 533
Timothy J. 131, 133, 138, 140
Walter H. 577
Wilburn C. 515, 522
Willard D. 577
William 9
William B. 83, 85, 87, 109, 369
William H. 480
William T. 533
William W. (b. 1806) 90
William W. (b. 1853) 157
William W. (b. 1862) 467, 563, 564
CAMPE, H.A. 580
CAMPHOR, Alexander P. 530
CANAS, Manuel, Jr. 457
CANBY, Richard S. 92
CANDLER
Allen D. 127, 129, 132, 134, 296
Asa G. 449, 545
Charles H. 545*
Ezekiel S., Jr. 151, 153, 156, 159, 162, 165, 168, 171, 174, 177
John W. 125, 135
Milton A. 118, 120
Warren A. 470*, 530
CANEVIN, John F.R. 528
CANFIELD
Gordon 214, 217, 220, 224, 227, 230, 233, 236, 239, 243
Harry C. 183, 187, 190, 193, 196
James H. 476, 478
CANHAM, Erwin D. 536, 573, 575, 601, 609
CANINE, Ralph J. 444
CANNON
Arthur P. 209, 213, 216, 219
Cavendish W. 429, 433, 435, 438, 439
Clarence 184, 187, 191, 194, 197, 201, 204, 207, 210, 214, 217, 220, 223, 227, 230, 233, 236, 239, 242, 246, 249
Frank J. 144, 146, 374
Howard W. 242, 246, 249, 252, 255, 259, 262, 265, 336, 612
Henry W. 545
James, Jr. 530
John K. 415, 416
John M. 526
Joseph G. 116, 118, 120, 122, 125, 127, 129, 132, 134, 139, 142, 145, 147, 150, 152, 153, 155, 156, 158*, 161*, 164, 170, 173, 176, 180
Marion 139
Newton 64, 66, 69, 70, 369
Raymond J. 202, 205, 209
Robert N. 405
Walter B. 563, 570, 603
William 291
William R. 531
CANTEY, James 396
CANTLON, John E. 575
CANTOR
Eddie 557, 559
Jacob A. 168
CANTRELL, Stephen, Jr. 457
CANTRILL, James C. 161, 164, 167, 170, 173, 177, 180
CANTWELL
James W. 478
John J. 523, 527
CAPA, Robert 607
CAPARN, Harold A. 573
CAPDEVILLE, Paul 457
CAPEHART
Homer E. 220, 223, 226, 229, 232, 235, 238, 242, 245, 303
James 139, 141
CAPEN
Elmer H. 483
Samuel B. 477, 575
CAPERS
Ellison 508, 521
John G. 444
William 530
William T. 510, 522
CAPERTON
Allen T. 120, 383, 393*
Hugh 64
CAPLAN, Harry 570
CAPLE, William G. 473
CAPLES, R.B. 595
CAPLIN, Mortimer M. 444
CAPOZZOLI, Louis J. 214, 217
CAPPER, Arthur 176, 180, 183, 187, 190, 193, 197, 200, 203, 206, 210, 213, 216, 220, 223, 306*
CAPPS
Edward 564, 570
Edwin M. 461*
W.L. 418
CAPRA, Frank 563, 575
CAPRON, Adin B. 146, 149, 152, 154, 157, 160, 163
CAPSTICK, John H. 171, 174
CARAWAY
Hattie W. 196, 199, 202, 206, 209, 212, 216, 282
Thaddeus H. 167, 170, 173, 176, 179, 183, 186, 189, 192, 196, 282
CARBERRY
John J. 523, 524, 525, 527
Thomas 462
CARBONERA, Victor E. 608
CARDEN, Cap R. 197, 200, 203
CARDOZO, Benjamin N. 270, 346, 609
CARDWELL, Richard H. 379
CAREW, John F. 168, 171, 174, 178, 181, 184, 188, 191, 194
CAREY
H. Lloyd 450
Hugh L. 246, 249, 252, 256, 259, 262, 265
J.M. 451
James B. 558, 559
Jeremiah T. 558
John 103
Joseph M. 136, 139, 141, 387*
P.V. 453
Robert D. 106, 199, 202, 205, 387*
W. Gibson, Jr. 575
Walter F. 575
CARGILL, O.A. 458
CARGO, David F. 343
CARHART, Henry S. 575
CARLAND, John E. 272
CARLETON
Alsie H. 531
Peter 60
CARLEY, Patrick J. 191, 194, 198, 201
CARLILE
John S. 99, 105*, 107, 379
Thomas 565
CARLIN
Charles C. 160, 163, 166, 169, 172, 175
James J. 472
Thomas 300
William P. 409, 410
CARLING, Thomas J. 576
CARLISLE
Floyd L. 545, 552
James H. 486
John G. 29, 30, 39, 121, 123, 125, 127*, 129, 130, 131, 132, 134, 137, 309
S.S. 424
CARLSEN, Emil 607, 610
CARLSON
Anton J. 563, 564, 570, 590
Chester F. 598, 601
Delmar R. 429
Frank 203, 206, 210, 213, 216, 220, 226, 229, 232, 235, 239, 242, 245, 248, 252, 255, 307*
George A. 285
Hjalmar G. 590, 598
Loren D. 571
Maxwell 549
Reinhold O. 453
Reynold E. 426
William D. 487
William H. 461
William S. 469, 477, 482, 484
CARLTON
Doyle E. 294
Ezra C. 128, 130
Henry H. 132, 134
Richard P. 549
CARLUCCI, Frank 444
CARLYLE, F. Ertel 227, 230, 234, 237
CARLYON, P.H. 458
CARMACK, Edward W. 146, 149, 152, 154, 157, 370
CARMALT, James W. 444
CARMAN
Edwin S. 573
James W.F. 516, 521
CARMER, Carl 580
CARMICHAEL
Archibald H. 199, 202
D.W. 460
Emmett B. 567
Leonard 483, 502, 570, 571
Oliver C. 465, 484
Richard B. 79
William 5, 437
CARNAHAN
Albert S.J. 220, 227, 230, 233, 236, 239, 242, 437
James 479
CARNAP, Rudolf 593
CARNEGIE, Andrew 603
CARNES
Thomas P. 52
W.D. 482
CARNEY
Charles J. 259, 262, 265
John E. 557
Leonard T. 536
Robert B. 416*, 417
Thomas 306
Thomas J. 552
CARNOVSKY, Leon 595
CARNS, Edwin H.J. 400
CAROLAN, John M. 461
CAROW, Edith Kermit 20
CARPENDER, Arthur S. 417
CARPENTER
Alonzo P. 338
Charles C.J. 513, 519
Cyrus C. 123, 125, 304
Davis 97
Edmund N. 188
Fred W. 433, 436
George T. 469
Homer W. 536
John A. 603
Kenneth 557
L.I. 536
Levi D. 88
Lewis 557*
Lewis C. 117
M. Scott 594, 599
Matthew H. 113, 115*, 117, 124, 385*
Newton H. 497
R.B. 462
Rhys 591
Terry M. 201
W.L. 453
Walter S., Jr. 546
Warren W. 612
William R. 200, 203
CARR
Archie 593
Caleb 9
Clark E. 427
Dabney S. 438
Elias 348
Eugene A. 406, 408
Francis 62
Harvey A. 571
Henry J. 568
Irving J. 403, 419
James 65
John 77, 79, 80, 84
Joseph B. 408
Nathan T. 118
Ralph L. 286
Robert K. 478
Stephen A. 557
Thomas H. 457
W.H. 450
Wilbur J. 426
William 566
Wooda N. 169
CARRAWAY, Gertrude S. 579
CARREL
Alexis 603, 605
George P. 452
CARRELL, George A. 480, 487, 525
CARRICK
Michael P. 558
Samuel 482
CARRIER
Chester O. 216
Wilbur O. 467
Willis H. 590
CARRIGG, Joseph L. 231, 234, 237, 240
CARRIKER, M.A., Jr. 592
CARRINGTON
Edward 7, 459
William C. 459
William J. 576
CARROLL
Beryl F. 304
Charles 3
Charles (of Carrollton) 3, 5, 51, 52, 316
Charles H. 88, 90
Coleman F. 523, 527
Daniel 4, 5, 51
Daniel L. 471
David W. 393
George W. 17
Howard J. 525
J. Roy, Jr. 567
James 84
John (bishop) 523, 525
John (artist) 589*
John A. (writer) 586
John A. (Rep.) 222, 226, 238, 241, 244, 286
John E. 461
John L. 317
John M. 115
John P. 526
Mark K. 529
Nicholas 449*
T.B. 456
T.C. 557
Thomas H. 471
Thomas K. 316
William 369*
CARRON, Malcolm 469
CARRUTHERS, Thomas 514, 521
CARSEY, J. Ben 564
CARSON
David W. 533
Hampton L. 564
Harry R. 511
Henderson H. 218, 224
James G. 533
John F. 532
John R. 594
Luella C. 475
Rachel 591, 593, 594, 602
Samuel P. 73, 75, 76, 78
CARSS, William L. 177, 187, 190
CARSWELL, G. Harrold 271
CARTER
Albert E. 186, 189, 193, 196, 199, 202, 206, 209, 212, 216
Amon G. 491
Amon G., Jr. 491
Arthur H. 578
B.F. 450
Benjamin C. 546
Bernard 474
Charles D. 160, 163, 166, 169, 172, 175, 178, 181, 185, 188
Charles W. 455
Dan T. 591
Elliott 586, 592, 603
F.G. 552
Franklin 486, 577

George H. 443
Harley W. 459
Herbert E. 604
Hodding 585
James C. 564, 579
James E. 455
James Earl 297
James M. 272
Jessie M. 402*
John 70, 72, 73, 75
John L., Jr. 477
John R. 423, 424*, 435, 436
Jonathan H. 396
Leslie D. 502
Luther C. 103
Marshall S. 444
Morris 499
N.H. 404
Raymond L. 482
Robert 9
Samuel P. 410
Steven V. 242
Thomas 531
Thomas H. 135, 143, 145, 148, 156, 159, 162, 331*
Tim Lee 252 255, 258, 261, 264
Timothy J. 82
Vincent M. 196, 199, 202
W. Beverly, Jr. 438
William 458
William B. 81, 83, 85
William H. 410
William H. (Rep.) 171, 174
William J. 578
William L. 486
CARTERET, Peter 8
CARTTER, David K. 93, 95, 424
CARTWRIGHT, Wilburn 191, 195, 198, 201, 205, 208, 211, 214
CARTY, John J. 595, 596*, 600
CARUSI, Ugo 443
CARUTH
Asher G. 132, 134, 137, 140
George W. 435
CARUTHERS
Robert L. 87, 392
Samuel 97, 99, 100
CARVEL, Elbert N. 292*
CARVER
A.M. 558
Eugene P. 580
Eugene P., Jr. 579
George Washington 609, 611
John 3, 8
Thomas 566
CARVILLE, Edward 220, 336*
CARY
Edward H. 569
Frank T. 548
George 71, 72
George B. 87
Glover H. 197, 200, 203
Irvan 557
Jeremiah E. 88
Samuel F. 17, 111
Shepard 87
Thomas 8*
William J. 161, 163, 166, 169, 172, 176
William N. 445
CASADY, Thomas 512, 521
CASE
Augustus L. 418
Charles 100, 102
Clarence E. 342
Clifford P. 220, 224, 227, 230, 233, 236, 239, 243, 246, 249, 252, 255, 259, 262, 265, 342
Everett 468, 493
Francis H. 208, 212, 215, 218, 221, 225, 228, 231, 234, 237, 240, 243, 247, 367
Francis M. 453
Harold C. 466
James H., Jr. 466, 485
Norman S. 363
Richard Y. 601
W.H. 462
Walter 68
William 452
CASER, Ettore 593
CASEY
James V. 523, 527
John J. 169, 172, 178, 185, 191, 195
Joseph 93, 273
Joseph E. 203, 207, 210, 213
Lawrence B. 527
Levi 58, 59
Lyman R. 135, 138, 350
Robert R. 244, 247, 250, 253, 260, 263, 266
Samuel 444
Samuel L. 104
Silas 407
T.L. 402
William J. 445
Zadoc 78, 80, 82, 84, 85
CASH, Albert D. 452
CASHMAN, Robert 534
CASKIE, John S. 96, 98, 99, 101
CASON, Thomas J. 116, 118
CASS
E.R. 565
Lewis 16, 25*, 27, 38, 40, 89, 91, 93, 95, 96, 97, 99, 322*
Lewis, Jr. 434*
Merwin P. 578
CASSADY, John H. 416, 417
CASSATA, John J. 526
CASSATT, Mary 607
CASSEDY
George 70, 71, 73
J. Albert 577
CASSEL, Henry B. 152, 154, 157, 160
CASSELS, George 451
CASSERLY, Eugene 111, 113, 115, 283
CASSIDY
Frederic G. 566
George W. 126, 128
James E. 526
James H. 163
Patrick F. 405
Richard T. 404
William F. 402
CASSINGHAM, John W. 151, 154
CASSODAY, John P. 385
CASTAGNA, Edwin 499, 586
CASTELLOW, Bryant T. 196, 200, 203
CASTLE
Curtis H. 144
Gordon B. 476
James N. 137
Latham 272
Nicholas 531
William B. 452
William R., Jr. 431
CASTLEMAN, Robert B. 457
CASTNER, Hamilton Y. 594
CASTO, Frank M. 566
CASTOR, George A. 154, 157
CASTRO, Raul H. 424, 427
CASWELL
Alexis 467
Lucien 120, 122, 124, 126, 131, 134, 136
Richard 6, 9
CATCHINGS, Thomas C. 130, 132, 135, 137, 140, 143, 145, 148
CATE
George W. 120
William H. 134, 136
CATES
Clifton B. 416
Louis S. 551*, 610
W.H. 462*
CATHCART, Charles W. 89, 91, 94, 302
CATHER, Willa 583, 598, 603
CATLEDGE, Turner 573
CATLIN
George 87
Theron E. 165
CATON, John D. 300
CATRON
John 269, 369
Thomas B. 165, 168, 171, 343, 461
CATT, Carrie Chapman 603
CATTELL
Alexander G. 108, 110, 112, 341
J. McKeen 563, 571
William C. 474
CATTERSON, Robert F. 455
CATTO, Henry E., Jr. 427
CATTON
Bruce 586, 602
Jack J. 415
CATTS, Sidney J. 293
CAULFIELD
Bernard G. 116, 118,
Genevieve 608
Henry S. 159, 330
CAUSEY
Beverly D. 472
John W. 137, 139
Peter F. 290
CAUSIN, John M.S. 87
CAVAGLIERI, Giorgio 591
CAVALCANTE, Anthony 228
CAVANAGH, Jerome P. 453
CAVANAUGH
James M. 100
John J. 478
John W. 478
Thomas 453
CAVE
Henry W. 565
Reuben L. 482
CAVEN, John 454*
CAVICCHIA, Peter A. 197, 201, 204
CECIL
Lester L. 272
Russell L. 590
CEDERBERG, Elford A. 233, 236, 239, 242, 245, 249, 252, 255, 258, 261, 264
CELEBREZZE, Anthony J. 36, 47, 272, 452
CELLER, Emanuel 184, 188, 191, 194, 198, 201, 204, 207, 211, 214, 217, 221, 224, 227, 230, 233, 236, 240, 243, 246, 249, 252, 256, 259, 262
CERMAK, Anton J. 451
CERVANTES, Alfonso J. 460
CESSNA, John 113, 117
CHABRAT, Guy I. 527
CHACE
Charles A. 455
Jonathan 126, 128*, 131, 133, 136, 362
CHADBOURNE, Paul A. 475*, 486*
CHADWICK
E. Wallace 224
French E. 419
George W. 603
Stephen F. 356, 568
Stephen J. 381
W.W. 460
Wallace L. 572
CHAFEE, John H. 326, 399
CHAFFEE
Adna R. 400
Calvin C. 99, 100
E. Leon 598, 600
Jerome B. 118, 120, 285
W.G. 493
CHAFIN, Eugene W. 17, 18
CHAHOON, George 459
CHAILLE-LONG, Charles 594
CHALLINOR, David 500
CHALMERS
E. Lawrence, Jr. 473, 497
Gordon K. 473
James R. 121, 123, 125, 128, 396
Joseph W. 89, 326
William W. 181, 188, 191, 195
CHAMBERLAIN
Abiram 288
Adrian R. 468
Charles E. 239, 242, 245, 249, 252, 255, 258, 261, 264
Clark W. 469
Daniel H. 365
Ebenezer M. 96
C.J. 557, 574
Francis L. 567
George E. 163, 166, 169, 172, 175, 178, 356*
Jacob P. 105
John C. 61
John L. 402
Joseph H. 474
Joshua L. 314, 466
M.H. 453
Owen 606
Samuel 590
W.I. 473
W. Edward 601
William 550*
William (Rep.) 58, 62
CHAMBERLIN
Henry E. 452
Stephen J. 400, 405
Thomas C. 486, 563, 575, 597, 607
CHAMBERS
A.B. 453
A.H. 458
Albert A. 516, 522
B.J. 17
C.M. 461
David 70
Ezekiel F. 72, 74, 76, 77, 79, 316
George 79, 81
Henry C. 392, 393
Henry H. 72, 277
John (Ky.) 74, 80, 82
John (N.Y.) 3
Lenoir 586
Richard H. 272
Robert 573
CHAMBLISS
Alex W. 371
John R. 393
CHAMIE, Alfred P. 568
CHAMOT, Emile 601
CHAMPION
Edwin V. 206
Epaphroditus 60, 61, 62, 63, 65
George 545*
John E. 470
CHAMPLIN
Christopher G. 55, 56, 62, 63, 361
James T. 468
CHANCE
Britton 596, 604
Edwin M. 600
Thomas M. 601
CHANCHE, John M.J. 527
CHANDLER
Albert B. 210, 213, 216, 220, 310*
Alvin D. 486
Charles F. 565*, 603
Dorothy B. 604
George 559
James F. 579
John (Mass.) 3
John (Maine) 59, 60, 68, 69, 71, 72, 74, 314
John W. 471
Joseph R. 93, 95, 97, 437
Julian A.C. 486
Otis 601
Robert F., Jr. 476
Thomas 76, 77
Thomas A. 175, 181
Walter 205, 208, 212, 456*
Walter M. 168, 171, 174, 181
William E. 29*, 42, 133, 135, 138, 140, 143, 146, 148, 338*
Zachariah 28, 44, 100, 102, 104, 106, 108, 110, 112, 114, 116, 123, 322*, 453
CHANDRASEKHAR, Subrahmanyan 604, 610
CHANEY
James E. 411
John 79, 81, 83
John C. 156, 158
Newcomb K. 607
CHANLER
John W. 107, 108, 110
Theodore W. 611
William A. 148
CHANNING
Edward 567, 583
William Ellery 597
CHANOCK, Robert M. 599
CHANUTE, Octave 572
CHAO, Edward C. 612
CHAPELLE
Dickey 607
Placide L. 524*
CHAPIN
Aaron L. 466
Alfred C. 138
Charles V. 572, 610
Chester W. 118
Daryl M. 612
F. Stuart 573
Graham H. 81
Herman A. 452
James P. 569
John P. 571
John Putnam 451
Marshall 453*
Roy D. 33, 46
Roy D., Jr. 543
Selden 430*, 433, 434, 435
Stephin 471
Vinton 432
W.F. 455
CHAPLIN
Charles 592
Jeremiah 468
Winfield S. 484
CHAPMAN
Albert K. 546*
Alger B. 492
Andrew G. 125
Augustus A. 88, 90

Carleton B. 567
Charles 94
Charles H. 478
Charles R. 454
Charles S. 610
Elbridge G. 411, 415
Frank 455
Frank M. 569, 592, 593, 609
Henry 101
J. Wilbur 532
John 55
John G. 89, 91
John L. 450
Jonathan 450
Leonard F., Jr. 416
Nathaniel 569, 570
Oscar L. 35, 44
Pleasant T. 156, 158, 161
Reuben 80, 82, 83, 85, 87, 89, 277
Reuben A. 320
Robert H. 477
Ross M. 571
Roy D. 33
Virgil M. 187, 190, 197, 200, 203, 206, 210, 213, 216, 220, 223, 226, 229, 310
William H. 455
CHAPPELL
Absalom H. 87
John J. 64, 66
Phil E. 455
William V., Jr. 257, 261, 264
CHARLES
Mrs. Allan E. 492
E. Otis 518, 522
William B. 171
CHARLESWORTH, James C. 563
CHARLTON, Robert M. 94, 295
CHARROTTE, J.C. 450
CHARTRAND, Joseph 526
CHASE
Carlton 505, 520
David W. 500
Dudley 64, 66, 67, 73, 75, 76, 375*
E.P. 584
George C. 466
George W. 97
H. Stephens 554*
Harrie B. 271
Harry W. 472, 477*
Horace 456
Ira J. 302
J. Mitchell 191, 195, 198
Jackson B. 236
Jere A. 476
Jeremiah T. 5, 316, 449
John W. 449
Lucia 593
Lucien B. 90, 92
Mary 585
Olin H. 452
Philander 468, 473, 505, 519, 521
Ray P. 200
Samuel (b. 1741) 3, 5, 269
Samuel (b. 1821) 74
Salmon P. 27, 39, 93, 95, 97, 105, 269, 352*
Thomas 472
W.H. 576
William C. 413
William M. 607
CHASTAIN, Elijah W. 94, 96
CHATARD, Francis S. 526
CHATELAIN
Leon, Jr. 567
Paul 500
CHATHAM, Richard T. 227, 230, 234, 237, 240
CHATTERTON, Fenimore 387
CHAUNCEY
Charles 501
Isaac 417
CHAUNCY, Charles 472
CHAUVENET, William 484, 563
CHAVES, Amado 461
CHAVEZ
David, Jr. 343, 461
Dennis 198, 201, 204, 207, 211, 214, 217, 221, 224, 227, 230, 233, 236, 239, 243, 246, 343
CHEADLE
Joseph B. 132, 134
Vernon I. 574
CHEATHAM
B. Franklin 403
Benjamin F. 394, 395*, 396*
Henry P. 135, 138
Richard 83
Richard B. 457
CHEEK
Donald B. 592
James E. 472
Leslie, Jr. 497, 502
CHEEVER
John 598, 602
R.E. 451
CHELF, Frank L. 220, 223, 226, 229, 232, 236, 239, 242, 245, 248, 252
CHEN, K.K. 609
CHENEY
Clarence O. 571
Louis R. 454, 575
Monroe G. 564
Oren B. 466
Person C. 130, 338*, 438
Walter L. 600
CHENNAULT, Claire L. 412
CHENOWETH
Alexander C. 600
J. Edgar 212, 216, 219, 222, 229, 232, 235, 238, 241, 244, 248
CHERRINGTON, Ben M. 469
CHERRY
Francis 282
R. Gregg 349
CHESBROUGH, Ellis S. 572
CHESHIRE, Joseph B., Jr. 508, 521
CHESLEY, Albert J. 572, 610
CHESNEY
Chester A. 226
Cummings C. 595
CHESNUT, James, Jr. 101, 103, 105, 365, 391, 392
CHESNUTT, Charles W. 611
CHESSER, Al H. 559
CHESTER
C.W. 578
Colby M. 547, 579
John 532
CHETHAM, Charles 502
CHETWOOD, William 81
CHEVES, Langdon 62, 63*, 64
CHEYNEY, Edward P. 567
CHI, Chen 591, 610
CHICHIZOLA, Antonio 544
CHICHLEY, Henry 9
CHICKERING, Charles A. 140, 143, 146, 148
CHIDLAW, Benjamin W. 415
CHILCOTT, George M. 124
CHILD
C.M. 573
F.J. 566
Jacob T. 436
Richard W. 431
CHILDRESS, Sarah 20
CHILDS
Barton 599
J. Rives 428, 436 439
Marquis 587
Orlo E. 564
Richard S. 579
Robert A. 139
Timothy 76, 81, 83, 86
Thomas W. 491
CHILES
L.F. 454
Lawton M., Jr. 261, 264, 294
CHILLMAN, James, Jr. 500*
CHILTON
C.M. 536
Horace 138, 144, 146, 149 372*
James 3
Samuel 88
Samuel B. 516
Thomas 74, 75, 79
William E. 166, 169, 172, 383
William P. 277, 391, 392*, 393
CHINARD, Gilbert 577
CHINDBLOM, Carl R. 176, 180, 183, 187, 190, 193, 196
CHING, Cyrus S. 443, 568
CHINN
Joseph W. 78, 80
Thomas W. 84, 436
William S. 453
CHIPERFIELD
Burnett M. 170, 193, 196
Robert B. 210, 213, 216, 219, 223, 226, 229, 232, 235, 238, 242, 245
CHIPMAN
Daniel 66
J. Logan 132, 135, 137, 140
John 572, 590, 595
John S. 89
Nathaniel 10, 55, 56, 57, 375*
CHISHOLM
Frank A. 580
Shirley 259, 262, 265
CHITTENDEN
Charles C. 566
Martin 58, 59, 61, 62, 63, 375
Russell H. 570
Simeon B. 117, 119, 121, 123
Thomas 9*, 375
Thomas C. 84, 86
CHLOPEK, Anthony 558
CHOATE
Mrs. Arthur O. 576
Joseph H. 429, 565
Rufus 77, 79, 84, 86, 87, 319, 597
Winfield S. 449
CHOLLAR, Robert G. 492
CHOPE, Harold D. 592
CHOY, Herbert Y.C. 272
CHRISFIELD J.A. Pearce 600
CHRISMAN
Charles S. 611
James S. 96, 392, 393
CHRIST, Benjamin C. 407
CHRISTENSEN
B.V. 570
Henry C. 609
P.P. 18
Val S. 451
Walter 460
CHRISTGAU, Victor 194, 197
CHRISTIAN
Henry A. 590
John 450
Letitia 20
CHRISTIANCY, Isaac P. 119, 121, 322, 435
CHRISTIANSON, Theodore 200, 204, 325
CHRISTIE
Alexander 524
Alexander G. 573
Gabriel 52, 53, 55
CHRIST-JANER, Arland F. 466, 468
CHRISTMAN, W.W. 593
CHRISTOPHER
George 461
George H. 227, 236, 239, 242
CHRISTOPHERSON, Charles A. 178, 182, 185, 188, 192, 195, 198
CHRISTY
John G. 455
Lloyd B. 459
CHUBB
Edwin W. 478*
Lewis W. 596
CHUDOFF, Earl 228, 231, 234, 237, 240
CHURCH
A.B. 445
Alonzo 471
Benjamin 403
Denver S. 167, 170, 173, 199
Frank 238, 241, 245, 248, 251, 254, 258, 261, 264, 299
Frederic E. 593
Marguerite Stitt 229, 232, 235, 238, 242, 245
Ralph E. 203, 206, 210, 216, 219, 223, 226
Samuel 287
Sanford E. 345
Thomas 590
CHURCHILL
Alfred V. 502
John C. 110, 112
Marlborough 400
Neil 450
Sylvester 402
Thomas J. 281
Winston 574
CHURCHWELL, William M. 96, 97
CIAMPI, Anthony F. 472*
CICATERRI, Felix 481
CILLEY
Bradbury 64, 65
Jonathan 82
Joseph 89, 337
CISLER, Walker L. 546*, 573, 595, 596, 598
CITRON, William M. 203, 206
CLAFLIN, William 121, 123, 320
CLAGETT, Clifton 58, 67, 68
CLAGGETT, John T. 505, 520
CLAGUE, Frank 180, 184, 187, 190, 194, 197
CLAIBORNE
James R. 201, 204
John 59, 61
John F.H. 81, 82
Nathaniel H. 73, 75, 77, 78, 80, 81
Randolph R., Jr. 515, 519
Mrs. Robert W. 502
Thomas (b. 1749) 53, 54, 55, 57, 58
Thomas (b. 1780) 67
William C.C. 55, 56, 66, 313*
CLAIR
James 486
Matthew W. 530
Matthew W., Jr. 531
CLAMER, Guilliam H. 594
CLANCY
Donald D. 246, 249, 253, 256, 259, 262, 265, 452
John M. 135, 138, 140
John R. 168
Robert H. 184, 190, 194, 197
CLAP, Thomas 487
CLAPHAM, A.R. 548
CLAPP
Almon M. 443
Asa W.H. 91
Charles H. 476
Frederick M. 499
Gordon R. 445
Henry W. 452
J.W. 392
Margaret 485, 585
Moses E. 148, 151, 153, 156, 159, 162, 165, 168, 171, 324
Verner W. 600
W.L. 456
CLARDY
John D. 142, 145
Kit F. 233
Martin L. 123, 125, 128, 130, 133
CLAREY, Bernard A. 417*
CLARK
Aaron 458
Abraham 3, 4, 6, 52, 53
Addison 482
Albert P. 483
Alex M. 454
Alonzo M. 387
Alvah A. 121, 123
Alvan 609
Ambrose W. 105, 107
Amos, Jr. 117
Barzilla W. 299
Bennett Champ 197, 200, 204, 207, 210, 214, 217, 272, 230
Champ (See Clark, James B.; Bennett Champ)
Charles (b. 1811) 326, 394
Charles (b. 1925) 271
Charles A. 299
Charles B. 134, 136
Charles E. 271
Charles N. 143
Christopher 58, 59
Clarence D. 136, 139, 141, 144, 147, 149, 152, 155, 158, 161, 163, 166, 169, 172, 387
D. Worth 203, 206, 209, 213, 216, 299
Daniel 101, 103, 105, 106, 107, 108, 338
David H. 418
Davis W. 530
Donald S. 572
Edward 372
Edward A. 423
Edward S. 491
Edward W. 570
Eleanor 602
Eliot 574, 577
Eugene C. 601
Ezra, Jr. 98, 100
Francine J.M. 491
Frank 155, 158, 161, 164, 167, 170, 173, 176, 180, 183
Frank M. 237, 240, 243, 246, 250, 253, 256, 259, 262, 265
Frank R. 564, 608

Franklin 91
Fred E. 568
G. Edward 428, 432, 436
George 457, 558
George C. 565
George H. 460
George R. 563
George R. (USN) 416
George Rogers 406
George T. 453
Georgia Neese 444
Grenville 589, 609
Harry C. 461
Henry A. 175
Henry S. 90
Henry T. 348
Herbert B. 534
Homer J. 465
Horace F. 101, 103, 554
J. Bayard 194, 198, 201, 204, 208, 211, 214, 218, 221, 224
J. Reuben, Jr. 433
James 472, 485
James (Rep.) 63, 65, 72, 74, 75, 308
James B. (Champ) 140, 145, 148, 151, 154, 156, 159, 162, 164, 165, 167, 168, 170, 171, 173, 174, 177
James G. 486
James W. 65
Jasper 558
Jesse 557
John (Del.) 290
John (Fla.) 454
John (Utah) 460
John B. (b. 1802) 100, 103, 105, 392, 393*, 533
John B. (b. 1831) 116, 119, 121, 123, 125
John B. (b. 1848) 566
John C. 74, 83, 84, 86
John M. 566
John Mason 597
Joseph 532
Joseph J. 417*
Joseph S. 240, 243, 246, 250, 253, 256, 360, 458
Kenneth B. 571, 611
Lewis W. 338
Lincoln 95
Linwood L. 193
Lot 71
Louise Bennett 497
Lucius C. 465
Mark W. 404*, 405*, 411, 412
Myron H. 345
Paul F. 548*
Ramsey 36, 41
Raymond M. 473
Richard 264, 305
Robert 68
Robert D. 478, 481
Robert Sterling 491
Rush 120, 123
S.H.H. 554
Samuel (Mich.) 97
Samuel (N.Y.) 79
Samuel M. 142, 145
Stephen C. 514, 522
Stephen Carlton 491
Stephen Carlton, Jr. 491
Thomas M. 506, 521
Tom C. 34, 35, 41, 270, 589, 598
Walter 348
Walter E. 476
Walton 575
Wilbur 444
William (b. 1774) 79, 81
William (b. 1891) 271
William A. 148, 151, 154, 156, 331*
William E. 480
William H. 600
William M. 604, 607
William S. 475
William T. 113, 115
William W. 392
CLARKE
Archibald S. 65
Bayard 99
Beverly L. 91, 429, 430
Bruce C. 404*, 405, 415
Caspar P. 499
Charles E. 93
Frank G. 146, 148
Frank W. 565
Frederick J. 402
Freeman 107, 115, 117
George 8
George L. 459
George W. 304
Gilmore D. 573
James C. 548
James P. 152, 155, 158, 161, 164, 167*, 170*, 281*
Jeremy 9
John (N.Y.) 501
John (Ga.) 295
John B. 118, 121
John D. 181, 184, 191, 194, 198, 201
John H. (b. 1789) 92, 94, 95 361
John H. (b. 1857) 270
John M. 576
Marian W. 201
Reader W. 109, 111
Richard 3
Richard H. 134, 136, 139, 142
Sidney 108, 110, 112
Simeon S. 610
Staley N. 86
Thomas C. 572
Walter 9*
CLARKSON
Matthew 7, 458
Matthew, Jr. 544
Percy W. 413, 414
Robert H. 506, 520
Robert L. 545
CLASON, Charles R. 207, 210, 213, 217, 220, 223
CLASSON, David G. 176, 179, 182
CLATON, Joshua 54
CLAUDE
Abram 449
Dennis 449*
Gordon 449
CLAUSE
R.L. 550*
W.L. 550*
CLAUSEN
A.W. 544
Don H. 248, 251, 254, 257, 260, 263
CLAUSON, Clinton A. 315
CLAWSON
Del 248, 251, 254, 257, 260, 263
Isaiah D. 99, 101
CLAXTON, Philander P. 444
CLAY
Alexander S. 145, 147, 150, 153, 155, 158, 161, 296
Brutus J. (b. 1808) 106
Brutus J. (b. 1847) 438
Cassius M. 436*
George 607
Clement Claiborne 96, 98, 100, 102, 104, 277, 392
Clement Comer 75, 77, 78, 82, 83, 85, 277*
Henry 16*, 25, 38, 59, 61, 62*, 63*, 65*, 66*, 67, 68, 70, 71, 77, 79, 82, 84, 85, 93, 95, 308*, 429, 597
James B. 100
James F. 127
John B. 435
John R. 435*, 436
Joseph (b. 1741) 5
Joseph (b. 1769) 58, 59, 60
Lucius D. 404, 596*, 598, 604, 609
Lucius D., Jr. 416
Matthew 55, 56, 57, 58, 59, 61, 62, 63, 66
Thomas H. 430, 434
William L. 258, 262, 265
CLAYPOOL
Harold K. 208, 211, 214
Haratio C. 166, 169, 175
CLAYTON
Alexander M 391, 392
Alvah 579
Augustin S. 77, 78
Bertram T. 148
Charles 115
Claude F. 271
Henry D. (b. 1827) 396, 465
Henry D. (b. 1857) 144, 147, 150, 152, 155, 158, 161, 164, 167
John M. 26, 38, 75, 77, 78, 80, 89, 90, 96, 98, 290*
Joshua 54, 290*
Powell 113, 115, 118, 281*, 433
Thomas 65, 70, 72, 80, 82, 83, 85, 87, 89, 290*
William M. 453
CLAYTOR, W. Graham, Jr. 552
CLEAR, Charles Val 497
CLEARY
James W. 481
John V. 545
Michael J. 550
Walter H. 377
William E. 174, 178, 184, 188
CLEAVES, Henry B. 314
CLEBURNE, Patrick R. 395*
CLELAND
Charles S. 533
Ralph E. 574
W.B. 552
CLEMENCE, G.M. 564
CLEMENS
Jeremiah 92, 94, 277
Paul 589
Samuel L. 597
Sherrard 96, 101, 103
CLEMENT
Frank 371*
Paul 576
Percival W. 376
CLEMENTE, L. Gary 227, 230
CLEMENTS
Andrew J. 105
Benjamin S. 461
Earle C. 220, 223, 226, 229, 232, 236, 310*
Isaac 116
James P. 516
Judson C. 125, 127, 129, 132, 134
Newton N. 122
Rufus 452
CLEMMER, John L. 572
CLEMSON, Thomas G. 423
CLENDENIN, David 64, 65
CLEVELAND
Chauncey F. 92, 94, 287
G.W. 453
Grover 13, 17*, 345, 451, 597
Harlan 472
J.T. 450
James C. 249, 252, 255, 259, 262, 265
Jesse F. 80, 82
Orestes 112
CLEVENGER
Cliff 211, 214, 218, 221, 224, 227, 230, 234, 237, 240
James 607
Raymond F. 252
CLEXTON, Edward W. 418
CLIFFORD
Clark M. 36, 47, 608
John H. 319
Nathan 26, 41, 84, 86, 269, 433
Thomas J. 477
CLIFT
David H. 600
Joseph W. 110
CLIFTON
Claiborne 452
Oliver 454*
William C. 452
CLINCH
Duncan L. 87
Edward S. 534
Harry A. 527
CLINCHY, Everett R. 578
CLINE
Cyrus 161, 164, 167, 170
Genevieve R. 273
Hugh F. 493
John W. 565, 569
Walter D. 579
CLINGAN, William 7
CLINGMAN
Charles 513, 520
Thomas L. 88, 91, 93, 95, 97, 99, 101, 103, 105, 348
CLINTON
De Witt 15, 57, 58, 344*, 458*
George 6, 8*, 14, 15*, 58, 60, 61, 62, 344*, 406
George, Jr. 58, 59, 60
George W. 450
Gordon S. 461
James 406
James G. 86, 88
CLIPPINGER
Arthur 531
Roy 219, 223
CLISBY, John H. 457
CLODIUS, Robert L. 486
CLOHESSY, Francis J. 577
CLOKEY, Joseph 533
CLOONAN, John J. 480
CLOOS, Ernst 564
CLOPTON
David 102, 392, 393
John 54, 55, 57, 58, 59, 61, 62, 63, 64, 66
CLOSE
Frederick J. 543
H. William 493
Harold C. 579
CLOSSON, Charles C. 461
CLOTHIER
Robert C. 480
Robert W. 476
CLOUD, Charles H. 469, 480
CLOUET, Alexander D. 392
CLOUGH
Charles A. 514, 522
David M. 324
CLOUSE, Wynne F. 182
CLOVER, Benjamin H. 137
CLOW, A.P. 493
CLOWNEY, William K. 80, 83
CLUETT
E. Harold 207, 211, 214
Sanford L. 598, 601
CLUNIE, Thomas J. 134
CLUSKEY, Michael W. 393
CLUTE, Oscar 475
CLUVERIUS, Wat Tyler 487
CLYDE, George D. 374
CLYMER
George 3, 4, 6, 51, 551
Hiester 117, 119, 122, 124
COAD, Merwin 239, 242, 245
COADY, Charles P. 168, 171, 174, 177
COAN, Mary F. 499
COATES, Edward H. 607
COATS
George F. 459
Marion 481
COBB
Amasa 107, 109, 111, 113, 333*, 455
Bernard C. 545, 546
Clinton L. 113, 115, 117
David 52
Frank I. 583
George T. 105
Howell (b. 1772) 60, 61, 62)
Howell (b. 1815) 27, 39, 87, 89, 91, 92*, 98, 295, 391*, 392
James E. 131, 134, 136, 139, 142
Nelson 306
Rufus W. 277
Samuel C. 450
Seth W. 138, 140, 143
Stanley 569, 595
Stephen A. 116
Thomas R. 120, 123, 125, 127, 130
Thomas R.R. 391, 392
Thomas W. 66, 68, 71, 72, 74, 295
William T. 315
Williamson R.W. 90, 92, 94, 96, 98, 100, 102
COBBS, Nicholas H. 505, 519
COBERLY, C.J. 601
COBINE, James D. 599
COBLE, Arthur B. 568
COBLEIGH, William M. 476
COBLENTZ, William W. 607, 610
COBO, Albert E. 453
COBURN
Abner 314
Frank P. 139
Frederic G. 544
John 110, 112, 114, 116
Stephen 102
COCHRAN
Alexander G. 119
Charles B. 451
Charles F. 145, 148, 151, 154
David H. 479
H. Merle 430, 434
Henry J. 544
Jacqueline 577
James (N.Y.) 55
James (N.C.) 61, 63
John 403
John J. 187, 191, 194, 197, 201, 204, 207, 210, 214, 217, 220
John P. 291
Robert L. 334
Thad 265
Thomas C. 192, 195, 198, 201
Thomas G. 567

COCHRANE
Aaron V. 146, 148
Alexander 543
Clark B. 101, 103
Edward L. 418*, 611
John 101, 103
COCKAYNE, Charles A. 482
COCKE
C. Francis 564
Erle 564
Erle, Jr. 568
John 69, 70, 72, 73
Norman A. 546
William 54, 55, 56, 57, 58, 369*
William M. 90, 92
William H. 484
COCKERILL, Joseph R. 101
COCKRAN, W. Bourke 133, 138, 140, 154, 157, 159, 181, 599
COCKRELL
Francis M. 119, 121, 123, 125, 128, 130, 133, 135, 138, 140, 143, 145, 148, 151, 153, 329
Jeremiah V. 141, 144
COCKRILL
B.D. 483
Sterling R. 281
COCKS, William W. 157, 159, 162
CODD, George P. 180
CODDING, James H. 143, 146, 453
CODDINGTON, William 9*
CODMAN, Robert 509, 520
CODY
Frank 485
John P. 523*, 524, 526
COE
Albert B. 535
Conway P. 444
Frank W. 402
George S. 564
Howard E. 579
Jonas 532
Robert D. 427
Wesley R. 573
COEFIELD, John 559
COEN, John R. 574
COERR, Wymberley D. 427, 439
COES, Harold V. 573
COFFEE
Harry B. 204, 207, 210, 214
John 78, 80
John M. 209, 212, 215, 219, 222
COFFEEN, Henry A. 141
COFFEY
Edward A. 460
Harry K. 577
Walter C. 471, 475
COFFIN
Charles 482
Charles D. 83
Charles E. 140, 142
Frank G. 534
Frank M. 239, 242, 271
Henry S. 532
Howard A. 223
Howard E. 577
Owen V. 288
Peleg, Jr. 52
Robert P. Tristram 584
Thomas C. 200
COFFMAN
George R. 577
Lotus D. 475
COFFROTH, Alexander H. 107, 109, 124
COFRAN, Rosswell T. 462*
COGEN, Charles 557
COGGESHALL
Arthur S. 502
John 9
John, Jr. 9
Lowell T. 565
William T. 427
COGGINS, L.W. 459
COGHLAN
John I. 487
John M. 113
COGSWELL
Parsons B. 452
William 132, 135, 137, 140, 460*
COHELAN, Jeffry 241, 244, 248, 251, 254, 257
COHEN
Herbert 500
Jerome B. 466
John S. 196, 297
Karl P. 569
Manuel F. 445
Mendes 572
Morris 572, 590
Paul J. 604
Seymour S. 599
Sheldon S. 444
Wilbur J. 36, 47, 592
William S. 264
William W. 191
COHN
Edwin J. 607, 609
Nathan 599, 612
COHU, LaMotte T. 553
COILE, Samuel A. 483
COIT
Joshua 52, 53, 54
Margaret L. 585
Thomas W. 482
COKE
Richard (b. 1790) 77
Richard (b. 1829) 122, 124, 126, 129, 131, 133, 136, 138, 141, 372*
COKER
E.G. 607
Francis W. 571
R.E. 573, 575
COLBERT, Richard C. 419
COLBURN
Burnham S. 575
Elbert B. 457
COLBY
Anthony 337
Bainbridge 31, 32, 38
Frank C. 536*
COLCLOUGH, Oswald S. 416, 471
COLCOCK, William F. 94, 96
COLCORD, Roswell K. 335
COLDEN
Cadwallader 8
Cadwallader D. 70, 458
Charles J. 199, 202, 206
COLE
Albert L. 596
Albert M. 220, 223, 226, 229
Charles W. 425, 465
Clarence A. 515, 522
Cornelius 106, 109, 111, 113, 283
Cyrenus 180, 183, 187, 190, 193, 197
David L. 443
Edward N. 547
Felix 425, 427
Francis W. 553
Fred C. 485
George B. 453
Henry O. 557
James R. 482
John 10
Jonathan O. 598
Kenneth S. 604
LaMont C. 575
Lawrence T. 466
Myron C. 536
Nathan 121, 460
Ned, Jr. 517, 519
Orsamus 94, 385
P.J. 459
R. Beverly 569
R. Clint 178, 181, 185
R. Taylor 571
Ralph D. 157, 160, 163
Russell D. 468
Stewart G. 473
Tom 609
W. Sterling 204, 207, 211, 214, 217, 221, 224, 227, 230, 233, 236, 240
Warner R. 534
Warren H. 565*, 590
Whitefoord R. 549
William C. 217, 220, 223, 233
William H. 130
William P. 190, 197, 200, 203, 207, 210, 213, 273*
COLEMAN
Arthur P. 576
C.T. 453*
Cyril 454
Frederick W.B. 427*, 431, 432
George W. 534
Glenn O. 607
Hamilton D. 135
James P. 271, 328
John 486
John C. 575
John F. 572
John R. 472
Joseph 484
Joseph (mayor) 457
Leighton 506, 519
Nicholas D. 75
Perez 457
Thomas B. 457
W.A. 452
Walter L. 457
William B. 572
William C. 534
William H. 172
COLEPEPPER, Thomas 9
COLERICK, Walpole G. 123, 125
COLES
Edward 300
Isaac 51, 53, 54
James S. 466, 492
Robert 598
Roswell S. 502
Walter 82, 83, 85, 87, 88
COLEY
Curtis G. 501
Edward H. 511, 519
COLFAX, Schuyler 14, 16, 98, 100, 102, 104, 106*, 107, 108, 109, 110, 111, 113
COLGLAZIER, Robert W., Jr. 401, 405
COLGROVE, Philip T. 576
COLHOUN, John E. 57, 364
COLLAMER, Jacob 26, 43, 88, 90, 92, 99, 101, 103, 105, 107, 109, 375
COLLENS, Arthur M. 551
COLLER, Frederick A. 565
COLLET, John C. 272
COLLETON, James 9
COLLETT, Joshua 352
COLLEY
James F. 501
Robert H. 544*
COLLIER
Abram T. 550
Charles A. 449
Charles F. 393
Harold R. 238, 242, 245, 248, 251, 255, 258, 261, 264
Henry D. 552
Henry W. 277*
Herman E., Jr. 476
James W. 162, 165, 168, 171, 174, 177, 181, 184, 187, 190, 194, 197
John A. 77
John H. 405, 415
William M. 425, 437, 471
COLLIGAN, Thomas 472
COLLIN, John F. 90
COLLINS
Amos M. 453
Barney W. 579
Charles 469, 470
Clem W. 536
Edgar T. 400
Ela 71
Evan R. 477
Francis D. 119, 122
Francis X. 460
Frank W. 600
G.G. 452
George W. 258, 261, 264
Henry A. 579
Henry J. 414
Henry W. 550
J. Lawton 400, 412, 413, 599
James F. 400, 404, 569
James M. 256, 260, 263, 266
John (Del.) 290
John (R.I.) 4, 7, 9, 361
John (Wash.) 461
John F. (b. 1874) 459
John F. (b. 1919) , 450
John J. 470
Joseph 569
Joseph B. 549
LeRoy 144, 578, 598
Lester E. 461
Linton M. 273
Michael 594*, 598, 608
Patrick A. 127, 130, 132, 450
Ross A. 181, 184, 187, 190, 194, 197, 200, 207, 210, 214
Samuel C. 591, 610, 611
Samuel L. 199, 202
Seaborn P. 568
Thomas 8
V.W. 578
W.H. ,576
William (b. 1818) 91
William (b. 1893) 579
COLLIS, Joseph F. 557
COLLISON, N. Harvey 550
COLLITZ, Hermann 577
COLLYER
Clayton , 557*
John M. 547
COLMAN
Howard D. 601
J. Douglas 578
Norman J. 29*, 45
Samuel ,574
COLMER, William M. 200, 204, 207, 210, 214, 217, 220, 223, 227, 230, 233, 236, 239, 242, 246, 249, 252, 255, 258, 262
COLMERY, Harry W. 568
COLMORE, Charles B. 510, 521
COLOVIN, Patrick 478
COLPITTS, Edwin H. 594
COLQUITT
Alfred H. 17, 96, 127, 129, 132, 134, 137, 139, 296*
Oscar B. 372
Walter T. 84, 85, 87, 89, 91, 295
COLSON
Charles F. 415
Clyde 485
David G. 142, 145
COLSTON
Edward 67
R.E. 395
COLT
LeBaron B. 169, 172, 175, 178, 182, 185, 271, 362
S. Sloan 544*
Samuel P. 554*
Thomas C., Jr. 498, 501, 502*
COLTMAN, John W. , 601
COLTON
Charles H. 525
Don B. 182, 185, 189, 192, 195, 199
COLUM, Padraic 580, 589
COLVARD, Dean W. 475
COLVE, Anthony 8
COLVIN
D. Leigh 18
George 474
Harvey D. 451
Howard T. 443
COLWELL
Howard G. 534
Richard S. 469
COLYAR, Arthur S. 393
COMAN, T. 458
COMBELLACK, Frederick M. 570
COMBS
Bert T. 272, 310, 599
George H., Jr. 191
Jesse M. 221, 225, 228, 231
Leslie 429, 430, 435
Thomas S. 417*
COMEGYS
Benjamin 551
Cornelius P. 290
Joseph P. 98, 290
COMER
Braxton B. 176, 278*
Gordon V. 536
COMERFORD, Matt 558
COMFORT
Howard 570
William W. 472
COMINGO, Abram 114, 116
COMINS, Linus B. 99, 100
COMLY, James M. 430
COMMAGER, Henry Steele 603
COMMONS, John R. 566
COMPTON
Alfred G. 468
Arthur H. 485, 563, 570, 596, 605, 609, 610
Barnes 130, 132, 135, 137, 140
Charles H. 568
Karl T. 475, 563, 570, 598, 610
Ranulf 216
Wilson M. 485
COMROE, Julius H., Jr. 571, 589
COMSTOCK
Ada L. 479
Charles C. 130
Daniel W. 173
George C. ,564
George F. 345
John P. 611
Oliver C. 64, 65, 67
Solomon G. 135
Theodore B. 465
W.D. 460

William A. 323
CONABLE, Barber B., Jr. 252, 256, 259, 262, 265
CONANT
James B. 428*, 472, 563, 590, 591, 596, 604, 608*, 609
Kenneth J. 574
Levi L. 486
CONARD
Grant 461
John 64
CONATY, Thomas J. 468, 527
CONCANEN, Richard L. 527
CONCORDIA, Charles 599
CONDICT
Ira 480
Lewis 62, 64, 65, 70, 71, 73, 74, 76, 77
Silas 6
Elbert N. 474*, 478
CONDIT
John 56, 57, 58, 59, 60, 61, 62, 64, 65, 68, 340*
Jonathan B. 532
Silas 77
CONDON
Edward U. 563, 570
Francis B. 195, 198, 202, 205, 363
James 457
Robert L. 232
William J. 526
CONE
Fred P. 294
Hutch I. 418
Orello 465
CONGDON, J.W. 483
CONGER
Edwin H. 130, 132, 134, 424, 425, 433
Harmon S. 91, 93
James L. 95
Omar D. 112, 114, 116, 119, 121, 123, 125, 128, 130, 322
CONGIATO, Nicholas 481*
CONIFF, Frank 586
CONKLIN
Edwin G. 563, 570*, 603
James 456*
CONKLING
Alfred 70, 433
Frederick A. 105
James C. 461
Mark L. 453
Roscoe 103, 105, 108, 110, 112, 115, 117, 119, 121, 123, 345
Wallace E. 513, 519
CONLAN, John B. 263
CONLEY
Benjamin 296
Edgar T. 401
R.E. 460
William G. 384
CONN
Charles G. 140
Jack T. 564
CONNABLE, A.B. 492
CONNALLY
John B. 36, 39, 373, 399
Tom T. 175, 179, 182, 185, 189, 192, 195, 198, 202, 205, 208, 212, 215, 218, 221, 225, 228, 231, 373
CONNARE, William G. 526
CONNELL
Arthur J. 568
Charles R. 182
George 458
George B. 475
James H. 478
Richard E. 165
Ted C. 580
William 146, 149, 152, 154
William J. 135
CONNELLY
John R. 167, 170, 173
Marc 574, 578, 583
CONNER
David 418
Fox 401, 404
James P. 148, 150, 153, 156, 159
John C. 113, 115
Martin S. 327
Samuel S. 65
W.C. 452
CONNERY
Lawrence J. 207, 210, 213
William P., Jr. 184, 187, 190, 194, 197, 200, 203, 207
CONNESS, John 106, 107, 109, 283
CONNOLLY
Daniel W. 128
Donal J. 462
Donald H. 411
James A. 142, 145
James J. 182, 185, 188, 192, 195, 198, 201
James L. 526
John 527
John F.X. 481
Maurice 167
Richard L. 416, 419
Thomas A. 524, 528
CONNOR
Albert O. 400, 405
Henry W. 70, 71, 73, 75, 76, 78, 79, 81, 83, 84
John T. 36, 46
Lewis A. 567
Morgan 401
Ralph 590, 608
Selden 314
William D. 401, 419, 483
William J. 462
CONNORS, J.J. 455
CONOVER, Simon B. 116, 118, 120, 293
CONRAD
Anthony L. 551
Charles M. 26, 27, 40, 86, 93, 311, 391, 392, 393
Frank 595, 599
Frederick 58, 59
John 64
Paul 587, 588
Robert T. 458
Thomas N. 484
CONRADI, Edward 470
CONROW, Aaron H. 392, 393*
CONROY
Joseph H. 525, 527
Perry J. 477
CONRY
Joseph A. 151
Michael F. 162, 165, 168, 171
CONSELMAN, Frank B. 564
CONSTABLE, Albert 89
CONSTANCE, Lincoln 574
CONTE, Silvio O. 242, 245, 249, 252, 255, 258, 261, 264
CONTEE, Benjamin 5, 51
CONVERS, Albert E. 546
CONVERSE
Edmund C. 544
George A. 418*
George L. 124, 126, 128
Julius 376
CONVEY, John 572
CONWAY
Albert 346
Asbury B. 387
Elias N. 281
Fred 591, 593
James F. 580
James S. 281
John R. 457
Katherine E. 599
Martin 102, 104
Theodore J. 404, 405
Thomas 402, 406
CONWELL
Henry 528
Russell H. 482
CONY
Daniel 449
Edward R. 586
Robert A. 449
Samuel 314, 449
CONYERS, John, Jr. 252, 255, 258, 261, 264
CONZETT, John V. 566
COOK
A.B. 417
Albert S. 577
Mrs. Anthony W. 579
Burton C. 108, 110, 112, 114
C.W. 547*
Charles A. 453
Daniel P. 68, 69, 71, 72
Donald C. 445, 543
Earle F. 403
Eli 451, 461
Ernest F. 609
George A. 444
George S. 536
George W. 158
Gilbert R. 412, 414
Howard 591
Ira 453
Joel 160, 163
John 461
John C. 127
John P. 96
Joseph P. 5
Kathryn F. 536
Levi 453*
Marlow W. 258, 261, 264, 310
Mercer 428, 434, 436
Orchard 59, 60, 61
P.S. 451
Paul W., Jr. 484
Philip (b. 1875) 511, 519
Philip (b. 1817) 116, 118, 120, 122, 125
Ransom M. 554*
Robert E. 243, 246
Roy B. 570, 609
Samuel A. 144
Samuel E. 183
Walter 567
Walter C. 564
Willard B. 580
William 457
William H. 608, 611
William M. 392
Willis C. 439
Zadock 65, 66
COOKE
Bates 77
Charles M., Jr. 417
E.N. 460
Edmund F. 194, 198
Edward 474
Edward D. 142, 145
Eleutheros 78
Francis 5
George 482
Josiah P. 563
Lorrin A. 288
Nicholas 9
R.D. 458
Richard J. 530
Robert E. 599*
Terence J. 523, 524
Thomas B. 62
COOLEDGE, Belle 460
COOLEY
Charles H. 573
Harold D. 201, 204, 208, 211, 214, 218, 221, 224, 227, 230, 234, 237, 240, 243, 246, 249, 253
James 435
Mortimer F. 573
Richard P. 554
Thomas M. 564
COOLIDGE
Calvin 13, 14, 18*, 320, 563, 603
Carlos 375
Frederick S. 137
Grace Goodhue 603
John 499
John G. 434
Marcus A. 197, 200, 203, 321
T. Jefferson 428
William D. 595, 596, 607, 610
COOMBE, A. Palmer 552
COOMBS
Frank L. 150, 431
George H. 536
William J. 138, 141
COON
Carlton S. 611
H.P. 461
Robert W. 572
Samuel H. 234, 237
COONEY
Frank H. 331
James 145, 148, 151
Joan Ganz 604
COONLEY, Howard 578
COONS
Albert H. 600, 607
Arthur G. 478
John 531
COONTZ, Robert E. 416, 580
COOPER
Allen F. 154, 157, 160, 163
Charles M. 139, 142
Edmund 109
Edward (N.Y.) 458
Edward (W. Va.) 172, 175
George B. 102
George W. 134, 137, 140
Grant B. 565
Henry 115, 117, 119, 370
Henry A. 141, 144, 147, 149, 152, 155, 158, 161, 163, 166, 169, 172, 176, 182, 186, 189, 192, 196
J.G. 497
J.T. 533
James 85, 86, 93, 95, 97, 358
James Fenimore 597
Jere 195, 198, 202, 205, 208, 212, 215, 218, 221, 225, 228, 231, 234, 237, 240
Job A. 285
John 6
John G. 172, 175, 178, 181, 185, 188, 191, 195, 198, 201, 204
John Sherman 223, 232, 236, 239, 242, 245, 248, 252, 255, 258, 261, 310*, 430, 433
John T. 449
Joseph A. 410
L. Gordon 594
Leon N. 606
Mario 574
Mark A. 84, 85, 87
Myers Y. 353
Myles 468
Oscar H. 466, 471
Peter 17, 597
Philip H. 483
Prentice 371, 435
Richard 588
Richard M. 76, 77
Robert A. 366
Samuel 401
Samuel B. 141, 144, 146, 149, 152, 155, 160
Thomas (S.C.) 481
Thomas (Del.) 63, 65
Thomas B. 105
Thomas P. 473
Tim E. 327
W.S. 600
William 54, 56
William B. 290
William C. 131, 133, 135
William J. 444
William R. 84
William S. 575, 595
COORS, D. Stanley 531
COOSEMANS, Ferdinand 474, 480
COOTE, Richard 8*
COOVER, M.S. 576
COOLBAUGH, Frank 543*
COPE
Arthur C. 565, 604
Edward D. 563, 597
COPELAND
Joseph J. 468
Kenneth W. 531
Lammot du Pont 546
Morris A. 566
Murray M. 565
Oren S. 214, 455
Royal S. 184, 188, 191, 194, 198, 201, 204, 207, 346
COPENHAVER, J.T. 451
COPLAND, Aaron 563, 585, 592, 603, 608
COPLEY
Ira C. 164, 167, 170, 173, 176, 180
Lionel 8
COPP, Owen 571
COPPEE, Henry 474
COPPER, S.M. 536
CORBALLY, John E., Jr. 472, 482
CORBETT
Henry W. 111, 113, 115, 356
Hunter 532
Robert J. 211, 221, 224, 228, 231, 234, 237, 240, 243, 246, 250, 253, 256, 259, 262
Roger B. 476
Timothy 525
CORBIN
Harry E. 486
Henry C. 401
CORBINO, Jon 610
CORBY, William 478*
CORCORAN, Francis V. 469
CORD, Erritt L. 544*
CORDELL, J.W. 462*
CORDIER, Andrew W. 468
CORDON, Guy 218, 221, 224, 227, 231, 234, 357
COREY
Wendell 563
William E. 554
CORI
Carl F. 596, 599, 605
Gerty T. 605
CORKER, Stephen A. 112
CORLETT, Charles H. 412,

413*
CORLEY, M. Simeon 111
CORLISS
George 501
George H. 609
John B. 143, 145, 148, 151
John O. 573
CORMAN, James C. 244, 248, 251, 254, 257, 260, 263
CORMENY, Alvin E. 487
CORN
N.S. 355
Samuel T. 387
CORNELL
Alonzo B. 345
Ezekiel 7
Gideon 10
Joseph 589, 592
Thomas 110, 126
CORNELY, Paul B. 572, 610
CORNER, George W. 607
CORNING
Charles R. 452
Erastus 101, 105, 449
Erastus, 2d 449
Parker 184, 188, 191, 194, 198, 201, 204
CORNISH
Johnston 140
Leslie 315
CORNWELL
Dean 591
John J. 383
CORONEL, Antonio F. 456
CORPER, Harry J. 572
CORPSTEIN, Peter 459
CORR, Frank J. 451
CORRADI, P. 418
CORRIGAN
Daniel 516
Frank P. 427, 434, 439
Joseph M. 468
Michael A. 524, 527
Robert F. 436
CORRY
Andrew V. 425, 432, 437
Frank M. 457
William 451
William F. 457
CORSCADEN, Thomas 594
CORSCOT, John 456
CORSE, John M. 409
CORSON
Bolton L. 601
Dale R. 468
Fred P. 469, 530
CORT, Stewart J. 544*, 595
CORTELYOU
George B. 30*, 31*, 39, 43, 45, 545
John R. 469
CORTESI, Arnaldo 585
CORTHELL, Elmer L. 572
CORWIN
Edward S. 571
Franklin 116
Moses B. 93, 97
Thomas 26, 27, 39, 78, 79, 81, 83, 84, 90, 92, 93, 103, 105, 352*, 433
CORWINE, Herbert J. 462
CORY
Abram E. 536
Charles B. 569
COSDEN, Jeremiah 69
COSGROVE
F.A. 548
Henry 525
James J. 546
John 128
Samuel G. 381
COSTAR, John C. 545
COSTELLO
John M. 202, 206, 209, 212, 216
Patrick H. 610
Peter E. 172, 175, 178
Timothy W. 465
William A. 438
COSTIGAN
Edward P. 196, 199, 203, 285
John E. 593, 610
COTA, Norman D. 413
COTHRAN
Andrew N. 483
James S. 133, 136
James W. 580
COTT, Perry 502
COTTAM
Clarence 591
Howard R. 431
COTTER
Joseph B. 529
William R. 260, 264
COTTERAL, John H. 272*
COTTERILL, George F. 461
COTTMAN, Joseph S. 95
COTTON
Aylett R. 114, 116
Francis R. 527
Norris 224, 227, 230, 233*, 236, 239, 243, 246, 249, 252, 255, 259, 262, 265, 339
COTTRELL
Frederick G. 590, 596, 598
James L. 89
Jesse B. 424
Leonard S., Jr. 573
COTZIAS, George C. 600
COUCH
Darius N. 407*, 408*, 410
Jessup N. 352
Richard B. 611
COUDEN, Robert 449*
COUDERT, Frederic R., Jr. 224, 227, 230, 233, 236, 240, 573
COUDREY, Harry M. 156, 159, 162
COUES
Elliott 569
Samuel E. 570
COUGHLIN
C.J. 557
Clarence D. 182
Howard 559
R. Lawrence 259, 262, 265
Timothy J. 467
COULTER
Cornelia C. 570
John B. 414
John L. 477
John M. 473, 563, 564, 574
L.E. 477
Richard 75, 76, 78, 79
W.J. 610
COUNTRYMAN, Gratia A. 568
COUNTS
George S. 557
J. Curtis 443
COURNAND, Andre F. 600, 606
COURSE, John M. 410
COURTENAY, William A. 451
COURTENEY, Edward H. 484
COUSE, E. Irving 598
COUSENS, John A. 483
COUSINARD, Edward 450
COUSINS
Robert G. 140, 142, 145, 148, 150, 153, 156, 159
William E. 523, 527
COUSLEY, Stanley W. 546
COUTANT, Frank R. 568
COURTNEY, W. Wirt 212, 215, 218, 221, 225
COUZENS
Frank 453
James 180, 184, 187, 190, 194, 197, 200, 203, 322, 453
COVERT
James W. 121, 123, 135, 138, 141
William C. 532
COVEY, Arthur 591
COVINGTON
George W. 125, 127
J. Harry 162, 165, 168
Joe E. 465
Leonard 59
Philip S. 486
COVODE, John 99, 101, 103, 105, 111, 113
COWAN
Donald R.G. 568
Edgar 105, 107, 109, 359
F.A. 599
George R. 612
Jacob P. 119
James P. 533
John C., Jr. 544
Richard S. 500
William P. 552
COWEN
Benjamin S. 86
John K. 142
Myron M. 423, 424, 435
Wilson 273
COWGER, William O. 255, 258, 261, 456
COWGILL
Calvin 123
James 455
COWHERD, William S. 145, 148, 151, 154, 455
COWLES
Alfred H. 594
Augustus W. 470
Charles H. 162
Edward 571
Eugene H. 594
George W. 112
Henry B. 76
Henry C. 574, 575
John G.W. 478, 545
Le Roy E. 484
William H.H. 131, 133, 135, 138
COWLEY
Malcolm 578*, 603
William H. 471
COWLING, Donald J. 467
COWPER, Edward A. 594
COX
Allyn 591
Catharine E.B. 499
Channing H. 320
Charles R. 548
Edward E. 186, 190, 193, 196, 200, 203, 206, 209, 213, 216, 219, 223, 226, 229
Edwin 590
George R. 451
Guy W. 548*
Harvey W. 470
Isaac N. 138
Jacob D. 28, 44, 121, 352, 407, 408, 409, 410*, 468, 600
James 61
James M. 18, 163, 166, 353*
John I. 370
Kenyon 591, 598
Leander M. 96, 98
N.W. 462
Nicholas N. 138, 141, 144, 146, 149
Reavis 568
Robert V. 587
Samuel H. 532
Samuel S. 101, 103, 105, 107, 112, 115, 117, 119, 121, 123, 126, 128, 131, 133
Sylvester W. 455*
William E. 158, 161, 164, 167, 170, 173
William R. 126, 128, 131
COXE
Alfred C. 271
Arthur C. 506, 522
Eckley B. 573
Macgrane 429, 430
Tench 7
William, Jr. 64
COY
Roy E. 498
Wayne 443
COYLE
Robert F. 532
William R. 188, 195, 198
COZZENS, James Gould 585, 598
CRABB
George W. 82, 83
Jeremiah 53
CRABTREE, John I. 580
CRACKSTON, John 3
CRADDOCK, John D. 193
CRAFT, Christopher C. 611
CRAFTS
James M. 475, 610
Samuel C. 67, 69, 70, 72, 87, 375*
Walter 572, 590
CRAGIN, Aaron H. 99, 101, 108, 110, 112, 114, 117, 119, 338
CRAGO, Thomas S. 166, 172, 175, 178, 182, 580
CRAIG
Alexander K. 138
Austin 465
Cleo F. 543*
George 303
George H. 127
George N. 568
Hector 71, 76
Henry K. 402
Howard A. 419
James 100, 103
Locke 348
Louis A. 402, 412, 413*, 414
Lyman C. 600
Malin 400*, 401, 419
Nancy Ellen 589
Oscar J. 476
Robert 77, 78, 82, 83, 85
Robert E. 558
Samuel A. 136
Walter E. 565
William B. (b. 1846) 469
William B. (b. 1877) 158, 161
Willis G. 532
CRAIGE, F. Burton 97, 99, 101, 103, 392
CRAIGHEAD, Edwin B. 468, 476, 483
CRAIGHILL
Lloyd R. 513
William P. 402, 572
CRAIK
James 403
William 53, 54, 55
CRAIL, Joe 189, 193, 196
CRAIN, William H. 131, 133, 136, 139, 141, 144
CRAINE, John P. 516, 520
CRAKER, John 79
CRALEY, N. Neiman, Jr. 253
CRAM
Ira H., Sr. 564, 608
Ralph A. 577
CRAMBLET
Thomas E. 466
W.H. 466
CRAMER
John 79, 81
Kenneth F. 402
Michael J. 427, 438
Myron C. 402
Robert V. 467
William C. 235, 238, 241, 245, 248, 251, 254, 257
CRAMPTON, George S. 601
CRAMTON, Louis C. 168, 171, 174, 177, 180, 184, 187, 190, 194
CRANDALL, Kenneth H. 564
CRANE
Arthur G. 387, 487
Bruce 607, 610
Charles H. 403
Charles R. 425
Charles S. 454
Clinton H. 610
E.J. 608
Frederick E. 346
Joseph C. 454
Joseph H. 76, 78, 79, 81
Philip M. 258, 261, 264
Richard 426
Stanley 610
Stephen 6
W. Murray 153, 156, 159, 162, 165, 320
William C. 466
William M. 418
CRANFIELD, Edward 8
CRANFILL, James B. 17
CRANFORD
Clarence W. 534
John W. 146
CRANSTON
Alan 257, 260, 263, 284
Earl 530
Henry Y. 88, 90
John 9
Robert B. 83, 85, 86, 92
Samuel 9
CRAPO
Henry H. 322
William W. 119, 121, 123, 125
CRAPSTER, T.G. 483
CRARY
Albert P. 594
Benjamin 471
Gerald D. 579
Isaac E. 82, 84
CRAWSHAW, William H. 468
CRAVATH, Paul D. 554
CRAVEN
Alfred 572
Charles 9
Elijah R. 532
J. Braxton, Jr. 271
CRAVENS
James A. 104, 106
James H. 85
Jordan E. 120, 122, 124
W. Fadjo 209, 212, 216, 219, 222
William B. 158, 161, 164, 199, 202, 206, 209
CRAVER, Harrison W. 568
CRAWFORD
Cheryl 592
Coe I. 163, 166, 169, 367
Corie I. 367
David L. 472
F.C. 578
Florence L. 538
Fred L. 204, 207, 210, 213, 217, 220, 223, 226,

230
Frederick C. 611, 612
George W. 26, 40, 85, 295
J.W. 460
James Y. 566
Joel 66, 68
Kenneth G. 557
M.L. 558
Martin J. 98, 100, 102, 391, 392
N.M. 475
Samuel J. 306
Samuel W. 408, 409
T.H. 456
Thomas H. 76, 78
Vernon D. 471
William 61, 63, 64, 65
William A. 436
William Harris 16, 24*, 39, 40, 60, 61, 62*, 63, 295, 428
William Henry 465
William T. 138, 144, 149, 160
CREAGER
Charles E. 163
Marvin H. 573
CREAL, Edward W. 203, 206, 210, 213, 216
CREAMER
J.J. 557
Thomas J. 117, 151
CREASY, William M. 402
CREBS, John M. 112, 114
CREECH, Harris 545
CREEDEN, John B. 471
CREEKMORE, J.H. 491
CREEL
Dana S. 492
Ralph L. 611
CREELY, John V. 115
CREESE, James 470
CREGIER, De Witt C. 451
CREGO, Ralph W. 455
CREIGHTON
Frank W. 512, 520
H. Jermain 575, 600, 607
Harriet B. 574
John A. 599
William, Jr. 64, 65, 75, 76, 78
William F. 516, 522
CREMIN, Lawrence A. 591
CRENSHAW, Bolling H. 466
CRESAP, Mark W., Jr. 554
CRESS, James B. 403
CRESSON, John C. 575
CRESWELL, John A. 28*, 43, 106, 108, 317
CRET, Paul P. 590, 591
CRETELLA, Albert W. 232, 235, 238
CRETIN, Joseph 528
CREVELING, Wesley 462
CREW
Henry 564, 570
William B. 353
CRIDER, John H. 585
CRILE
Austin D. 476
George W. 565, 603
CRIMMINS
Harry B. 480
John H. 427
CRIPPA, Edward D. 235, 388
CRISELL, E.H. 566
CRISFIELD, John W. 91, 104
CRISP
Arthur 591
Charles F. 127, 129, 132, 134, 136, 137, 142*
Charles R. 142, 167, 170, 173, 176, 180, 183, 186, 190, 193, 196
CRISSINGER, Daniel R. 443
CRIST, Henry 61
CRISWELL, W.A. 534
CRITCHER, John 115
CRITCHETT, James H. 575
CRITCHFIELD, Jack B. 480
CRITTENBERGER, Willis D. 405, 412*, 413, 415
CRITTENDEN
E.C. 580
John J. 26*, 27, 41, 66, 80, 82, 84, 85, 87, 89, 91, 98, 100, 102, 104, 308*
Thomas L. 407, 408, 409
Thomas T. 116, 121, 329
Thomas T., Jr. 455
William 515, 519
CRITZ
Harry H. 405
Hugh 475
CROCHERON
Henry 65
Jacob 76
CROCKER
Alvah 114, 116
Anna Belle 501
Edward S., 2d 430
Edwin B. 283
Herbert 572
Marcellus M. 408
Samuel L. 97
W.W. 546*
Walton L. 548
William 574
William H. 546*
CROCKETT
David 75, 76, 80
John M. 452*
John W. 83, 85, 392
Kennedy M. 434
Roy B. 576
CROES
John 505, 520
John J.R. 572
CROFT
Edward 402
George W. 154
Theodore G. 154
CROGHAN,
George 402
CROLL, William M. 185
CROMER, George W. 147, 150, 153, 156
CROMPTON, Alfred W. 501
CROMWELL
Frank H. 455
James H.R. 425
John 575
CROMMELIN, John H. 457
CRONBACH, Lee J. 571
CRONEIS, Carey 466, 480, 608
CRONIN
John W. 595
Joseph V. 454*
Paul W. 264
CRONK
Edward M. 437
George P. 574
CRONKHITE, Adelbert 410
CRONKITE, Walter 577
CROOK
A.N.J. 461
George 406, 409
Isaac 478, 479
Thurman C. 226
William H. 423
CROOKE, Philip S. 117
CROOKER, L.M. 450
CROOKS
Clayton J. 577
Harry M. 474
CROSBY
Charles N. 201, 205, 208
Edwin L. 578
Elisha O. 429
Herbert B. 401
Howard 477, 532, 570
John C. 137
Robert B. 334
William 8*
William G. 314
CROSLAND, David W. 579
CROSS
Bert S. 549*
Burton M. 315
Charles T. 437
Edward 83, 85
Edward M. 511, 522
George L. 478
Harry P. 575
James B. 456
M.S. 479
Oliver H. 195, 198, 202, 205
Richard E. 543
Robert D. 472, 482
Walter S. 536
Whitman 576
Wilbur L. 289, 578
CROSSER, Robert 169, 172, 175, 185, 188, 191, 195, 198, 201, 204, 208, 211, 214, 218, 221, 224, 227, 230, 234
CROSSFIELD, A.S. 594
CROSSLAND
Edward 114, 116
Charles E. 474, 482*
J.R.A. 432
CROSSLEY, M.L. 567*, 590
CROSSMAN
Abdil D. 457
Raymond M. 576
CROSWELL, Charles M. 322
CROTHERS, Austin L. 317
CROTTY
H.C. 557
John 455
CROUCH
Bill 585
Edward 64
Leslie E. 576
Parker L. 453
CROUNSE, Lorenzo 117, 119, 333
CROUSE
George W. 133
John N. 566
Russell 574, 585
CROW
Charles A. 162
Herman D. 381
William E. 182, 359
William J. 224
CROWDER
A.C. 454
Enoch H. 402, 426
CROWE
Eugene B. 196, 200, 203, 206, 210
Morrill M. 459
Philip K. 425, 434, 439
CROWELL
John (Ala.) 67
John (Ohio) 92, 93
John F. 470
CROWLEY
Archie H. 515
Joseph B. 147, 150, 153
Miles 144
Patrick F. 599
Mrs. Patrick F. 599
Richard 123, 126
CROWNINSHIELD
A.S. 418
Benjamin W. 24*, 42, 71, 72, 74, 76
Jacob 58, 59, 60
CROWTHER
Frank 178, 181, 184, 188, 191, 194, 198, 201, 204, 207, 211, 214
George C. 143
CROXTON
John T. 424
Thomas 131
CROZIER
John H. 90, 92
Robert 116, 306*
William 402, 410, 419
CRUCE, Lee 355
CRUDUP, Josiah 70
CRUFT, Charles 409
CRUGER
Daniel 67
John 458
John, Jr. 3, 458
CRUICKSHANK
Allan D. 393
Mrs. Allan D. 393
CRUIKSHANK, M.H. 393
CRUM, William D. 432
CRUMB, George 587
CRUMMEY, John D. 546*
CRUMP
Edward H. 198, 202, 456*
George W. 73
Rousseau O. 143, 145, 148
William 425
CRUMPACKER
Edgar D. 145, 147, 150, 153, 156, 158, 161, 164
Maurice E. 188
Shepard J., Jr. 229, 232, 235
CRUNDEN, Frederick M. 568
CRUTCHER, Thomas 457
CRUTCHFIELD, William 117
CRYER, George E. 456
CUBBISON, Donald 413
CUDAHY, John 424, 430, 432, 435
CUDDY, William 558
CUDWORTH
Grace F. 536
Luther P. 536
CULBERSON
Charles A. 149, 152, 155, 157, 160, 163, 166, 169, 172, 175, 178, 182, 372*
David B. 120, 122, 124, 126, 129, 131, 133, 136, 139, 141, 144
CULBERTSON
Clyde G. 572
William C. 136
William S. 425, 435
William W. 127
CULBRETH
E.E. 459
Thomas 66, 68
CULIN, Frank L., Jr. 414
CULKIN, Francis D. 191, 194, 198, 201, 204, 207, 211, 214, 217
CULLEN
Edgar M. 345
Elisha D. 98
George 485
Thomas H. 178, 181, 184, 188, 191, 194, 198, 201, 204, 207, 211, 214, 217
William 125, 127
CULLER, George D. 497, 502
CULLOM
Alvan 88, 90
Shelby M. 108, 110, 112, 127, 129, 132, 134, 137, 139, 142, 145, 147, 150, 153, 156, 158, 161, 164, 300*
William 96, 97
CULLOP, William A. 161, 164, 167, 170
CULLUM, George W. 483
CULMER, Mrs. Charles U. 576
CULP, Reed C. 576
CULPEPER, John 8
CULPEPPER, John 60, 64, 65, 68, 71, 75
CULVER
Charles V. 109
Erastus D. 90, 439
Essae M. 568, 600
John C. 252, 255, 258, 261, 264
CUMBACK, William 98
CUMMING
Burton 499*
Hugh S. 445, 572
Hugh S., Jr. 430
Thomas W. 97
William 6
CUMMINGS
Amos J. 133, 135, 138, 141, 143, 146, 148, 151
Byron 465, 497
Carlos E. 497
E.E. 589, 592, 610
Emerson L. 402, 405
Fred 199, 203, 206, 209
George A. 452
George B. 567
Hebert W. 185
Henry H. 600
Henry J.B. 120
Homer S. 33*, 41
J.E. 462
Joseph 478, 485
O. Sam 576
Thomas L. 457
Tilden 546
Virginia L. 497
Walter J. 272
Walter J., Sr. 546
CUMMINS
Albert B. 159, 161, 164, 167, 170, 173, 176, 179, 180, 183*, 186, 187, 304*
George D. 506
John D. 90, 92
CUNINGGIM, Merrimon 491
CUNNINGHAM
Charles C. 497, 502
Charles E. 17
David F. 529
Francis A. 90
G.I. 451
Glenn C. 239, 242, 246, 249, 252, 255, 259
James D. 573
John F. 528
John R. 469
Merce 592
Paul 572
Paul H. 216, 220, 223, 226, 229, 232, 235, 239
Ross M. 568
William J. 579
William M. 478
CURETON, Calvin M. 373
CURLEY
Daniel J. 529
Edward W. 204, 207, 211
James M. 165, 168, 217, 220, 321, 450*
Michael J. 523, 524, 528
CURLIN, William P., Jr. 261
CURME
George O. 577
George O., Jr. 594, 596
CURPHEY, Theodore J. 572
CURRAN
Charles C. 589, 593
Frank E. 461
Joseph E. 558
CURRELL, William S. 481
CURRENT, Richard N. 591

CURREY, Robert B. 457
CURRIE
Bruce 593
George R. 386
Gilbert A. 174, 177
CURRIER
Amos N. 473
Frank D. 151, 154, 157, 159, 162, 165
Moody 338
Stephen R. 493
CURRIGAN, Thomas G. 453
CURRIN, David M. 392, 393*
CURRY
Charles F. 167, 170, 173, 176, 179, 183, 186, 189, 193
Charles F., Jr. 196
Daniel 469
George 165
Jabez L.M. 100, 102, 391, 392*, 437
John S. 607
P.H. 551
CURTI, Merle 567, 585
CURTICE, Harlow H. 547
CURTIN
Andrew G. 126, 128, 131, 359, 436
John C. 454
Willard S. 240, 243, 246, 250, 253
CURTIS
Alfred A. 529
Benjamin R. 269
Carl T. 210, 214, 217, 220, 224, 227, 230, 233, 236, 239, 242, 246, 249, 252, 255, 258, 262, 265, 334
Carlton B. 95, 97, 117
Charles 14, 18*, 140, 142, 145, 148, 150, 153, 156, 159, 161, 164*, 170, 173, 176, 180, 183, 187, 190, 192, 306
Charles A. 478
Charles B. 427
Charles G. 598, 610
Charles M. 291
Edward 83, 84
Edward P. 594
Edwin U. 450
Ellwood F. 546
Fayette S. 572
George M. 142, 145
H. Holbrook 603
Harvey 473
Ivol I. 516, 521
James L. 432
Kenneth M. 315
Laurence 233, 236, 239, 242, 245
Newton M. 138, 141, 143
Oakley C. 315
Orrin 456
Samuel R. 100, 102, 104, 406
Thomas B. 230, 233, 236, 239, 242, 246, 249, 252, 255
W.C. 573
W.D. 456
Walter W. 525
William S. 473
CURTISS
Glenn H. 593*
James 451
CURWEN, John 571
CUSACK
Thomas 147
Thomas F. 525
CUSHING
Caleb 27*, 41, 81, 82, 84, 86, 425, 437
Courtland 427
Edmund L. 338
Frank 585
George H. 566
Harvey 565, 569, 583, 603
Howard G. 607
Jonathan P. 471
Richard 523*
Thomas 6
Thomas H. 401, 402
William 10, 269
CUSHMAN
Allerton S. 600
Austin T. 552
Charlotte S. 597
Francis W. 149, 152, 155, 158, 160, 163
John F. 423
John P. 67
Joshua 68, 69, 71
Joseph A. 597
Ralph S. 530
Robert E. 571
Robert E., Jr. 416
Samuel 81, 82
CUSICK, Peter 467
CUSTER, Benjamin A. 595
CUSTIS, Martha (Dandridge) 20
CUTCHEON, Byron M. 128, 130, 132, 135
CUTHBERT
Alfred 63, 65, 69, 71, 72, 78, 80, 82, 84, 85, 295
John A. 68
CUTLER
Augustus W. 119, 121
Carroll 485
John C. 374
Manasseh 56, 58
Nathan 314
Timothy 487
William P. 105
CUTRER, Lewis 454
CUTROW, Walter 591
CUTTEN, George B. 468
CUTTER
Charles A. 568
Leonard R. 450
CUTTING
Bronson M. 191, 194, 197, 201, 204, 343*
Churchill H. 565
Francis B. 97
Harmon S. 451
John T. 136
CUTTS
Charles 61, 62, 64, 337
Ernest A. 579
John 8
Marsena E. 125
Richard 56, 58, 59, 60, 61, 62
CUYLER
Abraham C. 449
Cornelis 449
Johannes 449
CYR, Leo G. 436

D

DABNEY
Charles W. 468, 482
Virginius 573, 585
DADDARIO, Emilio Q. 241, 244, 248, 251, 254, 257
DAEGER, Albert T. 524
DAGER, Holmes E. 415
DAGG, John L. 475
DAGUE, Paul B. 224, 228, 231, 234, 237, 240, 243, 246, 250, 253
DAGGETT
Athern P. 466
David 63, 65, 66, 287*
Frank S. 500
John D. 460
Naphtali 487
Rollin M. 123, 430
Samuel S. 550
DAGWELL, Benjamin D. 513, 521
DAHL, Robert A. 571
DAHLBERG, Edwin T. 534
DAHLE, Herman B. 149, 152
DAHLGREN
John A. 417, 418
Ulric 607
DAHLQUIST, John E. 404, 405, 413, 414
DAIL, Charles C. 461
DAILY, William M. 473
DAINGERFIELD, Eliott 593
DALBEY, Josiah T. 411
DALE
Charles M. 339
Harrison C. 472
Harry H. 168, 171, 174
Porter H. 172, 175, 179, 182, 185, 189, 192, 195, 199, 202, 377
Thomas 9*
Thomas H. 157
DALES, John B. 533
D'ALESANDRO
Thomas, Jr. 210, 213, 217, 220, 223, 450
Thomas J. 3d 450
DALEY
Arthur 586
E. Jerome 474*
John P. 404
Richard J. 451
DALLAS
Alexander J. 24, 39
George M. 14, 16, 78, 89, 90, 271, 358, 429, 458
John T. 512, 520
DALLDORF, Gilbert 600
DALLINGER, Frederick W. 171, 174, 177, 180, 184, 187, 190, 194, 197, 273
DALRYMPLE, Sherman H. 559
DALTON
Jack 600
John M. 330
Robert H. 612
Tristram 51, 319
DALY
Augustine 599
Charles P. 566
Edward C. 526
Edward J. 289
J. Burrwood 205, 208, 211
Marcus 543
Reginald A. 576, 597, 607
William D. 148
DALZELL, John 133, 136, 138, 141, 143, 146, 149, 152, 154, 157, 160, 163, 166
DAMEN, Arnold 474
DAMIANO, Celastine J. 525
DAMM, Walter J. 578
DAMON, Ralph S. 553, 611
DAMRELL, William S. 99, 100
DAMROSCH, Walter 563, 578, 603*
DANA
A.S. 600
Amasa 84, 88
Charles L. 569*
Daniel 469
Francis 4, 6, 319
James D. 563, 568, 575
John W. 314, 424
Judah 80, 314
Samuel 63
Samuel W. 53, 54, 55, 56, 57, 58, 60, 61*, 62, 63, 65, 66, 67, 287
DANAHER
Charles A. 272
John A. 209, 213, 216, 289
DANCIS, Joseph 592
DANCY, W. McLaws 454
DANDRIDGE, Edmund P. 513, 522
DANE
Joseph 68, 69
Nathan 6
DANFORD
Lorenzo 117, 119, 121, 143, 146
Robert M. 402
DANFORTH
Donald 551*
Henry G. 165, 168, 171
Walter R. 459
William H. 551*
William H. (b. 1926) 485
DANGERFIELD, George 586, 591
DANIEL
Charles E. 234, 366
Henry 74, 75, 77
John M. 436*
John R.J. 86, 88, 90, 91, 93, 95
John W. 131, 133, 136, 139, 141, 144, 147, 149, 152, 155, 158, 160, 163, 379
M. Price 234, 237, 240, 373*
Peter V. 269
Robert 8, 9
Robert W., Jr. 266
W.C. (Dan) 260, 263, 266, 568
William 17
DANIELL, Warren F. 138
DANIELS
Arthur H. 472
Charles 141, 143
Dominick V. 243, 246, 249, 252, 255, 259, 262, 265
Farrington 565, 596, 608
Gibson T. 534
Henry H. 513, 520
Josephus 31, 32*, 42, 433
Milton J. 152
Paul C. 427, 430
DANIELSON, George E. 260, 263
DANILOVA, Alexandra 593
DANNER, Joel B. 93
DARBY
Edwin T. 566
Ezra 59, 60
Harry 226, 307
John F. 95, 460*
D'ARCAMBAL, Alex. H. 572
D'ARCY, P.H. 460
DARCY, Thomas F. 587
DARDEN
Colgate W., Jr. 202, 205, 212, 215, 380, 484
Pretlow 458
Put 578
Stephen H. 393
DARGAN
Edmund S. 89, 277, 392
Edwin C. 534
George W. 129, 131, 133, 136
D'ARISTA, Robert 609
DARLEY, Ward 468
DARLING
Chester A. 465
George B. 492
Henry 471, 532
Jay N. 579, 583, 584, 591, 609
Louis 593
Mason C. 92
William A. 108
DARLINGTON
Charles F. 428
Edward 79, 81, 83
Gilbert 603
Isaac 67
James H. 509, 519
Smedley 133, 136
Urban V.W. 530
William 65, 68, 70
DARNELL, J.S. 453
DARR, Edward A. 552
DARRAGH
Alex 557
Archibald B. 151, 153, 156, 159
Cornelius 88, 90
John 459
DARRALL, Chester B. 112, 114, 116, 118, 121, 125
DARRELL, Norris 568
DARROW
Daniel C. 592
George P. 172, 175, 178, 182, 185, 188, 192, 195, 198, 201, 205, 208, 211
DARSIE, George 536
DARST
Joseph M. 460
Thomas C. 510, 519
DARTON, Nelson H. 595, 607
da SARACENA, Leo 480
DASBURG, Andrew 607
DASHIELL
John F. 571
Robert L. 469
DASPIT, Lawrence R. 419
DAU, William H.T. 484
DAUBENMIRE, Rexford 575
DAUBNEY, John E. 460
DAUGHERTY
Harry M. 32, 41
James A. 165
Jerome 471
DAUGHTON, Ralph H. 218, 222
DAVEE, Thomas 82, 84
DAVENPORT
Charles B. 573, 603
Franklin 55, 56, 340
Frederick M. 188, 191, 194, 198, 609
George W. 511, 519
Harry J. 228
Herbert J. 566
Horace W. 571
Ira 131, 133
James 53, 54
James S. 160, 166, 169, 172
John (b. 1752) 55, 56, 57, 58, 60, 61, 62, 63, 65
John (b. 1788) 75
Joseph J. 455
Samuel A. 146, 149
Stanley W. 149
Thomas 73, 75, 77, 78, 80
DAVES, John C. 580
DAVEY
Charles 480
Martin L. 175, 178, 185, 188, 191, 354
Peter 601
Randall 589, 593
Robert C. 140, 145, 148, 150, 153, 156, 159
DAVEZAC, Auguste 433*
DAVID, John B.M. 527
DAVIDOVSKY, Mario 588
DAVIDSON
A.T. 392*
Alexander C. 129, 131
Carter 473, 483
Garrison H. 405*, 419, 483

George (b. 1825) 594
George (b. 1889) 591
Howard C. 412
Irwin D. 236
Israel 572
James H. 147, 149, 152, 155, 158, 161, 163, 166, 176
James O. 385
John 449
John F. 483
Kenneth S.M. 611*
Levette J. 566
Philip 474
Phillip B., Jr. 400
Robert (b. 1750) 469, 532
Robert (b. 1808) 482
Robert C. 450
Robert H.M. 120, 122, 125, 127, 129, 132, 134
Robert L.D. 486
Roy E. 557
Thomas G. 98, 100, 102
Wilbur L. 465
William (b. 1778) 67, 68
William (b. 1919) 517, 522
William J. 473
William R. 568

DAVIE
Charles C. 452
William R. 4, 347, 428

DAVIES
A. Donald 518, 519
Arthur B. 593, 607
Charles E. 574
David C. 499
E.F.C. 573
E.P. 461
Edward 83, 85
George K. 483
Henry E. 345
John C. 227
Jacob G. 450
Joseph E. 424, 432, 439
Paul L. 546*
Samuel 479
Samuel W. 451
Thomas A. 407
Thomas F. (b. 1831) 508, 520
Thomas F. (b. 1872) 510, 522
Valentine 563
W.R. 486

DAVIS
Alexander M. 117
Amos 79
Archie K. 564, 575
Arthur C. 399
Arthur P. 572
Arthur V. 443*
Bette 563
Boothe C. 465
Cameron J. 512, 522
Charles H. 589, 593, 610
Charles Henry 417, 418
Charles J. 455
Charles P. 498
Charles R. 153, 156, 159, 162, 165, 168, 171, 174, 177, 180, 184
Charles S. 544*, 576
Clifford 212, 215, 218, 221, 225, 228, 231, 234, 237, 240, 243, 247, 250
Cushman K. 132, 135, 137, 140, 143, 145, 148, 324*
Daniel F. 314
David 17, 120, 122, 124, 125, 269, 300
David B. 587
David W. 299
Deane C. 377, 549, 550
Donald D. 547
Dwight F. 32, 33, 40
Edmund J. 372
Edward M. 502
Elmer 574
Ewin L. 178, 182, 185, 189, 192, 195, 198
Francis B. 554*
Finis E. 577
Frank H. 552
Garrett 84, 85, 87, 89, 104, 106, 108, 110, 112, 114, 309
George 391, 392*
George B. 402
George H. 575
George M. 416
George R. 122, 125, 127
George S. 472
George T. 95
George W. 569
Gladys Rockmore 598
Glenn R. 225, 228, 231, 235, 238, 254, 257, 260, 263, 266
H.L. 584
H. Winter 98, 100, 102, 106
Hal C. 557
Hallie Flanagan 592
Hallowell 571
Harry L. 353, 452
Harvey N. 573
Henry 471, 475
Henry G. 17, 115, 117, 120, 122, 124, 126, 383
Henry L. 480
Herbert J. 481
Horace 120, 122, 467
Horace G., Jr. 588
Howard R. 574
Howland 575, 580
Hyman D. 577
Ilus W. 455
Isaac 553
J.C. Bancroft 273*, 428
J.Z. 497
Jacob C. 98
Jacob E. 214
James 525
James C. 223, 226, 229, 232, 235, 238, 241, 245
James H. 172, 313*
James J. 32*, 33, 46, 195, 198, 201, 205, 208, 211, 215, 218, 360
James P. 524
Jeff 158, 161, 164, 281*
Jefferson 27, 40, 89, 91, 93, 95, 100, 102, 326*, 391
Jefferson C. 408, 409*, 410
Jerome C. 557
John (b. 1787) 72, 74, 76, 77, 79, 81, 82, 84, 89, 91, 93, 95, 319*, 553, 563
John (b. 1788) 85
John (b. 1826) 137, 140
John (b. 1851) 273
John A.G. 484*
John E. (b. 1895) 568
John E. (b. 1913) 351
John G. 94, 96, 100, 102
John J. (b. 1835) 115, 117
John J. (b. 1909) 400
John W. (b. 1789) 80, 84, 87, 89*, 425
John W. (b. 1826) 362*
John W. (b. 1867) 271
John W. (b. 1873) 18, 166, 169, 429, 565, 575, 603
John W. (b. 1916) 245, 248, 251, 254, 258, 261, 264
Jonathan M. 306
Joseph J. 119, 121, 124
Joseph S. 566
Kingsley 574
Leighton I. 419
Lewis 531
Lowndes H. 123, 125, 128
Loyal 565
M.M. 536
Mendel J. 163, 166
Monnett B. 417, 431, 434
Morgan J. 564, 576
Nathan S. 569
Nathan S., 3d 498
Nathaniel 424, 425, 426, 429, 430
Nathaniel M. 580
Nelson H. 402
Nicholas 392
Noah 112
Norman H. 569, 603
Oscar H. 273
Owen 574, 583
Reuben 100, 102, 392
Richard D. 86, 88
Richard H. 436
Robert C. 401
Robert L. 198
Robert T. 457
Robert Thompson 127, 130, 132
Robert Tyler 500, 501
Robert W. 145, 147, 150, 153
Roger 63, 64
Roy T. 426, 429*, 434
Russell C. 454
S.S. 451
Sammy, Jr. 611
Samuel 63
Shelby 438
Stillman S. 576
Stuart 590, 592
Thomas 97
Thomas A. 450
Thomas B. 158
Thomas F. 506, 521
Thomas T. (Ky.) 54, 55, 56
Thomas T. (N.Y.) 107, 108
Timothy (Iowa) 100
Timothy (Mass.) 99, 100
Tom J. 580
W.H. 462
W. True, Jr. 438
Warren R. 75, 76, 78, 80
Webster 455
Werter R. 466
Westmoreland 379
William M. 576, 594, 597, 599, 607
William M. (Pa.) 105
William T. 580
William W. 536
William Z. 353*

DAVISON
A.M. 455
Denver M. 355*
Edward 580
Frank E. 536
Fred C. 471
George M. 145
George S. 572
Henry P. 603
Mrs. Henry Pomeroy 603
Michael S. 404, 419

DAVISSON, Clinton J. 594, 605
DAVY, John M. 119

DAWES
Beman G. 157, 160
Charles G. 14, 18, 186, 189, 429, 444, 605
Henry L. 100, 102, 104, 106, 108, 110, 112, 114, 116, 118, 121, 123, 125, 127, 130, 132, 135, 137, 320
James W. 333
Rufus R. 126

DAWKINS, James B. 392

DAWLEY
Ernest J. 412, 413
Frank R. 457

DAWSON
Albert F. 156, 159, 161
D. Boone 451
Dana 531
G.M. 575
J. William 563, 575
John 7, 55, 56, 57, 58, 59, 61, 62, 63, 64
John, Jr. 451
John A. 534
John B. 86, 87
John L. 95, 97, 107, 109
John S. 307
Louis W. 549*
N.H.R. 444
Thomas 486
Thomas C. 426, 427, 434
William (Diplomat) 426, 427, 432, 439*
William (Educator) 486
William (Legislator) 130
William (Mayor) 460
William A. 225, 234, 237, 240
William C. 80, 82, 84, 85, 92, 94, 96, 295
William J. 53
William L. 502
William L. (Ill.) 216, 219, 223, 226, 229, 232, 235, 238, 242, 245, 248, 251, 255, 258
William M. 465
William M.O. 383
William W. 569

DAY
Arthur L. 576, 607
Dorothy 599
Edmund E. 468
Edward C. 286
Frank Miles 567
Frank P. 483
J. Edward 36, 43
James R. 482
Jeremiah 487
Luther Day 353
Price 585
Robert L. 450
Rowland 71, 79
Stephen A. 213
Timothy C. 99
W. Beach 493
William A. 546
William L. 547*
William R. 30, 38, 270, 271

DAYAN, Charles 77

DAYTON
Alston G. 144, 147, 149, 152, 155, 158
Jonathan 4, 6, 52, 53*, 54*, 55, 56, 57, 58, 340
Louis P. 451
William L. 16, 86, 88, 89, 91, 93, 340, 428
William L., Jr. 433

DEADERICK, James W. 370
DEAL, Joseph T. 182, 186, 189, 192

DEALEY
James W. 573
Patrick F. 470

DEAN
Amos 473
Arthur H. 573, 604, 609
Arthur L. 472
Bailey S. 472
Ben 576
Benjamin 121
Ezra 86, 88
Gilbert 95, 97
Gordon 443
H. Trendley 600
James 484
Josiah 60
Mason S. 566
R. Hal 551*
Sidney 98, 100
Walter C. 458
William F. 414

DEANE
Charles B. 224, 227, 230, 234, 237
Silas 5

DEAR, Cleveland 200, 203

DEARBORN
Henry 23, 24, 40, 52, 53, 400, 406, 435
Henry A.S. 77, 580

DEARDEN, John F. 523*, 528
DEARING, Fred M. 435*, 437
DeARMOND, David A. 138, 140, 143, 145, 148, 151, 154, 156, 159, 162
DEARMONT, R.L. 549
DEAS, David 451
DEASY, Luere B. 315
DEAVER, John B. 565
DEAVITT, Edward H. 457
DeBACA, Ezequiel C. 343
DeBAKEY, Michael E. 590, 600, 608
DeBELLIS, A.M. 599
DEBERRY, Edmund 76, 79, 81, 83, 84, 86, 88, 93
DeBLIECK, John 474, 487
DEBOE, William J. 145, 148, 150, 309
DeBOER, Joseph A. 549
DeBOLT, Rezin A. 119
DeBORE, Etienne 457
DeBORHEGYI, Stephan F. 500
DEBOSE, Laurance T. 418
DEBS, Eugene V. 17*, 18*

DeBUTTS
Harry A. 552
Henry 401, 402
John D. 543

DEBYE, Peter J.W. 596, 604, 605, 608
DeCAMP, Joseph 593
DeCARLO, Charles 481
DeCARVALHO, George 585
DECATUR, Stephen 417
DECELL, John L. 530
DeCHEVERUS, John L. 525

DECKER
A.S. 452
Charles T. 402
Clarence R. 580
George H. 400, 404, 405
Martin M. 577
Perl D. 168, 171, 174

DeCLUET, A. 391
DeCOE, Darold D., Sr. 580
DeCOURCY, William E. 429
DEEDS, Edward A. 549*
DEEMER, Elias 152, 154, 157
DEEN, Braswell D. 200, 203, 206

DEERE
Charles H. 546
John 546

DEERING
Charles 548
Nathaniel C. 120, 123, 125

DEES, Bowen C. 575
DEEVEY, Edward S. 575
DeFALCO, Lawrence M. 525
DeFORD, Earl H. 412
DeFOREST

Alfred V. 601, 608
Henry S. 165
Henry W. 552
Lee 594, 595, 598
Robert E. 137, 139
Robert W. 603
DEFREES
John D. 443
Joseph H. 108
Joseph H., Jr. 574
DeGARMO, Charles 482
DEGENER, Edward 113
DEGLER, Carl N. 588, 591
DeGOESBRIAND, Louis 525
DeGOLYER, E.L. 564, 596, 601, 608
DeGRAFF, John I. 74, 83
DeGRAFFENREID
Edward 225, 228
Reese C. 146, 149, 152
DeGRAMONT, Sanche 586
DeGRESS, J.C. 450
DeGRUYTER, J.A. 451
DeHART, John 6
DeHAVEN
Hugh 611
John J. 134
DEHON, Theodore 505, 521
DEHONEY
W.S. 453
W. Wayne 534
DEIBLER, Frederick S. 564
DEINES, John M. 566
DEITRICK, Frederick S. 168
DeJARNETTE, Daniel C. 103, 393*
DEJONG, Meindert 602
DeLONG, Russell N. 569
DeKIEWIET, Cornelis W. 468, 480
DeKNIGHT, Avel 591
DeKOONING, Willem 608
DELACOUR, Jean 500
DeLACY
Hugh 222
Phillip H. 570
DELAFIELD, Richard 402, 483
DeLaGARZA, Eligio, 2d 253, 256, 260, 263, 266
DeLAGUNA, Frederica 563
DeLaHOUSSAYE, Arthur A. 579
DeLAITTRE, John 457
DeLaMATER, Robert G. 601
DeLaMATYR, Gilbert 123
DeLaMontanya, James 84
DELANCEY
Etienne 3
James 3, 8, 10
William H. 479, 505, 522
DELANEY
A.K. 455
Edward K. 460
James J. 221, 227, 230, 233, 236, 240, 243, 246, 249, 252, 256, 259, 262, 265
John B. 527
John J. 174, 198, 201, 204, 207, 211, 214, 217, 221, 224
Joseph J. 558
R.R. 451
DELANO or DE LANO
Charles 102, 104
Columbus 28*, 44, 90, 109, 111, 444
Lyman 549
Milton 133, 135
Milton M. 453
William A. 590, 603
DELANOY, Peter 457
DELANY
Henry B. 511
Patrick B. 594
DELAPLAINE, Isaac C. 105
DELAPLANE, Stanton 584
DeLARGE, Robert C. 115
DELAVALL, Thomas 457*
DELBRUCK, Max 606
DeLeHAILANDIERE, Celestine 526
DeLEON, M.H. 452
DELGADO, Pedro 461
DELL, Roger L. 325
DELLAY, Vincent J. 239
DELLENBECK, John 256, 259, 262, 265
DELLET, James 83, 87
DELLINGER, John H. 598
DELLMUTH, Carl K. 546
DELLO JOIO, Norman 586
DELLUMS, Ronald V. 260, 263
DeLONG
C.J. 558
Charles E. 431*
Russell N. 569
DELORIT, Richard J. 486
DELPH, John M. 456
DelSESTO, Christopher 363
DeLUCCO, Dominick J. 454*
DeLUCE, Daniel 585
DeLUE, Donald 579, 591
DELUGACH, Albert L. 587
DELUREY, Lawrence 484
DEMARAY, Arthur E. 444
DeMARCO, Jean 591, 610
DEMENT, William C. 598
DEMAREST, William H.S. 480
DeMEYER, Nicholas 457
DeMILLE
Agnes 593
William 563
DEMING
Benjamin F. 80
Henry C. 106, 107, 453*, 457
Lucius P. 579
Olcott H. 438
William C. 445
DEMMLER, Ralph H. 445
DeMONTEBELLO, Philippe 500
DeMOTT, John 90
DeMOTTE, Mark L. 125
DEMPSEY
Edward J. 452
John 289
John J. 204, 207, 211, 230, 233, 236, 239, 343
S. Wallace 171, 174, 178, 181, 184, 188, 191, 194
DEMPSTER, Arthur J. 570
DEMSKE, James M. 467
DeMUTH, Peter J. 208
DENBY
Charles 425
Edward T. 511
Edwin 32, 42, 156, 159, 162
DeNECKERE, Leo R. 527
DENEEN, Charles S. 183, 186, 190, 193, 301*
DENFELD, Louis E. 416, 417, 418
DENHOLM, Frank E. 263, 266
DENIO, Hiram 345*
DENISON
Arthur C. 271
Charles 107, 109, 111
Dudley C. 120, 122
Edward E. 170, 173, 176, 180, 183, 187, 190, 193
George 68, 70
Joseph J. 466, 473
Rodger 564
DeNIVERNAIS, Edward J. (See Livernash, Edward)
DENMAN, William 272
DENNETT, Tyler 486, 584
DENNEY
C.E. 550
J.V. 564
Robert V. 255, 259
William D. 291
DENNING
Joseph M. 433
William 61
DENNIS
David W. 258, 261, 264
Fred L. 531
George R. 116, 118, 121, 317
John (b. 1771) 54, 55, 56, 57
John (b. 1807) 82, 84
John J. 461
Littleton P. 79
William C. 470
DENNISON
David S. 240
John H. 285
Robert L. 416, 417*
William 27*, 43, 352
DENNY
Allan 453
Caleb S. 454*
Charles R. 443
Collins 530
Ebenezer 459
Ebenezer (U.S. Army) 401*
Emery B. 349
George H. 465*, 485
George L. 454
Harmar 76, 78, 79, 81
Harmar D., Jr. 231
James W. 148, 153
Walter M. 143
William 9
DENNY-BROWN, Derek E. 569
DENOYELLES, Peter 64
DENSON, William H. 139
DENT
A.W. 578
Frederick B. 37, 46
George 52, 53, 54, 55
John H. 240, 243, 246, 250, 253, 256, 259, 262, 265
Josiah 462
Julia Boggs 20
S. Hubert, Jr. 161, 164, 167, 170, 173, 176
William B.W. 96
DENTON
George K. 173
Vachel 449*
Winfield K. 226, 229, 235, 239, 242, 245, 248, 251
DENVER
James W. 98
Mathew R. 160, 163, 166
DEPEW
Chauncey M. 148, 151, 154, 157, 159, 162, 345
Ganson 579
DePEYSTER
Abraham 10, 457
Frederic J. 575
Johannes 449*, 457
DePRIEST, Oscar 193, 196, 200
DEPUE, David A. 341
DERBIGNY, Pierre 311
DERBY
Samuel C. 465
Wilfrid N. 483
DERBYSHIRE, Arthur 500
DERCUM, Francis X. 569, 570
DeREIMER, Isaac 457
DERGARABEDIAN, Paul 564
DeRIVERA, Jose 592
DERN, George H. 33, 40, 374
DeROUEN, Rene L. 190, 193, 197, 200, 203, 207, 210
DeROULET, Vincent 431
DEROUNIAN, Steven B. 233, 236, 240, 243, 246, 249
DERSHEM, Frank L. 169
DERTHICK, Lawrence G. 444
DeRUSSY, Rene E. 483
DERVALL, William 457
DERWENT, Clarence 557
DERWINSKI, Edward J. 242, 245, 248, 251, 255, 258, 261, 264
DESANTIS, Ann 588
DeSAUSSURE
Henry W. 451
William F. 96, 452
DESCH, Carl W. 491
DeSCHWEINITZ, Edmund A. 476
DESFOR, Max 585
DESHA, Joseph 60, 61, 62, 63, 65, 66, 308
Robert 75, 76
DESHLER, Charles 600
DESMOND
Charles S. 346
Daniel F. 525
DES PORTES, Fay A. 424, 426, 429
DETHIER, Vincent G. 573
DETWEILER, Meade D. 574
DEUPREE, Richard R. 551*
DEUSSEN, Alexander 564, 608
DEUSTER, Peter V. 124, 126, 129
DEUTERMANN, Harold T. 417
DEUTSCH, Karl W. 571
DEVAN, R.P. 451
DEVANEY, John P. 325
DeVAUZ, William 558
DEVENS, Charles 28, 29, 41, 408
DEVER
Paul A. 321
William E. 451
DEVEREUX
Harry H. 461
James P.S. 229, 233, 236, 239
DEVERS, Jacob L. 404, 411*
DEVIN
William A. 349
William F. 461
DEVINE
J.M. 461*
John M. 415*
Joseph M. , 350
Samuel L. 243, 246, 249, 253, 256, 259, 262, 265
DEVINY, John J. 443
DEVITT or DE VITT
Edward I. 466
Edward J. 223
John H. 578
DEVLIN, William 466
DeVOE, W.R. 600
DeVORSS, Claude M. 577
DeVOTO, Bernard 585, 591, 602
DeWALD, Ernest T. 501
DEWALT, Arthur G. 172, 175, 178
DEWART
Lewis 78
William L. 101
D'EWART, Wesley A. 220, 224, 227, 230, 233
DeVRIES, Marion 144, 147, 272
DEW, Thomas R. 486
DEWEESE, John T. 111, 113
DEWEY
Bradley 565
Charles 549
Charles S. 213, 216
Daniel 64
Davis R. 566
John 564, 571, 593
Julius Y. 549
Martin 566
Melvil 568
Nelson 385
Richard 571
Thomas E. 18*, 346, 609
DEWING, Thomas W. 593, 607
DeWITT
Alexander 97, 99
Charles 6
Charles G. 76, 425
David M. 117
Francis B. 143
J. Doyle 553
Jacob H. 68
John L. 403, 405, 411, 419
Norman W. 570
Robert L. 516, 521
W.H. 392
DeWOLF, James 70, 72, 73, 361
DeWOLFE
Florence (Kling) 20
James P. 513, 520
DEXTER
Andrew 457
Gregory 9
Samuel 23*, 39, 40, 52, 55, 319
Walter F. 576
DEY, J. Ramsey 454
DeYOUNG, Russell 547*
DEZENDORF, John F. 126
D'HARNONCOURT, Rene 500
DIAL
Morse G. 553*
Nathaniel B. 178, 182, 185, 366
DIAMOND
Bernard 608
Louis K. 599*, 609
DIBBLE, Samuel 126, 129, 131, 133, 136
DIBRELL, George G. 120, 122, 124, 126, 129
DICE, Lee R. 575
DiCESNOLA, Louis Palma 499
DICHMAN, Ernst 426
DICK
Charles W. 146, 149, 151, 154*, 157, 160, 163, 353
John 97, 99, 101
Paul S. 554
Samuel 6
Samuel B. 124
William W., Jr. 401, 404
DICKE, Robert H. 604, 610
DICKENS
J.L. 483
Samuel 65
DICKERMAN, Charles H. 154
DICKERSON
Denver S. 335
Mahlon 25*, 42, 67, 68, 70, 71, 72, 74, 76, 77, 340*
Philemon 79, 81, 84, 340
William W. 134, 137
DICKERY, Charles D., Jr. 552*
DICKEY
Charles A. 532
Donald E. 592
Frank G. 473

Henry L. 121, 124
James 602
James E. 470, 530
Jesse C. 93
John 88, 92
John S. 469
Oliver J. 111, 113, 115
DICKIE, Samuel 465
DICKINSON
Andrew B. 434*
Baxter 532
Charles M. 424
Clement C. 162, 165, 168, 171, 174, 177, 184, 187, 191, 197, 201
Daniel S. 88, 90, 91, 93, 344
David W. 80, 88
Don M. 29*, 43
Dwight 438
Edward 97
Edward F. 113
Edwin 592
Edwin D. 573
H.C. 451
J.C. 499
Jacob M. 31, 40, 564, 576
James S. 393
John 2, 3, 4*, 5, 7, 8, 9
John D. 68, 70, 74, 76
Jonathan (Educator) 479
Jonathan (Mayor) 458*
Lauren D. 323
Lester J. 176, 180, 183, 187, 190, 193, 196, 200, 203, 305
Philemon 5, 51, 52, 340, 406
Rodolphus 92, 93
Sidney E. 589
William L. 251, 254, 257, 260, 263
DICKMAN
Franklin 353
Joseph T. 405. 410*
DICKMANN, Bernard F. 460
DICKSON
David 81
Frank S. 156
Janet S. 595
John 531
John (N.Y.) 77, 79
Joseph 56
Leonard E. 568
Samuel 99
Thomas H. 454
William 57, 58, 59
William A. 162, 165
DICKSTEIN, Samuel 184, 188, 191, 194, 198, 201, 204, 207, 211, 214, 217, 221
DICUS, Richard E. 515
DIEFENDORF, Charles H. 549*
DIEHL
Conrad 451
Michael 486
Samuel W.B. 416
William J. 459
DIEKEMA, Gerrit J. 159, 162, 433
DIELMAN, Frederick 577
DIERCKES, Albert A. 487
DIES
Martin 163, 166, 169, 172, 175
Martin, Jr. 198, 202, 205, 208, 212, 215, 218, 234, 237, 240
DIETERICH, William H. 196, 200, 203, 206, 301
DIETRICH
C. Elmer 205
Charles H. 151, 154, 333
Frank S. 272
DIETRIEK, William H. 591
DIETZ
David 584
William 73
DIFENDERFER, Robert E. 166, 169
DIGGES, Edward 9
DIGGS, Charles C., Jr. 236, 239, 242, 245, 249, 252, 255, 258, 261, 264
DILG, Will H. 576
DILL
Clarence C. 172, 175, 186, 189, 192, 195, 199, 202, 381
David B. 571
Franklin G. 483
DILLARD
Hardy C. 573
Irving 601
James H. 609
DILLIN, Harry L. 534
DILLING, George W. 461
DILLINGHAM
Paul, Jr. 88, 90, 376
William R. 149, 152, 155, 158, 160, 163, 166, 169, 172, 175, 179, 182, 376*
DILLON
C. Douglas 35, 39, 428
Charles H. 169, 172, 175
Francis J. 557, 559
George 584
John F. 564
Joseph E. 460
Patrick 478
Richard C. 343
Sidney 554*
DILWEG, LaVern R. 219
DILWORTH
Richard M. 610
Richardson 458
DIMAN, Byron 361
DIMITRY, Alexander 426, 434
DIMM, Jonathan R. 482
DIMMERLING, Harold J. 528
DIMMICK
Milo M. 93, 95
William H. 101, 103
DIMMOCK, Mary Scott (Lord) 20
DIMOCK, Davis, Jr. 86
DIMOND, Francis M. 361
DINAND, Joseph N. 472*
DINEEN, Robert E. 550*
DINGELL
John D. 200, 204, 207, 210, 213, 217, 220, 223, 226, 230, 233, 236, 261, 264
John D., Jr. 236, 239, 242, 245, 249, 252, 255, 258
DINGLE, John H. 600
DINGLEY, Nelson, Jr. 125, 127, 130, 132, 135, 137, 140, 142, 145, 314
DINGMAN
Harrison 579
Maurice J. 526
DINITZ, Simon 598
DINSMOOR
Samuel (b. 1766) 62, 337
Samuel (b. 1799) 337
William B. 574, 591
DINSMORE
Hugh A. 139, 142, 144, 147, 150, 152, 431
Ray P. 567
DINWIDDIE
Albert B. 483
Hardaway H. 482
Robert 9
DIRKSEN, Everett M. 200, 203, 206, 210, 213, 216, 219, 223, 229, 232, 235, 238, 242, 245, 248, 251, 254, 258, 301
DiSALLE, Michael V. 354
DISNEY
David T. 93, 95, 97
Walt 591, 608
Wesley E. 198, 201, 205, 208, 211, 214, 218
DISOSWAY, Gabriel P. 415, 416
DISQUE, Robert C. 470
DISTLER, Theodore A. 470
DITCHY, Clair W. 567
DITTER, J. William 201, 205, 208, 211, 215, 218
DITTMAR, George W. 566
DiVALENTIN, Louis 593
DIVEN
Alexander S. 105
Jeannette Murdock 497
DIVERS, William K. 443
DIX
John A. 27*, 39, 88, 90, 91, 344, 345, 428, 554
John Alden 345
William S. 568, 595
DIXON
Archibald 95, 96, 308
Frank M. 278
Frederick 536
Henry A. 237, 240, 244
James 89, 90, 100, 102, 104, 106, 107, 109, 287
James P., Jr. 465
Joseph 113
Joseph A. 208
Joseph M. 154, 156, 159, 162, 165, 331*
Lincoln 156, 158, 161, 164, 167, 170, 173
Luther S. 385
Nathan F. (b. 1774) 85, 86, 361
Nathan F. (b. 1812) 94, 107, 109, 111, 113
Nathan F. (b. 1847) 128, 136, 138, 141, 362
Robert E. 417
Samuel G. 563
Thomas 456
Thomas F. 597
William W. 138
DOAK
Stephenson 483
William N. 33, 46
DOAN
Charles A. 590
Herbert D. 546
Leland I. 546*
Robert E. 138
William 84, 86
DOANE
George W. 505, 520
John W. 546
William C. 506, 519
DOBBIN
C.E. 564
James C. 27*, 42, 90
DOBBINS
Donald C. 200, 203
J.S. 458
Samuel A. 117, 119
DOBBS
Arthur 9
Hoyt M. 530
Samuel C. 545
DOBIE
Armistead M. 271
J. Frank 608
DOBSON
Philip E. 467
Raymond C. 574
DOBZHANSKY, Theodosius 573, 604
DOCK, George 590
DOCKERY
Alexander M. 128, 130, 133, 135, 138, 140, 143, 145, 329
Alfred 90
Oliver H. 111, 113
DOCKING
George 307
Robert B. 307
DOCKSTADER
Frederick J. 500
Ralph W. 554
DOCKWEILER, John F. 199, 202, 206
DODD
Alvin E. 568
Edward 99, 101
Edwin D. 550
Francis J. 477
James B. 482
M.E. 534
Paul 481
Thomas J. 232, 235, 241, 244, 248, 251, 254, 257
Walter F. 571
William E. 428, 567
William H. 459
DODDRIDGE, Philip 77, 78
DODDS
Francis H. 162, 165
Harold W. 479, 579
Ozro J. 115
DODGE
Augustus C. 91, 93, 95, 96, 304, 437
Bayard 612
Charles G. 405
Cleveland H. 551, 603
Ebenezer 468
Ernest S. 501
Frederic 271
George E. 552
Grenville M. 110, 409
H. Percival 427, 430, 433, 434, 436*
Henry 92, 94, 96, 98, 99, 385
Homer L. 478
James M. 573, 594
Joseph M. 444, 564
R.L. 455
Ralph E. 531
Raymond 571
S.A. 577
Wallace H. 600
William E. 108
DODSON, Elmer H. 451
DOE
Charles 338
Jens A. 413
Nicholas B. 84
DOERFER, John C. 443
DOERFLINGER, Carl 500
DOERING, Otto C. 576
DOERMANN, Henry J. 482
DOGGETT, David S. 530
DOHAN, Edward G. 484
DOHERTY
Ann 499
Daniel J. 568
Grace 491
Henry L. 543, 545, 601
Robert E. 467, 599
William C. 431
DOIG, Andrew W. 84, 86
DOISY, Edward A. 596, 605
DOLAN
Francis J. 472
James H. 466
Margaret B. 578
Thomas 578
William D. 572
DOLBEY, Dorothy N. 452
DOLE
Albert M. 449
Robert J. 245, 248, 252, 255, 258, 261, 264, 307
DOLEMAN, Edgar C. 400
DOLGIN, George 423
D'OLIER, Franklin 551, 568
DOLL
Harry L. 515, 520
Henri G. 601
DOLLARD, Charles 491
DOLLEY, James C. 482
DOLLINGER, Isidore 227, 230, 233, 236, 240, 243
DOLLIVER
James I. 220, 223, 226, 229, 232, 235
Jonathan P. 134, 137, 140, 142, 145, 147, 148, 150, 153, 156, 159, 161, 304
DOLPH, Joseph N. 128, 131, 133, 136, 138, 141, 356
DOMENEC, Michael 528
DOMENGEAUX, James 213, 217, 220, 223
DOMENICI, Peter V. 265, 343
DOMINICK
Fred H. 175, 178, 182, 185, 188, 192, 195, 198
Peter H. 244, 248, 251, 254, 257, 260, 264, 286
DONAGHEY, George W. 281
DONAGHY, William A. 472
DONAHEY, A. Victor 204, 208, 211, 353, 354
DONAHUE
Donald J. 491, 543
Kenneth 499, 501
Maurice H. 271
Patrick J. 529
DONALD, David 586
DONALDSON
Henry H. 569
Jesse M. 34, 35, 43
Lee A. 574
DONDERO, George A. 200, 204, 207, 210, 213, 217, 220, 223, 226, 230, 233, 236
DONEGAN, Horace W.B. 514, 520
DONELSON, Andrew J. 16, 435, 438
DONEY, Carl G. 486
DONGAN, Thomas 8
DONGES, Ralph W.E. 577
DONHANSER, Robert 428
DONLEY
Charles S. 576
Joseph B. 113
Willis E. 577
DONLON
Alphonsus J. 471
Mary H. 273
DONNAN, William G. 114, 116
DONNELL
Forrest C. 220, 223, 227, 330*
James C. 549
James C., 2d 549
Lloyd H. 591
Otto D. 549, 590
Richard S. 91
DONNELLAN, Thomas A. 523, 527
DONNELLON, James A. 484
DONNELLY
Charles 550
Frederick W. 462
George J. 526
Ignatius 106, 108, 110
Michael 557
Mike 458

Phil M. 330*
Richard A. 462
Samuel B. 443, 558
Thomas J. 473
Walter J. 423, 426, 428, 439
DONNER, Frederic G. 547
DONOHOE
Michael 166, 169
Patrick A. 481
DONOHUE
F. Joseph 462
Harold D. 223, 226, 229, 233, 236, 239, 242, 245, 249, 252, 255, 258, 261, 264
Hugh A. 526, 529
Patrick 599
DONOVAN
Dennis D. 138, 141
Eileen R. 423
Herman L. 473
James B. 479
James G. 230, 233, 236
Jeremiah 167
Jerome F. 174, 178
John A. 529
Les 411
Richard 611
William 455
William J. 438
DONSON, Jerome 499
DOOB, Joseph L. 568
D'OOGE, Martin L. 570
DOOLEY
Edwin B. 240, 243, 246
Patrick J. 480
William F. 469
DOOLING, Peter J. 168, 171, 174, 178
DOOLITTLE
Dudley 167, 170, 173
Hilda 589, 592
James H. 412*, 597, 611, 612
James R. 101, 103, 105, 107, 109, 111, 385
John 455
Thomas B. 600
William H. 144, 144
DOONAN, James A. 471
DOORLEY, Joseph A., Jr. 459
DOORLY, John W. 536
DORAN
Frank B. 460
William T. 469
DORE, John F. 461*
DOREMUS, Frank E. 165, 168, 171, 174, 177, 453
DOREY, Halstead 404
DORFMAN
Albert 592, 599
Ben 445
DORHSTADER, Nicholas 452
DORMAN, Gerald D. 569
DORN
Francis E. 233, 236, 240, 243
W.J. Bryan 225, 231, 234, 237, 240, 243, 247, 250, 253, 256, 259, 263, 266
Walter E. 577
DORNBROOK, Fred L. 590
DORR
Balton 501
Charles P. 147
Goldthwaite H., 3d 501, 502
John V. 595
Robert E. 455
DORRANCE
Arthur 544*
Arthur C. 544
G. Morris Jr. 551*
George M. 544
John T. 544
John T., Jr. 544
DORRIS, A.P. 455
DORSEY
Anna H. 599
B.R. 548*
Clement 72, 74, 76
Frank J.G. 205, 208
George W.E. 130, 133, 135
Hugh M. 296
John L. 193
Stephen W. 115, 118, 120, 281
Thomas B. 316
DORSHEIMER, William 128
DORTCH, William T. 392, 393
DORVILLIER, William J. 586
DOSH, Thomas W. 480
DOS PASSOS, John 603
DOSTER, Frank 306
DOTY
James D. 94, 96
James E. 466
Paul 573
DOUBLEDAY
Abner 407*, 408*
Edgar A. 491
Ulysses F. 77, 81
DOUD, Mamie Geneva 20
DOUCET, Edward 470
DOUGALL, John B. 477
DOUGHERTY
Charles 129, 132
Charles J. 553
Daniel 599
Dennis J. 523, 524, 525
John 148, 151, 154
Joseph P. 529
Paul 589, 607
Proctor L. 462
Richard E. 572
DOUGHTON
I.M. 460
Robert L. 165, 168, 171, 175, 178, 181, 185, 188, 191, 194, 198, 201, 204, 208, 211, 214, 218, 221, 224, 227, 230
DOUGHTY
Alfred H. 455
John 400
DOUGLAS
Albert 160, 163
Beverly B. 120, 122
Davison M. 481
Donald W. 594, 596, 597, 610, 612
Emily T. 219
Fred J. 207, 211, 214, 217
Frederick 498
Helen Gahagan 219, 222, 225
James 551*, 596
James H., Jr. 399*, 608
John M. 548
Lewis W. 189, 192, 196, 429, 444, 549, 575, 603, 609
Paul H. 226, 229, 232, 235, 238, 242, 245, 248, 251, 301, 566, 597, 598
Stephen A. 16, 87, 89, 91, 92, 94, 96, 98, 100, 102, 104, 300
Thomas 293
Walter 551
William H. 154
William L. 320
William O. 270, 445, 591, 597
William W. 362
DOUGLASS
A.H. 456
Andrew E. 465
David B. 473
Frank P. 444
Howard 576
John J. 187, 190, 194, 197, 200, 612
John W. 444, 462
Malcolm 478
Paul F. 465
Robert W., Jr. 411, 412
William 497
DOUGTON, Robert L. 165
DOUTRICH, Isaac H. 192, 195, 198, 201, 205
DOUW
John 449
Volckert P. 449
DOVENER, Blackburn B. 144, 147, 149, 152, 155, 158
DOW
Alex 546, 573, 595
Frank 443
Herbert 546
James R. 549
John G. 252, 256, 262
Lorenzo 462
Sterling 574
Willard H. 546, 590
DOWD
Bernard J. 451
Clement 126, 128
John W. 482
DOWDELL
James F. 96, 98, 100, 465
James R. 278
DOWDNEY, Abraham 131
DOWDY, John V. 234, 237, 240, 244, 247, 250, 253, 256, 260, 263
DOWELL
Cassius C. 170, 173, 176, 180, 183, 187, 190, 193, 197, 200, 206, 210
Spright 466, 475*
DOWIE, John A. 538
DOWLING
Austin 524, 526
Michael P. 469*
Walter C. 428, 437
DOWMAN, Charles E. 470
DOWNEY
George E. 273
John G. 283
Sheridan 209, 212, 216, 219, 222, 225, 284
DOWNING
Finis E. 142
Robert W. 544
Thomas N. 244, 247, 250, 253, 257, 260, 263, 266
DOWNS
Charles R. 607
Lawrence A. 548*
LeRoy D. 213
Joseph 498
Robert B. 568, 600
Solomon W. 91, 93, 95, 311
DOWSE, Edward 68
DOX, Peter M. 111, 113
DOXEY
Charles T. 125
Wall 194, 197, 200, 204, 207, 210, 214, 328
DOYLE
Clyde G. 219, 225, 229, 232, 235, 238, 241, 244, 248
Edward J. 545
Thomas A. (Ill.) 183, 187, 190, 193
Thomas A. (R.I.) 459*
William C. 568
William E. 272
DOYTON, M.R. 456
DRACHMAN, Bernard 537
DRAGSTEDT, Lester R. 590
DRAHAM, George W. 458
DRAIN, James A. 568
DRAKE
Charles D. 110, 112, 273, 329
Francis M. 536
Francis M. (Gov.) 304
Harcourt C. 607
J. Frank 548, 590
Lauren J. 552
John R. 67
Marcus M. 451
Miles E. 465
W.S., Jr. 450
DRAKER, William F. 431
DRANE, Herbert J. 173, 176, 180, 183, 186, 189, 193, 196
DRAPER
Andrew S. 472
C.W. 600
Charles S. 597*, 598, 604*, 608
Eben S. 320
James 578
John W. 565, 609
Joseph 77, 78
William F. 140, 143
William H. 151, 154, 157, 159, 162, 165
William H., Jr. 610
DRAUGHON, Ralph B. 466
DRAYTON
John 364*, 451
Percival 418
William (b. 1776) 73, 75, 76, 78
William H. (b. 1742) 4, 7, 10, 364
DREHER
J. Clarence, Jr. 452
Julius D. 480
DREISER, Theodore 589
DRENNAN, Michael A. 477
DRESLER, Earl L. 554
DRESSER, Solomon R. 154, 157
DRETZKA, Sylvester H. 570
DREW
Charles J. 462
Charles R. 611
George F. 293
Gerald A. 424, 429, 431
Gilman A. 573
Ira W. 208
Irving W. 174, 338
James B. 360
John G. 549
Thomas S. 281
DREWRY
Patrick H. 179, 182, 186, 189, 192, 195, 199, 202, 205, 209, 212, 215, 218, 222, 225
William F. 571
DREYER, W.A. 575
DREYFUS
Camille 544
Lee S. 486
Louis G., Jr. 423*, 430*, 437
DRICK, John E. 547
DRIGGS
Edmund H. 146, 148
John D. 459
John F. 106, 108, 110
DRINAN, Robert F. 261, 264
DRINKER
Henry S. (b. 1850) 474
Henry S. (b. 1880) 589
DRISCOLL
Alfred E. 342, 579
D.J. 205
Daniel A. 162, 165, 168, 171
Francis A. 484
Justin A. 526
Michael E. 148, 151, 154, 157, 159, 162, 165
DRIVER
Samuel M. 381
William J. 179, 183, 186, 189, 193, 196, 199, 202, 206
DROMGOOLE, George C. 82, 83, 85, 88, 90, 92
DROPPERS, Garrett 429, 433, 481
DROSSAERTS, Jerome 524, 528
DROWN, Thomas M. 474
DRUCKMAN, Jacob 588
DRUKKER, Dow H. 168, 171, 174
DRUM
Augustus 97
Hugh A. 400, 402, 404, 405, 411, 419, 599
John S. 564
R.C. 401
DRUMM, Thomas W. 526
DRUMMOND, William 8
DRUMRIGHT, Everett F. 425
DRURY
Allen 586
Newton B. 444
Thomas J. 525, 528
DRUSHAL, J. Garber 486
DRYBURGH, John 454
DRYDEN
Hugh L. 594*, 596, 597*, 604, 608, 612
Forrest F. 551
John F. 151, 154, 157, 341, 551
DRYER, Thomas J. 430
DRYSDALE, Hugh 9
DRYTS, John B. 480
DUANE
J.C. 402
James 4, 6, 458
William J. (b. 1780) 25, 39
William J. (b. 1868) 470
DUBERMAN, Martin B. 591
DUBINSKY, David 558, 608
DUBLIN, Louis I. 572, 610
DUBOIS (or DuBOIS)
Charles A. 449
Charles G. 554
Cora 563
Edward C. 362
Fred T. 137, 139, 142, 150, 153, 155, 298*
Gaston 549
Guy Pene 589*, 593
James T. 426
John 527
William E.B. 611
DUBOS, Rene J. 587, 591, 599, 600, 607
DuBOSE
Dudley M. 114
Horace M. 530
Laurence T. 417
William G. 418
DuBOURG, Louis G. 471
DuBRIDGE, Lee A. 467, 570
DUBS, Rudolph 531
DUBUIS, Claude M. 526
DUBUISSON, Stephen J. 471
DUCH, Andrew J. 462
DUCHE, Jacob 458
DUCKWORTH
George E. 570
W.F. 458
William H. 297
DUDDY, Frank E., Jr. 474
DUDGEON, Farnham F. 453

DUDLEY
Charles B. 565
Charles E. 74, 76, 77, 344, 449*
Edward B. 76, 347
Edward R. 432*
Guilford, Jr. 427
Irving B. 424, 435
Joseph 8*, 10
Paul 10
Plimmon H. 594
R.H. 457
Thomas 8*
Thomas U. 507, 520
DUELL
Charles H. 444*
R. Holland 103, 105, 115, 117
DUER
William (b. 1747) 4, 6
William (b. 1805) 91, 93
William A. 468
DUFF
Charles B. 404
Hezekiah N. 580
James H. 231, 234, 237, 360*
John 554
DUFFIELD
Edward D. 551
George 532
DUFFEY, Warren J. 201, 204
DUFFY
Edmund 583, 584*
F. Ryan 202, 205, 209, 272, 386
James A. 526, 529
James M. 558
James P.B. 204
John A. 525
DUFRESNE, Armand A., Jr. 315
DUFROCQ, John R. 450
DUGAN, Alan 587, 602
DUGGAN, James 525
DUGGAR, Benjamin M. 574
DUGRO, P. Henry 126
DUKAS, Julius J. 537
DUKE
Angier Biddle 427*, 437
James B. 543, 546
Richard T.W. 113, 115
DULANY
Daniel 449
Walter 449
DULBECCO, Renato 600
DULEY, W.R. 455
DULIN, E.S. 482
DULL, Paul S. 501
DULLEA, Charles 481
DULLES
Allen 443
John Foster 35*, 38, 227, 346, 603, 608, 609
DULSKI, Thaddeus J. 243, 246, 249, 252, 256, 259, 262, 265
DUMAS, Woodrow 450
DUMBACH, Henry 474
DUMEZ, Andrew G. 570, 609
DUMMER, William 8*
DUMONT
Donald A. 424
Ebenezer 106, 108
DuMOULIN, Frank 510
DUN
Angus 514, 522
Edwin 431
DUNBAR
Charles F. 566
Clarence M. 579
Carl O. 501, 597
James W. 176, 180, 193
Ralph O. 381*
Walter 566
William 96
DUNCAN
Alexander 83, 84, 88
Asa N. 412
Charles K. 417*
Charles S. 589
Daniel 92
David S. 469
Donald B. 418
James A. 479
James H. 93, 95
James L. 516
James M. 558
John J. 253, 256, 260, 263, 266
Joseph 74, 75, 77, 78, 300
Luther N. 466*
Richard M. 201, 204, 207, 210, 214
Robert B. 250, 253
Mrs. Robert V.H. 579
W. Garnett 91
William A. 128
William C. 453
William W. 530
DUNGAN
D.R. 536
James I. 138
Ralph A. 425
DUNGLISON, Robley 484*
DUNHAM
Cyrus L. 93, 94, 96
John H. 546
Ransom W. 127, 129, 132
Sylvester C. 553
DUNIWAY
Ben C. 272, 492*
Clyde A. 476, 487
DUNKIN, Benjamin F. 365
DUNKLIN, Daniel 329
DUNLAP
George W. 104
James 485
John B. 444
John F. 465
Knight 571
Morey M. 577
Robert P. 87, 89, 314
William C. 80, 81
DUNLOP
George K. 507, 519, 520
John T. 459
R.G. 553*
DUNN
Aubert C. 204
Charles J. 315
David E. 457
Gano S. 595, 598
George G. 91, 98
George H. 82
Hugh E. 473
James, Jr. 576
James C. 424, 428, 437
Jesse J. 355
John H. 580
John R. 536
John T. 140
Matthew A. 201, 205, 208, 211
Poindexter 122, 124, 127, 129, 131
R. Loring 497
Ronald J. 574
Thomas B. 168, 171, 174, 178, 181
Thomas W. 405*, 419*
William C. 431
William M. 402
William McK. 102, 104
Winfield 371
DUNNE
Edmund M. 527
Edward F. 301, 451
Edward J. 525
Irene 599
James E. 459
William 481
DUNNELL, Mark H. 114, 116, 119, 121, 123, 125, 135
DUNNING
H.A.B. 609
Harrison F. 552*
Paris C. 302
William A. 567, 571
DUNPHY
Edward J. 135, 138, 141
J. Englebert 565
DUNSCOMB, Andrew 459
DUNSMORE, John W. 574
DUNSTER, Henry 472
DUNTEN, L.H. 576
DUNTLEY, S.Q. 580
DUNWELL, Charles T. 154, 157, 159
DuPEN, Everett G. 610
DUNPHY, J. Englebert 565
DuPONCEAU, Peter S. 570
DuPONT
Mrs. Alfred I. 492
Alfred Victor 546
Charles H. 293
Eleuthere Irenee 546
Eugene 546
Henry 546
Henry A. 155, 158, 161, 164, 167, 170, 291
Irenee 546
Lammot 546, 547
Pierre S. 546, 547*
Pierre S., 4th 261, 264
Richard C. 611
Samuel F. 417
T. Coleman 179, 186, 189, 291, 292, 546
DUPORTAIL, L.L. 402
DUPRE
H. Garland 162, 165, 167, 170, 174, 177, 180, 184
Jacques 311
Lucien J. 392, 393
DURAND
Asher B. 577
George H. 119
William F. 573, 590, 596*, 597, 612
DURANT
Ariel 587
Henry 467
Lionel 607
W.C. 547
Will 587
DURANTY, Walter 584
DURBIN
John P. 469
Winfield T. 302
DURBOROW, Allan C., Jr. 137, 139
DURBROW, Elbridge 439
DURELL
Daniel M. 60
E.H. 457
DUREY, Cyrus 159, 162
DURFEE
James R. 273
Job 70, 72, 361
Nathaniel B. 99, 101
Thomas 362
Walter H. 472
DURGAM, John S. 427
DURGAN, George R. 200
DURGIN, Samuel H. 572
DURHAM
Carl T. 211, 214, 218, 221, 224, 227, 230, 234, 237, 240, 243
G. Homer 465
George J. 450
John S. 429
Milton J. 116, 118, 121
Robert L. 567
DURICK, Joseph A. 527
DURIER, Anthony 525
DURKEE
Charles 94, 96, 99, 101, 103, 385
J. Stanley 472
DURKIN, Martin P. 35, 46, 559
DURNO, Edwin R. 246
DURRER, Robert 595
DUTILH, Charles 547
DUTTON, Henry 287
DUVAL
George L. 599
Isaac H. 113
William 459
William P. 63
DUVALL
Gabriel 51, 53, 269
John L. 454
Lewis 449
William P. 410
DuVIGNEAUD, Vincent 596, 600, 604, 606, 607
DWENGER, Joseph 526
DWIGHT
Arthur S. 595
Edward H. 499*, 500
Henry C. 454
Henry W. 69, 71, 72, 74, 76
Jeremiah W. 121, 123, 126
John W. 151, 154, 157, 159, 162, 165
Jonathan 569
Sereno E. 471
Theodore 58
Thomas 58
Timothy 487*
DWINELL
Justin 71
Lane 339
DWORSCHAK
Leo F. 526
Henry C. 209, 213, 216, 219, 223, 226, 229, 232, 235, 238, 241, 245, 299*
DWYER
Edward 460
Florence P. 239, 243, 246, 249, 252, 255, 259, 262
Robert E. 543
Robert J. 524, 528
DYE
Albert A. 456
Edward R. 611
DYER
Alexander B. 402
C.J. 459
David P. 112
David W. 271
Eliphalet 3, 5, 287
Elisha (b. 1811) 362
Elisha (b. 1839) 362, 459
Heman 479
J.P. 460
Leonidas C. 165, 168, 171, 174, 177, 181, 184, 187, 191, 194, 197
Rolla E. 610
Ross W. 371
Thomas 451
William H. 457
DYHRENFURTH, Norman G. 593, 599
DYKE
C.E. 462
William D. 456
DYKEMAN, Conrad V. 579
DYKES, Archie R. 482
DYKINGA, Jack 588
DYKSTRA
Clarence A. 445, 486, 571, 579
John 547
DYRE, William 457
DZIALYNSKI, Morris A. 454

E

EADS, James Buchanan 597
EAGAN, John J. 168, 171, 174, 177, 184
EAGER, Samuel W. 76
EAGLE
Harry 595
James P. 281, 534
Joe H. 169, 172, 175, 179, 198, 202, 205
EAGLES, William W. 414
EAGLESON
Ern G. 450*
William B., Jr. 547
EAGLETON
Thomas F. 258, 262, 265, 330
William L., Jr. 437
EAKER, Ira C. 412
EAKINS, Thomas 607
EAMES
Arthur J. 574
Benjamin T. 115, 117, 119
Charles 430, 439*
William S. 567
EARHART, Daniel S. 204
EARL
Mary-Ellen 497
Robert 345*
EARLE
Elias 59, 63, 64, 67, 69
F.S. 452
George H. 360, 423, 424
John B. 58
Joseph H. 146, 365
Pliny 571
Ralph 418, 487
S.B. 468
Samuel 54
EARLL
Jonas, Jr. 74, 76
Nehemiah H. 84
EARLY
John 471, 472, 530
Jubal A. 394, 395*
Peter 56, 57, 59, 295
Stephen T. 399
William A. 578
EARNEST
George B. 572
Herbert L. 414
EARTHMAN, Harold H. 221
EASBY, J.W. 418
EASLEY
Charles F. 461
Charles W. 604
EASTBURN, Manton 505, 520
EASTCHURCH, Thomas 8
EASTERBROOK, Edmund P. 401
EASTERWOOD, H.G. 462
EASTHAM, Melville 598
EASTLAND, James O. 214, 217, 220, 223, 227, 230, 233, 236, 239, 242, 245, 249, 252, 255, 258, 261, 265, 327, 328
EASTMAN
Ben C. 96, 98
George 546*, 590
Ira A. 84, 86
Linda A. 568
Nehemiah 73
EASTON
David 571
John 9
John S. 533
Nicholas 9*
Stanley A. 610
EASTWOOD, George A. 543*

EASUM, Donald B. 439
EATON
Benjamin H. 285
Charles A. 188, 191, 194, 197, 201, 204, 207, 211, 214, 217, 220, 224, 227, 230
Dorman B. 445
Edward D. 466
Francis 3
Fred 456
George W. 468
Horace 375
John 444, 474
John H. 25, 40, 67, 69, 70, 73, 76, 369, 437
Lewis 71
Marquis G. 567
Thomas M. 209
William J. 587
William R. 193, 196
William W. 116, 118, 120, 122, 127, 288
EAVENSON, Howard N. 610
EBAUGH, Franklin, Sr. 590
EBBOTT, Percy J. 545
EBERHARD, Harmon S. 544*
EBERHARDT
Charles C. 426, 434
Henry F. 600
EBERHART
Adolph O. 324
Richard 589, 592, 610
EBERHARTER, Herman P. 208, 211, 215, 218, 221, 224, 228, 231, 234, 237, 240
EBERLE
Edward R. 551*
Edward W. 416, 483
Eugene G. 609
EBERLEIN, Walter R. 599
EBERSOLE, William S. 468
EBERT, James D. 573
EBLE
Charles E. 545*
Francis X.A. 443
EBY, Maurice C. 453
ECCLES, Marriner S. 443
ECCLESTON, Samuel 523, 528
ECHOLS
Joseph H. 393
Leonard S. 179, 182
ECKER
Frederic W. 549*
Frederick H. 549*
ECKERT
Charles R. 205, 208
George N. 92
J. Presper 604, 608
ECKFELDT, Robert W. 413
ECKHARDT, Robert C. 256, 260, 263, 266
ECKLEY
Ephraim R. 107, 109, 111
Robert S. 473
ECKLUND, Coy G. 546
ECKMAN, Arthur W. 536
ECTON, Zales N. 224, 227, 230, 331
EDDISON, William B. 601
EDDLEMAN, Clyde D. 400, 401, 404, 405, 419
EDDY
Ansel D. 532
E.J. Foster 536
Edward D., Jr. 476
Frank M. 143, 145, 148, 151
Harrison P. 572
Henry T. 468*
Manton S. 404, 405, 412, 413, 419
Mary Baker 538
Norman 96
Paul D. 465
Samuel 68, 70, 72, 361
Spencer F. 423
William A. 436, 472
EDEL
Leon 587, 602
William W. 469
EDELMAN, Gerald M. 606
EDELSTEIN, M. Michael 211, 214
EDEN
Charles 8
John R. 106, 116, 118, 120
Robert 8
EDENS, Arthur H. 470
EDER, Donald G. 578
EDES, Robert T. 569
EDEY, Mrs. Frederick 576
EDGAR
George M. 465
John T. 532
EDGE
Arthur B., Jr. 491
Walter E. 177, 181, 184, 188, 191, 194, 341*, 342, 428
EDGELL, George H. 500
EDGERLY, Martin V.B. 549
EDGERTON
Alfred P. 95, 97, 445
Alonso J. 125, 324
Glen E. 443
Harold E. 593, 607
Henry W. 272
John E. 578
Joseph K. 106
Sidney 103, 105
EDIE, John R. 99, 101
EDINGER, Lois V. 578
EDISON
Charles 33, 42, 342, 579
Thomas A. 596*, 597, 600, 609
EDLEFSEN
J.L. 450
Russel E. 450
EDMANDS, J. Wiley 97
EDMISTON, Andrew 202, 205, 209, 212, 215
EDMOND, William 54, 55
EDMONDS
George W. 169, 172, 175, 178, 182, 185, 201
James B. 462
EDMONDSON
Edmond 234, 237, 240, 243, 246, 250, 253, 256, 259, 262
J. Howard 249, 355*
John 457*
EDMONSTON, Gabriel 559
EDMUNDS
Charles K. 479
George F. 109, 111, 113, 115, 117, 120, 122, 124*, 126, 127, 129, 131, 133, 136, 139, 376
J. Ollie 482
James R., Jr. 567
O.W. 577
Paul C. 136, 139, 141
EDMUNDSON, Henry A. 94, 96, 98, 99, 101, 103
EDSALL
John T. 607
Joseph E. 90, 91
Samuel C. 506, 520, 521
EDSON
Franklin 458
George L. 457
Winfield 534
EDWARDS
Benjamin 52
C.H. 462
Caldwell 151
Charles G. 158, 161, 164, 167, 170, 186, 190, 193
Clarence R. 410*
David 531
David M. 470
Don 248, 251, 254, 257, 260, 263
Don C. 156, 159, 161
E.L. 455
Edward I. 184, 188, 191, 340, 341
Edwin W. 252, 255, 258, 261, 264, 313
Elijah E. 468
Francis S. 99
Frank E. 461
George 272
George H. 455
Gordon 548*
Henry W. 67, 69, 70, 72, 287*
Horace H. 459
Howard 479
Idwal H. 401*
Ira 500
J.D. 454*
Jack 251, 254, 257, 260, 263
Jesse E. 567
John (Ark.) 113
John (Ky.) 51, 52, 308
John (N.Y.) 83
John (Pa.) 85, 86
John (S.C.) 451
John C. 86, 329
Jonathan (b. 1703) 479, 597
Jonathan (b. 1745) 483
Jonathan (b. 1817) 485
Joseph R. 455
Lena F. 608
Leverett 444*
Levi T. 600
Ninian 66, 68, 69, 71, 300*, 308
Oliver 453
Pierrepont 5
Ray O. 579
Robert C. 468
Samuel 68, 70, 71, 73
Thomas 402
Thomas M. 103, 105
Thomas O. 92
Walter A. 467
Weldon N. 65, 67, 68, 70, 71, 73
William F. 484
William P. 110
EELLS, James 532
EFFERSON, H. Manning 470
EFNER, Valentine 81
EGAN
Joseph 474
Louis H. 553
Maurice F. 427, 578, 599
Michael F. 528
Patrick 425
William A. 279*
William J. 577
EGBERT
Albert G. 119
James C. 574
Joseph 86
EGE
George 54, 55
Hettie B. 475
EGGAN, Fred 563, 611
EGGERS
Alfred J., Jr. 608
George W. 497, 498, 502
Melvin A. 482
EGGLESTON
Benjamin 109, 111
Edward 567
John W. 380
Joseph 55, 56
Joseph D. 471, 484
Max W. 570
EGLIN, William C.L. 575
EGLOFF, Gustav 567, 590
EGTVEDT, C.L. 544
EHRINGHAUS, John C.B. 349
EICHELBERGER, Robert L. 405, 412, 414, 483
EICHER, Edward C. 200, 203, 206, 445
EICHHORN, Rudolph J. 467
EIELSON, Harry 461
EICKHOFF, Anthony C. 121
EILBERG, Joshua 256, 259, 262, 266
EILERS, Louis K. 546*
EILTS, Herman F. 436
EINSTEIN
Albert 591, 596, 605
Edwin 123
Lewis 426*
EIS, Frederick 527
EISELEY, Loren 593
EISEMAN, Gertrude W. 536
EISENBERG, Leonard M. 576
EISENDRATH, Maurice 537
EISENHART, Luther P. 568
EISENHOWER
Dwight D. 13, 18*, 400*, 404*, 411*, 468, 596, 598*, 609
John S.D. 424
Milton S. 473*, 479
EISENMAN, William H. 590
EKLUND, John M. 557
EKSTROM, Clarence E. 417
EKWALL, William A. 205, 273
ELA, Jacob H. 110, 112
ELAM
James E. 450*
Joseph B. 121, 123
ELBERT
Edgar M. 577
John A. 469
Samuel 8
Samuel H. 285
ELBRICK, C. Burke 424, 435, 439
ELDER
Albert L. 565
J. Walter 168
William H. 523, 527
William V., 3d 497
ELDRED
Byron E. 594
Horace B. 499
Lewis 470
ELDREDGE
Charles A. 107, 109, 111, 113, 115
Nathaniel B. 128, 130
ELDRIDGE
Edwin C. 499
T.B. 459
ELEBASH, Huntley A. 517
ELET, John A. 480, 487
ELFSTROM, Robert L. 460
ELIOT
Charles W. 472, 563, 589, 603, 609
Martha M. 572, 610
Samuel 482
Samuel A. 93, 450
Thomas D. 97, 102, 104, 106, 108, 110
Thomas H. 213, 485
William G. 484
ELISCU, Frank 579
ELKO, Nicholas 523
ELKIN, Daniel C. 565
ELKINS
Davis 163, 179, 182, 186, 383*
Lloyd E. 567, 601
Stephen B. 29*, 40, 144, 147, 149, 152, 155, 158, 160, 163, 383
Wilson H. 475
ELKUS, Abram I. 438
ELL, Carl S. 477
ELLENBOGEN, Henry 201, 205, 208
ELLENDER, Allen J. 210, 213, 217, 220, 223, 226, 229, 232, 236, 239, 242, 245, 248, 252, 255, 258, 260, 261, 312
ELLERBE
J. Edwin 157, 160, 163, 166
William H. 365
ELLERHUSEN, Ulric 591
ELLERT, Levi R. 461
ELLERY
Christopher 57, 58, 361
Edward 483
William 34, 710
ELLET, Henry T. 89
ELLETT
Tazewell 144
Thomas H. 591
ELLICOTT, Benjamin 67
ELLINGSON, Mark 480
ELLINGTON
Arthur G. 449
Buford 371*
Edward (Duke) 608, 611
ELLIOT
Frank W. 578
James 58, 59, 61
Robert B. 115, 117
ELLIOTT
A. Marshall 577
Alfred J. 206, 209, 212, 216, 219, 222
Byron K. 548
David 532
Carl 225, 228, 232, 235, 238, 241, 244, 247
Douglas H. 243
Edward C. 479
George F. 416
Howard 550*
James 502
James T. 109
John 68, 69, 71, 295
John B. 481
John E. 601
John M. 557
John M. (Ky.) 96, 98, 100, 392*, 393
Lloyd H. 471, 474
Maude Howe 583
Mortimer F. 128
Richard N. 173, 176, 180, 183, 187, 190, 193
Robert W.B. 507, 522
Stephen 505, 519
W.D. 409
Washington L. 410
William 133, 136, 138, 144, 146, 149, 152
William A. 534
William S. 601
ELLIS
Alston 468, 478
Arthur W. 455
Bruce T. 501
Caleb 59
Carleton 600
Chesselden 88
Clyde T. 209, 212
E. John 118, 121, 123, 125, 127
Edgar C. 156, 159, 181, 194
Elmer 476

Hayne 416
Henry 8
Howard S. 566
Hubert S. 219, 222, 225
I.C. 458
John M. 478
John W. 348
Overton G. 381
Powhatan 73, 74, 76, 77, 326*, 433*
Vespasian 439
William C. 71
William E. 417
William R. 141, 143, 146, 160
William T. 135, 137, 140
ELLISON
Andrew 97
Daniel 217
Ralph 602, 608
ELLISTON
Herbert 585
Joseph T. 457
ELLMAKER, Amos 16, 65
ELLMAN, Richard 602
ELLSBERRY, William W. 131
ELLSWORTH
Charles C. 121
Franklin F. 171, 174, 177
Harris 218, 221, 224, 227, 231, 234, 237, 445
Henry L. 444, 453
Henry W. 437
Lincoln 598, 599
Oliver 4, 5, 15, 51*, 52, 53, 269, 287, 428
Robert F. 245, 248, 252
Samuel S. 90
William W. 75, 77, 78, 287
ELLWOOD
Charles A. 573
Reuben 127, 130
ELLYSON, J. Taylor 459
ELLZEY, Lawrence R. 197, 200
ELMEN, Gustaf W. 594
ELMENDORF
Henry 461
Lucas C. 55, 56, 57
Theresa West 568
ELMER
Ebenezer 57, 58, 59
John 578
Jonathan 6, 51, 340
Lucius Q.C. 88
William P. 217
ELMORE
Benjamin T. 452
Franklin H. 81, 83, 94, 364
ELROD, Samuel H. 367
ELSAESSER, Edward J. 221, 224
ELSBERG, Charles A. 569
ELSE, Gerald F. 570
ELSEY, George M. 569
ELSTON
Charles H. 211, 214, 218, 221, 224, 227, 230
John A. 170, 173, 176, 179
R.M. 459
ELTHON, Leo 305
ELTINGE, Leroy 400
ELTON, James O. 595
ELTSE, Ralph R. 199
ELVEHJEM, Conrad A. 486, 596, 600
ELVINS, Politte 162
ELWELL
Clarence E. 525
Helen Chaffee 536
Herbert 611
ELY
Alfred 103, 105
Ezra S. 532
Frederick D. 130
Hanson E. 419*
John 84
Joseph B. 321
Richard T. 566
Smith 458
Smith, Jr. 115, 119
Walter 272
William 59, 60, 61, 62, 64
EMANUEL
David 295
Victor 544*
EMBICK, Stanley D. 400, 405
EMBREE, Elisha 91
EMENS, John R. 466
EMERICH, Martin 153
EMERSON
Alfred E. 575
Benjamin K. 575
Frank C. 387
Haven 572, 610
Henry I. 172, 175, 178
J.N. 576
John 557
Kendall 578
Lee E. 377
Louis W. 148, 151
Oliver F. 566, 577
Ralph 574
Ralph Waldo 597
EMERY
Alden H. 590
Ernest 476
John G. 568
Lucilius A. 315
Matthew G. 462
Richard R. 515, 521
Willard P. 536
EMHARDT, Christian J. 454
EMMERICH, Fred J. 590
EMMERSON, Louis L. 301
EMMET
Grenville T. 423, 433
Lydia F. 593
Thomas A. 599
EMMETT
Lafayette 324
William L. 590, 594, 595, 611
EMMONS
Delos C. 404, 411, 419
S.F. 575
EMORY
John 530
Robert 469
EMOTT, James 61, 62
EMPIE, Adam 486
EMRICH, Richard S.M. 514, 520
EMRIE, Jonas R. 99
ENARSON, Harold L. 478
ENDACOTT, Paul 551
ENDERS
George W. 482
John F. 600, 606, 607, 608
Thomas O. 543
ENDICOTT
Carl E. 576
John 8*
Moredcai T. 418, 572
William C. 29*, 40, 498*
ENDIN, John P. 457
ENEMARK, William A. 402
ENGDAHL, Don E. 576
ENGEL
A.B. 483
Albert J. 204, 207, 210, 213, 217, 220, 223, 226
Anton J. 559
E.J. 543
E.W. 465
Jacob 538
ENGELHARDT, Fred 476
ENGER, W.M. 418
ENGERT, Cornelius Van H. 423, 427
ENGLAND
Edward T. 192
John 525
Stephen J. 536
ENGLE
Clair 216, 219, 222, 225, 229, 232, 235, 238, 241, 244, 247, 284
N.H. 568
ENGLEBRIGHT
Harry L. 186, 189, 193, 196, 199, 202, 206, 209, 212, 216
William F. 155, 158, 161
ENGLEMAN, James O. 473
ENGLER
Edmund A. 486
Jean E. 401
ENGLES, William M. 532
ENGLISH
Elbert H. 281*
James E. 104, 106, 118, 287*
James L. 460
James W. 449
Lorenzo 452
Thomas 3
Thomas D. 138, 140
Warren B. 139
William E. 127, 574
William H. 17, 96, 98, 100, 102
ENGSTROM, Elmer W. 551*
ENLOE
Benjamin A. 133, 136, 138, 141
W.G. 459
ENNIS
Cornelius 454
George P. 574
LeRoy M. 566
William P., Jr. 419
ENOCHS, William H. 138
ENSLEY, F. Gerald 531
ENT, Uzal G. 411
ENYART, William R. 577
EPES
James F. 139, 141
Sydney P. 147, 149
EPLEY
Marion 607
Marion J., Jr. 553*
EPPES, John W. 58, 59, 61, 62, 64, 67, 69, 378
EPPS, Francis 461, 462*
EPSTEIN
Ephraim M. 481
Herman 601
EPTON, Hicks 565
ERB
Donald M. 478
Jacob 531
ERBAN, Richard T. 601
ERBE, Norman A. 305
ERDMAN
Charles R. 532
Constantine J. 141, 143
Jacob 90
ERHARDT, John G. 423, 439
ERICKSON
Edgar C. 402
John E. 201, 331*
ERICSSON, John 609
ERIKSON, Erik H. 587, 602
ERK, Edmund F. 195, 198
ERLANGER, E. Joseph 570, 605
ERLENBORN, John N. 251, 255, 258, 261, 264
ERMENTROUT, Daniel 126, 128, 131, 133, 146
ERNESTENE, A. Carlton 567
ERNST
H.M. 549
Oswald H. 483
Richard P. 180, 184, 187, 309
ERRETT
Isaac 536
Rusell 122, 124, 126
ERSKINE
Alden J. 576
John 580
ERVAY, Henry S. 452
ERVIN
James 67, 69
Joe W. 221
Sam J., Jr. 221, 233, 237, 240, 243, 246, 249, 253, 256, 259, 262, 265, 349
ERVING, George W. 426, 437
ERWIN
E.B. 460
John D. 430*
John P. 457
ESAU, Katherine 574
ESCH
John J. (Pacifist) 570
John J. 149, 152, 155, 158, 161, 163, 166, 169, 172, 176, 179
Marvin L. 255, 258, 261, 265
ESHELMAN, Walter W. 578
ESHER, John 531
ESHLEMAN, Edwin D. 256, 259, 262, 266
ESHNER, Ann 589
ESKRIDGE, James B. 478
ESLICK
Edward E. 189, 192, 195, 198
Willa M.B. 198
ESPE, Carl 416
ESPELAGE, Bernard T. 526
ESPENSCHEID, Lloyd 598
ESQUIROL, John H. 516, 519
ESSEN, Frederick 174
ESSEX
Hiram E. 571
William L. 513, 521
ESTABROOK, Joseph 482
ESTEE, James B. 457
ESTEP, Harry A. 192, 195, 198
ESTERLY, Charles J. 188, 195
ESTES
David F. 476
Howell M., Jr. 415
Thomas S. 439
William L., Jr. 565
ESTIL, Benjamin 73
ESTOPINAL, Albert 159, 162, 165, 168, 171, 174
ESTY, Constantine C. 114
ETCHISON, Bruce 502
ETHERINGTON, Edwin D. 485
ETHRIDGE
Mark 578
Emerson 97, 99, 103
William N., Jr. 328
ETNIER, Stephen 610
ETRA, Max 537
EUBANK, Eugene L. 411
EURICH, Alvia C. 477
EUSTACE, Bartholomew J. 525
EUSTIS
Dorothy H. 603
George 311
George, Jr. 98, 100
James B. 118, 121, 130, 132, 135, 312*, 428
William 24, 40, 56, 58, 68, 69, 319, 433
William H. 457
EVANG, Karl 592
EVANS
Abbie Huston 600
Alexander 91, 93, 95
Alvin 152, 154
Arthur G. 478
Austin P. 577
Charles H. 570
Charles R. 177
Daniel J. 382
David A. 577
David J. 486
David R. 64
E. Lewis 559
Earle W. 565
Evan A. 272
Frank E. 251, 254, 257, 260, 264
Frederick W. 532
George 76, 77, 79, 80, 82, 84, 86, 87, 89, 314
Griffith C. 568
H. Clay 136
Henry C. 414
Herbert M. 607
Hiram K. 183
Horace M. 484
Hugh I. 532
I. Newton 122, 128, 131
James L. 118, 120
John (Del.) 5
John (Pa.) 9
John G. 365
John M. 168, 171, 174, 177, 184, 187, 191, 194, 197
Joshua, Jr. 76, 78
Josiah J. 97, 99, 101, 365
Lemuel D. 99, 372
Luther H. 444
Lynden 164
Marcellus H. 204, 207, 211
Margaret 497
N.W. 558
Nathan 92, 93
Richard L. 580
Robert B. 543
Robert D. 554*
Robert E. 177, 181
Robert K. 402, 404
S.H. 483
Silas 478
Thomas 55, 56
Walter 142, 145, 444
Walter H. 273
William A. 572
William E. 189, 193, 196, 199
William Lloyd 565, 590, 604
EVARTS, William M. 27, 28*, 38, 41, 130, 133, 135, 345
EVE
Joseph 438
Paul F. 569
EVELAND, William P. 530
EVELEIGH, Nicholas 7
EVELETH, Joseph J. 449
EVERARD, Richard 9
EVEREST
Frank F. 399, 415, 416
Harvey W. 467, 481
EVERETT
Alexander H. 425, 433, 437
Edward 16, 26, 38, 72, 74, 76, 77, 79, 97, 319*, 429, 472, 563, 580
Horace 76, 78, 80, 81, 83, 85, 87
John R. 477
Monroe G. 483
Robert A. 240, 244, 247, 250, 253, 256
Robert W. 137
William 140
EVERGOOD, Philip 593

EVERHART
James B. 128, 131
William 97
EVERITT, William L. 598
EVERMANN, Barton W. 497
EVERS
John W. 545
Medgar W. 596, 611
EVERSON, William G. 402
EVERSULL
F.L. 477
Harry K. 474
EVERTON, John S. 424, 473
EVERTS, Olrpheus 571
EVINS
Joe L. 225, 228, 231, 234, 237, 240, 244, 247, 250, 253, 256, 260, 263, 266
John H. 122, 124, 126, 129
EWALT, Jack R. 571
EWART, Hamilton G. 135
EWBANK, Thomas 444
EWELL
Benjamin S. 486*
Richard S. 394*, 395*
EWERS, John C. 500
EWERT, A.W. 459
EWING
Andrew 94
Ashley W. 455
Charles 340
D.R. 536
Edwin H. 90
Ephraim M. 308
George W. 392*, 393
H. Clay 455
Hugh 433
James 462
James (M.D.) 590
James F. 457
James S. 424
John (b. 1732) 479
John (b. 1789) 79, 82
John (b. 1857) 430
John H. 90
Mary G. 536
Maurice 567, 608
Oscar R. 597
Presley U. 95, 96
Robert 457
Robert B. 533
Thomas (b. 1789) 26*, 39, 44, 78, 79, 81, 93, 121, 124, 352*
Thomas (b. 1829) 121, 306
Thomas (b. 1852) 444
William L. 460
William L.D. 80, 300
William M. 594
EXLEY, Frederick 609
EXON, J. James 334
EXTON, William G. 572
EYRING, Henry 564, 565, 596, 604*
EYMAN, Henry C. 571
EZZARD, William 449*

F

FAAS, Horst 588, 607
FABER
H.E. 457
William F. 510, 520
FACCIOLI, Giuseppe 599
FACKENTHAL, Frank D. 468, 585
FADDIS, Charles I. 201, 205, 208, 211, 215
FADLING, J.E. 558
FAGG, Fred D., Jr. 481
FAHEY, John H. 443, 493, 574
FAHY
Charles 272
Edward J. 418
FAIN, J.L. 462
FAINSOD, Merle 571
FAIR
Elisha Y. 424
James G. 126, 128, 130, 335
FAIRBAIRN, Robert B. 466
FAIRBANK, John K. 567
FAIRBANKS
Arthur 500
Charles W. 14, 17, 18, 145, 147, 150, 153, 155, 158
Mrs. Charles W. 579
Douglas 563
Erastus 375, 376
Horace 376
FAIRCHILD
Benjamin L. 143, 174, 181, 185, 188
Charles G. 480
Charles S. 28*, 39
Edward 466
Edward T. (b. 1872) 386
Edward T. (b. 1854) 476
George T. 473
George W. 159, 162, 165, 168, 171, 174, 548
H.L. 576
Henry P. 573
Jairus C. 456
James H. 478*
Lucius 385, 437
Muir S. 415
Raymond W. 472
Thomas E. 272
FAIRCLOTH, William T. 348
FAIRFIELD
Edmund B. 476
F.W. 472*
John 80, 82, 86, 87, 89, 91, 314*
Louis W. 173, 176, 180, 183
FAIRLESS, Benjamin F. 554*, 568, 596*
FAIRLIE, John A. 571
FAIRMAN, James F. 576, 595
FAIRWEATHER, Thomas 453
FAISON
John M. 165, 168
S. Lane, Jr. 502
FALCONER, Jacob A. 169
FALES, Dean A., Jr. 498
FALK
Karl L. 470
Phillip H. 486
FALL
Albert B. 32, 44, 165, 168, 171, 174, 178, 181, 343
Paul H. 472
FALLON
George H. 223, 226, 229, 233, 236, 239, 242, 245, 248, 252, 255, 258
Walter A. 546
William H. 460
FALLOWS, Samuel J. 473
FANCHER, Frederick B. 350
FANNIN, Paul J. 251, 254, 257, 260, 263, 280*
FANNING
Joseph T., Jr. 574
Paulian 474
FARABEE, William C. 599
FARAGHER, T. Robert 549
FARAN, James J. 90, 92, 451
FARBER, Sidney 565, 600
FARBSTEIN, Leonard 240, 243, 246, 249, 252, 256, 259
FARD, W.D. 538
FARFEL, Aaron J. 491
FARGO, William G. 451
FARIS
Charles B. 272
Ellsworth 573
George W. 142, 145, 147
Robert E.L. 574
FARISH, William S. 553*, 570
FARLAND, Joseph S. 427, 430, 434*
FARLEE, Isaac G. 88
FARLEY
E. Wilder 97
Eliot 553*
James A. 33*, 43
James I. 200, 203, 206
James T. 122, 124, 127, 283
John H. 452*
John M. 523, 524
Joseph F. 445
Michael F. 171
FARLIN, Dudley 81
FARLOW
Alfred 536
William G. 563, 574
FARMER
E. Malcolm 576
Thomas 10
FARNAM, Henry W. 566
FARNER, Donald S. 592
FARNHAM
Henry 546
Roswell 376
FARNSLEY, Charles P. 252, 456
FARNSWORTH
Charles S. 402
Daniel D.T. 383
Hiram W. 462
Jerry 593, 598
John F. 100, 102, 106, 108, 110, 112, 114
Loring 462
FARNUM, Billie S. 252
FARQUHAR
J.M. 558
John H. 108
John M. 131, 133, 135
Norman H. 418
FARR
Evarts W. 123
John R. 166, 169, 172, 175, 178
Lee E. 599
FARRAGUT, David G. 417, 597
FARRAND
Ebenezer 396
Livingston 468*, 569, 578
Max 499, 567
FARRAR
Edgar H. 564
Frank L. 368
FARRELL
Francis D. 473
Francis W. 405
James A. 554*, 596
Raymond F. 443
FARRELLY
John P. 525
John W. 92
Patrick 70, 71, 73
FARRINGTON
James 82
Valerie 497
FARROW
James 393*
Samuel 64
FARWELL
Charles B. 114, 116, 118, 125, 129, 132, 134, 300
Leonard J. 385
Nathan A. 106, 314
Sewall S. 125
FASCELL, Dante B. 235, 238, 241, 245, 248, 251, 254, 257, 261, 264
FASI, Frank F. 454
FASSETT, J. Sloat 157, 159, 162
FAST, Gustave 611
FAUBUS, Orville 282
FAULKNER
Barry 591
Charles J. (b. 1806) 96, 98, 99, 101, 120, 428
Charles J. (b. 1847) 134, 136, 139, 141, 144, 147, 383
William 586, 587, 598, 602*, 603, 605
FAUNCE, William H.P. 467
FAUQUIER, Francis 9
FAUST
Charles L. (b. 1879) 181, 184, 187, 191
Charles L. (b. 1906) 575, 589
Daniel 452*
FAVILLE, William B. 567
FAVROT, George K. 159, 180, 184
FAWCETT
Jacob 333
M. Edward 509, 521
Novice G. 478
FAWICK, Thomas L. 611
FAY
C.N. 600
Eliphaz 468
Francis B. 95
Harold J.W. 601
James H. 211, 217
John 68
Sidney B. 567
Theodore S. 438
FEARN
J. Walker 429, 435, 436
Thomas M. 391, 392
FEATHERSTON
Lewis P. 91, 134
Winfield S. 93, 396
FEAZEL, William C. 223, 313
FECHET, James E. 401
FECHTELER, William M. 416, 417
FECTEAU, George O. 559
FEDERAL, J. Lennox 528
FEDIGAN, John 484
FEE
James A. 272
John G. 466
FEEHAN
Daniel F. 526
Patrick A. 523, 527
FEELY
Edward F. 424
John J. 150
FEENEY
Al G. 454
Daniel J. 528
FEESE, A.O. 575
FEIGHAN, Michael A. 218, 221, 224, 227, 230, 234, 237, 240, 243, 246, 249, 253, 256, 259
FEILD, Alexander L. 595
FEIN, Nathaniel 585
FEINBERG, Wilfred 271
FEINER, William 471
FEININGER, Lyonel 607
FEIS, Herbert 586
FEIST, Irving J. 574
FELCH, Alpheus 91, 93, 95, 322*
FELDER, John M. 78, 80
FELDMAN
George J. 432*
Herman 403
FELDMANN, Louis G. 580
FELIX, Robert H. 571, 592
FELKER, Samuel D. 338
FELL
D. Newlin 359
John 6
Thomas 480
Thomas B. 475
FELLER, William 604
FELLMAN, David 564
FELLOWS
Charles A. 462
Frank 213, 217, 220, 223, 226, 229
George E. 474
Harold E. 578
John A. 572
John R. 138, 141
Raymond 315
Samuel M. 468
FELMLEY, David 472
FELS
Samuel S. 491
William C. 466
FELT, Harry D. 416, 417
FELTON
Charles N. 129, 132, 136, 283
Cornelius C. 472
William H. 118, 120, 122
FENDALL, Josias 8
FENERTY, Clare G. 205
FENN
E. Hart 179, 183, 186, 189, 193
Wallace O. 571, 589
FENNEMAN, Nevin M. 576
FENNER
Arthur 361
Goodrich R. 513, 520
James 59, 60, 361*
FENTON
Frank 481
Ivor D. 211, 215, 218, 221, 224, 228, 231, 234, 237, 240, 243, 246
John 598
John E. 574
Lucien J. 143, 146
Reuben E. 97, 103, 105, 107, 112, 115, 117, 345*
William 501
FENTRESS, Calvin, Jr. 491
FENWICK
Benedict J. 471*, 525
Charles G. 573
Edward 525
Enoch 471
FERBER
Edna 583
Robert 568
FERDON, John W. 123
FERGUSON
Albert L. 575
Arthur D. 460
C. Vaughan 432
Mrs. C. Vaughan 576
Charles B. 501
Clarence C, Jr 438
Francis E. 550
Franklin L. 479
Glenn W. 431
Harley B. 419
Homer 217, 220, 223, 226, 230, 233, 323, 435
Homer L. 574
James 415
James E. 372
James L. 547
James M. 533
James S. 477
John 458
John H. 433
Margaret C. 574
Milton J. 568
Miriam A. 373*
Phil 205, 208, 211
R.G. 533
Roy K. 552

Samuel D. 507
Sydney 549*
Thomas B. 437
William S. 567
FERGUSSON, Harvey B. 165, 168
FERLE, Jacob W. 455*
FERMI, Enrico 570, 591 595, 596, 605, 609, 610
FERN, Joseph J. 454*
FERNALD
Bert M. 171, 174, 177, 180, 184 187, 315*
Merritt C. 474*
Merritt L. 574, 600
FERNANDEZ
Antonio M. 217, 221, 224, 227, 230 233, 236
Joachim O. 197, 200, 203, 207, 210
FERRE, Luis A. 595, 598
FERRELL
John A. 572
Joseph L. 594
Thomas M. 128
FERRERO, Edward 409
FERRIS
Charles G. 79, 86
David L. 511, 521, 522
Isaac 477
Scott 160, 163, 166, 169, 172, 175, 178
Woodbridge N. 184, 187, 190, 322, 323
FERRISS, Orange 110, 112
FERRY
Elisha P. 381
Frederick C. 471
Orris S. 102, 109, 111, 113, 116, 118, 288
Thomas W. 108, 110, 112, 114, 116, 118, 119, 120, 121, 123, 125 322
William M. 460
FESS, Simeon D. 169, 172, 175, 178 181, 185, 188, 191, 194, 198, 201, 353, 465
FESSENDEN
Edson 551
Reginald A. 598
Samuel C. 104
Thomas A.D. 104
William P. 27, 39, 86, 97, 98, 100, 102, 104, 106, 108, 110, 112, 314*
FESTGE, Otto 456
FETHERS, Ogden H. 576
FETTER, Frank A. 566
FETTERMAN, John 587
FETTERS, Karl L. 567
FEURERSTEIN, Moses I. 537
FEW
Ignatius A. 470
William 4, 5, 51*, 295, 547
William P. 470
FEWKES, John M. 557
FEY, John T. 484, 487, 549
FEYNMAN, Richard P. 595*, 606
FICKEL, Jacob E. 412
FICKEN, John F. 451
FICKLIN, Orlando B. 87, 89, 91, 94
FIEBACH, Albert H. 579
FIEDLER
George B. 140
William H.F. 128
FIELD
Allan B. 599
Charles L. 579
Charles W. 395
Crosby 590
David Dudley 119, 564
F.A. 454
Fred T. 321
George R. 486
James G. 17
Moses W. 116
Richard M. 566
Richard S. 105, 341
Scott 155, 157
Stanley 546
Stephen J. 269, 283
Thomas S. 486
Walbridge A. 121, 123, 320
William O. 595
FIELDER
George B. 140
James F. 341
FIELDS
J.J. 558
William C. 110
William J. 164, 167, 170, 173, 177, 180, 184, 310
FIESER, Louis F. 604
FIESINGER, William L. 198, 201, 204
FIFE
Ray 476
Robert H. 577
FIFER, Joseph W. 300
FIGGINS, Jessie D. 498
FILAN, Frank 585
FILBERT, William J. 596
FILBEY
Emery T. 501
Francis S. 559
FILENE, Edward A. 493
FILLER, Mervin G. 469
FILLERBROWN, Thomas 566
FILLEY
Chauncey I. 460
Oliver D. 460
FILLMORE
Charles 539
Millard 13, 14, 16*, 79, 83, 84, 86, 92, 94, 477
FILO, John Paul 588
FINAN, John M. 588
FINCH
Isaac 76
Robert H. 36, 47
William C. 470
William R. 434, 439
FINCHER, John A. 467
FINCK
Furman J. 589
William E. 107, 109, 117
FINDLAY
James 73, 75, 76, 78
John 70, 71, 73
John V.L. 127, 130
William 70, 71, 73
FINDLEY
Paul 245, 248, 251, 255, 258 261, 264
William 52, 53, 54, 55, 58, 59, 60, 61, 63, 64, 65, 358*
FINE
Henry B. 568
John 84
John S. 360
Sidney A. 230, 233, 236
FINERTY, John F. 127
FINGER
H. Ellis, Jr. 531
John W. 579
FINK
Albert 572
Colin G. 575, 589
George R. 598
Louis M. 526
FINKELNBURG, Gustavus A. 112, 114
FINLAY
James C. 470
Kirkman G. 511, 522
FINLAYSON, John D. 483, 486
FINLETTER, Thomas K. 399
FINLEY
Charles 193, 197
Clement A. 403
David E. (b. 1861) 149, 152, 154, 157, 160, 163, 166, 169, 172
David E. (b. 1890) 500, 609
Ebenezer B. 121, 124
Hugh F. 132, 135
Jesse J. 118, 120, 125, 456
John H. 468, 473, 566
Mark F. 566
Murray 557
Robert 471
Robert C. 382*
Samuel 479
Thomas D. 414
W.A. 478
W.W. 552
FINNEGAN
Edward R. 245, 248
Hugh M. 469
Joseph F. 443
Philip J. 272
FINNERAN, John G. 417
FINNEY
Benjamin F. 481
C.M. 577
Charles G. 478*
Darwin A. 111
John M.T. 565
Nat S. 585
Ross L. 592
FINNIGAN, George J. 526
FINO, Paul A. 233, 236, 240, 243, 246, 249, 252, 256
FIRESTONE, Floyd A. 601
FISCHELIS, Robert P. 609
FISCHER
Emil 594
Ernst G. 607
Fred 455
George D. 578
Israel F. 143, 146, 273
John 559
John S. 360
Louis 602
Louis E. 550
FISCHETTI, John 587
FISCHL, Louis J. 570
FISH
A.J. 462
Bert 427, 435, 436
Charles J. 497
Frederick P. 543
Hamilton (b. 1808) 28*, 38, 88, 95, 97, 99, 344*, 580
Hamilton (b. 1849) 162
Hamilton (b. 1888) 178, 181, 185, 188, 191, 194, 198, 201, 204, 207, 211, 214, 217
Hamilton, Jr. 259, 262, 265
Nicholas 424, 438
Stuyvesant 548
William H. 296
FISHBACK, William M. 281
FISHBOURN, William 458
FISHBURNE, John W. 199
FISHEL, Leslie H., Jr. 472
FISHER
Albert K. 569
C. Harold 567
Charles 67, 68, 84
David 92
Edward D. 569
Frederick B. 530
George 76
George P. 104, 567
Harry L. 565, 567
Hendrick 3
Horatio G. 124, 126
Hubert F. 175, 178, 182, 185, 189, 192, 195
Irving 566, 579
Jerome B. 574
John 112
Joseph A. 559
Joseph L. 492
Max M. 595
Michael M. 476, 485
O. Clark 218, 221, 225, 228, 231, 234, 237, 240, 244, 247, 250, 253, 256, 260, 263, 266
Samuel 532
Samuel S. 444
Samuel W. 471, 532
Spencer O. 130, 132
Stephen E. 536
W.C. 452
Walter C. 577
Walter L. 31*, 44
William 458
FISK
Clinton B. 17
Dwight 451
Ezra 532
James 59, 61, 63, 64, 67, 375
Jonathan 61, 64, 65
Lewis R. 475
Richmond 480
Wilbur 485
FISKE
Bradley A. 594
Charles 510, 519
Gertrude 593*
Haley 549
Lewis R. 465
Thomas S. 568
Wyman P. 578
FISTER, George M. 569
FITCH
Alvah R. 400
Asa 62
Ashbel P. 133, 135, 138, 141
Aubrey W. 483
Chauncey P. 566
Ebenezer 486
Graham N. 93, 94, 98, 100, 102, 302
Thomas (b. 1700) 8, 10
Thomas (b. 1855) 112
FITE
Daniel H. 467
Dean P. 492
FITHIAN, George W. 134, 137, 139
FITLER, Edwin H. 458
FITZELL, Lincoln 610
FITZGERALD (or FITZ GERALD)
Albert J. 559
C.B. 461
Desmond 572
Edmund 550
Edward 527
Edward A. 529
Francis A.J. 575
Frank D. 323*
James F. 558
James N. 530
John F. 143, 145, 148, 177, 450*
John J. 148, 151, 154, 157, 159, 162, 165, 168, 171, 174
Leslie M. 566
Oscar P. 530
Robert 610
Roy G. 181, 185, 188, 191, 195
Rufus H. 479
Thomas 91, 322
Thomas S. 469, 474*
William 78
William J. 206, 213
William S. 452
William T. 188, 191
FITZGIBBONS, John 201
FITZ HENRY, Louis 167, 272
FITZHUGH
Gilbert W. 549*
William 7
FITZMAURICE (or FITZ MAURICE)
Edmond J. 529
John E. 526
FITZPATRICK
Benjamin 90, 92, 94, 96, 98, 100*, 102*, 277*
Daniel R. 583, 586
James M. 191, 194, 198, 201, 204, 207, 211, 214, 217
John 457
Leo J. 578
M.F. 558
Morgan C. 154
P.F. 558
Thomas 587
Thomas B. 599
Thomas Y. 145, 148
William H. 585
FITZSIMMONS
Cantidius T. 474
Frank 558
Laurence J. 525
FITZSIMONS, Thomas 4, 7, 51, 52, 53
FITZWHYLSON, WilliaM H. 459
FJARE, Orvin B. 236
FLACK
Joseph 424, 426, 435
William H. 154, 157
FLAD, Henry 572
FLAGET, Benedict J. 527
FLAGG, F.H. 462
FLAGLER
Daniel W. 402
Henry M. 553*
Thomas T. 97, 99
FLAHERTY
Joseph A. 484
Lawrence J. 186
Peter F. 459
Thomas A. 207, 210, 213
FLAKE, Wilson C. 428
FLANAGAN
Bernard J. 527, 529
DeWitt C. 151
James W. 113, 115, 117, 372
FLANAGIN, Harris 281
FLANDERS
Benjamin F. 104, 301, 457
Ralph E. 222, 225, 228, 231, 234, 237, 240, 377, 573, 598, 601
Walter C. 493
FLANNAGAN, John W., Jr. 199, 202, 205, 209, 212, 215, 218, 222, 225
FLANNER, Janet 602
FLANNERY, J. Harold 208, 211, 215
FLASCH, Kilian C. 527
FLAVIN
Glennon P. 527
Martin 585
FLEEGER, George W. 131
FLEETWOOD, Frederick G. 185
FLEGER, Anthony A. 208

FLEISCHMAN, Julius 452
FLEISIG, Ross 564
FLEMING
Aretas B. 383
Dewey L. 585
Fenton B. 455
Francis P. 293
J.R. 459
James H. 569
John A. 598
Philip B. 426
Raymond H. 402
Robben W. 475
Robert V. 564
Sam M. 564
Samuel W. 453
Sandford 534
Wallace B. 466
Walter M. 579
William 7
William B. 120
William F. 378
William H. 145, 147, 150
William P. 549
FLEMMING, Arthur S. 35, 47, 474, 478
FLENNIKAN, Robert P. 426
FLENNIKEN, John C. 485*
FLESH, M.M. 455
FLETCHER
Albert 527
Allen M. 376
Andrew 567
Austin B. 579
Benjamin 8, 9
Charles K. 222
Duncan U. 161, 164, 167, 170, 173, 176, 180, 183, 186, 189, 193, 196, 199, 203, 293, 454*
E. Richmond 578
Esten A. 579
H.L. 455
Harvey 570
Henry (lawyer) 579
Henry (mayor) 459
Henry P. 424, 425, 431, 432, 433, 445
Isaac 83, 85
James C. 444, 484
Jean B. 591
Jefferson B. 577
John G. 455
John Gould 584
Loren 140, 143, 145, 148, 151, 156
Maurice J. 598
Moses 3
Norman 591
Richard (Mass.) 82
Richard (Miss.) 454
Ryland 375
Samuel H. 462
Stewart G. 572
Thomas (Ark.) 281
Thomas (Ky.) 65
Thomas B. 188, 191, 201, 204, 208
Thomas C. 329
William I. 568
FLETT, Lawrence 567, 590
FLEURE, Herbert J. 595
FLEXNER, Simon 563
FLICK
James P. 134, 137
Lawrence F. 599
FLICKINGER, Daniel 531
FLINN, Andre 532
FLINT
Austin, Sr. 569
Charles L. 475
Charles W. 468, 482, 530
Edward S. 452
Frank P. 155, 158, 161, 283
George W. 468
Leroy 497*
Willis H. 452
FLIPPIN, John R. 456
FLJOZDAL, F.H. 557
FLOCH, Joseph 598, 610
FLOERSH, John A. 523, 527
FLOOD
Daniel J. 221, 228, 231, 237, 240, 243, 246, 250, 253, 256, 259, 262, 266
Henry D. 152, 155, 158, 160, 163, 166, 169, 172, 175, 179
Joel W. 199
Thomas S. 133, 135
FLORA, A. Cline 578
FLORENCE
Elias 88
Fred F. 564
Thomas B. 95, 97, 99, 101, 103
FLORMAN, Irving 424
FLORY, Paul J. 594, 604
FLOURNOY, Thomas S. 92
FLOWER
Ebenezer 453
Roswell P. 126, 135, 345
Walter C. 457
FLOWERS
Robert L. 470
Walter 257, 260, 263
FLOYD
Charles A. 86
Charles M. 338
John (b. 1769) 74
John (b. 1783) 16, 67, 69, 70, 72, 73, 75, 378
John B. (b. 1806) 27, 40, 378, 451
John C. 155, 158, 161, 164, 167
John G. 84, 86, 95
William 3, 6, 51
FLUCKEY, Eugene B. 416
FLUNO, Francis J. 536
FLUOR, J. Robert 578
FLY, James L. 443
FLYE, Edwin 118
FLYNN
Edmund W. 363
Gerald T. 244
J.W. 453
John A. 480
Joseph V. 171, 174
Thomas D. 567
William S. 362
FLYNT, John J., Jr. 235, 238, 241, 245, 248, 251, 254, 258, 261, 264
FOARD, Fred T. 610
FOCHT
Benjamin K. 160, 163, 166, 172, 175, 178, 182, 201, 205, 208
John B. 482
FOCKE, Arthur E. 572
FOELKER, Otto G. 159, 162
FOERDERER, Robert H. 152
FOERY, Walter 529
FOGARTY, John E. 215, 218, 221, 225, 228, 231, 234, 237, 240, 243, 247, 250, 253, 599
FOGG
George G. 108, 338, 438
Sanford L. 449
Sanford L., Jr. 449*, 450
FOGHT H.W. 486
FOLDS Charles W. 576
FOLEY
B. Charles 474
Daniel F. 568
Eugene P. 445
Francis B. 572, 590
J.W. 553
James B. 100
James D. 469
John R. 242
John S. 526
Thomas S. 254, 257, 260, 263, 266
FOLGER
Alonzo D. 211, 214
Charles J. 29, 39, 345
Harry 558
John C. 424
John H. 214, 218, 221, 224
Walter, Jr. 66, 68
William M. 418
FOLINSBEE, John 589*
FOLK, Joseph W. 329
FOLKERS, Karl 565, 604
FOLKS, Homer 609
FOLLETT
John F. 128
W.I. 600
FOLLIARD, Edward T. 585, 608
FOLLIS, R. Gwin 552*, 590
FOLSOM
Frances 20*
Frank M. 551, 599
George 433
James E. 278*
Marion B. 35*, 47, 592, 595
Nathaniel 6
FOLTZ, J.M. 416
FOLWELL
William 518, 519
William W. 475
FOMAN, Samuel J. 592
FONG, Hiram L. 241, 245, 248, 251, 254, 158, 261, 264, 298
FONTANNE, Lynn 592, 608
FONVILLE, R.H. 454
FOORD, Alvin G. 572
FOOT, Solomon 88, 90, 96, 98, 99, 101, 102, 103, 104, 105, 106, 107, 109, 375
FOOTE
Andrew M. 417
Charles A. 71
Elisha 444
Ellsworth B. 222
Henry S. 91, 93, 95, 326*, 393*
J.H. 576
Lucius H. 431
Norman L. 516, 519
Patrick 481
Paul D. 570
Samuel A. 67, 70, 74, 75, 77, 78, 287*
Thomas M. 423, 425
Wallace T., Jr. 143, 146
William A. 545
FORAKER, Joseph B. 146, 149, 151, 154, 157, 160, 353*
FORAN, Martin A. 128, 131, 133
FORAND, Aime J. 208, 215, 218, 221, 225, 228, 231, 234, 237, 240, 243
FORBES
Edward W. 499
Esther 584
Gilbert 592
Harland C. 545*
James 5
John F. 482
John M. 423
John Murray 545
John S. 594, 600
Stephen A. 575
W. Cameron 431
FORCE
Juliana 502
Manning F. 410
Peter 462
Raymond C. 525
Roland W. 497
FORD
Aaron L. 204, 207, 210, 214
Cornelius 443
Edsel 491, 547
Edward 550
Elbert L. 402
Frederick W. 443
George 130
Gerald R., Jr. 226, 230, 233, 236, 239, 242, 245, 249, 252, 255, 258, 261, 265
Guy S. 475, 567
Henry 547*, 590, 594, 598
Henry, 2d 491, 547, 608
Henry J. 571
Henry P. 459
James 76, 78
Jeremiah D.M. 563, 577, 599
John H. 480*
John S. 450
John W. 577
L.H. 392
Leland M. 209, 212
Melbourne H. 132, 137
Morgan 273
Nicholas 123, 125
Peter S. 576
Sam C. 331
Seabury 352
Stanley H. 400
Thomas F. 199, 202, 206, 209, 212, 216, 300
William 550
William D. (Mich.) 252, 255, 258, 261, 265
William D. (N.Y.) 68
Worthington C. 567
Y.A. 474
FORDNEY, Joseph W. 148, 151, 153, 156, 159, 162, 165, 168, 171, 174, 177, 180
FOREMAN
A. Herbert 579
Edgar F. 259
Thomas M. 392
FOREST, John A. 528
FORESTER, John B. 80, 81
FORGAN, James B. 546, 547*
FORKER, Samuel C. 114
FORMAN
David 406
Edgar F. 250
Philip 271
W. St. John 134, 137, 139, 444
FORMENTO, Felix 572
FORMWALT, Moses W. 449
FORNANCE, Joseph 85, 86
FORNES, Charles V. 160, 162, 165
FORNEY
Daniel M. 65, 67
John H. 395
Peter 64
William H. 118, 120, 122, 124, 127, 129, 131, 134, 136
FORREST
French 396
George F. 455*
James T. 501
Matthew G. 611
Nathan B. 395
Thomas 68, 70
Uriah 5, 52
Wilbur 573
FORRESTAL, James V. 34*, 42, 47
FORRESTER
Elijah L. 229, 232, 235, 238, 241, 245, 248
Jay W. 598
FORSTER
George J. 456
J. Frank 552*
Robert E. 571
FORSYTH, John 25*, 38, 63, 65, 66, 71, 72, 74, 75, 77, 78, 295*, 433, 437
FORSYTHE
Albert P. 122
Donald T. 576
Edwin B. 259, 262, 265
George I. 404
W.E. 580
FORT
Franklin W. 188, 191, 194, 443
George F. 340
Greenbury L. 116, 118, 120, 123
John F. 341
Tomlison 74
FORTAS, Abe 270
FORTESCUE, Charles L. 594
FORTIER
Alcee 577
Louis J. 414
FORTUNE
Alonzo W. 536
Porter L., Jr. 475
William 570
FORWARD
Chauncey 73, 75, 76
Frank A. 595
John F., Jr. 461*
Walter 26, 39, 70, 71, 426
FORWOOD, William H. 403
FOSDICK
Harry Emerson 603
Nicoll 73
Raymond B. 492, 612
FOSS
Cyrus D. 485, 530
Eugene N. 162, 320
Frank H. 187, 190, 194, 197, 200
George E. 142, 145, 147, 150, 153, 156, 158, 161, 164, 170, 173
Harold L. 565
Joe 368
FOSTER
A. Lawrence 86
Abiel 6, 51, 53, 55, 56, 57
Addison G. 149, 152, 155, 381
Adriance S. 574
Alfred D. 550*
Ben 607
Charles 29*, 39, 115, 117, 119, 121, 353
Clyde T. 552*
David J. 152, 155, 158, 160, 163, 166
Dwight 52, 53, 54, 55*, 56, 319
E.D. 418
Ephraim H. 83, 88, 369*
George M., Jr. 499, 563
George P. 147, 150, 153
Henry A. 83, 88, 344
Henry D. 88, 90, 115
Hohen 459
Israel M. 178, 181, 185
J.P. 453
J.W. 563
James W., Jr. 499, 502
John 459

John G. 406
John H. 156, 158
John W. 29, 38, 433, 436, 437
Mrs. John W. 579
Kenneth C. 551
Lafayette L. 482
Lafayette S. 98, 100, 102, 104, 106, 107*, 287
Luther 476
Luther H. 483
Martin D. 158, 161, 164, 167, 170, 173
Matthew W. 566
Murphy J. 150, 153, 156, 159, 162, 164, 312*
Nathaniel G. 98
Randolph S. 530
Richard C. 465
Rufus E. 271
Sheppard W. 566
Stephen C. 100, 102, 456
Stephen Collins 597
Theodore 51, 52, 53, 54, 55, 56, 57, 361
Thomas 456
Thomas F. 75, 77, 78, 85
Thomas J. 392, 393
Wilder D. 114
Will 593
William C. 399, 443
William J. 599
FOUKE, Philip B. 102, 104
FOULKE, William D. 531, 579
FOULKES
George E. 200
William H. 532
FOULKROD, William W. 160, 163
FOULOIS, Benjamin D. 401
FOUNTAIN, Lawrence H. 234, 237, 240, 243, 246, 249, 253, 256, 259, 262, 265
FOURNACE, E. Gene 574
FOURNET, John B. 313
FOUSHEE, William 459
FOUST
Clifford M. 608
Julius I. 477
FOUT, Henry H. 531
FOWLE, Daniel G. 348
FOWLER
Charles H. 478, 530
Charles N. 143, 146, 148, 151, 154, 157, 159, 162
Cody 565*
Frederick H. 572
H. Robert 164, 167
Harlan D. 611
Harold N. 570
Henry H. 36, 39
John 54, 55, 56, 57, 59
John E. 146
Joseph S. 109, 111, 113, 370
Orin 93, 95
Philemon H. 532
Samuel (b. 1779) 79, 81
Samuel (b. 1851) 135, 138
William A. 591
FOX
Albert C. 474
Andrew F. 145, 148, 151
Charles W. 418
Daniel M. 458
Dixon R. 483
Herbert H.H. 511, 520
John 110, 112
John M. 472
Joseph J. 526
Kate 538
Margaret 538
Martin 558
Philip 500
Sylvan 587
William C. 427
William H. 497, 499
FOY, Lewis W. 544
FOYE, Arthur B. 567
FRALEY, Frederick 570
FRANCE, Joseph I. 174, 177, 180, 317
FRANCHER, Enoch L. 565
FRANCHESCHINI, Rocco 559
FRANCHOT, Richard 105
FRANCIS
Charles S. 423, 429, 435, 436
Clarence 547*
David R. 30*, 41, 329, 436, 460
George B. 174,
James B. 572
John B. 88, 361*
John M. 423, 429, 435
Joseph M. 508, 520
Josiah 461
Robert 610
Thomas, Jr. 599
William B. 166, 169
William T. 432
FRANCK, James 610
FRANCKE
Don E. 570, 609
Kuno 577
FRANK
August 103, 105, 107
Eugene M. 531
Glenn 486
Henry 538
Jerome N. 271, 445
Nathan 135
Tenney 570
Walter H. 412
FRANKE
Gustave H. 414
William B. 399
FRANKEL, L.K. 572, 578
FRANKFURTER, Felix 270, 589, 608
FRANKLIN
Benjamin 3*, 4, 7, 9, 570, 597
Benjamin J. 119, 121
Edward C. 565, 596, 604
James H. 534
Jesse 54, 56, 57*, 58, 60, 61, 62, 347*
John R. 97
Meshack 60, 61, 63, 64
William 8
William B. 407*, 408*
William H. 544
FRANKS, Lucinda 588
FRANTZ, Albert T. 286
FRANZ
John B. 526, 527
Shepherd I. 571
FRANZHEIM, Kenneth, 2d 433, 439
FRANZONI, F. Royce 570
FRARY
Francis C. 575, 589, 590, 595
Frank P. 461
FRASCA, John A. 587
FRASER
Donald M. 249, 252, 255, 258, 261, 265
James E. 579, 591, 603
John 473, 479
Joseph T., Jr. 501*, 607
Laura G. 610*
Peter M. 545
Thomas A., Jr. 516, 521
FRAWLEY, John F. 491
FRAYNE, John G. 580
FRAZER
Robert 427
Robert S. 360
FRAZIER
Arthur H. 423*
Charles H. 569
E. Franklin 573
James B. 157, 160, 163, 370*
James B., Jr. 228, 231, 234, 237, 240, 244, 247
Lynn J. 185, 188, 191, 194, 198, 201, 204, 208, 211, 350*
FREAR
J. Allen, Jr. 226, 229, 232, 235, 238, 241, 292
James A. 169, 172, 176, 179, 182, 186, 189, 192, 196, 199, 202
FREAS, Samuel T. 601
FRED, Edwin B. 486
FREDENDALL, Lloyd R. 405, 411, 412*
FREDERICK
Benjamin T. 127, 130
Robert T. 414
FREDERICKS
John D. 183, 186
Marshall M. 590, 591
FREDRIKSON, Roger L. 534
FREE
Arthur M. 179, 183, 186, 189, 193, 196
Lytle R. 533
FREED, Arthur 563
FREEDLEY, John 92, 93
FREEDMAN, Abraham L. 271
FREEHLING, William W. 591
FREEMAN
Alice 485
Allen W. 572
Chapman 119, 122
Charles Y. 545*
Douglas S. 584, 586
Fulton 426, 433
Gaylord 546, 547*
George W. 505, 519
Gordon M. 558
Howard E. 598
James 539
James C. 116
James E. 511, 522
John D. 95
John H. 491
John R. 572, 573, 590, 596
Jonathan 55, 56
Mary E. Wilkins 598
Nathaniel, Jr. 53, 54
Orville L. 36*, 45, 325
Paul L., Jr. 404*
Raymond L. 573
Richard P. 170, 173, 176, 179, 183, 186, 189, 193, 196
Ruth 578, 592
Thomas W. 392
FREER
Hamline H. 468
Romeo H. 149
FREIBERG
J. Walter 537
Julius 537
FREIBERGER, I.F. 545
FREKING, Frederick W. 527, 528
FRELEY, Jasper W. 485
FRELINGHUYSEN
Frederick 6, 53, 54, 340
Frederick T. 28, 29, 38, 108, 110, 114, 117, 119, 341*, 565
Joseph S. 174, 177, 181, 341
Peter H.B. 233, 236, 239, 243, 246, 249, 252, 255, 259, 262, 265
Theodore 16, 76, 77, 79, 340, 477, 480, 565, 570
FREMONT, John C. 16, 92, 283, 406
FRENCH
Augustus C. 300
Burton L. 153, 156, 158, 164, 167, 173, 176, 180, 183, 186, 190, 193, 196
C. Clement 485
Calvin H. 480
Carlos 132
Charles J. 452*
Daniel Chester 579, 591, 603
Ezra B. 102
Francis H. 410
Herbert J. 572
J. Stewart 470
James H. 461
John R. 111
Jonas H. 457
Philip 457
Richard 80, 87, 91
Samuel G. 396*
William H. 407*, 408*, 533
William M.R. 497
FRENSDORFF, Wesley 520
FRENZEL, Bill 261, 265
FRERET, William 457
FREUDENHEIM, Thomas 497
FREUND
Ernest 571
Jules 600
Paul A. 563
FREY
Albert W. 568
Fred C. 474
Gerald L. 528
Louis, Jr. 257, 261, 264
Oliver W. 201, 205, 208
William C. 517
FRICK
Bertha M. 595
Frederick 600
Henry 88
Thomas C. 567
FRIDAY
David 475
William C. 477
FRIDELL, Elmir A. 534
FRIEDEL, Samuel N. 233, 236, 239, 242, 245, 248, 252, 255, 258
FRIEDEN, John P. 469, 480, 481
FRIEDLANDER, Leo 579, 591
FRIEDMAN
Edmund 572
Herbert 604
Milton 566
FRIEDMANN, Herbert 500, 569, 592, 600
FRIEDRICH, Carl J. 571
FRIEL, Francis S. 572
FRIEND, Theodore W., III 482, 591
FRIENDLY
Alfred 587
Henry J. 271
FRIES
Amos A. 401
Edward D. 600
Frank W. 206, 210
George 90, 92
FRIESCKE, F.C. 593
FRIESELL, H. Edmund 566
FRIEZE, Henry S. 475
FRIIS, Harald T. 598
FRILEY
Charles E. 473
W.C. 471
FRINGS, Ketti 586
FRINK, Daniel A. 455
FRISBEE, Edward S. 485
FRISCH, Martin 591
FRITCHEY, John A. 453*
FRITCHMAN, Harry K. 450
FRITZ
John 573, 594, 596
Oscar M. 386
Roger J. 486
FRODERMAN, Edward 536
FROEHLKE, Robert F. 399
FROELICH, Harold V. 266
FROLICH, Per K. 565
FROMENTIN, Eligius 63, 65, 66, 311
FROMMEYER, Walter B., Jr. 567
FROSCH, Carl J. 601
FROST
Charles 595
Frances 610
Joel 71
John S. 557
Lawrence H. 416, 444
Marion F. 526
Richard G. 123, 125
Robert 583*, 584*, 589, 592, 600, 603, 609
Rufus S. 119
Wade H. 610
Wesley 434*
William G. 466
FROTHINGHAM, Louis A. 180, 184, 187, 190
FRUEAUFF
Harry D. 491
Harry D., Jr. 491
Lena R. 491
FRY
Charles M. 544
Frank R. 569
Franklin C. 535*
Jacob, Jr. 81, 83
James C. 414
Joseph, Jr. 75, 76
Joseph L. 451
Leslie M. 580
FRYE
Calvin A. 536
Jack 553
Walter 576
William P. 114, 116, 118, 121, 123, 125, 127, 130, 132, 135, 137, 140, 142*, 144, 147, 148, 150, 152, 153, 155, 156, 158, 159, 161, 162, 164, 165, 314
FUCHS, Ralph F. 564
FUGATE, Thomas B. 228, 231
FUHRMANN, Louis P. 451
FULBRIGHT
J. William 216, 219, 222, 225, 228, 232, 235, 238, 241, 244, 247, 251, 254, 257, 260, 263, 282, 465, 603
James F. 184, 191, 197
FULD, Stanley 346
FULKERSON
Abram 126
Frank B. 156
FULLAM, William F. 483
FULLER
Albert M. 500
Alvan T. 174, 177, 321
Ben H. 416
Benoni S. 118, 120
Calvin S. 612
Charles E. 153, 156, 158, 161, 164, 170, 173, 176, 180, 183, 187
Claude A. 193, 196, 199, 202, 206

Douglas R. 550
Edward 3
Edward C. 466
George 88
George D. 575
George W. 572, 600
Hadwen C. 217, 221, 224
Henry M. 95, 99
Homer T. 486
Horace H. 413, 419
J.O. 470
John W. 409
Levi K. 376
Melville W. 269
Nathan 454
Philo C. 79, 81
R. Buckminster 590, 592, 603
Richard 534
Richard E. 502
Robert 478
Samuel 3
T.P. 454
Thomas C. 393
Thomas J.D. 93, 95, 97, 98
Timothy 66, 68, 69, 71
W.D. 578
William E. 130, 132
William K. 79, 81
FULLERTON
Baxter P. 532
David 68
George S. 571
Mark A. 381*
FULMER
Hampton P. 182, 185, 188, 192, 195, 198, 202, 205, 208, 211, 215, 218
Willa L. 218
FULTON
Andrew 459
Andrew S. 92
Charles W. 154, 157, 160, 356
Elmer L. 160
James G. 221, 224, 228, 231, 234, 237, 240, 243, 246, 250, 253, 256, 259, 262
John H. 80
Richard H. 250, 253, 256, 260, 263, 266
Robert Fulton 597
Robert B. (Mass.) 466
Robert B. (Miss.) 467, 475
Robert D. 305
Samuel A. 533
William S. 80, 82, 83, 85, 87, 281
FUNK
Benjamin F. 139
Frank H. 180, 183, 187
Nevin E. 576, 590
FUNKHOUSER, Richard 428
FUNSTEN, James B. 508, 519, 522
FUNSTON
Edward H. 127, 130, 132, 134, 137, 140
Frederick 404, 419
G. Keith 482, 550, 604
FUQUA
Don 248, 251, 254, 257, 261, 264
Henry L. 312
Herbert B. 564
Stephen O. 402
FURAY, John B. 473, 474
FURBUSH, R.A. 543*
FURCHES, David M. 348
FURCOLO, Foster 226, 229, 321
FUREY, Francis J. 524, 528
FURLONG
Grant 218
William R. 418
FURLOW, Allen J. 187, 190
FURMAN
James C. 470
Moore 462
N. Howell 565
FURNAS
Clifford C. 477*
Robert W. 333
FURNISS, Henry W. 429
FUSHMAN, Arthur J. 549
FUSON, Reynold C. 604
FUSSLER, Herman H. 595
FUTRALL, John C. 465
FUTRELL, J. Marion 282
FUTTLE, Joseph F. 484
FYAN
Loleta Dawson 568
Robert W. 128, 138, 140
FRYING, Henry 594

G

GABBERT, William H. 285*
GABO, Naum 592
GABRIELS, Henry 527
GABRIELSON, Ira N. 591
GADDIS, M.P. 486
GADSBY, Edward N. 445
GADSDEN
Christopher 3, 7
Christopher E. 505, 521
James 401
John 451
GAERTNER
Carl 589*
William 607
GAFFEY, Hugh J. 413, 415*
GAGE
Henry T. 283, 435
Jack R. 388
John B. 455
Joshua 66
Lyman J. 30*, 39, 546, 564
Thomas 8
GAGER, C. Stuart 574, 579
GAHAN, Harry C. 181
GAILLARD
J. Palmer, Jr. 451
John 58, 59, 60, 61, 62, 63*, 64, 65, 66*, 67*, 69*, 70*, 72*, 73, 364
Peter C. 451
GAILOR, Thomas F. 481, 508, 522
GAINER, Joseph H. 459
GAINES
Absalom G. 480
Francis P. 484, 485, 486
John P. 91
John W. 146, 149, 152, 155, 157, 160
Joseph H. 152, 155, 158, 161, 163
Reuben R. 372
William E. 134
GAITHER
Burgess S. 392, 393
H. Rowan, Jr. 491
Nathan 75, 77
Ridgely 400, 405
GAJDUSEK, D. Carleton 599
GALANTIN, Ignatius J. 418
GALBERRY, Thomas 484, 526
GALBRAITH
Francis J. 430, 437
Frederick W., Jr. 568
J. Kenneth 430, 566
John 79, 81, 85
W.W. 416
William E. 568
GALE
Anthony 416
Benjamin F. 452
George 51
Henry G. 570
Levin 74
Richard P. 214, 217
Willis 545*
Zona 583
GALES, Joseph, Jr. 462
GALEY, Seth P. 455
GALIFIANAKIS, Nick 256, 259, 262
GALLAGHER
Buell G. 468*
Charles W. 474
Cornelius E. 243, 246, 249, 252, 255, 259, 262
Harold J. 565, 589
Henry M. 325
James 218, 224
Louis J. 460
Michael J. 526
Nicholas 526
Ralph W. 553*
Ray 580
Raymond J. 527
Thomas 161, 164, 167, 170, 173, 176
Thomas J. 459
Vernon F. 470
William J. 220
William M. 586
GALLALEE, John M. 465
GALLATIN, Albert 23, 24*, 39, 53, 54, 55, 56, 358, 428, 429*
GALLEHER, John N. 507, 520
GALLIE, Donald M. 566
GALLINGER, Jacob H. 130, 133, 138, 140, 143, 146, 148, 151, 154, 157, 159, 162, 164, 165, 168, 171, 174, 338
GALLIVAN, James A. 168, 171, 174, 177, 180, 184, 187, 190
GALLMAN, Waldemar J. 430, 435, 439
GALLOWAY
Alexander H. 552*
Charles B. 530
Irene O. 401
Joseph 7
Paul V. 531
Samuel 99
GALLUP
Albert 83
Anna B. 603
C. Stanton 534
Frank A. 480
George H. 579
GALPIN, Perrin C. 491
GALSTON
Arthur 574
Maltby 545
GALVIN, John 452*, 574
GAMBLE
Hamilton R. 329
James 95, 97
James L. 592
John R. 138
Kathryn E. 500
Ralph A. 207, 211, 214, 217, 221, 224, 227, 230, 233, 236
Robert 459
Robert J. 144, 149, 152, 154, 157, 160, 163, 166, 367
Roger L. 78, 85
GAMBRELL
David H. 261, 297
E. Smythe 565, 589
J.B. 475, 534
Mary L. 472
GAMBRILL, Stephen W. 184, 187, 190, 193, 197, 200, 203, 207
GAMERTSFELDER, Walter S. 478
GAMMAGE, Grady 465
GAMMON, Edgar G. 471
GAMSER, Howard G. 444*
GANDY, Harry L. 172, 175, 178
GANEY, J. Cullen 271
GANFIELD, William A. 467
GANLY, James V. 178
GANNETT
Barzillai 61, 62
Henry 578
GANNON
Robert I. 470
Thomas 470
GANONG, William F. 466, 574
GANSEVOORT, Leonard 6
GANSON, John 107
GANTT
Daniel 333
James B. 329, 330
GANTZ, Martin K. 138
GANZ, E. 459*
GARAND, John C. 598
GARBER
Daniel 589*, 593*, 607
F. Henry 459
Harvey C. 154, 157
Jacob A. 195
Milton C. 185, 188, 191, 195, 198
Paul N. 530
Robert S. 571
Roy O. 576
Silas 333
GARCELON, Alonzo 314
GARCIA VILLA, Jose 610
GARD, Warren 169, 172, 175, 178
GARDENHIER, E.L. 393
GARDENHIRE, J.B. 455
GARDENIER, Barent 60, 61
GARDINER
Addison 345
Henry G. 499
James B. 579
John 7
Julia 20
Richard 3
Sylvester 7
Theophilus M. 511
William C. 575
William T. 315
GARDNER
Archibald K. 272
Arthur 426
Augustus P. 151, 153, 156, 159, 162, 165, 168, 171, 174
Edward J. 24
Francis 60
Frank 183, 187, 190
Frederick D. 330
George W. 452*
Gideon 61
Henry B. 566
Henry J. 319
Hugh M. 476
Irvine C. 580
Isabella Stewart 499
James C. 256
John 10
John J. 140, 143, 146, 148, 151, 154, 157, 159, 162, 165
John W. 36, 47, 491, 595, 598, 603, 608
Joseph 7
Lester D. 597
Lucien D. 278
Lytt I. 599
Matthias B. 417*
Mills 121
O. Max 349
Obadiah 165, 315
Stephen S. 547*
Wallace J. 513, 520
Washington 148, 151, 153, 156, 159, 162
GAREY, Enoch B. 480
GARFIELD
Harry A. 486, 571
James A. 13, 17, 107, 109, 111, 113, 115, 117, 119, 121, 124
James R. 31*, 44
GARLAND
Augustus H. 29*, 41, 120, 122, 124, 127, 129, 281*, 392*, 393*
David S. 62
Hamlin 583, 609
James 82, 83, 85
James M. 461
Landon C. 465, 479, 484
Mahlon M. 172, 175, 178, 577
Peter A. 245
Rice 79, 80, 82, 84
Rufus K. 393
Thomas J. 510, 521
GARLINGTON, Ernest A. 402
GARMATZ, Edward A. 223, 226, 229, 233, 236, 239, 242, 245, 248, 252, 255, 258, 261
GARNER
Alfred B. 163
James W. 571
John Nance 14, 18*, 155, 157, 160, 163, 166, 169, 172, 175, 179, 182, 189, 192, 195, 196, 198, 199, 202, 206, 209, 212
Mabel Klockars 501
GARNETT
Alexander Y.P. 569
James M. (b. 1770) 59, 61
James M. (b. 1840) 480, 566, 570
Muscoe R.H. 99, 101, 103, 393
Robert S. 67, 69, 70, 72, 73
GARNSEY, Daniel G. 73, 74
GARRARD
James 308
Kenner 409
GARRECHT, Francis A. 272
GARRETSON, Ellis L. 579
GARRETT
Abraham E. 115
Alexander C. 507, 519
Amos 449
Augustus 451*
Clyde L. 208, 212
Daniel E. 169, 175, 182, 185, 189, 192, 195, 198
Finis J. 157, 160, 163, 166, 169, 172, 175, 178, 182, 185, 189, 192, 272*
George A. 430*
Henry E. 571
John W. 423, 431, 432, 433, 439
L.P. 564
Thomas E. 574
William A. 566
GARREY, Walter E. 571
GARRIGA, Mariano S. 525
GARRIGAN, Philip J. 529
GARRIGUES, James A. 285
GARRISON
Cornelius K. 461, 549
Daniel 71, 73
Earl G. 444

Edwin R. 531
George T. 126, 129
James H. 536
Lindley M. 31, 40
William C. 402
Winfred E. 467, 476
GARROW, Nathaniel 74
GARTH
Schuyler E. 531
William W. 120
GARTLAND, Francis X. 528
GARTNER, Fred C. 211
GARTRELL, Lucius J. 100, 102, 392
GARVAN
Francis P. 509, 608
Mrs. Francis P. 608
GARVER, J.M. 453
GARVEY
Dan E. 280
Eugene A. 525
Thomas V. 479
GARVIN
Clifton G., Jr. 553
Lucius F.C. 362
William S. 90
GARY
Elbert H. 554, 568
Eugene B. 365
Frank B. 160, 365
Hampson 427
J. Vaughan 222, 225, 228, 231, 234, 237, 241, 244, 247, 250
James A. 30, 43
John Y. 461
Raymond S. 355
GASAWAY, Ora 557
GASMAN, George A. 558
GASQUE
Allard H. 185, 188, 192, 195, 198, 202, 205, 208
Bessie H. 208
GASSAWAY, P.L. 205
GASSER
Herbert S. 605
Lorenzo D. 400
GASSON, Thomas I. 466
GASSWAY, Augustus 449
GASTON
Athelson 149
Herbert E. 443
J.B. 457
William 320, 450
William (N.C.) 64, 65
GATCH
Claude 460
Lee 593
T.M. 460
Thomas L. 416
Thomas M. 478, 484, 486*
GATES
Caleb F., Jr. 469
Charles W. 376
Frank C. 575
George A. 471, 479
Horatio 401
Merrill E. 465, 480
Noah P. 465*
Ralph E. 303
Robert M. 573
Samuel G. 486
Seth M. 84, 86
Thomas 9*
Thomas S. 479, 570
Thomas S., Jr. 35, 47, 399*, 608
William F., Jr. 517
GATEWOOD, Arthur R. 611
GATHERCOAL, Edmund N. 570, 609
GATHINGS, Ezekiel C. 209, 212, 216, 219, 222, 225, 229, 232, 235, 238, 241, 244, 247, 251, 254
GATHRIGHT, Thomas S. 482
GATLIN, Alfred M. 71
GATOS, Harry C. 575
GATTI, John 461
GATTON, Harper 576
GATZERT, Bailey 461
GAUD, William S. 443
GAUDIOSI, Albert V. 587
GAUGLER, R.C. 543
GAUL, Samuel 557
GAULEY, Robert D. 593
GAULT
Benjamin F. 481
Franklin B. 472
W.J. 458
GAUNT, John L., Jr. 586
GAUS
Charles H. 449
John M. 571
GAUSE, Lucien C. 118, 120
GAUSS, Clarence E. 425
GAVAGAN, Joseph A. 194, 198, 201, 204, 207, 211, 214, 217
GAVER, Mary V. 568
GAVIN
Frank J. 548
James M. 401*, 415, 428
John 559
Leon H. 218, 221, 224, 228, 231, 234, 237, 240, 243, 246, 250
GAWTRY, Harrison E. 545*
GAY
Clyde F. 548
Edward J. 130, 132, 173, 177, 312
Edwin F. 566
Frank B. 502
Peter 602
GAYDOS, Joseph M. 259, 262, 266
GAYLE
John 90, 277
June W. 148
R. Finley, Jr. 571
W.A. 457
GAYLER, Noel 416, 444
GAYLEY, James 594
GAYLORD
Edmund S. 566
James M. 95
R.M. 578
GAYNOR, William J. 458
GAZLAY, James W. 71
GEAR, John H. 132, 134, 140, 142, 145, 147, 304*
GEARHART, Bertrand W. 202, 206, 209, 212, 216, 219, 222
GEARIN, John M. 157, 356
GEARY
Edward R. 474
John W. 359, 408, 409*, 410, 461*
Thomas J. 134, 136, 139
GEBHARD
Bruno 498
John 70
GEDDES
George W. 124, 126, 128, 131
James 64
John 451*
GEE, Walter S. 578
GEELAN, James P. 219
GEER
Bennette E. 470
Theodore T. 356
GEHAN, Mark H. 460
GEHRING, C.F. 500*
GEHRMANN, Bernard J. 205, 209, 212, 215
GIEGENGACK, Augustus E. 443
GEIGER, John H. 568
GEIGLE, F.R. 472
GEISREITER, Bert E. 460
GEISSENHAINER, Jacob A. 135, 138, 140
GEISSLER, Arthur H. 429
GELL-MANN, Murray 596, 606
GENOIS, Charles 457
GENSMAN, Lorraine M. 181
GENTER, Albert L. 601
GENTH, Frederick A. 565
GENTNER
Philip 502
William E., Jr. 417
GENTON, Reuben E. 101
GENTRY
Brady P. 234, 237
Byron B. 580
Charles B. 468
Meredith P. 85, 87, 90, 92, 94, 96, 393
W.L. 467
GENZ, L.F. 491
GENZBERGER, Earle N. 576
GEORGE
Edwin O. 546
Enoch 530
Henry, Jr. 165, 168
Isaac D. 558
James Z. 125, 128, 130, 132, 135, 137, 140, 143, 145, 326, 327
Joseph L. 455
Leo E. 559
Melvin C. 126, 128
Myron V. 226, 229, 232, 236, 239
Newell A. 242
W.H. Krome 543
W. Kyle 533
Walter F. 180, 183, 186, 190, 193, 196, 200, 203, 206, 209, 213, 216, 219, 223, 226, 229, 232, 235, 297
GERALD, Park S. 599
GERAN, Elmer H. 184
GERARD
James W. 428
John 453
Ralph W. 571
GERCKE, Daniel J. 529
GEREN, Paul F. 482
GERETY, Peter L. 528
GERHARDT, Charles H. 413, 414
GERHART, Emanuel V. 470, 472
John K. 416
GERHOLZ, Robert P. 575
GERKEN, Rudolph A. 524, 525
GERLACH
Charles L. 211, 215, 218, 221, 224
Hal W. 462
GERMAN, Obadiah 61, 62, 64, 344
GERMER, Lester H. 594
GERNERD, Fred B. 182
GEROW
Leonard T. 400, 405, 412, 413, 419
Richard O. 527
GERRER
Dom Gregory 497
GERREY, T.H. 557
GERRITY, Thomas P. 415
GERRODETTE, Frank H. 497
GERRY
James 85, 86
Elbridge (b. 1744) 3, 4*, 6, 14, 15, 51, 52, 319, 428
Elbridge (b. 1813) 93
Peter G. 169, 175, 178, 182, 185, 188, 192, 205, 208, 211, 215, 218, 221, 362, 363
GERSHWIN, Ira 584
GERSTENBERG, Richard 547
GERTY, Francis J. 571
GERVAIS, John L. 7
GESKE, Norman 502
GESNER, Conrad H. 514, 521
GESSAMAN, Myron B. 452
GEST
Joseph H. 498
William H. 132, 134
GESTER, George C. 564
GETTELL, Richard G. 476
GETTY
George W. 408, 409
J. Paul 547
GETTYS
Tom S. 253, 256, 259, 263, 266
GETZ
J. Lawrence 111, 113, 115
John I. 432
GEUTING, Joseph T., Jr. 577
GEWIN, Walter P. 271
GEYELIN, Philip L. 587
GEYER
Henry S. 95, 97, 99, 329
John 458
Lee E. 209, 212
GEZORK, Herbert 534
GHELSTON, David 6
GHERARDI, Bancroft 595
GHIORSO, Albert 608
GHOLSON
James H. 80
Samuel J. 81, 82
Thomas S. 393
Thomas, Jr. 61, 62, 63, 64, 66
GHORMLEY
Alfred M. 544
Robert L. 416
GIAIMO, Robert N. 241, 244, 248, 251, 254, 257, 260, 264
GIANERA, William C. 481
GIANNINI
A.P. 544
Lawrence M. 544
GIAUQUE, William F. 594, 596, 605
GIBBENS, Ray V. 577
GIBBES
James G. 452
R.W. 452
Robert 9
T.H. 452
W.H. 452
GIBBIN, John H., Jr. 600
GIBBINS, Henry 403
GIBBON
John 408*, 409
John H., Jr. 589
GIBBONS
A.S. 479*
Edmund F. 525
J.L. 558
James 523*, 528
John H. 483
John J. 271
Sam M. 248, 251, 254, 257, 261, 264
William 5
GIBBS
Addison C. 356
David P. 403
Florence R. 209
Frederic A. 600
George S. 403
Josiah W. 597, 609
R.C. 580
Richard 424, 435
Thomas F. 449
W. Benjamin 209
William C. 361
William D. 476
William F. 596, 610, 611
Wolcott 563
GIBSON
A.R. 461
Charles H. 130, 132, 135, 137, 140, 142, 317
Ernest W. 185, 189, 192, 195, 199, 202, 205, 208, 377
Ernest W., Jr. 212, 377*
Eustace 129, 131
Floyd B. 272
Foye G. 470
George 403
Henry R. 144, 146, 149, 152, 155
Hugh S. 424*, 432*, 435, 438
James 455
James King 113
John 458
John B. 358
John S. 213, 216, 219
K.S. 580
Matthew M. 533
Norman R. 594, 598
Paris 151, 154, 331
Phil S. 284
Randall L. 118, 121, 123, 125, 127, 130, 132, 135, 137, 312
Robert A. 508, 522
Robert F., Jr. 515, 522
Robert W. 533
Thomas L. 355
Walter 577
GIDDENS, Paul H. 471
GIDDINGS
De Witt C. 115, 117, 122
Franklin H. 573
Joshua R. 83, 84, 86, 88, 90, 92, 93, 95, 97, 99, 101
GIDEONSE, Harry D. 467
GIESY, J.B. 460
GIFFEN
Hilliard R. 567
J. Kelly 533
William A. 566
GIFFORD
Charles L. 180, 184, 187, 190, 194, 197, 200, 203, 207, 210, 213, 217, 220, 223
Edward W. 499
Oscar S. 136
Walter S. 429, 543, 603
GIHON, Albert L. 572
GILBEAU, Francis 460
GILBERT
Abijah 111, 114, 116, 293
Cass 567, 577, 578, 591, 603
Charles B. 477
Charles K. 512, 520
Edward 92
Eliphalet W. 469*
Ezekiel 53, 54
Felix 591
George G. 148, 150, 153, 156
Grove K. 563, 575*, 578, 594, 598
Jacob H. 243, 246, 249, 252, 256, 259
Mahlon N. 507
Newton W. 156
Ralph W. 180, 184, 187, 190, 197
Sylvester 66

Sylvio J. 450
William A. 99
William B. 272
GILBERTSON, Lyle I. 575
GILBRETH, Lillian M. 598, 603
GILCHRIST
Albert W. 293
Fred C. 197, 200, 203, 206, 210, 213, 216
Gibb 482
Harry L. 401
John J. 273, 337
GILDEA, James H. 205, 208
GILDERSLEEVE
Basil L. 570*
Virginia Crocheron 466, 603
GILES
Barney M. 412
Benjamin F. 411
Howard 607
William B. 51, 52, 53, 54, 55, 57, 58, 59, 61, 62, 63, 64, 378*
William F. 89
William L. 475
GILFILLAN
Calvin W. 113
Francis 528
Francois A. 478
James 324*, 444
John B. 130
GILHAMS, Clarence C. 156, 158
GILKESON, Robert F. 551
GILL
D.W. 451*
E.G. 576
Hiram C. 461*
James P. 572
John, Jr. 156, 159, 162
Joseph J. 149, 151
Laura Drake 466
Michael J. 168
Patrick F. 162, 165
Theodore 563
Thomas P. 248
Turner A. 455
William H. 413, 414
Wilson L. 594
GILLEM, Alvan C., Jr. 405, 411, 412*, 415
GILLEN, Courtland C. 196
GILLER, Joseph A. 472
GILLESPIE
Cornelius 480*
Dean M. 216, 219
Eugene P. 138
Frank 200
George DeN. 507, 522
James 53, 54, 55, 58
Oscar W. 155, 157, 160, 163
Robert J. 570
GILLET
Charles W. 141, 143, 146, 148, 151, 154
Ransom H. 79, 81
GILLETT
Arthur D.S. 486
Frederick H. 140, 143, 145, 148, 151, 153, 156, 159, 162, 165, 168, 171, 174, 176, 177, 179, 180, 183, 184, 187, 190, 194, 321
James N. 152, 155, 283
GILLETTE
Edward H. 123
Francis 96, 287
Guy M. 200, 203, 206, 210, 213, 216, 226, 229, 232, 305*
John M. 573
Robert S. 550
William 603
Wilson D. 215, 218, 221, 224, 228, 231
GILLIAM, Jackson 517, 520
GILLIE, George W. 210, 213, 216, 220, 223
GILLIGAN
Frank P. 572
John J. 253, 354
GILLIN
John L. 573
John P. 563
GILLIS, James L. 101
GILLISPIE, Gregory 609
GILLON, Alexander 53
GILLULY, James 576, 607
GILMAN
Alfred A. 512
Benjamin A. 265
Charles J. 100
Daniel C. 467, 473, 565
John T. 6, 337*
Nicholas 6, 51, 52, 53, 59, 60, 61, 62, 64, 337
Richard C. 478
GILMER
Ben S. 543
George R. 69, 74, 78, 295*
John A. 101, 103, 393
Thomas E. 471
Thomas W. 26, 42, 87, 88, 378
William F. 227
GILMORE
Albert F. 536
Alfred 93, 95
Art 557
D.S. 492
Eddy 585
Edward 168
Eugene A. 473
F.C. 462*
Frank 557
John 76, 78
John W. 472
Joseph A. 338
Joseph M. 526
Samuel L. 162
W.S. 573
William J. 353
GILMOUR, Richard 525
GILPATRIC, Roswell L. 399
GILPIN
Charles 458
Charles S. 611
Henry D. 25, 41
GILROY
Frank D. 587
Thomas F. 458
GILRUTH, Robert R. 591, 594, 597, 608, 611
GILSON, Charles P. 516
GILSTRAP, Sam P. 432
GINDER, Philip D. 405
GINDRAT, John 457
GINGER, Lyman V. 578
GINGERY, Don 205, 208
GINGRICH
Arnold 596
John 418
GINN, R.B. 264
GINSBURG, Charles 608
GINZTON, Edward L. 598
GIPSON, Lawrence H. 587, 591
GIRARD, Frank 574
GIRDLER, Tom M. 568, 596
GIROD, Nicholas 457
GIST
Joseph 70, 72, 73
States R. 395*
William H. 365
GITLIN, David 592, 599
GITTINS, Robert H. 168
GLACKENS, William J. 607
GLADDEN, A.H. 452
GLADE, Earl J. 460
GLADFELTER, Millard E. 482
GLARNER, Fritz 593
GLASCOCK
John R. 127
Thomas 80, 82
GLASER, Donald A. 594, 606
GLASGOW
Ellen 584, 598
Hugh 64, 65
GLASPELL, Susan 583
GLASS
Carter 31, 39, 152, 155, 158, 160, 163, 166, 169, 172, 175, 179, 182, 186, 189, 192, 195, 199, 202, 205, 208, 212*, 215, 216, 218, 222, 380, 603, 609
H. Bentley 564*
Joseph S. 528
Presley T. 131, 133
Taylor 450
GLASSCOCK
Thomas O. 457
William E. 383
GLATFELTER, Samuel F. 185
GLEASON
Henry A. 574
James E. 590
John S., Jr. 568
Patrick H. 559
S. Everett 591
Thomas W. 558
GLEESON
Edward J. 480
Francis D. 526
Richard A. 481
GLEN
Henry 53, 54, 55, 56
James 9
John 449
Thomas L. 150
GLENDINNING, James 460
GLENN
James W. 552
John 493
John H., Jr. 594, 598, 599, 609
John T. 449
John W. 450
Laurence A. 525
Luther J. 449
Milton W. 239, 243, 246, 249
Otis F. 190, 193, 196, 301
Robert B. 348
William 567
GLENNAN, T. Keith 444
GLENNON, John J. 523, 524
GLICK
G. Wayne 470
George W. 306
GLIDDEN, William R. 572
GLONINGER, John 64
GLORIEUX, Alphonsus J. 525
GLOSSBRENNER
Adam J. 109, 111
Jacob 531
GLOSTER, Hugh M. 476
GLOVER
David D. 193, 196, 199
John 406
John M. (b. 1822) 116, 119, 121
John M. (b. 1852) 130, 133
Roy H. 543
William 8
GLOYD, Howard K. 498
GLUCK, Maxwell H. 425
GLUECK, Sheldon 608
GLUHAREFF, Michael E. 610
GLYNN
James P. 170, 173, 176, 179, 186, 189, 193
Martin H. 148, 345
William E. 454
GNICHTEL, Frederick W. 462
GOBBLE, Aaron 465
GOBIN
Hillary A. 466, 469
GOCKEL, Thomas R. 557*
GOCKELN, F. William 470
GODARD, Charles W. 449
GODBOLD, John C. 271
GODDARD
A.E. 460
Calvin 56, 57
Frederick P. 515
James L. 592
O.F. 331
Robert H. 597*
Samuel P. 280
William H. 566
GODDING, W.W. 571
GODEL, Kurt 595
GODFREY
Edward S., Jr. 572, 610
Hollis 470
GODLEY, G. McMurtrie 426, 431
GODOWSKY, Leopold, Jr. 601
GODSDEN, James 433
GODSHALK, William 124, 126
GODWIN
Blake-More 502
Hannibal L. 160, 162, 165, 168, 171, 175, 178
Mille E., Jr. 380
GOEBEL
Herman P. 157, 160, 163
Louis W. 534*
William 309
GOEBELL, P.W. 564
GOEKE, J. Henry 166, 169
GOEPPERT-MAYER, Maria 606
GOERTZ, Raymond C. 601
GOESSMANN, Charles A. 565
GOETHALS, George W. 401*, 594, 596, 603
GOETZE, Arthur B. 493, 554
GOETZMANN, William H. 587
GOFF
Abe M. 223
F.H. 545
Guy D. 189, 192, 195, 383
Milton B. 479*
Nathan 28, 29, 42, 129, 131, 134, 169, 172, 175, 271, 383
GOFORTH
John L. 572
N.B. 467*
GOGGIN, William L. 85, 87, 88, 92
GOHEEN, Robert F. 479
GOLAND, Martin 567
GOLD
Ivan 609
Nathan 3, 10
Thomas R. 61, 62, 65
GOLDBERG
Arthur J. 36, 46, 270, 595
Irving L. 271
Leo 564
Reuben L. 585
Solomon C. 598
GOLDBLATT
Harry 572, 589
Maurice 497
GOLDEN
Charles F. 531
James S. 226, 229, 232
GOLDENWEISER, Emanuel A. 566
GOLDER, Benjamin 188, 192, 195, 198
GOLDFOGLE, Henry M. 151, 154, 157, 160, 162, 165, 168, 178
GOLDMAN
Eric F. 591
Henry 600
Hetty 591
Robert P. 537
GOLDMARK, Peter C. 594
GOLDNER, Jacob H. 536
GOLDSBOROUGH
Charles 59, 60, 61, 62, 63, 65, 316
Louis M. 417, 483
Phillips Lee 193, 197, 200, 317, 318
Robert 5
Robert H. 63, 65, 66, 79, 80, 316*
T. Alan 180, 184, 187, 190, 193, 197, 200, 203, 207, 210
GOLDSMITH, Alfred N. 580, 598
GOLDSTEIN
Alvin H. 583
Herbert S. 537
I. 455*
GOLDTHWAITE, George T. 113, 115, 118, 277*
GOLDWATER
Barry, Jr. 257, 260, 263
Barry M. 19, 232, 235, 238, 241, 244, 247, 257, 260, 263, 280
GOLDWYN, Samuel 608
GOLDZIER, Julius 139
GOLLADAY
Edward I. 115
Jacob S. 110, 112
GOLTRA, Edward B. 559
GOLTZ, Gene 587
GOMBERG, Moses 565, 596, 603, 604
GONZALES
George A. 461
William E. 426, 435
GONZALEZ
Antonio C. 427, 434, 439
Henry B. 247, 250, 253, 256, 260, 263, 266
GOOCH
Daniel L. 150, 153
Daniel W. 100, 102, 104, 106, 116
William 9*
GOOD
James W. 30, 40, 161, 164, 167, 170, 173, 176, 180
Robert A. 599, 600
Robert C. 439
GOODALE, George L. 563
GOODALL, Louis B. 174, 177
GOODE
G. Brown 502
John, Jr. 120, 122, 124, 393*
Patrick G. 83, 84, 86
Samuel 56
William J. 574
William O. 87, 98, 99, 101, 103
GOODELL
Charles E. 243, 246, 249, 252, 256, 259, 346
David H. 338
Helen 597
Henry H. 475
Thomas D. 570
GOODEN

Reginald H. 514, 521
Robert B. 512
GOODENOW
Robert 95
Rufus K. 93
GOODHUE
Albert 498
Benjamin 51, 52*, 53*, 54, 55, 319
Bertram G. 590
F. Abbot 545
Grace 20
GOODIN, John R. 118
GOODING, Frank R. 176, 180, 183, 186, 190, 298, 299
GOODLAND, Walter S. 386
GOODLETT, John A. 457
GOODLING, George A. 246, 250, 256, 259, 262, 266
GOODLOE, William C. 424
GOODMAN
Aaron C. 551
John 3
Louis J. 537
Philip H. 450
GOODNIGHT
Cloyd 466
Isaac 135, 137, 140
James L. 485
GOODNOW, Frank J. 473, 571
GOODPASTER, Andrew J. 399, 404, 419
GOODPASTURE, Ernest W. 607, 610
GOODRICH
B.F. 547*
Caspar F. 419*
Chauncey 53, 54, 55, 60, 61, 62, 63, 287, 453
David M. 547
Elizur 55
Frances 586
Herbert F. 271
James P. 303
John Z. 95, 97
Lloyd 502, 592
Milo 115
GOODSELL
Charles T. 473
Daniel A. 530
GOODSON
Orr 499
W. Kenneth 531
GOODWILLIE, Eugene W. 491
GOODWIN
Angier L. 217, 220, 223, 226, 229, 233
Daniel R. 479, 482
Forrest 168
Frederick D. 512, 522
George E. 585
Godfrey G. 187, 190, 194, 197
Henry C. 97, 101
Ichabod 338
James 545*
John B. 449*
John N. 104
Philip A. 201, 204, 207
Philip L. 591
R.H. 452
Richard R. 449*
Robert C. 482
Robert K. 210
William N., Jr. 608
William S. 164, 167, 170, 173, 176
William W. 563, 570*
Williams F. 594
GOODWYN
Albert T. 142
James T. 452*
John L. 457
Peterson 58, 59, 61, 62, 63, 64, 66, 67
Thomas J. 452
GOODYEAR, Charles 90, 108, 600
GOODYKOONTZ, Wells 179, 182
GOOKIN, Charles 9
GORDON
Douglas H. 480
Edward C. 485
George A. 429, 433
George W. 160, 163, 166
Harry H. 592
Isaac G. 359
J.R. 595
James (b. 1739) 52, 53
James (b. 1833) 162, 327
James M. 483
James W. 322
John 472
John B. 116, 118, 120, 122, 137, 139, 142, 296*
John F. 547
Kermit 444
Lincoln 424, 473
Merritt J. 381
Patrick 9
Robert B. 149, 151
Samuel 86, 90
Thomas 10
Thomas S. 216, 219, 223, 226, 229, 232, 235, 238
William (b. 1763) 55, 56
William (b. 1862) 169, 172, 175
William F. 77, 78, 80
William J., Jr. 514, 519
GORDONE, Charles 587
GORE
Albert A. 212, 215, 218, 221, 225, 228, 231, 234, 237, 240, 243, 247, 250, 253, 256, 259, 371
Christopher 63, 65, 319*
George W. 470
Howard M. 32*, 45, 383
Thomas P. 160, 163, 166, 169, 172, 175, 178, 198, 201, 205, 355*
GORGAS
Josiah 465, 481
William C. 403, 569, 597, 603
William L. 453*
GORHAM
Benjamin 68, 69, 74, 76, 79
Charles T. 433
Nathaniel 4, 5, 6
GORMAN
Arthur P. 125, 127, 130, 132, 135, 137, 140, 142, 145, 153, 156, 317*
Daniel M. 525
Emily C. 401
George E. 167
James S. 137, 140
John J. 180, 187
Lawrence C. 471
Patrick E. 557
Paul A. 554
R.B. 462*
Thomas K. 525, 528
William P. 461
Willis A. 93, 94, 406
GORSKI
Chester C. 227
Martin 216, 219, 223, 226
GORSLINE, Douglas W. 593
GORST, Charles C. 593
GORTON
Lewis G. 475
Othniel 10, 361
Samuel 538
GOSHORN
Alfred T. 498
Jacob 451
GOSLINE, J.E. 552
GOSNELL, Harold C. 517, 522
GOSS
A.S. 578
Charles A. 333
Edward W. 196, 199
James Hamilton 111
Wesley P. 610
Wilbur H. 608
William F. 573
GOSSETT
Charles C. 219, 299*
Ed Lee 212, 215, 218, 221, 225, 228, 231
William T. 565
GOTT
Daniel 91, 93
E.N. 544
Edwin H. 493, 554
GOTTLIEB, Adolph 607
GOTTSCHALK
Louis 567
Robert 444
GOUCHER, John F. 471
Lewis K. 568
GOUGH, Lewis K. 568
GOULD
Arthur R. 187, 190, 193, 315
Benjamin A. 563
Charles H. 568
Curtis 436
Daughly 457
George J. 549
Gordon H.P. 552
Herman D. 93
Jay 549
Kingdon, Jr. 432
Laurence M. 467, 564
Norman J. 171, 174, 178, 181
Robert S. 372
Samuel B. 465, 477
Samuel W. 165
GOULDEN, Joseph A. 154, 157, 160, 162, 168, 171
GOURDIN, Theodore 64
GOURLEY, H.J. 459
GOUVERNEUR, Nicholas 544
GOVAN, Andrew R. 70, 72, 73
GOVE
Samuel F. 110
William P. 452
GOWANS, Alan 499
GOWDY, John 530
GOWEN, James 547*
GOWEY, J.F. 458
GRABACH, John R. 593
GRABAU, Amadens W. 597
GRABLE, E.F. 557
GRABOWSKI, Bernard F. 248, 251
GRACE
Eugene G. 544, 568, 596
J. Peter 599
John P. 451*
Thomas L. 469, 528
William R. 458*
GRAD, Arthur 479
GRADY
Benjamin F. 138, 141
Henry F. 429, 430*
J. Harold 450
Thomas E. 382
GRAF, Joseph 470
GRAFF
Frederic 572
Joseph V. 142, 145, 147, 150, 153, 156, 158, 161
GRAFLY, Charles 607
GRAFTON
Charles C. 508, 509
T.W. 536
GRAHAM
Charles K. 408
Clarence R. 568
Donald M. 546
Edward A. 457
Edward K. 477*
Evarts A. 565, 590
Frank A. 455
Frank P. 224, 349, 477, 597
Gene S. 587
George L. 471
George S. 169, 172, 175, 178, 182, 185, 188, 192, 195
Henry T. 471
Herbert W. 595
Horace F. 376
James 79, 81, 83, 84, 86, 90
James H. 103
James M. 161, 164, 167
John 435
John H. 141
Katherine 604
Lewis 558
Louis E. 211, 215, 218, 221, 224, 228, 231, 234
M.D. 393
Martha 592, 593
Milton H. 459
Robert B. 455*
Samuel J. 273
Walter S.F. 469
William (Ala.) 457
William (Ind.) 82
William (Va.) 485
William A. 16, 26, 42, 84, 86, 347*, 393
William F., Jr. 603
William H. 146, 149, 152, 157, 160, 163
William J. (b. 1872) 173, 176, 180, 183, 272*
William J. (b. 1877) 568
William P. 482
GRAINGER
Charles F. 456
Isaac B. 545
GRAKELOW, Charles H. 574
GRALLA, Arthur R. 418
GRAMMER, Elijah S. 199, 381
GRANAHAN
Kathryn O'Hay 240, 243, 246, 444
William T. 221, 228, 231, 234, 237
GRANATA, Peter C. 196
GRANBERRY, J.H. 600
GRANBERY, John C. 530
GRAND, Gordon 550*
GRANDGENT, Charles H. 566, 577
GRANFIELD, William J. 194, 197, 200, 203
GRANGE, Wallace B. 593
GRANGER
Amos P. 99, 101
Bradley F. 104
Daniel L.D. 154, 157, 160, 459
Francis 16, 26, 43, 81, 84, 86
Gideon 445
Gordon 409*
J.V.N. 576
Lester B. 579
Miles T. 132
Walter K. 215, 218, 222, 225, 228, 231
GRANJON, Henry 529
GRANT
A. Raymond 531
Abraham P. 83
Frederick D. 423, 424
George M. 206, 209, 212, 216, 219, 222, 225, 228, 232, 235, 238, 241, 244, 247
Heber J. 537
Hugh G. 423, 438
Hugh J. 458
James B. 285
Jedediah M. 460
John G. 162
Richard F. 575
Robert 578
Robert A. 210, 213, 216, 220, 223
Ulysses S. 13, 16, 17, 400, 406*, 407, 408, 409*, 597
Ulysses S. Grant, III 570
Walter S. 419
Whit M. 458
William T. 491
GRANTLAND, Seaton 80, 82
GRANT-SMITH, Ulysses 423, 439
GRANVILLE
Maurice F. 553
William A. 471
W. 589
GRANVILLE-SMITH, W. 589
GRASON, William 316
GRASSI, John A. 471
GRASSO, Ella T. 260, 264
GRATIAT, Charles 402
GRATZ
Hyman 547
William 559
GRAU, Shirley Ann 587
GRAUER, Gerhard W. 534
GRAVATT
John J. 513, 522
William L. 509, 522
GRAVE, Caswell 573
GRAVEL, Mike R. 257, 279, 260, 263
GRAVELY, Joseph J. 110
GRAVES
Alexander 128
Anson R. 508, 522
Benjamin B. 465
Charles H. 437
David Bibb 278*
Dixie Bibb 206, 278
Eugene S. 553
Frank P. 484, 487
Frederick R. 508
Gerald W. 455
Henry L. 466
Mortimer 566
R.B. 456
Samuel 476
Thomas A. 486
Walley W. 330
William J. 80, 82, 84
GRAY
Albert E. 498
Alexander 607
Asa 501, 563*, 597
Bowman 552*
Bowman, Jr. 552*
Campbell 512, 521
Carl R. 548, 554
Charles M. 451
Charles O. 483
Clifton D. 466
David 430
Duncan M. 513, 520
E.L. 455
Edward M. 476
Edward W. 171, 174
Edwin 56, 57, 58, 59, 61,

62, 63
Elisha 594
Finly H. 164, 167, 170, 200, 203, 206
G.W. 460
George 129, 132, 134, 137, 139, 142, 144, 271, 291
Gordon 399, 477, 608
Harold 466
Harold E. 550*
Harry J. 554
Henry 393
Henry P. 577
Hiram 83
Horace 269, 320
Isaac P. 302*, 433
James 457
James A. 552*
John C. 69
John H. 566
John P. 571
John S. 547
Joseph A. 205, 208
Joseph M.M. 465
Kenneth J. 235, 238, 242, 245, 248, 251, 255, 258, 261, 264
Landon C. 569
Mark R. 577
Norman B. 388
Oscar L. 170, 173
Peter F. 455
Peter W. 393
Ralph L. 543
Reid B. 611
Thomas T. 611
Tilbee D., II 575
W.H., Jr. 470
Walter H. 513, 519
William C. 508, 521
GRAYSON
Cary T. 569
William 7, 51, 378
William J. 80, 81
GRAZIANI, Sante 591
GRECO, Charles P. 525
GREDE, William J. 578
GREELEY
Edwin S. 579
Horace 17, 91
J.C. 454
GREELY, Adolphus W. 403, 594
GREEN
Allen J. 452
Ashbel 479, 532
Aubrey D. 577
Byram 88
Christopher 460
Clarence W. 474
Constance McLaughlin 587
Cordes B. 481
Dwight H. 301
Edith 237, 240, 243, 246, 250, 253, 256, 259, 262, 265
Edward 549
Ernest 558
Floyd F. 452
Francis J. 529
Fred W. 323
Frederick W. 95, 97
George H. 579
George J. 574
Grafton 370
Henry D. 149, 152, 359
Henry W. 340
Howard W. 568
Innis 75, 76
Isaiah L. 59, 60, 62
James S. 91, 93, 99, 100, 102, 329, 425
John 557
Joseph 528
Joseph A. 402, 411
Joseph C. 431*
Lewis W. 471, 482
Marshall 430
Otis W. 577
Paul 583
Richard 449
Robert A. 186, 189, 193, 196, 200, 203, 206, 209, 213, 216
Robert S. 130, 341
Roy M. 468
Rufus S. 470
Russell H. 552
Samuel A. 450
Samuel S. 568
Theodore F. 208, 211, 215, 218, 221, 224, 228, 231, 234, 237, 240, 243, 363*
Thomas 8
Thomas H. 402
Traill 474
W. Henry 532
Warren E. 367
Wharton J. 128, 131
William 609
William (Kans.) 462
William J. 250, 253, 256, 259, 262, 266
William J., Jr. 221, 228, 231, 234, 237, 240, 243, 246, 250
William M. (b. 1798) 506, 520
William M. (b. 1876) 511, 520
William R. 164, 167, 170, 173, 176, 180, 183, 187, 190, 273
Willis 84, 85, 87
GREENAWAY, Emerson 568
GREENBERG
Bernard G. 592
Max 559
Paul 587
GREENBLATT, Milton 597
GREENE
Albert C. 90, 92, 94, 361
Clarence W. 474, 571
Douglass T. 415*
Eugene H. 536
Evarts B. 567
Frank L. 166, 169, 172, 175, 179, 182, 185, 189, 192, 195, 377
George S. 407, 572
George W., 112
Henry A. 410, 419
Jacob L. 545
John P. 486
Michael F. 559
Nathaniel 403, 406
Nehemiah 306
Norman J. 575
R.H. 459
Ray 55, 56, 57, 361
Richard L. 485
Richard W. 361
S.H. 471*
Wallace M., Jr. 416
Walter K. 486
William 9*, 10
William C. 570
William L. 146
William S. 145, 148, 151, 153, 156, 159, 162, 165, 168, 171, 174, 177, 180, 184
GREENEBAUM, Robert J. 492
GREENEWALT, Crawford H. 546, 590, 596
GREENHALGE, Frederic T. 135, 320
GREENHOW, Robert 459
GREENLEAF
Halbert S. 128, 138
James L. 573
GREENLIEF, Francis F. 402
GREENLY, William L. 322
GREEMAN, Edward W. 133
GREENOUGH
John 475, 566
Robert B. 565*
GREENUP, Christopher 52*, 53, 308
GREENWAY
Emerson 600
G. Lauder 492
Isabella S. 199, 202
GREENWOOD
Alfred B. 96, 98, 100
Arthur H. 183, 187, 190, 193, 196, 200, 203, 206
Ernest 230
Marion 589
GREER, David H. 509, 520
GREEVER, Paul R. 205, 209
GREGG
Alexander (bishop) 506, 522
Alexander W. 155, 157, 160, 163, 166, 169, 172, 175
Andrew 52, 53, 54, 55, 56, 57, 58, 59, 60, 61*, 63, 358
Clifford C. 499*
Curtis H. 166, 577
David L. 430
David M. 408, 409*
Donald E. 589
Henry H. 570
Hugh 339
J.A. 486
James 452
James M. 100
John 392
Richard N. 499
GREGORY
Clint 459
D.T. 531
Dudley S. 91
Edmund B. 403
Elisha H. 569
Eugene J. 460
Herbert E. 497
Horace 589, 592, 600
J.C. 456
John 579, 591
John M. (b. 1804) 378
John M. (b. 1822) 472, 473
Luther E. 418
Noble J. 207, 210, 213, 216, 220, 223, 226, 229, 232, 236, 239
P.M. 460
Stephen S. 564
Tappan 565, 576
Thomas W. 31, 32, 41
William 362
William K. 611
William S. 455
William V. 190, 193, 197, 200, 203
GREIG, John 86
GREIGG, Stanley L. 252
GREINER, Russell F. 580
GRENNELL, George, Jr. 76, 77, 79, 81, 82
GRESHAM
Perry E. 466, 536
Walter 141
Walter Q. 29*, 38, 39, 43, 272, 409
GRESSLE, Lloyd E.D. 518, 519
GRETEMAN, Frank 529
GREULICH, William 611
GREVSTAD, Nicolay A. 434, 439
GREW, Joseph C. 431, 438*, 609
GREY
Benjamin E. 95, 96
Catherine 502
J.D. 534
GREYWACZ, Kathryn 500
GRIBBIN, Robert E. 512, 522
GRIBBLE, W.C., Jr. 401
GRIBBS, Roman S. 453
GRIDER
George W. 253, 570
Henry 87, 89, 104, 106, 108
GRIDLEY, Richard 402
GRIEPENTROG, Carl W. 557
GRIER
Harry D.M. 499
James H. 533
Robert C. 269
William 416
GRIEST, William W. 163, 166, 169, 172, 175, 178, 182, 185, 188, 194, 195
GRIEVE, Miller 426
GRIFFIN
Anthony J. 174, 178, 181, 185, 188, 191, 194, 198, 201, 204
Charles 408*, 409
Charles D. 416, 417
Charles H. 255, 258, 262
Cyrus 5, 7
Daniel J. 168, 171, 174
Edward D. 486
Herbert 580
Isaac 64, 65
James A. 529
James B. 611
James F. 577
James H. 484
James T. 493
John B. 459*
John K. 80, 81, 83, 85
Levi T. 140
Michael 141, 144, 147
Oscar O., Jr. 587
Robert P. 239, 242, 245, 249, 252*, 255, 258, 261, 264, 323
Robert S. 418
S. Marvin 297
Sam S. 450
Samuel 51, 52, 53
Thomas 58
Thomas J. 577
William A. 529
William V. 575
GRIFFING, Robert P., Jr. 499
GRIFFIS, Stanton 423, 427, 435, 437
GRIFFITH
Francis M. 145, 147, 150, 153
Harold M. 595
Ivor 570, 609
John K. 207, 210
L.A. 452
Paul H. 568
Samuel 115
Virgil 328
William 580
GRIFFITHS
David S. 461
Martha W. 236, 239, 242, 245, 249, 252, 255, 258, 261, 265
Percy W. 218, 221, 224
GRIFFITTS, Thomas 458*
GRIGGS
Herbert L. 544
James M. 145, 147, 150, 153, 155, 158, 161
John W. 30*, 41, 341
Robert F. 575, 593
GRIMES
J.E. 557
James W. 102, 104, 106, 108, 110, 112, 304*
John 529
Thomas W. 132, 134
William H. 585
William M. 415
GRIMKE
Archibald H. 611
John F. 451
GRIMM, H.P. 547
GRIMMELSMAN
Henry J. 526
Joseph 474*, 480, 487
GRIMSHAW
Arthur P. 455*
Jonathan 455
GRINER
George W., Jr. 413, 414, 415
John F. 557
GRINNELL
George B. 609
Henry 566
Joseph 87, 89, 91, 93, 569
Josiah B. 106, 108
Moses H. 84
GRINSTEAD, James F. 456
GRISCOM
Joseph H. 449
Lloyd C. 424, 431*, 435
Ludlow 591
W. Woodnut 594
GRISHAM, George 557
GRISSOM
Eugene 571
Virgil I. 594
GRISWOLD
A. Whitney 487
Alexander V. 505, 519
Dwight 233, 334*
Francis H. 419
Gaylord 58
Glenn H. 196, 200, 203, 206
Harry W. 212
Jared 453
John Ashley 112
John Augustus 107, 108, 110
John N.A. 548
Matthew (b. 1714) 8, 10
Matthew (b. 1833) 138, 143
Morley 336
Oscar W. 405*, 412*
Roger 53, 54, 55, 56, 57, 287
Sheldon M. 509, 519, 522
Stanley 61, 352
GROBMAN, Arnold B. 499
GROBSTEIN, Clifford 573
GROESBECK
Alexander J. 322
Herman V.S. 387
William S. 17, 101
GROGAN, John J. 557
GRONDAHL, Lars O. 607
GRONNA, Asle J. 157, 160, 162*, 165, 169, 171, 175, 178, 350
GRONOUSKI, John A. 36, 43, 435
GROOME, James B. 123, 125, 127, 317*
GROPIUS, Walter 590, 591
GROSE, George R. 469, 481, 530
GROSHANS, Werner 593
GROSS
Chaim 589
Chester H. 211, 218, 221, 224

Courtlandt S. 548*
Edward Z. 453
Ezra C. 68
Hal R. 517
Harold R. 226, 229, 232, 235, 239, 242, 245, 248, 252, 255, 258, 261, 264
Mason W. 480
Paul M. 564
Robert E. 589, 599, 600
Samuel 68, 70
Samuel D. 569
William H. 524, 528
Willis F. 536
GROSSCUP, Peter S. 272
GROSSMAN
Herman 558*
Marcus A. 572
Morton 591
GROSVENOR
Charles H. 131, 133, 135, 141, 143, 146, 149, 151, 154, 157
Gilbert H. 578, 609
Graham B. 544
Melville B. 578
Thomas P. 62, 64, 65
GROSZ, George 603
GROTE, Augustus R. 497
GROUCHY, Alex, Jr. 450
GROUT
Jonathan 51
Josiah 376
William W. 126, 131, 133, 136, 139, 141, 144, 147, 149
GROVE, William B. 52, 53, 54, 55, 56, 57
GROVER
Asa P. 110
D. Lawrence 272
James R., Jr. 249, 252, 256, 259, 262, 265
LaFayette 101, 121, 124, 126, 356*
Martin 90
GROVES
Mrs. Frederic A. 579
John W. 456
Robert W. 575
GROW
Galusha A. 95, 97, 99, 101, 103, 104, 105, 141, 143, 146, 149, 152
Robert W. 415*
GRUBBS, Daniel W. 454
GRUBER
Edmund L. 419
F. 498
GRUENEWALD, Max 493
GRUENING, Ernest 241, 244, 247, 251, 254, 279, 610
GRUENTHER, Alfred M. 399, 404, 569, 599, 603, 609
GRUMMAN
Leroy R. 597
Paul 499, 502
GRUMMOND, S.B. 453
GRUNDY
Felix 25, 41, 63, 64, 76, 78, 80, 81, 83, 85, 308, 369*
Joseph R. 195, 360
GRUNERT
George 411, 412
R.W. 551
GRUNSKY, Carl E. 497, 572
GRUPPE, Karl H. 579, 610
GRUTKA, Andrew G. 526
GUBBINS, George P. 557
GUBBRUD, Archie 368
GUBSER, Charles S. 232, 235, 238, 241, 244, 248, 251, 254, 257, 260, 263
GUDE, Gilbert 255, 258, 261, 264
GUDGER, James M. 154, 157, 165, 168
GUENTHER, Richard W. 126, 129, 131, 134
GUERNSEY
Frank E. 159, 162, 165, 168, 171
George H. 457
Mrs. George Thacher 579
S. Kendrick 580
GUERRARD, Benjamin 9
GUERRY
Alexander 481
William A. 509, 521
GUERTIN, George A. 527
GUEST, Raymond R. 430
GUFFEY
James M. 548
Joseph F. 205, 208, 211, 215, 218, 221, 360
GUFLER, Bernard A. 425, 428
GUGGENHEIM
Daniel 611
Harry F. 426, 491, 612
M. Robert 435
Mrs. Olga H. 491
Richard E. 492
Simon 158, 161, 164, 285, 491
Mrs. Simon 603
Solomon R. 491
GUILD
Curtis, Jr. 320
George B. 457
GUILFORD, J. Paul 571
GUILFOYLE
George H. 525
Merlin J. 529
Richard T. 525
GUILL, Ben H. 228
GUILLEMIN, Ernst A. 598
GUILLOTTE, J. Valsin 457
GUINAN, Matthew 5
GUION
John I. 326
Walter 173, 312
GUITERMAN, Arthur 580
GULBRANSEN, Earl A. 589
GULICK
Charles B. 570
John W. 402
Luther 571
GULLANDER, W.P. 578*
GULLINAN, Joseph S. 553
GUILLION
Alen W. 402, 403
Edmund A. 426, 439
GULLIVER, John P. 473
GUM, Walter C. 531
GUMMERE
Francis B. 577
Samuel J. 472
Samuel R. 433
William S. 341
GUMPEL, Hugh 591
GUMPERT, Emil 565
GUNCKEL, Lewis B. 117
GUND, George 545*
GUNDAKER, Guy 580
GUNDERSEN, Gunnar 569
GUNDERSON, Carl 367
GUNN
Calvin 455
Douglas 461
George P. 514, 522
James (Ga.) 51*, 52, 53, 54, 55, 295
James (Idaho) 145
John E. 527
GUNNELL, Francis M. 416
GUNNESS, Robert C. 552
GUNNISON, Almon 480
GUNTER
Gaston 457
Julius C. 285
Thomas M. 115, 118, 120, 122, 124
W.A. 457*
William D., Jr. 264
GUNTHER
C. Godfrey 458
Franklin M. 427, 435
GUPTON, William 457
GURKIN, John A. 458
GURLEY
Fred G. 543*
Henry H. 71, 72, 74, 75
John A. 103, 105
Phineas D. 532
GURNEE, Walter S. 451
GURNEY
Edward J. 248, 251, 254, 257, 261, 264, 294
J. Chandler 212, 215, 218, 221, 225, 228, 367
GUSTAFSON, George H. 564
GUSTAVSON, Reuben G. 476, 492
GUSTINE, Amos 86
GUSTON, Philip 589
GUTH, William W. 471, 479
GUTHE, Carl 501
GUTHMAN, Edwin O. 585
GUTHRIE
A.B., Jr. 585
Edwin R. 571
George W. 431, 459
Hunter 471
J.B. 459
James 27*, 39, 108, 110, 309, 549
Ramon 611
Robert G. 572
GUTTMACHER
Alan F. 592, 610
Manfred S. 608
GUY
Walter C. 579
William L. 351
GUYER
M.F. 573
Tennyson 265
Ulysses S. 183, 190, 193, 197, 200, 203, 206, 210, 213, 216
GUYON, James, Jr. 68
GUZZETTA, Dominic J. 465
GWALTER, L. Ivimy 536
GWILLIAM, George E. 577
GWIN, William M. 86, 92, 94, 96, 98, 100, 102, 283
GWINN
Ralph W. 221, 224, 227, 230, 233, 236, 240
William P. 554*
GWINNETT, Button 3, 4, 5, 8
GWYNNE, John W. 203, 206, 210, 213, 216, 220, 223
GYORGY, Paul 592

H

HAAN, William G. 410
HAAS
Francis J. 526
Harry J. 564
John A.W. 476
John C. 491
Leonard 486
Otto 491
HABACH, George F. 573
HABERLER, Gottfried 566
HABERLY, Loyd 580
HABERSHAM
John 5
Joseph 5, 445
Richard W. 84, 85
HACK, Howard 609
HACKER
Hilary B. 525
Joseph M. 576
HACKERMAN, Norman 480, 482, 575
HACKETT
Albert 586
Richard N. 160
Robert 404
Thomas C. 92
William S. 449
HACKLEY
Aaron, Jr. 68
Robert J. 461
HACKNEY, Thomas 159
HADDEN, D.P. 456
HADDOCK
Charles B. 435
Edward E. 459
HADDON, William, Jr. 592
HADEN, Clarence R. 516, 521
HADLEY
Arthur T. 487, 566, 578
Chalmers 568
Herbert S. 330, 484
Hiram E. 381, 476
Joshua 452
Lindley H. 172, 175, 179, 182, 186, 189, 192, 195, 199
Ozro A. 281
Rollin V. 499
William F.L. 142
HADLOCK, Wendell S. 498
HADSEL, Fred L. 428, 437
HADZSITS, George D. 570
HAFEY, William J. 528*
HAFFNER, Charles C., Jr. 414
HAGAMAN, Frank L. 307
HAGAN, G. Elliott 245, 248, 251, 254, 258, 261
HAGANS, John M. 117
HAGARTY, Frank A. 454
HAGEDORN, Herman 609
HAGEMEYER, W.A. 458
HAGEN
Harlan F. 232, 235, 238, 241, 244, 248, 251
Harold C. 217, 220, 223, 227, 230, 233
HAGER
Alva L. 140, 142, 145
George C. 580
John S. 115, 283
HAGERMAN
B.C. 466
James 564
HAGERTY, W.W. 470
HAGGARD, William D. 565, 569
HAGGERSON, Fred H. 553*
HAGGERTY, John 596
HAGGIN, James 543
HAGGOTT, Warren A. 158
HAGOOD
Johnson (b. 1829) 365
Johnson (b. 1873) 405
HAGUE
Arnold 575
Wesley M. 419
HAHN
John 65
Michael 104, 130, 311
Paul M. 543
Thomas M., Jr. 484
HAHNE, Ernest H. 475
HAIDER, Michael L. 553*, 567, 590, 596
HAIGHT
Charles 110, 112
Edward 105
Elizabeth H. 570
Henry H. 283
Thomas G. 271
HAIK, Raymond A. 576
HAILE
William (Miss.) 73, 74
William (N.H.) 338
HAINER, Eugene J. 140, 143
HAINES
Charles D. 141
Charles G. 571
Daniel 340*
Elwood L. 514, 520
Harry L. 198, 201, 205, 208, 215
Helen 600
John C. 451
John M. 298, 450
Ralph E., Jr. 404
William T. 315
HAIRE, Charles 461
HAIRFIELD, J.C. 471
HAISE, Fred W., Jr. 608
HAISLIP, Wade H. 400, 405, 412, 414
HAIT, James M. 546*
HALABY, Najeeb E. 550*
HALBACH, Edward A. 593
HALBERSTAM, David 587
HALBOUTY, Michel T. 564
HALDEMAN
Jacob S. 437
Richard J. 113, 115
Samuel 558
Samuel S. 570
HALDERMAN, J.A. 436
HALE
Artemas 89, 91
Benjamin 472
Benjamin E. 551
Charles R. 508
Edward E. 563
Edward J. 426
Eugene 112, 114, 116, 118, 121, 125, 127, 130, 132, 135, 137, 140, 142, 145, 148, 150, 153, 156, 159, 162, 314
Fletcher 188, 191, 194
Frederick 174, 177, 180, 184, 187, 190, 193, 197, 200, 203, 207, 210, 315
George E. 594, 596, 610
Horace M. 468
James T. 103, 105, 107
John B. 130
John P. (N.H.) 88, 91, 93, 95, 99, 101, 103, 105, 107, 337*, 437
John P. (W. Va.) 451
Lillian Wescott 589
Nathan W. 157, 160
Nathaniel C. 575
Robert 217, 220, 223, 226, 229, 233, 236, 239
Robert S. 108, 117
S.L. 391
Salma 67
Samuel W. 338
Stephen F. 392
William 61, 64, 65
William G. 570
Willis H. 412*
HALEY
Elisha 80, 82
George W. 449
James A. 232, 235, 238, 241, 245, 248, 251, 254, 257, 261, 264
James S. 457
John L. 550
Thomas P. 536
HALL
A.G. 483
A. Oakey 458
Albert R. 187, 190, 193
Allen A. 424, 439
Arnold B. 478
Arthur C.A. 508, 522

Asaph 563
Augustus 98
Benton J. 130, 444
Birney L. 457
Bolling 62, 63, 65
C.B. 419
Chapin 103
Charles B. 564
Charles F. 514, 520
Charles P. 401, 412, 414
D.A. 483
Daniel H. 477
Darwin S. 135
David 290, 355
David J. 480
David M. 243
Durward G. 246, 249, 252, 255, 258, 262
Edwin A. 211, 214, 217, 221, 224, 227, 230
Emmett M. 592
Florence Howe 583
Floyd D. 546*
Frank H. 286
Fred 307
Fred T. 497
Frederic A. 484
Frederick B. 288
George 68
George I. 574
George W. 461
Grant P. 451
G. Stanley 571*
Grover C. 583
Henry C. 426, 429, 430, 434, 436
Hiland 78, 80, 81, 83, 85, 87, 376*
Homer W. 190, 193, 196
Isaac H. 570
Jabez 536
James (b. 1750) 532
James (b. 1811) 501, 563, 575, 597
James K. 571
James K.P. 149, 152
Jeremiah 469
John 477
John (Md.) 5
John A. 549
John A.F. 453
John G. 543
John H. (Oreg.) 357
John H. (Wash.) 484
John L., Jr. 419
John W. 291, 475
Joseph 79, 80
Joshua G. 123, 126
Lawrence W. 101
Leonard W. 211, 214, 217, 221, 224, 227, 230
Luther E. 312
Lyman (b. 1724) 3, 5, 8
Lyman (b. 1859) 471
M.G. 455
Nathan K. 26, 43, 91
Norman 133
Obed 62
Osee M. 137, 140
Paul 559
Philo 160
Robert B. 99, 100
Robert Bruce 517
Robert H. 568
Robert S. 194, 197
Thomas 185, 188, 191, 194, 198
Thomas H. 67, 68, 70, 71, 75, 76, 78, 79
Uriel S. 140, 143
Wallace C. 579
Wesley W. 569
Willard 66, 68
Willard P. 91, 93, 95, 329
William 409
William (Rep.) 78, 369
William A. 105, 106
William B. 481
William E. 579, 603
William O. 428
William P. 401
William W. 470, 486
Wilton E. 218, 366
HALLAREN, Mary A. 401
HALLBECK, Elroy C. 559
HALLE, Louis J., Jr. 593
HALLECK
Charles A. 203, 206, 210, 213, 216, 220, 223, 226, 229, 232, 235, 239, 242, 245, 248, 251, 255
Henry W. 400, 406
HALLETT, Moses 285
HALLEY
Donald M., Jr. 499
Harry L.S. 355*
HALLIGAN, John, Jr. 418
HALLINAN
James T. 574
Paul J. 523, 525
HALLOCK
Donald H.V. 515, 520
John, Jr. 73, 74
HALLOWAY, Ransom 93
HALLOWELL
A. Irving 563, 611
Burton C. 483
Edwin 138
HALLOWS, E. Harold 386
HALPERN, Seymour 243, 246, 249, 252, 256, 259, 262
HALSELL, John E. 127, 130
HALSEY
Anthony P. 544
Frederick A. 590
George A. 110, 114
James H. 467
Jehiel H. 76
Milton B. 414
Nicoll 79
Robert H. 567
Silas 59
Thomas J. 194
William F. 609
HALSTEAD
Albert 423
William 82, 86
HALSTED, Caleb O. 545
HALTERMAN, Frederick 143
HALVORSEN, G.E. 460
HALVORSON
Kittel 137
Wilton L. 572
HAM, Roswell G. 476
HAMBLETON, Samuel 112, 114
HAMBURGER, Viktor 573
HAMER
Thomas L. 79, 81, 83
Thomas R. 161
Walter J. 575
HAMERSCHLAG, Arthur A. 467, 492
HAMERSLEY, William J. 453*
HAMILL
James A. 159, 162, 165, 168, 171, 174, 177
Patrick 112
HAMILTON
Alexander 4, 6, 23*, 39, 400, 402, 580, 597
Andrew 9
Andrew H. 118, 120
Andrew J. 103, 372
Charles M. (Fla.) 110, 111
Charles M. (N.Y.) 168, 171, 174
Charles S. 407
Charles S., Jr. 492
Cornelius S. 111
Daniel W. 159
Edward L. 145, 148, 151, 153, 156, 159, 162, 165, 168, 171, 174, 177
Elwood 271
Finley 200
Fowler 443
Franklin 465, 530
Frederick R. 466
Frederick W. 483
Harold L. 610
James 9*, 458
James, Jr. 70, 72, 73, 75, 364, 451
James M. 476
John (N.J.) 8*
John (Pa.) 59
John L. 564
John M. (Ill.) 300
John M. (W. Va.) 166
John McClure 607
John T. 137, 476
John W. 530
Lee H. 251, 255, 258, 261, 264
Maxwell M. 428
Morgan C. 113, 115, 117, 120, 372
Norman R. 209
Orris L. 382
Paul 24, 42, 364
Robert 117, 119
Samuel R. 462
Samuel W. 571
Thomas H. 472, 477
W.J., Jr. 575
William 454
William F. 571
William T. 93, 95, 97, 112, 114, 116, 317*
William W. 534
HAMITER, Joe B. 313
HAMLET
Harry G. 445, 483
O.C. 483
HAMLETT, Barksdale 400, 478
HAMLEY, Frederick G. 272, 382
HAMLIN
Charles S. 443
Courtney W. 154, 159, 162, 165, 168, 171, 174
Cyrus 475
Edward S. 88
Hannibal 14, 16, 87, 89, 91, 93, 95, 97, 98, 100, 102, 104, 106, 112, 114, 116, 118, 121, 123, 314*, 437
Oliver D. 272
Simon M. 203
Talbot F. 586
HAMLINE, Leonidas L. 530
HAMM, John 425
HAMMAKER, Wilbur E. 530
HAMMELL, James F. 455
HAMMER
Armand 550*
William C. 181, 185, 188, 191, 194
William J. 594*
HAMMERS, Karl R. 579
HAMMERSCHMIDT, John P. 254, 257, 260, 263
HAMMERSTEIN, Oscar, 2d 574, 585*
HAMMES, George A. 529
HAMMETT
Louis P. 596, 604*, 608
William H. 88
HAMMILL
James A. 159, 162, 165, 168, 171, 174
John 305
HAMMOCK, Cicero 449*
HAMMOND
Abram A. 302
Alonzo J. 572
Bray 586
C. Herrick 567
Creed C. 402
Dennis F. 449
Edward 93, 95
Graeme 569
Hall 318
Jabez D. 65
James B. 594
James H. 81, 101, 103, 364, 365
John 123, 126
John B. 445
John H. 610
Mrs. John H. 603
John H., Jr. 594, 598
Laurens 611
Matthew B. 566
Nathaniel J. 122, 125, 127, 129
Ogden H. 437
Rensellaer B. 467
Robert H. 83, 85
Samuel 57
Thomas 140
W.J. 558
William A. 403, 569
Winfield S. 159, 162, 165, 324
HAMMONS
David 91
Joseph 76, 77
HAMNETT, Jonathan 465*
HAMPDEN, Walter 603
HAMPSON
Joan G. 597
John L. 597
HAMPTON
James G. 90, 91
John R. 281
Moses 92, 93
Robert E. 445
Wade (b. 1752) 54, 58, 406
Wade (b. 1818) 124, 126, 128, 131, 133, 136, 365*, 395, 396
HANAWALT, Joseph D. 590
HANBACK, Lewis 127, 130
HANBURY, Harry A. 151
HANBY, William 530
HANCHER, Virgil M. 473
HANCHETT
Edwin L. 517, 519
Luther 105
HANCOCK
Clarence E. 191, 194, 198, 201, 204, 207, 211, 214, 217, 221
Franklin W., Jr. 194, 198, 201, 204, 208
George 3, 4, 53, 54
James D. 579
John (b. 1737) 3, 4, 5*, 6, 8*, 15, 319, 406
John (b. 1824) 115, 117, 120, 129
Lewis 450
Parker L. 566
Walker 607
Winfield S. 17, 408*, 409
HAND
Augustus C. 84
Augustus N. 271
Edward 7, 401, 406
Learned 271, 609
T. Millet 220, 224, 227, 230, 233, 236
HANDLEY
George 8
Harold W. 303
William A. 113
William J. 432, 438
HANDLIN, Oscar 585
HANDY
Alexander H. 326
Levin I. 144
Thomas T. 400, 404, 405
HANES, Robert M. 564
HANEY, Bert E. 272
HANFORD
Benjamin 17*
James H. 577
W.E. 567
HANKINS, Frank H. 573
HANKS
George J. 551*
James M. 113
HANLEY
Edward J. 595
James M. 253, 256, 259, 262, 265
John W. 549
William A. 573
HANLON, John J. 572
HANLY
J. Frank 18, 142, 303
Thomas B. 392, 393
HANNA
Bayless W. 423*
Clinton R. 599, 608
Edward J. 524
Ira L. 451
James R. 453
John 120
John A. 55, 56, 57, 58, 59
Katherine 502
Louis B. 162, 165, 350
Marcus A. 146, 149, 151, 154, 353
Matthew E. 429, 434
Richard T. 248, 251, 254, 257, 260, 263
Robert 77, 302
Septimus J. 536
Thomas H. 533
HANNAFORD, Jule M. 550*
HANNAH, John A. 443, 475
HANNAN, Jerome D. 524, 528
HANNEGAN
Edward A. 79, 80, 87, 89, 91, 302, 435
Robert E. 34, 43, 444
HANNETT, Arthur T. 343
HANRAHAN
Edmond N. 445
Robert P. 264
HANSBROUGH, Henry C. 135, 138, 141, 143, 146, 149, 151, 154, 157, 160, 350
HANSCOM, Isaiah 418
HANSELMAN, Joseph F. 472
HANSEN
Alvin H. 566
Arild E. 592
Arthur G. 471, 479
Clifford P. 257, 260, 263, 266, 388*
George V. 251, 254
Hendrick 449
Johannes 449*
John R. 252
Julia Butler 247, 250, 254, 257, 260, 263, 266
Orval 258, 261, 264
Robert E. 580
Walter F. 450
William C. 486
HANSFORD, Charles R. 457
HANSHUE, H.M. 553
HANSON
Abraham 432

Alexander C. 63, 65, 66, 68, 316
C. Arnold 471
George M. 576
H.C. 575
Harold E. 456
Henry W.A. 471
Howard 585
John 4, 5, 6
Marcus Lee 584
Ole 461
HAPGOOD
Norman 427
Powers 559
HARAHAN, James T. 548
HARALSON
Hugh 87, 89, 91, 92
Jeremiah 118
Jonathan 534
HARBACH, Otto A. 572
HARBERGER, John S. 545
HARBESON, John F. 577
HARBISON
Alexander 454
John 592
HARBORD, James G. 551*
HARD, Gideon 79, 81
HARDEE
Cary A. 294
William J. 394, 395*, 396
HARDEMAN, Thomas, Jr. 102, 127
HARDEN, Cecil M. 226, 229, 232, 235, 239
HARDENBERG, James R. 460*
HARDENBERGH
Augustus A. 119, 121, 126
Jacob R. 480
HARDENBROOK, Donald J. 578
HARDER
E.L. 599
Oscar E. 572
HARDIN
Adlai S. 579, 610
Benjamin 65, 68, 69, 79, 80
Charles H. 329
Clifford M. 36, 45, 476
J.M. 536
John J. 87
Martin D. 65, 308
Paul 481
Paul, Jr. 531
Paul, 3d 486
HARDING
Aaron 104, 106, 108
Abner C. 108, 110
Alfred 509, 522
Arthur M. 465
Benjamin F. 105, 107, 356
Bertrand 444
Edwin F. 413
George 591, 607
J. Eugene 160
Nelson 583*
Ralph R. 245, 248
W.P.G. 443
Warren G. 13, 18, 172, 175, 178, 353
William L. 304
HARDINGE, Harry W. 595, 601
HARDISON, O.B., Jr. 499
HARDMAN, Lamartine G. 297
HARDT
J. William 551
Robert A. 609
HARDWICK, Thomas W. 153, 155, 158, 161, 164, 167*, 170, 173, 296, 297
HARDY
Alexander M. 142
Arnold 585
Arthur C. 580, 601
Arthur S. 429, 435*, 436, 437, 438
Caldwell 564
Charles 8
Edward L. 480
F.A. 547
George 559
Guy U. 176, 179, 183, 186, 189, 193, 196
H.W. 455
John 126, 128
John C. 475
Josiah 8
Porter, Jr. 225, 228, 231, 234, 237, 241, 244, 247, 250, 253, 257
Rufus 160, 163, 166, 169, 172, 175, 179, 182
Samuel 7
Summers 355
HARE
Butler B. 188, 192, 195, 198, 211, 215, 218, 221
Dadius D. 138, 141
James B. 228
Raymond A. 427, 432, 436, 438, 439*
Robert 609
S. Herbert 573
Silas 133, 136
William H. 507, 521
HARFORD
Robert L. 466
W.G.W. 497
HARGIS, Denver D. 242
HARGRAVE
Thomas J. 546*
William L. 516, 521
HARGROVE, Robert K. 530
HARGROVES, V. Carney 534
HARING
Albert 568
John 6
HARITHAS, James 498
HARKEY, Ira B., Jr. 587
HARKINS
Matthew 528
Paul D. 401
William D. 596
HARKNESS
Albert 570
Edward S. 491
John 591
Sarah 591
William 563
HARLAN
Aaron 97, 99, 101
Allison W. 566
Andrew J. 93, 96
Byron B. 198, 201, 204, 208
James (Iowa) 27, 44, 98, 100, 102, 104, 106, 108, 110, 112, 114, 304*
James (Ky.) 80, 82
James E. 468
John M. (b. 1833) 269
John M. (b. 1899) 270, 271
Joseph G. 472
HARLESS
Richard F. 216, 219, 222
HARLEY
Herbert 589
J.E. 366
John 470
HARLFINGER, Frederick J. 416
HARLIN, Robert H. 461
HARLLEE, John 443
HARLOW
Harry F. 571, 604
James G. 485
James H. 573
HARMANSON, John H. 89, 91, 93
HARMAR, Josiah 400
HARMER, Alfred C. 115, 117, 122, 124, 126, 128, 131, 133, 136, 138, 141, 143, 146, 149
HARMON
Andrew D. 482, 536
Arthur L. 591
Austin M. 570
Ernest N. 405, 413, 415*, 478
Henry G. 469
Hubert R. 412*, 483
John H. 453
Judson 29, 30, 41, 353
L.L. 459
Nolan B. 531
Randall S. 242
HARMONY, David B. 418
HARMS, Oliver R. 535
HARNER, Nevin C. 472
HARNESS
Edward G. 551
Forest A. 210, 213, 216, 220, 223
HARNETT
Cornelius 4, 6
William 484*
HARNICK, Sheldon 586
HARNISH, J. Lester 534
HARNO, Albert J. 568
HARNSBERGER
Harry S. 388
Reynolds T. 576
HARNWELL, Gaylord P. 479
HARP, Reno S. 576
HARPER
Alexander 83, 88, 90, 95
Arthur C. 456
Arthur M. 414
Francis J. 83
Fred 574
George H. 468
Heber R. 469
J. Fletcher 572
James 533
James (N.Y.) 458
James (Pa.) 79, 81
James C. 115
John 453
John A. 62
John D. 543*
Joseph M. 77, 79
Paul A. 599
R.D. 533
Robert A. 574
Robert G. 15*, 53, 54, 55, 56, 65, 316
William 73, 364
William R. 466, 468
William S. 593
HARRAR, J. George 492
HARRELD, John W. 178, 181, 185, 188, 355
HARRELL
Ben 404, 405
Costen J. 531
HARRELSON, John W. 477
HARRIES, William H. 137
HARRIMAN
E. Roland 554, 569, 603
Edward H. 552, 554*
Florence Jaffray 434
Henry I. 575
Mrs. J. Borden 603
Job 17
Mary W. 603
W. Averell 34, 46, 346, 429, 439, 443, 544, 554, 595, 608
Walter 338
HARRINGTON
Emerson C. 317
Fred H. 486
George 438
George B. 610
Henry H. 482
Henry W. 106
Isaac R. 450
John L. 573
Joseph B. 460
Julian F. 434
Marion T. 482*
Mark W. 484
Michael J. 258, 261, 264
Russell C. 444
Samuel M. 291
Vincent F. 206, 210, 213
William W. 292
HARRIS
Abram W. 474, 478
Addison C. 423
Alexander L. 455*
Andrew L. 353
Arthur M. 534
Basil 443
Benjamin G. 106, 108
Benjamin W. 116, 119, 121, 123, 125
Bessom Smith 498
Bravid W. 514
Carleton 282
Charles C. 492
Charles M. 106
Christopher C. 167
Dave E. 550
Edward A. 585
Edwin B. 457
Elisha (b. 1791) 361
Elisha (b. 1824) 571
Franklin S. 467
Fred R. 249, 253, 256, 259, 262, 355
Frederic R. 418
George 465
George B. 545
George E. 112, 114
H.H. 480
Henry R. 116, 118, 120, 129
Henry S. 126
Hugh P. 404, 405
Hunter 416
Ira 105, 107, 108, 345, 480
Isham G. 94, 96, 122, 124, 126, 129, 131, 133, 136, 138, 139, 141, 144, 146, 369, 370
J. Morrison 98, 100, 102
John 416
John (N.Y.) 60
John H. 467
John S. 110, 112, 311
John T. 103, 115, 117, 120, 122, 124
Julian H. 590
Leavitt 428, 436
Leonard A. 451
Malcolm L. 569
Mark 69
Marquis L. 531
Merriman C. 530
Milton 567
Mitchell 458
Nathaniel E. 296
Oren 212, 216, 219, 222, 225, 229, 232, 235, 238, 241, 244, 247, 251
Patricia R. 432
Paul P. 580
Paul S. 502
Peter C. 401
Robert 545
Robert (Pa.) 71, 73
Robert LeR. 511, 521
Robert O. 165
Rufus C. 475, 483
Sampson W. 90, 92, 94, 96, 98
Samuel 466
Samuel S. 507, 520
Seale 590
Stephen R. 143
Steven R. 461
Thomas A. 392*
Thomas H. 456
Thomas K. 64
Thomas L. (b. 1816) 92, 98, 100
Thomas L. (b. 1823) 538
Thomas R. 466
Townsend 431
Vincent M. 525
Wiley P. 97, 391, 392
William 468
William A. (b. 1805) 87, 423
William A. (b. 1841) 140, 145, 148, 150, 306
William J. 176, 180, 183, 186, 190, 193, 196, 297
William L. 530
William O. 576
William T. 444
Winder R. 215, 218
HARRISON
Albert G. 81, 82, 84
Albertis S., Jr. 380
Alexander 607
Benjamin (b. 1726) 3, 7, 9
Benjamin (b. 1833) 13, 17*, 125, 127, 130, 302
Mrs. Benjamin 579
Burr P. 225, 228, 231, 234, 237, 241, 244, 247
Byron P. (See Harrison, Pat)
Carter B. 53, 54, 55
Carter H. 118, 120, 451*
Charles C. 479
Earl G. 443
Edwin D. 471
Fairfax 552
Francis B. 154, 160, 162, 165, 168
G.R. 580
George M. 379
George P. 139, 142
George R. 594, 610
Gessner 484*
Harold E. 592, 599
Helen C. 599
Henry 458
Henry B. 288
Henry C. 594
Horace H. 117
Hugh G. 456
James F. 484
James L. 443
James T. 332, 391, 392
Jason 455
John B. 355
John R. 587
John Scott 97, 99
Joseph, Jr. 609
Leland 435, 437, 438, 439
Pat 165, 168, 171, 174, 177, 181, 184, 187, 190, 194, 197, 200, 204, 207, 210, 212, 214, 327
R.W. 468
Richard A. 105
Richard B. 611
Robert D. 230, 233, 236, 239
Robert H. 15
Ross G. 573
Samuel S. 79, 81
Shelby 493
T.O.C. 333
Thomas S. 427
Thomas W. 172, 175, 179, 182, 186, 189, 192
Tinsley R. 567, 590

W. 462
W.H. 576
Wallace K. 590, 609
Walter M. 573
William, Jr. 6
William Henry (b. 1773) 13, 16*, 65, 67, 73, 75, 352, 406, 425
William Henry (b. 1892) 598
William Henry (b. 1896) 231, 235, 247, 250, 257
William K., Jr. 413
William S. 456
HARRITON, Abraham 611
HARROD, Benjamin M. 572
HARROLD
Joseph 558
Thomas L. 419
HARRY, Joseph E. 468
HARSHA, William H., Jr. 246, 249, 253, 256, 259, 262, 265
HARSHBERGER, J.W. 575
HARSHE, Robert B. 497
HARSHMAN, Ralph G. 466
HART
Albert B. 567, 571
Alden L. 554
Alphonso 128
Archibald C. 165, 168, 171
Charles 548
Charles B. 426
Charles C. 423, 435
Charles E. 404, 405
Charles S. 574
E. Kirke 121
Edward J. 204, 207, 211, 214, 217, 220, 224, 227, 230, 233
Emanuel B. 95
Ernest 546
Hastings H. 609
James M. 566, 577
Jesse C. 282
John 3, 6, 8
John F. 557
Joseph J. 143
Julian D. 470
Louis F. 381
Michael J. 197, 200
Moss 574, 584
Oliver J. 513, 521
Ossian B. 293
Parker T. 431, 436, 438, 439
Philip A. 242, 245, 249, 252, 255, 258, 261, 264, 323
Robert A. 450
Roswell 108
Samuel 570
Thomas B. 450
Thomas C. 219, 289, 483
Thomas N. 450*
William 574
William H. 403
HARTE, Joseph M. 515, 519
HARTENBOWER, J.J. 453
HARTER
Dow W. 201, 204, 208, 211, 214
Elmer E. 577
George A. 469
J. Francis 211
Michael D. 138, 141
HARTIGAN, John P. 271
HARTING, Darrell H. 601
HARTKE, Vance 242, 245, 248, 251, 255, 258, 261, 264, 303
HARTL, Leon 611
HARTLE, Russell P. 412, 413
HARTLEY
Fred A., Jr. 194, 197, 201, 204, 207, 211, 214, 217, 220, 224
Fred L. 554
James J. 525
Roland H. 381
Thomas 51, 52, 53, 54, 55, 56
HARTLINE, Haldan K. 606
HARTMAN
A.K. 455
Carl G. 573, 610
Charles S. 140, 143, 146, 427
Frank W. 572
Jesse L. 165
Leon W. 476
Leonard L. 466
Lewis O. 531
HARTMANN, John A. 462
HARTNESS
Harlan N. 413, 419
James 376, 573, 601
HARTNETT, Jeremiah A. 480
HARTRANFT, John F. 359
HARTRIDGE, Julian 118, 120, 392, 393
HARTSFIELD, William B. 449*
HARTSHORN, Edwin S. 403
HARTSHORNE, Richard 595
HARTT
Frederick C. 502
Samuel 418
HARTUNG
A.F. 558
Ernest W. 472
Gus E. 580
HARTY, Jeremiah J. 527
HARTZELL
Joseph C. 531
Thomas B. 566
William 118, 120
HARTZLER, Henry 530
HARTZOG
George B., Jr. 444
Henry S. 465, 468
HARVEY
E. Newton 573, 611
Edmund N. 610
George 429
James 245, 249, 252, 255, 258, 261, 265
James E. 435
James M. 116, 118, 306*
John 8*, 9*
Jonathan 73, 74, 76
Louis P. 385
Matthew 70, 71, 337
Ralph 223, 226, 229, 232, 235, 239, 245, 248, 251
Roger A. 565
W. Proctor 567
William G. 575
William W. 307
HARVIE, John 4, 7, 459
HARVILL, Richard A. 465
HARWOOD
Andrew A. 418
Richard 449
William 449
HASBROUCK
Abraham B. 73, 480
Abraham J. 64
Josiah 58, 67
Robert W. 415
Solomon 450
HASCALL
Augustus P. 95
Vincent C. 576
HASE, William F. 402
HASELL, Samuel 458*
HASELTON, Seneca 439
HASKEL, Daniel 484
HASKELL
Charles N. 355
Dudley C. 120, 123, 125, 127
Floyd K. 264, 286
Harry G., Jr. 238
Henry J. 585
Jonathan 401, 402
Reuben L. 171, 174, 178
Robert N. 315
William T. 92
HASKIN, John B. 101, 103
HASKINS
Charles H. 567, 577
Kittredge 152, 155, 158, 160
HASLER, Arthur D. 573, 575
HASLET, Joseph 290*
HASS
Firman H. 578
Henry B. 567, 590
HASSAM, Childe 589*, 593*, 607*, 610
HASSAUREK, Frederick 427
HASSETT, W.J. 460
HASTIE, William H. 271, 611
HASTINGS
Charles S. 594
Daniel H. 359
Daniel O. 189, 193, 196, 199, 203, 292
Edgar M. 572
George 97
George B. 534
James F. 259, 262, 265
John 84, 86
John S. 272
Kester L. 403
Robert F. 567
S. Clinton 89, 283
Seth 56, 58, 59
William S. 84, 86
William W. 172, 175, 178, 185, 188, 191, 195, 198, 201
HASTRICH, Jerome J. 526
HATCH
Carl A. 201, 204, 207, 211, 214, 217, 221, 224, 343
Edward 410
Francis W. 580
George 451
Herschel H. 128
Israel T. 101
J.H. 453
James H. 559*
Jethro A. 142
John Davis, Jr. 497, 502
Robert M. 515, 522
Theodore F. 592
William H. 123, 125, 128, 130, 133, 135, 138, 140
HATCHER
Harlan H. 475
Rhesa 454*
Robert A. 116, 119, 121, 393
Samuel C. 479
William B. 474
HATFIELD
Charles S. 272*
Edwin F. 532
H.G. 576
Henry D. 195, 199, 202, 383, 384
James T. 577
Mark O. 256, 259, 262, 265, 357*
HATHAWAY
Gail A. 572
Samuel G. 79
Stanley K. 388
William D. 252, 255, 258, 261, 264, 315
HATHORN
Henry H. 117, 119
John 51, 54
HATTON
Charles H. 576
Frank 29*, 43
Robert H. 103
HAUCK
Arthur A. 474
Herman J. 481
HAUG, John S. 601
HAUGEN
Einar 566
Gilbert N. 148, 150, 153, 156, 159, 161, 164, 167, 170, 173, 176, 180, 183, 187, 190, 193, 197
Nils P. 134, 136, 139, 141
HAUGHEY, Thomas 109
HAUGHS, George M.B. 455
HAUGHTON, Daniel J. 548*
HAUN, Henry P. 102, 283
HAUPERT, Raymond S. 476
HAUPT, Lewis M. 594
HAURY, Emil W. 497, 563, 611
HAUSER, Philip M. 574
HAUSS, Clarence E. 423
HAUSSLER, A.G. 466*
HAVEMEYER, William F. 458*
HAVEN
Erastus O. 475, 478, 482, 530
Gilbert 530
Nathaniel A. 61
Solomon G. 95, 97, 99, 451
HAVENNER, Franck R. 206, 209, 219, 222, 225, 229
HAVENS
Harrison E. 114, 116
James S. 162
Jonathan N. 54, 55, 56
Raymond M. 580
HAVILAND
C. Floyd 571
Marion 500
HAWES
Albert G. 77, 79, 80
Aylett 63, 64, 66
Harry B. 181, 184, 187*, 191, 194, 197, 330
Richard 82, 84
Richard S. 564
HAWK
N. Ray 478
Robert M.A. 123, 125
Rupert A. 471
HAWKES
Albert W. 217, 220, 224, 342, 575
James 70
HAWKINS
Alvin 370
Augustus F. 248, 251, 254, 257, 260, 263
Benjamin 6, 51, 52, 53, 347
Edler G. 533
George S. 100, 102
Hamilton S. 419
Isaac R. 109, 111, 113
Joseph 76
Joseph H. 63
Micajah T. 78, 79, 81, 83, 84
W.S. 574
William 347
HAWKS
Francis L. 483, 566
Charles, Jr. 212
Cicero S. 505, 520
HAWLEY
Claude E. 570
James H. 298, 450
John B. 112, 114, 116
Joseph R. 113, 116, 122, 125, 127, 129, 132, 134, 137, 139, 142, 144, 147, 150, 152, 288*
Robert B. 146, 149
Willis C. 160, 163, 166, 169, 172, 175, 178, 182, 185, 188, 191, 195, 198, 486
HAWORTH, Leland J. 444, 569
HAWS, J.H. Hobart 95
HAWTHORNE
Charles W. 589, 593*, 598*, 607
Nathaniel 597
HAY
Alexander 459
Andrew K. 93
Charles E. 461*
Edwin B. 574*
James 147, 149, 152, 155, 158, 160, 163, 166, 169, 172, 273
John 593
John B. 112, 114
John M. 30*, 38, 429
Marion E. 381
Philip C. 532
S.J. 452
Sam R. 530
HAYAKAWA, S.I. 481
HAYDEN
Carl 164, 167, 170, 173, 176, 179, 183, 186, 189, 192, 196, 199, 202, 206, 209, 212, 216, 219, 222, 225, 228, 232, 235, 238*, 241*, 244*, 247*, 251*, 254*, 280
Edward D. 130, 132
J. Willard 491
Moses 71, 73
Robert 600
HAYDN, Hiram C. 485
HAYES
A.B. 455
A.J. 557
Alexander 408
C.J. 557
Carlton J.H. 437, 567, 599
Charles F. 3d 502
Denis A. 557
Edward A. 568
Edward C. 573
Everis A. 155, 158, 161, 164, 167, 170, 173
Harvey C. 594
Helen 603
John S. 438
Max S. 18
Patrick J. 523, 524
Paul R. 271
Philip C. 120, 123
Ralph 492
Ralph L. 525, 526
Roland 611
Rutherford B. 13, 17, 109, 111, 353*
Samuel W. 355
Thomas G. 450
Walter I. 132, 134, 137, 140
William W. 453
HAYGOOD, Atticus G. 470, 530
HAYMAKER, J.N. 536
HAYMOND
Frank J. 589
Thomas S. 94
William S. 118
HAYNE
Arthur P. 101, 365
Robert Y. 72, 73, 75, 76,

78, 364*, 451
William E. 452
HAYNES
Caleb V. 411
Charles E. 72, 74, 75, 80, 82
George E. 579
J.C. 457*
J.J. 552
J. Manchester 449
John 8*
Landon C. 393*
Martin A. 128, 130
N.S. 536
Rowland 476
William E. 135, 138
HAYNIE, S.G. 450*
HAYNSWORTH
Clement F., Jr. 271
George 517
HAYS
Brooks 216, 219, 222, 225, 229, 232, 235, 238, 534
Calvin C. 532
Charles 111, 113, 115, 118
Charles M. 552
DeWitt C. 545
Edward D. 177, 181
Edward R. 134
George P. (b. 1838) 485, 532
George P. (b. 1892) 405, 413, 415
George W. 282
Isaac 563
S.H. 450
Samuel 8
Samuel L. 87
Silas B. 403
W.G. 459
Wayne L. 227, 230, 234, 237, 240, 243, 246, 249, 253, 256, 259, 262, 265
Will H. 32, 43, 577
HAYT, Charles D. 285
HAYTIN, John J. 454
HAYWARD
John T. 419, 601
Raymond W. 612
Richard 462*
William, Jr. 71
William S. 459
HAYWOOD
Nathan 575
Nelson 452
William H., Jr. 88, 90, 347
HAYWORTH, Don 236
HAZARD
Caroline 485
Henry T. 456
Jonathan J. 7
Nathaniel 68
HAZE, William H. 455
HAZELTINE
Abner 79, 81
Ira S. 125
HAZELTON
George C. 122, 124, 126
Gerry W. 115, 117
John W. 114, 117
HAZEN
Arlon G. 477
Melvin C. 462
William B. 403, 409, 410
HAZLETT, Theodore L., Jr. 492
HAZLEWOOD
Craig B. 564
John P. 416
HAZZARD
David 290
George W. 487
HEACOCK, B.C. 544
HEAD
J.M. 457
Natt 338
W.O. 456
Walter D. 580
Walter W. 564, 574
HEADY, Ferrel 476
HEALD
Henry T. 477, 491, 598, 603
K.C. 608
William H. 161, 164
HEALEY
Arthur D. 200, 203, 207, 210, 213
James C. 236, 240, 243, 246, 249
HEALY
George W., Jr. 573
James A. 528
Joseph 73, 74
Ned R. 219
Patrick F. 471
William 272
William J. 472
HEANEY, Gerald W. 272
HEANY, J. Allen 594
HEARD
Alexander 484
Augustine 431
J.W. 404
Jack W. 415
John T. 130, 133, 135, 138, 140
William H. 432
William W. 312
HEARN, W.A. 416
HEARNES, Warren E. 330
HEARST
George 129, 132, 134, 283
William Randolph 154, 157
William Randolph, Jr. 586
HEARTS, George 283
HEARTZ, John 557
HEATH
Donald R. 424*, 425, 431, 432, 436, 439*
Edward 457
James P. 79
John 53, 54
Lucien 460
Monroe 451
Perry S. 557
S. Burton 584
William 406
William W. 437
HEATHCOTE, Caleb 458
HEATON
David 111, 113
Earl 557
Leonard D. 403
Robert D. 172, 175
HEATWOLE, Joel P. 143, 145, 148, 151
HEAVENRICH
Samuel 498
Samuel W. 499
HEAVEY, John W. 402
HEBARD, William 94, 96
HEBB, Donald O. 571
HEBERT
F. Edward 213, 217, 220, 223, 226, 229, 233, 236, 239, 242, 245, 248, 252, 255, 258, 261, 264
Felix 195, 198, 202, 363
Louis 394
Paul M. 474
Paul O. 311
HECHLER, Kenneth 244, 247, 250, 254, 257, 260, 263, 266
HECHT
Anthony 587, 589, 600
Rudolph S. 564
HECK, N.N. 566
HECKEL, Charles W. 533
HECKERT
Charles G. 486
J. Brooks 578
HECKLER, Margaret M. 255, 258, 261, 264
HEDBERG, Hollis D. 576, 608
HEDDING, Elijah 530
HEDGE
Thomas 148, 150, 153, 156
Verne 455
William R. 580
HEDGES, William S. 578
HEDKE, Richard C. 580
HEDLEY, William J. 572
HEDRICH, Kenneth 590
HEDRICK
Earle R. 568
Erland H. 222, 225, 228, 231
George F. 558
Ira G. 609, 611
HEELAN, Edmond 529
HEFELBOWER, Samuel G. 471
HEFFERNAN, James J. 214, 217, 221, 224, 227, 230
HEFFNER, Ray L. 467
HEFFRON, Patrick R. 529
HEFLIN
Harry B. 485
Howell T. 279
J. Thomas 152, 155, 158, 161, 164, 167, 170, 173, 176*, 179, 183, 186, 189, 192, 278
Robert S. 111
HEFNER, R.A. 458
HEGEMAN, John R. 549
HEGENBERGER, Albert F. 412, 594
HEGNER, R.W. 573
HEHIR, Martin A. 470
HEIDELBERGER, Michael 600, 604
HEIDINGER, James V. 213, 216, 219
HEIERMANN, Francis 487
HEIL
Julius P. 386
Walter 497, 498
William 531
HEILMAN
E. Bruce 480
William 123, 125
HEILPRIN, Angelo 599, 600
HEIM, John B. 456
HEIMANN, Robert K. 543
HEIMBAUGH, Harold M. 576
HEIMBUCHER, Clifford V. 567
HEIMER, Jean 501
HEIMKE, William 429, 436
HEIMSCH, Charles 574
HEIN, C.C. 535
HEINDEL, Richard H. 479
HEINEMANN, Edward H. 594, 608
HEINER, Daniel B. 141, 143
HEINICKE, Christoph M. 597
HEININGER, H.R. 531
HEINKE, George H. 210
HEINRICHS, John F. 455
HEINSHEIMER, Alfred M. 492
HEINTZ, Victor 175
HEINTZELMAN
Samuel P. 407*
Stuart 400*, 401, 419
HEINZ
H. John, 3d 262, 266
Henry C. 576
John B. 570
HEINZERLING, Lyman 586
HEINZLE, J. Ulric 467
HEISE, George W. 575, 589
HEISER, Joseph M., Jr. 401
HEISKELL
John N. 164, 601
Joseph B. 393*
HEISLER, Charles W. 482
HEISS, Michael 523, 527
HEISTAND
John T. 513, 519
Samuel 531
HEISTER, Charles W. 482
HEITFELD, Henry 145, 147, 150, 298
HEITLAND, Emerton 591
HEITMAN
Charles E. 536
John H. 452
HEKKING, William M. 497
HEKTOEN, Ludvig 590
HELEVERING, Guy T. 444
HELFENSTEIN, Edward T. 512, 520
HELGESEN, Henry T. 165, 169, 172, 175
HELIKER, John E. 589, 593
HELLER
Louis B. 227, 230, 233
John L. 570
HELLMAN
I.W. 554
Lillian 592, 602, 603
Louis 610
HELLMANN, Claude B. 576
HELLMUND, Rudolf E. 599
HELLWEG, Frederick 601
HELM
Harold H. 545
Harvey 159, 161, 164, 167, 170, 173
James 10*
John L. 308, 309, 548
Joseph C. 285
HELMICK
Eli A. 402
William 103
HELMS
Jesse A. 265, 349
Richard M. 443
William 57, 58, 59, 60, 61
HELMSING, Charles H. 526, 529
HELPERN, Milton 590
HELSTOSKI, Henry 252, 256, 259, 262, 265
HELT, D.W. 557
HELTZER, Harry 549*
HELVERING, Guy T. 167, 170, 173
HELWIG, John B. 486
HEM, Halvor O. 611
HEMBEL, William 563
HEMENWAY, James A. 142, 145, 147, 150, 153, 156, 158, 303
HEMINGWAY
Ernest 586, 589, 606
W.L. 564
William 454
HEMLEY, Cecil 580
HEMPELMANN, John 266
HEMPHILL
John 103, 105, 372*, 392
John J. 129, 131, 136, 138
Joseph 57, 68, 70, 71, 73, 76
Robert W. 243, 247, 250
William A. 449
HEMPL, George 566, 570, 577
HEMPSTEAD, Stephen 304
HEMSLEY, William 6
HENCH
Atcheson L. 566
Philip S. 605, 607
HENCHEY, John E. 452
HENCKEN, Hugh 574
HENDEE, George W. 117, 120, 122
HENDERSON
Algo D. 465
Archibald (b. 1768) 56, 57
Archibald (b. 1785) 416
Bennet H. 66
Branton H. 575
Charles B. 174, 177, 278, 335
David B. 127, 130, 132, 134, 137, 140, 142, 145, 147, 148, 150*
David N. 246, 249, 253, 256, 259, 262, 265
Douglas 424
Elmer L. 569
Homer B. 530
J.T. 467
J.W. 372
Jack 593
J. Pinckney 101, 372*
James B. 553
James H. 109
John 84, 86, 88, 326
John B. 104, 106, 108, 110, 329
John E. 237, 240, 243
John S. 131, 133, 135, 138, 141
John W. (educator) 484
John W. (mayor) 462
Joseph 79, 81
Joseph W. 565
Junius 498
Leonard 347
Loy W. 430*, 433
Samuel (Ind.) 454
Samuel (Pa.) 64
Theodore S. 530
Thomas 54
Thomas J. 118, 120, 123, 125, 127, 130, 132, 134, 137, 139
William L. 318
HENDREN, H.H. 460
HENDRICK
Archer W. 476
Burton J. 583*
John K. 142
John T. 462
HENDRICKEN, Thomas F. 528
HENDRICKS
Joe 206, 209, 213, 216, 219, 222
Thomas A. 14, 17*, 94, 96, 106, 108, 110, 129, 302*
William 65, 66, 68, 72, 74, 75, 77, 79, 80, 302*
HENDRICKSON
George L. 570
Robert C. 227, 230, 233, 342, 433
Waino 455
HENDRIX
Eugene R. 530
Hal 587
Joseph C. 141, 564
HENKLE, Eli J. 118, 121, 123
HENLE
Gertrude 599
Robert J. 471
Werner 599
HENLEY
Barclay 127, 129
Thomas J. 87, 89, 91
James W. 531
HENN, Bernhart 95, 96
HENNE, Frances W. 600
HENNEKE, Ben G. 483
HENNESSY
John 523, 526
John J. 528, 529
William B. 570

HENNEY
Charles W. 202
William F. 454
HENNI, John M. 523, 527
HENNIKER-HEATON, Raymond 502
HENNING
Edward J. 577
G.C. 600
John F. 433
HENNINGS
F. Martin 598
Ivar 576
Thomas C., Jr. 204, 207, 210, 230, 233, 236, 239, 242, 330
HENRICKSON, Albert N. 497
HENRIQUES, J.A. 483
HENRY
Alexander 458
Charles L. 142, 145
Daniel M. 121, 123
David D. 472, 485
E. Stevens 142, 144, 147, 150, 153, 155, 158, 161, 164
E. William 443
Fred A. 536
Gustavus A. 393*
Guy V. 401
J. Addison 532
James 7
John (b. 1750) 6, 15, 51, 52*, 53, 54, 316*
John (b. 1800) 89
John F. 72
John W. 329
Joseph 502, 597
Lewis 181
Lou 20
Matthew G. 514, 522
Patrick (b. 1736) 7, 9*, 597
Patrick (b. 1843) 145, 148
Patrick (b. 1861) 151
Robert 481
Robert K. 222
Robert L. 146, 149, 152, 155, 157, 160, 163, 166, 169, 172
Robert P. 71, 72
Stephen G. 400, 415
Thomas 83, 85, 86, 92, 94
W. Laird 140
William (Miss.) 454
William (Pa.) 7
William (Vt.) 92, 94
William M. 608
William W. 567
HENSHAW
David 26, 42
John P.K. 505, 521
HENSLEY, Walter L. 165, 168, 171, 174
HENSON
Harold 456
Paul N. 554
HENTON, Willis R. 518
HEPBURN
A. Barton 545
A.J. 416
Andrew D. 469, 475
Joseph S. 600
William P. 125, 127, 130, 140, 142, 145, 148, 150, 153, 156, 159
HEPNER
Walter R. 480
William H. 453
HERBERMANN, Charles G. 599
HERBERT
Caleb C. 393*
Edward G. 601
Hardy 457
Hilary A. 30*, 42, 120, 122, 124, 127, 129, 131, 134, 136
John C. 65, 66
Paul A. 579
Philemon T. 98
Thomas J. 354
William C. 459
HERBSTER, Ben 534
HEREFORD, Frank 115, 117, 120, 122, 124, 383
HERGET, John F. 486
HERING
Carl 575
Hermann S. 536
Rudolph 572
HERKIMER
John 67, 71
Nicholas 406
HERLANDS, William B. 537
HERLONG, Albert S., Jr. 226, 229, 232, 235, 238, 241, 245, 248, 251, 254
HERMAN, John C. 453
HERMANN, Binger 131, 133, 136, 138, 141, 143, 154, 157
HERMANY, Charles 572
HERNANDEZ, Benigno C. 171, 178, 434
HERNDON
Ellen Lewis 20
Thomas H. 122, 124
William H. 461
William S. 115, 117
HERO, Andrew Jr. 402
HEROD, William 80, 82
HEROLD, J. Christopher 602
HEROM, Alexander R. 481
HERON, Raymond A. 513
HEROY
William B. 608
William B., Sr. 564
HERR
Edwin M. 554
Herbert T. 600
John 538
John K. 401
HERREID, Charles N. 367
HERREN, Thomas W. 405, 414
HERRICK
Anson 107
Clarence L. 476
Ebenezer 69, 71, 72
George M. 484
James B. 567, 590
John W. 481
Joshua 87
Manuel 181
Myron T. 353, 428*, 564
P.R. 452
Paul M. 531
Richard P. 90
Samuel 67
HERRING
Clyde L. 206, 210, 213, 305*
Pendleton 571
HERRMANN, August 574
HERRON
Charles D. 403, 404
Francis 532
Francis J. 406, 408
Helen 20
James H. 573
John S. 459
HERSCHEL, Clemens 572, 594
HERSETH, Ralph 368
HERSEY
Ira G. 174, 177, 180, 184, 187, 190
John 585
Mayo D. 591
Samuel F. 116
HERSH, Seymour M. 587
HERSHEY
Alfred D. 600, 606
Lewis B. 445
M.S. 491
HERSHOLT, Jean 563
HERSKOVITS, Melville 611
HERSMAN
Charles C. 485
Hugh 176
HERTER, Christian A. 35, 38, 217, 220, 223, 226, 230, 321, 608
HERTY
Charles H. 565, 590
Charles H., Jr. 572
HERVEY, Alpheus B. 480
HERWALD, Seymour W. 576
HERZOG, Raymond H. 549
HESBURGH, Theodore M. 478, 598, 604, 608
HESELTON, John W. 220, 223, 226, 230, 233, 236, 239
HESLIN, Thomas 527
HESS
Elmer 569
Harry H. 576, 607
Julius 592
Victor F. 605
Wendell F. 611
William E. 195, 198, 201, 204, 211, 214, 218, 221, 224, 230, 234, 237, 240, 243
HESSION, Cornelius M. 474
HESTER
H.I. 486
James M. 477
John H. 403, 414
HESTON
Charlton 559
J. Edgar 545
John W. 485
HETH, Henry 395*
HETRICK, Frank O. 566
HETZEL, Ralph D. 476, 479, 577
HEWES, Joseph 3, 4, 6
HEWETT
Donnel F. 607
Edgar L. 501
HEWITT
Abram S. 119, 121, 126, 128, 131, 458
Charles N. 572
Cyrus 455
George A. 578
Goldsmith W. 118, 120, 124, 127
H. Kent 416
John H. 486
Peter C. 594
William A. 546
HEWLETT, J. Monroe 591
HEWSTON, George 461
HEYBURN, Weldon B. 153, 155, 158, 161, 164, 298
HEYD
Charles G. 569
Norman G. 577
HEYDEN, Francis J. 593
HEYE, George G. 500
HEYER, Cornelius 544
HEYL, Paul R. 607
HEYMAN
D. John 492
David M. 492
HEYNS
Garrett 566
Roger 467
HEYWARD
Duncan C. 365
Thomas, Jr. 3, 4, 7
William, Jr. 71
HEYWOOD, Charles 416
HEYWORTH, Lawrence, Jr. 483
HIATT, Robert W. 472
HIBBARD
Aldro T. 589
Ellery A. 114
George A. 450
Harry 93, 95, 97
Lloyd J. 610
Walter R., Jr. 595
HIBBEN, John G. 479
HIBBERD, James F. 569
HIBBS, Louis E. 414
HIBSHMAN, Jacob 68
HICHBORN
Charles S. 449
Philip 418
HICKEL, Walter J. 36, 44, 279
HICKEN, Russell 500
HICKENLOOPER
Bourke B. 220, 223, 226, 229, 232, 235, 239, 242, 245, 248, 251, 255, 305*
Smith 271
HICKERNELL, L.F. 576
HICKERSON, John D. 428, 435
HICKEY
Alexander 480
Andrew J. 176, 180, 183, 187, 190, 193
Doyle O. 415
John J. 247, 272, 388*
Joseph A. 484
Patrick V. 599
Thomas F. (bishop) 528
Thomas F. 405*
William A. 528
HICKMAN
Clarence N. 612
E. 456*
George W., Jr. 402
J.E. 373
John 99, 101, 103, 105
Kenneth C.D. 611
HICKOK, Laurens P. 483, 532
HICKS
Elias 538
Floyd V. 254, 257, 260, 263, 266
Frederick C. 171, 174, 178, 181, 468
John 425, 435
Josiah 141, 143, 146
Louise Day 261
Marshall 461
Thomas H. 104, 106, 317*
Thomas W. 601
W.A. 460
Weimer K. 473
Whitehead 458
Xenophon 271
HICKSON, John L. 567
HIESTAND
Edgar W. 232, 235, 238, 241, 244
John A. 131, 133
HIESTER
Daniel (b. 1747) 51, 52, 53, 54, 56, 57
Daniel (b. 1774) 61
Isaac E. 97
John 10
Joseph 55, 56, 57, 58, 65, 67, 68, 358
William 78, 79, 81
HIBGY, William 106, 107, 109
HIGGINBOTTOM
Powers 450
Sam 532
Samuel I. 546
HIGGINS
Anthony 134, 137, 139, 291
Edward A. 474, 487
Edwin W. 155, 158, 161, 164
Eugene 589*, 593
Frank W. 345
George C. 597
H.B. 492
Harry B. 550
James H. 362
John P. 203, 207
John S. 515, 521
Marguerite 585, 607
Thomas J. 480
Victor 589*
William L. 199, 203
HIGGINSON, Stephen 6
HIGHTOWER
George R. 475
John B. 500
John M. 585
HIGLEY
Walter M. 514
William K. 498
HIGONNET, Rene A. 612
HILBERRY
Clarence 485
Norman 569
HILBORN, Samuel G. 136, 139, 142, 144
HILBUN, Benjamin F. 475
HILDEBRAND, Joel H. 565, 596, 604, 608
HILDEBRANDT
Fred H. 202, 205, 208
Theophil H. 568
HILDEBRANT, Charles Q. 151, 154
HILDRETH, Horace A. 315, 434, 467
HILGARD
Ernest R. 571
Julius L. 563
HILL
Albert R. 476
Ambrose P. 394*, 395*
Benjamin H. 118, 120, 122, 125, 296, 391, 392, 393
Charles A. 134
Charles G. 571
Charles L. 486
Clement S. 96
D.E. 547
Daniel B. 461
Daniel H. 394*, 395, 396, 465
David B. 138, 140, 143, 345*
David G. 492, 550
David J. 428, 432, 433, 438, 467
David S. 476
Delmas C. 272
Ebenezer J. 142, 144, 147, 150, 153, 155, 158, 161, 164, 170, 173
Eugene K. 484
Everett W. 580
Frank P. 568
Frederick B. 600
G.W. 568
George W. 543
Harry W. 419, 483
Hugh L. 92
Isaac 77, 79, 81, 337*
James B. 549
James J. 547
James L. 456
Jim D. 486
John (N.C.) 84
John (N.J.) 110, 112, 114, 126
John (Va.) 85
John A. 487
John F. 314

John P. 180, 184, 187
Joseph M. 281
Joshua 100, 102, 111, 114, 296
Knute 202, 205, 209, 212, 215
Lister 183, 186, 189, 192, 196, 199, 202, 206*, 209, 212, 216, 219, 222, 225, 228, 232, 235, 238, 241, 244, 247, 251, 254, 278, 590, 599
Louis C. 572
Louis W. 547, 548
Lyman 568
Mark L. 68, 69
Mason L. 564
Matthew W. 382
Nathaniel P. 122, 124, 127, 285
Percival S. 543
Ralph 108
Richard 458*
Robert C. 426, 427, 433, 437
Robert E. Lee 580
Robert P. 167, 208
Samuel B. 186, 189, 192, 195, 199, 202, 205
Thomas 465, 472
Thomas C. 427
W.H. 487
Walker 564
Walter B. 471
Whitmel 6
William 532
William A. 285
William D. 124, 128, 131
William H. (b. 1767) 56, 57
William H. (b. 1877) 178
William L. 203, 294
William M. 460
William S. 212, 216, 219, 222, 226, 229, 232, 235, 238
Wilson S. 153, 156, 159
HILLBOE, Herman E. 592
HILLDRING, John H. 400
HILLE, Einar 568
HILLEBOE, Herman E. 572, 592, 610
HILLEBRAND, William F. 565
HILLEGAS, Michael 444
HILLELSON, Jeffrey P. 233
HILLEN, Solomon, Jr. 84, 450
HILLENBRAND, Martin, J. 428, 430
HILLENKOETTER, Roscoe H. 443
HILLHARD, Henry W. 423
HILLHOUSE
James 51, 52, 53, 54, 55*, 56, 57, 58, 60, 61, 287
William 5
HILLIARD
Benjamin C. 170, 173, 286*
Henry W. 89, 90, 92, 424
William 461*
HILLIER, James 600
HILLINGER, Raymond P. 528
HILLINGS, Patrick J. 229, 232, 235, 238
HILLIS
Elwood 261, 264
Isaac L. 453
HILLKOWITZ, Philip 572
HILLMAN
James N. 470
Sidney 557
HILLS
Charles F. 498
Lee 573, 586
HILLSMAN, Matt 467
HILLYER
George 449
Junius 94, 96
Robert 580*, 584
HILTON
Frank C. 580
James H. 473
Robert B. 392, 393
Samuel L. 609
HIMES, Joseph H. 181
HIMMEL, Joseph J. 471
HIMROD, Charles 450*
HINCKLEY
Arthur T. 575
H.D. 483
Thomas 8*
HINCKS, Carroll C. 271
HINDMAN
Joseph A.E. 417
Thomas C. 102, 395, 396
William 6, 52*, 53, 54, 55, 56, 316
HINDS
Asher C. 165, 168, 171
Thomas 74, 76
HINE, Maynard K. 566
HINEBAUGH, William H. 167
HINES
Frank T. 434
Fred A. 579
John E. 514, 522
John L. 400*, 410
Linnaeus 473
Richard 73
Vincent J. 527
Walter D. 543
Wellington T. 417
William H. 141
HINITT, Frederick W. 485
HINKHOUSE, Forrest M. 501
HINKLE
James F. 343
John H. 452
HINKLEY, J. William 492
HINKS, Samuel 450
HINMAN
Clark T. 478
George W. 474
Joel 288
Thomas P. 566
HINRICHS
Amy 578
John H. 402
HINRICHSEN, William H. 145
HINSCH, Charles A. 564
HINSDALE
Burke A. 472
Robert G. 472
HINSHAW
Andrew J. 263
Carl 209, 212, 216, 219, 222, 225, 229, 232, 235, 612
David 609
Edmund H. 154, 156, 159, 162
HIPPLE, J.E. 459
HIRES, George 130, 133
HIRSCH
Hiram H. 600
Joseph 589*
Solomon 438
HIRSHFELD, Clarence F. 596
HIRSHSON, Louis M. 472
HIRST, A.C. 479
HISAW, F.L. 573
HISCOCK
Frank 121, 123, 126, 128, 131, 133, 135, 138, 345, 346
Ira V. 572, 578, 610
HISE
Elijah 108, 429
Frank 574
HITCH, Charles J. 467
HITCHCOCK
Albert E. 612
Albert S. 574
Edward 465
Ethan A. 30*, 31, 44, 436
Frank H. 31*, 43
Gilbert M. 154, 159, 162, 165, 168, 171, 174, 177, 181, 333
Henry (b. 1775) 277
Henry (b. 1829) 564
Henry E. 476
Henry L. 485
Henry-Russell 502
Herbert E. 205, 208, 367
Peter 67, 352*
Phineas W. 114, 117, 119, 333
HITCHINGS, George H. 607
HITE, Bert H. 601
HITT
R.S. Reynolds 429, 434
Robert R. 125, 127, 130, 132, 134, 137, 139, 142, 145, 147, 150, 153, 156
HITZ, William 272
HIXSON
Fred W. 465
George F. 576
HOADLEY
George 452
Horace G. 600
Jeremy 453
HOADLY, George 353
HOAG
Ella W. 536
Truman H. 113
HOAGLAND
Hudson 563
Jimmie Lee 588
Moses 93
HOAN, Daniel W. 456
HOAR
Ebenzer R. 28, 41, 116
George F. 112, 114, 116, 119, 121, 123, 125, 127, 130, 132, 135, 137, 140, 142, 145, 148, 150, 153, 320, 563, 567
Leonard 472
Rockwood 156
Samuel 81
Sherman 137
HOARD
Charles B. 101, 103
William D. 385
HOBAN
Edward F. 525, 528
Michael J. 528
HOBART
Aaron 68, 69, 71, 72
Donald M. 568
Garret A. 14, 17, 144, 147
John H. 505, 520
John S. 55, 344
Mrs. Lowell Fletcher 579
HOBBIE, Selah R. 74
HOBBINS, J.R. 543
HOBBS
A.I. 536
Barnabas C. 470
Herschel H. 534
Leland S. 413
Leonard S. 594
Nathaniel W. 452
Nicholas 571
Sam 202, 206, 209, 212, 216, 219, 222, 225
William J. 545
HOBBY
Oveta Culp 35, 47, 401, 603
William P. 372
HOBEN, Allan 473
HOBLITZELL
Bruce 456
Fetter S. 125, 127
John D., Jr. 241, 384
HOBSON
Henry W. 512, 522
Kenneth B. 415
Merk 476
Richmond P. 158, 161, 164, 167
HOCH
Daniel K. 218, 221
Edward W. 306
Homer 177, 180, 183, 187, 190, 193, 197
Lambert A. 525, 529
HOCHKLASSEN, H. 600
HOCHSCHILD, Walter 543*
HOCKENHULL, Andy W. 343
HOCKER, Lon 565
HODES
Henry I. 404, 405, 419
Horace L. 599
HODGDON
Daniel R. 484
Samuel 547
HODGE
Bachman G. 531
Benjamin L. 393
Charles 532
George B. 392*
John R. 405, 413*, 414
Maurice B. 534
HODGEN, John T. 569
HODGES
Alpheus P. 456
Arthur 450
Asa 115
Campbell B. 474
Charles D. 100
Courtney H. 402, 405*, 411, 412
Earle W. 576
George H. 306
George T. 99
Henry C., Jr. 410
J.C., Jr. 404
James 450
James L. 74, 76, 77
Joseph H. 529
Luther H. 36, 46, 349, 580
Nathaniel D.C. 568
Silas H. 444
Thomas E. 485
HODGKINS, Howard L. 471
HODGKINSON, Francis 594, 598
HODGMAN, Thomas M. 474
HODGSON
D.B. 483
James D. 36, 46
Laurence C. 460*
Percy 580
Samuel 403
Telfair 481
HODNETTE, John K. 595
HODSON, Kenneth J. 402
HOEBEL, E. Adamson 563
HOEFFER, James F.X. 469, 474, 480
HOEG, Halstead H. 454
HOEGH, Leo A. 305
HOEPPEL, John H. 199, 202
HOERNI, Jean A. 601
HOES, Hannah 20
HOEVEN, Charles B. 216, 220, 223, 226, 229, 232, 235, 239, 242, 245, 248
HOEY, Clyde R. 178, 221, 224, 227, 230, 233, 349*
HOF, Samuel 402
HOFF, Philip H. 377
HOFFA, James R. 558
HOFFACKER, Lewis 425, 427
HOFFECKER
John H. 147
Walter O. 147
HOFFMAN
Carl H. 221
Charles A. 569
Clare E. 204, 207, 210, 213, 217, 220, 223, 226, 230, 233, 236, 239, 242, 245
E.L. 594
Elmer J. 242, 245, 248
Harold G. 191, 194, 342*
Henry W. 98
Hugh F.T. 415
J. Ogden 83, 84
John T. 345, 458
Joseph 531
Michael 73, 74, 76, 77
Paul G. 443, 491, 596, 603
Philip G. 472
Ralph 502
Richard W. 226, 229, 232, 235
Sal B. 559
Samuel K. 597, 611
Wickham 427
Mrs. William H. 576
HOFFMAN
P.B. 548
Ralph 502
HOFFSTOT, Frank N. 553
HOFHEINZ, Roy 454
HOFSTADTER
Richard 586, 587
Robert 606
HOGAN
Aloysius J. 470
Bartholomew W. 416
Chester A. 579
Earl L. 242
Frank J. 565
Henry H. 550
James J. 525
John 108
John J. 526, 528
John P. 572
Joseph F. 546
Joseph L. 528
Lawrence J. 258, 261, 264
Michael J. 181
William 77
HOGE
James 532
John 58
John B. 126
Joseph P. 87, 89
Moses 471
Solomon L. 113, 119
William 57, 58, 60
William M. 404, 405*, 415
HOGEBOOM, James L. 71
HOGG
Charles E. 134
David 187, 190, 193, 196
Herschell M. 152, 155
James S. 372
Robert L. 195, 199
Samuel 67
HOGIN, P.E. 493
HOGLE, John F. 455
HOGUE, D.P. 462*
HOHLFELD, Alexander R. 577
HOIDALE, Einar 200
HOIE, Claus 591
HOIJER, Harry 563
HOISINGTON, Elizabeth B. 401
HOKE
R.F. 396
William A. 348
William E. 601*
HOLABIRD, Samuel B. 403
HOLADAY, William P. 183, 187, 190, 193, 196

HOLBORN, Hajo 567
HOLBROCK, Greg J. 214
HOLBROOK
Frederick 376
Lucius R. 419
Willard A. 401, 410
Willard A., Jr. 415
HOLCOMB
Glenn W. 572
Marcus H. 288
Silas A. 333*
Thomas 416, 438
HOLCOMBE
Arthur N. 571, 591
George 70, 71, 73, 74
James P. 393
John M. 551
Oscar 454*
HOLDEN
Edward S. 467
Hale 545*, 552
James S. 377
Louis E. 486
William W. 348
HOLDER, William D. 392, 393
HOLGATE, Thomas 478*
HOLIFIELD, Chet 216, 219, 222, 225, 229, 232, 235, 238, 241, 244, 248, 251, 254, 257, 260, 263
HOLLADAY
Alexander Q. 477
Alexander R. 94, 96
HOLLAND
Albert E. 472
Arthur J. 462*
Benjamin L. 551
Cornelius 76, 77
E.V. 286
Edward 449, 458
Edward E. 166, 169, 172, 175, 179
Elmer J. 215, 237, 240, 243, 246, 250, 253, 256
Ernest O. 485
F.P. 452
F.V. 286
Floyd 451
James 54, 57, 58, 59, 60, 61
Jerome H. 437, 598
R.A. 498
Rush L. 574
Spessard L. 219, 222, 226, 229, 232, 235, 238, 241, 245, 248, 251, 254, 257, 294*
W.M. 452
William J. 479, 497
HOLLANDER, Jacob H. 566
HOLLEMAN, Joel 85
HOLLENBECK, Conrad 333
HOLLERS, James P. 566
HOLLEY
Alexander H. 287
Horace 482
James A. 451
John M. 91
Robert W. 600, 606
HOLLICK, Arthur 502
HOLLIDAY
Cal 451
Cyrus K. 462*
Elias S. 150, 153, 156, 158
Frederick W.M. 379, 393
J.S. 501
Wallace T. 552*
HOLLING, Thomas L. 451
HOLLINGS, Ernest F. 256, 259, 263, 266, 366*
HOLLINGSHEAD, W.B. 600
HOLLINGSWORTH, David A. 163, 172, 175
HOLLINGWORTH, Harry L. 571
HOLLINS
George N. 396
J. Smith 450
HOLLINSWORTH
Henry 457
S.N. 457
HOLLIS
Henry F. 168, 171, 174, 338
Ira N. 486, 573
John H. 455
Orlando J. 478
Pat 461
Robert P. 419
HOLLISTER
Gideon H. 429
John B. 198, 201, 204, 443
HOLLOMON, John H. 478
HOLLORAN, Patrick J. 480
HOLLOWAY
Bruce K. 415*, 416
David P. 98, 444
Emory 583
Fred G. 531
James L., Jr. 416, 418, 483
James L. 3d 417
Josephus F. 573
Robert J. 568
William J. 272, 355
HOLLYDAY, R.C. 418
HOLM, Wilton R. 580
HOLMAN
Eugene 553*, 590
Frank E. 565, 589
Minard L. 573
Rufus C. 211, 214, 218, 357
William S. 102, 104, 106, 110, 112, 114, 116, 118, 125, 127, 130, 132, 134, 137, 140, 145
HOLMES
Adoniram J. 127, 130, 132
Arthur 469
Benjamin 455
Charles H. 112
David 55, 56, 57, 58, 59, 61, 68, 69, 71, 73, 326*
E. 498
Edward J. 500
Edwin R. 271
Elias B. 90, 91
Ephraim P. 417*
Gabriel 73, 75, 347
George F. 475
Hal 219, 222, 225, 228, 231, 234, 237, 241
Harry N. 565, 590
Isaac E. 85, 87, 88, 90, 92, 94
John (b. 1773) 66, 68*, 69, 71, 72, 74, 76, 77, 314*
John (b. 1891) 553
John B. 451
Julius C. 430, 433
Leslie A. 478
Merrill J. 473
Oliver Wendell (b. 1809) 597
Oliver Wendell (b. 1841) 270, 320, 589, 597, 609
Pehr G. 197, 200, 203, 207, 210, 213, 217, 220
Philip H. 594
Ralph C. 553*
Ralston S. 416
Robert D. 357
S.J. 573
Sidney T. 108
Theophilus H. 394
Thomas 597
Thomas H. 597
Uriel 66
William H. 500
William J., Jr. 481
HOLMSTEDT, Raleigh W. 473
HOLSEY, Hopkins 80, 82
HOLSHOUSER, James E., Jr. 349
HOLT
Andrew D. 482, 578
Cooper T. 580
Elmer 331
Grover J. 567
Hamilton 480, 576
Henry W. 380
Hines 84, 392
Homer A. 384
Ivan Lee 530
Jordan 450
Joseph 27*, 40, 43, 402, 444
Joseph F. 232, 235, 238, 241
L. Emmett, Jr. 592
Marjorie S. 264
O.T. 454
Orrin 80, 82
Rush D. 205, 209, 212, 384
Samuel D. 457*
Thomas M. 348
Victor, Jr. 547
HOLTEN, Samuel 4, 6, 52
HOLTON
Hart B. 127
Henry D. 572
Karl 608
Linwood 380
William B. 576
HOLTONER, J. Stanley 419
HOLTZCLAW, Jack G. 554
HOLTZMAN
Arnold H. 612
Elizabeth 265
John W. 454
Lester 233, 236, 240, 243, 246
HOLYOKE
Edward 472
Edward A. 563
HOLZAPFEL, E.W. 486
HOLZAPPLE, Joseph R. 416
HOLZINGER, Karl J. 591
HOMAN
Fletcher 486
Richard 580
W.K. 536
HOMANS, George C. 574
HOMER
Arthur B. 544*, 596
Winslow 607
HONAMAN, Earl M. 516, 519
HONE, Philip 458
HONES, Tiberius G. 480
HONEWELL, Arthur 559
HONEYMAN, Nan Wood 208
HONEYWELL, Mark C. 548
HONG
Edna 602
Howard 602
HOOD
Clifford F. 493, 554
George E. 171, 175
George H. 438
George J. 598
Graham S. 502
Harrison P. 611
John B. 394*, 395*, 396
Raymond M. 591
Solomon P. 432
HOOGKAMP, Herman F. 449
HOOK
Charles R. 578, 596
Enos 85, 86
Frank E. 204, 207, 210, 213, 220
H.M. 451
William C. 272
HOOKER
Charles E. 119, 121, 123, 125, 132, 135, 137, 140, 151
David G. 456
Edward P. 480
Edward W. 454
Elon H. 492
James M. 182, 186
John 452
Joseph 406, 407*, 408*, 409*
Warren B. 138, 141, 143, 146
HOOKS, Charles 65, 68, 70, 71
HOOPER
Alcaeus 450
Ben W. 370
Benjamin S. 129
Franklin W. 465, 497
Johnson J. 391*
Joseph L. 187, 190, 194, 197, 200
M.J. 557
Robert L. 10
Samuel 104, 106, 108, 110, 112, 114, 116
Stanford C. 594, 598
William (educator) 484
William (patriot) 3, 6
William L. 483
HOOTEN, Ernest A. 611
HOOVEN, M.D. 576
HOOVER
Calvin B. 566
Herbert C. 13, 18*, 32*, 46, 596, 598, 603, 609, 610
Mrs. Herbert C. 576*
Herbert, Jr. 598
J. Edgar 603, 609
Paul A. 546*
William H. 543
HOPE
Bob 604, 608
Clifford R. 190, 193, 197, 200, 203, 206, 210, 213, 216, 220, 223, 226, 229, 232, 236
J. William 567
John 476, 611
Stanley C. 578
HOPKINS
Albert C. 138, 141
Albert J. 130, 132, 134, 137, 139, 142, 145, 147, 150, 153, 156, 158, 300
Arthur F. 277
Arvah B. 462
Benjamin F. 111, 113
David W. 191, 194, 197
Edward (Conn.) 8*
Edward (Fla.) 454
Ernest M. 469, 549, 550
Esek 416
Frank A. 153, 156
George W. 82, 83, 85, 87, 88, 90, 101, 435
Harry L. 34, 46
Henry 486
Isaac S. 470, 471
J.W. 455
James 593
James H. 119, 128
John H. 505, 522
John Jay 547*
John P. 451
Louis B. 484
Mark 436, 487
Nathan T. 142
P.S. 500
Samuel 63
Samuel I. 134
Samuel M. 532
Samuel M. (Rep.) 64
Stephen 3, 4, 7, 9*, 10
Stephen T. 133
Thomas S. 575
William H. 471, 480
William R. 452
HOPKINSON
Charles 610
Francis (N.J.) 3, 4, 6
Francis (Pa.) 501
Joseph 65, 67
HOPPER, Edward 593, 603
HOPPES, Dale D. 612
HOPPIN, William W. 361
HOPPS, Walter, 498
HOPSON, W.H. 536
HOPWOOD
Erie C. 573
Herbert G. 417*
Robert F. 172
HORAN, Walter F. 219, 222, 225, 228, 231, 234, 237, 241, 244, 247, 250
HORD, Donal 589, 590
HORGAN, Paul 586, 591
HORKAN, George A. 403
HORLBECK, Henry B. 572
HORN
Carl, Jr. 546
Charles L. 492
Francis H. 479*
Henry 78
Nelson P. 466
Paul W. 482
Stephen 467
William 531
Williamson H. 457
HORNBEAK, Samuel L. 483
HORNBECK
John W. 92
Stanley K. 433
HORNBLOWER
Josiah 6
Joseph C. 340
HORNBY, Robert A. 550
HORNE
Edmund C. 473
John E. 443, 445
HORNER
Charles F. 577
H. Mansfield 554*, 597
Henry 301
John W. 466
Junius M. 508, 522
Matina S. 479
Richard E. 567
Wesley W. 572
HORNIBROOK, William H. 423, 426, 430, 435, 436
HORNIG, Donald F. 467
HORNOR, Lynn S. 199, 202
HORR
J.C. 458*
Ralph A. 199
Roswell G. 123, 125, 128
HORROCKS, James 486
HORRY, Elias 451*
HORSEY
Outerbridge (b. 1777) 61, 62, 63, 65, 66, 67, 290
Outerbridge (b. 1910) 426
HORSFORD, Jerediah 95
HORSKY
Charles A. 492
Edward 454
HORSMANDEN, Daniel 10
HORST, Louis 593
HORSTICK, William W. 514, 519
HORSTMANN, Ignatius F. 525
HORTON

Albert H. 306
Frank J. 249, 253, 256, 259, 262, 265
Frank O. 212
Henry H. 370
Jack K. 552*
Loton 548
Mildred M. 485
Thomas R. 99
Valentine 99, 101, 105
HOSEA, Addison 518, 520
HOSHOUR, Samuel 467
HOSKINS
Fred 534
George G. 117, 119
James D. 482
HOSMER
Craig 232, 235, 238, 241, 244, 248, 251, 254, 257, 260, 263
George W. 465
Hezekiah L. 55
James K. 568
Stephen T. 287
Titus 4, 5
HOSS, E. Embree 470, 530
HOSTETLER, Abraham J. 123
HOSTETTER
Jacob 67, 68
John C. 607
HOTCHKISS
Elisha 451
Giles W. 107, 108, 112
Julius 109
HOTT, James 531
HOTZ, Henry H., Jr. 501
HOUCHIN, John M. 551
HOUCK, Jacob, Jr. 86
HOUDRY, Eugene J. 608
HOUGH
Charles M. 271
David 58, 59
Harry 547
Harry B. 583
Henry H. 416
Lynn H. 478
Romeyn B. 594
Warwick 329
William J. 90
HOUGHTELING, James L. 443
HOUGHTON
Alanson B. 178, 181, 428, 429
Amory 428, 574
Arthur A., Jr. 575
Douglas 453
Herbert P. 467, 485
James C. 549
Sherman O. 113, 115
HOUK
George W. 138, 141
John C. 138, 141
Leonidas C. 124, 126, 129, 131, 133, 136
HOUSE
Charles L. 612
J. Cline 559
Jay E. 462
John F. 120, 122, 124, 126, 392
T.W., Sr. 454
HOUSEMAN, Julius 128
HOUSER, Theodore V. 493, 552
HOUSLEY, J. Elmer 576
HOUSTON
Charles H. 611
David F. 31*, 32, 39, 45, 482*, 484, 549
Frank K. 545
George S. 85, 87, 89, 90, 94, 96, 98, 100, 102, 122, 277*
Henry A. 153
John (Houstoun) 5, 8*
John M. 203, 206, 210, 213
John W. 89, 91, 92
P.D. 564
Robert G. 186, 189, 193, 196
Russell 549
Sam 72, 73, 90, 92, 94, 96, 98, 99, 101, 369, 372*
Thomas J. 579
Turner 459*
William 4, 5
William C. (N.J.) 4, 6
William C. (Tenn.) 157, 160, 163, 166, 169, 172, 175
William V. 480, 570
HOUSTOUN, John (See Houston)
HOUX, Frank L. 387
HOVDE
Frederick L. 479
Howard T. 568
HOVEN, Mathew J. 456*
HOVERTER, George A. 453
HOVEY, Alvin P. 132, 302, 408, 409, 435
HOVGAARD, William 611
HOVING
Thomas P.F. 499
Walter 579
HOW
John 460*
Samuel B. 469
HOWARD
Ada 485
Alan 591
Allen B. 449
Alfred T. 531
Arthur F. 460
Bart 584
Benjamin 60, 61
Benjamin C. 76, 77, 81, 82
Cecil 579, 591
Charles 453
Charles P. 558*
Edgar 184, 188, 191, 194, 197, 201
Edward D. 524
Ernest E. 572
Everette B. 178, 185, 191
Findley B. 434
Francis 9
Francis W. 525
George 316
George E., 573
Guy V. 204, 325
H. Clay 435
Henry (Mich.) 453
Henry (R.I.) 362
Hildegarde 592
J. Gordon 531
Jacob M. 86, 104, 106, 108, 110, 112, 322
James J. 252, 256, 259, 262, 265
John E. (b. 1752) 6, 8, 15, 53, 54, 55*, 56, 316*
John E. (b. 1902) 607
John R. 474
Jonas G. 130, 132
Leland O. 563
Martin, Jr. 3
Milford W. 142, 144
N.R. 573
Oliver O. 406, 408*, 409*, 410, 472, 483
Potter P. 450
Richard 587
Richard F. 498
Roger S. 478
Sidney 583
Solomon 478
Tilghman A. 84, 438
Timothy E. 599
Volney E. 94, 96
W.H.A. 470
W.J. 459
William 103
William A. 99, 100, 102
William G. 577
William M. 145, 147, 150, 153, 155, 158, 161, 164, 167, 170, 173
William W. 485
Willis E. 491
HOWARTH, Nelson O. 461*
HOWDEN, Frederick B. 510
HOWE
Albert R. 116
Albion P. 408*
Clarence D. 598
Elias 597
Harriet E. 595
Henry M. 594*, 596
Henry V. 608
Howard A. 599
George L. 608
Harold, 2d 444
James R. 143, 146
John W. 93, 95
Mark A. deW. (b. 1808) 507, 519
Mark A. deW. (b. 1864) 583
Percy R. 566
Robert 406
Thomas C. 497
Thomas Carr 467
Thomas M. 95, 97
Thomas Y., Jr. 95
Timothy O. 29, 43, 105, 107, 109, 111, 113, 115, 117, 120, 122, 385
Walter 425
William B.W. 507, 521
William W. 564
HOWELL
Albert S. 611
Benjamin F. 143, 146, 148, 151, 154, 157, 159, 162
Charles R. 227, 230, 233
David 7
Edward 79
Elias 81
Evan 213, 216, 219, 223, 273
Evan P. 449
George 154
Harry E. 578
J. Morton 427*
James B. 112, 304
Jeremiah B. 63, 64, 66, 361
John 418
John W. 595
Joseph 155, 157, 160, 163, 166, 169, 172
Leonard G. 456
Max D. 568
Morton B. 457
Nathaniel W. 64
R.B.C. 534
Richard 340
Robert B. 184, 187, 191, 194, 197, 201, 333
Roger, Jr. 466
William B. 273
William C. 462
William H. 570
William T. 444
HOWELLS
John M. 591
William Dean 563, 578, 603
William W. 563, 611
HOWES, Royce 586
HOWEY, Benjamin F. 128
HOWLAND
Benjamin 58, 59, 60, 361
Fred A. 549, 550
Henry E. 575
John 3
L. Paul 160, 163, 166
Leroy A. 485
HOWLEY, Richard 5
HOWRY, Charles B. 273
HOWSE, Hilary E. 457*
HOWSON, Louis R. 572
HOWZE
Hamilton H. 404, 405*
Robert L. 405
HOXWORTH, Stephen A. 167
HOYER, Eric G. 457
HOYLE
Eli D. 410
Rene E.D. 413
HOYT
Elton II 596
Francis S. 486
Henry A. 439
Henry M. 359
John P. 381
John W. 487
Joseph G. 484
Stephen 457
HRUSKA, Roman L. 233, 236, 239, 242, 246, 249, 252, 255, 258, 262, 265, 334
HSIA, David Y. 599
HUBARD, Edmund W. 87, 88, 90
HUBBARD
Asahel W. 106, 108, 110
C.H. 460
Chester D. 109, 111
David 83, 92
Demas, Jr. 108
Elbert H. 156, 159, 161, 164
Gardiner G. 578
Henry 76, 77, 79, 81, 82, 84, 337*
Henry V. 573
Joel D. 143
John 314
John H. 106, 107
John R. 481
Jonathan H. 62
Levi 64
Lucius F. 324
Richard B. 372, 431
Richard D. 109, 200
Russell S. 514, 522
Samuel D. 26, 27, 43, 89, 90
Thomas H. 67, 70
William P. 161, 163
HUBBELL
Alan F. 566
Edwin N. 109
James R. 109
Jay A. 116, 119, 121, 123, 125
William S. 88
HUBBERT, M. King 576
HUBBLE, Edwin P. 591, 596
HUBBS
Carl L. 600
Horace N. 472
Orlando 126
HUBER
Robert J. 265
Walter B. 221, 224, 227
Walter L. 572
William D. 559
HUBERT, Charles D. 476
HUBLEY, Edward B. 81, 83
HUCK, Winnifred S. 180
HUDD, Thomas R. 131, 134
HUDDELL, Arthur M. 558
HUDDLE, J. Klahr 424
HUDDLESTON
George 170, 173, 176, 179, 183, 186, 189, 192, 196, 199, 202
George, Jr. 235, 238, 241, 244, 247
Walter 264, 310
HUDGINS, Edward W. 380
HUDNUT, William H., 3d 264
HUDSON
Arthur J. 534
Barzillai 551
Charles, 86, 87, 89, 91
Charles L. 569
Claude S. 594, 596, 604, 609
Grant M. 184, 187, 190, 194
Henry 453
J.R. 461
John E. 543
Manley O. 573
Ralph P. 612
Silas A. 429
Thomas J. 140, 579
William 458
William M. 485
William W. 475*
HUDSPETH, Claude B. 179, 182, 185, 189, 192, 195
HUEBNER
Clarence R. 404, 412, 413
R.H. 476
Robert J. 604
HUEGLI, A.G. 484
HUEGY, Harvey W. 568
HUEY, Samuel C. 550
HUFF, George F. 138, 143, 154, 157, 160, 163
HUFFINES, Robert L., Jr. 553
HUFFMAN, James W. 221, 354
HUFSTEDLER, Shirley M. 272
HUFTY, Jacob 61, 62, 64
HUGER
Benjamin (b. 1768) 56, 57, 58, 66
Benjamin (b. 1806) 394
Daniel 7, 51, 52, 364
Daniel E. 88
Isaac 406
John 451
HUGGINS
Arthur 558
Charles B. 600, 606, 607
HUGHES
A.S. 558
Albert W. 551*
Alfred F. 471
Arthur H. 482, 483
Charles 97
Charles Evans 18, 32*, 38, 270*, 345, 534, 565, 568, 573, 579, 589, 603, 609
Charles F. 416
Charles J., Jr. 161, 285
Christopher 433*, 437
Dudley M. 161, 164, 167, 170
Edwin H. 469, 530
Everett C. 574
Everett S. 402
Frederick G. 572
George R. 501
George W. 102
Gordon A. 568
Harold E. 258, 261, 264, 305*
Hatcher 583
Howard 594
J. McCall 549
J.W.F. 462
James 100, 273
James A. 152, 155, 158,

161, 163, 166, 169, 192, 195
James F. 202
James H. 206, 209, 213, 292
James M. 88
John H. 400
John J. 524, 527
Langston 611
Matthew S. 530
R. John 587
Raymond M. 473, 475
Richard J. 342
Rowland R. 444
Sam S. 455
Simon P. 281
Thomas H. 76, 77
William 154, 159, 162, 165, 168, 171, 174, 341
William A.C. 530
HUGHSTON, Jonas A. 99
HUGUNIN, Daniel, Jr. 73
HUKRIEDE, Theodore W. 181
HULBERT
Calvin B. 475
Edmund D. 546
G. Murray 171, 174
Henry S. 611
John W. 65
Murray 574
HULBURD
Benjamin N. 377
Calvin T. 107, 109, 110
HULCY, Dechard A. 575
HULICK, George W. 141, 143
HULING, James H. 144, 451
HULINGS, Willis J. 169, 178
HULL
Albert W. 570, 598, 607
B.D. 576
Clark L. 571
Cordell 33*, 34, 38, 160, 163, 166, 169, 172, 175, 178, 185, 189, 192, 195, 198, 371, 573, 605, 609
David C. 475
Frank 558
Harry E. 170, 173, 176, 180, 183, 443
J.P.D. 608
John 481
John A. 402
John A.T. 137, 140, 142, 145, 148, 150, 153, 156, 159, 161
John E. 400, 404*
Mrs. Lytle 603
Merlin 196, 205, 209, 212, 215, 219, 222, 225, 228, 231, 235
Morton D. 183, 187, 190, 193, 196
Noble A. 122
Roger 549*
William 406
William E. 183, 187, 190, 193, 196
William R., Jr. 236, 239, 242, 246, 249, 252, 255, 258
HULLEY, Lincoln 482
HULLIHEN, Walter 469
HULM, John K. 612
HULSE, Hiram R. 510
HULSEY, William H. 449
HULTBERG, John 589, 593
HULTZ, Fred S. 477
HUMBERT, Russell J. 469
HUME
Alfred 475*
E.E. 453
Edgar E. 580
George S. 576
HUMES
John P. 423
Thomas D. 461
Thomas W. 482
William Y.C. 396
HUMMEL, Arthur W. 424
HUMPHRESS, John Y. 462
HUMPHREY
Augustin R. 181
Charles 73
Charles F. 403
Doris 593
Edward P. 532
Friend 449*
George D. 475, 487
George M. 35*, 39
Heman 465
Herman L. 122, 124, 126
Hubert H. 14, 19*, 227, 230, 233, 236, 239, 242, 245, 249, 251, 254, 261, 265, 325*, 457
James 103, 109
James M. 109, 110
Lyman U. 306
Moses 452*
Reuben 60
Stillman 452
William E. 155, 158, 160, 163, 166, 169, 172
Zephaniah M. 532
HUMPHREYS
Alex C. 573
Andrew 118
Andrew A. 408*
Benjamin G. 153, 156, 159, 162, 165, 168, 171, 174, 177, 181, 326
Cecil C. 475
Charles 7
David 435, 437
Harry E., Jr. 554*
Hector 480
Milton W. 570
Parry W. 64
Robert 236, 310
W.J. 566, 600, 607
William Y. 184
HUMPHRIES
A.A. 402
Rolfe 589, 610
HUMSTONE, Willard C. 543
HUN, Henry 569
HUNDLEY, W.B. 454
HUNGATE, William L. 249, 252, 255, 258, 262, 265
HUNGERFORD
H.B. 600
John N. 121
John P. 63, 64, 66
Orville 88, 90
HUNKELER, Edward J. 523, 526*
HUNN, John 291
HUNSAKER
Jerome C. 596, 597, 612
W.J. 461
HUNT
Alfred E. 543
Carleton 127
Charles W. 573
Duane G. 528
Earl G., Jr. 470, 531
Emory W. 467, 469, 534
Ezra M. 572
Frank W. 298
G. Carleton 580
George W.P. 280*
Henry A. 611
Henry F. 572
Henry J. 453
Henry T. 452
Hiram P. 81, 84, 86
I.P. 450
J. Ramsey 569
James B. 87, 89
Jesse 450
John E. 256, 259, 262, 265
John T. 154, 156
Jonathan 75, 76, 78
Joseph McV. 571
Juane G. 528
L. Clarence 465
Leigh 473
Lester C. 228, 231, 235, 387*
Paul C. 455
Phineas G.C. 566
Randell 483
Richard M. 567
Robert H. 455
Robert W. 573, 596
Roy A. 543
Samuel 57, 58
T. Sterry 563, 565*
Theodore G. 96
Thomas 483*
Ward 269, 345
Washington 88, 90, 91, 344
William H. (b. 1824) 29, 42, 273, 436
William H. (b. 1897) 272*
Wilson G. 548
HUNTER
Allan O. 229, 232
Andrew J. 139, 145
David 406, 407
Frank O. 411*
Fred H. 453
Frederick M. 469
James W. 514, 522
John 53, 54, 55, 364
John A. 474
John F. 208, 211, 214
John W. 109
Lemuel B. 492
Matthew A. 590
Morton C. 110, 116, 118, 120
Ralph M. 575
Richard C. 201, 334
Robert 8*
Robert M.T. 83*, 85, 87, 90, 92, 94, 96, 98, 99, 101, 103, 105, 378, 391, 392, 393*
Robert T. 382
Roy D. 476*
Sam 499
Thomas 472
W. Godfrey 132, 142, 153, 429, 430
Walter S. 571
Wilbur H. 501
William (b. 1754) 67
William (b. 1774) 63, 64, 66, 67, 68, 361, 424*
William F. 93, 95
William H. 83
William N. 396*
HUNTHAUSEN, Raymond 526
HUNTING, George C. 510
HUNTINGTON
Abel 79, 81
Anna Hyatt 589
Archer M. 566, 603
Arthur L. 460
Asahel 460, 498
Benjamin 5, 51
Collis P. 552
Daniel 577*
Daniel T. 510
Ebenezer 61, 66
Ellsworth 575, 599
Frederic D. 506, 519
George L. 461
Jabez W. 75, 77, 78, 83, 85, 87, 89, 90, 287
Samuel (b. 1731) 4, 5, 8, 15, 287
Samuel (b. 1765) 10, 352*
William E. 466
HUNTLEY
Elias D. 474
Robert E.R. 485
HUNTON
Eppa 117, 120, 122, 124, 139, 141, 379
Jonathan G. 314
HUNTSMAN, Adam 81
HUOT, T. Oliva 252
HURD
Frank H. 119, 124, 128
Henry M. 571
John G. 437
HURDIS, Charles E. 413
HURLBUT, Stephen A. 110, 118, 407, 426
HURLEY
Charles F. 321
Denis M. 143, 146
Edward N. 599
Francis D. 526
John F. 460*
Joseph P. 528
Mark J. 528
Patrick J. 33, 40, 425, 433
Robert E. 289
HUROK, Sol 593
HURST
J. Willis 567
John F. 465, 530
Thurman S. 355
William 601
HURTY, John N. 572
HUSA, Karel 587
HUSBAND, A.C. 418
HUSE, Emery 580
HUSS, H. Paul 461
HUSSEY
George F., Jr. 418
James T. 474
HUSTED, James W. 171, 174 178, 181
HUSTING, Paul O. 172, 175, 385
HUSTON
Joseph W. 444, 450
Simeon A. 512, 521
Tillinghast 580
HUTCHENS, Joseph W. 516, 519
HUTCHESON
John R. 484
Joseph C. 141, 144, 271
Joseph C., Jr. 454
Maurice A. 559
William L. 559
HUTCHIN, Claire E., Jr. 405
HUTCHINGS
Paul 559
Richard H. 571
HUTCHINS
Francis S. 466
Harry B. 475
John 103, 105
Robert M. 468, 597
W.J. 454
Waldo 123, 126, 128
Wells A. 107
William J. 466
HUTCHINSON
C.I. 460
Edward 249, 252, 255, 258, 261, 265
Elijah C. 171, 174, 177, 181
G. Evelyn 600
J. 457
John G. 451
Joseph 500
R.A. 533
Stuart N. 532
T. Leger 451*
Thomas 8, 10
Titus 375
Ralph C. 474, 485
HUTSON, Richard 4, 7, 451
HUTT, A.J. 455
HUTTIG, Charles H. 564
HUTTON
Edward F. 547
Frederick R. 573
John E. 130, 133
William F. 498
HUXMAN, Walter A. 272, 307
HUXTABLE, Ada Louise 587
HUYLER, John 101
HYATT
Alpheus 500
Anna V. 610*
Byron E. 450
Gerhardt W. 401
Gilbert E. 559
James W. 444
HYDE
Arthur M. 33, 45, 330
Charles C. 573
De Witt S. 233, 236, 239
E. Francis 565
E.P. 600
Edward 8*
Henry B. 546
Ira B. 116
James N. 573
John T.E. 449
Lillia Babbitt 492
Oliver M. 453*
Rosel H. 443*
Samuel C. 144
Tristram T. 451
W. Lewis 580
William A. 611
William D. 454, 466
HYER
Frank S. 486*
Julien C. 576
Robert S. 481
HYINK, Bernard L. 480
HYLAN, John F. 458
HYLAND
Francis F. 525
John J. 417*
Lawrence A. 594
HYLE, Michael 529
HYMAN
John A. 119
William B. 311
HYNDMAN, Donald E. 580
HYNEMAN
Charles S. 571
John M. 63, 64
HYNES
John B. 450
William J. 115

I

IACOCCA, Lee A. 547
ICHORD, Richard H. 246, 249, 252, 255, 258, 262, 265
ICKES, Harold L. 33*, 34*, 44
IDDINGS, Lewis M. 427
IDE, Henry C. 437
IGNATIUS, Paul R. 339
IGNATOW, David 610
IGOE
James T. 190, 193, 196
Michael L. 203
William L. 168, 171, 174, 177
IHLER, Henry 557
IHRIE, Peter, Jr. 76, 78
IKARD, Frank N. 231, 234, 237, 240, 244, 247, 570
IKIRT, George P. 141
ILES, Charles F. 453
ILSLEY, Daniel 60
IMBERTSON, Norman M. 601
IMHOFF, Lawrence E. 201,

204, 208, 214
IMLAY, James H. 55, 56
IMODA, Henry 481
IMPELLITTERI, Vincent R. 458
INGALLS
Jeremy 610
John J. 116, 118, 120, 123, 125, 127, 129, 130, 131, 132, 134*, 306
Rufus 403
INGE
Samuel W. 90, 92
William 586
William M. 80
INGERSOLL
Charles J. 64, 86, 88, 90, 92
Charles L. 468
Charles R. 288
Colin M. 94, 96
Ebon C. 106, 108, 110, 112
George P. 436
Howard L. 601
Jared 4, 7, 15
Joseph R. 81, 86, 88, 90, 92, 429
Ralph I. 72, 74, 75, 77
Ralph J. 436
Robert S. 431, 544*
Roy C. 544*
Royal E. 417
Stuart H. 417, 419
INGHAM
Samuel 80, 82
Samuel D. 25, 39, 64, 65, 67, 70, 71, 73, 75
INGLE, James A. 509
INGLEHEART, Austin S. 547*
INGLES, Harry C. 403
INGLEY, Fred 511, 519
INGLIS
Ernest A. 289
James 532
John B. 578
T.B. 416
INGOLDSBY, Richard 8*
INGRAHAM
Duncan N. 396, 418
Hollis S. 578
Joe 271
Mark H. 564
INGRAM
Jonas H. 417
Porter 392
William B., Jr. 456
INNES
Harry 308
Katherine 500
INOUYE, Daniel K. 241, 245, 248, 251, 254, 258, 261, 263, 298
INSKEEP, John 458*
INSULL, Samuel 545*
IPATIEFF, Vladimir 596
IRBY
John L.M. 138, 141, 144, 365
Richard 484
IREDELL
James (b. 1750) 15, 269
James (b. 1788) 74, 76, 347*
IRELAND
Clifford C. 173, 176, 180
John (b. 1827) 372
John (b. 1838) 524, 528
Mark L., Jr. 611
Merritte W. 403, 565
IRETON, Peter L. 528
IRION, Alfred B. 130
IRONES, Rutherford B. 461
IRONS
Ernest E. 569
John D. 476
IRVIN
Alexander 92
James 86, 88
Vivian R. 460
William A. 554
William W. 76, 78
IRVINE
James 478
Julia 485
S. G. 533
Samuel G. 476
William (b. 1741) 7, 53, 406
William (b. 1820) 103
William B. 474
IRVING
Frederick 430, 483
Frederick A. 413, 483
George W. 426,
Theodore L. 227, 230
Washington 437, 597
William 64, 65, 67
IRWIN
Donald J. 241, 251, 254
Edward M. 187, 190, 193
Harvey S. 150
Horace C. 461
Inez Haynes 574
James B. 594
Jared 64, 65, 295*
John N. 435
Nathaniel 532
Pat 355
Stafford L. 400, 412, 413
Thomas 76
Walter W. 594
William 283
William W. (Mason) 579
William W. (Rep.) 86, 426, 459
ISAACS, Norman E. 573, 609
ISACKS, Jacob C. 72, 73, 75, 76, 78
ISACSON, Leo 224
ISELEY, George A. 459
ISENBURGER, Eric 593
ISHERWOOD, Benjamin F. 417
ISRAEL
Charles R. 578
Rogers 510, 519
ISSENMANN, Clarence G. 525*
ITSCHNER, E.C. 402
ITTNER, Anthony F. 121
IVERSON, Alfred 91, 98, 100, 102, 296
IVES
Brayton 554
Charles 585
Eli 569
Frederic E. 594, 600, 610
Halsey C. 498
Herbert E. 580, 600*, 612
Hiram D. 402
Irving M. 224, 227, 230, 233, 236, 239, 346
Levi S. 505, 521
Willard 95
IVINS
E. 600
Benjamin F.P. 512, 520
IVY, Andrew C. 571
IZAC, Edouard V.M. 206, 209, 212, 216, 219
IZARD, Ralph 7, 51, 52, 53, 364
IZLAR, James F. 141

J

JACK
Summers M. 149, 152
William 86
JACKLIN, Edward G. 480
JACKLING, Daniel C. 596, 610
JACKSON
Abner 478, 482
Alfred M. 150
Amos H. 154
Andrew 13, 16*, 54, 55, 72, 73, 369*, 406, 597
Andrew L. 454
Archie B. 576
Charles 361
Chevalier 590, 594
Claiborne F. 329
David 7
David S. 91
Donald L. 222, 225, 229, 232, 235, 238, 241
Dugald C. 563, 595
Ed 303
Edward B. 69, 70
Elihu E. 317
Floyd L. 355
Frank D. 304
Fred S. 164
Frederick W. 610
George 54, 56, 57
George F. 576
Gordon T. 608
Hancock 329
Henry 508
Henry M. 215, 219, 222, 225, 228, 231, 234, 237, 241, 244, 247, 250, 254, 257, 260, 263, 266, 382
Henry R. 423*
Howard W. 450*
Howell E. 126, 129, 131, 269, 271, 370
Isaac R. 426
J. Hugh 576, 578
J. Monroe 136
Jabez N. 569
Jabez Y. 80, 82
Jacob B. 383
James (b. 1757) 51, 52, 53, 56, 57, 58, 295*
James (b. 1777) 563
James (b. 1819) 100, 102, 296
James S. 104
John B. 424*, 426, 429, 433, 435*, 436*
John G. 58, 59, 61, 62, 64, 66
John K. 395
John L. 513, 520
Jonathan 6
Joseph R. 273
Joseph W. 92, 94
Lee 593
N. Baxter 545*
Nathaniel J. 410
Oscar L. 131, 133
Richard, Jr. 60, 62, 63, 64
Robert H. 33, 34, 41, 270
Robert Hill 587
Robert T. 551
Russell L. 498
Samuel D. 216, 303
Sheldon 532
"Stonewall" (See Thomas J.)
Thomas B. 83, 84
Thomas J. 394*, 395, 597
W.A. 558
Walter C. 477
William (Mus. Dir.) 498
William (Rep.) 79, 81
William H. (Gen.) 396
William H. (Rep.) 150, 153, 159
William K. 575
William P. 165, 168, 317
William S. 286
William T. 93
JACOB
Charles 451
Charles D. 456*
John J. 383
JACOBI, Abraham 569, 603
JACOBS
Albert C. 469, 483
Andrew, Sr. 226
Andrew, Jr. 251, 255, 258, 261
Cyrus 450
Eastman N. 608
Ferris, Jr. 126
Israel 52
Joseph E. 426, 435
M.H. 573
Orange 461
Randall 418
Thornwell 478
W.V.E. 483*
JACOBSEN
Alfred 590
Bernhard M. 197, 200, 203
Einar W. 474
Thorkild P.R. 501
William S. 206, 210, 213
JACOBSON
Charles 558
Nathan 568
JACOBSTEIN, Meyer 185, 188, 191
JACOBUS, D.S. 573
JACOBY
Elias J. 579
George W. 569
JACOWAY, Henderson M. 164, 167, 170, 173, 176, 179
JADWIN
Cornelius C. 126
Edgar 402
JAFFA, Nathan 461
JAFFE, Louis I. 583
JAGGAR
Thomas A. 507, 522
Thomas A., Jr. 593
JAGOW, Elmer 472
JAICKS, Frederick G. 548
JAMES
Addison D. 159
Amaziah B. 121, 123
Arthur H. 360
Benjamin F. 228, 231, 234, 237, 240
Charles 604
Charles T. 95, 97, 99, 361
Darwin R. 128, 131
Earl D. 457
Earl E. 574
Edmund J. 472, 478, 563, 566
F. Don 479
Francis 85, 86
George 578, 592
Henry 583
Herman G. 478, 481
Hinton 194
Howard 587
Jack M. 597
John G. 482
John H. 449
L. Eldon 568
L. Stanley 599
Macgill 501
Marquis 583, 584
Ollie M. 153, 156, 159, 161, 164, 167, 170, 173, 309
Ralph K. 418
Rorer A. 179, 182
Thomas L. 29, 43
W. Frank 171, 174, 177, 180, 184, 187, 190, 194, 197, 200
Walter G. 476*
William 571*
William H. 333
JAMESON
J. Franklin 567
John 84, 88, 91
Samuel Y. 475
William J. 565, 568
JAMIESON
Francis A. 584
J. Kenneth 553*
William D. 161
JAMISON, David 10
JAMNBACK, Hugo 50
JANES
Edmund S. 530
Henry F. 80, 81
JANEWAY, Jacob J. 532
JANIS, Irving L. 598
JANNEY, Reynold 607
JANSEN
Johannes 458
Quinn 558
JANSON, Richard 499
JANSSEN, John 525
JANSSENS, Francis A. 524, 527
JANUARY, Lewis E. 567
JAQUES
Francis Lee 593
Mrs. Francis Lee 593
JARDINE, William M. 32, 33, 45, 427, 473, 486
JARK, Paul H. 405
JARMAN
John 231, 234, 237, 240, 243, 246, 250, 253, 256, 259, 262, 265
Pete 206, 209, 212, 216, 219, 222, 423
JARNAGIN, Spencer 88, 90, 369
JARRELL, Randall 602
JARRETT
Benjamin 208, 211, 215
John A. 451
JARVIS
Abraham 505, 519
Leonard 76, 77, 79, 80
Porter M. 553*
Thomas J. 8, 141, 348*, 424
JASTROW, Joseph 571
JAVITS, Jacob K. 224, 227, 230, 233, 239, 243, 246, 249, 252, 256, 259, 262, 265, 346
JAWORSKI, Leon 565*
JAY
John (b. 1745) 5, 6, 15*, 269, 344, 423, 428, 565
John (b. 1817) 423, 567
Peter A. 423, 427, 435
William 570
JAYNE, William 461*
JAYNES, G.H. 459
JEANMARD, Jules B. 527
JEARY, Clark 455
JEFFERIES, R.M. 366
JEFFERIS, Albert W. 177, 181
JEFFERS
Clyde G. 381
E.T. 533
Lamar 179, 183, 186, 189, 192, 196, 199
Robinson 589, 610
William M. 553
William N. 418
JEFFERSON
Benjamin L. 434
Frank A. 459
Mark 594

Thomas 3, 7, 9, 13, 14, 15*, 23*, 28, 54, 55, 570, 597
JEFFERY, Gordon 577
JEFFORDS
Elza 128
Olin M. 377
JEFFREY
Harry P. 218
Robert E. 439
Robert H. 452
JEFFREYS, Herbert 9
JEFFRIES
Edward J., Jr. 453
M.D. 467
Walter S. 211
Zay 572, 590, 595, 596
JELKS, William D. 278
JELLEY, Joseph F., Jr. 418
JELLIFFE, Smith E. 569
JEMISON, Robert, Jr. 392, 393
JENCKES
Joseph 9
Joseph S. 459
Thomas A. 107, 109, 111, 113
Virginia Ellis 200, 203, 206
JENCKS, Millard H. 480
JENIFER
Daniel (b. 1723) 4, 6
Daniel (b. 1791) 77, 81, 82, 84, 423
JENISON
Edward H. 223, 226, 229
Silas H. 375
JENKINS
Albert G. 101, 103, 393
Burris A. 482
C. Francis 580
Charles F. 594
Charles J. 17, 296
D. Abner 460
Daniel E. 476
Douglas 424
Earl W. 455
Elisha 449
Glenn L. 570, 609
Helen Hartley 579, 603
James G. 272
John 8*
John A. 580
John J. 144, 147, 149, 152, 155, 158, 161
Lawrence W. 501
Lemuel 71
Mitchell 224
Paul 593
Reuben E. 401
Robert 60, 61
T.A. 418
T. Atkinson 577
Thomas 512, 520
Thomas A. 188, 191, 195, 198, 201, 204, 208, 211, 214, 218, 221, 224, 227, 230, 234, 237, 240
Timothy 90, 91, 95
Warren 452
William F. 297
JENKS
Arthur B. 207, 211, 214
Chancellor L. 579
Downing B. 549
Frank W. 548
George A. 119
Jeremiah W. 566
Michael H. 88
Stephen M. 595
JENNER
Albert E., Jr. 565, 568
William E. 216, 223, 226, 229, 232, 235, 238, 303*
JENNESS, Benning W. 89, 337
JENNEWEIN, Paul 579, 591, 607, 610
JENNINGS
Alvin R. 567
David 73
Edmund 9
Elmer R. 572
Hal B., Jr. 403
Herbert S. 600
Jesse D. 611
John, Jr. 212, 215, 218, 221, 225, 228
Jonathan 71, 72, 74, 75, 302
Judson T. 568
O.E. 497
Obadiah 532
Paul 558
William 460
William N. 611
William P. 237, 241, 244, 247, 250, 253
William S. 293
JENSEN
Ben F. 210, 213, 216, 220, 223, 226, 229, 232, 235, 239, 242, 245, 248
Erling N. 476
James H. 479
Leslie 367
JERNICK, William J. 574
JERNIGAN, John D. 423, 430
JEROME
David H. 322
J. Hanson 450
William T. 3d 466
JERTBERG, Gilbert H. 272
JESSE, Richard H. 476*
JESSERICH, Paul H. 566
JESSUP
Henry H. 532
Morris K. 497
Philip C. 573
Walter A. 473, 491
JESTER, Beauford H. 373
JESUP, Thomas S. 403
JETER, Thomas B. 365
JETT
Robert C. 511, 522
Thomas M. 145, 147, 150
JEWELL
Gilbert 557
Marshall 28, 43, 288*, 436
JEWETT
Albert G. 435
Charles W. 454
Daniel T. 112, 329
Edgar B. 451
Frank B. 595, 596*, 598
Freeborn G. 77, 344
Hugh J. 117
Joshua H. 98, 100
Luther 66
Milo P. 484
JIMERSON, Earl W. 557
JINKS, J.R. 462
JOCELYN, George B. 465*
JOCOBUS, M.W. 532
JOECKEL, Carleton B. 600
JOELSON, Charles S. 246, 249, 252, 256, 259
JOHANNES, Francis 526
JOHANSEN
August E. 236, 239, 242, 245, 249
John C. 610
JOHANSSON, Carl E. 598
JOHN
David C. 471
John P.D. 469
JOHNS
Charley E. 294
Foster M. 572
John 486, 505, 522
John E. 482
Joshua L. 212, 215
Kensey 290
Kensey, Jr. 74, 75, 290
Richard E. 576
Robert 476, 480
JOHNSEN, Irving A. 596
JOHNSON
A.W. 416
Adna R. 163
Albert 169, 172, 175, 179, 182, 186, 189, 192, 195, 199
Albert W. 250, 253, 256, 259, 262, 266
Albinus A. 487
Alexander S. 345
Alvin S. 566
Andrew 13, 14, 16, 88, 90, 92, 94, 96, 101, 103, 105, 107, 119, 369*, 370
Anton J. 210, 213, 216, 219, 223
Ben 159, 161, 164, 167, 170, 173, 177, 180, 184, 187
Benjamin N. 579
Bert W. 577
Bushrod R. 395
Byron L. 241
C.E. 282
C. Oscar 534
Calvin D. 216
Cave 26*, 43, 76, 78, 80, 81, 85, 87, 88
Charles 57
Charles B. 554*
Charles E. 478
Charles F. 165, 168, 171, 271, 315
Charles N. 566
Charles P. 452
Charles W. 500
Clarence L. 594, 604, 608*, 611
Clarke H. 362
Davenport 411, 412*
David 364
Dewey W. 207
Donald E. 568
Douglas 576, 594, 599
Earl D. 547
Eben S. 530
Ebenezer 450*
Ed R. 580
Edward (Impresario) 603
Edward (mayor) 450*
Edward (soldier) 395*, 396
Edwin C. 206, 209, 212, 216, 219, 222, 226, 229, 232, 285, 286
Edwin S. 172, 175, 178, 367
Eldon L. 476
Emory R. 579, 603
Felix 416
Francis 68, 69, 71, 72
Frank B. 455
Franklin W. 468
Fred G. 194
Frederick A. 128, 131
Frederick F. 509, 520, 521
George K. 550
George W. 186, 202, 205, 209, 212, 215
Glen D. 224
Glendon E. 543
Grove L. 142
Hale 17
Hallett 426
Harold K. 400*, 419
Harold T. 241, 244, 248, 251, 254, 257, 260
Harry H. 414, 415
Harvey H. 97
Harvey M. 272
Haynes 587
Henry (b. 1783) 66, 68, 69, 71, 79, 80, 82, 87, 89, 91, 311*
Henry (b. 1855) 497
Henry U. 137, 140, 142, 145
Henry V. 453
Herman M. 469
Herrick 532
Herschel V. 16, 91, 295*, 392, 393, 424, 437
Hiram W. 18, 173, 176, 179, 183, 186, 189, 193, 196, 199, 202, 206, 209, 212, 216, 219, 283*
Hjalmar W. 595
Hosmer A. 572
Howard A. 331
Howard C. 594
Howard W. 475
Irving P. 510, 519
Isaac 311
J. Allen 576
J.T. 457
Jacob 169
James (Ga.) 94, 296
James (Ky.) 72
James (Va.) 64, 66, 67, 69
James A. 109, 111
James C. 458
James H. 89, 91
James I. 459*
James L. 93
James N. 283
James P. 264
James W. 548
James Weldon 578, 611
Jed 191, 195, 198, 201, 205, 208, 211, 214, 218, 221, 273
Jed, Jr. 253
Jeromus 73, 74
Jesse 476
John (Mo.) 455
John (Md.) 449*
John (N.Y.) 458
John (Ohio) 95
John (Tenn.) 456
John A. 324
John B. 590, 601, 611
John T. (b. 1788) 69, 71
John T. (b. 1856) 355
John W. 478
Joseph (S.C.) 451
Joseph (Va.) 72, 73, 78, 82, 83, 85, 90, 378
Joseph B. 377
Joseph H. 508, 520
Joseph L. 432
Joseph T. 152, 154, 157, 160, 163, 166, 169, 172
Josephine Winslow 583
Jotham 574
Keen 310
Lady Bird 20, 604
Leon H. 476
Leroy 216, 219, 222, 225, 229, 232, 235
Lester 443
Lester R. 235, 238, 241, 244, 247, 250
Louis A. 34, 47, 568
Louisa Catherine 20
Luther A. 185, 189, 192, 195, 198, 202, 205, 208, 212, 215, 218, 221
Luther A., Sr. 483
Lyndon B. 13, 14, 18, 19, 208, 212, 215, 218, 221, 225, 228, 231, 234, 237, 240, 244*, 247*, 373, 596, 610
Magnus 184, 200, 325
Malcolm 585
Martin N. 138, 141, 143, 146, 162, 350
Max S. 419
Mordecai W. 472, 611
N.B. 355
Nathaniel 9
Nels C. 399
Nelson T. 423, 425*
Noadia 79
Noble J. 187, 190, 193, 210, 213, 216, 220, 223, 273
P.G. 544*
Paul B. 177, 181, 327
Perley B. 88
Philip 591
Philip (Rep.) 105, 107, 109
R.P. 460
Robert W. 548*
Robert W., Jr. 548
Raymond D. 594, 598
Reverdy 26, 41, 89, 91, 93, 106, 108, 110, 316, 317, 429
Richard M. 14, 16*, 60, 61, 62, 63, 65, 66, 68, 69, 71, 72, 74, 75, 77, 79, 80, 82, 83, 308
Richard O. 455
Richard W. 408, 409*, 410
Robert (S.C.) 9*
Robert (Va.) 392, 393*
Robert D. 197
Robert E. 454
Robert L. 482
Robert W. (Bus. Exec.) 548*
Robert W. (Rep.) 90, 92, 94, 96, 98, 100, 102, 281, 392*, 393
Robert W., Jr. 548
Roy L. 417*
Royal C. 172, 175, 178, 182, 185, 188, 192, 195, 198
Samuel 468
Samuel W. 565
T.R. 576
Thomas (Ark.) 281
Thomas (Ky.) 392
Thomas (Md.) 6, 8, 269
Thomas C. 479
Thomas F. 245
Tom L. 138, 141, 452
Treat B. 567, 604
Treby 449
U. Alexis 426, 431, 438
Victor M. 576
W.H. 551
Waldo P. 104, 329, 392, 393
Walter W. 286
Ward 212, 216
Wayne 455
Wendell G. 472
William 269
Sir William 3
William B. (b. 1782) 534
William B. (b. 1919) 548*
William C. 79, 82, 84, 86
William R. 187, 190, 193, 196
William Roy 443
William S. (b. 1727) 3, 4, 5, 51*, 287, 468
William S. (b. 1913) 604
William T. 449
JOHNSTON
A. Langstaff 600
A.W. 459
Albert S. 394
Alva 583
Alvanley 557
C. Brooks 458
Charles 84

Charles C. 78
Clem D. 575
David E. 149
Eric A. 575, 577
Francis W. 339
Frontis W. 469
Gabriel 9
George W.C. 451
Henry S. 355
J. Bennett, Jr. 264, 313
James S. 508, 522
James T. 130, 132
John 575
John A. 410
John B. 178
John W. (Mo.) 460
John W. (Va.) 113, 115, 117, 120, 122, 124, 126, 379
Joseph E. 124, 394*, 395*, 396, 403
Joseph F. 158, 161, 164, 167, 278*
Josiah S. 69, 71, 72, 74, 75, 77, 79, 311
Leon H. 493
Logan T. 543
Olin D. 221, 225, 228, 231, 234, 237, 240, 243, 247, 250, 253, 366*
Percy H. 545*
Rienzi M. 166, 372
Robert S. 480
Rowland L. 194
S. Paul 500
Samuel 6, 9, 15, 51, 52, 347
Thomas D. 131, 133
Wayne A. 548*
William (Rep.) 107
William 533
William A. 306
William F. 358
William H. 557
William P. 474, 483
JOHNSTONE
George 138
William A. 476
JOLLEY, John L. 138
JOMINY, Walter E. 572
JONAS
Benjamin F. 123, 125, 127, 312
Charles A. 194
Charles R. 234, 237, 240, 243, 246, 249, 253, 256, 259, 262
Edgar A. 226, 229, 232
JONES
A.C. 453
A.H. 461
Aaron 578
Abner C. 577
Abraham G. 452
Alan W. 414
Alexander E. 467
Alexander F. 573
Alexander H. 111, 113
Allen 6
Andrieus A. 174, 178, 181, 184, 188, 191, 343
Arthur H. 577
Benjamin 79, 31
Benjamin F. 576
Bruce S. 451
Burr W. 129
C.G. 458*
C.P. 538
Catesby 580
Charles A. 360, 579
Charles W. 118, 120, 122, 125, 127, 129, 293
Clark A. 271
Clifford B. 482
D.C. 462
D.P. 457
Daniel T. 95, 97
Daniel W. 281
David C. 416
David R. 394*
De Garmo 453
E.D. 483
Ed 260, 263, 266
Edgar D. 536
Edward N. 482
Elmer A. 610
Eugene K. 579
Evan J. 178, 182
Everett H. 514, 522
Francis 67, 69, 70
Francis C. 593, 598
Frank (author) 602
Frank (Rep.) 119, 121
Frank C. 579
Fred H. 576
G.H. 486
G. Lewis 438
George 60, 295
George H. (b. 1856) 548
George H. (b. 1872) 553
George W. (b. 1804) 95, 96, 98, 100, 304, 425
George W. (b. 1806) 88, 90, 91, 92, 93, 94, 96, 97, 99, 101
George W. (b. 1828) 124, 126
Girault M. 514, 520
Griffith 458
Hamilton C. 224, 227, 230
Harrison 545
Harry C. 600
Henry L.L. 413
Herbert M. 401
Homer R. 225
Howard Mumford 563, 577, 587
Howard P. 430
Ira B. 365
Isaac (banker) 545
Isaac (mayor) 458
Isaac D. 86
J. Glancy 95, 97, 99, 101, 423
J.H. 486
J.R. 600
J. Russel 424
J. Wesley 432, 435
James (author) 602
James (Rep., Ga.) 55
James (Rep., Va.) 69, 70
James C. 96, 97, 99, 369*
James H. 129, 131
James K. 124, 127, 129, 131, 134, 136, 139, 142, 144, 147, 150, 281
James R. 265
James M. 455
James T. 120, 127, 129, 131
Jenkin L. 573, 575
Jesse H. 34*, 46, 443
John C. 476
John J. 102
John N. 456
John P. 117, 119, 121, 123, 126, 128, 130, 133, 135, 138, 140, 143, 146, 148, 151, 335
John Paul 416, 597
John Quentin 545
John R. 394
John S. (Nev.) 335
John S. (Ohio) 121
John T. 578
John T., Jr. 491
John W. (Ga.) 91
John W. (Va.) 82, 83, 85, 87*, 88
Joel 458
Joseph 7
Joshua L. 576
L.A. 580
Lewis R. 574
Lewis W. 465, 466, 480, 578
Lloyd A. 580
Lloyd E. 415
Marshall P. 432
Marvin 175, 179, 185, 189, 192, 195, 198, 202, 205, 208, 212, 273
Mattison B. 534
Minetry L. 486
Morgan 109
Nathaniel 83, 84
Nettie Marie 492
Noble W. 5
Owen 101
Paul 510, 522
Paul C. 223, 227, 230, 233, 236, 239, 242, 246, 249, 252, 255
Peter , 454*
Phineas 126
R.T. 280
R.W. 470
Richard 475
Richard C. 465
Richard L. 432
Robert E. 472, 530
Robert Edmond 590
Robert Emmet, Jr. 222, 225, 228, 232, 235, 238, 241, 244, 247, 251, 254, 257, 260, 263
Robert F. 211, 214, 218, 221, 224
Robert T. 608
Roger 401, 402
Roger W. 445
Roland 96
Rufus M. 609
Russell 586, 607
Sam Houston 313
Samuel 449*
Seaborn 78, 89
Seby B. 459
Stephen A. 476
T.D. 595
T. Sambola 430
Thomas 451
Thomas E. 470
Thomas F. 481
Thomas G. 278
Thomas L. 110, 112, 118
Thomas M. 392
Vincent S. 573
W. Alton 492, 545*
Walter 55, 58, 59, 61, 62
Walter B. 18, 253, 256, 259, 262, 265
Walter H. 518, 521
Warren L. 271
Wesley L. 149, 152, 155, 158, 160, 166, 169, 172, 175, 179, 182, 186, 189, 192, 195, 199, 381
William (b. 1753) 361
William (b. 1760) 24*, 42, 57
William A. 139, 141, 144, 147, 149, 152, 155, 158, 160, 163, 166, 169, 172, 175
William C. 478
William Carey 147
William H. 588
Willie 6
Woodrow W. 227, 230, 234, 237
JONKMAN, Bartel J. 210, 213, 217, 220, 223
JONSEN, Albert R. 481
JONSSON, Erik 453
JORDAN
B. Everett 240, 243, 246, 249, 253, 256, 259, 262, 349
Barbara 266
Bryce 482
Chester B. 338
Conrad N. 444
Cornelius T. 476
David S. 473, 481, 563
Donald L. 578
Edwin O. 610
George R. 576
Harry B. 419
Isaac M. 128
J.P. 577
John T. 461
Len B. 245, 248, 251, 254, 258, 261, 299*
Ray H. 551
Thomas W. 470
Vernon E., Jr. 579
Wilbur K. 479
William S. 454
Winthrop 591, 602
JORDEN, Edwin J. 141
JORGENSEN
Albert N. 468
Joseph 122, 124, 126
JOSEPH
E.B. 457
Thomas L. 595
William 8
JOSEPHS, Devereux C. 491
JOSEPHSON
Brian D. 594
Clarence E. 472
JOSLIN
Elliott P. 590
Jervis 451
JOST, Henry L. 184, 455
JOSTER, Samuel W. 483
JOUETT, Edward S. 536
JOVA, Joseph J. 430
JOVES, John 456
JOY
Alfred H. 564
C. Turner 483
Charles F. 140, 143, 145, 148, 151
James F. 545
JOYAL, Arnold E. 470
JOYCE
Charles H. 120, 122, 124, 126
Isaac W. 530
James 163
Kenyon A. 412
Robert F. 525
W. Seavey 466
JOYNER, W.R. 449
JUDA, Walter 612
JUDAH, Noble B. 426
JUDAY, Chancey 575, 600
JUDD
Bethel 480
Charles H. 571
Deane B. 580
E. Starr 569
Homer 566
Neil M. 593*
Norman B. 110, 112, 435
Paul 453
Walter H. 217, 220, 223, 227, 230, 233, 236, 239, 242, 245, 590
JUDGE, Thomas L. 332
JUDSON
Andrew T. 80
Edmund L. 449
Frederick N. 571
Harry P. 468, 534, 603
John P. 458
Thomas B. 455*
JUHAN, Frank A. 511, 519
JULIAN
George W. 93, 104, 106, 108, 110, 112
Ira 453
Mortimer 558
Percy L. 611
W.A. 444
JUNCKER, Henry D. 529
JUNEAU, Solomon 456
JUNGER, Aegidius 528
JUNKIN
Benjamin F. 103
George 474*, 475, 485, 532
JUST, Ernest E. 611
JUSTICE, William W. 501
JUSTREMSKI, Leon 450
JUUL, Niels 173, 176

K

KABIS, Dorothy Andrews 444
KACHADOORIAN, Zubel 609
KADING, Charles A. 192, 196, 199
KADISH, Sanford N. 564
KAEBNICK, H.W. 531
KAEMPFFERT, Waldemar 500
KAGAN, Jerome 598
KAGEY, Charles L. 428
KAHANE, Benjamin B. 563
KAHLENBERG
George E. 534
Louis 575
KAHN
Florence Prag 186, 189, 193, 196, 199, 202
Julius 147, 150, 155, 158, 161, 164, 167, 170, 173, 176, 179
Louis I. 592
KAIN
Bertha R. 477
John J. 524, 529
KAISER
Edgar F. 548, 598, 608
Henry J. 548
Philip M. 432, 436
Walter H. 595
KAISERMAN, J.R. 454
KALBFLEISCH, Martin 107
KALFBUS, Edward C. 419*
KALIJARVI, Thorsten V. 427
KALLOCH, Isaac S. 461
KALMBACH, Leland J. 549
KALODNER, Harry E. 271
KALTENBORN, Howard S. 493
KAMERICK, John J. 477, 478
KAMIHIRA, Ben 589*, 593
KAMM, Robert B. 478
KAMMERER, Herbert L. 579
KAMPMANN, Lewis L. 476
KAMPS, Louis 577
KANAVEL, Allen B. 565
KANE
Elias K. 72, 74, 75, 77, 78, 80, 300
George P. 450
John K. 570
Matthew J. 355*
Thomas F. 477, 484
William P. 484
KANN, Peter R. 588
KANTER, Charles A. 549*
KANTOR, MacKinlay 586
KANTROWITZ, Arthur 509
KAPITZKY, Frances 534
KAPLAN
Justin 587, 602
Kivie 578
KAPLOWITZ, Paul 445

KAPP, John W., Jr. 461
KAPPEL, Frederick R. 543*, 554, 596, 604, 608
KARAPETOFF, Vladimir 594
KARASICK, Joseph 537
KARB, George J. 452*
KARCH
Charles A. 196
George F. 545*
KARFIOL, Bernard 593
KARINSKA, Barbara 593
KARLING, E. Warner 580
KARMIN, Monroe W. 587
KARN, D.E. 545
KARR, Harry E. 576
KARRER, Enoch 600
KARST, Raymond W. 227
KARSTEN, Frank M. 224, 227, 230, 233, 236, 239, 242, 246, 249, 252, 255
KARTH, Joseph E. 242, 245, 249, 252, 255, 258, 261, 265
KASE, Max 585
KASEM, George A. 241
KASSABAUM, George E. 567
KASSON, John A. 106, 108, 116, 118, 125, 127, 423, 428
KASTENMEIR, Robert W. 244, 247, 250, 254, 257, 260, 263, 266
KATZ
Karl 499
Louis N. 567, 571, 589
Nathan K. 587
KATZENBACH
Frank S., Jr. 462
Nicholas deB. 36, 41, 612
KATZENBERGER, William E. 477
KATZER, Frederick X. 523, 526
KAUFFMAN, Draper L. 483
KAUFMAN
David E. 424, 436
David S. 90, 92, 94
George S. 584*
Irving R. 271
KAUFMANN, Aloys P. 460
KAUTZKY, Ted 591
KAVANAGH
Edward 77, 79, 314, 435
Patrick V. 477
Thomas C. 591
KAVANAUGH
Hubbard R. 530
William M. 164
KAY, Keith 607
KAYE
Danny 594, 604
Frederick A. 456*
William 456
KAYNOR, William K. 194
KAY-SCOTT, Cyril 498
KAYSER
A.H. 456
Stephen 499
KAZEN, Abraham, Jr. 256, 260, 263, 266
KEAN
Hamilton F. 194, 197, 201, 342
John (N.J.) 128, 133, 148, 151, 154, 157, 159, 162, 341
John (S.C.) 7
Robert W. 211, 214, 217, 220, 224, 227, 230, 233, 236, 239
William B. 405
KEANE
James J. 523, 525
John J. 468, 523, 528
Patrick J. 528
KEARNEY
Bernard W. 217, 221, 224, 227, 230, 233, 236, 240, 580
Dyre 5
Francis W. 480
James E. 528*
KEARNS
Carroll D. 224, 228, 231, 234, 237, 240, 243, 246
Charles C. 172, 175, 178, 181, 185, 188, 191, 195
Charles M. 601
Francis E. 531
Henry 443
Thomas 149, 152, 155, 374
KEARNY, Philip 407*
KEARSLEY, Jonathon 453*
KEAST, William R. 485
KEATING
Edward 167, 170, 173
Frank A. 414
Kenneth B. 224, 227, 230, 233, 236, 240, 243, 246, 249, 346, 430
Stephen F. 548
William J. 262, 265
KEATOR, Frederick W. 509, 521
KECK, Charles 579, 591
KEDZIE
Frank S. 475
Robert C. 572
KEE
James 254, 257, 260, 263
John 202, 205, 209, 212, 215, 219, 222, 225, 228, 231
Maude Elizabeth 231, 234, 238, 241, 244, 247, 250
KEEBLE, Edwin A. 393
KEEFE
Dan 558
Edward C. 576
Frank B. 212, 215, 219, 222, 225, 228
William J. 273
KEEFER, Thomas C. 572
KEEK, Charles 579
KEEL, Howard 559
KEELER
Charles A. 497
James E. 609
Richard W. 468
Stephen E. 512, 520
W.W. 551*, 578
KEELEY
James H., Jr. 438
Patrick C. 599
KEELY
George W. 566
George W., Jr. 468
KEEN, William W. 569, 570
KEENA, Leo J. 430, 438
KEENER
Jefferson W. 547*
John C. 530
KEENEY
Barnaby C. 467
Frederick T. 530
Russell W. 238
KEESE, Richard 74
KEETE, M.P. 451
KEFAUVER, Estes 18, 212, 215, 218, 221, 225, 228, 231, 234, 237, 240, 243, 247, 250, 371
KEHOE
A.H. 599
J. Walter 173
James N. 150, 153
KEHR
Edward C. 119
Louis 459
KEIDEL, Frederick A. 601
KEIFER, Warren 121, 124*, 126, 128, 157, 160, 163
KEIGHTLEY, Edwin W. 121
KEILEY
A.M. 459
Benjamin J. 528
KEIM
George deB. 575
George M. 83, 85, 86
William H. 101
KEISTER
Abraham L. 169, 172
Daniel L. 453
KEITH
Arthur 576
Charles S. 455
Hastings 242, 245, 249, 252, 255, 258, 261
James 379
Robert T.S. 417
William 9
KEITT, Laurence M. 97, 99, 101, 103, 392
KELEHER, William J. 466
KELIHER, John A. 153, 156, 159, 162
KELLEHER, Patrick J. 501
KELLENBERG, Walter P. 527, 528
KELLER
Arthur R. 472
Christopher, Jr. 517, 519
Ezra 486
Helen 603, 608, 609
Herbert P. 460
I. Wayne 578
Joseph E. 480
Joseph F. 601
Kent E. 196, 200, 203, 206
Oscar E. 177, 181, 184, 187
KELLETT, William R. 548
KELLEY
Augustine B. 215, 218, 221, 224, 228, 231, 234, 237, 240
B.F. 406
Claude D. 579
Francis C. 527
Harrison 134
John E. 146
John S. 559
Patrick H. 168, 171, 174, 177, 180
Robert 474, 480
Vincent C. 599
William D. 105, 107, 109, 111, 113, 115, 117, 119, 122, 124, 126, 128, 131, 133, 136
William F. 474
William M. 609
KELLINGER, Louis 469
KELLOGG
A. Remington 502
Albert 497
Charles 73
Francis W. 102, 104, 106, 109
Frank B. 32, 33, 38, 174, 177, 180, 324, 429, 564, 603, 605
Hamilton H. 515, 520
Henry 551
Hiram H. 473
Martin 467
Orlando 91, 107, 109
Paul A. 516
Stephen W. 111, 113, 116
Vernon L. 564
William 100, 102, 104
William P. 110, 112, 114, 121, 123, 125, 127, 311*, 312
KELLSTADT, Charles H. 552
KELLY
A. Way 454
Albert E. 533
Andrew 460
Cornelius F. 543*
Daniel A. 574
Edna F. 227, 230, 233, 236, 240, 243, 246, 249, 253, 256
Edward A. 196, 200, 203, 206, 210, 213, 219
Edward D. 526
Edward J. 525
Edward Joseph 451
Edward W. 531
Ellsworth 607
Evander F. 609
Everett L. 571
Francis M. 529
Frederick J. 472
George 583, 592
George B. 207
Harry F. 323
James 59, 60
James K. 115, 117, 119, 356
Joe W. 415
John (Md.) 449
John (N.Y.) 99, 101
John E. 419
John H. 396
Joseph J. 451
Joseph L. 380
M. Clyde 169, 175, 178, 182, 185, 188, 192, 195, 198, 201
Mervin J. 596, 598
Ralph 443
Raymond J. 568
Robert L. 470
William 69, 70, 277
William F. 547, 564
KELSEY
Francis W. 570, 574
Lorenzo A. 452
William H. 99, 101, 110, 112
KELSO
James L. 533
John R. 108
KELTON, J.C. 401
KEM
James P. 223, 227, 230, 330
Omer M. 138, 140, 143
KEMBLE, Gouverneur 83, 84
KEMENY, John G. 469
KEMERER, Benjamin T. 512, 519
KEMETZ, John T. 557
KEMMERER
Edwin W. 566
W.W. 472
KEMP
Bolivar E. 187, 190, 193, 197, 200
Jack F. 262, 265
James 474, 505, 520
James F. 576
Richard 9
Theodore 473
William E. 455
William S. 577
William W. 481, 601
KEMPE, C. Henry 599
KEMPER
Jackson 505, 520*
James L. 379, 394
James S. 424, 575
KEMPSHALL, Thomas 84
KENAN
Augustus H. 391, 392
Owen R. 392
Thomas 59, 60, 61
KENDALL
Amos 25*, 43
Charles W. 114, 117
Edward C. 605, 607
Edward H. 567
Elva R. 193
Henry H. 567
John W. 137
Jonas 68
Joseph G. 76, 77
Joseph M. 137, 142
Messmore 579
Paul W. 414
Samuel A. 178, 182, 185, 188, 192, 195, 198
Sergeant 598*
T.S. 533
William H. 549
William S. 502, 607
KENDEIGH, S. Charles 575, 592
KENDIG
H. Evert 609
Perry F. 480
KENDRICK
Asahel 570
J. Ryland 484
John B. 176, 179, 182, 186, 189, 192, 196, 199, 202, 387*
John M. 508, 519, 520
W. Freeland 458, 579
KENEFICK, John C. 554
KENIN, Herman 557
KENISON, Frank R. 339
KENISTON, Hayward 577
KENKEL, Frederick P. 599
KENNA
E. Douglas 578
John E. 122, 124, 126, 129, 131, 134, 136, 139, 383
Robert E. 481*
KENNAN, George F. 439, 563, 578, 586, 587, 591, 602*
KENNEDY
Ambrose 169, 172, 175, 178, 182
Ambrose J. 197, 200, 203, 207, 210
Andrew 85, 87, 89
Anthony 100, 102, 104, 317
Charles A. 159, 161, 164, 167, 170, 173, 176
Chase W. 410
David M. 36, 39, 546*, 591
Edward M. 245, 248, 252, 255, 258, 261, 264, 321, 492
Foster 569
Gerald H. 531
Gerald S. 547
Harry S. 514, 519
Hugh 457*
James 154, 157, 160, 163
John F. 13, 18, 223, 226, 230, 233, 236, 239, 242, 321, 492, 586, 599, 608
John L. 156
John P. 26, 27, 42, 82, 86, 87, 474
Joseph P. 429, 445
Julian 590, 596
Martin J. 198, 201, 204, 207, 210, 214, 217
Michael J. 211, 214
Robert 460
Robert F. 36, 41, 252, 346, 492
Robert P. 133, 135
W.P. 557
William (b. 1769) 58, 61, 63, 64

William (b. 1854) 167
X.J. 610
KENNELLY
Arthur E. 595, 598, 600, 607
Martin H. 451
KENNER, Duncan F. 391, 392*, 393
KENNERLY, David 588
KENNETT
John 408
Luther M. 99, 460
KENNEY
Edward A. 201, 204, 207
Edward C. 416
George C. 412*, 415
Richard R. 142, 144, 147, 291
T.A. 545
William P. 548
KENNON
Beverly 418
Robert F. 313
William, Jr. 92
William, Sr. 76, 78, 81
KENNY
T.E. 453
William J. 528
KENRICK
Francis P. 523, 528
Peter R. 524, 528, 529
KENT
Edward 314*
Everett 185, 192
Frank W. 498
Harry L. 476
James 344, 597
Joseph 62, 63, 68, 69, 71, 72, 79, 80, 82, 316*
Louis 610
Moss 64, 65
Ralph E. 567
Raymond A. 474
Robert H. 608
W. Wallace 272
Willard M. 576
William 164, 167, 170
KENYON
Alpheus B. 465
Helen 534
Wiley 460
William C. 465
William S. (b. 1820) 103
William S. (b. 1869) 164, 167, 170, 173, 176, 180, 272, 304
KEOGH
Andrew 568
Eugene J. 207, 211, 214, 217, 221, 224, 227, 230, 233, 236, 240, 243, 246, 249, 253
KEOUGH
Francis P. 523, 528
James 444
M.J. 558
KEPES, Gyorgy 590
KEPHART
Cyrus J. 531
Ezekiel 531
John W. 360
KEPNER
Wade H. 574
William E. 412*
KEPPEL
Francis 444
Frederick P. 491
KEPPELLE, Michael 458
KER, R.F. 461
KERCHEVAL, Thomas A. 457*
KERENS, Richard C. 423, 599
KERFOOT
John B. 482, 506, 521
John D. 452
Samuel F. 471
KERN
Frederick J. 150
John A. 479
John W. 164, 167, 170, 303
John W., Jr. 454
Paul B. 530
KERNAN, Francis 107, 119, 121, 123, 345
KERNER, Otto 272*, 301
KERR
Charles W. 532
Clark 467*
Daniel 132, 134
David R. 486, 533
Hugh T. 532
James 136
James R. 544*
James W. 589
Jean 599
John (Mayor) 452
John (Rep.) 64, 66
John, Jr. 97
John A. 455
John B. 93, 434
John H. 185, 188, 191, 194, 198, 201, 204, 208, 211, 214, 218, 221, 224, 227, 230
John L. 72, 74, 77, 84, 86, 316
Joseph 64, 352
Josiah L. 148
Michael C. 108, 110, 112, 114, 118*
Paul S. 493
Richard C. 454
Robert S. 227, 231, 234, 237, 240, 243, 246, 355*
Walter F. 599
William 459
William J. 478, 567
Winfield S. 143, 146, 149
KERRIGAN
James 105
John E. 450
KERSHAW
John 64
Joseph B. 395
KERSHEY, J.M. 466
KERSHNER, Frederick D. 482, 536
KERST, Donald W. 611
KERSTEN, Charles J. 225, 231, 235
KERSTETTER, William E. 469
KERWIN
Hugh L. 443
Walter T., Jr. 400
KESSLER
Karl G. 580
Louis M. 567
Silas G. 533
KESTER, Lenard 610
KETCHAM
John C. 180, 184, 187, 190, 194, 197
John H. 109, 110, 112, 115, 121, 123, 126, 128, 131, 133, 135, 138, 146, 148, 151, 154, 157
KETCHUM
Bostwick H. 575
Morris, Jr. 567
Omar B. 462
William 450
William M. 263
Winthrop W. 119
KETTER, Robert L. 477
KETTERING
Charles F. 492, 563, 590*, 595, 596*, 598, 603
Eugene W. 492, 610
KETTNER, William 167, 170, 173, 176
KEY
David M. 28, 43, 119, 370, 424
James L. 449*
John A. 169, 172, 175
Joseph S. 530
Philip 52
Philip B. 60, 61, 62
Robert E. 536
V.O., Jr. 571
William S. 411, 412, 414
KEYES
Charles H. 467, 481
Donald B. 567
Elias 70
Elisha W. 456
Erasmus D. 407*
Frederick G. 590, 609
Geoffrey 405*, 412, 415
Henry W. 177, 181, 184, 188, 191, 194, 197, 201, 204, 338*
Michael J. 528
Wade 391
Walter 460
KEYS, Clement M. 550*
KEYSER, F. Ray, Jr. 377
KHARASCH, Morris S. 609
KHORANA, F. Gobind 600, 606
KIBBEE, Robert J. 477
KIDD, Issac C., Jr. 417*, 418
KIDDER
Alfred V. 595, 611
David 71, 72
Randolph A. 425
KIDWELL, Zedekiah 98, 99
KIEFER
Andrew R. 140, 143, 460
Norvin C. 578
Paul W. 590
KIEFFER
John S. 480
Moses 472
KIEFNER, Charles E. 187, 194
KIEFT, William 8
KIEL, Henry W. 460
KIELY, Margaret V. 479
KIER, Porter M. 500
KIERAN
James 472
John 593
KIESS, Edgar R. 169, 172, 175, 178, 182, 185, 188, 192, 195
KIGAR, Donald F. 546
KILBOURN, Byron 456*
KILBOURNE
Arthur F. 571
Charles E. 400, 484
James 64, 65
KILBURN
Charles S. 415
Clarence E. 211, 214, 217, 221, 224, 227, 230, 233, 236, 240, 243, 246, 249
KILBY
Jack S. 604
Thomas E. 278
KILCOYNE, Francis P. 467
KILDAY, Paul J. 212, 215, 218, 221, 225, 228, 231, 234, 237, 240, 244, 247
KILDUFFE, Robert A. 572
KILEY
Moses E. 523, 529
Roger J. 272
KILGO, John C. 470, 530
KILGORE
Bernard 601
Constantine B. 133, 136, 139, 141
Daniel 79, 81, 83
David 100, 102
Harley M. 215, 219, 222, 225, 228, 231, 234, 238, 384
Joe M. 237, 240, 244, 247, 250
L. A. 599
Thomas, Jr. 534
KILKENNY, John F. 272
KILLE, Joseph 84
KILLEFER, Tom 491
KILLEN, William 10, 290
KILLIAN, James R., Jr. 475, 598, 603
KILLINGER, John W. 103, 105, 115, 117, 122, 124
KILPATRICK, Judson 409*, 410, 425
KIM, Earl 592
KIMBALL
Alanson M. 120
Charles D. 362
Dan A. 399
Dexter S. 573
Fiske 501
Henry M. 204
John 452
LeRoy S. 577
Nathan 408, 409, 410
Ralph 387*
Thomas R. 567
William P. 159
KIMBERLY
John A. 548
John R. 548*
KIMBREL, M. Monroe 564
KIMMEL, William 121, 123
KIMMELL, Husband E. 417
KIMPTON, Lawrence A. 468
KINCAID, John 75
KINCANNON, Andrew A. 475
KINCHELOE, David H. 170, 173, 177, 180, 184, 187, 190, 193, 273
KINDEL, George J. 167
KINDELBERGER, James H. 550*, 594, 597
KINDRED, John J. 165, 181, 185, 188, 191
KING
Adam 75, 76, 78
Andrew 114
Austin A. 106, 329
Bruce 343
C. F. 461
Campbell 400
Carleton J. 246, 249, 253, 256, 259, 262, 265
Cecil R. 212, 216, 219, 222, 225, 229, 232, 235, 238, 241, 244, 248, 251, 254
Charles 468
Charles F. 460
Charles G. 572
Clarence 443
Cyrus 64, 65
Daniel P. 87, 89, 91, 93
David S. 244, 247, 253, 432*
Edward J. 170, 173, 176, 180, 183, 187, 190
Edward L. 400, 419
Edward S. 502
Eli C. 452
Ernest J. 416, 417*
George G. 94, 96
Hamilton 436*
Hanford L., Jr. 519
Henry 78, 79
Henry C. 478*
Horatio 27*, 43
J. Floyd 123, 125, 127, 130
J. W. 417
James G. 93
John (Rep.) 77
John 532
John A. 93, 345
John E., Jr. 487
John H. (b. 1820) 409
John H. (b. 1900) 289
John P. 78, 80, 82, 295
John W. 339
Karl C. 231, 234, 237
Lorenzo H. 530
Martin Luther, Jr. 597, 606, 610, 611
Paul 589
Perkins 76
Philip B. 607
Philip C. 484
Porter 449
Preston 88, 90, 93, 95, 101, 103, 105, 345
Robert L. 567
Rufus (b. 1755) 4, 6, 15*, 51, 52, 53, 54, 64, 65, 67, 68, 70, 71, 344*, 428, 429
Rufus (b. 1814) 407, 434
Rufus H. 99
Samuel G. 458
Samuel W. 361
Spencer M. 429
Stanley 465
Thomas B. 84, 85, 89, 91, 92
W. Stirling 459
Washington 460
William 314
William F. 468
William H. 147, 149, 175, 179, 182, 185, 189, 192, 195, 199, 202, 205, 208, 209, 212, 215, 374
William Harrison 454
William R. 14, 16, 26, 63, 64, 65, 67, 69, 70, 72, 74, 75, 77, 78, 80*, 82*, 83*, 85*, 87, 90, 92*, 94*, 96, 277*, 428
William S. 119
Willis J. 531
Willis L. 596
Yelverton P. 425
KINGHAM, Herbert 451
KINGMAN
Dan C. 402
Eugene 499
Samuel A. 306
KINGSBURY
Albert 590, 594
Bernerd C. 566
Edward M. 583
Edwin P. 600
Joseph R. 484
Kenneth R. 552
KINGSLAKE, Rudolf 580
KINGSLAND
Ambrose S. 458
Lawrence C. 444
KINGSLEY
Calvin 530
Edwin R. 576
Sidney 584, 589
William H. 550, 551
KINKAID
Moses P. 154, 159, 162, 165, 168, 171, 174, 177, 181
Thomas C. 417
KINKEAD
Eugene F. 162, 165, 168
John H. 335
KINLEY, David 566, 572
KINLOCH, Francis 7
KINNA, John 454

KINNARD
George L. 79, 80
Harry W. O. 404
I. F. 599
KINNEAR, John C., Jr. 567
KINNELL, Galway 610
KINNEY
Dallas 587
William B. 436
KINSELLA
George B. 454
James H. 454
Richard J. 454*
Thomas 115
KINSEY
Charles 67, 68
James 6, 340
Oliver P. 484
V. Everett 600
William M. 135
KINSLEY, Martin 68
KINSMAN, Frederick J. 509, 519
KINSOLVING
Arthur II 514, 519
C. J. III 515, 520
George H. 508, 522
Lucien L. 508
KINYON, Alonzo G. 601
KINZEL, Augustus B. 567, 595
KINZER, J. Roland 195, 198, 201, 205, 208, 211, 215, 218, 221
KIP, William I. 506, 519
KIPHUTH, Robert J. 608
KIPP, George W. 160, 166
KIRBY
Abner 456
Ellwood 455
George H. 571
Hal P. 498
James 559
James T. 557
John, Jr. 578
Rollin 583*
William F. 170, 173, 176, 282
KIRCHHOFER, A. H. 573
KIRCHHOFFER, Richard A. 513, 520
KIRCHNER, Leon 587
KIRCHWEY, George W. 570
KIRK
Alan G. 416, 424, 425, 432, 439
Alexander C. 427, 429, 431, 436
Andrew J. 187
Claude R. 294
Grayson 468, 603
Norman T. 403
Raymond V. 470
Robert C. 423*, 439
Samuel A. 599
KIRKBRIDE, Thomas S. 571
KIRKER, Thomas 352
KIRKES, L.C. 483
KIRKLAND
Dorrance 67
Edward C. 564
James H. 484
John T. 472
Joseph 70
KIRKMAN, Henry N., Jr. 599
KIRKPATRICK
A.F. 533
Andrew 340
C.C. 483
Evron M. 570
G.R. 18
John L. 469
Littleton 88
Sanford 167
Sidney D. 575
Snyder S. 142
William 60
William H. 182
William S. 146, 474
KIRKSEY, James 462
KIRKWOOD
Daniel 469
James P. 572
John G. 609
Samuel J. 29, 44, 108, 120, 123, 125, 304*
KIRMAN, Richard 336
KIRSCH, Dwight 502
KIRSCHENBAUM, Jules 589
KIRSTEIN, Lincoln 593, 603
KIRWAN
Albert D. 473
Michael J. 208, 211, 214, 218, 221, 224, 227, 230, 234, 237, 240, 243, 246, 249, 253, 256, 259
KISSEL, John 181
KISTIAKOWSKY, George B. 596, 604, 608
KITCHEL, Harvey D. 475
KITCHELL
Aaron 52, 53, 54, 56, 59, 60, 61, 340
Horace Y. 579
KITCHEN, Bethuel M. 111
KITCHENS, Wade H. 206, 209
KITCHIN
A. Paul 243, 246
Claude 151, 154, 157, 160, 162, 165, 168, 171, 175, 178, 181
Thurman D. 484
William H. 124
William W. 124, 146, 149, 157, 348
KITSON, Arthur 600
KITTERA
John W. 52, 53, 54, 55, 56
Thomas 73
KITTLE, Charles M. 552
KITTLESON, I. Milo 456
KITTREDGE
Alfred B. 152, 154, 157, 160, 367
George L. 566, 577
George W. 97
William C. 549
KITTSON, Norman W. 460
KIVETTE, Frederick N. 417
KLAPPER, Paul 479
KLASSEN, Edwin T. 445
KLAUDER, Charles Z. 591
KLEBERG
Richard M. 198, 202, 205, 208, 212, 215, 218
Rudolph 144, 146, 149, 152
KLECZKA, John C. 179, 182
KLEIHAUER, Cleveland 536
KLEIN
Arthur G. 214, 217, 221, 224, 227, 230, 233, 236
Frank 578
Harry T. 553
J. Warren 465
John A. 401
Walter C. 517, 521
William 557
KLEINDIENST, Richard G. 36, 37
KLEINER, John J. 127, 130
KLEINPELL, Eugene H. 486
KLEINSCHMIDT
Edward E. 611
T.H. 454*
KLEKOTKA, John A. 484
KLENDA, Harry M. 566
KLEPPE, Thomas S. 256, 259, 445
KLEPPER
Frank B. 156
George M. 579
KLERMAN, Gerald L. 598
KLINE
Ardolph L. 181, 458
Charles H. 459
Clarice 578
George M. 571
Howard 577
I. Clinton 182
Marcus C.L. 154, 157
Marvin L. 457
Nathan S. 600*
Reamer 466
William F. 593
KLINGEL, Gilbert 593
KLINGENSMITH, John, Jr. 81, 83
KLIPSTEIN, Kenneth H. 543
KLIVER, W.H. 559
KLOEB, Frank L. 201, 204, 208
KLOPSTEG, Paul E. 563
KLOTSCHE, J. Martin 486
KLOTZ, Robert 124, 126
KLUCKHOHN, Clyde 563, 611
KLUCZYNSKI, John C. 229, 232, 235, 238, 242, 245, 248, 251, 255, 258, 261, 264
KLUMPH, Arch C. 580
KLUMPP, George L. 460
KLUTTZ, Theodore F. 149, 151, 154
KNABENSHUE, Paul 430
KNACHEL, Philip A. 499
KNAEBEL, John B. 610
KNAPP
A. Blair 469
Anthony L. 104, 106
Bliss 536
Bradford 466, 478, 482
C. Howard 578
Charles 112
Charles J. 135
Charles L. 151, 154, 157, 160, 162
Chauncy L. 99, 100
Edward F. 457
George O. 553
Isaac N. 600
Joseph F. 549
Martin A. 271
Philip C. 569
Ralph H. 536
Robert M. 116, 120
S.A. 473
KNAPPEN, Loyal E. 271
KNAPPENMEYER, Henry 473
KNATHS, Karl 589*, 592
KNAUSS, Francis J. 286
KNEBEL, G. Moses 564
KNEELAND
Fred 558
George J. 552
KNEIP, Richard F. 368
KNELLER, John W. 467
KNICKERBACKER, David B. 507, 520
KNICKERBOCKER
H.R. 583
Herman 61
KNIFFIN, Frank C. 198, 201, 204, 208
KNIGHT
Albion W. 481, 509
Austin M. 419
Charles L. 181
Charles M. 465
Cyrus F. 508, 520
D. Ridgeway 607
Douglas M. 470, 474
E. W. 454
Edward J. 509, 522
Erastus C. 451
Frank H. 566
Goodwin J. 284
Harry E. 400*
Henry G. 567, 590
Jabez C. 459
Jesse 387
John E. 455
John S. 573, 587, 601
Jonathan 99, 569
Nehemiah 58, 59, 60
Nehemiah R. 68, 70, 72, 73, 75, 76, 78, 80, 81, 83, 85, 361*
Raymond D. 454
Ridgeway B. 424, 435, 438
Samuel 375
KNIPE, J.F. 409, 410
KNIPLING, Edward F. 604
KNOCH, Win G. 272
KNOLES, Tully C. 479
KNOOP, Werner C. 456
KNOPF
Adolph 576, 607
Carl S. 486
Philip 153, 156, 158
KNOTT, J. Proctor 110, 112, 118, 121, 123, 125, 309
KNOUS, William L. 286*
KNOWLAND
Joseph R. 152, 155, 158, 161, 164, 167
William F. 219, 222, 225, 229, 232, 235, 238, 284
KNOWLES
Asa S. 477, 482
Edward P. 459
Freeman T. 146
Harvey C. 590
Horace G. 424*, 427, 435, 436
John H. 492, 609
Warren P. 386
KNOWLTON
Ebenezer 98
George W., Jr. 552
Horace A. 455
Marcus P. 320
Maud Briggs 498
William 483
KNOX
Clinton E. 426, 429
Frank 18, 33, 34, 42
Harley E. 461
Henry 23*, 40, 400, 406
James 96, 98
James H.M. 474
Philander C. 30, 31*, 38, 41, 154, 157, 160, 175, 178, 182, 359*
Samuel 106
Victor A. 233, 236, 239, 242, 245, 249
William E. 564
William R. 536
William S. 143, 145, 148, 151
KNUBEL, Frederick H. 535
KNUDSEN
Simon E. 547
William S. 547
KNUDSON, Bennett O. 576
KNUTSON
Coya G. 236, 239
Harold 174, 177, 181, 184, 187, 190, 194, 197, 200, 204, 207, 210, 214, 217, 220, 223
John W. 572, 578
Kent S. 535
Oscar R. 325
KOCH
Carl 591
Edward I. 259, 262, 265
John 610
John C. 456
KOCIALKOWSKI, Leo 200, 203, 206, 210, 213
KOELSCH, M. Oliver 272
KOENEKE, H.W. 564
KOERNER, Gustavus 437
KOESTER, Edward A. 564
KOFOID, C.A. 573
KOHLER
Foy D. 439
Fred 452
Walter J. 386
Walter J., Jr. 386
Wolfgang 571
KOHLMANN
Anthony 471
Hugo 491
KOHLMEIER, Louis M. 587
KOHLSAAT, Christian C. 272
KOHN
Robert D. 567
William 559
KOLAR, Edward J. 554*
KOLB
Delmar M. 501
Lawrence C. 571
KOLBE, Parke R. 465, 470, 479
KOLMER, John A. 572
KOLODNEY, William 593
KOLTHOFF, Izaak M. 596, 604
KOMER, Robert W. 438, 608
KONECCI, Eugene B. 564
KONIG, George 165, 168
KONOP, Thomas F. 166, 169, 172
KONRAD, Adolf 593
KONZELMANN, Frank W. 572
KOONTZ
Libby 578
William H. 109, 111
KOPP
Arthur W. 163, 166
William F. 180, 183, 187, 190, 193, 197
KOPPLEMANN, Herman P. 199, 203, 206, 213, 219
KORBLY, Charles A. 161, 164, 167
KORELL, Franklin F. 191, 195
KOREN, Henry L. 426
KORFF, Serge A. 566
KORNBERG, Arthur 606
KORNEGAY, Horace R. 246, 249, 253, 256
KORNFELD, Joseph S. 435
KORRY, Edward M. 425, 428
KORSTIAN, C.F. 575
KORTH, Fred 399
KORTHEUER, Mrs. Dayrell 500
KORTWRIGHT, Elizabeth 20
KOSINKI, Jerzy 602
KOSTER, Samuel W. 483
KOTCHIAN, A.C. 548
KOTHNY, Gottdank L. 601
KOUDELKA, Joseph M. 529
KOUWENHOVEN, William B. 595
KOWAL, Chester W. 451
KOWALSKI, Frank 241, 244
KOZOL, Jonathan 602
KRACKE, Roy R. 572
KRAEGE, F. Halsey 456
KRAELING, Carl H. 501
KRAFT, Christopher C., Jr. 597
KRAMER
Charles 199, 202, 206, 209, 212
Frank 461

Frederick 455*
Herman F. 414
Paul J. 574
KRAMM, Joseph 585
KRASCHEL, Nelson G. 305
KRAUS
Charles A. 565, 596*, 604, 608, 609
E.J. 574
Milton 173, 176, 180
KRAUSHAAR, Otto F. 471
KRAUSKOPF, Konrad B. 576
KRAUTBAUER, Francis X. 526
KRAUTH, Charles P. 471
KRAYER, Otto 589
KREBS
Jacob 73
John M. 532
Max V. 429
Paul J. 252
KREECK, George L. 434
KREGER, Edward A. 402
KREIDER, Aaron S. 169, 172, 175, 178
KREINHEDER, Oscar C. 484
KREIS, Frank 559
KREISMANN, Frederick 460
KREMER, George 71, 73, 75
KREMERS, Edward 609
KRENEK, Ernst 592
KRESGE, Stanley S. 492
KRESS
Rush H. 492
Samuel H. 492
KRETCHMER, Norman 592, 599
KRETSCHMER, Herman L. 569
KRETTEK, Germaine 600
KRETZMANN, Otto P. 484
KREUSSER, Otto T. 500
KREUZER, Barton 580
KREYMBORG, Alfred 580
KRIBBS, George F. 138, 141
KRIEGER, Alex D. 611
KRIM, George J. 467
KROCK, Arthur 584*, 604
KROEBER, Alfred L. 499, 611
KROGMAN, Wilton M. 611
KROGSTAD, Arnold N. 411
KROL, John J. 523, 524
KROLL
G. 600
Leon 589*, 593, 598, 607, 610
Leopold 513
William J. 589, 590, 595
KRONMILLER, John 162
KROON, Reinout P. 601, 611
KRUEGER
Otto 234, 237, 240
Walter 400, 405*, 411
KRUESI, Paul J. 575
KRUG, Julius A. 34*, 35, 44
KRUM
Howard L. 611
John M. 460
KRUMM, John M. 518, 522
KRUSE
Cornelius 566
Edward H., Jr. 226
KRUSEN, Frank H. 590
KRUTCH, Joseph Wood 593, 602
KRUTTSCHNITT, Julius 552
KUBICK, Gail 585
KUBLY, Herbert 602
KUCERA, Louis B. 527
KUCHEL, Thomas H. 232, 235, 238, 241, 244, 247, 251, 254, 284
KUEKES, Edward D. 586
KUHN
Edward W. 565
Joseph E. 419
V.E. 460
Wayne E. 567, 590
KUHNS, Joseph H. 95
KULP, Monroe H. 143, 146
KUMLER
Henry 531
Henry, Jr. 530
KUMP, Herman G. 384
KUMPF, Henry C. 455
KUNIN, Robert 608
KUNITZ, Stanley 586, 589, 592
KUNIYOSHI, Yasuo 607
KUNKEL
Jacob M. 100, 102
John C. (b. 1816) 99, 101
John C. (b. 1898) 211, 215, 218, 221, 224, 228, 246, 250, 253
KUNZ, Stanley H. 180, 183, 187, 190, 193, 196
KUNZE, William F. 457
KUNZLER, John E. 612
KUPFERMAN, Theodore 253, 256
KURKJIAN, Stephen A. 588
KURTZ
Charles M. 497
David B. 461
J. Banks 185, 188, 192, 195, 198, 201
William F. 547*
William H. 95, 97
KURTZMAN, David H. 479
KUSCH, Polykarp 606
KUSTERMANN, Gustav 161, 163
KUTER, Laurence S. 415, 416*
KUTZ, Charles W. 462
KUUSISTO, Allan A. 472, 477
KUYKENDALL
Andrew J. 108
Dan H. 256, 260, 263, 266
J. Edwin 461
Jerome K. 443
KUZELL, Charles R. 595
KUZNETS, Simon 566, 606
KVALE
Ole J. 184, 187, 190, 194
Paul J. 197, 200, 204, 207
KYES
Benjamin A. 455
Roger M. 399
KYL, John H. 242, 245, 248, 255, 258, 261
KYLE
Edwin J. 429
James H. 138, 141, 144, 146, 149, 152, 367
John C. 137, 140, 143
Joseph 533
Joseph B. 574
M.G. 533
Thomas B. 151, 154
KYRLE, Richard 9
KYROS, Peter N. 255, 258, 261, 264

L

LABAJ, Joseph J. 469
LABAREE, Benjamin 475
LaBARRE, George B. 462
LaBELL, Frank J. 577
LABOUISSE, Henry R. 429, 443
LaBRANCHE, Alcee 87, 438
LACEY
Edward S. 125, 128
John F. 134, 140, 142, 145, 148, 150, 153, 156
William N. 601
LACKEY, Dan V. 458
LACHMUND, Louis 460
LACOCK, Abner 63, 64, 65, 67, 358
LACOMBE, E. Henry 271
LaCOSS, Louis 585
LACY
Carleton 530
Drury 469, 532
William S.B. 437
LADD
David L. 444
Edwin F. 181, 185, 350, 477
George E. 476
George T. 571
George W. 123, 125
Herbert W. 362*
Jesse A. 413
William 570
William W. 575
LADEW, William 576
LADNER, Albert H., Jr. 577
LaDOW, George A. 119
LaDU, Blanche 565
LaDUE, John 453
LAERI, J. Howard 564
LaFARGE
John 591
Oliver 583
LAFEAN, Daniel F. 154, 157, 160, 163, 166, 172
LAFFERTY, Abraham W. 166, 169
LAFFOON
C.M. 599
Polk 130, 132
Ruby 310
LAFLIN, Addison H. 109, 110, 112
LaFOLLETTE
Charles M. 216, 220
Philip F. 386*
Robert M. 18, 131, 134, 136, 158, 161, 163, 166, 169, 172, 175, 179, 182, 186, 189, 385*
Robert M., Jr. 189, 192, 195, 199, 202, 205, 209, 212, 215, 219, 222, 386
William L. 166, 169, 172, 175
LAFORE, John A., Jr. 240, 243
LAFOUNTAINE, R.N. 451
LAGAN, Mathew D. 132, 137
LAGING, Duard 502
LaGORCE, John O. 578
LaGUARDIA, Fiorello H. 174, 178, 185, 188, 191, 194, 198, 458
LAHEE, Frederic H. 564, 608
LAHEY
Edwin A. 601
Frank H. 569
LAHM, Samuel 92
LAHR, E.V. 450
LAIDLAW, William G. 133, 135
LAING, R. Stanley 549
LAIR, Loren E. 36
LAIRD
James 128, 130, 133
John W. 465
William R., 3rd 384
LAISE, Carol C. 433
LAIST, Frederick 595
LAKE
Everett J. 288
George B. 333*
William A. 99
LAL, Gobind Behari 584
LALLY, Alexius V. 474
LALOR, Juvenal 480
LALUMIERE, Stanislaus P. 474
LAMAR
Henry G. 75, 77
J. Robert 154, 159
John B. 87
Joseph R. 270
Lucius Q.C. 100, 102, 116, 119, 121, 122, 123, 125, 128, 130, 269, 326
Mirabeau B. 426, 434
William B. 153, 155, 158
LAMB
Alfred W. 97
Arthur B. 565, 604, 608
Frederick H. 572
Hugh L. 526
John 147, 149, 152, 155, 158, 160, 163, 166
John E. 127
Ronald O. 548
Willis E., Jr. 606, 610
William F. 591
LAMBERT
Alexander 569
Charles E. 486
Joe C. 401
John (Ala.) 457
John (N.J.) 59, 60, 61, 62, 64, 340*
William (jour.) 586
William (mayor) 459
LAMBERSTON, William P. 193, 197, 200, 203, 206, 210, 213, 216
LAMBERTON
R.E. 458
Robert A. 474
LAMBETH, J. Walter 198, 201, 204, 208
LAMBUTH, Walter R. 530
LAMEREAUX, H.E. 453
LAMISON, Charles N. 115, 117
LAMM
A. Uno 599
Henry 330
LAMME, Benjamin G. 595
LAMNECK, Arthur P. 198, 201, 204, 208
LAMONT
Daniel S. 29, 30, 40
Robert P. 33, 46, 568
Thomas W. 492
LaMONTAINE, John 586
LaMOTHE, John D. 511, 519
LAMPE, William B. 532
LAMPERT
Florian 176, 179, 182, 186, 189, 192
James B. 483
LAMPKIN, John T. 393
LAMPORT, William H. 115, 117
LAMY, John B. 524, 528
LANCASTER, H. Carrington 577
LANCEFIELD, Rebecca C. 589
LAND
Edwin H. 563, 594, 598, 604, 608*, 610
Emory S. 418
Frank S. 579
William 460
LANDAU, George W. 434
LANDER, William 392
LANDERS
Franklin 118
George M. 118, 120
LANDES
Bertha K. 461
Henry 484
Silas Z. 130, 132
LANDGREBE, Earl F. 258, 261, 264
LANDIREU, Moon 457
LANDIS
Charles B. 145, 147, 150, 153, 156, 158
Eugene M. 571
Frederick (b. 1872) 153, 156
Frederick (b. 1912) 273
Gerald W. 210, 213, 216, 220, 223
James H. 471
James M. 445
James N. 573
John W. 569
Joseph F. 557
Walter S. 575, 590
LANDON
Alfred M. 18, 307
Judson 483
S. Whitney 493
Truman H. 416
LANDRETH, Clarence P. 607
LANDRITH, Ira 18
LANDRUM
Eugene M. 413, 414*
John M. 102
Phillip M. 232, 235, 238, 241, 245, 248, 251, 254, 258, 261, 264
LANDRY
J. Aristide 95
John T. 480
LANDSBURG, Helmut E. 567
LANDSDOWNE, J. Warren 570
LANDSTEINER, Karl 605
LANDY, James 101
LANE
Alfred C. 576
Amos 79, 80
Arthur Bliss 426*, 427, 431, 432, 434, 435, 439
C.C. 453
Donald E. 273
Ebenezer 352
Edward 132, 134, 137, 139
Franklin D. 459
Franklin K. 31, 32, 44
Frederic C. 567
George B. 458
Harriet 20
Harry 169, 172, 175, 356
Henry S. 84, 85, 104, 106, 108, 302*
James H. 96, 104, 106, 108, 306
John C. 454
John J. 558
John W. 452
Joseph 15, 101, 103, 356
Joseph R. 148
LaFayette 119
Loras T. 528
Robert E. 571
Samuel W. 449*
Thomas J. 213, 217, 220, 223, 226, 230, 233, 236, 239, 242, 245
William C. (librarian) 568
William C. (mayor) 460*
William P., Jr. 318
LANEY, Ben 282
LANGDALE, Noah, Jr. 471
LANGDON
Chauncey 66
George C. 453
John 4, 6, 8*, 15, 51*, 52*, 53, 54, 56, 337*
Samuel 472
Woodbury 6
LANGELOTH, Valeria 603
LANGEN, Odin 242, 245, 249, 252, 255, 258
LANGENBERG, Frederick

C. 601
LANGENHEIM, Ralph L. 483
LANGER
William 214, 218, 221, 224, 227, 230, 234, 237, 240, 243, 350*
William L. 567, 591
LANGEVIN, Thomas H. 467
LANGFELD, Herbert S. 571
LANGHAM, Jonathan N. 163, 166, 169
LANGLEY
James M. 434
John W. 159, 162, 164, 167, 170, 173, 176, 180, 184
Katherine G. 190, 193
Samuel P. 502, 563, 609
LANGLIE, Arthur B. 381*, 461
LANGLOIS, Harold V. 566
LANGMUIR
Alexander D. 592
Irving 563, 565, 596*, 598, 604*, 605, 610
LANGSAM, Walter C. 468, 471
LANGSTON, John M. 136, 427, 429, 472
LANGWORTHY, Edward 4, 5
LANHAM
Fritz G. 179, 182, 185, 189, 192, 195, 198, 202, 205, 208, 212, 215, 218, 221
Henderson L. 223, 226, 229, 232, 235, 238
Samuel W.T. 129, 131, 133, 136, 139, 146, 149, 152, 372
LANIER
Raphael O. 432
Sidney 597
LANING, J. Ford 160
LANKFORD
Menalcus 195, 199
Richard E. 236, 239, 242, 245, 248
William C. 176, 180, 183, 186, 190, 193, 196
LANMAN
Charles R. 570
James 67, 69, 70, 287
LANNING
Harris 4
R.L. 533
William M. 154, 271
LANPHIER, Thomas G., Jr. 577
LANSDEN, Dick L. 370
LANSING
Frederick 135
Gerrit Y. 77, 79, 81
John, Jr. 4, 6, 344, 449
Robert 31*, 38
William E. 105, 115, 117
LANSTON, Tolbert 594
LANTAFF, William C. 229, 232
LANTZ, Michael 579
LANYON, Wesley E. 592
LANZETTA, James J. 201, 207
LAPHAM
Elbridge G. 119, 121, 123, 126, 128, 345
Lewis A. 544
Oscar 138, 141
Roger D. 461
LAPORTE, John 79, 81
LAPRADE, W.T. 564
LaQUE, Francis L. 575, 589
LARAMORE, Don N. 273
LARCADE, Henry D., Jr. 217, 220, 223, 226, 229
LARDNER, James L. 417
LARIMER, Edgar B. 418
LARKIN
Arthur E., Jr. 547
John 470
Oliver W. 585
Thomas 449
Thomas B. 401, 403
LARMORE, Lewis 564
LARNED
John I.B. 512
Josephus N. 568
Samuel 425, 435
Simon 58
LaROE, Wilbur, Jr. 532
LARRABEE
Charles H. 103
William 304
William C. 469
William H. 196, 200, 203, 206, 210, 213
LARRAZOLO, Octaviano A. 191, 343*
LARSEN
Esper S., Jr. 607
Jakob A.O. 570
Roy E. 596
Stanley R. 405
William W. 173, 176, 180, 183, 186, 190, 193, 196
LARSON
Arthur 445
Laurence M. 567
Leonard W. 565, 569, 572
Morgan F. 342
Oscar J. 181, 184
Westside T. 412
LaRUE, Travis 450
LASCH, Robert 587
LASCOFF, J. Leon 570, 609
LaSERE, Emile 89, 91, 93
LASH
Israel G. 111, 113
Joseph P. 588, 602
LASHLEY, Karl S. 571
LASHLY, Jacob M. 565, 589
LASKER
Albert 492
Mary 492, 608
LASSEN, Helen Lee Wesel 491
LASSITER
Francis R. 149, 152, 160, 163
William 400, 404
LASSWELL, Harold D. 571, 573
LATCHER, Robert P. 433
LATHAM
Dana 444
George R. 109
Henry J. 221, 224, 227, 230, 233, 236, 240
Louis C. 126, 133
Milton S. 96, 102, 104, 283
Orval R. 478
LATHROP
Churchill P. 499
E. 600
Gertrude K. 610
John C. 536
John H. 473, 475, 476, 486
Samuel 68, 69, 71, 72
William 120
William L. 589, 607
LATIMER
Asbury C. 141, 144, 146, 149, 152, 154, 157, 160, 365
Henry 52*, 53, 54, 290
Julian L. 416
Thomas E. 457
Wendell M. 604
LATOURETTE, Kenneth S. 534, 567
LATROBE, F.C. 450*
LATSHAW, P.H.W. 453
LATTA
Delbert L. 243, 246, 249, 253, 256, 259, 262, 265
James 532
James P. 162, 165
LATTIMORE
John L. 572
Owen 599
Samuel A. 480
LATTING, Patience 458
LAUBACH, Frank C. 609
LAUBIN
Gladys 593
Reginald 593
LAUCK, Anthony J. 497
LAUER
Conrad N. 573
Walter F. 414
LAUFMAN, Sidney 589, 607
LAUGHLIN
Carl A. 566
George H. 472
Irwin B. 429, 437
LAUMAN, J.C. 408
LAURANCE, John 6, 51, 52, 54*, 55, 56, 344
LAURENCE
John 607
William L. 584, 585
LAURENS, Henry 4, 5, 7
LAURENT, Michael 588
LAURIE
James 572
James W. 483
M.B. 459
LAURITSEN, Charles C. 570
LAUSCHE, Frank J. 240, 243, 246, 249, 253, 256, 354*, 452
LAVELY, William 461
LAVIALLE, Peter J. 527
LAVIDGE, Robert J. 568
LAW
Charles B. 157, 160, 162, 300
Francis M. 564
James O. 450
James R. 456
John 104, 106
Lyman 62, 63, 65
Jonathan 8, 10
Richard 5, 10
Richard L. 418
Thomas C. 579
William 557
William A. 550, 564
LAWALL, Charles E. 485
LaWALL, Charles H. 609
LAWLER
Daniel W. 460
Frank 130, 132, 134
Joab 80, 82
John J. 528
Joseph H. 454
LAWLESS, Theodore K. 611
LAWLOR, Matthew 458
LAWRANCE, Charles L. 594
LAWRENCE
Abbott 81, 84, 429
Albert G. 426
Ambrose 566
Charles D. 273
Charles L. 594
Cornelius V. 79, 458
David 608
David L. 360, 459
Effingham 116
Ernest O. 594, 595, 598, 605
Frederic C. 516
George P. 145, 148, 151, 153, 156, 159, 162, 165
George V. 109, 111, 128
Henry F. 181
John 402
John (N.Y.) 457*
John (Pa.) 458
John W. 90
Joseph 73, 75, 86
Louise deKiriline 593
Robert 456
Rheuna D. 461
Samuel 71
Sidney 91
Thomas 458*
Thompson 414
William (b. 1814) 101
William (b. 1819) 109, 111, 113, 117, 119
William (b. 1850) 508, 520
William A. 513
William T. 91
LAWRIE, Lee 590, 591
LAWS
Bolitha J. 273
Gilbert L. 135
Samuel S. 476, 485
William R., Jr. 533
LAWSON
Andrew C. 576, 597, 607
Edward B. 430, 431
Ernest 589*, 593, 607, 610
John D. 117
John S. 549
John W. 139
Robert 406
Thomas 403
Thomas G. 137, 139, 142
Walter C. 610
LAWTHER, Joe E. 452
LAWTON
Alexander R. 394, 423, 564
Frederick J. 444
Samuel T. 413
LAWYER
James 459
Thomas 67
LAXALT, Paul 336
LAY
Alfred M. 123
Chester F. 481
Donald P. 272
George W. 79, 81, 437
Henry C. 506, 519*
Julius G. 430, 439
LAYDEN, Harry 558
LAYER, Robert 481
LAYTON
Caleb R. 176, 179
Fernando C. 138, 141, 143
Jack M. 572
Mrs. Roy F. 576
LAZARO, Ladislas 168, 171, 174, 177, 180, 184, 187
LAZARSFELD, Paul F. 574
LAZEAR, Jesse 105, 107
LAZZERINI, William A. 558
LEA
Benjamin J. 370
Clarence F. 173, 176, 179, 183, 186, 189, 193, 196, 199, 202, 206, 209, 212, 216, 219, 222
Henry C. 567
Isaac 563*
John M. 457
Luke (b. 1783) 80, 81
Luke (b. 1879) 166, 169, 172, 370
Preston 291
Pryor 75, 76
LEACH
Abby 570
DeWitt 100, 102
Edward 574
George E. 402, 457*
Hamilton E. 574
Henry G. 580
J.S. 553*
James M. 103, 115, 117, 393
James T. 393
Raymond H. 483
Robert H. 611
Robert M. 184
LEADBETTER, Daniel P. 83, 84
LEADER, George M. 360
LEAHY
Edward L. 228 363
William D. 416, 418*, 428
LEAKE
Chauncey D. 564
Eugene W. 159
Gerald 593, 598
Shelton F. 90, 103
Walter 66, 68, 326*
LEAKIN, Shepperd 450
LEAMY, F.A. 483
LEAR
Ben 404, 405, 411*
William P. 594
LEARNED
Amasa 51, 52
Marion D. 577
Stanley 551
LEARSON, T. Vincent 548
LEARY
Cornelius L. 104
Herbert F. 417
John 461
John J., Jr. 583
LEAS, W.H. 453
LEATHERS, W.S. 572
LEATHERWOOD, Elmer O. 182, 185, 189, 192, 195
LEAVELL
Hugh R. 572, 578, 610
James R. 546
William H. 429
LEAVENWORTH
Elias W. 119
T. M. 461
LEAVITT
Erasmus D. 573
Humphrey H. 76, 78, 79
John M. 474, 480
Scott 184, 187, 191, 194, 197
Thomas W. 502
LEAVY, Charles H. 209, 212, 215
LeBLANC, Fred S. 450
LeBLOND
Charles H. 528
Francis C. 107, 109
LEBRUN, Rico 589
LECHE, Richard W. 312
LeCLAIR, Titus G. 576
LECOMPTE (or LeCOMPTE)
Joseph 72, 74, 75, 77
Karl M. 210, 213, 216, 220, 223, 226, 229, 232, 235, 239
LeCONTE
John L. 467*, 563
Joseph 563, 575
LeCRAW, Roy 449
LEDBETTER, Donald N. 558
LEDDEN, W. Earl 531
LEDERBERG, Joshua 606
LEDERER, Jerome F. 597, 612
LEDERLE, John W. 475
LEDERMAN, Leon M. 604
LEDOUX, John W. 600
LEDVINA, Emmanuel B. 525
LEDYARD, Henry 453
LEE
Alfred 505, 519
Andrew E. 367
Ann 538

Arthur 7
Arthur (sculptor) 610
Benjamin 572
Benjamin F. 486
Blair 168, 171, 317
Charles 23*, 41, 406
Darryl A. 454
Edward W. 462
Edwin F. 530
Elmo P. 271
Everett S. 576
Fitzhugh (b. 1835) 379, 395
Fitzhugh (b. 1905) 419
Francis L. 3*, 7
Frank H. 201
Frederick B. 577
Frederick S. 570
George W. C. 485
Gideon 81, 458
Gordon 155, 158, 161, 164, 167, 170, 173, 176, 180, 183, 186
Harold B. 537
Harper 586
Henry (b. 1756) 17, 56, 378
Henry (b. 1782) 16
Henry W. 506, 520
J. Bracken 374, 460
J. R. E. 470
James A. 575
John 71
John A. 559*
John C. 480
John C. H. 411, 413
John F. 402
John S. 480
Joseph W. J. 427, 429
Josh 205, 208, 211, 214, 355
Joshua 81
Laurence F. 575
M. Lindley 103
Percy M. 328
Raymond E. 400
Richard Bland 51, 52, 53
Richard Henry 3, 4, 5, 7, 51*, 52, 378
Robert E. 394*, 395*, 483, 485, 597
Robert Emmet 166, 169
Robert G. 534
Robert M. 415
Robert Q. 195
Robert V. 401
Roger I. 569
Samuel P. 417*
Sherman E. 498
Silas 55, 56
Stephen D. 395, 396*, 475
T. George 543
Thomas (N. J.) 79, 81
Thomas (Va.) 9
Thomas Sim 6, 8, 316
Tsung-Dao 606
Umphrey 481
Wallace H. 474*
Warren I. 181
William 460
William C. 411, 415
William G. 557
William H. F. 134, 136, 395
William S. 453
LEEBRICK, Karl C. 473
LEECH
George L. 526
J. Russell 192, 195, 198
Margaret 584, 586, 591
LEEDOM, John P. 126
LEEDS
Charles J. 457
Morris E. 590, 595, 601
Winthrop M. 599
LEEDY, John W. 306
LEE-SMITH, Hughie 593
LEET, Isaac 85
LEETE
Frederick D. 530
William 8
LEFAVOUR, Henry 481
LeFEVER, Jacob 141, 143
LEFEVER, Joseph 63
LeFEVRE
Benjamin 124, 126, 128, 131
Frank J. 157
Jay 217, 221, 224, 227
LEFEVRE
George 573
Peter P. 526
LEFFERTS, John 64
LEFFINGWELL, Ernest de K. 594
LEFFLER
Isaac 75
Ross 579
Shepherd 91, 93
LEFSCHETZ, Solomon 568, 604
LEFTWICH
Jabez 70, 72
John W. 109, 456
LeGALLIENE, Eva 592
LEGARE
George S. 154, 157, 160, 163, 166
Hugh S. 26, 41, 83, 423
LEGGE, Alexander 548*
LEGGET, Robert F. 576
LEGGETT
Glenn 471
Mortimer D. 409, 410, 444
Robert L. 248, 251, 254, 257, 260, 263
Wilson D., Jr. 418, 611
LEGLER, Henry E. 568
LeGRAND, John C. 316
LeHALLE, Joseph 473
LEHLBACH
Frederick R. 171, 174, 177, 181, 184, 188, 191, 194, 197, 201, 204
Herman 130, 133, 135
LEHMAN
Edwin P. 565
Herbert H. 227, 230, 233, 236, 346*, 594, 597, 608
Irving 346
Raymond G. 414
William 264
William E. 105
LEHMANN
Frederick W. 564
Heinz E. 600
William F. 467
LEHR, John C. 200
LEHY, John F. 472
LEIB
Michael 56, 57, 58, 59, 60, 61, 63, 64, 358
Owen D. 90
LIEBOLD, Paul F. 523, 526
LEIDESDORF, Samuel D. 603
LEIDIG, Daniel G. 470
LEIDY
Joseph 563
Paul 101
LEIGH
Benjamin W. 80, 81, 378
Richard H. 418
Robert D. 466
LEIGHLY, John 594
LEIGHTON
David K. 517, 520
Moses R. 449
LEIGHTY, Jacob D. 142
LEIPER, George G. 76
LEIPZIG, Francis P. 525
LEISENRING, John 143
LEISER, Ernest 607
LEISERSON, William M. 444*
LEISHMAN, John G. A. 428, 430, 438*
LEISLER, Jacob 3, 8
LEITCH, William T. 456
LEITER, Benjamin F. 99, 101
LEITH, Charles K. 576, 607
LeJEUNE, John A. 416, 484
LEJINS, Peter P. 566
LELAND
Aaron W. 532
Timothy 588
Waldo 566
LeMAISTRE, Charles 482
LeMAY, Curtis E. 19, 415*, 416, 594
LEMKE, William 201, 204, 208, 211, 218, 221, 224, 227
LEMLEY, Harry J., Jr. 400, 419
LEMLY, Samuel C. 416
LEMMON
Clarence E. 536
Dal M. 272
LEMMONIER, August 478
LEMNITZER, Lyman L. 399, 400, 404*, 405
LeMOYNE, John V. 118
LEMP, John 450
LENAHAN, John T. 160
LENG, Charles W. 502
L'ENGLE, Claude 167
LENHART, A. P. 450*
LENIHAN
Mathias C. 526
Thomas M. 525
LENKER, Will G. 600
LENNETTE, Edwin H. 592
LENNON, Alton A. 233, 240, 243, 246, 249, 253, 256, 259, 349, 262
LENNOX, William G. 600
LENON, W. E. 455
LENOX
David 551
James 565
Walter 462
LENROOT
Irvine L. 163, 166, 169, 172, 176, 179, 182, 186, 189, 273, 385
Katherine F. 603
LENT
Frederick 470
James 76, 77
Norman F. 262, 265
LENTELLI, Leo 591
LENTHALL, John 418
LENTZ, John J. 146, 149
LEONARD
Abiel 3d 508, 520, 522*
Adna W. 530
Fred C. 143
George 51, 53
J. Paul 481
John E. 121
John W. 415*
Moses G. 88
Nathan R. 473
Stephen B. 81, 84
Vincent M. 528
William A. 508, 521
LEONHART, William 438, 439
LEONTIEF, Wassily 566
LEONTIS, Thomas E. 572
LEOPOLD
A. Starker 575, 591
Aldo 575
Luna B. 576, 594
LEOUGH, Francis P. 528
LePAGE, Wynn L. 575
LERAY, Francis X. 524, 525
LERCH, Archer L. 403
LeROY, Herman 544
LESHER, John V. 169, 172, 175, 178
LESINSKI
John 200, 204, 207, 210, 213, 217, 220, 223, 226
John, Jr. 230, 233, 236, 239, 242, 245, 249
LESLEY, J. P. 563
LESLIE
A. N. 450
Harry G. 303
Preston H. 309
LESSLER, Montague 151
LESSMANN, John B. 467
LESTER
E. F. 355
George N. 393
Posey G. 136, 139
R. L. 461
Rufus E. 134, 137, 139, 142, 145, 147, 150, 153, 155
LETCHER
John 96, 98, 99, 101, 379
John D. 478
Robert P. 71, 72, 74, 75, 77, 79, 308, 433
LETOURNEAU, Robert G. 610
LETSON, Elizabeth J. 497
LETTON, H. Hamblin 565
LETTS, F. Dickinson 187, 190, 193
LEUCHTENBURG, William E. 591
LEUSCHNER, A. O. 564
LEUTNER, William G. 485
LEVAN, Thomas F. 469
LeVANDER, Harold 325
LEVEE, M. C. 563
LEVEN, Stephen A. 528
LEVENE, Phoebus A. 596, 604
LEVENTHAL, Harold 272
LEVER, Asbury F. 152, 154, 157, 160, 163, 166, 169, 172, 175, 178
LEVERETT
John 8, 472
Miles C. 569
LEVERICH, Charles P. 544
LEVERING
Joshua 17, 534
Robert W. 243
LEVERMORE, Charles H. 465
LEVERONE, Louis E. 577
LEVI, Edward H. 468
LEVIERO, Anthony 585
LEVIN
Lewis C. 90, 92, 93
N. Gordon, Jr. 591
LEVINE
David 593
Jack 593
Jerome 598
Philip 599*, 607
S. Z. 592
Samuel A. 595
Seymour 598
LEVIS
J. P. 550
W. E. 550
LEVORSEN, A. I. 564, 576, 608
LEVY
David (see Yulee, David L.)
Ernest C. 572
Florence N. 497
Jefferson M. 148, 165, 168
John J. 449
Leonard W. 587
Louis E. 594*
Max 600
William M. 118
LEWELLING, Lorenzo D. 306
LEWINE, Robert F. 577*
LEWINSON, Minna 583
LEWIS
A. D. 557
Abner 90
Alexander 453
Alvin F. 485
Anthony 586, 587
Arnold M. 516, 522
B. B. 465
Barbour 117
Burwell B. 118, 122
Charles H. 435, 478
Charles S. 98
Charles W. 487
Clarence I. 593
Clarke 135, 137
Clyde A. 580
David A. 454*
David J. 165, 168, 171, 197, 200, 203, 207, 444
David P. 277, 391, 392
David S. 547, 549
David W. 392
Dean D. 569
Dixon H. 75, 77, 78, 80, 82, 83, 85, 87, 90, 277
Dwight N. 453*
E. P. C. 435
Earl R. 211, 218, 221, 224
Edmund H. 346
Edward 462*
Edward M. (b. 1863) 404
Edward M. (b. 1872) 475, 476
Edward T. 127
Edwin O. 575
Elijah B. 145, 147, 150, 153, 155, 158
Ellis 358
Eugene C. 600
Francis 3, 4, 6
Fred E. 169
G. E. 462
Geoffrey W. 425, 432
George D. 596
George W. 597, 611
Gilbert N. 596, 604, 609
J. Hamilton 147, 167, 170, 173, 196, 200, 203, 206, 209, 301*
Harrison L. 579
Isaac 594
Ivey F. 574
James O. 601
James T. 385
Janet 610
John E. 419
John F. 600
John F. (Sen.) 113, 115, 117, 379
John F., Jr. 607
John H. 125
John L. 457, 608
John T. (b. 1800) 501*
John T. (b. 1894) 405, 411
John W. (Ga.) 392
John W. (Ky.) 142
Joseph, Jr. 58, 59, 61, 63, 64, 66
Joseph H. 112, 114
Joseph J. 444
L. A. 574
L. H. 576
Lawrence 199, 202, 206, 209, 212, 216
Lowry L. 478
Lunsford L. 379
Morgan 344*, 403, 580
Nolan D. C. 590
Obed 461
Oscar 602

R. Allyn 459
Richard H. 572
Robert E. 272*
Robert J. 152
Roger 547*
Ross A. 584
Sinclair 583, 605
Thomas 58
W. 600
Warren K. 590*, 596, 604, 608
Wilfred 590, 601
Willard D. 474
William 223
William B. 569
William F. 513, 520, 521
William J. 67
William L. 471
William M. 474, 603
Wilson S. 530
LEWISOHN
Adolph 603
Sam A. 568
LEY, Henry A. 564
L'HOMMEDIEU, Ezra 6
LHOTA, Brian 480
LI, Choh H. 600
LIBBEY
Harry 129, 131
James A. 566
LIBBY
Charles F. 564
Ruthven E. 417
Willard F. 590, 594, 595, 596, 606
LIBONATI, Roland V. 238, 242, 245, 248
LICHT, Frank 363
LICHTENBERGER
Arthur C. 515, 520
James P. 573
LICHTENSTEIN, Parker E. 469
LICHTENWALNER, Norton L. 198
LICHTENWALTER, Franklin H. 224, 228
LICKFIELD, Francis W. 516, 521
LIDBURY, Frank A. 575
LIDDELL, St. John R. 395
LIDDON, Benjamin S. 293
LIDWELL, Walter 459
LIE, Jonas 577, 610*
LIEB
Charles 167, 170
John W. 595
LIEBEL, Michael, Jr. 172
LIEBER, G. Norman 402
LIEBLEIN, Seymour 596
LIEDTKE, William, Jr. 551
LIENHARD, Gustav O. 548
LIFTON, Robert J. 602
LIGGETT, Hunter 405, 410*, 419
LIGHT, Richard W. 566
LIGHTBURN, J.M.J. 409
LIGHTHALL, George 558
LIGHTNER
E. Allen 432
Milton C. 578
LIGON
Robert F. 120
Thomas W. 91, 316
LIKLY, William F. 477*
LILIENFELD, Abraham L. 592
LILIENTHAL, David E. 443, 445, 596
LILLEHEI, C. Walton 600
LILLEY
George 485
George L. 153, 155, 158, 288
Mial E. 157
Robert D. 493, 543
LILLIE, Dean K. 457
LILLIS, Thomas F. 526*
LILLY
Eli 492, 609
Josiah K. 492, 609
Josiah K., Jr. 492
Samuel 97
Thomas J. 186
William 141
LIMON, Jose 593
LINCOLN
Abraham 13, 15, 16*, 91, 597
Benjamin 406
C.S. 401
David C. 492
Enoch 66, 67, 69, 71, 72, 314
Francis H. 400
Frederic W., Jr. 450*
George G. 608
John C. 492
Lawrence J., Jr. 401, 405
Leroy A. 549*
Levi (b. 1749) 23, 41, 55, 56
Levi (b. 1782) 79, 81, 82, 84, 319
Robert T. 29, 40, 429
Waldo 563
William S. 110
LIND
George 459
James F. 228, 231
John 132, 135, 137, 153, 324
Samuel C. 565, 575, 604, 608
LINDABURY, Richard V. 580
LINDBERGH
Anne Morrow 598, 604
Charles A. (b. 1859) 159, 162, 165, 168, 171
Charles A. (b. 1902) 586, 597, 598, 604, 609, 612
LINDE, Karl P.G. 594
LINDELOF, Lawrence P. 558
LINDEMAN, Philip F. 403
LINDEN, Charles 497*
LINDER
Clarence H. 576*
Forrest E. 592
Harold F. 425, 443
LINDGREN, Waldemar 576, 607
LINDLEY
Ernest H. 472, 473
James J. 97, 99
Walter C. 272, 273
LINDLY, Jacob 478
LINDNER, Kenneth E. 486
LINDQUIST
Carl 331
Emory 486
Francis O. 168
LINDSAY
Alexander J. 578
Carroll 501
F.S.P. 454
George E. 497
George H. 151, 154, 157, 160, 162, 165
George W. 576
Howard 574, 585
John V. 243, 246, 249, 253, 458
Robert B. 277
Samuel M. 563
William 140, 142, 145, 148, 309
LINDSEY
Charles A. 572
Edward M. 577
Stephen D. 121, 123, 125
Washington E. 343
LINDSLEY
Henry D. 452
James G. 131
Ogden R. 598
Philip 532
William D. 97
LINDSLY, Harvey 569
LINDZEY, Gardner 571
LINEBARGER, Paul M.A. 570
LINEBERGER, Walter F. 179, 183, 186
LINEHAN, Neil J. 226
LINES, Edwin S. 509, 521
LINFORD, Henry B. 575, 589
LINFORTH, Ivan M. 570
LINGLE, William L. 469
LINK
Arthur A. 262, 351
Arthur S. 591*
Edwin A. 599, 608
Karl P. 589, 600
Theodore A. 564
William W. 219
LINN
Archibald L. 86
Henry W. 469
James 56
Lewis F. 79, 81, 82, 84, 86, 88, 329
John 67, 68
William 480
LINNARD, Lawrence G. 573
LINNEY
Robert J. 610
Romulus Z. 143, 146, 149
LINSLEY, Joel H. 474
LINTHICUM, J. Charles 165, 168, 171, 174, 177, 180, 184, 187, 190, 193, 197
LINTON
Edwin 600
John P. 576
M. Albert 551, 563
Ralph 611
William S. 140, 143
LINVILLE, Henry R. 557
LIONNI, Leo 591
LIPMANN, Fritz A. 604, 606
LIPPINCOTT, Joshua A. 473
LIPPITT
Charles W. 362, 580
Henry 362
Henry F. 166, 169, 172, 362
LIPPMANN, Walter 586, 587, 596, 603, 608
LIPPOLD, Richard 590
LIPPS, Evan 450
LIPSCOMB
Abner S. 277
Andrew A. 471
Glenard P. 232, 235, 238, 241, 244, 248, 251, 254, 257
T.J. 452
LISLE, Marcus C. 140
LISPENARD, Leonard 3
LISTER
Edward 3
Ernest 381
LITCHFIELD
Edward H. 479
Elisha 70, 71
Lawrence, Jr. 543*
Paul 611
Paul W. 547*
LITHGOW, James S. 456
LITTAUER, Lucius N. 146, 148, 151, 154, 157
LITTELL, Samuel H. 512, 519
LITTERER, William 457
LITTLE
Arthur D. 565
Charles 532
Chauncey B. 187
Clarence C. 474, 475
David B. 498
David M. 460
Edward C. 173, 177, 180, 183
Edward P. 95
Ernest 570, 609
Feramorz 460
Ganse 533
John 131
John S. 139, 142, 144, 147, 150, 152, 155, 281
Joseph J. 138
Peter 62, 65, 66, 68, 69, 71, 72, 74
Royal 553*
Samuel W. 455
Tom 586
William 459
LITTLEDALE, Harold A. 583
LITTLEFIELD
Alfred H. 362
Charles E. 148, 150, 153, 156, 159
Henry W. 467
Nathaniel S. 86, 93
LITTLEJOHN
Abram N. 506, 520
DeWitt C. 107
LITTLEPAGE, Adam B. 166, 172, 175
LITTLETON, Martin W. 165
LITTLEWOOD, William 597
LITTON, Jerry 265
LITTY, H.H. 456
LIVELY
G.W. 454
Robert M. 163
LIVERMORE
Arthur 67, 68, 71, 337
Edward S. 60, 61
Samuel 6, 51, 52*, 53*, 54, 55, 56, 57, 337
LIVERNASH, Edward J. 152
LIVERSIDGE, Horace P. 551
LIVESAY, William G. 414
LIVESLEY, T.A. 460
LIVINGSTON
Edward 25*, 38, 54, 55, 56, 71, 72, 74, 75, 77, 311, 428, 458
Henry B. 269
Henry W. 58, 59
Homer J. 546, 547*, 564
Robert R. 3, 4, 6
Rose 603
Vanbrugh 427
Walter 6
William 4, 6, 7, 340
LIVINGSTONE
Colin H. 574
William 564
LLOYD
Arthur S. 510
Edward (b. 1668) 8
Edward (b. 1740) 6
Edward (b. 1779) 59, 60, 68, 69, 71, 72, 316*
Frank 563
Harold 579
Harry 559
Henry 317
Hoyes 569
James (Mass.) 60, 61, 62, 63, 71, 72, 319*
James (Md.) 54, 55, 316
James H. 569
James T. 145, 148, 151, 154, 156, 159, 162, 165, 168, 171
John U. 609
Morton G. 600
Ralph W. 532
Sherman P. 250, 257, 260, 263, 266
Thomas 9*
Thomas J. 557
Wesley 202, 205
LOAN, Benjamin F. 106, 108, 110
LOBECK, Charles O. 165, 168, 171, 174
LOCHER
Cyrus 191, 353
Ralph S. 452
LOCHNER, Louis P. 584
LOCHRANE, Osborne A. 296
LOCKE
Charles E. 530
Eugene M. 434, 608
G.B. 456
George H. 568
John 71, 72, 74
John W. 466
Matthew 53, 54, 55
Samuel 472
LOCKER, Jesse D. 432
LOCKHARD, Earl T. 474
LOCKHART
Clinton 482
James 94, 100
James A. 143
LOCKMAN, DeWitt M. 577
LOCKWOOD
A.A. 461
A.I. 461
Benoni 547
Daniel N. 121, 138, 141
Francis C. 465
Henry W. 451
Mason G. 572
Theodore D. 483
Timothy T. 451
LOCY, William A. 573
LODER, Dwight H. 531
LODGE
George 600
Henry Cabot (b. 1850) 132, 135, 137, 140, 142, 145, 148, 150, 153, 156, 159, 162, 164, 165, 168, 171, 174, 177, 180, 184, 320
Henry Cabot (b. 1902) 18, 207, 210, 213, 217, 223, 226, 229, 321*, 428, 438*, 603, 609
John C. 453*
John Davis 222, 226, 289, 423, 437
John E. 499
LODWICK, Charles 457
LOEB
Henry 3d 456*
Isidor 571
James I. 429, 435
Morris 492
LOEFFLER, Charles M. 603
LOENING, Grover 594, 597, 612
LOESCH, Richards L., Jr. 611
LOESSER, Frank 587
LOEWI, Otto 605
LOFFLAND, William O. 456
LOFLAND, James R. 116
LOFT, George 168, 171
LOFTIN, Scott 203, 294, 565
LOFTSGARD, L.D. 477
LOGAN
Cornelius A. 425*, 426, 429, 430, 434, 436
George 57, 58, 59, 358
George W. 393
Henry 81, 83
James 9, 458
John A. 17, 102, 104, 114, 116, 118, 122, 125, 127, 129, 300*, 408, 409*,

410
Joshua 585
Marvel M. 197, 200, 203, 206, 310
Maurice 591
Sheridan A. 491
Thomas E. 450
Thomas M. 569
W. Turner 182, 185
Walter S. 579
William 68, 308
William H.G. 566
LOGUE
James W. 169
John 456
LOHNES, Grant R. 578
LOHR, Lenox R. 500
LOMAS, Bernard T. 465
LOMAX
John T. 484
Lunsford L. 484
LOMBARD
Richard D. 492
Warren P. 570
LOMBARDO, Joseph J. 580
LONDON, Meyer 171, 174, 181
LONDONER, Wolfe 453
LONERGAN
Augustine 167, 173, 176, 196, 199, 203, 206, 289
Frank J. 574
William 481
LONG
Alexander 107
Andrew T. 418
Armistead L. 395
Augustus C. 553*
Benjamin 452*
Boaz W. 426, 427*, 429, 434, 436, 501
Breckinridge 431
Chester I. 142, 148, 150, 153, 156, 159, 306, 565
Clarence D. 248, 252, 255, 258, 261, 264
Daniel A. 465
Earl K. 312, 313*
Edward H.C. 89
Edward V. 242, 246, 249, 252, 255, 330
Francis R. 455
George A. 533
George C., Jr. 551
George S. 233, 236, 239
Gillis W. 248, 264
Huey P. 197, 200, 203, 312*
Jefferson F. 112
John 70, 71, 73, 75
John B. 139
John D. 30*, 42, 128, 130, 132, 320, 580
John G. 427
John H. 565
John J. 480
Joseph 531
Lewis M. 206
Louis J. 485
Oren E. 241, 245, 298
Percy W. 577
Pierse 6
Robert A. 536*
Rose McConnell 203, 312
Russell B. 223, 226, 229, 232, 236, 239, 242, 245, 248, 252, 258, 261, 264, 313
Speedy O. 252, 255, 258, 261
William 452
LONGAKER, F.B. 458
LONGDEN, Henry B. 469
LONGENECKER, Herbert E. 483
LONGEST, Christopher 475
LONGFELLOW
Henry Wadsworth 597
Stephen 71
LONGGOOD, William 587
LONGHENRY, John 452
LONGID, Edward G. 516
LONGINO, Andrew H. 327
LONGLEY, Harry S. 510, 520
LONGMAN, Donald R. 568
LONGNECKER, Henry C. 103
LONGSTREET
Augustus B. 470, 475, 481
James 394*, 395*, 438
LONGWELL
Chester R. 576
J.H. 477
LONGWORTH, Nicholas 154, 157, 160, 163, 166, 172, 175, 178, 181, 185, 186, 188, 189, 191, 195
LONGYEAR, John W. 106, 108
LONSDALE, John G. 564
LOOFBOUROW, Frederick C. 195, 199
LOOKER, Othneil 352
LOOKSTEIN, Joseph H. 493
LOOMIS
Alfred L. 611
Andrew W. 83
Arphaxed 83
Charles P. 574
Dwight 102, 104
Francis B. 435, 439
Francis W. 570
George 465
James L. 545
Justin R. 467
Leverett M. 497
Simeon L. 551
LOORAM, Matthew 426, 437
LOOS, Charles L. 482, 536
LOPER, Vere V. 534
LOPEZ
Andrew 586
Celso 461
Joseph A. 471
LORAS, Peter J.M. 526
LORD
Arthur 580
Bert 204, 208, 211
C.J. 458
Chester S. 579
Clifford L. 472
Frederick W. 91
Henry W. 125
Herbert M. 444
I.C. 454
John C. 532
John W. 531
Louis E. 574
Mary Pilsbury 603
Milton E. 568
Nathan 469
Mrs. Oswald B. 578
Richard C. 580
Scott 119
William P. 356, 423
Willis 486
LORE, Charles B. 127, 129
LORIG
Clarence H. 572, 590
Edwin T. 612
LORIMER, William 142, 145, 147, 153, 156, 158, 161*, 164, 301
LORING
Charles 325
Charles G. 500
Charles H. 418, 573
Edward G. 213
George B. 121, 123
Oliver L. 513, 520
Richard T., Jr. 514, 522
William W. 395, 396
LORY
Charles A. 468
Milton M. 579
LOSCHE, Albert 454
LOSER, J. Carlton 240, 244, 247
LOTH, Morris 537
LOTHROP
George V.N. 436
S.K. 611
Stanley 498
LOTSHAW, Elmer 568
LOTT
Bushrod W. 460
Trent 265
LOUCKS, Alfred W. 460
LOUD
Eugene F. 136, 139, 142, 144, 147, 150
George A. 153, 156, 159, 162, 165, 171
LOUDENSLAGER, Henry C. 140, 143, 146, 148, 151, 154, 157, 159, 162, 165
LOUGH, Samuel A. 466
LOUGHLIN
John 525
K.C. 544
LOUGHRAN
John A. 346
Joshua 485
LOUGHRIDGE, William 110, 112, 116
LOUNSBERY
William 123
George E. 288
Phineas C. 288
LOUTTIT
Henry I. 514, 521
James A. 129
LOVE
Don L. 455*
Edgar A. 531
Francis J. 225
George C. 456
J. Spencer 544*
James 79
John 61, 62
John A. 286
Malcolm A. 476, 480
Peter E. 102
Rodney M. 253
Thomas C. 81
Thomas J. 480
William C. 65
William F. 145
LOVEBERRY, Clarence 501
LOVEJOY
Arthur O. 564
Frank W. 546
Owen 100, 102, 104, 106
LOVELACE
Francis 8
John 8*
W. Randolph 2d 597
LOVELESS, Herschel C. 305
LOVELL
Charence A. 608
James 4, 6
James A., Jr. 594, 598, 608
Joseph 403
Mansfield 394
Solomon 406
LOVERING
Henry B. 128, 130
Joseph 563*
Thomas S. 576
William C. 145, 148, 151, 153, 156, 159, 162
LOVETT
Edgar O. 480
John 64, 65
Robert A. 34, 47, 399, 552, 554*, 603, 608
LOVETTE, Oscar B. 198
LOVILL, Curtis D. 577
LOVRE, Harold O. 228, 231, 234, 237
LOW
Edmon 600
Fred R. 573
Frederick F. 104, 283, 425
George M. 597
Isaac 6
Joseph 452
Juliette 576
Philip B. 143, 146
Sanford 501
Seth 458, 468, 566, 574
LOWDEN, Frank O. 156, 158, 161, 301
LOWDERMILK, W.C. 567
LOWE
A.B. 557
David P. 114, 116
Enoch L. 316
Frank E. 403
Thaddeus S.C. 594
Thomas F. 449
Titus 530
William M. 122, 124
William S. 575
LOWELL
A. Lawrence 472, 571
Amy 583
Francis C. 271
James Russell 429, 437, 577, 597
John 6
Joshua A. 84, 86
Robert 585, 602
S.J. 578
LOWENSTEIN, Allard K. 259
LOWER, Christian 59
LOWERY
George H., Jr. 569, 592
Worth 558
LOWES, John L. 577
LOWETH, Charles F. 572
LOWIE, Robert H. 611
LOWNDES
Lloyd 116, 317
Rawlins 9, 451
Thomas 57, 58
William 63, 64, 66, 67, 69, 70
LOWRANCE, V.L. 416
LOWREY
Bill G. 181, 184, 187, 191
Mark B. 395
LOWRIE
Charles N. 573
John C. 532
Walter H. 68, 70, 71, 358, 359
LOWRY
Bates 500
Charles W. 570
D.M. 462
Fred N. 462
Howard F. 486
Raymond E. 557
Robert (Ind.) 127, 130
Robert (Miss.) 327
Robert J. 564
LOY, M. 467
LOYALL, George 77, 80, 82
LOYD, Alexander 451
LOZIER, Ralph F. 184, 187, 191, 194, 197, 201
LUBBOCK, Francis R. 372
LUBIN, Joseph I. 595
LUCAS
A.W. 450
Edward 80, 82
Francis F. 611
Frank 387
Frederic A. 497
Harry I. 455
Jim C. 586
John B.C. 58, 59
John P. 405, 412*, 413
Mabel E. 536
Robert 352
Robert H. 444
Scott W. 203, 206, 209, 213, 216, 219, 223, 301
William 85, 88
William V. 141
Wingate H. 225, 228, 231, 234
LUCCOCK, Naphtali 530
LUCE
Charles F. 545
Clare Boothe 216, 219, 431, 599, 603
Cyrus G. 322
Donald C. 551*
Henry R. 596
Robert 177, 180, 184, 187, 190, 194, 197, 200, 207, 210
Stephen B. 419
LUCEY
Patrick J. 386
Robert E. 524, 525
LUCKEY, Henry C. 204, 207
LUCKHARDT, Arno B. 570
LUCKIESH, Matthew 601
LUCKING, Alfred 153
LUDDEN, Patrick A. 529
LUDELING, John T. 311
LUDINGTON
Flora B. 568, 600
Harrison 385, 456*
Marshall I. 403
LUDLOW
Daniel 545
George C. 340
John 479
Louis 193, 196, 200, 203, 206, 210, 213, 216, 220, 223
Theodore R. 513
LUDWELL, Philip 9
LUDWIG, Arnold M. 598
LUECKE, John F. 207
LUERS, John H. 526
LUFKIN
Elgood C. 553*
Willfred W. 174, 177, 180
LUGAR, Richard G. 454
LUHNOW, Harold W. 493
LUHRING, Oscar R. 176, 180
LUJAN, Manuel, Jr. 259, 262, 265, 461
LUKAS, J. Anthony 587
LUKEN, Thomas 452
LUKENS
Donald E. 256, 259
Hiram S. 575
LUKS, George 593
LULL, Richard S. 501
LUMBARD, J. Edward 271, 589
LUMPKIN
Alva S. 576
John H. 87, 89, 91, 98
Joseph H. 296
Wilson 65, 74, 75, 82, 84, 295*
LUNA
Charles 557, 559
W. Bruce 558
LUND
Charles C. 565
F. Edward 473
Robert L. 578
LUNDBERG, George A. 573
LUNDEBERG, Harry 559
LUNDEEN, Ernest 174, 200, 203, 207, 210, 325
LUNDIN, Frederick 161

LUNDY, Robert F. 531
LUNEBURG, William V. 543
LUNGER, Irvin E. 482
LUNN, George R. 174
LUNT
Alfred 592, 608
William E. 577
LUPTON, Nathaniel T. 465
LURIA, Salvador E. 595, 606
LURTING, Robert 458
LURTON, Horace H. 270, 271, 370
LUSH, Jay L. 604
LUSK
Georgia Lee 224
Hall S. 243, 357
LUSKIN, Harold T. 567
LUTES, LeRoy 401, 405
LUTHER, Flavel S. 482
LUTKEWITTE, Lawrence 455
LUTTRELL, John K. 115, 118, 120
LUTZ
Dan 593
Ralph H. 564
LYBRAND
Archibald 146, 149
William M. 577
LYDENBERG, Harry M. 568, 600
LYDMAN, Jack W. 432
LYET, Jean P. 552
LYKINS, Johnston 455
LYLE
Aaron 61, 63, 64, 66
John E., Jr. 221, 225, 228, 231, 234
LYMAN
Charles 445
Daniel 361
Henry M. 569
Joseph 130, 132
Joseph S. 68
Lauren D. 584
Richard W. 482
Rufus A. 609
Samuel 53, 54, 55
Theodore (b. 1833) 128
Theodore (b. 1874) 563, 570, 594, 610
Theodore, Jr. 450
Theodore B. 507, 520
William 52, 53
LYNCH
Andrew G. 437
Charles 326
Daniel F. 566
Edmund C. 412
George A. 402
James K. 564
James M. 558*
John (Maine) 108, 110, 112, 114
John (Pa.) 133
John J. 477
John R. 116, 119, 125
Joseph P. 525
Kenneth M. 572
Patrick N. 525
Thomas 139, 141
Thomas, Jr. 3, 7
Tillman D. 572
Walter A. 211, 214, 217, 221, 224, 227
William F. 396*
LYND, William E. 412
LYNDE, William P. 92, 120, 122, 456
LYNDON, Josias 9
LYNN, James T. 37, 47
LYON
A.E. 557
Asa 66
Caleb 97
Cecil B. 425*
Chittenden 74, 75, 77, 79
E. Wilson 479
Ernest 432
Francis S. 80, 82, 84, 392, 393
Homer L. 181, 185, 188, 191
Lafayette A. 548
Lucius 82, 87, 322
Mary 597
Matthew 55, 56, 57, 59, 60, 61
T.L. 607
William P. 385
LYONS
Charles W. 466, 471, 480
Harry 566
Henry 452
Henry A. 283
Hugh 455
J.H. 461
James 393
James J. 481
John H. 557
John H., Jr. 557
Louis M. 601
Peter 378
Robert W. 459
William L. 456
LYTELL, Bert 557
LYTLE, Robert T. 79
LYTTLETON, William H. 9

M

MAAS, Melvin J. 190, 194, 197, 204, 207, 210, 214, 217
MABEE, Carleton 585
MABEY, Charles R. 374
MABIE, Hamilton W. 578
MABRY
Milton H. 293
Thomas J. 343
McADAM, Dunlap J., Jr. 601
MacADAM
David L. 580
Walter K. 576
McADAMS
Edward J. 543
Thomas B. 564
McADEN, C.A. 450
McADOO
William 128, 130, 133, 135
William Gibbs 31*, 39, 199, 202, 206, 283, 577
MACADIE, Donald 516
McAFEE
J.B. 462
Cleland B. 532
James W. 553, 554
Robert B. 425
McAFFEE, Mildred H. 603
McALEER
Owen C. 456
William 138, 141, 146, 149
McALISTER, Hill 371
MacALISTER, James 470
McALLISTER
Archibald 107
Edwin J. 600
James G. 471
Sydney G. 548
Thomas F. 271, 273
Walter W. 443, 461
McALMONT, J.J. 455
McALPINE, William J. 572
McANDREW, James W. 419*
McANDREWS
A. 559
James 150, 153, 167, 170, 173, 176, 203, 206, 210
McANULTY, Henry J. 470
McARDLE, Joseph A. 211, 215
McARTHUR
Clinton N. 172, 175, 178, 182
Duncan 71, 352
John 408
Samuel 476
MacARTHUR
Arthur 385
Douglas 400, 404*, 411, 483, 603, 609
Douglas, 2d 423, 424, 430, 431
MACARTNEY
Clarence E. 532
Thomas B. 482
McAULEY, Thomas 532
MACAULEY, Charles R. 583
McAULIFFE
Anthony C. 400, 402, 404, 405, 411, 414
Maurice F. 526
Michael F. 526
McAYEAL, R.A. 533
McBAIN, L. Doward 534
McBATH, James 482
MACBETH, Charles 451
MacBRIAR, Wallace N., Jr. 500
McBRIDE
George W. 143, 146, 149, 356
Henry 381
Horace L. 414, 419
James (diplomat) 430
James (neurologist) 569
Katherine E. 467, 604
Robert H. 426, 433
Thomas C. 601
William K. 453
MACBRIDE, Thomas H. 473
McBRYDE
Archibald 61, 63
John M. 481, 484
Warren H. 573
McCABE
Charles C. 465, 530
E.R. Warner 400
Edward W. 574
Francis X. 469
Gibson 596
James 474, 487
Thomas B. 443, 552*
William H. 469
McCAFFREY
John L. 548*
Stanley 479
William J. 419
McCAIN
Arthur W. 545
Charles S. 545, 550
Henry P. 401
J.S. 417
James A. 476, 473
John S., Jr. 416*
William A. 419
McCALEB, E. Howard 313
McCALL
Abner V. 466
George A. 407
Howard W., Jr. 545
John D. 450
John E. 144
Joseph B. 551
Peter 458
Samuel W. 140, 143, 145, 148, 151, 153, 156, 159, 162, 165, 320
Tom 357
McCALLA, Thomas 451
McCALLIM, William 459
McCALLUM
James 393
Philip 445
McCAMANT, Wallace 272, 579
McCANDLESS, James S. 579
McCARDLE, Eliza 20
McCARRAN, Patrick A. 201, 204, 207, 211, 214, 217, 220, 224, 227, 230, 233, 336
McCARTAN, Edward 591
McCARTER
Peter K. 478
Thomas N. 551*
McCARTHY
Carlton 459
Charles J. 594
Daniel J. 569
Dennis 110, 113
Edward A. 528
Eugene J. 227, 230, 233, 236, 239, 242, 245, 249, 252, 255, 258, 325
John H. 135
John J. 154, 156
Joseph E. 528
Joseph R. 225, 228, 231, 234, 238, 241, 386
Justin J. 525
Kathryn O'Loughlin (see O'Loughlin, Kathryn E.)
Patrick H. 461
Patrick J. 459
Raphael C. 474
Richard D. 253, 256, 259
W.S. 459
William 457
William C. 459
McCARTNEY, John A. 570
McCARTY
Andrew Z. 99
August 457
Charles F. 455
Charles P. 460
Dan 294
Earl H. 543
Jonathan 77, 79, 80
Richard 70
William M. 85
William T. 528
MacCARTY, William C. 572
McCARVER, C.P. 457
McCARVILLE, Paul E. 577
McCASKILL, A.P. 462
McCAULEY
Daniel 454
James 558
James A. 469
McCAUSLEN, William C. 88
McCAW, Robert H. 402
McCAWLEY, Charles G. 416
McCAY, Charles F. 481
MacCHESNEY, Brunson 573
MACHVER, Robert M. 573
McCLAMMY, Charles W. 133, 135
McCLARY, Nelson A. 579
McCLEAN, Moses 90
McCLEARY, James T. 140, 143, 145, 148, 151, 153, 156
McCLEERY, James 114
McCLELLAN
Abraham 83, 85, 87
Charles A.O. 134, 137
George 168
George B. (b. 1826) 15, 340, 400, 406*, 407*
George B. (b. 1865) 143, 146, 148, 151, 154, 458
H.C. 578
John L. 202, 206, 216, 219, 222, 225, 228, 232, 235, 238, 241, 244, 247, 251, 254, 257, 260, 263, 282
Robert 83, 86
T.R. 417
Thomas N. 278
William 553, 554
McCLELLAND
Charles M. 273
George W. 479
John S. 574
Robert 27, 44, 87, 89, 91, 322
Roswell D. 434
Thomas 473
William (b. 1842) 115
William (b. 1883) 513, 519*
McCLENACHAN, Blair 55
McCLENAHAN, D.A. 533
McCLENCH, William W. 549
McCLENE, James 7
McCLERNAND, John A. 87, 89, 91, 92, 102, 104, 407, 408
McCLINTIC, James V. 172, 175, 178, 181, 185, 188, 191, 195, 198, 201
McCLINTOCK
Barbara 604
Charles B. 195, 198
Emory 568
J.R. 459
Robert 423, 425, 432, 439
McCLISH, Eli 479
McCLORY
James E. 557
Robert 248, 251, 255, 258, 261, 264
McCLOSKEY
Augustus 195
John 470, 523, 524, 525
Matthew H. 430
Paul N., Jr. 254, 257, 260, 263
William B. 578
William G. 527
McCLOUD, Bentley G. 546
McCLOY, John J. 428, 545, 603, 608, 609
McCLUNG
Alexander K. 424
Clarence E. 573
Lee 444
McCLURE
Addison S. 126, 143
Charles 83, 85
James A. 254, 258, 261, 264, 299
James G.K. 603
John 281
P.F. 459
Robert B. 413, 414
Samuel S. 603
McCLURG
James 459*

Joseph W. 106, 108, 110, 329
McCLUSKEY, Thomas J. 470
McCOID, Moses A. 123, 125, 127
MacCOLL, Norah A. 595
McCOLLESTER
S.H. 465
John Y. 262, 265
McCOLLUM
Elmer V. 607
J. Brewster 359
Leonard F. 546*
McCOMAS
Louis E. 127, 130, 132, 135, 148, 150, 153, 317
William 80, 82
McCOMB, Eleazer 5
McCONAGHA, Glenn L. 476
McCONAUGHY
David 485
James L. 289, 473, 485
Walter P. 424, 425, 434, 437
McCONE, John A. 443*, 598
McCONIHE, Luther 454*
McCONNAUGHEY, George C. 443
McCONNELL
Felix G. 87, 89
Fowler B. 552*
Francis J. 469, 530
Frank C. 411
John P. 415*
John W. 476
Joseph H. 552
Samuel K., Jr. 218, 221, 224, 228, 231, 234, 237, 240
T. Raymond 477
W. Joseph 477
William J. 134, 298*
McCONNERY, James C. 461
McCOOK
Alexander M. 407, 408, 409, 419
Anson G. 121, 123, 126
Edward M. 409*, 430
McCOPPIN, Frank 461
McCORD
Andrew 58
David J. 452*
Jim Nance 218, 371
Guyte P. 462*
Leon P. 271
Myron H. 136
McCORKLE
Joseph W. 94
Paul 60, 172
MacCORKLE, William A. 383
McCORMACK
Arthur T. 572
Helen G. 502
John W. 190, 194, 197, 200, 203, 207, 210, 213, 217, 220, 223, 226, 230, 233, 236, 239, 242, 244, 245, 247, 249, 251, 252, 254, 255, 257*, 258, 599
Mike 263, 266
MacCORMACK, Daniel W. 443
McCORMICK
Andrew 461
Andrew P. 271
Anne O'Hare 584, 599, 603, 609
Brooks 548
Cyrus H. 548*
Edward J. 569, 574
Fowler 548*
Harold F. 548*
Harry B. 536
Henry C. 133, 136
J. Carroll 525, 528
James B. 465
James R. 110, 112, 114
John F. 469
John N. 509, 522
John W. 128
Lynde D. 417, 419
Medill 173, 176, 180, 183, 301
Nelson B. 145
Patrick J. 468
Richard C. 143
Robert S. 423, 428, 436
Ruth H. 193
Samuel B. 479
Thomas 499
Vance C. 453
Washington J. 181
William B. 462
MacCORMICK, Austin H. 565
McCORT, John J. 525
McCOSH, James 479
McCOSKER, Alfred J. 578
McCOSKRY, Samuel A. 505, 520
McCOWEN, Edward O. 218, 221, 224
McCOWN
E.C. 533
John P. 395
McCOY
Alex W. 564
Alvin S. 586
Charles B. 546
Cornelius J. 481
Frank R. 609
George W. 610
Herbert N. 596
James H. 530
Robert 78
Walter I. 165, 168
Whitley P. 443
William 63, 64, 66, 67, 69, 70, 72, 73, 75, 77, 78
William D. 432
McCRACKAN, William D. 536
McCRACKEN
Charles C. 468
Robert M. 170
MacCRACKEN
Henry M. 477, 479, 484
John H. 474, 485
William P., Jr. 612
McCRADY, Edward 481
McCRARY, George W. 20, 40, 112, 114, 116, 118
McCRATE, John D. 89
MacCRATE, John 178
McCRAY, Warren T. 303
McCREA
Samuel P. 476
Theodore H. 516
McCREADY
James 454
William U. 449
McCREARY
George D. 154, 157, 160, 163, 166
James B. 130, 132, 135, 137, 140, 142, 153, 156, 159, 309*
John (Ill.) 461*
John (S.C.) 69
McCREDIE, William W. 163
McCREE, Wade H., Jr. 272
McCREERY
Fenton R. 427, 430
Thomas C. 110, 112, 116, 118, 120, 309*
William (b. 1750) 57, 59, 60
William (b. 1786) 76
McCRILLIS, Arthur M. 579
McCRORY, James T. 533
McCUE, J.J. 450
McCUISH, John 307
McCULLOCH
Edgar A. 281
George 85
Hugh 27, 28, 29*, 39*
John 97
Philip D., Jr. 139, 142, 144, 147, 150
Roscoe C. 172, 175, 178, 194, 353
W.E. 533
William M. 224, 227, 231, 234, 237, 240, 243, 246, 249, 253, 256, 259, 262
McCULLOGH, Welty 133
McCULLOUGH
C. Rogers 569
Hiram 108, 110
John G. 376
Robert D. 577
Thomas G. 68
McCUMBER, Porter J. 149, 151, 154, 157, 160, 162, 165, 169, 171, 175, 178, 350
McCUNE, Shannon 484
McCURDY
Charles J. 423
Richard A. 549
Thomas A. 474
William F. 493
McCUTCHEON
George Barr 574
John T. 584
MacCUTCHEON, Aleck M. 576, 599
McDADE, Joseph M. 250, 253, 256, 259, 262, 266
McDANIEL
Edward H. 402
George W. 534
Henry D. 296
J.R. 462
Thomas M., Jr. 552
Walton B. 570
William 89
McDANNOLD, John J. 139
McDAVID
Horace W. 576
Raven I. 566
McDEARMON, James C. 141, 144
McDERMOTT
Allan L. 148, 151, 154, 157
George T. 272
James T. 158, 161, 164, 167, 170
Michael J. 427
Walsh 600, 612
McDEVITT
Joseph B. 416
Philip R. 526
McDIARMID
Errett W. 568
Hugh 466
McDILL
Alexander S. 117
James W. 116, 118, 125, 304
MacDILL, David 533
McDONALD
A.D. 552
Alexander (Sen.) 109, 111, 281
Alexander 435
Alfred J. 557
Charles 572
Charles J. 295
David J. 559
David L. 416, 417
Edward F. 138
Eugene F., Jr. 578
Harry A. 445
Howard S. 467
Hunter 572
J.S. 461
Jack H. 255, 258, 261
James G. 431
Jesse F. 285
John (Md.) 145
John (Tex.) 450
Joseph E. 93, 118, 120, 123, 302
Lyle 551
Ralph W. 466
William C. 343
William J. 468
MacDONALD
A.B. 583
Carlos F. 571
J. Clifford 608
Kenneth 573
John L. 132
William J. 168
MACDONALD
A.E. 571
Moses 95, 97
Torbert H. 236, 239, 242, 245, 249, 252, 255, 258, 261, 264
McDONNELL
Charles E. 525
James S. 549*, 594, 597
William A. 575
McDONOUGH
Gordon L. 219, 222, 225, 229, 232, 235, 238, 241, 244
John J. 460
Roger 568
MACDONOUGH, Thomas 417
McDOUGAL, Myres S. 573
McDOUGALL
Alexander 6, 406, 544
James A. 96, 104, 106, 107, 283
John 283
MacDOUGALL
Clinton D. 117, 119
Ellis C. 566
Frederick A. 456
McDOWELL
Abraham J. 452
Alexander 141
Alfred H., Jr. 554
Bert F. 455
Harris B., Jr. 235, 241, 245, 248, 251
Irvin 407*
Jack S. 585
James 90, 92, 94, 378
James F. 106
John (b. 1751) 479
John (b. 1771) 480*
John (b. 1780) 532
John (b. 1870) 532
John (b. 1905) 551
John A. 146, 149
John R. 211, 224
Joseph (b. 1756) 55
Joseph (b. 1758) 53
Joseph J. 88, 90
Samuel 80
Thomas D. 392
W.W. 430
William A. 532
William F. 469, 530
William G. 511, 519
MacDOWELL
Edward A. 597
Mrs. Edward 603
McDUFFIE
George 70, 72, 73, 75, 76, 78, 80, 86, 88, 364*
John 176, 179, 183, 186, 189, 192, 196, 199, 202
John V. 134
William C. 547
MACE, Daniel 94, 96, 98
McEACHRON, Karl B. 595, 601
McELHINEY, Thomas W. 428
McELHINNEY, C.F. 472
McELROY
Clarence H. 478
Neil H. 35, 47, 551*, 608
T.F. 458
William D. 444, 608, 610
McELWAIN, Frank A. 510, 520
MacELWANE, James B. 567
McENERY, Samuel D. 145, 148, 150, 153, 156, 159, 162, 312*
McENTEE, Edward M. 271
McENTEGART, Bryan J. 468, 525, 527
MacENULTY, J.F. 553*
McETTRICK, Michael J. 140
McEVOY, Christopher 484
McEWAN
James B. 449
Thomas, Jr. 143, 146
McEWEN
John A. 457
Robert C. 253, 256, 259, 262, 265
Robert W. 471
McFADDEN
James A. 529
Louis T. 172, 175, 178, 182, 185, 188, 192, 195, 198, 201
P.W. 450
McFALL
Jack K. 428
John J. 238, 241, 244, 248, 251, 254, 257, 260, 263
McFARLAN, Duncan 59
McFARLAND
Andrew 571
Carl 476, 589
Ernest W. 212, 216, 219, 222, 225, 228, 280*
Francis 532
James G. 574
James P. 547*
R.S. 564
Robert W. 475
William 120
MacFARLAND
Francis P. 526
Frank M. 497
W.H. 392
MACFARLAND, Henry B. 462
McFARLANE, William D. 202, 205, 208
MacFARLANE
Catharine 600
Janet R. 497
Robert S. 550*
McFAUL, James A. 529
McFEATTERS, Dale 493
McFETRIDGE, William L. 559
McGAFFEY, Albert B. 579
McGANN, Lawrence E. 137, 139, 142
McGARR, Lionel C. 419
McGARRY, William J. 466
McGARVEY, Robert N. 224
McGAUGHEY, Edward W. 89, 93
McGAVICK, Alexander J. 527
McGAVIN, Charles 156, 158
McGAVOCK
Randal 457
Randal W. 457
McGEE
Charles A.A. 577
Elijah M. 455
Gale W. 244, 247, 250, 254, 257, 260, 263, 266, 388
James 553

Richard A. 565
Tom E. 458
W.J. 563, 578
McGEHEE
Dan R. 204, 207, 210, 214, 217, 220
Francis 457
H. Coleman, Jr. 518
Harvey 328
McGHEE, George C. 428, 438
McGILL
Alexander T. 532
Andrew R. 324
George 193, 197, 200, 203, 206, 307
John (bishop) 528
John (mayor) 454
Ralph 586, 601, 608
William J. 468
McGILLICUDDY, Daniel J. 165, 168, 171
McGINLEY
Donald F. 242
J.P. 559
James J. 467
Laurence J. 470
Phyllis 586, 599
MacGINLEY, John B. 527
McGINTY, Bonaventure T. 474
McGIRK, Matthias 329
McGLACHLIN, Edward F., Jr. 419
McGLASSON, T.N.E. 459
McGLENNON, Cornelius A. 177
McGLINCHEY, Herbert J. 221
McGLOTHLIN, William J. 470, 534
McGOLRICK, James 526
McGOODWIN, Preston 439
McGOVERN
Francis E. 385
George S. 19, 240, 243, 250, 253, 256, 259, 263, 266, 368
John W. 554, 578
Patrick A. 525
Thomas 526
McGOWAN
Alexander 454*
Carl 272
Donald W. 402
James, Jr. 544*
Jonas H. 121, 123
Wallace A. 577
MacGOWAN, Thomas G. 568
McGRAIL, Richard P. 578
McGRANERY, James P. 35, 41, 208, 211, 215, 218
McGRATH
Christopher C. 227, 230
Earl J. 444
Frank 559
J. Howard 35, 41, 224, 228, 363*
John J. 199, 202, 206
Joseph F. 525
Thomas C., Jr. 252
McGRAW
E. Clyde 553*
John H. 381
McGREGOR
Ambrose M. 552
Douglas 465
J. Harry 211, 214, 218, 221, 224, 227, 230, 234, 237, 240
Jack R. 498
Louis D. 579
Malcolm F. 570
MacGREGOR
Clarence 178, 181, 185, 188, 191
Clark 245, 249, 252, 255, 258
Ian K. 491, 543*
McGREW, James C. 113, 115
McGROARTY, John S. 202
McGUCKEN, Joseph T. 524, 528
McGUFFEY, William H. 468, 478
McGUGIN, Harold C. 197, 200
McGUINNESS
Edwin D. 459
Eugene J. 527, 528
McGUIRE
Bird S. 160, 163, 166, 169
Eugene C. 579
Francis X.N. 484
Frederick B. 498
George A. 538
Hunter 569
John A. 226, 229
R.L. 461
William B. 546
McGUIRL, Hubert A. 566
McGURK
Edward A. 472
Joseph F. 427, 439
McGURN, John M. 554
McHALE, Patrick S. 477, 480
McHATTON, Robert L. 74
MACHACEK, John 588
MACHEBOEUF, Joseph P. 526
MACHEN
Harvey G. 252, 255
Willis B. 17, 114, 309, 392, 393
McHENRY
Henry D. 114
James 4, 6, 23*, 40
John G. 160, 163, 166
John H. 89
W.H. 453
MACHIR, James 55
MACHLET, Adolph W. 601
MACHLUP, Fritz 564, 566
MACHOLD
Earle J. 550
H. Edmund 550
MACHROWICZ, Thaddeus M. 230, 233, 236, 239, 242, 245
McHUGH, John 545
MACIEJEWSKI, Anton F. 210, 213
McILHENNY, John A. 445
McILVAINE
Abraham R. 88, 90, 92
Charles P. 473, 505, 521
George W. 353*
Joseph 71, 73, 340
Robinson 426, 429, 431
McILWAIN, Charles H. 567, 583
McILWAINE, Richard 471
McINDOE, Walter D. 105, 107, 109
McINERNEY, John J. 451
McINNERNEY, Thomas H. 548*
MacINNES, Duncan A. 575, 589, 604
McINNIS, Louis L. 482
McINTIRE
Albert W. 285
Clifford G. 229, 233, 236, 239, 242, 245, 248
Rufus 74, 76, 77, 79
William W. 145
McINTOSH
Carl W. 467, 476
Dempster 426, 439*
Lachlan 5, 406
Millicent C. 466, 603, 609
Robert J. 239
W.M., Jr. 462
McINTYRE
C.P. 457
Florence 497
James 523*
John J. 215, 388
Robert 530
Ross T. 416
Thomas J. 249, 252, 255, 259, 262, 265, 339
MacINTYRE
Archibald T. 114
Malcolm M. 546
MACIORA, Lucien J. 213
McIVER
Charles D. 477
Henry 365
MacIVER
Loren 593
Robert M. 573
McJUNKIN, Ebenezer 115, 117
MACK
Andrew 453
Jacob W. 537
Julian W. 271
Maynard 577
Peter F., Jr. 226, 229, 232, 235, 238, 242, 245
Russell V. 228, 231, 234, 237, 241, 244
William P. 483
McKAIG, William M. 137, 140
McKAY
David O. 537
Douglas 35, 44, 357, 460
Frederick S. 600
J.W. 485*
K. Gunn 263, 266
James I. 78, 79, 81, 83, 84, 86, 88, 90, 91
Neil R. 458
MACKAY
Clarence H. 603
Harry A. 458
James A. 251
John A. 532
Robert J. 575
Roland P. 569
William M. 600
MacKAYE, Percy 589, 610
McKAYLE, Donald 593
MACKAY-SMITH, Alexander 509, 521
McKEAN
Hugh F. 480
James B. 103, 105
Samuel 71, 73, 75, 79, 81, 83, 358
Thomas 3*, 4, 5, 10, 358*
Thomas J. 407
William R. 462
McKECHNIE, Robert 558
McKEE
Andrew I. 611
Charles J. 452*
David N. 536
George C. 112, 114, 116
James Y. 479
John 70, 72, 74
Joseph V. 458
Samuel (b. 1774) 61, 62, 63, 65
Samuel (b. 1833) 108, 110
Seth J. 416
William F. 415*
William L. 457
McKEEN, Joseph 466
McKEIGHAN, William A. 138, 140
McKEITHEN, John J. 313
McKELDIN, Theodore R. 318, 450*
McKELLAR, Kenneth D. 166, 169, 172, 175, 178, 182, 185, 188, 192, 195, 198, 202, 205, 208, 212, 215, 218, 219, 221, 225*, 228*, 231, 370
McKELLOPS, Henry J. 566
McKELVEY
Paul D. 533
Vincent E. 443
McKELVIE
Samuel R. 333
Jay W. 414
McKELWAY, B.M. 573
McKENDREE, William 530
McKENNA
Bernard 459
Joseph 30, 41, 129, 132, 134, 136, 269, 272
Philip M. 598
McKENNAN
Thomas M.T. 26, 44, 78, 79, 81, 83, 86
William 271
McKENNEY, William R. 144
McKENTY, Jacob K. 103
McKENSIE
Adelphus P. 474
Charles E. 217, 220
Daisette D.S. 536
James A. 121, 123, 125, 435
John 452
John C. 164, 167, 170, 173, 176, 180, 183
Lewis 105, 113
William P. 536*
MacKENZIE, A. Cameron 470
MACKENZIE
Alexander 402
Harold O. 436
Morley E. 579
McKEON, John 81, 86
McKEOUGH, Raymond S. 203, 206, 210, 213
McKEOWN
J.L.S. 465
Thomas D. 175, 178, 185, 188, 191, 195, 198, 201
McKERN, Will C. 500
McKESSON, John A., III 428
McKEVITT, James D. 260
MACKEY
Argyle R. 443
Edmund W.M. 119, 126, 129
George 558
Harry A. 458
Levi A. 119, 122
M. Cecil 481
McKIBBIN, Joseph C. 100
MACKIE, John C. 252
McKIERNON, John S. 363
McKIM
Alexander 61, 62, 63
Charles F. 567, 590
Isaac 69, 71, 79, 81, 82
John 508
McKINIRY, Richard F. 178
McKINLAY, Duncan E. 155, 158, 161
McKINLEY
Charles 571
Edward B. 419
James F. 401
John 72, 74, 75, 78, 269
John K. 553
William (Va.) 62
William, Jr. (Ohio) 13, 16*, 30*, 121, 124, 126, 128, 131, 133, 136, 353
William B. 156, 158, 161, 164, 170, 173, 176, 180, 183, 186, 301
McKINLY, John 8
McKINNEY
James 156, 158, 161, 164
James B. 460
James W. 558
John F. 107, 115
Luther F. 133, 138, 426
Philip W. 379
Robert M. 438
Roland J. 497, 500
Stewart B. 260, 264
McKINNON
Clinton D. 225, 229
Luther 469
MacKINNON
George E. 223, 272
Lee W. 482
McKINSTRY
Addis E. 548
Arthur R. 513, 519
MACKINTOSH
George L. 484
Kenneth 381
McKISSICK, James R. 481
McKISSOCK, Thomas 93
McKISSON, Robert E. 452
McKITRICK, E.S. 533
MACKLER, Bruce 592
McKNEALLY, Martin B. 259, 568
McKNIGHT
Colbert A. 573, 601
Felix R. 573
Harvey W. 471
John 469, 532
Robert 103, 105
Robert J. 497
William L. 549*
McLACHLAN, James 142, 150, 152, 155, 158, 161
MacLAFFERTY, James H. 179, 183
McLAIN
Frank A. 145, 148, 151, 153, 156, 159
Raymond F. 482*
Raymond S. 412, 414
McLANAHAN, James X. 93, 95
McLANATHAN, Richard B. 500
McLANE
Charles L. 470
John 338
Kathrine 499
Louis 25, 38, 39, 66, 68, 69, 70, 72, 74, 75, 290, 429*
Malcolm 452
Patrick 178
Robert M. (Mayor) 450
Robert M. (Rep.) 91, 93, 123, 125, 317, 425, 428, 433
MacLANE, Jean 589
McLAREN
John F. 479
William E. 507, 519
McLARIN, H.M. 558
McLARTY, Thomas 458
McLAUGHLIN
Allan J. 572
Andrew C. 567, 584
Bernard J. 525
Charles 528
Charles F. 204, 207, 210, 214
Donald H. 567
Gerald 271
J. Edd 580
J. Frank 554
James C. 159, 162, 165, 168, 171, 174, 177, 180, 184, 187, 190, 194, 197
Joseph 175, 182
Leo P. 470
Melvin O. 177, 181, 184,

188
Robert E. 462
Thomas H. 527
McLAURIN
Anselm J. 140, 151, 153, 156, 159, 162, 327*
John L. 138, 141, 144, 146*, 149, 152, 365
MacLAURIN, Richard C. 475
McLAWS, Lafayette 394*, 395*
MACLAY
Samuel 54, 58, 59, 60, 358
William (b. 1737) 51, 358
William (b. 1765) 66, 67
William B. 88, 90, 91, 101, 103
William J. 479
William P. 66, 67, 68
McLEAN
Alney 65, 68
Angus W. 349
Archibald 466
Daniel V. 474
Mrs. Donald 579
Donald H. 201, 204, 207, 211, 214, 217
Ernest L. 449
Finis E. 93
George E. 476
George P. 164, 167, 170, 173, 176, 179, 183, 186, 189, 288*
J.R. 392
James H. 125
John (b. 1795) 64, 65, 269, 445
John (b. 1791) 66, 71, 75, 300*
John G. 546
Joseph A. 455
Moses 90
Nathaniel C. 410
Ridley 416
Robert M. 428
W.R. 558
William 71, 73, 75
William P. 117
MacLEAN (or MACLEAN)
Alexander T. 549
Charles W. 516
Donald 569
George E. 473
J. Arthur 499
James A. 472
John 479
MACLEAY, Donald 554
MacLEISH, Archibald 444, 563, 584, 586*, 589, 592, 595, 602, 610
McLELLAN, Ralph 598
McLEMORE
Atkins J. 172, 175
Price C. 601
McLENE, Jeremiah 79, 81
MACLENNAN, Francis W. 610
McLEOD
Clarence J. 177, 184, 187, 190, 194, 197, 200, 204, 210
Scott 430
Thomas G. 366
MacLEOD, William 498
McLESKEY, B.G. 483
McLESTER, James S. 569
McLOSKEY, Robert T. 248
MACLURE, William 563
McMAHON
Brien 219, 222, 226, 229, 289
Gregory 224
Howard O. 601
John 558
John A. 119, 121, 124
John J. 529
Justin 474*
Laurence S. 526
Martin T. 434
Patrick 558
William C. 413
MACMAHON, Arthur W. 571
McMANAWAY, James G. 499
McMANUS, William 73
McMASTER
Erasmus D. 475
F.W. 452
John B. 567
John L. 454
William H. 188, 192, 195, 367*
MacMASTER, Daniel M. 500
McMATH
Francis C. 611
Robert R. 564, 611
Sid 282
McMENAMY, Francis X. 469
McMICHAEL
Morton (b. 1807) 458
Morton (b. 1836) 564
J.B. 533
T.H. 533
McMILLAN
Clara G. 211
Edwin M. 605
F.O. 576
James 135, 137, 140, 143, 145, 148, 151, 322
James B. 566
Jesse V. 474
John L. 211, 215, 218, 221, 225, 228, 231, 234, 237, 240, 243, 247, 250, 253, 256, 259, 263
John R. 567
Louis A. 591
Robert S. 591
Samuel 160
Samuel J.R. 119, 121, 123, 125, 128, 130, 324*
Thomas S. 188, 192, 195, 198, 202, 205, 208, 211
W.H. 533
William 485
MacMILLAN
Donald B. 593, 598
Douglas C. 611*
Douglas C. 611
Kerr D. 485
McMILLEN,
Rolla C. 216, 219, 223, 236
McMILLIN, Benton 124, 126, 129, 131, 133, 136, 138, 141, 144, 146, 370, 429, 435
McMINN, Joseph 369
McMORRAN, Henry G. 153, 156, 159, 162, 165
McMULLEN
Adam 333
Chester B. 229
Fayette 94, 96, 98, 99, 393
John 525
Richard C. 292
McMURLTRIE, William 565
McMURRAY
Howard J. 219
Joseph P. 443, 479
MacMURRAY, John Van A. 425, 427, 431, 432, 438
McMURRICH, J. Playfair 563
McMURRIN, Sterling M. 444
McMURRY
John F. 530
Thomas S. 453
McMURTY, Lewis S. 569
McNAGNY, William F. 140
McNAIR
Alexander 329
Edward 517
F.V. 483
John 95, 97
Lesley J. 404, 411, 419
Robert E. 366
William 459
William W. 456
McNAIRY, Philip F. 516, 520
McNAMAR, Michael 449*
McNAMARA
Andrew T. 403
Martin D. 526
Patrick V. 236, 239, 242, 245, 249, 252, 323
Robert S. 35, 36, 47, 547, 608
McNAMEE, Luke 416, 419
McNARNEY, Joseph T. 404, 411, 415
McNARRY, Philip F. 520
McNARY
Charles L. 18, 175, 178, 181, 185, 188, 191, 195, 198, 201, 205, 208, 211, 214, 218, 356
William S. 153, 156
McNAUGHER, John 533
McNAUGHT, James B. 572
McNAUGHTON, Ronald R. 567
MacNAUGHTON
Donald S. 551*
James 610
McNEALY, Robert 462
McNEELY
Eugene J. 543
Thompson W. 112, 114
McNEIL
Donald 474
Dudley B. 515, 522
MacNEIL
Mrs. Douglas H. 576
Hermon A. 579*, 591
McNEILL
Archibald 70, 73
Edwin R. 355
Neal E. 355
William H. 602
MacNEILL
John B. 599
MacNEISH, Richard S. 595
MACNELLY, Jeffrey K. 588
McNEMAR, Quinn 571
McNICHOLAS, John T. 523, 526
McNICHOLS
Stephen L.R. 286
William H., Jr. 453
MacNIDER, Hanford 425, 568
McNIERNEY, Francis 525
McNINCH, Frank R. 443*
McNULTA, John 116
McNULTY
Frank J. 184, 558
James A. 525, 527
McNUTT
Alexander G. 326
Patterson 466
Paul V. 303, 435, 568
MACOMB
Alexander 400, 401, 402
M.M. 404*, 419
MACOMBER
George E. 449
William B., Jr. 431
MACON
Nathaniel 16, 52, 53, 54, 55, 56*, 57*, 58*, 59, 60, 61, 63, 64, 65*, 67, 68, 70, 71, 72, 74, 347
Robert B. 152, 155, 158, 161, 164
Robert C. 414
McPARLAND, John 558
McPHAIL, George W. 469, 474
McPHERRON, J. Melville 478
McPHERSON
Edward 103, 105
Harry W. 473
Isaac V. 177, 181
James B. 406, 408, 409
John B. 271
John R. 121, 123, 126, 128, 130, 133, 135, 138, 140, 340
Smith 148
William 478, 565
McQUAID
Bernard J. 528
Patrick 454*
MacQUARRIE, Thomas W. 481
McQUEEN, John 92, 94, 96, 97, 99, 101, 103, 393
MacQUEEN, G.A. 451
McQUIGG, John R. 568
McQUILLEN, John H. 566
McQUOWN, Albert L. 572
McRAE
Colin J. 391, 392
James H. 400
John J. 95, 100, 102, 326*, 392
Milton A. 574
Thomas C. 129, 131, 134, 136, 139, 142, 144, 147, 150, 282
McREYNOLDS
James C. 31, 41, 270
Samuel D. 185, 189, 192, 195, 198, 202, 205, 208, 212
McROBERTS
Alexander 459
Samuel 85, 87, 300
McRUER, Donald C. 107
McSHANE
Andrew J. 457
Edward J. 568
Francis 484
John A. 133
McSHEA, Joseph 525
McSHERRY
James (b. 1776) 317
James (b. 1842) 70
William 471
McSORLEY, Edward 611
McSPADDEN, Clem R. 265
MacSPADDEN, H.L. 455
McSWAIN, John J. 182, 185, 188, 192, 195, 198, 202, 205
McSWEEN
Harold B. 242, 245
John 483
McSWEENEY
John 185, 188, 191, 208, 227
John M. 424
Miles B. 365
McSWINEY, James W. 549
McTYEIRE, Holland N. 530
McVAY, Charles B., Jr. 418
McVEAGH, Wayne 29, 41, 431, 438
MacVEAGH
Charles 431,
Franklin 31*, 39
Lincoln 429*, 430, 435, 437, 438, 439
McVEAN, Charles 79
McVEY
Frank L. 473, 477
Tyler 557
Walter L. 245
William E. 229, 232, 235, 238
McVICAR, John 558
MacVICAR
John 453*
John, Jr. 453
Peter 484
Robert W. 479
McVICKER
Roy H. 251
William N. 508, 521
McVINNEY, Russell J. 528
MacWHERTER, John E. 461
McWHORTER
Alexander 532
Ashton W. 471
George G. 293
McWILLIAMS
John D. 216
Robert H. 272, 286
McWILLIE, William 98, 326
MACY
Anne Sullivan 609
Jesse 571
John B. 98
John W., Jr. 445, 608
W. Kingsland 224, 227
MADDEN
J. Warren 273
James L. 477
Martin B. 156, 158, 161, 164, 167, 170, 173, 176, 180, 183, 187, 190
Ray J. 216, 220, 223, 226, 229, 232, 235, 239, 242, 245, 248, 251, 255, 258, 261, 264
Walter 462
MADDOCK, Walter 350
MADDOCKS
Moses R. 461
Ray T. 400
MADDOX
F.M. 450
John W. 139, 142, 145, 147, 150, 153
Lester 297
Robert F. 449, 564
William P. 479
MADIGAN, Edward R. 264
MADISON
Edmond H. 159, 161, 164
George 308
James (b. 1749) 486, 505, 522
James (b. 1751) 4, 7, 13, 15*, 23, 24, 38, 51, 52, 53, 54, 597
MAES, Camillus P. 525
MAESTRI, Robert S. 457
MAFFETT, James T. 133
MAGAFAN, Ethel 589
MAGATH, Thomas B. 572
MAGEE
Clare 227, 230
Frank L. 543*
J. Ralph 530
James C. 403
James M. 185, 188
James V. 587
John 74, 76
John A. 117
John B. 468
Rufus 437
Walter W. 171, 174, 178, 181, 185, 188
William A. 459*
William G. 473
William M. 474
MAGEVNEY, Eugene A. 469
MAGIE
William F. 570
William J. 340
MAGILL, Edward H. 482
MAGINNIS
Charles D. 567, 590, 599
S. Abbot 424
MAGLIN, William H. 403
MAGNA, Mrs. Russell W. 579

MAGNER
Francis 527
Thomas F. 135, 138, 141
MAGNUSEN, Henry 467
MAGNUSON
Donald H. 237, 241, 244, 247
Warren G. 209, 212, 215, 219*, 222, 225, 228, 231, 234, 237, 241, 244, 247, 250, 254, 257, 260, 263, 266, 381, 612
MAGOFFIN
Beriah 309
Ralph V.D. 574
MAGOON
Charles E. 434
Henry S. 120
MAGOUN
George F. 471
Horace W. 607
MAGOWAN, Frank A. 462
MAGRADY, Frederick W. 188, 192, 195, 198
MAGRATH, Andrew G. 365
MAGRUDER
Alexander C. 449
Allan B. 62, 311
Bruce 415
Calvert 271, 273
Carter B. 401, 404*, 405
George A. 418
John B. 394
John R. 449
Patrick 59, 444
William B. 462
MAGUIRE
Bernard A. 471*
George 460
George R. 574
James F. 474, 487
James G. 139, 142, 144
John A. 162, 165, 168
John J. 524
MAHAN
Alfred T. 419*, 567
Asa 478
Bryan F. 167
John W. 580
Patrick J. 469
MAHANY, Rowland B. 143, 146, 427
MAHER
Edward A. 449
Frank B. 548
James P. 165, 168, 171, 174, 177
Leo T. 528*
Stephen J. 599
Zacheus J. 481
MAHEY, John A. 498
MAHIN, Frank C. 413
MAHL, Alan R. 502
MAHON
G. Heyward, Jr. 205, 208
George H. 205, 208, 212, 215, 218, 221, 225, 228, 231, 234, 237, 240, 244, 247, 250, 253, 256, 260, 263, 266
Thaddeus M. 141, 143, 146, 149, 152, 154, 157
W. D. 557
MAHONE, William 126, 129, 131, 379
MAHONEY
Bernard J. 529
John C. 271
John F. 600
Peter P. 131, 133
William 460
William F. 150, 153
William J. 480
William P., Jr. 428
MAHOOL, J. Barry 450
MAHORNER, Howard 565
MAIER
Cornell C. 548
Henry W. 456
MAILER, Norman 587, 602
MAILLIARD, William S. 232, 235, 238, 241, 244, 248, 251, 254, 257, 260, 263
MAIN
Arthur E. 465
Charles E. 491
Charles T. 573, 590
John F. 381*
John H. T. 471*
Silas S. 455
Verner W. 204
MAISH, Levi 119, 122, 133, 136
MAISTER, William T. 450
MAJOR
Elliott W. 330
J. Earl 183, 190, 196, 200, 272
S. I. M. 435*
Samuel C. 177, 184, 187, 191
MAJORS, Thomas J. 121
MALAMUD
Bernard 587, 602*, 609
William 571
MALBONE, Francis 53, 54, 62, 361
MALBY, George R. 160, 162, 165
MALCOLM
Gilbert 469
Howard 467, 570
Wilbur G. 543*
MALETZ, Herbert N. 273
MALIK, Charles M. 604
MALIN, John H. 558
MALLALIEU, Willard F. 530
MALLARY
Richard W. 266
Rollin C. 69, 70, 72, 73, 75, 77
MALLERY
J. E. 459*
Joseph A. 381
MALLET, John W. 565
MALLETT, James R. 514, 521
MALLEY, John F. 574
MALLORY
Ernest 458
Francis 83, 85, 87
Lester D. 429, 431
Meredith 84
Robert 102, 104, 106
Rufus 111
Stephen R. 94, 96, 98, 100, 102, 104, 293, 391
Stephen R., Jr. 137, 139, 144, 147, 150, 153, 155, 158, 293
MALONE
George W. 224, 227, 230, 233, 236, 239, 336
James H. 456
James W. 529
Kemp 566, 577
Lee H. B. 498, 500
Ross L. 565
Thomas F. 567
MALONEY
David M. 529
Francis T. 199, 203, 206, 209, 213, 216, 219, 289
Franklin J. 224
Harry J. 400, 414
J. A. 558
James 557
John F. 455
Paul H. 197, 200, 203, 207, 210, 217, 220
Robert S. 180
William E. 558
William F. 480
MALOTT, Deane W. 468, 473
MALSTER, William T. 450
MALTBIE, William M. 289
MAMWARING, Rosser L. 572
MANAHAN, James 168
MANARD, B. O. 467
MANASCO, Carter 212, 216, 219, 222
MANDEL, Marvin 318
MANDERSON, Charles F. 128, 130, 133, 134, 135, 136, 138, 139, 140, 333, 564
MANEY, George 424, 434, 439
MANFULL, Melvin L. 425
MANGAN, Louis 453
MANGUM, Willie P. 71, 73, 78, 79, 81, 84, 85, 86, 87, 90, 91, 93, 95, 347*
MANHART, Franlin P. 482
MANHEIM, Ralph 602
MANIER, Will R., Jr. 580
MANKELL, Charles 318
MANKIEWICZ, Joseph L. 575
MANKIN, Helen Douglas 219
MANLEY
Harry S. 476
Joseph 474
Marian C. 600
MANLOVE, Joe J. 184, 187, 191, 194, 197
MANLY
B. C. 459
Basil (coll. pres.) 465
Basil 443
Charles 347, 470
John M. 577*
MANN
Abijah, Jr. 79, 81
Alexander 511, 521
C. B. 458
Cameron 509, 521*
Delbert 575
Edward C. 178
Frank C. 571
Frederic R. 423
Horace 91, 93, 95, 465, 597
James 110
James R. (Ill.) 145, 147, 150, 153, 156, 158, 161, 164, 167, 170, 173, 176, 180
James R. (S.C.) 259, 263, 266
Job 81, 92, 93
Joel K. 78, 79
Thomas C. 427, 433
William A. 402, 410
William H. 379
William M. 592
Mrs. William M. 592
Woodrow W. 456
MANNATT, James I. 476
MANNES, Leopold Damrosch 601
MANNING
Daniel 29, 39
Mrs. Daniel 579
James 7, 467
James M. 449
John, Jr. 113
John B. 451
John J. 418
John L. 364
Knox 557
Lucius B. 544*
Reginald W. 585
Richard I. (b. 1789) 80, 81, 364
Richard I. (b. 1859) 365
Thomas C. 312, 433
Thurston E. 467
Timothy 523, 526
Vannoy H. 121, 123, 125
Warren H. 573
William T. 511, 520
MANOGUE, Patrick 528
MANSFIELD
Joseph J. 175, 179, 182, 185, 189, 192, 195, 198, 202, 205, 208, 212, 215, 218, 221, 225
Frederick W. 450
M. J. Mike 217, 220, 224, 227, 230, 233, 236, 239, 242, 246, 249, 252, 255, 258, 262, 265, 331
Walter T. 271
MANSHIP
Charles H. 454
Paul 563, 579, 590, 603, 610
MANSON
John T. 565
Mahlon D. 114
MANSUR, Charles H. 133, 135, 138
MANTLE, Lee 140, 143, 145, 331
MANTON, Martin T. 271
MANUCY, Dominic 527
MAPES, Carl E. 168, 171, 174, 177, 180, 184, 187, 190, 194, 197, 200, 204, 207, 210
MAPOTHER, Wible 549
MARABLE, John H. 73, 75
MARAKLE, Willard A. 577
MARASCHI, Anthony 481
MARAZITI, Joseph J. 265
MARBLE
Edgar M. 444
Sebastian S. 314
Thomas L. 339
William A. 579
MARBURG, Theodore 424
MARBURY, Ogle 318
MARBUT, Curtis F. 594
MARCANTONIO, Vito 204, 211, 214, 217, 221, 224, 227
MARCEAU, Henri 501
MARCH
Alden 569
Francis A. 570*, 577
Peyton C. 400
MARCHAND
Albert G. 85, 86
David 67, 68
MARCHANT, Henry 4, 7
MARCHESSAULT, Damien 456*
MARCKWARDT, Albert H. 566
MARCUS
Louis 460
Marcia 609
MARCY
Daniel 107
Henry O. 569
Oliver 478
Randolph B. 402
William L. 26*, 27, 38, 40, 77, 344*
MARDAGA, Thomas 529
MARDEN
C. Carroll 577
Fred N. 452
John W. 589
Orison S. 565
MARDIAN, Sam 459
MARDIS, Samuel W. 77, 78
MARECHAL, Ambrose 523, 528
MARGESON, Edmund 3
MARIN, John 590
MARION
Francis 406
Robert 59, 60, 62
MARIS, Albert B. 271, 273
MARK, Herman F. 594, 604
MARKBREIT, Leopold 424, 452
MARKELL
Charles 318
Henry 73, 74
Jacob 64
MARKERT, Clement L. 573
MARKHAM
Charles H. 548*
Edward M. 402
Edwin 589
George C. 550
Henry H. 129, 283
Osmon G. 466
William (governor) 9*
William (mayor) 449
MARKLE
John 492
Willard A. 577
MARKLEY, Philip S. 71, 73
MARKS
Albert S. 370
George E. 594
Leonard H. 445
Wayne C. 547
William 73, 75, 76, 358
MARKWOOD
Jacob 531
Michael E. 558
MARLAND
Ernest W. 201, 355
William C. 384
MARLEY, James P. 413
MARLING
John L. 429
Joseph M. 526
MARLOWE, Donald E. 573
MARMADUKE, John S. 329
MARMION
Charles G. 515, 520
William H. 515, 522
MARQUAND
Allan 501
John P. 584
MARQUESS, William H. 485
MARQUETTE, Turner M. 108
MARQUIS
David C. 532
Donald G. 571
John A. 532
Robert L. 477
MARR
Alem 76
George W. L. 67
MARRIOTT, Richard H. 460
MARSALIS, John H. 226
MARSH
Albert L. 611
Benjamin F. 120, 123, 125, 139, 142, 145, 147, 153
Charles 66
Charles F. 486
Claudia H. 492
Daniel L. 466
E. B. 600
Ernest S. 543*
Fletcher O. 469
George P. 88, 90, 92, 94, 431, 438
James 484
John O., Jr. 250, 253, 257, 260
Othniel C. 501, 563
Reginald 593*, 603
William F. 578
MARSHAK, Robert E. 468
MARSHALL
Alexander K. 98

Alfred 86
Alfred C. 546
Anthony D. 432, 438
C. Morgan 502
Carrington T. 353
Edward C. 546
Edward C. (Rep.) 94
Ewing B. 577
Fred 227, 230, 233, 236, 239, 242, 245
Fred D. 452
George 575
George A. 146
George C. 34*, 38, 47*, 400*, 411, 569, 596, 603, 606, 609
George S. 452
Henry 391, 392
Henry R. 571
Humphrey (b. 1760) 53, 54, 55
Humphrey (b. 1812) 93, 95, 98, 100, 308, 393, 425
J. Stanley 470
James 472
James W. (b. 1822) 22, 43
James W. (b. 1844) 141
John 15, 23*, 38, 56, 269, 597
John P. 483
Lawrence 545
Leroy T. 201, 204
Louis 482, 485
Lycurgus L. 211
Orsamus H. 477
Paule 609
Richard J. 484
Robert J. 535
Samuel S. 98, 100, 108, 110, 112, 114, 116
Thomas A. 77, 79, 308
Thomas F. (Ky.) 85
Thomas F. (N.D.) 151, 154, 157, 160
Thomas R. 14, 18, 167, 170, 173, 176, 303
Thurgood 270, 271, 611
W. L. 462
Willard C. 460
William L. 402
William R. 324
MARSTON
Anson 572
Frank A. 572
Gilman 103, 105, 108, 338
MARTELL, Charles B. 417
MARTI, Lloyd 455
MARTIN
Alexander (b. 1740) 4, 9, 53, 54, 347*
Alexander (b. 1822) 469, 485
Augustus M. 525
Augustus N. 134, 137, 140
Augustus P. 450
Barclay 90
Benjamin F. 122, 124
Bennett S. 455
Burleigh 449
Charles 471
Charles (Ill.) 173
Charles D. 103
Charles E. 573
Charles H. (Ore.) 198, 201, 357, 400
Charles Henry (N.C.) 143, 146
Christopher 3
Clarence A. 413
Clarence D. 381
Clarence E. 565
D. D. 584
Daniel 316*
David 306
David G. 469
David T. 246, 249, 252, 255, 259, 262, 265
Eben W. 152, 154, 157, 160, 163, 166, 169
Edmund F. 544*, 595, 596
Edward 224, 228, 231, 234, 237, 240, 360*
Edward L. (Del.) 122, 125
Edward L. (Mo.) 455
Edwin M. 423, 424
Elbert S. 103
Fletcher 589, 593
Francois X. 311
Franklin H. 565
Frederick L. 411
Frederick S. 95
Gene C. 462
George B. 173, 309
George E. 272*
George I. 462
Glenn L. 594, 597
Graham A. 431, 438
Harold C. 483
Harold E. 587
Harold M. 417*
Harold R. 532*
Harry 557
Homer 557, 559
I. Jack 273
J. A. 557
J. H. 451
J. L. 434
James D. 251
James G. 265
James R. 549
James S. 116
John (b. 1730) 8
John (b. 1833) 140
John (b. 1893) 593
John A. (b. 1839) 306*
John A. (b. 1868) 161, 164, 199, 202, 206, 209
John Bartlow 427
John C. 210
John D. 271
John E. 386
John F. 458
John J. 469
John M. 129, 392
John P. 89
John W. 294, 454
Joseph 586
Joseph A. 453
Joseph J. 124
Joseph W., Jr. 187, 190, 194, 197, 200, 203, 207, 210, 213, 217, 220, 222, 223, 226, 230, 232, 233, 236, 239, 242, 245, 249, 252
Joshua L. 80, 82, 277
Josiah 9
Lewis J. 168
Luther 4, 6
Nathaniel 452
Noah 337
Pat M. 248
Paul E. 531
Preston 443
Richard B. 517
Robert N. 72
Roy B., Jr. 458
S. Walter 470
Thomas 549
Thomas E. (Iowa) 210, 213, 216, 220, 223, 226, 229, 232, 235, 239, 242, 305
Thomas E. (Md.) 449
Thomas S. 144, 147, 149, 152, 155, 158, 160, 163, 166, 169, 172, 175, 179, 379
W. F. 551
Walter B. 569
Walter R. 579
Whitmell P. 171, 174, 177, 180, 184, 187, 190
Will T. 395, 396
William C. 530
William D. 75, 76
William H. 133, 136
William J. 469*
William I. 417
William McChesney, Jr. 443*
William T. 452
MARTINDALE
Henry C. 71, 73, 74, 76, 79
Joseph B. 545
MARTINE, James E. 165, 168, 171, 340
MARTINEAU, John E. 282
MARTINO, Antonio P. 589, 610
MARTS, Arnaud C. 467
MARTY
Martin 528, 529
Martin E. 602
MARVEL
Carl S. 565, 590, 596, 604, 608
Josiah 565
Josiah, Jr. 427*
MARVIL, Joshua H. 291
MARVIN
Cloyd H. 465, 471
Dudley 71, 73, 74, 91
Dwight 573
Enoch M. 530
Francis 141
H. M. 567
James 473
James M. 107, 109, 111
Richard P. 83, 84
Thomas O. 445
William 293
MARX
Alexander 499
Charles D. 572
Oscar B. 453
Roberto B. 590
MARYE, George T. 436
MARZALL, John A. 444
MASCAREL, Jose 456
MASLOW, Abraham H. 571
MASNATA, Aloysius 481*
MASON
Armistead T. 66, 378
Arthur J. 611
Birny, Jr. 553*
Charles 444
Charles A. 514, 519
Charles W. 355
E. S. 544
Edward S. 566
George W. 543*
Harry H. 203
James B. 66, 67
James M. 83, 90, 92, 94, 96, 98*, 99, 100, 101, 103, 105, 378, 392
James T. 569
Jeremiah 64, 65, 67, 337
John 545
John C. 93, 95, 100
John M. 469
John T. 86
John W. 444
John Y. 26*, 41, 42, 78, 80, 82, 428
Jonathan 55, 56, 66, 68, 319
Joseph 123, 126
Max 468, 492
Moses, Jr. 79, 80
Newton E. 418
Noah M. 206, 210, 213, 216, 219, 223, 226, 229, 232, 235, 238, 242, 245
Oliver P. 333
Philip H. 458
Richard S. 469, 472
Roswell B. 451
Roy 591
Russell Z. 474
Samson 81, 83, 84, 86
Steven 578
Stevens T. (Mich.) 322
Stevens T. (Va.) 53, 54, 55, 56, 57, 58, 378
Warren P. 599
Wilbur N. 466
Wiley R. 513
William 81
William C. 589, 607
William E. 132, 134, 145, 147, 150, 173, 176, 180, 300
William H. 611
MASSELL, Sam 449
MASSEY
Otis 454
William A. 165, 335
Zachary D. 163
MASSINGDALE, Sam C. 205, 208, 211, 214
MAST, Samuel O. 573
MASTEN, Joseph G. 450*
MASTER, Henry B. 532
MASTERS
Dorotha McClurkin 497
Edgar Lee 589, 610
Harry V. 465
Irving U. 452
J. E. 574
Josiah 59, 60
Thomas 458
MASTERSON, Kleber S. 417*
MASTERTON, George 559
MASUDA, George T. 517, 521
MATARAZZO, Joseph D. 598
MATAS, Rudolph 565, 590
MATHER
Frank J., Jr. 501
Increase 472
James J. 457
Jean Paul 475
Kirtley F. 563*, 578, 594
Robert 554
Stephen T. 444, 603
MATHERS, Frank C. 575
MATHERY, John 474
MATHESON, Kenneth G. 470, 471
MATHEWS
Arthur F. 590
Clifton 272
David 465
Elbert G. 432, 434
Frank A., Jr. 220, 224
George (b. 1739) 8, 51, 295
George (b. 1774) 311
George (b. 1850) 531
Henry M. 383
James 86, 88
James K. 531
James M. 477
John 7, 9
Joseph M. 569
Shailer 534
Vincent 61
MATHEWSON
Champion H. 567, 590, 595
Elisha 60, 62, 361
Lemuel 399, 405
MATHIAS
Charles McC., Jr. 245, 248, 252, 255, 258, 261, 264, 318
Robert B. 254, 257, 260, 263
MATHIOT, Joshua 86
MATHIS
A. J. 453
M. Dawson 261, 264
MATLACK
James 70, 71
Timothy 7
MATSON
Aaron 70, 71
Courtland C. 125, 127, 130, 132
George C. 564
Greta 589
MATSUNAGA, Spark M. 248, 251, 254, 258, 261, 264
MATTERN, George W. 453
MATTERS, Margaret M. G. 536
MATTES, William F. 600
MATTESON
Charles 362
Joel A. 300
Orsamus B. 93, 97, 99, 101
MATTHES, Marion C. 272
MATTHEWS
Arthur J. 465
Brander 577, 578
Charles 166
Claude 302
David 458
Donald R. (Billy) 232, 235, 238, 241, 245, 248, 251
Edmund O. 418
Francis P. 399, 430
George H. 476
H. Freeman 423, 433, 437
Herbert 607
James C. 477
Joe L. 568
Joseph W. 326
Mark A. 532
Nathan, Jr. 450
Nelson E. 172
Paul 510, 520
Samuel 9
Stanley 121, 269, 353
William 471
William (Rep.) 54
MATTHIAS, Bernd T. 612
MATTINGLY, Garrett 586
MATTISON, George A., Jr. 579
MATTOCKS, John 70, 73, 87, 375
MATTOON, Ebenezer 55, 56
MATTSON, Henry E. 593, 607
MATZ, Nicholas C. 526
MAUBORGNE, Joseph O. 403
MAUCHLY, John W. 608
MAUCK, Joseph W. 481
MAUCKER, James W. 478
MAUERMAN, R. J. 483
MAUERMANN, Gus B. 461
MAULDIN, William 585, 586
MAULL, Baldwin 549*
MAUPIN, Socrates 484
MAURAN, John L. 567
MAURER
Alfred H. 607
David W. 566
Oscar E. 534
W. Irving 466
MAURICE, James 97
MAURY
Abram P. 81, 83
Dabney H. 394, 426
John W. 462
Matthew F. 597
Reuben 584
MAUTHE, James L. 595
MAUZY, Wayne L. 501
MAVERICK
Maury 205, 208, 461
S. A. 460, 461

MAW, Herbert B. 374
MAWBY, Russell G. 492
MAXCY
E. H. 452*
Jonathan 467, 481, 483
Kenneth F. 610
Virgil 423
MAXEY
George 360
Powhattan W. 457
Samuel B. 120, 122, 124, 126, 129, 131, 372
MAXFIELD, James T. 460*
MAXON
James M. 511, 522
John 497
MAXWELL
Augustus E. 96, 98, 293, 392, 393
David F. 565
George 572
George C. 62
John P. B. 82, 86
Joseph R. N. 466, 472
Lewis 75, 77, 78
Russell L. 401, 411
Samuel 146, 333*
Samuel D. 454
Thomas 76
William 406
William (b. 1884) 471
William (b. 1908) 78
MAY
Andrew J. 197, 200, 203, 207, 210, 213, 216, 220
Catherine 244, 250, 254, 257, 260
Charles D. 592, 599
Edgar 586
Edwin H., Jr. 238
Henry 97, 104
James V. 571
John L. 527
Mitchell 148
Orville E. 590
William L. 78, 80, 82, 461
MAYALL, Samuel 97
MAYBANK, Burnet R. 215, 218, 221, 225, 228, 231, 234, 366*, 451
MAYBECK, Bernard R. 590
MAYBERRY, William A. 549*
MAYBIN, William 452
MAYBURY, William C. 128, 130, 453
MAYER
Ferdinand L. 429
George V. L. 431
Julius M. 271
MAYERSON, Hymen S. 571
MAYES
Edward 475
Robert B. 327
MAYFIELD
Earle B. 185, 189, 192, 373
Harold F. 569, 592
MAYHAM, Stephen L. 113, 121
MAYHEW
Edgar deN. 497
Richard 589
MAYNARD
Carl W. 572
Douglas 472
Harry L. 152, 155, 158, 160, 163
Horace 28, 29, 43, 101, 103, 105, 109, 111, 113, 115, 117, 438
John 74, 86
MAYNE
F. Blair 480
Wiley 255, 261, 264
MAYO
Alfred M. 564
Charles H. 565, 569
Joseph 459*
Robert B. 502
Robert M. 129
Robert P. 444
William J. 565, 569, 603
William T. 462
Wyndham R. 458
MAYR, Ernst 569, 592, 600, 604
MAYRANT, William 66
MAYS
Benjamin E. 476
Dannite H. 161, 164
Donald J. 586
James H. 172, 175, 179
MAZZARINI, Richard 608
MAZZOLI, Romano L. 261, 264
MEACHAM, James 94, 96, 98, 99
MEAD
Albert E. 381
Charles L. 530
Cowles 59
Daniel W. 572
Elizabeth S. 476
George H. 549*
George J. 608
Giles W. 500
Glenn C. 580
Harold G. 601
James M. 178, 181, 185, 188, 191, 198, 201, 204, 207, 208, 211, 214, 217, 221, 346
John A. 376
Leonard C. 483
Margaret 563, 611
Nelson P. 468
Sterling V. 566
W. Rutherford 603
William E. 566
William H. 517, 519
MEADE
Edwin R. 119
Francis L. 477
George G. 406, 407*, 408*, 409
Hugh A. 223
Richard K. 92, 94, 96, 424
Robert H. 418
W. Howes 223
William 505, 522
MEADER, George 230, 233, 236, 239, 242, 245, 249
MEADOWS, Clarence W. 384
MEALS, Ezra S. 453*
MEANS
Mrs. Alan H. 576
Alexander 470
John H. 364
Rice W. 183, 186, 285, 580
William 451
MEANY, George 599, 608
MEBANE, Alexander 53
MECHAU, Frank 589
MECHEM
Edwin L. 246, 249, 343*
Merritt C. 343
MEDARY, Milton B. 567, 590
MEDBURY, Charles S. 536
MEDEIROS, Humberto S. 523
MEDFORD, Richard C. 501
MEDILL
Joseph 451
William 84, 86, 352
MEDINA, Harold R. 271, 603
MEDSGER, Oliver P. 593
MEECH, Ezra 69, 73
MEEDS, Lloyd 254, 257, 260, 263, 266
MEEHAN, John S. 444
MEEHL, Paul E. 571
MEEK, Walter J. 571
MEEKER
George H. 600
George W. 452
Jacob E. 171, 174
Leonard C. 436
MEEKINSON, David 146, 149
MEEKS
Everett V. 502
James A. 200, 203, 206
MEERSCHAERT, Theophile 527
MEES
C. E. Kenneth 596, 610
Otto 467
MEESE, William G. 546
MEGEL, Carl J. 557
MEGGERS, William F. 580, 594
MEGINNISS, B. A. 462
MEGOWEN, C. R. 550
MEHAFFY, Pat 272
MEHL, Robert F. 590, 595
MEHLHOUSE, H. G. 493
MEIER
E. D. 573
Julius 357
Walter F. 574
MEIERE, Hildreth 590, 591
MEIGS
Henry 68
Josiah 471
Matthew 469
Montgomery C. 403
Return J., Jr. 60, 61, 352*, 403, 445
MEIKLEJOHN
Alexander 465, 608
George D. 140, 143
MEIN, John G. 429
MEINZER, O. E. 567
MELADY, Thomas P. 424, 438
MELASKY, Harris M. 414
MELBY, Ernest O. 476
MELCORTH, Edward 589, 593
MELCHER
John 258, 262, 265
Joseph 526
Louis C. 514
MELCHERS, Gari 593, 603
MELDRIM, Peter W. 564
MELENDY, Arthur R. 566
MELHAM, Thomas W. 579
MELHOUSE, Harvey G. 554
MELICK, Balthazar P. 545
MELISH, William B. 579*
MELL, Patrick H. 468, 471, 534*
MELLEN
Charles S. 550
Prentiss 66, 68, 314, 319
MELLETTE, Arthur C. 367
MELLISH, David B. 117
MELLON
Andrew W. 32*, 33, 39, 429, 548, 590
Paul 492, 603
Richard B. 543, 590
Richard K. 609
W. L. 548
MELLUS, Henry 456
MELOCHE, Daniel H. 601
MELOY
Francis E., Jr. 427
Guy S., Jr. 404, 405*
William T. 533
MELSON, Charles L. 417, 419, 483
MELTON, William D. 481
MELTZER, Samuel J. 570
MELVILLE, George W. 418, 573, 599
MELVIN
Henry A. 574
Marion E. 486
MEMMINGER, Christopher G. 391*, 392
MENAGH, Louis R. 551
MENCHACA, Antonio 460
MENCKEN, Henry L. 603
MENDEL, Lafayette B. 590
MENDELSON, Jack H. 598
MENDENHALL
Charles E. 570
George 569
Joseph A. 432
Thomas C. 486, 563, 594, 596
Thomas C. 2d 481
Walter C. 443, 576
MENDES, H. Pereira 537
MENEES, Thomas 393*
MENENDEZ, Joseph C. 580
MENG, John J. 472
MENGE, Edward 558
MENGES, Franklin 188, 192, 195
MENIFEE, Richard H. 82
MENK, Louis W. 544*, 545, 550
MENKES, Sigmund 593*
MENNINGER
Karl 590, 603, 608
William C. 571, 603
MENOHER, Charles T. 401, 404, 410
MENOTTI, Gian-Carlo 585, 586
MENTZER, William C. 597
MENUET, Robert L. 483
MENZEL, Donald H. 564
MENZIES, John W. 104
MERCER
Asa S. 484
Charles F. 67, 69, 70, 72, 73, 75, 77, 78, 80, 82, 83, 85
David H. 140, 143, 146, 148, 151
James 7
John F. 4, 7, 52, 316
MERCHANT, Livingston T. 425*
MERCIER, A. T. 552
MERCUR, Ulysses 109, 111, 113, 115, 359
MEREDITH
Edwin T. 32*, 45
Elisha E. 139, 141, 144
James E., Jr. 578
Samuel 7, 444
William 600
William M. 26, 39
MERGENTHALER, Ottmar 594
MERICA, Paul D. 590, 595, 596*
MERITT, Benjamin D. 570
MERIWETHER
David (Ga.) 56, 57, 59
David (Ky.) 95
James 72
James A. 85
MERRELL
George R. 423, 427, 428, 430
Jack G. 415
John P. 419
MERRETT, William 457
MERRIAM
Augustus C. 570
C. Hart 569, 609
Charles E. 571
Clinton L. 115, 117
Frank F. 284
J. C. 576
John F. 550*
William R. 324
MERRICK
Edwin T. 311
F. 486
Frank A. 554
J. Vaughan 575
Mary V. 599
Samuel V. 575
Thomas D. 455
William D. 82, 84, 86, 87, 316
William M. 559
William M. (Rep.) 114
MERRIFIELD
Bruce 600
Webster 477
MERRILL
Ayres P. 424
Charles M. 272
Charles W. 595
D. Bailey 232
E. D. 574
Edward F. 315
Edwin G. 544
Eleanor (Brown) 578
Elmer T. 570
Frederick J. H. 501
George E. 468
George W. 430
James 592, 602
Josiah L., Jr. 601
Malcolm E. 592
Malcolm H. 572
Orsamus C. 67, 69
Paul 564
Perry H. 457
Robert T. 580
Samuel 451
Samuel (b. 1822) 304
Stephen M. 530
Walter M. 498
MERRIMAN
O. C. 456*, 457
Truman A. 131, 133
MERRIMON, Augustus S. 117, 119, 121, 348*
MERRIT, Edwin A., Jr. 165, 168
MERRITT
Arthur H. 566
Edward A. 536
Ernest 570

H. Houston 569
Matthew J. 204, 208, 211, 214, 217
Schuyler 173, 176, 179, 183, 186, 189, 193, 199, 203
W. H. 453
Wesley 483
William 457
MERROW, Chester E. 217, 220, 224, 227, 230, 233, 236, 239, 243, 246
MERRY, William L. 426, 434, 436
MERTON, Robert K. 574
MERWIN
Bruce W. 481
Orange 72, 74
William S. 588
MESERVE, Robert W. 565*
MESICK, William S. 145, 148
MESKILL, Thomas J. 254, 289
MESSENBAUGH, J. F. 458
MESSER, Asa 467
MESSERSMITH, George S. 423*, 426, 433
MESSERVY, William S. 460
MESSMER
Sebastian G. 523, 526
Thomas 499
MESTA, Perle 432
MESTRE, Harold 466
MESTROVIC, Ivan 589, 590, 603
METCALF
Albert A. 536
Arunah 62
Bryce 580
Elizabeth 500
Gordon M. 552
Henry B. 17
Jesse H. 185, 188, 192, 195, 198, 202, 205, 363
Keyes D. 568, 600
Lee 233, 236, 239, 242, 246, 249, 252, 255, 258, 262, 265, 332
M. M. 573
Ralph 337
Victor H. 30, 31*, 42, 45, 147, 150, 152
Willard L. 593, 607
William 572
Z. P. 575
METCALFE
Henry B. 119
Lyne S. 121
Ralph H. 261, 264
Thomas 68, 69, 71, 72, 74, 91, 308*
METSKER, D. C. 462
METTEN, John F. 611
METZ
Christian 538
Herman A. 168
METZGER
Sidney M. 526
Stanley D. 445
METZLER, Dwight F. 572
MEWHORT, Roland A. 549*
MEY, Cornelius J. 8
MEYER
A. Leonard 459
Adolf 569, 571
Adolph 137, 140, 142, 145, 148, 150, 153, 156, 159
Albert G. 523*, 529
Andrew J. 480
Armin H. 430, 431, 432
E. B. 576
Eugene 443
Frederick A. 587
George R. 411
George von L. 31*, 42, 43, 436
Harry M., Jr. 599
Herbert A. 223, 226
Herman H. B. 568
John A. 213
John C. 415*
Karl W. 486, 600*, 610
Rudolph J. 474, 480, 487
William H. 244
MEYERHOF, Otto F. 605
MEYERS
Benjamin F. 115
F. J. 558
Grant U. 578
J. E. 457
William G. 574
MEYERSON, Martin 477, 479
MEYNER, Robert B. 342
MEZES, Sidney E. 468, 482
MEZVINSKY, Edward 264
MICHAELIS, John H. 405
MICHAELSON, M. Alfred 180, 183, 187, 190, 193
MICHALEK, Anthony 156
MICHALIS, Clarence G. 579, 603
MICHAUD, John S. 525
MICHEL, Robert H. 238, 242, 245, 248, 251, 255, 258, 261, 264
MICHELS, Agnes K. L. 570
MICHELSON, Albert A. 563, 570, 594, 596, 597, 605, 609
MICHENER
Earl C. 177, 180, 184, 187, 190, 194, 197, 204, 207, 210, 213, 217, 220, 223, 226
James A. 585, 595
MICKELSON
George T. 367
Stanley R. 404
MICKEY
J. Ross 150
John H. 333
MICKLE, Andrew H. 458
MIDDAUGH, John T. 467
MIDDENDORF, J. William, II 433
MIDDLEBUSH, Frederick A. 476
MIDDLEKAUFF, Robert 591
MIDDLESWARTH, Ner 97
MIDDLETON
Arthur 3, 7, 9
George 107
Henry (b. 1717) 5, 7
Henry (b. 1770) 66, 67, 364, 436
Thomas 484
Troy H. 412, 414, 474
W. Vernon 531
MIEGE, John B. 469
MIDGLEY, Thomas, Jr. 565, 596, 601, 604, 608
MIELZINER, Jo 592
MIERS, Robert W. 145, 147, 150, 153
MIES van der ROHE, Ludwig 590, 591, 592, 598, 603, 608
MIFFLIN, Thomas 4, 5, 7, 9, 358, 403*, 406
MIKELL, Henry J. 511, 519
MIKVA, Abner J. 258, 261
MILAM, Carl H. 600
MILBANK, Jeremiah 609
MILBURN, Frank W. 413, 414
MILES
Arthur C. 418
Clarence G. 455
D. S. 407
Francis H., Jr. 419
Frank T. 569
Frederick 122, 125, 134
John Eoten 343
Josephine 610
Joshua W. 142
L. C. 547
Leland W. 465
Nelson A. 400
Richard P. 527
Samuel 458
Sherman 400
Thomas H. 469, 474
W. Porcher 101, 103, 391, 392, 393*, 451, 481
Walter R. 571
MILEY
Henry M. 600
Michael 600
William M. 415
MILFORD, Dale 266
MILHOLLAND, James 479
MILHOUSE, Paul W. 531
MILLARD
Arnold A. 459
Charles D. 198, 201, 204, 208
G. Richard 516
Joseph H. 151, 154, 156, 333
Stephen C. 128, 131
Willard J. 381*
MILLAY, Edna St. Vincent 583
MILLEDGE, John 51, 53, 54, 56, 58, 60*, 61, 295*
MILLEDOLER, Philip 480, 532
MILLEN, John 87
MILLENKOETTER, Roscoe H. 443
MILLER
Alden H. 569, 592
Alfred B. 485
Allen J. 515, 519
Alten S. 553
Alton L. 534
Arjay 547
Arthur 585, 592, 603
Arthur L. (churchman) 533
Arthur L. 217, 220, 224, 227, 230, 233, 236, 239
Augustine A. 467
Augustus S. 459
Benjamin M. 278
Bert H. 226, 299
Bradford 462
C. Jeff 565
C. O. G. 550*
Campbell E. 573
Carl F. 593
Carl P. 580
Carl W. 593
Caroline 584
Charles A. 453
Charles E. 472
Charles R. 291
Clarence B. 162, 165, 168, 171, 174
Clarence E. 256, 259, 262, 265
Clement W. 241, 244
Daniel F. 93
Daniel H. 71, 73, 75, 76
Daniel L. 550
Darius 545
Dayton C. 570, 594, 600
Edward T. 223, 226, 229, 233, 236, 239
F. John 410
Floyd C. 461
Frank 587
Fred J. 573
Fred W. 414
Fredric W. 498
G. William 553
Gene 587
George A. (b. 1868) 530, 536
George A. (b. 1920) 571
George F. 109, 111
George P. 219, 222, 225, 229, 235, 238, 241, 244, 248, 251, 254, 257, 260
George S. 483
George W. 553*
Gerald E. 417
Gerrit S., Jr. 600
Glenn L. 574
H. B. 478
Henry (labor leader) 558
Henry (physician) 569
Homer V. M. 111, 296
Horace H. 424
Howard S. 232
J. Cloyd 578
J. Hillis 470
J. Irwin 491
Jack R. 245, 248, 251, 255, 258, 261, 305
Jacob W. 86, 88, 89, 91, 93, 95, 340
James F. 457*
James F. (Rep.) 129, 131
James M. 148, 150, 153, 156, 159, 161
James R. 478
James W. 485
Jesse 79, 81
John (Mo.) 82, 84, 86, 329
John (Md.) 449
John (N.Y.) 73
John (N.D.) 350
John B. 552*
John E. 455
John Elvis 196, 199, 202, 206*, 209, 212, 282
John F. (Wash.) 175, 179, 182, 186, 189, 192, 195, 461
John F. (Calif.) 124, 127, 129, 283, 410
John G. 452
John G. 95, 97
John K. 92, 93
Joseph 101
Joseph S. 444*
Justin 272, 578
Keith J. 279
Kenneth H. 610
Killian 99
Lee P. 564
Leslie A. 387
Louis E. 217
Lucas M. 139
Luther D. 401
Maynard M. 593
Morris S. 64
N. Edd 476
Nathan 7
Nathan L. 346
Neal E. 571, 604
Neville 456, 578
Norman C. 587
Orrin L. 142
Osborn M. 595
Otto N. 552*
Owen 557
Paul A. (educator) 480, 485
Paul A. (executor) 550
Perry 587
Pleasant M. 62
Ralph R. 500
Raphael H. 536
Ray T. 452
Rene H. 608
Richard E. 593
Robert A. 553
Robert C. 497
Robert W. 550*
Rutger B. 81
Samuel 532
Samuel A. 393*
Samuel F. 107, 269
Samuel H. 126, 128, 172
Shackelford, Jr. 272
Smith 96, 98
Stephen 324
Stephen D. 66, 67, 78, 364*
Thomas 8
Thomas B. 215, 218
Thomas E. 136
Thomas W. 170
Tom 450*
Vern W. 460
Victor J. 460
W. W. 458
Warner 123, 126, 128, 130, 345
Warren 144, 147
Watson B. 443
Wilbur C. 469
Wilbur K. 272
William (b. 1770) 347
William (b. 1782) 538
William B. 583
William E. (b. 1908) 272
William E. (b. 1914) 19, 230, 233, 237, 240, 243, 246, 249
William H. 107
William H. H. 29*, 41
William J. 209, 216, 222
William P. 476
William R. 281
William S. 90
MILLETT
Fred B. 564
John D. 475
MILLIGAN
Alexander R. 482
Edward 551
Jacob L. 177, 184, 187, 191, 194, 197, 201
John 476
John J. 77, 78, 80, 82
Mary L. 401
Samuel 273
MILLIKAN
Charles Van O. 601
Clark B. 608
Robert A. 467, 563, 570, 590, 595, 596, 605, 609
MILLIKEN
Carl E. 315, 534
Charles A. 449
Charles W. 116, 118
Earl 461
Frank R. 548
Howard E. 453

Isaac L. 451
John 412, 413
Seth L. 127, 130, 132, 135, 137, 140, 142, 145
William G. 323
William H., Jr. 243, 246, 250
William M. 498
MILLIKIN
Eugene D. 212, 216, 219, 222, 226, 229, 232, 235, 286
John 412, 413, 415
MILLIMAN, Elmer E. 557
MILLINGTON
Charles S. 162
E. J. 534
MILLIS
Harry A. 566
John S. 484, 485
MILLOR, William J. 469
MILLS
Albert L. 402, 419, 483
Cedric Earl 517
Charles K. 569*
Clyde M. 443
Cyrus T. 475
Daniel W. 145
Earl C. 579
Earle W. 418, 611
Elijah H. 65, 66, 68, 69, 71, 72, 319
Frederick C. 566
Franklin S. 462*
George G. 458
Jesse T. 458
Job 531
John 401, 402
Joshua 452*
Joseph J. 470
Merrill I. 453
Newt V. 207, 210, 213
Ogden L. 33, 39, 181, 185, 188
Paul C. 502
Ray 453
Roger Q. 117, 120, 122, 124, 126, 129, 131, 133, 136, 138, 139, 141, 144, 146, 372
Samuel M. 401
Sheldon T. 423, 427, 431
Susan T. 475
Thomas B. 574
Thornton A. 532
Wilbur D. 209, 212, 216, 219, 222, 225, 229, 232, 235, 238, 241, 244, 247, 251, 254, 257, 260, 263
William C. 501*
William F. R. 453
William O. 261, 264
MILLSON, John S. 94, 96, 98, 99, 101, 103
MILLSOP, Thomas E. 595
MILLSPAUGH
Frank C. 181
Frank R. 508, 520
Frederick W. 579
William H. 601
MILLWARD, William 99, 103
MILNE
J. Scott 558
William J. 477
MILNER, Robert T. 482
MILNES
Alfred 143
William, Jr. 113
MILNOR
James 63
John W. 604
William 60, 61, 66, 70
MILTON
Hugh M. II 403, 476*
John (gov.) 292
John 15
John G. 207, 342
William H., Jr. 484
William H. 158, 293
MILTONBERGER, Butler B. 402
MIMS
John F. 449
Livingston 449
MINAHAN, Daniel F. 177, 184
MINARD
A. E. 477
Guy M. 548*
MINER
Ahiman L. 96
Alonzo A. 483
C. W. 419
Charles 73, 75
Henry C. 143
Leroy M. S. 566
Phineas 78
Robert G. 437, 438
MINGES, Clyde E. 566
MINGLEDORFF, C. Glenn 470
MINISH, Joseph G. 249, 252, 256, 259, 262, 265
MINK, Patsy T. 251, 254, 258, 261, 264
MINNICH, D. E. 573
MINNIGERODE, C. Powell 498
MINNIS, Joseph S. 515, 519
MINOR
Benjamin B. 476
Charles L. C. 484
Edward S. 144, 147, 149, 152, 155, 158
Mrs. George Maynard 579
Harold B. 431, 432
Thomas T. 461
William T. 287
MINOT
Charles S. 563
George R. 590, 603, 605
MINOW, Newton N. 443
MINSHALL
Thaddeus A. 353*
William E. 237, 240, 243, 246, 253, 256, 259, 262, 265
MINSSEN, Herman F. 481
MINTER, Charles S., Jr. 483
MINTON
Henry C. 532
Lee W. 557
Sherman 203, 206, 210, 270, 272, 303
MINTZING, Jacob F. 451
MINUIT, Peter 8
MINVIELLE, Gabriel 457
MIRIANI, Louis C. 453
MIRICK, Carlos B. 601
MISCH, Frank W. 491
MITCHEL
Charles B. 104, 281, 392, 393
John P. 458
MITCHELL
Alex 564
Alexander 115, 117
Alexander C. 164
Anderson 86
Arthur W. 203, 206, 210, 213
Charles B. (b. 1863) 530
Charles E. (b. 1837) 444
Charles E. (b. 1877) 432, 547*
Charles F. 83, 84
Charles L. 127, 129
Charles S. 545*
Clarence M., Jr. 611
David B. 295
Don G. 568
Donald J. 265
Edward A. 223
Frank W. 457
Fred T. 475
George E. 71, 72, 76, 77
H. Walton 533
Harlan E. 238, 241
Harry B. 445*
Henry 572
Henry (Rep.) 79
Henry L. 293
Henry W. 571
Hugh B. 222, 228, 231, 381
James C. 73, 75
James L. 454
James P. 35*, 46
James S. 70, 71, 73
James T. 359
John 73, 75
John H. 117, 119, 121, 131, 133, 136, 138, 141, 143, 151, 154, 157, 356*
John I. 122, 124, 126, 128, 131, 359
John J. 546
John J. (Rep.) 162, 168
John K. 396*
John L. 139, 141, 144, 147, 385
John M. 143, 146
John N. 36, 41
John P. 603
John R. (b. 1861) 381
John R. (b. 1877) 198, 202, 205, 208
Margaret 584
Maria 597
Maurice B. 469
Nahum 58
Nathaniel 5, 290
Parren J. 261, 264
Rexford S. 486
Richard B. 513, 519
Robert (Ohio) 79
Robert (Va.) 459*
Robert B. 409
S. A. 564
S. T. 486
S. Weir 569, 570
Samuel C. 469, 481
Stephen M. 5, 52, 287*
Thomas R. 70, 73, 75, 78
Walter 512, 519
Wesley C. 563, 566, 603
William 104
William D. 445
William DeWitt 33, 41
William L. 445
MITCHILL, Samuel L. 57, 58*, 59, 60, 61, 62, 344
MITSCHER
Marc A. 417*
O. A. 458
MITTY, John J. 524, 528
MIXER, Frederick K. 497
MIZE
Chester L. 252, 255, 258, 445
Robert H. 511, 522
MIZELL, Wilmer D. 259, 262, 265
MIZNER, John K. 407
MOAKLEY, John J. 264
MOBLEY, W. Carlton 196
MOCK, Vernon P. 400, 405
MODJESKI, Ralph 596*, 607
MODLIN, George M. 480
MOE, Henry A. 491, 570, 603
MOELLER
Henry 480, 487, 523, 525
Walter H. 243, 246, 253
MOEN, Philip L. 553
MOEUR, Benjamin B. 280
MOFFAT
Douglas M. 423
Hugh 453
James D. 485, 532
Jay Pierrepont 425, 432
MOFFATT, Seth C. 130
MOFFET, John 113
MOFFETT
Elwood 557
James A. II 493
Robert 536
William A. 417
MOFFITT
Hosea 64, 65
James K. 546
John H. 133, 135
MOHLER, A. L. 554
MOHRHARDT, Foster E. 568
MOLE, Peter 580
MOLER, James M. 576
MOLEY, Raymond 608
MOLINA, Edward C. 594
MOLL, John L. 608
MOLLENHOFF, Clark R. 586, 601
MOLLISON
Irvin C. 273
James A. 412
MOLLOHAN, Robert H. 234, 238, 260, 263, 266, 577
MOLLOY, Thomas E. 525
MOLONY, Richard S. 94
MOLYNEUX, Robert 471*
MOMADAY, M. Scott 587
MOMPESSON, Roger 10*
MOMYER, William W. 415
MONAGAN, John S. 241, 244, 248, 251, 254, 257, 260
MONAGHAN
Francis J. 527
Frank B. 558
James C. 599
John J. 529
Joseph P. 201, 204
MONAHAN
Frank J. 577
James G. 179
MONAN, J. Donald 466
MONAST, Louis 192
MONCKTON, Robert 8
MONCURE, Richard C. L. 379
MONDALE, Walter F. 252, 255, 258, 261, 265, 325
MONDELL, Frank W. 144, 149, 152, 155, 158, 161, 163, 166, 169, 172, 176, 179, 182
MONELL, Robert 68, 76
MONEY
Hernando D. 119, 121, 123, 125, 128, 140, 143, 145, 148, 151, 153, 156, 159, 162, 327
John 597
MONGAN, Agnes 499
MONGET, Joseph 450
MONIHAN, J. O. 459
MONK, Tom B. 460
MONKIEWICZ, Boleslaus J. 209, 216
MONNET, Julien C. 478
MONNETT, Victor E. 608
MONROE
A. J. 460
Frank A. 312
James (b. 1758) 7, 13, 15*, 24*, 38, 40, 51, 52, 53, 378*, 428*, 429, 597
James (b. 1821) 115, 117, 119, 121, 124
James (b. 1799) 84
John T. 457*
Logan 578
Thomas 392
MONRONEY, A. S. Mike 211, 214, 218, 221, 224, 227, 231, 234, 237, 240, 243, 246, 249, 253, 256, 355, 577, 612
MONTAGU, Charles G. 9*
MONTAGUE
Andrew J. 169, 172, 175, 179, 182, 186, 189, 192, 195, 199, 202, 205, 209, 379, 570
Andrew P. 470
Robert L. 393
MONTEGUT, Joseph E. 457
MONTEITH
Alexander C. 576, 595
Walter E. 454
William J. 474
MONTET, Numa F. 193, 196, 200, 203
MONTEVERDE, F. L. 456
MONTGOMERIE, John 8*
MONTGOMERY
Alexander B. 132, 135, 137, 140
Alfred E. 417
Charles F. 498
Daniel, Jr. 60
Deane 568
Edward S. 585
Gillespie V. 255, 258, 262, 265
George T. 527
Helen Barrett 534
Henry 477
J. B. 577
J. K. 533
James W. 516
John (Md.) 60, 61, 62, 450
John (Mo.) 485
John F. 430
John G. 101
John K. 476
Joseph 7
Lall G. 572
Martin V. B. 444
Richard 406
Riley B. 536
Robert 559*
Robert M. 272
Robert N. 476, 533
Samuel J. 188
Thomas 63, 68, 69
Thomas L. 568
W. A. 467
William (b. 1736) 53
William (b. 1789) 81, 83, 84
William (b. 1818) 101, 103
MONTOYA
Joseph M. 239, 243, 246, 249, 252, 256, 259, 262, 265, 343
Nestor 181
MOODIE, Thomas H. 350
MOODY
Arthur Blair 230, 323
Clarence L. 564, 608
Dan 373
Gideon C. 136, 367
Graham B. 564
James M. 151
Lewis F. 594
Malcolm A. 149, 151
Paul D. 475
Ralph E. 554
William H. 30*, 41, 42, 143, 145, 148, 151, 270
William L., Jr. 543
William R. 514, 520
Zenas F. 356
MOON
John A. 146, 149, 152, 155, 157, 160, 163, 166, 169, 172, 175, 178
John W. 140

Reuben O. 154, 157, 160, 163, 166
Thomas E. 598
MOONEY
Charles A. 178, 185, 188, 191, 195
Daniel F. 434
Edward A. 523*, 528
William C. 172
MOONLIGHT, Thomas 424
MOOR
Frank D. 462
William L. 462
Wyman B. 91, 314
MOORE
Allan F. 180, 183
Alexander P. 435, 437
Alfred 269
Andrew 51, 52, 53, 54, 58*, 59, 61, 370
Andrew B. 277
Arch O., Jr. 241, 244, 247, 250, 254, 257, 384
A. Harry 204, 207, 342*
Arthur J. 530
Barrington 575
Benjamin 468*, 505, 520
Bryant E. 413, 483
C. Ellis 178, 181, 185, 188, 191, 195, 198
C. Robert 425, 432
Charles C. 299
Charles H. 499
Clifford H. 570
Constance 498
Daniel K. 349
David H. 469, 530
Douglas 563, 578, 585
Edward B. 444
Edward H. 218, 221, 224, 355
Edward M. 569
Eliakim H. 563, 568
Eliakim H. (Rep.) 113
Elizabeth Luce 603
Ely 81, 83
Francis, Jr. 454*
Frank G. 570
Frank M. 499
Gabriel 69, 70, 72, 74, 77, 78, 80, 277*
George E. 592
George F. (b. 1822) 372*
George F. (b. 1851) 563
George F. (b. 1887) 404
George Stevens 547*
George Sylvester 611
H. Guy 486
Harry T. 611
Harry T. (b. 1874) 511, 519
Heman A. 88
Henry 8
Henry D. 93, 95
Henry T. 481
Hollis A. 466
Horace L. 140
J. Hampton 157, 160, 163, 166, 169, 172, 175, 178, 458*
James (b. 1641) 9*
James (b. 1764) 482
James E. 400, 419
James W. 392, 393
Jere A. 483
Jeremiah 483
Jesse H. 112, 114
John (b. 1788) 84, 86, 95
John (b. 1826) 403
John (b. 1835) 528
John B. 571, 609
John C. 453
John D. J. 430
John M. (b. 1862) 157, 160, 163, 166
John M. (b. 1867) 530
John W. (Ky.) 187, 190, 193
John W. (educator) 480
John W. (mayor) 455
Joseph 470
Laban T. 102
Lamont 502
Leonard P. 271
Littleton W. 133, 136, 139
Marianne 585, 589, 592*, 602, 603, 604, 610
Martin A. 578
Meredith 557
Nathaniel F. 468
Nicholas R. 57, 59, 60, 61, 63, 65
Noah W., Jr. 531
O. Otto 286*
Orlando H. 410
Orren C. 135
Oscar F. 99
Paul, Jr. 517, 520
Paul J. 191
Pius 481
Preston J. 568
R. Lee 183
Raymond C. 576, 597, 608
Richard B. 600, 607
Richard C. 505, 522
Robert (b. 1778) 67, 68
Robert (b. 1838) 572
Robert E. 455
Robert J. 567
Robert L. 568
Robert M. 451
R. Walton 179, 182, 186, 189, 192, 195
Samuel 67, 68, 70
Samuel B. 277
Samuel M. 80
Stanford 606
Sydenham 100, 102
T. Justin, Jr. 554
Thomas 57, 58, 59, 60, 61, 62, 66
Thomas L. 69, 70
Thomas O. 311
Thomas P. 71, 72, 74, 425
W. F. 373
Wendell F. 612
Wilbert E. 573
William (N.J.) 110, 112
William (Pa.) 9
William C. 575
William D. 475
William E. 532
William H. (banker) 544*
William H. (mayor) 461
William M. 517
William R. 126
William S. 117
Willis L. 578
Zephaniah S. 465, 486
MOOREHEAD
Tom 246
Warren K. 501
William S. 243, 246, 250, 253, 256, 259, 262, 266
MOORER, Thomas H. 399, 416, 417*
MOORES
John H. 460*
Merrill 170, 173, 176, 180, 183
MOORFIELD, Storey 578
MOORHEAD
Carlos J. 263
James K. 103, 105, 107, 109, 111
MOORMAN
Charles H. 271
Henry D. 190
Thomas S. 483
MOOS, Malcolm 475
MOOSE, James S., Jr. 436, 437, 438
MOOT, Robert C. 445
MORA, Francis 527
MORALES, Franklin E. 430
MORAN
Benjamin 435
Dan 546
Edward C., Jr. 200, 203
M.J. 559
Robert 461
T. Donald 466
MORANO, Albert P. 229, 232, 235, 238
MORE, Hermon 502
MOREELL, Ben 428*, 596
MOREHEAD
Charles S. 91, 93, 308
James T. (Ky.) 85, 87, 89, 308*
James T. (N.C.) 95
John A. 480
John H. 184, 188, 191, 194, 197, 201, 333
John M. 347
John M. (b. 1866) 162
John M. (b. 1870) 437
John P. 392
MOREHOUSE
Allen P. 329
Daniel W. 469, 536
MORELAND
Jesse E. 479
William H. 508, 521
MORELL, George W. 407*, 408
MORENO, Francis G.D.S. 527
MORENON, Ernest 591
MOREY
Frank 112, 114, 116, 118
George W. 608
Henry L. 126, 128, 136
John H. 476
Lloyd 472
MORGAN
Arthur E. 445, 465
Cecil 579
Charles H. (b. 1831) 573
Charles H. (b. 1872) 119, 121, 128, 140, 162
Charles H. (b. 1902) 499
Christopher 84, 86
David H. 482
D.N. 444
Daniel (S. Car.) 452
Daniel (Va.) 55, 406
Daniel E. 452
David H. 482
David W.R. 573
Dick T. 163, 166, 169, 172, 175, 178
Edmund M. 589
Edwin B. 97, 99, 101
Edwin D. 107, 108, 110, 345*
Edwin V. 424, 426, 431, 434, 435, 439
Ephraim F. 383
Frank A. 564
George A. 431
George S. 451
George W. 111, 113, 115, 435
Gilbert 479
Harcourt A. 445, 481
J. Pierpont 492, 554, 603
James 62
James B. 130, 132, 135
James D. 409, 410
James H. 469*
John (b. 1735) 403
John (b. 1803) 478
John H. 456
John J. 70, 71, 79
John T. (b. 1824) 120, 122, 124, 127, 129, 131, 134, 136, 139, 142, 144, 147, 150, 152, 155, 158, 277
Lewis H. 563
Lewis L. 165, 168, 171
Lewis R. 271
Marshall M. 546
Nathaniel H. 551
P.H. 433
Ralph 559*
S.W.K. 595
Simpson H. 393
Stephen 149, 151, 154
Thomas A. 550
Thomas E. 221, 224, 228, 231, 234, 237, 240, 243, 246, 250, 253, 256, 259, 262, 266
Thomas H. 563, 605
William E. 468
William G. 569
William H. 566
William M. 181, 185, 188, 191
William S. 82, 83
MORGENS, Howard J. 551*
MORGENTHALER, George W. 564
MORGENTHAU
Henry 438
Henry, Jr. 33*, 34*, 39
MORIARTY, Patrick E. 484
MORILL, Edmund N. 306
MORIN
John M. 169, 172, 175, 178, 182, 185, 188, 192
Relman 585, 586
MORISON
George S. 572
Samuel Eliot 563, 567, 584, 586, 591, 603, 608, 609
Thomas L. 578
MORITZ, Theodore L. 205
MORKOVSKY, John L. 525
MORLAND, Jesse E. 479
MORLEY
Clarence J. 285
Edward W. 563, 565, 594, 596
Felix 584
Felix M. 472
Frank 568
Grace L. McC. 502
S. Griswold 577
Sylvanus G. 501
MORPHIS, Joseph L. 112, 114
MORRELL
Daniel J. 111, 113
Edward de V. 149, 152, 154, 157
MORRES, Nora K. 502*
MORREY
Charles B. 568
Humphrey 458
MORRILL
Amos 372
Anson P. 104, 314
David L. 67, 68, 70, 337*
Edmund N. 127, 130, 132, 134
James L. 475, 487
Justin S. 99, 101, 103, 105, 107, 109, 111, 113, 115, 117, 120, 122, 124, 126, 129, 131, 133, 136, 139, 141, 144, 147, 376
Lot M. 28*, 39, 102, 104, 106, 108, 110, 112, 114, 116, 118, 314*
Samuel P. 112
MORRIN, P.J. 557
MORRIS
Anthony 458
Anthony, Sr. 458
B.J. 479
Benjamin W., II 506, 521*
Benjamin W. 591
Brewster H. 425
Buckner S. 451
Cadwalader 7
Calvary (b. 1798) 83, 84, 86
Calvary (b. 1851) 545*
Charles 418*
Daniel 107, 109
Dave H. 424, 432
Delyte W. 481
Donald F. 549
Earl F. 565
Edward D. 532
Edward J. 88, 101, 103, 105, 436, 438
Edward M. 412
Edward P. 570
Effingham B. 563
Emory W. 492
George E. 381
George M. 565, 589
Gouverneur 4, 6, 56, 57, 344, 428
Harrison S. 501
Ira N. 437
Isaac N. 100, 102
J.G. 501
James C. 511, 520, 521
James R. 105, 107
John B. 527
Jonathan D. 92, 93
Joseph 88, 90
Joseph R. 454
Joseph W. 184
Kindred J. 457
Leland B. 430*
Lewis (b. 1725) 3, 6
Lewis (b. 1671) 8*, 10
Lewis R. 55, 56, 57
Luzon B. 288
Mathias 81, 83
Richard 344
Richard B. 591
Richard P. 460
Robert (Pa.) 3, 4, 7, 51, 52, 53, 358
Robert (Colo.) 453
Robert (N.J.) 10
Robert H. 458
Robert Hunter 9, 10
R. Page W. 145, 148, 151
Roland S. 431, 570
Samuel W. 83, 85
T.O. 457
Thomas (N.Y.) 57
Thomas (Ohio) 79, 81, 83, 352
Thomas A. 530
Thomas G. 243, 246, 249, 252, 256
Toby 224, 227, 231, 240, 243
Victor P. 478
William H. H., Jr. 412*, 415*
Wright 602
MORRISETT, Lloyd N. 492
MORRISH, William F. 544
MORRISON
Cameron 194, 198, 219, 348, 349
deLesseps S. 457
Donald E. 578
Dorilus 456*
Frank B. 334
George W. 93, 97
Henry C. 530
James D. 508, 519
James H. 217, 220, 223,

226, 229, 233, 236, 230, 242, 245, 248, 252
James L.D. 98
James M. 545
John A. 95
John F. 410, 419
John H. 532
John T. 298
Martin A. 161, 164, 167, 170, 445
N.J. 486
Robert F. 283
Robert H. 469
Theodore N. 508, 520
William M. 451
William R. 106, 116, 118, 120, 123, 125, 127, 130
MORRISSEY
Andrew 478
Andrew H. 333
James P. 481
John 111, 113
P.H. 557
MORROW
Dwight W. 194, 197, 342, 433
Edwin P. 309
Elizabeth S. 481
George E. 478
Jeremiah 58, 59, 60, 61, 63, 64, 65, 67, 84, 86, 352*
John (N.M.) 184, 188, 191
John (Va.) 59, 61
John H. 429
William W. 29, 132, 134
MORSCH, Lucile M. 568, 595
MORSE
Byron R. 456
Edward S. 501, 563
Elijah A. 135, 137, 140, 143
Elmer A. 161, 163, 166
F. Bradford 245, 249, 252, 255, 258, 261
Freeman H. 87, 100, 102
Hermann N. 532
Isaac E. 87, 89, 91, 93
Leopold 121, 123, 125, 128, 132
Marston 568, 604
Oliver A. 101
Robert W. 468
Samuel F.B. 577*, 597
Wayne L. 221, 224, 227, 231, 234, 237, 240, 243, 246, 250, 253, 256, 357, 597
MORSELL, W.F.C. 600
MORTENSEN
S.H. 599
William H. 454
MORTIMER
Charles G. 547*
J.D. 550, 553
MORTON
Charles G. 404, 410
Florrinell F. 568
Jackson 92, 94, 96, 293, 391, 392
James M., Jr. 271
Jeremiah 94
John 3*, 7
John J., Jr. 565
Joseph 9*
Levi P. 14, 123, 126, 134, 136, 345, 428
Marcus 66, 68, 319*
Marcus, Jr. 320
Oliver H.P.T. 110, 112, 114, 116, 118, 120, 302*
Paul 29, 30, 42, 546
Rogers C.B. 36, 37, 44, 248, 252, 255, 258
Roy J. 572
Samuel G. 563
J. Sterling 30*, 45
Thruston B. 223, 226, 229, 239, 242, 245, 248, 252, 255, 310
William T.G. 597
MORYSON, Francis 9
MOSBY, John B. 452
MOSCOSO, Teodoro 439
MOSEL, Tad 586
MOSELEY
George V. 405
John O. 476
Jonathan O. 58, 60, 61, 62, 63, 65, 66, 67
William A. 88, 90
William D. 293
MOSER, Guy L. 208, 211, 215
MOSES
Andrew 400, 404
Charles L. 137, 139, 142
Franklin J. 365
George H. 174, 177, 181, 184, 186, 188, 189, 191, 192, 194, 196, 197, 338, 429, 433
John 221, 350*
M.L. 457
Raymond G. 401
Robert 603*, 609
William F. 516
MOSGROVE, James 126
MOSHER
Charles A. 246, 249, 253, 256, 259, 262, 265
Gouveneur F. 511, 521
Ira 578
Samuel B. 552
MOSIER, Harold G. 208
MOSLEY, J. Brooke 515, 519
MOSS
Emma S. 572
F.B. 459*
Frank E. 244, 247, 250, 253, 256, 260, 263, 266, 374
Howard 602
Howard A. 598
Hunter H., Jr. 169. 172
J. McKenzie 150
John E., Jr. 232, 235, 238, 241, 244, 248, 251, 254, 257, 260, 263
John H. 576
Joseph R. 366
Lemuel 473
McKenzie 273
Ralph W. 161, 164, 167, 170
Robert V. 534
Sanford A. 594, 598, 608*
MOSSER, J. Belmont 576
MOSTEL, Zero 595
MOTLEY
Arthur H. 575
Constance Baker 598
J. Lothrop 423, 429, 597
MOTON, Robert R. 483, 611
MOTT
C.S. Harding 492
Charles Stewart 492
Frank E. 492
Frank Luther 584, 591
Gershom 409
James 57, 58
James W. 201, 205, 208, 211, 215, 218, 221
John R. 605
Lewis F. 566, 577
Luther W. 165, 168, 171, 174, 178, 181
Richard 99, 101
W.C. 416
MOTTE, Isaac 7
MOTTMAN, G.A. 458
MOUDRY, Frank W. 609
MOUDY, James M. 482, 536
MOULDER
Morgan M. 227, 230, 233, 236, 239, 242, 246
Peter V. 548
MOULTON
Arthur W. 511, 522
Edward O. 481
George A. 570
H.N. 456
Mace 89
Samuel W. 108, 125, 127
Sherman R. 377
MOULTRIE
James 569
William 9, 364
MOULTROP, Irving E. 594
MOUNT
Arnold J. 544
James A. 302
Wallace 381
MOUNTAIN, W.W. 574
MOUNTCASTLE, Katharine B. 491
MOUSER
Grant E. 157, 160
Grant E., Jr. 195, 198
MOUTON
Alexander 80, 96, 311*
Robert L. 207, 210
MOUZON, Edwin D. 530
MOVER, Rober W. 449
MOVIUS, Hallum L., Jr. 611
MOWBRAY, H. Siddons 590, 593
MOWER, Joseph A. 410
MOWERY, Edward J. 586
MOWRER
Edgar Ansel 584
Orral H. 571
Paul S. 583
MOWREY, Corma A. 578
MOWRY, Daniel, Jr. 7
MOXLEY, William J. 161
MOYER, Charles B. 455
MOYLAN
Cornelius A. 454
Edward B. 576
Stephen 403
William 470
MOYLE, James H. 443
MOYNIHAN
Daniel P. 430
Patrick H. 200
MOYRAUD, Louis 612
MOZLEY, Norman A. 143
MRAK, Ignatius 527
MRUK, Joseph 217, 451
MUCCIO, John J. 429, 430*, 437
MUDD
Mrs. Harvey S. 576
Sydney E. (b. 1858) 135, 145, 148, 150, 153, 156, 159, 162
Sydney E. (b.1885) 171, 174, 177, 180, 184
MUDGE
Lewis S. 532
Verne D. 415
MUELLER
Erwin H. 608
Frederick H. 35, 46
George E. 604
Joseph M. 529
Paul J. 414
Reuben H. 531
MUENCH, Aloisius J. 523, 526
MUENSTERBERG, H. 571
MUGAVARO, Francis J. 525
MUHLENBERG
Francis S. 75
Frederick A. (b. 1818) 476
Frederick A. (b. 1887) 224
Frederick A.C. 7, 51*, 52, 53, 54
Henry A. 97
Henry A.P. 76, 78, 79, 81, 83, 423
John Peter G. 51, 53, 56, 57, 358
Peter 406
MUIR
Charles H. 410, 413, 419
James I. 414
MULDOON
Hugh C. 609
Peter J. 528
MULDOWNEY, Michael J. 201
MULDROW, Henry L. 121, 123, 125, 128
MULFORD, R.H. 550*
MULHOLLAND, Frank L. 580
MULKEY
Frederick W. 157, 356
William O. 167
MULLAN, W.J. Reid 466
MULLANEY, James 403
MULLANPHY, Bryan 460
MULLEDY
Samuel 471
Thomas F. 471*
MULLEN
Ambrose 484
Tobias 526
MULLENDORE, William C. 552
MULLER
George P. 565
Henry N. 573
Hermann J. 605
Nicholas 121, 123, 128, 131, 148, 151
Steven 473
MULLIGAN
James H., Jr. 576
John J. 77, 78, 80, 82
William H. 271
MULLIKEN, Robert S. 596, 606, 609
MULLIN, Joseph 95
MULLINS
Charles L., Jr. 413
David W. 465
Edgar Y. 534
James 111
Robert D. 587
William 3
MULLON, James I. 487
MULLOY, William T. 525
MULOCH, E.H. 453
MULROY, James W. 583
MULRY
Joseph A. 470
Thomas M. 599
MULTER
Abraham J. 224, 227, 230, 233, 237, 240, 243, 246, 249, 253, 256
Smith L. 579
MULTHAUF, Robert P. 500
MUMA, Edith N. 492
MUMFORD
George 67
Gurdon S. 59, 60, 61
L. Quincy 444, 568
Lewis 563, 592, 602, 603, 608
Paul 10*, 361
MUMMA
Albert G. 418
Walter M. 231, 234, 237, 240, 243
MUNCK, A.E. 459
MUNDELEIN, George W. 523*
MUNDT, Karl E. 212, 215, 218, 221, 225*, 228, 231, 234, 237, 240, 243, 247, 250, 253, 256, 259, 263, 367
MUNDY, George W. 419
MUNFORD, Walter F. 554
MUNGEN, William 111, 113
MUNGER, William R. 559
MUNI, Paul 595
MUNK, Max M. 609
MUNN, Ralph 568
MUNNERLYN, Charles J. 392
MUNOZ-MARIN, Luis 608
MUNRO
Dana C. 567, 577
Dana G. 429
William B. 564, 571
MUNROE
A.J. 460
Addison P. 575
Charles E. 565
George B. 551*
James 449
MUNSELL, Oliver S. 473
MUNSON, Loveland 376
MURCH, Thompson H. 123, 125
MURCHIE
Guy 593
Harold H. 315
MURDAUGH, Edmund D. 478
MURDOCK
Abe (Orrice A.) 202, 205, 208, 212, 215, 218, 222, 374
George P. 563, 611
John R. 206, 209, 212, 216, 219, 222, 225, 228
Victor 153, 156, 159, 161, 164, 167
William 3
MURFEE, Edward H. 465
MURFIN, Orrin G. 416
MURFREE, William H. 64, 65
MURIE
Adolph 593
Olaus J. 591
MURKLAND, Charles S. 476
MURLIN, Lemuel H. 466*, 469
MURNINGHAN, Max E. 455
MURPHEY, Charles 94
MURPHREE
Albert A. 470*
Dennis 327, 328
MURPHY
Arthur P. 156, 162
B. Frank 178, 181, 185, 188, 191, 195, 198
Carl 611
Daniel J. 417
Edward, Jr. 40, 143, 146, 345
Ernest 553
Everett J. 142
Francis P. 339
Frank (b. 1890) 33, 41, 270, 323, 453
Frank (Ariz.) 459
Franklin 340, 579
Franklin D. 473, 492
Gardner 571
George 251, 254, 257, 284, 559
Harry C. 545
Henry C. 88, 91, 433
Herschel S. 579
Isaac 281
J.J. 460
James J. 227, 230
James W. 161
Jeremiah H. 127, 130
John 78, 277
John B. 569, 599
John J. 557
John M. 249, 253, 256,

259, 262, 265
John T. 470
John W. 218, 221
Joseph S. 479
Leo T. 461
Maurice, Jr. 246, 339
Morgan F. (b. 1932) 261, 264
Morgan F. (b. 1905) 545
Patrick 474
Ray 568
Ray D. 546
Richard L. 200, 203, 305
Robert C. 569, 592, 593, 594
Robert D. 424, 428, 431, 599, 609
Thomas E. 472
Thomas F. 557
Timothy J. 580
Timothy L. 481
Walter J. 590
William B. 544
William F. 528
William J. 466
William P. 605
William S. 425, 438
William T. 242, 245, 248, 251, 255, 258

MURRAH
Alfred P. 272
Pendleton 372
William B. 530

MURRAY
Ambrose S. 99, 101
Arthur 401, 402, 410
Don 586
Dwight H. 569
George D. 417
George M. 515, 519
George W. 141, 144
Grover E. 482, 564
Hugh C. 283
J.L. 451
J. Ralph 470
James C. 235
James E. 201, 204, 207, 210, 214, 217, 220, 224, 227, 230, 233, 236, 239, 242, 331
John (b. 1732) 8, 9
John (b. 1741) 538, 539
John (b. 1768) 67, 68
John G. 510, 520
John G. (b. 1877) 524, 528
John L. 82
John P. 393
Johnston 355
Joseph 3
Logan C. 564
M.M. 459
Maxwell 413*
Milton 557
Nicholas 532
Philip 559
Reid F. 212, 215, 219, 222, 225, 228, 231
Robert 403
Robert M. 128
Thomas, Jr. 70
Thomas E. 599
Thomas J. 218, 221, 225, 228, 231, 234, 237, 240, 244, 247, 250, 253
Wallace 430
William 95, 97
William F. (b. 1881) 165, 168
William H. 169, 172
William J. 355
William Vans 52, 53, 428, 433

MURRIN, L. 451
MURROW, Edward R. 445, 595, 596, 608
MUSCHENHEIM, Carl 600
MUSGRAVE, George W. 532
MUSICK, James B. 498
MUSKAT, Morris 601
MUSKIE, Edmund S. 19, 242, 245, 248, 252, 255, 258, 261, 264, 315*, 592, 596
MUSSELWHITE, Harry W. 200

MUSSER
George W. 285
John H. 569

MUSSEY, Reuben D. 569
MUSSIO, John K. 529
MUSTARD, Harry S. 572

MUTCHLER
Howard 141, 152
William 119, 126, 128, 136, 138

MUTCHMORE, S.A. 532
MUTER, George 308
MUTZ, Sterling F. 579

MYER
Albert J. 403*
John W. 500

MYERS
Amos 107
C. Kilmer 517, 519
Charles F., Jr. 544*
Charles W. 578
Donald J. 413
Francis J. 211, 215, 218, 221, 224, 228, 360
Henry L. 165, 168, 171, 174, 177, 181, 331
Jerome 593, 598
John A. 501
John T. 255, 258, 261, 264
Leonard 107, 109, 111, 113, 115, 117
Louis W. 284
William M. 452
William R. 123

MYLONAS, George E. 574

N

NABERS, Benjamin D. 95
NABOKOV, Vladimir 589, 592
NABRIT, James M., Jr. 472
NACHOD, Carl P. 601
NADAI, Arpad L. 594
NADER, Ralph 612
NAFEW, J.S. 558
NAFFZIGER, Howard C. 565
NAFTALIN, Arthur 457

NAGEL
Carlos R. 501
Charles (b. 1849) 31*, 45
Charles (b. 1899) 497, 498, 500
Conrad 563

NAGLER, Fred 589, 593, 611
NAIDEN, Earl L. 412
NAIR, John H. 567, 590
NAJJAR, Victor A. 599
NALL, T. Otto 531

NALLE
Joseph 450
Richard T. 575

NALLY, Edward J. 551
NANCE, Albinus 333
NAPHEN, Henry F. 148, 151

NAPTON
William 462*
William B. 329

NAREY, Harry E. 213

NASH
Abner 6, 9
C.W. 453
Charles E. 449
Charles E. (La.) 118
Charles W. 543*
Francis 406
Frederick 347
George K. 353
John W. 462
Norman B. 514, 520
Philip C. 482
Royal 578

NASON
Henry B. 565
John W. 467, 482

NASSAU, Charles W. 474
NASSIKAS, John N. 443
NATCHER, William H. 236, 239, 242, 245, 248, 252, 255, 258, 261, 264
NATION, Bill 451
NAUDAIN, Arnold 75, 77, 78, 80, 290
NAUMBERG, Robert 611
NAVAGH, James J. 527*
NAVE, M.C. 558
NAY, Mary L. Gough 536

NAYLOR
Charles 83, 85
Isaac 452
Kirk E. 476
William K. 400
Wilson S. 474

NAZZARO, Joseph J. 415, 416

NEAL
Henry S. 121, 124, 126
Herbert V. 573
James A. 536
John R. 131, 133
Lawrence T. 117, 119
Leonard 471
William E. 234, 241

NEALE
Francis 471*
Leonard 523
Mervin G. 472
Raphael 68, 69, 71

NEALL, Isaac J. 558
NEBECKER, Enos H. 444
NEDZI, Lucien N. 245, 249, 252, 255, 258, 261, 265
NEECE, William H. 127, 130

NEEDHAM
Charles W. 471
James C. 147, 150, 152, 155, 158, 161, 164

NEEDLES
Edward M. 550
Enoch R. 572

NEEL
Alice 589
James V. 600

NEELEY, George A. 164, 167

NEELY
Henry A. 506, 520
Matthew M. 169, 172, 175, 179, 186, 189, 192, 199, 202, 205, 209, 212, 215, 222, 228, 231, 234, 238, 241, 383, 384*, 577
Thomas B. 530

NEFF
Charles T., Jr. 485
Jay H. 455
Lewis E. 575
Pat M. 373, 466, 534
Paul J. 549

NEGLEY, James S. 113, 115, 117, 131, 408, 409
NEHRLING, Henry 500

NEIL
A.B. 370
Matt M. 370

NEILAN, Edwin P. 575

NEILL
Charles R. 599
Edward D. 474
Robert 139, 142
William 469, 532

NEILSON
John 4
Nellie 567
William A. 577

NELAN, Augustine P. 474
NELSEN, Ancher 242, 245, 249, 252, 255, 258, 261, 265

NELSON
Adolphus P. 176, 179, 182
Alfred C. 469
Allison 449
Arthur E. 213, 325, 460
Aven 487, 574
Ben 451
Charles B. 450
Charles C. 460
Charles J. 424, 432, 437
Charles P. 226, 229, 233, 236
Cleland K. (bishop) 508, 519*
Cleland K. (col. pres.) 480
Donald M. 603
Edward W. 569
Frank 557
Frank A. 534
Gaylord 250, 254, 257, 260, 263, 266, 386*
George L. 598
Harry M. 565
Henry A. 532
Homer A. 107
Hugh 63, 64, 66, 67, 69, 70, 437
Jack 586
James 557
Jeremiah 59, 65, 66, 68, 69, 71, 77
John 26*, 41, 69, 436
John E. 180, 184, 187, 190, 193, 196
John H. 473
John M. (b. 1876) 604
John M. (b. 1870) 158, 161, 163, 166, 169, 172, 176, 182, 186, 189, 192, 196, 199
Knute 128, 130, 132, 143, 145, 148, 151, 153, 156, 159, 162, 165, 168, 171, 174, 177, 180, 324*
Milton G. 477
Oscar F. 559
Ralph T. 403
Richard H. 509, 519
Roger 57, 59, 60, 61
Samuel 269, 344
Theodore 473*
Thomas, Jr. 3, 4, 7, 9
Thomas A.R. 103, 425
Thomas H. 425, 433
Thomas M. 66, 67
William 407
William (b. 1711) 9
William (b. 1784) 91, 93
William L. 177, 187, 191, 194, 197, 204, 207, 210, 214

NEMIROFF, Howard 589
NERAZ, John C. 528

NES
Charles M., Jr. 567
Henry 88, 92, 94

NESBETT, Buell A. 279

NESBIT
Reed M. 565
Walter 200
Wilson 67

NESMITH, James W. 105, 109, 117, 356
NESS, Frederick W. 470
NESSELRODE, Clifford C. 565
NESSEN, Ron 607
NESTINGEN, Ivan A. 456
NESTOS, Ragnvald A. 350
NETTING, M. Graham 497
NEUBAUER, Joseph A. 492, 550

NEUBERGER
Maurine B. 246, 250, 253, 357
Richard L. 237, 240, 243, 357

NEUMANN
Gerhard 594
John N. 528
Robert G. 423

NEUMILLER, Louis B. 544*
NEUSTICH, John B. 473
NEVELSON, Louise 592

NEVILLE
Arthur C. 500
Edwin L. 438
Harvey A. 474
Joseph 53
Keith 333
Wendell C. 416
William 148, 151

NEVILS, W. Coleman 471

NEVIN
Crocker 549*
John W. 470*
Robert M. 151, 154, 157

NEVINS, Allan 563, 567, 584*, 591, 602, 603

NEW
Anthony 53, 54, 55, 56, 57, 58, 62, 66, 69
Harry S. 32*, 33, 43, 173, 176, 180, 303
Jeptha D. 118, 123
John C. 444

NEWBEGIN, Robert 429, 430

NEWBERRY
J.S. (b. 1822) 563
John S. (b. 1826) 123
Truman H. 31*, 42, 177, 180, 322
Walter C. 137

NEWBERT, Elmer E. 449

NEWBOLD
Joshua G. 304
Thomas 60, 61, 62

NEWBRANCH, Harvey E. 583
NEWBURN, Harry K. 465, 476, 478

NEWCOMB
Carman A. 110
Edwin L. 609
Horatio C. 454
Horatio D. 549*
John L. 484
Simon 563, 564, 568, 597
Theodore M. 571

NEWCOMBE, F.C. 574
NEWCOMER, Christian 531
NEWEL, Stanford 432, 433

NEWELL
Barbara W. 485
Frederick B. 531
Frederick H. 594
Homer E. 567
Hubert M. 525
James M. 591
John 548
Norman D. 597
William A. 91, 93, 108, 341

NEWGARDEN, Paul W. 415

NEWHALL
Beaumont 498
C.S. 547
J. Lincoln 193

NEWHARD, Peter 85, 86
NEWHAUSER, Edward B.D. 599
NEWLANDS, Francis G. 140, 143, 146, 148, 151, 154, 157, 159, 162, 165, 168, 171, 174, 335

NEWLIN
Ellis J. 469
Gurney E. 565
NEWLUN, Chester O. 486
NEWMAN
Alexander 94
Barnett 592
Bernard 273
James H. 465
John P. 530
Oliver P. 462
Stephen M. 472
Walter S. 484
NEWMARK, Nathan M. 604
NEWNAM, Frank H., Jr. 572
NEWNAN, Daniel 77
NEWSHAM, Joseph P. 110, 112
NEWSOM
Carroll V. 477
David D. 432
Herschel D. 578
Isaac E. 468
M. Eugene 580
NEWSOME, John P. 216
NEWTON
A. 453
Cherubusco 132
Cleveland A. 177, 181, 184, 187
Eben 95
Francis J. 501
H.A. 563
Howard C. 570
James Q. 453, 468, 491
James T. 444
John 402, 408*, 409, 599
John B. 508
Louie D. 534
Norman T. 573
Roy C. 590
S.G. 461
Thomas, Jr. 57, 58, 59, 61, 62, 63, 64, 66, 67, 69, 70, 72, 73, 75, 77, 78
Thomas W. 89
Walter H. 177, 181, 184, 187, 190, 194
Willoughby 88
NEYMAN, Jerzy 604
NIBLACK
Albert P. 416
Silas L. 114
William E. 100, 102, 108, 110, 112, 114, 116
NICCOLLS, Samuel J. 532
NICE
Harry W. 318
Margaret Morse 592
NICHOL, William 457
NICHOLAS
George 459*
John 53, 54, 55, 56
Robert C. 80, 82, 84, 311
Tom 591
Wilson C. 56, 57, 58, 61, 62, 378*
NICHOLL
A.Y. 401
Louise Townsend 589, 610
NICHOLLS
Francis T. 312*
John C. 122, 127
Samuel J. 172, 175, 178
Thomas D. 160, 163
NICHOLS
Charles A. 171, 174, 177
Charles H. 571
Charles L. 563
Edward L. 563, 570, 594, 610
Edward T. 418
Edward W. 484
Ernest F. 475, 469, 610
Ernest R. 473
G.E. 575
H.L. 460
Hobart 574, 577, 589*
Hugh L. 353
Jesse E. 565
John 133
John C. (Jack) 205, 208, 211, 214, 218
John G. 456*
John P. 469
John R. 476
John W. 512
Malcolm E. 450
Matthias H. 97, 99, 101
Philip, Jr. 272, 273*, 443
Roy C. 531
Roy F. 567, 585
Shirley H. 512, 522
Thomas S. 550*
William 254, 257, 260, 263
William F. 508, 519
William H. 565
NICHOLSON
Alfred O.P. 85, 87, 103, 105, 369*, 370
Donald W. 223, 226, 230, 233, 236, 239
Francis 8*, 9*
George M. 355
H. Burke 545*
Isaac L. 508, 520
J. Lee 577
James R. 574
James W. 474
John 61
John A. 108, 109
John R. 291
Joseph H. 55, 56, 57, 59
Meredith 434*, 439
R.F. 418
Samuel D. 179, 183, 285
Thomas 530
Thomas D. 497
Will F. 453
NICKERSON
Ruth 610
Samuel M. 546*
NICKS, Jess 543
NICODEMUS, William J.L. 403
NICOLL
Abimael Y. 402
Henry 91
James C. 574
NICOLLS
Matthias 457
Richard 8
NICOLSON, Marjorie Hope 577
NIEBUHR, Reinhold 608
NIEDERMAIR, John C. 611
NIEDRINGHAUS
Frederick G. 135
Henry F. 191, 194, 197, 579
NIEL, Francis 480
NIELDS, James F. 577
NIELSEN
Johannes M. 569
M. 611
NIELSON
Hazel B. 578
William A. 481
NIEUWLAND, Julius A. 604
NILAN, John J. 526
NILES
Addison C. 283
Jason 116
Jeremiah 10
John M. 25, 43, 80, 82, 87, 89, 90, 287*
Nathaniel (Vt.) 52, 53
Nathaniel 436
Thomas M. 572
William W. 507, 520
NIMITZ
Chester N. 609
Chester W. 416, 417, 418
NIMTZ, F. Jay 239
NINDE, William X. 530
NINFO, Salvatore 558*
NIRENBERG, Marshall W. 595, 596, 600, 604*, 606
NIRENSTEIN, Samuel 537
NISBET
Charles 469
Eugenius A. 84, 85, 391, 392
NITZE
Paul H. 399*
William A. 577
NIVEN, Archibald C. 90
NIVOLA, Constantino 590
NIX
Lucile 600
Robert N.C. 240, 243, 246, 250, 253, 256, 259, 262, 266
NIXON
George S. 157, 159, 162, 165, 335
John 406
John T. 103, 105
Richard M. 13, 14, 18*, 19*, 222, 225*, 229, 232, 235, 238, 241, 284
NOA, Thomas L. 527
NOAH, Phil B. 543*
NOBILI, John 481
NOBLE
Albert G. 418*
Alfred 572, 594
Andrew J. 457
David A. 97
Earl B. 564
Edward J. 492
Eugene A. 469, 471
James 65, 66, 68, 69, 71, 72, 74, 75, 302
John W. 29, 30, 44
Joseph V. 500
Noah 302
Patrick 364
Warren P. 105, 107
William H. 83
NOCE
Daniel 402
Robert H. 600
NODAR, Robert J., Jr. 224
NOE, James A. 312
NOEL
Edmund F. 327
Frank 584
John S. 576
Llewellyn G. 566
Philip W. 363
NOELL
John W. 103, 105, 106
Thomas 457
Thomas E. 108, 110
NOGUCHI, Isamu 590, 591, 592
NOLAN
Dennis E. 400, 401
George M. 454
John I. 167, 170, 173, 176, 179
Mae E. 179, 183
Michael N. 126, 449
Thomas B. 443, 576
William I. 194, 197
NOLAND
Iveson B. 515, 520
James E. 226
NOLD, Wendelin J. 526
NOLEN, C.C. 477
NOLL, John F. 526
NOLLEN, John S. 471
NOLTE, Richard H. 439
NOLTING, Frederick E., Jr. 439
NOOE, Roger T. 536
NOONAN
Edward A. 460
Edward T. 147
George H. 144
Herbert C. 474
J.P. 558
Joseph M. 477
NORBECK, Peter 182, 185, 188, 192, 195, 198, 202, 205, 367*
NORBLAD
A. Walter, Jr. 221, 224, 227, 231, 234, 237, 240, 243, 246, 250
Albin W. 357
NORCROSS
Amasa 121, 123, 125
Jonathan 449
Otis 450
NORDBERG, Martin E. 611
NORDEN, Carl L. 598
NORDLAND, Gerald 502
NORDMEYER, Henry W. 577
NOREM, Owen J.C. 432
NORICK, James H. 458*
NORLIN, George 468
NORMAN, Fred 219, 225
NORRELL
Catherine D. 244
William F. 209, 212, 216, 219, 222, 225, 229, 232, 235, 238, 241
NORRIS
Benjamin W. 109
Edwin L. 331
Ernest E. 552
Frank W. 419
George W. 154, 156, 159, 162, 165, 168, 171, 174, 177, 181, 184, 187, 191, 194, 197, 201, 204, 207, 210, 214, 333
Isaac 3, 458
James F. 565, 590
Louis W. 465
Moses, Jr. 88, 89, 93, 95, 97, 337
NORSTAD, Lauris P. 400, 404, 415, 416, 604
NORTH
Cecil J. 549
Edward W. 451
James W. 449*
John A. 551
S. Taylor 172
Simeon 471
William 55, 344, 401*, 402
NORTHCOTT
Elliott 271, 426, 434, 439
H. Clifford 531
NORTHEN, William J. 296, 534
NORTHERN, Mary Moody 543
NORTHOP, Cyrus 475
NORTHROP
Aaron L. 566
Henry P. 525
John H. 605
John K. 611
William 554
NORTHRUP, Edwin F. 589, 594, 600
NORTHWAY, Stephen A. 141, 143, 146
NORTON
Charles E. 574
Charles P. 477
Clarence C. 486
Daniel S. 108, 110, 112, 324
Ebenezer F. 76
Eckstein 549
Elijah H. 105, 329
James 146, 149
James A. 146, 149, 151
Jesse O. 96, 98, 106
John 404
John (artist) 591
John N. 191, 197
John W.R. 572
M.E. 459
Mary T. 188, 191, 194, 197, 201, 204, 207, 211, 214, 217, 220, 224, 227
Miner G. 181
Nelson I. 119
Patrick D. 169, 172, 175
R.L. 393
Richard H. 135, 138
Thomas H. 454
William A. 469
NORVAL, Theophilus L. 333*
NORVELL, John 82, 84, 322
NORWEB, R. Henry 424, 426, 427, 435*
NORWOOD
Elisabeth 536
John N. 465
Thomas M. 114, 116, 118, 129, 132, 296
NOTLEY, Thomas 8
NOTSON, Robert C. 573
NOTT
Abraham 56, 452
Charles C. 273*
Edward 9
Eliphalet 483, 532
NOTTE, John A., Jr. 363
NOTTINGHAM, J. Curtis 570
NOURSE
Amos 98, 314
C.J. 401
Edwin G. 566
Elizabeth 599
NOWICKI, Matthew 591
NOYES
Arthur A. 475, 563, 565, 596, 609
Arthur P. 571
Charles F. 492
Edward F. 353, 428
Henry S. 478*
John 66
John H. 538*
Joseph C. 82
Newbold 573
Reuel J. 449
W. Albert, Jr. 565, 596, 608
Walter C. 271
William A. 565, 596, 604, 608
NUCKOLLS, William T. 75, 76, 78
NUELSON, John L. 530
NUFER, Albert F. 423, 427, 435
NUGEN, Robert H. 105
NUGENT
Gregory 474
John F. 173, 176, 298
NULL, Lester H. 558
NULTON, Louis M. 483
NUNAN, Joseph D., Jr. 444
NUNN
David A. 111, 117
Ira H. 416
Louie B. 310
Sam 264, 297
NUNNALLY, G.A. 475

NUSSBAUM, Paul J. 525, 527
NUTE
Alonzo 135
Monroe L. 577
NUTT, Cyrus 469*, 473
NUTTER
Donald G. 332
Harold P. 577
NUTTING
Charles B. 479
Newton W. 128, 133
P.G. 580
NYE
Frank M. 159, 162, 165
Gerald P. 188, 191, 194, 198, 201, 204, 208, 211, 214, 218, 350
James W. 106, 108, 110, 112, 114, 335
Russell B. 585
Wallace G. 457
NYGAARD, Hjalmar C. 246, 249
NYQUIST, Harry 598

O

OAKES
James L. 271
John B. 612
John C. 400, 405
Urian 472
OAKEY, Peter D. 170
OAKLEY
M. 487
Thomas J. 64, 74
Violet 591, 607
OAKMAN, Charles G. 233
OAKS, Dallin H. 467
OATES
James F., Jr. 546*
Joyce Carol 602, 609
William C. 124, 127, 129, 131, 134, 136, 139, 278
OATIS, William 607
OBER, Edgar B. 549*
OBERHOLTZER, Edison E. 472
OBERLY
Henry S. 480
John H. 558
OBEY, David R. 260, 263, 266
O'BOYLE
Francis B. 480
Patrick 523, 524
O'BRIEN
Brian 580
Charles F.X. 181, 184
Christopher D. 460
Edward C. 434, 439
Eugene W. 573
Frank M. 583
George D. 207, 213, 217, 220, 226, 230, 233
George M. 264
Henry J. 523, 526
Hugh 450
James 124
James H. 168
Jeremiah 71, 72, 74
John A. 472
John D. 577
John P. 458
Joseph J. 211, 214, 217
Lawrence F. 36, 43
Leo W. 230, 233, 237, 240, 243, 246, 249, 253
R.G. 458
Robert L. 445
Thomas H. 559
Thomas J. (b. 1842) 427, 431*
Thomas J. (b. 1878) 200, 203, 206, 216, 219, 223, 226, 229, 232, 235, 238, 242, 245, 248
William J. 116, 118
William J., Jr. 574
William S. 192
O'BYRNE
John J. 477
Mrs. Roscoe C. 579
O'CALLAGHAN, Mike 336
OCHILTREE
David 461
Thomas P. 129
William B. 392
OCHOA, Servero 606
OCHS, Adolph S. 603
OCHSNER
Albert J. 565
Alton 565*, 590
OCKERSON, John A. 572
O'CONNELL
Ambrose 273
David J. 178, 185, 188, 191, 194
Denis J. 468, 528
Eugene 528
James 557
James D. 403
Jeremiah E. 185, 188, 195
Jerry J. 207
John J. 271
John M. 202, 205, 208
Joseph F. 159, 162
M.F. 558
Michael J. 469
Stephen C. 470
William H. 523*, 528
O'CONNOR
Basil 569, 578, 603
Charles 195
Dennis P. 454
Edwin 587
Flannery 602
Herbert R. 223, 226, 229
James (b. 1870) 177, 180, 184, 187, 190, 193
James (b. 1823) 527
James F. 207, 210, 214, 217, 220
Jeremiah 466
John J. 185, 188, 191, 194, 198, 201, 204, 207
John J. (b. 1855) 527
Michael 526, 528
Michael J. (St. Louis) 480
Michael J. (Cincinnati) 487
Michael P. 124, 126
Paul L. 487
T.V. 558
William A. 529
William P. 527, 529
O'CONOR, Herbert R. 318*
O'DANIEL
John W. 404, 413
W. Lee 215, 218, 221, 225, 373*
O'DAY
Caroline 204, 208, 211, 214
John 557
Timothy 455
ODDIE, Tasker L. 181, 184, 188, 191, 194, 197, 335*
O'DEA, Edward J. 528
ODEGAARD
Charles 566
Charles E. 484
ODEGARD, Peter H. 571
ODELL
Arthur G., Jr. 567
Benjamin B., Jr. 143, 146, 345
Gerard P. 599
John J.P. 564
Morgan S. 474
Moses F. 105, 107
N. Holmes 114
O'DELL, William F. 568
ODENHEIMER, William H. 506, 520, 521
ODETS, Clifford 589
ODGERS, Merle M. 467
ODIN, Jean Marie 524, 526
ODLIN, Reno 564
O'DONAGHUE, Denis 527
O'DONNELL
Charles L. 478
Cletus F. 527
Edward J. 474
Emmett, Jr. 416
J. Hugh 478
James 130, 132, 135, 137
T.A. 570
ODUM
Eugene P. 575
Howard W. 573
O'DWYER
Fred J. 558
John P. 484*
William 433, 458
OELMAN
Robert S. 492
Robert S. 549*
O'FERRALL, Charles T. 29, 131, 134, 136, 139, 141, 379
O'FARRELL, Michael J. 529
OFFENHAUER, Roy E. 466
O'FLANAGAN, Dermot 526
OFSTIE, Ralph A. 417*
OGANOFF, Ida 589
OGBURN
Charlton 593
William F. 573
OGDEN
Aaron 580
Aaron 56, 57, 340*
Charles F. 177, 180
David A. 67
David A.D. 402
Henry W. 140, 142, 145
Michael J. 573
Robert 3
Wesley 372
William B. 451, 554
OGG, Frederic A. 571
OGILBY
Lyman C. 515, 521
Remsen B. 482
OGILVIE, Richard B. 301
OGLE
Alexander 67
Andrew J. 94
Benjamin 316
Charles 83, 85
Marbury B. 570
Samuel 8*
OGLESBY
Richard 116, 118, 120, 300*
Woodson R. 168, 171
OGLETHORPE, James E. 8
O'GORMAN
James A. 165, 168, 171, 345
Patrick F. 480
Thomas 529
O'GRADY, James M.E. 148
O'HAGAN, Joseph B. 472
O'HAIR
Frank T. 167
Robert C. 576
O'HARA
Barratt 226, 232, 235, 238, 242, 245, 248, 251, 255
Edwin V. 526*
Frank 602
Gerald P. 528
James 403
James E. 128, 131
James G. 242, 245, 249, 252, 255, 258, 261, 265
John 589, 602
John F. 478, 523, 524, 525
Joseph P. 214, 217, 220, 223, 227, 230, 233, 236, 239
William 528
O'HARE, John 559
O'HERN, John F. 528
OHLIGER, Lewis P. 138
O'KANE, Michael 472
O'KEEFE
Arthur J. 457
Georgia 592, 603
Gerald F. 525
John 557
Lawrence 558
Matthias J. 460
Vincent T. 470
O'KELLY, James 538
OKEY, John W. 353
O'KONSKI, Alvin E. 219, 222, 225, 228, 231, 235, 238, 241, 244, 247, 250, 254, 257, 260, 263
OLCOTT
Ben W. 356
J. Van Vechten 157, 160, 162
Simeon 57, 58, 337*
OLDEN, Charles S. 340
OLDENBURG
Claes 592
Richard 500
OLDFATHER, William A. 570
OLDFIELD
Pearl P. 189, 193
William A. 161, 164, 167, 170, 173, 176, 179, 183, 186, 189
OLDHAM
George A. 511, 519
J.P. 454*
William F. 530
William S. 392, 393*
OLDS
Edson B. 93, 95, 97
George D. 465
Glenn A. 473
Irving S. 554, 609
James 598
Leland 443*
Robert 411
O'LEARY
Arthur A. 471
Denis 168
Edward J. 492
James A. 204, 208, 211, 214, 217
James L. 569
John W. 575
Thomas M. 529
OLGEERT, Benjamin H., Jr. 434
OLENDORF, George F. 579
OLIN
Abram B. 101, 103, 105
Franklin W. 491
Gideon 58, 59
Henry 72
John M. 550
Stephen 479, 485*
OLINSKY, Ivan G. 593
OLIPHANT
Patrick B. 587
Walter T. 567
OLITSKI, Jules 593, 607
OLIVER
Allen L. 579
Andrew 97, 99
Bernard M. 576
Covey T. 426
Daniel C. 174
E.L. 595
Frank 185, 188, 191, 194, 198, 201
George T. 163, 166, 169, 172, 359
Henry K. 460
James 416
James A. 497
James C. 207, 210, 213, 242
Lunsford E. 415
Mary 610
Mordecai 97, 99
Oren A. 566
Peter 10
Robert T. 566
Robert W. 473
S. Addison 118, 120
Webster J. 273
William B. 170, 173, 176, 179, 183, 186, 189, 192, 196, 199, 202
William M. 86
OLMSTEAD
Dawson 403
Philo H. 452*
OLMSTED
Charles E. 575
Charles S. 509, 519
Charles T. 509, 519
David 460
Frederick L., Jr. 573*, 590, 603
John C. 573*
Marlin E. 146, 149, 152, 154, 157, 160, 163, 166
Robert G. 468
OLNEY
Frank F. 459
Richard 29*, 30, 38, 41
Richard 171, 174, 177
O'LOUGHLIN, Kathryn E. 200
OLPIN, A. Ray 484
OLPP, Archibald E. 181
OLSEN
Arnold 246, 249, 252, 255, 258
Henry S. 557
James K. 479
OLSON
Alec G. 249, 252
B.G. 486
Clinton J. 437
Culbert L. 284
Edward 481
Floyd B. 325
H. Everett 544*
Harry 568
Harry F. 599
Obert 450
Ole H. 350
O'MAHONEY, Joseph C. 202, 205, 209, 212, 215, 219, 222, 225, 228, 231, 235, 238, 241, 244, 387, 388
O'MALLEY
Comerford J. 469
Francis A. 467
Thomas D. 202, 205, 209
O'MEARA, Andrew P. 404
ONAHAN, William J. 599
ONDERDONK
Benjamin T. 505, 520
Henry U. 505, 521
O'NEAL
Edward A., 277, 278
Edward A., Jr. 549
Emmet 278
Emmet (b. 1887) 203, 207, 210, 213, 216, 220, 435
Joseph T. 456
Matson, Jr. 251, 254, 258
R. 452
O'NEALL
Charles F. 461
John B. 365

John H. 132
O'NEIL
Charles 418
Henry P. 574
James F. 568
Joseph H. 135, 137, 140
Ralph T. 568
O'NEILL
Arthur J. 528
C. William 354*
Charles 107, 109, 111, 113, 117, 119, 122, 124, 126, 128, 131, 133, 136, 138, 141
Charles A. 312
Edward 456*
Edward J. 405
Edward L. 207
Eugene 583*, 586, 603, 605
Francis A., Jr. 444*
Gerard M. 588
Harry P. 228, 231
James A. 550
John 107
John J. (journalist) 584
John J. 128, 130, 133, 138, 140
Merlin 445
Thomas 474
Thomas P., Jr. 233, 236, 239, 242, 245, 249, 252, 255, 258, 261, 264
ONG, William A. 577
ONSAGER, Lars 596, 604, 606, 609, 610
OOMS, Casper W. 444
OOSTING, Henry J. 575
OOTHOUT, John 544
OPDYKE, George 458
OPLER, Marvin K. 563
OPPEN, George 587
OPPENHEIMER, J. Robert 570, 595
OPPICE, Harold W. 566
ORD
Edward O.C. 408
George 563
J. Garsche 413
O'REAR, John D. 424
O'REGAN
Anthony 525, 529
Patrick M. 480
O'REILLY
Bernard 526
Bernard P. 469*
Charles J. 525, 527
Daniel 124
James 526
John 477
Patrick T. 529
Robert M. 403, 569
Thomas C. 528
OREM, Charles R. 543
ORGILL, Edmund 456
ORMAN, James B. 285
ORMANDY, Eugene 608
ORMSBEE, Ebenezer J. 376
ORMSBY, Stephen 62, 63, 65
O'ROURK, E.J. 557
ORR
Alexander D. 52*, 53
Benjamin 66
Benjamin G. 462
Carey 586
Douglas W. 567
J. Alvin 533
Jackson 114, 116
James L. 94, 96, 97, 99, 100, 101, 365, 392, 393*, 436
John A. 392, 393
Louis M. 569
Robert, Jr. 73, 75
William E. 272
ORT, Samuel A. 486*
ORTH, Godlove S. 106, 108, 110, 112, 116, 123, 125, 423
ORTIZ, Alfredo 461*
ORTON
Edward 465, 478, 563, 575
Harlow S. 385, 456
O.M. 558
Samuel T. 571
William 444
ORWIG, William 531
OSBORN
Chase S. 322
Elizabeth 609
Fairfield 591, 609
Henry F. 563, 594, 597, 603, 609
Henry L. 471
Monroe 355
Ronald E. 536
Sidney P. 280
Thomas A. 306
Thomas O. 423, 424, 425
Thomas W. 109, 111, 114, 293
William C. ,603
William H. (b. 1825) 548
William H. (b. 1856) 444
OSBORNE
Danvers 8
Edward W. 509, 522
Edwin S. 131, 133, 136
George 501
Harold S. 576, 595
Henry Z. 173, 176, 179
John E. 147, 387
Lithgow 434
Stanley deJ. 550*
Thomas B. 83, 85
OSENBAUGH, Richard J. 576
OSGOOD
Charles E. 571
Gayton P. 79
Jacob 538
Joseph B. 460
Samuel 6, 445, 547
William F. 568
O'SHAUNESSY, George F. 166, 169, 172, 175
O'SHAUGHNESSY, I.A. 599
O'SHEA, Benjamin 553
OSMER, James H. 124
OSMERS, Frank C., Jr. 211, 214, 230, 233, 236, 239, 243, 246, 249
OSMUNDSON, Theodore 573
OSTERHAUS, Peter J. 408, 409*
OSTERTAG, Harold C. 230, 233, 237, 240, 243, 246, 249
OSTRANDER
Floyd D. 566
N. 458
Russell C. 455
OSTREICHER, Robert T. 452
O'SULLIVAN
Clifford 272
Dean T. 480
Eugene D. 227
Jeremiah 527
John L. 435
Patrick B. 183, 289
OSWALD
Genevieve 593
John W. 473, 479
OTEY
James H. 505, 522
Peter J. 144, 147, 149, 152
OTIL, Elwell S. 419
OTIS
Charles W. 452
George L. 460
Harris F. 462
Harrison Gray 54, 55, 66, 68, 69, 319, 450
James 461
James (Mass.) 3
John 93
John G. 137
Merrill E. 568
Norton P. 154
Samuel A. 6
OTJEN, Theobald 144, 147, 149, 152, 155, 158
O'TOOLE
Donald L. 208, 211, 214, 217, 221, 224, 227, 230
William J. 434
OTT
Emil 567
Isaac 569
Phillip 455
Richard B. 382
OTTENBERG, Miriam 586
OTTERBEIN, Philip W. 531
OTTESEN, Schuyler F. 568
OTTING, Bernard J. 480
OTTINGER
Lawrence 553
Richard L. 253, 256, 259
OUTERBRIDGE, Alexander E., Jr. 594
OUTHWAITE, Joseph H. 131, 133, 136, 138, 141
OUTLAND, George E. 216, 219
OUTLAW
David 91, 93, 95
George 71
OVENSHIRE, Charles E. 579
OVERBERGER, Charles G. 565
OVERHOLSER
Ed 458
Winfred 571, 608
OVERMAN
Lee S. 154, 157, 160, 162, 165, 168, 171, 174, 178, 181, 185, 188, 191, 194, 348
Richard E. 455
OVERMYER, Arthur W. 172, 175
OVERS, Walter H. 511
OVERSTOLZ, Henry 460
OVERSTREET
James 69, 70
James W. 155, 173, 176, 180
Jesse 142, 145, 147, 150, 153, 156, 158
OVERTON
Anthony 611
Edward, Jr. 122, 124
John H. 197, 200, 203, 207, 210, 213, 217, 220, 223, 312
John, Jr. 456
Walter H. 75
Watkins 456*
OWEN
Alfred 469
Allen F. 92
Daniel 361
David B. 466
Edgar W. 564, 608
Emmett M. 200, 203, 206, 209
George W. 70, 72, 74
James 67
James H. 459
John 347
Richard 479
Robert D. 87, 89, 436, 437
Robert L. 160, 163, 166, 169, 172, 175, 178, 181, 185, 355
Russell D. 583
Ruth Bryan 193, 196, 427
Selwyn N. 353*
Thomas H. 355
Vaux 558
William D. 130, 132, 134
OWENS
Charles B. 559
Frank C. 452
George W. 80, 82
Hubert B. 573
James B. 391, 392
James W. 136, 138
Jesse N. 455
John W. 584
L.B. 452
Michael J. 594
Thomas L. 223
William C. 142
OWSLEY
Alvin M. 427, 430, 435, 568
Bryan Y. 85
William 308
OXNAM
G. Bromley 469, 530
Robert 479

P

PACA, William 3, 6, 8
PACE
Charles N. 411
Eric 607
Frank, Jr. 399, 444, 547*, 579*
Stephen 206, 209, 213, 216, 219, 223, 226
PACHECO, Romualdo 120, 122, 124, 283, 429, 430
PACHLER, William J. 559
PACK, John Paul 536
PACKARD
Alpheus S. 501
Arthur W. 492
C.S.W. 547
David 399
Jasper 112, 114, 116
Lewis R. 570
PACKER
Asa 97, 99
Fred L. 585
Horace B. 146, 149
John B. 113, 115, 117, 119
William F. 359
PACKWOOD, Robert W. 259, 262, 265, 357
PADDOCK
Algernon S. 119, 121, 123, 133, 135, 138, 333*
Benjamin H. 507, 520
F.J. 459*
George A. 213, 216
George W. 466
John A. 507, 521
Robert L. 509, 519
PADELFORD
Frederick M. 577
Seth 362
PADGETT, Lemuel P. 152, 155, 157, 160, 163, 166, 169, 172, 175, 178, 182
PAGE
Addison F. 502
Carroll S. 160, 163, 166, 169, 172, 175, 179, 182, 376*
Charles G. 501
Charles H. 131, 138, 141
Curtis H. 580
Daniel D. 460
Edward, Jr. 424
George T. 272, 564
Henry 137
Herman 510, 520, 521, 522
Herman L. 456
Herman R. 513
Hilliard W. 547
Horace F. 115, 118, 120, 122, 124
Irvine H. 567, 589, 590, 607
John (N.H.) 81, 337*
John (Va.) 51, 52, 53, 54, 378
John B. 376
Mann 7
Marie Danforth 598
Richard L. 396
Robert 56
Robert G. 551*
Robert N. 154, 157, 160, 162, 165, 168, 171
Sherman 79, 81
Thomas N. 431
Thomas W. 445
Walter H. 429
William 577
PAHLS, John 469, 474
PAIGE
Calvin D. 168, 171, 174, 177, 180, 184
David R. 128
John K. 449
PAINE
Charles (b. 1799) 375
Charles (b. 1830) 572
Charles J. 410
Edward H. 576
Elijah 55, 56, 57, 375
Halbert E. 109, 111, 113, 444
Rowlett 456
Robert 530
Robert Treat (b. 1731) 3, 6
Robert Treat (b. 1835) 570
Robert Treat (b. 1812) 99
Rowlett 456
Thomas 597
Thomas O. 444
Ephraim 6
William W. 112
PAINTER, Theophilus S. 482, 573
PALACHE, Charles 576
PALADE, George E. 600, 607
PALAMOUNTAIN, Joseph C., Jr. 481
PALEN, Rufus 84
PALFREY, John G. 91
PALLADINO
N. Joseph 569
Ralph A. 403
PALMER
A. Mitchell 32*, 41, 163, 166, 169
Albert 450
Albert W. 534
Alice Freeman 597
Anthony 9
Beriah 58
Bruce, Jr. 400
Charles D. 405
Cyrus M. 192
Ely E. 423*
Everett W. 531
Frank W. 112, 114, 443*
George W. 101, 103
Harold D. 572
Henry L. 550
Henry W. 152, 154, 157, 163
James S. 417
John 17
John (b. 1785) 67, 83
John M. 17, 137, 139, 142, 300*, 408, 409*
John W. 194
Joseph II 432, 434

Joseph C. 416
L.E. 558
Leigh C. 418
Lester E. 450
Potter 497
Ralph S. 592
Richard E. 572
Robert M. 423
Robert R. 567, 591
Samuel S. 532
T. Chalkley 563
Thomas W. 128, 130, 132, 322
William A. 69, 70, 72, 375*
Williston B. 401
PALMISANO, Vincent L. 190, 193, 197, 200, 203, 207
PANKOW, Steven 451
PANOFSKY, Wolfgang K.H. 596, 604
PANTZER, Robert T. 476
PAPANICOLAOU, George 607
PAPENFOTH, Herman A. 578
PAPPENHEIMER, John R. 571
PARCELL, Malcolm 610
PARDEE
Don A. 271
George C. 283
PARDUE, Austin 514, 521
PARET, William 507, 520
PARISH, Francis D. 478
PARK
Edwards A. 592
Frank 167, 170, 173, 176, 180, 183
Guy B. 330
John 456
John D. 288
Marion Edwards 467
Orlando 575
Robert E. 573
Robert H. 599
Samuel C. 460
Thomas 564, 575
William E. 481
William H. 572, 603, 609, 610
PARKE, John G. 408, 483
PARKER
Abraham X. 126, 128, 131, 133
Albert 462
Alton B. 17, 345, 564
Amasa J. 83
Andrew 95
Arthur C. 502
Ben H. 564
Cola G. 548*, 578
Cortlandt (b. 1818) 564
Cortlandt (b. 1884) 413
Daniel (bus. exec.) 578
Daniel 401, 402
Dorothy 611
Earl 572
Edward M. 509, 520
Edwin P., Jr. 414
Edwin W. 530
Emmett N. 381
F.A. 483
Frank 400
Gail Thain 466
George B. 584
George H. 563
Glenn 388
Homer C. 196, 200
Hosea W. 114, 117
Isaac 54, 319
Isaac C. 114, 116
James (N.J.) 79, 81
James (Mass.) 64, 68
James E. 412*
James S. 168, 171, 174, 178, 181, 185, 188, 191, 194, 198, 201
James K. 486
James W. 546, 573
Jay S. 307
Joel (b. 1795) 337
Joel (b. 1813) 341*
John 7
John C. (b. 1865) 594
John C. (b. 1879) 576
John J. 271, 589
John M. (b. 1805) 99, 101
John M. (b. 1863) 312
Josiah 51, 52, 53, 54, 55, 56
Lauris S. 455*
Lawton 589
Linus 530
Matthew H. 558
Millard M. 465
Moses G. 579
Nahum 60, 61, 337
Paul 498
R. Hunt 349
Ralph D. 610
Richard 94
Richard E. 81, 83, 378
Richard W. 143, 146, 148, 151, 154, 157, 159, 162, 168, 171, 174, 181
Robert Andrew 609
Robert C. 462
Roy H. 401
Samuel 505, 520
Samuel W. 94, 96
Severn E. 69
T. Nelson 459
Theodore W. 400
Torrance 536
William H. 160
William R. 577
PARKHILL, James W. 478
PARKHURST
Charles 497*
Christopher F. 362
Frederick H. 315
John G. 424
PARKINSON
C. Jay 543*
Daniel B. 481
David B. 608
Thomas I. 546
W. Lynn 272
PARKMAN
Francis 597
Paul D. 599
PARKS
Charles W. 418
Floyd L. 404, 405
Gordon 611
Gorham 79, 80
Harry S. 601
Lloyd M. 570
Robert J. 597
Robert O. 502
Tilman B. 179, 183, 186, 189, 193, 196, 199, 202
W. George 567, 590
W. Robert 473
PARMELEE
Howard C. 575
William 449*
PARMENTER, William 82, 84, 86, 87
PARNELL, Harvey 282
PARR
Albert E. 497, 501
Samuel W. 565
PARRAN
Thomas (b. 1860) 165
Thomas (b. 1892) 445, 492, 572, 610
PARRETT, William F. 134, 137
PARRINGTON, Vernon L. 583
PARRIS
Albion K. 65, 66, 74, 314*
Stanford E. 266
Viril D. 82, 84
PARRISH
Edward 482
Isaac 85, 90
Lucian W. 179, 182
Maxfield 591
Samuel L. 603
PARROTT, John F. 67, 68, 70, 71, 337
PARRY, D.M. 578
PARSON, Samuel, Jr. 573*
PARSONS
Andrew 322
Archibald L. 418
Charles 564
Charles L. 604, 608
Claude V. 193, 196, 200, 203, 206, 210
Edward L. 511, 519
Edward S. 474
Edward Y. 118
Ernest 455
Frank N. 338
Geoffrey 584
Herbert 157, 160, 162
J. Graham 431, 436
Lewis E. 277
Richard C. 117
Robert W. 492
Robert W., Jr. 492
Samuel 406
Talcott 563, 573
Theophilus 319
William W. 473
PARTCH, Harry 611
PARTRIDGE
Alden 478, 483
Charlotte 499
Donald B. 197
Earle E. 412, 415, 416*
Frank C. 195, 377, 439
George 6, 51
James R. 424, 430, 436, 439
Oliver 3*
Richard C. 400
Samuel 86
Sidney C. 509, 522
PARVIN, Theophilus 569
PASAMANICK, Benjamin 597, 598
PASCHAL
George 461
Thomas M. 141
PASCHALL
Davis Y. 486
H. Franklin 534
PASCHANG, John L. 526
PASCO, Samuel 132, 134, 137, 139, 142, 144, 147, 293
PASSMAN, Otto E. 223, 226, 229, 233, 236, 239, 242, 245, 248, 252, 255, 258, 261, 264
PASSOC, Peter 569
PASTORE, John O. 228, 231, 234, 237, 240, 243, 247, 250, 253, 259, 262, 266, 363*
PASTORIZA, Joseph J. 454
PATCH
Alexander M., Jr. 405*, 412*, 413, 414
Joseph D. 414
PATCHEN, Kenneth 603, 610
PATE, Randolph M. 416
PATERSON
John 58
William 4, 51, 269, 340*
PATMAN, Wright 195, 198, 202, 205, 208, 212, 215, 218, 221, 225, 228, 231, 234, 237, 240, 244, 247, 250, 253, 256, 260, 263, 266
PATRICK
Edwin D. 413
Hugh T. 569
J. Milton 568
John 586
Joseph C. 594
Luther 206, 209, 212, 219
Mason M. 401
PATRIDGE
Donald B. 197
Frank C. 195, 199
PATTANGALL, William R. 315
PATTEN
Edward J. 249, 252, 256, 259, 262, 265
Harold A. 225, 228, 232
John 5, 52, 53
Simon N. 566
Thomas G. 165, 168, 171
PATTERSON
Alex E. 549
Boyd C. 485
David T. 109, 111, 370
Edward G. 450
Edward W. 203, 206
Ellis E. 219
Ernest M. 563
Eugene 587
Francis F., Jr. 177, 181, 184, 188
Frederick B. 549, 577
Frederick D. 483
George R. 152, 154, 157
George W. 121
Gilbert B. 154, 157
Grove 573
Herbert P. 545
Howard A. 565
Isaac L. 357
J.T. 573
James K. 473
James O. 157, 160, 163
James T. 222, 226, 229, 232, 235, 238
James W. 107, 108, 110, 112, 114, 338
Jefferson 439
John (Ohio) 71, 406
John D. (Pa.) 453*, 566
John H. 549
John J. 117, 119, 122, 365
John L. 474
John M. 278
Joseph W. 449*
Josiah 138, 141, 144
LaFayette L. 189, 192, 196
Malcom R. 152, 155, 157, 370
Paul L. 357
Perry S. 576
Richard C., Jr. 429, 438, 439
Robert 570
Robert M. 484, 570*
Robert P. 34, 40, 271
Robert U. (b. 1877) 403
Robert U. 547
Robert W. 532
Roscoe C. 181, 194, 197, 200, 330
Thomas 67, 68, 70, 71
Thomas J. 88
Thomas M. 120, 150, 152, 155, 285
Walter 70
William (N.Y.) 83
William (Ohio) 79, 81
Okey L. 384
John M. 138, 353
Robert E. (b. 1800) 468*
Robert E. (b. 1850) 359*
PATTON
Alexander 452*
Carl S. 534
Charles E. 166, 169
Charles H. 566
David H. 137
Francis L. 479
George S., Jr. 404, 405*, 412, 413, 415
Henry 485
Isaac W. 457
Mrs. James B. 579
John (Pa.) 105, 133
John (Mich.) 453
John, Jr. (Mich.) 140, 322
John D. 128
John M. 77, 78, 80, 82, 83
Kenneth S. 433
Leslie K. 483
Nat 205, 208, 212, 215, 218
Robert M. 277
Thomas F. 596
William M. 472
PATY, Raymond R. 465
PATZ, Arnall 599, 600
PAUL
Arloe W. 491
David 476, 533
Henry N. 547
James 547
John (b. 1839) 126
John (b. 1883) 182
Oglesby 567
Thomas 538
Willard S. 400, 413, 414, 471
PAULDING
James K. 25, 42
William, Jr. 62, 458*
PAULEN, Ben S. 306
PAULI, Wolfgang 605
PAULIN, Richard C. 501
PAULING, Linus 565, 596, 606*, 609
PAULLIN, James E. 569
PAULSON, Stanley 481
PAUND, Louise 577
PAWLEY, William D. 424, 435
PAWLING, Levi 67
PAXSON
Edward M. 359
Frederic L. 567, 583
PAXTON, William M. 532
PAYNE
D.A. 486
Eugene Gray 587
Fernandus 573
Frederick G. 233, 236, 239, 315*, 449
Henry B. 119, 131, 133, 135, 353
Henry C. 30, 43
John 506
John Barton 32*, 44, 569
Milton J. 455*
Melvin M. 578
Nathan F. 452
Sereno E. 128, 131, 135, 138, 141, 143, 146, 148, 151, 154, 157, 160, 162, 165, 168
Virginia 557
William W. 85, 87, 89
PAYNTER
Lemuel 83, 85
Samuel 290
Thomas H. 135, 137, 140, 159, 161, 164, 309
PAYSON, Lewis E. 125, 127, 130, 132, 134
PAYTON
Daniel 460
Robert L. 425

PEABODY
Charles 549
Charles A. 548
Endicott 321
Francis 498
George 597
James H. 285*
Malcolm E. 513, 519
Nathaniel 6
Paul E. 413
Robert S. 567
Selim H. 472, 498
PEACE, Roger C. 215, 366
PEACOCK, Leslie C. 546
PEAK, John L. 438
PEAKE, Alonzo W. 552
PEARCE
Charles C. 462
Charles E. 145, 148
Dutee J. 73, 75, 76, 78, 80, 81
James A. 81, 82, 86, 87, 89, 91, 93, 95, 97, 98, 100, 102, 104, 316
John J. 99
P.T. 462
PEARL, William A. 485
PEARLSTEIN, Seymour 598
PEARRE, George A. 148, 150, 153, 156, 159, 162
PEARSE, A.S. 573, 575
PEARSON
Albert J. 138, 141
Alfred J. 428, 435
Gerald L. 612
Herron 205, 208, 212, 215
James B. 245, 248, 252, 255, 258, 261, 264, 307
Jay F.W. 475
John 557
John J. 81
Joseph 61, 63, 64
Joseph T., Jr. 610
Raymond A. 473, 475
Richmond 143, 146, 149, 429, 433, 435*
Richmond M. 348
T. Gilbert 593
PEARTREE, William 457
PEARY
Robert E. 566, 594*, 598, 599
Mrs. Robert E. 593
PEASE
Arthur S. 465, 570
Calvin (b. 1776) 352
Calvin (b. 1813) 484
Elisha M. 372*
Henry R. 116, 326
Lute 585
PEASLEE
Amos J. 570
Charles H. 91, 93, 95
Robert J. 339
PEASLEY, Amos J. 423
PEAT, Wilbur D. 497, 499
PEAVEY, Hubert H. 186, 189, 192, 196, 199, 202
PEAVY, George W. 478
PEAY
Austin 370
Gordon N. 455
PECK
Adelbert H. 566
Asahel 376
E.R. 450
Ebenezer 273
Elijah W. 277
Erasmus D. 113, 115
George R. 564
George W. (b. 1818) 99, 455
George W. (b. 1840) 385
Gregory 563, 608
H.E. 429*
Jared V. 97
Jesse T. 469, 530
John J. 407
John W. 272
Lucius B. 92, 94
Luther C. 83, 84
Tracy 570
Willys R. 438
PECKHAM
Rufus W. (b. 1809) 97
Rufus W. (b. 1833) 269
PECKOVER, J. 594
PECORA, William T. 443
PEDEN
James A. 423
Preston E. 224
PEDERSEN, P.O. 598
PEDDIE, Thomas B. 121
PEEK
Burton F. 546
George N. 433
Harmanus 68
PEEL, Samuel W. 127, 129, 131, 134, 136
PEELE, William W. 530
PEELER, W.B. 482
PEELLE, Stanton J. 125, 127, 273
PEERS, Benjamin O. 482
PEERY
George C. 186, 189, 192, 380
Thomas M. 572
William 5
PEET, Raymond E. 417
PEETZ, John E. 501
PEFFER, William A. 137, 140, 142, 306
PEFLEY, Peter J. 450
PEGLER, Westbrook 584
PEGRAM
George B. 570
George H. 572
John 67
PEIRCE
Benjamin 563
G.J. 574
Herbert H.D. 434
Joseph 57
Robert B.F. 125
William F. 473
William H. 595
PELHAM, Charles 115
PELIKAN, Alfred G. 499
PELL
Claiborne 247, 250, 253, 256, 259, 262, 266, 363
Herbert Claiborne 178, 430, 435, 436
Howland 575
Philip 6
Wilbur F., Jr. 272
PELLETIER, Lawrence L. 465
PELLICER, Anthony D. 528
PELLY, Thomas M. 234, 237, 241, 244, 247, 250, 254, 257, 260, 263
PELTIER, Eugene J. 418
PELTON
F.W. 452
Guy R. 99
Lester A. 594
PEMBERTON
J.B. 451
John C. 395
William Y. 331
PENCE
J.T. 450
Lafayette 139
PENDER, William D. 395
PENDERGRAFT, Caro 459
PENDERGRASS
Edward J. 531
Eugene P. 565
PENDLETON
Edmund 7, 10
Edmund H. 77, 378
Ellen F. 485
George C. 141, 144
George H. 16, 101, 103, 105, 107, 124, 126, 128, 353, 428
James M. 115, 117
John O. 136, 139, 141
John S. 90, 92, 423, 425
Nathaniel 4, 5
Nathaniel G. (b. 1793) 86
William K. 466, 536
William N. 394*
PENEZ, Charles 498
PENFIELD
Frederic C. 423, 427
James K. 430
R.C. 547
PENICK
Charles C. 507
Edwin A. 511, 521
PENINGTON, John B. 132, 134
PENN
Alexander G. 93, 95
John 4, 5
John (Pa.) 9*
Richard 9
Stanley W. 587
William 9, 597
PENNELL
Maynard L. 611
Ralph M. 413
PENNEWILL, Simeon S. 291
PENNEY
Gaylord W. 611
James C. 551*
Joseph 471
Louis H. 567
PENNIMAN
Ebenezer J. 95
Josiah H. 479
PENNINGTON
Alexander C. 97, 99
William (N.J.) 102, 103, 340*
William 572
PENNOCK, William 459
PENNOYER, Sylvester 356
PENNYBACKER, Isaac S. 83, 90, 378
PENNYPACKER
Isaac A. 580
Samuel W. 359
PENROSE
Boies 146, 149, 151, 154, 157, 160, 163, 166, 169, 172, 175, 178, 182, 359
Richard A.F., Jr. 563, 576
Julie V.L. 491
Spencer 491
PENTUFF, J.R. 482
PEPPER
Claude D. 203, 206, 209, 213, 216, 219, 222, 226, 248, 251, 254, 257, 261, 264, 294
G. Willing 552
George D.B. 468
George Wharton 182, 185, 188, 359, 568, 589, 603
Irving St. C. 164, 167
William 479
William P. 501*
PEPPIATT, Guy S. 578
PERCE, Legrand W. 112, 114
PERCHE, Napoleon J. 524
PERCY
Charles H. 254, 258, 261, 264, 301
Earl H. 406
George 9*
LeRoy 162, 165, 327
Walker 602
PEREGOY, J.W. 558
PEREGRINE, P.A. 558
PERHAM, Sidney 106, 108, 110, 314
PERK, Ralph J. 452
PERKINS
Bishop 97
Bishop W. 127, 130, 132, 134, 137, 306
Bradford 591
Carl D. 226, 229, 232, 236, 239, 242, 245, 248, 252, 255, 258, 261, 264
Charles E. 545
Charles E., Jr. 545
Courtland D. 567
D.T. 554
Dexter 567
Elias 56
Frances 33, 34*, 46
G.T. 547*
George C. 139, 142, 144, 147, 150, 152, 155, 158, 161, 162, 167, 283*
George D. 137, 140, 142, 145
Henry A. 482
Henry F. 499
Herbert F. 548
James A. 468, 604
James B. 151, 154, 157, 160, 162
James E. 578, 592
James H. 547
James M. 453
Jared 95
John, Jr. 96, 391, 392, 393
John A. 469
Randolph 181, 184, 188, 191, 194, 197, 201, 204
Thomas J. 462
Thomas L. 491, 543, 546
PERKY, Kirtland I. 164, 298
PERLEY, Ira 337*, 338
PERLIK, Charles A., Jr. 557
PERLIS, Donald 609
PERLITZ, Charles A., Jr. 546
PERLMAN, Nathaniel D. 178, 181, 185, 188
PERRILL, Augustus L. 90
PERRIN
Bernadotte 570
Herbert T. 414
Leslie N. 547
PERRY
Aaron F. 115
Alfred T. 474
Benjamin F. 365
Benjamin L., Jr. 470
Bertrand J. 549
Edwin A. 574
Edward A. 293
Eli 115, 117, 449
Helen 500
James DeWolf 510, 521
John J. 98, 102
John R. 418
Madison S. 293
Marvin B., Jr. 471
Nehemiah 105, 107
Oliver H. 417
Ralph B. 584
Thomas J. 89
William H. 131, 133, 136
William S. 472, 507, 528
PERSELL, Charles B., Jr. 517
PERSHING, John J. 400, 405, 410*, 584, 609
PERSICO, Ignatius 528
PERSON
H.T. 487
Henry 122
Seymour H. 197
PERSONS
Gordon 278
John C. 413
PESCHGES, John H. 525
PETER, George 65, 66, 72
PETERKIN
George W. 507, 522
Julia 583
PETERS
Andrew J. 159, 162, 165, 168, 450
Frank, Jr. 588
George S. 452
James L. 569, 592
John A. (b. 1822) 110, 112, 114, 314
John A. (b. 1864) 168, 171, 174, 177, 180
John A. (coll. pres.) 472
John F. 595, 601
John S. 287
Mason S. 145
Richard 3, 7
Samuel R. 127, 130, 132, 134
Thomas M. 277
PETERSEN
Andrew N. 181
Dean H. 455
Forrest 594
Norman V. 564
Theodore S. 552
PETERSON
Burt A. 601
Clifford 502
F. Raymond 564
Frederick 569
Hjalmar 325
Howard C. 546*
Hugh 203, 206, 209, 213, 216, 219
John B. 527
J. Hardin 200, 203, 206, 209, 213, 216, 219, 222, 226
John B. 167
Joseph 571
Joseph N. 460
M. Blaine 247
Martha E. 466
Merrill D. 591
P. Kenneth 457
P. Victor 467
Peter G. 36, 46
R.A. 544
Roger Tory 591, 592, 593
Russell W. 292
Val 334, 427, 428
Virgil L. 402
Walter 339
PETIT, George A. 470
PETRIE
George 91
Lester 454
PETRIKIN, David 83, 85
PETRILLO, James C. 557
PETRY, Herb C., Jr. 577
PETTEE, Charles H. 476*
PETTENGILL
Charles W. 580
Samuel B. 196, 200, 203, 206
PETTIBONE, Augustus H. 126, 129, 131
PETTIGREW
Ebenezer 81
Richard F. 136, 138, 141, 144, 146, 149, 367
Samuel 459
PETTINGILL, John A. 449
PETTIS
Andrew A. 557
Jerry L. 254, 257, 260, 263
S. Newton 111, 424

Spencer D. 76
PETTIT
Charles 7
John 87, 89, 91, 94, 96, 302
John U. 98, 100, 102
Joseph M. 471
W.J. 557
PETTUS
Edmund W. 144, 147, 150, 152, 155, 158, 278
John J. 326*
PETTY, O.A. 451
PEURIFOY, John E. 429*, 438
PEW
J. Edgar 570, 601
J. Howard 553*, 590
Joseph N. 553
Joseph N., Jr. 553
PEYRE, Henry M. 577
PEYSER
Peter A. 262, 265
Theodore A. 201, 204, 208
PEYTON
Balie 80, 81, 425
Ephraim G. 326
Joseph H. 88, 90
Philip B. 419
Robert L.Y. 392*
Samuel O. 91, 100, 102
PFEIFER
Joseph L. 204, 208, 211, 214, 217, 221, 224, 227
William L. 227
PFEIFFER
George 559
Gustavus A. 492
Richard C. 534
PFEIL, Aloysius J. 467
PFOHL, Frank 558
PFOST, George B. 232, 235, 238, 242, 245
PFOTENHAUER, F. 535
PFUND, A. Herman 580, 601
PHEIFFER, William T. 214, 427
PHELAN
James (b. 1821) 392
James (b. 1856) 133, 136
James D. 170, 173, 176, 283, 461
James J. 599
John H. 599
Michael F. 168, 171, 174, 177
Richard 528
PHELPS
Anson G. 570
Byron 461
Charles E. 108, 110
D. Maynard 568
Darwin 113
Edward J. 429, 564
Elisha 67, 72, 74
Guy R. 545
James 118, 120, 122, 125
John S. 89, 91, 93, 95, 97, 99, 100, 103, 105, 329
Lancelot 80, 82
Oliver 59
Phelps 427
Samuel S. 85, 87, 88, 90, 92, 94, 96, 98, 375*
Seth L. 435, 462
Timothy G. 104
William Lyon 578, 603
William W. 101
William W. 117, 128, 130, 133, 428
PHEMISTER, Dallas B. 565
PHILBIN, Philip J. 217, 220, 223, 226, 230, 233, 236, 239, 242, 245, 249, 252, 255, 258
PHILBROOK, Alden W. 449
PHILIP, Hoffman 423, 425, 426, 434, 435, 439
PHILIPP
Emanuel L. 385
Robert 589, 593*
PHILIPS
Ferdinand 594
John F. 119, 123
PHILLIPS
A.A. 458
Albert J. 590, 595
Alfred N. 206
Asa E., Jr. 575
C. Hooper 457
Charles F. 466
Dayton E. 225, 228
Frank 551*
Fremont O. 149
Glenn R. 531
Harry 272
Henry D. 513, 522
Henry M. 101
J.H. 453
Jay A. 567
John 70
John (Calif.) 216, 219, 222, 226, 229, 232, 235
John (Miss.) 450
John C. (b. 1870) 280
John C. (b. 1876) 592
John G. 548
John L. 461
John Marshall 502*
Joseph (Ill.) 300
Joseph (Wisc.) 456
Leon C. 355
Nelson 372
Orie L. 272, 589
Paul L. 558, 559
Percy T. 566
Philip 96
Ray E. 534
Robert A. 600
Samuel C. 444
Solomon 449
Stephen C. 79, 81, 82, 460
Stephen W. 498
T.M. 536
Thomas L. 552
Thomas W. 141, 143
Thomas W., Jr. 185, 188
Wendell C. 569
Willard 550
William 424, 425, 431, 432*, 433
William A. 116, 118, 120
William H. 572
William K. 417
William W. 532
PHILPOT, Harry M. 466
PHILPUTT, A.B. 536
PHILSON, Robert 68
PHIPPEN, George D. 501
PHIPPS
Lawrence C. 176, 179, 183, 186, 189, 193, 285
Louis N. 449
Spencer 8*
PHIPS, William 8
PHISTER, Elijah C. 123, 125
PHOENIX, J. Phillips 88, 93
PHRANER, Wilson 470
PHYTHIAN, Robert L. 483
PICCIRILLI, Attilio 610
PICCONE, Camilo 591
PICHER, Oliver S. 399
PICK, Lewis A. 402
PICKARD
Greenleaf W. 598
Josiah L. 473
William L. 475
PICKEL, George J. 473*
PICKENS
Andrew 53, 364, 406
Francis W. 80, 91, 83, 85, 87, 365, 436
Israel 63, 64, 65, 72, 277*
PICKERING
Donald E. 599
Edward C. 563, 564, 609
John 4, 337, 563
Timothy 23*, 38, 40, 57, 59, 60, 61, 64, 65, 319, 401, 403, 406, 445
William H. 567, 595, 597, 611
PICKETT
Charles E. 161, 164, 574
George E. 394, 395
J.C. 435
J. Waskom 530
John C. 272
Joseph D. 473
Neal C. 454
Thomas A. 221, 225, 228, 231
PICKLE, J.J. 250, 253, 256, 260, 263, 266
PICKLER, John A. 136, 138, 141, 144
PICKMAN, Benjamin, Jr. 61
PIDCOCK, James N. 130, 133
PIDGEON
John, Jr. 453
Walter 559
PIEL, Gerard 591
PIEPER, Franz 535
PIERCE
B.O. 570
Benjamin 337*
Clifford D. 576
Cyrus N. 566
Earle V. 534
Franklin 13, 15, 79, 81, 82, 84, 86, 337
George E. 485
George F. 470, 530
George W. 596, 598
Gilbert A. 135, 350, 435
Henry A. 430
Henry L. 116, 119, 450*
Henry N. 507, 519
John L. 415
John R. 595, 604
P.E. 401
Ray V. 124
Rice A. 129, 136, 138, 146, 149, 152, 155
Wallace E. 211
Walter E. 450
Walter M. 201, 205, 208, 211, 215, 356
William 4, 5
William H. 576
William H. (metal eng.) 595
Willis M. 567
Winslow S. 554*
PIERPOINT, John 376
PIERPONT, Francis H. 379
PIERREPONT, Edwards 28, 41, 429
PIERSON
Abraham 487
Albert 402
Fritz A. 566
Isaac 74, 76
J. Willis 577
Jeremiah H. 70
Job 78, 79
Lewis E. 564, 575
W.W., Jr. 477
Warren L. 443
PIETENPOL, Clarence J. 469
PIEZ, Charles 573
PIFER, Alan 491
PIGOTT
James P. 139
Reginald J.S. 573, 594
Stephen J. 590
PIKE
Austin F. 117, 128, 130, 338
Frederick A. 104, 106, 108, 110
James 99, 101
James A. 516, 519
James S. 433
Jarvis 452
Otis G. 246, 249, 253, 256, 259, 262, 265
Sumner T. 443
Zebulon M. 401, 402, 406
PILCH, John J. 558
PILCHER
John L. 232, 235, 238, 241, 245, 248
W.S. 456
PILE, William A. 110, 439
PILES, Samuel H. 158, 160, 163, 381, 426
PILGARD, John A. 454
PILGRIM, Charles W. 571
PILIE, Louis H. 567
PILLARD, Charles H. 558
PILLIOD, Charles J., Jr. 547
PILLION, John R. 233, 237, 240, 243, 246, 249
PILLSBURY
George A. (Minn.) 457
George A. (N.H.) 452
Gilbert 451
John E. 418, 578
John S. 324
Walter B. 571
PILSBRY, Henry A. 600
PILSBURY
Edward 457
Timothy 90, 92
PIMPER, James 443
PINASCO, John 481*
PINCHBACK, P.B.S. 311
PINCHOT, Gifford 360*, 609
PINCKNEY
Charles (b. 1730) 7
Charles (b. 1758) 4, 55, 56, 57, 69, 437
Charles C. 4, 15*, 580
Henry L. 80, 81, 451*
John A. 517, 522
John M. 155
Joseph C. 574
Thomas 9, 15, 55, 56, 428, 437, 580
PINDALL
James 67, 69
Xenophon O. 281
PINDAR, John S. 131, 135
PINE
J. 483
William B. 188, 191, 195, 355
PING, Charles J. 483
PINGREE
David 460
Hazen S. 322, 453
Samuel E. 376
PINKERTON, Lowell C. 430, 431, 437
PINKHAM, William P. 470
PINKNEY
Robert F. 396
William (b. 1764) 24*, 41, 52, 65, 68, 69, 316, 428, 429, 436*, 449
William (b. 1810) 507, 520
PINNEY
James A. 450
Silas U. 456
PINNOCK, Thomas 460
PINTEN, Joseph G. 526, 529
PINTER, Lawrence J. 502
PIPER
James H. 482
William 63, 64, 66
William A. 118
PIRCE, William A. 131
PIRIE, Robert B. 417
PIRNIE
Alexander 243, 246, 249, 253, 256, 259, 262
Malcolm 572, 598
PISKOR, Frank P. 480
PISTON, Walter 585, 586, 592
PITAVAL, John B. 524
PITCAIRN
Harold 594
John 550*
PITCHER
James 455
Nathaniel 68, 70, 78, 344
Thomas G. 483
Zina 453*, 569
PITCHFORD, John H. 355
PITHAN, Athalicio T. 513
PITKIN
Albert J. 600
Frederick W. 285
John R.G. 423
Timothy 58, 60, 61, 62, 63, 65, 66
William 3, 8, 10*
PITMAN, Charles W. 94
PITNEY, Mahlon 143, 146, 270
PITOT, James 457
PITTENGER
Lemuel A. 466, 473
William A. 194, 197, 204, 210, 214, 217, 220
PITTMAN
Beatrice T. 536
Hobson 593, 610
Key 165, 168, 171, 174, 177, 181, 184, 188, 191, 194, 197, 201, 202, 204, 206, 207, 209, 211
Vail M. 336
PITTS
Herman C. 565
Robert F. 571
PITZER, Kenneth S. 480, 482, 608
PLACE, John B.M. 543*
PLAGENS, Joseph C. 526, 527
PLAISTED
Frederick W. 315, 449*
Harris M. 118, 314
PLANK, E.T. 558
PLANT, David 74
PLANTS, Tobias A. 109, 111
PLANTZ, Samuel 474
PLASS, Norman 484
PLASSMANN, Thomas 480
PLATE, Walter 593
PLATER
George 6, 316
Thomas 56, 57
PLATNER, Samuel B. 570
PLATT
Charles Adams 603
Edmund 168, 171, 174, 178
James H., Jr. 113, 115, 117
Jonas 56
Orville H. 122, 125, 127, 129, 132, 134, 137, 139, 142, 144, 147, 150, 152, 155, 288
Robert B. 575
Rutherford 593
Thomas C. 117, 119, 146, 148, 151, 154, 157, 159, 345
Zephania 6
PLATTEN, John W. 545
PLAUCHE, Vance 213
PLEASANT, Ruffin G. 312
PLEASANTON, Alfred 408*,

409
PLEASANTS
James 63, 64, 66, 67, 69*, 70, 378*
James J., Jr. 456
PLEHN, Carl C. 566
PLEISSNER, Ogden 591*
PLEPPE, Tom 450
PLIMPTON, Calvin H. 465
PLITT, Edwin A. 433
PLOESER, Walter C. 214, 217, 220, 224, 426, 434
PLOSCOWE, Morris 608
PLOWMAN, Thomas S. 144
PLUMB
Preston B. 120, 123, 125, 127, 130, 132, 134, 137, 306
Ralph 130, 132
PLUMER
Arnold 83, 86
George 70, 71, 73
William 57, 58, 59, 337*
William, Jr. 68, 70, 71
William S. 532
PLUMLEY
Charles A. 202, 205, 208, 212, 215, 218, 222, 225, 228, 478
Frank 163, 166, 169
H. Ladd 553*, 575
PLUMMER
Edward H. 410
Franklin E. 77, 79
Mary W. 568
PLUMSTED
Clement 458*
William 458*
PLUNKETT
Robert 471
Willis H. 459
PLYLER, John L. 470
POAGE, William R. 208, 212, 215, 218, 222, 225, 228, 231, 234, 237, 240, 244, 247, 250, 253, 256, 260, 263, 266
PODELL, Bertram L. 256, 259, 262, 265
POE
Edgar Allan 597
Philip L. 575
POEHLER, Henry 123
POETKER, Albert H. 469
POFF, Richard H. 237, 241, 244, 247, 250, 253, 257, 263
POFFENBERGER, Albert T. 571
POGUE, L. Welch 577
POHL, LaVera 499
POHLMAN, Julius 497
POILLON, Howard A. 492
POINDEXTER
George 66, 76, 77, 78, 79, 326*
Miles 163, 166, 169, 172, 175, 179, 182, 381, 435
POINSETT
Joel R. 25, 40, 432
Joel R. 70, 72, 73
POLAND
Luke P. 109, 111, 113, 115, 117, 129, 376*
Reginald R. 498, 499
POLETTI, Charles 346
POLIER, Justine Wise 608
POLK
Albert F. 173
Charles 290*
Frank L. 578
James G. 198, 201, 204, 208, 211, 227, 231, 237, 240, 243
James H. 404
James K. 13, 15*, 73, 75, 76, 78, 80*, 81, 82, 83, 369
Leonidas 394*, 395, 396, 505, 519, 520
Rufus K. 149, 152
Sylvanus 456
Trusten 100, 102, 104, 329*
William H. 96, 436
POLLARD
Charles L. 502
Ernest M. 156, 159
H. Marvin 565
Henry M. 121
John G. 380
Mrs. John Garland 502
Ramsey 534
Richard 425
POLLOCK
Howard W. 254, 257
James 88, 90, 92, 358
James K. 571
Lewis J. 569
P.D. 475
Thomas 8*
Thomas C. 533
William 559
William P. 175, 366
POLSGROVE, James 453
POLSLEY, Daniel H. 111
POMERENE, Atlee 166, 169, 172, 175, 178, 353
POMEROY
Allan 461
Charles 112
Samuel C. 104, 106, 108, 110, 112, 114, 306
Seth 406
Theodore M. 105, 107, 109*, 111
POMFRET, John E. 486, 499
POND
Benjamin 62
Charles H. 287
Edward B. 461
Irving K. 567
Theodore H. 497, 498
PONDER, James 291
PONTIUS, Clarence I. 483
POOL
Eugene H. 565
Joe R. 250, 253, 256
John 111, 113, 115, 348
Solomon S. 477
Walter F. 128
POOLE
Abram 589*
Ernest 583
John 580
R.F. 468
Theodore L. 143
William F. 567, 568
POOLER, J.S. 584
POOR
Alfred E. 577
Anne 589
Enoch 406
Henry V. 607
POPE
Arthur 499
Bayard F. 603
Charles A. 569
George 578
Jack M. 546
James P. 200, 203, 206, 299, 450
James S. 573, 601
John (b. 1770) 60, 61*, 62, 82, 84, 85, 308
John (b. 1823) 406, 407
John A. 499
John Russell 591
O.C. 471
Patrick H. 79
W. Kenneth 531
Walter L. 272
Willia T. 472
Young J. 365
POPEJOY, Thomas L. 476
POPHAM, William 580
POPMA, Alfred M. 565
POPPEN, Emanuel 535
POPPER, David H. 426
POPPLETON, Early F. 119
PORT, Martin 467
PORTER
A.W. Noel 512, 521
Albert G. 102, 104, 302, 431
Alexander 79, 80, 311
Augustus A. 453
Augustus S. 84, 86, 87, 322
Charles H. 113, 115
Charles O. 240, 243
Charles T. 596
D.T. 456
Daniel R., III 501
David 417, 438*
David D. 417*, 418, 483
David R. 358
De Forest 459*
Dwight J. 432
Frank M. 570
Fitz-John 407*, 408
Gilchrist 95, 99
Henry K. 154
Horace 579
James 67
James D. 370, 425
James M. 26, 40
John 59, 60, 61
John C. 456
Joseph E. 548
Katherine Anne 587, 602, 603
Keith R. 607
Lawrence C. 580*
Lester G. 544
Marshall M. 579
Noah 487
Paul A. 443
Peter A. 160
Peter B. 25, 40, 61, 62, 65
Quincy 586
Ray E. 401, 414
Robert W., Jr. 405
Stephen G. 166, 169, 172, 175, 178, 182, 185, 188, 192, 195
Timothy H. 73
William H. 545
William J. 423, 433, 437
William N. 402
PORTERFIELD, John D. 572
PORTH, J.P. 455
PORTEUS, Morgan 518
PORTIER, Michael 527
POSEY
Francis B. 132
Thomas 62, 311
POSPISILIK, Theophilus 480
POSSEHL, John 558
POST
A.M. 333
George A. 128
George B. 567, 590
James D. 166, 169
James H. 603
Jotham, Jr. 64
Levi A. 570
Philip S. 132, 134, 137, 139
POSVAR, Wesley W. 479
POTEAT
Edwin M. 470
Hubert M. 579
William L. 484
POTHIER, Aram J. 362, 363
POTOFSKY, Jacob S. 557
POTT
John 9
W.S.A. 470
POTTER
A.A. 573
Allen 119
Alonzo 506, 521
Charles E. 223, 226, 230, 233, 236, 239, 323
Charles N. 387
Clarkson N. 113, 115, 117, 121, 564
David M. 567, 601
Eliphalet N. 472, 483
Elisha R. 54, 55, 62, 63, 64
Elisha R., Jr. 88
Emery D. 88, 93
George W. 585
Henry C. 507, 520
Horatio 506, 520
Howard 590
Howard W. 557
John F. 101, 103, 105
John M. 472
Orlando B. 128
Robert 76, 78
Robert B. 408, 409
Samuel J. 58, 361
William 431
William K. 459
William P. 418
William W. 83
POTTHAST, Edward H. 593
POTTLE, Emory B. 101, 103
POTTS
Charles E. 479
David, Jr. 78, 79, 81, 83
David M. 224
Frederick A. 551*
R.D. 419
Richard 6, 52*, 53, 316
Stacy 462
Thomas R. 460
POTZGER, John E. 575
POU, Edward W. 151, 154, 157, 160, 162, 165, 168, 171, 175, 178, 181, 185, 188, 191, 194, 198, 201
POUCH, Mrs. William H. 579
POUGH, Frederick H. 502
POULLADA, Leon B. 438
POULSON, Norris 216, 222, 226, 229, 232, 456
POUND
Cuthbert W. 346
Ezra 589
Roscoe 563, 589
Thaddenus C. 122, 124, 126
POUSETTE-DART, Richard 593
POVICH, Kenneth J. 525
POWEL
C.A. 576
Samuel 458*
POWELL
A.M. 459
Adam Clayton, Jr. 221, 224, 227, 230, 233, 237, 240, 243, 246, 249, 253, 256, 259
Alfred H. 73
Ben H. 579
Benjamin E. 568
Chilton 515, 521
Cuthbert 87
David 265
Dawn 611
E. Burnley 590
E.I. 536
Herbert B. 404, 405, 433
James W. 563, 574
John W. 443
Joseph 119
Lazarus 102, 104, 106, 308, 309
Leonard J. 484
Levin 56
Lewis F., Jr. 270, 565*
Lyman P. 472
Noble C. 513, 520
Paulus 94, 95, 98, 99, 101
Radford G. 559
Samuel 66
Sumner Chilton 587
Theophilus O. 571
Thomas R. 571
Walter E. 262, 265
Wesley 339
William F. 427, 429
POWELSON, W.V.N. 553
POWER
Cornelius M. 529
F.D. 536
J.B. 477
Thomas C. 135, 138, 140, 331
Thomas S. 415*
W. 470
POWERS
Abigail 20
Caleb 164, 167, 170, 173
Charles A. 565
D. Lane 201, 204, 207, 211, 214, 217, 220
E.B. 575
George M. 376, 377
Gershom 76
Grover F. 592, 599
H. Henry 139, 141, 144, 147, 149
J.D. 564
J.F. 602
James E. 568
James K. 465
Joseph N. 475*
Justin L. 609
Llewellyn 121, 150, 153, 156, 159, 314
Ridgley C. 326
Samuel L. 151, 153
Sanger R. 566
Sidney 564
Thomas 588
Winn 460
POWNALL, Thomas 8
POYNTER, William A. 333
PRACHT, C. Frederick 218
PRAEGER, Emil H. 591
PRALL, Anning S. 185, 188, 191, 194, 198, 201, 443
PRASSE, Arthur T. 566
PRATHER, William L. 482
PRATOR, Ralph 481
PRATT
Benjamin 10
Charles 479
Charles C. 163
Daniel D. 112, 114, 116, 302, 444
E. Spencer 434
Eliza Jane 221
Frederick 502
George O., Jr. 502
Haraden 598
Harcourt J. 188, 191, 194, 198
Harry H. 171, 174
Harry N. 498
Henry C. 411*
Henry O. 116, 118
Hiram 450*
James T. 96
John (coll. pres.) 469
John (Mil.) 401
Joseph M. 218
Le Gage 159
Nathan P. 471

Perry W. 596
Richardson, Jr. 479
Robert 457
Ruth S.B. 194, 198
Thomas G. 93, 95, 97, 98, 316*
Wallace E. 564, 590, 601, 608
Walter M. 575*
William V. 416, 419
Zadock 83, 88
PRATTE, Bernard 460
PRAY
Charles N. 159, 162, 165
James S. 573
PREBLE, William P. 433
PRELLWITZ, Henry 593
PRENDERGAST, Edmond F. 524
PRENTER, William B. 557
PRENTICE
Donald B. 474
Samuel O. 288
PRENTIS
H.W., Jr. 578
Robert R. 380
PRENTISS
Benjamin M. 407
John H. 83, 84
Samuel 78, 80, 81, 83, 85, 87, 375
Sergeant S. 82
William A. 456
PRESCOTT
Albert B. 563, 565
Benjamin F. 338
Cyrus D. 124, 126
Henry W. 570
Kenneth W. 500
Stedman 318
W.B. 558
PRESS, Ernst 534
PRESSEY, Julia C. 595
PRESSLY, John T. 533
PRESTON
Francis 53, 54
G. Merritt 611
Jacob A. 87
James H. 450, 579
James P. 378
John F. 402
Maurice A. 416
Miles B. 454
Prince H., Jr. 223, 226, 229, 232, 235, 238, 241
Robert J. 571
Samuel 458
Thomas J., Jr. 485
Thomas R. 564
Walter 392, 393
Willard 484
William 95, 96, 395, 437
William B. 26, 42, 92, 392, 393
William C. 80, 81, 83, 85, 86, 364, 452, 481
PRESTOPINO, Gregorio 589
PRETTYMAN
Cornelius W. 469
E. Barrett 272
PREUS
J.A.O. 535
Jacob A.O. 324
PREUSS, Edward 599
PREWITT, Alan M. 371
PREYER, L. Richardson 259, 262, 265
PRICE
Alan 610
Andrew (Rep.) 135, 137, 140, 142
Andrew 549
Byron 585
C. Melvin 219, 223, 226, 229, 232, 235, 242, 245, 248, 251, 255, 258, 261, 264
Charles C. 565
Don K. 564
Emory H. 216, 219, 222
Gwilym A. 554*, 596
Hiram 106, 108, 110, 120, 123
Hollis F. 534
Mrs. Holton R., Jr. 576
Hugh H. 131
James F. 469
James H. 380
James L. 353
Jesse D. 168, 171, 174
John G. 574
Leontyne 608, 611
Malcolm 478
Robert D. 256, 260, 263, 266
Robert T. 307
Rodman M. 95, 340
Samuel 120, 383
Sterling 89, 329, 394
Thomas L. 105, 455
Thomas R. 577
William C. 444
William J. 434
William P. 112, 114
William T. 129, 131
PRICHARD, Vernon E. 415*
PRICKETT
Fay B. 414, 415
H.E. 450
PRIDE, Alfred M. 417*
PRIDEMORE, Auburn L. 122
PRIDGEON, John, Jr. 453
PRIDMORE, Howard J. 491
PRIEST
Degory 3
I.G. 580
Ira A. 465
Ivy Baker 444
J. Percy 215, 218, 221, 225, 228, 231, 234, 237
John W. 461*
PRIESTLEY, James T. 565
PRIEUR, Denis 457
PRIME, S. Irenaeus 485
PRIMEAU, Ernest J. 527
PRIMM, James N. 472
PRINCE
Charles H. 110
David C. 576, 599
Frederick H. 543
Frederick O. 450*
George W. 142, 145, 147, 150, 153, 156, 158, 161, 164
John D. 427, 436, 439
John S. 460*
Morton 569
Oliver H. 74, 295
Thomas 8*
William 71
William Wood 543*
PRINDLE, Elizur H. 115
PRINGEY, Joseph C. 181
PRINGLE
Benjamin 97, 99
Edward E. 286*
George H. 549
Henry F. 584
James R. 451
Joel R.P. 419
William H. 576
PRIOLEAU, Samuel 451
PRIOR
Frank O. 552*
Harris K. 500*
PRITCHARD
George M. 194
Jeter C. 141, 143, 146, 149, 151, 271, 348
Stuart 492
Thomas H. 484
PRITCHETT
C. Herman 571
Harold 558
Henry S. 475, 491
PRITZLAFF, John C., Jr. 432
PROBST, Charles O. 572
PROCHNOW, Herbert V. 547
PROCTER, William C. 551*
PROCTOR
A. Philmister 591
Carlton S. 572
Fletcher D. 376
James M. 272
John R. 445
Mortimer R. 377
Ralph E. 462
Redfield 29, 40, 139, 141, 144, 147, 149, 152, 155, 158, 160, 376*, 377
W. Theodore 462
PROFFIT, George H. 84, 85, 424
PROFFITT, David W. 532
PROKNOW, Donald E. 554
PROKOP, Stanley A. 243
PROKOSCH, Eduard 577
PROMISEL, N.E. 572
PROSSER
C. Ladd 571, 573
Seward 544
William F. 113
PROUDFIT, Andrew 456
PROUT, Frank J. 466
PROUTY
George H. 376
Solomon F. 164, 167
Winston L. 231, 234, 237, 240, 244, 247, 250, 253, 257, 260, 263, 377
PROVOOST, Samuel 505, 520
PROVOST, David 457
PROVOSTY, Oliver O. 312
PROXMIRE, William 241, 244, 247, 250, 254, 257, 260, 263, 266, 386
PRUDEN, Edward H. 534
PRUGH, George S. 402
PRUIS, John J. 466
PRUITT, Robert G. 574
PRUYN
John V. L. 107, 111
Robert H. 431
Robert L. 450
PRYER, Thomas M. 531
PRYOR
David H. 254, 257, 260
Luke 122, 127, 277
Roger A. 103, 392, 393
Samuel B. 452
PUCHTA, George 452
PUCINSKI, Roman C. 242, 245, 248, 251, 255, 258, 261
PUCK, Theodore 600
PUCKETT, Allen E. 567
PUELICHER, John H. 564
PUGH
George E. 99, 101, 103, 352
Herbert L. 416
James L. 102, 122, 124, 127, 129, 131, 134, 136, 139, 142, 277, 392, 393
John 59, 60
John H. 121
Samuel J. 142, 145, 148
PUGSLEY
Cornelius A. 151, 579
Jacob J. 133, 136
PUHAN, Alfred 430
PUJO, Arsene P. 153, 156, 159, 162, 165
PULESTON
Dennis 608
W.D. 416
PULITZER, Joseph 131
PULLEN, Eugene H. 564
PULLIAM
Roscoe 481
Samuel 459
PULSIFER, Harold T. 580
PUMPELLY, Raphael 575
PUPIN, Michael I. 563, 583, 594, 596, 598, 603
PURCELL
Clare 530
Edward M. 570, 606
Ganson 445
Graham 247, 250, 253, 256, 260, 263
John B. 487, 523, 525
R.R. 454*
William E. 162, 350
PURDOM, W.A. 454
PURDY
Lawson 579
Smith M. 88
PURINTON, Daniel B. 469, 485*
PURMAN, William J. 116, 118
PURNELL
Benjamin 538
Fred S. 173, 176, 180, 183, 187, 190, 193, 196
William H. 469
PURSLEY, Leo A. 526
PURTELL, William A. 232, 235, 238, 289*
PURVIANCE
Samuel A. 99, 101
Samuel D. 58
PURYEAR
Bennett 480*
Charles 482
Richard C. 97, 99, 392
PUSEY
Merlo J. 585, 591
Nathan M. 472, 474, 604
William A. 569
William H.M. 127
William W., 3d 485
PUSHKAREV, Boris 602
PUTNAM
C.A. 578
Daniel 473
Emily James (Smith) 466
Frederic W. 499, 501*, 563, 595
Frederick W., Jr. 517
Harvey 83, 91, 93
Herbert 444, 568, 600, 609
Israel 406
James J. 569
James O. 424, 477
James W. (b. 1860) 569
James W. (b. 1865) 467*
Rufus 402
William L. 271
PUTT, Donald R. 415
PYE, William S. 419
PYLE
Ernest T. (Ernie) 585
Gladys 208, 367
Howard 280
Howard C. 567
PYLES, Thomas 566
PYNCHON
Thomas 609
Thomas R. 482
PYNE, Percy R. 547

Q

QUA, Stanley E. 321
QUACKENBUSH, John A. 135, 138
QUAIN, Edwin A. 471
QUARLES
Donald A. 399, 576, 608
James M. 103
Joseph V. 149, 152, 155, 385
Julian M. 149
Louis 491
Tunstall 66, 68
QUARRY, Robert 9
QUARTER, William 525
QUARTERMAN, George H. 514, 521
QUAY, Mathew S. 133, 136, 138, 141, 143, 146, 149, 151, 154, 359*
QUAYLE
John F. 185, 188, 191, 194
William A. 466, 530
QUEEN
Frank B. 572
Stuart A. 573
QUEENAN, John W. 567
QUEENY
Edgar Monsanto 549*
John F. 549*
QUENEAU, Paul 595
QUENSTEDT, Walter E. 449
QUESADA, Elwood R. 415
QUIE, Albert H. 239, 242, 245, 249, 252, 255, 258, 261, 265
QUIGG, Lemuel E. 141, 143, 146
QUIGLEY
James E. 523, 525
James M. 237, 243
QUILL, Michael J. 559
QUILLEN, James H. 250, 253, 256, 260, 263, 266
QUIMBY, J.F. 408
QUIN
C.K. 461*
Clinton S. 511, 522
Percy E. 168, 171, 174, 181, 184, 187, 191, 194, 197
QUINAN, Matthew 559
QUINBY
Henry B. 338
William E. 433
QUINCY
Josiah (b. 1772) 59, 60, 61, 62, 450, 472
Josiah, Jr. 450
Josiah P. (b. 1859) 450
Samuel M. 457
QUINE, Williard V. 593
QUINETTE, E.N. 458
QUINLAN
Francis J. 599
John 527
Patrick J. 559
QUINLIN, Simon 574
QUINN
Daniel J. 470
Huston 456
J. Herbert 452
James L. (Rep.) 205, 208
James L. 500
John 135
John R. 568
Peter A. 221
Robert E. 363
T. Vincent 227, 230
Terence J. 121
W. William 405
William F. 298
William J. 545
QUINTARD, Charles T. 481, 506, 522
QUINTON
Cornelia B. Sage 497*
Harold 552*
QUISENBERRY, H.N. 482
QUITMAN, John A. 99, 100, 326*

QUYNN, Allen 449*

R

RAAB, George 499
RABASSA, Gregory 602
RABAUT, Louis C. 204, 207, 210, 213, 217, 220, 226, 230, 233, 236, 239, 242, 245
RABI, Isidor I. 570, 591, 594, 605
RABIN, Benjamin J. 221, 224
RABING, Albert 580
RABINOW, Jacob 601
RABINOWITZ, Jay A. 279
RABORN, William F. 594
RABUN, William 295
RACE, John A. 254
RADCLIFF
Jacob 458*
Wallace 532
RADCLIFFE
Amos H. 177, 181
George L. 203, 207, 210, 213, 217, 220, 318
RADDIN, Charles S. 498
RADEMACHER, Joseph 526, 527
RADER
Frank 456
I. Andrew 491
RADFORD
Arthur W. 399, 416, 417*
William 107, 109
William A. 443
RADWAN, Edmund P. 230, 233, 237, 240
RAE, C.W. 418
RAFFEL, Mrs. Alvin 498
RAFFERTY, William 480
RAFTERY
Lawrence M. 558
S. Frank 558
RAGEN, Joseph E. 566
RAGON, Heartsill 183, 186, 189, 193, 196, 199
RAGSDALE
B.A. 462
Isaac N. 449
J. Williard 169, 172, 175, 178
RAGUET, Condy 547
RAHN
A.A.D. 579
Herman 571
RAICHLE, Frank G. 565
RAILSBACK, Thomas F. 255, 258, 261, 264
RAIN, Frank L. 574
RAINE, Herbert W. 452
RAINES
John 135, 138
Richard C. 531
RAINEY
Henry T. 153, 156, 158, 161, 164, 167, 170, 173, 176, 183, 187, 190, 193, 196, 199, 200
Homer P. 467, 482*
John W. 173, 176, 180
Joseph H. 113, 115, 117, 119, 122
Lilius B. 176, 179
Robert M. 355
RAINIE, Herbert W. 452
RAINS, Albert 219, 222, 225, 228, 232, 235, 238, 241, 244, 247
RAINWATER, Herbert R. 580
RAKER, John E. 164, 167, 170, 173, 176, 179, 183
RALLS
Charles C. 580
John P. 392
RALSTON
Samuel M. 183, 303*
William E. 580
RAMAGE, Lawson P. 417
RAMALEY, Francis 575
RAMBAUT, Thomas 486
RAMBIN, J. Howard, Jr. 553*
RAMER, John E. 434
RAMEY
Frank M. 193
Homer A. 218, 221, 224
RAMMELKAMP, Charles H., Jr. 589
RAMPTON, Calvin L. 374
RAMSAY
David 7
Erskine 610
Francis M. 418, 483
George D. 402
Nathaniel 6
Robert H. 594
Robert L. 202, 205, 209, 215, 228, 231
RAMSDELL, George A. 338
RAMSEUR, S.D. 395
RAMSEY
Alexander 28, 29, 40, 88, 90, 106, 108, 110, 112, 114, 116, 324*, 460
DeWitt C. 417*
James G. 393
John R. 174, 177
Lloyd B. 403
Robert 79, 86
William 75, 76
William M. 460
William S. 85
RAMSEYER, C. William 170, 173, 176, 180, 183, 187, 190, 193, 197
RAMSPECK, Robert C.W. 193, 196, 200, 203, 206, 209, 213, 216, 219, 445
RAND
A.C. 457*
Austin L. 569
Edward K. 570, 577
George F. 549
Robert L. 443
William McN. 549
RANDALL
Alexander 86
Alexander W. 27, 43, 385, 434
Benjamin (b. 1789) 84, 86
Benjamin (b. 1749) 538
Blanchard 580
Charles H. 170, 173, 176
Charles S. 135, 137, 140
Clarence B. 548*, 608, 609
Clifford A. 580
Clifford E. 179
Edwin J. 513
Edwin M. 293
George M. 506, 519
Harrison M. 570
James G. 567, 591
Jesse W. 553
John 449*
John D. 565
Richard H. 502
Samuel J. 107, 109, 111, 113, 115, 117, 118, 119, 120, 122*, 124, 126, 128, 131, 133, 136
William H. 106, 108
William J. 242, 246, 249, 252, 255, 258, 262, 265
RANDELL, Choice B. 152, 155, 157, 160, 163, 166
RANDOLPH
A. Philip 608, 611
Alfred M. 507, 522
Beverly 9, 378
Edmund (b. 1753) 4, 7, 9, 23*, 38, 41
Evan 551
George W. 391
Isham 594
James F. 74, 76, 77
James H. 122
Jennings 202, 205, 209, 212, 215, 219, 222, 241, 244, 247, 250, 254, 257, 260, 263, 266, 384
John 56, 57, 58, 59, 61, 62, 63, 66, 69, 70, 72, 73*, 75, 80, 378, 436
Joseph F. 82, 84, 86
Lucretia 20
Peyton 5, 7
Theodore F. 119, 121, 123, 340*
Thomas M. 58, 59, 378
Victor M. 396
Wallace F. 401
Woodruff 558
RANEY
George P. 293
J.A. 576
John H. 143
RANGEL, Charles B. 262, 265
RANKIN
Alan C. 473
Christopher 68, 69, 71, 73
Fred W. 565, 569
George A. 600
James D. 533
Jeannette 174, 214
Jeremiah 472
John E. 181, 184, 187, 191, 194, 197, 200, 204, 207, 210, 214, 217, 220, 227, 230
Joseph 129 131
Karl L. 425*, 439
Raymond C. 483
Walter L. 467*
Watson S. 572
William J. 454
RANKINE, James 472
RANNEY
Ambrose A. 125, 128, 130
Rufus P. 352
RANSDELL, Joseph E. 148, 150, 153, 156, 159, 162, 165, 167, 170, 173, 177, 180, 184, 187, 190, 193, 312
RANSIER, Alonzo J. 117
RANSLEY, Harry C. 178, 182, 185, 188, 192, 195, 198, 201, 205
RANSOM
Epaphroditus 322
Harry H. 482
John Crowe 589, 592*, 600, 602, 603
Matt W. 115, 117, 119, 121, 124, 126, 128, 131, 133, 135, 138, 139, 141, 348, 433
Paul L. 414
Robert 394
Thomas E.G. 409*
Truman B. 478
William L. 565, 589
RANTOUL
Robert, Jr. 93, 95, 319
Robert S. 460, 498
RAO, Paul P. 273
RAPIER, James T. 115
RAPINE, Daniel 462
RAPP, George 538
RAPPE, Amedeus 525
RAQUET, Condy 424
RARICK, John R. 255, 258, 261, 264
RARIDEN, James 82, 84
RASSWEILER, C.F. 565
RATCHFORD, C. Brice 476
RATCLIFFE, John 9
RATH, George E. 517
RATHBONE
Henry R. 183, 187, 190
Jared L. 449
Josephine A. 568
M.J. 553*, 590
Perry T. 498, 500
RATHBUN
George O. 88, 90
Richard 502
RATHJE, Frank C. 564
RATHVON, Lora C. 536
RATLIFF, Fred 576
RATNER, Payne H. 307
RATSHESKY, Abraham C. 426
RATTNER, Abraham 593
RAUB, Albert N. 469
RAUCH
Frederick A. 470
George W. 158, 161, 164, 167, 170
Henry E. 544
John Henry 571
RAUDEBAUGH, Robert 572
RAUM, Green B. 110, 444
RAUSCH, C.J. 454
RAUSCHENBERG, Robert 593
RAUSCHENBERGER, William G. 456
RAUSCHER, Russell T. 516, 520
RAUSHENBUSH, Esther 481
RAVDIN, Isidor S. 565*
RAVENEL
Mazyck P. 572
William deC 502
RAVENSCROFT, John S. 505, 521
RAVNDAL, Christian M. 426, 427, 430, 439
RAWLE, Francis 564
RAWLINGS
Edwin W. 415, 547*
Isaac 456*
Marjorie Kinnan 584
RAWLINS
John A. 28, 40
Joseph L. 146, 149, 152, 374
RAWLS, Morgan 116
RAWSON, Charles A. 180, 305
RAY
George W. 128, 138, 141, 143, 146, 148, 151
Gordon N. 491
Isaac 571
James B. 302
John H. 233, 237, 240, 243, 246
Joseph W. 136
Means R. 455
Ossian 123, 126, 128
Reid H. 580
Robert D. (Ia.) 305
Robert D. (Mo.) 329
Walter J.L. 576
William H. 116
RAYBURN, Sam 169, 172, 175, 182, 185, 189, 192, 195, 199, 202, 205, 208, 209, 212, 215, 216, 218, 219, 222, 225*, 228*, 231, 234, 235, 237, 238, 240, 241, 244*, 247
RAYFIEL, Leo F. 221, 224
RAYMOND
Andrew Van V. 483
Arthur E. 597, 608, 611
Benjamin W. 451*
Bradford P. 474, 485
Henry J. 109
Jerome H. 482, 485
John H. 484
John M. 460
RAYNER
Isidor 132, 137, 140, 156, 159, 162, 165, 317
Kenneth 84, 86, 88
RAYNOR, John P. 474
RAYTON, W.B. 580
RE, Edward D. 273
REA
David 119, 121
George P. 470
John (Pa.) 58, 59, 60, 61, 64
John (Fla.) 461
Paul M. 502
Samuel 596
William C. 558
READ
Allen W. 566
Almon H. 86, 88
Charles 10, 458
Conyers 567
Daniel 476
George 3, 4, 5, 51*, 52, 290
George W. 410
George W., Jr. 405, 415
Granville M. 590
Harold J. 575
Henry E. 393
Jacob 7, 54*, 55, 56, 364
John 551
John M. 359, 429
Nathan 55, 56
William B. 114, 116
READE, Edwin G. 99, 392
READING
John 8
John R. 113
Richard W. 453
READY
Charles 97, 99, 101
Michael J. 525
Thomas J., Jr. 548
REAGAN
John H. 101, 103, 120, 122, 124, 126, 129, 131, 133, 136, 138, 372, 391, 392
Ronald 284, 559*
REAMER, W.S. 452
REAMES, Alfred E. 208, 357
REAMS
Henry F. 231, 234
R. Borden 426, 431, 434, 438, 439
REARDON, Lambert J. 455
REAVIS
C. Frank 171, 174, 177, 181
James B. 381
REBAY, Hilla 499
REBER
Grote 594
John 178, 182
W.H. 454
RECK, John 455
RECTANUS, Earl F. 416
RECTOR, Henry M. 281
RED, John W., Jr. 492
REDDEN, Monroe M. 224, 227, 230
REDDING
B.B. 460
Charles S. 575
REDFIELD
Alfred C. 575
Edward W. 589, 593, 607*, 610
Isaac F. 375
Robert 611

William C. 31, 32, 46, 165, 579, 603
REDFORD, Emmette S. 571
REDING, John R. 86, 88
REDINGTON, Alfred 449
REDLIN, Rolland 253
REDLON, Reginald 480
REDMAN, L.V. 565
REDMOND
Ernest R. 402
Roland L. 566
William P. 559
REECE
B. Carroll 182, 185, 189, 192, 195, 202, 205, 208, 212, 215, 218, 221, 231, 234, 237, 240, 244, 247
Louise G. 247
Roy R. 461
REED
Alfred 462
B.L. 483
Charles A.L. 569
Charles M. 88
Chauncey W. 203, 206, 210, 213, 216, 219, 223, 226, 229, 232, 235
Clyde M. 210, 213, 216, 220, 223, 226, 306, 307
D.C. 461
Daniel A. 178, 181, 185, 188, 191, 194, 198, 201, 204, 208, 211, 214, 217, 221, 224, 227, 230, 233, 237, 240, 243
David A. 182, 185, 188, 191, 195, 201, 359
David B. 517
Edward C. 78
Elmer E. 486
Eugene E. 168
Geroge E. 469
Harrison 293
Isaac 95
J. Theodore ,563
James A. 165, 168, 171, 174, 177, 181, 184, 187, 191, 330, 455
James B. 183, 186, 189
James W. 458
John (b. 1751) 54, 55
John (b. 1781) 64, 65, 69, 71, 72, 74, 76, 77, 79, 81, 82, 84
John F. 476, 575
John H. 315
John S. 543
Joseph 4, 7, 9, 401
Joseph R. 134
Lowell J. 473, 572, 610
Marshall R. 531
P. Barker 456
Philip 59, 60, 61, 62, 66, 69, 316
R. Glenn, Jr. 576
Ralph D. 564
Robert R. 94
S. Albert 594
Samuel 576
Stanley F. 270
Stuart F. 175, 179, 182, 186
Vergil D. 568
Victor J. 527
Walter 597
Walter L. 402
William B. 425
REEDER
John W. 536
William A. 148, 150, 153, 156, 159, 161
REEL, A.H. 451
REES
Edward H. 206, 210, 213, 216, 220, 223, 226, 229, 232, 236, 239, 242
Mina 564
Rollin R. 164
Thomas M. 251, 254, 257, 260, 263
REESE
B.D. 600
Charles L. 565
David A. 96
Everett D. 564
Frederick F. 509, 519
Hans H.F. 569
Lizette W. 610
Manoah B. 333*
Seaborn 125, 127, 129
Theodore I. 510, 522
W.S. 457
William B. 482
REESER, Edwin B. 570
REEVE, Tapping 287
REEVES
Albert L., Jr. 224
Charles F. 484
George P. 517, 519
Henry A. 113
Ira L. 478
James E. 572
James H. 400
Jesse S. 571
Milton O. 600
Raymond J. 416
Walter 142, 145, 147, 150
REFFIELD, William C. 563
REGAN
H.C., Jr. 600
Kenneth M. 225, 228, 231, 234
REGULA, Ralph S. 265
REH, Francis F. 525, 528
REHAK, Peter 607
REHNQUIST, William H. 270
REHRING, George J. 529
REHWINKEL, Frederick H. 566
REICHELDERFER, Luther H. 462
REICHER, Louis J. 525
REID
Benjamin L. 587
C.C. 576
Charles C. 150, 152, 155, 158, 161
Charles S. 297
Charlotte T. 248, 251, 255, 258, 261
David S. 88, 90, 97, 347*
Frank R. 183, 187, 190, 193, 196, 200
Harry F. 566
Helen Rogers 609
James 476
James R. 7
James W. (b. 1849) 128, 131
James W. (b. 1900) 459
John W. 105
Joseph H. 610
Ogden R. 249, 253, 256, 259, 262, 265, 431
Richard 599
Robert 593
Robert R. 66, 68, 69
Whitelaw 17, 429
William S. 471
William T. 467
REIFEL, Benjamin 247, 250, 253, 256, 259
REIFF, Evan A. 471
REIFSNIDER, Charles S. 511
REILLY
George R. 577
George V. 552
James B. 119, 122, 136, 138, 141
James W. 410
John 119
John W. 589
Michael K. 169, 172, 196, 199, 202, 205, 209
Thomas L. 164, 167
Wilson 101
REILY, Luther 83
REIMANN, Stanley P. 572
REINARTZ, Leo F. 567, 595
REINBURG, J.E. 483
REINECKE, Ed 251, 254
REINERT
Carl M. 469
Paul C. 480
REINHARDT
Aurelia H. 475
Emil F. 412*, 414*
G. Frederick 431, 439*
John E. 434
REINHART
C.S. 458
Stanley E. 413, 414
REINHEIMER, Bartel H. 513, 521
REINSCH, Paul S. 425, 571
REISCHAUER, Edwin O. 431
REISMAN, Philip 598
REISTLE, Carl E., Jr. 567, 601
REITT, L.M. 391
REITZ, J. Wayne 470
RELFE, James H. 89, 90
REMEY, William B. 416
REMINGTON
Harvey F. 579
John W. 564
William P. 511, 519
REMINICK, Seymour 589
REMMEL, Pratt C. 456
REMSEN
Henry 545
Ira 473, 563, 565, 596, 608
RENCHARD
George W. 424
William S. 545*
RENCHER, Abraham 76, 78, 79, 81, 83, 86, 435
RENCKER, Robert W. 553
RENNE, Roland R. 476
RENNEBOHM, Oscar 386
RENNEKER, George J. 469
RENO, Jesse L. 407
RENOUARD, Edward I. 610
RENQUIST, William H. 270
RENTSCHLER
Frederick B. 554, 597
Gordon S. 547*
REPHLO, Louis S. 455
REPLOGLE, Luther J. 430
REPPLIER, Agnes 599, 603
RESA, Alexander J. 219
RESE, Frederick 526
RESNICK, Joseph Y. 253, 256
RESOR, Stanley R. 399
RESSLER, Herschel 558
RESTARICK, Henry B. 509, 519
RESTON, James 585, 586, 595
RETTGER, Robert E. 564
REUS-FROYLAN, Francisco 521
REUSS, Henry S. 238, 241, 244, 247, 250, 254, 257, 260, 263, 266
REUTER, Edward B. 573
REUTHER, Walter P. 559
REUTTER, J.G. 455
REVELEY, W. Taylor 471
REVELS, Hiram R. 112, 326
REVERCOMB, W. Chapman 219, 222, 225, 238, 241, 384*
REVERMAN, Theodore H. 529
REX, George 353
REXFORD, E.L. 465
REXROTH, Kenneth 610
REYBOLD, Eugene 401, 402
REYBURN
John E. 136, 138, 141, 143, 157, 458
William S. 166
REYERSON, Lloyd H. 567
REYNOLDS
Arthur 546, 564
Charles R. 403
Edward (b. 1860) 501
Edward 565
Edwin 573
Edwin R. 103
Fidelis 480
George M. 564
Gideon 91, 93
Henry E. 456
Ignatius A. 525
James B. 66, 72
John (Ga.) 8
John (Ill.) 78, 80, 84, 85, 300
John F. 407, 408*
John H. 612
John H. (Rep.) 103
John M. 157, 160, 163
John W. 386
Joseph 81
Joseph J. 409
Powell B. 485*
Richard J. 552
Richard S., Sr. 552*
Richard S., Jr. 552*
Robert J. 291
Robert M. 424
Robert R. 198, 201, 204, 208, 211, 214, 218, 349
Samuel W. 233, 334
Thomas (Ill.) 300, 329
Thomas H. 466
W.E. 483
W.M. 467
Walter H. 459
William F. 445
William N. 552*
RHAWN, William H. 564
RHEA
Frank A. 513, 519
John 58, 59, 60, 62, 63, 64, 67, 69, 70
John S. 145, 148, 150, 153
William F. 149, 152
RHEEM, Richard S. 498
RHEES, Rush 480
RHETT
John T. 452
R. Goodwin 451, 574
R. Barnwell 83, 85, 87, 88, 90, 92, 94, 364, 391, 392
RHETTS, Charles E. 432
RHINELANDER, Philip M. 510
RHINOCK, Joseph L. 156, 159, 162
RHOADES
Donald A. 548
Edward H., Jr. 534
RHOADS
James E. 467
Jonathan E. 565*
Samuel 7, 458
RHODE, Paul P. 526
RHODES
Allen F. 573
George M. 228, 231, 234, 237, 240, 243, 246, 250, 253, 256
James A. 354, 452
James Ford 567, 583, 603
John J. 232, 235, 238, 241, 244, 247, 251, 254, 257, 260, 263
Marion E. 156, 177, 181
Stephen H. 548
RHYNE, Charles S. 565, 589
RIBICOFF, Abraham A. 36, 47, 226, 229, 248, 251, 254, 257, 260, 264, 289*
RICAUD, James B. 98, 100
RICE
A.D. 452
A. Hamilton 599
Alexander H. 102, 104, 106, 108, 320, 450
Americus V. 119, 121
Baldwin 454*
Benjamin F. 109, 111, 113, 281
Benjamin H. 532
Caleb 549
David B. 474
Donald B. 576
E. Wilbur, Jr. 595
Edmund 132, 460*
Edward Y. 114
Elial J. 466
Elliott W. 409
Elmer 574, 583
Harvey M. 474
Henry M. 100, 102, 104, 324
John B. (b. 1832) 126
John B. (b. 1809) 116, 451
John H. (Me.) 104, 106, 108, 532
John J. 485*, 486
John L. 572
John M. 112, 114
John S. 433
Joseph J. 525
M.C. 454
Nathan L. 485, 532
Nathaniel 9
Norman S. 497
Paul N. 568
Robert E. 477
Samuel F. 277
Theron M. 125
Thomas 65, 66
Walter L. 423
William 462
William W. 121, 123, 125, 128, 130
RICH
Adrienne 610
Bennett M. 485
Carl W. 249, 452*
Charles 64, 67, 69, 70, 72
Charles W.G. 405
Daniel C. 497, 502
Giles S. 273
John T. 125, 322
Raymond A. 544
Robert F. 195, 198, 201, 205, 208, 211, 215, 221, 224, 228
RICHARD, Paul 458
RICHARDS
Arthur L. 428
Benjamin W. 458
Charles L. 184
Charles R. 474
Cyril F. 469
D.W. 606
David E. 515
DeForest 387
G.M. 600
George W. 534
I.A. 592, 600
J.H. 450
J. Havens 471
Jacob 58, 59, 60
James 532
James A.D. 141
James P. 202, 205, 208,

211, 215, 218, 221, 225, 228, 231, 234, 237
John (Pa.) 54
John (N.Y.) 71
John G. 366
John K. 271
John N. 567
John S. 568
Joseph W. 575
Laura E. 583
Mark 67, 69
Matthias 60, 61
Paul B. 564
R.Q. 570
Theodore W. 563*, 565, 596*, 605, 609
W.C. 584
Wallace 497
Wayne E. 580
William A. 387
William T. 607
RICHARDSON
A.R. 462
David P. 124, 126
Dean E. 549
Edgar P. 498
Elliot L. 36, 37, 47
Ernest C. 568
Ernest G. 530
Friend W. 284
George F. 140
H.G. 458
H. Smith, Jr. 492
Harold D. 465
Harry A. 158, 161, 164, 291
Israel B. 407*
J.A. 460
J. Milton 517, 522
James A., 3d 402
James D. 131, 133, 136, 138, 141, 144, 146, 149, 152, 155
James L., Jr. 400
James M. 156, 579
James O. 418
James R. 364
James T., Jr. 405
John P. 81, 83, 364, 365
John S. 124, 126
Joseph 74, 76
Robert C., Jr. 404, 411, 412
Rupert N. 471
Scovel 273
Tobias G. 569
W.R. 536
Wayne 607
William (Ala.) 147, 150, 152, 155, 158, 161, 164, 167
William (Va.) 459
William A. (b. 1811) 91, 92, 94, 96, 98, 104*, 106, 300
William A. (b. 1821) 39, 273
William E. 201, 205
William F. 536
William S. 547
RICHERT, William 453
RICHESON, Forrest L. 536
RICHEY, Thomas 466
RICHMAN, Arthur 574
RICHMOND
Alfred C. 445
Carleton R. 563
Charles A. 483
James B. 124
Hiram L. 117
Jonathan 68
Lewis 435
RICHTER
Conrad 585, 602
Gisela M.A. 591
Henry J. 526
Richard B. 569
RICHTMYER, Floyd K. 570, 580
RICKARDS
George C. 402
John E. 331
RICKENBACKER, Edward V. 546*
RICKETTS
Claude V. 417
Edwin D. 172, 178, 181
Forrest E. 599
James B. 407*, 409
Louis D. 595
RICKEY, George 590
RICKOVER, Hyman G. 595, 609
RICKS
Earl T. 402
Jesse J. 553
RIDDICK
Carl W. 177, 181
F.G. 458
Wallace C. 477
Walter G. 272
RIDDLE
Albert G. 105
David H. 479, 485, 532
George R. 94, 96, 106, 107, 109, 291
Haywood Y. 120, 122
John W. 423, 427, 435, 436*
RIDDLEBERGER
Harrison H. 129, 131, 133, 379
James W. 443
RIDDLER, John G. 455
RIDER
Ira E. 154
R.P. 482
RIDGE
Albert A. 272
Lola 610*
RIDGEDALE, John 3
RIDGELY
Charles C. 316
Henry M. 62, 63, 72, 74, 290
Nicholas 290
Richard 6
RIDGLEY
Edwin R. 145, 148
R., Jr. 483
RIDGWAY
Joseph 83, 85, 86
Matthew B. 400, 404*, 405, 412, 415, 596
Raymond R. 575
Robert (b. 1823) 113
Robert (civil eng.) 572
RIDLEY
Clarence S. 413
J.J. 482
RIDOUT, Samuel 449*
RIEBER, Torkild 553
RIECK, Edward E. 548
RIEGEL, Byron 565
RIEGGER, Wallingford 592
RIEGLE, Donald W., Jr. 255, 258, 261, 265
RIEHLMAN, R. Walter 224, 227, 230, 233, 237, 240, 243, 246, 249
RIES, Heinrich 576
RIETI, Vittorio 611
RIEVE, Emil 559
RIFE, John W. 136, 138
RIGBY, W.O. 462
RIGGE, Joseph 474
RIGGIO, Vincent 543
RIGGS
C.E. 416
Henry E. 572
James M. 127, 130
Jetur R. 103
Lewis 86
Walter M. 468
RIGHTER, Walter C. 520
RIGHTMIRE, George W. 478
RIGHTOR, Edward 574
RIGNEY, Hugh M. 206
RIHL, Charles H. 557
RIKER
C.L. 600
Samuel 58, 60
RILEY
Corinne B. 247
Fletcher 355
Henry A. 569
Herbert D. 399
James Whitcomb 603
John J. 221, 225, 231, 234, 237, 240, 243, 247
Ray L. 576
RINAKER, John I. 142
RINALDO, Matthew J. 265
RINCLIFFE, Roy G. 551
RINER
C.W. 451
William A. 387*, 388
RING, Harold 481
RINGGOLD
Samuel 61, 62, 63, 65
Thomas 3
RINGLAND
Adam W. 474
Albert 600
RINGO, Daniel 281
RIORDAN
Daniel J. 148, 157, 160, 162, 165, 168, 171, 174, 178, 181
Joseph W. 481
Patrick W. 524
RIOTTE, Charles N. 426, 434
RIPLEY
Christopher G. 324
Edward P. 543*
Eleazar W. 80, 82
James W. 402
James W. (Me.) 72, 74, 76
Philip 453
S. Dillon 501, 502
Thomas C. 90
William Z. 566
RIPPEL, Julius A. 492
RISK, Charles F. 205, 211
RISLEY
Elijah 93
John E. 427
RITCHEY, Thomas 92, 97
RITCHIE
Albert C. 317
Andrew C. 497, 502
Byron F. 141
David 97, 99, 101
James M. 126
John 114
Walter B. 576
RITER, C.H., 3d 578
RITNER, Joseph 358
RITTENHOUSE, David 570
RITTER
Burwell C. 108
George 451
John 88, 90
Joseph E. 523*, 524, 526
Louis 454
RITTLE, R.M. 459
RIVERA, Victor M. 517, 521
RIVERO, Horacio 437
RIVERS
Eurith D. 297
L. Mendel 215, 218, 221, 225, 228, 231, 234, 237, 240, 243, 247, 250, 253, 256, 259
Ralph J. 241, 244, 247, 251
Thomas 99
William C. 402
RIVES
Francis E. 83, 85
Lloyd M. 425
Richard T. 271
William C. 72, 73, 75, 77, 78, 80, 81, 83, 85, 87, 88, 378* 392, 393, 428*
Zeno J. 156
RIVKIN, William R. 428, 432, 436
RIVLIN, Harry N. 468
RIX, Carl B. 565
RIXEY, John F. 147, 149, 152, 155, 158
RIXFORD, Gulian P. 497
RIXLEY, Presley M. 416
RIZZO, Frank L. 458
RIZLEY, Ross 214, 218, 221, 224
ROACH
Isaac 458
Sidney C. 181, 184
William N. 141, 143, 146, 350
ROANE
Archibald 369
John 62, 63, 64, 75, 77, 82
John J. 78
John S. 281
William H. 66, 83, 85, 378
ROBARDS, Rachel (Donelson) 20
ROBATHAN, Dorothy M. 570
ROBB
Charles H. 272
Edward 145, 148, 151, 154
Roger 272
ROBBINS
Asher 73, 75, 76, 78, 80, 81, 83, 361
Edward E. 146, 175
Franklin 593
Frederick C. 599, 606
Gaston A. 139, 142, 147
George R. 99, 101
Gilbert F. 459
James J. 465
Jerome 592
John, Jr. 94, 95, 97, 119
Joseph C. 534
Richard W. 553
Thomas J., Jr. 419*
Warren D. 425, 427, 436
William J. 570, 574
William M. (b. 1828) 117, 119, 121
William M. 491
ROBERDEAU, Daniel 4, 7
ROBERT
Mrs. Henry, Jr. 579
Joseph C. 471
Joseph T. 476
ROBERTS
A.J. 454
Albert H. 370
Alexander C. 481
Anthony E. 99, 101
Arthur J. 468
Charles B. 118, 121
David 460
Dennis J. 363, 459
Edward 458
Edwin E. 165, 168, 171, 174
Ellis H. 115, 117, 444
Ernest W. 148, 151, 153, 156, 159, 162, 165, 168, 171
Frank H.H., Jr. 611
George A. 572
Godfrey M. 459*
H. Ray 247, 250, 253, 256, 260
Henry 288
J. Milnor, Jr. 403
John W. 530
Jonathan 63, 64*, 65, 67, 68, 358
Kenneth 586
Kenneth A. 228, 232, 235, 238, 241, 244, 247
Laurance P. 497
Mrs. Laurance P. 497
Morton 589, 591, 593
Oran M. 372*
Owen J. 270, 570
Priscilla 607
Ray 263, 266
Robert R. 530
Robert W. 88, 89
Roy A. 573
Stewart R. 567
Thomas H. 363
Thomas S. 592
W.A. 491
W. Lyn 415
Walter O. 564
William B. 511, 521
Wiliam C. 532
William H. 532
William M. 572
William P. 513
William R. 115, 117, 425
ROBERTSON
A. Willis 202, 205, 209, 212, 215, 218, 222, 225, 228, 231, 234, 237, 241, 244, 247, 250, 253, 380
Albert J. 443
Alice M. 181
Charles F. 506, 520
Charles R. 214, 221, 224
Daniel A. 460
David A. 471
E. Jeff 458
Edward V. 219, 222, 225, 387
Edward W. 121, 123, 125
Elgin B. 576
Felix 457*
George 66, 68, 69, 308
Gustavus A. 449
Howard 500
J.W. 450
James B.A. 355
James Y. 459
John 80, 82, 83
John E. 452
R.E. 455
Reuben B., Jr. 399
Ronald V. 570
Samuel B. 547
Samuel M. 132, 135, 137, 140, 142, 145, 148, 150, 153, 156
T. Hart 594
Thomas A. 127, 130
Thomas B. (La.) 62, 63, 65, 66, 311
Thomas B. 499
Thomas E. 444
Thomas J. 111, 113, 115, 117, 119, 365
W.T. 457
Walter M. 412, 413
William H. 111
Wyndham 378
ROBESON
Edward J., Jr. 228, 231, 234, 237, 241
George M. 28*, 42, 123, 126
Paul 611
ROBEY, William H. 567
ROBIE
Frederick 314

Reuben 95
ROBINS
C.A. 299
Claude R. 453
Henry E. 468
Thomas 551
ROBINSON
Arthur R. 187, 190, 193, 196, 200, 303, 533
Boardman 591
C. Ray 565
Charles 306
Charles H. 533
Christopher 103, 435
Cornelius 392
Daniel S. 467
Edward (b. 1796) 82
Edward (b. 1858) 499, 500
Edwin Arlington 583*, 603
Elmer E. 461
Ezekiel G. 467
Franklin C. 572
Fred N. 577*
Frederick B. 468
George D. 121, 123, 125, 128, 320
Harold 517
Henry (N.H.) 452
Henry (Fla.) 454
Henry C. 454
Henry D. 509, 520
Henry S. 545
J. Ben 566
J. Kenneth 263, 266
J..W. 458
J.W. (Utah) 202, 205, 208, 212, 215, 218, 222
Jack R. 611
James 452
James A. 474
James C. 102, 104, 106, 114, 116
James F. 309
James H. 567
James M. 145, 147, 150, 153
James S. 126, 128
James W. 117
Jeremiah W. 450
Jesse 576
John (Va.) 9
John 585
John B. 138, 141, 144
John C. 408*, 409
John E. 530
John K. 418
John L. 91, 93, 94
John M. (Ill.) 75, 77, 78, 80, 82, 84, 300
John M. (Md.) 317
John N. 414
John S. (b. 1804) 375
John S. (b. 1856) 148, 151
John S. (b. 1880) 381
John W. 530
Jonathan 61, 62, 63, 64, 375
Joseph T. 18, 152, 155, 158, 161, 164, 167, 170, 173, 176, 179, 183, 186, 189, 192, 196, 199, 202, 206, 282
Leonidas D. 175, 178
Lucius 345
Maurice R. 596
Milton S. 118, 120
Morris 549
Moses 9, 10*, 375
Noel 551
Orville 88
Pat L. 455
Robert 608
Robert P. 292
Samuel M. 418*, 611
Spottswood W., III 272
Thomas, Jr. 84
Thomas J.B. 183, 187, 190, 193, 197
W.D. 557
Waltour M. 329
Wilfred H. 566
William E. (b. 1814) 111, 126, 128
William E. (b. 1900) 545*
William J. 533
William S. 574, 589
William S.O., Jr. 546
ROBISON
David F. 99
Howard W. 240, 243, 246, 249, 253, 256, 259, 262, 265
Samuel S. 483
William F. 480
ROBITZEK, Edward H. 600
ROBSION
John M. 177, 180, 184, 187, 190, 193*, 203, 207, 210, 213, 216, 220, 223, 310
John M., Jr. 232, 236, 239
ROBSON, John 455*
ROBY, Henry W. 600
ROCH, George 458
ROCHE
James M. 547*
John A. 451
John P. 468
Philip Q. 608
ROCHEFONTAINE, Stephen 402
ROCHESTER, William B. 70, 425
ROCK, George H. 418
ROCKEFELLER
David 545*, 604
James S. 547*
John D. 552, 553, 603
John D., Jr. 492, 591, 603
John D., 3d 604, 610
Laurance S. 591, 603, 604, 608, 609
Lewis K. 208, 211, 214
Nelson A. 346, 598, 604
Winthrop 282, 604
ROCKEY, Clement D. 530
ROCKHILL
William 91
William W. 425, 429, 435, 436*, 438, 594
ROCKLIFF, James A. 467
ROCKWELL
Francis W. 128, 130, 132, 135
Hosea H. 138
John A. 89, 90
Julius 87, 89, 91, 93, 97, 319
Norman 595
Robert F. 212, 216, 219, 222
Stuart W. 433
Willard F., Jr. 550
RODDAN, Edward L. 439
RODDENBERY, Seaborn A. 161, 164, 167
RODDEY, Philip D. 396
RODDIS, Louis H., Jr. 545, 569
RODECK, Hugo G. 498
RODEN, Carl B. 568
RODENBERG, William A. 147, 153, 156, 158, 161, 164, 170, 173, 176, 180
RODERT, Lewis A. 594, 611
RODES
Harold P. 466
Robert E. 395
RODGERS
C.R.P. 418, 483*
G.F. 460
George W. 417
John 532
John (Geologist) 576
Raymond P. 419
Richard 585*, 592
Robert L. 211, 215, 218, 221
W.S.S. 553*, 590
William C. 466
William L. 419
Woodall 453
RODINO, Peter W., Jr. 227, 230, 233, 236, 239, 243, 246, 249, 252, 256, 259, 262, 265
RODMAN
Benedict J. 473
Isaac P. 407, 408
William 63
William L. 569
William M. 459
RODNEY
Caesar A. 3, 5, 8, 24, 41, 57, 69*, 290, 423
Caleb 290
Daniel 15, 69, 72, 290*
George B. 85, 87
Thomas 5
ROE
Azel 532
Dudley G. 220
James A. 221
Kenneth 573
Robert A. 259, 262, 265
ROEBER, Eugene F. 575
ROEDER
Bernard F. 417
J.E. 600
ROESCH
Charles E. 451
Raymond A. 469
ROESSLER, John E. 484
ROETHKE, Theodore 586, 592, 602, 610
ROFFIGNOC, Joseph 457
ROGERS
Andrew J. 107, 108
Anthony A.C. 111
Bruce 589
Byron G. 229, 232, 235, 238, 241, 244, 248, 251, 254, 257
C.J. 388
Carl R. 571
Charles 88
Daniel 290
Dwight L. 219, 222, 226, 229, 232
Edith Nourse 187, 190, 194, 197, 200, 203, 207, 210, 213, 217, 220, 223, 226, 230, 233, 236, 239, 242
Edward 84
Ernest E. 579
Frank B. 595
George F. 221
H. Gold 436
Harry H. 536, 580
Harry L. 403
Henry S. 479
Henry W. 478
Howard G. 612
J. Justin 576
Jacob S. 549
James 81, 85, 87
Jefferson T. 455*
John (b. 1631) 472
John (b. 1813) 6, 115
John (b. 1890) 536
John H. 127, 129, 131, 134
John I. 573
John Jacob 168, 171, 174, 177, 180, 184
John R. 381
John T. 583
John W. 498
Jonathan C. 471
Joseph G. 571
Leo J. 462
Meyric C. 497, 498
Nat S. 564
Paul G. 235, 238, 241, 245, 248, 251, 254, 257, 261, 264
Platt 453
Robert E. 575
Robert S. 570
S. St. George 393
Sion H. 97, 115
Thomas 3
Thomas J. 67, 68, 70, 71
Walter E. 231, 234, 237, 240, 244, 247, 250, 253
Warren L. 512
Will (b. 1879) 611
Will (b. 1898) 201, 205, 208, 211, 214
Will, Jr. 216
William B. (b. 1804) 475*, 484, 563*
William B. (b. 1857) 474, 480
William F. 128
William H. 456
William N. 184, 197, 201, 204
William O. 483
William P. 35, 36, 37, 38, 41, 604
Woodall 453
ROGOFF
Fannie 492
Julius M. 492
ROHLFS, Marcus 534
ROHLMAN, Henry P. 523, 525
ROHRBOUGH, Edward G. 219, 225
ROLAND, Edwin J. 445
ROLEY, Ronald F. 558
ROLFE, John C. 570
ROLLINS
Edward A. 444
Edward H. 105, 107, 108, 121, 123, 126, 338
Frank W. 338
James S. 105, 106
Lloyd 497, 498
Walter H. 486
ROLPH
James, Jr. 284, 461
S. Wyman 575
Thomas 212, 216
ROLVAAG, Karl F. 325, 430
ROMAN
Andre B. 311*
J. Dixon 91
ROMANO, Umberto 598, 610
ROMANOFF, Paul 499
ROMBOUTS, Francis 457
ROME, Howard P. 571
ROMEIS, Jacob 131, 133
ROMER, Alfred S. 564, 573, 597, 607
ROMEYN, John B. 532
ROMJUE, Milton A. 174, 177, 184, 187, 191, 194, 197, 201, 204, 207, 210, 214
ROMNES, Haakon I. 543*, 554
ROMNEY, George W. 36, 47, 323, 543*, 598
ROMULO, Carlos P. 584
RONALD, James T. 461
RONALDSON, James 575
RONAN, Daniel J. 251, 254, 255, 258
RONCALIO, Teno 254, 263, 266
RONCALLO, Angelo D. 265
RONDON, Hector 587
RONDOU, Rene 559
RONEY, Paul H. ,271
RONNE, Finn 599
RONNEBECK, Arnold 498
ROOD, Florence 557
ROOK, Edward F. 607
ROOKS, Lowell W. 414
ROOME, Charles 545
ROONEY
Fred B. 250, 253, 256, 259, 262, 266
John J. 218, 221, 224, 227, 230, 233, 237, 240, 243, 246, 249, 253, 256, 259, 262, 265
ROOP, J. Clawson 444
ROOSEVELT
Eleanor 3, 30, 597
Franklin Delano 13, 18*
Franklin D., Jr. 227, 230, 233, 346
Isaac 544
James 235, 238, 241, 244, 248, 251
James I. 86
Nicholas 430
Robert B. 115, 433
Theodore 13, 14, 17*, 18, 150, 345, 567, 578, 597, 605
Theodore, Jr. 609
ROOT
Azariah S. 568
Elihu 30*, 38, 40, 162, 165, 168, 345, 564, 573, 589, 603, 605, 609
Erastus 58, 61, 65, 78
Jesse 5, 287
John F. 431
John G. 454
John W. 590
Joseph Moseley 90, 92, 93
Joseph P. 425
ROOTS, Logan H. 109, 111, 509
ROPER
Albert L. 458
Charles 600
Daniel C. 33, 34, 46, 425, 444
John W. 418
Sheldon M. 576
Thomas 451
RORIMER, James J. 499
RORTY, Malcolm C. 568
ROSA, Edward B. 594
ROSANOFF, Martin A. 604
ROSATI, Joseph 527, 528
ROSE
Alex 559
Arnold M. 574
Augustus S. 569
Charles G., 3d 265
David S. 456*
David S. (Bishop) 516
Frank A. 465, 482
Henry R. 456
John C. 271
John M. 175, 182
Maurice 415
Robert L. 91, 93
Robert S. 71, 73, 76
Rufus E. 419
U.M. 564
William 598
William C. 596, 604
William G. 452*
ROSECRANS
Sylvester H. 525
William S. 124, 127, 400*, 407, 408, 409, 433, 599

ROSELLINI
Albert D. 382
Hugh J. 382
ROSEN
Charles (b. 1878) 589
Charles 602
Donn E. 600
ROSENAU, Milton J. 610
ROSENBERG
Abraham 558
Adolph 537
Emanuel 608
Louis C. 590
ROSENBERRY, Marvin B. 386
ROSENBLOOM, Benjamin L. 182, 186
ROSENBLUTH, Marshall N. 595
ROSENGARTEN, George D. 565
ROSENHAUPT, Hans 493
ROSENN, Max 271
ROSENSTEIN, Samuel M. 273
ROSENSTOCK, Arthur 557
ROSENTHAL
A.M. 586
Benjamin S. 246, 249, 253, 256, 259, 262, 265
Doris 593
Joe 585
ROSENWALD
Julius 552*
Lessing 552
ROSIER, Joseph 215, 384
ROSIN, Joseph 609
ROSS
Bennett B. 466
C. Ben 299
Charles G. 584
Clarence F. 465*
Claude G. 425, 429, 438
David 6
Donald R. 272
Edmund G. 108, 110, 112, 306
Edward A. 573
Erskine M. 272
Frank E. 611
George 3, 7
Harold D. 577
Heck 453
Henry H. 73
James 15, 53, 54*, 55, 56, 57, 358
John (Md.) 449*
John (Pa.) 61, 66, 67
John W. 462
Jonathan 147, 149, 376*
Lawrence S. 372, 482
Lewis W. 106, 108, 110
Maurice O. 467
Miles 119, 121, 123, 126
Morrill 415
Nellie T. 387
Robert T. 224, 230
Sobieski 117, 119
Thomas 94, 96
Thomas R. 68, 70, 71
W.W. 462
William B. 387
William H.H. 290
ROSSBY, C.G. 608
ROSSDALE, Albert B. 181
ROSSELL, William T. 402
ROSSI, Angelo J. 461
ROSSIN, R.S. 459
ROSSINI, Frederick D. 599, 604, 608, 612
ROSSITER
Clinton 591
Percival S. 416
ROSSON
W.S. 453
William B. 404
ROSTENKOWSKI, Dan 242, 245, 248, 251, 255, 258, 261, 264
ROSTOW, Walt W. 608
ROTH
Almon E. 580
F.G.R. 579
Philip 602
William V., Jr. 254, 257, 261, 264, 292
ROTHENBURGER, William F. 536
ROTHERMEL, John H. 160, 163, 166, 169
ROTHKO, Mark 592
ROTHROCK, Mary U. 568, 600
ROTHSCHILD, Jerome J. 491
ROTHWELL
Charles E. 475
Gideon F. 123
William R. 486
ROUDEBUSH, Richard L. 245, 248, 251, 255, 258, 580
ROUMFORT, Augustus L. 453
ROUNDS
Nelson 486
Sterling P. 443
ROUNDY, Frank C. 579
ROUNTREE, William M. 424, 434, 437
ROUS
Francis P. 604, 606
Peyton 600
ROUSE
Arthur B. 164, 167, 170, 173, 177, 180, 184, 187
Irving B. 563, 611
Milford O. 569
William 451
ROUSH, J. Edward 245, 248, 251, 255, 261, 264
ROUSSEAU
Lawrence 396
Lovell H. 108, 408
Richard H. 430
ROUSSEL, Willis J. 600
ROUSSELOT, John H. 244, 257, 260, 263
ROUTT, John L. 285*, 453
ROUTZOHN, Harry N. 211
ROUX, Jules 450
ROUZIE, Richard L. 611
ROWAN
Carl T. 428, 445, 601
John (Rep.) 60, 72, 74, 75, 308
John (Dipl.) 436
Joseph 178
Matthew 9
Stephen N. 532
Thomas E. 456
William A. 216, 219
ROWBOTTOM, Harry E. 187, 190, 193
ROWCLIFF, Gilbert J. 416
ROWE
Ed 218
Frederick W. 171, 174, 178
George H. 579
James 493
Leo S. 563, 571
Peter 97
Peter T. 508, 519
Roscoe C. 449
ROWELL
Chester H. 609
John W. 376
Henry T. 574
Jonathan H. 127, 130, 132, 134
Lyman S. 484
ROWLAND
Alfred 133, 135
Charles H. 172, 175
D.P. 559
David 3
Henry A. 570, 609
Raymond E. 551*
ROWLEY
Howard C. 579
Louis N. 573
Park A. 545
T.A. 408
ROWLINSON, C.C. 472
ROY
Alphonse 207
William R. 261, 264
ROYAL, John K. 453
ROYALL, Kenneth C. 34, 40, 399
ROYAR, M.L. 418
ROYBAL, Edward R. 248, 251, 254, 257, 260, 263
ROYCE
Asa M. 486
Homer E. 101, 103, 376
Josiah 571
Ralph 411*
Stephen 375*
ROYKO, Mike 588
ROYS, Francis W. 487*
ROYSE, Lemuel W. 142, 145
ROYSTER, Vermont C. 573, 586
ROYSTON, Grandison D. 392
RUBEL, Albert C. 554*, 590, 601
RUBEN, Samuel A. 601
RUBENDALL, Howard L. 469
RUBEY
Thomas L. 165, 168, 171, 174, 177, 184, 187, 191
William W. 576, 604, 607
RUBIN, Harry 600
RUBLEE, Horace 438*
RUBOTTOM, Roy R., Jr. 423
RUBY, John C. 451
RUCKER
Atterson W. 161, 164
Daniel H. 403
Tinsley W. 170
William W. 148, 151, 154, 156, 159, 162, 165, 168, 171, 174, 177, 181
RUCKMAN, John W. 410*
RUDD
John A. 462
Stephen A. 198, 201, 204
Thomas B. 471
RUDDER, James E. 482
RUDENBERG, Reinhold 594
RUDER, Melvin H. 587
RUDESILL, C.E. 451
RUDKIN, Frank H. 272, 381
RUDOLPH
Abraham M. 599
C. Hugo 462*
Louis C. 481
Michael 401, 402
RUE, Levi L. 551*
REUHLMANN, Eugene P. 452
RUEPPEL, Merrill C. 498
RUESCH, Jurgen 597
RUFF, Walter S. 577
RUFFIN
Ben A. 576
James E. 201
Thomas (b. 1787) 347
Thomas (b. 1820) 97, 99, 101, 103, 392
William H. 578
RUFFNER
Clark L. 404, 405
Henry 485
RUGER
Thomas H. 296, 410, 419, 483
William C. 345
RUGG, Arthur P. 320, 563
RUGGLES
Arthur H. 571
Benjamin 65, 67, 68, 70, 71, 73, 75, 76, 78, 352
Carl 592
Charles H. 70, 344
Daniel 394
G.D. 401
John 79, 80, 82, 84, 314
Nathaniel 64, 65, 66
Timothy 3
RUHM, Herman D., Jr. 544
RULISON, Nelson S. 507, 519
RUMBOUGH, J. Wright, Jr. 493
RUMMEL, Joseph F. 524, 527
RUMPLE, John N.W. 150
RUMSEY
Benjamin 6, 10, 316
David, Jr. 91, 93
Edward 82
Julian S. 451
RUMSFELD, Donald 248, 251, 255, 258, 444
RUNGIUS, Carl 610
RUNK, John 90
RUNKLE, John D. 475
RUNNELS
Hardin R. 372
Harold 262, 265
Hiram G. 326
RUNYON
Theodore 407, 428*
William N. 340
RUPERT, Joseph 453
RUPLEY, Arthur R. 169
RUPP, Lawrence H. 574
RUPPE, Philip E. 255, 258, 261, 265
RUPPERT, Jacob, Jr. 148, 151, 154, 157
RUSACK, Robert C. 517
RUSBY
J.M. 600
Henry H. 609
RUSCHENBERGER, William S.W. 563
RUSH
Benjamin 3, 7
Kenneth 399, 428, 553
Orville F. 579
Richard 15, 16, 24, 25, 39, 41, 428, 429
RUSHTON, Kenneth 600
RUSK
Dean 10, 35, 38, 492, 604, 608
Harry W. 130, 132, 135, 137, 140, 142
Howard A. 603
Jeremiah M. 29, 30, 45, 115, 117, 120, 385
Ralph L. 602
Thomas J. 90, 92, 94, 96, 98, 99, 100, 101, 372
RUSS
John 67, 69
William M. 459
RUSSEL, George H. 564
RUSSELL
Benjamin E. 139, 142
Bruce A. 585
Charles A. 132, 134, 137, 139, 142, 144, 147, 150
Charles E. 583
Charles H. 224, 336
Charles T. 538
Charles W. 392, 393*
Charles W. (Dipl.) 435
Daniel L. 124, 348
David A. 81, 83, 84
Donald J. 552*
Donald S. 253, 271, 366*, 481
Ernest J. 567
Francis H. 428, 433, 438
Frederick F. 565, 610
George L. 416
Gordon J. 152, 155, 157, 160, 163
Henry D. 413
Henry N. 563, 564, 570, 596, 610
Israel C. 575
J. Edward 172
James McP. 86
James S. 417, 594
Jeremiah 88
John (Bishop) 531
John (Rep.) 59, 60
John E. 132
John H. 416
John J. 525, 528
John M. 492
Jonathan 69, 428, 429*, 437
Joseph (b. 1702) 10
Joseph (b. 1800) 90, 95
Joseph J. 159, 165, 168, 171, 174
Lee M. 327
Nelson V. 467
Norman F.S. 601
R.M. 533
Richard B. 196, 200, 203, 206, 209, 213, 216, 219, 223, 226, 229, 232, 235, 238, 241, 245, 248, 251, 254, 257*, 297*
Richard J. 576, 594
Richard M. 203
Robert L. 416
Robert L. 271
Robert P. 590
Sam M. 215, 218, 222
Samuel L. 97
Thomas 580
William 75, 76, 78, 86
William A. 123, 125, 128
William E. 320
William F. 101
William L. 571
William O. 572
William T. 525
William W. 426, 427*, 436, 439
RUSSO, Nicholas 466
RUST
Albert 98, 102, 392
Richard S. 486
RUTENBER, C.G. 534
RUTER, Martin 465
RUTH, Earl B. 259, 262, 265
RUTHERFORD
Albert G. 208, 211, 215
Griffith 406
J.T. 237, 240, 244, 247
John 378, 501
Robert 53, 54
Samuel 186, 190, 193, 196
RUTHERFURD
John 52, 53, 54, 55, 340
Lewis M. 609
RUTHRAUFF, John M. 486
RUTHVEN, Alexander G. 475
RUTLEDGE
Archibald 593
Edward 3, 4, 7, 364
Francis H. 506, 519
John 3, 4, 7, 9*, 15, 269*, 364
John, Jr. 55, 56, 57
Wiley B., Jr. 270, 272
RYALL, Daniel B. 84
RYAN
Edward F. 525
Edward G. 385
Edward J. 557

Elmer J. 204, 207, 210
Frank M. 557
George 9
Harold M. 245, 249
Harris J. 595
Hewson A. 430
J. Harold 578
James 529
James H. 468, 524, 527
James W. 149
John D. (b. 1864) 543*
John D. (b. 1915) 415*, 416
John D. 415
John T., Jr. 405
John W. 473, 475
Joseph P. 558
Joseph T. 523
L. Harold 578
Leo J. 263
Leo W. 577
Lewis C. 565
Patrick J. (b. 1831) 524
Patrick J. (b. 1902) 401
Robert J. 434
Stephen V. 525
Thelma Catherine Patricia 20
Thomas 120, 123, 125, 127, 130, 132, 433
Thomas F. 480
Thomas J. 181
Vincent J. 525
William 141
William F. 573
William Fitts 246, 249, 253, 256, 259, 262
William H. 148, 151, 154, 157, 160
RYBERG, Inez S. 570
RYCKMAN
Albert Jan 449
Charles S. 583
RYDER
Charles W. 412, 413
Chauncey F. 589
James 471*, 480
Loren L. 580
Oscar B. 445
RYE, Thomas C. 370
RYERSON, Edward L. 492, 548, 596
RYLAND, Robert 480
RYON
Augustus M. 476
John W. 124
RYORS, Alfred 473, 478
RYSKAMP, Charles A. 500
RYSKIND, Morrie 584
RYTER, Joseph F. 219

S

SAARINEN
Eero 590
Eliel 590, 591
SABATH, Adolph J. 158, 161, 164, 167, 170, 173, 176, 180, 183, 187, 190, 193, 196, 200, 203, 206, 210, 213, 216, 219, 223, 226, 229
SABIN
Albert B. 599, 600, 604
Alvah 98, 99
Dwight M. 128, 130, 132, 324
SABINE, Lorenzo 95
SACCIO, Leonard J. 426
SACHAR, Abram B. 466
SACHS
Bernard 569*
Ernest 569
George 590
Herman 498
Julius 570
SACK, Leo R. 426
SACKET, Delos B. 402
SACKETT
Frederic, Jr. 187, 190, 193, 310, 428
William A. 93, 95
SACKLER, Howard 587
SACKS, Leon 208, 211, 215
SADIK, Marvin S. 497, 500
SADLAK, Antoni N. 222, 226, 229, 232, 235, 238
SADLER
McGruder E. 482, 536
Marion 543
Reinhold 335
Thomas W. 129
SADLIER, Mary A. 599
SADOWSKI, George G. 200, 204, 207, 217, 220, 223, 226
SADTLER, Benjamin 476
SAFER, Morley 607
SAFFIN, William 558
SAFFOLD
Reuben 277
William B. 465
SAFFORD, Edward L. 461
SAGE
Bruce H. 601
Cornelia B. 497
Ebenezer 61, 62, 64
John C. 511, 522
John H. 569
Russell 97, 99
SAHS, Adolph L. 569
SAILLY, Peter 59
SAILOR, Joseph 567
ST. CLAIR
Arthur 5, 7, 400, 401, 406
Leonard P. 554
ST. DENIS, Ruth 593
SAINT-GAUDENS
Augustus 597, 603
Homer 498
ST. GEORGE
Armin V. 572
Katharine 224, 227, 230, 233, 237, 240, 243, 246, 249
ST. GERMAIN, Fernand J. 247, 250, 253, 256, 259, 262, 266
ST. JOHN
Bruce 498, 500
Charles 115, 117
Daniel B. 91
Henry 88, 90
John P. 17, 306
ST. JOHNS, Adela Rogers 608
ST. MARTIN, Louis 95, 130
ST. ONGE, William L. 248, 251, 254, 257
ST. PALAIS, James M. 526
SAISA, Joseph 481*
SALATKA, Charles A. 527
SALE
George 476
W.W. 451
SALET, Eugene A. 419
SALINGER, Pierre 247, 284
SALISBURY
Harrison E. 586
Stephen 563
Stephen, Jr. 563
SALK, Jonas E. 600, 603
SALLADA, Harold B. 417
SALLAS, George M. 436
SALLMON, William H. 467
SALLNESS, Fritchof T. 577
SALMON
Edward T. 570
Joshua S. 148, 151
Thomas 377
Thomas W. 571
William C. 185
SALOMON, Edward 385
SALPOINTE, John B. 524
SALSICH, LeRoy 610
SALTONSTALL
Dudley 416
Gurdon 8, 10
Leverett (b. 1783) 82, 84, 86, 460
Leverett (b. 1892) 220, 223, 226, 229, 233, 236, 239, 242, 245, 248, 252, 321*
SALTZMAN
Charles E. 575
Charles M. 403
Henry 479
SAMANS, Carl 572
SAMFORD
John A. 444
William J. 122, 278
SAMMARTINO, Peter 470
SAMMIS, J.U. 574
SAMMONS
Edward C. 554*
Thomas 58, 59, 61, 62
SAMPEY, John E. 534
SAMPLE
Chester A. 558
Paul 589, 598
Robert F. 532
Samuel C. 87
Thomas G. 576
SAMPSON
Archibald J. 427
Ezekiel S. 118, 120
Flem D. 310
Francis L. 401
John J. 567
W.T. 483
William T. 418
Zabdiel 66, 68
SAMS
Earl C. 551*
Oscar E. 467
SAMSON, George W. 471
SAMSTAG, Gordon 593
SAMUEL
Bernard 458
Edmund W. 157
SAMUELS
Ernest 587, 591
Green B. 85
Howard J. 445
SAMUELSON
Don 299
Paul A. 566, 595, 606
SANBORN
Alden S. 456
John B. 272
John C. 223, 226
Richard B. 450
Walter H. 272
SANCHEZ, Phillip 444
SANDAGE, Allan R. 604
SANDAGER, Harry 211
SANDBURG, Carl 583, 584, 585, 595*, 603, 608, 609
SANDEFER, Jefferson D. 471
SANDEMAN, Robert 538
SANDERS
Archie D. 174, 178, 181, 185, 188, 191, 194, 198
B.M. 475
Carl E. 297
Daniel C. 484
Everett 173, 176, 180, 183
Frank K. 484
Frederic W. 476
Henry A. 570
Jared Y. 174, 177, 312
Jared Y., Jr. 200, 203, 213
Jennings B. 475
Morgan G. 182, 185, 189, 192, 195, 199, 202, 205, 208
Newell 166, 370
Robert 449
Thomas H. 578
Wilbur F. 135, 138, 331
William F. 516
SANDERSON
Dwight 573
George H. 461
Henry S. 574
John A. 580
John F. 392
Silas W. 283
SANDFORD
James T. 72
Thomas 57, 59
SANDIDGE, John M. 98, 100
SANDLIN, John N. 180, 184, 187, 190, 193, 197, 200, 203
SANDMAN, Charles W., Jr. 256, 259, 262, 265
SANDOVAL, Hilary J., Jr. 445
SANDRICH, Mark 575
SANDS
James H. 483
Joshua 58, 73
Thomas J. 419
W.B. 331
William F. 429
SANDY, William C. 571
SANER, R.E.L. 565
SANFORD
Alfred 455
Arthur H. 572
Edmund C. 571
Edward T. 270
Henry G. 575
Henry S. 424
John (b. 1803) 86
John (b. 1851) 135, 138
John W.A. 80
Jonah 76
Louis C. 510, 521
Nathan 16, 65, 67, 68, 73, 74, 76, 344*
Peleg 9
Rollin B. 171, 174, 178
Steadman V. 471
Stephen 113
Terry 349, 470
SANGER
George P. 548
Henry H. 549*
SANGREN, Paul V. 485
SANKEY, James P. 533
SANSBURY, Marvin O. 536
SANSOM, William 558
SAN SOUCI, Emery J. 362
SANTANGELO, Alfred E. 240, 243, 246
SANTAYANA, George 593
SANTORA, Philip 586
SAPHORE, Edwin W. 510, 519
SAPP
Arthur H. 580
William F. 120, 123
William R. 97, 99
SAPPINGTON, G. Ridgely 579
SARASIN, Ronald A. 264
SARBACHER, George W., Jr. 224
SARBANES, Paul S. 261, 264
SARDELLA, Lou 598
SARGEANT
George 453
Nathaniel P. 319
William H. 549
SARGENT
Aaron A. 104, 111, 113, 115, 118, 120, 283
Aaron 428
Francis W. 321
Harry G. 452
John G. 32, 33, 41
John Singer 590, 603, 607
Jonathan E. 338
William G. 461
Winthrop 401
SARLES, Elmore Y. 350
SARNOFF
David 551*, 604
Robert W. 551*
SAROYAN, William 584
SARTAIN, John 501*
SARTORI, Albert J. 577
SASIA, Joseph 481*
SASMETT, William J. 465
SASSCER, Lansdale G. 210, 213, 217, 220, 223, 226, 229
SATTERFIELD
Dave E. 209, 212, 215, 218, 222
David E., 3rd 253, 257, 260, 263, 266
J.V., Jr. 455
John C. 565
SATTERLEE
Henry Y. 508, 522
Walter 593
SATTERTHWAITE, Joseph C. 424, 425, 433, 437
SAUER, Carl O. 595
SAUERHERING, Edward 144, 147
SAUL, Thomas 501
SAULNIER, Edmond 480
SAULSBURY
Eli 114, 116, 118, 120, 122, 125, 127, 129, 132, 291
Gove 291
Willard 102, 104, 106, 107, 109, 111, 291*
Willard, Jr. 167, 170, 173*, 291
SAUND, Dalip S. 238, 241, 244
SAUNDERS
Alvin 121, 123, 126, 333
Arnold E. 474*
Carl M. 585
David J. 459
Edward W. 158, 160, 163, 166, 169, 172, 175, 179
Harold E. 611
Robert 486
Romulus M. 70, 71, 73, 86, 88, 437
William 578
SAUTHOFF, Harry 205, 209, 215, 219
SAUVEUR, Albert 594, 596
SAVAGE
Albert R. 315
Charles R. 222
Eugene F. 591*, 593, 598, 610
Ezra P. 333
Howard P. 568
John 65, 67, 344
John A. 467
John H. 94, 96, 99, 101
John L. 596
John S. 119
Marion A. 599
Wallace H. 453
SAVIN, Albert B. 599
SAWHILL, W.R. 533
SAWTELLE
Charles G. 403
Cullen 89, 93
William H. 272
SAWYER
Andrew J. 455
B.C. 459
Charles 34, 35, 46, 424,

432
Charles H. (b. 1840) 338
Charles H. (b. 1907) 502
Donald H. 572
Frederick A. 111, 113, 115, 365
Grant 336
Harold E. 514, 519
John E. 486
John G. 131, 133, 135
Lemuel 60, 61, 63, 67, 68, 70, 73, 75
Philetus 109, 111, 113, 115, 117, 126, 129, 131, 134, 136, 139, 385
Ralph A. 580
Samuel L. 123
Samuel T. 83
W.C. 479
William 90, 92
SAXBE, William B. 259, 262, 265, 354
SAXTON, Ida 20
SAY, Benjamin 60, 62
SAYERS
Frances C. 600
Joseph D. 131, 133, 136, 139, 141, 144, 146, 372
SAYLE
George C. 456
William 9
SAYLER
Henry B. 116
Milton 117, 119, 121
SAYLES, John M. 477
SAYLOR
John P. 228, 231, 234, 237, 240, 243, 246, 250, 253, 256, 259, 262, 266
W.A. 450
SAYRE
Harry D. 559
Lewis A. 569
Morris 578
Robert M. 434, 439
William 457*
SCADDING, Charles 509, 521
SCAIFE
Alan M. 493
Lauriston L. 514, 522
SCALES
Alfred M. 101, 119, 121, 124, 126, 128, 348
Archibald H. 483
Henry M. 458
James R. 484
SCAMMAN, John F. 89
SCAMMEL, Alexander 401
SCANLAN
John J. 526
Lawrence 528
SCANLON
Apelles J. 474
Thomas E. 215, 218
Timothy H. 454
William 543
SCANNELL, Richard 527, 528
SCARBOROUGH
John 507, 520
Lee R. 534
Robert B. 152, 154
W.S. 486
William J. 466
SCARBROUGH, Cleve K. 500
SCARBURGH, George P. 273
SCARLETT, William 512, 520
SCARPITTI, Frank 598
SCATCHARD, George 609
SCATENA, Lorenzo 544
SCATES, Walter B. 300
SCERRA, Joseph A. 580
SCHAAFF, Charles H. 549
SCHAAPMAN, Henry A. 469
SCHACHTER, Oscar 573
SCHADE, Henry A. 611
SCHADEBERG, Henry C. 247, 250, 257, 260
SCHAEFER
Adolph O. 572
Edwin M. 200, 203, 206, 210, 213
Hugo H. 609
John C. 186, 189, 192, 196, 199, 212
John P. 465
Ralph A. 575
Walter V. 589
William D. 450
SCHAEFFER
Charles A. 473
John A. 470
SCHAFFER
Nile C. 499
William I. 360
SCHAIRER, George S. 597, 608, 611
SCHALL, Thomas D. 171, 174, 177, 181, 184, 187, 190, 194, 197, 200, 204, 325
SCHALLER, Walter F. 569
SCHAPIRO, Meyer 592
SCHAPMAN, Henry 487
SCHATTSCHNEIDER, E.E. 571
SCHATZ, Edward 467
SCHAU, Mrs. Walter M. 586
SCHAUFELE, William E., Jr. 439
SCHEEL, Nivard 468
SCHEELE, Leonard A. 445
SCHEFFER, Victor B. 593
SCHEIBERLING, Edward N. 568
SCHEIL, Merrill A. 572
SCHELL
Joseph O. 473
Richard 117
SCHELLENBACH, William L. 600
SCHELLING, Felix E. 577
SCHENCK
Abraham H. 65
Edgar C. 497*, 499, 502
Ferdinand S. 79, 81
Paul F. 231, 234, 237, 240, 243, 246, 249
Robert C. 88, 90, 92, 93, 107, 109, 111, 113, 407, 424, 429
SCHENK, Francis J. 525, 526
SCHENKEN, John R. 572
SCHER, Philip G. 527
SCHERER
Gordon H. 234, 237, 240, 243, 246
James A.B. 467
Walter H. 566
SCHERESCHEWSKY, Samuel I.J. 507
SCHERFFIUS, Henry 454
SCHERLE, William J. 255, 258, 261, 264
SCHERMERHORN
Abraham M. 93, 95
Simon J. 141
W. George 600
SCHEU, Solomon 451
SCHEUCH, Frederick C. 476*
SCHEUER, James H. 253, 256, 259, 262
SCHEVILL, Rudolph 577
SCHEXNAYDER, Maurice 527
SCHIFF
John M. 574
Mortimer L. 574
SCHIFFLER
Andrew C. 212, 219
SCHILLING, Hugo K. 577
SCHINDLER, Alex 537
SCHINNER, Augustine F. 529*
SCHIOTZ, Fredrik A. 535
SCHIRM, Charles R. 150
SCHIRO, Victor H. 457
SCHIRRA, Walter M., Jr. 594
SCHISLER, Gale 251
SCHLADWEILER, Alphonse J. 527
SCHLAGETER, Robert W. 500
SCHLAGLE, Frank L. 578
SCHLAIKJER, J.W. 589
SCHLARMAN, Joseph H. 527
SCHLATTER, David M. 415, 419
SCHLEICHER, Gustave 120, 122
SCHLESINGER
Arthur M., Sr. 567
Arthur M., Jr. 585, 587, 591, 602, 603
Benjamin 558*
Frank 564
Hermann I. 596, 608
James R. 443*
SCHLEY
Julian L. 402
William 78, 80, 295
SCHLINK, Frederick J. 600
SCHLOSINGER, Hermann I. 608
SCHLUEDERBERG, Carl G. 575
SCHLUMBERGER
Conrad 601
Marcel 601
SCHMEDEMAN, Albert G. 386, 434, 456
SCHMIDHAUSER, John R. 252
SCHMIDT
Adolph W. 425, 492
Dana Adams 607
Frank 455
Maarten 610
Max E. 600
William R. 413, 414
SCHMIED, Kenneth A. 456
SCHMITS, John G. 91, 92
SCHMITT
Bernadotte E. 567, 583
Francis O. 600
Henry J. 600
Otto H. 612
SCHMITZ
Eugene E. 461
Henry 484
John G. 257, 260
SCHMUCK, Elmer N. 512, 522
SCHNACKENBERG, Elmer J. 272
SCHNADER, William A. 589
SCHNALL, Thomas D. 177
SCHNEEBELI
Gustav A. 157
Herman T. 243, 246, 250, 253, 256, 262, 266
SCHNEIDER
C.J. 469
Charles C. 572
George J. 186, 189, 192, 196, 199, 205, 209
Herman 468
Jean 586
SCHNELLBECKER, George G. 462
SCHNEPP, John S. 461
SCHNIERLE, John 451*
SCHNITGER, W.R. 451
SCHOCKLEY, William 598
SCHOECH, William A. 417, 418
SCHOELLKOPF
Alfred H. 550
J. Fred 549
SCHOEMANN, Peter T. 559
SCHOENFELD
H.F. Arthur 424, 426, 427, 428, 430
Rudolf E. 426, 429, 432, 436
SCHOENEMAN, George J. 444
SCHOENFUSS, Frank 600
SCHOENINGER, Carl J. 580
SCHOENSTEIN, Paul 585
SCHOEPPEL
Andrew F. 226, 229, 232, 235, 239, 242, 245, 307*
Malcolm F. 418
SCHOFIELD
Harvey A. 486
John M. 27, 28, 40, 400, 406*, 409, 410*
Lemuel B. 443
W. Elmer 589, 593, 607
William 271
SCHOLLE, Hardinge 500
SCHOLTZ, Joseph D. 456
SCHOMBURG, August 419
SCHONBERG, Harold C. 588
SCHOOLCRAFT, John L. 93, 95
SCHOONMAKER
Cornelius 52
Marius 95
SCHOONOVER
Draper T. 474
SCHORGER, Arlie W. 592
SCHORTEN, Henry 450*
SCHOTTLAND, Charles I. 445, 466
SCHOULER, James 567
SCHOUTEN, Raymond W. 467
SCHOW, Robert A. 400
SCHRADER, Franz 573
SCHRAMM, Jacob R. 574
SCHRECKENGOST, Viktor 590
SCHREIBER, Raemer 569
SCHREINER, Oswald 600
SCHREIVER, Bernard A. 415
SCHREMBS, Joseph 525, 529
SCHRENK, Matthew H. 601
SCHREYVOGEL, Charles 593
SCHRICKER, Henry F. 303*
SCHRIEFFER, John R. 606
SCHROEDER
Francis 437*
John W. 454
Patricia 264
SCHUBAUER, Galen B. 608
SCHUBERT, Joseph C. 456
SCHUCHERT, Charles 501, 576, 597, 607
SCHUCK, Charles J. 576
SCHUETTE, C.H. 467
SCHUETZ, Leonard W. 196, 200, 203, 206, 210, 213, 216
SCHUH
Henry F. 535
L.H. 467
SCHUHMANN, Reinhardt, Jr. 595
SCHUIRMANN, R.E. 416
SCHULER, Anthony J. 526
SCHULMAN, Irving 599
SCHULTE
Godfrey V. 473
Paul C. 523, 526
William T. 200, 203, 206, 210, 213
SCHULTZ
Adolph H. 611
Arthur L. 465
George P. 36, 46, 444, 612
John 487
John R. 465
Theodore W. 566
SCHULTZE
Augustus 476
Charles L. 444
SCHULZE, John A. 358
SCHUMACHER, Howard 596
SCHUMAKER, John G. 113, 117, 119
SCHUMAN, William 584, 592
SCHUMPETER, Joseph A. 566
SCHUNEMAN, Martin G. 59
SCHUREMAN, James 6, 51, 55, 56, 64
SCHURMAN, Jacob G. 425, 428, 429, 433, 468
SCHURZ, Carl 28, 29, 44, 112, 114, 116, 329, 437, 407, 408, 409*
SCHUSTER, Eldon B. 526
SCHUYLER
David 449
Eugene 429, 435, 436
Johannes 449*
Karl C. 196, 285
Louisa L. 609
Montgomery 436
Myndert 449*
Philip (b. 1733) 6, 51, 55, 344, 406
Philip (b. 1768) 67
Pieter 449
Robert 548
Robert L. 567
W.S. 404
William E., Jr. 444
SCHWAB
Charles M. 544*, 554, 568, 573, 596
Frank X. 451
Louis 452
Sidney I. 569
SCHWABE
George B. 221, 224, 231
Max 217, 220, 224
SCHWADA, John W. 465
SCHWAN, H.C. 535
SCHWARTZ
Delmore 592, 610
Harry H. 209, 212, 215, 387, 444
John 103
Samuel J. 452
SCHWARTZKOPF, Sam 455
SCHWARZE, William 476
SCHWARZSCHILD, Martin 564
SCHWEBACH, James 527
SCHWEIKER, Richard S. 246, 250, 253, 256, 259, 265, 360
SCHWEINITZ, George E. 569
SCHWELLENBACH
E.W. 381
Lewis B. 34, 46, 205, 209, 212, 381
SCHWEMLEIN, William 601
SCHWENGEL
Frank R. 552
Fred 235, 239, 242, 245, 248, 255, 258, 261, 264
SCHWERT, Pius L. 211, 214
SCHWETNER, Augustus J. 529
SCHWINGER, Julian 595, 604, 606
SCOBLICK, James P. 224
SCOFIELD
Edward 385
Glenni W. 107, 109, 111, 113, 115, 117, 273
SCOLLAN, Thomas P. 460

SCOTT
Abram M. 326
Angelo C. 478
Arthur H. 552
Austin 480
Byron N. 202, 206
Caroline Lavinia 20
Charles 308, 406
Charles F. (b. 1860) 153, 156, 159, 161
Charles F. (b. 1864) 595
Charles L. (b. 1827) 100, 102, 439
Charles L. (b. 1883) 411, 413
David R. 594
David W. 500
Donald 501
Elmon 381
Frank D. 171, 174, 177, 180, 184, 187
Fred N. 577
George C. 164, 167, 173
George M. 460
Gustavus 6
Hardie 224, 228, 231
Harold W. 578
Harvey D. 98
Hugh 215, 218, 224, 228, 231, 234, 237, 240, 243, 246, 250, 253, 256, 259, 262, 265, 360
Hugh L. 400, 483
Isaiah B. 530
James B. 573
John (b. 1784) 76
John (b. 1785) 69, 71, 73
John (b. 1824) 113, 115, 117
John A. 570
John F. 462
John F.R. 580
John G. 106
John M. 458
John Morin 6
John R.K. 172, 175, 359
John Thad, Jr. 444
John W. (b. 1807) 485*
John W. (b. 1908) 578
Joseph 599
Josiah 353
L.S. 460
Levi 530
Lon A. 182
M.G. 558
Marshal L. 533
Mrs. Matthew T. 579
Nathan B. 149, 152, 155, 158, 160, 163, 383, 444
Orange 539
Owen 137
Ralph J. 240, 243, 246, 249, 253
Richard H. 387
Robert E. 392
Robert K. 365
Robert W. 349
Roy W. 567
Stanley L. 401
Thomas (b. 1772) 352
Thomas (b. 1739) 51, 53
Thomas A. 554
Thomas F. 506, 521*
Tully 285
Upton 449
W. Kerr 233, 237, 240, 349*
Walter 454
Walter D. 478, 571
Walter Q. 478
Wendell G. 565
William 329
William A. 532
William B. 570, 576, 597, 599, 607
William H. 478*
William L. (b. 1828) 131, 133
William L. (b. 1915) 257, 260, 263, 266, 380
Winfield 16, 400, 406*
Winfield T. 610
SCOTTEN, Robert M. 426, 427*, 433
SCOULLER
John C. 533
John Y. 533
SCOVEL, Sylvester F. 486
SCOVELL, Clinton H. 577
SCOVILLE
Jonathan 124, 126, 451
Wilbur L. 609
SCOY, Thomas V. 486
SCRANTON
George W. 103, 105
Joseph A. 126, 131, 136, 141, 144
William W. 246, 360, 579
SCRIPTURE, Edward E. 600
SCRIVEN, George P. 403
SCRIVNER
Errett P. 216, 220, 223, 226, 229, 232, 236, 239
Eugene M. 459
SCROGGY, Thomas E. 167
SCRUGGS, William L. 426*, 439
SCRUGHAM, James G. 201, 204, 207, 211, 214*, 217, 220, 335, 336
SCUDDER
Caleb 454
Henry J. 117
Hubert B. 226, 229, 232, 235, 238
Isaac W. 117
John A. 61
Kenyon J. 566
Nathaniel 4, 6
Samuel H. 500
Townsend 148, 154
Tredwell 67
Zeno 95, 97
SCULL, Edward 133, 136, 138
SCULLY
Cornelius 459
John 470
Thomas J. 165, 168, 171, 174, 177
William A. 525
SCUPIN, Carl A. 554
SCURRY, Richardson 96
SEABORG, Glenn T. 443, 467, 564, 591, 595, 596*, 604, 605
SEABROOK, Whitemarsh B. 364
SEABURY
Paul 591
Samuel 505, 519
Samuel (b. 1873) 603, 609
SEAGER, Henry R. 566
SEALOCK, William E. 476
SEAMAN
Eugene C. 512, 521
Henry J. 90
Jonathan O. 405
William 586
William H. 272
SEAMENS, Robert C., Jr. 399
SEAMSTER, Lee 282
SEARCH, Theodore C. 578
SEARCY, James T. 571
SEARING
Hudson R. 545*
John A. 101
SEARLE, James 7
SEARLES, Colbert 577
SEARLS
Fred, Jr. 610
Niles 283
SEARS
Barnabas F. 565
Barnas 467
Clinton W. 473
Paul B. 563, 575, 595
Richard W. 552
Robert R. 571
Samuel P. 565
William J. 170, 173, 176, 179, 183, 186, 189, 200, 203
Willis G. 184, 188, 191, 194
SEASHORE, Carl E. 571
SEASONGOOD, Murray 452, 579
SEATON
Frederick A. 35, 44, 230, 334
George 563
John L. 465, 479
William W. 462
SEAVER
Benjamin 450
Ebenezer 58, 59, 60, 61, 62
Esther I. 498
SEAVEY, Clyde L. 443
SEAWELL, William T. 550*
SEAY
Thomas 277
Thomas F. 579
William A. 424
SEBALD
W.W. 543
William J. 423, 424, 431
SEBASTIAN
Charles E. 456
William K. 90, 92, 94, 96, 98, 100, 102, 104, 281
SEBELIUS, Keith G. 258, 261, 264
SEBREE, Edmund B. 413, 414
SEBRELL, John N. 579
SEBRING, William H. 454
SECCOMBE, James 211
SECREST, Robert T. 201, 204, 208, 211, 214, 227, 231, 234, 249, 253
SEDDON, James A. 90, 94, 391, 392
SEDGWICK
Charles B. 103, 105
John 407*, 408*, 409
Samuel H. 333
Theodore 51, 52*, 53*, 54*, 55, 56, 319
William T. 572
SEDITA, Frank A. 451*
SEE, Horace 573
SEEBOLD, Andrew L. 469
SEEGERS, J. Conrad 476
SEELEY
Elias P. 340
John E. 115
Paul S. 536
SEELYE
Julius H. 119, 465
Laurens H. 480
Laurenus 481
Talcott W. 438
SEELY-BROWN, Horace, Jr. 222, 229, 232, 235, 238, 244
SEEP, Joseph 551
SEERLY, John J. 137
SEES, John V. 534*
SEGAL, Bernard G. 565*
SEGAR, Joseph E. 105
SEGER, George N. 184, 188, 191, 194, 197, 201, 204, 207, 211
SEGHERS, Charles J. 524
SEGRE, Emilio G. 606
SEGUIN, Edouard C. 569
SEHON, John L. 461
SEIBELS, John J. 423, 424
SEIBERLING
Francis 195, 198
Frank A. 547
John F. 262, 265
SEIBOLD, Louis 583
SEIDEL, Emil 18, 456
SEIDENSTICKER, Edward G. 602
SEIDEWITZ, Edwin A. 449
SEIDMAN, J.S. 567
SEIMES, Mrs. Erwin F. 579
SEIP, Theodore L. 476
SEITZ
Collins J. 271
Frederick 570, 596
Henry J. 600
Philip F.D. 597
SELBY
Thomas H. 461
Thomas J. 150
SELDEN
Armistead I., Jr. 232, 235, 238, 241, 244, 247, 251, 254
David 557
Dudley 79
John E. 551*
Samuel L. 345
William 444
SELDOMRIDGE, Harry H. 167
SELECMAN
Charles C. 481, 530
Charles E. 553
SELIG, Lester N. 553
SELIGMAN
Arthur 343, 461
Edwin R.A. 564, 566
SELIKOFF, Irving 600
SELLARS, Richard B. 548
SELLECK, John K. 476
SELLER, David F. 416
SELLERS
Charles 591*
Coleman 573, 575
David F. 483
Robert V. 545
William 575
SELLERY, George C. 486
SELLS, Sam R. 166, 169, 172, 175, 178
SELMON, A.C. 492
SELVIG
Conrad G. 190, 194, 197
Forrest 497
SELWAY, George R. 517, 521
SELYE, Lewis 111
SEMMES
Benedict J. 76, 77
Benedict J., Jr. 417, 418, 419
Raphael (b. 1809) 396
Raphael (b. 1895) 501
Thomas J. 392, 393, 564
SEMON, Waldo L. 594
SEMPLE
Ellen C. 594
James 87, 89, 300, 425
W.T. 564
SENA, Jose D. 461
SENER, James B. 117
SENEY
George A. 128, 131, 133, 136
Joshua 6, 51, 52
SENN, Nicholas 569
SENNER, George F., Jr. 247, 251
SENSENBRENNER
Frank J. 548*
Maynard E. 452*
SENSENICH, R.L. 569
SENTER
DeWitt C. 370
George B. 452
John H. 457
William T. 88
SEQUIN, Juan N. 460
SERBER, Robert 570
SERENA, Joseph A. 466
SERGEANT
George 453
John 16, 66, 67, 68, 70, 75, 83, 85, 86
Jonathan D. 6
SERKIN, Rudolf 608
SERLES, Earl R. 570
SERLEY, Homer H. 478
SERLING, Rod 577
SERVIES, John W. 580
SESSIONS
Edson O. 427, 428
James P. 454
Roger 592, 603
Walter L. 115, 117, 131
SESSUMS
Davis 508 520
John W., Jr. 415
SETH, Oliver 272
SETON, Ernest Thompson 593
SETTLE
Evan E. 145
Thomas (b. 1789) 67, 68
Thomas (b. 1831) 435
Thomas (b. 1865) 141, 143
SETZLER, Frank M. 593
SEUBERT, Edward G. 552
SEVERANCE
Cordenio A. 565
Luther 87, 89, 430
SEVEREID, Eric 604
SEVERNS, Henry F. 271
SEVIER
Ambrose H. 80, 82, 83, 85, 87, 89*, 90, 281, 433
Hal H. 425
John 51, 63, 64, 66, 369*
SEWALL
Arthur 17
Charles S. 77, 86
Harold M. 430
Joseph A. 468
Jotham B. 570
Samuel (b. 1652) 3, 10
Samuel (b. 1757) 53, 54, 56, 319
Stephen 10
Sumner 315
SEWARD
George F. 425
James L. 96, 98, 100
William H. 93, 95, 97, 99, 101, 103, 344*
SEWELL
Lydia Amanda 593
William H. 574
William J. 126, 128, 130, 143, 146, 148, 151, 340*
SEXTON
Anne 587, 610
Frank B. 393*
Leonidas 120
Lester , 550
SEYBERT
Adam 62, 63, 64, 67
John 531
SEYFERTH, Otto A. 575
SEYFFERT, Leopold 598
SEYMOUR
Charles 487
David L. 88, 95
Edward 127, 129
Forrest W. 584
George F. 466, 507, 522
Henry W. 132
Horatio (b. 1778) 70, 72, 73, 75, 76, 78, 375

Horatio (b. 1810) 16, 345*
John 8
John S. 444
L.D. 543
Origen S. 94, 96, 288
Thaddeus 484
Thomas 453
Thomas D. 570, 574
Thomas H. 87, 287, 436
Whitney North 565*, 589
William 81
SEYS, Jahn 432
SHACKELFORD, John W. 126
SHACKLEFORD
Dorsey W. 148, 151, 154, 156, 159, 162, 165, 168, 171, 174
Thomas G. 326
SHAEFFER, James H. 579
SHAFER
George F. 350
Helen 485
Paul W. 207, 210, 213, 217, 220, 223, 226, 230, 233
Raymond P. 360
SHAFFEL, Romanus A. 469
SHAFFER
Joseph C. 195
Laurence F. 571
Philip C. 579
Roy L. 477
SHAFROTH, John F. 142, 144, 147, 150, 152, 167, 170, 173, 285*
SHAHAN, Thomas J. 468
SHAHN, Ben 590, 603
SHAKESPEARE, Frank 445
SHAKSPEARE, Joseph A. 457*
SHALER
Charles B. 579
N.S. 575
SHALKOP, Robert L. 497
SHALLENBERGER
Ashton C. 151, 171, 174, 184, 188, 191, 197, 201, 333
William S. 122, 124, 126
SHAMBAUGH, Benjamin F. 571
SHANAHAN
Jeremiah F. 526
John W. 526
SHANK
Corwin S. 534
Samuel L. 454*
SHANKLIN
George S. 108
John A. 451
William A. 485
SHANKS
Bruce M. 586
Carrol M. 551
John P.C. 104, 110, 112, 114, 116
SHANLEY
James A. 203, 206, 209, 213
John 526
SHANNON
Anthony 587
Claude E. 598, 604
Edgar F., Jr. 484
Fred A. 583
James 475
James C. 289
Joseph B. 197, 201, 204, 207, 210, 214
Michael F. 574
Patrick 455
Paul E.V. 531
Richard C. 143, 146, 426, 434, 436
Thomas 73
Thomas B. 106
Wilson 97, 352*, 433
SHANTZ
Harold 436
Homer L. 465, 575
SHAPIRO
Charles H. 537
Harry L. 563, 609
Karl 585, 592, 610
Samuel H. 301
SHAPLEY, Harlow 563*, 564, 596, 610
SHAPP, Milton J. 360
SHARBAUGH, H. Robert 553
SHARFMAN, I.L. 566
SHARKEY, William L. 326
SHARON, William 119, 121, 123, 335
SHARP
Aaron J. 574
E. Preston 566
Edgar A. 221
George G. 611
James 460
John F. 355
L.W. 574
Paul F. 469, 472, 478
Robert 483
Solomon P. 63, 65
Ulysses S.G. 416, 417*
William G. 163, 166, 169, 428
SHARPE
Dudley C. 399
Henry G. 403, 410
Horatio 8
M.Q. 367
Percy 457
Peter 71
William 7
SHARPLESS, Isaac 472
SHARPLEY, William H. 453
SHARSWOOD, George 359
SHARTEL, Cassius M. 156
SHATTUC, William B. 146, 149, 151
SHATTUCK, W. 460
SHAUCK, John A. 353*
SHAUGHNESSY, Gerald ,528
SHAW
Aaron 100, 127
Albert 571
Albert D. 148
Alexander P. 530
Avery A. 469, 534
Edwin 594
Francis T. 459
Frank L. 456
Frank T. 130, 132
G. Howland 599
George B. 141, 576
George P. 427, 434*
Guy L. 180
H.M. 600
Harry 578
Henry 66, 68
Henry M. 97, 101
Howard V. 590
James B. 532
John A. 557
John B. 470
John G. 143
John W. 524, 528
Joseph B. 462
Lemuel 319
Leslie M. 30*, 39, 304
Lucien 284
Ralph R. 568, 595
Robert S. 475
Samuel 61, 62, 63
Tristram 84, 86
William E. 473
SHAWN, Ted 593
SHAYLER, Ernest V. 511, 520
SHEA
Cornelius 558
Francis R. 526
John G. 599
Joseph 470
Joseph H. 425
Marion E. 479
T.E. 493
SHEAFE, James 56, 57, 337
SHEAHAN, Marion W. 572, 610
SHEAKLEY, James 119
SHEAR, Byron D. 458
SHEARER, John B. 469
SHEDD
Fred F. 573
William E. 400
SHEEHAN
Daniel E. 524
Timothy P. 229, 232, 235, 238
SHEELER, Charles 589
SHEEN
Milton R. 601
Fulton J. 528
SHEERAN, Francis 484
SHEFFER, Daniel 83
SHEFFEY, Daniel 62, 63, 64, 66
SHEFFIELD
James R. 433
William P. (b. 1859) 163
William P. (b. 1820) 105, 128, 362
SHEHAN, Lawrence J. 523*, 525
SHEIL, Bernard J. 597
SHELBY
David D. 271
Isaac 308*
SHELDEN, Carlos D. 145, 148, 151
SHELDON
Charles H. 367
David N. 468
Edward S. 566, 577
George L. 333
Lionel A. 112, 114, 116
Porter 113
SHELFORD, V.E. 575
SHELL
George R.E. 484
George W. 138, 141
SHELLABARGER, Samuel 105, 109, 111, 115, 435
SHELLEY
Charles M. 120, 122, 124, 127
George M. 455
John F. 226, 229, 232, 235, 238, 241, 244, 248, 461
W.D. 450
SHELLWORTH, Eugene W. 450
SHELTON
James E. 564
Samuel A. 181
Turner B. 434
SHEPARD
Alan B., Jr. 594, 609
Charles B. 83, 84
Donald D. 492*
Frederick M. 554
L.G. 483
Luther D. 566
Odell 584
Roger B. 493
Silas E. 472
Walter J. 571
William 54, 56*
William B. 76, 78, 79, 81
William O. 530
William P. 572
SHEPERD, Howard C. 547*
SHEPHARD, Richard G. 491
SHEPHERD
Benjamin F. 572
James E. 348
Lemuel C. 416
William G. 576
SHEPLER, Matthias 83
SHEPLEY
Ethan A.H. 485
Ether 79, 80, 314*
George F. 311, 457
Henry R. 591, 603
SHEPPARD
Eleanor P. 459
Harry R. 206, 209, 212, 216, 219, 222, 226, 229, 232, 235, 238, 241, 244, 248
John C. 365
Morris 152, 155, 157, 160, 163, 166*, 169, 172, 175, 178, 182, 185, 189, 192, 195, 198, 202, 205, 208, 212, 215, 372
John L. 149, 152
Samuel L. 604
SHEPPERD
Augustine H. 75, 76, 78, 79, 81, 83, 86, 91, 93
J.H. 477
SHERA, Jesse H. 595
SHERBORNE, John E. 601
SHERBURN, George W. 577
SHERBURNE
Henry, Jr. 3
John C. 377
John S. 53*
SHEREDINE, Upton 52
SHERER
Albert W., Jr. 426, 427, 429, 438
Samuel L. 498
SHERIDAN
George A. 116
Harry R. 457
John E. 211, 215, 218, 221
Leo J. 430
Philip H. 400, 406, 408, 409*
SHERLEY, J. Swagar 153, 156, 159, 162, 164, 167, 170, 173
SHERMAN
Alson S. 451
Buren R. 304
David A. 482
Eugene B. 450
Forest P. 416, 417
Francis C. 451*
Frederick C. 417
H.W. 558
Henry C. 590, 596, 604
James S. 14, 17, 31, 133, 135, 141, 143, 146, 149, 151, 154, 157, 160, 161, 164
John 28, 30, 38, 39, 99, 101, 103, 105, 107, 109, 111, 113, 115, 117, 119, 126, 128, 129, 131, 133, 135, 138, 141, 143, 352, 353
Jonathan G. 514, 520
Judson W. 101
L.P. 453
Lawrence Y. 167, 170, 173, 176, 301
Matthew 461
Roger 4*, 5, 51, 52, 287
Socrates N. 105
William P. 462
William T. 400, 406, 407, 408, 409*, 474, 597
SHERO, Lucius R. 570
SHERRILL
Charles H. 423, 438
Eliakim 91
Edmund K. 516
Henry K. 512, 520
SHERROD, William C. 111
SHERWIN, John C. 123, 125
SHERWOOD
George H. 497
Granville H. 510, 522
Henry (Rep.) 115
Henry 578
Isaac R. 117, 160, 163, 166, 169, 172, 175, 178, 185
Robert E. 584*, 585, 591, 603
Samuel 64
Samuel B. 66
Thomas A. 329
Thomas E. 452
SHESTACK, Alan 502
SHETRONE, Henry C. 501
SHEWHART, Walter A. 598
SHEWMAKE, John T. 393
SHIEL, George K. 105
SHIELDS
Benjamin G. 85, 439
Ebenezer J. 81, 83
J.P. 557
James (b. 1762) 76
James (b. 1810) 92, 94, 96, 100, 121, 300, 324, 329
John K. 169, 172, 175, 178, 182, 185, 370*
William J. 559
SHIKLER, Aaron 593
SHILLADY, John 578
SHIMER, William A. 474
SHINN
Allen M. 417
Richard R. 549
William N. 79, 81
William P. 572
SHINO, R.A. 462
SHIPHERD, Zebulon R. 64
SHIPLEY
F.W. 574
George E. 242, 245, 248, 251, 255, 258, 261, 264
Samuel R. 551
SHIPMAN
Emma C. 536
Herbert 511
Nathaniel 271
SHIPP
Albert M. 486
Scott 484
SHIPPEN
Edward 358
Edward (b. ca. 1700) 458*
Edward (b. 1639) 9
William, Jr. 403
William 7
SHIPSTEAD, Henrik 184, 187, 190, 194, 197, 200, 204, 207, 210, 213, 217, 220, 325
SHIRAS
George, Jr. 269
George, 3d 154
SHIRER, William L. 602
SHIRES, Henry H. 515
SHIRK, George H. 458
SHIRLEY
John W. 469
William 8*
SHIVELEY
Charles E. 576
Benjamin F. 127, 132, 134, 137, 161, 164, 167, 170, 303
SHIVERS, Allan 373, 575
SHMUCKER, Samuel S. 471

SHOBER
Francis Edwin 113, 115
Francis Emanuel 154
SHOCK, W.H. 417
SHOCKLEY, William B. 598, 606
SHOEMAKER
Benjamin 458*
Eugene Merle 612
Francis H. 200
Henry W. 424
Lazarus D. 115, 117
Samuel 458
Vaughn 584, 585
William R. 418
SHOHOL, Charles 537
SHOLES, Z.G. 600
SHOLTZ
David (governor) 294
David 574
SHONK, George W. 138
SHOREY, Paul 570
SHORT
Charles 473
Dewey 194, 204, 207, 210, 214, 217, 220, 224, 227, 230, 233, 236
Don L. 243, 246, 249
Roy H. 531
Walter 404
William 428, 433, 437
SHORTER
Eli S. 98, 100
John G. 277, 391, 392
SHORTLIDGE, Joseph 479
SHORTRIDGE
Abram C. 479
Eli C.D. 350
G.D. 457
N. Parker 551*
Samuel M. 179, 183, 186, 189, 193, 196, 284
SHOTT, Hugh I. 195, 199, 215, 384
SHOTWELL, James T. 603
SHOUDY, William H. 461
SHOULDERS, Harrison H. 569
SHOUP
A.C. 455
David M. 416
George L. 134, 137, 139, 142, 145, 147, 298*
Oliver H. 285
Paul 552
Richard G. 262, 265
SHOUPP, William E. 569
SHOUSE, Jouett 170
SHOWALTER
John W. 272
Joseph B. 146, 149, 152
SHOWER, Jacob 97
SHOWERS, J. Balmer 531
SHRADER, James E. 611
SHREVE
Earl O. 575
Forest 575
Levin L. 548
Milton W. 169, 178, 182, 185, 188, 192, 195, 198
R.H. 567
SHRIVER
Garner E. 245, 148, 152, 255, 258, 261, 264
Phillip R. 475
R. Sargent 19, 428, 444, 595, 599
SHRYOCK
L.B. 476
Richard H. 564, 566
SHUBRICK, William B. 418
SHUCK, Daniel 531
SHUFORD
Alonzo C. 143, 146
George A. 234, 237, 240
SHULL
D.C. 534
Joseph H. 154
Martha A. 578
SHULLENBERGER, William S. 536
SHULTZ
Emanuel 126
George P. 36, 37, 39, 46
Jacob F. 455
SHUMAKER, Clifford H. 573
SHUMAN, Otto R. 576
SHUMWAY
F. Ritter 575
Forrest N. 552
SHUNK
Francis R. 358
William A. 419
SHUPE, Reed 459
SHURCLIFF, Arthur A. 573
SHURTLEFF
Harry C. 457
Nathaniel B. 450
SHUSTER
E.G. 266
George N. 472, 580, 599
SHUTE
Atwood 458
Samuel 8*
SHUTT, William E. 461
SHWACHMAN, Harry 599
SHYROCK, Henry W. 481
SIBAL, Agner W. 244, 248
SIBERT
Franklin C. 412, 413
William L. 401, 410
SIBLEY
Charles G. 501
Georgiana F. 603
Harper 575
Henry J. 324
Jonas 71
Joseph C. 141, 149, 152, 154, 157
Samuel H. 271
Mark H. 83
SICARD, Montgomery 418
SICKEL, Welling G. 462
SICKELS, Carlton R. 248, 252
SICKLES
Daniel E. 101, 103, 141, 408*, 437
Nicholas 81
SIDDALL, Kelly Y. 492
SIDEBOTHAM, Harold 502
SIDELL, William 559
SIDES, John H. 417
SIDNEY, George, 575*
SIEBECKER, Robert C. 385
SIEBER, Joseph 600
SIEG, Lee P. 484
SIEGEL
Isaac 171, 174, 178, 181
Sidney 569
SIEGFRIED, Charles A. 549
SIEGMUND, J.C. 460
SIEKMANN, Robert H. 558
SIEMILLER, P.L. 557
SIEMINSKI, Alfred D. 230, 233, 236, 239
SIGEL, Franz 406, 407
SIGLER
Kim 323
Maurice H. 566
SIGMAN, Morris 558
SIKES
Enoch W. 468
Robert L.F. 213, 216, 219, 222, 226, 229, 232, 235, 238, 241, 245, 248, 251, 254, 257, 261, 264
SIKORSKY, Igor I. 591, 596, 597, 604, 607, 608, 610, 612
SILBER
John R. 466
William B. 465
SILER, Eugene 236, 239, 242, 245, 248
SILL
Edward 452
John M.B. 431
Thomas H. 73, 76
SILLARS, Malcolm O. 481
SILLCOX, Lewis K. 573, 590
SILLIMAN, Gold 406
SILLS, Kenneth C.M. 466
SILSBEE
Nathaniel 66, 68, 72, 74, 76, 77, 79, 319
Nathaniel, Jr. 460*
SILVER
Arthur E. 599
Edwin 455
Robert D., Jr. 455*
SILVERMAN
Burton 589, 598
William A. 599
SILVERSTEIN, Abe 597, 608
SILVESTER
Lindsay M. 415
Peter 51, 52
Peter H. 91, 93
SILZER, George 342
SIME, Frederick W. 380
SIMKIN, William E. 443
SIMKINS, Eldred 67, 69
SIMMONDS, Albert C. 544*
SIMMONS
David A. 565, 568
Edward 591
Edward E., Jr. 601
Furnifold M. 133, 151, 154, 157, 160, 162, 165, 168, 171, 174, 178, 181, 185, 188, 191, 194, 348
George A. 97, 99
G.C. 460
George F. 476
Hezzleton E. 465
Jack W. 462
James F. 86, 88, 90, 101, 103, 105, 361, 362
James S. (Rep.) 162, 165
James S. 610
John F. 427*
Norwood L. 580
Ozzie G. 598
Robert G. 184, 188, 191, 194, 197, 334
Thomas J. 296
SIMMS
Albert G. 194
Dudley L. 577
John F. 343
Stephen C. 499
William E. 102, 392, 393
SIMON
Irving M. 559
John G. 493
Joseph 146, 149, 151, 356
SIMONDS
G.F. 594
George S. 400, 405, 419
John O. 573
John W. 481
Ossian C. 573
William E. 134, 444
SIMONS
Charles C. 271
Samuel 87
SIMONSEN, Donald 467
SIMONSON, Joseph 428
SIMONTON
Charles B. 124, 126
Charles H. 271
William 85, 86
SIMPKINS, John 143, 145
SIMPSON
A.B. 538
Alan 484
Bryan 271
Burton T. 565
Edna Oakes 242
Ernest C. 596
George B. 381*
George G. 573, 597, 604, 607
James 545
James, Jr. 200
Jeremiah 137, 140, 145
John A. 466
John W. 474
Kenneth F. 214
Kirke L. 583
Louis 587
Matthew 469, 530
Milward L. 250, 254, 388*
Oramel H. 312
Richard F. 88, 90, 92
Richard M. 208, 211, 215, 218, 221, 224, 228, 231, 234, 237, 240, 243
Samuel 557
Sidney E. 216, 219, 223, 226, 229, 232, 235, 238
Walter M. 572
William D. 365*, 393*
William H. 405*, 412, 413*
SIMRALL, Horatio F. 326
SIMS
Alexander D. 90, 92
Bennett J. 518, 519
Charles N. 482
Henry Upson 565
Hugo S., Jr. 228
J. Marion 569
Leonard H. 89
Thetus W. 146, 149, 152, 155, 157, 160, 163, 166, 169, 172, 175
Walter A. 449
William S. 419, 583, 609
SINCLAIR
Duncan 536
Gregg M., 472
James H. 178, 181, 185, 188, 191, 194, 198, 201
Upton 584
SINEX, Thomas H. 465, 479
SINGER
H. Douglas 569
Isaac Bashevis 592, 602
Margaret Thaler 598
Max 580
SINGLETARY, Otis A. 473, 477
SINGLETON
James W. 123, 125
Otho R. 97, 100, 102, 119, 121, 123, 125, 128, 130, 392, 393
SINKLER, Wharton 569
SINNICKSON
Clement H. 119, 121
Thomas (b. 1744) 51, 55
Thomas (b. 1786) 74
SINNOTT
Edmund W. 563, 574
Nicholas J. 169, 172, 175, 178, 182, 185, 188, 191, 273
SINSLOW, Warren 347
SIPE, William A. 138, 141
SIPLE
Paul A. 598
Walter H. 498, 502
SIPPY, John J. 572
SIRACUSA, Ernest V. 424
SIROVICH, William I. 191, 194, 198, 201, 204, 208, 211
SISK, B.F. 235, 238, 241, 244, 248, 251, 254, 257, 260, 263
SISSON
Edward O. 476
Francis H. 564
Frederick J. 201, 204
Thomas U. 162, 165, 168, 171, 174, 177, 181
SITES, Frank C. 185
SITGREAVES
Charles 108, 110
John 7
Samuel 54, 55
SITTLER, Edward L., Jr. 231
SIVARD, Robert 593
SIVERD, Clifford D. 543*
SIZER, Theodore 502
SKEELS, Harold 599
SKEEN, D.A. 576
SKELLY, William G. 547
SKELTON
Byron 273
Charles 95, 97
Martha (Wayles) 20
SKIDMORE, Louis 590
SKIFF, Frederick J.V. 499
SKILES
Elwin L. 471
William W. 151, 154
SKILTON, D.W.C. 551
SKINNER
Burrhus F. 604
Charles R. 126, 128
Charles W. 418
Elliott P. 439
Harry 143, 146
Joshua J. 601
Onias 300
Richard 64, 375*
Robert P. 427, 429, 431, 432, 438
Thomas G. 128, 131, 135
Thomas H. 532
Thomas J. 53, 54, 58
W.W. 460
SKIRM, Anthony 462
SKODAK, Marie P. 599
SKOLFIELD, O.P. 450
SKROMSTAD, Harold K. 608
SKUBITZ, Joe 248, 252, 255, 258, 261, 264
SKUTCH, Alexander 592
SLACK
Elijah 468*
John 244, 247, 250, 254, 257, 260, 263, 266
L. Ert 454
SLADE
Charles 78
William 78, 80, 81, 83, 85, 87, 375
William A. 499
SLADEN, Fred W. 483
SLAGLE
Christian W. 473
Robert L. 481
SLATER
James H. 115, 124, 126, 128, 356
John C. 604
O. Eugene 531
Robert E. 548*
SLATON, John M. 296
SLATTERY
Charles L. 511, 520
James M. 209, 301
Kenneth F. 477
SLAUGHTER
Gabriel 308
Roger C. 217, 220
W. M. 451
SLAVENS, James W. L. 455
SLAYDEN, James L. 146, 149, 152, 155, 157, 160, 163, 166, 169, 172, 175, 570
SLAYMAKER, Amos 64

SLAYTER, Games 601
SLAYTON, Donald K. 594
SLEDD, Andrew 470
SLEEPER
Albert E. 322
Joseph A. 550
SLEET, Moneta, Jr. 587
SLEMMONS, William E. 485
SLEMONS, William F. 118, 120, 122
SLEMP
Campbell 155, 158
C. Bascom 160, 163, 166, 169, 172, 175, 179, 182
SLEPIAN, Joseph 595, 599
SLEVIN, Richard D. 469
SLEYSTER, Rock 569
SLICHTER
Donald C. 550*
Sumner H. 566
SLIDELL
John 87, 89, 96, 98, 100, 102, 311
Thomas 311
SLIGH, Charles R., Jr. 578
SLINGERLAND, John I. 91
SLOAN
A. Scott 105
Alexander K. 430
Alfred P., Jr. 493, 547, 598, 603
Andrew 116
Benjamin M. 481
Charles H. 165, 168, 171, 174
Clay 281
Ithamar C. 107, 109
J. H. 461*
James 58, 59, 60
John 603
John E. 414
M. 451
W. McB. 452
SLOANE
John 68, 70, 71, 73, 75
John 444
Jonathan 79, 81
William M. 563, 567, 578, 603
SLOCTEMYER, Hugo F. 487
SLOCUM
A. Gaylord 473
Henry W. 113, 115, 128, 406, 407*, 408*, 409*, 410
SLOCUMB, Jesse 67, 68
SLOSS, Joseph H. 113, 115
SLOVER, S. L. 458
SMADEL, Joseph 600
SMALL
Albion W. 468, 573
Frank, Jr. 233
George L. 602
Jacob 450
John H. 149, 151, 154, 157, 160, 162, 165, 168, 171, 175, 178
Len 301
William B. 117
SMALLS, Robert 119, 122, 126, 129, 131
SMALLWOOD
Samuel N. 462*
William 8
William 406
SMART
Ephraim K. 91, 95
Jacob E. 416
James H. 479
James S. 117
SMATHERS
Eugene 533
George A. 222, 226, 229, 232, 235, 238, 241, 245, 248, 251, 254, 294
James F. 601
William H. 207, 211, 214, 342
SMEDBERG, William R. 3d 417, 418, 483
SMELT
Dennis 59, 60, 61
Ronald 567
SMILEY
Charles H. 593
Elmer E. 487
Joseph R. 468, 482
W. B. 533
SMILIE, John 53, 56, 57, 58, 59, 60, 62, 63
SMILLIE
James D. 574
Wilson G. 610
SMITH
A. C. 500
A. Coke 530
A. Donaldson 594, 599
A. Ervine 521
A. Frank 530
Abigail 20
A. Herr 117, 119, 122, 124, 126, 128
Acheson 575
Addison T. 167, 170, 173, 176, 180, 183, 186, 190, 193, 196
Albert C. 405, 415
Albert (Me.) 84
Albert (N.Y.) 88, 90
Alexander 565
Alfred E. 18, 346*, 599, 603
Alfred T. 400
Allen E. 419
Alphonse J. 527
Amanda B. 458
Amor, Jr. 451
Andrew J. 408
Anthony 590
Arthur 70, 72
Arthur E. 554*
Arthur M. 273
Augustus W. 485
Asa D. 469
B. Holly 566
Ballard 66, 67, 69
Benjamin 347
Benjamin A. II 245, 321
Benjamin B. 505, 520
Bernard 68
Bryce B. 455
Byron L. 550
C. B. 454
C. R. 543
Caleb B. 27, 44, 87, 89, 91
Campbell 402
Carlos G. 465
Charles B. (N.Y.) 165, 168, 171, 174
Charles B. (W. Va.) 136
Charles E. 592
Charles Emory 30*, 43
Charles F. (b. 1807) 407
Charles F. (b. 1852) 570
Charles J. 480
Charles L. (educator) 475
Charles L. (mayor) 461
Charles M. 377
Charles S. 459
Charles W. (bishop) 530
Charles W. (mayor) 449*
Charles W. (business executive) 568
Clement A. 592
Clement L. 570
Clifford P. 536*
Clyde H. 207, 210
Cotesworth P. 326
Courtney C. 482
Curtis P. 452
Cyril S. 590, 595
Cyrus R. 36, 46
D. D. 453*
Daniel 55, 59, 60, 62, 369*
Daniel C. 454
Darwin E. 548
David 592
David H. 145, 148, 150, 153, 156
Delazon 101, 356, 427
Dietrich C. 125
Earl E. T. 426
Earle C. 590
Edgar F. 479, 565*, 570, 594, 608
Edgar M. 473
Edward Byron 550
Edward C. 376
Edward H. 105
Edward L. 454
Edward P. 472
Edward W. 403
Edwin O. 468
Elizabeth Rudel 444
Ellison D. 163, 166, 169, 172, 175, 178, 182, 185, 188, 192, 195, 198, 202, 205, 208, 211, 215, 218, 365
Elmo 357
Ernest A. 482
Ernest T. 486
Erwin F. 574
Eugene A. 576
Everett 565
Everett P. 568
Everett W. 545
Ezekiel 432
Floyd E. 557
Forrest 330
Francis H. 484
Francis O. J. 79, 80, 82
Francis P. 470
Francis R. 215
Frank E. 233, 236, 239, 242, 246
Frank L. 176, 190
Frank O. 168
Frank W. 545
Fred W. 576
Frederic H., Jr. 415, 416
Frederick C. 211, 214, 218, 221, 224, 227
Frederick R. 579
G. A. 396, 409
G. Morris 482
Geoffrey S. 547*
George 62, 63
George A. 537
George B. 456*
George F. 548
George F. B. 545
George H. 486
George J. 154
George L. 116
George O. 443*, 594
George R. 168, 171
George W. (business exec.) 550*
George W. (educator) 468, 482
George W. (governor) 378
George W. (legislator) 134, 137, 139, 142, 145, 147, 150, 153, 156
George W. (mayor) 456
Gerrit 97
Gertrude E. 570
Gilbert M. 574
Giles A. 410
Goldwin 567
Gomer G. 208
Gordon M. 497, 498
Gordon V. 515, 520
Green C. 106, 108
Griffin 282
Gustavos W. 394
H. A. 566
H. Alexander 217, 220, 224, 227, 230, 233, 236, 239, 342
H. Allen 238, 241, 244, 248, 251, 254, 257, 260
H. Armour 499
H. Boardman 115, 117
H. Lester 530
H. Page 418
Hal M. 461
Harold D. 444
Harold P. 416, 417
Harold T. 473
Harry A. 400, 419
Harry D. 536
Harry P. 572
Hazel Brannan 587
Henry 474
Henry (Wis.) 134
Henry B. 532
Henry C. 148, 151
Henry K. 451
Henry L. 469, 485
Henry N. 577, 591
Henry P. 3d 253, 256, 259, 262, 265
Herbert B. 532
Herbert E. 554*
Hezekiah B. 123
Hiram H. 455
Hiram Y. 127
Hoke 30, 44, 164, 167, 170, 173, 176, 296*
Homer W. 599, 607
Horace 460
Horace H. 431
Howard E. 598
Howard Van 586
Howard W. 199, 202, 205, 209, 212, 215, 218, 222, 225, 228, 231, 234, 237, 241, 244, 247, 250, 253
Huldah M. 498
Hulett C. 384
Isaac (b. 1740) 54
Isaac (b. 1761) 64
Israel 52, 53, 54, 57, 58, 59, 61, 375*
J. A. 396
J. Ambler 117
J. Emil 461
J. Frank 532
J. Henry 546*
J. Joseph 203, 206, 209, 213, 271
J. L. 452
J. Lawrence 563, 565
J. Millard 475
J. Russell 594
J. W. 460
J. Waldo 596
James 3, 7
James, Jr. 140, 143, 146, 340
James F. 272*
James H., Jr. 443
James M. (educator) 474
James M. (legislator) 393
James S. 67, 68
James V. 256
James W. (mayor) 450
James W. (business exec.) 545
James Y. 362, 459
Jedediah K. 60
Jeremiah 52, 53*, 55, 337*
Jerome V. C. 450
Jesse M. 573
Joe L. 195, 199, 202, 205, 209, 212, 215, 219
Joel P. 469
John (colonist) 9
John (N.Y.) 56, 57, 58*, 59, 60, 61, 62, 344
John (Ohio) 58, 59, 60, 352
John (R.I.) 9*
John (Va.) 57, 58, 59, 61, 62, 63, 64
John (Vt.) 85
John A. 486
John A. (Rep.) 113, 115
John B. (b. 1756) 471, 483, 532
John B. (b. 1838) 338
John C. 533
John Cotton 55, 56, 57, 58, 287, 565
John Cotton, Jr. 424
John E. 408, 409*, 410
John F., Jr. 548
John G. 376
John Hugh 457*
John Hyatt 126
John J. (see J. Joseph Smith)
John Lee 576
John M. C. 165, 168, 171, 174, 177, 180
John Q. 117
John S. 69
John T. 88
John W. (Mich.) 453
John W. (Tex.) 460*
John W. (Ill.) 461*
John Walter 148, 159, 162, 165, 168, 171, 174, 177, 317*
Jonathan B. 4, 7
Joseph (b. 1790) 418
Joseph (b. 1805) 537, 538
Joseph (b. 1901) 415
Joseph F. 537
Joseph Fielding 537
Joseph M. 296
Joseph S. 113
Joseph T. 532
Josiah 7
Justin H. 583
Kenneth G. 579
Kingsbury 586
L. P. 461
Lauren H. 590
Lawrence H. 215, 219, 222, 225, 228, 231, 235, 238, 241
Len Y. 579
Leo R. 527
Leslie R. 536
Luther M. 470
Madison R. 159, 429
Marcus A. 164, 167, 170, 173, 176, 280
Margaret Chase 210, 213, 217, 220, 223, 226, 229, 233, 236, 239, 242, 245, 248, 252, 255, 258, 261, 315, 604
Margaret H. D. 599
Margaret Mackall 20
Marion 454
Mark A. 576
Martin F. 202, 205, 209, 212, 215
Martin L. 395, 409*
Mason 578
Mathew C. 409
Melancthon 6
Meriwether 7
Merriman 587, 608
Milton H. 549*
Munroe 571
Myrtle Holm 536
Nathan 78, 80, 287
Nathaniel 53, 54
Neal E. 242, 245, 248, 252, 255, 258, 261, 264

Nels H. 387
Nelson Lee 443
Norman M. 418, 481
Oberlin 573
O'Brien 59
Olcott D. 543*
Oliver H. 74, 82, 84, 85, 302
Orson 546
Osborn L. 470
Otis 475
Owen L. W. 432
Page 591
Perry 82, 83, 85, 287
Philip A. 517
Preston 373
R. C. 558
R. Rundle 501
Ralph C. 413, 414
Ralph T. 258, 301
Reginald H. 589
Rhoten A. 478
Richard 6
Richard T. 599
Robert (b. 1732) 505, 521, 532
Robert (b. 1757) 23, 24*, 38, 42, 474
Robert (b. 1802) 87, 89, 91, 100
Robert A. 460*
Robert B. 331
Robert H. 391, 392
Robert I. 551
Ronald B. 573
S. S. 460
S. Stanhope 471, 479, 532
Samuel (Md.) 52, 53, 54, 55, 56, 57, 58, 59, 60*, 61, 62, 63, 65, 66, 68, 69*, 71, 72, 74*, 75, 76, 77, 316*, 450
Samuel (N.H.) 64
Samuel (Pa.) 59, 60, 62
Samuel A. (Pa.) 76, 78
Samuel A. (Tenn.) 97, 99, 101
Samuel E. (b. 1788) 314
Samuel E. (b. 1861) 571
Samuel F. 551
Samuel W. 145, 148, 151, 153, 156, 159, 162, 165, 168
Seymour A. 482
Solomon A. 546, 550*
Stephen 571
Sydney 327
Sylvester C. 155, 158, 161, 164
Sylvester C., Jr. 565
Theobald 610
Thomas (Ind.) 84, 87, 89
Thomas (Pa.) 7, 66
Thomas (S.C.) 9*
Thomas A. 156
Thomas B. 458
Thomas F. 174, 178
Thomas J. (Niagara, Univ.) 477
Thomas J. (John Carroll Univ.) 473
Thomas L. 547
Thomas M. 473
Thomas R. 451
Thomas S. 474
Thomas V. 210
Tom K. 564
Thorowgood 450
Truman 83, 85, 89, 90, 287
W. Angie 531
W. Herman 451
W. J. 483
W. N. H. 392*, 393
W. Warren 559
Walter Bedell 405, 439, 443, 603
Walter G. 564, 599
Walter I. 148, 150, 153, 156, 159, 161, 164, 272
Wendell L. 492
Wendell R. 568
Willard J. 445
William (b. 1727) 479
William (Va) 70, 72, 73
William (b. 1797) 87, 98, 99, 101, 103, 378, 379, 393
William (b. 1751) 55
William (b. 1762) 16*, 66, 67, 69, 70, 73, 75, 76, 364*
William (b. 1728) 6, 51
William (b. 1697) 3
William (b. 1655) 10*
William 501
William A. (artist) 574, 591*
William A. (educator) 479*
William A. (justice) ,307
William Alden 143, 145, 148, 151, 153, 156*, 159, 162, 165, 168, 171, 174
William A. (N.C.) 117
William B. (Phila.) 458
William E. (Ga.) 118, 120, 122, 393
William E. (Wis.) 385
William F. (b. 1824) 407*, 408*
William F. (b. 1904) 271
William H. (b. 1826) 277
William H. (b. 1848) 475
William Henry 545
William J. 113
William L. 51, 52, 53, 54, 55, 435
William N. H. 103, 348
William O. 154, 157
William R. (b. 1868) 404, 483
William R. (b. 1815) 94, 96, 98, 392, 393
William R. (b. 1863) 155, 157, 160, 163, 166, 169, 172
William R. (union leader) 558
William S. (b. 1907) 322
William S. (N.Y.) (b. 1755) 64
William S. (soldier) 408
William S., Jr. 552
William W. 479
Willis (lawyer) 565
Willis (b. 1887) 227, 230, 233, 349
Wint 223, 226, 229, 232, 236, 239, 242
Worthington 484
Worthington C. 111, 113, 115
SMITHERS, Nathaniel B. 106
SMITHWICK, John H. 176, 180, 183, 186
SMOOT
Abraham O. 460
Reed 155, 157, 160, 163, 166, 169, 172, 175, 182, 185, 189, 192, 195, 199, 374
William A.S. 554
SMYLIE, Robert E. 299
SMYSER
Hamilton M. 577
Martin L. 136, 157
SMYTH
Alexander (b. 1765) 67, 69, 70, 72, 75, 77, 402, 406
Charles P. 604
Constantine J. 272
Frederick 10
Frederick (gov.) 338
George W. 98
Henry D. 570, 612
Herbert W. 570
J. Adger 451
John H. 432
Lindley 547
Timothy C. 526
W. Frank 566
William 112
SMYTHE
F. R. 450
Henry M. 427, 429
Hugh H. 432, 438
SNAPP
Henry 114
Howard M. 153, 156, 158, 161
SNAVELY, Guy 474
SNEAD
Harold F. 380
Thomas L. 393
SNEATH, William S. 553
SNEDECOR, Estes 580
SNEED
Thomas E. 450
William H. 99
SNEER, George 453*
SNELBAKER, David T. 451
SNELL
Bertrand H. 171, 174, 178, 181, 185, 188, 191, 194, 198, 201, 204, 208
Earl 357
Foster D. 567
SNELLING
Charles M. 471
Milton 558
Walter O. 601
SNIDER
Luther C. 564
Samuel P. 135
SNIPES, P. D. 459
SNODGRASS
Charles E. 149, 152
David L. 370
George M. 486
Henry C. 138, 141
John F. 98
Robert E. 600
Roy D. 536
W. D. 586
SNOOK
Homer C. 601
John S. 151, 154, 175
SNOVER, Horace G. 143, 145
SNOW
Donald F. 193, 197
Edwin M. 571
Francis H. 473
Glenn E. 578
Henry S. 479
Herman W. 137
Lorenzo 537
Marshall S. 484*
Wilbert 289
William F. 578
William J. 402
William P. 424, 434
William W. 95
SNOWDEN
A. Landon 435, 437
J. M. 459
SNYDER
Adam W. 82
Charles P. (b. 1847) 129, 131, 134, 451
Charles P. (b. 1879) 419
Edwin H. 551*
Edwin R. 481
Franklyn B. 478
Gerald C. 568
Henry F. 449
Henry N. 486
Homer P. 171, 174, 178, 181, 185
J. Y. 564
J. Buell 201, 205, 208, 211, 215, 218, 221
John 86
John I. 553*
John W. 34*, 39
Jonathan L. 475
Laurence H. 472, 563
M. G. (Gene) 248, 255, 258, 261, 264
Melvin C. 225
Meredith P. 456*
Oliver P. 113, 115
Simon 358
Virgil 568
SOBELOFF, Simon E. 271, 318
SOCKMAN, Ralph W. 604
SODERBERG, C. Richard 591
SOENNEKER, Henry J. 527
SOLBERT, Oscar N. 498
SOLLENBERGER, Paul 601
SOLLERS, Augustus R. 86, 97
SOLOMON
Alan 499
Emmett G. 546*
Harry C. 569, 571
SOLOV, Zachary 593
SOMERS
Andrew L. 188, 191, 194, 198, 201, 204, 208, 211, 214, 218, 221, 224, 227
Peter J. 141, 456
SOMERVELL, Brehon B. 401
SOMES, Daniel E. 102
SOMMER
Charles H. 549*
Clifford C. 564
SOMMERHAUSER, William B. 473
SOMMERS, Davidson 492, 546
SONDERN, Frederic F. 572
SONENSHEIN, N. 418
SONFIELD, Robert L. 579
SONNA, Peter 450
SONNEBORN, Tracy M. 573
SONNECKEN, Edwin H. 568
SONNEDECKER, Glenn 609
SONNEMANN, Roger C. 491
SONONDS, William E. 444
SOPER
Fred L. 610
Morris A. 271
SOPRIS, Richard 453
SORENSEN, R. W. 576
SORENSON
Edgar P. 412
Roy 492
SORG, Paul J. 141, 143
SORIN, Edward F. 478
SORLIE, Arthur G. 350
SOROKIN, Pitirim A. 574
SORRICK, Karl M. 576
SORSBY, William B. 424, 430
SOSNOWSKI, John B. 187
SOTH, Lauren K. 586
SOTHELL
John 9
Seth 8*
SOUCER, Appolo 417
SOUERS, Loren E. 579
SOULE
George 3
Joshua 530
Nathan 78
Pierre 89, 93, 95, 96, 311*, 437
SOUTH
Charles L. 205, 208, 212, 215
John G. 434, 435
SOUTHALL
J. P. C. 580
Robert G. 155, 158
SOUTHARD
Addison E. 427
Elmer E. 571
Henry 57, 58, 59, 60, 61, 65, 67, 68
Isaac 77
James H. 143, 146, 149, 151, 154, 157
Milton I. 117, 119, 121
Samuel L. 25*, 42, 68, 70, 79, 81, 82, 84, 85, 340*
SOUTHERLAND, Clarence A. 292
SOUTHGATE
Horatio 505
William W. 82
SOUTHWICK, George N. 143, 146, 151, 154, 157, 160, 162
SOUTHWORTH, George C. 598
SOWDEN, William H. 131, 133
SOWDON, Arthur J. C. 575
SOWER, Frank W. 453
SOWERBY, Leo 585
SOWLE, Claude R. 478
SOYER
Moses 593
Raphael 589, 593*, 610
SPAATZ, Carl A. 412, 415, 594
SPAFFORD, Edward P. 568
SPAHR, Charles E. 552*
SPAIGHT
Richard D. 4, 7, 55, 56, 347
Richard D., Jr. 71, 347
SPAIN
Frances L. 568
Frank E. 580
SPALDING
Burleigh F. 149, 154
Christopher W. 566
Franklin S. 509, 522*
George 143, 145
George R. 401
John F. 507, 519
John L. 527
Keith 470
Martin J. 523, 527
Rufus P. 107, 109, 111
Thomas 59
William A. 533
SPANGENBERG, Augustus G. 538
SPANGLER
David 79, 81
Jacob 67
W. C. 473*
SPARGO, John 497
SPARKMAN
John J. 18, 206, 209, 212, 216, 219*, 222, 225, 228, 232, 235, 238, 241, 244, 247, 251, 254, 257, 260, 263, 278
Stephen M. 142, 145, 147, 150, 153, 155, 158, 161, 164, 167, 170
SPARKS
Charles I. 193, 197
Chauncey 278
Edward J. 424, 429, 439*
Edwin E. 479
Frank H. 484
Fred 585
George M. 471
I. 461
Jared 472
John 335

W. Maynard 531
William A. J. 118, 120, 123, 125
William J. 565, 590, 608
William M. 272
SPARROW
Edward 391, 392, 393
Patrick J. 471
SPATER, George A. 543
SPAULDING
Elbridge G. 93, 103, 105, 451
Huntley N. 339
John J. 599
Oliver L. 125
Rolland H. 338
SPEAKS, John C. 181, 185, 188, 191, 195
SPEAR
Ellis 444
William T. 353*
SPEARING, J. Zach[arie] 184, 187, 190, 193
SPEARMAN, Francis H. 599
SPEARS, Robert R. 517, 521
SPECHT, Frederick W. 543*
SPEDDING, Frank H. 595, 604
SPEED
Hattie B. 502
James 19, 20, 41
James 456
Leland 454
Thomas 66
SPEER
Edgar B. 493, 554
Emory 122, 125
Peter M. 166
Robert E. 532
R. Milton 115, 117
Robert W. 453*
Thomas J. 114
SPEICHER, Eugene 593*, 607*
SPEIGHT
Francis 589*, 607
Jesse 76, 78, 79, 81, 89, 91, 326
SPEISS, Fred N. 612
SPELLACY, Thomas J. 454
SPELLER, Frank N. 601
SPELLMAN, Francis J. 523, 524, 604
SPELLMEYER, Henry 530
SPELTZ, George H. 528
SPENCE
Adolphus N. II 443
Brent 197, 200, 203, 207, 210, 213, 216, 220, 223, 226, 229, 232, 236, 239, 242, 245
Carroll 438
Edward F. 456
Floyd D. 263, 266
John S. 71, 77, 80, 82, 84, 316
Thomas A. 87
SPENCER
Ambrose 76, 344, 449
Bunyan 469
Mrs. C. Lorillard 603
Charles L. 493
Elijah 70
Elizabeth 609
F. M. 533
Frank M. 476
George E. 109, 111, 113, 115, 118, 120, 277
George L. 212, 282
Henry E. 451
Henry R. 571
Herbert L. 467
I. J. 536
James B. 83
James G. 143
John C. 26*, 39, 40, 67
John R. 497
Joseph 5, 406
Matthew L. 484
Nicholas 9
Oliver 473
Richard 71
Robert 598, 607
Robert M. 512, 522
S. B. 449
Samuel (b. 1847) 552
Samuel (b. 1910) 462
Samuel R., Jr. 469
Selden R. 174, 177, 181, 184, 330
Warren P. 600
William B. 118
William I. 547
SPENGLER, Joseph J. 566
SPERAKIS, Nicholas 609
SPERRY
Charles S. 419
Elmer A. 573, 593, 594*, 596, 598
Elmer A., Jr. 601
Jacob 547
Lewis 137, 139
Nehemiah D. 142, 144, 147, 150, 153, 155, 158, 161
Watson R. 435
SPEYER, Leonora 580, 583
SPICER, Mrs. Donald 579
SPICKERNAGLE, William 456
SPIEGEL, Frederick S. 452
SPIELMANN, C. 467
SPIER, Leslie 611
SPIES, Tom D. 590
SPIESS, Charles A. 461
SPIGHT, Thomas 145, 148, 151, 153, 156, 159, 162
SPILHAUS, Athelstan F. 564, 575
SPILLER, William G. 569
SPINGARN
Arthur B. 578
Joel E. 578
SPINNER, Francis E. 99, 101, 103, 444
SPINOLA, Francis B. 133, 135
SPITZER, Lyman, Jr. 564
SPITZGLASS, Jacob M. 601
SPITZKA, Edward C. 569
SPIVY, Berton E., Jr. 399
SPLAWN, Walter M. W. 482
SPOCK, Benjamin M. 599
SPOEHR, Alexander 497, 563
SPOFFORD
Ainsworth R. 444
S. F. 453
William, Jr. 517, 519
SPONABLE, Earl I. 580
SPONBERG, Harold E. 484
SPONG, William B., Jr. 257, 260, 380
SPOONER
Charles H. 478
Henry J. 126, 128, 131, 133, 136
John C. 131, 134, 136, 147, 149, 152, 155, 158, 161, 385*
Paul 10
Philip L., Jr. 456
SPORN, Philip 543, 591, 595, 596
SPOTSWOOD, Alexander 9
SPRADLING, A. L. 557
SPRAGENS, Thomas A. 482
SPRAGINS, Robert L. 414*
SPRAGUE
Charles A. 357, 601
Charles F. 145, 148
E. Carleton 477
Frank J. 594, 595, 596*
George A. 453
Homer B. 475, 477
Howard B. 567
Joseph H. 454
Oliver M. W. 566
Peleg (b. 1793) 72, 74, 76, 77, 79, 314
Peleg (b. 1756) 55
Robert J. 480
Thomas L. 418
William (b. 1799) 81, 86, 88, 361*
William (b. 1809) 93
William (b. 1830) 107, 109, 111, 113, 115, 117, 362*
William P. 115, 117
SPRECHER
Robert A. 272
Samuel 486
SPRENG, Samuel 531
SPRICK, Dan T. 456
SPRIGG
James C. 85
Michael C. 74, 76
Richard, Jr. 53, 54, 56
Samuel 316
Thomas 52, 53
William 352
SPRIGGS, John T. 128, 131
SPRIGLE, Raymond 584
SPRING, Gardiner 532
SPRINGER
John M. 530
Raymond S. 210, 213, 216, 220, 223
William L. 229, 232, 235, 238, 242, 245, 248, 251, 255, 258, 261
William M. 118, 120, 123, 125, 127, 130, 132, 134, 137, 139
SPRINGS, Elliott White 493
SPROUL
Elliott W. 180, 183, 187, 190, 193
Robert G. 467
Stanley E. 450
William C. 359
William H. 183, 187, 190, 193
SPROULE
John C. 564
William 552*
SPROUSE, Philip D. 425
SPRUANCE
Presley 90, 92, 94, 290
Raymond A. 417, 419, 435
SPRY, William 374
SQUIER
E. George 429
George O. 403, 594, 596
J. Bentley 565
SQUIRE, Watson C. 136, 139, 141, 144, 381
SQUIERS, Herbert G. 426, 434
SQUYERS, Scott P. 580
STAATS, Barent P. 449
STABLER, John G. 366
STACK
Edmund J. 164
John 594*, 608, 612
Joseph M. 580
Michael J. 205, 208
Thomas H. 466
STACKHOUSE, Eli T. 138
STACY, Walter P. 349
STADELMAN, G. M. 547
STAEBLER, Neil 249
STAFFORD
Ethelred M. 577
Jean 587
Mrs. Marie Peary 593
Robert T. 247, 250, 253, 257, 260, 263*, 266, 377
William 602, 610
William H. 155, 158, 161, 163, 169, 172, 176, 182, 196, 199
STAGER, Anson 554
STAGG, Peter 547
STAGGERS, Harley O. 228, 231, 234, 238, 241, 244, 247, 250, 254, 257, 260, 263, 266
STAHL
Ben 610
Eddie R. 557
STAHLE
Edward F. 451
James A. 144
STAHLNECKER, William G. 131, 133, 135, 138
STAHR
Elvis J. 399, 473, 485
John S. 470
STAIR, Mrs. Ralph M. 533
STAKEM, Thomas E., Jr. 443
STAKMAN, Elvin C. 563
STALBAUM, Lynn E. 254
STALEY, Austin L. 271
STALKER, Gale H. 185, 188, 191, 194, 198, 201
STALLINGS, Jesse F. 139, 142, 144, 147
STALLO, John B. 431
STALLWORTH, James A. 100, 102
STAMBAUGH
Armstrong A. 552
Lynn U. 568
STAMM
Frederick W. 474
John S. 531
STAMPER
John 458
Malcolm T. 544
STANARD, Edwin O. 116
STANBERY
Henry 27, 41
William 75, 76, 78
STANBURY, Nathan 458
STANDIFER, James 72, 76, 78, 80, 81, 83
STANDIFORD, Elisha D. 116, 549
STANDISH, Myles 3
STANDLEY, William H. 416, 439
STANFIELD, Robert N. 181, 185, 188, 356
STANFILL, William A. 220, 310
STANFORD
Ann 610
Edward V. 484
Henry K. 475
Homer R. 418
Leland 129, 132, 134, 136, 139, 283*, 552
R.C. 280
Richard 55, 56, 57, 58, 59, 60, 61, 63, 64, 65
STANG, William 526
STANLEY
Augustus O. 153, 156, 159, 162, 164, 167, 177, 180, 184, 309*
David S. 407, 408, 409
Edward L. 551
Thomas B. 225, 228, 231, 234, 380
W.B. 452
Wendell M. 596*, 604, 605
William 595
William B. 452
William E. 306
Winifred C. 218
STANLY
Edward 83, 84, 86, 93, 95
John 57, 61
STANNARD, E.T. 548
STANS, Maurice H. 36, 46, 444, 567
STANSBURY, Elijah 450
STANTON
Benjamin 95, 99, 101, 103
Edwin F. 438*
Edwin M. 27*, 40, 41
Frank 604
Frederick P. 90, 92, 94, 96, 97
Glenn 567
J. William 253, 256, 259, 262, 265
James V. 262, 265
Joseph, Jr. 51, 52, 57, 58, 59, 361
Patrick 484
Richard H. 93, 95, 96
Robert L. 475, 532
William H. 119
STANWELL-FLETCHER, Theodora 593
STAPLES
D.T. 547
P.A. 491
Philip C. 575
Waller R. 392, 393*
William R. 361
STAPLETON, Benjamin F. 453*
STAPP, E. Lee 576
STARCHER, George W. 477
STARCK, Taylor 577
STARECK, Jesse E. , 601
STARIHA, John N. 528
STARIN, John H. 121, 124
STARK
Benjamin 105, 356
Dudley S. 515, 521
Fortney H. 263
Harold R. 416*, 418
Leland 515, 521
Lloyd C. 330
Louis 584
Louis H. 598
Robert 452
William L. 146, 148, 151
STARKEY
Frank T. 220
Thomas A. 507, 521
STARKWEATHER
David A. 85, 90, 425
George A. 91
Henry H. 109, 111, 113, 116, 118
Samuel 452*
STARNES, Joe 202, 206, 209, 212, 216
STARR
Chauncy 569
Eliza A. 599
Isaac 589
John F. 107, 108
Louis E. 580
M. Kenneth 500
Moses A. 569
Richard C. 574
Steve 587
William G. 479
START
Charles N. 324
Theodore 452
STASSEN, Harold E. 325, 443*, 479, 534
STATTON, Arthur 531
STAUFFER
John N. 486
S. Walter 234, 240
STAUNTON, E.W. 451
STAUPERS, Mabel Keaton 611
STAVER, LeRoy B. 554*

STAYTON, John W. 372
STEADMAN, David 501
STEAGALL, Henry B. 170, 173, 176, 179, 183, 186, 189, 192, 196, 199, 202, 206, 209, 212, 216
STEARLY, Wilson R. 510, 521
STEARMAN, Lloyd 548
STEARNS
Asahel 65
Charles F. 363
Foster 211, 214, 217
Frederic P. 572
H.P. 571
Jonathan F. 532
Marcellus L. 293
Onslow 338
Ozora P. 112, 324
Raymond P. 602
Robert E.C. 497
Robert L. 468
William A. 465
STEBBINS
Ernest L. 572, 578
G. Ledyard, Jr. 574
Henry E. 433, 438
Henry G. 107
Joel 564, 610
STECK
Amos 453
Daniel F. 187, 190, 193, 305
STEDMAN
Charles M. 165, 168, 171, 175, 178, 181, 185, 188, 191, 194
Edmund C. 578
Henry R. 569
Seymour 18
William 58, 59, 60, 61
STEED, Thomas J. 227, 231, 234, 237, 240, 243, 246, 250, 253, 256, 259, 262, 265
STEEDMAN, James B. 409
STEEGMULLER, Francis 602
STEEL, Alfred G.B. 607
STEELE
E.N. 458
Edwin G. 611
Frederick 408
George McK. 474
George W. 125, 127, 130, 132, 142, 145, 147, 150
Harry L. 402
Henry J. 172, 175, 178
Holmes 454
Isaac N. 439
James H. 592
John 51, 52
John B. 105, 107
John H. 337
John N. 79, 81
Leslie J. 190, 193
Robert D. 467
Robert H. 257, 260, 264
Robert W. 285
Thomas J. 170
W.L. 454*
Walter L. 611
Walter L. (Rep.) 121, 124
William G. 105, 107
STEELMAN, John R. 443
STEENERSON, Halvor 153, 156, 159, 162, 165, 168, 171, 174, 177, 181
STEENROD, Lewis 85, 87, 88
STEENWYCK, Cornelius 457*
STEERE, William C. 574
STEEVES
B.L. 460
John M. 423
STEFAN, Karl 204, 207, 210, 214, 217, 220, 224, 227, 230
STEFANSSON, Vilhjalmur 594, 598, 599
STEGNER, Wallace E. 588
STEICHEN, Edward 590, 608
STEIGER
Sam 254, 257, 260, 263
William A. 257, 260, 263, 266
STEIN
Clarence S. 590
William H. 606
STEINBACH, H. Burr 573
STEINBECK, John 584, 606, 608
STEINBROCKER, Ann 609
STEINER
Celestin J. 469, 487
John E. 611
STEINERT, William J. 381
STEINFELD, Jesse L. 445
STEINHARDT, Laurence A. 425, 426, 435, 437, 438, 439
STEINKRAUS, Herman W. 575
STEINMAN, B.U. 460
STEINMETZ, Charles P. 594
STEIWER, Frederick 191, 195, 198, 201, 205, 208, 357
STELLE, John H. 301, 568
STELLHORN, William F. 467
STELOFF, Frances ,603
STEMPF, Victor H. 578
STENGER, William S. 119, 122
STENGLE, Charles I. 185, 557
STENNIS, John C. 223, 227, 230, 233, 236, 239, 242, 245, 249, 252, 258, 261, 265, 328
STENVIG, Charles 457
STEPHANSKY, Ben S. 424
STEPHEN, Adam 406
STEPHENS
Abraham P. 95
Albert L. 272
Alexander H. 87, 89, 91, 92, 94, 96, 98, 100, 116, 118, 120, 122, 125, 296, 391, 392
Ambrose E.B. 178, 181, 185, 188
Daniel V. 165, 168, 171, 174
E.W. 534
Frederick 451
H. Morse 567
Harold M. 272
Hubert D. 165, 168, 171, 174, 177, 184, 187, 190, 194, 197, 200, 327
John H. 146, 149, 152, 155, 157, 160, 163, 166, 169, 172
John L. 425
L.L. 459
Lon V. 329
Olin J., 2nd 611
Philander 76, 78
Robert G., Jr. 245, 248, 251, 254, 258, 261, 264
Samuel 8
Thomas J. 451
William 8
William D. 164, 167, 170, 283, 456
STEPHENSON
Isaac 129, 131, 134, 161, 163, 166, 169, 385
James 58, 62, 70, 72
John G. 444
Rome C. 564
Samuel M. 135, 137, 140, 143
William B. 567
STERETT
James P. 359
Samuel 52
STERIGERE, John B. 75, 76
STERLING
Ansel 69, 70
Bruce F. 175
Chandler W. 516, 520
Donald J. 573
Frederick A. 424, 427, 430, 431, 437
J.E. Wallace 482, 499
John A. 153, 156, 158, 161, 164, 170, 173
John W. 486
Micah 70
Ross S. 373
Theodore 473
Thomas 169, 172, 175, 178, 182, 185, 367
Walter G. 579
STERN
Curt 573
Horace 360
Otto 605
Sam 574
STERNBERG, George M. 403, 569, 572
STERNE, Maurice 593*
STERNER, James H. 578
STERRETT, Frank W. 511, 519
STETSON
Charles 93
Herbert L. 473
John B., Jr. 428, 435
Lemuel 88
STETTINIUS, Edward R., Jr. 34*, 38, 554, 603
STEUART, Leonard P. 579
STEUNENBERG, Frank 298
STEVENS
Aaron F. 110, 112
Albert W. 592*, 598
Alexander H. 569
Benjamin F. 550
Bradford N. 114
Breese J. 456
Daniel 451
Edmund 585
Eugene M. 546
Frederick C. 145, 148, 151, 153, 156, 159, 162, 165, 168
George 563, 575*
George W. 502
Harvey A. 599
Henry L., Jr. 568
Hestor L. 97
Isaac I. 407
J. Putnam 579
James 67
James H. 454
John 6
John C. 572
John F. 572, 596*, 598
John L. 430, 434, 437, 439
John P. 272
Joseph W. 449
Lewis M. 491
Lyman D. 452, 476
Moses T. 137, 140
Neil E. 574
Norman C. 454
Raymond 590
Raymond B. 168, 445
Robert S. 128
Robert T. 399
Samuel N. 471
Samuel, Jr. 316
Thaddeus 94, 95, 103, 105, 107, 109, 111
Theodore F. 257, 260, 263, 279
Wallace 586, 592, 602*
William B. (b. 1915) 501
William B. (b. 1815) 506, 521
William B. (b. 1884) 511, 520
STEVENSON
Adlai E. 14, 17, 18*, 118, 123, 139, 142, 301, 612
Adlai E., 3d 258, 261, 264, 301
Mrs. Adlai E. 579*
Andrew 70, 72, 73, 74, 75, 77, 78*, 80, 429
Carter L. 395*, 396*
Charles C. 335
Charles R. 577
Coke R. 373
Dean T. 517, 519
Elizabeth 591
George H. 571
George S. 571, 578
Harry 558
J. Ross 532
James 449
James S. 73, 75
Job E. 113, 115
Joel 452
John A. 550
John R. 573
John V. 575
John W. 100, 102, 114, 116, 118, 309*, 564
Markley 573
R.S. 491
Thomas G. 409
William E. (b. 1820) 383
William E. (b. 1900) 435, 478
William F. 175, 178, 182, 185, 188, 192, 195, 198, 443
William H. 215, 219, 222, 225
STEVER, H. Guyford 444, 467
STEVES, Sam B. 461
STEWARD
Julian H. 611
Lewis 137
Luther C. 558
STEWARDSON, Langdon C. 472
STEWART
A. Tom 208, 212, 215, 218, 221, 225, 371
Adiel F. 460
Alexander (Wic.) 144, 147, 149
Alexander D. 518, 522
Alexander P. 394, 395*, 396*, 475
Andrew (b. 1791) 70, 71, 73, 75, 78, 80, 88, 90, 92
Andrew (b. 1836) 138
B.D. 455
C. Allan 439
Charles 6
Charles (Tex.) 129, 131, 133, 136, 139
David 93, 316
David W. 187, 305
Douglas 497
E.E. 548*
Edwin L. 611
George 449*
George C. 512, 519
George D. 565
George W. 570
Irvin 485
J. Harold 567
Jacob H. 121, 460*
James 67
James A. 98, 100, 102
James B. 434*
James F. 143, 146, 149, 151
James G. 452
John (Conn.) 87
John (Pa.) 56, 57, 58
John D. 132, 134
John G. 203
John K. 149, 151
John W. 129, 131, 133, 136, 160, 376*
Lyman 554
Merch B. 483
Newell 459, 570
Paul 218, 221
Paul R. 485
Percy H. 197
Potter 270, 272
Robert M. 329
Robert W. 552
Samuel V. 331
T. Dale 500, 611
Thomas E. 111
W.L. 554
William (Md.) 450
William (Pa.) 101, 103
William H. (b. 1921) 445
William M. 106, 108, 110, 112, 114, 117, 133, 135, 138, 140, 143, 146, 148, 151, 154, 335*
STHAL, David 271
STICKLEY, John L. 577
STICKNEY, William W. 376
STICHTER, Wayne E. 565
STIEGLITZ, Julius 565, 596
STIFLE, Ethan M. 580
STIGLER
George J. 566
William G. 218, 221, 224, 227, 231
STILES
Baxter B. 453*
Ezra 487
George 450
John D. 105, 107, 113
William H. 87, 423
STILL, Clyfford 589
STILLE
Alfred 569
Charles J. 479
STILLINGS, Charles A. 443
STILLMAN
Allyn S. 454
Charles B. 557
James 547*
James A. 547*
STILLWAGEN, Colin A. 578
STILLWELL
Lewis B. 599
Thomas N. 108, 439
Willis B. 595
STILWELL
Joseph W. 404, 405, 411*, 412
Richard G. 400
STIMPSON, Harry F., Jr. 434
STIMSON
Frederic J. 423
Henry L. 31*, 33*, 34*, 38, 40*, 609
Rufus W. 468
STINCHFIELD, Frederick H. 565
STINESS
John H. 362
Walter R. 172, 175, 178, 182
STINSON, Bill 250
STIRES, Ernest M. 512, 520
STIRLING
Matthew W. 592*, 593
Mrs. Matthew W. 592
STITH

Gerald 457
Gerard 558
William 486
STITT
E.R. 416
Theodore 580
STIVERS, Moses D. 135
STOAN, D. Lindley 318
STOBBS, George R. 187, 190, 194
STOCK, Chester 576
STOCKARD, Charles R. 573
STOCKBRIDGE
Francis B. 132, 135, 137, 140, 322, 443
H.E. 477
Henry 135, 474, 579
Levi 475
STOCKDALE
Edward G. 430
Thomas R. 132, 135, 137, 140
STOCKING
George W. 566
Jay T. 534
STOCKLEY, Charles C. 291
STOCKMAN, Lowell 218, 221, 224, 227, 231
STOCKSLAGER, Strother M. 125, 127
STOCKTON
Charles H. 419, 471
Gilchrist B. 423
John P. 108, 112, 114, 117, 340*, 434
Richard 3, 6, 15, 54, 55, 65, 340
Robert F. 95, 340
Thomas 290
STOCKWELL, B. Foster 531
STODDARD
A.E. 554
Alice Kent 593, 598
Ebenezer 69, 70
Francis R. 575*
George D. 472
Herbert L. 592
STODDERT
Benjamin 23*, 42
John T. 79
STODIECK, Wilbur H. 459
STOESSEL, Walter J., Jr. 435
STOESSINGER, John G. 591
STOFFER, Bryan S. 484
STOKE, Harold W. 474, 476, 479
STOKELY, Samuel 86
STOKES
Anson P., Jr. 515, 520
Carl B. 452
Charles F. 416
Colin 552
Edward C. 340
Edward L. 198, 201
J. Stogdell 601
J. William 144, 146, 149
Louis 259, 262, 265
Montfort 65, 67, 68, 70, 347*
Rembert 486
Thomas L. 584
William B. 103, 109, 111, 113
STOKLEY, William S. 458
STOKOWSKI, Leopold 590, 603
STOLK, W.C. 491
STOLL
Clarence G. 554
Philip H. 178, 182
STOLTZ, Merton P. 467
STOLTZFUS, William A., Jr. 431
STONE
Alfred P. 88
Calvin P. 571
Charles B. 412
Charles W. 136, 138, 141, 144, 146
Claudius U. 164, 167, 170
Corliss P. 461
David 56, 57, 58, 59, 64, 347*
David L. 403
Eben F. 125, 128, 130
Edward Durrel 591*, 603
Edward W. 451
Frederick 110, 112
George C. 595
George W. 277
George W., Jr. 577
Harlan F. 32, 41, 270*
J.A.B. 473
James K. 472, 473
James W. 87, 95
John 452
John H. 316
John M. 326, 327, 475
John S. 600
John T. 532
John W. 121, 123
Joseph C. 120
Judson F. 548
Kimbrough 272
Lyndes B. 551
Marshall H. 568
Marvin L. 567
Michael J. 51
Mortimer 286
Ruth 610
Thomas 3, 4, 6
Ulysses S. 195
W. Clement 493
Warren S. 557
William (Md.) 8
William (Tenn.) 83
William A. 138, 141, 144, 146, 359
William H. 116, 119
William J. (Mo.) 130, 133, 135, 153, 156, 159, 162, 165, 168, 171, 174, 329*
William J. (Ken.) 130, 132, 135, 137, 140
William M. (b. 1779) 505, 520
William M. 304
William S. 483
Winthrop E. 479
Witmer 569, 592
STONEMAN, George 283, 408*, 409
STONER, R.B. 491
STONES, George C. 595
STONESTREET, Charles H. 471
STONEY
James M. 513, 520
Thomas P. 451
STOOKEY, S. Donald 612*
STOOPS, Herbert M. 598
STOPPEL, Arthur E. 455
STORER
Bellamy (b. 1796) 81
Bellamy (b. 1847) 138, 141, 423, 424, 437
Clement 60, 67, 337
D. Humphreys 569
James W. 534
Norman W. 599
Robert W. 569
STOREY
Moorfield 564
Robert G. 565, 589
William B. 543
STORK, Charles W. 580
STORKE
Harry P. 487
Thomas M. 206, 284, 587, 601
STORM
Frederic 151
John B. 115, 117, 128, 131
STORMS, A.B. 473
STORROW, James J. 543, 574
STORRS
Charles B. 485
Henry R. 67, 68, 71, 73, 74, 76
John W. 452
Richard S. 567
William L. 75, 77, 83, 287
STORY
Ala 502
John P. 401
Joseph 60, 269, 597
Mrs. William Cumming 579
Worth 451
STOUFFER, Samuel A. 573
STOUGH, Fruman C. 518, 519
STOUGHTON
Bradley 572, 575
Clarence C. 486
E.W. 436
William 3, 8*, 10
William L. 112, 114
STOUT
Byron G. 137
Ernest G. 608
George L. 499, 502
Jacob 290
Lansing 103
Minard W. 476
Rex 574*
Richard F. 416
Samuel V.D. 457
Tom 168, 171
STOVALL, Pleasant A. 438
STOVER
Elias S. 476
Fred 580
John H. 110
STOW
Alexander W. 385
Silas 62
STOWE
A. Monroe 482
Allen B. 473
Harriet Beecher 597
Leland 583
W. McFerrin 531
STOWELL
John M. 456
William H.H. 115, 117, 120
STOWER, John G. 74
STRADER, Peter W. 113
STRADLING, George F. 600
STRAIGHT, James L. 450
STRAIT
Horace B. 116, 119, 121, 125, 128, 130
Thomas J. 141, 144, 146
STRANAHAN, James S.T. 99
STRAND, August L. 476, 478
STRANGE
James F. 449
Robert (b. 1796) 81, 83, 84, 347
Robert (b. 1857) 509, 519
STRATEMEYER, George E. 416
STRATTON
C.S. 475, 479
Charles C. 82, 86
Charles G. 340
George M. 571
George O. 457
Howard W. 474
John 57
John L.N. 103, 105
Julius A. 475, 598
Nathan T. 95, 97
Samuel S. (b. 1898) 475
Samuel S. (b. 1916) 243, 246, 249, 253, 256, 259, 262, 265
Samuel W. 475, 594
William G. 213, 223, 301
STRAUB
Albert H. 453
Christian M. 97
STRAUGHN, James H. 530
STRAUGHTON, William 471
STRAUS
Aaron 493
Isidor 141
Jesse I. 428
Nathan 603
Oscar S. 31*, 45, 438*
William L., Jr. 611
STRAUSS
Israel 569
Joseph 418
Lewis L. 35, 46, 443, 598, 608
Willis A. 550*
STRAUSZ-HUPE, Robert 424, 425, 432
STRAVINSKY, Igor 603
STRAW, Ezekiel A. 338
STRAWBRIDGE, James D. 117
STRAWN, Silas H. 565, 575
STRAYER
Frank T. 580
Joseph R. 567, 577
STRECKER
Edward A. 571
Ignatius J. 523
Ignatius H. 529
STREET
Allen 458
Charles L. 515
George L. 579
Randall S. 68
STREETER
Alson J. 17
D.R. 558
Thomas W. 563
STREETT, St. Clair 411, 412*
STREIBERT, Theodore 445
STRETTELL, Robert 458
STRIBLING
C.K. 483
T.S. 584
STRICKLAND
Hardy 392
Randolph 112
STRICKLER, Woodrow M. 474
STRIDER
Robert E. 511, 522
Robert E.L., 2d 468
STRIGHAM, Silas H. 417
STRINGER, Lawrence B. 167
STRINGFELLOW
Douglas R. 234
George E. 579
STRITCH, Samuel A. 523*, 529
STROBEL, Edward H. 425
STRODE
H.A. 468
Jesse B. 143, 146
STROH
Donald A. 413, 414
Nicholas W. 607
STROHM
Adam 568
John 90, 92
STROHMEYER, Joseph 588
STROM, Carl W. 424, 425
STRONG
Benjamin 544
Caleb 4, 51, 52*, 53, 319*
Edward W. 467
Frank 473, 478
Frederick S. 404, 410
George V. 400*
Henry A. 546
James 68, 71, 73, 74, 76
James G. 177, 180, 183, 187, 190, 193, 197
James W. 467
Jedediah 5
John 580
John D. 601
Jonathan 609
Julius L. 111, 113
L. Corrin 434
Luther M. 141, 143
Nathan L. 175, 178, 182, 185, 188, 192, 195, 198, 201
Robert C. 430
Selah B. 88
Soloman 65, 66
Stephen 90
Sterling P. 202
Theron R. 84
Thomas C. 485
Willard R. 457
William (b. 1763) 63, 64, 69
William (b. 1808) 92, 94, 269
William D. 611
William L. 458
STROOP, Paul D. 417*, 418
STROTHER
Dean C. 416
George F. 67, 69
James F. (b. 1811) 96
James F. (b. 1868) 189, 192
Samuel B. 455
STROTZ, Robert H. 478
STROUD, William D. 567
STROUSE, Myer 107, 109
STROWD, William F. 143, 146
STROZIER, Robert M. 470
STRUBLE
Arthur D. 417
Isaac S. 127, 130, 132, 134
STRUDWICK, William F. 54
STRUGHOLD, Hubertus 597
STRUM, Louie W. 271
STRUSS, James H. 471
STRUVE
Henry G. 461
Otto 564
STRYKER, Melanchthon W. 471
STUART
Albert R. 515, 519
Alexander H.H. 26, 27, 44, 87
Andrew 97
Archibald 83
Charles E. 91, 95, 97, 98, 99, 100, 322
David 97
Elbridge A. 544*
Elbridge H. 544*
Edwin S. 359, 458
Francis L. 572
Gilbert 597
Granville 434, 439
Harold C. 592
Henry C. 379
J. Leighton 425
James E.B. 394*, 395*
Jeb (See James E.B.)
Jesse 589
John T. 84, 85, 106
Philip 62, 63, 65, 66
R. Douglas 425
R. Marvin 531
STUBBLEFIELD, Frank A. 242, 245, 248, 252, 255, 258, 261, 264
STUBBS
Henry E. 199, 202, 206
Joseph E. 476

Marshall 402
Walter R. 306
STUBER, William G. 546*
STUCKEY, W.S., Jr. 254, 258, 261, 264
STUDDS, Gerry E. 264
STUDEBAKER
Clement, Jr. 550
John W. 444
Mabel 578
STUDLEY, Elmer E. 201
STUEMPFIG, Walter 589, 593
STUKES, Taylor H. 366
STULBERG, Louis 558
STULL, Howard W. 198
STULTS, Allen P. 564
STUMP
Felix B. 416, 417*
Herman 135, 137
STUMPF, Samuel E. 468
STUNKARD, Albert J. 598
STUNTEBECK, Francis F. 480
STUNTZ, Homer C. 530
STURGEON, Daniel 85, 86, 88, 90, 92, 93, 358
STURGES
Jonathan 5, 51
Lewis B. 58, 60, 61, 62, 63, 65
STURGIS
Guy H. 315
R. Clipston 567
Samuel D. 407*, 408*
Samuel D., Jr. 402
STURGISS, George C. 161, 163
STURM, Clarence L. 577
STURTEVANT
Alfred H. 573, 604
Harwood 512, 519
John C. 146
STUTESMAN, James F. 424
STUYVESANT, Peter 8
STYRON, William 587, 598
SUCZEK, Robert 601
SUGARMAN, George 607
SUGDEN, Walter S. 579
SULLINS, David 470
SULLIVAN
A.M. 580*
Christopher D. 174, 178, 181, 185, 188, 191, 194, 198, 201, 204, 208, 211
David 559
Denis J. 460
Donal M. 557
E. Mark 574
Ed 577
Eugene C. 607
George 62
Ignatius A. 454
James (Mass.) 6, 319
James (Conn.) 454
James H. 558
James J. 480
James M. 427
Jerd F., Jr. 546
Jerry B. 273
John 6, 8, 337, 406
John A. 153, 156
John B. 214, 220, 227, 230
John L. (Judge) 333
John L. (Gen.) 399
John P. 574
Leon 611
Leonor Kretzer 233, 236, 239, 242, 246, 249, 252, 255, 258, 262, 265
Louis H. 590
Max W. 501
Matt I. 283
Maurice J. 217
Mortimer A. 484
Patrick J. (Pa.) 195, 198
Patrick J. (Wyo.) 196, 387
Peter J. 425
Reginald H. 454*
Thomas L. 454
Timothy D. 154, 157, 168
William H. 431
Mrs. William H., Jr. 579
William V. 145*, 148, 327
SULLOWAY, Cyrus A. 143, 146, 148, 151, 154, 157, 159, 162, 165, 171, 174
SULTAN, Daniel I. 402, 411, 413
SULZBERGER
Arthur Hays 601, 609
Cyrus L. 585
SULZER, William 143, 146, 149, 151, 154, 157, 160, 162, 165, 345
SUMAN, John R. 567, 596, 601
SUMMER, James A. 547
SUMMERALL, Charles P. 400, 404, 410
SUMMERFIELD, Arthur E. 35*, 43
SUMMERLIN, George T. 430, 434, 439
SUMMERS
A. Burke 432
Augustus N. 353
George W. 87, 88
John W. 179, 182, 186, 189, 192, 195, 199
SUMMERSKILL, John 481
SUMMITT, H.C. 462
SUMNER
Arthur P. 579
Charles 95, 97, 98, 100, 102, 104, 106, 108, 110, 112, 114, 116, 319
Charles A. 127
Daniel H. 129
Edwin V. 407*, 408
George G. 454
Increase 319
James B. 605
Jessie 210, 213, 216, 219
Jethro 406
Walter T. 510, 521
William G. 573
SUMNERS, Hatton W. 169, 172, 175, 182, 185, 189, 192, 195, 199, 202, 205, 208, 212, 215, 218, 222, 589
SUMWALT, Robert L. 481
SUMTER
Thomas 51, 52, 55, 56, 57*, 58, 59, 60, 62, 364, 406
Thomas, Jr. 435
Thomas D. 85, 87
SUN, Chen 608
SUND, R.J. 491
SUNDERLAND, Byron 472
SUNDERMAN, F. William 572
SUNDSTROM, Frank L. 217, 220, 224
SUPER, Charles W. 478*
SUPPLEE, Henderson, Jr. 544*
SURFACE, James R. 473
SURLES, Alexander D., Jr. 405
SUTHERLAND
Archibald H. 402
Charles 403
Earl W., Jr. 600, 606
Edwin H. 573
George 152, 157, 160, 163, 166, 169, 172, 270, 374, 564
Howard 169, 172, 175, 179, 182, 383
Jabez G. 114
Joel B. 75, 76, 78, 80, 81
Josiah 95
Roderick D. 146, 148
SUTPHIN, William H. 197, 201, 204, 207, 211, 214
SUTRO, Adolph 461
SUTTON
George M. 593
Glenn W. 445
Goyn A. 461
Henry M. 611
James P. 228, 231, 234
Joseph L. 473
Leonard B. 286*
William J. 403
William S. 482
SUZZALLO, Henry 484
SWAIM
David G. 402
H. Nathan 272
SWAIN
Charles A. 576
David L. 347, 477
George F. 572
Joseph 473, 482
Leslie E. 534
Robert L. 609
W.W. 454
SWAINSON, John B. 323
SWALLOW, Silas C. 17
SWAN
John 7
Joseph R. 352
Samuel 70, 71, 73, 74, 76
Thomas W. 271
William G. 393*
SWANK
Emory C. 425
Fletcher B. 181, 185, 188, 191, 198, 201
SWANN
Sherlock, Jr. 575
Edward 151
Richard 449*
Thomas 112, 114, 116, 118, 121, 317, 450
William F.G. 594
SWANSEN, Raymond 559
SWANSON
Charles E. 193, 197
Claude A. 33*, 42, 141, 144, 147, 149, 152, 155, 158, 163, 166, 169, 172, 175, 179, 182, 186, 189, 192, 195, 199, 379*
Clifford A. 416
Harold A. 453
Ralph A. 458
SWANTON, John R. 611
SWANWICK, John 54, 55
SWART, Peter 60
SWARTS, Gardner T. 572
SWARTWOUT
Mary Cooke 500
Robert 403
SWARTZ
Carl E. 572, 590
Joshua W. 188
SWASEY
Ambrose 573, 590, 596, 598
John P. 159
SWAYNE, Noah H. 269
SWEARER, Howard R. 467
SWEARINGEN
Eugene L. 483
Henry 83, 85
Henry C. 532
John E. 552*
Van C. 454
SWEAT, Lorenzo D.M. 106
SWEATT, H.W. 548
SWEAZEY, George E. 533
SWEENEY
James J. 526
James Johnson 499, 500
James P. 467
Martin L. 198, 201, 204, 208, 211, 214
Robert E. 253
Thomas W. 409
Walter C., Jr. 415
William N. 112
Zachary T. 536
SWEENY
Edward C. 577
George 85, 86
SWEET
Burton E. 170, 173, 176, 180
Edwin F. 165
Frederick A. 501
James R. 461*
John E. 573, 596
John E., Jr. 534
John H. 210
Thaddeus C. 185, 188, 191
William E. 285
William H. 466
Willis 134, 137, 139
SWEETLAND, William H. 362
SWEETSER
Charles 93, 95
Frank L. 568, 577
SWENEY, Joseph H. 134
SWENGEL, Uriah 531
SWENSON
Eric P. 547
Laurits S. 427, 433, 434*, 438
May 610
Orvar 599
SWENSRUD, S.A. 548
SWETMAN, Ralph W. 465
SWETT, Josiah 478
SWICK, J. Howard 192, 195, 198, 201
SWIDLER, Joseph C. 443
SWIFT
A. Ervine 515
Benjamin 75, 76, 80, 81, 83, 375
C.H. 460
Eben 419
George Bell 451*
George R. 219, 278
Gustavus 553
Gustavus F., Jr. 553*
H.A. 324
Innis P. 412, 415
John 458*
Joseph G. 402, 483
Louis F. 553*
Oscar W. 171, 174
Willis E. 449
Zephaniah 52, 53, 287
SWIGER, Ernest G. 578
SWIGERT
John L., Jr. 608
Phillip 453
SWINBURNE, John 131, 449
SWINDALL, Charles 178
SWING
Joseph M. 405, 415, 419, 443
Philip D. 179, 183, 186, 189, 193, 196
SWINNEY, E.F. 564
SWINT, John J. 529
SWISHER, Carl B. 571
SWITZER, Robert M. 166, 169, 172, 175
SWOOPE
Jacob 62
William I. 185, 188
SWOPE
Gerard 598, 603
Guy J. 208
Herbert Bayard 583
John A. 128, 131
King 177
Samuel F. 98
SWORDS
Raymond J. 472
Vincent T. 477
SWYGERT, Luther M. 272
SYKES
Eugene O. 443
George 407*, 408*
George (N.J.) 88, 90
Richard E. 480
James 5, 290
William E. 601
Wilfred 548
SYLVIS, William H. 558
SYMES, George G. 129, 132
SYMMES
Anna T. 20
Harrison M. 431
John C. 6
SYMINGTON
J. Fife, Jr. 438
James W. 258, 262, 265
Stuart 233, 236, 239, 242, 246, 249, 252, 255, 258, 262, 265, 330, 399, 612
SYMMS, Steven D. 264
SYMONS, Gardner 610
SYMONDS, Gene 607
SYPHER, J. Hale 110, 112, 114, 116
SYPHERD, Wilbur O. 469
SYRETT, Harold C. 467
SZENT-GYORGYI, Albert von 589, 605
SZILARD, Leo 595*

T

TABER
John 185, 188, 191, 194, 198, 201, 204, 208, 211, 214, 218, 221, 224, 227, 230, 233, 237, 240, 243, 246
L.J. 578
Stephen 109, 111
Thomas 74
TABOR, Horace A.W. 124, 285
TACKETT, Boyd 225, 229
TAFEL, Gustav 452
TAFF, George S. 462*
TAFFE, John 110, 112, 114
TAFT
Alphonso 28*, 40, 41, 423, 436
Charles P. 143, 452
Jonathan 566
Kingsley A. 221, 354*
Robert A. 211, 214, 218, 221, 224, 227, 230, 234, 354
Robert, Jr. 249, 256, 259, 262, 265
Royal C. 362
Russell S. 376
William Howard 13, 17, 18, 30*, 44, 270, 271, 564, 569, 575, 603
William Howard, 3d 430
TAGGART
Joseph 164, 167, 170
Samuel 58, 59, 60, 61, 62, 64, 65
Thomas 170, 454
TAGUE, Peter F. 171, 174, 177, 180, 184
TAILER, William 8*
TAINTOR, C.C. 600
TAIT
Charles 61, 62, 63, 65, 66, 295
Watson F., Jr. 551

  William 457
TAITT, Francis M. 512, 521
TAKASAKI, Richard S. 472
TALBERT
  Mary B. 611
  W. Jasper 141, 144, 146, 149, 152
TALBOT
  Arthur N. 572, 596
  Beatrice 597
  Ethelbert 507, 519*, 522
  Harold E. 399, 550
  Isham 63, 65, 66, 68, 69, 71, 308
  Joseph C. 506, 520, 521
  Joseph E. 213, 216, 219, 445
  Nathan B. 592, 599
  Phillips 429
  Ray H. 285
  Samson 469
  Silas 3
  Thomas 320
  Thomas W. 557
  Walter 459
TALBOTT
  Albert G. 98, 100
  J. Fred C. 123, 125, 127, 140, 153, 156, 159, 162, 165, 168, 171, 174
  Leander J. 455
  Philip M. 575
TALBURT, Harold M. 584
TALCOTT
  Burt L. 248, 251, 254, 257, 260, 263
  Charles A. 165, 168
  George 402
  J. Frederick 565
  Joseph 8
TALIAFERRO
  Benjamin 55, 56
  James P. 147, 150, 153, 155, 158, 161, 293
  John 57, 63, 72, 73, 75, 77, 82, 83, 85, 87
  William B. 394*
TALLCHIEF, Maria 593
TALLE, Henry O. 210, 213, 216, 220, 223, 226, 229, 232, 235, 239
TALLEY, Lee 545*
TALLMADGE
  Benjamin 56, 57, 58, 60, 61, 62, 63, 65
  Frederick A. 91
  James, Jr. 67
  John J. 456
  Nathaniel P. 79, 81, 83, 84, 86, 88, 344
TALLMAN, Peleg 62
TALLON, William T. 480
TALLY, J.O., Jr. 576
TALMA, Louise 611
TALMADGE
  Eugene 297*
  Herman E. 238, 241, 245, 248, 251, 254, 257, 261, 264, 297*
  Mrs. Julius Y. 579
TALMAGE
  James E. 484
  Samuel K. 478
TAMM, Edward 272
TANEY, Roger B. 25*, 39, 41, 269
TANNEHILL, Adamson 64
TANNER
  Adolphus H. 113
  Edmund E. 577
  John R. 300
  Paul F. 528
  Robert H. 576
TANZLER, Hans, Jr. 454
TAPPAN
  Benjamin 84, 86, 88, 352
  David S. 475
  Eli T. 473
  Henry P. 475
  Mason W. 99, 101, 103
TAPPIN, John L. 432
TAPSCOTT, Ralph H. 545*
TARADASH, Daniel 563
TARBELL, Edmund C. 593*, 598, 607*, 610
TARBOX
  Frank K. 550
  George E., Jr. 579
  John K. 119
TARKINGTON
  Andrew W. 546
  Booth 583*, 598, 603, 609
TARR
  Christian 67, 68
  Curtis W. 445, 474
TARSNEY
  John C. 135, 138, 140, 143
  Timothy E. 130, 132
TARVER, Malcolm C. 190, 193, 196, 200, 203, 206, 213, 216, 219
TASCA, Henry J. 429, 433
TASKER
  Benjamin 3, 8, 449
  Homer G. 580
TATE
  Allen 578, 589, 592*
  Benjamin 459
  Farish C. 139, 142, 145, 147, 150, 153
  H.T. 444
  J. Waddy 453
  James H.J. 458
  John A. 536
  John T. 570
  Joseph 459
  Magnus 66
  Willis M. 481
TATGENHORST, Charles Jr. 191
TATHAM, William P. 575
TATLOCK, John S.P. 577*
TATLOW, Richard H. 572
TATNALL
  Edward F. 69, 71, 72, 74
  Josiah 53, 54, 295*, 396*
TATOM, Absalom 54
TATUM
  Edward L. 606
  M.B. 457
  T.P. 462
TAUBER, Maurice F. 595
TAUL, Micah 65
TAULBEE, William P. 130, 132
TAURIELLO, Anthony F. 227
TAURO, G. Joseph 321
TAUSSIG
  Frank W. 445, 566
  Helen B. 567, 599, 600, 607, 608
  John H. 600
TAVENNER, Clyde H. 167, 170
TAWES, J. Millard 318
TAWNEY, James A. 140, 143, 145, 148, 151, 153, 156, 159, 162
TAX, Sol 563, 611
TAYLER, Robert W. 143, 146, 149, 151
TAYLOR
  A.B. 456
  A.H. 598
  Abner 134, 137
  Albert D. 573
  Alexander W. 117
  Alfred A. 136, 138, 141, 370
  Archer 577
  Archibald A.E. 486
  Arthur H. 140
  Benjamin I. 168
  Caleb N. 111, 113
  Carl C. 573
  Charles E. 455, 484
  Charles G., Jr. 549
  Chester W. 179
  Claude A. 366
  Claudia Alta 20, 604
  Daniel G. 460
  David W. 418, 596*, 611
  Dean P. 218, 221, 224, 227, 230, 233, 237, 240, 243
  Deems 572
  E.H., Jr. 453*
  E. Leland 456
  Ed R. 451
  Edward L., Jr. 157, 160, 163, 166
  Edward R. 594
  Edward R. (Mayor) 461
  Edward S. 608
  Edward T. 161, 164, 167, 170, 173, 176, 179, 183, 186, 189, 193, 196, 199, 203, 206, 209, 212
  Edward W. 569
  Ezra B. 124, 126, 128, 131, 133, 136, 138
  F.A. 500
  Francis Henry 499, 502*, 603
  Frank A. 500
  Fred M. 566
  Fred W. 594
  Frederick E. 534
  Frederick W. (bishop) 509, 521
  Frederick W. 573
  Gene 265
  George (Rep.) 101
  George 3, 7
  George A. 517, 519
  George W. 608
  George Washington 144, 147, 150, 152, 155, 158, 161, 164, 167
  Glen H. 18, 219, 223, 226, 299
  H. Birchard 594
  H.M. 454
  Hannis 437
  Harold 481
  Harry 402
  Henry 607
  Henry J. 438
  Henry O. 567
  Herbert J. 580
  Henry C. 418, 419
  Herbert W. 181, 188
  Horace D. 454
  Howard C. 565
  Howard C., Jr. 565
  Hugh S. 493, 596, 604
  Isaac H. 131
  J. Alfred 186, 189
  J. Will 178, 182, 185, 189, 192, 195, 198, 202, 205, 208, 212
  J. Winthrop 416
  Jack D. 551
  James M. 484
  John (N.Y.) 344
  John (Albany) 449
  John (Va.) 52, 53, 58, 70, 72, 378*
  John (S.C.) 60, 62*, 63, 64, 66, 364*, 452
  John (Utah) 537
  John C. 202, 205, 208
  John J. 97
  John L. (N.C.) 347
  John L. (Ohio) 92, 93, 95, 97
  John M. (bus. exec.) 545
  John M. (Rep.) 129, 131
  John M. (U.S.N.) 417
  John N. 591
  John W. (Rep.) 64, 65, 67*, 68, 70, 71, 72, 73, 74, 76, 78
  John W. (b. 1906) 474
  Jonathan 85
  Joseph 607
  Joseph D. 126, 128, 133, 136, 138
  Joshua C. 500
  Lady Bird 20, 604
  Leon 340
  Lily R. 570
  Mark P. 451
  Maxwell D. 399, 400, 401, 404*, 405, 415, 439, 483, 604
  Miles 98, 100, 102
  Moses 547
  Moulton B. 601
  Myron C. 554*
  Nathaniel G. 97, 109
  Nelson 109
  Paul 593
  Prince A., Jr. 531
  R.L. 416
  Reese H. 554*
  Richard M. 459
  Robert 73
  Robert F. 293
  Robert L. 124, 160, 163, 166, 370*
  Robert Lewis 586
  Robert W. 143, 146, 149, 151
  Roy A. 243, 246, 249, 253, 256, 259, 262, 265
  Russell J. 559
  S.J. 454
  Sam F. 482
  Samuel M. 164, 167, 170, 173, 176, 179
  Simon 452*
  Stephen W. 468
  Theophilus M. 533
  Vincent A. 138
  W.R.L. 458
  Waller 65, 66, 68, 69, 71, 302
  Walter P. 575
  Wayne C. 443
  William (Rep. Va.) 88, 90
  William (Rep. N.Y.) 79, 81, 83
  William (bishop) 530
  William C. 607
  William H. (mayor) 454
  William H. (bus. exec.) 551
  William H. 584
  William P. 80
  William R. 385
  William S. 309
  Zachary 13, 16, 131
TAZEWELL
  Henry 52, 53*, 54, 55, 378
  Littleton W. 16, 56, 72, 73, 75, 76, 77, 78, 378*
TEAGLE, Walter C. 493, 552, 553*, 590
TEAGUE
  Charles M. 235, 238, 241, 244, 248, 251, 254, 257, 260, 264
  Donald 591*
  Olin E. 225, 228, 231, 234, 237, 240, 244, 247, 250, 253, 256, 260, 263, 266
  Sam E., Jr. 462
  W.M. 457
TEAL
  B.F. 600
  Gordon K. 598
TEALE
  Edward L., Jr. 611
  Edwin W. 587, 593
TEARE, B.R., Jr. 576
TEASDALE, Sara 583
TEBBETTS, George P. 461
TEEL, Warren F. 465
TEESE, Frederick H. 119
TEIGAN, Henry G. 207
TEITZ, Richard S. 502
TELFAIR
  Edward 4, 5, 8*, 295
  Thomas 63, 65
TELFORD, William C. 461
TELLER
  Edward 595*
  Henry M. 29, 44, 118, 120, 122, 124, 129, 132, 134, 137, 139, 142, 144, 147, 150, 152, 155, 158, 284, 285
  Isaac 97
  James H. 285
  Ludwig 240, 243
TELLES, Raymond 426
TELLIER, Remigius I. 470
TEMPLE
  Edward A. 510, 521
  Gray 516, 521
  Henry W. 169, 172, 175, 178, 182, 185, 188, 192, 195, 198
  J.R. 453
  Jackson 283
  William 290
TEMPLETON
  B.J. 459
  Charles A. 288
  Max A. 455
  Thomas W. 175
TEMPLIN, Richard L. 601
TEN BROECK, Abraham 449*
TENCH, Thomas 8
TENER, John K. 163, 359, 574
TENEROWICZ, Rudolph G. 210, 213
TEN EYCK
  Anthony 430
  Egbert 71, 73
  Jacob C. 449
  John C. 103, 105, 107, 340
  Peter G. 168, 181
TENNEHILL, Wilkins 457
TENNENT
  Charles G. 580
  David H. 573
  William M. 532
TENNEY
  Henry M. 478*
  John S. 314
  Samuel 56, 57, 58, 59
TENZER, Herbert 253, 256
TERMAN
  Frederick E. 598
  Lewis M. 571
TERRAL, Thomas J. 282
TERRELL
  Alexander W. 438
  Daniel V. 572
  Edwin E. 424
  George B. 202
  Henry, Jr. 413, 414
  James C. 80
  Joseph M. 161, 164, 296*
  W. Glenn, Jr. 485
  William 66, 68
TERRES, John K. 593
TERRIS, Milton 572
TERRY
  Alfred H. 410
  Charles L., Jr. 292*
  David D. 199, 202, 206,

209, 212
David S. 283
John H. 262
Luther L. 445
Lyon F. 601
Nathaniel 66, 453
Thomas A. 411
Thomas D. 481
William 115, 120
William L. 136, 139, 142, 144, 147
TESCHEMACHER, H.F. 461
TELSA, Nikola 594, 595
TEST, John 71, 72, 75
TETZLAFF, Joseph 469
TEW, James D. 547
TEWES, Donald E. 241
TEWKSBURY
Donald G. 466
Howard H. 434
TEYRAL, Hazel J. 593
THACH
Charles C. 466
John S. 416
THACHER
George 473
George (Rep.) 6, 51, 52*, 53, 54, 56
George H. 449*
John B. 449*
John B., 2d 449
John M. 444
Nicholas G. 436
Thomas C. 168
THALER, Louis K. 577
THALHEIMER, Walter J. 459
THARP, William 290
THATCHER
George O. 471
H.M. 460
Henry C. 285
Henry K. 417
Maurice H. 184, 187, 190, 193, 196
Roscoe W. 475
Samuel 56, 58
THAXTER
Benjamin A. 474
Roland 574
THAYER
Abbott H. 593, 607, 610
Amos M. 272
Andrew J. 105
Benjamin B. 543
Edwin B. 516, 519
Eli 100, 102
Harry B. 543, 554
Harry I. 187
Henry E. 486
John A. 165
John M. 108, 110, 112, 333*
John R. 148, 151, 153
M. Russell 107, 109
Robert H. 436
Samuel R. 433
Sylvanus 483, 597
William R. 567, 603
William S. 569
William W. 356
THEAKER, Thomas C. 103, 444
THEBAUD
Augustus 470*
Hewlett 416
THEILER, Max 600, 605
THEIS, John B. 467
THELEN
Max 491
Max, Jr. 491
THEOBALD, John J. 479
THEOPHILUS, Donald R. 472
THEUERER, Henry C. 601
THIBODEAUX, Bannon G. 89, 91
THIELE, Walter G. ,307
THIELEPAPE, W.C.A. 461
THIEME, Frederick P. 468
THILL
Frank A. 528
Lewis D. 212, 215
THILLY, Frank 564
THIMANN, Kenneth V. 574
THIRKFIELD, Wilbur P. 472, 530
THISTLEWOOD, Napoleon B. 158, 161, 164
THOBURN, James M. 530
THOM
Cameron E. 456
Horace B. 491
William R. 201, 204, 208, 214, 221
THOMAS
A.G. 536
Albert 208, 212, 215, 218, 222, 225, 228, 231, 234, 237, 240, 244, 247, 250, 253
Albert S. 512, 521
Allen 439
Augustus 578, 603
Benjamin F. 104
C.G. 600
C.W. 455*
Calvin 566, 577
Charles A. 549*, 565, 590, 608
Charles R. 115, 117, 149, 151, 154, 157, 160, 162
Charles S. (Sen.) 164, 167, 170, 173, 176, 285*
Charles S. 399, 553
Christopher Y. 117
David 57, 58, 59, 60
Dorothy S. 573
Edwin J. 547*
Elbert D. 202, 205, 208, 212, 215, 218, 222, 225, 228, 374
Elisha S. 507, 520
Francis 77, 79, 81, 82, 84, 104, 106, 108, 110, 316, 435
Frank W. 470
Franklin 572
George (b. 1705) 9
George (b. 1866) 484
George H. 406, 408, 409*, 410
George M. 132
Gerald W. 476
Henry F. 140, 143
Henry M. 569
Isaac 66
Isaiah 563
J. Elmer 564
J. Parnell 207, 211, 214, 217, 220, 224, 227
James 316
James E. 462
James H. 92, 94, 103
James J. 452
James R. 470
James S. (mayor) 460
James S. (bishop) 531
Jesse B. 66, 68, 69, 71, 72, 74, 300
John (b. 1725) 406
John (b. 1805) 538
John (b. 1874) 190, 193, 196, 209, 213, 216, 219, 299*
John C. 55
John H. 449
John J. 392
John L. 591
John Lewis Jr. 108
John M. 475
John M. 478, 479, 480
John R. 123, 125, 127, 130, 132
John W. 590
J.W. Elmer 185, 188, 191, 195, 198, 201, 205, 208, 211, 214, 218, 221, 224, 227, 355
Joshua 580
Lera M. 253
Lorenzo 401
Lot 148, 150, 153
M. Carey 467
Marion B. 483
Nathaniel S. 509, 522
Nicholas W. 451
Ormsby B. 131, 134, 136
Philemon 77, 79
Phillip F. 27, 39, 84, 118, 316, 444
Richard 54, 55, 56
Robert S. 486
Robert Y., Jr. 162, 164, 167, 170, 173, 177, 180, 184
Samuel F. 466
Seth 272
W. Stephen 502
Walter S. 572
William A. 154, 157, 160, 163
William D. 201, 204
William I. 573
William M.M. 512
William S. 515
William W., Jr. 437*
Wray 452
THOMASON
Hugh F. 392
R. Ewing 199, 202, 205, 208, 212, 215, 218, 222, 225
THOMASSON, William P. 87, 89
THOMPSON
Al A. 459
Albert C. 131, 133, 136
Alexis W. 548*
Allen C. 454
Arthur W. 551
Benjamin 591
Benjamin (Rep.) 89, 95
Carmi A. 444
Charles F. 403, 411, 412
Charles J. 178, 181, 185, 188, 191, 195
Charles L. 532
Charles O. 486
Charles P. 119
Charles W. 150, 152
Chester C. 200, 203, 206
Clark W. 202, 225, 228, 231, 234, 237, 240, 244, 247, 250, 253
David E. 424, 433
David P. 438
Dorothy 603
Earl A. 610
Edwin J. 474
Ernest O. 590
Ezra 460*
Fletcher 254, 258, 261
Floyd E. 574
Floyd L. 567
Fountain L. 162, 350
Frank, Jr. 236, 239, 243, 246, 249, 252, 256, 262, 265
George A. 558
George W. 96
Glenn W. 469
Guy A. 565
Hedge 20
Hugh M. 507, 520
Hugh S. 365
J.A. 533
J. Eric S. 595, 611
J.F. 483
Jacob 27, 44, 84, 86, 88, 89, 91, 93
James (mayor) 459
James (judge) 90, 92, 94, 359
James W. 567
Joel 64
John (banker) 545
John (b. 1749) 56, 60, 61
John (b. 1809) 101
John B. 84, 85, 91, 93, 96, 98, 100, 308
John E.W. 427, 429
John M. 117, 122
John R. 485
Johnathan 545
Joseph B. 169, 172, 175, 178
Joseph W. 271
Lawrance R. 588
Leslie A. 461*
Llewellyn E. 423, 439*
Margaret 574
Marvin R. 492
Matthew L.P. 532
Melvin E. 297
Orrel 497
Paul 473
Paul W. 492
Philip 71
Philip B., Jr. 123, 125, 127
Philip R. 57, 58, 59
Raymond H. 497
Richard W. 28, 42, 85, 91
Robert A. 92
Robert W. 533
Rupert C., Jr. 553*
Ruth 230, 233, 236
Samuel C. 545
Sheldon 450
Smith 24, 25, 42, 269, 344
Theo A. 233, 236, 239, 242, 245, 248, 252
Thomas L. 132, 424
Thomas W. 59, 64, 65, 337
Tyler 428, 430
Waddy, Jr. 81, 83, 85, 433
Wanna F. 454
Wiley 69, 71, 72, 74, 75, 77
William (coll. pres.) 486
William (Rep.) 91, 93
William G. (mayor) 453*
William G. (Rep.) 123, 125
William H. (Kans.) 167, 170, 173, 201, 306
William H. (Ill.) 451*
William H. (Nebr.) 334
William O. (coll. pres.) 475, 478
William O. 532
William P. 533
THOMSON
Alexander , 72, 73
Arthur C. 510, 522
Charles M. 167
David 484
Edward 530
E. Keith 238, 241, 244
Elihu 594, 595, 596*, 609
John 73, 76, 78, 79, 81
John R. 97, 99, 101, 103, 105, 340
Mark 54
Meldrim, Jr. 339
Thaddeus A. 426
Vernon W. 247, 250, 254, 257, 260, 263, 266, 386
Virgil 585, 592, 603
THON, William 589*
THONE, Charles 262, 265
THOREAU, Henry David 597
THORINGTON
J.H. 457*
James 98
THORKELSON, Jacob 210
THORNBER, John J. 497
THORNBERRY
David R. 517, 522
W. Homer 228, 231, 234, 237, 240, 244, 247, 250, 271
THORNBURGH, Jacob M. 117, 120, 122
THORNDIKE
Ashley H. 577
Edward L. 563, 571, 593
Lynn 567
THORNELL, Jack R. 587
THORNTHWAITE, Charles W. 594
THORNTON
Anthony 108
Dan 286
George 548
George T. 557
James B. 435
John R. 162, 164, 167, 312
Matthew 3, 6
R.L. 453
Ray 263
Walter F. 481
William 559
William M. 484
William T. 461
THORNWELL, James H. 481, 532
THORP, Robert T. 144, 147
THORPE
Burton L. 566
James 499
Roy H. 181
THOURON, Henry J. 607
THROCKMORTON
James W. 120, 122, 129, 131, 372
John L. 404, 405
THROOP
Enos T. 344, 436
George R. 485
THROPP, Joseph E. 149
THROWER, Randolph W. 444
THRUSTON
Buckner 59, 60, 61, 308
R.C. Ballard 579
THURLOW, Oscar G. 607
THURMAN
Allen G. 17, 90, 113, 115, 117, 119, 121, 122, 124, 353
J.M. 452
John R. 93
THURMOND, J. Strom 18, 237, 240, 243, 247, 250, 253, 256, 259, 263, 266, 366
THURNAUER, Hans 575
THURSTON
Benjamin B. 92, 96, 97, 99
John M. 143, 146, 148, 333
Lee M. 444
Lloyd 187, 190, 193, 200, 203, 206
Raymond L. 429, 437
Robert H. 573
Theodore P. 510, 519, 521
Walter 424, 427*, 433
THURSTONE, Louis L. 571
THWAITE, Reuben G. 568
THWING, Charles F. 485
THYE, Edward J. 223, 227, 230, 233, 236, 239, 325*
TIBBATTS, John W. 87, 89
TIBBETT, Lawrence 557
TIBBETTS, Margaret J. 434

TIBBITS, George 58
TIBBLES, Thomas H. 17
TIBBOTT, Harve 211, 215, 218, 221, 224
TIBBS, William H. 393
TICE
Linwood F. 570, 609
Merton B. 580
TICHENOR
Isaac 54, 55, 67, 68, 69, 375*
Isaac T. 465
TIDD, George N. 543
TIDINGS, Joseph 610
TIDRICK, R.L. 453
TIEF, Francis J., 528
TIEMANN
Daniel F. 458
Norbert T. 334
TIERNAN
Frances 599
Martin F. 601
Robert O. 256, 259, 262, 266
TIERNEY
Michael 526
William L. 196
TIFFIN, Edward 60, 352*
TIFT, Nelson 110
TIGERT, John J. 444, 470, 530
TIGHT, William G. 476
TIHEN, John H. 526, 527
TILDEN
Daniel R. 88, 90
John P. 575
Samuel J. 17, 345
TILFORD
Henry M. 552
John E. 549
TILGHMAN
Benjamin C. 594
Edward 3
Matthew 6
William 358, 570
TILL, William 458
TILLER, Carl W. 534
TILLETT, William S. 600
TILLEY
Edward 3
John 3
TILLINGHAST
Charles S., Jr. 553*
Joseph L. 83, 85, 86
Pardon E. 362
Thomas 55, 57
TILLMAN
Benjamin R. 144, 146, 149, 152, 154, 157, 160, 163, 166, 169, 172, 175, 365*
George D. 124, 126, 129, 131, 133, 136, 138
James D. 427
John B. 483
John N. 465
John N. (Rep.) 170, 173, 176, 179, 183, 186, 189
Lewis 113
Samuel E. 483
TILLOTSON, David 57
TILNEY
A.A. 544
Frederick 569
TILSON
John Q. 161, 164, 170, 173, 176, 179, 183, 186, 189, 193, 196
William J. 273
TILTON, James 5, 403
TIMANUS, E. Clay 450
TIMBERLAKE
Charles B. 170, 173, 176, 179, 183, 186, 189, 193, 196
Clare H. 426
TIMBERS, William H. 271
TIMKEN
Edith 493
Henry H. 493
Henry H., Jr. 493
W.R. 493
TIMMERMAN, George Bell, Jr. 366
TIMMONS
Benson E.L., 3d 429
Gerald D. 566
TIMON, John 525
TIMOSHENKO, Stephen P. 594
TINCHER, Jasper N. 177, 180, 183, 187
TINDALE, John J. 574
TINDELL, S.W. 467
TINGLEY
Clyde 343
Katherine 539
TINKER
Clarence L. 412
Isaac 457
Thomas 3
TINKHAM, George H. 171, 174, 177, 180, 184, 187, 190, 194, 197, 200, 203, 207, 210, 213
TINSLEY, Harry C. 566
TIPPETT, Donald H. 531
TIPPO, Oswald 574
TIPTON
John 77, 79, 80, 82, 302
Thomas F. 120
Thomas W. 108, 110, 112, 114, 117, 333
TIREY, Ralph W. 473
TIRRELL, Charles Q. 151, 153, 156, 159, 162
TISDEL, Frederick M. 487
TISHLER, Max 608
TITCOMB
Lendall 449
Samuel 449
TITSWORTH, Paul E. 465
TITTMANN
Harold H., Jr. 429, 435
O.H. 578
TITTLE, H.M. 558
TITUS, Obadiah 83
TIVNAN, Edward P. 470
TLOURDE, Gary 596
TOBERMAN, James R. 456*
TOBEY
Charles W. 201, 204, 207, 211, 214, 217, 220, 224, 227, 230, 233, 339
Edward S. 570, 580
F.T. 456
Frank A. 401
Mark 590, 607
TOBIAS
Channing H. 611
Charles W. 575
TOBIN
Daniel J. 558
James 566
John W. 576
John W. (mayor) 461
Maurice J. 34, 35, 46, 321, 450
Richard 453
Richard H. 433
TOBRINER, Walter N. 431, 462
TOCH
Ernest 586
Maxmilian 567
TOD
David 352, 424
John 70, 71
TODD
Albert M. 145
Charles S. 436
Dolly [Dorothea] (Payne) 20
George D. 456
Henry A. 577
James M. 573
Lemuel 99, 117
Mary Ann 20
Paul H., Jr. 252
Thomas 269, 308
W.E. Clyde 592*
TODMAN, Terence A. 425, 429
TOEBBE, Augustus M. 525
TOEPFER, Louis A. 468
TOLAN, John H. 202, 206, 209, 212, 216, 219
TOLAND
George W. 83, 85, 86
John 588
Terrence 480
TOLISCHUS, Otto D. 584
TOLL
Herman 243, 246, 250, 253
William E. 510
TOLLEFSON, Thor C. 225, 228, 231, 234, 237, 241, 244, 247, 250
TOLLEY
Harold S. 188
William P. 465, 482
TOLMAN
Carl 485
Edgar B. 589
Edgar C. 571
Ruel P. 500
Warren W. 381*
TOMLINSON
C.W. 564
Elizabeth 536
Gideon 67, 69, 70, 72, 77, 78, 80, 287*
Irving C. 536*
Thomas A. 86
Travis H. 459
TOMPKINS
Arthur S. 149, 151
Caleb 67, 68
Christopher 77, 79
Cydnor B. 101, 103
Daniel D. 14, 15, 66, 67, 69, 70, 344
Emmett 151
George 329
Harvey J. 571
Patrick W. 91
TOMPPERT, Phil 456*
TONE, Frank J. 575, 589
TONELLI, Joseph P. 558
TONER, Joseph M. 569, 571
TONGUE, Thomas H. 146, 149, 151
TONRY, Richard J. 204
TOOKER
John S. 455*
Sterling T. 553
TOOLE
Joseph K. 331*
K. Ross 500, 501
TOOLEN, Thomas J. 527
TOOLEY, William H. 599
TOOMBS, Robert 89, 91, 92, 94, 96, 98, 100, 102, 295, 391*, 392
TOON, Malcolm 426, 439
TOPEL, Bernard J. 529
TOPPING, Norman 481
TORBERT
Alfred T.A. 406, 409, 436
Horace G., Jr. 424, 437
TORBET, Robert G. 534
TORCHIO, Philip 595
TORNEY, George H. 403
TORRANCE, David 288
TORRENCE
John F. 451
Ridgely 589, 610
TORRENS, James H. 218, 221
TORREY
John 563
Joseph 484
TOTTEN
J.G. 402
Ralph J. 438
Silas 473, 482
TOUCEY, Isaac 26, 27*, 41, 42, 80, 82, 94, 96, 98, 287*
TOULMIN, Harry 482
TOURET, Frank H. 510, 519, 522
TOU VELLE, William E. 160, 163
TOWAR, James D. 487
TOWE
Harry L. 217, 220, 224, 227, 230
Kenneth C. 543*
TOWER
Charlemagne 423, 428, 436
Dudley 554
John G. 247, 250, 253, 256, 260, 263, 266, 373
Walter S. 568, 596
John G. 247, 373
Zealous B. 483
TOWERS
John H. 417*
John T. 462
TOWERY, Roland K. 586
TOWEY
Frank W., Jr. 207
James F. 550
TOWLE, Simon 461
TOWN, Charles F. 558
TOWNE
Charles A. 143, 148, 157, 324
Henry R. 573
TOWNER, Horace M. 164, 167, 170, 173, 176, 180
TOWNES, Charles H. 570, 598, 606, 610
TOWNS, George W.B. 80, 82, 89, 295
TOWNSEND
Amos 121, 124, 126
Charles C. 136
Charles E. 153, 156, 159, 162, 165, 168, 171, 174, 177, 180, 322
Charles H. 497
Dwight 107, 115
E.D. 401
Edward W. 165, 168
Edwin F. 419
Franklin 449
George 65, 67
H. Clifford 303
Hosea 134, 137
J. 461
John 449*
John G., Jr. 193, 196, 199, 203, 206, 209, 291, 292
Lawrence 424, 435
M. Ernest 477
Martin I. 119, 121
Robert L. 417
Washington 113, 115, 117, 119
William K. 271
TOWNSHEND
Norton S. 95
Richard W. 120, 123, 125, 127, 130, 132
TOWNSLEY, Clarence P. 483
TOY, Crawford H. 570
TRABANT, Edward A. 469
TRACEWELL, Robert J. 142
TRACEY
B. Peter 474
Charles 133, 135, 138, 141
John P. 143
TRACY
Albert H. 68, 70, 71
Andrew 98
Benjamin F. 29, 30, 42
D.W. 558*
Henry W. 107
Joseph P. 400
Phineas L. 74, 76, 78
Robert E. 525
Uri 59, 61, 62
Uriah 52, 53*, 54, 55, 56, 57, 58, 60, 287
TRADEWELL, James D. 452
TRAEGER, William I. 199
TRAFTON, Mark 99
TRAHUE, Charles C. 457
TRAIN
Arthur 574, 578
Charles R. 102, 104
H.C. 416
William F. 405*, 419
TRAMBURG, John W. 445
TRAMMELL, Park 173, 176, 180, 183, 186, 189, 193, 196, 199, 203, 293*
TRANSEAU, Edgar N. 574, 575
TRANSUE, Andrew J. 207
TRAPHAGEN, John C. 544
TRAPIER, Paul 7
TRAPNELL, Thomas J.H. 405
TRAPP
Frank A. 499
Martin E. 355
TRAQUAIR, James 550
TRASK
Harry A. 586
John E.D. 499, 501
Ozell M. 272
Willard 602
TRAUTMAN, Gerald H. 543
TRAVER, William A. 553*
TRAVERS, Howard K. 429
TRAYLOR
John H. 452
Melvin A. 546, 547, 564
TRAYNOR
Philip A. 213, 219
Roger J. 284, 589
TRAYWICK, Leland 476
TREACEY, John B. 527
TREADWAY, Allen T. 168, 171, 174, 177, 180, 184, 187, 190, 194, 197, 200, 203, 207, 210, 213, 217
TREADWELL
Daniel 609
J.W.F. 575
John 5, 287
TREANOR, Walter E. 272
TREAT
Charles G. 404, 410
Charles H. 444
John F. 579
Robert 8*
Samuel H. 300
TREDTIN, Walter S. 469
TREDWAY, William M. 90
TREDWELL, Thomas 52, 53
TREE, Lambert 424, 436
TREEN, David C. 264
TREGASKIS, Richard 607
TREINEN, Sylvester W. 525
TRELEASE
Richard M., Jr. 520
William 574
TRELOAR, William M. 143
TREMAIN, Lyman 117
TRENHOLM
George A. 391
W.L. 554
TRENOR, Henry H. 559
TRENT, William 10

TRESIDDER, Donald B. 482
TREUTLEN, John A. 8
TREZVANT, James 73, 75, 77
TRIBBITT, Sherman W. 292
TRIBBLE
Harold W. 484
Samuel J. 164, 167, 170
TRIGG
Abram 55, 56, 57, 58, 59, 61
Connally F. 131
John J. 55, 56, 57, 58
TRILLING, Lionel 592
TRIMBLE
Allen 352
Carey A. 103, 105
David 66, 68, 69, 71, 72
James W. 219, 222, 225, 229, 232, 235, 238, 241, 244, 247, 251
John 111
Lawrence S. 108, 110, 112
Robert 269
South 150, 153, 156
Vana 586
William A. 68, 70, 352
William C. 425
TRINKLE, E. Lee 380
TRIPLETT
George W. 393
Philip 84, 85
TRIPP
Bartlett 423
Guy E. 554
H.T. 455
TRIPPE
Juan T. 550*, 597, 598, 603, 612
Robert 98, 100, 392
TRIPPET, Byron K. 484
TRIST, Nicholas P. 433
TRIVELLI, Albert 481
TROBEE, James 528
TROOST
George W. 491
Gerard 563
TROTH, Joseph D. 557
TROTTER
Frank B. 485
James F. 82, 326
Mildred 611
TROTTI, Samuel W. 87
TROUP, George M. 60, 61, 62, 63, 65, 66, 75, 77, 78, 295*
TROUSDALE, William 369, 424
TROUT
Douglas G. 483
Michael C. 97
TROUTMAN, William I. 218
TROWBRIDGE
Alexander B. 36, 46, 568
Alvah 564
C.C. 453
John 563
Josiah 450
Rowland E. 104, 108, 110
TROLAND, L.T. 580
TROXEL, Oliver L. 439
TROY, William 602
TROYER, Laird J. 455
TRUAX, Charles V. 201, 204
TRUBACH, Ernest 593
TRUDEAU
Arthur G. 400, 401
Charles 457
TRUEBLOOD, Robert M. 567
TRUEHEART, William C. 434
TRUESDELL, Karl 419
TRUETT, George W. 534
TRUITT, George 290
TRULLINGER, J.T. 458
TRUMAN
David B. 476, 571
Harry S 204, 207, 210, 214, 217, 219, 220, 330, 596, 597, 598
James 566
Louis W. 405
TRUMBO, Andrew 89
TRUMBULL
James H. 570
John H. 289
Jonathan (b. 1710) 8, 10
Jonathan (b. 1740) 51*, 52, 53, 287*
Joseph (b. 1737) 5
Joseph (b. 1782) 78, 83, 85, 287
Lyman 98, 100, 102, 104, 106, 108, 110, 112, 114, 300
Merlin L. 572
TRUMP, John G. 599
TRUESCOTT, Lucien K., Jr. 405, 412, 413
TRUSLOW, John A. 451
TRUSSEL, C.P. 585
TRYON
Dwight W. 607
J.R. 416
William 8, 9
TSCHAPPAT, William H. 402
TSCHOEPE, Thomas 525, 528
TUCHMAN, Barbara W. 587, 588
TUCK
Amos 91, 93, 95
S. Pinkney 427*
William M. 234, 237, 241, 244, 247, 250, 253, 257, 380
TUCKER
Beverly D. 509, 513, 521, 522
Ebenezer 73, 74
George 69, 70, 72, 484
Henry H. 471, 475
Henry St. George (b. 1780) 66, 67, 378, 484
Henry St. George (b. 1853) 136, 139, 141, 144, 182, 186, 189, 192, 195, 199, 485, 564
Henry St. George (b. 1874) 510, 522
John R. 396
John R. (N.J.) 462*
John R. (Va.) 120, 122, 124, 126, 129, 131, 564
Merle H. 576
Raymond R. 460
Robert H. 485
Starling 67, 69, 70, 72, 73, 75, 76
Thomas T. 7, 51, 52, 444
Tilghman M. 88, 326
William H. 600
William J. 469
TUCKERMAN
Charles K. 429
Louis B. 611
TUDOR
William (law.) 402
William (dipl.) 424
TUFTS, John Q. 118
TUGWELL, Rexford Guy 591
TUIGG, John 528
TULLOSS, Ress E. 486
TULLY
Albert J. 576
Pleasant B. 127
TUMULTY, T. James 236
TUNNARD, Christopher 602
TUNNELL
Elbe W. 291
James M. 213, 216, 219, 292
TUNNER, William H. 415, 416
TUNNEY, John V. 251, 254, 257, 260, 263, 284
TUOHY, William 587
TUPPER
Frederick 577
Stanley R. 245, 248, 252
TURCK, Charles J. 474
TURLEY, Thomas B. 146, 149, 370
TURNBULL, Robert 163, 166
TURNER
A. Francis 580
Archelaus E. 483, 485
Benjamin S. 113
Carl C. 403
Charles, Jr. 61, 62
Charles E. 453
Charles H. 135
Charles Y. 591
Clarence W. 182, 202, 205, 208, 212
Dan W. 305
Daniel 75
Edward C. 516, 520
Eli M. 485
Erastus J. 132, 134
Evan H. 501
Ewald 578
Frederick Jackson 567, 584
G.H. 453*
George 147, 149, 152, 381
Henry G. 125, 127, 129, 132, 134, 137, 139, 142
Herman L. 533
J. Milton 432
Jabez 460
James (N.C.) 59, 60, 61, 62, 64, 65, 347*
James (Md.) 79, 81
James M. 455*
James H. 460*
Joel H. 456
John 3
John B. 355
John R. 485
Josiah 393
Oscar 123, 125, 127, 148
Ralph H. 574
Roy J. 355
Scott 567, 598
Smith S. 141, 144
Thomas 121, 123
Thomas G. 362
Thomas J. 91
Vines E. 566
Wallace 586
Walter V. 594, 600
William 525
TURNEY
Hopkins L. 83, 85, 87, 90, 92, 94, 369
Jacob 119, 122
Peter 370
TURPIE, David 104, 132, 134, 137, 139, 142, 145, 302*
TURPIN
C. Murray 195, 198, 201, 205
Edward A. 439
Louis W. 134, 136, 139
TURRELL
Herbert 493
Margaret 493
TURRILL, Joel 79, 81
TUSTIN, Ernest L. 534
TUTEN, J. Russell 248, 251
TUTHILL
John W. 424
Joseph H. 115
Selah 70
TUTT
Charles L. 491
William T. 491
TUTTLE
Arthur S. 572
Daniel S. 506, 519, 520*, 522
Elbert P. 271
Emerson 502
Hiram A. 338
James M. 408
Martin 453
William E., Jr. 165, 168
TUTWILER, Carrington C. 600
TUVE, Merle A. 591, 608
TWADDLE, Harry L. 414
TWAIN, Mark 597
TWEED
Benjamin 484
Charles H. 552
Harrison 481, 568, 589
William M. 97
TWEEDY, Samuel 78
TWICHELL, Ginery 110, 112, 114
TWINING
Nathan C. 418
Nathan F. 399, 400, 401, 412*, 415*, 594
TWIST, Oliver S. 577
TWITCHELL
George M. 450
Herbert K. 545*
R.E. 461
TWITTY, Victor C. 573
TWOMBLY, John 486
TWORKOV, Jack 593
TWYMAN
Frank 611
Joseph 483
Robert J. 223
TYDINGS
Joseph D. 252, 255, 258, 318
Millard E. 184, 187, 190, 193, 197, 200, 203, 207, 210, 213, 217, 220, 223, 226, 318
TYLER
Alice S. 568
Asher 88
B.B. 536
Bennett T. 469
Daniel 407
D. Gardiner 141, 144
Henry S. 456
J. Hoge 379
James M. 124, 126
John (b. 1790) 13, 14, 16*, 66, 67, 69, 75, 76, 78*, 80, 81, 85, 87, 378, 392
John (b. 1747) 378
John P. 510, 521
Lyon G. 486
Priscilla Cooper 20
Richard G. 478
Royall 375
S. Heth 458
William 526
William R. 433
TYNDALL
Robert 454
William T. 156
TYNER
George P. 400, 401
James N. 28*, 43
James N. 112, 114, 116
TYNTE, Edward 9
TYRELL, W. Bradley 466
TYRRELL
D.L. 455
John 546
TYSON
Charles R. 550, 551
Jacob 71
Job R. 99
John R. 179, 278
Lawrence D. 189, 192, 195, 370
Levering 476
TYTUS, John B. 596

U

UBBY, Winthrop C. 474
UCELLO, Antonina P. 454
UDALL
Morris K. 244, 247, 251, 254, 257, 260, 263
John H. 459
Nicholas 459
Stewart L. 36*, 44, 235, 238, 241, 591
UDREE, Daniel 64, 68, 70, 72
UDY, Marvin J. 575
UHL, Edwin F. 428
UFER, Walter 589, 593, 598, 607
UHLENBECK, George E. 570
UHLIG, Herbert H. 575
UHLMAN, Wesley C. 461
ULIO, James A. 401
ULLMAN
Albert C. 240, 243, 246, 250, 253, 256, 259, 262, 265
Berthold L. 570, 577
ULLSVIK, Bjarne R. 486
ULRICH
Charles F. 593
Edward O. 607
Frederick L. 600
ULTANY, Don 585
ULVELING, Ralph A. 568, 600
UMBECK, Sharvy G. 473
UMSTEAD, William B. 201, 204, 208, 224, 349*
UNDERHILL
Charles L. 180, 184, 187, 190, 194, 197
Edwin S. 165, 168
John Q. 149
Walter 93
UNDERWOOD
Cecil 384
Felix J. 572
G.V., Jr. 405
John W.H. 102
Joseph R. 80, 82, 84, 85, 91, 93, 95, 308
Julius E. 578
L. Wesley 474
Mell G. 185, 188, 191, 195, 198, 201, 204
Oscar W. 142, 144, 147, 150, 152, 155, 158, 161, 164, 167, 170, 173, 176, 179, 183, 186, 278
Thomas R. 226, 229*, 310
Warner L. 98, 100
UNGER
Irwin 587
Leonard 431, 438
UNTERKOEFLER, Ernest L. 525
UPDEGRAFF
Harlan 468
Jonathan T. 124, 126
Thomas 123, 125, 140, 142, 145
UPDIKE
John 602, 609
Ralph E. 187, 190
UPFOLD, George 506, 520
UPHAM
Alfred H. 472, 475
Charles W. 297, 460
Don A.J. 456
Frank B. 418
George B. 57
Jabez 60, 61
John H.J. 569
John S., Jr. 405, 419

Nathaniel 67, 68, 70
William 88, 90, 92, 94, 96, 375
William H. 385
UPJOHN
Richard 567
W.H. 492
UPLINGER, Robert J. 577
UPSHAW, William D. 176, 180, 183, 186
UPSHUR
Abel P. 26*, 38, 42
George P. 483
UPSON
Charles 106, 108, 110
Christopher C. 124, 126
Maxwell M. 601
William H. 113, 115
UPTON
Charles H. 105
Miller 466
Robert W. 233, 339
URBAHN, Max O. 567
URBAN
Ralph E. 512
Thomas N., Jr. 453
UREY, Harold C. 596*, 604, 605
URNER, Milton G. 123, 125
USHER, John P. 27, 44
UTLEY
George B. 568
Henry M. 568
UTT, James B. 232, 235, 238, 241, 244, 248, 251, 254, 257
UTTER, George H. 166, 362
UTTERBACK
Hubert 203
John G. 200

V

VACQUIER, Victor 612
VAIL
Aaron 429, 437
George 97, 99
Henry 83
Richard B. 223, 229
Theodore N. 543*
Thomas H. 506, 520
VAILE, William N. 176, 179, 183, 186
VAKY, Viron P. 426
VALDEZ, Manuel 461
VALE, Roy E. 532
VALENTI, Jack 577
VALENTINE
Alan 480
Edward K. 123, 126, 128
Emery 455*
Joseph F. 558
Milton 471
Warren P. 601
VALETTE, Eugene 558
VALK, William W. 99
VALLANDIGHAM, Clement L. 101, 103, 105
VALLIANT, Leroy B. 330
VALTMAN, Edmund S. 587
VAN AERNAM, Henry 109, 111, 124, 126
VAN ALEN
James I. 60
John E. 53, 54, 55
VAN ALLEN
James A. 594, 597
John T. 427
VAN ALSTYNE
Norman 558
Thomas J. 128, 449
VANAMAN, Arthur W. 419
VAN AMRINGE, John H. 568
VAN ANTWERP
Eugene I. 453, 580
Lee D. 575
VAN ARSDALE, T.W., Jr. 466
VAN AUKEN, Daniel M. 111, 113
VAN BEUREN, Archbold 575
VAN BIESBROECK, George 593
VAN BOMEL, Leroy A. 548*
VAN BRUGH, Pieter 449*
VAN BRUNT, Henry 567
VAN BUREN
James H. 509, 521
John 86
Martin 13, 14, 16*, 25, 38, 70, 71, 73, 74, 78, 80, 344*, 429
William H. 455
VANCE
Cyrus R. 399*, 608
John L. 119
Joseph 70, 71, 73, 75, 76, 78, 79, 88, 90, 352
Joseph A. 532
Robert B. (b. 1793) 71
Robert B. (b. 1828) 117, 119, 121, 124, 126, 128
Robert J. 132
Rupert B. 573
S.B.H. 458
Sheldon B. 425, 426
William F. 456
Zebulon B. 101, 103, 124, 126, 128, 131, 133, 135, 138, 141, 348*
VAN CLEAVE, J.W. 578
VAN CLEVE, H.P. 408, 409
VAN CORTLANDT
Jacobus 458*
Philip 53, 54, 55, 56, 57, 58, 59, 60
Pierre, Jr. 62
Stephanus 10, 457*
VAN DAM, Rip 8
VAN DE CARR, C.R., Jr. 549
VAN DEERLIN, Lionel 248, 251, 254, 260, 264
VAN DE GRAFF, Robert J. 594
VANDEGRIFT, Alexander A. 416
VAN DEMAN, Ralph H. 400
VANDENBERG
Arthur H. 190, 194, 197, 200, 203, 207 210, 213, 217, 220, 222, 223, 226, 230, 323, 596, 609
Hoyt S. 400, 412, 415*
VANDERBILT
Arthur T. 342, 565, 568, 589
William 363
VANDERHOFF, V.L. 502
VANDERHORST
Arnoldus 364, 451*
John 515, 522
VANDER JAGT, Guy 255, 258, 261, 265
VANDERLIP, F.A. 547
VANDER LUGHT, Gerrit T. 467
VANDERPOEL, Aaron 79, 81, 84
VAN DEVANTER, Willis 270, 272, 387
VANDERVEER, Abraham 83
VAN DE VELDE, James O. 525, 527, 480
VAN DE VEN, Cornelius 525
VANDEVER, William 102, 104, 132, 134
VAN DE VYVER, Augustine 528
VANDIVER
Frank E. 480
Samuel E., Jr. 297
Willard D. 145, 148, 151, 154
VAN DOREN
Carl 584
Mark 563, 584, 589
VAN DORN, Earl 394
VAN DRESER, Joseph 453
VAN DUSEN, Francis L. 271
VAN DUYN, Mona 592, 602
VAN DUZER
Albert W. 517
Clarence D. 154
VAN DYCK, Vedder 513, 522
VAN DYKE
Carl C. 171, 174, 177
Henry 432, 433, 532, 578
Henry J. 532
James A. 453
John 91, 93
John C. 578
John H. 550
Nicholas (b. 1738) 4, 5, 8
Nicholas (b. 1769) 60, 61, 66, 67, 69, 70, 72, 290
William D. 550
VANE, Henry 8
VAN EATON, Henry S. 128, 130
VAN ETTEN, Nathan B. 569
VAN EVERDINGEN, Antonius F. 601
VAN FLEET
Frederick A. 575
James A. 405*, 412, 413, 414
VAN GAASBECK, Peter 53
VAN HARLINGEN, Ernest 498
VAN HISE, Charles R. 486, 563, 575
VAN HOLLEN, Christopher 425
VAN HORN
Burt 105, 109, 111
George 138
Kent R. 572
Marion D. 453
Robert T. 108, 110, 112, 125, 143, 455*
William H. 601
VAN HORNE
Archibald 60, 61
Espy 73, 75
Isaac 57, 58
VAN HOUTEN, Isaac B. 79
VAN HYNING, Thompson 499
VANIK, Charles A. 237, 240, 243, 246, 249, 253, 256, 259, 262, 265
VAN KEUREN, Alexander H. 418*
VAN LAER, Alex T. 574
VAN LEAR, Thomas 457
VAN LEER, Blake R. 471
VAN METER, Ralph A. 475
VANMETER, John I. 88
VANN, John Paul 608
VAN NESS
Cornelius P. 375*, 437
James 461
John P. (mayor) 462
John P. (Rep.) 57
VAN NIEL, Cornelis B. 604, 610
VAN NORDEN, Charles 470
VAN NORTWICK, John 545
VAN NUYS, Frederick 200, 203, 206, 210, 213, 216, 303
VAN ORSDEL, Josiah A. 272, 579
VAN OSTERHOUT, Martin D. 272
VAN OSTRAND, Archie E. 536
VAN PELT
John R. 500
William K. 231, 235, 238, 241, 244, 247, 250
VAN QUICKENBORNE, Charles F. 480
VAN RAVENSWAAY, Charles 498
VAN RENSSELAER
Cortlandt 532
Henry B. 86
Jeremiah 51
Killian K. 57, 58, 59, 60, 61
Mariana Griswold 589
Maunsell 472
Philip S. 449*
Robert 406
Solomon V. 68, 70
Stephen 70, 71, 73, 74, 406
VAN REYPEN, William K. 416, 569
VAN ROSSEM, Adrian J. 592
VAN ROSSUM, Theodore 467
VAN SANT
James E. 246
Joshua 97, 450
Samuel R. 324
VAN SCHAICK
Isaac W. 131, 136
Sybrant G. 449
VAN SLYKE, Donald D. 594, 596, 604
VAN SOELEN, Theodore 589
VAN SWEARINGEN, Thomas 69, 70
VAN TRUMP, Philadelph 111, 113, 115
VAN TWILLER, Wouter 8
VAN TYNE
Claude H. 583
Josselyn 569
VAN VALKENBERG, John 576
VAN VALKENBURGH
Arba S. 272
Robert B. 105, 107, 431
VAN VECHTEN, Teunis 449*
VAN VLECK
Edward B. 568
John H. 570, 604
John M. 485
VAN VOORHIS
Henry C. 141, 143, 146, 149, 151, 154
John 124, 126, 141
VAN VORHES, Nelson H. 119, 121
VAN WAGONER, Murray D. 323
VAN WINKLE
Lee 458*
Marshall 157
Peter G. 107, 109, 111, 383
VAN WYCK
Charles H. 103, 105, 111, 113, 126, 128, 130, 333
Robert A. 458
William W. 70, 71
VAN ZANDT
Charles C. 362
James E. 211, 215, 218, 224, 228, 231, 234, 237, 240, 243, 246, 580
VARCO, Richard L. 600
VARDAMAN, James K. 168, 171, 174, 327*
VARE, William S. 166, 169, 172, 175, 178, 182, 185, 188, 360
VARESE, Edgard 592
VARIAN
Isaac L. 458
Russell H. 611
Sigurd F. 611
VARICK, Richard 458, 565
VARLEY, Robert P. 518, 520
VARNER, Durward B. 476
VARNUM
James M. 7, 406
John 72, 74, 76
Joseph B. 53, 54, 56*, 58, 59, 60*, 61*, 62*, 63, 64, 65, 319
VARSI, Aloysius 481
VATH, Joseph G. 525
VATHIS, Paul 587
VAUGHAN
Henry F. 572, 610
Horace W. 169
T. Wayland 576, 607
Victor C. 569
William W. 115
VAUGHN
Albert C., Sr. 231
Jack H. 426, 434
William S. 546*
VAUGHT, Edward S. 576
VAUX, Richard 136, 458
VAVOULIS, George J. 460
VAY, G.L. 450*
VEATCH, James C. 409
VEAZEY
Thomas W. 316
William R. 575
VEBLEN, Oswald 568
VEEDER, William D. 121
VEHR, Urban J. 526
VEHSLAGE, John H.G. 146
VELDE, Harold H. 226, 229, 232, 235
VENABLE
A.W. 392
Abraham B. 52, 53, 54, 55, 58, 378
Abraham W. 91, 93, 95
Charles S. 484
Edward C. 136
Emerson 567
Francis P. 477, 565
William W. 171, 174, 177
VERBEKE, William K. 453
VERDIN, John S. 480
VERHAEGEN, Peter J. 480
VERHULST, William 8
VERITY
C. William, Jr. 543
George M. 543
VERNIER, Robert L. 599
VEROT, Augustin 528*
VERPLANCK
Daniel C. 58, 59, 60
Gulian C. 73, 74, 76, 78, 544
VERREE, John P. 103, 105
VERTIN, John 527
VESSEY, Robert S. 367
VEST, George G. 123, 125, 128, 130, 133, 135, 138, 140, 143, 145, 148, 151, 329, 392*, 393
VESTAL, Albert H. 173, 176, 180, 183, 187, 190, 193, 196
VETHAKE, Henry 479, 485
VEVIER, Charles 465
VEYSEY, Victor V. 260, 264
VIBBARD, Chauncey 105
VICITIES, Joseph L. 580
VICKERS
George 110, 112, 114, 317
Harry F. 552*, 590

Thomas 468
VICKERY
Frederick P. 498
Peleg O. 449
VICKREY, Robert 598
VICTORY, John F. 612
VIDAL, Michael 110
VIDOR, King 575
VIELE, Egbert L. 131
VIERECK, Peter 585
VIGNES, Clement V. 566
VIGORITO, Joseph O. 253, 256, 259, 262, 266
VILA, George R. 554*
VILAS
Levi B. 456
William F. 29*, 43, 44, 139, 141, 144, 385
VILES, Blaine S. 449
VILLANI, Ralph A. 577
VILLARD, Henry S. 432*, 436
VILLERE
Charles J. 393
Jacques P. 311
VILLIGER, Burchard 480, 481*
VINAL, George W. 589
VINCENT
Beverly M. 207, 210, 213, 216
Bird J. 184, 187, 190, 194
Boyd 508, 522
Earl W. 190
George E. 475, 492, 573, 603
John A. 461
John Carter 433, 438
John H. 530
William D. 145
VINER, Jacob 566
VINING, John 5, 51*, 52, 53, 54, 290
VINJE, Aad J. 386
VINSON
Carl 167, 170, 173, 176, 180, 183, 186, 190, 193, 196, 200, 203, 206, 209, 213, 216, 219, 223, 226, 229, 232, 235, 238, 241, 245, 248, 608
Fred M. 34, 39, 184, 187, 190, 197, 200, 203, 207, 270, 272
Robert E. 482, 485
VINTON
Alexander H. 509, 522
Samuel F. 71, 73, 75, 76, 78, 79, 81, 88, 90, 92, 94
VIOLETTE, Anthony 450
VISCARDI, Henry, Jr. 609
VISSANI, Charles 480
VISSCHER, Maurice B. 571, 589
VITTRUP, Russell L. 400
VITZ, Carl 568, 600
VIVIAN
John C. 286
Weston E. 252
VOEGELI, Charles A. 514
VOGEL
Arthur A. 518
Charles J. 272
Cyril J. 528
Herbert D. 445
VOGELSTEIN
Hans A. 543
Ludwig 537
VOGLER, William L. 543*
VOGT
Howard W. 559
John W., Jr. 399
VOIGT
Edward 176, 179, 182, 186, 189
Edwin E. 531
VOLA, Vicki 557
VOLK
Douglas 610
Lester D. 178, 181
VOLKER
Joseph 465
William 493
VOLL, John A. 557
VOLLAND, Roscoe H. 566
VOLLMER, Henry 167
VOLPE, John A. 36, 47, 321*, 431
VOLSTEAD, Andrew J. 153, 156, 159, 162, 165, 168, 171, 174, 177, 181
VOLTZ, R.E. 459
VOLWILER, Ernest H. 565, 590, 608
VON BEKESY, George 606
VON BRAUN, Wernher 594, 597
VON CULIN, G.M. 594
VON GROSCHWITZ, Gustave 498
VON JAGEMANN, Hans C.G. 577
VONK, Paul K. 478
VON KARMAN, Theodore 590, 596*, 597, 604, 608, 612
VON KELLER, Beatrice 502
VON KLEINSMID, Rufus B. 465, 481, 603
VON MOSCHZISKER, Robert 359
VON NEUMANN, John 568, 595*, 608
VON OHAIN, Hans J.P. 596
VON PITTLER, J.W. 600
VON RECKLINGHAUSEN, Max 600
VON REINHOLD-JAMESSON, J.R. 497
VON STEINWEHR, Adolph 407, 408, 409*
VON STEUBEN, F.W.A. 402
VOORHEES
Daniel W. 104, 106, 108, 112, 114, 120, 123, 125, 127, 130, 132, 134, 137, 139, 142, 302
Foster M. 341
Stephen F. 567
Paul W. 492
VOORHIS
Charles H. 123
H. Jerry 206, 209, 212, 216, 219
VOPICKA, Charles J. 424, 435, 436
VORHEES, Edward B. 604
VORHIES, Charles T. 575
VORYS, John M. 211, 214, 218, 221, 224, 227, 231, 234, 237, 240
VOSBURGH, Warren C. 589
VOSE, Roger 64, 65
VOSPER, Robert 568
VOTER, Thomas W. 499
VREDENBURGH, John S. 461
VREELAND
Albert L. 211, 214
Edward B. 149, 151, 154, 157, 160, 162, 165
VROOM
Garret D.W. 462
Peter D. 84, 340, 402, 435
VURSELL, Charles W. 216, 219, 223, 226, 229, 232, 235, 238

W

WACHENFELD, William T. 491
WACHTER, Frank C. 148, 150, 153, 156
WADDEL
John N. 475
Moses 471
WADDELL, Alfred M. 115, 117, 119, 121
WADDILL
Edmund, Jr. 136, 271
James R. 123
WADDLE, Benjamin 476*
WADE
Benjamin 32, 40, 95, 97, 99, 101, 103, 105, 107*, 109*, 111, 352
Edward 97, 99, 101, 103
Horace M. 415, 416
Martin J. 153
Preston A. 565
Raymond J. 530
William H. 130, 133, 135
WADHAM, James E. 461
WADHAMS, Edgar P. 527
WADLEIGH
Bainbridge 117, 119, 121, 338
L.B. 459
WADSWORTH
Benjamin 472
Decius 402
George 426, 430, 431*, 436, 438*, 439
Guy W. 478
James (Conn.) 5
James (N.Y.) 451
James S. 408*, 409
James W. 126, 128, 138, 141, 143, 146, 149, 151, 154, 157
James W., Jr. 171, 174, 178, 181, 184, 188, 201, 204, 208, 211, 214, 218, 221, 224, 227, 345
Jeremiah 5, 51*, 52, 544
Peleg 52, 53, 54, 56*, 58, 59
William H. 104, 106, 130
WAEHNER, Louis C. 574
WAESCHE, Russell R. 445
WAGENER
David D. 80, 81, 83, 85
John A. 451
WAGERS, Ralph E. 536
WAGGAMAN, George A. 77, 79, 311
WAGGENER, Leslie 482
WAGGNER, Benjamin G. 600
WAGGONER, Raymond W. 571
WAGGONNER, Joe D., Jr. 245, 248, 252, 255, 258, 261, 264
WAGLEY, Charles 563
WAGMAN, Frederick H. 568
WAGNER
Aubrey J. 445
Charles F. 595
Charles G. 571
David 329
Earl T. 227
Edmund F. 565
J. Addington 568
James E. 534*
Martin 557
Paul A. 480
Peter J. 84
Richard 575
Robert F. 191, 194, 198, 201, 204, 207, 211, 214, 217, 221, 224, 227, 346, 437, 458
WAGONER
George C.R. 151
W.E. 466
WAHL, Lutz 401
WAHLQUIST, John T. 481
WAHNISH, S.A. 462
WAID, Dan Everet 567
WAILES, Edward T. 426, 430*, 439
WAINHOUSE, Austryn 602
WAINWRIGHT
Jonathan M. (b. 1792) 506, 520
Jonathan M. (b. 1864) 185, 188, 191, 194, 565
Jonathan M. (b. 1883) 405, 411
Louie L. 566
Richard 483
Stuyvesant, 2d 233, 237, 240, 243
WAIT
John T. 118, 120, 122, 125, 127, 129
Orin J. 465
Samuel 484
T.B. 460
WAITE
Byron S. 273
Davis H. 285
Henry (b. 1787) 287
Henry M. (b. 1869) 579
Morrison R. 269
WAITS, Edward M. 482
WAITT, Alden H. 402
WAKEFIELD
Edmund B. 472
James B. 128, 130
WAKELEE, Edmund W. 551
WAKEMAN
Abram 99
Seth 115
WAKSMAN, Selman A. 595, 600, 606, 607
WALBRIDGE
Cyrus P. 460
David S. 99, 100
Henry S. 95
Hiram 95, 97
William S. 550
WALCOTT
Charles D. 443, 502*, 563, 570, 575, 597
Frederic C. 193, 196, 199, 289
Harry M. 593
Henry P. 563, 572
WALCUTT, Charles C. 452
WALD
George 595, 600, 606, 610
Lillian D. 597
WALDEN
Ebenezer 450
Hiram 93
John M. 530
Madison M. 114
W.R. 559
WALDIE, Jerome R. 251, 254, 257, 260, 264
WALDO
Dwight B. 485
George E. 157, 160
Loren P. 92
William F. 174
WALDORF, Ernest L. 530
WALDRON
Alfred M. 201
Henry 99, 100, 102, 114, 116, 119
Richard 8
WALDVOGEL, Edward N. 452
WALES
George E. 73, 75
John 92, 290
P.S. 416
William W. 456*
WALK, William E., Jr. 580
WALKER
A. Earl 569
Abram J. 277
Amasa 104
Austin A. 450
Benjamin 57
Buz M. 475
Charles C.B. 119
Clement A. 571
Clifford 297
Cranville T. 536
D. Ormonde 486
Daniel 301
David (Ky.) 66, 68
David (Ark.) 281
David S. 293, 462
David S., Jr. 462*
Donald 480
E.S. Johnny 252, 256
Eric A. 479
Felix 67, 68, 70
Francis 53
Francis A. 475, 566
Frank C. 33, 34*, 43, 599
Fred L. 413
Freeman 68, 69, 295
George 308
George H. 456*
George W. 462
Gilbert C. 120, 122, 379
Henderson 8
Henry O. 593
Horatio 607
Hugh K. 532
Isaac P. 92, 94, 96, 98, 385
James 472
James A. 144, 147
James D. 122, 124, 127, 281
James J. 458
James M. 545
James P. 133, 135
John (b. 1744) 51, 378
John (b. 1906) 500
John C. 394
John D.G. 418
John L. 574
John M. 513, 519
John R. 167, 170, 173
John T. 518
John W. 67, 69
Joseph A. 594
Joseph H. 135, 137, 140, 143, 145
Joseph M. 311
Leroy P. 391
Lewis L. 193
M.B. 408
Paul A. 443
Percy 98
Pinkney H. 300
Prentiss 252
R.L. 451
R. Lindsay 395
Ralph 567, 590
Ralph T. 591
Richard W. 391, 392, 393
Richard W., Jr. 271
Robert B. 543*
Robert F. 330
Robert J. 26, 39, 81, 82, 84, 86, 88, 89, 126, 326
Ronald H. 445
Samuel 462
Shelby 452

Stephen L. 480
T.J. 417
Thomas J. 273
Thomas W. 478
Tom P. 553*
Walter 196
Walton H. 405*, 412, 413, 415
Waurine 578
William A. 97
William B. 547
William D. 507, 521, 522
William H. 575, 604
William H.T. 395*
William W. 566
WALKOWITZ, Abraham 611
WALL
Garret D. 81, 82, 84, 340
James W. 105, 340
Joseph F. 591
William 105
William A. 574
WALLACE
Alexander S. 113, 115, 117, 119
Anthony F.C. 563
Bess [Elizabeth Virginia] 20
Charles F. 601
D.A. 533
Daniel 92, 94, 96
David 85, 302
David A. 476
DeWitt 492, 596, 609
Mrs. DeWitt 609
Fred C. 413
George C. 19, 279*
Harry B. 485
Harry R. 454
Henry A. 14, 18*, 33*, 34, 45, 46, 212, 216
Henry C. 32, 45
Hugh C. 428
James 474
James M. 66, 67, 68
John F. 572
John M. 460
John W. 105, 119
Jonathan H. 128
Lew 407, 438
Lurleen B. 279
Nathaniel D. 130
Robert M. 152, 155, 158, 161
Rodney 135
Tom 573, 576
William A. 119, 122, 124, 359
William C. 135
William H.L. 407
William J. 271, 454
William M. 599
WALLACH, Richard 462
WALLACK, Walter M. 566
WALLAU, H.J. 455
WALLBER, Emil 456
WALLEEN, Hans A. 574
WALLENWEIN, Henry F. 577
WALLER
C. Richard 611
Curtis L. 271
Edwin N. 450
Thomas M. 288
William L. 328
WALLEY, Samuel H. 97
WALLGREN, Monrad C. 202, 205, 209, 212*, 215, 219, 381, 443
WALLHAUSER, George M. 243, 246, 249
WALLIN
Homer N. 418
Samuel 168
WALLING, Ansel T. 119
WALLIS
Severn T. 474
W. Allen 480*
WALLS, Josiah T. 114, 116, 118
WALMSLEY
T. Semmes 457
Walter N., Jr. 438
WALN, Robert 55, 56
WALSH
Allan B. 168
Arthur 217, 342
Charles J. 481
David I. 177, 180, 184, 187, 190, 194, 197, 200, 203, 207, 210, 213, 217, 220, 320*, 321
Denny 587
Don 609
Edward J. 477, 480
Emmet M. 525, 529
James J. 143, 599
John P. 431
John R. 226
Joseph 171, 174, 177, 180
Joseph L. 568
Julius S. 553
Louis S. 528
Matthew J. 478
Michael 97
Michael P. 466, 470
Patrick 139, 296
Redmond J. 480
Robert L. 411
Robert M. 426
Thomas E. 478
Thomas J. (b. 1859) 168, 171, 174, 177, 181, 184, 187, 191, 194, 197, 331
Thomas J. (b. 1873) 523, 527, 529
Thomas Y. 95
William 118, 121
William B. 599, 609
William F. 265
William T. 599
Willimina R. 610
WALSHE, James J. 469
WALTER
Francis E. 201, 205, 208, 211, 215, 218, 221, 224, 228, 231, 234, 237, 240, 243, 246, 250
Paul A.F. 501
Thomas U. 567
WALTERS
Anderson H. 169, 178, 182, 188
Basil L. 573
Henry 549
Herbert S. 250, 371
Jack E. 465
Johnnie M. 444
Raymond 468
Robert 458
Sumner F.D. 514, 521
WALTHALL, Edward C. 130, 132, 135, 137, 140, 143, 145, 327*, 396*
WALTHER, C.F.W. 535*
WALTHOUR, John B. 515, 519
WALTON
Aubrey G. 531
Charles W. 104
Clarence C. 468
Eliakin P. 101, 103, 105
George 3, 4*, 5, 8, 53, 295
George L. 569
James C. 355, 458
John 5
Lester A. 432
Matthew 57, 59
Thomas O. 482
William B. 174
WALWORTH
Arthur 586
Reuben H. 70
WALZ, John A. 577
WAMPLER
Fred 242
William C. 234, 257, 260, 263, 266
WANAMAKER
John 29, 30, 43
Pearl 578
WANGENSTEEN, Owen H. 565, 590, 607
WANGER
Irving P. 141, 144, 146, 149, 152, 154, 157, 160, 163
Walter 563*
WANTON
Gideon 9*
John 9
Joseph 9
William 9
WARBURG, Felix M. 492
WARBURTON
Herbert B. 232
Stanton 166
WARD
Aaron 73, 74, 78, 79, 81, 86
Aileen 602
Alfred G. 417
Andrew H. 108
Angus 423
Artemas 6, 52*, 406
Artemas, Jr. 64, 65
Charles B. 171, 174, 178, 181, 185
Chester 416
Clarence 497
David J. 210, 213, 217
Elijah 101, 105, 107, 119
George C. 552
George M. 480*, 485
George T. 392
Hallett S. 181, 185
Hamilton 109, 111, 113
Henry Ward 3
Henry B. 576
Henry G. 271
J.O.A. 577, 579
Henry L. 500*
J. Harris 545
J. Truman 578
James A. 480
James H. 130
Jasper D. 116
John (bishop) 526
John (mayor) 451
John C. 511, 519
John E. 425
John Q.A. 591
John W. 465
Jonathan 65
Lester F. 573
Malthus A. 501
Marcus L. (Rep.) 117, 340
Marcus L. 566
Matthias 101, 103, 372
Orlando 415*
Paul 481
Paul W. 585
Ralph A. 530
Richard 9
Robert 587
Samuel 7, 9*, 10
Seth 530
Thomas 64, 65
Thomas B. 127, 130
Thomas W. 450*
W. Ralph 531
William 122, 124, 126, 576
William L. 146
William T. 95, 410
WARDEN, Herbert E. 600
WARWELL, Daniel 78, 79, 81
WARE
John H. 259, 262, 266
John H., 3d 259, 262, 266
Nicholas 69, 71, 295
Orie S. 190
WARFIELD
Edwin 317, 579
Ethelbert D. 474, 475
Henry R. 68, 69, 71
WARING, Roane 568
WARKANY, Josef 592, 599
WARMOTH, Henry C. 311
WARNE, Frank W. 530
WARNECKE, Frederick J. 515, 519
WARNER
Adoniram J. 124, 128, 131
Charles D. 578
Edward P. 597, 612
Frederick M. 322
Gertrude Bass 501
Hiram 98, 296
Harry B. 547
Henry C. 574
Hiram 296*
Ira D. 531
J.C. 467, 565, 575, 590
J. DeWitt 138, 141
John W. 399
Joseph E. 455
Langdon 501
Levi 118, 120
Milo J. 568
Philip J. 578
Richard 126, 129
Samuel L. 107
Vespasian 142, 145, 147, 150, 153
W.B. 578
Willard 109, 111, 277
William 130, 133, 156, 159, 162, 329, 455
Worcester R. 573
WARNOCK, William R. 151, 154
WARREN
Althea H. 568
Avra M. 427*, 428, 433, 434*, 438
Casper C. 534
Charles 583
Charles B. 431, 433
Charles H. 580
Constance 481
Cornelius 91
Earl 18, 270, 284, 596, 598
Ed 451*
Edgar L. 443
Edward A. 96, 100
F.E. 451
Fletcher 434*, 438, 439
Fitz Henry 429
Francis E. 136, 139, 144, 147, 149, 152, 155, 158, 161, 163, 166, 169, 172, 176, 179, 182, 186, 189, 192, 196, 387*
Frank J. 462
Frederick M. (b. 1858) 577
Frederick M. (b. 1903) 403
Fuller 294
Glenn B. 573, 590, 596, 611
Gouverneur K. 409
Henry E. 599, 611
Henry W. 530
Howard C. 571
J. Edward 545
James T. 467
James W. 567
John 460
John C. 569
John E. 590
Joseph M. 115
Lindsay C. 188, 191, 194, 198, 201, 204, 208, 211
Lott 84, 85
Minton 570
Richard 3, 580
Robert H. 483
Robert Penn 585, 586, 592, 602, 604, 610
Royal K. 474
Shields 595*
Stafford L. 595
William F. 466
William W. 119
Winslow 580
WARRINGTON
John K. 271
Lewis 418*
WARWICK
Charles F. 458
John G. 138
WASH, Carlyle H. 412
WASHBURN
Albert H. 423
Alfred 592
Benjamin M. 512, 521
Bradford 500, 592, 593
Cadwallader C. 99, 101, 103, 111, 113, 385, 408
Charles A. 434*
Charles G. 156, 159, 162
Emory 319
Frank S. 543
Gordon B. 497, 498
Harvey B. 566
Henry D. 108, 110
Israel, Jr. 95, 97, 98, 100, 102, 314
John D. 438
John H. 479
Lester 557
Margaret F. 571
Paul A. 531
Peter T. 376
Sherwood L. 563, 611
William B. 106, 108, 110, 112, 114, 116, 320*
William D. 123, 125, 128, 135, 137, 140, 324
WASHBURNE
Elihu B. 28, 38, 96, 98, 100, 102, 104, 106, 108, 110, 112, 428
Hempstead 451
WASHINGER, William 531
WASHINGTON
Booker T. 483, 597
Bushrod 269
George 4, 7, 13, 15*, 400*, 580, 597
George C. 74, 76, 77, 81
George T. 272
Joseph E. 133, 136, 138, 141, 144
Thomas 418
W.S. 566
Walter E. 462, 598
William H. 86
WASIELEWSKI, Thaddeus F.B. 215, 219, 222
WASILEWSKI, Vincent T. 578
WASON
Edward H. 171, 174, 177, 181, 184, 188, 191, 194, 197
R.R. 578
WASSELL
John 455
Sam M. 456
WASTE, William H. 284
WATERBURY
David, Jr. 406
L.E. 491
WATERHOUSE
A.G. 594
George B. 572
R.G. 470

WATERMAN
Alan T. 444, 564, 608
Charles M. 457
Charles W. 189, 193, 196, 285
Robert W. 283
Sterry R. 271, 568
WATERS
David P. 460
F.W. 460
Henry J. 473
John K. 404*, 405
Russell J. 147
Vincent S. 528
William E. 485
WATKINS
Aaron S. 17, 18*
Albert G. 94, 96, 99, 101
Arthur V. 225, 228, 231, 234, 237, 240, 374
David O. 341
Elton 185
Franklin C. 593, 607*
George C. 281
G. Roberts 253, 256, 259
John 457
John T. 156, 159, 162, 165, 168, 171, 174, 177
Victor M. 493
W.W. 392
William T. 530
WATMOUGH, John G. 78, 80
WATRES, Laurence H. 185, 188, 192, 195
WATROUS, Harry W. 577, 589, 593, 610
WATSON
Albert, II 405
Albert W. 250, 253, 256, 259
Alfred A. 507, 519
Alfred M. 526
Andrew 533
Arthur K. 428, 579, 604
Burl S. 545*
Clarence W. 163, 166, 383
Cooper K. 99
David K. 143
Dudley C. 499
Henry W. 172, 175, 178, 182, 185, 188, 192, 195, 198, 201
James 55, 56, 344
James D. 600, 606
James E. 142, 147, 150, 153, 156, 158, 170, 173, 176, 180, 183, 187, 190, 193, 196, 303
James L. 273
James M. 572
John 485, 580
John B. 571
John H. 376
John W.C. 393
Joseph 458
LeRoy H. 414, 415
Lewis F. 122, 126, 136
M. Marvin 36, 43
Mark S. 585, 608
Richard S. 515, 522
Robert C. 444
Thomas E. 17, 137, 180, 297
Thomas J. 548, 603
Thomas J., Jr. 548, 574, 604, 608
Walter A. 169, 172, 175, 179
WATT
George 566
James 592
James R. 449
Richard M. 418
WATTERS
A.F. 491
Loras J. 529
WATTERSON
Harvey M. 85, 87
Henry 118
John A. 525
WATTERSTON, George 444
WATTS
Charles H., II 467
F.O. 564
H. Bascom 531
Henry M. 423
John 53
John C. 229, 232, 236, 239, 242, 245, 248, 252, 255, 258, 261
Ralph J. 474
Richard C. 366
Thomas H. 277, 391
William C. 416
WAUGH
Beverly 530
Daniel W. 137, 140
Frederick J. 593
Karl T. 469
Samuel C. 443
Sidney 579
WAUL, Thomas N. 392
WAUNEKA, Annie D. 608
WAX, John J. 450
WAY, Stewart 601
WAYLAND, Francis 467, 570
WAYMACK, W.W. 584
WAYMAN, H.C. 486
WAYNE
Anthony 51, 400, 406
Isaac 72
James M. 75, 77, 78, 269
Joseph, Jr. 551*
William 580
WAYNICK, Capus M. 426, 434
WEADOCK, Thomas A.E. 137, 140
WEAKLEY
Robert 62
Samuel D. 278
WEAR, Frank L. 483
WEARE, Mesech 3, 8
WEARIN, Otha D. 200, 203, 206
WEATHERBY
Samuel S. 466
William H. 437
WEATHERFORD
Willis D. 466
Zadoc L. 209
WEATHERLY, Ulysses G. 573
WEAVER
Archibald J. 128, 130
Arthur J. 334
C.C. 470
Charles P. 456
Claude 169
Erasmus M. 402*
Frank P. 382
H.A. 459
J.E. 575
James B. 17, 123, 130, 132
James D. 250
John 458
John C. 476, 486
Jonathan 531
Paul 564, 608
Phillip H. 236, 239, 242, 246
Ralph C. 580
Robert C. 36, 47, 466, 595, 611
Rufus W. 475
Walter L. 146, 149
Warren 563, 591
William 602
William G. 413
Zebulon 175, 178, 181, 185, 188, 191, 198, 201, 204, 208, 211, 214, 218, 221
WEBB
Alexander 468
Edwin Y. 154, 157, 160, 162, 165, 168, 171, 175, 178
F.D. 584
James E. 444*, 594, 608
James W. 423, 424
Jesse L., Jr. 450
Mrs. Jesse L., Jr. 450
Lance 531
Lucy Ware 20
S.H. 455*
S.P. 461
Stephen T. 460*
W.H., Jr. 450
Walter P. 567
William A. 396
William B. 462
William R. 166, 370
William S. 579
William W. 509, 520
WEBBER
Amos R. 154, 157
Donald 534
E. Leland 499
George W. 125
Samuel 472
WEBER
Ernst 479, 576
Gustave W. 482
Henry C.P. 604
John B. 131, 133
Joseph N. 557
Robert F. 576
WEBERT, Paul 471
WEBSTER
Arthur G. 570
Cecil 577
Clyde I. 579
Daniel 16, 26*, 38*, 64, 65, 71, 72, 74, 76, 77, 79, 81, 82, 84, 89, 91, 93, 319*, 597
Donald D. 577
Edwin H. 102, 104, 106, 108
George S. 572
Harrison E. 483
Horace 468
J. Stanley 179, 182
John 8
Taylor 79, 81, 83
WECHSLER, Israel S. 569
WEDDELL, Alexander W. 423, 437
WEDEMEYER
Albert C. 400, 405*, 411
William W. 165
WEECH, A. Ashley 592
WEED
Clyde E. 543*, 610
E.D. 454
Edwin G. 507, 519
Gideon A. 461
John E. 414
WEEDON, George 401
WEEKLEY, William 531
WEEKS
Edgar 148, 151
Edward 596
Frank B. 288
George E. 449
George M. 403
I.D. 481
John E. 199, 377
John W. (N.H.) 76, 77
John W. (Mass.) 156, 159, 162, 165, 168, 171, 174, 320
Joseph 81, 82
Lewis G. 564, 608
Raymond 566, 577
Sinclair 35*, 46, 217, 321
William F. 510
WEEMS
Capell L. 154, 157, 160
John C. 72, 74
Katharine L. 610
WEETHEE, Jonathan P. 485
WEFALD, Knud 184, 187
WEGMAN, Myron E. 592
WEHMAN, E. Edward, Jr. 451
WEHRLE, Vincent 525
WEHRWEIN, Austin 586
WEIBEL, Walter L. 400
WEICHEL, Alvin F. 218, 221, 224, 227, 231, 234
WEICK
Fred E. 608
Paul C. 272
WEICKER, Lowell P., Jr. 257, 260, 264, 289
WEIDEMAN, Carl M. 200
WEIDENREICH, Franz 611
WEIDLEIN, Edward R. 565, 608
WEIDLOG, Charles B. 600
WEIDMAN, Jerome 574, 586
WEIGAND, Hermann J. 577
WEIGHTMAN, Roger C. 462
WEIGLE, Richard D. 480
WEIHOFEN, Henry 608
WEILER
Herold J. 402
Jack D. 595
WEINBERG, Alvin M. 569
WEINBERGER, Caspar W. 37, 47, 444
WEINER, Mort 577
WEINHARDT, Carl J., Jr. 499
WEINMAN, Adolph A. 579, 590, 591
WEINSTEIN, Jacob 597
WEINGRAUB, Joseph T. 342
WEIR
A.H. 455
Ernest T. 568, 596
J. Alden 577, 593, 607*
John F. 502
Samuel C. 533
William C. 480
WEIS
Carl A. 577
Jessica McC. 243, 246
WEISENBURGH, Theodore H. 569
WEISNER
Jerome B. 475
Maurice F. 417
WEISS
J.M. 607
Nathan 477
Samuel A. 215, 218, 221
William 537
WEISSE, Charles H. 155, 158, 161, 163
WEISSKOPF, Victor F. 570
WEITZEL
George T. 434
Godfrey 457*
WELBORN, John 156
WELCH
Adonijah S. 109, 293
Archibald A. 551
Ashbel 572
Charles W. 532
Earl 355*
Frank 121
Herbert 530
John 95, 353*
Leo D. 553
Louie 454
Norman A. 569
Orin T. 462*
Philip J. 227, 230
Richard J. 186, 189, 193, 196, 199, 202, 206, 209, 212, 216, 219, 222, 226
Thomas 457
Thomas A. 526
William H. 563, 569, 603
William W. 98
WELD, William E. 485
WELDON
Christopher J. 529
Lawrence 273
WELFLE, Frederick E. 473
WELFORD, Walter 350
WELKER
Herman 229, 232, 235, 299
Martin 109, 111, 113
WELLBORN
Charles, Jr. 417, 419
Marshall J. 92
Olin 124, 126, 129, 131
WELLER
George 585
John B. 85, 86, 88, 94, 96, 98, 283, 433
Luman H. 127
Ovington E. 180, 184, 187, 317
Philip 557
Reginald H. 509, 519
Royal H. 185, 188, 191
Samuel H. 478
Thomas H. 599, 606
WELLES
Charles B. 570
Edward R. 507, 515, 520, 522
Gideon 27*, 42
H.T. 456
Roger 416
Samuel 3
Sumner 426, 596
Thomas 8*
WELLFORD, Beverly R. 569
WELLING
James C. 471, 480
Milton H. 175, 179
WELLINGTON, George L. 142, 145, 148, 150, 317
WELLMAN
Frederick C. 498
Harry R. 467
Hiller C. 568
Samuel T. 573
WELLS
Alexander T. 576
Alfred 103
Arthur W. 449
Briant H. 400, 401, 404
Chandler J. 451
Charles 450
Charles R. 566
Cord O. 486
Daniel, Jr. 98, 99
Daniel H. 460
Erastus 112, 114, 116, 119, 123
Frances S. 536
G. Wiley 119
George E. 273
H.N. 456
Heber M. 374
Henry H. 379
Herman B. 473
James M. 311
John 95
John S. 97, 337
L.N.D. 536
Lemuel H. 508, 522
Oscar 564
Owen A. 141
Richard H. 580
Rolla 460
Samuel 314
William H. 54, 55, 56, 57, 63, 65, 290*
WELMAN, J.C. 564
WELSH

A.S. 473
George A. 185, 188, 192, 195, 198
Israel 392, 393
John S. 429
Martin I. 460
Matthew E. 303
Robert J. 484
Thomas 408
W.A. 536
WELTER, John M. 558
WELTNER
Charles L. 248, 251
Philip 478
WELTY
Benjamin F. 175, 178
Eudora 592, 598, 603
WEMPLE, Edward 128
WENDELL, Cornelius 443
WENDOVER, Peter H. 65, 67, 68
WENDT, Waldemar F. 416
WENE, Elmer H. 207, 214, 217
WENG, Siegfried R. 498
WENLEY, Archibald G. 499
WENNER, Frank 611
WENT, Frits W. 574
WENTE
C.F. 544
Edward C. 611
WENTWORTH
Benning 8
C.C. 600
Elmer M. 579
John (Ill.) 87, 89, 91, 92, 96, 108, 451
John (N.H.) 4, 6, 8
Tappan 97
Walter A. 579
WERDEL, Thomas H. 226, 229
WERNER
Adolph 468
Charles G. 584
Hazen G. 531
Mary Lou 586
Mort 577
Theodore B. 202, 205
WERNETTE, John P. 476
WERT, Robert J. 475
WERTENBAKER, Thomas J. 567
WERTS, George T. 340
WERTZ
D. Frederick 531
George M. 185
William H.H. 576
William W. 451
WESBROOK, Frank F. 572
WESCOE, W. Clarke 473
WESCOTT, Glenway 578
WESLEY
Arthur F. 531
Charles H. 486*
WESSELL, Nils Y. 483, 493
WESSON
Charles M. 402
L.A. 462*
WEST
A.M. 17
Andrew F. 570
Ben 457
Charles F. 198, 201
Edward H. 514, 519
Francis 9
George 126, 131, 133
Guy A. 480
Hamilton 519
Harry F. 550
Henry F. 454
Herbert B. 492
Howard 567
James E. 603
John 9
John C. (b. 1885) 477
John C. (b. 1925) 366
Joseph 9*
Joseph R. 462
J. Rodman 114, 116, 118, 311
Milton H. 202, 205, 208, 212, 215, 218, 222, 225
Oswald 356
Richard V. 497
Roy O. 32, 33, 44
William S. 167, 296
WESTBROOK
John 86
Theodoric R. 33
WESTCOTT, James D., Jr. 89, 91, 293
WESTENDORP, Willem F. 611
WESTERFIELD, Samuel Z., Jr. 432
WESTERLO, Rensselaer 67
WESTERMANN, William L. 567
WESTERVELT, Jacob A. 458
WESTFALL, William A. 576
WESTHEIMER, Frank H. 596
WESTINGHOUSE, George 554, 573, 595, 596, 597
WESTLAKE, W. Ralston 452
WESTLAND, Alfred J. 234, 237, 241, 244, 247, 250
WESTMORELAND, William C. 400, 483
WESTON
Edward 594, 596, 599
Horace C. 580
James A. 338*
John B. 465*
Karl E. 502
Nathan 314
WESTOVER
Oscar 401
Wendell 403
WETENHALL, J. Huber 548
WETHERBY, Lawrence W. 310
WETHERED, John 87
WETHERILL, Henry E. 600
WETMORE
Alexander 502*, 569, 592, 593
Charles W. 546, 553
Edmund 564
Frank O. 546, 547*
George P. 144, 146, 149, 152, 154, 157, 160, 163, 166, 362*
James S. 516
Ralph H. 574
WEVER, John M. 138, 141
WEXLER, Jacqueline G. 472
WEYBRECHT, J.F. 451
WEYER, Henry A. 601
WEYGANDT, Carl V. 354
WEYL
Charles N. 601
F. Joachim 472
WEYLAND, Otto P. 412, 415, 416
WEYMOUTH, George W. 145, 148
WHALEN
Charles W., Jr. 256, 259, 262, 265
John P. 468
WHALEY
C. Forrest 455
Kellian V. 105, 107, 109
Richard S. 169, 172, 175, 178, 273
Storm H. 465
WHALLEY, J. Irving 246, 250, 253, 256, 259, 262
WHALLON, Reuben 79
WHARTON
A.O. 557
Charles H. 468
Charles S. 156
Clifton R. 434, 436
Clifton R., Jr. 475
Edith 583, 589, 603
Franklin 416
Hunter P. 558
J. Ernest 230, 233, 237, 240, 243, 246, 249
Jesse 60, 64, 66, 369
John A. 395
Ramsey 454*
Robert 458*
Samuel 15
Thomas 9
WHATCOAT, Richard 530
WHEALON, John F. 523, 526
WHEAT
John J. 475
William H. 210, 213, 216
WHEATLAND
Henry 498, 501
Stephen G. 460
WHEATLEY
E.L. 558
Seth 456
WHEATON
Henry S. 426, 435, 478
Horace 88, 90
Laban 61, 62, 64, 65
Nathaniel S. 482
William W. 453
WHEEDON, George 406
WHEELER
Benjamin I. 467
Burton K. 18, 184, 187, 191, 194, 201, 204, 207, 210, 214, 217, 220, 331
Charles B., Jr. 455
Charles K. 145, 148, 150
Charles L. 580
David H. 465, 478
Earle G. 399*, 400
Edward J. 580
Ezra 109
Frank W. 135
Fred B. 459
George A. 600
George W. 288
Grattan H. 78
Hamilton K. 139
Harold A. 598
Harrison H. 137
Harry A. 574*
Homer J. 479
John (Coll. Pres.) 484
John (Rep.) 97, 99
John A. 570, 595*, 596, 604
John H. 434
Joseph 124, 129, 131, 134, 136, 139, 142, 144, 147, 395*, 396
Joseph L. 600
Loren E. 170, 173, 176, 180, 187, 461
Martha S. 566
Nelson P. 160, 163
Post 423, 434
Raymond A. 402, 411*, 598
Robert C. 497
Royal T. 372
T.B. 450
Thomas 558
William A. 14, 17, 105, 113, 115, 117, 119, 120, 122
William M. 223, 226, 229, 232
William M. 500
William M., Jr. 600, 608
WHEELOCK
Charles D. 611
Eleazar 469
John 469
John Hall 592
WHEELWRIGHT, Thomas S. 554
WHELAN
Charles E. 456
Edward 481
James 527
Richard V. 528, 529
Robert L. 526
Thomas E. 434
WHELCHEL, B. Frank 203, 206, 209, 213, 216
WHELPLEY
Edward W. 340
Henry M. 609
WHELTON, Daniel A. 450
WHERRETT, H.S. 550
WHERRY
Arthur C. 566
Kenneth S. 217, 220, 224, 227, 230, 334
WHETCROFT, Burton 449*
WHETSTONE, Karl F. 476
WHIDDEN, Benjamin F. 429
WHILLOCK, H. Westerman 450*
WHIPPLE
Allen O. 590, 612
Amiel W. 408*
George H. 605
Henry B. 506, 520
J.C. 451
Thomas, Jr. 70, 71, 73, 74
William 3, 6
William G. 455
WHISTLER, James A. McNeill 597, 607
WHITACRE, John J. 166, 169
WHITAKER
Benjamin P. 483
D.M. 573
Frederic 574
George 486
H.E. 549*
Jard I. 449
John A. 223, 226, 229
John C. 552*
Martin D. 474
Ozi W. 506, 519, 520, 521
Samuel 273
WHITCOMB
Edgar 303
James 93, 302*
Richard T. 594, 609
WHITE
A.C. 461*
Addison 95
Albert B. 383
Albert E. 572
Albert S. 82, 84, 85, 87, 104, 302
Alden P. 498
Alexander (Va.) 51, 52
Alexander (Ala.) 94
Alexander C. 131
Allison 101
Alma B. 538
Andrew D. 428*, 436, 468, 567
Arthur A. 414
Mrs. Ashmead 579
Bartow 73
Benjamin 87
Byron R. 270
Campbell P. 76, 78, 79
Cecil F. 226
Charles 484
Charles B. 571
Charles D. 529
Charles Dunning 430
Charles H. 412, 413
Charles L. 468
Charles M. 595, 596
Charles T. 574
Chilton A. 105, 107
Clinton I. 460
Compton I. 200, 203, 206, 209, 213, 216, 219, 226
Compton I., Jr. 248, 251
Daniel A. 498
Daniel P. 392
David (Rep.) 71
David 576
Deane R. 580
Doris 591
Dudley A. 208, 211
E.B. 603, 604, 608
Edward D. (b. 1795) 75, 77, 79, 84, 86, 311, 312
Edward D. (b. 1845) 137, 140, 269, 270, 599
Emerson E. 479
F. Edson 543
Francis (Va.) 64
Francis (Dipl.) 426, 433, 437
Frank 350, 444
Frank S. 167, 278
Frank X. 491
Frederick E. 137
George 166, 169, 175, 353
George A. 553
George B. 418
George E. 142, 145
George H. 146, 149
George W. 481
Gideon 449
Gilbert F. 472, 595
Goodrich C. 470
H.O. 460
Harry (Pa.) 122, 124
Harry (Wash.) 461
Hays B. 177, 180, 183, 187, 190
Helen C. 564, 599
Henry 428, 431
Henry H. 482
Henry S. 568
Horace 345
Hugh 90, 91, 93
Hugh L. 327, 328
Hugh L. (Tenn.) 16, 73, 75, 76, 77, 78*, 80, 81, 83, 85, 369
I.C. 564
Ian McKibbin 497, 498
Isaac D. 404*, 405*, 415
Israel C. 576
James 533
James (N.C.) 7
James (Ind.) 132
James B. (Ky.) 150
John 80, 82, 84, 85*, 87
John A. 557
John B. 484
John C. 511, 522
John Campbell 429*, 433, 435, 486
John D. (Ky.) 118, 125, 127
John H. 508, 520, 521
John J. 600
John T. 330
John W. 574
Joseph L. 85
Joseph W. 107
Julius 423
K. Owen 534
Katharine E. 427
Kevin H. 450
Lawrence G. 577
Lee C. 443
Leonard 62
Leonard D. 571, 586, 591
Leslie A. 563, 611
Luther W., III 479

Lynn T., Jr. 475
M.M. 564
Magner 583
Maunsel 594
Michael D. 120
Miller G. 400
Milo 128, 130
Paul Dudley 567, 589, 590, 608
Paul W. 334
Philip B. 593*
Phillips 6
Philo 427*
Phineas 70
R.E. 450
R.N. 461
Richard C. 253, 256, 260, 263, 266
Robert 460
Robert I. 473
Robert M. 594
S. Harrison 189, 285
Samuel 55, 56, 57, 58, 60, 61, 290
Stafford G. 379
Stephen M. 139, 142, 144, 283
Stephen V. 133
Theodore H. 587
Thomas D. 412, 415*
Wallace H., Jr. 174, 177, 180, 184, 187, 190, 193, 197, 200, 203, 207, 210, 213, 217, 220, 223, 315
Walter 578, 611
Walter M. 536
Wilbur M. ,198
Wilbur W. 482
William (b. 1580) 3
William (b. 1748) 505, 521
William (b. 1822) 353*
William Alanson 571
William Allen 573, 583, 585*, 609
William J. 141
William R. 466, 471
William S. 586, 608
WHITEAKER, John , 124, 356
WHITEFORD, William K. 548*
WHITEHEAD
Alfred North 593
C. Frank 454
Cortlandt 507, 521
Don 585, 586
Ennis C. 412, 416
Frank 419
James L. 502
John B. 594, 595, 600
Joseph 189, 192, 195
Robert F. 444
Thomas 117
WHITEHILL
Alexander R. 485
James 64
John 58, 59
Robert 59, 60, 62, 63, 64
WHITEHORN, John C. 571
WHITEHOUSE
Alton W., Jr. 552
Henry J. 506, 519
John O. 117, 119
Seth C. 449
Sheldon 426, 429
William P. 315
William W. 465
WHITEHURST, G. William 260, 263, 266
WHITELAW, Robert H. 135
WHITELEY
Richard H. 112, 114, 116
William G. 100, 102
WHITENER, Basil L. 240, 243, 246, 249, 253, 256
WHITESIDE
Jenkin 62, 63, 369
John 66, 67
WHITFIELD
Albert H. 327
Henry L. 327
James (b. 1770) 523, 528
James (b. 1791) 326
Robert L. 393
Willis J. 598
WHITFORD, Greeley W. 285
WHITING
Frederic A. 498, 499
Justin R. 545, 546
Justin R. (Mich.) 132, 135, 137, 140
Richard H. ,118
William (b. 1813) 116
William (b. 1841) 128, 130, 132
William D. 418
William F. 32, 33, 46
William H., Jr. 471
William H.C. 394*
WHITLEY, James L. 194, 198, 201
WHITLOCK
Brand 424
Roger H. 482*
Benaiah 468, 471
WHITMAN
Charles S. 345, 565
Ezekial 61, 66, 68, 69, 314
Ezra B. 572
Frederic B. 492
Lemuel 70
Walt 597
WHITEMARSH, Thomas 454
WHITMER, George C. 453
WHITMORE
Elias 73
Frank C. 565, 596, 604
George W. 113
WHITNEY
A.F. 557
Cornelius V. 550
Eli 597
George 492
John D. 471
John Hay 429, 595, 601
Louis B. 459
Thomas R. 99
William C. 29*, 42
William D. 570
Willis R. 565, 575, 595, 596*, 603
WHITON, Edward V. 385
WHITSON
G.S. 564
William O. 564
WHITTAKER, Charles E. 270, 272
WHITTEMORE
B. Frank 111, 113
Herbert L. 601
Lewis B. 513
Reed 589, 603
WHITTEN
Jamie L. 214, 217, 220, 223, 227, 230, 233, 236, 239, 242, 246, 249, 252, 255, 258, 262, 265
William R. 570
WHITTHORNE, Washington C. 115, 117, 120, 122, 124, 126, 131, 133, 136, 370
WHITTIER, John Greenleaf 597
WHITTINGHAM, William R. 505, 520
WHITTINGTON, William M. 187, 191, 194, 197, 200, 204, 207, 210, 214, 217, 220, 223, 227
WHITTLE, Francis McN. 506, 522
WHITTLESEY
Elisha 71, 73, 75, 76, 78, 79, 81, 83
Frederick 78, 79
Thomas T. 80, 82
William A. 93
WHITTMORE, Don Juan 572
WHITTREDGE, Worthington 577
WHITVORD, A.E. 564
WHITWORTH, George F. 484*
WHYBURN
Gordon T. 568
William M. 482
WHYTE, William P. 110, 118, 121, 123, 156, 159, 317*, 450
WIBIRD, Richard 3
WICK, William W. 84, 89, 91
WICKARD, Claude R. 33, 34*, 45
WICKE, Lloyd C. 531
WICKENDEN, W.E. 576
WICKERSHAM
George W. 31*, 41, 568, 589
J.P. 427
Victor 214, 218, 221, 227, 231, 234, 237, 246, 250
WICKES, Eliphalet 59
WICKHAM
Charles P. 133, 136
Kenneth J. 401
William C. 393
William H. 458
William T. 472
WICKLIFFE
Charles A. 26, 43, 71, 72, 74, 75, 77, 104, 308
Robert C. 162, 165, 311
Robert, Jr. 436
WIDDEMER, Margaret 583
WIDGERY
John 455
William 62
WIDMER, Robert H. 611
WIDNALL, William B. 227, 230, 233, 236, 239, 243, 246, 249, 252, 256, 259, 262, 265
WIDNEY, Joseph P. 481
WIDSOE, John A. 484
WIEGAND, Karl M. 574
WIENECKE, Robert 419
WIENER
Alexander S. 599, 607
Norbert ,602, 604
WIER, Roy W. 227, 230, 233, 236, 239, 242
WIGFALL, Louis T. 103, 105, 372, 392, 393*
WIGGER, Winand M. 527
WIGGERS, Carl J. 571, 589
WIGGIN, Albert H. 545
WIGGINS
A.L.M. 549, 564
Benjamin L. 481
Charles E. 254, 257, 260, 264
Dossie M. 482
James R. 573, 601
WIGGINTON, Peter D. 118, 120
WIGGLE, Peter 558
WIGGLESWORTH
Edward 500
Richard B. 190, 194, 197, 200, 203, 207, 210, 213, 217, 220, 223, 226, 230, 233, 236, 239, 425
WIGHTMAN
Clair S. 479
Joseph M. 450
William M. 486, 530
WIGMORE, John H. 564, 589
WIGNER, Eugene P. 570, 595*, 596, 604, 606
WIKE, Scott 118, 134, 137
WILBER
David 117, 124, 133, 135
David F. 143, 146
WILBOUR, Isaac 60
WILBUR
Alroy A. 455
Curtis D. 32*, 33, 42, 272, 284
Dwight L. 569
Ray L. 33, 44, 482, 569
Richard 586, 592*, 602
WILBY, Francis B. 483
WILCOMB, C.P. 498
WILCOX
Cadmus M. 394, 395
J. Mark 200, 203, 206
Jeduthun 64, 65
John A. 95, 393
Joseph 458
Leonard 86, 337
Perry 546
WILDE
Arthur H. 465
Louis J. 461
Richard H. 65, 71, 74, 75, 77, 78
WILDER
A. Carter 106
Burt G. 569
Charlotte 610
H.H. 573
Mitchell A. 498, 502
Raymond L. 568
Thornton 583, 584*, 592, 602, 603, 604, 608
William H. 473
William Henry 165, 168
WILDHABER, Ernest 601
WILDMAN
Clyde E. 469
Zalmon 80
WILDRICK, Isaac 93, 95
WILES, Irving 593
WILEY
Alexander 212, 215, 219, 222, 225, 228, 231, 234, 238, 241, 244, 247, 386
Ariosto A. 150, 152, 155, 158
E.E. 470
Harvey W. 565, 594
Isaac W. 530
James S. 91
John C. 426, 427, 430, 431, 434, 435
John McC. 135
Oliver C. 158
William H. 154, 157, 162
WILFLEY, Xenophon P. 174, 330
WILINSKY, Charles F. 572
WILKE, Kenneth W. 462
WILKES
Charles 544
Charles (b. 1798) 417
Jack S. 458
Peter S. 393
WILKESON, Samuel 450
WILKEY, Malcolm R. 272
WILKIE, Wendell L. 603
WILKIN
James W. 65, 67
Samuel J. 78
WILKINS
Beriah 128, 131, 133
Ernest H. 478, 577*
Eugene G. 477
Fraser 426
John, Jr. 403
Lawson 592
Raymond S. 321
Robert W. 567, 600
Roger C. 553*
Roy 578, 596, 608, 609, 611
William 16, 26*, 40, 78, 79, 88, 358, 436
WILKINSON
Ernest L. 467
James 400*, 406
Morton S. 102, 104, 106, 112, 324
S.E. 557
T.S. 416
Theodore S. 132, 135
WILKOWSKI, Jean M. 439
WILL
Arthur A. 456
Erwin H. 554
Philip, Jr. 567
Thomas E. 473
WILLARD
Ammiel J. 365
Arthur C. ,472
Ashbel P. 302
Charles W. 113, 115, 117
Daniel 603
Emma 597
Frances E. 597
George 116, 119
Joseph 472
Joseph E. 437
Moses T. 452
WILLAUER, Whiting 426, 430
WILLCOX
Monson A. 473
Orlando B. 407, 408*, 409
Walter F. 566
Washington F. 134, 137
William B. 591
WILLENBROCK, F. Karl 576
WILLENS, John M. 400
WILLERS, Thomas F. 550, 553
WILLETT
Francis 10
H.G. 608
Marinus 458
Thomas 457*
William F., Jr. 160, 162
WILLEY
Calvin 72, 74, 75, 287
Earle D. 216
Gordon R. 563, 611
John W. 452
Norman B. 298
Waitman T. 105, 107, 109, 111, 113, 379, 383
WILLFORD, Albert C. 200
WILLGING, Joseph C. 528
WILLHAM, Oliver S. 478
WILLIAMS
A.S. 457
Abram P. 129, 283
Albert J., Jr. 611
Albert L. 548
Alfred M. 474
Alpheus S. 119, 121, 407, 408, 409*, 410, 436
Andrew 119, 121
Archibald H.A. 138
Arthur B. 184
Arthur L. 509, 520
Ashbel C. 565
Ben T. 355
Benjamin 3, 347*
C. Fred 571
Channing M. 506
Charles D. 509, 520
Charles G. 117, 120, 122, 124, 126
Charles K. 375*
Christopher H. 83, 85, 87, 94, 96
Clanton W. 472

Clarence C. 402
Clarence S. 419
Clarke 569
Claude A. 553
Clement C. 474
Clyde 567, 595
Clyde (Mo.) 191, 197, 201, 204, 207, 210
Dana S. 579
Daniel 449
David E. 547
David R. 59, 60, 63, 364
David W. 482
E.A. 450
Edgar I. 577
Edward T. 405
Elihu S. 133, 136
Elisha 3, 487
Franklin H. 428
Frederick B. 598
G. Mennen 323, 435
George 460
George F. 137
George G. 545
George H. (b. 1823) 28*, 41, 109, 111, 113, 356
George H. (b. 1871) 187, 330
George H. (b. 1914) 465
George S. 209
Gershom M. 508, 521
Guinn 182, 185, 189, 192, 195, 199
Harrison A., Jr. 233, 236, 243, 246, 249, 252, 255, 259, 262, 265, 342
Harvey D. 607
Henry 84, 87
Henry D. 600
Henry L. 460
Hermann W., Jr. 498
Hezekiah 89, 91
Homer B. 466
Hugh E., Jr. 462*
Isaac, Jr. 64, 67, 71
J.J. 456
J.T. 462
Jack 280, 459
Jack K. 482
James (Del.) 118, 120
James (Diplomat) 438
James (Md.) 449*
James D. 118, 302
James E. 449
James R. 134, 137, 139, 147, 150, 153
James W. 86
Jared 69, 70, 72
Jared W. 82, 84, 97, 337*
Jeremiah N. ,118, 120
Jesse Lynch 574, 583
John (b. 1731) 4, 7
John (b. 1752) 54, 55
John (b. 1778) 66, 67, 69, 70, 369, 425
John (b. 1807) 99
John (b. 1817) 482, 506, 519
John (Labor) 559
John (W. Va.) 451*
John A. 473
John Bell 223, 227, 230, 233, 236, 239, 242, 246, 249, 252, 255, 328
John D. 475
John F. 402*
John H. 570
John Henry 566
John J. (archbishop) 523, 525
John J. (Sen.) 222, 226, 229, 232, 235, 238, 241, 245, 248, 251, 254, 257, 292
John M.S. 116
John R. 453*
John Sharp 140, 143, 145, 148, 151, 153, 156, 159, 165, 168, 171, 174, 177, 181
John S. 123, 125, 127, 309, 327
Jonathan 66, 402, 483*
Joseph H. 314
Joseph L. 83, 85, 87
Joseph R. 475
Lawrence G. 256, 259, 262, 266
Lemuel 56*, 58
Levi T. 450
Lewis 65, 66, 68, 70, 71, 73, 75, 76, 78, 79, 81, 83, 84, 86
Marmaduke 58, 59, 60
Marshall J. 353*
Morgan B. 146
Murat W. 427
Nathan 59
Paul R. 611
Randolph P. 592
Ransome J. 366
Reuel 82, 84, 86, 314
Richard 121
Robert 55, 56, 57
Robert B. 411
Robert C. 486
Robert L. 355*
Robert Lee 272
Robert R. 594, 596
Robin M., Jr. 574
Robley C. 601
Roger 9, 597
Roger J. 565
Roy H. 577
S. Clay 552*
S. Wells 565
Samuel T. 405
Seward H. 172
Sherrod 80, 82, 84
Stephen 501
T. Harry 587, 602
Tennessee 585, 586, 592, 603
Thomas 3
Thomas (Ala.) 122, 124, 127
Thomas (Pa.) 107, 109, 111
Thomas Hickman 82, 326*
Thomas Hill 66, 68, 69, 71, 73, 74
Thomas S. (b. 1777) 66, 287, 453
Thomas S. (b. 1872) 170, 173, 176, 180, 183, 187, 190, 193, 273
Thomas W. 83, 85
Van Zandt 580
Walter 476
Walter C. 608
Wheeler 579
Wilbur G. 465
William (b. 1815) 115
William (b. 1731) 3, 5
William (b. 1821) 110, 112, 114, 116, 434, 439
William B. 116, 119
William Carlos 587, 589, 592*, 600, 602, 603
William E. 147, 167, 170
William M. 444
William R. 230, 233, 237, 240
William T.B. 611
WILLIAMSON
Andrew 406
Ben M. 193, 310
E.D. 601
Edgar, Jr. 579
Frederick E. 545
George 426, 429, 430, 434, 436
Hugh 4, 7, 51, 52
Isaac H. 340
James D. 485
John G.A. 439
John N. 154
Robert B. 315
Samuel 469
William 182, 185, 188, 192, 195
William C. 533
William D. 69, 314
WILLIARD, George W. 472
WILLIE, Asa H. 117, 372
WILLIFORD, E. Allan 580
WILLING
Charles 458*
Thomas 7, 458
WILLINGER, Aloysius J. 527
WILLIS
Albert S. 121, 123, 125, 127, 130, 430
Bailey 576, 607
Benjamin A. 119, 121
Edwin E. 226, 229, 233, 236, 239, 242, 245, 248, 252, 255
Frances E. 425, 434, 438*
Francis 51
Frank B. 166, 169, 178, 181, 185, 188, 191, 353*
John B. 536
Jonathan S. 142
Raymond E. 213, 216, 220, 303
Simeon S. 310
William S. 477
WILLISTON, Samuel 589
WILLITS
Edwin 121, 123, 125, 475
Oliver G. 544
WILLKIE, Wendell L. 18, 546, 603
WILLMS, John 470
WILLOUGHBY
Charles C. 501
W.F. 571
Westel, Jr. 14
Westel W. 571
WILLS
David 478
William H. 377
WILLSON
Augustus E. 309
Russell 483
WILLWEBER, Christian 427
WILLYS, John N. 435
WILMER
E.G. 547
Joseph R.P. 506, 520
Richard H. (b. 1816) 506, 519
Richard H. (b. 1892) 580
William H. 486
WILMORE, John J. 466
WILMOT, David 90, 92, 94, 105, 273, 359
WILNER, Robert F. 513
WILSHIRE, William W. 115, 118, 281
WILSON
Alexander 58, 59, 61
Alpheus W. 530
Benjamin 120, 122, 124, 126
Benjamin D. 456
Benjamin J. 601
Charles (Rep. Tex.) 266
Charles (union leader) 557
Charles E. 35*, 47, 547, 608
Charles H. 248, 251, 254, 257, 260, 264
David J. 273
Charles S. 424, 435, 439
Charles T.R. 607
Donald 400
Donald R. 478, 568
Durward S. 413*
Earl 213, 216, 220, 223, 226, 229, 232, 235, 239, 245, 248
Ebenezer 457
Edgar 142, 147
Edgar C. 80
Edmond B. 498
Edmund 603, 604, 608
Edmund B. 563
Edward T. 546
Edward W. 543
Edwin B. 563
Edwin C. 434, 438, 439
Emanuel W. 383
Emmett 167, 170
Ephraim K. (b. 1771) 74, 76
Ephraim K. (b. 1821) 116, 130, 132, 135, 317
Eugene E. 554
Eugene H. 468
Eugene M. 112, 457*
F. Perry 553*
Felix Z. 457
Forrest 584
Francis 557
Francis H. 143, 146
Frank E. 512, 519
Frank E. (N.Y.) 149, 151, 154, 165, 168
George (educator) 478
George (mayor) 459
George (physician) 569
George A. 216, 220, 223, 305*
George H. 227
George W. (IRS) 444
George W. (Rep.) 141, 143
Gill R. 577
Halsey W. 600
Harry L. 574
Henry (b. 1812) 14, 17, 97, 98, 100, 102, 104, 106, 108, 110, 112, 114, 115, 118, 319
Henry (b. 1778) 72, 73
Henry B. 483
Henry L. 424, 425, 433
Hugh R. 428, 438
I.W. 543*
Isaac 71
J. Frank 225, 228, 231, 234
J.Q. 460
J. Walter 573
James (b. 1835) 7, 269, 314
James (b. 1835) 30*, 31*, 45, 116, 118, 127
James (b. 1825) 100, 102, 439
James (b. 1797) 91, 93
James (b. 1766) 64
James (b. 1779) 72, 73, 75
James C. (b. 1830) 533
James C. (b. 1874) 175
James F. 104, 106, 108, 110, 127, 130, 132, 134, 137, 140, 304
James M. 409, 410
James J. 65, 67, 68, 340
James P. 469
James T.D. 454*
Jeremiah M. 114, 116
John (Mass.) 64, 66
John (So. Car.) 70, 72, 73
John A. (b. 1850) 533
John A. (b. 1890) 604
John A. (b. 1897) 501*
John D. 485
John H. (Haw.) 454*
John H. (Pa.) 178
John H. (Ken.) 135, 137
John L. (S.C.) 364
John L. (Wash.) 136, 139, 141, 144, 147, 150, 381
John M. 402, 483
John T. 557
John T. (Ohio) 111, 113, 115
Joseph C. 462
Joseph G. 117
Joseph M. 575
Joshua L. 532
Kendrick R., Jr. 544*
Leroy A. 543
Logan 482
Louis R. 568
Luther B. 530
Margaret 583
Nathan 60
O.J. 460
O. Meredith 478
Oliver 578
Oren E. 449
Orme 429
Owen M. 475
Ralph L. 572
Rathmell 469
Richard 586
Riley J. 171, 174, 177, 180, 184, 187, 190, 193, 197, 200, 203
Robert 104, 106, 329
Robert C. 232, 235, 238, 241, 244, 248, 251, 254, 257, 260, 264
Robert E. 552
Robert G. 478
Robert G., Jr. 579
Robert P.C. 135, 138
Robert R. (Pa.) (b. 1898) 573
Robert R. (b. 1914) 594
Russell 452
S. Davis 458
Samuel 476
Samuel B. 325
Samuel J. 485, 532
Samuel K. 474
Scott 271, 315
Simon C. 453
Stanley C. 377
Stanyarne 144, 146, 149
Stephen F. 109, 111
Theodore D. 418
Thomas (b. 1765) 63, 459*
Thomas (b. 1772) 64, 66
Thomas (b. 1827) 132, 324
Thomas B. 563
Thomas M. 430
T. Webber 184, 187
Thornton A. 544
Val H. 481
W. Bruce 533
W.T. 391
Walter K. 412
Walter K., Jr. 402
Willard 472
William (Fla.) 461
William (Ill.) 300
William (Ohio) 71, 73, 75
William (Pa.) 66, 67
William B. 31, 32*, 46, 160, 163, 166
William E. 183
William H. 205
William L. 30*, 43, 129, 131, 134, 136, 139, 141, 485*
William S. 392
William W. 153, 156, 158, 161, 164, 170, 173, 176
Winston P. 402

Woodrow 13, 18*, 340, 479, 571, 597, 605
WILSTACH, Charles F. 451
WILTNER, Charles L. 248, 251
WILTZ, Louis A. 312, 457
WIMAN, Charles Deere 546*
WIMBERLY, George 456
WIMER, John M. 460*
WIMPRESS, Duncan 483
WINANS
Edwin B. 404, 483
Edwin B. (Mich.) 128, 130, 322
James J. 113
John 129
WINANT, John G. 339*, 429, 445, 579
WINBORNE, J. Wallace 349
WINCHELL
Alexander 482, 575
Newton H. 575
WINCHESTER
Boyd 112, 114, 438
James R. 510, 519
M.B. 456
WINDER
Levin 316
William H. 401, 402
WINDING, Charles A. 549*
WINDLE, William F. 600
WINDOM, William 29*, 39*, 102, 104, 106, 108, 110, 112, 114, 116, 119, 121, 123, 125, 324*
WINE
J.R., Jr. 454
James W. 431, 432
WINEBRENNER, John 538
WINER, Donald A. 500
WINFIELD, Charles H. 107, 109
WING
Asa S. 551
E. Rumsey 427
George W. 457
John D. 512, 521
Leonard F. 414
WINGATE
Joseph F. 74, 76
Paine 6, 51*, 52, 337
Washington M. 484
WINGFIELD
Clyde J. 466
Edward M. 9
J.W. 451
John H.D. 507, 521
WINGO
Effiegene (Locke) 193, 196
Otis T. 167, 170, 173, 176, 179, 183, 186, 189, 193
WINICK, Myron 599
WINKELMANN, Christian H. 529
WINLOCK, Herbert E. 499
WINN
A.M. 460
Courtland S. 449
Larry, Jr. 255, 261, 264
Richard 53, 54, 57, 58, 59, 60, 62, 63
Thomas E. 137
WINNE, Harry A. 596
WINNET, Nochem S. 491
WINNETT, H.J. 455
WINSHIP
Blanton 402
North 438, 439
WINSLOW
Charles-Edward A. 572, 610
Edward 3, 8
Gilbert 3
John B. 385
Josiah 8
Loa Elizabeth 584
Samuel E. 168, 171, 174, 177, 180, 184
Warren 99, 101, 103, 347
WINSOR
Justin 567, 568*
Lou B. 579
WINSTANLEY, Thomas 451
WINSTEAD, W. Arthur 217, 220, 223, 230, 233, 239, 242, 249
WINSTEIN, Saul 604, 609
WINSTON
Frederick S. 549
George T. 477, 482
John A. 277
Joseph 53, 58, 59
Phillip B. 457
WINTER
Andrew 598, 610
Charles E. 179, 186, 189, 192
Edwin W. 550
Elisha I. 64
Ezra 591
George Ben W. 566
Harrison L. 271
John G. 570
T.Z. 461
Thomas D. 210, 213, 216, 220
WINTERLE, Fred S. 462*
WINTERS
Robert W. 599
Yvor 592*, 603
WINTERSTEINER, Oskar 604
WINTHROP
Fitz-John 8
Francis B. 462
John 8*
John, Jr. 8*
Robert C. 84, 86, 87, 89, 90, 91, 93*, 319
Thomas L. 563
Waitsill 10*
WIRT, William 16, 24, 25*, 41
WIRTH
Conrad L. 444, 609
Louis 573
WIRTZ, W. Willard 36, 46, 597
WISDOM, John M. 271
WISE
George D. 126, 129, 131, 134, 136, 139, 141
Henry A. 80, 82, 83, 85, 87, 88, 379, 418, 424
James 510, 520
James W. 170, 173, 176, 180
John S. 129
Morgan R. 124, 126
Peter M. 571
Raleigh J. 601
Richard A. 147, 149
Robert 575
Wes 453
WISELY, H.R. 574
WISER, F.C., Jr. 553
WISEWELL, George F. 469
WISHART
Charles F. 486, 532
P.B. 548
W.I. 533
WISNER
Henry 6
Moses 322
William 532
William C. 532
WISSER, John P. 404*, 410
WISTAR
Caspar 570
Isaac J. 563, 570
WISTER, Owen 609
WISWELL, Andrew P. 314
WITCHER, John S. 113
WITHERELL, James 61
WITHEROW, W.P. 578
WITHERS
Charles D. 436
Garrett L. 226, 232, 310
Jones M. 394, 395
Robert E. 120, 122, 124, 379
Thomas J. 391, 392
WITHERSPOON
James H. 393
James W. 533
John (b. 1723) 3, 4, 6, 532
John (b. 1790) 532
John A. 569
Robert 62
Samuel A. 165, 168, 171
William H. 400
WITHINGTON, Frederic S. 418
WITHROW
Gardner R. 199, 202, 205, 209, 228, 231, 235, 238, 241, 244
John L. 532
WITHYCOMBE, James 356
WITMAN, William, II 438
WITMER
C. Paul 491
Percy 454
WITSCHEY, Robert E. 567
WITSCHI, Emil 573
WITSELL, Edward F. 401*
WITTE
Edwin E. 566
Richard S. 576
William H. 97
WITTEMORE, Lewis B. 522
WITTER, R.H. 558
WITTHUHN, I.R. 576
WITTMAN, Otto 502
WOFFORD
Harris L., Jr. 467
Thomas A. 237, 366
WOGAN, John B. 415
WOHLSTETTER, Roberta 591
WOLCHOK, Samuel 559
WOLCOTT
Daniel F. 292*
Edward O. 134, 137, 139, 142, 144, 147, 285
James L. 291
Jesse P. 197, 200, 204, 207, 210, 213, 217, 220, 223, 226, 230, 233, 236
Josiah O. 173, 176, 179, 291*
Oliver 3, 4, 5, 287*
Oliver, Jr. 23*, 39, 287
Roger (b. 1679) 3, 8*
Roger (b. 1847) 320
WOLD, John S. 260
WOLF
George 72, 73, 75, 358
Harry B. 159
Leonard G. 242
Robert A. 611
Sidney K. 580
Stewart 597
William P. 112
WOLFE
Albert B. 566
Frederick B. 517, 520
Linnis March 585
Simeon K. 116
WOLFENDEN, James 192, 195, 198, 201, 205, 208, 211, 215, 218, 221
WOLFF
Harold G. 569, 597
Irving 594
J. Scott 184
Lester L. 253, 256, 259, 262, 265
Miles H. 573
Stewart 597
WOLFORD, Frank L. 127, 130
WOLFSON, Albert 592
WOLKOMIR, Nathan T. 558
WOLLAN, Ernest O. 612
WOLLEY
John 3
Mary E. 476
WOLLMAN, Mary Schenck 603
WOLMAN
Abel 572, 610
Paul C. 580
WOLPE, Stefan 592
WOLPERT, Ira 584
WOLTMAN
Frederick 585
Henry W. 569
WOLVERTON
Charles A. 191, 194, 197, 201, 204, 207, 211, 214, 217, 220, 224, 227, 230, 233, 236, 239
John M. 189, 195
Simon P. 138, 141
WOMER, Parley P. 484
WONG, Jason D. 499
WOOD
Abiel 64
Alan, Jr. 119
Amos E. 93
Arthur M. 552
Benjamin 105, 107, 126
Benson 142
Bradford R. 90, 426
C. Tyler 612
David A. 565
Ernest E. 156
Fernando 86, 107, 111, 113, 115, 117, 119, 121, 124, 458*
George B. 569, 570
George T. 372
George W. 576
Gordon S. 591
H.A. Wise 594
Harold S. 466
Howard T. 536
Ira W. 154, 157, 159, 162, 165
J.S. 415
J. Harris 545
James (b. 1747) 378
James (b. 1799) 532
James (b. 1839) 565
James F.B. 524, 528
James M. 482
John (Ill.) 300
John (Pa.) 103
John E. (b. 1780) 402
John J. 74
John M. 98, 100
John S. 196, 200, 219, 223, 226, 229
John T. (Rep. Idaho) 229
John T. 558
Joseph (colonist) 5
Joseph (mayor) 462
Joseph D. 458
Leonard 400, 410*, 575, 609
Leslie E. 460
Marquis L. 470
Milton L. 517
Reuben 352*
Reuben T. 201, 204, 207, 210, 352*
Robert 475
Robert C. 36, 47
Robert E. 493, 552*
Robert J. 404
Robert W. 570, 610
Silas 68, 70, 71, 73, 74
Thomas J. 127, 407, 408, 409*, 410
Thomas W. 574, 577
W.D. 461
W.W. 417
Walter A. (b. 1815) 124, 126
Walter A. (b. 1907) 566
William E. 554
William M. 416
William R. (b. 1861) 170, 173, 176, 180, 183, 187, 190, 193, 196
WOODARD
Clifford A. 536
Frederick A. 141, 143
WOODBRIDGE
Enoch 375
Frederick E. 107, 109, 111
William 86, 87, 89, 322*
WOODBURN, William 119, 130, 133
WOODBURY
Charles H. 593
Levi 25*, 39, 42, 73, 74, 76, 86, 88, 89, 269, 337*
Peter 271
Urban A. 376
WOODCOCK
Amos W.W. 480
Charles E. 509, 520
David 70, 74
Leonard 559
WOODFIELD, William H., Jr. 579
WOODFORD
Stewart L. 117, 437
William 406
WOODHALL, Barnes 470
WOODHOUSE
Chase Going 226
Samuel W., Jr. 501
WOODHULL
Caleb S. 458
John 532
WOODIN, William H. 33, 39
WOODLOCK, Thomas F. 599
WOODMAN
Charles W. 142
Edgar H. 452
Frederick T. 456
J.J. 578
WOODRING
Harry H. 33, 40, 307
James D. 465
Wendell P. 576, 607
WOODROUGH, Joseph W. 272
WOODROW
Herbert 571
James 481
WOODRUFF
Aaron D. 462
David B. 576
George C. 104
John 98, 102
L.L. 573
Marion U. 461
Robert W. 545*
Rollin S. 288
Roscoe B. 405, 412, 413, 414
Roy O. 168, 180, 184, 187, 190, 194, 197, 200, 204, 207, 210, 213, 217, 220, 223, 226, 230
Thomas M. 90
Wilford 537
WOODRUM, Clifton A. 186, 189, 192, 195, 199, 202, 205, 209, 212, 215, 218, 222
WOODS
Albert F. 475
Alva 482, 465

Andrew S. 337
Charles A. 271
Charles R. 409*, 410
Cyrus E. 431, 435, 437
Frank P. 161, 164, 167, 170, 173
George 479
George L. 356
Henry 56, 57
James B. 557
James P. 175, 179, 182
John 73
Leonard 466
M.W. 418
Samuel D. 147, 150
Smith D. 455
Thomas H. 327*
W.O. 444
W.P. 576
Walter A. 272
William 71
William B. 269
WOODSIDE
Jonathan F. 426
Robert G. 580
William P. 572
WOODSON
Archelaus M. 330*
Carter 611
James A. 455
Samuel H. (Ky.) 69
Samuel H. (Mo.) 100, 103
Silas 329
Walter B. 416
WOODWARD
C.M. 563
C. Vann 567, 591
Carl R. 479
Claude W. 459
Frank C. 481
Frederic C. 468
George W. 111, 113, 359
Gilbert M. 129
J.D. 501
James G. 449*
Joseph A. 88, 90, 92, 94, 96
Joseph J. 569
Luther T. 486
R.S. 563
Robert B. 596, 604*, 606, 609
Robert F. 425, 426, 437, 439
Robert S. 568
Samuel B. 571
Stanley 425
Tyler 554
William 66
William C. 572
WOODWORTH
Albert B. 452
James H. 98, 451
John M. 445
Laurin D. 117, 119
Newell B. 579
Robert S. 571
William W. 90
WOODYARD, Harry C. 155, 158, 161, 163, 172, 175, 179, 182, 189
WOOLARD, George P. 567
WOOLDRIDGE
A.P. 450
Edmund F. 419
Edmund T. 417
WOOLERY, W.H. 466
WOOLEY, Samuel H. 544*
WOOLFENDEN, Henry L. 568
WOOLFLEY, Francis A. 414
WOOLFORD, John D. 454
WOOLLEN, Evans, Jr. 564
WOOLLEY
John G. 17
Mary E. 476
Victor B. 271
WOOLNER, Samuel 537
WOOLNOUGH, James K. 400, 404
WOOLRIDGE, A.P. 450
WOOLSEY
Lester H. 573
Theodore D. 487
WOOLVERTON, John 462
WOOLWORTH, James M. 564
WOOMER, Ephraim M. 141, 144
WOOSTER, David 406
WOOTEN
Dudley G. 152
Ralph H. 411, 412
William P. 419
WORCESTER
David 471
Samuel T. 105
WORD, Thomas J. 82
WORDEN
Alfred M. 594
John L. 483
WORK
Bertram G. 547*
Harold K. 572
Hubert 32*, 43, 44, 569, 571
Lincoln T. 567
WORKER, Francis 459
WORKING, Lincoln 454
WORKMAN, William H. 456
WORKS
George A. 468
John D. 164, 167, 170, 283
WORLEY
F. Eugene 215, 218, 222, 225, 228, 273
Henry W. 452
WORMAN, Ludwig 70
WORMLEY, Stanton L. 472
WORSHAM, James B. 596
WORST, J.H. 477
WORTENDYKE, Jacob R. 101
WORTH
Gorham A. 547
Jonathan 348
WORTHEN, William E. 572
WORTHING, A.G. 580
WORTHINGTON
Brice T.B. 449
George 507, 520
Henry G. 107, 423, 439
John 3
John T.H. 77, 82, 84
Leslie B. 493, 554, 596
Nicholas E. 127, 130
Thomas 58, 59, 61, 63, 64, 352*
Thomas C. 72
WORTHY, J.C. 493
WORTIS, S. Bernard 569
WOTHERSPOON, William W. 400, 419
WOUK, Herman 585
WOZENCRAFT, Frank W. 452
WOZNICKI, Stephen S. 528
WRAITH, William 595
WRATHER, William E. 443, 564, 596, 601, 608
WREN, Thomas 121
WRIGHT
Ashley B. 140, 143, 145
Augustus R. 100, 391, 392*
Benjamin D. 293
Benjamin F. 481
Burton H. 553
Carroll D. 563
Cecil L. 551
Charles F. 149, 152, 154
Charles W., Jr. 462
Daniel B. 97, 99
Don 587
Donald R. 284
Earl 500
Edward L. 565
Edwin R.V. 108
Eugene A. 272
F.E. 580
Fielding L. 18, 328
Francis M. 273
Frank Lloyd 590, 603
Frederick P. 460
George F. 454
George G. 114, 116, 118, 304, 564
George W. 92
Harry N. 468
Hendrick B. 97, 105, 122, 124
Henry L. 567
Horatio G. 402, 406, 408, 409
Irving S. 567, 589
Isaac 547
J. Butler 426*, 430, 439
J. Skelly 272
James 588, 589, 592
James (Ga.) 8*
James A. 215, 218
James C., Jr. 237, 240, 244, 247, 250, 253, 256, 260, 263, 266
Jerauld 416, 417, 425
John B. (D.C.) 462
John B. (Neb.) 455
John C. 71, 73, 75
John G. 460
John H. 570
John J. 523, 528, 529
John K. 595
John V. 99, 101, 103, 393
Joseph A. 87, 104, 302*, 435*
Joshua 462
Louis B. 499
Louis T. 611
Loyd 565
Luke E. 30, 31, 40, 431
M.A. 575
Milton 531
Myron B. 136, 138, 141
Orville 593, 594, 596*, 597*
Paul S. 532
Quincy 564, 571, 573
R.R., Jr. 486*
Richard 611
Robert 56, 58, 59, 61, 62, 63, 65, 69, 316*
Robert R. 453
Roberts J. 566
Roy V. 573
Ruth S. 578
Samuel G. 90
Sewall 573, 604
Silas, Jr. 74, 77, 79, 81, 83, 84, 86, 88, 344*
Smithson E. 452
Solomon W. 455
Theodore P. 468, 597
Thomas H. 514, 519
Thomas K. 432
Turbutt 6
Wilbur 597
William 88, 90, 97, 99, 101, 107, 108, 340*
William C. 173, 176, 180, 183, 186, 190, 193, 196
William G. 516, 520
William M. 401, 410*
Wyllis E. 595
WRISTON
Henry M. 467, 474
Walter B. 547*
WROTH, Edward P. 514, 519
WU, Chien-Shiung 612
WUORINEN, Charles W. 587
WURDEMANN, Audrey 584
WURSTER, William W. 590
WURTS, John 73
WURTSMITH, Paul B. 412
WURZBACH, Harry M. 182, 185, 189, 192, 195
WYANT, Adam M. 182, 185, 188, 192, 195
WYATT
Francis 9*
John R. 517, 522
Robert H. 578
Wendell 253, 256, 259, 262, 265
Wilson W. 456
WYATT-BROWN, Hunter 512, 519
WYCHE, Ira T. 402, 414
WYCISLO, Aloysius J. 526
WYCKOFF
Charles T. 466
John 567
Joseph C. 474
Ralph D. 601
WYDLER, John W. 249, 253, 259, 262, 265
WYER
James I. 568
Malcolm G. 568
WYETH
Andrew 589, 591, 595, 603, 607, 608
John W. 569
WYLIE
Andrew 473, 485*
Chalmers P. 256, 259, 262, 265
WYLLYS, George 8
WYMAN
A.U. 444*
J. 457
Jeffries 501, 563
Louis C. 249, 255, 259, 262, 265
Walker D. 486
Walter 445, 572
Willard G. 404, 405, 414
William S. 465*
WYNEKEN, F.C.D. 535
WYNKOOP, Henry 7, 51
WYNN, William J. 152
WYNNE
J.S. 459
Kenneth 289
Lyman C. 598
Robert J. 30, 31, 43
WYNNS, Thomas 57, 58, 59
WYTHE
George 3, 4, 7
Joseph H. 486

Y

YADEN, James G. 557
YAEGER, H.J. 462
YAHR, Melvin D. 569
YANCEY
Bartlett 64, 65
Benjamin C. 423
Joel 74, 75
William L. 87, 89, 392
YANDELL, David W. 569
YANG, Chen Ning 606
YANOFSKY, Charles 600
YAPLE, George L. 128
YARBOROUGH
Ralph W. 240, 244, 241, 250, 253, 256, 260, 373
William P. 400
YARD, Emory N. 462
YARDLEY, Robert M. 133, 136
YARNALL, D. Robert 573, 598
YARNELL, H.E. 418
YATES
Abraham 6, 449
John B. 65
Joseph C. 344
Julian E. 401
Peter W. 6
Richard 94, 96, 108, 110, 112, 300*
Richard, Jr. 176, 180, 183, 187, 190, 193, 196
Robert 4, 344
Sidney R. 226, 229, 232, 235, 238, 242, 245, 251, 255, 258, 261, 264
William 486
YATRON, Gus 259, 262, 266
YEAGER
Charles E. 594
Ernest B. 575
YEAKEL, Reuben 531
YEAMAN, George H. 104, 106, 427
YEAMANS, John 9
YEARDLEY, George 9*
YEATES, Jesse J. 119, 121, 124
YEATMAN, Pope 610
YELL, Archibald 80, 82, 89, 281
YEOMANS, John W. 474, 532
YERGAN, Max 611
YERKES
John W. 444
Robert M. 571
YERXA, Thomas 593*
YESLER, Henry L. 461*
YETT, W.D. 450
YLITALO, J. Raymond 434
YOAKUM, Charles H. 144
YOCHUM, Harold L. 467
YOCUM, Seth H. 124
YODER
Claude M. 486
Samuel S. 133, 135
YOGMAN, John 552
YOKE, F. Roy 577
YON, Thomas A. 189, 193, 196
YORK
Robert 586
Tyre 128
YORKE
Samuel 547
Thomas J. 82, 86
YORTY, Samuel W. 229, 232, 456
YOST
Casper S. 573
Charles W. 431*, 433, 438
Jacob 134, 147
Jacob S. 88, 90
Robert L. 424
YOUMANS, Henry M. 137
YOUNG
A. 533
Albert 558
Allyn A. 566
Andrew 264
Arthur M. 601
Augustus 87
Brig S. 576
Brigham 537
Bryan R. 89
C.W. (Bill) 261, 264
Charles 611
Charles A. 563
Charles D. 600
Clement C. 284
Clifton 233, 236
David W. 567
Donald 493, 574
Dwight 573

E.T. 458
Ebenezer 75, 77, 78
Edward L. 266
Evan E. 424, 427*
Frederick G. 474
G.M. 572
George M. 169, 172, 175, 178, 181, 185, 273
George U. 459
George W. 577
H. Casey 120, 122, 124, 129
H. Edwin 474
H. Olin 153, 156, 159, 162, 165, 168
Isaac D. 164
J. Russel 425
James 166, 169, 172, 175, 179
James R. 146, 149, 152
James S. 591
John (N.Y.) 81, 86, 344
John (univ. pres.) 467
John A. 240, 244, 247, 250, 253, 256, 260, 263, 266
John C. 532
John C. (jur.) 286
John D. 116
John F. 506, 519
John R. (b. 1841) 444
John R. (b. 1900) 462
John S. 121
Josue M. 526
Karl 577
Kenneth T. 438
Kimball 573
L.W., Jr. 551
Lafayette 161, 304
Mahonri S. 498, 500
Milton R. 221, 224, 227, 230, 234, 237, 240, 243, 246, 253, 256, 262, 265, 350
N.B. 470
Owen D. 551, 609
Philip 433, 445
Pierce M.B. 110, 112, 114, 116, 429, 430
Richard 162
Richard M. 82, 84, 85, 300
Robert N. 400, 405
Rodney S. 574
Roy A. (b. 1882) 443
Roy A. (b. 1921) 479
Samuel B.M. 400, 419
Samuel H. 264
Stark 592
Stephen M. 201, 204, 214, 227, 243, 246, 249, 253, 256, 259, 354
Thomas L. 124, 126, 353
Timothy R. 92
Whitney M., Jr. 579, 608
William A. 147, 149
William C. 532
William G. 608
William L. 532
William S. (Ky.) 72, 74
William S. 478
Winthrop 456
YOUNGBLOOD, Harold F. 223
YOUNGDAHL
Luther W. 325
Oscar F. 210, 214
YOUNGER
J. Arthur 232, 235, 238, 241, 244, 248, 251, 254
John E. 611
YOUNGSON, A.B. 557
YOUNGWORTH, Leo V. 579
YOUNT, Robert C. 453
YOUTZ, Philip N. 497
YULEE, David Levy 89, 91, 92, 98, 100, 102, 293*

Z

ZABLOCKI, Clement J. 228, 231, 235, 238, 241, 244, 247, 250, 254, 257, 260, 263, 266
ZABRISKIE
Edwin G. 569
Robert 485
ZACH, Leon 573
ZACHER, L. Edmund 553
ZAHM
Albert F. 599
John I. 467
ZAIS, Melvin 405
ZALESKI, Alexander M. 527
ZAMECNIK, Paul C. 607
ZANDMAN, Felix 601
ZARDETTI, Otto 528
ZARISKI, Oscar 568, 604
ZARITSKY, Max 559
ZATURENSKA, Marya 584, 610
ZEALAND, Joseph , 469, 474, 480
ZEBLEY, John H., Jr. 567
ZEEK, Charles F. 600
ZEHRUNG, Frank C. 455*
ZEIDLER
Carl F. 456
Frank P. 456
ZEILIN, Jacob 416
ZELENKO, Herbert 237, 240, 243, 246
ZELENY
Charles 573
John 570
ZELLER, Andrew 531
ZELLERBACH, James D. 431, 491
ZENER, Clarence 612
ZENNECK, Jonathan 598
ZENOR, William T. 145, 147, 150, 153, 156
ZENTMAYER, Joseph 594
ZEPP, Erwin C. 501
ZIEGENHEIN, Henry 460
ZIEGLER
Edward D. 149
Nolan F. 453
Winfred H. 513, 522
ZIHLMAN, Frederick N. 174, 177, 180, 184, 187, 190, 193, 577
ZILBOORG, Gregory 608
ZIMMER, John T. 592
ZIMMERMAN
Charles J. 545
Fred R. 386
George J. 451
James F. 476
John E. 551*
Orville 204, 207, 210, 214, 217, 220, 224
Paul W. 589
Percy W. 612
Wayne C. 402
ZIMMERMANN, William F. 601
ZINDEL, Paul 588
ZINN
Charles J. 570
Donald J. 579
Walter H. 595
ZINSSER, Hans 610
ZINZENDORF, Nicholas 538
ZION, Roger H. 255, 258, 261, 264
ZIONCHECK, Marion A. 202, 205
ZNANIECKI, Florian 573
ZOLL, Samuel E. 460
ZOLLARS, Ely V. 472, 482
ZOLLICOFFER, Felix K. 97, 99, 101
ZOLLINGER, Robert M. 565
ZOOK, George F. 444, 465
ZORACH, William 603
ZORNOW, Gerald B. 546
ZSISSLY, 589*, 593
ZUBLY, John J. 5
ZUCKERT, Eugene M. 399
ZUELZER, Wolf W. 599
ZUERCHER, Joseph P. 469
ZUMBERGE, James H. 476
ZUMWALT, Elmo R., Jr. 416
ZUROWESTE, Albert R. 525
ZWACH, John M. 255, 258, 261, 265
ZWICK, Charles J. 444
ZWORYKIN, Vladimir K. 595, 598, 599, 604, 608, 610